ISBN 978-0-428-46146-1
PIBN 11221785

FB &c Ltd, Dalton House, 60 Windsor Avenue, London, SW19 2RR.
Company number 08720141. Registered in England and Wales.

For support please visit www.forgottenbooks.com

A COMPENDIUM

OF

THE NINTH CENSUS

(JUNE 1, 1870,)

COMPILED PURSUANT TO A

CONCURRENT RESOLUTION OF CONGRESS,

AND UNDER THE DIRECTION OF THE

SECRETARY OF THE INTERIOR,

BY

FRANCIS A. WALKER,
SUPERINTENDENT OF CENSUS

WASHINGTON:
GOVERNMENT PRINTING OFFICE.
1872.

CONTENTS.

SCHOOL ATTENDANCE AND ILLITERACY.

SCHOOLS, LIBRARIES, NEWSPAPERS, AND CHURCHES.

PAUPERISM AND CRIME.

AREAS, FAMILIES, AND DWELLINGS.

SEX, AND SCHOOL, MILITARY, AND CITIZENSHIP AGES.

OCCUPATIONS.

THE BLIND, DEAF AND DUMB, INSANE, AND IDIOTIC.

WEALTH, TAXATION, AND PUBLIC INDEBTEDNESS.

AGRICULTURE.

MANUFACTURES.

REPORT

OF

THE SUPERINTENDENT OF THE NINTH CENSUS.

DEPARTMENT OF THE INTERIOR, CENSUS OFFICE,
November 1, 1872.

SIR: I have the honor to advise the Department of the completion of the work of the Ninth Census; and I take the occasion of the annual report, required by law to be rendered at this time, to submit the entire material for the Compendium authorized by the concurrent resolution of May 31, 1872. The extended tables, to be comprised in the quarto volumes authorized by the resolution of April 19, 1871, are in the hands of the Congressional Printer, and nearly all are in type. Both the text and the tables of the Population volume have been for some time awaiting the completion of the maps designed to illustrate this volume; and it is anticipated that bound copies will be upon the desks of members at the assembling of Congress in December. The two remaining quarto volumes are complete in the Congressional Printing Office; one of them, the volume on Vital Statistics, being in type. Of the other volume, that on the industry of the United States, about one hundred pages remain as yet untouched.

I am advised that it is probable, notwithstanding the enormous pressure on the Printing Office from the legislative matter thrown upon it in the first weeks of the session, that the last of the quarto volumes of the census will be completed early in January.

I cannot pass this point without acknowledging the advantage which this Office has derived from the manner in which its necessarily heavy demands upon the Congressional Printing Office have been met. The intelligent interest taken in the work by the Hon. A. M. Clapp, Congressional Printer, and the zeal and efficiency of his subordinate officers, have amounted to a positive re-enforcement of the Census Office. But for facilities far beyond what any Bureau officer has a right to claim, the publication of the census volumes must have been carried far over into the next year.

In the course of the census, occasion has been found but too frequently to note defects in the act of 1850, under which, notwithstanding the vast changes which the country has undergone, both in the conditions of enumeration and in the proper subjects of statistical inquiry, the census of the United States continues to be taken.

In the report rendered from this Office on the 26th of December of last year, which report is made a part of the Population volume soon to issue from the press, a full discussion was had of the general system of enumeration now in force, while the particular deficiencies in the schedules of 1850, and in the agencies provided for the collection of the material relating thereto, have been discussed in immediate connection with the individual tables of the several quarto volumes, nearly every important table being prefaced by a body of remarks in which are set forth the errors known or suspected to exist therein, with such explanations as could be afforded of the reason of such errors, whether it be found in the nature of the subject, in the scheme of inquiry, or in the machinery created for the purpose by the act of 1850. The limits of a Compendium will not allow of the reproduction of these remarks at length, nor could they generally be abridged to advantage. It has, therefore, been deemed desirable to accompany the tables of the present publication with references to the extended tables on the same subjects, and the discussions relating thereto, in the several quarto volumes, so that those who have occasion to use the statistics of the census for purposes requiring great exactness of detail and nicety of treatment, may be assisted to consult the fuller reports at libraries and public offices, should they not be personally in possession of them.

The appropriation of $25,000 made at the last session of Congress for preparing and publishing maps for illustrating the quarto volumes of the census, has been expended with results which it is believed will meet the hearty approval of Congress and the country. The greater portion of the maps printed under this appropriation were prepared at the Census Office, out of its own material. For the purpose, however, of illustrating more completely the sanitary and industrial conditions of the country, certain other maps have been prepared, in respect to which the Census Office has been the recipient of favors from individuals and institutions, whose names and titles the Superintendent feels it a high honor to be allowed to associate with his work. To that eminent and venerable scholar, Professor Joseph Henry, Secretary of the Smithsonian Institution, and to Professor Charles A. Schott, of the Coast Survey Office, acknowledgment is due for maps showing, severally, the annual distribution of rain and the courses of the lines of equal temperature; charts eloquent with instruction upon the agricultural capabilities of the country and the conditions of human life among us. Professor A. Guyot, of Princeton College, through his publishers, Messrs. Scribner, Welford & Co., of New York, kindly placed at the disposal of this Office the plates of his valuable physical map of the country, to which Professor Schott has, with the permission of the Superintendent of the United States Coast Survey, added by far the most complete and accurate series of elevations yet attained. These three maps have been used to illustrate the volume on Vital Statistics.

Professor Charles H. Hitchcock, of Dartmouth College, assisted by

Professor William P. Blake, of New Haven, has prepared a geological map, to be found in the volume on Industry, upon which are laid down eight principal formations, with a comprehensiveness, a precision, and a degree of detail never before attempted in the geological description of the United States. All the work thus kindly contributed to the publications of the census has been reproduced in the best style of the engraving art, and the Superintendent can feel no hesitation in claiming for the results the highest value, both in popular instruction and in the positive increase of scientific knowledge.

Of the maps prepared at the Census Office, seven have been assigned to the illustration of the Population volume, four to the volume on Vital Statistics, and four to the volume on Industry. Most of these maps are double, presenting two distinct subjects, generally selected for purposes of direct contrast. The maps in the Population volume exhibit the density of total population ; the distribution severally of the colored and the foreign elements of population; the dispersion over the States of the natives of certain specified foreign countries, viz: Germany, Ireland, Sweden and Norway, England and Wales, China, and British America; the illiteracy and the wealth of each section in contrast; and, finally, the geographical and political divisions of the United States at each period of its existence, from the organization of the Government to the latest census year.

The maps illustrative of the volume on Vital Statistics show the range, and, within the range, the degree of prevalence of four specific diseases, or groups of diseases, viz: 1st, consumption; 2d, typhoid, typhus, and enteric fevers; 3d, malarial diseases; 4th, dysentery, diarrhea, and enteritis.

The maps illustrative of the volume on Industry exhibit the range and degree of cultivation of five principal crops, viz: cotton, corn, wheat, hay, and tobacco, and also the dairy products of each State and section.

The possibilities of this style of illustration are practically without limit. The present, as the first attempt of the kind in the United States, may be found to contain faults of treatment in some particulars; but it is not doubted that this will hereafter be an essential part of the census report. A thousand persons will thus obtain, without effort, just and vivid impressions in respect to the most important features of their country, physically, socially, and industrially, where one will, by long and painful study of the tables of the census, create such a series of pictures in his own mind.

The cordiality with which the press and the country have recognized the early publication of the prime results of the census has afforded ample compensation to the Superintendent for all the effort that has been required to accomplish the completion of the work of compilation within two years from the conclusion of the enumeration. There is no reason, however, why, with such modifications of existing laws as would insure that the material should come originally to the Census Office in proper shape for tabulation, the entire compilation should not be concluded within a year from the date of the first receipt of returns. It is not possible for one who has had such painful occasion as the present Superintendent to observe the workings of the census law of 1850, to characterize it otherwise than as clumsy, antiquated, and barbarous. The machinery it provides is as unfit for use in the census of the United States, in this day of advanced statistical science, as the smooth-bore, muzzle-loading "Queen's-arm" of the Revolution would be for service against the repeating-rifle of the present time. It ought not to be possible that another census should be taken under this law: such a thing ought not to be seriously proposed. The country has suffered more than enough already of discredit and of loss on account of the wretched insufficiency and inappropriateness of the provisions of this ill-constructed and outgrown statute.

I do earnestly recommend that the attention of Congress be especially invited to the propriety and expediency of an intermediate census, to be taken in 1875, in preparation for the approaching centennial celebration of the political birth of the nation. A census of the United States taken under a system and with a management which would secure the publication of the results by the 1st of June, 1876, would be a noble monument to erect at the end of a century of the nation's life. It would mark off the first grand stage in an industrial and social progress altogether unprecedented in history, and serve as the starting-point of a fresh career which we have, under Providence, reason to believe shall be greater and happier yet.

Another consideration, which strongly influences me in this recommendation, is the belief that a census in 1875 would secure the taking of the Federal census thereafter at intervals of five years only. The interval of ten years fixed by the Constitution has been found to be far too long for all the uses to which the statistics of the census are put, except only for the redistribution of congressional representation.

So rapid are the internal changes of the country, oftentimes setting calculation at naught, so fierce and vast the growth of the nation as a whole, that the hiatus in the statistical information at the command of the legislator, the pamphleteer, the journalist, and the social and political philosopher, becomes positively painful five or six years after the date of the census. Whoever will call to mind the estimates as to the population and wealth of cities, States, and sections which immediately before the occurrence of the last census were popularly put forth, were made the material of political and industrial speculation, and were even taken as the basis of State and national legislation, will hardly be disposed to question that the cost of a census once in five years would be amply repaid by the light it would shed upon the condition of the people and the progress of the nation in population and wealth. Were the country once to learn by practical experience the advantages of a quinquennial enumeration, it is not likely that a longer period would ever thereafter be allowed to intervene between the Federal censuses.

In the report rendered from this Office December 26, 1871, mention was made by name of several gentlemen connected with the Office, to whom acknowledgments were due for highly meritorious services. In closing the work of the Ninth Census, it is now my pleasant duty to publicly recognize the zeal and activity of George D. Harrington, esq., the chief clerk of the Bureau, and the intelligent and spirited co-operation of Messrs. Henry Stone, C. S. Mixter, and S. A. Galpin. More than a formal acknowledgment is due from me to Mr. S. W. Stocking, the chief of the Division of Results, from whose hands has gone to press every page of the census reports of 1870. A projector by nature, of large resource and indefinite capacity for work, he has proved a most valuable assistant in devising the forms and methods of compilation and of publication. The first clerk appointed at my instance, after my own appointment as Superintendent, in February, 1870, I respectfully recommend him to you as a person eminently qualified to discharge the duties of census clerk of the Interior Department during the interval between the Ninth and the Tenth Census.

Mr. A. S. Boernstein has "cast" nearly every table of the present census, and has superintended the reading of the proof. One of the most capable printers in the United States, an artist in his craft, the typographical excellence of the series of volumes of which this now submitted is the last, has been in no small measure due to his industry and taste.

To yourself, honored sir, I have again to tender heartfelt thanks for generous and cordial support in the duties of my office.

Very respectfully, your obedient servant,

FRANCIS A. WALKER,
Superintendent.

Hon. COLUMBUS DELANO,
Secretary of the Interior.

POPULATION. WITH RACE.

TABLE I.—*Aggregate Population at each Census.*

	States and Territories.		1870.		1860.		185
	The United States		38, 558, 371		31, 443, 321		23,
	The States		38, 115, 641		31, 183, 744		23,
1	Alabama	16	996, 992	13	964, 201	12	
2	Arkansas	26	484, 471	25	435, 450	26	
3	California	24	560, 247	26	379, 994	29	
4	Connecticut	25	537, 454	24	460, 147	21	
5	Delaware	34	125, 015	32	112, 216	30	
6	Florida	33	187, 748	31	140, 424	31	
7	Georgia	12	1, 184, 109	11	1, 057, 286	9	
8	Illinois	4	2, 539, 891	4	1, 711, 951	11	
9	Indiana	6	1, 680, 637	6	1, 350, 428	7	
10	Iowa	11	1, 194, 020	20	674, 913	27	
11	Kansas	29	364, 399	33	107, 206	...	...
12	Kentucky	8	1, 321, 011	9	1, 155, 684	8	
13	Louisiana	21	726, 915	17	708, 002	18	
14	Maine	23	626, 915	22	628, 279	16	
15	Maryland	20	780, 894	19	687, 049	17	
16	Massachusetts	7	1, 457, 351	7	1, 231, 066	6	
17	Michigan	13	1, 184, 059	16	749, 113	20	
18	Minnesota	28	439, 706	30	172, 023	33	
19	Mississippi	18	827, 922	14	791, 305	15	
20	Missouri	5	1, 721, 295	8	1, 182, 012	13	
21	Nebraska	35	122, 993	35	28, 841	...	...
22	Nevada	37	42, 491	36	6, 857	...	...
23	New Hampshire	31	318, 300	27	326, 073	22	
24	New Jersey	17	906, 096	21	672, 035	19	
25	New York	1	4, 382, 759	1	3, 880, 735	1	3,
26	North Carolina	14	1, 071, 361	12	992, 622	10	
27	Ohio	3	2, 665, 260	3	2, 339, 511	3	1,
28	Oregon	36	90, 923	34	52, 465	32	
29	Pennsylvania	2	3, 521, 951	2	2, 906, 215	2	2,
30	Rhode Island	32	217, 353	29	174, 620	28	
31	South Carolina	22	705, 606	18	703, 708	14	
32	Tennessee	9	1, 258, 520	10	1, 109, 801	5	1,
33	Texas	19	818, 579	23	604, 215	25	
34	Vermont	30	330, 551	28	315, 098	23	
35	Virginia	10	1, 225, 163	5	1, 596, 318	4	1,
36	West Virginia	27	442, 014	...	...	...	...
37	Wisconsin	15	1, 054, 670	15	775, 881	24	
	The Territories		442, 730		259, 577		
1	Arizona	9	9, 658	...	...	...	...
2	Colorado	4	39, 864	4	34, 277	...	...
3	Dakota	8	14, 181	6	4, 837	...	...
4	District of Columbia	1	131, 700	2	75, 080	2	
5	Idaho	7	14, 999	...	...	...	...
6	Montana	6	20, 595	...	...	...	...
7	New Mexico	2	91, 874	1	93, 516	1	
8	Utah	3	86, 786	3	40, 273	3	
9	Washington	5	23, 955	5	11, 594	...	...
10	Wyoming	10	9, 118	...	...	...	...
	On public ships in service of the United States		...		...		...

NOTE.—The narrow column under each census year shows the order of the States and Territor arranged according to magnitude of population in the aggregate or in each class.

TABLE I.—*Aggregate Population at each Census.*

	1840.		1830.		1820.		1810.		1800.		1790.	
	17,069,453		12,866,020		*4,631 9,633,822		7,239,881		5,308,483		3,929,214	
	17,019,641		12,820,868		*4,631 9,600,783		7,215,858		5,294,390		3,929,214	
12	590,756	15	309,527	19	127,901	...	...	...	...	...	...	1
25	97,574	27	30,388	25	*18 14,255	...	...	...	...	...	...	2
...	...	...	...	...	...	...	...	...	...	...	...	3
20	309,978	16	297,675	14	*100 275,148	9	261,942	8	251,002	8	237,946	4
26	78,085	24	76,748	22	72,749	19	72,674	17	64,273	16	59,096	5
27	54,477	25	34,730	...	...	...	...	...	...	...	...	6
9	691,392	10	516,823	11	*4 340,985	11	252,433	12	162,686	13	82,548	7
14	476,183	20	157,445	24	*49 55,162	23	12,282	...	...	...	...	8
10	685,866	13	343,031	18	147,178	21	24,520	20	5,641	...	...	9
28	43,112	...	...	...	...	...	...	...	...	...	...	10
...	...	...	...	...	...	...	...	...	...	...	...	11
6	779,828	6	687,917	6	*188 564,135	7	406,511	9	220,955	14	73,677	12
19	352,411	19	215,739	17	*484 152,923	18	76,556	...	...	...	...	13
13	501,793	12	399,455	12	*66 208,269	14	228,705	14	151,719	11	96,540	14
15	470,019	11	447,040	10	407,350	8	380,546	7	341,548	6	319,728	15
8	737,699	8	610,408	7	*128 523,159	5	472,040	5	422,845	4	378,787	16
23	212,267	28	31,639	26	*131 8,765	24	4,762	...	...	...	...	17
...	...	...	...	...	...	...	...	...	...	...	...	18
17	373,651	22	136,621	21	75,448	20	40,352	19	8,850	...	...	19
16	383,702	21	140,455	23	*29 66,557	22	20,845	...	...	...	...	20
...	...	...	...	...	...	...	...	...	...	...	...	21
...	...	...	...	...	...	...	...	...	...	...	...	22
22	284,574	18	269,328	15	*139 244,022	16	214,460	11	183,858	10	141,885	23
18	373,306	14	320,823	13	*149 277,426	12	245,562	10	211,149	9	184,139	24
1	2,428,921	1	1,918,608	1	*701 1,372,111	2	959,049	3	589,051	5	340,120	25
7	753,419	5	737,987	4	638,829	4	555,500	4	478,103	3	393,751	26
3	1,519,467	4	937,903	5	*139 581,295	13	230,760	18	45,365	...	...	27
...	...	...	...	...	...	...	...	...	...	...	...	28
2	1,724,033	2	1,348,233	3	*1,951 1,047,507	3	810,091	2	602,365	2	434,373	29
24	108,830	23	97,199	20	*44 83,015	17	76,931	16	69,122	15	68,825	30
11	594,398	9	581,185	8	502,741	6	415,115	6	345,591	7	249,073	31
5	829,210	7	681,904	9	*52 422,771	10	261,727	15	105,602	17	35,691	32
...	...	...	...	...	...	...	...	...	...	...	...	33
21	291,948	17	280,652	16	*15 235,966	15	217,895	13	154,465	12	85,425	34
4	1,239,797	3	1,211,405	2	*255 1,065,116	1	974,600	1	880,200	1	747,610	35
...	...	...	...	...	...	...	...	...	...	...	...	36
29	30,945	...	...	...	...	...	...	...	...	...	...	37
	43,712		39,834		33,039		24,023		14,093		...	
...	...	...	...	...	...	...	...	...	...	...	...	1
...	...	...	...	...	...	...	...	...	...	...	...	2
...	...	...	...	...	...	...	...	...	...	...	...	3
1	43,712	1	39,834	1	33,039	1	24,023	1	14,093	...	...	4
...	...	...	...	...	...	...	...	...	...	...	...	5
...	...	...	...	...	...	...	...	...	...	...	...	6
...	...	...	...	...	...	...	...	...	...	...	...	7
...	...	...	...	...	...	...	...	...	...	...	...	8
...	...	...	...	...	...	...	...	...	...	...	...	9
...	...	...	...	...	...	...	...	...	...	...	...	10
	6,100		5,318		...		...		...		...	

* All other persons, except Indians not taxed.

TABLE II.—*White Population at each Census.*

	States and Territories.		1870.		1860.		1850.
	The United States		33, 589, 377		26, 922, 537		19, 553, 068
	The States		33, 203, 128		26, 690, 780		19, 442, 272
1	Alabama	21	521, 384	18	526, 271	15	426, 514
2	Arkansas	26	362, 115	25	324, 143	26	162, 189
3	California	22	499, 424	26	323, 177	29	91, 635
4	Connecticut	20	527, 549	20	451, 504	18	363, 099
5	Delaware	34	102, 221	32	90, 589	30	71, 169
6	Florida	35	96, 057	33	77, 746	31	47, 203
7	Georgia	16	638, 926	17	591, 550	13	521, 572
8	Illinois	4	2, 511, 096	4	1, 704, 291	7	846, 034
9	Indiana	5	1, 655, 837	5	1, 338, 710	5	977, 154
10	Iowa	8	1, 188, 207	13	673, 779	25	191, 881
11	Kansas	28	346, 377	31	106, 390	...	.....
12	Kentucky	10	1, 098, 692	9	919, 484	8	761, 413
13	Louisiana	27	362, 065	22	357, 456	24	255, 491
14	Maine	17	624, 809	16	626, 947	11	581, 813
15	Maryland	18	605, 497	19	515, 918	16	417, 943
16	Massachusetts	7	1, 443, 156	6	1, 221, 432	4	985, 450
17	Michigan	9	1, 167, 282	12	736, 142	17	395, 071
18	Minnesota	23	438, 257	30	169, 395	33	6, 038
19	Mississippi	25	382, 896	23	353, 899	22	295, 718
20	Missouri	6	1, 603, 146	7	1, 063, 489	10	592, 004
21	Nebraska	33	122, 117	35	28, 696	...	.....
22	Nevada	37	38, 959	36	6, 812	...	.....
23	New Hampshire	30	317, 697	24	325, 579	19	317, 456
24	New Jersey	13	875, 407	14	646, 699	14	465, 509
25	New York	1	4, 330, 210	1	3, 831, 590	1	3, 048, 325
26	North Carolina	15	678, 470	15	629, 942	12	553, 028
27	Ohio	3	2, 601, 946	3	2, 302, 808	3	1, 955, 050
28	Oregon	36	86, 929	34	52, 160	32	13, 087
29	Pennsylvania	2	3, 456, 609	2	2, 849, 259	2	2, 258, 160
30	Rhode Island	32	212, 219	29	170, 649	28	143, 875
31	South Carolina	31	289, 667	28	291, 300	23	274, 563
32	Tennessee	12	936, 119	10	826, 722	9	756, 836
33	Texas	19	564, 700	21	420, 891	27	154, 034
34	Vermont	29	329, 613	27	314, 369	20	313, 402
35	Virginia	14	712, 089	8	1, 047, 299	6	894, 800
36	West Virginia	24	424, 033	...	.....	...	.....
37	Wisconsin	11	1, 051, 351	11	773, 693	21	304, 756
	The Territories		386, 249		231, 757		110, 796
1	Arizona	9	9, 581	...	.....	...	.....
2	Colorado	4	39, 221	4	34, 231	...	.....
3	Dakota	7	12, 887	6	2, 576	...	.....
4	District of Columbia	2	88, 278	2	60, 763	2	37, 941
5	Idaho	8	10, 618	...	.....	...	.....
6	Montana	6	18, 306	...	.....	...	.....
7	New Mexico	1	90, 393	1	82, 924	1	61, 525
8	Utah	3	86, 044	3	40, 125	3	11, 330
9	Washington	5	22, 195	5	11, 138	...	.....
10	Wyoming	10	8, 726	...	.....	...	.....
	On public ships in service of the United States		.....		.....		.....

TABLE II.—*White Population at each Census.*

1840.		1830.		1820.		1810.		1800.		1790.		
	14,195,805		10,537,378		7,862,166		5,862,073		4,306,446		3,172,006	
	14,158,048		10,504,497		7,839,552		5,845,904		4,296,380		3,172,006	
14	335,185	18	190,406	18	85,451	...	...	...	...	...	...	1
25	77,174	26	25,671	25	12,579	...	...	...	...	...	...	2
...	...	...	...	...	...	...	...	...	...	...	...	3
17	301,856	14	289,603	10	267,181	7	255,179	6	244,721	6	232,374	4
26	58,561	24	57,601	22	55,282	18	55,361	17	49,852	16	46,310	5
29	27,943	27	18,385	...	...	...	...	...	...	...	...	6
12	407,695	12	296,806	16	180,566	16	145,414	14	102,261	15	52,886	7
11	472,254	19	155,061	23	53,788	23	11,501	...	...	...	...	8
6	678,698	10	339,399	17	145,758	20	23,890	19	5,343	...	...	9
27	42,924	...	...	...	...	...	...	...	...	...	...	10
...	...	...	...	...	...	...	...	...	...	...	...	11
8	590,253	7	517,787	6	434,644	6	324,237	11	179,873	14	61,133	12
23	158,457	22	89,441	20	73,383	19	34,311	...	...	...	...	13
9	500,438	9	398,263	9	297,340	10	227,736	13	150,901	11	96,002	14
16	318,204	13	291,108	11	260,223	8	235,117	7	216,326	7	208,649	15
5	729,030	5	603,359	5	516,419	4	465,303	4	416,393	3	373,324	16
21	211,560	25	31,346	26	8,591	24	4,618	...	...	...	...	17
...	...	...	...	...	...	...	...	...	...	...	...	18
22	179,074	23	70,443	24	42,176	21	23,024	20	5,179	...	...	19
15	323,888	20	114,795	21	55,988	22	17,227	...	...	...	...	20
...	...	...	...	...	...	...	...	...	...	...	...	21
...	...	...	...	...	...	...	...	...	...	...	...	22
19	284,036	16	268,721	13	243,236	15	213,490	10	182,898	9	141,097	23
13	351,588	11	300,266	12	257,409	11	226,868	9	194,325	8	169,954	24
1	2,378,890	1	1,873,663	1	1,332,744	1	918,699	2	557,731	4	314,142	25
10	484,870	8	472,843	7	419,200	5	376,410	5	337,764	5	288,204	26
3	1,502,122	3	928,329	4	576,572	9	228,861	18	45,028	...	...	27
...	...	...	...	...	...	...	...	...	...	...	...	28
2	1,676,115	2	1,309,900	2	1,017,094	2	786,804	1	586,095	2	424,099	29
24	105,587	21	93,621	19	79,413	17	73,214	16	65,438	13	64,470	30
20	259,084	17	257,863	14	237,440	14	214,196	8	196,255	10	140,178	31
7	640,627	6	535,746	8	339,927	13	215,875	15	91,709	17	31,913	32
...	...	...	...	...	...	...	...	...	...	...	...	33
18	291,218	15	279,771	15	235,063	12	217,145	12	153,908	12	85,154	34
4	740,968	4	694,300	3	603,085	3	551,514	3	514,280	1	442,117	35
...	...	...	...	...	...	...	...	...	...	...	...	36
28	30,749	...	...	...	...	...	...	...	...	...	...	37
	30,657		27,563		22,614		16,079		10,066		...	
...	...	...	...	...	...	...	...	...	...	...	...	1
...	...	...	...	...	...	...	...	...	...	...	...	2
...	...	...	...	...	...	...	...	...	...	...	...	3
1	30,657	1	27,563	1	22,614	1	16,079	1	10,066	...	...	4
...	...	...	...	...	...	...	...	...	...	...	...	5
...	...	...	...	...	...	...	...	...	...	...	...	6
...	...	...	...	...	...	...	...	...	...	...	...	7
...	...	...	...	...	...	...	...	...	...	...	...	8
...	...	...	...	...	...	...	...	...	...	...	...	9
...	...	...	...	...	...	...	...	...	...	...	...	10
	6,100		5,318		...		...		...		...	

TABLE III.—*Colored Population at each Census.*

	States and Territories.	1870.		1860.		185[illegible]	
	The United States		4, 880, 009		4, 441, 830		3, 6
	The States		4, 835, 106		4, 427, 294		3, 6
1	Alabama	3	475, 510	3	437, 770	4	3
2	Arkansas	12	122, 169	13	111, 259	15	
3	California	29	4, 272	25	4, 086	27	
4	Connecticut	26	9, 668	22	8, 627	22	
5	Delaware	21	22, 794	19	21, 627	19	
6	Florida	14	91, 689	14	62, 677	16	
7	Georgia	1	545, 142	2	465, 698	3	3
8	Illinois	19	28, 762	23	7, 628	23	
9	Indiana	20	24, 560	20	11, 428	20	
10	Iowa	27	5, 762	29	1, 069	31	
11	Kansas	23	17, 108	31	627	....	....
12	Kentucky	10	222, 210	9	236, 167	9	2
13	Louisiana	7	364, 210	7	350, 373	7	2
14	Maine	31	1, 606	27	1, 327	26	
15	Maryland	11	175, 391	11	171, 131	10	1
16	Massachusetts	24	13, 947	21	9, 602	21	
17	Michigan	25	11, 849	24	6, 799	25	
18	Minnesota	34	759	33	259	33	
19	Mississippi	4	444, 201	4	437, 404	6	3
20	Missouri	13	118, 071	12	118, 503	11	
21	Nebraska	33	789	35	82	....	....
22	Nevada	36	357	36	45	....	....
23	New Hampshire	35	580	32	494	30	
24	New Jersey	18	30, 658	18	25, 336	18	
25	New York	17	52, 081	16	49, 005	14	
26	North Carolina	6	391, 650	6	361, 522	5	3
27	Ohio	16	63, 213	17	36, 673	17	
28	Oregon	37	346	34	128	32	
29	Pennsylvania	15	65, 294	15	56, 949	13	
30	Rhode Island	28	4, 980	26	3, 952	24	
31	South Carolina	5	415, 814	5	412, 320	2	3
32	Tennessee	8	322, 331	8	283, 019	8	2
33	Texas	9	253, 475	10	182, 921	12	
34	Vermont	32	924	30	709	28	
35	Virginia	2	512, 841	1	548, 907	1	5
36	West Virginia	22	17, 980	....	....	....	....
37	Wisconsin	30	2, 113	28	1, 171	29	
	The Territories		44, 903		14, 536		1
1	Arizona	9	26	....	....	....	....
2	Colorado	2	456	4	46	....	....
3	Dakota	7	94	....	....	....	....
4	District of Columbia	1	43, 404	1	14, 316	1	1
5	Idaho	8	60	....	....	....	....
6	Montana	4	183	....	....	....	....
7	New Mexico	5	172	2	85	3	
8	Utah	6	118	3	59	2	
9	Washington	3	207	5	30	....	....
10	Wyoming	4	183	....	....	....	....
	On public ships in service of the United States.	....	....	....	....	....	....

TABLE III.—*Colored Population at each Census.*

1840.		1830.		1820.		1810.		1800.		1790.		
	2,873,648		2,328,642		1,771,656		1,377,808		1,002,037		757,208	
	2,860,593		2,316,371		1,761,231		1,369,864		998,010		757,208	
5	255,571	9	119,121	9	42,450	...	...	...	...	...	...	1
16	20,400	20	4,717	20	1,676	...	...	...	...	...	...	2
...	...	...	...	...	...	...	...	...	...	...	...	3
20	8,122	18	8,072	16	7,967	14	6,763	13	6,281	11	5,572	4
17	19,524	15	19,147	14	17,467	13	17,313	10	14,421	8	12,786	5
14	26,534	16	16,345	...	...	...	...	...	...	...	...	6
3	283,697	4	220,017	4	151,419	5	107,019	5	60,425	5	29,662	7
22	3,929	23	2,384	22	1,374	21	781	...	...	...	...	8
21	7,168	21	3,632	21	1,420	23	630	20	298	...	...	9
29	188	...	...	...	...	...	...	...	...	...	...	10
...	...	...	...	...	...	...	...	...	...	...	...	11
8	189,575	5	170,130	6	129,491	6	82,274	6	41,082	9	12,544	12
7	193,954	8	126,298	8	79,540	8	42,245	...	...	...	...	13
24	1,355	24	1,192	23	929	20	969	17	818	16	538	14
10	151,815	6	155,932	5	147,127	4	145,429	4	125,222	2	111,079	15
19	8,669	19	7,049	17	6,740	15	6,737	12	6,452	12	5,463	16
26	707	27	293	26	174	24	144	...	...	...	...	17
...	...	...	...	...	...	...	...	...	...	...	...	18
6	196,577	10	66,178	11	33,272	12	17,328	15	3,671	...	...	19
11	59,814	13	25,660	15	10,569	17	3,618	...	...	...	...	20
...	...	...	...	...	...	...	...	...	...	...	...	21
...	...	...	...	...	...	...	...	...	...	...	...	22
27	538	26	607	25	786	19	970	16	860	15	788	23
15	21,718	14	20,557	13	20,017	11	18,694	8	16,824	7	14,185	24
12	50,031	11	44,945	10	39,367	9	40,350	7	31,320	6	25,978	25
4	268,549	3	265,144	3	219,629	3	179,090	3	140,339	4	105,547	26
18	17,345	17	9,574	18	4,723	18	1,899	19	337	...	...	27
...	...	...	...	...	...	...	...	...	...	...	...	28
13	47,918	12	38,333	12	30,413	10	23,287	9	16,270	10	10,274	29
23	3,243	22	3,578	19	3,602	16	3,717	14	3,684	13	4,355	30
2	335,314	2	323,322	2	265,301	2	200,919	2	149,336	3	108,895	31
9	188,583	7	146,158	7	82,844	7	45,852	11	13,893	14	3,778	32
...	...	...	...	...	...	...	...	...	...	...	...	33
25	730	25	881	24	903	22	750	18	557	17	271	34
1	498,829	1	517,105	1	462,031	1	423,086	1	365,920	1	305,493	35
...	...	...	...	...	...	...	...	...	...	...	...	36
28	196	...	...	...	...	...	...	...	...	...	...	37
	13,055		12,271		10,425		7,944		4,027		...	
...	...	...	...	...	...	...	...	...	...	...	...	1
...	...	...	...	...	...	...	...	...	...	...	...	2
...	...	...	...	...	...	...	...	...	...	...	...	3
1	13,055	1	12,271	1	10,425	1	7,944	1	4,027	...	...	4
...	...	...	...	...	...	...	...	...	...	...	...	5
...	...	...	...	...	...	...	...	...	...	...	...	6
...	...	...	...	...	...	...	...	...	...	...	...	7
...	...	...	...	...	...	...	...	...	...	...	...	8
...	...	...	...	...	...	...	...	...	...	...	...	9
...	...	...	...	...	...	...	...	...	...	...	...	10
	...		...		...		...		...		...	

TABLE IV.—*Free Colored Population at each Census.*

	States and Territories.	1870.		1860.		185
	The United States		4,880,009		488,070	4
	The States		4,835,106		476,748	4
1	Alabama	3	475,510	22	2,690	21
2	Arkansas	12	122,169	33	144	28
3	California	29	4,272	18	4,086	23
4	Connecticut	26	9,668	14	8,627	14
5	Delaware	21	22,794	8	19,829	8
6	Florida	14	91,689	26	932	24
7	Georgia	1	545,142	21	3,500	18
8	Illinois	19	28,762	15	7,628	16
9	Indiana	20	24,560	10	11,428	10
10	Iowa	27	5,762	25	1,069	31
11	Kansas	23	17,108	29	625	...
12	Kentucky	10	222,210	11	10,684	11
13	Louisiana	7	364,210	9	18,647	9
14	Maine	31	1,606	23	1,327	22
15	Maryland	11	175,391	1	83,942	1
16	Massachusetts	24	13,947	13	9,602	12
17	Michigan	25	11,849	17	6,799	20
18	Minnesota	34	759	32	259	33
19	Mississippi	4	444,201	27	773	25
20	Missouri	13	118,071	20	3,572	19
21	Nebraska	33	789	35	67	...
22	Nevada	36	357	36	45	...
23	New Hampshire	35	580	30	494	20
24	New Jersey	18	30,658	7	25,318	7
25	New York	17	52,081	4	49,005	4
26	North Carolina	6	391,650	6	30,463	5
27	Ohio	16	63,213	5	36,673	6
28	Oregon	37	346	34	128	32
29	Pennsylvania	15	65,294	3	56,949	3
30	Rhode Island	28	4,980	19	3,952	17
31	South Carolina	5	415,814	12	9,914	13
32	Tennessee	8	322,331	16	7,300	15
33	Texas	9	253,475	31	355	30
34	Vermont	32	924	28	709	26
35	Virginia	2	512,841	2	58,042	2
36	West Virginia	22	17,980	...	...	...
37	Wisconsin	30	2,113	24	1,171	27
	The Territories		44,903		11,322	
1	Arizona	9	26	...	...	...
2	Colorado	2	456	3	46	...
3	Dakota	7	94	...	...	...
4	District of Columbia	1	43,404	1	11,131	1
5	Idaho	8	60	...	...	...
6	Montana	4	183	...	...	...
7	New Mexico	5	172	2	85	3
8	Utah	6	118	4	30	2
9	Washington	3	207	4	30	...
10	Wyoming	4	183	...	...	...
	On public ships in service of the United States	...	...	...	...	...

TABLE IV.—*Free Colored Population at each Census.*

	1840.		1830.		1820.		1810.		1800.		1790.	
	386,293		319,599		233,634		186,446		108,435		59,527	
	377,932		313,447		229,586		183,897		107,652		59,527	
19	2,039	19	1,572	21	571							1
27	465	27	141	26	59							2
												3
12	8,105	10	8,047	9	7,870	10	6,453	8	5,330	9	2,808	4
9	16,919	8	15,855	6	12,958	5	13,136	5	8,268	7	3,899	5
23	817	22	844									6
18	2,753	17	2,486	16	1,763	14	1,801	12	1,019	14	398	7
16	3,598	18	1,637	23	457	20	613					8
14	7,165	15	3,629	17	1,230	22	393	20	163			9
29	172											10
												11
13	7,317	13	4,917	14	2,759	15	1,713	15	739	17	114	12
5	25,502	7	16,710	8	10,476	8	7,585					13
22	1,355	20	1,190	18	929	18	969	14	818	13	538	14
1	62,078	1	52,938	1	39,730	1	33,927	2	19,587	2	8,043	15
10	8,669	12	7,048	11	6,740	9	6,737	7	6,452	4	5,463	16
25	707	26	261	25	174	24	120					17
												18
21	1,366	25	519	22	458	23	240	19	182			19
20	1,574	24	569	24	347	21	607					20
												21
												22
26	537	23	604	20	786	17	970	13	858	12	630	23
7	21,044	6	18,303	7	12,460	7	7,843	9	4,402	10	2,762	24
2	50,027	3	44,870	4	29,279	3	25,333	4	10,417	6	4,654	25
6	22,732	5	19,543	5	14,712	6	10,266	6	7,043	5	4,975	26
8	17,342	9	9,568	12	4,723	13	1,899	17	337			27
												28
4	47,854	4	37,930	3	30,202	4	22,492	3	14,564	3	6,537	29
17	3,238	16	3,561	13	3,554	12	3,609	10	3,304	8	3,407	30
11	8,276	11	7,921	10	6,826	11	4,554	11	3,185	11	1,801	31
15	5,524	14	4,555	15	2,737	16	1,317	18	309	15	361	32
												33
24	730	21	881	19	903	19	750	16	557	16	271	34
3	49,842	2	47,348	2	36,883	2	30,570	1	20,124	1	12,866	35
												36
28	185											37
	8,361		6,152		4,048		2,549		783			
												1
												2
												3
1	8,361	1	6,152	1	4,048	1	2,549	1	783			4
												5
												6
												7
												8
												9
												10

TABLE V.—*Slave Population at each Census.*

	States and Territories.	1870.		1860.		1850.	
	The United States				3,953,760		3,204,
	The States				3,950,546		3,200,
1	Alabama			4	435,080	4	342,
2	Arkansas			12	111,115	13	47,
3	California						
4	Connecticut						
5	Delaware			15	1,798	15	2,
6	Florida			14	61,745	14	39,
7	Georgia			2	462,198	3	381,
8	Illinois						
9	Indiana						
10	Iowa						
11	Kansas			18	2		
12	Kentucky			9	225,483	9	210,
13	Louisiana			6	331,726	7	244,
14	Maine						
15	Maryland			13	87,189	10	90,
16	Massachusetts						
17	Michigan						
18	Minnesota						
19	Mississippi			3	436,631	5	309,
20	Missouri			11	114,931	11	87,
21	Nebraska			17	15		
22	Nevada						
23	New Hampshire						
24	New Jersey			16	(a)18	16	
25	New York						
26	North Carolina			7	331,059	6	288,
27	Ohio						
28	Oregon						
29	Pennsylvania						
30	Rhode Island						
31	South Carolina			5	402,406	2	384,
32	Tennessee			8	275,719	8	239,
33	Texas			10	182,566	12	58,
34	Vermont						
35	Virginia			1	490,865	1	472,
36	West Virginia						
37	Wisconsin						
	The Territories				3,214		3,
1	Arizona						
2	Colorado						
3	Dakota						
4	District of Columbia			1	3,185	1	3,
5	Idaho						
6	Montana						
7	New Mexico						
8	Utah			2	29	2	
9	Washington						
10	Wyoming						
	On public ships in service of the United States						

(a) Colored apprentices for life, by the act to abolish slavery, passed April 18, 1846.

TABLE V.—*Slave Population at each Census.*

1840.		1830.		1820.		1810.		1800.		1790.		
	2,487,355		2,009,043		1,538,022		1,191,362		893,602		697,681	
	2,482,661		2,002,924		1,531,645		1,185,967		890,358		697,681	
4	253,532	7	117,549	9	41,879	...	...	...	...	...	...	1
13	19,935	13	4,576	15	1,617	...	...	...	...	...	...	2
...	...	...	...	...	...	...	...	...	...	...	...	3
18	17	20	25	19	97	15	310	13	951	12	2,764	4
14	2,605	14	3,292	14	4,509	12	4,177	10	6,153	9	8,887	5
12	25,717	12	15,501	...	...	...	...	...	...	...	...	6
3	280,944	4	217,531	4	149,656	5	105,218	5	59,406	5	29,264	7
16	331	16	747	16	917	17	168	...	...	...	...	8
22	3	23	3	18	190	16	237	15	135	...	...	9
19	16	...	...	...	...	...	...	...	...	...	...	10
...	...	...	...	...	...	...	...	...	...	...	...	11
8	182,258	5	165,213	5	126,732	6	80,561	6	40,343	7	12,430	12
9	168,452	8	109,588	8	69,064	8	34,660	...	...	...	...	13
...	...	24	2	...	...	...	...	...	...	...	...	14
10	89,737	9	102,994	6	107,307	4	111,502	4	105,635	3	103,036	15
...	...	25	1	...	...	...	...	...	...	...	...	16
...	...	19	32	...	...	19	24	...	...	...	...	17
...	...	...	...	...	...	...	...	...	...	...	...	18
6	195,211	10	65,659	10	32,814	9	17,088	11	3,489	...	...	19
11	58,240	11	25,091	11	10,222	13	3,011	...	...	...	...	20
...	...	...	...	...	...	...	...	...	...	...	...	21
...	...	...	...	...	...	...	...	...	...	...	...	22
24	1	23	3	...	...	...	...	16	8	14	158	23
15	674	15	2,254	13	7,557	11	10,851	9	12,422	8	11,423	24
22	4	18	75	12	10,088	10	15,017	7	20,903	6	21,324	25
5	245,817	3	245,601	3	204,917	3	168,824	3	133,296	4	100,572	26
23	3	22	6	...	...	...	...	...	...	...	...	27
...	...	...	...	...	...	...	...	...	...	...	...	28
17	64	17	403	17	211	14	795	12	1,706	10	3,737	29
21	5	21	17	20	48	18	108	14	380	13	948	30
2	327,038	2	315,401	2	258,475	2	196,365	2	146,151	2	107,094	31
7	183,059	6	141,603	7	80,107	7	44,535	8	13,584	11	3,417	32
...	...	...	...	...	...	...	...	...	...	...	...	33
...	...	...	...	...	...	...	...	...	...	...	...	34
1	448,987	1	469,757	1	425,148	1	392,516	1	345,796	1	292,627	35
...	...	...	...	...	...	...	...	...	...	...	...	36
20	11	...	...	...	...	...	...	...	...	...	...	37
	4,694		6,119		6,377		5,395		3,244		...	
...	...	...	...	...	...	...	...	...	...	...	...	1
...	...	...	...	...	...	...	...	...	...	...	...	2
...	...	...	...	...	...	...	...	...	...	...	...	3
1	4,694	1	6,119	1	6,377	1	5,395	1	3,244	...	...	4
...	...	...	...	...	...	...	...	...	...	...	...	5
...	...	...	...	...	...	...	...	...	...	...	...	6
...	...	...	...	...	...	...	...	...	...	...	...	7
...	...	...	...	...	...	...	...	...	...	...	...	8
...	...	...	...	...	...	...	...	...	...	...	...	9
...	...	...	...	...	...	...	...	...	...	...	...	10
...		...		...		...		...		...		

TABLE VI.—*Chinese, Japanese, and Civilized Indian Population at each Census.*

States and Territories.	Chinese.				Japanese.		Civilized Indian.			
	1870.		1860.		1870.		1870.		1860.	
The United States		63, 199		34, 933		55		25, 731		44, 021
The States		56, 124		34, 933		55		21, 228		30, 737
Alabama							21	98	11	160
Arkansas	4	98					22	89	18	48
California	1	49, 277	1	34, 933	1	33	1	7, 241	1	17, 798
Connecticut	14	2					14	235	25	16
Delaware										
Florida							34	2	29	1
Georgia	15	1					27	40	19	38
Illinois	15	1					29	32	21	32
Indiana							13	240	7	290
Iowa	13	3					26	48	15	65
Kansas							5	914	8	189
Kentucky	15	1					19	108	20	33
Louisiana	6	71					8	569	10	173
Maine	15	1					9	499	27	5
Maryland	14	2					33	4		
Massachusetts	5	87			2	10	17	151	21	32
Michigan	15	1			3	1	2	4, 926	2	6, 172
Minnesota							7	690	3	2, 369
Mississippi	9	16					6	809	28	2
Missouri	13	3					24	75	23	20
Nebraska							23	87	16	63
Nevada	3	3, 152					30	23		
New Hampshire							30	23		
New Jersey	11	5			2	10	31	16		
New York	7	29					10	439	12	140
North Carolina							3	1, 241	4	1, 158
Ohio	15	1					20	100	22	30
Oregon	2	3, 330					12	318	9	177
Pennsylvania	10	13			3	1	28	34	26	7
Rhode Island							16	154	24	19
South Carolina	15	1					18	124	14	88
Tennessee							25	70	17	60
Texas	8	25					11	379	6	403
Vermont							32	14	23	20
Virginia	12	4					15	229	13	112
West Virginia							35	1		
Wisconsin							4	1, 206	5	1, 017
The Territories		7, 075						4, 503		13, 284
Arizona	6	20					9	31		
Colorado	7	7					4	180		
Dakota							3	1, 200	2	2, 261
District of Columbia	8	3					10	15	5	1
Idaho	1	4, 274					8	47		
Montana	2	1, 949					6	157		
New Mexico							2	1, 309	1	10, 507
Utah	3	445					5	179	4	89
Washington	4	234					1	1, 319	3	426
Wyoming	5	143					7	66		
On public ships in service of the United States										

TREATMENT OF INDIANS IN THE CENSUS.

[Extract from report of the Superintendent, in Vol. I, Ninth Census.]

Indians taxed.—In the absence of any constitutional, legal, or judicial definition of the phrase "Indians not taxed," as found in the Constitution and in the census law of 1850, it has been held for census purposes to apply only to Indians maintaining their tribal relations and living upon Government reservations.

The broken bands and the scattered remnants of tribes still to be found in many States of the Union, though generally in a condition of pauperism, have been included in the enumeration of the people. By the fact of breaking away from their tribal relations, they are regarded as having entered the body of citizens and as subject to taxation, from the point of view of the Constitution, although they may be exempted actually from taxation by local legislation or by the accident of pauperism. It has been held that it was not necessary that a member of this race should be proved to have actually paid taxes, in order to take him out of the class "Indians not taxed," but only that he should be found in a position, so far as the authorities or agents of the census can know, to be taxed were he in possession of property. His pauperism has been regarded as an individual accident, which cannot possibly affect his constitutional relations. Even where the lands formerly belonging to a tribe have been granted in severalty, without the right of alienation or sale, and the land itself exempted from taxation, such special provisions have been regarded rather as an exception to ordinary legislation in respect to personal rights and personal obligations, made in the interest of the community, than as creating a class to be excluded from the enumeration of the people. The provisions of the Constitution in regard to the enumeration of Indians, being invidious, and opposed to the general spirit of that instrument, and even more emphatically opposed to the spirit of recent legislation and of the late constitutional amendments, should be construed strictly and not liberally.

In 1860 the same principle appears to have been applied in determining the representative population of the States. Reference to pages 598 and 599 of the Population volume of the Eighth Census will show that all the Indians embraced in the table of General Population were included in the representative population of their respective States, except for the State of California.

The reason for excluding Indians in making up the representative population of California was undoubtedly found in the fact that in 1860 the Indians of that State were mainly upon Government reservations, some of which have since been abolished. There appears no longer to be any reason for treating the State of California exceptionally in respect to the Indians found upon its territory. To have made the treatment of this class at the census of 1860 consistent throughout, the 17,798 Indians of California should not have been included at all in the statements of constitutional population.

The number of Indians in each State returned under this construction, as forming a part of the constitutional population, is found in the table on the preceding page.

Half-breeds.—Another question seriously affecting the return of Indians in the census is the treatment of half-breeds, in which term persons with any perceptible trace of Indian blood, whether mixed with white or with negro stock, are popularly included. How shall these be treated? Shall they be regarded as following the condition of the father or of the mother? Or, again, shall they be classified with respect to the superior or to the inferior blood? When it is considered how few of pure Indian race are to be found outside of Government reservations, and how variously mixed are even the camps and settlements, popularly known as Indian, in the older States of the Union, it will be seen that the decision of the question must affect, in an important degree, the numbers of this class to be returned in the census.

It has been held that, in treating this question, the Census Office is not to be concluded or in the least constrained by analogy from laws or judicial decisions relating to the former slave population of the country. The rule that the child should follow the condition of the mother was the bad necessity of a bad cause, which required every point to be construed against freedom. Something very nearly opposed to this would seem to be in accordance with the present spirit of our laws, as well as to be the dictate of common sense. The principle which has governed in the classification of persons of part Indian blood in the present census has been as follows: Where persons reported as "half-breeds" are found residing with whites, adopting their habits of life and methods of industry, such persons are to be treated as belonging to the white population. Where, on the other hand, they are found in communities composed wholly or mainly of Indians, the opposite construction is taken. In a word, in the equilibrium produced by the equal division of blood, the habits, tastes, and associations of the half-breed are allowed to determine his gravitation to the one class or the other. It is believed that this is at once the most logical and the least cumbersome treatment of the subject, in the manifest inexpediency of attempting to trace and record all the varieties of this race, especially considering the small and fast-decreasing numbers in which it is found within the States of the Union. [For the treatment of Indians other than taxed, see page 22.]

TABLE VII.—*True Population of the United States*—1870.

	States and Territories.	Aggregate.	White.	Colored.	Chines
	The United States	38, 925, 598	33, 592, 245	4, 886, 387	63
	The States	38, 205, 598	33, 203, 128	4, 835, 106	56
1	Alabama	996, 992	521, 384	475, 510	....
2	Arkansas	484, 471	362, 115	122, 169	
3	California	582, 031	499, 424	4, 272	49
4	Connecticut	537, 454	527, 549	9, 668	
5	Delaware	125, 015	102, 221	22, 794	....
6	Florida	188, 248	96, 057	91, 689	....
7	Georgia	1, 184, 109	638, 926	545, 142	
8	Illinois	2, 539, 891	2, 511, 096	28, 762	
9	Indiana	1, 680, 637	1, 655, 837	24, 560	....
10	Iowa	1, 194, 320	1, 188, 207	5, 762	
11	Kansas	373, 299	346, 377	17, 108	....
12	Kentucky	1, 321, 011	1, 098, 692	222, 210	
13	Louisiana	726, 915	362, 065	364, 210	
14	Maine	626, 915	624, 809	1, 606	
15	Maryland	780, 894	605, 497	175, 391	
16	Massachusetts	1, 457, 351	1, 443, 156	13, 947	
17	Michigan	1, 187, 234	1, 167, 282	11, 849	
18	Minnesota	446, 056	438, 257	759	....
19	Mississippi	827, 922	382, 896	444, 201	
20	Missouri	1, 721, 295	1, 603, 146	118, 071	
21	Nebraska	120, 322	122, 117	789	....
22	Nevada	58, 711	38, 959	357	3
23	New Hampshire	318, 300	317, 697	580	....
24	New Jersey	906, 096	875, 407	30, 658	
25	New York	4, 387, 464	4, 330, 210	52, 081	
26	North Carolina	1, 071, 361	678, 470	391, 650	....
27	Ohio	2, 665, 260	2, 601, 946	63, 213	
28	Oregon	101, 883	86, 929	346	
29	Pennsylvania	3, 522, 050	3, 456, 609	65, 294	
30	Rhode Island	217, 353	212, 219	4, 980	....
31	South Carolina	705, 606	289, 667	415, 814	
32	Tennessee	1, 258, 520	936, 119	322, 331	....
33	Texas	818, 899	564, 700	253, 475	
34	Vermont	330, 551	329, 613	924	....
35	Virginia	1, 225, 163	712, 089	512, 841	
36	West Virginia	442, 014	424, 033	17, 980	....
37	Wisconsin	1, 064, 985	1, 051, 351	2, 113	....
	The Territories	720, 000	389, 117	51, 281	7
1	Alaska	70, 461	461	....	....
2	Arizona	41, 710	9, 581	26	
3	Colorado	47, 164	39, 221	456	
4	Dakota	40, 501	12, 887	94	....
5	District of Columbia	131, 700	88, 278	43, 404	
6	Idaho	20, 583	10, 618	60	
7	Indian Country	68, 152	2, 407	6, 378	....
8	Montana	39, 895	18, 306	183	1
9	New Mexico	111, 303	90, 393	172	....
10	Utah	99, 581	86, 044	118	
11	Washington	37, 432	22, 195	207	
12	Wyoming	11, 518	8, 726	183	

TABLE VII.—*True Population of the United States*—1870.

INDIAN.										
Total.	Out of tribal relations.	SUSTAINING TRIBAL RELATIONS.								
		Total.	On reservations and at agencies.						Nomadic, (estimated.)	
			Enumerated.					Estimated.		
			Total.	Men.	Women.	Male children.	Female children.			
383,712	25,731	357,961	96,366	26,583	30,464	19,740	19,579	26,875	234,740	
111,185	21,228	89,957	33,642	9,506	11,329	6,590	6,127	18,575	37,740	
98	98									1
89	89									2
29,025	7,241	21,784	5,784	1,966	2,181	865	772	2,500	13,500	3
235	235									4
										5
502	2	500							500	6
40	40									7
32	32									8
240	240									9
348	48	300						300		10
9,814	914	8,900	5,900	1,985	1,850	1,089	976		3,000	11
108	108									12
569	569									13
499	499									14
4	4									15
151	151									16
8,101	4,926	3,175						3,175		17
7,040	690	6,330						6,350		18
809	809									19
75	75									20
6,416	87	6,329	6,329	1,667	2,321	1,279	1,062			21
16,243	23	16,220							16,220	22
23	23									23
16	16									24
5,144	439	4,705	4,705	1,144	1,196	1,154	1,211			25
1,241	1,241									26
100	100									27
11,278	318	10,960	6,110	1,705	2,404	1,024	977	650	4,200	28
133	34	99	99	21	25	29	24			29
154	154									30
124	124									31
70	70									32
699	379	320							320	33
14	14									34
229	229									35
1	1									36
11,521	1,206	10,315	4,715	1,108	1,352	1,150	1,105	5,600		37
272,527	4,503	268,024	62,724	16,987	19,135	13,130	13,452	8,300	197,000	
70,000		70,000							70,000	1
32,083	31	32,052	4,352	1,277	1,396	925	754		27,700	2
7,450	150	7,300							7,300	3
27,520	1,200	26,320							26,320	4
15	15									5
5,631	47	5,584	3,284	1,006	1,203	549	526		2,300	6
59,367		59,367	19,067	3,884	4,445	5,146	5,592	5,900	34,400	7
19,457	157	19,300							19,300	8
20,738	1,309	19,429	14,349	4,278	5,326	2,150	2,595		5,080	9
12,974	179	12,795	8,195	2,715	2,620	1,526	1,334		4,600	10
14,796	1,319	13,477	13,477	3,827	4,145	2,854	2,651			11
2,466	66	2,400						2,400		12

NOTE TO THE TABLE OF TRUE POPULATION. (Page 20.)

(From the report of the Superintendent, in Vol. I, Ninth Census.)

The Territories.—The Constitution, as a matter of course, contains no requirement for any enumeration of persons outside the *States* of the Union. The census law of 1850, however, makes provision for enumerating the inhabitants of the several Territories upon the same terms as the inhabitants of the States; and such enumeration has been made in connection with the Ninth Census. The results will be found in detail in the other tables of the present volume, and in the aggregate, as well as with certain distinctions of race and color, in the preceding table.

Alaska.—No special provision of law exists for any enumeration within the newly acquired district of Alaska; nor was it found practicable to organize the census service there under the general powers conferred by the act of 1850, or as an incident to the operations of the Treasury or the War Departments. In order, however, to present the statistics of the true population of the country formally complete, that district has been included in the table preceding the population of the several classes, being there stated according to the best available data, consisting mainly of reports, nominal lists, &c., from officers of the Army on duty in that military department.

Indians not taxed.—It is to be regretted that the census law of 1850, while extending the enumeration required by the Constitution to the inhabitants of the Territories, should have followed the narrower rule of that instrument in respect to the Indian population. The phrase of the Constitution, "Indians not taxed," seems to have been adopted by the framers of the census law as a matter of course. Now, the fact that the Constitution excludes from the basis of representation "Indians not taxed," affords no possible reason why, in a census which is on its face taken with equal reference to statistical as to political interests, such persons should be excluded from the population of the country. They should, of course, appear separately, so that the provisions of the Constitution in regard to the apportionment of Representatives may be carried out; but they should appear, nevertheless, as a constituent part of the population of the country, viewed in the light of all social, economical, and moral principles. An Indian not taxed should, to put it upon the lowest possible ground, be reported in the census just as truly as the vagabond or pauper of the white or the colored race. The fact that he sustains a vague political relation is no reason why he should not be recognized as a human being by a census which counts even the cattle and horses of the country. The practical exclusion of Indians from the census creates a hiatus which is wholly unnecessary, and which goes to impair that completeness which affords a great part of the satisfaction of any statistical work. With a view, therefore, to reaching the true population of the country as nearly as is practicable, in the absence of distinct authority for the appointment of assistant marshals to enumerate the several tribes and bands of Indians, inquiries were conducted extensively through the agents of the Indian Office during the year 1870, the result of which, it is believed, has been to secure a closer approximation to the true numbers of this class of the population than has ever before been effected. [By the same agency the population of the Indian Country was ascertained.]

The preceding table, therefore, in which these several elements, omitted from the enumeration, are made to appear, presents the ultimate facts of the population of the United States, so far as it is possible to reach them by all the agencies directly or indirectly at the command of the authorities of the census. In this table, however, no attempt has been made to allow for omissions occurring in the enumeration of the classes of persons recognized by the census law and embraced on the schedule of inhabitants. It is one of the faults of the present system that not only will such omissions occur, but they occur so erratically and irrationally as to make it impossible to reach anything like a satisfactory estimate of their extent, or their distribution between classes of the population or sections of the country.

TABLE VIII.—*Population by Counties at each Census—ALABAMA.*

	Counties.	AGGREGATE.								WHITE.		
		1870.	1860.	1850.	1840.	1830.	1820.	1810.	1800.	1870.	1860.	1850.
	The State	996992	964201	771623	590756	309527	127901	a9046	a1250	521384	526271	426514
1	Autauga (b) (k)	11623	16739	15023	14342	11874	3853			4329	7105	6274
2	Baker (b)	6194								5057		
3	Baldwin (l)	6004	7530	4414	2951	2324	1713	a1427		3159	3585	2100
4	Barbour (d)	29309	30812	23632	12024					12143	14629	12842
5	Benton (c)			17163	14260							13397
6	Bibb (b)	7469	11894	9969	8284	6306	3676			5061	8027	7097
7	Blount (m)	9945	10865	7367	5570	4233	2415			9263	10193	6941
8	Bullock (d)	24474								7223		
9	Butler (e) (j)	14981	18122	10836	8685	5650	1405			8590	11260	7162
10	Calhoun (c) (h) (m)	13980	21539							10088	17169	
11	Cataco (f)						5263					
12	Chambers (q)	17562	23214	23960	17333					8974	11315	12784
13	Cherokee (m)	11132	18360	13884	8773					9652	15321	12170
14	Choctaw	12676	13877	8389						5802	6767	4620
15	Clarke	14663	15049	9786	8640	7595	5839			7098	7599	4901
16	Clay (g)	9560								8823		
17	Cleburne (h)	8017								7441		
18	Coffee (j) (n)	6171	9623	5940						5151	8200	5320
19	Colbert (i)	12537								7898		
20	Conecuh (l)	9574	11311	9322	8197	7444	5713			4667	6419	4925
21	Coosa (k)	11945	19273	14543	6995					8544	14044	10414
22	Covington (j)	4868	6469	3645	2435	1522				4269	5631	3077
23	Crenshaw (j)	11156								8950		
24	Dale (n)	11325	12197	6382	7397	2031				9528	10379	5622
25	Dallas	40705	33625	29727	25199	14017	6003			8552	7785	7461
26	De Kalb (m)	7126	10705	8245	5929					6656	9853	7730
27	Elmore (k)	14477								7747		
28	Escambia (l)	4041								3047		
29	Etowah (m)	10109								8401		
30	Fayette (r)	7136	12850	9681	6942	3547				6059	11145	8451
31	Franklin (i)	8006	18627	19610	14270	11078	4988			6693	10119	11398
32	Geneva (n)	2959								2732		
33	Greene (o)	18399	30859	31441	24024	15026	4554			3858	7251	9265
34	Hale (o)	21792								4802		
35	Hancock (p)			1542								1480
36	Henry	14191	14918	9019	5787	4020	2638			9534	10464	6776
37	Jackson	19410	18283	14088	15715	12700	8751			16350	14811	11754
38	Jefferson	12345	11746	8989	7131	6855				9839	9078	6714
39	Lauderdale	15091	17420	17172	14485	11781	4963			9921	10639	11097
40	Lawrence	16658	13975	15258	13313	14984				10096	7173	8342
41	Lee (q)	21750								10151		
42	Limestone	15017	15306	16483	14374	14807	9871			7764	7215	8399
43	Lowndes (c) (j)	25719	27716	21915	19539	9410				5986	8362	7258
44	Macon (d) (q)	17727	26802	26898	11247					5103	8624	11286
45	Madison	31267	26451	26427	25706	27990	17481	a4699		15527	11685	11937
46	Marengo (o)	26151	31171	27831	17264	7700	2933			6090	6761	7101
47	Marion (r)	6059	11182	7833	5847	4058				5835	9293	6922
48	Marshall (m)	9871	11472	8846	7553					8504	9596	7952
49	Mobile	49311	41131	27600	18741	6267	2672			28195	28559	17303
50	Monroe	14214	15667	12013	10680	8782	8838			6625	6878	5648
51	Montgomery (d) (k)	43704	35904	29711	24574	12695	6604			12419	12122	10169
52	Morgan (f)	12187	11335	10125	9841	9062				8829	7592	6637
53	Perry (b) (o)	24975	27724	22285	19086	11490				7142	9479	8342
54	Pickens	17690	22316	21512	17118	6622				8052	10117	10972
55	Pike (d) (j)	17423	24435	15920	10108	7108				12798	15646	12102
56	Randolph (g) (h)	12006	20059	11581	4973					10365	18132	10616
57	Russell (q)	21636	26592	19548	13513					5946	10936	8405
58	Sanford (r)	8893								7230		
59	Shelby (b)	12218	12618	9536	6112	5704	2416			8840	8970	7153
60	St. Clair (m)	9360	11013	6829	5638	5975	4166			7295	9236	5501
61	Sumter	24109	24035	22250	29937					5202	5919	7369
62	Talladega (g) (h)	18064	23520	18624	12587					8469	14634	11617
63	Tallapoosa (k) (q)	16963	23827	15584	6444					12772	17154	11511
64	Tuscaloosa (o)	20081	23200	18056	16583	13646	8229			11787	12971	10571
65	Walker	6543	7980	5124	4032	2202				6235	7461	4857
66	Washington	3912	4669	2713	5300	3474		a2920	a1250	2125	2119	1195
67	Wilcox	28377	24618	17352	15278	9548	2917			6767	6795	5517
68	Winston (p)	4155	3576							4134	3454	

(*a*) Then in the Territory of Mississippi. (*b*) In 1868 Baker from Autauga, Bibb, Perry, and Shelby. (*c*) In 1858 name changed from Benton to Calhoun. (*d*) In 1866 Bullock from Barbour, Macon, Montgomery, and Pike. (*e*) In 1866 west half township 11, range 16, from Lowndes. (*f*) In 1821 name changed from Cataco to Morgan. (*g*) In 1866 Clay from Randolph and Talladega. (*h*) In 1866 Cleburne from Calhoun, Randolph, and Talladega. (*i*) In 1867 Colbert from Franklin. (*j*) In 1866 Crenshaw from Butler, Coffee, Covington, Lowndes, and Pike. (*k*) In 1866 Elmore from Autauga, Coosa, Montgomery,

Table VIII.—*Population by Counties at each Census—ALABAMA.*

White—Continued.				Colored.								Indian.		
1830.	1820.	1810.	1800.	1870.	1860.	1850.	1840.	1830.	1820.	1810.	1800.	1870.	1860.	
190406	85451	a6422	a733	475510	437770	345109	253571	119121	42450	a2624	a517	98	160	
5867	2203			7292	9621	8749	8125	6007	1650			2	13	1
				1137										2
965	651	a667		2845	3854	2314	1790	1359	1062	a760			91	3
				17165	16183	10790	5555					1		4
						3766	2900							5
5113	2930			2408	3867	2872	2028	1193	746					6
3882	2239			682	672	426	345	351	176					7
				17251										8
3904	835			6391	6862	3674	2493	1746	570					9
				3892	4370									10
	4394								869					11
				8588	11899	11176	7143							12
				1480	3039	1714	1121							13
				6872	7110	3769						2		14
3894	3778			7565	7450	4885	4412	3701	2061					15
				737										16
				576										17
				1020	1423	560								18
				4639										19
3812	3769			4901	4892	4397	3821	3632	1944			6		20
				3394	5223	4129	2137					7	6	21
1118				509	838	568	380	404						22
				2206										23
1757				1797	1816	760	588	274					2	24
6794	3324			32152	25840	22266	17277	7223	2679			1		25
				470	852	515	340							26
				6730										27
				951								43		28
				1708										29
3035				1077	1705	1230	981	512						30
6069	3308			1313	8508	8212	6034	5009	1680					31
				227										32
7585	2861			14541	23608	22176	16468	7441	1693					33
				16990										34
						62								35
3005	2011			4657	4454	2243	1086	1015	627					36
11418	8129			3060	3472	2334	1852	1282	622					37
5121				2506	2668	2275	1645	1734						38
7960	3556			5170	6781	6075	5638	3821	1407					39
8361				6542	6802	6916	6170	6623						40
				11507								2		41
8077	6922			7253	8091	8084	6876	6730	2949					42
5001				20633	19354	14657	12583	4409						43
				12620	18177	15612	5878					4	1	44
13855	8813	a3745		15740	14765	14490	13409	14135	8668	a954			1	45
4549	2052			20058	24410	20730	11914	3151	881			3		46
3472				221	1288	911	733	606					1	47
				1367	1872	894	865						4	48
3440	1653			21107	12571	10297	6978	2827	1019			9	1	49
5165	5014			7572	8751	6365	5310	3617	3824			17	38	50
6180	3941			31285	23780	19542	15602	6515	2663				2	51
6126				3358	3743	3488	3261	2936						52
7149				17833	18245	13943	10365	4341						53
4974				9638	12199	10540	7771	1648						54
5204				4625	8789	3818	2121	1904						55
				1641	1927	965	527							56
				15690	15656	11143	7269							57
				15[illegible]										58
4549	2011			3378	3648	2383	1618	1155	405					59
4818	3607			2065	1777	1328	1133	1157	559					60
				18907	18116	14881	16036							61
				9595	8886	7007	4924							62
				4190	6673	4073	2020					1		63
8807	5894			8294	10229	7485	6640	4839	2335					64
2044				308	519	267	212	168						65
1924		a2010	a733	1787	2550	1518	2457	1550		a910	a517			66
5442	1556			21610	17823	11835	9318	4106	1361					67
				21	122									68

llapoosa. (*l*) In 1868 Escambia from Baldwin and Conecuh. (*m*) In 1866 Etowah from Blount, n, Cherokee, DeKalb, Marshall, and St. Clair. (*n*) In 1868 Geneva from Coffee and Dale; in 1869-'70 ed to Florida line. (*o*) In 1867 Hale from Greene, Marengo, Perry, and Tuscaloosa. (*p*) In 1850 k, name changed to Winston. (*q*) In 1866 Lee from Chambers, Macon, Russell, and Tallapoosa. 867 Sanford from Fayette and Marion.

TABLE VIII.—*Population by Counties at each Census—ARKANSAS.*

	Counties.	AGGREGATE.							WHITE.	
		1870.	1860.	1850.	1840.	1830.	1820.	1810.	1870.	1860.
	The State	484471	435450	209897	97574	30388	[*18] 14255	a1062	362115	324143
1	Arkansas	8268	8844	3245	1346	1426	1260	a1062	3982	3923
2	Ashley	8042	8590	2058					4278	4829
3	Benton	13831	9306	3710	2228				13640	8905
4	Boone (c)	7032							6958	
5	Bradley	8646	8388	3829					6117	5698
6	Calhoun	3853	4103						2753	3122
7	Carroll (c) (d)	5780	9383	4614	2844				5743	9053
8	Chicot	7214	9234	5115	3806	1165			1816	1722
9	Clarke	11953	9735	4070	2309	1369	1040		8461	7510
10	Columbia	11397	12449						7679	8843
11	Conway	8112	6697	3583	2892	982			7482	5895
12	Craighead	4577	3066						4334	2978
13	Crawford	8957	7850	7960	4266	2440			7961	6996
14	Crittenden (h)	3831	4920	2648	1561	1272			1253	2573
15	Cross (h)	3915							2626	
16	Dallas	5707	8283	6877					3956	4788
17	Desha	6125	6459	2911	1598				2185	2655
18	Drew	9960	9078	3276					6106	5581
19	Franklin	9627	7298	3972	2665				8976	6330
20	Fulton	4843	4024	1819					4758	3926
21	Grant (e)	3943							3604	
22	Greene	7573	5843	2593	1586				7417	5654
23	Hempstead (f)	13768	13989	7672	4921	2512	[*2] 2246		7439	8589
24	Hot Springs (e)	5877	5635	3609	1907	458			5626	5019
25	Independence	14566	14307	7767	3669	2031			13658	12970
26	Izard	6806	7215	3213	2240	1266			6624	6831
27	Jackson (j)	7268	10493	3086	1540	333			5656	7957
28	Jefferson (e)	15733	14971	5834	2566	772			5356	7813
29	Johnson	9152	7612	5227	3433				8539	6639
30	Lafayette	9139	8464	5220	2200	748			3981	4146
31	Lawrence (i)	5981	9372	5274	2835	2806	[*10] 5592		5735	8875
32	Little River (f)	3236							1358	
33	Madison (d)	8231	7740	4823	2775				8081	7444
34	Marion (c)	3979	6192	2308	1325				3960	5993
35	Miller (g)					356	999			
36	Mississippi	3633	3895	2368	1410				2662	2434
37	Monroe	8336	5657	2049	936	461			5135	3431
38	Montgomery	2984	3633	1958					2864	3541
39	Newton	4374	3393	1758					4365	3369
40	Ouachita	12975	12936	9591					7511	8457
41	Perry	2685	2465	978					2395	2162
42	Phillips	15372	14877	6935	3547	1152	[*4] 1197		4871	5931
43	Pike	3788	4025	1861	969				3367	3798
44	Poinsett (h)	1720	3621	2308	1320				1494	2535
45	Polk	3376	4262	1263					3323	4090
46	Pope	8386	7883	4710	2850	1483			7811	6965
47	Prairie	5604	8854	2097					3793	6015
48	Pulaski	32066	11699	5657	5350	2395	[*2] 1921		18348	8187
49	Randolph	7466	6261	3275	2196				7109	5902
50	Saline (e)	3911	6640	3903	2061				3726	5891
51	Scott	7483	5145	3083	1694				7362	4930
52	Searcy	5614	5271	1979	936				5584	5178
53	Sebastian	12940	9238						11545	8555
54	Sevier (f)	4492	10516	4240	2810	634			3523	7150
55	Sharpe (i)	5400							5286	
56	St. Francis (h) (j)	6714	8672	4479	2499	1505			4368	6031
57	Union	10571	12288	10298	2889	640			5673	5957
58	Van Buren	5107	5357	2864	1518				4988	5157
59	Washington	17266	14673	9970	7148	2182			16590	13106
60	White	10347	8316	2619	929				9146	6881
61	Woodruff (j)	6891							4205	
62	Yell	8048	6333	3341					7281	5335

(*) All other persons, except Indians not taxed.

(a) Then in the Territory of Louisiana, and returned as follows: "Settlements of Hopefield and St. Francis, white 159, free colored 0, slave 29, total 188; settlements on the *Arkansas*, white 765, free colored 2, slave 107, total 874."

(c) In 1869 Boone from Carroll and Marion.

TABLE VIII.—*Population by Counties at each Census—ARKANSAS.*

ITE—Continued.				COLORED.							CHI-NESE.	INDIAN.		
0.	1830.	1820.	1810.	1870.	1860.	1850.	1840.	1830.	1820.	1810.	1870.	1870.	1860.	
74	25671	12579	a924	122169	111259	47708	20400	4717	1076	138	98	89	48	
80	1044	1076	a924	4212	4921	1531	366	382	184	138	74			1
				3764	3761	649								2
50				182	385	202	178					9	16	3
				74										4
				2529	2690	1228								5
				1100	981									6
07				37	330	223	137							7
05	868			5393	7512	3993	2701	277			5			8
22	1264	970		3492	2219	957	687	105	70					9
				3718	3604									10
95	895			630	802	244	197	87						11
				253	88									12
14	2080			989	864	1025	652	360				8		13
96	1101			2575	2347	806	465	171				3		14
				1280										15
				1751	3495	2544								16
55				3934	3804	1226	443				5	1		17
				3854	3497	915								18
57				651	968	475	408							19
				85	88	51								20
				339										21
36				156	189	63	50							22
23	1987	1753		6329	5400	2492	1998	525	493					23
55	404			650	616	372	252	54				1		24
46	1724			908	1337	840	523	307						25
99	1177			182	382	196	141	89					2	26
58	316			1612	2536	569	282	17						27
51	606			10167	7158	2637	1015	166			10			28
39				613	973	738	594							29
55	405			5158	4318	3320	1645	343						30
62	2473	5073		246	497	392	273	333	519					31
				1878										32
92				150	296	164	83							33
21				19	269	255	104							34
	301	917						55	82					35
90				971	1461	872	510							36
96	386			3200	2226	398	150	75				1		37
				120	92	67								38
				9	24	54								39
				5458	4479	3306						6		40
				290	303	21								41
25	1015	1052		10501	8945	2594	922	137	145				1	42
50				421	227	110	109							43
53				225	1086	282	67					1		44
				45	172	67						8		45
26	1272			575	978	479	224	211						46
				1811	2839	285								47
61	1928	1738		13708	3512	1151	1389	467	183		4	6		48
73				357	359	246	223							49
92				185	749	509	399							50
42				121	215	162	152							51
43				30	93	29	3							52
				1354	681							41	2	53
76	568			968	3366	1403	734	66				1		54
				114										55
92	1368			2446	2621	709	367	137						56
41	462			4896	6331	4772	908	178						57
59				119	200	103	59							58
46	2007			674	1540	1213	902	175				2	27	59
41				1200	1435	310	88					1		60
				2686										61
				767	998	439								62

0 part of Madison attached to Carroll.
9 Grant from Hot Springs, Jefferson, and Saline.
57 Little River from Hempstead and Sevier.
southwestern county of the State. The part of it north of Red River now in Indian Terri- part south of Red River now in Texas.
2 Cross from Crittenden, Poinsett, and St. Francis.
8 Sharpe from Lawrence.
2 Woodruff from Jackson and St. Francis.

TABLE VIII.—*Population by Counties at each Census—CALIFORNIA.*

	Counties.	AGGREGATE.			WHITE.		
		1870.	1860.	1850.	1870.	1860.	1850.
	The State	560247	379994	92597	499424	323177	91635
1	Alameda	24237	8927	....	22106	8548	....
2	Alpine (d)	685	....	....	676	....	....
3	Amador (d)	9582	10930	....	7883	8252	....
4	Butte	11403	12106	3574	9197	9737	3541
5	Calaveras (d)	8895	16299	16884	7405	12546	16802
6	Colusa	6165	2274	115	5389	2165	115
7	Contra Costa	8461	5328	(e)	8271	5185	....
8	Del Norte	2022	1993	....	1009	1341	....
9	El Dorado (d)	10309	20562	20057	8589	15515	19908
10	Fresno	6336	4605	....	3259	909	....
11	Humboldt	6140	2694	....	6025	2498	....
12	Inyo	1956	....	....	1608	....	....
13	Kern (g)	2925	....	....	2193	....	....
14	Klamath	1686	1803	....	1081	1220	....
15	Lake (h)	2969	....	....	2925	....	....
16	Lassen (i)	1327	....	....	1309	....	....
17	Los Angeles	15309	11333	3530	14720	9221	3518
18	Marin	6903	3334	323	6394	3097	321
19	Mariposa	4572	6243	4379	3364	4303	4184
20	Mendocino (k)	7545	3967	55	6865	2905	55
21	Merced	2807	1141	....	2548	1114	....
22	Mono (d) (l)	430	....	....	386	....	....
23	Monterey	9876	4739	1872	9429	4305	1854
24	Napa (h)	7163	5521	405	6725	5448	405
25	Nevada	19134	16446	....	16334	14138	....
26	Placer	11357	13270	....	8850	10819	....
27	Plumas (g) (i)	4489	4363	....	3571	3851	....
28	Sacramento	26830	24142	9087	22725	21692	8875
29	San Bernardino	3988	5551	....	3964	2504	....
30	San Diego	4951	4324	798	4838	1249	790
31	San Francisco (o)	149473	56802	(e)	136059	52866	....
32	San Joaquin (p)	21050	9435	3647	19193	9166	3616
33	San Luis Obispo	4772	1782	336	4567	1621	335
34	San Mateo (o)	6635	3214	....	6098	3088	....
35	Santa Barbara	7784	3543	1185	7484	3178	1181
36	Santa Clara	26246	11912	(e)	24536	11646	....
37	Santa Cruz	8743	4944	643	8532	4688	643
38	Shasta (i)	4173	4360	378	3529	3895	378
39	Sierra	5619	11387	....	4781	9192	....
40	Siskiyou	6848	7629	....	5329	6992	....
41	Solano	16871	7169	580	15870	7092	543
42	Sonoma	19819	11867	560	19184	11587	559
43	Stanislaus (p)	6499	2245	....	6189	2002	....
44	Sutter (g)	5030	3390	3444	4791	3348	3424
45	Tehama	3587	4044	....	3166	3342	....
46	Trinity	3213	5125	1635	1951	3370	1617
47	Tulare	4533	4638	....	4391	3202	....
48	Tuolumne (p)	8150	16229	8351	6556	14095	8288
49	Yolo (g)	9899	4716	1086	9318	4683	1076
50	Yuba	10851	13668	9673	8362	11582	9007

(*a*) Including 33 Japanese.
(*d*) In 1863 Alpine from Amador, Calaveras, El Dorado, and Mono.
(*e*) The returns of 1850 for Contra Costa and Santa Clara were lost on the way to the Census Office, and those for San Francisco were destroyed by fire. The corrected State census of 1852 gives the population of these three counties as follows: Contra Costa, 2,786; San Francisco, 36,154; and Santa Clara, 6,764; and gives the total population of the State (save El Dorado, not returned) at 215,122. El Dorado was estimated at 40,000, which would make the total probable population at that date 255,122. (*Vide* Doc. No. 14, Appendix to Senate Journal, 4th session legislature of California.)
(*f*) Including 22 Japanese.
(*g*) In 1865 organized.

TABLE VIII.—*Population by Counties at each Census—CALIFORNIA.*

COLORED.			CHINESE.		INDIAN.		
1870.	1860.	1850.	1870.	1860.	1870.	1860.	
4272	4086	962	a49310	34933	7241	17798	
81	55	....	1939	193	111	131	1
1	....	....	8	....	....	....	2
73	88	....	1627	2568	....	29	3
84	71	32	2082	2177	40	121	4
31	95	99	1441	3657	18	1	5
81	95	....	271	9	494	75	6
21	27	....	160	2	9	114	7
12	49	....	217	338	784	395	8
129	277	140	f1589	4762	6	8	9
15	3	....	487	369	2635	3994	10
....	6	....	39	37	76	153	11
8	....	....	29	....	311	....	12
4	....	....	143	....	585	....	13
2	4	....	549	533	61	49	14
2	....	....	119	....	23	....	15
....	....	....	17	....	1	....	16
124	87	12	f236	11	219	2814	17
22	23	2	361	4	126	219	18
99	90	195	1084	1843	34	7	19
9	3	....	129	5	542	1054	20
36	23	....	186	....	37	4	21
....	....	....	42	....	2	....	22
16	17	18	230	6	201	411	23
109	55	....	263	17	66	1	24
165	156	....	2627	2147	8	8	25
95	52	....	2410	2392	2	7	26
2	5	....	911	369	5	166	27
475	468	212	m3596	1731	34	251	28
8	19	....	16	....	....	[illegible]	29
15	8	8	70	....	28	[illegible]	30
[illegible]	1176	....	n12030	2719	54	41	31
283	126	31	[illegible]	139	5	4	32
9	12	1	59	....	137	142	33
10	68	....	519	6	8	52	34
38	....	4	109	....	153	365	35
173	87	....	1525	22	12	157	36
53	32	....	156	6	2	218	37
44	42	....	574	415	26	8	38
28	57	....	810	2206	....	....	39
29	71	....	1440	515	50	51	40
78	42	37	920	14	3	21	41
77	85	1	473	51	85	144	42
4	45	....	306	192	....	6	43
31	30	20	208	2	....	10	44
73	42	....	294	104	54	656	45
23	17	18	1099	1638	140	100	46
39	23	....	99	13	4	1340	47
67	166	63	1524	1962	3	6	48
69	27	10	395	6	117	....	49
152	233	66	2337	1781	....	72	50

) In 1863 Lake from Napa.
In 1863 Lassen from Plumas and Shasta.
) Including 2 Japanese.
) In 1860 organized.
In 1863 organized.
) Including 1 Japanese.
) Including 8 Japanese.
) In 1857 San Mateo from San Francisco.
) In 1854 Stanislaus from San Joaquin and Tuolumne.

TABLE VIII.—*Population by Counties at each Census—CONNECTICUT.*

	Counties.	AGGREGATE.									WHITE.		
		1870.	1860.	1850.	1840.	1830.	1820.	1810.	1800.	1790.	1870.	1860.	1850.
	The State	537454	460147	370792	309978	297675	*100 275148	261942	251002	237946	527549	451504	363099
1	Fairfield	95276	77476	59775	49917	47010	*5 42734	40950	38208	36250	93582	75800	58319
2	Hartford	109007	89962	69967	55629	51131	47264	44733	42147	38029	107252	88643	68707
3	Litchfield	48727	47318	45253	40448	42858	*94 41173	41375	41214	38755	47648	46207	44222
4	Middlesex	36099	30859	27216	24879	24844	*1 22404	20723	19847	18855	35722	30522	26927
5	New Haven	121257	97345	65588	48582	43847	39616	37064	32162	30830	118517	95223	64159
6	New London	66570	61731	51821	44463	42201	35943	34707	34883	33200	65010	60387	50313
7	Tolland (*a*)	22000	21177	20091	17980	18702	14330	13779	14319	13106	21801	20920	19946
8	Windham (*a*)	38518	34279	31081	28080	27082	31684	28611	28222	28921	38017	33802	30506

(*) All other persons, except Indians not taxed.

(*a*) In the official census of 1860, 468 whites, belonging to the town of Mansfield, Tolland County, were published as of Windham, Windham County. The totals of Tolland County have here been increased 468, and those of Windham County decreased 468.

TABLE VIII.—*Population by Counties at each Census—DELAWARE.*

	Counties.	AGGREGATE.									WHITE.		
		1870.	1860.	1850.	1840.	1830.	1820.	1810.	1800.	1790.	1870.	1860.	1850.
	The State	125015	112216	91532	78085	76748	72749	72674	64273	*a*59094	102221	90589	71169
1	Kent	29804	27804	22816	19872	19913	20793	20495	19554	18920	22640	20330	16084
2	New Castle	63515	54797	42780	33120	29720	27899	24429	25361	*a*19686	53323	46355	34765
3	Sussex	31696	29615	25936	25093	27115	24057	27750	19358	20488	26258	23904	20320

(*a*) It will be observed that the several classes of New Castle County (white, free colored, and slave) exceed the total of the county here given by 2. The error comes from the original return of the marshal in respect to this county. It is impossible to ascertain, by reference to any printed or written document, whether the error is in the items or the totals. The totals of the county and of the State

TABLE VIII.—*Population by Counties at each Census—CONNECTICUT.*

White—Continued.						Colored. (c) (d)									
1840.	1830.	1820.	1810.	1800.	1790.	1870.	1860.	1850.	1840.	1830.	1820.	1810.	1800.	1790.	
301856	289603	267181	255179	244721	232374	9668	8627	7693	8122	8072	7967	6763	6281	5572	
48380	45614	41353	39682	36975	35126	1680	1676	1456	1337	1306	1381	1268	1233	1124	1
54347	49989	46057	43796	41337	57336	1732	1319	1260	1282	1142	1207	937	810	693	2
39410	41772	40288	40587	40511	38199	1052	1114	1031	1038	1086	885	788	703	556	3
24439	24322	21895	20353	19524	18494	372	337	289	440	522	509	370	323	361	4
47135	42670	38378	36163	31276	29072	2734	2113	1429	1447	1177	1238	901	886	858	5
42723	40368	34249	33051	33438	31885	1419	1344	1508	1740	1833	1694	1656	1445	1315	6
17741	18436	14080	13550	14107	12965	199	256	145	239	266	250	220	212	141	7
27481	26432	30881	27988	27553	28307	460	471	575	599	650	803	623	669	524	8

(c) At 1870, Chinese 2, Indians 235, as follows: Fairfield, 14 Indians; Hartford, 2 Indians and 1 Chinese; Litchfield, 97 Indians; Middlesex, 5 Indians; New Haven, 6 Indians; New London, 141 Indians; Windham, 40 Indians and 1 Chinese. At 1860, 16 Indians, as follows: in New Haven, 9; in Tolland, 1; in Windham, 6.

(d) At the census of 1840 thirty-seven other slaves were returned by the marshal, which have been omitted from this table, being then captured in the slaver Amistad and not a portion of the population of Connecticut.

TABLE VIII.—*Population by Counties at each Census—DELAWARE.*

White—Continued.						Colored.									
1840.	1830.	1820.	1810.	1800.	1790.	1870.	1860.	1850.	1840.	1830.	1820.	1810.	1800.	1790.	
58561	57601	55282	55361	49852	46310	22794	21627	20363	19524	19147	17467	17313	14421	12786	
13618	13654	14190	14151	13823	14050	7164	7474	6732	6254	6259	6603	6344	5731	4870	1
25806	23226	22360	19463	20769	16487	10192	8442	8015	7314	6494	5539	4966	4592	3201	2
19137	20721	18732	21747	15260	15773	5438	5711	5616	5956	6394	5325	6003	4098	4715	3

have, therefore, been allowed to stand as they were printed in the official census of 1790. In Table I the items have been assumed to be correct, and the totals, 19,098 and 58,090, have been taken to be the correct totals of the county and of the State.

TABLE VIII.—Population by Counties at each Census—FLORIDA.

	Counties.	AGGREGATE.				
		1870.	1860.	1850.	1840.	1830.
	The State	187748	140424	87445	54477	34730
1	Alachua	17328	8232	2524	2282	2204
2	Baker (d)	1325				
3	Benton (a)			926		
4	Bradford (d)	3671				
5	Brevard (f)	1216	246			
6	Calhoun	998	1446	1377	1142	
7	Clay	2098	1914			
8	Columbia	7335	4646	4808	2102	
9	Dade (f)	85	83	159	446	
10	Duval	11921	5074	4539	4156	1970
11	Escambia	7817	5768	4351	3993	b2518
12	Franklin	1256	1904	1561	1030	
13	Gadsden	9802	9396	8784	5992	4895
14	Hamilton	5749	4154	2511	1464	553
15	Hernando (a)	2938	*1200			
16	Hillsborough	3216	2981	2377	452	
17	Holmes	1572	1386	1305		
18	Jackson	9528	10209	6639	4681	c3907
19	Jefferson	13398	9876	7718	5713	3312
20	La Fayette	1783	2068			
21	Leon	15236	12343	11442	10713	6494
22	Levy	2018	1781	465		
23	Liberty	1050	1457			
24	Madison	11121	7779	5490	2644	585
25	Manatee	1931	854			
26	Marion	10804	8609	3338		
27	Monroe	5657	2913	2645	f688	517
28	Mosquito (e)				73	733
29	Nassau	4247	3644	2164	1892	1511
30	New River (d)		3820			
31	Orange (e)	2195	987	466		
32	Polk (f)	3169				
33	Putnam	3821	2712	687		
34	Santa Rosa	3312	5480	2883		g868
35	St. John's	2618	3038	2525	2694	2538
36	St. Lucie (f)			139		
37	Sumter	2952	1549			
38	Suwannee	3556	2303			
39	Taylor	1453	1384			
40	Volusia (f)	1723	1158			
41	Wakulla	2506	2839	1955		
42	Walton	3041	3037	1817	1461	h1207
43	Washington	2302	2154	1950	859	i978

(*) Estimated.
(a) In 1850, Benton, now Hernando.
(b) West of Escambia River, including Santa Rosa Island.
(c) Excepting that part of Holmes Creek, and including that part of Washington on the Chipola and Appalachicola Rivers.
(d) Since 1860 New River absorbed by Baker and Bradford.
(e) Mosquito, now Orange.

TABLE VIII.—*Population by Counties at each Census—FLORIDA.*

WHITE.					COLORED.					INDIAN.	
1870.	1860.	1850.	1840.	1830.	1870.	1860.	1850.	1840.	1830.	1870.	No.
96057	77746	47203	27943	18385	91689	62677	40242	26534	16345	k2	
4935	3767	1617	1719	1592	12393	4465	907	563	612	....	1
1033	....	....	....	....	290	....	....	....	....	....	2
....	....	604	....	....	....	....	322	....	....	....	3
2247	....	....	....	....	824	....	....	....	....	....	4
1197	224	....	....	....	19	22	....	....	....	....	5
754	895	886	705	....	244	551	491	437	....	....	6
1699	1388	....	....	....	309	526	....	....	....	....	7
4107	2582	3541	1649	....	3228	2064	1267	453	....	....	8
72	80	147	412	....	13	3	12	34	....	....	9
5141	2925	2338	2250	866	6780	2149	2201	1906	1104	....	10
4937	3853	2644	2330	b1319	2880	2114	1707	1063	1199	....	11
781	1378	1184	782	....	475	526	377	248	....	....	12
3764	3981	3897	2637	2388	6038	5415	4887	3355	2307	....	13
3346	2734	1817	1034	492	2363	1420	694	430	61	....	14
2083	*1000	....	....	....	854	200	....	....	....	1	15
2670	2415	1706	437	....	546	566	671	15	....	....	16
1435	1871	1037	....	....	137	115	168	....	....	....	17
3930	5263	3075	2002	c2040	5598	4946	3564	2679	1867	....	18
3501	3498	2775	2162	1695	9897	6378	4943	3551	1617	....	19
1526	1490	....	....	....	197	578	....	....	....	....	20
2895	3194	3183	3461	3336	12341	9149	8259	7252	3158	....	21
1623	1331	320	....	....	395	430	145	....	....	....	22
797	935	....	....	....	323	522	....	....	....	....	23
4429	3521	2802	1442	262	6692	4258	2688	1202	263	....	24
1843	601	....	....	....	88	253	....	....	....	....	25
2946	3294	2068	....	....	7878	5315	1270	....	....	....	26
4631	2302	2088	516	368	1026	611	557	172	149	....	27
....	....	....	73	49	....	....	....	....	684	....	28
2277	1978	1061	954	672	1970	1066	1103	938	839	....	29
....	3075	....	....	....	....	745	....	....	....	....	30
1997	823	238	....	....	198	164	228	....	....	....	31
2687	....	....	....	....	482	....	....	....	....	....	32
2487	1634	473	....	....	1334	1078	214	....	....	....	33
2750	4048	2095	....	g506	562	1432	788	....	362	....	34
1937	1953	1417	1685	1336	681	1085	1108	1009	1202	....	35
....	....	111	....	....	....	....	28	....	....	....	36
1972	1000	....	....	....	980	549	....	....	....	....	37
2121	1467	....	....	....	1435	836	....	....	....	....	38
1374	1259	....	....	....	79	125	....	....	....	....	39
1395	861	....	....	....	328	297	....	....	....	....	40
1562	1672	1164	....	....	944	1167	791	....	....	....	41
2636	2584	1481	1189	h882	405	433	336	272	325	....	42
1928	1670	1434	504	i382	373	484	516	355	396	1	43

(*f*) Since 1850 Brevard, and parts of Dade, Polk, and Volusia have absorbed St. Lucie.
(*g*) Escambia and Walton, between Yellow and Escambia Rivers.
(*h*) Walton and Washington, between Choctawatchee and Yellow Rivers, including isthmus south of Choctawatchee, being in Washington.
(*i*) Washington, excepting that part on Chipola and Appalachicola Rivers, and including that part of Jackson west of Holmes Creek.
(*j*) City of Key West.
(*k*) At the census of 1860 only 1 Indian was returned who was on the schedule for Escambia County.

TABLE VIII.—*Population by Counties at each Census—GEORGIA.*

	Counties.	AGGREGATE.									WHITE.		
		1870.	1860.	1850.	1840.	1830.	1820.	1810.	1800.	1790.	1870.	1860.	1850.
	The State	1184109	1057286	906185	691392	516823	340985	252433	162686	82548	638926	591550	521572
1	Appling	5086	4190	2949	2052	1468	1264	.....	.....	.....	4110	3442	2529
2	Baker	6843	4985	8120	4226	1253	.....	.....	.....	.....	1868	1103	4351
3	Baldwin	10618	9078	8148	7250	7295	7734	6356	.....	.....	3844	4057	3513
4	Banks	4973	4707	.....	.....	.....	.....	.....	.....	.....	4032	3610	.....
5	Bartow	16566	.....	.....	.....	.....	.....	.....	.....	.....	11646	.....	.....
6	Berrien	4518	3475	.....	.....	.....	.....	.....	.....	.....	4037	3041	.....
7	Bibb	21255	16291	12699	9802	7154	.....	.....	.....	.....	9801	9456	7009
8	Brooks	8342	6356	.....	.....	.....	.....	.....	.....	.....	4111	3067	.....
9	Bryan	5252	4015	3424	3182	3139	3021	2827	2836	.....	1647	1636	1164
10	Bulloch	5610	5668	4300	3102	2587	2578	2305	1913	.....	3868	3506	2540
11	Burke	17679	17165	16100	13176	11833	11577	10858	9504	9467	4213	5013	5118
12	Butts	6941	6455	6488	5308	4944	.....	.....	.....	.....	3490	3373	3060
13	Calhoun	5503	4913	.....	.....	.....	.....	.....	.....	.....	2026	2174	.....
14	Camden	4615	5420	6319	6075	4578	4311	3941	1681	305	1458	1276	2060
15	Campbell	9176	8301	7232	5370	3323	.....	.....	.....	.....	6560	6289	5718
16	Carroll	11782	11991	9357	5252	3419	.....	.....	.....	.....	10473	10116	8222
17	Cass (a)	.....	15724	13300	9390	.....	.....	.....	.....	.....	.....	11433	10271
18	Catoosa	4409	5082	.....	.....	.....	.....	.....	.....	.....	3793	4368	.....
19	Charlton	1897	1780	.....	.....	.....	.....	.....	.....	.....	1406	1223	.....
20	Chatham	41279	31043	23901	18801	14127	14737	13540	12946	10769	16760	15511	9152
21	Chattahoochee	6059	5797	.....	.....	.....	.....	.....	.....	.....	2854	3034	.....
22	Chattooga	6902	7165	6815	3438	.....	.....	.....	.....	.....	5209	5107	5131
23	Cherokee	10399	11291	12800	5895	.....	.....	.....	.....	.....	9117	10047	11630
24	Clarke	12941	11218	11119	10522	10176	8767	7628	.....	.....	6488	5539	5513
25	Clay	5493	4893	.....	.....	.....	.....	.....	.....	.....	2644	2626	.....
26	Clayton	5477	4466	.....	.....	.....	.....	.....	.....	.....	3734	3240	.....
27	Clinch	3945	3063	637	.....	.....	.....	.....	.....	.....	3437	2609	506
28	Cobb	13814	14242	13843	7539	.....	.....	.....	.....	.....	10503	10410	11568
29	Coffee	3192	2879	.....	.....	.....	.....	.....	.....	.....	2514	2206	.....
30	Colquitt	1654	1316	.....	.....	.....	.....	.....	.....	.....	1517	1195	.....
31	Columbia	13529	11860	11961	11356	12606	12695	11242	8345	.....	4080	3511	3617
32	Coweta	15875	14703	13635	10364	5003	.....	.....	.....	.....	7856	7433	8202
33	Crawford	7557	7693	8984	7981	5313	.....	.....	.....	.....	3234	3407	4342
34	Dade	3033	3069	2680	1364	.....	.....	.....	.....	.....	2788	2765	2532
35	Dawson	4369	3856	.....	.....	.....	.....	.....	.....	.....	4032	3526	.....
36	Decatur	15183	11922	8262	5872	3854	.....	.....	.....	.....	7465	5085	4615
37	De Kalb	10014	7806	14328	10467	10042	.....	.....	.....	.....	7352	5798	11372
38	Dooly	9790	8017	8361	4427	2135	.....	.....	.....	.....	4035	4845	5580
39	Dougherty	11517	8295	.....	.....	.....	.....	.....	.....	.....	2093	2207	.....
40	Early	6998	6149	7246	5444	2051	768	.....	.....	.....	2826	2092	3716
41	Echols	1978	1491	.....	.....	.....	.....	.....	.....	.....	1513	1177	.....
42	Effingham	4214	4755	3864	3075	2924	3018	2586	2072	2424	2507	2572	2007
43	Elbert	9249	10433	12959	11125	12354	11788	12156	10094	.....	4386	4697	6676
44	Emanuel	6134	5081	4577	3129	2673	2928	.....	.....	.....	4431	3748	3301
45	Fannin	5429	5139	.....	.....	.....	.....	.....	.....	.....	5285	4966	.....
46	Fayette	8221	7047	8709	6191	5504	.....	.....	.....	.....	5683	5022	6741
47	Floyd	17230	15195	8205	4441	.....	.....	.....	.....	.....	11473	9209	5202
48	Forsyth	7983	7749	8850	5619	.....	.....	.....	.....	.....	6862	6851	7812
49	Franklin	7893	7393	11513	9886	10107	9040	10815	6859	1041	6034	6038	9076
50	Fulton	33446	14427	.....	.....	.....	.....	.....	.....	.....	18104	11441	.....
51	Gilmer	6644	6724	8440	2536	.....	.....	.....	.....	.....	6527	6553	8236
52	Glascock	2736	2437	.....	.....	.....	.....	.....	.....	.....	1917	1654	.....
53	Glynn	5376	3889	4933	5302	4567	3418	3417	1874	413	1926	1048	696
54	Gordon	9268	10146	5984	.....	.....	.....	.....	.....	.....	7726	8001	5156
55	Greene	12454	12652	13068	11690	12549	13589	11679	10761	5405	4298	4229	4744
56	Gwinnett	12431	12940	11257	10804	13289	4589	.....	.....	.....	10272	10358	8052
57	Habersham	6322	5966	8895	7961	10671	3145	.....	.....	.....	5373	5136	7675
58	Hall	9607	9366	8713	7875	11748	5086	.....	.....	.....	8317	8091	7370
59	Hancock	11317	12044	11578	9659	11820	12734	13330	14456	.....	3645	3871	4210
60	Haralson	4004	3039	.....	.....	.....	.....	.....	.....	.....	3685	2816	.....
61	Harris	13284	13736	14721	13933	5105	.....	.....	.....	.....	5791	5979	6700
62	Hart	6783	6137	.....	.....	.....	.....	.....	.....	.....	4841	4603	.....
63	Heard	7866	7805	6923	5329	.....	.....	.....	.....	.....	5218	4979	4520
64	Henry	10102	10702	14726	11756	10566	.....	.....	.....	.....	6269	6175	9742
65	Houston	20406	15611	16450	9711	7369	.....	.....	.....	.....	5071	4828	6510
66	Irwin	1837	1699	3334	2038	1180	411	.....	.....	.....	1541	1459	2983
67	Jackson	11181	10605	9768	8522	9004	8355	10569	7736	.....	7471	7249	6808
68	Jasper	10439	10743	11486	11111	13131	14614	7573	.....	.....	3884	3771	4321
69	Jefferson	12190	10219	9131	7254	7309	7054	6111	5684	.....	4247	4133	3717
70	Johnson	2964	2919	.....	.....	.....	.....	.....	.....	.....	2049	2003	.....
71	Jones	9436	9107	10224	10065	13345	16570	8597	.....	.....	2991	3034	3699
72	Laurens	7834	6998	6442	5585	5580	5436	2210	.....	.....	4180	3723	3479
73	Lee	9567	7196	6660	4520	1680	.....	.....	.....	.....	1924	2242	3023
74	Liberty	7688	8367	7926	7241	7233	6695	6228	5313	5355	2428	2284	2002

TABLE VIII.—*Population by Counties at each Census*—*GEORGIA.*

White—Continued.						Colored. (b)									
1840.	1830.	1820.	1810.	1800.	1790.	1870.	1860.	1850.	1840.	1830.	1820.	1810.	1800.	1790.	
407695	296806	189566	145414	102261	52886	545142	465698	384613	283697	220017	151419	107019	60425	29662	
1752	1284	1176	......	......	......	976	748	429	297	184	86	......	......	......	1
2447	977	......	......	......	......	4955	3492	3780	1779	270	......	......	......	......	2
3075	2726	3487	3790	......	......	6774	5021	4628	4173	4538	4247	2568	......	......	3
......	......	......	......	......	......	921	1037	......	......	......	......	......	......	......	4
......	......	......	......	......	......	4719	......	......	......	......	......	......	......	......	5
......	......	......	......	......	......	460	434	......	......	......	......	......	......	......	6
5355	4139	......	......	......	......	11424	6831	5690	4447	3015	......	......	......	......	7
......	......	......	......	......	......	4231	5284	......	......	......	......	......	......	......	8
897	729	750	557	528	......	3005	2379	2260	2285	2416	2262	2270	2308	......	9
2147	1933	1877	1861	1629	......	1744	2162	1460	955	654	701	444	284	......	10
4609	3066	5673	6091	6323	7064	13436	19132	10382	8567	6787	5904	4767	2981	2403	11
3285	3254	......	......	......	......	3448	3082	2808	2023	1630	......	......	......	......	12
......	......	......	......	......	......	3477	2730	......	......	......	......	......	......	......	13
2004	1438	1808	1207	936	221	3157	4144	4250	4071	3120	2533	2734	745	84	14
4626	2204	......	......	......	......	2587	2012	1514	844	620	......	......	......	......	15
4725	2724	......	......	......	......	1309	1875	1105	527	695	......	......	......	......	16
7381	......	......	......	......	......	......	4291	3029	2009	......	......	......	......	......	17
......	......	......	......	......	......	616	714	......	......	......	......	......	......	......	18
......	......	......	......	......	......	401	557	......	......	......	......	......	......	......	19
6601	4236	4509	3214	3673	2456	24518	15532	14749	12000	9901	10168	10326	9273	8313	20
......	......	......	......	......	......	3405	2763	......	......	......	......	......	......	......	21
2624	......	......	......	......	......	1303	2058	1684	814	......	......	......	......	......	22
5401	......	......	......	......	......	1281	1244	1170	494	......	......	......	......	......	23
5603	5438	5285	5000	......	......	6453	5679	5606	4919	4738	3482	2698	......	......	24
......	......	......	......	......	......	2649	2267	......	......	......	......	......	......	......	25
......	......	......	......	......	......	1743	1226	......	......	......	......	......	......	......	26
......	......	......	......	......	......	507	454	131	......	......	......	......	......	......	27
6630	......	......	......	......	......	3217	3832	2275	909	......	......	......	......	......	28
......	......	......	......	......	......	678	673	......	......	......	......	......	......	......	29
......	......	......	......	......	......	137	121	......	......	......	......	......	......	......	30
3920	4467	5213	5220	5321	......	9449	8349	8344	7436	8130	7482	6013	3024	......	31
7263	3631	......	......	......	......	8019	7270	5433	3101	1372	......	......	......	......	32
4412	3501	......	......	......	......	4273	4286	4643	3569	1732	......	......	......	......	33
1285	......	......	......	......	......	245	304	148	79	......	......	......	......	......	34
......	......	......	......	......	......	337	336	......	......	......	......	......	......	......	35
3478	2541	......	......	......	......	7718	5937	3641	2394	1313	......	......	......	......	36
8456	6376	......	......	......	......	2662	2008	2956	2011	1606	......	......	......	......	37
3234	1787	......	......	......	......	4855	4072	2781	1193	348	......	......	......	......	38
......	......	......	......	......	......	9424	6088	......	......	......	......	......	......	......	39
3120	1505	551	......	......	......	4172	4057	3330	2324	546	217	......	......	......	40
......	......	......	......	......	......	465	314	......	......	......	......	......	......	......	41
1633	1707	1654	1575	1310	1674	1704	2183	1857	1142	1217	1364	1011	762	750	42
6077	6501	6629	7532	7255	......	4868	5736	6283	5048	5853	5150	4624	2630	......	43
2500	2179	2526	......	......	......	1703	1333	996	629	494	402	......	......	......	44
......	......	......	......	......	......	144	144	......	......	......	......	......	......	......	45
4827	4266	......	......	......	......	2538	2025	1568	1361	1238	......	......	......	......	46
3165	......	......	......	......	......	5753	5936	3003	1275	......	......	......	......	......	47
5060	......	......	......	......	......	1121	838	1038	559	......	......	......	......	......	48
7754	7094	7240	9143	5292	885	1859	1355	2437	2132	2413	1800	1672	967	156	49
......	......	......	......	......	......	15282	2986	......	......	......	......	......	......	......	50
2441	......	......	......	......	......	117	170	204	95	......	......	......	......	......	51
......	......	......	......	......	......	819	783	......	......	......	......	......	......	......	52
891	597	643	564	779	193	3450	2841	4237	4411	3970	2775	2853	1095	220	53
......	......	......	......	......	......	1536	2145	822	......	......	......	......	......	......	54
4641	5026	6509	6308	7097	4020	8156	8423	8324	7019	7523	6090	5281	3064	1385	55
8552	10249	4070	......	......	......	2159	2582	2305	2252	2340	539	......	......	......	56
7007	9457	2868	......	......	......	949	830	1250	954	914	277	......	......	......	57
6773	10563	4681	......	......	......	1200	1275	1343	1102	1165	405	......	......	......	58
3697	4603	5847	6849	9605	......	7672	8173	7368	5962	7217	6887	6481	4851	......	59
......	......	......	......	......	......	319	223	......	......	......	......	......	......	......	60
7482	2831	......	......	......	......	7493	7757	8012	6451	2274	......	......	......	......	61
......	......	......	......	......	......	1942	1534	......	......	......	......	......	......	......	62
3749	......	......	......	......	......	2648	2826	2403	158	......	......	......	......	......	63
8424	7989	......	......	......	......	3823	4527	4984	3332	2377	......	......	......	......	64
4861	5161	......	......	......	......	13282	10783	9046	1830	2208	......	......	......	......	65
1772	1066	372	......	......	......	296	246	451	266	114	39	......	......	......	66
5094	6180	6346	8712	6828	......	3710	3356	2960	2528	2821	2003	1827	1408	......	67
4921	6767	9086	5713	......	......	6555	6072	7165	6100	6364	5528	1830	......	......	68
2477	3603	3932	3746	4004	......	7943	6088	5411	4377	3706	3122	2365	1676	......	69
......	......	......	......	......	......	917	856	......	......	......	......	......	......	......	70
4117	6471	9620	5571	......	......	6445	6023	6725	5618	6874	6250	3026	......	......	71
3078	3290	3450	1714	......	......	3654	2277	[illegible]	2767	2889	1986	[illegible]	......	......	72
2402	1369	......	......	......	......	7613	4971	3555	2051	311	......	......	......	......	73
1643	1588	1641	1352	1346	1567	5260	6095	5821	5536	5615	5654	1876	3967	4032	74

TABLE VIII.—*Population by Counties at each Census—GEORGIA*—Continued.

	Counties.	AGGREGATE.									WHITE.		
		1870.	1860.	1850.	1840.	1830.	1820.	1810.	1800.	1790.	1870.	1860.	1850.
75	Lincoln	5413	5466	5998	5895	6145	6458	4555	4766	......	1797	1675	2187
76	Lowndes	8321	5249	7714	5574	2453	......	......	......	......	4276	2850	5339
77	Lumpkin	5161	4626	8955	5671	......	......	......	......	......	4629	4156	7995
78	Macon	11458	8449	7052	5045	......	......	......	......	......	3975	3575	4088
79	Madison	5227	5933	5703	4510	4646	3735	......	......	......	3646	3924	3763
80	Marion	8000	7390	10280	4812	1436	......	......	......	......	4169	3854	6667
81	McIntosh	4491	5546	6027	5360	4998	5129	3739	2660	......	1196	1429	1326
82	Meriwether	13756	15330	16476	14132	4422	......	......	......	......	6387	6578	8481
83	Miller	3091	1791	......	......	......	......	......	......	......	2135	1151	......
84	Milton	4284	4602	......	......	......	......	......	......	......	3818	3984	......
85	Mitchell	6633	4308	......	......	......	......	......	......	......	3683	2716	......
86	Monroe	17213	15953	16985	16275	16202	......	......	......	......	6409	5753	6810
87	Montgomery	3586	2997	2154	1616	1269	1869	2954	3180	......	2478	2014	1541
88	Morgan	10696	9997	10744	9121	12046	13520	8369	......	......	3637	2983	3034
89	Murray	6500	7083	14433	4695	......	......	......	......	......	5743	5639	12499
90	Muscogee	16663	16584	18578	11699	3508	......	......	......	......	7441	8906	10355
91	Newton	14615	14320	13296	11628	11155	......	......	......	......	8601	7822	8077
92	Oglethorpe	11782	11549	12259	10868	13618	14046	12297	9780	......	4641	4014	4382
93	Paulding	7639	7038	7039	2556	......	......	......	......	......	7083	6460	5560
94	Pickens	5317	4951	......	......	......	......	......	......	......	5188	4705	......
95	Pierce	2778	1973	......	......	......	......	......	......	......	1964	1740	......
96	Pike	10905	10078	14306	9176	6149	......	......	......	......	5099	5332	8689
97	Polk	7822	6295	......	......	......	......	......	......	......	5244	3853	......
98	Pulaski	11940	8744	6627	5389	4906	5283	2093	......	......	5055	4607	3784
99	Putnam	10461	10125	10794	10260	13261	15475	10029	......	......	3016	2956	3300
100	Quitman	4150	3499	......	......	......	......	......	......	......	1773	1870	......
101	Rabun	3256	3271	2448	1912	2176	524	......	......	......	3137	3061	2338
102	Randolph	10561	9571	12868	8276	2191	......	......	......	......	5084	5103	7857
103	Richmond	25724	21284	16246	11932	11644	8608	6189	5475	11317	13157	12405	8153
104	Schley	5129	4633	......	......	......	......	......	......	......	2278	2274	......
105	Scriven	9175	8274	6847	4794	4776	3941	4477	3019	......	4287	3742	3173
106	Spalding	10205	8699	......	......	......	......	......	......	......	5327	4826	......
107	Stewart	14204	13422	16027	12933	......	......	......	......	......	5104	5534	8649
108	Sumter	16559	9428	10322	5759	......	......	......	......	......	5020	4536	6469
109	Talbot	11913	13616	16534	15627	5940	......	......	......	......	4761	4994	7793
110	Taliaferro	4796	4583	5146	5190	4934	......	......	......	......	1809	1693	2031
111	Tatnall	4860	4352	3227	2724	2040	2644	2206	......	......	3580	3191	2378
112	Taylor	7143	5998	......	......	......	......	......	......	......	4181	3601	......
113	Telfair	3245	2713	3026	2763	2136	2104	744	......	......	2100	1877	2096
114	Terrell	9053	6232	......	......	......	......	......	......	......	3769	3343	......
115	Thomas	14523	10766	10103	6766	3299	......	......	......	......	6160	4488	4943
116	Towns	2780	2459	......	......	......	......	......	......	......	2623	2346	......
117	Troup	17632	16262	16879	15733	5799	......	......	......	......	6408	6223	7791
118	Twiggs	8545	8320	8179	8422	8031	10640	3405	......	......	2913	2930	3517
119	Union	5267	4413	7234	3152	......	......	......	......	......	5153	4295	6955
120	Upson	9430	9910	9424	9408	7013	......	......	......	......	4865	5015	4720
121	Walker	9925	10082	13109	6572	......	......	......	......	......	8396	8517	11408
122	Walton	11038	11074	10821	10209	10929	4192	1026	......	......	6876	6447	6895
123	Ware	2286	2200	3888	2323	1205	......	......	......	......	1834	1818	3397
124	Warren	10545	9820	12425	9789	10946	10630	8725	8329	......	4285	4347	6158
125	Washington	15842	13698	11766	10565	9820	10627	9940	10300	4552	7530	6143	5991
126	Wayne	2177	2268	1499	1258	963	1010	676	......	......	1798	1617	1088
127	Webster	4677	5030	......	......	......	......	......	......	......	2439	2741	......
128	White	4606	3315	......	......	......	......	......	......	......	4042	3041	......
129	Whitfield	10117	10047	......	......	......	......	......	......	......	8606	8314	......
130	Wilcox	2439	2115	......	......	......	......	......	......	......	1902	1692	......
131	Wilkes	11796	11420	12107	10148	14237	[*1] 17666	14887	13103	31500	3969	3434	3805
132	Wilkinson	9383	9376	8296	6842	6513	6992	2154	......	......	4684	5472	5551
133	Worth	3778	2763	......	......	......	......	......	......	......	2673	2118	......

(*) All other persons except Indians not taxed.
(*a*) Name changed to Bartow.

TABLE VIII.—*Population by Counties at each Census—GEORGIA*—Continued.

WHITE—Continued.						COLORED. (*b*)									
1840.	1830.	1820.	1810.	1800.	1790.	1870.	1860.	1850.	1840.	1830.	1820.	1810.	1800.	1790.	
2327	2824	3378	2331	3326	......	3616	3791	3811	3368	3321	3080	2224	1440	......	75
4304	2113	......	......	......	......	4045	2390	2375	1180	340	......	......	......	......	76
5143	......	......	......	......	......	462	470	960	528	......	......	......	......	......	77
3553	......	......	......	......	......	7483	4874	2964	1492	......	......	......	......	......	78
3185	3385	2829	......	......	......	1581	2009	1940	1385	1261	906	......	......	......	79
3741	1327	......	......	......	......	3830	3536	3613	1071	109	......	......	......	......	80
1348	1095	1343	761	831	......	3288	4117	4701	4012	3903	3786	2978	1829	......	81
8725	3018	......	......	......	......	7369	8752	7995	5407	1404	......	......	......	......	82
......	......	......	......	......	......	956	640	......	......	......	......	......	......	......	83
......	......	......	......	......	......	466	618	......	......	......	......	......	......	......	84
......	......	......	......	......	......	2950	1592	......	......	......	......	......	......	......	85
7804	8838	......	......	......	......	10804	10200	10175	8471	7364	......	......	......	......	86
1279	934	1165	2190	2742	......	1108	983	613	337	335	704	764	438	......	87
3461	5211	7463	5949	......	......	7058	7013	7110	5660	6835	6057	2420	......	......	88
3896	......	......	......	......	......	757	1444	1941	709	......	......	......	......	......	89
6930	2260	......	......	......	......	9220	7618	8223	4760	1248	......	......	......	......	90
7890	8122	......	......	......	......	6014	6498	5219	3738	3027	......	......	......	......	91
4506	5659	6703	6857	6686	......	7141	7535	7877	6362	7959	7343	5440	3094	......	92
2102	......	......	......	......	......	556	578	c1479	454	......	......	......	......	......	93
......	......	......	......	......	......	129	246	......	......	......	......	......	......	......	94
......	......	......	......	......	......	814	233	(*c*)	......	......	......	......	......	......	95
6595	4356	......	......	......	......	4906	4746	5620	2581	1793	......	......	......	......	96
......	......	......	......	......	......	2578	2442	......	......	......	......	......	......	......	97
2972	3123	3237	1553	......	......	5984	4137	2843	2417	1783	2046	540	......	......	98
3741	5513	8208	6771	......	......	7443	7169	7494	6519	7748	7267	3258	......	......	99
......	......	......	......	......	......	2377	1629	......	......	......	......	......	......	......	100
1828	2115	509	......	......	......	119	210	110	84	61	15	......	......	......	101
5586	1508	......	......	......	......	5477	4468	5011	2690	683	......	......	......	......	102
5630	5163	3667	2081	2728	7162	12565	8679	8093	6282	6481	4941	3508	2747	4155	103
......	......	......	......	......	......	2851	2359	......	......	......	......	......	......	......	104
2162	2387	2090	2657	2253	......	4888	4532	3674	2632	2389	1851	1820	766	......	105
......	......	......	......	......	......	4878	3873	......	......	......	......	......	......	......	106
8174	......	......	......	......	......	9100	7888	7378	4759	......	......	......	......	......	107
4115	......	......	......	......	......	10639	4892	3853	1644	......	......	......	......	......	108
8861	3839	......	......	......	......	7152	8622	8741	6766	2101	......	......	......	......	109
2295	2162	......	......	......	......	2987	2890	3095	2895	2772	......	......	......	......	110
1878	1520	2063	1600	......	......	1280	1161	849	846	520	581	606	......	......	111
......	......	......	......	......	......	2962	2397	......	......	......	......	......	......	......	112
2001	1569	1423	525	......	......	1145	836	930	762	567	681	219	......	......	113
......	......	......	......	......	......	5284	2889	......	......	......	......	......	......	......	114
3810	2127	......	......	......	......	8363	6278	5160	2956	1172	......	......	......	......	115
......	......	......	......	......	......	155	113	......	......	......	......	......	......	......	116
8682	3607	......	......	......	......	11224	10039	9088	7051	2192	......	......	......	......	117
4214	4495	7096	2756	......	......	5632	5390	4662	4208	3536	3544	649	......	......	118
3065	......	......	......	......	......	114	118	279	87	......	......	......	......	......	119
5536	4444	......	......	......	......	4565	4895	4704	3872	2569	......	......	......	......	120
5583	......	......	......	......	......	1529	1565	1701	989	......	......	......	......	......	121
6583	7762	3556	964	......	......	4162	4627	3926	3636	3167	636	62	......	......	122
2189	1141	......	......	......	......	452	382	291	134	64	......	......	......	......	123
5176	6152	6530	5659	6252	......	6260	5473	6267	4613	4794	4100	3066	2077	......	124
5962	5895	6697	6423	7181	3856	8312	6555	5775	4603	3925	3930	3517	3119	696	125
877	676	671	421	......	......	379	651	411	381	287	339	255	......	......	126
......	......	......	......	......	......	2238	2289	......	......	......	......	......	......	......	127
......	......	......	......	......	......	564	274	......	......	......	......	......	......	......	128
......	......	......	......	......	......	1511	1733	......	......	......	......	......	......	......	129
......	......	......	......	......	......	537	423	......	......	......	......	......	......	......	130
3630	5265	7838	7602	8032	24052	7827	7986	8302	6518	8972	9768	7285	5071	7448	131
4957	4598	5516	1836	......	......	4699	3904	2745	1885	1925	1476	318	......	......	132
......	......	......	......	......	......	1105	645	......	......	......	......	......	......	......	133

(*b*) At 1870, Chinese, 1; Indians, 40, as follows: Bartow, 1 Indian; Berrien, 1 Indian; Chatham, 1 Indian; Cherokee, 1 Indian; Clinch, 1 Chinese; Cobb, 4 Indians; Effingham, 3 Indians; Floyd, 4 Indians; Gordon, 6 Indians; Houston, 3 Indians; Marion, 1 Indian; McIntosh, 7 Indians; Morgan, 1 Indian; Muscogee, 2 Indians; Pulaski, 1 Indian; Richmond, 2 Indians; Towns, 2 Indians. At 1860, 38 Indians, as follows: In Bibb, 2 Indians; Brooks, 5 Indians; Fannin, 29 Indians; Gilmer, 1 Indian; Morgan, 1 Indian.

(*c*) In Table II of Vol. 1 of the Ninth Census, 2 free colored in the line for the county of Pierce belong to the county of Paulding.

TABLE VIII.—*Population by Counties at each Census—ILLINOIS.*

	Counties.	AGGREGATE.								WHITE.		
		1870.	1860.	1850.	1840.	1830.	1820.	1810.	1800.	1870.	1860.	1850.
	The State	2539891	1711951	851470	476183	157445	*49 55162	12282	*a*2458	2511096	1704291	846034
1	Adams	56362	41323	26508	14476	2186	......	......	......	54794	41144	26360
2	Alexander	10564	4707	2484	3313	1390	626	......	......	8268	4632	2464
3	Bond	13152	9815	6144	5060	3124	2931	......	......	13042	9767	6136
4	Boone	12942	11678	7624	1705	......	......	......	......	12907	11670	7618
5	Brown	12205	9938	7198	4183	......	......	......	......	12179	9919	7182
6	Bureau	32415	26426	8841	3067	......	......	......	......	32272	26415	8831
7	Calhoun	6562	5144	3231	1741	1090	......	......	......	6550	5143	3230
8	Carroll	16705	11733	4586	1023	......	......	......	......	16675	11718	4583
9	Cass	11580	11325	7253	2981	......	......	......	......	11570	11313	7248
10	Champaign	32737	14629	2649	1475	......	......	......	......	32504	14581	2647
11	Christian	20363	10492	3203	1878	......	......	......	......	20318	10473	3203
12	Clark	18719	14987	9532	7453	3940	931	......	......	18698	14948	9494
13	Clay	15875	9336	4289	3228	755	......	......	......	15818	9309	4268
14	Clinton	16285	10941	5139	3718	2330	......	......	......	16262	10729	5002
15	Coles	25235	14203	9335	9616	......	......	......	......	25015	14174	9209
16	Cook	349966	144954	43385	10201	......	......	......	......	346102	143947	43007
17	Crawford	13889	11551	7135	4422	3117	*23 2999	......	......	13885	11529	7118
18	Cumberland	12223	8311	3718	......	......	......	......	......	12220	8309	3718
19	De Kalb	23265	19086	7540	1697	......	......	......	......	23212	19079	7539
20	De Witt	14768	10820	5002	3247	......	......	......	......	14712	10814	5001
21	Douglas	13484	7140	......	......	......	......	......	......	13387	7109	......
22	Du Page	16685	14701	9290	3535	......	......	......	......	16632	14696	9287
23	Edgar	21450	16925	10692	8225	4071	......	......	......	21339	16888	10646
24	Edwards	7565	5454	3524	3070	1649	3444	......	......	7498	5379	3490
25	Effingham	15653	7816	3799	1675	......	......	......	......	15643	7805	3792
26	Fayette	19638	11189	8075	6328	2704	......	......	......	19583	11146	8027
27	Ford	9103	1979	......	......	......	......	......	......	9089	1979	......
28	Franklin	12652	9393	5681	3682	4083	1763	......	......	12646	9367	5646
29	Fulton	38291	33338	22508	13142	1841	......	......	......	38226	33289	22492
30	Gallatin	11134	8055	5448	10760	7405	3155	......	......	10522	7639	5093
31	Greene	20277	16093	12429	11951	7674	......	......	......	20255	16067	12369
32	Grundy	14938	10379	3023	......	......	......	......	......	14843	10362	3021
33	Hamilton	13014	9915	6362	3945	2616	......	......	......	12993	9849	6310
34	Hancock	35935	29061	14652	9946	483	......	......	......	35807	29040	14633
35	Hardin	5113	3759	2887	1378	......	......	......	......	5024	3704	2808
36	Henderson	12582	9501	4612	......	......	......	......	......	12575	9499	4610
37	Henry	35506	20660	3807	1260	41	......	......	......	35413	20658	3807
38	Iroquois	25782	12325	4149	1695	......	......	......	......	25618	12285	4070
39	Jackson	19634	9589	5862	3566	1828	1542	......	......	18639	9560	5829
40	Jasper	11234	8364	3220	1472	......	......	......	......	11211	8350	3206
41	Jefferson	17864	12965	8109	5762	2555	691	......	......	17826	12931	8083
42	Jersey	15054	12051	7354	4535	......	......	......	*a*100	14823	11942	7300
43	Jo Daviess	27820	27325	18604	6180	2111	......	......	......	27727	27147	18386
44	Johnson	11248	9342	4114	3626	1596	843	......	......	11196	9306	4097
45	Kane	39091	30062	16703	6501	......	......	......	......	38724	30024	16697
46	Kankakee	24352	15412	......	......	......	......	......	......	24282	15393	......
47	Kendall	12399	13074	7730	......	......	......	......	......	12345	13073	7724
48	Knox	39522	28663	13279	7060	274	......	......	......	38713	28512	13197
49	Lake	21014	18257	14226	2634	......	......	......	......	20948	18248	14187
50	La Salle	60792	48332	17815	9348	......	......	......	......	60722	48272	17799
51	Lawrence	12533	9214	6121	7092	3668	......	......	......	12243	8976	5843
52	Lee	27171	17651	5292	2035	......	......	......	......	27123	17643	5288
53	Livingston	31471	11637	1552	759	......	......	......	......	31360	11632	1552
54	Logan	23053	14272	5128	2333	......	......	......	......	22937	14247	5128
55	Macon	26481	13738	3988	3039	1122	......	......	......	26246	13655	3985
56	Macoupin	32726	24602	12355	7826	1990	......	......	......	32406	24504	12272
57	Madison	44131	31251	20441	14433	6221	13550	......	......	41917	30679	19992
58	Marion	20622	12739	6720	4742	2125	......	......	......	20407	12730	6716
59	Marshall	16956	13437	5180	1849	......	......	......	......	16943	13437	5178
60	Mason	16184	10931	5921	......	......	......	......	......	16181	10920	5898
61	Massac	9581	6213	4092	......	......	......	......	......	8025	6101	4070
62	McDonough	26509	20069	7616	5308	(*b*)	......	......	......	26467	20061	7611
63	McHenry	23762	22089	14978	2578	......	......	......	......	23698	22085	14975
64	McLean	53988	28772	10163	6565	......	......	......	......	53561	28580	10121
65	Menard	11735	9584	6349	4431	......	......	......	......	11727	9577	6298
66	Mercer	18769	15042	5246	2352	26	......	......	......	18741	15037	5244
67	Monroe	12982	12832	7679	4481	2000	*21 1516	......	......	12913	12815	7633
68	Montgomery	25314	13979	6277	4490	2953	......	......	......	25162	13881	6258
69	Morgan	28463	22112	16064	19547	12714	......	......	......	27869	21937	15939

TABLE VIII.—*Population by Counties at each Census*—*ILLINOIS.*

White—Continued.					Colored.								Indian.		
1840.	1830.	1820.	1810.	1800.	1870.	1860.	1850.	1840.	1830.	1820.	1810.	1800.	1870.	1860.	
472254	155061	53788	11501	a2275	28762	7628	5436	3929	2384	1374	781	183	32	32	
14443	2181	.....	.....	.....	1567	179	139	33	5	.....	.....	.....	1	.....	1
3304	1378	626	.....	.....	2296	55	20	9	12	.....	.....	.....	.....	.....	2
5042	3122	2882	.....	.....	110	48	8	12	2	49	.....	.....	.....	.....	3
1705	.....	.....	.....	.....	35	8	6	.....	.....	.....	.....	.....	.....	.....	4
4176	.....	.....	.....	.....	26	19	16	7	.....	.....	.....	.....	.....	.....	5
3061	.....	.....	.....	.....	143	11	10	6	.....	.....	.....	.....	.....	.....	6
1736	1090	.....	.....	.....	3	1	1	15	.....	.....	.....	.....	.....	.....	7
1019	.....	.....	.....	.....	30	15	3	4	.....	.....	.....	.....	.....	.....	8
2970	.....	.....	.....	.....	4	12	5	11	.....	.....	.....	.....	.....	.....	9
1475	.....	.....	.....	.....	233	48	2	.....	.....	.....	.....	.....	.....	.....	10
1878	.....	.....	.....	.....	45	17	.....	.....	.....	.....	.....	.....	.....	.....	11
7420	2021	933	.....	.....	21	39	38	27	19	1	.....	.....	.....	.....	12
3205	753	.....	.....	.....	56	27	21	23	2	.....	.....	.....	1	.....	13
3597	2243	.....	.....	.....	321	212	137	121	87	.....	.....	.....	.....	.....	14
9583	.....	.....	.....	.....	230	29	36	33	.....	.....	.....	.....	.....	.....	15
10146	.....	.....	.....	.....	3858	1007	378	55	.....	.....	.....	.....	6	.....	16
4389	3103	2927	.....	.....	4	22	17	40	14	72	.....	.....	.....	.....	17
.....	.....	.....	.....	.....	3	2	.....	.....	.....	.....	.....	.....	.....	.....	18
1697	.....	.....	.....	.....	53	7	1	.....	.....	.....	.....	.....	.....	.....	19
3946	.....	.....	.....	.....	56	6	1	1	.....	.....	.....	.....	.....	.....	20
.....	.....	.....	.....	.....	97	31	.....	.....	.....	.....	.....	.....	.....	.....	21
3531	.....	.....	.....	.....	33	5	3	4	.....	.....	.....	.....	.....	.....	22
8181	4056	.....	.....	.....	111	37	52	44	15	.....	.....	.....	.....	.....	23
2027	1609	3422	.....	.....	67	75	34	42	40	22	.....	.....	.....	.....	24
1670	.....	.....	.....	.....	10	11	7	5	.....	.....	.....	.....	.....	.....	25
6902	2669	.....	.....	.....	53	43	48	66	35	.....	.....	.....	.....	.....	26
.....	.....	.....	.....	.....	14	.....	.....	.....	.....	.....	.....	.....	.....	.....	27
3071	4036	1691	.....	.....	6	26	35	11	47	72	.....	.....	.....	.....	28
13110	1841	.....	.....	.....	65	49	16	32	.....	.....	.....	.....	.....	.....	29
10065	6939	2860	.....	.....	612	426	353	695	466	295	.....	.....	.....	.....	30
11901	7634	.....	.....	.....	22	26	60	50	40	.....	.....	.....	.....	.....	31
.....	.....	.....	.....	.....	94	7	9	.....	.....	.....	.....	.....	1	10	32
3928	2606	.....	.....	.....	21	66	52	17	10	.....	.....	.....	.....	.....	33
9031	483	.....	.....	.....	128	20	19	15	.....	.....	.....	.....	.....	1	34
1330	.....	.....	.....	.....	89	55	79	48	.....	.....	.....	.....	.....	.....	35
.....	.....	.....	.....	.....	7	2	2	.....	.....	.....	.....	.....	.....	.....	36
1256	41	.....	.....	.....	93	2	.....	4	.....	.....	.....	.....	.....	.....	37
1694	.....	.....	.....	.....	164	40	79	1	.....	.....	.....	.....	.....	.....	38
3523	1766	1503	.....	.....	995	29	33	43	62	30	.....	.....	.....	.....	39
1430	.....	.....	.....	.....	23	14	14	42	.....	.....	.....	.....	.....	.....	40
5753	2532	689	.....	.....	38	34	26	9	3	2	.....	.....	.....	.....	41
4513	.....	.....	.....	a100	231	109	54	22	.....	.....	.....	.....	.....	.....	42
6040	2047	.....	.....	.....	92	178	218	140	64	.....	.....	.....	1	.....	43
3608	1584	829	.....	.....	52	36	17	18	12	14	.....	.....	.....	.....	44
6497	.....	.....	.....	.....	367	38	6	4	.....	.....	.....	.....	.....	.....	45
.....	.....	.....	.....	.....	69	19	.....	.....	.....	.....	.....	.....	1	.....	46
.....	.....	.....	.....	.....	54	1	6	.....	.....	.....	.....	.....	.....	.....	47
7057	274	.....	.....	.....	809	151	82	3	.....	.....	.....	.....	.....	.....	48
2623	.....	.....	.....	.....	62	9	39	6	.....	.....	.....	.....	4	.....	49
9,346	.....	.....	.....	.....	69	60	16	2	.....	.....	.....	.....	1	.....	50
6407	3495	.....	.....	.....	290	238	278	225	173	.....	.....	.....	.....	.....	51
2029	.....	.....	.....	.....	48	8	4	6	.....	.....	.....	.....	.....	.....	52
757	.....	.....	.....	.....	111	5	.....	2	.....	.....	.....	.....	.....	.....	53
2334	.....	.....	.....	.....	116	25	.....	1	.....	.....	.....	.....	.....	.....	54
3030	1122	.....	.....	.....	235	83	3	3	.....	.....	.....	.....	.....	.....	55
7791	1990	.....	.....	.....	320	98	83	33	.....	.....	.....	.....	.....	.....	56
14000	6104	13423	.....	.....	2214	502	449	343	117	127	.....	.....	.....	10	57
4740	2121	.....	.....	.....	215	9	4	2	4	.....	.....	.....	.....	.....	58
1849	.....	.....	.....	.....	13	.....	2	.....	.....	.....	.....	.....	.....	.....	59
.....	.....	.....	.....	.....	3	2	23	.....	.....	.....	.....	.....	.....	.....	60
.....	.....	.....	.....	.....	956	112	22	.....	.....	.....	.....	.....	.....	.....	61
5308	(b)	.....	.....	.....	42	8	5	.....	.....	.....	.....	.....	.....	.....	62
2578	.....	.....	.....	.....	64	4	3	.....	.....	.....	.....	.....	.....	.....	63
6556	.....	.....	.....	.....	427	192	42	9	.....	.....	.....	.....	.....	.....	64
4421	.....	.....	.....	.....	8	7	21	10	.....	.....	.....	.....	.....	.....	65
2352	26	.....	.....	.....	28	5	2	.....	.....	.....	.....	.....	.....	.....	66
4400	1959	1493	.....	.....	69	17	46	81	41	23	.....	.....	.....	.....	67
4478	2945	.....	.....	.....	152	98	19	12	8	.....	.....	.....	.....	.....	68
19479	12682	.....	.....	.....	503	175	125	68	39	.....	.....	.....	.....	.....	69

TABLE VIII.—*Population by Counties at each Census—ILLINOIS*—Continued.

	Counties.	AGGREGATE.								WHITE.		
		1870.	1860.	1850.	1840.	1830.	1820.	1810.	1800.	1870.	1860.	1850.
70	Moultrie	10385	6385	3234						10384	6384	3225
71	Ogle	27492	22888	10020	3479					27407	22863	9990
72	Peoria	47540	36601	17547	6153	(c)				47385	36475	17461
73	Perry	13723	9552	5278	3222	1215				13332	9508	5267
74	Piatt	10953	6127	1606						10947	6124	1606
75	Pike	30768	27249	18819	11728	2396				30661	27182	18776
76	Pope	11437	6742	3975	4094	3316	2610			10955	6546	3871
77	Pulaski	8752	3943	2265						6358	3904	2257
78	Putnam	6280	5587	3924	2131	c1310				6215	5579	3920
79	Randolph	20859	17205	11079	7944	4429	3492	7275	a1103	19722	16766	10696
80	Richland	12803	9711	4012						12771	9709	4002
81	Rock Island	29783	21005	6937	2610					29646	20981	6935
82	Saline	12714	9331	5588						12483	9152	5495
83	Sangamon	46352	32274	19228	14716	12960				45186	31963	18975
84	Schuyler	17419	14684	10573	6972	b2959				17394	14670	10547
85	Scott	10530	9069	7914	6215					10515	9047	7902
86	Shelby	25476	14613	7807	6659	2972				25416	14590	7762
87	Stark	10751	9004	3710	1573					10730	9003	3710
88	St. Clair	51068	37694	20180	13631	7078	*5 5248	5007	a1255	49771	37169	19599
89	Stephenson	30608	25112	11666	2800					30596	25112	11658
90	Tazewell	27903	21470	12052	7221	4716				27839	21427	12016
91	Union	16518	11181	7615	5524	3239	2362			16370	11145	7570
92	Vermilion	30388	19800	11492	9303	5836				30338	19779	11481
93	Wabash	8841	7313	4690	4240	2710				8778	7233	4640
94	Warren	23174	18336	8176	6739	308				22051	18293	8162
95	Washington	17599	13731	6953	4810	1675	1517			17463	13725	6929
96	Wayne	19758	12223	6825	5133	2553	1114			19729	12222	6822
97	White	16846	12403	8925	7919	6091	4828			16673	12274	8816
98	Whitesides	27503	18737	5361	2514					27444	18727	5359
99	Will	43013	29321	16703	10167					42771	29264	16670
100	Williamson	17329	12205	7216	4457					17223	12087	7149
101	Winnebago	29301	24491	11773	4609					29180	24457	11761
102	Woodford	18956	13282	4415						18946	13281	4415

(*) All other persons, except Indians not taxed.
(*a*) Then in Indiana Territory. The 100 placed opposite Jersey County was reported to be at "Opee, on the Illinois River."

TABLE VIII.—*Population by Counties at each Census—INDIANA*.

	Counties.	AGGREGATE.								WHITE.		
		1870.	1860.	1850.	1840.	1830.	1820.	1810.	1800.	1870.	1860.	1850.
	The State	1680637	1350428	988416	685866	343031	147178	24520	b766 a5124 2517	1655837	1338710	977154
1	Adams	11382	9252	5797	2264					11382	9246	5789
2	Allen	43494	29328	16919	5942	996				43428	29243	16817
3	Bartholomew	21133	17865	12428	1226	5476				21122	17858	12346
4	Benton	5615	2809	1144						5615	2809	1144
5	Blackford	6272	4122	2860	10042					6258	4122	2849
6	Boone	22593	16751	11631	8121	621				22353	16663	11611
7	Brown	8681	6507	4846	2364					8680	6503	4827
8	Carroll	16152	13489	11015	7819	1611				16128	13476	10982
9	Cass	24193	16843	11021	5480	1162				24082	16770	10960
10	Clarke	24770	20502	15828	14595	10686	8709	5670		22800	19982	15246
11	Clay	19084	12161	7944	5567	1616				19054	12139	7926
12	Clinton	17330	14505	11869	7508	1423				17323	14485	11845
13	Crawford	9851	8226	6524	5282	3238	2583			9848	8226	6523
14	Daviess	16747	13323	10352	6720	4543	3432			16618	13249	10308
15	Dearborn	24116	24406	20166	19327	13974	11468	7310		24058	24332	20019
16	Decatur	19053	17294	15107	12171	5887				18966	17270	14951
17	De Kalb	17167	13880	8251	1968					17163	13865	8241
18	Delaware	19030	15753	10843	8843	2374	3677			18976	15737	10839
19	Dubois	12597	10394	6321	3632	1778	1168			12562	10382	6300

TABLE VIII.—*Population by Counties at each Census—ILLINOIS*—Continued.

White—Continued.					Colored.								Indian.†		
1840.	1830.	1820.	1810.	1800.	1870.	1860.	1850.	1840.	1830.	1820.	1810.	1800.	1870.	1860.	
......	......	......	......	......	1	1	9	......	......	......	......	......	......	......	70
3473	......	......	......	......	85	25	30	6	......	......	......	......	......	......	71
6144	(c)	......	......	......	155	126	86	9	......	......	......	......	......	......	72
3230	1211	......	......	......	391	44	11	2	4	......	......	......	......	......	73
......	......	......	......	......	6	3	......	......	......	......	......	......	......	......	74
11716	2393	......	......	......	106	67	43	12	3	......	......	......	1	......	75
4036	3232	2576	......	......	471	196	104	58	84	34	......	......	11	......	76
......	......	......	......	......	2394	39	8	......	......	......	......	......	......	......	77
2129	c1269	......	......	......	65	8	4	2	41	......	......	......	......	......	78
7627	4066	3175	6647	a962	1137	430	383	317	363	317	628	141	......	......	79
......	......	......	......	......	30	2	10	......	......	......	......	......	......	......	80
2602	......	......	......	......	137	21	2	8	......	......	......	......	......	......	81
......	......	......	......	......	231	170	93	......	......	......	......	......	......	9	82
14541	12913	......	......	......	1166	311	253	175	47	......	......	......	......	......	83
6949	b2957	......	......	......	25	14	26	23	2	......	......	......	......	......	84
6210	......	......	......	......	15	22	12	5	......	......	......	......	......	......	85
6643	2970	......	......	......	60	23	45	26	2	......	......	......	......	......	86
1573	......	......	......	......	21	1	......	......	......	......	......	......	......	......	87
13171	6771	5068	4854	a1213	1297	525	581	460	307	180	153	42	......	......	88
2797	......	......	......	......	12	......	8	3	......	......	......	......	......	......	89
7201	4701	......	......	......	64	43	36	20	16	......	......	......	......	......	90
5494	3204	2338	......	......	148	36	45	30	35	24	......	......	......	......	91
9288	5830	......	......	......	49	21	11	15	6	......	......	......	1	......	92
4304	2093	......	......	......	63	80	50	36	17	......	......	......	......	......	93
6708	308	......	......	......	223	43	14	31	......	......	......	......	......	......	94
4763	1639	1484	......	......	133	6	24	47	36	33	......	......	3	......	95
5127	2547	1111	......	......	29	1	3	6	6	3	......	......	......	......	96
7842	5085	4761	......	......	173	129	109	77	106	67	......	......	......	......	97
2514	......	......	......	......	59	8	2	......	......	......	......	......	......	2	98
10157	......	......	......	......	242	57	33	10	......	......	......	......	......	......	99
4428	......	......	......	......	106	118	67	29	......	......	......	......	......	......	100
4605	......	......	......	......	121	34	12	4	......	......	......	......	......	......	101
......	......	......	......	......	10	1	......	......	......	......	......	......	......	......	102

(†) Chinese, at 1870: Morgan, 1.
(b) Schuyler and McDonough reported together and here tabulated in the line of Schuyler County.
(c) Peoria and Putnam reported together and here tabulated in the line of Putnam County.

TABLE VIII.—*Population by Counties at each Census—INDIANA.*

White—Continued.					Colored.								Indian.		
1840.	1830.	1820.	1810.	1800.	1870.	1860.	1850.	1840.	1830.	1820.	1810.	1800.	1870.	1860.	
678698	339399	145758	23890	b767 a b2941 2402	24560	11428	11262	7168	3632	1420	630	a298	240	290	
2247	......	......	......	......	......	6	8	17	......	......	......	......	......	......	1
5924	992	......	......	......	42	63	102	18	4	......	......	......	24	22	2
1213	5470	......	......	......	11	7	82	13	6	......	......	......	......	......	3
......	......	......	......	......	......	......	......	......	......	......	......	......	......	......	4
1000[illegible]	......	......	......	......	14	......	11	34	......	......	......	......	......	......	5
8102	619	......	......	......	240	90	20	19	2	......	......	......	......	......	6
2341	......	......	......	......	1	......	19	23	......	......	......	......	......	4	7
7813	1611	......	......	......	24	13	33	6	......	......	......	......	......	......	8
5440	1146	......	......	......	111	65	61	40	16	......	......	......	......	8	9
14207	10443	8571	5519	......	1970	520	582	388	243	138	121	......	......	......	10
5564	1615	......	......	......	26	22	18	3	1	......	......	......	4	......	11
7499	1422	......	......	......	7	20	24	9	1	......	......	......	......	......	12
5270	3238	2583	......	......	3	......	1	12	......	......	......	......	......	......	13
6695	4490	3400	......	......	129	74	41	25	44	32	......	......	......	......	14
19152	13912	11396	7218	......	58	74	147	135	62	72	92	......	......	......	15
12108	5277	......	......	......	87	24	156	63	10	......	......	......	......	......	16
1961	......	......	......	......	4	15	10	7	......	......	......	......	......	......	17
8840	2372	3674	......	......	53	16	4	3	2	3	......	......	1	......	18
3625	1776	1160	......	......	33	12	21	7	2	8	......	......	......	......	19

TABLE VIII.—*Population by Counties at each Census—INDIANA*—Continued.

	Counties.	Aggregate.								White.		
		1870.	1860.	1850.	1840.	1830.	1820.	1810.	1800.	1870.	1860.	1850.
20	Elkhart	26026	20986	12690	6660	935	......	......	......	25901	20966	[illegible]
21	Fayette	10476	10225	10217	9837	9112	5950	......	......	10384	10138	[illegible]
22	Floyd	23300	20183	14875	9454	6361	2776	......	......	21438	19426	[illegible]
23	Fountain	16389	15566	13253	11218	7619	......	......	......	16342	15482	[illegible]
24	Franklin	20223	19549	17968	13349	10190	10763	......	......	20199	19446	[illegible]
25	Fulton	12726	9422	5982	1993	......	......	......	......	12710	9416	[illegible]
26	Gibson	17371	14532	10771	8977	5418	3876	......	......	16934	14236	[illegible]
27	Grant	18487	15797	11092	4875	......	......	......	......	17750	15413	[illegible]
28	Greene	19514	16041	12313	8321	4242	......	......	......	19493	[illegible]	[illegible]
29	Hamilton	20882	17310	12684	9855	1757	......	......	......	20367	16900	[illegible]
30	Hancock	15123	12802	9698	7535	1436	......	......	......	15069	12700	[illegible]
31	Harrison	19913	18521	15286	12459	10273	7875	3595	......	19564	18407	[illegible]
32	Hendricks	20277	16953	14083	11264	3975	......	......	......	20005	16908	[illegible]
33	Henry	22986	20119	17605	15128	6497	......	......	......	22545	19636	[illegible]
34	Howard	15847	12524	6657	......	......	......	......	......	15541	12359	[illegible]
35	Huntington	19036	14867	7850	1579	......	......	......	......	19028	14865	[illegible]
36	Jackson	18974	16286	11047	8961	4870	4010	......	......	18810	16107	[illegible]
37	Jasper	6354	4291	3540	1267	......	......	......	......	6351	4290	[illegible]
38	Jay	15000	11399	7047	3863	......	......	......	......	14979	11378	[illegible]
39	Jefferson	29741	25036	23916	16614	11465	8038	......	......	28636	24538	[illegible]
40	Jennings	16218	14749	12096	8829	3974	2000	......	......	15706	14598	[illegible]
41	Johnson	18366	14854	12101	9352	4019	......	......	......	18251	14835	[illegible]
42	Knox	21562	16056	11084	10657	6525	5437	7945	2517	21182	15807	[illegible]
43	Kosciusko	23531	17418	10243	4170	......	......	......	......	23521	17416	[illegible]
44	La Grange	14148	11366	8387	3664	......	......	......	......	14123	11350	[illegible]
45	Lake	12339	9145	3991	1468	......	......	......	......	12336	9140	[illegible]
46	La Porte	27062	22919	12145	8184	......	......	......	......	26834	22764	[illegible]
47	Lawrence	14628	13692	12097	11782	9234	4116	......	......	14378	13574	[illegible]
48	Madison	22770	16518	12375	8874	2238	......	......	......	22682	16458	[illegible]
49	Marion	71939	39855	24103	16080	7192	......	......	......	67997	39030	[illegible]
50	Marshall	20211	12722	5348	1651	......	......	......	......	20211	12719	[illegible]
51	Martin	11103	8975	5941	3875	2010	1032	......	......	11067	8923	[illegible]
52	Miami	21052	16851	11304	3048	......	......	......	......	20856	16631	[illegible]
53	Monroe	14168	12847	11286	10143	6577	2679	......	......	13909	12822	[illegible]
54	Montgomery	23765	20888	18084	14438	7317	......	......	......	23597	20738	17941
55	Morgan	17528	16110	14576	10741	5593	......	......	......	17454	16003	14501
56	Newton	5829	2360	......	......	......	......	......	......	5796	2360	......
57	Noble	20389	14915	7946	2702	......	......	......	......	20376	14907	7946
58	Ohio	5837	5462	5308	......	......	......	......	......	5618	5439	5271
59	Orange	13497	12076	10809	9602	7901	5368	......	......	13138	11816	10556
60	Owen	16137	14376	12106	8359	4017	838	......	......	16078	14291	11950
61	Parke	18166	15538	14968	13499	7535	......	......	......	18014	15342	14740
62	Perry	14801	11847	7268	4655	3369	2330	......	......	14631	11844	7259
63	Pike	13779	10078	7720	4769	2475	1472	......	......	13765	10064	7710
64	Porter	13942	10313	5234	2162	......	......	......	......	13903	10298	5229
65	Posey	19185	16167	12549	9683	6549	4061	......	......	18621	16031	12451
66	Pulaski	7801	5711	2595	561	......	......	......	......	7801	5711	2595
67	Putnam	21514	20681	18615	16843	8262	......	......	......	21409	20062	18581
68	Randolph	22862	18997	14725	10684	3912	1808	......	a1103	22217	18172	14063
69	Ripley	20977	19054	14820	10392	3989	1822	......	......	20874	18967	14794
70	Rush	17626	16193	16445	16456	9707	......	......	......	17162	15774	16018
71	Scott	7873	7303	5885	4242	3092	2334	......	......	7864	7301	5870
72	Shelby	21892	19569	15502	12005	6295	......	......	......	21764	19548	15453
73	Spencer	17998	14556	8616	6305	3196	1882	......	......	17049	14554	8602
74	Starke	3888	2195	557	149	......	......	......	......	3888	2194	557
75	St. Clair	......	......	......	......	......	......	......	a1255	......	......	......
76	Steuben	12854	10374	6104	2578	......	......	......	......	12849	10372	6102
77	St. Joseph	25322	18455	10954	6425	287	......	......	......	25195	18338	10985
78	Sullivan	18453	15064	10141	8315	4630	3498	......	......	18345	14944	10103
79	Switzerland	12134	12698	12932	9920	7028	3934	......	......	12013	12656	12906
80	Tippecanoe	33515	25726	19377	13724	7187	......	......	......	33343	25582	19216
81	Tipton	11953	8170	3532	......	......	......	......	......	11892	8135	3532
82	Union	6341	7109	6944	8017	7944	......	......	......	6329	7063	6906
83	Vanderburgh	33145	20552	11414	6250	2611	1798	......	......	30994	20423	11187
84	Vermillion	10840	9422	8661	8274	5692	......	......	......	10792	9394	8642
85	Vigo	33549	22517	15289	12076	5766	3390	......	......	32417	21811	14541
86	Wabash	21305	17547	12138	2756	......	147	......	......	21174	17469	12124
87	Warren	10204	10057	7387	5656	2861	......	......	......	10181	10040	7476
88	Warrick	17653	13261	8811	6321	2877	1749	......	......	17166	13242	8792
89	Washington	18495	17909	17040	15269	13064	9039	......	......	18477	17722	16786
90	Wayne	34048	29558	25320	23290	18571	12119	......	......	32810	28684	24984
91	Wells	13585	10844	6152	1822	......	......	......	......	13585	10843	6141
92	White	10554	8258	4761	1832	......	......	......	......	10551	8217	4762
93	Whitley	14399	10730	5190	1237	......	......	......	......	14303	10637	5095

(*a*) These counties now parts of the State of Illinois.

TABLE VIII.—*Population by Counties at each Census—INDIANA*—Continued.

White—Continued.					Colored.								Indian.		
1840.	1830.	1820.	1810.	1800.	1870.	1860.	1850.	1840.	1830.	1820.	1810.	1800.	1870.	1860.	
6656	935				35	20	16	2							20
9784	9081	5041			92	87	72	53	31	9					21
9032	6096	2707			1402	757	574	402	265	69					22
11185	7610				47	73	58	33	9						23
13367	10009	10298			24	103	209	82	91	65					24
1592					16	6	2	1							25
4840	5363	3801			437	274	217	137	53	75					26
4675					737	384	147							1	27
8239	4201				21	79	75	82	41						28
9788	1756				515	350	182	67	1						29
7496	1436				54	93	104	39							30
12370	10150	7806	3562		349	114	91	89	123	69	33				31
11847	3970				182	45	36	17	5						32
14983	6456				441	283	287	145	41						33
					304	165	105								34
1565					5	2	3	14					3		35
8771	4750	3974			164	179	214	190	190	30					36
1985					3	5	1	2							37
3952					91	21	30	11							38
16185	11285	7990			1105	512	568	429	240	112					39
8671	3916	1955			422	151	324	158	58	45					40
9332	4013				115	19	15	20	6						41
10096	6078	5153	7561	2402	380	449	530	561	447	284	384	115			42
4170					10	2	1								43
3961					25	16	18	3							44
1466					3	5	1	2							45
8152					226	135	78	32							46
11678	9175	4101			250	118	94	106	50	15					47
8868	2227				88	60	14	6	11						48
15825	7119				3938	826	650	255	73				4		49
1650						3	2	1							50
2852	1009	1028			36	52	96	23	11	4					51
3044					51	47	11	4					145	173	52
10130	6507	2071			259	25	27	13	70	8					53
14344	7308				107	150	143	94	9						54
10651	5502				74	107	75	90	31						55
					33										56
2702					13	8	6								57
					189	23	37								58
9444	7776	5272			159	260	251	158	125	96					59
8211	3092	927			59	85	156	148	25	11					60
13436	7319				152	196	225	63	16						61
4651	3356	2314			150	3	9	4	13	16					62
4749	2461	1465			14	14	10	20	14	7					63
2155					39	17	5	7							64
9642	6523	4044			564	136	98	41	26	17					65
561															66
16815	8256				105	19	31	28	6						67
10180	3789	1803		a962	617	825	662	504	123	5		a141			68
10349	3981	1890			103	87	96	43	8	2					69
15973	9600				463	419	427	483	107				1		70
4227	3077	2328			5	2	15	15	15	6					71
11985	8287				128	21	19	20	8						72
6278	3182	1877			949	2	14	27	14	5					73
149						1									74
				a1213								a42			75
2578					5	2	2								76
6416	287				120	68	29	9					7	20	77
8239	4591	3470			105	120	32	26	30	28					78
9678	7015	3925			121	42	66	42	13	9					79
13670	7187				172	143	161	54						1	80
					61	35	7								81
7856	7867				112	40	38	61	77					6	82
6136	2563	1787			2151	127	227	114	48	11					83
8251	5673				48	30	18	23	19						84
11651	5643	3364			1099	706	748	425	123	26			3		85
2746		142			84	33	14	10		5			47	45	86
5656	2861				22	17	9						1		87
6113	2875	1742			487	19	29	8	2	7					88
15076	12858	8060			18	187	252	193	206	59					89
22054	18154	12033			1238	870	1036	626	417	66					90
1609						1	11	13							91
1830					3	21	9	2							92
1221					97	92	95	16						1	93

(*b*) Then in Indiana Territory, but now in parts in Illinois, Michigan, and Wisconsin.

TABLE VIII.—*Population by Counties at each Census—IOWA.*

	Counties.	Aggregate.				White.		
		1870.	1860.	1850.	1840.	1870.	1860.	1850.
	The State	1194020	674913	192214	43112	1188207	673779	191881
1	Adair	3982	984			3981	984	
2	Adams	4614	1533			4590	1533	
3	Allamakee	17868	12237	777		17860	12231	777
4	Appanoose	16456	11931	3131		16421	11918	3124
5	Audubon	1212	454			1211	454	
6	Benton	22454	8496	672		22430	8495	672
7	Black Hawk	21706	8244	135		21688	8226	135
8	Boone	14584	4232	735		14572	4232	735
9	Bremer	12528	4915			12510	4910	
10	Buchanan	17034	7906	517		17025	7904	517
11	Buena Vista	1585	57			1585	57	
12	Buncombe (*a*)							
13	Butler	9951	3724			9951	3723	
14	Calhoun	1602	147			1602	147	
15	Carroll	2451	281			2451	281	
16	Cass	5464	1612			5459	1612	
17	Cedar	19731	12949	3941	1253	19689	12937	3939
18	Cerro Gordo	4722	940			4718	940	
19	Cherokee	1967	58			1961	58	
20	Chickasaw	10180	4336			10177	4331	
21	Clarke	8735	5427	79		8709	5427	79
22	Clay	1523	52			1523	52	
23	Clayton	27771	20728	3873	1101	27744	20703	3871
24	Clinton	35357	18938	2822	821	35226	18925	2802
25	Crawford	2530	383			2529	383	
26	Dallas	12019	5244	854		11994	5244	854
27	Davis	15565	12764	7264		15535	13702	7257
28	Decatur	12018	8677	965		11977	8670	964
29	Delaware	17432	11024	1759	168	17411	11023	1759
30	Des Moines	27256	19611	12988	5577	27020	19583	12963
31	Dickinson	1389	180			1389	180	
32	Dubuque	38969	31164	10841	3059	38802	31083	10813
33	Emmet	1392	105			1389	105	
34	Fayette	16973	12073	825		16964	12019	825
35	Floyd	10768	3744			10765	3744	
36	Franklin	4738	1309			4733	1309	
37	Fremont	11174	5074	1244		11144	5069	1244
38	Greene	4627	1374			4624	1374	
39	Grundy	6399	793			6399	793	
40	Guthrie	7061	3058			7056	3058	
41	Hamilton	6055	1699			6052	1699	
42	Hancock	999	179			994	179	
43	Hardin	13684	5440			13651	5449	
44	Harrison	8931	3621			8930	3620	
45	Henry	21463	18701	8707	3772	20980	18677	8695
46	Howard	6282	3168			6270	3167	
47	Humboldt	2596	332			2596	332	
48	Ida	226	43			226	43	
49	Iowa	16644	8029	822		16633	8029	821
50	Jackson	22619	18493	7210	1411	22594	18482	7201
51	Jasper	22116	9883	1280		22047	9882	1280
52	Jefferson	17839	15038	9904	2773	17786	15030	9903
53	Johnson	24898	17573	4472	1491	24890	17535	4450
54	Jones	19731	13306	3007	471	19690	13299	3006
55	Keokuk	19434	13271	4822		19431	13271	4822
56	Kossuth	3351	416			3351	416	
57	Lee	37210	29232	18861	6093	35647	28987	18809
58	Linn	31080	18947	5444	1373	31032	18936	5441
59	Louisa	12877	10370	4939	1927	12818	10276	4923
60	Lucas	10388	5766	471		10357	5764	471
61	Lyon (*a*)	221				221		
62	Madison	13884	7339	1179		13881	7339	1179
63	Mahaska	22508	14816	5989		22356	14800	5988
64	Marion	24436	16813	5482		24403	16780	5453
65	Marshall	17576	6015	338		17536	6015	338
66	Mills	8718	4481			8713	4462	
67	Mitchell	9582	3409			9581	3409	
68	Monona	3654	832			3612	828	
69	Monroe	12724	8612	2884		12675	8610	2884
70	Montgomery	5934	1256			5921	1245	
71	Muscatine	21688	16444	5731	1942	21525	16332	5662
72	O'Brien	715	8			709	8	
73	Osceola (*b*)							

TABLE VIII.—*Population by Counties at each Census—IOWA.*

Colored.				Chinese.	Indian.		
1870.	1860.	1850.	1840.	1870.	1870.	1860.	
5762	1069	333	188	3	48	65	
1							1
24							2
8	6						3
35	13	7					4
1							5
24	1						6
18	18						7
11					1		8
17	5				1		9
9	2						10
							11
	1						12
							13
							14
							15
5							16
42	12	2					17
4							18
6							19
3	5						20
26							21
							22
26	25	2	7		1		23
129	13	20	10		2		24
1							25
25							26
30	2	7					27
41	7	1					28
21	1						29
227	28	25	6				30
							31
167	81	28	72				32
8							33
70	54						34
3							35
5							36
29	5				1		37
3							38
							39
5							40
3							41
5							42
23					10		43
1	1						44
465	24	12	16		18		45
12	1						46
							47
							48
11		*a*1					49
25	11	9	10				50
69	1						51
53	8	1					52
98	37	22	3				53
32	7	1					54
3							55
							56
1,563	245	52	11				57
48	11	3	1				58
50	94	16	17				59
31	2						60
							61
3							62
150	16	1					63
36	33	29					64
37				3			65
5	16					3	66
1							67
42	1					3	68
49	2						69
13						11	70
163	112	69	25				71
6							72
							73

TABLE VIII.—*Population by Counties at each Census—IOWA*—Continued.

	Counties.	AGGREGATE.				WHITE.		
		1870.	1860.	1850.	1840.	1870.	1860.	1850.
74	Page	9975	4419	551		9829	4418	551
75	Palo Alto	1336	132			1336	132	
76	Plymouth	2199	148			2199	138	
77	Pocahontas	1446	103			1446	103	
78	Polk	27857	11625	4513		27554	11612	4513
79	Pottawattamie	16893	4968	7828		16725	4959	7828
80	Poweshiek	15581	5668	615		15502	5661	615
81	Ringgold	5691	2923			5686	2922	
82	Sac	1411	246			1410	246	
83	Scott	38599	25959	5986	2140	38353	25930	5972
84	Shelby	2540	818			2534	817	
85	Sioux	576	10			576	10	
86	Story	11651	4051			11649	4051	
87	Tama	16131	5285	8		16086	5285	8
88	Taylor	6989	3590	204		6988	3590	204
89	Union	5986	2012			5973	2012	
90	Van Buren	17672	17081	12270	6146	17461	17077	12265
91	Wapello	22346	14518	8471		22153	14471	8466
92	Warren	17980	10281	961		17899	10267	961
93	Washington	18952	14235	4957	1594	18899	14222	4957
94	Wayne	11287	6409	340		11286	6398	339
95	Webster	10484	2504			10475	2500	
96	Winnebago	1562	168			1561	168	
97	Winneshiek	23570	13942	546		23545	13942	546
98	Woodbury	6172	1119			6119	1078	
99	Worth	2892	756			2892	756	
100	Wright	2392	653			2390	653	

(a) In 1862 name changed from Buncombe to Lyon.
(b) Unorganized; no population.

TABLE VIII.—*Population by Counties at each Census—KANSAS.*

	Counties.	AGGREGATE.					WHITE.			
		1870.	1860.	1850.	1840.	1830.	1870.	1860.	1850.	1840.
	The State	364399	107206				346377	106390		
1	Allen	7022	3082				6869	3079		
2	Anderson	5220	2400				5108	2398		
3	Atchison	15507	7729				14368	7693		
4	Barton	2					2			
5	Bourbon	15076	6101				14297	6035		
6	Breckenridge		3197					3197		
7	Brown	6823	2607				6721	2607		
8	Butler	3035	437				3002	432		
9	Chase	1975	808				1969	808		
10	Cherokee	11038					10899			
11	Clay	2942	163				2932	163		
12	Cloud	2323					2316			
13	Coffey	6201	2842				6045	2842		
14	Cowley	1175					1175			
15	Crawford	8160					8158			
16	Davis	5526	1163				5394	1162		
17	Dickinson	3043	378				3026	378		
18	Doniphan	13969	8083				13135	8026		
19	Dorn		88					88		
20	Douglas	20592	8637				19232	8633		
21	Ellis	1336					1304			
22	Ellsworth	1185					1159			
23	Ford	427					317			
24	Franklin	10385	3030				9961	3030		
25	Godfrey		19					19		
26	Greenwood	3484	759				3440	759		
27	Howard	2794					2794			
28	Hunter		158					150		
29	Jackson	6053	1936				5937	1936		
30	Jefferson	12526	4459				11901	4439		

TABLE VIII.—*Population by Counties at each Census—IOWA*—Continued.

Colored.				Chinese.	Indian.		
1870.	1860.	1850.	1840.	1870.	1870.	1860.	
153	1						74
							75
						10	76
							77
303	13						78
163	9				5		79
79	7						80
5	1						81
1							82
246	39	14	8				83
6	1						84
							85
2							86
45							87
101							88
13							89
211	4	5	2				90
193	47	5					91
81	14						92
53	13						93
1	11	1					94
9	4						95
1							96
25							97
44	3				9	38	98
							99
2							100

(c) In table 2, quarto volume, census of 1850, 1 free colored reported erroneously as in Howard County instead of Iowa County.

TABLE VIII.—*Population by Counties at each Census—KANSAS.*

Colored.					Indian.					
1870.	1860.	1850.	1840.	1830.	1870.	1860.	1850.	1840.	1830.	
17108	627				914	189				
152	3				1					1
112	2									2
1136	36				3					3
										4
770	65				9	1				5
										6
95					7					7
30	5				3					8
6										9
134					5					10
10										11
7										12
156										13
										14
2										15
122	1				4					16
17										17
833	41				1	16				18
										19
2352	4				8					20
31					1					21
28										22
109					1					23
364					60					24
										25
35										26
										27
	8									28
45					71					29
625	20									30

TABLE VIII.—*Population by Counties at each Census—KANSAS*—Continue

	Counties.	Aggregate.					White.			
		1870.	1860.	1850.	1840.	1830.	1870.	1860.	1850.	184
31	Jewell	207					207			
32	Johnson	13684	4364				13241	4364		
33	Labette	9973					9879			
34	Leavenworth	32444	12606				28148	12311		
35	Lincoln	516					516			
36	Linn	12174	6336				11504	6313		
37	Lykins		4980					4978		
38	Lyon	8014					7888			
39	Madison		636					636		
40	Marion	768	74				766	74		
41	Marshall	6901	2280				6893	2280		
42	McGhee		1501					1428		
43	McPherson	738					727			
44	Miami	11725					11248			
45	Mitchell	485					485			
46	Montgomery	7564					7496			
47	Morris	2225	770				2152	770		
48	Nemaha	7339	2436				7316	2436		
49	Neosho	10206					10130			
50	Ness	2					2			
51	Osage	7648	1113				7530	1113		
52	Osborne	33					33			
53	Otoe		238					214		
54	Ottawa	2127					2125			
55	Pawnee	179					173			
56	Pottawattamie	7848	1529				7255	1529		
57	Republic	1281					1281			
58	Rice	5					5			
59	Riley	5105	1224				5035	1224		
60	Russell	156					143			
61	Saline	4246					4240			
62	Sedgwick	1095					1085			
63	Shawnee	13121	3513				12032	3505		
64	Smith	66					66			
65	Sumner	22					22			
66	Trego	166					165			
67	Wabaunsee	3362	1023				3183	1023		
68	Wallace	538					536			
69	Washington	4081	383				4079	383		
70	Wilson	6694	27				6689	27		
71	Woodson	3827	1488				3793	1488		
72	Wyandotte	10015	2609				7839	2420		

TABLE VIII.—*Population by Counties at each Census—KENTUCKY.*

	Counties.	Aggregate.									Whi	
		1870.	1860.	1850.	1840.	1830.	1820.	1810.	1800.	1790.	1870.	186
	The State	1321011	1155684	982405	779828	687917	*182 564135	406511	220955	73677	1098692	9194
1	Adair	11065	9509	9898	8466	8217	8765	6011			9229	78
2	Allen	10296	9187	8742	7329	6485	5327				9192	76
3	Anderson	5449	7404	6260	5452	4520					4751	60
4	Ballard	12576	8692	5496							11099	69
5	Barren	17780	16665	20240	17288	15079	10328	11286	4784		14157	125
6	Bath	10145	12113	12115	9763	8799	7961				8443	94
7	Boone	10696	11196	11185	10034	9075	6542	3608	1534		9684	94
8	Bourbon	14863	14860	14466	14478	18436	17664	18009	12825	7837	8186	77
9	Boyd	8573	6044								8282	56
10	Boyle	9515	9304	9116							5836	55
11	Bracken	11409	11021	8903	7053	6518	5280	3700	2606		10773	101
12	Breathitt	5672	4980	3785	2195						5491	47
13	Breckenridge	13440	13236	10593	8944	7345	7485	3430	807		11758	108
14	Bullitt	7781	7289	6774	6334	5652	5831	4311	3542		6587	58
15	Butler	9404	7927	5755	3898	3058	3083	2181			8761	71
16	Caldwell	10826	9318	13048	10365	8324	9022	4268			8748	68
17	Calloway	9410	9915	8096	9794	5164					8598	84

TABLE VIII.—*Population by Counties at each Census—KANSAS*—Continued.

COLORED.					INDIAN.					
1870.	1860.	1850.	1840.	1830.	1870.	1860.	1850.	1840.	1830.	
...	...	...	...	...	...	...	...	...	...	31
438	...	...	...	...	5	...	...	...	...	32
94	...	...	...	...	...	...	...	...	...	33
4284	295	...	...	...	12	...	...	...	...	34
...	...	...	...	...	...	...	...	...	...	35
655	1	...	...	...	15	22	...	...	...	36
...	...	...	...	...	...	2	...	...	...	37
126	...	...	...	...	...	...	...	...	...	38
...	...	...	...	...	...	...	...	...	...	39
1	...	...	...	...	1	...	...	...	...	40
8	...	...	...	...	...	...	...	...	...	41
...	66	...	...	...	...	7	...	...	...	42
11	...	...	...	...	...	...	...	...	...	43
466	...	...	...	...	11	...	...	...	...	44
...	...	...	...	...	...	...	...	...	...	45
65	...	...	...	...	3	...	...	...	...	46
72	...	...	...	...	1	...	...	...	...	47
23	...	...	...	...	...	...	...	...	...	48
45	...	...	...	...	31	...	...	...	...	49
...	...	...	...	...	...	...	...	...	...	50
118	...	...	...	...	...	...	...	...	...	51
...	...	...	...	...	...	...	...	...	...	52
...	24	...	...	...	...	...	...	...	...	53
2	...	...	...	...	...	...	...	...	...	54
6	...	...	...	...	...	...	...	...	...	55
443	...	...	...	...	150	...	...	...	...	56
...	...	...	...	...	...	...	...	...	...	57
...	...	...	...	...	...	...	...	...	...	58
70	...	...	...	...	...	...	...	...	...	59
13	...	...	...	...	...	...	...	...	...	60
6	...	...	...	...	...	...	...	...	...	61
9	...	...	...	...	1	...	...	...	...	62
729	8	...	...	...	360	...	...	...	...	63
...	...	...	...	...	...	...	...	...	...	64
...	...	...	...	...	...	...	...	...	...	65
1	...	...	...	...	...	...	...	...	...	66
85	...	...	...	...	94	...	...	...	...	67
2	...	...	...	...	...	...	...	...	...	68
2	...	...	...	...	...	...	...	...	...	69
5	...	...	...	...	...	...	...	...	...	70
34	...	...	...	...	...	...	...	...	...	71
2120	48	...	...	...	56	141	...	...	...	72

TABLE VIII.—*Population by Counties at each Census—KENTUCKY.*

WHITE—Continued.						COLORED. (a)									
1840.	1830.	1820.	1810.	1800.	1790.	1870.	1860.	1850.	1840.	1830.	1820.	1810.	1800.	1790.	
590253	517787	434644	324237	179873	61133	222210	236167	220992	189575	170130	129491	82274	41082	12544	
6769	6451	7249	5050	...	...	1836	1662	1815	1697	1766	1516	961	...	...	1
6375	5321	4594	...	...	...	1104	1562	1357	954	964	731	...	...	...	2
4372	3518	...	...	...	...	698	1371	1312	1080	1002	...	...	...	...	3
...	...	...	...	...	...	1477	1749	868	...	...	...	...	...	...	4
13147	11316	7875	9552	4279	...	3623	4126	4697	4141	3763	2453	1734	505	...	5
7706	7186	6685	...	...	...	2702	2641	2651	2055	1613	1276	...	...	...	6
7924	7214	5227	2924	1194	...	1012	1793	2141	2210	1861	1315	684	340	...	7
7845	11272	12369	13650	10627	6929	6677	7067	7311	6653	7164	5295	4359	2198	908	8
...	...	...	...	...	...	291	173	...	...	...	...	...	...	...	9
...	...	...	...	...	...	3679	3714	3741	...	...	...	...	...	...	10
6083	5575	4560	3317	2349	...	636	833	954	970	943	730	389	257	...	11
2076	...	...	...	...	...	181	215	182	119	...	...	...	...	...	12
7239	5849	6217	2919	765	...	1682	2357	1977	1705	1496	1268	511	42	...	13
4906	4503	4578	3321	2564	...	1194	1474	1382	1338	1149	1253	990	978	...	14
3379	2601	2611	1899	...	...	643	795	700	519	457	472	282	...	...	15
8091	6527	7567	3685	...	...	2078	2445	3246	2274	1797	1455	583	...	...	16
8870	4732	...	...	...	...	812	1506	1008	924	432	...	...	...	...	17

4 C C

TABLE VIII.—*Population by Counties at each Census—KENTUCKY*—Continued.

	Counties.	AGGREGATE.									WHITE.		
		1870.	1860.	1850.	1840.	1830.	1820.	1810.	1800.	1790.	1870.	1860.	1850.
18	Campbell	27406	20909	13127	5214	9883	7022	3473	1903	......	27123	20701	12871
19	Carroll	6189	6578	5526	3966	......	......	......	......	......	5649	5491	4549
20	Carter	7509	8516	6241	2905	......	......	......	......	......	7400	8170	5969
21	Casey	8884	6466	6556	4939	4342	4349	3285	......	......	8340	5743	5882
22	Christian	23227	21627	19580	15587	12684	10459	11020	2318	......	13415	11619	11290
23	Clark	10882	11484	12683	10802	13051	11449	11519	7653	......	7167	6598	7703
24	Clay	8297	6652	5421	4607	3548	4393	2398	......	......	7802	6041	4734
25	Clinton	6497	5781	4889	3863	......	......	......	......	......	6205	5503	4589
26	Crittenden	9381	8796	6351	......	......	......	......	......	......	8572	7838	5471
27	Cumberland	7690	7340	7005	6090	8624	8058	6191	3284	......	6181	5874	5476
28	Daviess	20714	15549	12362	8331	5209	3876	......	......	......	17111	11958	9419
29	Edmondson	4459	4645	4088	2914	2642	......	......	......	......	4233	4361	3748
30	Elliott	4433	......	......	......	......	......	......	......	......	4411	......	......
31	Estill	9198	6886	5985	5535	4618	3507	2082	......	......	8590	6363	5568
32	Fayette	26656	22599	22735	22194	25098	23250	21370	14028	18410	14142	11889	11178
33	Fleming	13398	12489	13914	13268	13499	12186	8947	5016	......	11842	10350	11617
34	Floyd	7877	6388	5714	6302	4347	3207	3485	478	......	7706	6168	5309
							*74						
35	Franklin	15300	12694	12462	9420	9254	10950	8013	5078	......	10637	8860	8749
36	Fulton	6161	5317	4446	......	......	......	......	......	......	5824	4220	3428
37	Gallatin	5074	5056	5137	4003	6674	7075	3307	1291	......	4474	4334	4299
38	Garrard	10376	10531	10237	10480	11871	10851	9186	6186	......	6972	6857	7026
39	Grant	9529	8356	6531	4192	2986	1805	......	......	......	9020	7630	5993
40	Graves	19398	16233	11397	7465	2504	......	......	......	......	17069	13386	9959
41	Grayson	11580	7982	6837	4461	3880	4055	2301	......	......	11173	7628	6397
42	Green	9379	8806	9060	14212	13138	11943	6735	6096	......	7442	6323	6339
43	Greenup	11463	8760	9654	6297	5852	4311	2369	......	......	11002	8350	8994
44	Hancock	6591	6213	3853	2581	1515	......	......	......	......	5861	5882	3316
45	Hardin	15705	15189	14525	16357	12849	10498	7531	3653	......	13429	13026	12022
46	Harlan	4415	5494	4268	3015	2929	1961	......	......	......	4304	5352	4108
47	Harrison	12993	13779	13064	12472	13234	12278	7752	4350	......	10615	10341	9733
48	Hart	13687	10348	9093	7031	5191	4184	......	......	......	11495	8878	7739
49	Henderson	18457	14262	12171	9548	6659	5714	4703	1468	......	12467	8405	7651
50	Henry	11066	11949	11442	10015	11387	10816	6777	3258	......	8828	8602	8073
51	Hickman	8453	7008	4791	8968	5198	......	......	......	......	6818	5739	3002
52	Hopkins	13827	11875	12441	9171	6763	5322	2964	......	......	11958	9836	10199
53	Jackson	4547	3087	......	......	......	......	......	......	......	4496	3050	......
							*2						
54	Jefferson	118953	89404	59831	36346	23979	20766	13399	8754	4765	99606	77093	47283
55	Jessamine	8638	9465	10249	9396	9960	9297	8377	5461	......	5190	5671	6256
56	Johnson	7494	5306	3873	......	......	......	......	......	......	7373	5960	3843
57	Josh Bell	3731	......	......	......	......	......	......	......	......	3620	......	......
58	Kenton	36096	25467	17038	7816	......	......	......	......	......	34430	24815	16117
59	Knox	8294	7707	7050	5722	4315	3661	5875	1109	......	7737	7034	6236
60	La Rue	8235	6891	5859	......	......	......	......	......	......	7270	5987	5177
61	Laurel	6016	5488	4145	3079	2206	......	......	......	......	5872	5301	3947
62	Lawrence	8497	7601	6281	4730	3900	......	......	......	......	8376	7443	6142
63	Lee	3055	......	......	......	......	......	......	......	......	2994	......	......
64	Letcher	4608	3904	2512	......	......	......	......	......	......	4479	3787	2440
65	Lewis	9115	8361	7202	6306	5229	3973	2357	......	......	8697	8114	6872
							*6						
66	Lincoln	10947	10647	10093	10187	11002	9975	8676	8621	6548	7871	7059	6634
67	Livingston	8200	7213	6578	9025	5971	5824	3674	2856	......	7147	5065	5401
68	Logan	20429	19021	16581	13615	13012	14423	12123	5807	......	14706	12295	10750
69	Lyon	6233	5307	......	......	......	......	......	......	......	4814	4167	......
70	Madison	19543	17207	15727	16355	18751	15954	15540	10490	5772	13271	11025	10209
71	Magoffin	4684	3485	......	......	......	......	......	......	......	4505	3338	......
72	Marion	12838	12593	11765	11032	......	......	......	......	......	9495	9004	8508
73	Marshall	9455	6982	5269	......	......	......	......	......	......	9070	6596	5000
74	Mason	18126	18222	18344	15719	16199	13588	12450	12182	2729	14514	14065	13674
75	McCracken	13988	10360	6067	4745	1297	......	......	......	......	10699	8554	5037
76	McLean	7614	6144	......	......	......	......	......	......	......	6800	5227	......
77	Meade	9485	8898	7393	5780	4131	......	......	......	......	8191	6944	5790
78	Menifee	1986	......	......	......	......	......	......	......	......	1970	......	......
							*190						
79	Mercer	13144	13701	14067	18720	17694	15487	12630	9646	7091	9834	10149	10471
80	Metcalfe	7934	6745	......	......	......	......	......	......	......	7073	5014	......
81	Monroe	9231	8551	7756	6526	5340	4956	......	......	......	8442	7619	6962
82	Montgomery	7557	7859	9903	9332	10240	9587	12975	7082	......	4858	4967	6686
83	Morgan	5975	9237	7620	4603	2857	......	......	......	......	5931	8986	7395
84	Muhlenburg	12638	10725	9809	6964	5340	4979	4181	1443	......	11005	9101	8250
85	Nelson	14804	15799	14789	13637	14932	16273	14078	9860	11315	10886	10160	9541
86	Nicholas	9129	11030	10361	8745	8834	7973	4898	2925	......	7885	9261	8682
87	Ohio	15561	12209	9749	6592	4715	3879	3792	1223	......	14108	10888	8365
88	Oldham	9027	7283	7629	7380	9588	......	......	......	......	6217	4915	5156
89	Owen	14309	12719	10444	8232	5786	2031	......	......	......	13133	10989	6882
90	Owsley	3889	5335	3774	......	......	......	......	......	......	3812	5205	3616
91	Pendleton	14030	10443	6774	4455	3863	3086	3061	1613	......	13389	9977	6230

TABLE VIII.—*Population by Counties at each Census—KENTUCKY*—Continued.

WHITE—Continued.					COLORED. (a)									
1830.	1820.	1810.	1800.	1790.	1870.	1860.	1850.	1840.	1830.	1820.	1810.	1800.	1790.	
8828	6115	2991	1612	......	282	204	256	293	1055	907	482	291	......	18
......	......	......	......	......	540	1087	977	754	......	......	......	......	......	19
......	......	......	......	......	100	346	281	194	......	......	......	......	......	20
3943	3876	3039	......	......	544	723	693	568	499	473	246	......	......	21
8283	6943	9235	2021	......	9812	10008	8290	6096	4401	3516	1785	297	......	22
8489	7945	8562	6075	......	3715	4886	4974	4047	4502	3504	2957	1578	......	23
3117	4018	2257	......	......	495	611	687	653	431	375	141	......	......	24
......	......	......	......	......	292	278	300	189	......	......	......	......	......	25
......	......	......	......	......	809	958	878	......	......	......	......	......	......	26
6918	6712	5266	3012	......	1500	1466	1529	1519	1706	1346	925	272	......	27
3274	3017	......	......	......	3603	3501	2943	2004	1335	859	......	......	......	28
2305	......	......	......	......	226	284	340	335	337	......	......	......	......	29
......	......	......	......	......	22	......	......	......	......	......	......	......	......	30
4147	3218	1948	......	......	509	523	417	575	471	289	134	......	......	31
13688	13728	13498	9715	14626	12513	10700	11557	11309	11410	9522	7872	4313	3784	32
11663	11011	8381	4752	......	1556	2130	2207	2110	1836	1175	566	264	......	33
4190	7867	3370	447	......	171	220	211	199	157	340	115	31	......	34
5922	7261	5756	3687	......	4663	3834	3722	3083	3279	3689	2257	1301	......	35
......	......	......	......	......	937	1097	947	......	......	......	......	......	......	36
5466	5817	2607	960	......	600	722	738	649	1208	1258	700	331	......	37
8242	7901	7088	4921	......	3404	3674	3208	3370	3629	2050	2098	1265	......	38
2717	1666	......	......	......	509	726	538	354	260	139	......	......	......	39
2222	......	......	......	......	2320	2847	1447	821	282	......	......	......	......	40
3631	3836	2198	......	......	407	354	330	199	249	219	103	......	......	41
9502	8683	5265	5257	......	1937	2483	2725	3949	3636	3260	1470	839	......	42
4832	3730	1874	......	......	461	410	662	818	1020	581	495	......	......	43
1165	......	......	......	......	729	831	637	542	350	......	......	......	......	44
10757	9009	6563	3317	......	2276	2563	2502	2528	2092	1489	968	336	......	45
2786	1851	......	......	......	99	142	160	87	143	110	......	......	......	46
10342	10051	6638	3925	......	2378	3432	3331	3477	2892	2227	1114	425	......	47
4366	3572	......	......	......	2192	1470	1354	1053	825	612	......	......	......	48
4078	3419	3160	1076	......	5990	5644	4520	3367	2581	2295	1534	392	......	49
8880	8808	5629	2848	......	2438	3347	3067	2778	2507	2008	1148	410	......	50
4324	......	......	......	......	1635	1269	859	1623	874	......	......	......	......	51
5427	4334	2551	......	......	1869	2039	2242	1754	1336	988	413	......	......	52
......	......	......	......	......	51	28	......	......	......	......	......	......	......	53
16714	13665	8938	6325	3857	19140	12311	12548	9350	7265	7101	4461	2429	908	54
6437	6395	5858	3879	......	3439	3794	3993	3616	3523	2902	2519	1582	......	55
......	......	......	......	......	37	46	30	......	......	......	......	......	......	56
......	......	......	......	......	111	......	......	......	......	......	......	......	......	57
......	......	......	......	......	1657	652	921	785	......	......	......	......	......	58
3781	3305	5528	1044	......	557	673	812	700	534	356	347	65	......	59
......	......	......	......	......	965	904	682	......	......	......	......	......	......	60
2077	......	......	......	......	144	187	198	115	125	......	......	......	......	61
3806	......	......	......	......	121	158	139	78	94	......	......	......	......	62
......	......	......	......	......	131	......	......	......	......	......	......	......	......	63
......	......	......	......	......	129	117	72	......	......	......	......	......	......	64
4751	3505	2072	......	......	298	247	330	433	478	468	285	......	......	65
7245	6862	6307	6822	5446	3076	3588	3459	3605	3757	3111	2369	1799	1102	66
4801	4770	2932	2306	......	1052	1258	1177	1687	1170	1054	742	460	......	67
8282	9590	9468	4939	......	5723	6726	5831	5136	4730	4833	2655	868	......	68
......	......	......	......	......	1419	1140	......	......	......	......	......	......	......	69
12629	11738	12481	8761	5035	6272	6182	5458	5495	6122	4216	3059	1729	737	70
......	......	......	......	......	179	147	......	......	......	......	......	......	......	71
......	......	......	......	......	3343	3589	3167	2602	......	......	......	......	......	72
......	......	......	......	......	385	386	269	......	......	......	......	......	......	73
11649	10160	9992	10347	2500	3582	4157	4670	4581	4560	3128	2467	1835	229	74
1149	......	......	......	......	3289	1806	830	681	149	......	......	......	......	75
......	......	......	......	......	814	917	......	......	......	......	......	......	......	76
3181	......	......	......	......	1294	1954	1504	1414	950	......	......	......	......	77
......	......	......	......	......	16	......	......	......	......	......	......	......	......	78
12596	11530	9290	7297	3745	3310	3552	3596	5659	5008	3957	3340	2349	1346	79
......	......	......	......	......	861	831	......	......	......	......	......	......	......	80
4690	4453	......	......	......	789	939	854	715	650	503	......	......	......	81
7506	7504	11171	6304	......	2609	2892	3237	2023	2734	2083	1804	778	......	82
2809	......	......	......	......	44	251	225	64	48	......	......	......	......	83
4227	4302	3698	1313	......	1633	1624	1559	1209	1015	677	483	130	......	84
10207	12340	10940	7948	10032	3918	5639	5246	4759	4725	3933	3138	1018	1283	85
7519	7021	4368	2597	......	1244	1769	1679	1435	1315	952	530	328	......	86
4104	3392	3245	1069	......	1393	1321	1181	845	611	487	547	154	......	87
6913	......	......	......	......	2810	2468	2473	2522	2673	......	......	......	......	88
4501	1823	......	......	......	1176	1730	1562	1317	885	208	......	......	......	89
......	......	......	......	......	75	130	158	......	......	......	......	......	......	90
3424	2758	2674	1371	......	641	466	544	442	439	328	387	242	......	91

TABLE VIII.—*Population by Counties at each Census—KENTUCKY*—**Continued.**

	Counties.	AGGREGATE.									WHITE.		
		1870.	1860.	1850.	1840.	1830.	1820.	1810.	1800.	1790.	1870.	1860.	1850.
92	Perry	4274	3950	3092	3089	3330	......	......	......	......	4173	3863	2972
93	Pike	9562	7384	5365	3567	2677	......	......	......	......	9460	7247	5258
94	Powell	2599	2257	......	......	......	......	......	......	......	2360	2108	......
95	Pulaski	17670	17201	14195	9620	9500	7597	6897	3161	......	16305	15819	12861
96	Robertson	5399	......	......	......	......	......	......	......	......	5142	......	......
97	Rock Castle	7145	5343	4697	3409	2865	2249	1731	......	......	6776	4946	4289
98	Rowan	2991	2282	......	......	......	......	......	......	......	2950	2139	......
99	Russell	5809	6024	5349	4238	3879	......	......	......	......	5516	5453	4901
100	Scott	11607	14417	14946	13668	14677	14219	12419	8007	......	7651	8441	8891
101	Shelby	15733	16433	17095	17768	19030	21047	14877	8191	......	10350	9634	10289
102	Simpson	9573	8146	7733	6537	5815	4852	......	......	......	7406	5743	5758
103	Spencer	5956	6188	6842	6581	6812	......	......	......	......	4477	3974	4650
104	Taylor	8226	7481	7250	......	......	......	......	......	......	6376	5755	5462
105	Todd	12612	11575	12268	9991	8680	5089	......	......	......	7752	6681	7361
106	Trigg	13686	11051	10129	7716	5916	3874	......	......	......	9880	7362	7232
107	Trimble	5577	5880	5963	4480	......	......	......	......	......	5121	5044	4993
108	Union	13640	12791	9012	6673	4764	3470	......	......	......	11066	9666	6704
109	Warren	21742	17320	15123	15446	10949	11776	11937	4686	......	15375	11790	10597
110	Washington	12464	11575	12194	10596	19017	15947	13248	9050	......	10354	8707	9080
111	Wayne	10602	10259	8692	7399	8685	7951	5430	......	......	9927	9244	7855
112	Webster	10937	7533	......	......	......	......	......	......	......	9582	6417	......
113	Whitley	8278	7762	7447	4673	3806	2340	......	......	......	8140	7552	7222
114	Wolfe	3603	......	......	......	......	......	......	......	......	3575	......	......
115	Woodford	8240	11219	12423	11740	12273	12207	9659	6624	9210	4415	5270	5858

(*) All other persons, except Indians not taxed.

TABLE VIII.—*Population by Counties at each Census—LOUISIANA.*

	Parishes.	AGGREGATE.							WHITE.		
		1870.	1860.	1850.	1840.	1830.	1820.	1810.	1870.	1860.	1850.
	The State	726915	708002	517762	352411	a210 215529	*484 152923	76556	362065	357456	255491
1	Ascension	11577	11484	10752	6951	5426	3728	2219	4265	3940	3340
2	Assumption	13234	15379	10538	7141	5669	3576	2472	6247	7189	5170
3	Avoyelles	12926	13167	9326	6616	3484	2245	1209	6751	5904	4059
4	Bienville	10636	†11000	5539	......	......	......	......	5589	†5000	3683
5	Bossier	12675	11348	6962	......	......	......	......	3505	3348	2307
6	Caddo	21714	12140	8884	5282	......	......	......	5913	4733	3634
7	Calcasieu (b)	6733	5928	3914	2057	......	......	......	5171	4451	2718
8	Caldwell	4820	4833	2815	2017	......	......	......	2596	2888	1584
9	Cameron (b)	1591	......	......	......	......	......	......	1249	......	......
10	Carroll	10110	18052	8789	4237	......	......	......	2390	4124	2336
11	Catahoula	8475	11651	7132	4955	2581	2287	1164	4381	5492	3585
12	Claiborne	20240	16848	7471	6185	1764	......	......	9630	8996	4949
13	Concordia	9977	13805	7758	9414	4662	2626	2895	720	1242	823
14	De Soto	14962	13298	8023	......	......	......	......	5111	4777	3549
15	East Baton Rouge	17816	16046	11977	8138	6698	*412 4808	1463	6471	6944	5347
16	East Feliciana	13499	14697	13598	11893	8247	*65 c12667	......	4106	4081	4060
17	Franklin	5078	6162	3251	......	......	......	......	2233	2738	1664
18	Grant (d)	4517	......	......	......	......	......	......	2078	......	......
19	Iberia (f)	9042	......	......	......	......	......	......	4531	......	......
20	Iberville	12347	14661	12278	8495	7049	4414	2679	3669	3793	3568
21	Jackson	7646	9465	5566	......	......	......	......	4203	5367	3406
22	Jefferson	17767	15372	25093	10470	6846	......	......	6709	9964	18046
23	Lafayette	10388	9003	6720	7841	5653	......	......	5631	4307	3390
24	Lafourche	14719	14044	9532	7303	5503	*7 3748	1995	8060	7500	5142
25	Livingston (g)	4026	4431	3385	2315	......	......	......	3085	3120	2584
26	Madison	8600	14133	8773	5142	......	......	......	936	1640	1416
27	Morehouse	9387	10357	3913	......	......	......	......	3012	3784	1577
28	Natchitoches	18265	16699	14228	14350	7905	7486	2870	7312	6304	5466
29	Orleans	191418	174491	119460	102193	49826	41351	24552	140923	149063	91431
30	Ouachita	11582	4727	5008	4640	5140	2896	1077	3759	1887	2292

TABLE VIII.—*Population by Counties at each Census—KENTUCKY*—Continued.

WHITE—Continued.						COLORED. (a)									
1840.	1830.	1820.	1810.	1800.	1790.	1870.	1860.	1850.	1840.	1830.	1820.	1810.	1800.	1790.	
2923	3150	.....	.....	.....	.....	96	87	120	166	180	.....	.....	.....	.....	92
3469	2599	.....	.....	.....	.....	102	137	115	98	78	.....	.....	.....	.....	93
.....	.....	.....	.....	.....	.....	239	149	.....	.....	.....	.....	.....	.....	.....	94
8383	8473	6951	6429	2928	.....	1075	1382	1334	1037	1027	646	468	233	.....	95
.....	.....	.....	.....	.....	.....	257	.....	.....	.....	.....	.....	.....	.....	.....	96
3023	2575	2098	1568	.....	.....	369	* 397	408	386	200	161	163	.....	.....	97
.....	.....	.....	.....	.....	.....	32	143	.....	.....	.....	.....	.....	.....	.....	98
3828	3419	.....	.....	.....	.....	293	571	448	410	460	.....	.....	.....	.....	99
8230	9146	9545	8509	6085	.....	3955	5976	6055	5448	5531	4074	3820	1922	.....	100
11256	13015	15796	11721	6681	.....	5383	6799	6806	6512	6015	5251	3156	1510	.....	101
5004	4570	4032	.....	.....	.....	2167	2403	1977	1533	1245	820	.....	.....	.....	102
4650	5281	.....	.....	.....	.....	1479	2214	2183	1931	1531	.....	.....	.....	.....	103
.....	.....	.....	.....	.....	.....	1850	1720	1788	.....	.....	.....	.....	.....	.....	104
6070	5459	3356	.....	.....	.....	4860	4894	4907	3921	3221	1733	.....	.....	.....	105
5614	4467	3039	.....	.....	.....	3606	3489	2877	2102	1449	835	.....	.....	.....	106
3787	.....	.....	.....	.....	.....	456	836	970	693	.....	.....	.....	.....	.....	107
4999	3388	2429	.....	.....	.....	2574	3125	2308	1764	1376	1041	.....	.....	.....	108
11078	7989	9169	10422	4251	.....	6367	5521	4526	4368	2960	2607	1515	435	.....	109
7900	14218	12159	10981	7611	.....	2110	2868	3108	2696	4799	3788	2267	1439	.....	110
6754	8046	7393	5200	.....	.....	675	1015	837	645	639	558	230	.....	.....	111
.....	.....	.....	.....	.....	.....	1355	1116	.....	.....	.....	.....	.....	.....	.....	112
4508	3665	2232	.....	.....	.....	138	209	225	165	141	108	.....	.....	.....	113
.....	.....	.....	.....	.....	.....	28	.....	.....	.....	.....	.....	.....	.....	.....	114
5816	6498	7422	6153	4502	6963	3825	5943	6545	5924	5775	4785	3506	2122	2247	115

(a) At 1870: Chinese, 1; Indians, 108, as follows: Campbell, 1 Indian; Fayette, 1 Indian; Hancock, Chinese; Harlan, 12 Indians; Jefferson, 1 Indian; Johnson, 84 Indians; Livingston, 1 Indian; Owsley, 2 Indians; Perry, 5 Indians; Scott, 1 Indian. At 1860, Indians, 33, as follows: Breathitt, 15 Indians; Campbell, 4 Indians; Henderson, 13 Indians; Whitley, 1 Indian.

TABLE VIII.—*Population by Counties at each Census—LOUISIANA.*

WHITE—Continued.				COLORED.							CHINESE.	INDIAN.		
1840.	1830.	1820.	1810.	1870.	1860.	1850.	1840.	1830.	1820.	1810.	1870.	1870.	1860.	
158457	a210 89231	73383	34311	364210	350373	262271	193954	126298	79540	42245	71	569	173	
2255	1725	1495	1141	7310	7544	7412	4696	3701	2233	1078	2	3	.....	1
4103	3760	2409	1915	6984	8190	5368	3038	1909	1167	557	.....	.....	.....	2
3066	2114	1438	783	6175	7259	5267	3550	1370	807	426	.....	.....	4	3
.....	.....	.....	.....	5047	15100	1916	.....	.....	.....	.....	.....	.....	.....	4
.....	.....	.....	.....	9170	8000	4455	.....	.....	.....	.....	.....	.....	.....	5
2416	.....	.....	.....	15799	7407	5250	2866	.....	.....	.....	1	1	.....	6
1349	.....	.....	.....	1457	1476	1196	708	.....	.....	.....	.....	105	1	7
1354	.....	.....	.....	2224	1945	1231	663	.....	.....	.....	.....	.....	.....	8
.....	.....	.....	.....	342	.....	.....	.....	.....	.....	.....	.....	.....	.....	9
1146	.....	.....	.....	7718	13928	6453	3091	.....	.....	.....	12	.....	.....	10
2035	1643	1524	808	4083	6159	3547	2020	938	763	356	.....	11	.....	11
3846	1539	.....	.....	10008	7852	2522	2339	225	.....	.....	.....	2	.....	12
1380	1025	827	1279	9257	12563	6935	8031	3637	1799	1616	.....	.....	.....	13
.....	.....	.....	.....	9851	8521	4471	.....	.....	.....	.....	.....	.....	.....	14
3750	3162	2600	706	11343	9102	6630	4388	3530	2208	757	.....	2	.....	15
3992	3571	c5434	.....	9393	10616	9538	7901	4676	c7233	.....	.....	.....	.....	16
.....	.....	.....	.....	2844	3404	1587	.....	.....	.....	.....	.....	1	.....	17
.....	.....	.....	.....	2414	.....	.....	.....	.....	.....	.....	.....	25	.....	18
.....	.....	.....	.....	4510	.....	.....	.....	.....	.....	.....	1	.....	.....	19
2523	2380	2019	1429	8675	10868	8710	5972	4669	2395	1250	2	1	.....	20
.....	.....	.....	.....	3443	4098	2160	.....	.....	.....	.....	.....	.....	.....	21
4866	1596	.....	.....	11054	5407	7047	5604	5250	.....	.....	4	.....	1	22
4474	3177	.....	.....	4755	4694	3330	3367	2476	.....	.....	.....	2	2	23
3986	3310	2652	1691	6659	6544	4390	3317	2193	1096	304	.....	.....	.....	24
1533	.....	.....	.....	933	1311	861	782	.....	.....	.....	.....	8	.....	25
1210	.....	.....	.....	7663	12493	7357	3932	.....	.....	.....	.....	1	.....	26
.....	.....	.....	.....	6375	6573	2036	.....	.....	.....	.....	.....	.....	.....	27
7042	3892	4745	1213	10929	10393	8762	7308	4103	2741	1657	19	5	2	28
52519	21281	19244	8001	50456	25423	28029	42674	28545	22107	16551	23	16	5	29
2188	2938	2016	794	7823	2840	2716	2452	2202	880	293	.....	.....	.....	30

TABLE VIII.—*Population by Counties at each Census—LOUISIANA*—Continued.

	Parishes.	Aggregate.							White.		
		1870.	1860.	1850.	1840.	1830.	1820.	1810.	1870.	1860.	1850.
31	Plaquemines	10552	8494	7390	5060	4489	2354	1549	3703	2595	[illegible]
32	Point Coupée	12981	17718	11339	7898	5936	4912	4539	3752	4094	[illegible]
33	Rapides (d)	18015	25360	16561	14132	7575	6065	2200	7742	9711	5037
34	Richland (e)	5110	......	......	......	......	......	......	2405	......	......
35	Sabine	6456	5828	4515	......	......	......	......	4592	4115	3347
36	St. Bernard	3553	4076	3802	*3237	3356	2635	1020	1640	1771	[illegible]
37	St. Charles	4867	5297	5120	4700	5147	3862	3291	897	938	867
38	St. Helena (g)	5423	7130	4561	3525	4028	3026	......	2509	3413	[illegible]
39	St. James	10152	11499	11098	8548	7646	5660	3955	3275	3348	[illegible]
40	St. John the Baptist	6762	7930	7317	5776	5677	3854	2990	2715	3037	[illegible]
41	St. Landry	25553	23104	22253	15233	12591	10085	5048	13776	10703	10149
42	St. Martin (f)	9370	12674	11761	8674	7205	12063	7369	4280	4984	[illegible]
43	St. Mary (f)	13860	16816	13697	8950	6442	......	......	4203	3475	[illegible]
44	St. Tammany (g)	5586	5406	6364	4598	2864	1723	......	3411	3153	[illegible]
45	Tangipahoa (g)	7928	......	......	......	......	......	......	4934	......	......
46	Tensas	12419	16078	9040	......	......	......	......	1400	1479	906
47	Terrebonne	12451	12091	7724	4410	2121	......	......	6080	5131	[illegible]
48	Union	11685	10389	8203	1838	......	......	......	7311	6641	[illegible]
49	Vermillion (b)	4528	4324	3409	......	......	......	......	3480	3001	[illegible]
50	Washington (g)	3330	4708	3408	2649	2286	2517	......	2391	2996	[illegible]
51	West Baton Rouge	5114	7312	6270	4638	3084	2335	......	1710	1859	1815
52	West Feliciana	10499	11671	13245	10910	8629	......	......	1583	2036	[illegible]
53	Winn (d)	4954	6876	......	......	......	......	......	4044	5480	......

(*) All other persons, except Indians not taxed.
(†) Estimated.
(a) White deaf, dumb, blind, and aliens omitted erroneously by the assistant marshals, and returned by the marshal in the aggregate only.
(b) In 1870 Cameron from Calcasieu and Vermillion.

TABLE VIII.—*Population by Counties at each Census—MAINE.*

	Counties.	Aggregate.									White.		
		1870.	1860.	1850.	1840.	1830.	1820.	1810.	1800.	1790.	1870.	1860.	1850.
	The State	626915	628279	583169	501793	399455	[*66] 298269	228705	151719	96540	624809	626947	581813
1	Androscoggin	35866	29726	......	......	......	......	......	......	......	35826	29715	......
2	Aroostook	29609	22479	12529	9413	......	......	......	......	......	29353	22453	12529
3	Cumberland	82021	75591	79538	68658	60102	[*66] 49379	42831	38208	26105	81503	75116	78939
4	Franklin	18807	20403	20027	20801	......	......	......	......	......	18796	20398	20008
5	Hancock	36495	37757	34372	28605	24336	31290	30031	16358	9549	36444	37717	34343
6	Kennebec	53203	55655	62521	55823	52485	42623	32564	24571	......	53019	55511	62382
7	Knox	30823	32716	......	......	......	......	......	......	......	30707	32596	......
8	Lincoln	25597	27860	74875	63517	57192	53189	42992	30225	29236	25531	27814	74603
9	Oxford	33488	36698	39763	38351	35219	27104	17630	......	......	33465	36696	39758
10	Penobscot	75150	72731	63089	45705	31530	13870	......	......	......	74581	72632	63022
11	Piscataquis	14403	15032	14735	13138	......	......	......	......	......	14398	15032	14732
12	Sagadahoc	18803	21790	......	......	......	......	......	......	......	18693	21702	......
13	Somerset	34611	36753	35581	33912	35787	21787	12910	......	......	34582	36738	35567
14	Waldo	34522	38447	47230	41509	29788	......	......	......	......	34493	38423	47191
15	Washington	43343	42534	38811	28327	21294	12744	7870	4461	2758	43188	42360	38085
16	York	60174	62107	60098	54034	51722	46283	41877	37896	28892	60100	62054	60068

(*) All other persons, except Indians not taxed.

TABLE VIII.—*Population by Counties at each Census—LOUISIANA*—Continued.

WHITE—Continued.				COLORED.							CHINESE.	INDIAN.		
1840.	1830.	1820.	1810.	1870.	1860.	1850.	1840.	1830.	1820.	1810.	1870.	1870.	1860.	
1351	1082	637	557	6845	5899	5109	3709	3407	1717	902	......	4	......	31
2057	1471	1092	1248	9229	13624	8371	5811	4465	3820	3201	......	......	......	32
3343	2133	2491	986	10267	15649	11524	10880	5442	3574	1904	......	6	......	33
......	......	......	......	2705	......	......	......	......	......	......	......	......	......	34
......	......	......	......	1847	1713	1168	......	......	......	......	......	17	......	35
1035	790	637	628	1913	2305	2396	2202	2576	1908	392	......	......	......	36
874	871	727	880	3963	4359	4253	3896	4276	3135	2471	7	......	......	37
1945	2884	2164	......	2914	3717	2307	1580	1404	862	......	......	......	......	38
2769	2567	2522	1902	6877	8151	7813	5786	5089	3138	1993	......	......	......	39
2141	1980	1532	1402	4044	4893	4731	3635	3697	2722	1588	......	3	......	40
7179	6712	5368	2289	11694	12401	12113	8054	5879	4717	2059	......	83	......	41
3349	2810	5802	3950	5064	7669	7018	5125	4395	6201	3410	......	20	21	42
2366	1912	......	......	9607	13408	10274	6584	4530	......	......	......	50	33	43
2353	1318	1053	......	2175	2253	2722	2245	1546	670	......	......	......	......	44
......	......	......	......	2994	......	......	......	......	......	......	......	......	......	45
......	......	......	......	11018	14599	8140	......	......	......	......	......	1	......	46
2075	1063	......	......	6172	6857	4419	2335	1058	......	......	......	109	103	47
1273	......	......	......	4374	3748	3485	565	......	......	......	......	......	......	48
......	......	......	......	1047	1323	1081	......	......	......	......	......	1	......	49
1856	1695	1957	......	939	1712	1041	793	501	560	......	......	......	......	50
1371	1004	908	......	3404	5453	4455	3267	2080	1497	......	......	......	......	51
2064	2190	......	......	8915	9635	10772	8846	6439	......	......	......	1	......	52
......	......	......	......	909	1395	......	......	......	......	......	......	1	1	53

(c) East and West Feliciana.
(d) In 1869 Grant from Rapides and Winn.
(e) In 1868 organized.
(f) In 1868 Iberia from St. Martin and St. Mary.
(g) In 1869 Tangipahoa from Livingston, St. Helena, St. Tammany, and Washington.

TABLE VIII.—*Population by Counties at each Census—MAINE.*

WHITE—Continued.						COLORED (a.)									
1840.	1830.	1820.	1810.	1800.	1790.	1870.	1860.	1850.	1840.	1830.	1820.	1810.	1800.	1790.	
500438	398263	297340	227736	150901	96002	1606	1327	1356	1355	1192	929	969	818	538	
......	......	......	......	......	......	40	11	......	......	......	......	......	......	......	1
9410	......	......	......	......	......	56	26	6	3	......	......	......	......	......	2
62117	59649	49030	42465	37918	25919	517	475	599	511	453	349	366	200	186	3
20783	......	......	......	......	......	10	5	19	18	......	......	......	......	......	4
29581	24312	31249	29940	16316	9511	49	40	29	24	24	41	91	42	38	5
55624	52262	42457	32380	24402	......	184	144	139	199	223	166	174	169	......	6
......	......	......	......	......	......	116	130	......	......	......	......	......	......	......	7
63582	56964	53020	42828	30100	29096	58	46	272	235	228	169	161	125	140	8
38344	35188	27086	17617	......	......	23	2	5	7	31	18	13	......	......	9
45575	31489	13854	......	......	......	108	99	67	130	41	16	......	......	......	10
13137	......	......	......	......	......	54	......	3	1	......	......	......	......	......	11
......	......	......	......	......	......	109	83	......	......	......	......	......	......	......	12
33869	35763	21775	12910	......	......	24	15	14	23	22	12	......	......	......	13
41457	29739	......	......	......	......	29	24	30	52	29	......	......	......	......	14
22287	21233	12688	7834	4436	2738	155	174	128	60	61	56	36	25	20	15
52972	51642	46181	41752	37729	29738	74	53	36	62	80	102	125	167	154	16

(a) At 1870, Chinese, 1; Indians, 499, as follows: Cumberland, 1 Indian; Franklin, 1 Indian; Hancock, 1 Chinese and 1 Indian; Lincoln, 8 Indians; Penobscot, 461 Indians; Piscataquis, 21 Indians; Sagadahoc, 1 Indian; Somerset, 5 Indians. At 1860, Indians, 5, as follows: Sagadahoc, 5 Indians.

TABLE VIII.—*Population by Counties at each Census—MARYLAND.*

	Counties.	AGGREGATE.									WHITE.		
		1870.	1860.	1850.	1840.	1830.	1820.	1810.	1800.	1790.	1870.	1860.	1850.
	The State	780894	687049	583034	470019	447040	407350	380546	341548	319728	605497	515918	417943
1	Allegany	38536	28348	22769	15690	10609	8654	6909	6303	4809	37370	27215	21633
2	Anne Arundel	24457	23900	32393	29532	28295	27165	26668	22623	22598	12725	11704	16542
3	Baltimore	330741	266553	210646	134379	120870	96201	75810	59030	38937	282818	231242	174853
4	Calvert	9865	10447	9646	9229	8900	8073	8005	8297	8652	4332	3997	3630
5	Caroline	12101	11129	9692	7806	9070	10108	9453	9226	9506	8343	7604	6096
6	Carroll	28619	24533	20616	17241	......	......	......	......	......	26444	22525	18667
7	Cecil	25874	23862	18939	17232	15432	16048	13066	9018	13625	21860	19994	15472
8	Charles	15738	16517	16162	16023	17769	16500	20245	19172	20613	6418	5796	5665
9	Dorchester	19458	20461	18877	18843	18686	17759	18108	16346	15875	11902	11654	10747
10	Frederick	47572	46591	40987	36405	45789	40459	34437	31523	30791	39999	38391	33314
11	Harford	22605	23415	19356	17120	16319	15924	21258	17626	14976	17750	17971	14413
12	Howard	14150	13338	......	......	......	......	......	......	......	10676	9081	......
13	Kent	17102	13267	11386	10842	10501	11453	11450	11771	12836	9370	7347	5616
14	Montgomery	20563	18322	15860	15456	19816	16400	17980	15058	18003	13128	11349	9435
15	Prince George's	21138	23327	21549	19539	20474	20216	20589	21185	21344	11358	9650	8901
16	Queen Anne	16171	15961	14484	12633	14397	14952	16648	14857	15463	9579	8415	6936
17	Saint Mary's	14944	15213	13698	13224	13459	12974	12794	13699	15544	7218	6798	6223
18	Somerset (a)	18190	24992	22456	19508	20166	19579	17195	17358	15610	10916	15332	13386
19	Talbot	16137	14795	13811	12090	12947	14389	14230	13436	13084	9471	8106	7084
20	Washington	34712	31417	30848	28850	25268	23075	18730	18650	15822	31874	28305	26930
21	Wicomico (a)	15802	......	......	......	......	......	......	......	......	11396	......	......
22	Worcester (a)	16419	20661	18859	18377	18273	17421	16971	16370	11640	10550	13442	12401

(a) In 1867, Wicomico from Somerset and Worcester.

TABLE VIII.—*Population by Counties at each Census—MASSACHUSETTS.*

	Counties.	AGGREGATE.									WHITE.		
		1870.	1860.	1850.	1840.	1830.	1820.	1810.	1800.	1790.	1870.	1860.	1850.
	The State	1457351	1231066	994514	737699	610408	*128 523159	472040	422845	378787	1443156	1221432	985450
1	Barnstable	32774	35990	35276	32548	28514	24026	22211	19293	17354	32310	35890	35153
2	Berkshire	64827	55120	49591	41745	37835	35720	35907	33885	30291	63427	53910	48258
3	Bristol	102886	93794	76192	60164	49592	40908	37168	33880	31709	100777	91858	74650
4	Dukes	3787	4403	4540	3958	3517	3292	3290	3118	3265	3541	4385	4487
5	Essex	200843	165611	131300	94987	82859	74655	71888	61196	57913	199600	164952	130682
6	Franklin	32635	31434	30870	28812	29501	29268	......	......	......	32543	31370	30779
7	Hampden	78409	57366	51283	37366	31639	28021	......	......	......	77590	56883	50780
8	Hampshire	44388	37823	35732	30897	30254	26487	76275	72432	59681	44036	37509	35403
9	Middlesex	274353	216354	161383	106611	77961	61472	52789	46928	42737	272594	215458	160676
10	Nantucket	4123	6094	8452	9012	7202	*27 7239	6807	5617	4620	4038	5966	8058
11	Norfolk	89443	109950	78892	53140	41972	36471	31245	27216	......	89058	109702	78643
12	Plymouth	65365	64768	55697	47373	43044	*30 38106	35169	30073	29535	64834	64329	55241
13	Suffolk	270802	192700	144517	95773	62163	*50 43890	34381	28015	44875	267048	190279	142479
14	Worcester	192716	159659	130789	95313	84355	*21 73604	64910	61192	56807	191550	158881	130132

(*) All other persons, except Indians not taxed.

(a) At 1870, Chinese 97, Japanese 10, Indians 151, as follows: Barnstable, 4 Indians; Berkshire, 75 Chinese and 3 Indians; Bristol, 1 Chinese and 41 Indians; Essex, 3 Chinese and 2 Indians; Franklin, 1 Indian; Hampden, 6 Indians; Hampshire, 1 Japanese; Middlesex, 3 Chinese and 7 Indians; Nantucket,

TABLE VIII.—*Population by Counties at each Census—MARYLAND.*

White—Continued.						Colored. (b)									
1840.	1830.	1820.	1810.	1800.	1790.	1870.	1860.	1850.	1840.	1830.	1820.	1810.	1800.	1790.	
318204	291108	260223	235117	216326	208649	175391	171131	165091	151815	155932	147127	145429	125222	111079	
14663	9569	7664	6176	5703	4539	1166	1133	1136	1027	1040	990	733	600	270	1
14636	13872	13482	12439	11030	11664	11732	12196	15851	14902	14423	13681	14229	11593	10934	2
105331	92329	72635	57233	45050	30878	47921	35311	35793	29048	28541	23506	18577	13980	8059	3
3585	3788	3711	3680	3889	4211	5533	6450	6016	5644	5112	4362	4325	4408	4441	4
3334	6241	7144	6932	6759	7028	3758	3525	3596	2472	2829	2964	2521	2467	2478	5
15221	......	......	......	......	......	2175	2008	1949	2020	......	......	......	......	......	6
13329	11478	11923	9652	6542	10055	4014	3868	3467	3903	3954	4125	3414	2476	3570	7
6022	6789	6514	7398	9043	10124	9318	10721	10497	10001	10980	9986	12847	10129	10489	8
10629	10685	10095	10415	9415	10010	7556	8807	8130	8214	8001	7664	7693	6931	5863	9
28975	36703	31997	27983	26478	26937	7572	8200	7673	7430	9086	8462	6454	5045	3854	10
13041	11314	11217	14606	12018	10784	4855	5444	4943	5079	5005	4707	6632	5608	4192	11
......	......	......	......	......	......	3474	4257	......	......	......	......	......	......	......	12
5616	5044	5315	5222	5311	6748	7732	5020	5770	5226	5457	6138	6228	6260	6088	13
8706	12103	9082	9731	8508	11679	7434	6973	6425	6690	7713	7318	8249	6550	6324	14
7823	7687	7935	6471	8346	10004	9780	13677	12648	11716	12787	12281	14118	12839	11340	15
6132	6659	7226	7529	7315	8171	6592	7546	7548	6501	7738	7726	9119	7542	7292	16
6070	6097	6633	6158	6678	8216	7726	8415	7475	7154	7362	6941	6636	7021	7328	17
11485	11371	10384	9162	9340	8272	7274	9660	9071	8023	8795	9195	8033	8018	7338	18
6063	6291	7387	7249	7070	7231	6666	6689	6727	6027	6656	7002	6981	6366	5853	19
24724	21277	19247	15591	16108	14472	2838	3112	3918	4126	3991	3828	3139	2542	1350	20
......	......	......	......	......	......	4406	......	......	......	......	......	......	......	......	21
11765	11811	11232	11490	11523	7626	5869	7219	6458	6612	6462	6189	5481	4847	4014	22

(b) At 1870, Chinese 2, Indians 4, as follows: Baltimore, 1 Chinese and 1 Indian; Charles, 2 Indians; Frederick, 1 Chinese; Montgomery, 1 Indian.

TABLE VIII.—*Population by Counties at each Census—MASSACHUSETTS.*

White—Continued.						Colored. (a)									
1840.	1830.	1820.	1810.	1800.	1790.	1870.	1860.	1850.	1840.	1830.	1820.	1810.	1800.	1790.	
729030	603330	516419	465303	416393	373324	13947	9602	9064	8669	7049	6740	6737	6452	5463	
32111	28346	23845	21975	19030	16982	460	100	123	437	168	181	236	263	372	1
40467	36844	34858	35254	33301	29068	1322	1210	1333	1278	991	862	653	494	323	2
52934	48664	40110	36244	33072	30980	2067	1936	1533	1230	928	798	924	808	729	3
3938	3469	3195	3134	2916	3232	246	18	53	20	48	97	156	202	33	4
94480	82336	74060	71028	60285	57033	1038	659	618	507	523	655	860	911	880	5
28724	28310	29133	......	......	......	91	64	91	88	191	135	......	......	......	6
37054	31292	27715	......	......	......	813	483	503	312	347	306	......	......	......	7
30896	30029	26271	75669	71867	59230	351	254	329	201	225	216	606	565	451	8
106118	77444	61057	52415	46458	42140	1749	896	707	493	517	415	374	470	597	9
8433	6923	6992	6507	5389	4510	80	128	394	579	279	247	300	228	110	10
32880	41803	36214	30980	25890	......	353	218	249	160	169	257	256	326	......	11
47020	42633	37718	34749	29616	29032	506	439	456	353	411	388	420	457	503	12
93335	60280	42164	32897	26777	43819	3735	2398	2038	2438	1883	1726	1484	1238	1056	13
94740	83986	73147	64442	60702	56398	1136	769	637	573	369	457	468	490	409	14

5 Indians; Norfolk, 2 Chinese and 20 Indians; Plymouth, 1 Chinese and 24 Indians; Suffolk, 2 Chinese, 5 Japanese, and 12 Indians; Worcester, 26 Indians and 4 Japanese. At 1860, Indians 32, as follows: Suffolk, 23 Indians; Worcester, 9 Indians.

TABLE VIII.—*Population by Counties at each Census—MICHIGAN.*

	Counties.	AGGREGATE.								WHITE.	
		1870.	1860.	1850.	1840.	1830.	1820.	1810.	1800.	1870.	1860.
	The State	1184059	749113	397654	212267	31639	*131 8765	4762	a551	1167282	736142
1	Alcona	696	185							690	185
2	Allegan	32105	16087	5125	1783					31668	15993
3	Alpona	2756	290							2754	290
4	Antrim	1985	179							1920	178
5	Barry	22199	13858	5072	1078					22110	13785
6	Bay	15900	3164							15701	3166
7	Benzie (b)	2184								2155	
8	Berrien	35104	22378	11417	5011	325				34507	21931
9	Branch	26226	20981	12472	5715					26173	20948
10	Brown (c)					1356	952				
11	Calhoun	36569	29564	19162	10599					35954	29180
12	Cass	21094	17721	10907	5710	919				19351	16291
13	Charlevoix (d)	1724								1502	
14	Cheboygan	2196	517							2025	393
15	Chippewa	1689	1603	898	534	626				950	1351
16	Clare	366								366	
17	Clinton	22845	13916	5102	1614					22784	13902
18	Crawford (c)					692	*131 361				
19	Delta	2542	1172							2523	1052
20	Eaton	25171	16476	7058	2379					25093	16454
21	Emmet	1211	1149							111	123
22	Genesee	33900	22498	12031	4268					33779	22407
23	Gladwin (e)		14								14
24	Grand Traverse	4443	1286							4427	1263
25	Gratiot	11810	4042							11772	4034
26	Hillsdale	31684	25675	16159	7240					31615	25642
27	Houghton	13879	9234	708						13778	9203
28	Huron	9049	3165	210						8989	3164
29	Ingham	25268	17435	8631	2498					25109	17398
30	Ionia	27681	16682	7597	1923					27627	16612
31	Iosco	3163	175							3149	175
32	Iowa (c)					1587					
33	Isabella	4113	1443							4095	585
34	Jackson	36047	26671	19431	13130					35620	26480
35	Kalamazoo	32054	24646	13179	7380					31528	24327
36	Kalkaska	424								423	
37	Kent	50403	30716	12016	2587					50237	30500
38	Keweenaw (f)	4205								4200	
39	Lake	548								548	
40	Lapeer	21345	14754	7029	4265					21261	14685
41	Leelanaw	4576	2158							4047	1327
42	Lenawee	45595	38112	26372	17889	1491				45204	37861
43	Livingston	19336	16851	13485	7430					19279	16825
44	Mackinac (k)	1716								1406	
45	Macomb	27616	22843	15530	9716	2413	898	A580		27498	22780
46	Manistee	6074	975							6060	971
47	Manitou	891	1042							891	862
48	Marquette (r)	15033	2821	136						14900	2734
49	Mason	3263	831	93						3023	419
50	Mecosta	5642	970							6500	965
51	Menominee (j)	1791								*1777	
52	Michilimackinac (k)		1938	a3598	923	877	819	i615	a551		1011
53	Midland	3285	787	65						3269	786
54	Missaukee	130								130	
55	Monroe	27483	21593	14698	9922	3187	1831	m1340		27405	21504
56	Montcalm	13629	3968	891						13561	3957
57	Montmorenci (e)										
58	Muskegon	14894	3947							14854	3923
59	Newaygo	7294	2760	510						7159	2661
60	Oakland	40867	38261	31270	23646	4911	330			40402	37953
61	Oceana	7222	1816	300	496					6616	1236
62	Ogemaw	12								12	
63	Ontonagon	2845	4568	389						2813	4544
64	Osceola	2093	27							2076	27
65	Oscoda	70								70	
66	Otsego (e)										
67	Ottawa	26651	13215	5587	208					26541	13167
68	Presque Isle	355	26							354	26
69	Roscommon (e)										
70	Saginaw	39097	12693	2609	892					38683	12537
71	Sanilac	14562	7599	2112						14527	7599
72	Schoolcraft (t)		78	16							52
73	Shiawassee	20858	12349	5230	2103					20823	12334
74	St. Clair	36661	26604	10420	4606	1114				36593	26551

TABLE VIII.—*Population by Counties at each Census—MICHIGAN.*

White—Continued.					Colored.							Indian.		
40.	1830.	1820.	1810.	1800.	1870.	1860.	1850.	1840.	1830.	1820.	1810.	1870.	1860.	
1360	31346	8591	4618	a551	11849	6799	2583	707	293	174	144	p4926	6172	
....	......	......	......	......	......	......	......	......	......	......	......	......	......	1
1782	......	......	......	......	345	58	5	1	......	......	......	92	106	2
....	......	......	......	......	2	......	......	......	......	......	......	......	......	3
....	......	......	......	......	1	......	......	......	......	......	......	64	1	4
1078	......	......	......	......	89	58	39	......	......	......	......	......	15	5
....	......	......	......	......	116	6	......	......	......	......	......	83	52	6
....	......	......	......	......	29	......	......	......	......	......	......	......	......	7
4972	323	......	......	......	596	410	239	39	2	......	......	1	37	8
5710	......	......	......	......	53	33	16	5	......	......	......	......	......	9
....	1344	951	......	......	......	......	......	......	12	1	......	......	......	10
6576	......	......	......	......	560	376	207	23	......	......	......	55	8	11
5702	918	......	......	......	1690	1368	389	8	1	......	......	53	62	12
....	......	......	......	......	9	......	......	......	......	......	......	213	......	13
....	......	......	......	......	8	......	......	......	......	......	......	163	124	14
529	624	......	......	......	5	8	8	5	2	......	......	734	244	15
....	......	......	......	......	......	......	......	......	......	......	......	......	......	16
1614	......	......	......	......	60	14	2	......	......	......	......	1	......	17
....	680	345	......	......	......	......	......	......	12	16	......	......	......	18
....	......	......	......	......	4	......	......	......	......	......	......	15	120	19
2379	......	......	......	......	78	16	3	......	......	......	......	......	6	20
....	......	......	......	......	......	......	......	......	......	......	......	1100	1026	21
4259	......	......	......	......	104	44	28	9	......	......	......	17	47	22
....	......	......	......	......	......	......	......	......	......	......	......	......	......	23
....	......	......	......	......	11	......	......	......	......	......	......	5	43	24
....	......	......	......	......	32	9	......	......	......	......	......	6	9	25
7224	......	......	......	......	69	33	6	16	......	......	......	......	......	26
....	......	......	......	......	28	62	1	......	......	......	......	73	279	27
....	......	......	......	......	3	1	......	......	......	......	......	57	......	28
2497	......	......	......	......	158	37	25	1	......	......	......	81	......	29
1922	......	......	......	......	51	30	8	1	......	......	......	......	40	30
....	......	......	......	......	9	......	......	......	......	......	......	5	......	31
....	1547	......	......	......	......	......	......	......	40	......	......	......	......	32
....	......	......	......	......	18	......	......	......	......	......	......	......	848	33
3104	......	......	......	......	421	185	85	26	......	......	......	4	......	34
7366	......	......	......	......	525	319	99	14	......	......	......	1	......	35
....	......	......	......	......	......	......	......	......	......	......	......	1	......	36
2585	......	......	......	......	157	125	34	2	......	......	......	9	1	37
....	......	......	......	......	2	......	......	......	......	......	......	3	......	38
....	......	......	......	......	......	......	......	......	......	......	......	......	......	39
4249	......	......	......	......	81	52	22	16	......	......	......	......	17	40
....	......	......	......	......	17	3	......	......	......	......	......	512	628	41
7856	1490	......	......	......	380	243	92	33	1	......	......	2	8	42
7426	......	......	......	......	57	26	4	4	......	......	......	......	......	43
....	......	......	......	......	25	......	......	......	......	......	......	285	......	44
9693	2412	896	h578	......	118	63	29	23	1	2	2	......	......	45
....	......	......	......	......	14	4	......	......	......	......	......	......	......	46
....	......	......	......	......	......	......	......	......	......	......	......	......	160	47
....	......	......	......	......	61	60	......	......	......	......	......	72	27	48
....	......	......	......	......	10	1	......	......	......	......	......	230	411	49
....	......	......	......	......	127	5	......	......	......	......	......	9	......	50
....	......	......	......	......	9	......	......	......	......	......	......	5	......	51
922	871	814	i599	a551	......	20	37	1	6	5	16	......	907	52
....	......	......	......	......	14	1	1	......	......	......	......	2	......	53
....	......	......	......	......	......	......	......	......	......	......	......	......	......	54
9867	3169	1823	m1327	......	78	29	56	55	18	8	13	......	......	55
....	......	......	......	......	68	11	......	......	......	......	......	......	......	56
....	......	......	......	......	......	......	......	......	......	......	......	......	......	57
....	......	......	......	......	40	24	......	......	......	......	......	......	......	58
....	......	......	......	......	5	50	1	......	......	......	......	130	49	59
3590	4892	321	......	......	465	309	61	56	10	9	......	......	......	60
494	......	......	......	......	13	10	19	2	......	......	......	503	570	61
....	......	......	......	......	......	......	......	......	......	......	......	......	......	62
....	......	......	......	......	13	24	6	......	......	......	......	19	......	63
...	......	......	......	......	1	......	......	......	......	......	......	16	......	64
....	......	......	......	......	......	......	......	......	......	......	......	......	......	65
....	......	......	......	......	......	......	......	......	......	......	......	......	......	66
208	......	......	......	......	95	43	39	......	......	......	......	q14	5	67
....	......	......	......	......	......	......	......	......	......	......	......	1	......	68
....	......	......	......	......	......	......	......	......	......	......	......	......	......	69
892	......	......	......	......	288	38	......	......	......	......	......	120	98	70
....	......	......	......	......	28	......	......	......	......	......	......	7	......	71
....	......	......	......	......	......	4	......	......	......	......	......	......	22	72
2102	......	......	......	......	35	14	......	1	......	......	......	......	1	73
4590	1112	......	......	......	66	53	94	10	2	......	......	2	......	74

TABLE VIII.—*Population by Counties at each Census—MICHIGAN*—Continued.

	Counties.	AGGREGATE.								WHITE.	
		1870.	1860.	1850.	1840.	1830.	1820.	1810.	1800.	1870.	1860.
75	St. Joseph	26275	21262	12725	7068	1313	......	......	......	26142	[illegible]
76	Tuscola	13714	4886	291	......	......	......	......	......	13704	[illegible]
77	Van Buren	28829	15224	5800	1910	5	......	......	......	28152	[illegible]
78	Washtenaw	41434	35686	28567	23571	4042	......	......	......	40307	[illegible]
79	Wayne	119038	75547	42756	24173	6781	3574	a2227	......	116351	[illegible]
80	Wexford	650	......	......	......	......	......	......	......	647	......

(*) All other persons, except Indians not taxed.
(*a*) Following the return of "Indiana Territory," A. D. 1800, is this note: "At Machilamacanac, on the 1st of August, 1800, there were 251 souls; boatmen from Canada, etc., 300 souls."
(*b*) In 1869 organized.
(*c*) In 1837 annexed to Wisconsin.
(*d*) In 1869 organized.
(*e*) Returned as having no population.
(*f*) In 1861 organized.
(*h*) Civil district of Huron.
(*i*) Civil district of Michilimackinac.

TABLE VIII.—*Population by Counties at each Census—MINNESOTA.*

	Counties.	AGGREGATE.						WHITE.		
		1870.	1860.	1850.	1840.	1830.	1820.	1870.	1860.	1850.
	The State	439706	172023	6077	......	......	......	438257	169395	6038
1	Aitkin	178	2	......	......	......	......	18	2	......
2	Anoka	3940	2106	......	......	......	......	3925	2106	......
3	Becker	308	386	......	......	......	......	308	77	......
4	Beltrami (*a*)	80	......	......	......	......	......	80	......	......
5	Benton	1558	627	418	......	......	......	1556	626	416
6	Big Stone (*b*)	24	......	......	......	......	......	24	......	......
7	Blue Earth	17302	4803	......	......	......	......	17282	4802	......
8	Breckenridge (*c*) (*f*)	......	79	......	......	......	......	......	72	......
9	Brown (*o*)	6396	2339	......	......	......	......	6396	2256	......
10	Buchanan (*d*)	......	26	......	......	......	......	......	26	......
11	Carlton	286	51	......	......	......	......	274	51	......
12	Carver	11586	5106	......	......	......	......	11585	5106	......
13	Cass (*n*)	380	150	......	......	......	......	172	62	......
14	Chippewa (*e*)	1467	......	......	......	......	......	1433	......	......
15	Chisago	4358	1743	......	......	......	......	4309	1729	......
16	Clay (*f*)	92	......	......	......	......	......	92	......	......
17	Cottonwood	534	12	......	......	......	......	534	12	......
18	Crow Wing	200	269	......	......	......	......	199	189	......
19	Dakota	16312	9093	584	......	......	......	16264	9052	[illegible]
20	Dodge	8598	3797	......	......	......	......	8593	3797	......
21	Douglas	4239	195	......	......	......	......	4230	195	......
22	Faribault	9940	1335	......	......	......	......	9938	1335	......
23	Fillmore	24887	13542	......	......	......	......	24870	13542	......
24	Freeborn	10578	3367	......	......	......	......	10571	3367	......
25	Goodhue	22618	8977	......	......	......	......	22596	8971	......
26	Grant (*g*)	340	......	......	......	......	......	321	......	......
27	Hennepin	31566	12849	......	......	......	......	31329	12835	......
28	Houston	14936	6645	......	......	......	......	14926	6645	......
29	Isanti	2035	284	......	......	......	......	2035	284	......
30	Itasca (*a*)	96	51	97	......	......	......	78	7	97
31	Jackson	1825	181	......	......	......	......	1823	181	......
32	Kanabec	93	30	......	......	......	......	93	30	......
33	Kandiyohi	1760	76	......	......	......	......	1760	76	......
34	Lac qui Parle	145	......	......	......	......	......	145	......	......
35	Lake	135	248	......	......	......	......	134	248	......
36	Le Sueur	11607	5318	......	......	......	......	11590	5278	......
37	Lincoln (*h*)	......	......	......	......	......	......	......	......	......
38	Mankahta	......	......	158	......	......	......	......	......	[illegible]
39	Manomin	......	136	......	......	......	......	......	135	......
40	Martin	3867	151	......	......	......	......	3867	151	......

TABLE VIII.—*Population by Counties at each Census—MICHIGAN*—Continued.

WHITE—Continued.						COLORED.							INDIAN.		
1850.	1840.	1830.	1820.	1810.	1800.	1870.	1860.	1850.	1840.	1830.	1820.	1810.	1870.	1860.	
12699	7064	1310				133	62	26	4	3					75
291						9							1	4	76
5786	1900	5				538	151	14	1				139	172	77
28336	23501	4035				1125	634	231	70	7			2	3	78
42032	23898	6614	3441	n2114		2683	1673	724	275	167	133	113	4	2	79
						3									80

(j) In 1863 name changed from Bleeker to Menominee.
(k) Name changed from Michilimackinac to Mackinac.
(m) Civil district of Erie.
(n) Civil district of Detroit.
(o) In the census of 1850 "Michilimackinac" and twenty-one unorganized counties were tabulated together in amounts as above.
(p) Also 1 Japanese and 1 Chinese.
(q) Also 1 Japanese.
(r) Including Schoolcraft.
(s) Chinese.
(t) Population included in Marquette, to which Schoolcraft is attached for judicial purposes.

TABLE VIII.—*Population by Counties at each Census—MINNESOTA.*

WHITE—Contin'd.			COLORED.						INDIAN.						
1840.	1830.	1820.	1870.	1860.	1850.	1840.	1830.	1820.	1870.	1860.	1850.	1840.	1830.	1820.	
			759	259	39				690	2369					
									160						1
			15												2
										380					3
															4
			1		2				1	1					5
															6
			20	1											7
										7					8
										81					9
															10
									12						11
			1												12
			12	13					196	75					13
									34						14
			1	12					48	2					15
															16
															17
									1	80					18
			46	30	2				2	2					19
			5												20
									9						21
			2												22
			17												23
			7												24
			22	6											25
									19						26
			190	13					47	1					27
			10												28
															29
				1					18	43					30
			2												31
															32
															33
															34
									1						35
			5	20					12	20					36
															37
															38
				1											39
															40

TABLE VIII.—*Population by Counties at each Census—MINNESOTA*—Continued.

	Counties.	AGGREGATE.						WHITE.		
		1870.	1860.	1850.	1840.	1830.	1820.	1870.	1860.	1850.
41	McLeod	5643	1286					5643	1286	
42	McPhail									
43	Meeker	6090	928					6088	928	
44	Mille Lac	1109	73					1107	70	
45	Monongalia	3161	350					3161	350	
46	Morrison	1681	618					1681	587	
47	Mower	10447	3217					10447	3216	
48	Murray	209	29					209	29	
49	Nicollet	8362	3773					8327	3712	
50	Nobles	117	35					117	33	
51	Olmsted	19793	9524					19766	9524	
52	Otter Tail	1968	240					1966	178	
53	Pembina	64	1612	1134				64	336	1134
54	Pierce (*b*) (*c*) (*i*) (*l*)		11						10	
55	Pine	648	92					645	75	
56	Pipestone (*k*)		23						23	
57	Polk (*f*) (*q*)		240						146	
58	Pope	2691						2690		
59	Ramsey	23085	12150	2227				22836	12060	2197
60	Redwood (*j*)	1829						1826		
61	Renville (*e*)	3219	245					3219	240	
62	Rice	16083	7543					16025	7532	
63	Rock (*k*)	138						138		
64	Scott	11042	4595					11024	4594	
65	Sherburne	2050	723					2050	723	
66	Sibley	6725	3609					6724	3609	
67	Stearns	14206	4505					14201	4502	
68	Steele	8271	2863					8258	2863	
69	Stevens (*l*)	174						161		
70	St. Louis	4561	406					4529	262	
71	Todd (*n*)	2036	430					2035	430	
72	Traverse (*m*)	13						5		
73	Wabashaw	15859	7228	243				15836	7214	242
74	Wadena (*n*)	6						5		
75	Wahnata			160						160
76	Waseca	7854	2601					7852	2598	
77	Washington	11809	6123	1056				11775	6043	1052
78	Watonwan (*o*)	2426						2426		
79	Wilkin (*p*)	295	40					295	40	
80	Winona	22319	9208					22269	9188	
81	Wright	9457	3729					9457	3722	

(*a*) In 1866 Beltrami from Itasca.
(*b*) In 1862 Big Stone from Pierce.
(*c*) In 1862 part of Breckenridge to Clay, and in 1868 remainder to Wilkin.
(*d*) Absorbed by Pine.
(*e*) In 1862 Chippewa from Pierce and Renville.
(*f*) In 1862 Clay from Breckenridge and Polk.
(*g*) In 1868 Grant from Toombs, and original territory not included in any county.
(*h*) The status of this county is doubtful, the legality of its formation out of Renville County being questioned.

TABLE VIII.—*Population by Counties at each Census—MISSISSIPPI.*

	Counties.	AGGREGATE.								WHITE.			
		1870.	1860.	1850.	1840.	1830.	1820.	1810.	1800.	1870.	1860.	1850.	1840.
	The State	827922	791305	606526	375651	136621	75448	a9046 31306	a1250 7600	382896	353899	295718	179074
1	Adams	19084	20165	18601	19434	14937	12076	10002	4660	4797	5648	3948	4910
2	Alcorn (*b*)	10431								7663			
3	Amite (*c*)	10973	12336	9694	9511	7934	6853	4750		4196	4427	3641	3741
4	Attala	14776	14169	10991	4303					8828	9142	7571	2965
5	Baldwin							a427					
6	Bolivar	9732	10471	2577	1356					1900	1393	395	384
7	Calhoun	10561	9518							8561	7695		

TABLE VIII.—*Population by Counties at each Census—MINNESOTA*—Continued.

White—Contin'd.			Colored.						Indian.						
1840.	1830.	1820.	1870.	1860.	1850.	1840.	1830.	1820.	1870.	1860.	1850.	1840.	1830.	1820.	
															41
															42
			2												43
			2	2						1					44
															45
				1						30					46
				1											47
															48
			4	1					31	60					49
															50
			27												51
									2	62					52
										1274					53
										1					54
			2	16					1	1					55
															56
										94					57
			1												58
			198	70	30				1						59
			1						2						60
										5					61
			19	11					39						62
															63
			8						10	1					64
															65
			1												66
			5	3											67
			13												68
									13						69
			22						10	144					70
			1	4											71
									8						72
			23	14	1										73
			1												74
															75
			2	1						2					76
			21	7	4				13	73					77
															78
															79
			50	19											80
				7											81

(i) Absorbed by Big Stone, Chippewa, Pope, Stevens, and Swift.
(j) In 1862 from Brown.
(k) In 1857 Rock. In 1860 erroneously reported as Pipestone.
(l) In 1862 Stevens from Pierce.
(m) In 1862 from Toombs, and original territory not included in any county.
(n) In 1858 Wadena from Cass and Todd.
(o) In 1860 Watonwan from Brown.
(p) In 1856 established as Toombs; in 1868 name changed to Andy Johnson, and in 1868 to Wilkin.
(q) Returned as having no population.

TABLE VIII.—*Population by Counties at each Census—MISSISSIPPI.*

White—Continued.				Colored.								Chinese.	Indian.		
1830.	1820.	1810.	1800.	1870.	1860.	1850.	1840.	1830.	1820.	1810.	1800.	1870.	1870.	1860.	
70443	42176	a6422 16602	a733 4446	444201	437404	310808	196577	66178	33272	a2624 14704	a517 3154	16	809	2	
3860	4005	4255	2248	14287	14517	14053	14524	11077	8071	5747	2412				1
				2768											2
3816	4006	3312		6777	7909	6053	5770	4118	2847	1438					3
				5948	5025	3120	1348							2	4
		a667								a760					5
				7816	9078	2182	972					16			6
				2000	1823										7

TABLE VIII.—*Population by Counties at each Census—MISSISSIPPI*—Continu

	Counties.	Aggregate.										
		1870.	1860.	1850.	1840.	1830.	1820.	1810.	1800.	1870.	1860.	1850.
8	Carroll (c)	21047	22035	18491	10481	.....	.....	.....	.....	9497	8214	8653
9	Chickasaw	19899	16426	16369	2955	.....	.....	.....	.....	9830	7338	9887
10	Choctaw (c)	16988	15722	11402	6010	.....	.....	.....	.....	12526	11525	8420
11	Claiborne	13386	15679	14941	13078	9787	5963	3102	.....	3390	3339	3449
12	Clark	7505	10771	5477	2980	.....	.....	.....	.....	4073	5692	3823
13	Coahoma	7144	6606	2780	1290	.....	.....	.....	.....	1763	1521	1387
14	Copiah (e)	20608	15398	11794	9854	7001	.....	.....	.....	10217	7432	6303
15	Covington	4753	4408	3338	2717	2551	2230	.....	.....	3106	2815	2222
16	De Soto	32021	23336	19042	7002	.....	.....	.....	.....	14276	9349	9487
17	Franklin (e)	7498	8265	5904	4775	4622	3821	2016	.....	3698	3495	2540
18	Greene	2038	2232	2018	1636	1854	1445	.....	.....	1666	1526	1379
19	Grenada (c)	10571	.....	.....	.....	.....	.....	.....	.....	3929	.....	.....
20	Hancock	4239	3139	3672	3367	1962	1504	.....	.....	3053	2222	2444
21	Harrison	5795	4819	4875	.....	.....	.....	.....	.....	4368	3751	3378
22	Hinds	30488	31339	25340	19098	8645	.....	.....	.....	9820	8940	8690
23	Holmes	19370	17791	13928	9452	.....	.....	.....	.....	6145	5806	5547
24	Issaquena	6887	7831	4478	.....	.....	.....	.....	.....	741	587	366
25	Itawamba	7812	17695	13528	5375	.....	.....	.....	.....	6820	14156	11305
26	Jackson	4362	4122	3196	1965	1792	1682	.....	.....	3167	2955	2266
27	Jasper	10884	11007	6184	3958	.....	.....	.....	.....	5801	6453	4293
28	Jefferson (d)	1384	15349	13193	11650	9755	6822	4001	2940	3215	2918	2634
29	Jones	3313	3323	2164	1258	1471	.....	.....	.....	3005	2916	1887
30	Kemper	12920	11682	12517	7663	.....	.....	.....	.....	5706	5936	7138
31	Lafayette	18802	16125	14069	6531	.....	.....	.....	.....	10819	8989	8346
32	Lauderdale	13462	13313	8717	5358	.....	.....	.....	.....	7051	8224	6052
33	Lawrence (e)	6720	9213	6478	5920	5293	4916	.....	.....	3678	5513	3549
34	Leake	8496	9324	5533	2162	.....	.....	.....	.....	5491	6266	3982
35	Lee	15955	.....	.....	.....	.....	.....	.....	.....	11100	.....	.....
36	Lincoln (e)	10184	.....	.....	.....	.....	.....	.....	.....	6022	.....	.....
37	Lowndes	30502	23625	19544	14513	3173	.....	.....	.....	7480	6291	6523
38	Madison	20948	23382	18173	15530	4973	.....	a4699	.....	5809	5260	4328
39	Marion	4211	4686	4410	3830	3691	3116	.....	.....	2562	2500	2215
40	Marshall	29416	28823	29689	17526	.....	.....	.....	.....	12917	11376	14271
41	Monroe	22631	21283	21172	9250	3861	2721	.....	.....	8631	8545	9416
42	Neshoba	7439	8343	4728	2437	.....	.....	.....	.....	5419	6131	3393
43	Newton	10067	9661	4465	2527	.....	.....	.....	.....	6386	6279	3432
44	Noxubee	20905	20667	16299	9975	.....	.....	.....	.....	5107	5171	4976
45	Oktibbeha	14891	12977	9171	4276	.....	.....	.....	.....	5587	5328	4309
46	Panola	20754	13794	11444	4657	.....	.....	.....	.....	8169	5237	5021
47	Perry	2694	2606	2438	1889	2300	2037	.....	.....	1971	1858	1673
48	Pike (e)	11303	11135	7300	6151	5402	4438	.....	.....	5930	6174	4225
49	Pontotoc	12525	22113	17112	4491	.....	.....	.....	.....	9513	14513	12136
50	Prentiss (f)	9348	.....	.....	.....	.....	.....	.....	.....	7504	.....	.....
51	Rankin	12977	13635	7227	4631	2083	.....	.....	.....	5704	6530	3940
52	Scott	7847	8139	3961	1653	.....	.....	.....	.....	4680	5180	2778
53	Simpson	5718	6080	4734	3380	2680	.....	.....	.....	3569	3744	3190
54	Smith	7126	7638	4071	1961	.....	.....	.....	.....	5415	5135	3073
55	Sunflower	5015	5019	1102	.....	.....	.....	.....	.....	1772	1102	348
56	Tallahatchie (c)	7852	7890	4643	2985	.....	.....	.....	.....	3215	2835	2396
57	Tippah (b)	20727	22550	20741	9444	.....	.....	.....	.....	15636	16206	15807
58	Tishemingo (b) (f)	7350	24149	15490	6681	.....	.....	.....	.....	6609	19150	13528
59	Tunica	5358	4366	1314	821	.....	.....	.....	.....	1231	883	396
60	Warren	26769	27690	18120	15920	7861	2693	1114	.....	7907	6896	5996
61	Washington	14569	15679	8389	7287	1976	.....	a2920	a1250	2164	1212	546
62	Wayne	4206	3691	2892	2120	2781	3324	1253	.....	2370	1744	1499
63	Wilkinson	12705	15933	10914	14193	11686	9718	5068	.....	2698	2779	3624
64	Winston	8984	9811	7956	4650	.....	.....	.....	.....	5572	5583	5178
65	Yalabusha (c)	13254	16952	17258	12248	.....	.....	.....	.....	6292	7415	8052
66	Yazoo	17279	22373	14418	10480	6550	.....	.....	.....	4824	5657	4069

(a) Now in Alabama.
(b) In 1870 Alcorn from Tippah and Tishemingo.
(c) In 1870 Grenada from Carroll, Choctaw, Tallahatchie, and Yalabusha.

VIII.—*Population by Counties at each Census—MISSISSIPPI*—Continued.

—Continued.			COLORED.								CHINESE.	INDIAN.		
.	1810.	1800.	1870.	1860.	1850.	1840.	1830.	1820.	1810.	1800.	1870.	1870.	1860.	
			11550	13821	9638	5345								8
			10069	9088	6482	807								9
			4462	4197	2982	1567								10
40	1552		9996	12340	11492	9846	6228	3123	1550					11
			3432	5079	1654	910								12
			5381	5085	1393	524								13
			10390	7966	5491	3793	1763					1		14
24			1647	1563	1116	856	702	406						15
			17745	13987	9555	3027								16
77	1263		3800	4767	3364	2712	2210	1514	748					17
63			372	706	639	429	538	382						18
			6642											19
42			1186	857	1228	1130	617	452						20
			1427	1068	1497									21
			20659	22399	16650	12320	3236							22
			13225	11985	8381	5600								23
			6146	7244	4112									24
			986	3539	2133	723								25
00			1194	1167	930	506	439	382				1		26
			4898	4554	1891	1257						185		27
54	2189	2198	10633	12431	10559	9261	6717	3668	1812	742				28
			308	407	277	164	102							29
			7214	5746	5379	3051								30
			7983	7136	5723	2855								31
			6411	5089	2665	1306								32
19			3042	3700	2929	2272	1816	997						33
			3005	3058	1551	548								34
			4855											35
			4162											36
			23022	16734	13921	8783	1009							37
	a3745		15139	18122	13845	11544	2192		a954					38
84			1649	2186	2195	1709	1721	1232						39
			16499	17447	15418	8268								40
92			14000	12738	11754	4104	957	529						41
			1703	2212	1335	744						317		42
			3386	3382	1033	547						295		43
			15798	15496	14323	6158								44
			9304	7649	4862	2212								45
			12585	8557	6423	2420								46
39			723	748	759	464	835	498						47
43			5312	4961	3135	2395	1605	995				1		48
			3012	7600	4976	1596								49
			1751											50
			7273	7105	3287	1854	388							51
			3167	2959	1183	464								52
			2149	2336	1544	907	666							53
			1711	2203	998	419								54
			3243	3917	754									55
			4637	5055	2547	1593								56
			5091	6344	4934	2135								57
			711	4990	1962	820								58
			4127	3483	918	255								59
01	622		18862	13800	12124	10597	4505	1292	492					60
	a2010	a733	12405	14467	7843	6633	1191		a910	a517				61
50	972		1636	1947	1393	979	1077	1073	281					62
37	2432		10007	13154	13290	10924	7887	5781	2636					63
			3403	4228	2778	1589						2		64
			7058	9537	8606	5608								65
			12395	16716	10349	7364	2472							66

2 name changed from Pickering to Jefferson.
0 Lincoln from Amite, Copiah, Franklin, Lawrence, and Pike.
0 Prentiss from Tishemingo.

TABLE VIII.—*Population by Counties at each Census—MISSOURI.*

	Counties.	Aggregate.							White.	
		1870.	1860.	1850.	1840.	1830.	1820.	1810.	1870.	1860.
	The State	1721295	1182012	682044	383702	140455	*29 66557	20845	1603146	1063489
1	Adair	11448	8531	2342	......	......	......	......	11305	[illegible]
2	Andrew	15137	11850	9433	......	......	......	......	14736	10049
3	Atchison	8440	4649	1678	......	......	......	......	8405	[illegible]
4	Andrain	12307	8075	3506	1949	......	......	......	11237	[illegible]
5	Barry	10373	7995	3467	4705	......	......	......	10320	[illegible]
6	Barton	5087	1817	......	......	......	......	......	5068	1798
7	Bates (c)	15960	7215	3669	......	......	......	......	15840	6765
8	Benton	11322	9072	5015	4205	......	......	......	11009	8469
9	Bollinger	8162	7371	......	......	......	......	......	8116	7128
10	Boone	20765	19486	14979	13561	8859	......	......	16727	14399
11	Buchanan	35109	23861	12975	6237	......	......	......	33155	21799
12	Butler	4298	2891	1616	......	......	......	......	4275	2857
13	Caldwell	11390	5034	2316	1458	......	......	......	11106	4810
14	Callaway	19202	17449	13827	11765	6159	......	......	15768	12695
15	Camden	6108	4975	2338	......	......	......	......	5950	4769
16	Cape Girardeau	17558	15547	13912	9359	7445	5968	3888	15012	13961
17	Carroll	17446	9763	5441	2423	......	......	......	16619	8692
18	Carter	1455	1235	......	......	......	......	......	1425	1200
19	Cass (c)	19296	9794	6090	......	......	......	......	18793	8731
20	Cedar	9474	6637	3361	......	......	......	......	9363	6439
21	Chariton	19136	12562	7514	4746	1780	......	......	16336	9672
22	Christian	6707	5491	......	......	......	......	......	6592	5362
23	Clarke	13667	11684	5527	2846	......	......	......	13372	11216
24	Clay	15564	13023	10332	8282	5338	......	......	13718	9595
25	Clinton	14063	7848	3786	2724	......	......	......	13380	6955
26	Cole	10292	9697	6696	9286	3023	......	......	9041	8645
27	Cooper	20692	17356	12950	10484	6904	6959	......	17340	13398
28	Crawford	7982	5823	6397	3561	1712	......	......	7896	5640
29	Dade	8683	7072	4246	......	......	......	......	8479	6721
30	Dallas	8383	5892	3648	......	......	......	......	8294	5777
31	Daviess	14410	9606	5298	2736	......	......	......	14086	9248
32	De Kalb	9858	5224	2075	......	......	......	......	9736	5081
33	Dent	6357	5654	......	......	......	......	......	6326	5408
34	Dodge (a)	......	......	375	......	......	......	......	......	......
35	Douglas	3915	2414	......	......	......	......	......	3898	2414
36	Dunklin	5982	5026	1229	......	......	......	......	5816	4555
37	Franklin	30098	18085	11021	7515	3484	2379	......	27925	16465
38	Gasconade	10093	8727	4996	5330	1545	......	......	10013	8641
39	Gentry (d)	11607	11980	4248	......	......	......	......	11551	11862
40	Greene	21549	13186	12785	5372	......	......	......	19693	11599
41	Grundy	10567	7887	3006	......	......	......	......	10432	7596
42	Harrison	14635	10626	2447	......	......	......	......	14625	10601
43	Henry (b)	17401	9866	4052	......	......	......	......	16750	8620
44	Hickory	6452	4705	2329	......	......	......	......	6362	4503
45	Holt	11652	6550	3957	......	......	......	......	11468	6241
46	Howard	17233	15946	13969	13108	10854	13426	......	13040	9986
47	Howell	4218	3169	......	......	......	......	......	4193	3132
48	Iron	6278	5842	......	......	......	......	......	5926	5569
49	Jackson	55041	22913	14000	7612	2823	......	......	49810	18882
50	Jasper	14928	6883	4223	......	......	......	......	14700	6533
51	Jefferson	15380	10344	6928	4296	2592	1835	......	14617	9763
52	Johnson	24648	14644	7464	4471	......	......	......	23180	12743
53	Knox	10974	8727	2894	......	......	......	......	10774	8436
54	Laclede	9380	5182	2498	......	......	......	......	9216	4875
55	Lafayette	22623	20098	13690	6815	2912	......	......	18582	13698
56	Lawrence	13067	8846	4859	......	......	......	......	12808	8550
57	Lewis	15114	12286	6578	6040	......	......	......	13033	10063
58	Lincoln	15960	14210	9421	7449	4059	1662	......	13972	11347
59	Linn	15900	9112	4058	2245	......	......	......	15158	8509
60	Livingston	16730	7417	4247	4325	......	......	......	15774	6812
61	Macon	23230	14346	6565	6034	......	......	......	21734	13673
62	Madison	5849	5664	6003	3395	2371	2047	......	5688	5178
63	Maries	5916	4901	......	......	......	......	......	5894	4830
64	Marion	23780	18838	12230	9623	4837	......	......	20187	15732
65	McDonald	5226	4038	2236	......	......	......	......	5189	3957
66	Mercer	11557	9300	2691	......	......	......	......	11464	9274
67	Miller	6616	6812	3834	2282	......	......	......	6440	6572
68	Mississippi	4982	4859	3123	......	......	......	......	4063	3849
69	Moniteau	11375	10124	6004	......	......	......	......	10496	9975
70	Monroe	17149	14785	10541	9505	......	......	......	15144	11722
71	Montgomery	10405	9718	5489	4371	3902	3074	......	9406	8061
72	Morgan	8434	8202	4650	4407	......	......	......	8127	7542
73	New Madrid	6357	5654	5541	4554	2350	2296	3165	4931	3861
74	Newton	12821	9319	4268	3790	......	......	......	12471	8842
75	Nodaway	14751	5252	2118	......	......	......	......	14663	5122

TABLE VIII.—*Population by Counties at each Census—MISSOURI.*

	White—Continued.				Colored.							Indian.		
.	1840.	1830.	1820.	1810.	1870.	1860.	1850.	1840.	1830.	1820.	1810.	1870.	1860.	
34	323888	114795	55988	17227	118071	118503	90040	59814	25660	10569	3618	75	20	
23					143	95	59							1
57					401	901	676							2
11					34	71	37					1		3
18	1752				1070	1166	458	197						4
17	4518				52	257	150	277				1		5
..					19	21								6
30					120	450	149							7
17	3944				320	612	468	261						8
					46	245								9
30	10529	6935			4038	5087	3679	3032	1924					10
22	6004				1953	2002	903	233				1		11
3					21	54	53					2		12
76	1397				284	224	140	61						13
35	8601	4702			3434	4554	3932	3164	1457					14
18					149	206	130							15
13	8020	6398	5058	3201	1646	1586	1709	1339	1047	910	507			16
12	2155				827	1071	629	268						17
					30	35								18
0					502	1013	480					1		19
8					111	217	83							20
5	3709	1479			2800	2890	1829	1037	301					21
					114	229						1		22
3	2423				295	468	514	423						23
5	6373	4443			1846	3498	2747	1900	895					24
6	2530				683	1163	440	194						25
9	8073	2718			1251	1052	997	1213	305					26
7	8312	5876	6307		3352	3828	3113	2172	1028	650				27
2	3377	1647			86	183	285	184	65					28
1					204	351	275							29
2					89	115	96							30
6	2600				324	358	242	136						31
0					122	143	65							32
					31	156								33
3							2							34
					27									35
5					166	171	24							36
2	6447	3084	2170		2173	1620	1479	1068	400	209				37
4	4987	1401			80	85	112	343	144				1	38
5					56	118	53							39
8	4693				2156	1077	1237	679						40
6					115	291	150							41
4					10	25	13							42
7					642	1246	675							43
3					90	202	186							44
7					184	309	130							45
9	9381	8177	11319		5193	5960	4930	3727	2077	2107				46
					21	36						1		47
					352	313								48
0	6245	2630			5223	4014	3010	1367	193			8	17	49
9					138	350	214							50
7	3960	2344	1620		763	581	521	336	248	215				51
3	3911				1458	1901	891	560				1		52
6					200	291	268							53
7					162	307	141							54
5	4799	2181			4039	6410	4685	2016	431			2		55
7					259	287	251							56
7	4966				1181	1303	1221	1074						57
9	5873	3306	1419		1987	2863	2032	1576	753	243		1		58
7	2102				742	603	379	143						59
3	4082				956	605	314	243						60
2	5808				1196	673	303	226						61
8	2762	1936	1672		159	485	725	633	435	375				62
					22	71								63
2	7289	3506			3592	3106	2908	2384	1331			1		64
2					37	81	104							65
1					93	26	20							66
5	2170				176	240	189	112						67
3					919	1010	750							68
4					879	749	570							69
1	7813				2005	3063	2080	1692						70
9	3524	3296	2547		939	1657	1040	847	606	527				71
2	3891				307	657	458	516						72
3	3748	1875	2001	2735	1425	1791	1488	806	475	295	430	1		73
2	3616				350	477	256	171						74
2					87	129	70					1		75

TABLE VIII.—*Population by Counties at each Census—MISSOURI*—Continued.

	Counties.	AGGREGATE.							WHITE.	
		1870.	1860.	1850.	1840.	1830.	1820.	1810.	1870.	1860.
76	Oregon	3287	3009	1432					3283	[illegible]
77	Osage	10793	7879	6704					10467	[illegible]
78	Ozark	3363	2447	2294					3351	[illegible]
79	Pemiscot	2059	2362						1911	[illegible]
80	Perry	9877	9128	7215	5760	3349			9477	[illegible]
81	Pettis	18706	9392	5150	2930				16580	[illegible]
82	Phelps	10506	5714						10212	[illegible]
83	Pike	23076	18417	13609	10646	6129	3747		18881	[illegible]
84	Platte	17352	18350	16845	8913				16160	[illegible]
85	Polk	12445	9995	6186	8449				12186	[illegible]
86	Pulaski	4714	3835	3998	6529				4689	[illegible]
87	Putnam (*a*)	11217	9207	1636					11208	[illegible]
88	Ralls	10510	8592	6151	5670	4375			9255	[illegible]
89	Randolph	15908	11407	9439	7198	2942			13774	[illegible]
90	Ray	18700	14092	10373	6553	2657			16867	[illegible]
91	Reynolds	3756	3173	1849					3745	[illegible]
92	Ripley	3175	3747	2830	2856				3165	[illegible]
93	Rives (*b*)				4726					
94	Saline	21672	14699	8843	5258	2873			17918	[illegible]
95	Schuyler	8820	6697	3287					8806	[illegible]
96	Scotland	10670	8873	3782					10541	[illegible]
97	Scott	7317	5247	3182	5974	2136			6991	[illegible]
98	Shannon	2339	2284	1199					2336	[illegible]
99	Shelby	10119	7301	4253	3056				9540	[illegible]
100	St. Charles	21304	16523	11454	7911	4320	3970	3505	19381	[illegible]
101	St. Clair	6742	6812	3556					6590	[illegible]
102	Ste. Genevieve	8384	8029	4964	3148	2186	4962	4620	7953	[illegible]
103	St. François	9742	7249	5313	3211	2366			9294	[illegible]
104	St. Louis	351189	190524	104978	35979	14125	*39 10020	5667	324700	[illegible]
105	Stoddard	8535	7877	4277	3153				8465	[illegible]
106	Stone	3253	2400						3233	[illegible]
107	Sullivan	11907	9198	2983					11865	[illegible]
108	Taney	4407	3576	4373	3264				4397	[illegible]
109	Texas	9618	6067	2312					9523	[illegible]
110	Van Buren (*c*)				4693					
111	Vernon	11247	4850						11165	4701
112	Warren	9673	8839	5860	4253				8931	[illegible]
113	Washington	11719	9723	8811	7213	6784	2769		10748	[illegible]
114	Wayne	6068	5629	4518	3403	3264	1443		6001	[illegible]
115	Webster	10434	7099						10185	[illegible]
116	Worth (*d*)	5004							5004	
117	Wright	5684	4508	3387					5658	4441

(*) All other persons, except Indians not taxed.
(†) Chinese, at 1870: Total, 3—Madison, 2; St. Louis, 1.
(*a*) Formerly western half of Putnam, afterward restored to Putnam.

TABLE VIII.—*Population by Counties at each Census—NEBRASKA.*

	Counties.	AGGREGATE.					WHITE.	
		1870.	1860.	1850.	1840.	1830.	1870.	1860.
	The State	122993	28841				122117	[illegible]
1	Adams	19					19	
2	Blackbird	31					31	
3	Buffalo	193	114				192	114
4	Burt	2847	388				2847	388
5	Butler	1290	27				1286	27
6	Calhoun		41					41
7	Cass	8151	3369				8127	3369
8	Cedar	1032	246				1030	[illegible]
9	Cheyenne	190					187	
10	Clay	54	165				54	165
11	Colfax	1424					1417	
12	Cuming	2964	67				2964	67
13	Dakota	2040	819				2040	[illegible]
14	Dawson	103	16				103	16
15	Dixon	1345	247				1345	247

TABLE VIII.—*Population by Counties at each Census—MISSOURI*—Continued.

WHITE—Continued.					COLORED.							INDIAN.		
1850.	1840.	1830.	1820.	1810.	1870.	1860.	1850.	1840.	1830.	1820.	1810.	1870.	1860.	
1392					4	26	40							76
6434					326	256	270							77
2279					12	86	15							78
					148	280								79
6393	4969	2810			400	762	820	792	539					80
4261	2377				2126	1888	889	553						81
					294	86								82
10290	8157	4932	3071		4195	4115	3310	2480	1197	676				83
13996	8049				1192	3369	2849	864						84
5804	7978				259	527	382	471						85
3885	6338				25	56	113	191						86
1617					9	31	19							87
4775	4450	3328			1255	1804	1376	1220	847					88
7202	5749	2447			2134	2030	2177	1449	495					89
6833	5714	2487			1833	2054	1540	839	170					90
1824					11	38	25							91
2731	2777				10	81	99	79						92
	4086							640						93
6105	3635	2141			3754	4899	2738	1623	732					94
3230					14	39	57							95
3631					199	131	151							96
2773	5028	1765			326	517	409	946	371					97
1190					3	13	9							98
3744	2587				571	730	509	469				8		99
9492	6286	3337	3275	3221	1922	2210	1962	1625	983	695	284	1		100
3107					152	583	449							101
4233	2563	1612	3932	3173	431	706	731	585	574	1030	1447			102
4636	2694	1929			518	957	677	517	437					103
97540	30505	11109	8014	4807	26387	6211	7437	5474	3016	2006	860	41		104
4221	3081				70	218	56	72						105
					20	16								106
2995					42	103	88							107
4274	3212				10	87	99	52						108
2270					95	58	42							109
	4148							245						110
					82	138							1	111
4921	3555				741	1041	939	698				1		112
7713	6248	5582	2344		971	1053	1098	965	1202	425				113
4152	3069	2882	1239		67	268	366	334	382	204				114
					248	220						1		115
														116
3205					26	66	82						1	117

(b) Name changed from Rives to Henry.
(c) Van Buren formerly comprised what is now Bates and Cass.
(d) In 1861 Worth from Gentry.

TABLE VIII.—*Population by Counties at each Census—NEBRASKA.*

WHITE—Continued.			COLORED.					INDIAN.					
1850.	1840.	1830.	1870.	1860.	1850.	1840.	1830.	1870.	1860.	1850.	1840.	1830.	
			789	82				87	63				
													1
													2
			1										3
													4
			4										5
													6
			24										7
			1	3				1					8
			3										9
													10
			7										11
													12
				13									13
													14
													15

TABLE VIII.—*Population by Counties at each Census*—NEBRASKA—Continued.

	Counties.	Aggregate. 1870.	Aggregate. 1860.	Aggregate. 1850.	Aggregate. 1840.	Aggregate. 1830.	White. 1870.	White. 1860.
16	Dodge	4212	309				4206	[illegible]
17	Douglas	19982	4328				[illegible]	[illegible]
18	Fillmore	238					238	
19	Fort Randall		355					[illegible]
20	Franklin	26					26	
21	Gage	3359	421				3357	[illegible]
22	Grant	484					475	
23	Green		16					16
24	Hall	1057	116				1057	116
25	Hamilton	130					130	
26	Harrison	631					625	
27	Jackson	9					9	
28	Jefferson (*a*)	2440					2440	
29	Johnson	3429	528				3429	[illegible]
30	Jones (*a*)		122					[illegible]
31	Kearney	58	474				58	[illegible]
32	Lancaster	7074	153				7050	[illegible]
33	L'Eau qui Court	261	152				258	[illegible]
34	Lincoln	17					17	
35	Lyon	78					78	
36	Madison	1133	(*b*)				1133	(*b*)
37	Merrick	557	109				557	[illegible]
38	Monroe	235					235	
39	Nemaha	7593	3139				7563	[illegible]
40	Nuckolls	8	22				8	[illegible]
41	Otoe	12345	4211				12123	[illegible]
42	Pawnee	4171	882				4171	[illegible]
43	Pierce	152					152	
44	Platte	1899	*b*782				1895	[illegible]
45	Polk	136	19				136	19
46	Richardson	9780	2835				9692	[illegible]
47	Saline	3106	39				3106	[illegible]
48	Sarpy	2913	1201				2911	[illegible]
49	Saunders	4547					4537	
50	Seward	2953					2953	
51	Shorter		117					116
52	Stanton	636					636	
53	Taylor	97					97	
54	Washington	4452	1249				4451	[illegible]
55	Wayne	182					182	
56	Webster	16					16	
57	York	604					604	
58	Unorganized Northwest Territory (*c*)	52	1765				52	[illegible]
59	Unorganized Territory west of Madison County	183					183	
60	Winnebago Indian reservation	31					31	
61	Pawnee Indian reservation	44					44	

(*a*) Since 1860 Jones merged in Jefferson.
(*b*) In 1860 Madison and Platte were reported together; totals are herein placed opposite Platte.

TABLE VIII.—*Population by Counties at each Census—NEBRASKA*—Continued.

White—Continued.			Colored.					Indian.					
1850.	1840.	1830.	1870.	1860.	1850.	1840.	1830.	1870.	1860.	1850.	1840.	1830.	
			4										16
			459	21					2				17
													18
				2									19
													20
			2										21
			9										22
													23
													24
													25
			6										26
													27
													28
													29
													30
				9									31
			15										32
				14				3	3				33
													34
													35
									(b)				36
									2				37
													38
			8	5				2	37				39
													40
			219	14				3	3				41
													42
													43
			4						b7				44
													45
			10	1				78					46
													47
			2						2				48
			10										49
													50
									3				51
													52
													53
			1										54
													55
													56
													57
									4				58
													59
													60
													61

(c) North of latitude 40° and west of longitude 103°; also, north by latitude 42°, east by longitude [illegible]1° 30', south by latitude 40°, and west by longitude 103°.

TABLE VIII.—*Population by Counties at each Census—NEVADA.*

	Counties.	AGGREGATE.				WHITE.	
		1870.	1860.	1850.	1840.	1870.	1860.
	The State	42491	6857			38959	6812
1	Carson		6712				6667
2	Churchill	196				180	
3	Douglas	1215				1157	
4	Elko	3447				2975	
5	Esmeralda	1553				1489	
6	Humboldt	1916	40			1684	40
7	Lander	2815				2566	
8	Lincoln	2985				2937	
9	Lyon	1837				1719	
10	Nye	1087				1080	
11	Ormsby	3668				2868	
12	Pah Ute (*a*)						
13	Roop	133				129	
14	St. Mary's		105				105
15	Storey	11359				10514	
16	Washoe	3091				2831	
17	White Pine	7189				6830	

(*a*) At 1870 Pah Ute included in the returns of Lincoln.

TABLE VIII.—*Population by Counties at each Census—NEW HAMPSHIRE.*

	Counties.	AGGREGATE.									WHITE.		
		1870.	1860.	1850.	1840.	1830.	1820.	1810.	1800.	1790.	1870.	1860.	1850.
	The State	318300	326073	317976	284574	269328	†139 244022	214460	183858	141885	317697	325579	317456
1	Belknap	17681	18549	17721							17640	18510	17692
2	Carroll	17332	20465	20157							17316	20465	20155
3	Cheshire	27265	27434	30144	26429	27016	45376	40988	38825	28772	27250	27399	30110
4	Coos	14932	13161	11853	9849	8388	5549	3991			14909	13154	11849
5	Grafton	39103	42260	42343	42311	38682	32989	28462	23093	13472	39062	42237	42316
6	Hillsborough	64238	62140	57478	42494	37724	53884	49249	43899	32871	64109	62033	57356
7	Merrimack	42151	41408	40337	36253	34614					42055	41286	40244
8	Rockingham	47297	50122	49194	45771	44325	†139 55107	50175	45427	43169	47143	50095	49057
9	Strafford	30243	31493	29374	61127	58910	51117	41595	32614	23601	30199	31462	29364
10	Sullivan	18058	19041	19375	20340	19669					18014	19008	19334

(*) All other persons, except Indians not taxed.

(†) In Table II, Volume I, of Ninth Census, 1 slave on the line of Rockingham County should be in Hillsborough County.

TABLE VIII.—*Population by Counties at each Census—NEVADA.*

White—Continued. 1850.	White—Continued. 1840.	Colored. 1870.	Colored. 1860.	Colored. 1850.	Colored. 1840.	Chinese. 1870.	Chinese. 1860.	Chinese. 1850.	Chinese. 1840.	Indian. 1870.	Indian. 1860.	Indian. 1850.	Indian. 1840.	
......	......	357	45	......	......	3152	......	......	......	23	......	......	......	
......	......	......	45	......	......	......	......	......	......	......	......	......	......	1
......	......	......	......	......	......	16	......	......	......	......	......	......	......	2
......	......	32	......	......	......	23	......	......	......	3	......	......	......	3
......	......	33	......	......	......	430	......	......	......	......	......	......	......	4
......	......	8	......	......	......	56	......	......	......	......	......	......	......	5
......	......	9	......	......	......	240	......	......	......	3	......	......	......	6
......	......	31	......	......	......	218	......	......	......	......	......	......	......	7
......	......	11	......	......	......	23	......	......	......	14	......	......	......	8
......	......	2	......	......	......	116	......	......	......	......	......	......	......	9
......	......	1	......	......	......	6	......	......	......	......	......	......	......	10
......	......	31	......	......	......	769	......	......	......	......	......	......	......	11
......	......	......	......	......	......	......	......	......	......	......	......	......	......	12
......	......	......	......	......	......	4	......	......	......	......	......	......	......	13
......	......	......	......	......	......	......	......	......	......	......	......	......	......	14
......	......	96	......	......	......	749	......	......	......	......	......	......	......	15
......	......	36	......	......	......	221	......	......	......	3	......	......	......	16
......	......	67	......	......	......	292	......	......	......	......	......	......	......	17

TABLE VIII.—*Population by Counties at each Census—NEW HAMPSHIRE.*

White—Continued. 1840.	1830.	1820.	1810.	1800.	1790.	Colored. (a) 1870.	1860.	1850.	1840.	1830.	1820.	1810.	1800.	1790.	
284036	268721	243236	213490	182998	141097	580	494	520	538	607	786	970	860	788	
......	......	......	......	......	......	41	39	29	......	......	......	......	......	......	1
......	......	......	......	......	......	13	......	2	......	......	......	......	......	......	2
26389	26973	45296	40927	38713	28687	15	35	28	40	43	80	61	112	85	3
9846	8380	5545	3971	......	......	10	7	4	3	8	4	20	......	......	4
42280	38653	32942	28398	23023	13423	41	23	27	31	29	47	64	70	49	5
42298	37609	53651	49020	43694	32694	124	107	119	196	115	233	229	205	177	6
36147	34488	......	......	......	......	96	122	93	106	126	......	......	......	......	7
45572	44137	54752	49665	45067	42778	153	97	127	199	188	355	510	360	391	8
61095	58840	51050	41509	32501	23515	44	31	50	32	70	67	86	113	86	9
20309	19641	......	......	......	......	43	33	41	31	28	......	......	......	......	10

(a) At 1870, Indians 23, as follows: Carroll, 3; Coos, 13; Hillsborough, 5; Rockingham, 1; Sullivan, 1.

TABLE VIII.—*Population by Counties at each Census—NEW JERSEY.*

	Counties.	AGGREGATE.									WHITE.		
		1870.	1860.	1850.	1840.	1830.	1820.	1810.	1800.	1790.	1870.	1860.	1850.
	The State	906096	672035	489555	373306	320823	*149 277426	245562	211149	184139	875407	646699	465509
1	Atlantic	14093	11786	8961	8726	......	......	......	......	......	13909	11592	8743
2	Bergen	30122	21618	14725	13223	22412	*40 18138	16603	15156	12601	28489	19955	13000
3	Burlington	53639	49730	43203	32831	31107	28822	24979	21521	18095	51098	47506	41094
4	Camden	46193	34457	25422	......	......	......	......	......	......	41751	31883	23192
5	Cape May	8349	7130	6433	5324	4936	4265	3632	3066	2571	7922	6857	6186
6	Cumberland	34665	22605	17189	14374	14098	12668	12670	9529	8248	33898	21310	16029
7	Essex	143839	98877	73950	44621	41911	30793	25984	22269	17785	141296	97120	71616
8	Gloucester	21562	18444	14655	25438	28431	*18 23071	19744	16115	13363	20589	17737	14025
9	Hudson	129067	62717	21822	9483	......	......	......	......	......	128016	62064	21319
10	Hunterdon	36963	33654	28990	24789	31060	*91 28513	24556	21261	20153	36020	32854	28173
11	Mercer	46386	37419	27992	21502	......	......	......	......	......	44018	35194	25959
12	Middlesex	45029	34812	28635	21893	23157	21470	20381	17890	15956	43474	33504	27222
13	Monmouth	46195	39346	30313	32909	29233	25038	22150	19872	16918	43285	36058	27915
14	Morris	43137	34677	30158	25844	23666	21368	21828	17750	16216	42403	33960	29131
15	Ocean	13628	11176	10032	......	......	......	......	......	......	13511	11052	9892
16	Passaic	46416	29013	22569	16734	......	......	......	......	......	45741	28454	21923
17	Salem	23940	22458	19467	16024	14155	14022	12761	11371	10437	21203	19996	17392
18	Somerset	23510	22057	19692	17455	17689	16506	14725	12815	12296	21985	20460	17950
19	Sussex	23168	23846	22989	21770	20346	32752	25549	22534	19500	22972	23522	22648
20	Union	41859	27780	......	......	......	......	......	......	......	40563	26915	......
21	Warren	34336	28433	22358	20366	18627	......	......	......	......	33955	28046	21976

(*) All other persons, except Indians not taxed.
(a) Colored apprentices for life by the act to abolish slavery passed April 18, 1846.

TABLE VIII.—*Population by Counties at each Census—NEW YORK.*

	Counties.	AGGREGATE.									WHITE.	
		1870.	1860.	1850.	1840.	1830.	1820.	1810.	1800.	1790.	1870.	1860.
	The State	4382759	3880735	3097394	2428921	1918608	*701 1372111	959049	589051	340120	4330210	3831590
1	Albany	133052	113917	93279	68593	53520	38116	34661	34103	75736	131957	112978
2	Allegany	40814	41881	37808	40975	26276	9330	1942	......	......	40465	41617
3	Broome	44103	35906	30660	22338	17579	14343	8130	......	......	43624	35462
4	Cattaraugus	43909	43886	38950	28872	16724	4090	......	......	......	43745	43735
5	Cayuga	59550	55767	55458	50338	47948	38897	29843	15907	......	58890	55316
6	Chautauqua	59327	58422	50493	47975	34671	12568	......	......	......	59187	58213
7	Chemung	35281	26917	28821	20732	......	......	......	......	......	34484	26345
8	Chenango	40564	40934	40311	40785	37238	31215	21704	16087	......	40259	40671
9	Clinton	47947	45735	40047	28157	19344	12070	8002	a8516	1614	47819	45607
10	Columbia	47044	47172	43073	43252	39907	38330	32390	35472	27732	45730	45798
11	Cortland	25173	26294	25140	24607	23791	16507	8869	......	......	25115	26278
12	Delaware	42972	42465	39834	35396	33024	26587	20303	10228	......	42740	42379
13	Dutchess	74041	64941	58992	52398	50926	46615	51363	47775	45266	71996	62990
14	Erie	178699	141971	100993	62465	35719	......	......	......	......	177841	141083
15	Essex	29042	28214	31148	23634	19287	12811	9477	(a)	......	28962	28091
16	Franklin	30271	30837	25102	16518	11312	4439	2617	......	......	30244	30818
17	Fulton	27064	24162	20171	18049	......	......	......	......	......	26835	23977
18	Genesee	31606	32189	28488	59587	52147	*28 58065	12588	......	......	31453	32103
19	Greene	31832	31930	33126	30446	29525	22996	19536	13074	......	31293	31111
20	Hamilton	2960	3024	2188	1907	1325	1251	......	......	......	2958	3019
21	Herkimer	39929	40561	38244	37477	35870	*72 30945	22046	14503	......	39696	40360
22	Jefferson	65415	69825	68153	60984	48493	32952	15140	......	......	65178	69611
23	Kings	419921	279122	138882	47613	20535	11187	8303	5740	4495	414254	274129
24	Lewis	28699	28580	24564	17830	15239	9227	6433	......	......	28642	28541
25	Livingston	38309	39546	40875	35140	27729	......	......	......	......	38094	39368
26	Madison	43522	43545	43072	40008	39038	32208	25144	......	......	43124	43169
27	Monroe	117868	100648	87650	64902	49855	......	......	......	......	117303	[illegible]

TABLE VIII.—*Population by Counties at each Census—NEW JERSEY.*

	WHITE—Continued.					COLORED. (b)									
0.	1830.	1820.	1810.	1800.	1790.	1870.	1860.	1850.	1840.	1830.	1820.	1810.	1800.	1790.	
588	300266	257409	226868	194325	169954	30658	a25336	24046	21718	20557	20017	18694	16824	14185	
492	......	......	......	......	......	181	194	218	234	......	......	......	......	......	1
472	19934	15396	13638	12129	10108	1632	1663	1665	1751	2476	2742	2965	3027	2493	2
187	29729	27479	23940	20563	17270	2540	2234	2109	1644	1378	1343	1039	958	825	3
...	......	......	......	......	......	4430	2574	2230	......	......	......	......	......	......	4
126	4708	4032	3440	2888	2416	427	273	247	198	228	233	192	178	155	5
178	13305	12045	12081	9183	7990	1767	1295	1130	806	788	623	589	346	258	6
203	39754	28744	24097	20550	16454	2539	1757	2334	1928	2157	2049	1887	1719	1331	7
907	28878	21968	18784	15408	12830	973	707	620	1631	1553	1103	960	707	539	8
153	......	......	......	......	......	1050	653	503	330	......	......	......	......	......	9
976	29118	26454	22750	19521	18661	634	800	817	813	1942	2059	1806	1740	1492	10
161	......	......	......	......	......	2362	2225	2042	2341	......	......	......	......	......	11
330	21630	19425	18418	16063	14498	1545	1308	1380	1563	2127	2045	1963	1827	1458	12
544	26934	22808	20014	17771	14969	2910	2658	2398	2265	2209	2230	2136	2101	1949	13
896	23699	20254	20768	16875	15532	733	687	1027	948	967	1114	1060	875	684	14
...	......	......	......	......	......	117	124	140	......	......	......	......	......	......	15
942	......	......	......	......	......	675	559	646	792	......	......	......	......	......	16
227	19743	13006	11695	10679	9891	2737	2462	2075	1797	1412	1016	1066	692	546	17
998	15382	13897	12441	10777	10339	1524	1597	1742	1757	2307	2609	2284	2036	1957	18
403	19894	31901	24602	21918	18996	196	324	341	367	452	851	747	616	504	19
...	......	......	......	......	......	1296	865	......	......	......	......	......	......	......	20
903	18158	......	......	......	......	381	387	382	463	460	......	......	......	......	21

At 1870, Chinese 5, Japanese 10, Indians 16, as follows: Bergen, 1 Chinese; Burlington, 1 Indian; den, 12 Indians; Essex, 2 Chinese and 2 Indians; Hudson, 1 Indian; Middlesex, 1 Chinese and 9 Japan- Morris, 1 Chinese; Somerset, 1 Japanese.

TABLE VIII.—*Population by Counties at each Census—NEW YORK.*

	WHITE—Continued.						COLORED. (c)									
0.	1840.	1830.	1820.	1810.	1800.	1790.	1870.	1860.	1850.	1840.	1830.	1820.	1810.	1800.	1790.	
325	2378890	1873663	1332744	918699	557731	314142	52081	49005	49069	50031	44945	39367	40350	31320	25978	
085	67279	51925	36845	33023	31942	71642	1095	938	1194	1314	1595	1271	1638	2161	4094	1
680	40833	26197	9301	1921	......	......	349	264	128	142	79	20	21	....	....	2
229	22115	17483	14255	8077	......	......	481	464	431	223	96	88	53	....	....	3
848	28834	16703	4084	.....	......	......	164	151	102	38	21	6	....	....	....	4
915	49903	47579	38658	29682	15835	.....	657	451	543	435	369	239	161	72	....	5
353	47851	34571	12555	......	......	......	195	205	140	124	100	13	....	....	....	6
535	20619	......	......	......	......	......	793	572	286	113	....	....	....	....	....	7
047	40512	30969	31019	21615	16031	......	302	263	261	273	269	196	89	56	....	8
935	28071	19262	11972	7941	a8395	1581	128	128	112	86	82	93	61	b121	33	9
761	41696	38325	35516	30661	33481	26054	1312	1380	1312	1556	1582	1814	1729	1991	1678	10
098	24561	23753	16456	8867	......	......	58	16	42	46	38	51	2	....	....	11
633	35206	32821	26449	20171	10182	......	232	186	201	190	203	138	132	46	....	12
022	50128	48440	44158	48977	45235	42970	2113	2051	1970	2270	2486	2457	2386	2540	2296	13
168	61857	35476	......	......	......	......	858	878	825	608	243	....	....	....	....	14
098	23556	19227	12780	9474	(a)	......	80	123	50	78	60	31	3	(b)	....	15
040	16515	11288	4439	2614	......	......	27	19	62	3	24	....	3	....	....	16
069	17935	......	......	......	......	......	221	185	102	114	....	....	....	....	....	17
411	59472	52055	57948	12563	......	......	153	84	77	115	92	117	25	....	....	18
231	29553	28531	22225	18798	12157	......	629	819	895	893	904	771	738	617	....	19
186	1904	1324	1249	......	......	......	1	3	2	3	1	2	....	....	....	20
041	37190	35518	30685	21905	14434	......	226	251	203	287	352	260	141	69	....	21
962	60843	48354	32812	15100	......	......	236	209	191	141	139	140	40	....	....	22
817	44767	18528	9426	6450	3929	3017	5653	4999	4065	2846	2007	1761	1853	1811	1478	23
522	17777	15156	9184	6404	......	......	54	39	42	53	83	43	29	....	....	24
666	35000	27595	......	......	......	......	215	184	209	140	134	....	....	....	....	25
774	39785	38811	32016	24932	......	......	313	300	298	223	227	192	212	....	....	26
951	64247	49390	......	......	......	......	605	567	699	655	465	....	....	....	....	27

TABLE VIII.—*Population by Counties at each Census*—*NEW YORK*—**Continued.**

	Counties.	AGGREGATE.									WHITE.	
		1870.	1860.	1850.	1840.	1830.	1820.	1810.	1800.	1790.	1870.	1860.
28	Montgomery (*b*) ...	34457	30866	31992	35818	43715	*8 37561	41214	22051	28848	34102	30509
29	New York	942292	813669	515547	312710	202589	123706	96373	60515	33131	929199	801088
30	Niagara	50437	50399	42276	31132	18482	22990	8971	......	......	49989	49982
31	Oneida............	110008	105202	99566	85310	71326	50997	33792	22258	......	109358	104563
32	Onondaga.........	104183	90686	85890	67911	58973	41467	25987	7608	......	103475	90131
33	Ontario	45108	44563	43929	43501	40288	88267	42032	15218	1075	44578	43994
34	Orange	80902	63812	57145	50739	45366	41213	34347	29355	18492	78370	61708
35	Orleans	27689	28717	28501	25127	17732	......	......	......	......	27517	28588
36	Oswego	77941	75958	62198	43619	27119	12374	......	......	......	77633	75023
37	Otsego	48967	50157	48638	49628	51372	44856	38802	21343	......	48732	49850
38	Putnam	15420	14002	14138	12825	12628	11268	......	......	......	15300	13819
39	Queens	73803	57391	36833	30324	22460	21519	19336	16916	16014	70007	54004
40	Rensselaer.........	99549	86328	73363	60259	49424	*39 40114	36309	30351	......	98765	85967
41	Richmond..........	33029	25492	15061	10965	7082	6135	5347	4564	3835	32242	24633
42	Rockland	25213	22492	16962	11975	9388	8837	7758	6353	......	24484	21943
43	Saratoga...........	51529	51729	45646	40553	38679	36052	33147	24564	......	50839	51036
44	Schenectady	21347	20002	20054	17387	12347	*205 12876	10201	......	......	21179	19758
45	Schoharie..........	33340	34469	33548	32358	27902	*7 23147	18945	9808	......	32914	33965
46	Schuyler...........	18989	18840	......	......	......	......	......	......	......	18803	18740
47	Seneca.............	27823	28138	25441	24874	21041	23619	16609	......	......	27584	27925
48	Steuben............	67717	66690	63771	46138	33851	21989	7246	1788	......	67330	66814
49	St. Lawrence (*c*) ...	84826	83689	68617	56706	36354	16037	7885	......	......	84746	83099
50	Suffolk.............	46924	43275	36922	32469	26780	*312 23930	21113	19735	16440	44956	41461
51	Sullivan	34550	32385	25088	15629	12364	8900	6108	......	......	34451	32291
52	Tioga..............	30572	28748	24880	20527	27690	16971	7899	7109	......	30206	28469
53	Tompkins	33178	31409	38746	37948	36545	20681	......	......	......	32777	31119
54	Ulster	84075	76381	59384	45822	36550	30934	26576	24855	29397	82638	74772
55	Warren.............	22592	21434	17199	13422	11796	9453	......	......	......	22528	21376
56	Washington (*d*)....	49568	45904	44750	41080	42635	38831	44289	35792	14042	49186	45643
57	Wayne	47710	47762	44953	42057	33643	......	......	......	......	47355	47489
58	Westchester	131348	99497	58263	48686	36456	32638	30272	27373	24003	128830	97227
59	Wyoming...........	29164	31968	31981	......	......	......	......	......	......	29082	31913
60	Yates..............	19595	20290	20590	20444	19009	......	......	......	......	19429	20133

(*) All other persons, except Indians not taxed.
(*a*) Clinton and Essex opposite Clinton.
(*b*) At first Tryon; in 1784 name changed to Montgomery.
(*c*) Parts of Herkimer, Montgomery, and Oneida, provisionally annexed.
(*d*) At first Charlotte; in 1784 name changed to Washington.
(*e*) At 1870, Chinese 29, Indians 439, as follows: Cayuga, 3 Indians; Chautauqua, 5 Indians; Chemung, 4 Indians; Chenango, 3 Indians; Columbia, 1 Chinese and 1 Indian; Dutchess, 2 Chinese; Fulton, 8 Indians; Hamilton, 1 Indian; Herkimer, 7 Indians; Jefferson, 1 Indian; Kings, 7 Chinese and 7 Indians; Lewis, 3 Indians; Madison, 85 Indians; Montgomery, 4 Indians; New York, 12 Chinese and 9 Indians;

ABLE VIII.—*Population by Counties at each Census—NEW YORK—Continued.*

White—Continued.						Colored. (c)									
1840.	1830.	1820.	1810.	1800.	1790.	1870.	1860.	1850.	1840.	1830.	1820.	1810.	1800.	1790.	
35230	43004	36641	40137	21577	28219	351	357	474	588	711	920	1077	474	620	28
296352	188613	112820	86550	54133	29661	13072	12574	13815	16358	13976	10886	9823	6382	3470	29
30891	18380	22208	8932	......	......	448	317	317	241	102	82	39	......	......	30
84666	70858	50620	33581	22133	......	509	638	672	614	468	377	211	125	......	31
67434	58461	41213	25823	7669	......	707	555	613	477	492	254	164	29	......	32
42837	38833	87540	41521	15052	1058	530	639	616	664	455	727	511	166	17	33
48447	43143	39119	32454	27676	17325	2744	2112	2464	2262	2223	2094	1893	1079	1167	34
25056	17705	......	......	......	......	173	131	108	69	27	......	......	......	......	35
43404	26973	12342	......	......	......	306	315	215	215	144	32	......	......	......	36
49406	51108	44605	38595	21251	......	229	307	175	222	264	251	207	92	......	37
12657	12464	11053	......	......	......	190	183	138	168	164	215	......	......	......	38
26815	19332	18312	16173	13945	12897	3791	3387	3451	3509	3108	3207	3163	2971	3117	39
59669	48388	39049	35197	29340	......	783	1058	1019	1190	1036	1065	1112	1011	......	40
10462	6530	5525	4636	3806	2949	787	650	590	483	552	610	711	758	886	41
11343	8837	8301	7150	5734	......	728	549	596	432	451	536	608	619	......	42
39904	38067	35425	32475	24133	......	683	691	618	649	592	627	672	431	......	43
16977	12043	12329	9695	......	......	168	241	388	410	304	556	506	......	......	44
31865	27335	22581	18394	9443	......	426	484	478	493	567	566	551	365	......	45
......	......	......	......	......	......	185	100	......	......	......	......	......	......	......	46
24675	20864	23335	16464	......	......	207	213	181	199	177	264	145	......	......	47
45850	33643	21813	7130	1766	......	383	475	371	288	298	176	116	22	......	48
56671	36294	16015	7863	......	......	72	50	39	35	60	22	22	......	......	49
30292	24767	22441	19327	17833	14216	1806	1798	2117	2177	2013	1489	1786	1902	2224	50
15549	12245	8798	6054	......	......	99	94	100	80	119	102	54	......	......	51
20363	27527	16835	7799	7060	......	359	248	197	162	163	136	100	49	......	52
37695	36311	20600	......	......	......	491	237	325	233	234	72	......	......	......	53
44018	34780	28814	24073	22262	26334	1433	1609	1585	1804	1770	2120	2303	2593	3063	54
13390	11774	9436	......	......	......	54	58	46	32	22	17	......	......	......	55
40808	42242	38427	41150	35393	13992	379	259	350	272	393	404	3130	399	50	56
41833	33455	......	......	......	......	344	270	268	222	188	......	......	......	......	57
46386	34341	30795	28342	25604	22227	2513	2270	2075	2300	2113	1843	1930	1769	1776	58
......	......	......	......	......	......	82	52	64	......	......	......	......	......	......	59
20310	18903	......	......	......	......	166	157	165	134	106	......	......	......	......	60

, 60 Indians; Onondaga, 1 Indian; Orange, 8 Indians; Oswego, 2 Indians; Otsego, 6 Indians; , 1 Chinese and 4 Indians; Rensselaer, 1 Indian; Rockland, 1 Indian; Saratoga, 7 Indians; Sten- ndians; St. Lawrence, 8 Indians; Suffolk, 162 Indians; Tioga, 7 Indians; Ulster, 1 Chinese and ns; Warren, 10 Indians; Washington, 3 Indians; Wayne, 11 Indians; Westchester, 5 Chinese, , Indians 140, as follows: Albany, 1 Indian; Chautauqua, 4 Indians; Hamilton, 2 Indians; Her- 1 Indian; Jefferson, 5 Indians; Madison, 85 Indians; New York, 7 Indians; Oneida, 1 Indian; laer, 3 Indians; Schenectady, 3 Indians; Steuben, 1 Indian; St. Lawrence, 2 Indians; Suffolk, 16 ; Tioga, 1 Indian; Washington, 2 Indians; Wayne, 3 Indians; Wyoming, 3 Indians.

TABLE VIII.—*Population by Counties at each Census—NORTH CAROLINA.*

	Counties.	AGGREGATE.									WHITE.		
		1870.	1860.	1850.	1840.	1830.	1820.	1810.	1800.	1790.	1870.	1860.	1850.
	The State	1071361	992622	869039	753419	737987	638829	555500	478103	393751	678470	629942	553028
1	Alamance	11874	11852	11444	.....	.....	.....	.....	.....	.....	8234	7985	7921
2	Alexander (a)	6868	6022	5220	.....	.....	.....	.....	.....	.....	6034	5387	4653
3	Alleghany	3691	3590	.....	.....	.....	.....	.....	.....	.....	3401	3351	.....
4	Anson (a)	12428	13664	13489	15077	14095	12534	8831	8146	5133	6350	6561	6554
5	Ashe	9573	7956	8777	7467	6987	4335	3694	2783	.....	8991	7423	7896
6	Beaufort	13011	14766	13816	12225	10969	9850	7203	6242	5462	8379	8109	7964
7	Bertie	12950	14310	12851	12175	12262	10805	11218	11249	12606	5513	5806	5335
8	Bladen	12831	11995	9767	8022	7811	7276	5671	7028	5084	6729	6233	3049
9	Brunswick	7754	8406	7272	5265	6516	5480	4778	4110	3071	4448	4515	3631
10	Buncombe	15412	12654	13425	10084	16281	10542	9277	5812	.....	13109	10010	11601
11	Burke	9777	9237	7772	15799	17888	13411	11007	9929	8118	7463	6645	5477
12	Cabarrus	11954	10546	9747	9259	8810	7248	6158	5094	.....	8025	7301	6042
13	Caldwell	8476	7497	6317	.....	.....	.....	.....	.....	.....	7006	6295	5005
14	Camden	5361	5343	6049	5663	6733	6347	5347	4191	4033	3230	2912	3563
15	Carteret	9010	8186	6939	6591	6597	5609	4823	4399	3732	6285	6064	5166
16	Caswell	16081	16215	15269	14693	15185	13253	11757	8701	10096	6587	6578	7076
17	Catawba	10984	10729	8862	.....	.....	.....	.....	.....	.....	9281	9033	7375
18	Chatham	19723	19101	18449	16242	15405	12661	12977	11861	9221	12893	12549	12161
19	Cherokee	8080	9166	6838	3427	.....	.....	.....	.....	.....	7296	8383	6490
20	Chowan	6450	6842	6721	6690	6697	6464	5297	5132	5011	3081	2979	[illegible]
21	Clay	2461	.....	.....	.....	.....	.....	.....	.....	.....	2319	.....	.....
22	Cleaveland	12696	12348	10396	.....	.....	.....	.....	.....	.....	10633	10106	8501
23	Columbus	8474	8597	5909	3941	4141	3912	3022	.....	.....	5398	5779	4653
24	Craven	20516	16268	14709	13438	13734	13394	12676	10245	10469	8400	8747	[illegible]
25	Cumberland	17035	16369	20610	15284	14834	14446	9382	9264	8671	9580	9554	12447
26	Currituck (b)	5131	7415	7236	6703	7655	8098	6985	6928	5219	3991	4668	4590
27	Dare (b)	2778	.....	.....	.....	.....	.....	.....	.....	.....	2401	.....	.....
28	Davidson	17414	16601	15320	14606	13389	.....	.....	.....	.....	13808	13376	12137
29	Davie	9620	8494	7866	7574	.....	.....	.....	.....	.....	6327	6001	5612
30	Duplin	15542	15784	13514	11182	11291	9744	7863	6796	5662	8770	8280	7182
31	Edgecombe	22970	17376	17189	15708	14935	13276	12423	10421	10255	7858	6879	8350
32	Forsyth	13050	12692	11168	.....	.....	.....	.....	.....	.....	10716	10710	9681
33	Franklin	14134	14107	11713	10980	10665	9741	10166	8529	7559	6633	6465	5642
34	Gaston	12602	9307	8073	.....	.....	.....	.....	.....	.....	8430	6097	5835
35	Gates	7724	8443	8426	8161	7866	6837	5965	5881	5392	4517	4181	4136
36	Granville	24831	23396	21249	18817	19355	18222	15576	14015	10982	11476	11187	10894
37	Greene	8687	7925	6619	6595	6413	4533	4867	4218	6893	4166	3824	3320
38	Guilford	21736	20056	19754	19175	18737	14511	11420	9442	7191	15650	15738	15874
39	Halifax	20408	19442	16589	16865	17739	17237	13620	13945	13965	6418	6641	5765
40	Harnett	8895	8039	.....	.....	.....	.....	.....	.....	.....	5857	5358	.....
41	Haywood	7921	5801	7074	4975	4578	4073	2780	.....	.....	7400	5474	6841
42	Henderson (c)	7706	10448	6853	5129	.....	.....	.....	.....	.....	6496	8981	5682
43	Hertford	9273	9504	8142	7484	8537	7712	6052	6701	5828	4321	3947	3553
44	Hyde (b)	6445	7732	7636	6458	6184	4967	6029	4829	4120	4067	4682	4756
45	Iredell	16931	15347	14719	15685	14918	13071	10972	8856	5435	12288	11141	10347
46	Jackson	6683	5515	.....	.....	.....	.....	.....	.....	.....	5898	4179	.....
47	Johnston	16897	15656	13726	10599	10938	9607	6867	6301	5634	11703	10545	8879
48	Jones	5002	5730	5039	4945	5608	5216	4968	4339	4822	2346	2304	2130
49	Lenoir	10434	10220	7828	7605	7723	6799	5572	4005	.....	4902	4902	3567
50	Lincoln	9573	8195	7746	25160	22455	18147	16359	12660	9224	6814	5999	5655
51	Macon	6615	6004	6389	4869	5333	.....	.....	.....	.....	6173	5313	5734
52	Madison	8192	5908	.....	.....	.....	.....	.....	.....	.....	7858	5678	.....
53	Martin	9647	10195	8307	7637	8539	6320	5987	5629	6080	5064	5435	4617
54	McDowell	7592	7120	6246	.....	.....	.....	.....	.....	.....	5820	5542	4771
55	Mecklenburg	24299	17374	13914	18273	20073	16895	14272	10439	11395	13578	10534	8985
56	Mitchell	4705	.....	.....	.....	.....	.....	.....	.....	.....	4492	.....	.....
57	Montgomery	7487	7649	6872	10780	10919	8693	8430	7677	4725	5359	5780	5055
58	Moore	12040	11427	9342	7988	7745	7128	6367	4767	3770	9021	8725	7196
59	Nash	11077	11687	10657	9047	8490	8185	7268	6975	7393	6356	6320	5072
60	New Hanover	27978	21715	17668	13312	10959	10866	11465	7060	6831	11779	10615	8201
61	Northampton	14749	13372	13335	13369	13391	13242	13082	12353	9981	6229	5009	5004
62	Onslow	7569	8856	8283	7527	7814	7016	6669	5623	5387	5173	5195	5003
63	Orange	17507	16947	17055	24356	23908	23492	20135	16362	12216	11087	11311	11330
64	Pasquotank	8131	8940	8950	8514	8641	8008	7674	5379	5497	4180	4150	4610
65	Perquimans (d)	7945	7238	7332	9790	7419	6857	6052	5708	5440	3947	3285	3630
66	Person (d)	11170	11221	10781	7346	10027	9029	6642	6402	.....	6066	5708	5303
67	Pitt	17276	16080	13397	11806	12093	10001	9169	9084	8275	8892	7480	6664
68	Polk	4319	4043	.....	.....	.....	.....	.....	.....	.....	3341	3312	.....
69	Randolph	17551	16793	15832	12875	12406	11331	10112	9234	7276	14945	14716	13787
70	Richmond	12882	11009	9818	8909	9396	7537	6695	5623	5055	6284	5211	4869
71	Robeson	16262	15489	12826	10370	9433	8204	7528	6839	5326	8892	8572	7231
72	Rockingham	15708	16746	14495	13442	12935	11474	10316	8277	6187	9493	10019	8747
73	Rowan	16810	14589	13870	12109	20786	26009	21543	20060	15828	11503	10523	9900
74	Rutherford	13121	11573	13550	19202	17557	15351	13202	10753	7808	10479	9050	10493
75	Sampson	16436	16624	14585	12157	11634	8908	6620	6719	6065	9953	9108	8427
76	Stanley	8315	7801	6922	.....	.....	.....	.....	.....	.....	7026	6587	5437

TABLE VIII.—*Population by Counties at each Census—NORTH CAROLINA.*

	WHITE—Continued.					COLORED. (e)									
	1830.	1820.	1810.	1800.	1790.	1870.	1860.	1850.	1840.	1830.	1820.	1810.	1800.	1790.	
0	472843	419200	376410	337764	288204	391650	361522	316011	268549	265144	219629	179090	140339	105547	
	......	......	......	......	......	3640	3867	3523	......	......	......	......	......	......	1
	......	......	......	......	......	834	635	567	......	......	......	......	......	......	2
	......	......	......	......	......	290	239	......	......	......	......	......	......	......	3
3	9157	8011	6418	6725	4264	6078	7103	6935	5444	4938	3623	2413	1421	869	4
1	6398	4045	3541	2043	......	582	533	681	556	394	290	153	140	......	5
0	6317	5869	4369	4008	3701	4632	6606	6152	5175	4652	3981	2834	2234	1761	6
4	5238	4830	4945	5534	7117	7437	8504	7516	7031	7004	5975	6273	5715	5489	7
7	4301	4346	3572	4577	3350	6102	5762	4718	3705	3310	2830	2099	2451	1734	8
2	3001	2937	2314	2333	1557	3306	3891	3621	2493	3515	2543	2464	1777	1514	9
8	14523	9467	8564	5431	......	2103	2044	1824	1286	1758	1075	713	381	......	10
9	14060	11419	9514	9051	7512	2314	2502	2295	3480	3828	1992	1493	878	606	11
1	6508	5632	4921	4393	......	3929	3155	2805	2282	2302	1616	1237	701	......	12
	......	......	......	......	......	1380	1202	1312	......	......	......	......	......	......	13
4	4508	4481	3888	2905	2965	2121	2401	2461	1819	2225	1866	1459	1196	1068	14
7	4865	4171	3545	3373	2927	2725	2122	1773	1504	1732	1438	1278	1026	805	15
3	8309	7543	7368	5887	7282	9494	9637	8193	7350	6786	5710	4389	2814	2808	16
	......	......	......	......	......	1703	1096	1587	......	......	......	......	......	......	17
9	10073	8670	9100	8950	7580	6830	6572	6288	5633	5332	3991	3877	2911	1641	18
5	......	......	......	......	......	301	557	345	222	......	......	......	......	......	19
5	2761	2839	2409	2592	2382	3369	3863	3782	3825	3936	3625	2888	2540	2629	20
	......	......	......	......	......	142	......	......	......	......	......	......	......	......	21
	......	......	......	......	......	2063	2240	1805	......	......	......	......	......	......	22
9	3030	2922	2292	......	......	2948	2818	1654	1142	1141	990	730	......	......	23
4	6602	6563	6501	5756	6474	12116	7521	7489	6814	7132	6831	6175	4489	3995	24
0	9091	9131	6491	6422	6407	7515	6815	8163	6254	5743	5315	2891	2842	2264	25
4	5335	6098	5234	5284	4001	1140	2746	2637	2249	2320	2000	1751	1644	1218	26
	......	......	......	......	......	377	......	......	......	......	......	......	......	......	27
7	11321	......	......	......	......	3546	3225	3183	2669	2068	......	......	......	......	28
4	......	......	......	......	......	3093	2493	2254	1980	......	......	......	......	......	29
4	6628	6084	5418	4677	4276	6766	7495	6352	4938	4603	3660	2445	1919	1386	30
5	7632	7273	7079	6410	7033	15112	10497	8830	7793	7303	6003	5344	4011	3222	31
	......	......	......	......	......	2334	1982	1307	......	......	......	......	......	......	32
7	5337	4873	4665	4831	4805	7501	7642	6070	5753	5328	4868	5501	3698	2754	33
	......	......	......	......	......	4172	2310	2138	......	......	......	......	......	......	34
7	3891	3969	3062	3111	3080	3207	4262	4267	4024	3975	2848	2903	2770	2312	35
9	9430	8630	7363	7580	6504	13155	12209	10955	9508	9925	9592	8213	6135	4478	36
5	3433	2294	2970	2695	4933	4521	4101	3360	3220	2080	2239	1897	1523	1960	37
1	15761	12692	9850	8497	6648	6080	4318	3880	3224	2976	1819	1570	945	543	38
3	5870	6236	5760	6071	7016	13990	12801	10824	11242	11869	11001	7860	7874	6949	39
	......	......	......	......	......	3038	2687	......	......	......	......	......	......	......	40
0	4224	3780	2602	......	......	515	327	433	325	354	293	178	......	......	41
8	......	......	......	......	......	1208	1467	961	501	......	......	......	......	......	42
4	3874	3680	2943	3102	3170	4952	5557	4589	4100	4063	4032	3109	3299	2658	43
9	4081	3241	4067	3379	3035	2376	3048	2880	2449	2103	1726	1942	1450	1085	44
0	11206	10058	8535	7331	4574	4643	4206	4172	3755	3712	3013	2437	1525	861	45
	......	......	......	......	......	274	274	......	......	......	......	......	......	......	46
6	7174	6406	4509	4504	4241	5194	5111	4847	3603	3764	3201	2358	1797	1393	47
7	2347	2300	2502	2326	3071	2656	3526	2890	2998	3261	2916	2166	2013	1731	48
7	3678	3331	3019	2124	......	5532	5318	4261	3918	4045	3468	2553	1581	......	49
8	17506	14791	13862	11119	8289	2759	2196	2091	5502	4949	3356	2497	1541	935	50
6	4837	......	......	......	......	403	634	655	423	496	......	......	......	......	51
	......	......	......	......	......	334	230	......	......	......	......	......	......	......	52
8	4941	3378	3515	3660	4095	4583	4760	3690	3199	3598	2942	2472	1909	1985	53
	......	......	......	......	......	1772	1578	1475	......	......	......	......	......	......	54
0	12787	11685	10744	8436	9722	10721	6834	5629	6423	7286	3210	3528	2003	1073	55
	......	......	......	......	......	213	......	......	......	......	......	......	......	......	56
1	8514	6860	6700	6284	3986	2128	1869	1817	2559	2405	1833	1730	1393	839	57
3	5996	5778	5367	4128	3387	3019	2702	2146	1545	1749	1350	1000	639	383	58
1	4501	4522	4244	4236	3196	4721	5367	4685	4106	3989	3863	3624	2739	2197	59
1	5007	5086	4891	2908	3026	16199	11098	9467	6941	5952	5780	6574	4152	3805	60
8	5213	5254	5244	5605	3110	8516	7463	7341	7551	8178	7988	7838	6748	4871	61
5	1569	4179	4329	3809	3555	2396	3661	3280	2852	3245	2837	2310	1814	1832	62
1	15916	16777	15102	12681	10055	6420	5698	5725	7585	7002	6715	5033	3681	2161	63
0	4382	4860	4829	3390	3795	3951	4490	4340	3864	3659	3118	2845	1989	1703	64
6	4327	4179	3916	3627	3525	3988	3953	3702	3250	3092	2678	2136	2081	1915	65
9	5447	5275	3987	4197	......	5104	5313	5188	4561	4580	3754	2655	2205	......	66
	6668	5731	5580	6167	5883	8414	8600	6733	5672	5425	4270	3589	2917	2392	67
	......	......	......	......	......	978	726	......	......	......	......	......	......	......	68
7	10594	10017	9109	8425	6800	2606	2077	2045	1768	1812	1314	1003	809	476	69
3	5731	5459	5372	4723	4417	6598	5798	4929	4215	3665	2078	1323	900	638	70
2	6329	5677	5771	5500	4516	7370	6917	5505	4108	3104	2527	1757	1339	810	71
5	8428	8350	8159	6528	5077	9215	6727	5748	4847	4507	3124	2157	1749	1110	72
6	11462	20480	17697	17186	13989	5307	4066	3970	3163	6324	5520	3846	2874	1839	73
5	14074	11989	12184	9668	7192	2642	2511	3125	3327	3483	3362	1018	1085	616	74
5	7509	3872	4562	4870	4742	6483	7516	6162	4682	4125	3030	2058	1849	1323	75
	......	......	......	......	......	1289	1214	1485	......	......	......	......	......	......	76

TABLE VIII.—*Population by Counties at each Census—NORTH CAROLINA*—Continued.

	Counties.	AGGREGATE.									WHITE.		
		1870.	1860.	1850.	1840.	1830.	1820.	1810.	1800.	1790.	1870.	1860.	1850.
77	Stokes	11208	10402	9206	16265	16196	14033	11645	11026	8528	8600	7847	[illegible]
78	Surry	11252	10380	18443	15079	14504	12320	10366	9505	7191	9693	8956	16139
79	Transylvania (c)	3536	......	......	......	......	......	......	......	......	3227	......	......
80	Tyrrell (b)	4173	4944	5133	4657	4732	4319	3364	3395	4744	2871	3204	3391
81	Union	12217	11202	10051	......	......	......	......	......	......	9523	8903	8018
82	Wake	35617	28627	24888	21118	20398	20102	17086	13437	10192	19426	16448	14173
83	Warren	17768	15726	13912	12919	11877	11158	11004	11284	9397	5276	4923	4601
84	Washington	6516	6357	5664	4525	4552	3986	3464	2422	......	3739	3503	3303
85	Watauga	5287	4957	3400	......	......	......	......	......	......	5061	4772	3242
86	Wayne	18144	14905	13486	10891	10331	9040	8687	6772	6133	10004	8717	7801
87	Wilkes	15539	14749	12099	12577	11968	9967	9054	7247	8143	13877	13280	10733
88	Wilson	12258	9720	......	......	......	......	......	......	......	7185	5043	......
89	Yadkin	10697	10714	......	......	......	......	......	......	......	9353	9106	......
90	Yancey (c)	5909	8655	8205	5962	......	......	......	......	......	5601	8236	7809

(a) In the Census Report of 1850, the white and free colored population of Alexander County was published as of Anson County, and *vice versa*.
(b) Since 1860 Dare from Currituck, Hyde, and Tyrrell.
(c) In 1861 Transylvania from Henderson and Yancey.
(d) In Table II, of Volume I of the Ninth Census, the aggregates of Perquimans and Person Counties for the census of 1840 are transposed.

TABLE VIII.—*Population by Counties at each Census—OHIO.*

	Counties.	AGGREGATE.								WHITE.		
		1870.	1860.	1850.	1840.	1830.	1820.	1810.	1800.	1870.	1860.	1850.
	The State	2665260	2339511	1980329	1519467	937903	[179] 581295	230760	45365	2601946	2302808	1955050
1	Adams	20750	20309	18883	13183	12281	10406	9434	3432	20377	20304	[illegible]
2	Allen	23623	19185	12109	9079	578	......	......	......	23410	19115	[illegible]
3	Ashland	21933	22951	23813	......	......	......	......	......	21907	22935	23810
4	Ashtabula	32517	31814	28767	23724	14584	[7] 7375	......	......	32365	31789	[illegible]
5	Athens	23768	21364	18215	19109	9787	6338	2791	......	22095	20976	[illegible]
6	Auglaize	20041	17187	11338	......	......	......	......	......	19979	17123	11951
7	Belmont	39714	36398	34600	30901	28627	20329	11097	......	38406	35401	[illegible]
8	Brown	30802	29958	27332	22715	17867	13356	......	......	28735	28842	[illegible]
9	Butler	39912	35840	30789	28173	27142	21746	11150	......	38921	35111	[illegible]
10	Carroll	14491	15738	17685	18108	......	......	......	......	14433	15697	[illegible]
11	Champaign	24188	22698	19782	16721	12131	8479	6303	......	23078	21910	[illegible]
12	Clark	32070	25300	22178	16882	13114	9533	......	......	30014	24808	21856
13	Clermont	34268	33034	30455	23106	20466	15820	9965	......	32638	32901	[illegible]
14	Clinton	21914	21461	18838	15719	11436	8085	2674	......	20769	20638	[illegible]
15	Columbiana	38299	32836	33621	40378	35592	22033	10878	......	37814	32556	[illegible]
16	Coshocton	23600	25032	25674	21590	11161	7086	......	......	23567	25008	[illegible]
17	Crawford	25556	23881	18177	13152	4791	......	......	......	25454	23841	18167
18	Cuyahoga	132010	78033	48099	26506	10373	6328	1459	......	130564	77139	[illegible]
19	Darke	32278	26009	20276	13282	6204	3717	......	......	31717	25598	[illegible]
20	Defiance	15719	11886	6966	......	......	......	......	......	15608	11808	6947
21	Delaware	25175	23902	21817	22060	11504	7639	2000	......	24618	23771	[illegible]
22	Erie	28188	24474	18568	12599	......	......	......	......	27845	24325	[illegible]
23	Fairfield	31138	30538	30264	31924	24786	16633	11361	......	30824	30281	[illegible]
24	Fayette	17170	15935	12726	10984	8182	6316	1854	......	16095	15246	[illegible]
25	Franklin	63019	50361	42909	25049	14741	[120] 10172	3486	......	60251	48783	[illegible]
26	Fulton	17789	14043	7781	......	......	......	......	......	17766	14034	[illegible]
27	Gallia	25545	22043	17063	13444	9733	7098	4181	......	22743	20453	15963
28	Geauga	14190	15817	17827	16297	15813	7791	2917	......	14169	15810	[illegible]
29	Greene	28038	26197	21946	17528	14801	[8] 10521	5870	......	24190	24728	[illegible]
30	Guernsey	23838	24474	30438	27748	18036	9292	3051	......	23483	24197	[illegible]
31	Hamilton	260370	216410	156844	80145	52317	31764	15258	14692	252934	211808	[illegible]
32	Hancock	23847	22886	16751	9986	813	......	......	......	23730	22836	[illegible]
33	Hardin	18714	13570	8251	4598	210	......	......	......	18440	13460	[illegible]
34	Harrison	18682	19110	20157	20099	20916	14345	......	......	18197	18953	[illegible]

TABLE VIII.—*Population by Counties at each Census—NORTH CAROLINA*—Continued.

White—Continued.						Colored. (e)									
1840.	1830.	1820.	1810.	1800.	1790.	1870.	1860.	1850.	1840.	1830.	1820.	1810.	1800.	1790.	
13418	13122	11634	9777	9524	7728	2608	2555	1942	2847	3074	2309	1868	1502	800	77
16003	12374	10843	8813	8479	6476	1560	1430	2284	1966	2130	1477	1553	1020	715	78
......	......	......	......	......	......	309	......	......	......	......	......	......	......	......	79
3160	3283	3007	2420	2523	3543	1302	1740	1832	1497	1449	1319	944	872	1201	80
......	......	......	......	......	......	2694	2226	2033	......	......	......	......	......	......	81
12113	11456	11951	10689	8672	7549	16184	12179	10715	9005	8942	8151	6397	4565	2643	82
4390	4258	4214	4491	5136	4600	12492	10803	9311	8729	7619	6944	6613	6148	4768	83
2639	2704	2242	2114	1508	......	2777	2764	2455	1886	1848	1744	1350	824	......	84
......	......	......	......	......	......	226	185	158	......	......	......	......	......	......	85
6734	6670	5721	5220	4700	4539	8140	6188	5685	4137	3661	3340	2867	2072	1394	86
10976	10339	8633	7772	6353	7592	1662	1469	1366	1601	1629	1334	1282	854	551	87
......	......	......	......	......	......	5073	3771	......	......	......	......	......	......	......	88
......	......	......	......	......	......	1444	1608	......	......	......	......	......	......	......	89
5661	......	......	......	......	......	308	429	396	281	......	......	......	......	......	90

(e) At 1870, Indians 1,241, as follows: Camden, 1 Indian; Cherokee, 483 Indians; Jackson, 711 Indians; Macon, 39 Indians; Wake, 7 Indians. At 1860, Indians 1,158, as follows: Cherokee, 26 Indians; Hyde, 2 Indians; Jackson, 1,002 Indians; Macon, 53 Indians; Mecklenburg, 6 Indians; New Hanover, 2 Indians; Polk, 5 Indians.

TABLE VIII.—*Population by Counties at each Census—OHIO.*

White—Continued.					Colored. (a)								Indian.		
1840.	1830.	1820.	1810.	1800.	1870.	1860.	1850.	1840.	1830.	1820.	1810.	1800.	1870.	1860.	
1502122	928329	576572	228861	45028	63213	36673	25279	17345	9574	4723	1899	337	100	30	
13120	12210	10356	9413	3417	373	105	55	63	71	56	21	15	......	......	1
9056	578	......	......	......	213	70	27	23	......	......	......	......	......	......	2
......	......	......	......	......	26	16	3	......	......	......	......	......	......	......	3
23707	14573	7371	......	......	151	25	43	17	11	4	......	......	1	......	4
19054	9774	6312	2787	......	773	386	106	55	13	26	4	......	......	2	5
......	......	......	......	......	61	64	87	......	......	......	......	......	1	......	6
30179	25030	20102	11009	......	1307	997	778	722	597	227	88	......	1	......	7
22101	17347	13018	......	......	2967	1116	863	614	520	338	......	......	......	......	8
37919	26956	21588	11071	......	988	729	367	254	184	158	79	......	3	......	9
18059	......	......	......	......	58	41	52	49	......	......	......	......	......	......	10
16393	11924	8330	6218	......	1110	768	494	328	207	149	65	......	......	......	11
16622	12963	9491	......	......	2056	492	323	200	151	42	......	......	......	......	12
22954	20374	15791	9928	......	1629	833	412	122	92	29	37	......	1	......	13
15342	11322	8039	2665	......	1145	823	596	377	114	46	9	......	......	......	14
39961	35240	21873	10770	......	485	280	182	417	352	160	99	......	......	......	15
21552	11118	7067	......	......	33	24	44	38	43	19	......	......	......	......	16
13147	4770	......	......	......	101	40	10	5	21	......	......	......	1	......	17
26385	10297	6274	1445	......	1443	894	359	121	76	54	11	......	1	......	18
13082	6131	3699	......	......	561	481	248	200	73	18	......	......	......	......	19
......	......	......	......	......	111	78	19	......	......	......	......	......	......	......	20
21984	11452	7602	1956	......	557	131	135	76	52	37	44	......	......	......	21
12502	......	......	......	......	342	149	202	97	......	......	......	......	1	......	22
31562	24580	16611	11326	......	314	257	280	342	206	22	35	......	......	......	23
10748	8129	6291	1850	......	1074	629	291	236	53	25	4	......	1	......	24
24244	14453	10040	3443	......	2768	1578	1607	805	288	132	43	......	......	......	25
......	......	......	......	......	23	1	1	......	......	......	......	......	......	8	26
19645	9211	6957	4166	......	2802	1590	1198	709	522	141	15	......	......	......	27
16204	15792	7785	2914	......	21	7	7	3	21	6	3	......	......	......	28
17184	14639	10469	5834	......	3815	1473	654	344	162	53	36	......	24	......	29
27852	17800	9240	3044	......	345	277	168	190	146	52	7	......	......	......	30
77569	51017	31131	15100	14692	7432	4606	3600	2576	1306	633	158	......	4	......	31
9078	804	......	......	......	117	50	26	8	9	......	......	......	......	......	32
4304	210	......	......	......	274	110	14	4	......	......	......	......	......	......	33
19956	20841	14317	......	......	485	157	287	163	75	28	......	......	......	......	34

TABLE VIII.—*Population by Counties at each Census—OHIO*—Continued.

Counties.	AGGREGATE.								WHITE.		
	1870.	1860. (a)	1850.	1840.	1830.	1820.	1810.	1800.	1870.	1860.	1850.
Henry	14028	8901	3434	2503	262	......	......	......	14017	8900	[illegible]
Highland	29133	27773	25781	22269	16345	12308	5766	......	27449	26815	[illegible]
Hocking	17925	17057	14119	9741	4008	2130	......	......	17783	16838	[illegible]
Holmes	18177	20589	20452	18088	9135	......	......	......	18173	20564	[illegible]
Huron	28532	29616	26203	23933	13341	6675	......	......	28332	29537	[illegible]
Jackson	21759	17941	12719	9744	5941	3746	......	......	20970	17845	[illegible]
Jefferson	29188	26115	29133	25030	22489	18531	17260	8766	28183	25408	[illegible]
Knox	26333	27735	28872	29579	17085	8326	2149	......	26144	27870	[illegible]
Lake	15935	15576	14654	13719	......	......	......	......	15835	15540	[illegible]
Lawrence	31380	23249	15246	9738	5367	3499	......	......	30120	22564	[illegible]
Licking	35756	37011	38846	35096	20869	11861	3852	......	35513	36868	[illegible]
Logan	23028	20996	19162	14015	6440	3181	......	......	22066	20341	[illegible]
Lorain	30308	29744	26086	18467	5696	......	......	......	29196	29195	[illegible]
Lucas	46722	25831	12363	9382	......	......	......	......	45044	25555	[illegible]
Madison	15633	13015	10015	9025	6190	4799	1603	......	14928	12730	[illegible]
Mahoning	31001	25894	23735	......	......	......	......	......	30744	25888	[illegible]
Marion	16184	15490	12618	14765	6551	......	......	......	16067	15444	[illegible]
Medina	20092	22517	24441	18352	7560	3082	......	......	20042	22479	[illegible]
Meigs	31465	26534	17971	11452	6158	4480	......	......	29841	26043	[illegible]
Mercer	17254	14104	7712	8277	1110	......	......	......	16810	13408	[illegible]
Miami	32740	29959	24999	19688	12807	8851	3941	......	31691	29157	[illegible]
Monroe	25779	25741	28351	18521	8768	4645	......	......	25670	25657	[illegible]
Montgomery	64006	52230	38218	31938	24362	15999	7722	......	63107	51634	[illegible]
Morgan	20363	22119	28585	20852	11800	5297	......	......	20127	21970	[illegible]
Morrow	18583	20445	20280	......	......	......	......	......	18440	20356	[illegible]
Muskingum	44886	44416	45049	38749	29334	17824	10036	......	43719	[illegible]	[illegible]
Noble	19949	20751	......	......	......	......	......	......	19864	20722	......
Ottawa	13364	7016	3308	2248	......	......	......	......	13272	7016	[illegible]
Paulding	8544	4945	1766	1034	161	......	......	......	8069	4811	[illegible]
Perry	18453	19678	20775	19344	13970	8429	......	......	18366	[illegible]	[illegible]
Pickaway	24875	23469	21006	19725	16001	13149	7124	......	23795	[illegible]	[illegible]
Pike	15447	13643	10953	7626	6024	4253	......	......	14304	13301	[illegible]
Portage	24584	24208	24419	22965	18826	10095	2995	......	24479	[illegible]	[illegible]
Preble	21809	21820	21736	19482	16291	10237	3304	......	21390	[illegible]	[illegible]
Putnam	17081	12808	7221	5189	230	......	......	......	17008	12808	[illegible]
Richland	32516	31158	30879	44532	24006	9169	......	......	32372	31140	[illegible]
Ross	37097	35071	32074	27460	24068	20619	15514	8540	33862	[illegible]	[illegible]
Sandusky	25503	21429	14305	10182	2851	852	......	......	25360	21374	[illegible]
Scioto	29302	24297	18428	11192	8740	5750	3399	......	28389	23974	[illegible]
Seneca	30827	30868	27104	18128	5159	......	......	......	30668	30744	[illegible]
Shelby	20748	17493	13958	12154	3671	2106	......	......	20142	16913	[illegible]
Stark	52508	42978	39878	34603	26588	12406	2734	......	52190	[illegible]	[illegible]
Summit	34674	27344	27485	22560	......	......	......	......	34373	27251	[illegible]
Trumbull	38659	30656	30490	38107	26153	15542	8671	1302	38425	30576	[illegible]
Tuscarawas	33840	32463	31761	25631	14298	8328	3045	......	33724	[illegible]	[illegible]
Union	18730	16507	12204	8422	3192	1996	......	......	18387	16984	[illegible]
Van Wert	15823	10238	4793	1577	49	......	......	......	15619	10170	[illegible]
Vinton	15027	13631	9353	......	......	......	......	......	14819	13478	[illegible]
Warren	26689	26902	25560	23141	21468	17837	9925	......	25511	26219	[illegible]
Washington	40609	36268	29540	20823	11731	10425	5991	5427	39551	[illegible]	[illegible]
Wayne	35116	32483	32981	35808	23333	11933	......	3206	35001	32456	[illegible]
Williams	20991	16633	8018	4465	387	......	......	......	20049	[illegible]	[illegible]
Wood	24596	17886	9157	5357	1102	733	......	......	24553	[illegible]	[illegible]
Wyandot	18553	15596	11194	......	......	......	......	......	18402	15551	[illegible]

(a) At 1870, Chinese, 1, as follows: Lawrence, 1 Chinese.

TABLE VIII.—*Population by Counties at each Census*—*OHIO*—Continued.

WHITE—Continued.				COLORED.								INDIAN. (a)		
30.	1820.	1810.	1800.	1870.	1860.	1850.	1840.	1830.	1820.	1810.	1800.	1870.	1860.	
309	......	......	......	11	1	......	6	......	......	......	......	......	......	35
16832	12137	5640	......	1684	958	898	786	314	171	126	......	......	......	36
6991	2130	......	......	149	219	117	46	7	......	......	......	......	......	37
9422	......	......	......	4	5	3	3	10	......	......	......	......	......	38
13285	6648	......	......	200	79	39	106	56	7	......	......	......	......	39
5617	3710	......	......	789	696	301	318	194	36	......	......	......	......	40
22106	16314	17136	8731	1603	707	665	497	381	217	194	35	......	......	41
17941	6804	2137	......	186	50	69	65	44	90	12	......	3	......	42
......	......	......	......	100	36	38	21	......	......	......	......	......	......	43
3[illegible]	3476	......	......	1941	665	302	140	107	33	......	......	16	......	44
20799	11863	3844	......	943	149	122	140	77	36	8	......	......	......	45
6345	3103	......	......	969	655	536	407	86	78	......	......	......	......	46
5662	......	......	......	1106	549	254	88	3	......	......	......	9	......	47
......	......	......	......	776	278	139	56	......	......	......	......	2	......	48
6145	4777	1590	......	705	276	78	97	46	22	13	......	......	......	49
......	......	......	......	257	61	98	......	......	......	......	......	......	1	50
6551	......	......	......	97	46	21	36	......	......	......	......	......	......	51
7546	3866	......	......	56	35	35	13	12	14	......	......	......	......	52
6158	4477	......	......	1684	291	52	26	2	3	......	......	......	......	53
1166	......	......	......	444	606	308	204	1	......	......	......	......	......	54
18758	8791	3090	......	1049	600	602	211	48	60	21	......	......	2	55
8738	4634	......	......	103	84	69	12	13	11	......	......	......	......	56
[illegible]	15[illegible]	7088	......	808	388	349	376	140	73	54	......	......	1	57
11731	[illegible]	......	......	236	143	96	65	68	15	......	......	......	......	58
......	......	......	......	143	89	18	......	......	......	......	......	......	......	59
[illegible]	17631	9051	......	1166	1000	631	583	366	193	75	......	1	......	60
......	......	......	......	85	28	......	......	......	......	......	......	......	......	61
......	......	......	......	92	......	1	5	......	......	......	......	......	......	62
161	......	......	......	475	134	1	......	......	......	......	......	......	......	63
13[illegible]	8411	......	......	80	49	39	47	19	18	......	......	7	......	64
15837	13011	7055	......	1060	839	412	333	164	138	60	......	......	......	65
8846	4131	......	......	1142	849	618	320	175	198	......	......	1	......	66
16760	10073	3986	......	105	76	55	39	66	29	7	......	......	......	67
[illegible]	10805	3279	......	419	124	77	60	53	32	25	......	......	......	68
230	......	......	......	73	6	11	1	......	......	......	......	......	......	69
23975	9130	......	......	144	18	67	65	31	30	......	......	......	......	70
23171	20117	15144	6415	3230	2791	1906	1195	887	509	370	125	5	......	71
2832	849	......	......	143	55	47	41	19	3	......	......	......	......	72
8542	5714	3370	......	1013	323	211	206	92	36	29	......	......	......	73
5097	......	......	......	159	123	151	65	62	......	......	......	......	1	74
3629	2007	......	......	600	580	407	252	42	9	......	......	6	......	75
26407	12380	2727	......	318	172	159	204	181	26	7	......	......	......	76
......	......	......	......	209	88	121	42	......	......	......	......	2	5	77
26110	15492	8616	1297	233	80	65	70	43	50	55	5	1	......	78
14242	8324	3039	......	116	70	80	71	56	4	6	......	......	......	79
3190	1988	......	......	343	223	128	78	2	8	......	......	......	......	80
49	......	......	......	304	68	47	......	......	......	......	......	......	......	81
......	......	......	......	208	153	107	......	......	......	......	......	......	......	82
21279	17650	9636	......	1178	676	602	341	189	167	89	......	......	7	83
11592	10396	5943	5400	1056	646	390	289	139	90	48	18	......	......	84
23291	11933	......	3007	55	27	28	41	42	......	......	139	......	......	85
396	......	......	......	42	1	......	2	1	......	......	......	......	......	86
1000	732	......	......	43	3	18	32	12	1	......	......	......	......	87
......	......	......	......	88	42	49	......	......	......	......	......	9	3	88

TABLE VIII.—*Population by Counties at each Census—OREGON.*

	Counties.	AGGREGATE.					WHITE.				
		1870.	1860.	1850.	1840.	1830.	1870.	1860.	1850.	1840.	1830.
	The State	90923	52465	13294	......	......	86929	52160	13087	......	......
1	Baker (a)	2804	......	......	......	......	2121	......	......	......	......
2	Benton	4584	3074	814	......	......	4569	3059	810	......	......
3	Clackamas	5993	3466	1859	......	......	5914	3464	1836	......	......
4	Clarke (d)	......	......	643	......	......	......	......	502	......	......
5	Clatsop	1255	498	462	......	......	1221	496	458	......	......
6	Columbia	863	532	......	......	......	860	532	......	......	......
7	Coos	1644	445	......	......	......	1619	421	......	......	......
8	Curry	504	393	......	......	......	481	376	......	......	......
9	Douglas (c)	6066	3203	......	......	......	5926	3167	......	......	......
10	Grant (b)	2251	......	......	......	......	1304	......	......	......	......
11	Jackson	4778	3736	......	......	......	4064	3689	......	......	......
12	Josephine	1204	1623	......	......	......	955	1609	......	......	......
13	Lane	6426	4780	......	......	......	6417	4779	......	......	......
14	Lewis (d)	......	......	558	......	......	......	......	457	......	......
15	Linn	8717	6772	994	......	......	8708	6763	994	......	......
16	Marion	9965	7088	2749	......	......	9854	7022	2740	......	......
17	Multnomah	11510	4150	......	......	......	10806	4126	......	......	......
18	Polk	4701	3625	1051	......	......	4693	3623	1046	......	......
19	Tillamook	408	95	......	......	......	391	95	......	......	......
20	Umatilla (a)	2916	......	......	......	......	2840	......	......	......	......
21	Umpqua (c)	......	1250	......	......	......	......	1242	......	......	......
22	Union (b)	2552	......	......	......	......	2505	......	......	......	......
23	Wasco (a) (b)	2509	1689	......	......	......	2452	1673	......	......	......
24	Washington	4261	2801	2652	......	......	4222	2780	2643	......	......
25	Yam Hill	5012	3245	1512	......	......	5007	3244	1511	......	......

(*a*) In 1862 Baker and Umatilla from Wasco.
(*b*) In 1864 Grant and Union from Wasco.

TABLE VIII.—*Population by Counties at each Census—PENNSYLVANIA.*

	Counties.	AGGREGATE.									WHITE.	
		1870.	1860.	1850.	1840.	1830.	1820.	1810.	1800.	1790.	1870.	1860.
	The State	3521951	2906215	2311786	1724033	1348233	*1951 1047507	810091	602365	434373	3456609	2849259
1	Adams	30315	28006	25981	23044	21379	19370	15152	13172	......	29750	27532
2	Allegheny	262204	178831	138290	81235	50552	34921	25317	15087	10309	257743	176102
3	Armstrong	43382	35797	29560	28365	17701	10324	6143	2399	......	43203	35619
4	Beaver	36148	29140	26689	29368	24183	15340	12168	5776	......	35818	29866
5	Bedford	29635	26736	23052	29335	24502	20248	15746	12039	13124	29150	26242
6	Berks	106701	93818	77129	64569	53152	46275	43146	32407	30179	106269	93321
7	Blair	38051	27829	21777	......	......	......	......	......	......	37063	27546
8	Bradford	53204	48734	42831	32769	19746	11554	......	......	......	52715	48531
9	Bucks	64336	63578	56091	48107	45745	37842	32371	27496	25401	62532	61950
10	Butler	36510	35594	30346	22378	14581	10193	7346	3916	......	36468	35536
11	Cambria	36569	29155	17773	11256	7076	3287	2117	......	......	36471	29040
12	Cameron (a)	4273	......	......	......	......	......	......	......	......	4261	......
13	Carbon	28144	21033	15686	......	......	......	......	......	......	28079	21024
14	Centre	34418	27000	23355	20492	18879	13796	10681	b13609	b7562	34152	26739
15	Chester	77805	74578	66438	57515	50910	44451	39596	32093	27937	71560	68671
16	Clarion	26537	24988	23565	......	......	......	......	......	......	26511	24925
17	Clearfield	25741	18759	12586	7834	4803	2342	875	......	......	25600	18678
18	Clinton (a)	23211	17723	11207	8323	......	......	......	......	......	23016	17586
19	Columbia	28766	25065	17710	24267	20059	17621	......	......	......	28622	24962
20	Crawford	63832	48755	37849	31724	16030	9397	6178	2346	......	63350	48574
21	Cumberland	43912	40098	34327	30953	29226	23606	26757	25386	18243	41895	38758
22	Dauphin	60740	46756	35754	30118	25243	21653	31883	22270	18177	57768	45047
23	Delaware	39403	30597	24679	19791	17323	14810	14734	12809	9483	36650	28048
24	Elk (a)	8488	5915	3531	......	......	......	......	......	......	8424	5904
25	Erie	65973	49432	38742	31344	17041	*12 8541	3758	1468	......	65584	49251
26	Fayette	43284	39909	39112	33574	29172	27285	24714	20159	13325	41780	38360
27	Forest	4010	898	......	......	......	......	......	......	......	4003	898

TABLE VIII.—*Population by Counties at each Census—OREGON.*

COLORED.					CHINESE.					INDIAN.					
…0.	1860.	1850.	1840.	1830.	1870.	1860.	1850.	1840.	1830.	1870.	1860.	1850.	1840.	1830.	
346	128	207	......	......	3330	......	......	......	......	318	177	......	......	......	
1	......	......	......	......	680	......	......	......	......	2	......	......	......	......	1
10	10	4	......	......	......	......	......	......	......	5	5	......	......	......	2
23	1	23	......	......	50	......	......	......	......	6	1	......	......	......	3
..	......	51	......	......	......	......	......	......	......	......	......	......	......	......	4
8	2	4	......	......	13	......	......	......	......	13	......	......	......	......	5
..	......	......	......	......	......	......	......	......	......	3	......	......	......	......	6
..	......	......	......	......	13	......	......	......	......	12	24	......	......	......	7
2	......	......	......	......	12	......	......	......	......	8	17	......	......	......	8
4	9	......	......	......	76	......	......	......	......	60	27	......	......	......	9
5	......	......	......	......	940	......	......	......	......	2	......	......	......	......	10
26	42	......	......	......	634	......	......	......	......	52	5	......	......	......	11
..	4	......	......	......	223	......	......	......	......	26	10	......	......	......	12
..	1	......	......	......	7	......	......	......	......	2	......	......	......	......	13
..	......	101	......	......	......	......	......	......	......	......	......	......	......	......	14
7	7	......	......	......	2	......	......	......	......	......	2	......	......	......	15
62	20	9	......	......	27	......	......	......	......	22	46	......	......	......	16
163	17	......	......	......	508	......	......	......	......	33	7	......	......	......	17
6	2	5	......	......	2	......	......	......	......	......	......	......	......	......	18
..	......	......	......	......	......	......	......	......	......	17	......	......	......	......	19
2	......	......	......	......	70	......	......	......	......	4	......	......	......	......	20
..	3	......	......	......	......	......	......	......	......	......	5	......	......	......	21
1	......	......	......	......	45	......	......	......	......	1	......	......	......	......	22
21	9	......	......	......	27	......	......	......	......	9	7	......	......	......	23
..	......	9	......	......	......	......	......	......	......	39	21	......	......	......	24
2	1	1	......	......	1	......	......	......	......	2	......	......	......	......	25

In 1862 Umpqua consolidated with Douglas.
Since 1850 to Territory of Washington.

TABLE VIII.—*Population by Counties at each Census—PENNSYLVANIA.*

WHITE—Continued.							COLORED. (c)									
…0.	1840.	1830.	1820.	1810.	1800.	1790.	1870.	1860.	1850.	1840.	1830.	1820.	1810.	1800.	1790.	
…160	1676115	1309900	1017094	786804	586095	424099	63294	56949	53626	47918	38333	30413	23287	16270	10274	
…126	22352	20742	18741	14743	12869	......	565	474	555	692	637	629	409	303	......	1
…859	79117	49356	34236	24879	14752	10141	4459	2725	3431	2818	1196	695	438	335	166	2
…131	28253	17605	10282	6139	2398	......	179	178	129	112	96	42	4	1	......	3
…144	29102	24044	15234	12085	5737	......	330	274	245	266	139	106	83	39	......	4
…337	28865	24076	19902	15625	12010	13044	485	494	415	470	426	346	121	29	80	5
…579	64043	52366	45797	42618	32223	29913	424	497	530	526	586	478	528	184	266	6
…317	......	......	......	......	......	......	386	283	260	......	......	......	......	......	......	7
…334	32608	19664	11519	......	......	......	489	203	197	161	84	35	......	......	......	8
…869	46368	44026	36558	31377	26887	24559	1803	1618	1722	1739	1419	1284	994	660	842	9
…292	22317	14555	10180	7336	3913	......	42	56	84	61	26	13	10	3	......	10
…545	11158	7014	3267	2078	......	......	98	115	128	98	62	20	39	......	......	11
...	......	......	......	......	......	......	12	......	......	......	......	......	......	......	......	12
…156	......	......	......	......	......	......	65	9	30	......	......	......	......	......	......	13
…112	20191	18617	13676	10566	b13460	b7461	266	261	243	301	262	130	115	b149	b101	14
…215	53372	47911	41710	37775	30002	27249	6233	5907	5223	4143	2909	2741	1821	1191	688	15
…148	......	......	......	......	......	......	26	63	117	......	......	......	......	......	......	16
…182	7777	4750	2307	840	......	......	135	81	104	57	53	35	35	......	......	17
…355	8247	......	......	......	......	......	195	137	152	76	......	......	......	......	......	18
…307	24198	19964	17558	......	......	......	144	103	103	75	95	63	......	......	......	19
…750	31609	15096	9356	6156	2336	......	481	182	99	113	34	41	22	10	......	20
…470	29933	28291	22861	26185	24826	17814	2015	1340	957	1020	935	745	572	537	429	21
…176	29161	24332	21147	31604	22011	17908	2972	1709	1278	957	911	506	279	259	269	22
…122	18458	16062	13701	13912	12157	9144	2744	1649	1557	1333	1261	1109	822	652	339	23
…329	......	......	......	......	......	......	64	11	2	......	......	......	......	......	......	24
…393	31944	10996	8469	3709	1449	......	389	181	149	100	115	72	49	19	......	25
…443	32109	28166	26385	24066	19740	12905	1503	1549	1669	1465	1006	900	648	419	330	26
...	......	......	......	......	......	......	7	......	......	......	......	......	......	......	......	27

TABLE VIII.—*Population by Counties at each Census*—*PENNSYLVANIA*—Continued.

	Counties.	Aggregate.									White.	
		1870.	1860.	1850.	1840.	1830.	1820.	1810.	1800.	1790.	1870.	1860.
28	Franklin	45365	42126	39904	37793	35037	31892	23083	19638	15655	42903	40[illegible]
29	Fulton	9360	9131	7567	......	......	......	......	......	......	9309	90[illegible]
30	Greene	25887	24343	22136	19147	18028	15554	12544	8605	......	25374	23816
31	Huntingdon	31251	28100	24786	35484	27145	*3 20139	14778	13008	7565	30952	27810
32	Indiana	36138	33687	27170	20782	14252	8882	6214	......	......	35952	3358[illegible]
33	Jefferson	21656	18270	13518	7253	2025	561	161	......	......	21588	181[illegible]
34	Juniata	17390	16986	13029	11080	......	......	......	......	......	17164	167[illegible]
35	Lancaster	121340	116314	98944	84203	76631	*361 67975	53927	43403	36147	118479	112854
36	Lawrence	27298	22999	21079	......	......	......	......	......	......	27181	[illegible]
37	Lebanon	34096	31831	26071	21872	20557	*13 16975	......	......	......	34022	31746
38	Lehigh	56796	43753	32479	25787	22256	18895	......	......	......	56756	[illegible]
39	Luzerne	160915	90244	56072	44006	27379	20027	18109	12839	4904	160149	89794
40	Lycoming	47626	37399	26257	22649	17636	13517	11006	5414	......	46775	[illegible]
41	McKean (*a*)	8825	8859	5254	2975	1439	728	142	......	......	8801	[illegible]
42	Mercer	49977	36856	33172	32873	19729	11681	8277	3228	......	49700	[illegible]
43	Mifflin	17508	16340	14980	13092	21690	16618	12132	(*b*)	(*b*)	17985	[illegible]
44	Monroe	18362	16758	13270	9879	......	......	......	......	......	18157	[illegible]
45	Montgomery	81612	70500	58291	47241	39406	35793	29703	24150	22929	80375	[illegible]
46	Montour	15344	13053	13239	......	......	......	......	......	......	15265	[illegible]
47	Northampton	61432	47904	40235	40996	39482	31765	38145	30062	24250	61245	[illegible]
48	Northumberland	41444	28922	23272	20027	18133	15424	36327	27797	17161	41311	[illegible]
49	Perry	25447	22793	20088	17096	14261	*58 11284	......	......	......	25307	[illegible]
50	Philadelphia	674022	565529	408762	258037	188797	*1460 135637	111210	81009	54391	651854	543344
51	Pike	8436	7155	5881	3832	4843	*4 2890	......	......	......	8383	7018
52	Potter (*a*)	11265	11470	6048	3371	1265	186	29	......	......	11943	11455
53	Schuylkill	116428	89510	60713	29053	20744	*28 11311	......	......	......	116044	8915[illegible]
54	Snyder	15606	15035	......	......	......	......	......	......	......	15573	[illegible]
55	Somerset	28226	26778	24416	19650	17762	13974	11284	10188	......	28181	26731
56	Sullivan	6191	5637	3694	......	......	......	......	......	......	6186	[illegible]
57	Susquehanna	37523	36267	28688	21195	16787	9960	......	......	......	37874	[illegible]
58	Tioga	35097	31044	23987	15498	8978	4021	1687	......	......	35003	[illegible]
59	Union	15565	14145	26083	22787	20795	18619	......	......	......	15403	[illegible]
60	Venango	47925	25043	18310	17900	9470	4915	3060	1130	......	47492	[illegible]
61	Warren	23897	19190	13671	9278	4697	1976	827	233	......	23787	1912[illegible]
62	Washington	48483	46805	44939	41279	42784	40038	36289	28298	23866	46452	4507[illegible]
63	Wayne	33188	32239	21890	11848	7663	4127	4125	2562	......	33147	3219[illegible]
64	Westmoreland	58719	53736	51726	42699	38400	30540	26392	22726	16018	58160	[illegible]
65	Wyoming	14585	12540	10655	......	......	......	......	......	......	14575	[illegible]
66	York	76134	68200	57450	47010	42859	*12 38747	31958	25643	37747	74900	[illegible]

(*) All other persons, except Indians not taxed.
(*a*) In 1860, Cameron from Clinton, Elk, McKean, and Potter.
(*b*) Centre and Mifflin were tabulated together in 1790 and 1800, and are here placed in the line of Centre.

TABLE VIII.—*Population by Counties at each Census*—*RHODE ISLAND.*

	Counties.	Aggregate.									White.		
		1870.	1860.	1850.	1840.	1830.	1820.	1810.	1800.	1790.	1870.	1860.	1850.
	The State	217353	174620	147545	108830	97199	*44 83015	76931	69122	68825	212219	170649	143875
1	Bristol	9421	8907	8514	6476	5446	5637	5072	3801	3211	9233	8309	[illegible]
2	Kent	18595	17303	15068	13083	12789	*1 10227	9834	8487	8848	18257	17038	148[illegible]
3	Newport	20050	21896	20007	16874	16535	*1 15770	16294	14845	14300	19113	21074	19[illegible]
4	Providence	149190	107799	87526	58073	47018	*38 35698	30769	25854	24391	146246	103821	85708
5	Washington	20097	18715	16430	14324	15411	*4 15683	14962	16135	18075	19368	18117	15909

(*) All other persons, except Indians not taxed.

VIII.—*Population by Counties at each Census*—*PENNSYLVANIA*—Continued.

White—Continued.						Colored. (c)									
840.	1830.	1820.	1810.	1800.	1790.	1870.	1860.	1850.	1840.	1830.	1820.	1810.	1800.	1790.	
35760	33220	30326	22072	18793	15052	2462	1799	1948	2033	1817	1566	1011	845	603	28
....	......	......	......	......	......	151	101	93	......	......	......	......	......	......	29
18733	17715	13293	12462	8525	......	513	526	476	414	313	261	82	80	......	30
34977	26813	19866	14668	12876	7498	299	290	335	507	332	273	110	132	67	31
30027	14144	8821	6200	......	......	186	186	254	153	108	61	14	......	......	32
7196	2003	551	160	......	......	68	81	94	57	22	10	1	......	......	33
10971	......	......	......	......	......	226	261	131	109	......	......	......	......	......	34
81196	74086	65748	52326	42439	33254	2361	3459	3614	3005	2545	2227	1691	964	893	35
....	......	......	......	......	......	117	102	132	......	......	......	......	......	......	36
21769	20464	16968	......	......	......	74	83	86	103	93	107	......	......	......	37
25754	22166	18846	......	......	......	40	57	48	33	90	49	......	......	......	38
40811	27193	19914	18016	12743	4880	766	450	373	195	186	113	99	96	24	39
22230	17388	13375	10940	5112	......	831	399	367	350	248	142	66	302	......	40
2970	1438	727	141	......	......	24	......	36	5	1	1	1	......	......	41
32543	19522	11590	8230	3315	......	277	291	291	328	267	91	47	13	......	42
12644	21331	16441	12016	(b)	(b)	223	415	410	446	359	177	116	(b)	(b)	43
8829	......	......	......	......	......	205	197	100	50	......	......	......	......	......	44
46561	38662	34916	29029	25590	22375	1237	904	857	689	744	877	674	560	554	45
....	......	......	......	......	......	79	114	84	......	......	......	......	......	......	46
40832	32290	31565	37956	29813	24094	186	141	136	164	192	200	189	249	156	47
19922	18033	15310	36130	27633	16963	133	115	92	105	109	114	197	164	198	48
16042	14148	11216	......	......	......	140	119	135	154	113	68	......	......	......	49
38204	173173	123746	100688	74129	51902	22147	22185	19761	19833	15624	11891	10522	6880	2489	50
3983	4743	2839	......	......	......	113	137	189	149	100	51	......	......	......	51
3370	1262	185	28	......	......	22	15	6	1	3	1	1	......	......	52
28728	20506	11216	......	......	......	384	357	408	320	236	95	......	......	......	53
....	......	......	......	......	......	33	35	......	......	......	......	......	......	......	54
19568	17678	13888	11270	10163	......	45	47	99	82	84	86	14	25	......	55
....	......	......	......	......	......	5	9	11	......	......	......	......	......	......	56
21006	16714	9910	......	......	......	249	209	160	97	73	50	......	......	......	57
15429	8949	4004	1687	......	......	94	102	98	69	29	17	......	......	......	58
22700	20738	18545	......	......	......	162	55	101	87	57	74	......	......	......	59
17873	9437	4887	3054	1124	......	433	69	40	27	33	28	6	6	......	60
9238	4683	1975	827	233	......	104	51	72	40	14	1	......	......	......	61
40164	41931	39291	35683	27874	23591	2031	1726	1559	1115	853	747	606	424	275	62
11809	7632	4111	4078	2507	......	41	40	49	39	31	16	47	55	......	63
42406	38022	30288	26127	22499	13851	559	432	446	291	378	252	265	227	167	64
....	......	......	......	......	......	10	5	5	......	......	......	......	......	......	65
46036	41851	37960	31329	25214	36411	1233	1366	1125	974	1098	787	629	429	1336	66

870, Chinese 14, Indians 34, as follows: Allegheny, 2 Indians; Armstrong, 1 Indian; Berks, 8 ucks, 1 Indian; Chester, 3 Indians; Crawford, 1 Indian; Cumberland, 2 Indians; Fayette, 1 Northampton, 1 Indian; Philadelphia, 13 Chinese and 8 Indians; Warren, 6 Indians; York, 1 t 1860, 7 Indians, as follows: Allegheny, 4 Indians; Bucks, 1 Indian; Greene, 1 Indian; Lan- dian.

TABLE VIII.—*Population by Counties at each Census*—*RHODE ISLAND*.

White—Continued.					Colored.									Indian.		
0.	1820.	1810.	1800.	1790.	1870.	1860.	1850.	1840.	1830.	1820.	1810.	1800.	1790.	1870	1860.	
321	79413	73214	65438	64470	4980	3952	3670	3243	3578	3602	3717	3684	4355	154	19	
162	5333	4814	3610	3021	187	308	311	245	264	304	258	191	190	1	....	1
188	9888	9476	6060	6434	337	259	229	312	301	330	358	427	414	1	6	2
321	14890	15346	13768	13120	931	822	782	581	714	880	948	1077	1180	4	....	3
154	34327	29493	24878	23531	2011	1977	1818	1594	1564	1371	1276	976	860	33	1	4
376	14975	14085	15122	16364	614	586	530	311	735	708	877	1013	1711	115	12	5

TABLE VIII.—*Population by Counties at each Census—SOUTH CAROLINA.*

	Counties.	Aggregate.									White.		
		1870.	1860.	1850.	1840.	1830.	1820.	1810.	1800.	1790.	1870.	1860.	1850.
	The State	705606	703708	668507	594398	581185	502741	415115	345591	249073	289667	291300	274563
1	Abbeville	31129	32385	32318	29351	28149	23167	21156	13553	9197	10916	11516	[illegible]
2	Anderson (b)	24049	22873	21475	18493	17169	......	......	......	......	14436	14286	13867
3	Barnwell	35724	30743	26608	21471	19236	14750	12280	7376	......	13578	12702	12289
4	Beaufort	34359	40053	38805	35794	37032	32199	25887	20428	18753	5309	6714	5947
5	Charleston	88863	70100	83844	82661	86338	80212	63179	57480	46647	28204	29136	25208
6	Chester	18805	18122	18038	17747	17182	14189	11479	8185	6866	6290	7096	8003
7	Chesterfield	10584	11834	10790	8574	8472	6645	5564	5216	......	6275	7354	6678
8	Clarendon	14038	13095	......				......	......	......	4660	4378	......
9	Colleton	25410	41916	25466	25548	27256	26404	26359	24903	20338	8909	9255	6775
10	Darlington	26243	20361	16830	14822	13728	10949	9047	7631	......	10097	8421	6747
11	Edgefield	42486	39887	39262	32852	30509	25119	23160	18130	13289	17040	15653	16252
12	Fairfield	19888	22111	21404	20165	21546	17174	11857	10067	7623	5787	6373	7008
13	Georgetown	16161	21305	20647	18274	19943	17603	15679	22938	22122	2773	3013	2193
14	Greenville	22262	21892	20156	17839	16476	14530	13133	11504	6503	15121	14631	13370
15	Horry	10721	7962	7646	5755	5245	5025	4349	......	......	7486	5564	5522
16	Kershaw	11754	13086	14473	12281	13545	12432	9867	7340	......	3909	5026	4681
17	Lancaster	12087	11797	10988	9907	10361	8716	6318	6012	6302	6159	6054	5857
18	Laurens	22536	23858	23407	21584	20863	17682	14982	12809	9337	9904	10529	11370
19	Lexington	12988	15579	12930	12111	9065	8083	6641	......	......	8432	9333	7350
20	Marion	22160	21190	17407	13932	11208	10201	8884	6914	......	11428	11007	9581
21	Marlborough	11814	12434	10789	8408	8582	6425	4966	5452	10706	5140	5373	5033
22	Newberry	20775	20879	20143	18350	17441	16104	13964	12006	9342	7457	7000	7242
23	Oconee (a)	10536									8114	......	......
24	Orangeburg	16865	24896	23582	18519	18453	15653	13229	15766	18513	5709	8108	8190
25	Pendleton (b)				......	......	27022	22897	20052	9568	......	......	......
26	Pickens (a) (b)	10269	19639	16904	14356	14473	......	......	......	......	7730	15335	13105
27	Richland	23025	18307	20243	16397	14772	12321	9027	6097	3930	7842	6863	6764
28	Spartanburg	25784	26919	26400	23669	21150	16989	14259	12122	8800	17375	18537	18311
29	Sumter	25268	23859	33220	27892	28277	25369	19054	13103	6940	7463	6857	9813
30	Union	19248	19635	19852	18936	17906	14126	10995	10237	7693	8718	8670	9317
31	Williamsburgh	15489	15489	12447	10327	9018	8716	6871	......	......	5346	5187	3902
32	York	24286	21502	19433	18383	17790	14936	10032	10250	6604	12114	11329	11209

(a) In 1869 Oconee from Pickens.
(b) In 1826 Anderson and Pickens from all of Pendleton.
(c) At 1870, Chinese, 1; Indians, 124, as follows: Charleston, 56 Indians; Chester, 2 Indians; Clarendon, 12 Indians; Colleton, 9 Indians; Edgefield, 29 Indians; Lancaster, 4 Indians; Pickens, 1 Indian; Rich-

---

TABLE VIII.—*Population by Counties at each Census—TENNESSEE.*

	Counties.	Aggregate.									White.		
		1870.	1860.	1850.	1840.	1830.	1820.	1810.	1800.	1790.	1870.	1860.	1850.
	The State	1258520	1109801	1002717	829210	681904	422771	261727	105602	35691	936119	826722	756836
1	Anderson	8704	7068	6938	5658	5310	4668	3959	......	......	7773	6477	6391
2	Bedford	24333	21584	21511	20546	30396	16012	8242	......	......	17849	14788	15837
3	Benton	8234	8463	6315	4772	......	......	......	......	......	7782	7918	5931
4	Bledsoe	4870	4459	5959	5676	4648	4005	3259	......	......	4161	3643	5036
5	Blount	14237	13270	12424	11745	11028	11258	8839	5587	......	12781	11711	11213
6	Bradley	11652	11701	12259	7385	......	......	......	......	......	9952	10470	11478
7	Campbell	7445	6712	6068	6149	5110	4244	2668	......	......	7017	6281	5651
8	Cannon	10502	9509	8982	7193	......	......	......	......	......	9575	8530	8115
9	Carroll	19447	17437	15967	12362	9397	......	......	......	......	14648	13339	12815
10	Carter	7909	7124	6296	5372	6414	4835	4190	4813	......	7336	6727	5911
11	Cheatham	6678	7258	......	......	......	......	......	......	......	5208	5376	......
12	Claiborne	9321	9643	9369	9474	8470	5508	4798	......	......	8563	8724	8610
13	Cocke	12458	10408	8300	6992	6017	4892	5154	(a)	......	11194	9482	7501
14	Coffee	10237	9689	8351	8184	......	......	......	......	......	8736	8150	7074
15	Cumberland	3461	3460	......	......	......	......	......	......	......	3363	3321	......
16	Davidson	62897	47055	38882	30509	28122	20154	15608	9965	3459	37468	31056	23853
17	Decatur	7772	6276	6003	......	......	......	......	......	......	6716	5477	5863
18	De Kalb	11425	10573	8016	5868	......	......	......	......	......	10321	8533	7331
19	Dickson	9340	9982	8404	7074	7265	5190	4516	......	......	7993	7774	6985

TABLE VIII.—*Population by Counties at each Census—SOUTH CAROLINA.*

WHITE—Continued.					COLORED. (c)									
1830.	1820.	1810.	1800.	1790.	1870.	1860.	1850.	1840.	1830.	1820.	1810.	1800.	1790.	
257863	237440	214196	196255	140178	415814	412320	393944	335314	323322	265301	200919	149336	108895	
14861	13488	14396	10548	7505	20213	20869	19619	15471	13288	9679	6760	3005	1692	1
12704	......	......	......	......	9593	8587	7608	5746	4465	......	......	......	......	2
10456	8162	7969	5575	......	22146	18041	14319	10938	8780	6358	4311	1801	......	3
5364	4679	4792	4199	4364	29050	33339	32858	30144	31368	27530	21095	16429	14389	4
20804	19376	16011	14374	11801	66603	40912	58636	61740	65534	60836	47168	43106	34846	5
9946	9611	8722	7019	5891	12513	11024	10035	7858	7236	4378	3737	1166	985	6
5356	4412	3867	3995	......	4309	4480	4112	3037	3116	2233	1697	1221	......	7
......	......	......	......	......	9366	8717	......	......	......	......	......	......	......	8
5354	4341	4290	4394	3601	16492	32661	21691	19674	21902	22063	22069	20509	16737	9
6714	6407	6259	5263	......	16146	11929	10083	7653	7014	4549	2788	2368	......	10
14957	12864	14433	13063	9005	25417	24233	23010	17832	15552	12255	8727	5067	3684	11
9705	9378	7786	8096	6138	14101	15738	14336	12578	11841	7796	4071	1901	1485	12
1931	1830	1710	6275	8878	13388	18292	18454	16181	18012	15773	13969	10063	13244	13
11380	11017	10739	10029	5888	7141	7261	6786	5348	5096	3513	2394	1475	615	14
3513	3568	2933	......	......	3235	2398	2124	1601	1732	1457	1416	......	......	15
5016	5628	4942	4706	......	7945	8038	9792	8293	8329	6804	4925	2834	......	16
6165	5848	4300	4898	4864	5924	5743	5131	4342	4196	2808	2016	1114	1438	17
13564	12755	11645	10870	8210	12632	13329	13037	9012	7229	4927	3337	1939	1127	18
5239	5267	4713	......	......	4536	6246	5580	4710	3820	2816	1928	......	......	19
7358	6652	6019	4621	......	10732	10183	7626	5339	3870	3549	2805	2293	......	20
4194	3250	3173	3880	7418	6668	7061	5756	4220	4388	3175	1793	1572	3288	21
6919	10177	9848	9707	8186	13318	13879	12901	10142	8522	5927	4116	2299	1156	22
......	......	......	......	......	2422	......	......	......	......	......	......	......	......	23
7316	6760	6639	10315	12412	11156	16786	15462	12198	10037	8893	6590	5451	6101	24
......	22140	19364	17760	8731	......	......	......	......	......	4882	3533	2292	837	25
11464	......	......	......	......	2538	4304	3799	2808	3009	......	......	......	......	26
5238	4499	3458	2929	2479	15177	11444	13479	11071	9534	7822	5550	3168	1451	27
16144	13655	11835	10609	7907	8408	8382	8089	5745	5006	3334	2424	1513	893	28
9184	8844	7128	6239	4228	17805	17092	23407	19248	19093	16525	11986	6864	2712	29
10654	9786	8081	8472	6420	10580	10965	10535	8451	7252	4340	2914	1765	1263	30
2829	2795	2306	......	......	10143	10302	8545	7000	6180	5921	4565	......	......	31
11054	10251	6828	8419	5652	12167	10173	8134	6934	6736	4685	3204	1831	952	32

Chinese and 5 Indians; Spartanburg, 1 Indian; York, 5 Indians. At 1860 Indians, 88, as follows: ston, 58 Indians; Chester, 2 Indians; Darlington, 11 Indians; Edgefield, 1 Indian; Kershaw, 22 s.

TABLE VIII.—*Population by Counties at each Census—TENNESSEE.*

WHITE—Continued.					COLORED. (c)									
1830.	1820.	1810.	1800.	1790.	1870.	1860.	1850.	1840.	1830.	1820.	1810.	1800.	1790.	
535746	339927	215875	91709	31913	322331	283019	245881	188583	146158	82844	45852	13893	3778	
4813	4295	3694	......	......	928	591	547	440	497	373	265	......	......	1
24683	12334	7057	......	......	6484	6796	5574	4354	5733	3678	1185	......	......	2
......	......	......	......	......	452	545	384	255	......	......	......	......	......	3
4165	3616	3050	......	......	709	816	923	666	483	389	209	......	......	4
9915	10154	8008	5240	......	1436	1559	1211	1081	1113	1104	831	347	......	5
......	......	......	......	......	1700	1231	781	414	......	......	......	......	......	6
4794	4093	2507	......	......	428	431	417	318	316	151	163	......	......	7
......	......	......	......	......	927	979	867	635	......	......	......	......	......	8
7694	......	......	......	......	4799	4098	3152	2248	1703	......	......	......	......	9
5940	4484	3928	4509	......	573	396	385	374	474	351	202	304	......	10
......	......	......	......	......	1470	1882	......	......	......	......	......	......	......	11
7763	5101	4436	......	......	758	919	759	709	707	407	362	......	......	12
5309	4409	4702	(a)	......	1274	926	799	793	708	483	452	......	......	13
......	......	......	......	......	1501	1539	1277	1127	......	......	......	......	......	14
......	......	......	......	......	98	139	......	......	......	......	......	......	......	15
15989	12066	9173	6861	2722	25412	15009	15069	13052	12133	8088	6435	3104	677	16
......	......	......	......	......	1056	799	740	......	......	......	......	......	......	17
......	......	......	......	......	1104	1040	625	470	......	......	......	......	......	18
5574	3861	3536	......	......	1677	2208	2119	1704	1691	1329	980	......	......	19

TABLE VIII.—*Population by Counties at each Census—TENNESSEE*—Continued.

	Counties.	AGGREGATE.									WHITE.		
		1870.	1860.	1850.	1840.	1830.	1820.	1810.	1800.	1790.	1870.	1860.	1850.
20	Dyer	13706	10536	6361	4484	1904	......	......	......	......	10813	7889	4889
21	Fayette	26145	24327	26719	21501	8652	......	......	......	......	9156	*8820	11416
22	Fentress	4717	5054	4454	3550	2748	......	......	......	......	4547	4865	4322
23	Franklin	14970	13848	13768	12033	15620	16571	5730	......	......	11098	10249	10087
24	Gibson	25666	21777	19548	13689	5801	......	......	......	......	18801	15543	15280
25	Giles	32413	26166	25949	21494	18703	12558	4546	......	......	19675	15293	16518
26	Grainger	12421	10902	12370	10572	10066	7651	6397	7367	......	11391	9727	11179
27	Greene	21668	19004	17824	16076	14410	11324	9713	7610	7741	19604	17485	16398
28	Grundy	3250	3093	2773	......	......	......	......	......	......	3113	2813	2522
29	Hamilton	17241	13258	10075	8175	2276	821	......	......	......	13053	11641	9216
30	Hancock	7148	7020	5660	......	......	......	......	......	......	6563	6700	5447
31	Hardeman	18074	17769	17456	14563	11655	......	......	......	......	11218	10505	10298
32	Hardin	11768	11214	10328	8245	4868	1462	......	......	......	10321	9554	9040
33	Hawkins	15837	16162	13370	15035	13683	10949	7643	6563	6970	13947	14032	11567
34	Haywood	25094	19232	17259	13870	5334	......	......	......	......	11261	8163	8711
35	Henderson	14217	14491	13164	11875	8748	......	......	......	......	11809	11189	10578
36	Henry	20380	19133	18233	14906	12249	......	......	......	......	15176	13292	13387
37	Hickman	9856	9312	9397	8618	8119	6080	2583	......	......	8385	7532	7559
38	Humphreys	9326	9096	6422	5195	6187	4067	1511	......	......	8031	7619	5304
39	Jackson	12583	11725	15673	12872	9698	7593	5401	......	......	11816	10467	14006
40	Jefferson	19476	16043	13204	12076	11801	8953	7309	a9017	......	16566	13777	11458
41	Johnson	5852	5018	3705	2658	......	......	......	......	......	5434	4737	3485
42	Knox	28990	22813	18807	15485	14498	13034	10171	12446	......	24150	20020	16385
43	Lake (b)	2428	......	......	......	......	......	......	......	......	2035	......	......
44	Lauderdale	10838	7559	5169	3435	......	......	......	......	......	7354	4684	3397
45	Lawrence	7601	9320	9280	7121	5411	3271	......	......	......	7036	8136	8604
46	Lewis	1986	2241	4438	......	......	......	......	......	......	1798	1992	3894
47	Lincoln	28050	22828	23492	21493	22075	14761	6104	......	......	22097	15926	17802
48	Macon	6633	7290	6948	......	......	......	......	......	......	5842	6244	6122
49	Madison	23480	21535	21470	16530	11594	......	......	......	......	13328	11440	12857
50	Marion	6841	6190	6314	6070	5508	3888	......	......	......	5098	5487	5718
51	Marshall	16207	14592	15616	14555	......	......	......	......	......	11822	10064	11915
52	Maury	36289	32498	29520	28186	27665	*32 22089	10359		......	20022	17701	16759
53	McMinn	13969	13555	13906	12719	14460	1623	......	......	......	12130	11547	12286
54	McNairy	12726	14732	12864	9385	5697	......	......	......	......	11226	12810	11447
55	Meigs	4511	4667	4879	4794	......	......	......	......	......	4075	4021	4480
56	Monroe	12589	12607	11874	12056	13708	2529	......	......	......	11339	10890	10623
57	Montgomery	24747	20895	21045	16927	14349	12219	8021	2899	1387	13077	11235	11060
58	Morgan	2969	3353	3430	2660	2582	1676	......	......	......	2868	3192	3301
59	Obion (b)	15584	12817	7633	4814	2099	......	......	......	......	13402	10380	6572
60	Overton	11297	12637	11211	9279	8242	7128	5643	......	......	10747	11452	10088
61	Perry	6925	6042	5821	7419	7094	2384	......	......	......	6453	5486	5503
62	Polk	7369	8726	6338	3570	......	......	......	......	......	7049	8228	5884
63	Putnam	8698	8558	......	......	......	......	......	......	......	8168	7840	......
64	Rhea	5538	4991	4415	3985	8186	4215	2504	......	......	5007	4346	3951
65	Roane	15622	13583	12185	10948	11341	7895	5581	......	......	13494	11730	10325
66	Robertson	16166	15265	16145	13801	13272	9938	7270	4280	......	11353	10375	11303
67	Rutherford	33289	27918	29122	24280	26134	19552	10265	......	......	16807	14743	16910
68	Scott	4054	3519	1905	......	......	......	......	......	......	4015	3446	1868
69	Sequatchie	2335	2120	......	......	......	......	......	......	......	2100	1918	......
70	Sevier	11028	9122	6920	6442	5717	4772	4505	3419	3619	10495	8520	6450
71	Shelby	76378	48092	31157	14721	5648	364	......	......	......	39737	30861	16579
72	Smith	15994	16357	18412	21179	19906	17580	11649	4294	......	12458	12015	13709
73	Stewart	12019	9896	9719	8587	6968	8397	4262	......	......	9319	7404	7017
74	Sullivan	13136	13552	11742	10736	10073	7015	6847	10218	4447	12279	12309	10603
75	Sumner	23711	22030	22717	22445	20569	19211	13792	4616	2196	15934	14227	14487
76	Tipton	14884	10705	8887	6800	5317	......	......	......	......	7988	5408	4673
77	Union	7605	6117	......	......	......	......	......	......	......	7391	5853	......
78	Van Buren	2725	2581	2674	......	......	......	......	......	......	2509	2334	2481
79	Warren	12714	11147	10179	10803	15210	10348	5725	......	......	10753	8760	8986
80	Washington	16317	14829	13861	11751	10995	9557	7740	6379	5872	14703	13580	12671
81	Wayne	10209	9115	8170	7705	6013	2459	......	......	......	9316	7841	7232
82	Weakley	20755	18216	14608	9870	4797	......	......	......	......	16856	13985	11525
83	White	9375	9381	11444	10747	9967	8701	4028	......	......	8895	8074	10101
84	Williamson	25328	23827	27201	27006	26638	20640	13153	2868	......	13917	11415	14286
85	Wilson	25881	26072	27443	24460	25472	18730	11952	3261	......	18544	17787	19913

(*) All other persons, except Indians not taxed.
(a) In 1800 Cocke and Jefferson reported together.
(b) In 1870 Lake from Obion.

TABLE VIII.—*Population by Counties at each Census—TENNESSEE*—Continued.

White—Continued.						Colored. (c)									
1840.	1830.	1820.	1810.	1800.	1790.	1870.	1860.	1850.	1840.	1830.	1820.	1810.	1800.	1790.	
3427	1388	......	......	......	......	2893	2647	1477	1057	616	......	......	......	......	20
10573	5427	......	......	......	......	10987	15501	15303	10928	3225	......	......	......	......	21
3465	2655	......	......	......	......	170	159	149	85	120	......	......	......	......	22
8835	12034	12338	5080	......	......	2972	3599	3683	3098	3586	4253	710	......	......	23
10612	4497	......	......	......	......	6865	6232	4262	3077	1304	......	......	......	......	24
14485	12738	9272	3813	......	......	12738	10871	9431	7069	5965	3286	733	......	......	25
9521	8894	6796	5678	6871	......	1030	1235	1200	1051	1172	855	719	496	......	26
14919	13343	10465	9046	7137	7247	2064	1519	1298	1157	1167	859	667	473	404	27
......	......	......	......	......	......	137	280	251	......	......	......	......	......	......	28
7498	2136	766	......	......	......	4188	1611	850	677	140	55	......	......	......	29
......	......	......	......	......	......	585	314	213	......	......	......	......	......	......	30
9091	7970	......	......	......	......	6854	7204	7148	5472	3685	......	......	......	......	31
7287	4380	1317	......	......	......	1447	1600	1288	858	478	145	......	......	......	32
13408	11638	9308	6697	5667	6095	1889	2119	1803	1627	2045	1641	946	896	875	33
7575	3498	......	......	......	......	13832	11067	8548	6295	1842	......	......	......	......	34
9811	7300	......	......	......	......	2408	3302	2594	1964	1439	......	......	......	......	35
11214	9279	......	......	......	......	5804	5541	4846	3692	3020	......	......	......	......	36
7230	6891	5371	2132	......	......	1471	1780	1838	1398	1228	709	251	......	......	37
4446	3438	3528	1366	......	......	1295	1477	1118	747	755	545	145	......	......	38
11536	8533	6734	4012	......	......	707	1258	1673	1336	1165	859	489	......	......	39
10688	10486	8030	6453	a8995	......	2910	2366	1746	1414	1305	923	857	722	......	40
9493	......	......	......	......	......	418	261	220	105	......	......	......	......	......	41
13378	12337	11136	8870	11129	......	4840	2793	2422	2107	2141	1908	1205	1317	......	42
......	......	......	......	......	......	393	......	......	......	......	......	......	......	......	43
3483	......	......	......	......	......	3494	2875	1772	1012	......	......	......	......	......	44
6370	4851	3086	......	......	......	565	1184	1186	731	560	205	......	......	......	45
......	......	......	......	......	......	188	249	744	......	......	......	......	......	......	46
17217	17880	12506	5382	......	......	5953	6902	5690	4376	4155	2255	722	......	......	47
......	......	......	......	......	......	791	1046	826	......	......	......	......	......	......	48
10490	7384	......	......	......	......	10152	10095	8613	6110	4210	......	......	......	......	49
8658	5836	3719	......	......	......	915	703	596	412	272	169	......	......	......	50
11498	......	......	......	......	......	4385	4328	3701	3087	......	......	......	......	......	51
17090	18800	15620	7792	......	......	16865	14797	12761	11006	9465	6460	2637	......	......	52
11430	13156	1452	......	......	......	1830	2005	1620	1269	1304	171	......	......	......	53
8589	5316	......	......	......	......	1500	1922	1417	796	381	......	......	......	......	54
4492	......	......	......	......	......	436	645	399	206	......	......	......	......	......	55
11125	12610	2351	......	......	......	1235	1708	1251	931	1090	178	......	......	......	56
9702	8485	7491	5866	2078	1191	11670	9640	9145	7165	5864	4728	2635	821	196	57
2534	2516	1630	......	......	......	101	161	129	126	66	46	......	......	......	58
4219	1761	......	......	......	......	2182	2437	1061	595	338	......	......	......	......	59
8334	7333	6431	5282	......	......	550	1185	1123	945	909	697	361	......	......	60
6713	6681	2161	......	......	......	472	556	318	706	413	221	......	......	......	61
3249	......	......	......	......	......	313	465	454	321	......	......	......	......	......	62
......	......	......	......	......	......	530	718	......	......	......	......	......	......	......	63
3580	7536	3858	2290	......	......	531	645	464	405	650	357	214	......	......	64
9590	10130	7025	4896	......	......	2128	1853	1660	1358	1211	870	685	......	......	65
9977	9576	7379	5623	3414	......	4813	4890	4642	3824	3696	2539	1647	866	......	66
15042	17324	14165	7527	......	......	16478	13174	12212	9336	8810	5387	2738	......	......	67
......	......	......	......	......	......	39	73	37	......	......	......	......	......	......	68
......	......	......	......	......	......	175	202	......	......	......	......	......	......	......	69
6048	5323	4409	4296	3255	3390	533	602	470	394	394	303	299	164	229	70
7605	3537	251	......	......	......	36640	17229	14578	7116	2111	113	......	......	......	71
16627	15427	13938	9424	3693	......	3536	4348	4703	4552	4479	3642	2225	601	......	72
6317	5469	6097	3465	......	......	2700	2491	2702	2270	1499	1400	797	......	......	73
9504	8682	6063	6071	9710	4043	857	1243	1139	1232	1301	938	770	508	404	74
14891	13179	13301	9961	3332	1840	7777	7803	8230	7554	7390	5910	3831	1284	356	75
3637	3566	......	......	......	......	6891	5207	4214	3163	1749	......	......	......	......	76
......	......	......	......	......	......	214	264	......	......	......	......	......	......	......	77
......	......	......	......	......	......	156	247	193	......	......	......	......	......	......	78
9366	13614	9385	5241	......	......	1955	2386	1793	1437	1596	963	484	......	......	79
10600	9810	8506	6854	5821	5325	1614	1249	1190	1151	1185	1051	886	558	547	80
7151	5721	2387	......	......	......	893	1274	938	554	292	72	......	......	......	81
8072	3944	......	......	......	......	3299	4231	3083	1798	853	......	......	......	......	82
9640	6977	7981	3745	......	......	1080	1307	1343	1107	990	720	283	......	......	83
13641	10004	13503	9156	2174	......	11411	12412	12035	11365	10634	7047	3997	694	......	84
12303	19267	14724	9271	2523	......	7331	8285	7530	6257	6245	4006	2681	738	......	85

(c) At 1870, Indians, 70, as follows: Anderson, 3; Davidson, 17; Hardeman, 2; Hawkins, 1; Haywood, 1; Maury, 2; Monroe, 15; Polk, 7; Rutherford, 4; Shelby, 1; Tipton, 5; Warren, 6; Wilson, 6. At 1860 Indians, 60, as follows: Carter, 1; Hamilton, 6; Hawkins, 11; McMinn, 3; Meigs, 1; Polk, 33; Rutherford, 1; Shelby, 2; Stewart, 1; Warren, 1.

TABLE VIII.—*Population by Counties at each Census*—*TEXAS.*

	Counties.	AGGREGATE.			WHITE.		
		1870.	1860.	1850.	1870.	1860.	1850.
	The State	818579	604215	212592	564700	420891	154034
1	Anderson	9229	10398	2884	4793	6730	[illegible]
2	Angelina	3985	4271	1165	3243	3575	942
3	Archer (g)	....	....	....	....	....	....
4	Atascosa	2915	1578	....	2733	1471	....
5	Austin	15087	10139	3841	8513	6225	[illegible]
6	Bandera (e)	649	399	....	631	387	....
7	Bastrop	12290	7006	3099	7056	4415	[illegible]
8	Baylor (g)	....	....	....	....	....	(a)
9	Bee	1082	910	....	1013	802	....
10	Bell	9771	4799	....	8667	3794	....
11	Bexar	16043	14454	6052	13739	13057	[illegible]
12	Bexar District	1077	....	....	1014	....	....
13	Blanco	1187	1281	....	1143	1183	....
14	Bosque (d)	4981	2005	....	4453	1712	....
15	Bowie	4684	5052	2912	2434	2401	1271
16	Brazoria	7527	7143	4841	1791	2027	1329
17	Brazos	9205	2776	614	5446	1713	466
18	Brown	544	244	....	507	244	....
19	Buchanan (f)	....	230	....	....	198	....
20	Burleson	8072	5683	1713	5051	3679	1213
21	Burnet	3688	2487	....	3330	2252	....
22	Caldwell	6572	4481	1329	4041	2870	1054
23	Calhoun	3443	2642	1110	2536	2228	867
24	Callahan (g)	....	....	....	....	....	(a)
25	Cameron	10999	6028	8541	10842	5953	8469
26	Cass (c)	....	8411	4991	....	4936	3089
27	Chambers	1503	1508	....	1051	995	....
28	Cherokee	11079	12098	6673	7794	8849	5389
29	Clay (g)	....	109	....	....	107	....
30	Coleman	347	....	....	340	....	....
31	Collin	14013	9264	1950	12348	8217	1816
32	Colorado	8326	7885	2257	4625	4396	1534
33	Comal	5283	4030	1723	4906	3837	1662
34	Comanche	1001	709	....	977	648	....
35	Concho (g)	....	....	....	....	....	(a)
36	Cook	5315	3760	220	4827	3391	219
37	Coryell	4124	2666	....	3845	2360	....
38	Dallas	13314	8665	2743	11197	7591	2536
39	Davis (c)	8875	....	....	5496	....	....
40	Dawson	....	281	....	....	281	....
41	Demmit	109	....	....	103	....	(a)
42	Denton	7251	5031	641	6751	4780	631
43	De Witt	6443	5108	1716	4686	3465	1148
44	Duval	1083	....	....	1080	....	(a)
45	Eastland	88	99	....	87	99	....
46	Edwards (g)	....	....	....	....	....	(a)
47	Ellis	7514	5246	989	6008	4136	902
48	El Paso	3671	4051	....	3529	3626	....
49	Ensinal	427	43	....	427	43	....
50	Erath (d)	1801	2425	....	1712	2307	....
51	Falls	9851	3614	....	5145	1895	....
52	Fannin	13207	9217	3788	10721	7496	3360
53	Fayette	16863	11604	3756	10953	7808	2740
54	Fort Bend	7114	6143	2533	1604	2007	974
55	Freestone	8139	6881	....	4771	3268	....
56	Frio	309	42	....	294	40	....
57	Galveston	15290	8229	4529	12053	6707	3785
58	Gillespie (c)	3566	2736	1240	3489	2703	1235
59	Goliad	3628	3384	648	2751	2541	435
60	Gonzales	8951	8059	1492	5269	4891	891
61	Grayson	14387	8184	2008	12237	6892	1822
62	Grimes	13218	10307	4008	5294	4832	2326
63	Guadalupe	7282	5444	1511	4748	3689	1171
64	Hamilton	733	489	....	715	463	....
65	Hardeman (g)	....	....	....	....	....	(a)
66	Hardin	1460	1353	....	1218	1162	....
67	Harris	17375	9070	4668	10865	7008	3756
68	Harrison	13241	15001	11822	4310	6217	5604
69	Haskell (g)	....	....	....	....	....	(a)
70	Hays	4088	2126	387	2871	1329	259
71	Henderson	6786	4595	1237	5132	3478	1155
72	Hidalgo	2387	1192	....	2345	1155	....
73	Hill	7453	3653	....	6647	3003	....
74	Hood (d)	2585	....	....	2477	....	....
75	Hopkins	12651	7745	2623	11030	6749	2409
76	Houston	8147	8058	2721	4605	5239	2036

COMPENDIUM OF THE NINTH CENSUS.

TABLE VIII.—*Population by Counties at each Census—TEXAS.*

COLORED.			CHINESE.	INDIAN.		
1870.	1860.	1850.	1870.	1870.	1860.	
253475	182921	58558	25	379	403	
4430	3668	600	....	....	....	1
742	696	220	....	....	....	2
....	....	....	....	....	....	3
160	107	....	....	22	....	4
6371	3914	1555	....	....	....	5
18	12	....	....	....	....	6
5234	2591	919	....	1	....	7
....	....	....	....	....	....	8
69	79	....	....	....	29	9
1104	1005	....	....	....	....	10
2303	1397	419	....	1	....	11
63	....	....	....	....	....	12
41	98	....	....	....	....	13
528	233	....	....	....	....	14
2249	2631	1641	....	1	....	15
5736	5116	3512	....	....	....	16
3759	1063	148	....	....	....	17
37	....	....	....	....	....	18
....	32	....	....	....	....	19
3021	2003	500	....	....	1	20
358	235	....	....	....	....	21
2531	1611	275	....	....	....	22
907	414	243	....	....	....	23
....	....	....	....	....	....	24
157	73	72	....	....	2	25
....	3475	1902	....	....	....	26
452	513	....	....	....	....	27
3285	3249	1284	....	....	....	28
....	2	....	....	....	....	29
7	....	....	....	....	....	30
1653	1047	134	....	12	....	31
3701	3559	723	....	....	....	32
377	193	61	....	....	....	33
24	61	....	....	....	....	34
....	....	....	....	....	....	35
471	369	1	....	17	....	36
279	306	....	....	....	....	37
2109	1074	207	....	8	....	38
3179	....	....	....	....	....	39
....	....	....	....	....	....	40
6	....	....	....	....	....	41
500	251	10	....	....	....	42
1757	1643	568	....	....	....	43
3	....	....	....	....	....	44
1	....	....	....	....	....	45
....	....	....	....	....	....	46
1506	1104	87	....	....	6	47
306	29	....	....	136	196	48
....	....	....	....	....	....	49
69	118	....	....	....	....	50
4081	1718	....	....	23	1	51
2484	1721	528	....	2	....	52
5901	3796	1016	....	9	....	53
5310	4136	1550	....	....	....	54
3368	3613	....	....	....	....	55
15	2	....	....	....	....	56
3236	1522	744	....	1	....	57
77	33	5	....	....	....	58
876	843	213	....	1	....	59
3670	3168	601	....	12	....	60
2145	1292	186	....	5	....	61
7921	5469	1082	....	....	....	62
2534	1735	340	....	....	....	63
17	20	....	....	....	....	64
....	....	....	....	....	....	65
242	191	....	....	....	....	66
6509	2062	912	....	....	....	67
8331	6784	6218	....	....	....	68
....	....	....	....	....	....	69
1217	797	128	....	....	....	70
1654	1117	82	....	....	....	71
41	35	....	....	....	....	72
806	650	....	....	....	....	73
97	....	....	11	....	....	74
1020	990	154	....	....	....	75
3542	2819	685	....	....	....	76

		[illegible]	1890.	[illegible]	[illegible]	[illegible]	[illegible]
	[illegible]	[illegible]	[illegible]	[illegible]	[illegible]	2022	2400
	[illegible]	[illegible]	[illegible]	[illegible]	[illegible]	[illegible]	....
	[illegible]	[illegible]	[illegible]	[illegible]	[illegible]	[illegible]	169
	[illegible]	[illegible]	[illegible]	[illegible]	[illegible]	[illegible]	3338
	[illegible]	[illegible]	[illegible]	[illegible]	[illegible]	[illegible]	1947
	[illegible]	[illegible]	[illegible]	[illegible]	[illegible]	[illegible]	1555
	[illegible]	[illegible]	[illegible]	[illegible]	[illegible]	[illegible]	650
	[illegible]	[illegible]	[illegible]	[illegible]	[illegible]	[illegible]	....
	[illegible]	[illegible]	[illegible]	[illegible]	[illegible]	[illegible]	....
	[illegible]	[illegible]	[illegible]	[illegible]	[illegible]	[illegible]	2976
	[illegible]	[illegible]	[illegible]	[illegible]	[illegible]	[illegible]	....
	[illegible]	[illegible]	[illegible]	[illegible]	[illegible]	4226	1548
	[illegible]	[illegible]	[illegible]	[illegible]	[illegible]	[illegible]	....
	[illegible]	[illegible]	[illegible]	[illegible]	[illegible]	[illegible]	2403
	[illegible]	[illegible]	[illegible]	[illegible]	[illegible]	[illegible]	390
	[illegible]	[illegible]	[illegible]	[illegible]	[illegible]	[illegible]	670
	[illegible]						(a)
	[illegible]	[illegible]	[illegible]	[illegible]	[illegible]	[illegible]	6012
	[illegible]	[illegible]	[illegible]	[illegible]	[illegible]	[illegible]	1556
	[illegible]	[illegible]	[illegible]	[illegible]	[illegible]	[illegible]	2087
	[illegible]	[illegible]	[illegible]	[illegible]	[illegible]	[illegible]	197
	[illegible]	[illegible]	[illegible]	......	[illegible]	[illegible]	....
	[illegible]	[illegible]	44		[illegible]	35	....
	[illegible]	[illegible]	[illegible]	[illegible]	[illegible]	[illegible]	3278
	[illegible]	[illegible]	[illegible]	[illegible]	[illegible]	[illegible]	3575
	[illegible]	[illegible]	[illegible]	......	[illegible]	[illegible]	(b)
	[illegible]	[illegible]	......	......	[illegible]	....	....
	[illegible]	[illegible]	[illegible]	[illegible]	[illegible]	5170	[illegible]
	[illegible]	....	....	....	....	....	(a)
140	Time reservation (g)	....	324	....	....	124	....
141	[illegible]	[illegible]	[illegible]	[illegible]	[illegible]	7209	3168
142	[illegible]	[illegible]	[illegible]	[illegible]	[illegible]	4931	2336
143	[illegible]	4141	[illegible]	....	[illegible]	[illegible]	....
144	[illegible]	5010	[illegible]	[illegible]	[illegible]	[illegible]	[illegible]
[illegible]	[illegible]	[illegible]	10645	[illegible]	7172	6671	[illegible]
	[illegible]	651	[illegible]	....	[illegible]	479	....
	[illegible]	6494	[illegible]	[illegible]	[illegible]	3453	1308
	[illegible]	4860	4171	2019	3092	2757	[illegible]
	[illegible]	9776	8191	3964	3951	4036	[illegible]
	[illegible]	23104	13215	5063	10863	7268	3168
	[illegible]	9615	1397	....	2613	1397	(b)
	[illegible]	3426	[illegible]	[illegible]	514	646	[illegible]
	[illegible]	....	....	....	....	....	....
	[illegible]	....	....	....	....	....	....

TABLE VIII.—*Population by Counties at each Census—TEXAS*—Continued.

COLORED.			CHINESE.	INDIAN.		
1870.	1860.	1850.	1870.	1870.	1860.	
1078	577	43	.....	.....	.....	77
72	50	.....	1	.....	.....	78
1164	1216	369	.....	.....	.....	79
1759	1611	541	.....	.....	.....	80
498	311	332	.....	.....	.....	81
279	513	.....	.....	.....	.....	82
.....	.....	.....	.....	.....	.....	83
279	387	.....	.....	.....	.....	84
838	533	65	.....	.....	.....	85
101	.....	.....	.....	.....	.....	86
90	49	.....	.....	.....	.....	87
.....	.....	.....	.....	.....	.....	88
418	15	.....	.....	.....	.....	89
.....	.....	.....	.....	.....	.....	90
4410	2842	1085	.....	.....	.....	91
64	154	.....	.....	.....	.....	92
1	.....	.....	.....	.....	.....	93
2707	1707	432	.....	.....	.....	94
2708	2620	631	.....	.....	.....	95
1975	1067	899	.....	.....	.....	96
1919	1073	618	10	.....	.....	97
22	85	.....	.....	.....	.....	98
18	54	.....	.....	.....	.....	99
1470	675	.....	.....	.....	.....	100
4262	2017	.....	.....	.....	.....	101
26	24	.....	.....	.....	.....	102
2190	2107	1211	.....	.....	.....	103
281	22	.....	.....	.....	.....	104
2	.....	.....	.....	.....	.....	105
4887	2404	.....	.....	.....	.....	106
12	.....	.....	.....	.....	.....	107
92	106	26	.....	.....	.....	108
372	.....	.....	.....	.....	.....	109
.....	.....	.....	.....	.....	.....	110
2977	1543	438	.....	.....	.....	111
94	35	.....	.....	.....	.....	112
3351	2811	945	.....	.....	.....	113
3275	2362	1435	.....	.....	.....	114
2245	1891	247	.....	.....	.....	115
831	1013	434	.....	.....	.....	116
332	217	48	.....	.....	.....	117
250	421	.....	.....	.....	.....	118
.....	130	.....	.....	.....	.....	119
3727	3058	1195	.....	.....	.....	120
293	222	.....	.....	.....	.....	121
4298	4202	806	.....	.....	.....	122
489	6	.....	.....	.....	.....	123
4148	3044	1413	.....	.....	.....	124
246	249	19	.....	.....	.....	125
4530	2258	264	3	.....	.....	126
.....	.....	.....	.....	.....	.....	127
7715	6133	2136	.....	.....	.....	128
1107	1150	942	.....	.....	.....	129
1964	1717	1561	.....	.....	.....	130
64	95	3	.....	.....	.....	131
144	89	.....	.....	.....	.....	132
55	9	.....	.....	.....	.....	133
1755	1477	961	.....	.....	.....	134
7131	4984	717	.....	.....	.....	135
18	10	.....	.....	.....	.....	136
24	.....	.....	.....	.....	.....	137
705	850	65	.....	.....	.....	138
.....	.....	.....	.....	.....	.....	139
.....	.....	.....	.....	.....	.....	140
2818	2439	468	.....	.....	.....	141
4647	3149	202	.....	.....	.....	142
1084	960	.....	.....	.....	.....	143
1479	1148	418	.....	.....	.....	144
4867	3794	682	.....	.....	.....	145
73	27	.....	.....	.....	.....	146
642	324	40	.....	.....	.....	147
1768	1414	623	.....	.....	.....	148
5823	4135	1301	.....	.....	.....	149
12241	7944	2817	.....	.....	.....	150
2	.....	.....	.....	.....	.....	151
2910	2734	1242	.....	.....	.....	152
.....	.....	.....	.....	.....	.....	153
.....	.....	.....	.....	.....	.....	154

TABLE VIII.—*Population by Counties at each Census—TEXAS*—Continued.

	Counties.	AGGREGATE.			WHITE.		
		1870.	1860.	1850.	1870.	1860.	1850.
155	Williamson	6368	4529	1568	5563	3638	1418
156	Wilson	2556	....	....	2093	....	....
157	Wise	1450	3160	....	1390	3031	....
158	Wood	6894	4968	....	5647	3963	....
159	Young	135	592	....	131	500	....
160	Young Territory	....	....	....	....	....	....
161	Zapata	1188	1248	....	1488	1248	....
162	Zavala	133	26	....	129	26	....

(a) In 1850 no population returned.
(b) In 1850 Cameron, Starr, and Webb reported together.
(c) In 1862 name changed from Cass to Davis.

TABLE VIII.—*Population by Counties at each Census—VERMONT.*

	Counties.	AGGREGATE.									WHITE.		
		1870.	1860.	1850.	1840.	1830.	1820.	1810.	1800.	1790.	1870.	1860.	1850.
	The State....	330551	315098	314120	291948	280652	[*15] 235966	217895	154465	85425	329613	314369	313402
1	Addison	23484	24010	26549	23583	24940	20469	19993	13417	6449	23378	23921	26441
2	Bennington	21325	19436	18589	16872	17468	16125	15893	14617	12254	21176	19345	18511
3	Caledonia	22235	21698	23595	21891	20967	16669	18730	9377	......	22220	21674	23584
4	Chittenden	36480	28171	29036	22977	21765	16272	18120	12778	7295	36350	28052	28927
5	Essex	6811	5786	4650	4226	3981	3284	3087	1479	......	6805	5786	4647
6	Franklin	30291	27231	28586	24531	24525	17192	16427	8782	......	30193	27193	28500
7	Grand Isle	4082	4276	4145	3883	3696	3527	3445	......	......	4071	4271	4142
8	Lamoille	12448	12311	10872	10475	......	......	......	......	......	12438	12310	10869
9	Orange	23090	25455	27296	27873	27285	24681	25247	18238	10526	23077	25431	27277
10	Orleans	21035	18981	15707	13634	13980	6976	5830	1439	......	21006	18961	15694
11	Rutland	40651	35946	33059	30699	31294	[*8] 29975	29486	23813	15591	40469	35806	32938
12	Washington	26520	27622	24654	23506	21378	[*7] 14106	......	......	......	26491	27605	24640
13	Windham	26036	26982	29062	27442	28748	28457	26760	23581	17570	25086	26949	29025
14	Windsor	36063	37193	38320	40356	40625	38233	34877	26944	15740	35953	37065	38207

(*) All other persons, except Indians not taxed.

TABLE VIII.—*Population by Counties at each Census—TEXAS*—Continued.

COLORED.			CHINESE.	INDIAN.		
1870.	1860.	1850.	1870.	1870.	1860.	
801	891	158	.....	.....	.....	155
463	.....	.....	.....	.....	.....	156
51	129	.....	.....	.....	.....	157
1247	1005	.....	.....	.....	.....	158
4	92	.....	.....	.....	.....	159
.....	.....	.....	.....	.....	.....	160
.....	.....	.....	.....	.....	.....	161
4	.....	.....	.....	.....	.....	162

(*d*) In 1866 Hood from Bosque, Erath, and Johnson.
(*e*) In 1862 Kendall from Bandera and Gillespie.
(*f*) In 1862 name changed from Buchanan to Stephens.
(*g*) Returned as having no population.

TABLE VIII.—*Population by Counties at each Census—VERMONT.*

WHITE—Continued.						COLORED.									INDIAN.		
1840.	1830.	1820.	1810.	1800.	1790.	1870.	1860.	1850.	1840.	1830.	1820.	1810.	1800.	1790.	1870.	1860.	
291218	279771	235063	217145	153908	85154	924	709	718	730	881	903	750	557	271	14	20	
23472	24853	20350	19877	13351	6412	106	89	108	111	87	119	116	66	37	.....	.....	1
16771	17360	16046	15848	14539	12218	149	91	78	101	108	79	45	78	36	.....	.....	2
21877	20039	16641	18701	9301	.....	15	24	11	14	28	28	29	16	.....	.....	.....	3
22895	21653	16159	18053	12732	7272	130	99	109	82	112	122	67	46	23	.....	20	4
4218	3965	3274	3081	1476	.....	3	.....	3	8	16	10	6	3	.....	3	.....	5
24473	24429	17098	16327	8762	.....	98	38	86	58	96	94	100	20	.....	.....	.....	6
3883	3696	3518	3431	.....	.....	5	5	3	.....	.....	9	14	.....	.....	6	.....	7
10472	.....	.....	.....	.....	.....	5	1	3	3	.....	.....	.....	.....	.....	5	.....	8
27852	27256	24633	25196	18152	10485	13	24	19	21	29	48	51	86	41	.....	.....	9
13623	13944	6940	5803	1422	.....	29	20	13	11	36	36	27	17	.....	.....	.....	10
30569	31183	29855	29387	23723	16560	182	140	121	130	111	120	99	90	31	.....	.....	11
23485	21354	14001	.....	.....	.....	29	17	14	21	24	15	.....	.....	.....	.....	.....	12
27408	28710	28402	26709	23541	17512	50	33	37	34	38	55	51	40	58	.....	.....	13
40220	40429	38065	34732	26849	15695	110	128	113	136	156	168	145	95	45	.....	.....	14

TABLE VIII.—*Population by Counties at each Census—VIRGINIA.*

	Counties.	AGGREGATE.									WHITE.		
		1870.	1860.	1850.	1840.	1830.	1820.	1810.	1800.	1790.	1870.	1860.	1850.
	The State..	1225163	1219630	1119348	a9967 1015260	a9573 1034481	*210 a9703 928348	a8552 869131	a5049 801608	691737	712089	691773	61[illegible]
1	Accomack	20409	18586	17890	17096	16656	15966	15743	15693	13959	12367	10661	96[illegible]
2	Albemarle	27544	26625	25800	22924	22618	*3 19747	18268	16439	12585	12530	12103	118[illegible]
3	Alexandria	16755	12652	10008	a9967	a9573	a9703	a8552	a5049	......	9444	9851	7217
4	Alleghany	3674	6765	3515	2749	2816	......	......	......	......	3005	5643	276[illegible]
5	Amelia	9878	10741	9770	10320	11036	*110 10994	10594	9432	b18097	3055	2897	278[illegible]
6	Amherst.........	14900	13742	12699	12576	12071	10423	10548	16801	13703	8184	7167	63[illegible]
7	Appomattox	8950	8889	9193	......	......	......	......	......	......	4414	4118	[illegible]
8	Augusta.........	28763	27749	24610	19628	19926	10742	14308	11712	10886	22026	21547	1898[illegible]
9	Bath...........	3795	3676	3426	4300	4002	*6 5231	4837	5508	......	2906	2652	2434
10	Bedford.........	25327	25068	24080	20203	20246	19305	16148	14125	10531	14557	14388	13556
11	Bland (c)........	400	......	......	......	......	......	......	......	......	3783	......	......
12	Botetourt	11329	11516	14908	11679	16354	13589	13301	10427	10524	8166	8441	10746
13	Brunswick.......	13427	14809	13894	14346	15767	16687	15411	16339	12827	4325	4992	48[illegible]
14	Buchanan........	3777	2793	......	......	......	......	......	......	......	3730	2762	......
15	Buckingham	13371	15212	13837	18786	18351	17569	20059	13389	9779	5680	6041	54[illegible]
16	Campbell	28384	26197	23245	21030	20350	16569	11001	9866	7685	14041	13588	11533
17	Caroline	15128	18464	18456	17813	17760	*26 17982	17544	17438	17489	7077	6948	6891
18	Carroll..........	9147	8012	5909	......	......	......	......	......	......	8819	7719	57[illegible]
19	Charles City....	4975	5609	5200	4774	5500	5255	5186	5365	5588	1822	1806	1664
20	Charlotte	14513	14471	13955	14595	15252	13290	13161	11912	10078	4900	4981	4615
21	Chesterfield.....	18470	19016	17489	17148	18637	18003	9979	14488	14214	9730	10019	8406
22	Clarke	6670	7146	7352	6353	......	......	......	......	......	4511	3707	3614
23	Craig	2942	3553	......	......	......	......	......	......	......	2712	3103	......
24	Culpeper	12227	12063	12282	11393	24027	*2 20942	18967	18100	22105	6058	4959	5112
25	Cumberland	8142	9961	9751	10399	11690	11023	9992	9839	8153	2709	2946	308[illegible]
26	Dinwiddie	30702	30198	25118	22558	21901	20482	18190	15374	13934	13017	13678	10942
27	Elizabeth City..	8303	5798	4586	3706	5053	3789	3608	2778	3450	2830	3180	2341
28	Essex...........	9927	10469	10206	11309	10521	9909	9376	9508	9122	3477	3296	3035
29	Fairfax	12952	11834	10682	9370	9204	11404	13111	13317	12320	8667	8046	6835
30	Fauquier	19690	21706	20868	21897	26086	23103	22689	21329	17892	11834	10430	9875
31	Floyd...........	9824	8236	6458	4453	......	......	......	......	......	8827	7745	6001
32	Fluvanna.......	9875	10353	9487	8812	8221	6704	4775	4623	3921	4778	5093	4319
33	Franklin.........	18264	20098	17430	15832	14911	12017	10724	9302	6842	12208	13642	1163[illegible]
34	Frederick........	16596	16546	15975	14242	26046	24706	22574	24744	19681	13863	13079	12769
35	Giles (c)	5875	6883	6570	5307	5274	4521	3745	......	......	5272	6038	5859
36	Gloucester	10211	10956	10527	10715	10608	9678	10427	8181	13498	4782	4517	4290
37	Goochland	10313	10656	10352	9760	10369	10007	10203	9696	9053	3711	3814	3863
38	Grayson	9587	8252	6677	9087	7675	5598	4941	3912	......	8833	7653	6142
39	Greene	4634	5022	4400	4232	......	......	......	......	......	3182	3015	2067
40	Greenville	6362	6374	5639	6366	7117	6858	6853	6727	6362	2155	1974	1731
41	Halifax	27828	26520	25962	25936	28034	19060	22133	19377	14722	11502	11060	10976
42	Hanover.........	16455	17222	15153	14968	16253	15267	15082	14403	14754	7893	7482	6539
43	Henrico.........	66179	61616	43572	33076	28797	23667	19680	14886	12000	35148	37966	23826
44	Henry	12303	12105	8872	7335	7100	5624	5611	5259	8479	6722	6773	5324
45	Highland	4151	4319	4227	......	......	......	......	......	......	3803	3890	3837
46	Isle of Wight...	8320	9977	9353	9972	10517	*21 10118	9186	9342	9028	4974	5037	4710
47	James City	4425	5798	4020	3779	3838	4563	4094	3931	4070	1985	2167	1469
48	King and Queen.	9709	10328	10319	10862	11644	11798	10988	9879	9377	4221	3801	4094
49	King George....	5742	6571	5971	5927	6397	6116	6454	6749	7366	2927	2510	2301
50	King William...	7515	8530	8779	9258	9812	9697	9285	9035	8128	2943	2589	2701
51	Lancaster.......	5355	5151	4708	4628	4801	5517	5592	5375	5638	2198	1981	1802
52	Lee.............	13268	11032	10267	8441	6461	4256	4694	3538	......	12263	10185	9440
53	Loudon	20929	21774	22079	20431	21939	22702	21338	20523	18962	13288	15021	15081
54	Louisa	16332	16701	16691	15433	16151	13746	11900	11892	8467	6269	6183	6423
55	Lunenburg	10403	11983	11692	11055	11957	10662	12265	10381	8959	4144	4421	4314
56	Madison	8670	8854	9331	8107	9236	8490	8381	8322	......	4959	4360	4456
57	Matthews	6200	7091	6714	7442	7664	6920	4227	5806	......	4104	3865	3642
58	Mecklenburg ...	21318	20096	20630	20724	20477	19786	18453	17008	14733	7162	6778	7256
59	Middlesex	4981	4364	4394	4392	4122	4057	4414	4203	4140	2459	1863	1923
60	Montgomery....	12556	10617	8359	7405	12306	8733	8409	9044	13228	9674	8251	6822
61	Nansemond.....	11576	13693	12283	10795	11784	10494	10324	11127	9010	6059	5732	5424
62	Nelson..........	13898	13015	12758	12287	11254	10137	9684	......	......	7586	6649	6478
63	New Kent	4381	5884	6064	6230	6458	6630	6478	6363	6239	2003	2145	2222
64	Norfolk.........	46702	36227	33036	27569	24806	*7 23936	22872	19419	14524	24380	24357	20329
65	Northampton ...	8046	7832	7498	7715	8641	7705	7474	6763	6889	3196	2998	3105
66	Northumberland	6863	7531	7346	7924	7953	8016	8308	7803	9163	3808	3870	3072
67	Nottoway.......	9291	8836	8437	9719	10130	*4 9656	9278	9401	(b)	2241	2270	2234

TABLE VIII.—*Population by Counties at each Census—VIRGINIA.*

WHITE—Continued.					COLORED. (e)									
1830.	1820.	1810.	1800.	1790.	1870.	1860.	1850.	1840.	1830.	1820.	1810.	1800.	1790.	
a6411 537216	a6556 482849	a5734 458139	a4394 443386	391524	512841	527763	503279	a3236 477.108	a3162 497265	a3147 445499	a2818 410972	a1555 358222	300203	
9458	9386	9341	9723	8976	7842	7925	8282	7478	7198	6580	6402	5970	4983	1
10455	8715	8642	8796	6835	14994	14522	13925	12412	12163	11032	9626	7643	5750	2
a6411	a6556	a5734	a4394	......	7310	2801	2791	a3236	a3162	a3147	a2818	a1555	......	3
2197	......	......	......	......	579	1122	752	607	619	......	......	......	......	4
3203	3407	3233	2789	b6684	6823	7844	6985	7246	7743	7587	7341	6643	11413	5
5883	4610	5143	9205	8286	6704	6575	6347	6150	6188	5813	5405	7596	5417	6
......	......	......	......	......	4536	4771	4984	......	......	......	......	......	......	7
13257	12963	11232	9671	9260	6737	6202	5627	4556	4669	3779	3076	2041	1626	8
2797	3965	3906	4830	......	889	1024	992	1130	1205	1266	931	678	......	9
11123	10953	9789	9826	7725	10770	10680	10524	9187	9123	8252	6359	4299	2806	10
......	......	......	......	......	217	......	......	......	......	......	......	......	......	11
11798	10493	10726	8773	9241	3163	3075	4162	3302	4556	3096	2375	1654	1283	12
5397	5889	5665	6647	5019	8902	9817	9009	9368	10370	10798	9746	9692	6908	13
......	......	......	......	......	47	31	......	......	......	......	......	......	......	14
7177	7345	7780	6824	5496	7711	9171	8411	11463	11174	10224	12279	6565	4283	15
9995	8447	5370	5893	4946	14343	12609	11712	10817	10355	8122	5631	3973	2739	16
6499	6497	6452	6492	6994	8038	11516	11565	11088	11261	11485	11092	10046	10495	17
......	......	......	......	......	328	293	183	......	......	......	......	......	......	18
1782	1750	1776	1954	2084	3153	3803	3536	3103	3718	3505	3410	3411	3504	19
5583	5005	5354	5506	5199	9613	9490	9340	9565	9609	8285	7807	6406	4879	20
7700	7543	3692	6317	6358	8733	8997	9083	9289	10928	10460	6287	8171	7856	21
......	......	......	......	......	2139	3439	3738	3486	......	......	......	......	......	22
......	......	......	......	......	230	450	......	......	......	......	......	......	......	23
12046	11136	10391	10479	13809	6169	7104	7170	6460	11981	9806	8576	7621	8296	24
4054	3966	3715	3945	3577	5433	7015	6669	7136	7636	7057	6277	5894	4576	25
8655	8470	7010	6347	6049	17664	16520	14176	12711	13246	12012	11180	9027	7895	26
2704	2076	1799	1298	1556	5471	2618	2245	1752	2349	1713	1809	1540	1894	27
3647	3490	3411	3465	3543	6650	7173	7171	7354	6874	6410	5965	6043	5579	28
4892	6224	6626	7035	7611	4284	3788	3847	3901	4312	5180	6485	6282	4709	29
12950	11429	11984	12444	11157	7856	11276	10993	11296	13136	11674	10705	4885	6735	30
......	......	......	......	......	997	491	457	330	......	......	......	......	......	31
4223	3375	2576	2650	2430	5097	5260	4948	4367	3998	3329	2199	1964	1491	32
9728	8227	7966	7701	5735	5996	6456	5792	5332	5183	3790	2758	1601	1107	33
17361	16557	15547	18628	15315	2733	3467	3206	3124	8685	8149	7027	6116	4366	34
4760	4174	3478	......	......	598	845	712	623	514	347	267	......	......	35
4314	4008	4183	3237	6225	5429	6439	6237	6303	6204	5670	6244	4944	7279	36
3857	3796	4230	4480	4140	6601	6842	6489	6190	6512	6211	5973	5216	4913	37
7161	5170	4641	3741	......	754	599	535	545	514	428	300	171	......	38
......	......	......	......	......	1452	2007	1733	*1785	......	......	......	......	......	39
2104	2056	2254	2398	2730	4207	4400	3908	4418	5013	4802	4709	4349	3832	40
12916	8758	12117	11168	8931	16266	15460	14986	14791	15118	10302	10016	8209	5791	41
6526	6130	6219	5052	6291	8562	9740	8614	8706	9727	9137	8863	8451	8463	42
13471	11763	9182	6836	5600	31031	23631	19746	16176	15326	11904	10498	8050	6400	43
4058	3321	3641	3715	6763	5581	5332	3548	3092	3042	2303	1970	1544	1716	44
......	......	......	......	......	348	429	390	......	......	......	......	......	......	45
5023	4883	4447	4735	4786	3446	4940	4643	5054	5494	5235	4730	4607	4242	46
1283	1551	1354	1374	1519	2440	3631	2531	2454	2555	3012	2740	2557	2551	47
4714	5460	4718	4335	4159	5488	6527	6225	6436	6930	6338	6270	5544	5218	48
2475	2349	2381	2598	3123	2815	4061	3670	3658	3922	3767	4073	4151	4243	49
3155	3449	3294	3139	2893	4455	5941	6078	6108	6657	6248	5991	5916	5235	50
1976	2488	2276	2090	2259	3157	3170	2906	2725	2825	3129	3316	3285	3379	51
5830	3885	4337	3292	......	1005	837	827	612	631	371	357	246	......	52
15497	16144	15577	15200	14749	5691	6753	6998	6591	6142	6558	5761	5923	4213	53
6468	5967	5253	5768	3880	10063	10518	10268	9386	9681	7779	6647	6124	4587	54
4479	3873	4933	4372	4547	6059	7562	7358	6924	7478	6789	7332	6090	4412	55
4289	3800	4323	4636	......	3711	4494	4875	4378	4947	4690	4058	3486	......	56
3994	3616	2118	2985	......	2036	3226	3072	3473	3670	3304	2109	2821	......	57
7471	7710	7696	7779	7555	14156	13318	13374	12970	13006	12076	10753	9229	7178	58
1868	1756	1811	1603	1531	2522	2501	2491	2351	2254	2361	2303	2300	2600	59
10224	7447	7253	8037	12394	2882	2366	1537	1580	2082	1436	1156	1007	811	60
5143	4575	4593	5809	4713	5517	7961	6859	5847	6641	5919	5731	5118	4207	61
5186	4395	4897	......	......	6312	6366	6280	6119	6068	5742	4787	......	......	62
2586	2537	2445	2523	2391	2361	3738	3842	3758	3872	4033	3533	3840	3848	63
13314	13260	12221	11401	8028	22320	11807	12707	12125	11492	10676	10551	8018	5596	64
3574	3369	3216	2931	3181	4848	4834	4393	4374	5067	4336	4258	3892	3708	65
4829	4134	4162	3679	4506	3054	3661	4274	3890	3984	3882	4146	4124	4657	66
2965	2805	2730	3311	(b)	7050	6566	6203	7289	7165	6851	6548	6090	(b)	67

TABLE VIII.—*Population by Counties at each Census—VIRGINIA*—Continued.

	Counties.	AGGREGATE.									WHITE.		
		1870.	1860.	1850.	1840.	1830.	1820.	1810.	1800.	1790.	1870.	1860.	1850.
68	Orange	10396	10851	10067	9125	14637	*33 12880	12323	11449	9921	4938	4553	3962
69	Page	8462	8109	7600	6194	......	......	......	......	......	7476	6875	6332
70	Patrick	10161	9359	9609	8032	7395	5089	4695	4331	......	7836	7158	7187
71	Pittsylvania	31343	32104	28796	26398	26034	21323	17172	12697	11579	15250	17105	15363
72	Powhatan	7667	8392	8178	7924	8517	8292	8073	7769	6822	2552	2580	2513
73	Prince Edward	12004	11844	11857	14069	14107	12577	12409	10962	8100	4106	4037	4177
74	Prince George	7820	8411	7596	7175	8367	8030	8050	7425	8173	2774	2899	2678
75	Princess Anne	8273	7714	7669	7285	9102	8768	9498	8859	7793	4369	4333	4280
76	Prince William	7504	8565	8129	8144	9330	9419	11311	12733	11615	5691	5690	5079
77	Pulaski	6538	5416	5118	3739	......	......	......	......	......	4729	3844	3613
78	Rappahannock	8261	8850	9782	9257	......	......	......	......	......	5195	5018	5642
79	Richmond	6503	6856	6448	5065	6055	5706	6214	d13744	6985	3475	3570	3463
80	Roanoke	9350	8048	8477	5499	......	......	......	......	......	6218	5250	3612
81	Rockbridge	16058	17248	16045	14284	14244	11945	10318	8945	6548	12162	12841	11484
82	Rockingham	23668	23408	20294	17344	20683	14784	12753	10374	7449	21152	20489	17496
83	Russell	11103	10280	11919	7878	6714	5536	6319	4808	3338	9936	9130	10886
84	Scott	13036	12072	9829	7303	5724	4263	......	......	......	12512	11530	9322
85	Shenandoah	14936	13896	13768	11618	19750	18926	13646	13823	10510	14260	12827	12563
86	Smyth	8898	8952	8162	6522	......	......	......	......	......	7654	7732	6898
87	Southampton	12285	12915	13521	14525	16074	14170	13497	13925	12864	5468	5713	5940
88	Spottsylvania	11728	16076	14911	15161	15134	14254	13296	13002	11252	7069	7716	6894
89	Stafford	6420	8555	8044	8454	9362	9517	9830	9971	9588	4935	4922	4415
90	Surry	5585	6133	5679	6480	7109	6594	6855	6535	6227	2393	2334	2215
91	Sussex	7885	10175	9820	11229	12720	11884	11362	11062	10549	2962	3118	3086
92	Tazewell (c)	10791	9920	9942	6290	5749	3916	3007	2127	......	9193	8625	8807
93	Warren	5716	6442	6607	5627	......	......	......	......	......	4611	4583	4493
94	Warwick	1672	1740	1546	1456	1570	1608	1835	1650	1690	620	662	599
95	Washington	16816	16892	14612	13001	15614	12444	12156	9536	5625	14156	14095	12939
96	Westmoreland	7682	8282	8080	8019	8396	6901	8102	(d)	7722	3531	3387	3376
97	Wise	4785	4508	......	......	......	......	......	......	......	4717	4416	......
98	Wythe (c)	11611	12305	12024	9375	12163	9692	8356	6380	......	9269	9986	9618
99	York	7198	4949	4460	4720	5354	4384	5187	3231	5233	2507	2342	1825

(*) All other persons, except Indians not taxed.
(*a*) Then in the District of Columbia.
(*b*) Amelia and Nottoway tabulated together, and here placed opposite Amelia.
(*c*) In 1861 Bland from Giles, Tazewell, and Wythe.
(*d*) Richmond and Westmoreland tabulated together, opposite Richmond.

TABLE VIII.—*Population by Counties at each Census—WEST VIRGINIA.* (*a*)

	Counties.	AGGREGATE.									WHITE.		
		1870.	1860.	1850.	1840.	1830.	1820.	1810.	1800.	1790.	1870.	1860.	1850.
	The State	442014	376688	302313	224537	176924	*40 136768	105469	78592	55873	424033	355526	278731
1	Barbour	10312	8958	9005	......	......	......	......	......	......	9926	8728	8670
2	Berkeley	14900	12525	11771	10972	10518	11211	11479	22006	19713	13228	10589	9566
3	Boone (d)	4553	4840	3237	......	......	......	......	......	......	4400	4681	3054
4	Braxton	6480	4992	4212	2575	......	......	......	......	......	6393	4885	4123
5	Brooke	5464	5494	5054	7948	7041	6631	5843	4706	......	5367	5425	4923
6	Cabell (d)	6429	8020	6299	8163	5884	4789	2717	......	......	6306	7691	5002
7	Calhoun	2939	2502	......	......	......	......	......	......	......	2931	2492	......
8	Clay	2196	1787	......	......	......	......	......	......	......	2192	1761	......
9	Doddridge	7076	5203	2750	......	......	......	......	......	......	7041	5168	2718
10	Fayette	6647	5997	3955	3924	......	......	......	......	......	6529	5716	3780
11	Gilmer	4338	3759	3475	......	......	......	......	......	......	4311	3685	3403
12	Grant (b)	4467	......	......	......	......	......	......	......	......	4136	......	......
13	Greenbrier	11417	12211	10022	8695	9006	7041	5914	4345	e6015	10314	10500	8549
14	Hampshire (e)	7643	13913	14036	12295	11279	10889	9784	8348	7346	7003	12478	12379
15	Hancock	4363	4445	4050	......	......	......	......	......	......	4336	4442	4040
16	Hardy (b)	5518	9864	9543	7622	6798	5700	5525	6627	7336	4902	8521	7927
17	Harrison	16714	13790	11728	17669	14722	10932	9958	4848	2080	16058	13176	11213
18	Jackson	10300	8306	6544	4890	......	......	......	......	......	10242	8240	6480
19	Jefferson	13219	14535	15357	14082	12927	13087	11851	......	......	9731	10064	10476

TABLE VIII—*Population by Counties at each Census—VIRGINIA*—Continued.

White—Continued.						Colored. (e)									
1840.	1830.	1820.	1810.	1800.	1790.	1870.	1860.	1850.	1840.	1830.	1820.	1810.	1800.	1790.	
3575	6456	5219	5711	6160	5436	5458	6298	6105	5550	8181	7661	6612	5289	4485	68
5197	......	......	......	......	......	986	1234	1268	997	......	......	......	......	......	69
6087	5496	3776	3696	3552	......	2325	2301	2422	1945	1899	1313	999	779	......	70
14283	14694	12636	10710	8503	8538	16084	14999	13533	12115	11340	8687	6462	4194	3041	71
2432	2661	2492	2484	2393	2356	5115	5812	5665	5492	5856	5800	5589	5376	4536	72
4923	5039	4627	5264	4978	4082	7898	7807	7680	9146	9068	7950	7145	5984	4018	73
2692	3069	3119	3101	2795	3387	5046	5512	4926	4483	5298	4911	4949	4630	4786	74
3096	5023	4812	5305	5200	4527	3902	3381	3389	3289	4077	3956	4193	3659	3266	75
4867	5127	4761	5733	6975	6744	1813	[illegible]	3050	3277	4203	4658	5578	5758	4871	76
2768	......	......	......	......	......	1809	1602	1505	971	......	......	......	......	......	77
5307	......	......	......	......	......	3066	3832	4140	3950	......	......	......	......	......	78
3092	2975	2749	2775	*d*5334	2918	3028	3286	2985	2873	3080	2957	3439	*d*8410	4067	79
3845	......	......	......	......	......	3132	2798	2665	1654	......	......	......	......	......	80
10448	10465	9038	8445	7778	5825	3890	4407	4561	3836	3779	2907	1873	1167	723	81
14944	17814	12646	11049	9266	6677	2516	2919	2798	2400	2869	2138	1704	1108	772	82
7152	6002	4989	5897	4443	3143	1167	1150	1053	726	712	547	422	365	195	83
6911	5378	3992	......	......	......	524	542	507	392	346	271	......	......	......	84
10320	16809	16708	12461	12947	9979	676	1069	1203	1298	2881	2218	1185	876	531	85
5539	......	......	......	......	......	1244	1220	1264	983	......	......	......	......	......	86
6171	6573	6127	5982	6461	6312	6795	7202	7581	8354	9501	8043	7515	7464	6552	87
6786	6384	5639	5506	5875	5171	4659	8360	8017	8375	8750	8315	7700	7127	6081	88
4489	4713	4788	5319	5435	5465	1485	3633	3629	3965	4649	4729	4511	4536	4123	89
2557	2865	2642	2751	2777	2762	3192	3799	3464	3923	4244	3952	4104	3758	3465	90
3564	4118	4155	4436	4532	4771	4923	7057	6734	7645	8602	7729	6926	6530	5778	91
5466	4911	3435	2661	1895	......	1598	1295	1135	824	838	481	346	232	......	92
3851	......	......	......	......	......	1105	1859	2114	1776	......	......	......	......	......	93
604	633	620	697	614	667	1052	1078	947	852	937	988	1138	1045	1023	94
10731	12785	10393	10581	8250	5167	2653	2806	2243	2270	2829	2051	1575	1286	458	95
3466	3710	3031	3401	(*d*)	3183	4151	4895	4704	4553	4686	3870	4701	(*d*)	4539	96
......	......	......	......	......	......	68	92	......	......	......	......	......	......	......	97
7632	9932	8111	7180	5538	......	2342	2319	2406	1743	2211	1581	1176	842	......	98
1958	2129	1568	1798	1166	2115	4691	2607	2635	2762	2045	2790	3389	2065	3118	99

(*e*) At 1870 Chinese 4, Indians 229, as follows: Alexandria, 1 Chinese; Amherst, 12 Indians; Caroline, 13 Indians; Chesterfield, 7 Indians; Dinwiddie, 21 Indians; Fairfax, 1 Chinese; Giles, 5 Indians; Goochland, 1 Indian; King William, 117 Indians; New Kent, 15 Indians; Norfolk, 2 Indians; Northumberland, 1 Indian; Princess Anne, 2 Chinese; Rockbridge, 6 Indians; Southampton, 22 Indians; Washington, 7 Indians. At 1860, Indians 94, as follows: Henrico, 19 Indians; Lee, 10 Indians; New Kent, 1 Indian; Norfolk, 63 Indians; Washington, 1 Indian.

TABLE VIII.—*Population by Counties at each Census—WEST VIRGINIA.* (*a*)

White—Continued.						Colored.									Indian.		
1840.	1830.	1820.	1810.	1800.	1790.	1870.	1860.	1850.	1840.	1830.	1820.	1810.	1800.	1790.	1870.	1860.	
203016	157084	120236	93355	70894	50593	17980	21144	23582	21521	19840	16332	12114	7698	5280	1	18	
......	......	......	......	......	......	386	230	335	......	......	......	......	......	......	......	......	1
8760	8323	9085	9760	17832	16650	1672	1936	2205	2212	2195	2126	1719	4174	3063	......	......	2
......	......	......	......	......	......	153	159	183	......	......	......	......	......	......	......	......	3
2509	......	......	......	......	......	87	107	89	66	......	......	......	......	......	......	......	4
7760	6774	* 6190	5472	4402	......	97	69	131	168	267	441	371	304	......	......	......	5
7574	5207	4388	2471	......	......	123	329	397	589	617	401	246	......	......	......	......	6
......	......	......	......	......	......	8	10	......	......	......	......	......	......	......	......	......	7
......	......	......	......	......	......	4	26	......	......	......	......	......	......	......	......	......	8
......	......	......	......	......	......	35	35	32	......	......	......	......	......	......	......	......	9
3773	......	......	......	......	......	118	281	175	151	......	......	......	......	......	......	......	10
......	......	......	......	......	......	24	74	72	......	......	......	......	......	......	......	......	11
......	......	......	......	......	......	331	......	......	......	......	......	......	......	......	......	......	12
7267	7722	6163	5390	4046	*c*5676	1103	1711	1473	1408	1224	878	524	299	339	......	......	13
10703	9796	9507	8731	7598	6879	640	1435	1657	1592	1453	1382	1053	750	467	......	......	14
......	......	......	......	......	......	27	3	10	......	......	......	......	......	......	......	......	15
6100	5408	4606	4579	5893	6556	616	1343	1616	1522	1390	1094	946	734	780	......	......	16
10850	13887	10300	9448	4598	2013	655	614	515	819	835	632	510	250	67	1	......	17
4803	......	......	......	......	......	58	66	64	87	......	......	......	......	......	......	......	18
9223	8435	8707	7967	......	......	3488	4471	4881	4739	4492	4380	3884	......	......	......	......	19

TABLE VIII.—*Population by Counties at each Census—WEST VIRGINIA*—Continued.

	Counties.	AGGREGATE.									WHITE.		
		1870.	1860.	1850.	1840.	1830.	1820.	1810.	1800.	1790.	1870.	1860.	1850.
20	Kanawha (*d*)	22349	16150	15353	13567	9326	6399	3866	3239	(*c*)	20111	13785	[illegible]
21	Lewis	10175	7999	10031	8151	6241	4247	......	......	......	9979	7736	[illegible]
22	Lincoln (*d*)	5053	......	......	......	......	......	......	......	......	5017	......	......
23	Logan (*d*)	5124	4938	3620	4309	3680	......	......	......	......	5022	4789	[illegible]
24	Marion	12107	12722	10552	......	......	......	......	......	......	12020	12656	[illegible]
25	Marshall	14941	12997	10138	6937	......	......	......	......	......	14821	12911	[illegible]
26	Mason	15978	9173	7539	6777	6534	4868	1991	......	......	15444	8750	[illegible]
27	McDowell	1952	1535	......	......	......	......	......	......	......	1952	1535	......
28	Mercer	7064	6819	4222	2233	......	......	......	......	......	6670	6428	4018
29	Mineral (*e*)	6332	......	......	......	......	......	......	......	......	5954	......	......
30	Monongalia	13547	13048	12387	17368	14056	11060 *40	12793	8540	4768	13316	12901	[illegible]
31	Monroe	11124	10757	10204	8422	7798	6580	5444	4188	......	10121	9536	[illegible]
32	Morgan	4315	3732	3557	4253	2694	2500	......	......	......	4199	3614	[illegible]
33	Nicholas	4458	4627	3963	2515	3346	1853	......	......	......	4427	4471	[illegible]
34	Ohio	28831	22422	18006	13357	15584	9182	8175	4740	5212	28387	22196	[illegible]
35	Pendleton	6455	6164	5795	6940	6271	4846	4239	3962	2452	6361	5870	[illegible]
36	Pleasants	3012	2945	......	......	......	......	......	......	......	2996	2925	......
37	Pocahontas	4069	3958	3598	2922	2542	......	......	......	......	3810	3686	[illegible]
38	Preston	14555	13312	11708	6866	5144	3422	......	......	......	14437	13182	[illegible]
39	Putnam (*d*)	7794	6301	5335	......	......	......	......	......	......	7534	5708	[illegible]
40	Raleigh	3673	3367	1765	......	......	......	......	......	......	3657	3291	[illegible]
41	Randolph	5563	4990	5243	6208	5000	3357	2854	1826	951	5460	4793	[illegible]
42	Ritchie	9055	6847	3902	......	......	......	......	......	......	8992	6809	[illegible]
43	Roane	7232	5381	......	......	......	......	......	......	......	7209	5307	......
44	Taylor	9367	7463	5367	......	......	......	......	......	......	9024	7300	5130
45	Tucker	1907	1428	......	......	......	......	......	......	......	1880	1392	......
46	Tyler	7832	6517	5498	6954	4104	2314	......	......	......	7822	6488	5456
47	Upshur	8023	7292	......	......	......	......	......	......	......	7851	7064	......
48	Wayne (*d*)	7852	6747	4760	......	......	......	......	......	......	7699	6604	4564
49	Webster	1730	1555	......	......	......	......	......	......	......	1730	1552	......
50	Wetzel	8595	6703	4284	......	......	......	......	......	......	8584	6691	[illegible]
51	Wirt	4804	3751	3353	......	......	......	......	......	......	4775	3728	[illegible]
52	Wood	19000	11046	9450	7923	6429	5860	3036	1217	......	18287	10791	[illegible]
53	Wyoming	3171	2861	1645	......	......	......	......	......	......	3130	2795	[illegible]

(*) All other persons, except Indians not taxed.
(*a*) In 1863 organized from Virginia.
(*b*) Grant from Hardy.

TABLE VIII.—*Population by Counties at each Census—WISCONSIN.*

	Counties.	AGGREGATE.								WHITE.	
		1870.	1860.	1850.	1840.	1830.	1820.	1810.	1800.	1870.	1860.
	The State	1054670	775881	305391	30945	......	......	......	*a*115	1051351	773693
1	Adams	6601	6492	187	......	......	......	......	......	6597	6472
2	Ashland (*e*)	221	515	......	......	......	......	......	......	221	515
3	Bad Ax (*b*)	......	11007	......	......	......	......	......	......	......	10968
4	Barron	538	......	......	......	......	......	......	......	530	......
5	Bayfield	344	......	......	......	......	......	......	......	341	......
6	Brown	25168	11795	6215	2107	......	......	......	*a*50	25006	11774
7	Buffalo	11123	3864	......	......	......	......	......	......	11120	3864
8	Burnett	706	12	......	......	......	......	......	......	695	12
9	Calumet	12335	7895	1743	275	......	......	......	......	11088	7179
10	Chippewa	8311	1895	615	......	......	......	......	......	8269	1766
11	Clark	3450	789	......	......	......	......	......	......	3444	789
12	Columbia	28802	24441	9565	......	......	......	......	......	28769	24421
13	Crawford	13075	8068	2498	1502	......	......	......	*a*65	13054	8040
14	Dallas (*c*)	......	13	......	......	......	......	......	......	......	13

III.—*Population by Counties at each Census—WEST VIRGINIA*—Continued.

White—Continued.					Colored.									Indian.		
0.	1820.	1810.	1800.	1790.	1870.	1860.	1850.	1840.	1830.	1820.	1810.	1800.	1790.	1870.	1860.	
31	5297	3468	3001	(e)	2238	2365	3352	2637	1793	1102	398	238				20
56	4122				196	263	411	162	185	125						21
					36											22
11					162	149	87	150	169							23
					78	66	113									24
					120	86	88	83								25
76	4245	1742			534	423	698	854	758	621	249					26
																27
					394	391	204	106								28
					378											29
75	10568	12405	8359	4602	231	147	295	406	481	492	388	181	166			30
33	6009	4998	3987		1093	1221	1142	965	765	571	446	201				31
19	2367				116	118	126	140	175	133						32
24	1805				31	156	74	75	122	48						33
29	8720	7081	4468	4907	444	226	394	515	555	462	494	272	305			34
52	4451	3952	3816	2378	94	294	352	495	519	392	287	146	74			35
					16	20										36
98					259	272	293	238	244							37
88	3336				118	112	146	123	156	86					18	38
					260	593	642									39
					16	76	36									40
26	3166	2706	1739	932	103	197	240	400	374	191	148	87	19			41
					63	38	16									42
					23	74										43
					343	161	237									44
					27	36										45
91	2203				10	29	42	90	113	111						46
					172	228										47
					153	143	196									48
						3										49
					11	12	23									50
					29	23	34									51
01	4998	2585	1155		713	255	442	680	928	862	451	62				52
					41	66	62									53

nbrier and Kanawha opposite Greenbrier.
oln from Boone, Cabell, Kanawha, Logan, Putnam, and Wayne.
ral from Hampshire.

TABLE VIII.—*Population by Counties at each Census—WISCONSIN.*

White—Continued.					Colored.								Indian.		
40.	1830.	1820.	1810.	1800.	1870.	1860.	1850.	1840.	1830.	1820.	1810.	1800.	1870.	1860.	
0749				a115	2113	1171	635	196					1206	f1017	
					3	20							1		1
															2
						39									3
					4								4		4
					1								2		5
2083				a50	67	20	45	24					93	1	6
													3		7
													11		8
249					50		123	26					597	g716	9
					13		1						29	h129	10
					2								4		11
					30	20	18						3		12
1497				a65	15	28	17	5					6		13
															14

TABLE VIII.—*Population by Counties at each Census—WISCONSIN*—Continued.

	Counties.	AGGREGATE.								WHITE.	
		1870.	1860.	1850.	1840.	1830.	1820.	1810.	1800.	1870.	1860.
15	Dane	53096	43922	16639	314	......	......	......	......	52990	[illegible]
16	Dodge	47035	42818	19138	67	......	......	......	......	46941	[illegible]
17	Door	4919	2948	......	......	......	......	......	......	4919	2947
18	Douglas	1122	812	......	......	......	......	......	......	1111	[illegible]
19	Dunn	9488	2704	......	......	......	......	......	......	9485	[illegible]
20	Eau Claire	10769	3162	......	......	......	......	......	......	10743	[illegible]
21	Fond du Lac	46273	34154	14510	139	......	......	......	......	46047	[illegible]
22	Grant	37979	31189	16169	3926	......	......	......	......	37881	[illegible]
23	Green	23611	19808	8566	933	......	......	......	......	23587	[illegible]
24	Green Lake (*j*)	13195	12663	......	......	......	......	......	......	13176	[illegible]
25	Iowa	24544	18967	9525	3978	......	......	......	......	24490	[illegible]
26	Jackson	7687	4170	......	......	......	......	......	......	7686	4166
27	Jefferson	34040	30438	15317	914	......	......	......	......	33970	[illegible]
28	Juneau	12372	8770	......	......	......	......	......	......	12356	8709
29	Kenosha	13147	13900	10734	......	......	......	......	......	13117	[illegible]
30	Kewaunee	10128	5530	......	......	......	......	......	......	10127	5530
31	La Crosse	20297	12186	......	......	......	......	......	......	20192	12149
32	La Fayette	22659	18134	11531	......	......	......	......	......	22646	18108
33	La Pointe (*d*)(*e*)	......	353	489	......	......	......	......	......	......	332
34	Manitowoc	33364	22416	3702	235	......	......	......	......	33349	22412
35	Marathon	5885	2892	508	......	......	......	......	......	5879	2853
36	Marquette (*j*)	8056	8233	8641	18	......	......	......	......	8053	8233
37	Milwaukee	89930	62518	31077	5605	......	......	......	......	89739	62411
38	Monroe	16550	8410	......	......	......	......	......	......	16515	8407
39	Oconto	8321	3592	......	......	......	......	......	......	8254	3537
40	Outagamie	18430	9587	......	......	......	......	......	......	18371	9547
41	Ozaukee	15564	15682	......	......	......	......	......	......	15563	[illegible]
42	Pepin	4659	2392	......	......	......	......	......	......	4659	2392
43	Pierce	9958	4672	......	......	......	......	......	......	9909	4639
44	Polk	3422	1400	......	......	......	......	......	......	3363	1369
45	Portage	10634	7507	1250	1623	......	......	......	......	10617	7496
46	Racine	26740	21360	14973	3475	......	......	......	......	26543	21225
47	Richland	15731	9732	903	......	......	......	......	......	15712	9722
48	Rock	39030	36090	20750	1701	......	......	......	......	38829	36396
49	Sauk	23860	18963	4371	102	......	......	......	......	23808	18916
50	Shawano (*i*)	3166	829	......	......	......	......	......	......	3080	779
51	Sheboygan	31749	26875	8379	133	......	......	......	......	31745	26870
52	St. Croix	11035	5392	624	809	......	......	......	......	11016	5388
53	Trempealeau	10732	2560	......	......	......	......	......	......	10728	2558
54	Vernon	18645	......	......	......	......	......	......	......	18574	......
55	Walworth	25972	26496	17862	2611	......	......	......	......	25935	26436
56	Washington	23919	23622	19485	343	......	......	......	......	23911	[illegible]
57	Waukesha	28274	26831	19258	......	......	......	......	......	28213	26797
58	Waupaca	15539	8851	......	......	......	......	......	......	15507	8850
59	Waushara	11279	8770	......	......	......	......	......	......	11260	8760
60	Winnebago	37279	23770	10167	135	......	......	......	......	37131	23700
61	Wood	3912	2425	......	......	......	......	......	......	3890	2424

(*a*) In a note to the return of the "Territory of Indiana" appears the following: "On the 1st of August, 1800, at Prairie du Chien, on the Mississippi, there were 65 souls; at Green Bay, on Lake Michigan, there were 50 souls."

(*b*) In 1862 name changed from Bad Ax to Vernon.

(*c*) In 1869 name changed from Dallas to Barron.

(*d*) In 1866 name changed from La Pointe to Bayfield.

TABLE VIII.—*Population by Counties at each Census—WISCONSIN*—Continued.

WHITE—Continued.						COLORED.								INDIAN.		
1850.	1840.	1830.	1820.	1810.	1800.	1870.	1860.	1850.	1840.	1830.	1820.	1810.	1800.	1870.	1860.	
16613	313					106	72	26	1							15
19126	63					77	19	12	4					17	24	16
							1									17
						7	4							4		18
						2	18							1		19
						26	9									20
14507	136					909	59	3	3					17		21
16139	2879					98	35	30	48							22
8566	933					24										23
						16	31							3		24
9496	3045					45	23	29	33							25
						1	4									26
15314	913					66	5	3	1					4		27
						7	1							9		28
10716						30	28	18								29
														1		30
						105	37									31
11517						13	26	14								32
483							1	6								33
3702	234					8	4		1					7		34
508														15	39	35
8634	18					2		7						1		36
30965	5573					185	107	111	32					6		37
						33	3							2		38
						7	27							60	28	39
						30	10							29	30	40
						1										41
																42
						49	33									43
														59	11	44
1249	1619					1	7	1	4					16	4	45
14907	3467					194	135	66	8					3		46
902						18	9	1						1		47
29727	1700					104	93	23	1					7	1	48
4370	102					51	36	1						1	11	49
						3	47							83	3	50
8372	133					4	5	7								51
619	805					16	2	5	4					3	2	52
						4	1									53
						71										54
17859	2610					37	60	3	1							55
19485	343					8										56
19213						58	34	45						3		57
						3	1							29		58
						1	4							18		59
10147	135					113	52	20						35	18	60
						5	1							17		61

(*e*) Since 1860 part of Ashland annexed to La Pointe.
(*f*) Including 404 half-breeds.
(*g*) Including 296 half-breeds.
(*h*) Including 118 half-breeds.
(*i*) In 1864 name changed from Shawanaw to Shawano.
(*j*) In 1858 Green Lake from Marquette.

TABLE VIII.—*Population by Counties at each Census—TERRITORY OF ARIZONA.*

Counties.	AGGREGATE.			WHITE.			COLORED.			CHINESE.	INDIAN.	
	1870.	1860.	1850.	1870.	1860.	1850.	1870.	1860.	1850.	1870.	1870.	1860.
The Territory	9658	a6482	......	9581	a2421	......	26	a21	......	20	31	a4040
Mohave	179	......	......	175	......	......	4	......	......	......	......	......
Pima	5716	......	......	5698	......	......	12	......	......	......	6	......
Yavapai	2142	......	......	2116	......	......	8	......	......	12	6	......
Yuma	1621	......	......	1592	......	......	2	......	......	8	19	......

TERRITORY OF COLORADO.

Counties.	Aggregate 1870.	Aggregate 1860.	Aggregate 1850.	White 1870.	White 1860.	White 1850.	Colored 1870.	Colored 1860.	Colored 1850.	Chinese 1870.	Indian 1870.	Indian 1860.
The Territory	39864	34277	......	39221	34231	......	456	46	......	7	180	......
Arapahoe	6829	......	......	6566	......	......	257	......	......	4	2	......
Bent	592	......	......	570	......	......	11	......	......	......	11	......
Boulder	1939	......	......	1938	......	......	1	......	......	......	......	......
Clear Creek	1596	......	......	1572	......	......	22	......	......	2	......	......
Conejos	2504	......	......	2470	......	......	......	......	......	......	34	......
Costilla	1779	......	......	1761	......	......	1	......	......	......	17	......
Douglas	1388	......	......	1385	......	......	2	......	......	......	1	......
El Paso	987	......	......	986	......	......	1	......	......	......	......	......
Fremont	1064	......	......	1063	......	......	1	......	......	......	......	......
Gilpin	5490	......	......	5429	......	......	60	......	......	1	......	......
Greenwood	510	......	......	479	......	......	31	......	......	......	......	......
Huerfano	2250	......	......	2217	......	......	2	......	......	......	31	......
Jefferson	2390	......	......	2370	......	......	20	......	......	......	......	......
Lake	522	......	......	521	......	......	1	......	......	......	......	......
Larimer	838	......	......	828	......	......	......	......	......	......	10	......
Las Animas	4276	......	......	4191	......	......	13	......	......	......	72	......
Park	447	......	......	446	......	......	1	......	......	......	......	......
Pueblo	2265	......	......	2237	......	......	27	......	......	......	1	......
Saguache	304	......	......	304	......	......	......	......	......	......	......	......
Summit	258	......	......	253	......	......	5	......	......	......	......	......
Weld	1636	......	......	1635	......	......	......	......	......	......	1	......

TERRITORY OF DAKOTA.

Counties.	Aggregate 1870.	Aggregate 1860.	Aggregate 1850.	White 1870.	White 1860.	White 1850.	Colored 1870.	Colored 1860.	Colored 1850.	Chinese 1870.	Indian 1870.	Indian 1860.
The Territory	14181	4837	......	12887	2576	......	94	......	......	......	1200	2261
Bonhomme	608	......	......	* 592	......	......	4	......	......	......	12	......
Brookings	163	......	......	18	......	......	......	......	......	......	145	......
Buffalo	246	......	......	214	......	......	9	......	......	......	23	......
Charles Mix	152	......	......	35	......	......	......	......	......	......	117	......
Clay	2621	......	......	2618	......	......	2	......	......	......	1	......
Deuel	37	......	......	17	......	......	......	......	......	......	20	......
Hutchinson	37	......	......	37	......	......	......	......	......	......	......	......
Jayne	5	......	......	3	......	......	2	......	......	......	......	......
Lincoln	712	......	......	712	......	......	......	......	......	......	......	......
Minnehaha	355	......	......	301	......	......	......	......	......	......	54	......
Pembina	1213	......	......	404	......	......	1	......	......	......	808	......
Todd	337	......	......	321	......	......	16	......	......	......	......	......
Union	3507	......	......	3496	......	......	......	......	......	......	11	......
Yankton	2097	......	......	2077	......	......	19	......	......	......	1	......
Unorganized portion of Territory.	2091	......	......	2042	......	......	41	......	......	......	8	......

(*a*) Then the county of Arizona, in the Territory of New Mexico.

TABLE VIII.—*Population by Counties at each Census*—*DISTRICT OF COLUMBIA.*

Cities, etc.	AGGREGATE.								
	1870.	1860.	1850.	1840.	1830.	1820.	1810.	1800.	1790.
The District	131700	75080	51687	a9967 33745	a9573 30261	a9703 23336	a8552 15471	a3949 8144	......
Georgetown City	11384	8733	8366	7312	8441	7360	4948	b8144	......
Washington City	109199	61122	40001	23364	18826	13247	8208		......
Remainder of the District	11117	5225	3320	3069	2994	2729	2315		......
Alexandria County	......	......	......	a9967	a9573	a9703	a8552	a3949	......

Cities, etc.	WHITE.								
	1870.	1866.	1850.	1840.	1830.	1820.	1810.	1800.	1790.
The District	88278	60763	37941	a6731 23926	a6411 21152	a6556 16058	a5734 10345	a4394 5672	......
Georgetown City	8113	6798	6080	5124	6057	4940	3235	b5672	......
Washington City	73731	50138	29730	16843	13367	9606	5904		......
Remainder of the District	6434	3827	2131	1959	1728	1512	1206		......
Alexandria County	......	......	......	a6731	a6411	a6556	a5734	a4394	......

Cities, etc.	COLORED.								
	1870.	1860.	1850.	1840.	1830.	1820.	1810.	1800.	1790.
The District	43404	14316	13746	a3236 9819	a3162 9109	a3147 7278	a2818 5126	a1555 2472	......
Georgetown City	3271	1935	2296	2188	2384	2420	1713	b2472	......
Washington City	35455	10983	10271	6521	5459	3641	2304		......
Remainder of the District	4678	1398	1189	1110	1266	1217	1109		......
Alexandria County	......	......	......	a3236	a3162	a3147	a2818	a1555	......

Cities, etc.	CHINESE.								
	1870.	1860.	1850.	1840.	1830.	1820.	1810.	1800.	1790.
The District	3	......	......	......	......	......	......	......	......
Georgetown City	......	......	......	......	......	......	......	......	......
Washington City	......	......	......	......	......	......	......	......	......
Remainder of the District	3	......	......	......	......	......	......	......	......
Alexandria County	......	......	......	......	......	......	......	......	......

Cities, etc.	INDIAN.								
	1870.	1860.	1850.	1840.	1830.	1820.	1810.	1800.	1790.
The District	15	1	......	......	......	......	......	......	......
Georgetown City	......	......	......	......	......	......	......	......	......
Washington City	13	1	......	......	......	......	......	......	......
Remainder of the District	2	......	......	......	......	......	......	......	......
Alexandria County	......	......	......	......	......	......	......	......	......

(*a*) Then in the District of Columbia, now in Virginia.
(*b*) All of Washington County.

TABLE VIII.—*Population by Counties at each Census*—*TERRITORY OF IDAHO.*

Counties.	AGGREGATE.			WHITE.			COLORED.			CHINESE.	INDIAN.	
	1870.	1860.	1850.	1870.	1860.	1850.	1870.	1860.	1850.	1870.	1870.	1860.
The Territory	14999			10618			60			4274	47	
Ada	2675			2569			20			78	8	
Alturas	689			369			5			314	1	
Boise	3834			2057			15			1754	8	
Idaho	849			415			2			425	7	
Lemhi	988			864			2			120	2	
Nez Percés	1607			837			4			747	19	
Oneida	1922			1921			1					
Owyhee	1713			1334			9			368	2	
Shoshone	722			252			2			468		

TERRITORY OF MONTANA.

Counties.	Aggregate 1870.	Aggregate 1860.	Aggregate 1850.	White 1870.	White 1860.	White 1850.	Colored 1870.	Colored 1860.	Colored 1850.	Chinese 1870.	Indian 1870.	Indian 1860.
The Territory	20595			18306			183			1949	157	
Beaver Head	722			714			2			6		
Big Horn	38			38								
Choteau	517			476			20			3	18	
Dawson	177			161			4				12	
Deer Lodge	4367			3551			15			776	25	
Gallatin	1578			1554			13			4	7	
Jefferson	1531			1406			2			122	1	
Lewis and Clarke	5040			4279			92			666	3	
Madison	2684			2361			20			299	4	
Meagher	1387			1346			4			29	8	
Missoula	2554			2420			11			44	79	

TERRITORY OF NEW MEXICO.

Counties.	Aggregate 1870.	Aggregate 1860.	Aggregate 1850.	White 1870.	White 1860.	White 1850.	Colored 1870.	Colored 1860.	Colored 1850.	Chinese 1870.	Indian 1870.	Indian 1860.
The Territory	91874	93516	61547	90393	82924	61525	172	85	22		1309	10507
Arizona (a)		6482			2421			21				4040
Bernalillo	7591	8769	7751	7473	8574	7749	7	9	2		111	186
Colfax (b)	1992			1960			10				22	
Doña-Aña (c)	5864	6239		5862	6239		1				1	
Grant (c)	1143			1134			9					
Lincoln (d)	1803			1789			14					
Mora (b)	8056	5566		7986	5524		18	14			52	28
Rio Arriba	9294	9849	10668	8976	9329	10667	2		1		316	520
San Miguel	16058	13714	7074	15924	13670	7070	17	1	4		117	43
Santa Aña	2599	3572	4645	2534	1505	4644	24		1		41	2067
Santa Fé	9699	8114	7713	9585	7995	7699	38	27	14		76	92
Socorro (d)	6603	5787		6537	5706		19	6			47	75
Taos	12079	14103	9507	11792	13479	9507	3	7			284	617
Valencia	9093	11321	14189	8841	8482	14189	10				242	2839

(a) Originally embraced the country now constituting the Territory of Arizona.
(b) In 1869 Colfax from Mora.
(c) In 1868 Grant from Doña-Aña.
(d) In 1869 Lincoln from Socorro.

TERRITORY OF UTAH.

Counties.	Aggregate 1870.	Aggregate 1860.	Aggregate 1850.	White 1870.	White 1860.	White 1850.	Colored 1870.	Colored 1860.	Colored 1850.	Chinese 1870.	Indian 1870.	Indian 1860.
The Territory	86786	40273	11380	86044	40125	11330	118	59	50	445	179	89
Beaver	2007	785		2005	785						2	
Box Elder	4855	1608		4429	1608		19			403	4	
Cache	8229	2605		8219	2601		5				5	4
Cedar		741			741							
Davis	4459	2904	1134	4454	2886	1134		10			5	8
Deseret (a)												
Greasewood (a)												
Green River (b)		141			133							8
Iron	2277	1010	360	2262	1010	359			1		15	
Juab	2034	672		2028	672		4				2	
Kane	1513			1505			1				7	

TABLE VIII.—*Population by Counties at each Census—TERRITORY OF UTAH*—Contin'd.

Counties.	AGGREGATE.			WHITE.			COLORED.			CHINESE.	INDIAN.	
	1870.	1860.	1850.	1870.	1860.	1850.	1870.	1860.	1850.	1870.	1870.	1860.
Malade (*f*)												
Millard	2753	715		2665	715		1				87	
Morgan	1972			1970			2					
Piute	82			80							2	
Rich (*c*)	1955			1953							2	
Rio Virgin (*d*)	450			449							1	
Salt Lake	18337	11295	6157	18277	11200	6142	51	45	15		9	50
San Pete	6786	3815	365	6771	3806	365					15	9
Sevier	19			19								
Shambip (*e*)		162			162							
Summit	2512	198		2467	198		4			39	2	
Tooele	2177	1008	152	2177	1000	152						8
Utah	12203	8248	2026	12185	8243	1992	6	4	34		12	1
Wasatch (*g*)	1244			1244								
Washington	3064	691		3052	691		4				8	
Weber	7858	3675	1186	7833	3674	1186	21			3	1	1

(*a*) In 1866 set off to Nevada, except small portions of each attached to Tooele County.
(*b*) Since 1860 set off to Wyoming Territory.
(*c*) In 1863 organized.
(*d*) In 1867 organized. By the survey of 1871 this county is set off to Nevada.
(*e*) Since 1860 absorbed by Juab, Tooele, and Utah.
(*f*) Merged in Box Elder.
(*g*) In 1862 organized.

TERRITORY OF WASHINGTON.

Counties.	Aggregate 1870.	Aggregate 1860.	Aggregate 1850.	White 1870.	White 1860.	White 1850.	Colored 1870.	Colored 1860.	Colored 1850.	Chinese 1870.	Indian 1870.	Indian 1860.
The Territory	23955	11594		22195	11138		207	30		234	1319	426
Chehalis	401	285		397	283						4	2
Clallam	408	149		374	149					2	32	
Clarke	3081	2384		3013	2367			1			68	16
Cowlitz	730	406		709	405		7			1	13	1
Island (*e*)	626	294		594	292		2			7	23	2
Jefferson	1268	531		1126	523		12	8		19	111	
King	2120	302		1809	301		34	1		33	244	
Kitsap	866	544		839	540		14	4		13		
Klikitat	329	230		326	230						3	
Lewis	888	384		868	336		8	1		1	11	47
Mason (*a*)	289			275			5			1	8	
Pacific	738	420		607	406		1			6	124	14
Pierce	1409	1115		1149	1114		75			7	178	1
Sawamish (*a*)		162			162							
Skamania	133	173		129	171						4	2
Snohomish (*e*)	599			529			2			3	65	
Spokane (*b*)		996			674			2				320
Stevens (*b*) (*c*)	734			567						42	125	
Thurston	2246	1507		2193	1495		27	12		19	7	
Wahkiakum	270	42		165	41		1			15	89	1
Walla-Walla (*c*)	5300	1318		5174	1297		11	1		42	73	20
Whatcom	534	352		451	352		1			21	61	
Yakima (*d*)	432			428							4	
The Disputed Islands	554			473			7			2	72	

(*a*) In 1864 name changed from Sawamish to Mason.
(*b*) In 1864 Spokane merged in Stevens.
(*c*) In 1863 Stevens from Walla-Walla.
(*d*) In 1865 organized.
(*e*) In 1861 Snohomish from Island.

TERRITORY OF WYOMING.

Counties.	Aggregate 1870.	Aggregate 1860.	Aggregate 1850.	White 1870.	White 1860.	White 1850.	Colored 1870.	Colored 1860.	Colored 1850.	Chinese 1870.	Indian 1870.	Indian 1860.
The Territory	9118			8726			183			143	66	
Albany	2021			1971			40			2	8	
Carbon	1368			1360			7			1		
Laramie	2957			2822			109			13	13	
Sweetwater	1916			1777			24			95	20	
Uintah	856			796			3			32	25	

TABLE IX.—*Population of Minor Civil Divisions, with General Nativity and Race*—*ALABAMA*

NOTE.—The marginal column marks beats, precincts, or land-surveyed townships; the first indentation, cities; the second, towns. Names of towns are placed under the names of the precincts or beats in which they are respectively situated. The population of each beat or precinct includes that of all towns situated in it.

Counties.	Total.	Nativity.		Race.	
		Native.	Foreign.	White.	Colored.
AUTAUGA.					
1. Prattville	3675	3660	15	1393	2282
Prattville	1346	......	......	1346	......
2. Autaugaville	2387	2376	11	541	1846
3. Mulberry	1551	1549	2	318	1233
4. Milton	1595	1593	2	616	979
5. Independence	1137	1135	2	561	576
6. Kingston	1278	1277	1	900	a376
BAKER.					
1. Mims's Cross R.	788	788	......	733	55
2. Providence C'h	1024	1023	1	848	176
3. Bugbie's Mill	1436	1436	......	1068	368
4. Grantville	1859	1854	5	1663	196
Grantville	1761	1756	5	1573	188
5. Maplesville	1087	1086	1	745	342
BALDWIN.					
Townships 1 S.	160	158	2	101	59
Townships 2 S.	278	276	2	197	81
Townships 3 S.	480	474	6	248	232
Townships 4 S.	480	467	13	174	306
Townships 5 S.	640	619	21	288	352
Townships 6 S.	1120	1079	41	474	646
Townships 7 S.	640	613	27	447	193
Townships 8 S.	320	317	3	262	58
Townships 9 S.	320	291	29	281	39
Townships 1 N.	320	318	2	218	102
Townships 2 N.	480	476	4	161	319
Townships 3 N.	320	319	1	86	234
Townships 4 N.	446	446	......	222	224
BARBOUR.					
Eufaula	3185	3072	113	1545	1640
Township 8, R. 24	640	640	......	485	155
Township 9, R. 24	1280	1279	1	637	643
Township 10, R. 24	450	449	1	295	155
Township 11, R. 24	320	320	......	161	159
Township 13, R. 24	40	40	......	12	28
Township 8, R. 25	752	751	1	634	118
Township 9, R. 25	960	958	2	635	325
Township 10, R. 25	757	756	1	446	311
Township 11, R. 25	944	943	1	677	267
Township 12, R. 25	160	160	......	98	62
Township 8, R. 26	480	480	......	403	77
Township 9, R. 26	634	633	1	488	146
Township 10, R. 26	1334	1327	7	794	540
Township 11, R. 26	1440	1440	......	454	986
Township 12, R. 26	760	760	......	57	703
Township 13, R. 26	320	320	......	56	264
Township 9, R. 27	792	784	8	655	137
Township 10, R. 27	800	800	......	467	333
Township 11, R. 27	1720	1718	2	491	1229
Township 12, R. 27	1800	1800	......	312	1488
Township 13, R. 27	2238	2237	1	286	1952
Township 9, R. 28	776	776	......	384	392
Township 10, R. 28	1522	1517	5	599	923
Township 11, R. 28	842	842	......	232	b609
Township 12, R. 28	1352	1352	......	193	1159
Township 13, R. 28	240	240	......	27	213
Township 9, R. 29	135	135	......	44	91
Township 10, R. 29	40	40	......	17	23
Township 11, R. 29	1676	1672	4	369	1307
Township 12, R. 29	920	918	2	190	730

(a) Also 2 Indians.

Counties.	Total.	Nativity.		Race.	
		Native.	Foreign.	White.	Colored.
BIBB.					
1. Kingdom	835	835	......	550	285
2. Scottsville	955	954	1	750	205
3. Hawlmon	788	788	......	599	189
4. James	859	859	......	363	496
5. Centreville	1285	1285	......	746	539
6. Six Mile	709	707	2	525	184
7. Randolph	2038	2019	19	1546	496
BLOUNT.					
5. Blountsville	539	539	......	490	49
6. Brookville	510	510	......	466	44
7. Summit	630	630	......	590	40
8. Geo. White	232	232	......	220	12
9. Murfree's Val'y	630	630	......	530	100
10. Foster's Chapel	310	310	......	300	10
11. Cross Roads	770	770	......	690	80
12. Dry Creek	442	442	......	440	2
13. White's	252	252	......	240	12
14. Village Springs	700	700	......	590	110
Town. 9, R. 1 E.	461	461	......	449	12
Town. 9, R. 1 W.	87	87	......	87	......
Town. 10, R. 1 W.	147	147	......	147	......
Town. 10, R. 1 E.	111	111	......	105	6
Town. 11, R. 1 W.	541	540	1	489	52
Town. 12, R. 1 W.	499	499	......	497	2
Town. 13, R. 1 W.	228	227	1	210	18
Town. 14, R. 1 W.	137	137	......	128	9
Town. 9, R. 2 W.	127	127	......	127	......
Town. 10, R. 2 W.	60	60	......	60	......
Town. 11, R. 2 W.	218	218	......	218	......
Town. 12, R. 2 W.	337	337	......	316	21
Town. 13, R. 2 W.	468	467	1	441	27
Town, 14, R. 2 W.	255	255	......	250	5
Town. 9, R. 3 W.	297	290	7	297	......
Town. 10, R. 3 W.	85	85	......	85	......
Town. 11, R. 3 W.	240	240	......	240	......
Town. 12, R. 3 W.	368	368	......	318	50
Town. 13, R. 3 W.	264	263	1	243	21
BULLOCK.					
1. Midway	3036	3027	9	884	2152
2. Indian Creek	1162	1158	4	582	580
3. Perote	1538	1535	3	739	799
4. Scotland	760	759	1	370	390
5. Bughall	1823	1821	2	905	918
6. Union Church	1307	1306	1	570	737
7. Greenwood	3396	3393	3	643	2753
8. Bruceville	862	862	......	226	636
9. Sardis	1218	1217	1	301	917
10. Union Springs	4664	4614	50	1119	3545
Union Spr'gs	1455	1413	42	752	703
11. Ridgeley	2080	2075	5	528	1552
12. Enon	1748	1743	5	206	1542
13. Suspension	880	878	2	150	730
BUTLER.					
Townships 7	1459	1459	......	1151	308
Townships 8	1494	1492	2	963	531
Townships 9	942	942	......	661	281
Townships 10	6126	6055	71	3440	2686
Greenville	2856	2790	66	1555	1301
Townships 11	4960	4954	6	2369	2591

(b) Also 1 Indian.

TABLE IX.—*Population of Minor Civil Divisions, &c.—ALABAMA*—Continued.

Counties.	Total.	Nativity. Native.	Nativity. Foreign.	Race. White.	Race. Colored.
CALHOUN.(*)					
ksonville	1849	1792	57	1155	694
Jacksonville	958	918	40	603	355
xandria	1669	1669	......	980	709
	379	378	1	284	95
ldox	1280	1279	1	973	307
kville	434	434	......	410	24
itchie	857	856	1	727	130
Grove	520	520	......	449	71
lden's	1070	1069	1	850	220
liga	1665	1658	7	1250	415
	559	557	2	411	148
	908	907	1	594	314
	867	865	2	610	257
ford	1147	1138	9	867	280
phur Spr'gs	560	560	......	397	163
CHAMBERS.					
kory Flat	1460	1455	5	1004	456
vell	848	848	......	627	221
l Town	1206	1206	......	864	342
pville	909	907	2	700	209
kely's	1162	1158	4	801	361
donia	1186	1186	......	654	532
fton	2259	2234	25	775	1484
Fayette	1694	1685	9	813	881
La Fayette	1382	1373	9	704	678
od's Shop	1231	1231	......	687	544
w Harmony	1240	1237	3	655	585
t Bowery	1144	1144	......	372	772
weta	1205	1205	......	347	858
lin	2018	2008	10	675	1343
CHEROKEE.					
ford's	574	572	2	523	51
rd's	379	379	......	368	11
ng Garden	161	160	1	151	10
ard's	135	135	......	130	5
ship 9, R. 7	16	16	......	16	......
ship 10, R. 7	40	40	......	40	......
ship 9, R. 8	590	590	......	588	2
ship 10, R. 8	870	869	1	706	164
ship 11, R. 8	195	195	......	117	78
ship 7, R. 9	125	124	1	125	......
ship 8, R. 9	152	152	......	141	11
ship 9, R. 9	557	557	......	490	67
ship 10, R. 9	1049	1047	2	783	266
ship 11, R. 9	393	392	1	337	56
ship 12, R. 9	340	340	......	326	14
ship 7, R. 10	273	273	......	243	30
ship 8, R. 10	585	584	1	534	51
ship 9, R. 10	1274	1263	11	1044	230
ship 10, R. 10	781	773	8	658	123
ship 11, R. 10	469	469	......	453	16
ship 12, R. 10	677	677	......	589	88
ship 6, R. 11	155	155	......	146	9
ship 7, R. 11	158	158	......	144	14
ship 8, R. 11	477	477	......	451	26
ship 9, R. 11	81	81	......	81	......
ship 10, R. 11	626	626	......	468	158
CHOCTAW.					
ships 9	1915	1904	11	1009	906
ships 10	874	866	8	572	302
ships 11	2079	2078	1	1196	a881
ships 12	484	483	1	231	253
ships 13	2242	2236	6	898	1344
ships 14	2810	2798	12	946	1864
ships 15	2272	2268	4	950	1322

Counties.	Total.	Nativity. Native.	Nativity. Foreign.	Race. White.	Race. Colored.
CLARKE.					
Bashi	640	640	......	360	280
Campbell's	401	401	......	220	181
Cane Creek	480	478	2	355	125
Choctaw Corner	891	889	2	512	379
Clarksville	200	200	......	92	108
Coffeeville	1200	1189	11	571	629
Coffeeville	280	280	......	162	118
Gainestown	2409	2384	25	381	2028
Gates	640	640	......	352	288
Good Springs	559	558	1	422	137
Gosport	600	600	......	99	501
Grove Hill	1360	1358	2	971	389
Grove Hill	200	200	......	160	40
Indian Ridge	316	315	1	149	167
Jackson	1360	1355	5	662	698
Jackson Creek	393	393	......	133	260
Mitcham's	960	952	8	787	173
Pleasant Hill	520	518	2	283	237
Suggsville	935	933	2	274	661
Webb's Mill	799	798	1	475	324
CLAY.					
1. Delta	924	923	1	825	99
2. Flat Rock	945	944	1	875	70
3. Fox Creek	839	837	2	776	63
4. Wesobulga	907	907	......	869	38
5. Colleta	411	411	......	391	20
6. Ashland	1499	1499	......	1394	105
Ashland	118	118	......	117	1
7. Bowden	274	273	1	236	38
8. Brownville	795	794	1	646	149
9. McConatha	972	972	......	931	41
10. Wicker's	770	770	......	723	47
11. Almond	967	966	1	912	55
12. Mountain	257	257	......	245	12
CLEBURNE.					
Township 17, R. 8	211	211	......	183	28
Township 17, R. 9	753	753	......	696	57
Township 15, R. 10	445	445	......	384	61
Township 16, R. 10	679	678	1	573	106
Township 17, R. 10	909	909	......	814	95
Township 13, R. 11	587	587	......	555	32
Township 14, R. 11	435	435	......	434	1
Township 15, R. 11	640	640	......	606	34
Township 16, R. 11	425	425	......	422	3
Township 17, R. 11	555	550	5	455	100
Township 14, R. 12	635	635	......	629	6
Township 15, R. 12	617	616	1	601	16
Township 16, R. 12	509	509	......	490	19
Township 17, R. 12	617	617	......	599	18
COFFEE.					
Township 3, R. 19	212	212	......	178	34
Township 4, R. 19	80	80	......	63	17
Township 5, R. 19	327	326	1	312	15
Township 6, R. 19	377	377	......	324	53
Township 7, R. 19	432	432	......	422	10
Township 3, R. 20	136	136	......	128	8
Township 4, R. 20	206	206	......	184	22
Township 5, R. 20	1045	1045	......	615	430
Township 6, R. 20	475	475	......	429	46
Township 7, R. 20	342	342	......	319	23
Township 4, R. 21	58	58	......	58	......
Township 5, R. 21	476	476	......	340	136
Township 6, R. 21	558	558	......	495	63
Township 7, R. 21	56	56	......	51	5
Township 4, R. 22	120	120	......	75	45

(*) Incomplete; the other principal civil divisions were not separately returned.
(a) Also 2 Indians.

TABLE IX.—*Population of Minor Civil Divisions, &c.—ALABAMA*—Continued.

Counties.	Total.	Nativity.		Race.	
		Native.	Foreign.	White.	Colored.
COFFEE—Cont'd.					
Township 5, R. 22.	599	599	......	522	77
Township 6, R. 22.	360	359	1	344	16
Township 7, R. 22.	312	312	......	292	20
COLBERT.					
Township 3, R. 10.	960	958	2	346	614
Township 4, R. 10.	1438	1429	9	469	969
Township 5, R. 10	615	615	......	496	119
Township 6, R. 10	633	632	1	589	44
Township 3, R. 11.	320	317	3	126	194
Township 4, R. 11*a*	1150	1144	6	456	694
Township 5, R. 11.	285	285	......	258	27
Township 6, R. 11.	291	291	......	265	26
Township 4, R. 12.	509	506	3	290	219
Township 5, R. 12.	382	381	1	366	16
Township 3, R. 13.	247	246	1	158	89
Township 4, R. 13.	799	797	2	408	391
Township 5, R. 13	340	340	......	338	2
Township 3, R. 14.	929	915	14	695	234
Township 4, R. 14.	411	410	1	361	50
Township 5, R. 14.	166	166	......	153	13
Township 2, R. 15.	470	467	3	359	111
Township 3, R. 15.	503	503	......	387	116
Township 4, R. 15.	588	588	......	367	221
Township 5, R. 15.	287	285	2	247	40
Tuscumbia.....	1214	1177	37	764	450
CONECUH.					
1. Sepulga........	1600	1599	1	1127	473
2. Mill............	1031	1031	......	588	*b*437
3. Belleville.......	1584	1578	6	651	933
4. Evergreen......	1760	1751	9	624	1136
5. Sparta	913	913	......	264	649
6. Old Town	1749	1746	3	1024	725
7. Brooklyn.......	937	936	1	389	548
COOSA.					
1. Brookville.....	689	689	......	431	258
2. Nixburg.......	2249	2248	1	1059	1190
3. Socopatoy	1267	1267	......	709	558
4. Atkins	543	541	2	452	91
5. Hanover	545	545	......	483	62
6. Vincent	511	511	......	425	86
7. Rockford	1068	1068	......	910	158
8. Concord	754	754	......	468	286
9. McCord's......	873	873	......	576	297
10. Flint Hill......	637	637	......	578	*b*33
11. Weogufka.....	404	403	1	366	38
12. Jordan's	568	567	1	436	132
13. Marble Valley.	634	634	......	532	102
14. Lewis	367	366	1	337	*c*29
15. Traveler's Rest	836	836	......	782	54
COVINGTON.					
Township 1, R. 14.	73	73	......	73	......
Township 2, R. 14.	18	18	......	18	......
Township 3, R. 14.	401	401	......	287	114
Township 4, R. 14.	208	208	......	166	42
Township 5, R. 14.	432	432	......	296	136
Township 6, R. 14.	216	216	......	208	8
Township 2, R. 15.	26	26	......	26	......
Township 3, R. 15	103	103	......	88	15
Township 4, R. 15.	160	160	......	121	39
Township 5, R. 15.	120	120	......	120	......
Township 6, R. 15.	160	160	......	160	......
Township 1, R. 16.	71	71	......	71	......
Township 2, R. 16	70	70	......	70	......
Township 3, R. 16	37	37	......	37	......
Township 4, R. 16.	192	192	......	180	12
COVINGTON—Cont'd.					
Township 5, R. 16.	309	309	......	279	30
Township 6, R. 16.	448	448	......	371	77
Township 1, R. 17.	100	100	......	84	16
Township 2, R. 17.	106	106	......	105	1
Township 3, R. 17.	143	143	......	131	12
Township 4, R. 17.	147	147	......	144	3
Township 5, R. 17.	123	123	......	118	5
Township 6, R. 17.	643	643	......	566	77
Township 1, R. 18.	129	129	......	129	......
Township 2, R. 18	90	90	......	80	10
Township 3, R. 18.	127	127	......	127	......
Township 4, R. 18.	155	155	......	153	2
Township 5, R. 18.	61	61	......	61	......
DALE.					
1. Ozark	1720	1718	2	1383	337
2. Westville	1014	1014	......	726	288
3. Daleville......	997	997	......	738	259
4. Newton.......	640	640	......	531	109
5. Gilley's	400	400	......	388	12
6. Beaver Creek.	400	399	1	387	13
7. Reynolds	560	560	......	443	117
8. Sylvan Grove.	524	524	......	460	64
9. Echo..........	950	947	3	809	141
10. Cloptin	800	800	......	643	157
11. Skippersville .	1720	1720	......	1534	186
12. Barnes's Cross Roads	800	798	2	722	78
13. Rocky Head ..	830	800	......	764	36
DALLAS.					
Athens...........	3565	3557	8	361	3204
Belleview	1535	1533	2	110	1425
Burnsville........	1497	1491	6	155	*c*1341
Cahawba	1859	1833	26	258	1601
Cahawba	431	414	17	129	302
Carlowville.......	800	800	......	293	507
Dublin	707	706	1	481	226
Harrell's Cross Roads	3778	3771	7	430	3348
Lexington........	650	650	......	54	596
Old Town	983	974	9	318	665
Orrville	2124	2120	4	490	1634
Pencis............	942	941	1	145	797
Pine Flat.........	1558	1545	13	250	1308
Plantersville	854	854	......	409	445
Pleasant Hill.....	2003	1992	11	330	1673
Portland	1740	1731	9	205	1535
River.............	1457	1453	4	154	1303
Selma (*d*)	1651	1646	5	114	1537
Selma	6484	6183	301	2824	3660
Summerfield......	1467	1457	10	393	1074
Union	2949	2938	11	297	2652
Warrenton	1057	1046	11	246	811
Woodlawn........	1045	1045	......	325	720
DE KALB.					
Township 8, R. 5..	480	479	1	443	37
Township 9, R. 5..	207	207	......	203	4
Township 6, R. 6..	80	80	......	80	......
Township 7, R. 6..	96	95	1	96	......
Township 9, R. 6..	160	160	......	152	8
Township 10, R. 6..	200	200	......	199	1
Township 6, R. 7..	160	160	......	160	......
Township 7, R. 7..	348	347	1	348	......
Township 8, R. 7..	480	479	1	445	35
Township 9, R. 7..	480	479	1	411	69
Township 5, R. 8..	158	158	......	158	......
Township 6, R. 8..	80	80	......	80	......
Township 7, R. 8..	707	706	1	646	61

(*a*) Exclusive of city of Tuscumbia.
(*b*) Also 6 Indians.
(*c*) Also 1 Indian.
(*d*) Exclusive of city of Selma.

TABLE IX.—*Population of Minor Civil Divisions, &c.—ALABAMA*—Continued.

Counties.	Total.	Nativity. Native.	Nativity. Foreign.	Race. White.	Race. Colored.
[CALHOUN?]—Cont'd.					
hip 8, R. 8.	371	371	......	319	52
hip 3, R. 9	53	53	......	53	......
hip 4, R. 9.	270	270	......	270	......
hip 5, R. 9	297	297	......	293	4
hip 6, R. 9	960	958	2	856	104
hip 7, R. 9.	306	305	1	274	32
hip 2, R. 10	61	61	......	61	......
hip 3, R. 10	40	40	......	40	......
hip 4, R. 10.	841	798	43	784	57
hip 6, R. 10.	291	290	1	285	6
[E]LMORE.					
leman	868	866	2	632	236
anahatchee.	1095	1095	......	992	103
llassee	2048	2039	9	1104	944
tchell's Mills	640	640	......	107	533
dtuck	1421	1421	......	928	493
ntral Institute	907	907	......	715	192
yokville ...	806	804	2	520	286
etumpka ...	3820	3788	32	1695	2125
Wetumpka	1137	1119	18	543	594
ntington ...	1317	1314	3	386	931
bison Sp'gs.	774	752	22	110	664
wn Creek ..	411	411	......	248	163
e Points ...	370	370	......	310	60
[ES]CAMBIA.					
's Spring ..	196	194	2	130	*a*26
ne	479	476	3	359	*b*117
ker's	967	964	3	662	305
ard	1087	1074	13	909	178
rton	1312	1295	17	987	325
[ET]OWAH.					
sden	2203	2171	32	1549	654
illipps's ...	477	477	......	341	136
nsas	481	481	......	407	74
ke's Bluff ..	1049	1047	2	867	182
l Play	327	327	......	241	86
rkey Town .	685	681	4	509	176
ck's	490	489	1	489	1
rdin's	445	445	......	443	2
lker's	524	524	......	480	44
ck Spring ..	372	371	1	325	47
te's	274	267	7	212	62
vell's	122	122	......	122	......
yne's	522	522	......	481	41
ss Roads ..	345	345	......	295	50
lard's	962	962	......	911	51
ra Spring ..	722	720	2	624	98
hip 12, R. 3 ..	109	109	......	105	4
[FAY]ETTE. (*)					
....	1173	1168	5	1008	165
's	411	411	......	371	40
....	286	286	......	201	85
....	389	388	1	339	50
n	252	252	......	179	73
l's	247	247	......	232	15
er	647	646	1	583	64
hips 13, 14 ..	135	135	......	108	27
hips 14	934	934	......	776	158

Counties.	Total.	Nativity. Native.	Nativity. Foreign.	Race. White.	Race. Colored.
FAYETTE (*)—Con.					
Townships 15	639	639	......	616	23
Townships 16	1070	1070	......	927	143
Townships 17	389	389	......	282	107
FRANKLIN.					
Burleson	1050	1050	......	970	80
Frankfort	1517	1517	......	1399	118
Frankfort	162	162	......	141	21
Mountain Springs.	820	818	2	631	189
Nauvoo	1289	1280	9	1168	121
Newburg	725	724	1	564	161
Pleasant Site	1053	1053	......	910	143
Russellville	1484	1481	3	983	501
Russellville ..	180	180	......	146	34
Tennent's	68	68	......	68	......
GENEVA.					
Townships 1	1629	1624	5	1472	157
Townships 2	1330	1328	2	1260	70
Geneva (*c*)	126	......	......	104	22
GREENE.					
Boligee	1770	1756	14	206	1564
Clinton	2224	2215	9	481	1743
Eutaw	1920	1890	30	429	1491
Forkland	2789	2786	3	331	2458
Knoxville	1032	1030	2	390	642
Mantua	1598	1597	1	660	938
Mount Hebron ...	2049	2048	1	242	1807
Pleasant Ridge ...	1547	1545	2	328	1219
Springfield	915	911	4	166	749
Tishabee, or Garrett's Shop	1440	1438	2	137	1303
Union	1115	1111	4	488	627
HALE.					
1. Havana	1440	1438	2	599	841
2. New Prospect.	1280	1253	27	292	988
3. Harrison	800	800	......	357	443
4. Greensboro ...	2400	2363	37	975	1425
Greensboro	1760	1724	36	788	972
5. Newbern	2400	2387	13	275	2125
6. Hollow Square	3360	3356	4	558	2802
7. Cedarville	1920	1912	8	146	1774
8. Macon	3426	3415	11	187	3239
9. Laneville	2560	2560	......	81	2479
10. Warren's Store	480	480	......	294	186
11. Five-Mile	766	766	......	626	140
12. Carthage	960	957	3	412	548
HENRY.					
1. Gordon	1823	1821	2	982	841
2. Chipola	732	732	......	707	25
3. Columbia	1382	1381	1	932	450
4. Hilson's	774	774	......	745	29
5. Roeville	890	890	......	713	177
6. Green's Mills .	816	815	1	459	357
7. Franklin	1040	1040	......	657	383
8. Abbeville	1267	1264	3	787	480
9. Woodhams ..	600	600	......	445	155
10. Brock's	663	662	1	509	154
11. Lawrenceville	1194	1194	......	659	535
12. Hilliardsville .	1867	1865	2	922	945
13. Saunders	1143	1142	1	1017	126

(*) Incomplete: the other principal civil divisions were not separately returned.
(*a*) Also 40 Indians.
(*b*) Also 3 Indians.
(*c*) Its township not ascertained.

TABLE IX.—*Population of Minor Civil Divisions, &c.*—*ALABAMA*—Continued.

Counties.	Total.	Nativity. Native.	Nativity. Foreign.	Race. White.	Race. Colored.
JACKSON.					
1. Bridgeport	1002	1000	2	919	83
3. Stevenson (a)	1348	1338	10	907	441
4. Carpenter	903	889	14	857	46
5. Kaskes	729	728	1	665	64
6. Fackler's Sta'n	760	756	4	547	213
7. Pleasant Grove	730	730	......	472	258
8. Cave Spring	378	378	......	316	62
9. Allison's Mills	564	562	2	493	71
10. Bellefonte	957	955	2	692	265
Bellefonte	72	72	......	45	27
11. Hawk's Spring	386	386	......	385	1
12. Coffee Town	640	640	......	587	53
13. Berry's Store	660	658	2	557	103
14. Larkinsville	2098	2098	......	1614	484
15. Perry's	621	621	......	560	61
16. Woodville	993	992	1	856	137
17. Nashville	557	557	......	474	83
18. Collins	1520	1520	......	1490	30
19. Trice's	709	709	......	639	70
20. Kyle's Spring	467	467	......	386	81
21. Scottsboro	1443	1436	7	1297	146
Scottsboro	357	350	7	309	48
22. Sanders's	158	158	......	158	......
23. Paint Rock	1502	1500	2	1194	308
24. Kirby's Mill	285	285	......	285	......
JEFFERSON.					
Town. 15, R. 1 E	426	426	......	396	30
Town. 16, R. 1 E	273	272	1	213	60
Town. 17, R. 1 E	260	260	......	208	52
Town. 15, R. 1 W	717	716	1	597	120
Town. 16, R. 1 W	698	698	......	549	149
Town. 17, R. 1 W	297	296	1	271	26
Town. 18, R. 1 W	246	246	......	218	28
Town. 14, R. 2 W	303	303	......	291	12
Town. 15, R. 2 W	301	301	......	274	27
Town. 16, R. 2 W	456	456	......	253	203
Town. 17, R. 2 W	923	920	3	545	378
Town. 18, R. 2 W	47	46	1	31	16
Town. 14, R. 3 W	378	378	......	372	6
Town. 15, R. 3 W	255	255	......	254	1
Town. 16, R. 2 W	179	179	......	169	10
Town. 17, R. 3 W	438	432	6	207	231
Town. 18, R. 3 W	1055	1043	12	661	394
Town. 19, R. 3 W	42	42	......	36	6
Town. 20, R. 3 W	196	196	......	175	21
Town. 14, R. 4 W	101	101	......	96	5
Town. 15, R. 4 W	395	393	......	388	7
Town. 16, R. 4 W	188	188	......	171	17
Town. 17, R. 4 W	551	551	......	534	17
Town. 18, R. 4 W	274	274	......	169	105
Town. 19, R. 4 W	533	531	2	288	245
Town. 20, R. 4 W	339	339	......	289	50
Town. 15, R. 5 W	139	139	......	138	1
Town. 16, R. 5 W	232	232	......	232	......
Town. 17, R. 5 W	130	130	......	130	......
Town. 18, R. 5 W	319	319	......	315	4
Town. 19, R. 5 W	281	281	......	159	122
Town. 20, R. 5 W	358	355	3	278	80
Town. 16, R. 6 W	103	103	......	99	4
Town. 17, R. 6 W	222	221	1	221	1
Town. 18, R. 6 W	241	241	......	219	22
Town. 19, R. 6 W	290	290	......	251	39
Town. 18, R. 7 W	159	159	......	149	10
LAUDERDALE.					
1. Florence	2528	2464	64	1393	1135
Florence	2003	1947	56	1118	885
2. Center Star	1627	1624	3	1086	541
3. Ingram Cross R.	511	511	......	433	78
LAUDERDALE—C'd.					
4. Rogersville	1501	1501	......	961	[illegible]
Rogersville	435	435	......	277	158
5. Stutt's	1028	1022	6	978	50
6. Lexington	1236	1235	1	1205	31
7. Waterloo	1186	1184	2	1027	159
8. Blackburn's	672	669	3	563	[illegible]
9. Raw Hide	757	757	......	631	126
10. Oakland	2887	2877	10	902	[illegible]
11. Gravelly Sp'gs	862	862	......	421	441
12. Spain's	296	296	......	285	11
LAWRENCE.					
1. Hillsboro	1863	1858	5	1031	832
2. Courtland	2553	2533	20	912	1641
3. Jonesboro	1087	1087	......	502	585
4. Brickville	656	654	2	346	310
5. Landersville	631	631	......	448	183
6. Mount Hope	1077	1077	......	819	258
7. Moulton	2006	1995	11	1515	491
8. Pin Hook	407	404	3	354	53
9. Oakville	1709	1708	1	1486	[illegible]
10. Mountain Sp'ng	228	228	......	226	2
11. Leighton	1283	1280	3	502	781
12. Avoca	936	936	......	684	[illegible]
13. Wolf Spring	601	600	1	561	40
14. Kinlock	1621	1619	2	500	[illegible]
LEE.					
1. Beulah	1299	1298	1	849	450
2. Opelika	5085	5072	13	2515	2570
5. Loochapoka	3456	3453	3	1254	[illegible]
6. Auburn	3822	3806	16	1490	[illegible]
Auburn	1018	1016	2	273	745
7. Providence Ch.	382	382	......	303	79
8. Salem	2963	2961	2	1356	b[illegible]
9. White's School-house	120	120	......	96	24
10. Brownsville	1425	1413	12	838	[illegible]
10. Whitten's	2019	2009	10	771	[illegible]
11. Wacoochee	1179	1178	1	682	497
LIMESTONE.					
1. Athens	2618	2603	15	1024	1594
Athens	887	874	13	549	338
2. Shoalford	1536	1528	8	681	855
3. Sand Springs	588	588	......	543	45
4. Pettusville	1659	1658	1	947	712
5. Legg's	1216	1213	3	690	[illegible]
6. Wickham	882	882	......	792	90
7. Pleasant Grove	649	648	1	598	51
8. Big Creek	1140	1137	3	621	519
9. Georgia	958	956	2	693	265
10. Slough	1468	1461	7	501	967
11. Mooresville	2303	2299	4	674	1629
Mooresville	165	165	......	117	48
LOWNDES.					
1. Haynesville	3484	3465	19	507	2977
2. Lowndesboro	4882	4862	20	472	4410
3. Benton	2627	2616	11	401	[illegible]
4. Colorine	2951	2936	15	565	2386
5. Farmersville	1116	1115	1	272	844
6. Bragg's Store	1035	1034	1	522	513
7. Mount Willing	2125	2119	6	415	1710
8. Calhoun	2781	2775	6	848	1933
9. Letohatchee	2538	2532	6	319	2219
10. Sandy Ridge	2180	2179	1	765	1415

(a) Beat No. 2 annexed to beat No. 3. (b) Also 2 Indians.

TABLE IX.—*Population of Minor Civil Divisions, &c.—ALABAMA*—Continued.

Counties.	Total.	Nativity. Native.	Nativity. Foreign.	Race. White.	Race. Colored.
MACON.					
1. Tuskegee	4392	4359	33	1481	2911
2. Texas	598	598	......	347	251
3. Society Hill	1185	1185	......	422	763
4. Warrior Stand	2179	2179	......	426	1753
9. Cotton Valley	2120	2120	......	224	1896
10. Honey Cut	1708	1706	2	186	1522
11. Cross Keys	2560	2556	4	478	a2078
12. Franklin	1294	1288	6	617	677
13. Notasulga	1691	1686	5	922	769
MADISON.					
Cluttsville	1311	1310	1	563	748
Collier's Store	933	932	1	635	298
Cross Roads	336	334	2	210	126
Huntsville (b)	3511	3484	27	1387	2124
Huntsville	4907	4741	166	2532	2375
Kelly's Mills	1525	1524	1	1123	402
Madison Station	1647	1643	4	731	916
Maysville	2682	2672	10	1803	879
Meridianville	3842	3839	3	1609	2233
New Market	2825	2817	8	1685	1140
Poplar Ridge	611	611	......	492	119
Triana	2540	2538	2	334	2206
Vienna	1660	1658	2	1463	197
Whitesburg	2937	2920	17	960	1977
MARENGO.					
Dayton	6731	6726	5	615	6116
Dayton	426	423	3	185	241
Demopolis	4245	4174	71	730	3515
Demopolis	1539	1475	64	574	965
Dixon Mills	1000	994	6	533	c466
Dixon Mills	120	120	......	40	80
Hampden	742	742	......	284	458
Hampden	40	40	......	4	36
Hill's	756	754	2	313	443
Horse Creek	1337	1335	2	665	c671
Jefferson	2445	2430	15	400	2045
Jefferson	233	233	......	90	143
Linden	1927	1926	1	387	1540
Linden	300	300	......	147	153
McKinley	1481	1478	3	344	1137
Nanafalia	724	723	1	403	321
Pineville	400	400	......	221	179
Shiloh	1391	1390	1	747	c643
Spring Hill	2972	2963	9	448	2524
MARION. (*)					
8. Allen's Factory	587	586	1	562	25
9. Wylie's	400	400	......	375	25
MARSHALL.					
1.	822	817	5	688	134
2.	470	470	......	462	8
3.	275	274	1	202	73
5.	506	506	......	495	11
6.	482	481	1	417	65
7. Claysville	827	827	......	557	270
MARSHALL—Con.					
8. Boshart	464	464	......	431	33
9. Kennamer's	412	412	......	366	46
10. Honeycomb	247	246	1	216	31
11. Paint Rock	471	469	2	296	175
12. Oleander	870	868	2	806	64
13. Board's Bluff	373	369	4	341	32
14. Warrenton	863	862	1	621	242
Warrenton	60	60	......	42	18
15. Red Hill	428	428	......	392	36
16.	353	353	......	353	......
17.	761	761	......	676	85
18.	613	613	......	612	1
19. Buckswort	390	390	......	382	8
Guntersville (d)	244	243	1	191	53
MOBILE.					
1.	3823	3649	174	2096	1727
2.	3334	3089	245	2189	1145
3.	2479	2213	266	1716	763
4.	2111	2072	39	788	e1314
5.	3627	3582	45	2137	1490
6.	946	828	118	584	362
7.	957	884	73	570	387
Mobile	32034	27795	4239	18115	13919
MONROE.					
1. Little River	748	746	2	280	f458
2. Claiborne	2245	2230	15	963	c1281
3. Monroeville	1597	1595	2	1000	597
4. Burnt Corn	959	958	1	347	g607
5. East	859	855	4	386	473
6. Ridge	1190	1188	2	608	582
7. McKinley	960	959	1	454	506
8. Bell's Landing	1310	1310	......	397	c912
9. Old Texas	1067	1063	4	418	649
10. Germany	1537	1536	1	525	1012
11. Pineville	853	853	......	632	221
12. Midway	889	887	2	615	274
MONTGOMERY.					
1.	2400	2398	2	1580	820
2.	6240	6239	1	2536	3704
3. Mount Meigs	3999	3993	6	356	3643
4. Court-House (h)	9194	9095	99	1093	8101
5. Exch'ge Hot'l (i)	1600	1587	13	183	1417
6. Rives	1800	1790	10	232	1568
7. Barnes's	3680	3674	6	280	3400
8. Robinson's R'ds	2639	2639	......	504	2135
9. Porter's	1564	1563	1	250	1314
Montgomery	10588	9802	786	5405	5183
MORGAN.					
1. Decatur	2821	2779	42	1358	1463
Decatur	671	648	23	419	252
2. Lane's	722	721	1	516	206
3. Danville	1159	1159	......	955	204
4. Gibson	1274	1273	1	1047	227
5. Falkville	1198	1186	12	1054	144

(*) Incomplete; the other principal civil divisions were not separately returned.
(a) Also 4 Indians.
(b) Exclusive of city of Huntsville.
(c) Also 1 Indian.
(d) Its beat not ascertained.
(e) Also 9 Indians.
(f) Also 10 Indians.
(g) Also 5 Indians.
(h) Exclusive of 3d, 4th, 5th, and part of the 6th wards of the city of Montgomery.
(i) Exclusive of 1st, 2d, and part of the 6th wards of the city of Montgomery.

TABLE IX.—*Population of Minor Civil Divisions, &c.*—*ALABAMA*—Continued.

Counties.	Total.	Nativity. Native.	Nativity. Foreign.	Race. White.	Race. Colored.
MORGAN—Cont'd.					
6. Weaver's Mill	494	494	......	486	8
7. Applegrove	1379	1342	37	1087	292
8. Valhermosa	1037	1030	7	752	285
9. Somerville	1786	1783	3	1282	504
Somerville	115	115	......	89	26
10. Hartsell's	317	315	2	292	25
PERRY.					
Township 16, R. 6	1695	1695	......	158	1537
Township 17, R. 6	2635	2614	21	439	2196
Uniontown	1444	1425	19	301	1143
Township 18, R. 6	1440	1439	1	66	1374
Township 19, R. 6	1343	1335	8	126	1217
Township 20, R. 6	1883	1881	2	491	1392
Township 19, R. 7	3605	3553	52	1576	2029
Marion	2646	2595	51	1191	1455
Township 20, R. 7	960	958	2	641	319
Township 21, R. 7	2117	2116	1	232	1885
Township 18, R. 8	1120	1119	1	113	1007
Township 19, R. 8	902	901	1	181	721
Township 20, R. 8	1119	1114	5	145	974
Township 21, R. 8	826	826	......	247	579
Township 18, R. 9	1232	1231	1	356	876
Township 19, R. 9	1098	1098	......	464	631
Township 20, R. 9	1049	1047	2	614	435
Township 21, R. 9	903	903	......	713	190
Township 19, R. 10	433	433	......	170	263
Heard's Beat	615	614	1	410	205
PICKENS.					
1. Shelton's	218	218	......	173	45
2. Palmetto	581	580	1	491	90
3. Vaile's	456	454	2	306	150
4. Providence	775	774	1	440	335
5. Henry's	589	589	......	367	222
6. Corr's	495	495	......	407	88
7. Reform	495	492	3	337	158
8. Beard's	446	446	......	268	178
9. Yorkville	1593	1589	4	764	829
10. Gordo	517	517	......	407	110
11. Bostick's	479	479	......	330	149
12. Spring Hill	942	942	......	416	526
13. Raleigh	476	473	3	334	142
14. Speed's Mill	198	198	......	148	50
15. Carrollton	1841	1839	2	986	855
16. Pickensville	1111	1106	5	433	678
17. King's Store	212	212	......	157	55
18. Olney	959	957	2	324	635
19. Bridgeville	1265	1265	......	269	996
20. Memphis	475	472	3	152	323
21. Vienna	1435	1433	2	304	1131
22. Fairfield	2132	2125	7	239	1893
PIKE.					
1. Troy	2650	2634	16	1887	763
Troy	1058	1044	14	818	240
2. Orion	1530	1529	1	1117	413
3. China Grove	1080	1080	......	583	497
4. Cross Roads	1120	1120	......	899	221
5. Monticello	569	569	......	500	69
6. Tan Yard	1440	1440	......	990	450
7. Dixon's	2240	2237	3	1641	599
8. Grimes's	1600	1596	4	1311	289
9. Darby's	1743	1738	5	1260	483
10. Goshen Hill	1268	1267	1	974	294
11. Mitchell's	1251	1251	......	927	324
12. Pleasant Hill	640	640	......	556	84
13. Linwood	292	291	1	153	139

Counties.	Total.	Nativity. Native.	Nativity. Foreign.	Race. White.	Race. Colored.
RANDOLPH.					
1. Saxon's	827	824	3	772	55
2. Morrison's	707	707	......	670	37
3. Rock Dale	624	624	......	570	54
4. Lamar	617	617	......	546	71
5. Barson's	1214	1214	......	1140	74
6. Wedowee	1791	1787	4	1479	312
Wedowee	130	129	1	122	8
7. Fox Creek	972	972	......	947	25
8. Flat Rock	901	901	......	803	98
9. Louina	1159	1158	1	826	333
10. Roanoke	1750	1749	1	1397	353
11. Rock Mill	929	927	2	795	134
12. Bacon Level	515	515	......	420	95
RUSSELL.					
Fort Mitchell	2032	2024	8	648	1384
Girard	3984	3956	28	1759	2225
Glenville	1712	1709	3	322	1390
Hogg Island	885	881	4	109	776
Hurtesville	1440	1438	2	316	1124
Hynes	1120	1120	......	407	713
North Carolina	720	718	2	194	526
Oswichee	1920	1919	1	198	1722
Silver Run	4305	4296	9	1368	2937
Traywick's	1280	1279	1	388	892
Uchee	2238	2233	5	337	1901
SANFORD.					
1. Town	1078	1076	2	930	148
2. Lawrence	537	537	......	478	59
3. Sizemore's	242	242	......	187	55
4. Brown's	459	459	......	452	7
5. Henson Spring	334	334	......	183	151
6. Millerville	504	504	......	440	64
7. Pine Spring	447	447	......	389	58
8. Moscow	855	854	1	630	225
9. Bett's	1048	1047	1	850	198
10. Trull's	712	710	2	452	260
11. Wilson's	957	956	1	882	75
12. Strickland's	658	658	......	595	63
13. Sheen's	567	566	1	498	69
14. Milport	495	492	3	358	137
SHELBY. (a)					
1. Montevallo	1276	1209	67	792	484
2. Johnson's	729	721	8	587	142
3. Elliottsville	501	500	1	367	134
4. Highland	657	657	......	521	136
5. Hillsboro	522	507	15	285	237
6. Mud Town	1228	1216	12	844	384
8. Columbiana	1040	1033	7	662	378
9. Wilsonville	560	559	1	269	291
10. Harpersville	1334	1325	9	662	672
11. Bear Creek	693	692	1	667	26
12. Upper Yellow Leaf	438	435	3	437	1
13. Camp Branch	637	636	1	587	50
14. Spring Creek	1183	1178	5	835	348
15. Tyler's	383	376	7	368	15
16. Bold Spring	537	537	......	483	54
17. Spearman's	500	499	1	464	36
ST. CLAIR. (b)					
1. Ashville	922	922	......	677	245
2. Free Chapel	873	872	1	654	219
3. Branchville	1419	1419	......	1306	113

(a) Beat No. 7 to Baker County.
(b) In 1866 precincts Nos. 6 and 7, St. Clair, annexed to Etowah County.

TABLE IX.—*Population of Minor Civil Divisions, &c.—ALABAMA*—Continued.

Counties.	Total.	Nativity. Native.	Nativity. Foreign.	Race. White.	Race. Colored.
ST. CLAIR—Cont'd.					
4. Springville	1080	1077	3	818	262
5. Benson's Store	305	305	......	279	26
8. Greensport	548	547	1	373	175
9. Trout Creek	933	933	......	840	93
10. Broken Arrow	760	760	......	664	96
11. Cropwell	1080	1080	......	764	316
12. Mondines	1440	1438	2	920	520
SUMTER.					
1. Black Bluff	640	636	4	200	440
2. Gaston	480	479	1	138	342
3. Rosserville	1154	1153	1	531	623
4. Earbees	520	520	......	192	328
5. Intercourse	440	438	2	169	271
6. Anville	410	408	2	78	332
7. Livingston	2320	2295	25	673	1647
Livingston	500	500	......	300	200
8. Brewersville	1520	1517	3	221	1299
9. Belmont	2916	2906	10	642	2274
10. Bluff Port	555	551	4	171	384
11. Jones's Bluff	2134	2130	4	231	1903
12. Sumterville	1577	1577	......	264	1313
13. Payneville	1405	1402	3	128	1277
14. Gainesville	3916	3889	27	667	3249
16. Preston	1562	1555	7	272	1290
18. Cuba	480	479	1	333	147
19. Warsaw	2080	2077	3	292	1788
TALLADEGA.					
1. Blue Eye	1414	1412	2	773	641
2. Eastaboga	973	967	6	383	590
3. Buckhorn	1614	1607	7	977	637
4. Chinabee	810	806	4	257	553
5. Talladega (*a*)	2640	2611	29	1198	1442
Talladega	1933	1897	36	920	1013
6. Mardisville	1357	1357	......	463	894
7. Cask's	737	734	3	511	226
8. Kymulger	1615	1615	......	593	1022
9. Riser's	1488	1486	2	500	988
10. Fayetteville	1337	1335	2	695	642
11. Syllacages	1034	1027	7	695	339
12. Childresburg	1112	1109	3	504	608
TALLAPOOSA.					
1. Gold Branch	680	679	1	497	183
2. Youngville	1680	1679	1	1281	399
3. Hackney	1755	1753	2	1306	449
4. Poplar Springs	638	636	2	612	26
5. New Site	800	798	2	711	89
6. Duffy's	1273	1272	1	1002	271
7. Dadeville	1266	1263	3	813	453
8. Oakfuska	417	417	......	355	62
9. Red Ridge	520	520	......	416	104
10. Eufaula	595	593	2	572	23
11. Walnut Hill	762	762	......	525	237
12. Reeltown	1200	1199	1	771	429
13. Kinderhook	800	800	......	617	183
14. Rome	1026	1026	......	576	450
15. Camp Hill	373	373	......	261	112
16. Dudleyville	1600	1599	1	1169	*b*430
17. Daviston	1578	1578	......	1288	290
TUSCALOOSA.					
1. Dunn's	556	555	1	516	40
2. New Lexington	557	557	......	424	133
TUSCAL'A—Cont'd.					
3. Moore's Bridge	556	556	......	518	38
4. Squire's Store	518	516	2	475	43
5. Aker's	367	367	......	335	32
6. Hassell's	355	355	......	302	53
7. Dodson's	924	923	1	597	327
8. Mrs. Bell's	304	303	1	287	17
9. Hugh's	637	635	2	505	132
10. Northport	2273	2261	12	1310	963
Northport	604	602	2	436	168
11. Faver's	467	467	......	398	69
12. McMath's	497	497	......	337	160
13. White's	715	691	24	545	170
14. Smith's	616	613	3	411	205
15. Kennedale	1262	1186	76	818	444
16. Tuscaloosa (*c*)	3340	3267	73	983	2357
Tuscaloosa	1689	1594	95	902	787
17. Hickman's	592	592	......	410	182
18. Frierson's	946	920	26	261	685
19. Blocker's	950	948	2	507	443
20. Crosland's	316	315	1	304	12
21. Romulus	540	539	1	312	228
22. Foster's Store	1104	1103	1	330	774
WALKER.					
Townships 12	662	661	1	639	23
Townships 13	1747	1747	......	1607	140
Townships 14	1942	1939	3	1871	71
Townships 15	1295	1292	3	1245	50
Townships 16	644	644	......	630	14
Townships 17	253	253	......	243	10
WASHINGTON.					
1. Lewis Creek	1250	1250	......	431	819
2. St. Stephens	1214	1208	6	685	529
3. Warrick's Mill	863	859	4	600	263
4. Escatawba	585	583	2	409	176
WILCOX.					
1. Camden	3060	3029	31	835	2225
2. Canton	1528	1526	2	263	1265
3. Rehoboth	1842	1840	2	284	1558
4. Prairie Bluff	2960	2952	8	272	2688
5. Clifton	1696	1695	1	348	1348
6. Bethel	2456	2452	4	600	1856
7. Lower Peach Tree	1831	1821	10	552	1279
8. Black's Bluff	1586	1583	3	281	1305
9. Allenton	1954	1944	10	418	1536
10. Bonham's	1709	1707	2	482	1227
11. Pine Apple	1960	1957	3	849	1111
12. Snow Hill	4115	4112	3	622	3493
13. Mims's	960	956	4	519	441
14. Fox Mills	720	717	3	442	278
WINSTON.					
1. Houston	498	......	......	......	......
2. Jones	299	......	......	......	......
3. Harville	365	......	......	......	......
4. Spiegle	493	......	......	......	......
5. Allen's	553	553	......	550	3
6. Black Swamp	632	632	......	631	1
7. Pond	411	411	......	408	3
8. Nesmith	380	......	......	......	......
9. Sandy	302	301	1	300	2
10. Looney's Tav'n	222	......	......	......	......

(*a*) Exclusive of city of Talladega.
(*b*) Also 1 Indian.
(*c*) Exclusive of city of Tuscaloosa.

TABLE IX.—*Population of Minor Civil Divisions, &c.*—*ARIZONA.*

Counties.	Total.	Nativity. Native.	Nativity. Foreign.	Race. White.	Race. Colored.
MOHAVE.					
Hardyville	20	20	.....	18	2
Mohave City	159	102	57	157	2
PIMA. (a)					
Adamsville	400	54	346	400	.....
Apache Pass	400	175	225	400	.....
Calabasas	62	16	46	62	.....
Casa Blanca	52	24	28	49	1
Cerro Colorado	58	9	49	58	.....
Crittenden, (camp)	215	100	115	215	.....
Florence	218	77	141	216	1
Goodwin, (camp)	200	82	118	200	.....
Grant, (camp)	340	148	192	340	.....
Maricopa Wells	68	39	29	66	1
Rieletto	32	9	23	32	.....
Saguano	71	9	62	71	.....
San Pedro	80	17	63	80	.....
San Xavier	118	60	58	116	.....
Tubac	178	55	123	178	.....
Tucson	3224	1026	2198	3215	9
YAVAPAI. (b)					
Big Bug, Woolsey Valley, & Lower Lynx Creek	96	66	30	96	.....
YAVAPAI—Cont'd.					
Camp Toll Gate & Walnut Creek	107	46	61	107	.....
China Valley and Lower Granite Creek	80	63	17	79	.....
Date Creek, Kirkland, and Skull Valleys	90	62	28	89	.....
People's Valley and vicinity	45	18	27	45	.....
Prescott	668	462	206	657	4
Rio Verdo	174	81	93	174	.....
Salt River Valley	240	98	142	235	3
Vulture City	155	70	85	149	1
Vulture Mine	113	32	81	112	.....
Walnut Grove	40	28	12	40	.....
Wickenburg	174	65	109	174	.....
Williamson's Valley	160	117	43	159	.....
YUMA. (c)					
Arizona City	1144	449	695	1121	1
Ehrenberg	223	81	142	219	.....
La Paz	251	89	165	[illegible]	1

(a) Pima County: Casa Blanca also includes 2 Indians; Florence, 1 Indian; Maricopa Wells, 1 Indian; San Xavier, 2 Indians.

(b) Yavapai County: China Valley and Lower Granite Creek also includes 1 Indian; Date Creek, Kirkland, and Skull Valleys, 1 Chinese; Prescott, 2 Indians and 5 Chinese; Salt River Valley, 2 Indians; Vulture City, 5 Chinese; Vulture Mine, 1 Chinese; Williamson's Valley, 1 Indian.

(c) Yuma County: Arizona City also includes 15 Indians and 7 Chinese; Ehrenberg, 3 Indians and 1 Chinese; La Paz, 1 Indian.

TABLE IX.—*Population of Minor Civil Divisions, &c.*—*ARKANSAS.*

NOTE.—The marginal column marks townships; the first indentation, cities; the second, towns. Names of towns are placed under the names of the townships in which they are respectively situated. The population of each township includes that of all towns situated in it.

Counties.	Total.	Nativity. Native.	Nativity. Foreign.	Race. White.	Race. Colored.
ARKANSAS.					
Arkansas	683	674	9	429	a253
Bayou Metor	306	306	.....	296	10
Choctaw	860	825	35	258	b572
Crockett	637	633	4	455	182
Cr'kett's Bluff	37	35	2	27	10
Cypress Bayou	318	316	2	303	15
Douglas	760	747	13	85	c663
Kimbrough	611	595	16	138	d463
La Greux	355	348	7	339	16
Old River	981	974	7	282	699
Polk	613	605	8	376	237
Prairie	1035	1030	5	786	249
ARKANSAS—Cont'd.					
Silver Lake	702	680	22	97	e584
Villemont	407	404	3	138	269
ASHLEY.					
Bear House	525	525	.....	424	101
Beech Creek	269	269	.....	186	83
Carter	960	948	12	715	245
De Bastrop	1386	1369	17	488	898
Egypt	513	512	1	387	126
Extra	603	600	3	363	240
Longview	432	429	3	276	156

(a) Also 1 Chinese.
(b) Also 30 Chinese.
(c) Also 12 Chinese.
(d) Also 10 Chinese.
(e) Also 21 Chinese.

BLE IX.—*Population of Minor Civil Divisions, &c.—ARKANSAS*—Continued.

nties.	Total.	Nativity. Native.	Nativity. Foreign.	Race. White.	Race. Colored.
—Cont'd.					
line	450	444	6	235	215
ek	998	998	......	421	577
	984	978	6	280	704
	480	478	2	183	297
	442	441	1	320	122
TON.					
	1701	1695	6	1689	a11
	5384	5370	14	5319	65
rairie	3443	3426	17	3377	b58
eek	1988	1979	9	1980	8
iver	1315	1312	3	1275	40
ONE.					
ek	314	313	1	312	2
n	577	577	......	577	......
Creek	646	644	2	644	2
	826	818	8	807	19
	320	320	......	315	5
	1649	1648	1	1618	31
ek	214	214	......	214	......
	1214	1212	2	1204	10
af	827	827	......	825	2
ton	445	445	......	442	3
LEY.					
	630	628	2	377	253
	255	255	......	168	87
e	689	688	1	621	68
	248	248	......	216	32
	889	882	7	621	268
	311	311	......	229	82
	718	715	3	571	147
	656	654	2	302	354
ou	1806	1802	4	1315	491
l	997	996	1	696	301
	792	790	2	499	293
ton	655	655	......	502	153
OUN.					
	220	220	......	178	42
nolle	505	502	3	240	265
	383	383	......	276	107
	220	220	......	180	40
	438	436	2	303	135
	153	153	......	151	2
	365	364	1	244	121
	194	193	1	171	23
ayou	608	607	1	447	161
pton	138	138	......	118	20
	481	481	......	333	148
	286	286	......	230	56
OLL.					
n	808	808	......	791	17
lton	113	113	......	112	1
ek	511	507	4	505	6
	660	660	......	660	......
ver	686	684	2	686	......
	253	253	......	252	1
ek	452	451	1	448	4
	842	842	......	839	3
	1368	1366	2	1362	6
OT.					
con	753	747	6	308	445
	207	205	2	123	84

Counties.	Total.	Nativity. Native.	Nativity. Foreign.	Race. White.	Race. Colored.
CHICOT—Cont'd.					
Franklin	344	315	29	156	188
Louisiana	1059	1041	18	123	936
Masona	215	209	6	92	c118
McConnell	1773	1734	39	352	1421
Oden	1523	1480	43	216	1306
Planter	332	329	3	196	136
Rail Road	1008	994	14	248	760
CLARKE.					
Alpine	828	828	......	789	39
Anderson	504	504	......	312	192
Antoine	1835	1827	8	1320	515
Arkadelphia	948	940	8	680	268
Beech Creek	448	448	......	302	146
Caddo	2717	2711	6	1518	1199
Cedar	897	897	......	861	36
Cold Bath	645	645	......	632	13
Elkins	584	583	1	377	207
Greenville	749	749	......	614	135
Manchester	770	769	1	279	491
Missouri	502	502	......	342	160
South Fork	898	897	1	581	317
Terre Noire	576	575	1	534	42
COLUMBIA.					
Alabama	866	863	3	668	198
Boone	827	825	2	520	307
Brown	1090	1090	......	608	482
Buena Vista	538	538	......	439	99
Calhoun	806	805	1	609	197
Clay	357	357	......	222	135
Cornio	413	413	......	309	104
Georgia	783	779	4	541	242
Harrison	960	955	5	637	323
Magnolia	1946	1944	2	1164	782
Magnolia	259	257	2	207	52
Mississippi	829	828	1	515	314
Moss	346	346	......	307	39
Smith	282	282	......	239	43
Taylor	830	830	......	463	367
Warren	524	523	1	438	86
CONWAY.					
Benton	583	583	......	564	19
Cadron	502	483	19	457	45
East Fork	410	408	2	387	23
Griffin	458	457	1	456	2
Hardin	730	729	1	703	27
Howard	745	740	5	542	203
Lick Mountain	518	516	2	515	3
Muddy Bayou	583	580	3	570	13
Newton	514	506	8	513	1
Union	1085	1081	4	1079	6
Walker	222	222	......	222	......
Washington	487	487	......	486	1
Welborn	1275	1253	22	988	287
Lewisburg	239	225	14	199	40
CRAIGHEAD.					
Big Creek	487	487	......	485	2
Buffalo	221	220	1	204	17
Jonesboro	2094	2092	2	1991	103
Jonesboro	155	155	......	141	14
Mamelle	496	494	2	404	92
Powell	1098	1098	......	1076	22
Texas	181	180	1	164	17

(a) Also 1 Indian. (b) Also 8 Indians. (c) Also 5 Chinese.

TABLE IX.—*Population of Minor Civil Divisions, &c.*—*ARKANSAS*—Continued.

Counties.	Total.	Nativity. Native.	Nativity. Foreign.	Race. White.	Race. Colored.
CRAWFORD.					
Cedar Creek	952	950	2	936	16
Jasper	688	686	2	688	......
Lafayette	902	902	......	899	3
Lee Creek	654	646	8	614	40
Mountain	508	508	......	504	4
Richland	927	923	4	816	111
Shepard	335	334	1	335	......
Upper	357	357	......	335	22
Van Buren	3296	3223	73	2521	*a*768
Van Buren	985	948	37	695	*b*285
Vine Prairie	338	338	......	313	*d*24
CRITTENDEN.					
Council	312	307	5	165	147
Edmonson	160	158	2	15	145
Hopefield	157	152	5	99	58
Jackson	316	311	5	218	98
Jasper	1416	1406	10	333	*c*1080
Lucas	190	190	......	38	152
Proctor	650	647	3	127	523
Tyranga	150	149	1	124	26
Walnut Grove	160	155	5	100	60
Wappanocca	320	320	......	34	286
CROSS.					
Bedford	319	318	1	280	39
Brushy Lake	313	312	1	300	13
Mitchell	670	663	7	424	246
Searcy	1018	1013	5	593	425
Smith	1515	1508	7	975	540
Wittsburg	113	109	4	101	12
Tyrongia	80	80	......	54	26
DALLAS.					
Chester	510	510	......	343	167
Holly Springs	636	635	1	511	125
Jackson	637	637	......	516	121
Manchester	574	573	1	404	170
Owens	690	689	1	408	282
Princeton	1142	1138	4	726	416
Saline	488	487	1	461	27
Smith	1030	1029	1	587	443
DESHA.					
Chester	260	250	10	206	54
Island	400	389	11	112	288
Jefferson	773	768	5	382	391
Mississippi	1600	1570	30	340	*d*1259
Red Fork	2078	2037	41	577	*e*1496
Richland	445	365	80	306	139
Wilkinson	569	546	23	262	307
DREW.					
Bartholomew	560	556	4	295	265
Bear House	458	457	1	384	74
Beauregard	598	598	......	292	306
Clear Creek	776	774	2	562	214
Collins	463	460	3	238	225
Ferguson	400	400	......	126	274
Franklin	567	567	......	469	98
Marion	2100	2088	12	1001	1099
Mill Creek	808	808	......	717	91
Prairie	266	266	......	219	47
Salem	677	676	1	374	303
Smith	502	501	1	479	23
Spring Hill	1128	1125	3	546	582
Veasey	657	657	......	404	253

Counties.	Total.	Nativity. Native.	Nativity. Foreign.	Race. White.	Race. Colored.
FRANKLIN.					
Boston	289	288	1	288	1
Limestone	240	240	......	236	4
Lower	960	956	4	638	322
Roseville	92	91	1	89	3
Middle	840	840	......	677	163
Mill Creek	883	871	12	861	22
Mulberry	1280	1274	6	1261	19
Prairie	1440	1422	18	1387	53
Short Mountain	375	374	1	358	17
Six Mile	880	880	......	877	3
White Oak	2160	2145	15	2122	37
Ozark	210	206	4	201	9
White Rock	280	279	1	280	......
FULTON.					
Bennett's Bayou	427	424	3	427	......
Benton	461	461	......	458	3
Big Creek	535	534	1	535	......
Big North Fork	473	473	......	442	31
Big Spring	228	228	......	222	6
Franklin	580	580	......	548	32
Myatt	516	515	1	516	......
Pleasant Ridge	330	330	......	328	2
South Fork	518	518	......	510	8
Union	775	775	......	772	3
GRANT.					
Calvert	476	476	......	403	73
Darysaw	357	355	2	339	18
Davis	578	577	1	476	102
De Kalb	529	529	......	476	53
Fenter	173	173	......	172	1
Franklin	298	298	......	298	......
Madison	635	635	......	580	55
Merry Green	278	278	......	275	3
Simpson	311	309	2	308	3
Tennessee	308	307	1	277	31
GREENE.					
Black River	131	131	......	131	......
Bradshaw	535	535	......	533	2
Cache	766	766	......	731	35
Chalk Bluff	1030	1029	1	1024	6
Clark	500	499	1	488	12
Concord	960	959	1	937	23
Friendship	394	394	......	392	2
Hurricane	385	385	......	382	3
Johnson	683	683	......	678	5
Salem	676	676	......	670	6
St. Francis	970	970	......	929	41
Union	543	543	......	522	21
HEMPSTEAD.					
Bois d'Arc	632	628	4	201	431
Mine Creek	2560	2559	1	1414	1116
Missouri	1267	1265	2	889	378
Ozan	4405	4386	19	1708	2697
Redland	960	958	2	805	155
Saline	1265	1265	......	522	743
Spring Hill	1240	1235	5	780	460
Terre Rouge	1439	1437	2	1090	349
HOT SPRINGS.					
Antioch	320	320	......	307	13
Big Creek	158	157	1	158	......

(*a*) Also 7 Indians.
(*b*) Also 5 Indians.
(*c*) Also 3 Indians.
(*d*) Also 1 Indian.
(*e*) Also 3 Chinese.

TABLE IX.—*Population of Minor Civil Divisions, &c.—ARKANSAS*—Continued.

Counties.	Total.	Nativity. Native.	Nativity. Foreign.	Race. White.	Race. Colored.
PRINGS—C'd.					
Creek	231	231	.....	209	22
r	1057	1051	6	916	141
prings	1604	1566	38	1289	315
ot Springs	1276	1241	35	980	296
ita	542	541	1	482	a59
ps	239	239	.....	238	1
e Bayou	859	858	1	780	79
	444	442	2	431	13
	423	423	.....	416	7
PENDENCE.					
y	702	701	1	693	9
n	887	887	.....	880	7
ottom	938	935	3	836	102
River	1358	1356	2	1332	26
	177	176	1	158	19
ian	1327	1326	1	1229	98
iow	243	242	1	238	5
lin	559	558	1	544	15
sboro	618	617	1	617	1
Brier	1369	1366	3	1234	135
ng Springs	320	320	.....	320	.....
son	777	777	.....	744	33
ty	455	454	1	451	4
le	1656	1634	22	1340	316
atesville	881	862	19	647	234
	531	531	.....	528	3
ce	308	307	1	308	.....
ington	869	866	3	809	60
River	1472	1468	4	1397	75
IZARD.					
Mountain	454	454	.....	454	.....
	275	275	.....	274	1
ay	768	768	.....	736	32
lin	660	659	1	626	34
s	122	121	1	117	5
reek	897	896	1	893	4
Fork	454	452	2	454	.....
wood	280	280	.....	279	1
y Bayou	720	719	1	696	24
nore	400	398	2	399	1
Rock	257	255	2	223	34
	1153	1153	.....	1148	5
River	366	366	.....	325	41
ACKSON.					
n	290	289	1	284	6
	1313	1311	2	1108	205
enridge	694	693	1	499	195
	377	377	.....	309	68
Lake	189	189	.....	182	7
l Glaize	447	445	2	379	68
son	1976	1937	39	1342	634
acksonport	769	739	30	552	217
Woods	261	261	.....	260	1
	1061	1057	4	692	369
	660	658	2	601	59
FFERSON.					
an	615	613	2	297	318
olomew	459	459	.....	240	219
	1321	1308	13	158	b1160
ar	1732	1706	26	654	c1073
y Lake	292	292	.....	86	206
n	800	798	2	332	468
Bayou	1597	1592	5	360	1237
and	933	918	15	247	686

(a) Also 1 Indian.
(b) Also 3 Chinese.

Counties.	Total.	Nativity. Native.	Nativity. Foreign.	Race. White.	Race. Colored.
JEFFERSON—Co'd.					
Spring	406	405	1	296	110
Talladega	526	523	3	329	197
Vaughn	4735	4550	185	1614	d3119
Pine Bluff	2081	1902	179	1279	d800
Victoria	1263	1256	7	102	1161
Washington	231	228	3	200	31
White Oak	210	209	1	210	.....
Whiteville	613	612	1	431	182
JOHNSON.					
Clark	1399	1399	.....	1314	85
Grant	960	956	4	853	107
Horsehead	995	992	3	971	24
Mountain	296	294	2	278	18
Mulberry	341	341	.....	341	.....
Perry	495	493	2	474	21
Pilot Rock	164	164	.....	164	.....
Piney	176	175	1	175	1
Pittsburg	959	953	6	848	111
Sherman	107	107	.....	107	.....
Shoal Creek	1355	1348	7	1225	130
Spadra	1905	1889	16	1789	116
Clarksville	466	459	7	413	53
LAFAYETTE.					
Beech	984	984	.....	690	294
La Grange	2784	2775	9	850	1934
Red River	2131	2129	2	622	1509
Roane	1150	1143	7	486	664
Sulphur Fork	1570	1563	7	1070	500
Walker Creek	520	518	2	263	257
LAWRENCE.					
Ashland	147	147	.....	139	8
Black River	1189	1182	7	1147	42
Cache	128	128	.....	114	14
Campbell	576	576	.....	568	8
Duty	573	572	1	522	51
Lawrence	244	244	.....	244	.....
Marion	440	439	1	426	14
Reed's Creek	811	810	1	796	15
Spring River	729	729	.....	720	9
Strawberry	1144	1143	1	1059	85
Smithville	126	126	.....	116	10
LITTLE RIVER.					
Franklin	388	388	.....	169	219
Jackson	820	807	13	358	462
Johnson	274	272	2	82	192
Lick Creek	361	358	3	231	130
Little River	160	160	.....	125	35
Red River	1233	1231	2	393	840
MADISON.					
Bowen	1023	1023	.....	999	24
California	313	313	.....	299	14
Hilburn	424	424	.....	404	20
King's River	958	958	.....	946	12
Kingston	65	65	.....	65	.....
Marble	338	337	1	335	3
Piney	270	270	.....	270	.....
Prairie	1251	1249	2	1247	4
Richland	1362	1362	.....	1338	24
Valley	743	742	1	736	7
War Eagle	1465	1465	.....	1423	42
Huntsville	224	224	.....	205	19
Wharton's Creek	84	84	.....	84	.....

(c) Also 5 Chinese.
(d) Also 2 Chinese.

TABLE IX.—*Population of Minor Civil Divisions, &c.—ARKANSAS*—Continued.

Counties.	Total.	Nativity. Native.	Nativity. Foreign.	Race. White.	Race. Colored.
MARION.					
Barren Creek	320	320	......	320	......
Blythe	190	190	......	190	......
Buffalo	268	267	1	268	......
Flippen Barren	330	330	......	330	......
Hampton	217	217	......	216	1
Independence	226	226	......	226	......
James's Creek	183	183	......	182	1
Little North Fork	303	303	......	299	4
Rapp's Barren	480	480	......	477	3
Sugar Loaf	130	130	......	130	......
Union	998	997	1	988	10
Yellville	96	96	......	96	......
Whiteville	314	313	1	314	......
MISSISSIPPI.					
Big Lake	211	211	......	205	6
Canadian	330	326	4	242	88
Carson Lake	74	74	......	71	3
Chickasauba	448	446	2	410	38
Clear Lake	126	123	3	125	1
Little River	54	54	......	54	......
Monroe	1133	1123	10	736	397
Pecan	155	153	2	150	5
Scott	659	649	10	478	181
Swayne	93	89	4	81	12
Troy	350	347	3	110	240
MONROE.					
Cache	1452	1433	19	1057	395
Cypress	655	652	3	479	176
Duncan	1334	1323	11	586	748
Eve	297	271	26	281	16
Hampton	794	790	4	697	97
Hickory Ridge	778	770	8	587	a190
Jackson	784	784	......	402	382
Montgomery	1123	1109	14	313	810
Plain	220	217	3	184	36
Richland	899	894	5	549	350
MONTGOMERY.					
Big Fork	206	206	......	202	4
Caddo	234	234	......	234	......
Gap	528	527	1	493	35
Mazarne	387	387	......	387	......
Mountain	509	509	......	462	47
Polk	304	304	......	304	......
South Fork	624	620	4	599	25
Sulphur Springs	192	192	......	183	9
NEWTON.					
Boston	109	109	......	109	......
Jackson	850	849	1	850	......
Jasper	72	72	......	72	......
Jefferson	334	332	2	334	......
Mill Creek	313	313	......	313	......
Osage	248	247	1	248	......
Pleasant Hill	352	352	......	352	......
Polk	369	369	......	366	3
Prairie	501	500	1	500	1
Richland	161	159	2	161	......
Union	203	203	......	202	1
Van Buren	319	318	1	317	2
White	615	615	......	613	2
OUACHITA.					
Sebastian	306	305	1	284	22
Bridge Creek	375	374	1	214	161
Caney	845	845	......	760	85
Carouse	528	528	......	374	154
Carroll	713	713	......	212	501
Ecore Fabre	2325	2246	79	1184	b1138
Camden	1612	1537	75	998	c612
Freeo	868	868	......	392	476
Fremont	242	242	......	131	111
Jackson	580	580	......	299	281
Jefferson	782	782	......	406	a374
Lafayette	1131	1124	7	617	514
Liberty	908	906	2	392	a515
Marion	643	642	1	414	229
Missouri	720	719	1	555	165
Red Hill	476	476	......	388	88
Smackover	660	659	1	276	384
Union	382	382	......	315	67
Washington	401	400	1	271	130
PERRY.					
Aplin	439	436	3	357	82
Bentley	345	341	4	341	4
Cossa	240	237	3	240	......
Fourche Lefave	403	400	3	365	38
Higgins	292	288	4	273	19
McCool	131	131	......	131	......
Perry	366	361	5	219	147
Petite Jean	228	228	......	228	......
Rose Creek	241	241	......	241	......
PHILLIPS.					
Bear Creek	170	170	......	50	120
Big Creek	1699	1674	25	680	1019
Independence	638	631	7	290	348
L'Anguille	800	788	12	295	505
Marion	735	728	7	545	190
Mooney	300	294	6	187	113
Planter's	1102	1095	7	165	937
Richland	1929	1915	14	631	1298
Lagrange	62	......	......	......	......
Searcy	1375	1363	12	177	1198
Spring Creek	1563	1554	9	581	982
St. Francis	5061	4873	188	1370	3691
Helena	2249	2098	151	1140	1109
PIKE.					
Antoine	238	238	......	238	......
Brewer	597	597	......	493	104
Caney Fork	199	198	1	157	42
Missouri	770	769	1	676	94
Mountain	238	238	......	236	2
Muddy Fork	477	477	......	405	72
Thompson	868	865	3	782	86
White	401	401	......	380	21
POINSETT.					
Bolivar	867	861	6	794	a72
Greenfield	261	261	......	252	9
Scott	592	591	1	448	144
POLK.					
Big Fork	274	274	......	272	2
Centre	614	614	......	598	16
Cove	456	456	......	447	9
Freedom	257	257	......	245	d4

(*a*) Also 1 Indian.
(*b*) Also 3 Indians.
(*c*) Also 2 Indians.
(*d*) Also 8 Indians.

TABLE IX.—*Population of Minor Civil Divisions, &c.—ARKANSAS*—Continued.

Counties.	Total.	Nativity.		Race.	
		Native.	Foreign.	White.	Colored.
POLK—Continued.					
Fulton	196	195	1	196	.....
Mountain	281	281	.....	281	.....
Ouachita	237	237	.....	233	4
Sulphur Springs	768	766	2	758	10
White	293	292	1	293	.....
POPE.					
Allen	225	225	.....	225	.....
Clark	966	952	14	916	50
Dover	1063	1058	5	1007	56
Galla Rock	1163	1144	19	936	227
Griffin	479	478	1	477	2
Gum Log	646	646	.....	634	12
Illinois	1657	1644	13	1535	122
Independence	240	240	.....	240	.....
Liberty	741	739	2	728	13
Martin	360	359	1	270	90
Moreland	299	299	.....	297	2
North Fork	215	214	1	215	.....
Witson	332	332	.....	331	1
PRAIRIE.					
Centre	772	772	.....	518	254
Hamilton	582	571	11	468	114
Hickory Plains	1030	1026	4	736	294
Lonoke	371	369	2	278	93
Richwoods	280	278	2	179	101
Rock Roe	277	275	2	204	73
Surrounded Hills	635	634	1	94	541
Wattensaw	660	628	32	528	132
White River	997	984	13	788	209
PULASKI.					
Ashley	2110	2074	36	561	1549
Bayou	509	507	2	448	61
Big Rock	3990	3932	58	1046	a2943
Campbell	1304	1287	17	358	b942
Caroline	2802	2798	4	2469	333
Clear Lake	378	368	10	160	218
Cypress	369	369	.....	359	10
Eagle	889	877	12	481	408
Eastmann	1731	1604	127	671	1060
Fourche	601	587	14	413	188
Grey	704	701	3	588	116
Little Rock	12380	11044	1336	7101	c5274
Maumelle	422	416	6	367	55
Mineral	191	181	10	182	9
Owen	505	491	14	474	31
Payatte	650	631	28	465	194
Plant	461	456	5	457	4
Prairie	1292	1292	.....	1169	123
Richwoods	409	407	2	270	139
Union	360	348	12	309	51
RANDOLPH.					
Current River	1378	1375	3	1326	52
De Mun	1764	1750	14	1576	188
Little Black	2710	2706	4	2673	37
Roanoke	1614	1613	1	1534	80
SALINE.					
Beaver	240	240	.....	231	9
Dyer	512	510	2	509	3
SALINE—Cont'd.					
Hurricane	390	390	.....	365	25
Jefferson	169	168	1	167	2
Marble	493	492	1	492	1
Owen	283	282	1	246	37
Saline	1194	1187	7	1108	86
Union	279	279	.....	257	22
Wills	351	351	.....	351	.....
SCOTT.					
Black Fork	160	160	.....	160	.....
Blancet	325	325	.....	323	2
Boone	937	934	3	898	39
Brawley	183	183	.....	182	1
Hickman	1310	1302	8	1293	17
Waldron	162	158	4	153	9
Hunt	280	280	.....	280	.....
Lafave	175	175	.....	173	2
Lafayette	400	399	1	370	30
Mountain	277	277	.....	277	.....
Park	495	495	.....	487	8
Reveille	882	879	3	867	15
Sugar Creek	476	474	2	473	3
Tumbleston	1084	1083	1	1080	4
Washburn	499	499	.....	499	.....
SEARCY.					
Bear Creek	865	862	3	855	10
Burrowsv'e (*d*)	84	84	.....	84	.....
Big Flat	472	472	.....	472	.....
Buffalo	195	195	.....	195	.....
Calf Creek	511	511	.....	505	6
Campbell	350	350	.....	350	.....
Locust Grove	524	524	.....	524	.....
Mount Pleasant	167	167	.....	167	.....
Prairie	202	201	1	201	1
Red River	240	240	.....	240	.....
Richland	471	471	.....	465	6
Sulphur Springs	226	226	.....	226	.....
Tomahawk	719	719	.....	712	7
Wiley's Cove	663	663	.....	663	.....
SEBASTIAN.					
Bates	623	621	2	611	12
Big Creek	1062	1049	13	1005	e48
Centre	1903	1892	11	1870	33
Cole	527	524	3	509	18
Ft. Smith Res	64	46	18	62	2
Marion	1315	1275	40	1212	f96
Mississippi	530	527	3	530	.....
Sugar Loaf	2059	2042	17	1889	170
Sulphur	713	692	21	675	38
Upper	3666	3150	516	2714	g927
Ft. Smith (*h*)	2227	1816	411	1682	e536
Washburne	478	474	4	468	10
SEVIER.					
Bear Creek	159	159	.....	157	2
Blue Bayou	840	840	.....	601	239
Cedar Creek	117	117	.....	81	36
Clear Creek	238	238	.....	225	13
Jefferson	347	346	1	336	11
Madison	468	468	.....	466	2
Monroe	309	309	.....	267	42
Paraclifta	579	576	3	413	a165
Paraclifta	45	45	.....	18	27

(*a*) Also 1 Indian.
(*b*) Also 4 Chinese.
(*c*) Also 5 Indians.
(*d*) Or Marshall.
(*e*) Also 9 Indians.
(*f*) Also 7 Indians.
(*g*) Also 25 Indians.
(*h*) On Government reservation.

TABLE IX.—*Population of Minor Civil Divisions, &c.*—*ARKANSAS*—Continued.

Counties.	Total.	Nativity.		Race.	
		Native.	Foreign.	White.	Colored.
SEVIER—Cont'd.					
Red Colony	463	461	2	316	147
Saline	353	349	4	275	78
Washington	619	619		386	233
SHARPE.					
Big Creek	414	411	3	411	3
Jackson	275	275		275	
Lebanon	509	509		509	
Morgan	371	371		362	9
North	295	292	3	294	1
Piney Fork	1454	1451	3	1374	80
Richwood	722	721	1	719	3
Scott	680	679	1	679	1
Union	177	177		160	17
Washington	503	501	2	503	
ST. FRANCIS.					
Franks	1906	1876	30	1271	632
Griggs	160	150	10	148	12
Johnson	788	783	5	459	329
L'Anguille	306	304	2	295	11
Liberty	273	269	4	74	199
St. Francis	513	498	15	339	174
Texas	710	703	7	422	288
Tillico	733	729	4	451	282
Union	1325	1296	29	786	539
UNION.					
Boone	642	638	4	304	338
Cornie	752	750	2	440	312
Eldorado	2349	2339	10	1105	1244
Franklin	799	798	1	427	372
Garner	456	456		307	149
Harrison	729	725	4	420	309
Jackson	814	813	1	449	365
Johnson	1309	1307	2	574	735
Lassile	782	782		543	239
Pigeon Hill	236	233	3	175	61
Tubal	351	349	2	240	111
Van Buren	1032	1030	2	525	507
Wilmington	320	308	12	166	154
VAN BUREN.					
Cadiou	587	586	1	559	28
Craig	282	282		282	
Davis	488	487	1	488	
Giles	611	610	1	551	60
Griggs	593	593		586	7
Hartanggs	297	297		297	
Holly	153	153		153	
Liberty	295	295		295	
Mountain	80	80		80	
Peter Creek	149	149		149	
Piney	160	160		158	2
Red River	516	516		516	
Sugar Loaf	259	259		238	21
Turkey Creek	80	80		80	
Union	216	216		215	1
Valley	224	224		224	
Washington	117	117		117	

Counties.	Total.	Nativity.		Race.	
		Native.	Foreign.	White.	Colored.
WASHINGTON.					
Brush Creek	740	739	1	722	18
Cane Hill	1611	1604	7	1503	108
Clear Creek	1199	1195	4	1191	8
Cove Creek	514	514		505	9
Elm Spring	1071	1065	6	1063	8
Illinois	1200	1197	3	1146	(a) 52
Marr's Hill	1280	1279	1	1272	8
Mountain	936	935	1	882	54
Prairie	3884	3835	49	3554	330
Fayetteville	955	930	25	803	152
Richland	1156	1154	2	1139	17
Vineyard	887	874	13	871	16
West Fork	1243	1242	1	1226	17
White River	1545	1542	3	1516	29
WHITE.					
Caldwell	451	450	1	445	6
Clay	517	510	7	516	1
Des Arc	861	860	1	725	(b) 136
Dogwood	513	513		447	66
Gray	2252	2241	11	1719	533
Searcy	874	863	11	746	128
Harrison	972	968	4	932	40
Jackson	355	353	2	354	1
Kentucky	443	443		411	32
Liberty	368	367	1	357	11
Marion	382	381	1	371	11
Marshall	429	428	1	392	37
Mingo	80	79	1	75	5
Negro Hill	57	57		44	13
Pine	149	149		149	
Red River	713	711	2	558	155
Royal	732	732		699	33
Union	1013	1012	1	892	121
White River	60	58	2	60	
WOODRUFF.					
Augusta	2213	2183	30	1283	930
Cotton Plant	1007	1000	7	723	284
Deview	1201	1196	5	942	259
Freman	487	483	4	298	189
Point	788	787	1	272	516
Surrounded Hill	248	243	5	155	93
White River	944	943	1	529	415
YELL.					
Chickalah	175	175		175	
Crawford	211	211		211	
Dardanelle	1838	1828	10	1440	398
Dardanelle	926	917	9	745	181
Delaware	550	550		513	37
Dutch Creek	466	464	2	459	7
Gally Rock	687	684	3	554	133
Lower Lafave	457	457		441	16
Magazine	729	729		723	6
Mountain	144	144		144	
Riley	545	544	1	519	26
Rover	394	394		380	14
Spring Creek	778	777	1	710	68
Upper Lafave	715	715		673	42
Ward	359	359		359	

(a) Also 2 Indians. (b) Also 1 Indian.

TABLE IX.—*Population of Minor Civil Divisions, &c.—CALIFORNIA.*

TE.—The marginal column marks townships or supervisor's districts, precincts, and land-survey ships; the first indentation, cities; the second, towns. Names of towns are placed under the names e townships or supervisor's districts, precincts, and land-survey townships in which they are respect- situated. The population of each township or supervisor's district, precinct, and land-survey ship, includes that of all towns situated in it.

Counties.	Total.	NATIVITY. Native.	NATIVITY. Foreign.	RACE. White.	RACE. Colored.
AMEDA. (a)					
eda	1557	869	688	1407	8
klyn	2810	1632	1178	2539	11
Brooklyn	1603	1002	601	1500	3
	3341	1773	1568	3138	......
Hayward	504	305	199	487	......
San Leandro	426	254	172	412	......
ray	2400	1467	933	2159	3
and	11104	6940	4164	10142	53
kland	10500	......	......	......	......
hington	3019	1695	1324	2721	4
Alvarado	315	177	138	259	......
LPINE. (b)					
	44	39	5	44	......
	102	56	46	102	......
	114	97	17	112	......
	261	186	75	257	......
	130	84	46	127	1
	34	23	11	34	......
MADOR. (c)					
ckson	2408	1170	1238	1988	3
ne	1779	1094	685	1330	24
lcano	1357	840	517	1218	2
tter	1966	1157	809	1858	36
ytown	853	486	367	640	2
ddletown	1219	702	517	849	5
BUTTE. (d)					
ell	337	178	159	243	2
ow	490	163	327	255	......
o	3714	2790	924	3175	33
ilton	1130	569	561	649	2
shew	857	472	385	660	......
ntain Spring	264	166	98	199	4
r	2430	1558	872	2054	28
Oroville	1425	......	......	......	......
on	1169	813	356	1122	4
	281	215	66	253	......
ndotte	731	504	227	587	11

Counties.	Total.	NATIVITY. Native.	NATIVITY. Foreign.	RACE. White.	RACE. Colored.
CALAVERAS. (c)					
4.	960	522	438	744	......
5.	1800	730	1070	1289	11
6.	1600	765	835	1335	9
7.	1178	694	484	1084	......
8.	1748	1041	707	1519	4
9.	1129	661	468	1040	3
10.	480	264	216	394	4
COLUSA. (f)					
Butte	604	500	104	565	10
Colusa	2193	1770	423	1961	38
Colusa	1051	750	292	866	30
Grand Island	702	571	131	619	4
Monroe	1130	926	204	979	13
Princeton	132	87	45	109	2
Stoney Creek	686	634	52	538	3
Spring Valley	850	687	163	727	15
CONTRA COSTA. (g)					
1.	2001	1278	723	1966	7
Martinez	560	431	129	542	7
San Pablo	1075	641	434	1069	......
2.	1850	1498	352	1828	5
3.	4610	3015	1595	4477	9
DEL NORTE. (h)					
Crescent	977	832	145	536	3
Crescent City	458	353	105	369	2
Happy Camp	382	178	204	118	3
Mountain	99	42	57	74	......
Smith's River	564	528	36	281	6
EL DORADO. (i)					
Coloma	925	499	426	663	24
Cosumnes	542	372	170	467	4
Diamond Spring	1055	635	420	882	3
Georgetown	1023	669	354	835	21
Greenwood	557	297	260	469	2
Kelsey's	315	218	97	296	2
Lake Valley	246	198	48	244	......

Alameda County: Alameda also includes 142 Chinese; Brooklyn, 266 Chinese; Eden, 203 Chinese; ray, 128 Chinese and 110 Indians; Oakland, 906 Chinese and 1 Indian; Washington, 294 Chinese.

Alpine County: Township 3 also includes 2 Chinese; township 4, 4 Chinese; township 5, 2 Chinese.

Amador County: Jackson also includes 417 Chinese; Ione, 425 Chinese; Volcano, 137 Chinese; er, 72 Chinese; Drytown, 211 Chinese; Fiddletown, 365 Chinese.

Butte County: Bidwell also includes 83 Chinese and 4 Indians; Concow, 235 Chinese; Chico, 506 ese; Hamilton, 479 Chinese; Kimshew, 197 Chinese; Mountain Spring, 46 Chinese and 15 ndians r, 348 Chinese; Oregon 43 Chinese; Oro, 19 Chinese and 9 Indians; Wyandotte, 121 Chinese and 12 ans.

Calaveras County: Township 4 also includes 216 Chinese; township 5, 500 Chinese; township 6, Chinese ownship 7, 94 Chinese; township 8, 222 Chinese and 3 Indians; township 9, 71 Chinese 15 Indians; township 10, 82 Chinese. Townships Nos. 1, 2, and 3 annexed to Amador County in 1855, no change made in the remaining numbers.

Colusa County: Butte also includes 11 Chinese and 18 Indians; Colusa, 153 Chinese and 43 Indians; d Island, 30 Chinese and 49 Indians; Monroe, 60 Chinese and 78 Indians; Stoney Creek, 1 Chinese 144 Indians; Spring Valley, 16 Chinese and 92 Indians. Butte and Union returned together, there g no defined line of boundary between them.

Contra Costa County: Township 1 also includes 26 Chinese and 2 Indians; township 2, 17 Chinese; ship 3, 117 Chinese and 7 Indians.

Del Norte County: Crescent also includes 31 Chinese and 407 Indians; Happy Camp, 163 Chinese 98 Indians; Mountain, 20 Chinese and 5 Indians; Smith's River, 3 Chinese and 274 Indians.

El Dorado County: Coloma also includes 215 Chinese, 1 Indian, and 22 Japanese; Cosumnes, 70 ese and 1 Indian; Diamond Spring, 166 Chinese and 4 Indians; Georgetown, 147 Chinese; Green-l, 86 Chinese; Kelsey's, 17 Chinese; Lake Valley, 2 Chinese; Mountain, 59 Chinese; Mud Spring, Chinese; Placerville, 290 Chinese; Salmon Falls, 117 Chinese; White Oak, 78 Chinese.

TABLE IX.—*Population of Minor Civil Divisions, &c.*—*CALIFORNIA*—Continued.

Counties.	Total.	Nativity.		Race.	
		Native.	Foreign.	White.	Colored.
EL DORADO—Con.					
Mountain	271	136	135	212	......
Mud Springs	1572	953	619	1244	24
Placerville	2624	1670	954	2296	29
Placerville	1562	991	571	1318	26
Salmon Falls	428	184	244	290	21
White Oak	751	456	295	671	2
FRESNO. (a)					
1.	2836	2001	835	1879	......
2.	1760	1318	442	533	3
3.	1740	1655	85	847	12
HUMBOLDT. (b)					
Arcata	924	693	231	915	......
Buckport	388	267	121	384	......
Eel River	827	725	102	825	......
Eureka	2049	1282	767	1999	......
Mattole	453	404	49	443	......
Pacific	818	697	121	810	......
South Fork	273	231	42	252	......
Table Bluff	408	327	81	397	......
INYO. (c)					
Bishop Creek	624	480	144	616	2
Cerro Gordo	474	152	322	295	2
Independence	400	263	137	378	3
Lone Pine	458	269	189	319	1
KERN. (d)					
1.	629	477	152	398	3
2.	510	460	50	474	......
3.	120	82	38	85	1
4.	616	496	120	372	......
5.	820	477	343	728	......
6.	230	165	65	136	......
KLAMATH. (e)					
Dillon	79	45	34	41	......
Hoopa Valley Indian Reservation	12	10	2	12	......
Klamath	278	160	118	226	1
Camp Gaston	118	60	58	116	1
Liberty	348	106	242	197	......
Sawyer's Bar	160	81	79	120	......
KLAMATH—Cont'd.					
Orleans	173	109	64	111	......
Salmon	136	31	105	40	......
South Fork	286	75	211	99	......
Trinidad	374	257	117	355	1
Trinidad	160	109	51	153	1
LAKE. (f)					
1st Supervis's dist.	1156	885	271	1131	1
Knoxv'e Mines	164	37	127	164	......
Lower Lake	692	530	162	582	1
2d Supervis's dist.	880	821	59	874	......
Lakeport	248	225	23	245	1
3d Supervis's dist.	933	777	156	820	1
LASSEN. (g)					
Janesville	441	401	40	440	......
Long Valley	135	112	23	132	......
Milford	113	104	9	112	......
Susanville	638	561	77	625	......
LOS ANGELES. (h)					
El Monte	1254	1064	190	1245	3
Azusa	320	248	72	317	......
Los Angeles	2776	1997	779	2645	22
Los Angeles	5728	3724	2004	5349	93
Los Nietos	1544	1274	270	1535	4
San Gabriel	436	332	104	426	1
Santa Aña	1445	1025	420	1427	2
Anaheim	881	680	201	878	3
San José	474	410	64	470	4
San Juan	445	349	96	440	......
Soledad	265	162	103	264	......
Wilmington	942	647	295	910	5
Compton	160	141	19	160	......
MARIN. (i)					
Bolinas	625	390	235	598	......
Novato	417	213	204	364	4
Nicassio	592	308	284	555	......
Point Reyes	271	165	106	242	......
San Rafael	2695	1480	1215	2455	15
San Rafael	841	540	301	833	8
San Antonio	451	231	220	450	......
Sancelito	731	319	412	717	3
Tomales	1121	655	466	1013	......

(*a*) Fresno County: Township 1 also includes 23 Chinese and 934 Indians; township 2, 306 Chinese and 828 Indians; township 3, 8 Chinese and 873 Indians.

(*b*) Humboldt County: Arcata also includes 6 Chinese and 3 Indians; Bucksport, 4 Indians; Eel River, 2 Indians; Eureka, 33 Chinese and 17 Indians; Mattole, 10 Indians; Pacific, 8 Indians; South Fork, 21 Indians; Table Bluff, 11 Indians.

(*c*) Inyo County: Bishop Creek also includes 6 Indians; Cerro Gordo, 10 Chinese and 167 Indians; Independence, 14 Chinese and 5 Indians; Lone Pine, 5 Chinese and 133 Indians.

(*d*) Kern County: Township 1 also includes 38 Chinese and 190 Indians; township 2, 11 Chinese and 25 Indians; township 3, 4 Chinese and 30 Indians; township 4, 19 Chinese and 225 Indians; township 5, 52 Chinese and 40 Indians; township 6, 19 Chinese and 75 Indians.

(*e*) Klamath County: Dillon also includes 28 Chinese and 10 Indians; Klamath, 33 Chinese and 18 Indians; Liberty, 151 Chinese; Orleans, 46 Chinese and 16 Indians; Salmon, 90 Chinese and 6 Indians; South Fork, 185 Chinese and 2 Indians; Trinidad, 9 Chinese and 9 Indians.

(*f*) Lake County: 1st Supervisor's district also includes 18 Chinese and 6 Indians; 2d Supervisor's district, 1 Chinese and 5 Indians; 3d Supervisor's district, 100 Chinese and 12 Indians; Lower Lake, 101 Chinese and 8 Indians; Lakeport, 2 Indians. Part of Lower Lake and part of Lakeport in 3d district.

(*g*) Lassen County: Janesville also includes 1 Chinese; Long Valley, 2 Chinese and 1 Indian; Milford, 1 Chinese; Susanville, 13 Chinese.

(*h*) Los Angeles County: El Monte also includes 6 Chinese; Los Angeles, 10 Chinese and 90 Indians; Los Angeles City, 172 Chinese and 114 Indians; Los Nietos, 5 Chinese; San Gabriel, 7 Chinese and 2 Japanese; Santa Aña, 15 Chinese and 1 Indian; Soladad, 1 Chinese; Wilmington, 18 Chinese. Los Angeles exclusive of city of Los Angeles.

(*i*) Marin County: Bolinas also includes 11 Chinese and 16 Indians; Novato, 32 Chinese and 17 Indians; Nicassio, 4 Chinese and 33 Indians; Point Reyes, 11 Chinese and 18 Indians; San Rafael, 199 Chinese and 26 Indians; San Antonio, 1 Chinese; Sancelito, 6 Chinese and 5 Indians; Tomales, 97 Chinese and 11 Indians.

TABLE IX.—*Population of Minor Civil Divisions, &c.—CALIFORNIA*—Continued.

Counties.	Total.	Nativity. Native.	Nativity. Foreign.	Race. White.	Race. Colored.
MARIPOSA. (a)					
1.	1420	624	796	1016	25
2.	585	248	337	463	7
3.	1732	912	820	1289	34
4.	835	408	427	506	24
MENDOCINO. (b)					
Anderson	679	590	89	617	1
Anderson	623	534	89	617	1
Big River	1911	1284	627	1545	6
Albion	115	74	41	111	......
Big River (*)	473	318	155	456	6
Casper	196	60	136	195	......
Cuffy's Cove	158	108	50	158	......
Little River	158	96	62	158	......
Noyo	80	50	30	76	......
Novarro	315	179	136	311	......
Ten-Mile Riv'r	80	63	17	80	......
Calpella	807	780	27	807	......
Little Lake	946	886	60	939	......
Punta Arenas	1406	977	429	1173	......
Bourn's Lan'g.	40	18	22	32	......
Furgus's Cove	40	36	4	40	......
Gualala	236	126	110	196	......
Punta Arenas	956	663	293	905	......
Round Valley	444	383	61	438	2
Round Valley Reservation	15	13	2	15	......
Sanel	371	333	38	370	......
Ukiah	966	901	65	961	......
MONO. (c)					
Antelope	162	146	16	160	......
Benton	94	66	28	91	......
Bridgeport	174	93	81	135	......
Bridgeport	60	40	20	59	......
MONTEREY. (d)					
Alisa	2723	2108	615	2625	6
Salinas City	599	454	145	581	2
San Antonio	761	585	176	730	......
Castroville	1302	1004	298	1248	2
Castroville	436	371	65	425	2
Monterey	1923	1504	419	1737	1
Monterey	1112	895	217	1056	1
Pajaro	761	590	171	760	......
San Benito	529	406	123	516	......
San Juan	2638	2058	580	2543	7
NAPA. (e)					
Hot Springs	2120	1686	434	1997	6
Napa	3791	2657	1134	3510	92
Napa City	1879	1268	611	1743	67
Yount	1252	1051	201	1218	11
NEVADA. (f)					
Bloomfield	636	384	252	588	1
Bridgeport	1829	1034	795	1517	4
Eureka	1249	538	711	908	2
Grass Valley	7063	3696	3367	6608	60
Little York	868	501	367	739	1
Meadow Lake	1655	918	737	1239	14
Nevada	3986	2345	1641	3244	72
Rough and Ready	1210	782	428	1016	10
Washington	638	281	357	475	1
PLACER. (g)					
1.	663	474	189	606	1
Roseville	115	92	23	112	......
2.	693	337	356	481	1
3.	1439	760	679	1022	24
Auburn	800	400	400	550	10
4.	2860	1499	1361	2047	12
5.	1122	676	446	966	40
6.	923	345	578	609	1
7.	754	400	354	661	6
8.	330	175	155	295	5
9.	1284	727	557	1091	5
Newcastle	551	261	290	433	1
Pino	191	104	87	151	2
Rocklin	542	362	180	507	2
10.	1030	670	360	846	......
11.	259	104	155	225	......
PLUMAS. (h)					
Goodwin	639	223	416	391	......
Indian	880	611	269	817	1
Mineral	400	129	271	225	1
Plumas	640	383	257	505	......
Quincy	208	......	......	......	......
Quartz	810	569	241	785	......
Rich Bar	200	69	131	144	......
Seneca	400	262	138	327	......
Washington	520	168	352	377	......

(a) Mariposa County: Township 1 also includes 372 Chinese and 7 Indians; township 2, 115 Chinese; township 3, 383 Chinese and 26 Indians; township 4, 214 Chinese and 1 Indian.

(b) Mendocino County: Anderson also includes 5 Chinese and 56 Indians: Big River, 21 Chinese and 339 Indians; Little Lake, 7 Indians; Punta Arenas, 99 Chinese and 134 Indians; Round Valley, 4 Indians; Sanel, 1 Indian; Ukiah, 4 Chinese and 1 Indian.

(c) Mono County: Antelope also includes 2 Indians; Benton, 3 Chinese; Bridgeport, 39 Chinese.

(d) Monterey County: Alisa also includes 32 Chinese and 60 Indians; Castroville, 43 Chinese and 9 Indians; Monterey, 92 Chinese and 93 Indians; Pajaro, 1 Chinese; San Benito, 13 Indians; San Juan, 62 Chinese and 26 Indians.

(e) Napa County: Hot Springs also includes 113 Chinese and 4 Indians; Napa, 143 Chinese and 46 Indians; Yount, 7 Chinese and 16 Indians.

(f) Nevada County: Bloomfield also includes 47 Chinese; Bridgeport, 306 Chinese and 2 Indians; Eureka, 339 Chinese; Grass Valley, 391 Chinese and 4 Indians; Little York, 128 Chinese; Meadow Lake, 402 Chinese; Nevada, 669 Chinese and 1 Indian; Rough and Ready, 183 Chinese and 1 Indian; Washington, 162 Chinese.

(g) Placer County: Township 1 also includes 56 Chinese; township 2, 211 Chinese; township 3, 393 Chinese; township 4, 800 Chinese and 1 Indian; township 5, 116 Chinese; township 6, 313 Chinese; township 7, 87 Chinese; township 8, 30 Chinese; township 9, 187 Chinese and 1 Indian; township 10, 184 Chinese; township 11, 34 Chinese.

(h) Plumas County: Goodwin also includes 248 Chinese; Indian, 57 Chinese and 5 Indians; Mineral, 174 Chinese; Plumas, 135 Chinese; Quartz, 25 Chinese; Rich Bar, 56 Chinese; Seneca, 73 Chinese; Washington, 143 Chinese.

(*) Or Mendocino.

TABLE IX.—*Population of Minor Civil Divisions, &c.—CALIFORNIA*—Continued.

Counties.	Total.	Nativity. Native.	Nativity. Foreign.	Race. White.	Race. Colored.
SACRAMENTO. (*a*)					
Alabama	336	276	60	332	......
American	416	219	197	339	......
Brighton	909	713	196	877	2
Center	461	211	250	301	......
Cosumnes	694	404	290	474	15
Dry Creek	603	457	146	559	6
Franklin	1272	869	403	1132	1
Georgiana	1056	274	782	459	......
Granite	1579	553	1026	859	22
Lee	376	307	69	369	1
Mississippi	171	89	82	134	......
Natoma	523	280	243	391	......
Sacramento	16283	10081	6202	14485	418
San Joaquin	1073	823	250	1014	10
Sutter	1078	672	406	1000	......
SAN BERNARDINO. (*b*)					
Belleville	56	19	37	56	......
Chino	308	264	44	308	......
San Bernardino	3064	2575	489	3040	8
San Salvador	560	470	90	560	......
SAN DIEGO. (*c*)					
Fort Yuma	331	120	211	330	......
Colorado	229	77	152	229	......
Julian	531	421	110	526	......
La Pala	120	85	35	120	......
Milquaty	324	302	22	324	......
Pala Valley Reservation	46	29	17	46	......
Powy	91	75	16	89	1
San Diego	2300	1748	552	2234	1
San Jacinto	92	85	7	92	......
San Luis Rey	335	306	29	309	......
San Pasqual	275	207	68	275	......
San Pasqual Valley Res	117	58	59	117	......
Temacula	140	111	29	130	10
Warner's Ranch	246	193	53	243	3
SAN FRANCISCO. (*d*)					
San Francisco	149473	75754	73719	136059	1330
SAN JOAQUIN. (*e*)					
Castoria	1184	960	224	1092	5
Dent	1115	951	164	1097	......
Douglas	1751	1396	355	1695	25
Elkhorn	1428	1215	213	1371	9
Elliott	954	813	141	924	2
Liberty	1231	1029	202	1160	5
O'Neal	1719	1224	495	1469	11
Stockton	10066	5964	4102	8820	16
Tulare	1269	992	277	1246	1
Union	333	280	53	319	......
S'N LUIS OBISPO. (*f*)					
Arroyo Grande	776	601	175	732	1
Moro	627	571	56	605	......
Salinas	679	477	202	644	3
San Luis Obispo	1579	1172	407	1500	4
Santa Rosa	1111	1012	99	1086	1
SAN MATEO. (*g*)					
1. San Bruno	1269	367	902	1088	......
2. San Mateo	977	478	499	835	......
3. Pulgas	1438	800	638	1381	......
4. Redwood	627	409	218	614	......
Redwood City	727	448	279	712	......
5. Half-Moon Bay	1665	1012	653	1561	5
6. Pescadero	659	431	228	619	5
S'TA BARBARA. (*h*)					
1. San Buonaventura	2491	2119	372	2394	3
2. Santa Barbara	4255	3561	694	4109	31
3. Santa Inez	1038	858	180	981	2
SANTA CLARA. (*i*)					
Almaden	1647	880	767	1630	4
Alviso	588	314	274	466	1
Burnett	802	533	269	792	......
Fremont	2018	1252	766	1904	14
Gilroy	3195	2474	721	3090	15
Gilroy	1625	1200	425	1544	12
Milpitas	665	488	177	658	......
Redwood	1353	1048	305	1334	4

(*a*) Sacramento County: Alabama also includes 3 Chinese and 1 Indian; American, 76 Chinese and 1 Indian; Brighton, 29 Chinese and 1 Indian; Center, 160 Chinese; Cosumnes, 198 Chinese and 7 Indians; Dry Creek, 31 Chinese and 7 Indians; Franklin, 137 Chinese and 2 Indians: Georgiana, 597 Chinese; Granite, 697 Chinese and 1 Indian; Lee, 5 Chinese and 1 Indian; Mississippi, 37 Chinese; Natoma, 132 Chinese; Sacramento, 1,370 Chinese, 9 Indians, and 1 Japanese; San Joaquin, 48 Chinese and 1 Indian; Sutter, 75 Chinese and 3 Indians.

(*b*) San Bernardino County: San Bernardino also includes 16 Chinese.

(*c*) San Diego County: Fort Yuma also includes 1 Chinese; Julian, 5 Chinese; Powy, 1 Chinese; San Diego City, 63 Chinese and 2 Indians; San Luis Rey, 26 Indians.

(*d*) San Francisco County: San Francisco, 12,022 Chinese, 54 Indians, and 8 Japanese.

(*e*) San Joaquin County: Castoria also includes 87 Chinese; Dent, 18 Chinese; Douglas, 31 Chinese; Elkhorn, 48 Chinese; Elliott, 28 Chinese; Liberty, 66 Chinese; O'Neal, 239 Chinese; Stockton, 1,076 Chinese and 5 Indians; Tulare, 22 Chinese; Union, 14 Chinese.

(*f*) San Luis Obispo County: Arroyo Grande also includes 34 Chinese and 9 Indians; Moro, 22 Indians; Salin[illegible] Chinese and 23 Indians; San Luis Obispo, 15 Chinese and 60 Indians; Santa Rosa, 1 Chinese and [illegible]dians.

(*g*) San Mateo County: San Bruno also includes 181 Chinese; San Mateo, 136 Chinese and 6 Indians; Pulgas, 56 Chinese and 1 Indian; Redwood, 13 Chinese; Redwood City, 14 Chinese and 1 Indian; Half-Moon Bay, 98 Chinese and 1 Indian; Pescadero, 35 Chinese.

(*h*) Santa Barbara County: San Buonaventura also includes 14 Chinese and 78 Indians; Santa Barbara, 82 Chinese and 33 Indians; Santa Ires, 13 Chinese and 42 Indians.

(*i*) Santa Clara County: Almaden also includes 6 Chinese and 7 Indians; Alviso, 121 Chinese; Burnett, 9 Chinese and 1 Indian; Fremont, 100 Chinese; Gilroy, 89 Chinese and 1 Indian: Milpitas, 7 Chinese; Redwood, 15 Chinese; Santa Clara, 175 Chinese; San José, 289 Chinese and 3 Indians; San José City, 714 Chinese.

TABLE IX.—*Population of Minor Civil Divisions, &c.—CALIFORNIA*—Continued.

Counties.	Total.	Nativity. Native.	Nativity. Foreign.	Race. White.	Race. Colored.
SANTA CLARA—Continued.					
Santa Clara	3469	2544	925	3276	18
San José (a)	3420	2374	1046	3116	12
San José	9089	5334	3755	8270	105
SANTA CRUZ. (b)					
Pajaro	3114	2449	665	3004	45
Watsonville	1151	900	251	1098	23
Santa Cruz	4436	3346	1090	4349	8
Santa Cruz	2561	1935	626	2500	8
Soquel	1193	963	230	1179	......
SHASTA. (c)					
1.	924	611	313	796	36
2.	559	197	362	285	2
3.	113	93	20	104	......
4.	359	325	34	359	......
5.	356	305	51	352	3
6.	957	922	35	954	......
7.	359	142	217	206	1
8.	546	342	204	473	2
SIERRA. (d)					
Butte	1182	534	648	999	25
Downieville	704	393	311	571	25
Eureka	350	117	233	236	......
Forest	748	400	348	634	1
Allegheny	240	145	95	223	......
Forest City	152	92	60	141	......
Gibson	520	249	271	476	......
Lincoln	616	292	324	463	1
Sears	758	318	440	639	......
Sierra	686	566	120	679	......
Table Rock	759	340	419	655	1
SISKIYOU. (e)					
Big Valley	246	240	6	246	......
Butte	410	342	68	373	......
Cottonwood	421	161	260	230	2
Humbug	251	71	180	131	......
Klamath	84	33	51	40	......
Scott River	446	171	275	221	......
Scott Valley	1259	798	461	983	5
South	939	532	407	729	......
Surprise Valley	649	590	59	648	......
Table Rock	327	286	41	322	......
Yreka	1816	1097	719	1422	22
Yreka City	1063	732	331	881	22

Counties.	Total.	Nativity. Native.	Nativity. Foreign.	Race. White.	Race. Colored.
SOLANO. (f)					
Benicia	1656	1045	611	1609	18
Denverton	470	287	183	465	1
Green Valley	592	405	187	512	......
Bridgeport	80	63	17	78	......
Main Prairie	761	613	148	760	......
Binghamton	80	73	7	80	......
Main Prairie	160	142	18	160	......
Montezuma	347	233	114	323	......
Rio Vista	888	517	371	790	......
Rio Vista	319	216	103	312	......
Silveyville	1583	1134	449	1536	6
Batavia	200	156	44	190	3
Dixon	317	199	118	293	2
Silveyville	279	207	72	267	1
Suisun	1842	1268	574	1557	4
Fairfield	329	244	85	325	4
Suisun City	462	363	99	443	......
Tremont	640	439	201	632	......
Vacaville	1701	1307	394	1530	......
Vaca Station	120	76	44	115	......
Vacaville	343	289	54	332	......
Vallejo	6391	4015	2376	6156	49
SONOMA. (g)					
Annaly	2374	2004	370	2343	1
Bodega	1407	1000	407	1367	2
Cloverdale	612	538	74	609	......
Healdsburg	959	838	121	939	8
Mendocino	2690	2417	273	2659	17
Petaluma	4588	3372	1216	4422	45
Russian River	987	877	110	978	......
Salt Point	1088	640	448	947	......
Santa Rosa	2898	2569	329	2850	11
Sonoma	1513	957	556	1371	1
Vallejo	1114	770	344	1093	......
Washington	548	512	36	545	......
Geyserville	68	54	14	65	......
STANISLAUS. (h)					
Branch	787	597	190	733	1
Buena Vista	357	248	109	316	......
Emory	843	507	336	692	1
Empire	2993	2573	420	2946	2
North	223	187	36	220	......
San Joaquin	1015	803	212	1006	......
Washington	281	232	49	276	......

(a) Exclusive of city of San José.

(b) Santa Cruz County: Pajaro also includes 65 Chinese; Santa Cruz, 77 Chinese and 2 Indians; Soquel, 14 Chinese.

(c) Shasta County: Township 1 also includes 79 Chinese and 13 Indians; township 2, 272 Chinese; township 3, 9 Indians; township 5, 1 Indian; township 6, 2 Chinese and 1 Indian; township 7, 151 Chinese and 1 Indian; township 8, 70 Chinese and 1 Indian.

(d) Sierra County: Butte also includes 158 Chinese; Eureka, 114 Chinese; Forest, 113 Chinese; Gibson, 44 Chinese; Lincoln, 152 Chinese; Sears, 119 Chinese; Sierra, 7 Chinese; Table Rock, 103 Chinese.

(e) Siskiyou County: Butte also includes 34 Chinese and 3 Indians; Cottonwood, 184 Chinese and 5 Indians; Humbug, 120 Chinese; Klamath, 42 Chinese and 2 Indians; Scott River, 224 Chinese and 1 Indian; Scott Valley, 282 Chinese and 5 Indians; South, 206 Chinese and 4 Indians; Surprise Valley, 1 Indian; Table Rock, 1 Chinese and 4 Indians; Yreka, 347 Chinese and 25 Indians.

(f) Solano County: Benicia also includes 29 Chinese; Denverton, 4 Chinese; Green Valley, 77 Chinese and 3 Indians; Main Prairie, 1 Chinese; Montezuma, 24 Chinese; Rio Vista, 98 Chinese; Silveyville, 41 Chinese; Suisun, 281 Chinese; Tremont, 8 Chinese; Vacaville, 171 Chinese; Vallejo, 186 Chinese.

(g) Sonoma County: Annaly also includes 11 Chinese and 19 Indians; Bodega, 21 Chinese and 17 Indians; Cloverdale, 3 Chinese; Healdsburg, 12 Chinese; Mendocino, 14 Chinese; Petaluma, 121 Chinese; Russian River, 7 Chinese and 2 Indians; Salt Point, 96 Chinese and 45 Indians; Santa Rosa, 35 Chinese and 2 Indians; Sonoma, 141 Chinese; Vallejo, 21 Chinese; Washington, 3 Chinese.

(h) Stanislaus County: Branch also includes 53 Chinese; Buena Vista, 41 Chinese; Emory, 150 Chinese; Empire, 45 Chinese; North, 3 Chinese; San Joaquin, 9 Chinese; Washington, 5 Chinese.

TABLE IX.—*Population of Minor Civil Divisions, &c.—CALIFORNIA*—Continued.

Counties.	Total.	Nativity.		Race.	
		Native.	Foreign.	White.	Colored.
SUTTER. (a)					
Butte	1359	1083	276	1298	5
Nicholaus	799	634	165	773	5
Sutter	1075	776	299	1025	1
Vernon	799	650	149	744	16
Yuba	998	806	192	951	4
TEHAMA. (b)					
Antelope	320	279	41	298	1
Battle Creek	199	181	18	189	3
Bell Mills	79	76	3	78	......
Cottonwood	240	190	50	237	1
Hunter's	40	37	3	38	......
Lassen	240	178	62	208	......
Mill Creek	80	76	4	80	......
Molino (c)	......	......	......	......	......
Toomes's Gr't	40	37	3	38	......
Paskenta	356	315	41	353	1
Stoney Creek	76	68	8	75	......
Payne's Creek	80	80	......	80	......
Red Bluff	1032	793	239	943	29
Red Bluff	992	755	237	904	29
Tehama	881	592	289	624	38
Merrill's	124	103	21	117	......
TRINITY. (d)					
Indian Creek	783	364	419	513	......
Indian Creek	183	57	126	109	......
Lewiston	338	146	192	199	......
Minersville	102	54	48	76	......
Trinity Centre	160	107	53	136	......
Junction City	570	198	372	329	1
Cañon City	130	37	93	81	1
Junction City	440	161	279	248	......
North Fork	461	188	273	230	......
Weaverville	1399	647	752	879	22
Douglas City	411	120	291	187	......
Hay Fork Valley	172	142	30	128	......
Weaverville	816	385	431	561	22
TULARE. (e)					
Farmersville	807	755	52	796	9
TULARE—Cont'd.					
King's River	166	148	18	162	......
Packwood	214	172	42	214	......
Tule River	1098	953	145	1082	1
Tule Indian Reservation	12	10	2	12	......
Venice	490	475	15	487	......
Visalia	1626	1377	249	1540	29
Visalia	913	707	206	855	4
White River	120	87	33	98	......
TUOLUMNE. (f)					
1. Sonora	2489	1383	1106	2211	39
Sonora	1322	787	535	1170	32
2. Columbia	2192	1235	957	1944	10
Columbia	1125	625	500	1017	3
3. Chinese Camp	2220	1016	1204	1540	16
4. Big Oak Flat	1249	548	701	861	3
YOLO. (g)					
Buckeye	860	739	121	788	22
Cache Creek	3067	2462	605	2943	15
Cottonwood	1319	1152	167	1253	19
Fremont	91	75	16	89	......
Grafton	1861	1486	375	1741	8
Merritt	480	282	198	432	......
Putah	1412	1020	392	1326	2
Washington	809	562	247	740	3
YUBA. (h)					
East Bear River	603	425	178	500	6
Foster's Bar	524	286	238	393	1
Linda	401	283	118	374	5
Long Bar	519	378	141	471	6
Marysville (i)	433	314	119	374	27
Marysville	4738	2358	2380	3225	96
New York	542	371	171	507	......
North East	363	152	211	196	......
Parke Bar	250	153	97	243	......
Rose's Bar	1191	679	512	1112	5
Slate Range	880	441	439	599	3
West Bear River	407	304	103	368	3

(a) Sutter County: Butte also includes 56 Chinese; Nicholaus, 21 Chinese; Sutter, 49 Chinese; Vernon, 39 Chinese; Yuba, 43 Chinese.

(b) Tehama County: Antelope also includes 19 Chinese and 2 Indians; Battle Creek, 1 Chinese and 6 Indians; Bell Mills, 1 Chinese; Cottonwood, 2 Indians; Hunter's, 2 Indians; Lassen, 31 Chinese and 1 Indian; Toomes's Grant, 2 Chinese; Pasakenta, 1 Chinese and 1 Indian; Red Bluff, 56 Chinese and 4 Indians; Tehama, 183 Chinese and 36 Indians.

(c) Returned with Lassen and Tehama.

(d) Trinity County: Indian Creek also includes 251 Chinese and 19 Indians; Junction City, 216 Chinese and 24 Indians; North Fork, 178 Chinese and 53 Indians; Weaverville, 454 Chinese and 44 Indians.

(e) Tulare County: Farmersville also includes 2 Chinese; King's River, 4 Chinese; Tule River, 15 Chinese; Venice, 3 Chinese; Visalia, 57 Chinese; White River, 18 Chinese and 4 Indians.

(f) Tuolumne County: Sonora also includes 236 Chinese and 3 Indians; Columbia, 238 Chinese; Chinese Camp, 664 Chinese; Big Oak Flat, 385 Chinese.

(g) Yolo County: Buckeye also includes 26 Chinese and 24 Indians; Cache Creek, 88 Chinese and 21 Indians; Cottonwood, 16 Chinese and 31 Indians; Fremont, 2 Chinese; Grafton, 78 Chinese and 34 Indians; Merritt, 48 Chinese; Putah, 78 Chinese and 6 Indians; Washington, 65 Chinese and 1 Indian.

(h) Yuba County: East Bear River, 97 Chinese; Foster's Bar, 130 Chinese; Linda, 22 Chinese; Long Bar, 42 Chinese; Marysville, 32 Chinese; Marysville City, 1,417 Chinese; New York, 35 Chinese; North East, 167 Chinese; Parke Bar, 7 Chinese; Rose's Bar, 74 Chinese; Slate Range, 278 Chinese; West Bear River, 36 Chinese.

(i) Exclusive of city of Marysville.

TABLE IX.—*Population of Minor Civil Divisions, &c.*—CONNECTICUT.

—The marginal column marks towns; the first indentation, cities; the second, villages. Names …ges are placed under the names of the towns in which they are respectively situated. The …ion of each town includes that of all villages situated in it.

…nties.	Total.	NATIVITY. Native.	NATIVITY. Foreign.	RACE. White.	RACE. Colored.
…FIELD.					
…………	2311	[illegible]	[illegible]	[illegible]	11
…rt …………	[illegible]	14916	[illegible]	[illegible]	[illegible]
…eport …………	[illegible]	[illegible]	[illegible]	[illegible]	[illegible]
…ld …………	[illegible]	1651	148	1167	a34
…y …………	8753	7175	1578	[illegible]	[illegible]
…bury …………	6542	5199	1343	[illegible]	b106
…………	1808	1630	178	1799	9
…………	1988	1913	75	1930	58
…l …………	5645	4430	1215	[illegible]	213
…sh …………	7644	[illegible]	[illegible]	7440	204
…son …………	1587	1407	180	1490	97
…………	[illegible]	1183	43	[illegible]	b12
…naan …………	2497	[illegible]	[illegible]	2461	36
…rfield …………	670	[illegible]	42	[illegible]	5
…n …………	3681	[illegible]	715	3640	41
…………	12119	[illegible]	[illegible]	11941	178
…ld …………	[illegible]	1471	153	[illegible]	78
…ld …………	1919	1747	[illegible]	[illegible]	[illegible]
…………	846	[illegible]	37	814	[illegible]
…………	9714	7446	[illegible]	[illegible]	112
…………	[illegible]	2081	351	[illegible]	134
…H …………	1336	1259	77	[illegible]	a10
…………	1656	1611	[illegible]	[illegible]	[illegible]
…t …………	3361	2744	617	[illegible]	[illegible]
…………	1804	1674	130	1793	11
…TFORD.					
…………	987	878	109	982	5
…………	2436	2064	372	2424	12
…ld …………	1473	1206	267	1448	25
…………	3788	3256	532	3776	12
…on …………	1319	969	350	1314	5
…………	2639	2101	538	2617	22
…anby …………	853	732	121	827	26
…rtford …………	3007	2581	426	3000	7
…ndsor …………	2822	2097	725	2808	14
…………	6322	4037	2285	6301	21
…ton …………	2616	2086	530	[illegible]	b91
…ury …………	3560	3102	458	3525	35
…………	1517	1418	99	1485	32
…l …………	37743	26779	10964	36778	d963
…rd …………	37180	26363	10817	36239	d940
…l …………	789	770	19	770	19
…ter …………	4223	3021	1202	4191	32
…ough …………	476	451	25	454	22
…tain …………	9480	6318	3162	9425	55
…e …………	1433	1202	231	1407	26
…ill …………	971	857	114	966	5
…y …………	2051	1543	508	2039	12
…ton …………	4314	3573	741	4277	37
…indsor …………	1688	1527	161	1682	6
…………	3277	2875	402	3241	36
…artford …………	1533	1293	240	1489	44
…field …………	2693	2306	387	2620	73
…ington So-…ty …………	778	653	125	775	3
…………	2783	2233	550	2673	110
… Locks …………	2154	1441	713	2149	5
…FIELD.					
…sted …………	1439	1315	124	1427	12
…on …………	750	689	61	745	5

Counties.	Total.	NATIVITY. Native.	NATIVITY. Foreign.	RACE. White.	RACE. Colored.
LITCHFIELD—Con.					
Bridgewater …………	877	793	[illegible]	[illegible]	3
Canaan …………	[illegible]	[illegible]	[illegible]	[illegible]	[illegible]
Colebrook …………	1141	[illegible]	[illegible]	[illegible]	6
Cornwall …………	1772	1561	211	[illegible]	[illegible]
Goshen …………	[illegible]	[illegible]	[illegible]	[illegible]	[illegible]
Harwinton …………	1044	[illegible]	[illegible]	[illegible]	[illegible]
Kent …………	1744	1615	129	[illegible]	[illegible]
Litchfield …………	3113	2701	412	[illegible]	[illegible]
Morris …………	701	657	44	[illegible]	[illegible]
New Hartford …………	[illegible]	[illegible]	[illegible]	[illegible]	[illegible]
New Milford …………	[illegible]	[illegible]	[illegible]	[illegible]	[illegible]
Norfolk …………	1641	[illegible]	[illegible]	[illegible]	[illegible]
North Canaan …………	[illegible]	[illegible]	[illegible]	[illegible]	[illegible]
Plymouth …………	[illegible]	[illegible]	[illegible]	[illegible]	30
Roxbury …………	919	[illegible]	84	[illegible]	1
Salisbury …………	[illegible]	[illegible]	[illegible]	[illegible]	[illegible]
Sharon …………	2441	[illegible]	[illegible]	[illegible]	145
Torrington …………	[illegible]	[illegible]	[illegible]	[illegible]	[illegible]
Warren …………	673	[illegible]	[illegible]	[illegible]	1
Washington …………	[illegible]	1480	[illegible]	[illegible]	3
Watertown …………	[illegible]	[illegible]	[illegible]	[illegible]	45
Winchester …………	[illegible]	[illegible]	[illegible]	[illegible]	[illegible]
Woodbury …………	1931	[illegible]	[illegible]	[illegible]	[illegible]
MIDDLESEX.					
Chatham …………	2771	[illegible]	[illegible]	[illegible]	24
Chester …………	1094	945	149	[illegible]	6
Clinton …………	1404	1357	47	1400	4
Cromwell …………	1856	1358	498	1856	……
Durham …………	1086	971	115	1070	[illegible]
East Haddam …………	2951	2729	222	[illegible]	43
Essex …………	1669	1598	71	1664	5
Haddam …………	2071	1917	154	2060	11
Killingworth …………	856	849	7	856	……
Middlefield …………	1053	813	240	1015	38
Middletown(f) …………	4203	3175	1028	4190	b12
Middletown …………	6923	5005	1918	6769	a152
Old Saybrook …………	1215	1073	142	1194	21
Portland …………	4693	2775	1918	4692	1
Saybrook …………	1267	1126	141	1222	45
Westbrook …………	987	961	26	985	2
NEW HAVEN.					
Bethany …………	1135	874	261	1133	2
Branford …………	2488	2113	375	2473	15
Cheshire …………	2344	1853	491	2294	50
Derby …………	8020	5913	2107	7887	133
Ansonia …………	2749	1847	902	2719	30
Birmingham …………	2103	1399	704	2081	22
Derby Narrows, (E. of river) …………	1907	1460	447	1868	39
Derby Narrows, (W. of river) …………	1261	917	344	1219	42
East Haven …………	2714	2419	295	2679	b34
Guilford …………	2576	2441	135	2518	58
Hamden …………	3028	2566	462	2863	165
Madison …………	1814	1717	97	1796	18
Meriden …………	10495	7473	3022	10418	77
Middlebury …………	696	621	75	682	b13
Milford …………	3405	3056	349	3333	a70

(a) Also 2 Indians.
(b) Also 1 Indian.
(c) Also 7 Indians.

(d) Also 1 Chinese and 1 Indian.
(e) Also 24 Indians.
(f) Exclusive of city of Middletown.

TABLE IX.—*Population of Minor Civil Divisions, &c.—CONNECTICUT*—Continued.

Counties.	Total.	Nativity. Native.	Nativity. Foreign.	Race. White.	Race. Colored.
NEW HAVEN—Con.					
Naugatuck	2830	2024	806	2812	18
New Haven (a)	50840	36484	14356	49090	b1749
North Branford	1035	955	80	1026	9
North Haven	1771	1476	295	1768	3
Orange	2634	2257	377	2525	b108
Orange	782	654	128	750	b31
West Haven	1852	1603	249	1775	77
Oxford	1338	1200	138	1318	20
Prospect	551	520	31	545	6
Seymour	2122	1678	444	2097	25
Southbury	1318	1218	100	1291	27
Wallingford	3676	2956	720	3613	63
Waterbury	13106	8650	4456	13041	65
Buck Hill School Dist.	117	103	14	115	2
Waterville School Dist.	426	337	89	426	.....
Waterbury	10826	6933	3893	10765	61
Wolcott	491	470	21	490	1
Woodbridge	830	774	56	825	5
NEW LONDON.					
Bozrah	984	828	156	970	b13
Colchester	3383	2506	877	3320	63
Colchester	1321	1035	286	1306	15
East Lyme	1506	1426	80	1505	1
Franklin	731	657	74	704	27
Griswold	2575	2070	505	2480	c85
Groton	5124	4738	386	5039	85
Lebanon	2211	1914	297	2129	d80
Ledyard	1392	1354	38	1373	e6
Lisbon	502	445	57	485	17
Lyme	1181	1146	35	1162	19
Montville	2495	2177	318	2465	f23
New London	9576	7881	1695	9344	g224
North Stonington	1759	1714	45	1699	h32
Norwich (i)	16653	12025	4628	16255	j387
Norwich (i)	16653	12025	4628	16255	j387
Old Lyme	1362	1282	80	1355	7
Preston	2161	1887	274	2131	b29
Salem	717	691	26	693	24
Sprague	3463	1450	2013	3444	19
NEW LONDON—Con.					
Stonington	6313	5199	1114	6053	260
1st voting dist.	473	443	30	430	43
2d voting dist	2072	1495	577	2059	13
3d voting dist	1877	1615	262	1707	170
Stonington, (3d district)	1561	1328	233	1412	149
4th voting dist.	1369	1149	220	1360	9
5th voting dist.	522	497	25	477	45
Waterford	2482	2278	204	2464	18
TOLLAND.					
Andover	461	447	14	452	9
Bolton	576	555	21	559	17
Columbia	891	814	77	868	23
Coventry	2057	1767	290	2047	10
Ellington	1452	1224	228	1426	26
Hebron	1279	1165	114	1256	23
Mansfield	2401	2157	244	2386	15
Somers	1247	1177	70	1235	12
Stafford	3405	2982	423	3397	8
Tolland	1216	1089	127	1210	6
Union	627	583	44	624	3
Vernon	5446	3626	1820	5406	40
Willington	942	883	59	941	1
WINDHAM.					
Ashford	1241	1186	55	1236	5
Brooklyn	2354	1548	806	2299	55
Canterbury	1543	1408	135	1508	35
Chaplin	704	641	63	702	2
Eastford	984	949	35	942	k37
Hampton	891	811	80	864	27
Killingly	5712	4538	1174	5674	38
Plainfield	4521	3040	1481	4459	l50
Pomfret	1488	1321	167	1426	62
Putnam	4192	2608	1584	4171	k16
Scotland	643	626	17	636	7
Sterling	1022	873	149	1020	2
Thompson	3804	2752	1052	3770	34
Voluntown	1052	920	132	1042	10
Windham	5412	4017	1395	5383	m28
Woodstock	2955	2709	246	2885	n49

(a) The city of New Haven comprises all of New Haven Township.
(b) Also 1 Indian.
(c) Also 10 Indians.
(d) Also 2 Indians.
(e) Also 13 Indians.
(f) Also 8 Indians, and 59 Indians on the reservation.
(g) Also 8 Indians.
(h) Also 28 Indians.
(i) In 1860 and 1870 the city of Norwich includes the whole township.
(j) Also 11 Indians.
(k) Also 5 Indians.
(l) Also 12 Indians.
(m) Also 1 Chinese.
(n) Also 21 Indians.

TABLE IX.—*Population of Minor Civil Divisions, &c.*—*COLORADO.*

Counties.	Total.	Nativity.		Race.	
		Native.	Foreign.	White.	Colored.
ARAPAHOE. (*) (a)					
Denver	4759	3621	1138	4518	237
BOULDER.					
Boulder Valley	663	608	55	663	......
Boulder City	343	307	36	343	......
Left Hand	213	182	31	212	1
South Boulder Valley	282	222	60	282	......
St. Vrain	781	709	72	781	......
CLEAR CREEK. (*) (b)					
Georgetown	802	621	181	783	17
Idaho	229	187	42	224	5
CONEJOS. (*)					
Utah Reservation	25	20	5	25	......
COSTILLA. (c)					
1.	359	355	4	345	......
3.	253	205	48	252	1
4.	425	425	......	425	......
5.	235	232	3	235	......
6.	356	353	3	353	......
7.	151	151	......	151	......
EL PASO.					
Colorado City	81	73	8	81	......
FREMONT. (*)					
Cañon City	229	213	16	228	1
Wet Mountain Valley	352	155	197	352	......
German Colony	230	59	171	230	......
GILPIN. (*) (d)					
Black Hawk	1068	771	297	1065	3
Central City	2360	1605	755	2305	51
Nevada	973	571	402	970	3
GREENWOOD. (*)					
Kit Carson	473	316	157	442	31
HUERFANO. (e)					
Cucharis River & tributaries	1142	1124	18	1116	2
Huerfano & tributaries	1108	1084	24	1101	......
JEFFERSON. (*)					
Golden City	587	484	103	575	12
Mount Vernon	31	28	3	31	......
LARIMER. (f)					
Big Thompson	315	277	38	313	......
Cache à la Poudre	363	309	54	355	......
Sherwood	160	136	24	160	......
LAS ANIMAS. (g)					
Apishapa Valley	893	870	23	865	1
Purgatoire Valley, east of Trinidad	1597	1562	35	1577	1
Purgatoire Valley, west of Trinidad	1224	1213	11	1206	3
Trinidad	562	506	56	543	8
PUEBLO. (*)					
Fort Reynolds	54	33	21	54	......
Pueblo	666	590	76	652	14
SUMMIT. (*)					
Breckenridge	51	37	14	51	......
Montezuma	22	15	7	22	......
St. John's	71	38	33	71	......
WELD. (h)					
1.	253	195	58	253	......
2. (i)	240	223	17	240	......
St. Vrain (i)	240	223	17	240	......
3.	75	66	9	75	......
4.	81	63	18	81	......
5.	640	539	101	640	......
Evans (j)	189	161	28	188	......
Greeley	480	403	77	480	......
N. E. Corner	158	69	89	158	......

(*) Incomplete; the other principal civil divisions were not separately returned.
(a) Arapahoe County: Denver also includes 4 Chinese.
(b) Clear Creek County: Georgetown also includes 2 Chinese.
(c) Costillo County: Township 1 also includes 14 Indians; township 6, 3 Indians.
(d) Gilpin County: Central City also includes 1 Chinese.
(e) Huerfano County: Cucharis River and tributaries also includes 24 Indians; Huerfano and tributaries, 7 Indians.
(f) Larimer County: Big Thompson also includes 2 Indians; Cache à la Poudre, 8 Indians.
(g) Las Animas County: Apishapa Valley also contains 27 Indians; Purgatoire Valley, east of Trinidad, 19 Indians; Purgatoire Valley, west of Trinidad, 15 Indians; Trinidad, 11 Indians.
(h) Weld County: Evans also includes 1 Indian.
(i) St. Vrain village comprises all of district No. 2.
(j) Its district not ascertained.

TABLE IX.—*Population of Minor Civil Divisions, &c.*—*DAKOTA.*

Counties.	Total.	Nativity. Native.	Nativity. Foreign.	Race. White.	Race. Colored.
UNION.					
Big Sioux Town	388	327	61	378	(a)
Brule Creek Town	600	324	276	600	......
Civil Bend Town	570	466	104	570	......
Elk Point Town	775	651	124	775	......
Jefferson Town	616	416	200	615	(b)
Sioux Vall'y Town	558	319	239	558	......
YANKTON. (*)					
Yankton	737	571	166	718	(c) 18
East of James River	540	310	230	539	1
North of James River	55	12	43	55	......
West of James River	155	115	40	155	......

Counties.	Total.	Nativity. Native.	Nativity. Foreign.	Race. White.	Race. Colored.
IN UNORGANIZED TERRITORY.					
Cheyenne and vicinity	132	56	76	125	7
Fort Buford and vicinity	454	240	214	440	15
Fort Rice and vicinity	215	118	97	211	4
Fort Stevenson and vicinity	151	77	74	147	(d)
Fort Sully and vicinity	745	393	352	710	35
Fort Totten and vicinity	240	157	83	239	1
Grand River and vicinity	154	92	62	153	1

(*) Incomplete; the other principal civil divisions were not separately returned.
(a) Also 10 Indians.
(b) Also 1 Indian.
(c) Also 3 Indians.
(d) Also 4 Indians.

TABLE IX.—*Population of Minor Civil Divisions, &c.*—*DELAWARE.*

NOTE.—The marginal column marks hundreds; the first indentation, cities; the second, towns. Names of towns are placed under the names of the hundreds in which they are respectively situated. The population of each hundred includes that of all towns situated in it.

Counties.	Total.	Nativity. Native.	Nativity. Foreign.	Race. White.	Race. Colored.
KENT.					
Dover	6394	6267	127	4555	1839
Dover	1906	1834	72	1405	501
Duck Creek	4279	4154	125	3406	873
Clayton, (E. S.)	80	71	9	79	1
Salisbury	97	97	......	62	35
Smyrna	2110	2018	92	1791	319
Smyrna Land.	158	155	3	158	......
Kenton	2655	2602	53	1851	804
Clayt'n, (W.S.)	34	31	3	32	2
Little Creek	1892	1876	16	1399	493
Milford	3093	3062	31	2305	788
North Milford	1150	1121	29	798	352
Mispillion	3478	3444	34	2990	488
North Murderkill	3631	3573	58	2706	925
Camden	657	653	4	489	168
Wyoming	280	274	6	255	25
South Murderkill	4382	4306	76	3428	954
Felton	437	416	21	420	17
Frederica	588	583	5	522	66
NEW CASTLE.					
Appoquinimink	4299	4184	115	3010	1289
Brandywine	3180	2668	512	3094	86
Christiana	5370	4262	1108	4832	538
Mill Creek	3302	2993	309	2944	358
New Castle	3682	3234	448	2906	776
New Castle	1916	1619	297	1604	312
Pencader	2542	2390	152	1652	890

Counties.	Total.	Nativity. Native.	Nativity. Foreign.	Race. White.	Race. Colored.
NEW CASTLE—Con.					
Red Lion	2604	2277	327	2075	529
Delaware City	1059	885	174	1000	59
Fort Delaware	153	88	65	153	......
St. George	265	244	21	241	24
St. George	5075	4862	213	3075	2000
South St. G'rge	111	107	4	100	11
Middletown	915	883	32	788	127
Odessa	695	652	43	519	176
Port Penn	320	307	13	244	76
White Clay Creek	2620	2437	183	2105	515
Christiana	443	417	26	309	134
Newark	915	848	67	770	145
Wilmington	30841	25689	3152	27630	3211
SUSSEX.					
Baltimore	3380	3377	3	3001	379
Roxana	114	114	......	114	......
Broad Creek	3480	3480	......	3089	391
Broadkiln	2419	2412	7	2020	399
Milton	824	820	4	711	113
Cedar Creek	3544	3512	32	2883	661
Lincoln	130	126	4	125	5
South Milford	800	789	11	708	92
Dagsborough	2599	2597	2	2223	376
Frankfort	149	149	......	142	7
Millsborough	194	193	1	148	46
Georgetown	1863	1851	12	1569	294
Georgetown	710	701	9	572	138

TABLE IX.—*Population of Minor Civil Divisions, &c.—DELAWARE*—Continued.

Counties.	Total.	Nativity. Native.	Nativity. Foreign.	Race. White.	Race. Colored.	Counties.	Total.	Nativity. Native.	Nativity. Foreign.	Race. White.	Race. Colored.
SUSSEX—Cont'd.						SUSSEX—Cont'd.					
Indian River	1667	1665	2	1304	363	Nanticoke	2076	2071	5	1795	281
Lewes & Rehoboth	2128	2117	11	1520	608	Northwest Fork	2071	2066	5	1567	504
Lewes	1090	1080	10	852	238	Bridgeville	300	300	......	247	53
Little Creek	3770	3769	1	3194	576	Seaford	2699	2682	17	2093	606
Laurel	1080	1080	......	814	266	Seaford	1304	1290	14	1007	297

TABLE IX.—*Population of Minor Civil Divisions, &c.—DISTRICT OF COLUMBIA.*

Cities, etc.	Total.	Nativity. Native.	Nativity. Foreign.	Race. White.	Race. Colored.	Cities, etc.	Total.	Nativity. Native.	Nativity. Foreign.	Race. White.	Race. Colored.
Georgetown, (city)	11384	10364	1020	8113	3271	East of 7th st. turnpike	7032	6089	943	3023	4004
Washington, (city)	109199	95442	13757	73731	a35455	West of 7th st. turnpike	4085	3551	534	2811	1274
Remainder of District	11117	9640	1477	6434	b4678						

(a) Also 13 Indians. (b) Also 2 Indians and 3 Chinese.

TABLE IX.—*Population of Minor Civil Divisions, &c.—FLORIDA.*

NOTE.—The marginal column marks precincts, which in some counties were returned according to their former boundaries. In other counties the names in the marginal column are only names of polling-places around which voters and their families have been grouped. The first indentation marks cities; the second towns. Names of towns are placed under the names of the precincts in which they are respectively situated. The population of each precinct includes that of all towns situated in it.

Counties.	Total.	Nativity. Native.	Nativity. Foreign.	Race. White.	Race. Colored.	Counties.	Total.	Nativity. Native.	Nativity. Foreign.	Race. White.	Race. Colored.
ALACHUA. (*)						CLAY.					
Gainesville	1444	1400	44	679	765	Fleming's Island	133	133	......	127	6
BAKER.						GreenCoveSprings	373	368	5	240	133
						Kingsley's	297	297	......	283	14
						Middleburg	940	930	10	717	223
Johnsville	312	312	......	295	17	Trail Ridge	200	198	2	189	11
McClenny's Still	98	98	......	43	55	Whitesville (town)	155	155	......	143	12
Olustee	219	219	......	152	67						
Sanderson, (town)	696	691	5	545	151	COLUMBIA.					
BRADFORD.						Benton	733	732	1	484	249
						Ellesville	1484	1479	5	944	540
Lake Butler, (t'wn)	1073	1073	......	861	212	Lake City	5118	5092	26	2679	2439
Rediah's	80	79	1	68	12	Lake City	964	954	10	520	444
Providence	1101	1101	......	706	395						
Starke	1417	1412	5	1212	205	DUVAL.					
BREVARD.						Baldwin	694	692	2	447	247
						Fort George	148	145	3	53	95
Fort Capron	1216	1216	......	1197	19	Jacksonville	6912	6485	427	2923	3989

(*) Incomplete; the precincts were not separately returned.

TABLE IX.—*Population of Minor Civil Divisions, &c.*—FLORIDA—Continued.

Counties.	Total.	Nativity. Native.	Nativity. Foreign.	Race. White.	Race. Colored.
DUVAL—Cont'd.					
La Villa	1078	1051	27	243	835
Mandarin	2040	1989	51	859	1181
Yellow Bluff	1049	1040	9	616	433
ESCAMBIA. (†)					
Molino	266	258	8	113	153
Pensacola	3347	3066	281	2083	1264
Warrington	1697	1448	249	982	715
FRANKLIN.					
Appalachicola	127	117	10	108	19
Appalachicola	1129	987	142	673	456
GADSDEN.					
Concord	1744	1742	2	881	863
Concord	176	176	......	144	32
Chattahoochee	1249	1242	7	555	604
Midway	1136	1135	1	234	902
Quincy	3993	3965	28	1299	2694
Quincy	743	724	19	367	376
St. Bernard	1680	1678	2	795	885
HAMILTON.					
Barlow	1925	1923	2	1121	804
Jasper	835	834	1	506	329
Jasper	138	138	......	95	43
Taylor	1069	1066	3	661	408
White Springs	1920	1918	2	1098	822
HERNANDO.					
Aucloke	120	118	2	109	11
Brookville	1112	1109	3	541	571
Crystal River	283	277	6	230	53
Fort Dade	955	953	2	786	169
Lake Lindsey	265	264	1	256	(a) 8
Stage Pond	203	199	4	161	42
HILLSBOROUGH.					
Alifia	422	419	3	355	67
Crawford Mill	774	772	2	568	206
Hurrah	446	445	1	426	20
Tampa, (town)	796	751	45	574	222
Taylor's School-house	778	750	28	747	31
HOLMES.					
Cerro Gordo	727	727	......	642	85
Cerro Gordo	672	672	......	597	75
Elmore	200	200	......	200	......
Harold	485	484	1	439	46
Harris	160	160	......	154	6
JACKSON. (*)					
Marianna	663	653	10	279	384
JEFFERSON.					
1.	2317	2310	7	723	1594
2.	3863	3835	28	1082	2781
Monticello	1052	1029	23	472	580
3.	532	527	5	113	419
JEFFERSON—C'd.					
4.	1468	1466	2	213	1255
5.	1126	1120	6	345	781
Williamsburg	253	250	3	204	49
6.	788	788	......	35	753
7.	712	709	3	396	316
8.	2592	2586	6	604	1988
LAFAYETTE.					
California	313	312	1	307	6
Cook's Hammock	237	237	......	228	9
Governor's Hill	275	275	......	263	12
New Troy	497	496	1	461	36
Summerville	461	461	......	327	134
LEON.					
Centerville	1581	1581	......	185	1396
Claire's	979	976	3	30	949
Jamonia	2977	2971	6	449	2528
Lake Jackson	1618	1615	3	96	1522
Lloyd Station	219	219	......	21	198
Miccosukie	1026	1024	2	176	850
Tallahassee	4813	4797	16	1118	3695
Tallahassee	2023	1946	77	890	1203
LEVY.					
Black	169	167	2	158	11
Brownson, (town)	375	374	1	339	36
Cedar Keys (b)	440	421	19	329	111
Cow Creek	92	92	......	88	4
Levyville	794	783	11	584	210
Otter Creek	148	147	1	125	23
LIBERTY.					
Bear Creek	319	319	......	270	49
Bristol	330	328	2	265	65
Oak Grove	401	401	......	192	209
MADISON. (*)					
Madison	924	905	19	415	509
MANATEE.					
Townships 33	438	434	4	419	19
Townships 34	640	621	19	598	42
Townships 35	232	232	......	223	9
Townships 36	140	140	......	139	1
Townships 37	71	71	......	71	......
Townships 38	142	142	......	135	7
Townships 39	196	192	4	186	10
Townships 40	39	38	1	39	......
Fort Thompson's Settlement	33	33	......	33	......
MARION.					
Camp Izard	1277	1276	1	518	759
Flemmington	1097	1095	2	189	908
Ocala	6835	6807	28	1929	4906
Ocala	600	......	......	......	......
Orange Springs	1595	1595	......	290	1305

(*) Incomplete; the precincts were not separately returned.
(†) Incomplete; the other principal civil divisions were not separately returned.
(a) Also 1 Indian.
(b) Its precinct not ascertained.

…ABLE IX.—*Population of Minor Civil Divisions, &c.—FLORIDA*—Continued.

…nties.	Total.	Nativity. Native.	Nativity. Foreign.	Race. White.	Race. Colored.
…NROE.					
…ugas	237	161	76	219	18
…st	5016	2733	2283	4027	989
…st of Key …	300	168	132	290	10
…northeast …e Roman)	104	87	17	95	9
…AU. (*)					
…andina	1722	1594	128	763	959
…ANGE.					
…rings	374	372	2	314	60
…sville	315	314	1	296	19
…lle	415	406	9	369	46
…	1091	1082	9	1018	73
…LK.					
…	464	462	2	350	114
…ad	1189	1180	9	1075	114
…rn	640	640	.....	572	68
…ain	876	875	1	690	186
…NAM.					
…	443	443	.....	420	23
…Springs	349	336	13	235	114
…geSprings	40	40	.....	23	17
…	1120	1079	41	588	532
…tka	720	682	38	359	361
…'s Mills	760	755	5	383	377
…son's Mills	120	120	.....	72	48
…'s	512	511	1	289	223
…	637	610	27	572	65
…A ROSA.					
…ll	372	370	2	328	44
…y	234	232	2	219	15
…s Ferry	253	252	1	226	27
…ck Pond	94	94	.....	90	4
…	1574	1527	47	1252	322
…on	1014	978	36	809	205
…ton	272	263	9	220	52
…vel	173	173	.....	117	56
…k	170	166	4	151	19
…	170	162	8	147	23
…OHN'S.					
…	343	322	21	291	52
…a	220	219	1	205	15

Counties.	Total.	Nativity. Native.	Nativity. Foreign.	Race. White.	Race. Colored.
ST. JOHN'S—Con'd.					
St. Augustine	336	330	6	316	20
St. Augustine	1717	1610	107	1123	594
SUMTER.					
Curry's Store	280	280	.....	205	75
Leesburg	932	929	3	500	432
Okahumka	320	320	.....	278	42
Sumterville	1360	1356	4	869	491
SUWANEE.					
Houston	915	913	2	429	486
Live Oak	1396	1394	2	705	691
Wellborn	1945	1943	2	[illegible]	[illegible]
TAYLOR.					
1.	355	355	.....	334	21
2.	317	317	.....	287	30
3.	641	640	1	613	28
4.	140	140	.....	140	.....
VOLUSIA.					
Cabbage Point	89	89	.....	87	2
Enterprise	485	483	2	261	224
Fort Orange	157	147	10	106	51
Sand Point	245	235	10	224	21
Smyrna	64	60	4	55	9
Volusia	623	621	2	602	21
WAKULLA.					
Crawfordville	709	703	6	554	155
Newport	199	198	1	104	95
Oklokonee	255	253	2	214	41
Sopchoppy	387	387	.....	261	126
St. Mark's	130	124	6	78	52
Wakulla River, E.	289	283	6	146	143
Wakulla River, W	537	535	2	205	332
WALTON.					
Boggy Bayou	358	356	2	349	9
Chesnut	306	304	2	284	22
Cleary's	406	401	5	361	45
Four-Mile Land'g.	768	765	3	662	106
Freeport	281	279	2	264	17
Uchee Anna (a)	922	913	9	716	206
WASHINGTON. (*)					
Vernon	53	50	3	47	6

(*) Incomplete; the precincts were not separately returned.
(a) Its precinct not ascertained.

TABLE IX.—*Population of Minor Civil Divisions, &c.—GEORGIA.*

NOTE.—The marginal column marks militia districts, whose numbers are official; the names are those in general use. The first indentation marks cities; the second, towns. Names of towns are placed under the names of the militia districts in which they are respectively situated. The population of each militia district includes that of all towns situated in it.

Counties.	Total.	Nativity. Native.	Nativity. Foreign.	Race. White.	Race. Colored.
APPLING.					
442. Fifth (a)	986	981	5	923	63
443. Third (a)	863	862	1	716	147
456. Second (a)	993	992	1	810	183
457. Holmesville	721	718	3	639	82
483. Fourth (a)	1232	1230	2	755	477
1239. Louisville	291	288	3	267	24
BAKER.					
956. Seventh (a)	2751	2749	2	987	1764
971. Eighth (a)	3126	3119	7	671	2455
Newton	145	143	2	84	61
1183. Twelfth (a)	966	965	1	230	736
BALDWIN.					
105. Gumm's	615	614	1	220	395
115. Salem	1780	1779	1	718	1062
318. Smith's	1444	1440	4	269	1175
319. Pittsburgh	1208	1207	1	230	978
320. Milledgeville	2750	2700	50	1203	1547
321. Scottsboro	1389	1376	13	626	763
322. Hall's	1432	1419	13	578	854
BANKS.					
207. David's	582	582	......	462	120
208. Bushville	830	830	......	566	264
265. Homer	726	726	......	577	149
Homer	120	120	......	105	15
284. Washington	586	586	......	556	30
371. Columbia	474	474	......	383	91
448. Golden Hill	668	668	......	604	64
912. Poplar Sp'gs	509	509	......	457	52
1206. Wilmot's	302	302	......	233	69
1210. Berlin	296	295	1	214	82
BARTOW.					
819. Allatoona	686	679	7	571	115
822. Cartersville	4115	4089	26	2707	1408
Cartersv'le	2232	2220	12	1567	665
827. Pine Log	1199	1198	1	977	222
828. Cassville	2462	2456	6	1755	b706
851. Euharlee	2555	2535	20	1544	1011
856. Adairsville	1662	1657	5	1322	340
Adairsv'le	603	602	1	475	128
936. Little Prairie	597	597	......	546	51
952. Kingston	1923	1919	4	1265	658
1011. Wolf Run	965	959	6	864	101
Kingston	402	402	......	295	107
BERRIEN.					
518. Fifth (a)	413	409	4	398	15
1144. Upp'r 10th (a)	1265	1263	2	1067	198
1145. Lower 9th (a)	870	869	1	779	b90
1146. Upper 9th (a)	211	211	......	205	6
1148. Low'r 10th (a)	298	298	......	295	3
1156. Sixth (a)	507	507	......	485	22
1157. Nashville	954	953	1	828	126
Nashville	95	95	......	88	7
BIBB.					
481. Godfrey	2096	2019	77	941	1155
482. Warrior	1548	1545	3	833	715
483. Howard	938	930	8	230	708
514. East Macon c	1504	1491	13	502	1002
519. Hazzard	1121	1119	2	377	744
520. Rutland	1594	1589	5	814	780
1085. Vineville	1644	1620	24	498	1146
Macon (d)	10810	10179	631	5627	5183
BROOKS.					
659. Nankin	1217	1216	1	739	478
660. Morven	1217	1215	2	599	618
780. Tallokas	242	242	......	114	128
1198. Groverville	2134	2134	......	853	1281
1199. Quitman	2304	2283	21	1261	1043
Quitman	784	779	5	438	346
1230. Dry Lake	1228	1227	1	555	673
BULLOCK.					
44. Sink Hole	536	536	......	350	186
45. Club House	907	906	1	611	296
46. Lockhart	1087	1086	1	865	222
47. Brier Patch	1510	1508	2	887	623
48. Hagan's	885	879	6	618	267
1309. Statesboro'	685	684	1	535	150
Statesboro	33	32	1	29	4
BURKE. (*)					
61. Lester's	928	928	......	187	741
62. Waynesboro	843	832	11	206	637
63. Alexander	1187	1185	2	265	922
Alexander	227	226	1	103	124
64. Sapp's	1156	1154	2	454	702
65. Tarver's	887	882	5	312	575
66. Gordon's	1116	1115	1	206	910
67. Knight's	1174	1174	......	125	1049
68. Brigham's	1473	1470	3	777	696
69.	707	706	1	75	632
70. Sodom	1022	1022	......	182	840
71. Ireland	1534	1533	1	291	1243
72. Ballard's	818	817	1	70	748
73.	1799	1796	3	604	1195
74. Bar Camp	1426	1426	......	258	1168
75.	810	809	1	90	720
BUTTS. (†)					
Indian Springs	248	247	1	121	127
CALHOUN.					
574.	1596	1592	4	552	1044
626.	2034	2032	2	1008	1026
Morgan	126	125	1	94	32
1123.	1873	1872	1	466	1407
CAMDEN.					
Bayley's Mills	458	453	5	66	392
Horse Stamp	717	713	4	253	464

(*) Incomplete; some militia districts were not separately returned.
(†) Incomplete; the militia districts were not separately returned.
(a) County number.
(b) Also 1 Indian.
(c) Exclusive of part of Macon City.
(d) Includes the 56th and 716th militia districts, and portion of the 514th.

TABLE IX.—*Population of Minor Civil Divisions, &c.—GEORGIA*—Continued.

Counties.	Total.	Nativity.		Race.	
		Native.	Foreign.	White.	Colored.
CAMDEN—Cont'd.					
Jeffersonton	729	719	10	168	561
Rose Creek	1084	1074	10	393	691
St. Mary's	836	814	22	319	517
St. Mary's	702	685	17	284	418
Ward's Store	791	786	5	259	532
CAMPBELL.					
652. Palmetto	604	600	4	470	134
Palmetto	294	291	3	195	99
730. Dark Corner	790	790	......	633	157
731. Sand Town	784	777	7	488	296
733. Campbellton	887	884	3	582	305
Camp'ton	119	119	......	87	32
736. Pumpkin T'n	802	796	6	705	97
757. Good's	1625	1625	......	1017	608
784. Chestnut Log	1390	1390	......	1128	262
1134. Fairburn	1430	1427	3	1014	416
Fairburn	305	305	......	208	97
1165. Cross Anchor	864	862	2	552	312
CARROLL.					
642. Villa Rica	959	954	5	876	83
649.	1395	1393	2	1210	185
682.	1038	1037	1	911	127
713.	338	338	......	315	23
714. Carrollton	1943	1940	3	1652	291
729.	1252	1251	1	1155	97
1096.	950	949	1	893	57
1111. Bowdon	1831	1831	......	1631	200
Bowdon	350	350	......	313	37
1122. Fairplay	979	979	......	838	141
1152. Kansas	412	412	......	371	41
1163. Trickum's	331	331	......	303	28
1240. Turkey Cr'k	354	353	1	318	36
CATOOSA.					
908. Ringgold	1158	1155	3	971	187
Ringgold	316	315	1	235	81
1084. Cross Roads	799	791	8	687	112
1094. Chambers	563	563	......	492	71
1095. Black Stock	558	558	......	495	63
1096. Bloody Ninth	240	239	1	188	52
1109. Catoosa	771	770	1	716	55
1110. Wood Station	320	319	1	244	76
CHATHAM.					
Savannah	28235	24564	3671	15166	*a*13068
5. Thunderbolt	2244	2117	127	405	1839
6. White Bluff	3621	3565	56	490	3131
7. Ogeechee	4612	4568	44	411	4201
8. Cherokee Hill	2567	2549	18	288	2279
CHATTAHOOCHEE.					
672. Gobler's Hill	713	713	......	396	317
787. Halloca	505	505	......	254	251
1104. Cusseta	1090	1086	4	208	882
Cusseta	216	215	1	164	52
1106. Jamestown	956	956	......	205	751
1107. Pine Knot	595	592	3	336	259
1108. Coleman's	1218	1218	......	400	818
1153. Big Sandy	382	382	......	255	127
CHATTOOGA.					
870. Trion Fact'ry	1280	1278	2	1133	147
925. Summerville	800	798	2	562	238
Summer'le	281	281	......	203	78
CHATTOOGA—Con.					
940. Dirt Town	960	958	2	777	183
962. Dirt Town	960	960	......	714	246
961. Millville (*b*)	800	800	......	544	256
962. Broom Town	1462	1460	2	1190	272
1083. Millville	640	639	1	479	161
CHEROKEE.					
792. Canton	894	893	1	751	143
Canton	214	214	......	188	26
817. Bell's	909	906	3	764	145
818. Mullin's	459	458	1	390	69
890. Woodstock	891	891	......	648	243
960. Salacoe	359	359	......	297	62
971. Shakerag	503	503	......	491	*a*11
1000. Cross Roads	981	975	6	903	78
1008. Harbin's	963	963	......	903	60
1010. Hickory Flat	821	821	......	730	91
1015. Lick Skillet	640	639	1	454	186
1019. Wild Cat	640	636	4	594	46
1028. Fairplay	800	799	1	745	55
1031. Con's Creek	640	637	3	624	16
1032. Ball Ground	553	553	......	492	61
1174. Little River	346	345	1	331	15
CLARKE.					
216. Athens (*c*)	692	690	2	312	380
Athens	4251	4147	104	2284	1967
217. Georgia Fac'y	870	866	4	573	297
218. Puryear's	368	368	......	168	200
219. Sandy Creek	619	616	3	299	320
220. Buck Branch	624	621	3	125	499
221. Watkinsville	917	916	1	388	529
Watkins'le	643	642	1	325	318
222. Farmington	527	527	......	178	349
223. Scull Shoals	688	688	......	358	330
224. Dark Corners	501	501	......	276	225
225. Wild Cat	528	528	......	277	251
239. High Shoals	707	707	......	400	307
240. Buncomb	649	648	1	339	310
241. Barber Creek	531	528	3	310	221
261. Salem	469	467	2	201	268
CLAY.					
431. Town	1506	1492	14	677	829
Ft. Gaines	758	745	13	397	361
749. Cotton Hill	2531	2524	7	1068	1463
Cotton Hill	143	143	......	43	100
969. McElvey's Mill	1456	1453	3	899	557
CLAYTON.					
532. Chambers	816	814	2	402	414
548. Poplar Spr'g	1511	1510	1	1124	387
1088. Town	1915	1908	7	1336	579
Jonesboro	531	529	2	406	125
1159. Adamson	1235	1229	6	872	363
CLINCH.					
526. Johnson's	1530	1523	7	1242	288
970. Magnolia	341	338	3	299	42
1092. Stockton	476	476	......	411	65
1061. Griffin	372	372	......	358	14
1141. Ribron	421	419	2	421	......
1219. Lowdiver	361	357	4	336	*d*24
1224. Homerville	444	443	1	370	74

(*a*) Also 1 Indian.
(*b*) Or Seminole.
(*c*) Exclusive of city of Athens.
(*d*) Also 1 Chinese.

TABLE IX.—*Population of Minor Civil Divisions, &c.*—*GEORGIA*—Continued.

Counties.	Total.	Nativity. Native.	Nativity. Foreign.	Race. White.	Race. Colored.
COBB.					
845. Roswell	479	473	6	443	36
846. Powder Sp'gs	959	959	......	706	253
851. Acworth	2504	2502	2	2028	476
891. Merritt's	471	471	......	420	51
895. Cox	1440	1439	1	1140	300
898. Marietta	4376	4332	44	2968	a1405
Marietta	1888	1860	28	1196	b690
911. Gritter	1282	1278	4	1013	c268
991. Kenesaw	635	635	......	516	119
992. Lemon's	823	823	......	694	129
1017. Oregon	845	845	......	665	180
COFFEE.					
437. Pickrens	554	554	......	383	171
748. Court House	643	643	......	590	53
1026. Roberts	618	617	1	473	145
1127. Curry's	315	313	2	258	57
1130. Mills's	579	579	......	395	184
1170. Tanner's	483	482	1	415	68
COLQUITT.					
799.	513	512	1	475	38
1020.	172	172	......	169	3
1151.	598	595	3	550	48
1184.	371	370	1	323	48
COLUMBIA.					
125. Nebraska	1239	1236	3	205	1034
126. Smith's	1796	1789	7	290	1506
127. Marshall's	737	736	1	106	631
128. Saw Dust	1808	1802	6	658	1150
129. Appling	1512	1508	4	344	1168
130. Cobham	1058	1057	1	291	767
131. Academy	596	596	......	176	420
132. Shield's	477	474	3	105	372
133. Lombardy	1787	1782	5	1003	784
Thompson	369	365	4	263	106
134. Thompson	1274	1260	14	592	682
135. Luke's Store	652	652	......	110	542
174. Wrightsboro	593	592	1	200	393
COWETA.					
645. Sixth Land	2049	2044	5	801	1248
646. Town	2910	2883	27	1322	1588
Newnan	1917	1890	27	1170	847
647. Fourth Land	1174	1174	......	821	353
601. First Land	2407	2405	2	1493	914
693. Third Land	2155	2152	3	815	1340
742. Cedar Creek	1022	1021	1	626	396
755. Hurricane	550	550	......	174	376
806. Second Land	2055	2053	2	919	1136
992. Panther Cr'k	808	808	......	553	255
1139. Grantville	745	745	......	332	413
CRAWFORD.					
497. Castlebury's	1023	1023	......	385	638
521. Hammock's	1252	1252	......	357	895
529. Tabor's	1115	1115	......	316	799
532. Roger's	843	843	......	545	298
577. Towell's	529	529	......	469	60
593. Knoxville	1381	1379	2	659	722
594. Beasley's	787	787	......	335	452
630. Webb's	627	627	......	218	409
DADE.					
873. Sligo	377	......	......	377	......

Counties.	Total.	Nativity. Native.	Nativity. Foreign.	Race. White.	Race. Colored.
DADE—Continued.					
875. Empire Iron Works	357	......	......	357	......
960. Trenton	489	......	......	489	......
Trenton	223	222	1	196	27
974. Creek	278	277	1	233	45
1037. Sutten's	342	......	......	342	......
1038. Rising Fawn	333	329	4	305	28
1089. Egypt	171	......	......	171	......
1129. Stephen's Mill	365	361	4	337	28
1214. Lookout Mountain	126	......	......	126	......
1222. Sand Mountain	195	......	......	195	......
DAWSON.					
820. Sanford's	366	365	1	357	9
830. Armacalola	433	433	......	402	31
916. Savannah	315	314	1	257	58
931. Shoal Creek	326	325	1	314	12
979. Cut Off	405	405	......	399	6
989. Yellow Creek	463	462	1	391	72
1016. Black's	439	438	1	393	46
1022. Barrett's	394	392	2	344	50
1028. Kilough's	352	352	......	316	36
1178. Town	522	522	......	513	9
1180. Purdy's	354	354	......	346	8
DECATUR.					
513. Bainbridge	2026	1982	44	960	1066
Bainbr'ge	1351	1309	42	844	507
553. Harrison's	1088	1085	3	766	322
621. Limesink	2143	2142	1	1241	902
635. Lower Spring Creek	1114	1114	......	671	443
694. Attapulgus	1488	1487	1	521	967
Attapulgus	267	267	......	140	127
720. Jones	1575	1570	5	881	694
914. Faceville	1657	1657	......	566	1091
1005. Cooper's	1263	1262	1	585	678
1046. Rock Pond	1430	1428	2	739	691
1188. Pine Hill	1399	1399	......	535	864
DE KALB.					
487. Barnes	882	882	......	679	203
524. Shallowford	277	277	......	264	13
531. Decatur	2080	2071	9	1362	718
Decatur	401	400	1	299	102
536. Pantherville	1798	1786	12	1224	574
563. Diamond	814	811	3	657	157
572. Browning's	774	773	1	668	106
637. Evans	618	618	......	413	205
683. Lithonia	639	639	......	437	202
686. Cross Keys	761	760	1	599	162
1045. Stone Mountain	1371	1359	12	1049	322
Stone M'n	690	678	12	523	167
DOOLY.					
516. Millwood	1360	1355	5	833	527
535. Vienna	1516	1515	1	663	853
585. Byron	1189	1185	4	547	642
633. Drayton	1553	1551	2	561	992
640. Fohe's	971	969	2	390	581
732. Bedgood	291	291	......	291	......
945. Green	688	687	1	596	92
1004. Gum Creek	1343	1343	......	473	870

(a) Also 3 Indians. (b) Also 2 Indians. (c) Also 1 Indian.

TABLE IX.—*Population of Minor Civil Divisions, &c.—GEORGIA*.

ounties.	Total.	NATIVITY. Native.	Foreign.	RACE. White.	Colored.
LY—Cont'd.					
'arille's	487	485	2	392	95
'ohnson.....	392	392	......	389	3
OUERTY. (*)					
Albany (to'n)	2101	1974	127	1114	987
EARLY.					
'edar Spring	1148	1148	......	520	628
tiver	1201	1200	1	594	607
Damascus ...	2096	2090	6	675	1421
Blakely	1056	1049	7	512	544
'rquharts ..	767	767	......	270	497
'uba	730	730	......	255	475
CHOLS.					
Gilmore's	548	548	......	537	11
Howell's	105	105	......	78	27
Statenville ..	681	681	......	426	255
Statenville	61	61	......	39	22
Kinsey's	644	644	......	472	172
FINGHAM.					
....	610	605	5	414	196
....	1592	1583	9	1019	a571
....	1364	1364	......	737	627
Springfield	32	32	......	23	9
....	648	647	1	337	b310
LBERT.					
berton	512	509	3	278	234
ngstreet ...	613	612	1	203	410
iam	929	927	2	412	517
tersburg ...	925	922	3	276	649
'yeke's	800	799	1	220	580
ackersville .	1077	1076	1	284	793
oss	425	425	......	152	273
ko	741	741	......	519	222
aines's......	363	363	......	239	124
oshen......	880	880	......	740	140
ebbsburgh .	1090	1086	4	508	582
ntreville ...	894	893	1	555	339
MANUEL.					
ohnson	1208	1206	2	710	498
'rog Pond ..	314	314	......	231	83
wainsboro..	1044	1043	1	889	155
Swainsbo	108	107	1	94	14
pence's	1061	1053	8	567	494
'denfield	612	611	1	562	50
Lick Skillet	799	797	2	632	167
cotland	637	635	2	515	122
Gum Log	459	459	......	325	134
FANNIN.					
'oontooley..	513	513	......	481	32
Morganton ..	1635	1633	2	1567	68
olwell......	418	418	......	417	1
'airplay	337	337	......	324	13
ketuah	414	414	......	414	......
Hot House ..	487	483	4	487	......
ugar Creek	508	508	......	493	15
Mobile	396	396	......	396	......

Counties.	Total.	NA' Native.	FO		
FANNIN—Cont'd.					
1205. Flint Hill ...	542	540	2	527	15
1242. Rock Creek .	179	179	......	179	......
FAYETTE.					
495. Sixth (c)	1368	1365	3	818	550
496. Fifth, or Town (c) ...	1444	1441	3	881	563
499. Ninth (c)....	787	784	3	657	130
538. Fourth (c) ..	795	795	......	503	292
549. Upper Seventh (c) ...	1240	1239	1	872	361
624. Lower Seventh (e)	1010	1009	1	773	237
709. Black Rock..	613	613	......	443	170
1204. Union	964	963	1	729	235
FLOYD.					
820. Cave Spring.	2078	2069	9	1306	772
855. No. Carolina.	1175	1173	2	716	459
859. Walter's	1128	1124	4	795	333
919. Rome (d)	3199	3161	38	1923	e1272
923. Texas Valley	782	782	......	628	154
924. Barker's	1302	1299	3	833	469
949. Floyd Sprin's	1000	999	1	791	209
962. Chulio.......	1761	1759	2	1217	544
1048. Etowah.....	672	672	......	534	138
1059. Livingston ..	800	800	......	522	278
1120. Flatwoods...	585	570	15	465	120
Rome	2748	2662	86	1743	1005
FORSYTH.					
795. Big Creek	1525	1525	......	1338	187
835. High Tower..	959	955	4	839	120
841. Chestatee	1165	1165	......	1082	83
870. Coal Mountain	1112	1112	......	1014	98
879. Cumming	1434	1434	......	1108	326
Cumming	267	267	......	238	29
880. Vickery's Cr'k	940	940	......	773	167
885. Chattahoochee	848	848	......	708	140
FRANKLIN.					
206. Bryant's......	398	398	......	290	108
211. Flintsville....	800	800	......	618	182
212. Byrom's......	482	482	......	390	92
213. Gum Log	1199	1198	1	973	226
215. Big Smith's ..	561	561	......	404	157
218. Gunnel's	789	789	......	423	366
263. Dooley's	677	677	......	531	146
264. Carnesville...	990	989	1	657	333
Carnesville.	266	266	......	181	85
267. Wolf Pit	474	472	2	424	50
370. Manley's	799	799	......	689	110
812. Strange's.....	724	723	1	635	89
FULTON. (*)					
Atlanta	21789	20699	1090	11860	9929
West End	621	613	8	319	302
GILMER.					
850. Ellijay	1288	1288	......	1279	9
864. Tekenetley..	1047	1047	......	1022	25
907. Board Town	595	595	......	590	5
932. Carticay	857	857	......	818	39

ncomplete; the militia districts were not separately returned.
ncomplete; some militia districts were not separately returned.
Also 2 Indians.
Also 1 Indian.

(c) County number.
(d) Exclusive of city of Rome.
(e) Also 4 Indians.

TABLE IX.—*Population of Minor Civil Divisions, &c.*—*GEORGIA*—**Continued.**

Counties.	Total.	Nativity. Native.	Nativity. Foreign.	Race. White.	Race. Colored.
GILMER—Cont'd.					
958. Mount. Town	691	691	......	682	9
1009. Tails Creek	769	769	......	742	27
1035. Leaches	409	409	......	406	3
1091. Ball Ground	366	366	......	366	......
1135. Town Creek	307	307	......	307	......
1136. Cherry Dog	315	315	......	315	......
GLASCOCK.					
1167. Gibson's	739	739	......	572	167
1168. Down's	829	827	2	636	193
1169. Kent's	700	700	......	461	239
1234.	468	466	2	268	200
GLYNN.					
24. Brunswick	2348	2233	115	1455	893
25.	602	595	7	30	572
26.	1210	1200	10	204	1006
27.	1216	1197	19	237	979
GORDON.					
849. Calhoun	832	820	12	504	328
Calhoun	427	427	......	372	55
856. Fifteenth (a)	639	638	1	536	103
874. Fairmount	1036	1032	4	963	73
973. Seventh (a)	619	618	1	425	194
980. Resaca	839	836	3	701	138
1050. Springtown	599	597	2	513	86
1054. Sugar Valley	884	881	......	820	64
1056. Sonora	1002	1002	......	888	114
1057. Twenty-fourth (a)	517	517	......	447	664
1063. Eighth (a)	793	792	1	642	151
1064. Oothcalooga	601	598	3	522	79
1235. Coosawattee	480	478	2	393	87
GREENE.					
137. Holtzclaw's	361	361	......	173	188
138. Woodville	400	397	3	153	247
140. Crutchfield's	519	516	3	179	340
141. Caldwell's	645	644	1	165	480
142. Astin's	1275	1275	......	480	795
143. Greensboro	1713	1704	9	651	1062
Greensboro	913	905	8	390	523
144. White Plains	857	856	1	311	546
White Pl'ns	374	373	1	180	194
145. Winfield's	477	476	1	103	374
146. Branch's	320	318	2	89	231
147. Partee's	800	800	......	256	544
148. Penfield	767	760	7	376	391
Penfield	447	440	7	261	186
149. Foster's	1200	1200	......	611	589
160. Winslet's	1360	1358	2	335	1025
161. Park's	877	876	1	222	655
162. Credille's	563	563	......	87	476
163. Hutcheson's	320	320	......	107	213
GWINNETT.					
316. Ben Smith	1298	1297	1	1181	117
399. Harbin's	1050	1050	......	900	150
404. Goodwin's	480	478	2	242	238
405. Berkshire	1352	1350	2	1202	150
406. Pickneyv'e (c)	1120	1116	4	850	270
407. Lawrenceville	1201	1200	1	1001	200
408. Rockbridge	851	850	1	700	151
409. Cate's	1201	1200	1	1000	201
GWINNETT—C't'd.					
444. Hog Mountain	1006	1005	1	905	101
544. Martin's	1151	1150	1	1000	151
555. Sugar Hill	847	847	......	534	313
562. Cain's	874	874	......	757	117
HABERSHAM.					
402. Curriher	1066	1065	1	1001	65
409. Clarksville	727	716	11	582	145
Clarksvil'e	263	261	2	215	48
414. Mud Creek	810	810	......	740	70
422. Deep Creek	812	812	......	556	256
448. Toccoah	713	705	8	477	236
501. Batesville	561	558	3	530	31
666. Cool Spring	375	375	......	330	45
732. Centre Hill	590	590	......	505	85
977. Fair Play	362	361	1	326	36
1021. Fork	306	306	......	294	12
HALL.					
268. Tadmor	669	664	5	581	88
385. Morgan	951	948	3	744	207
392. Clinchem	756	754	2	635	121
403. Glade	950	950	......	806	144
410. Narramore's	318	318	......	278	40
411. Town	1058	1051	7	861	197
Gainesville	472	466	6	407	65
413. Robert's	794	794	......	711	83
434. Thomason's	709	709	......	648	61
565. Wilson's	877	876	1	779	98
569. Bark Camp	588	587	1	517	71
570. Whelchel's	429	428	1	382	47
575. Fork	533	533	......	486	47
803. Big Hickory	308	308	......	213	95
810. Polkville	667	667	......	586	81
HANCOCK. (*)					
112. Medlock	159	159	......	58	101
113. Burlington	320	319	1	123	197
114. Rachel	799	799	......	179	620
118. Fair Play	896	894	2	364	532
HARALSON.					
653. Tallapoosa	708	707	1	653	55
813. Price	761	761	......	742	19
1077. Waldroop	770	770	......	727	43
1078. Newnan	729	729	......	655	74
1143. Buchanan, (town)	768	766	2	662	106
1225. Walton	268	267	1	246	22
HARRIS.					
672. Hamilton	1358	1358	......	677	681
Hamilton	359	359	......	219	140
679. Whittaker's	813	812	1	319	494
695. Ellerslee	992	991	1	338	654
696. Cataula	994	993	1	435	559
703. Goodman's	895	895	......	454	441
707. Lower 19th (a)	845	844	1	542	303
717. Blue Spring	1004	1003	1	387	617
781. Negro Heel	949	949	......	350	599
782. Dowdles	781	781	......	325	456
786. Valley Plains	1051	1051	......	412	639
920. Whitesville	969	968	1	383	586
934. Waverly Hall	877	877	......	356	521
1186. Upper 10th (a)	890	890	......	427	463

(*) Incomplete; some militia districts were not separately returned.
(a) County number.
(b) Also 6 Indians.
(c) Or "Norcross."

ABLE IX.—*Population of Minor Civil Divisions, &c.*—*GEORGIA*—Continued.

Counties.	Total.	Nativity. Native.	Nativity. Foreign.	Race. White.	Race. Colored.
s—Cont'd.					
iith's......	866	864	2	377	489
ART.					
rtwell	909	909	......	731	178
Hartwell	154	154	......	123	31
s's........	1132	1132	......	856	276
iith's......	880	880	......	399	481
d Creek..	642	641	1	532	110
ll's	393	393	......	298	95
oal Creek.	1135	1134	1	898	237
Curry's ..	945	945	......	606	339
oley's	747	747	......	521	226
ARD.					
Cloud.....	649	649	......	365	284
ston......	1092	1092	......	601	491
as	947	945	2	679	268
bone	792	791	1	464	328
nklin	1335	1334	1	815	520
k Ankle..	715	715	......	621	94
loth	693	693	......	267	426
ica........	772	772	......	606	166
e Shin	871	870	1	800	71
NRY.					
phen......	640	632	1	378	262
aw	476	475	1	329	147
e's........	474	471	3	308	166
ust Grove	991	990	1	531	460
Donough ..	983	982	1	627	356
McDono'h	320	319	1	223	97
sheba.....	809	809	......	604	205
r's........	2028	2027	1	1147	881
r Creek...	1849	1848	1	985	864
Mullin's...	762	761	1	575	187
Johnson ..	662	661	1	452	210
Shakerag	428	427	1	333	95
STON.					
ver 14th (a)	1556	1555	1	153	1403
er 11th (a)	903	901	2	234	669
np's......	1795	1791	4	643	1152
t Valley ..	3369	3355	14	859	2510
Fort Val'y	1333	1322	11	546	787
k'ry Grove	1390	1385	5	236	1154
ynoville ...	1401	1398	3	197	b1201
ver Town	1473	1472	1	389	1084
er 14th (a)	1001	1000	1	160	841
ver 5th (a)	1200	1199	1	507	693
er 5th (a)	1035	1033	2	434	601
h (a)......	1376	1375	1	294	1082
iderson's..	797	797	......	179	618
er Town..	1803	1791	12	604	1199
Perry	836	825	11	381	455
ancey's ore......	1307	1307	......	182	1125
WIN.					
....	693	......	......	633	......
....	358	......	......	358	......
....	320	......	......	320	......
....	277	......	......	277	......
....	189	......	......	189	......

Counties.	Total.	Nativity. Native.	Nativity. Foreign.	Race. White.	Race. Colored.
JACKSON. (*)					
242. Clarksboro'h	1010	1010	......	565	445
243. House's......	994	992	2	614	380
245. Jefferson.....	988	988	......	632	356
246. Chandler's...	918	917	1	610	308
248. J. Randolph .	1394	1393	1	1184	210
253. Newtown.....	579	579	......	312	267
255. Minish	327	327	......	201	126
257. Harrisburgh	1214	1213	1	780	434
428. Cuningham's	899	899	......	548	351
455. Miller	303	303	......	202	101
465. Wilson	944	944	......	707	237
1042. Santa Fé	445	445	......	373	72
JASPER.					
191. Lane & Fear's	908	908	......	357	551
262. Lazenby......	396	396	......	100	296
289. Goolsby & Horeb's....	1081	1079	2	186	895
291. Wyatt's.......	450	448	2	162	288
291. Fish..........	478	478	......	140	338
292. Henderson & Cooke......	355	355	......	174	181
293. Hillsboro.....	527	525	2	130	397
295. Monticello....	808	803	5	316	492
296. White & Martin's........	639	638	1	386	253
297. Thompson & Barnes	404	403	1	216	188
363. Whitfield's ...	797	796	1	168	629
364. Langston & Heod's......	561	561	......	183	378
365. Lawrence	509	509	......	209	300
373. Grubb & Niblett's	892	892	......	477	415
379. Gilstrap & Benton's....	798	798	......	360	438
380. Robinson & Kelly's	639	639	......	164	475
904. Water's	197	197	......	156	41
JEFFERSON.					
76. Sylvan Grove..	1767	1763	4	644	1123
77. } 81. } Pope Hill....	3156	3153	3	1423	1733
78. } 82. } Louisville ...	1078	1072	6	316	762
Louisville	356	350	6	162	194
79. Tenn's Bridge.	1433	1432	1	290	1143
83. Bethany	2360	2356	4	1134	1226
84. Alexander's ...	1244	1237	7	244	1000
85. Barton	1152	1150	2	196	956
JOHNSON.					
55.	642	642	......	520	122
56.	321	321	......	296	25
1201.	661	600	1	548	53
1202.	1400	1399	1	685	715
JONES.					
202. Wallace	576	576	......	211	365
299. Finney's	461	460	1	92	369
300. Barron	137	137	......	9	128
301. Tranquilla ...	711	711	......	120	591
304. Roberts	677	676	1	202	475

(*) Incomplete; some militia districts were not separately returned.
(a) County number.
(b) Also 3 Indians.

TABLE IX.—*Population of Minor Civil Divisions, &c.—GEORGIA*—Continued.

Counties.	Total.	Nativity: Native.	Nativity: Foreign.	Race: White.	Race: Colored.
JONES—Cont'd.					
305. Lester	715	714	1	168	547
337. Hammock's	928	928	......	435	493
347. Towle's	927	927	......	358	569
358. Pope's	200	200	......	76	124
359. Flower's	581	579	2	156	425
360. White's	1214	1214	......	392	822
361. Hawkins	585	585	......	220	365
378. Etheridge	185	185	......	70	115
447. Sanders	699	699	......	277	422
450. Clinton	492	491	1	131	361
Clinton	362	361	1	119	243
459. Davison	348	347	1	74	274
LAURENS.					
52. Smith's	1092	1090	2	857	235
86. Royal's	685	685	......	329	356
87. Buckeye	522	522	......	137	385
342. Dublin	1345	1339	6	707	638
343. Pinetuckey	870	870	......	696	174
344. Hampton Mills	984	983	1	540	444
345. Harvard	941	938	3	218	723
391. Bailey's	878	876	2	428	450
392. Burgamy's	517	517	......	268	249
LEE.					
915. Starkville	1800	1797	3	209	1591
938. Palmyra	2007	2006	1	169	1838
975. Redbone	2000	1999	1	529	1471
976. Smithville	2000	1994	6	648	1352
1238. Chokee	1760	1759	1	369	1391
LIBERTY. (*)					
15. Mount Hope	4709	4693	16	640	4069
St. Catharine	128	127	1	1	127
16.	1116	1116	......	739	377
17. Taylor's Cr'k	1101	1098	3	655	446
1132.	762	762	......	394	368
LINCOLN.					
182. Shady Hill	605	605	......	181	424
183. Winn's	804	804	......	280	524
184. Samuel's	614	612	2	307	307
185. Sybert's	422	422	......	114	308
186. Lincolnton	862	861	1	369	493
Lincolnton	92	92	......	61	31
187. Goshen	906	906	......	243	663
188. Lisbon	737	735	2	112	625
269. Parks	463	463	......	191	272
LOWNDES. (*)					
663. Valdosta	1598	1588	10	784	814
Valdosta	1199	1189	10	646	553
LUMPKIN.					
821. Auraria	797	795	2	707	90
831. Martin's Ford	160	160	......	114	46
837. Dahlonega	749	743	6	591	158
Dahlonega	471	468	3	367	104
838. Shoal Creek	480	480	......	420	60
840. Nimble Will	417	417	......	396	21
900. Yahoola	747	747	......	729	18
935. Davis	612	610	2	572	40
990. Crumley's	330	330	......	302	28
1051. Wahoo	84	84	......	84	......
1116. Chestatee	640	640	......	639	1
1244. Frogtown	145	145	......	145	......
MACON.					
543. Marshallville	3212	3203	9	710	[illegible]
Marshallville	424	418	6	[illegible]	[illegible]
740. Edge's	619	619	......	[illegible]	[illegible]
757. Gatlin's	1589	1589	......	[illegible]	[illegible]
770. Montezuma	1597	1594	3	331	[illegible]
814. Lanier	721	716	5	314	[illegible]
Lanier	......	......	......	......	......
1002. Hicks	2034	2028	6	[illegible]	[illegible]
1070. Oglethorpe	1686	1681	5	631	[illegible]
Oglethorpe	400	396	4	[illegible]	[illegible]
MADISON.					
203. Fork	397	397	......	[illegible]	170
204. Town	403	403	......	246	157
205. Paoli	1042	1042	......	[illegible]	[illegible]
262. Pocataligo	919	919	......	[illegible]	[illegible]
382. Grove Hill	922	922	......	[illegible]	[illegible]
383. Nowhere	795	795	......	615	[illegible]
438. Mill	520	520	......	437	83
591. Harrison	229	229	......	197	32
MARION.					
710. Kitchafoonee	1837	1834	3	547	a[illegible]
807. Buena Vista	1632	1631	1	907	[illegible]
Buena Vista	525	525	......	[illegible]	[illegible]
808. Tazewell	1203	1203	......	654	[illegible]
948. Redbone	1075	1074	1	776	[illegible]
955. Fort Perry	601	599	2	[illegible]	79
1034. Jacksonville	1652	1650	2	763	889
MC'INTOSH.					
22.	438	434	4	90	348
24.	1006	995	11	644	[illegible]
Jonesville	99	99	......	80	19
271.	3047	2986	61	462	a2584
Black Isl'd	15	15	......	......	15
Broughton Island	71	71	......	1	70
Butler's Is	216	216	......	1	215
Ceylon	63	63	......	......	63
Chambers's Isl	115	115	......	1	114
Champney's Isl	137	136	1	1	136
Darien	547	523	24	111	a435
General's Island	49	49	......	......	49
Herd's Isl.	13	13	......	8	5
Potosi Isl.	36	36	......	......	36
Ridgeville	413	390	23	192	221
Sapelo Isl.	336	326	10	24	312
Stage Road	36	36	......	1	35
MERIWETHER.					
1.	2080	2079	1	1126	954
3.	2240	2240	......	660	1580
8.	1756	1753	3	629	1127
9.	4000	3995	5	1867	2133
10.	1440	1437	3	884	556
11.	2240	2238	2	1221	1019
MILLER.					
903.	1615	......	......	1615	......
1029.	661	......	......	661	......
1160.	815	......	......	815	......

(*) Incomplete; some militia districts were not separately returned.
(*a*) Also 1 Indian. (*b*) Also 6 Indians.

TABLE IX.—*Population of Minor Civil Divisions, &c.—GEORGIA*—Continued.

Counties.	Total.	Nativity. Native.	Nativity. Foreign.	Race. White.	Race. Colored.
MILTON.					
827. Double Br'ch.	630	638	1	595	44
842. First (a)	432	432	......	410	22
892. Little River	875	874	1	826	49
1172. Newtown	356	356	......	249	107
1175. Crossville	677	677	......	580	97
1176. Alpharetta	595	595	......	530	65
Alpharet'a	126	126	......	115	11
1226. Crogan's	395	395	......	339	56
1227. Big Creek	315	315	......	289	26
MITCHELL.					
9. Gum Pond	1439	1437	2	617	822
10. Jones's	1568	1554	14	1210	358
Camilla	289	279	10	211	78
11. McElvinville	3626	3622	4	1856	1770
MONROE.					
466. Middlebrooks	1032	1032	......	385	647
468. New Market	1112	1111	1	389	723
473. Benton's	628	627	1	129	499
478. Kelsey's	797	796	1	177	620
480. Forsyth	1510	1497	13	710	800
504. Johnstonville	1293	1293	......	620	673
523. Unionville	1604	1604	......	864	740
539. Redbone	1148	1148	......	518	630
554. Burgay's	1117	1112	5	275	842
557. Culloden	1509	1508	1	451	1058
595. Ever's	755	754	1	228	527
596. Dillard's	1268	1264	4	381	887
599. Russelville	887	887	......	302	585
618. Brantley's	865	865	......	318	547
632. Proctor's	604	604	......	348	256
634. Coxe's	1064	1084	......	314	770
MONTGOMERY.					
51.	842	832	10	590	252
275.	788	786	2	457	331
393.	799	797	2	595	204
394.	483	480	3	343	140
1221.	674	674	......	493	181
MORGAN. (*)					
Madison	1389	1374	15	619	770
Rutledge	235	235	......	203	32
MURRAY.					
824. Town	1168	1165	3	1042	126
Spr. Place	248	245	3	201	47
825. Ball Ground	957	956	1	718	239
874. Eighth (a)	800	800	......	760	40
972. Doolittle	480	480	......	437	43
984. Tenth (a)	878	878	......	812	66
1011. Alaculsa	519	519	......	486	33
1013. McDonald's	840	830	10	774	66
1030. Shuck Pen	858	854	4	714	144
MUSCOGEE. (*)					
Columbus	7401	7037	364	4196	(b)3204
Wynton	754	748	6	348	406
NEWTON.					
420. Brick Store	1031	1030	1	419	612
460. Brewer's	659	656	3	368	291
461. Stansell's	1312	1308	4	858	454

Counties.	Total.	Nativity. Native.	Nativity. Foreign.	Race. White.	Race. Colored.
NEWTON—Cont'd.					
462. Town	2772	2768	4	1634	1138
Covington	1121	1118	3	637	484
Oxford	665	664	1	375	290
463. Wyatt's	1356	1354	2	711	645
476. Rock Dale	1760	1758	2	1280	480
Conyer's	637	635	2	518	119
477. Hay's	1266	1266	......	633	633
546. Gaither's	549	549	......	199	350
547. Downs, or Oak Hill	920	919	1	606	314
566. Ball Rock	1070	1070	......	643	427
567. Rocky Plains	738	737	1	437	301
575. Sheffield	1182	1178	4	813	369
PAULDING.					
832. Burnt Hickory	1111	1111	......	1097	14
839. Ninet'nth (a)	959	958	1	927	32
942. Weddington	745	744	1	645	100
951. Cain's	439	439	......	350	89
1003. Acorn Tree	718	718	......	688	30
1080. Dallas	1067	1067	......	971	96
1081. Twentieth (a)	723	722	1	657	66
1087. P'mpk'n Vine	520	520	......	504	16
1143. California	952	952	......	861	91
1218. Umphrey's	405	404	1	383	22
PICKENS.					
794. Talking Rock	937	932	5	913	24
899. Dug Road	574	573	1	574	......
1026. P'rsim'n Tree	483	482	1	474	9
1036. Truckwheel	770	770	......	754	16
1098. Town	713	713	......	703	10
1099. Grassy Knob	299	299	......	297	2
1101. Jerusalem	638	638	......	603	35
1129. Townsend's	453	453	......	420	33
1182. Sharp Top	450	447	3	450	......
PIERCE.					
584. Stewart's	1410	1407	3	983	427
Blackshear	490	488	2	283	207
590. Jones	800	797	3	676	124
1181. Wall's	568	567	1	305	263
PIKE.					
505. Ninth (a)	1588	1588	......	735	853
533. Barnesville	2326	2315	11	1219	1107
Barnesville	754	746	8	498	256
534. First (a)	1107	1105	2	410	697
540. Liberty Hill	1164	1162	2	748	416
545. Driver's	628	628	......	337	291
551. Eighth (a)	1264	1263	1	690	574
580. Zebulon	745	745	......	429	316
581. McDowell	1102	1102	......	772	330
592.	981	981	......	659	322
POLK.					
1072. Van Wert	2145	2126	19	1433	712
1073. Buncombe	368	368	......	324	44
1074. Fish Creek	876	875	1	686	190
1075. Cedar Town	2269	2263	6	1265	1004
Cedar T'n	323	319	4	212	111
1076. Hampton's	871	868	3	621	250
1079. Garrison's	939	936	3	656	283
1223. Young's	354	354	......	259	95

(*) Incomplete; some militia districts were not separately returned.
(a) County number.
(b) Also 1 Indian.

TABLE IX.—*Population of Minor Civil Divisions, &c.*—*GEORGIA*—**Continued.**

Counties.	Total.	Nativity. Native.	Nativity. Foreign.	Race. White.	Race. Colored.
PULASKI. (*)					
396. Cochran..	132	132	.....	70	62
511.	848	846	2	484	364
542.	2616	2598	18	792	a1823
Hawkinsville....	813	798	15	437	376
764.	436	436	.....	258	178
1236.	636	636	.....	227	400
PUTNAM.					
306. Glade's.......	701	699	2	247	454
307. Rockville	694	693	1	155	539
308. Ashbank	528	528	.....	159	369
309. Tompkins's ..	551	551	.....	60	491
310. Avalona......	779	779	.....	219	560
311. Opposition ...	503	501	2	146	357
312. Garrard's	599	599	.....	104	495
313. Johnson's	535	533	2	176	359
314. Hendrick's ...	613	612	1	231	382
367. Fork	461	460	1	105	356
368. Eatonton	1601	1574	27	589	1012
Eatonton.	1240	1215	25	496	744
369. Half-Acre	747	746	1	196	551
374. Harrison's ...	562	562	.....	170	392
375. Patrick's	497	497	.....	128	369
389. Pop Castle ...	532	532	.....	209	323
390. Hawkins's....	558	558	.....	122	436
QUITMAN.					
811. Eighth (b) ...	2247	2243	4	832	1415
Georget'n	263	259	4	125	138
1195. N'th Carolina	867	861	6	434	433
1196. Florida......	339	339	.....	164	175
1197. Bumbleton ..	697	697	.....	343	354
RABUN. (†)					
Clayton	70	70	.....	63	7
RANDOLPH.					
718. Town	3235	3192	43	1513	1722
Cuthbert .	2210	2169	41	1094	1116
777. Tenth (b)....	1598	1598	.....	692	906
934. Sixth (b)	1039	1039	.....	643	396
947. Fifth (b)	1436	1435	1	830	606
954. Ninth (b)....	1180	1176	4	421	759
998. Fourth (b) ...	960	958	2	508	452
1131. Seventh (b)..	1113	1111	2	477	636
RICHMOND. (*)					
121. Poor House ..	854	854	.....	524	330
123.	1703	1657	46	488	1215
124. Fairer's	1756	1746	10	636	a1120
Augusta ...	15389	13937	1452	8957	a6431
120. 1st w.	4242	3970	272	2435	1807
122. 2d w..	3399	2959	440	2072	a1326
398. 3d w..	3228	2778	450	1878	1350
600. 4th w.	4520	4230	290	2572	1948
SCHLEY.					
785. Lick Skillet ..	1440	1439	1	476	964
882. Bump Head ..	1279	1279	.....	575	704
946. Buck Creek ..	991	990	1	625	366
961. Town	1419	1416	3	602	817
Ellaville .	157	155	2	65	92
SPALDING.					
490. Cabin	1559	1557	2	[illegible]	[illegible]
1001. Griffin City..	3421	3374	47	1803	[illegible]
1065. Orr's	804	799	5	384	[illegible]
1066. Akin's	716	714	2	498	218
1067. Mount Zion .	760	759	1	354	406
1068. Union	1346	1345	1	806	540
1069. Africa	1080	1078	2	399	681
1149. Line Creek..	519	518	1	263	256
STEWART.					
725. Mineral Spr'g	1507	1501	6	347	1160
727. Richland.....	989	988	1	406	583
747. Sardin's	838	837	1	[illegible]	[illegible]
796. Lumpkin.....	2856	2846	10	1275	1581
Lumpkin.	778	768	10	438	340
807. Florence	2140	2138	2	390	1750
816. Scienceville ..	949	949	.....	347	602
905. Green Hill ...	545	545	.....	191	354
906. Pan Handle ..	749	748	1	335	414
980. Antioch	2924	2917	7	[illegible]	[illegible]
988. Bumbleton ...	1407	1406	1	697	710
SUMTER.					
687. Tallow Town	1120	1119	1	309	811
745. Danville	1830	1822	8	541	1289
756. Brown's.....	2193	2189	4	424	1769
759. Botsford.....	1127	1125	2	451	676
789. Town	5221	5161	60	2168	[illegible]
Americus	3259	3205	54	1655	1604
884. Friendship ..	1011	1010	1	321	690
993. Andersonv'le	1366	1364	2	640	726
1007. Hammond's .	1327	1325	2	560	767
1185. Tabernacle ..	1364	1363	1	509	855
TALBOT.					
681. Pleasant Hill.	1234	1232	2	608	626
685. Talbotton	1596	1592	4	698	898
Talbotton	796	795	1	433	363
688. Wilkinson ...	1160	1159	1	350	810
689. Flint Hill	1074	1072	2	394	680
876. Redbone	515	515	.....	244	271
877. Centerville ...	920	919	1	356	564
883. Pratsburgh...	960	959	1	257	703
886. Hart's........	603	603	.....	243	360
889. Geneva.......	1119	1118	1	498	621
894. O'Neill's......	759	759	.....	316	443
902. Valley	1094	1094	.....	427	667
904. Roughedge ...	879	876	3	390	489
TATNALL. (†)					
41. Reedsville.....	55	55	.....	34	21
TAYLOR.					
737. Daviston ...	320	319	1	212	108
741. Reynolds....	1171	1171	.....	630	542
743. Carsonville..	1120	1120	.....	366	754
757. Butler.......	2479	2472	7	1628	851
768. Pan Handle .	800	798	2	378	422
843. Howard	360	360	.....	315	45
1071. Cedar Creek.	893	893	.....	623	270
TELFAIR.					
337.	601	601	.....	390	211
338.	960	959	1	570	390

(*) Incomplete; some militia districts were not separately returned.
(†) Incomplete; the militia districts were not separately returned.
(a) Also 1 Indian.
(b) County number.

TABLE IX.—*Population of Minor Civil Divisions, &c.—GEORGIA*—Continued.

Counties.	Total.	Nativity.		Race.	
		Native.	Foreign.	White.	Colored.
TELFAIR—Cont'd.					
Jacksonville	40	39	1	28	12
339.	1088	1086	2	686	402
340.	596	594	2	454	142
TERRELL.					
811. Daniel's C't Ground ...	889	887	2	502	387
909. Chickasaw Hatchet ...	1953	1951	2	520	1433
941. 11th Court Ground ...	988	987	1	540	448
1143. Brown's Sta'n	1579	1577	2	602	977
1150. Dover	1754	1752	2	621	1133
1154. Town	1890	1871	19	984	906
Dawson .	1099	1082	17	730	369
THOMAS.					
579. Duncanville .	2429	2428	1	546	1883
637. Thomasville .	2517	2498	19	750	1767
Thomasville (a) .	1651	1509	52	606	985
753. Eighteenth, (part of) (b)	1907	1906	1	1084	823
754. Ancella	2750	2747	3	1088	1662
783. Ways	1285	1281	4	649	636
891. Glasgow	1547	1547	......	388	1159
1212. Murphy's ...	272	271	1	226	46
1227. Bullock's	865	863	2	763	102
TOWNS.					
833. Lower Hiawassee	365	365	......	309	56
918. Brasstown ...	876	876	......	832	c42
980. Town's	640	640	......	626	14
1133. Hitower	620	619	1	619	1
1263. Up. Hiawas'e	279	279	......	237	42
TROUP. (*)					
La Grange	2053	2021	32	895	1158
677. Troup Fact'ry	1498	1497	1	694	804
692. Mountville ...	1471	1467	4	382	1089
699. O'Neal's	1248	1247	1	562	686
West P'nt	1405	1386	19	601	804
Long Cane	560	560	......	178	382
TWIGGS.					
323. Pierson's	1363	1363	......	498	865
324. Ware's	736	735	1	106	630
325. Jeffersonville .	672	671	1	166	506
326. Shady Grove .	472	470	2	148	324
354. Higgsville	1583	1581	2	679	904
355. Smith's	1360	1359	1	752	608
356. McDonald's ..	719	719	......	302	417
372. Bluff	485	485	......	146	339
396. Tarversville ..	890	890	......	71	819
425. Marion	265	265	......	45	220
UNION.					
834. Choestoe	703	703	......	660	43
843. Ivy Log	463	463	......	463	......
UNION—Cont'd.					
865. Blairsville ..	616	615	1	586	30
994. Canada	242	242	......	242	......
995. Gaddistown .	365	365	......	364	1
996. Arkaqua	584	584	......	581	3
1018. Young Cane.	291	291	......	289	2
1024. Gum Log	348	348	......	344	4
1050. Lower Young Cane	440	440	......	438	2
1147. Brasstown ..	218	218	......	199	19
1155. Dooley	386	385	1	382	4
1162. Coosa	457	457	......	451	6
1241. Cooper's Cr'k	154	154	......	154	......
UPSON. (†)					
Thomaston	630	629	1	342	288
WALKER.					
826. Crawfish	547	531	16	511	36
869. Chestnut Flat	416	416	......	372	44
871. Lafayette ...	1217	1216	1	916	301
Lafayette	251	251	......	193	58
881. Pond Spring .	1150	1150	......	988	162
943. Wilson's	651	651	......	549	102
944. Pea Vine	972	971	1	852	120
953. E. Armuchee	1061	1060	1	937	124
956. Chattanooga Valley	984	967	17	753	231
960. Cain Creek ..	493	493	......	453	40
971. Upper Cove .	1443	1442	1	1311	132
1053. W. Armuchee	680	678	2	443	237
1161. Mountain ...	311	306	5	311	......
WALTON.					
249. Cut-off	980	980	......	759	221
250. Brantley's	556	555	1	381	175
415. Lindley's	833	833	......	630	203
416. Broken Arrow	745	745	......	506	239
417. Buncombe ..	1266	1266	......	913	353
418. Social Circle ..	1015	1014	1	595	420
So'l Circle	405	404	1	250	155
419. Town	1161	1161	......	591	570
Monroe ..	438	438	......	260	178
421. Brooks's	709	709	......	343	366
454. Mountain	1137	1137	......	635	502
502. Allen's	726	726	......	403	323
503. Blasingame ..	969	969	......	577	392
559. Richardson ...	941	941	......	543	398
WARE.					
451. Waresboro ..	819	813	6	606	213
1030. Sweat's	186	186	......	152	34
1060. Stewart's	396	396	......	363	33
1082. Guess	434	434	......	386	48
1231. Tebeauville .	451	451	......	327	124
WARREN. (*)					
Warrenton	620	611	9	261	359
Gar'son at War'ton	68	47	21	63	5

(*) Incomplete; some militia districts were not separately returned.
(†) Incomplete; the militia districts were not separately returned.
(a) Its militia district not ascertained.
(b) County number.
(c) Also 2 Indians.

TABLE IX.—*Population of Minor Civil Divisions, &c.—GEORGIA*—Continued.

Counties.	Total.	Nativity. Native.	Nativity. Foreign.	Race. White.	Race. Colored.
WASHINGTON.					
88. McBride's	1015	1011	4	431	584
89. Wammock's	262	262	......	255	7
90. Robson's	813	810	3	403	410
91. Peacock	1701	1698	3	1088	613
92. Lamb's	1753	1753	......	879	874
93. Farmer's	1189	1189	......	397	792
94. Davisboro	1248	1244	4	357	891
95. Cato's	1461	1457	4	705	756
96. Giles	1355	1353	2	794	561
97. Sandersville	1989	1973	16	807	1182
98. Buck's	1044	1044	......	376	668
99. Prosser's	702	702	......	452	250
100. Clay's	751	751	......	347	404
136. Carter's Mill	559	558	1	239	320
WAYNE.					
333. Phinholaway	926	920	6	718	208
334. Waynesville	468	463	5	341	127
335. Over River	405	405	......	402	3
1217. Court House	378	378	......	337	41
WEBSTER.					
802.	477	476	1	274	203
978.	2102	2102	......	893	1209
Preston	186	186	......	115	71
1092.	974	973	1	523	451
Weston	66	65	1	53	13
1093.	647	647	......	437	210
1105.	477	477	......	312	165
WHITE.					
426. Mossy Creek	760	760	......	669	91
427. Nacoochee	794	785	9	700	94
558. Tessentee	718	717	1	601	117
761. Blue Creek	520	515	5	407	113
836. Town Creek	640	640	......	575	65
861. Mount Yonah	785	785	......	712	73
Cleveland	145	145	......	139	6
862. Shoal Creek	389	388	1	378	11
WHITFIELD.					
627. Tilton	1255	1246	9	1119	136
629. Tenth (a)	1043	1041	2	982	61
631. Ninth (a)	655	654	1	629	26
640. Mill Creek	696	694	2	638	58
868. Trickum	788	785	3	660	128
872. Dalton	4285	4200	85	3388	897
Dalton	1809	1753	56	1370	439
WHITFIELD—C'd.					
1070. Varnell's Station	511	510	1	446	65
1233. Tunnel Hill	884	883	1	744	140
WILCOX.					
443. Bower's Mills	668	667	1	391	277
1103. Gin House	384	384	......	349	35
1158. Abbeville	613	613	......	479	134
1171. Shakerag	361	360	1	347	14
1177. McDuffie Mill	413	412	1	336	77
WILKES.					
164. Town	2412	2368	44	742	1670
Washington	1506	1463	43	599	907
165. Newton	552	550	2	160	[illegible]
166. Limeford's	765	764	1	279	[illegible]
167. Mallorysville	441	440	1	148	[illegible]
168. Centerville	561	561	......	272	[illegible]
169. Tyrone	684	681	3	218	[illegible]
171. Irwin's	452	452	......	227	[illegible]
174. Upton's	571	571	......	169	[illegible]
175. Cross Roads	877	875	2	309	[illegible]
176. Pente	806	805	1	213	[illegible]
177. Bussey's	558	556	2	199	[illegible]
178. Danburg	697	696	1	252	445
179. Anderson's	883	883	......	172	711
180. Delhi	564	562	2	247	317
181. Williams	973	970	3	353	[illegible]
WILKINSON.					
327. Irwinton	1067	1063	4	439	[illegible]
Irwinton	241	237	4	165	76
328. Bloodworth	818	818	......	476	342
329. Lord's	1806	1802	4	1023	783
331. Ramah	1512	1504	8	970	542
332. Griffin's	1045	1045	......	488	557
352. High Hill	1480	1480	......	573	907
353. Turkey Creek	709	709	......	227	482
1245. Bethel	946	945	1	488	458
WORTH.					
512.	982	981	1	526	456
867.	1155	1153	2	901	254
Isabella	54	54	......	54	......
1044.	534	534	......	449	85
1121.	833	832	1	529	304
1124.	40	40	......	34	6
1125.	234	234	......	234	......

(a) County number.

TABLE IX.—*Population of Minor Civil Divisions, &c.—IDAHO.*

Counties.	Total.	Nativity.		Race.	
		Native.	Foreign.	White.	Colored.
ADA. (*) (*a*)					
Boisé City	995	739	256	912	13
Boisé Valley	76	62	14	72	2
ALTURAS. (*) (*b*)					
Atlanta, (town)	72	48	24	71	......
Boisé River Dist't	40	......	40	......	......
Boisé River Mining District	40	25	15	30	......
Overland Road and Snake River	28	23	5	28	......
Overland Road and vicinity	83	68	15	81	......
South Boisé River Mining District	16	......	16	......	......
Yuba and Middle Boisé District	80	11	69	20	......
BOISÉ. (*c*)					
Beaver Creek	80	2	78	5	......
Buena Vista	880	100	780	147	......
Centreville	474	124	350	202	1
Deadwood Basin	40	17	23	27	......
Gold Hill	111	21	90	59	......
Granite Creek	299	91	208	217	4
Idaho City	889	402	487	632	4
Payette Mines	39	28	11	38	......
Payette Valley	118	89	29	116	......
Pioneer	477	114	363	271	4
Placerville	318	117	201	235	2
Squaw Creek Valley	30	26	4	30	......
Upper Payette Valley	79	52	27	78	......
IDAHO. (*d*)					
Florence Precinct	154	47	107	121	......
Miller's Camp Precinct	6	3	3	6	......
Slate Creek Precinct	13	9	4	10	......
Warren Precinct	22	17	5	22	......
Washington Precinct	543	92	451	190	2
White Bird Precinct	71	17	54	41	......
South Fork Salmon River	40	20	20	25	......
LEMHI. (*e*)					
Fort Lemhi Dist't	37	32	5	37	......
Leesburg Mining District	180	85	95	137	1
Loon Creek Mining District	480	242	238	470	1
Salmon River Mining District	87	55	32	86	......
Salmon City and vicinity	186	88	98	116	......
Stanley Basin Mining District	18	7	11	18	......
NEZ PERCÉ. (*f*)					
First District	512	301	211	422	3
Lapwai, (garrison)	91	50	41	91	......
Kootenai District	31	23	8	31	......
Nez Percé Reservation	112	80	32	107	1
Second District	225	126	99	149	......
Third District	727	79	648	128	......
ONEIDA.					
Bear River Valley, (geographical)	314	216	98	314	......
Montpelia	120	83	37	120	......
Lincoln Valley, (geographical)	156	87	69	156	......
Fort Hull	77	37	40	77	......
Malade Valley, (geographical)	994	534	460	993	1
Malade City	591	311	280	590	1
Snake River Mining District	159	120	39	159	......
Soda Spring (town)	144	107	37	144	......
Upper Snake River Mining District	155	125	30	155	......
OWYHEE. (*) (*g*)					
Booneville Mining District	160	27	133	69	......
Bruno District	40	38	2	38	......
Camp Three Forks, (garrison)	89	45	44	89	......

(*) Incomplete; some civil divisions were not separately returned.

(*a*) Ada County: Boisé City also contains 65 Chinese and 5 Indians; Boisé Valley, 2 Chinese.

(*b*) Alturas County: Atlanta (town) also includes 1 Chinese; Boisé River District, 40 Chinese; Boisé River Mining District, 9 Chinese and 1 Indian; Overland Road and vicinity, 2 Chinese; South Boisé River Mining District, 16 Chinese; Yuba and Middle Boisé District, 60 Chinese.

(*c*) Boisé County: Beaver Creek also includes 75 Chinese; Buena Vista, 733 Chinese; Centreville, 271 Chinese; Deadwood Basin, 12 Chinese and 1 Indian; Gold Hill, 49 Chinese and 3 Indians; Granite Creek, 77 Chinese and 1 Indian; Idaho City, 253 Chinese; Payette Mines, 1 Indian; Payette Valley, 1 Chinese and 1 Indian; Pioneer, 202 Chinese; Placerville, 80 Chinese and 1 Indian; Upper Payette Valley, 1 Chinese.

(*d*) Idaho County: Florence Precinct also includes 33 Chinese; Slate Creek Precinct, 3 Chinese; Washington Precinct, 348 Chinese and 3 Indians; White Bird Precinct, 26 Chinese and 4 Indians; South Fork Salmon River, 15 Chinese.

(*e*) Lemhi County: Leesburg Mining District also includes 42 Chinese; Loon Creek Mining District, 7 Chinese and 2 Indians; Salmon River Mining District, 1 Chinese; Salmon City and vicinity, 70 Chinese.

(*f*) Nez Percé County: First District also includes 72 Chinese and 15 Indians; Nez Percé Reservation, 4 Chinese; Second District, 72 Chinese and 4 Indians; Third District, 599 Chinese.

(*g*) Owyhee County: Booneville Mining District also includes 91 Chinese; Bruno District, 1 Chinese and 1 Indian; Flint Mining District, 3 Chinese; Oro Fino Mining District, 6 Chinese; Reynold's Creek Mining District, 3 Chinese and 1 Indian; Silver City Mining District, 179 Chinese; Wagontown Mining District, 85 Chinese.

TABLE IX.—*Population of Minor Civil Divisions, &c.*—*IDAHO*—Continued.

Counties.	Total.	NATIVITY. Native.	NATIVITY. Foreign.	RACE. White.	RACE. Colored.	Counties.	Total.	NATIVITY. Native.	NATIVITY. Foreign.	RACE. White.	RACE. Colored.
OWYHEE—Cont'd.						OWYHEE—Cont'd.					
Flint Mining Dist't	30	18	12	27	......	Wagontown Mining District	160	53	107	73	......
Oro Fino Mining District	113	24	89	107	......	SHOSHONE. (a)					
Reynold's Creek District	77	60	17	73	......	First Election Precinct	598	54	544	136	1
Silver City Mining District	873	460	413	685	9	Second Election Precinct	4	......	4	4	......
Silver City ...	599	350	249	472	8	Third Election Precinct	120	39	81	112	1
Snake River Mining District	120	93	27	120	......						

(a) Shoshone County: First Election Precinct also includes 461 Chinese; Third Election Precinct, 7 Chinese.

TABLE IX.—*Population of Minor Civil Divisions, &c.*—*ILLINOIS.*

NOTE.—The marginal column marks townships, precincts, and land-survey townships; the first indentation, cities; the second, towns. Names of towns are placed under the name of the township, precinct, or land-survey township in which they are respectively situated. The population of each township, precinct, or land-survey township includes that of all towns situated in it.

Counties.	Total.	NATIVITY. Native.	NATIVITY. Foreign.	RACE. White.	RACE. Colored.	Counties.	Total.	NATIVITY. Native.	NATIVITY. Foreign.	RACE. White.	RACE. Colored.
ADAMS.						ALEXANDER.					
Beverly	1173	1088	85	1173	......	Cairo (c)	6267	5022	1245	4418	1849
Burton	1423	1228	195	1421	2	Clear Creek	1068	1042	26	1023	45
Camp Point	2130	1937	193	2116	14	Dog Tooth	301	295	6	210	91
Clayton	2063	1765	298	2033	30	Grove Island	553	537	16	448	105
Columbus	975	808	167	975	......	Hazlewood	674	671	3	656	18
Concord	1140	1023	117	1123	17	North Cairo (d) ...	58	58	......	20	38
Ellington (a)	2298	1777	521	2138	160	Santa Fé	600	565	35	555	45
Fall Creek	990	858	132	990	......	Thebes	473	443	30	472	1
Gilmer	1425	1161	264	1397	28	Unity	570	530	40	466	104
Honey Creek	1495	1341	154	1453	42						
Coatsburg	192	160	32	192	......	BOND.					
Houston	1239	1118	121	1234	5						
Keene	1283	1219	64	1283	......						
Liberty	1623	1479	144	1623	......	Beaver Creek	1490	1295	195	1489	1
Lima	1462	1410	52	1457	5	Fairview	1044	1023	21	1044	......
Lima	285	281	4	284	1	Greenville	1989	1800	189	1970	19
McKee	1410	1286	124	1409	1	La Grange	1060	1031	29	1059	1
Melrose (a)	2076	1464	612	1927	140	McCord	1433	1324	109	1353	80
Mendon	1796	1634	162	1766	30	Mulberry Grove ..	1738	1700	38	1730	8
Mendon	501	474	27	495	6	Okaw	945	844	101	945	......
North East	1521	1180	341	1519	2	Pocahontas	1535	1216	319	1534	1
Payson	1881	1764	117	1881	......	Ripley	972	817	155	972	......
Quincy	24052	16319	7733	22978	b1073	7 north, R. 2 west.	336	334	2	336	......
Richfield	1496	1417	79	1496	......	7 north, R. 3 west.	367	361	6	367	......
Ursa	1411	1346	65	1402	9	7 north, R. 4 west.	243	235	8	243	......

(a) Exclusive of part of city of Quincy.
(b) Also 1 Indian.
(c) City of Cairo includes all of South Cairo and part of North Cairo Precincts.
(d) Exclusive of part of city of Cairo.

'ABLE IX.—*Population of Minor Civil Divisions, &c.—ILLINOIS*—Continued.

unties.	Total.	Nativity. Native.	Nativity. Foreign.	Race. White.	Race. Colored.
OONE.					
re	4410	3501	909	4379	31
videre	3231	2573	658	3209	22
....	1164	1019	145	1163	1
....	1536	1135	401	1536	......
ia	1345	955	390	1345	......
....	1273	1125	148	1270	3
....	1002	844	158	1002	......
ster	1144	758	386	1144	......
....	1068	808	260	1068	......
OWN.					
rn	1050	1017	33	1050	......
stown	1522	1477	45	1522	......
n..........	1150	1061	89	1150	......
....	1560	1471	89	1560	......
i	1145	1011	134	1145	......
Sterling...	2703	2422	281	2677	26
nt Sterling	1352	1179	173	1344	8
lge........	1011	906	105	1011	......
....	593	580	13	593	......
ies	1471	1412	59	1471	......
REAU.					
(a)	1216	980	236	1215	1
kilwa (a) ..	761	676	85	759	2
b).........	1469	1295	174	1456	13
....	1145	938	207	1145	......
....	1023	756	267	1023	......
l..........	2309	1944	365	2309	......
ffield......	771	617	154	771	......
b)	1402	1226	176	1394	8
er (b).....	304	291	13	299	5
d	748	650	98	748	......
....	392	276	116	392	......
ille........	901	804	97	896	5
....	1059	744	315	1059	......
Town (a)..	1660	1373	287	1643	17
e	1408	1188	220	1406	2
own	387	293	94	387	......
....	839	703	136	839	......
....	973	799	174	973	......
....	1118	1014	104	1118	......
....	1034	841	193	1033	1
et	1510	1174	336	1508	2
....	1137	912	225	1137	......
on	4363	3313	1050	4307	56
oeton	3264	2467	797	3212	52
....	1497	1109	388	1496	1
....	1187	1015	172	1187	......
ld	1396	978	418	1396	......
and	492	411	81	492	......
....	1750	1446	304	1713	37
HOUN.					
w	947	901	46	946	1
....	534	433	101	534	......
....	564	393	171	564	......
....	498	452	46	496	2
rg	707	643	64	707	......
....	650	518	132	650	......
....	1551	1104	447	1551	......
od	1111	903	208	1111	......
RROLL.					
Grove.....	1154	1022	132	1154	......
CARROLL—Cont'd.					
Elk Horn Grove..	662	595	67	654	8
Fair Haven.......	1169	835	334	1168	1
Freedom	811	741	70	811	......
Lima	531	453	76	531	......
Mount Carroll	2815	2458	357	2813	2
Mount Carroll	1736	1552	204	1754	2
Rock Creek.......	2056	1859	197	2046	10
Lanark.......	972	863	109	963	9
Salem	839	653	186	835	4
Savanna..........	1236	999	237	1233	3
Savanna......	971	778	193	970	1
Shannon	1102	856	246	1102	......
Shannon	635	522	113	635	......
Washington......	603	395	208	602	1
Woodland	906	772	134	906	......
Wysox	1331	1243	88	1330	1
Milledgeville .	238	213	25	238	......
York	1490	1332	158	1490	......
CASS.					
Arenzville.......	884	650	234	884	......
Beardstown	3582	2690	892	3582	......
Beardstown ..	2528	1856	672	2528	......
Ravenswood..	55	45	10	55	......
Chandlerville	1047	888	159	1047	......
Chandlerville.	401	333	68	401	......
Hickory	513	444	69	513	......
Indian Creek	433	366	67	433	......
Lancaster	1239	1163	76	1235	4
Ashland......	203	185	18	200	3
Monroe	630	563	67	630	......
Princeton	348	325	23	348	......
Richmond	1115	1060	55	1115	......
Virginia.........	1789	1562	227	1789	......
Virginia......	954	833	121	954	......
CHAMPAIGN.					
Brown	486	434	52	486	......
Champaign (c)....	710	620	90	708	2
Champaign....	4625	3667	958	4502	123
Colfax...........	633	522	111	633	......
Compromise......	707	616	91	707	......
Condit	755	676	79	755	......
Crittenden	870	782	88	870	......
East Bend........	643	547	96	643	......
Harwood	779	665	114	779	......
Hensley	804	720	84	804	......
Kerr	361	342	19	361	......
Ludlow	920	757	163	920	......
Middletown	1401	1318	83	1396	5
Newcomb	897	862	35	897	......
North Homer (d) .	641	619	22	641	......
Pesotum	919	781	138	919	......
Philo	1184	1091	93	1184	......
Philo	291	285	6	291	......
Rantoul	1628	1355	273	1627	1
Raymond.........	323	231	92	323	......
Sadorus	1458	1236	222	1458	......
Sadorus	300	254	46	300	......
Scott	755	676	79	755	......
Sidney	1560	1425	135	1528	32
Sidney	480	447	33	480	......
Somer	1120	1025	95	1098	22
South Homer (d) .	1510	1320	190	1509	1
Homer	767	694	73	766	1
Stanton	1088	1055	33	1088	......
St. Joseph	1222	1205	17	1222	......
Tolono	1413	1195	218	1412	1
Tolono	777	626	151	776	1

Tiskilwa Village 390 in Arispe and 371 in Indian Town.
Dover Village 35 in Berlin and 269 in Dover. (c) Exclusive of city of Champaign.
orth and South Homer together constitute the township of South Homer.

TABLE IX.—*Population of Minor Civil Divisions, &c.*—ILLINOIS—Continued.

Counties.	Total.	Nativity. Native.	Nativity. Foreign.	Race. White.	Race. Colored.
CHAMPAIGN—Con.					
Urbana	3325	2982	343	3279	46
Urbana	2277	2017	260	2237	40
CHRISTIAN.					
Assumption	1246	933	313	1246	......
Assumption	590	461	129	590	......
Bear Creek	720	650	70	720	......
Buckhart	2028	1981	47	2027	1
Greenwood	776	698	78	776	......
Johnson	640	615	25	640	......
King	413	342	71	413	......
Locust	825	714	111	825	......
May	681	629	52	681	......
Morrisonville	128	111	17	128	......
Mosquito	1270	1206	64	1270	......
Mount Auburn	1640	1610	30	1640	......
Pana	3096	2761	335	3081	15
Pana	2207	1945	262	2192	15
Ricks	414	322	92	413	1
Rosemond	1107	992	115	1107	......
South Fork	1279	1115	164	1270	9
Stonington	738	656	82	738	......
Tacusah	1182	1105	77	1181	1
Taylorville	2180	2004	176	2162	18
CLARK.					
Anderson	947	859	88	947	......
Auburn	602	575	27	602	......
Cumberland	1469	1440	29	1469	......
Darwin	1012	919	93	1012	......
Dolson	1221	1179	42	1221	......
Douglas	555	503	52	555	......
Johnson	823	814	9	823	......
Marshall	2541	2226	315	2528	13
Martinsville	1572	1507	65	1572	......
Melrose	989	983	6	989	......
Orange	924	918	6	924	......
Parker	863	860	3	863	......
Wabash	2945	2790	155	2937	8
Westfield	1166	1148	18	1166	......
York	1090	1079	11	1090	......
CLAY.					
Bible Grove	998	967	31	998	......
Blair	857	840	17	857	......
Clay City	1364	1291	73	1346	18
Clay City	594	544	50	587	7
Harter	2785	2672	113	2771	a13
Flora	1339	1289	50	1326	13
Hoosier Prairie	1179	1171	8	1179	......
Larkinsburg	976	931	45	976	......
Louisville	1200	1161	39	1198	2
Louisville	529	511	18	529	......
Oskaloosa	1171	1129	42	1152	19
Pixley	1517	1396	121	1517	......
Stanford	1349	1311	38	1347	2
Xenia	2479	2432	47	2477	2
Xenia	916	876	40	914	2
CLINTON.					
Town. 1 N., R. 1 W	991	877	114	960	31
Town. 2 N., R. 1 W	919	704	215	915	4
Town. 3 N., R. 1 W	617	553	64	617	......
Town. 1 N., R. 2 W	522	464	58	517	5
Town. 2 N., R. 2 W	2402	1930	472	2310	92
CLINTON—Cont'd.					
Carlyle	1364	1045	319	1337	27
Town. 3 N., R. 2 W	698	594	104	698	......
Town. 1 N., R. 3 W	513	432	81	485	28
Town. 2 N., R. 3 W	919	671	248	914	5
Town. 3 N., R. 3 W	874	689	185	868	6
Town. 1 N., R. 4 W	1054	562	492	1054	......
Hanover	391	191	200	391	......
Town. 2 N., R. 4 W	1512	892	620	1478	34
Breese	489	258	231	485	4
Town. 3 N., R. 4 W	1032	695	337	922	110
Jamestown	120	81	39	120	......
Town. 1 N., R. 5 W	1353	750	603	1353	......
Town. 1 S., R. 5 W	520	328	192	520	......
Town. 2 N., R. 5 W	2359	1605	754	2351	8
Hull	300	177	123	300	......
Trenton	948	626	322	948	......
COLES.					
Ashmore	2088	2059	29	2088	......
Charleston	4472	4278	194	4457	15
Charleston	2849	2702	147	2834	15
East Oakland	1500	1477	23	1478	22
Hickory	1402	1339	63	1402	......
Humboldt	2023	1896	127	2023	......
Hutton	2196	2176	20	2196	......
Lafayette	1265	1229	36	1257	8
Mattoon	4967	4517	450	4793	174
Morgan	818	801	17	818	......
Okaw	1711	1645	66	1711	......
Paradise	1220	1208	12	1219	1
Pleasant Grove	1573	1557	16	1573	......
COOK.					
Barrington	1490	1034	456	1485	5
Bloom	1213	693	520	1213	......
Bremen	1501	729	772	1501	......
Bremen	164	78	86	164	......
Calumet	1253	652	601	1251	2
Chicago	298977	154420	144557	295281	3691
Cicero	1545	1011	534	1541	4
Elk Grove	1120	664	456	1120	......
Evanston	3062	2162	900	3019	43
Hanover	1098	593	505	1097	1
Hyde Park	3644	2238	1406	3616	28
Jefferson	1813	893	920	1769	44
Lake	3360	1883	1477	3359	1
Lake View	1841	1049	792	1839	2
Lemont	3573	1772	1801	3572	1
Leyden	1437	830	607	1436	(a)
Lyons	2427	1275	1152	2426	1
Maine	1808	1068	740	1806	2
New Trier	1105	742	363	1105	......
Niles	1791	850	941	1782	9
Northfield	1705	1004	701	1703	2
Orland	1130	579	551	1127	3
Palatine	1855	1218	637	1854	1
Palos	853	523	330	851	2
Proviso	2091	981	1110	2078	13
Rich	1339	722	617	1339	......
Shaumburg	931	456	475	931	......
Thornton	2222	1100	1122	2221	1
Thornton	301	156	145	301	......
Wheeling	1835	1067	768	1833	2
Worth	1747	986	761	1747	......
CRAWFORD.					
Honey Creek	1868	1865	3	1868	......
Hutsonville	1851	1836	15	1851	......
Licking	1625	1609	16	1625	......

(a) Also 1 Indian.

(b) Also 5 Indians.

TABLE IX.—*Population of Minor Civil Divisions, &c.—ILLINOIS*—Continued.

Counties.	Total.	Nativity. Native.	Nativity. Foreign.	Race. White.	Race. Colored.
CRAWFORD—Con.					
Martin	1099	1093	6	1099	......
Montgomery	1792	1775	17	1792	......
Oblong	1490	1474	16	1490	......
Palestine	1988	1959	29	1984	4
Robinson	1851	1826	25	1851	......
South West	325	325	......	325	......
CUMBERLAND.					
Cottonwood	1342	1334	8	1342	......
Crooked Creek	981	963	18	980	1
Greenup	2128	2083	45	2127	1
Greenup	535	509	26	535	......
Neoga	2285	2220	65	2284	1
Neoga	540	534	6	539	1
Spring Point	833	717	116	833	......
Sumpter	1751	1724	27	1751	......
Prairie City	305	297	8	305	......
Union	1836	1829	7	1836	......
Woodbury	1067	1017	50	1067	......
DE KALB.					
Afton	873	649	224	873	......
Clinton	1004	863	141	1003	1
Courtland	1293	1108	185	1292	1
De Kalb	2164	1653	511	2145	19
Franklin	1004	813	191	1004	......
Genoa	993	859	134	992	1
Kingston	975	848	127	975	......
Malta	1157	840	317	1153	4
Mayfield	941	786	155	941	......
Milan	857	573	284	855	2
Paw-Paw	978	849	129	977	1
Pierce	1003	744	259	1003	......
Shabbona	1205	909	296	1205	......
Somonauk	3359	2845	514	3339	20
Sandwich	1844	1615	229	1829	15
South Grove	795	602	193	795	......
Squaw Grove	886	706	180	886	......
Sycamore	2852	2328	524	2848	4
Sycamore	1967	1624	343	1967	......
Victor	926	696	230	926	......
DE WITT.					
Barnett	1078	1053	25	1078	......
Clintonia	2338	2119	219	2283	55
Clinton	1800	......	......	......	......
Creek	1022	987	35	1022	......
De Witt	1061	1034	27	1061	......
Harp	1164	1127	37	1164	......
Nixon	649	613	36	649	......
Rutledge	664	645	19	664	......
Santa Anna	1276	1231	45	1276	......
Farmer City	537	506	31	537	......
Texas	1064	1007	57	1064	......
Turnbridge	1105	1039	66	1105	......
Wapella	1437	1255	182	1436	1
Waynesville	970	953	17	970	......
Wilson	640	600	40	640	......
DOUGLAS.					
Arcola	2332	2081	251	2332	......
Bourbon	1457	1380	77	1457	......
Bowdre	1313	1277	36	1313	......
Camargo	1808	1781	27	1785	23
Garrett	1599	1488	111	1599	......
Newman	1077	1047	30	1075	2
Sargent	1035	1024	11	991	44
Tuscola	2863	2718	145	2835	28
DU PAGE.					
Addison	1613	799	814	1613	......
Bloomingdale	1141	732	409	1141	......
Downer's Grove	2518	1701	817	2507	11
Lisle (a)	1270	908	362	1270	......
Milton	2175	1714	461	2159	16
Wheaton	998	852	146	985	13
Naperville (a)	1226	968	258	1226	......
Naperville	1713	1314	399	1713	......
Wayne	1019	734	285	1019	......
Winfield	2211	1585	626	2211	......
York	1799	1017	782	1793	6
Elmhurst	329	164	165	323	6
EDGAR.					
Bruellett's	1086	1077	9	1086	......
Buck	794	752	42	794	......
Edgar	1617	1580	37	1617	......
Elbridge	1807	1789	18	1807	......
Embarras	1280	1247	33	1271	9
Grandview	1899	1825	74	1890	9
Hunter	1029	973	56	1029	......
Kansas	1618	1580	38	1615	3
Paris	4522	4253	269	4446	76
Paris	3057	2846	211	3000	57
Prairie	829	823	6	829	......
Ross	731	713	18	729	2
Shiloh	745	728	17	745	......
Stratton	1621	1580	41	1618	3
Symmes	1185	1166	19	1179	6
Young America	687	678	9	684	3
EDWARDS.					
Albion	2856	2400	456	2815	41
Albion	613	474	139	613	......
Dixon	526	465	61	526	......
French Creek	1132	977	155	1106	26
Salem	1582	1368	214	1582	......
Shelby	1469	1355	114	1469	......
EFFINGHAM.					
Bishop	564	422	142	564	......
Douglas	3222	2481	741	3220	2
Effingham	2383	1864	519	2381	2
Jackson	1028	987	41	1028	......
Liberty	504	484	20	504	......
Lucas	592	522	70	592	......
Mason	1908	1789	119	1902	6
Mason	490	467	23	486	4
Moccasin	1088	882	206	1088	......
Mound	1211	868	343	1211	......
Saint Francis	509	322	187	509	......
Summit	1432	1254	178	1432	......
Teutopolis	1033	641	392	1033	......
Union	637	608	29	637	......
Watson	1066	959	107	1064	2
West	859	639	220	859	......
FAYETTE.					
Avena	1182	1130	52	1182	......
St. Elmo	273	254	19	273	......
Bear Grove	992	966	26	984	8
Bowling Green	1097	1067	30	1097	......
Hurricane	1333	1242	91	1333	......
Kaskaskia	1220	1144	76	1218	2
Shobonier	143	137	16	143	......
Laclede	1242	1062	180	1242	......
Farnia	232	197	35	232	......
Laclede	159	135	24	159	......

(a) Exclusive of part of village of Naperville.

TABLE IX.—*Population of Minor Civil Divisions, &c.*—ILLINOIS—Continued.

Counties.	Total.	Nativity.		Race.	
		Native.	Foreign.	White.	Colored.
FAYETTE—Cont'd.					
London	1186	1177	9	1186	......
Otego	903	864	39	903	......
Ramsey	1862	1743	119	1862	......
Sefton	1227	1174	53	1227	......
Seminary	920	895	25	918	2
Sharon	1663	1530	133	1660	3
Vandalia	2431	2073	358	2392	39
Vandalia	1771	1443	328	1754	17
Wheatland	871	823	48	871	......
Wilburton	1509	1232	277	1509	......
FORD.					
Brenton	1073	915	158	1072	1
Piper City	302	267	35	302	......
Button	610	521	89	610	......
Dix	782	683	99	782	......
Drummer	568	509	59	568	......
Lyman	740	559	181	740	......
Mona	356	249	107	356	......
Patton	2726	1957	769	2714	12
Paxton	1456	1037	419	1445	11
Peach Orchard	374	254	120	374	......
Pella	552	464	88	552	......
Rogers	593	444	149	593	......
Sullivant	141	64	77	140	1
Wall	588	486	102	588	......
FRANKLIN.					
Town. 5 S., R. 1 E.	1040	1040	......	1040	......
Town. 6 S., R. 1 E.	960	948	12	960	......
Town. 7 S., R. 1 E.	788	784	4	788	......
Town. 5 S., R. 2 E.	660	660	......	660	......
Town. 6 S., R. 2 E.	1036	1033	3	1036	......
Town. 7 S., R. 2 E.	909	907	2	909	......
Town. 5 S., R. 3 E.	1224	1212	12	1224	......
Town. 6 S., R. 3 E.	1458	1443	15	1458	......
Benton	615	600	15	615	......
Town. 7 S., R. 3 E.	1270	1266	4	1270	......
Town. 5 S., R. 4 E.	988	985	3	988	......
Town. 6 S., R. 4 E.	1015	1004	11	1015	......
Town. 7 S., R. 4 E.	1304	1298	6	1298	6
FULTON.					
Astoria	2118	2031	87	2118	......
Banner	1104	1079	25	1104	......
Bernadotte	1253	1213	40	1253	......
Buckhart	1577	1467	110	1577	......
Canton	4472	4119	353	4452	20
Canton	3308	2995	313	3290	18
Cass	1283	1260	23	1283	......
Deerfield	907	830	77	907	......
Ellisville	657	633	24	657	......
Fairview	1317	1271	46	1317	......
Farmers	1058	1013	45	1058	......
Farmington	2066	1946	120	2066	......
Harris	1029	980	49	1029	......
Marietta	110	109	1	110	......
Isabel	715	687	28	712	3
Joshua	1175	1128	47	1175	......
Kerton	504	490	14	504	......
Lee	1296	1269	27	1296	......
Lewistown	2952	2739	213	2939	13
Liverpool	1336	1297	39	1327	9
Orion	1082	1002	80	1082	......
Pleasant	1685	1597	88	1676	9
Ipava	488	450	38	488	......
Putnam	1654	1537	117	1654	......
Cuba	568	492	76	568	......
Union	1914	1744	170	1914	......
Avon	672	611	61	672	......
FULTON—Cont'd.					
Vermont	2289	2174	115	2278	11
Waterford	454	438	16	454	......
Woodland	1602	1585	17	1602	......
Young Hickory	792	769	23	792	......
GALLATIN.					
Township 7, R. 8	610	609	1	610	......
Township 8, R. 8	1332	1307	25	1311	21
Township 9, R. 8	1199	1153	46	1092	107
Equality	356	337	19	338	18
Township 10, R. 8	799	786	13	797	2
Township 7, R. 9	309	309	......	309	......
Township 8, R. 9	1438	1405	33	1438	......
Township 9, R. 9	1037	1015	22	969	68
Township 10, R. 9	1485	1382	103	1420	65
Township 7, R. 10	675	645	30	675	......
New Haven	356	328	28	356	......
Township 8, R. 10	347	342	5	313	34
Township 9, R. 10	1813	1684	129	1498	315
Shawneetown	1309	1192	117	1088	221
GREENE.					
Bluff Dale	1440	1274	166	1440	......
Carrollton	2760	2357	403	2748	12
Kane	957	894	63	956	1
Mineral Springs	1181	1129	52	1181	......
Mount Airy	1320	1269	51	1320	......
New Providence	480	452	28	480	......
Walkerville	800	781	19	800	......
White Hall	1600	1431	169	1600	......
White Hall	1200	1057	143	1200	......
Woodville	1352	1251	101	1352	......
Town. 9, R. 10 W.	308	296	12	308	......
Town. 10, R. 10 W.	1706	1586	120	1706	......
Town. 11, R. 10 W.	920	886	34	920	......
Town. 9, R. 11 W.	1119	1019	100	1119	......
Town. 10, R. 11 W.	1240	1085	155	1232	8
Town. 11, R. 11 W.	1101	995	106	1101	......
Township 12 S., R. 11 W.	275	259	16	275	......
Township 12 S., R. 12 W.	1137	1097	40	1136	1
Township 12 S., R. 13 W.	581	569	12	581	......
GRUNDY.					
Auxsable	927	663	264	906	21
Braceville	1188	778	410	1183	5
Erienna	337	259	78	337	......
Felix	616	445	171	615	1
Goodfarm	803	599	204	802	1
Greenfield	1645	1222	423	1644	1
Gardner	940	681	259	939	1
Highland	980	781	199	979	1
Mazon	1005	886	119	1005	......
Morris (a)	113	59	54	113	......
Morris	3138	2312	826	3119	19
Nettle Creek	916	569	347	916	......
Norman	417	344	73	416	(b)
Saratoga	1233	740	493	1219	14
Vienna	900	665	235	900	......
Wauponsee	720	622	98	689	31
HAMILTON.					
Town. 3 S., R. 5 E.	351	350	1	351	......
Town. 4 S., R. 5 E.	1218	1182	36	1218	......
Town. 5 S., R. 5 E.	1420	1415	5	1419	1
Town. 6 S., R. 5 E.	1211	1211	......	1198	13
Town. 7 S., R. 5 E.	607	606	1	607	......

(*a*) Exclusive of city of Morris.

(*b*) Also 1 Indian.

TABLE IX.—*Population of Minor Civil Divisions, &c.—ILLINOIS*—Continued.

...nties.	Total.	Nativity. Native.	Nativity. Foreign.	Race. White.	Race. Colored.
...ON—Con.					
...S., R. 6 E.	379	367	12	373	6
...Prairie ...ty	160	148	12	154	6
...S., R. 6 E.	908	854	54	908	......
...S., R. 6 E.	1924	1894	30	1922	2
...eansboro	683	667	16	681	2
...S., R. 6 E.	960	943	17	960	......
...S., R. 6 E.	511	510	1	511	......
...S., R. 7 E.	122	122	......	122	......
...S., R. 7 E.	625	623	2	625	......
...S., R. 7 E.	1413	1387	26	1413	......
...S., R. 7 E.	720	717	3	720	......
...S., R. 7 E.	645	643	2	645	......
...OCK.					
...e	1018	835	183	1018	......
...	1992	1858	134	1974	18
...eek	1117	959	158	1116	1
...	2448	2282	166	2446	2
...hage	1448	1329	119	1446	2
...	1601	1502	99	1599	2
...	1019	982	37	1019	......
...a Green	1475	1413	62	1475	......
...n	1019	901	118	1003	16
...	926	903	23	926	......
...y	1457	1366	91	1457	......
...e	1741	1638	103	1735	6
...lle	1111	974	137	1101	10
...	1578	1031	547	1578	......
...ove	1217	1174	43	1217	......
...lo	1946	1762	184	1946	......
...	1380	1209	171	1380	......
...eek	1201	1085	116	1201	......
...tun	656	608	48	654	2
...	1485	1178	307	1484	1
...as	1147	1075	72	1147	......
...'s	1650	1629	21	1650	......
...	1474	1245	229	1467	7
...	4058	3079	979	4014	44
...saw	3583	2698	885	3539	44
...	1219	1089	130	1200	19
...RDIN.					
...ock	869	863	6	829	40
...n	827	792	35	783	44
...	1468	1407	61	1465	3
...eek	856	841	15	856	......
...re	533	474	59	531	2
...	560	552	8	560	......
...ERSON.					
...ip 8 N., ...	1126	1059	67	1126	......
...tnn	201	188	13	201	......
...ip 9 N., ...	953	806	147	953	......
...ip 10 N., ...	1406	1199	207	1405	1
...sville	353	290	63	353	......
...ip 11 N., ...	1224	1119	105	1223	1
...ip 12 N., ...	1028	929	99	1027	1
...p 8 N., ...	1132	1056	76	1131	1
...e Haute	139	138	1	130	......
...ip 9 N., ...	1072	982	90	1070	2
...a	127	115	12	127	......

Counties.	Total.	Nativity. Native.	Nativity. Foreign.	Race. White.	Race. Colored.
HENDERSON—Con.					
Warren	84	83	1	82	2
Township 10 N., R. 5 W	1438	1032	406	1438	......
Lynn	251	131	120	251	......
Sagetown	332	221	111	332	......
Township 11 N., R. 5 W	1723	1456	267	1722	1
Oquawka	1370	1128	242	1369	1
Township 12 N., R. 5 W	143	135	8	143	......
Township 8 N., R. 6 W	709	633	76	709	......
Township 9 N., R. 6 W	433	377	56	433	......
Shokokon	79	74	5	79	......
Township 10 N., R. 6 W	86	69	17	86	......
Township 8 N., R. 7 W	100	94	15	109	......
Dallas City	78	71	7	78	......
HENRY.					
Alba	295	213	82	295	......
Annawan	1261	1043	218	1258	3
Andover	1767	780	987	1759	8
Atkinson	1132	898	234	1132	......
Burns	1144	967	177	1143	1
Cambridge	1682	1276	406	1679	3
Clover	1695	1328	367	1695	......
Colona	1223	935	318	1223	......
Cornwall	952	808	144	952	......
Edford	948	657	291	948	......
Galva	3096	2251	845	3079	17
Galva	2160	1582	578	2143	17
Genesco	4081	3155	926	4068	13
Geneseo	3042	2353	689	3031	11
Hanna	964	680	284	964	......
Kewanee	4225	2869	1356	4188	37
Loraine	577	433	144	577	......
Lynn	1119	466	653	1112	7
Munson	1171	936	235	1171	......
Osco	1216	880	336	1216	......
Oxford	1327	860	467	1327	......
Phœnix	793	688	105	793	......
Weller	1560	682	878	1559	1
Western	1372	929	443	1372	......
Wethersfield	1247	1047	200	1244	3
Yorktown	659	477	182	659	......
IROQUOIS.					
Artesia	1269	1114	155	1268	1
Ash Grove	1146	1056	90	1141	5
Ashkum	1315	875	440	1315	......
Beaver	1278	849	429	1278	......
Belmont	833	818	15	833	......
Concord	878	848	30	859	19
Douglas	2399	1891	508	2399	......
Fountain Creek	503	435	68	503	......
Grenard	541	522	19	541	......
Iroquois	679	584	95	669	10
Loda	1921	1495	426	1909	12
Lovejoy	240	213	27	240	......
Martinton	866	620	246	866	......
Middleport (a)	861	790	71	861	......
Milford	1107	1037	70	1107	......
Milford	230	194	36	230	......
Onarga	2822	2537	285	2748	74
Papineau	1064	631	433	1036	28
Prairie Green	480	451	29	479	1
Shebanco	2530	1686	844	2526	4

(a) Exclusive of city of Watseka.

TABLE IX.—*Population of Minor Civil Divisions, &c.—ILLINOIS*—Continued.

Counties.	Total.	Nativity.		Race.	
		Native.	Foreign.	White.	Colored.
IROQUOIS—Cont'd.					
Sheldon	812	743	69	807	5
Sheldon	231	203	28	231	......
Stockland	687	662	25	687	......
Watseka	1551	1372	179	1546	5
JACKSON.					
Bradley	1297	1222	75	1297	......
Carbondale	3370	3226	144	2987	383
Degonia	470	428	42	464	6
De Soto	1433	1398	35	1396	37
Elk Prairie	1354	1320	34	1249	105
Grand Tower	2181	1785	396	1973	208
Killon	959	876	83	959	......
Kincaid	1049	1026	23	1044	5
Levan	1321	1285	36	1305	16
Makanda	1680	1644	36	1578	102
Murphysboro	3464	2647	817	3339	125
Ridge	1056	1045	11	1048	8
JASPER.					
Crooked Creek	1568	1546	22	1568	......
Granville	1260	1247	13	1260	......
Grove	1094	1044	50	1094	......
North Muddy	867	838	29	867	......
Smallwood	993	969	24	993	......
South Muddy	584	560	24	584	......
St. Marie	1452	1231	221	1452	......
Wade	1864	1752	112	1841	23
Willow Hill	1552	1520	32	1552	......
JEFFERSON.					
Town. 1 S., R. 1 E.	778	769	9	767	11
Town. 2 S., R. 1 E.	905	891	14	905	......
Town. 3 S., R. 1 E.	869	854	15	863	6
Town. 4 S., R. 1 E.	576	573	3	576	......
Town. 1 S., R. 2 E.	1289	1271	18	1289	......
Town. 2 S., R. 2 E.	1175	1168	7	1175	......
Town. 3 S., R. 2 E.	986	983	3	986	......
Town. 4 S., R. 2 E.	1175	1168	7	1173	2
Town. 1 S., R. 3 E.	1099	1086	13	1099	......
Town. 2 S., R. 3 E.	2540	2467	73	2531	9
Mt. Vernon	1167	1110	57	1159	8
Town. 3 S., R. 3 E.	979	963	16	975	4
Town. 4 S., R. 3 E.	1337	1333	4	1332	5
Spr'g Garden	205	204	1	205	......
Town. 1 S., R. 4 E.	850	847	3	850	......
Town. 2 S., R. 4 E.	960	953	7	959	1
Town. 3 S., R. 4 E.	1086	1081	5	1086	......
Town. 4 S., R. 4 E.	1260	1250	10	1260	......
JERSEY.					
Town. 7, R. 10 W.	1345	880	465	1271	74
Town. 8, R. 10 W.	1242	1019	223	1241	1
Town. 9, R. 10 W.	562	506	56	562	......
Town. 6, R. 11 W.	1034	866	168	1020	14
Town. 7, R. 11 W.	1166	986	180	1159	7
Town. 8, R. 11 W.	3576	3027	549	3457	119
Jerseyville	2576	2142	434	2460	116
Town. 9, R. 11 W.	324	320	4	324	......
Town. 6, R. 12 W.	1328	940	388	1319	9
Town. 7, R. 12 W.	1269	1192	77	1267	2
Town. 8, R. 12 W.	1381	1130	251	1376	5
Town. 6, R. 13 W.	272	240	32	272	......
Town. 7, R. 13 W.	592	546	46	592	......
Town. 8, R. 13 W.	963	850	113	963	......
JO DAVIESS.					
Apple River	1108	804	304	1108	......
Berreman	559	494	65	559	......
Council Hill	725	470	255	725	......
Derinda	804	501	303	803	1
Dunleith	1352	950	402	1351	(a)
East Galena	856	520	336	856	......
Elizabeth	1618	1163	455	1618	......
Galena	7019	4546	2473	6941	78
Guilford	1079	752	327	1079	......
Hanover	1191	960	231	1191	......
Menomonee	593	364	229	593	......
Nora	1046	918	128	1046	......
Pleasant Valley	943	764	179	943	......
Rice	570	382	188	570	......
Rush	1036	867	169	1023	13
Scales Mound	748	489	259	748	......
Stockton	1214	1027	187	1214	......
Thompson	800	522	278	800	......
Vinegar Hill	693	432	261	693	......
Ward's Grove	530	474	56	530	......
Warren	1786	1533	253	1786	......
Warren	1666	1434	232	1666	......
West Galena (b)	591	374	217	591	......
Woodbine	959	660	299	959	......
JOHNSON.					
Axley	1199	1193	6	1179	20
Bluff	1325	1322	3	1323	2
Buncomb	1385	1382	3	1370	15
Elvira	1268	1268	......	1268	......
Flat Lick	1180	1179	1	1175	5
Saline	1282	1269	13	1282	......
Simpson	916	915	1	916	......
Sulphur Springs	1197	1195	2	1197	......
Vienna	1496	1463	33	1486	10
Vienna	550	523	27	545	5
KANE.					
Aurora (c)	2033	1274	759	2017	16
Aurora	11162	8091	3071	11013	149
Batavia	3018	2231	787	2972	46
Big Rock	829	645	184	829	......
Blackberry	1173	985	188	1171	2
Burlington	919	687	232	919	......
Campton	957	745	212	956	1
Dundee	2079	1320	759	2079	......
Elgin (d)	1298	997	301	1298	......
Elgin	5441	3989	1452	5369	72
Geneva	1829	1350	479	1789	40
Hampshire	1049	815	234	1049	......
Kaneville	999	840	159	998	1
Plato	1004	773	231	1002	2
Rutland	960	682	278	960	......
St. Charles	2281	1720	561	2261	20
Sugar Grove	787	667	120	779	8
Virgil	1273	944	329	1272	1
KANKAKEE.					
Aroma	1100	902	198	1092	8
Bourbonnais	2068	1205	863	2068	......
Essex	990	719	271	990	......
Ganier	1582	1149	433	1582	......
Kankakee	5189	3308	1881	5151	38
Limestone	840	605	235	839	1
Manteno	1681	1090	591	1676	5
Momence	1291	1005	286	1280	11

(a) Also 1 Indian.
(b) Exclusive of city of Galena.
(c) Exclusive of city of Aurora.
(d) Exclusive of city of Elgin.

TABLE IX.—*Population of Minor Civil Divisions, &c.—ILLINOIS*—Continued.

Counties.	Total.	Nativity. Native.	Nativity. Foreign.	Race. White.	Race. Colored.
AKEE—Con'd					
m	1180	924	256	1180	......
	1356	927	429	1356	......
	1140	716	424	1139	1
ville	1112	915	197	1112	......
a	865	614	251	864	1
nne	1385	813	572	1385	......
er	1081	708	373	1079	a1
whead	1492	1072	420	1489	3
ENDALL.					
rove	1726	1322	404	1718	8
d	1352	1113	239	1345	7
	1265	966	299	1265	......
all	1445	1096	349	1445	......
n	1150	844	306	1149	1
Rock	1843	1560	283	1842	1
ay	918	701	217	896	22
go	1756	1378	378	1741	15
d	944	735	209	944	......
KNOX.					
	2153	2017	136	2127	26
bingdon (b)	948	886	62	947	1
nut	1144	1115	29	1144	......
y	1219	891	328	1219	......
	1045	968	77	1045	......
burg (c)	878	717	161	823	55
esburg	10158	7022	3136	9583	575
Creek	1056	1009	47	1056	......
erson	1742	1317	425	1741	1
n Point	1854	1762	92	1854	......
	2881	2434	447	2769	112
noxville	1883	1571	312	1807	76
	966	734	232	966	......
on	1426	1366	60	1425	1
io	1942	1486	456	1933	9
neida	1034	861	173	1027	7
e	1167	1079	88	1161	6
ler	853	806	47	853	......
	1133	981	152	1133	......
	1906	1761	145	1904	2
a	1950	1365	585	1937	13
'ataga	1205	839	366	1198	7
	899	784	115	899	......
ria	1190	941	249	1187	3
nt Grove	1960	1288	672	1954	6
ltona	902	574	328	897	5
LAKE.					
ch	1595	1248	347	1595	......
	1005	791	214	1005	......
n	640	538	102	640	......
	970	667	303	970	......
eld	1525	981	544	1517	d4
	1277	745	532	1277	......
ont	1015	760	255	1011	4
	572	397	175	572	......
tyville	1236	945	291	1234	2
ort	1289	957	332	1289	......
s	1262	868	394	1233	29
m	1259	803	456	1258	1
en	1235	1013	222	1227	8
onda	1120	886	234	1120	......

Counties.	Total.	Nativity. Native.	Nativity. Foreign.	Race. White.	Race. Colored.
LAKE—Continued.					
Waukegan (e)	507	376	131	506	1
Waukegan	4507	3321	1186	4494	13
LA SALLE.					
Adams	1662	1118	544	1661	1
Allen	877	635	242	876	1
Brookfield	1230	982	248	1230	......
Bruce	1921	1494	427	1918	3
Streator	1486	1136	350	1483	3
Dayton	653	526	127	651	2
Dayton	163	115	48	161	2
Deer Park	894	775	119	893	1
Dimmick	1222	846	376	1222	......
Eagle	870	636	234	869	1
Earl	2129	1703	426	2128	1
Eden	1523	1267	256	1523	......
Fall River	523	458	65	523	......
Farm Ridge	1042	887	155	1042	......
Freedom	1262	1012	250	1261	1
Grand Rapids	1148	871	277	1147	1
Groveland	1561	1368	193	1559	2
Hope	1437	1193	244	1435	2
La Salle (f)	5452	3120	2332	5452	......
La Salle	5200	......	......	......	......
Manlius	2463	1968	495	2463	......
Crotty	691	532	159	691	......
Marseilles	758	606	152	758	......
Mendota (g)	1043	777	266	1039	4
Mendota	3546	2596	950	3514	32
Meriden	1069	918	151	1066	3
Mission	1596	1005	591	1596	......
Northville	1187	838	349	1187	......
Ophir	1085	857	228	1085	......
Osage	1176	946	230	1176	......
Ottawa (h)	463	306	157	462	1
Ottawa	7736	5556	2180	7726	10
Otter Creek	1009	796	213	1008	(a)
Peru (i)	3945	2444	1501	3944	1
Peru	3650	......	......	......	......
Richland	730	410	320	730	......
Rutland	1499	1232	267	1499	......
Rutland	412	388	24	410	2
Serena	1076	769	307	1076	......
South Ottawa	597	491	106	597	......
Troy Grove	1501	1067	434	1501	......
Utica	1145	816	329	1145	......
Vermillion	671	577	94	670	1
Wallace	734	507	227	733	1
Waltham	1115	763	352	1115	......
LAWRENCE.					
Allison	855	828	27	817	38
Bond	1087	1084	3	1003	84
Christy	2904	2799	105	2893	11
Bridgeport	435	406	29	435	......
Sumner	672	652	20	667	5
Denison	1668	1586	82	1666	2
St. Francisv'e.	131	116	15	131	......
Lawrence	1492	1456	36	1408	84
Lawrenceville	435	422	13	423	12
Lukin	1755	1685	70	1755	......
Petty	1591	1565	26	1591	......
Russell	1181	1173	8	1110	71
Russellville	311	309	2	311	......

) Also 1 Indian.
) Also of Abingdon, in Indian Point, 752; total of Abingdon, 1,700.
) Exclusive of city of Galesburg.
) Also 4 Indians.
(e) Exclusive of city of Waukegan.
(f) Inclusive of city of La Salle.
(g) Exclusive of city of Mendota.
(h) Exclusive of city of Ottawa.
(i) Inclusive of Peru City.

TABLE IX.—*Population of Minor Civil Divisions, &c.*—ILLINOIS—Continued.

Counties.	Total.	Nativity.		Race.		Counties.	Total.	Nativity.		Race.	
		Native.	Foreign.	White.	Colored.			Native.	Foreign.	White.	Colored.
LEE.						**LOGAN—Cont'd.**					
Alto	832	537	295	831	1	Corwine	1069	997	72	1069	......
Amboy (a)	1279	1003	276	1279	......	Middletown	223	215	8	223	......
Amboy	2825	2147	678	2820	5	East Lincoln	3397	2976	421	3344	53
Ashton	1007	816	191	1004	3	Elkhart	1325	1173	152	1318	7
Bradford	1086	789	297	1086	......	Elkhart	378	335	43	371	7
Brooklyn	1235	880	355	1235	......	Eminence	1362	1291	71	1357	5
China	2351	1989	362	2345	6	Hurlbut	476	393	83	474	2
Franklin Gro.	757	636	121	752	5	Laenna	691	598	93	691	......
Dixon (b)	632	555	77	631	1	Lake Fork	398	383	15	398	......
Dixon	4055	3158	897	4029	26	Mount Pulaski	1910	1680	230	1905	5
East Grove	765	517	248	765	......	Mount Pulaski	653	515	138	648	5
Hamilton	186	165	21	186	......	Oran	769	678	91	769	......
Harmon	542	419	123	542	......	Orvil	1196	1040	156	1196	......
Lee Centre	1028	777	251	1028	......	Prairie Creek	1164	877	287	1164	......
Marion	747	551	196	747	......	Sheridan	1002	882	120	1002	......
May	1007	666	341	1007	......	West Lincoln	3053	2348	705	3027	26
Nelson	600	504	96	600	......						
Palmyra	1109	927	182	1103	6	**MACON.**					
Reynolds	742	483	259	742	......						
South Dixon	905	743	162	905	......	Austin	713	654	59	713	......
Sublette	1300	989	311	1300	......	Blue Mound	1089	953	136	1089	......
Viola	639	533	106	639	......	Decatur (c)	1337	1221	116	1316	21
Willow Creek	1019	734	285	1019	......	Decatur	7161	6164	997	6998	163
Wyoming	1280	1185	95	1280	......	Friends' Creek	1538	1437	101	1538	......
						Harristown	984	940	44	978	6
LIVINGSTON.						Hickory Point	1136	1096	40	1133	3
						Illini	821	750	71	818	3
Amity	790	700	90	790	......	Long Creek	1372	1330	42	1372	......
Avoca	825	732	93	818	7	Macon	1549	1431	118	1535	14
Belle Prairie	630	547	83	630	......	Maroa	1824	1709	115	1821	3
Broughton	823	660	163	823	......	Maroa	766	710	56	766	......
Charlotte	746	568	178	746	......	Milan	322	310	12	322	......
Chatsworth	1622	1211	411	1618	4	Mount Zion	1096	1077	19	1096	......
Chatsworth	999	706	293	995	4	Niantic	977	915	62	977	......
Dwight	1804	1435	369	1798	6	Oakley	1137	1118	19	1137	......
Dwight	1044	857	187	1038	6	Pleasant View	899	788	111	886	13
Eppard's Point	861	739	122	844	17	South Macon	79	75	4	79	......
Esmen	917	740	177	914	3	Wheatland	1336	1248	88	1327	9
Fayette	257	163	94	256	1	Whitmore	1111	1067	44	1111	......
Forest	1084	882	202	1082	2						
Germantown	369	245	124	369	......	**MACOUPIN.**					
Indian Grove	2635	2138	497	2635	......						
Fairbury	1493	1276	217	1493	......	Barr's Store	999	956	43	998	1
Long Point	970	828	142	970	......	Carlinville	5808	4598	1210	5730	78
Nebraska	1162	796	366	1162	......	Palmyra	2400	2321	79	2400	......
Nevada	877	629	248	877	......	Scottsville	1440	1429	11	1440	......
Newtown	1114	998	116	1112	2	Township 7, R. 6	1604	1177	427	1604	......
Odell	1435	1162	273	1431	4	Township 8, R. 6	853	690	163	853	......
Odell	739	616	123	735	4	Township 9, R. 6	710	653	57	707	3
Owego	800	652	148	800	......	Township 10, R. 6	870	803	67	865	5
Pike	847	622	225	847	......	Township 11, R. 6	1211	1133	78	1211	......
Pleasant Ridge	809	633	176	808	1	Township 12, R. 6	3075	2741	334	3050	25
Pontiac	2438	2103	335	2374	64	Township 7, R. 7	877	783	94	869	8
Pontiac	1657	1430	227	1605	52	Township 8, R. 7	1085	902	183	1080	5
Reading	1503	1358	145	1503	......	Township 11, R. 7	695	622	73	695	......
Ancona	250	215	35	250	......	Township 12, R. 7	1250	1228	22	1250	......
Reading	70	65	5	70	......	Township 7, R. 8	2884	2229	655	2837	47
Rook's Creek	945	724	221	945	......	Township 8, R. 8	1072	919	153	1070	2
Round Grove	640	506	134	640	......	Township 9, R. 8	643	536	107	642	1
Saunemin	974	811	163	974	......	Township 7, R. 9	1794	1319	475	1753	41
Sullivan	921	700	221	921	......	Township 8, R. 9	1517	1291	226	1415	102
Sunbury	891	724	167	891	......	Township 9, R. 9	1048	873	175	1046	2
Union	711	534	177	711	......	Township 10, R. 9	891	745	146	891	......
Waldo	1051	770	281	1051	......						
						MADISON.					
LOGAN.											
						Township 3, R. 5	2707	1410	1297	2706	1
Ætna	920	802	118	919	1	Highland	1737	871	866	1737	......
Atlanta	2339	2152	187	2313	26	Township 4, R. 5	800	495	305	800	......
Broadwell	920	809	111	920	......	Township 5, R. 5	629	474	155	629	......
Broadwell	194	160	34	194	......	Township 6, R. 5	776	664	112	776	......
Chester	1062	944	118	1061	1	Township 3, R. 6	1246	873	371	1240	6

(a) Exclusive of city of Amboy.
(b) Exclusive of city of Dixon.
(c) Exclusive of city of Decatur.

'ABLE IX.—*Population of Minor Civil Divisions, &c.—ILLINOIS*—Continued.

ounties.	Total.	Nativity. Native.	Nativity. Foreign.	Race. White.	Race. Colored.
x—Cont'd.					
hip 4, R. 6	1919	1281	638	1911	8
rine	858	506	352	858	......
hip 5, R. 6	1061	791	270	1057	4
ambra	101	60	41	101	......
en Castle	120	99	21	120	......
hip 5, R. 6	872	697	175	872	......
hip 3, R. 7	1880	1445	435	1841	39
hip 4, R. 7	1024	777	247	826	198
hip 5, R. 7	980	635	345	980	......
hip 6, R. 7	1115	783	332	1115	......
hip 3, R. 8	3002	2148	854	2876	126
hip 4, R. 8	3486	2431	1055	3257	229
wardsville	2193	1480	713	2140	53
hip 5, R. 8	1492	1020	472	1467	25
hip 6, R. 8	1308	828	480	1302	6
ro	184	124	60	184	......
hip 3, R. 9	1421	971	450	1218	203
hip 4, R. 9	920	718	202	880	40
hip 5, R. 9(a)	3326	2806	520	3011	315
	8665	6013	2652	8285	380
halto	67	56	11	67	......
hip 6, R. 9	1688	1191	497	1565	123
hip 3, R. 10	792	560	232	714	78
hip 5, R. 10	869	577	292	781	88
hip 6, R. 10	2153	1661	492	1808	345
ARION.					
..	794	759	35	791	3
ia (b)	389	380	9	389	......
alia	3190	2694	496	3069	121
City	833	638	195	825	8
ndy	1895	1799	96	1895	......
e	1161	1120	41	1161	......
m	835	779	56	811	24
ork	822	773	49	820	2
	1268	1103	165	1243	25
	1298	1278	20	1298	......
	1294	1247	47	1294	......
n	1139	1127	12	1135	4
	893	880	13	893	......
	3132	3041	91	3107	25
em	1182	1125	57	1158	24
al	958	883	75	956	2
Hill	721	706	15	720	1
SHALL.					
lain	1092	914	178	1092	......
gton	1020	815	205	1020	......
	1989	1747	242	1989	......
nona	879	772	107	879	......
	2613	2025	588	2603	10
ary	2162	1687	475	2152	10
ell	753	602	151	753	......
	2440	1951	489	2438	2
son	2105	1653	452	2103	2
irie	1400	1145	255	1399	1
nd	920	774	146	920	......
s	883	689	194	883	......
ta	1163	941	222	1163	......
a	1478	1236	242	1478	......
rland	558	470	88	558	......
ield	1205	1019	186	1205	......
ASON.					
Grove	1199	1027	172	1199	......
	2124	1802	322	2124	......
h	464	425	39	464	......

(a) Exclusive of city of Alton.
(b) Exclusive of city of Centralia.

Counties.	Total.	Nativity. Native.	Nativity. Foreign.	Race. White.	Race. Colored.
MASON—Cont'd.					
Crane Creek	1068	1020	48	1068	......
Havana	2933	2406	527	2930	3
Havana	1785	1465	320	1782	3
Lynchburg	804	692	112	804	......
Manito	1352	1088	264	1352	......
Manito	375	332	43	375	......
Mason City	2387	2244	143	2387	......
Mason City	1615	1537	78	1615	......
Mason Plains	800	639	161	800	......
Pennsylvania	932	875	57	932	......
Quiver	893	788	105	893	......
Salt Creek	1102	1044	58	1102	......
Sherman	590	492	98	590	......
MASSAC.					
Township 14, R. 3	424	421	3	395	29
Township 14, R. 4	1060	998	62	1048	12
Township 14, R. 5	632	498	134	628	4
Township 15, R. 3	276	273	3	265	11
Township 15, R. 4	997	914	83	930	67
Township 15, R. 5	1458	1298	160	1337	121
Township 15, R. 6	668	644	24	661	7
Township 16, R. 5	374	366	8	221	153
Township 16, R. 6	1098	1089	9	839	259
Brooklyn	104	102	2	104	......
Metropolis	2490	2291	199	2197	293
MC'DONOUGH.					
Bethel	1040	1035	5	1040	......
Blandensville	1707	1616	91	1699	8
Bushnell (c)	578	565	13	578	......
Bushnell	2003	1820	183	2003	......
Chalmers (d)	1484	1321	163	1484	......
Eldorado	1105	1073	32	1105	......
Emmett	957	870	87	957	......
Hire	1186	1169	17	1186	......
Blandensville	1565	1541	24	1563	2
Industry	1533	1493	40	1533	......
Industry	378	372	6	378	......
La Moin	1167	1130	37	1166	1
Macomb (d)	1219	1186	33	1218	1
Macomb	2748	2469	279	2732	16
Randolph	346	338	8	346	......
Mound	1350	1288	62	1346	4
New Salem	1233	1198	35	1222	11
Prairie City	1645	1589	56	1644	1
Prairie City	1078	1032	46	1077	1
Sciota	1138	1098	40	1138	......
Scotland	1162	1044	118	1162	......
Tennessee	2126	1770	356	2126	......
Walnut Grove	1128	1050	78	1128	......
MC'HENRY.					
Alden	722	609	113	722	......
Algonquin	2157	1573	584	2156	1
Burton	281	201	80	281	......
Chemung	2222	1845	377	2198	24
Harvard	1120	920	200	1102	18
Coral	1345	1170	175	1339	6
Dorr	2681	2179	502	2670	11
Woodstock	1574	1255	319	1563	11
Dunham	999	754	245	999	......
Grafton	1361	1020	341	1359	2
Greenwood	925	759	166	924	1
Hartland	1037	678	359	1036	1
Hebron	930	841	89	929	1
Marengo	2253	1991	262	2242	11
Marengo	1327	1209	118	1317	10
McHenry	1988	1531	457	1983	5

(c) Exclusive of city of Bushnell.
(d) Exclusive of part of city of Macomb.

TABLE IX.—*Population of Minor Civil Divisions, &c.—ILLINOIS*—Continued.

Counties.	Total.	Nativity. Native.	Nativity. Foreign.	Race. White.	Race. Colored.
McHENRY—Con.					
Nunda	1548	1248	300	1548	......
Richmond	1404	1115	289	1403	1
Riley	882	746	136	882	......
Seneca	1027	874	153	1027	......
MC'LEAN.					
Allen	1224	1050	174	1224	......
Stanford	274	249	25	274	......
Arrowsmith	927	870	57	927	......
Bell Flower	659	584	75	659	......
Bloomington (a)	1829	1394	435	1810	19
Bloomington	14590	10692	3898	14355	235
Blue Mound	1219	1082	137	1219	......
Cheney's Grove	1164	1130	34	1164	......
Saybrook	389	375	14	389	......
Chenoa	2351	2022	329	2350	1
Cropsey	859	752	107	858	1
Dale	1188	1128	60	1162	26
Shirley	163	155	8	163	......
Danvers	1760	1502	258	1750	1
Danvers	356	312	44	356	......
Downs	1196	1167	29	1196	......
Dry Grove	1267	1079	188	1247	20
Empire	2133	2061	72	2129	4
Le Roy	862	826	36	858	4
Funk's Grove	818	736	82	818	......
Gridley	1709	1523	186	1709	......
Hudson	1392	1187	205	1392	......
Lawndale	835	786	49	835	......
Lexington	2404	2204	200	2399	5
Martin	687	657	30	686	1
Money Creek	999	960	39	999	......
Mount Hope	1550	1438	112	1549	1
McLean	600	547	53	600	......
Normal	3156	2768	388	3044	112
Normal	1116	1021	95	1081	35
Old Town	1109	995	114	1109	......
Padua	1249	1188	61	1249	......
Randolph	1958	1850	108	1958	......
Heyworth	300	294	6	300	......
Towanda	1235	947	288	1235	......
West	941	909	32	940	1
White Oak	532	487	45	532	......
Yates	1048	878	170	1048	......
MENARD.					
Town. 18, R. 5 W	793	677	116	793	......
Town. 19, R. 5 W	1243	1068	175	1243	......
Sweet Water	230	204	26	230	......
Town. 17, R. 6 W. (b)	1172	1059	113	1172	......
Athens (b)	351	318	33	350	1
Town. 18, R. 6 W. (b)	1271	1184	87	1270	1
Town. 19, R. 6 W	1239	1052	187	1239	......
Greenview	373	311	62	373	......
Town. 17, R. 7 W. (c)	880	803	77	880	......
Town. 18, R. 7 W	2821	2380	441	2814	7
Petersburg	1792	1465	327	1787	5
Town. 19, R. 7 W	941	797	144	941	......
Town. 17, R. 8 W (c)	472	402	70	472	......
Tallula (c)	339	289	50	339	......
Town. 18, R. 8 W	477	417	60	477	......
Town. 19, R. 8 W	426	393	33	426	......
MERCER.					
Abingtou	931	883	48	931	......
Duncan	974	901	73	966	8
Eliza	767	698	69	767	......
MERCER—Cont'd.					
Green	1326	1201	125	1315	11
Viola	407	380	27	399	8
Keithsburg	1579	1455	124	1579	......
Keithsburg	1179	1087	92	1179	......
Mercer	1949	1783	166	1940	9
Aledo	1076	959	117	1071	5
Millersburg	1134	1069	65	1134	......
Millersburg	277	268	9	277	......
New Boston	1758	1603	155	1758	......
New Boston	779	679	100	779	......
North Henderson	1062	974	88	1062	......
Ohio Grove	1125	1053	72	1125	......
Perryton	1085	996	89	1085	......
Preëmption	1161	853	308	1161	......
Richland Grove	1444	937	507	1444	......
Swedona	359	183	176	359	......
Rivoli	1298	1077	221	1298	......
New Windsor	379	301	78	379	......
Suez	1176	1025	151	1176	......
MONROE.					
Bluff	925	625	300	910	15
Eagle	2388	1575	813	2382	6
Columbia	1246	768	478	1246	......
Fountain	2977	1894	1083	2977	......
Waterloo	1537	979	558	1537	......
Harrisonville	478	387	91	473	5
Mitchie	799	600	199	799	......
Moredock	636	506	130	594	42
New Design	2016	1265	751	2015	1
Prairie du Long	1146	739	407	1146	......
Renault	1617	1079	538	1617	......
MONTGOMERY.					
Audubon	1250	1215	35	1250	......
Bear Creek	1650	1603	47	1650	......
Bois D'Arc	1177	1019	158	1176	1
Butler	2107	1826	281	2049	58
Butler	1648	1418	230	1644	4
East Fork	1421	1383	38	1421	......
Hillsboro	3417	3172	245	3367	50
Hurricane	724	699	25	724	......
Irving	1591	1542	49	1584	7
Irving	751	714	37	750	1
Litchfield (d)	1746	1633	113	1740	6
Litchfield	3852	3101	751	3830	22
Nokomis	2738	2455	283	2730	8
Nokomis	893	705	188	887	6
Walshville	1740	1556	184	1740	......
Zanesville	1901	1716	185	1901	......
MORGAN.					
Arcadia	1251	1130	121	1246	5
Bethel	1468	1176	292	1464	4
Concord	1280	1139	141	1279	1
Franklin	2057	1936	121	2056	1
Jacksonville (e)	3890	3205	685	3801	89
Jacksonville	9203	7105	2098	8792	f 410
Lynnville	643	456	187	643	......
Mauvaise Terre	736	592	144	688	48
Meredosia	1383	1142	241	1383	......
Sulphur Springs	627	478	149	625	2
Waverly	2463	2350	113	2433	30
Wright's	2022	1823	199	2022	......
Yatesville	1440	1273	167	1437	3

(a) Exclusive of city of Bloomington.
(b) Of Athens, 198 in T. 17, range 6 W; 153 in T. 18, range 6 W.
(c) Of Tallula, 186 in T. 17, range 8 W; 153 in T. 17, range 7 W.
(d) Exclusive of city of Litchfield.
(e) Exclusive of city of Jacksonville.
(f) Also 1 Chinese.

ABLE IX.—*Population of Minor Civil Divisions, &c.—ILLINOIS*—Continued.

...nties.	Total.	Nativity. Native.	Nativity. Foreign.	Race. White.	Race. Colored.
LTRIE.					
....	924	822	102	924	......
lson	1021	994	27	1021	......
n Creek ..	1001	993	8	1000	1
on........	1588	1547	41	1588	......
....	786	728	58	786	......
bone	1127	1031	96	1127	......
....	2658	2582	76	2658	......
van......	742	699	43	742	......
's	1280	1246	34	1280	......
ILE.					
lle........	746	644	102	746	......
....	3524	3176	348	3513	11
....	1805	1621	184	1796	9
....	1093	915	178	1087	6
....	1120	899	221	1118	2
int	777	721	56	777	......
....	2288	1919	369	2276	12
l	2177	1427	750	2175	2
Detour....	605	524	81	605	......
....	1265	1017	248	1265	......
e	467	393	74	467	......
er	1057	948	109	1057	......
le	726	535	191	726	......
....	1030	818	212	1029	1
d	1181	878	303	1181	......
....	923	785	138	923	......
Morris....	1455	1307	148	1445	10
....	483	366	117	483	......
....	1325	1122	203	1298	27
eek.......	1215	1194	21	1214	1
ck	1048	854	194	1041	7
le........	737	635	102	733	4
....	829	578	251	828	1
....	402	318	84	401	1
ock......	999	737	262	999	......
ORIA.					
....	1185	1001	184	1185	......
d........	1547	1343	204	1547	......
he	1486	1208	278	1482	4
d..........	2410	2101	309	2410	......
wood.....	1476	1234	242	1476	......
....	1094	985	109	1091	3
....	980	753	227	980	......
....	837	657	180	837	......
o..........	1440	1035	405	1439	1
ne	2302	1534	768	2292	10
....	1065	992	73	1065	......
....	905	749	156	905	......
k	1075	960	115	1075	......
z)	794	474	320	794	......
....	22849	15492	7357	22719	130
lle	1335	1207	128	1335	......
ceville ...	424	386	38	424	......
....	948	810	138	948	......
d	1239	961	278	1232	7
l	1108	901	207	1108	......
....	1707	1549	158	1707	......
....	1234	1155	79	1234	......
ERRY.					
S.,R.1 W.	1670	1579	91	1670	......
arva	937	878	59	937	......
S.,R.1 W.	1371	1234	137	1357	14
S.,R.1 W.	1381	1120	261	1296	85

Counties.	Total.	Nativity. Native.	Nativity. Foreign.	Race. White.	Race. Colored.
PERRY—Cont'd.					
Du Quoin.......	2212	1861	351	2027	185
St. John's	356	194	162	308	48
Town. 4 S., R. 2 W.	409	369	40	409	......
Town. 5 S., R. 2 W.	684	634	50	684	......
Town. 6 S., R. 2 W	898	753	143	873	25
Town. 4 S., R. 3 W.	420	357	63	420	......
Town. 5 S., R. 3 W.	1637	1432	205	1597	40
Pinckneyville	773	669	104	736	37
Town. 6 S., R. 3 W.	657	591	66	644	13
Town. 4 S., R. 4 W.	829	661	168	804	25
Town. 5 S., R. 4 W.	785	638	147	781	4
Town. 6 S., R. 4 W.	770	701	69	770	......
PIATT.					
Bement	1471	1310	161	1471	......
Blue Ridge	1120	1072	48	1120	......
Cerro Gordo	1650	1550	100	1648	2
Goose Creek.......	1120	1081	39	1120	......
Monticello	1840	1725	115	1836	4
Monticello ...	871	816	55	867	4
Sangamon	1380	1351	29	1380	......
Unity	934	877	57	934	......
Willow Branch...	1438	1384	54	1438	......
PIKE.					
Atlas...............	1584	1552	32	1570	14
Barry	2496	2375	121	2496	......
Chambersburg ...	788	765	23	788	......
Derry	1327	1237	90	1325	2
Detroit	1056	996	60	1056	......
Detroit	160	152	8	160	......
Fairmount	1120	1073	47	1120	......
Flint	403	356	47	403	......
Griggsville	2645	2420	225	2645	......
Griggsville...	1456	1322	134	1456	......
Hadley............	1309	1256	53	1234	75
Hardin.............	1468	1440	28	1468	......
Kinderhook	1454	1379	75	1454	......
Martinsburg	1466	1389	77	1466	......
Montezuma	1498	1420	78	1496	2
Milton	354	331	23	354	......
Newburgh	1540	1413	127	1540	......
New Salem........	1418	1350	68	1418	......
New Salem...	316	301	15	316	......
Pearl..............	628	622	6	627	1
Perry	2161	1969	192	2153	8
Perry	798	715	83	796	2
Pittsfield	2799	2377	422	2797	b1
Pittsfield	1621	1367	254	1620	1
Pleasant Hill	1411	1388	23	1411	......
Pleasant Hill .	230	228	2	230	......
Pleasant Vale	1188	1139	49	1185	3
Spring Creek.....	1009	1003	6	1009	......
POPE.					
Town. 11, R. 5 E ..	945	939	6	945	......
Town. 12, R. 5 E ..	781	757	24	680	101
Town. 13, R. 5 E ..	1198	1190	8	1177	21
Town. 14, R. 5 E ..	762	753	9	654	108
Town. 11, R. 6 E ..	580	572	8	580	......
Town. 12, R. 6 E ..	1037	1030	7	1037	......
Town. 13, R. 6 E ..	1233	1131	102	1222	c5
Town. 14, R. 6 E ..	1111	1087	24	1109	2
Town. 15, R. 6 E ..	800	767	33	793	7
Town. 11, R. 7 E ..	480	472	8	480	......
Town. 12, R. 7 E ..	632	612	20	632	......

(*a*) Exclusive of city of Peoria. (*b*) Also 1 Indian. (*c*) Also 6 Indians.

TABLE IX.—*Population of Minor Civil Divisions, &c.—ILLINOIS*—Continued.

Counties.	Total.	Nativity.		Race.	
		Native.	Foreign.	White.	Colored.
POPE—Continued.					
Town. 13, R. 7 E	994	808	186	914	*a*75
Golconda	858	687	171	783	75
Town. 15, R. 7 E	122	122	.....	109	13
Town. 16, R. 7 E	762	751	11	623	139
PULASKI.					
Town. 14, R. 1 E	546	528	18	509	37
Town. 15, R. 1 E	1498	1468	30	988	510
Caledonia	222	218	4	175	47
Town. 16, R. 1 E (*b*)	400	395	5	197	203
Town. 14, R. 2 E	796	789	7	494	302
Town. 15, R. 2 E	319	316	3	225	94
Town. 14, R. 1 W	800	774	26	707	93
Town. 15, R. 1 W	1435	1401	34	1180	255
Town. 16, R. 1 W	1327	1254	73	713	614
Mound City	1631	1382	249	1345	286
PUTNAM.					
Granville	1668	1270	398	1630	38
Hennepin	2144	1848	296	2117	27
Magnolia	1667	1476	191	1667	.....
Senachwine	801	654	147	801	.....
RANDOLPH.					
Town. 4 S., R. 5 W	1426	1177	249	1242	184
Town. 5 S., R. 5 W	1942	1713	229	1644	298
Sparta (*c*)	1335	1198	137	1172	163
Town. 6 S., R. 5 W *c*	1185	936	249	1185	.....
Town. 7 S., R. 5 W	785	633	152	784	1
Town. 8 S., R. 5 W	466	423	43	466	.....
Town. 4 S., R. 6 W	1019	839	180	945	74
Town. 5 S., R. 6 W *c*	1667	1495	172	1495	172
Town. 6 S., R. 6 W	1152	839	313	1145	7
Town. 7 S., R. 6 W	955	761	194	836	119
Town. 8 S., R. 6 W	217	216	1	217	.....
Town. 4 S., R. 7 W	818	667	151	818	.....
Town. 5 S., R. 7 W	920	749	171	920	.....
Town. 6 S., R. 7 W	1182	999	183	1182	.....
Town. 7 S., R. 7 W	1831	1440	391	1720	111
Chester	1615	1249	366	1529	86
Town. 4 S., R. 8 W	2008	1299	709	2008	.....
Red Bud	880	582	298	880	.....
Town. 5 S., R. 8 W	947	651	296	947	.....
Town. 6 S., R. 8 W	1186	1082	104	1120	66
Town. 5 S., R. 9 W	1153	986	167	1048	105
RICHLAND.					
Bonpas	891	851	40	891	.....
Claremont	1278	1204	74	1278	.....
Claremont	120	116	4	120	.....
Decker	971	958	13	971	.....
Denver	952	933	19	950	2
Germany	1040	948	92	1040	.....
Madison	1163	1104	59	1162	1
Noble	1333	1309	24	1333	.....
Noble	380	376	4	380	.....
Olney (*d*)	1412	1309	103	1408	4
Olney	2680	2332	348	2657	23
Preston	1083	996	87	1083	.....
ROCK ISLAND.					
Andalusia	878	759	119	878	.....
Black Hawk	1723	1351	372	1696	27
Camden Mills	818	675	143	810	8
Bowling	952	650	302	952	.....
ROCK ISLAND—C'd.					
Buffalo Prairie	1291	1120	171	1291	.....
Canoe Creek	413	349	64	413	.....
Coal Valley	2545	1511	1034	2537	8
Coe	1175	1001	174	1175	.....
Cordova	935	856	79	935	.....
Drury	1331	1160	171	1331	.....
Edgington	1106	984	122	1104	2
Govern't Isl'd	165	85	80	163	2
Hampton	2006	1477	529	2006	.....
Moline	5754	3318	2436	5716	38
Moline	4166	2431	1735	4141	25
Port Byron (*e*)	832	747	85	832	.....
Port Byron	576	517	59	576	.....
Rock Island	7890	5145	2745	7830	60
Zuma	787	601	186	787	.....
SALINE.					
Brushy	1040	1032	8	1034	6
Cottage Grove	713	712	1	707	6
Douglas	1437	1436	1	1338	99
Eldorado	1691	1680	11	1617	74
Galatia	1319	1315	4	1316	3
Harrisburg	1710	1689	21	1663	47
Harrisburg	590	580	10	590	.....
Independence	648	646	2	648	.....
Plainview	450	446	4	450	.....
Raleigh	2108	2103	5	2095	13
Summerset	800	784	16	797	3
Stonefort	798	792	6	798	.....
SANGAMON.					
Auburn	1303	1216	87	1291	12
Ball	966	928	58	964	2
Buffalo Heart	538	488	50	537	1
Cartwright	1851	1646	205	1797	54
Chatham	1460	1290	170	1458	2
Clear Lake	1566	1388	178	1524	42
Cooper	785	749	36	784	1
Cotton Hill	754	732	22	752	2
Curran	1000	856	144	998	2
Falkington	973	896	77	973	.....
Fancy Creek	1195	1107	88	1185	10
Gardner	1270	1081	189	1269	1
Illiopolis	1829	1691	138	1825	4
Illiopolis	395	368	27	392	3
Island Grove	1069	939	130	1053	16
Loami	1470	1391	79	1453	17
Mechanicsburg	1443	1335	108	1421	22
Buffalo	263	222	41	256	7
Mechanicsb'g	366	360	6	361	5
New Berlin	954	732	222	948	6
Pawnee	1293	1167	126	1293	.....
Rochester	1440	1368	72	1414	26
Sackett	698	622	76	698	.....
Springfield (*f*)	2447	1825	622	2369	78
Springfield	17364	12908	4456	16556	808
Williams	1279	1164	115	1274	5
Woodside	1385	1056	329	1330	55
SCHUYLER.					
Bainbridge	1200	1159	41	1200	.....
Birmingham	1253	1230	23	1253	.....
Brooklyn	1071	1052	19	1071	.....
Browning	2139	1636	503	2139	.....
Browning	214	207	7	214	.....
Buena Vista	1152	1088	64	1140	12

(*a*) Also 5 Indians.
(*b*) Exclusive of Mound City.
(*c*) Of Sparta, 872 in township 6 S., R. 5 W., and 463 in township 5 S., R. 6 W.
(*d*) Exclusive of city of Olney.
(*e*) Exclusive of city of Rock Island.
(*f*) Exclusive of city of Springfield.

TABLE IX.—*Population of Minor Civil Divisions, &c.—ILLINOIS*—Continued.

Counties.	Total.	Nativity. Native.	Nativity. Foreign.	Race. White.	Race. Colored.
CHUYLER—Cont'd					
amden	1173	1127	46	1173	......
rederick	956	629	327	956	......
Frederick	669	376	293	669	......
Iickory	557	547	10	557	......
Iuntsville	1228	1199	29	1228	......
ittleton	1140	1081	59	1140	......
akland	1026	984	42	1026	......
ushville	3021	2779	242	3008	13
Rushville	1539	1383	156	1533	6
Voodstock	1503	1376	127	1503	......
SCOTT.					
aples	597	536	61	595	2
Vinchester	1661	1382	279	1659	2
ownship 13, R. 11	1071	937	134	1069	2
ownship 14, R. 11	267	197	70	267	......
ownship 13, R. 12	1615	1449	166	1615	......
ownship 14, R. 12	1154	1035	119	1153	1
ownship 15, R. 12	734	626	108	727	7
ownship 13, R. 13	583	562	21	583	......
ownship 14, R. 13	1269	1230	39	1269	......
ownship 15, R. 13	1512	1347	165	1511	1
ownship 15, R. 14	67	53	14	67	......
SHELBY.					
Ashgrove	1499	1468	31	1499	......
Big Spring	1755	1442	313	1755	......
Cold Spring	1656	1639	17	1655	1
Dry Point	1671	1629	42	1671	......
Flat Branch	989	938	51	989	......
Holland	1352	1321	31	1352	......
Mowequa	869	800	69	869	......
Oconee	1558	1450	108	1558	......
Okaw	1280	1211	69	1279	1
Penn	428	414	14	428	......
Pickaway	728	699	29	728	......
Prairie	1218	885	333	1218	......
Richland	1053	1005	48	1053	......
Ridge	1139	1119	20	1139	......
Rose	1494	1376	118	1494	......
Moulton	106	92	14	106	......
Rural	909	789	120	902	7
Shelby (a)	1058	1016	42	1037	21
Shelbyville	2051	1917	134	2024	27
Tower Hill	1176	1083	93	1176	......
Windsor	1593	1564	29	1590	3
Windsor	518	493	25	518	......
STARK.					
Bradford (b)	280	252	28	280	......
Elmira	1108	891	217	1104	4
Essex	1538	1431	107	1538	......
Wyoming	640	602	38	640	......
Goshen	1270	1123	147	1270	......
La Fayette	284	274	10	284	......
Osceola	1278	1148	130	1278	......
Penn	1121	972	149	1121	......
Toulon	2060	1842	218	2051	9
Toulon	904	835	69	896	8
Valley	1061	845	216	1057	4
West Jersey	1315	1223	92	1311	4
ST. CLAIR.					
E. St. Louis (b)	5644	3291	2353	5544	100

Counties.	Total.	Nativity. Native.	Nativity. Foreign.	Race. White.	Race. Colored.
ST. CLAIR—Cont'd.					
Town. 1 N., R. 6 W	3750	2196	1554	3745	5
Mascoutah	2790	1597	1193	2785	5
Town. 1 S., R. 6 W	887	570	317	887	......
Town. 2 N., R. 6 W	3952	2981	971	3808	144
Lebanon	2117	1668	449	1983	134
Summerfield	770	489	281	770	......
Town. 2 S., R. 6 W	1508	912	596	1508	......
Town. 3 S., R. 6 W	1139	753	386	1139	......
Town. 1 N., R. 7 W	1817	1224	593	1779	38
Shiloh	298	172	126	293	5
Town. 1 S., R. 7 W	2056	1398	658	1986	70
Freburg	920	601	319	920	......
Town. 2 N., R. 7 W	2077	1394	683	1967	110
O'Fallon	1117	675	442	1096	21
Town. 2 S., R. 7 W	1522	994	528	1522	......
Town. 3 S., R. 7 W	669	457	212	669	......
T'n. 1 N., R. 8 W (c)	3673	2130	1543	3638	35
Belleville	8146	5060	3086	7989	157
W. Belleville	1679	906	773	1679	......
Town. 1 S., R. 8 W	1620	1131	489	1620	......
Town. 2 N., R. 8 W	2486	1466	1020	2428	58
Town. 2 S., R. 8 W	1106	792	314	1106	......
Town. 1 N., R. 9 W	1998	1067	931	1995	3
Town. 1 S., R. 9 W	2296	1549	747	2296	......
Centreville	1116	698	418	1116	......
Town. 2 N., R. 9 W	896	572	324	884	12
Town. 2 S., R. 9 W	540	320	220	540	......
Townships 1 and 2 N., R. 10 W	3073	2335	738	2508	565
Town. 1 S., R. 10 W	213	155	58	213	......
STEPHENSON.					
Buckeye	1761	1605	156	1761	......
Dakota	952	872	80	952	......
Erin	877	649	228	876	1
Florence	1185	897	288	1177	8
Freeport	7889	5602	2287	7888	1
Harlem	1243	1029	214	1243	......
Jefferson	546	403	143	546	......
Kent	1116	891	225	1116	......
Lancaster (d)	986	842	144	986	......
Loran	1200	987	213	1200	......
Oneco	1401	1327	74	1401	......
Orangeville	255	242	13	255	......
Ridott	1915	1161	754	1915	......
Rock Grove	1096	928	168	1096	......
Rock Run	2242	1725	517	2241	1
Silver Creek	1309	753	556	1308	1
Waddams	1359	1157	202	1359	......
West Point	2602	2135	467	2602	......
Lena	1294	1075	219	1294	......
Winslow	929	857	72	929	......
TAZEWELL.					
Boynton	820	714	106	819	1
Cincinnati (e)	758	560	198	758	......
Deer Creek	763	679	84	763	......
Delavan	1957	1737	220	1931	26
Dillon	1126	989	137	1122	4
Elm Grove	1072	844	228	1071	1
Fond du Lac	889	707	182	889	......
Groveland	1323	994	329	1323	......
Hittle	940	906	34	940	......
Hopedale	1096	979	117	1096	......
Little Mackinaw	1256	1048	208	1256	......

(a) Exclusive of city of Shelbyville.
(b) Its township not ascertained.
(c) Exclusive of city of Belleville.
(d) Exclusive of city of Freeport.
(e) Exclusive of part of city of Pekin.

TABLE IX.—*Population of Minor Civil Divisions, &c.*—*ILLINOIS*—Continued.

Counties.	Total.	Nativity. Native.	Nativity. Foreign.	Race. White.	Race. Colored.
TAZEWELL—Con.					
Mackinaw	1379	1272	107	1379	......
Mackinaw	496	433	63	496	......
Malone	710	646	64	709	1
Morton	1228	922	306	1225	3
Pekin (a)	166	125	41	166	......
Pekin	5696	3915	1781	5669	27
Sand Prairie	1046	846	200	1046	......
Spring Lake	857	793	64	857	......
Tremont	1365	1115	250	1365	......
Tremont	437	357	80	437	......
Washington	3456	2781	675	3455	1
Washington	1607	1310	297	1606	1
UNION.					
Anna	2697	2577	120	2653	44
Anna	1269	1169	100	1244	25
Casper	2718	2553	165	2652	66
Dongola	3095	2972	123	3089	6
Jonesboro	1577	1462	115	1576	1
Jonesboro	1108	1010	98	1108	......
Messenheimer	1076	992	84	1066	10
Preston	629	624	5	628	1
Rich	1432	1417	15	1432	......
Ridge	940	938	2	939	1
Stokes	1573	1561	12	1560	13
Union	781	770	11	775	6
VERMILION.					
Blount	1532	1514	18	1531	1
Butler	925	801	124	925	......
Carroll	2032	1995	37	2029	3
Catlin	1826	1675	151	1821	b4
Danville (c)	2434	2107	327	2434	......
Danville	4751	3785	966	4737	14
Elwood	1987	1963	24	1976	11
Georgetown	2237	2216	21	2235	2
Grant	1204	1147	57	1203	1
Middle Fork	1440	1381	59	1439	1
Newell	1909	1809	100	1898	11
Oakwood	2364	2311	53	2364	......
Pilot	1332	1293	39	1332	......
Ross	1738	1645	93	1738	......
Sidell	1165	1111	54	1165	......
Vance	1512	1470	42	1511	1
WABASH.					
Bon Pas	1000	915	85	960	40
Coffee	1502	1437	65	1496	6
Friendsville	1216	1190	26	1215	1
Lancaster	956	922	34	956	......
Lick Prairie	527	512	15	527	......
Mount Carmel	880	788	92	876	4
Mount Carmel	1640	1442	198	1628	12
Wabash	1120	1084	36	1120	......
WARREN.					
Berwick	1066	985	81	1065	1
Cold Brook	1256	1108	148	1251	5
Ellison	1258	1188	70	1258	......
Floyd	1146	1039	107	1146	......
Greenbush	1270	1185	85	1270	......
Hale	1212	1094	118	1211	1
Kelly	1295	1098	197	1294	1
Lenox	948	846	102	929	19
Monmouth (d)	1574	1374	200	1549	25
Monmouth	4662	4084	578	4492	170
Point Pleasant	1004	915	89	1004	......
WARREN—Cont'd.					
Roseville	1153	1048	105	1153	......
Spring Grove	1080	963	117	1080	......
Sumner	998	933	65	998	......
Swan	1007	949	58	1007	......
Tompkins	2245	2075	170	2244	1
Y'ng America	1145	1076	69	1144	1
WASHINGTON.					
Town. 1 S., R. 1 W.	1652	1520	132	1635	17
Town. 2 S., R. 1 W.	2787	2685	102	2752	[illegible]
Ashley	1030	......	......	......	......
Richview	1080	......	......	......	......
Town. 3 S., R. 1 W.	933	842	91	880	[illegible]
Town. 1 S., R. 2 W.	1072	550	522	1072	......
Town. 1 N., R. 2 W.	208	122	86	202	6
Town. 2 S., R. 2 W.	781	714	67	781	......
Town. 3 S., R. 2 W.	632	605	27	632	......
Town. 1 S., R. 3 W.	782	451	331	782	......
Town. 2 S., R. 3 W.	2279	1802	477	2275	4
Nashville	1640	1339	301	1636	4
Town. 3 S., R. 3 W.	722	599	123	722	......
Town. 1 S., R. 4 W.	1521	989	532	1520	1
Bridgeport	511	380	131	510	1
Town. 2 S., R. 4 W.	792	526	266	792	......
Town. 3 S., R. 4 W.	892	705	187	876	16
Elkton	160	129	31	155	5
Town. 1 S., R. 5 W.	564	286	278	564	......
Venedy	230	121	109	230	......
Town. 2 S., R. 5 W.	1211	761	450	1211	......
Johannesb'rg	101	67	34	101	......
Petersburg	35	21	14	35	......
Town. 3 S., R. 5 W.	771	577	194	767	4
Oakdale	116	84	32	116	......
WAYNE.					
Arrington	1640	1586	54	1640	......
Barnhill	2632	2539	93	2628	4
Fairfield	719	695	24	715	4
Bedford	1336	1324	12	1336	......
Big Mound	1168	1121	47	1144	24
Brush Creek	1470	1457	13	1470	......
Elm	968	902	66	968	......
Four Mile	1817	1804	13	1816	1
Hickory Hill	878	871	7	878	......
Indian Prairie	1727	1713	14	1727	......
Jasper	1016	996	20	1016	......
La Mard	1349	1312	37	1349	......
Leech	1258	1193	65	1258	......
Massilon	781	742	39	781	......
Mount Erie	1238	1214	24	1238	......
Zif	480	464	16	480	......
WHITE.					
Burnt Prairie	2186	2148	38	2185	1
Carmi	3669	3377	292	3577	92
Enfield	2426	2395	31	2426	......
Fox River	1867	1812	55	1817	50
Grayville	1925	1791	134	1918	7
Herald's Prairie	1160	1149	11	1160	......
Indian Creek	2010	1993	17	2010	......
Prairie	1603	1576	27	1580	23
WHITESIDES.					
Albany	805	706	99	805	......
Albany	606	561	45	606	......
Clyde	1093	884	209	1093	......
Coloma	856	746	110	856	......

(a) Exclusive of part of city of Pekin.
(b) Also 1 Indian.
(c) Exclusive of city of Danville.
(d) Exclusive of city of Monmouth.
(e) Also 3 Indians.

TABLE IX.—*Population of Minor Civil Divisions, &c.—ILLINOIS*—Continued.

Counties.	Total.	Nativity. Native.	Nativity. Foreign.	Race. White.	Race. Colored.
WHITESIDES—Con.					
k Falls ...	471	412	59	471	......
....	695	618	77	695	......
....	758	654	104	758	......
....	2162	1624	538	2145	17
lton	1875	1428	447	1858	17
Plain	1091	905	186	1091	......
e	1271	1081	190	1271	......
nan	624	423	201	624	......
s	1436	1130	306	1435	1
....	676	603	73	676	......
....	1196	904	292	1196	......
....	1039	963	76	1035	4
orency	668	543	125	668	......
Pleasant ..	2553	2175	378	2543	10
....	880	789	91	880	......
d	986	882	104	986	......
tstown	1274	1151	123	1273	1
phetstown.	276	261	15	276	......
(a)	712	600	112	710	2
ng	3998	3288	710	3974	21
o	634	565	69	634	......
Grove	1070	903	167	1070	......
....	1026	776	250	1026	......
WILL.					
hon	1164	926	238	1162	2
....	1468	856	612	1467	1
e	1118	810	308	1117	1
e	875	644	231	875	......
rt	1924	1055	869	1924	......
Garden	1202	646	556	1202	......
....	1279	946	333	1257	22
n	1485	1189	296	1483	2
(b)	2940	2093	847	2815	125
....	7263	4959	2304	7228	35
rt	3584	2368	1216	3566	18
kport	1772	1180	592	1766	6
tan	922	604	318	922	......
....	1600	879	721	1591	9
nee	598	332	266	591	7
nox	1121	808	313	1107	14
e	1213	761	452	1213	......
ld	1750	1300	450	1750	......
infield ...	723	667	56	723	......
....	2771	1184	1587	2771	......
....	918	617	301	918	......
ngton	1564	722	842	1563	1
....	924	776	148	923	1
land	1133	823	310	1132	1
....	911	485	426	911	......
ngton	2766	1971	795	2757	9
lmington ..	1828	1378	450	1819	9
....	1118	804	314	1117	1
LIAMSON.					
ip 8, R. 1	616	606	10	615	1

Counties.	Total.	Nativity. Native.	Nativity. Foreign.	Race. White.	Race. Colored.
WILLIAMSON—Con.					
Township 9, R. 1	1440	1425	15	1427	13
Township 10, R. 1	1597	1597	......	1597	......
Township 8, R. 2	639	638	1	639	......
Township 9, R. 2	1461	1433	28	1452	9
Township 10, R. 2	1413	1410	3	1413	......
Township 8, R. 3	2057	1986	71	2056	1
Township 9, R. 3	1760	1753	7	1728	32
Township 10, R. 3	1564	1561	3	1563	1
Township 8, R. 4	2062	2058	4	2013	49
Township 9, R. 4	1280	1264	16	1280	......
Township 10, R. 4	1440	1435	5	1440	......
WINNEBAGO.					
Burritt	991	717	274	984	7
Cherry Valley	1421	1069	352	1421	......
Durand	1578	1347	231	1575	3
Guilford	1062	795	267	1057	5
Harlem	781	544	237	779	2
Harrison	725	586	139	725	......
Laona	742	601	141	742	......
New Milford	915	723	192	915	......
Owen	929	654	275	929	......
Pecatonica	1780	1454	326	1778	2
Rockford (c)	1383	1089	294	1375	8
Rockford	11049	8008	3041	10966	83
Rockton	1827	1486	341	1826	1
Roscoe	1135	992	143	1127	8
Seward	997	824	173	996	1
Shirland	559	501	58	558	1
Winnebago	1427	1198	229	1427	......
Elida	468	394	74	468	......
WOODFORD.					
Cazenovia	990	890	100	990	......
Washburn	272	210	62	272	......
Clayton	1022	695	327	1022	......
El Paso (d)	852	669	183	852	......
El Paso	1564	1341	223	1561	3
Green	933	769	164	933	......
Kansas	349	328	21	349	......
Lynn	800	571	229	800	......
Metamora	1718	1397	321	1717	1
Metamora	702	609	93	701	1
Minonk	2115	1498	617	2115	......
Minonk	1122	850	272	1122	......
Montgomery	652	497	155	651	1
Olio	2508	2218	290	2503	5
Eureka	1233	1154	79	1228	5
Palestine	1325	1131	194	1325	......
Secor	407	349	58	407	......
Panola	1260	981	279	1260	......
Partridge	395	314	81	395	......
Roanoke	998	723	275	998	......
Spring Bay	475	376	99	475	......
Spring Bay	235	178	57	235	......
Worth	1000	553	447	1000	......

(a) Exclusive of city of Sterling.
(b) Exclusive of city of Joliet.
(c) Exclusive of city of Rockford.
(d) Exclusive of city of El Paso.

TABLE IX.—*Population of Minor Civil Divisions, &c.*—*INDIANA.*

NOTE.—The margin townships; the first indentation, cities; the second, towns. Names of towns are placed under the names of the townships in which they are respectively situated. The population of each township includes that of all towns situated in it.

Counties.	Total.	Nativity. Native.	Nativity. Foreign.	Race. White.	Race. Colored.
ADAMS.					
Blue Creek	820	806	14	820	......
French	824	634	190	824	......
Hartford	935	848	87	935	......
Jefferson	494	463	31	494	......
Kirkland	508	471	37	508	......
Monroe	960	835	125	960	......
Preble	996	726	270	996	......
Root	1252	1094	158	1252	......
St. Mary's	925	897	28	925	......
Pleasant Mills	80	76	4	80	......
Union	865	776	89	865	......
Wabash	957	865	92	957	......
Washington	1846	1646	200	1846	......
Decatur	858	754	104	858	......
ALLEN.					
Aboite	906	842	64	896	10
Adams	2388	1791	597	2388	......
New Haven	912	692	220	912	......
Cedar Creek	1713	1551	162	1713	......
Eel River	1217	1168	49	1211	6
Fort Wayne	17718	12677	5041	17692	26
Jackson	202	170	32	202	......
Jefferson	1445	1124	321	1445	......
Lafayette	1471	1411	60	1471	......
Lake	1309	1080	229	1309	......
Madison	1278	1106	172	1278	......
Marion	1319	1100	219	1319	......
Maumee	394	366	28	394	......
Milan	1183	1033	150	1183	......
Monroe	1479	1385	94	1479	......
Monroeville	630	589	41	630	......
Perry	1280	1126	154	1280	......
Pleasant	1280	1091	189	1280	......
Scipio	420	400	20	420	......
Springfield	1749	1656	93	1749	......
St. Joseph	1373	1067	306	1373	......
Washington	1628	1238	390	1628	......
Wayne (a)	1742	1353	389	1718	(b)
BARTHOLOMEW.					
Clay	778	744	34	778	......
Clifty	1133	1095	38	1133	......
Columbus	5187	4634	553	5180	7
Columbus	3359	2926	433	3353	6
Flat Rock	1543	1500	43	1542	1
German	1302	1272	30	1301	1
Taylorsville	350	327	23	350	......
Harrison	1228	1149	79	1228	......
Bethany	54	53	1	54	......
Haw Creek	2634	2535	99	2634	......
Hartsville	433	426	7	433	......
Hope	765	703	62	765	......
Jackson	618	474	144	618	......
Waymansville	55	37	18	55	......
Nineveh	767	749	18	767	......
Ohio	747	686	61	745	2
Rock Creek	1203	1176	27	1203	......
Sand Creek	1149	1123	26	1149	......
Azalia	91	91	......	91	......
Elizabethtown	294	282	12	294	......
Union	1008	934	74	1008	......
Wayne	1836	1629	207	1836	......
Jonesville	206	193	13	206	......
Waylesburg	101	95	6	101	......
Waynesville	104	96	8	104	......
BENTON.					
Bolivar	776	686	90	776	......
Gilboa	452	428	24	452	......
Grant	835	783	52	835	......
Oak Grove	1239	1128	111	1239	......
Oxford	519	484	35	519	......
Parish Grove	193	153	40	193	......
Pine	523	469	54	523	......
Prairie	278	231	46	278	......
Richland	546	443	103	546	......
Union	340	305	35	340	......
York	433	303	130	433	......
BLACKFORD.					
Harrison	1680	1645	35	1680	......
Jackson	1399	1376	23	1399	......
Trenton	80	80	......	80	......
Licking	2185	2089	96	2171	14
Hartford	878	835	43	867	11
Washington	1008	971	37	1008	......
BOONE.					
Center	3885	3787	98	3843	42
Lebanon	1572	1512	60	1544	28
Clinton	1220	1213	7	1220	......
Eagle	2327	2260	67	2320	7
Zionsville	956	933	23	949	7
Harrison	1209	1196	13	1209	......
Jackson	2453	2405	48	2452	1
Jamestown	603	563	40	602	1
Jefferson	1675	1664	11	1673	2
Marion	1786	1766	20	1775	11
Perry	1109	1073	36	1109	......
Sugar Creek	3138	3080	58	2960	178
Thorntown	1526	1495	31	1449	77
Union	1057	1046	11	1057	......
Washington	1391	1375	16	1386	5
Worth	1343	1323	20	1343	......
BROWN.					
Hamblin	2011	1967	44	2011	......
Jackson	1750	1717	33	1750	......
Johnson	685	677	8	685	......
Van Buren	2048	2021	27	2048	......
Washington	2187	2147	40	2186	1
Nashville	270	260	10	269	1
CARROLL.					
Adams	1149	1124	25	1149	......
Lockport	176	174	2	176	......
Burlington	1198	1194	4	1198	......
Carrollton	1046	1035	11	1046	......
Clay	949	919	30	948	1
Deer Creek	3458	3029	429	3435	23
Delphi	1614	1341	273	1607	7
Mortonsville	80	67	13	80	......
South Delphi	160	144	16	160	......
West Delphi	253	185	68	239	14
Democrat	1122	1093	29	1122	......
Jackson	1301	1290	11	1301	......
Camden	476	471	5	476	......
Jefferson	947	924	23	947	......
Madison	727	681	46	727	......
Monroe	910	903	7	910	......
Rock Creek	1316	1278	38	1316	......
Rockfield	289	277	12	289	......
Tippecanoe	1109	1062	47	1109	......
Pittsburg	320	306	14	320	......
Washington	920	873	47	920	......

(a) Exclusive of city of Fort Wayne.

(b) Also 24 Indians.

.BLE IX.—*Population of Minor Civil Divisions, &c.*—*INDIANA*—Continued.

...ties.	Total.	NATIVITY. Native.	NATIVITY. Foreign.	RACE. White.	RACE. Colored.
...SS.					
....	807	793	14	807	......
...m	993	969	24	993	......
....	1262	1180	82	1262	......
...l Center.	306	276	30	306	......
....	814	797	17	814	......
....	1021	982	39	1021	......
...ek.......	1271	1245	26	1271	......
....	160	139	21	160	......
....	1171	1045	126	1171	......
....	1519	1475	44	1519	......
...ston	390	365	25	390	......
....	1285	1216	69	1285	......
...port	8950	6994	1956	8830	111
...ntown (b)	903	663	240	856	47
of Old-...rn (b)....	25	22	3	25	......
...own (b)..	260	214	46	252	8
...wn (b)...	349	308	41	344	5
Jerusa-...(b)......	231	138	93	231	......
...rtown (b).	447	333	114	447	......
of Browns-...rs (b)....	48	42	6	48	......
...Logan (b)	978	688	290	978	......
....	1008	992	16	1008	......
....	904	844	60	904	......
....	1808	1748	60	1808	......
...ton......	1220	1154	66	1220	......
...RKE.					
...m	763	745	18	763	......
....	692	636	56	692	......
...wn......	3294	3061	233	2878	416
...lestown..	2204	2040	164	1974	230
...ville (c)..	3042	2653	389	2623	419
...nville...	7254	5957	1297	6452	802
....	1863	1698	165	1837	26
....	1360	1267	93	1360	......
....	679	655	24	673	6
...eck......	1116	916	200	1099	17
....	1022	946	76	926	96
....	1598	1517	81	1419	179
...ton......	1357	1351	6	1348	9
....	730	673	57	730	......
...AY.					
....	2772	2351	421	2761	11
...l........	2186	1896	290	2175	11
....	470	457	13	470	......
...d	126	124	2	126	......
...nson	868	835	33	868	......
....	2241	2178	63	2241	......
....	1711	1561	150	1711	......
....	1220	1203	17	1217	(d)
....	1340	1288	52	1340	......
....	2132	1980	152	2128	4
...rland ..	136	135	1	136	......
...urg.....	200	189	11	200	......
...ton ...	589	523	66	589	......
...amstown	65	62	3	65	......
...dge......	1140	1105	35	1140	......
...oro......	137	134	3	137	......
...e Point	226	222	4	226	......
...n	3323	2583	740	3319	4
...htsville..	1071	605	466	1068	3
...ony ...	597	522	75	597	......
...Mines ...	199	137	62	199	......

Counties.	Total.	NATIVITY. Native.	NATIVITY. Foreign.	RACE. White.	RACE. Colored.
CLAY—Cont'd.					
Washington	1867	1757	110	1859	e7
Bowling Green	606	567	39	599	7
CLINTON.					
Jackson	3932	3878	54	3929	3
Frankfort	1300	......	......	......	......
Johnson..........	1666	1647	19	1666	......
Kirklin	1266	1259	7	1266	......
Kirklin......	141	138	3	141	......
Madison..........	865	853	12	865	......
Michigan..........	1732	1718	14	1732	......
Michigantown	315	311	4	315	......
Owen	1118	1111	7	1118	......
Perry	1220	1189	31	1220	......
Colfax........	187	173	14	187	......
Ross	1741	1714	27	1741	......
Rossville.....	389	384	5	389	......
Sugar Creek......	964	953	11	960	4
Warren	1692	1685	7	1692	......
Washington	1134	1120	14	1134	......
Jefferson	253	248	5	253	......
CRAWFORD.					
Boone	494	483	11	492	2
Alton	137	137	......	136	1
Jennings	2081	2036	45	2081	......
Leavenworth.	567	557	10	567	......
Magnolia.....	33	33	......	33	......
Johnson...........	652	645	7	652	......
Liberty	757	754	3	757	......
Ohio	1078	1058	20	1077	1
Fredonia	72	69	3	72	......
Patoka...........	1253	1199	54	1253	......
Sterling	1327	1319	8	1327	......
Union	1082	1032	50	1082	......
Whisky Run	1127	1083	44	1127	......
Milltown	87	83	4	87	......
DAVIESS.					
Barr	2758	2575	183	2758	......
Montgomery .	135	125	10	135	......
Bogard	1170	1160	10	1170	......
Elmore	865	861	4	865	......
Harrison	1084	1049	35	1084	......
Madison	1440	1429	11	1440	......
Clarksburg...	160	156	4	160	......
Reeve	1671	1560	111	1671	......
Alfordsville ..	128	127	1	128	......
Steele	738	705	33	717	21
Van Buren	1172	1147	25	1172	......
Raglesville ..	53	53	......	53	......
Veale	893	879	14	890	3
Washington	4956	4475	481	4851	105
Washington ..	2901	2493	408	2856	45
DEARBORN.					
Cesar Creek	556	407	149	556	......
Centre	4699	3701	998	4695	4
Aurora......	3304	2581	723	3300	4
Cochran	675	484	191	675	......
Clay..............	1269	1106	163	1269	......
Harrison	1086	887	199	1081	5
Hogan	949	880	69	949	......

(a) Exclusive of city of Logansport.
(b) Localities constituting the new limits of the city of Logansport.
(c) Exclusive of city of Jeffersonville.
(d) Also 3 Indians.
(e) Also 1 Indian.

TABLE IX.—*Population of Minor Civil Divisions, &c.*—*INDIANA*—Continued.

Counties.	Total.	Nativity.		Race.	
		Native.	Foreign.	White.	Colored.
DEARBORN—Con.					
Wilmington	301	297	4	301	......
Jackson	1366	942	424	1366	......
Kelso	1908	1298	610	1908	......
Lawrenceburg (a)	1708	1450	258	1707	1
Lawrenceburg	3159	2472	687	3134	25
Logan	832	669	163	832	......
Manchester	2029	1734	295	2029	......
Miller	1120	1022	98	1100	20
Sparta	1939	1767	172	1938	1
Moore's Hill	617	592	25	617	......
Washington	510	464	46	508	2
York	986	721	265	986	......
DECATUR.					
Adams	2162	2041	121	2154	8
St. Omer	169	168	1	169	......
Clay	2065	2027	38	2064	1
Milford	316	309	7	316	......
Clinton	828	828	......	828	......
Fugit	1630	1481	149	1620	10
Jackson	1746	1694	52	1746	......
Marion	2315	1971	344	2315	......
Salt Creek	1687	1470	217	1687	......
Sand Creek	2029	1988	41	2029	......
Washington	4591	4320	271	4523	68
DE KALB.					
Butler	1209	1129	80	1209	......
Concord	1472	1453	19	1472	......
Fairfield	1554	1441	113	1554	......
Franklin	1243	1201	42	1243	......
Jackson	1141	1116	25	1141	......
Newville	842	819	23	842	......
Richland	1825	1686	139	1824	1
Corunna	242	230	12	242	......
Lawrence	176	156	20	175	1
Smithfield	1342	1255	87	1342	......
Stafford	584	549	35	584	......
Troy	600	591	9	600	......
Union	3059	2787	272	3056	3
Waterloo	1259	1159	100	1256	3
Auburn	677	......	......	......	......
Wilmington	2296	2176	120	2296	......
DELAWARE.					
Centre	4375	4106	269	4327	48
Muncie	2992	2752	240	2944	48
Delaware	1210	1197	13	1209	1
Hamilton	1129	1080	49	1129	......
Harrison	1400	1393	7	1400	......
Liberty	1639	1625	14	1639	......
Monroe	1247	1236	11	1247	......
Mount Pleasant	1880	1841	39	1877	3
Niles	1140	1132	8	1140	......
Perry	1163	1156	7	1162	(b)
Salem	1413	1370	43	1413	......
Union	1244	1217	27	1243	1
Washington	1190	1176	14	1190	......
DUBOIS.					
Bainbridge	2521	2013	508	2516	5
Jasper	547	393	154	547	......
Columbia	1622	1437	185	1622	......
Ferdinand	1732	1169	563	1732	......
DUBOIS—Cont'd.					
Hall	2046	1736	310	2046	......
Harbison	1390	1373	217	1390	......
Patoka	3086	2408	678	3056	30
ELKHART.					
Baugo	749	717	32	749	......
Benton	1188	1153	35	1188	......
Benton	203	192	11	203	......
Cleveland	549	522	27	549	......
Clinton	2099	1972	127	2099	......
Millersburg	52	52	......	52	......
Concord	4725	4319	406	4706	19
Elkhart	3265	2910	355	3246	19
Elkhart (c)	1477	1415	62	1474	3
Goshen	3133	2661	472	3125	8
Harrison	1655	1555	100	1655	......
Jackson	1289	1220	69	1289	......
New Paris	145	140	5	145	......
Jefferson	982	944	38	981	1
Locke	882	818	64	882	......
Locke	167	132	35	167	......
Middlebury	1709	1640	69	1709	......
Olive	1149	1075	74	1149	......
Wakarusa	245	226	19	245	......
Osolo	922	900	22	921	1
Union	1221	1119	102	1221	......
Washington	1391	1347	44	1388	3
Bristol	681	648	33	678	3
York	906	872	34	906	......
FAYETTE.					
Columbia	929	893	36	929	......
Connersville (d)	1211	1125	86	1180	31
Connersville	2496	2036	460	2441	55
Fairview	601	576	25	601	......
Harrison	867	831	36	866	1
Jackson	1037	1000	37	1037	......
Everton	149	133	16	149	......
Jennings	836	822	14	835	1
Orange	881	845	36	880	1
Posey	947	929	18	944	3
Waterloo	•671	655	16	671	......
FLOYD.					
Franklin	793	711	82	779	14
Georgetown	1424	1286	138	1414	10
Greenville	1814	1701	113	1809	5
Lafayette	1576	1272	304	1552	24
New Albany (e)	2297	1901	396	2081	216
New Albany	15396	12734	2662	14203	1193
FOUNTAIN.					
Cain	1802	1711	91	1802	......
Davis	663	625	38	663	......
Fulton	916	906	10	916	......
Jackson	1321	1316	5	1321	......
Logan	2608	2238	370	2581	27
Attica	2273	1939	334	2259	14
Mill Creek	1491	1482	9	1491	......
Richland	1759	1741	18	1759	......
Shawnee	867	833	34	867	......
Troy	3156	2802	354	3136	20
Covington	1888	1570	318	1868	20
Van Buren	522	521	1	522	......
Wabash	1284	1266	18	1284	......

(a) Exclusive of city of Lawrenceburg.
(b) Also 1 Indian.
(c) Exclusive of city of Goshen.
(d) Exclusive of city of Connersville.
(e) Exclusive of city of New Albany.

BLE IX.—*Population of Minor Civil Divisions, &c.—INDIANA*—Continued.

ntles.	Total.	NATIVITY. Native.	NATIVITY. Foreign.	RACE. White.	RACE. Colored.
KLIN.					
....	675	651	24	674	1
Grove..	801	758	43	801	......
le........	4207	3604	603	4207	......
....	1488	1128	360	1488	......
....	845	823	22	845	......
l	1796	1292	504	1796	......
....	1942	1833	109	1921	21
el	741	694	47	729	12
rset.....	94	88	6	94	......
n........	1222	1143	79	1222	......
....	974	958	16	974	......
....	2070	1378	692	2070	......
burg....	160	112	48	160	......
k........	1223	1040	183	1222	1
ld	1513	1400	113	1513	......
ter	1467	1287	180	1466	1
TON.					
aubbee..	745	707	38	745	......
....	1919	1878	41	1919	......
....	1429	1352	77	1429	......
tlo.......	1262	1249	13	1262	......
....	1314	1254	60	1314	......
r.........	3726	3553	173	3710	16
ester	1528	1425	103	1512	16
....	1200	1157	43	1200	......
....	1131	1062	69	1131	......
SON.					
....	1626	1467	159	1626	......
....	2238	2198	40	2232	6
....	2616	2186	430	2614	2
ery	3121	3063	58	3088	33
sville ..	522	493	29	522	......
....	4397	3972	425	4085	312
eton ...	1847	1630	217	1724	123
....	442	436	6	442	......
ton	757	748	9	757	......
ver	2174	2108	66	2090	84
ton	356	346	10	356	......
a	844	808	36	838	6
NT.					
....	2641	2542	99	2572	69
n........	1658	1572	86	1619	39
t	1573	1543	30	1520	53
nonut ..	337	334	3	331	6
....	1471	1466	5	1366	105
....	1115	1111	4	1115	......
....	1398	1378	20	1398	......
....	1989	1981	8	1533	456
....	1523	1499	24	1469	54
boro ...	581	563	18	571	10
....	1047	1026	21	1047	......
....	1575	1563	12	1575	......
....	1065	1038	27	1065	......
....	841	830	11	841	......
n	1110	1076	34	1110	......
on.......	1139	1120	19	1139	......
NE.					
ek	2059	2049	10	2058	1
....	819	812	7	819	......
....	1870	1861	9	1870	......
....	501	495	6	500	1
....	780	755	25	780	......
....	532	513	19	532	......
....	1321	1319	2	1317	4
....	1969	1965	4	1969	......
....	1348	1310	38	1334	14

Counties.	Total.	NATIVITY. Native.	NATIVITY. Foreign.	RACE. White.	RACE. Colored.
GREENE—Cont'd.					
Richland	2143	2114	29	2142	1
Bloomfield....	656	636	20	655	1
Smith	670	666	4	670	......
Stafford	841	827	14	841	......
Stockton...	1240	1171	69	1240	......
Taylor	1677	1639	38	1677	......
Washington.......	640	630	10	640	......
Wright.............	1104	1092	12	1104	......
HAMILTON.					
Adams	2178	2161	17	2099	79
Clay	1413	1403	10	1397	16
Delaware	1434	1426	8	1419	15
Fall Creek.........	1530	1520	10	1530	......
Jackson	3724	3605	119	3586	138
Cicero	422	382	40	422	......
Noblesville	3568	3465	103	3368	200
Noblesville...	1435	1377	58	1364	71
Washington	3590	3580	10	3523	67
Westfield	608	604	4	560	48
Wayne	1398	1376	22	1398	......
White River	2047	1955	92	2047	......
HANCOCK.					
Blue River	1125	1115	10	1122	3
Brandywine	1061	1042	19	1060	1
Brown	1329	1318	11	1329	......
Buck Creek	1227	1196	31	1227	......
Center	3495	3401	94	3464	31
Greenfield....	1203	1140	63	1173	30
Green	1177	1155	22	1177	......
Harrison	......	......	......	......	......
Jackson	1849	1813	36	1847	2
Charlottesville	414	407	7	414	......
Cleveland	118	108	10	118	......
Jones	......	......	......	......	......
Sugar Creek.......	1897	1652	245	1886	11
Union	......	......	......	......	......
Vernon.............	1963	1888	75	1957	6
Fortville	387	353	34	387	......
McCord'rsv'le	168	160	8	168	......
Worth	......	......	......	......	......
HARRISON.					
Blue River	1198	1158	40	1198	......
Boone	1870	1776	94	1828	42
Franklin	1402	1130	272	1402	......
Lanesville....	157	120	37	157	......
Harrison	3462	3334	128	3275	187
Corydon.......	747	714	33	646	101
Heth	1615	1597	18	1564	51
Jackson	1400	1276	124	1400	......
Morgan	1426	1240	186	1423	3
Posey	1774	1693	81	1766	8
Elizabeth	216	209	7	216	......
Scott	996	980	16	996	......
Spencer	1310	1207	103	1310	......
Taylor	1259	1174	85	1259	......
Washington	1176	1167	9	1168	8
Webster	1025	926	99	975	50
HENDRICKS.					
Brown	1233	1149	84	1233	......
Centre	2795	2699	96	2765	30
Danville......	1040	969	71	1036	4
Clay...............	1571	1564	7	1569	2
Eel River	1676	1666	10	1676	......
North Salem..	261	258	3	261	......
Franklin	1316	1299	17	1316	......
Stilesville	295	295	......	295	......

TABLE IX.—*Population of Minor Civil Divisions, &c.—INDIANA*—Continued.

Counties.	Total.	Nativity. Native.	Nativity. Foreign.	Race. White.	Race. Colored.
HENDRICKS—Con.					
Guilford	2193	2170	23	2085	108
Plainfield	795	782	13	790	5
Liberty	2478	2452	26	2465	13
Bellville	264	262	2	264	......
Lincoln	1502	1385	117	1502	......
Brownsburg	551	499	52	551	......
Marion	1263	1260	3	1256	7
New Winchester	124	122	2	124	......
Middle	1422	1384	38	1422	......
Pittsborough	201	197	4	201	......
Union	1326	1294	32	1325	1
Washington	1502	1440	62	1481	21
HENRY.					
Blue River	862	855	7	849	13
Dudley	1339	1321	18	1311	28
Fall Creek	2005	1974	31	1997	8
Honey Creek	100	94	6	100	......
Mechanicsburg	133	133	......	133	......
Middletown	711	699	12	703	8
Franklin	1579	1537	42	1549	30
Lewisville	416	386	30	416	......
Greensboro	1488	1482	6	1404	84
Harrison	1888	1877	11	1857	31
Henry	2818	2693	125	2749	69
New Castle	1556	1462	94	1512	44
Jefferson	1234	1210	24	1234	......
Sulphur Sp'gs	246	233	13	246	......
Liberty	1884	1859	25	1876	8
Prairie	1623	1600	23	1623	......
Hillsboro	95	93	2	95	......
Luray	66	66	......	66	......
Summit	108	105	3	108	......
Spiceland	2014	1996	18	1947	67
Spiceland	370	368	2	351	19
Stony Creek	934	929	5	920	14
Bluntsville	178	176	2	171	7
Wayne	3318	3199	119	3229	89
Knightstown	1528	1475	53	1486	42
HOWARD.					
Centre	2857	2737	120	2761	96
Kokomo	2177	2078	99	2094	83
Clay	1350	1318	32	1309	41
Harrison	807	806	1	803	4
Honey Creek	732	730	2	714	18
Russiaville	160	160	......	146	14
Howard	1707	1672	35	1707	......
Irvin	1316	1294	22	1217	99
Jackson	1000	986	14	1000	......
Liberty	1697	1662	35	1697	......
Monroe	891	887	4	845	46
New London	240	237	3	212	28
Taylor	1745	1711	34	1745	......
Union	1745	1739	6	1745	......
HUNTINGTON.					
Clear Creek	1273	1212	61	1273	......
Dallas	1483	1351	132	1483	......
Antioch	449	435	14	449	......
Huntington	4449	3732	717	4445	*a*1
Huntington	2925	2415	510	2923	(*b*)
Jackson	2257	2126	131	2254	3
Roanoke	627	599	28	627	......
Jefferson (*c*)	1227	1223	4	1227	......
HUNTINGTON—Con.					
Lancaster (*d*)	1492	1443	49	1491	1
Mount Etna (*c*) (*e*) (*f*) (*d*)	231	230	1	231	......
Polk (*e*)	960	942	18	960	......
Rock Creek	1639	1620	19	1639	......
Markle	218	215	3	218	......
Salamonie	1485	1468	17	1485	......
Warren	358	354	4	358	......
Union	1016	963	53	1016	......
Warren	951	864	87	951	......
Wayne (*f*)	804	802	2	804	......
JACKSON.					
Brownstown	2580	2314	266	2578	2
Brownstown	572	539	33	571	1
Carr	1665	1627	38	1665	......
Driftwood	922	850	72	922	......
Grassy Fork	1188	1035	153	1188	......
Hamilton	1565	1435	130	1565	......
Jackson (*g*)	1137	979	158	1053	84
Owen	1589	1582	7	1589	......
Redding	1525	1409	116	1521	4
Salt Creek	1963	1898	65	1963	......
Seymour	2372	2074	298	2305	67
Vernon	1508	1437	71	1508	......
Washington	960	739	221	953	7
JASPER.					
Barkley	832	805	27	831	1
Carpenter	1081	1019	62	1081	......
Remington	390	366	24	390	......
Gillam	635	624	11	634	1
Hanging Grove	393	365	28	393	......
Jordan	327	312	15	327	......
Kankakee	215	203	12	215	......
Keener	71	66	5	71	......
Marion	1629	1554	75	1629	......
Rensselaer	617	579	38	617	......
Milroy	123	118	5	122	1
Newton	468	432	36	468	......
Union	196	177	19	196	......
Walker	281	247	34	281	......
Wheatfield	103	92	11	103	......
JAY.					
Bear Creek	1247	1217	30	1247	......
Green	1115	1091	24	1115	......
Jackson	989	978	11	989	......
Jefferson	1640	1608	32	1640	......
Knox	685	681	4	685	......
Madison	1279	1196	83	1279	......
Noble	1218	1141	77	1218	......
Penn	1441	1426	15	1431	10
Pike	1585	1558	27	1585	......
Richland	1342	1326	16	1342	......
Wabash	933	768	165	933	......
Wayne	1526	1502	24	1515	11
Portland	462	453	9	451	11
JEFFERSON.					
Graham	1408	1352	56	1408	......
Hanover	1390	1229	161	1167	223
Hanover	564	494	70	506	58
Lancaster	1442	1378	64	1407	35
Madison (*h*)	4865	4296	569	4576	289
North Madison	1007	861	146	1007	......

(*a*) Also 3 Indians.
(*b*) Also 2 Indians.
(*c*) Of Mount Etna in Jefferson, 32.
(*d*) Of Mount Etna in Lancaster, 102.
(*e*) Of Mount Etna in Polk, 22.
(*f*) Of Mount Etna in Wayne, 5.
(*g*) Exclusive of city of Seymour.
(*h*) Exclusive of city of Madison.

…BLE IX.—*Population of Minor Civil Divisions, &c.—INDIANA*—Continued.

…ties.	Total.	Nativity. Native.	Nativity. Foreign.	Race. White.	Race. Colored.
…N—Con.					
…n	10709	8515	2194	10363	346
…	1975	1905	70	1975	......
…	1760	1558	202	1741	19
…an	1125	1053	72	1117	8
…	309	277	32	301	8
…	1682	1639	43	1581	101
…	1890	1818	72	1890	......
…	1486	1411	75	1411	75
…NGS.					
…	945	905	40	884	61
…	1563	1437	126	1453	110
…	2633	2104	529	2563	70
… Vernon	1758	1374	384	1709	49
…	1272	1189	83	1272	......
…	2037	1936	101	2032	5
…	1200	1120	80	1191	9
…ery	1326	1263	63	1325	1
…k	930	830	100	929	1
…	1927	1684	243	1927	......
…	2385	2176	209	2220	165
…on	673	625	48	650	23
…SON.					
…r	2573	2415	158	2548	25
…urg	1799	1650	149	1775	24
…	1474	1418	56	1473	1
…(a)	2903	2867	36	2893	10
…n City	2707	2539	168	2631	76
…	1668	1658	10	1668	......
…	1650	1642	8	1650	......
…	2170	2153	17	2169	1
…	1466	1460	6	1464	2
…ver	1755	1730	25	1755	......
…OX.					
…	1283	1260	23	1229	54
…	837	830	7	837	......
…	2812	2785	27	2797	15
…	1543	1365	178	1543	......
…	1269	1241	25	1231	38
…	1285	1265	20	1285	......
…	2426	2162	264	2426	......
…s (b)	1426	1244	182	1382	44
…nce	5440	4344	1096	5238	202
…on	1537	1512	25	1523	14
…	1704	1437	267	1691	13
…USKO.					
…	1973	1922	51	1973	......
…	1007	981	26	1007	......
…Green	397	384	13	397	......
…	1280	1266	14	1280	......
…	1745	1723	22	1745	......
…	1043	1030	13	1043	......
…	711	685	26	711	......
…	990	968	22	990	......
…	1490	1462	28	1490	......
…urg	320	309	11	320	......
…quet	92	87	5	92	......
…go	116	116	......	116	......
…	1248	1222	26	1248	......
…	700	650	50	700	......
…	1353	1332	21	1353	......
…oe	1236	1175	61	1236	......
…ter	87	73	14	87	......
…reek	1336	1287	49	1336	......
…use	227	215	12	227	......
…n	1467	1424	43	1467	......

Counties.	Total.	Nativity. Native.	Nativity. Foreign.	Race. White.	Race. Colored.
KOSCIUSKO—Con.					
Milford	432	414	18	432	......
Washington	2288	2211	77	2288	......
Pierceton	1063	1023	40	1063	......
Wayne	3664	3465	199	3654	10
Warsaw	2206	2035	171	2196	10
LA GRANGE.					
Bloomfield	2254	2165	89	2250	4
La Grange	1038	985	53	1034	4
Clay	1248	1202	46	1248	......
Clearspring	1223	1193	30	1212	11
Eden	930	903	27	930	......
Greenfield	1078	1004	74	1078	......
Johnson	1322	1266	56	1322	......
Lima	1371	1280	91	1361	10
Lima	419	395	24	409	10
Ontario	277	258	19	277	......
Milford	1288	1227	61	1288	......
Newbury	1159	1117	42	1159	......
Springfield	928	894	34	928	......
Van Buren	1347	1204	143	1347	......
LAKE.					
Cedar Creek	1326	1207	119	1326	......
Center	1932	1455	477	1932	......
Eagle Creek	737	632	105	736	1
Hanover	973	577	396	973	......
Hobart	1037	623	414	1037	......
North	1593	730	863	1591	2
Ross	1625	1278	347	1625	......
St. John's	1442	890	552	1442	......
West Creek	1158	907	251	1158	......
Winfield	516	443	73	516	......
LA PORTE.					
Cass	1214	725	489	1213	1
Centre (c)	1147	904	243	1130	17
Clinton	797	696	101	797	......
Cool Spring	1328	898	430	1327	1
Dewey	202	96	106	202	......
Galena	867	812	55	867	......
Hanna	486	411	75	486	......
Hudson	636	602	34	636	......
Johnson	170	161	9	170	......
Kankakee	1185	1124	61	1184	1
La Porte	6581	4576	2005	6469	112
Lincoln	558	474	84	543	15
Michigan	4688	2927	1761	4623	65
Michigan City	3985	2400	1585	3940	45
New Durham	1984	1603	381	1982	2
Westville City	640	577	63	638	2
Noble	1008	901	107	1006	2
Pleasant	814	696	118	814	......
Scipio	856	696	160	848	8
Springfield	1072	813	259	1068	4
Union	585	493	92	585	......
Wills	884	812	72	884	......
LAWRENCE.					
Bono	1005	998	7	1005	......
Flinn	967	962	5	967	......
Guthrie	1292	1274	18	1291	1
Indian Creek	1348	1340	8	1339	9
Marion	3006	2950	56	2897	109
Mitchell	1087	1050	37	1025	62
Marshall	830	827	3	826	4
Perry	982	977	5	967	15
Pleasant Run	699	698	1	699	......
Shawswick	2560	2442	118	2494	66
Spice Valley	1939	1923	16	1893	46

…sive of city of Franklin. (b) Exclusive of city of Vincennes. (c) Exclusive of city of La Porte.

TABLE IX.—*Population of Minor Civil Divisions, &c.—INDIANA*—Continued.

Counties.	Total.	Nativity. Native.	Nativity. Foreign.	Race. White.	Race. Colored.
MADISON.					
Adams	1564	1552	12	1564	......
Markleville	83	80	3	83	......
New Columbus	135	135	......	135	......
Anderson	4713	4342	371	4653	60
Anderson	3126	2787	339	3066	60
Boone	1078	1070	8	1078	......
Independence	40	40	......	40	......
Duck Creek	789	773	16	779	10
Fall Creek	2483	2436	47	2481	2
Huntsville	202	200	2	202	......
Pendleton	675	657	18	673	2
Green	954	942	12	954	......
Alfont	76	76	......	76	......
Jackson	1344	1329	15	1339	5
Lafayette	1452	1427	25	1449	3
Monroe	2221	2195	26	2221	......
Alexandria	287	282	5	287	......
Pipe Creek	2300	2257	43	2293	7
Ellwood	310	291	19	310	......
Frankton	270	265	5	270	......
Richland	1065	1039	26	1065	......
Stoney Creek	1082	1067	15	1082	......
Fishersburg	96	95	1	96	......
Union	851	838	13	850	1
Chesterfield	203	201	2	202	1
Van Buren	874	870	4	874	......
MARION.					
Centre (a)	4274	3519	755	3841	433
Decatur	1559	1517	42	1550	9
Franklin	2376	2219	157	2352	24
Acton	210	162	48	210	......
Indianapolis	48244	37587	10657	45309	b2931
Lawrence	2360	2294	66	2294	66
Perry	2452	2351	101	2340	112
Pike	2206	2153	53	2160	46
Warren	2291	1927	364	2261	30
Cumberland	276	250	26	276	......
Washington	2439	2383	56	2326	113
Allisonville	62	62	......	62	......
Millersville	64	64	......	64	......
Wayne	3738	3342	396	3564	174
MARSHALL.					
Bourbon	2794	2616	178	2794	......
Bourbon	874	829	45	874	......
Centre	4830	4318	512	4830	......
Plymouth	2482	2095	387	2482	......
German	2233	1918	315	2233	......
Green	1097	1074	23	1097	......
North	1484	1422	62	1484	......
Polk	1812	1754	58	1812	......
Tippecanoe	1165	1146	19	1165	......
Union	1335	1262	73	1335	......
Walnut	1972	1921	51	1972	......
West	1489	1405	84	1489	......
MARTIN.					
Baker	1018	1017	1	1018	......
Brown	1048	1043	5	1048	......
Center	1170	1141	29	1170	......
Columbia	831	813	18	831	......
Halbert	1336	1296	40	1303	33
Shoals	513	498	15	513	......
Lost River	899	892	7	899	......
McCameron	985	974	11	985	......
Mitcheltree	1026	1020	6	1026	......
Perry	1760	1639	121	1757	3
Loogootee	748	690	58	746	2
Rutherford	1030	1011	19	1030	......

Counties.	Total.	Nativity. Native.	Nativity. Foreign.	Race. White.	Race. Colored.
MIAMI.					
Allen	1042	1025	17	1042	......
Butler	1535	1503	32	1397	(e)
Peoria	119	115	4	119	......
Santa Fé	115	115	......	115	......
Clay	972	933	39	972	......
Deer Creek	1173	1139	34	1173	......
Erie	599	573	26	599	......
Harrison	1202	1147	55	1197	5
Jackson	1645	1619	26	1645	......
Jefferson	1370	1333	37	1370	......
Perry	1667	1619	48	1667	......
Peru (d)	1115	1045	70	1104	11
Peru	3617	3114	503	3587	30
Pipe Creek	1227	1173	54	1226	1
Richland	1600	1564	36	1600	......
Union	982	965	17	982	......
Washington	1306	1197	109	1295	11
MONROE.					
Bean Blossom	1316	1284	32	1310	6
Mount Tabor	66	63	3	66	......
Stinesville	140	129	11	140	......
Benton	867	846	21	867	......
Bloomington	2860	2710	150	2738	122
Bloomington	1032	1000	32	981	51
Clear Creek	1325	1310	15	1325	......
Indian Creek	988	980	8	987	1
Marion	372	362	10	372	......
Perry	1513	1460	53	1482	31
Polk	843	838	5	843	......
Richland	1486	1446	40	1415	71
Salt Creek	636	622	14	636	......
Van Buren	972	956	16	953	19
Washington	990	979	11	981	9
MONTGOMERY.					
Brown	2126	2103	23	2126	......
Clark	2175	2113	62	2167	8
Ladoga	878	834	44	870	8
Coal Creek	1773	1732	41	1772	1
Crawfordsville	3701	3241	460	3607	94
Franklin	1683	1675	8	1678	5
Madison	974	924	50	974	......
Ripley	1433	1409	24	1427	6
Scott	1111	1085	26	1107	4
Sugar Creek	1176	1165	11	1170	......
Union (f)	4746	4606	140	4698	48
Whiteville	129	125	4	129	......
Walnut	1449	1431	18	1448	1
Wayne	1418	1394	24	1418	......
MORGAN.					
Adams	1207	1206	1	1207	......
Ashland	969	963	6	969	......
Baker	436	454	2	436	......
Brown	1673	1657	16	1663	10
Mooresville	1229	1216	13	1223	6
Clay	1234	1232	2	1233	1
Green	1345	1306	39	1345	......
Gregg	1041	1026	15	1041	......
Harrison	378	368	10	378	......
Jackson	1723	1663	60	1723	......
Jefferson	1081	1037	44	1080	1
Madison	1042	1026	16	1042	......
Monroe	1467	1465	2	1467	......
Monrovia	348	347	1	348	......
Ray	761	761	......	761	......
Washington	3151	3036	115	3089	62
Martinsville	1131	1076	55	1107	24

(a) Exclusive of city of Indianapolis.
(b) Also 4 Indians.
(c) Also 138 Indians.
(d) Exclusive of city of Peru.
(e) Also 7 Indians.
(f) Exclusive of city of Crawfordsville.

TABLE IX.—*Population of Minor Civil Divisions, &c.—INDIANA*—Continued.

Counties.	Total.	Nativity. Native.	Nativity. Foreign.	Race. White.	Race. Colored.
NEWTON.					
Beaver	637	604	33	635	2
Grant	609	582	117	603	6
Iroquois	619	588	31	619	......
Jackson	766	737	29	766	......
Jefferson	1606	1459	147	1601	5
Kentland	802	720	82	797	5
Lake	378	338	40	378	......
McClellan	141	140	1	122	19
Washington	983	941	42	982	1
NOBLE.					
Albion	598	588	10	598	......
Albion	476	......	......	......	......
Allen	1754	1551	203	1754	......
Avilla	138	134	4	138	......
Lisbon	142	139	3	142	......
Elkhart	1541	1427	114	1541	......
Wawaka	252	243	9	252	......
Green	1106	1088	18	1106	......
Jefferson	1293	1257	36	1293	......
Kendallville	2164	1727	437	2158	6
Noble	1013	993	20	1013	......
Orange	2066	1922	144	2065	1
Brimfield	247	236	11	247	......
Rome City	351	332	19	350	1
Wolcottville	80	78	2	80	......
Perry	3135	2923	212	3129	6
Ligonier	1514	1356	158	1508	6
Sparta	1381	1362	19	1381	......
Swan	1295	1208	87	1295	......
Washington	766	754	12	766	......
Wayne (a)	1236	1079	157	1236	......
York	1041	1010	31	1041	......
OHIO.					
Cass	772	715	57	772	......
Pike	921	715	206	921	......
Randolph	3475	3317	158	3291	184
Rising Sun	1760	1692	68	1667	93
Union	669	637	32	664	5
ORANGE.					
French Lick	1599	1585	14	1590	9
Greenfield	1439	1438	1	1439	......
Jackson	1148	1143	5	1147	1
Newton Stewart	90	88	2	90	......
North East	930	920	10	930	......
North West	879	870	9	875	4
Orangeville	904	900	4	887	17
Orleans	1865	1847	18	1845	20
Orleans	905	893	12	885	20
Paoli	2350	2322	28	2275	75
Paoli	628	606	22	597	31
South East	1556	1552	4	1540	16
Stamper's Creek	827	821	6	810	17
OWEN.					
Clay	1284	1280	4	1284	......
Franklin	1512	1499	13	1512	......
Harrison	451	450	1	451	......
Jackson	757	721	36	757	......
Jefferson	2018	1973	45	2018	......
Jennings	801	796	5	801	......
Lafayette	1071	1057	14	1068	3
Marion	1767	1641	126	1767	......
Montgomery	808	807	1	808	......
Morgan	1031	1013	18	1031	......
Taylor	757	744	13	757	......
OWEN—Cont'd.					
Washington	2547	2496	51	2497	50
Spencer	971	930	41	945	26
Wayne	1333	1281	52	1327	6
Gosport	860	813	47	854	6
PARKE.					
Adams	3286	3211	75	3212	74
Rockville	1187	1134	53	1132	55
Florida	2110	2075	35	2110	......
Greene	1122	1109	13	1122	......
Howard	554	553	1	554	......
Jackson	1377	1355	22	1377	......
Liberty	1540	1533	7	1540	......
Penn	1335	1317	18	1315	20
Annapolis	279	279	......	277	2
Racoon	1327	1320	7	1286	41
Reserve	1387	1336	51	1375	12
Montezuma	624	575	49	624	......
Sugar Creek	878	872	6	878	......
Union	1256	1245	11	1256	......
Wabash	781	767	14	781	......
Washington	1213	1202	11	1208	5
PERRY.					
Anderson	1136	1023	113	1136	......
Clark	1567	1492	75	1567	......
Leopold	862	638	224	862	......
Oil	1440	1237	203	1440	......
Tobin	2345	2188	157	2318	27
Rome	221	210	11	221	......
Troy	6086	4153	1933	5974	112
Cannelton	2481	1781	700	2419	62
Rock Island	241	134	107	241	......
Tell City	1660	912	748	1650	10
Troy	480	392	88	480	......
Union	1365	1334	31	1354	11
PIKE.					
Clay	747	747	......	747	......
Jefferson	2188	2167	21	2188	......
Lockhart	1829	1673	156	1829	......
Logan	921	917	4	921	......
Madison	723	719	4	723	......
Marion	1428	1424	4	1428	......
Monroe	1820	1756	64	1820	......
Patoka	1760	1747	13	1760	......
Washington	2363	2260	103	2349	14
Petersburg	923	858	65	910	13
PORTER.					
Boone	1215	1128	87	1213	2
Centre (b)	1394	1122	272	1394	......
Essex	228	171	57	228	......
Jackson	1072	885	187	1049	23
Liberty	798	657	141	797	1
Morgan	579	505	74	579	......
Pine	474	292	182	474	......
Pleasant	615	524	91	615	......
Portage	728	455	273	723	5
Porter	1006	886	120	1006	......
Union	1057	899	158	1057	......
Valparaiso	2765	2203	562	2760	5
Washington	647	588	59	647	......
Westchester	1364	788	576	1361	3
POSEY.					
Bethel	581	567	14	581	......

(a) Exclusive of city of Kendallville

(b) Exclusive of city of Valparaiso.

TABLE IX.—*Population of Minor Civil Divisions, &c.*—*INDIANA*—Continued.

Counties.	Total.	Nativity.		Race.	
		Native.	Foreign.	White.	Colored.
POSEY—Cont'd.					
Black	6291	5654	637	5799	492
Mount Vernon	2880	2451	429	2642	238
Center	955	908	47	955	......
Harmony	2231	2020	211	2219	12
New Harmony	836	705	131	832	4
Lynn	1666	1630	36	1652	14
Marr's	2029	1489	540	2029	......
Point	980	946	34	935	45
Robb	1781	1717	64	1780	1
Poseyville	213	208	5	213	......
Stewartsville	135	126	9	135	......
Robinson	1683	1087	596	1683	......
Smith	988	913	75	988	......
PULASKI.					
Beaver	489	442	47	489	......
Cass	460	349	111	460	......
Franklin	226	188	38	226	......
Harrison	753	739	14	753	......
Indian Creek	812	727	85	812	......
Pulaski	123	104	19	123	......
Jefferson	171	160	11	171	......
Monroe	1418	1260	158	1418	......
Winamac	906	783	123	906	......
Rich Grove	315	222	93	315	......
Salem	567	493	74	567	......
Francisville	281	242	39	281	......
Tippecanoe	833	720	113	833	......
Monterey	210	183	27	210	......
Van Buren	972	948	24	972	......
Rosedale	88	78	10	88	......
Star City	115	115	......	115	......
White Post	785	605	180	785	......
Medaryville	193	147	46	193	......
PUTNAM.					
Clinton	1036	1033	3	1036	......
Cloverdale	1740	1712	28	1740	......
Cloverdale	317	301	16	317	......
Floyd	1336	1301	35	1336	......
Groveland	67	67	......	67	......
Franklin	1266	1249	17	1266	......
Greencastle (a)	1716	1565	151	1699	17
Greencastle	3227	2861	366	3185	42
Jackson	1431	1428	3	1431	......
New Marysville	109	109	......	109	......
Jefferson	990	983	7	960	30
Mt. Meridian	90	86	4	90	......
Madison	1043	1008	35	1042	1
Marion	1453	1407	46	1453	......
Fillmore	217	198	19	217	......
Mill Creek	492	492	......	492	......
Monroe	1608	1569	39	1595	13
Russell	1246	1218	28	1244	2
Warren	1087	1071	16	1087	......
Putnamville	219	214	5	219	......
Washington	1843	1827	16	1843	......
RANDOLPH.					
Franklin	1537	1479	58	1536	1
Ridgeville	716	676	40	715	1
Greene	1034	1020	14	1034	......
Fairview	142	141	1	142	......
Emmettsville	67	61	6	67	......
Green's Fork	2043	2022	21	1800	243
Spartansburg	192	190	2	185	7
Jackson	1349	1315	34	1349	......
RANDOLPH—Cont'd.					
Monroe	1662	1618	44	1649	13
Farmland	532	519	13	519	13
Morristown	257	243	14	257	......
Nettle Creek	1459	1454	5	1310	149
Stony Creek	1212	1203	9	1176	36
Ward	1614	1584	30	1614	......
Deerfield	239	237	2	239	......
Washington	2051	2044	7	1970	81
Wayne	3220	3053	167	3210	10
Union City	1439	1324	115	1437	2
West River	1612	1584	28	1562	50
Huntsville	130	127	3	130	......
White River	4069	3926	143	4035	34
Winchester	1456	1369	87	1442	14
RIPLEY.					
Adams	2703	1924	779	2702	1
Brown	2234	1918	316	2192	42
Centre	1581	1390	191	1581	......
Delaware	1559	1227	332	1559	......
Franklin	1961	1600	361	1960	1
Jackson	1401	1100	301	1401	......
Johnson	2409	2279	130	2389	20
Versailles	495	455	40	495	......
Laughery	1874	1266	608	1874	......
Otter Creek	1637	1562	75	1632	5
Shelby	2412	2178	234	2383	29
Washington	1206	1129	77	1201	5
RUSH.					
Anderson	1452	1447	5	1444	8
Centre	1645	1605	40	1629	16
Jackson	770	756	14	764	6
Noble	1203	1189	14	1189	14
Orange	1273	1260	13	1273	......
Posey	1763	1737	26	1749	14
Burlington	218	212	6	218	......
Richland	917	892	25	910	7
Ripley	1841	1832	9	1502	339
Carthage	481	477	4	418	63
Rushville	3327	3068	259	2780	547
Rushville	1696	1476	220	1263	433
Union	1206	1142	64	1201	5
Walker	1081	1045	36	1081	......
Manilla	163	159	4	163	......
Washington	1148	1123	25	1141	7
Raleigh	89	86	3	89	......
SCOTT.					
Finley	1102	1085	17	1101	1
Jennings	1278	1263	15	1278	......
Austin	321	311	10	321	......
Johnson	1454	1441	13	1454	......
New Frankfort	79	77	2	79	......
Wooster	111	111	......	111	......
Lexington	2529	2399	130	2527	2
Lexington	440	415	25	439	1
Vienna	1510	1458	52	1508	2
Vienna	166	158	8	166	......
SHELBY.					
Addison (c)	2677	2602	75	2619	58
Brandywine	1224	1175	49	1224	......
Hanover	1572	1540	32	1571	1
Hendricks	1704	1672	32	1704	......
Jackson	1305	1278	27	1305	......

(a) Exclusive of city of Greencastle.
(b) Also 1 Indian.
(c) Exclusive of city of Shelbyville.

BLE IX.—*Population of Minor Civil Divisions, &c.—INDIANA*—Continued.

...ties.	Total.	NATIVITY. Native.	Foreign.	RACE. White.	Colored.
—Cont'd.					
...uburn ..	89	89	......	89	......
....	1463	1394	71	1464	1
....	940	920	20	940	......
....	1730	1661	50	1730	......
....	1733	1696	37	1733	......
...ville	2731	2440	291	2663	68
...eek	1028	1015	13	1028	......
....	1200	1133	67	1200	......
...m	1194	1181	13	1194	......
...ton	1390	1373	17	1390	......
...CER.					
....	1420	1196	224	1408	12
....	1385	1224	161	1378	7
....	1871	1693	178	1849	22
...d	2426	2321	105	2323	103
....	1977	1390	587	1977	......
....	1569	1329	240	1569	......
....	926	900	26	914	12
....	2381	2314	67	2247	134
....	3843	3575	268	3184	659
...port	1720	1693	27	1515	205
...KE.					
...a	251	240	11	251	......
....	555	546	9	555	......
...t	244	242	2	244	......
....	244	197	47	244	......
...let	47	38	9	47	......
....	125	123	2	125	......
...end	505	472	33	505	......
....	524	483	41	524	......
...ertown ..	71	61	10	71	......
...d	532	428	104	532	......
...Pierre ...	105	79	26	105	......
...ton	546	530	16	546	......
....	606	527	79	606	......
...h Judson.	115	101	14	115	......
...BEN.					
...ke	455	446	9	455	......
....	962	936	26	962	......
...mont	392	385	7	392	......
....	1122	1096	26	1122	......
...wn	779	751	28	779	......
...o	975	935	40	975	......
....	1318	1273	45	1318	......
....	2071	1929	142	2066	5
...ola	1072	990	82	1070	2
....	653	644	9	653	......
....	1385	1333	52	1385	......
....	1024	998	26	1024	......
....	1253	1226	27	1253	......
....	857	840	17	857	......
...OSEPH.					
....	717	686	31	717	......
....	1442	1024	418	1442	......
....	551	538	13	551	......
....	964	914	50	964	......
....	408	352	56	408	......
....	1394	1339	55	1394	......
...h Liberty	223	214	9	223	......
....	1063	1001	62	1063	......
....	1697	1363	334	1697	......
....	1560	1425	135	1558	(a)
....	4982	4159	823	4969	13
...awaka .	2617	2090	527	2604	13

(a) Also 2 Indians.
(b) Exclusive of city of South Bend.

Counties.	Total.	NATIVITY. Native.	Foreign.	RACE. White.	Colored.
ST. JOSEPH—Cont'd					
Portage (b)	777	677	100	756	c16
South Bend	7206	5841	1365	7133	73
Union	1801	1695	106	1783	18
Warren	760	736	24	760	......
SULLIVAN.					
Cass	1488	1478	10	1488	......
Curry	2171	2096	75	2170	1
Fairbanks	1234	1231	3	1234	......
Gill	2135	2105	30	2113	22
Merom	496	490	6	496	......
Haddon	2750	2717	33	2683	67
Carlisle	499	486	13	499	......
Hamilton	3759	3702	57	3744	15
Sullivan	1396	1348	48	1389	7
Jackson	1732	1696	36	1732	......
Jefferson	1251	1233	18	1251	......
Turman	1933	1926	7	1933	......
SWITZERLAND.					
Cotton	1700	1673	27	1695	5
Craig	1843	1802	41	1843	......
Jefferson	3368	3194	144	3334	34
Pleasant	2145	2039	106	2130	15
Posey	2183	2120	63	2139	44
York	995	961	34	972	23
TIPPECANOE.					
Fairfield (d)	2230	1684	546	2218	12
Linwood	548	398	150	548	......
Jackson	1081	1007	74	1074	7
Lafayette	13506	9867	3639	13372	134
Lauramie	2444	2308	136	2444	......
Clarkville	191	170	21	191	......
Colburn	148	142	6	148	......
Concord	51	50	1	51	......
Stockwell	403	369	34	403	......
Perry	1481	1366	115	1481	......
Randolph	948	862	86	947	1
Romney	104	98	6	104	......
Sheffield	1599	1524	75	1599	......
Dayton	385	363	22	385	......
Shelby	1395	1292	103	1393	......
Tippecanoe	2274	2166	108	2272	2
Wabash	2129	1952	177	2129	......
Washington	1376	1333	43	1375	1
Americus	143	141	2	143	......
Transitville ..	205	193	12	205	......
Wayne	1801	1643	158	1786	15
West Point ...	246	231	15	246	......
Wheaton	87	86	1	87	......
Wea	1251	1137	114	1251	......
TIPTON.					
Cicero	3646	3516	130	3609	37
Tipton	892	853	39	875	17
Jefferson	1738	1703	35	1738	......
Liberty	1746	1730	16	1746	......
Madison	1729	1713	16	1705	24
Prairie	1547	1535	12	1547	......
Wildcat	1547	1534	13	1547	......
UNION.					
Brownsville	900	832	68	900	......
Brownsvile ...	320	281	39	320	......
Centre	1896	1811	85	1853	43
Liberty	700	677	23	692	8

(c) Also 5 Indians.
(d) Exclusive of city of Lafayette.

TABLE IX.—*Population of Minor Civil Divisions, &c.—INDIANA*—Continued.

Counties.	Total.	Nativity. Native.	Nativity. Foreign.	Race. White.	Race. Colored.
UNION—Cont'd.					
Harmony	734	722	12	722	12
Harrison	759	712	47	759	......
Liberty	763	738	25	752	11
Union	1289	1235	54	1243	46
VANDERBURGH.					
Armstrong	1290	868	422	1290	......
Centre	1689	1258	431	1577	112
Evansville	21830	15554	6276	20403	1427
German	1683	1062	621	1680	3
Knight	1342	1194	148	1097	245
Perry	1719	1176	543	1550	169
Pigeon (a)	875	597	278	793	82
Scott	1677	1202	475	1631	46
Union	1040	911	129	973	67
VERMILLION.					
Clinton	2223	2177	46	2184	39
Clinton	564	554	10	535	29
Eugene	1396	1362	34	1396	......
Eugene	347	328	19	347	......
Helt	2794	2740	54	2794	......
Highland	2294	2236	58	2286	8
Perrysville	690	669	21	683	7
Vermillion	2133	2089	44	2132	1
Newport	398	385	13	397	1
VIGO.					
Fayette	1912	1847	65	1908	4
Harrison (b)	870	791	79	870	......
Honey Creek	1519	1474	45	1495	24
Linton	1437	1430	7	1335	102
Lost Creek	1914	1850	64	1705	209
Nevins	1299	1289	10	1203	96
Otter Creek	1269	1246	23	1026	243
Pierson	1489	1476	13	1488	1
Prairie Creek	1236	1223	13	1230	6
Prairieton	955	932	23	955	......
Riley	1492	1452	40	1492	......
Sugar Creek	2054	1830	224	2054	......
Terre Haute	16103	13002	3101	15686	c414
WABASH.					
Chester	3143	3049	94	3142	1
La Gro	4066	3774	292	4048	18
La Gro	519	448	71	519	......
Liberty	1816	1812	4	1792	d4
Noble (e)	4485	4334	151	4468	17
Pleasant	2553	2493	60	2553	......
Wabash City	2881	2586	295	2838	43
Waltz	2361	2351	10	2333	f1
Somerset	371	366	5	371	......
WARREN.					
Jordan	448	443	5	448	......
J. Q. Adams	809	779	30	804	5
Kent	601	585	16	601	......
Liberty	1176	1144	32	1176	......
Medina	609	575	34	609	......
Mound	394	386	8	394	......
Pike	941	879	62	936	5
Pine	1032	994	38	1028	4
Prairie	667	599	68	667	......
Steuben	1068	1009	59	1068	......
WARREN—Cont'd.					
Warren	1208	1170	38	1206	g1
Independence	183	182	1	183	......
Washington	1251	1181	70	1244	7
Williamsport	988	948	40	987	1
WARRICK.					
Anderson	842	794	48	811	31
Boone	4042	3725	317	3883	159
Booneville	1039	836	203	1039	......
Campbell	1437	1163	274	1393	44
Greer	864	675	189	860	4
Hart	1892	1805	87	1892	......
Lane	870	867	3	870	......
Ohio	3290	2923	367	3055	235
Newburg	1464	1217	247	1409	55
Owen	1440	1432	8	1439	1
Pigeon	1646	1631	15	1646	......
Skelton	1330	1250	80	1317	13
WASHINGTON.					
Brown	1521	1486	35	1521	......
Franklin	1366	1353	13	1359	7
Gibson	1525	1507	18	1525	......
Howard	1158	1157	1	1158	......
Jackson	779	757	22	779	......
Martinsburg	123	119	4	123	......
Jefferson	1532	1496	36	1531	1
Madison	835	822	13	835	......
Monroe	1058	1046	12	1058	......
Pierce	1179	1177	2	1178	1
Polk	920	893	27	920	......
Posey	1349	1331	18	1349	......
Fredericksb'g	160	159	1	160	......
Hardinsburg	199	196	3	199	......
Vernon	1101	1090	11	1101	......
Washington	4172	4028	144	4163	9
Salem	1294	1217	77	1285	9
WAYNE.					
Abington	833	803	30	833	......
Abington	161	153	8	161	......
Boston	894	852	42	888	6
Centre	2855	2718	137	2788	67
Centreville	1077	1004	73	1058	19
Clay	1094	1064	30	1081	13
Washington	379	358	21	379	......
Dalton	766	756	10	748	18
Dalton	73	73	......	73	......
Franklin	1385	1356	29	1327	58
Franklin	80	80	......	80	......
Bethel	88	88	......	88	......
White Water	144	144	......	143	1
Green	1293	1270	23	1291	2
Williamsburg	248	246	2	248	......
Harrison	580	560	20	579	1
Jackson	4949	4605	344	4726	223
Jacksonburg	109	101	8	109	......
Cambridge City	2162	1903	259	2059	103
Dublin	1076	1062	14	1023	53
East Germantown	536	512	24	536	......
Jefferson	1785	1731	54	1783	2
Hagerstown	830	792	38	830	......
New Garden	1519	1477	42	1351	168
Fairfax	21	21	......	20	1
Newport	343	340	3	286	57

(a) Exclusive of city of Evansville.
(b) Exclusive of city of Terre Haute.
(c) Also 3 Indians.
(d) Also 20 Indians.
(e) Exclusive of Wabash City.
(f) Also 27 Indians.
(g) Also 1 Indian.

[T]ABLE IX.—*Population of Minor Civil Divisions, &c.—INDIANA*—Continued.

[Co]unties.	Total.	NATIVITY. Native.	NATIVITY. Foreign.	RACE. White.	RACE. Colored.
[WAYN]E—Cont'd.					
....	876	871	5	841	35
[Ec]onomy	229	225	4	228	1
[Rich]mond	9445	7745	1700	8975	470
[Washi]ngton	2040	1938	102	2024	16
[Mi]lton	823	768	55	813	10
[Wayn]e (a)	3734	3354	380	3574	160
[W]ELLS.					
[Chester]	1212	1177	35	1212	......
[Harris]on	2961	2733	228	2961	......
[Bl]uffton	1131	1075	56	1131	......
[Jackso]n	1140	1127	13	1140	......
[Jeffers]on	1773	1686	87	1773	......
[Lancas]ter	1381	1337	44	1381	......
[Liberty]	1097	1072	25	1097	......
[Nottin]gham	1432	1382	50	1432	......
[Rock C]reek	1326	1272	54	1326	......
....	1263	1243	20	1263	......
[W]HITE.					
[Big Cr]eek	584	532	32	582	2
....	451	426	25	451	......
[Honey] Creek	611	471	140	611	......
[Re]ynolds	306	221	85	306	......
[Jackso]n	1358	1328	30	1358	......
[Bu]rnettsville.	270	262	8	270	......

Counties.	Total.	NATIVITY. Native.	NATIVITY. Foreign.	RACE. White.	RACE. Colored.
WHITE—Cont'd.					
Idaville	197	193	4	197	......
Liberty	888	869	19	888	......
Monon	969	938	31	969	......
New Bradford	196	180	16	196	......
Prairie	1998	1897	101	1998	......
Brookston	406	370	36	406	......
Princeton	851	818	33	850	1
Wolcott	109	91	18	109	......
Round Grove.....	401	358	43	401	......
Union	1832	1755	77	1832	......
Monticello....	887	832	55	887	......
West Point	611	574	37	611	......
WHITLEY.					
Cleveland	2041	1999	42	2041	......
Columbia (b)	1271	1177	94	1269	2
Columbia.......	1663	1400	263	1663	......
Etna	429	427	2	429	......
Jefferson	1263	1199	64	1263	......
Richland	1723	1659	64	1723	......
Smith	1232	1211	21	1138	94
Thorn Creek	1343	1253	90	1343	......
Troy	894	886	8	893	1
Union	1294	1204	90	1294	......
Coesse	192	168	24	192	......
Washington......	1246	1138	108	1246	......

(a) Exclusive of city of Richmond.

(b) Exclusive of city of Columbia.

TABLE IX.—*Population of Minor Civil Divisions, &c.—IOWA.*

[NOTE].—The marginal column marks townships; the first indentation, cities; the second, towns. [Names] of towns are placed under the names of the townships in which they are respectively situated. [The po]pulation of each township includes that of all towns situated in it.

[Co]unties.	Total.	NATIVITY. Native.	NATIVITY. Foreign.	RACE. White.	RACE. Colored.
[A]DAIR.					
....	139	136	3	139	......
[...] River	235	203	32	235	......
[...]eld.........	197	188	9	197	......
....	137	123	14	137	......
[...]n	434	420	14	434	......
[...]n	339	314	25	339	......
[...]n	362	334	28	362	......
....	531	457	74	531	......
[...]d	292	279	13	291	1
[Some]rset........	439	406	33	439	......
....	169	154	15	169	......
....	213	183	30	213	......
[Washi]ngton.......	495	481	14	495	......
[A]DAMS.					
....	301	294	7	301	......
....	190	177	13	190	......
[...]s	333	319	14	333	......
....	438	399	39	438	......

Counties.	Total.	NATIVITY. Native.	NATIVITY. Foreign.	RACE. White.	RACE. Colored.
ADAMS—Cont'd.					
Lincoln	170	161	9	170	......
Mercer	138	124	14	138	......
Nodaway.........	628	591	37	628	......
Queen City	398	338	60	398	......
Quincy	1090	1027	63	1066	24
Quincy	283	275	8	283	......
Union	393	375	18	393	......
Washington	535	532	3	535	......
ALAMAKEE.					
Center	1048	429	619	1048	......
Fairview	630	439	191	630	......
Franklin	850	753	97	850	......
French Creek	791	521	270	791	......
Hanover	550	290	260	550	......
Iowa	347	254	93	347	......
Jefferson	1015	802	213	1014	1
Lafayette	1120	688	432	1120	......
Lansing	2519	1524	995	2518	1

TABLE IX.—*Population of Minor Civil Divisions, &c.*—*IOWA*—Continued.

Counties.	Total.	Nativity. Native.	Nativity. Foreign.	Race. White.	Race. Colored.
ALLAMAKEE—Con.					
Lansing	1755	1065	690	1754	1
Linton	712	557	155	712	......
Ludlow	1038	723	315	1038	......
Makee	1784	1259	525	1783	1
Paint Creek	1141	616	525	1141	......
Post	1223	1054	169	1223	......
Taylor	863	574	289	863	......
Union City	578	344	234	578	......
Union Prairie	912	602	310	912	......
Waterloo	747	336	411	742	5
APPANOOSE.					
Bellair	655	644	11	653	2
Caldwell	1201	1171	30	1194	7
Center	1723	1672	51	1708	15
Centerville	1037	1002	35	1022	15
Chariton	888	877	11	888	......
Douglas	590	585	5	590	......
Franklin	888	863	25	888	......
Independence	1030	1016	14	1030	......
John's	895	877	18	895	......
Lincoln	586	582	4	585	1
Pleasant	1101	1073	28	1101	......
Sharon	661	636	25	661	......
Taylor	1059	1036	23	1059	......
Moravia	161	157	4	161	......
Udell	907	896	11	907	......
Unionville	183	180	3	183	......
Union	668	668	......	668	......
Walnut	778	768	10	778	......
Washington (*a*)	1873	1804	69	1872	1
Moulton (*a*)	678	642	*36	677	1
Orleans	38	37	1	38	......
Wells (*a*)	953	943	10	944	9
AUDUBON.					
Audubon	381	344	37	381	......
Exira	426	378	48	426	......
Exira	161	137	24	161	......
Oakfield	405	381	24	404	1
BENTON.					
Benton	601	566	35	601	......
Big Grove	856	808	48	856	......
Bruce	567	481	86	566	1
Canton	1509	1423	86	1509	......
Cedar	1041	971	70	1040	1
Eden	804	723	81	804	......
Eldorado	777	517	260	777	......
Florence	1290	792	498	1289	1
Florence	313	198	115	313	......
Fremont	946	566	380	946	......
Harrison	502	491	11	502	......
Homer	567	455	112	567	......
Iowa	2639	2118	521	2635	4
Belle Plain	1488	1199	289	1488	......
East Irving	84	80	4	84	......
Jackson	963	871	92	963	......
Kane	763	493	270	763	......
Leroy	1807	1496	311	1796	11
Blairstown	682	596	86	671	11
Luzerne	144	115	29	144	......
Monroe	759	667	92	759	......
Polk	1196	1122	74	1196	......
St. Clair	811	656	155	810	1
Taylor	3331	3146	185	3326	5
Vinton	2460	2311	149	2455	5
Union	725	487	238	725	......

Counties.	Total.	Nativity. Native.	Nativity. Foreign.	Race. White.	Race. Colored.
BLACK HAWK.					
Barclay	861	687	174	861	......
Bennington	654	518	136	654	......
Big Creek	1394	1227	167	1394	......
Black Hawk	716	563	153	716	......
Cedar (*b*)	731	578	153	731	......
Cedar Falls	1311	1139	172	1308	3
Cedar Falls	3070	2316	754	3065	5
Eagle	507	357	150	507	......
East Waterloo	913	811	102	913	......
Fox	812	612	200	811	1
Lester	844	679	165	844	......
Lincoln	462	380	82	461	1
Mount Vernon	1035	852	183	1035	......
Orange	864	786	78	864	......
Poyner	1063	869	194	1063	......
Spring Creek	707	658	49	707	......
Union	419	386	33	419	......
Washington	548	507	41	548	......
Waterloo (*c*)	458	397	61	458	......
Waterloo	4337	3628	709	4329	8
BOONE.					
Cass	895	760	135	895	......
Des Moines	5241	4255	986	5230	11
Booneesboro	1518	1349	169	1518	......
Montana	2415	1864	551	2404	11
Dodge	1297	1098	199	1297	......
Douglas	879	627	252	879	......
Jackson	798	690	108	797	(*d*)
Marcy	2015	1443	572	2015	......
Pilot Mound	747	410	337	747	......
Union	398	364	34	398	......
Worth	975	886	89	975	......
Yell	1339	1143	196	1339	......
BREMER.					
Dayton	419	299	120	419	......
Douglas	587	429	158	587	......
Franklin	643	490	153	643	......
Frederika	389	338	51	389	......
Fremont	613	401	212	612	1
Jackson	1131	1062	69	1121	10
Jefferson	766	555	211	766	......
Lafayette	867	767	100	866	(*d*)
Leroy	363	270	93	363	......
Maxfield	735	360	375	735	......
Polk	1267	1167	100	1265	2
Sumner	582	488	94	580	2
Warren	927	603	324	927	......
Washington (*e*)	948	841	107	948	......
Waverly	2291	1986	305	2289	2
BUCHANAN.					
Buffalo	598	527	71	598	......
Byron	1195	1035	160	1195	......
Cono	579	476	103	579	......
Fairbank	1238	1037	201	1238	......
Fremont	554	484	70	553	1
Hazelton	885	744	141	885	......
Homer	581	502	79	581	......
Independence	2945	2400	545	2938	7
Jefferson	918	791	127	918	......
Liberty	1272	1200	72	1272	......
Madison	661	591	70	661	......
Middlefield	666	508	158	666	......
Newton	981	778	203	981	......

(*a*) Of Moulton, 612 in Washington, 66 in Wells.
(*b*) Exclusive of city of Cedar Falls.
(*c*) Exclusive of city of Waterloo.
(*d*) Also 1 Indian.
(*e*) Exclusive of city of Waverly.

TABLE IX.—*Population of Minor Civil Divisions, &c.—IOWA*—Continued.

Counties.	Total.	Nativity. Native.	Nativity. Foreign.	Race. White.	Race. Colored.
[B]ANAN—Con.					
....	1633	1416	217	1633	......
er	550	481	69	550	......
ington (a) ...	1259	1000	259	1258	1
burg	519	432	87	519	......
[BUE]NA VISTA.					
e (b)	233	129	104	233	......
s	71	51	20	71	......
....	385	278	107	385	......
)	302	244	58	302	......
x Rapids (b)	61	33	28	61	......
nus	278	228	50	278	......
d	60	47	13	60	......
Lake	256	204	52	256	......
BUTLER.					
n	1039	916	123	1039	......
r	1084	956	128	1084	......
zette	206	175	31	206	......
r	1329	1219	110	1329	......
Water	461	404	57	461	......
n	383	*349	34	383	......
ont	655	503	152	655	......
on	569	523	46	569	......
son	613	445	168	613	......
utler Center	152	112	40	152	......
son	293	208	85	293	......
oe	644	508	136	644	......
ord	512	477	35	512	......
y	299	264	35	299	......
Rock	1142	1055	87	1142	......
ington	402	268	134	402	......
Point	320	257	63	320	......
[C]ALHOUN.					
nn	263	258	5	263	......
ake City	103	102	1	103	......
on	367	349	18	367	......
ln	427	343	84	427	......
nan	545	398	147	545	......
[C]ARROLL.					
ll	578	492	86	578	......
arroll	384	342	42	384	......
en	408	364	44	408	......
lidden	177	144	33	177	......
r	157	152	5	157	......
on	400	395	5	400	......
lan	472	303	169	472	......
n	436	428	8	436	......
CASS.					
Grove	163	148	15	162	1
ton	337	204	133	336	1
....	1200	1140	60	1200	......
ewis	400	......	......	......	......
....	367	316	51	367	......
sa	2120	1780	340	2117	3
tlantic	1200	......	......	......	......
ey Grove	1166	1006	160	1166	......
n	111	105	6	111	......
CEDAR.					
....	591	537	54	591	......
r	2899	2738	161	2882	17
ipton	1246	1161	85	1231	15
CEDAR—Cont'd.					
Dayton	1546	1337	209	1546	......
Clarence	726	630	96	726	......
Fairfield	754	617	137	754	......
Farmington	1249	996	253	1249	......
Durant	373	316	57	373	......
Fremont	1160	1049	111	1160	......
Stanwood	257	243	14	257	......
Gower	957	859	98	945	12
Inland	1112	986	126	1112	......
Iowa	1168	1083	85	1164	4
Linn	521	495	26	521	......
Massillon	974	793	181	974	......
Pioneer	1622	1494	128	1616	6
Mechanicsville	628	583	45	623	5
Red Oak	594	489	105	594	......
Rochester	797	739	58	797	......
Rochester	174	167	7	174	......
Springdale	1539	1399	140	1538	1
Springfield	1509	1133	376	1507	2
London	486	346	140	486	......
Sugar Creek	739	645	94	739	......
CERRO GORDO.					
Clear Lake	175	143	32	175	......
Falls	553	423	130	553	......
Geneseo	240	198	42	240	......
Grant	95	80	15	95	......
Lake	1164	893	271	1163	1
Clear Lake	775	575	200	774	1
Lincoln	279	244	35	277	2
Mason	1784	1435	349	1783	1
Mason City	1183	955	228	1182	1
Owen	211	186	25	211	......
Portland	221	165	56	221	......
CHEROKEE.					
Afton	263	238	25	263	......
Cedar	250	172	78	245	5
Cherokee	719	516	203	718	1
Cherokee	438	......	......	......	......
Pilot Rock	280	256	24	280	......
Pitcher	144	120	24	144	......
Spring	33	33	......	33	......
Willow	278	265	13	278	......
CHICKASAW.					
Bradford	2076	1812	264	2076	......
Nashua	817	728	89	817	......
Chickasaw	1076	954	122	1074	2
Dayton	543	381	162	543	......
Deerfield	599	460	139	599	......
Dresden	535	479	56	535	......
Fredericksburg ..	611	571	40	611	......
Jacksonville	828	540	288	828	......
New Hampton	947	753	194	947	......
New Hampton	455	391	64	455	......
Richland	566	503	63	566	......
Stapleton	800	557	243	799	1
Utica	931	574	357	931	......
Washington	668	455	213	668	......
CLARKE.					
Doyle	965	958	7	965	......
Franklin	677	668	9	677	......
Fremont	484	475	9	484	......
Green Bay	507	492	15	507	......
Jackson	798	760	38	798	......
Knox	777	757	20	777	......

(a) Exclusive of city of Independence.

(b) Of Sioux Rapids, 40 in Lee and 21 in Barnes.

TABLE IX.—*Population of Minor Civil Divisions, &c.*—*IOWA*—Continued.

Counties.	Total.	Nativity. Native.	Nativity. Foreign.	Race. White.	Race. Colored.
CLARKE—Cont'd.					
Liberty	778	774	4	778	......
Madison	419	380	39	419	......
Osceola	1889	1816	73	1863	26
Osceola	1298	1236	62	1272	26
Troy	426	388	38	426	......
Ward	421	406	15	421	......
Washington	594	588	6	594	......
CLAY.					
Clay	310	243	67	310	......
Peterson	44	35	9	44	......
Douglas	320	290	30	320	......
Lincoln	299	252	47	299	......
Spencer	594	519	75	594	......
CLAYTON.					
Boardman	1806	1300	506	1805	1
El Kader	697	528	169	696	1
Buena Vista	308	228	80	308	......
Cass	1272	1059	213	1272	......
Clayton	954	611	343	954	......
Cox Creek	989	633	356	989	......
Elk	901	791	110	901	......
Farmersburg	1236	858	378	1236	......
Garnavillo	1226	742	484	1226	......
Giard	1294	866	428	1289	5
Grand Meadow	945	608	337	945	......
Highland	834	533	301	834	......
Jefferson	2245	1173	1072	2244	1
Guttenberg	1040	548	492	1040	......
Lodomillo	1002	934	68	1002	......
Mallory	945	870	75	945	......
Marion	1066	462	604	1066	......
McGregor	2074	1538	536	2071	*a*2
Mendon (*b*)	2029	1374	655	2024	5
Millville	842	675	167	842	......
Monona	1656	1340	316	1656	......
Read	840	453	387	839	1
Sperry	1141	947	194	1130	11
Volga	1178	663	515	1178	......
Wagner	988	592	396	988	......
CLINTON.					
Berlin	805	515	290	805	......
Bloomfield	1231	997	234	1231	......
Brookfield	1040	851	189	1040	......
Camanche	1453	1132	321	1453	......
Camanche	840	642	198	840	......
Center	1317	668	649	1317	......
Clinton (*c*)	1841	1349	492	1834	7
Clinton	6129	4344	1785	6047	*a*81
Deep Creek	1081	601	480	1081	......
De Witt	3186	2605	581	3172	14
De Witt	1749	1402	347	1736	13
Eden	985	689	296	985	......
Elk River	1296	769	527	1296	......
Hampshire	1030	543	487	1030	......
Liberty	931	640	291	931	......
Lyons (*d*)	389	282	107	388	1
Lyons	4088	2844	1244	4070	*a*17
Olive	1580	1086	494	1579	1
Orange	1018	760	258	1018	......
Sharon	1152	867	285	1152	......
Spring Rock	1694	1119	575	1686	8
Wheatland	788	548	24	780	......
Washington	995	584	411	995	......
Waterford	1160	729	431	1160	......
Welton	956	726	230	956	......
CRAWFORD.					
Boyer	135	120	15	135	......
Charter Oak	67	58	9	66	1
Denison	633	493	140	633	......
Denison	326	236	90	326	......
East Boyer	231	161	70	231	......
Jackson	246	125	121	246	......
Milford	663	575	88	663	......
Deloit	103	100	3	103	......
Union	555	438	117	555	......
DALLAS.					
Adams	1015	1003	12	1015	......
Adel	1563	1460	103	1563	......
Adel	711	672	39	711	......
Dallas Centre	133	113	20	133	......
Beaver	343	267	76	343	......
Boone	552	485	67	552	......
Colfax	582	546	36	582	......
Dallas	338	316	22	338	......
Des Moines	802	694	108	801	1
Grant	382	312	70	382	......
Lincoln	213	207	6	213	......
Linn	762	749	13	762	......
Spring Valley	908	853	55	908	......
Sugar Grove	506	448	58	498	8
Union	1663	1600	63	1663	......
Van Meter	1433	1307	126	1417	16
Walnut	489	446	43	489	......
Washington	468	446	22	468	......
DAVIS.					
Bloomfield	2543	2435	108	2516	27
Bloomfield	1553	1489	64	1531	22
Drakeville	534	523	11	534	......
Drakeville	207	200	7	207	......
Fabius	1494	1474	20	1494	......
Fox River	1256	1233	23	1256	......
West Grove	109	104	5	109	......
Grove	1230	1143	87	1230	......
Lick Creek	1246	1210	36	1246	......
Marion	798	783	15	798	......
Perry	722	705	17	721	1
Prairie	600	569	31	600	......
Roscoe	570	518	52	568	2
Salt Creek	889	862	27	889	......
Soap Creek	817	775	42	817	......
Union	1225	1164	61	1225	......
Wycondah	1641	1629	12	1641	......
DECATUR.					
Bloomington	266	263	3	266	......
Burrell	852	834	18	848	4
Center	1738	1710	28	1736	2
Leon	820	......	......	......	......
Decatur	1046	1025	21	1045	1
Eden	1065	1046	19	1065	......
Fayette	318	303	15	318	......
Franklin	466	449	17	466	......
Garden Grove	859	809	50	851	8
Grand River	345	326	19	334	11
Hamilton	846	824	22	846	......
High Point	796	774	22	789	7
Long Creek	714	705	9	707	7
Morgan	529	523	6	528	1
New Buda	547	499	48	547	......
Richland	849	822	27	849	......
Woodland	782	742	40	782	......

(*a*) Also 1 Indian.
(*b*) Exclusive of city of McGregor.
(*c*) Exclusive of city of Clinton.
(*d*) Exclusive of city of Lyons.

TABLE IX.—*Population of Minor Civil Divisions, &c.—IOWA*—Continued.

›unties.	Total.	Nativity. Native.	Nativity. Foreign.	Race. White.	Race. Colored.
.AWARE.					
....	730	516	214	730	......
ı	821	489	332	821	......
Grove....	1003	865	138	1003	......
....	1400	1020	380	1400	......
re.........	2727	2410	317	2721	6
nchester ..	1492	1311	181	1488	4
....	1174	1009	165	1172	2
hi	413	360	53	413	......
....	927	799	128	927	......
;reen......	752	644	108	752	......
Creek.....	1088	975	113	1088	......
....	767	691	76	767	......
'ork.......	912	626	286	911	1
....	1484	1241	243	1479	5
....	474	380	94	473	1
ıd	874	673	201	874	......
'ork.......	1610	1374	236	1604	6
....	689	593	96	689	......
MOINES.					
a.....	584	516	68	584	......
....	1192	923	269	1189	3
ington (*a*) .	14930	10173	4757	14725	205
e	1604	1490	114	1603	1
iver.......	1278	1026	252	1275	3
n	1549	1303	246	1548	1
....	807	642	165	807	......
ı	103	89	14	103	......
ıt Grove...	1023	843	180	1023	......
....	1362	1031	331	1350	12
;gton......	1081	963	118	1081	......
Springs...	1743	1538	205	1741	2
KINSON.					
Grove.....	283	244	39	283	......
rit Lake...	76	69	7	76	......
ove	172	153	19	172	......
....	236	217	19	236	......
ako.......	268	240	28	268	......
ım	430	342	88	430	......
BUQUE.					
....	1289	885	404	1289	......
....	1039	646	393	1039	......
l	1109	730	379	1109	......
....	979	679	300	978	1
ıque	18134	11910	6524	17979	155
....	878	615	263	878	......
n	1550	942	608	1550	......
....	1415	974	441	1414	1
....	1102	649	453	1102	......
n	972	610	362	964	8
ine	2046	1105	941	2046	......
....	889	485	404	889	......
Creek.....	1022	689	333	1022	......
lound.....	1137	742	395	1137	......
....	1742	1362	380	1742	......
....	1243	832	411	1241	2
;gton......	963	746	217	963	......
'ater	1160	804	356	1160	......
MMET.					
ong's Gro'e	45	19	26	45	......
....	146	83	63	146	......
th	98	87	11	98	......
....	232	176	56	232	......
'illo	480	402	78	477	3
berville...	168	159	9	168	......
w	56	55	1	56	......

Counties.	Total.	Nativity. Native.	Nativity. Foreign.	Race. White.	Race. Colored.
EMMET—Cont'd.					
High Lake	182	92	90	182	......
Peterson	153	76	77	153	......
FAYETTE.					
Auburn	1059	856	203	1059	......
Banks.............	223	180	43	223	......
Center	504	469	35	504	......
Clermont..........	1263	847	416	1262	1
Dover	1150	790	360	1150	......
Eden	927	765	162	927	......
Fairfield	1026	898	128	1026	......
Fremont	499	422	77	499	......
Harlan	312	290	22	312	......
Illyria............	851	750	101	844	7
Jefferson	639	528	111	639	......
Oran	715	590	125	715	......
Pleasant Valley ..	1119	841	278	1119	......
Putnam	766	658	108	766	......
Richland	405	371	34	405	......
Scott	337	261	76	337	......
Smithfield	638	561	77	638	......
Westfield..........	1708	1526	182	1653	55
West Union	2032	1811	221	2026	6
West Union ..	1489	1325	164	1483	6
Windsor...........	800	702	98	799	1
FLOYD.					
Cedar	415	365	50	415	......
Floyd	1328	1179	149	1328	......
Niles..............	561	447	114	559	2
Pleasant Grove ...	442	371	71	442	......
Riverton	953	800	153	953	......
Rockford	732	670	62	732	......
Rock Grove	1289	1087	202	1289	......
St. Charles	3374	2590	784	3373	1
Charles City ..	2166	1684	482	2166	......
Scott	196	180	16	196	......
Ulster.............	500	368	132	500	......
Union	978	908	70	978	......
FRANKLIN.					
Clinton............	475	377	98	475	......
Genova............	445	354	91	445	......
Grant	156	125	31	156	......
Ingham	293	255	38	291	2
Iowa	125	109	16	125	......
Morgan	240	185	55	240	......
Oakland...........	319	267	52	319	......
Osceola...........	617	407	210	616	1
Reeve	704	643	61	703	1
Washington	1079	849	230	1078	1
Hampton	588	496	92	587	1
West Fork	285	243	42	285	......
FREMONT.					
Benton	904	855	49	903	1
Fisher.............	748	712	36	748	......
Franklin	2232	1986	246	2211	*b*20
Hamburg.....	1431	1264	167	1420	*b*10
Madison...........	1277	1214	63	1275	2
Monroe............	901	885	16	901	......
Ross..............	1314	1237	77	1311	3
Tabor	310	287	23	307	3
Scott	1277	1244	33	1277	......
Sidney	2521	2456	65	2518	3
Sidney........	817	783	34	814	3
GREENE.					
Cedar	306	243	63	306	......

(*a*) Includes the whole of Burlington Township.

(*b*) Also 1 Indian.

TABLE IX.—*Population of Minor Civil Divisions, &c.—IOWA*—**Continued.**

Counties.	Total.	NATIVITY.		RACE.	
		Native.	Foreign.	White.	Colored.
GREENE—Cont'd.					
Hardin	195	165	30	195	......
Jefferson	1828	1712	116	1828	......
Jefferson	779	728	51	779	......
Kendrick	887	835	52	887	......
Washington	1411	1276	135	1408	3
Grand Junct'n	444	361	83	441	3
GRUNDY.					
Beaver	401	335	66	401	......
Black Hawk	396	289	107	396	......
Clay	329	303	26	329	......
Colfax	278	163	115	278	......
Fairfield	720	536	184	720	......
Felix	656	635	21	656	......
German	839	323	516	839	......
Grant	436	282	154	436	......
Lincoln	206	125	81	206	......
Melrose	513	459	54	513	......
Palermo	684	582	102	684	......
Pleasant Valley	402	257	145	402	......
Shiloh	539	261	278	539	......
GUTHRIE.					
Bear Grove	417	390	27	417	......
Beaver	520	505	15	520	......
Cass	1754	1693	61	1752	2
Panora	504	478	26	503	1
Center	924	875	49	924	......
Dodge	293	279	14	292	1
Grant	104	73	31	104	......
Highland	229	220	9	229	......
Jackson	875	846	29	875	......
Orange	212	207	5	212	......
Penn	676	620	56	675	1
Richland	218	210	8	218	......
Thompson	671	543	128	670	1
Union	168	162	6	168	......
HAMILTON.					
Blairsburg	310	236	74	310	......
Boone	1837	1574	263	1835	2
Webster	1339	1180	159	1337	2
Cass	433	406	27	433	......
Clear Lake	131	85	46	131	......
Ellsworth	186	101	85	186	......
Fremont	390	343	47	389	1
Hamilton	546	513	33	546	......
Lyon	188	175	13	188	......
Marion	885	554	331	885	......
Rose Grove	68	55	13	68	......
Scott	270	125	145	270	......
Webster	811	764	47	811	......
HANCOCK.					
Amsterdam	259	236	23	254	5
Concord	149	122	27	149	......
Crystal	58	48	10	58	......
Ellington	342	292	50	342	......
Madison	191	165	26	191	......
HARDIN.					
Alden	739	647	92	739	......
Buckeye	159	149	10	159	......
Clay	1394	1123	271	1384	(a)
Eldora	2070	1897	173	2070	......
Eldora	1268	1154	114	1268	......
Ellis	518	468	50	518	......
HARDIN—Cont'd.					
Etna	1849	1217	632	1848	1
Grant	148	137	11	148	......
Hardin	2013	1810	203	1998	15
Jackson	867	749	118	864	3
Pleasant	842	747	95	842	......
Providence	1335	1304	31	1335	......
Sherman	77	48	29	77	......
Tipton	397	362	35	397	......
Union	1276	1245	31	1272	4
HARRISON.					
Boyer	589	532	57	588	1
Calhoun	371	331	40	371	......
Cass	217	203	14	217	......
Cincinnati	447	392	55	447	......
Clay	456	440	16	456	......
Douglas	185	155	30	185	......
Harrison	830	674	156	830	......
Jackson	206	188	18	206	......
Jefferson	694	632	62	694	......
Lagrange	308	287	21	308	......
Lincoln	88	83	5	88	......
Little Sioux	644	592	52	644	......
Magnolia	828	736	92	828	......
Magnolia	450	......	......	......	......
Morgan	464	439	25	464	......
Raglan	334	307	27	334	......
St. John	1507	1360	147	1507	......
Taylor	525	464	61	525	......
Union	238	195	43	238	......
HENRY.					
Baltimore	1114	1074	40	1090	(b)13
Canaan	784	730	54	771	(c)6
Centre	6310	5577	733	6027	283
Mt. Pleasant	4245	3824	421	3906	339
Jackson	1262	1183	79	1208	54
Jefferson	1438	1316	122	1438	......
Marion	1371	1292	79	1360	11
New London	1746	1681	65	1735	11
Salem	1882	1820	62	1871	11
Scott	1113	1070	43	1112	1
Tippecanoe	1750	1663	87	1706	44
Trenton	1435	1353	82	1406	29
Wayne	1258	993	265	1256	2
HOWARD.					
Afton	474	333	141	474	......
Albion	682	574	108	682	......
Chester	324	279	45	324	......
Forest City	832	617	215	832	......
Howard	204	151	53	204	......
Howard Center	294	209	85	294	......
Jamestown	312	269	43	312	......
New Oregon	996	704	292	996	......
Oakdale	176	149	27	176	......
Paris	434	311	123	434	......
Saratoga	104	90	14	104	......
Vernon Springs	1450	1137	313	1438	12
Cresco	912	712	200	909	3
HUMBOLDT.					
Dakota	676	538	138	676	......
Dakota City	162	133	29	162	......
Delano (d)	145	100	45	145	......
Humboldt (d)	334	263	71	334	......
Lott's Creek (d)	291	228	63	291	......
Rutland	422	354	68	422	......

(*a*) Also 10 Indians.
(*b*) Also 11 Indians.
(*c*) Also 7 Indians.
(*d*) Of Lott's Creek, 122 in Delano and 169 in Humboldt.

TABLE IX.—*Population of Minor Civil Divisions, &c.*—*IOWA*—Continued.

·unties.	Total.	Nativity. Native.	Nativity. Foreign.	Race. White.	Race. Colored.
·LDT—Con.					
Vale	533	440	93	533	......
ing Vale	335	......	......	......	......
....	393	331	62	393	......
sta	93	64	29	93	......
IDA.					
....	165	151	14	165	......
....	30	......	......	......	......
s	61	57	4	61	......
OWA.					
....	1441	351	1090	1441	......
....	235	230	5	235	......
....	939	854	85	939	......
....	1627	1495	132	1627	......
e	1004	826	178	1004	......
....	1040	876	164	1040	......
d	1234	1065	169	1233	1
....	563	375	188	563	......
Creek	1081	1023	58	1081	......
....	962	538	424	962	......
....	445	314	131	445	......
....	394	336	58	394	......
o	2329	1970	359	2321	8
ᴇngo City	1693	1464	229	1685	8
....	623	518	105	623	......
....	692	526	166	692	......
....	862	614	248	862	......
gton	619	494	125	617	2
....	554	437	117	554	......
KSON.					
e	2402	1717	685	2392	10
evue City	1353	990	363	1343	10
a	1103	1037	66	1103	......
....	857	548	309	857	......
y Owen	12	12	......	12	......
d	889	663	226	889	......
's Creek	1502	1388	114	1501	1
....	1209	686	523	1209	......
....	862	598	264	862	......
eta (a)	1071	937	134	1071	......
oketa	1756	1512	244	1743	13
ath	1137	904	233	1137	......
reek	902	651	251	902	......
....	1273	1124	149	1273	......
lrew City	352	328	24	352	......
Springs	1161	696	465	1160	1
d	1141	848	293	1141	......
'ork	1014	942	72	1014	......
s Morts	920	469	451	920	......
....	1214	915	299	1214	......
ula	920	710	210	920	......
ren	1155	828	327	1155	......
gton	1051	734	317	1051	......
SPER.					
Vista	1073	1035	38	1072	1
reek	1125	1094	31	1125	......
ines	2105	2004	101	2101	4
ek	1180	1074	106	1180	......
w	2332	2118	214	2331	1
Grove	462	432	30	462	......
dence	834	770	64	833	1
....	1507	1305	202	1504	3
rove	1342	1318	24	1342	......
....	1010	904	106	1007	3

Counties.	Total.	Nativity. Native.	Nativity. Foreign.	Race. White.	Race. Colored.
JASPER—Cont'd.					
Mariposa	407	321	86	407	......
Mound Prairie	1016	974	42	1016	......
Newton	2686	2486	200	2630	56
Newton	1983	1829	154	1934	49
Palo Alto	1064	855	209	1064	......
Poweshiek	1239	1196	43	1239	......
Richland	749	689	60	749	......
Rock Creek	480	446	34	480	......
Sherman	1007	942	65	1007	......
Washington	498	458	40	498	......
JEFFERSON.					
Black Hawk	1019	983	36	1019	......
Buchanan	1499	1312	187	1499	......
Cedar	816	716	100	805	11
Des Moines	1280	1255	25	1277	3
Fairfield (b)	1640	1507	133	1640	......
Fairfield	2226	1933	293	2205	21
Liberty	1082	1019	63	1082	......
Lockridge	1680	1069	611	1674	6
Locust Grove	1486	1435	51	1486	......
Batavia	310	289	21	310	......
Penn	1616	1490	126	1614	2
Polk	1211	1167	44	1211	......
Abingdon	222	219	3	222	......
Pound Prairie	1085	960	125	1075	10
Walnut	1199	979	220	1199	......
JOHNSON.					
Big Grove	1358	951	407	1354	4
Cedar	1094	729	365	1094	......
Clear Creek	728	593	135	728	......
Fremont	965	865	100	964	1
Graham	1019	801	218	1018	1
Hardin	737	575	162	737	......
Iowa City (c)	2180	1557	623	2173	7
Iowa City	5914	4308	1606	5842	72
Jefferson	900	504	396	900	......
Liberty	640	486	154	639	1
Madison	800	669	131	800	......
Monroe	1034	640	394	1034	......
Newport	814	545	269	814	......
Oxford	1043	768	275	1043	......
Penn	676	571	105	676	......
Pleasant Valley	1189	981	208	1189	......
Scott	964	843	121	954	10
Sharon	1120	834	286	1120	......
Union	790	533	257	789	1
Washington	933	820	113	932	1
JONES.					
Cass	913	826	87	910	3
Castle Grove	839	612	227	839	......
Clay	925	792	133	925	......
Fairview	3085	2787	298	3076	9
Anamosa	2083	1814	269	2074	9
Fairview	238	231	7	238	......
Greenfield	1083	1010	73	1083	......
Hale	997	914	83	997	......
Jackson	899	796	103	899	......
Madison	1067	933	134	1066	1
Monticello	2241	1839	402	2238	3
Monticello	1337	1092	245	1337	......
Oxford	1121	797	324	1120	1
Richland	794	562	232	793	1
Rome	1067	1039	28	1060	7
Scotch Grove	929	787	142	929	......
Washington	860	567	293	860	......

(a) Exclusive of city of Maquoketa.
(b) Exclusive of city of Fairfield.
(c) Exclusive of Iowa City

TABLE IX.—*Population of Minor Civil Divisions, &c.*—*IOWA*—Continued.

Counties.	Total.	Nativity. Native.	Nativity. Foreign.	Race. White.	Race. Colored.
JONES—Cont'd.					
Wayne	1178	944	234	1178	......
Wyoming	1733	1561	172	1726	7
KEOKUK.					
Adams	866	830	36	866	......
Benton	1309	1232	77	1309	......
Clear Creek	1118	867	251	1118	......
English River	1221	1151	70	1221	......
German	1512	1094	418	1512	......
Jackson	1528	1509	19	1528	......
Lafayette	959	789	170	959	......
Lancaster	1525	1467	58	1525	......
Lancaster	135	127	8	135	......
Liberty	1135	1079	56	1135	......
Prairie	704	660	44	704	......
Richland	1585	1553	32	1585	......
Sigourney	1637	1511	126	1634	3
Sigourney	992	911	81	989	3
Steady Run	1038	1002	36	1038	......
Van Buren	1031	949	82	1031	......
Warren	799	786	13	799	......
Washington	1467	1373	94	1467	......
KOSSUTH.					
Algona	2157	1775	382	2157	......
Algona	860	679	181	860	......
Cresco	309	229	80	309	......
Greenwood	280	220	60	280	......
Irvington	605	556	49	605	......
LEE.					
Cedar	1196	1116	80	1177	19
Charleston	1241	1083	158	1241	......
Charleston	188	178	10	188	......
Denmark	1011	972	39	964	47
Denmark	276	263	13	255	21
Des Moines	1104	953	151	1016	88
Fort Madison	4011	2843	1168	3947	64
Franklin	1872	1234	638	1866	6
Franklin	628	372	256	628	......
Green Bay	664	548	116	664	......
Harrison	988	870	118	953	35
Jackson (*a*)	1460	1077	383	1310	150
Jefferson	1059	902	157	1045	14
Keokuk	12766	9229	3537	11751	1015
Madison (*b*)	219	163	56	206	13
Marion	1335	1057	278	1333	2
Montrose	3387	2356	1031	3297	90
Montrose	905	838	67	904	1
Pleasant Ridge	972	856	116	968	4
Van Buren	956	886	70	956	......
Washington	1075	919	156	1066	9
West Point	1894	1345	549	1887	7
West Point	794	547	247	794	......
LINN.					
Bertram	827	748	79	827	......
Boulden	937	789	148	937	......
Prairieburg	116	111	5	116	......
Brown	1581	1526	55	1581	......
Buffalo	508	400	108	508	......
Cedar Rapids	5940	4560	1380	5899	41
Clinton	1205	1015	190	1205	......
College	1468	1116	352	1468	......
Fairfax	1193	923	270	1193	......
Fayette	914	849	65	914	......
LINN—Cont'd.					
Franklin	2738	2502	236	2734	4
Mount Vernon	910	854	56	906	4
Jackson	996	933	63	996	......
Linn	1083	1047	36	1083	......
Maine	1263	1193	69	1263	......
Waubeck	222	201	21	222	......
Marion	3854	3573	281	3851	3
Marion	1822	1644	178	1822	......
Monroe	868	824	44	868	......
Otter Creek	1600	1450	150	1600	......
Putnam	760	477	283	760	......
Rapids (*c*)	1068	941	127	1068	......
Spring Grove	795	737	58	795	......
Washington	1483	1384	99	1483	......
Center Point	443	420	23	443	......
LOUISA.					
Columbus City	2344	2016	328	2339	5
Clifton	200	......	......	......	......
Columbus Jun	850	......	......	......	......
Hillsboro	46	......	......	......	......
Concord	892	825	67	892	......
Fredonia	150	100	50	150	......
Elliott	370	330	40	370	......
Elm Grove	701	675	26	693	8
Grandview	1635	1483	152	1612	23
Grandview	422	400	22	421	1
Lett's	88	68	20	88	......
Jefferson	846	787	59	829	17
Toolsborough	160	140	20	160	......
Marshall	967	921	46	967	......
Morning Sun	1258	1215	43	1258	......
Morning Sun	314	295	19	314	......
Oakland	604	560	44	604	......
Port Allen	50	40	10	50	......
Port Louisa	774	683	91	768	6
Port Louisa	75	60	15	75	......
Union	616	596	20	616	......
Wapello	1870	1675	195	1869	1
Wapello	870	762	108	869	1
LUCAS.					
Benton	696	664	32	696	......
Cedar	764	753	11	764	......
La Grange	150	......	......	......	......
Chariton	2601	2365	236	2571	30
Chariton	1728	......	......	......	......
English	960	922	38	960	......
Jackson	460	418	42	460	......
Liberty	600	566	34	600	......
Otter Creek	711	695	16	711	......
Pleasant	632	601	31	632	......
Union	658	638	20	658	......
Warren	963	916	47	963	......
Washington	753	728	25	752	1
Russell	175	......	......	......	......
White Breast	590	551	39	590	......
MADISON.					
Crawford	739	597	142	739	......
Douglas	938	905	33	938	......
Grand River	598	589	9	598	......
Jackson	534	513	21	534	......
Jefferson	655	623	32	655	......
Lee	426	347	79	426	......
Lincoln	954	908	46	954	......
Madison	1036	985	51	1036	......

(*a*) Exclusive of city of Keokuk.
(*b*) Exclusive of city of Fort Madison.
(*c*) Exclusive of city of Cedar Rapids.

TABLE IX.—*Population of Minor Civil Divisions, &c.—IOWA*—Continued.

[illegible]unties.	Total.	Nativity. Native.	Nativity. Foreign.	Race. White.	Race. Colored.
x—Cont'd					
lham	222	203	19	222	......
....	495	465	30	495	......
....	705	694	11	705	......
....	651	625	26	651	......
....	1229	1206	23	1228	1
....	1040	1022	18	1039	1
....	1044	1006	38	1044	......
....	869	861	8	869	......
r..........	486	459	27	486	......
rset	1485	1416	69	1484	1
HASKA.					
....	835	814	21	835	......
ak........	936	739	197	935	1
....	1265	1239	26	1256	9
ines	1101	1053	48	1101	......
n	1270	1192	78	1264	6
n	1174	1144	30	1174	......
ı..........	953	926	27	948	5
....	1258	1234	24	1258	......
a (a)......	3387	3096	291	3371	16
oosa	3204	2990	214	3126	78
t Grove...	875	841	34	875	......
....	1364	1269	95	1338	26
d..	1561	1395	166	1561	......
....	1103	1060	43	1103	......
....	1190	1078	112	1181	9
ak	1032	1021	11	1032	......
RION.					
....	1372	1342	30	1372	......
....	1066	936	130	1066	......
rbern	190	188	2	190	......
n	768	723	45	768	......
....	1332	1321	11	1303	29
ica	181	176	5	181	......
le	4750	4609	141	4743	7
xville	800	775	25	800	......
airie	4958	3066	1892	4958	......
sterdam ..	43	21	22	43	......
th Pella ..	87	53	34	87	......
a..........	1909	1091	818	1909	......
ast Pella.	147	114	33	147	......
th Pella ..	191	163	28	191	......
....	1532	1499	33	1532	......
ilton.....	133	129	4	133	......
ysville ...	266	261	5	266	......
....	465	450	15	465	......
t Grove...	1445	1415	30	1445	......
....	879	794	85	879	......
k	1334	1308	26	1334	......
Rock	255	255	......	255	......
....	1484	1262	222	1484	......
y..........	176	151	25	176	......
....	1001	978	23	1001	......
....	765	755	10	765	......
gton.......	1285	1273	12	1285	......
mbia	104	98	6	104	......
port	108	108	......	108	......
SHALL.					
....	838	811	27	831	7
....	649	592	57	649	......
astle	764	692	72	763	1
....	1123	1100	23	1123	......
ion	475	463	12	475	......
n..........	691	601	90	691	......
d..	1537	1218	319	1537	......

Exclusive of city of Oskaloosa,
Also 1 Chinese.
Exclusive of city of Marshalltown.

Counties.	Total.	Nativity. Native.	Nativity. Foreign.	Race. White.	Race. Colored.
MARSHALL—Con.					
Liberty	709	661	48	709	......
Liscomb..........	836	796	40	835	(b)
Logan............	273	222	51	273	......
Marietta	1005	909	96	1004	1
Marion	853	801	52	853	......
Marshall (c)......	727	679	48	714	13
Marshalltown ..	3218	2644	574	3201	d15
Minerva..........	680	509	171	680	......
State Center	1076	977	99	1076	......
State Center..	559	495	64	559	......
Timber Creek	886	793	93	886	......
Vienna	905	796	109	905	......
Washington......	806	662	144	806	......
MILLS.					
Anderson	531	477	54	531	......
Glenwood (e)	842	802	40	840	2
Glenwood	1291	1229	62	1289	2
Indian Creek.....	690	638	52	690	......
Ingraham	318	296	22	318	......
Lyons............	895	877	18	895	......
Oak	748	460	288	748	......
Platteville	762	599	163	761	1
Rawles	781	734	47	781	......
Silver Creek......	1019	929	90	1019	......
St. Mary's........	279	214	65	279	......
White Cloud	562	529	33	562	......
MITCHELL.					
Burr Oak.........	425	364	61	425	......
Cedar	733	498	235	733	......
Douglas	282	219	63	282	......
Jenkins	587	497	90	587	......
Liberty	173	152	21	173	......
Lincoln	493	413	80	493	......
Mitchell..........	1228	1017	211	1228	......
Mitchell......	829	699	130	829	......
Newburg..........	536	273	263	536	......
Osage	2158	1831	327	2158	......
Osage	1400	1174	226	1400	......
Otranto	596	336	260	596	......
Rock	474	288	186	474	......
Stacyville	344	274	70	344	......
St. Ansgar........	893	552	341	893	......
St. Ansgar....	360	272	88	360	......
Union	355	246	109	355	......
Wayne............	305	230	75	304	1
MONONA.					
Ashton............	106	89	17	106	......
Belvidere	272	226	46	233	39
Center	138	137	1	138	......
Fairview	281	145	136	281	......
Franklin	856	705	151	856	......
Onaw	478	388	90	478	......
Grant	252	239	13	252	......
Kennebec	333	312	21	333	......
Lake	178	158	20	178	......
Lincoln	308	274	34	308	......
Maple............	345	316	29	343	2
Sherman	196	165	31	196	......
Soldier	193	156	37	192	1
Spring Valley	142	109	33	142	......
West Fork	54	46	8	54	......
MONROE.					
Bluff Creek.......	1015	966	49	1015	......

(d) Also 2 Chinese.
(e) Exclusive of city of Glenwood.

TABLE IX.—*Population of Minor Civil Divisions, &c.*—*IOWA*—**Continued.**

Counties.	Total.	Nativity. Native.	Nativity. Foreign.	Race. White.	Race. Colored.
MONROE—Cont'd.					
Cedar	831	786	45	831	......
Franklin	613	544	69	612	1
Guilford	873	612	261	873	......
Jackson	942	834	108	942	......
Mantua	1185	1079	106	1185	......
Cuba	84	82	2	84	......
Monroe	773	744	29	773	......
Pleasant	1299	1122	177	1299	......
Troy	2490	2375	115	2443	47
Albia	1621	1535	86	1582	39
Union	1161	1109	52	1160	1
Urbana	887	851	36	887	......
Wayne	655	553	102	655	......
MONTGOMERY.					
Douglas	467	449	18	467	......
Frankfort	437	405	32	437	......
Grant	351	284	67	351	......
Jackson	1109	1030	79	1108	1
Villisca	457	402	55	456	1
Lincoln	195	180	15	195	......
Red Oak	2222	1856	366	2211	11
Red Oak Junc.	1315	1011	304	1305	10
Sherman	295	272	23	294	1
Washington	426	404	22	426	......
West	432	378	54	432	......
MUSCATINE.					
Bloomington (*a*)	1411	1223	188	1407	4
Cedar	421	395	26	421	......
Fulton	1276	911	365	1274	2
Fulton or Stockton	108	68	40	108	......
Goshen	1381	1244	137	1380	1
Lake	843	672	171	827	16
Montpelier	735	511	224	735	......
Moscow	1033	818	215	1033	......
Moscow	346	298	48	346	......
Muscatine	6718	4991	1727	6611	107
Orono	372	366	6	372	......
Pike	740	639	101	740	......
Seventy-Six	959	832	127	951	8
Sweetland	1510	1239	271	1510	......
Fairport	136	128	8	136	......
Wapsinonoc	1944	1735	209	1923	21
Wilton	2345	1873	472	2341	4
Wilton Junc	1317	1079	238	1314	3
O'BRIEN.					
Liberty	715	649	66	709	6
O'Brien	79	70	9	79	......
PAGE.					
Amity	1010	913	97	988	22
Amity	217	204	13	202	15
Buchanan	771	753	18	769	2
Douglas	503	408	95	503	......
East River	977	967	10	975	2
Fremont	307	268	39	307	......
Grant	201	194	7	200	1
Harlan	756	679	77	737	19
Lincoln	645	589	56	645	......
Nebraska	620	612	8	605	15
Hawleyville	200	198	2	191	9
Nodaway	2150	2046	104	2060	90
Clarinda	1022	980	42	964	58
PAGE—Cont'd.					
Pierce	430	413	17	430	......
Tarkio	363	350	13	362	1
Valley	636	612	24	636	......
Washington	606	531	75	605	1
PALO ALTO.					
Emmetsburg	316	205	111	316	......
Emmetsburg	44	33	11	44	......
Freedom	161	122	39	161	......
Great Oak	240	164	76	240	......
Nevada	142	110	32	142	......
Rush Lake	245	188	57	245	......
West Bend	232	200	32	232	......
PLYMOUTH.					
Elgin	429	291	138	429	......
Johnson	80	44	36	80	......
Le Mars	152	124	28	152	......
Lincoln	440	320	120	440	......
Perry	74	52	22	74	......
Plymouth	357	218	139	357	......
Sioux	311	230	81	311	......
Stanton	356	271	85	356	......
POCAHONTAS.					
Clinton	53	46	7	53	......
Des Moines	256	194	62	256	......
Lizard	955	558	397	955	......
Powhatan	180	150	30	180	......
POLK.					
Allen	739	695	37	720	19
Beaver	1213	1148	65	1203	10
Bloomfield	1132	986	146	1125	7
Camp	1558	1531	27	1558	......
Delaware	865	809	56	865	......
Des Moines	12035	9557	2478	11807	228
Douglas	613	553	60	613	......
Elkhart	744	650	94	738	6
Four-Mile	531	518	13	531	......
Franklin	654	627	27	654	......
Jefferson	832	779	53	825	7
Lee (*b*)	729	688	41	706	23
Madison	2626	2175	451	2626	......
Saylor	1007	938	69	1007	......
Valley	715	636	79	713	2
Walnut	1231	1072	159	1223	8
Washington	640	582	58	640	......
POTTAWATTAMIE.					
Boomer	611	450	161	611	......
Center	528	518	10	528	......
Council Bluffs	10020	7206	2814	9589	426
Crescent	1117	850	267	1117	......
Grove	356	345	11	356	......
Hardin	122	105	17	121	1
James	309	287	22	309	......
Kane (*d*)	1086	854	232	1085	1
Knox	961	868	93	960	1
Macedonia	321	301	20	321	......
Rockford	623	560	63	623	......
Silver Creek	231	180	51	231	......
Walnut Creek	382	369	13	382	......
York	226	177	49	226	......

(*a*) Exclusive of city of Muscatine.
(*b*) Exclusive of 5th, 6th, and 7th wards of city of Des Moines.
(*c*) Also 5 Indians.
(*d*) Exclusive of city of Council Bluffs.

TABLE IX.—*Population of Minor Civil Divisions, &c.—IOWA*—Continued.

ounties.	Total.	Nativity.		Race.	
		Native.	Foreign.	White.	Colored.
[POW]ESHIEK.					
[C]reek	1852	1675	177	1848	4
[Br]ooklyn	971	852	119	969	2
[...]r	568	580	41	566	2
[Bear] River	799	750	49	798	1
[...]ll	2389	2108	281	2344	45
[Gr]innell	1482	1309	173	1440	42
[...]n	1629	1535	94	1622	7
[M]ontezuma	555	500	55	551	4
[...]on	900	849	51	900	.....
[...]n	658	494	164	658	.....
[...]n	769	662	107	768	1
[...]m	804	653	151	804	.....
[...]nt	646	581	65	636	10
	512	451	61	512	.....
[...]an	558	456	102	558	.....
[...] Creek	910	836	74	909	1
	824	814	10	818	6
[...]n	1137	1049	88	1137	.....
[Washi]ngton	626	516	110	624	2
[RIN]GGOLD.					
[...]s	502	492	10	502	.....
[...]n	367	354	13	367	.....
[...]a	341	335	6	341	.....
	290	281	9	290	.....
[...]on	527	498	29	527	.....
[...]y	243	236	7	243	.....
[...]n	205	192	13	205	.....
[...] Creek	709	680	29	709	.....
[...] Fork	457	426	31	457	.....
[...]e	268	254	14	268	.....
[...] Ayr	827	781	46	822	5
[M]ount Ayr	422	408	14	417	5
[...]y	112	103	9	112	.....
	325	315	10	325	.....
[Washi]ngton	518	454	64	518	.....
SAC.					
[...]s	358	303	55	358	.....
[...]n	469	436	33	469	.....
[...] City	156	143	13	156	.....
	584	508	76	583	1
[S]COTT.					
[...] Grove	646	466	180	646	.....
[...]rass	1420	747	673	1420	.....
[...]	1435	999	436	1434	1
[Bu]ffalo	368	228	140	368	.....
	889	650	239	889	.....
	847	407	440	847	.....
[Daven]port (*a*)	3414	2202	1212	3396	18
[Dave]nport	20038	11737	8301	19828	210
[...]y Grove	1298	727	571	1298	.....
[...]ire	1940	1650	290	1937	3
[...] Claire	1093	918	175	1091	2
[...]y	1193	818	375	1192	1
[...]n	1038	698	340	1038	.....
[...]nt Valley	751	583	168	743	8
[...]ton	1197	1068	129	1197	.....
[Pr]inceton	498	456	42	498	.....
[...]gham	280	152	128	279	1
[...]an	1222	610	612	1221	1
[...]ld	991	557	434	988	3
[SH]ELBY.					
	120	100	20	120	.....
	129	103	26	129	.....

Counties.	Total.	Nativity.		Race.	
		Native.	Foreign.	White.	Colored.
SHELBY—Cont'd.					
Fairview	647	465	182	647	.....
Galland's Grove	692	638	54	689	3
Manteno	50	49	1	47	3
Harlan	466	439	27	463	3
Harlan	128	123	5	128	.....
Jackson	486	442	44	486	.....
SIOUX. (*)					
Calliope	40	40	.....	40	.....
STORY.					
Collins	611	603	8	611	.....
Franklin	924	836	88	924	.....
Grant	406	376	30	406	.....
Howard	968	469	499	968	.....
Indian Creek	1074	1020	54	1074	.....
Iowa Center	248	241	7	248	.....
La Fayette	401	166	235	401	.....
Lincoln	243	183	60	243	.....
Milford	503	431	72	503	.....
Nevada	1611	1436	175	1610	1
Nevada	982	829	153	981	1
New Albany	1003	921	82	1003	.....
Colo	226	203	23	226	.....
Palestine	732	470	262	732	.....
Sherman	420	382	38	420	.....
Union	1089	897	192	1089	.....
Cambridge	200	182	18	200	.....
Washington	1666	1452	214	1665	1
Ames	636	562	74	636	.....
TAMA.					
Buckingham	634	482	152	634	.....
Carlton	812	754	58	811	1
Carroll	382	326	56	382	.....
Clark	336	272	64	336	.....
Columbia	718	652	66	718	.....
Crystal	542	401	141	541	1
Genesco	580	537	43	580	.....
Grant	211	116	95	211	.....
Highland	503	471	32	503	.....
Howard	1043	973	70	1043	.....
Indian Village	1523	1395	128	1522	1
Lincoln	220	105	115	220	.....
Oneida	715	517	198	715	.....
Otter Creek	2046	1640	406	2045	1
Tama	1161	989	172	1160	1
Perry	713	568	145	711	2
Richland	888	818	70	888	.....
Salt Creek	1113	861	252	1113	.....
Spring Creek	573	417	156	573	.....
Toledo	1579	1463	116	1540	39
Toledo	888	821	67	849	39
York	1000	528	472	1000	.....
TAYLOR.					
Benton	1055	1028	27	1021	34
Bedford	720	.....	.....	.....	.....
Clayton	530	515	15	530	.....
Dallas	604	599	5	590	14
Gay	248	237	11	248	.....
Grant	173	171	2	173	.....
Holt	356	318	38	337	19
Jackson	351	344	7	343	8
Jefferson	542	536	6	540	2
Marshall (*b*)	309	298	11	302	7
Mason	580	555	25	578	2

(*) Incomplete; the other principal subdivisions were not separately returned.
(*a*) Exclusive of city of Davenport.
(*b*) Including the new township of Grove, which was not separately returned.

TABLE IX.—*Population of Minor Civil Divisions, &c.—IOWA—*Continued.

Counties.	Total.	Nativity. Native.	Nativity. Foreign.	Race. White.	Race. Colored.
TAYLOR—Cont'd.					
Nodaway	422	395	27	407	15
Platte	163	146	17	163	......
Polk	724	711	13	724	......
Ross	531	523	8	531	......
Washington	401	390	11	401	......
UNION.					
Dodge	229	226	3	229	......
Douglas	824	637	187	824	......
Creston	411	284	127	411	......
Cromwell	166	136	30	166	......
Highland	247	235	12	247	......
Jones	840	790	50	840	......
Thayer	114	88	26	114	......
Lincoln	560	528	32	560	......
New Hope	299	292	7	299	......
Platte	565	541	24	565	......
Pleasant	563	539	24	563	......
Sand Creek	328	298	30	321	7
Union	1531	1448	83	1525	6
Afton	961	912	49	9.9	2
VAN BUREN.					
Bonaparte	1341	1214	127	1328	13
Cedar	1090	1060	30	1090	......
Chequest	967	930	37	967	......
Des Moines	1078	1029	49	1076	2
Farmington	1439	1291	148	1420	19
Farmington	640	564	76	639	1
Harrisburgh	1089	1028	61	1089	......
Jackson	1292	1269	23	1290	2
Lick Creek	1199	1116	83	1180	19
Union	1672	1623	49	1646	26
Birmingham	626	618	8	610	16
Van Buren	2455	2343	112	2333	122
Keosauqua	869	834	35	778	91
Vernon	1474	1406	68	1474	......
Village	1540	1460	80	1540	......
Washington	1036	977	59	1028	8
Bentonsport	432	394	38	431	1
WAPELLO.					
Adams	1363	1327	36	1363	......
Blakesburg	236	231	5	236	......
Agency	1223	1153	70	1213	10
Agency	630	594	36	630	......
Cass	859	750	109	859	......
Chillicothe	211	192	19	211	......
Center (*a*)	1693	1491	202	1686	7
Port Richm'nd	85	83	2	85	......
Columbia	2101	1919	182	2086	15
Eddyville	1212	1076	136	1202	10
Competine	1033	1001	32	1033	......
Marysville	42	41	1	42	......
Dahlonega	623	603	20	622	1
Dahlonega	148	145	3	148	......
Green	1252	1191	61	1252	......
Highland	959	928	31	959	......
Keokuk	700	656	44	698	2
Ottumwa	5214	4275	939	5101	113
Pleasant	1166	1145	21	1166	......
Polk	1113	867	246	1113	......
Richland	1451	1367	84	1406	45
Kirkville	236	232	4	223	13
Washington	1596	1495	101	1596	......
Ashland	181	177	4	181	......
WARREN.					
Allen	788	735	53	788	......
Carlisle	200	193	7	200	......
Belmont	1048	1026	22	1048	......
Greenfield	1514	1420	94	1490	[illegible]
Greenbush	129	125	4	129	......
Jackson	639	604	35	639	......
Jefferson	1012	849	163	1011	1
Liberty	891	883	8	891	......
Lynn	1020	941	79	1020	......
Otter	929	916	13	921	[illegible]
Hammondsb'g	59	59	......	59	......
Palmyra	1347	1319	28	1346	1
Palmyra	226	225	1	226	......
Richland	1381	1349	32	1381	......
Hartford	295	293	2	295	......
Squaw	695	685	10	695	......
Union	1112	1097	15	1112	......
Virginia	524	512	12	524	......
Washington	3379	3285	94	[illegible]	[illegible]
Indianola	1428	1374	54	1390	[illegible]
White Breast	1016	960	56	1016	......
White Oak	685	671	14	685	......
WASHINGTON.					
Brighton	1384	1326	58	1384	......
Brighton	785	754	31	785	......
Cedar	957	925	32	957	......
Clay	788	768	20	787	1
Crawford	1317	1251	66	1317	......
Crawfordsville	249	243	6	249	......
Dutch Creek	1228	1124	104	1228	......
English River	1501	1144	357	1497	4
Franklin	816	784	32	816	......
Highland	753	667	86	753	......
Iowa	1062	863	199	1062	......
Jackson	879	780	99	878	1
Lime Creek	1333	1209	124	1333	......
Marion	1124	1017	107	1124	......
Oregon	1318	1252	66	1318	......
Seventy-Six	449	416	33	449	......
Washington	4043	3728	315	3996	47
Washington	2575	2359	216	2540	35
WAYNE.					
Benton	852	841	11	852	......
Clay	473	442	31	473	......
Clinton	643	639	4	643	......
Corydon	1277	1205	72	1277	......
Corydon	618	588	30	618	......
Grand River	833	829	4	833	......
Howard	575	553	22	575	......
Jackson	356	339	17	356	......
Jefferson	704	694	10	704	......
Monroe	587	585	2	587	......
Genoa	87	86	1	87	......
Richman	374	357	17	374	......
South Fork	774	760	14	774	......
Union	1005	994	11	1004	1
Walnut	674	647	27	674	......
Warren	514	502	12	514	......
Washington	693	673	20	693	......
Wright	953	941	12	953	......
WEBSTER.					
Badger	431	230	201	431	......
Dayton	975	462	513	975	......

(*a*) Exclusive of city of Ottumwa.

[T]ABLE IX.—*Population of Minor Civil Divisions, &c.—IOWA*—Continued.

[Coun]ties.	Total.	NATIVITY. Native.	NATIVITY. Foreign.	RACE. White.	RACE. Colored.
[...]E—Con.					
[...]ek	266	188	78	266	......
	513	414	99	513	......
[...]odge	3095	2224	871	3087	8
	106	71	35	106	......
	432	148	284	432	......
	380	287	93	380	......
	402	298	104	402	......
[...]ve	119	26	93	119	......
	596	476	120	595	1
	574	496	78	574	......
[...]a (a)	921	660	261	921	......
[...]ton	765	644	121	765	......
	560	508	52	560	......
	349	335	14	349	......
[...]BAGO.					
	432	278	154	432	......
	179	159	20	179	......
[...]t City	155	......	......	......	......
	436	178	258	436	......
	214	86	128	214	......
	301	195	106	300	1
[...]SHIEK.					
[...]ld	1183	1027	156	1182	1
	809	534	275	809	......
	960	755	205	960	......
	1864	816	1048	1862	2
	864	577	287	864	......
	3723	2389	1334	3705	18
[...]rah	2110	1369	741	2092	18
[...]le	1154	820	334	1153	1
	661	498	163	661	......
[...]d	1196	539	657	1196	......
	1041	707	334	1039	2
[...]l	922	401	521	922	......
	668	374	294	668	......
	822	397	425	822	......
	891	372	519	891	......

Counties.	Total.	NATIVITY. Native.	NATIVITY. Foreign.	RACE. White.	RACE. Colored.
WINNESHIEK—Con.					
Military	1515	831	684	1515	......
Orleans	674	495	179	674	......
Pleasant	994	496	498	994	......
Springfield	1260	538	722	1260	......
Sumner	909	351	558	909	......
Washington	1460	894	566	1459	1
WOODBURY.					
Correctionville	600	510	90	600	......
Little Sioux	900	765	135	900	......
Sioux City (b)	800	680	120	789	c2
Sioux City	3401	2259	1142	3359	42
Woodbury	471	439	32	471	......
WORTH.					
Bristol	503	363	140	503	......
Brookfield	274	167	107	274	......
Fertile	164	142	22	164	......
Hartland	575	282	293	575	......
Northwood	725	473	252	725	......
Northwood	289	229	60	289	......
Silver Lake	354	171	183	354	......
Union	297	201	96	297	......
WRIGHT.					
Belmond	327	288	39	326	1
Boone	146	132	14	145	1
Clarion	153	136	17	153	......
Clarion	37	35	2	37	......
Eagle Grove	195	157	38	195	......
Iowa	204	183	21	204	......
Liberty	269	243	26	269	......
Pleasant	332	285	47	332	......
Troy	248	225	23	248	......
Vernon	175	142	33	175	......
Wall Lake	199	176	23	199	......
Woodstock	144	127	17	144	......

[(a) E]xclusive of city of Fort Dodge. (b) Exclusive of Sioux City. (c) Also 9 Indians.

TABLE IX.—*Population of Minor Civil Divisions, &c.—KANSAS.*

[...]-The marginal column marks townships and land-survey townships; the first indentation, [th]e second, towns. Names of towns are placed under the names of the townships or land-survey [...]s in which they are respectively situated. The population of each township or land-survey [...] includes that of all towns situated in it.

[Coun]ties.	Total.	NATIVITY. Native.	NATIVITY. Foreign.	RACE. White.	RACE. Colored.
[AL]LEN.					
[...]Grove	794	656	138	791	3
[...]eek	614	607	7	600	a13
	452	407	45	452	......
	634	619	15	608	26
[...]lt	2035	1701	334	1998	37

Counties.	Total.	NATIVITY. Native.	NATIVITY. Foreign.	RACE. White.	RACE. Colored.
ALLEN—Cont'd.					
Humboldt	1202	937	265	1180	22
Iola	1759	1689	70	1694	65
Osage	463	441	22	463	......
Salem	271	245	26	263	8

(a) Also 1 Indian.

TABLE IX.—*Population of Minor Civil Divisions, &c.—KANSAS—Continued.*

Counties.	Total.	Nativity. Native.	Nativity. Foreign.	Race. White.	Race. Colored.
ANDERSON.					
Jackson	539	516	23	521	18
Monroe	2044	1806	238	1956	88
Garnett	1219	1047	172	1145	74
Ozark	617	591	26	617	......
Reeder	702	631	71	702	......
Walker	891	830	61	891	......
Greeley	145	142	3	145	......
Washington	427	408	19	421	6
ATCHISON.					
Atchison	7054	5248	1806	6214	840
Centre	1605	1447	158	1581	24
Grasshopper	1145	1018	127	1140	5
Kaplone	775	671	104	772	(a)
Lancaster	909	763	146	863	46
Mount Pleasant	1344	1160	184	1300	44
Shannon	1301	1004	297	1246	55
Walnut	1374	1207	167	1252	122
BOURBON.					
Drywood	1199	1147	52	1194	b4
Franklin	1207	1175	32	1207	......
Freedom	815	756	59	761	54
Fort Scott	4174	3480	694	3711	a460
Marion	1182	1149	33	1175	7
Marmaton	904	894	10	878	26
Mill Creek	859	827	32	811	48
Osage	1053	991	62	1036	c12
Pawnee	630	564	66	630	......
Scott	1729	1596	133	1672	57
Timber Hill	1035	1011	24	933	102
Walnut	289	278	11	289	......
BROWN.					
Claytonville	2048	1712	336	2040	d1
Irwin	2300	2075	225	2243	57
Lochnain	914	791	123	897	17
Walnut Creek	1561	1405	156	1541	20
BUTLER.					
Augusta	515	471	44	513	2
Chelsea	277	266	11	272	5
Eldorado	797	744	53	781	16
Towanda	597	560	37	597	......
Walnut	849	818	31	839	a7
CHASE.					
Bazaar	364	346	18	363	1
Cottonwood	315	289	26	313	2
Diamond Creek	469	401	68	469	......
Falls	459	420	39	457	2
Toledo	368	340	28	367	1
CHEROKEE.					
Cherokee	370	327	43	370	......
Crawford	593	556	37	589	4
Lola	650	632	18	650	......
Lowell	1612	1576	36	1592	e16
Lyon	378	341	37	378	......
Neosho	900	873	27	889	11
Pleasant View	971	933	38	970	1
Ross	449	428	21	449	......
Salamanca	708	653	55	693	15
CHEROKEE—Con.					
Columbus	402	360	42	387	[illegible]
Shawnee	894	874	20	891	[illegible]
Sheridan	1149	1116	33	1148	[illegible]
Spring Valley (f)	1080	1013	67	1076	[illegible]
Baxter Springs	1284	1121	163	1204	[illegible]
CLAY.					
Clay Centre	1134	940	194	1125	[illegible]
Republican	856	461	395	855	[illegible]
Sherman	952	656	296	952	......
CLOUD.					
Buffalo	303	251	52	303	......
Elk	561	459	102	561	[illegible]
Shirley	637	540	97	637	......
Sibley	309	237	72	309	......
Solomon	513	433	80	512	[illegible]
COFFEY.					
Avon	905	848	57	888	[illegible]
Burlington	1600	1444	156	1563	[illegible]
Burlington	960	848	112	928	[illegible]
California	645	622	23	645	......
Leroy	1094	1041	53	1038	[illegible]
Leroy	410	370	40	410	......
Neosho	604	564	40	604	......
Ottumwa	833	799	34	770	[illegible]
Ottumwa	263	262	1	255	[illegible]
Pottawatamie	520	472	48	520	......
COWLEY.					
Cedar Creek	79	74	5	79	......
Creswell	214	186	28	214	......
Grouse Creek	153	147	6	153	......
Rock Creek	160	155	5	160	......
Timber Creek	97	93	4	97	......
Winfield	472	439	33	472	......
CRAWFORD.					
Baker	962	909	53	962	......
Crawford	1535	1408	127	1533	[illegible]
Grant	421	339	82	421	......
Lincoln	1490	1427	63	1490	......
Osage	980	949	31	980	......
Sheridan	1042	969	73	1042	......
Sherman	567	485	82	567	......
Walnut	568	509	59	568	......
Washington	595	584	11	595	......
DAVIS.					
Davis	2748	1889	859	2715	[illegible]
Fort Riley, (garrison)	560	317	243	559	[illegible]
Junction City	2778	1615	1163	2679	[illegible]
DICKINSON.					
Grant	849	726	123	838	[illegible]
Lamb	462	365	97	462	......
Lincoln	398	290	108	397	[illegible]
Newbern	583	396	187	579	[illegible]
Sherman	177	100	77	176	[illegible]
Union	574	299	275	574	......

(a) Also 3 Indians.
(b) Also 1 Indian.
(c) Also 5 Indians.
(d) Also 7 Indians.
(e) Also 4 Indians.
(f) Exclusive of city of Baxter Springs.

LE IX.—*Population of Minor Civil Divisions, &c.—KANSAS*—Continued.

...es.	Total.	Nativity: Native.	Nativity: Foreign.	Race: White.	Race: Colored.
...AN.					
....	1015	867	148	969	46
....	2248	2033	215	2159	89
te....	54	53	1	54	......
....	639	584	55	589	50
....	3531	3379	152	3283	248
oint...	242	222	20	235	7
d.....	282	269	13	242	40
Cloud	843	798	45	783	60
....	658	495	163	635	3
)....	138	126	12	138	......
1....	2513	2204	309	2136	a376
t.....	79	69	10	72	7
....	2070	1841	229	2019	51
an....	528	478	50	516	12
City...	102	87	15	102	......
....	1934	1563	371	1914	20
...AS.					
....	1030	971	59	944	86
....	1901	1497	404	1602	b291
....	583	555	28	437	146
....	913	804	109	870	43
....	8320	6886	1434	6908	1412
....	971	903	68	904	67
....	879	808	71	879	......
....	2431	2171	260	2402	29
....	2401	2127	274	2134	267
ngs...	1163	1064	99	1152	11
.					
....	6	6	......	6	......
Cav-line..	80	35	45	80	......
gis....	320	181	139	320	......
cho..	17	10	7	17	......
a....	120	46	74	120	......
....	320	180	140	315	5
....	320	215	105	293	a26
of Big	33	17	16	33	......
Big	12	10	2	12	......
Big	15	14	1	15	......
moky.	9	8	1	9	......
....	43	29	14	43	......
....	18	8	10	18	......
ek....	23	20	3	23	......
...TH.					
....	448	276	172	429	19
r......	293	173	120	293	......
Creek	444	334	110	437	7
.					
....	427	308	119	317	a109
...IN.					
....	1034	967	67	1025	9
....	1021	962	59	1020	1
....	1115	995	120	1053	c10
....	923	863	60	910	a12
....	575	523	52	570	5
....	877	834	43	824	d48
....	2941	2538	403	2677	e262

Counties.	Total.	Nativity: Native.	Nativity: Foreign.	Race: White.	Race: Colored.
FRANKLIN—Cont'd.					
Peoria..............	1160	1123	37	1156	4
Pottawattamie ...	695	666	29	683	12
South Ottawa	44	40	4	43	1
GREENWOOD.					
Eureka..............	1040	878	162	1011	29
Fall River.........	1119	1052	67	1114	5
Janesville	259	250	9	258	1
Lane	320	306	14	320	......
Madison	284	275	9	284	......
Pleasant Grove...	462	457	5	462	......
HOWARD.					
Bellville...........	1240	1170	70	1240	......
Elk Falls..........	1160	1104	56	1160	......
Liberty.............	394	375	19	394	......
JACKSON.					
Douglas	1760	1662	98	1675	f14
Franklin	2325	1951	374	2315	10
Holton	426	381	45	406	20
Jefferson	1542	1433	109	1541	1
JEFFERSON.					
Grasshopper Falls	1943	1775	168	1773	170
Grasshopper Falls.......	603	568	35	513	90
Jefferson	1680	1580	100	1665	15
Kaw	749	682	67	723	26
Kentucky	1976	1845	131	1850	126
Medina.........	197	180	17	197	......
Perry	403	382	21	340	63
Oskaloosa	1613	1556	57	1436	177
Oskaloosa	640	615	25	560	80
Ozawkie............	1600	1541	59	1545	55
Rock Creek	441	402	39	441	......
Sarcoxie............	1876	1806	70	1823	53
Union	648	613	35	645	3
JOHNSON.					
Aubrey	1125	1068	57	1123	2
Gardner............	944	791	153	938	6
Lexington..........	1256	1148	108	1238	18
Monticello	1093	1023	70	1037	56
McCamish	908	785	123	887	21
Olathe..............	3022	2680	342	2885	137
Olathe.........	1817	1606	211	1707	110
Oxford	1926	1849	77	1917	9
Shawnee	2451	2171	280	2271	d175
Spring Hill........	959	915	44	945	14
LABETTE.					
Canada..............	480	427	53	474	6
Fairview	464	439	25	464	......
Hackberry	637	598	39	637	......
Labette	282	268	14	281	1
Liberty	720	686	34	715	5
Montana	783	763	20	783	......
Mound Valley....	275	216	59	275	......
Mount Pleasant ..	249	240	9	249	......
Neosho	515	492	23	515	......
North	581	557	24	581	......
Oswego	1836	1701	135	1805	31
Oswego	1196	1086	110	1166	30

(a) Also 1 Indian.
(b) Also 8 Indians.
(c) Also 52 Indians.
(d) Also 5 Indians.
(e) Also 2 Indians.
(f) Also 71 Indians.

TABLE IX.—*Population of Minor Civil Divisions, &c.*—*KANSAS*—Continued.

Counties.	Total.	Nativity.		Race.	
		Native.	Foreign.	White.	Colored.
LABETTE—Cont'd.					
Osage	930	855	75	930	......
Richland	1744	1648	96	1693	51
Chotopah	960	891	69	909	51
Walton	477	363	114	477	......
LEAVENWORTH.					
Alexandria	1179	1087	92	1097	82
Delaware	1641	1406	235	1380	a258
Easton	1169	1052	117	1133	36
Fairmount	749	666	83	699	50
Fort Leavenworth Reserve (b)	1975	1145	830	1957	18
High Prairie	1300	1092	208	1149	c150
Kickapoo	1855	1524	331	1642	213
Leavenworth	17873	13363	4510	14848	c3024
Reno	946	858	88	789	d151
Sherman	834	790	44	820	14
Stranger	1323	1057	266	1155	168
Tonganoxie	1600	1489	111	1479	c120
LINCOLN.					
Lincoln	516	393	123	516	......
LINN.					
Blue Mound	341	330	11	333	8
Centreville	1034	1007	27	998	e35
Liberty	480	470	10	464	16
Lincoln	2012	1887	125	1930	e68
Mound City	1374	1326	48	1164	210
Mound City	635	619	16	533	102
Paris	1396	1357	39	1244	152
Potosi	1779	1684	95	1763	16
Scott	1306	1271	35	1246	60
Stanton	528	513	15	517	11
Sheridan	828	759	69	828	......
Valley	1096	1043	53	1017	79
LYON.					
Agnes City	143	123	20	138	5
Americus	884	818	66	883	1
Center	126	124	2	126	......
Emporia	1182	950	232	1174	8
Emporia	2168	1856	312	2063	105
Elmendaro	533	496	37	533	......
Fremont	549	496	53	549	......
Jackson	1079	953	126	1077	2
Pike	693	666	27	692	1
Waterloo	657	603	54	653	4
MARION.					
Cedar Creek	105	94	11	105	......
Centre	539	502	37	537	c1
Doyle	124	109	15	124	......
MARSHALL.					
Blue Rapids	1247	1085	162	1247	......
Guitland	707	521	186	707	......
Marysville	1625	1057	568	1625	......
Marysville	300	211	89	300	......
Vermillion	1738	1507	231	1738	......
Waterville	1584	1237	347	1576	8

Counties.	Total.	Nativity.		Race.
		Native.	Foreign.	White.
MC'PHERSON.				
Gypsum Creek	117	103	14	109
Sharp Creek	199	81	118	196
Smoky Hill	348	94	254	348
Turkey Creek	74	35	39	74
MIAMI.				
Marysville	1383	1299	84	1259
Miami	725	678	47	706
Middle Creek	650	583	67	650
Mound	498	471	27	498
Osage	1396	1226	170	1347
Osawatomie	1182	1117	65	1064
Paola (g)	624	564	60	618
Paola	1811	1663	148	1613
Richland	844	790	54	844
Stanton	844	800	44	793
Sugar Creek	444	436	8	444
Wea	1324	1230	94	1312
MITCHELL.				
Asherville	144	110	34	144
Beloit	173	157	16	173
Cawker City	38	31	7	38
Glen Elder	25	24	1	25
Salt Creek	40	40	......	40
Solomon Rapids	65	49	16	65
MONTGOMERY.				
Carny	361	340	21	354
Cherry	802	706	96	798
Fawn Creek	505	479	26	505
Independence	1394	1291	103	1333
Independence	435	400	35	434
Lewisburg	827	804	23	825
Parker	474	408	66	462
Rutland	485	466	19	476
Sycamore	547	530	17	547
Verdigris	1052	990	62	1050
Westralia	1117	1074	43	1086
Westralia	104	102	2	93
MORRIS.				
Clarke's Creek	320	261	59	318
Council Grove	1080	982	98	1014
Council Grove	712	649	63	661
Neosho	825	733	92	820
NEMAHA.				
Clear Creek	367	266	101	359
Copioma	424	383	41	424
Granada	893	757	136	891
Home	719	645	74	719
Nemaha	491	346	145	491
Red Vermillion	775	646	129	774
Richmond	2153	1499	654	2152
Rock Creek	740	624	116	729
Valley	777	714	63	777
NEOSHO.				
Big Creek	1077	1041	36	1076
Canville	1070	1013	57	1057
Centerville	889	839	50	888

(a) Also 3 Indians.
(b) Government reservation.
(c) Also 1 Indian.
(d) Also 6 Indians.
(e) Also 14 Indians
(f) Also 8 Indians.
(g) Exclusive of city of Paola.
(h) Also 2 Indians.
(i) Also 13 Indians.

BLE IX.—*Population of Minor Civil Divisions, &c.—KANSAS*—Continued.

...ies.	Total.	Nativity. Native.	Nativity. Foreign.	Race. White.	Race. Colored.
Cont'd.					
....	921	743	78	812	9
....	1350	1288	62	1330	a14
....	418	397	21	417	1
....	839	760	79	839	......
....	745	720	25	740	5
....	1732	1433	299	1700	b12
Mission	791	638	153	786	5
....	907	802	105	903	4
rove....	686	616	70	686	......
E.					
....	1865	1712	153	1844	21
....	588	335	253	582	6
e	1549	1398	151	1518	31
game ..	655	591	64	639	16
....	1141	865	276	1140	1
....	966	766	200	954	12
ok.....	1539	1431	108	1492	47
NE.					
. 11 W..	12	7	5	12	......
. 13 W..	21	19	2	21	......
WA.					
....	720	596	124	720	......
....	359	254	105	359	......
....	708	507	201	706	2
....	250	215	35	250	......
EE.					
d......	179	98	81	173	6
TTAMIE.					
....	544	411	133	544	......
....	2409	2014	395	2183	c155
ille	344	295	49	342	2
amie ...	1155	968	187	1153	2
....	812	541	271	812	......
....	435	383	52	435	......
rge	118	103	15	118	......
....	1205	938	267	852	d280
....	1288	1049	239	1276	a6
LIC.					
n	219	207	12	219	......
....	292	276	16	292	......
....	770	622	148	770	......
E.					
Corner.	5	4	1	5	......
Y.					
....	616	527	89	616	......
....	1249	751	498	1249	......
n	1969	1633	336	1900	69
ttan ...	1173	967	206	1108	65
....	741	586	155	741	......
....	530	434	96	529	1

Counties.	Total.	Nativity. Native.	Nativity. Foreign.	Race. White.	Race. Colored.
RUSSELL.					
Coal Mines	156	94	62	143	13
SALINE.					
Elm Creek	2027	1492	535	2024	3
Salina	918	593	325	915	3
Spring Creek	726	502	224	724	2
Brookville....	201	137	64	200	1
Solomon	581	428	153	580	1
Walnut Grove....	912	349	563	912	......
SEDGWICK.					
Rockford.........	197	166	31	196	(e)
Waneulla	209	198	11	209	......
Wichita	689	572	117	680	9
SHAWNEE.					
Auburn	662	586	76	628	34
Dover	611	545	66	527	f1
Monmouth	713	638	75	713	......
Silver Lake.......	1416	1304	112	1142	g2
Silver Lake City	159	127	32	132	(h)
Soldier	1430	1318	112	1288	142
Tecumseh	854	782	72	833	i19
Topeka...........	1079	969	110	1022	57
Topeka.........	5790	4978	812	5314	j473
Williamsport.....	566	537	29	565	1
TREGO.					
Coyote	17	9	8	17	......
Grinnell	40	16	24	40	......
Park's Fork......	34	14	20	34	......
Saline	35	19	16	34	1
Smoky	40	27	13	40	......
WABAUNSEE.					
Alma...............	890	485	405	850	40
Mission Creek....	445	354	91	442	3
Newbury..........	475	396	79	377	k5
Wabaunsee	517	461	56	488	29
Wilmington	662	621	41	655	e6
Zeandale	373	349	24	371	2
WALLACE.					
Buffalo Station ...	10	1	9	10	......
Fort Wallace......	396	238	158	394	2
Monument Station	12	4	8	12	......
Phil. Sheridan....	80	49	31	80	......
Pond City	40	29	11	40	......
WASHINGTON.					
Clifton	713	619	94	713	......
Lincoln...........	1533	1287	246	1532	1
Mill Creek........	597	573	24	597	......
Washington	1238	1034	204	1238	......
WILSON.					
Cedar	539	511	28	538	1

(a) Also 6 Indians.
(b) Also 11 Indians.
(c) Also 71 Indians.
(d) Also 73 Indians.
(e) Also 1 Indian.
(f) Also 83 Indians.
(g) Also 272 Indians.
(h) Also 27 Indians.
(i) Also 2 Indians.
(j) Also 3 Indians.
(k) Also 93 Indians.

TABLE IX.—*Population of Minor Civil Divisions, &c.—KANSAS*—Continued.

Counties.	Total.	Nativity. Native.	Nativity. Foreign.	Race. White.	Race. Colored.
WILSON—Cont'd.					
Centre	855	790	65	852	3
Chetopah	580	551	29	580	......
Clifton	918	809	109	917	1
Fall River	896	839	57	896	......
Guilford	604	585	19	604	......
Pleasant Valley	470	426	44	470	......
Neodesha	1145	1079	66	1145	......
Verdigris	687	665	22	687	......
WOODSON.					
Belmont	622	583	39	622	......
WOODSON—Cont'd.					
Liberty	363	313	50	363	......
Neosho Falls	1406	1285	121	1381	25
Neosho Falls	532	468	64	523	9
Owl Creek	1096	960	136	1096	......
Toronto	340	295	45	331	9
WYANDOTTE.					
Delaware	926	863	63	811	115
Prairie	916	771	145	878	38
Quindaro	2139	1994	145	1437	(a) [illegible]
Shawnee	1243	1075	168	1079	(b) [illegible]
Wyandotte	1851	1633	218	1435	(c) [illegible]
Wyandotte	2940	2430	510	2201	(d) [illegible]

(a) Also 8 Indians. (b) Also 16 Indians. (c) Also 30 Indians. (d) Also 2 Indians.

TABLE IX.—*Population of Minor Civil Divisions, &c.—KENTUCKY.*

NOTE.—The marginal column marks precincts, or election districts, whose numbers are official; the names are those in general use. The first indentation marks cities; the second towns. Names of towns are placed under the names of the precincts or election districts in which they are respectively situated. The population of each precinct or election district includes that of all towns situated in it.

Counties.	Total.	Nativity. Native.	Nativity. Foreign.	Race. White.	Race. Colored.
ADAIR.					
Casey's Creek	552	552	......	492	60
Columbia	3616	3613	3	2635	981
Columbia	506	505	1	429	77
Gradyville	1713	1712	1	1442	271
Harmony	1434	1433	1	1225	209
Leatherwood	1309	1308	1	1215	94
Neatsville	1204	1204	......	1065	139
White Oak	1237	1236	1	1155	82
ALLEN.					
1. Scottsville	2529	2525	4	2156	373
Scottsville	217	215	2	185	32
2. Butlersville	1862	1862	......	1758	104
3. Raleigh	1690	1686	4	1528	162
4. Spillman	930	929	1	757	173
5.	907	907	......	851	56
6.	1751	1751	......	1608	143
New Roe	145	145	......	108	37
7.	627	627	......	534	93
ANDERSON.					
Chesher's	639	637	2	603	36
Goodnight's	1353	1351	2	1297	56
Lawrenceburg	2048	2025	23	1598	450
Lawrenceb'g	393	386	7	279	114
Palmer's	631	628	3	587	44
Rough and Ready	778	771	7	666	112
Rough and Ready	160	158	2	153	7
BALLARD.					
1. McCuistian	1333	1321	12	1055	278
2. Tharp's	1541	1510	31	1294	247
3. Blandville	2017	1999	18	1819	198
Blandville	385	384	1	321	64
4. Cobb's	1440	1438	2	1323	117
5. Pickett's	1227	1217	10	1174	53
6. Lovelaceville	1939	1932	7	1583	356
7. Milburn	1753	1746	7	1591	162
Milburn	314	313	1	299	15
8. Sullinger's	1326	1321	5	1290	36
BARREN.					
Cave City	1945	1925	20	1454	491
Cave City	387	376	11	256	131
Glasgow	6057	6032	25	4631	1426
Glasgow	733	720	13	472	261
Glasgow Junction	1315	1311	4	1113	202
Hiseville	2190	2185	5	1652	538
Rocky Hill	1974	1968	6	1483	491
Sartain's	846	846	......	740	106
Saunders'	947	947	......	883	64
Tracy	2506	2504	2	2181	325
BATH.					
Bethel	1600	1560	40	1241	359
Mud Lick	1855	1854	1	1686	169
Owingsville	1947	1933	14	1569	378
Owingsville	550	543	7	351	199
Sharpsburg	1785	1757	28	1134	651

IX.—*Population of Minor Civil Divisions, &c.—KENTUCKY*—Continued.

...	Total.	Nativity. Native.	Nativity. Foreign.	Race. White.	Race. Colored.
...nt'd.					
...urg...	319	310	9	228	91
...hur...	1520	1519	1	1441	79
......	1438	1432	6	1372	66
...g ...	120	119	1	114	6
.					
......	615	586	29	563	52
...r	61	50	11	61	......
......	1257	1218	39	1176	81
......	1557	1529	28	1333	224
...ton ...	277	268	9	247	30
......	844	824	20	800	44
......	1472	1380	92	1298	174
......	374	335	39	331	43
......	1162	1084	78	1068	94
...urg ...	400	363	37	384	16
......	1298	1223	75	1194	104
...port ...	120	109	11	118	2
......	827	813	14	720	107
......	777	728	49	735	42
......	887	846	41	797	90
...x.					
......	1117	1084	33	668	449
......	638	619	19	316	322
......	1040	1032	8	699	341
......	636	616	20	317	310
......	492	486	6	252	240
......	1635	1612	23	962	673
...urg ..	675	663	12	498	177
...etown	1560	1526	34	852	708
...iddle-					
......	320	312	8	152	168
......	4220	4068	152	1881	2339
...ris ...	212	183	29	151	61
......	2655	2443	212	1647	1008
...lls ...	870	848	22	592	278
......	570	569	1	567	3
......	1225	1195	30	1218	7
...'gs (b)	1276	1081	195	1238	38
...urg ...	876	848	28	855	21
......	2462	2207	255	2407	55
...d	1459	1248	211	1405	54
...rg ...	2164	2109	55	1997	167
...sburg	1019	983	36	907	112
.					
......	2169	2150	19	1642	527
...ille ..	173	172	1	110	63
......	1451	1438	13	1060	391
...le (c) .	2542	2463	79	1332	1210
...ille ..	479	479	......	375	104
...City .	223	213	10	159	64
......	1675	1663	12	925	750
......	1678	1655	23	877	801
...x.					
......	3031	2688	343	2719	312
......	960	894	66	794	166
......	2281	2178	103	2173	108
......	125	123	2	125	......
......	2406	2319	87	2322	84
...ille ...	348	329	19	303	45

Counties.	Total.	Nativity. Native.	Nativity. Foreign.	Race. White.	Race. Colored.
BRACKEN—Cont'd.					
Fairview	792	765	27	768	24
Foster	1103	1060	43	1092	11
Foster	191	188	3	189	2
Germantown	989	963	26	953	36
Germantown	191	188	3	180	11
Milford	807	796	11	746	61
Milford	108	108	......	106	2
BREATHITT.					
1. Jackson	1028	1028	......	959	69
Jackson	54	54	......	53	1
2. George's Branch	489	489	......	479	10
3. Troublesome ...	701	701	......	665	36
4. Bradley's	599	599	......	599	......
5. Elliottsville	474	474	......	457	17
6. Frozen	780	780	......	773	7
7. Crawford's	674	674	......	633	41
8. Crockettsville ..	936	936	......	935	1
BRECKENRIDGE.					
Bowleyville	1524	1515	9	1333	191
Bowleyville ..	96	96	......	75	21
Big Spring, pt. of (e)	42	41	1	32	10
Clifton Mill	1045	1042	3	855	190
Cloverport	2678	2584	94	2137	541
Cloverport ...	849	823	26	679	170
Dehaven's	319	318	1	295	24
Hardinsburg	2504	2474	30	2128	376
Hardinsburg .	455	446	9	331	124
Hayne's	456	453	3	433	23
Hudsonville	1082	1078	4	1064	18
Locust Hill	479	473	6	449	30
McDaniel's	473	468	5	446	27
Stephensport	593	587	6	558	35
Stephensport .	160	156	4	150	10
Union Star	1429	1405	24	1322	107
Union Star ...	104	102	2	96	8
Wheatley	856	855	1	748	108
BULLITT.					
Leache's	1155	1134	21	994	161
Mount Washington	1400	1384	16	1216	184
Mount Washington	340	332	8	274	66
Pine Tavern	2147	2064	83	1918	229
Pitt's Point ..	98	96	2	93	5
Shepherdsville ...	3079	2996	83	2459	620
Shepherdsville	257	248	9	188	69
BUTLER.					
Burden's	1655	1655	......	1647	8
London's	1780	1779	1	1664	116
Morgantown	1340	1331	9	1115	225
Morgantown .	125	125	......	107	18
Renfrow's	1141	1136	5	1125	16
Rochester	2104	2104	......	2011	93
Rochester	228	228	......	222	6
Woodbury	1184	1175	9	999	185
Woodbury ...	171	166	5	130	41
CALDWELL.					
Bucksnort	898	855	43	867	31

...sive of city of Paris.
...alled Buena Vista.
...lle lies in Precincts Nos. 3 and 4, about half in each.

(d) Exclusive of part of village of Danville.
(e) See note (b) Hardin County, and (e) Meade County.

TABLE IX.—*Population of Minor Civil Divisions, &c.—KENTUCKY*—Continued.

Counties.	Total.	Nativity. Native.	Nativity. Foreign.	Race. White.	Race. Colored.
CALDWELL—Con.					
Farmersville	788	787	1	688	100
Fredonia	1585	1581	4	1233	352
Fredonia	155	155	.....	110	45
Harmony	1139	1138	1	873	266
Princeton	4441	4400	41	3335	1106
Princeton	1012	992	20	694	318
Tennessee	1201	1201	.....	1028	173
William's Mill	774	773	1	724	50
CALLOWAY.					
Brinkley	1477	1477	.....	1419	58
Brinkley	165	165	.....	162	3
Liberty	960	960	.....	925	35
Murray	2024	2023	1	1750	274
Murray	179	179	.....	136	43
New Concord	2558	2555	3	2283	275
Swan's	1243	1240	3	1133	110
Wadesborough	1148	1148	.....	1088	60
CAMPBELL. (*)					
Alexandria	2727	2156	571	2677	50
Alexandria	381	299	82	366	15
Bellview	381	263	118	381	.....
Carthage	1084	1003	81	1066	18
Cold Springs	1053	873	180	1040	13
Dayton	2367	1761	606	2324	43
Dayton	1749	1337	412	1727	22
Eight-Mile	538	428	110	537	(a)
Grant's Lick	1782	1651	131	1780	2
Gupser's Mill	876	756	120	868	8
Highland	617	499	118	600	17
John Hill's	579	375	204	572	7
Newport	15087	10290	4797	14965	122
CARROLL.					
Carrollton	2246	2058	188	2049	197
Carrollton	1098	951	147	1006	92
Ghent	1415	1375	40	1251	164
Ghent	464	448	16	425	39
Jordan	326	311	15	326	.....
Locust	1030	1014	16	965	65
Mill Creek	701	675	26	691	10
Prestonville	239	223	16	234	5
Worthville	471	466	5	367	104
CARTER.					
1. Grayson	1407	1401	6	1343	64
Grayson	152	152	.....	142	10
2. Buffalo	1300	1266	34	1296	4
3. Olive Hill	737	736	1	737	.....
4. Upper Tygret	638	638	.....	638	.....
5. Count's	758	757	1	752	6
6. Doer Creek	849	849	.....	849	.....
7. Little Fork	1062	1059	3	1037	25
8. Star Furnace	758	717	41	757	1
CASEY.					
Casey's Creek	923	921	2	918	5
Jenkins	1626	1625	1	1592	34
Leo	564	564	.....	511	53
Liberty	1981	1976	5	1756	225
Rolling Fork	2238	2233	5	2081	157
Tate's	1552	1549	3	1482	70
CHRISTIAN.					
Fruit Hill	3199	3173	26	2549	650
CHRISTIAN—Cont'd.					
Garrettsburg	1737	1734	3	604	1133
Hamby	1851	1743	108	1684	167
Hopkinsville	3136	2978	158	1676	1460
Lafayette	1333	1328	5	661	672
Lafayette	215	213	2	148	67
Long View	2400	2382	18	869	1531
Mount Vernon	1600	1598	2	1048	552
Pembroke	4276	4240	36	1963	2313
Pembroke	278	276	2	157	121
States Mill	1920	1915	5	1645	275
Union Sch'l Home	1755	1755	.....	716	1039
CLARK.					
Blue Ball	1759	1722	37	1138	621
Germantown	1594	1580	14	940	654
Goode's	2236	2227	9	1889	347
Kiddville	957	956	1	681	276
Pinchem	1035	1035	.....	851	184
Winchester	3301	3225	76	1668	1633
Winchester	1616	1578	38	654	962
CLAY.					
1. Manchester	2506	2498	8	2095	411
2. Cornett's	800	799	1	799	1
3. Allen's	951	951	.....	938	13
4. Big Creek	800	800	.....	783	17
5. Rockhouse	440	440	.....	437	3
6. Beech Fork	480	480	.....	480	.....
7. Asher's	320	319	1	302	18
8. Otter Creek	640	640	.....	613	27
9. Bullskin	400	400	.....	397	3
10. Pigeon Roost	640	639	1	633	7
11. Phillip's Fork	320	320	.....	319	1
CLINTON.					
1. Albany	1629	1629	.....	1512	117
Albany	163	163	.....	153	10
2. Piney Woods	1361	1339	22	1306	55
3. Neathery	1244	1241	3	1210	34
4. Ill Will	1237	1237	.....	1223	14
5. Hay's	1026	1024	2	954	72
CRITTENDEN.					
1. Marion	2370	2365	11	2117	259
Marion	102	102	.....	79	23
2. Dycersburg	1247	1237	10	1152	95
3. Union	906	904	2	870	36
4. Hurricane	1437	1434	3	1303	134
5. Ford's Ferry	765	764	1	638	127
6. Bell's Mines	1315	1276	39	1204	111
7. Piney	1335	1335	.....	1288	47
CUMBERLAND.					
Burkesville	2774	2767	7	2035	739
Carver	650	650	.....	641	9
Elliot	823	823	.....	662	161
Kettle Creek	919	919	.....	901	18
Marrowbone	1914	1913	1	1441	473
Whetstone	610	610	.....	511	99
DAVIESS.					
Boston	1452	1448	4	1353	99
Whitesville	257	253	4	238	19
Curdsville	2154	2121	33	2013	141
Knottsville	1831	1822	9	1693	138
Lowertown, No. 1	2960	2862	98	2131	829

(*) Incomplete; some civil divisions were not separately returned.
(a) Also 1 Indian.

TABLE IX.—*Population of Minor Civil Divisions, &c.—KENTUCKY*—Continued.

Counties.	Total.	Nativity. Native.	Nativity. Foreign.	Race. White.	Race. Colored.
DAVIESS—Cont'd.					
Masonville	766	763	3	663	103
Murry	1640	1624	16	1272	368
Oakford	988	967	21	795	193
Owensboro	3437	3128	309	2783	654
Uppertown, No. 2	2597	2511	86	1965	632
Vanover	1088	1081	7	1024	64
Velvington	1801	1781	20	1419	382
EDMONDSON.					
1. Brownsville	1088	1085	3	1045	43
2. Durbin's	1120	1120	......	1117	3
3. Chameleon Spr's	813	812	1	732	81
4. Parker	1063	1059	4	964	99
5. Fork	375	373	2	375	......
ELLIOTT.					
1. Martinsburg	1662	1662	......	1660	2
Martinsbu'g	62	62	......	62	......
2. Devil Fork	320	319	1	300	20
3. Newcomb	639	639	......	639	......
4. Little Fork	879	879	......	879	......
5. Lower	933	933	......	933	......
ESTILL.					
Crooked Creek	1503	1500	3	1355	148
Fork's	1045	1044	1	1015	30
Hardwick's Creek	896	896	......	873	23
Irvine	2013	2002	11	1843	170
Irvine	224	223	1	172	52
Miller's Creek	2612	2532	80	2413	199
Station Camp	1129	1128	1	1100	29
FAYETTE.					
1. Athens	2271	2226	45	1163	1108
2. Briar Hill (*a*)	1300	1267	33	608	692
3. Dog Fennel	1919	1837	82	1025	894
4. Sandersville	2562	2490	72	1471	1091
5. South Elkhorn	1660	1621	39	991	669
6. East Hickman	2143	2083	60	1255	888
Lexington	14801	13717	1084	7629	*b*7171
FLEMING.					
Centerville	1576	1533	43	1492	84
Elizaville	1341	1310	31	1117	224
Elizaville	180	178	2	160	20
Flemingsburg	2790	2680	110	2035	755
Flemingsburg	425	411	14	359	66
Fox Springs	480	479	1	476	4
Hillsboro	2020	2014	6	1984	36
Hillsboro	1464	1459	5	1442	22
Mount Carmel	1396	1363	33	1269	127
Mount Carmel	1196	1167	29	1094	102
Poplar Plains	2034	2024	10	1846	188
Poplar Plains	1565	1558	7	1491	74
Sherburne	801	792	9	749	52
Sherburne	158	152	6	112	46
Tilton	960	952	8	874	86
Tilton	125	125	......	107	18
FLOYD.					
Middle Creek	737	737	......	728	9
Allen's	1351	1349	2	1334	17
Dry Creek	556	556	......	540	16
Mouth of Mud	1160	1160	......	1123	37

Counties.	Total.	Nativity. Native.	Nativity. Foreign.	Race. White.	Race. Colored.
FLOYD—Continued.					
6. Mouth of Beaver	832	831	1	808	24
7. John's Creek	1072	1072	......	1070	2
8. Prestonsburg	1564	1561	3	1516	48
Prestonsburg	179	178	1	172	7
9. John B. Harris	605	605	......	587	18
FRANKLIN.					
Bald Knob	1732	1730	2	1505	227
Benson	1071	1060	11	997	74
Bridgeport	1766	1751	15	1213	553
Court House	1090	1026	64	750	340
Forks of Elkhorn	1375	1362	13	904	471
Frankfort	5396	4999	397	3061	2335
Market House	885	861	24	539	346
Bell Point	91	91	......	81	10
Peak's Mill	1985	1966	19	1668	317
FULTON.					
1. Lodgton	810	807	3	776	34
2. Johnson's	1562	1558	4	1170	392
3. Hickman	2730	2556	174	2354	376
Hickman	1120	979	141	939	181
4. Madrid Bend	303	297	6	284	19
5. Fulton Station	756	753	3	640	116
GALLATIN.					
1. Hogin's	1570	1517	53	1361	209
2. Warsaw	2101	2057	44	1786	315
Warsaw	715	694	21	535	180
3. Napoleon	1403	1370	33	1327	76
GARRARD.					
1. Brandy Springs	2083	2076	7	1437	646
2. Buckeye	1567	1566	1	1286	281
3. Lancaster	4070	4048	22	2547	1523
Lancaster	741	730	11	410	331
4. Bryantsville	2656	2648	8	1702	954
GRANT.					
Cordova	1597	1589	8	1585	12
Crittenden	1407	1376	31	1271	136
Crittenden	295	288	7	230	65
Downingsville	1504	1489	15	1460	44
Flat Creek	925	879	46	901	24
Mount Zion	776	754	22	731	45
Williamstown	3320	3239	81	3072	248
Williamstown	281	273	8	240	41
GRAVES.					
Boswell's	2474	2468	6	2155	319
Cuba	1735	1735	......	1474	261
Farmington	1440	1439	1	1294	146
Feliciana	2242	2225	17	1981	261
Haynes's	2317	2307	10	2140	177
Houseman's	1471	1442	29	1393	78
Lynnville	1311	1309	2	1235	76
Mayfield	4042	4006	36	3245	797
Mayfield	779	762	17	625	154
Ozment's	273	273	......	216	57
Panther, or Pryor's	1174	1174	......	1068	106
Symsonia	919	919	......	868	51
GRAYSON.					
Cany	2268	2176	92	2203	65
Haynes	2020	2017	3	1949	71

(*a*) Exclusive of city of Lexington.

(*b*) Also 1 Indian.

TABLE IX.—*Population of Minor Civil Divisions, &c.*—*KENTUCKY*—Continued.

Counties.	Total.	Nativity. Native.	Nativity. Foreign.	Race. White.	Race. Colored.
GRAYSON—Cont'd.					
Litchfield	5270	5028	242	5051	219
Litchfield	314	302	12	257	57
Rock Creek	2022	2011	11	1970	52
Millerstown	80	79	1	76	4
GREEN.					
1. Greensburg	2662	2661	1	1583	1079
Greensburg	351	351	......	201	150
2. Grove	1312	1307	5	897	415
3. Bruersburg	2453	2452	1	2253	200
Oscoola	89	89	......	82	7
4. Low. Brush Cr'k	1525	1524	1	1381	144
5. Up. Brush Creek	1427	1425	2	1328	99
GREENUP.					
1. Greenup C'rt Ho	3001	2916	85	2736	265
Greenupsb'rg	507	478	29	428	79
2. Globe School Ho	1968	1920	48	1940	28
3. Liberty	1446	1427	19	1397	49
4. Old Town	1939	1909	30	1882	57
5. Hunnewell Furnace	2315	2008	307	2277	38
6. Barn	794	781	13	770	24
HANCOCK.					
Hawesville	2446	2322	124	2097	a348
Hawesville	855	764	91	718	a136
Indian Creek	724	698	26	686	38
Lewis Lane's	617	582	35	589	28
Lewisport	1948	1924	24	1649	299
Lewisport	308	303	5	275	33
Pelville	856	847	9	840	16
Pelville	84	84	......	84	......
HARDIN.					
Allison	1901	1896	5	1742	159
Big Spring, part of (b)	49	47	2	35	14
Atcher	747	736	11	638	109
Colesburg	638	597	41	620	18
Elizabethtown	4740	4565	175	3687	1053
Elizabethtown	1743	1606	137	1083	660
Haycraft's	919	891	28	830	89
Meeting Creek	945	945	......	940	5
Nolynn	1257	1225	32	994	263
Stephensburg	1724	1692	32	1497	227
Wallingsford	1621	1606	15	1451	170
Sonora	266	266	......	214	52
West Point	1213	1194	19	1030	183
West Point	206	203	3	139	67
HARLAN.					
1. Mount Pleasant	902	902	......	846	56
2. Martin's Fork	462	462	......	433	29
3. Clover Fork	412	412	......	410	2
4. Upper Poor Fork	419	419	......	419	......
5. New Harlan	414	414	......	412	2
6. Wallen's Creek	579	579	......	579	......
7. Puckett's Creek	520	520	......	516	4
8. Lower Poor Fork	168	168	......	164	4
9. Slater's Fork	539	539	......	535	c2
HARRISON.					
Berry's	2211	2164	47	1903	308
HARRISON—Cont'd.					
Berryville	235	222	13	191	44
Colemansville	77	77	......	47	30
Buena Vista	1580	1568	12	1409	171
Cason's	1033	1016	17	824	209
Claysville	932	929	3	832	100
Claysville	115	115	......	93	22
Cynthiana	3615	3309	306	2531	1084
Baltzell	153	144	9	46	107
Cynthiana	1771	1579	192	1194	577
Leesburg	1373	1342	31	961	412
Leesburg	144	135	9	104	40
Richland	1271	1267	4	1255	16
Rutland	978	975	3	890	88
HART.					
Caverna	1919	1908	11	1425	494
Caverna	479	473	6	398	81
Hammondville	1538	1536	2	1379	159
Hardyville	3197	3192	5	2532	665
Hardyville	68	68	......	63	5
Mumfordsville	1671	1632	39	1075	596
Mumfordsville	249	243	6	159	90
No. 6	1114	1112	2	1096	18
Powder Mill	1234	1233	1	1103	131
Priceville	1594	1582	12	1429	165
Woodsonville	1420	1411	9	1136	284
Woodsonville	140	140	......	110	30
HENDERSON.					
Cairo	2096	2078	18	1737	359
Corydon	1872	1852	20	1108	764
Corydon	247	235	12	196	51
Hebbardsville	1975	1962	13	1536	439
Henderson	1262	1215	47	653	609
Henderson	4171	3750	421	2682	1489
Lo'r Henderson (d)	620	617	3	321	299
Point	714	701	13	476	238
Smith's Mills	1853	1831	22	1347	506
Spottsville	949	922	27	734	215
Tillotson's	1440	1414	26	1094	346
Upper Town (d)	1505	1427	78	785	720
HENRY.					
Bethlehem	507	503	4	464	43
Blackwell's	634	628	6	572	62
Campbellsburg	795	777	18	584	211
Drennon's Ridge	797	783	14	711	86
Eminence	1118	1088	30	764	354
Guestville	304	296	8	287	17
Jericho	800	793	7	551	249
Lockport	1513	1490	23	1379	134
New Castle	1599	1579	20	905	694
New Castle	670	653	17	500	170
Pendleton	479	457	22	341	138
Pleasureville	1172	1155	17	884	288
Port Royal	1028	1019	9	874	154
Turner	320	320	......	312	8
HICKMAN.					
Clinton	1644	1642	2	1438	206
Clinton	272	270	2	189	83
Columbus	2573	2485	88	1479	1094
Columbus	1574	1492	82	813	761
Hays	1560	1558	2	1470	90
McAllister	798	797	1	712	86
Moscow	1282	1271	11	1170	112

(a) Also 1 Chinese.
(b) See note (e) Breckenridge County, and (e) Meade County. Total 134 13 native, 3 foreign, 108 white, 26 colored.
(c) Also 12 Indians.
(d) Exclusive of city of Henderson.

BLE IX.—*Population of Minor Civil Divisions, &c.—KENTUCKY—Continued.*

unties.	Total.	Nativity. Native.	Nativity. Foreign.	Race. White.	Race. Colored.
N—Cont'd.					
scow	350	345	5	308	42
Hill	501	501	......	488	13
land	95	95	......	61	34
PKINS.					
il	1416	1411	5	1298	118
House ...	2268	2264	4	1800	468
rsville ...	1264	1257	7	1136	128
....	1772	1769	3	1407	365
ston	1949	1944	5	1826	123
r Springs..	1353	1353	......	1293	60
ary	2104	2088	16	1756	348
rsburg	679	677	2	636	43
dlisonville (a)	1022	1002	20	806	216
NSON.					
....	661	660	1	652	9
ick	497	497	......	466	31
ugh	596	596	......	596	......
....	623	623	......	618	5
reek	724	724	......	724	......
....	346	346	......	342	4
n	1100	1100	......	1098	2
RSON.					
baker's ..	605	429	176	529	76
....	652	554	98	506	146
m	643	514	129	437	206
oads	783	754	29	604	179
int	389	381	8	347	42
ille	1085	1078	7	886	199
's	1685	1334	351	1287	398
s Creek ...	876	795	81	558	318
....	385	381	4	363	22
ntown	1620	1543	77	1338	282
ville	100753	75085	25668	85706	b14956
Pond	1353	1295	58	1026	327
own	2074	1923	151	1472	602
dletown ..	244	241	3	213	31
o's	835	655	180	560	275
's	738	635	103	632	106
Dale	792	737	55	475	317
Garden ...	827	633	194	684	143
le House..	2340	1932	408	1798	542
....	518	485	33	508	10
AMINE.					
Nicholas- (c)	1265	1245	20	635	630
Nicholas- (c)	1525	1510	15	955	570
cholasville	1089	1072	17	487	602
e Creek ...	1439	1426	13	1026	413
Hickman.	680	680	......	544	136
....	1363	1358	5	699	664
....	1277	1270	7	853	424
NSON.					
Creek ...	1098	1098	......	1046	d11
p	1338	1338	......	1338	......
Fork	851	850	1	851	......
reek	720	717	3	710	10
lle	1714	1712	2	1650	e12
tsville ...	247	247	......	247	......

Counties.	Total.	Nativity. Native.	Nativity. Foreign.	Race. White.	Race. Colored.
JOHNSON—Cont'd.					
Rock Castle	648	648	......	648	......
Tom's Creek	1125	1123	2	1121	4
JOSH BELL.					
1. Pensville	974	973	1	884	90
2. Big Clear Creek	259	259	......	259	......
3. Yellow Creek ...	890	890	......	878	12
4. Browney's Cre'k	614	614	......	609	5
5. Straight Creek, right fork	273	273	......	270	3
6. Straight Creek, left fork	483	483	......	482	1
7. Little Clear Cr'k	238	238	......	238	......
KENTON.					
Bromley	121	89	32	121	......
Buena Vista	1449	989	460	1361	88
Coke's	1753	1605	148	1721	32
Covington	24505	17453	7052	23401	1104
Independence	1577	1420	157	1481	96
Independence.	134	123	11	132	2
Ludlow	817	577	240	814	3
Scott's	1954	1619	335	1808	146
Stephenson	1833	1725	108	1714	119
West Covington .	993	650	343	989	4
Western Reserve .	1094	883	211	1029	65
KNOX.					
1. Barboursville ...	1360	1358	2	1146	214
Barboursv'le	438	437	1	370	68
2. Flat Lick	1566	1566	......	1515	51
3. Pain's	1105	1105	......	1058	47
4. Poplar Creek ...	1113	1113	......	1051	62
5. Indian Creek ...	1283	1282	1	1175	108
6. Greasy Creek ...	794	794	......	739	55
7. Stinking Creek..	1073	1073	......	1053	20
LA RUE.					
Buffalo	1230	1225	5	1123	107
Edlin	513	508	5	421	92
Hodgenville	2501	2478	23	2020	481
Hodgenville ..	404	401	3	315	89
Magnolia	752	752	......	717	35
Otter Creek	885	881	4	853	32
Price's	1109	1098	11	1001	108
Upton	1245	1240	5	1135	110
LAUREL.					
Bush	881	881	......	881	......
Kemper	284	280	4	283	1
London	1686	1684	2	1579	107
London	165	164	1	151	14
McHargue	917	917	......	900	17
Newcomb	381	381	......	378	3
Racoon	1398	1397	1	1382	16
Rock House	272	272	......	272	......
Stepping Rock ...	197	197	......	197	......
LAWRENCE.					
1. Seed Tick	825	823	2	825	......
2. Dry Fork	147	147	......	146	1
3. Cat Fork	759	757	2	759	......
4. Big Blaine	960	960	......	960	......
5. Little Blaine ...	800	799	1	799	1

precinct not ascertained.
so 1 Indian.
clusive of part of village of Nicholasville.

(d) Also 41 Indians.
(e) Also 43 Indians.

TABLE IX.—*Population of Minor Civil Divisions, &c.*—*KENTUCKY*—Continued.

Counties.	Total.	Nativity. Native.	Nativity. Foreign.	Race. White.	Race. Colored.
LAWRENCE—Con.					
6. Peach Orchard	871	862	9	837	34
7. Rocastle	726	726	.....	726	.....
8. Warfield	522	521	1	518	4
9. Louisa	1621	1610	11	1540	81
Louisa	425	419	6	402	23
10. George's Creek	692	691	1	692	.....
11. Clayton	574	574	.....	574	.....
LEE.					
Beattyville	668	664	4	592	76
Beattyville	123	120	3	117	6
Coal Branch	540	540	.....	509	31
Old Landing	315	315	.....	314	1
Proctor	580	578	2	557	23
Proctor	100	99	1	95	5
Sturgeon	214	214	.....	214	.....
Thomas	738	738	.....	738	.....
LETCHER.					
1. Whitesburg	1050	1050	.....	1036	14
2. Millstone	716	716	.....	707	9
3. Nat. Collins	634	633	1	631	3
4. Car's Fork	800	800	.....	760	40
5. Mouth of Rock-house	545	545	.....	492	53
6. Cumberland	503	503	.....	503	.....
7. Sine Fork	360	360	.....	350	10
LEWIS.					
Concord	1236	1208	28	1194	42
Concord	228	220	8	222	6
Elk Fork	672	649	23	670	2
Esculapia	1138	1120	18	1110	28
Kinniconick	1375	1361	14	1346	29
Laurel	714	707	7	708	6
Mower's	810	803	7	809	1
Poplar Flat	738	734	4	720	18
Tolesboro	887	884	3	852	35
Vanceburg	1545	1507	38	1478	67
Vanceburg	513	506	7	468	45
LINCOLN.					
Crab Orchard	2039	2031	8	1448	591
Crab Orchard	631	628	3	376	255
Highland	1019	1015	4	998	21
Hustonville	1625	1615	10	1150	475
Hustonville	320	315	5	190	130
Stanford	4214	4170	44	2621	1593
Stanford	752	740	12	414	338
Turnersville	743	743	.....	533	210
Walnut Flat	484	479	5	329	155
Waynesburg	823	823	.....	792	31
LIVINGSTON.					
1. Smithland	1842	1804	38	1413	429
Smithland	690	668	22	515	175
2. Driskill (a)	2809	2744	65	2606	(b) 202
3. Salem	1359	1353	6	1180	179
Salem	50	49	1	49	1
5. Carrsville	1870	1850	20	1730	140
6. Panhandle	320	313	7	218	102
LOGAN.					
Adairsville	2531	2515	16	1720	811
Adairsville	214	211	3	171	43
LOGAN—Cont'd.					
Clay	2883	2847	36	2237	646
Auburn	610	584	26	489	121
Fillmore	1950	1948	2	1680	270
Gordonsville	1782	1780	2	1356	426
Gordonsville	221	221	.....	161	60
Hardison	2496	2494	2	2217	279
Hogan	1405	1398	7	869	536
Keysburg	1595	1590	5	924	671
Keysburg	133	133	.....	106	27
Russellville	4706	4590	116	2922	1784
Russellville	1843	1798	45	1026	817
Shocco	1081	1071	10	781	300
South Union	263	256	7	263	.....
LYON.					
1. Eddyville	3514	3499	15	2697	817
Eddyville	386	383	3	269	117
2. Parkersville	1879	1851	28	1396	483
3. Ladies' Spring	840	837	3	718	122
MADISON.					
Elliston	2397	2384	13	1773	624
Foxtown	1872	1855	17	1133	739
Glade	2181	2172	9	1633	548
Kirksville	2327	2306	21	1488	839
Million	1717	1713	4	1314	403
Posey	877	877	.....	759	118
Richmond	3046	2979	67	1537	1509
Richmond	1629	1594	35	880	749
Union	2543	2525	18	1829	714
Yates	2583	2580	3	1805	778
MAGOFFIN.					
1. Salyersville	1387	1387	.....	1292	95
2. Bloomington	655	655	.....	621	34
3. Johnson Fork	640	640	.....	640	.....
4. Middle Fork	563	563	.....	562	1
5. Whitaker's	847	847	.....	802	45
6. Trace	486	486	.....	486	.....
Salyersville (c)	106	105	1	102	4
MARION.					
Bradfordsville	1488	1483	5	1263	225
Bradfordsville	155	153	2	142	13
Haysville	1505	1492	13	1141	364
Lebanon	4617	4475	142	2772	1845
Lebanon	1925	1832	93	1102	823
Loretto	1675	1632	43	1455	220
Loretto	42	42	.....	35	7
New Market	1572	1543	29	1307	265
Raywick	1231	1229	2	1017	214
Raywick	160	158	2	137	23
St. Mary's	750	746	4	560	190
St. Mary's	113	111	2	106	7
MARSHALL.					
1. Reed's	636	636	.....	585	51
2. Smith's	559	558	1	540	19
3. Darnell	1022	1018	4	985	37
4. Benton	158	158	.....	158	.....
5. Benton	556	556	.....	543	13
6. Benton's School	745	745	.....	733	12
7. Briensburg	634	630	4	571	63
8. Birmingham	2094	2065	29	1995	99
Birm'gham	322	306	16	292	30
9. Staton's	1156	1149	7	1117	39
10. Bishop	1895	1894	1	1843	52

(a) Including 4. Dyer's Hill.
(b) Also 1 Indian.
(c) Its precinct not ascertained.

LE IX.—*Population of Minor Civil Divisions, &c.—KENTUCKY*—Continued.

...nties.	Total.	Nativity. Native.	Nativity. Foreign.	Race. White.	Race. Colored.
...SON.					
....	1332	1243	89	1127	205
...er	532	505	27	465	67
...town.	1173	1139	34	1000	173
...nantown .	160	*158	2	138	22
...rg	1532	1474	58	1123	409
...isburg ...	151	138	13	133	18
...ick........	2041	1937	104	1293	748
...'s Lick...	199	173	26	128	71
...lo (a).....	1726	1600	126	1437	289
...ille	4705	4149	556	4024	681
....	794	732	62	603	191
...erva.......	159	153	6	130	29
...sville	789	765	24	682	107
...urg	1610	1566	44	1496	114
....	871	855	16	803	68
...is.........	149	147	2	146	3
...ton.......	1553	1475	78	956	597
...hington ..	240	223	17	106	134
...ACKEN.					
...r's........	966	817	149	798	168
....	2144	2030	114	1689	455
...n's........	1257	1161	96	1106	151
...Roads.....	602	602	......	503	99
...ville.......	1893	1879	14	1530	363
...oodville..	68	68	......	54	14
....	260	242	18	208	52
...cah (c) ..	6866	6255	611	4865	2001
...LEAN.					
....	2728	2701	24	2303	425
....	1115	1109	6	1068	47
...o's Chapel	438	437	1	398	40
...re	1264	1246	18	1130	134
...rmore....	302	294	8	235	67
....	980	970	10	918	62
...sey	216	209	7	187	29
...nto	1089	1087	2	983	106
...amento ..	195	193	2	171	24
...ADE.					
...aft's (d) ..	1117	1112	5	916	201
...Branch ..	603	597	6	572	31
...rlia	984	964	20	913	71
...House (d).	1275	1265	10	960	315
...randenb'rg	427	410	17	297	130
...ttsville...	2055	2023	32	1931	124
...ring	1018	1011	7	774	244
...g Spring, pt. of (e) ..	43	43	......	41	2
...Creek	662	659	3	583	79
...ille	842	836	6	794	48
...tt's.......	502	502	......	451	51
...NIFER.					
...idge......	639	634	5	639	......
...r	336	336	......	335	1
...hburg	531	531	......	531	......
....	480	479	1	465	15

Counties.	Total.	Nativity. Native.	Nativity. Foreign.	Race. White.	Race. Colored.
MERCER.					
1. Dicksville	1126	1096	30	960	166
Nevada	14	14	......	14	......
2.	1486	1485	1	1418	68
Cornishville	151	151	......	150	1
3.	426	425	1	339	87
4. Salvisa.........	1650	1645	5	1231	419
Salvisa	153	153	......	124	29
5. (f)............	2397	2298	99	1794	603
Pleas'nt Hill	362	305	57	344	18
6. (f)............	1719	1704	15	1383	336
7. Eldorado	1655	1647	8	1176	479
8. Baton Rouge....	480	480	......	429	51
Harrodsb'g.	2205	2158	47	1104	1101
METCALFE.					
East Fork.........	730	730	......	608	122
Edmonton	2547	2541	6	2322	225
Edmonton	146	144	2	116	30
Fairview	430	430	......	410	20
Flat Rock	691	691	......	683	8
La Fayette	2040	2039	1	1690	350
La Fayette ...	53	53	......	44	9
Sartain	1496	1496	......	1360	136
MONROE.					
1. Gum's...........	1280	1280	......	1191	89
2. Turner's	1699	1699	......	1513	186
3. Brush	1106	1106	......	1031	75
4. Centre Point ...	1010	1010	......	830	180
5. Martinsburg	523	523	......	472	51
6. Tompkinsville ..	2773	2772	1	2649	124
Tompkinsv'e	218	217	1	188	30
7. Union	840	839	1	756	84
MONTGOMERY.					
Aaron's Run	1120	1114	6	694	426
Camargo	960	928	32	721	239
Jeffersonville	997	990	7	825	172
Levee	960	942	18	549	411
Mount Sterling ...	3520	3428	92	2069	1451
M't Sterling ..	1040	996	44	597	443
MORGAN.					
1. West Liberty ...	1635	1632	3	1625	10
W't Liberty.	142	142	......	141	1
2. Caney	821	821	......	812	9
3. Grassy	760	760	......	751	9
4. Blackwater.....	720	720	......	716	4
5. Hampton's Mill.	384	383	1	384	......
6. Blair's.........	430	430	......	428	2
7. Paint...........	701	701	......	699	2
8. River	524	524	......	516	8
MUHLENBURG.					
1. South Carrollton	2962	2818	144	2575	387
S. Carrollton	240	230	10	199	41
2. Boggess (g)	2349	2337	12	1960	389
3. Court House (g)	4320	4312	8	3975	345
Greenville..	557	550	7	390	167
4. Paradise	779	736	43	563	216
6. Summers	1671	1667	4	1542	129

(a) Exclusive of city of Maysville.
(b) Exclusive of part of city of Paducah.
(c) The city of Paducah constitutes the whole of Precinct No. 1 and part of No. 7.
(d) Exclusive of part of village of Brandenburg.
(e) See note (b) Hardin County, and (e) Breckenridge County.
(f) Exclusive of part of village of Harrodsburg.
(g) Exclusive of part of village of Greenville.

TABLE IX.—*Population of Minor Civil Divisions, &c.*—*KENTUCKY*—Continued.

Counties.	Total.	Nativity. Native.	Nativity. Foreign.	Race. White.	Race. Colored.
NELSON.					
Ballard's	892	890	2	855	37
Balltown	237	236	1	183	54
Bardstown	5187	4938	249	3768	1419
Bardstown	1835	1746	89	1125	710
Bloomfield	1555	1513	42	812	743
Bloomfield	435	431	4	266	169
Boston	448	443	5	363	85
Chaplin	1225	1217	8	955	270
Fairfield	897	865	32	612	285
Fairfield	167	152	15	100	67
High Grove	403	399	4	258	145
New Haven	3171	3069	102	2445	726
New Haven	99	96	3	69	30
Sands	789	778	11	635	154
NICHOLAS.					
1. Blue Lick Sp'gs	751	738	13	742	9
2. Headquarters	1807	1799	8	1634	173
3. Ellisville	1089	1055	34	1025	64
4. Carlisle	2802	2660	142	2173	629
Carlisle	606	567	39	445	161
5. East Union	1000	996	4	829	171
6. Buzzard's Roost	1680	1635	45	1482	198
OHIO.					
Bartlett's	1082	1078	4	1037	45
Bell's	1057	1053	4	928	129
Caney	1205	1195	10	1203	2
Centerville	1765	1752	13	1693	72
Ceralvo	60	60	.....	59	1
Cool Spring, No. 2	1410	1342	68	1310	100
Rockport	173	165	8	169	4
Cromwell, No. 8	2250	2241	9	2064	186
Cromwell	149	143	6	124	25
Ellis	993	993	.....	987	6
Fordsville	1437	1435	2	1354	83
Hartford, Nos. 7 and 9	3263	3210	53	2611	652
Hartford	511	484	27	409	102
Sulphur Springs	926	925	1	812	114
OLDHAM.					
Ballardsville	1144	1063	81	810	334
Brownsboro	1277	1237	40	837	440
Floydsburg	800	769	31	563	237
La Grange	2137	2071	66	1423	714
La Grange	612	589	23	372	240
Rollington	891	788	103	581	310
Saltillo	1194	1116	78	689	505
West Point	1584	1569	15	1314	270
OWEN.					
Caney	979	978	1	923	56
Dallasburg	820	812	8	705	115
Gratz	1520	1500	20	1390	130
Harmony	849	848	1	849	.....
Lusby's Mill	1737	1734	3	1710	27
Monterey	1598	1592	6	1555	43
New Columbus	1088	1088	.....	983	105
New Liberty	1946	1909	37	1561	385
New Liberty	304	300	4	264	40
Owenton	2432	2403	29	2204	228
Owenton	297	283	14	227	70
Poplar Grove	1340	1334	6	1253	87
OWSLEY.					
Booneville	1282	1281	1	1254	28
Booneville	111	111	.....	108	3
OWSLEY—Cont'd.					
Buffalo	416	416	.....	401	15
Indian Creek	317	317	.....	312	5
Island Creek	442	442	.....	434	8
Traveller's Rest	1432	1430	2	1411	21
PENDLETON.					
1. Falmouth	4258	3942	316	3886	372
Falmouth	614	522	92	521	93
2. McKenneysb'rg	589	588	1	556	33
3. Bonais	1524	1482	42	1460	64
4. Sand Luck	1539	1394	145	1521	18
5. Grassy Creek	1757	1658	99	1755	2
6. Collinsville	1152	1114	38	1148	4
7. Hughes	1422	1357	65	1321	101
8. Butler	1789	1679	110	1762	27
Butler	144	113	31	144	.....
PERRY.					
Bolin's	328	328	.....	325	3
Campbell	393	393	.....	385	8
Hazard	1065	1065	.....	1000	65
Leatherwood	347	347	.....	343	4
Lost Creek	385	385	.....	385	.....
Maggard	439	439	.....	439	.....
McIntosh	546	546	.....	536	10
Troublesome	571	571	.....	555	16
PIKE.					
1. Town	1809	1807	2	1746	63
Pikeville	140	140	.....	128	12
2. Shelby	1115	1115	.....	1115	.....
3. Marrowbone	688	687	1	687	1
4. Grapevine	1039	1038	1	1026	13
5. Lower John Creek	713	713	.....	706	7
6. Pond	1088	1088	.....	1082	6
7. Peter	912	912	.....	905	7
8. Upper John Creek	727	727	.....	723	4
9. Elkhorn	679	679	.....	679	.....
10. Big Creek	792	791	1	791	1
POWELL.					
1. West Bend	667	664	3	603	64
2. Stanton	808	805	3	766	42
Stanton (c)	73	73	.....	71	2
3. North Fork	266	266	.....	222	44
4. South Fork	785	785	.....	698	87
PULASKI.					
Bent	530	530	.....	530	.....
Buncombe	380	380	.....	374	6
Burdine	585	581	4	585	.....
Dallas	1060	1060	.....	1000	60
Gaines	1204	1196	8	1162	42
Gladd's	1572	1572	.....	1556	16
Grundy	1019	1015	4	949	70
Harrison	1694	1692	2	1673	21
Juggernaut	682	681	1	671	11
Mount Gilead	1533	1532	1	1504	29
Point	1509	1506	3	1454	55
Price	979	979	.....	932	47
Somerset	4276	4265	11	3558	718
Somerset	587	584	3	434	153
Texas	647	645	2	647	.....

(a) Also 2 Indians. (b) Also 5 Indians. (c) Its precinct not ascertained.

ABLE IX.—*Population of Minor Civil Divisions, &c.—KENTUCKY—Continued.*

Counties.	Total.	Nativity. Native.	Nativity. Foreign.	Race. White.	Race. Colored.
ROBERTSON.					
...town	1103	1099	4	1049	54
...ll's Mill	1151	1142	9	1074	77
...Olivet	2146	2124	22	2085	61
...ount Olivet	254	249	5	248	6
...k	999	998	1	934	65
ROCK CASTLE.					
...nt Vernon	2650	2641	9	2452	198
Mt. Vernon	252	244	8	223	29
...er Creek	1054	1053	1	1006	48
...bld Cane	980	978	2	930	50
...adstone	611	610	1	598	13
...	793	793	......	788	5
...	1057	1055	2	1002	55
ROWAN.					
...y Creek	624	624	......	624	......
...Roads	617	616	1	596	21
...ead	716	716	......	706	10
...	569	569	......	568	1
...rove	465	464	1	465	......
RUSSELL.					
...stown	2342	2341	1	2199	143
Jamestown	138	138	......	100	38
...lsborough	800	800	......	741	59
...ena	805	805	......	772	33
Wilson's	1068	1066	2	1024	44
...'s Mills	794	793	1	780	14
SCOTT.					
...gle, No. 5	1279	1274	5	1001	278
...town, No. 1	4071	4003	68	1901	2170
...orgetown	1570	1537	33	842	728
...Fork, No. 4	1634	1623	11	1490	144
...wn, No. 8	479	472	7	304	175
..., No. 7	637	635	2	438	199
...ing Ground, ...	1600	1590	10	1240	360
...yfoot, No. 6	791	776	15	630	161
Sulphur, ...	1116	1068	48	647	a468
SHELBY.					
...yville	4822	4596	226	2710	2112
Shelbyville	2180	2075	105	1219	961
...	1111	1093	18	808	303
Clay	88	86	2	75	13
...tiansburg	2102	2052	50	1394	708
...'s	1512	1499	13	832	680
...sonville	2237	2193	44	1477	760
Simpsonv'e	239	213	26	195	44
...s	1136	1123	13	682	454
...isonville	988	976	12	809	179
...insville	876	871	5	791	85
Hardinsville	88	88	......	83	5
...sonville	949	938	11	847	102
SIMPSON.					
Franklin (b)	1808	1755	53	1239	569
...Spring	1690	1688	11	1260	430
Knob	1581	1560	21	1111	470
...	1455	1449	6	1314	141
...d Pond	1112	1107	5	1017	95
...leton	1918	1916	2	1456	462

Counties.	Total.	Nativity. Native.	Nativity. Foreign.	Race. White.	Race. Colored.
SPENCER.					
Camp Branch	796	790	6	500	296
Elk Creek	997	985	12	654	343
Nation's	1119	1105	14	1037	82
Taylorsville	1873	1823	50	1382	491
Waterford	1171	1151	20	904	267
TAYLOR.					
Campbellsville	2577	2571	6	1784	793
Campbellsv'e	512	511	1	369	143
Ireland	1505	1504	1	1071	434
Mannsville	1452	1452	......	1375	77
Pitman's Creek	1385	1385	......	1216	169
Saloma	1307	1304	3	930	377
Saloma	73	73	......	73	......
TODD.					
Allensville	812	809	3	393	419
Allensville	310	307	3	166	144
Clifty	468	468	......	468	......
Elkton	3306	3296	10	2131	1175
Fairview	1967	1964	3	1263	704
Hadensville	1499	1483	16	716	783
Kirkmansv'e(c)	889	889	......	787	102
Sharon	897	897	......	871	26
Trenton	2774	2756	18	1123	1651
Trenton	221	219	2	104	117
TRIGG.					
Bethesda	320	320	......	310	10
Cadiz	3960	3946	14	2213	1747
Cadiz	680	675	5	358	322
Canton	1214	1210	4	900	314
Canton	320	317	3	208	112
Furguson	720	720	......	505	215
Futrill	480	476	4	471	9
Golden Pond	1124	1118	6	884	240
Linton	800	800	......	718	82
Roaring Spring	2680	2678	2	1940	740
Roaring Spr'g.	120	119	1	81	39
Rock Castle	560	560	......	515	45
Rock Castle	80	80	......	67	13
Wallonia	1828	1825	3	1424	404
TRIMBLE.					
Bedford	1852	1829	23	1619	233
Bedford	200	197	3	167	33
Burrows	725	721	4	666	59
Milton	1709	1663	46	1586	123
Kingston	59	52	7	58	1
Milton	223	203	20	202	21
Palmyra	574	568	6	564	10
Providence	717	716	1	686	31
UNION.					
Caseyville	2952	2726	226	2555	397
Caseyville	520	491	29	389	131
Hill's	1207	1196	11	1108	99
Lindle's	906	899	7	804	102
Morganfield	2813	2789	24	2058	755
Morganfield	300	295	5	236	64
Raleigh	838	833	5	543	295
Shiloh	792	785	7	684	108
Uniontown	2899	2823	76	2230	669
Uniontown	896	857	39	705	191
Waller's	1233	1225	8	1084	149

(a) Also 1 Indian. (b) Franklin comprises Precinct No. 1. (c) Its precinct not ascertained.

TABLE IX.—*Population of Minor Civil Divisions, &c.—KENTUCKY*—**Continued.**

Counties.	Total.	Nativity. Native.	Nativity. Foreign.	Race. White.	Race. Colored.
WARREN.					
Bowling Green	7235	6778	457	4470	2765
Bowling Green	4574	4153	421	2904	1670
Covington	1997	1968	29	1377	620
Elk Spring	2699	2690	9	1993	706
Goshen	2329	2325	4	1994	335
Green Castle	1479	1471	8	1334	145
Hadley	959	958	1	858	101
Lucas	2604	2581	23	1684	920
Potter	1088	1081	7	701	387
Woodburn	1352	1346	6	964	388
WASHINGTON.					
Fredesburg	1063	1056	7	888	175
Glenville	838	829	9	653	185
Mackville	2326	2326	......	2020	306
Mackville	180	180	......	156	24
North	2280	2279	1	2258	22
Pottsville	1304	1297	7	1051	253
Springfield	3268	3145	123	2181	1087
Springfield	502	490	12	334	168
Willisburg	1385	1379	6	1303	82
WAYNE.					
1. Monticello	2759	2743	16	2436	323
2. Mullentown	1302	1301	1	1251	51
3. Slickford	1718	1717	1	1672	46
4. South Fork	1117	1115	2	1103	14
5. Linkin	1427	1425	2	1424	3
6. Mill Springs	1940	1935	5	1702	238
7. Rock Creek	339	339	......	339	......
WEBSTER.					
1. Petersburg	2270	2259	11	2125	145
2. Dixon	2880	2872	8	2532	348
Dixon	330	326	4	273	57
WEBSTER—Cont'd.					
3. Slaughtersville	1414	1405	9	1221	[illegible]
Slaughters'e	130	122	8	108	[illegible]
4. Vandersburg	1132	1130	2	1004	[illegible]
5. Clay	1903	1902	1	1706	[illegible]
Clay	170	170	......	132	[illegible]
6. Providence	1338	1336	2	994	344
WHITLEY.					
1. South America	640	639	1	637	3
2. Boston	1027	1027	......	1013	14
3. London	960	960	......	[illegible]	[illegible]
4. Williamsburg	1210	1209	1	[illegible]	[illegible]
Williamsb'g	139	139	......	134	5
5. Jofield	526	526	......	526	......
6. Martin Spring	789	789	......	789	......
7. Lower Region	812	812	......	795	17
8. Marsh Creek	1639	1637	2	1614	25
9. Watt's Creek	675	675	......	644	31
WOLFE.					
1. Clefty	362	362	......	362	......
2. Hazel Green	1030	1030	......	1009	[illegible]
Hazel Green	77	77	......	72	[illegible]
3. Campton	1868	1868	......	1861	7
Campton	67	67	......	66	1
4. Devil's Creek	343	343	......	343	......
WOODFORD.					
Clover Bottom	947	947	......	[illegible]	[illegible]
Midway	1370	1337	33	[illegible]	[illegible]
Midway	532	510	22	[illegible]	[illegible]
Millville	641	610	31	435	[illegible]
Mortonsville	744	740	4	403	[illegible]
Versailles	4538	4476	62	2199	[illegible]
Versailles	3268	3214	54	1532	[illegible]

TABLE IX.—*Population of Minor Civil Divisions, &c.—LOUISIANA.*

NOTE.—The marginal column marks wards, whose numbers are official; the names are those in general use. The first indentation marks cities; the second, towns. Names of towns are placed under the names of the wards in which they are respectively situated. The population of each ward includes that of all towns situated in it.

Parishes.	Total.	Nativity. Native.	Nativity. Foreign.	Race. White.	Race. Colored.
ASCENSION.					
1st ward	1143	1133	10	262	881
2d ward	1494	1456	38	414	a1079
3d ward	640	635	5	328	312
4th ward (b)	1244	1218	26	337	a906
Donaldsonville	1573	1445	128	777	796
5th ward	2029	2010	19	299	1730
6th ward	1106	1102	4	123	983
7th ward	1458	1440	18	1054	404
8th ward	890	873	17	671	219
ASSUMPTION					
1st ward	1103	1089	14	542	561
2d ward	960	953	7	345	615
3d ward	1160	1142	18	403	757
4th ward	760	756	4	203	557
5th ward	800	794	6	514	286
6th ward	1600	1533	67	612	[illegible]
7th ward	1280	1254	26	431	849
8th ward	1734	1707	27	801	933
9th ward	818	788	30	492	326

(a) Also 1 Chinese.

(b) Exclusive of city of Donaldsonville.

TABLE IX.—*Population of Minor Civil Divisions, &c.—LOUISIANA*—Continued.

Parishes.	Total.	Nativity: Native.	Nativity: Foreign.	Race: White.	Race: Colored.
ASSUMPTION—Con.					
[illegible] ward	642	632	10	356	*a*283
[illegible] ward	475	470	5	283	192
[illegible] ward	959	950	9	625	334
[illegible] ward	639	637	2	396	243
[illegible] ward	304	289	15	244	60
AVOYELLES.					
1st ward	658	621	37	470	188
2d ward	1522	1451	71	1015	507
Marksville	437	381	56	336	101
3d ward	1350	1306	44	767	583
4th ward	939	929	10	814	125
5th ward	3506	3396	110	1537	1969
6th ward	2576	2554	22	1368	1208
7th ward	2375	2356	19	780	1595
BIENVILLE.					
1st ward	2387	2383	4	1391	996
2d ward	1463	1459	4	558	905
3d ward	1440	1435	5	654	786
4th ward	2003	1993	10	1120	883
5th ward	950	950	......	558	392
6th ward	1118	1113	5	602	516
7th ward	1275	1268	7	706	569
BOSSIER.					
1st ward	1280	1260	20	249	1031
2d ward	2238	2231	7	250	1988
3d ward	3997	3981	16	1403	2594
4th ward	1600	1593	7	441	1159
5th ward	1600	1598	2	437	1163
6th ward	1960	1953	7	725	1235
CADDO.					
1st ward	2706	2685	21	730	1976
2d ward	2588	2578	10	359	*b*2228
3d ward	2377	2372	5	447	1930
4th ward (*c*)	2195	2132	63	589	1606
5th ward	1755	1746	9	343	1412
6th ward	3092	3057	35	291	*d*2800
7th ward	2394	2381	13	715	1679
Shreveport	4607	3982	625	2439	2168
CALCASIEU. (*e*)					
1st ward	483	475	8	411	72
2d ward	597	589	8	528	69
3d ward	1493	1423	70	987	*f*403
4th ward	521	507	14	368	*g*151
5th ward	1549	1534	15	1062	*g*485
6th ward	994	991	3	913	81
7th ward	1096	1089	7	902	194
CALDWELL.					
1st ward	894	893	1	246	648
2d ward	540	540	......	183	357
3d ward	259	259	......	222	37
4th ward	1028	1020	8	566	462
Columbia	235	231	4	116	119
5th ward	592	591	1	400	192
6th ward	154	154	......	132	22
7th ward	448	447	1	159	289
8th ward	207	204	3	102	105
9th ward	306	306	......	261	45
10th ward	392	390	2	325	67

Parishes.	Total.	Nativity: Native.	Nativity: Foreign.	Race: White.	Race: Colored.
CARROLL.					
1st ward	2200	2136	64	280	*h*1908
2d ward	3120	3019	101	465	2655
Lake Providence	320	269	51	223	97
3d ward	1920	1913	7	102	1818
4th ward	75	74	1	15	60
5th ward	1154	1141	13	718	436
6th ward	1641	1634	7	800	841
Floyd	157	156	1	107	50
CATAHOULA.					
1st ward	640	639	1	506	*i*125
2d ward or Trinity	958	947	11	708	*g*248
3d ward	762	757	5	559	203
4th ward	612	610	2	551	61
5th ward	361	357	4	263	98
6th ward	429	409	20	340	89
Harrisonburg	217	197	20	158	59
7th ward	938	920	18	300	638
8th ward	659	654	5	105	554
9th ward	209	209	......	46	163
10th ward	358	358	......	139	219
11th ward	208	183	25	156	52
12th ward	1225	1221	4	352	873
13th ward	874	867	7	211	663
14th ward	242	235	7	145	97
CLAIBORNE.					
1st ward	1847	1846	1	1073	774
2d ward	2479	2479	......	872	*g*1605
3d ward	3215	3206	9	1959	1256
4th ward	3530	3447	83	1589	1941
Minden	1100	1071	29	800	300
5th ward	1399	1398	1	788	611
6th ward	1231	1231	......	679	552
7th ward	4619	4600	19	1844	2775
Arizona	400	398	2	271	129
Homer	80	80	......	22	58
8th ward	1920	1918	2	826	1094
CONCORDIA.					
1st ward	640	626	14	88	552
2d ward	1248	1241	7	63	1185
3d ward	1899	1894	5	37	1862
4th ward	2828	2789	39	168	2660
5th ward	1557	1548	9	57	1500
6th ward	669	665	4	56	613
7th ward	751	738	13	72	679
8th ward	160	157	3	64	96
9th ward	225	220	5	115	110
DE SOTO.					
1st ward	3040	3016	24	1126	1914
2d ward	2400	2391	9	589	1811
3d ward	952	950	2	460	492
4th ward	2554	2526	28	1095	1459
Mansfield	813	792	21	511	302
5th ward	1600	1589	11	556	1044
6th ward	1219	1211	8	215	1004
7th ward	1757	1748	9	529	1228
8th ward	1440	1437	3	541	899
EAST BATON ROUGE.					
1st ward (*j*)	3798	3540	258	1698	2100

(*a*) Also 3 Indians.
(*b*) Also 1 Indian.
(*c*) Exclusive of city of Shreveport.
(*d*) Also 1 Chinese.
(*e*) In 1870, 7th and 8th wards to Cameron Parish.
(*f*) Also 101 Indians.
(*g*) Also 2 Indians.
(*h*) Also 12 Chinese.
(*i*) Also 9 Indians.
(*j*) 1st and 2d wards comprise city of Baton Rouge.

TABLE IX.—*Population of Minor Civil Divisions, &c.*—*LOUISIANA*—**Continued.**

Parishes.	Total.	Nativity. Native.	Nativity. Foreign.	Race. White.	Race. Colored.
EAST BATON ROUGE—Continued.					
2d ward (*a*)	2700	2342	358	1443	*b*1256
3d ward	1600	1581	19	583	1017
4th ward	891	874	17	489	402
5th ward	320	311	9	61	259
6th ward	819	799	20	137	682
7th ward	984	961	23	150	*b*833
8th ward	921	910	11	170	751
9th ward	779	775	4	119	660
10th ward	2720	2695	25	578	2142
11th ward	959	944	15	596	363
12th ward	1325	1311	14	447	878
Baton Rouge	6498	5882	616	3141	*b*3356
EAST FELICIANA.					
1st ward	2397	2359	38	464	1933
2d ward	1230	1222	8	406	824
3d ward	3249	3127	122	1119	2130
Jackson	934	816	118	716	218
4th ward	1000	999	1	125	875
5th ward	1966	1869	97	890	1076
Clinton	930	840	90	633	297
6th ward	1273	1271	2	467	806
7th ward	1200	1188	12	234	966
8th ward	1184	1179	5	401	783
FRANKLIN. (*c*)					
1st ward	569	557	12	184	*b*384
2d ward	1040	1036	4	384	656
3d ward	616	609	7	259	357
4th ward	823	790	33	551	272
5th ward	464	460	4	159	305
8th ward	425	424	1	138	287
10th ward	353	352	1	158	195
11th ward	580	577	3	235	345
12th ward	208	208	.....	165	43
GRANT.					
1st ward	1795	1783	12	217	*d*1575
Colfax	40	36	4	19	21
2d ward	709	706	3	382	327
3d ward	325	325	.....	291	34
4th ward	308	308	.....	252	*b*55
5th ward	168	168	.....	139	*e*19
6th ward	634	633	1	411	223
7th ward	578	565	13	386	*f*181
Montgomery	160	150	10	121	39
IBERIA.					
1st ward	2864	2794	70	1101	1763
2d ward	2427	2207	220	1501	926
New Iberia	1472	1285	187	1004	468
3d ward	2396	2355	41	1171	*g*1224
4th ward	1355	1329	26	758	597
IBERVILLE.					
1st ward	3016	2942	74	718	2298
2d ward	1920	1765	155	974	946
Plaquemines	1460	1316	144	892	568
3d ward	1089	1082	7	207	882
4th ward	1581	1544	37	552	1029
IBERVILLE—Cont'd.					
5th ward	1247	1210	37	333	[illegible]
6th ward	457	448	9	[illegible]	[illegible]
7th ward	1545	1527	18	412	[illegible]
8th ward	1492	1482	10	[illegible]	[illegible]
JACKSON.					
1st ward	1138	1136	2	598	540
2d ward	2062	2053	9	1132	930
3d ward	927	926	1	445	482
4th ward	1065	1065	.....	435	630
5th ward	612	612	.....	496	116
6th ward	1348	1346	2	[illegible]	[illegible]
7th ward	494	493	1	269	225
JEFFERSON.					
1st ward, east of Miss. River	1020	902	118	330	[illegible]
2d ward, east of Miss. River	1303	1028	275	846	457
3d ward, east of Miss. River	343	321	22	138	[illegible]
4th ward, east of Miss. River	590	555	35	137	[illegible]
5th ward, east of Miss. River	735	714	21	107	[illegible]
6th ward, east of Miss. River	856	837	19	134	[illegible]
7th ward, east of Miss. River	574	543	31	[illegible]	[illegible]
8th ward, east of Miss. River	610	393	217	556	[illegible]
Bath (*j*)	614	586	28	[illegible]	[illegible]
Carrollton (*j*)	6495	5518	977	3153	[illegible]
Harlem (*j*)	291	277	14	70	[illegible]
Kennerville (*j*)	2028	1942	86	294	1734
Left Bank (*j*)	1218	1170	48	204	1014
Metairie Ridge (*j*)	456	416	40	166	[illegible]
Shrewsbury	634	622	12	147	487
LAFAYETTE.					
1st ward	1435	1405	30	765	670
2d ward	1486	1460	26	750	[illegible]
3d ward	1629	1537	92	864	765
Vermillionv'e	777	685	92	454	323
4th ward	1376	1362	14	780	596
5th ward	1515	1496	19	810	705
6th ward	1502	1477	25	817	685
7th ward	1445	1420	25	835	610
LAFOURCHE.					
1st ward	2486	2458	28	841	1645
2d ward	960	932	28	753	207
3d ward	3496	3469	27	[illegible]	[illegible]
4th ward	480	472	8	321	159
5th ward	1200	1185	15	969	231
6th ward	1435	1421	14	624	811
7th ward	2338	2173	165	1363	975
Thibodeaux	1922	1779	143	1149	773
8th ward	750	742	8	609	141
9th ward	1574	1560	14	1378	196

(*a*) 1st and 2d wards comprise city of Baton Rouge.
(*b*) Also 1 Indian.
(*c*) In 1868, 6th, 7th, and 9th wards to Richland Parish.
(*d*) Also 3 Indians.
(*e*) Also 10 Indians.
(*f*) Also 11 Indians.
(*g*) Also 1 Chinese.
(*h*) Also 2 Chinese.
(*i*) Also 4 Chinese.
(*j*) The places named constitute the parish west of the Mississippi River.
(*k*) Also 2 Indians.

[...]LE IX.—*Population of Minor Civil Divisions, &c.—LOUISIANA*—Continued.

[...]shes.	Total.	Nativity: Native.	Nativity: Foreign.	Race: White.	Race: Colored.
[...]STON.					
[...]l	354	551	3	354	200
[...]l	551	549	2	427	124
[...]l	586	568	18	519	67
[...]l	542	520	22	469	133
[...]l	501	500	1	328	173
[...]l	399	395	4	337	62
[...]l	199	199	......	185	a6
[...]l	359	323	36	256	103
[...]l	335	332	3	270	65
[...]BON.					
[...]	800	780	20	80	720
[...]	1526	1493	33	156	1370
[...]	2001	1959	42	188	b1812
[...]	2138	2129	9	176	1962
[...]	1693	1671	22	166	1527
[...]	202	183	19	63	139
[...]	240	228	12	107	133
[...]HOUSE.					
[...]l	1167	1163	4	164	1003
[...]l	664	662	2	362	302
[...]l	400	398	2	174	226
[...]l	1146	1090	56	684	462
[...]up	521	472	49	382	139
[...]l	1710	1707	3	408	1302
[...]l	1665	1655	10	399	1266
[...]l	478	478	......	149	329
[...]l	972	965	7	244	728
[...]l	146	145	1	104	42
[...]d	1039	1039	......	324	715
[...]TOCHES.					
[...]d	1439	1418	21	657	782
[...]d	1007	994	13	629	378
[...]d	1930	1910	20	536	1394
[...]d	2693	2651	42	755	e1925
[...]d	1085	1084	1	608	477
[...]d	851	841	10	455	396
[...]d	374	373	1	346	b27
[...]d	287	285	2	281	6
[...]d	619	610	9	174	445
[...]d	1896	1871	25	747	d1144
[...]d	2498	2472	26	497	c1996
[...]d	2962	2786	176	1128	1834
[...]chitoches	1401	1242	159	837	564
[...]d	624	624	......	499	125
[...]EANS.					
[...]rleans	191418	142943	48475	140923	f50456
[...]HITA.					
[...]	1953	1943	10	290	1663
[...]	1379	1369	10	232	1147
[...]	4213	3981	232	1183	3030
[...]roe	1949	1741	208	919	1030
[...]	493	492	1	115	378
[...]	798	798	......	499	299
[...]	1228	1225	3	777	451
[...]	1089	1075	14	446	643
[...], Trenton.	429	416	13	217	212
[...]EMINES.					
[...]d	815	783	32	94	g717
[...]d	840	787	53	116	724

Parishes.	Total.	Nativity: Native.	Nativity: Foreign.	Race: White.	Race: Colored.
PLAQUEMINES—Cont'd.					
3d ward	529	507	22	40	489
4th ward	1259	1194	65	541	718
5th ward	570	554	16	221	349
6th ward	695	540	155	536	159
7th ward	798	778	20	85	713
8th ward	822	795	27	170	652
9th ward	1220	1164	56	194	1026
10th ward	1608	1509	99	516	1092
11th ward	945	706	239	760	185
12th ward	451	318	133	430	21
POINT COUPÉE.					
1st ward	145	140	5	94	51
2d ward	638	631	7	233	405
3d ward	1251	1224	27	247	1004
4th ward	1918	1877	41	334	1584
5th ward	837	812	25	250	587
6th ward	765	734	31	168	597
7th ward	926	869	57	234	692
8th ward	1745	1696	49	255	1490
9th ward	936	908	28	269	667
10th ward	656	632	24	284	372
11th ward	910	894	16	438	472
12th ward	485	484	1	258	227
13th ward	945	940	5	357	588
14th ward	824	810	14	271	553
RAPIDES.					
Alexandria	1985	1778	207	869	1116
Alexandria	1218	1019	199	770	448
Anacoca	1640	1634	6	1506	134
Bayou Rapides	1208	1190	18	250	958
Calcasieu	1022	1010	12	869	153
Cheneyville	2617	2603	14	479	2138
Cotile	1280	1267	13	369	911
Lamourie	2485	2464	21	438	2047
Pineville	2079	2004	75	1404	h669
Pineville	414	372	42	283	131
Rapides	1330	1326	4	154	1176
Spring Hill	1593	1584	9	641	952
West	776	776	......	763	13
RICHLAND.					
1st ward	902	881	21	478	424
Delhi	186	174	12	131	55
2d ward	779	767	12	417	362
Rayville	106	101	5	78	28
3d ward	1153	1098	55	473	680
4th ward	1051	1040	11	482	569
5th ward	1225	1217	8	555	670
SABINE.					
1st ward	826	820	6	666	160
2d ward	494	494	......	352	142
3d ward	701	699	2	496	205
4th ward	1313	1293	20	691	b621
5th ward	320	318	2	299	h13
6th ward	727	718	9	576	144
7th ward	716	715	1	383	333
8th ward	569	567	2	485	84
9th ward	572	569	3	442	130
10th ward	225	225	......	192	i23
ST. BERNARD.					
1st ward	1291	1142	149	432	859
2d ward	492	473	19	308	184

[...]lso 8 Indians.
[...]lso 1 Indian.
[...]lso 13 Chinese.
(*d*) Also 1 Chinese and 4 Indians.
(*e*) Also 5 Chinese.
(*f*) Also 16 Indians and 23 Chinese.
(*g*) Also 4 Indians.
(*h*) Also 6 Indians.
(*i*) Also 10 Indians.

TABLE IX.—*Population of Minor Civil Divisions, &c.*—*LOUISIANA*—**Continued.**

Parishes.	Total.	Nativity.		Race.	
		Native.	Foreign.	White.	Colored.
ST. BERNARD—Cont'd.					
3d ward	269	264	5	165	104
4th ward	463	450	13	146	317
5th ward	516	486	30	410	106
6th ward	522	458	64	179	343
ST. CHARLES.					
1st ward	1197	1173	24	198	999
2d ward	797	772	25	228	a562
3d ward	1120	1106	14	213	907
4th ward	576	555	21	125	451
5th ward	1177	1160	17	133	1044
ST. HELENA.					
1st ward	769	765	4	291	478
2d ward	1600	1582	18	621	979
Greensburg	160	159	1	61	99
3d ward	571	569	2	264	307
4th ward	1054	1052	2	624	430
5th ward	320	310	10	168	152
6th ward	1109	1108	1	541	568
ST. JAMES.					
1st ward	1120	1094	26	372	748
2d ward	1691	1631	60	743	948
3d ward	1169	1159	10	404	765
4th ward	860	837	23	341	519
5th ward	1774	1742	32	352	1422
6th ward	1577	1544	33	373	1204
7th ward	1583	1549	34	443	1140
8th ward	378	371	7	247	131
ST. JOHN THE BAPTIST.					
1st ward	773	752	21	308	b463
2d ward	1109	1068	41	543	566
3d ward	960	945	15	455	c504
4th ward	1240	1226	14	352	888
5th ward	1760	1712	48	756	1004
6th ward	920	903	17	301	619
ST. LANDRY.					
1st ward	4199	4065	134	1562	2637
Opelousas	1546	1428	118	880	666
2d ward	2370	2273	97	1206	1164
Grand Coteau	470	396	74	328	142
3d ward	8316	8136	180	3097	d5136
Washington	907	818	89	643	264
4th ward	4246	4210	36	2995	1251
Ville Platte	135	128	7	98	37
5th ward	3778	3747	31	2816	962
6th ward	2644	2604	40	2100	544
ST. MARTIN.					
1st ward	320	312	8	269	51
2d ward	5193	5025	168	2072	b3119
St. Martinsv'e	1190	1077	113	635	555
3d ward	1119	1077	42	592	527
4th ward	2738	2720	18	1353	e1367
ST. MARY.					
1st ward	1971	1932	39	547	f1382
2d ward	1421	1405	16	433	988
3d ward	4159	3981	178	1217	[illegible]
Franklin	1265	1131	134	700	565
4th ward	3790	3722	68	900	g2886
5th ward	2519	2309	210	1076	i1440
Brashear City	776	642	134	500	276
ST. TAMMANY.					
1st ward	479	474	5	436	43
2d ward	644	633	11	468	176
3d ward	854	840	14	296	558
4th ward	691	602	89	469	222
Madisonville	398	353	45	218	180
5th ward	80	62	18	58	22
6th ward	1461	1315	146	868	593
Covington	585	535	50	325	260
7th ward	104	99	5	104	......
9th ward	1273	1085	188	784	489
Lewisburg	110	97	13	81	29
Mandeville	541	422	119	363	178
TANGIPAHOA.					
1st ward	3373	3219	154	1816	1557
Amite City	910	852	58	503	407
Tangipahoa	236	217	19	157	79
2d ward	1845	1830	15	1113	732
3d ward	1565	1449	116	1078	487
Ponchatoula	320	291	29	185	135
4th ward	1145	1094	51	927	218
TENSAS.					
1st ward	2700	2669	31	231	j2440
2d ward	1938	1924	14	146	1792
3d ward	4058	3932	126	473	3585
4th ward	1006	992	14	141	865
6th ward	1495	1431	64	271	1224
7th ward	1222	1203	19	138	1084
TERREBONNE.					
1st ward	688	679	9	260	428
2d ward	858	851	7	360	498
3d ward	908	903	5	150	758
4th ward	667	651	16	540	127
5th ward	273	272	1	227	[illegible]
6th ward	1791	1705	86	765	1026
Houma	593	528	65	347	246
7th ward	746	732	14	266	480
8th ward	1081	1058	23	786	k245
9th ward	687	682	5	355	332
10th ward	760	757	3	671	[illegible]
11th ward	1570	1552	18	528	j1013
12th ward	759	757	2	439	c319
13th ward	594	582	12	247	347
14th ward	1069	1056	13	486	583
UNION.					
1st ward	1942	1917	25	1008	934
Farmersville	272	250	22	176	96

(*a*) Also 7 Chinese.
(*b*) Also 2 Indians.
(*c*) Also 1 Indian.
(*d*) Also 83 Indians.
(*e*) Also 18 Indians.
(*f*) Also 42 Indians.
(*g*) Also 4 Indians.
(*h*) Also 114 Indians.
(*i*) Also 3 Indians.
(*j*) Also 29 Indians.
(*k*) Also 50 Indians.

TABLE IX.—*Population of Minor Civil Divisions, &c.—LOUISIANA*—Continued.

Counties.	Total.	NATIVITY.		RACE.	
		Native.	Foreign.	White.	Colored.
UNION—Cont'd.					
d ward	1729	1725	4	1090	639
d ward	1760	1759	1	1183	577
th ward	2111	2111	......	1405	706
th ward	2703	2697	6	1894	809
th ward	1440	1437	3	731	709
VERMILLION.					
1st ward	441	437	4	394	47
2d ward	486	478	8	329	157
3d ward	1544	1499	45	999	545
Abbeville	545	509	36	335	210
4th ward	636	632	4	618	18
5th ward	364	364	......	273	91
6th ward	519	501	18	440	a78
7th ward	538	536	2	427	111
WASHINGTON.					
1st ward	632	631	1	487	145
2d ward	628	627	1	465	163
3d ward	572	567	5	482	90
Franklinton	121	118	3	94	27
4th ward	470	469	1	232	238
5th ward	458	455	3	358	100
6th ward	570	570	......	367	203

Counties.	Total.	NATIVITY.		RACE.	
		Native.	Foreign.	White.	Colored.
WEST FELICIANA.					
1st ward	640	586	54	333	a306
2d ward	680	662	18	95	585
3d ward	1837	1828	9	187	1650
4th ward	840	829	11	107	733
5th ward	965	963	2	123	842
6th ward	155	154	1	69	86
7th ward	906	905	1	50	856
8th ward	826	822	4	64	762
9th ward, or Bayou Sara	440	374	66	262	178
10th ward	1483	1477	6	49	1434
11th ward	607	605	2	122	485
12th ward	1120	1116	4	122	998
WINN.					
1st ward	960	954	6	860	a99
Winfield	94	92	2	82	12
2d ward	637	636	1	604	33
3d ward	542	542	......	466	76
4th ward	640	636	4	370	270
5th ward	485	484	1	421	64
6th ward	741	738	3	473	268
8th ward	456	453	3	387	69
9th ward	493	492	1	463	30

(*a*) Also 1 Indian.

TABLE IX.—*Population of Minor Civil Divisions, &c.—MAINE.*

NOTE.—The marginal column marks towns, unless otherwise designated; the first indentation, cities; the second, villages. Names of villages are placed under the names of the towns in which they are respectively situated. The population of each town includes that of all villages situated in it.

Counties.	Total.	NATIVITY.		RACE.	
		Native.	Foreign.	White.	Colored.
ANDROSCOGGIN.					
Auburn	6169	5992	177	6163	6
Durham	1350	1336	14	1348	2
East Livermore	1004	985	19	1004	......
Greene	1094	1082	12	1092	2
Leeds	1288	1270	18	1279	9
Lewiston	13600	10592	3008	13581	19
Lisbon	2014	1817	197	2013	1
Livermore	1467	1456	11	1467	......
Minot	1569	1539	30	1568	1
Poland	2436	2393	43	2436	......
Turner	2380	2356	24	2380	......
Wales	556	553	3	556	......
Webster	939	865	74	939	......
AROOSTOOK.					
Above St. Francis Plantation (*a*)	156	101	55	156	......
Alva Plantation	496	297	199	496	......
Amity	311	247	64	311	......

Counties.	Total.	NATIVITY.		RACE.	
		Native.	Foreign.	White.	Colored.
AROOSTOOK—Con.					
Bancroft Plant'n	177	129	48	177	......
Benedicta	413	316	97	413	......
Bridgewater	605	354	251	605	......
Castle Hill Plant'n	237	190	47	237	......
Crystal	250	230	20	250	......
Cyr	376	274	102	376	......
Dalton	445	391	54	445	......
Dickeyville	1851	1408	443	1851	......
Eagle Lake Plan'n	143	95	48	143	......
Eaton	522	412	110	522	......
Fort Fairfield	1893	1459	434	1892	1
Fort Kent	1034	709	325	1034	......
Glenwood	185	171	14	185	......
Grant Isle	688	513	175	688	......
Greenwood Plan'n	47	41	6	47	......
Hamlin Plantat'n	558	448	110	558	......
Haynesville Pl'n	165	141	24	165	......
Hodgdon	989	643	346	988	1
Houlton	2850	1665	1185	2814	36
Island Falls Pl'n	183	173	10	183	......
Limestone	263	186	77	263	......

(*a*) Unorganized territory.

TABLE IX.—*Population of Minor Civil Divisions, &c.—MAINE—Continued.*

Counties.	Total.	Nativity.		Race.	
		Native.	Foreign.	White.	Colored.
AROOSTOOK—Con.					
Linneus	1008	760	248	1002	6
Littleton	700	491	209	700	......
Ludlow	371	250	121	371	......
Lyndon	1410	1090	320	1410	......
Macwahoc Plan'n	170	147	23	160	10
Madawaska	1041	854	187	1041	......
Mapleton Plan'n	444	345	99	444	......
Mars Hill	399	256	143	398	1
Marsardis	169	135	34	169	......
Maysville	758	610	148	758	......
Molunkus Plan'n	61	52	9	61	......
Monticello	760	467	293	760	......
New Limerick	308	237	71	307	1
Oakfield Plan'n	559	426	133	559	......
Orient	219	150	69	219	......
Perham Plantat'n	79	78	1	79	......
Portage Lake Pl'n	124	90	34	124	......
Presque Isle	970	770	200	970	......
Reed Plantation	54	52	2	54	......
Sherman	701	667	34	701	......
Smyrna	159	113	46	159	......
St. Francis Plan'n	253	204	49	253	......
St. John's Plan'n	127	85	42	127	......
Van Buren Plan'n	922	692	230	922	......
Wade Plantation	76	56	20	76	......
Wallagrass Plan'n	297	214	83	297	......
Washburn	449	331	118	449	......
Westfield Plan'n	76	68	8	76	......
Weston	394	360	34	394	......
Woodland Plan'n	174	153	21	174	......
Township F, R. 1	67	33	34	67	......
Township 11, R. 1	274	203	71	274	......
Township B, R. 2	46	33	13	46	......
Township C, R. 2	6	6	......	6	......
Township K, R. 2	132	74	58	132	......
Township 11, R. 3	40	40	......	40	......
Township 5, R. 4	129	114	15	129	......
Township 6, R. 4	118	93	25	118	......
Township 1, R. 5	38	27	11	38	......
Township 5, R. 5	107	100	7	107	......
Township 6, R. 5	121	116	5	121	......
Township 7, R. 5	16	13	3	16	......
Township 8, R. 5	29	22	7	29	......
Township 9, R. 5	25	20	5	25	......
Township 12, R. 5	69	67	2	69	......
Township 9, R. 6	100	84	16	100	......
Township 11, R. 6	51	31	20	51	......
Township 12, R. 6	30	21	9	30	......
Township 13, R. 6	2	2	......	2	......
Township 17, R. 6	83	58	25	83	......
Township 15, R. 7	6	5	1	6	......
Township 18, R. 10	51	44	7	51	......
CUMBERLAND.					
Baldwin	1101	1092	9	1101	......
Bridgeton	2685	2563	122	2685	......
Brunswick	4687	4148	539	4604	83
Brunswick	1449	1383	66	1440	9
Cape Elizabeth	5106	4462	644	5090	16
Casco	998	995	3	997	1
Cumberland	1626	1606	20	1626	......
Falmouth	1730	1698	32	1729	1
Freeport	2457	2428	29	2455	2
Gorham	3351	3186	165	3347	4
Gray	1738	1699	39	1738	......
Harpswell	1749	1716	33	1721	28
Harrison	1219	1191	28	1219	......
Naples	1058	1054	4	1058	......
New Gloucester	1496	1460	36	1494	2
North Yarmouth	940	934	6	939	1
Otisfield	1099	1090	9	1099	......
CUMBERLAND—Con.					
Portland	31413	24401	7012	31078	a[illegible]
Pownal	981	963	18	981	......
Raymond	1120	1118	2	1120	......
Scarborough	1692	1656	36	1692	......
Sebago	803	795	8	802	1
Standish	2089	1921	168	2089	......
Westbrook	6583	5819	764	6569	[illegible]
Windham	2428	2390	38	2425	3
Yarmouth	1872	1797	75	[illegible]	[illegible]
FRANKLIN.					
Avon	610	607	3	610	......
Carthage	486	485	1	486	......
Chesterville	1011	1008	3	1011	......
Dallas Plantation	159	159	......	159	......
Farmington	3251	3072	179	3247	4
Freeman	608	608	......	608	......
Industry	725	719	6	725	......
Jay	1490	1475	15	1489	a1
Jerusalem Township	32	31	1	32	......
Kingfield	560	552	8	560	......
Lang Plantation	36	36	......	36	......
Madrid	394	393	1	394	......
New Sharon	1451	1447	4	1450	1
New Vineyard	755	747	8	755	......
Perkins Plantation	149	149	......	149	......
Phillips	1373	1360	13	1373	......
Rangely	313	312	1	313	......
Rangely Plantation	45	45	......	45	......
Salem	307	301	6	307	......
Sandy River Plantation	111	111	......	111	......
Strong	634	624	10	634	......
Temple	640	635	5	639	1
Washington Plantation	62	62	......	62	......
Weld	1130	1127	3	1129	1
Wilton	1906	1880	26	1906	......
Township E	93	92	1	91	2
Township 4, R. 2	9	9	......	9	......
Township 1, R. 3	69	69	......	69	......
Township 4, R. 3	25	25	......	25	......
Township 1, R. 4	342	340	2	342	......
Township 6, Plantation	31	31	......	31	......
HANCOCK.					
Amherst	350	338	12	350	......
Aurora	212	209	3	212	......
Beach Isle	9	9	......	9	......
Bear Isle	13	13	......	13	......
Bluehill	1707	1692	15	1707	......
Bradbury Isle	6	6	......	6	......
Brooklyn	966	955	11	966	......
Brooksville	1275	1265	10	1275	......
Bucksport	3433	3258	175	3422	11
Butler's Isle	12	12	......	12	......
Castine	1303	1257	46	1297	6
Cranberry Isles	350	343	7	350	......
Dedham	448	442	6	448	......
Deer Isle	3414	3364	50	3404	10
Eagle Isle	30	29	1	30	......
Eastbrook	187	182	5	187	......
Eden	1195	1184	11	1182	13
Ellsworth	5257	4925	332	5256	1
Franklin	1042	1025	17	1042	......
Gouldsborough	1709	1675	34	1705	a3

(a) Also 1 Indian.

...LE IX.—*Population of Minor Civil Divisions, &c.—MAINE*—Continued.

...s.	Total.	NATIVITY. Native.	NATIVITY. Foreign.	RACE. White.	RACE. Colored.
...ont'd.					
......	974	950	24	972	2
......	6	6	......	6	......
......	612	608	4	612	......
Plant-					
......	177	174	3	177	......
......	369	368	1	369	......
e.....	5	5	......	5	......
rt....	918	894	24	918	......
Isle ..	13	12	1	13	......
......	1701	1691	10	1701	......
......	246	242	4	246	......
......	1418	1416	2	1418	......
Isle ..	3	2	1	3	......
......	1113	1107	6	1113	......
Isle.	22	22	......	22	......
......	796	764	32	796	......
......	1242	1237	5	1241	1
......	451	449	2	451	......
......	1822	1772	50	1821	(a)
......	678	673	5	678	......
......	352	333	19	352	......
......	366	361	5	366	......
......	25	23	2	25	......
n....	69	60	9	67	2
n....	10	9	1	10	......
n....	56	54	2	56	......
n....	12	12	......	12	......
n....	19	19	......	19	......
n....	102	101	1	102	......
...x.					
......	1356	1345	11	1356	......
......	7808	7357	451	7730	78
......	1485	1481	4	1484	1
......	1180	1158	22	1180	......
......	1238	949	289	1237	1
......	2118	2084	34	2107	11
......	1766	1747	19	1765	1
......	257	230	27	257	......
......	859	844	15	859	......
......	900	886	14	900	......
......	4497	4314	183	4440	57
......	3007	2802	205	3003	4
......	1506	1499	7	1504	2
......	732	722	10	732	......
......	1744	1710	34	1744	......
on ...	1252	1247	5	1252	......
......	2353	2292	61	2353	......
......	1456	1419	37	1456	......
......	725	722	3	725	......
......	1471	1455	16	1471	......
ation.	68	67	1	68	......
gh ...	2919	2722	197	2917	2
......	740	734	6	739	1
......	4852	4305	547	4842	10
......	938	938	......	938	......
er ...	1044	1041	3	1038	6
......	1266	1252	14	1266	......
......	1437	1394	43	1432	5
......	2229	2198	31	2224	5
......	1485	1467	18	1484	1
......	4512	4448	64	4502	10
......	704	696	8	704	......
......	890	885	5	886	4
......	907	905	2	907	......
...lan'n.	277	276	1	277	......
Island	13	13	......	13	......
...ns Is'd	250	249	1	250	......
...cenI'd	14	14	......	14	......

(a) Also 1 Chinese.

Counties.	Total.	NATIVITY. Native.	NATIVITY. Foreign.	RACE. White.	RACE. Colored.
KNOX—Continued.					
Muscle Ridge Pl'n	263	169	94	263	......
North Haven......	806	788	18	806	......
Rockland.......	7074	6754	320	7058	16
South Thomaston.	1693	1596	97	1692	1
St. George........	2318	2261	57	2315	3
Thomaston	3092	2832	260	3086	6
Union	1701	1695	6	1701	......
Vinal Haven	1851	1747	104	1851	......
Warren...........	1974	1957	17	1899	75
Washington	1276	1269	7	1276	......
LINCOLN.					
Alna	747	740	7	747	......
Boothbay.........	3200	3094	106	3200	......
Bremen	797	783	14	797	......
Bristol	2916	2884	32	2883	33
Cow Island	19	19	......	19	......
Damariscotta.....	1232	1209	23	1227	5
Dresden	990	979	11	988	2
Edgecomb........	1056	1046	10	1055	1
Jefferson	1821	1805	16	1821	......
Marsh Island	20	18	2	20	......
Monhegan Island	145	145	......	145	......
Muscongus Island.	142	141	1	142	......
New Castle.......	1729	1643	86	1723	6
Nobleborough	1150	1141	9	1150	......
Somerville........	505	505	......	504	1
Southport	684	653	31	684	......
Waldoborough....	4174	4127	47	4165	9
Westport.........	699	678	21	691	(b)
Whitefield	1594	1480	114	1594	......
Wiscasset........	1977	1883	94	1976	1
OXFORD.					
Albany...........	651	632	19	651	......
Andover	757	744	13	756	1
Andover, North Surplus	38	38	......	38	......
Andover, West Surplus	4	4	......	4	......
Bethel............	2286	2259	27	2283	3
Brownfield	1323	1265	58	1321	2
Buckfield	1494	1484	10	1494	......
Byron	242	232	10	242	......
Canton	984	974	10	984	......
Denmark	1069	1059	10	1069	......
Dixfield	1049	1040	9	1049	......
Franklin Plant'n	178	172	6	178	......
Fryeburg.........	1507	1482	25	1507	......
Fryeburg Academy Grant........	38	37	1	38	......
Gilead............	329	328	1	329	......
Grafton	94	94	......	94	......
Greenwood	845	823	22	845	......
Hamlin's Grant ..	95	95	......	94	1
Hanover	188	188	......	188	......
Hartford	996	994	2	996	......
Hebron...........	744	733	11	744	......
Hiram............	1393	1285	108	1393	......
Lincoln Plantat'n.	30	30	......	30	......
Lovell	1018	1014	4	1018	......
Mason...........	127	126	1	127	......
Mexico	458	447	11	458	......
Milton Plantation.	258	249	9	258	......
Newry	416	409	7	416	......
Norway	1954	1928	26	1952	2
Norway	916	896	20	916	......
Oxford	1631	1570	61	1623	8
Paris	2765	2703	62	2765	......
Peru	931	924	7	930	1
Porter............	1104	1099	5	1103	1

(b) Also 8 Indians.

TABLE IX.—*Population of Minor Civil Divisions, &c.*—MAINE—Continued.

Counties.	Total.	Nativity. Native.	Nativity. Foreign.	Race. White.	Race. Colored.
OXFORD—Cont'd.					
Riley Plantation	32	32	......	32	......
Roxbury	162	158	4	162	......
Rumford	1212	1208	4	1209	3
Stoneham	425	425	......	425	......
Stow	427	425	2	427	......
Sumner	1170	1163	7	1169	1
Sweden	549	549	......	549	......
Upton	187	187	......	187	......
Waterford	1286	1277	9	1286	......
Woodstock	994	987	7	994	......
Township C	3	3	......	3	......
Township 5, R. 1	45	45	......	45	......
PENOBSCOT.					
Alton	508	480	28	507	1
Argyle	307	297	10	307	......
Bangor	18289	15275	3014	18205	84
Bradford	1487	1456	31	1487	......
Bradley	866	742	124	866	......
Brewer	3214	2812	402	3209	5
Burlington	553	525	28	553	......
Carmel	1348	1295	53	1348	......
Carroll	632	596	36	632	......
Charleston	1191	1175	16	1191	......
Chester	350	329	21	350	......
Clifton	348	330	18	348	......
Corinna	1513	1509	4	1513	......
Corinth	1462	1455	7	1462	......
Dexter	2875	2658	217	2874	1
Dixmont	1309	1300	9	1309	......
Drew Plantation	85	80	5	85	......
Eddington	776	726	50	776	......
Edinburg	55	55	......	55	......
Enfield	545	531	14	545	......
Etna	844	842	2	844	......
Exeter	1424	1416	8	1423	1
Garland	1306	1283	23	1306	......
Glenburn	720	703	17	720	......
Greenbush	621	581	40	621	......
Greenfield	317	309	8	317	......
Hampden	3068	2894	174	3065	3
Hermon	1489	1453	36	1489	......
Holden	758	729	29	758	......
Howland	176	176	......	176	......
Hudson	739	722	17	739	......
Independence Plantation	185	66	119	185	......
Kenduskeag	770	763	7	770	......
La Grange	622	613	9	621	1
Lakeville Plantation	108	104	4	108	......
Lee	960	939	21	960	......
Levant	1159	1153	6	1159	......
Lincoln	1530	1429	101	1530	......
Lowell	448	423	25	448	......
Mattamiscontis Plantation	51	51	......	51	......
Mattawamkeag	356	294	62	356	......
Maxfield	156	156	......	156	......
Medway Plantation	321	308	13	320	1
Milford	827	702	125	826	1
Mount Chase	262	210	52	262	......
Newburg	1115	1088	27	1115	......
Newport	1559	1521	38	1559	......
Oldtown	4529	3695	834	4067	a3
Orono	2888	2321	567	2888	......
Orrington	1768	1728	40	1766	2
Passadumkeag	243	228	15	243	......
Pattagumpus Plantation	94	93	1	94	......
PENOBSCOT—Con.					
Patten	704	644	60	702	(b)
Plymouth	941	935	6	941	......
Prentiss	387	382	5	387	......
Springfield	879	847	32	879	......
Staceyville Plantation	138	125	13	138	......
Stetson	937	916	21	936	1
Veazie	810	757	53	810	......
Webster Plantation	28	24	4	28	......
West Indian Plantation	13	13	......	13	......
Whitney Ridge	18	18	......	18	......
Winn	714	480	234	710	4
Woodville Plantation	170	154	16	170	......
Township 3, R. 1	25	25	......	25	......
Township 2, R. 6	61	48	13	61	......
Township A, R. 7	19	19	......	19	......
Township 2, R. 9	14	14	......	14	......
1. Plantation	66	65	1	66	......
2. Plantation	100	98	2	100	......
PISCATAQUIS.					
Abbot	712	707	5	712	......
Atkinson	810	794	16	810	......
Barnard	149	140	9	149	......
Blanchard	164	164	......	164	......
Bowerbank Plantation	83	81	2	83	......
Brownville	860	784	76	835	25
Dover	1983	1941	42	1983	......
Elliottsville Plantation	42	40	2	42	......
Foxcroft	1178	1149	29	1178	......
Greenville	369	317	52	346	c3
Guilford	818	809	9	818	......
Katahdin Iron Works Plantation	35	33	2	35	......
Kingsbury	174	174	......	174	......
Medford	294	291	3	294	......
Milo	938	896	42	938	......
Monson	604	603	1	604	......
Orneville	575	546	29	575	......
Parkman	1105	1101	4	1105	......
Sangerville	1140	1129	11	1140	......
Sebec	954	891	63	954	......
Shirley	206	206	......	206	......
Wellington	681	680	1	681	......
Williamsburg	176	164	12	160	16
Township 4, R. 4	5	5	......	5	......
Township 8, R. 8	173	164	9	173	......
All north of Elliottsville, Greenville, and Shirley	175	133	42	174	(d)
SAGADAHOC.					
Arrowsic	252	251	1	251	1
Bath	7371	6754	617	7313	[illegible]
Bowdoin	1345	1344	1	1340	5
Bowdoinham	1804	1781	23	1803	1
Georgetown	1135	1119	16	1135	......
Perkins	71	70	1	71	......
Phipsburg	1344	1316	28	1312	[illegible]
Richmond	2442	2381	61	2440	2
Topsham	1498	1461	37	1493	5
West Bath	[illegible]	379	1	379	......
Woolwich	1168	1119	49	1161	7

(a) Also 459 Indians.
(b) Also 2 Indians.
(c) Also 20 Indians.
(d) Also 1 Indian.

E IX.—*Population of Minor Civil Divisions, &c.*—*MAINE*—Continued.

	Total.	Nativity. Native.	Nativity. Foreign.	Race. White.	Race. Colored.
.....	1745	1719	26	1743	2
.....	1540	1512	28	1540	......
.....	1	......	1	1	......
tain					
.....	8	7	1	8	......
.....	826	773	53	826	......
lan-					
.....	2	1	1	2	......
nta-					
.....	14	14	......	14	......
.....	627	624	3	627	......
.....	472	471	1	472	......
.....	1472	1447	25	1471	1
lan-					
.....	214	192	22	214	......
.....	452	438	14	452	......
.....	959	936	23	958	1
lan-					
.....	100	99	1	100	......
.....	37	31	6	37	......
.....	690	687	3	690	......
.....	803	800	3	803	......
.....	2998	2730	268	2997	1
nta-					
.....	112	111	1	112	......
tion.	159	126	33	159	......
.....	978	972	6	973	5
.....	1120	1071	49	1120	......
.....	1	1	......	1	......
wn					
.....	65	54	11	65	......
.....	397	397	......	397	......
.....	1401	1380	21	1401	......
.....	96	83	13	96	......
.....	846	843	3	846	......
lan-					
.....	104	79	25	104	......
.....	528	454	74	528	......
l.....	1454	1448	6	1454	......
.....	1756	1702	54	1753	3
vock	546	531	15	545	1
.....	1322	1309	13	1321	1
lan-					
.....	11	11	......	11	......
.....	1813	1761	52	1812	1
dge					
.....	135	134	1	135	......
.....	584	580	4	584	......
nta-					
.....	15	15	......	15	......
.....	3893	3473	420	3881	b7
.....	704	702	2	704	......
.....	1176	1108	68	1176	......
.....	1675	1663	12	1674	1
.....	1083	1080	3	1083	......
lan-					
.....	73	69	4	73	......
. 7..	6	6	......	6	......
. 2..	128	126	2	127	1
. 3..	16	6	10	16	......
.....	5278	5063	215	5270	8
.....	628	627	1	628	......
.....	868	859	9	868	......
.....	788	786	2	788	......
.....	1152	1115	37	1152	......
.....	716	714	2	716	......
.....	1230	1220	10	1230	......
.....	707	703	4	707	......
.....	889	885	4	889	......
.....	907	898	9	902	5

Counties.	Total.	Nativity. Native.	Nativity. Foreign.	Race. White.	Race. Colored.
WALDO—Cont'd.					
Lincolnville	1900	1891	9	1900	......
Monroe	1375	1362	13	1375	......
Montville	1467	1454	13	1467	......
Morrill	523	523	......	520	3
Northport	902	895	7	902	......
Palermo	1223	1217	6	1222	1
Prospect	886	870	16	880	6
Searsmont	1418	1405	13	1418	......
Searsport	2282	2204	78	2280	2
Stockton	2089	2057	32	2086	3
Swanville	770	762	8	770	......
Thorndike	730	722	8	730	......
Troy	1201	1197	4	1201	......
Unity	1201	1198	3	1200	1
Waldo	648	645	3	648	......
Winterport	2744	2615	129	2744	......
WASHINGTON.					
Addison	1201	1182	19	1201	......
Alexander	456	396	60	456	......
Baileyville	377	293	84	375	2
Baring	364	257	107	364	......
Beddington	134	134	......	134	......
Calais	5944	3558	2386	5900	44
Centerville	145	145	......	145	......
Charlotte	467	420	47	467	......
Cherryfield	1760	1622	138	1759	1
Codyville Plantation	62	57	5	62	......
Columbia	668	656	12	668	......
Columbia Falls	608	602	6	605	3
Cooper	360	322	38	360	......
Crawford	209	198	11	209	......
Cutler	925	890	35	925	......
Danforth	313	280	33	313	......
Deblois	139	137	2	139	......
Dennysville	488	467	21	487	1
Devereaux	8	8	......	8	......
Dyer	24	20	4	24	......
East Machias	2017	1830	187	2017	......
Eastport	3736	2605	1131	3702	34
Edmunds	448	413	35	448	......
Forest City Plantation	81	43	38	81	......
Harrington	1142	1118	24	1142	......
Hinkley	19	19	......	19	......
Indian	14	7	7	14	......
Jackson Brook Plantation	206	132	74	206	......
Jonesborough	522	517	5	514	8
Jonesport	1305	1288	17	1305	......
Lubec	2136	1759	377	2135	1
Machias	2525	2294	231	2508	17
Machiasport	1526	1466	60	1525	1
Marion	213	195	18	211	2
Marshfield	350	334	16	350	......
Meddybemps	200	175	25	200	......
Milbridge	1558	1533	25	1553	5
Northfield	190	186	4	190	......
Pembroke	2551	2098	453	2550	1
Perry	1149	970	179	1143	6
Princeton	1072	898	174	1061	11
Robbins' Plantation	4	......	4	4	......
Robbinston	926	716	210	916	10
Steuben	1062	1030	32	1056	6
Talmadge Plantation	80	65	15	80	......
Tapsfield	463	417	46	463	......
Trescott	603	423	180	603	......
Vanceboro Plantation	329	101	228	329	......

(a) Unincorporated.

(b) Also 5 Indians.

TABLE IX.—*Population of Minor Civil Divisions, &c.—MAINE*—Continued.

Counties.	Total.	Nativity. Native.	Nativity. Foreign.	Race. White.	Race. Colored.
WASH'GTON—Con.					
Waite Plantation	122	95	27	122	......
Wesley	336	309	27	335	1
Whiting	414	399	15	414	......
Whitneyville	569	487	82	569	......
Township 1	246	24	222	245	1
Township 7, R. 2	119	110	9	119	......
Township 9, R. 4	71	66	5	71	......
Towns'p 14, E. div.	149	132	17	149	......
Towns'p 18, E. div.	42	42	......	42	......
Towns'p 19, E. div.	20	18	2	20	......
Township 21	168	152	16	168	......
Township 26	8	8	......	8	......
YORK.					
Acton	1008	969	39	1008	......
Alfred	1224	1146	78	1222	2
Berwick	2291	2040	251	2283	8
Biddeford	10282	7540	2742	10282	......
Buxton	2546	2500	46	2546	......
YORK—Cont'd.					
Cornish	1100	1085	15	1100	......
Dayton	611	600	11	611	......
Elliot	1769	1743	26	1765	4
Hollis	1541	1524	17	1540	1
Kennebunk	2603	2481	122	2601	2
Kennebunkport	2372	2307	65	2372	......
Kittery	3333	3159	174	3309	24
Lebanon	1953	1838	115	1953	......
Limerick	1425	1413	12	1423	2
Limington	1630	1630	......	1630	......
Lyman	1052	1050	2	1050	2
Newfield	1193	1182	11	1193	......
North Berwick	1623	1599	24	1622	1
Parsonsfield	1894	1892	2	1894	......
Saco	5755	5384	371	5742	13
Sanford	2397	2224	173	2397	......
Shapleigh	1087	1067	20	1087	......
South Berwick	2510	2402	108	2498	12
Waterborough	1548	1539	9	1542	6
Wells	2773	2728	45	2773	......
York	2654	2619	35	2654	......

TABLE IX.—*Population of Minor Civil Divisions, &c.—MARYLAND.*

NOTE.—The marginal column marks election districts, whose numbers are official; the names are those in general use. The first indentation marks cities; the second, towns. Names of towns are placed under the names of the election districts in which they are respectively situated. The population of each election district includes that of all towns situated in it.

Counties.	Total.	Nativity. Native.	Nativity. Foreign.	Race. White.	Race. Colored.
ALLEGANY.					
1. Altamount	1133	1062	71	1097	36
2. Selbysport	1419	1386	33	1419	......
3. Grantsville	1786	1672	114	1784	2
4. Westernport	4687	3522	1165	4643	44
5. Frostburg	6131	4212	1919	5909	222
6. Cumberland (a)	1272	1121	151	1238	34
7. Old Town	851	818	33	806	45
8. Orleans	633	601	32	588	45
9. Flintstone	1284	1261	23	1249	35
10. Ryan Glade	851	790	61	848	3
11. Accident	1006	849	157	1005	1
12. Mount Savage	2051	1576	475	2045	6
13. Cumberland (a)	1324	1165	159	1288	36
14. Sang Run	673	663	10	670	3
15. Oakland	1396	1268	128	1365	31
16. Lonaconing	3983	2016	1967	3983	......
Cumberland	8056	6585	1471	7433	623
ANNE ARUNDELL.					
1.	4171	4134	37	1576	2595
2.	2759	2710	49	1014	1745
3.	3103	3043	60	1449	1654
4.	2799	2753	46	1867	932
5.	2218	2042	176	1328	890
ANNE ARUNDEL—Continued.					
6. Annapolis, (city)	5744	5238	506	3892	1852
8.	3663	3642	21	1609	2054
BALTIMORE.					
1.	9328	7463	1865	8005	1323
Ellicott City, part of (b)	77	74	3	76	1
2.	3127	2732	395	2736	391
3.	6149	5115	1034	5360	789
4.	3634	3427	207	2951	683
Reisterstown	479	462	17	426	53
Woodensburg	54	53	1	52	2
5.	2014	1973	41	1874	140
6.	2235	2128	107	2216	19
7.	2823	2755	68	2552	271
8.	5720	4882	838	4909	811
Luthervi'e	382	340	42	316	66
Texas	640	414	226	616	24
Warren	317	308	9	316	1
9.	10731	9194	1537	9635	1096

(a) Exclusive of part of city of Cumberland.
(b) See note (a,) Howard County. Total, 1,722: Native, 1,544; foreign, 178; white, 1,367; colored, 355.

IX.—*Population of Minor Civil Divisions, &c.—MARYLAND*—Continued.

ies.	Total.	Nativity: Native.	Nativity: Foreign.	Race: White.	Race: Colored.
—Con.					
....	2556	2360	196	2019	537
....	4231	3673	558	3575	656
....	8663	6562	2101	7340	1323
....	2176	1849	327	1849	327
more...	267354	210870	56484	227794	a39558
RT.					
....	3226	3215	11	1296	1930
....	3063	3055	8	1403	1660
Fred-cktown	64	64	......	50	14
....	3576	3570	6	1633	1943
NE.					
....	1498	1497	1	948	550
rough	2473	2459	14	1499	974
nsboro'	561	557	4	431	130
....	4097	4069	28	2850	1247
ons...	431	426	5	321	110
'......	2527	2515	12	1840	687
ourg...	1506	1486	20	1206	300
LL.					
wn....	2368	2306	62	2293	75
mpt'wn	41	41	......	33	8
eytown	413	374	39	391	22
wn....	3058	2981	77	2861	197
zleeb'g	161	161	......	160	1
Brid'e	323	319	4	317	6
ontown	319	318	1	289	30
....	1953	1902	51	1944	9
rsville.	159	159	......	159	......
's.....	2448	2305	143	2317	131
......	3008	2852	156	2477	531
ster...	3268	3093	275	3253	15
ebest'r	755	699	56	754	1
nster..	5227	4973	254	4669	558
tmin-er.....	2310	2208	102	2039	271
ead....	1742	1656	86	1714	28
pstead	235	235	......	234	1
....	2037	2007	30	1734	303
urg...	1276	1253	23	1240	36
ndsor	2134	2088	46	1842	292
Vernon	51	49	2	51	......
Wid-r......	396	374	22	363	33
—					
....	3337	3252	85	2274	1063
ton....	462	453	9	285	177
rick...	320	311	9	274	46
ke City	2683	2543	140	2084	599
apo'e-ty.....	1008	926	82	945	63
....	4170	3962	208	3627	543
m.....	1797	1725	72	1422	375
....	2219	2105	114	2102	117
t......	3645	3516	129	3327	318
est'wn	223	221	2	215	8
easant..	748	733	15	735	13
n.....	2618	2546	72	2493	125
g Sun.	277	273	4	276	1
osit...	4198	3994	204	3334	864
Deposit.	1839	1707	132	1352	487

Counties.	Total.	Nativity: Native.	Nativity: Foreign.	Race: White.	Race: Colored.
CECIL—Cont'd.					
8. Mount Pleasant.	1440	1392	48	1141	299
9. Brick Meeting-House.....	1564	1504	60	1478	86
CHARLES.					
1. Hill Top	4040	4029	11	1692	2348
2. Allen's Fresh ..	4584	4568	16	1739	2845
Port Tobacco (b).....	215	211	4	121	94
3. Duffield	3485	3456	29	1461	2024
4. Bryantown	3629	3608	21	1526	c2101
DORCHESTER.					
1. Northw't Fork.	1652	1650	2	1389	263
2. E. New Market	2347	2346	1	1139	1208
3. Vienna	1568	1568	......	874	694
4. Parson's Creek	1748	1746	2	1046	702
5. Lake	1409	1409	......	933	476
6. Hooper's Island	760	760	......	625	135
7. Cambridge	3203	3188	15	1638	1565
Cambridge.	1642	1631	11	881	761
8. Neck	1280	1280	......	949	331
9. Church Creek .	1144	1141	3	506	638
10. Strait	987	987	......	934	53
11. Drawbridge ..	1087	1085	2	512	575
12. Williamsburg .	1247	1241	6	914	333
13. Bucktown.....	885	884	1	310	575
14. Holland Island.	141	141	......	133	8
FREDERICK.					
1. Buckeystown..	2414	2397	17	1711	703
2. Frederick (d)..	3378	3266	112	2906	472
Frederick ...	8526	7884	642	6703	e1822
3. Middletown ...	2874	2851	23	2633	241
Middlet'wn	746	740	6	659	87
4. Creagerstown	2006	1992	14	1924	82
5. Emmettsburg	3168	2967	201	3030	138
Emmettsburg	706	682	24	675	31
6. Catoctin.......	1326	1313	13	1308	18
7. Urbana	2359	2316	43	1636	723
8. Liberty	3281	3221	60	2586	695
9. New Market ..	3476	3438	38	2636	840
10. Hauvers	1389	1373	16	1367	22
11. Woodsboro....	2064	2040	24	1950	114
12. Petersville	2574	2516	58	1781	793
Berlin	208	205	3	163	45
Burkittsv'e	293	288	5	272	21
Knoxville	320	306	14	254	66
Petersville.	159	147	12	87	72
13. Mount Pleasant	1565	1547	18	1176	389
14. Jefferson	1491	1477	14	1224	267
Jefferson ..	257	257	......	239	18
15. Mechanicst'wn	2340	2255	85	2276	64
Mech'nicstown	583	577	6	562	21
16. Jackson	1699	1684	15	1676	23
Myersville.	139	139	......	139	......
17. Johnsville.....	1642	1624	18	1476	166
HARFORD.					
1. Abingdon	2598	2303	295	2076	522
Abingdon ..	106	103	3	84	22
2. Hall's Cross R'ds	3805	3700	105	2671	1134
Oakington ..	158	154	4	118	40

(*a*) Also 1 Chinese and 1 Indian.
(*b*) Of Port Tobacco 204 in Allen's Fresh; 11 in Duffield.
(*c*) Also 2 Indians.
(*d*) Exclusive of city of Frederick.
(*e*) Also 1 Chinese.

TABLE IX.—*Population of Minor Civil Divisions, &c.—MARYLAND*—Continu

Counties.	Total.	Nativity. Native.	Nativity. Foreign.	Race. White.	Race. Colored.
HARFORD—Con.					
3. Belair	5650	5333	317	4406	1244
Belair	633	592	41	497	136
4. Marshall's	4409	4236	173	3639	770
5. Dublin	3862	3777	85	3118	744
Darlington	168	164	4	141	27
Dublin	123	123	......	119	4
Pylesville	38	38	......	38	......
6. Havre de Grace, (town)	2281	2050	231	1840	441
HOWARD.					
1.	1936	1718	218	1478	458
2.	3604	3211	393	2750	854
Ellicott City, part of (a)	1645	1470	175	1291	354
Elysville	302	287	15	302	......
3. Cross	1734	1590	144	1366	368
4. Lisbon	2492	2432	60	1857	635
5.	2086	1992	94	1492	594
6.	2298	2189	109	1733	565
KENT.					
1. Millington	4419	4323	96	2379	2040
Galena	307	300	7	270	37
Massey's Cross R'ds	75	75	......	72	3
Millington	420	414	6	254	166
Sassafras	281	273	8	157	124
2. Kennedyville	3247	3183	64	1685	1562
Chesterville	81	77	4	69	12
3. Worton	2454	2391	63	1248	1206
4. Chestertown	3639	3590	49	1854	1785
Chestert'wn	1871	1843	28	1063	808
5. Edesville	3343	3293	50	2204	1139
MONTGOMERY.					
1. Cracklin's	3477	3424	53	1911	1566
2. Clarksburg	3064	3006	58	2457	607
3. Medley's	3885	3808	77	2304	b1580
4. Rockville	5437	5282	155	3706	1731
Rockville	660	649	11	429	231
5. Berry's	4700	4551	149	2750	1950
PRINCE GEORGE'S.					
1. Vansville	2273	2130	143	1494	779
2. Bladensburg	3006	2870	136	1795	1211
Bladensb'g.	410	382	28	297	113
3. Marlborough	3239	3177	62	1213	2026
Marlboro'	492	473	19	255	237
4. Nottingham	2476	2456	20	1084	1392
5. Piscataway	1999	1987	12	1132	867
6. Spaulding	1687	1634	53	1229	458
7. Queen Anne	2276	2247	29	819	1457
8. Aquasco	1723	1713	10	746	977
9. Surratt	775	773	2	484	291
10. Laurel	1684	1622	62	1362	322
Laurel	1148	1110	38	1066	82
QUEEN ANNE.					
1. Dixon's Tavern	3626	3574	52	2542	1084
2. Church Hill	3655	3622	33	2347	1308
3. Centreville	5360	5339	21	2825	2535
Centreville	915	906	9	574	341
4. Kent Island	1847	1837	10	940	907
5. Queenstown	1683	1682	1	925	758

Counties.	Total.	Nativity. Native.	Nativity. Foreign.	R[ace]. White.
SAINT MARY'S.				
1. St. Inigoes	1897	1878	19	79
2. Clifton Factory	3001	2977	24	146
3. Leonardtown	2957	2945	12	162
Leonardto'n	485	476	9	27
4. Chaptico	3553	3529	24	174
5. Charlotte Hall	1601	1598	3	67
6. Patuxent	1935	1933	2	99
SOMERSET.				
1. Princess Anne	4120	4108	12	205
Princess Anne	805	803	2	43
2. Dame's Quarter	1565	1562	3	107
3. Brinkley's	2536	2524	12	137
4. Dublin	1454	1453	1	75
5. Hungary Neck	938	935	3	58
6. Potato Neck	2266	2256	10	119
7. Smith's Island	399	399	......	36
8. Lawson's	3349	3338	11	249
9. Tangier	1563	1562	1	104
TALBOT.				
1. Easton	4637	4584	53	245
Easton	2110	2088	22	119
2. St. Michael's	3448	3435	13	219
St. Michael's	1095	1091	4	89
3. Trappe	3939	3893	46	217
Oxford	227	227	......	18
Trappe	272	270	2	211
4. Chapel	2791	2743	48	172
5. Bay Hundred	1322	1313	9	92
WASHINGTON.				
1. Sharpsburg	2478	2450	19	230
Sharpsbu'g	1001	1000	1	94
2. Williamsport	3123	3026	97	2749
Williams-port	1283	1255	28	1077
3. Hagerstown	6471	6105	366	5389
Hagerstown	5779	5442	337	4910
4. Clear Spring	2763	2716	47	2495
Clear Spr'g	702	687	15	559
5. Hancock	2139	2056	83	1886
Hancock	860	817	43	73
6. Boonsboro	2579	2556	23	2465
Boonsboro	835	822	13	812
7. Cavetown	1899	1873	26	187
Cavetown	181	178	3	181
Smithburg	459	448	11	453
8. Pleasant Valley	1183	1175	8	1140
9. Leitersburg	1673	1638	35	165
Leitersbu'g	335	333	2	335
10. Funkstown	1649	1627	22	1544
Funkst'wn	671	655	16	69
11. Sandy Hook	1316	1280	36	117
12. Tilghmanton	1489	1480	9	139
13. Conococheague	1402	1387	15	138
14. Ringgold	763	746	17	76
15. Indian Spring	1565	1542	23	150
16. Beaver Creek	1366	1360	6	129
17. Antietam (c)	854	835	19	851
WICOMICO.				
1. Barren Creek	1572	1572	......	125
2. Quantico	1453	1448	5	83
3. Tyaskin	2601	2596	5	151
4. Pittsburg	2132	2132	......	193

(a) See note (b,) Baltimore County. Total, 1,722: Native, 1,544; foreign, 178; white, 1,367; color
(b) Also 1 Indian.
(c) Exclusive of city of Hagerstown.

TABLE IX.—*Population of Minor Civil Divisions, &c.—MARYLAND*—Continued.

Counties.	Total.	Nativity. Native.	Nativity. Foreign.	Race. White.	Race. Colored.	Counties.	Total.	Nativity. Native.	Nativity. Foreign.	Race. White.	Race. Colored.
WICOMICO—Con.						WORCESTER—Con.					
5. Dennis	683	683	......	617	66	Snow Hill	960	949	11	560	400
6. Parson's	1106	1106	......	877	229	3. Berlin	4330	4322	8	2666	1664
7. Trappe	1288	1286	2	894	394	Berlin	697	692	5	497	200
8. Nutter's	870	870	......	697	173	Whaleysvi'e	150	150	......	117	33
9. Salisbury	3312	3291	21	2239	1073	4. Newark	941	941	......	583	358
Salisbury	2064	2043	21	1430	634	5. St. Martin's	1133	1133	......	940	193
10. Sharptown	695	691	4	529	166	Bishopsville	35	35	......	35	......
WORCESTER.						6. Colbourne	861	861	......	694	167
						7. Atkinson	1312	1312	......	1029	283
						8. Sandy Hill	2176	2170	6	1418	758
1. Coston	2832	2828	4	1639	1193	Girdletree Hill	74	74	......	67	7
Newtown	1195	1191	4	867	328	Lindseyville	54	54	......	45	9
2. Snow Hill	2834	2823	11	1581	1253	Sandy Hill	146	145	1	129	17

TABLE IX.—*Population of Minor Civil Divisions, &c.—MASSACHUSETTS.*

NOTE.—The marginal column marks towns; the first indentation, cities.

Counties.	Total.	Nativity. Native.	Nativity. Foreign.	Race. White.	Race. Colored.	Counties.	Total.	Nativity. Native.	Nativity. Foreign.	Race. White.	Race. Colored.
BARNSTABLE.						BERKSHIRE—Con.					
Barnstable	4793	4646	147	4725	68	Otis	960	891	69	928	32
Brewster	1259	1200	59	1253	6	Peru	455	389	66	445	10
Chatham	2411	2395	16	2410	1	Pittsfield	11112	7947	3165	10800	c311
Dennis	3269	3179	90	3269	......	Richmond	1091	770	321	1089	2
Eastham	668	652	16	668	......	Sandisfield	1482	1324	158	1481	1
Falmouth	2237	2114	123	2224	a11	Savoy	861	813	48	861	......
Harwich	3080	3003	77	3074	6	Sheffield	2535	2197	338	2372	163
Mashpee	348	343	5	39	a307	Stockbridge	2003	1605	398	1932	71
Orleans	1323	1304	19	1323	......	Tyringham	557	517	40	539	18
Provincetown	3865	3076	789	3864	1	Washington	694	534	160	677	17
Sandwich	3694	3364	330	3656	38	West Stockbridge	1924	1442	482	1887	37
Truro	1269	1195	74	1269	......	Williamstown	3559	2963	596	3492	67
Wellfleet	2135	2070	65	2131	4	Windsor	686	649	37	685	1
Yarmouth	2423	2384	39	2405	18						
BERKSHIRE.						BRISTOL.					
						Acushnet	1132	1123	9	1127	5
Adams	12090	8146	3944	11957	b57	Attleborough	6769	5337	1432	6719	50
Alford	430	408	22	429	1	Berkley	744	731	13	742	2
Becket	1346	1104	242	1337	9	Dartmouth	3367	3251	116	3280	d81
Cheshire	1758	1376	382	1751	7	Dighton	1817	1663	154	1799	18
Clarksburg	686	565	121	686	......	Easton	3668	2913	755	3656	12
Dalton	1252	957	295	1231	21	Fairhaven	2626	2565	61	2609	17
Egremont	931	878	53	920	11	Fall River	26766	15288	11478	26635	e106
Florida	1322	686	636	1322	......	Freetown	1372	1346	26	1360	12
Great Barrington	4320	3489	831	4226	c93	Mansfield	2432	2165	267	2422	10
Hancock	882	731	151	861	21	New Bedford	21320	17645	3675	19806	f1505
Hinsdale	1695	1121	574	1653	42	Norton	1821	1671	150	1810	11
Lanesborough	1393	1087	306	1333	60	Raynham	1713	1599	114	1689	24
Lee	3866	3007	859	3736	130	Rehoboth	1895	1830	65	1881	c13
Lenox	1965	1507	458	1861	104	Seekonk	1021	965	56	1004	17
Monterey	653	602	51	628	25	Somerset	1776	1559	217	1759	17
Mount Washing'n	256	242	14	255	1	Swanzey	1294	1214	80	1277	17
New Ashford	208	175	33	208	......	Taunton	18629	14024	4605	18508	121
New Marlborough	1855	1570	285	1845	10	Westport	2724	2685	39	2694	c29

(a) Also 2 Indians.
(b) Also 75 Chinese and 1 Indian.
(c) Also 1 Indian.
(d) Also 5 Indians and 1 Chinese.
(e) Also 25 Indians.
(f) Also 9 Indians.

TABLE IX.—*Population of Minor Civil Divisions, &c.—MASSACHUSETTS*—Continued.

Counties.	Total.	Nativity. Native.	Nativity. Foreign.	Race. White.	Race. Colored.
DUKES.					
Chilmark	476	467	9	474	2
Edgartown	1516	1472	44	1464	52
Gay Head	160	159	1	9	151
Gosnold	99	88	11	99	.....
Tisbury	1536	1496	40	1495	41
ESSEX.					
Amesbury	5581	4058	1523	5570	11
Andover	4873	3684	1189	4843	30
Beverly	6507	5826	681	6500	a6
Boxford	847	791	56	845	2
Bradford	2014	1813	201	1985	29
Danvers	5600	4633	967	5582	18
Essex	1614	1513	101	1594	20
Georgetown	2088	1896	192	2088	.....
Gloucester	15389	11382	4007	15378	11
Groveland	1776	1521	255	1776	.....
Hamilton	790	721	69	786	4
Haverhill	13092	11089	2003	13071	21
Ipswich	3720	3292	428	3713	b6
Lawrence	28921	16204	12717	28814	b106
Lynn	28233	23298	4935	27862	371
Lynnfield	818	750	68	817	1
Manchester	1665	1475	190	1665	.....
Marblehead	7703	6803	900	7692	11
Methuen	2959	2455	504	2952	7
Middleton	1010	933	77	1010	.....
Nahant	475	359	116	466	9
Newbury	1430	1340	90	1424	6
Newburyport	12595	10666	1929	12514	81
North Andover	2549	1839	710	2547	2
Peabody	7343	5693	1650	7327	16
Rockport	3904	3334	570	3902	2
Rowley	1157	1119	38	1157	.....
Salem	24117	18033	6084	23874	c243
Salisbury	3776	3341	435	3775	1
Saugus	2247	1869	378	2246	1
Swampscott	1846	1574	272	1838	8
Topsfield	1213	1146	67	1212	1
Wenham	985	925	60	982	3
West Newbury	2006	1690	316	1995	11
FRANKLIN.					
Ashfield	1180	1149	31	1177	a2
Bernardston	961	942	19	961	.....
Buckland	1946	1430	516	1946	.....
Charlemont	1005	971	34	994	11
Colrain	1742	1610	132	1741	1
Conway	1460	1304	156	1458	2
Deerfield	3632	2752	880	3592	40
Erving	579	531	48	579	.....
Gill	653	636	17	653	.....
Greenfield	3589	2947	642	3566	23
Hawley	672	659	13	671	1
Heath	613	598	15	612	1
Leverett	877	859	18	877	.....
Leyden	518	474	44	518	.....
Monroe	201	196	5	201	.....
Montague	2224	1786	438	2221	3
New Salem	987	984	3	987	.....
Northfield	1720	1611	109	1718	2
Orange	2091	2004	87	2091	.....
Rowe	581	564	17	581	.....
Shelburne	1582	1480	102	1578	4
Shutesbury	614	610	4	613	1
Sunderland	832	782	50	832	.....
Warwick	769	745	24	769	.....
Wendell	539	510	29	539	.....
Whately	1068	907	161	1068	.....

Counties.	Total.	Nativity. Native.	Nativity. Foreign.	Race. White.	Race. Colored.
HAMPDEN.					
Agawam	2001	1411	590	1983	[illegible]
Blandford	1026	995	31	1015	11
Brimfield	1288	1162	126	1285	3
Chester	1253	1111	142	1249	4
Chicopee	9607	6103	3504	9601	6
Granville	1293	1188	105	1196	d6
Holland	344	338	6	344	.....
Holyoke	10733	5243	5490	10715	18
Longmeadow	1342	1174	168	1338	4
Ludlow	1136	1002	134	1109	27
Monson	3204	2783	421	3145	59
Montgomery	318	301	17	311	7
Palmer	3631	2578	1053	3612	d15
Russell	635	542	93	622	13
Southwick	1100	1031	69	1098	2
Springfield	26703	19773	6930	26136	567
Tolland	509	458	51	507	2
Wales	831	754	77	831	.....
Westfield	6519	5542	977	6481	38
West Springfield	2606	1999	607	2600	6
Wilbraham	2330	2128	202	2319	11
HAMPSHIRE.					
Amherst	4035	3701	334	3947	d87
Belchertown	2428	2231	197	2411	17
Chesterfield	811	776	35	811	.....
Cummington	1037	963	74	1031	6
Easthampton	3620	2536	1084	3619	1
Enfield	1023	888	135	1019	4
Goshen	368	358	10	368	.....
Granby	863	793	70	861	2
Greenwich	665	656	9	664	1
Hadley	2301	1809	492	2275	26
Hatfield	1594	1183	411	1576	18
Huntington	1156	997	159	1153	3
Middlefield	728	573	155	722	6
Northampton	10160	7441	2719	10002	158
Pelham	673	663	10	672	1
Plainfield	521	518	3	520	1
Prescott	541	532	9	541	.....
South Hadley	2840	2113	727	2832	8
Southampton	1159	1023	136	1159	.....
Ware	4259	2727	1532	4251	8
Westhampton	587	539	48	586	1
Williamsburg	2159	1711	448	2150	9
Worthington	860	833	27	854	6
MIDDLESEX.					
Acton	1593	1449	144	1590	3
Arlington	3261	2309	952	3228	33
Ashby	994	956	38	994	.....
Ashland	2186	1839	347	2185	1
Bedford	849	757	92	846	3
Belmont	1513	1043	470	1505	8
Billerica	1833	1478	355	1829	4
Boxborough	338	313	25	325	13
Brighton	4967	3361	1006	4903	64
Burlington	626	502	124	625	1
Cambridge	39634	27579	12055	38785	[illegible]
Carlisle	569	532	37	569	.....
Charlestown	28323	21399	6924	28196	[illegible]
Chelmsford	2374	1968	406	2372	[illegible]
Concord	2412	1912	500	2392	[illegible]
Dracut	2078	1666	412	2064	[illegible]
Dunstable	471	452	19	471	.....
Everett	2220	1826	394	2203	
Framingham	4968	3898	1070	4956	
Groton	3584	3059	525	3546	
Holliston	3073	2577	496	3071	

(a) Also 1 Indian.
(b) Also 1 Chinese.
(c) Also 1 Indian and 1 Chinese.
(d) Also 4 Indians.
(e) Also 1 Japanese.

X.—*Population of Minor Civil Divisions, &c.*—*MASSACHUSETTS*—Continued.

ies.	Total.	Nativity.		Race.	
		Native.	Foreign.	White.	Colored.
:—Con.					
....	4419	3260	1159	4416	3
....	3389	2637	752	3385	4
....	2277	1778	499	2265	12
....	791	657	134	783	8
....	983	839	144	972	11
....	40928	26493	14435	40815	a111
....	7367	5653	1714	7333	b31
gh	8474	5908	2566	8463	11
....	5717	4402	1315	5694	23
....	3414	2858	556	3405	9
....	6404	5000	1404	6372	e31
....	12825	9469	3356	12735	a88
ling ...	942	893	49	937	5
....	1842	1686	156	1839	3
....	2664	2442	222	2661	3
....	1062	960	102	1054	8
....	1451	1162	289	1450	1
....	14685	10553	4132	14658	b26
....	4513	3722	791	4483	30
....	1813	1416	397	1811	2
....	2091	1558	533	2086	5
....	1944	1260	684	1913	e30
....	1962	1845	117	1947	15
agh ...	629	570	59	623	6
....	4135	3347	788	4127	8
....	9065	6460	2605	9056	9
....	4336	3093	1243	4311	15
....	1240	1092	148	1233	b6
....	1803	1497	306	1797	6
....	1261	1078	183	1261	......
n	866	773	93	860	6
r	2645	1991	654	2635	10
....	8560	6124	2436	8557	3
KET.					
....	4123	3920	203	4038	d80
LK.					
....	1282	1133	149	1282	......
....	3948	3127	821	3942	6
....	6650	4357	2293	6626	b23
....	3879	2829	1050	3848	e14
....	2130	1851	279	2130	......
....	7342	5432	1910	7295	f44
....	645	515	130	645	......
h	3057	2784	273	3046	11
....	2512	2155	357	2502	10
....	4136	2909	1227	4120	16
....	1142	1013	129	1139	3
....	3721	3134	587	3713	8
....	2683	1991	692	2654	b28
....	3607	2648	959	3593	14
....	1081	868	213	1074	7
....	7442	5648	1794	7427	15
....	5642	4643	999	5627	15
....	1508	1324	184	1507	1
....	4914	4121	793	4893	21
....	2137	1767	370	2136	1
ury ...	8683	6021	2662	8625	58
....	9010	7719	1291	8979	31
....	2292	2044	248	2265	27
TH.					
....	9308	7962	1346	9265	c42
er	3660	2961	699	3611	49

2 Indians.
1 Chinese.
1 Indian.
5 Indians.
17 Indians.
3 Indians.

Counties.	Total.	Nativity.		Race.	
		Native.	Foreign.	White.	Colored.
PLYMOUTH—Cont'd.					
Carver	1092	1042	50	1087	5
Duxbury	2341	2278	63	2336	5
East Bridgewater.	3017	2725	292	3010	7
Halifax	619	611	8	619	......
Hanover	1628	1548	80	1615	13
Hanson	1219	1178	41	1219	......
Hingham	4422	3803	619	4379	43
Hull	261	232	29	261	......
Kingston	1604	1467	137	1603	1
Lakeville	1159	1109	50	1148	11
Marion	896	873	23	896	......
Marshfield	1659	1617	42	1654	5
Mattapoisett	1361	1346	15	1346	15
Middleborough ...	4687	4400	287	4669	18
North Bridgewat'r	8007	6701	1306	7966	41
Pembroke	1447	1398	49	1433	14
Plymouth	6238	5699	539	6096	g119
Plympton	804	794	10	804	......
Rochester	1024	1013	11	1019	5
Scituate	2350	2109	241	2350	......
South Scituate....	1661	1610	51	1582	79
Wareham	3098	2649	449	3078	20
West Bridgewater	1803	1555	248	1789	c14
SUFFOLK.					
Boston	250526	162540	87986	247013	h3496
Chelsea	18547	14595	3952	18307	i238
North Chelsea....	1197	924	273	1196	1
Winthrop	532	455	77	532	......
WORCESTER.					
Ashburnham	2172	1888	284	2165	7
Athol	3517	3244	273	3513	4
Auburn	1178	887	291	1173	5
Barre	2572	2289	283	2562	10
Berlin	1016	965	51	1009	7
Blackstone	5421	3372	2049	5416	5
Bolton	1014	943	71	1009	5
Boylston	800	697	103	783	17
Brookfield	2527	2145	382	2513	14
Charlton	1878	1761	117	1872	6
Clinton	5429	3340	2089	5427	2
Dana	758	749	9	757	1
Douglas	2182	1722	460	2174	8
Dudley	2388	1445	943	2365	23
Fitchburg	11260	8743	2517	11214	j42
Gardner	3333	2783	550	3275	58
Grafton	4594	3367	1227	4570	24
Hardwick	2219	1555	664	2213	6
Harvard	1341	1229	112	1330	11
Holden	2062	1641	421	2054	(k)
Hubbardston	1654	1540	114	1632	22
Lancaster	1845	1546	299	1816	29
Leicester	2768	1950	818	2768	......
Leominster...........	3894	3505	389	3894	......
Lunenburg	1121	1086	35	1121	......
Mendon	1175	1065	110	1129	j42
Milford	9890	7313	2577	9850	40
Millbury	4397	2679	1718	4388	9
New Braintree ...	640	542	98	640	......
Northborough	1504	1357	147	1504	......
Northbridge.......	3774	2457	1317	3767	c6
North Brookfield.	3343	2555	788	3338	5
Oakham	860	803	57	860	......
Oxford	2669	2224	445	2631	38
Paxton	646	582	64	643	3

(g) Also 22 Indians and 1 Chinese.
(h) Also 12 Indians and 5 Japanese.
(i) Also 2 Chinese.
(j) Also 4 Indians.
(k) Also 8 Indians.

TABLE IX.—*Population of Minor Civil Divisions, &c.—MASSACHUSETTS*—Continued.

Counties.	Total.	Nativity. Native.	Nativity. Foreign.	Race. White.	Race. Colored.	Counties.	Total.	Nativity. Native.	Nativity. Foreign.	Race. White.	Race. Colored.
WORCESTER—Con.						WORCESTER—Con.					
Petersham	1335	1268	67	1323	12	Templeton	2802	2334	468	2797	5
Phillipston	693	661	32	693	......	Upton	1989	1750	239	1986	3
Princeton	1279	1120	159	1277	2	Uxbridge	3058	2322	736	3042	16
Royalston	1354	1262	92	1353	1	Warren	2625	2019	606	2607	18
Rutland	1024	928	96	1024	......	Webster	4763	2694	2069	4751	12
Shrewsbury	1610	1408	202	1609	1	Westborough	3601	2942	659	3578	23
Southborough	2135	1707	428	2134	1	West Boylston	2862	1935	927	2855	7
Southbridge	5208	2921	2287	5200	a3	West Brookfield	1842	1584	258	1833	9
Spencer	3952	2747	1205	3950	2	Westminster	1770	1625	145	1765	5
Sterling	1670	1551	119	1648	22	Winchenden	3398	2849	549	3393	5
Sturbridge	2101	1644	457	2076	25	Worcester	41105	29159	11946	40388	c713
Sutton	2699	1966	733	2693	6						

(*a*) Also 5 Indians.
(*b*) Also 4 Indians.
(*c*) Also 4 Japanese.

TABLE IX.—*Population of Minor Civil Divisions, &c.—MICHIGAN.*

NOTE.—The marginal column marks townships; the first indentation, cities; the second, towns. Names of towns are placed under the names of the townships in which they are respectively situated. The population of each township includes that of all towns situated in it.

Counties.	Total.	Nativity. Native.	Nativity. Foreign.	Race. White.	Race. Colored.	Counties.	Total.	Nativity. Native.	Nativity. Foreign.	Race. White.	Race. Colored.
ALCONA.						ALLEGAN—Cont'd.					
Alcona	146	78	68	146	......	Saugatuck	1026	747	279	1026	......
Greenbush	86	21	65	86	......	Trowbridge	1337	1174	163	1306	31
Harrisville	464	283	181	464	......	Watson	1220	1004	216	1220	......
ALLEGAN.						Wayland	1963	1824	139	1890	d8
Allegan	3642	3090	552	3600	42	Wayland	585	553	32	582	3
Allegan	2374	2000	374	2342	32	ALPENA.					
Casco	1264	1170	94	1263	1	Alpena	2612	1209	1403	2612	......
Cheshire	1443	1373	70	1229	a211	Ossineke	144	57	87	142	2
Clyde	298	283	15	274	24	ANTRIM.					
Dorr	1518	1182	336	1518	......	Banks	504	347	157	504	......
Fillmore	1436	723	713	1436	......	Elk Rapids	370	214	156	369	1
Ganges	1255	1086	169	1255	......	Helena	483	325	158	483	......
Gunplain	2238	1918	320	2235	3	Milton	359	217	142	295	(e)
Plainwell	1035	927	108	1032	3	Torch Lake	269	185	84	269	......
Heath	1000	903	97	1000	......	BARRY.					
Hopkins	1271	1123	148	1271	......	Assyria	1175	1063	112	1175	......
Laketown	660	409	251	660	......	Baltimore	1155	1060	95	1144	11
Lee	249	219	30	232	b8	Barry	1297	1153	144	1259	38
Leighton	1206	978	228	1.05	1	Carlton	1125	1078	47	1125	......
Manlius	541	455	86	541	......	Castleton	1738	1596	142	1738	......
Martin	963	869	94	963	......	Nashville	642	602	40	642	......
Monterey	1284	1161	123	1283	1	Hastings	2919	2641	278	2918	1
Otsego	2396	2142	254	2381	15	Hastings	1793	1605	188	1792	1
Otsego	994	910	84	989	5	Hope	1143	1026	117	1135	8
Overisel	1060	513	547	1060	......						
Pine Plains	180	164	16	180	......						
Salem	1143	893	250	1143	......						
Saugatuck	2538	1863	675	2523	(c)						

(*a*) Also 3 Indians.
(*b*) Also 9 Indians.
(*c*) Also 15 Indians.
(*d*) Also 65 Indians.
(*e*) Also 64 Indians.

ABLE IX.—*Population of Minor Civil Divisions, &c.*—*MICHIGAN*—Continued.

ounties.	Total.	Nativity. Native.	Nativity. Foreign.	Race. White.	Race. Colored.
Y—Cent'd.					
	1248	1112	136	1248	......
own	1296	1144	152	1296	......
Grove	1328	1210	118	1301	27
ville	1145	1019	126	1144	1
ville	1280	1154	126	1280	......
d	1156	1061	95	1156	......
apple	1795	1509	286	1793	2
ddleville	541	482	59	541	......
and	1376	1203	173	1376	......
e Springs	1023	953	70	1022	1
BAY.					
s	459	295	164	459	......
es	255	105	150	255	......
r	3606	1913	1693	3585	a16
City	7064	3789	3275	6981	83
	141	84	57	141	......
on	946	522	424	938	8
wlin	756	434	322	671	b7
r	568	359	209	568	......
outh	1660	1088	572	1658	2
rtsmouth	1243	822	421	1241	2
ms	445	279	166	445	......
ENZIE.					
a	393	371	22	393	......
nia	214	194	20	213	1
	71	60	11	71	......
d Lake	585	433	152	585	......
re	169	138	31	167	2
tead	163	136	27	151	12
	204	191	13	204	......
d	130	119	11	121	9
	181	140	41	181	......
n	74	60	14	69	5
RRIEN.					
idge	1337	1111	226	1337	......
	3116	2689	427	3095	21
nton Harbor	661	563	98	656	5
n	1405	1332	73	1361	c43
nd	1522	1386	136	1517	5
nan	2857	2617	240	2840	17
chanan	1702	1580	122	1688	14
ming	992	803	189	989	3
	856	761	95	856	......
	834	761	73	833	1
	1002	881	121	980	22
n	1188	1019	169	1182	6
uffalo	1289	828	461	1264	25
w Buffalo	683	418	265	670	13
d)	1909	1713	196	1881	28
s	4630	3656	974	4463	167
ko	1615	1539	76	1609	6
rrien Spr'gs	662	638	24	656	6
ene	1379	1248	131	1312	67
ton	1040	902	138	1040	......
	906	842	64	885	21
eph	2994	2256	738	2848	146
Oaks	1316	1052	264	1304	12
hree Oaks	499	444	55	487	12
nliet	1674	1505	169	1668	6
aw	1243	1146	97	1243	......

Also 5 Indians.
Also 78 Indian.
Also 1 Indian.
Exclusive of city of Niles.
Exclusive of city of Coldwater.

Counties.	Total.	Nativity. Native.	Nativity. Foreign.	Race. White.	Race. Colored.
BRANCH.					
Alganse	1421	1349	72	1421	......
Batavia	1308	1257	51	1308	......
Bethel	1511	1439	72	1506	5
Bronson	2100	1862	238	2100	......
Butler	1430	1345	85	1430	......
California	803	742	61	802	1
Coldwater (e)	1525	1399	126	1521	4
Coldwater	4381	3868	513	4352	29
Gilead	794	780	14	794	......
Girard	1230	1165	65	1229	1
Kinderhook	637	617	20	637	......
Matteson	1305	1261	44	1305	......
Noble	756	709	47	755	1
Ovid	1230	1156	74	1230	......
Quincy	2586	2492	94	2582	4
Quincy	1092	1059	33	1089	8
Sherwood	1088	1049	39	1087	1
Union	2121	2028	93	2114	7
CALHOUN.					
Albion	2409	2130	279	2378	f27
Athens	1294	1236	58	1243	(g)
Battle Creek (h)	1188	1046	142	1163	25
Battle Creek	5838	5140	698	5523	315
Bedford	1466	1282	184	1450	16
Burlington	1485	1412	73	1485	......
Clarence	1075	1003	72	1075	......
Clarendon	1150	1073	77	1150	......
Convis	1015	923	92	1014	1
Eckford	1011	937	74	1009	2
Emmett	1309	1168	141	1301	8
Fredonia	1031	894	137	1023	8
Homer	1575	1397	178	1573	2
Homer	685	641	44	685	......
Lee	1123	1033	90	1105	18
Leroy	1303	1230	73	1302	1
Marengo	1329	1217	112	1327	2
Marshall (i)	984	850	134	982	2
Marshall	4925	3862	1063	4816	109
Newton	975	841	134	975	......
Pennfield	1132	993	139	1121	11
Sheridan	1619	1444	175	1607	12
Tekonsha	1333	1255	78	1332	1
CASS.					
Calvin	1788	1750	38	694	1094
Howard	1171	1038	133	1163	8
Jefferson	1047	1001	46	1046	1
La Grange	1884	1748	136	1824	60
Cassopolis	728	708	20	678	50
Marcellus	1255	1172	84	1251	4
Mason	809	788	21	809	......
Milton	594	547	47	594	......
Newburg	1314	1176	138	1260	54
Ontwa	995	956	39	995	......
Adamsville	104	95	9	104	......
Edwardsburg	297	290	7	297	......
Penn	1421	1338	83	1326	95
Pokagon	1386	1299	87	1357	29
Pokagon	228	211	17	228	......
Summerville	184	172	12	168	16
Porter	1933	1859	74	1697	236
Silver Creek	3084	2787	297	2968	j63
Dowagiac	1932	1771	161	1873	a54
Volinia	1414	1332	82	1369	45
Wayne	999	886	113	998	1

(f) Also 4 Indians.
(g) Also 51 Indians.
(h) Exclusive of city of Battle Creek.
(i) Exclusive of city of Marshall.
(j) Also 53 Indians.

TABLE IX.—*Population of Minor Civil Divisions, &c.*—MICHIGAN—Continued.

Counties.	Total.	Nativity. Native.	Nativity. Foreign.	Race. White.	Race. Colored.
CHARLEVOIX.					
Charlevoix	456	390	66	235	a8
Evangeline	90	64	26	90	.....
Eveline	294	192	102	294	.....
Marion	302	196	106	302	.....
Norwood	182	134	48	182	.....
South Ann	400	212	188	399	1
CHEBOYGAN.					
Burt	72	65	7	7	(b)
Duncan	831	437	394	783	c2
Inverness	1293	743	550	1235	d6
CHIPPEWA.					
Sault Ste. Marie	1213	932	281	610	e3
Sugar Island	238	126	112	162	(f)
Warner	238	139	99	178	g2
CLARK.					
Big Rapids	132	76	56	132	.....
Grant	147	97	50	147	.....
Sheridan	87	80	7	87	.....
CLINTON.					
Bath	1125	1037	88	1125	.....
Bengal	1086	943	143	1086	.....
Bingham	2910	2512	398	2894	16
Dallas	1360	1035	325	1360	.....
De Witt	1306	1147	159	1306	.....
Duplain	1493	1301	192	1493	.....
Eagle	1008	947	61	1008	.....
Essex	1501	1420	81	1500	1
Greenbush	1486	1403	83	1481	h4
Lebanon	1119	1035	84	1119	.....
Olive	1156	1057	99	1156	.....
Ovid	2420	2188	232	2400	20
Riley	1139	1032	107	1120	19
Victor	940	847	93	940	.....
Watertown	1297	1175	122	1297	.....
Westphalia	1499	1017	482	1499	.....
DELTA.					
Centreville	86	43	43	86	.....
Delton	833	406	427	828	(i)
Escanaba	1370	774	596	1356	j4
Masonville	152	62	90	152	.....
St. Martin's Island	101	78	23	101	.....
EATON.					
Bellevue	1985	1843	142	1971	14
Bellevue	608	568	40	599	9
Benton	1355	1262	93	1355	.....
Brookfield	1057	1006	51	1057	.....
Carmel (k)	2504	2350	154	2479	25
Charlotte (k)	2253	2068	185	2227	26
Chester	1117	1056	61	1117	.....
Delta	1154	1032	122	1153	1
Eaton (k)	2035	1926	109	2034	1
Eaton Rapids	3636	3490	146	3617	19
EATON—Cont'd.					
Eaton Rapids	1221	1149	72	1203	18
Kalamo	1363	1282	81	1362	1
Oneida	2047	1907	140	2042	5
Roxand	1144	1055	89	1144	.....
Sunfield	1106	1015	91	1106	.....
Vermontville	1801	1685	116	1796	5
Vermontville	544	499	45	539	5
Walton	1645	1546	99	1638	7
Olivet	526	475	51	520	6
Windsor	1222	1167	55	1222	.....
EMMIT.					
Bear Creek	254	250	4	25	[illegible]
La Croix	663	624	39	64	[illegible]
Little Traverse	294	286	8	27	[illegible]
GENESEE.					
Argentine	1061	973	88	1060	1
Atlas	1501	1378	123	1501	.....
Burton (o)	1667	1356	311	1661	6
Clayton	1047	898	149	1047	.....
Davison	1124	943	181	1124	.....
Fenton	3965	3554	411	3950	15
Fenton	2353	2085	268	2338	15
Linden	565	523	42	565	.....
Flint (o)	2142	1656	486	2142	.....
Flint	5386	4194	1192	5334	52
Flushing	1919	1616	303	1913	6
Flushing	687	593	94	684	3
Forest	1564	1179	385	1564	.....
Gaines	1316	1131	185	1299	(p)
Genesee	1666	1492	174	1659	7
Grand Blanc	1367	1226	141	1366	1
Montrose	805	686	119	796	9
Mount Morris	1402	1087	315	1402	.....
Mundy	1371	1285	86	1370	1
Richfield	1421	1229	192	1421	.....
Thetford	1260	1058	202	1257	3
Vienna	1916	1577	339	1913	3
GRAND TRAVERSE.					
Blair	383	297	86	383	.....
East Bay	466	338	128	466	.....
Grant	293	202	91	293	.....
Long Lake	333	277	56	333	.....
Mayfield	250	205	45	250	.....
Paradise	266	203	63	266	.....
Peninsula	667	480	187	664	3
Traverse	1275	900	375	1262	[illegible]
Whitewater	510	397	113	510	.....
GRATIOT.					
Arcada	1202	1059	143	1194	8
Alma	402	346	56	402	.....
Bethany	1462	1310	152	1455	q1
St. Louis	888	804	84	887	1
Elba	323	300	23	323	.....
Emerson	590	499	91	590	.....
Fulton	1170	1108	62	1160	10
Hamilton	294	277	17	294	.....
La Fayette	288	258	30	288	.....

(a) Also 213 Indians.
(b) Also 65 Indians.
(c) Also 46 Indians.
(d) Also 52 Indians.
(e) Also 600 Indians.
(f) Also 76 Indians.
(g) Also 58 Indians.
(h) Also 1 Indian.
(i) Also 5 Indians.
(j) Also 10 Indians.
(k) Of Charlotte, 1,356 in Carmel; 897 in Eaton.
(l) Also 234 Indians.
(m) Also 599 Indians.
(n) Also 267 Indians.
(o) Exclusive of part of city of Flint.
(p) Also 17 Indians.
(q) Also 6 Indians.

e IX.—*Population of Minor Civil Divisions, &c.—MICHIGAN*—Continued.

ies.	Total.	Nativity: Native.	Nativity: Foreign.	Race: White.	Race: Colored.
Cont'd.					
....	1006	925	81	1001	5
1	586	522	64	586	......
ie.......	890	738	152	888	2
....	846	795	51	846	......
....	981	879	102	981	......
....	575	521	54	575	......
....	815	708	107	809	6
a	551	508	43	551	......
....	231	206	25	231	......
LE.					
....	1797	1660	137	1789	8
....	1759	1536	223	1756	3
....	1160	1111	49	1160	......
....	1683	1559	124	1670	13
....	1883	1812	71	1883	......
....	2172	1932	240	2163	9
t).......	562	534	28	562	......
....	3518	3057	461	3497	21
....	1973	1865	108	1973	......
....	1946	1819	127	1945	1
....	1223	1148	75	1223	......
....	1675	1583	92	1675	......
....	1624	1582	42	1624	......
....	1657	1573	84	1657	......
....	1107	1033	74	1100	7
....	1297	1218	79	1297	......
....	1513	1457	56	1513	......
e.......	1321	1277	44	1314	7
....	1814	1732	82	1814	......
ON.					
....	670	253	417	670	......
....	160	100	60	155	(b)
....	3182	1131	2051	3175	b2
....	2163	1052	1111	2145	(c)
....	2700	1113	1587	2693	d6
....	769	373	396	769	......
....	33	23	10	33	......
....	1540	841	699	1520	f12
....	1117	432	685	1117	......
....	669	225	444	629	g4
....	876	467	409	872	4
N.					
....	441	170	271	441	......
....	116	59	57	116	......
....	382	209	173	382	......
....	91	40	51	91	......
....	335	154	181	335	......
1.......	528	270	258	512	h1
....	173	89	84	173	......
....	309	172	137	309	......
....	475	209	266	475	......
....	403	174	229	403	......
....	325	156	169	325	......
....	213	78	135	213	......
....	891	362	529	891	......
a	778	346	432	777	1
....	746	346	400	746	......
1	666	345	321	665	1
....	158	37	121	150	(f)
....	385	173	212	385	......
....	907	526	381	907	......
....	181	91	90	147	(i)
....	276	104	172	276	......
k.......	270	153	117	270	......

Counties.	Total.	Nativity: Native.	Nativity: Foreign.	Race: White.	Race: Colored.
INGHAM.					
Alaiedon	1296	1204	92	1294	2
Aurelius	1506	1396	110	1501	5
Bunker Hill	957	855	102	957	......
Delhi	1259	1065	194	1259	......
Ingham	1392	1268	124	1383	9
Dansville	443	419	24	442	1
Lansing (j)	823	714	109	823	......
Lansing	5241	4403	838	5163	k77
Leroy	859	834	25	859	......
Leslie	1996	1844	152	1958	38
Locke	1115	1011	104	1115	......
Meridian	1374	1238	136	1374	......
Onondaga	1229	1140	89	1228	1
Stockbridge	892	834	58	892	......
Vevay	2332	2163	169	2307	25
Mason	1212	1123	89	1207	5
Wheatfield	781	687	94	781	......
White Oak	979	914	65	978	1
Williamstown	1237	1098	139	1237	......
IONIA.					
Berlin	1587	1373	214	1587	......
Boston	1947	1697	250	1943	4
Saranac	724	641	83	720	4
Campbell	1120	915	205	1120	......
Danby	1176	1117	59	1176	......
Easton	1401	1208	193	1401	......
Ionia	4158	3434	724	4129	29
Ionia	2500	1991	509	2487	13
Keene	1271	983	288	1271	......
Lyons	2855	2531	324	2854	1
Lyons	704	623	81	703	1
North Plains	1976	1654	322	1968	8
Hubbardston	531	456	75	527	4
Odessa	959	884	75	959	......
Orange	1382	1194	188	1382	......
Orleans	1426	1267	159	1419	7
Otisco	1578	1381	197	1578	......
Portland	2353	2130	223	2349	4
Portland	1060	988	72	1056	4
Ronald	1353	1214	139	1352	1
Sebewa	1139	1045	94	1139	......
IOSCO.					
Alabaster	235	137	98	235	......
Grant	107	80	27	107	......
Oscoda	476	165	311	476	......
Plainfield	122	106	16	122	......
Sable	842	445	397	833	b4
Tawas	1381	805	576	1376	5
ISABELLA.					
Broomfield	118	73	45	118	......
Chippewa	315	283	32	315	......
Coe	987	930	57	981	6
Coldwater	151	137	14	151	......
Fremont	342	295	47	342	......
Gillmore	88	75	13	88	......
Isabella	56	49	7	56	......
Lincoln	672	588	84	672	......
Rolland	210	198	12	198	12
Sherman	134	104	30	134	......
Union	657	566	91	657	......
Vernon	383	242	141	383	......

lusive of city of Hillsdale.
5 Indians.
18 Indians.
1 Indian.
870 the population of Portage Township
d Houghton Village returned as identical.

(f) Also 8 Indians.
(g) Also 36 Indians.
(h) Also 15 Indians.
(i) Also 34 Indians.
(j) Exclusive of city of Lansing.
(k) Also 1 Chinese.

TABLE IX.—*Population of Minor Civil Divisions, &c.*—*MICHIGAN*—*Continued.*

Counties.	Total.	Nativity. Native.	Nativity. Foreign.	Race. White.	Race. Colored.
JACKSON.					
Blackman	1470	1175	295	1459	a10
Brooklyn	1691	1504	187	1678	13
Brooklyn	544	476	68	543	1
Columbia	1002	955	47	1001	1
Concord	1465	1259	206	1465	......
Grass Lake	2042	1806	236	2038	4
Hanover	1093	993	100	1093	......
Henrietta	976	893	83	976	......
Jackson (b)	11447	8999	2448	11085	c359
Leoni	1376	1283	93	1369	7
Liberty	1070	1019	51	1070	......
Napoleon	1030	981	49	1029	1
Parma	1514	1401	113	1508	6
Pulaski	1165	1060	105	1164	1
Rives	1345	1167	178	1342	3
Sandstone	1598	1428	170	1591	7
Spring Arbor	1117	1023	94	1114	3
Springport	1292	1222	70	1291	1
Summit	863	759	104	856	7
Tompkins	1262	1124	138	1262	......
Waterloo	1229	1001	228	1229	......
KALAMAZOO.					
Alamo	1148	1051	97	1148	......
Augusta	608	570	38	606	2
Brady	1382	1268	114	1342	40
Charleston	1369	1269	100	1363	6
Galesburg	140	131	9	140	......
Cooper	1254	1090	164	1254	......
Climax	1389	1278	111	1389	......
Comstock	2018	1839	179	2009	9
Kalamazoo	10447	7871	2576	10085	a361
Kalamazoo	9181	6845	2336	8848	a332
Oshtemo	1594	1394	200	1558	36
Pavilion	1208	1062	146	1204	4
Portage	1050	956	94	1035	15
Prairie Ronde	1163	1081	82	1162	1
Richland	1381	1190	191	1374	7
Ross	1397	1279	118	1372	25
Schoolcraft	2136	1961	175	2122	14
Schoolcraft	932	832	100	932	......
Texas	1109	955	154	1107	2
Wakeshma	1401	1292	109	1398	3
KALCASKA.					
Rapid River	424	237	187	423	(a)
KENT.					
Ada	1427	1080	347	1418	(d)
Algoma	1959	1770	189	1952	7
Rockford	582	522	60	575	7
Alpine	1445	1179	266	1445	......
Bowne	1275	1022	253	1275	......
Byron	1326	1136	190	1320	6
Caledonia	1599	1125	474	1599	......
Cannon	1206	1036	170	1205	1
Cascade	1157	996	161	1156	1
Courtland	1338	1191	147	1338	......
Gaines	1205	936	269	1193	12
Grand Rapids (e)	1650	1150	500	1650	......
Grand Rapids	16507	10782	5725	16407	100
Grattan	1297	1051	246	1297	......
Lowell	3086	2576	510	3083	3
KENT—Cont'd.					
Lowell	1503	1283	220	1500	3
Nelson	1102	987	115	1102	......
Oakfield	1092	932	160	1092	......
Paris	1543	1202	341	1533	10
Plainfield	1499	1234	265	1499	......
Solon	911	804	107	911	......
Sparta	1666	1349	317	1666	......
Spencer	580	502	78	580	......
Tyrone	730	633	97	717	13
Vergennes	1342	1053	289	1342	......
Walker	1675	1237	438	1675	......
Wyoming	1786	1346	440	1782	4
KEWEENAW.					
Clifton	615	285	330	615	......
Copper Harbor	359	173	186	358	[illegible]
Eagle Harbor	778	374	404	778	......
Amygdaloid Mine	61	33	28	61	......
Copper Falls Mine	454	183	271	454	......
Eagle Harbor	233	142	91	233	......
Grant	152	83	69	152	......
Houghton	1325	665	660	1321	f3
Sherman	929	449	480	929	......
Sibley	47	30	17	47	......
LAKE.					
Chase	520	377	143	520	......
Lake	28	24	4	28	......
LAPEER.					
Almont	2298	1702	596	2283	15
Arcada	418	308	110	418	......
Attica	1620	1217	403	1620	......
Burlington	880	400	480	879	1
Burnside	1173	599	574	1173	......
Deerfield	419	292	127	419	......
Dryden	1695	1432	263	1695	......
Elba	1001	855	146	1001	......
Goodland	811	543	268	811	......
Hadley	1461	1288	173	1461	......
Imlay	1243	807	436	1242	1
Lapeer (g)	1092	859	233	1091	1
Lapeer	1772	1392	380	1758	14
Marathon	986	747	239	986	......
Mayfield	1028	858	170	994	34
Metamora	1310	1106	204	1310	......
North Branch	762	389	373	744	18
Oregon	877	675	202	877	......
Rich	499	315	184	499	......
LEELANAW.					
Bingham	637	460	177	388	(h)
Centreville	939	524	415	869	(i)
Glen Arbor	405	221	184	405	......
Elmwood	535	340	195	528	7
Empire	450	261	189	449	1
Kasson	440	358	82	440	......
Leelanaw	830	638	192	635	(j)
North Port	238	178	60	221	k1
Sleeping Bear	340	242	98	333	7

(a) Also 1 Indian.
(b) The city of Jackson constitutes Jackson Township.
(c) Also 3 Indians.
(d) Also 9 Indians.
(e) Exclusive of city of Grand Rapids.
(f) Also 2 Indians.
(g) Exclusive of city of Lapeer.
(h) Also 249 Indians.
(i) Also 69 Indians.
(j) Also 194 Indians.
(k) Also 16 Indians.

TABLE IX.—*Population of Minor Civil Divisions, &c.—MICHIGAN*—Continued.

Counties.	Total.	Nativity. Native.	Nativity. Foreign.	Race. White.	Race. Colored.
LENAWEE.					
Adrian (a)	1451	1340	111	1435	16
Adrian	8438	6779	1659	8247	b189
Blissfield	1766	1574	192	1749	17
Cambridge	1110	973	137	1110	......
Clinton	1356	1174	182	1353	3
Clinton	752	634	118	750	2
Deerfield	1234	1073	161	1229	5
Dover	1494	1422	72	1493	1
Fairfield	1725	1649	76	1724	1
Franklin	1459	1339	120	1441	18
Hudson	4094	3671	423	4060	34
Hudson	2459	2229	230	2429	30
Macon	1439	1272	167	1436	3
Madison (a)	1294	1173	121	1288	6
Medina	1973	1830	143	1972	1
Ogden	1515	1299	216	1515	......
Palmyra	1757	1563	194	1750	7
Raisin	1645	1431	214	1623	22
Ridgeway	992	852	140	983	9
Riga	1540	1119	421	1535	5
Rollin	1515	1432	83	1514	1
Rome	1454	1389	65	1452	2
Seneca	2396	2305	91	2396	......
Tecumseh	2583	2288	295	2544	39
Tecumseh	2039	1812	227	2004	35
Woodstock	1365	1309	56	1355	10
LIVINGSTON.					
Brighton	1440	1192	248	1438	2
Brighton	454	383	71	453	1
Cohoctah	1176	1042	134	1176	......
Conway	1020	934	86	1020	......
Deerfield	1128	988	140	1128	......
Genoa	992	775	217	984	8
Green Oak	994	823	171	990	4
Hamburg	907	792	115	907	......
Hamburg	81	67	14	81	......
Handy	1306	1216	90	1306	......
Hartland	1159	1024	135	1158	1
Howell	2563	2230	333	2538	25
Iosco	904	816	88	903	1
Marion	1111	968	143	1107	4
Osceola	1012	878	134	1012	......
Putnam	1361	1185	176	1359	2
Pinckney	446	405	41	446	......
Tyrone	1222	1089	133	1218	4
Unadilla	1041	943	98	1035	6
Milan	143	130	13	141	2
MACKINAC.					
Holmes	938	722	216	837	c2
Moran	373	312	61	315	d4
St. Ignace	405	349	56	254	e19
MACOMB.					
Armada	1721	1371	350	1706	15
Armada	494	398	96	481	13
Bruce	2145	1672	473	2143	2
Chesterfield	2175	1644	531	2175	......
Clinton	3590	2458	1132	3564	26
Mt. Clemenes	1768	1331	437	1757	11
Erin	2466	1542	924	2466	......
Harrison	605	558	47	604	1

Counties.	Total.	Nativity. Native.	Nativity. Foreign.	Race. White.	Race. Colored.
MACOMB—Cont'd.					
Lenox	2134	1542	592	2115	19
New Haven	413	333	80	413	......
Macomb	1805	1204	601	1805	......
Ray	1555	1307	248	1555	......
Richmond	2181	1615	566	2165	16
Memphis	385	244	141	379	6
Shelby	1695	1492	203	1695	......
Sterling	1549	1077	472	1533	16
Warren	1938	1150	788	1932	6
Washington	2057	1683	374	2040	17
MANISTEE.					
Arcadia	175	155	20	175	......
Bear Lake	417	291	126	417	......
Brown	459	297	162	459	......
Cleon	85	71	14	85	......
Filer	376	181	195	376	......
Manistee (f)	271	137	134	271	......
Manistee	3343	1686	1657	3334	9
Marilla	129	100	29	129	......
Onekama	255	204	51	255	......
Pleasanton	283	182	101	278	5
Stronach	281	104	177	281	......
MANITOU.					
Chandler	190	117	73	190	......
Fox Island	44	34	10	44	......
Galilee	203	125	78	203	......
North Manitou Island	91	21	70	91	......
Payenno	287	130	157	287	......
South Manitou Island	76	51	25	76	......
MARQUETTE.					
Chocolay	260	95	165	260	......
Ishpeming	6103	1757	4346	6094	g1
Marquette	4617	2186	2431	4497	h58
Marquette	4000	1927	2073	3880	h58
Munissing (i)	799	305	494	797	(b)
Negaunee	3254	1450	1804	3252	2
Negaunee	2559	1214	1345	2557	2
MASON.					
Amber	492	418	74	396	(j)
Freesoil	142	114	28	142	......
Grant	125	68	57	125	......
Hamlin	124	63	61	116	(g)
Lincoln	165	92	73	165	......
Pere Marquette	954	560	394	954	......
Riverton	538	467	71	442	(j)
Sherman	152	114	38	152	......
Summit	257	186	71	256	1
Victory	314	246	68	275	k9
MECOSTA.					
Ætna	335	248	87	335	......
Austin	346	203	143	346	......
Big Rapids (l)	465	360	105	465	......
Big Rapids	1237	961	276	1223	14
Chippewa	140	111	29	140	......

(a) Exclusive of part of city of Adrian.
(b) Also 2 Indians.
(c) Also 99 Indians.
(d) Also 54 Indians.
(e) Also 132 Indians.
(f) Exclusive of city of Manistee.
(g) Also 8 Indians.
(h) Also 62 Indians.
(i) Comprises all of the unorganized county of Schoolcraft, which is attached to Marquette County for judicial purposes.
(j) Also 96 Indians.
(k) Also 30 Indians.
(l) Exclusive of city of Big Rapids.

TABLE IX.—*Population of Minor Civil Divisions, &c.*—MICHIGAN—Continued.

Counties.	Total.	Nativity.		Race.		Counties.	Total.	Nativity.		Race.	
		Native.	Foreign.	White.	Colored.			Native.	Foreign.	White.	Colored.
MECOSTA—Cont'd.						MONTCALM—Con'd.					
Colfax	146	117	29	146	......	Montcalm	1006	662	344	1000	6
Deerfield	564	378	186	562	2	Pierson	755	607	148	755	......
Fork	162	135	27	162	......	Pine	283	226	57	283	......
Grant	144	130	14	144	......	Reynolds	457	387	70	457	......
Green	616	455	161	616	......	Richland	88	81	7	88	......
Hinton	390	292	98	390	......	Sidney (*f*)	611	564	47	611	......
Mecosta	262	206	56	257	(*a*)	Winfield	326	246	80	322	4
Millbrook	301	202	99	279	22	MUSKEGON.					
Sheridan	134	115	19	134	......	Blue Lake	381	325	56	381	......
Wheatland	400	287	113	307	*b*89	Casenovia	1094	925	169	1094	......
MENOMINEE.						Cedar Creek	660	534	126	660	......
Cedarville	194	109	85	192	(*c*)	Dalton	401	337	64	401	......
Menominee	1597	809	788	1585	*d*9	Egelston	233	194	39	233	......
MIDLAND.						Fruitland	228	185	43	228	......
Gladwin	122	69	53	122	......	Laketon	1039	559	480	1039	......
Homer	247	202	45	247	......	Lovell	167	127	40	167	......
Ingersoll	402	267	135	402	......	Moorland	194	168	26	194	......
Jasper	139	110	29	139	......	Muskegon (*g*)	401	217	184	401	......
Jerome	355	260	95	355	......	Muskegon	6002	3158	2844	5973	29
Lincoln	322	210	112	322	......	Norton	688	472	216	687	1
Midland	1616	1264	352	1600	*c*14	Oceana	919	599	320	919	......
Midland	1160	883	277	1146	14	Ravenna	1035	783	252	1035	......
Porter	82	66	16	82	......	White River	1452	866	586	1446	6
MISSAUKEE.						Whitehall	842	535	307	836	6
Reeder	130	43	87	130	......	NEWAYGO.					
MONROE.						Ashland	770	653	117	770	......
Ash	1451	1163	288	1451	......	Barton	383	349	34	383	......
Bedford	1459	1265	194	1452	7	Beaver	142	124	18	142	......
Berlin	1844	1606	238	1844	......	Big Prairie	403	344	59	403	......
Dundee	2384	2060	324	2383	1	Bridgeton	397	332	65	372	(*h*)
Erie	1527	1433	94	1518	9	Brooks	974	817	157	910	64
Exeter	1067	834	233	1067	......	Newaygo	703	579	124	698	5
Frenchtown	2115	1710	405	2115	......	Croton	923	778	145	923	......
Ida	1020	781	239	1018	2	Dayton	771	648	123	771	......
La Salle	1392	1215	177	1392	......	Denver	777	672	105	777	......
London	1031	893	138	1031	......	Ensley	606	514	92	606	......
Milan	1420	1316	104	1419	1	Everett	231	214	17	231	......
Monroe (*c*)	1003	832	171	1000	3	Grant	77	75	2	77	......
Monroe	5086	3777	1309	5044	42	Sheridan	458	383	75	412	(*j*)
Raisinville	1793	1355	438	1793	......	Sherman	382	342	40	382	......
Summerfield	1464	1315	149	1464	......	OAKLAND.					
Whiteford	1427	1235	192	1414	13	Addison	1063	960	103	1063	......
MONTCALM.						Avon	1850	1621	229	1850	......
Belvidere	54	50	4	54	......	Bloomfield	2105	1812	293	2084	21
Bloomer	1422	1294	128	1413	9	Brandon	1284	1186	98	1284	......
Bushnell	1266	1159	107	1250	16	Commerce	1392	1159	233	1392	......
Cato	523	434	89	523	......	Farmington	1927	1604	323	1917	10
Crystal	746	706	40	746	......	Groveland	1180	1024	156	1179	1
Day (*f*)	510	486	24	510	......	Highland	1241	1125	116	1239	2
Stanton (*f*)	600	576	24	600	......	Holly	2437	2103	334	2424	13
Douglass (*f*)	215	182	33	215	......	Holly	1429	1204	225	1416	13
Eureka	2775	2371	404	2765	10	Independence	1586	1343	243	1585	1
Greenville	1807	1529	278	1798	9	Clarkston	471	420	51	471	......
Evergreen (*f*)	489	455	34	489	......	Lyon	1298	1101	197	1291	7
Fairplains	974	847	127	951	23	Milford	1767	1493	274	1744	23
Ferris	494	455	39	494	......	Novi	1351	1219	132	1336	15
Home	173	161	12	173	......	Oakland	1086	976	110	1086	......
Maple Valley	462	335	127	462	......	Orion	1151	1017	134	1150	1
						Orion	304	270	34	303	1
						Oxford	1367	1243	124	1362	5
						Pontiac (*k*)	1075	912	163	1072	3
						Pontiac	4867	3914	953	4501	366

(*a*) Also 3 Indians.
(*b*) Also 4 Indians.
(*c*) Also 2 Indians.
(*d*) Also 3 Indians.
(*e*) Exclusive of city of Monroe.
(*f*) Of Stanton Village, 331 in Day; 7 in Douglass; 13 in Evergreen; and 249 in Sidney.
(*g*) Exclusive of city of Muskegon.
(*h*) Also 25 Indians.
(*i*) Also 59 Indians.
(*j*) Also 46 Indians.
(*k*) Exclusive of city of Pontiac.

TABLE IX.—*Population of Minor Civil Divisions, &c.—MICHIGAN*—Continued.

Counties.	Total.	Nativity.		Race.	
		Native.	Foreign.	White.	Colored.
OAKLAND—Cont'd.					
Rose	1169	1035	134	1168	1
Royal Oak	1520	1160	360	1489	31
Southfield	1547	1260	287	1540	7
Springfield	1378	1161	217	1376	2
Troy	1541	1253	288	1525	16
Waterford	1362	1163	199	1360	2
West Bloomfield	1143	986	157	1126	17
White Lake	1180	940	240	1179	1
OCEANA.					
Benona	637	477	160	637	......
Clay Banks	462	331	131	462	......
Colfax	77	74	3	77	......
Crystal	181	171	10	72	(a)
Elbridge	524	517	7	50	(b)
Ferry	366	327	39	366	......
Golden	335	258	77	335	......
Grant	208	160	48	208	......
Greenwood	249	216	33	249	......
Hart	1004	930	74	1000	4
Leavitt	316	286	30	316	......
Newfield	265	234	31	265	......
Otto	135	118	17	128	7
Pentwater	1414	1031	383	1409	d 2
Pentwater	1294	940	354	1292	d 2
Shelby	557	432	125	557	......
Ware	492	380	112	492	......
ONTONAGON.					
Algonquin	54	32	22	54	......
Carp Lake	25	17	8	23	(f)
Greenland	548	295	253	548	......
Ontonagon	739	512	227	711	g 13
Rockland	1479	858	621	1477	(f)
OSCEOLA.					
Evart	168	148	20	168	......
Hartwick	47	46	1	47	......
Hersey	286	195	91	270	(h)
Highland	58	45	13	58	......
Leroy	148	129	19	148	......
Lincoln	334	253	81	334	......
Middle Branch	49	35	14	49	......
Orient	54	45	9	54	......
Osceola	137	112	25	137	......
Richmond	653	281	372	652	1
Sherman	116	104	12	116	......
Sylvan	43	42	1	43	......
OTTAWA.					
Allendale	799	660	139	799	......
Blendon	718	480	238	718	......
Chester	1405	1096	309	1405	......
Crockery	1125	843	282	1118	(i)
Georgetown	1474	1154	320	1474	......
Grand Haven (j)	558	328	230	558	......
Grand Haven	3147	1639	1508	3079	i 61
Holland (k)	2353	1192	1161	2352	1
Holland	2319	1146	1173	2315	l 3
Jamestown	1612	1199	413	1606	6
OTTAWA—Cont'd.					
Olive	612	346	266	612	......
Polkton	2416	1889	527	2416	......
Robinson	406	326	80	406	......
Spring Lake	1836	1050	786	1812	24
Spring Lake	1156	619	537	1147	9
Tallmadge	1451	1176	275	1451	......
Wright	2077	1738	339	2077	......
Zeeland	2343	1185	1158	2343	......
PRESQUE ISLE.					
Rogers	355	96	259	354	(m)
Presque Isle	66	41	25	65	(m)
SAGINAW.					
Albee	197	165	32	197	......
Birch Run	925	788	137	925	......
Blumfield	1074	640	434	1074	......
Brady	471	384	87	470	1
Brant	331	222	109	331	......
Bridgeport	1171	854	317	1168	3
Buena Vista (n)	1005	528	477	1004	(m)
Carrolton	1564	756	808	1557	7
Chapin	258	230	28	258	......
Chesaning	1507	1288	219	1505	2
Chesaning	721	610	111	719	2
East Saginaw	11350	6284	5066	11171	179
Frankinmuth	1488	974	514	1488	......
Fremont	170	123	47	170	......
Kochville	1070	697	373	1070	......
Maple Grove	505	418	87	505	......
Richland	466	296	170	466	......
Saginaw (o)	1004	641	363	1004	......
Saginaw	7460	4329	3131	7368	92
Spaulding	2117	1400	717	2117	......
So'th Saginaw	1875	1253	622	1875	......
St. Charles	1185	984	201	1127	p3
Swan Creek	427	275	152	426	1
Taymouth	638	478	160	568	(q)
Thomastown	697	392	305	697	......
Tittabawassee	864	700	164	864	......
Zilwaukee	1153	488	665	1153	......
SANILAC.					
Argyle	151	44	107	151	......
Austin	349	119	230	349	......
Bridgehampton	936	435	501	928	8
Buel	216	104	112	216	......
Delaware	741	343	398	741	......
Forestville	121	43	78	121	......
Elk	633	329	304	633	......
Flynn	131	58	73	131	......
Forester	670	327	343	667	3
Forester	233	110	123	230	3
Richmondville	83	44	39	83	......
Fremont	640	266	374	640	......
Greenleaf	336	167	169	336	......
Lamotte	94	45	49	94	......
Lexington	2433	1312	1121	2424	9
Maple Valley	335	126	209	335	......
Marion	665	267	398	664	1
Marlette	705	289	416	705	......

(a) Also 109 Indians.
(b) Also 474 Indians.
(d) Also 10 Indians.
(f) Also 2 Indians.
(g) Also 15 Indians.
(h) Also 16 Indians.
(i) Also 7 Indians.
(j) Exclusive of city of Grand Haven.
(k) Exclusive of city of Holland.
(l) Also 1 Japanese.
(m) Also 1 Indian.
(n) Exclusive of city of East Saginaw.
(o) Exclusive of city of Saginaw.
(p) Also 55 Indians.
(q) Also 70 Indians.

TABLE IX.—*Population of Minor Civil Divisions, &c.—MICHIGAN*—Continued.

Counties.	Total.	Nativity. Native.	Nativity. Foreign.	Race. White.	Race. Colored.
SANILAC—Cont'd.					
Minden	456	174	282	456	......
Moore	112	38	74	105	(a)
Sanilac	1988	956	1032	1988	......
Speaker	1118	504	614	1118	......
Washington	370	185	185	370	......
Watertown	49	32	17	49	......
Worth	1434	732	702	1427	7
SHIAWASSEE.					
Antrim	992	875	117	992	......
Bennington	1424	1217	207	1416	8
Burns	1557	1441	116	1557	......
Caledonia (b)	891	771	120	891	......
Corunna	1408	1245	163	1401	7
Fairfield	632	560	72	632	......
Hazelton	822	676	146	820	2
Middlebury	1018	883	135	1016	2
New Haven	999	768	231	999	......
Owasso (c)	1058	822	236	1058	......
Owasso	2065	1630	435	2052	13
Perry	1058	945	113	1058	......
Rush	683	552	131	683	......
Sciota	1270	1088	182	1267	3
Shiawassee	1422	1304	118	1422	......
Venice	986	883	103	986	......
Vernon	1797	1623	174	1797	......
Woodhull	776	703	73	776	......
ST. CLAIR.					
Berlin	1231	891	340	1231	......
Brockway	1330	709	621	1330	......
Burtchville	726	360	366	726	......
Casco	1991	1084	907	1991	......
China	1637	1093	544	1630	7
Clay	1475	1104	371	1473	(d)
Algonac	754	559	195	752	(d)
Clyde	1176	698	478	1176	......
Columbus	1218	800	418	1218	......
Cottrellville	2372	1645	727	2372	......
Marine City	1240	870	370	1240	......
East China	297	222	75	297	......
Emmet	960	510	450	960	......
Fort Gratiot	1032	513	519	1032	......
Grant	1143	614	529	1140	3
Greenwood	898	370	528	898	......
Ira	1580	990	590	1580	......
Kenockee	1229	640	589	1229	......
Kimball	1091	621	470	1091	......
Lynn	539	264	275	539	......
Mussey	1117	570	547	1117	......
Port Huron (e)	832	450	382	832	......
Port Huron	5973	3113	2860	5958	15
Riley	1664	1092	572	1664	......
St. Clair (f)	2002	1325	677	2000	2
St. Clair	1790	1108	682	1751	39
Wales	1358	908	450	1358	......
ST. JOSEPH.					
Burr Oak	1911	1733	178	1903	8
Burr Oak	724	663	61	722	2
Colon	1504	1413	91	1504	......
Colon	398	387	11	398	......
Constantine	2406	2178	228	2368	38
Constantine	1290	1148	142	1271	19
Fabius	1277	1109	168	1277	......

Counties.	Total.	Nativity. Native.	Nativity. Foreign.	Race. White.	Race. Colored.
ST. JOSEPH—Con'd.					
Fawn River	680	616	64	666	14
Florence	970	853	117	970	......
Flowerfield	1538	1395	143	1538	......
Flowerfield	210	198	12	210	......
Leonidas	1463	1401	62	1463	......
Lockport	3456	3115	341	3421	35
Lockport	1553	1419	134	1549	4
Three Rivers	1189	1082	107	1158	31
Mendon	1908	1786	122	1892	16
Mendon	660	624	36	644	16
Mottville	721	682	39	721	......
Nottawa	1868	1665	203	1855	13
Centreville	749	665	84	741	8
Park	1274	1239	35	1274	......
Sherman	1160	850	310	1160	......
Sturgis	2406	1957	349	2400	6
Sturgis	1768	1479	289	1762	6
White Pigeon	1833	1599	234	1830	3
White Pigeon	922	811	111	919	3
TUSCOLA.					
Akron	585	465	120	585	......
Almer	671	537	134	671	......
Arbela	870	722	148	870	......
Columbia	424	318	106	424	......
Dayton	660	396	264	660	......
Denmark	816	593	223	816	......
Elkland	511	298	213	511	......
Ellington	452	286	166	452	......
Elmwood	369	198	171	368	1
Fairgrove	928	772	156	928	......
Fremont	664	376	288	664	......
Geneva	152	110	42	146	6
Gilford	353	278	75	353	......
Indian Fields	825	685	140	824	1
Juniata	1042	930	112	1041	(g)
Watrousville	213	185	28	213	......
Kingston	324	157	167	324	......
Koylton	422	235	187	422	......
Millington	613	490	123	612	1
Novesta	105	89	16	105	......
Tuscola	1110	932	178	1110	......
Vassar	775	660	115	775	......
Watertown	684	438	246	684	......
Wells	194	155	39	194	......
Wisner	165	141	24	165	......
VAN BUREN.					
Almena	980	917	63	951	29
Antwerp	2690	2499	191	2674	16
Lawton	1081	984	97	1073	8
Arlington	1360	1250	110	1257	103
Bangor	1525	1416	109	1499	(h)
Bloomingdale	1496	1387	109	1482	14
Columbia	1269	1137	132	1262	7
Breedsville	255	223	32	255	......
Decatur	2512	2267	245	2426	86
Decatur	1420	1273	147	1392	28
Deerfield	677	591	86	601	76
Geneva	1086	976	110	1080	6
Hamilton	1172	1099	73	1128	44
Hartford	1709	1560	149	1614	(j)
Keeler	1303	1182	121	1303	......
Lawrence	1927	1806	121	1923	4
Lawrence	555	509	46	555	......
Paw Paw	2670	2419	251	2590	80

(a) Also 7 Indians.
(b) Exclusive of city of Corunna.
(c) Exclusive of city of Owasso.
(d) Also 2 Indians.
(e) Exclusive of city of Port Huron.
(f) Exclusive of city of St. Clair.
(g) Also 1 Indian.
(h) Also 26 Indians.
(i) Also 18 Indians.
(j) Also 95 Indians.

BLE IX.—*Population of Minor Civil Divisions, &c.—MICHIGAN*—Continued.

nties.	Total.	Nativity. Native.	Nativity. Foreign.	Race. White.	Race. Colored.
REN—Con.					
Paw....	1428	1291	137	1416	12
ove.......	1700	1522	178	1699	1
....	1316	1203	113	1280	36
aven.....	2203	1844	359	2167	36
h Haven.	1576	1289	287	1569	7
....	1234	1167	67	1216	18
TENAW.					
or (a)....	1383	1013	370	1360	23
Arbor.....	7363	5575	1788	7131	232
....	1470	1202	268	1412	58
ater......	1379	1070	309	1372	7
....	889	688	201	888	1
a.........	1261	717	544	1260	1
....	1052	877	175	1051	1
....	1344	948	396	1308	36
....	823	655	168	823	......
ster......	2516	2039	477	2488	28
ld........	1300	956	344	1300	......
d.........	1121	922	199	1076	45
....	1216	1058	158	1190	26
....	1955	1617	338	1928	27
....	2495	1896	599	2468	27
ter.......	1161	949	212	1151	10
....	1087	877	210	1080	7
r.........	1268	1064	204	1244	24
....	1931	1530	401	1926	5
lsea......	1013	810	203	1010	3
r.........	974	799	175	974	......
....	1575	1407	168	1544	31
ti (b).....	1561	1335	226	1413	148
anti......	5471	4463	1008	5071	c398

Counties.	Total.	Nativity. Native.	Nativity. Foreign.	Race. White.	Race. Colored.
WAYNE.					
Brownstown.....	2037	1703	334	1985	52
Canton..........	1392	1197	195	1339	53
Dearborn........	2302	1555	747	2272	30
Dearborn.....	530	......	......	......	......
Betroit........	79577	44196	35381	77338	d2235
Ecorse (e).......	2211	1521	690	2200	11
Greenfield......	2406	1482	924	2366	40
Grosse Point.....	2230	1519	711	2222	8
Hamtranck.......	2998	1695	1303	2946	52
Huron...........	1263	1099	164	1263	......
Livonia.........	1679	1359	320	1679	......
Monguagon......	1475	1016	459	1457	18
Nankin..........	2955	2353	602	2917	38
Wayno......	833	674	159	829	4
Plymouth........	3016	2630	386	2962	54
Northville....	626	557	69	623	3
Plymouth....	969	831	138	953	16
Redford..........	1872	1425	447	1868	4
Romulus.........	1463	1183	280	1423	40
Springwells......	3488	1753	1735	3462	26
Fort Wayne..	188	75	113	188	......
Sumpter.........	1106	947	159	1100	6
Taylor..........	867	520	347	862	5
Van Buren.......	1970	1719	251	1959	11
Wyandotte....	2731	1581	1150	2731	......
WEXFORD.					
Colfax..........	172	153	19	169	3
Hanover.........	112	98	14	112	......
Springville......	107	91	16	107	......
Wexford........	259	246	13	259	......

xclusive of city of Ann Arbor.
xclusive of city of Ypsilanti.
lso 2 Indians.

(d) Also 4 Indians.
(e) Exclusive of city of Wyandotte.

TABLE IX.—*Population of Minor Civil Divisions, &c.—MINNESOTA.*

:—The marginal column marks townships and land-survey townships; the first indentation, the second, towns. Names of towns are placed under the names of the townships or land-survey ips in which they are respectively situated. The population of each township or land-survey ip includes that of all towns situated in it.

nnties.	Total.	Nativity. Native.	Nativity. Foreign.	Race. White.	Race. Colored.
NOKA.					
....	1498	1188	310	1488	10
....	216	139	77	216	......
....	340	228	112	340	......
ville......	687	397	290	682	5
bns.......	71	47	24	71	......
....	396	285	111	396	......
in........	103	74	29	103	......
rove......	198	149	49	198	......

Counties.	Total.	Nativity. Native.	Nativity. Foreign.	Race. White.	Race. Colored.
ANOKA—Cont'd.					
Ramsey..........	265	237	28	265	......
St. Francis.......	166	124	42	166	......
BENTON.					
Alberta..........	158	103	55	158	......
Gilmanton.......	193	126	67	193	......
Glendorado......	139	102	37	139	......

TABLE IX.—*Population of Minor Civil Divisions, &c.*—*MINNESOTA*—**Continued.**

Counties.	Total.	Nativity. Native.	Nativity. Foreign.	Race. White.	Race. Colored.
BENTON—Cont'd.					
Langola	85	73	12	85	.....
Maywood	83	58	25	83	.....
Minden	81	60	21	81	.....
Sauk Rapids	444	343	101	443	1
Sauk Rapids	412	318	94	411	1
St. George	317	166	151	317	.....
Watab	58	44	14	57	(a)
Watab	22	15	7	22	.....
BLUE EARTH.					
Beauford	336	201	135	336	.....
Butternut Valley	590	266	324	590	.....
Cambria	339	223	116	339	.....
Ceresco	313	227	86	313	.....
Danville	557	359	198	557	.....
Decoria	262	190	72	262	.....
Garden City	1391	1154	237	1391	.....
Crystal Lake	360	247	113	360	.....
Garden City	368	341	27	368	.....
Jamestown	234	135	99	234	.....
Judson	661	418	243	661	.....
Loray	448	308	140	442	6
Lime	744	321	423	744	.....
Lincoln	495	332	163	495	.....
Lyra	433	318	115	433	.....
Mankato (b)	1272	810	462	1270	2
Mankato	3482	2309	1173	3476	6
Mapleton	583	501	82	583	.....
McPherson	903	725	178	901	2
Winnebago Agency	195	154	41	193	2
Medo	712	581	131	711	1
Pleasant Mound	448	301	147	448	.....
Rapidan	449	339	110	447	2
Shelby	728	612	116	728	.....
South Bend	596	363	233	596	.....
South Bend	301	142	159	301	.....
Sterling	661	558	103	660	1
Vernon	665	597	68	665	.....
BROWN.					
Albin	194	109	85	194	.....
Cottonwood	607	310	297	607	.....
Eden	431	250	181	431	.....
Home	779	455	324	779	.....
Lake Hanskah	215	73	142	215	.....
Leavenworth	433	269	164	433	.....
Linden	457	161	296	457	.....
Milford	632	324	308	632	.....
New Ulm	1310	679	631	1310	.....
Prairieville	214	69	145	214	.....
Sigel	379	155	224	379	.....
Stark	447	323	124	447	.....
Township 108 N., R. 33 W	97	47	50	97	.....
Township 108 N., R. 34 W	17	2	15	17	.....
Township 109 N., R. 34 W	174	79	95	174	.....
Township 109 N., R. 35 W	10	6	4	10	.....
CARLTON.					
Little Moose Lake	24	16	8	24	.....
Moose Lake	51	26	25	39	(c)
Railroad Junction	27	10	17	27	.....
Thompson	163	48	115	163	.....
Twin Lakes	21	18	3	21	.....
CARVER.					
Benton	1297	609	688	1297	.....
Camden	414	222	192	414	.....
Carver	521	274	247	521	.....
Chanhassen	1064	585	499	1063	1
Chaska	847	423	424	847	.....
Dahlgreen	1303	555	748	1303	.....
Hancock	632	331	301	632	.....
Hollywood	534	291	243	534	.....
Laketown	1039	510	529	1039	.....
San Francisco	754	319	435	754	.....
Waconia	1097	480	617	1097	.....
Watertown	1241	638	603	1241	.....
Young America	823	431	392	823	.....
CHIPPEWA.					
Benson	628	208	420	628	.....
Granite Falls	373	199	174	346	(d)
Sparta	275	207	68	275	.....
Tunsburg	191	84	107	184	(e)
CHISAGO.					
Amador	77	69	8	77	.....
Chisago Lake	775	270	505	775	.....
Fish Lake	385	80	305	385	.....
Franconia	650	279	371	650	.....
Rusheba	706	316	390	692	(f)
Sunrise	240	213	27	227	d
Taylor's Falls	1003	658	345	981	(g)
Wyoming	522	279	243	522	.....
DAKOTA.					
Burnsville	361	231	130	361	.....
Castle Rock	703	553	150	703	.....
Douglas	707	361	346	706	1
Egan	670	424	246	670	.....
Empire	995	731	264	995	.....
Eureka	924	504	420	924	.....
Greenvale	725	396	329	725	.....
Hampton	930	551	379	930	.....
Hastings	3458	2383	1075	3418	40
Inver Grove	971	622	349	971	.....
Lakeville	780	591	189	775	5
Lebanon	216	135	81	216	.....
Marshan	527	321	206	527	.....
Mendota	444	269	175	444	.....
Ninniger	400	327	73	400	.....
Randolph	170	130	40	170	.....
Ravenna	236	206	30	236	.....
Rosemount	681	467	214	681	.....
Sciota	328	222	106	328	.....
Vermillion	652	395	257	652	.....
Waterford	331	290	41	331	.....
West St. Paul	1103	658	445	1101	(h)
DODGE.					
Ashland	611	482	129	611	.....
Canisteo	880	474	406	880	.....
Claremont	538	461	77	538	.....
Rice Lake	51	49	2	51	.....
Concord	792	705	87	792	.....
Ellington	258	187	71	258	.....
Hayfield	18	2	16	18	.....
Mantorville	1969	1646	323	1964	5
Kasson	515	421	94	515	.....
Mantorville	622	514	108	618	4
Milton	912	760	152	912	.....
Ripley	294	213	81	294	.....

(a) Also 1 Indian.
(b) Exclusive of city of Mankato.
(c) Also 12 Indians.
(d) Also 27 Indians.
(e) Also 7 Indians.
(f) Also 14 Indians.
(g) Also 22 Indians.
(h) Also 2 Indians.

BLE IX.—*Population of Minor Civil Divisions, &c.—MINNESOTA*—Continued.

[Co]unties.	Total.	Nativity. Native.	Nativity. Foreign.	Race. White.	Race. Colored.
—Cont'd.					
....	850	359	491	850	......
i..........	1134	1030	104	1134	......
sioja......	324	300	24	324	......
ld	342	196	146	342	......
UGLAS.					
Iria.......	503	301	202	494	(a)
....	116	88	28	116	......
vn	164	85	79	164	......
lle	250	96	154	250	......
City	452	182	270	452	......
....	448	374	74	448	......
....	224	110	114	224	......
ary.......	244	217	27	244	......
lley	232	138	94	232	......
lle........	285	128	157	285	......
....	235	66	169	235	......
....	178	135	43	178	......
....	400	242	158	400	......
k	145	32	113	145	......
lo	155	75	80	155	......
....	208	47	161	208	......
IBAULT.					
....	561	380	181	561	......
rth City..	1121	859	262	1191	......
reek......	422	272	150	422	......
)	347	269	78	347	......
....	203	135	68	203	......
....	470	425	45	470	......
l	748	365	383	748	......
....	304	238	66	304	......
....	550	369	181	550	......
ess	477	368	109	477	......
....	61	50	11	61	......
....	621	491	130	620	1
ta Lake..	564	417	147	563	1
rove	390	241	149	390	......
t..........	552	461	91	552	......
....	396	211	185	396	......
....	266	171	95	266	......
....	607	579	28	607	......
Lake	500	431	69	500	......
ago City..	780	690	90	780	......
nnebago City........	326	284	42	326	......
MORE.					
t..........	1115	561	554	1115	......
hl.........	853	279	574	853	......
....	419	285	134	419	......
eld	888	569	319	888	......
....	933	673	260	933	......
....	1012	726	286	1012	......
na	788	585	203	788	......
on	1646	790	856	1644	2
esborough	655	333	322	653	2
ll	1661	1243	418	1656	5
e..........	987	814	173	987	......
ille	599	467	132	599	......
in	1037	647	390	1037	......
ay.........	890	491	399	890	......
....	784	330	454	784	......
....	683	626	57	681	2
rg.........	1047	610	437	1047	......
y	1380	452	928	1380	......

Counties.	Total.	Nativity. Native.	Nativity. Foreign.	Race. White.	Race. Colored.
FILLMORE—Con'd.					
Pilot Mound......	945	456	489	945	......
Preble............	670	302	368	670	......
Preston	1498	930	568	1498	......
Preston	600	434	166	600	......
Rushford	1973	979	994	1973	......
Rushford.....	1245	688	557	1245	......
Spring Valley	1279	1037	242	1271	8
Sumner	988	855	133	988	......
York	812	471	341	812	......
FREEBORN.					
Albert Lea.......	1167	719	448	1162	5
Alden	381	348	33	380	1
Bancroft	799	375	424	799	......
Bath	404	152	252	404	......
Carlston..........	378	295	83	378	......
Freeborn	362	318	44	362	......
Freeman	694	322	372	694	......
Geneva...........	378	295	83	378	......
Hartland.........	485	261	224	484	1
Hayward.........	382	220	102	382	......
London...........	311	236	75	311	......
Manchester	701	387	314	701	......
Mansfield	379	204	175	379	......
Moscow	592	477	115	592	......
Newry	596	294	302	596	......
Nunda	675	412	263	675	......
Oakland	412	304	108	412	......
Pickerel Lake....	337	221	116	337	......
Riceland	633	243	390	633	......
Shell Rock	512	435	77	512	......
GOODHUE.					
Bell Creek	820	424	396	820	......
Belvidere........	626	341	285	626	......
Burnside.........	396	244	152	389	7
Cannon Falls ...	957	446	511	957	......
Central Point	160	140	20	160	......
Cherry Grove	884	623	261	884	......
Featherstone	850	415	435	850	......
Florence	760	514	246	753	7
Goodhue	750	378	372	750	......
Grant	338	219	119	337	1
Hay Creek	901	421	480	900	1
Holden	1199	504	695	1199	......
Kenyon	633	267	366	633	......
Leon	970	445	525	970	......
Lillian	489	347	142	489	......
Minneola	1089	522	567	1088	1
Pine Island	1140	880	260	1139	1
Red Wing......	4260	2335	1925	4257	3
Roscoe	811	527	284	810	1
Vasa	1218	430	788	1218	......
Wacota	88	57	31	88	......
Wanamingo......	1468	581	887	1468	......
Warsaw..........	1027	465	562	1027	......
Zumbrota	784	639	145	784	......
HENNEPIN.					
Bloomington	738	519	219	721	c2
Brooklyn.........	1024	767	257	1021	d1
Champlin	292	248	44	292	......
Corcoran	914	530	384	902	(e)
Crystal Lake.....	718	532	186	718	......
Dayton	951	650	301	951	......
Eden Prairie......	576	410	166	576	......

lso 9 Indians.
ormerly Cobb.
lso 15 Indians.

(d) Also 2 Indians.
(e) Also 12 Indians.

TABLE IX.—*Population of Minor Civil Divisions, &c.*—*MINNESOTA*—Continued.

Counties.	Total.	Nativity. Native.	Nativity. Foreign.	Race. White.	Race. Colored.
HENNEPIN—Con'd.					
Excelsior	335	282	53	335	......
Greenwood	425	264	161	424	1
Hassan	551	362	189	551	......
Independence	502	390	112	502	......
Maple Grove	1014	682	332	996	(a)
Medina	1058	670	388	1058	......
Minneapolis (b)	1173	834	339	1158	15
Minneapolis	13066	8613	4453	12957	109
Minnetonka	552	372	180	552	......
Minnetrista	626	407	219	626	......
Plymouth	872	516	356	872	......
Richfield	930	668	262	920	10
St. Anthony (c)	236	169	67	235	1
St. Anthony	5013	3453	1560	4962	51
HOUSTON.					
Blackhammer	709	342	367	709	......
Brownsville	1589	949	640	1588	1
Brownsville	625	......	......	......	......
Caledonia	1628	1013	615	1628	......
Caledonia	470	332	138	470	......
Crooked Creek	465	261	204	465	......
Hokah	1038	629	409	1038	......
Hokah (d)	525	......	......	......	......
Houston	1075	592	483	1074	1
Jefferson	372	217	155	372	......
La Crescent	961	619	342	961	......
La Crescent	380	......	......	......	......
Mayville	611	285	326	611	......
Money Creek	609	444	165	609	......
Hamilton	50	42	8	50	......
Mound Prairie	650	304	346	650	......
Sheldon	828	385	443	828	......
Spring Grove	1331	593	738	1331	......
Union	456	260	196	448	8
Wilmington	1200	564	636	1200	......
Winnebago	804	426	378	804	......
Yucatan	610	293	317	610	......
ISANTI.					
Cambridge	374	90	284	374	......
Isanti	458	115	343	458	......
Maple Ridge	268	128	140	268	......
North Branch	224	122	102	224	......
Spencer Brook	403	253	150	403	......
Spring Vale	93	51	42	93	......
Stanford	215	106	109	215	......
JACKSON.					
Bellmont	625	231	394	625	......
Des Moines	548	429	119	546	2
Middletown	165	129	36	165	......
Minnesota	126	115	11	126	......
Petersburg	168	122	46	168	......
Wisconsin	193	166	27	193	......
KANABEC.					
Brunswick	93	85	8	93	......
KANDIYOHI.					
Elizabeth	77	33	44	77	......
Gennesee	361	148	213	361	......
Kandiyohi	538	161	377	538	......
Lake Lillian	238	67	171	238	......
Whitefield	77	40	37	77	......
Willman	449	199	250	449	......
LAKE.					
Beaver Bay	119	100	19	119	......
Pigeon River	16	14	2	15	(e)
LE SUEUR.					
Cleveland	1052	809	243	1052	......
Cordova	539	439	100	539	......
Derrynane	739	431	308	739	......
Elysian	852	628	224	849	3
Kasota	903	687	216	903	......
Kilkenny	730	496	234	730	......
Lanesburg	1123	389	734	1123	......
Le Sueur	1009	674	335	1009	......
Lexington	507	398	109	507	......
Montgomery	609	284	325	597	(f)
Ottawa	613	442	171	613	......
Sharon	924	628	296	922	2
Tyrone	830	500	330	830	......
Washington	359	264	95	359	......
Waterville	798	621	177	798	......
MARTIN.					
Centre Creek	377	339	38	377	......
Elm Creek	188	163	25	188	......
Fairmount	699	621	78	699	......
Lake Belt	296	248	48	296	......
Mangaska	141	125	16	141	......
Nashville	508	422	86	508	......
Pleasant Prairie	408	346	62	408	......
Rutland	196	164	32	196	......
Silver Lake	487	434	53	487	......
Tenhassen	314	289	25	314	......
Waverly	253	189	64	253	......
MC'LEOD.					
Acoma	392	232	160	392	......
Bergen	588	294	294	588	......
Collins	191	181	10	191	......
Glencoe	487	389	98	487	......
Glendale	527	377	150	527	......
Hale	399	320	79	399	......
Helen	476	223	253	476	......
Hutchinson	440	349	91	440	......
Lynn	243	138	105	243	......
Penn	420	312	108	420	......
Rich Valley	527	344	183	527	......
Sumter	315	227	88	315	......
Winsted	638	371	267	638	......
MEEKER.					
Acton	486	125	361	486	......
Collingwood	30	28	2	30	......
Ellsworth	270	177	93	270	......
Forest City	401	300	101	401	......
Forest City	181	136	45	181	......
Forest Prairie	315	249	66	315	......
Greenleaf	392	225	167	391	1
Greenleaf	54	35	19	54	......
Harvey	364	219	145	364	......
Kingston	530	432	98	530	......
Kingston	56	50	6	56	......
Litchfield	841	438	403	840	1
Litchfield	353	241	112	352	1
Mannanah	375	239	136	375	......
New Virginia	428	308	120	428	......
Rice City	359	244	115	359	......
Swan Lake	539	356	183	539	......
Swede Grove	446	140	306	446	......
Union Grove	314	257	57	314	......

(a) Also 18 Indians.
(b) Exclusive of city of Minneapolis.
(c) Exclusive of city of St. Anthony.
(d) Its township not ascertained.
(e) Also 1 Indian.
(f) Also 12 Indians.

BLE IX.—*Population of Minor Civil Divisions, &c.—MINNESOTA*—Continued.

unties.	Total.	Nativity. Native.	Foreign.	Race. White.	Colored.
LE LAC.					
nsh	294	230	64	294	......
....	153	105	48	153	......
on	662	583	79	660	2
ONGALIA.					
k	523	246	277	523	......
....	266	58	208	266	......
Lake	234	102	132	234	......
n	356	214	142	356	......
....	276	154	122	276	......
larme	196	28	168	196	......
ondon	319	179	140	319	......
Lake	669	223	446	669	......
le	322	250	63	322	......
RRISON.					
rairie	344	213	131	344	......
ew	92	70	22	92	......
Prairie	201	124	77	201	......
Falls	457	330	127	457	......
....	151	82	69	151	......
ivers	436	294	142	436	......
OWER.					
....	576	226	350	576	......
....	2631	1915	716	2631	......
stin	2039	1421	618	2039	......
or Marshall	101	58	43	101	......
gton	257	136	121	257	......
....	120	50	70	120	......
ord	674	501	173	674	......
Meadow	444	228	216	444	......
g	773	587	186	773	......
....	1057	790	267	1057	......
....	480	394	86	480	......
....	637	290	347	637	......
t Valley ..	319	264	55	319	......
....	813	607	206	813	......
ck	602	458	144	602	......
o	380	251	129	380	......
m	179	148	31	179	......
n	404	335	69	404	......
COLLET.					
le	414	280	134	414	......
otte	214	66	148	214	......
nd	640	308	332	640	......
....	566	257	309	566	......
ette	594	241	353	594	......
rairie	828	391	437	828	......
veden	568	190	378	568	......
t	658	387	271	658	......
....	2640	1446	1194	2633	*a*4
Peter	2124	1198	926	2117	*a*4
se	537	339	198	513	(*b*)
ewton	703	376	327	679	(*c*)
MSTED.					
....	1055	860	195	1055	......
e (*d*)	812	688	124	812	......
....	822	640	182	820	2
....	1140	938	202	1139	1
gton	937	618	319	936	1
OLMSTED—Cont'd.					
Haverhill	650	514	136	650	......
High Forest	1243	931	312	1241	2
High Forest ..	249	229	20	248	1
Kolmar	972	825	147	972	......
Marion	929	739	190	928	1
New Haven	860	758	102	860	......
Oronoco	753	666	87	752	1
Orion	637	529	108	637	......
Pleasant Grove ...	1071	926	145	1071	......
Quincy	807	655	152	807	......
Rochester (*d*)	591	417	174	590	1
Rochester	3953	3022	931	3935	18
Rock Dell	837	426	411	837	......
Salem	996	568	428	996	......
Viola	728	644	84	728	......
OTTER TAIL.					
Aardal	85	20	65	85	......
Clitheral	220	142	78	219	(*e*)
Lane Prairie	80	7	73	80	......
Eagle Lake	80	30	50	80	......
Fordenskjold	140	20	120	140	......
Otter Tail City ...	52	32	20	51	(*e*)
Range 43	376	161	215	376	......
Rush Lake	167	118	49	167	......
St. Olaf	408	172	236	408	......
Townships 21 E ..	221	143	78	221	......
Tumoli	139	43	96	139	......
PINE.					
Chengwatana	99	81	18	99	......
Hinckley	255	133	122	252	*e*2
Kettle River	74	20	54	74	......
Pine City	220	90	130	220	......
POPE.					
Anderson	74	15	59	74	......
Barnsness	153	57	96	153	......
Ben Wade	240	53	187	240	......
Chippewa	116	29	87	116	......
Gilchrist	169	58	111	169	......
Glenwood	214	142	72	213	1
Grove Lake	292	225	67	292	......
Lake Johanna	219	101	118	219	......
Levan	150	119	31	150	......
Nora	99	32	67	99	......
Reno	254	124	130	254	......
Rolling Fork	211	49	162	211	......
Westport	238	200	38	238	......
White Bear Lake	202	106	156	262	......
RAMSEY.					
McLean	442	264	178	442	......
Mount View	215	144	71	215	......
New Canada	789	512	277	782	7
Reserve	429	238	191	429	......
Rose	750	453	297	741	9
St. Paul	20030	11343	8687	19849	*e* 180
White Bear	430	292	138	428	2
REDWOOD.					
Lac qui Parle	307	115	192	307	......
Lynd	268	235	33	266	(*f*)

Also 3 Indians.
Also 24 Indians.
Also 4 Indians.

(*d*) Exclusive of part of city of Rochester.
(*e*) Also 1 Indian.
(*f*) Also 2 Indians.

TABLE IX.—*Population of Minor Civil Divisions, &c.—MINNESOTA—Continued.*

Counties.	Total.	Nativity. Native.	Nativity. Foreign.	Race. White.	Race. Colored.
REDWOOD—Con'd.					
Redwood Falls	691	492	199	691	......
Sheridan	111	52	59	111	......
Sherman	67	50	17	66	1
Yellow Medicine	385	203	182	385	......
RENVILLE.					
Beaver	569	401	168	569	......
Birch Cooley	503	306	197	503	......
Cairo	326	227	99	326	......
Camp	418	154	264	418	......
Cedar Mills	205	180	25	205	......
Cosmos	62	41	21	62	......
Flora	269	186	83	269	......
Hawk Creek	353	91	250	353	......
Preston Lake	198	133	65	198	......
Sacred Heart	316	86	230	316	......
RICE.					
Bridgewater	957	693	264	957	......
Cannon City	510	459	51	510	......
Erin	526	317	209	526	......
Faribault	4103	2842	1261	4064	a3
Faribault	3045	2127	918	3042	3
Forest	577	390	187	577	......
Morristown	1090	961	129	1090	......
Morristown	317	288	29	317	......
Northfield	2278	1753	525	2264	14
Richland	773	515	258	773	......
Shieldsville	558	307	251	558	......
Shieldsville	110	57	53	110	......
Walcott	599	497	102	598	1
Warsaw	1000	787	213	999	1
Webster	414	264	150	414	......
Wells	1153	808	345	1152	(b)
Wheatland	681	295	386	679	(c)
Wheeling	864	461	403	864	......
SCOTT.					
Belle Plaine	2375	1484	891	2375	......
Belle Plaine	497	307	190	497	......
Cedar Lake	756	490	266	756	......
Credit River	448	272	176	448	......
Eagle Creek (d)	1120	709	411	1110	(e)
Glendale	387	224	163	387	......
Helena	1089	503	586	1089	......
Louisville	358	212	146	351	7
New Market	472	227	245	472	......
Sand Creek	1520	886	634	1520	......
Shakopee	1263	759	504	1262	1
Shakopee City (d)	1349	861	488	1345	f1
Spring Lake	939	665	274	939	......
St. Lawrence	315	194	121	315	......
SHERBURNE.					
Baldwin	234	188	46	234	......
Big Lake	571	364	207	571	......
Clear Lake	137	122	15	137	......
Clinton Lake	152	95	57	152	......
Elk River	537	458	79	537	......
Livonia	263	200	63	263	......
Santiago	156	97	59	156	......
SIBLEY.					
Alfsborg	264	71	193	264	......
SIBLEY—Cont'd.					
Arlington	732	393	339	732	......
Clear Lake	156	43	113	156	......
Dryden	443	206	237	443	......
Faxon	587	325	262	587	......
Green Isle	437	218	219	437	......
Henderson	1291	718	573	1290	1
Henderson	706	382	324	706	......
Jesson Land	749	437	312	749	......
Kelso	442	231	211	442	......
New Auburn	300	240	60	300	......
Sibley	272	150	122	272	......
Transit	424	242	182	424	......
Washington Lake	608	388	220	608	......
STEARNS.					
Albany	231	63	168	231	......
Avon	211	92	119	211	......
Brockway	478	318	160	478	......
Crow Creek	197	75	122	197	......
Eden Lake	244	178	66	244	......
Fair Haven	320	254	66	320	......
Getty	366	263	103	361	5
Grove	424	226	198	424	......
Lake Henry	159	82	77	159	......
Le Sauk	268	179	89	268	......
Luxemburg	237	109	128	237	......
Lynden	270	225	45	270	......
Main Prairie	621	540	81	621	......
Melrose	269	198	71	269	......
Munson	795	431	364	795	......
North Fork	280	132	148	280	......
Oak	478	249	229	478	......
Painesville	318	243	75	318	......
Raymond	305	219	86	305	......
Rockville	403	238	165	403	......
Sauk Centre	1155	976	179	1155	......
St. Augusta	570	315	255	570	......
St. Cloud (g)	582	379	203	582	......
St. Cloud	2161	1446	715	2161	......
St. Joseph	868	478	390	868	......
St. Martin	556	313	243	556	......
St. Wendell	356	209	147	356	......
Wakefield	613	336	277	613	......
Zion	471	223	248	471	......
STEELE.					
Aurora	422	303	119	422	......
Berlin	409	257	152	409	......
Clinton Falls	338	289	49	337	1
Deerfield	438	275	163	438	......
Havana	636	409	227	636	......
Lemond	417	271	146	417	......
Medford	520	463	57	519	1
Meriden	739	527	212	739	......
Merton	548	404	144	548	......
Oak Glen	344	271	73	344	......
Owatonna (h)	502	338	164	501	1
Owatonna	2070	1693	377	2060	10
Somerset	566	334	232	566	......
Summit	322	254	68	322	......
ST. LOUIS.					
Duluth	3131	1266	1865	3109	22
Fond du Lac	800	240	560	790	(e)
Oneota	504	198	306	504	......
Rice Lake	36	4	32	36	......

(a) Also 36 Indians.
(b) Also 1 Indian.
(c) Also 2 Indians.
(d) Of Shakopee City; 1,029 in Shakopee; 320 in Eagle Creek.
(e) Also 10 Indians.
(f) Also 3 Indians.
(g) Exclusive of city of St. Cloud.
(h) Exclusive of city of Owatonna.

...—*Population of Minor Civil Divisions, &c.—MINNESOTA*—Continued.

	Total.	Nativity. Native.	Nativity. Foreign.	Race. White.	Race. Colored.
...	124	92	32	124	......
...	195	173	22	195	......
...	269	164	105	269	......
...	94	56	38	94	......
...	202	106	96	201	1
...	643	484	159	643	......
...	202	159	43	202	......
...	307	265	42	307	......
...	835	625	210	835	......
...	878	707	171	878	......
...	1769	1014	755	1769	......
...	336	171	165	336	......
d'g	782	493	289	782	......
...	590	412	178	589	1
...	812	676	136	812	......
...	716	462	254	716	......
...	380	260	120	380	......
...	2608	1952	656	2602	6
...	681	609	72	678	3
...	393	236	157	393	......
...	217	134	83	217	......
t..	642	519	123	642	......
...	1365	1134	231	1365	......
...	637	545	92	637	......
...	740	451	289	740	......
...	1739	1262	477	1726	13
...	460	294	166	460	......
...	793	414	379	793	......
...	458	294	164	458	......
...	429	337	92	429	......
e..	676	386	290	676	......
...	253	202	51	253	......
..	832	655	177	832	......
...	913	567	346	913	......
...	947	774	173	947	......
...	532	216	316	532	......
...	531	273	258	531	......
...	737	451	286	737	......
...	305	229	76	304	1
...	668	499	169	667	1
...	1031	791	240	1031	......
...	551	414	137	551	......
...	825	462	363	825	(a)
...	594	387	207	594	......
...	705	503	202	705	......
...	824	488	336	822	2
...	309	166	143	309	......
...	595	387	208	594	1
...	1698	764	934	1697	(b)
...	307	219	88	297	(c)
...	456	233	223	456	......
...	4506	2253	2253	4488	18
...	4124	2052	2072	4106	18
...	990	578	412	990	......
...	263	188	75	263	......

Counties.	Total.	Nativity. Native.	Nativity. Foreign.	Race. White.	Race. Colored.
WATONWAN—Con.					
Fieldon	254	196	58	254	......
Long Lake	225	76	149	225	......
Madelia	675	451	224	675	......
Riverdale	259	129	130	259	......
South Branch	146	135	11	146	......
St. James	141	58	83	141	......
Town. 105, R. 33 (d)	61	17	44	61	......
Town. 106, R. 31 (e)	215	120	95	215	......
Town. 106, R. 33 (g)	17	10	7	17	......
Town. 107, R. 32 (f)	123	24	99	123	......
Town. 107, R. 33 (f)	47	20	27	47	......
WILKIN.					
McCauleyville	117	57	60	117	......
Pomme de Terre	178	46	132	178	......
WINONA.					
Dresbach	311	238	73	311	......
Elba	681	443	238	681	......
Fremont	1006	695	311	1006	......
Hart	859	366	493	859	......
Hillsdale	417	275	142	417	......
Homer	837	640	197	837	......
Homer	91	83	8	91	......
Jefferson	640	320	320	640	......
Mount Vernon	559	299	260	559	......
New Hartford	692	521	171	692	......
Pleasant Hill	643	508	135	643	......
Richmond	219	161	58	219	......
Rolling Stone	595	385	210	595	......
Saratoga	1058	861	197	1058	......
St. Charles	1960	1546	414	1954	6
St. Charles	1151	917	234	1145	6
Utica	1370	964	406	1370	......
Warren	819	628	191	819	......
Whitewater	435	371	64	435	......
Wilson	1016	698	318	1016	......
Winona (h)	487	316	171	487	......
Winona	7192	4512	2680	7148	44
Wiscoy	523	421	102	523	......
WRIGHT.					
Albion	281	210	71	281	......
Buffalo	508	340	168	508	......
Chatham	161	99	62	161	......
Clear Water	552	444	108	552	......
Cokato	452	161	291	452	......
Corrinna	220	195	25	220	......
Frankfort	564	335	229	564	......
Franklin	797	509	288	797	......
French Lake	221	122	99	221	......
Maple Lake	381	222	159	381	......
Marysville	527	319	208	527	......
Middleville	362	313	49	362	......
Monticello	903	755	148	903	......
Otsego	595	509	86	595	......
Rockford	782	543	239	782	......
Silver Creek	285	223	62	285	......
South Side	143	127	16	143	......
Stockholm	534	212	322	534	......
Victor	596	441	155	596	......
Woodland	593	389	204	593	......

...lians.
...lian.
...dians.
...to Long Lake.

(e) Attached to Madelia.
(f) Attached to Riverdale.
(g) Attached to St. James.
(h) Exclusive of city of Winona.

TABLE IX.—*Population of Minor Civil Divisions, &c.—MISSISSIPPI.*

NOTE.—The marginal column marks beats, districts, precincts, or land-survey townships; the first indentation, cities; the second, towns. Names of towns are placed under the names of the civil divisions of the county in which they are respectively situated. The population of each beat, district, precinct, or land-survey township includes that of all towns situated in it.

Counties.	Total.	Nativity. Native.	Nativity. Foreign.	Race. White.	Race. Colored.
ADAMS. (*)					
Natchez	9057	8475	582	3728	5329
ALCORN. (*)					
Corinth	1512	1477	35	833	679
AMITE.					
Liberty	2639	2613	26	1140	1499
Liberty	560	540	20	337	223
Smithdale	1320	1317	3	556	764
Talbert's	2068	2062	6	994	1074
Thickwoods	2511	2509	2	596	1915
Tickfau	2435	2425	*10	910	1525
ATTALA.					
Beat 1	2595	2584	11	1599	996
Kosciusko	577	569	8	394	183
Beat 2	2507	2501	6	1670	837
Beat 3	2346	2340	6	1516	830
Beat 4	4477	4441	36	2068	2409
Beat 5	2851	2845	6	1975	876
CALHOUN.					
Town. 12, R. 1 E.	400	399	1	387	13
Town. 13, R. 1 E.	836	836	......	731	105
Town. 11, R. 1 W.	1116	1114	2	946	170
Town. 12, R. 1 W.	400	400	......	360	40
Town. 13, R. 1 W.	826	826	......	692	134
Pittsboro	186	186	......	156	30
Town. 14, R. 1 W.	1440	1436	4	1079	361
Town. 11, R. 2 W.	678	676	2	580	98
Town. 12, R. 2 W.	560	551	9	466	94
Town. 13, R. 2 W.	680	679	1	623	57
Town. 11, R. 3 W.	280	279	1	259	21
Town. 12, R. 3 W.	320	319	1	263	57
Town. 22, R. 8 E.	538	537	1	362	176
Town. 23, R. 8 E.	640	640	......	424	216
Town. 24, R. 8 E.	247	247	......	156	91
Town. 22, R. 9 E.	800	798	2	632	168
Town. 23, R. 9 E.	480	476	4	348	132
Town. 22, R. 10 E.	320	320	......	253	67
CARROLL.					
Beat 1, Abatanpaubogue	3537	3478	59	1733	1804
Beat 2, Puttuccocoah	847	844	3	318	529
Beat 3, Biacco	4532	4444	88	1492	3040
Beat 4, Big Sands	4581	4538	43	2492	2086
Carrollton	377	371	6	257	120
Beat 5, Hayes Cr'k	7550	7437	113	3459	4091
CHICKASAW. (*)					
Houston	400	397	3	259	141
Okalona	1410	1348	62	680	730
Sparta	99	99	......	37	62
CHOCTAW.					
Town. 17, R. 6	459	459	......	390	69
Town. 17, R. 7	828	828	......	581	247
Town. 18, R. 7	767	767	......	472	295
CHOCTAW—Cont'd.					
Town. 19, R. 7	934	930	4	469	465
Town. 20, R. 7	841	841	......	537	304
Town. 21, R. 7	309	309	......	147	162
Town. 17, R. 8	894	894	......	588	306
Town. 18, R. 8	623	622	1	526	97
Town. 19, R. 8	794	790	4	483	311
Town. 20, R. 8	563	563	......	392	171
Town. 21, R. 8	676	675	1	534	142
Town. 17, R. 9	840	836	4	521	319
Town. 18, R. 9	586	582	4	519	67
Town. 19, R. 9	676	675	1	436	240
Town. 20, R. 9	583	582	1	444	139
Town. 21, R. 9	734	734	......	552	182
Town. 17, R. 10	585	578	7	485	100
Town. 18, R. 10	671	661	10	565	106
Town. 19, R. 10	507	507	......	408	99
Town. 20, R. 10	579	577	2	438	141
Town. 21, R. 10	607	607	......	567	40
Town. 17, R. 11	609	606	3	492	117
Town. 18, R. 11	527	527	......	460	67
Town. 19, R. 11	552	551	1	498	54
Town. 20, R. 11	566	566	......	484	82
Town. 21, R. 11	678	676	2	568	110
CLAIBORNE.					
Beat 1	3393	3363	30	435	2958
Brandywine District	2029	2019	10	666	1363
Grand Gulf Precinct	2058	2031	27	455	1603
Grand Gulf	190	179	11	94	96
Pattona District	2813	2783	30	661	2152
Port Gibson	1088	979	109	617	471
Rock Springs District	2005	2000	5	556	1449
CLARK.					
District 1	1428	1418	10	817	611
District 2	2536	2525	11	1340	1196
District 3	2118	2074	44	1134	984
District 4	792	788	4	447	345
District 5	631	629	2	335	296
COAHOMA.					
Beat 1, Moon Lake	972	968	4	250	722
Beat 2, Friar's P't	1489	1441	48	490	999
Beat 3, Swan Lake	1967	1951	16	320	1647
Beat 4, Clarksdale	1931	1908	23	446	1485
Beat 5, Robersonville	785	771	14	257	528
COPIAH.					
District 1	2205	2169	36	1131	1074
Hazlehurst	662	630	32	478	184
District 3	2713	2703	10	1218	1495
District 4	629	627	2	197	432
Town'ps 1 and 2	8959	8924	35	3932	a5026
Town'ps 9 and 10	4459	4438	21	2647	1812
Beauregard	315	302	13	221	94
Crystal Sp'ngs	864	814	50	538	326
Wesson	464	448	16	333	131

(*) Incomplete; the other principal civil divisions were not separately returned.
(a) Also 1 Indian.

...LE IX.—*Population of Minor Civil Divisions, &c.—MISSISSIPPI*—Continued.

...nties.	Total.	Nativity. Native.	Nativity. Foreign.	Race. White.	Race. Colored.
...GTON.					
...Williams-	440	433	7	343	97
...Watt's	960	958	2	814	146
...Holloday	920	917	3	537	383
...ount Car-	1400	1393	7	639	761
...coha	1033	1029	4	773	260
...OTO.					
....	6844	6791	53	2948	3896
....	7840	7816	24	4043	3797
....	5831	5777	54	3127	2704
....	3557	3472	85	1251	2306
....	7949	7845	104	2907	5042
...ando	730	687	43	457	273
...ENE.					
..., Leakes-	406	406	......	357	49
...2, State	491	491	......	367	124
..., Smith's	373	371	2	361	12
...Lamlem	365	364	1	250	115
..., Vernal	403	400	3	331	72
...ADA.					
...s 21	2140	2115	25	706	1434
...s 22	5727	5531	196	2452	3275
...a	1887	1698	189	1133	754
...s 23	2704	2687	17	771	1933
...OCK.					
....	999	959	40	590	409
...wn	160	157	3	82	78
...ngton ..	479	465	14	194	285
....	400	398	2	326	74
...sville ...	71	71	......	21	50
....	40	38	2	25	15
....	1520	1497	23	1196	324
....	1280	1133	147	916	364
...SON.					
....	1320	1111	209	1167	153
....	954	763	191	838	116
....	1134	1029	105	741	393
...sboro ...	459	403	56	324	135
...ppi City	252	222	30	135	117
....	2688	2404	284	1923	765
...Christian	1951	1693	258	1318	633
....	404	404	......	293	111
....	249	248	1	244	5
...DS.					
...R. 1 E. ..	1439	1416	23	268	1171
...R. 1 W. ..	1480	1474	6	437	1043
...R. 1 W. ..	2844	2816	28	789	2055
...R. 1 W. ..	1359	1324	35	395	964
...R. 1 W. ..	628	618	10	340	288
...R. 1 W. ..	1679	1660	19	258	1421
...R. 2 W. ..	353	349	4	110	243
...R. 2 W. ..	2560	2549	11	875	1685
...R. 2 W. ..	439	403	36	302	137
...R. 2 W.	1200	1168	32	323	877

Counties.	Total.	Nativity. Native.	Nativity. Foreign.	Race. White.	Race. Colored.
HINDS—Cont'd.					
Town. 7, R. 2 W.	1979	1965	14	654	1325
Town. 3, R. 3 W.	452	451	1	211	241
Town. 4, R. 3 W.	320	319	1	44	276
Town. 5, R. 3 W.	480	477	3	83	397
Town. 6, R. 3 W.	200	195	5	55	145
Town. 7, R. 3 W.	1561	1554	7	321	1240
Town. 3, R. 4 W.	1600	1585	15	565	1035
Town. 4, R. 4 W.	840	839	1	252	588
Town. 5, R. 4 W.	2484	2463	21	519	1965
Town. 6, R. 4 W.	760	758	2	179	581
Town. 5, R. 5 W.	279	270	9	98	181
Town. 13, R. 5 W.	468	467	1	175	293
Town. 14, R. 5 W.	850	843	7	306	544
Jackson	4234	3830	404	2270	1964
HOLMES.					
Durant District ..	4861	4831	30	1957	2004
Durant	375	......	......	......	......
Eulogy District ..	1509	1500	9	478	1031
Lexingt'n District	3099	3055	44	907	2102
Lexington	744	......	......	......	......
Richland District.	5584	5540	44	1787	3797
Tchula District...	4317	4266	51	926	3391
ISSAQUENA.					
Dunbarton Precinct	604	601	3	71	533
Rolling Fork Precinct	1380	1333	47	280	1100
Schola Precinct ..	1285	1270	15	140	1145
Skipwith Precinct	2349	2332	17	165	2184
Tallula Precinct..	1269	1249	20	105	1164
ITAWAMBA.(a)					
Fulton	132	132	......	108	24
JACKSON.(a)					
Duck Bayou .	283	257	26	245	38
Mossy Point.	440	416	24	168	272
Ocean Spring	560	502	58	411	149
Pascagoula ...	480	449	31	277	203
JASPER.					
Center Beat......	3160	3114	46	1838	b1297
Paulding	262	256	6	154	108
Northeast Beat...	2407	2401	6	1066	c1244
Northwest Beat ..	832	828	4	491	341
Southeast Beat...	2395	2392	3	1080	d1252
Southwest Beat ..	2090	2089	1	1326	764
JEFFERSON.					
Beat 1, Union Ch..	440	438	2	220	220
Union Church	120	119	1	94	26
Beat 2, Ebenezer.	4563	4527	36	973	3500
Beat 3, Fayette ...	200	193	7	59	141
Fayette	120	113	7	47	73
Beat 4, Church Hill	5888	5849	39	1300	4588
Beat 5, Rodney ...	2757	2655	102	663	2094
Rodney	573	505	68	317	256
LAFAYETTE.(a)					
Oxford	1422	1341	81	980	442

...omplete; the other principal civil divisions were not separately returned.
...e incorporated city of Shieldsborough.
...so 23 Indians.
(c) Also 97 Indians.
(d) Also 63 Indians.

TABLE IX.—*Population of Minor Civil Divisions, &c.*—*MISSISSIPPI*—Continued.

Counties.	Total.	NATIVITY.		RACE.	
		Native.	Foreign.	White.	Colored.
LAUDERDALE.					
Beat 1 (a)	5990	5823	167	2963	3027
Beat 2	2440	2424	16	1235	1205
Beat 3 (a)	2265	2257	8	1356	903
Beat 4	1387	1385	2	658	729
Beat 5 (a)	1380	1375	5	839	541
Meridian	2709	2575	134	1547	1162
LAWRENCE.					
Town. 5, R. 10 E	600	600	......	307	293
Town. 6, R. 10 E	160	160	......	99	61
Town. 7, R. 10 E	160	159	1	86	74
Town. 8, R. 10 E	120	120	......	78	42
Town. 9, R. 10 E	200	200	......	116	84
Town. 5, R. 11 E	360	356	4	173	187
Town. 6, R. 11 E	280	280	......	130	150
Town. 7, R. 11 E	440	433	7	204	236
Monticello	200	194	6	95	105
Town. 8, R. 11 E	40	40	......	16	24
Town. 9, R. 11 E	200	200	......	83	117
Town. 5, R. 18 W	400	400	......	282	118
Town. 6, R. 18 W	880	880	......	511	369
Town. 7, R. 18 W	480	480	......	255	225
Town. 8, R. 18 W	400	400	......	282	118
Town. 9, R. 18 W	360	360	......	226	134
Town. 5, R. 19 W	560	554	6	238	322
Town. 6, R. 19 W	600	597	3	316	284
Town. 7, R. 19 W	240	240	......	112	128
Town. 8, R. 19 W	200	200	......	137	63
Town. 9, R. 19 W	40	40	......	27	13
LEE.					
District 1	3661	3656	5	2915	746
Baldwin	133	133	......	106	27
Gumtown	240	238	2	172	68
District 2	2417	2386	31	1764	653
Saltillo	148	144	4	128	20
District 3	3298	3285	13	2348	950
Tupelo	618	608	10	367	251
District 4	2459	2456	3	1520	939
District 5	4120	4100	20	2553	1567
LINCOLN.					
District 5	1703	1698	5	1175	528
Bogue Chitto	104	101	3	83	21
District 6	1962	1960	2	1326	636
District 7	3652	3548	104	2068	1584
Brookhaven	1614	1522	92	926	688
District 8	2867	2860	7	1453	1414
LOWNDES.					
District 1	2856	2851	5	554	2302
District 2	2555	2516	39	1282	1273
Columbus	4812	4633	179	2074	2738
District 3	2545	2526	19	692	1853
District 4	6708	6695	13	885	5823
District 5	11026	10955	71	1993	9033
West Point	1392	1360	32	711	681
MADISON.					
District 1	5640	5557	83	1109	4531
District 2	2205	2190	15	495	1810
District 3	4569	4507	62	984	3585
District 4	3102	3054	48	1077	2025
District 5	3379	3350	29	1069	2310
Canton	1963	1802	161	1085	878

Counties.	Total.	NATIVITY.		RACE.	
		Native.	Foreign.	White.	Colored.
MARION.					
Beat 1	1548	1543	5	767	781
Columbia	66	63	3	56	10
Beat 2	412	411	1	348	64
Beat 3	441	441	......	287	154
Beat 4	1127	1127	......	688	[illegible]
Beat 5	683	682	1	475	[illegible]
MARSHALL.					
Towns. 1, 2, and 3, range 1	3329	3310	19	873	2456
Town. 4, range 1	635	632	3	500	135
Town. 5, range 1	319	319	......	289	30
Town. 6, range 1	440	440	......	386	54
Towns. 1, 2, and 3, range 2	3011	2955	56	1190	1821
Town. 4, range 2	3046	2884	162	1805	1241
Holly Springs	2406	2261	140	1483	923
Town. 5, range 2	480	478	2	223	257
Town. 6, range 2	1158	1155	3	667	491
Towns. 1, 2, and 3, range 3	4396	4381	15	1869	2527
Town. 4, range 3	320	313	7	103	217
Town. 5, range 3	1106	1103	3	449	657
Waterford	40	40	......	36	4
Town. 6, range 3	478	478	......	279	199
Towns. 1, 2, and 3, range 4	2900	2875	25	1028	1872
Town. 4, range 4	1245	1241	4	427	818
Town. 5, range 4	2217	2202	15	695	1522
Chulahoma	139	133	6	114	25
Town. 6, range 4	800	797	3	392	408
Towns. 1, 2, and 3, range 5	2042	2001	41	885	1157
Town. 4, range 5	399	397	2	222	177
Town. 5, range 5	399	398	1	205	194
Town. 6, range 5	696	687	9	450	246
MONROE.					
District 4	14566	14472	94	4734	9832
Aberdeen	2022	1982	40	909	1113
District 5	8065	8040	25	3607	4458
NESHOBA.					
Beat 1	1497	1420	7	1060	[illegible]
Beat 2	1552	1546	6	903	[illegible]
Beat 3	1550	1547	3	1149	[illegible]
Beat 4	2056	2050	6	1547	[illegible]
Beat 5	854	850	4	734	[illegible]
NEWTON. (c)					
Beat 1. Centre	2597	2590	7	1713	f856
Hickory	155	153	2	120	35
Newton	154	154	......	131	23
Beat 2. Northeast	1293	1292	1	969	324
Beat 3. Northwest	2000	1948	52	1578	422
Beat 4. Southwest	1883	1865	18	868	1015
Beat 5. Southeast	2034	2027	7	1258	g769
NOXUBEE.					
District 1	4719	4682	37	710	4009
District 2	4161	4153	8	944	3217
District 3 (h)	6288	6254	34	1502	4786
District 4	2462	2449	13	865	1597
District 5	2300	2275	25	579	1721
Macon	975	945	30	487	488

(a) Exclusive of village of Meridian.
(b) Also 70 Indians.
(c) Also 143 Indians.
(d) Also 101 Indians.
(e) Also 260 Indians in the county at large.
(f) Also 28 Indians.
(g) Also 7 Indians.
(h) Exclusive of part of city of Macon.

L.—*Population of Minor Civil Divisions, &c.—MISSISSIPPI*—Continued.

	Total.	Nativity: Native.	Nativity: Foreign.	Race: White.	Race: Colored.
lle	3160	3137	23	959	2201
....	475	466	9	300	175
....	3847	3823	24	1206	2641
l e					
....	1996	1994	2	1466	530
ield	1728	1728	......	1169	559
s w					
...	4160	4155	5	787	3373
....	3717	3691	26	1088	2629
....	4468	4423	45	1575	2893
....	2714	2698	16	1270	1444
....	3628	3598	30	1958	1670
....	6227	6154	73	2277	3950
....	227	216	11	150	77
....	192	190	2	108	84
....	80	79	1	58	22
k..	492	492	......	405	87
C'k	240	240	......	203	37
Hill.	40	40	......	32	8
....	82	82	......	71	11
...	720	720	......	382	338
asta	120	118	2	57	63
roo	120	120	......	117	3
....	360	359	1	274	86
....	80	79	1	73	7
C'k	280	279	1	224	56
n's					
....	80	80	......	75	5
E...	795	684	111	627	168
E...	960	911	49	458	502
E...	640	630	10	241	b398
E...	1651	1486	165	1029	622
E...	634	615	19	285	349
and					
...	1230	1203	27	528	702
...	578	575	3	226	352
...	318	318	......	208	110
...	616	613	3	283	333
...	426	415	11	198	228
...	240	240	......	161	79
and					
....	791	791	......	435	356
E ..	295	290	5	129	166
E ..	638	635	3	396	242
E ..	265	265	......	121	144
E ..	102	102	......	66	36
E .	622	622	......	374	248
E ..	270	268	2	160	110
E ..	232	232	......	65	167
....	384	383	1	239	145
.6..	925	923	2	772	153
.6..	1942	1939	3	1487	455
.6..	1779	1774	5	1072	707
.7..	640	637	3	475	165
.7..	768	765	3	637	131
...	458	456	2	343	115
.7..	600	598	2	549	51
.8..	317	317	......	311	6

Counties.	Total.	Nativity: Native.	Nativity: Foreign.	Race: White.	Race: Colored.
PRENTISS—Cont'd.					
Township 5, R. 8..	615	615	......	579	36
Township 6, R. 8..	566	566	......	560	6
Township 7, R. 8..	280	280	......	275	5
Township 4, R. 9..	185	185	......	180	5
Township 5, R. 9..	280	280	......	272	8
Township 6, R. 9..	238	238	......	229	9
Township 7, R. 9..	213	213	......	196	17
RANKIN.					
Beat 1. Steen's C'k	2713	2686	27	1030	1683
Beat 2. Brandon ..	2978	2932	46	922	2056
Brandon......	756	731	25	431	325
Beat 3. Fannin ...	2679	2656	23	1479	1200
Bt. 4. Pelahatchee.	2229	2210	19	801	1428
Beat 5. Cato	2378	2376	2	1472	906
SCOTT.					
Precinct 1. Hillsboro, (V)	2514	2498	16	1459	1055
Precinct 2. Sherman Hill	1479	1478	1	550	929
Prec. 3. Morton...	1446	1442	4	971	475
Prec. 4. Ludlow ..	777	776	1	495	282
Prec. 5. Damascus	1631	1623	8	1205	426
SIMPSON.					
Beat 1............	1040	1037	3	699	341
Beat 2............	1120	1120	......	630	490
Beat 3............	1518	1513	5	916	602
Beat 4............	880	880	......	481	399
Beat 5............	1160	1159	1	843	317
SMITH.					
Beat 1............	1700	1694	6	1215	485
Raleigh	111	107	4	94	17
Beat 2............	985	981	4	757	228
Beat 3............	1279	1278	1	1090	189
Beat 4............	1862	1860	2	1440	422
Beat 5............	1300	1297	3	913	387
SUNFLOWER.					
District 1.........	1552	1498	54	484	1068
McNutt	44	39	5	44	......
District 2.........	1266	1233	33	421	845
District 3.........	1163	1091	72	462	701
District 4.........	778	772	6	290	488
District 5.........	256	254	2	115	141
TALLAHATCHIE.					
District 1	1788	1762	26	882	906
District 2.........	1960	1942	18	881	1079
District 3.........	1329	1327	2	499	830
District 4.........	1802	1793	9	727	1075
District 5.........	973	967	6	226	747
TIPPAH.					
Township 1, R. 1..	551	550	1	185	366
Township 2, R. 1..	1069	1066	3	429	640
Township 3, R. 1..	1031	1028	3	592	439
Township 4, R. 1..	565	563	2	456	109
Township 5, R. 1..	635	634	1	470	165
Township 6, R. 1..	672	670	2	605	67
Township 1, R. 2..	620	616	4	315	305
Township 2, R. 2..	771	768	3	712	59
Township 3, R. 2..	551	551	......	524	27
Township 4, R. 2..	538	538	......	394	144

places named constitute the county as returned.

(b) Also 1 Indian.

TABLE IX.—*Population of Minor Civil Divisions, &c.—MISSISSIPPI*—Continued.

Counties.	Total.	Nativity. Native.	Nativity. Foreign.	Race. White.	Race. Colored.
TIPPAH—Cont'd.					
Township 5, R. 2..	666	666	......	470	196
Township 6, R. 2..	717	716	1	483	234
Township 1, R. 3..	392	392	......	372	20
Township 2, R. 3..	831	830	1	740	91
Township 3, R. 3..	836	835	1	790	46
Township 4, R. 3..	1361	1353	8	857	504
Ripley	422	416	6	264	158
Township 5, R. 3..	1120	1119	1	592	528
Township 6, R. 3..	1120	1116	4	794	326
Township 1, R. 4..	476	475	1	418	58
Township 2, R. 4..	852	852	......	762	90
Township 3, R. 4..	790	790	......	634	156
Township 4, R. 4..	663	659	4	483	180
Township 5, R. 4..	1212	1211	1	1066	146
Township 6, R. 4..	764	764	......	724	40
Township 3, R. 5..	353	353	......	353	......
Township 4, R. 5..	316	316	......	291	25
Township 5, R. 5..	483	482	1	439	44
Township 6, R. 5..	772	768	4	686	86
TISHOMINGO.					
Beat 1. Iuka......	2754	2735	19	2366	388
Beat 2. Eastport..	1650	1647	3	1522	128
Bt. 3. Cartersville.	1045	1045	......	936	109
Beat 4. Highland .	846	842	4	768	78
Bt. 5. Bay Springs	1055	1054	1	1017	38
TUNICA.					
District 1.........	1483	1461	22	223	1260
District 2.........	613	612	1	123	490
District 3.........	2203	2179	24	420	1783
District 4.........	319	316	3	211	108
District 5.........	740	737	3	254	486
WARREN.					
Bovina Precinct..	4043	4017	26	458	3585
Davis' Bend Prec't	1600	1584	16	40	1560
Meredith Precinct	745	741	4	73	672
Mildale Precinct .	480	466	14	194	286
Oak Ridge Prec't .	1160	1150	10	442	718
Red Bone Precinct	3001	2979	22	601	2400
Vicksburg	12443	11027	1416	5638	6805
Warrenton Prec't.	1760	1734	26	247	1513
Yazoo Precinct...	1537	1485	52	214	1323
WASHINGTON. (*)					
Greenville....	890	756	134	489	401
WAYNE.					
Beat 1............	636	630	6	372	264
Beat 2............	668	664	4	376	292
Winchester ..	14	14	......	11	3
Beat 3............	1398	1396	2	656	742
Beat 4............	986	986	......	697	289
Beat 5............	518	516	2	469	49
WILKINSON.					
District 1.........	3426	3339	87	912	2514
District 2.........	3840	3830	10	439	3401
District 3.........	1519	1510	9	283	1236
District 4........	2480	2442	38	473	2007
District 5.........	1440	1437	3	501	939
WINSTON.					
Town. 13, R. 10 E..	497	478	1	412	85
Town. 14, R. 10 E..	792	780	12	543	249
Town. 16, R. 10 E..	640	633	7	304	336
Town. 13, R. 11 E..	880	880	......	523	(a)348
Town. 14, R. 11 E..	800	799	1	420	380
Town. 16, R. 11 E..	797	779	18	304	493
Town. 13, R. 12 E..	480	474	6	298	182
Town. 14, R. 12 E..	559	558	1	347	212
Town. 15, R. 12 E..	507	503	4	308	199
Louisville	385	381	4	256	129
Town. 16, R. 12 E..	454	450	4	318	136
Town. 13, R. 13 E..	159	159	......	138	21
Town. 14, R. 13 E..	74	74	......	38	36
Town. 15, R. 13 E..	558	558	......	336	222
Town. 16, R. 13 E..	630	630	......	428	202
Town. 13, R. 14 E..	272	271	1	182	90
Town. 14, R. 14 E..	160	160	......	77	83
Town. 15, R. 14 E..	265	264	1	189	76
Town. 16, R. 14 E..	478	476	2	407	71
YAZOO.					
District 1.........	4381	4353	28	525	3856
District 2.........	6191	6044	147	2334	3857
District 3.........	6707	6655	52	2035	4672

(*) Incomplete; the other principal civil divisions were not separately returned.
(*a*) Also 9 Indians.

TABLE IX.—Population of Minor Civil Divisions, &c.—MISSOURI.

...e marginal column marks townships or land-survey townships; the first indentation, ...econd, towns. Names of towns are placed under the names of the townships or land-sur...ps in which they are respectively situated. The population of each township or land-sur...p includes that of all towns situated in it.

...s.	Total.	Nativity: Native.	Nativity: Foreign.	Race: White.	Race: Colored.
......	3369	3260	109	3254	115
...le	1471	1411	60	1404	67
......	1340	1273	67	1340	......
......	854	823	31	853	1
......	877	867	10	877	......
......	420	407	13	417	3
......	1041	1008	33	1036	5
......	769	758	11	754	15
......	1164	1010	54	1162	2
...e	100	97	3	100	......
......	495	477	18	495	......
......	1119	1089	30	1117	2
......	32	32	......	32	......
...r.					
......	2401	2339	62	2333	68
......	271	267	4	263	8
......	1605	1509	96	1516	89
......	2680	2469	211	2663	17
...y City	286	260	26	286	......
......	2363	2231	132	2203	160
...h	1257	1159	98	1126	131
......	3416	3254	162	3398	18
......	2672	2459	213	2624	49
...er	218	205	13	216	2
...N.					
......	680	511	169	674	6
......	905	861	44	904	1
......	1276	1197	79	1274	2
......	1673	1513	160	1662	11
...ns	1250	1178	72	1250	......
......	75	74	1	75	......
......	562	539	23	561	1
......	1120	1015	105	1110	10
...t	490	450	40	480	10
......	265	253	12	265	......
......	974	898	76	970	a3
...City ..	252	225	27	252	......
...N.					
......	1480	1409	71	1423	57
......	300	277	23	283	17
......	1003	940	63	969	34
......	1191	1147	44	1111	80
......	5602	5339	263	4809	793
......	2602	2434	168	2097	505
......	991	924	67	943	48
......	1740	1684	56	1699	41
...					
...k	984	982	2	984	......
...k	527	527	......	513	14
......	1571	1567	4	1565	6
...o	287	287	......	283	4
...rie	857	847	10	857	......
......	509	509	......	507	a1
......	704	704	......	704	......
...ver	667	661	6	667	......
......	1686	1682	4	1679	7
...k	2112	2110	2	2088	24
...r	756	756	......	756	......

Counties.	Total.	Nativity: Native.	Nativity: Foreign.	Race: White.	Race: Colored.
BARTON.					
Barton City	270	256	14	270	......
Doylesport	385	359	26	385	......
East Fork	452	446	6	452	......
Golden Grove	405	400	5	401	4
Lamar	1611	1551	60	1599	12
Nashville	466	453	13	465	1
Newton	802	788	14	802	......
North Fork	544	532	12	544	......
Union	152	146	6	150	2
BATES.					
Boone	1257	1232	25	1252	5
Charlotte	1289	1256	33	1285	4
Deer Creek	1057	1045	12	1055	2
Grand River	1024	1009	15	1021	3
Lone Oak	1360	1320	40	1360	......
Mingo	789	775	14	789	......
Mount Pleasant ..	2688	2587	101	2623	65
Butler	1064	1013	51	1027	37
Osage	500	495	5	498	2
Prairie City	1786	1612	174	1776	10
Pleasant Gap	1634	1572	62	1630	4
Spruce	1506	1457	49	1483	23
Walnut Creek	1070	1062	8	1068	2
BENTON.					
Alexander	921	917	4	904	17
Cole	865	734	131	865	......
Fristoe	1401	1374	27	1391	10
Lindsey	1383	1338	45	1294	89
Tom	799	786	13	779	20
Union	1185	1162	23	1183	2
Warsaw Landing	498	491	7	435	63
White	1993	1848	145	1955	38
Williams	2277	1548	729	2196	81
BOLLINGER.					
Fillmore	427	424	3	413	14
German	1117	1100	17	1117	......
Lorance	2872	2748	124	2864	8
Liberty	1680	1557	123	1676	4
Union	143	1368	68	1430	6
Wayne	630	626	4	616	14
BOONE.					
Bourbon	2384	2314	70	2268	116
Cedar	5020	4967	53	4204	816
Columbia	5560	5422	138	3810	1750
Columbia	2236	2151	85	1438	798
Missouri	2812	2777	35	2022	790
Rocheport	823	797	26	562	261
Perche	3119	3104	15	2903	216
Rocky Fork	1870	1855	15	1520	350
BUCHANAN.					
Bloomington	1487	1457	30	1343	144
De Kalb	224	214	10	202	22
Center	1918	1763	155	1870	48
Crawford	1516	1508	8	1436	80
Jackson	890	876	14	878	12
Lake	297	287	10	297	......

(a) Also 1 Indian.

300

TABLE IX.—*Population of Minor Civil Divisions, &c.*—MISSOURI—Continued.

Counties.	Total.	Nativity. Native.	Nativity. Foreign.	Race. White.	Race. Colored.
BUCHANAN—Con.					
Marion	1697	1517	180	1679	18
Easton	318	293	25	314	4
Platte	1159	1135	24	1150	9
Rush	1629	1562	67	1591	38
St. Joseph	19565	14339	5226	18052	a1512
Tremont	1106	1074	32	1095	11
Washington (b)	3042	2511	531	2967	75
Wayne	803	767	36	797	6
BUTLER.					
Ash Hills	491	490	1	491	......
Black River	492	483	9	492	......
Beaver Dam	786	776	10	772	14
Cane Creek	323	322	1	323	......
Epps	263	259	4	263	......
Gillis Bluff	203	202	1	203	......
Poplar Bluff	840	834	6	833	c5
St. Francis	246	246	......	246	......
Thomas	654	653	1	652	2
CALDWELL.					
Breckinridge	1336	1244	92	1332	4
Breckinridge	515	491	24	512	3
Davis	573	549	24	569	4
Fairview	910	840	70	909	1
Proctorville	60	57	3	60	......
Gomer	558	514	44	534	24
Grant	909	866	43	893	16
Hamilton	1658	1540	118	1580	78
Hamilton	975	918	57	925	50
Kidder	922	820	102	922	......
Kidder	195	166	29	195	......
Kingston	1277	1226	51	1130	147
Kingston	414	398	16	357	57
Lincoln	589	552	37	589	......
Mirabile	931	908	23	926	5
Mirabile	140	137	3	138	2
New York	857	811	46	857	......
Rockford	870	845	25	865	5
CALLAWAY.					
Auxvasse	2050	1882	168	1613	437
Portland	121	101	20	110	11
Bourbon	1590	1573	17	1306	284
Cedar	2453	2387	66	1907	546
Côte sans Dessein	869	858	11	756	113
Fulton	4565	4270	295	3622	943
Fulton	1585	1442	143	1155	430
Liberty	1646	1635	11	1350	296
Nine-Mile Prairie	3679	3637	42	3123	556
Round Prairie	1211	1126	85	999	212
St. Aubert	1139	1130	9	1032	107
CAMDEN.					
Adair	637	632	5	637	......
Auglaize	1330	1307	23	1313	17
Jackson	810	808	2	800	10
Jasper	292	288	4	285	7
Osage	1426	1397	29	1336	90
Linn Creek	132	129	3	106	26
Russell	1141	1131	10	1141	......
Warren	472	469	3	447	25
CAPE GIRARDEAU.					
Apple Creek	2626	2247	379	2498	128
Byrd	2112	1830	282	1812	300
Jackson	459	381	78	421	38

Counties.	Total.	Nativity. Native.	Nativity. Foreign.	Race. White.	Race. Colored.
CAPE GIRARD'U—C'd.					
Cape Girardeau (d)	1651	1427	224	1319	332
Cape Girardeau	3585	2527	1058	3083	502
Hubble	1689	1294	395	1536	153
Liberty	870	841	29	865	5
Randol	1534	1331	203	1423	111
Shawnee	1676	1493	183	1528	148
Welch	589	550	39	587	2
White Water	1226	1181	45	1220	6
CARROLL.					
Grand River	3802	3678	124	3604	198
De Witt	317	311	6	317	......
Hurricane	2285	2203	82	2275	10
Morris	3831	3658	173	3810	21
Sugartree Bottom	2186	2022	164	2046	140
Norborne	148	125	23	148	......
Wakanda	5342	5063	279	4914	428
Carrollton	1832	1711	121	1597	235
CARTER.					
Carter	760	755	5	741	19
Jackson	695	689	6	684	11
CASS.					
Austin	1366	1330	36	1360	6
Big Creek	1097	1070	27	1089	8
Camp Branch	1258	1231	27	1258	......
Cold Water	439	425	14	438	1
Dolan	1475	1377	98	1472	3
Everett	905	896	9	889	16
Grand River	3978	3830	148	3840	138
Harrisonville	1032	967	65	954	78
Index	795	761	34	789	6
Mount Pleasant	712	700	12	702	10
North Dolan	903	894	9	895	8
Pleasant Hill	3502	3245	257	3231	c271
Pleasant Hill	2554	2328	226	2309	c245
Polk	1307	1269	38	1293	14
Sugar Creek	1559	1529	30	1538	21
CEDAR.					
Benton	1130	1122	8	1128	2
Box	1307	1271	36	1307	......
Cedar	788	777	11	784	4
Jefferson	1040	1036	4	1016	24
Lynn	2670	2638	32	2638	32
Madison	1561	1554	7	1533	28
Washington	978	972	6	957	21
CHARITON.					
Bee Branch	1593	1437	156	1575	18
Bowling Green	1496	1349	147	941	555
Brunswick	4576	4225	351	3810	766
Brunswick	1645	1444	201	1175	470
Buffalo Lick	1267	1240	27	1083	184
Chariton	651	608	43	423	228
Clarke	939	909	30	926	13
Cunningham	761	714	47	759	2
Keytesville	1663	1602	61	1351	312
Keytesville	529	498	31	385	144
Missouri	820	802	18	634	186
Muscle Fork	710	702	8	692	18
Prairie	1473	1370	103	1160	313
Salisbury	1497	1366	131	1370	127
Salisbury	626	567	59	539	87
Wayland	674	651	23	631	43
Yellow Creek	1016	966	50	961	55

(a) Also 1 Indian.
(b) Exclusive of city of St. Joseph.
(c) Also 2 Indians.
(d) Exclusive of city of Cape Girardeau.

ABLE IX.—*Population of Minor Civil Divisions, &c.*—*MISSOURI*—Continued.

…unties.	Total.	Nativity. Native.	Nativity. Foreign.	Race. White.	Race. Colored.
…ISTIAN.					
…………	527	526	1	527	……
…………	1276	1275	1	1183	93
…y………	480	478	2	475	5
…………	1440	1436	4	1439	1
…den…….	81	80	1	81	……
…………	309	309	……	304	5
…………	473	472	1	473	……
…………	1243	1217	26	1238	5
…………	959	957	2	953	a5
…ARKE.					
…………	1119	1046	73	1079	40
…ines……	1235	1206	29	1170	65
…Francisv'e.	408	398	10	403	5
…………	824	809	15	824	……
…………	756	699	57	745	11
…………	1472	1317	155	1466	6
…a………	843	802	41	843	……
…………	1100	1002	98	1097	3
…)………	1060	1017	43	972	88
…ome……	1000	967	33	972	28
…………	1155	1051	104	1150	5
…………	902	832	70	886	16
…xandria ..	688	627	61	673	13
…rton……	1316	1271	45	1294	22
…da…….	885	832	53	874	11
…LAY.					
…River….	2798	2727	71	2577	221
…souri…..	572	551	21	484	88
…………	2241	2126	115	1944	297
…………	4831	4527	304	4034	797
…rty…….	1700	1558	142	1358	342
…………	3085	3032	53	2641	444
…gton……	2609	2545	64	2522	87
…rney……	396	375	21	386	10
…STON.					
…………	2491	2201	290	2265	226
…tsburg …	1067	956	111	908	159
…………	1925	1627	298	1785	140
…………	1752	1733	19	1624	128
…esville…	27	27	……	26	1
…esville…	248	246	2	245	3
…le…….	2007	1949	58	1970	37
…………	1782	1682	100	1755	27
…rop……	523	467	56	516	7
…………	1631	1565	66	1583	48
…………	2475	2279	196	2398	77
…eron…..	1428	1325	103	1366	62
…OLE.					
…………	800	732	68	781	19
…(b)…….	1839	1557	282	1483	356
…on City …	4420	3374	1046	3704	716
…………	901	607	294	850	51
…………	1108	1015	93	1048	60
…………	620	500	120	587	33
…………	604	449	155	588	16
…OPER.					
…ter……	548	544	4	466	82
…e………	5319	4397	922	4096	1223
…ville…..	3506	2844	662	2671	835
…Fork…..	1126	1011	115	1046	80
…eck…….	1198	963	235	1078	120
…………	1372	1327	45	1139	233

Counties.	Total.	Nativity. Native.	Nativity. Foreign.	Race. White.	Race. Colored.
COOPER—Cont'd.					
La Mine……….	1088	1060	28	853	235
Lebanon……….	3316	2984	332	2974	342
Moniteau……….	1373	1314	59	1275	98
Palestine……….	2430	2299	131	1976	454
Pilot Grove…….	1086	973	113	964	122
Saline………….	1836	1725	111	1473	363
CRAWFORD.					
Benton………….	1184	1060	124	1158	26
Boone………….	839	796	43	838	1
Courtois……….	960	943	17	953	7
Knob View…….	515	430	85	511	4
Liberty……….	1071	1028	43	1064	7
Meramec……….	907	886	21	876	31
Steelville….	232	226	6	212	20
Oak Hill ………	707	673	34	700	7
Osage………….	784	770	14	784	……
Union………….	1015	1003	12	1012	3
DADE.					
Centre………….	1568	1554	14	1505	63
Greenfield….	364	359	5	356	8
Grant………….	279	260	19	279	……
Horse Creek……	597	584	13	597	……
Marion…………	414	395	19	412	2
Morgan………..	2114	2111	3	2026	88
North…………	725	723	2	716	9
Polk………….	1453	1443	10	1442	11
Smith…………	504	503	1	490	14
South…………	1029	1025	4	1012	17
DALLAS.					
Benton………	2055	2032	23	2014	41
Buffalo…….	278	274	4	273	5
Grant…………	1002	996	6	994	8
Jackson………	1432	1431	1	1401	31
Jasper………..	933	913	20	933	……
Lincoln……….	943	942	1	943	……
Miller………..	548	548	……	548	……
Washington…..	1470	1459	11	1461	9
DAVIESS.					
Benton…………	1199	1196	3	1194	5
Colfax…………	584	564	20	584	……
Grand River……	1093	1086	7	1092	1
Grant………….	784	775	9	779	5
Harrison……….	831	803	28	804	27
Jackson……….	1059	1050	9	1053	6
Jefferson……….	1059	1018	41	1030	29
Liberty……….	781	749	32	777	4
Lincoln……….	736	730	6	723	13
Marion…………	1321	1307	14	1287	34
Monroe…………	729	712	17	707	22
Salem………….	986	981	5	982	4
Sheridan……….	923	899	24	913	10
Union………….	1515	1494	21	1354	161
Washington……	810	803	7	807	3
DE KALB.					
Adams………….	879	831	48	869	10
Camden……….	1359	1259	100	1342	17
Colfax…………	796	669	127	791	5
Dallas………….	807	782	25	807	……
Grand River……	959	926	33	952	7
Grant………….	956	924	32	956	……
Polk…………..	957	919	38	956	1
Sherman……….	1116	1082	34	1116	……
Washington……	2029	1863	166	1947	82

(a) Also 1 Indian.

(b) Exclusive of Jefferson City.

TABLE IX.—*Population of Minor Civil Divisions, &c.—MISSOURI*—**Continued.**

Counties.	Total.	Nativity.		Race.	
		Native.	Foreign.	White.	Colored.
DENT.					
Current	467	463	4	459	8
Franklin	848	842	6	846	2
Linn	403	398	5	398	5
Marameo	374	365	9	371	3
Norman	730	721	9	729	1
Osage	288	287	1	282	6
Spring Creek	1281	1255	26	1278	3
Salem	280	271	9	280	......
Texas	870	870	......	869	1
Watkins	816	781	35	814	2
DOUGLAS.					
Benton	379	378	1	379	......
Boone	480	478	2	479	1
Buchanan	430	427	3	430	......
Campbell	413	411	2	413	......
Cass	410	410	......	410	......
Clay	333	333	......	333	......
Finley	332	331	1	331	1
Jackson	330	330	......	310	20
Lincoln	209	209	......	209	......
Spring Creek	386	385	1	381	5
Washington	213	213	......	213	......
DUNKLIN.					
Clay	1426	1419	7	1380	46
Freeborn	1104	1100	4	1033	71
Four-Mile	830	828	2	828	2
Holcomb's	608	607	1	583	25
Independence	747	740	7	735	12
Salem	470	470	......	468	2
Union	797	794	3	789	8
FRANKLIN.					
Bœuf	3910	2925	985	3559	351
Boone	1655	1359	96	1649	6
Boles	5183	4022	1161	4588	595
Pacific	1208	918	290	1028	180
Calvy	2100	1946	154	1943	157
Central	2271	2062	209	2067	204
Lyon	3528	2362	1166	3434	94
Meramec	1480	1314	166	1461	19
Prairie	1502	1435	67	1353	149
Union	2855	1951	904	2694	161
Washington	5614	3807	1807	5177	437
GASCONADE.					
Bœuf	1277	851	426	1277	......
Boulware	983	656	327	977	6
Brush Creek	566	460	106	566	......
Barbois	800	736	64	799	1
Canaan	1107	898	209	1107	......
Richland	1099	634	465	1064	35
Roark	3033	1771	1262	2995	38
Hermann	1335	738	597	1322	13
Third Creek	1228	841	387	1228	......
Third Creek	200	121	79	200	......
GENTRY.					
Athens	2211	2158	53	2187	24
Albany	607	591	16	586	21
Bogle	991	951	40	988	3
Cooper	1498	1450	48	1494	4
Howard	1310	1301	9	1306	4
Huggins	1112	1090	22	1112	......
Jackson	1037	976	61	1035	2
Miller	2596	2533	63	2577	19
Gentryville	255	250	5	249	6
Wilson	852	839	13	852	......
GREENE.					
Boone	1692	1648	44	1604	88
Campbell	8694	8067	627	7088	1606
Springfield	5555	5089	466	4465	1090
Cass	1531	1526	5	1484	47
Center	1681	1647	34	1679	2
Clay	840	834	6	786	54
Jackson	1759	1741	18	1700	59
Pond Creek	882	842	40	868	14
Robinson	2419	2392	27	2292	127
Taylor	998	995	3	953	45
Wilson	1053	1039	14	939	114
GRUNDY.					
Franklin	1029	993	36	1029	......
Jefferson	874	858	16	869	5
Liberty	1036	1016	20	1036	......
Madison	1396	1366	30	1372	24
Marion	2284	2236	48	2267	17
Trenton	2934	2799	135	2865	69
Trenton	920	875	45	884	36
Washington	1014	1008	6	1014	......
HARRISON.					
Bethany	2460	2417	43	2451	9
Butler	748	742	6	748	......
Clay	911	894	17	911	......
Cypress	1230	1226	4	1230	......
Dallas	551	524	27	551	......
Lincoln	555	530	25	555	......
Madison	861	828	33	861	......
Marion	2567	2496	71	2567	......
Sugar Creek	1133	1116	17	1132	1
Trail Creek	1085	1075	10	1085	......
Union	1193	1176	17	1193	......
Washington	469	453	16	469	......
White Oak	872	869	3	872	......
HENRY.					
Big Creek	1390	1369	21	1363	27
Bogard	1117	1057	60	1080	37
Deep Water	2055	1898	157	2011	44
Grand River	5450	5129	321	5127	323
Clinton	640	574	66	621	19
Osage	828	809	19	826	2
Springfield	1896	1876	20	1869	27
Tebo	3308	3196	112	3156	152
White Oak	1357	1298	59	1327	30
HICKORY.					
Centre	1245	1208	37	1195	50
Green	1217	1201	16	1203	14
Montgomery	1575	1449	126	1560	15
Quincy	80	80	......	80	......
Wheatland	80	73	7	80	......
Stark	1130	1113	17	1125	5
Tyler	1285	1231	54	1279	6
HOLT.					
Benton	2226	2145	81	2205	21
Clay	887	866	21	887	......
Dallas	1285	1225	60	1278	7
Lewis	4081	3843	238	3962	119
Forest City	676	629	47	654	22
Oregon	824	766	58	770	54
Nodaway	2055	1919	136	2022	33
Union	1118	1005	113	1114	4

IX.—*Population of Minor Civil Divisions, &c.—MISSOURI*—Continued.

	Total.	Nativity. Native.	Nativity. Foreign.	Race. White.	Race. Colored.
....	1249	1239	10	1141	108
....	1686	1679	7	1366	320
....	4043	3769	274	2578	1465
....	1795	1582	213	1137	658
....	2474	2372	102	1704	770
klin	227	221	6	217	10
....	2317	2304	13	1542	775
....	2476	2420	56	1793	683
....	220	209	11	148	72
....	2988	2896	92	1916	1072
....	815	778	37	552	263
....	809	806	3	804	5
....	177	176	1	172	5
....	349	346	3	349	......
....	976	966	10	965	11
ns..	130	123	7	129	1
....	421	406	15	420	1
....	430	427	3	430	......
....	448	444	4	447	(a)
s ..	608	606	2	606	2
....	3058	2634	424	2741	317
....	250	237	13	215	35
...	573	501	72	528	45
) ..	581	392	189	476	105
....	417	415	2	417	......
....	1118	1051	67	1088	30
....	463	456	7	463	......
....	479	469	10	479	......
....	743	731	12	738	5
....	3603	3433	170	3425	178
....	1695	1650	45	1582	113
e ..	3184	2824	360	2553	631
....	32260	24581	7679	28484	b3770
....	1612	1345	267	1484	128
....	3493	3310	183	3375	118
....	2707	2668	39	2650	57
....	2036	2018	18	2012	24
....	2305	2201	104	2250	55
....	1051	962	89	989	d60
....	1095	924	171	1006	89
....	765	743	22	765	......
....	948	889	59	942	6
....	1238	1226	12	1237	1
....	758	721	37	752	6
....	3964	3811	153	3922	42
....	2035	1996	39	2012	23
....	1195	1170	25	1192	3
....	868	856	12	867	1
....	1174	1134	40	1159	15
....	1983	1964	19	1942	41
....	2033	1873	160	1975	58
....	1789	1543	246	1763	26
....	1865	1604	261	1622	243
....	2764	2143	621	2712	52
....	1217	1104	113	1138	79
....	2896	1994	902	2804	92
....	2816	2410	406	2603	213

...so 1 Indian.
...so 6 Indians.

Counties.	Total.	Nativity. Native.	Nativity. Foreign.	Race. White.	Race. Colored.
JOHNSON.					
Chilhowie	1362	1335	27	1340	22
Chilhowie	185	180	5	184	1
Columbus	1394	1386	8	1279	115
Columbus	168	167	1	147	21
Grover	1233	1157	76	1204	29
Hazle Hill........	1904	1878	26	1798	106
Fayetteville..	139	136	3	133	6
Jackson	2200	2176	24	2150	50
Kingsville.........	1360	1317	43	1347	13
Kingsville....	298	295	3	293	5
Madison...........	3329	3083	246	3176	153
Holden	1576	1410	166	1514	62
Post Oak	2631	2589	42	2516	a114
Cornelia	57	57	......	57	......
Eldorado	24	24	......	23	1
Rose Hill..........	1439	1416	23	1400	39
Rose Hill.....	199	197	2	186	13
Warrensburg.....	4804	4519	285	4151	653
Warrensburg	2945	2722	223	2447	498
Washington......	2992	2809	183	2828	164
Knob Noster	914	847	67	879	35
KNOX.					
Benton	1602	1481	121	1596	6
Centre............	2416	2194	222	2368	48
Edina	807	728	79	784	23
Fabius	1587	1557	30	1510	77
Newark	354	339	15	304	50
Greensburg	994	874	120	986	8
Jeddo	1134	1092	42	1115	19
Lyon	1121	1084	37	1113	8
Salt River........	2120	2086	34	2086	34
LACLEDE.					
Gasconade........	655	654	1	652	3
Hooker	1114	1096	18	1094	20
Lebanon..........	3358	3123	235	3228	130
Lebanon......	1090	1000	90	1012	78
Osage	1257	1225	32	1255	2
Smith	1146	1120	26	1144	2
Union	1850	1818	32	1845	5
LAFAYETTE.					
Clay..............	3508	3408	100	3019	489
Davis	1723	1526	197	1479	244
Dover	2251	2195	56	1680	571
Dover	320	303	17	254	66
Freedom	2539	1907	632	2363	196
Lexington........	6336	5606	730	4447	d1887
Lexington....	4373	3766	607	3193	d1178
Middleton...	2163	2071	92	1744	419
Waverly	887	845	42	726	161
Sniabar	1550	1530	20	1515	35
Washington	2533	2449	84	2335	198
LAWRENCE.					
Buck Prairie	1514	1483	31	1505	9
Marionsville..	272	261	11	272	......
Green	1434	1417	17	1397	37
Mount Pleasant..	1853	1793	60	1833	20
Pierce........	432	380	52	430	2
Mount Vernon....	3030	2961	69	2840	190
Mount Vernon	558	533	25	471	87
Ozark	1752	1746	6	1752	......
Spring River	1098	1062	36	1098	......

(c) Exclusive of city of Westport.
(d) Also 2 Indians.

TABLE IX.—*Population of Minor Civil Divisions, &c.*—*MISSOURI*—Continued.

Counties.	Total.	Nativity. Native.	Nativity. Foreign.	Race. White.	Race. Colored.	Counties.	Total.	Nativity. Native.	Nativity. Foreign.	Race. White.	Race. Colored.
LAWRENCE—Con.						MACON.					
Verona	240	214	26	240	......	Bevier	1531	1067	464	1488	43
Turnback	967	961	6	967	......	Bevier	833	441	392	832	1
Vineyard	1419	1406	13	1416	3	Bloomington	156	150	6	156	......
Lyons	80	77	3	80	......	Callao	1643	1586	57	1514	129
LEWIS.						Callao	310	300	10	260	50
Canton	3434	3132	302	3118	316	Chariton	1269	1252	17	1221	48
Canton	2363	2116	247	2087	276	College Mound	183	183	......	164	19
Dickerson	204	198	6	189	15	Hudson	1376	1211	165	1252	124
Lyon	820	782	38	777	43	Independence	1120	1107	13	1117	3
Township 60, R. 6	960	913	47	853	107	Jackson	1755	1658	97	1714	41
Township 61, R. 6	2623	2292	331	2266	357	La Plata	1566	1505	61	1552	14
Lagrange	1576	1344	232	1298	278	La Plata	546	527	19	540	6
Township 60, R. 7	793	770	23	758	35	Liberty	1210	1169	41	1184	[illegible]
Township 61, R. 7	1111	1077	34	1045	66	Macon	3678	3238	440	2758	[illegible]
Monticello	301	293	8	285	16	Middle Fork	1134	1079	55	1065	69
Township 60, R. 8	511	479	32	497	14	Narrows	1132	1102	30	1117	15
Township 61, R. 8	788	765	23	723	65	Richland	1180	1170	10	1173	7
Township 62, R. 8	540	496	44	517	23	Mercyville	79	79	......	79	......
Township 63, R. 8	634	626	8	624	10	Russell	1658	1285	373	1653	5
Williamstown	180	180	......	180	......	Ten Mile	1518	1421	97	1469	49
Township 60, R. 9	625	595	30	559	66	Walnut Creek	1304	1198	106	1302	2
Township 61, R. 9	732	715	17	702	30	MADISON.					
Township 62, R. 9	922	898	24	893	29	Castor	1000	967	33	964	36
Township 63, R. 9	417	408	9	412	5	Fredericktown	601	556	45	546	55
LINCOLN.						German	868	830	38	857	11
Bedford	2325	2197	128	1917	a407	Liberty	480	475	5	480	......
Troy	703	675	28	500	203	Polk	320	306	14	320	......
Clark	1887	1683	204	1622	265	St. Francis	386	379	7	383	3
Hurricane	3712	3670	42	3084	628	St. Michael's	1325	1097	228	1271	54
New Hope	186	185	1	152	34	Twelve-Mile	869	861	8	867	2
Millwood	1479	1385	94	1381	98	MARIES.					
Monroe	2616	2268	348	2429	187	Boone	692	654	38	692	......
Cape au Gris	56	50	6	54	2	Dry Creek	422	415	7	422	......
Prairie	1241	1164	77	1172	69	Jackson	1419	1284	135	1412	7
Union	1361	1314	47	1193	168	Jefferson	1123	1050	73	1118	5
Waverly	1339	1321	18	1174	165	Johnson	1257	1234	23	1254	3
LINN.						Miller	759	722	37	750	......
Baker	1269	1100	169	1269	......	Spring Creek	244	239	5	237	7
Benton	696	685	11	691	5	MARION.					
Brookfield	2321	1949	372	2229	92	Fabius	1908	1761	147	1676	232
Brookfield	402	365	37	388	14	Hannibal	10125	8493	1632	8508	a1616
Clay	939	923	16	914	25	Liberty	3871	3420	451	3022	849
Enterprise	322	270	52	322	......	Palmyra	2615	2231	384	2040	575
Jackson	948	933	15	933	15	Mason (d)	600	533	67	498	102
Jefferson	1810	1707	103	1634	176	Miller	1273	1224	49	1036	237
Locust Creek	2398	2264	134	2194	204	Round Grove	1379	1339	40	1324	55
North Salem	953	868	85	923	30	South River	728	652	76	632	96
Parson's Creek	1118	1063	55	1037	81	Union	1471	1428	43	1327	144
Yellow Creek	3126	2737	389	3012	114	Warren	2425	2314	111	2163	262
LIVINGSTON.						MC'DONALD.					
Blue Mound	1048	828	220	1044	4	Elk	941	929	12	940	1
Chillicothe (b)	2118	1943	175	2036	82	Erie	615	612	3	608	7
Chillicothe	3978	3554	424	3483	495	Fox	529	527	2	525	4
Cream Ridge	956	899	57	945	11	Pineville	1057	1045	12	1051	6
Fairview	1006	944	62	1005	1	Prairie	907	892	15	888	19
Grand River	1160	1127	33	1059	101	Richwood	833	832	1	833	......
Green	903	825	78	794	109	White Rock	344	344	......	344	......
Utica	722	655	67	633	89	MERCER.					
Jackson	2603	2547	56	2548	55						
Medicine	901	817	84	885	16						
Monroe	716	658	58	705	11	Harrison	914	910	4	914	......
Mooresville	1092	1001	91	1021	71	Lindley	1519	1504	15	1510	9
Wheeling	249	233	16	249	......	Madison	2021	1999	22	2020	

(a) Also 1 Indian.
(b) Exclusive of city of Chillicothe.

(c) Also 2 Chinese.
(d) Exclusive of city of Hannibal.

IX.—*Population of Minor Civil Divisions, &c.*—MISSOURI—Continued.

	Total.	Nativity. Native.	Nativity. Foreign.	Race. White.	Race. Colored.
...nt'd.					
.....	1006	1003	3	990	16
.....	839	823	16	839	......
.....	2107	2058	49	2098	9
.....	389	379	10	389	......
.....	1129	1116	13	1119	10
.....	1114	1096	18	1069	45
.....	808	808	......	805	3
.....	608	604	4	585	23
.....	1068	1040	28	1052	16
a...	125	120	5	119	6
.....	622	619	3	622	......
.....	542	495	47	539	3
.....	695	677	18	695	......
.....	1361	1352	9	1325	36
.....	1720	1702	18	1622	98
nt.	122	118	4	122	......
.					
.....	361	353	8	344	17
.....	697	676	21	684	13
.....	357	349	8	261	96
.....	632	616	16	373	259
.....	505	499	6	489	16
.....	1778	1658	120	1482	296
a...	635	579	56	535	100
.....	652	646	6	430	222
.					
.....	1585	1531	54	1481	104
.....	1948	1726	222	1824	124
.....	1084	1034	50	971	113
.....	1024	1002	22	1013	11
.....	3492	2987	505	3318	174
.....	2242	1923	319	1889	353
.....	1518	1495	23	1252	266
.....	71	71	......	67	4
.....	654	612	42	640	14
.....	4367	4225	142	3541	826
.....	895	857	38	680	215
.....	2147	2032	115	2040	107
.....	120	119	1	117	3
.....	2107	2092	15	1991	116
.....	880	827	53	831	49
.....	353	331	22	333	20
.....	1463	1442	21	1324	139
.....	1566	1533	33	1404	162
.....	1512	1440	72	1247	265
.....	935	926	9	874	61
Y.					
.....	2200	2050	150	2028	172
.....	2254	2179	75	1924	330
.....	1835	1524	311	1699	136
.....	1658	1641	17	1557	101
.....	2458	2253	205	2258	200
.....	543	521	22	543	......
.....	1731	1500	231	1667	64
.....	53	43	10	53	......
.....	917	876	41	861	56
.....	2168	2106	62	2100	68

Counties.	Total.	Nativity. Native.	Nativity. Foreign.	Race. White.	Race. Colored.
MORGAN—Cont'd.					
Osage	787	760	27	785	2
Richland	1785	1485	300	1775	10
Versailles	503	487	16	396	107
NEW MADRID.					
Big Prairie	1039	1032	7	938	101
La Sieur	2004	1997	7	1705	299
New Madrid	2861	2793	68	1853	a1007
New Madrid	634	592	42	439	195
St. John	403	402	1	385	18
NEWTON.					
Benton	968	939	29	935	33
Buffalo	785	778	7	780	5
Franklin	1238	1233	5	1218	20
Granby	1889	1845	44	1884	5
Lost Creek	1093	1070	23	1093	......
Seneca	285	265	20	285	......
Marion	1166	1145	21	1150	16
Neosho	2022	1935	87	1899	123
Neosho	875	824	51	833	42
Newtonia	1609	1596	13	1471	138
Newtonia	463	457	6	383	80
Shoal Creek	763	749	14	754	9
Van Buren	1288	1255	33	1287	1
NODAWAY.					
Atchison	1219	1205	14	1215	4
Grant	1105	1014	91	1104	1
Green	1613	1584	29	1610	3
Hughes	1420	1378	42	1416	4
Independence	670	643	27	670	......
Jackson	895	844	51	895	......
Lincoln	1042	1029	13	1042	......
Polk	3427	3031	396	3352	a74
Maryville	1682	1423	259	1603	79
Union	1308	1281	27	1308	......
Washington	1058	943	115	1058	......
White Cloud	994	949	45	993	1
OREGON.					
Jobe	848	847	1	845	3
Moore	921	920	1	921	......
Oak Grove	1081	1079	2	1081	......
Piney	437	433	4	436	1
Alton	76	76	......	75	1
OSAGE.					
Benton	2513	2086	427	2340	173
Crawford	2438	2079	359	2399	39
Jackson	1104	782	322	1068	36
Jefferson	1390	1163	227	1372	18
Linn	1757	1217	540	1721	36
Washington	1591	1065	526	1567	24
OZARK.					
Bayou	480	480	......	473	7
Bridges	532	531	1	532	......
Jackson	353	353	......	352	1
Jasper	618	615	3	615	3
Marion	745	743	2	745	......
Richland	635	635	......	634	1
PEMISCOT.					
Braggadocio	90	90	......	90	......

(a) Also 1 Indian.

TABLE IX.—*Population of Minor Civil Divisions, &c.—MISSOURI*—Continued.

Counties.	Total.	Nativity. Native.	Nativity. Foreign.	Race. White.	Race. Colored.
PEMISCOT—Cont'd.					
Butler	298	296	2	291	7
Gayoso	463	456	7	441	22
Little Prairie	492	488	4	398	94
Little River	120	120	......	120	......
Pemiscot	226	223	3	202	24
Virginia	370	369	1	369	1
PERRY.					
Bois Brule	1337	1224	113	1279	58
Brazeau	2281	1652	629	2218	63
Altenburg	200	128	72	200	......
Wittenberg	116	72	44	116	......
Cinque Hommes	2910	2401	509	2747	163
Perryville	501	414	87	481	20
Saline	1409	1373	36	1304	105
St. Mary's	1940	1684	256	1929	11
PETTIS.					
Blackwater	1603	1564	39	1544	59
Dunksburg	39	39	......	39	......
Bowling Green	2467	2085	382	2194	273
Smith's City	309	278	31	270	39
Elk Fork	2404	2295	109	2160	244
Dresden	348	307	41	283	65
Lamonte	184	171	13	170	14
Flat Creek	1651	1430	221	1603	48
Heath's Creek	2523	2482	41	2266	257
Mount Sterling	6305	5640	665	5087	1218
Sedalia	4560	3968	592	3715	845
Washington	1753	1660	93	1726	27
PHELPS.					
Arlington	1190	1128	62	1177	13
Cold Spring	964	866	98	964	......
Liberty	470	429	41	470	......
Maramec	1048	961	87	1047	1
Rolla	4184	3765	419	3957	227
Rolla	1354	1179	175	1231	123
Spring Creek	1119	1109	10	1109	10
St. James	1531	1434	97	1488	43
PIKE.					
Ashley	1222	1213	9	859	363
Ashley	368	363	5	282	86
Buffalo	2880	2800	80	2367	513
Calumet	5185	5030	155	3718	1467
Clarksville	1152	1093	59	907	245
Cuivre	3271	3083	188	2676	595
Bowling Green	599	554	45	533	66
Hartford	1583	1563	20	1456	127
Indian Creek	1103	1093	10	1060	43
Louisiana	3639	3333	306	2964	675
Peno	2160	2118	42	1932	228
Salt River	379	359	20	367	12
Spencer	1654	1641	13	1482	172
PLATTE.					
Carroll	2691	2631	60	2414	277
Platte City	599	563	36	513	86
Greene	2245	2179	66	2158	87
Camden Point	77	74	3	75	2
New Market	167	162	5	159	8
Lee	2290	2135	155	2161	129
Marshall	2038	1987	51	1918	120
Iatan	129	120	9	118	11
Pettis	3943	3746	197	3800	143
Preston	1692	1654	38	1635	57
Ridgeley	121	119	2	119	2
PLATTE—Cont'd.					
Weston	2453	2027	426	2074	379
Weston	1614	1252	362	1340	274
POLK.					
Benton	1650	1626	24	1649	1
Green	1074	1069	5	1067	7
Jackson	1483	1472	11	1456	27
Jefferson	480	477	3	458	22
Johnson	898	892	6	848	50
Looney	1750	1744	6	1687	63
Madison	1361	1359	2	1333	28
Marion	2489	2470	19	2428	61
Bolivar	635	629	6	601	34
Mooney	1260	1255	5	1259	1
PULASKI.					
Big Piney	541	529	12	541	......
Cullen	849	845	4	828	21
Liberty	893	874	19	893	......
Robideaux	677	675	2	674	3
Tavern	796	764	32	796	......
Union	958	935	23	957	1
PUTNAM.					
Elm	1040	1027	13	1038	2
Grant	638	634	4	636	2
Jackson	799	782	17	799	......
Liberty	1174	1161	13	1173	1
Lincoln	1057	1021	36	1057	......
Medicine	665	659	6	665	......
Richland	720	705	15	719	1
Sherman	987	978	9	986	1
Union	2053	2015	38	2051	2
Unionville	462	460	2	460	2
York	1484	1464	20	1484	......
RALLS.					
Center	726	711	15	679	47
Clay	1701	1588	113	1365	336
Jasper	1394	1348	46	1246	148
Saline	1634	1566	68	1535	99
Salt River	1337	1283	54	1211	126
Saverton	1599	1525	74	1458	141
Spencer	2119	2070	49	1767	352
New London	410	395	15	357	53
RANDOLPH.					
Chariton	1699	1672	27	1534	165
Jackson	1175	1147	28	1096	79
Prairie	2863	2779	84	2548	315
Salt River	782	775	7	752	30
Salt Spring	3526	3385	141	2804	722
Silver Creek	1831	1806	25	1321	510
Sugar Creek	2896	2654	202	2602	294
Moberly	1514	1297	217	1401	113
Union	1136	1119	17	1027	109
RAY.					
Camden	3347	3211	136	3065	282
Camden	357	316	41	336	21
Crooked River	1622	1574	48	1475	147
Fishing River	1653	1630	23	1596	57
Grape Grove	2660	2614	46	2499	161
Knoxville	2469	2423	46	2421	48
Polk	1368	1343	25	1315	53
Richmond	5581	5340	241	4496	1085
Richmond	1218	1108	110	993	225

IX.—*Population of Minor Civil Divisions, &c.—MISSOURI*—Continued.

	Total.	Nativity.		Race.	
		Native.	Foreign.	White.	Colored.
....	1280	1270	10	1280	....
....	605	599	6	605	....
....	32	29	3	32	....
....	327	324	3	327	....
....	910	906	4	909	1
....	634	634	....	624	10
....	960	933	27	956	4
....	146	145	1	146	....
....	160	160	....	160	....
....	280	273	7	280	....
....	240	238	2	240	....
....	855	843	12	850	5
....	680	674	6	679	1
....	3174	3138	36	2463	711
....	1798	1780	18	1498	296
(a)	373	....	....	....	....
....	1536	1450	86	1320	216
....	1956	1883	73	1672	284
....	3002	2758	244	2555	447
....	3701	3478	223	2830	871
....	3622	3513	109	2879	743
....	742	705	37	558	184
....	2895	2689	206	2711	184
....	833	817	16	823	10
....	1474	1438	36	1474	....
....	1101	1065	36	1100	1
....	1115	1078	37	1115	....
....	1529	1490	39	1528	1
....	427	406	21	427	....
....	1653	1515	138	1653	....
....	1115	1097	18	1113	2
....	1491	1360	131	1484	7
....	3297	3229	68	3189	108
....	1007	977	30	957	50
....	1219	1179	40	1219	....
....	1245	1239	6	1245	....
it ..	1230	1212	18	1219	11
....	784	768	16	781	3
....	1404	1394	10	1404	....
....	1267	1161	106	1062	205
....	1000	798	202	967	33
....	2613	2262	351	2585	28
....	1080	1069	11	1052	28
....	777	760	17	775	2
....	580	572	8	530	30
....	312	312	....	312	....
....	156	156	....	156	....
....	325	325	....	325	....
....	198	196	2	198	....
....	370	368	2	367	3
....	95	95	....	93	....
....	290	290	....	286	....
....	193	193	....	193	....
....	155	155	....	155	....
....	251	249	2	251	....

township not ascertained.
merly Birch Prairie.
o 8 Indians.
clusive of city of St. Charles.

Counties.	Total.	Nativity.		Race.	
		Native.	Foreign.	White.	Colored.
SHELBY.					
Bethel	1224	1143	79	1152	82
Black Creek	1418	1338	80	1276	142
Shelbyville	530	518	12	440	90
Clay	1433	1330	103	1398	35
Clarence	444	410	34	432	12
Jackson	1410	1354	56	1352	58
Hunnewell	327	295	32	316	11
Jefferson	867	838	29	857	10
Salt River	1986	1852	134	1793	(e)193
Shelbina	1145	1069	76	989	156
Taylor	920	881	39	891	29
Tiger Fork	855	835	20	780	75
ST. CHARLES.					
Callaway	1745	1340	405	1524	221
Cuvier	3174	2726	448	2714	460
Dardenne	3092	2376	716	2800	292
Femme Osage	2383	1739	644	2231	152
Portage des Sioux	1801	1417	384	1719	82
Portage	160	153	7	159	1
St. Charles (d)	3479	2344	1135	3038	(f)438
St. Charles	5570	3761	1769	5136	434
ST. CLAIR.					
Butler	646	636	10	640	6
Chalk Level	651	640	11	640	11
Jackson	411	409	2	410	1
Monegaw	1434	1377	57	1432	2
Osceola	957	921	36	882	75
Osceola	331	298	33	286	45
Polk	316	315	1	316	....
Roscoe	922	898	24	873	49
Roscoe	302	296	6	302	....
Speedwell	606	600	6	603	3
Taberville	160	156	4	157	3
Washington	589	585	4	583	6
STE. GENEVIEVE.					
Beauvais	1306	1115	191	1198	108
St. Mary	397	335	62	357	40
Jackson	1112	967	145	1098	14
Saline	980	937	43	920	60
Ste. Genevieve	3409	2674	735	3174	235
Ste. Genevieve	1521	1283	238	1345	176
Union	1577	1515	62	1363	14
ST. FRANÇOIS.					
Big River	436	432	4	366	70
Iron	2555	1629	926	2542	13
Iron Mount	2018	1161	857	2017	1
Liberty	1405	1360	45	1323	82
Marion	854	799	55	830	24
Pendleton	851	781	70	851	....
Perry	1351	1307	44	1245	106
Randolph	676	664	12	663	13
St. François	1614	1481	133	1404	210
Farmington	393	332	61	340	53
ST. LOUIS.					
Bonhomme	6108	4708	1400	5303	805
Carondelet	5387	3608	1779	5080	307
Central	8923	6017	2906	8120	803
Meramec	3436	2705	731	2853	583
St. Ferdinand	7314	5346	1968	6382	932
St. Louis	9203	5818	3385	8395	(g)808
St. Louis	310864	198615	112249	288737	22088

(e) Also 1 Indian.
(f) Also 3 Indians.
(g) Also 38 Indians and 1 Chinese.

TABLE IX.—*Population of Minor Civil Divisions, &c.*—*MISSOURI*—Continued.

Counties.	Total.	Nativity. Native.	Nativity. Foreign.	Race. White.	Race. Colored.
STODDARD.					
Castor	2785	2750	35	2729	56
Bloomfield	379	365	14	344	35
Duck Creek	781	779	2	781	......
Elk	621	619	2	621	......
Liberty	1307	1302	5	1301	6
New Lisbon	1182	1174	8	1182	......
Pike	1421	1410	11	1413	8
Richland	438	437	1	438	......
STONE.					
Cass	592	590	2	592	......
Flat Creek	595	593	2	593	2
James	447	445	2	444	3
Pierce	781	779	2	766	15
Washington	506	504	2	506	......
Galena	27	27	......	27	......
Williams	332	332	......	332	......
SULLIVAN.					
Bowman	581	580	1	579	2
Buchanan	1104	1079	25	1104	......
Clay	877	870	7	875	2
Duncan	1064	1054	10	1054	10
Jackson	902	878	24	902	......
Liberty	772	751	21	772	......
Morris	964	934	30	964	......
Penn	1744	1704	40	1744	......
Pleasant Hill	634	609	25	634	......
Polk	1415	1375	40	1400	15
Milan	319	309	10	304	15
Taylor	628	614	14	615	13
Union	1222	1207	15	1222	......
TANEY.					
Beaver	581	578	3	581	......
Big Creek	267	262	5	266	1
Jasper	615	614	1	615	......
Newton	603	597	6	602	1
Scott	554	553	1	554	......
Swann	1787	1781	6	1779	8
Forsyth	87	87	......	87	......
TEXAS.					
Boone	323	313	10	323	......
Burdine	316	313	3	316	......
Carroll	519	517	2	519	......
Cass	779	778	1	779	......
Clinton	721	719	2	721	......
Jackson	537	522	15	537	......
Lynch	522	507	15	511	11
Morris	539	538	1	539	......
Ozark	638	633	5	633	5
Pierce	366	364	2	364	2
Piney	866	854	12	864	2
Roubidoux	617	609	8	598	19
Sherrill	1399	1347	52	1364	35
Upton	642	629	13	632	10
Wood and Richland	834	834	......	823	11
VERNON.					
Bacon	813	786	27	809	4
Center	2603	2540	63	2567	36
Clear Creek	445	444	1	436	9
VERNON—Cont'd.					
Deerfield	506	484	22	506	......
Dry Wood	475	468	7	475	......
Harrison	415	408	7	414	1
Henry	680	666	14	670	10
Montevallo	1349	1331	18	1346	3
Moundville	897	878	19	896	1
Osage	1538	1521	17	1531	7
Richland	547	544	3	541	6
Virgil	979	952	27	974	5
WARREN.					
Bridgeport	822	697	125	717	105
Camp Branch	901	782	119	858	43
Charrette	2690	1686	1004	2571	119
Dutzow	72	43	29	62	10
Marthasville	178	123	55	150	28
Elkhorn	2479	1892	587	2274	(a)204
Warrenton	588	465	123	553	35
Hickory Grove	1763	1499	264	1552	211
Pinkney	1018	626	392	965	53
WASHINGTON.					
Belleview	1867	1834	33	1741	126
Breton	2396	2161	235	2069	327
Potosi	897	......	......	......	......
Concord	1343	1254	89	1262	81
Harmony	1485	1470	15	1363	122
Johnson	717	705	12	702	15
Kingston	1085	1067	18	1040	45
Liberty	879	821	58	835	44
Richwood	760	693	67	739	21
Union	1187	1138	49	967	220
WAYNE.					
Benton	1291	1290	1	1274	17
Black River	743	739	4	743	......
Cedar Creek	379	379	......	367	12
Cowan	492	485	7	486	6
Jefferson	371	362	9	348	23
Logan	1057	1040	17	1053	4
St. François	1735	1727	8	1730	5
WEBSTER.					
Benton	768	765	3	765	3
Dallas	1255	1245	10	1230	25
Findley	625	621	4	620	5
Hazlewood	1267	1246	21	1213	54
Ozark	3488	3263	225	3349	(a)138
Marshfield	809	725	84	746	63
Union	1593	1565	28	1575	18
Washington	1438	1431	7	1433	5
WORTH.					
Allen	1352	1332	20	1352	......
Fletchall	582	559	23	582	......
Green	703	692	11	703	......
Middle Fork	279	272	7	279	......
Smith	889	874	15	889	......
Union	1199	1177	22	1199	......
WRIGHT. (*)					
Boone	123	122	1	123	......

(*) Incomplete; the other principal civil divisions were not separately returned.
(a) Also 1 Indian.

TABLE IX.—*Population of Minor Civil Divisions, &c.—MONTANA.*

ties.	Total.	Nativity. Native.	Nativity. Foreign.	Race. White.	Race. Colored.
IEAD. (a)					
....	37	28	9	37	......
nt'n and le	80	44	36	79	......
....	381	255	126	375	1
ead Val-	144	99	45	143	1
....	27	22	5	27	......
'rairie	53	40	7	53	......
ORN.					
ncy	14	8	6	14	......
one River	24	18	6	24	......
AU. (b)					
City, or nton....	367	294	73	330	18
Benton, River....	40	28	12	38	2
on, (gar-	68	32	36	68	......
r Valley.	42	25	17	40	......
ON. (c)					
y, mouth Creek, d River.	18	13	5	18	......
River, ...	159	127	32	143	4
DGE. (d)					
....	355	133	222	317	1
....	499	232	267	386	1
y	241	83	158	142	1
y.......	260	116	144	181	1
ge.......	788	559	229	751	5
burg	133	68	65	131	1
ulch ...	155	36	119	126	......
Gulch....	239	122	117	234	......
k	72	60	12	72	......
. Moose, Gulches	171	111	60	169	......
....	40	27	13	39	1
....	187	109	78	185	......
n	56	23	33	56	......
urg	59	35	24	59	......
nd Pike's	560	230	330	317	2
nd Mod- ulches ...	35	25	10	35	......
w	425	151	274	260	2
ton......	92	18	74	91	......

Counties.	Total.	Nativity. Native.	Nativity. Foreign.	Race. White.	Race. Colored.
GALLATIN. (e)					
Bozeman	574	413	161	559	11
Bozeman City.	168	130	38	159	5
East Gallatin.....	310	254	56	308	1
Gallatin City.....	152	123	29	150	......
Gallatin City.	53	39	14	52	......
Noble	221	186	35	218	......
West Gallatin.....	205	169	36	204	......
Willow Creek	116	105	11	115	1
JEFFERSON. (f)					
Basin..............	144	80	64	103	......
Beaver Creek	82	65	17	82	......
Jefferson City....	104	76	28	100	1
Jefferson Valley..	167	121	46	155	......
Lower Boulder ...	100	61	39	100	......
Prickly Pear	223	129	94	183	......
Radersburg	311	234	77	311	......
Springville	86	61	25	81	......
Three Forks......	31	30	1	30	1
Upper Boulder ...	182	124	58	162	......
Upper Indian Cr'k	101	76	25	99	......
LEWIS AND CLARKE. (g)					
Caddett's Pass, (near)	71	40	31	71	......
Cañon Creek	39	31	8	39	......
Fork Greenhorn..	40	19	21	40	......
Fort Shaw........	473	215	258	468	5
Greenhorn Creek.	39	8	31	33	......
Grizzly Gulch....	38	31	7	38	......
Grizzly and Silver Creek	38	26	12	38	......
Helena	3106	1747	1359	2391	71
Helena, (1st dist).	736	509	227	714	9
Lump Gulch......	20	16	4	20	......
Mouth of Sun River, (near) ..	22	20	2	22	......
Prickly Pear Valley	479	374	105	473	6
Quartz Gulch and Greenhorn	40	28	12	40	......
Silver City and vicinity	64	29	35	64	......
Silver Creek and Trinity.........	80	47	33	76	3
South Fork Cañon Creek and Little Prickly Pear ...	39	25	14	39	......
Sun-River Valley	176	138	38	79	......
Ten-Mile Cr'k and Nelson Gulch...	79	51	28	78	......
Trinity, Pelyan, and Cañon Cr'ks.	39	17	22	31	......
Unionville........	158	104	54	148	7

ver Head County: Bald Mountain and Big Hole also includes 1 Chinese; Bannock, 5 Chinese.
teau County: Benton City or Fort Benton also includes 3 Chinese and 16 Indians; Sun River Indians.
rson County: Missouri River (near) also includes 12 Indians.
r Lodge County: Beartown also includes 37 Chinese; Blackfoot, 112 Chinese; Butte City, 98 Cable City, 75 Chinese and 3 Indians; Deer Lodge, 15 Chinese and 17 Indians; Emmettsburg, ; French Gulch, 27 Chinese and 2 Indians; German Gulch, 5 Chinese; Highland, Moose, and lches, 1 Chinese and 1 Indian; Pioneer and Pike's Peak, 240 Chinese and 1 Indian; Silver Chinese; Washington, 1 Chinese.
latin County: Boseman also includes 4 Chinese; East Gallatin, 1 Indian; Gallatin City, 2 Noble, 3 Indians; West Gallatin, 1 Indian.
ferson County: Basin also includes 41 Chinese; Jefferson City, 3 Chinese; Jefferson Valley, e; Prickly Pear, 40 Chinese; Springville, 5 Chinese; Upper Boulder, 19 Chinese and 1 Indian; dian Creek, 2 Chinese.
wis and Clarke County: Greenhorn Creek also includes 6 Chinese; Helena, 641 Chinese and 3 Helena, (first district,) 11 Chinese and 2 Indians; Silver Creek and Trinity, 1 Chinese; Sun-lley, 6 Chinese; Ten-Mile Creek and Nelson Gulch, 1 Chinese; Trinity, Pelyan, and Cañon Chinese; Unionville, 3 Chinese.

TABLE IX.—*Population of Minor Civil Divisions, &c.*—*MONTANA*—Continued.

Counties.	Total.	Nativity. Native.	Nativity. Foreign.	Race. White.	Race. Colored.
MADISON. (*) (a)					
Virginia City	867	444	423	569	19
MEAGHER. (b)					
Diamond City	460	295	165	451	4
Missouri Valley and South Deep Creek	359	275	84	357	......
New York Gulch and vicinity	343	214	129	319	......
MEAGHER—Cont'd.					
Thompson Gulch and North Deep Creek Valley	225	157	68	219	......
MISSOULA. (*) (c)					
Bitter Root Valley	314	273	41	299	......
Cedar Creek Mines	1486	625	861	1446	3

(*) Incomplete; the other principal civil divisions were not separately returned.
(a) Madison County: Virginia City also includes 279 Chinese.
(b) Meagher County: Diamond City also includes 5 Chinese; Missouri Valley and South Deep Creek, 2 Indians; New York Gulch and vicinity, 24 Chinese; Thompson Gulch and North Deep Creek Valley, 6 Indians.
(c) Missoula County: Bitter Root Valley also includes 15 Indians; Cedar Creek Mines, 32 Chinese and 5 Indians.

TABLE IX.—*Population of Minor Civil Divisions, &c.*—*NEBRASKA.*

NOTE.—The marginal column marks precincts and land-survey townships; the first indentation cities; the second, towns. Names of towns are placed under the names of the precincts or land-survey townships in which they are respectively situated. The population of each precinct or land-survey township includes that of all towns situated in it.

Counties.	Total.	Nativity. Native.	Nativity. Foreign.	Race. White.	Race. Colored.
BLACK BIRD.					
Omaha Agency	31	26	5	31	......
BUFFALO.					
Precinct 1	105	55	50	105	......
Precinct 2	35	19	16	34	1
Precinct 3	53	26	27	53	......
BURT.					
Arizona	534	501	33	534	......
Belt Creek	287	167	120	287	......
Decatur	614	558	56	614	......
Everett	277	245	32	277	......
Oakland	227	97	130	227	......
Riverside	139	119	20	139	......
Silver Creek	271	196	75	271	......
Tekamah	498	451	47	498	......
BUTLER.					
Bone Creek	384	351	33	384	......
Oak Creek	119	113	6	119	......
Pepperville	197	166	31	197	......
Skull Creek	238	167	71	236	2
Ulysses	352	305	47	350	2
CASS.					
Avoca	480	398	82	480	......
Eight-Mile Grove	480	394	86	480	......
Elmwood	317	290	27	317	......
Liberty	400	385	15	400	......
Louisville	636	474	162	636	......
Mount Pleasant	320	297	23	320	......
Oreopolis	249	206	43	249	......
Plattsmouth	2448	1831	617	2425	23
Plattsmouth	1944	1396	548	1921	23
Rock Bluffs	756	726	30	755	1
Salt Creek	478	438	40	478	......
South Bend	311	235	76	311	......
Stove Creek	480	439	41	480	......
Tipton	315	287	28	315	......
Weeping Water	481	443	38	481	......
CEDAR.					
Brooks	40	23	17	40	......
St. Helena	665	312	353	665	......
St. James	327	237	90	325	(a) 1
CUMING.					
Townships 21 and 22, R. 4 and 5	626	252	374	626	......

(a) Also 1 Indian.

IX.—*Population of Minor Civil Divisions, &c.—NEBRASKA*—Continued.

	Total.	Nativity.		Race.	
		Native.	Foreign.	White.	Colored.
nt'd.					
R.					
....	480	278	202	480	......
R.					
....	1032	622	410	1032	......
t (a)	520	......	......	......	......
E..	72	26	46	72	......
R. 5.	232	160	72	232	......
R. 6	144	90	54	144	......
R. 7	108	27	81	108	......
R. 4	156	106	50	156	......
R. 5	84	65	19	84	......
R. 6	15	4	11	15	......
R. 7.	15	11	4	15	......
....	225	172	53	225	......
....	194	148	46	194	......
....	595	555	40	595	......
....	300	282	18	300	......
....	668	446	222	668	......
....	552	454	98	552	......
....	168	82	86	168	......
....	334	279	55	334	......
....	843	638	205	843	......
....	1703	1127	576	1700	3
....	1195	777	418	1193	2
....	723	281	442	723	......
....	456	319	137	456	......
....	809	613	196	808	1
....	521	216	305	521	......
....	260	......	......	......	......
....	174	......	......	......	......
....	296	......	......	......	......
....	395	......	......	......	......
....	440	......	......	......	......
....	444	......	......	......	......
....	1042	......	......	......	......
....	16083	9763	6320	15637	446
....	631	......	......	......	......
....	217	......	......	......	......
....	624	518	106	623	1
....	354	331	23	354	......
....	770	722	48	770	......
....	13	13	......	13	......
....	650	319	331	650	......
....	213	107	106	213	......
....	194	115	79	194	......
ver.	89	64	25	89	......
t....	41	30	11	41	......

Counties.	Total.	Nativity.		Race.	
		Native.	Foreign.	White.	Colored.
JEFFERSON.					
Antelope	296	276	20	296	......
Big Sandy	693	533	160	693	......
Cubb Creek	261	216	45	261	......
Fairbury	370	316	54	370	......
Hobbs	378	356	22	378	......
Jenkins	442	388	54	442	......
JOHNSON.					
Helena	333	299	34	333	......
Spring Creek	521	488	33	521	......
Sterling	480	363	117	480	......
Tecumseh	722	657	65	722	......
Todd Creek	542	495	47	542	......
Vesta	639	593	46	639	......
Weston	192	168	24	192	......
LANCASTER. (*)					
Lincoln	2141	1702	739	2426	15
L'EAU QUI COURT.					
Frankfort	63	36	27	63	......
Niobrara	171	52	119	168	(b)
Santee Agency	27	26	1	27	......
MADISON.					
Battle Creek	284	239	45	284	......
Norfolk	593	363	230	593	......
Union Creek	256	170	86	256	......
MERRICK.					
Precinct 1	136	100	36	136	......
Precinct 2	243	186	57	243	......
Precinct 3	178	100	78	178	......
NEMAHA.					
Aspinwall	572	513	59	572	......
Bedford	195	171	24	195	......
Benton	456	355	101	456	......
Brownville	2386	2190	196	2376	c8
Brownville	1305	1162	143	1295	c8
Douglas	393	315	78	393	......
Glenrock	582	493	89	582	......
Lafayette	618	533	85	618	......
Nemaha	628	603	25	628	......
Peru	1164	1099	65	1164	......
St. Deroin	276	268	8	276	......
Washington	323	207	116	323	......
OTOE.					
Belmont	508	403	105	501	7
Delaware	597	454	143	597	......
Four-Mile	571	491	80	571	......
Hendricks	440	380	60	440	......
McWilliams	480	325	155	480	......
Nebraska	6050	4664	1386	5840	b207
Osage	218	172	46	218	......
Otoe	1044	842	202	1044	......
Palmyra	886	617	269	886	......
Syracuse	640	557	83	640	......
Wyoming	911	704	207	906	5

(*) Incomplete; the other principal civil divisions were not separately returned.
(a) Situated in township 22, range 6.
(b) Also 3 Indians.
(c) Also 2 Indians.

TABLE IX.—*Population of Minor Civil Divisions, &c.—NEBRASKA*—Continued.

Counties.	Total.	Nativity.		Race.	
		Native.	Foreign.	White.	Colored.
PAWNEE.					
Township 1, R. 9 E	141	115	26	141	......
Township 1, R. 10	289	222	67	289	......
Township 1, R. 11	507	467	40	507	......
Township 1, R. 12	597	537	60	597	......
Township 2, R. 9	337	304	33	337	......
Township 2, R. 10	197	176	21	197	......
Township 2, R. 11	815	745	70	815	......
Township 2, R. 12	427	354	73	427	......
Township 3, R. 9	30	30	......	30	......
Township 3, R. 9 and 12	40	39	1	40	......
Township 3, R. 9, 10, 11, and 12	40	38	2	40	......
Township 3, R. 10	158	103	55	158	......
Township 3, R. 10 and 11	39	22	17	39	......
Township 3, R. 11	238	139	99	238	......
Township 3, R. 12	316	265	51	316	......
PIERCE.					
Pierce	152	44	108	152	......
PLATTE.					
Butler	328	165	163	328	......
Columbus	1233	649	584	1230	3
Columbus	526	342	184	523	3
Monroe	338	174	164	337	1
POLK.					
North Blue	92	80	12	92	......
Platte River	44	42	2	44	......
RICHARDSON.					
Arago	1245	769	476	1223	(a)
Arago	364	247	117	364	......
Barrada	886	798	88	834	(b)
Falls City	1166	1089	77	1163	3
Falls City	607	558	49	605	2
Franklin	225	212	13	225	......
Grant	515	439	76	514	1
Great Nemaha Agency	33	26	7	33	......
Humboldt	605	493	112	605	......
Liberty	506	477	29	506	......
Muddy	408	345	63	403	5
Nemaha	404	369	35	404	......
Ohio	622	521	101	622	......
Porter	219	204	15	219	......
Rulo	1326	1085	241	1323	c1
Rulo	611	461	150	610	(d)
Salem	681	645	36	681	......
Salem	304	289	15	304	......
Speiser	338	297	41	338	......
St. Stephens	601	484	117	599	(c)
SALINE.					
Precinct 1. Big Blue	818	741	77	818	......
Precinct 2. Camden	741	411	330	741	......
Precinct 3. Turkey Creek	394	359	35	394	......
Precinct 4. Swan Creek	448	395	53	448	......
Precinct 5. Swan City	418	403	15	418	......
Precinct 6. Monroe	287	90	197	287	......
SARPY.					
Bellevue	961	......	......	959	2
Fairview	381	......	......	......	......
Forest City	383	......	......	......	......
La Platte	299	......	......	......	......
Papillion	333	......	......	......	......
Plattford	556	......	......	......	......
SAUNDERS.					
Township 13, R. 5	63	62	1	63	......
Township 14, R. 5	148	94	54	148	......
Township 15, R. 5	109	23	84	109	......
Township 17, R. 5	114	29	85	114	......
Township 13, R. 6	125	122	3	125	......
Township 14, R. 6	88	52	36	88	......
Township 15, R. 6	132	32	100	132	......
Township 16, R. 6	106	52	54	106	......
Township 17, R. 6	89	68	21	89	......
Township 13, R. 7	155	70	85	155	......
Township 14, R. 7	207	178	29	207	......
Township 15, R. 7	137	56	81	137	......
Township 16, R. 7	165	99	66	165	......
Township 17, R. 7	144	96	48	144	......
Township 13, R. 8	177	143	34	177	......
Township 14, R. 8	232	141	91	232	......
Township 15, R. 8	147	83	64	147	......
Township 16, R. 8	213	133	80	213	......
Township 17, R. 8	26	14	12	26	......
Township 12, R. 9	731	661	70	721	10
Ashland	653	584	69	643	10
Township 13, R. 9	420	368	52	420	......
Township 14, R. 9	425	326	99	425	......
Township 15, R. 9	250	198	52	250	......
Township 16, R. 9	144	112	32	144	......
SEWARD.					
Beaver Creek	565	507	58	565	......
Camden	309	280	29	309	......
Milford	659	579	80	659	......
Oak Grove	213	195	18	213	......
Seward	1207	1017	190	1207	......
WASHINGTON.					
Bell Creek	200	149	51	200	......
Blair	917	768	149	917	......
Blair	494	416	78	494	......
Cuming City	543	475	68	543	......
De Soto	288	245	43	288	......
Fontenelle	400	269	131	399	1
Fort Calhoun	868	625	243	868	......
Fort Calhoun	236	223	13	236	......
Grant	479	353	126	479	......
Lincoln	276	197	79	276	......
Richland	221	174	47	221	......
Sheridan	260	187	73	260	......
WAYNE.					
Taffe	182	124	58	182	......
YORK.					
Beaver Creek	129	122	7	129	......
Blue River	258	242	16	258	......
Lincoln Creek	217	190	27	217	......

(a) Also 22 Indians.
(b) Also 52 Indians.
(c) Also 2 Indians.
(d) Also 1 Indian.

TABLE IX.—*Population of Minor Civil Divisions, &c.—NEVADA.*

-The marginal column marks precincts or townships; the first indentation, cities: the second, ocalities, whose names are placed under the names of the precincts or townships in which espectively situated. The population of each precinct or township includes that of all locali-ted in it.

ties.	Total.	NATIVITY. Native.	NATIVITY. Foreign.	RACE. White.	RACE. Colored.
AS. (a)					
k	120	......	......	117	......
k........	132	......	......	130	......
....	462	......	......	460	8
lley.....	140	......	......	138	......
ley......	11	......	......	11	......
....	280	......	......	260	24
iver	41	......	......	41	......
. (b)					
ty.......	122	93	29	121	......
....	43	33	10	43	......
llock....	160	86	74	159	1
....	295	168	127	241	5
alley	80	67	13	80	......
....	1160	723	437	1028	24
t Wells..	42	5	37	9	......
Valley..	134	98	36	133	......
Hill	212	114	98	206	2
alley....	88	64	24	87	......
City....	467	275	162	420	1
ey	35	27	8	34	......
e.......	160	26	134	38	......
l	110	81	29	108	......
lley	153	114	39	152	......
ey.......	69	34	35	48	......
....	117	46	71	68	......
LDA. (c)					
....	280	204	76	262	......
rora	160	127	33	154	......
water....	120	82	38	112	......
gton	135	110	25	128	6
....	245	145	90	218	1
....	625	404	221	612	1
o Grove	305	214	91	301	1
e Grove					
ockland	40	20	20	40	......
ckland...	120	68	52	113	......
....	158	120	38	157	......
DT. (d)					
ountain..	261	146	115	244	2
sta......	520	306	214	464	2
ville ...	470	271	199	414	2
....	23	10	13	15	......
ak	11	3	8	10	1
....	80	50	30	66	......
lley....	27	26	1	26	1
t........	136	69	67	106	......
....	117	49	68	93	1

Counties.	Total.	NATIVITY. Native.	NATIVITY. Foreign.	RACE. White.	RACE. Colored.
HUMBOLDT—Con.					
Paradise Valley ..	230	152	78	228	......
Queen's River....	76	41	35	76	......
Sacramento	25	13	12	24	......
Sierra	84	51	33	68	......
Star City.........	36	11	25	30	......
Winnemucca	290	138	152	234	3
LANDER. (e)					
Austin	1324	754	570	1291	27
Battle Mt. Station	150	81	69	103	2
Beowawe.....	54	23	31	33	......
Cortez District	46	22	24	45	......
Eureka District.......	640	375	265	624	2
Garden Valley	28	24	4	27	......
Grass Valley..	26	20	6	26	......
Northern Reese River Valley......	106	72	34	105	......
Palisade......	39	22	17	26	......
Secret Cañon.	95	57	38	95	......
Smoking Valley	19	11	8	19	......
Southern Reese River Valley......	113	81	32	112	......
Tuscarora, Independence Valley......	119	12	107	15	......
Yankee Blade.	56	26	30	55	......
LINCOLN. (f)					
Hiko	110	83	27	108	1
Hiko	54	40	14	53	......
Pahranagat Valley......	39	35	4	38	1
Tampinte	17	8	9	17	......
Panaca	493	379	114	488	2
Bullionville...	96	73	23	96	......
Clover Valley.	32	29	3	32	......
Meadow Valley	365	277	88	360	2
Proche	1620	1067	553	1587	8
Dry Valley...	133	105	28	131	......
Eagle Valley .	159	139	20	158	......
Highland	21	15	6	21	......
Proche City ..	1141	665	479	1116	6
Rose Valley ..	27	19	8	27	......
Spring Valley.	136	124	12	134	2
Rio Virgin	762	619	143	754	......

-Wherever in Nevada the items of a locality fail to make the total the deficiency represents se and Indians.

uglas County: Cave Rock also includes 3 Chinese; East Fork, 2 Chinese; Genoa, 14 Chinese; alley, 2 Chinese; Mattsville, 2 Chinese and 3 Indians.

o County: Bruno City also includes 1 Chinese; Carlin, 49 Chinese; Elko, 108 Chinese; Hum-ils, 33 Chinese; Lamoille Valley, 1 Chinese; Mineral Hill, 4 Chinese; Mound Valley, 1 Chi-ountain City, 46 Chinese; Pine Valley, 1 Chinese; Placerville, 122 Chinese; Rail Road, 2 Chi-by Valley, 1 Chinese; Star Valley, 21 Chinese; Tuano, 49 Chinese.

eralda County: Township 1 also includes 18 Chinese; Sweetwater, 8 Chinese; Wellington, 1 Townships 4 and 5, 16 Chinese; Township 6, 12 Chinese; Township 7, 1 Chinese.

mboldt County: Battle Mountain also includes 15 Chinese; Buena Vista, 54 Chinese; Central, ; Golconda, 13 Chinese and 1 Indian; Humboldt, 30 Chinese; Lake, 23 Chinese; Paradise Val-nese and 1 Indian; Sacramento, 1 Chinese; Sierra, 15 Chinese and 1 Indian; Star City, 6 Chi-innemucca, 53 Chinese.

der County: Austin also includes 16 Chinese; Battle Mt. Station, 45 Chinese; Beowawe, 21 Cortez District, 1 Chinese; Eureka District, 14 Chinese; Garden Valley, 1 Chinese; Northern ver Valley, 1 Chinese; Palisade, 13 Chinese; Southern Reese River Valley, 1 Chinese; Tusca-pendence Valley, 104 Chinese; Yankee Blade, 1 Chinese.

ncoln County: Hiko also includes 1 Indian; Panaca, 3 Indians; Proche, 23 Chinese and 2 In-io Virgin, 8 Indians.

TABLE IX.—*Population of Minor Civil Divisions, &c.—NEVADA*—Continued.

Counties.	Total.	Nativity.		Race.	
		Native.	Foreign.	White.	Colored.
LINCOLN—Cont'd.					
Colville	4	3	1	2	......
Junction of Rio Virgin	13	13	......	13	......
Las Vegas Valley	8	8	......	5	......
Overton	149	117	32	149	......
St. Joseph	198	157	41	198	......
St. Thomas	252	197	55	252	......
West Point	138	124	14	135	......
LYON. (a)					
Churchill	40	19	21	40	......
Dayton	918	457	461	843	1
Silver City	879	417	462	836	1
NYE. (b)					
Belmont	244	154	90	243	1
Duckwater	145	105	40	145	......
Ellsworth	54	41	13	53	......
Hot Creek	40	33	7	40	......
Ione	52	37	15	52	......
Patterson	40	27	13	40	......
Reveille	80	52	28	78	......
Silver Park	263	189	74	260	......
Smoky Valley	57	33	24	57	......
Washington	49	33	16	49	......
White River	63	56	7	63	......
ORMSBY. (c)					
Carson City	3042	1436	1606	2316	29
Empire City	626	324	302	552	2
STOREY. (d)					
Gold Hill	4311	1965	2346	4096	5
STOREY—Cont'd.					
Virginia	7048	3592	3456	6418	91
WASHOE. (e)					
Clark's Station	46	1	15	45	......
Crystal Peak	120	90	30	108	1
Franktown	271	139	132	264	......
Geiger Grade	55	19	36	50	1
Glendale	129	94	35	125	......
Long Valley	45	39	6	45	......
Mill Station	129	76	53	124	3
Ophir	110	91	19	109	......
Pea Vine	10	9	1	10	......
Red Rock	6	......	6	......	......
Reno	1035	695	340	929	22
Truckee Meadows	320	224	96	293	1
Verdi	40	27	13	40	......
Wadsworth	253	173	80	209	8
Washoe City	552	320	232	510	......
WHITE PINE. (f)					
Diamond Valley	26	16	10	26	......
Egan Cañon	93	45	48	93	......
Hamilton	3913	2147	1766	3698	55
Kern	36	16	20	36	......
Newark Valley	75	53	22	75	......
Piermont	18	9	9	18	......
Pinto	51	31	20	51	......
Robinson	67	42	25	67	......
Shermantown	932	583	349	930	1
Spring Valley	19	13	6	19	......
Steptoe Valley	39	26	13	39	......
Treasure	1920	791	1129	1778	11

(a) *Lyon County:* Dayton also includes 74 Chinese; Silver City, 42 Chinese.
(b) *Nye County:* Ellsworth also includes 1 Chinese; Reveille, 2 Chinese; Silver Park, 3 Chinese.
(c) *Ormsby County:* Carson City also includes 697 Chinese; Empire City, 72 Chinese.
(d) *Storey County:* Gold Hill also includes 210 Chinese; Virginia, 539 Chinese.
(e) *Washoe County:* Clark's Station also includes 1 Chinese; Crystal Peak, 11 Chinese; Franktown, 7 Chinese; Geiger Grade, 4 Chinese; Glendale, 4 Chinese; Mill Station, 2 Chinese; Ophir, 1 Chinese; Red Rock, 6 Chinese; Reno, 81 Chinese and 3 Indians; Truckee Meadows, 26 Chinese; Wadsworth, 36 Chinese; Washoe City, 42 Chinese.
(f) *White Pine County:* Hamilton city also includes 160 Chinese; Shermantown city, 1 Chinese; Treasure city, 131 Chinese.

TABLE IX.—*Population of Minor Civil Divisions, &c.—NEW HAMPSHIRE.*

NOTE.—The marginal column marks towns; the first indentation, cities; the second, villages. Names of villages are placed under the names of the towns in which they are respectively situated. The population of each town includes that of all villages situated in it.

Counties.	Total.	Nativity.		Race.	
		Native.	Foreign.	White.	Colored.
BELKNAP.					
Alton	1768	1708	60	1768	......
Barnstead	1543	1534	9	1542	1
Belmont	1165	1152	13	1161	4
BELKNAP—Cont'd.					
Center Harbor	446	444	2	445	1
Gilford	3361	3190	171	3346	15
Gilmanton	1642	1628	14	1629	13

X.—*Population of Minor Civil Divisions, &c.—NEW HAMPSHIRE*—Continued.

...ties.	Total.	NATIVITY. Native.	NATIVITY. Foreign.	RACE. White.	RACE. Colored.
—Cont'd.					
....	2309	1988	321	2306	3
....	1807	1781	26	1806	1
...ipton	1257	1217	40	1257	......
...on	1236	1229	7	1233	3
....	1147	1123	24	1147	......
...OLL.					
....	339	336	3	339	......
....	629	626	3	629	......
...l	416	415	1	416	......
....	445	445	......	445	......
....	1607	1585	22	1605	2
....	657	657	......	657	......
....	904	896	8	902	2
....	737	735	2	736	1
...s Locat'n	4	4	......	4	......
...s Locat'n	26	26	......	26	......
....	474	471	3	474	......
....	646	633	13	643	(a)
...orough ..	1299	1280	19	1297	2
....	1822	1812	10	1821	1
....	1854	1823	31	1853	1
...h	1344	1333	11	1342	2
...rough ...	949	943	6	949	......
...l	1185	1157	28	1181	1
...ough	1995	1979	16	1994	1
...HIRE.					
....	1213	1194	19	1213	......
...eld	1289	1274	15	1289	......
....	930	833	97	930	......
...an	1140	1096	44	1140	......
....	590	563	27	590	......
....	1342	1246	96	1342	......
....	1256	1172	84	1256	......
....	5971	5304	667	5967	4
...agh	1017	996	21	1010	7
....	716	712	4	716	......
....	744	653	91	743	1
...d	868	855	13	868	......
....	1107	1027	80	1107	......
....	174	162	12	173	1
....	637	626	11	636	1
....	347	326	21	347	......
....	318	313	5	318	......
....	1626	1548	78	1625	1
....	767	736	31	767	......
....	1830	1721	109	1830	......
...eland ..	1256	1200	56	1256	......
...ter	2097	1906	191	2097	......
...os					
....	529	318	211	529	......
...ge	28	27	1	28	......
....	378	338	40	378	......
...le	269	250	19	269	......
...k	1372	1207	165	1372	......
....	752	673	79	752	......
....	773	670	103	773	......
...mouth					
...ge Grant	11	11	......	11	......
...ille	8	8	......	8	......
....	317	310	7	317	......
....	178	174	4	178	......
....	1167	915	252	1161	(b)
...n's Grant	71	34	37	64	(c)
....	826	788	38	826	......
...r	2248	1925	323	2246	2
...in's Gra't	17	16	1	17	......

Counties.	Total.	NATIVITY. Native.	NATIVITY. Foreign.	RACE. White.	RACE. Colored.
COOS—Cont'd.					
Milan	710	640	70	710	......
Millsfield...	28	27	1	28	......
Northumberland .	955	693	262	954	1
Pittsburg	400	355	45	399	1
Randolph.........	138	121	17	138	......
Shelburne.........	259	252	7	259	......
Stark	464	399	65	464	......
Stewartstown	909	788	121	903	6
Stratford	886	763	123	886	......
Success	5	5	......	5	......
Wentworth Location ...	38	37	1	38	......
Whitefield	1196	1038	158	1196	......
GRAFTON.					
Alexandria.......	876	868	8	876	......
Ashland..........	885	800	85	885	......
Bath	1168	1095	73	1168	......
Benton............	375	339	36	375	......
Bethlehem	998	872	126	998	......
Bridgewater	453	449	4	453	......
Bristol	1416	1398	18	1416	......
Campton	1226	1209	17	1225	1
Canaan...........	1877	1705	172	1877	......
Danbury	796	776	20	796	......
Dorchester	689	648	41	689	......
Ellsworth	193	192	1	193	......
Enfield...........	1662	1580	82	1658	4
Franconia........	549	514	35	549	......
Grafton	907	894	13	907	......
Groton	583	570	13	583	......
Hanover	2085	1955	130	2075	10
Haverhill	2271	2126	145	2266	5
Hebron...........	382	371	11	382	......
Holderness	793	782	11	791	2
Landaff	882	858	24	881	1
Lebanon..........	3094	2761	333	3093	1
Lincoln	71	70	1	71	......
Lisbon	1844	1782	62	1844	......
Littleton	2446	2152	294	2440	6
Lyman	658	624	34	658	......
Lyme	1358	1307	51	1356	2
Monroe...........	532	483	49	532	......
Orange...........	340	335	5	340	......
Orford............	1119	1079	40	1119	......
Piermont.........	792	739	53	791	1
Plymouth	1409	1369	40	1408	1
Rumney..........	1165	1105	60	1163	2
Thornton	840	823	17	840	......
Warren	960	877	83	955	5
Waterville	33	28	5	33	......
Wentworth	971	920	51	971	......
Woodstock	405	392	13	405	......
HILLSBOROUGH.					
Amherst	1353	1270	83	1351	2
Antrim	904	896	8	904	......
Bedford	1221	1112	109	1221	......
Bennington	401	393	8	401	......
Brookline	741	717	24	741	......
Deering	722	702	20	722	......
Francestown	932	907	25	932	......
Goffstown	1656	1587	69	1644	12
Greenfield........	527	503	24	527	......
Hancock	692	680	12	692	......
Hillsborough.....	1595	1579	16	1595	......
Hollis	1079	1043	36	1077	2
Hudson	1066	1015	51	1065	1
Litchfield	345	330	15	339	6
Lyndeborough ...	820	797	23	820	......

(a) Also 3 Indians. (b) Also 6 Indians. (c) Also 7 Indians.

TABLE IX.—*Population of Minor Civil Divisions, &c.—NEW HAMPSHIRE—Continued.*

Counties.	Total.	Nativity. Native.	Nativity. Foreign.	Race. White.	Race. Colored.
HILLSBORO'—Con.					
Manchester	23536	16378	7158	23481	*a*50
Mason	1364	1185	179	1358	6
Merrimack	1066	976	90	1066	......
Milford	2606	2311	295	2606	......
Mont Vernon	601	588	13	600	1
Nashua	10543	8218	2325	10518	25
New Boston	1241	1205	36	1234	7
New Ipswich	1380	1234	146	1377	3
Pelham	861	788	73	861	......
Peterborough	2236	2089	147	2228	8
Sharon	182	171	11	182	......
Temple	421	394	27	421	......
Weare	2092	2009	83	2091	1
Wilton	1974	1608	366	1974	......
Windsor	81	81	......	81	......
MERRIMACK.					
Allenstown	804	486	318	804	......
Andover	1206	1163	43	1206	......
Boscawen	1637	1383	254	1635	2
Bow	745	741	4	745	......
Bradford	1081	1067	14	1079	2
Canterbury	1169	1144	25	1151	18
Chichester	871	866	5	870	1
Concord	12241	10577	1664	12205	36
Dunbarton	778	757	21	777	1
Epsom	993	990	3	993	......
Franklin	2301	2024	277	2299	2
Henniker	1288	1263	25	1287	1
Hill	620	606	14	620	......
Hooksett	1330	1024	306	1329	1
Hopkinton	1814	1761	53	1813	1
Loudon	1282	1260	22	1277	5
Newbury	601	597	4	601	......
New London	959	935	24	959	......
Northfield	833	820	13	833	......
Pembroke	2518	1736	782	2518	......
Pittsfield	1600	1589	11	1596	4
Salisbury	897	884	13	897	......
Sutton	1155	1143	12	1136	19
Warner	1667	1653	14	1664	3
Webster	689	674	15	689	......
Wilmot	1072	1059	13	1072	......
ROCKINGHAM.					
Atkinson	488	474	14	488	......
Auburn	815	780	35	815	......
Brentwood	895	865	30	889	6
Candia	1456	1409	47	1456	......
Chester	1153	1133	20	1152	1
Danville	548	545	3	548	......
Deerfield	1768	1736	32	1756	*b*11
Derry	1809	1693	116	1808	1
East Kingston	553	534	19	553	......
Epping	1270	1236	34	1267	3
Exeter	3437	3060	377	3386	51
Fremont	527	519	8	527	......
Gosport	94	94	......	94	......
ROCK'GHAM—Con.					
Greenland	695	668	27	693	2
Hampstead	935	915	20	935	......
Hampton	1177	1155	22	1174	3
Hampton Falls	679	602	77	678	1
Kensington	642	631	11	642	......
Kingston	1054	1019	35	1048	6
Londonderry	1405	1362	43	1404	1
New Castle	667	649	18	667	......
Newington	414	406	8	414	......
New Market	1987	1722	265	1987	......
Newton	856	825	31	855	1
North Hampton	723	718	5	723	......
Northwood	1430	1421	9	1430	......
Nottingham	1130	1107	23	1129	1
Plaistow	879	695	184	879	......
Portsmouth	9211	8205	1006	9155	56
Raymond	1121	1108	13	1120	1
Rye	993	987	6	991	2
Salem	1603	1515	88	1602	1
Sandown	496	492	4	496	......
Seabrook	1609	1591	18	1609	......
South Hampton	448	444	4	448	......
South Newmarket	808	702	106	806	2
Stratham	769	744	25	769	......
Windham	753	717	36	753	......
STRAFFORD.					
Barrington	1581	1567	14	1580	1
Dover	9294	7848	1446	9261	33
Durham	1298	1235	63	1297	1
Farmington	2063	2034	29	2062	1
Lee	776	763	13	775	1
Madbury	408	401	7	408	......
Middleton	476	470	6	473	3
Milton	1598	1513	85	1598	......
New Durham	973	938	35	973	......
Rochester	4103	3712	391	4103	......
Rollinsford	1500	1251	249	1498	2
Somersworth	4504	3572	932	4504	......
Strafford	1669	1654	15	1667	2
SULLIVAN.					
Acworth	1050	1034	16	1050	......
Charlestown	1741	1560	181	1738	3
Claremont	4053	3518	535	4046	7
Cornish	1334	1298	36	1334	......
Croydon	652	652	......	652	......
Goshen	507	495	12	507	......
Grantham	608	589	19	608	......
Langdon	411	392	19	402	9
Lempster	678	659	19	678	......
Newport	2163	2059	104	2148	15
Plainfield	1589	1559	30	1588	(*b*)
Springfield	781	775	6	779	2
Sunapee	808	797	11	808	......
Unity	844	826	18	841	3
Washington	839	830	9	835	4

(*a*) Also 5 Indians. (*b*) Also 1 Indian.

'ABLE IX.—*Population of Minor Civil Divisions, &c.*—*NEW JERSEY.*

he marginal column marks townships; the first indentation, cities; the second, towns. 'owns are placed under the names of the townships in which they are respectively situated. ion of each township includes that of all towns situated in it.

s.	Total.	Nativity. Native.	Nativity. Foreign.	Race. White.	Race. Colored.
IC.					
ity ...	1043	929	114	1028	15
......	948	755	193	929	19
......	3585	3552	33	3535	50
......	2860	2572	288	2822	38
rbor ..	1311	649	662	1294	17
......	1271	1185	86	1260	11
......	2265	1954	311	2231	34
nton ..	1404	1202	202	1382	22
......	810	805	5	810	......
f.					
......	2899	2468	431	2827	72
......	8038	5828	2210	7705	a333
......	2664	2195	469	2438	226
......	2632	2433	199	2392	240
......	3221	1765	1456	3081	140
loes ..	4929	3991	938	4616	313
r	1168	907	261	1099	69
......	2057	1331	726	1986	71
......	2514	2355	150	2345	169
ON.					
......	807	793	14	794	13
......	2438	2151	287	2390	30
......	1418	1239	179	1400	18
......	5.0	......	......	......	......
......	6041	5327	714	5835	206
......	1025	916	109	969	56
......	5817	5358	459	5243	574
......	2586	2325	261	2427	159
......	1748	1663	85	1665	83
......	3112	2613	499	3001	111
......	3351	3034	317	2994	357
arbor.	1779	1746	33	1774	5
......	1718	1552	166	1656	62
......	2880	2731	149	2841	39
......	2189	2117	72	2111	78
er	2536	2492	44	2358	178
n	4018	3738	280	3801	217
......	2743	2654	89	2700	43
on	797	774	23	789	8
......	450	446	4	449	1
......	1149	1059	90	1108	b40
n	2374	2301	73	2361	13
......	1761	1661	100	1711	50
......	609	584	25	600	9
on	1369	1283	86	1191	178
ugh ..	750	693	57	739	11
......	389	360	29	371	18
s.					
......	20045	17462	2583	19218	b826
......	1718	1643	75	916	802
......	1625	1448	177	1455	170
le	86	78	8	86	......
......	2710	2557	153	2567	143
......	1926	1774	152	1697	229
field ..	1075	1007	68	1011	64
......	1663	1524	139	1632	31
......	8437	6880	1557	6929	c1497
r City	3682	2736	946	3656	c15
......	2381	2126	255	1747	634
atville	245	221	24	225	20

Counties.	Total.	Nativity. Native.	Nativity. Foreign.	Race. White.	Race. Colored.
CAMDEN—Cont'd.					
Washington	1567	1450	117	1525	42
Waterford	2071	1891	180	2031	40
Winslow	2050	1837	213	2034	16
CAPE MAY.					
Dennis	1640	1617	23	1638	2
Lower	1783	1748	35	1576	207
Middle	3443	3305	138	3232	211
Cape May	1248	1129	119	1102	146
Upper	1483	1478	5	1476	7
CUMBERLAND.					
Bridgeton	6830	6476	354	6402	428
Deerfield	1518	1443	75	1517	1
Downe	3385	3376	9	3368	17
Fairfield	3011	2973	38	2596	415
Greenwich	1262	1239	23	903	359
Hopewell	1857	1791	66	1734	123
Landis	7079	6243	836	6837	242
Maurice River	2500	2489	11	2467	33
Millville	6101	5591	510	5998	103
Stow Creek	1122	1093	29	1076	46
ESSEX.					
Belleville	3644	2534	1110	3574	70
Bloomfield	4580	3366	1214	4457	123
Caldwell	2727	2416	311	2698	29
Clinton	2240	1734	506	2204	36
East Orange	4315	3458	857	4240	75
Livingston	1157	978	179	1149	8
Millburn	1675	1157	518	1664	11
Montclair	2853	2049	804	2817	36
Newark	105059	69175	35884	103267	d1789
Orange	9348	6117	3231	9116	b231
South Orange	2963	2157	806	2931	32
West Orange	2106	1457	649	2059	47
Woodside	1172	906	266	1120	52
GLOUCESTER.					
Clayton	3674	3369	305	3650	24
Deptford	4963	4627	336	4176	487
Woodbury	1965	1822	143	1694	271
Franklin	2188	2054	134	2121	67
Greenwich	2342	2221	121	2266	76
Harrison	3038	2756	282	2950	79
Mantua	1897	1733	164	1885	12
Woolwich	3760	3405	355	3332	428
HUDSON.					
Bayonne	3834	2626	1208	3784	50
Greenville	2789	1647	1142	2702	87
Harrison	4129	2239	1890	4107	22
Hoboken	20297	9963	10334	20255	42
Jersey City	82546	50711	31835	81840	b705
Kearney	974	560	414	971	3
North Bergen	2032	1020	1112	1945	87
Union	6737	3499	3238	6733	4
Union	4640	2362	2278	4636	4
Weehawken	597	342	255	596	1
West Hoboken ...	4132	2396	1736	4083	49

1 Chinese.
1 Indian.

(c) Also 11 Indians.
(d) Also 1 Indian and 2 Chinese.

TABLE IX.—*Population of Minor Civil Divisions, &c.—NEW JERSEY*—Continued.

Counties.	Total.	Nativity. Native.	Nativity. Foreign.	Race. White.	Race. Colored.
HUNTERDON.					
Alexandria	1253	1191	62	1228	25
Frenchtown, (borough)	912	905	7	912	.....
Bethlehem	2211	2073	138	2182	29
Clinton	3919	3674	245	3853	66
Clinton (boro')	785	739	46	756	29
Delaware	2959	2885	74	2927	32
East Amwell	1802	1759	43	1708	94
Franklin	1342	1332	10	1335	7
Kingwood	1942	1921	21	1940	2
Lebanon	3561	3273	288	3539	22
Raritan	3654	3442	212	3517	137
Flemington	1412	1306	106	1356	56
Readington	3070	3002	68	3008	62
Tewksbury	2327	2289	38	2246	81
Union	1051	1026	25	1041	10
West Amwell	4872	4199	673	4805	67
Lambertville	3842	3209	633	3815	27
MERCER.					
East Windsor	2383	2284	99	2293	90
Hightstown, (borough)	1347	1296	51	1311	36
Ewing	2477	1818	659	2344	133
Hamilton	5417	4456	961	5245	172
Hopewell	4276	4104	172	3989	287
Lawrence	2251	1769	482	2073	178
Millham	677	406	271	666	11
Princeton	3986	3517	469	3419	567
Princeton, (borough)	2798	2459	339	2350	448
Trenton	22874	17855	5019	22069	805
Washington	1294	1209	85	1226	68
West Windsor	1428	1351	77	1360	68
MIDDLESEX.					
East Brunswick	2861	2336	525	2788	73
Madison	1634	1429	205	1603	31
Monroe	3253	3008	245	3134	119
N'w Brunsw'k (a)	15058	11684	3374	14472	b577
North Brunswick	1124	957	167	1076	48
Perth Amboy	2861	2170	691	2815	46
Piscataway	2757	2389	368	2579	178
Raritan	3460	2798	662	3346	114
South Amboy	4525	3070	1455	4515	c9
South Brunswick	3779	3473	306	3564	215
Woodbridge	3717	2596	1121	3582	135
MONMOUTH.					
Atlantic	1713	1471	242	1553	160
Freehold	4231	3756	475	3912	319
Holmdel	1415	1160	255	1352	63
Howell	3371	3248	123	3356	15
Manalapan	2286	2079	207	2091	195
Marlborough	2231	1831	400	2095	136
Matawan	2839	2246	593	2640	199
Middletown	4639	4017	622	4230	409
Millstone	2087	1947	140	2014	73
Ocean	6189	5777	412	5803	386
Raritan	3443	3097	346	3367	76
Keyport	2366	2111	255	2317	49
Shrewsbury	5440	4855	585	4849	591
Red Bank	2086	1866	220	1991	95
Upper Freehold	3640	3411	229	3368	272
Wall	2671	2601	70	2655	16
MORRIS.					
Boonton	3458	2696	762	3432	26
Chatham	3715	2883	832	3602	113
MORRIS—Cont'd.					
Chester	1743	1577	166	1728	15
Hanover	3623	3049	574	3519	104
Jefferson	1430	1250	180	1430	.....
Mendham	1553	1425	128	1532	21
Mountville	1403	1320	83	1358	45
Morris	5674	4522	1152	5432	242
Passaic	1624	1395	229	1610	14
Pequannock	1534	1499	35	1486	48
Randolph	5111	3357	1754	5076	d34
Rockaway	6445	4138	2307	6431	14
Roxbury	3320	2967	353	3306	14
Washington	2484	2442	42	2449	35
OCEAN.					
Brick	2724	2619	105	2706	18
Dover	3044	2912	132	3038	6
Jackson	1755	1730	25	1752	3
Manchester	1102	898	204	1090	12
Plumstead	1566	1509	57	1495	71
Stafford	1514	1499	15	1507	7
Maunahawkinsville	629	620	9	624	5
Union	1923	1897	26	1923	.....
PASSAIC.					
Acquackanonck	4368	2996	1372	4264	104
Little Falls	1282	896	386	1277	5
Manchester	1166	899	267	1129	37
Paterson	33579	20711	12868	33218	361
Pompton	1840	1733	107	1779	61
Wayne	1521	1306	215	1473	48
West Milford	2660	2527	133	2601	59
SALEM.					
Elsinborough	700	677	23	596	104
Lower Alloway's Creek	1485	1452	33	1295	190
Low'r Penn's Neck	1452	1406	46	1224	228
Mannington	2351	2249	102	1896	455
Pilesgrove	3385	3246	139	2910	475
Sharpstown	296	282	14	277	19
Woodstown	1611	1544	67	1578	33
Pittsgrove	1667	1590	77	1663	4
Centerton	155	151	4	155	.....
Elmer	347	334	13	345	2
Salem	4555	4185	370	4295	260
Upper Alloway's Creek	3062	2991	71	2722	340
Upp'r Penn's Neck	3178	3063	115	3117	61
Upper Pittsgrove	2087	2005	82	2045	42
SOMERSET.					
Bedminster	1881	1802	79	1788	93
Bernard's	2369	2143	226	2328	41
Branchburg	1251	1198	53	1192	59
Bridgewater	5883	4885	998	5504	379
Bound Brook	556	484	72	547	9
Raritan	1009	744	265	1006	3
Somerville	2236	1969	267	1959	277
Franklin	3912	3366	546	3537	375
Hillsborough	3443	3209	234	3173	d269
Montgomery	2066	1938	128	1817	249
Warren	2705	2179	526	2649	56
SUSSEX.					
Andover	1126	1115	11	1123	3
Byram	1332	1243	89	1320	12

(a) Comprises both city and township of New Brunswick.
(b) Also 9 Japanese.
(c) Also 1 Chinese.
(d) Also 1 Japanese.

: IX.—*Population of Minor Civil Divisions, &c.—NEW JERSEY*—Continued.

ies.	Total.	Nativity. Native.	Nativity. Foreign.	Race. White.	Race. Colored.
Cont'd.					
....	1776	1746	30	1758	18
....	868	843	25	865	3
....	1023	1006	17	1019	4
....	1668	1479	189	1661	7
....	884	863	21	873	11
....	932	920	12	915	17
n	2403	2111	292	2362	41
....	1230	1215	15	1213	17
....	2032	1890	142	2031	1
....	1632	1615	17	1632	......
....	1979	1937	42	1973	6
....	647	645	2	631	16
....	3636	3441	195	3596	40
x.					
....	331	249	82	331	......
1......	20832	14080	6752	20261	571
....	1396	1058	338	1303	93
dence..	934	744	190	918	16
d	5095	4189	906	4892	203
....	6258	5076	1182	6012	246
l.......	770	663	107	743	27
....	1176	820	356	1169	7

Counties.	Total.	Nativity. Native.	Nativity. Foreign.	Race. White.	Race. Colored.
UNION—Cont'd.					
Union	2314	1849	465	2267	47
Westfield	2753	2214	539	2667	86
WARREN.					
Belvidere..........	1882	1760	122	1819	63
Blairstown	1379	1361	18	1369	10
Franklin	1655	1627	28	1635	20
Frelinghuysen ...	1113	1094	19	1108	5
Greenwich	2587	2489	98	2558	29
Hackettstown	2202	1885	317	2193	9
Hardwick	638	634	4	638	......
Harmony..........	1405	1378	27	1396	9
Hope.............	1542	1530	12	1540	2
Independence	1766	1654	112	1759	7
Knowlton	1691	1610	81	1690	1
Lapatcong	1150	1012	138	1147	3
Mansfield	1997	1852	145	1955	42
Oxford	2952	2626	326	2902	50
Pahaquarry	405	399	6	405	......
Phillipsburg	5932	4709	1223	5907	25
Washington	4040	3426	614	3934	106
Washington, (borough) ..	1880	1694	186	1795	85

TABLE IX.—*Population of Minor Civil Divisions, &c.—NEW MEXICO.*

The marginal column marks precincts; the first indentation, cities; the second, all other whose names are placed under the names of the precincts in which they are respectively The population of each precinct includes that of all localities situated in it. Wherever in a lity the items fail to make the total, there the deficiency represents the Indians.

ies.	Total.	Nativity. Native.	Nativity. Foreign.	Race. White.	Race. Colored.
LO. (a)					
da	648	645	3	645	......
nerque.	1307	1253	54	1279	6
o.......	103	103	......	101	......
s.......	309	309	......	308	......
illo	745	739	6	725	......
l.......	49	49	......	49	......
Carmel.	21	21	......	21	......
cito	61	61	......	61	......
....	291	286	5	289	......
s.......	687	686	1	670	......
acho....	336	336	......	326	......
....	12	10	2	12	......
Pueblo rvation.	12	9	3	12	......
eñora dalupe .	65	65	......	63	......
andela-	200	200	......	200	......
riegos ..	285	285	......	285	......
asitos..	212	211	1	212	......

Counties.	Total.	Nativity. Native.	Nativity. Foreign.	Race. White.	Race. Colored.
BERNALILLO—Con.					
Los Ranchos..	480	479	1	471	......
Madera.......	20	20	......	20	......
Padilla	309	309	......	304	......
Pajarita	308	304	4	300	......
Ranchos de Atrisco.....	304	304	......	299	......
Sandia Indian Reservation	10	10	......	10	......
San Antonio..	177	177	......	176	1
San Antonita.	131	131	......	131	......
San Francisco.	180	180	......	177	......
San Ignacio ..	221	220	1	219	......
Tijera	108	107	1	108	......
COLFAX. (b)					
Precinct 1........	800	619	181	792	7
Precinct 2........	132	97	35	123	......
Precinct 3........	1060	1009	51	1045	3

alillo County: Alameda also includes 3 Indians; Albuquerque, 22 Indians; Atrisco, 2 Indians, 1 Indian; Bernalillo, 20 Indians; Chilili, 2 Indians; Corales, 17 Indians; El Rancho, 10 La Señora Guadalupe, 2 Indians; Los Ranchos, 9 Indians; Padilla, 5 Indians; Pajarita, 8 Ranchos de Atrisco, 5 Indians; San Francisco, 3 Indians; San Ignacio, 2 Indians.
x County: Precinct 1 also includes 1 Indian; Precinct 2, 9 Indians; Precinct 3, 12 Indians.

TABLE IX.—*Population of Minor Civil Divisions, &c.*—*NEW MEXICO*—Continued.

Counties.	Total.	Nativity. Native.	Nativity. Foreign.	Race. White.	Race. Colored.
DOÑA AÑA. (a)					
Chamberino	463	207	256	463	......
Doña Aña	728	387	341	728	......
Fort Selden, (garrison)	153	92	61	153	......
La Mesa	370	163	207	370	......
Las Cruces	1304	631	673	1304	......
Leasburg	24	10	14	23	(a)
Los Chulos	125	46	79	125	......
Martin's, or Jornado del Muerto	11	11	......	10	1
Mesilla	1578	742	836	1578	......
Picacho	210	163	47	210	......
Rio Polomas	186	175	11	186	......
San Agustine Springs	7	7	......	7	......
Santo Tomas	114	40	74	114	......
Sloc'm's R'nch, or Water Holes	6	5	1	6	......
Tortugas R'ch	298	115	183	298	......
Union	287	62	225	287	......
GRANT.					
Apache Tegua Ranche	5	3	2	4	1
Central City	89	43	46	89	......
Cow Springs Ranche	2	2	......	2	......
F't Cummings, (garrison)	70	30	40	68	2
Fort Bayard, (garrison)	241	118	123	237	4
Lacy's, or Hot Sp'gs Ranch	3	1	2	3	......
Los Mimbres	184	124	60	183	1
Pinos Altos	246	94	152	246	......
Ralston	174	113	61	174	......
San Lorenzo	49	13	36	49	......
Silver City	80	51	29	79	1
LINCOLN.					
Precinct 1	631	558	73	622	9
Precinct 2	160	160	......	159	1
Precinct 3	372	365	7	369	3
Precinct 4	640	603	37	639	1
MORA. (b)					
1. Mora	1083	1045	38	1057	6
2. San Antonio	470	465	5	466	......
3. Guadalupita	511	509	2	507	......
4. (c)	......	......	......	......	......
MORA—Cont'd.					
5. La Cueba	640	636	4	638	......
6. La Cebolla	903	898	5	903	......
7. Golondrinas	366	350	16	366	......
8. Ocate	1200	1179	21	1193	......
9. Agua Negra	415	412	3	408	......
10. El Coyote	538	530	8	536	......
11. La Junta	1107	953	154	1092	[illegible]
12. Santa Clara	411	400	11	409	......
13. Loma Parda	412	398	14	409	......
RIO ARRIBA. (d)					
1. Embudo	653	651	2	646	......
Embudo	516	514	2	509	......
Ojo Sarco	137	137	......	137	......
2. La Joya	789	781	8	755	1
La Joya	274	272	2	257	......
Los Luceros	119	117	2	115	......
Plaza Alcaldo	196	196	......	195	1
San Juan	80	73	7	76	......
Villita	120	120	......	111	......
3. Vallecito	549	547	2	528	......
Cerbilletta	113	113	......	113	......
Petaca	40	40	......	40	......
Vallecito	396	393	3	375	......
4. El Rito	805	801	4	771	......
5. Abiquiu	725	718	7	680	1
6. Chama Abajo	570	570	......	550	......
7. Santa Cruz	686	681	5	668	......
8. Chimayo	566	566	......	566	......
9. Cañones	206	204	2	200	......
10. Tierra Azul	232	232	......	219	......
11. El Tunque	276	276	......	264	......
12. Ojo Caliente	245	245	......	234	......
13. Huique	349	348	1	333	......
Bosque	40	40	......	39	......
Huique	309	308	1	294	......
14. San José	431	428	3	429	......
15. (e)	......	......	......	......	......
16. Tierra Amarilla	559	555	4	530	......
Nambe Pueblo Res'n.	175	175	......	175	......
San Juan Pueblo Reserv'n.	1031	1022	9	994	......
Santa Clara Pueblo Reserv'n.	447	445	2	435	......
SAN MIGUEL (f)					
Apache Sp'gs.	13	12	1	13	..
Agua Negra	92	91	1	90	..

(a) Doña Aña County: Leasburg also includes 1 Indian.

(b) Mora County: Mora also includes 20 Indians; San Antonio, 4 Indians; Guadalupita, 4 Indi[ans]; La Cueba, 2 Indians; Ocate, 5 Indians; Agua Negra, 7 Indians; El Coyote, 2 Indians; La Junta, [illegible] [In]dians; Santa Clara, 2 Indians; Loma Parda, 3 Indians.

(c) In 1868 to Colfax County.

(d) Rio Arriba County: Embudo also includes 7 Indians; La Joya, 33 Indians; Vallecito, 21 India[ns]; El Rito, 34 Indians; Abiquiu, 44 Indians; Chama Abajo, 20 Indians; Santa Cruz, 18 Indians; Cañon[es], 6 Indians; Tierra Azul, 13 Indians; El Tunque, 12 Indians; Ojo Caliente, 11 Indians; Huique, 16 [In]dians; San José, 2 Indians; Tierra Amarilla, 29 Indians; San Juan Pueblo Reservation, 37 India[ns]; Santa Clara Pueblo Reservation, 12 Indians.

(e) Precinct No. 15 abolished.

(f) San Miguel County: Agua Negra also includes 2 Indians; Cañada de Aguilar, 1 Indian; Colon[ias] de San José, 3 Indians; El Macho, 1 Indian; El Pueblo, 5 Indians; El Puertecito, 2 Indians; El Teco[lo]tito, 1 Indian; Gallinas Crossing, 1 Indian; Joya Larga, 2 Indians; La Cuesta, 4 Indians; La Estanc[ia], 2 Indians; La Lagunita, 1 Indian; Las Gallinas, 1 Indian; Las Tuzas, 4 Indians; Los Torres, 1 In[]dian; Lower Anton Chico, 2 Indians; Lower Las Vegas, 25 Indians; Monton de Alamos, 9 Indians; Pecos, 6 Indians; Puerto de Luna, 2 Indians; Rincon de Tecolote, 3 Indians; Rio Colorado, 9 Indians; San Geronimo, 1 Indian; San José, 2 Indians; San Miguel, 4 Indians; Sapello, 7 Indians; Tecolote, 4 Indians; Upper Colonias, 1 Indian; Upper Las Vegas, 11 Indians.

TABLE IX.—*Population of Minor Civil Divisions, &c.*—*NEW MEXICO*—Continued.

Counties.	Total.	Nativity: Native.	Nativity: Foreign.	Race: White.	Race: Colored.
SAN MIGUEL—Con.					
Aroyo de Conchas	150	151	[illegible]	150	......
Berna	128	128	......	128	......
Cañada de Aguilar	56	54	2	55	......
Cedar Springs	17	15	2	17	......
Colonias de San José	492	490	2	489	......
Chaperito	429	427	2	429	......
El Aguila	131	133	1	134	......
El Burro	144	142	2	144	......
El Guzano	67	67	......	67	......
El Macho	131	134	......	133	......
El Pueblo	292	292	......	287	......
El Puertecito	349	349	......	347	......
El Sonito	90	89	1	90	......
El Tecolotito	125	125	......	124	......
Fort Bascom	88	69	19	84	4
Fort Summer	12	9	3	12	......
Gallinas Crossing	119	118	1	118	......
Hatch	66	65	1	66	......
Jorupa	120	119	1	120	......
Joya Larga	200	193	7	198	......
La Cuesta	660	660	......	656	......
La Entrañosa	73	72	1	73	......
La Estancia	107	102	5	105	......
La Junta	176	173	3	176	......
La Lagunita	54	54	......	53	......
Las Gallinas	112	110	2	111	......
Las Mulas	85	85	......	85	......
Las Ruedas	84	83	1	84	......
Las Tuzas	239	239	......	235	......
Los Esteritos	63	63	......	63	......
Los Frigos	123	123	......	123	......
Los Ritos	40	40	......	40	......
Los Tecoloteños	175	171	4	175	......
Los Torres	174	174	......	173	......
Los Valles de San Antonio	242	240	2	242	......
Los Valles de San Agustin	399	396	3	399	......
Lower Anton Chico	556	547	9	554	......
Lower Cueva	114	114	......	111	......
Lower Las Vegas	1730	1649	81	1695	10
Montoya de Alamos	792	788	4	793	......
Ojitos Frios	210	209	1	210	......
Pecos	354	348	8	350	......
Pu'rto de Luna	713	699	11	711	......
Rincon de Tecolote	313	312	1	312	......
Rio Colorado	714	704	10	701	1
Rio La Vaca	56	56	......	56	......
San Geronimo	442	437	5	441	......
San José	489	486	3	487	......
San Miguel	563	557	6	559	......
Sapello	937	924	13	929	1
Tecolote	634	621	13	630	......
Tres Hermanos	54	54	......	54	......
Upper Anton Chico	186	184	2	186	......
Upper Colonias	112	112	......	111	......
Upper La Cueva	154	152	2	154	......
Upper Las Vegas	796	789	7	784	1
SANTA AÑA. (a)					
Algodones	229	226	3	224	......
Angostura	138	138	......	138	......
Bajado	146	146	......	146	......
Cañada de Cochita	202	202	......	201	1
Cili	105	104	1	101	2
Cocheta Puebla Reserv'n	361	360	1	354	......
Cañon de Gemes	319	316	3	316	2
Cubero	59	59	......	53	1
Lemitas	52	52	......	52	......
Ojo del Espiritu Santo y Nacimiento	57	57	......	56	......
Peña Blanca	427	424	3	405	13
San Domingo Pueblo Res	105	105	......	98	1
San Isidro	130	130	......	127	......
Santa Aña Pueblo Res	9	9	......	9	......
Tejon	96	96	......	92	4
Uña de Gato	59	58	1	59	......
Vallecito	105	105	......	103	......
SANTA FÉ. (b)					
1. Rio Pojoaque	676	675	1	675	......
2. Rio Tesuque	262	261	1	262	......
3. (c)	2527	2375	152	2492	16
4. (c)	2238	2112	126	2195	18
5. Agua Fria	483	480	3	483	......
6. Cienega	421	415	6	416	......
7. Real de Dolores	183	179	4	181	2
8. Galisteo	504	497	7	497	2
9. San Ildefonso	428	424	4	425	......
10. Quimado	752	762	......	742	......
Quimado	288	288	......	285	......
11. Los Truches	376	376	......	371	......
Los Truches (d)	840	840	......	828	......
12. Real de San Francisco	80	74	0	80	......
Pojoaque Pueblo Reserv'n.	397	395	2	396	......
San Ildefonso Res	372	368	4	370	......
Sante Fé (c)	4765	4487	278	4687	34

(a) Santa Aña County: Algodones also includes 5 Indians; Cili, 2 Indians; Cocheta Puebla Reservation, 7 Indians; Cañon de Gemes, 1 Indian; Cubero, 5 Indians; Ojo del Espiritu Santo y Nacimiento, 1 Indian; Peña Blanca, 9 Indians; San Domingo Pueblo Reservation, 6 Indians; San Isidro, 3 Indians; Vallecito, 2 Indians.

(b) Santa Fé County: Rio Pojoaque also includes 1 Indian; Precincts 3 and 4, (indentical with city of Santa Fé,) 44 Indians; Cienega, 5 Indians; Galisteo, 5 Indians; San Ildefonso, 3 Indians; Quimado, 10 Indians; Los Truches, 5 Indians; Los Truches City, 12 Indians; Pojoaque Pueblo Reservation, 1 Indian; San Ildefonso Reservation, 2 Indians.

(c) Santa Fé City reported as being identical with Precincts 3 and 4.

(d) Los Truches in Precincts Nos. 10 and 11.

TABLE IX.—*Population of Minor Civil Divisions, &c.*—*NEW MEXICO*—**Continued.**

Counties.	Total.	Nativity. Native.	Nativity. Foreign.	Race. White.	Race. Colored.
SOCORRO. (*a*)					
1. Socorro	921	877	44	891	4
2. Limitar	640	638	2	635	1
3. Pulvedero	437	436	1	434	......
4. Savinal	488	487	1	487	......
5. La Jolla	495	492	3	491	......
6. La Jollita	351	349	2	350	1
7. San Antonio	565	561	4	561	2
8. Contadero	514	412	102	504	10
9. Parajo	527	519	8	527	......
10. Alamosita	278	237	41	275	1
11. Cañada La Mosa	205	200	5	205	......
12. Tajo	70	70	......	69	......
13. San Marcial	397	392	5	397	......
14. (*b*)	......	......	......	......	......
15. Valverdo	239	239	......	238	......
16. Las Nutrias	283	283	......	280	......
Southern Apache country	193	192	1	193	......
TAOS. (*c*)					
Arroyo Hondo	477	465	12	469	......
Arroyo Seco	958	951	7	929	......
Chamisal	335	335	......	335	......
Cordovas	789	787	2	733	......
Costilla	631	624	7	625	......
El Llano	716	714	2	709	......
El Rancho	1329	1324	5	1325	......
Fernando de Taos	1302	1273	29	1266	......
TAOS—Continued.					
Peñasco	544	541	3	531	......
Picuris Pueblo Reservation	773	771	2	756	......
Pinos	349	349	......	343	......
Placita	830	826	4	788	......
Red Willow Pueblo Res.	1600	1578	22	1553	3
Rio Colorado	514	511	3	503	......
Rio del Pueblo	219	218	1	218	......
Serro	390	390	......	386	......
Trampas	323	323	......	323	......
VALENCIA. (*d*)					
1. Valencia	581	570	11	562	......
2. Las Lunas	598	561	37	538	1
3. Tomé	1035	1018	17	1012	......
4. Casa Colorado	235	234	1	226	......
5. Mansano	738	733	5	732	......
6. Tajiqua	534	530	4	531	......
7. Belin	720	713	7	708	1
8. Sevolleta	581	573	8	558	......
9. Cubero	630	601	29	611	......
10. Jarales	897	891	6	885	......
11. Punta del Agua	338	335	3	336	......
12. Fort Wingate	464	268	196	463	1
13. San Mateo	224	222	2	224	......
14. El Rito	256	248	8	247	......
15. Peralta	616	598	18	574	6
16. Gabaldones	478	471	7	473	......
Pueblo de Laguna Reserv'n.	168	166	2	161	1

(*a*) Socorro County: Socorro also includes 26 Indians; Limitar, 4 Indians; Pulvedero, 3 Indians; Savinal, 1 Indian; La Jolla, 4 Indians; San Antonio, 2 Indians; Alamosita, 2 Indians; Tajo, 1 Indian; Valverdo, 1 Indian; Las Nutrias, 3 Indians.

(*b*) In 1870 Precinct No. 14 to Doña Aña County.

(*c*) Taos County: Arroyo Hondo also includes 8 Indians; Arroyo Seco, 29 Indians; Cordovas, 56 Indians; Costilla, 6 Indians; El Llano, 7 Indians; El Rancho, 4 Indians; Fernando de Taos, 36 Indians; Peñasco, 13 Indians; Picuris Pueblo Reservation, 17 Indians; Pinos, 6 Indians; Placita, 42 Indians; Red Willow Pueblo Reservation, 44 Indians; Rio Colorado, 11 Indians; Rio del Pueblo, 1 Indian; Serro, 4 Indians.

(*d*) Valencia County: Valencia also includes 19 Indians; Las Lunas, 59 Indians; Tomé, 23 Indians; Casa Colorado, 9 Indians; Mansano, 6 Indians; Tajiqua, 3 Indians; Belin, 11 Indians; Sevolleta, 23 Indians; Cubero, 19 Indians; Jarales, 12 Indians; Punta del Agua, 2 Indians; El Rito, 9 Indians; Peralta, 36 Indians; Gabaldones, 5 Indians; Pueblo de Laguna Reservation, 6 Indians.

TABLE IX.—*Population of Minor Civil Divisions, &c.—NEW YORK.*

NOTE.—The marginal column marks towns; the first indentation, cities; the second, villages. Names of villages are placed under the names of the towns in which they are respectively situated. The population of each town includes that of all villages situated in it.

Counties.	Total.	Nativity.		Race.	
		Native.	Foreign.	White.	Colored.
ALBANY.					
Albany (*)	69422	47215	22207	68658	764
Berne	2562	2490	72	2561	1
Berneville	250	......	......	......	......
South Berne	50	......	......	......	......
West Berne	100	......	......	......	......
Bethlehem	6950	4979	1971	6859	91
Coeymans	3077	2857	220	3018	59
Cohoes	15357	7947	7410	15340	17
Guilderland	3132	2894	238	3130	2
Knox	1656	1624	32	1654	2
New Scotland	3411	3238	173	3386	25
Clarksville	236	231	5	236	......
New Salem	219	213	6	219	......
New Scotland	103	71	32	103	......
Rensselaerville	2492	2440	52	2492	......
Cooksburg	67	......	......	......	......
Medusa	94	......	......	......	......
Potter's Hollow	138	......	......	......	......
Preston Hollow	284	......	......	......	......
Rensselaerville	526	......	......	......	......
Watervliet (a)	22609	15721	6888	22478	131
Green Island	3135	2197	938	3135	......
West Troy	10693	7139	3554	10609	84
Westerlo	2384	2333	51	2381	3
Chesterville	247	......	......	......	......
S'th Westerlo	147	......	......	......	......
ALLEGANY.					
Alfred	1555	1499	56	1546	9
Allen	794	703	91	787	7
Alma	766	665	101	741	25
Almond	1686	1642	44	1678	8
Amity	2087	1948	139	2082	5
Belmont	795	734	61	792	3
Andover	1873	1618	255	1873	......
Angelica	1643	1431	212	1612	31
Angelica	991	849	142	980	11
Belfast	1488	1367	121	1488	......
Birdsall	755	652	103	755	......
Bolivar	959	944	15	956	3
Burns	1340	1221	119	1340	......
Caneadea	1869	1683	186	1822	47
Caneadea	236	......	......	......	......
Oramel	289	......	......	......	......
Centreville	1043	912	131	1042	1
Centreville	167	......	......	......	......
Clarksville	784	762	22	782	2
Cuba	2397	2186	211	2357	40
Friendship	1528	1460	68	1527	1
Friendship	474	444	30	474	......
Genesee	888	881	7	886	2
Granger	1050	938	112	1044	6
Grove	1056	924	132	1056	......
Hume	1920	1775	145	1917	3
Fillmore	215	......	......	......	......
Hume	254	......	......	......	......
Wiscoy	193	......	......	......	......
Independence	1175	1133	42	1174	1
New Hudson	1142	1083	59	1141	1
ALLEGANY—Con.					
Rushford	1636	1528	108	1622	14
Rushford	543	......	......	......	......
Scio	1652	1551	101	1576	76
Ward	745	693	52	745	......
Wellsville	3781	3010	771	3768	13
Wellsville	2034	1625	409	2027	7
West Almond	799	774	25	799	......
Willing	1199	1093	106	1199	......
Wirt	1204	1192	12	1150	54
BROOME.					
Barker	1396	1373	23	1396	......
Binghamton (b)	2066	1860	206	2043	23
Binghamton	12692	10350	2342	12382	310
Chenango	1680	1585	95	1680	......
Colesville	3400	3295	105	3397	3
Centre	146	142	4	146	......
Harpersville	218	214	4	218	......
Nineveh, part of (c)	93	92	1	93	......
Conklin	1440	1300	140	1439	1
Fenton	1499	1475	24	1498	1
Kirkwood	1402	1261	141	1388	14
Lisle	2525	2401	124	2513	12
Maine	2035	1933	102	2035	......
Maine	303	278	25	303	......
Nanticoke	1058	1001	57	1058	......
Sanford	3249	2939	310	3209	40
Deposit, part of (d)	790	656	134	774	16
Triangle	1944	1868	76	1927	17
Triangle	273	263	10	273	......
Upper Lisle	247	231	16	246	1
Whitney's P't	480	462	18	473	7
Union	2538	2430	108	2500	38
Vestal	2221	2094	127	2199	22
Windsor	2958	2893	65	2958	......
Windsor	325	315	10	325	......
CATTARAUGUS.					
Allegany	2485	1878	607	2483	2
Allegany	746	538	208	746	......
Ashford	1801	1594	207	1793	8
Carrollton	1142	892	250	1132	10
Cold Spring	835	773	62	831	4
Conewango	1281	1219	62	1281	......
Dayton	1267	1124	143	1267	......
East Otto	1164	1044	120	1163	1
Ellicottville	1833	1435	398	1820	13
Ellicottville	579	517	62	567	12
Farmersville	1114	1036	78	1113	1
Franklinville	1559	1377	182	1557	2
Freedom	1371	1125	246	1371	......
Great Valley	1641	1388	253	1641	......
Hinsdale	1491	1375	116	1488	3
Hinsdale	321	310	11	321	......
Humphrey	1065	936	129	1065	......
Ischua	872	836	36	872	......
Leon	1204	1143	61	1203	1
Little Valley	1108	979	129	1108	......
Lyndon	894	791	103	894	......

(*) The text gives the city of Albany as it was previous to the recent legislation changing its limits. The population of the city as now bounded is 76,216.

(a) Exclusive of city of Cohoes.

(b) Exclusive of city of Binghamton.

(c) See note (b,) Chenango County. Total, 127; Native, 126; foreign, 1; white, 127.

(d) See note (a,) Delaware County. Total, 1,286; Native, 1,109; foreign, 177; white, 1,248; colored, 38.

TABLE IX.—*Population of Minor Civil Divisions, &c.—NEW YORK*—Continued.

Counties.	Total.	Nativity: Native.	Nativity: Foreign.	Race: White.	Race: Colored.
CATTARAUGUS—Continued.					
Machias	1170	1063	107	1167	3
Mansfield	1135	981	154	1135	......
Napoli	1174	1125	49	1171	......
New Albion	1487	1351	136	1484	3
Olean	2668	2122	546	2610	58
Olean	1327	1113	214	1281	43
Otto	1028	908	120	1024	4
Perrysburgh	1313	1249	64	1312	1
Persia	1220	1051	169	1206	14
Gowanda, part of (a)	581	503	78	573	8
Portville	1814	1583	231	1803	11
Portville	450	......	......	......	......
Randolph	2167	1953	214	2165	2
Red House	407	367	40	407	......
Salamanca	1881	1448	433	1879	2
South Valley	743	656	87	743	......
Yorkshire	1575	1532	43	1554	21
CAYUGA.					
Auburn	17225	12583	4642	16581	b641
Aurelius	1952	1601	351	1950	2
Cayuga	435	333	102	435	......
Brutus	2621	2290	331	2592	29
Weedsport	1348	1183	165	1333	15
Cato	2091	1921	170	2088	3
Meridian	249	243	6	249	......
Conquest	1821	1708	113	1821	......
Fleming	1207	1021	186	1185	22
Genoa	2295	2118	177	2286	9
Ira	2014	1918	96	2011	3
Ledyard	2221	1874	347	2131	90
Aurora	450	......	......	......	......
Locke	1077	1032	45	1074	3
Mentz	2278	2025	253	2250	28
Port Byron	1089	986	103	1067	22
Montezuma	1292	1140	152	1285	7
Montezuma	473	419	54	472	1
Moravia	2169	2024	145	2159	10
Niles	1912	1751	161	1909	3
Owasco	1261	1085	176	1235	26
Scipio	2070	1738	332	2049	21
Sempronius	1165	1087	78	1160	5
Sennett	1748	1405	343	1741	7
Springport	2175	1905	270	2152	23
Union Springs	1150	......	......	......	......
Sterling	2840	2483	357	2840	......
Fairhaven	532	488	44	532	......
Martville	126	121	5	126	......
Sterling	237	224	13	237	......
Sterling Val'y	172	152	20	172	......
Summer Hill	1036	998	38	1036	......
Throop	1302	1090	212	1302	......
Throopsville	126	117	9	126	......
Venice	1880	1707	173	1856	24
Victory	1898	1808	90	1897	1
Victory	170	165	5	170	......
Westbury	152	150	2	152	......
CHAUTAUQUA.					
Arkwright	1030	923	107	1025	5
Busti	1844	1586	258	1824	20
Busti Corners	278	259	19	278	......
Carroll	1548	1417	131	1548	......

Counties.	Total.	Nativity: Native.	Nativity: Foreign.	Race: White.	Race: Colored.
CHAUTAUQUA—Continued.					
Fentonville	82	79	3	82	......
Frewsburgh	379	349	30	379	......
Charlotte	1682	1501	181	1676	6
Chautauqua	3064	2547	517	3058	6
De Wittville	262	208	54	260	2
Hartfield	59	54	5	59	......
Mayville	701	579	122	698	3
Cherry Creek	1359	1316	43	1358	1
Cherry Creek	271	266	5	271	......
Clymer	1486	1187	299	1479	7
Clymer	400	......	......	......	......
Dunkirk	6912	4493	2419	6895	17
Dunkirk	5231	3366	1865	5214	17
Ellery	1616	1581	35	1614	(d)
Ellicott	6679	5177	1502	6627	b49
Jamestown	5336	4028	1308	5289	d45
Ellington	1556	1519	37	1554	2
Ellington	314	307	7	314	......
French Creek	973	815	158	973	......
Gerry	1096	1027	69	1096	......
Hanover	4037	3526	511	4015	22
Forestville	722	663	59	718	4
Irving	355	276	79	354	1
Silver Creek	666	538	128	666	......
Smith's Mills	128	121	7	128	......
Harmony	3416	3213	203	3408	8
Ashville	350	......	......	......	......
Blockville	200	......	......	......	......
Panama	650	......	......	......	......
Kiantone	539	453	86	539	......
Kiantone	62	57	5	62	......
Mina	1092	951	141	1092	......
Poland	1418	1287	131	1415	3
Pomfret	4306	3656	650	4294	12
Fredonia	2546	2212	334	2535	11
Laona	218	186	32	218	......
Portland	1887	1693	194	1885	2
Brocton	329	297	32	329	......
Centreville	141	134	7	141	......
Ripley	1943	1702	241	1941	5
Quincy	350	......	......	......	......
Sheridan	1686	1363	323	1686	......
Sherman	1470	1328	142	1468	2
Sherman	610	545	65	608	2
Stockton	1639	1556	83	1637	2
Cassadaga	225	206	19	225	......
Delanti	245	242	3	245	......
Villenova	1401	1343	58	1396	5
Hamlet	155	147	8	155	......
Westfield	3645	2885	760	3624	21
Westfield	3000	......	......	......	......
CHEMUNG.					
Ashland	1558	1400	158	1550	8
Wellsburgh	542	452	90	537	5
Baldwin	969	950	19	969	......
Big Flats	1902	1755	147	1870	32
Catlin (e)	1342	1316	26	1342	......
Chemung	1907	1824	83	1905	2
Elmira (f)	1190	1089	101	1162	28
Elmira	15863	12472	3391	15267	g595
Erin	1392	1372	20	1382	10
Horseheads	2961	2774	187	2855	b103
Breesport	292	275	17	290	2
Horseheads	1410	1303	107	1321	89•

(a) See note (c.) Erie County. Total, 994; Native, 829; foreign, 165; white, 985; colored, 9.
(b) Also 3 Indians.
(c) Also 4 Indians.
(d) Also 2 Indians.
(e) Of Pine Valley: 171 in Veteran, 89 in Catlin.
(f) Exclusive of city of Elmira.
(g) Also 1 Indian.

TABLE IX.—*Population of Minor Civil Divisions, &c.—NEW YORK*—Continued.

Counties.	Total.	Nativity. Native.	Nativity. Foreign.	Race. White.	Race. Colored.
CHEMUNG—Con'd.					
Southport	2185	1911	274	2182	3
Van Etten	1533	1495	38	1533	.....
Veteran (a)	2479	2370	109	2467	12
Millport	741	696	45	736	5
Pine Valley (a)	260	248	12	260	.....
Sullivanville	157	156	1	157	.....
CHENANGO.					
Afton	1931	1896	35	1922	9
Afton	457	443	14	457	.....
Nineveh, part of (b)	34	34	.....	34	.....
Bainbridge	1793	1732	61	1784	9
Bainbridge	681	659	22	676	5
Columbus	1197	1127	70	1197	.....
Coventry	1490	1464	26	1490	.....
German	712	689	23	711	1
Greene	3537	3417	120	3511	26
Greene	1025	1010	15	1002	23
Guilford	2806	2615	191	2796	c8
Guilford	331	303	28	331	.....
Lincklaen	926	899	27	924	2
McDonough	1280	1225	55	1279	1
McDonough	256	234	22	256	.....
New Berlin	2460	2347	113	2454	6
North Norwich	1075	1034	41	1074	1
Norwich	5601	4847	754	5441	160
Norwich	4279	3637	642	4122	157
Otselic	1733	1522	211	1722	11
Oxford	3278	2899	379	3247	31
Oxford	1278	1167	111	1266	12
Pharsalia	1141	1118	23	1140	1
Pitcher	1124	1106	18	1124	.....
Pitcher	148	147	1	148	.....
Plymouth	1523	1438	85	1521	2
Plymouth	179	170	9	178	1
Preston	957	884	73	951	d5
Preston Corners	102	98	4	100	2
Sherburne	2927	2648	279	2899	28
Earlville, part of (e)	183	170	13	182	1
Smithville	1405	1283	122	1404	1
Smyrna	1668	1595	73	1668	.....
CLINTON.					
Altona	2759	1857	902	2750	9
Ausable	2863	2248	615	2859	4
Beekmantown	2552	2015	537	2527	25
Blackbrook	3561	2533	1028	3558	3
Champlain	5080	3434	1646	5070	10
Champlain	1850	.....	.....	.....	.....
Coopersville	205	.....	.....	.....	.....
Perry's Mills	276	.....	.....	.....	.....
Rouse's Point	1266	.....	.....	.....	.....
Chazy	3206	2605	601	3199	7
Clinton	2206	1300	906	2206	.....
Dannemora	1512	995	517	1480	32
Ellenburgh	3042	2280	762	3028	14
Mooers	4634	3175	1459	4634	.....
Peru	2632	2224	408	2629	3
Plattsburgh	8414	6228	2186	8403	11
Plattsburgh	5139	3524	1615	5129	10
Saranac	3802	2937	865	3792	10
Schuyler's Falls	1684	1439	245	1684	.....

Counties.	Total.	Nativity. Native.	Nativity. Foreign.	Race. White.	Race. Colored.
COLUMBIA.					
Ancram	1793	1687	106	1783	10
Austerlitz	1442	1295	147	1393	49
Canaan	1877	1650	227	1849	28
Chatham (f)	4372	3732	640	4230	142
Chatham (f)	1387	1135	252	1376	11
Claverack	3671	3345	326	3607	64
Philmont	699	612	87	699	.....
Clermont	1021	956	65	1014	7
Copake	1847	1685	162	1837	10
Gallatin	1416	1375	41	1412	4
Germantown	1393	1319	74	1374	19
Ghent (f)	2886	2470	416	2731	155
Greenport (g)	1325	1141	184	1267	58
Hudson	8615	7001	1614	8274	h339
Hillsdale	2083	1949	134	2077	6
Kinderhook	4055	3500	555	3842	213
Livingston	1938	1843	95	1923	15
New Lebanon	2124	1794	330	2111	13
Stockport	1438	1166	272	1383	55
Stuyvesant	2263	1846	417	2143	120
Taghkanic	1485	1431	54	1480	5
CORTLAND.					
Cincinnatus	1155	1130	25	1155	.....
Cincinnatus	350	347	3	350	.....
Cortlandville	6082	5627	455	6065	17
Cortland	3066	2775	291	3050	16
McGrawville	517	506	11	517	.....
South Cortl'nd	54	53	1	54	.....
Cuyler	1357	1265	92	1357	.....
Cuyler	90	90	.....	90	.....
Freetown	906	848	58	905	1
Harford	997	962	35	993	4
Homer	3813	3424	389	3789	24
Homer	2008	1793	215	1985	23
Lapeer	735	722	13	735	.....
Marathon	1611	1509	102	1609	2
Marathon	871	807	64	869	2
Preble	1150	1034	116	1150	.....
Preble	195	187	8	195	.....
Scott	1083	1034	49	1075	8
Solon	872	779	93	872	.....
Taylor	1016	1000	16	1014	2
Truxton	1618	1291	327	1618	.....
Truxton	314	280	34	314	.....
Virgil	1889	1797	92	1889	.....
Willett	889	873	16	889	.....
Willett	120	120	.....	120	.....
DELAWARE.					
Andes	2840	2515	325	2836	4
Bovina	1022	897	125	1019	3
Colchester	2652	2512	140	2646	6
Davenport	2187	2087	100	2186	1
Delhi	2920	2444	476	2845	75
Delhi	1223	1065	158	1202	21
Franklin	3283	3131	152	3280	3
Franklin	681	662	19	680	1
Hamden	1762	1518	244	1743	19
Hamden	133	112	21	133	.....
Lansingville	110	96	14	107	3
Hancock	3069	2899	170	3065	4
Harpersfield	1485	1421	64	1483	2
Kortright	1812	1675	137	1807	5
Masonville	1738	1704	34	1735	3

(a) Of Pine Valley: 171 in Veteran, 89 in Catlin.
(b) See note (c,) Broome County.
(c) Also 2 Indians.
(d) Also 1 Indian.
(e) See note (f,) Madison County.
(f) Of Chatham Village: 818 in Chatham and 569 in Ghent.
(g) Exclusive of city of Hudson.
(h) Also 1 Indian and 1 Chinese.

TABLE IX.—*Population of Minor Civil Divisions, &c.*—*NEW YORK*—Continued.

Counties.	Total.	Nativity. Native.	Nativity. Foreign.	Race. White.	Race. Colored.
DELAWARE—Con.					
Masonville	200	197	3	200	......
Meredith	1462	1348	114	1462	......
Middletown	3035	2894	141	3029	6
Roxbury	2188	2069	119	2174	14
Sidney	2597	2244	353	2589	8
Sidney Plains	405	312	93	405	......
Stamford	1658	1549	109	1645	13
Tompkins	4046	3864	182	4022	24
Cannonsville	319	306	13	319	......
Deposit, part of (*a*)	496	453	43	474	22
Walton	3216	3032	184	3174	42
Walton	866	825	41	862	4
DUTCHESS.					
Amenia	2662	2145	517	2574	88
Beekman	1486	1363	123	1415	71
Clinton	1708	1628	80	1701	7
Dover	2279	2035	244	2246	33
East Fishkill	2306	2145	161	2234	72
Fishkill (*b*)	11752	9279	2473	11329	423
Fishkill	737	701	36	686	51
Fishkill Landing	2992	2186	806	2867	125
Glenham	924	539	385	918	6
Matteawan	2406	2027	379	2393	13
New Carthage	241	218	23	216	25
Wappinger's Falls (*b*)	2263	1626	637	2245	13
Hyde Park	2695	2261	434	2615	80
Hyde Park	600	......	......	......	......
La Grange	1774	1611	163	1721	53
Milan	1474	1413	61	1454	20
Northeast	2179	1757	422	2126	53
Pawling	1760	1616	144	1746	14
Pine Plains	1503	1297	206	1474	29
Pine Plains	401	364	37	397	4
Pleasant Valley	1963	1825	138	1912	51
Poughkeepsie (*b*) (*c*)	4009	3054	955	3941	68
Channingville	1350	......	......	......	......
New Hamburg	400	......	......	......	......
Rockdale	75	......	......	......	......
Poughkeepsie	20080	15655	4425	19388	*d*690
Red Hook	4350	3960	390	4242	108
Annandale	347	......	......	......	......
Barrytown	248	......	......	......	......
Madalin	629	605	24	621	8
Red Hook	861	791	70	843	18
Tivoli	452	367	85	443	9
Upper Red Hook	206	204	2	198	8
Rhinebeck	3719	3221	498	3664	55
Rhinebeck	1322	1195	127	1308	14
Stanford	2116	1955	161	2072	44
Union Vale	1434	1329	105	1411	23
Washington	2792	2389	403	2661	131
ERIE.					
Alden	2547	1897	650	2543	4
Amherst	4555	3289	1266	4544	11
Williamsville	912	702	210	910	2
Aurora	2573	2173	400	2572	1
Boston	1633	1253	380	1633	......
Brandt	1359	1018	341	1357	2
Buffalo	117714	71477	46237	117018	696
Cheektowaga	2465	1578	887	2453	12
ERIE—Continued.					
Clarence	3147	2271	876	3146	1
Colden	1472	1234	238	1472	......
Collins	2100	1883	217	2071	29
Gowanda, part of (*e*)	413	326	87	412	1
Concord	3171	2719	452	3167	4
Springville	1006	......	......	......	......
East Hamburg	2270	1743	527	2262	8
Eden	2270	1717	553	2259	11
Elma	2827	1980	847	2823	4
Blossom's Mills	99	49	50	99	......
East Elma	112	99	13	112	......
Elma	165	136	29	165	......
Evans	2593	2159	434	2588	5
Angola	600	......	......	......	......
East Evans	100	......	......	......	......
Evans Centre	150	......	......	......	......
North Evans	150	......	......	......	......
Pontiac	100	......	......	......	......
Grand Island	1126	747	379	1097	29
Hamburg	2934	2187	747	2933	1
Holland	1451	1309	142	1451	......
Lancaster	4336	2981	1355	4326	10
Lancaster	1697	1161	536	1697	......
Marilla	1804	1468	336	1804	......
Marilla	250	......	......	......	......
Newstead	3380	2672	708	3370	10
Akron	444	398	46	441	3
North Collins	1617	1332	285	1616	1
Sardinia	1704	1595	109	1696	8
Tonawanda	3039	2094	945	3038	1
Tonawanda, part of (*f*)	2125	1458	667	2124	1
Wales	1416	1226	190	1411	5
West Seneca	3196	1790	1406	3191	5
Ebenezer	449	......	......	......	......
ESSEX.					
Chesterfield	2795	2244	551	2786	9
Crown Point	2149	2255	194	2448	1
Elizabethtown	1488	1269	219	1482	6
Essex	1600	1429	171	1595	5
Jay	2496	2162	334	2495	1
Keene	720	650	70	720	......
Lewis	1724	1486	238	1708	16
Minerva	908	713	195	908	......
Moriah	4683	3398	1285	4683	......
Newcomb	178	165	13	178	......
North Elba	349	333	16	334	15
North Hudson	738	608	130	738	......
Schroon	1899	1631	268	1899	......
Schroon	300	......	......	......	......
St. Armand	335	312	23	327	8
Ticonderoga	2590	2241	349	2584	6
Alexandria	680	......	......	......	......
Westport	1577	1441	136	1565	12
Willsborough	1719	1356	363	1718	1
Wilmington	794	716	78	794	......
FRANKLIN.					
Bangor	2431	2000	431	2430	1
Belmont	1619	1188	431	1619	......
Bombay	1488	1084	404	1488	......
Brandon	692	623	69	692	......
Brighton	204	176	28	204	......
Burke	2141	1649	492	2141	......

(*a*) See note (*d*,) Broome County.
(*b*) Of Wappinger's Falls: 1,612 in Fishkill and 651 in Poughkeepsie.
(*c*) Exclusive of city of Poughkeepsie.
(*d*) Also 2 Chinese.
(*e*) See note (*a*,) Cattaraugus County.
(*f*) See note (*g*,) Niagara County. Total, 2,812: Native, 1,888; foreign, 924; white, 2,811; colored, 1.

TABLE IX.—*Population of Minor Civil Divisions, &c.*—*NEW YORK*—Continued.

Counties.	Total.	Nativity: Native.	Nativity: Foreign.	Race: White.	Race: Colored.
[FRANK]LIN—Con'd.					
[Ch]auguay	2971	2199	772	2971	......
[Const]able	1546	1118	428	1546	......
[Dick]ason	1990	1814	176	1990	......
......	234	199	35	234	......
[Ft.] Covington ...	2436	1813	623	2436	.....
[W.] Covington.	953	669	284	953	......
[Frank]lin	1195	974	221	1183	12
[Har]ietstown	416	381	35	416	......
...e	7186	5155	2031	7182	4
......	2064	1682	382	2054	10
...ville	1658	1266	392	1658	......
[F]ULTON.					
...ker	970	659	311	970	....
...albin	2492	2331	161	2471	a16
[F]onda's Bush.	987	......	......	......	....
...a	828	731	97	816	12
...tah	2207	2145	62	2199	8
...town	12273	10866	1407	12107	166
[G]loversville ..	4518	4056	462	4447	71
[Jo]hnstown ...	3282	2719	563	3228	54
...eld	2241	2131	110	2228	13
...ampton	1927	1881	46	1923	4
...heim	1950	1882	68	1913	b1
......	1013	871	142	1012	1
...ord	1163	1052	111	1163	....
[G]ENESEE.					
...ma	1805	1487	318	1763	42
...nder	1605	1388	217	1602	3
...ia (c)	6485	5014	1471	6423	62
...tavia	3890	2975	915	3840	50
...n	1997	1679	318	1986	11
...ardville	788	672	116	778	10
...ny	1652	1459	193	1647	5
......	1734	1376	358	1734	......
......	2054	1774	280	2053	1
......	1905	1577	328	1905	......
...y	4627	3686	941	4605	22
[Le] Roy	2634	2091	543	2613	21
...ld	1471	1166	305	1471	......
...on	1614	1382	232	1612	2
[Pemb]roke (c)	2810	2443	367	2807	3
[E.] Pembr'e (c)	156	140	16	147	9
...rd	1847	1342	505	1845	2
[G]REENE.					
...ud	992	978	14	992	......
...s	2942	2716	226	2862	80
[A]thens	1793	1654	139	1763	30
......	2283	2214	69	2258	25
...ill	7677	6478	1199	7437	240
[C]atskill	3791	3149	642	3615	176
...eds	847	554	293	844	3
...ckie	3829	3480	349	3650	179
...an	2257	2212	45	2236	21
...ville	2084	2007	77	2058	26
...tt	426	418	8	425	1
...r	1524	1353	171	1517	7
...t	1105	1088	17	1105	......
...gton	1371	1341	30	1370	1
[New] Baltimore...	2617	2464	153	2581	36
...sville	1240	1151	89	1229	11
[Pr]attsville....	489	463	26	482	7
[Dur]ham	1485	1446	39	1483	2

Counties.	Total.	Nativity: Native.	Nativity: Foreign.	Race: White.	Race: Colored.
HAMILTON.					
Arietta	136	121	15	136	......
Benson	320	300	20	320	......
Hope	698	643	55	698	......
Indian Lake	202	187	15	202	......
Lake Pleasant....	318	292	26	318	......
Long Lake	280	265	15	279	(d)
Morehouse	186	116	70	186	......
Wells	817	727	90	816	1
HERKIMER.					
Columbia	1637	1545	92	1629	8
Danube (e)	1324	1226	98	1321	3
Newville	112	103	9	112	......
Fairfield (f)	1653	1348	305	1652	1
Fairfield	281	224	57	281	......
Frankfort	3065	2587	478	3061	4
Frankfort	1083	874	209	1080	3
German Flatts ...	5718	4697	1021	5664	54
Ilion	2876	2116	760	2840	36
Mohawk	1404	1199	205	1388	16
Herkimer	2949	2550	399	2929	20
Herkimer	1220	1084	136	1214	6
Litchfield	1384	1176	208	1375	9
Little Falls (e)....	5612	4486	1126	5536	a76
Little Falls (e)	5387	4078	1309	5309	a76
Manheim (e)......	2000	1623	377	1996	4
Newport (f)......	1954	1682	272	1927	27
Middleville (f)	406	342	64	405	1
Newport	651	598	53	632	19
Norway	1117	942	175	1116	1
Ohio	1009	891	118	1009	......
Russia	2220	1989	231	2218	2
Cold Brook ...	170	160	10	170	......
Grant	71	65	6	71	......
Gravesville ...	67	66	1	67	......
Russia Corn'rs.	58	56	2	58	......
Salisbury	1933	1671	262	1932	1
Schuyler	1558	1352	206	1556	2
Stark	1541	1492	49	1540	1
Starkville	174	170	4	174	......
Van Hornesv'e	169	157	12	169	......
Warren	1503	1419	84	1488	g10
Wilmurt	191	152	39	191	......
Winfield	1561	1316	245	1561	......
JEFFERSON.					
Adams	3348	3062	286	3283	65
Adams	1352	1213	139	1296	56
Alexandria	3087	2562	525	3087	......
Antwerp	3310	2785	525	3310	......
Antwerp	773	627	146	773	......
Brownville	3219	2868	351	3211	8
Brownville ...	450	380	70	446	4
Cape Vincent	3342	2488	854	3340	2
Cape Vincent	1269	897	372	1268	1
Champion	2156	1941	215	2153	d2
Clayton	4082	3389	693	4080	2
Clayton	1020	......	......	......	......
Depauville ...	225	......	......	......	......
Gardner's I'd	7	......	......	......	......
Grindstone I'd	330	......	......	......	......
Grinnell's I'd	3	......	......	......	......
Robin's Island	5	......	......	......	......
Washington Island	4	......	......	......	......
Ellisburgh	4822	4484	338	4808	14

[(a)] Also 2 Indians.
[(b)] Also 6 Indians.
[(c)] Of East Pembroke: 38 in Batavia and 118 in Pembroke.
[(d)] Also 1 Indian.
(e) Of Little Falls: 6 in Danube, 4,786 in Little Falls, and 595 in Manheim.
(f) Of Middleville: 152 in Fairfield and 254 in Newport.
(g) Also 5 Indians.

TABLE IX.—*Population of Minor Civil Divisions, &c.*—*NEW YORK*—Continued.

Counties.	Total.	Nativity. Native.	Nativity. Foreign.	Race. White.	Race. Colored.
JEFFERSON—Con.					
Henderson	1926	1721	205	1923	3
Henderson	339	322	17	338	1
Hounsfield	2636	2178	458	2621	15
Sackett's Har'r	713	581	132	706	7
Le Ray	2862	2586	276	2854	8
Evans's Mills	500	459	41	500	......
Lorraine	1377	1296	81	1376	1
Lyme	2465	2151	314	2465	......
Chaumont	370	304	66	370	......
Three-Mile Bay	417	364	53	417	......
Orleans	2445	2107	338	2444	1
Pamelia	1292	1114	178	1289	3
Philadelphia	1679	1504	175	1679	......
Philadelphia	384	343	41	384	......
Rodman	1604	1497	107	1602	2
Rutland	1903	1659	244	1901	2
Black River	181	171	10	181	......
Felt's Mills	235	211	24	235	......
Theresa	2364	2078	286	2362	2
Theresa	798	705	93	796	2
Watertown	1373	1164	209	1373	......
Watertown	9336	6707	2629	9258	78
Wilna	4060	3427	633	4040	20
Worth	727	651	76	719	8
KINGS.					
Brooklyn	396099	251381	144718	391142	a4944
Flatbush	6309	3251	3058	6106	203
Flatlands	2286	1805	481	2152	134
Gravesend	2131	1506	625	1956	175
New Lots	9800	6010	3790	9671	129
New Utrecht	3296	2157	1139	3227	b68
LEWIS.					
Croghan	2433	1638	795	2425	8
Denmark	2109	1898	211	2100	9
Copenhagen	575	518	57	575	......
Diana	1778	1449	329	1778	......
Greig (d)	2638	2149	489	2634	c1
Harrisburgh	1090	920	170	1083	7
High Market	1051	755	296	1051	......
Lewis	1252	884	368	1252	......
Leyden (d)	2048	1675	373	2045	3
P'rt Leyden (d)	977	748	229	974	3
Lowville	2805	2454	351	2793	12
Martinsburgh	2282	1987	295	2268	14
Montague	718	603	115	718	......
New Bremen	1908	1373	535	1908	......
Osceola	688	532	156	688	......
Pinckney	1149	981	168	1149	......
Turin	1493	1365	128	1493	......
Turin	552	504	48	552	......
Watson	1146	1063	83	1146	......
West Turin	2111	1741	370	2111	......
Constableville	712	......	......	......	......
LIVINGSTON.					
Avon	3038	2324	714	3002	36
Avon	900	......	......	......	......
Caledonia	1813	1294	519	1811	2
Caledonia	597	440	157	597	......
Conesus	1362	1262	100	1357	5
LIVINGSTON—Con.					
Conesus C'ntre	231	......	......	......	......
Geneseo	3032	2427	605	2986	46
Groveland	1455	1265	190	1455	......
Leicester	1744	1574	170	1707	37
Moscow	245	241	4	243	2
Lima	2912	2355	557	2896	16
Lima	1257	1069	188	1249	8
Livonia	2705	2402	303	2693	12
Hemlock Lake	257	......	......	......	......
Lakeville	130	......	......	......	......
Livonia Centre	193	......	......	......	......
Livonia Stat'n	399	......	......	......	......
Mount Morris	3877	3318	559	3861	16
Mount Morris	1930	1515	415	1916	14
North Dansville	4015	3258	757	4010	5
Dansville	3387	2707	680	3383	4
Nunda	2686	2445	241	2670	16
Nunda	1189	979	210	1173	16
Ossian	1168	1073	95	1168	......
Portage	1338	1187	151	1334	4
Sparta	1182	1080	102	1182	......
Springwater	2174	2078	96	2172	2
West Sparta	1244	1144	100	1244	......
York	2564	1986	578	2546	18
MADISON.					
Brookfield	3565	3302	263	3565	......
Clarkville	322	315	7	322	......
NorthBrookf'd	226	212	14	226	......
Cazenovia	4265	3802	463	4222	43
Cazenovia	1718	1518	200	1691	27
De Ruyter	2009	1716	293	2004	5
De Ruyter	605	576	29	601	4
Eaton	3690	3165	525	3671	e17
Morrisville	570	547	23	563	7
Fenner	1381	1209	172	1374	7
Georgetown	1423	1359	64	1419	4
Hamilton	3687	3336	351	3669	18
Earlville, part of (f)	216	207	9	216	......
East Hamilton	53	51	2	53	......
Hamilton	1529	1370	159	1512	17
Hubbardsville	117	104	13	117	......
Poolville	163	152	11	163	......
Lebanon	1559	1459	100	1544	15
Lenox	9816	8645	1171	9657	g78
Canastota	1492	1317	175	1472	20
Durhamville, part of (h)	148	115	33	148	......
Oneida	3262	2714	548	3238	24
OneidaValley	273	222	51	273	......
Madison	2402	2090	312	2394	8
Nelson	1730	1489	241	1730	......
Smithfield	1227	1171	56	1147	80
Peterboro	368	357	11	326	42
Stockbridge	1847	1666	181	1784	63
Knoxville	241	214	27	241	......
Munnsville	313	279	34	311	2
Sullivan	4921	4297	624	4855	66
Bridgeport	217	207	10	217	......
Chittenango	968	812	156	952	16
Chittenango Station	92	62	30	92	......
Lakeport	134	130	4	134	......

(a) Also 6 Indians and 7 Chinese.
(b) Also 1 Indian.
(c) Also 3 Indians.
(d) Of Port Leyden: 254 in Greig and 723 in Leyden.
(e) Also 2 Indians.
(f) See note (c) Chenango County. Total, 399: Native, 377; foreign, 22; white, 398; colored, 1.
(g) Also 81 Indians.
(h) See note (g,) Oneida County.

: IX.—*Population of Minor Civil Divisions, &c.*—*NEW YORK*—Continued.

s.	Total.	Nativity. Native.	Nativity. Foreign.	Race. White.	Race. Colored.
s.					
......	4304	2767	1537	4282	22
......	2367	1757	610	2356	11
hill...	104	75	29	104	......
......	1884	1627	257	1880	4
......	3541	2451	1090	3537	4
......	4314	3073	1241	4309	5
......	737	411	326	737	......
......	2304	1921	383	2297	7
......	2280	1734	546	2277	3
......	3990	2936	1054	3973	17
......	2900	2372	528	2891	9
e Falls	921	776	145	921	......
......	2874	2409	465	2870	4
port..	591	501	90	591	......
......	2864	2450	414	2860	4
......	2928	2345	583	2921	7
......	3261	2678	583	3240	21
......	1974	1512	462	1973	1
d.....	505	404	101	505	......
......	2171	1652	519	2171	......
......	62386	41202	21184	61959	427
......	1654	1263	391	1651	3
......	4558	3694	864	4531	27
rt....	2817	2238	579	2791	26
......	2749	2316	433	2730	19
r......	291	259	32	287	4
......	2565	1945	620	2555	10
lle....	119	90	29	118	1
ERY.					
(a)...	7706	6172	1534	7618	b87
dam..	5426	4264	1162	5375	b50
nan's					
......	250	......	......	......	......
......	4256	3714	542	4210	46
......	150	......	......	......	......
arie..	1822	1543	279	1790	32
......	1601	1562	39	1601	......
ille...	160	145	15	160	......
......	3002	2595	407	2975	27
unter..	200	140	60	200	......
le....	130	105	25	130	......
ckson	446	300	146	446	......
Bush..	120	100	20	120	......
......	2782	2543	239	2749	33
ille...	96	96	......	96	......
ille...	1117	1016	101	1100	17
......	145	140	5	145	......
......	4600	4109	491	4549	51
ain....	1797	1602	195	1765	32
......	3015	2686	329	2955	c57
......	1092	942	150	1073	19
Hill (a)	365	......	......	......	......
......	2814	2476	338	2800	14
ine					
e.....	493	......	......	......	......
......	2492	2360	132	2474	18
le....	2189	1960	229	2171	18
sville	1376	......	......	......	......
RK.					
......	942292	523198	419094	929199	d13073

Counties.	Total.	Nativity. Native.	Nativity. Foreign.	Race. White.	Race. Colored.
NIAGARA.					
Cambria..........	2145	1764	381	2141	4
Hartland (e)......	3226	2687	539	3222	4
Lewiston.........	2959	2169	790	2944	15
Lewiston......	770	531	239	758	12
Lockport (f)......	3032	2289	743	3017	15
Lockport.......	12426	8937	3489	12205	221
Newfane..........	3097	2620	477	3095	2
Niagara..........	6832	4258	2574	6666	166
Niagara City	2276	1458	818	2267	9
Niagara Falls	3006	1853	1153	2866	140
Pendleton........	1772	1298	474	1771	1
Pendleton.....	214	177	37	214	......
Porter...........	2042	1607	435	2041	1
Youngstown	476	334	142	476	......
Royalton (e)......	4726	3597	1129	4720	6
Middleport (e)	731	596	135	730	1
Wolcottsville	756	353	403	756	......
Somerset.........	1862	1546	316	1857	5
Wheatfield.......	3406	2000	1406	3406	......
Tonawanda, part of (g)..	687	430	257	687	......
Wilson...........	2912	2438	474	2904	8
Wilson.......	661	584	77	655	6
ONEIDA.					
Annsville........	2716	2288	428	2716	......
Taberg.......	400	300	100	400	......
Augusta (h)......	2067	1754	313	2063	4
Augusta Centre.......	147	131	16	147	......
Knox Corners.	208	182	26	208	......
Oriskany Falls (h)....	628	515	113	626	2
Ava..............	1160	971	189	1159	1
Boonville........	4106	3418	688	4105	1
Boonville.....	1418	1168	250	1418	......
Hawkinsville.	150	......	......	......	......
Bridgewater......	1258	991	267	1258	......
Bridgewater..	230	202	28	230	......
Camden..........	3687	3234	453	3674	13
Camden.......	1703	1465	238	1699	4
Deerfield.........	2045	1440	605	2041	4
Florence.........	2299	1714	585	2288	11
Floyd............	1209	960	249	1209	......
Floyd Corners	95	79	16	95	......
Forestport.......	1276	1011	265	1272	4
Kirkland (i)......	4912	3944	968	4846	66
Clark's Mill (i)...	420	318	102	413	7
Clinton.......	1640	1375	265	1603	37
Franklin.....	379	261	118	379	......
Manchester...	158	131	27	158	......
Lee (j)...........	2636	2392	244	2615	21
Delta (j).....	270	262	8	270	......
Lee Center...	355	333	22	355	......
West Branch	97	82	15	97	......
Marcy (k)........	1451	1067	384	1451	......
Marshall (h) (l)...	2145	1699	446	2133	m10
Deansville....	195	181	14	194	1
New Hartford....	4037	2984	1053	4031	6
New Hartford	743	574	169	737	6
Paris............	3575	2835	740	3571	4
Cassville.....	152	140	12	152	......

ibe's Hill: 150 in Amsterdam and 215 in awk.
Indian.
Indians.
Indians and 12 Chinese.
iddleport: 109 in Hartland and 622 in alton.
sive of city of Lockport.
ite (f,) Erie County.

(h) Of Oriskany Falls: 599 in Augusta and 29 in Marshall.
(i) Of Clark's Mills: 395 in Kirkland and 25 in Whitestown.
(j) Of Delta: 220 in Lee and 50 in Western.
(k) Of Stittville: 28 in Marcy and 215 in Trenton.
(l) Of Waterville: 152 in Marshall and 1,030 in Saugerfield.
(m) Also 2 Indians.

TABLE IX.—*Population of Minor Civil Divisions, &c.*—*NEW YORK*—Continued.

Counties.	Total.	Nativity. Native.	Nativity. Foreign.	Race. White.	Race. Colored.
ONEIDA—Cont'd.					
Clayville	944	667	277	944	......
Holman City	75	75	......	73	2
Sauquoit	459	397	62	459	......
Remsen	1184	906	278	1183	1
Remsen	289	208	81	288	1
Rome (a)	11000	8239	2761	10918	b71
Sangerfield (c)	2513	2061	452	2473	40
Waterville (c)	1182	956	226	1177	5
Steuben	1261	1023	238	1261	......
Trenton (d)	3156	2542	614	3151	5
Gang Mills	104	84	20	104	......
Holland Patent	320	277	43	320	......
Prospect	312	253	59	312	......
South Trenton	206	155	51	206	......
Stittville (d)	243	203	40	243	......
Trenton	294	241	53	293	1
Trenton Falls	128	107	21	125	3
Utica	28804	18955	9849	28583	e219
Vernon	2840	2379	461	2760	f35
Oneida Castle	262	241	21	262	......
Vernon	391	332	59	382	9
Verona	5757	4720	1037	5750	7
Durhamville, part of (g)	711	594	117	711	......
Higginsville	219	189	30	219	......
New London	453	416	37	453	......
Verona	229	205	24	229	......
Vienna	3180	2896	284	3176	4
McConnellsville	118	111	7	118	......
North Bay	348	312	36	345	3
Vienna	156	140	16	155	1
West Vienna	113	110	3	113	......
Western (h)	2423	2130	293	2387	36
Westernville	235	......	......	......	......
Westmoreland	2952	2426	526	2940	12
Hampton	444	363	81	442	2
Hecla	125	93	32	125	......
Lowell	171	151	20	164	7
Whitestown (i)	4339	3322	1017	4324	15
New York Mills	1264	859	405	1264	......
Oriskany	584	462	122	583	1
Pleasa't Valley	87	55	32	87	......
Walesville	115	103	12	113	2
Whitesboro	964	798	166	962	2
Yorkville	213	181	32	212	1
ONONDAGA.					
Camillus	2423	2075	348	2416	7
Amboy	128	121	7	128	......
Belle Isle	68	57	11	68	......
Camillus	598	507	91	598	......
Cicero (j)	2902	2673	229	2884	k17
Brewerton, part of (l)	322	303	19	315	7
Cicero Corners	212	184	28	212	......
Clay (j)	3156	2830	326	3143	13
Belgium	166	151	15	165	1
Centerville (j)	289	273	16	287	2
Euclid	138	126	12	138	......
Three River Point	43	39	4	43	......
De Witt	3105	2487	618	3103	2
ONONDAGA—Cont'd.					
Jamesville	402	345	57	402	......
Orville	157	146	11	157	......
Elbridge	3796	3196	600	3770	26
Elbridge	463	423	40	462	1
Jordan	1263	1104	159	1246	17
Fabius	2047	1872	175	2046	1
Apulia	181	167	14	181	......
Fabius	378	356	22	378	......
Geddes	4505	3075	1430	4496	9
Geddes	3629	2443	1186	3620	9
La Fayette	2233	2001	232	2226	7
Cardiff	147	145	2	147	......
La Fayette	135	128	7	135	......
Lysander (m)	4944	4369	575	4889	55
Baldwinsville (m)	2130	1831	299	2107	23
Lysander	268	250	18	268	......
Plainville	161	143	18	161	......
Manlius	5833	5019	814	5814	19
Fayetteville	1402	1195	207	1393	9
Kirkville	150	144	6	150	......
Manlius	879	772	107	879	......
Manlius Cent'r	100	90	10	100	......
Manlius Stat'n	200	175	25	200	......
Marcellus	2337	1850	487	2333	4
Marcellus	428	362	66	427	1
Marcellus Falls	140	109	31	140	......
Onondaga	5530	4453	1077	5455	75
Navarino	83	80	3	83	......
Onondaga	176	147	29	176	......
Onondaga Valley	571	479	92	562	9
South Onondaga	242	231	11	231	11
Otisco	1602	1353	249	1596	6
Pompey	3314	2894	420	3313	1
Salina	2688	1992	696	2681	7
Liverpool	1555	1248	307	1555	......
Skaneateles	4524	3304	1220	4499	25
Mottville	276	198	78	276	......
Skaneateles	1409	1081	328	1391	18
Spafford	1595	1441	154	1595	......
Syracuse	43051	29061	13990	42616	435
Tully	1560	1441	119	1558	2
Van Buren (m)	3038	2724	314	3036	2
Canton	223	197	26	223	......
ONTARIO.					
Bristol	1551	1428	123	1551	......
Canadice	905	859	46	900	5
Canandaigua	7274	5804	1470	7160	114
Canandaigua	4862	3714	1148	4754	108
East Bloomfield	2250	1812	438	2195	55
East Bl'mfield	320	262	58	320	......
Farmington	1896	1588	308	1891	5
Gorham	2489	2196	293	2488	1
Hopewell	1863	1588	275	1844	19
Manchester (n)	3546	3021	525	3497	49
Clifton Springs (n)	746	624	122	722	24
Naples	2188	2093	95	2179	9
Naples	902	836	66	896	6
Phelps (n)	5130	4504	626	5106	24
Phelps	1355	1195	160	1345	10

(a) Includes the whole town.
(b) Also 11 Indians.
(c) Of Waterville: 152 in Marshall and 1,030 in Sangerfield.
(d) Of Stittville: 28 in Marcy and 215 in Trenton.
(e) Also 2 Indians.
(f) Also 45 Indians.
(g) See note (h,) Madison County. Total 859: Native, 709; foreign, 150; white, 859.
(h) Of Delta: 220 in Lee and 50 in Western.
(i) Of Clark's Mills: 305 in Kirkland and 25 in Whitestown.
(j) Of Centerville: 46 in Cicero and 242 in Clay.
(k) Also 1 Indian.
(l) See note (f,) Oswego County. Total, 518: Native, 484; foreign, 34; white, 511; colored, 7.
(m) Of Baldwinsville: 1,401 in Lysander and 729 in Van Buren.
(n) Of Clifton Springs: 641 in Manchester and 105 in Phelps.

LE IX.—*Population of Minor Civil Divisions, &c.*—NEW YORK—Continued.

ties.	Total.	Nativity: Native.	Nativity: Foreign.	Race: White.	Race: Colored.
—Cont'd.					
l	1622	1389	233	1617	5
	9188	7048	2140	8976	212
ra	5521	4176	1345	5325	196
stol	1218	1147	71	1218	......
	2437	2003	434	2419	18
r	506	444	62	502	4
omfield	1651	1378	273	1637	14
GE.					
Grove	2502	2164	338	2349	a145
	2113	1825	288	1939	174
er	666	587	79	656	10
	5989	4570	1419	5861	128
n wall ding	200	......	......	......	......
Point	942	527	415	937	5
	2024	1782	242	2009	15
	9387	7701	1686	9250	137
Jervis	6377	5226	1151	6343	34
	3903	3295	608	3596	307
n	2205	1833	372	2013	192
e	1123	1080	43	1123	......
burgh	1224	1039	185	1111	113
	1443	1353	90	1429	14
	4666	3993	673	4619	47
ery	4536	3777	759	4367	169
gomery	960	862	98	898	62
on	1254	961	293	1252	2
pe	1842	1622	220	1825	17
h (b)	3541	2920	621	3405	136
gh	17014	12668	4346	16457	557
dsor	2482	1952	530	2432	50
	9477	7846	1631	9228	249
etown	6049	4878	1171	5892	157
	5736	5284	452	5551	185
a	459	430	29	422	37
ick	938	852	86	920	18
da	1900	1772	128	1828	72
ANS.					
	6756	5732	1024	6691	65
	3322	2736	586	3266	56
	2327	2044	283	2319	8
	1668	1467	201	1660	8
	2196	1907	289	2190	6
Har- (c)	315	......	......	......	......
s	250	......	......	......	......
	1744	1547	197	1744	......
	2522	2179	343	2519	3
(d)	5096	4067	1029	5047	49
	124	97	27	124	......
na (d)	2821	2152	669	2776	45
way	118	106	12	118	......
	3366	2801	565	3341	25
	2014	1702	312	2006	8
onville	100	......	......	......	......
GO.					
	2359	2187	172	2356	3
	1431	1272	159	1431	......
	1053	983	70	1053	......
a	3437	2970	467	3406	31
land	895	711	184	886	9
antia	587	500	87	587	......

Counties.	Total.	Nativity: Native.	Nativity: Foreign.	Race: White.	Race: Colored.
OSWEGO—Cont'd.					
Granby	3972	3308	664	3964	e7
Oswego Falls	1119	751	368	1119	......
Hannibal	3234	3002	232	3221	13
Hannibal	454	416	38	451	3
Hastings	3058	2724	334	3058	......
Brewerton, part of (f)	196	181	15	196	......
Caughdenoy	220	204	16	220	......
Central Sq're	359	323	36	359	......
Mexico	3802	3488	314	3773	29
Mexico	1204	1120	84	1183	21
Texas	150	......	......	......	......
New Haven	1764	1617	147	1761	3
Orwell	1215	1161	54	1215	......
Oswego	3043	2447	596	3039	4
Oswego	20910	13989	6921	20777	e132
Palermo	2052	1925	127	2050	2
Parish	1929	1860	69	1929	......
Redfield	1324	962	362	1322	2
Richland	3975	3627	348	3972	3
Sandy Creek	2629	2486	143	2627	2
Sandy Creek	986	937	49	985	1
Schroeppel	3987	3644	343	3972	15
Hinmansville	154	145	9	154	......
Phoenix	1418	1314	104	1418	......
Scriba	3065	2698	367	3058	7
Volney	6565	5716	849	6512	53
Fulton	3507	2984	523	3484	23
West Monroe	1304	1183	121	1304	......
Williamstown	1833	1434	399	1833	......
OTSEGO.					
Burlington	1476	1417	59	1476	......
Butternuts	2174	2045	129	2165	9
Butternuts	675	654	21	671	4
Cherry Valley	2337	2101	236	2336	1
Cherry Valley	930	787	143	930	......
Decatur	802	797	5	801	1
Edmeston	1744	1692	52	1744	......
Exeter	1256	1167	89	1255	1
Hartwick	2339	2264	75	2338	1
Laurens	1919	1888	31	1917	2
Maryland	2402	2305	97	2388	14
Schenevus	549	518	31	548	1
Middlefield	2868	2599	269	2843	25
Milford	2301	2214	87	2297	4
Morris	2253	2155	98	2240	13
New Lisbon	1545	1467	78	1544	1
Oneonta	2568	2497	71	2568	......
Oneonta	1061	1000	61	1061	......
Otego	2052	2007	45	2047	5
Otsego	4590	4132	458	4526	64
Pittsfield	1469	1391	78	1422	47
Plainfield	1248	1066	182	1242	(g)
Richfield	1831	1676	155	1811	20
Richfield Sp'gs	696	644	52	679	17
Roseboom	1589	1522	67	1589	......
Springfield	2022	1842	180	2022	......
Unadilla	2555	2483	72	2542	13
Unadilla	875	847	28	864	11
Westford	1300	1276	24	1300	......
Worcester	2327	2231	96	2319	8
PUTNAM.					
Carmel	2797	2342	455	2785	12
Carmel	590	505	85	590	......

8 Indians.
nsive of city of Newburgh.
Eagle Harbor: 50 in Barre and 265 in
aines.

(d) Of Medina: 1,968 in Ridgeway and 853 in Shelby.
(e) Also 1 Indian.
(f) See note (l.) Onondaga County.
(g) Also 6 Indians.

TABLE IX.—*Population of Minor Civil Divisions, &c.—NEW YORK*—Continued.

Counties.	Total.	Nativity. Native.	Nativity. Foreign.	Race. White.	Race. Colored.
PUTNAM—Cont'd.					
Kent	1547	1411	136	1536	11
Patterson	1418	1257	161	1400	18
Phillipstown	5117	4094	1023	5110	7
Cold Spring	3086	2317	769	3084	2
Putnam Valley	1566	1503	63	1566	......
Southeast	2975	2362	613	2933	42
QUEENS.					
Flushing	14650	9984	4666	13834	816
College Point	3652	1980	1672	3626	26
Flushing	6223	4625	1598	5703	520
White Stone	1907	1322	585	1892	15
Hempstead	13999	12619	1380	13588	a409
Hempstead	2316	2063	253	2185	a129
Jamaica	7745	5884	1861	7334	b410
Jamaica	3791	2917	874	3504	287
Newtown	20274	12539	7735	19845	b428
Astoria	5204	3213	1991	5122	82
Columbusville	1251	813	438	1150	101
Hunter's Poi't	1596	935	661	1566	30
Long Isl'd City	3867	2300	1567	3865	2
Newtownville	2108	1485	623	2031	77
Ravenswood	1536	958	578	1503	33
North Hempstead	6540	5301	1239	5046	c893
Port Wash'ton	804	741	63	746	58
Roslyn	655	558	97	580	75
Oyster Bay	10595	8401	2194	9760	835
Oyster Bay	889	810	79	851	35
RENSSELAER.					
Berlin	2088	1791	297	2088	......
Brunswick	3128	2709	419	3121	7
East Greenbush	1845	1449	396	1832	13
Grafton	1599	1485	114	1597	2
Greenbush	6202	4655	1547	6161	41
Hoosick	5728	4417	1311	5694	34
Lansingburgh	6804	5153	1651	6688	116
Lansingburgh	6372	4796	1576	6256	116
Nassau	2705	2525	180	2698	7
Brainard	168	160	8	167	1
East Nassau	192	190	2	192	......
Nassau	348	312	36	347	1
North Greenbush	3058	2562	496	3025	b32
Bath	1465	1269	196	1439	b25
Winant's Kill	140	127	13	140	......
Petersburgh	1732	1612	90	1732	......
Pittstown (d)	4033	3136	657	[illegible]	34
Johnsonville	500	20.	300	499	1
Valley Falls (d)	600	......	......	......	......
Poestenkill	1769	1547	222	1769	......
Sand Lake	2633	2209	424	2632	1
Sand Lake	503	440	63	503	......
West S'd Lake	315	273	42	315	......
Schaghticoke (d)	3125	[illegible]	636	3102	23
Hart's Falls	1111	806	305	[illegible]	8
Schodack	4442	3635	807	4403	39
Castleton	580	300	280	578	2
Stephentown	2133	1978	155	2117	16
Troy	46465	30246	16219	46047	418
RICHMOND.					
Castleton	9504	5922	3582	9427	77
RICHMOND—Cont'd.					
New Brighton	7495	4591	2904	7467	[illegible]
Middletown	7589	4743	2846	7389	[illegible]
Northfield	5949	4895	1054	5830	119
Port Richm'nd	3028	2393	635	2955	73
Southfield	5082	3284	1798	5014	[illegible]
Westfield	4905	4072	833	4582	[illegible]
Tottenville	1571	1422	149	1508	[illegible]
ROCKLAND.					
Clarkstown (e)	4137	3403	734	4014	123
Rockland Lake	510	386	124	495	15
Haverstraw	6412	4188	2224	6297	115
Warren	3469	2314	1155	[illegible]	[illegible]
Orangetown (e)	6810	5687	1123	6384	[illegible]
Nyack (e)	3438	2944	494	3237	[illegible]
Piermont	1703	1296	407	1602	[illegible]
Ramapo	4649	4155	494	[illegible]	[illegible]
Stony Point	3205	2430	775	3200	5
SARATOGA.					
Ballston (f)	2180	1859	321	2168	12
Charlton	1607	1400	207	1587	[illegible]
Clifton Park	2657	2336	321	2615	[illegible]
Corinth	1500	1399	101	1499	1
Day	1127	1066	61	1127	......
Edinburgh	1405	1380	25	1405	......
Bachellorsv'le	216	215	1	216	......
Galway	2174	1867	307	2172	2
Greenfield	2698	2440	258	2672	26
Hadley	1039	892	147	1037	2
Halfmoon (g)	3093	2683	410	3088	5
Mechanicsville (g)	1075	830	245	1065	10
Malta	1212	1071	141	1196	16
Milton (f)	4946	4094	852	4884	62
Ballst'n Spa (f)	2970	2480	490	2931	39
Moreau	2256	1904	352	2241	[illegible]
So. Glens Falls	1047	787	260	1047	......
Northumberland	1655	1490	165	1630	25
Providence	1155	1084	71	1150	5
Saratoga	4052	3222	830	4031	21
Schuylerville	1367	1172	195	1361	6
Victory Mills	870	504	366	870	......
Saratoga Springs	8537	6892	1645	[illegible]	[illegible]
Saratoga Spr	7516	5989	1527	[illegible]	[illegible]
Stillwater (g)	3401	2833	568	3345	[illegible]
Stillwater	737	654	83	716	21
Waterford	3631	2757	874	3572	59
Waterford	3071	2334	737	3017	54
Wilton	1204	1151	53	1197	7
SCHENECTADY.					
Duanesburgh	3042	2922	120	3040	2
Glenville	2973	2572	401	2956	17
Niskayuna (i)	1105	891	214	1103	2
Princetown	846	804	42	846	......
Rotterdam	2355	2060	295	2344	11
Schenectady	11026	8412	2614	10890	136
SCHOHARIE.					
Blenheim	1437	1410	27	1434	3

(a) Also 2 Indians.
(b) Also 1 Indian.
(c) Also 1 Chinese.
(d) Of Valley Falls: 400 in Pittstown and 200 in Schaghticoke.
(e) Of Nyack: 432 in Clarkstown and 3,006 in Orangetown.
(f) Of Ballston Spa: 344 in Ballston and 2,626 in Milton.
(g) Of Mechanicsville: 581 in Halfmoon and 494 in Stillwater.
(h) Also 5 Indians.
(i) Exclusive of city of Schenectady.

TABLE IX.—*Population of Minor Civil Divisions, &c.—NEW YORK*—Continued.

Counties.	Total.	Nativity. Native.	Nativity. Foreign.	Race. White.	Race. Colored.
SCHOHARIE—Con.					
Broome	1834	1821	13	1834	......
Carlisle	1730	1707	23	1727	3
Cobleskill	2847	2708	139	2798	49
Cobleskill	1030	951	79	990	40
Conesville	1314	1291	23	1313	1
Esperance	1276	1236	40	1261	15
Fulton	2700	2675	25	2696	4
Gilboa	2227	2156	71	2226	1
Jefferson	1712	1680	32	1711	1
Middleburgh	3180	3085	95	3124	56
Middleburgh	863	834	29	822	41
Richmondville	2307	2256	51	2297	10
Richmondville	630	621	9	630	......
Schoharie	3207	3055	152	2963	244
Schoharie	1200	......	......	......	......
Seward	1765	1733	32	1761	4
Sharon	2648	2540	108	2626	22
Shar'n Springs	520	......	......	......	......
Summit	1631	1599	32	1631	......
Wright	1525	1487	38	1512	13
SCHUYLER.					
Catharine	1629	1612	17	1602	27
Cayuta	641	635	6	634	7
Dix (a)	4282	3910	372	4237	45
Watkins	2639	2325	314	2595	44
Hector	4905	4745	160	4874	31
Montour (a)	1828	1725	103	1789	39
Havana (a)	1273	1174	99	1235	38
Orange	1960	1843	117	1952	8
Reading	1751	1543	208	1728	23
Tyrone	1993	1928	65	1987	6
SENECA.					
Covert	2238	1933	305	2230	8
Fayette (b)	3364	3114	250	3351	13
Junius	1420	1294	126	1403	17
Lodi	1825	1725	100	1812	13
Ovid	2403	2122	281	2354	49
Ovid	724	646	78	698	26
Romulus	2223	1892	331	2221	2
Seneca Falls	6860	5507	1353	6814	46
Seneca Falls	5890	4999	891	5854	36
Tyre	1280	1166	114	1277	3
Varick	1741	1631	110	1715	26
Waterloo (b)	4469	3594	875	4407	62
Waterloo (b)	4086	3286	800	4042	44
STEUBEN.					
Addison	2218	2017	201	2186	32
Avoca	1740	1675	65	1735	5
Avoca	492	475	17	489	3
Bath	6236	5669	567	6112	124
Kanona	190	......	......	......	......
Bradford	1080	1077	3	1069	11
Cameron	1334	1283	51	1331	......
Cameron	161	150	11	161	......
Campbell	1989	1828	161	1986	3
Canisteo	2435	2318	117	2434	1
Caton	1544	1460	84	1541	3
Cohocton	2710	2413	297	2699	11
Corning	6502	5397	1105	6419	83
Corning	4018	3084	934	3974	44
Gibson	372	360	12	360	12
Knoxville	785	735	50	766	19
Dansville	1981	1791	190	1981	......
Erwin	1977	1771	206	1969	8
Fremont	1119	1091	28	1114	5
STEUBEN—Cont'd.					
Greenwood	1394	1275	119	1393	1
Gr'nw'dC'ntre	100	......	......	......	......
Hartsville	993	948	45	993	......
Hornby	1202	1156	46	1202	......
Hornellsville	5837	4949	888	5821	16
Hornellsville	4552	3770	782	4542	10
Howard	2122	1976	146	2122	......
Howard	167	......	......	......	......
Jasper	1683	1655	28	1682	1
Jasper Four Corners	200	......	......	......	......
Lindley	1251	1189	62	1246	5
Prattsburgh	2479	2367	112	2440	39
Prattsburgh	639	605	34	633	6
Pulteney	1393	1355	38	1391	2
Rathbone	1357	1237	120	1353	(c)
Thurston	1215	1173	42	1214	1
Troupsburgh	2281	2213	68	2281	......
Troupsburgh Centre	100	......	......	......	......
Tuscarora	1528	1457	71	1528	......
Urbana	2082	1917	165	2072	10
Hammondsp't	602	529	73	593	9
Wayland	2553	2017	536	2553	......
Wayne	891	868	23	889	2
West Union	1264	1017	247	1264	......
Wheeler	1330	1314	16	1311	19
Woodhull	1997	1960	37	1996	1
Woodhull	392	381	11	392	......
ST. LAWRENCE.					
Brasher	3342	2511	831	3342	......
Brasher Falls	450	......	......	......	......
Brasher Iron Works	250	......	......	......	......
Helena	150	......	......	......	......
Canton	6014	4871	1143	6011	3
Canton	1681	1401	280	1680	1
RensselaerF'ls	395	308	87	395	......
Clifton	221	142	79	220	1
Colton	1719	1403	316	1719	......
Colton	633	518	115	633	......
De Kalb	3116	2585	531	3111	5
De Peyster	1138	889	249	1138	......
Edwards	1076	961	115	1076	......
Fine	603	511	92	603	......
Fowler	1785	1609	176	1784	1
Fullersville	149	137	12	148	1
Hailesboro	177	164	13	177	......
Little York	117	112	5	117	......
Gouverneur	3539	2834	705	3536	3
Gouverneur	1627	1252	375	1626	1
Hammond	1757	1345	412	1756	1
Hermon*	1792	1610	182	1792	......
Hermon	573	521	52	573	......
Hopkinton	1907	1674	233	1902	5
Hopkinton	200	185	15	200	......
Lawrence	2577	2142	435	2577	......
Lawrenceville	350	315	35	350	......
Nicholville	300	275	25	300	......
N'rthL'wr'nce	550	440	110	550	......
Lisbon	4475	3335	1140	4475	......
Louisville	2132	1556	576	2131	1
Macomb	1673	1391	282	1673	......
Pope's Mills	76	56	20	76	......
Madrid	2071	1648	423	2063	8
Madrid	670	540	130	670	......
Massena	2560	2047	513	2547	13
Massena	483	364	119	478	5
Morristown	1954	1624	330	1953	1

(a) Of Havana: 100 in Dix and 1,173 in Montour.
(b) Of Waterloo: 646 in Fayette and 3,440 in Waterloo.
(c) Also 4 Indians.

TABLE IX.—*Population of Minor Civil Divisions, &c.*—*NEW YORK*—**Continued.**

Counties.	Total.	Nativity. Native.	Nativity. Foreign.	Race. White.	Race. Colored.
ST. LAWRENCE—C'd					
Norfolk	2441	1918	523	2436	5
Norfolk	540	413	127	540	......
Ogdensburg	10076	6004	4072	10058	18
Oswegatchie (a)	3018	2135	883	3016	2
Parishville	2241	1976	265	2240	1
Parishville	312	289	23	311	1
Pierrepont	2391	2127	264	2391	......
Ellsworth	179	166	13	179	......
Pitcairn	667	635	32	666	1
Potsdam	7774	6188	1586	7763	b3
Potsdam	2891	2294	597	2881	b2
Potsdam Junc	966	701	265	965	1
Rossie	1661	1321	340	1661	......
Rossie	149	127	22	149	......
Somerville	113	109	4	113	......
Wegatchie	201	157	44	201	......
Russell	2688	2395	293	2688	......
Russell	335	308	27	335	......
Stockholm	3819	3312	507	3819	......
Waddington	2599	1908	691	2599	......
Waddington	710	487	223	710	......
SUFFOLK.					
Brookhaven	10159	9619	540	9771	c365
East Hampton	2372	2212	160	2181	d159
Huntington	10704	9225	1479	10230	e473
Amityville	500	......	......	......	......
Babylon	1225	......	......	......	......
Cold Springs	730	......	......	......	......
Huntington	2433	......	......	......	......
Northport	1060	......	......	......	......
Islip	4597	3688	909	4435	162
Bay Shore	1200	......	......	......	......
Sayville	1290	......	......	......	......
Riverhead	3461	3190	271	3403	58
Jamesport	323	312	11	321	2
Riverhead (f)	1296	1189	107	1252	44
Shelter Island	645	571	74	632	13
Smithtown	2136	1890	246	1921	g213
Southampton (f)	6135	5704	431	5847	h188
Atlanticville	179	176	3	179	......
Bridgeh'mpt'n	1334	1237	97	1264	c47
Eastport	135	134	1	135	......
Flanders	160	160	......	160	......
Good Ground	504	500	4	503	1
North Haven	112	104	8	112	......
Quogue	137	130	7	104	33
Red Creek	46	46	......	46	......
Sag Harbor	1723	1464	259	1700	23
Shinnecock	97	97	......	......	(i)
Southampton	943	904	39	922	g19
Speonk	174	173	1	174	......
West Hampt'n	439	431	8	411	28
Southold	6715	5948	767	6536	j175
Greenport	1819	1615	204	1715	e103
SULLIVAN.					
Bethel	2736	2343	393	2735	1
Callicoon	2763	1912	851	2763	......
Cochecton	1190	1064	126	1190	......
SULLIVAN—Cont'd.					
Delaware	1998	1440	558	1993	5
Fallsburgh	3206	2829	377	3189	17
Forrestburgh	915	748	167	915	......
Fremont	2218	1674	544	2218	......
Highland	958	800	158	944	14
Liberty	3389	2994	395	3377	12
Lumberland	1065	911	154	1064	1
Mamakating	4866	4064	802	4827	39
Wurtsboro	797	656	141	790	7
Neversink	2458	2345	113	2456	2
Rockland	1946	1717	229	1944	2
Thompson	3514	3105	409	3508	6
Monticello	912	......	......	......	......
Tusten	1028	782	246	1028	......
TIOGA.					
Barton	5087	4697	390	5030	57
Factoryville	318	289	29	313	5
Waverly	2239	2008	231	2192	47
Berkshire	1240	1194	46	1237	3
Candor	4250	4105	145	4232	18
Newark Valley	2321	2198	123	2320	1
Nichols	1663	1637	26	1645	18
Nichols	281	275	6	280	1
Owego	9442	8622	820	9250	192
Apalachin	300	295	5	299	1
Flemingville	91	91	......	87	4
Owego	4756	4174	582	4594	162
Richford	1434	1403	31	1415	19
Spencer	1863	1819	44	1832	31
Tioga	3272	2995	277	3244	28
Halsey Valley	103	103	......	102	1
Smithborough	304	277	27	304	......
Tioga Centre	304	268	36	300	4
TOMPKINS.					
Caroline	2175	2133	42	2151	24
Speedsville	153	144	9	153	......
Danby	2126	2065	61	2114	12
Dryden (l)	4818	4524	294	4805	13
Dryden	672	......	......	......	......
Etna	230	......	......	......	......
Enfield	1693	1637	56	1692	1
Groton (l)	3512	3323	189	3505	7
Groton	863	818	45	859	4
McLean (l)	405	......	......	......	......
Ithaca	10107	8970	1137	9831	276
Ithaca	8462	7427	1035	8191	271
Lansing	2874	2803	71	2862	12
Lansingville	67	65	2	67	......
Ludlowville	376	369	7	368	8
Newfield	2602	2542	60	2602	......
Ulysses	3271	3054	217	3215	56
Trumansburg	1246	1181	65	1193	53
ULSTER.					
Denning	1044	966	78	1044	......
Esopus	4557	3825	732	4548	9
Sleightsburgh	203	191	12	203	......

(a) Exclusive of city of Ogdensburg.
(b) Also 8 Indians.
(c) Also 23 Indians.
(d) Also 32 Indians.
(e) Also 1 Indian.
(f) Of Riverhead: 1,144 in Riverhead and 152 in Southampton.
(g) Also 2 Indians.
(h) Also 100 Indians.
(i) Also 97 Indians.
(j) Also 4 Indians.
(k) Also 7 Indians.
(l) Of McLean: 105 in Dryden and 300 in Groton.

LE IX.—*Population of Minor Civil Divisions, &c.*—NEW YORK—Continued.

...ties.	Total.	Nativity. Native.	Nativity. Foreign.	Race. White.	Race. Colored.
—Cont'd.					
Esen ...	1251	894	367	1251	......
...Rondout	405	303	102	405	......
....	1991	1770	221	1895	96
...urgh	628	617	11	628	......
....	2987	2496	491	2908	79
....	21943	16058	5885	21497	a442
...ston	6315	5506	809	6056	259
...out	10114	6519	3595	9981	a129
....	2658	2512	146	2643	15
...wn	4223	4065	158	4006	217
...ugh	2975	2611	364	2938	37
...ts	2040	1853	187	1942	98
...Paltz	485	......	......	......	......
....	3083	3020	63	3054	29
...l	2031	1914	117	1980	51
...r	4088	4012	76	4065	23
...e	3625	2725	900	3607	18
...s	10455	8636	1819	10351	104
...erties	3731	2964	767	3731	......
...a	2751	2311	440	2744	7
...unk	2823	2668	155	2779	44
...ng	8151	7320	831	8001	150
...ek	2022	1956	66	2008	14
...REN.					
....	1135	1098	37	1135	......
....	1041	975	66	1028	[illegible]
....	2329	2118	211	2329	......
....	637	615	22	632	5
....	1500	1429	71	1492	8
...g	2599	2290	309	2595	4
....	1174	1075	99	1174	......
...ury	8387	6865	1522	8358	29
...'s Falls ..	4500	......	......	......	......
...eek	1127	1077	50	1127	......
....	1084	1034	50	1084	......
...burgh ...	1579	1438	141	1574	5
...rensb'rgh	715	616	99	713	2
...NGTON.					
....	2850	2442	408	2839	11
...le	351	315	36	350	1
...ge (d) ...	2589	2195	394	2580	9
....	684	625	59	678	e5
....	3072	2583	489	3006	66
....	3329	3062	267	3315	14
...Ann	639	599	40	636	3
...ard	5125	4241	884	5100	25
...Edward	3492	2787	705	3487	5
....	4003	3088	915	3988	15
...ch	4030	3489	541	3978	52
....	955	728	227	953	2
....	1989	1707	282	1984	5
....	2399	2062	337	2398	1
....	1662	1361	301	1637	25
...ry	4277	3514	763	4240	37
...y Hill ...	2347	1811	536	2332	15
....	603	547	56	601	2
....	3556	2906	650	3528	f26
...n	1239	......	......	......	......
...reek (d) ..	2881	2498	383	2852	29
...bridge (d)	1530	1381	149	1511	19
...ll	5564	4256	1308	5509	55
...hall	4322	3136	1186	4273	49

Counties.	Total.	Nativity. Native.	Nativity. Foreign.	Race. White.	Race. Colored.
WAYNE.					
Arcadia	5271	4477	794	5245	26
Fairville	154	128	26	154	......
Newark	2248	1964	284	2235	13
Butler	2023	1919	104	2023	......
Galen	5706	4709	997	5658	b41
Clyde	2735	2193	542	2710	25
Huron	2000	1842	158	1968	32
Lyons	5115	3938	1177	5051	c63
Lyons	3350	2545	805	3298	c51
Macedon	2636	2119	517	2626	10
Macedon	451	390	61	443	8
Marion	1967	1591	376	1966	1
Marion	432	399	33	432	......
Ontario	2295	1896	399	2278	17
Palmyra	4188	3457	731	4140	e45
Palmyra	2152	2033	119	2131	21
Rose	2066	1864	192	2035	31
Savannah	1933	1700	233	1929	4
Sodus	4631	4030	601	4562	69
Sodus	516	468	48	515	1
Joy	122	103	19	122	......
Walworth	2236	1837	399	2231	5
Walworth	362	313	49	362	......
Williamson	2430	1872	558	2430	......
Wolcott	3223	3048	175	3213	10
Red Creek	529	496	33	526	3
Wolcott	658	629	29	652	6
WESTCHESTER.					
Bedford	3697	3291	406	3597	100
Cortlandt	11694	9482	2212	11521	173
Peekskill	6500	......	......	......	......
Verplank	1500	......	......	......	......
East Chester	7491	4845	2646	7410	81
Central Mount Vernon	450	......	......	......	......
E. Mt. Vernon	500	......	......	......	......
Mount Vernon	2700	......	......	......	......
W. Mt. Vernon	1200	......	......	......	......
Greenburgh	10790	7415	3375	10628	g160
Harrison	787	668	119	660	127
Lewisborough	1601	1436	165	1589	12
Mamaroneck	1483	969	514	1433	50
Morrisania	19609	12206	7403	19322	287
Mount Pleasant ..	5210	4010	1200	5058	152
Beekmantown	2206	1587	619	2104	102
New Castle	2152	1903	249	2121	31
New Rochelle	3915	2771	1144	3761	154
New Rochelle	279	213	66	276	3
North Castle	1996	1874	122	1951	45
North Salem	1754	1502	252	1710	44
Ossining	7798	5859	1939	7595	h202
Sing Sing	4696	3504	1192	4552	h143
Pelham	1790	1426	364	1780	10
Poundridge	1194	1167	27	1192	2
Rye	7150	5361	1789	6891	259
Port Chester .	3797	......	......	......	......
Scarsdale	517	365	152	501	16
Somers	1721	1455	266	1673	48
Westchester	6015	4038	1977	5916	99
West Farms	9372	6044	3328	9249	g121
Belmont	171	107	64	171	......
Clairmont	158	101	57	158	......
Fairmount ...	508	370	138	494	14
Fordham	2151	1350	801	2140	11

(a) Also 3 Indians and 1 Chinese.
(b) Also 7 Indians.
(c) Also 3 Indians.
(d) Of Cambridge: 563 in Cambridge and 967 in White Creek.
(e) Also 1 Indian.
(f) Also 2 Indians.
(g) Also 2 Chinese.
(h) Also 1 Chinese.

TABLE IX.—*Population of Minor Civil Divisions, &c.—NEW YORK*—Continued.

Counties.	Total.	NATIVITY.		RACE.		Counties.	Total.	NATIVITY.		RACE.	
		Native.	Foreign.	White.	Colored.			Native.	Foreign.	White.	Colored.
WESTCHESTER—C'd.						WYOMING—Cont'd.					
Monterey	118	63	55	117	1	Java	1956	1631	325	1956	......
Mount Eden	116	70	46	116	......	Middlebury	1620	1493	127	1620	......
Mount Hope	487	315	172	482	5	Wyoming	338	319	19	338	......
Tremont	2025	1407	618	2012	13	Orangeville	1217	1040	177	1208	9
West Farms	1761	1089	672	1758	3	Perry	2342	2108	234	2335	7
Wm.'s Bridge	144	78	66	144	......	Perry Centre	183	175	8	183	......
Woodstock	307	201	106	284	23	Perry	867	771	96	861	6
White Plains	2630	1909	721	2586	44	Pike	1730	1639	91	1727	3
Yonkers	18357	11645	6712	18127	230	Pike	551	528	23	550	1
Yonkers	12733	8080	4653	12575	158	Sheldon	2258	1655	603	2257	1
Yorktown	2625	2363	262	2559	66	Warsaw	3143	2790	353	3104	39
WYOMING.						Warsaw	1631	1496	135	1593	38
						Wethersfield	1219	1141	78	1219	......
						Wethersfield	170	165	5	170	......
Arcade	1742	1488	254	1739	3						
Arcade	573	......	......	......	......	YATES.					
Attica	2546	2048	498	2543	3						
Attica	1333	1054	279	1331	2	Barrington	1506	1447	59	1497	9
Bennington	2385	1837	548	2385	......	Benton (a)	2422	2116	306	2411	11
Castile	2186	1984	202	2179	7	Italy	1341	1260	81	1337	4
Castile	712	669	43	708	4	Jerusalem	2612	2376	236	2599	13
Covington	1189	988	201	1189	......	Middlesex	1314	1256	58	1311	3
Eagle	1040	964	76	1040	......	Milo (a)	4779	4132	647	4715	64
Eagle	110	......	......	......	......	Penn Yan (a)	3488	3002	486	3423	65
Gainesville	1612	1509	103	1602	10	Potter	1970	1827	143	1958	12
Gainesville	114	111	3	114	......	Starkey	2370	2269	101	2343	27
Geneseo Falls	979	798	181	979	......	Dundee	730	......	......	......	......
Portageville	491	383	108	491	......	Torrey	1281	1157	124	1264	17

(a) Of Penn Yan: 485 in Benton and 3,003 in Milo.

TABLE IX.—*Population of Minor Civil Divisions, &c.—NORTH CAROLINA.*

NOTE.—The marginal column marks townships, their names and numbers being official; the first indentation, cities; the second, towns. Names of towns are placed under the names of the townships in which they are respectively situated. The population of each township includes that of all towns situated in it.

Counties.	Total.	NATIVITY.		RACE.		Counties.	Total.	NATIVITY.		RACE.	
		Native.	Foreign.	White.	Colored.			Native.	Foreign.	White.	Colored.
ALAMANCE.						ALEXANDER—Con.					
Albright's, No. 7	625	625	......	440	185	Gaultney's, No. 3	1126	1126	......	904	222
Boon's Stat'n, No. 3	1100	1099	1	894	206	Little River, No. 1	635	635	......	598	37
Coble's, No. 2	875	875	......	718	157	Miller, No. 8	741	741	......	582	159
Faucett's, No. 5	1327	1324	3	894	433	Sharpe, No. 4	825	825	......	734	91
Graham, No. 6	2332	2286	46	1375	957	Sugar Loaf, No. 2	707	707	......	673	34
Graham	502	462	40	311	191	Taylorsville, No. 6	1078	1078	......	892	186
Melville, No. 10	1221	1220	1	690	531	Taylorsville	169	169	......	143	26
Morton's, No. 4	794	794	......	587	207	Wittenb'rg's, No. 7	848	848	......	794	54
Newlin's, No. 8	862	862	......	706	156						
Patterson's, No. 1	717	716	1	645	72	ALLEGHANY.					
Pleasant Grove, No. 11	1246	1246	......	692	554	Cherry Lane, No. 6	309	309	......	289	20
Thompson's, No. 9	775	775	......	593	182	Cranberry, No. 3	458	457	1	445	13
						Gap Civil, No. 4	958	957	1	881	77
ALEXANDER.						Glade Creek, No. 5	640	640	......	587	53
						Piney Creek, No. 1	689	689	......	630	59
Ellendale, No. 5	908	908	......	867	41	Plather's Cr'k, No. 2	637	635	2	569	68

TABLE IX.—*Population of Minor Civil Divisions, &c.—NORTH CAROLINA*—Continued.

Counties.	Total.	Nativity. Native.	Nativity. Foreign.	Race. White.	Race. Colored.
ANSON.					
Ansonville, No. 6	1843	1840	3	797	1046
Burnsville, No. 5	1038	1038	......	744	294
Gulledge's, No. 2	1519	1515	4	853	666
Lanesboro, No. 4	1293	1293	......	772	521
Lilesville, No. 7	1715	1713	2	762	953
Morven, No. 8	1325	1324	1	601	724
Wadesboro, No. 1	2337	2327	10	1174	1163
Wadesboro	480	477	3	334	146
White's Store, No. 3	1358	1356	2	647	711
ASHE.					
Chestnut Hill, No. 3	1412	1412	......	1264	148
Helton, No. 4	1004	1004	......	978	26
Horse Creek, No. 6	813	813	......	792	21
Jefferson, No. 1	1228	1226	2	1079	149
Laurel, No. 8	456	456	......	437	19
North Fork, No. 9	951	951	......	903	48
Old Field, No. 10	595	595	......	532	63
Peak Creek, No. 2	1005	1003	2	949	56
Pine Swamp, No. 11	409	409	......	399	10
Piney, No. 5	839	839	......	810	29
Stagg's Creek, No. 7	861	861	......	848	13
BEAUFORT.					
Bath, No. 3	1969	1967	2	1217	752
Chocowinity, No. 5	1630	1629	1	1168	462
Long Acre, No. 2	1651	1651	......	1368	283
Pamplico, No. 7	568	568	......	521	47
Pantego, No. 4	1792	1788	4	1144	648
Richland, No. 6	2097	2096	1	1159	938
Washington, No. 1	3304	3289	15	1802	1502
Washington	2094	2079	15	987	1107
BERTIE.					
Colerain, No. 4	1968	1967	1	976	992
Merry Hill, No. 2	1114	1114	......	546	568
Mitchell's No. 5	856	856	......	533	323
Roxibel, No. 6	1384	1384	......	672	712
Snakebite, No. 8	1336	1336	......	688	648
White's, No. 3	1025	1025	......	504	521
Windsor, No. 1	3732	3730	2	1306	2426
Windsor	427	426	1	199	228
Woodville, No. 7	1535	1535	......	288	1247
BLADEN.					
Abbottsburg, No. 4	716	716	......	384	332
Beaver Dam, No. 11	619	619	......	433	186
Bladenboro, No. 2	1005	1002	3	713	292
Brown Marsh, No. 5	800	799	1	396	404
Carver's Cr'k, No. 7	996	994	2	378	618
Colly, No. 9	1220	1219	1	604	616
Elizabetht'n, No. 3	1904	1903	1	719	1185
Elizab'thtown	62	62	......	59	3
French's Cr'k, No. 8	1176	1173	3	692	484
Hollow, No. 1	1243	1240	3	577	666
Turnbull, No. 10	447	447	......	381	66
White Oak, No. 12	1265	1263	2	852	413
White's Cr'k, No. 6	1440	1438	2	600	840
BRUNSWICK.					
Lockwood's Folly, No. 3	874	870	4	702	172
North West, No. 6	2030	2029	1	808	1222
Shallotte, No. 2	1035	1033	2	771	264
Smithville, No. 4	1583	1567	16	943	640
Smithville	810	796	14	571	239
Town Creek, No. 5	1780	1776	4	788	992
Waccamaw, No. 1	452	452	......	436	16
BUNCOMBE.					
Asheville, No. 9	2593	2531	62	1759	834
Asheville	1400	1370	30	829	571
Avery's Creek, No. 1	655	654	1	585	70
Big Ivy, No. 12	1270	1270	......	1154	116
Fairview No. 7	779	779	......	656	123
Flat Creek, No. 11	1168	1167	1	1061	107
Limeston, No. 6	688	688	......	568	120
Lower Hominy, No. 2	1215	1212	3	1002	213
Leicester, No. 4	2180	2157	23	2001	179
Reem's Creek, No. 10	1121	1119	2	967	154
Sandy Mush, No. 5	894	894	......	788	106
Swannanoa, No. 8	1526	1524	2	1271	255
Upper Hominy, No. 3	1323	1323	......	1227	96
BURKE.					
Icard, No. 3	929	929	......	885	44
Love Lady, No. 2	597	597	......	529	68
Lower Creek, No. 9	750	750	......	493	257
Lower Fork, No. 4	616	616	......	614	2
Lynville, No. 7	1020	1020	......	621	399
Morganton, No. 1	2221	2212	9	1552	669
Morganton	551	551	3	330	224
Silver Creek, No. 6	1314	1313	1	937	377
Upper Creek, No. 8	1736	1735	1	1238	498
Upper Fork, No. 5	594	594	......	594	......
CABARRUS.					
Baptist Church, No. 11	1032	1026	6	660	372
Bethel, No. 10	1095	1095	......	763	332
Concord, No. 12	1259	1255	4	868	391
Concord	878	875	3	617	261
Ducast's, No. 3	1015	1013	2	615	400
Faggert's, No. 6	619	618	1	559	60
Holdbrook's, No. 4	1115	1111	4	737	378
Livengood's, No. 5	662	661	1	559	103
Miller's, No. 7	422	422	......	315	107
Mount Pleasant, No. 8	1021	1021	......	815	206
Plott's, No. 9	913	908	5	713	200
Poplar Tent, No. 2	1280	1270	10	546	734
Rocky River, No. 1	1521	1519	2	875	646
CALDWELL.					
Buffalo, No. 6	792	792	......	540	252
John's River, No. 8	883	883	......	689	194
King's Creek, No. 5	625	625	......	512	113
Lenoir, No. 2 (a)	2054	2053	1	1669	385
Lenoir (a)	446	442	4	382	64
Little River, No. 4	888	888	......	828	60
Lower Creek, No. 1 (a)	1092	1089	3	943	149
Patterson, No. 7	789	789	......	657	132
Summers's, No. 3	1353	1353	......	1258	95
CAMDEN.					
Court House, No. 2	1759	1759	......	1098	661
Shiloh, No. 1	1546	1546	......	1099	447
South Mills	2056	2048	8	1042	(b) 1013
CARTERET.					
Beaufort, No. 4	2850	2787	63	1492	1358
Beaufort	2430	2420	10	1188	1242
Fort Macon, (garrison)	121	68	53	118	3

(a) Of Lenoir: 301 in Lenoir and 145 in Lower Creek.
(b) Also 1 Indian.

TABLE IX.—*Population of Minor Civil Divisions, &c.*—*NEW YORK*—Continued.

Counties.	Total.	Nativity. Native.	Nativity. Foreign.	Race. White.	Race. Colored.	Counties.	Total.	Nativity. Native.	Nativity. Foreign.	Race. White.	Race. Colored.
WESTCHESTER—C'd.						WYOMING—Cont'd.					
Monterey	118	63	55	117	1	Java	1956	1631	325	1956	......
Mount Eden	116	70	46	116	......	Middlebury	1620	1493	127	1620	......
Mount Hope	487	315	172	482	5	Wyoming	338	319	19	338	......
Tremont	2025	1407	618	2012	13	Orangeville	1217	1040	177	1208	9
West Farms	1761	1089	672	1758	3	Perry	2342	2108	234	2335	7
Wm.'s Bridge	144	78	66	144	......	Perry Centre	183	175	8	183	......
Woodstock	307	201	106	284	23	Perry	867	771	96	861	6
White Plains	2630	1909	721	2586	44	Pike	1730	1639	91	1727	3
Yonkers	18357	11645	6712	18127	230	Pike	551	528	23	550	1
Yonkers	12733	8080	4653	12575	158	Sheldon	2258	1655	603	2257	1
Yorktown	2625	2363	262	2559	66	Warsaw	3143	2790	353	3104	39
						Warsaw	1631	1496	135	1593	38
WYOMING.						Wethersfield	1219	1141	78	1219	......
						Wethersfield	170	165	5	170	......
Arcade	1742	1488	254	1739	3						
Arcade	573	......	......	......	......	YATES.					
Attica	2546	2048	498	2543	3						
Attica	1333	1054	279	1331	2	Barrington	1506	1447	59	1497	9
Bennington	2385	1837	548	2385	......	Benton (a)	2422	2116	306	2411	11
Castile	2186	1984	202	2179	7	Italy	1341	1260	81	1337	4
Castile	712	669	43	708	4	Jerusalem	2612	2376	236	2599	13
Covington	1189	988	201	1189	......	Middlesex	1314	1256	58	1311	3
Eagle	1040	964	76	1040	......	Milo (a)	4779	4132	647	4715	64
Eagle	110	......	......	......	......	Penn Yan (a)	3488	3002	486	3423	65
Gainesville	1612	1509	103	1602	10	Potter	1970	1827	143	1952	18
Gainesville	114	111	3	114	......	Starkey	2370	2269	101	2343	27
Genesee Falls	979	798	181	979	......	Dundee	730	......	......	......	......
Portageville	491	383	108	491	......	Torrey	1281	1157	124	1264	17

(a) Of Penn Yan: 485 in Benton and 3,003 in Milo.

TABLE IX.—*Population of Minor Civil Divisions, &c.*—*NORTH CAROLINA.*

NOTE.—The marginal column marks townships, their names and numbers being official; the first indentation, cities; the second, towns. Names of towns are placed under the names of the townships in which they are respectively situated. The population of each township includes that of all towns situated in it.

Counties.	Total.	Nativity. Native.	Nativity. Foreign.	Race. White.	Race. Colored.
ALAMANCE.					
Albright's, No. 7	625	625	......	440	185
Boon's Stat'n, No. 3	1100	1099	1	894	206
Coble's, No. 2	875	875	......	718	157
Faucett's, No. 5	1327	1324	3	[illegible]	[illegible]
Graham, No. 6	2332	2286	46	[illegible]	[illegible]
Graham	502	462	40	311	[illegible]
Melville, No. 10	1221	1220	1	[illegible]	[illegible]
Morton's, No. 4	794	794	......	[illegible]	[illegible]
Newlin's, No. 8	862	862	......	[illegible]	[illegible]
Patterson's, No. 1	717	716	1	[illegible]	[illegible]
Pleasant Grove, No. 11	1246	1246	......	[illegible]	[illegible]
Thompson's, No. 9	775	775	......	[illegible]	[illegible]
ALEXANDER.					
Ellendale, No. 5	905	[illegible]	[illegible]	[illegible]	[illegible]

TABLE IX.—*Population of Minor Civil Divisions, &c.—NORTH CAROLINA*—**Continued.**

Counties.	Total.	Nativity.		Race.	
		Native.	Foreign.	White.	Colored.
CARTERET—Cont'd					
Hunting Quarter, No. 7	945	945	......	938	7
Morehead, No. 2	1168	1166	2	635	533
Morehead	267	267	......	184	83
Newport, No. 3	968	968	......	597	371
Newport	121	121	......	103	18
Portsmouth, No. 8	341	341	......	335	6
Smyrna, No. 6	905	903	2	843	62
Strait's, No. 5	991	990	1	928	63
White Oak, No. 1	842	840	2	517	325
CASWELL.					
Anderson's, No. 8	1544	1544	......	873	671
Dan River, No. 2	1910	1910	......	613	1297
Hightowers, No. 7	1502	1501	1	648	854
Leasburg, No. 6	1461	1459	2	430	1031
Locust Hill, No. 4	1781	1780	1	760	1021
Milton, No. 1	2752	2749	3	1014	1738
Pelham, No. 3	1560	1559	1	691	869
Stoney Creek, No. 9	1368	1367	1	732	636
Yanceyville, No. 5	2203	2203	......	826	1377
CATAWBA.					
Bandy's, No. 1	727	727	......	652	75
Caldwell's, No. 2	1101	1100	1	956	145
Cline's, No. 3	1904	1902	2	1684	220
Hamilton's, No. 4	1562	1562	......	1211	351
Hickory Tavern, No. 5	1591	1587	4	1481	110
Jacob's Fork, No. 6	1106	1104	2	896	210
Mountain Creek, No. 7	1298	1298	......	957	341
Newton, No. 8	1695	1694	1	1444	251
Newton	323	323	......	264	59
CHATHAM. (*)					
Bear Creek, No. 3	1328	1328	......	1196	132
Cape Fear, No. 12	2285	2285	......	1225	1060
Centre, No. 8 (a)	1255	1253	2	669	586
Gulf, No. 6	1786	1783	3	1174	612
Hickory Mountain, No. 5 (a)	960	960	......	510	450
Matthews, No. 2 (a)	873	873	......	577	296
New Hope, No. 11 a	1760	1759	1	1225	535
Oakland, No. 9	1593	1525	68	1096	497
CHEROKEE.					
Beaver Dam, No. 5	763	762	1	655	b2
Cheoah, No. 7	1427	1426	1	1113	c21
Hot House, No. 3	645	644	1	617	28
Murphy, No. 1	1545	1542	3	1380	d94
Murphy	175	175	......	167	8
Nottla, No. 2	940	940	......	862	78
Shoal Creek, No. 4	1332	1332	......	1323	9
Sticoah, No. 8	398	398	......	398	......
Valley Town, No. 9	1030	1026	4	948	e69
CHOWAN.					
Edenton or Lower, No. 1	3664	3655	9	1133	2531
Edenton	1243	......	......	......	......
Middle, No. 2	1610	1607	3	1086	524
Upper, No. 3	1176	1176	......	862	314
CLAY.					
Brasstown, No. 1	395	394	1	394	1
Hayesville, No. 2	884	884	......	846	[illegible]
Hayesville	35	35	......	32	3
Hiwassee, No. 4	418	417	1	387	31
Shooting Crk, No. 5	423	423	......	415	8
Tusquittee, No. 3	341	341	......	307	34
CLEAVELAND.					
Double Shoal, No. 9	1410	1410	......	1190	220
Duncan and Hinton Creek, No. 8	1242	1242	......	1067	175
King's Mountain, No. 4	1248	1243	5	1003	245
Knob Creek, No. 10	638	638	......	605	33
Rich Mountain, No. 11	751	750	1	731	20
Sandy Run, No. 7	1191	1191	......	1048	143
Shelby, No. 6	1849	1848	1	1377	472
Sulphur Spring, No. 3	1222	1222	......	1030	192
Township No. 1 (f)	471	471	......	390	81
Township No. 2 (f)	1167	1166	1	1036	131
Township No. 5 (f)	1507	1503	4	1166	341
COLUMBUS.					
Bogue, No. 1	1393	1393	......	635	758
Bug Hill, No. 7	513	513	......	424	89
Fair Bluff, No. 5	1309	1309	......	922	387
Lee's, No. 8	631	630	1	538	93
Taton's, No. 4	879	878	1	548	331
Welches Creek, No. 2	818	818	......	381	437
Williams' No. 6	905	905	......	839	66
Whiteville, No. 3	2026	2024	2	1289	737
Whiteville	104	104	......	86	18
CRAVEN.					
Adam's Cr'k, No. 5	1352	1351	1	432	920
Croatan, No. 6	656	656	......	148	508
Dover, No. 9	2206	2201	5	931	1275
New Berne, No. 8 (g)	1606	1603	3	225	1381
New Berne	5849	5736	113	2020	3829
Wildwood, No. 7	2241	2238	3	108	2133
Township No. 1 (h)	2447	2446	1	1527	920
Township No. 2 (h)	1666	1666	......	1349	317
Township No. 3 (h)	909	907	2	681	228
Township No. 4 (h)	1584	1584	......	979	605
CUMBERLAND.					
Black River, No. 8	760	760	......	531	229
Carver's Creek, No. 2	1391	1383	8	658	733
Cedar Creek, No. 6	2358	2358	......	1668	690
Cross Creek, No. 4 (i)	147	147	......	38	109
Fayetteville	4660	4598	62	2342	2318
Flea Hill, No. 7	1899	1897	2	942	957
Quewhiffle, No. 1	954	949	5	632	322
Rock Fish, No. 5	2982	2976	6	1723	1259
Seventy-first, No. 3	1884	1847	37	986	898
CURRITUCK.					
Atlantic	320	320	......	303	17

(*) Incomplete; see note (a).
(a) That part of township south of Pittsboro road.
(b) Also 106 Indians.
(c) Also 293 Indians.
(d) Also 71 Indians.
(e) Also 13 Indians.
(f) No name.
(g) Exclusive of city of New Berne.
(h) No name.
(i) Exclusive of city of Fayetteville.

L—*Population of Minor Civil Divisions, &c.—NORTH CAROLINA*—Continued.

ies.	Total.	Nativity: Native.	Nativity: Foreign.	Race: White.	Race: Colored.
k—Con.					
No. 2..	1867	1866	1	1286	581
No. 3...	600	600	......	583	17
o. 1	1204	1203	1	910	294
Branch, ...	1140	1139	1	909	231
E.					
o. 5	255	255	......	231	24
, No. 4..	251	251	......	250	1
No. 1 ...	673	673	......	647	26
, No. 2	599	599	......	595	4
d. No. 3.	1000	996	4	678	322
SON.					
, No. 8..	436	436	......	397	39
o. 10 ...	720	720	......	682	38
16	1311	1311	......	670	641
n, No. 1.	987	987	......	887	100
ll, No. 3	1115	1111	4	1019	96
ville, ...	978	978	......	738	240
ve, No.	868	863	5	469	390
No. 4 ...	941	936	5	901	40
prings, ...	675	675	......	560	115
Hill, ...	637	637	......	570	67
, No. 14.	2289	2279	10	1590	699
ton	475	466	9	324	151
o. 9 ...	1026	1026	......	881	145
, No. 5..	975	958	17	905	70
le, No. 2	2517	2517	......	2073	444
sville ..	214	214	......	146	68
13	985	984	1	733	252
o. 12 ..	954	954	......	793	161
[illegible].					
No. 1. ..	1232	1232	......	1000	232
, No. 5 .	919	918	1	784	135
n, No. 4.	2047	2047	......	1443	604
. 3	2320	2317	3	1415	905
, No. 2 ..	1544	1544	......	1021	523
, No. 6	1558	1557	1	914	644
ville ...	300	300	......	250	50
IN.					
, No. 4	667	666	1	520	147
Creek, ...	1024	1024	......	758	266
No. 1 ...	1918	1908	10	650	1268
No. 3 ...	481	481	......	379	102
....	381	380	1	228	153
ek, No. 8	1449	1447	2	875	574
le, No. 12	2878	2862	16	1298	1580
, No. 6..	709	709	......	605	104
No. 10 ..	1606	1603	3	875	731
, No. 9..	1380	1379	1	701	679
o. 5	662	660	2	449	213
No. 11...	1362	1359	3	708	654
e, No. 2.	1025	1021	4	730	295
OMBE.					
. 13	1281	1281	......	454	827
k, No. 4	1706	1704	2	322	1384
eto, No. 2	2000	1999	1	572	1428
shing o. 5	1629	1629	......	468	1161

Counties.	Total.	Nativity: Native.	Nativity: Foreign.	Race: White.	Race: Colored.
EDGECOMBE—Con.					
Lower Town Cr'k, No. 10	937	937	......	471	466
Otter's Cr'k, No. 9.	651	651	......	465	186
Rocky Mount, No. 12	2158	2146	12	1024	1134
Rocky Mount.	357	347	10	190	167
Sparta, No. 8......	1522	1521	1	589	933
Swift Creek, No. 7.	2383	2382	1	456	1927
Tarboro, No. 1	3102	3060	42	1008	2094
Tarboro	1340	1308	32	687	653
Upper Coneto, No. 3	1437	1436	1	418	1019
Upper Town Cr'k, No. 14	1092	1091	1	650	442
Upper Fishing Creek, No. 6	2064	2064	......	683	1381
Walnut Creek, No. 11	1008	1005	3	278	730
FORSYTH.					
Abbott's Creek, No. 9	753	753	......	674	79
Bethania, No. 3 ...	1162	1162	......	838	324
Belew's Cr'k, No. 1	817	816	1	602	215
Broad Bay, No. 11	993	993	......	843	150
Kearnersville, No. 5	995	995	......	720	275
Lewisville, No. 13	816	816	......	644	172
Middle Fork, No. 6	1046	1044	2	873	173
Old Richmond, No. 4	833	833	......	700	133
Old Town, No. 7 ..	860	860	......	781	79
Salem Chapel, No. 2	848	848	......	616	232
South Fork, No. 12	1398	1397	1	1294	104
Vienna, No. 8	836	836	......	678	158
Winston, No. 10...	1693	1681	12	1453	240
Winston......	443	438	5	348	95
FRANKLIN.					
Cedar Rock, No. 4.	1112	1112	......	631	481
Cypress Cr'k, No. 9	1087	1087	......	596	491
Dunn's, No. 10 ...	838	838	......	512	326
Franklinton, No. 6.	1956	1955	1	765	1191
Franklinton ..	305	305	......	200	105
Freeman's No. 7 ..	1318	1318	......	613	705
Harris', No. 8.....	1266	1266	......	764	502
Hayesville, No. 1..	1630	1624	6	739	891
Louisburg, No. 5..	2542	2542	......	830	1712
Louisburg ...	750	750	......	350	400
Sandy Creek, No. 2	1453	1450	3	739	714
The Gold Mines, No. 3	932	928	4	444	488
GASTON.					
Cherryville, No. 1	2003	1999	4	1658	345
Crowder's Mountain, No. 5	1931	1930	1	1304	627
Dallas, No. 2	4006	3994	12	2628	1378
Dallas	299	293	6	196	103
River Bend, No. 3	2248	2238	10	1398	850
South Point, No. 4	2414	2407	7	1442	972
GATES.					
Gatesville, No. 1 ..	1155	1155	......	599	556
Gatesville	156	156	......	107	49
Hall, No. 2........	778	778	......	617	161
Haslett's, No. 4 ...	946	946	......	513	433
Holly Grove, No. 5.	1213	1213	......	744	469
Hunter's Mill, No. 6	1461	1461	......	859	602
Mintonsville, No. 7	1183	1183	......	642	541
Reynoldson, No. 3.	988	988	......	543	445

TABLE IX.—*Population of Minor Civil Divisions, &c.—NORTH CAROLINA*—Continued.

Counties.	Total.	Nativity. Native.	Nativity. Foreign.	Race. White.	Race. Colored.
GRANVILLE.					
Brassfield's, No. 11	3015	3015	......	1815	1200
Dutchville, No. 10	1752	1752	......	1110	642
Fishing Cr'k, No. 8	2413	2411	2	1018	1395
Henderson, No. 6	3033	3031	2	1247	1786
[1] Henderson	545	543	2	244	301
Kittrell's, No. 7	1829	1828	1	909	920
Oak Hill, No. 3	2183	2183	......	951	1232
Oxford, No. 5	2724	2723	1	1101	1623
Oxford	916	915	1	463	453
Sassafras Fork, No. 2	1859	1859	......	772	1087
Tally Ho, No. 9	2138	2138	......	1240	898
Townsville, No. 1	2187	2186	1	548	1639
Walnut Grove, No. 4	1698	1698	......	765	933
GREENE.					
Hookerton	1286	1286	......	673	613
Hookerton	163	163	......	87	76
Olds	2931	2930	1	1346	1585
Snow Hill	2650	2650	......	1251	1399
Snow Hill	320	320	......	137	183
Spreight Bridge	1820	1820	......	896	924
GUILFORD.					
Bruce, No. 13	1034	1034	......	681	353
Centre Grove, No. 10	1110	1110	......	637	473
Clay, No. 6	835	835	......	726	109
Deep River, No. 17	1071	1071	......	861	210
Fentriss, No. 9	866	866	......	705	161
Friendship, No. 14	1348	1302	46	968	380
Gilmer, No. 8 (a)	2311	2288	23	1319	992
Greensboro (a)	497	484	13	369	128
Green, No. 3	1119	1119	......	979	140
High Point, No. 18	1627	1622	5	1343	284
Jamestown, No. 15	1539	1509	30	1327	212
Jefferson, No. 5	1045	1044	1	815	230
Madison, No. 4	840	839	1	575	265
Monroe, No. 7	840	840	......	484	356
Morehead, No. 11 (a)	2104	2077	27	1209	895
Oak Ridge, No. 16	1022	1020	2	778	244
Rock Creek, No. 2	1082	1081	1	710	372
Sumner, No. 12	1120	1105	15	904	216
Washington, No. 1	823	823	......	635	188
HALIFAX.					
Arcadia, No. 1	2898	2894	4	604	2294
Halifax	429	425	4	129	300
Buckaria, No. 2	1782	1781	1	668	1114
Caledonia, No. 3	2118	2117	1	503	1615
Dalmatia, No. 4	2796	2794	2	1009	1787
Etruria, No. 5	2038	2038	......	1099	1839
Formosa, No. 6	2957	2957	......	903	2054
Palmyra, No. 7	2345	2344	1	832	1513
Rapides, No. 8	2574	2570	4	800	1774
Weldon	208	208	......	74	134
HARNETT.					
Averasboro, No. 9	716	716	......	599	117
Barbecue, No. 6	1111	1100	11	592	519
Buckhorn, No. 3	1438	1436	2	1133	305
Grove, No. 1	1093	1093	......	915	178
Johnsonville, No. 8	483	475	8	312	171
Lillington, No. 4	699	698	1	256	443
Neill's Creek, No. 2	1137	1136	1	822	315
HARNETT—Cont'd.					
Stewart's Creek, No. 7	997	994	3	413	[illegible]
Upper Little River, No. 5	1221	1216	5	815	[illegible]
HAYWOOD.					
Beaver Dam, No. 4	1745	1734	11	1654	91
Cataloochee, No. 8	198	198	......	198	......
Crabtree, No. 5	1048	1048	......	1032	16
East Fork, No. 3	286	286	......	251	35
Fines Creek, No. 6	1048	1047	1	1044	4
Jonathan's Creek, No. 7	987	987	......	957	30
Upper Pigeon, No. 2	1066	1066	......	991	75
Waynesville, No. 1	1543	1538	5	1279	[illegible]
HENDERSON.					
Blue Ridge, No. 2	1354	1352	2	1179	175
Crab Creek, No. 6	607	607	......	555	[illegible]
Edneyville, No. 1	1125	1123	2	1020	105
Green River, No. 5	709	709	......	702	7
Hendersonville, No. 4	1636	1626	10	1208	[illegible]
Hendersonv'e	278	277	1	209	[illegible]
Hooper's Creek, No. 3	755	750	5	569	186
Mill's River, No. 7	1520	1518	2	1267	253
HERTFORD.					
Harrellsville, No. 5	1743	1741	2	692	1051
Manney's Neck, No. 1	1313	1313	......	578	735
Murfreesboro, No. 2	1961	1953	8	1033	928
Murfreesboro	753	750	3	451	302
St. John's, No. 3	2016	2016	......	1072	944
Winton, No. 4	2240	2239	1	946	1294
HYDE.					
Currituck, No. 1	1582	1578	4	1008	574
Fairfield, No. 4	1145	1145	......	642	503
Lake Landing, No. 3	2235	2235	......	1421	814
Ocracoke, No. 5	368	368	......	361	7
Swan Quarter, No. 2	1115	1115	......	635	480
IREDELL.					
Barringer's, No. 13	998	997	1	744	254
Bethany, No. 8	506	504	2	296	210
Chambersburg, No. 10	949	949	......	646	303
Concord, No. 9	869	867	2	696	173
Coodle Creek, No. 15	1629	1628	1	915	714
Cool Spring, No. 7	711	711	......	497	214
Davidson's, No. 16	1540	1540	......	987	553
Eagle Mills, No. 1	1090	1089	1	848	[illegible]
Fallstown, No. 14	879	879	......	711	[illegible]
Turnersburg, No. 4	796	795	1	525	[illegible]
New Hope, No. 3	871	871	......	756	[illegible]
Olin, No. 5	923	918	2	642	[illegible]
Sharpesburg, No. 6	947	947	......	746	[illegible]
Shiloh, No. 12	1541	1540	1	1336	[illegible]

(a) Of Greensboro: 280 in Gilmor and 217 in Morehead.

(b) Also 39 Indians.

[.]—*Population of Minor Civil Divisions, &c.—NORTH CAROLINA*—Continued.

[...]ies.	Total.	NATIVITY. Native.	NATIVITY. Foreign.	RACE. White.	RACE. Colored.
-Cont'd.					
, No. 11	1656	1645	11	986	670
ville....	644	635	9	421	223
re, No. 2	1029	1028	1	957	72
ON.					
k	951	950	1	926	25
alley ..	509	507	2	503	6
....	520	518	2	486	34
k	555	555	......	532	23
rn	1697	1697	......	950	a36
....	515	515	......	509	6
eek	529	527	2	504	25
....	1407	1407	......	1288	119
ON.					
le, No. 5	922	922	......	638	284
. 10	1105	1105	......	950	155
No. 8...	1445	1436	9	1061	384
o. 1	1534	1533	1	908	626
No. 3 ..	1450	1450	......	1373	77
No. 6 ...	1326	1326	......	1146	180
o. 4....	1043	1043	......	825	218
o. 11...	1294	1294	......	1057	237
Grove, ...	1535	1535	......	1141	394
9	1167	1164	3	632	535
No. 7..	2864	2861	3	1336	1528
ield	415	414	1	213	202
o. 12 ..	1203	1203	......	627	576
S.					
ek......	1108	1108	......	562	546
eek....	541	540	1	284	257
......	1263	1261	2	466	797
....	814	812	2	373	441
....	616	615	1	375	241
....	660	660	......	286	374
R.					
, No. 2.	1470	1470	......	665	805
o. 1	4604	4590	14	1909	2695
....	1103	1089	14	486	617
ll, No. 3	2627	2627	......	1132	1495
No. 5..	572	572	......	450	122
No. 6...	400	400	......	204	196
....	761	760	1	542	219
N.					
rings, ...	2097	2094	3	1337	760
o. 6 ...	2162	2158	4	1233	929
, No. 1	430	430	......	412	18
o. 3	1170	1168	2	996	174
. 4 (b)	886	880	6	538	348
s, No. 7	625	625	......	551	74
, No. 2.	872	871	1	767	105
5......	1331	1327	4	980	351
(.					
. 10 ...	542	542	......	541	1
, No. 5	157	155	2	156	1
Town, ...	320	320	......	320	......
haye, ...	480	480	......	428	c13

Counties.	Total.	NATIVITY. Native.	NATIVITY. Foreign.	RACE. White.	RACE. Colored.
MACON—Cont'd.					
Cowee, No. 9......	760	759	1	672	88
Ellijay, No. 3	525	524	1	473	52
Franklin, No. 1	1310	1309	1	1203	107
Mill Shoal, No. 2 ..	528	528	......	453	75
Nantahala, No. 11	383	383	......	382	1
Smith's Bridge, No. 6	708	708	......	671	37
Sugar Fork, No. 4	356	356	......	356	......
Welches...........	546	546	......	518	28
MADISON.					
Gabriel's Creek, No. 3	1372	1372	......	1311	61
Laurell, No. 2.....	992	991	1	981	11
Marshall, No. 1 ...	1502	1501	1	1408	94
Middle Fork of Ivy, No. 4	793	791	2	748	45
Pine Creek, No. 7	887	887	......	843	44
Sandy Mush, No. 6	458	458	......	458	......
Spring Cr'k, No. 8.	944	944	......	943	1
Warm Sp'gs, No. 9.	498	497	1	431	67
West Fork of Ivy, No. 5	746	745	1	735	11
MARTIN.					
Hamilton, No. 3...	3957	3957	......	1720	2237
Hamilton.....	200	200	......	80	120
Jamesville, No. 1..	2530	2524	6	1525	1005
Jamesville....	150	147	3	101	49
Williamston, No. 2	3160	3153	7	1819	1341
Williamston ..	520	520	......	309	211
MC'DOWELL.					
Broad River, No. 8.	399	399	......	383	16
Crooked Cr'k, No. 7	389	389	......	323	66
Dysartsville, No. 4.	767	767	......	668	99
Finley, No. 3	580	580	......	437	143
Higgins, No. 10 ...	401	401	......	346	55
Jamestown, No. 6	412	412	......	355	57
Marion, No. 1	1943	1938	5	1386	557
North Cove, No. 2	874	873	1	721	153
Old Fort, No. 9....	1280	1241	39	686	594
Sugar Hill, No. 5..	547	546	1	515	32
MECKLENBURG.					
Berryhill's, No. 2..	1414	1404	10	757	657
Charlotte, No. 1 ...	2212	2194	18	841	1371
Charlotte	4473	4305	168	2593	1880
Clear Creek, No. 6	615	611	4	422	193
Crab Orchard, No. 7	1522	1516	6	806	716
Deweese, No. 9....	1606	1599	7	967	639
Lemley's, No. 10 ..	971	968	3	635	336
Long Creek, No. 11	1457	1454	3	963	494
Mallard Cr'k, No. 8.	1436	1430	6	937	499
Morning Star	918	914	4	703	215
Paw Creek, No. 12.	1591	1586	5	993	598
Providence, No. 5	1936	1929	7	826	1110
Sharon, No. 4	2197	2189	8	1125	1072
Steele Creek, No. 3.	1951	1948	3	1010	941
MITCHELL.					
Bakersville, No. 1.	1101	1099	2	1037	64
Bee Creek, No. 4..	189	189	......	188	1
Brummet's Creek, No. 11	217	217	......	217	......
Cranberry, No. 7..	158	158	......	147	11

[...]711 Indians.
[...]ical with Lincolnton Village.

(c) Also 39 Indians.

TABLE IX.—*Population of Minor Civil Divisions, &c.—NORTH CAROLINA*—Continued.

Counties.	Total.	Nativity. Native.	Nativity. Foreign.	Race. White.	Race. Colored.
MITCHELL—Cont'd					
Grassy Cr'k, No. 3	514	511	......	507	7
Harrel's, No. 10	479	479	......	479	......
Linville, No. 6	347	347	......	337	10
Little Rock Cr'k, No. 8	397	397	......	397	......
Red Hill, No. 9	299	299	......	276	23
Snow Creek, No. 2	385	385	......	385	......
Toe River, No. 5	619	619	......	522	97
MONTGOMERY.					
Cheek's Cr'k, No. 2	960	960	......	511	449
Eldorado, No. 9	887	887	......	771	116
Hill, No. 5	477	477	......	448	29
Hollongsworth, No. 4	695	695	......	527	168
Little River, No. 6	415	414	1	376	39
Mount Gilead, No. 8	1280	1280	......	770	510
Ophor, No. 7	451	451	......	419	32
Pedee, No. 10	640	640	......	351	289
Rocky Sp'g, No. 3	320	320	......	181	139
Troy, No. 1	882	882	......	591	291
Troy	67	67	......	64	3
Uharrie, No. 11	480	480	......	414	66
MOORE.					
Bensalem, No. 2	1032	1027	5	896	136
Carthage, No. 1	1786	1772	14	1267	519
Greenwood, No. 7	1523	1514	9	1098	425
Jackson Springs, No. 10	537	537	......	412	125
McNeill's, No. 8	532	529	3	389	143
Pocket, No. 5	1362	1360	2	895	467
Ritter, No. 4	1524	1522	2	1189	335
Sand Hill, No. 9	268	265	3	208	60
Shuffield, No. 3	1270	1270	......	1140	130
Sloan's, No. 6	2206	2206	......	1527	679
NASH.					
Chesterfield, No. 6	863	863	......	522	341
Liberty, No. 2	2860	2855	5	1221	1639
Middleton, No. 4	1465	1465	......	988	477
Springfield, No. 5	2111	2111	......	1516	595
Union, No. 3	1639	1639	......	1003	636
Washington, No. 1	2139	2139	......	1106	1033
NEW HANOVER.					
Cape Fear, No. 5	996	992	4	190	806
Caswell, No. 9	1057	1055	2	538	519
Columbia, No. 10	1715	1711	4	845	870
Federal Pt., No. 1	410	410	......	210	200
Franklin, No. 11	1309	1307	2	543	706
Grant, No. 6	1119	1118	1	474	645
Harnett, No. 4	1543	1533	10	520	1023
Holden, No. 7	2056	2047	9	689	1367
Holly, No. 13	1016	1015	1	455	561
Lincoln, No. 8	1359	1358	1	619	740
Masonboro, No. 2	541	532	9	371	170
Union, No. 12	1391	1379	12	799	592
Wilmington (a)	13446	12876	570	5526	7920
NORTHAMPTON.					
Gaston, No. 1	2310	2310	......	668	1642
Gaston	11	11	......	5	6
Jackson, No. 5	523	519	4	251	272
Jackson	181	178	3	97	84
Kirby	1844	1843	1	1057	787
NORTHAMPTON—Cont'd.					
Occoneechee	1944	1944	......	463	1481
Rich Square, No. 10	3133	3133	......	1322	1811
Roanoke	1778	1778	......	977	801
Seaboard, No. 4	1576	1574	2	665	911
Wickacanee	1641	1641	......	836	805
ONSLOW.					
Jacksonville, No. 1	1166	1164	2	860	306
Jacksonville	60	60	......	39	21
Richland, No. 3	2133	2131	2	1296	837
Stump Sound, No. 2	1515	1514	1	1138	377
Swansboro, No. 4	1475	1470	5	992	483
Swansboro	141	138	3	129	12
White Oaks, No. 5	1280	1280	......	897	383
ORANGE.					
Bingham, No. 7	1604	1604	......	1254	350
Cedar Grove, No. 4	2047	2047	......	1330	717
Chapel Hill, No. 2	2799	2792	7	1684	1115
Durham, No. 6	2323	2323	......	1635	688
Hillsborough, No. 1	3624	3621	3	1995	1629
Hillsborough	809	807	2	405	404
Little River, No. 3	1553	1553	......	1114	439
Mangum, No. 5	2465	2465	......	1402	1063
Patterson, No. 8	1092	1092	......	653	439
PASQUOTANK.					
Elizabeth City, No. 3 (b)	2006	1979	27	1043	963
Elizabeth City (b)	930	922	8	509	421
Mt. Hermon, No. 4	1184	1184	......	702	482
Newland, No. 6	1481	1481	......	758	723
Nixonton, No. 2 (b)	1626	1626	......	656	970
Providence, No. 5	520	520	......	442	78
Salem, No. 1	1314	1312	2	609	705
PERQUIMANS.					
Belvidere, No. 3	2403	2403	......	1381	1022
Bethel, No. 5	1128	1128	......	505	623
Hertford, No. 4	1188	1188	......	610	578
Hertford	486	486	......	254	232
New Hope, No. 1	1933	1931	2	799	1134
Parksville, No. 2	1293	1292	1	632	661
PERSON.					
Allensville, No. 8	1120	1120	......	660	460
Bushy Fork, No. 1	1425	1425	......	952	473
Cunningham's, No. 3	1119	1119	......	488	631
Flat River, No. 4	958	957	1	548	410
Holloway's, No. 9	1279	1279	......	643	636
Mt. Tirzah, No. 7	1117	1117	......	665	452
Olive Hill, No. 2	1439	1439	......	716	723
Roxboro, No. 5	1117	1116	1	718	399
Woodsdale, No. 6	1596	1594	2	676	920
PITT.					
Belvin, No. 6	2151	2151	......	1178	973
California, No. 2	3826	3826	......	1582	2244
Chicoa, No. 5	1683	1683	......	939	744
Contentnea, No. 3	2118	2118	......	1413	705
Greenville, No. 1	3838	3831	7	1828	2010
Greenville	601	596	5	305	296

(a) Identical with Township No. 3, same name.
(b) Of Elizabeth City: 801 in Elizabeth City and 129 in Nixonton.

—*Population of Minor Civil Divisions, &c.—NORTH CAROLINA*—Continued.

	Total.	Nativity. Native.	Nativity. Foreign.	Race. White.	Race. Colored.
ued.					
7...	2060	2060	......	911	1149
No. 4.	1800	1799	1	1011	789
No. 5.	1179	1176	3	878	301
.1...	744	744	......	601	143
No. 3	797	797	......	658	139
....	640	640	......	525	115
o. 2.	959	959	......	679	280
L.					
11...	1172	1169	3	968	204
.....	182	182	......	155	27
No. 10	1212	1212	......	1018	194
1....	781	781	......	624	157
.3...	1254	1254	......	1064	190
5...	1028	1028	......	873	155
lle,					
.....	1528	1527	1	1406	122
.....	949	949	......	832	117
....	1009	1008	1	874	135
o. 16.	1095	1094	1	893	202
No. 9	1297	1294	3	1155	142
o. 5.	931	931	......	844	87
ove,					
.....	1218	1218	......	946	272
8...	713	713	......	678	35
o. 14	1296	1296	......	1125	171
3....	1471	1470	1	1074	397
....	597	596	1	571	26
.					
No. 3	635	634	1	325	310
o. 4.	799	799	......	373	426
o. 8.	2127	2105	22	860	1367
ngs,					
....	1040	1037	3	618	422
No. 5	1455	1450	5	823	632
am..	454	453	1	278	176
.....	1656	1656	......	566	1090
No. 9	1887	1873	14	810	1077
No. 7	2044	2035	9	1372	672
6...	1239	1238	1	537	702
No. 4.	1041	1039	2	519	522
No.					
.....	800	800	......	359	441
No. 1.	1014	1014	......	399	615
.....	1159	1158	1	961	198
No.					
.....	1511	1508	3	473	1038
No.					
.....	1023	1023	......	782	241
dge,					
.....	1075	1072	3	630	445
o. 15	1339	1330	9	659	680
n...	615	606	9	331	284
3..	460	460	......	159	301
....	1684	1676	8	635	1049
ill,					
.....	1088	1088	......	837	251
11..	1052	1044	8	658	394
No. 5	1708	1703	5	889	819
No.					
.....	684	683	1	401	283
.9..	624	623	1	531	93
M.					
.....	1880	1880	......	1357	523

Counties.	Total.	Nativity. Native.	Nativity. Foreign.	Race. White.	Race. Colored.
ROCKINGHAM—Con.					
Leaksville........	2031	2019	12	1101	930
Mayo	3339	3335	4	2025	1314
Madison......	295	295	......	142	143
Oregonville	2561	2560	1	1401	1160
Simpsonville	1590	1590	......	1152	438
Wentworth	1767	1766	1	1085	682
Williamsboro	2340	2339	1	1372	968
ROWAN.					
Atwell, No. 7	2051	2049	2	1663	388
Franklin, No. 2 ...	1184	1184	......	914	270
Gold Hill, No. 9...	959	945	14	849	110
Litaker, No. 8	1508	1508	......	1284	224
Locke, No. 6.......	1119	1119	......	615	504
Morgan, No. 10 ...	1064	1062	2	1003	61
Mount Ulla, No. 5	1720	1719	1	892	828
Providence, No. 11	1516	1513	3	1145	371
Salisbury, No. 1...	3327	3308	19	1767	1560
Salisbury.....	168	165	3	67	101
Scotch-Irish, No. 4.	1469	1469	......	817	652
Unity, No. 3	893	893	......	554	339
RUTHERFORD.					
Camp Creek, No. 11	1007	1006	1	817	190
Chimney Rock, No. 13	1024	1022	2	825	199
Colfax, No. 6......	964	964	......	841	123
Cool Springs, No. 7	1031	1031	......	826	205
Duncan's Creek, No. 8	999	999	......	812	187
Golden Valley, No. 9	1122	1122	......	1083	39
Green Hill, No. 2 .	1186	1186	......	874	312
High Shoals, No. 5	904	903	1	774	130
Logan's Store, No. 10	1597	1597	......	1262	335
Morgan, No. 12 ...	731	731	......	661	70
Rutherfordtom, No. 1	1097	1093	4	632	465
Rutherfordton	479	476	3	262	217
Sulphur Spring, No. 4	967	967	......	756	211
Union, No. 3	492	492	......	316	176
SAMPSON.					
Clinton, No. 1	2777	2766	11	1391	1386
Clinton.......	204	199	5	143	61
Dismal, No. 7......	746	745	1	657	89
Hall's, No. 4	1010	1010	......	652	358
Honeycutt's, No. 8	1283	1282	1	880	403
Lisbon, No. 11	1389	1388	1	661	728
Little Coharie, No. 9	1235	1235	......	937	298
McDaniel, No. 10 .	843	843	......	438	405
Mingo, No. 6.......	1240	1240	......	1127	113
Piney Grove, No. 3	1776	1775	1	937	839
Taylor's Bridge, No 12	1521	1520	1	774	747
Turkey, No. 2.....	1167	1166	1	475	692
Westbrooks, No. 5	1449	1449	......	1024	425
STANLEY.					
Albemarle, No. 2..	1600	1593	7	1232	368
Almonds, No. 5 ...	792	792	......	770	22
Big Lick, No. 6 ...	1354	1354	......	1298	56

TABLE IX.—*Population of Minor Civil Divisions, &c.—NORTH CAROLINA*—Continued.

Counties.	Total.	Nativity. Native.	Nativity. Foreign.	Race. White.	Race. Colored.
STANLEY—Cont'd.					
Centre, No. 1	1065	1065	......	715	350
Furr, No. 7	1044	1044	......	968	76
Harris, No. 3	924	924	......	714	210
Ridenhouse, No. 4	656	656	......	576	80
Tyson, No. 8	880	879	1	653	227
STOKES.					
Beaver Island, No. 7	1247	1247	......	802	445
Meadows, No. 5	2065	2064	1	1626	439
Peter's Creek, No. 2	1491	1491	......	1251	240
Quaker Gap, No. 3	1749	1749	......	1462	287
Saura Town, No. 6	1117	1117	......	546	571
Snow Creek, No. 1	1781	1781	......	1269	512
Yadkin, No. 4	1758	1757	1	1644	114
SURRY.					
Bryan, No. 10	1032	1031	1	944	88
Dobson, No. 7	1255	1255	......	1083	172
Eldora, No. 4	858	858	......	836	22
Franklin, No. 11	629	629	......	597	32
Hotel, No. 9	709	709	......	613	96
Marsh, No. 8	619	619	......	568	51
Mount Airy, No. 5	2353	2345	8	1750	603
Pilot, No. 2	1311	1310	1	1156	155
Rockford, No. 3	890	890	......	777	113
Stewart's Creek, No. 6	796	794	2	649	147
Westfield, No. 1	800	800	......	719	81
TRANSYLVANIA.					
Boyd, No. 1	448	443	......	391	57
Brevard	784	783	1	642	142
Cathey's Creek, No. 5	515	515	......	470	45
Dunn's Rock, No. 4	420	420	......	371	49
Eastatoee, No. 6	351	351	......	351	......
Gloucester, No. 8	372	372	......	371	1
Hogback, No. 7	243	243	......	243	......
Little River, No. 2	403	403	......	388	15
TYRRELL.					
Alligator, No. 4	778	778	......	513	265
Columbia, No. 3	1206	1203	3	1045	161
Gum Neck, No. 2	1068	1068	......	764	304
Scuppernong, No. 1	1121	1117	4	549	572
UNION.					
Buford, No. 2	1158	1156	2	1024	134
Goose Creek, No. 6	2207	2207	......	1926	281
Jackson, No. 3	1010	1009	1	623	387
Lane's Creek, No. 1	1575	1573	2	1230	345
Monroe, No. 5	2386	2385	1	1816	570
Monroe	448	447	1	358	90
New Salem, No. 7	2191	2189	2	1711	480
Sandy Ridge, No. 4	1690	1690	......	1193	497
WAKE.					
Barton's Creek, No. 4	1585	1583	2	1040	545
Buckhorn, No. 14	1694	1694	......	1019	675
Cedar Fork, No. 7	1533	1532	1	979	554
House's Creek, No. 8	2098	2093	5	1183	a908
Little River, No. 6	1315	1315	......	796	519
WAKE—Cont'd.					
Mark's Creek, No. 10	1396	1396	......	745	[illegible]
Middle Creek, No. 15	1477	1477	......	[illegible]	[illegible]
New Light, No. 2	798	798	......	[illegible]	[illegible]
Oak Grove, No. 3	2075	2075	......	1333	[illegible]
Panther Branch, No. 16	921	921	......	[illegible]	[illegible]
Raleigh, No. 1 (b)	2359	2302	57	[illegible]	[illegible]
Raleigh	7790	7651	139	[illegible]	[illegible]
St. Mary's, No. 13	2124	2123	1	1128	[illegible]
St. Matthew's, No. 9	2192	2190	2	704	[illegible]
Swift Creek, No. 12	1445	1426	19	[illegible]	[illegible]
Wake Forest, No. 5	3135	3133	2	1564	[illegible]
White Oak, No. 11	1680	1678	2	1154	[illegible]
WARREN.					
Fishing Cr'k, No. 8	1598	1598	......	367	[illegible]
Haw Tree, No. 3	1540	1537	3	582	[illegible]
Judkins, No. 9	1432	1421	11	481	[illegible]
Nut Bush, No. 5	2430	2429	1	651	1779
River, No. 1	1500	1498	2	518	[illegible]
Sandy Cr'k, No. 6	2753	2752	1	1107	[illegible]
Shocco, No. 7	1637	1636	1	[illegible]	[illegible]
Six-Pound, No. 2	930	930	......	257	[illegible]
Smith's Cr'k, No. 4	1062	1059	3	[illegible]	[illegible]
Warrenton, No. 10	2886	2870	16	776	[illegible]
Warrenton	941	934	7	407	534
WASHINGTON.					
Cool Spring	1561	1559	2	989	572
Lee's Mill	1522	1522	......	820	702
Plymouth	2565	2559	6	1988	1377
Plymouth	1389	1384	5	582	807
Skinnersville	868	868	......	642	226
WATAUGA.					
Ball Mountain, No. 3	320	320	......	319	1
Beaver Dam, No. 8	413	413	......	401	12
Blue Ridge, No. 10	460	460	......	441	19
Boone, No. 1	737	737	......	615	119
Cove Creek, No. 4	887	887	......	864	23
Elk Creek, No. 6	265	265	......	255	10
Laurel Cr'k, No. 9	585	585	......	575	10
Meat Camp, No. 7	370	370	......	369	1
Shanouehaw, No. 11	328	328	......	309	19
Stoney Fork, No. 6	366	365	1	366	......
Watauga, No. 2	556	556	......	544	12
WAYNE.					
Brogden, No. 2	2560	2553	7	1240	1320
Fork River, No. 4	1611	1601	10	851	760
Fork River	811	810	1	495	316
Goldsboro, No. 5	3886	3828	58	1908	1978
Goldsboro	1134	1086	48	687	447
Grantham, No. 1	1823	1823	......	1349	474
Holden	751	751	......	513	238
Indian Sp'gs, No. 3	1280	1280	......	858	422
Nahunta, No. 9	1874	1869	5	972	902
New Hope, No. 6	1520	1520	......	758	762
Pikeville, No. 8	1720	1715	5	1031	689
Saulston, No. 7	1119	1119	......	530	589
WILKES.					
Antioch, No. 15	704	704	......	608	96

(a) Also 7 Indians.
(b) Exclusive of city of Raleigh.

IX.—*Population of Minor Civil Divisions, &c.—NORTH CAROLINA*—Continued.

...ties.	Total.	Nativity. Native.	Nativity. Foreign.	Race. White.	Race. Colored.
—Cont'd.					
r'k, No. 10	960	900	......	835	125
Mountain.	434	434	......	434	......
, No. 1 ...	1556	1556	......	1408	148
9	675	675	......	605	70
Cr'k, No.	542	542	......	390	152
in, No. 8	606	606	......	589	17
ork, No. 7	1062	1062	......	1013	49
's, No. 14	627	627	......	609	18
y, No. 5 ..	1362	1359	3	1241	121
tle, No. 16	1120	1120	......	868	252
ek, No. 3	960	960	......	847	113
, No. 17 ..	760	760	......	691	69
l, No. 2 ...	972	972	......	903	69
o. 6	894	893	1	816	78
Grove, ...	1005	1005	......	943	62
ro, No. 11	1300	1300	......	1077	223
SON.					
eek, No. 2	1474	1466	8	833	641
Creek ..	77	73	4	59	18
ads, No. 3	694	694	......	581	113
s, No. 8 ..	1178	1178	......	657	521
wn, No. 7	1271	1265	6	728	543
l, No. 5 ..	1165	1165	......	942	223
, No. 9 ...	1108	1103	5	575	533
ill, No. 4	636	636	......	497	139
burg, No.	1007	998	9	424	583

Counties.	Total.	Nativity. Native.	Nativity. Foreign.	Race. White.	Race. Colored.
Wilson—Cont'd.					
Taylor's, No. 6	555	555	......	299	256
Wilson, No. 1	3170	3149	21	1649	1521
Wilson	1036	1019	17	749	287
YADKIN.					
Boonville, No. 4 ...	1058	1058	......	957	101
Buck Shoal, No. 1	1390	1390	......	1343	47
Deep Creek, No. 3	1236	1236	......	1089	147
East Bend, No. 8 ..	1353	1352	1	1197	156
Fall Creek, No. 6 ..	1192	1192	......	1046	146
Forbush, No. 7	1429	1429	......	947	482
Knob's, No. 2	1451	1451	......	1296	155
Liberty, No. 5	1588	1587	1	1378	210
Yadkinville ..	133	133	......	119	14
YANCY.					
Brush Creek, No. 7	495	495	......	454	41
Burnsville, No. 1 ..	505	505	......	444	61
Caney River, No. 2	1202	1202	......	1114	88
Egypt, No. 3	781	781	......	762	19
Hollow Poplar, No. 5	382	382	......	382	......
Jack's Creek, No. 6	946	946	......	917	29
Little Crabtree, No. 8	483	483	......	447	36
Pensacola, No. 10	319	319	......	318	1
Ramsey Town, No. 4	452	452	......	430	22
South Tar River, No. 9	344	344	......	333	11

TABLE IX.—*Population of Minor Civil Divisions, &c.—OHIO.*

-The marginal column marks townships; the first indentation, cities; the second, incorporated ...nd villages, whose names are placed under and their population included in that of the town... ...hich they are situated.

...ties.	Total.	Nativity. Native.	Nativity. Foreign.	Race. White.	Race. Colored.
...AMS.					
....	2172	2162	10	2164	8
st Grove ..	103	102	1	103	......
....	1833	1684	149	1830	3
mercial ..	64	54	10	63	1
ville	937	819	118	936	1
e	471	460	11	471	......
....	2268	2208	60	2255	13
....	1377	1342	35	1296	81
ter	982	961	21	958	24
chester ..	942	921	21	919	23
....	1748	1728	20	1748	......
....	1304	1288	16	1302	2
htsville .	63	62	1	63	......
....	1069	1053	16	1069	......
kinsville ..	65	64	1	65	......
y	36	36	......	36	......
....	1409	1390	19	1397	12
....	2086	2066	20	2045	41
onville ..	310	308	2	309	1

Counties.	Total.	Nativity. Native.	Nativity. Foreign.	Race. White.	Race. Colored.
Adams—Cont'd.					
Tiffin	1858	1752	106	1848	10
West Union ..	486	457	29	481	5
Wayne	1169	1133	36	1062	107
Winchester	1475	1442	33	1403	72
Winchester ..	416	399	17	381	35
ALLEN.					
Amanda	1376	1338	38	1375	1
Auglaize	1696	1679	17	1696	......
Bath	1255	1197	58	1254	1
German	1462	1425	37	1458	4
Allentown	90	90	......	90	......
Elida	533	522	11	529	4
Jackson	1801	1733	68	1801	......
Lafayette	337	316	21	337	......
Marion	2920	2452	468	2917	3
Delphos	1027	768	259	1024	3
Monroe	1739	1681	58	1739	......

TABLE IX.—*Population of Minor Civil Divisions, &c.—OHIO—Continued.*

Counties.	Total.	Nativity. Native.	Nativity. Foreign.	Race. White.	Race. Colored.
ALLEN—Cont'd.					
Ottawa	4662	3993	669	4475	187
Lima	4500	3832	668	4313	187
Perry	1235	1209	26	1235	......
Richland	2139	1850	289	2138	1
Bluffton	489	448	41	488	1
Shawnee	1169	1136	33	1153	16
Spencer	1153	1035	118	1153	......
Spencerville	364	343	21	364	......
Sugar Creek	1016	829	187	1016	......
ASHLAND.					
Clear Creek	1198	1089	109	1198	......
Savannah	394	357	37	394	......
Green	1818	1773	45	1815	3
Hanover	1832	1623	209	1832	......
Loudonville	811	703	108	811	......
Jackson	1409	1379	30	1409	......
Lake	701	627	74	701	......
Mifflin	781	760	21	781	......
Milton	1240	1189	51	1240	......
Mohican	1561	1533	28	1561	......
Jeromeville	328	322	6	328	......
Montgomery	4029	3777	252	4018	11
Ashland	2601	2386	215	2590	11
Orange	1485	1428	57	1485	......
Orange	271	243	28	271	......
Perry	1452	1418	34	1452	......
Ruggles	758	697	61	757	1
Sullivan	825	782	43	824	1
Troy	757	706	51	757	......
Vermillion	2087	1937	150	2077	10
Haysville	576	540	36	566	10
ASHTABULA.					
Andover	921	889	32	921	......
Ashtabula	3394	2867	527	3374	20
Ashtabula	1999	1638	361	1984	15
Austinburg	1111	1037	74	1091	20
Cherry Valley	726	710	16	723	3
Colebrook	800	749	51	800	......
Conneaut	3010	2776	234	2992	a17
Conneaut	1163	1033	130	1149	14
Denmark	544	524	20	544	......
Dorset	372	356	16	371	1
Geneva	2298	2146	152	2290	8
Geneva	1090	992	98	1088	2
Harpersfield	1120	1046	74	1119	1
Hartsgrove	799	760	39	799	......
Jefferson	1712	1584	128	1670	42
Jefferson	869	822	47	835	34
Kingsville	1758	1658	100	1751	7
Lenox	752	730	22	746	6
Monroe	1419	1347	72	1417	2
Morgan	1083	1021	62	1071	12
Rock Creek	491	461	30	488	3
New Lyme	708	671	37	708	......
Orwell	936	843	93	927	9
Pierpont	990	963	27	988	2
Plymouth	657	614	43	657	......
Richmond	883	842	41	883	......
Rome	669	631	38	669	......
Saybrook	1421	1295	126	1420	1
Sheffield	770	740	30	770	......
Trumbull	1084	1000	84	1084	......
Wayne	817	772	45	817	......
Williamsfield	892	882	10	892	......
Windsor	871	847	24	871	......
ATHENS.					
Alexander	1511	1502	9	1506	5

Counties.	Total.	Nativity. Native.	Nativity. Foreign.	Race. White.	Race. Colored.
ATHENS—Cont'd.					
Ames	1220	1220	9	1196	24
Amesville	162	162	......	161	1
Athens	3277	3063	214	3031	246
Athens	1696	1577	119	1553	143
Bern	1014	1007	7	990	24
Canaan	1543	1461	82	1543	......
Carthage	1272	1231	41	1272	......
Dover	1697	1648	49	1689	8
Chauncy	201	201	......	200	1
Milfield	94	92	2	94	......
Salina	90	89	1	90	......
Slabby	63	63	......	63	......
Lee	1146	1133	13	888	258
Albany	480	468	12	300	180
Lodi	1551	1528	23	1551	......
Rome	1972	1897	75	1861	111
Trimble	1379	1365	14	1373	6
Trimble	81	81	......	81	......
Troy	1830	1809	21	1815	15
Coolville	334	324	10	334	......
Waterloo	1695	1587	108	1663	32
Marshfield	240	237	3	240	......
York	2652	2465	187	2618	34
Nelsonville	1080	981	99	1067	13
AUGLAIZE.					
Clay	1095	1018	77	1095	......
Duchouquet	3959	3360	599	3945	14
Criderville	167	163	4	167	......
Wapakoneta	2150	1732	418	2136	14
German	1750	1196	554	1749	1
New Bremen	528	337	191	528	......
Ober-Bremen	423	296	127	422	1
Goshen	524	515	9	524	......
Jackson	1502	976	526	1501	1
Minster	868	564	304	867	1
Logan	900	829	71	900	......
Moulton	1252	1101	151	1239	a12
Noble	1159	968	191	1152	7
Pusheta	1290	1016	274	1290	......
Salem	877	772	105	877	......
Kossuth	112	90	22	112	......
St. Mary's	2420	1988	432	2405	15
St. Mary's	1370	1104	266	1358	12
Union	1462	1448	14	1462	......
Washington	840	671	169	840	......
Wayne	1011	1002	9	1000	11
BELMONT.					
Colerain	1308	1280	28	1232	76
Flushing	1484	1479	5	1352	132
Flushing	206	206	......	195	11
Goshen	2163	2086	77	2103	60
Belmont	287	273	14	265	22
Fairmount	125	112	13	125	......
Kirkwood	1792	1768	24	1791	1
Sewelsville	84	79	5	84	......
Mead	1850	1790	60	1849	1
Pease	5211	4688	523	5008	203
Bridgeport	1178	1076	102	1076	102
Martinsville	1835	1626	209	1792	43
Pultney	6319	5212	1107	6171	148
Bellaire	4033	3165	868	3917	116
West Wheeling	407	373	34	405	2
Richland	4170	3873	297	4025	a144
St. Clairsville	1056	983	73	978	78
Smith	1777	1721	56	1777	......
Demos	167	164	3	167	......
Jacobsburgh	89	85	4	89	......

(a) Also 1 Indian.

TABLE IX.—*Population of Minor Civil Divisions, &c.*—OHIO—Continued.

...ties.	Total.	Nativity: Native.	Nativity: Foreign.	Race: White.	Race: Colored.
—Cont'd.					
....	2042	1967	75	1895	147
...n	91	91	......	91	......
...set	197	194	3	193	4
...erance- ...	120	98	22	120	......
....	1684	1650	34	1667	17
...stown...	423	404	19	423	......
....	4099	3954	145	3776	323
...sville...	2063	1985	78	1921	142
...Olivet.	84	82	2	84	......
...on	1367	1334	33	1355	12
....	1700	1680	20	1675	25
....	1240	1221	19	1222	18
...herds- ...n	44	40	4	44	......
...town ...	156	153	3	156	......
....	1508	1397	111	1508	......
...ry	58	58	......	58	......
...hatan ...t	201	180	21	201	......
...rsville ..	73	60	13	73	......
...rx.					
....	1251	1228	23	1103	148
...ir	204	198	6	168	36
....	1691	1678	13	1683	8
...urg.....	201	197	4	201	......
...rsville ..	151	149	2	151	......
....	1166	1096	70	1011	155
...sle	140	139	1	140	......
....	1225	1092	133	1195	30
...im a ...	117	90	27	117	......
....	1490	1445	45	1480	10
...n	31	31	......	31	......
...bush	42	42	......	42	......
...n	3020	2869	151	2842	178
...een	871	808	63	774	97
....	995	941	54	971	24
...le	87	83	4	87	......
....	1267	1238	29	1182	85
...lville...	359	346	13	358	1
....	2817	2631	186	2674	143
...nsport ..	530	487	43	530	......
....	3016	2444	572	3012	4
...eville ..	397	301	96	397	......
....	1314	1286	28	1313	1
....	2605	2455	150	2397	208
...town ..	1037	956	81	965	72
....	1070	1057	13	976	94
...Hope	145	144	1	145	......
....	1394	1360	34	1327	67
....	5399	4793	606	4505	894
...na	104	81	23	101	3
....	2323	2062	261	1874	449
...on	1082	1018	64	1064	18
...ia	164	163	1	164	......
...ER.					
...t)	2431	1969	462	2403	28
...r's Cor-	127	111	16	127	......
...n	11081	8019	3062	10844	b236
....	1460	1262	198	1432	28
....	5242	4320	922	5177	65
...da	226	188	38	226	......
...town ..	3046	2476	570	2997	49
...e	324	268	56	323	1

Counties.	Total.	Nativity: Native.	Nativity: Foreign.	Race: White.	Race: Colored.
BUTLER—Cont'd.					
Liberty	1443	1347	96	1443	......
Bethany	98	96	2	98	......
Madison	2450	2084	366	2430	20
Madison	158	142	16	158	......
Miltonville ...	179	169	10	178	1
Trenton	340	230	110	340	......
Milford	1828	1589	239	1816	12
Collinsville ...	140	112	28	140	......
Darrtown	258	213	45	257	1
Somerville	389	348	41	389	......
Morgan	1807	1638	169	1807	......
Oxford	3959	3466	493	3461	c496
Oxford	1738	1498	240	1452	b285
Riley	1612	1492	120	1606	6
Ross	1705	1495	210	1670	35
St. Clair	1187	1009	178	1167	20
Union	2013	1780	233	2013	......
Westchester ..	257	232	25	257	......
Wayne	1694	1532	162	1652	42
Jacksonburgh	127	124	3	127	......
Seven-Mile ...	229	197	32	229	......
CARROLL.					
Augusta	1015	972	43	1011	4
Brown	2022	1839	183	2012	10
Malvern	269	250	19	269	......
Minerva	210	204	6	210	......
Centre	1227	1179	48	1215	12
Carrollton	813	775	38	807	6
East	827	762	65	811	16
Fox	1119	1015	104	1119	......
Harrison	1024	977	47	1024	......
Lee	901	863	38	898	3
Louden	831	808	23	831	......
Monroe	931	917	14	931	......
Orange	1207	1169	38	1195	12
Perry	932	906	26	931	1
Rose	1106	1006	100	1106	......
Union	609	573	36	609	......
Washington	740	720	20	740	......
CHAMPAIGN.					
Adams	1238	1204	34	1204	34
Concord	1035	1027	8	1009	26
Goshen	1965	1870	95	1860	105
Mechanicsb'rg	940	873	67	887	53
Harrison	944	917	27	938	6
Spring Hills ..	172	167	5	172	......
Jackson	1831	1775	56	1825	6
Johnson	2297	2242	55	2284	13
Mad River	1803	1758	45	1803	......
Rush	1789	1696	93	1723	66
Lewisburg	733	701	32	697	36
Salem	1854	1730	124	1789	65
Kennard	70	59	11	70	......
Union	1600	1570	30	1536	64
Urbana (d)	1827	1664	163	1559	268
Urbana	4276	3632	644	3867	409
Wayne	1729	1639	90	1681	48
CLARK.					
Bethel	3086	2924	162	3068	18
German	1918	1824	94	1906	12
Fremont	218	202	16	218	......
Noblesville ...	60	57	3	60	......
Greene	1464	1396	68	1308	156

...) Exclusive of city of Hamilton.
...) Also 1 Indian.

(c) Also 2 Indians.
(d) Exclusive of city of Urbana.

9 0 0

TABLE IX.—*Population of Minor Civil Divisions, &c.—OHIO*—Continued.

Counties.	Total.	Nativity. Native.	Nativity. Foreign.	Race. White.	Race. Colored.
CLARK—Cont'd.					
Harmony	1821	1656	165	1789	32
Plattsburg	87	80	7	87	......
Vienna	239	238	1	239	......
Madison	1965	1742	223	1806	159
South Charleston	818	741	77	764	51
Mad River	1873	1705	168	1754	119
Moorefield	1268	1187	81	1204	64
Pike	1582	1531	51	1581	1
Dialton	61	59	2	61	......
North Hampton	205	192	13	205	......
Pleasant	1553	1509	44	1481	72
Catawba	318	316	2	300	18
Springfield (a)	2888	2557	331	2692	196
Springfield	12652	10483	2169	11425	1227
CLERMONT.					
Batavia	3334	3160	174	3239	95
Batavia	827	786	41	767	60
Franklin	3298	3158	140	3018	280
Chilo	160	157	3	160	......
Felicity	955	919	36	807	148
Rural	119	117	2	119	......
Utopia	80	70	10	80	......
Goshen	1876	1735	141	1867	9
Goshen	274	263	11	274	......
Jackson	1658	1608	50	1640	18
Miami	3491	3055	436	3326	165
Milford	620	492	128	610	10
Monroe	2088	1974	114	2052	36
Laurel	126	126	......	118	8
Point Pleasant	137	126	11	131	6
Ohio	3381	3031	350	2666	b714
New Richmond	2516	2249	267	1886	630
Pierce	1773	1628	145	1751	22
Stone Lick	1880	1643	237	1879	1
Owensville	377	317	60	377	......
Tate	2678	2592	86	2584	94
Bethel	634	619	15	610	24
Union	1920	1768	152	1917	3
Mount Carmel	192	172	20	192	......
Withamsville	254	248	6	254	......
Washington	2818	2645	173	2722	96
Moscow	443	406	37	437	6
Neville	422	400	22	414	8
Point Isabel	160	158	2	160	......
Wayne	1690	1657	33	1690	......
Edenton	86	82	4	86	......
Georgetown	65	65	......	65	......
Newtonsville	120	117	3	120	......
Woodville	72	72	......	72	......
Williamsburg	2383	2327	56	2288	95
Williamsburg	773	754	19	732	41
CLINTON.					
Adams	883	860	23	802	81
Chester	1173	1150	23	1106	67
New Burlington, pt. of (c)	184	181	3	184	......
Clarke	1877	1810	67	1759	118
Martinsville	261	261	......	231	30
Green	2492	2451	41	2452	40
New Vienna	573	554	19	562	11
Jefferson	1445	1391	54	1432	13
Westboro	237	229	8	237	......
Liberty	1184	1166	18	1120	64
Port William	184	179	5	175	9
CLINTON—Cont'd.					
Marion	1592	1548	44	1591	1
Blanchester	513	485	28	512	1
Richland	1854	1781	73	1819	35
Union	4227	4065	162	3617	610
Wilmington	2023	1919	104	1580	443
Verona	1513	1455	58	1483	30
Clarksville	389	369	20	384	5
Washington	1250	1239	11	1250	......
Cuba	76	73	3	76	......
Morrisville	39	37	2	39	......
Wayne	1267	1227	40	1194	73
Wilson	1157	1089	68	1144	13
Bloomington	119	118	1	119	......
COLUMBIANA.					
Butler	1558	1493	65	1543	15
Damascus	94	89	5	86	8
Center	2895	2672	223	2881	14
New Lisbon	1569	1445	124	1565	4
Elk Run	1335	1271	64	1335	......
Fairfield	2652	2517	135	2642	10
Columbiana	870	822	48	860	10
Franklin	866	718	148	866	......
Hanover	2310	2163	147	2290	20
Dungamon	129	......	......	......	......
Hanover	481	456	25	465	16
Knox	2151	1936	215	2138	13
North Georgetown	173	......	......	......	......
Winchester (d)	235	......	......	......	......
Liverpool	2907	2379	528	2876	31
East Liverpool	2105	1643	462	2103	2
Madison	1202	1138	64	1201	1
Middleton	1327	1306	21	1327	......
Perry	4388	4068	320	4091	297
Salem	3700	3420	280	3425	275
Salem	3199	2510	689	3188	11
Leetonia	1200	801	399	1195	5
Washingtonville	517	348	169	517	......
St. Clair	1156	1131	25	1143	13
Unity	2286	2050	236	2286	......
Washington	2228	1769	459	2209	19
Salineville	1429	1090	339	1426	3
Wayne	766	719	47	766	......
West	1985	1922	63	1978	7
Bayard	89	87	2	89	......
Moultrie	19	......	......	......	......
New Chambersburg	131	......	......	......	......
Yellow Creek	3088	2752	336	3054	34
Wellsville	2313	2044	269	2290	23
COSHOCTON.					
Adams	1113	1019	94	1113	......
Bedford	918	899	19	918	......
West Bedford	152	150	2	152	......
Bethlehem	850	807	43	838	12
Clarke	867	806	61	867	......
Crawford	1245	1026	219	1245	......
Franklin	972	875	97	971	1
Jackson	1767	1624	143	1766	1
Jefferson	1059	932	127	1059	......
Keene	787	733	54	787	......
Lafayette	920	878	42	920	......
Linton	1600	1479	121	1598	2
Millcreek	586	554	32	586	......
Monroe	832	766	66	832	......

(a) Exclusive of city of Springfield.
(b) Also 1 Indian.
(c) See note (d,) Greene County. Total, 227; native, 224; foreign, 3; white, 227.
(d) Or Homeworth.

…E IX.—*Population of Minor Civil Divisions, &c.—OHIO*—Continued.

	Total.	Nativity: Native.	Nativity: Foreign.	Race: White.	Race: Colored.
on.					
....	1005	976	29	1005	......
....	1110	1067	73	1140	......
....	932	921	11	932	......
l....	80	78	2	80	......
....	773	755	18	773	......
sle	175	171	4	175	......
....	804	735	69	804	......
....	2725	2356	369	2708	17
....	1754	1535	219	1738	16
....	1014	947	67	1014	......
....	768	754	14	768	......
....	923	859	64	923	......
....	910	805	105	910	......
rg..	63	48	15	63	......
....	4184	3553	631	4150	34
....	3066	2519	547	3032	34
....	1247	980	267	1247	......
..	1281	996	285	1281	......
ing.					
....	273	186	87	273	......
....	370	346	24	365	5
....	1572	1393	179	1572	......
....	4021	3312	709	3981	a39
....	2279	1892	387	2240	a38
....	1597	1469	128	1597	......
....	253	232	21	253	......
....	1140	986	154	1140	......
....	4369	3527	842	4347	22
....	3523	2814	709	3501	22
....	665	632	33	665	......
....	566	530	36	566	......
....	1156	1043	113	1156	......
....	988	790	198	988	......
....	70	65	5	70	......
....	1190	1052	138	1189	1
ies.					
....	52	46	6	52	......
....	1788	1381	407	1776	12
....	828	596	232	825	3
....	1007	867	140	1001	6
....	3712	2260	1452	3702	10
...	648	526	122	644	4
....	1321	1108	213	1319	2
lls	1016	864	152	1015	1
....	92829	54011	38818	91535	a1293
....	1445	1016	429	1443	2
l....	5050	3684	1366	4982	68
....	2188	1585	603	2188	......
...	1761	1160	601	1735	26
....	892	788	104	892	......
....	3662	2302	1360	3659	3
....	1628	1101	527	1625	3
....	6227	3694	2533	6221	6
....	1570	1196	374	1566	4
....	383	265	118	380	3
....	812	632	180	812	......
....	1432	953	479	1432	......
....	2001	1409	592	1989	12
...	1089	830	259	1088	1
....	899	769	130	899	......
....	896	697	199	896	......
....	1429	969	460	1429	......
....	2201	2106	95	2199	2

Counties.	Total.	Nativity: Native.	Nativity: Foreign.	Race: White.	Race: Colored.
DARKE—Cont'd.					
Bradford	243	220	23	243	......
Gettysburg ...	228	211	17	226	2
Allen	781	745	36	781	......
Brown	1239	1157	82	1239	......
Dallas	221	203	18	221	......
Butler	1524	1491	33	1524	......
Castine	177	169	8	177	......
Franklin	1366	1318	48	1366	......
German	1743	1718	25	1339	404
Palestine	264	255	9	264	......
Tampico	67	65	2	24	43
Greenville	5688	5069	619	5637	51
Cole Town. ..	86	85	1	86	......
Greenville ...	2520	2161	359	2497	23
Pikeville	356	304	52	355	1
Harrison	2007	1947	60	2007	......
Hollansburg ..	239	239	......	239	......
New Madison .	452	408	44	452	......
Jackson	2088	1953	135	2088	......
Union City ...	792	686	106	792	......
Mississinawa	798	757	41	798	......
Monroe	1226	1138	88	1226	......
Neave	1093	1072	21	1093	......
Jefferson	107	99	8	107	......
Sampson	346	346	......	346	......
Patterson	978	857	121	978	......
Richland	1105	1066	39	1105	......
Twin	1998	1931	67	1998	......
Arcanum	450	443	7	450	......
Gordon	87	82	5	87	......
Ithaca	150	146	4	150	......
Van Buren	1212	1189	23	1198	11
Wabash	824	797	27	819	5
Washington	1537	1498	39	1471	63
Hillgrove ...	117	104	13	117	......
Wayne	1983	1736	247	1961	22
York	797	762	35	797	......
DEFIANCE.					
Adams	1220	884	336	1220	......
Defiance	3615	2812	803	3568	47
Defiance	2750	2072	678	2709	41
Delaware	1160	1012	148	1160	......
Farmer	1184	1156	28	1184	......
Hicksville	1287	1247	40	1287	......
Highland	946	837	109	898	48
Mark	595	547	48	595	......
Milford	1555	1448	107	1546	9
Noble	867	693	174	867	......
Brunersburg ..	185	150	35	185	......
Richland	1194	1014	180	1187	7
Tiffin	1080	974	106	1080	......
Evansport	191	188	3	191	......
Washington	1016	898	118	1016	......
DELAWARE.					
Berkshire	1336	1322	14	1330	6
Sunbury	236	230	6	235	1
Berlin	1330	1266	64	1325	5
Brown	1108	1046	62	1105	3
Eden	191	190	1	191	......
Concord	1092	1053	39	1062	30
Delaware	6861	5851	1010	6472	389
Delaware ...	5641	4739	902	5275	366
Genoa	1050	1012	38	1046	4
Harlem	1149	1141	8	1143	6
Kingston	587	585	2	587	......
Liberty	1395	1353	42	1392	3
Marlboro	562	521	41	562	......
Orange	1266	1217	49	1233	33

(*a*) Also 1 Indian.

TABLE IX.—*Population of Minor Civil Divisions, &c.*—OHIO—Continued.

Counties.	Total.	Nativity. Native.	Nativity. Foreign.	Race. White.	Race. Colored.
DELAWARE—Con.					
Oxford	1250	1185	65	1218	32
Ashley	454	428	26	434	20
Porter	819	786	33	819	......
Radnor	1255	1057	198	1221	34
Scioto	1542	1514	28	1535	7
Thompson	866	857	9	866	......
Trenton	907	899	8	902	5
Troy	800	761	39	800	......
ERIE.					
Berlin	1741	1601	140	1738	3
Florence	1341	1212	129	1336	5
Groton	910	740	170	907	3
Huron	1483	1221	262	1481	2
Huron	697	583	114	696	1
Kelley's Island	838	532	306	838	......
Margaretta	1622	1307	315	1565	57
Milan	2210	1900	310	2192	18
Milan	774	654	120	768	6
Oxford	1238	949	289	1231	7
Perkins	1291	977	314	1242	49
Portland (a)	681	447	234	654	27
Sandusky	13000	8396	4604	12831	b168
Vermillion	1833	1504	329	1830	3
Vermillion	721	571	150	721	......
FAIRFIELD.					
Amanda	1547	1502	45	1544	3
New Strasburg	44	44	......	44	......
Royalton	158	157	1	158	......
Berne	3056	2734	322	3019	37
East Lancaster	566	485	81	541	25
Sugar Grove	254	242	12	254	......
Bloom	2071	1956	115	2071	......
Greencastle	59	55	4	59	......
Jefferson	76	68	8	76	......
Lithopolis	394	374	20	394	......
Clear Creek	1743	1731	12	1743	......
Oakland	152	149	3	152	......
Stoutsville	160	160	......	160	......
Greenfield	1944	1841	103	1932	12
Carroll	187	170	17	187	......
Dumontville	10	9	1	10	......
Gesellsville	58	58	......	58	......
Havensport	83	82	1	83	......
Hocking (c)	2005	1839	166	1974	31
Lancaster	4725	4005	720	4510	215
Liberty	3000	2856	144	3000	......
Baltimore	489	471	18	489	......
Basil	220	197	23	220	......
Madison	1292	1242	50	1287	5
Pleasant	2327	2216	111	2318	9
Richland	1517	1497	20	1517	......
East Rushville	221	217	4	221	......
West Rushville	185	181	4	185	......
Rush Creek	1752	1714	38	1752	......
Bremen	265	258	7	265	......
Violet	2087	2015	72	2085	2
Lockville	131	113	18	131	......
Pickerington	195	195	......	194	1
Waterloo	85	84	1	85	......
Walnut	2072	2042	30	2072	......
Millersport	149	148	1	149	......
New Salem	177	176	1	177	......
FAYETTE.					
Concord	981	959	22	981	......
Greene	879	865	14	870	9
FAYETTE—Cont'd.					
Jasper	1992	1952	40	1868	124
Jefferson	2532	2435	97	2442	90
Jeffersonville	212	196	16	210	2
Madison	1300	1282	18	1280	20
Waterloo	120	116	4	120	......
Marion	743	727	16	695	48
Paint	1742	1703	39	1571	b170
Bloomingburg	312	311	1	276	36
Perry	1194	1167	27	1057	137
Union	4471	4235	236	4079	392
Washington	2117	1945	172	1864	253
Wayne	1336	1297	39	1252	84
Good Hope	118	118	......	104	14
FRANKLIN.					
Blendon	1771	1701	70	1726	45
Westerville	741	721	20	711	30
Brown	819	741	78	809	10
Clinton	1800	1507	293	1725	75
Columbus	31274	23663	7611	29427	1847
Franklin	2629	2255	374	2564	65
Franklinton	690	568	122	690	......
Hamilton	1827	1645	182	1786	41
Lockbourne	281	254	27	281	......
Shadeville	124	117	7	123	1
Jackson	1923	1748	175	1900	23
Grove City	143	123	20	143	......
Jefferson	1405	1303	102	1394	11
Madison	3440	3266	174	3434	6
Groveport	627	590	37	625	2
Winchester	633	601	32	633	......
Mifflin	1562	1416	146	1512	50
Montgomery (d)	2470	1937	533	2289	181
Piqua	2364	1859	505	2183	181
Norwich	1632	1507	125	1567	65
Hilliard	282	267	15	276	6
Perry	1297	1239	58	1227	70
Plain	1293	1273	20	1293	......
Pleasant	1833	1718	115	1801	32
Georgiesville	22	22	......	18	4
Harrisburg	153	141	12	153	......
Prairie	1364	1213	151	1316	48
Sharon	1480	1415	65	1388	92
Truro	1866	1691	175	1793	73
Reynoldsburg	457	440	17	450	7
Washington	1334	1274	60	1300	34
FULTON.					
Amboy	1089	953	136	1089	......
Chesterfield	926	895	31	922	4
Clinton	3235	2948	287	3227	8
Wauseon	1474	1307	167	1466	8
Dover	930	883	47	929	1
Franklin	999	835	164	998	1
Fulton	1328	1223	105	1328	......
German	2479	1797	682	2478	1
Archbold	373	247	126	372	1
Gorham	1655	1611	44	1655	......
Pike	878	831	47	876	2
Royalton	871	813	58	869	2
Swan Creek	1100	1022	78	1099	1
York	2299	2135	164	2296	3
Delta	753	644	100	750	3
GALLIA.					
Addison	1340	1329	11	1133	207
Cheshire	1895	1870	25	1712	183
Cheshire	276	273	3	264	12

(a) Exclusive of city of Sandusky.
(b) Also 1 Indian.
(c) Exclusive of city of Lancaster.
(d) Exclusive of city of Columbus.

'ABLE IX.—*Population of Minor Civil Divisions, &c.—OHIO*—Continued.

ies.	Total.	Nativity. Native.	Nativity. Foreign.	Race. White.	Race. Colored.
'ont'd.					
....	1400	1391	9	1399	1
)	868	820	48	626	242
....	3711	3456	255	2965	746
....	1577	1503	74	1333	244
....	1386	1243	143	1324	62
....	1279	1273	6	1279	......
....	1329	1304	25	1329	......
1	1609	1575	34	1461	148
on	191	189	2	175	16
....	137	135	2	136	1
....	1403	1393	10	1256	147
....	978	965	13	978	......
....	1514	1319	195	1478	36
....	1700	1511	189	1389	311
....	1824	1788	36	1350	474
....	1732	1649	83	1731	1
A.					
....	783	743	40	782	1
....	660	624	36	660	......
....	1004	983	21	1004	......
....	1772	1640	132	1769	3
1	885	789	96	884	1
....	727	671	56	725	2
....	909	866	43	908	1
....	767	735	32	766	1
....	824	809	15	821	3
....	732	716	16	732	......
....	705	682	23	705	......
....	761	722	39	760	1
....	861	833	28	860	1
....	953	931	22	948	5
....	805	735	70	804	1
....	1095	975	120	1095	......
....	832	814	18	830	2
E.					
....	2684	2528	156	2657	27
l......	397	381	16	397	......
....	639	577	62	629	10
k	2289	2179	110	2265	24
ck....	1114	1104	10	1072	42
....	2361	2240	121	1964	b373
lle	753	693	60	713	c34
....	1277	1248	29	1246	31
ille ..	193	191	2	183	10
....	2784	2594	190	2399	385
....	253	233	20	248	5
prings	1435	1326	109	1201	234
....	1084	1071	13	904	180
....	1076	1061	15	943	133
......	1701	1660	41	1544	157
wn	532	520	12	468	64
s	1555	1517	38	1485	70
rlings					
t of(d)	43	43	......	43	......
Valley.	290	266	24	290	......
....	1482	1438	44	1467	15
ok	369	343	26	369	......
....	2254	2154	100	1566	688

Counties.	Total.	Nativity. Native.	Nativity. Foreign.	Race. White.	Race. Colored.
GREENE—Cont'd.					
Xenia	6377	5686	691	4687	1690
GUERNSEY.					
Adams	762	732	30	762	......
Cambridge	3624	3389	235	3476	148
Cambridge ...	2193	2071	122	2060	133
Centre...........	1016	926	90	989	27
Jackson	867	848	19	845	22
Byesville	25	25	......	25	......
Jefferson	904	888	16	904	......
Knox............	810	758	52	808	2
Liberty...........	1163	1132	31	1163	......
Liberty.......	169	166	3	169	......
Salem	93	91	2	93	......
Londonderry	1313	1276	37	1313	......
Londonderry .	69	67	2	69	......
Madison	1170	1151	19	1169	1
Antrim.......	160	159	1	160	......
Winchester ..	179	174	5	178	1
Millwood	1524	1491	33	1523	1
Millwood	367	361	6	367	......
Salesville.....	172	168	4	172	......
Monroe...........	1018	985	33	1017	1
Birmingham..	210	203	7	209	1
Oxford	1709	1649	60	1689	20
Fairview	377	352	25	361	16
Middletown ..	166	159	7	166	......
Richland	1404	1385	19	1396	8
NewGottingen	33	31	2	33	......
Senecaville ...	376	374	2	370	6
Spencer	1359	1343	16	1328	31
Cumberland..	319	311	8	319	......
Valley...........	834	824	10	834	......
Hartford	98	98	......	98	......
Point Pleasant	138	136	2	138	......
Washington	712	698	14	712	......
Westland.........	889	856	33	889	......
Claysville	118	112	6	118	......
Wheeling	1090	1055	35	1089	1
Bridgeville ...	40	40	......	40	......
Wills.............	1670	1630	40	1587	83
Elizabethtown	44	44	......	44	......
Washington ..	554	544	10	498	56
HAMILTON.					
Anderson	4077	3513	564	4048	29
Cincinnati......	216239	136627	79612	210335	f5900
Addition of May 16, '70(g)	1446	977	469	1365	h80
Addition of May 16, '70 (i)	484	321	163	483	1
Addition of May 16, '70(j)	859	618	241	818	41
Addition of May 16, '70(k)	4602	2875	1727	4552	50
Addition of May 16, '70 (l)	4108	2747	1361	4025	83
Addition of May 16, '70(m)	2908	1884	1024	2821	87

sive of city of Gallipolis.
4 Indians.
Indians.
ote (c.) Clinton County.
sive of city of Xenia.
Indians.
nded sections 2 and 8 of Mill Creek.
Indian.
f Riverside, in Delhi Township, and Delhi Township at large.
ns 21, 22, 27, 28, 33, and 34, Columbia and Columbia at large.
f Mill Creek west of Colerain pike, and south of section 35; also Mill Creek west of Cole-
large.
f Mill Creek north of Colerain pike and Mill Creek and Mill Creek at large.
f Mill Creek between Colerain pike, Mill Creek, and Carthage pike.

TABLE IX.—*Population of Minor Civil Divisions, &c.—OHIO*—Continued.

Counties.	Total.	Nativity. Native.	Nativity. Foreign.	Race. White.	Race. Colored.
HAMILTON—Con.					
Addition of May 16, '70 (a)	1546	1064	482	1459	87
Colerain	3689	2806	883	3662	27
Georgetown	172	144	28	172	......
Columbia	3184	2636	548	3102	82
Crosby	2514	2186	328	2473	41
Harrison	1417	1192	225	1400	17
New Baltimore	96	74	22	96	......
New Haven	161	154	7	161	......
Shaker or Whitewater	123	102	21	123	......
Delhi	2620	1841	779	2577	43
Green	4356	3334	1022	4258	98
Harrison	758	661	97	749	9
Miami	2105	1882	223	1907	198
Mill Creek	3291	2368	923	3091	200
Spencer	2543	2000	543	2508	35
Columbia	1105	912	193	1091	14
Springfield (b)	6548	5085	1463	5954	594
Glendale	1780	1330	450	1682	98
Hartwell	67	61	6	63	4
Springdale	382	354	28	355	27
Sycamore (b)	5460	4291	1169	5395	65
Lockland (b)	1299	1164	135	1008	291
Reading	1575	940	635	1575	......
Symmes	1377	1174	203	1340	37
Whitewater	1609	1467	142	1535	74
HANCOCK.					
Allen	969	933	36	969	......
Van Buren	157	146	11	157	......
Amanda	1469	1444	25	1469	......
Big Lick	1179	1118	61	1179	......
Blanchard	1304	1258	46	1304	......
Cass	759	708	51	759	......
Delaware	1280	1261	19	1218	62
Eagle	1330	1283	47	1330	......
Findlay	4073	3641	432	4018	55
Findlay	3315	2898	417	3261	54
Jackson	1209	1188	21	1209	......
Liberty	1011	991	20	1011	......
Madison	967	890	77	967	......
Marion	990	934	56	990	......
Orange	1167	1119	48	1167	......
Pleasant	1336	1287	49	1336	......
McComb	319	316	3	319	......
Portage	899	862	37	899	......
Union	1546	1485	61	1546	......
Van Buren	780	678	102	780	......
Washington	1579	1466	113	1579	......
Arcadia	288	282	6	288	......
HARDIN.					
Blanchard	1250	1189	61	1187	63
Buck	1259	1151	108	1186	73
Cessna	732	644	88	719	13
Dudley	1008	952	56	1002	6
Goshen	928	848	80	928	......
Hale	1254	1213	41	1240	14
Ridgeway	177	169	8	177	......
Jackson	1412	1308	104	1409	3
Liberty	2308	2239	69	2303	5
Lynn	457	426	31	457	......
Marion	671	645	26	671	......
McDonald	900	860	40	894	6
HARDIN—Cont'd.					
Pleasant	4002	3313	689	3935	67
Kenton	2616	2128	488	2547	69
Round Head	759	740	19	750	9
Round Head	117	115	2	117	......
Taylor Creek	891	823	68	884	7
Washington	883	764	119	875	8
HARRISON.					
Archer	726	712	14	724	2
Athens	1232	1216	16	1209	23
New Athens	354	347	7	335	19
Cadiz	2704	2605	99	2431	273
Cadiz	1435	1371	64	1196	239
Franklin	1153	1124	29	1138	15
Deersville	306	291	15	300	6
Freeport	1015	985	30	1015	......
German	1227	1188	39	1226	1
Greene	1547	1525	22	1535	12
Hopedale	359	353	6	357	2
Monroe	1012	961	51	1012	......
Moorefield	1117	1105	12	1117	......
Moorefield	289	284	5	289	......
North	1202	1158	44	1177	25
Nottingham	921	908	13	921	......
Rumley	1158	1137	21	1158	......
Short Creek	1799	1763	36	1703	96
Harrisville	258	244	14	258	......
Stock	771	751	20	733	38
Washington	1092	1080	12	1092	......
HENRY.					
Bartlow	126	107	19	122	4
Damascus	1179	1088	91	1179	......
Flat Rock	1184	925	259	1184	......
Freedom	812	625	187	812	......
Harrison	1295	1240	55	1295	......
Liberty	1766	1692	74	1766	......
Marion	513	430	83	513	......
Monroe	658	534	124	658	......
Napoleon	3334	2621	713	3327	7
Napoleon	2018	1703	315	2011	7
Pleasant	860	573	287	860	......
Richfield	396	369	27	396	......
Ridgeville	764	613	151	764	......
Washington	1141	1040	101	1141	......
HIGHLAND.					
Brush Creek	1601	1592	9	1554	47
Sinking Sp'ngs	200	195	5	199	1
Clay	1345	1258	87	1336	9
Buford	120	120	......	120	......
Concord (c)	1262	1236	26	1239	23
Sugar-Tree Ridge	88	85	3	85	3
Dodson	1710	1612	98	1705	5
Lynchburg	476	447	29	474	2
Fairfield	2565	2504	61	2544	21
Centerfield	128	127	1	128	......
East Monroe	163	163	......	162	1
Leesburg	508	480	28	462	46
New Lexing'n	242	231	11	236	6
Hamer	959	948	11	959	......
Danville	157	149	8	157	......
Jackson (c)	905	903	2	905	......
Belfast	72	72	......	72	......
Fairfax (c)	84	84	......	84	......

(a) Part of Mill Creek east of Carthage pike and south of the south line of sections 5 and 11: also remainder of that portion of Mill Creek being east of Carthage pike and Mill Creek, and north of south line of sections 5 and 11.

(b) Of Lockland: 456 in Springfield and 552 in Sycamore.

(c) Of Fairfax: 39 in Concord and 45 in Jackson.

LE IX.—*Population of Minor Civil Divisions, &c.*—OHIO—Continued.

	Total.	Nativity. Native.	Nativity. Foreign.	Race. White.	Race. Colored.
-Con.					
lon-					
.....	8	8	.....	8	.....
.....	5189	4817	372	4470	719
ugh .	2818	2515	303	2430	388
.....	3261	3090	171	2888	373
d	1712	1582	130	1525	187
.....	821	813	8	821	.....
.....	112	111	1	112	.....
.....	1107	1094	13	1091	16
ket..	143	140	3	143	.....
.....	2429	2394	35	2376	53
ton ..	111	106	5	111	.....
rsb'g	216	216	.....	216	.....
ough.	220	219	1	220	.....
.....	1471	1410	61	1260	211
.....	1029	987	42	1022	7
vn ...	117	115	2	117	.....
.....	1455	1447	8	1450	5
.....	972	947	25	971	1
e	78	77	1	78	.....
.....	1052	941	111	1052	.....
own	414	333	81	414	.....
lle ..	52	52	.....	52	.....
.					
.....	1448	1436	12	1448	.....
ville.	133	130	3	133	.....
.....	3760	3480	280	3714	46
.....	1827	1633	194	1800	27
.....	986	911	75	986	.....
.....	1513	1427	86	1511	2
.....	1343	1267	76	1343	.....
lle...	67	63	4	67	.....
.....	1561	1433	128	1561	.....
.....	1745	1698	47	1745	.....
sta..	56	52	4	56	.....
rry..	136	132	4	136	.....
.....	1179	1159	20	1179	.....
.....	1551	1527	24	1551	.....
.....	1305	1268	37	1211	94
.....	1534	1456	78	1534	.....
.....	50	50	.....	50	.....
.....	62	62	.....	62	.....
ount					
t ...	67	64	3	67	.....
.....	1007	920	87	1007	.....
.....	224	199	25	224	.....
.....	1408	1319	89	1407	1
.....	2857	2607	250	2856	1
rg ..	1457	1312	145	1456	1
.....	1121	1042	79	1121	.....
.....	116	110	6	116	.....
.....	964	870	94	964	.....
.....	1066	1002	64	1066	.....
.....	921	894	27	921	.....
.....	1212	970	242	1212	.....
rg..	260	170	90	260	.....
.....	1413	1338	75	1413	.....
lle ..	299	282	17	299	.....
...	1242	1057	185	1240	2
.....	1101	1076	25	1101	.....
.....	1259	1128	131	1259	.....
.....	99	90	9	99	.....
wn ..	150	135	15	150	.....
k...	1321	1175	146	1321	.....
.....	1285	1168	117	1285	.....
.....	208	202	6	208	.....

Counties.	Total.	Nativity. Native.	Nativity. Foreign.	Race. White.	Race. Colored.
HURON.					
Bronson	980	900	80	978	2
Clarksfield	1062	1028	34	1061	1
Fairfield	1332	1257	75	1318	14
Fitchville	795	753	42	785	10
Greenfield	954	868	86	954	.....
Greenwich	881	846	35	880	1
Hartland	953	900	53	952	1
Lyme	2380	1681	699	2375	5
Bellevue	1219	871	348	1214	5
New Haven	1221	1121	100	1221	.....
New London	1475	1386	89	1465	10
New London	678	633	45	677	1
Norwalk	5752	4777	975	5646	106
Norwalk	4498	3666	832	4406	92
Norwich	1172	1051	121	1171	1
Peru	1297	1003	294	1296	1
Richmond	880	823	57	880	.....
Ridgefield	2533	1929	604	2530	3
Monroeville	1344	1016	328	1344	.....
Ripley	1089	1038	51	1088	1
Sherman	1260	880	380	1257	3
Townsend	1300	1211	89	1290	10
Wakeman	1216	1100	116	1185	31
JACKSON.					
Bloomfield	1775	1661	114	1775	.....
Vega	65	61	4	65	.....
Pattensville	38	38	.....	38	.....
Winchester	89	87	2	89	.....
Franklin	1665	1619	46	1609	56
Hamilton	1108	1053	55	1088	20
Jackson	1532	1502	30	1325	207
Jefferson	3002	2547	455	3002	.....
Liberty	1747	1698	49	1550	197
Lick	3746	3370	376	3602	144
Jackson	2016	1764	252	1951	65
Madison	2174	1729	445	2134	40
Milton	2372	2273	99	2247	125
Berlin Cross Roads	233	219	14	220	13
Middleton	71	71	.....	71	.....
Scioto	1505	1419	86	1505	.....
Washington	1133	1094	39	1133	.....
JEFFERSON.					
Brush Creek	697	654	43	697	.....
Monroeville	82	81	1	82	.....
Cross Creek	1800	1690	110	1768	32
New Alexandria	167	163	4	164	3
Wintersville	113	110	3	113	.....
Island Creek	1626	1572	54	1622	4
Knox	1301	1243	58	1300	1
Knoxville	165	147	18	165	.....
Shanghai	76	73	3	76	.....
Somerset	77	75	2	77	.....
Mount Pleasant	1564	1534	30	1204	360
Mt. Pleasant	563	550	13	447	116
Ross	685	675	10	685	.....
Salem	1708	1634	74	1697	11
Annapolis	139	134	5	139	.....
East Springfield	170	161	9	170	.....
Richmond	405	383	22	404	1
Saline	1922	1379	543	1921	1
Hammondsv'e	504	379	125	503	1
Irondale	751	396	355	751	.....
Sloan's Station	470	454	22	462	8
Smithfield	1761	1735	26	1658	103

TABLE IX.—*Population of Minor Civil Divisions, &c.*—OHIO—Continued.

Counties.	Total.	Nativity.		Race.	
		Native.	Foreign.	White.	Colored.
JEFFERSON—Con.					
Smithfield	515	499	16	469	46
York	89	......	......	......	......
Springfield	826	779	47	826	......
Amsterdam	89	67	22	89	......
Steubenville (a)	2100	1670	430	2072	28
Steubenville	8107	6460	1647	7831	276
Warren	1637	1560	77	1609	28
Warrenton	241	232	9	241	......
Wayne	1564	1536	28	1452	112
Bloomfield	146	145	1	146	......
Wells	1414	1368	46	1373	41
La Grange	228	207	21	222	6
KNOX.					
Berlin	887	875	12	887	......
Brown	1242	1177	65	1242	......
Brownsville	160	158	2	160	......
Butler	701	671	30	701	......
Clay	940	932	8	940	......
Clinton (b)	984	915	69	984	......
College	926	825	101	923	(c)
Gambier	581	506	75	578	(c)
Harrison	687	685	2	686	1
Hillear	931	900	31	930	1
Howard	800	792	8	800	......
Jackson	818	815	3	818	......
Jefferson	1308	1202	106	1308	......
Greersville	73	61	12	73	......
Mount Holly	159	155	4	159	......
Liberty	959	921	38	959	......
Middlebury	929	917	12	929	......
Milford	1024	1022	2	1024	......
Miller	902	890	12	902	......
Monroe	1087	1059	28	1086	1
Morgan	645	631	14	645	......
Morris	860	841	19	850	10
Mount Vernon	4876	4327	549	4726	150
Pike	1301	1286	15	1301	......
Pleasant	851	810	41	851	......
Union	1017	980	37	1017	......
Danville	134	130	4	134	......
Millwood	122	120	2	122	......
Wayne	1658	1615	43	1635	23
Fredericktown	690	667	23	672	18
LAKE.					
Concord	797	760	37	792	5
Kirtland	1029	987	42	1029	......
Leroy	811	735	76	811	......
Madison	2913	2724	189	2896	17
Madison	757	682	75	749	8
Mentor	1666	1487	179	1664	2
Mentor	416	362	54	415	1
Painesville	4995	4233	762	4926	69
Painesville	3728	3171	557	3673	55
Perry	1208	1125	83	1207	1
Willoughby	2516	2212	304	2510	6
Willoughby	867	778	89	862	5
LAWRENCE.					
Aid	1476	1466	10	1467	9
Decatur	1761	1528	233	1727	34
Elizabeth	3357	2790	567	3323	34
Fayette	2082	2066	16	1667	d414
Hamilton	1108	985	123	1078	30
Ironton	5686	4604	1082	5380	306
LAWRENCE—Con.					
Lawrence	1245	1229	16	1212	33
Mason	1884	1867	17	1884	......
Perry	2215	2110	105	2183	32
Rome	2096	2071	25	1974	e116
Symmes	995	987	8	971	24
Union	1940	1928	12	1855	f73
Upper (g)	2146	1973	173	2078	68
Washington	1446	1281	165	1380	66
Windsor	1943	1913	30	1943	......
LICKING.					
Bennington	907	900	7	907	......
Appleton	56	55	1	56	......
Bowling Green	1042	1019	23	1042	......
Brownsville	384	371	13	384	......
Linnville	100	95	5	100	......
Burlington	1061	1026	35	1060	1
Homer	226	216	10	226	......
Eden	782	775	7	782	......
Etna	1224	1101	123	1222	2
Etna	258	245	13	257	1
Fallsburg	865	855	10	865	......
Franklin	847	835	12	847	......
Granville	2127	1911	216	2072	55
Granville	1109	1002	107	1080	29
Hanover	1165	1130	35	1165	......
Hanover	322	307	15	322	......
Harrison	1242	1202	40	1240	2
Kirkersville	295	288	7	294	1
Hartford	1917	1009	8	1017	......
Hartford	229	226	3	229	......
Hopewell	1009	997	12	1002	7
Gratiot, part of (h)	154	154	......	154	......
Jersey	1253	1225	28	1253	......
Jersey	101	97	4	101	......
Liberty	837	813	24	837	......
Licking	850	834	16	849	1
Jackson	438	428	10	437	1
Lima	1642	1579	63	1639	3
Columbia Centre	205	180	25	205	......
Pataskala	462	457	5	459	3
Madison	959	895	64	959	......
Mary Ann	804	772	32	804	......
McKean	990	956	34	990	......
Fredonia	99	99	......	99	......
Monroe	1119	1108	11	1119	......
Johnson	241	237	4	241	......
Newark (i)	919	790	129	919	......
Newark	6698	5413	1285	6543	155
Newton	1283	1244	39	1283	......
Chatham	156	152	4	156	......
St. Louisville	166	158	8	166	......
Vantallar	70	70	......	70	......
Perry	897	891	6	892	5
Elizabetht'wn	113	113	......	113	......
St. Albans	1110	1064	46	1108	2
Alexandria	303	297	6	302	1
Union	1855	1793	62	1854	1
Hebron	478	471	7	477	1
Luray	55	47	8	55	......
Washington	1252	1185	67	1243	9
Utica	384	361	23	383	1
LOGAN.					
Bloomfield	655	636	19	655	......

(a) Exclusive of city of Steubenville.
(b) Exclusive of city of Mount Vernon.
(c) Also 3 Indians.
(d) Also 1 Chinese.
(e) Also 6 Indians.
(f) Also 12 Indians.
(g) Exclusive of city of Ironton.
(h) See note (b.) Muskingum County. Total, 228. Native, 227; foreign, 1; white, 228.
(i) Exclusive of city of Newark.

TABLE IX.—*Population of Minor Civil Divisions, &c.*—*OHIO*—Continued.

…nties.	Total.	Nativity: Native.	Nativity: Foreign.	Race: White.	Race: Colored.
—Cont'd.					
Creek	1344	1333	11	1125	219
t Ridgway	100	92	8	88	12
n	994	956	38	979	15
n	1634	1588	46	1588	46
esfield	282	279	3	280	2
…	3733	3367	386	3496	237
efontaine	3182	2843	339	2944	238
…	1624	1537	87	1571	53
t Liberty	741	704	37	709	32
mr	1406	1365	41	1371	35
tsville	322	315	7	309	13
…	1768	1715	53	1762	6
Graff	624	587	37	620	4
ncy	320	317	3	320	……
…	1372	1349	23	1191	181
…	922	905	17	900	22
t	994	969	25	994	……
d	1401	1339	62	1357	44
o Centre	276	264	12	275	1
eek	2044	1964	80	1995	49
hsylvania	310	293	17	271	39
…	673	667	6	656	17
…	753	721	32	750	3
gton	812	804	8	798	14
…	879	847	32	878	1
RAIN.					
t	2482	1692	790	2482	……
…	1924	1308	616	1924	……
iver	838	618	220	822	16
n	508	483	25	508	……
elm	1461	1029	432	1458	3
…	858	764	94	854	4
…	1219	963	256	1219	……
ia	892	713	179	892	……
…	1052	842	210	1052	……
…	4076	3113	963	4007	69
ria	3038	2339	699	2976	62
…	960	810	150	951	9
ta	927	768	159	898	29
gton	834	790	44	832	2
ge	1309	1200	109	1306	(a).
l	749	726	23	739	10
d	980	851	129	913	67
lle	1477	1140	337	1472	5
er	691	648	43	691	……
…	4207	3832	375	3343	864
thm	2888	2691	197	2276	612
d	973	737	236	964	9
ton	1891	1724	167	1862	a19
llington	1281	1149	132	1263	a15
CAS.					
…	959	645	314	950	9
tan	1394	1092	302	1352	42
va	833	748	85	825	8
…	1863	1320	543	1841	b20
nce	863	741	122	863	……
d	822	670	152	822	……
…	653	519	134	653	……
ield	701	628	73	689	12
n	447	383	64	442	5
a	1400	1201	199	1366	34
o	31584	20485	11099	30972	612
gton (c)	1549	1166	383	1525	24
ille	1609	1344	265	1608	1
field	2945	1661	284	2936	9
umee City	1779	1459	320	1773	6

so 3 Indians.
so 2 Indians.
clusive of city of Toledo.

Counties.	Total.	Nativity: Native.	Nativity: Foreign.	Race: White.	Race: Colored.
MADISON.					
Canaan	729	695	34	724	5
Amity	106	105	1	106	……
Darby	988	900	88	965	21
Pleasant Val'y	467	415	52	465	2
Deer Creek	823	727	96	764	59
Lafayette	143	132	11	142	1
Fairfield	1210	1151	59	1199	11
California	112	110	2	112	……
Jefferson	1888	1717	171	1726	162
Jefferson	577	497	80	549	28
Monroe	463	413	50	441	22
Oak Run	456	422	34	394	62
Paint	955	855	100	937	18
Pike	394	373	21	380	14
Liverpool	67	66	1	67	……
Pleasant	1330	1302	28	1291	39
Mt. Sterling	389	377	12	382	7
Range	1367	1263	104	1325	42
Somerford	935	872	63	935	……
Tradersville	25	25	……	25	……
Stokes	986	892	94	973	13
Union	3109	2707	402	2874	235
London	2066	1737	329	1910	156
MAHONING.					
Austintown	1948	1485	463	1943	5
Beaver	1933	1820	113	1933	……
East Lewiston	105	97	8	105	……
Lima	160	156	4	160	……
Berlin	963	938	25	963	……
Boardman (d)	817	775	42	817	……
Canfield	1513	1392	121	1502	11
Canfield	640	597	43	635	5
Coitsville	1161	927	234	1160	1
Ellsworth	652	615	37	652	……
Goshen	1475	1437	38	1442	33
Damascoville	208	202	6	208	……
Green	1733	1606	127	1726	7
Green	146	131	15	146	……
New Albany	100	82	18	100	……
Washingtonville	232	197	35	232	……
Jackson	909	876	33	906	3
Milton	744	733	11	744	……
Poland (d)	2481	2141	340	2465	16
Lowellville	722	632	90	715	7
Poland (d)	453	436	17	452	1
Smith	1685	1526	159	1677	8
Beloit	80	80	……	80	……
East Alliance	288	203	85	288	……
North Benton	138	131	7	138	……
Springfield	2150	1981	169	2147	3
New Middletown	147	143	4	147	……
New Springfield	142	127	15	142	……
Petersburg	218	193	25	218	……
Youngstown (e)	2762	1682	1080	2724	38
Youngstown	8075	5258	2817	7943	132
MARION.					
Big Island	940	848	92	935	5
Bowling Green	903	880	23	903	……
Claridon	1483	1298	185	1481	2
Caledonia	419	370	49	419	……
Grand	403	381	22	403	……
Grand Prairie	370	351	19	370	……
Green Camp	999	869	130	985	14

(d) Of Poland: 53 in Boardman and 400 in Poland.
(e) Exclusive of city of Youngstown.

TABLE IX.—*Population of Minor Civil Divisions, &c.*—*OHIO*—Continued.

Counties.	Total.	NATIVITY.		RACE.	
		Native.	Foreign.	White.	Colored.
MARION—Cont'd.					
Marion	3486	2889	597	3467	19
Marion	2531	2063	468	2513	18
Montgomery	1451	1319	132	1445	6
Pleasant	1078	927	151	1055	23
Prospect	1280	1196	84	1266	14
Richland	1146	900	246	1146	......
Salt Rock	351	328	23	351	......
Scott	495	464	31	495	......
Tully	770	688	82	758	12
Waldo	1029	935	94	1027	2
Waldo	247	244	3	247	......
MEDINA.					
Brunswick	980	888	92	980	......
Chatham	980	947	33	971	9
Granger	987	929	58	987	......
Guilford	1809	1753	56	1800	9
Seville	597	582	15	589	8
Harrisville	1182	1115	67	1182	......
Hinckley	972	909	63	972	......
Homer	886	852	34	886	......
La Fayette	1109	1067	42	1103	6
Litchfield	860	813	47	860	......
Liverpool	1425	1014	411	1425	......
Medina (*a*)	1553	1399	154	1536	17
Medina (*a*)	1159	1063	96	1143	16
Montville (*a*)	1097	1041	56	1095	2
Sharon	1131	1067	64	1130	1
Spencer	929	906	23	929	......
Wadsworth	2283	2102	181	2277	6
Wadsworth	949	853	96	944	5
Westfield	1023	993	30	1023	......
York	886	764	122	886	......
MEIGS.					
Bedford	1645	1612	33	1636	9
Chester	1656	1527	129	1648	8
Chester	172	172	......	172	......
Columbia	1286	1276	10	1281	5
Lebanon	1823	1799	24	1803	20
Letart	1319	1286	33	1303	16
Antiquity	280	263	17	280	......
Olive	1863	1818	45	1858	5
Reedville	129	129	......	129	......
Orange	828	783	45	828	......
Pomeroy	5824	4173	1651	5370	454
Rutland	2471	2435	36	2223	248
Salem	1718	1686	32	1684	34
Salisbury (*b*)	4902	4486	416	4152	750
Middleport	2236	1994	242	1849	387
Scipio	1761	1741	20	1750	11
Harrisonville	160	156	4	160	......
Pageville	80	77	3	80	......
Sutton	4369	3558	811	4305	64
Minersville	1000	639	361	970	30
Racine	560	553	7	537	23
Syracuse	1273	932	341	1271	2
MERCER.					
Black Creek	1087	1035	52	1087	......
Butler	1301	1133	168	1143	158
Center	1255	1210	45	1255	......
Neptune	96	90	6	96	......
Dublin	1599	1575	24	1599	......
Mercer	73	73	......	73	......
Shane's Crossing	246	240	6	246	......
Franklin	831	760	71	800	31
MERCER—Cont'd.					
Gibson	1100	969	131	1100	......
Granville	1234	893	341	1083	151
Fort Henry	153	106	47	153	......
Hopewell	894	776	118	894	......
Jefferson	1557	1412	145	1554	3
Celina	859	769	90	856	3
Liberty	779	647	132	779	......
Marion	1876	1303	573	1777	99
Chickasaw	386	281	105	302	84
Kopel	305	212	93	305	......
St. John's	105	72	33	105	......
Recovery	1118	903	215	1117	1
Fort Recovery	89	87	2	89	......
Union	1475	1424	51	1474	1
Mendon	164	160	4	164	......
Washington	1148	999	149	1148	......
MIAMI.					
Bethel	1801	1764	37	1798	3
Brandt	240	238	2	240	......
Charleston	130	123	7	130	......
Brown	1639	1582	57	1639	......
Fletcher	306	292	14	306	......
Lena	144	143	1	144	......
Concord	4701	4389	312	4323	378
Troy	3005	2767	238	2667	338
Elizabeth	1236	1212	24	1235	1
Lost Creek	1367	1345	22	1367	......
Casstown	241	237	4	241	......
Monroe	2704	2508	196	2674	30
Tippecanoe City	1204	1059	145	1192	12
Newberry	3565	3359	206	3554	11
Bradford	166	152	14	164	2
Clayton	101	100	1	101	......
Covington	1010	892	118	1009	1
Newton	2241	2175	66	2187	54
Pleasant Hill	324	320	4	324	......
Piqua	5967	4840	1127	5716	251
Spring Creek	1606	1433	173	1490	116
Huntersville	233	158	75	233	......
Rossville	91	62	29	91	......
Staunton	1317	1249	68	1310	7
Union	3291	3198	93	3155	136
Milton	455	447	8	455	......
Washington (*c*)	1305	1177	128	1243	62
MONROE.					
Adams	1201	1153	48	1201	......
Cameron	145	129	16	145	......
Benton	987	902	85	987	......
Bethel	1284	1212	72	1266	18
Lebanon	124	119	5	124	......
Centre	2585	2318	267	2585	......
Woodsfield	753	656	97	753	......
Franklin	1418	1375	43	1354	64
Stafford	150	144	6	142	8
Green	1282	1175	107	1282	......
New Castle	99	95	4	99	......
Jackson	1354	1257	97	1354	......
Cochransville	112	112	......	112	......
Lee	1114	888	226	1114	......
Sardis	170	157	13	170	......
Malaga	1577	1346	231	1577	......
Jerusalem	91	91	......	91	......
Malaga	114	110	4	114	......
Miltonsburg	176	125	51	176	......
Ohio	1801	1428	373	1787	14
Baresville	359	314	45	359	......

(*a*) Of Medina: 865 in Medina and 294 in Montville.
(*b*) Exclusive of city of Pomeroy.
(*c*) Exclusive of city of Piqua.

TABLE IX.—*Population of Minor Civil Divisions, &c.—OHIO*—Continued.

Counties.	Total.	Nativity.		Race.	
		Native.	Foreign.	White.	Colored.
MONROE—Cont'd.					
Perry	1116	1083	33	1116	......
Antioch	165	164	1	165	......
Salem	2106	1866	240	2106	......
Clarington	728	643	85	728	......
Seneca	1242	1177	65	1242	......
Calais	126	122	4	126	......
Summit	970	795	175	970	......
Lewisville	124	103	21	124	......
Sunsbury	1428	1406	22	1428	......
Beallsville	324	318	6	324	......
Switzerland	1342	1091	251	1335	7
Washington	1720	1679	41	1720	......
Graysville	199	194	5	199	......
Wayne	1252	1174	78	1252	......
MONTGOMERY.					
Butler	2153	1960	193	2070	83
Chamb'rsburg	165	155	10	128	37
Little York	111	96	15	111	......
Vandalia	313	285	28	310	3
Clay	2541	2392	149	2541	......
Bachman	67	65	2	67	......
Dodson	47	32	15	47	......
Phillipsburg	187	172	15	187	......
South Arl'gton	124	122	2	124	......
West Baltim'e	69	57	12	69	......
Dayton	30473	23050	7423	29925	548
German	3197	3000	197	3128	69
Germantown	1440	1362	78	1436	4
Harrison (a)	2116	1811	305	2111	5
Jackson	2170	2096	71	2170	......
Farmersville	312	303	9	312	......
Jefferson	3350	2545	805	3316	34
Madison	2097	1856	241	2097	......
Amity	29	28	1	29	......
Post Town	37	35	2	37	......
Trotwood	42	38	4	42	......
Mad River	1867	1528	339	1855	12
Miami	4418	3903	515	4388	30
Alexandria	180	......	......	......	......
Carrollton	370	......	......	......	......
Miamisburg	1425	1242	183	1421	4
Perry	2029	1988	41	2020	9
Randolph	2077	1987	90	2077	......
Salem	312	308	4	312	......
Union	212	202	10	212	......
Van Buren	2600	2156	444	2587	13
Shakerstown	54	44	10	53	1
Washington	1758	1685	73	1752	6
Wayne	1160	1070	90	1160	......
MORGAN.					
Bloom	987	963	24	980	7
Eagleport	79	79	......	72	7
Bristol	1469	1448	21	1468	1
Centre	1353	1309	44	1353	......
Elizabeth	1325	1282	43	1325	......
Deerfield	981	952	29	975	6
Triadelphia	34	34	......	34	......
Homer	1690	1678	12	1678	12
Mountsville	33	33	......	33	......
Malta	1625	1609	16	1625	......
Malta	513	502	11	513	......
Manchester	712	704	8	712	......
Marion	2074	2067	7	1903	171
Chesterfield	354	352	2	354	......
Meigsville	1295	1228	67	1295	......
New Castle	57	54	3	57	......
MORGAN—Cont'd.					
Unionville	92	92	......	92	......
Morgan	2185	2097	88	2162	23
McConn'sville	1646	1575	71	1624	22
Penn	1242	1236	6	1241	1
Pennsville	189	189	......	189	......
Union	1583	1572	11	1578	5
Morganville	77	77	......	77	......
Ringgold	79	79	......	79	......
Rosseau	49	49	......	49	......
Windsor	2251	2194	57	2242	9
Stockport	289	282	7	289	......
York	916	816	100	915	1
Deavertown	160	144	16	160	......
MORROW.					
Bennington	899	885	14	892	7
Canaan	1109	1088	21	1109	......
Cardington	2199	2088	111	2178	21
Cardington	918	866	52	911	7
Chester	1073	1038	35	1069	4
Chesterville	282	274	8	279	3
Congress	1347	1291	56	1347	......
Franklin	1011	995	16	1011	......
Gilead	2017	1971	46	1976	41
Mount Gilead	1087	1063	24	1057	30
Harmony	773	755	18	773	......
Lincoln	915	899	16	888	27
North Bloomfield	1194	1094	100	1193	1
Bl'ming Grove	113	110	3	113	......
Perry	1044	1017	27	1044	......
Johnsville	159	145	14	159	......
North Woodbury	118	118	......	118	......
Peru	953	947	6	918	35
South Bloomfield	1115	1099	16	1114	1
Sparta	197	196	1	196	1
Troy	696	657	39	696	......
Washington	916	863	53	911	5
Iberia	238	224	14	234	4
Westfield	1322	1233	89	1321	1
MUSKINGUM.					
Adams	727	659	68	727	......
Blue Rock	1093	1085	8	1092	1
Brush Creek	1292	1219	73	1289	3
Cass	851	781	70	836	15
Clay	776	751	25	776	......
Roseville	426	414	12	426	......
Falls	3361	2852	509	3181	180
West Zanesville	1744	1384	360	1707	37
Harrison	1197	1072	125	1197	......
Taylorsville	544	471	73	544	......
Highland	784	758	26	784	......
Bloomfield	98	91	7	98	......
Hopewell	1763	1732	31	1741	22
Gratiot, part of (b)	74	73	1	74	......
Hopewell	75	75	......	75	......
Mt. Sterling	210	207	3	210	......
Jackson	1174	1143	31	1174	......
Frazeysburg	325	321	4	325	......
Dresden (c)	1156	1045	111	1137	19
Licking	992	953	39	974	18
Madison	1072	1036	36	1072	......
Meigs	1412	1386	26	1310	102
Monroe	876	852	24	876	......
Otsego	111	109	2	111	......

(a) Exclusive of city of Dayton.
(b) See note (h.) Licking County.
(c) The village of Dresden comprises the whole of the population of Jefferson township.

TABLE IX.—*Population of Minor Civil Divisions, &c.—OHIO*—Continued.

Counties.	Total.	Nativity. Native.	Nativity. Foreign.	Race. White.	Race. Colored.
MUSKINGUM—Con.					
Muskingum	1078	1056	22	1076	2
Shannon	44	44	......	44	......
Newton	2389	2347	42	2320	69
Uniontown	287	287	......	287	......
Perry	991	948	43	991	......
Bridgeville	45	43	2	45	......
Sonora	97	97	......	97	......
Rich Hill	1404	1356	48	1396	8
Salem	941	900	41	940	1
Adamsville	280	269	11	280	......
Salt Creek	1131	1119	12	1131	......
Chandlersville	241	237	4	241	......
Springfield	4022	3748	274	3656	366
Putnam	2050	1923	127	1807	243
Union	1643	1567	76	1621	22
New Concord	488	464	24	486	2
Norwich	268	264	4	268	......
Washington (*a*)	1242	1203	39	1225	17
Jackson	56	54	2	56	......
Wayne	1508	1369	139	1486	22
Duncan's Falls	194	183	11	194	......
Zanesville	10011	8448	1563	9711	*b*299
NOBLE.					
Beaver	1684	1663	21	1684	......
Williamsburg	213	211	2	213	......
Brookfield	978	969	9	953	25
Buffalo	780	772	8	780	......
Center	1703	1671	32	1701	2
Sarahsville	256	254	2	256	......
Elk	1655	1477	178	1637	18
Enoch	1362	1222	140	1362	......
Jackson	1190	1140	50	1190	......
Jefferson	1278	1239	39	1272	6
Middleburg	116	113	3	116	......
Marion	1733	1660	73	1724	9
Summerfield	470	458	12	462	8
Noble	1121	1113	8	1121	......
Olive	1810	1793	17	1809	1
Caldwell	318	312	6	317	1
Seneca	982	971	11	982	......
Mt. Ephraim	171	167	4	171	......
Sharon	1227	1203	24	1227	......
Stock	1650	1599	51	1626	24
Carlisle	218	217	1	218	......
East Union	857	811	46	854	3
Wayne	796	793	3	796	......
Kennonsburg	94	93	1	94	......
OTTAWA.					
Bay	509	378	131	509	......
Benton	1152	742	410	1145	7
Carroll	1036	931	105	1036	......
Catawba Island	515	417	98	515	......
Clay	2174	1654	520	2172	2
Genoa	558	420	138	556	2
Danbury	1252	810	442	1250	2
Erie	455	387	68	455	......
Harris	2190	1789	401	2179	11
Elmore	1131	925	206	1120	11
Portage	1246	895	351	1246	......
Port Clinton	543	428	115	543	......
Put-in-Bay	1148	797	351	1078	70
Salem	1687	1089	598	1687	......
PAULDING.					
Anglaize	788	691	97	788	......
Benton	404	368	36	404	......
PAULDING—Cont'd.					
Blue Creek	163	162	1	99	64
Brown	1140	1100	40	1139	1
Carryall	1087	1027	60	1063	24
Crane	1686	1497	189	1588	98
Antwerp	717	647	70	710	7
Emerald	717	577	140	683	34
Harrison	304	287	17	304	......
Jackson	556	511	45	541	15
Latty	294	291	3	277	17
Paulding	448	433	15	448	......
Washington	957	946	11	737	220
PERRY.					
Bearfield	901	872	29	901	......
Clayton	1195	1156	39	1195	......
Rehoboth	156	147	9	156	......
Saltillo	83	82	1	83	......
Harrison	1202	1152	50	1202	......
Hopewell	1260	1248	12	1260	......
Jackson	1539	1432	107	1539	......
Madison	685	621	4	676	9
Mount Perry	71	70	1	71	......
Sego	33	33	......	33	......
Monday Creek	1165	1132	33	1129	36
Monroe	1120	1046	74	1095	*c*18
Pike	2319	2198	121	2314	5
New Lexi'gton	953	915	38	948	5
Pleasant	655	635	20	655	......
Reading	3334	3121	213	3327	7
New Reading	95	95	......	95	......
Somerset	1153	1049	104	1146	7
Salt Lick	1349	1318	31	1344	5
Thorne	1729	1714	15	1729	......
PICKAWAY.					
Circleville (*d*)	515	474	41	509	6
Circleville	5407	4845	562	4717	690
Darby	1548	1507	41	1547	1
Palestine	81	81	......	81	......
Deer Creek	1458	1420	38	1431	27
Williamsport	514	499	15	500	14
Harrison	1271	1226	45	1218	53
South Bloomfield	283	270	13	283	......
Jackson	1202	1154	48	1111	91
Madison	883	858	25	883	......
Monroe	1870	1818	52	1853	17
Muhlenburg	957	930	27	885	72
Darbyville	233	230	3	232	1
Perry	1415	1382	33	1413	2
New Holland	326	312	14	326	......
Pickaway	1632	1569	63	1615	17
Salt Creek	1750	1734	16	1747	3
Stringtown	71	71	......	71	......
Tarlton	407	404	3	404	3
Scioto	1545	1522	23	1517	28
Genoa	154	153	1	154	......
Walnut	1636	1604	32	1624	12
Ringgold	121	117	4	121	......
Washington	996	978	18	991	5
Wayne	790	762	28	734	56
PIKE.					
Beaver	694	575	119	689	5
Benton	1119	1116	3	1026	93
Camp Creek	743	731	12	743	......
Jackson	1840	1779	61	1196	*b*643
Marion	813	741	72	809	4

(*a*) Exclusive of city of Zanesville.
(*b*) Also 1 Indian.
(*c*) Also 7 Indians.
(*d*) Exclusive of city of Circleville.

ABLE IX.—*Population of Minor Civil Divisions, &c.*—*OHIO*—Continued.

…ies.	Total.	Nativity. Native.	Nativity. Foreign.	Race. White.	Race. Colored.
…ont'd.					
………	1108	1094	14	1108	……
………	1138	1116	22	1128	10
………	181	174	7	181	……
………	1422	1385	37	1145	277
………	2320	1955	365	2320	……
…ly ………	1202	976	226	1202	……
………	748	742	6	734	14
………	772	764	8	756	16
………	1451	1338	113	1371	80
…n ………	638	588	50	588	50
………	628	623	5	628	……
………	651	589	62	651	……
…RE.					
………	1180	1075	105	1131	29
………	642	594	48	642	……
………	913	878	35	912	1
…n………	675	643	32	675	……
………	1025	947	78	1023	2
………	929	861	68	929	……
………	3037	2582	455	3020	17
………	781	756	25	781	……
………	1234	1179	55	1232	2
………	1126	1039	87	1126	……
………	1355	1300	55	1355	……
…ville (a)	658	605	53	658	……
………	848	712	136	848	……
………	691	541	150	691	……
………	1564	1337	227	1560	4
………	3423	2979	444	3377	46
…a ………	2188	1872	316	2159	29
………	1169	1049	120	1165	4
…n ………	977	924	53	977	……
…n………	706	669	37	706	……
………	1444	1243	201	1444	……
………	865	823	42	865	……
…E.					
………	1123	1041	82	1096	27
………	895	876	19	844	51
………	2023	1961	62	1963	60
…nash ………	53	51	2	53	……
…Elkton	156	155	1	137	19
…ester …	430	424	6	426	4
………	2264	2211	53	2264	……
…nia ……	107	99	8	107	……
…burg …	391	376	15	391	……
………	1751	1639	112	1651	100
………	1430	1331	99	1360	70
………	1953	1856	97	1909	44
………	1634	1531	103	1634	……
…rise …	61	58	3	61	……
………	1631	1600	31	1631	……
………	1862	1780	82	1849	13
…n ………	648	628	20	641	7
………	1799	1696	103	1799	……
…Alexan-…(b) ………	455	432	23	455	……
…a………	3414	3184	230	3360	54
………	1748	1613	135	1726	22
…M.					
………	1593	1537	56	1584	9
………	315	306	9	314	1
…g ………	779	617	162	779	……
………	737	648	89	737	……
………	1059	808	251	1058	1

Counties.	Total.	Nativity. Native.	Nativity. Foreign.	Race. White.	Race. Colored.
PUTNAM—Cont'd.					
Liberty ………	1120	1009	111	1110	10
Leipsic ………	200	196	4	200	……
Monroe ………	451	441	10	449	2
Monterey ………	979	729	250	972	7
Ottawa ………	2837	2293	544	2825	12
Ottawa ………	1129	1027	102	1117	12
Palmer ………	434	362	72	434	……
Perry ………	637	623	14	637	……
Pleasant ………	1953	1848	105	1931	22
Columbus Grove ………	578	557	21	578	……
Riley ………	1084	976	108	1084	……
Pendleton ………	145	127	18	145	……
Sugar Creek ………	1037	904	133	1031	6
Union ………	1031	973	58	1031	……
Kalida ………	290	281	9	290	……
Van Buren ………	1350	1265	85	1346	4
Bellmore ………	261	235	26	261	……
RICHLAND.					
Blooming Grove ………	1199	1165	34	1199	……
Butler ………	768	714	54	768	……
Cass ………	1274	1224	50	1272	2
Shiloh ………	297	282	15	297	……
Franklin ………	943	916	27	943	……
Jackson ………	934	905	29	934	……
Jefferson ………	2251	2183	68	2222	29
Belleville ………	720	687	33	713	7
Madison (c) ………	1521	1394	127	1521	……
Mansfield ………	8029	6507	1522	7949	80
Mifflin ………	898	851	47	898	……
Monroe ………	1572	1545	27	1572	……
Lucas ………	312	295	17	312	……
Perry ………	686	683	3	686	……
Plymouth ………	1609	1466	143	1609	……
Plymouth ………	703	611	92	703	……
Sandusky ………	682	568	114	682	……
Sharon ………	2762	2389	373	2758	4
Shelby ………	1807	1608	199	1803	4
Springfield ………	2046	1962	84	2020	26
Lexington ………	482	462	20	482	……
Troy ………	830	783	47	828	2
Washington ………	1496	1361	135	1495	1
Weller ………	1140	1068	72	1140	……
Worthington ………	1870	1802	68	1870	……
ROSS.					
Buckskin ………	2229	2156	73	1981	248
Chillicothe ………	8920	7111	1809	8146	774
Colerain ………	1635	1586	49	1629	6
Adelphia ………	417	409	8	417	……
Economy ………	166	160	6	166	……
Concord ………	2772	2716	56	2448	324
Frankfort ………	519	504	15	389	130
Deerfield ………	1223	1201	22	1191	32
Franklin ………	1082	1049	33	1053	d25
Green ………	1898	1813	85	1865	33
Kingston ………	345	332	13	339	6
Harrison ………	1150	1091	59	1142	8
Mooresville ………	52	52	……	52	……
Huntington ………	2367	2139	228	2192	175
Jefferson ………	1013	1001	12	871	142
Richmond ………	227	226	1	227	……
Liberty ………	1460	1444	16	1387	73
Londonderry ………	163	162	1	163	……
London Station ………	57	56	1	57	……
Paint ………	1001	973	28	979	22

…arrettsville: 187 in Hiram and 471 in Nelson.
…est Alexandria: 165 in Lanier and 290 in Twin.

(c) Exclusive of city of Mansfield.
(d) Also 4 Indiana.

TABLE IX.—*Population of Minor Civil Divisions, &c.*—*OHIO*—**Continued.**

Counties.	Total.	Nativity. Native.	Nativity. Foreign.	Race. White.	Race. Colored.
Ross—Cont'd.					
Paxton	1738	1713	25	1585	153
Bainbridge	647	628	19	619	28
Scioto (a)	2318	1915	403	1998	320
Massieville	119	113	6	82	37
Springfield	1238	1133	105	1109	b128
Twin	2263	2215	48	1958	305
Bourneville	208	202	6	207	1
Union	2790	2683	107	2328	462
SANDUSKY.					
Ballville	1731	1526	205	1729	2
Fremont	5455	4383	1072	5403	52
Green Creek	3666	3292	374	3623	43
Jackson	1350	1209	141	1350	......
Madison	985	900	85	985	......
Rice	927	723	204	927	......
Riley	1461	1187	274	1451	10
Sandusky (c)	1570	1304	266	1569	1
Scott	1274	1184	90	1274	......
Townsend	1290	1108	182	1264	26
Washington	2282	1916	366	2274	8
Woodville	1418	1006	412	1418	......
York	2094	1806	288	2093	1
SCIOTO.					
Bloom	2203	2027	176	2203	......
Webster	200	188	12	200	......
Brush Creek	1410	1336	74	1410	......
Clay	927	797	130	881	46
Green	1882	1715	167	1882	......
Harrison	1032	917	115	1032	......
Jefferson	559	525	34	559	......
Madison	1578	1527	51	1577	1
Morgan	758	747	11	751	7
Nile	1473	1360	113	1457	16
Porter	1965	1746	219	1965	......
Sciotoville	480	429	51	480	......
Wheelersburg	358	337	21	358	......
Portsmouth (d)	10592	8530	2062	9722	870
Rush	638	593	45	624	14
Union	552	445	107	552	......
Valley	724	684	40	723	1
Vernon	1924	1779	145	1924	......
Washington	1085	999	86	1027	58
SENECA.					
Adams	1537	1447	90	1529	8
Big Spring	2084	1581	503	2075	9
Adrian	257	236	21	257	......
New Riegel	236	157	79	236	......
Bloom	1492	1381	111	1488	1
Clinton (e)	1526	1370	156	1526	......
Eden	1483	1400	83	1474	9
Melmore	188	184	4	188	......
Hopewell	1370	1179	191	1370	......
Bascom	107	95	12	107	......
Jackson	1131	1080	51	1131	......
Liberty	1668	1566	102	1668	......
London	3133	2736	397	3126	7
Fostoria	1733	1580	153	1726	7
Pleasant	1352	1257	95	1352	......
SENECA—Cont'd.					
Reed	1334	1200	134	1334	......
Scipio	1635	1537	98	1610	25
Republic	481	454	27	464	17
Seneca	1583	1376	207	1561	22
Berwick	188	162	26	188	......
Thompson	2070	1794	276	2070	......
Tiffin	5648	4490	1158	5573	75
Venice	1781	1555	226	1781	......
Attica	370	331	39	370	......
SHELBY.					
Clinton	3591	3097	494	3453	138
Sidney	2808	2390	418	2718	90
Cynthian	1597	1419	178	1596	1
Centre Point	444	403	41	444	......
Newport	307	262	45	307	......
Dinsmore	1700	1491	209	1631	69
Franklin	839	762	77	830	9
Green	1254	1218	36	1254	......
Palestine	86	86	......	86	......
Plattsville	94	93	1	94	......
Jackson	1461	1349	112	1461	......
Jacks'n Centre	60	60	......	60	......
Montra	110	101	9	110	......
Loramie	1707	1457	250	1704	3
Houston	56	49	7	56	......
North Houst'n	44	42	2	44	......
Russia	53	34	19	53	......
McLean	1309	925	384	1305	4
Berlin	266	196	70	266	......
Orange	951	904	47	925	26
Perry	1208	1173	35	1208	......
Pemberton	157	146	11	157	......
Salem	1428	1377	51	1428	......
Port Jefferson	410	401	9	410	......
Turtle Creek	1230	1145	85	1197	33
Hardin	87	83	4	86	1
Van Buren	1381	1114	267	1070	f305
Washington	1092	1054	38	1080	12
Lockington	214	209	5	214	......
Newburn	239	235	4	227	12
STARK.					
Bethlehem	2148	1851	297	2147	1
Canton (g)	1952	1678	274	1951	1
Canton	8660	7037	1623	8638	22
Jackson	1616	1371	245	1608	8
Lake	2113	1991	122	2113	......
Lawrence	3366	2489	877	3366	......
Canal Fulton	1048	770	278	1048	......
Lexington	5700	4984	716	5567	133
Alliance	4063	3495	568	3995	68
Limaville	204	167	37	193	11
Mount Union	315	307	8	311	4
Marlboro	1870	1759	111	1865	5
Massillon	5185	3952	1233	5079	106
Nimishillen	2645	2182	463	2645	......
Osnaburg	2046	1883	163	2035	11
Paris	2625	2402	223	2625	......
Perry (h)	1736	1474	262	1723	13
Pike	1333	1245	88	1333	......
Plain	2226	2037	189	2223	3

(a) Exclusive of city of Chillicothe.
(b) Also 1 Indian.
(c) Exclusive of city of Fremont.
(d) City of Portsmouth comprises the whole of Wayne township.
(e) Exclusive of city of Tiffin.
(f) Also 6 Indians.
(g) Exclusive of city of Canton.
(h) Exclusive of city of Massillon.

'ABLE IX.—*Population of Minor Civil Divisions, &c.—OHIO*—Continued.

ties.	Total.	Nativity. Native.	Nativity. Foreign.	Race. White.	Race. Colored.
Cont'd.					
....	1116	1031	85	1114	2
esburg .	425	390	35	423	2
ek......	1779	1582	197	1771	8
as......	2412	2036	376	2412	......
on......	1980	1744	236	1975	5
IIT.					
....	10006	7402	2604	9810	196
....	1034	984	50	1034	......
....	1142	954	188	1142	......
....	1233	1194	39	1233	......
....	1817	1312	505	1817	......
hoga s (a)....	1861	1494	367	1828	b31
....	1887	1717	170	1887	......
....	1740	1666	74	1740	......
....	1520	1278	242	1494	26
y	994	722	272	987	7
ton	982	885	97	981	1
l........	1009	891	118	1008	1
....	1821	1548	273	1821	......
)	1594	1270	324	1578	16
....	1018	942	76	1011	7
d.......	2085	1782	303	2085	......
....	925	841	84	918	7
....	1277	1055	222	1274	3
g.......	729	676	53	725	4
ULL.					
....	1240	1150	90	1239	1
sburg ..	446	416	30	445	1
l.	798	618	180	796	2
....	954	876	78	954	......
....	983	964	19	982	1
l........	2657	1642	1015	2657	......
....	820	750	70	813	7
on	1056	1017	39	1046	10
....	871	839	32	871	......
....	915	845	70	907	8
....	938	866	72	932	6
....	1314	1234	80	1265	49
eville ..	260	235	25	253	7
....	664	616	48	664	......
....	4588	2513	2075	4578	9
ard	1126	635	491	1125	(d)
....	893	798	95	891	2
....	1029	953	76	1028	1
....	2420	1572	848	2420	......
a	858	816	42	858	......
....	935	892	43	930	5
nia	796	752	44	796	......
....	1280	1226	54	1276	4
on	799	785	14	798	1
....	930	830	100	930	......
....	1132	1032	100	1131	1
)........	1148	934	214	1129	19
....	3457	2896	561	3362	95
field	5184	3152	2032	5172	12
AWAS.					
....	1251	906	345	1251	......
sville ...	160	123	37	160	......
....	1127	867	260	1127	......
....	1205	987	218	1205	......
nhutten	284	263	21	284	......
....	3515	2815	700	3514	1
Dover .	1593	1204	389	1593	......
ld	126	121	5	126	......

Counties.	Total.	Nativity. Native.	Nativity. Foreign.	Race. White.	Race. Colored.
TUSCARAWAS–Con.					
Fairfield	781	698	83	781	......
Franklin	998	894	104	998	......
Strasbourg ..	142	116	26	142	......
Goshen	4650	3957	693	4626	24
Lockport	250	125	125	250	......
New Philadelphia.....	3143	2686	457	3119	24
Jefferson	1058	848	210	1058	......
Lawrence	1479	1136	343	1475	4
Bolivar........	413	358	55	410	3
Zoar	326	213	113	325	1
Mill	3436	3197	239	3360	76
Dennison.....	828	725	103	825	3
Eastport	25	23	2	25	......
Uhrichsville ..	1541	1430	111	1482	59
Oxford	1667	1588	79	1667	......
New Comerstown	791	759	32	791	......
Perry	1089	1084	5	1089	......
Westchester	198	198	......	198	......
Rush	977	949	28	973	4
Salem	1725	1525	200	1725	......
Port Washington......	425	351	74	425	......
Sandy............	1163	975	188	1161	2
Mineral City .	175	140	35	173	2
Sandyville ...	227	209	18	227	......
Sugar Creek......	1482	1291	191	1482	......
Shanesville...	360	317	43	360	......
Union	742	684	58	742	......
Warren	822	808	14	822	......
New Cumberland........	160	......	......	......	......
Warwick.........	1387	1165	222	1383	4
Trenton	292	250	42	292	......
Washington	1113	1085	28	1113	......
Gilmore	133	122	11	133	......
Newtown	98	97	1	98	......
Wayne	1132	975	157	1131	1
Dundee	106	92	14	106	......
York	1041	770	271	1041	......
UNION.					
Allen	1198	1130	68	1197	1
Claiborne	1947	1873	74	1908	39
Richwood	436	419	17	434	2
Darby............	1142	1021	121	1139	3
Dover	929	901	28	929	......
Jackson	935	910	25	935	......
Jerome	1462	1397	65	1400	62
Leesburg.........	1410	1390	20	1410	......
Liberty	1414	1387	27	1387	27
Mill Creek	798	787	11	796	2
Paris	2838	2641	197	2726	112
Marysville ...	1441	1348	93	1404	37
Taylor	1141	1118	23	1073	68
Union	1336	1241	95	1315	21
Milford Centre	372	332	40	366	6
Washington......	819	799	20	817	2
York	1361	1334	27	1355	6
VAN WERT.					
Harrison	1319	1191	128	1319	......
Hoaglin	622	599	23	622	......
Jackson	249	244	5	249	......
Jennings	914	762	152	914	......
Liberty	1174	1118	56	1173	1
Pleasant (f)	3683	3509	174	3605	78
Van Wert (f).	2625	2487	138	2547	78

ahoga Falls (village) embraces the whole wnship of same name.
2 Indians.
usive of city of Akron.

(d) Also 1 Indian.
(e) Exclusive of city of Warren.
(f) Of Van Wert: 2,403 in Pleasant and 222 in Ridge.

TABLE IX.—*Population of Minor Civil Divisions, &c.*—OHIO—Continued.

Counties.	Total.	Nativity.		Race.	
		Native.	Foreign.	White.	Colored.
VAN WERT—Con.					
Ridge (a)	1406	1362	44	1379	27
Tully	1064	995	69	1064	......
Union	524	499	25	516	8
Washington	2241	1865	376	2241	......
Delphos	640	557	83	640	......
Middle Point	119	105	14	119	......
Straghn	68	64	4	68	......
Willshire	1644	1529	115	1554	90
Willshire	268	255	13	268	......
York	983	834	149	983	......
VINTON.					
Brown	1297	1207	90	1296	1
Clinton	1724	1560	164	1724	......
Hamden	364	326	38	364	......
Eagle	681	677	4	678	3
Elk	2063	1958	105	2048	15
McArthur	861	819	42	846	15
Harrison	782	770	12	761	21
Jackson	1294	1286	8	1294	......
Knox	559	556	3	522	37
Madison	1623	1412	211	1621	2
Zaleski	690	548	142	688	2
Richland	1814	1780	34	1808	6
Swan	1062	1050	12	1062	......
Vinton	656	637	19	655	1
Wilkesville	1472	1372	100	1350	122
WARREN.					
Clear Creek	2605	2509	96	2502	103
Springborough	477	448	29	458	19
Deerfield	1965	1804	161	1886	79
Mason	387	359	28	374	13
Franklin	3012	2799	213	2959	53
Franklin	1832	1710	122	1802	30
Hamilton	2466	2308	158	2268	198
Maineville	290	282	8	286	4
Harlan	2396	2238	158	2392	4
Butlerville	191	180	11	191	......
New Columbia	70	68	2	70	......
Massie	1270	1237	33	1053	217
Harveysburg	388	384	4	300	88
Salem	2102	1882	220	2064	38
East Morrow	262	235	27	262	......
Fredericksb'g	64	50	14	64	......
Morrow	708	578	130	705	3
Roachester	155	147	8	134	21
Turtle Creek	5650	5290	360	5354	296
Lebanon	2749	2580	169	2531	218
Union Village	232	175	57	232	......
Union	1089	1021	68	1081	8
Deerfield	274	253	21	274	......
Washington	1229	1173	56	1207	22
Fort Ancient	43	36	7	42	1
Freeport	37	32	5	37	......
Wayne	2905	2785	120	2745	160
Corwin	135	119	16	134	1
Crosswicks	48	46	2	34	14
Mount Holly	205	193	12	203	2
Waynesville	745	716	29	743	2
WASHINGTON.					
Adams	1786	1592	194	1786	......
Buell's Lowell	350	298	52	350	......
WASHINGTON—Con.					
Aurelius	799	756	43	799	......
Barlow	1194	1111	83	1064	130
Vincent	162	155	7	162	......
Belpre	2462	2279	183	2318	144
Belpre	911	791	120	807	104
Decatur	1437	1359	78	1217	220
Dunham	755	651	104	755	......
Fairfield	824	749	75	824	......
Fearing	1358	1069	289	1358	......
Grand View	2273	2128	145	2257	16
Grand View	193	193	......	184	9
Matamoras	406	361	45	406	......
Independence	1395	1290	105	1395	......
Lawrence	2860	2665	195	2860	......
Liberty	1632	1485	147	1632	......
Ludlow	1082	1043	39	1082	......
Marietta (b)	2697	2371	326	2600	97
Harmer	1511	1285	226	1416	95
Marietta	5218	4353	865	5083	135
Muskingum	1136	945	191	1106	30
Newport	2002	1934	68	1997	5
Palmer	671	654	17	667	4
Plymouth	84	84	......	84	......
Salem	1610	1355	255	1610	......
Salem	187	167	20	187	......
Union	862	679	183	849	13
Warren	1604	1438	166	1591	13
Waterford	2046	2012	34	2037	9
Beverly City	814	791	23	805	9
Coal Run River	203	202	1	203	......
Watertown	1456	1323	133	1435	21
Watertown	181	158	23	181	......
Wesley	1450	1438	12	1229	221
Pleasanton	109	108	1	109	......
WAYNE.					
Baughman (c)(d)	2067	1853	214	2067	......
M'rsh'lville(d)	322	267	55	322	......
Canaan	1997	1888	109	1997	......
Burbank	258	248	10	258	......
Chester	1921	1875	46	1921	......
Chippewa (d)	2510	2119	391	2507	3
Doylestown	551	497	54	549	2
Clinton	1502	1437	65	1502	......
Shreve	479	455	24	479	......
Congress	2581	2502	79	2580	1
Congress	309	305	4	309	......
West Salem	713	668	45	712	1
East Union	1865	1731	134	1865	......
Apple Creek	300	278	22	300	......
Franklin	1302	1253	49	1302	......
Moorland	69	66	3	69	......
Green (c)	2715	2493	222	2713	2
Orrville (c)	745	679	66	744	1
Milton	1524	1386	138	1524	......
Paint	1418	1094	324	1418	......
Mount Eaton	296	182	114	296	......
West Lebanon	164	158	6	164	......
Plain	1837	1750	87	1829	8
Salt Creek	1593	1392	201	1593	......
Fredericksb'g	539	491	48	539	......
Maysville	88	74	14	88	......
Sugar Creek	2006	1789	217	2005	1
Dalton	412	385	27	411	1
Wayne	1714	1645	69	1711	3
Wooster (e)	1145	1051	94	1137	8
Wooster	5419	4730	689	5390	29

(*a*) Of Van Wert: 2,403 in Pleasant and 222 in Ridge.
(*b*) Exclusive of city of Marietta.
(*c*) Of Orville: 329 in Baughman and 416 in Green.
(*d*) Of Marshallville: 298 in Baughman and 24 in Chippewa.
(*e*) Exclusive of city of Wooster.

ABLE IX.—*Population of Minor Civil Divisions, &c.*—*OHIO*—Continued.

ies.	Total.	Nativity: Native.	Nativity: Foreign.	Race: White.	Race: Colored.
AMS.					
....	1681	1580	101	1676	5
Unity ..	537	523	14	537	......
er......	1207	1155	52	1207	......
....	1628	1531	97	1628	......
....	1678	1476	202	1678	......
....	1564	1515	49	1559	5
....	1532	1485	47	1532	......
r	338	331	7	338	......
....	1181	1133	48	1181	......
....	1521	1467	54	1521	......
....	3547	3276	271	3525	22
....	2284	2007	187	2264	20
l.......	1981	1686	295	1971	10
r	671	595	76	671	......
....	1844	1580	264	1844	......
ton.....	690	579	111	690	......
....	1627	1600	27	1627	......
D.					
....	1394	1352	42	1394	......
....	1331	1196	135	1329	2
;Gr'n(a)	906	823	83	904	2
....	1089	846	243	1089	......
....	685	668	17	685	......
....	347	318	29	347	......
....	1120	845	275	1120	......
....	965	912	53	965	......
n	1221	1029	192	1221	......
ns......	243	223	20	243	......
....	1464	1233	231	1464	......

Counties.	Total.	Nativity: Native.	Nativity: Foreign.	Race: White.	Race: Colored.
WOOD—Cont'd.					
Montgomery	1636	1560	76	1636	......
Perry	1323	1287	36	1323	......
Perrysburg.......	4100	3145	955	4070	30
Perrysburg...	1835	1481	354	1812	23
Plain (a)	1719	1562	157	1719	......
Portage	1069	1009	60	1069	......
Troy	1057	770	287	1057	......
Washington	1321	1204	117	1311	10
Webster..........	922	784	138	922	......
Weston...........	1833	1725	108	1832	1
WYANDOT.					
Antrim (b)........	1061	1006	55	1061	......
Crane	3876	3273	603	3819	57
Up'r Sandusky	2564	2096	468	2519	45
Crawford.........	1860	1744	116	1859	1
Carey	692	648	44	691	1
Eden (b)...........	1423	1330	93	1411	12
Jackson...........	771	718	53	771	......
Kirby	835	673	162	831	4
Marseilles	603	584	19	603	......
Marseilles	251	247	4	251	......
Mifflin	866	786	80	866	......
Nevada (b) ...	828	764	64	823	5
Pitt	991	856	135	991	......
Richland	1271	1224	47	1268	3
Ridge	584	562	22	584	......
Salem	1103	918	185	1103	......
Sycamore	850	826	24	850	......
Tymochtee	1631	1578	53	1622	(c)

owling Green: 471 in Centre and 435 in am.

(b) Exclusive of part of village of Nevada.
(c) Also 9 Indians.

TABLE IX.—*Population of Minor Civil Divisions, &c.*—*OREGON.*

The marginal column marks precincts; the first indentation, cities; the second, all other whose names are placed under the names of the precincts in which they are respectively The population of each precinct includes that of all localities situated in it. Wherever the ny locality fail to make the total, the deficiency represents the Chinese and Indians.

ies.	Total.	Nativity: Native.	Nativity: Foreign.	Race: White.	Race: Colored.
. (a)					
....	69	35	34	55	......
....	442	157	285	209	......
er......	79	70	9	78	......
s	342	95	247	140	......
....	269	102	167	133	......
lley	54	53	1	54	......
r River ey (b) ..	1095	904	191	1027	1

Counties.	Total.	Nativity: Native.	Nativity: Foreign.	Race: White.	Race: Colored.
BAKER—Cont'd.					
Baker City ...	312	233	79	292	1
Rye Valley	73	51	22	73	......
Shasta	320	231	89	291	......
Willow C'k Valley	61	59	2	61	......
BENTON. (*)					
Siletz Reser'n.	32	32	......	32	......

nplete; the other principal civil divisions were not separately reported.
r County: Amelia also includes 14 Chinese; Auburn, 233 Chinese; Burnt River, 1 Chinese; ., 202 Chinese; Humboldt, 135 Chinese and 1 Indian; Powder River Valley, 66 Chinese and Shasta, 29 Chinese.
ographical valley containing the village of Baker City.

TABLE IX.—*Population of Minor Civil Divisions, &c.—OREGON—Continued.*

Counties.	Total.	NATIVITY. Native.	NATIVITY. Foreign.	RACE. White.	RACE. Colored.
CLACKAMAS. (a)					
Beaver	310	293	17	310	......
Canemah	381	340	41	381	......
Cascades	240	232	8	240	......
Cutting's	279	273	6	277	2
Harding's	238	233	5	238	......
Lower Molalla	318	303	15	315	3
Marshfield	240	204	36	240	......
Marquam's	397	388	9	397	......
Milwaukie	217	185	32	217	......
Oregon City	1382	1116	266	1317	10
Oswego	145	132	13	137	7
Pleasant Hill	200	192	8	200	......
Rock Creek	219	212	7	219	......
Springwater	239	236	3	239	......
Tualitan	234	223	11	234	......
Union	316	257	59	316	......
Upper Molalla	358	342	16	357	1
Young's	280	275	5	280	......
CLATSOP. (b)					
Astoria	903	676	227	882	4
Astoria	639	496	143	620	4
Cathalamet Bay	121	73	48	121	......
Nehalem Val'y	42	37	5	41	......
Young's River Valley	101	70	31	100	......
Clatsop	266	224	42	255	2
Clatsop Plains	200	175	25	195	2
Lewis and Clarke's River, (near)	15	8	7	15	......
Lexington	23	18	5	23	......
Lower Nehalem Valley	28	23	5	28	......
Westport	86	52	34	84	2
COLUMBIA. (c)					
Deer Island	117	108	9	117	......
Oak Point	177	137	40	174	......
Rainier	116	94	22	116	......
Sauvie's	72	68	4	72	......
Scappoose	237	220	17	237	......
St. Helen's	144	117	27	144	......
COOS.					
Beaver Slough	122	......	......	......	......
Coos River	196	......	......	......	......
Coquille	210	......	......	......	......
Empire City	381	......	......	......	......
Enchanted Prairie	41	......	......	......	......
Johnson's	73	......	......	......	......
Marshfield	402	......	......	......	......
North Coquille	67	......	......	......	......
Randolph	152	......	......	......	......
CURRY.					
Chetco	129	......	......	......	......
Port Orford	168	......	......	......	......
Rogue River	207	......	......	......	......
DOUGLAS. (d)					
Calapooya	1116	1047	69	1107	......
Camas Valley	106	102	4	106	......
Canyonville	788	723	65	713	......
Cole's Valley	312	300	12	312	......
Cow Creek	165	136	29	140	......
Deer Creek	949	892	57	941	......
Elkton	196	178	18	195	......
Gardiner	206	146	60	203	......
Looking-Glass	480	470	10	476	......
Mount Scott	273	268	5	268	2
Myrtle Creek	504	486	18	497	5
Scottsburg	101	95	6	101	......
Ten-Mile	223	214	9	223	......
Wilbur	243	233	10	241	......
Yoncalla	404	394	10	404	......
GRANT. (e)					
Bull Run	46	30	16	45	......
Camp Harney	40	35	5	37	1
Elk	103	34	69	43	......
Granite	448	64	384	83	......
John Day	279	164	115	193	......
Low'r Canyon City	168	55	113	75	3
Marysville	127	72	55	102	......
Olive Creek	135	53	82	97	......
Rock Creek	30	26	4	28	......
South Fork	49	48	1	49	......
Union	523	270	253	323	......
Up'r Canyon City	255	119	136	182	1
Winter's	48	31	17	47	......
JACKSON. (*)					
Fort Klamath, (U.S. garri'n)	48	16	32	48	......
Klamath Reservation	19	15	4	19	......
LANE. (f)					
Camp Creek	208	204	4	208	......
Coast Fork	835	826	9	835	......
Eugene	1852	1775	77	1844	......
Eugene City	861	802	59	854	......
Fall Creek	174	172	2	174	......
Landcaster	738	725	13	738	......
Long Tom	232	231	1	232	......
Lost Valley	171	169	2	171	......
Mohawk	159	155	4	159	......
Pleasant Hill	399	398	1	398	......
Richardson	370	369	1	370	......

(*) Incomplete: the other principal civil divisions were not separately reported.

(a) Clackamas County: Oregon City also includes 50 Chinese and 5 Indians; Oswego, 1 Indian.

(b) Clatsop County: Astoria also includes 13 Chinese and 4 Indians; Clatsop, 9 Indians.

(c) Columbia County: Oak Point also includes 3 Indians.

(d) Douglas County: Calapooya also includes 5 Chinese and 4 Indians; Canyonville, 36 Chinese and 39 Indians; Cow Creek, 21 Chinese and [illegible] Indian; Deer Creek, 7 Chinese and 1 Indian; Elkton, 1 Chinese; Gardiner, [illegible] Chinese and 3 Indians; Looking-Glass, 4 Indians; Mount Scott, 3 Indians; Myrtle Creek, 2 Chinese and [illegible] Indians; Wilbur, 2 Indians.

(e) Grant County: Bull Run also includes [illegible] Chinese; Camp Harney, 2 Chinese; Elk, 60 Chinese; Granite, 365 Chinese; John Day, 85 Chinese and 1 Indian; Lower Canyon City, 90 Chinese; Marysville, 25 Chinese; Olive Creek, 38 Chinese; Rock Creek, 2 Chinese; Union Fork, 199 Chinese and 1 Indian; Upper Canyon City, 72 Chinese; Winter's, 1 Chinese.

(f) Lane County: Eugene also includes 7 Chinese and 1 Indian; Pleasant Hill, 1 Indian.

ABLE IX.—*Population of Minor Civil Divisions, &c.—OREGON*—Continued.

ıtiee.	Total.	Native.	Foreign.	White.	Colored.
		NATIVITY.		RACE.	
-Cont'd.					
....	240	238	2	240	......
....	144	138	6	144	......
id	640	632	8	640	......
tte.......	264	259	5	264	......
S. (a)					
....	1902	1886	106	1988	2
ille	788	766	22	786	2
eek......	295	292	3	295	......
Butte...	270	268	2	270	......
ırg.......	1014	985	29	1014	......
....	515	509	6	513	2
....	380	362	18	380	......
....	751	745	6	751	......
....	451	446	5	451	......
lgo......	730	705	25	730	......
....	925	914	11	924	1
ɔino......	199	196	3	199	......
....	187	183	4	187	......
)..........	220	217	3	220	......
ON. (b)					
....	592	572	20	592	......
le........	118	118	......	113	5
....	304	232	72	304	......
....	188	175	13	188	......
le	439	371	68	437	......
rg.........	586	463	123	577	......
em.......	1218	1080	138	1175	32
....	613	552	61	605	6
Prairie ...	231	229	2	231	......
....	596	569	27	595	......
....	623	605	18	621	1
lem......	784	731	50	778	5
....	1139	947	192	1108	13
a.........	801	782	19	801	......
lem	840	753	87	837	......
y	726	715	11	726	......
a..........	237	222	15	236	......
MAH. (c)					
Portland	830	653	177	811	12
....	212	163	49	197	......
ah	218	180	38	218	......
nd	8293	5715	2578	7060	149
Valley ..	193	183	10	193	......
....	376	352	24	369	......
Island...	274	238	36	270	1
's	275	238	37	273	......
tte.......	313	285	28	307	......

Counties.	Total.	Native.	Foreign.	White.	Colored.
		NATIVITY.		RACE.	
POLK. (d)					
Dallas............	795	773	22	794	......
La Creole	157	154	3	157	......
Monmouth	3749	3646	103	3742	6
TILLAMOOK. (e)					
Nestocton	142	137	5	140	......
Tillamook........	266	243	23	251	......
UMATILLA. (f)					
Alta..............	318	314	4	315	2
Butler Creek	107	97	10	107	......
Meadows..........	363	350	13	363	......
Pendleton	243	217	26	233	......
Umatilla	206	122	84	150	......
Umatilla Reservation....	41	30	11	39	......
Walla Walla	900	849	51	897	......
Weston	605	589	16	603	......
Willow Creek	133	124	9	133	......
UNION. (g)					
Cove	593	566	27	592	......
Eagle Creek......	160	147	13	160	......
Grand Ronde.....	119	77	42	85	......
Iowa	320	299	21	320	......
La Grande	640	588	52	633	1
Summerville	320	297	23	316	......
Union	400	364	36	399	......
WASCO. (h)					
Antelope Valley..	131	125	6	130	1
Bridge Creek.....	74	67	7	74	......
Celilo	44	28	16	37	3
East Dalles (i) ...	600	494	106	592	4
Dalles (i)	942	......	......	......	......
Falls	24	15	9	24	......
Fifteen-Mile	257	245	12	256	......
Hood River.......	85	79	6	77	7
Mosier	40	35	5	40	......
Ochoco	191	187	4	191	......
Rock Creek.......	195	181	14	195	......
Tygh Valley	142	140	2	141	......
Warm Springs Agency	21	21	......	21	......
West Dalles (i) ...	705	514	191	674	6
WASHINGTON. (j)					
Beaver Dam......	182	162	20	182	......
Butte	724	675	49	724	......

omplete; the other principal civil divisions were not separately reported.
an County: Albany also includes 2 Chinese.
arion County: Butteville also includes 2 Indians; Champoeg, 1 Chinese and 8 Indians; East Chinese and 5 Indians; Fairfield, 2 Indians; Jefferson, 1 Chinese; Lincoln, 1 Indian; North Chinese; Salem, 17 Chinese and 1 Indian; South Salem, 1 Chinese and 2 Indians; Waconda,
ultnomah County: East Portland also includes 6 Chinese and 1 Indian; Fulton, 15 Chinese; l, 456 Chinese and 28 Indians; Sandy, 7 Chinese; Sauvie's Island, 2 Chinese and 1 Indian; St. 2 Chinese; Willamette, 3 Chinese and 3 Indians.
lk County: Dallas also includes 1 Chinese; Monmouth, 1 Chinese.
lamook County: Nestocton also includes 2 Indians; Tillamook, 15 Indians.
matilla County: Alta also includes 1 Indian; Pendleton, 9 Chinese and 1 Indian; Umatilla, 56 ; Walla Walla, 1 Chinese and 2 Indians; Weston, 2 Chinese.
nion County: Cove also includes 1 Chinese; Grand Ronde, 34 Chinese; La Grande, 6 Chinese; rville, 3 Chinese and 1 Indian; Union, 1 Chinese.
asco County: Celilo also includes 4 Chinese; East Dalles, 1 Chinese and 3 Indians; Fifteen- Indian; Hood River, 1 Indian; Tygh Valley, 1 Indian; West Dalles, 22 Chinese and 3 Indians.
lles village lies in the precincts of East Dalles and West Dalles.
ashington County: Centreville also includes 19 Indians; Hillsboro, 20 Indians.

TABLE IX.—*Population of Minor Civil Divisions, &c.*—*OREGON*—Continued.

Counties.	Total.	Nativity. Native.	Nativity. Foreign.	Race. White.	Race. Colored.
WASHINGTON-Con.					
Cedar Creek	211	199	12	211	......
Centreville	457	421	36	438	......
Dairy Creek	304	297	7	304	......
Forest Grove	922	893	29	922	......
Hillsboro	796	757	39	776	......
South Tualitin	298	283	15	298	......
Wapatoo	367	351	16	367	......
YAM HILL. (a)					
Amity	432	424	8	432	......
YAM HILL—Con.					
Dayton	587	550	37	586	1
East Chehalem	234	216	18	234	......
Grande Ronde Agency	23	23	......	23	......
Lafayette	655	643	12	654	1
McMinnville	1125	1061	64	1124	......
McMinnville	388	350	38	388	......
North Fork	553	527	26	553	......
Sheridan	692	669	23	692	......
West Chehalem	378	364	14	377	......
Willamette	333	321	12	333	......

(a) Yam Hill County: Dayton also includes 1 Chinese; McMinnville, 1 Indian; West Chehalem, 1 Indian.

TABLE IX.—*Population of Minor Civil Divisions, &c.*—*PENNSYLVANIA.*

marks townships and boroughs: the first indentation, cities: the second, towns. Names of towns are placed under the names of the townships in which they are respectively situated. The population of each township of all towns situated in it, but not that of the boroughs.

Counties.	Total.	Nativity. Native.	Nativity. Foreign.	Race. White.	Race. Colored.
ADAMS.					
Berwick	507	494	13	507	......
Berwick, (boro'gh)	325	309	16	324	1
Butler	1333	1326	7	1313	20
Conowago	1029	976	53	1020	9
McSherryst'n	291	269	22	291	......
Cumberland	1455	1402	53	1364	91
Gettysburg, (boro')	3074	2945	129	2835	239
Franklin	2176	2117	59	2163	13
Freedom	449	444	5	437	12
Germany	880	844	36	879	1
Littlesto'n, (boro')	847	832	15	844	3
Hamilton	1118	1108	10	1118	......
Hamiltonban	1418	1403	15	1388	30
Fairfield	258	255	3	245	13
Highland	421	419	2	408	13
Huntington	1595	1583	12	1585	10
York Springs, (borough)	356	351	5	350	6
Latimore	1230	1227	3	1224	6
Liberty	860	844	16	838	22
Menallen	1814	1802	12	1760	54
Mount Joy	1172	1147	25	1172	......
Mount Pleasant	1947	1878	69	1946	1
Oxford	1322	1263	59	1315	7
Reading	1326	1319	7	1324	2
Straban	1547	1533	14	1536	11
Tyrone	1009	1007	2	1005	4
Union	1105	1049	56	1095	10
ALLEGHENY.					
Allegheny	53180	37872	15308	52018	1162
Baldwin	3104	2154	950	3075	29
Chartiers	2269	1712	557	2240	29
Temperanceville, (borough)	2069	1422	647	2046	23
ALLEGHENY—Con.					
Crescent	364	332	32	364	......
East Deer	1390	1211	179	1390	......
Elizabeth	2937	2463	474	2847	90
Elizabeth, (boro')	1196	1114	82	1094	102
Fawn	681	622	59	673	8
Tarentum, (boro')	944	867	77	934	10
Findley	1170	1139	31	1148	22
Forward	1300	1156	144	1257	43
Franklin	716	626	90	716	......
Hampton	938	753	185	937	1
Harrison	1870	1476	394	1869	1
Indiana	2806	2188	618	2790	16
Sharpsburg, (boro')	2176	1600	576	2175	1
Jefferson	2066	1725	341	2053	13
West Elizabeth, (borough)	590	471	119	570	20
Killbuck	1919	1367	552	1910	9
Leet	629	524	105	621	8
Lincoln	1399	1066	333	1397	2
Lower St. Clair	5322	3155	2167	5256	66
Allentown, (boro')	772	455	317	772	......
Birmingham, (borough)	8603	5945	2658	8506	97
East Birmingham, (borough)	9488	6306	3182	9426	62
Monongahela, (borough)	1153	664	489	1153	......
Mount Washington, (borough)	1988	1331	657	1962	26
Ormsby, (borough)	2225	1244	981	2207	18
South Pittsburgh, (borough)	3095	1955	1140	3088	7
West Pittsburgh, (borough)	2095	1087	1008	2095	......
Marshall	705	543	162	705	......
McCandless	957	729	228	956	1

—Population of Minor Civil Divisions, &c.—PENNSYLVANIA—Continued.

	Total.	Nativity. Native.	Nativity. Foreign.	Race. White.	Race. Colored.
Con.					
....	3816	2371	1445	3774	42
....	5058	3338	1720	5034	a23
') ..	668	434	234	666	a1
....	1230	1134	96	1230	......
....	289	245	44	289	......
....	1482	1280	202	1437	45
les .	2461	1770	691	2450	11
....	685	555	130	683	2
....	1193	1078	115	1190	3
....	2685	2003	682	2666	19
oro')	380	288	92	372	8
....	718	608	110	714	4
....	86076	58254	27822	84061	2015
....	1300	1152	148	1283	17
....	1600	1107	493	1560	40
....	707	617	90	706	1
....	2275	1640	635	2228	47
....	1623	1218	405	1602	21
o')..	384	303	81	377	7
....	1807	1335	472	1739	68
....	443	351	92	434	9
ro').	1472	1310	162	1416	56
....	1473	1107	366	1472	1
a) ..	1447	974	473	1439	8
....	1258	1137	121	1249	9
....	1927	1345	582	1907	20
es..	2194	1701	493	2184	10
bor-					
....	2523	2153	370	2520	3
....	739	581	158	715	24
....	1986	1189	797	1972	14
gh)	1335	867	468	1329	6
r...	810	748	62	800	10
....	1299	1074	225	1297	2
....	3455	2706	749	3414	41
o') .	1290	1060	230	1290	......
s.					
....	2539	2396	143	2534	5
ugh)	29	23	6	29	......
bor-					
....	368	350	18	367	1
....	3619	2529	1090	3614	5
....	964	941	23	964	......
k ..	2246	2155	91	2246	......
....	1451	1391	60	1448	3
....	1728	1666	62	1716	12
gh).	764	643	121	762	2
....	1504	1431	73	1504	......
....	1621	1485	136	1621	......
....	1402	1333	69	1401	1
....	1071	1013	58	1071	......
oro')	330	316	14	330	......
....	1057	1024	33	1057	......
....	3577	3176	401	3550	a26
oro')	201	143	58	201	......
....	1642	1562	80	1549	93
....	1738	1684	54	1738	......
o')...	235	232	3	234	1
....	1341	1335	6	1341	......
....	1127	1116	11	1126	1
....	1633	1522	111	1629	4
o')..	1640	1475	165	1632	8
....	1023	969	54	1023	......
....	1821	1665	156	1821	......
oro')	1889	1669	220	1872	17
....	1180	1140	40	1180	......
....	2028	1939	89	2028	......
n ...	1098	1003	95	1098	......
n ,					
....	216	202	14	216	......

Counties.	Total.	Nativity. Native.	Nativity. Foreign.	Race. White.	Race. Colored.
BEAVER.					
Big Beaver	1559	1273	286	1546	13
New Galileo	241	218	23	241	......
Borough	379	354	25	379	......
Brighton	844	790	54	844	......
Beaver, (borough)	1120	1044	76	1102	18
Bridgewater, (borough)	1119	992	127	1051	68
Fallston, (boro')	629	575	54	629	......
Chippewa	817	738	79	806	11
Darlington	1811	1443	368	1804	7
Darlington	280	266	14	278	2
Economy	1324	1089	235	1324	......
Franklin	676	619	57	676	......
Greene	1836	1815	21	1786	50
Georgetown	297	288	9	297	......
Hookstown	259	256	3	250	9
Hanover	1500	1482	18	1490	10
Frankfort Springs	155	150	5	154	1
Harmony	225	72	153	225	......
Hopewell	1015	985	30	1011	4
Independence	728	710	18	719	9
Industry	796	740	56	796	......
Marion	307	237	70	307	......
Moon	936	863	73	936	......
Phillipsburg, (borough)	554	472	82	554	......
New Sewickley	1602	1354	248	1602	......
Freedom, (boro')	634	571	63	633	1
North Sewickley	1108	1046	62	1100	8
Ohio	1534	1471	63	1520	14
Patterson	74	67	7	74	......
Beaver Falls, (borough)	3112	2634	478	3082	30
Pulaski	943	816	127	941	2
New Brighton, (borough)	4037	3415	622	3974	63
Raccoon	1012	999	13	1003	9
Rochester	620	508	112	619	1
Rochester, (boro')	2091	1889	202	2081	10
South Beaver	1206	1131	75	1204	2
St. Clair	232	192	40	232	......
BEDFORD.					
Bedford	2333	2294	39	2129	204
Bedford, (borough)	1247	1219	28	1192	55
Broad Top	1626	1293	333	1604	22
Coaldale	262	137	125	262	......
Colerain	1204	1194	10	1204	......
Rainsburg	250	249	1	250	......
Cumberl'nd Valley	1357	1340	17	1282	75
East Providence	1274	1256	18	1273	1
Harrison	783	738	45	782	1
Hopewell	1078	1008	70	1078	......
Juniata	1437	1358	79	1415	22
Liberty	806	789	17	794	12
Saxton, (borough)	318	290	28	317	1
Londonderry	1255	1081	174	1254	1
Middle Woodberry	1483	1456	27	1478	5
Woodberry, (boro')	294	287	7	293	1
Monroe	1719	1713	6	1718	1
Napier	1825	1811	14	1810	15
Schellsburg, (borough)	342	339	3	342	......
Snake Spring	631	619	12	621	10
Southampton	1647	1642	5	1647	......
South Woodberry	1439	1422	17	1419	20
St. Clair	2219	2202	17	2212	7
St. Clairsville	144	140	4	142	2
Union	1791	1780	11	1791	......

ndian.
e of part of Sewickley, (borough.)

(c) Exclusive of part of Edgewater, (borough.)

TABLE IX.—*Population of Minor Civil Divisions, &c.*—*PENNSYLVANIA*—Continued.

Counties.	Total.	Nativity.		Race.	
		Native.	Foreign.	White.	Colored.
BEDFORD—Cont'd.					
West Providence	970	903	67	957	13
Bloody Run, (borough)	557	528	29	538	19
BERKS.					
Albany	1510	1494	16	1504	6
Alsace	1294	1234	60	1294	......
Amity	1646	1620	26	1645	1
Bern	2124	2091	33	2124	......
Bethel	2285	2271	14	2285	......
Brecknock	813	794	19	807	6
Caernarvon	927	914	13	926	1
Centre	1529	1523	6	1529	......
Colebrookdale	1660	1569	91	1635	5
Boyertown	690	628	62	685	5
Cumru	2573	2396	177	2570	3
District	724	715	9	724	......
Douglass	1072	1052	20	1071	1
Earl	1022	1018	4	1020	2
Exeter	2239	2192	47	2238	1
Greenwich	2151	2022	129	2151	......
Heidelberg	1193	1186	7	1193	......
Womelsdorf, (borough)	1031	1029	2	1026	5
Hereford	1260	1252	8	1260	......
Jefferson	1133	1132	1	1130	3
Long Swamp	2910	2833	77	2908	2
Lower Heidelberg	2480	2459	21	2480	......
Maiden Creek	1615	1602	13	1611	4
Marion	1440	1432	8	1437	3
Stouchsburg	397	394	3	397	......
Maxatawney	2531	2482	49	2531	......
Kutztown, (boro')	945	917	28	945	......
Muhlenberg	1547	1521	26	1547	......
North Heidelberg	979	974	5	979	......
Oley	1986	1974	12	1986	......
Ontelaunee	1339	1306	33	1339	......
Penn	1515	1506	9	1514	1
Bernville, (boro')	457	455	2	457	......
Perry	1680	1620	60	1680	......
Pike	925	922	3	925	......
Reading	33930	30059	3871	33611	*a*311
Richmond	2874	2814	60	2874	......
Robeson	2458	2415	43	2450	8
Rockland	1451	1438	13	1448	3
Ruscomb Manor	1408	1389	19	1408	......
Spring	2253	2229	24	2253	......
Tulpehocken	2013	2005	8	2008	5
Union	2165	2079	86	2115	50
Upper Bern	2008	1980	28	2005	3
Up'r Tulpehocken	1196	1195	1	1196	......
Washington	1609	1520	89	1609	......
Windsor	1211	1144	67	1211	......
Hamburg, (boro')	1590	1541	49	1590	......
BLAIR.					
Allegheny	1915	1666	247	1902	11
Altoona	10610	9119	1491	10462	148
Antes	1893	1831	62	1893	......
Blair	1571	1410	161	1561	10
Gaysport, (boro')	799	667	132	790	9
Hollidaysburg, (borough)	2952	2487	465	2815	137
Catharine	907	891	16	907	......
Frankstown	1553	1505	48	1551	2
Freedom	1020	997	23	1020	......
Greenfield	1233	1225	8	1229	4
Huston	1335	1297	38	1335	......
Juniata	621	587	34	621	......
BLAIR—Cont'd.					
Logan (*b*)	2422	2247	175	2409	13
North Woodberry	933	917	16	933	......
Martinsb'g, (boro')	536	522	14	531	5
Snyder	1412	1282	130	1412	......
Tyrone, (borough)	1840	1639	201	1810	30
Taylor	1368	1337	31	1368	......
Tyrone	1006	985	21	1005	1
Woodberry	2107	2080	27	2091	16
Williamsburg	821	811	10	815	6
BRADFORD.					
Albany	1379	1281	98	1377	2
Armenia	391	389	2	386	5
Asylum	1155	1108	47	1095	60
Athens	2256	2019	237	2242	14
Athens, (borough)	965	862	103	944	21
Barclay	2009	905	1104	2009	......
Burlington	1375	1326	49	1374	1
Burlington	203	191	12	203	......
Canton	1840	1762	78	1834	6
Alba	222	205	17	222	......
Canton, (borough)	710	675	35	708	[illegible]
Columbia	1521	1479	42	1505	16
Sylvania	212	207	5	212	......
Franklin	705	685	20	705	......
Granville	1375	1307	68	1375	......
Herrick	1009	937	72	1008	1
Le Roy	1144	1117	27	1126	18
Litchfield	1256	1231	25	1256	......
Monroe	1221	1143	78	1182	39
Monroe, (borough)	293	287	6	292	1
North Towanda	592	522	70	588	4
Orwell	1296	1268	28	1296	......
Overton	550	468	82	549	1
Pike	1814	1732	82	1813	1
Le Raysville	284	275	9	284	......
Ridgebury	1476	1282	194	1475	1
Rome	1333	1283	50	1333	......
Rome	230	227	3	230	......
Sheshequin	1596	1521	75	1589	7
Smithfield	1790	1684	106	1780	10
South Creek	1070	1007	63	1064	6
Springfield	1455	1421	34	1454	1
Standing Stone	905	849	56	904	1
Terry	1079	1048	31	1014	65
Towanda	916	816	100	871	45
Towanda, (boro')	2696	2373	323	2609	[illegible]
Troy	1479	1429	50	1476	3
Troy, (borough)	1081	959	122	1053	[illegible]
Tuscarora	1224	1214	10	1206	18
Ulster	1174	1058	116	1172	2
Warren	1421	1291	130	1417	4
Wells	1207	1175	32	1205	2
West Burlington	896	887	9	895	1
Wilmot	1365	1230	135	1365	......
Windham	1188	1158	30	1188	......
Wyalusing	1707	1577	130	1706	1
Wysox	1290	1213	77	1283	[illegible]
BUCKS.					
Bedminster	2370	2330	40	2364	6
Bensalem	2353	2057	296	2183	*c*169
Bristol	2040	1839	201	1774	266
Bristol, (borough)	3269	2849	420	3142	127
Buckingham	2910	2809	101	2767	143
Doylestown	1954	1768	186	1926	28
Doylest'wn, (boro')	1601	1462	139	1590	11
Durham	1209	1084	125	1209	......
Falls	2298	2104	194	2188	110

(*a*) Also 8 Indians.
(*b*) Exclusive of city of Altoona.
(*c*) Also 1 Indian.

IX.—*Population of Minor Civil Divisions, &c.*—*PENNSYLVANIA*—Continued.

...ties.	Total.	Nativity. Native.	Nativity. Foreign.	Race. White.	Race. Colored.
-Cont'd.					
...ngton....	211	......	......	......	......
...lle,(boro')	813	762	51	788	25
...rtown ...	150	......	......	......	......
....	1250	1208	42	1250	......
....	2869	2740	129	2864	5
...akefield .	2066	1839	227	1862	204
...wn	2360	2238	122	2150	210
....	2900	2836	64	2893	5
...ain......	1707	1595	112	1692	13
...n	933	838	95	883	50
...a, (boro')	859	824	35	815	44
...xon	1528	1418	110	1528	......
...n, (boro') .	944	888	56	941	3
...pton	1896	1785	111	1875	21
...d........	2617	2544	73	2607	10
....	2111	2018	93	2104	7
...n, (boro') .	863	836	27	856	7
....	3363	3172	191	3342	21
....	2791	2635	156	2666	125
...pe, (boro')	1225	1046	179	1150	75
...pton.....	1393	1335	58	1390	3
...ld	2551	2506	45	2551	......
....	2401	2284	117	2401	......
...lakefield.	1505	1420	85	1445	60
...ster......	840	808	32	816	24
...ton	949	889	60	940	9
....	775	756	19	767	8
...town	823	771	52	811	12
...LER.					
....	973	873	100	972	1
...y........	890	845	45	890	......
....	600	582	18	600	......
....	1495	1189	306	1493	2
....	981	842	139	980	1
...borough)	1935	1636	299	1933	2
....	843	787	56	836	7
....	903	882	21	903	......
....	1062	1039	23	1062	......
...nry.......	216	214	2	216	......
...l	847	692	155	847	......
...esville ...	75	......	......	......	......
....	1132	1027	105	1132	......
....	926	910	16	926	......
...euessing	1051	991	60	1051	......
...y........	945	837	108	945	......
....	852	750	102	850	2
...'n,(boro')	207	164	43	207	......
...r	1078	1029	49	1078	......
....	1025	870	155	1024	1
...n	1047	994	53	1047	......
...pect	271	257	14	271	......
....	1137	979	158	1136	1
...r, (boro')	414	369	45	414	......
...le, (boro')	387	315	72	387	......
...n	1234	923	311	1234	......
...rg, (boro')	295	188	107	295	......
...er	1053	897	156	1051	2
....	850	804	46	850	......
....	478	449	29	470	8
...lle, (boro')	352	347	5	352	......
...x........	1010	940	70	1009	1
...reek......	972	924	48	969	3
...ersville ..	198	193	5	198	......
....	926	811	115	918	8
....	1309	1237	72	1309	......
....	837	768	69	837	......
...Rock....	879	839	40	879	......
...lle, (boro')	366	357	9	366	......
....	1304	907	397	1303	1
....	902	835	67	902	......
...gton	996	956	40	996	......

Counties.	Total.	Nativity. Native.	Nativity. Foreign.	Race. White.	Race. Colored.
BUTLER—Cont'd.					
Winfield	1121	921	200	1119	2
Worth	893	852	41	893	......
CAMBRIA.					
Adams	836	799	37	836	......
Allegheny........	1230	1041	189	1230	......
Loretto, (borough)	280	244	36	278	2
Blacklick.........	646	582	64	646	......
Cambria..........	1086	857	229	1086	......
Ebensburg, (boro')	1240	1082	158	1221	19
Carroll	1780	1458	322	1780	......
Carrollto'n, (boro')	416	312	104	416	......
Chest	870	712	158	870	......
Clearfield (a)	1531	1419	112	1531	......
Chest Sp'gs, (boro')	269	257	12	260	9
Conemaugh	728	632	96	728	......
Conema'gh, (boro')	2336	1540	796	2336	......
Franklin, (boro')..	426	392	34	426	......
Johnstown, (boro')	6028	4566	1462	5991	37
Croyle............	886	768	118	886	......
Gallitzin	977	775	202	977	......
Jackson	906	849	57	906	......
Munster..........	598	501	97	598	......
Richland	868	809	59	868	......
Summerhill	752	681	71	750	2
Wilmore, (boro')..	393	350	43	383	10
Susquehanna	1106	1060	46	1106	......
Taylor	1670	1438	232	1670	......
Cooperdale ...	246	234	12	246	......
East Conemaugh, (borough)	381	331	50	381	......
Millville, (boro') ..	2105	1276	829	2105	......
Prospect, (boro') ..	576	308	268	576	......
Washington	1904	1586	318	1899	5
Summitville ..	177	150	27	177	......
White............	969	933	36	969	......
Yoder............	1032	863	169	1018	14
Cambria, (boro') ..	1744	1049	695	1744	......
CAMERON.					
Gibson	1236	857	379	1236	......
Grove	440	410	30	440	......
Lumber	674	562	112	673	1
Portage	99	96	3	99	......
Shippen	1824	1582	242	1813	11
Emporium ...	898	765	133	887	11
CARBON.					
Banks............	3982	2223	1759	3982	......
East Penn........	862	841	21	862	......
Franklin	1912	1780	132	1912	......
Weissport, (boro')	359	323	36	359	......
Kidder	1417	1236	181	1409	8
Lausanne	1416	887	529	1415	1
Weatherly, (boro')	1076	904	172	1076	......
Lower Towamensing	1552	1466	86	1551	1
Mahoning	1589	1470	119	1588	1
Lehighton, (boro')	1485	1343	142	1463	22
Mauch Chunk	5210	3181	2029	5210	......
E. Mauch Chunk, (borough)	1585	1084	501	1585	......
Mauch Chunk, (borough)	3841	2752	1089	3809	32
Packer	441	399	42	441	......
Penn Forest......	504	452	52	504	......
Upper Towamensing	913	842	71	913	......

(a) Exclusive of part of Chest Springs, (borough.)

TABLE IX.—*Population of Minor Civil Divisions, &c.—PENNSYLVANIA*—Continued.

Counties.	Total.	Nativity. Native.	Nativity. Foreign.	Race. White.	Race. Colored.
CENTRE.					
Benner	1362	1300	62	1362	......
Boggs	2135	2074	61	2132	3
Milesburg, (boro')	600	574	26	595	5
Burnside	386	368	18	386	......
Curtin	459	440	19	459	......
Ferguson	2111	2076	35	2109	2
Gregg	1636	1627	9	1636	......
Haines	1354	1347	7	1353	1
Half-Moon	698	689	9	696	2
Harris	1999	1980	19	1999	......
Boalsburg	371	367	4	371	......
Howard	875	846	29	875	......
Howard, (borough)	334	312	22	334	......
Huston	863	845	18	862	1
Liberty	1062	1042	20	1062	......
Marion	823	796	27	820	3
Miles	1325	1311	14	1323	2
Patton	721	700	21	695	26
Penn	1158	1156	2	1158	......
Potter	2358	2329	29	2358	......
Rush	1963	1564	399	1962	1
Philipsb'rg, (boro')	1086	1015	71	1050	36
Snow Shoe	1162	970	192	1162	......
Spring	1608	1526	82	1571	37
Bellefonte, (boro')	2655	2374	281	2509	146
Taylor	512	510	2	512	......
Union	847	827	20	847	......
Unionville, (boro')	320	313	7	319	1
Walker	1356	1332	24	1356	......
Worth	650	645	5	650	......
CHESTER.					
Birmingham	450	379	71	400	50
Cain	984	912	72	900	84
Charleston	907	877	30	846	61
East Bradford	1033	897	136	945	*a*87
East Brandywine	1011	894	117	983	28
East Cain	232	209	23	210	22
Downingtown, (borough)	1077	963	114	1040	37
East Coventry	1318	1280	38	1298	20
East Fallowfield	1291	1262	29	1188	103
East Goshen	696	653	43	649	47
East Marlborough	1401	1370	31	1141	*a*259
East Nantmeal	920	908	12	896	24
E't Nottingham (*b*)	1400	1337	63	1319	81
East Pikeland	826	772	54	817	9
Easttown	736	680	56	694	42
East Vincent	1961	1873	88	1946	15
East Whiteland	1222	1014	208	1124	98
Elk	839	794	45	829	10
Franklin	922	886	36	840	82
Highland	958	936	22	843	115
Honeybrook	1957	1907	50	1887	70
Hopewell, (boro')	268	262	6	260	8
Kennett	1308	1208	100	1138	170
Kennett, (boro')	884	841	43	726	158
London Britain	663	617	46	615	48
Londonderry	714	683	31	677	37
London Grove	1804	1668	136	1515	289
Lower Oxford (*b*)	1449	1396	53	1141	*a*307
Oxford, (borough)	1151	1084	67	1060	91
New Garden	1790	1609	181	1462	328
Newlin	775	732	43	709	66
New London	911	878	33	805	106
North Coventry	1251	1218	33	1248	3
Penn	692	656	36	612	80
Pennsbury	767	710	57	670	97
Pocopson	573	526	47	441	132
Sadsbury	2400	2260	140	2221	179
Coatesville, (boro')	2025	1885	140	1897	128
CHESTER—Cont'd.					
Schuylkill	1593	1430	163	1506	87
Phœnixv'e, (boro')	5292	3810	1482	5268	24
South Coventry	649	637	12	599	50
Thornbury	235	205	30	211	24
Tredyffrin	1897	1675	222	1778	119
Upper Oxford	1079	1053	26	956	123
Upper Uwchlan	781	759	22	772	9
Uwchlan	794	775	19	698	96
Valley	1165	1043	122	1040	125
Wallace	746	725	21	738	8
Warwick	1266	1250	16	1250	16
West Bradford	1336	1454	82	1361	175
West Brandywine	933	900	33	921	12
West Cain	1398	1321	77	1307	91
West Fallowfield	1159	1077	82	1115	44
West Goshen	944	838	106	753	191
Westchester, (b'ro')	5630	5150	480	4708	922
West Marlb'rough	1189	1073	116	1021	168
West Nantmeal	1070	1054	16	1069	1
West Nottingham	879	845	34	840	39
West Pikeland	1201	1095	106	1178	23
Westtown	818	728	90	747	71
West Vincent	1256	1237	19	1231	25
West Whiteland	1177	1039	138	1021	156
Willistown	1552	1440	112	1495	57
CLARION.					
Ashland	758	696	62	758	......
Beaver	1338	1274	64	1338	......
Brady	263	244	19	263	......
East Brady, (boro')	728	552	176	727	1
Clarion	1059	1036	23	1059	......
Clarion, (boro')	709	648	61	699	10
Strattonv'e, (boro')	356	349	7	356	......
Elk	1055	945	110	1055	......
Farmington	1642	1499	143	1642	......
Highland	524	512	12	524	......
Knox	656	505	151	656	......
Licking	1218	1184	34	1218	......
Callensburg	255	251	4	255	......
Limestone	1375	1343	32	1375	......
Madison	1935	1795	140	1935	......
Mill Creek	517	496	21	517	......
Monroe	1334	1308	26	1332	2
Curllsville	208	201	7	208	......
Paint	346	305	41	334	12
Perry	1568	1525	43	1568	......
Piney	1160	1083	77	1160	......
Porter	1546	1520	26	1546	......
New Bethlehem, (borough)	348	342	6	348	......
Red Bank	1434	1388	46	1434	......
Richland	1015	983	32	1014	1
Salem	949	925	24	949	......
Toby	1140	1122	18	1140	......
Rimersburg, (boro')	324	313	11	324	......
Washington	1240	1045	195	1240	......
CLEARFIELD.					
Beccaria	1239	1205	34	1239	......
Bell	918	903	15	918	......
Bloom	315	301	14	315	......
Boggs	784	749	35	784	......
Bradford	1172	1148	24	1168	4
Brady	2009	1830	179	2008	1
Burnside	1024	1003	21	1024	......
New Washington	211	210	1	211	......
Chest	1178	1152	26	1178	......
Covington	701	561	140	701	......

(*a*) Also 1 Indian.

(*b*) Exclusive of part of Hopewell, (borough.)

.—*Population of Minor Civil Divisions, &c.—PENNSYLVANIA*—Continued.

...	Total.	Nativity. Native.	Nativity. Foreign.	Race. White.	Race. Colored.
—Con.					
......	1461	1107	354	1431	10
ough)	813	687	126	805	8
......	585	582	3	585	......
......	601	543	58	600	1
......	490	414	76	490	......
......	468	448	20	468	......
......	638	619	19	638	......
......	587	518	69	587	......
......	561	520	41	561	......
......	452	416	36	414	38
......	587	562	25	587	......
......	1720	1613	107	1718	2
oro').	1361	1237	124	1351	10
......	1480	1200	280	1455	25
......	639	601	38	622	17
,(b'ro'	230	228	2	230	......
......	1138	1126	12	1125	13
(boro'	556	545	11	550	6
......	400	386	14	400	......
......	1034	847	187	1034	......
......	950	822	128	943	7
oro') .	452	429	23	452	......
......	887	857	30	887	......
,(b'ro'	384	370	14	384	......
......	1301	1105	196	1301	......
ough)	1940	1541	399	1930	10
......	332	279	53	330	2
......	400	387	13	394	6
......	515	454	61	505	10
......	252	212	40	252	......
......	1102	1074	28	1100	2
oro').	414	410	4	414	......
......	295	266	29	295	......
......	439	372	67	380	59
......	1391	1371	20	1387	4
......	515	490	25	515	......
......	6986	6103	883	6899	87
......	823	817	6	817	6
......	970	911	59	969	1
......	1101	1092	9	1101	......
......	701	668	33	701	......
......	1061	867	194	1060	1
......	958	933	25	958	......
......	1053	1045	8	1052	1
(bor-.					
......	3341	2998	343	3262	79
......	1077	1063	14	1077	......
ro') ..	923	892	31	922	1
......	1614	1577	37	1601	13
......	1322	1312	10	1317	5
......	1943	1119	824	1943	......
oro') ..	1342	889	453	1341	1
k....	1372	1367	5	1372	......
......	506	501	5	500	6
......	1588	1575	13	1588	......
......	1170	1024	146	1167	3
......	565	557	8	565	......
......	1534	1502	32	1534	......
......	1086	1070	16	1086	......
......	599	591	8	594	5
......	1029	1027	2	1029	......
......	627	553	74	627	......
ant..	751	739	12	751	......
......	905	896	9	904	1
......	751	741	10	749	2

Counties.	Total.	Nativity. Native.	Nativity. Foreign.	Race. White.	Race. Colored.
COLUMBIA—Con.					
Roaring Creek ...	486	462	24	486	......
Scott	1465	1429	36	1438	27
Sugar Loaf	739	731	8	739	......
CRAWFORD.					
Athens	1317	1290	27	1317	......
Beaver	1177	1101	76	1177	......
Bloomfield	1262	1238	24	1262	......
Riceville, (boro')	301	290	11	301	......
Cambridge	747	700	47	747	......
Cambridge, (boro')	452	436	16	451	1
Conneaut	1729	1667	62	1729	......
Cussewago	1674	1578	96	1662	12
East Fallowfield ..	1167	1098	69	1167	......
East Fairfield	741	661	80	741	......
Cochranton, (boro')	459	398	61	458	1
Fairfield	871	822	49	871	......
Greenwood	1782	1761	21	1771	11
Hayfield	1824	1732	92	1821	3
Mead (*b*)	2421	2073	348	2398	23
Meadville	7103	5744	1359	6917	*c*185
North Shenango ..	901	866	35	898	3
Oil Creek (*d*)	2041	1768	273	2040	1
Oil Creek, (boro').	428	353	75	428	......
Pine	343	328	15	343	......
Linesville, (boro').	434	421	13	429	5
Randolph	1732	1566	166	1731	1
Richmond	1399	1376	23	1398	1
Rockdale	1664	1591	73	1659	5
Rome	1274	1140	134	1274	......
Centreville, (boro')	322	314	8	322	......
Sadsbury	894	865	29	893	1
Evansburg, (boro')	174	171	3	174	......
South Shenango ..	1042	965	77	1042	......
Sparta	1131	1088	43	1128	3
Spartansburg, (borough)	457	391	66	457	......
Spring	1522	1457	65	1521	1
Conneautville, (borough)	1000	908	92	985	15
Spring, (borough)	323	319	4	323	......
Steuben	1020	968	52	1020	......
Townsville, (boro')	280	269	11	280	......
Summerhill	1232	1153	79	1232	......
Summit	1034	991	43	1034	......
Titusville	8639	6185	2454	8432	207
Troy	983	954	29	983	......
Union	622	508	114	622	......
Venango	623	571	52	623	......
Venango, (boro')..	318	286	32	318	......
Vernon	1615	1353	262	1615	......
Vallonia, (boro') ..	462	307	155	462	......
Wayne	1464	1359	105	1464	......
West Fallowfield	503	481	22	503	......
Hartstown, (boro')	188	183	5	188	......
West Shenango ...	357	344	13	357	......
Woodcock	1723	1633	90	1723	......
Saegert'wn, (boro')	441	412	29	439	2
Woodcock, (boro')	220	214	6	220	......
Blooming Val'y	209	202	7	209	......
CUMBERLAND.					
Dickinson	1617	1596	21	1489	128
E. Pennsborough .	2719	2635	84	2712	7
Frankford	1369	1358	11	1357	12
Hampden	1199	1186	13	1196	3
Hopewell	977	971	6	958	19
Newburg, (boro')	392	392	......	392	......
Lower Allen	1336	1320	16	1332	4

...ed as indentical with Bloom Township.
...ve of city of Meadville.

(*c*) Also 1 Indian.
(*d*) Exclusive of city of Titusville.

TABLE IX.—*Population of Minor Civil Divisions, &c.—PENNSYLVANIA—Continued.*

Counties.	Total.	Nativity. Native.	Nativity. Foreign.	Race. White.	Race. Colored.
CUMBERLAND—Cont'd.					
Middlesex	1417	1375	42	1398	19
Mifflin	1455	1442	13	1445	*a*9
Monroe	1832	1815	17	1829	3
Newton	2345	2309	36	2237	108
Newville, (boro')	907	898	9	872	35
North Middleton	1223	1182	41	1196	27
Carlisle, (boro')	6650	6249	401	5596	*a*1053
Penn	1888	1844	44	1853	35
Shippensburg	381	376	5	311	70
Shippensburg, (borough)	2065	2050	15	1894	171
Silver Spring	2259	2233	26	2248	11
Mechanicsburg, (borough)	2569	2519	50	2459	110
Southampton	2050	2030	20	2028	22
South Middleton	3226	3184	42	3148	78
Upper Allen	1341	1316	25	1317	24
New Cumberland, (borough)	515	514	1	515	......
W. Pennsborough	2180	2172	8	2113	67
DAUPHIN.					
Conowago	831	826	5	830	1
Derry	2877	2795	82	2849	28
Derry	216	215	1	216	......
Hummelstown	837	818	19	821	16
East Hanover	1723	1712	11	1712	11
Halifax	1905	1883	22	1892	13
Halifax	568	555	13	568	......
Harrisburg	23104	20309	2795	20817	2287
Jackson	1036	1033	3	1036	......
Jefferson	843	835	8	843	......
Londonderry	1935	1854	81	1852	83
Lower Paxton	1623	1602	21	1617	6
Lower Swatara	1290	1275	15	1258	32
Highspire	612	601	11	597	15
Middleton, (boro')	2980	2880	100	2810	170
Lykens	1246	1235	11	1245	1
Gratz, (borough)	386	382	4	372	14
Matamoras	143	......	......	......	......
Middle Paxton	1317	1298	19	1288	29
Dauphin, (boro')	739	727	12	733	6
Mifflin	614	614	......	614	......
Berrysburg, (boro')	451	447	4	451	......
Uniontown, (boro')	299	298	1	299	......
Reed	353	353	......	352	1
Rush	105	101	4	105	......
South Hanover	1196	1183	13	1196	......
Susquehanna	2264	2049	215	2189	75
Rockville	259	253	6	258	1
Upper Paxton	1371	1360	11	1370	1
Millersb'rg, (boro')	1518	1497	21	1503	15
Upper Swatara (*b*)	1991	1775	216	1799	192
Baldwin	477	327	150	457	20
Church Hill	159	157	2	159	......
Washington	1255	1250	5	1255	......
West Hanover	1044	1031	13	1042	2
Wiconisco	2993	2319	674	2988	5
Williams	1451	1080	371	1451	......
DELAWARE.					
Aston	1845	1536	309	1776	69
Bethel	554	519	35	543	11
Birmingham	765	649	116	663	102
Chester (*c*)	1452	1121	331	1355	97
Chester	9485	7492	1993	8773	712
S. Chester, (boro')	1242	1004	238	956	286
Upland, (borough)	1341	905	436	1332	9
Concord	1293	1180	113	1121	172
Darby	995	862	133	855	140
DELAWARE—Con.					
Darby, (borough)	1205	978	227	1084	[illegible]
Edgemont	678	647	31	651	[illegible]
Haverford	1338	1038	300	1309	[illegible]
Lower Chichester	1129	1020	109	1054	[illegible]
Marple	858	807	51	823	[illegible]
Middletown	2578	2123	455	2378	[illegible]
Nether Providence	1448	1091	357	1405	[illegible]
Newtown	748	704	44	703	[illegible]
Radnor	1431	1132	299	1384	[illegible]
Ridley	1142	914	228	1104	[illegible]
Springfield	1267	1126	141	1228	[illegible]
Thornbury	990	878	112	889	[illegible]
Tinicum	147	116	31	125	[illegible]
Upper Chichester	539	498	41	494	[illegible]
Upper Darby	3130	2511	629	[illegible]	[illegible]
Upper Providence	758	612	146	682	[illegible]
Media, (borough)	1015	921	124	[illegible]	108
ELK.					
Bennezette	902	553	349	902	......
Benzinger	1630	924	706	1630	......
St. Mary's, (boro')	1084	728	356	1082	2
Fox	1188	896	292	1188	......
Highland	98	86	12	98	......
Horton	631	570	61	631	......
Jay	534	475	59	534	......
Jones	1091	681	410	1031	60
Millstone	173	166	7	173	......
Ridgway	800	635	165	798	2
Spring Creek	357	340	17	357	......
ERIE.					
Amity	924	901	23	924	......
Concord	1436	1303	133	1425	11
Conneaut	1538	1489	49	1533	5
Albion, (borough)	452	418	34	452	......
Corry	6809	5080	1729	6726	83
Elk Creek	1462	1346	116	1462	......
Erie	19646	12718	6928	19446	200
Fairview	1674	1367	307	1671	3
Fairview, (boro')	480	402	78	480	......
Franklin	994	926	68	994	......
Girard	2018	1819	199	2015	3
Girard, (borough)	704	614	90	700	4
Lockport, (boro')	405	398	7	405	......
Green	1395	1074	321	1391	4
Greenfield	1039	946	93	1039	......
Harbor Creek	1974	1682	292	1951	23
Le Bœuf	1748	1660	88	1742	6
McKean	1426	1154	272	1426	......
Middleboro'gh	126	105	21	126	......
Mill Creek (*d*)	2744	2080	664	2726	18
Northeast	2213	1805	408	2207	6
Northeast, (boro')	900	816	84	896	[illegible]
Springfield	1742	1665	77	1740	[illegible]
Summit	1047	802	245	1047	......
Union	1334	1209	125	1332	[illegible]
Union, (borough)	1500	1226	274	1495	[illegible]
Venango	1370	1307	63	1370	......
Wattsburg, (boro')	286	277	9	284	[illegible]
Washington	1943	1816	127	1943	......
Edinboro, (boro')	801	765	36	801	......
Waterford	1884	1669	215	1879	[illegible]
Waterford, (boro')	790	723	67	785	[illegible]
Wayne	1295	1242	53	1295	......
FAYETTE.					
Brownsville	286	273	13	257	29

(*a*) Also 1 Indian.
(*b*) Exclusive of city of Harrisburg.
(*c*) Exclusive of city of Chester.
(*d*) Exclusive of city of Erie.

.—*Population of Minor Civil Divisions, &c.—PENNSYLVANIA*—Continued.

s.	Total.	NATIVITY. Native.	NATIVITY. Foreign.	RACE. White.	RACE. Colored.
ont'd.					
boro')	1749	1599	150	1573	176
......	1657	1635	22	1656	1
......	1163	990	173	1156	7
boro')	1292	1206	86	1273	19
......	2972	2736	236	2911	61
boro')	333	326	7	287	46
......	1299	1293	6	1268	31
......	2544	2523	21	2532	12
......	1911	1908	3	1909	2
......	951	936	15	951	......
......	1381	1344	37	1329	52
......	1807	1772	35	1626	181
boro')	1199	1154	45	961	238
......	1376	1359	17	1342	34
......	1359	1356	3	1304	55
......	1683	1660	23	1613	70
......	1445	1430	15	1417	28
......	1152	1121	31	1099	53
......	1209	1199	10	1208	1
......	860	851	9	832	28
boro')	2503	2416	87	2239	a263
......	1629	1554	75	1628	1
......	1644	1630	14	1634	10
......	1266	1095	171	1261	5
......	2276	2222	54	2271	5
......	1065	959	106	1018	47
boro')	906	880	26	887	19
ity,					
......	889	844	45	879	10
......	1478	1397	81	1459	19
......	504	485	19	504	......
......	226	176	50	225	1
......	1226	1040	186	1225	1
......	513	489	24	508	5
......	78	47	31	78	......
......	118	108	10	118	......
......	575	520	55	575	......
......	450	391	59	450	......
ro')...	320	304	16	320	......
:.					
......	3762	3657	105	3629	133
tle,					
......	1650	1616	34	1502	148
......	2146	2138	8	2118	28
......	3357	3304	53	3209	148
......	3097	3015	82	2960	137
urg,					
......	6308	5793	515	5441	867
......	1630	1597	33	1518	112
......	2178	2155	23	2164	14
......	1326	1320	6	1320	6
......	1419	1387	32	1400	19
......	3611	3566	45	3261	350
urg,					
......	971	938	33	862	109
......	2603	2546	57	2457	146
......	315	308	7	313	2
......	3127	3047	80	3039	88
......	1963	1949	14	1860	103
......	305	......	......	......	......
......	1902	1880	22	1886	16
as...	389	385	4	389	......
......	606	600	6	606	......
......	2364	2321	43	2337	27
ro',					
......	1345	1314	31	1334	11

Counties.	Total.	NATIVITY. Native.	NATIVITY. Foreign.	RACE. White.	RACE. Colored.
FULTON.					
Ayr	1247	1211	36	1196	51
Belfast	856	855	1	856	......
Bethel	861	839	22	828	33
Brush Creek	876	862	14	870	6
Dublin	879	851	28	865	14
Licking Creek	925	916	9	925	......
Taylor	868	865	3	866	2
Thompson	649	641	8	641	8
Todd	634	589	45	605	29
McConnellsburg, (borough)	552	536	16	545	7
Union	424	363	61	424	......
Wells	589	587	2	588	1
GREENE.					
Aleppo	1382	1373	9	1361	21
Centre	1777	1773	4	1723	54
Cumberland	1768	1751	17	1739	29
Carmichael's, (borough)	491	489	2	490	1
Dunkard	1520	1520	......	1516	4
Franklin	1500	1404	6	1453	47
Gilmore	703	702	1	701	2
Green	739	734	5	730	......
Jackson	964	962	2	925	39
Jefferson	1322	1307	15	1317	5
Marion	1349	1318	31	1267	82
Waynesburg, (borough)	1272	......	......	......	......
Monongahela	1424	1420	4	1373	51
Morgan	1101	1095	6	1099	2
Morris	1296	1287	9	1295	1
Perry	1292	1291	1	1249	43
Rich Hill	2470	2454	16	2447	23
Spring Hill	1484	1468	16	1431	33
Washington	765	761	4	765	......
Wayne	1563	1563	......	1527	36
Whitely	977	973	4	957	20
HUNTINGDON.					
Barree	1237	1211	26	1237	......
Brady	904	894	10	904	......
Carbon	2233	1508	725	2231	2
Bro'd Top City	327	258	69	326	1
Coal Mont	189	165	24	189	......
Cass	599	596	3	583	16
Cassville, (boro)	416	413	3	416	......
Clay	818	808	10	811	7
Three Springs, (borough)	189	183	6	189	......
Cromwell	1380	1361	19	1379	1
Orbisonia	177	173	4	177	......
Dublin	984	968	16	975	9
Franklin	1355	1319	36	1347	8
Henderson	661	624	37	661	......
Hopewell	412	404	8	412	......
Jackson	1662	1635	27	1662	......
Juniata	393	371	22	393	......
Lincoln	532	522	10	532	......
Morris	688	664	24	687	1
Oneida	386	359	27	384	2
Huntingdon, (borough)	3034	2787	247	2865	169
Penn	1143	1098	45	1139	4
Porter	1253	1241	12	1212	41
Alexandria, (boro')	556	532	24	555	1
Shirley	1633	1603	30	1623	10
Mt. Union, (boro')	535	511	24	535	......
Shirleysb'g, (boro')	329	311	18	329	......

(*a*) Also 1 Chinese.

TABLE IX.—*Population of Minor Civil Divisions, &c.—PENNSYLVANIA—Continued.*

Counties.	Total.	NATIVITY.		RACE.	
		Native.	Foreign.	White.	Colored.
LUZERNE—Cont'd.					
Scott	1132	1092	40	1127	5
Scranton	35092	19205	15887	35043	49
Slocum	317	314	3	317	......
Spring Brook	426	317	109	426	......
Sugar Loaf	1240	1162	78	1240	......
Union	1637	1623	14	1632	5
Wilkesbarre	7090	3928	3162	7003	87
Wilkesbarre, (borough)	10174	7517	2657	9758	416
Wright	603	494	109	603	......
LYCOMING.					
Anthony	543	525	18	543	......
Armstrong	1424	1269	155	1421	3
Bastress	251	173	78	251	......
Brady	394	388	6	394	......
Brown	347	343	4	347	......
Cascade	595	463	132	595	......
Clinton	1315	1278	37	1315	......
Cogan House	599	555	44	594	5
Cummings	277	276	1	277	......
Eldred	739	705	34	739	......
Fairfield	479	450	29	479	......
Montoursville, (borough)	1048	1005	43	1046	2
Franklin	739	736	3	739	......
Hepburn	971	884	87	971	......
Jackson	542	521	21	542	......
Jordan	473	459	14	473	......
Lewis	963	854	109	961	2
Limestone (a)	1256	1128	128	1256	......
Loyalsock	1475	1323	152	1412	63
Lycoming	642	594	48	642	......
McHenry	309	305	4	309	......
McIntyre	674	574	100	670	4
Mifflin	1004	923	81	1004	......
Moreland	815	810	5	815	......
Muncy	978	939	39	969	9
Muncy Creek	1510	1466	44	1503	7
Muncy, (borough)	1040	1013	27	1029	11
Nippenose	567	498	69	554	13
Old Lycoming	475	462	13	475	......
Penn	701	694	7	701	......
Piatt	493	479	14	493	......
Pine	527	493	34	527	......
Plunkett's Creek	415	399	16	415	......
Porter	650	600	50	606	44
Jersey Shore, (borough)	1394	1322	72	1352	42
Shrewsbury	442	433	9	442	......
Susquehanna	346	304	42	346	......
Upper Fairfield	770	702	68	770	......
Washington	1122	1099	23	1122	......
Watson	280	268	12	280	......
Williamsport	16030	13404	2626	15386	644
Wolf	819	797	22	817	2
Hughesville, (borough)	456	447	9	456	......
Woodward	737	708	29	737	......
McKEAN.					
Annin	760	642	118	760	......
Bradford	1446	1347	99	1445	1
Ceres	798	668	130	798	......
Corydon	169	160	9	169	......
Eldred	897	835	62	896	1
Hamilton	120	110	10	120	......
Hamlin	121	112	9	121	......
Keating	1435	1300	135	1431	4
Smethport	231	212	19	228	3
Lafayette	591	392	199	591	......
McKEAN—Cont'd.					
Liberty	1093	1062	31	1089	4
Norwich	257	234	23	257	......
Otto	298	296	2	298	......
Sergeant	119	88	31	119	......
Wetmore	721	430	291	707	14
MERCER.					
Cool Spring	865	769	96	860	5
Deer Creek	579	575	4	579	......
Delaware	1703	1630	73	1703	......
E. Lackawannock	672	613	59	640	32
Fairview	920	814	106	920	......
Findley	1710	1421	289	1692	18
Mercer, (borough)	1235	1153	82	1196	39
French Creek	999	932	67	999	......
Green	832	790	42	832	......
Jamestown, (boro')	572	498	74	571	1
Hempfield	1119	1008	111	1119	......
Greenville, (boro')	1848	1661	187	1845	3
Hickory	7700	4790	2910	7675	25
Sharon, (borough)	4221	2990	1231	4201	20
Jackson	752	704	48	752	......
Jefferson	1292	1205	87	1271	21
Lackawannock	1079	1018	61	1071	8
Lake	524	479	45	524	......
Liberty	634	605	29	631	3
Mill Creek	1086	1069	17	1085	1
New Lebanon	273	273	......	273	......
New Vernon	796	745	51	796	......
Otter Creek	560	532	28	560	......
Perry	914	848	66	914	......
Pine	1235	1164	71	1235	......
Pymatuning	2549	2053	496	2506	43
Clarksville, (boro')	350	337	22	358	1
Salem	686	657	29	686	......
Sandy Creek	734	706	28	733	1
Sheakleyville, (borough)	273	263	10	272	1
Sandy Lake	1028	930	98	1020	8
Sandy L'ke, (boro')	428	407	21	428	......
Shenango	2616	1865	751	2615	1
West Middlesex, (borough)	888	805	83	883	5
Springfield	1318	1252	66	1312	6
Stoneboro, (boro')	471	281	190	463	8
Sugar Grove	511	486	25	511	......
West Salem	2082	1818	264	2075	7
Wilmington	548	522	26	540	8
Wolf Creek	555	506	49	555	......
Worth	1084	1041	43	1072	12
MIFFLIN.					
Armagh	1873	1844	29	1864	9
Bratton	852	839	13	852	......
Brown	1192	1150	42	1184	[illegible]
Decatur	1171	1158	13	1171	......
Derry	1901	1806	95	1901	......
Granville	1297	1252	45	1292	[illegible]
Lewistown, (boro')	2737	2588	149	2590	[illegible]
Menno	1173	1164	9	1172	[illegible]
Oliver	1355	1296	59	1333	[illegible]
McVeyto'n, (boro')	685	645	40	670	[illegible]
Union	1469	1439	30	1466	[illegible]
Wayne	1453	1410	43	1440	[illegible]
Newton Hamilton, (borough)	350	339	11	350	......
MONROE.					
Barrett	930	762	168	930	......
Chestnut Hill	1419	1385	34	1419	......
Coolbaugh	1028	830	198	1028	......
Eldred	937	934	3	936	1
Hamilton	1892	1879	13	1892	......

(a) Exclusive of city of Williamsport.

: IX.—*Population of Minor Civil Divisions, &c.—PENNSYLVANIA*—Continued.

...nties.	Total.	NATIVITY. Native.	NATIVITY. Foreign.	RACE. White.	RACE. Colored.
...E—Cont'd.					
....	851	834	17	850	1
...Smithfield	1359	1320	39	1359	......
... .	622	566	56	622	......
....	1119	1059	60	1119	......
....	1076	995	81	1076	......
....	259	250	9	259	......
....	734	724	10	734	......
...eld........	1443	1373	70	1396	47
....	2160	2032	128	2122	38
...burg, (bo-...)	1793	1719	74	1675	118
...ana	477	442	35	477	......
...nnock	263	252	11	263	......
...GOMERY.					
...n.........	2440	2018	422	2375	65
...ham	2462	1926	536	2404	58
....	1604	1571	33	1602	2
...ia	1959	1910	49	1958	1
...k	1818	1705	113	1818	......
...d	2094	1964	130	2070	24
...Wales, (bo-...)	407	385	22	407	......
....	1512	1381	131	1510	2
...n.........	1382	1292	90	1361	21
...k	2600	2483	117	2598	2
...derion	4886	3885	1001	4765	121
...Providence	1572	1491	81	1559	13
...Salford ...	1645	1570	75	1645	......
...ough	1303	1191	112	1303	......
...mery.	922	857	65	911	11
...ld	2207	2069	138	2146	61
...anover	1900	1838	62	1899	1
...n	1335	1218	117	1318	17
...wn, (boro')	10753	9133	1620	10339	414
...ien	2056	1999	57	2054	2
...th	2025	1645	380	1999	26
...hocken, (borough).	3071	2175	896	3047	24
...ove	2895	2782	113	2887	8
...wn, (boro')	4125	3861	264	4096	29
...eld	1222	998	224	1213	9
...ensing	1209	1184	25	1208	1
...Dublin	1588	1427	161	1528	60
...Hanover..	2197	2128	69	2197	......
...derion	3870	2944	926	3740	130
...ego Mingo	470	333	137	470	......
...ort, (boro')	1578	1216	362	1553	25
...shohocken	470	310	160	469	1
...hinactes..	173	150	23	173	......
...tton Hill ..	50	27	23	50	......
...Kennedy	516	365	151	472	44
...desburg ..	386	256	130	386	......
...ley Forge	119	94	25	119	......
...Providence	3202	2989	213	3158	44
...Salford	1705	1621	84	1704	1
...Marsh.....	3151	2687	464	3100	51
...ino	1330	1227	103	1318	12
...tor........	1587	1552	35	1585	2
...NTOUR.					
...y.	959	942	17	959	......
....	414	393	21	413	1
....	716	712	4	716	......
...gtonville, (borough)	172	170	2	172	......
....	1229	1205	24	1229	......
...ono	710	709	1	709	1
...ag	1036	832	204	1016	20
...e, (boro')..	8436	6372	2064	8379	57

Counties.	Total.	NATIVITY. Native.	NATIVITY. Foreign.	RACE. White.	RACE. Colored.
MONTOUR—Cont'd.					
Mayberry	215	213	2	215	......
Valley	1061	884	177	1061	......
West Hemlock ...	396	392	4	396	......
NORTHAMPTON.					
Allen	2040	1804	236	2040	......
Bethlehem	2230	2142	88	2223	7
Bethlehem, (boro')	4512	4117	395	4477	a34
Freemansburg, (borough)	643	601	42	640	3
South Bethlehem, (borough)	3556	2450	1106	3537	19
Bushkill..........	1901	1789	112	1899	2
East Allen	1180	1157	23	1180	......
Bath, (borough) ..	707	690	17	707	......
Forks	1450	1412	38	1445	5
Easton, (borough)	10987	9664	1323	10889	98
Hanover	499	495	4	499	......
Lehigh	3496	3247	249	3496	......
Lower Mt. Bethel	3641	3474	167	3641	......
Lower Nazareth..	1086	1061	25	1086	......
Lower Saucon	4991	4463	528	4979	12
Moore	2938	2812	126	2938	......
Chapman, (boro').	388	195	193	386	2
Palmer...........	1444	1335	109	1444	......
Plainfield	1988	1816	172	1988	......
Upper Mt Bethel	3764	3568	196	3763	1
Upper Nazareth..	740	688	52	740	......
Nazareth, (boro')	949	879	70	948	1
Williams	2428	2274	154	2428	......
Glendon, (boro') ..	707	444	263	707	......
South Easton, (borough)	3167	2481	686	3165	2
NORTHUMBERLAND.					
Cameron	603	572	31	603	......
Chillisquaque	1597	1572	25	1597	......
Milton, (borough).	1909	1829	80	1878	31
Coal......... ...	2920	1882	1038	2890	30
Shamokin (boro')	4320	3488	832	4300	20
Delaware	1879	1859	20	1875	4
McEwinsville, (borough)	342	338	4	342	......
Watsontown, (borough)	1181	1147	34	1180	1
Jackson	886	884	2	886	......
Jordan	924	923	1	924	......
Lewis	1228	1212	16	1225	3
Turbotville, (borough)	417	406	11	417	......
Little Mahanoy ..	269	266	3	269	......
Lower Augusta ..	1802	1794	8	1802	......
Lower Mahanoy..	1790	1784	6	1789	1
Mount Carmel ...	2451	1366	1085	2439	12
Mt. Carmel, (boro')	1289	978	311	1289	......
Point	938	901	37	938	......
Northumberland, (borough)	1788	1710	78	1784	4
Rush	1324	1286	38	1322	2
Shamokin	2282	2255	27	2281	1
Turbot	1803	1777	26	1803	......
Upper Augusta..	1246	1225	21	1245	1
Sunbury, (boro')..	3131	3021	110	3108	23
Upper Mahanoy ..	878	878	......	878	......
Washington	801	798	3	801	......
Zerbo	1446	968	478	1446	......
PERRY.					
Buffalo..........	770	765	5	770	......

(a) Also 1 Indian.

TABLE IX.—*Population of Minor Civil Divisions, &c.*—*PENNSYLVANIA*—Continued.

Counties.	Total.	Nativity. Native.	Nativity. Foreign.	Race. White.	Race. Colored.
PERRY—Cont'd.					
Carroll	1425	1399	26	1425	......
Centre	1121	1007	21	1121	......
Bloomfield, (boro')	655	653	2	654	1
Greenwood	1080	1061	19	1064	16
Millerstown, (borough)	533	508	25	515	18
Howe	410	406	4	402	8
Jackson	1103	1101	2	1100	3
Juniata	983	976	7	983	......
Liverpool	859	857	2	853	6
Liverpool, (boro')	823	822	1	823	......
Madison	1577	1573	4	1575	2
Miller	438	430	8	431	7
Oliver	511	505	6	511	......
Newport, (boro')	945	919	26	939	6
Penn	1529	1463	66	1520	9
Marysville, (boro')	863	848	15	837	26
Petersburg, (boro')	960	935	25	959	1
Rye	703	693	10	687	16
Saville	1693	1670	23	1691	2
Spring	1492	1474	18	1492	......
Toboyne	914	907	7	914	......
New Germantown	133	......	......	......	......
Tuscarora	899	884	15	884	15
Tyrone	1287	1278	9	1283	4
Landisburg, (borough)	369	366	3	369	......
Watts	725	709	16	725	......
New Buffalo	259	257	2	259	......
Wheatfield	780	727	53	780	......
PHILADELPHIA.					
Philadelphia	674022	490398	183624	651854	*a*22147
PIKE.					
Blooming Grove	378	292	86	378	......
Delaware	758	683	75	730	28
Dingman	519	393	126	507	12
Green	919	742	177	919	......
Lackawaxen	1757	1424	333	1737	20
Lehman	832	805	27	823	9
Milford	912	772	140	882	30
Milford	746	634	112	716	30
Palmyra	570	467	103	570	......
Porter	102	93	9	102	......
Shohola	729	513	216	729	......
Westfall	960	756	204	946	14
POTTER.					
Abbot	534	289	245	534	......
Allegheny	625	615	10	624	1
Bingham	773	769	4	773	......
Clara	195	193	2	187	8
Eulalia	353	307	46	353	......
Coudersport, (borough)	471	403	68	471	......
Genesee	767	628	139	756	11
Harrison	1052	1041	11	1052	......
Hebron	754	739	15	754	......
Hector	651	640	11	651	......
Homer	160	141	19	159	1
Jackson	49	49	......	49	......
Keating	78	75	3	78	......
Oswayo	629	591	38	629	......
Pike	184	183	1	184	......
Pleasant Valley	140	134	6	139	1
Roulet	525	453	72	525	......

Counties.	Total.	Nativity. Native.	Nativity. Foreign.	Race. White.	Race. Colored.
POTTER—Cont'd.					
Sharon	968	944	24	968	......
Stewardson	210	185	25	210	......
Summit	145	143	2	145	......
Sweden	357	319	38	357	......
Sylvania	267	248	19	267	......
Ulysses	789	772	17	789	......
Lewisville	226	223	3	226	......
West Branch	302	221	81	302	......
Wharton	287	286	1	287	......
SCHUYLKILL.					
Barry	950	886	64	935	15
Blythe	1924	1281	643	1924	......
Middleport, (boro')	377	252	125	377	......
New Philadelphia, (borough)	558	371	187	558	......
Branch	1200	946	254	1200	......
Butler	5905	3637	2268	5904	1
Ashland, (boro')	5714	3775	1939	5699	15
Cass	4621	2902	1719	4621	......
East Brunswick	1661	1600	61	1659	2
East Norwegian	983	623	360	983	......
East Union	614	572	42	614	......
Eldred	968	946	22	968	......
Foster	1001	622	379	1001	......
Frailey	1322	989	333	1318	4
Hegins	1154	1133	21	1153	1
Hubley	547	535	12	542	5
Mahanoy	9400	5472	3928	9400	......
Mahanoy, (boro')	5533	3372	2161	5532	1
Shenandoah, (borough)	2951	1679	1272	2951	......
New Castle	2229	1441	788	2229	......
St. Clair, (boro')	5726	3437	2289	5726	......
North Manheim	2420	1956	464	2405	15
Cressona, (boro')	1507	1364	143	1507	......
Mt. Carbon, (boro')	364	245	119	357	7
Palo Alto, (boro')	1740	1206	534	1740	......
Schuylkill Haven, (borough)	2940	2646	294	2934	6
North Union	666	655	11	666	......
Norwegian	1390	902	488	1390	......
Minersville, (borough)	3699	2530	1169	3698	1
Port Carbon, (borough)	2251	1746	505	2249	2
Yorkville, (boro')	553	371	182	553	......
Pine Grove	2274	2217	57	2266	8
Pine Grove, (boro')	845	808	37	844	1
Porter	1167	995	172	1167	......
Johnstown	70	53	17	70	......
Reiner City	116	96	20	116	......
Tower City	358	306	52	358	......
Williams Valley	425	407	18	425	......
Pottsville, (boro')	12384	9672	2712	12184	200
Rahn	1227	734	493	1227	......
Reilly	1890	1136	754	1890	......
Rush	2291	1438	853	2290	1
Ryan	600	532	68	600	......
Schuylkill	1840	1312	528	1840	......
Tamaqua, (boro')	5960	4382	1578	5932	28
South Manheim	929	891	38	928	1
Auburn, (boro')	511	493	18	511	......
Tremont	754	556	198	739	15
Tremont, (boro')	1709	1356	353	1709	......
Union	1110	1056	54	1110	......
Up'er Mahantango	761	758	3	761	......
Washington	1313	1301	12	1307	6
Wayne	1549	1503	43	1546	......
West Brunswick	1163	1148	15	1156	7

(*a*) Also 12 Chinese, 1 Japanese, and 8 Indians.

: IX.—*Population of Minor Civil Divisions, &c.—PENNSYLVANIA*—Continued.

…nties.	Total.	Nativity. Native.	Nativity. Foreign.	Race. White.	Race. Colored.
…KILL—Con.					
…burg, (bo-…)	728	706	22	728	......
…nton, (bo-…)	578	532	46	536	42
…enn	1980	1954	26	1980	......
…YDER.					
…	1766	1761	5	1766	......
…	885	885	......	872	13
…n	1007	1004	3	1007	......
…n	934	926	8	929	5
…burg, (bo-…)	370	370	......	370	......
…i	712	704	8	712	......
…Creek	574	574	......	574	......
…	1126	1123	3	1121	5
…	1415	1411	4	1414	1
…Grove, (bo-…)	1453	1433	20	1444	9
…	1016	1009	7	1016	......
…	1091	1086	5	1091	......
…gton	1541	1533	8	1541	......
…eaver	1131	1124	7	1131	......
…erry	585	584	1	585	......
…MERSET.					
…n	1456	1431	25	1454	2
…eny	1133	982	151	1133	......
…svalley	1597	1526	71	1597	......
…(borough)	640	579	61	640	......
…ugh	1172	1128	44	1172	......
…	1012	968	44	1011	1
…ry, (boro')	291	281	10	291	......
…ille	494	441	53	494	......
…on	706	673	33	706	......
…	1703	1647	56	1696	7
…r	951	714	237	947	4
…Turkeyfoot	1264	1117	147	1263	1
…creek	580	568	12	580	......
…l	1409	1375	34	1409	......
…entreville, (…ugh)	196	195	1	196	......
…mpton	1137	865	272	1136	1
…	923	908	15	923	......
…boning	1213	1200	13	1213	......
…wn, (boro')	288	284	4	287	1
…	1287	1269	18	1287	......
…et	2836	2725	111	2834	2
…et, (boro')	945	920	25	944	1
…mpton	673	610	63	673	......
…sburg, (bo-…h)	290	254	36	286	4
…creek	1526	1498	28	1526	......
…t	1493	1325	168	1492	1
…Turkeyfoot	1011	944	67	991	20
…LLIVAN.					
…	1710	1327	383	1710	......
…re, (boro')	376	325	51	376	......
…	336	286	50	334	2
…on	634	619	15	634	......
…d	705	608	97	703	2
…	854	749	105	854	......
…	443	421	22	443	......
…rove	249	237	12	249	......
…o	530	395	135	530	......
…e, (boro')	145	132	13	145	......
…bury	209	192	17	208	1
…UEHANNA.					
…on	528	386	142	528	......

Counties.	Total.	Nativity. Native.	Nativity. Foreign.	Race. White.	Race. Colored.
SUSQUEHANNA—Continued.					
Ararat	771	606	165	769	2
Auburn	2006	1891	115	2006	......
Bridgewater	1459	1410	49	1455	1
Montrose, (boro')	1463	1395	68	1293	170
Brooklyn	1128	1103	25	1118	10
Choconut	939	743	196	939	......
Friendsville	223	182	41	223	......
Little Meadows	133	123	10	133	......
Clifford	1532	1391	141	1532	......
Dundaff	187	181	6	187	......
Dimock	1124	1075	49	1124	......
Forest Lake	995	883	112	995	......
Franklin	849	775	74	847	2
Gibson	1368	1303	65	1366	2
Great Bend	1431	1280	151	1427	4
Great Bend, (borough)	855	681	174	854	1
Harford	1595	1517	78	1579	16
Harmony	1212	989	223	1211	1
Herrick	950	778	172	950	......
Jackson	1175	1153	22	1175	......
Jessup	804	786	18	802	2
Lathrop	983	955	28	983	......
Lenox	1751	1653	98	1751	......
Liberty	1030	947	83	1030	......
Middletown	871	682	189	871	......
New Milford	1647	1566	81	1642	5
New Milford, (borough)	600	548	52	600	......
Oakland	1106	887	219	1102	4
Susquehanna, (borough)	2729	1948	781	2729	......
Rush	1418	1320	98	1418	......
Silver Lake	1079	839	240	1079	......
Springville	1424	1406	18	1400	24
Thompson	701	623	78	699	2
TIOGA.					
Bloss	4008	2249	1759	4006	2
Brookfield	885	875	10	877	8
Charleston	2014	1877	137	2009	5
Chatham	1575	1562	13	1575	......
Clymer	1079	1068	11	1079	......
Covington	811	765	46	806	5
Covington, (boro')	315	292	23	315	......
Deerfield	665	654	11	664	1
Knoxville, (boro')	400	395	5	400	......
Delmar	1885	1812	73	1877	8
Wellsboro, (boro')	1465	1318	147	1436	29
Elk	172	143	29	172	......
Elkland, (boro')	332	330	2	331	1
Farmington	997	985	12	997	......
Gaines	440	433	7	440	......
Jackson	1531	1490	41	1530	1
Lawrence	957	933	24	957	......
Lawrenceville, (borough)	478	462	16	474	4
Liberty	1379	1258	121	1379	......
Middlebury	1500	1470	30	1496	4
Morris	423	405	18	423	......
Nelson	456	447	9	454	2
Osceola	523	507	16	521	2
Richmond	1558	1517	41	1555	3
Mansfield, (boro')	616	595	21	610	6
Rutland	1157	1131	26	1157	......
Shippen	270	266	4	270	......
Sullivan	1637	1622	15	1637	......
Mainsburg	212	210	2	212	......
Tioga	1074	930	144	1073	1
Tioga, (borough)	440	390	50	429	11
Union	1098	983	115	1097	1
Ward	285	280	5	285	......

TABLE IX.—*Population of Minor Civil Divisions, &c.—PENNSYLVANIA*—Continued.

Counties.	Total.	Nativity. Native.	Nativity. Foreign.	Race. White.	Race. Colored.
TIOGA—Cont'd.					
Fall Brook, (boro')	1390	597	793	1390	......
Westfield	912	900	12	912	......
Westfield, (boro')	370	357	13	370	......
UNION.					
Buffalo	1521	1514	7	1521	......
East Buffalo	1011	1004	7	1004	7
Lewisburg, (boro')	3121	3021	100	3020	101
Gregg	821	813	8	821	......
Hartley	1143	1132	11	1122	21
Kelly	942	938	4	938	4
Lewis	1007	1002	5	1007	......
Hartleton	292	291	1	292	......
Limestone	880	869	11	873	7
Mifflinburg, (borough)	911	904	7	910	1
Union	840	813	27	822	18
New Berlin, (borough)	646	639	7	644	2
West Buffalo	1046	1041	5	1046	......
White Door	1676	1610	66	1675	1
VENANGO.					
Allegheny	1485	1279	206	1469	16
Pleasantville, (borough)	1598	1358	240	1576	22
Canal	980	970	10	970	10
Utica, (borough)	225	212	13	225	......
Cherrytree	2326	1972	354	2319	7
Clinton	901	863	38	900	1
Cornplanter	9863	8104	1759	9769	94
Pit Hole City, (borough)	237	189	48	225	12
Cranberry	2337	2153	184	2337	......
Venango City, (borough)	1550	1414	136	1543	7
French Creek	1330	1216	114	1324	6
Franklin	3908	3313	595	3738	170
Irwin	1489	1445	44	1489	......
Jackson	720	709	11	720	......
Cooperstown, (borough)	264	250	14	264	......
Oakland	1082	1051	31	1082	......
Oil Creek	5098	4232	866	5075	23
Oil City, (borough)	2276	1824	452	2217	59
Pine Grove	875	816	59	875	......
Plum	1140	1096	44	1140	......
President	618	544	74	618	......
Richland	1023	1003	20	1023	......
Rockland	2068	1971	97	2067	1
Sandy Creek	1391	1311	80	1391	......
Scrub Grass	997	980	17	997	......
Emberton, (boro')	488	445	43	486	2
Sugar Creek	1656	1419	237	1653	3
WARREN.					
Brokenstraw	1048	853	195	1040	8
Youngsville, (borough)	462	416	46	462	......
Cherry Grove	61	57	4	61	......
Columbus	1257	1120	137	1248	a5
Columbus, (boro')	466	398	68	466	......
Conewango	1212	933	279	1209	3
Warren, (borough)	2014	1524	490	2009	5
Corydon	411	395	16	411	......
Deerfield	2324	1969	355	2307	17
Tidioute, (boro')	1638	1293	345	1618	20
Eldred	557	537	20	556	1
Elk	469	401	68	469	......
Farmington	1101	959	142	1101	......
WARREN—Cont'd.					
Freehold	1316	1158	158	1311	5
Glade	899	724	175	875	24
Kinzua	318	302	16	318	......
Limestone	848	721	127	845	3
Mead	463	325	138	462	1
Pine Grove	1206	1099	107	1206	......
Pittsfield	1260	1044	216	1257	3
Pleasant	385	287	98	383	(b)
Sheffield	660	490	170	659	1
Southwest	677	655	22	677	......
Spring Creek	1116	1066	50	1108	8
Sugar Grove	1729	1265	464	1729	......
WASHINGTON.					
Allen	815	736	79	802	13
Amwell	1879	1861	18	1871	8
Buffalo	1189	1156	33	1185	4
Taylorstown	98	95	3	98	......
Canton	592	573	19	577	15
Carroll	3178	2518	660	3020	158
Monongahela, (borough)	1078	1035	43	1020	58
Cecil	1102	1004	98	[illegible]	[illegible]
Chartiers	1870	1703	167	1696	[illegible]
Cannonsburg, (borough)	641	609	32	563	78
Cross Creek	1034	982	52	969	65
Cross Creek	134	133	1	134	......
Donegal	2068	2005	63	2030	38
Claysville	284	276	8	284	......
East Bethlehem	1621	1586	35	1606	15
Millboro, (boro')	324	322	2	324	......
East Finley	1186	1175	11	1186	......
East Pike Run	817	783	34	799	18
California, (boro')	659	656	3	653	6
Greenfield, (boro')	386	367	19	385	1
West Brownsv'e, (borough)	547	534	13	536	11
Fallowfield	834	821	13	801	33
Franklin	1074	1046	28	1010	64
Washington, (borough)	3571	3364	207	3141	[illegible]
Hanover	1898	1829	69	1786	112
Hopewell	804	775	29	710	94
West Middleto'n, (borough)	346	328	18	303	43
Independence	977	946	31	921	56
Independence	144	138	6	137	7
Jefferson	880	860	20	867	13
Morris	1050	1040	10	1048	2
Mount Pleasant	1321	1230	91	1298	23
North Strabane	1273	1192	81	1144	129
Nottingham	924	886	38	910	14
Peters	943	888	55	940	3
Robinson	937	861	76	921	16
Smith	2067	1815	252	2034	33
Somerset	1325	1309	16	1303	22
Bentleysville	277	277	......	268	9
South Strabane	1159	1108	51	1089	70
Union	1418	1168	250	1404	14
West Bethlehem	1964	1933	31	1963	1
West Finley	1471	1448	23	1441	30
West Pike Run	1252	1238	14	1147	105
Beallville	297	296	1	286	11
WAYNE.					
Berlin	1295	965	330	1295	......
Buckingham	1127	944	183	1125	2
Canaan	680	527	153	680	......
Waymart, (boro')	567	501	66	561	6
Cherry Ridge	1101	800	301	1100	1

(*a*) Also 4 Indians.

(*b*) Also 2 Indians.

X.—*Population of Minor Civil Divisions, &c.—PENNSYLVANIA*—Continued.

…s.	Total.	Nativity. Native.	Nativity. Foreign.	Race. White.	Race. Colored.
…ont'd.					
……	1178	958	220	1178	……
……	2823	2474	349	2823	……
……	1196	914	282	1182	14
…y……	202	147	55	201	1
……	628	538	90	627	1
…' ……	1269	1135	134	1269	……
…sant ..	1952	1590	362	1951	1
……	690	510	180	690	……
……	2481	1749	732	2477	4
……	642	534	108	638	4
……	1400	1230	170	1400	……
……	2607	2402	205	2607	……
……	817	764	53	817	……
…an ….	1308	1208	100	1308	……
……	1454	1250	204	1454	……
……	4449	2818	1631	4442	7
…(boro').	2654	1931	723	2653	1
…(boro').	394	323	71	394	……
…rough)	476	404	72	476	……
…LAND.					
……	1710	1560	150	1709	1
……	810	786	24	793	17
……	1819	1715	104	1812	7
……	875	853	22	874	1
……	4959	4663	296	4918	41
…rough)	1127	1021	106	1122	5
… (boro')					
…andria,	211	209	2	208	3
…) ……	305	296	9	305	……
……	1112	1086	26	1112	……
…oro') ..	192	189	3	192	……
…ngton.	2134	2099	35	2104	30
……	1895	1815	80	1880	15
…'……	298	269	29	298	……
……	1796	1748	48	1793	3
……	5819	5584	235	5786	33
…burg ..	229	227	2	229	……
…, (bor-					
……	1642	1569	73	1601	41
…boro')..	533	523	10	533	……
……	2434	2380	54	2433	1
…boro')..	317	310	7	316	1
…a ……	813	785	28	804	9
…sant ..	2547	2492	55	2492	55
…asant,					
…) ……	717	713	4	689	28
…tington	3493	2589	904	3456	37
…ough)..	833	712	121	826	7
……	2423	2240	183	2419	4
…ugh) ..	820	583	237	820	……
……	2786	2583	203	2597	189
……	2124	2085	39	2106	18
…ough) .	448	438	10	447	1
……	2372	2096	276	2367	5
…tington	2210	2151	59	2210	……
…ewton,					
…) ……	992	858	134	991	1
……	777	747	30	773	4
…nce(bo')	333	326	7	333	……
……	3624	3301	323	3624	……
…own,					
…) ……	301	285	16	301	……
…n……	1416	1391	25	1414	2
…NG.					
……	620	588	32	619	1

Counties.	Total.	Nativity. Native.	Nativity. Foreign.	Race. White.	Race. Colored.
WYOMING—Cont'd.					
Clinton	834	796	38	834	……
Eaton	830	826	4	829	1
Exeter	211	211	……	211	……
Falls	1096	1064	32	1095	1
Forkston	576	555	21	576	……
Lemon	531	523	8	531	……
Mehoopany	888	873	15	888	……
Meshoppen	1239	1137	102	1238	1
Monroe	974	937	37	974	……
Nicholson	1546	1463	83	1541	5
North Branch	358	336	22	358	……
North Moreland	831	803	28	830	1
Overfield	433	409	24	433	……
Tunkhannock	1212	1157	55	1212	……
Tunkhannock, (borough)	953	889	64	953	……
Washington	793	748	45	793	……
Windham	660	645	15	660	……
YORK.					
Carroll	898	895	3	896	2
Dillsburg, (boro')	281	273	8	277	4
Chanceford	2501	2434	67	2442	59
Conowago	1382	1363	19	1382	……
Dover	2281	2267	14	2281	……
Dover, (borough)	418	418	……	418	……
Fairview	1941	1895	46	1920	21
Fawn	1457	1432	25	1387	70
Franklin	910	902	8	908	2
Franklintown, (borough)	181	181	……	181	……
Heidelburg	2266	2143	123	2260	6
Hanover, (boro')	1839	1728	111	1828	11
Hellam	1639	1620	19	1617	22
Wrightsville, (borough)	1544	1452	92	1406	138
Hopewell	3830	3669	161	3746	84
Stewartstown	212	210	2	212	……
Jackson	1499	1476	23	1499	……
Lower Chanceford	2306	2289	17	2086	220
Lower Windsor	2429	2361	68	2428	1
Manchester	2427	2383	44	2423	4
Manchester, (borough)	406	403	3	405	1
Manheim	1159	1134	25	1159	……
Monaghan	1028	1019	9	1024	4
Newberry	2412	2377	35	2406	6
Goldsboro', (boro')	310	306	4	309	1
Lewisberry	268	267	1	268	……
North Codorus	2476	2391	85	2473	3
Paradise	1300	1296	4	1299	1
Peach Bottom	2366	2063	303	2233	133
Shrewsbury	3559	3298	261	3535	24
Glen Rock	537	488	49	537	……
Shrewsbury	600	585	15	600	……
South Codorus	2002	1952	50	2002	……
Jefferson, (boro')	327	320	7	327	……
Springfield	1958	1858	100	1953	5
Logansville	256	252	4	256	……
Spring Garden (b)	3040	2729	311	2994	46
Upper Windsor	2024	1974	50	2014	10
Warrington	1726	1716	10	1724	2
Washington	1444	1443	1	1444	……
West Manchester	1824	1747	77	1821	3
West Manheim	1147	1112	35	1137	10
York	2594	2450	144	2591	3
Dallastown	287	267	20	287	……
York	11003	9855	1148	10665	c337

(a) Exclusive of part of Wayne, (borough.)
(b) Exclusive of city of York.
(c) Also 1 Indian.

TABLE IX.—*Population of Minor Civil Divisions, &c.*—RHODE ISLAND.

NOTE.—The marginal column marks towns; the first indentation, cities.

Counties.	Total.	Nativity. Native.	Nativity. Foreign.	Race. White.	Race. Colored.
BRISTOL.					
Barrington	1111	816	295	1095	a15
Bristol	5302	4288	1014	5167	135
Warren	3008	2251	757	2971	37
KENT.					
Coventry	4349	3654	695	4337	12
East Greenwich	2660	2232	428	2559	101
Warwick	10453	7066	3387	10229	a223
West Greenwich	1133	1088	45	1132	1
NEWPORT.					
Jamestown	378	363	15	370	8
Little Compton	1166	1098	68	1127	39
Middletown	971	892	79	965	6
Newport	12521	9741	2780	11728	b789
New Shoreham	1113	1108	5	1079	34
Portsmouth	2003	1766	237	1974	29
Tiverton	1898	1818	80	1872	26
PROVIDENCE.					
Burrillville	4674	3250	1424	4646	b24
PROVIDENCE—Con.					
Cranston	4822	3313	1509	4745	[illegible]
Cumberland	3882	2611	1271	[illegible]	[illegible]
East Providence	2668	2316	352	[illegible]	[illegible]
Foster	1630	1621	9	1629	[illegible]
Glocester	2385	2160	225	2377	[illegible]
Johnston	4192	3211	981	4172	[illegible]
Lincoln	7889	4569	3320	[illegible]	[illegible]
North Providence	20495	13151	7344	20414	[illegible]
North Smithfield	3052	1781	1271	[illegible]	[illegible]
Pawtucket	6619	4350	2269	6602	[illegible]
Providence	68904	51727	17177	[illegible]	[illegible]
Scituate	3846	3604	242	3832	[illegible]
Smithfield	2605	1973	632	2581	[illegible]
Woonsocket	11527	5933	5594	[illegible]	[illegible]
WASHINGTON.					
Charlestown	1119	1066	53	[illegible]	[illegible]
Exeter	1462	1445	17	[illegible]	[illegible]
Hopkinton	2682	2578	104	2651	[illegible]
North Kingstown	3568	3137	431	3472	[illegible]
Richmond	2064	1886	178	[illegible]	[illegible]
South Kingstown	4493	4212	281	4179	[illegible]
Westerly	4709	3873	836	4625	[illegible]

(a) Also 1 Indian.
(b) Also 4 Indians.
(c) Also 3 Indians.
(d) Also 25 Indians.
(e) Also 115 Indians.

TABLE IX.—*Population of Minor Civil Divisions, &c.*—SOUTH CAROLINA.

NOTE.—The marginal column marks townships, as they existed June 1, 1870; the first indentation, cities; the second, towns. Names of towns are placed under the names of the townships in which they are respectively situated. The population of each township includes that of all towns situated in it.

Counties.	Total.	Nativity. Native.	Nativity. Foreign.	Race. White.	Race. Colored.
ABBEVILLE.					
Abbeville	3034	2994	40	1001	2033
Bordeaux	2232	2227	5	834	1398
Calhoun Mills	2208	2198	10	510	1698
Cedar Springs	1503	1496	7	447	1056
Cokesbury	2179	2179	.....	915	1264
Cokesbury	700	.....	.....	.....	.....
Diamond Hill	1760	1752	8	811	949
Donnaldsville	1155	1152	3	581	574
Due West	1030	1029	1	608	422
Due West	400	.....	.....	.....	.....
Greenwood	2817	2808	9	912	1905
Greenwood	700	.....	.....	.....	.....
ABBEVILLE—Con.					
Indian Hill	1920	1914	6	798	1122
Long Cain	1400	1400	.....	687	713
Lowndesville	2480	2477	3	1025	1455
Magnolia	1790	1790	.....	300	1490
Ninety-Six	2586	2586	.....	747	1839
Smithville	1519	1517	2	378	1141
Whitehall	1516	1516	.....	362	1154
ANDERSON.					
Belton	1364	1364	.....	898	466
Broadway	1378	1375	3	750	625

…—*Population of Minor Civil Divisions, &c.*—*SOUTH CAROLINA*—Continued.

…ies.	Total.	Nativity. Native.	Nativity. Foreign.	Race. White.	Race. Colored.
…—Con.					
…eek	1752	1750	2	1199	553
…(a)	1880	1855	25	1096	784
…er	1178	1177	1	743	435
…	1562	1561	1	1074	488
…	1577	1574	3	959	618
…	1240	1239	1	684	556
…h	1926	1923	3	1009	917
…	1296	1293	3	799	497
…	1525	1521	4	1056	469
…	2115	2103	12	1122	993
…ton	985	984	1	530	455
…	871	870	1	517	354
…	1067	1066	1	629	438
…a)	1892	1869	23	968	924
…oor (a)	1432	1404	28	673	759
…on	1426	1425	1	953	473
…ELL.					
…	2259	2214	45	1163	1096
…	1847	1845	2	504	1343
…	1907	1901	6	672	1235
…	1181	1166	15	543	638
…	1176	1174	2	362	814
…ing	1742	1741	1	388	1354
…	2327	2305	22	1074	1253
…dgo	1385	1383	2	351	1034
…	2400	2396	4	442	1958
…	1120	1115	5	608	512
…	1935	1927	8	345	1590
…reek	1295	1283	12	719	576
…ress	1620	1617	3	695	925
…	1218	1203	15	402	816
…	1280	1269	11	735	545
…	1849	1842	7	575	1274
…	987	987	......	371	616
…	618	616	2	381	237
…	1513	1512	1	380	1133
…low	1219	1219	......	505	714
…	1359	1352	7	725	631
…	1087	1087	......	334	753
…	1379	1376	3	692	687
…	1021	1018	3	612	409
…RT.					
…	5511	5437	74	513	4998
…rt	1739	1677	62	466	1273
…	2047	2032	15	116	1931
…chie	2573	2554	19	1092	1481
…	2319	2318	1	984	1335
…d	3073	3044	29	71	3002
…	3905	3896	9	806	3099
…	1400	1400	......	777	623
…	605	605	......	252	353
…	1771	1767	4	387	1384
…	2225	2224	1	65	2160
…	6152	6145	7	87	6065
…	2778	2778	......	159	2619
…ON. (b)					
…on	48956	44064	4892	22749	e26173
…rch	4493	4416	77	673	3820
…s	3277	3272	5	83	3194
…Island	1808	1803	5	55	1753
…Goose …	7795	7763	32	2115	5680
…Santee	2657	2656	1	447	2210
…Berkley	7868	7867	1	663	d7201

…nderson: 593 in Centerville and 839 in …ennes.

…major civil divisions of this county are …ishes.

…4 Indians.

Counties.	Total.	Nativity. Native.	Nativity. Foreign.	Race. White.	Race. Colored.
CHARLEST'N—Con.					
St. John's, Colleton	8604	8593	11	441	8163
Edisto Island	2762	2754	8	128	2634
John's Island	2016	2015	1	144	1872
Wadmalaw Island	3826	3824	2	169	3657
St. Stephen's	3094	3086	8	866	e2210
St. Thomas and St. Dennis	2119	2109	10	167	1952
Cainhoy	318	312	6	94	224
CHESTER.					
Baton Rouge	3098	3091	7	1130	1968
Blackstock	479	470	9	173	306
Chester	944	915	29	489	455
East Chester	732	712	20	254	478
Hallsville	1416	1413	3	279	1137
Hazlewood	1556	1549	7	560	996
Landsford	2400	2394	6	856	1544
Lewisville	2507	2502	5	756	f1749
Rossville	1600	1598	2	548	1052
West Blackstock	1278	1266	12	508	770
West Chester	2795	2777	18	737	2058
CHESTERFIELD.					
Alligator	659	659	......	531	128
Cheraw	2258	2210	48	685	1573
Cheraw	960	916	44	472	488
Cole Hill	710	708	2	617	93
Court House	1708	1706	2	1125	583
Jefferson	1101	1097	4	804	297
Mount Croghan	1682	1681	1	1072	610
Old Store	1921	1897	24	1315	606
Steerpen	545	545	......	126	419
CLARENDON.					
Brewington	199	199	......	109	90
Calvary	1152	1149	3	299	853
Concord	800	796	4	226	574
Douglas	310	310	......	248	62
Friendship	1440	1439	1	294	g1134
Fulton	1087	1087	......	200	887
Harmony	480	480	......	172	308
Manning	1278	1267	11	577	701
Midway	425	425	......	171	254
Mott's	600	600	......	439	161
Mount Zion	440	439	1	256	184
New Zion	640	640	......	202	438
Plowden's Mill	853	853	......	300	553
Sammy Swamp	960	957	3	415	545
Sandy Grove	317	317	......	210	107
Santee	977	977	......	151	826
St. James	640	639	1	129	511
St. Mark's	480	478	2	158	322
St. Paul's	960	960	......	104	856
COLLETON.					
Blake	2255	2248	7	36	2219
Bowen	1467	1464	3	855	612
Braxton	1971	1971	......	1165	806
Frazer	827	826	1	82	745
Glover	1102	1101	1	174	928
Lowndes	1850	1845	5	69	1781
Scott	1361	1361	......	945	416
Sheridan	1121	1113	8	573	548
St. George's Par'h	3993	3989	4	2098	1895
St. Paul's Parish	4656	4655	1	792	h3855

(d) Also 4 Indians.
(e) Also 18 Indians.
(f) Also 2 Indians.
(g) Also 12 Indians.
(h) Also 9 Indians.

TABLE IX.—*Population of Minor Civil Divisions, &c.*—*SOUTH CAROLINA*—Contin

Counties.	Total.	Nativity.		Race.	
		Native.	Foreign.	White.	Colored.
COLLETON—Con.					
Verdiere	3176	3158	18	1274	1902
Walterboro	636	623	13	307	329
Warren	1631	1631	......	846	785
DARLINGTON.					
Boston	1913	1913	......	910	1003
Brown	1598	1598	......	753	845
Butler	1099	1098	1	336	763
Colfax	1418	1416	2	138	1280
Flood	862	859	3	196	666
Grant	2172	2146	26	505	1667
Hamilton	1814	1812	2	318	1496
Holliman	1590	1590	......	898	692
Humphrey	896	896	......	543	353
Lang's	1214	1211	3	254	960
Lincoln	1845	1843	2	923	922
Sherman	1385	1385	......	837	548
Snetter's	771	771	......	113	658
Stevens's	1918	1917	1	950	968
Lunney	609	667	2	413	256
Thomas	1558	1555	3	825	733
Timmonsville	477	474	3	235	242
Whittemore	1986	1960	26	534	1452
Wright	1535	1535	......	651	884
EDGEFIELD.					
Blocker's	1035	1035	......	363	672
Butler's	2080	2071	9	448	1632
Coleman's	2243	2242	1	929	1314
Collins	733	733	......	303	430
Cooper's	1795	1792	3	714	1081
Dean's	1320	1320	......	539	a780
Grant	1116	1114	2	252	864
Gray	2533	2530	3	1192	1341
Gregg	3200	3164	36	2369	b811
Hamburg	1120	1099	21	273	c842
Hammond	2560	2550	10	662	a1897
Hibler	1607	1605	2	724	883
Horn's Creek (d)	1945	1935	10	409	1536
Huiet's	2556	2553	3	1305	1251
Mobley's	1278	1273	5	455	823
Norris	1485	1481	4	838	647
Pickens (d)	1559	1555	4	601	958
Edgefield (d)	846	836	10	344	502
Rhinehart's	1438	1421	17	862	576
Ryan	836	835	1	357	479
Schultz	848	835	13	236	612
Shaw's Creek	1760	1755	5	891	e867
Springfield (d)	1861	1857	4	431	1430
Spring Grove	2477	2473	4	1095	1382
Talbert's	1117	1117	......	283	834
Turkey Creek	959	958	1	264	695
Washington	1025	1025	......	245	780
FAIRFIELD.					
1	2236	2232	4	697	1539
2	2159	2127	32	471	1688
3	1600	1598	2	363	1237
4	1554	1518	36	646	908
Winnsboro'	1124	1090	34	483	641
5	932	932	......	136	796
6	1120	1119	1	482	638
7	1280	1269	11	332	948
8	1562	1562	......	790	772
9	1600	1592	8	520	1080
10	1059	1053	6	283	776
11	1280	1278	2	259	1021
12	1266	1257	9	314	952
13	2240	2232	8	494	1746

(a) Also 1 Indian.
(b) Also 20 Indians.
(c) Also 5 Indians.

Counties.	Total.	Nativity.		Race.
		Native.	Foreign.	White.
GEORGETOWN.				
Black River	960	959	1	96
Collins	1440	1439	1	730
Georgetown	3520	3474	46	745
Georgetown	2080	2034	46	63
Pee Dee	2400	2398	2	174
Sampit	960	958	2	68
Santee	2571	2571	......	261
Waccamaw	4310	4303	7	513
GREENVILLE.				
Austin	1512	1499	13	1086
Bates	1400	1396	4	962
Butler	1646	1640	6	1005
Chick's Springs	1226	1223	3	903
Cleveland	814	814	......	733
Dunklin	1457	1447	10	837
Fairview	1749	1740	9	976
Gantt	844	843	1	531
Grassy Mountain	1335	1334	1	1268
Greenville	3135	3087	48	1553
Greenville	2757	2712	45	1388
Grove	1089	1086	3	565
Highland	1261	1259	2	1041
Oak Lawn	905	904	1	894
O'Neal	1348	1342	6	1098
Paris Mountain	690	680	10	510
Saluda	1701	1700	1	1493
HORRY.				
Bayboro	885	883	2	808
Buck's	1481	1478	3	661
Conwayborough	1610	1600	10	1094
Conwaybor'gh	606	596	10	389
Dog Bluff	789	789	......	672
Dogwood Neck	573	573	......	429
Floyd's	630	630	......	516
Gallivant's Ferry	1069	1067	2	872
Green Sea	1043	1042	1	937
Little River	951	948	3	496
Simpson's Creek	945	945	......	736
Socastee	725	724	1	410
KERSHAW.				
Buffalo	1764	1760	4	1222
De Kalb	2578	2537	41	588
Camden	1007	970	37	432
Flat Rock	3755	3752	3	957
Wateree	3657	3646	11	1042
LANCASTER.				
Cane Creek	1759	1752	7	350
Cedar Creek	1505	1503	2	361
Flat Creek	2088	2088	......	1548
Gills Creek	2040	2030	10	1009
Lancaster	591	587	4	291
Indian Land	969	966	3	532
Pleasant Hill	1624	1621	3	1035
Spring Hill	1142	1138	4	952
Waxhaw	960	960	......	292
LAURENS.				
Cross Hill	2393	2371	22	733
Dial	2529	2528	1	1643
Hunter	2557	2550	7	700
Jack's	2720	2709	11	697
Laurens	4289	4271	18	1841
Scuffletown	1797	1795	2	818

(d) Of Edgefield: 268 in Horn's Creek, Pickens, and 262 in Springfield.
(e) Also 2 Indians.
(f) Also 4 Indians.

X.—*Population of Minor Civil Divisions, &c.—SOUTH CAROLINA*—Continued.

…ties.	Total.	Nativity. Native.	Nativity. Foreign.	Race. White.	Race. Colored.
—Cont'd.					
....	2132	2128	4	1222	910
....	2158	2148	10	1091	1067
....	1961	1958	3	1159	802
…ON. (*)					
…ek......	474	474	......	408	66
…rings...	354	354	......	322	32
…er......	1116	1114	2	798	318
…ap......	933	931	2	675	258
…in......	253	253	......	175	78
....	1095	1089	6	670	425
…k......	1352	1350	2	634	718
…amp....	358	358	......	247	111
…ollow...	872	869	3	564	308
…eek....	1315	1315	......	890	425
…l........	1563	1554	9	1082	481
…l Creek.	28	28	......	28	......
....	703	703	......	503	200
…ngs.....	679	670	9	337	342
…ings....	458	458	......	368	90
....	792	791	1	572	220
…n.......	643	638	5	179	464
…ON.					
....	767	766	1	469	298
…Neck...	884	884	......	448	436
....	1007	1007	......	517	490
…el.......	919	912	7	609	310
…e........	1314	1313	1	613	701
....	1318	1316	2	913	405
....	2005	2002	3	624	1381
....	1155	1155	......	585	570
....	1365	1365	......	749	616
....	858	858	......	557	301
....	2490	2459	31	1206	1284
…n........	968	938	30	468	500
…s........	1635	1633	2	635	1000
....	985	985	......	611	374
....	1113	1113	......	649	464
....	1815	1814	1	1088	727
....	891	891	......	437	454
....	1429	1429	......	590	839
....	210	210	......	128	82
…BORO.					
…le.......	1407	1406	1	757	650
…ille.....	1736	1734	2	553	1183
…lle......	857	854	3	526	331
…lle......	1597	1594	3	762	835
....	1581	1579	2	830	751
....	1308	1308	......	686	622
....	1505	1503	2	388	1117
....	1823	1819	4	644	1179
…ERRY.					
....	1791	1770	21	428	1363
....	1224	1199	25	695	529
....	2224	2215	9	579	1645
....	2133	2116	17	615	1518
....	2061	2032	29	880	1181
…n's......	1171	1166	5	363	808
…ll's.....	1675	1665	10	536	1139
....	1513	1510	3	375	1138
....	2792	2754	38	1250	1542
…erry....	1891	1860	31	822	1069
....	2290	2290	......	463	1827
…attery..	1901	1900	1	1273	628

Counties.	Total.	Nativity. Native.	Nativity. Foreign.	Race. White.	Race. Colored.
OCONEE.					
Centre............	1910	1909	1	1515	395
Chattooga.........	596	586	10	579	17
Keowee...........	1120	1093	27	897	223
Pulaski..........	653	652	1	638	15
Seneca...........	2313	2303	10	1382	931
Tugaloo..........	1436	1434	2	1112	324
Wagoner..........	1982	1909	73	1529	453
Walhalla......	716	653	63	557	159
Whitewater.......	526	518	8	462	64
ORANGEBURGH.					
Amelia...........	2040	2015	25	295	1745
Branchville.......	1339	1336	3	543	796
Branchville...	366	363	3	187	179
Caw Caw..........	934	932	2	336	598
Cow Castle.......	720	720	......	274	446
Goodby's.........	719	719	......	256	463
Goodland.........	955	954	1	545	410
Hebron...........	311	311	......	146	165
Hopewell.........	293	286	7	237	56
Liberty...........	408	406	2	229	179
Lyons............	1537	1529	8	306	1231
Middle...........	1104	1101	3	380	724
New Hope.........	951	951	......	208	743
Orange...........	1243	1235	8	478	765
Orangeburgh.	246	239	7	133	113
Pine Grove.......	827	826	1	211	616
Poplar...........	730	730	......	207	523
Providence.......	880	880	......	304	576
Rocky Grove......	697	694	3	369	328
Tabernacle.......	355	355	......	209	146
Vance's..........	822	822	......	176	646
PICKENS.					
Dacusville........	1356	1356	......	1059	297
Easley...........	1089	1088	1	909	180
Eastaloe.........	1099	1098	1	1013	86
Garvin...........	1478	1473	5	925	553
Pickensville......	3164	3163	1	2227	a936
Pickensville..	1222	1222	......	817	a405
Pumpkintown.....	716	716	......	518	198
Salubrity.........	1367	1365	2	1079	288
RICHLAND.					
Centre............	1124	1092	32	564	560
Columbia.........	832	812	20	370	462
Columbia.......	9298	8722	576	4002	b5295
Fourth...........	7687	7663	24	1236	6451
Lower............	307	307	......	3	304
Third............	1815	1803	12	906	c904
Upper............	1962	1957	5	761	1201
SPARTANBURG.					
Beech Spring.....	3280	3278	2	2369	911
Campo Bello......	2951	2946	5	2144	807
Cherokee.........	1675	1675	......	1375	300
Court House......	1229	1196	33	778	451
Cross Anchor.....	1833	1832	1	1133	700
Fair Forest.......	1129	1128	1	652	477
Glenn Spring.....	1814	1810	4	1150	664
Limestone........	2463	2454	9	1611	852
Pacolett..........	1312	1308	4	864	448
Riedsville........	2679	2679	......	1647	1032
Spartanburg......	2669	2650	19	1945	724
Spartanburg..	1080	1071	9	685	395
White Plain......	1342	1340	2	920	422
Woodruff.........	1408	1408	......	787	a621

…omplete; the other principal civil divis…ns were not separately returned.

…o 1 Indian.

(b) Also 1 Chinese.

(c) Also 5 Indians.

TABLE IX.—*Population of Minor Civil Divisions, &c.—SOUTH CAROLINA*—Continued.

Counties.	Total.	NATIVITY. Native.	NATIVITY. Foreign.	RACE. White.	RACE. Colored.	Counties.	Total.	NATIVITY. Native.	NATIVITY. Foreign.	RACE. White.	RACE. Colored.
SUMTER.						WILLIAMSBURG.					
Bishopville	1701	1698	3	723	978	Anderson	576	576	......	355	221
Bradford Springs	1142	1141	1	621	521	Hope	1591	1591	......	444	1147
Carter's Crossing	947	945	2	267	680	Indian	1147	1147	......	304	843
Concord	1519	1518	1	431	1088	Johnson	1218	1217	1	421	797
Lynchburg	1598	1992	6	566	1432	Kings	1774	1750	24	392	1382
Manchester	320	302	18	98	222	Lake	873	873	......	524	349
Maysville	1763	1759	4	365	1308	Laws	1274	1271	3	202	1072
Middleton	649	646	3	147	502	Lee	1181	1181	......	933	248
Mount Clio	1574	1574	......	371	1203	Mingo	627	627	......	158	469
Privateer	1679	1679	......	549	1130	Penn	676	675	1	158	518
Providence	1485	1481	4	266	1219	Ridge	1426	1423	3	288	1138
Rafting Creek	1585	1585	......	283	1302	Sumter	1679	1674	5	745	934
Shiloh	1518	1518	......	668	850	Sutton's	466	466	......	188	278
Stateburg	2095	2091	4	299	1796	Turkey	981	981	......	234	747
Sumter	3659	3596	63	1411	2248						
Sumter	1807	1747	60	991	816	YORK.					
Swimming Pens	1634	1632	2	398	1236						
UNION.						Bethel	2330	2320	10	1170	1160
Bogansville	1891	1885	6	814	1077	Bethesda	2997	2967	10	1077	1920
Cross Keys	1349	1349	......	736	613	Broad River	1455	1451	4	769	686
Draytonsville	1864	1856	8	1052	812	Bullock's Creek	3068	3056	12	1381	1687
Fishdam	1120	1119	1	180	940	Blairsville	487	484	3	232	255
Goshen Hill	1431	1427	4	316	1115	Catawba	2893	2879	14	1404	1489
Gowdeysville	2647	2645	2	1220	1427	Cherokee	1895	1892	3	1296	599
Jonesville	1809	1800	9	931	878	Ebenezer	2157	2153	4	814	1343
Pinkney	2413	2412	1	1451	962	Fort Mill	2473	2457	16	1309	a1159
Santuck	1879	1878	1	657	1222	King's Mountain	1818	1817	1	1217	601
Union	2845	2812	33	1361	1484	York	3200	3165	35	1677	1523

(*a*) Also 5 Indians.

TABLE IX.—*Population of Minor Civil Divisions, &c.—TENNESSEE.*

NOTE.—The marginal column marks civil districts. Their numbers are official; their names are those in general use. The first indentation marks cities; the second, towns. Names of towns are placed under the names of the civil districts in which they are respectively situated. The population of each civil district includes that of all towns situated in it.

Counties.	Total.	NATIVITY. Native.	NATIVITY. Foreign.	RACE. White.	RACE. Colored.	Counties.	Total.	NATIVITY. Native.	NATIVITY. Foreign.	RACE. White.	RACE. Colored.
ANDERSON.						BEDFORD.					
1. Long's	537	535	2	502	35	1. Wood's	790	766	24	567	[illegible]
2. Wallace's Cross Roads	791	791	......	778	13	2. Davidson's	1476	1474	2	1036	[illegible]
3. Adkin's	593	592	1	548	45	3. Yell's	1828	1826	2	1185	[illegible]
4. Hall's	1192	1192	......	1029	163	4. Bellbuckle	1303	1301	2	835	[illegible]
5. Ross's	1289	1219	70	1133	156	5. Deason's	1135	1134	1	696	[illegible]
6. Clinton	903	902	1	689	214	6. Sulphur Sp'ngs	1108	1101	7	683	[illegible]
Clinton	325	324	1	242	83	7. Shelbyville	3177	3119	58	2015	1[illegible]
7. Hog	476	473	3	458	a15	Shelbyville	1719	1674	45	1137	[illegible]
8. Peck	719	718	1	619	100	8. Head's	668	668	......	577	[illegible]
9. Scarborough	731	731	......	618	113	9. Puckett's	869	868	1	630	[illegible]
10. New River	382	382	......	382	......	10. Rover	1348	1347	1	1013	[illegible]
11. Moore	477	476	1	448	29	11. Poplin's Cross Roads	1757	1756	1	1360	[illegible]
12. Robbins	614	614	......	569	45						

(*a*) Also 3 Indians.

X.—*Population of Minor Civil Divisions, &c.*—*TENNESSEE*—Continued.

	Total.	Nativity. Native.	Nativity. Foreign.	Race. White.	Race. Colored.
nt'd.					
ing ..	1235	1229	6	1084	151
.....	812	812	.....	725	87
.....	1131	1130	1	912	219
n's					
.....	855	847	8	518	337
.....	1403	1403	.....	1142	261
.....	1216	1216	.....	928	288
.....	1141	1141	.....	1013	128
.....	1082	1081	1	921	161
ek ..	552	549	3	484	68
.....	940	939	1	895	45
rel ..	657	657	.....	626	31
rot..	644	641	3	632	12
.....	1107	1104	3	1027	80
en ..	148	147	1	138	10
.....	1061	1058	3	1047	14
C'k.	536	535	1	515	21
pec					
.....	923	920	3	859	64
k ...	888	879	9	839	49
Dam					
.....	609	667	2	611	58
.....	257	257	.....	247	10
.....	275	255	.....	252	3
.....	327	327	.....	325	2
Mill .	469	469	.....	391	78
ton..	586	586	.....	510	76
ng...	538	538	.....	433	105
.....	763	755	8	588	175
ville.	188	186	2	148	40
.....	608	606	2	464	144
.....	601	599	2	538	63
.....	593	593	.....	530	63
.....	130	130	.....	130	.....
.....	917	917	.....	870	47
wn..	720	718	2	634	86
.....	833	833	.....	719	114
.....	945	944	1	810	135
lle ..	810	810	.....	752	58
ll ...	776	775	1	688	88
.....	671	662	9	633	38
.....	711	708	3	689	22
.....	1620	1595	25	1298	322
ville.	811	800	11	708	103
.....	967	964	3	752	215
.....	872	869	3	739	133
.....	640	633	7	533	107
.....	1046	1046	.....	1018	28
.....	932	931	1	875	57
chee.	930	928	2	928	2
ve ...	382	382	.....	382	.....
e	465	465	.....	461	4
.					
chool-					
.....	793	792	1	673	120
ey's .	795	795	.....	765	30
eek ..	959	952	7	882	77
.....	480	478	2	458	22
ng...	773	773	.....	692	81
l	1734	1708	26	1234	500
land.	1658	1632	26	1158	500
.....	794	789	5	573	221
n....	800	799	1	595	205

Counties.	Total.	Nativity. Native.	Nativity. Foreign.	Race. White.	Race. Colored.
BRADLEY—Cont'd.					
9. Eureka	824	824	.....	651	173
10. Marler's	1076	1076	.....	978	98
11. W. Wood's....	870	870	.....	771	99
12. Samuel Howard's	955	954	1	921	34
13. Davidson's ...	799	797	2	759	40
CAMPBELL.					
1. Craig's	752	752	.....	725	27
2. Hatmaker's...	637	637	.....	634	3
3. Lindsey's	430	428	2	415	15
4. Town.........	1153	1127	26	1065	88
Jacksonborough	178	177	1	173	5
5. Walker's	520	520	.....	420	100
6. Fincastle	322	322	.....	273	49
7. Dry Branch...	640	640	.....	568	72
8. Page's	640	639	1	591	49
9. Low	574	574	.....	570	4
10. Upper Elk F'k	609	609	.....	601	8
11. Lower Elk F'k	473	473	.....	472	1
12. Henderson's ..	216	216	.....	204	12
13. Straight Fork.	200	200	.....	200	.....
14. Beach Fork...	279	279	.....	279	.....
CANNON.					
1. McKnight's...	790	789	1	619	171
2. Smith's	640	639	1	538	102
3. Brawley's F'rk	566	566	.....	504	62
4. Brady's Rock.	1126	1124	2	1072	54
5. Lemay's	703	702	1	693	10
6. Woodbury	1565	1563	2	1261	304
Woodbury	329	329	.....	254	75
7. Bailey's.......	786	786	.....	748	38
8. Bear Wallow .	551	551	.....	551	.....
9. Short Mount'n	640	640	.....	620	20
10. Clear Fork....	822	821	1	794	28
11. Auburn.......	1373	1373	.....	1267	106
12. Bradyville	940	939	1	908	32
CARROLL.					
1. Lavinia.......	1915	1909	6	1306	609
2. Trezevant	2128	2113	15	1489	639
3. Christmasville	647	642	5	548	99
4. McKinzie.....	1450	1424	26	893	557
5. McLemorsville	1228	1222	6	735	493
6. Hickory Flat .	831	828	3	628	203
7. Puntatock	552	552	.....	483	69
8. Sugar Hill....	610	609	1	524	86
9. Macedonia....	768	767	1	466	302
10. Shaffner's.....	924	924	.....	831	93
11. Huntingdon ..	1913	1900	13	1394	519
Huntingd'n	609	606	3	410	199
12. Watsons's	628	628	.....	441	187
13. Clarksburg ...	951	950	1	770	181
14. Maple Creek ..	1014	1014	.....	850	164
15. Buena Vista ..	666	665	1	505	161
16. Hollow Rock ..	1053	1052	1	849	204
17. Marlborough .	1063	1063	.....	990	73
18. Butler's.......	540	540	.....	495	45
19. Newbill's Cross Roads	566	564	2	451	115
CARTER.					
1. Elk	587	587	.....	576	11
2. Crab Orchard.	609	608	1	561	48
3. Doe River Cove	578	577	1	523	55
4. Ellis Mill.	402	402	.....	366	36
5. William's Tan Yard	800	799	1	767	33

TABLE IX.—*Population of Minor Civil Divisions, &c.—TENNESSEE—Continued.*

Counties.	Total.	Nativity.		Race.	
		Native.	Foreign.	White.	Colored.
CARTER—Cont'd.					
6. Taylor's Mount	638	635	3	521	117
7. Elizabethtown	970	965	5	871	99
Elizabethtown	321	321	......	298	23
8. Turkeytown	959	955	4	890	69
9. Miller's Mill	903	901	2	819	84
10. Stoney Creek	1035	1035	......	1035	......
11. Limest'ne Cove	428	423	5	407	21
CHEATHAM.					
1. Ashland City	862	858	4	765	97
Ashland	121	121	......	111	10
2. Blue Spring	462	458	4	413	49
3. Sycamore Mills	814	811	3	665	149
4. Shaw's	594	594	......	487	107
5. Cheap Hill	546	546	......	426	120
6. Gupton	437	434	3	324	113
7. Smith's Shop	572	572	......	457	115
8. Hagewood's	240	240	......	140	100
9. Crouch's	705	702	3	577	128
10. Narrows Harpeth	638	636	2	399	239
11. Kingston Sp'gs	652	647	5	418	234
12. Henry's	156	154	2	137	19
CLAIBORNE.					
1. Clear Fork	473	473	......	473	......
2. Rogers's	533	533	......	518	15
3. Thomas's	1052	1052	......	904	148
4. Brick House	759	757	2	706	53
5. Widow Rogers'	530	530	......	521	9
6. Runion's	939	939	......	772	167
7. Pearson's	507	507	......	480	27
8. Big Springs	933	933	......	862	71
9. Tazewell	1830	1818	12	1581	249
Tazewell	345	341	4	218	127
10. Lone Mountain	519	519	......	509	10
11. Sand Lick	627	627	......	618	9
12. Keck's	619	619	......	619	......
COCKE.					
1. Big Creek	1236	1227	9	1138	98
2. Grass	926	926	......	822	104
3. Parrottsville	1095	1088	7	1037	58
4. Knobb's	1397	1396	1	1220	177
5. Irish Bottom	946	946	......	798	148
6. Newport	1123	1122	1	802	321
Newport Depot	281	281	......	204	77
7. Dutch Bottom	1344	1343	1	1100	244
8. Sweetwater	714	712	2	660	54
9. English Creek	783	783	......	779	4
10. Lower Causby	800	800	......	780	20
11. Bridgeport	521	521	......	475	46
12. Upper Causby	1002	1001	1	1002	......
13. Grassy Fork	571	571	......	571	......
COFFEE.					
1. Garrison	758	758	......	666	92
2. Beech Grove	767	766	1	627	140
3. Noah's Fork	1257	1253	4	1032	225
4. Riley's Creek	745	745	......	708	37
5. Blackman's Precinct	738	736	2	669	69
6. Manchester	1687	1676	11	1531	156
Manchester	500	496	4	435	65
COFFEE—Cont'd.					
7. Hillsborough	693	692	1	611	[illegible]
8. Charles	319	319	......	303	16
9. Hickory Creek	489	488	1	390	[illegible]
10. Flat Mountain	665	662	3	586	79
11. Cunningham	581	581	......	448	133
12. Prairie	468	468	......	319	149
13. Tullahoma (a)	589	583	6	399	190
14. Concord	481	475	6	447	34
CUMBERLAND.					
1. Camp Ground	190	188	2	189	1
2. Webb's Mill	290	286	4	285	5
3. Cracker's Neck	484	478	6	474	10
4. Valley	651	648	3	609	42
5. Town	574	564	10	567	7
Crossville	95	93	2	94	1
6. Shelling	285	285	......	285	......
7. Flamby's Mill	332	330	2	323	9
8. Cove	344	341	3	341	3
9. Flat Rock	311	305	6	290	21
DAVIDSON.					
2.	1690	1663	27	1083	607
3.	950	946	4	[illegible]	[illegible]
4.	1699	1685	14	798	901
5.	1618	1575	43	1036	[illegible]
6.	1022	1016	6	712	[illegible]
7.	1056	1051	5	717	[illegible]
8.	1940	1936	4	[illegible]	711
9.	1645	1584	61	839	806
10.	3167	2900	267	1486	1681
11.	1325	1275	50	662	[illegible]
12.	858	829	29	447	411
13.	4492	3958	534	2067	[illegible]
14.	1433	1388	45	822	611
15.	740	725	15	379	361
16.	538	538	......	413	125
17.	4439	4131	308	2891	1548
18.	1877	1826	51	988	889
19.	1052	1031	21	547	505
20.	1464	1442	22	979	485
21.	800	759	41	476	324
22.	1008	994	14	686	[illegible]
23.	1096	1072	24	714	382
24.	739	733	6	618	127
25.	1084	1064	20	601	454
Nashville (c)	25865	23056	2809	16149	9709
DECATUR.					
1.	748	746	2	648	100
2. Shannonsville	739	739	......	630	109
3. Mount Zion	886	868	18	693	[illegible]
4. Decaturville	1293	1292	1	1126	[illegible]
Decaturville	188	188	......	173	[illegible]
5.	494	494	......	456	[illegible]
6.	540	539	1	449	[illegible]
7.	521	516	5	451	[illegible]
8.	271	268	3	274	......
9.	530	523	7	501	[illegible]
10.	468	466	2	431	[illegible]
11.	693	691	2	513	[illegible]
12.	586	586	......	544	[illegible]
DE KALB.					
1. Alexandria	907	906	1	673	[illegible]
2. Liberty	780	778	2	661	[illegible]
3. Clear Fork	574	574	......	527	[illegible]

(a) Tullahoma (town) comprises whole of 13th district.
(b) Also 10 Indians.
(c) City of Nashville comprises 1st district for this county.
(d) Also 7 Indians.

…LE IX.—*Population of Minor Civil Divisions, &c.—TENNESSEE*—Continued.

…nties.	Total.	Nativity. Native.	Nativity. Foreign.	Race. White.	Race. Colored.
…n—Cont'd.					
Creek	946	946	......	864	82
....	714	714	......	703	11
....	591	591	......	587	4
....	715	715	......	695	20
....	491	491	......	436	55
…hville	1504	1501	3	1417	87
…an Creek..	688	688	......	672	16
…che's ...	464	464	......	411	53
…ner's Br'h	422	422	......	381	41
…s of the Pike	388	388	......	294	94
....	488	488	......	430	58
…on's Tan Yard	421	421	......	379	42
…el Hill...	856	856	......	765	91
…perance Hall.......	476	476	......	426	50
…KSON.					
…n........	654	647	7	501	153
…y........	630	629	1	610	20
…er's	444	443	1	426	18
…bull	657	642	15	612	45
…dsville ...	727	727	......	593	134
…lotte......	1420	1411	9	1164	256
…Charlotte..	276	276	......	176	100
…-Roads ...	737	736	1	552	185
…Acre	1110	1099	11	732	378
…ard's......	720	715	5	584	136
…n Valley..	873	872	1	722	151
…rville	746	744	2	664	82
…e Bluff ...	622	615	7	503	119
…TER.					
… Cross Roads	1229	1227	2	929	300
…r's Chapel	1085	1085	......	801	284
…nut Bluff	1044	1042	2	979	65
…sburg	1693	1675	18	1160	533
…versburg .	683	669	14	464	219
…icane Hill Church.......	1055	1054	1	828	227
…ern	1760	1748	12	1387	373
… Union Church	843	842	1	616	227
…ville	862	861	1	730	132
…America	1487	1487	......	1269	218
…ce's Chapel	783	782	1	627	156
…ell's Ferry	227	226	1	188	39
… Springs	445	441	1	353	92
…on's	157	157	......	140	17
…dship	1036	1036	......	806	230
…ETTE.					
…rville	2106	2075	31	914	1192
…erville ...	954	931	23	524	430
…n...	1046	1044	2	598	448
…ford's	1346	1343	3	536	810
…ersville ..	2436	2427	9	499	1937
…onte......	1576	1561	15	272	1304
…en's	1626	1614	12	709	917
…ory Wythe	1684	1667	17	587	1097
…and.......	2018	2010	8	565	1453
....	1699	1698	1	365	1334
…ayette....	2840	2829	11	847	1993
…n	1380	1378	2	479	901
…ow	920	917	3	450	470
…ange	1040	1008	32	551	489
…a Grange	760	729	31	469	291
…ston......	2346	2338	10	1076	1270
…ty........	2080	2075	5	708	1372

Counties.	Total.	Nativity. Native.	Nativity. Foreign.	Race. White.	Race. Colored.
FENTRESS.					
1. Indian Creek..	552	552	......	539	13
2. Poplar Cove...	537	536	1	517	20
3. Jamestown....	344	339	5	309	35
4. Taylor's	359	359	......	350	9
5. Station Camp..	103	103	......	103	......
6. Singleton......	554	554	......	517	37
7. Academy......	604	604	......	595	9
8. Three Forks of Wolf River..	591	591	......	559	32
9. Ramsey's......	174	174	......	174	......
10. Paul	135	135	......	135	......
11. Tadpole	548	548	......	533	15
12. North Carolina	216	216	......	216	......
FRANKLIN.					
1. Winchester ...	2539	2472	67	1663	876
2. Owl Hollow....	908	880	28	695	213
3. South Salem...	979	978	1	885	94
4. Hunt's Station.	1238	1235	3	882	356
5. Pond	630	620	10	360	270
6. Marble Hill....	669	667	2	615	54
7. Rock Creek....	938	919	19	846	92
8. Stricker's Mill.	1112	1074	38	876	236
9. Hawkeville....	1200	1200	......	969	231
10. Cowan's Stat'n.	1393	1381	12	1065	328
11. Grosse's.......	376	371	5	318	58
12. Anderson's....	776	774	2	666	110
13. Linking Cove .	265	265	......	264	1
14. Hurricane.....	594	590	4	565	29
15. Ridgeville.....	1063	1060	3	1039	24
16. Rico's	290	290	......	290	......
GIBSON.					
1. Heath's	1076	1076	......	814	262
2. South Gibson..	1075	1074	1	706	369
3. Humboldt	2296	2209	87	1531	765
4. Quincy	816	815	1	609	207
5. Brazil	1732	1728	4	1088	644
6. Eaton	1710	1709	1	1051	659
7. Trenton	3816	3773	43	2151	1665
Trenton ...	1909	1870	39	1125	784
8. Yorkville......	1272	1270	2	1053	219
9. Rutherford Station	938	933	5	826	112
10. Possum Pond..	995	994	1	958	37
11. Grist's	813	813	......	742	71
12. Tuckerville ...	622	617	5	519	103
13. Milan	1548	1536	12	1052	496
14. Lynn Point....	655	655	......	571	84
15. Skull Bone	640	640	......	591	49
16. McLeary's	705	705	......	612	93
17. North Gibson..	664	662	2	640	24
18. Pickett's	831	831	......	468	363
19. Walnut Grove.	717	715	2	651	66
20. Robertson's Store........	707	704	3	429	278
21. Dyer Station ..	990	989	1	830	160
22. Thetford's.....	444	444	......	427	17
23. Evans.........	604	603	1	482	122
GILES.					
1. Elkmont Spr'gs	1454	1454	......	832	622
2. Prospect	1714	1711	3	888	826
3. Hanna	1397	1397	......	1109	288
4. Hammond's Store	790	790	......	696	94
5. Slate Springs..	1542	1538	4	1021	521
6. Coopertown ...	1554	1551	3	742	812
7. Pulaski	3041	2964	77	1462	1579
Pulaski ...	2070	2003	67	1158	912
8. McNairy's.....	2232	2227	5	1084	1148

TABLE IX.—*Population of Minor Civil Divisions, &c.—TENNESSEE—Continued.*

Counties.	Total.	Nativity.		Race.	
		Native.	Foreign.	White.	Colored.
GILES—Cont'd.					
9. Elkton	1677	1675	2	922	755
10. Garrott's	1316	1314	2	1032	284
11. Buchanan's	1268	1268	......	921	347
12. Maxwell's Schoolhouse	1859	1852	7	606	1253
13. Wilsford	1346	1342	4	783	563
14. Campbellsv'e *a*	1373	1372	1	1157	216
15. Lynnv'e Stat'n	2397	2393	4	1568	829
Lynnville	154	154	......	92	62
Lynnville Station	204	203	1	177	27
16. Odd Fellows' Hall	1747	1744	3	882	865
17. Cornersville	2141	2135	6	1442	699
18. Shaw's	1190	1190	......	806	384
19. Campbellsv'e *a*	1044	1044	......	752	292
Campbellsville (*a*)	124	124	......	107	17
20. Bunker's Hill	1331	1328	3	970	361
GRAINGER.					
1. Morristown	1265	1255	10	1115	150
2. Noe's Mill	968	968	......	885	83
3. Country	546	546	......	513	33
4. Turley's Mill	874	871	3	839	35
5. James	993	993	......	958	35
6. Buffaloes Mills	694	694	......	669	25
7. Harris	691	691	......	665	26
8. Cross-Roads	1120	1119	1	948	172
9. Bean's Station	905	905	......	740	165
10. Thorn Hill	910	910	......	769	141
Rutledge	107	107	......	94	13
11. Hipsher	780	780	......	741	39
12. Lewis Mills	944	944	......	942	2
13. Hogskin	538	538	......	528	10
14. Lennis	465	465	......	447	18
15. Nash	728	728	......	632	96
GREENE.					
1. Broylis	890	889	1	840	50
2. Lintz	596	595	1	570	26
3. Caney Branch	1170	1170	......	1043	127
4. Warrensburg	1100	1098	2	930	170
5. Bigg's	650	650	......	600	50
6. Guthrie's	907	903	4	868	39
7. Moore's	717	717	......	694	23
8. Hartman's	702	701	1	635	67
9. Bower's	747	744	3	633	114
10. Greeneville	1679	1663	16	1199	480
Greeneville	1039	1028	11	786	253
11. Morelock	1132	1132	......	1094	38
12. Hankins	857	856	1	765	92
13. Doak's	957	949	8	771	186
14. D. R. Johnson	720	720	......	661	59
15. Crawford	1151	1148	3	1078	73
16. Rush	858	856	2	837	21
17. English	1349	1349	......	1288	61
18. Love's	1337	1330	7	1214	123
19. Midway	752	749	3	713	39
20. Cotter	556	556	......	520	36
21. Harvey	532	532	......	532	......
22. Camp Creek	849	845	4	807	42
23. McGuffin's	638	634	4	558	80
24. Caverner's	461	460	1	408	53
25. Evans's	361	361	......	346	15

Counties.	Total.	Nativity.		Race.	
		Native.	Foreign.	White.	Colored.
GRUNDY.					
1. Hubbard'sCove	343	343	......	311	32
2. Meyers' or Fult's Cove	87	87	......	81	6
3. Northcut'sCove	195	195	......	195	......
4. Collins's River	373	373	......	373	......
5. Tate	231	110	121	231	......
6. Johnson's	141	139	2	141	......
7. Lovan's	369	364	5	356	13
8. Burrow's Cove	270	270	......	168	2
9. Pelham	374	373	1	341	33
10. Altamont	217	188	29	207	10
11.	650	599	51	629	21
HAMILTON.					
1. Dallas	711	711	......	654	57
2. Brown's	767	764	3	659	108
3. Stringer's	686	683	3	413	273
4. Lookout	691	688	3	488	203
5. Chicamauga	737	730	7	548	189
6. Hobb's	430	428	2	357	73
7. Harrison	892	884	8	701	191
Harrison	421	418	3	324	97
8. Ooltewah	1102	1101	1	931	171
9. Long Savannah	548	547	1	467	81
10. Grasshopper	961	961	......	898	63
11. Sale Creek	763	736	27	706	57
12. Soddy	726	693	33	684	42
13. ProspectCh'rch	513	513	......	468	45
15. Tynersville	793	787	6	555	238
16. Fairmount	177	173	4	177	......
17. Halfway House	651	642	9	475	176
Chattanooga (*e*)	6093	5618	475	3872	2221
HANCOCK.					
1. Mills, or War Creek	466	466	......	442	24
2. Murrell	457	457	......	411	46
3. Click	569	569	......	541	28
4. Wallen, or Bend	502	502	......	453	49
5. Davies	440	440	......	382	58
6. Town	916	916	......	818	98
Sneedsville	177	177	......	162	15
7. Brier Creek	493	493	......	466	27
8. Sumter	370	369	1	354	16
9. Mulberry Gap	418	418	......	361	57
10. Holland, or Walker's	588	588	......	558	30
11. Panther Creek	459	459	......	386	73
12. Livisay	418	417	1	412	6
13. Walker, or Mills	441	441	......	417	24
14. Four-Mile	611	611	......	562	49
HARDEMAN.					
1. GrandJunction	1805	1766	39	871	934
Junction	460	......	......	......	......
Saulsb'ry (*b*)	400	......	......	......	......
2. Middleburg	920	920	......	473	447
3. New Castle	1424	1422	2	420	1004
4. Whiteville	1572	1568	4	707	865
Whitev'e (*d*)	80	......	......	......	......
5. Clinton	741	735	6	339	402
6. Bolivar	1600	1558	42	831	769
Bolivar	889	879	10	591	298
7. White's Schoolhouse	448	435	13	247	201

(*a*) Of Campbellsville (village:) 29 in 14th district and 95 in 19th district.
(*b*) Also partly in 10th district.
(*c*) Also 2 Indians.
(*d*) Also partly in 3d and 5th districts.
(*e*) Chattanooga comprises the 14th district.

TABLE IX.—*Population of Minor Civil Divisions, &c.—TENNESSEE*—Continued.

Counties.	Total.	Nativity. Native.	Nativity. Foreign.	Race. White.	Race. Colored.
HARDEMAN—Con.					
8. Drake's	745	745		471	274
9. Van Buren	661	661		348	313
Van Buren	16				
10. Saulsbury	950	947	3	680	270
11. Middleton	1508	1501	7	1263	245
Middleton	150				
Pocahontas	225				
12. Sweet Gum	625	624	1	503	122
13. Hanna's	1228	1216	12	1016	212
14. Smith's	664	662	2	523	141
15. Toone's Station	1487	1465	22	1089	398
16. Doyle's	884	884		833	51
17. Ubet	722	722		604	118
HARDIN.					
1. Gore's	617	615	2	539	78
2. Laden's Mills	662	660	2	557	105
3. Old Town	1130	1129	1	944	186
4. Savannah	1336	1330	6	1034	302
Savannah	328	324	4	272	56
5. Harbour's	517	517		449	68
6. Bethel	1033	1033		950	83
7. McGee's	588	581	7	528	60
8. Quall's	1065	1065		979	86
9. Monticello	516	514	2	505	11
10. Hamburg	446	445	1	387	59
11. Bone Yard	830	827	3	760	70
12. Liberty	967	966	1	835	132
13. Saltillo	1159	1157	2	1065	94
14. Pine Grove	482	482		393	89
15. Pittsburg	420	414	6	396	24
HAWKINS.					
1. St. Clair	974	972	2	896	78
2. Lower Clinch	752	752		691	61
3. Upper Clinch	577	577		537	40
4. Lower Beech Creek	881	881		841	40
5. McPheter's Bent	702	702		669	33
6. Crew's	1126	1122	4	971	155
7. Wallace's	1080	1078	2	938	142
8. Surgoinsville	1447	1447		1084	363
9. Waterson's	855	853	2	795	60
10. Rogersville	1902	1894	8	1467	*a*431
Rogersville	657	650	7	495	162
11. Choptack	965	959	6	906	59
12. Mooreburg	875	873	2	744	131
13. Hartsman's	789	787	2	679	110
14. Whitehorn	731	731		695	36
15. Dodson's Creek	1102	1101	1	989	113
16. Upper Beech Creek	414	414		414	
17. Sulphur Sprin's	662	662		628	34
HAYWOOD.					
1. Williams's Mill	1119	1117	2	438	681
2. Dancyville	1554	1553	1	671	883
3. Stanton	1421	1393	28	451	970
4. Gray's School-house	1598	1588	10	705	893
5. Allen's	2048	2034	14	947	*a*1100
6. Morton's	1350	1347	3	476	874
7. Brownsville	4262	4153	109	1957	2305
Brownsville	2457	2361	96	1441	1016
8. Wright's Sch'l-house	1812	1809	3	618	1194
9. Haywood's	2060	2057	3	359	1701
10. Woodville	1200	1200		658	542
11. Bell's Station	1641	1624	17	1180	461
HAYWOOD—Con.					
12. Lanefield	1586	1585	1	956	630
13. Cageville	972	970	2	749	223
14. Foster's	1112	1111	1	755	357
15. Hart	1359	1359		341	1018
HENDERSON.					
1.	421	421		368	53
2. Crucifix	662	662		595	67
3. Mifiin	778	777	1	548	230
4. Henderson	551	550	1	399	152
5. Jack Creek	843	843		750	93
6.	775	775		648	127
7.	941	939	2	710	231
8. Rhodes	799	798	1	482	317
9. Farmville	696	696		515	181
10.	947	938	9	755	192
11.	1045	1045		999	46
12.	594	594		571	23
13.	930	929	1	905	25
14.	1021	1020	1	932	89
15.	697	697		668	29
16. Lone Elm	481	481		436	45
17.	794	794		395	399
18. Poplar Springs	450	450		449	1
19.	386	386		322	64
20.	406	406		362	44
HENRY.					
1. Paris	1797	1768	29	1063	734
2. Langford's	590	581	9	483	107
3. Bridge's	982	981	1	627	355
4. Beard's	750	749	1	611	139
5. Cowan's	1334	1325	9	852	482
6. Hagle Ridge	1000	996	4	852	148
7. Manlyville	1049	1048	1	784	265
8. Haglerville	790	788	2	693	97
9. Henry Station	1362	1355	7	864	498
10. Caledonia	1460	1457	3	1046	414
11. Cottage Grove	1407	1407		975	432
12. North Fork	1198	1197	1	976	222
13.	1120	1120		878	242
14. Conyersville	1258	1255	3	978	280
15. Mouth of Sandy	596	596		569	27
16.	1166	1165	1	856	310
17. Porter's Station	563	560	3	484	79
18.	835	835		698	137
19. Mansfield	571	571		352	219
20. Paris Landing	552	550	2	535	17
HICKMAN.					
1. Centreville	1425	1425		932	493
Centreville	175	175		100	75
2. Little Lot	781	780	1	714	67
3. Shady Grove	616	616		458	158
4. Mayberry's	750	749	1	714	36
5. McMinn's	637	636	1	615	22
6. Pine Wood	827	826	1	692	135
7. Vernon	733	731	2	599	134
8. Sugar Creek	516	515	1	481	35
9. Whitfield	840	840		647	193
10. McClaren	688	688		660	28
11. Peeler's	516	516		503	13
12. Sharp's	400	400		397	3
13. Leather Wood	446	446		410	36
14. Wheat's	348	348		296	52
15. Poplar Union	333	333		267	66
HUMPHREYS.					
1. Hall's Creek	735	735		671	64

(*a*) Also 1 Indian.

TABLE IX.—*Population of Minor Civil Divisions, &c.—TENNESSEE*—Continued.

Counties.	Total.	Nativity. Native.	Nativity. Foreign.	Race. White.	Race. Colored.
HUMPHREYS—Con.					
2. Johnsonville	979	962	17	545	434
3. Big Bottom	1079	1079	......	947	132
4. Upper Buffalo	978	977	1	948	30
5. Upper White Oak	750	741	9	636	114
6. Waverly	680	645	35	528	152
Waverly	207	206	1	151	56
7. Blue Creek	468	467	1	405	63
8. Big Hurricane	738	727	11	637	101
9. TumblingCre'k	506	506	......	483	23
10. McEwen's	1012	911	101	967	45
11. Lower White Oak	357	355	2	322	35
12. Lower Buffalo	1044	1041	......	962	82
JACKSON.					
1. Gainsboro	1285	1285	......	1204	81
2. Sadler's Mills	580	580	......	569	11
3. Salt Lick	1194	1194	......	1078	116
4. Gum Springs	530	530	......	499	31
5. Centreville	932	932	......	917	15
6. Celina	583	583	......	485	98
7. Butler's Landing	751	751	......	683	68
8. Sugar Creek	485	485	......	473	12
9. Roaring River	906	906	......	879	27
10. Cummin's Mill	561	561	......	561	......
11. Flynn's Lick	1211	1211	......	1130	81
12. Walnut Stump	556	556	......	556	......
13. Big Springs	704	704	......	681	23
14. Double Cabin	799	799	......	787	12
15. Granville	1154	1154	......	963	191
16. Tick	352	352	......	351	1
JEFFERSON.					
1. French's	1194	1192	2	1146	48
2. Dandridge	1532	1527	5	1242	290
3. Muddy Creek	1508	1508	......	1427	81
4. McGuire	958	957	1	801	157
5. Copeland's	1618	1618	......	1288	330
6. Hodge's	1145	1144	1	867	278
7. New Market	1440	1435	5	1223	217
8. New Market	926	924	2	737	189
9. Mossy Creek	1920	1911	9	1545	375
10. Talbott's	1505	1501	4	1335	170
11. Sulphur Spring	1438	1428	10	1256	182
12. Morristown	988	985	3	840	148
13. McDaniel	1120	1118	2	909	211
14. Bewley	546	546	......	454	92
15. Russellville	647	641	6	528	119
16. Whitesburg	518	517	1	495	23
17. Woollard's	473	472	1	473	......
JOHNSON.					
1. Laurel	630	629	1	615	15
2. Taylorsville	1164	1164	......	952	212
Taylorsville	236	236	......	194	42
3. Lower Mount'n	531	529	2	520	11
4. Vaught's	754	754	......	701	53
5. Wagner's	602	602	......	565	37
6. Pine Orchard	474	474	......	445	29
7. Little Doe	668	668	......	632	36
8. Shady	178	178	......	173	5
9. Upper Mount'n	529	529	......	525	4
10. Dugger's	322	322	......	306	16
KNOX.					
1. Knoxville	8008	7385	623	5725	2283
2. Carns	1889	1838	51	1375	514
3. Shipe's	1090	1084	6	966	124
KNOX—Cont'd.					
4. Mynott's	708	708	......	631	77
5. Tuster's	675	675	......	628	47
6. Cox's	868	864	4	857	11
7. Mynott's	958	948	10	872	86
8. Bell's	935	935	10	843	92
9. Harden	746	744	2	592	154
10. Campbell's Station	1807	1803	4	1579	228
11. McClellan's	1581	1566	15	1371	210
12. Lonas	1304	1249	55	1050	254
13. Rudder's	642	641	1	577	65
14. Temperance Hall	1308	1307	1	1227	81
15. Dearmond's	1214	1212	2	1091	123
16. Cannon's	1667	1665	2	1542	125
17. Stonehouse	1244	1220	24	1134	110
18. Mayor's	917	903	14	787	130
19. Trotter	929	928	1	824	105
20. Marvel Hill	500	500	......	483	17
Knoxville	8682	8050	632	6073	2609
LAKE.					
1.	540	528	12	494	46
2.	957	937	20	706	251
3.	494	491	3	412	82
4.	218	216	2	206	12
5.	102	101	1	100	2
6.	117	116	1	117	......
LAUDERDALE.					
1. Durhamville	1790	1785	5	706	1084
2. Ripley	1841	1823	18	1348	493
Ripley	532	520	12	402	130
3. Barefield's	1280	1276	4	916	364
4. Fulton	484	476	8	260	224
5. Ashport	317	311	6	224	93
6. Rickman's	1026	1024	2	908	118
7. Double Br'ches	1484	1484	......	1106	378
8. Double Bridges	1483	1479	4	1010	473
9. Hale's Point	159	159	......	106	53
10. Gimpsoville	974	972	2	770	204
LAWRENCE.					
1. Wayland's Springs	725	725	......	686	39
2. Belew	360	359	1	359	1
3. Legg's	757	757	......	739	18
4. Oglesby	343	342	1	322	21
5. Springer	482	480	2	437	45
6. Sims	492	491	1	460	32
7. Taylor's	473	473	......	464	9
8. Lawrenceburg	857	822	35	722	135
Lawrenceburg	351	335	16	291	60
9. Dodson	520	510	10	456	64
10. West	756	751	5	634	122
11. Henryville	273	273	......	257	16
12. Laurel Hill	293	291	2	288	5
13. Burlison	272	272	......	265	7
14. McMillon	309	308	1	303	6
15. West Point	689	689	......	624	65
LEWIS.					
1. Cathey's Creek	219	219	......	200	19
2. Rocky Branch	151	151	......	141	10
3. Cane Creek	175	175	......	173	2
4. West Fork of Bigby	170	170	......	167	3
5. Newburg	262	262	......	219	43
Newburg	11	11	......	11	......

—*Population of Minor Civil Divisions, &c.—TENNESSEE*—Continued.

Total.	Nativity: Native.	Nativity: Foreign.	Race: White.	Race: Colored.
400	400	......	352	48
241	241	......	241	......
368	367	1	307	61
1755	1755	......	1488	267
1283	1283	......	1039	244
788	787	1	684	104
1094	1093	1	852	242
1302	1302	......	1177	125
1700	1695	5	1391	309
124	124	......	105	19
1358	1357	1	804	554
2145	2114	31	1264	881
1206	1184	22	756	450
988	986	2	750	238
1257	1255	2	1061	196
695	694	1	511	184
1225	1222	3	841	384
1069	1067	2	798	271
953	953	......	676	277
844	842	2	687	157
1033	1032	1	850	183
1156	1154	2	997	159
1310	1305	5	1266	244
1077	1076	1	1001	76
1282	1280	2	988	294
842	841	1	527	315
446	444	2	425	21
1026	1019	7	850	176
454	454	......	433	21
768	767	1	737	31
772	771	1	685	87
161	161	......	147	14
502	502	......	486	16
819	818	1	573	246
817	817	......	712	105
423	423	......	413	10
508	508	......	491	17
636	636	......	603	33
280	280	......	273	7
543	543	......	488	55
359	359	......	348	11
510	510	......	428	82
464	464	......	342	122
1331	1329	2	931	400
1167	1167	......	694	473
854	854	......	475	379
1493	1493	......	768	725
880	880	......	309	571
775	775	......	262	513
1418	1418	......	436	982
1200	1200	......	540	660
1400	1400	......	821	579
1482	1482	......	724	758
823	823	......	403	420
1412	1411	1	782	630
529	529	......	401	128
590	590	......	379	211
4682	4479	203	2800	1882
4119	3923	196	2619	1500
960	960	......	744	216
1024	1021	3	706	318
1400	1400	......	1183	217

Counties.	Total.	Nativity: Native.	Nativity: Foreign.	Race: White.	Race: Colored.
MARION.					
3. Looney's Creek	906	905	1	872	34
4. Dadsville	706	705	1	681	25
5. Lewis	636	636	......	565	71
6. Mullins Cove	421	420	1	416	5
7. Jasper	1410	1408	2	1077	333
Jasper	375	......	......	......	......
8. Shell Mound	491	488	3	414	77
9. Sweeton's Cove	276	276	......	224	52
10. Head of Battle Creek	672	650	2	585	87
11. Battle Creek	747	740	7	627	120
13. Running Water	596	543	53	485	111
MARSHALL.					
1. Baptist Church	1354	1352	2	1119	235
2. Spring Place	843	843	......	709	134
3. Catalpa Grove	818	817	1	768	50
4. New Hope	1087	1085	2	895	192
5. Belfast	1011	1007	4	696	315
6. Farmington	919	918	1	658	261
7. Rich Creek	767	766	1	479	288
8. Chapel Hill	1514	1513	1	862	652
9. Corlett's	1090	1090	......	676	414
10. Caney Spring	796	796	......	632	164
11. Berlin	706	703	3	472	234
12. McCrady	882	882	......	631	251
13. Mooresville	1063	1053	10	783	280
14. Wilson Hill	882	882	......	539	343
15. Lewisburg	1686	1684	2	1277	409
Lewisburg	322	321	1	276	46
16. Verona	789	789	......	626	163
MAURY.					
1. Kinderhook	581	579	2	537	44
2. Love's	626	624	2	369	257
3. Fox's House	558	558	......	373	185
4. Park's	805	805	......	609	196
5. Hurricane Switch	1132	1132	......	515	a616
6. Culleoka	2071	2061	10	1467	604
7. Bigbyville	1651	1648	3	981	970
8. Bigbyville	1488	1475	13	640	a847
9. Columbia	4838	4738	100	2320	2518
Columbia	2550	2482	68	1442	1108
10. Poplar Top	2023	2010	13	798	1225
11. New York	1822	1801	21	917	905
12. Mount Pleasant	1730	1725	5	1221	509
13. Mount Pleasant	1304	1302	2	500	804
14. Williamsport	1256	1254	2	613	643
15. Hampshire	677	677	......	495	182
16. Hampshire	869	867	2	569	300
17. Leper's Creek	1462	1457	5	858	604
18. Santa Fé	972	972	......	687	285
19. Gravel Hill	1445	1441	4	873	572
20. Partee's	1633	1631	2	822	811
21. Bear Creek	1515	1510	5	813	702
22. Spring Hill	2483	2469	14	967	1516
23. Kedron	1256	1256	......	683	573
24. Rock Creek	1108	1107	1	745	363
25. Rally Hill	984	984	......	650	334
MC'MINN.					
1. Small's	668	667	1	551	117
2. Kyker's	768	767	1	754	14
3. Thomas	646	646	......	595	51
4. Mouse Creek	625	621	4	482	143
5. Lowery's	653	652	1	496	157
6. Barnet	855	855	......	774	81
7. Athens	1768	1764	4	1310	458

(a) Also 1 Indian.

TABLE IX.—*Population of Minor Civil Divisions, &c.*—*TENNESSEE*—Continued.

Counties.	Total.	Nativity.		Race.	
		Native.	Foreign.	White.	Colored.
McMINN—Cont'd.					
Athens	974	970	4	733	241
8. Gregory	897	896	1	833	64
9. Morris	772	772	......	740	32
10. Riceville	1187	1187	......	1013	174
11. Wildcat	850	849	1	760	90
12. Firestone	844	844	......	767	77
13. Knob	712	712	......	703	9
14. Carlock	745	744	1	635	110
15. Shoddy	827	827	......	773	54
16. Calhoun	716	714	2	563	153
Calhoun	232	232	......	184	48
17. Cracker's Neck	436	436	......	390	46
MC'NAIRY.					
1. Big Hill	832	830	2	812	20
2. Camden	1090	1086	4	1027	63
3. Sobby	1029	1023	6	914	115
4. Montezuma	769	769	......	645	124
5.	1162	1161	1	969	193
6.	452	451	1	386	66
7.	1308	1296	12	1070	238
8. Cotton Ridge	960	957	3	771	189
9. Monterey	905	905	......	837	68
10. Stantonville	974	974	......	902	72
11. Swaim's	604	604	......	571	33
12.	354	354	......	315	39
13. Bogan Ray's	593	592	1	515	78
14. Jones	639	639	......	505	134
15.	624	624	......	567	57
16.	431	431	......	420	11
MEIGS.					
1.	640	640	......	594	46
2.	626	626	......	549	77
3.	542	541	1	513	29
4.	633	633	......	612	21
Decatur	99	99	......	98	1
5.	406	405	1	375	31
6.	555	554	1	488	67
7.	619	616	3	525	94
8.	490	490	......	419	71
MONROE.					
1. Sweetwater	1069	1064	5	874	195
2. Head of Fork Creek	479	479	......	409	70
3. Fork Creek	710	709	1	619	91
4. Philadelphia	953	953	......	707	246
5. Knox	858	858	......	702	a154
6. McGill's	415	415	......	384	31
7. Watson	800	799	1	790	10
8. Kelsoe	719	718	1	661	58
9. Hall's	706	705	1	655	51
10. Madisonville	563	562	1	482	81
Madisonv'e	324	323	1	280	44
11. Dyer's	357	356	1	300	57
12. Kimbrough	934	934	......	886	48
13. Big Creek	794	793	1	787	7
14. Tellico Plains	683	680	3	667	16
15. Toco	640	640	......	547	93
16. Ball Play	478	478	......	470	8
17. Citico	460	460	......	449	11
18. Dry Creek	545	545	......	537	8
19. Coker Creek	228	228	......	228	......
20. Cain Creek	198	198	......	185	(b)
MONTGOMERY.					
1.	1877	1863	14	678	1199
MONTGOMERY—Con.					
2. Rollow's Shop	786	778	8	340	446
3. Ringold	1116	1115	1	357	759
4. Jordan Springs	1735	1730	5	777	958
5. Party Royal	1258	1248	10	616	642
6. Cherry's Stat'n	1128	1125	3	363	765
7. New Provid'ce	1122	1113	9	504	618
8. Woodlawn	1126	1126	......	594	532
9. Oakwood	1495	1488	7	809	686
10. Weakley's	402	402	......	273	129
11. Swift's	609	607	2	365	244
12. Clarksville	2549	2469	80	990	1559
13. Clarksv'e (c)	3200	3012	188	1721	1479
14. Major's	440	439	1	344	96
15. Bagnell's	665	659	6	511	154
16.	867	866	1	597	270
17.	1480	1476	4	975	505
18.	1249	1206	43	931	318
19.	1080	1056	24	828	252
20.	563	562	1	444	119
MORGAN.					
1. Est's	426	418	8	419	7
2. Jones's	463	441	22	442	21
3. Delin's	272	259	13	272	......
4. Wartburg	871	803	68	825	46
Montgom'y	30	30	......	30	......
5. Morris	373	370	3	357	16
6. Davidson's	121	120	1	121	......
7. Lee's School-house	223	223	......	223	......
8. White's	220	215	5	209	11
OBION.					
1. Jacksonville	1490	1489	1	1188	302
2. P. Hamilton	1547	1543	4	1227	320
3. Wildcat	1280	1273	7	1202	78
5. Black Oak	1074	1074	......	1061	13
6. Troy	2595	2585	10	2225	370
Troy	500	......	......	......	......
7. Dickerson's	1211	1210	1	974	237
8. Kenton's Stat'n	1063	1059	4	993	70
9. Texas	820	811	9	801	19
11. Boyett's Store	598	598	......	555	43
12. Massengale's Old Store	492	492	......	382	110
13. Union City	2479	2446	33	1969	510
14. Palestine Ch'ch	935	935	......	825	110
OVERTON.					
1.	567	567	......	529	38
2.	822	822	......	813	9
3.	921	921	......	910	11
4. Pea Ridge	587	587	......	511	76
5.	692	692	......	676	16
6.	1297	1295	2	1158	139
Livingston	240	238	2	196	44
7. Sourwood	919	919	......	909	10
8. Iron's Creek	900	900	......	845	55
9.	541	541	......	519	22
10. Nettle Carrier	737	737	......	700	37
11. Monroe	831	831	......	783	48
12. Olympus	821	821	......	783	38
13. Mitchel's Creek	507	507	......	487	20
14.	308	308	......	304	4
15. Hill	462	462	......	453	9
16. Mill Creek	385	383	2	367	18

(*a*) Also 2 Indians.
(*b*) Also 13 Indians.
(*c*) The 13th district comprises all of town of Clarksville.

X.—*Population of Minor Civil Divisions, &c.*—*TENNESSEE*—Continued.

	Total.	Nativity. Native.	Nativity. Foreign.	Race. White.	Race. Colored.
....	503	501	2	459	44
k...	739	737	2	717	22
ek..	709	693	16	656	53
lling	932	926	6	895	37
s...	279	279	......	259	20
....	1013	1012	1	829	184
....	149	148	1	113	36
n...	627	620	7	602	25
....	884	874	10	844	40
o...	344	344	......	340	4
....	461	461	......	456	5
k..	434	428	6	396	38
....	676	675	1	578	98
....	1238	1236	2	1170	a61
....	250	249	1	242	a1
....	920	916	4	905	15
....	628	627	1	589	39
....	351	343	8	351	......
....	425	422	3	422	3
....	344	342	2	344	......
....	1730	1569	161	1715	15
....	405	405	......	405	......
....	652	618	34	570	82
....	1189	1189	......	1103	86
llo..	156	156	......	129	27
....	491	491	......	482	9
....	715	715	......	672	43
....	557	557	......	533	24
....	277	277	......	275	2
....	293	293	......	283	10
....	607	607	......	585	22
g...	707	707	......	695	12
lley.	330	330	......	309	21
....	702	702	......	640	62
....	830	830	......	781	49
....	476	476	......	373	103
....	350	350	......	350	......
....	160	158	2	160	......
....	574	574	......	502	72
....	440	439	1	425	15
s...	900	900	......	829	71
....	684	679	5	594	90
ck..	818	816	2	758	60
....	692	692	......	638	54
....	406	406	......	356	50
n...	680	679	1	578	102
igt'n	223	222	1	180	43
....	315	315	......	304	11
ls ..	883	881	2	809	74
n ..	160	160	......	141	19
.....	1429	1393	36	1118	311
on ..	739	709	30	517	222
.....	1027	1017	10	919	108
.....	873	862	11	826	37
rove	1373	1367	6	1234	139
.....	1357	1354	3	1017	340
k ...	526	526	......	403	123
alley	541	541	......	498	43
.....	598	598	......	588	10

ndians.

C C

Counties.	Total.	Nativity. Native.	Nativity. Foreign.	Race. White.	Race. Colored.
ROANE—Cont'd.					
9. Stamp's Creek.	719	719	......	667	52
10. Riley's Creek..	423	423	......	375	48
11. Johnson's	825	825	......	624	201
12. White Creek ..	794	793	1	707	87
13. Post Oak Spr'gs	1769	1671	98	1433	336
14. May's	999	997	2	939	60
15. McGill	1083	1083	......	996	87
16. Cooper's.......	765	761	4	679	86
17. Kelley's	521	521	......	461	60
ROBERTSON.					
1. Mitchelville ..	866	863	3	668	198
2. Black Jack....	1186	1185	1	819	367
3.	855	855	......	583	272
4.	829	826	3	538	291
5.	495	495	......	319	176
6.	740	740	......	502	238
7.	857	853	4	486	371
8. Cedar Hill.....	1010	1004	6	629	381
9. Springfield	2140	2104	36	1356	784
10. Hilliard's	1120	1118	2	881	239
11. Whitehill	868	868	......	700	168
12. Greenbrior State*......	1000	986	14	919	81
13.	913	910	3	739	174
14.	561	561	......	490	71
15. Cross Plains...	1260	1257	3	834	426
16. Binkley's......	666	664	2	563	103
17.	800	799	1	327	473
RUTHERFORD.					
1. Sanders	614	613	1	399	215
2. Booth Spring..	874	871	......	412	462
3. Gambrel's	1343	1340	3	676	667
4. Mechanicsville.	881	881	......	575	306
5. Fall Creek.....	1574	1567	7	686	888
6. Jefferson	1055	1055	......	635	420
7. Wilkerson Cross Roads	1608	1608	......	553	1055
8. Eagleville	1142	1137	5	592	550
9. Sulphur Spr'gs.	2000	1995	5	488	1512
10. Versailles	1285	1285	......	884	401
11. Barfield	2063	2054	9	526	1537
12. Windrow......	995	994	1	569	426
13. Murfreesboro .	3993	3887	106	1799	2194
Murfreesboro.....	3502	3402	100	1697	b1805
14. Middleton	1045	1045	......	676	369
15. Valley	1208	1208	......	685	523
16. Milton	720	720	......	568	152
17. Trimble's	910	909	1	602	308
18. Fox Camps....	1758	1758	......	440	1318
19. McCrackin's...	922	922	......	608	314
20. Fosterville	1427	1424	3	768	659
21. Bushnell's Cr'k	1317	1310	7	603	714
22. Brown's Mill ..	723	723	......	478	245
23. Yourie's.......	1178	1177	1	956	222
24. Big Spring	1160	1159	1	952	208
25. Millersburg ...	1494	1487	7	685	809
SCOTT.					
1. Big South Fork	238	238	......	238	......
2. Huntsville	705	705	......	687	18
Huntsville.	85	85	......	84	1
3. Black Creek...	317	317	......	309	8
4. Straight Fork .	382	382	......	380	2
5. Smokey Creek	145	145	......	144	1
6. Buffalo	495	495	......	491	4

(*b*) Also 4 Indians.

. TABLE IX.—*Population of Minor Civil Divisions, &c.—TENNESSEE*—Continued.

Counties.	Total.	Nativity.		Race.	
		Native.	Foreign.	White.	Colored.
SCOTT—Cont'd.					
7. Jellico	415	415	......	415	......
8. Chitwoods	712	706	6	708	4
9. Brimstone	429	429	......	427	2
10. Bull Creek	216	216	......	216	......
SEQUATCHIE.					
1. Jefferson Graham's	429	429	......	384	45
2. Geo. Walker's	132	132	......	132	......
3. W.R. Henson's	289	289	......	274	15
4. Dunlap	472	472	......	426	46
5. C. Gott's	311	311	......	271	40
6. J. B. Pickett's	361	361	......	332	29
7. Sam. Fennel's	208	200	8	208	......
8. Schoolhouse	133	133	......	133	......
SEVIER.					
1. Jones's Cove	939	939	......	939	......
2. Emert's Cove	561	559	2	555	6
3. Fair Garden	1276	1275	1	1244	32
4. Bush's Mill	916	916	......	845	71
5. Sevierville	950	950	......	850	100
Sevierville	159	159	......	126	33
6. Wear's Cove	683	681	2	677	6
7. Carlett's Mill	978	978	......	910	68
8. Henry's Cross Roads	1002	1001	1	932	70
9. Boyd's Creek	607	606	1	544	63
10. Nob's	945	945	......	945	......
11. White Oak Flats	614	614	......	614	......
12. Paw Paw Hollow	475	475	......	444	31
13. Bird's Creek	478	478	......	463	15
14. Cowan's School-house	604	604	......	533	71
SHELBY.					
1. Sulphur Well	2361	2344	17	1160	1201
2.	2087	2060	27	828	1259
3.	1614	1574	40	665	949
4.	1100	1091	9	766	334
5.	2129	1850	279	1162	967
6.	3358	3238	120	1425	a1932
7. Wythe	2700	2685	15	803	1897
Bartlett	244	241	3	140	104
8. Oakland	1738	1717	21	709	1029
9.	2293	2290	3	1031	1262
10.	2775	2744	31	980	1795
Colliersville	274	269	5	186	88
11. Macon	1872	1840	32	663	1209
Germantown	197	184	13	162	35
12.	2289	2245	44	711	1578
13.	3039	2953	86	666	2373
14.	2442	2262	180	1350	1092
15.	1840	1609	231	1058	782
16.	1777	1754	23	549	1228
17.	738	713	25	456	282
Memphis	40226	33446	6780	24755	15471
SMITH.					
1. Carthage	1021	1015	6	601	420
Carthage	477	471	6	254	223
2. Hogg's Store	1105	1105	......	934	171
3. Taylor's	639	637	2	548	91
4. Dixon Springs	1777	1774	3	1108	669
5. Williams's	860	860	......	792	68
SMITH—Cont'd.					
6. Upper Peyton's Creek	707	707	......	629	78
7. Dixon Creek	938	938	......	697	241
8. Goose Creek	673	670	3	516	157
9. Lancaster	311	311	......	245	66
10. Scrugg's	653	653	......	564	89
11. Hurricane C'k	649	649	......	550	99
12. Upper Rome	573	573	......	405	168
13. Lower Rome	624	624	......	505	119
14. Hogan's Creek	782	782	......	575	207
15. Gordonsville	830	830	......	660	170
16. Snow Creek	763	763	......	610	153
17. New Middleton	1176	1176	......	951	225
18. Buena Vista	394	393	1	257	137
19. Brush Creek	456	456	......	393	63
20. Hughes' Mill	486	486	......	447	39
21. Chestn't Mound	577	577	......	462	115
STEWART.					
1. Lee's	1096	1084	12	666	430
2. Parker	915	914	1	733	182
3. Big Rock	949	949	......	610	339
4. Tobacco Port	920	919	1	787	133
5. Lockhart	1331	1308	23	948	383
6. Dover Furnace	860	837	23	583	277
7. Dover	1798	1761	37	1358	440
Dover	270	264	6	225	45
8. Panther Creek	966	964	2	891	75
9. Great Western Furnace	616	616	......	503	113
10. John McClish	608	596	12	523	85
11. Vickers	1055	990	65	906	149
12. Barnes	905	896	9	811	94
SULLIVAN.					
1. Carmack's	956	956	......	892	64
2. Paperville	488	486	2	466	22
3. Crumby's	642	642	......	631	11
4. Thomas's	556	555	1	515	41
5. Blountsville	1050	1048	2	969	81
Blountsv'le	180	179	1	179	1
6. White	652	651	1	624	28
7. Roller	721	721	......	688	33
8. Spurgin	884	884	......	875	9
9. Fork	798	797	1	769	29
10. Faust	577	575	2	511	66
11. Gott's	812	812	......	742	70
12. Kingsport	534	533	1	460	74
13. Easley	692	692	......	614	78
14. Branstuller	638	637	1	614	24
15. Peoples	757	757	......	723	34
16. Union	772	771	1	751	21
17. Bristol	853	848	5	719	134
18. Yeokley	754	754	......	716	38
SUMNER.					
1. Hartsville	1477	1469	8	924	553
2. Rocky Mount	876	872	4	673	203
3. Castilian Spr'gs	1216	1215	1	715	501
4. Cairo	629	626	3	350	279
5. Gallatin	3049	2994	55	1417	1632
Gallatin	2123	2076	47	982	1141
6. Baber's	866	865	1	398	468
7. Saundersville	1573	1535	38	746	827
8. Joyner's	1087	1084	3	743	344
9. Shackle Island	1119	1109	10	817	302
10. Gamblin's	967	964	3	709	258
11. Salem	1523	1519	4	725	798
12. Shiloh	1337	1337	......	749	588

(*a*) Also 1 Indian.

IX.—*Population of Minor Civil Divisions, &c.—TENNESSEE*—Continued.

…es.	Total.	Nativity. Native.	Nativity. Foreign.	Race. White.	Race. Colored.
…ont'd.					
………	1139	1138	1	921	218
………	602	602	……	418	184
…s……	1373	1372	1	1360	13
………	1263	1263	……	1184	79
………	1334	1327	7	1173	161
………	1102	1100	2	965	137
…s ……	1179	1164	15	947	232
….					
…n….	2772	2719	53	1347	1425
…ngton.	447	422	25	337	110
………	436	436	……	371	65
………	487	481	6	434	53
…1……	867	853	14	478	a384
………	1000	995	5	700	300
…ion …	1518	1496	22	1079	439
…ille …	1279	1249	30	824	455
………	1630	1604	26	812	818
…epot..	1187	1166	21	365	822
…own ..	1333	1328	5	344	989
………	345	344	1	115	230
………	969	963	6	779	190
…cle….	1061	1057	4	340	721
….					
…ville..	662	660	2	636	26
…ard-					
…le…..	155	154	1	142	13
…lo…..	636	636	……	613	23
………	734	734	……	731	3
…l…..	808	808	……	786	22
…s…..	480	477	3	463	17
………	562	562	……	535	27
…kCross					
………	733	732	1	706	27
…ross					
………	468	468	……	451	17
…ck….	543	543	……	531	12
…Chapel	682	682	……	647	35
…line					
………	565	565	……	563	2
…llow..	712	712	……	709	3
…EN.					
………	283	283	……	262	21
…n …	254	253	1	233	21
………	278	278	……	238	40
…eek..	359	358	1	359	……
…reek .	197	197	……	193	4
…dge…	318	318	……	279	39
………	614	612	2	606	8
…eer ..	147	147	……	142	5
…iver..	422	422	……	399	23
…N.					
…ville..	2850	2796	54	2105	a740
…innv'e	1172	1140	32	846	a321
…'s ….	580	579	1	489	91
………	489	488	1	433	56
………	638	630	2	564	74
…'s ….	851	846	5	809	42
………	656	636	……	622	34
………	679	679	……	570	109
…ield's					
…ard…	957	957	……	713	244
…(b)…	944	934	10	727	217
…o ….	684	683	1	601	c82

Counties.	Total.	Nativity. Native.	Nativity. Foreign.	Race. White.	Race. Colored.
WARREN—Cont'd.					
11. Bilo's………	761	753	8	672	89
12. Van Hooser's .	512	509	3	469	43
13. Mitchell's…..	706	702	4	654	52
14. Poplar Grove.	641	638	3	572	69
15. Cope's ………	766	764	2	753	13
WASHINGTON.					
1. Mauk's …….	875	875	……	854	21
2. Bricker's …..	736	736	……	638	98
3. McAllister's ..	989	989	……	860	129
4. Williams'…..	807	807	……	755	52
5. Taylor's …….	722	722	……	654	68
6. Embreeville ..	595	593	2	542	53
7. Grease Cove..	652	652	……	633	19
8. Fine's ………	997	997	……	954	46
9. Brush Creek..	1281	1280	1	1037	244
10. Knob Creek ..	588	588	……	513	75
11. Boon's Creek .	976	975	1	896	80
12. Buffalo Ridge.	835	834	1	697	138
13. Hogarth's…..	954	954	……	918	36
14. Swaney's …..	920	920	……	837	83
15. Jonesboro ….	1445	1427	18	1129	316
16. Leesburg …..	583	577	6	545	38
17. Campbell's….	923	923	……	870	53
18. Flag Pond ….	1247	1246	1	1197	50
19. Fall Branch ..	192	192	……	177	13
WAYNE.					
1. Beech Creek..	801	801	……	764	37
2. Clifton………	1004	1000	4	702	302
3. Opossum Creek	667	667	……	602	65
4. Waynesboro ..	1531	1525	6	1374	157
5. Hardin's Creek	814	813	1	683	131
6. Ashland …….	894	893	1	849	45
7. Martin's Mill.	958	957	1	880	78
8. Harbor's Cave Spring……	757	757	……	723	34
9. Second Creek.	478	478	……	467	11
10. Holte's …….	758	758	……	743	15
11. Butler's Creek	932	931	1	914	18
12. Factory's Fork	615	615	……	615	……
WEAKLEY.					
1. Boydsville ….	876	876	……	788	88
2. Pierce's…….	1558	1553	5	1217	341
3. Gardner …….	1162	1160	2	875	287
4. Latham's ……	1042	1042	……	931	111
5. Palmersville ..	1404	1403	1	1151	253
6. Thompson's Creek…….	1028	1028	……	848	180
7. Dresden …….	2608	2602	6	1737	871
Dresden	355	350	5	221	134
8. Tansel's …….	968	965	3	828	140
9. Kemp's…….	1058	1058	……	950	108
10. Parks………	1187	1184	3	853	334
11. Oakwood …..	1477	1466	11	1257	220
12. Hays ……….	786	784	2	628	158
13. Dukedom…..	923	923	……	813	110
14. Collers………	1440	1439	1	1239	201
15. Jonesboro ….	759	759	……	678	81
16. Golden Spring	540	540	……	525	15
17. Rucker's……	996	995	1	799	197
18. Jones………	943	942	1	739	204
WHITE.					
1. Sparta…….	1655	1651	4	1238	417
Sparta ….	414	……	……	……	……

(a) Also 5 Indians.
(b) The population of the village of Viola comprises district No. 9.
(c) Also 1 Indian.

TABLE IX.—*Population of Minor Civil Divisions, &c.—TENNESSEE*—Continued.

Counties.	Total.	NATIVITY. Native.	Foreign.	RACE. White.	Colored.
WHITE—Con. (a)					
2. Hickory Valley	989	989		881	108
3. Doyle	737	737		683	54
4. Sparkman	713	709	4	644	69
5. Darkey Spring	1012	1012		1000	12
6. Arnold's	1017	1017		914	103
7. Bunker Hill	612	612		578	34
8. Matlock's	525	524	1	472	53
9. Farley	498	498		450	48
11. Big Spring Church	641	640	1	625	16
12. Yankeytown	829	825	4	664	165
13. Clarktown	147	145	2	146	1
WILLIAMSON.					
1. Smith's Sp'ngs	979	973	6	933	46
2. Thompson Davis	704	704		639	65
3. Hillsboro	1238	1237	1	723	515
4. Cayce's Spring	1678	1666	12	721	957
5. Southall's	1824	1812	12	836	988
6. Hill's	1002	983	19	472	530
7. Pryor Smith	762	759	3	481	281
8. Beech's Stand	1207	1202	5	654	553
9. Franklin	2002	1969	33	1021	981
Franklin	1552	1522	30	869	683
10. Douglas	1677	1670	7	599	1078
11. Ridge Meetinghouse	1799	1788	11	872	927
12. Bethesda	782	782		591	191
13. Peytonsville	1073	1070	3	572	501
14. Carother's Mill	1170	1168	2	708	462
15. Brentwood	1141	1133	8	627	514
16. Winstead's	974	972	2	601	373
17. Nolensville	1024	1018	6	613	411

Counties.	Total.	NATIVITY. Native.	Foreign.	RACE. White.	Colored.
WILLIAMSON—Con.					
18. Triune	1054	1050	4	435	619
19. Knobb	852	850	2	562	290
20. College Grove	666	664	2	347	319
21. Owen Hill	1083	1078	5	497	586
22. Flat Creek	637	637		413	224
WILSON.					
1. Green Hill	1405	1399	6	761	644
2. Silver Springs	1158	1157	1	800	358
3. Forestville	903	900	3	573	330
4. Lagnardo	1388	1388		946	442
5. Cedar Grove	1167	1162	5	904	263
6. Lyon's	861	858	3	611	250
7. Young's	826	826		531	295
8. Belcher's	723	723		443	280
9. Pursley	699	698	1	442	257
10. Lebanon	2806	2774	32	1598	b1202
Lebanon	2073	2046	27	1156	917
11. Linwood	807	807		569	238
12. Commerce	1035	1035		716	319
13. Turner's	868	868		756	112
14. Shelton's	575	574	1	467	108
15. Statesville	1260	1259	1	1164	96
16. Cherry Valley	1045	1045		761	284
17. Cainsville	1330	1328	2	988	342
18. Henderson's Cross Roads	756	756		638	118
19. Doak's	851	851		642	209
20. Hurricane	1039	1033	6	887	152
21. Flat Rock	889	889		693	196
22. Ligon	956	952	4	686	270
23. Oak Grove	788	788		652	136
24. Lohman's Store	937	936	1	678	259
25. Alford's Campground	809	808	1	658	151

(a) District No. 10 since 1850 to Putnam County.

(b) Also 6 Indians.

TABLE IX.—*Population of Minor Civil Divisions, &c.—TEXAS.*

NOTE.—The marginal column marks beats and precincts; the first indentation, cities: the second, towns. Names of towns are placed under the beats or precincts in which they are respectively situated. The population of each beat or precinct includes that of all towns situated in it.

Counties.	Total.	NATIVITY. Native.	Foreign.	RACE. White.	Colored.
ANGELINA. (*)					
Homer	216	215	1	194	22
ATASCOSA.					
1.	1310	1161	149	1226	a65
Pleasanton	206	203	3	186	b13
2.	1136	1018	118	1057	c76
3.	81	71	10	81	
4.	388	351	37	369	19

Counties.	Total.	NATIVITY. Native.	Foreign.	RACE. White.	Colored.
AUSTIN.					
1.	3907	3345	562	2062	1845
2.	3321	3197	124	1046	2275
3.	2129	2073	56	702	1427
San Felipe	238	211	27	163	75
4. Cat Spring	1172	615	557	1074	98
5.	4558	2847	1711	3629	929

(*) Incomplete; the other principal civil divisions were not separately returned.
(a) Also 19 Indians.
(b) Also 7 Indians.
(c) Also 3 Indians.

TABLE IX.—*Population of Minor Civil Divisions, &c.—TEXAS*—Continued.

Counties.	Total.	Nativity. Native.	Nativity. Foreign.	Race. White.	Race. Colored.
BANDERA.					
1.	237	176	61	234	3
2.	105	91	14	94	11
3.	240	227	13	237	3
4.	67	51	16	66	1
BASTROP. (*)					
Bastrop	1199	1006	193	833	366
BELL.					
1. Belton	1058	1039	19	885	173
Belton	281	281	......	206	75
2. Aiken	1106	1095	11	965	141
3. Harrisville	2480	2462	18	2165	315
4. Salado	2555	2529	26	2214	341
5. Nolan	2572	2562	10	2438	134
BEXAR. (*)					
San Antonio	12256	8136	4120	10298	*a*1957
BEXAR DISTRICT.					
Bismarck Farm	42	10	32	42	......
Concho Mail Station	34	25	9	24	10
Fort Chadbourne	1	1	......	1	......
Fort Concho and vic'ty	913	548	365	864	49
Jone's Ran'e	13	11	2	12	1
Kickapoo Springs	12	11	1	10	2
Lispan Sp'gs	21	18	3	20	1
San Angela	41	29	12	41	......
BLANCO.					
1.	492	467	25	465	27
2.	201	190	11	189	12
3.	227	213	14	222	5
4.	106	102	4	106	......
5.	161	107	54	161	......
BOWIE.					
1.	394	391	3	273	121
2.	1193	1191	2	355	838
3.	1000	995	5	571	429
4.	1072	1064	8	427	*a*644
5.	752	746	6	627	125
Boston	273	267	6	181	92
BRAZORIA.					
1. Brazoria	2637	2482	155	580	2057
Brazoria	725	644	81	261	464
2. Columbia	1873	1795	78	482	1391
Colombia	426	398	28	257	169
3. Sandy Point	1763	1736	27	125	1638
4. Liverpool	649	584	65	316	333
5. Quintana	605	568	37	288	317
BURLESON.					
1. Caldwell	319	316	3	231	88
2. Brazos Bottom	2391	2337	54	847	1544
BURLESON—Cont'd.					
3. Chance's Prairie	2927	2886	41	2046	881
4. Lexington	1800	1760	40	1342	458
Lexington	157	140	17	138	19
5. Blue Branch	635	598	37	585	50
BURNET.					
1. Burnet	962	954	8	859	103
Burnet	280	276	4	241	39
2. North Gabriel	799	793	6	745	54
3. Oatmeal	801	794	7	731	70
4. Buckbone Valley	719	691	28	621	98
5. Hickory Creek	407	400	7	374	33
CALDWELL.					
1.	1372	......	......	......	......
Lockhart	560	527	33	403	157
2.	1800	......	......	......	......
3.	2000	......	......	......	......
4.	1100	......	......	......	......
5.	300	......	......	......	......
CALHOUN.					
1.	2169	1618	551	1669	500
Indianola	1900	1452	448	1408	492
Indianola, (Old)	206	128	78	203	......
2.	936	874	62	565	371
Lavacca	768	721	47	429	339
3.	182	146	36	156	26
4. Matagorda Is'ld	156	136	20	146	10
CAMERON.					
1.	1335	532	803	1330	5
2. (*b*)	1275	482	793	1254	21
3.	1559	688	871	1540	19
4.	1115	397	718	1081	34
5.	810	316	494	810	......
Brownsville	4905	1612	3293	4827	78
CHAMBERS.					
1. Smith's Point	93	86	7	92	1
2. Double Bayou	523	492	31	330	193
3. Wallisville	528	520	8	304	224
Wallisville	27	27	......	12	15
4. Old River	256	242	14	233	23
5. Cedar Bayou	103	98	5	92	11
CHEROKEE.					
1.	1908	1902	6	1437	471
Alto	61	60	1	58	3
2.	2787	2779	8	2024	763
3.	1825	1813	12	1496	329
Rusk	545	533	12	416	129
4.	2222	2221	1	1253	969
5.	2337	2332	5	1584	753
COLLIN.					
1.	4642	4608	34	3798	*c*832
McKinney	503	491	12	403	100
2.	3761	3758	3	3560	201

(*) Incomplete; the other principal civil divisions were not separately returned.
(*a*) Also 1 Indian.
(*b*) Exclusive of city of Brownsville.
(*c*) Also 12 Indians.

TABLE IX.—*Population of Minor Civil Divisions, &c.*—*TEXAS*—Continued.

Counties.	Total.	Nativity.		Race.	
		Native.	Foreign.	White.	Colored.
COLLIN—Cont'd.					
Farmersville	114	114	.....	114	.....
3.	1620	1617	3	1373	247
Mantua	86	85	1	70	16
4.	1565	1554	11	1434	131
Weston	157	157	.....	136	21
5.	2425	2404	21	2183	242
Plano	155	155	.....	126	29
COLORADO.					
1. Columbus	2745	2591	154	1370	1375
2.	1161	1113	48	725	436
3.	2032	1412	620	1480	552
4. Alleytown	1512	1249	263	945	567
5.	876	854	22	105	771
COMAL.					
1. New Braunfels	2261	1291	970	2171	90
2.	918	565	353	905	13
3.	702	449	253	688	14
4.	315	214	101	301	14
5.	1087	763	324	841	246
COMANCHE. (*)					
Beasley's Creek	1001	1000	1	977	24
COOK.					
1.	1822	1805	17	1567	a252
2.	1237	1231	6	1164	73
3.	1309	1301	8	1273	b22
4.	355	354	1	291	64
5.	592	583	9	532	60
CORYELL.					
1. Gatesville	1455	1451	4	1355	100
2. Coryell	558	558	.....	525	33
3. Leonville	175	173	2	139	36
4. Sugar Loaf	770	769	1	726	44
5. Station Creek	1166	1162	4	1100	66
DALLAS.					
1.	2967	2832	135	2145	c821
2.	3356	3321	35	3024	332
3.	1111	1072	39	992	119
4.	3358	3328	30	2729	629
5.	2522	2513	9	2307	d208
DAVIS.					
1.	2271	2265	6	1397	874
2.	942	938	4	648	294
3.	3170	3167	3	1871	1299
4.	2135	2132	3	1326	809
5.	357	356	1	254	103
DENTON.					
1. Denton	1898	1887	11	1796	102
Denton	361	354	7	329	32
2. Pilot Point	2200	2192	8	2106	94
3. Lewisville	1662	1647	15	1497	165
4. Elizabethtown	1104	1102	2	1018	86
5. Bolivar	387	384	3	334	53
DE WITT.					
1. Clinton	1559	1410	149	1179	380
Clinton	217	195	22	196	21
2. Concrete	1598	1522	76	851	747
3. Yorktown	1626	1099	527	1473	153
4. Meyersville	669	437	232	582	87
5. Terryville	1000	987	13	721	279
DUVAL.					
4. Concepcion	1083	483	600	1080	3
EASTLAND.					
Eastland	88	87	1	87	1
ELLIS.					
Burnham	1599	1594	5	1083	516
Milford	995	991	4	797	198
Red Oak	2442	2428	14	2219	223
Waxahac'ie	2478	2453	25	1909	569
EL PASO.					
El Paso	764	352	412	696	e62
Ft. Quitman	361	290	71	127	234
San Elizario	1120	876	244	1116	4
Socorro	627	489	138	627	.....
Yolita	799	594	205	669	(f)
ERATH.					
Alarm and Green C'k	120	120	.....	120	.....
Armstrong Creek	75	75	.....	75	.....
Bosque C'k	575	575	.....	535	40
Duffin's C'k.	476	476	.....	466	10
North Fork Bosque Cr	78	78	.....	72	6
Willow Sp'g	238	238	.....	228	10
Dublin	77	77	.....	77	.....
Stephens-v'e, (town)	162	159	3	139	23
FALLS.					
1.	3120	3031	89	1281	1839
Marlin	602	581	21	436	166
2.	1523	1503	20	1145	d378
3.	1650	1645	5	573	1077
4.	1075	1066	9	760	315
5.	2483	2457	26	1386	g1078
FANNIN.					
1.	3072	3049	23	2455	617
Bonham	928	913	15	622	306
2.	2692	2689	3	2530	162
3.	1703	1688	15	1382	h319
Ladonia	516	508	8	429	h85
4.	3774	3770	4	3134	640
Honey Grove	382	381	1	281	101
5.	1966	1960	6	1220	746
FAYETTE.					
1.	2732	2392	340	1254	1478

(*) Incomplete; the other principal civil divisions were not separately returned.
(a) Also 3 Indians.
(b) Also 14 Indians.
(c) Also 1 Indian.
(d) Also 7 Indians.
(e) Also 6 Indians.
(f) Also 130 Indians.
(g) Also 19 Indians.
(h) Also 2 Indians.

TABLE IX.—*Population of Minor Civil Divisions, &c.—TEXAS*—Continued.

Counties.	Total.	Nativity. Native.	Nativity. Foreign.	Race. White.	Race. Colored.
AYETTE—Cont'd.					
....	1836	1248	588	1239	597
....	2550	1831	719	1843	707
nd 5	8261	6874	1387	5550	a2705
Fayette....	319	248	71	273	46
La Grange.	1165	1000	165	794	b368
FORT BEND.					
....	1339	1319	20	167	1172
....	2398	2373	25	324	2074
....	1541	1519	22	258	1283
....	1692	1604	88	743	949
Richmond .	816	742	74	458	358
....	144	135	9	112	32
FREESTONE.					
Fairfield	1998	1986	12	1041	957
Fairfield...	800	789	11	476	324
Cotton Gin	1793	1789	4	1173	620
Butler	1806	1806	......	861	945
Pine Bluff......	1515	1511	4	1102	413
Woodland	1027	1023	4	594	433
FRIO.					
....	309	293	16	294	15
GALVESTON.					
....	458	377	81	397	61
....	825	608	217	662	163
....	189	174	15	184	5
Galveston (c).	13818	10204	3614	10810	d3007
GILLESPIE.					
....	1626	947	679	1624	2
Fredericksburg.......	1164	659	505	1163	1
....	1077	745	332	1024	53
....	320	204	116	320	......
....	317	216	101	297	20
....	226	166	60	224	2
GONZALES.					
Gonzales....	1255	1163	92	737	d517
Belmont	1746	1731	15	735	e1001
....	2829	2807	22	1473	1356
....	1849	1837	12	1387	d461
....	1272	1266	6	937	335
GRAYSON.					
Sherman.......	6348	6306	42	4986	f1360
Sherman...	1439	1413	26	949	490
....	1386	1375	11	1293	93
....	2432	2423	9	2263	f167
....	3427	3418	9	2953	474
....	794	788	6	742	d51
GRIMES.					
....	4659	4602	57	1723	2936
Anderson..	495	468	27	364	131

Counties.	Total.	Nativity. Native.	Nativity. Foreign.	Race. White.	Race. Colored.
GRIMES—Cont'd.					
Prairie Plains ...	642	638	4	366	276
2.	1771	1759	12	716	1055
3.	3941	3838	103	1626	2315
Navasota...	1509	1421	88	733	776
4.	1005	996	9	275	b727
5.	1842	1810	32	954	888
GUADALUPE.					
1.	3044	2777	267	1637	1407
Seguin.....	988	878	110	729	259
2.	1036	657	379	930	106
3.	1004	933	71	687	317
4.	1337	1279	58	858	479
5.	861	697	164	636	225
HARDIN.					
1.	209	208	1	170	39
2.	164	164	......	110	54
3.	358	349	9	327	31
4.	495	492	3	393	102
5.	234	232	2	218	16
HARRIS. (*)					
Harrisburg.	571	513	58	273	298
Houston......	9382	7811	1571	5691	3691
Lynchburg .	79	75	4	60	19
San Jacinto	172	148	24	103	69
HARRISON.					
1.	1764	1758	6	353	1411
2.	1755	1749	6	351	1404
3.	5412	5302	110	1985	3427
Marshall...	1920	1820	100	1069	851
4.	2951	2942	9	1041	1910
5.	1359	1359	......	580	779
HAYS.					
1. San Marcos	1776	1706	69	1009	767
San Marcos	742	723	19	502	240
2. Stringtown ...	745	647	98	517	228
3. Heaton's.......	316	305	11	313	3
4. Dripping Sp'ng.	456	447	9	445	11
5. Mountain City.	795	775	20	587	208
HENDERSON.					
1. Athens	1507	1506	1	1041	466
Athens	545	545	......	394	151
2. Price's.........	1011	1010	1	784	227
3. Goshen	1123	1120	3	989	134
4. Brownsboro....	1541	1501	40	1397	144
5. Fincastle	1604	1598	6	921	683
HIDALGO.					
1.	749	263	486	714	d34
2.	558	234	324	553	5
3. } 4. }	555	139	416	553	2
5.	525	132	393	525	......

(*) Incomplete; the other principal civil divisions were not separately returned.
(a) Also 6 Indians.
(b) Also 3 Indians.
(c) The city of Galveston comprises all of precincts 3 and 4, and part of 1, 2, and 5.
(d) Also 1 Indian.
(e) Also 10 Indians.
(f) Also 2 Indians.

TABLE IX.—*Population of Minor Civil Divisions, &c.*—*TEXAS*—Continued.

Counties.	Total.	Nativity. Native.	Nativity. Foreign.	Race. White.	Race. Colored.
HILL.					
1. Cleburne	2796	2785	11	2457	339
Hillsboro	313	312	1	246	67
Peoria	234	234	......	223	11
2. Wilbankes	574	572	2	455	119
3. Caddo	1617	1612	5	1496	121
4. Alvarado	1724	1721	3	1591	133
5. Grandview	742	739	3	648	94
HOPKINS.					
1.	3371	3350	21	2865	*a*505
2.	2707	2701	6	2266	441
3.	2279	2278	1	1964	315
4.	1848	1845	3	1699	149
5.	1525	1524	1	1434	91
Sulphur Sp'ngs (*b*)	921	910	11	802	119
HOUSTON.					
1.	2699	2684	15	1303	1396
Crockett	538	526	12	365	173
2.	1300	1297	3	901	399
3.	1465	1457	8	957	508
4.	1581	1576	5	936	645
5.	1102	1099	3	508	594
HUNT.					
1.	2023	2001	22	1548	475
2.	2285	2277	8	2163	122
3.	957	956	1	858	99
4.	2878	2867	11	2667	211
5.	2148	2142	6	1977	171
JACK.					
1.	550	529	21	477	*c*71
2.	53	53	......	53	......
3.	23	23	......	23	......
5.	68	65	3	67	1
JASPER.					
1.	399	398	1	309	90
2.	1601	1598	3	994	607
3.	1120	1119	1	725	395
4.	480	478	2	216	264
5.	618	618	......	215	403
JEFFERSON.					
1.	799	785	14	448	351
2.	144	121	23	139	5
3. Sabine City (*d*)	457	425	32	385	72
4.	342	332	10	282	60
5.	164	163	1	154	10
JOHNSON.					
1.	1714	1702	12	1585	129
Cleburne	686	679	7	611	75
2.	218	217	1	214	4
3.	777	775	2	746	31
4.	971	971	......	929	42

Counties.	Total.	Nativity. Native.	Nativity. Foreign.	Race. White.	Race. Colored.
JOHNSON—Cont'd.					
5.	1243	1235	8	1165	[illegible]
KENDALL.					
1.	571	372	199	509	
2.	143	103	40	141	
3.	226	200	26	199	
4.	230	131	99	230	
5.	366	255	111	366	....
KERR.					
1. Kerrsville	453	402	51	430	
2. Zanzenburg	244	231	13	185	
3. Cypress Creek	126	68	58	121	
4. Johnson's Creek	86	83	3	86	....
5. Tezener's Mills	133	127	6	130	
KINNEY. (*)					
Brackettsv'e	232	135	97	195	
Fort Clark	395	380	15	45	[illegible]
San Filipo	161	52	109	15[illegible]	
LAMAR.					
1.	4010	3954	56	2753	[illegible]
2.	3880	3874	6	2742	[illegible]
3.	4344	4334	10	3366	[illegible]
4.	1736	1733	3	900	[illegible]
5.	1820	1812	8	1604	[illegible]
LAMPASAS.					
1. Town	780	769	11	699	
2 & 3. McAnelly's	262	262	......	261	
4. Patterson	150	150	......	148	
5. Taylor's	152	151	1	150	
LAVACA. (*)					
Hallettsville	431	359	72	329	[illegible]
LEON.					
1.	1296	1288	8	629	[illegible]
Centreville	221	217	4	151	
2.	1545	1539	6	651	[illegible]
3.	1022	1021	1	464	[illegible]
4.	345	344	1	262	[illegible]
5.	2315	2309	6	1809	[illegible]
LIBERTY.					
1. Liberty	2123	2070	53	1101	*g*1[illegible]
Liberty	458	432	26	300	[illegible]
2. Grand Cave	330	330	......	127	[illegible]
3. Fash'ton Prairie	1003	999	4	676	[illegible]
4. West Liberty	525	502	23	252	[illegible]
West Lib'ty	230	227	3	127	[illegible]
5. Shiloh Church	433	424	9	259	[illegible]
LLANO.					
1. Llano (*j*)	188	176	12	183	
2.	411	409	2	405	

(*) Incomplete; the other principal civil divisions were not separately returned.
(*a*) Also 1 Indian.
(*b*) Its precinct not ascertained.
(*c*) Also 1 Chinese and 1 Indian.
(*d*) Comprises all of precinct 3.
(*e*) Also 5 Indians.
(*f*) Also 14 Indians.
(*g*) Also 6 Indians.
(*h*) Also 15 Indians.
(*i*) Also 3 Indians.
(*j*) Comprises the whole of precinct 1.

TABLE IX.—*Population of Minor Civil Divisions, &c.*—*TEXAS*—Continued.

Counties.	Total.	Nativity. Native.	Nativity. Foreign.	Race. White.	Race. Colored.
LLANO—Cont'd.					
....	388	386	2	382	6
....	340	265	75	339	1
....	52	52	......	52	......
MADISON. (*)					
....	1216	1208	8	516	700
Mad'ville (a)	98	95	3	89	9
MARION.					
....	279	279	......	106	173
....	1516	1499	17	774	742
....	1710	1704	6	656	1054
....	867	862	5	299	568
Jefferson	4190	3816	374	2365	1825
MASON.					
Mason (b) ..	296	261	35	275	c19
....	166	104	62	166	......
....	131	97	34	124	7
....	85	49	36	85	......
MATAGORDA.					
Peninsula......	722	614	108	554	168
Matagorda.	386	345	41	244	142
....	1036	1001	35	183	e851
Kenner's Prairie...	65	64	1	37	28
....	574	552	22	177	d396
....	669	635	34	36	633
Linville....	40	39	1	......	40
....	376	329	47	304	72
Palacios ...	35	27	8	32	3
Tres Palacios	226	195	31	186	40
MAVERICK. (*)					
Eagle Pass	1240	421	819	1198	42
Fort Duncan	294	278	16	58	236
M'LENNAN. (*)					
East Waco .	612	608	4	293	d318
Waco	3008	2804	204	1914	e1091
MEDINA.					
1.	784	479	305	784	......
Castroville	515	299	216	515	......
2.	394	221	173	394	......
3.	212	149	63	164	48
4.	376	247	129	362	14
D'Hanis ...	213	213	......	199	14
5.	312	284	28	282	30
MILAM.					
1. Cameron	3697	3662	35	2213	d1483
2. Bryant Station	260	258	2	122	138
3. Port Sullivan..	1423	1407	16	1053	370
4. Maysfield	1890	1883	7	1206	d683
5. Devilla	1714	1707	7	1411	303
MONTAGUE.					
1.	79	79	......	78	1
MONTAGUE—Con.					
2.	240	238	2	231	f4
3.	200	200	......	193	7
4.	240	240	......	228	12
5.	131	131	......	131	......
MONTGOMERY. (g)					
Boggy	640	634	6	490	150
Danville	2020	2018	2	687	1333
Longstreet	320	320	......	234	86
Montgomery ...	2863	2846	17	1258	d1604
Tillis Prairie ...	640	595	45	462	178
NACOGDOCHES.					
1.	3188	3149	39	1731	e1454
Nac'doches.	500	492	8	300	200
2.	1807	1805	2	1208	599
3.	1734	1731	3	1171	563
4.	1099	1099	......	826	273
5.	1786	1771	15	1371	h386
NAVARRO.					
1.	2685	2667	18	1808	877
Corsicana ..	80	80	......	55	25
2.	848	847	1	601	247
3.	1018	1015	3	669	349
4.	1956	1947	9	1558	398
5.	2372	2361	11	1998	374
NEWTON.					
1.	958	955	3	530	428
2.	640	639	1	389	251
3.	200	200	......	153	47
4.	201	201	......	185	16
5.	188	188	......	99	89
NUECES.					
1. Corpus Christi (b)	2140	1433	707	1852	288
2. Banquetto	506	360	146	501	5
3. San Diego......	784	252	532	780	4
5. Santa Gertrude.	545	268	277	510	35
ORANGE.					
1.	420	409	11	296	124
2.	275	265	10	247	28
3.	303	297	6	236	67
4.	167	167	......	151	16
5.	90	89	1	75	15
PANOLA.					
1. Carthage	2559	2554	5	1908	651
2. Beckville	2240	2239	1	1515	725
3. Evergreen	1920	1919	1	960	960
4. Harmony	1760	1759	1	981	779
5. Allen's	1640	1638	2	1028	612
PARKER.					
1.	2112	2097	15	1898	214
2.	1052	1048	4	1001	51
3.	151	147	4	150	1
4.	579	577	2	567	12

(*) Incomplete; the other principal civil divisions were not separately returned.
(a) Its beat not ascertained.
(b) Comprises the whole of precinct 1.
(c) Also 2 Indians.
(d) Also 1 Indian.
(e) Also 3 Indians.
(f) Also 5 Indians.
(g) Precincts returned without numbers.
(h) Also 29 Indians.

TABLE IX.—*Population of Minor Civil Divisions, &c.*—*TEXAS*—Continued.

Counties.	Total.	Nativity. Native.	Nativity. Foreign.	Race. White.	Race. Colored.
PARKER—Cont'd.					
5.	292	292	.....	277	15
POLK.					
1.	3553	3540	13	1395	2158
2.	1983	1982	1	1083	900
3.	1197	1190	7	670	527
4.	1070	1063	7	808	262
5.	904	903	1	452	*a*451
PRESIDIO.					
Fort Davis	615	416	199	290	325
Ft. Stockton	458	265	193	298	160
Lylesville	124	20	104	124	.....
Presidio del Norte	439	96	343	435	4
RED RIVER.					
1.	3335	3308	27	1767	1568
Clarksville	613	589	24	417	196
2.	3163	3143	20	2421	742
3.	1333	1330	3	680	653
4.	2067	2053	14	1117	950
5.	755	754	1	520	235
REFUGIO.					
1. Rockport	480	443	37	421	59
2. St. Mary's	311	303	8	276	35
3. Refugio	1053	898	155	1006	47
4. Hines Bay	216	194	22	190	26
5. St. Joseph Isl'd.	264	242	22	185	79
ROBERTSON.					
1.	3728	3475	253	1736	*b*1991
2.	1555	1525	30	539	1016
3.	1457	1448	9	1072	385
4.	1660	1651	9	1125	535
5.	1590	1478	112	985	*c*603
RUSK.					
1.	2880	2875	5	1503	1377
2.	3198	3191	7	1669	1529
3.	3200	3184	16	1347	1853
4.	3520	3502	18	2311	1209
5.	3200	3191	9	1773	1427
Hend'son (*d*)	918	906	12	598	320
SABINE.					
1.	480	472	8	452	28
2.	955	951	4	552	403
3.	707	705	2	563	144
4.	480	478	2	303	177
5.	634	634	.....	279	355
SAN AUGUSTINE. (*)					
San Augus'e	250	.....	.....	.....	.....
SAN SABA.					
1.	102	102	.....	101	1
2.	765	756	9	669	96
San Saba	168	166	2	143	25
SAN SABA—Cont'd.					
3.	295	294	1	249	46
4.	154	153	1	153	1
5.	119	119	.....	119	.....
SHACKLEFORD.					
Beasley's Cr	79	76	3	56	23
Clear F'k of the Brazos	79	74	5	63	16
Fort Griffin	297	158	139	281	16
SHELBY.					
1.	1463	1460	3	1186	277
2.	1080	1075	5	571	509
3.	1000	998	2	562	438
4.	682	679	3	597	85
5.	1507	1503	4	1061	446
SMITH.					
1. Tyler	1750	1716	34	974	776
2. Canton, or Troupe	3891	3885	6	2424	1467
3. Etna	2888	2883	5	1680	1208
4. Garden Valley	3977	3966	11	2392	1585
5. Starrville	4026	4023	3	1985	2041
STARR. (*)					
Ring'ld Barracks	377	170	207	368	9
STEPHENS.					
Big Sandy Cr	36	36	.....	35	1
Cedar Creek	137	134	3	122	15
Lynch's R'e.	42	39	3	34	8
Pickettsv'e.	115	114	1	115	.....
TARRANT.					
1.	1628	1606	22	1303	325
2.	1827	1819	8	1700	127
3.	866	861	5	803	63
4.	880	875	5	736	144
5.	467	465	2	440	27
6.	120	120	.....	101	19
TITUS. (*)					
Daingerfield	272	271	1	222	50
Mt. Pleasant	275	272	3	210	65
Mt. Vernon	223	222	1	154	69
TRAVIS. (*)					
1.	1033	1008	25	646	387
Webb'rville	330	324	6	208	122
4.	1400	1241	159	1082	*a*317
5.	1600	1517	83	993	607
Austin	4428	3812	616	2813	1615
TRINITY. (*)					
Pennington	193	191	2	181	12
Sumpter	145	144	1	100	45

(*) Incomplete: the other principal civil divisions were not separately returned.
(*a*) Also 1 Indian.
(*b*) Also 1 Chinese.
(*c*) Also 2 Chinese.
(*d*) Its precinct not ascertained.

TABLE IX.—*Population of Minor Civil Divisions, &c.*—*TEXAS*—Continued.

Counties.	Total.	Nativity. Native.	Nativity. Foreign.	Race. White.	Race. Colored.
UPSHUR.					
1.	2880	2880	......	1514	1366
2.	2399	2398	1	1352	1047
3.	2400	2394	6	1565	835
4.	2129	2127	2	1333	796
5.	2231	2227	4	1408	823
UVALDE. (*)					
Uvalde	163	146	17	137	26
VAN ZANDT.					
1.	1698	1694	4	1394	304
Canton	183	182	1	161	22
2.	1400	1390	10	1292	108
3.	853	837	16	785	68
4.	1504	1498	6	1382	122
5.	1039	1037	2	959	80
VICTORIA.					
1.	2731	2142	589	1743	988
Victoria	2534	1971	563	1639	895
2.	721	623	98	461	260
3.	312	261	51	223	89
4.	748	711	37	348	400
5.	348	263	85	317	31
WALKER.					
1.	3609	3409	200	1342	a2265
Huntsville	1599	1432	167	959	a638
2.	765	763	2	424	341
3.	2079	2068	11	875	1204
4.	1914	1887	27	573	1341
5.	1349	1337	12	677	672
WASHINGTON.					
1. Washington	4354	4283	71	1151	3203
2. Chapel Hill	3943	3829	114	1115	2828
Chapel Hill	602	583	19	342	260
3. Brenham	9716	8527	1189	4884	4832
Brenham	2221	1941	280	1288	933
4. Union Hill	3908	3157	751	2623	1285
5. Evergreen	1183	1130	53	1090	93
WEBB.					
1.	2233	1343	890	2231	2
Laredo	2046	1241	805	2046	......
2.	150	71	79	150	......
3.	232	124	108	232	......
WHARTON.					
1.	1110	1105	5	91	1019
2.	1105	1094	11	130	975
3.	790	784	6	100	690
4.	315	310	5	154	a159
5.	106	104	2	39	67
WILLIAMSON.					
1.	1750	......	......	......	......
Georgetown	479	475	4	371	b107
2.	1650	......	......	......	......
3.	1506	......	......	......	......
4.	802	......	......	......	......
Liberty Hill	47	47	......	46	1
5.	660	......	......	......	......
WILSON.					
1.	128	125	3	83	45
2.	459	441	18	230	229
3.	637	580	57	601	36
4.	904	653	251	817	87
5.	428	416	12	362	66
WISE.					
1.	688	684	4	657	31
2.	36	36	......	36	......
3.	165	161	4	161	4
4.	401	399	2	387	14
5.	160	159	1	158	2
WOOD.					
1.	1699	1694	5	1130	569
Quitman	320	315	5	234	86
2.	687	687	......	639	48
3.	1590	1589	1	1378	212
4.	2130	2124	6	1920	210
5.	788	786	2	580	208
YOUNG.					
Belknap	67	67	......	63	4
George Lembrig's R'ch	20	20	......	20	......
Medlan's R.	28	28	......	28	......
Saltworks	20	20	......	20	......
ZAPATA.					
1. R'nch Sabrinitos	455	84	371	455	......
2. Rameriano	393	148	245	393	......
3. San Pedro	376	55	321	376	......
4. Salomonio	64	6	58	64	......
5. Los Albercos	200	28	172	200	......

(*) Incomplete: the other principal civil divisions were not separately returned.
(a) Also 2 Indians.
(b) Also 1 Indian.

TABLE IX.—*Population of Minor Civil Divisions, &c.*—*UTAH.*

NOTE.—The marginal column marks precincts; the first indentation, cities; the second, all other localities, whose names are placed under the names of the precincts in which they are respectively situated. The population of each precinct includes that of all localities situated in it. Whenever the items of any locality fail to make the total, the deficiency represents the Chinese and Indians.

Counties.	Total.	Nativity.		Race.	
		Native.	Foreign.	White.	Colored.
BEAVER. (a)					
Adamsville	179	105	74	179	......
Beaver City	1207	864	343	1207	......
Greenville	175	100	75	175	......
Minersville	446	336	110	444	......
BOX ELDER. (b)					
Bear River	317	107	210	317	......
Bear River City	289	94	195	289	......
Point Lookout	28	13	15	28	......
Box Elder	2080	1369	711	2058	......
Brigham City	1315	820	495	1313	......
Three-Mile Creek	222	140	82	203	......
Towns'p 9, N., range 2 W.	35	30	5	35	......
Corinne	806	475	331	699	18
Corinne City	783	473	310	697	18
Little Mountain	23	2	21	2	......
Kelton	453	216	237	317	1
Bovine	19	1	18	2	......
Curlew Valley	54	46	8	54	......
Kelton	101	54	47	74	......
Lake Station	17	1	16	2	......
Lucine	21	3	18	7	......
Matlin	15	1	14	2	......
Park Valley	70	56	14	69	1
Sections 135 and 136	17	1	16	2	......
Tecoma	14	......	14	3	......
Terrace	125	53	72	102	......
Mantua	184	84	100	184	......
Portage	158	99	59	157	......
Promontory	172	28	144	55	......
Blue Creek	90	14	76	31	......
Monument	14	1	13	3	......
Promontory Station	43	12	31	17	......
Rozel	25	1	24	4	......
Willard	685	417	268	642	......
Willard City	552	317	235	521	......
CACHE. (c)					
Clarkston	153	84	69	153	......
Franklin	558	381	177	557	......
Hyde Park	343	212	131	343	......
Hyrum City	708	352	356	708	......
Logan (d)	1757	965	792	1756	......
Mendon	345	224	121	345	......
Millville	402	278	124	396	5
Newton	195	114	81	195	......
Oxford	260	227	33	260	......
Bridgeport	29	28	1	29	......
CACHE—Cont'd.					
Clifton	82	69	13	82	......
Oxford	149	130	19	149	......
Paradise	346	214	132	345	......
Providence	481	262	219	480	......
Richmond	817	637	180	817	......
Smithfield	744	492	252	744	......
Wellsville	885	556	329	885	......
Weston	235	123	112	235	......
DAVIS. (e)					
Bountiful	1517	1031	486	1516	......
Centreville	544	390	154	542	......
Farmington	976	739	237	974	......
Kaysville	1422	850	572	1422	......
IRON. (f)					
Cedar City	517	304	213	512	......
Eagleville	422	355	67	420	......
Iron City	92	70	22	91	......
Paragoonah	211	152	59	211	......
Parowan	861	588	273	854	......
Summit	174	141	33	174	......
JUAB. (g)					
Chicken Creek	113	104	9	113	......
Levan	320	178	142	318	2
Mona	315	255	60	315	......
Nephi City	1286	807	479	1284	2
KANE. (h)					
Belleview	44	38	6	44	......
Duncan's Retreat	71	56	15	71	......
Grafton	38	30	8	38	......
Harmony	243	225	18	241	1
Kanab	73	65	8	72	......
Kanorah	280	251	29	280	......
Rockville	225	190	35	223	......
Shonesburg	51	48	3	51	......
Tokerville	264	208	56	261	......
Virgin City	224	181	43	224	......
MILLARD. (i)					
Corn Creek	83	83	......	......	......
Cove Creek	26	22	4	26	......
Deseret	150	97	53	150	......
Fillmore	905	660	245	902	......
Holden	266	181	85	265	......
Komash	520	401	119	519	1
Meadow Creek	193	121	72	193	......
Petersburg	145	127	18	145	......
Scipio	465	282	183	465	......

(a) Beaver County: Minersville also includes 2 Indians.
(b) Box Elder County: Box Elder also includes 19 Chinese and 3 Indians; Corinne, 89 Chinese; Kelton, 135 Chinese; Portage, 1 Indian; Promontory, 117 Chinese; Willard, 43 Chinese.
(c) Cache County: Franklin also includes 1 Indian; Logan, 1 Indian; Millville, 1 Indian; Paradise, 1 Indian; Providence, 1 Indian.
(d) Logan City comprises all of Logan precinct.
(e) Davis County: Bountiful also includes 1 Indian; Centreville, 2 Indians; Farmington, 2 Indians.
(f) Iron County: Cedar City also includes 5 Indians; Eagleville, 2 Indians; Iron City, 1 Indian; Parowan, 7 Indians.
(g) Juab County: Nephi City also includes 2 Indians.
(h) Kane County: Harmony also includes 1 Indian; Kanab, 1 Indian; Rockville, 2 Indians; Tokerville, 3 Indians.
(i) Millard County: Corn Creek also includes 83 Indians; Fillmore, 3 Indians; Holden, 1 Indian.

TABLE IX.—*Population of Minor Civil Divisions, &c.—UTAH*—Continued.

Counties.	Total.	Nativity. Native.	Nativity. Foreign.	Race. White.	Race. Colored.
MORGAN.					
Morgan	1972	1215	757	1970	2
PIUTE. (a)					
Bullion City	82	54	28	80	......
RICH. (b)					
Bennington	57	48	9	57	......
Bloomington	316	197	119	316	......
Fish Haven	52	29	23	52	......
Kimballsville	60	47	13	60	......
Laketown	127	78	49	126	......
Liberty	86	62	24	86	......
Montpelier	299	216	83	299	......
Ovid	66	15	51	66	......
Paris	502	342	160	501	......
Randolph	76	49	27	76	......
St. Charles	294	188	106	294	......
Swan Creek	20	20	......	20	......
RIO VIRGEN. (c)					
Overton	119	93	26	119	......
St. Joseph	193	150	43	193	......
West Point	138	125	13	137	......
SALT LAKE. (d)					
Big Cottonw'd Cañon	200	117	83	200	......
Big Cottonw'd Ward	570	330	240	569	......
Bingham Cañon	276	182	94	275	......
Camp Douglas, (U. S. garrison)	107	60	47	107	......
Little Cottonwood Cañon	216	118	98	213	3
Mill Creek Ward	918	595	323	918	......
South Cottonwood Ward	1144	653	491	1132	12
Sugarhouse Ward	641	337	304	641	......
West Jordan Ward	639	389	250	637	......
Willow Creek Ward	480	328	152	480	......
Brighton	292	181	111	292	......
Salt Lake City	12854	7604	5250	12813	36
SAN PETE. (e)					
Ephraim City (f)	1167	501	666	1164	......
Fairview	531	399	132	530	......
SAN PETE—Cont'd.					
Fountain Green	562	322	240	560	......
Gunnison (f)	475	243	232	474	......
Manti	1239	784	455	1232	......
Moroni City	633	366	267	633	......
M't Pleasant (f)	1346	752	504	1345	......
Spring City	623	399	224	623	......
Wales	83	45	38	83	......
Warren Creek	127	79	48	127	......
SEVIER.					
Glen Cove	15	......	15	15	......
Richfield	4	......	4	4	......
SUMMIT. (g)					
Coalville	626	325	301	626	......
Echo City	139	79	60	122	1
Hennefersville	172	70	102	172	......
Hoytsville	228	133	95	228	......
Parley's Park	164	125	39	163	1
Peva	149	86	63	149	......
Rhodes Valley	345	228	117	345	......
Rockport	113	57	56	113	......
Wanship	315	205	110	312	2
Wasatch	261	140	121	237	......
TOOELE.					
East Tooele City	114	57	57	114	......
Grantsville	755	496	259	755	......
Mount Vernon	111	60	51	111	......
St. John's	150	86	73	159	......
Stockton	80	56	24	80	......
Tooele City	958	595	363	958	......
UTAH. (h)					
Alpine City	208	119	89	208	......
American Fork	1115	678	437	1114	......
Cedar Fork	272	227	45	271	......
Fairfield	223	150	73	223	......
Lehigh City	1058	667	391	1058	......
Newton	458	262	196	458	......
Payson	1436	1095	341	1435	......
Pleasant Gr've	930	591	339	930	......
Pondtown (f)	353	290	63	352	......
Provo	2384	1745	639	2383	......
Santaquin	602	402	200	601	......
Spanish Fork (i)	1450	877	573	1441	6
Springville	1661	1301	360	1658	......
WASATCH.					
Heber City (j)	658	457	201	658	......
Midway	378	285	93	378	......

(a) Piute County: Bullion City also includes 2 Indians.
(b) Rich County: Laketown also includes 1 Indian; Paris, 1 Indian.
(c) Rio Virgin County: West Point also includes 1 Indian.
(d) Salt Lake County: Big Cottonwood Ward also includes 1 Indian; Bingham Cañon, 1 Indian; Salt Lake City, 5 Indians; West Jordan Ward, 2 Indians.
(e) San Pete County: Ephraim City also includes 3 Indians; Fairview, 1 Indian; Fountain Green, 2 Indians; Gunnison, 1 Indian; Manti, 7 Indians; Mount Pleasant, 1 Indian.
(f) Comprises village of same name.
(g) Summit County: Echo City also includes 15 Chinese and 1 Indian; Wanship, 1 Indian; Wasatch, 24 Chinese.
(h) Utah County: American Fork also includes 1 Indian; Cedar Fork, 1 Indian; Payson, 1 Indian; Pondtown, 1 Indian; Provo, 1 Indian; Santaquin, 1 Indian; Spanish Fork, 3 Indians; Springville, 3 Indians.
(i) The incorporated town of Spanish Fork includes Spanish Fork City.
(j) Its precinct not ascertained.

TABLE IX.—*Population of Minor Civil Divisions, &c.*—*UTAH*—Continued.

Counties.	Total.	Nativity. Native.	Nativity. Foreign.	Race. White.	Race. Colored.	Counties.	Total.	Nativity. Native.	Nativity. Foreign.	Race. White.	Race. Colored.
WASATCH—Cont'd.						WASHINGTON—Con.					
Round Valley	208	145	63	208	......	St. George	1142	900	242	1138	1
WASHINGTON. (a)						Washington	463	358	105	463	......
Claratown	233	156	77	232	1	WEBER. (b)					
Clover Valley	83	78	5	83	......	East Weber	343	215	128	343	......
Harrisburg	105	96	9	103	......	Hooper's	1189	794	395	1189	......
Hebron	111	106	5	111	......	Hulverson's	203	123	80	203	......
Leeds	104	96	8	104	......	Huntsville	1051	726	325	1051	......
Mountain Meadow	42	41	1	42	......	Lynn	314	247	67	314	......
Panaca	350	266	84	346	2	North Ogden	683	488	195	683	......
Pine Valley	326	283	43	325	......	Ogden	3127	2066	1061	3102	21
Pinto	105	75	30	105	......	Plain City	440	262	178	440	......
						Slatersville	508	321	187	508	......

(a) Washington County: Harrisburg also includes 2 Indians; Panaca, 2 Indians; Pine Valley, 1 Indian; St. George, 3 Indians.
(b) Weber County: Ogden also includes 3 Chinese and 1 Indian.

TABLE IX.—*Population of Minor Civil Divisions, &c.*—*VERMONT.*

NOTE.—The marginal column marks towns; the first indentation, cities; the second, villages. Names of villages are placed under the names of the towns in which they are respectively situated. The population of each town includes that of all villages situated in it.

Counties.	Total.	Nativity. Native.	Nativity. Foreign.	Race. White.	Race. Colored.	Counties.	Total.	Nativity. Native.	Nativity. Foreign.	Race. White.	Race. Colored.
ADDISON.						BENNINGTON—Con.					
Addison	911	815	96	911	......	Manchester	1897	1655	242	1885	12
Bridport	1171	1061	110	1170	1	Peru	500	456	44	500	......
Bristol	1365	1259	106	1319	46	Pownal	1705	1582	123	1684	21
Cornwall	969	820	149	967	2	Readsboro	828	813	15	822	6
Ferrisburgh	1768	1543	225	1766	2	Rupert	1017	903	114	1017	......
Goshen	330	297	33	330	......	Sandgate	705	667	38	700	5
Granville	726	655	71	726	......	Searsburgh	235	226	9	235	......
Hancock	430	414	16	430	......	Shaftsbury	2027	1845	182	2012	15
Leicester	630	514	116	622	8	Stamford	633	588	45	631	2
Lincoln	1174	1089	85	1174	......	Sunderland	553	513	40	553	......
Middlebury	3086	2551	535	3081	5	Winhall	842	754	88	833	9
Monkton	1006	875	131	1004	2	Woodford	371	365	6	371	......
New Haven	1355	1198	157	1345	10						
Orwell	1192	981	211	1191	1	CALEDONIA.					
Panton	390	352	38	384	6						
Ripton	617	555	62	613	4	Barnet	1945	1724	221	1945	......
Salisbury	902	782	120	901	1	Burke	1162	1049	113	1162	......
Shoreham	1225	1049	176	1224	1	Danville	2216	1952	264	2215	1
Starksboro	1361	1254	107	1361	......	Groton	811	792	19	811	......
Vergennes	1570	1205	365	1557	13	Hardwick	1519	1438	81	1519	......
Waltham	249	222	27	249	......	Kirby	417	381	36	417	......
Weybridge	627	556	71	623	4	Lyndon	2179	1875	304	2179	......
Whiting	430	398	32	430	......	Newark	593	537	56	593	......
						Peacham	1141	1045	96	1141	......
BENNINGTON.						Ryegate	935	834	101	935	......
						Sheffield	811	758	53	811	......
Arlington	1636	1349	287	1636	......	Stannard	228	214	14	228	......
Bennington	5760	4713	1047	5685	75	St. Johnsbury	4665	3607	1058	4659	6
Bennington	2501	1949	552	2478	23	Sutton	920	881	39	920	......
Dorset	2195	1757	438	2194	1	Walden	992	917	75	992	......
Glastenbury	119	94	25	118	1	Waterford	879	789	90	879	......
Landgrove	302	294	8	302	......	Whelock	822	751	71	814	8

ABLE IX.—*Population of Minor Civil Divisions, &c.*—*VERMONT*—Continued.

...nties.	Total.	Nativity. Native.	Nativity. Foreign.	Race. White.	Race. Colored.
TENDEN.					
	711	554	157	710	1
Goro	29	29	......	29	......
ngton	14387	8219	6168	14310	77
te	1430	1215	215	1429	1
ster	3911	2527	1384	3907	4
	2022	1692	330	2014	8
urgh	1573	1340	233	1562	11
gton	864	815	49	864	......
	1757	1509	248	1757	......
	2062	1702	360	2062	......
nd	1309	1021	288	1308	1
rne	1190	931	259	1181	9
Burlington	791	569	222	786	5
rge	111	97	14	111	......
ill	1655	1362	293	1655	......
rd	1237	1129	108	1236	1
on	1441	1191	250	1429	12
SSEX.					
l	14	14	......	14	......
ield	455	362	93	455	......
on	1535	900	635	1535	......
rick	221	147	74	221	......
n	419	353	66	419	......
d	1276	1191	85	1275	(a)
Haven	191	173	18	191	......
and	33	6	27	33	......
y	174	166	8	174	......
all	483	451	32	482	1
gton	191	157	34	191	......
burg	999	965	34	997	(b)
one	254	243	11	254	......
	303	73	230	303	......
y	263	211	52	261	2
ANKLIN.					
's Gore	34	28	6	34	......
field	1403	1183	220	1403	......
iro	1609	1199	410	1608	1
urg	2077	1641	436	2077	......
x	1956	1714	242	1954	2
ld	2391	1912	479	2390	1
er	865	789	76	865	......
lin	1612	1205	407	1611	1
ia	1603	1441	162	1603	......
ate	2260	1741	519	2259	1
gomery	1423	1207	216	1423	......
rd	1481	1141	340	1481	......
n	1697	1327	370	1697	......
bans	7014	4831	2183	6928	86
on	2866	2177	689	2860	6
AND ISLE.					
g	1716	1224	492	1714	2
Isle	682	591	91	680	(b)
a Motte	497	379	118	494	3
Hero	601	484	117	601	......
Hero	586	493	93	582	(c)
AMOILLE.					
lere	369	339	30	368	1
ridge	1651	1488	163	1651	......
	958	877	81	958	......
e	637	591	46	637	......
Park	1624	1552	72	1621	......
on	1558	1423	135	1558	......
stown	1897	1786	111	1895	2
	2049	1871	178	2043	d1

(*a*) Also 1 Indian.
(*b*) Also 2 Indians.

Counties.	Total.	Nativity. Native.	Nativity. Foreign.	Race. White.	Race. Colored.
LAMOILLE—Cont'd.					
Waterville	573	534	39	573	......
Wolcott	1132	1083	49	1131	1
ORANGE.					
Bradford	1492	1399	93	1491	1
Braintree	1066	1006	60	1065	1
Brookfield	1269	1225	44	1269	......
Chelsea	1526	1489	37	1524	2
Corinth	1470	1414	56	1469	1
Fairlee	416	397	19	416	......
Newbury	2241	2053	188	2240	1
Orange	733	716	17	733	......
Randolph	2829	2660	169	2827	2
Strafford	1290	1281	9	1290	......
Thetford	1613	1585	28	1611	2
Topsham	1418	1346	72	1418	......
Tunbridge	1405	1391	14	1404	1
Vershire	1140	922	218	1138	2
Washington	1113	1092	21	1113	......
West Fairlee	833	762	71	833	......
Williamstown	1236	1205	31	1236	......
ORLEANS.					
Albany	1151	1010	141	1151	......
Barton	1911	1598	313	1911	......
Brownington	901	760	141	901	......
Charleston	1278	1105	173	1277	1
Coventry	914	775	139	914	......
Craftsbury	1330	1229	101	1330	......
Derby	2039	1364	675	2038	1
Glover	1178	1047	131	1178	......
Greensboro	1027	876	151	1027	......
Holland	881	585	296	881	......
Irasburgh	1085	952	133	1070	15
Jay	553	447	106	553	......
Lowell	942	808	134	942	......
Morgan	614	490	124	614	......
Newport	2050	1674	376	2049	1
Salem	693	486	207	682	11
Troy	1355	1161	194	1355	......
Westfield	721	578	143	721	......
Westmore	412	328	84	412	......
RUTLAND.					
Benson	1244	1112	132	1234	10
Brandon	3571	2957	614	3570	1
Castleton	3243	2495	748	3185	58
Chittenden	802	720	82	802	......
Clarendon	1173	1070	103	1170	3
Danby	1319	1222	97	1317	2
Fair Haven	2208	1551	657	2203	5
Hubbardton	606	530	76	603	3
Ira	413	353	60	413	......
Mendon	612	496	116	612	......
Middletown	777	728	49	777	......
Mount Holly	1582	1404	178	1579	3
Mount Tabor	301	262	39	300	1
Pawlet	1505	1394	111	1494	11
Pittsfield	482	475	7	482	......
Pittsford	2127	1766	361	2126	1
Poultney	2836	2267	569	2823	13
Rutland	9834	6871	2963	9765	69
Sherburne	462	459	3	462	......
Shrewsbury	1145	1003	142	1144	1
Sudbury	601	543	58	601	......
Tinmouth	589	553	36	589	......
Wallingford	2023	1827	196	2022	1
Wells	713	649	64	713	......
West Haven	483	437	46	483	......

(*c*) Also 4 Indians.
(*d*) Also 5 Indians.

TABLE IX.—*Population of Minor Civil Divisions, &c.—VERMONT*—Continued.

Counties.	Total.	NATIVITY. Native.	NATIVITY. Foreign.	RACE. White.	RACE. Colored.
WASHINGTON.					
Barre	1882	1827	55	1881	1
Berlin	1474	1306	168	1469	5
Cabot	1279	1225	54	1278	1
Calais	1309	1288	21	1308	1
Duxbury	893	750	143	891	2
East Montpelier	1130	1071	59	1130	......
Fayston	694	566	128	694	......
Harris Gore	12	11	1	12	......
Marshfield	1072	1051	21	1071	1
Middlesex	1171	1074	97	1170	1
Montpelier	3023	2583	440	3013	10
Moretown	1263	1120	143	1263	......
Northfield	3410	2971	439	3408	2
Plainfield	726	713	13	725	1
Roxbury	916	825	91	916	......
Waitsfield	948	847	101	948	......
Warren	1008	978	30	1008	......
Waterbury	2633	2336	297	2631	2
Woodbury	902	890	12	902	......
Worcester	775	732	43	773	2
WINDHAM.					
Athens	295	288	7	294	1
Brattleboro	4933	4387	546	4923	10
Brookline	203	202	1	203	......
Dover	635	633	2	635	......
Dummerston	916	875	41	916	......
Grafton	1008	1001	7	1008	......
Guilford	1277	1163	114	1277	......
Halifax	1029	1017	12	1029	......
Jamaica	1223	1211	12	1223	......
Londonderry	1252	1232	20	1252	......
Marlboro	665	659	6	665	......
Newfane	1113	1106	7	1111	2
Putney	1167	1071	96	1164	3
Rockingham	2854	2613	241	2853	1
Bellows Falls	697	581	116	697	......
WINDHAM—Cont'd.					
Somerset	80	80	......	80	......
Stratton	294	293	1	294	......
Townshend	1171	1163	8	1169	2
Vernon	764	704	60	760	4
Wardsboro	866	858	8	865	1
Westminster	1238	1188	50	1219	19
Whitingham	1263	1257	6	1256	7
Wilmington	1246	1239	7	1246	......
Windham	544	541	3	544	......
WINDSOR.					
Andover	588	573	15	586	2
Baltimore	83	80	3	83	......
Barnard	1208	1161	47	1207	1
Bethel	1817	1726	91	1817	......
Bridgewater	1141	1128	13	1141	......
Cavendish	1823	1508	315	1820	3
Chester	2052	1967	85	2051	1
Hartford	2480	2214	266	2474	6
Hartland	1710	1635	75	1707	3
Ludlow	1827	1621	206	1826	1
Norwich	1639	1606	33	1638	1
Plymouth	1285	1111	174	1284	1
Pomfret	1251	1219	32	1247	4
Reading	1012	995	17	1010	2
Rochester	1444	1418	26	1441	3
Royalton	1679	1612	67	1678	1
Sharon	1013	978	35	1013	......
Springfield	2937	2828	109	2933	4
Springfield	1337	1262	75	1334	3
Stockbridge	1269	1231	38	1268	1
Weathersfield	1557	1485	72	1557	......
Weston	931	898	33	931	......
West Windsor	708	698	10	708	......
Windsor	1699	1554	145	1673	26
Woodstock	2910	2717	193	2880	30

TABLE IX.—*Population of Minor Civil Divisions, &c.—VIRGINIA.*

NOTE.—The marginal column marks townships; the first indentation, cities; the second, towns. Names of towns are placed under the names of the townships in which they are respectively situated. The population of each township includes that of all towns situated in it.

Counties.	Total.	NATIVITY. Native.	NATIVITY. Foreign.	RACE. White.	RACE. Colored.
ACCOMACK.					
Atlantic	4111	4108	3	2513	1598
Islands	1122	1120	2	1046	76
Lee	6183	6178	5	3703	2480
Metompkin	4450	4449	1	3148	1302
Pungoteague	4543	4537	6	2157	2386
ALBEMARLE.					
Charlottesville	7145	7008	137	2899	4246
Charlottesville	2838	2748	90	1365	1473
ALBEMARLE—Con.					
Rivanna	4697	4683	14	1988	2709
Sam Miller	4959	4933	26	2738	2221
Scottsville	5994	5964	30	2609	3385
Howardsville	83	83	......	56	27
Scottsville	388	382	6	252	136
Whitehall	4749	4747	2	2316	2433
ALEXANDRIA.					
Alexandria	13570	12763	807	8269	a5300

(a) Also 1 Chinese.

…LE IX.—*Population of Minor Civil Divisions, &c.*—VIRGINIA—Continued.

…ties.	Total.	Nativity. Native.	Nativity. Foreign.	Race. White.	Race. Colored.
…IA—C'd					
....	1374	1317	57	517	857
....	1256	1161	95	383	873
…on	555	531	24	275	280
…IANY.					
…ring....	1388	1331	57	1291	97
....	1018	994	24	822	196
....	1268	1241	27	982	286
…IA.					
....	3597	3402	195	1130	2467
....	2827	2823	4	812	2015
....	3454	3448	6	1113	2341
…RST.					
....	3632	3611	21	1795	1837
....	3193	3126	67	1705	1488
....	4628	4602	26	2925	a1701
…co......	3447	3447	......	1859	1588
…TTOX.					
…ll.......	3840	3831	9	1828	2012
....	2551	2551	......	1369	1182
....	2559	2558	1	1217	1342
…STA.					
…Manor...	8071	7780	291	5656	2415
…ton	5120	4895	225	3585	1535
…ver......	4376	4364	12	3592	784
…or.......	4163	4134	29	3722	441
....	3292	3272	20	2524	768
…ds......	4380	4362	18	3462	918
…Heads..	886	886	......	742	144
…er......	4481	4464	17	3070	1411
…esboro'h	536	531	5	347	189
…H.					
…ek......	903	891	12	617	286
…gh	1004	994	10	790	214
…ings ...	890	880	10	689	201
…ille	998	985	13	810	188
…ORD.					
…burg ...	3428	3422	6	2676	752
…nt	2820	2818	2	1525	1295
....	2809	2799	10	1193	1616
....	5840	5824	16	2962	2878
…y	1208	1202	6	519	689
....	3175	3171	4	1917	1258
....	4004	3992	12	2036	1968
....	3251	3251	......	2248	1003
…ID.					
…sburg...	1233	1225	8	1166	67
…p.......	1000	999	1	931	69
....	828	825	3	760	68
....	939	937	2	926	13

Counties.	Total.	Nativity. Native.	Nativity. Foreign.	Race. White.	Race. Colored.
BOTETOURT.					
Amsterdam	3828	3812	16	2876	952
Buchanan	4000	3986	14	2809	1191
Fincastle.........	3501	3498	3	2481	1020
BRUNSWICK.					
Meherrin.........	5019	5019	......	1844	3175
Red Oak..........	3365	3364	1	1009	2356
Totaro	5043	5039	4	1672	3371
BUCHANAN.					
Garden............	1045	1045	......	1045	......
Grundy	1152	1152	......	1149	3
Sand Lick........	1580	1580	......	1536	44
BUCKINGHAM.					
Curdsville.........	2101	2101	......	658	1443
Francisco	1615	1607	8	619	996
James River	3033	3028	5	1435	1598
Marshall	2605	2508	97	1209	1396
Maysville	1916	1912	4	811	1105
Slate River.......	2101	2101	......	928	1173
CAMPBELL. (*)					
Brookville........	4960	4799	161	2390	2570
Lynchburg	6825	6554	271	3472	3353
CAROLINE.					
Bowling Green...	4765	4744	21	2574	b2178
BowlingGreen	395	392	3	241	154
Madison...........	3682	3676	6	1649	2033
Port Royal	3543	3527	16	1498	2045
Port Royal ...	435	435	......	221	214
Reedy Church....	3138	3129	9	1356	1782
CARROLL.					
Fancy Gap	1530	1527	3	1492	38
Laurel Fork (c)...	2197	2196	1	2163	34
Pine Creek (c)	1969	1967	2	1919	50
Hillsville (c)..	268	......	......	......	......
Piper's Gap (c) ...	1605	1603	2	1564	41
Sulphur Springs(c)	1846	1842	4	1681	165
CHARLES CITY.					
Chickahominy ...	1372	1365	7	695	677
Harrison..........	1684	1671	13	535	1149
Tyler	1919	1909	10	592	1327
CHARLOTTE.					
Bacon	3683	3671	12	1157	2526
Madison..........	3222	3222	......	1067	2155
Roanoke	4830	4825	5	1531	3299
Walton	2778	2770	8	1145	1633
CHESTERFIELD.					
Bermuda	877	871	6	227	d643
Chester	2313	2289	24	1230	1083

…mplete; the other principal civil divisions were not separately returned.
… 12 Indians.
… 13 Indians.
…Hillsville: 50 in Laurel Fork, 82 in Pine Creek, 61 in Piper's Gap, and 69 in Sulphur Springs.
… 7 Indians.

TABLE IX.—*Population of Minor Civil Divisions, &c.—VIRGINIA*—Continued.

Counties.	Total.	Nativity. Native.	Nativity. Foreign.	Race. White.	Race. Colored.
CHESTERFIELD—C'd					
Clover Hill	3210	3155	55	1667	1543
Dale	1803	1788	15	1051	752
Manchester	5043	4942	101	2610	2433
Manchester	2599	2559	40	1517	1082
Matoaca	2595	2588	7	1650	945
Mid Lothian	2629	2552	77	1245	1384
CLARKE.					
Battletown	1884	1878	6	1259	625
Berryville	580	575	5	353	227
Chapel	1793	1788	5	1282	511
Millwood	213	213	......	143	70
Greenway	1570	1563	7	976	594
White Post	192	191	1	108	84
Long Marsh	1423	1390	33	994	429
CRAIG.					
Alleghany	938	938	......	879	59
New Castle	1189	1185	4	1045	144
New Castle	199	198	1	151	48
Summonsville	815	815	......	788	27
CULPEPER.					
Catalpa	3388	3351	37	1652	1736
Fairfax	1800	1740	60	1000	800
Cedar Mountain	1708	1697	11	672	1036
Jeffersonton	2953	2932	21	1311	1642
Jeffersonton	400	389	11	280	120
Salem	2178	2167	11	1185	993
Stevensburg	2000	1989	11	1238	762
Stevensburg	150	144	6	95	55
CUMBERLAND.					
Hamilton	2990	2990	......	1081	1909
Madison	2752	2745	7	928	1824
Randolph	2400	2394	6	700	1700
DINWIDDIE.					
Darvilles	3082	3074	8	1126	1956
Namozine	3310	3291	19	1266	2044
Petersburg	18950	18505	445	8744	a10185
Rowanty	3274	3259	15	1208	2066
Sapony	2086	2086	......	673	1413
ELIZABETH CITY.					
Chesapeake	2703	2663	40	783	1920
Fortr'ss Monroe (b)	589	318	271	563	26
Hampton (c)	2300	2282	18	460	1840
Old P't Comfort (b)	313	269	44	262	51
Southfield	1766	1753	13	423	1343
Wythe	2932	2924	8	801	2131
ESSEX.					
Central	3149	3140	9	1221	2228
Occupacia	3270	3269	1	859	2411
Rappahannock	3208	3206	2	1197	2011
FAIRFAX.					
Centreville	1721	1687	34	1137	584
FAIRFAX—Cont'd.					
Dranesville	2055	2000	55	1579	476
Falls Church	2461	2326	135	1566	d894
Lee	1346	1292	54	1040	306
Mount Vernon	2233	2167	66	1266	967
Providence	3136	3053	83	2079	1057
FAUQUIER.					
Cedar Run	2145	2110	35	1194	951
Center	4356	4265	91	2465	1891
Warrenton	1256	1214	42	704	552
Marshall	4312	4297	15	2777	1535
Rappahannock	3132	3111	21	1816	1316
Scott	5745	5686	59	3582	2163
Upperville	422	421	1	197	225
FLOYD.					
Alum Ridge	1035	1034	1	986	49
Burk's Fork	671	671	......	630	41
Indian Valley	1475	1475	......	1382	93
Jacksonville	2773	2768	5	2473	300
Jacksonville	321	320	1	255	66
Little River	1879	1879	......	1617	262
Locust Grove	1991	1988	3	1739	252
FLUVANNA.					
Columbia	2331	2325	6	1120	1211
Columbiana	311	308	3	113	198
Cunningham	2771	2768	3	1582	1189
Fork Union	2794	2790	4	926	1868
Palmyra	1979	1979	......	1150	829
FRANKLIN.					
Black Water	1796	1796	......	989	807
Boonsbrook	2078	2078	......	1643	435
Brown Hill	1692	1691	1	1250	442
Gill's Creek	2453	2453	......	1675	778
Long Branch	1877	1876	1	1564	313
Magoder	1879	1879	......	1363	516
Rocky Mount	2034	2034	......	1231	803
Snow Creek	2549	2547	2	1432	1117
Union Hall	1906	1905	1	1121	785
FREDERICK.					
Back Creek	1895	1875	20	1860	35
Gainesboro	2422	2420	2	2337	85
Opequan	4414	4343	71	3779	635
Newtown	625	614	11	529	96
Stonewall	3388	3327	61	2787	601
Winchester (c)	4477	4375	102	3100	1377
GILES.					
Newport	1007	1007	......	949	58
Pearisburg	1653	1641	12	1434	219
Pembroke	1327	1327	......	1214	113
Staffordsville	1888	1873	15	1675	f208
GLOUCESTER.					
Abingdon	4506	4493	13	2440	2066
Petsworth	2692	2686	6	1234	1458
Ware	3013	3004	9	1108	1905

(a) Also 21 Indians.
(b) Belongs to United States; not included in any township.
(c) Its population included in one or more townships not ascertained.
(d) Also 1 Chinese.
(e) Its township not ascertained.
(f) Also 5 Indians.

[TA]BLE IX.—*Population of Minor Civil Divisions, &c.—VIRGINIA*—Continued.

[Cou]nties.	Total.	Nativity. Native.	Nativity. Foreign.	Race. White.	Race. Colored.
[...]ULAND.					
....	3216	3212	4	1155	2061
....	3667	3650	17	1332	2335
[...]hole	3430	3419	11	1224	a2205
[...]YSON.					
[...]ek	4116	4103	13	3685	431
[...]n	2240	2234	6	2087	153
[...]Creek	3231	3225	6	3061	170
[...]ENE.					
....	1331	1330	1	1079	252
[...]ville	1514	1498	16	913	601
[...]lsville	1789	1781	8	1190	599
[...]NVILLE.					
....	2809	2809	......	802	2007
[...]rd	2367	2364	3	908	1459
[...]ksford	116	116	......	30	86
....	1186	1186	......	445	741
[...]IFAX.					
....	3731	3728	3	1423	2308
[...]reek	5563	5563	......	2162	3401
....	3576	3569	7	1961	1615
[...]Carmel	4861	4857	4	1721	3140
....	6182	6179	3	2327	3855
[...]a	3915	3914	1	1968	1947
[...]OVER.					
[...]Creek	2844	2838	6	1165	1679
....	3942	3923	19	2032	1910
[...]land	491	486	5	290	201
[...]Dam	3237	3233	4	1524	1713
....	3085	3065	20	1451	1634
....	3347	3334	13	1721	1626
[...]RICO.					
[...]nd	3612	3426	186	1953	1659
[...]l	4980	4785	195	2257	2723
[...]ond	51038	47260	3778	27928	23110
[...]e	3339	3221	118	1625	1714
....	3210	3128	82	1385	1825
[...]NBY.					
[...]asture	2302	2299	3	1218	1081
[...]wood	3673	3669	4	1988	1685
[...]ville	3157	3155	2	1607	1550
[...]ay	3171	3168	3	1909	1262
[...]HLAND.					
[...]ass	1418	1414	4	1342	76
[...]y	1101	1094	7	1067	34
[...]ll	1632	1630	2	1394	238
[...]F WIGHT.					
....	3171	3167	4	1649	1522
[...]t	2906	2901	5	1594	1312
[...]hfield	652	652	......	367	285
[...]r	2243	2239	4	1631	612
[...]S CITY.					
[...]wn	1088	1079	9	365	723

Counties.	Total.	Nativity. Native.	Nativity. Foreign.	Race. White.	Race. Colored.
JAMES CITY—Con'd					
Powhatan	1117	1116	1	381	736
Stonehouse	828	825	3	346	482
Williamsburg	1392	1340	52	893	499
KING AND QUEEN.					
Buena Vista	2985	2978	7	1333	1652
Newtown	2647	2643	4	1179	1468
Stevensville	4077	4076	1	1709	2368
KING GEORGE.					
Chotank	2814	2810	4	1327	1487
Passpatangy	1131	1123	8	656	475
Shiloh	1797	1793	4	944	853
KING WILLIAM.					
Acquinton	2960	2952	8	1024	1936
King William	44	44	......	9	35
Mangohick	2362	2359	3	1022	1340
West Point	2193	2185	8	897	b1179
LANCASTER.					
Mantua	1608	1606	2	700	908
White Chapel	1669	1664	5	614	1055
Whitestone	2078	2070	8	884	1194
LEE.					
Jonesville	3369	3367	2	3216	153
Jonesville	274	273	1	242	32
Rocky Station....	2304	2303	1	2177	127
Rose Hill	3023	3022	1	2667	356
White Shoals.....	2750	2748	2	2490	260
Yokum Station...	1822	1821	1	1713	109
LOUDON.					
Broad Run	2582	2537	45	1925	657
Jefferson	3355	3325	30	2534	821
Hillsboro	246	245	1	186	60
Waterford ...	419	415	4	321	98
Leesburg..........	4075	4042	33	2857	1218
Leesburg.....	1144	1134	10	791	353
Lovettsville	3020	2998	22	2756	264
Lovettsville ..	155	152	3	139	16
Mercer...........	4360	4304	56	2727	1633
Mount Gilead	3537	3518	19	2439	1098
LOUISA. (*)					
Cuckoo...........	2199	2181	18	819	1380
Green Spring	2018	1998	20	834	1184
Jackson	1525	1513	12	741	784
LouisaCo'rt House	2559	2547	12	970	1589
LUNENBURG.					
Brown's Store	2147	2146	1	839	1308
Columbian Grove.	1422	1420	2	535	887
Lewiston..........	1805	1801	4	668	1137
Lochleven.........	1681	1681	......	804	877
Pleasant Grove...	1778	1767	11	724	1054
Rehoboth	1570	1568	2	771	799
MADISON.					
Locust Dale......	3484	3481	3	1778	1706
Rapidan..........	2306	2295	11	1275	1031
Robertson........	2880	2878	2	1906	974

(*) Incomplete; the other principal civil divisions were not separately returned.
(a) Also 1 Indian.
(b) Also 117 Indians.

TABLE IX.—*Population of Minor Civil Divisions, &c.—VIRGINIA—Continued.*

Counties.	Total.	Nativity.		Race.	
		Native.	Foreign.	White.	Colored.
MATTHEWS.					
Chesapeake	1700	1699	1	1212	488
Piankatank	2024	2024	.....	1391	633
Westville	2476	2473	3	1501	975
MECKLENBURG.					
Boydton	4708	4706	2	1365	3343
Boydton	261	261	.....	115	146
Blue Stone	1984	1979	5	580	1404
Buckthorn	2046	2045	1	959	1087
Christiansville	2550	2542	8	754	1796
Christiansville	106	101	5	63	43
Clarksville	3700	3698	2	1605	2095
Flat Creek	2328	2327	1	573	1755
Palmer's Springs	1618	1618	.....	324	1294
South Hill	2384	2383	1	1002	1382
MIDDLESEX.					
Jamaica	1298	1292	6	566	732
Pine Top	1968	1966	2	1160	808
Saluda	1715	1713	2	733	982
MONTGOMERY.					
Allegany	2504	2499	5	2014	490
Auburn	3171	3164	7	2385	786
Blacksburg	3565	3532	33	2887	678
Christiansburg	3316	3300	16	2388	928
Christiansb'rg	864	860	4	571	293
NANSEMOND.					
Chickatuck	2709	2694	15	1527	1182
Cypress	2550	2543	7	1527	1023
Holly Neck	3275	3275	.....	1675	1600
Sleepy Hole	2112	2104	8	788	1324
Suffolk (*a*)	930	927	3	542	388
NELSON.					
Lovingston	5511	5469	42	2734	2777
Massie's Mills	4546	4545	1	2749	1797
Rockfish	3841	3836	5	2103	1738
NEW KENT.					
Black Creek	998	993	5	453	*b*536
Cumberland	1249	1237	12	603	*c*640
St. Peter's	1122	1110	12	402	720
Ware Creek	1012	1004	8	547	465
NORFOLK.					
Butts's Road	2039	2039	.....	779	1260
Deep Creek	2202	2195	7	725	1477
Norfolk	19229	18490	739	10462	*d*8766
Navy Yard, (garrison)	98	66	32	86	12
Pleasant Grove	2429	2427	2	1454	975
Portsmouth	10492	10016	476	6874	*d*3617
Tanner's Creek	2989	2922	67	1247	1742
Washington	2124	2098	26	1064	1060
Western Branch	5100	5056	44	1689	3411
NORTHAMPTON.					
Capeville	2381	2381	.....	1101	1280
Eastville	3395	3393	2	1136	2259
Franktown	2270	2265	5	961	1309
NORTHUMBERLAND.					
Fairfield	1645	1643	2	904	741
Heathville	1996	1989	7	1077	*d*918
Lottsburg	1777	1775	2	1187	590
Wicomico	1445	1445	.....	640	805
NOTTOWAY.					
Bellefonte	2837	2834	3	898	1939
Blendon	3026	3012	14	600	2426
Hatoka	3428	3426	2	742	2686
ORANGE.					
Barbour	1323	1322	1	655	668
Gordon	1343	1328	15	893	450
Madison	3773	3734	39	1773	2000
Orange Ct. Ho	731	715	16	351	380
Taylor	3957	3952	5	1617	2340
PAGE.					
Luray	2144	2139	5	1738	406
Marksville	2208	2203	5	2009	199
Shenandoah Iron Works	2175	2157	18	1942	233
Springfield	1935	1925	10	1787	148
PATRICK.					
Dan River	2778	2776	2	2448	330
Mayo River	4017	4017	.....	2546	1471
Smith's River	3366	3365	1	2842	524
PITTSYLVANIA.					
Bannister	3347	3346	1	1502	1845
Calland's	2848	2844	4	1777	1071
Chatham	4262	4251	11	2390	1872
Dan River	10306	10271	35	4153	6153
Danville	3463	3433	30	1398	2065
Pigg River	2686	2683	3	1398	1288
Staunton	3270	3270	.....	1954	1316
Tunstalls	4624	4622	2	2085	2539
POWHATAN.					
Huguenot	2527	2518	9	1014	1513
Macon	2745	2735	10	854	1891
Spencer	2395	2387	8	684	1711
PRINCE EDWARD.					
Buffalo	3415	3400	15	1262	2153
Farmville	2496	2469	27	832	1664
Farmville	1543	1518	25	598	945
Hampton	2702	2699	3	923	1779
Leigh	3391	3363	28	1089	2302
PRINCE GEORGE.					
Blackwater	911	889	22	473	438
Bland	2260	2232	28	643	1617
Brandon	1600	1588	12	564	1036
Rives	1723	1711	12	508	1215
Templeton	1326	1320	6	586	740
PRINCESS ANNE.					
Kempsville	3100	3093	7	962	*e*2137
Pungo	2120	2117	3	1558	562
Seaboard	3053	3036	17	1849	*e*1203

(*a*) In no township.
(*b*) Also 9 Indians.
(*c*) Also 6 Indians.
(*d*) Also 1 Indian.
(*e*) Also 1 Chinese.

TABLE IX.—*Population of Minor Civil Divisions, &c.—VIRGINIA*—Continued.

Counties.	Total.	Nativity. Native.	Nativity. Foreign.	Race. White.	Race. Colored.
PRINCE WILLIAM.					
Brentsville	937	909	28	694	243
Cole's	1279	1272	7	1138	141
Dumfries	844	828	16	678	166
Dumfries	167	166	1	155	12
Gainesville	1908	1880	28	1294	614
Manassas	1645	1588	57	1089	556
Occoquan	891	885	6	798	93
Occoquan	228	228	.....	199	29
PULASKI.					
Dublin	2722	2705	17	1784	938
High Wassie	1897	1890	7	1569	328
Newbern	1919	1910	9	1376	543
RAPPAHANNOCK.					
Hampton	1934	1933	1	1024	910
Jackson	1568	1561	7	958	610
Piedmont	1634	1631	3	1252	382
Stonewall	1763	1754	9	1179	584
Wakefield	1362	1357	5	782	580
RICHMOND.					
Farnham	1354	1348	6	773	581
Marshall	1992	1978	14	916	1076
Stonewall	1397	1397	.....	890	507
Washington	1760	1753	7	896	864
ROANOKE.					
Big Lick	2592	2590	2	1526	1066
Catawba	845	843	2	705	140
Cave Spring	2261	2257	4	1754	507
Salem	3652	3638	14	2233	1419
Salem	1355	1346	9	855	500
ROCKBRIDGE.					
Buffalo	2445	2444	1	2077	a362
Kerr's Creek	1833	1830	3	1449	384
Lexington	3948	3861	87	2577	1371
Lexington	2873	2810	63	1982	891
Natural Bridge	2792	2776	16	1989	803
South River	2573	2567	6	2076	497
Walker's Creek	2467	2465	2	1994	473
ROCKINGHAM.					
Ashby	2268	2267	1	2136	132
Brock's Gap	1366	1362	4	1358	8
Central	2882	2854	28	2705	177
Elk Run	2341	2339	2	1907	434
Franklin	3200	3191	9	3015	185
Mt. Crawford	901	898	3	845	56
Harrisonburg	2828	2759	69	2157	671
Harrisonburg	2036	1978	58	1409	627
Linville	3536	3522	14	3323	213
Plains	3035	3018	17	2879	156
Stonewall	2212	2204	8	1672	540
RUSSELL.					
Castlewood's	1886	1886	.....	1634	252
Copper Creek	1339	1338	1	1222	117
Elk Garden	2023	2022	1	1754	269
Lebanon	2246	2244	2	2005	241
Lebanon	209	209	.....	164	45
Moccasin	1229	1227	2	1088	141
New Garden	2380	2376	4	2233	147

Counties.	Total.	Nativity. Native.	Nativity. Foreign.	Race. White.	Race. Colored.
SCOTT.					
De Kalb	1975	1974	1	1882	93
Estillville	2400	2397	3	2180	220
Estillville	106	106	.....	80	26
Floyd	1171	1169	2	1134	37
Fulkerson	1576	1575	1	1524	52
Johnston	1870	1869	1	1827	43
Powell	2261	2261	.....	2238	23
Taylor	1783	1782	1	1727	56
SHENANDOAH.					
Ashby	2645	2619	26	2452	193
Mt. Jackson	270	264	6	220	50
Davis	2293	2277	16	2159	134
Strasburg	580	575	5	525	55
Johnston (b)	1889	1850	39	1818	71
Powell's Fort	704	699	5	702	2
Lee	2698	2668	30	2565	133
New Market	600	588	12	538	62
Madison	3001	2975	26	2949	52
Edenburg	452	450	2	438	14
Stonewall (b)	2410	2393	17	2317	93
Woodstock (b)	859	824	35	731	128
SMYTH.					
Marion	3779	3769	10	3202	577
Marion	368	366	2	288	80
Rich Valley	3572	3557	15	3062	510
St. Clair	1547	1544	3	1390	157
SOUTHAMPTON.					
Berlin and Ivor	2674	2673	1	1318	1356
Boykins	2292	2287	5	914	c1356
Drewrysville	1811	1810	1	613	1198
Franklin	1564	1562	2	719	845
Jerusalem	2061	2059	2	1030	1031
Newsom's	1883	1877	6	874	1009
SPOTTSYLVANIA.					
Berkley	1801	1797	4	924	877
Courtland	2222	2185	37	1090	1132
Chancellor	1446	1392	54	999	447
Fredericksburg	4046	3867	179	2715	1331
Livingston	2213	2208	5	1341	872
STAFFORD.					
Aquia	2085	2059	26	1502	583
Falmouth	1694	1683	11	1315	379
Hartwood	1536	1522	14	1301	235
Rock Hill	1105	1105	.....	817	288
SURRY.					
Blackwater	1235	1235	.....	545	690
Cobham	2110	2107	3	923	1187
Guilford	2240	2232	8	925	1315
SUSSEX.					
Henry	1220	1220	.....	500	720
Newville	1369	1365	4	467	902
Stoney Creek	1510	1510	.....	449	1061
Sussex C't House	1778	1775	3	624	1154
Wakefield	1063	1063	.....	471	592
Waverly	945	943	2	451	494

(a) Also 6 Indians.
(b) Of Woodstock: 382 in Johnston and 477 in Stonewall.
(c) Also 22 Indians.

TABLE IX.—*Population of Minor Civil Divisions, &c.—VIRGINIA*—Continued.

Counties.	Total.	Nativity. Native.	Nativity. Foreign.	Race. White.	Race. Colored.
TAZEWELL.					
Clear Fork	3415	3404	11	3022	393
Jeffersonville	3682	3675	7	2939	743
Maiden Spring	3694	3693	1	3232	462
WARREN.					
Cedarville	1734	1718	16	1348	386
Front Royal	1872	1849	23	1424	448
Front Royal	705	700	5	486	219
South River	2110	2108	2	1839	271
WARWICK.					
Denbigh	391	391	.....	164	227
Warwick	21	21	.....	18	3
Newport	733	729	4	288	445
Stanley	548	546	2	168	380
WASHINGTON.					
Abingdon	3163	3135	28	2367	796
Abingdon	715	703	12	469	246
Glade Spring	2898	2898	.....	2481	417
Goodson	3835	3805	30	3113	722
Kinderhook	2391	2386	5	2274	117
North Fork	2058	2058	.....	1958	a99
Saltville	2471	2455	16	1963	b502
WESTMORELAND.					
Cople	3353	3338	15	1301	2052
Montross	1862	1859	3	1065	797
Washington	2467	2457	10	1165	1302
WISE.					
Gladeville	1252	1251	1	1247	5
Richmond	743	743	.....	732	11
Robinson	769	766	3	762	7
Tipps	985	985	.....	940	45
Walker	1036	1036	.....	1036	.....
WYTHE.					
Black Lick (c)	3489	3468	21	3046	443
Fort Chiswell (c)	4034	3982	52	2761	1273
Wytheville (c)	1671	1635	36	1198	473
Speedwell	4088	4041	47	3462	626
YORK.					
Bruton	1839	1821	18	371	1468
Grafton	1431	1418	13	844	587
Nelson	2218	2208	10	272	1946
Pocoson	1710	1702	8	1030	680

(a) Also 1 Indian. (b) Also 6 Indians.
(c) Of Wytheville: 726 in Black Lick and 945 in Fort Chiswell.

TABLE IX.—*Population of Minor Civil Divisions, &c.—WASHINGTON.*

Counties.	Total.	Nativity. Native.	Nativity. Foreign.	Race. White.	Race. Colored.
CHEHALIS.(*)					
Chehalis Res.	19	18	1	19	......
Quinaielt Res	5	4	1	5	......
CLALLAM.(*)					
Neeah Bay Reservation.	11	14	......	14	......
ISLAND.(a)					
Camano Island	157	36	121	148	1
Whidby Island	469	364	105	446	1
JEFFERSON.(b)					
Chemicum	133	75	58	120	1
Port Discovery	152	64	88	141	1
Port Ludlow	259	105	154	200	6
Port Townsend	593	367	226	537	4
Quilcine	131	79	52	128	......
KING.(*)					
Cedar River locality	40	34	6	40	......
Dwamish Riv.	80	59	21	80	......
Freeport	40	17	23	40	......
Lake Washington locality	120	68	52	119	1
Puyallup Res.	5	5	......	5	......
Seattle	1107	828	279	1094	13
Squak & Snoqualmie	40	24	16	40	......
White River locality	277	224	53	275	2
KITSAP.(c)					
Port Blakeley	61	24	37	61	......
Port Gamble	326	177	149	311	2
Port Madison	249	108	141	244	5
Port Orchard	80	47	33	73	7
Seabeck	150	78	72	150	......

(*) Incomplete: the other principal civil divisions were not separately returned.
(a) Island County: Camano also includes 5 Chinese and 3 Indians; Whidby Island, 2 Chinese and 20 Indians.
(b) Jefferson County: Chemicum also includes 12 Indians; Port Discovery, 5 Chinese and 5 Indians; Port Ludlow, 7 Chinese and 46 Indians; Port Townsend, 7 Chinese and 45 Indians; Quilcine, 3 Indians.
(c) Kitsap County: Port Gamble also includes 13 Chinese.

X.—*Population of Minor Civil Divisions, &c.—WASHINGTON*—Continued.

…s.	Total.	Nativity. Native.	Nativity. Foreign.	Race. White.	Race. Colored.
…z)					
……	96	91	5	94	1
……	147	137	10	147	……
…rie…	278	234	44	268	1
……	172	134	38	170	……
…uck…	195	183	12	189	6
…b)					
……	73	62	11	70	……
……	59	58	1	59	……
…d's Ms	17	15	2	16	……
…sh Re.	16	12	4	16	……
…ity…	124	78	46	114	5
…) (c)					
…lle…	104	72	32	94	……
…*)					
…Val.	312	278	34	304	8
…m…	314	230	84	305	9
……	73	50	23	71	2
…(d)					
……	142	95	47	121	1
…a…	433	302	131	384	1
…Res'n	24	16	8	24	……
…(f)					
……	587	363	224	451	……
…ville, …on)…	57	21	36	57	……
…Plain	29	21	8	11	……
……	118	104	14	105	……
…(g)					
……	91	90	1	91	……
…airie.	208	192	16	208	……

Counties.	Total.	Nativity. Native.	Nativity. Foreign.	Race. White.	Race. Colored.
THURSTON—Con'd.					
Coal Bank	168	153	15	168	……
Grand Mound	149	138	11	148	……
Olympia	1203	966	237	1158	24
Tumwater	354	330	24	349	3
Tumwater	206	192	14	205	……
Yelm	73	62	11	71	……
WALLA-WALLA. (h)					
Frenchtown	2612	2393	219	2555	1
Waitsburg	1174	1121	53	1165	……
Waitsburg	107	101	6	104	……
Walla-Walla	1514	1178	336	1454	10
Walla-Walla	1394	1081	313	1346	10
WHATCOM. (i)					
Fidalgo	79	74	5	62	……
Samish	71	48	23	62	……
Skagit	86	55	31	74	……
Swinimish	40	27	13	38	……
Whatcom	258	137	121	215	1
"*The disputed islands.*" (j)					
Blakeley Island	2	2	……	1	……
Decatur Island	8	5	3	7	……
Henry's Island	2	……	2	1	……
Lope's Island	48	24	24	41	……
Orcas Island	108	71	37	85	……
San Juan Island (k)	376	189	187	333	7
American garrison	98	38	60	98	……
Shaw's Island	1	1	……	……	……
Spiedan Island	2	……	2	1	……
Stuart's Island	1	1	……	……	……
Waldron Island	6	4	2	4	……
YAKIMA. (*)					
Yakima Res'n	23	22	1	23	……

…lete; the other principal civil divisions were not separately returned.
…County: Bois Fort also includes 1 Indian; Cowlitz Prairie, 9 Indians; Newakum, 1 Chinese …

…County: Arcadia also includes 1 Chinese and 2 Indians; Sherwood's Mills, 1 Indian; Union …ns.
…County: Oysterville also includes 3 Chinese and 7 Indians.
…ish County: Precinct also includes 20 Indians; Stuliquamish, 3 Chinese and 45 Indians. …ed without name.
…County: Fort Colville also includes 41 Chinese and 95 Indians; Spokane Plain, (village,) …d 17 Indians; Union Flat, 13 Indians.
…on County: Grand Mound also includes 1 Indian; Olympia, 18 Chinese and 3 Indians; Tum… …nct,) 1 Chinese and 1 Indian; Tumwater, (village,) 1 Chinese; Yelm, 2 Indians.
…Walla County: Frenchtown also includes 3 Chinese and 53 Indians; Waitsburg, 6 Chinese …s; Waitsburg, (village,) 3 Chinese; Walla-Walla, 33 Chinese and 17 Indians; Walla-Walla, …Chinese and 8 Indians.
…om County: Fidalgo also includes 17 Indians; Samish, 9 Indians; Skagit, 1 Chinese and 11 …nimish, 2 Indians; Whatcom, 20 Chinese and 22 Indians.
…puted islands, (so styled on the return of the assistant marshal:) Blakeley Island also …dian; Decatur Island, 1 Indian; Henry's Island, 1 Indian; Lope's Island, 7 Indians; Orcas …lians; San Juan Island, 2 Chinese and 34 Indians; Shaw's Island, 1 Indian; Spiedan Island, …uart's Island, 1 Indian; Waldron Island, 2 Indians.
…nt to an arrangement between the authorities of the United States and those of her Brit… …y, entered into in November, 1859, a temporary joint military occupation of the Island of …s agreed to. This occupation still exists. Consequently, in the enumeration of the inhab… …island, both citizens of the United States and British subjects are included. San Juan …e given, includes all the population of the island except the British garrison.

TABLE IX.—*Population of Minor Civil Divisions, &c.—WEST VIRGINIA.*

NOTE.—The marginal column marks townships; the first indentation, cities; the second, towns. Names of towns are placed under the names of the townships in which they are respectively situated. The population of each township includes that of all towns situated in it.

Counties.	Total.	Nativity. Native.	Nativity. Foreign.	Race. White.	Race. Colored.
BARBOUR.					
Barker	1961	1913	48	1955	6
Cove	1657	1656	1	1607	50
Elk	1010	1010	.....	1000	10
Glade	1302	1296	6	1302	.....
Philippi	1605	1602	3	1413	192
Pleasant	1395	1389	6	1279	116
Union	1382	1365	17	1370	12
BERKELEY.					
Arden	1528	1479	49	1297	231
Falling Water	1218	1199	19	1067	151
Gerardtown	1857	1853	4	1681	176
Hedgesville	2499	2456	43	2272	227
Martinsb'g (a)	4863	4375	488	4387	476
Mill Creek	1270	1260	10	1072	198
Opequan	1665	1639	26	1452	213
BOONE.					
Crook	702	702	.....	631	71
Peytona	1166	1121	45	1152	14
Scott	792	790	2	751	41
Sherman	878	875	3	869	9
Washington	1015	1014	1	997	18
BRAXTON.					
Clay	2164	2140	24	2117	47
Franklin	1279	1276	3	1259	20
Lincoln	1642	1624	18	1623	19
Washington	1395	1390	5	1394	1
BROOKE.					
Buffalo	2191	2070	121	2132	59
Cross Creek	1907	1764	143	1883	24
Wellsburg	1366	1232	134	1352	14
CABELL.					
Barboursville	1228	1187	41	1183	45
Barboursville	371	356	15	357	14
Grant	980	944	36	975	5
Guyandotte	2095	2059	36	2037	58
Guyandotte	427	412	15	419	8
McComas	1149	1138	11	1139	10
Union	977	932	45	972	5
CALHOUN.					
Centre	520	520	.....	520	.....
Lee	608	606	2	608	.....
Arnoldsburg	22	21	1	22	.....
Sheridan	589	589	.....	589	.....
Sherman	640	634	6	634	6
Washington	582	577	5	580	2
CLAY.					
Buffalo	790	790	.....	786	4
Henry	484	484	.....	484	.....
Pleasant	488	488	.....	488	.....
Union	434	434	.....	434	.....
DODDRIDGE.					
Central	833	808	25	820	13
Grant	1128	1087	41	1127	1
McClellan	939	933	6	939	.....
New Milton	1777	1760	17	1777	.....
Southwest	1251	1154	97	1249	2
West Union	1128	1069	59	1109	19
FAYETTE.					
Falls	1414	1400	14	1373	41
Fayetteville	1977	1969	8	1943	34
Mountain Cove	1923	1915	8	1895	28
Sewell	1333	1331	2	1318	15
GILMER.					
Centre	1201	1195	6	1201	.....
De Kalb	848	845	3	848	.....
Glenville	1422	1407	15	1399	23
Glenville	174	169	5	171	3
Troy	867	866	1	863	4
GRANT.					
Grant	1598	1572	26	1455	143
Milroy	1836	1831	5	1651	185
Union	1033	979	54	1030	3
GREENBRIER.					
Anthony's Creek	632	627	5	612	20
Big Level	1589	1559	30	1407	182
Blue Sulphur	2148	2130	18	2064	84
Falling Spring	1138	1130	8	1024	114
Fort Spring	901	875	26	819	82
Irish Corner	840	790	50	801	39
Lewisburg (b)	875	854	21	586	289
Meadow Bluff	1306	1286	20	1272	34
White Sulphur	976	924	52	812	164
Williamsburg	1012	1003	9	917	95
HAMPSHIRE.					
Blooming	1195	1186	9	1115	80
Capon	1160	1151	9	1128	32
Gore	1895	1878	17	1829	66
Romney	1031	1022	9	798	233
Romney	482	474	8	353	129
Sherman	1089	1086	3	1071	18
Springfield	1273	1245	28	1062	211
HANCOCK.					
Butler	979	907	72	976	3
Clay	1507	1389	118	1506	1
Grant	1005	983	22	984	21
Poe	872	853	19	870	2
HARDY.					
Capon	1541	1536	5	1431	110
Lost River	1301	1296	5	1267	34
Moorefield	2676	2645	31	2204	472

(a) Comprises township of same name.
(b) Comprises entire township of same name.

[TAB]LE IX.—*Population of Minor Civil Divisions, &c.—WEST VIRGINIA*—Continued.

Counties.	Total.	Nativity. Native.	Nativity. Foreign.	Race. White.	Race. Colored.
[H]ARRISON.					
k	2085	1989	96	1853	232
	1574	1571	3	1540	34
	2058	1819	239	1904	154
e	1560	1559	1	1482	78
	1361	1358	3	1329	32
t	1547	1543	4	1518	29
is	1599	1593	6	1589	10
son	1474	1439	35	1422	52
Mile	1736	1704	32	1724	a11
n	1720	1717	3	1697	23
JACKSON.					
ore	2169	2137	32	2144	25
Ravenswood	362	352	10	357	5
t	2031	2022	9	2019	12
Creek	2821	2776	45	2801	20
Ripley	226	212	14	224	2
n	1830	1793	37	1830	.....
hington	1449	1449	.....	1448	1
[J]EFFERSON.					
ill	2030	2011	19	1467	563
Smithfield	361	359	2	267	94
ar	2892	2744	148	2455	437
line	1867	1852	15	1411	456
t	4571	4525	46	2957	1614
Charlestown	1593	1570	23	1056	537
herd	1859	1826	33	1441	418
herdstown	1389	1380	9	1041	348
[K]ANAWHA.					
Sandy	876	874	2	876	.....
n Creek	2437	2278	159	2287	150
leston	3857	3620	237	3038	819
Charleston	3162	2948	214	2401	761
	2451	2369	82	2434	17
rson	1635	1592	43	1495	140
ion	2792	2749	43	2375	417
on	3190	3117	73	2638	552
talico	1597	1592	5	1566	31
n	2449	2421	28	2349	100
hington	1065	1050	15	1053	12
LEWIS.					
elle	2002	1966	36	1998	4
Lew (b)	2174	2153	21	2153	21
oln	1164	1160	4	1158	6
idan (b)	2320	2017	303	2210	110
Weston (b)	1111	986	125	1043	68
ey (b)	2515	2357	158	2460	55
LINCOLN.					
ell	1123	1122	1	1095	28
d	604	601	3	604	.....
s Creek	858	857	1	857	1
son	508	508	.....	508	.....
dan	949	942	7	948	1
n	468	468	.....	462	6
ington	543	541	2	543	.....
LOGAN.					
manville	924	923	1	876	48
y	1472	1470	2	1460	12
n	1220	1218	2	1184	36
racoma	43	43	.....	43	.....
LOGAN—Cont'd.					
Magnolia	a 667	667	.....	667	.....
Triadelphia	841	839	2	835	6
MARION.					
Fairmount	1781	1723	58	1717	64
Barrackville	114	114	.....	114	.....
Fairmont	621	606	15	578	4
Johnton	55	52	3	47	83
Grant	530	530	.....	529	1
Boothsville	125	125	.....	124	1
Lincoln	2127	2101	26	2126	1
Farmington	85	85	.....	85	.....
Worthington	127	127	.....	127	.....
Mannington	2924	2872	52	2915	9
Mannington	411	402	9	403	8
Paw Paw	1653	1653	.....	1653	.....
Barnettville	54	54	.....	54	.....
Fairview	72	72	.....	72	.....
Riversville	63	63	.....	63	.....
Union	1739	1690	49	1736	3
Palatine	558	525	33	558	.....
Winfield	1353	1348	5	1353	.....
Houltown	33	33	.....	33	.....
Newport	68	68	.....	68	.....
Winfield	47	47	.....	47	.....
MARSHALL.					
Cameron	1627	1563	64	1625	2
Clay (c)	1005	967	38	1004	1
Franklin	1610	1574	36	1603	7
Liberty	2062	1954	108	2034	28
Meade	1308	1246	62	1308	.....
Moundsville c	1500	1397	103	1444	56
Sand Hill	951	915	36	945	6
Union	2742	2336	406	2736	6
Washington (c)	993	971	22	979	14
Webster	1143	1109	34	1143	.....
MASON.					
Arbuckle	1301	1294	7	1187	114
Clendennin	1657	1646	11	1589	68
Cologne	1023	994	29	1023	.....
Cooper	1204	1184	20	1199	5
Graham	2325	2117	208	2319	6
Hartford	918	913	5	912	6
New Haven	489	440	49	489	.....
Hannon	1551	1541	10	1523	28
Lewis	1364	1335	29	1165	199
P't Pleasant	773	750	23	648	125
Robinson	1145	1137	8	1093	52
Union	1084	1075	9	1080	4
Waggoner	3324	2702	622	3266	58
Clifton	693	495	198	691	2
Mason	1182	878	304	1139	43
W. Columbia	778	714	64	775	3
MC'DOWELL.					
Big Creek	688	685	3	688	.....
Elkhorn	416	416	.....	416	.....
Sandy River	848	848	.....	848	.....
MERCER.					
Beaver Pond	1277	1273	4	1149	128
East River	1419	1417	2	1364	55
Jumping Branch	1441	1441	.....	1433	8
Plymouth	1687	1680	7	1535	152
Rock	1240	1236	4	1189	51

(a) Also 1 Indian.
(b) Of Weston: 193 in Jane Lew, 753 in Sheridan, and 165 in Willey.
(c) Clay and *Washington* exclusive of Moundsville.

TABLE IX.—*Population of Minor Civil Divisions, &c.—WEST VIRGINIA*—Continued.

Counties.	Total.	Nativity. Native.	Nativity. Foreign.	Race. White.	Race. Colored.
MINERAL.					
Cabin Run	822	817	5	760	62
Elk	423	412	11	409	14
Frankfort	957	924	33	838	119
Mill Creek	598	596	2	569	29
New Creek	1120	1088	32	1045	75
Piedmont	1785	1453	332	1758	27
Piedmont	1366	1162	204	1340	26
Welton	627	616	11	575	52
MONONGALIA.					
Battelle	1856	1850	6	1841	15
Cass	1449	1442	7	1448	1
Clay	1972	1971	1	1963	9
Clinton	1900	1880	20	1870	30
Grant	2216	2202	14	2186	30
Morgan	2536	2512	24	2397	139
Morgantown	797	787	10	741	56
Union	1618	1598	20	1611	7
MONROE.					
Forest Hill	1920	1899	21	1846	74
Red Sulphur Spr'g	1904	1892	12	1719	185
Second Creek	1222	1213	9	1077	145
Springfield	1624	1618	6	1527	97
Sweet Springs	1354	1340	14	1212	142
Union	1676	1649	27	1363	313
Union	419	408	11	299	120
Wolf Creek	1424	1411	13	1377	47
MORGAN.					
Allen	766	736	30	755	11
Bath	925	904	21	876	49
Bath	407	398	9	364	43
Cacapon	958	924	34	906	52
Rock Gap	635	627	8	633	2
Sleepy Creek	374	365	9	373	1
Timber Ridge	657	652	5	656	1
NICHOLAS.					
Grant	729	726	3	729	......
Jefferson	649	649	......	645	4
Kentucky	615	613	2	608	7
Mumble-the-peg	996	985	11	994	2
Summerville	645	621	24	630	15
Wilderness	824	821	3	821	3
OHIO.					
Liberty	1362	1327	35	1336	26
West Liberty	251	248	3	239	12
Richland	1389	1238	151	1377	12
Clinton	257	207	50	257	......
Ritchie	4126	2819	1307	4125	1
S. Wheeling	3158	2075	1083	3157	1
Triadelphia	2141	1933	208	2126	15
Triadelphia	239	209	30	238	1
Washington	533	367	166	533	......
Fulton	333	224	109	333	......
Wheeling (a)	19280	15127	4153	18890	390
PENDLETON.					
Bethel	714	713	1	692	22
Circleville	1108	1108	......	1106	2
Franklin	1209	1209	......	1189	20
Mill Run	1160	1160	......	1136	24
Sugar Grove	984	984	......	967	17
Union	1280	1275	5	1271	9

Counties.	Total.	Nativity. Native.	Nativity. Foreign.	Race. White.	Race. Colored.
PLEASANTS.					
Grant	601	595	6	587	14
Jefferson	407	404	3	407	......
La Fayette	397	397	......	396	1
McKim	449	449	......	449	......
Union	338	328	10	338	......
Washington	820	795	25	819	1
POCAHONTAS.					
Grant	837	833	4	774	63
Lincoln	1015	1008	7	997	18
Meade	887	885	2	874	13
Union	1330	1309	21	1165	165
PRESTON.					
Grant	1733	1701	32	1730	3
Brandonville	100	99	1	100	......
Kingwood	1581	1464	117	1539	42
Lyon	2612	2319	293	2565	47
Pleasant	1570	1545	25	1570	......
Portland	1997	1931	66	1989	8
Reno	2536	2424	112	2522	14
Union	1395	1332	63	1391	4
Valley	1131	1122	9	1131	......
PUTNAM.					
Buffalo	1448	1424	24	1374	74
Buffalo	321	313	8	298	23
Curry	1162	1160	2	1140	22
Grant	1146	1141	5	1085	61
Hutton	1568	1485	83	1546	22
Scott	1794	1770	24	1713	81
Union	676	675	1	676	......
RALEIGH.					
Clear Fork	552	552	......	551	1
Marsh Fork	736	736	......	735	1
Richman	389	376	13	387	2
Shady Spring	686	686	......	680	6
Town	811	806	5	810	1
Trap Hill	499	499	......	494	5
RANDOLPH.					
Beverly	847	845	2	824	23
Clay	540	540	......	537	3
Clark	496	492	4	479	17
Dry Fork	659	658	1	650	......
Green	893	889	4	869	24
Mingo	537	535	2	531	6
Reynolds	657	656	1	631	26
Scott	594	492	102	594	......
Union	340	319	21	336	4
RITCHIE.					
Clay	2746	2668	78	2706	40
Grant	2552	2370	182	2547	5
Murphy	1605	1565	40	1604	1
Union	2152	2144	8	2135	17
Harrisville	140	138	2	136	4
ROANE.					
Curtis	580	580	......	580	......
Geary	950	949	1	946	4
Harper	955	954	1	955	......
Reedy	964	963	1	961	3
Smithfield	1406	1044	2	1034	12

(a) City of Wheeling comprises the townships of Centre, Clay, Madison, Union, Webster, and Washington.

X.—*Population of Minor Civil Divisions, &c.—WEST VIRGINIA*—Continued.

…ies.	Total.	Nativity. Native.	Nativity. Foreign.	Race. White.	Race. Colored.
…Cont'd.					
…........	1366	1359	7	1362	4
…r	143	141	2	142	1
…........	1371	1371	......	1371	......
…on.					
…eek....	1134	1133	1	1104	30
…........	738	720	12	703	35
…ise	753	750	3	717	36
…........	958	927	31	944	14
…n	942	936	6	875	67
…n (a)...	1927	1725	202	1948	39
…........	934	896	38	929	5
…........	966	890	76	918	48
…........	955	900	55	886	69
…er.					
…k.......	610	609	1	596	14
…ille.....	433	429	4	425	8
…........	864	849	15	859	5
…n.					
…........	1079	1073	6	1078	1
…........	1890	1876	14	1890	......
…bourne.	182	182	......	182	......
…........	1645	1586	59	1638	7
…ville ...	364	353	11	364	......
…........	1316	1307	9	1314	2
…........	817	812	5	817	......
…........	1085	1070	15	1085	......
…ur.					
…........	1272	1268	4	1267	5
…on	1674	1661	13	1574	100
…annon..	475	469	6	428	47
…........	1284	1281	3	1278	6
…........	1176	1122	54	1137	39
…........	1601	1598	3	1579	22
…n	1016	1008	8	1016	......
…se.					
…........	1992	1983	9	1943	49
…........	1297	1290	7	1271	26
…........	1314	1314	......	1286	28
…........	1559	1558	1	1539	20
…........	1690	1679	11	1660	30

Counties.	Total.	Nativity. Native.	Nativity. Foreign.	Race. White.	Race. Colored.
WEBSTER.					
Fork Lick........	671	667	4	671	......
Glade	447	447	......	447	......
Holly	612	612	......	612	......
WETZEL.					
Centre	1336	1317	19	1336	......
Church	1607	1535	72	1606	1
Grant	1021	1012	9	1017	4
Green	931	920	11	931	......
Magnolia	1598	1486	112	1595	3
New Martinsville........	260	254	6	260	......
Proctor	2102	2011	91	2099	3
WIRT.					
Burning Springs..	1368	1343	25	1346	22
Clay.............	533	519	14	531	2
Elizabeth	804	792	12	800	4
Newark	580	577	3	579	1
Reedy	489	487	2	489	......
Spring Creek	490	478	12	490	......
Tucker	540	537	3	540	......
WOOD.					
Clay.............	1108	1059	49	1098	10
Claysville	123	113	10	120	3
Harris	1699	1650	49	1698	1
Lubeck	2009	1860	149	1971	38
Parkersburg (b) ..	1095	1048	47	934	161
Parkersburg ...	5546	4745	801	5099	447
Slate	878	876	2	865	13
Steele	1562	1549	13	1562	......
Taggarts	1050	1016	34	1038	12
Union	1362	1324	38	1362	......
Walker	1205	1134	71	1198	7
Williams	1486	1452	34	1462	24
Williamstown	282	272	10	281	1
WYOMING.					
Barker's Ridge...	407	407	......	407	......
Centre...........	622	622	......	622	......
Clear Fork	529	526	3	498	31
Huff's Creek.....	342	342	......	342	......
Oceana	791	791	......	782	9
Slab Fork	480	480	......	479	1

…mprises township of same name.

(b) Exclusive of city of Parkersburg.

TABLE IX.—*Population of Minor Civil Divisions, &c.*—*WISCONSIN.*

NOTE.—The marginal column marks townships; the first indentation, cities; the second, towns. Names of towns are placed under the names of the townships in which they are respectively situated. The population of each township includes that of all towns situated in it.

Counties.	Total.	Nativity. Native.	Nativity. Foreign.	Race. White.	Race. Colored.
ADAMS.					
Adams	425	363	62	425	......
Friendship	76	67	9	76	......
Big Flats	89	80	9	89	......
Dell Prairie	534	470	64	534	......
Easton	338	306	32	338	......
Jackson	481	414	67	481	......
Leola	185	179	6	185	......
Lincoln	433	389	44	433	......
Monroe	416	350	66	414	2
New Chester	329	296	33	329	......
New Haven	894	737	157	893	(a)
Preston	161	148	13	161	......
Quincy	272	213	59	271	1
Richfield	266	244	22	266	......
Rome	143	119	24	143	......
Springville	386	341	45	386	......
Strong's Prairie	1043	540	503	1043	......
White Creek	206	162	44	206	......
ASHLAND.					
La Pointe	221	174	47	221	......
BARRON.					
Barron	538	246	292	530	b4
BAYFIELD.					
Bayfield	341	285	56	341	c1
BROWN.					
Bellevue	822	419	403	822	......
Depere	2800	1641	1159	2784	d10
Depere	1372	836	536	1366	a5
West Depere	875	516	359	868	e2
Eaton	358	210	148	358	......
Glenmore	730	420	310	730	......
Green Bay (f)	1073	483	590	1073	......
Green Bay	4666	2851	1815	4637	29
Holland	1279	760	519	1279	......
Howard	3620	2101	1519	3585	g5
Fort Howard	2462	1376	1086	2456	c4
Humboldt	735	351	384	735	......
Lawrence	750	507	243	723	h1
Morrison	1169	668	501	1169	......
New Denmark	815	336	479	815	......
Pittsfield	585	396	189	583	(c)
Preble	1108	564	544	1101	7
Rockland	753	439	314	752	(a)
Scott	1385	897	488	1381	(b)
Suamico	1074	706	368	1064	b6
Wrightstown	1446	979	467	1415	i9
BUFFALO.					
Alma	1049	525	524	1046	(j)
Alma	565	297	268	565	......
BUFFALO—Cont'd.					
Belvidere	632	297	335	632	......
Buffalo	1594	842	752	1594	......
Buffalo City	268	151	117	268	......
Fountain City	867	453	414	867	......
Canton	648	518	130	648	......
Cross	564	316	248	564	......
Gilmanton	715	580	135	715	......
Glencoe	676	417	259	676	......
Maxville	434	379	55	434	......
Milton	244	107	137	244	......
Modena	621	388	233	621	......
Montana	508	278	230	508	......
Naples	1009	807	202	1009	......
Nelson	1291	834	457	1291	......
Waumanda	1138	566	572	1138	......
BURNETT.					
Grantsburg	706	144	562	695	(k)
CALUMET.					
Brillion	672	380	292	672	......
Brothertown	1605	1070	535	1279	l9
Charlestown	1250	869	381	1218	m12
Chilton	1517	1049	468	1510	(n)
Chilton	363	229	134	356	(n)
Harrison	1562	914	648	1561	(e)
New Holstein	1813	906	907	1813	......
Rantoul	915	434	481	915	......
Stockbridge	1978	1532	446	1697	o29
Woodville	1023	507	516	1023	......
CHIPPEWA.					
Anson	455	268	187	432	(p)
Bloomer	1559	1034	525	1559	......
Chippewa Falls (q)	2507	1209	1298	2502	5
Eagle Point	1667	945	722	1659	8
Edson	231	167	64	231	......
Lafayette	970	556	414	964	(d)
Sigel	123	76	47	123	......
Wheaton	799	470	329	799	......
CLARK.					
Eaton	316	186	130	311	(e)
Grant	386	264	122	383	(j)
Levis	203	168	35	203	......
Loyal	543	476	67	543	......
Lynn	108	74	34	108	......
Mentor	441	369	72	441	......
Pine Valley	953	782	171	952	1
Weston	500	432	68	499	1
COLUMBIA.					
Arlington	822	520	302	822	......

(a) Also 1 Indian.
(b) Also 4 Indians.
(c) Also 2 Indians.
(d) Also 6 Indians.
(e) Also 5 Indians.
(f) Exclusive of city of Green Bay.
(g) Also 30 Indians.
(h) Also 26 Indians.
(i) Also 22 Indians.
(j) Also 3 Indians.
(k) Also 11 Indians.
(l) Also 317 Indians.
(m) Also 20 Indians.
(n) Also 7 Indians.
(o) Also 252 Indians.
(p) Also 23 Indians.
(q) Includes entire population of township of same name.

.E IX.—*Population of Minor Civil Divisions, &c.—WISCONSIN*—Continued.

ies.	Total.	Nativity: Native.	Nativity: Foreign.	Race: White.	Race: Colored.
.—Con.					
....	1180	626	554	1176	a1
....	2840	1956	884	2840	......
bus	1888	1286	602	1888	......
(b)	1449	872	577	1449	......
ia (b) ...	502	267	235	502	......
ph	61	50	11	61	......
....	1397	1077	320	1397	......
ra	85	74	11	85	......
te	300	226	74	300	......
bago...	709	488	221	702	7
Prairie .	1286	984	302	1286	......
iver....	259	239	20	259	......
....	1000	640	360	998	2
....	1098	620	478	1097	1
....	1031	606	425	1031	......
....	1566	1285	281	1564	2
....	725	575	150	725	......
....	879	650	229	879	......
....	920	750	170	920	......
....	1702	1180	522	1701	1
rn	1114	819	295	1114	......
....	1715	1102	613	1715	......
town ...	100	73	27	100	......
....	300	220	80	300	......
....	247	190	57	247	......
....	3945	2432	1513	3932	13
b)......	1157	728	429	1157	......
....	832	574	258	832	......
....	797	499	298	797	......
t........	949	794	155	947	2
....	1281	1079	202	1280	1
ville...	205	171	34	204	1
na	270	228	42	270	......
)RD.					
....	1416	1137	279	1416	......
....	1214	779	435	1214	......
....	1279	753	526	1279	......
....	489	452	37	488	1
....	452	411	41	452	......
Chien..	3661	2458	1203	3642	d13
ie du					
u	2700	......	......	......	......
....	800	740	60	799	1
....	1233	930	303	1233	......
....	348	331	17	348	......
....	1260	945	315	1260	......
....	923	676	247	923	......
..					
....	1142	924	218	1141	1
....	1155	556	599	1154	1
n	966	614	352	966	......
rove...	1011	614	397	1011	......
nd......	1165	586	579	1165	......
....	1274	830	444	1274	......
....	1127	716	411	1127	......
....	1342	713	629	1342	......
ove....	955	670	285	955	......
ns......	1506	833	673	1506	......
....	1043	673	370	1043	......
....	1040	525	515	1040	......
....	2179	1409	770	2165	14

Counties.	Total.	Nativity: Native.	Nativity: Foreign.	Race: White.	Race: Colored.
DANE—Cont'd.					
Stoughton....	985	565	420	982	3
Dunn	1172	696	476	1172	......
Fitchburg.........	1152	850	302	1150	2
Madison (e)	857	601	256	843	14
Madison.........	9176	6062	3114	9114	62
Mazomanie.........	1713	1162	551	1712	1
Mazomanie...	1143	726	417	1142	1
Medina............	1525	1054	471	1524	1
Middleton.........	1821	1033	788	1819	2
Middleton Station	285	177	108	284	1
Pleasant Br'ch	173	85	88	172	1
Montrose..........	1155	816	339	1153	2
Bellville......	132	102	30	132	......
Oregon............	1498	1277	221	1497	1
Perry	1051	503	548	1051	......
Pheasant Springs.	1065	547	518	1064	1
Primrose	1015	543	472	1015	......
Roxbury.	1207	734	473	1207	......
Rutland	1139	928	211	1139	......
Springdale	1138	664	474	1138	......
Springfield	1439	779	660	1439	......
Sun Prairie.......	1610	1235	375	1610	......
Sun Prairie...	626	498	128	626	......
Vermont	1244	500	744	1244	......
Verona...........	1125	777	348	1124	1
Vienna...........	1176	678	498	1176	......
Westport	1589	827	762	1588	1
Windsor	1256	727	529	1255	1
York..............	1068	800	268	1067	1
DODGE.					
Ashippun	1623	970	653	1623	......
Beaver Dam (f)...	1461	1019	442	1456	(g)
Beaver Dam....	3265	2378	887	3259	6
Burnett	981	688	293	981	......
Calamus..........	1140	696	444	1140	......
Chester	1876	1438	438	1846	h18
Waupun, part of (i).	1011	777	234	990	g16
Clyman	1426	856	570	1426	......
Elba..............	1496	988	508	1496	......
Emmett (j)	1375	702	673	1375	......
Fox Lake...... ..	1916	1354	562	1878	38
Fox Lake.....	1086	838	248	1053	33
Herman	1935	984	951	1935	......
Hubbard	3008	1697	1311	3008	......
Hustisford	1696	821	875	1696	......
Lebanon	1621	877	744	1621	......
Leroy	1576	1045	531	1566	10
Lomira............	1905	1005	900	1905	......
Lowell	2415	1482	933	2415	......
Oak Grove	2105	1631	474	2104	1
Juneau.......	300	237	63	300	......
Oak Grove....	80	65	15	80	......
Portland	1286	788	498	1286	......
Rubicon...........	1995	1302	693	1995	......
Shields	1119	633	486	1119	......
Theresa	2248	1083	1165	2248	......
Trenton	1735	1174	561	1733	2
Watertown, part of (k)	2186	980	1206	2186	......
Westford..........	1341	876	465	1340	1
Williamstown	2305	1241	1064	2304	1

3 Indians.
ambria: 430 in Courtland and 72 in Ran-
ph.
isive of city of Portage.
6 Indians.
isive of city of Madison.
isive of city of Beaver Dam.
5 Indians.

(h) Also 12 Indians.
(i) See note (g,) Fond du Lac County. Total, 1,935: Native, 1,440; foreign, 495; white, 1,914; colored, 21.
(j) Exclusive of 5th and 6th wards of Watertown.
(k) See page 367, note (d,) Jefferson County.

TABLE IX.—*Population of Minor Civil Divisions, &c.—WISCONSIN—Continued.*

Counties.	Total.	Nativity. Native.	Nativity. Foreign.	Race. White.	Race. Colored.
DOOR.					
Bailey's Harbor	297	191	106	297	......
Brussells	406	161	245	406	......
Clay Banks	319	221	98	319	......
Egg Harbor	165	114	51	165	......
Forestville	351	190	161	351	......
Gardner	403	193	210	403	......
Gibraltar	466	288	178	466	......
Jacksonport	139	92	47	139	......
Liberty Grove	333	126	207	333	......
Nasawaupee	346	190	156	346	......
Sevastopol	326	204	122	326	......
Sturgeon Bay	690	454	236	690	......
Union	294	124	170	294	......
Washington	384	258	126	384	......
DOUGLAS.					
Superior	1122	712	410	1111	*a*7
DUNN.					
Colfax	233	124	109	233	......
Dunn	990	679	311	990	......
Eau Gallo	978	688	290	978	......
Elk Mound	433	166	267	433	......
Grant	588	315	273	588	......
Lucas	317	277	40	317	......
Menomonee	2210	1210	1000	2210	......
New Haven	554	474	80	552	*b*1
Peru	242	185	57	242	......
Red Cedar	648	375	273	648	......
Rock Creek	267	212	55	267	......
Sheridan	117	70	47	117	......
Sherman	305	277	28	305	......
Spring Brook	1061	801	260	1061	......
Tainter	206	144	62	206	......
Weston	339	271	68	338	1
EAU CLAIRE.					
Bridge Creek	1538	1273	265	1538	......
Augusta	761	615	146	761	......
Brunswick	575	401	174	574	1
Eau Claire (*c*)	1476	1040	436	1453	23
Lincoln	911	539	372	911	......
North Eau Claire	1127	517	610	1127	......
North Eau Claire	965	408	557	965	......
Oak Grove	895	659	236	895	......
Oak Grove	376	296	80	376	......
Otter Creek	920	684	236	920	......
Pleasant Valley	348	258	90	348	......
Washington	527	384	143	527	......
West Eau Claire	2452	1639	813	2450	2
Eau Claire City	2293	1529	764	2291	2
FOND DU LAC.					
Alto	1448	770	678	1448	......
Ashford	1799	1156	643	1799	......
Auburn	1626	1016	610	1626	......
Byron	1441	1104	337	1441	......
Calumet	1460	865	595	1460	......
Eden	1448	1052	396	1448	......
Eldorado	1674	987	687	1666	8
Empire	1055	686	369	1047	*b*7
Fond du Lac (*d*)	1266	914	352	1258	*b*7
Fond du Lac	12764	8735	4029	12583	*e*179

(*a*) Also 4 Indians.
(*b*) Also 1 Indian.
(*c*) The village of Eau Claire comprises the township of Eau Claire.

Counties.	Total.	Nativity. Native.	Nativity. Foreign.	Ra[ce.] White.
FOND DU LAC—Continued.				
Forest	1417	870	547	1417
Friendship	1101	662	439	1101
Lamartine	1367	1102	265	1367
Marshfield	1593	900	693	1593
Metomen	1898	1315	583	1898
Oakfield	1361	1118	243	1360
Osceola	1209	858	351	1209
Ripon	4119	2919	1200	4116
Ripon	2976	2211	765	2973
Rosendale	1298	904	394	1284
Springvale	1246	952	294	1244
Taycheedah	1522	961	561	1521
Waupun	2161	1631	530	2161
Waupun, part of (*g*)	924	663	261	924
GRANT.				
Beetown	1624	1366	258	1580
Beetown	505	421	84	505
Bloomington	1245	1071	174	1241
Bloomington	365	324	41	365
Blue River	660	277	383	660
Boscobel	1650	1367	283	1649
Boscobel	1509	1246	263	1499
Cassville	1318	922	396	1318
Cassville	551	411	140	551
Clifton	1076	792	284	1076
Ellenboro	803	676	127	803
Fennimore	1794	1471	323	1794
Glen Haven	1177	844	333	1177
Glen Haven	163	119	44	163
Harrison	1045	872	173	1045
Hazel Green	2161	1355	806	2161
Hazel Green	723	434	289	723
Hickory Grove	907	594	313	907
Jamestown	1114	734	380	1113
Lancaster	2716	2167	549	2695
Liberty	907	615	292	906
Lima	1085	932	153	1085
Little Grant	813	611	202	813
Marion	675	547	128	675
Millville	223	192	31	223
Mount Hope	758	636	122	758
Muscoda	911	584	327	911
Paris	907	611	296	907
Patch Grove	829	700	129	810
Patch Grove	177	158	19	158
Platteville	3683	2628	1055	3677
Platteville	2537	1811	726	2531
Potosi	2686	1868	818	2686
Smelser	1291	991	300	1291
Waterloo	951	756	195	950
Watterstown	580	445	135	580
Wingville	1031	797	234	1031
Woodman	559	452	107	559
Wyalusing	800	692	108	800
GREEN.				
Adams	1007	637	370	1007
Albany	1374	1077	297	1374
Brooklyn	1111	889	222	1111
Cadiz	1401	1264	137	1401
Clarno	1637	1335	302	1637
Decatur	2459	2095	364	2459
Brodhead	1548	1328	220	1548
Exeter	949	767	182	949

(*d*) Exclusive of city of Fond du Lac.
(*e*) Also 2 Indians.
(*f*) Also 12 Indians.
(*g*) See note (*i*,) Dodge County.

TABLE IX.—*Population of Minor Civil Divisions, &c.—WISCONSIN*—Continued.

Counties.	Total.	Nativity. Native.	Nativity. Foreign.	Race. White.	Race. Colored.
GREEN—Cont'd.					
Jefferson	1673	1415	258	1673	......
Jordan	1083	819	264	1083	......
Monroe	4536	3638	898	4518	18
Monroe	3408	2709	699	3390	18
Mount Pleasant	1164	953	211	1163	1
New Glarus	958	491	467	958	......
Spring Grove	1236	1078	158	1236	......
Sylvester	1034	819	215	1032	2
Washington	901	611	290	901	......
York	1088	644	444	1088	......
GREEN LAKE.					
Berlin	3800	2989	811	3797	3
Berlin	2777	2106	671	2775	2
Brooklyn	1339	981	358	1334	5
Green Lake	1102	780	322	1092	a7
Kingston	807	605	202	806	1
Mackford	1251	942	309	1251	......
Manchester	1140	645	495	1140	......
Marquette	928	588	340	928	......
Princeton	1709	969	740	1709	......
Princeton	705	483	222	705	......
Seneca	414	232	182	414	......
St. Marie	705	367	338	705	......
IOWA.					
Arena	2131	1348	783	2130	1
Clyde	1124	801	323	1120	4
Avoca	418	325	93	418	......
Dodgeville	3708	2161	1547	3707	1
Dodgeville	1407	827	580	1406	1
Highland	3016	1848	1168	3016	......
Highland	482	267	215	482	......
Linden	2054	1339	715	2047	7
Mifflin	1490	1081	409	1484	6
Mineral Point	4825	3056	1769	4800	25
Mineral Point	3275	2021	1254	3257	18
Moscow	955	502	453	955	......
Pulaski	1082	714	368	1082	......
Ridgeway	2489	1379	1110	2488	1
Waldwick	935	586	349	935	......
Wyoming	735	551	184	735	......
JACKSON.					
Albion	1991	1536	455	1990	1
Black River Falls	1101	859	242	1101	......
Alma	731	630	101	731	......
Garden Valley	678	568	110	678	......
Hixton	899	661	238	899	......
Irving	828	631	197	828	......
Manchester	421	338	83	421	......
Melrose	929	676	253	929	......
Northfield	499	295	204	499	......
Springfield	711	429	282	711	......
JEFFERSON.					
Aztalan	1261	810	451	1258	3
Cold Spring	740	578	162	734	6
Concord	1627	992	635	1624	3
Farmington	2416	1402	1014	2405	11
Hebron	1372	1047	325	1367	5
Ixonia	1777	927	850	1777	......
Jefferson	4408	2875	1533	4406	b1
Jefferson	2176	1411	765	2175	1
JEFFERSON—Con.					
Koshkonong	3202	2544	658	3195	a4
Fort Atkinson	2010	1604	406	2006	a1
Lake Mills	1509	1055	454	1485	24
Lake Mills	590	473	117	573	17
Milford	1608	977	631	1604	4
Oakland	1071	746	325	1069	2
Palmyra	1621	1234	387	1619	2
Palmyra	703	601	102	702	1
Sullivan	1556	1021	535	1556	......
Sumner	468	289	179	468	......
Waterloo	1818	1117	701	1818	......
Waterloo	727	494	233	727	......
Watertown (c)	2222	1147	1075	2222	......
Watertown, part of (d)	5364	2986	2378	5363	1
JUNEAU.					
Armenia	254	203	51	254	......
Clearfield	203	126	77	203	......
Fountain	599	394	205	599	......
Germantown	593	448	145	593	......
Kildare	585	395	190	585	......
Lemonweir	1947	1546	401	1946	1
Mauston	952	767	185	951	1
Lindina	1065	860	205	1064	1
Lisbon	1670	1285	385	1669	1
New Lisbon	1221	927	294	1220	1
Lyndon	479	355	124	475	4
Marion	284	194	90	284	......
Necedah	1186	856	330	1177	(e)
Necedah	944	662	282	944	......
Orange	235	196	39	235	......
Plymouth	795	598	197	795	......
Seven-Mile Creek	825	565	260	825	......
Summit	722	615	107	722	......
Wonewoc	930	725	205	930	......
KENOSHA.					
Brighton	1185	703	482	1185	......
Bristol	1140	947	193	1140	......
Kenosha	4309	2995	1314	4300	9
Paris	1015	620	395	1014	1
Pleasant Prairie	1377	920	457	1359	18
Randall	533	410	123	533	......
Salem	1386	1022	364	1384	2
Somers (f)	1359	933	426	1359	......
Wheatland	843	516	327	843	......
KEWAUNEE.					
Ahnepee	1544	833	711	1544	......
Carlton	1185	539	646	1185	......
Casco	794	372	422	794	......
Franklin	1280	496	784	1280	......
Kewaunee	1681	776	905	1681	......
Lincoln	680	308	372	680	......
Montpelier	877	329	548	877	......
Pierce	1130	532	598	1130	......
Red River	957	457	500	956	(b)
LA CROSSE.					
Bangor	1151	675	476	1151	......
Burns	943	727	216	943	......
Campbell (g)	2084	1242	842	2083	1
N'th La Crosse	1494	928	566	1493	1
Farmington	1522	1011	511	1520	2

(a) Also 3 Indians.
(b) Also 1 Indian.
(c) Exclusive of part of city of Watertown.
(d) See note (k,) Dodge County. Total, 7,550: Native, 3,967; foreign, 3,583; white, 7,549; colored, 1.
(e) Also 9 Indians.
(f) Exclusive of city of Kenosha.
(g) Exclusive of city of La Crosse.

TABLE IX.—*Population of Minor Civil Divisions, &c.*—*WISCONSIN*—Continued.

Counties.	Total.	Nativity. Native.	Nativity. Foreign.	Race. White.	Race. Colored.
LA CROSSE—Con.					
Greenfield	676	291	385	676	......
Hamilton	2261	1374	887	2260	1
Holland	819	436	383	819	......
La Crosse	7785	4336	3449	7684	101
Onalaska	1532	936	596	1532	......
Shelby	654	319	335	654	......
Washington	870	348	522	870	......
LA FAYETTE.					
Argyle	1634	1026	608	1634	......
Blanchard	455	270	185	455	......
Belmont	1303	890	413	1301	2
Benton	1723	1070	653	1721	2
Darlington	2773	2203	570	2770	3
Elk Grove	1377	904	473	1377	......
Fayette	1193	916	277	1192	1
Gratiot	1718	1362	356	1716	2
Kendall	1131	774	357	1131	......
Monticello	480	371	109	479	1
New Diggings	1794	1112	682	1794	......
Seymour	419	228	191	419	......
Shullsburg	2702	1763	939	2701	1
Wayne	1056	929	127	1056	......
White Oak Spr'gs	540	387	153	540	......
Willow Springs	1117	781	336	1117	......
Wiota	1699	1219	480	1698	1
MANITOWOC.					
Cato	1675	947	728	1675	......
Centerville	1650	841	809	1650	......
Coooperstown	1563	748	815	1563	......
Eaton	1468	657	811	1463	(a)
Franklin	1597	783	814	1597	......
Gibson	1638	760	878	1638	......
Kossuth	2186	1050	1136	2186	......
Liberty	1430	711	719	1430	......
Manitowoc (b)	1016	594	422	1016	......
Manitowoc	5168	2591	2577	5161	c5
Manitowoc Rapids	1860	1003	857	1860	......
Maple Grove	1147	591	556	1147	......
Meeme	1579	856	723	1576	3
Mishicott	1551	782	769	1551	......
Newton	1992	1019	973	1992	......
Rockland	889	398	491	889	......
Schleswig	1718	870	848	1718	......
Two Creeks	472	214	258	472	......
Two Rivers	2765	1453	1312	2765	......
Two Rivers	1365	761	604	1365	......
MARATHON.					
Bergen	86	68	18	84	(c)
Berlin	879	334	545	879	......
Jenny	215	167	48	209	(d)
Knowlton	166	119	47	166	......
Maine	694	306	388	691	(e)
Marathon	344	221	123	344	......
Mosinee	334	238	96	331	(e)
Stettin	712	269	443	712	......
Texas	284	177	107	284	......
Wausau	1797	983	814	1796	(f)
Wausau	1349	755	594	1349	......
Wien	109	44	65	109	......
Weston	265	213	52	265	......
MARQUETTE.					
Buffalo	812	594	218	811	1
Crystal Lake	550	234	316	550	......
Douglas	616	470	146	615	(f)
Harris	498	339	159	498	......
Mecan	712	223	489	712	......
Montello	834	556	278	834	......
Moundville	408	275	133	407	1
Neshkoro	436	236	200	436	......
Newton	609	324	285	609	......
Oxford	608	527	81	608	......
Packwaukee	612	496	116	612	......
Shields	566	303	263	566	......
Springfield	261	180	81	261	......
Westfield	534	371	163	534	......
MILWAUKEE.					
Franklin	2090	1225	865	2090	......
Granville	2401	1363	1038	2396	(a)
Greenfield	2281	1192	1089	2281	......
Lake (g)	2974	1573	1401	2974	......
Milwaukee (g)	3096	1479	1617	3096	......
Milwaukee	71440	37667	33773	71263	f176
Oak Creek	1959	1162	797	1958	1
Wauwatosa (g)	3689	2036	1653	3681	8
MONROE.					
Adrian	603	431	172	602	1
Angelo	461	396	65	455	6
Clifton	501	300	201	501	......
Eaton	392	334	58	391	(f)
Glendale	679	578	101	679	......
Greenfield	519	407	112	517	2
Jefferson	764	446	318	764	......
Lafayette	492	392	100	491	(f)
Leon	1241	903	338	1241	......
Lincoln	1137	998	139	1137	......
Little Falls	621	500	121	621	......
Oakdale	619	438	181	605	14
Portland	630	291	339	630	......
Ridgeville	829	502	327	829	......
Sheldon	615	446	169	615	......
Sparta	3461	2894	567	3451	10
Sparta	2314	1924	390	2305	9
Tomah	1666	1271	395	1666	......
Tomah	837	706	131	837	......
Wellington	502	401	101	502	......
Wilton	818	584	234	818	......
OCONTO.					
Gillett	268	198	70	266	(c)
Little Suamico	542	287	255	542	......
Marinette	1334	612	722	1315	h3
Oconto	3278	1814	1464	3264	i1
Oconto	2655	1431	1224	2654	1
Pensaukee	777	546	231	777	......
Peshtigo	1749	930	819	1731	j3
Stiles	373	204	169	359	(k)
OUTAGAMIE.					
Appleton	4518	2990	1528	4496	d16
Black Creek	528	349	179	528	......
Bovina	437	345	92	411	l5

(a) Also 5 Indians.
(b) Exclusive of city of Manitowoc.
(c) Also 2 Indians.
(d) Also 6 Indians.
(e) Also 3 Indians.
(f) Also 1 Indian.
(g) Exclusive of part of city of Milwaukee.
(h) Also 16 Indians.
(i) Also 13 Indians.
(j) Also 15 Indians.
(k) Also 14 Indians.
(l) Also 21 Indians.

TABLE IX.—*Population of Minor Civil Divisions, &c.*—*WISCONSIN*—Continued.

Counties.	Total.	Nativity. Native.	Nativity. Foreign.	Race. White.	Race. Colored.
OUTAGAMIE—Con.					
Buchanan	823	437	386	823	......
Center	1201	694	507	1201	......
Dale	991	767	224	991	......
Deer Creek	134	96	38	134	......
Ellington	1248	809	439	1238	*a*8
Freedom	1330	753	577	1330	......
Grand Chute (*b*)	1390	895	495	1389	1
Greenville	1460	789	671	1460	......
Hortonia	1080	776	304	1080	......
Kaukauna	1429	837	592	1429	......
Liberty	461	299	162	461	......
Maine	101	86	15	101	......
Maple Creek	631	375	256	631	......
Osborn	417	268	149	417	......
Seymour	251	176	75	251	......
OZAUKEE.					
Belgium	1979	1114	865	1979	......
Cedarburg	2557	1358	1199	2557	......
Fredonia	1688	995	693	1688	......
Grafton	1864	998	866	1864	......
Mequon	3156	1739	1417	3156	......
Port Washington	2390	1386	1004	2390	......
Saukville	1930	1138	792	1929	1
PEPIN.					
Albany	275	204	71	275	......
Durand	917	773	144	917	......
Frankfort	340	292	48	340	......
Lima	477	364	113	477	......
Pepin	956	654	302	956	......
Stockholm	499	154	345	499	......
Waterville	835	645	190	835	......
Waubeck	360	265	95	360	......
PIERCE.					
Clifton	615	551	64	615	......
Diamond Bluff	475	390	85	475	......
Ellsworth	747	573	174	747	......
El Paso	248	134	114	248	......
Gilman	503	221	282	503	......
Hartland	574	416	158	574	......
Maiden Rock	501	307	194	501	......
Martell	717	359	358	717	......
Oak Grove	839	593	246	839	......
Prescott (*c*)	1138	905	233	1099	39
River Falls	1217	1062	155	1217	......
River Falls	741	669	72	741	......
Rock Elm	554	461	93	554	......
Salem	241	207	34	241	......
Spring Lake	386	314	72	386	......
Trenton	304	248	56	304	......
Trimbelle	633	547	86	623	10
Union	266	172	94	266	......
POLK.					
Alden	390	211	179	383	(*d*)
Balsam Lake	192	142	50	158	(*e*)
Black Brook	323	215	108	316	(*d*)
Farmington	593	382	211	590	(*f*)
Lincoln	287	243	44	287	......
Luck	68	10	58	64	(*g*)
Milltown	66	43	23	66	......
POLK—Cont'd.					
Osceola	710	499	211	709	(*h*)
St. Croix Falls	288	231	57	288	......
St. Croix Falls	543	352	191	540	(*f*)
Sterling	250	152	98	250	......
PORTAGE.					
Almond	651	491	160	651	......
Amherst	982	622	360	982	......
Belmont	508	437	71	508	......
Buena Vista	624	530	94	624	......
Eau Plaine	333	236	97	333	......
Grant	240	122	118	240	......
Hull	621	332	289	621	......
Lanark	471	317	154	471	......
Linwood	388	282	106	372	(*i*)
New Hope	751	345	406	751	......
Pine Grove	318	290	28	318	......
Plover	881	806	75	881	......
Sharon	948	346	602	948	......
Steven's Point	1895	1313	582	1895	......
Steven's Point	1810	1243	567	1810	......
Stockton	1023	744	279	1022	1
RACINE.					
Burlington	2762	1681	1081	2761	1
Burlington	1589	960	629	1588	1
Caledonia	2800	1508	1292	2791	9
Dover	1047	655	392	1047	......
Mount Pleasant	3560	2233	1327	3533	27
Norway	1040	462	578	1026	14
Racine	9880	5889	3991	9736	*f*141
Raymond	1608	877	731	1608	......
Rochester	876	637	239	876	......
Rochester	392	280	112	392	......
Waterford	1580	1067	513	1580	......
Waterford	545	324	221	545	......
Yorkville	1587	940	647	1585	2
RICHLAND.					
Akan	675	559	116	675	......
Bloom	1171	1128	43	1171	......
Buena Vista	1044	939	105	1044	......
Dayton	968	829	139	968	......
Eagle	1083	987	96	1079	4
Forest	926	903	23	926	......
Henrietta	754	610	144	754	......
Ithica	1266	1059	207	1266	......
Marshall	847	762	85	847	......
Orion	697	588	109	697	......
Richland	1572	1427	145	1569	3
Richwood	1378	1230	148	1377	1
Rockbridge	994	918	76	993	(*h*)
Sylvant	888	859	29	888	......
Westford	801	576	225	801	......
Willow	667	580	87	657	10
ROCK.					
Avon	886	620	266	883	3
Beloit (*j*)	743	594	149	743	......
Beloit	4396	3518	878	4330	66
Bradford	1006	794	212	1006	......
Center	1064	867	197	1063	1
Clinton	1943	1518	425	1940	3

(*a*) Also 2 Indians.
(*b*) Exclusive of city of Appleton.
(*c*) Comprises the whole of Prescott Township.
(*d*) Also 7 Indians.
(*e*) Also 34 Indians.
(*f*) Also 3 Indians.
(*g*) Also 4 Indians.
(*h*) Also 1 Indian.
(*i*) Also 16 Indians.
(*j*) Exclusive of city of Beloit.

TABLE IX.—*Population of Minor Civil Divisions, &c.—WISCONSIN*—Continued.

Counties.	Total.	Nativity. Native.	Nativity. Foreign.	Race. White.	Race. Colored.
ROCK—Cont'd.					
Fulton	2168	1716	452	2157	11
Harmony	1214	924	290	1214	......
Janesville (a)	926	723	203	922	4
Janesville	8789	6554	2235	8727	62
Johnstown	1299	1029	270	1295	4
La Prairie	867	734	133	865	2
Lima	1136	940	196	1136	......
Magnolia	1156	927	229	1153	3
Milton	2010	1773	237	1998	12
Newark	1074	838	236	1073	1
Plymouth	1396	1039	357	1396	......
Porter	1223	923	300	1223	......
Rock (a)	1062	814	248	1055	(b)
Spring Valley	1253	841	412	1246	7
Turtle	1274	1088	186	1273	1
Union	2145	1928	217	2131	14
SAUK.					
Baraboo	2758	2314	444	2754	4
Baraboo	1528	1254	274	1527	1
Bear Creek	858	615	243	857	1
Delona	536	391	145	536	......
Excelsior	874	664	210	874	......
Fairfield	689	610	79	688	1
Franklin	786	486	300	786	......
Freedom	778	511	267	778	......
Greenfield	746	568	178	746	......
Honey Creek	1180	559	621	1180	......
Ironton	1245	1009	236	1244	1
Lavalle	881	716	165	881	......
Merrimac	765	560	205	765	......
New Buffalo	956	859	97	955	(c)
Prairie du Sac	2258	1373	885	2258	......
Reedsburg	1631	1074	557	1631	......
Reedsburg	547	406	141	547	......
Spring Green	1156	884	272	1151	5
Spring Green	422	335	87	419	3
Sumter	847	675	172	847	......
Troy	995	575	420	995	......
Washington	1042	859	183	1042	......
Westfield	1230	702	528	1212	18
Winfield	758	545	213	758	......
Woodland	891	759	132	870	21
SHAWANO.					
Angelica	233	127	106	216	(d)
Belle Plaine	576	360	216	575	1
Grant	226	112	114	226	......
Hartland	541	211	330	540	(c)
Keshena	49	49	......	30	(e)
Pella	318	125	193	318	......
Richmond	539	325	214	506	(f)
Shawanaw	298	208	90	295	g1
Washington	71	31	40	60	(h)
Waukechon	315	140	175	314	1
SHEBOYGAN.					
Greenbush	1939	1446	493	1939	......
Herman	2252	1116	1136	2255	......
Holland	2704	1516	1188	2704	......
Lima	2190	1387	803	2189	1
Lynden	1552	1215	337	1550	2
Mitchell	1124	784	340	1124	......
Moselle	1088	525	563	1088	......
SHEBOYGAN—Con.					
Plymouth	2280	1530	750	2280	......
Rhine	1672	934	738	1672	......
Russell	623	361	262	623	......
Scott	1448	931	517	1447	1
Sheboygan (i)	1403	744	659	1403	......
Sheboygan	5310	2920	2390	5310	......
Sheboygan Falls	3223	2083	1140	3223	......
Sheboygan Falls	1174	872	302	1174	......
Sherman	1664	1000	664	1664	......
Wilson	1277	700	577	1277	......
ST. CROIX.					
Ceylon	348	171	177	348	......
Eau Galle	535	326	209	534	(c)
Emerald	206	147	59	206	......
Erin	1024	595	429	1024	......
Hammond	895	632	263	895	......
Hudson	2203	1576	627	2194	g7
Hudson	1748	1274	474	1740	g6
Kinnickinick	628	495	133	628	......
Pleasant Valley	592	321	271	592	......
Richmond	875	677	198	874	1
Rush River	549	312	237	549	......
St. Joseph	265	143	122	265	......
Somerset	491	295	196	491	......
Springfield	372	232	140	372	......
Star Prairie	773	595	178	773	......
Troy	812	604	208	805	7
Warren	467	330	137	466	1
TREMPEALEAU.					
Arcadia	1651	922	729	1651	......
Burnside	542	312	230	542	......
Caledonia	507	384	123	507	......
Ettrick	1214	465	749	1214	......
Gale	1450	947	503	1449	1
Galesville	1068	747	321	1068	......
Hale	616	315	301	616	......
Lincoln	822	477	345	821	1
Preston	955	378	577	953	2
Sumner	889	624	265	889	......
Trempealeau	2086	1515	571	2086	......
VERNON.					
Bergen	795	435	360	795	......
Christiana	1133	464	669	1133	......
Clinton	823	692	131	823	......
Coon	708	277	431	708	......
Forest	662	634	28	660	2
Franklin	1231	884	347	1231	......
Genoa	685	539	146	683	2
Greenwood	744	545	199	744	......
Hamburg	1208	529	679	1208	......
Harmony	781	612	169	781	......
Hillsboro	985	802	183	983	2
Jefferson	1108	843	265	1108	......
Kickapoo	912	806	106	912	......
Liberty	414	369	45	414	......
Stark	756	731	25	756	......
Sterling	1060	723	337	1060	......
Union	506	354	152	505	1
Viroqua	1988	1477	511	1988	......
Webster	812	742	70	812	......

(a) Exclusive of a part of city of Janesville.
(b) Also 7 Indians.
(c) Also 1 Indian.
(d) Also 17 Indians.
(e) Also 19 Indians.
(f) Also 33 Indians.
(g) Also 2 Indians.
(h) Also 11 Indians.
(i) Exclusive of city of Sheboygan

[TABLE I]X.—*Population of Minor Civil Divisions, &c.—WISCONSIN*—Continued.

	Total.	Nativity: Native.	Nativity: Foreign.	Race: White.	Race: Colored.
…nt'd.					
......	697	604	93	697	......
......	637	543	94	633	4
…H.					
......	1091	870	221	1091	......
......	1583	1369	214	1582	1
......	2509	2205	304	2509	......
......	1688	1488	200	1688	......
......	1431	1072	359	1430	......
…a (a) .	1205	966	239	1202	3
......	1040	863	177	1039	1
......	1312	972	340	1312	......
......	1032	777	255	1032	......
......	1039	773	266	1039	......
......	895	727	168	895	......
......	1017	750	267	1016	1
......	1865	1605	260	1852	13
…e....	1209	968	241	1209	......
......	992	745	247	992	......
......	1176	896	280	1176	......
......	2291	2040	251	2291	......
…Bay ..	997	875	122	997	......
......	4285	3224	1061	4268	17
…ON.					
......	1833	1048	785	1833	......
......	1376	825	551	1370	6
......	1266	790	476	1266	......
......	1885	1158	727	1885	......
......	1954	1119	835	1954	......
......	2685	1735	950	2683	2
......	1978	1051	927	1978	......
......	1309	716	593	1309	......
......	2220	1261	959	2220	......
......	1654	961	693	1654	......
......	2035	1103	932	2035	......
......	1710	926	784	1710	......
......	2014	1172	842	2014	......
…nd	1058	610	448	1058	......
.					
......	2281	1387	894	2278	3
......	1364	819	545	1364	......
......	1256	900	356	1252	4
......	1462	912	550	1462	......
......	1384	841	543	1384	......
......	2350	1467	883	2349	1
......	1612	993	619	1612	......
......	1261	918	313	1257	4
......	1409	809	600	1408	(b)
......	1809	1136	673	1809	......
......	2931	2604	327	2930	1
…woc .	1408	1004	404	1407	1
......	922	586	336	918	4
......	1818	1122	696	1814	4
......	1358	947	411	1352	6
......	1180	789	391	1180	......
......	3877	2708	1169	3844	c31
…a ...	2633	1938	695	2605	28
.					
......	462	265	197	462	......
......	661	397	264	661	......

Counties.	Total.	Nativity: Native.	Nativity: Foreign.	Race: White.	Race: Colored.
WAUPACA—Con.					
Dayton	871	754	117	871	......
Dupont	150	129	21	127	(d)
Farmington	734	536	198	734	......
Fremont	651	488	163	651	......
Helvetia	148	46	102	148	......
Iola	729	384	345	729	......
Larrabee	362	265	97	362	......
Lebanon	657	375	282	657	......
Lind	1017	792	225	1017	......
Little Wolf	716	555	161	716	......
Matteson	289	213	76	289	......
Mukwa	1819	1389	430	1812	e2
New London	1015	789	226	1008	e2
Royalton	953	788	165	953	......
Scandinavia	1065	497	568	1065	......
St. Lawrence	759	523	236	759	......
Union	211	183	28	211	......
Waupaca	2042	1485	557	2041	1
Weyauwega	1243	947	296	1242	(b)
WAUSHARA.					
Aurora	967	815	152	948	f1
Bloomfield	1123	580	543	1123	......
Coloma	309	287	22	309	......
Dakota	477	374	103	477	......
Deerfield	234	203	31	234	......
Hancock	438	412	26	438	......
Leon	869	692	177	869	......
Marion	565	466	99	565	......
Mount Morris	584	369	215	584	......
Oasis	634	570	64	634	......
Plainfield	997	929	68	997	......
Poysippi	612	466	146	612	......
Richford	428	357	71	428	......
Rose	397	249	148	397	......
Saxeville	746	424	322	746	......
Springwater	466	320	146	466	......
Warren	632	463	169	632	......
Wautonra	801	726	75	801	......
WINNEBAGO.					
Algoma (g)	807	667	140	807	......
Black Wolf	847	457	390	847	......
Clayton	1340	809	531	1340	......
Menasha	3107	2002	1105	3095	h8
Menasha	2484	1632	852	2479	b4
Nekimi	1278	717	561	1278	......
Neenah	3123	2092	1031	3097	26
Neenah	2655	1773	882	2637	18
Nepeuskin	1129	876	253	1129	......
Omro	3216	2752	464	3200	(i)
Omro	1838	1584	254	1830	(j)
Oshkosh (k)	729	471	258	726	3
Oshkosh	12663	8122	4541	12592	l68
Poygan	843	621	222	843	......
Rushford	2019	1713	300	2001	m6
Eureka	317	263	54	317	......
Utica	1039	723	316	1038	1
Vinland	1040	743	297	1040	......
Winchester	1439	671	768	1439	......
Winneconne	2155	1530	625	2154	1
Butte des Morts	166	117	49	166	......
Winneconne	1159	829	330	1158	1
Wolf River	505	243	262	505	......

…es township of same name.
…ndian.
…ndians.
…Indians.
…ndians.
…Indians.
…ve of 2d and 3d wards of city of Oshkosh.

(h) Also 4 Indians.
(i) Also 16 Indians.
(j) Also 8 Indians.
(k) Exclusive of 1st, 4th, and 5th wards of city of Oshkosh.
(l) Also 3 Indians.
(m) Also 12 Indians.

TABLE IX.—*Population of Minor Civil Divisions, &c.—WISCONSIN*—**Continued.**

Counties.	Total.	Nativity. Native.	Nativity. Foreign.	Race. White.	Race. Colored.	Counties.	Total.	Nativity. Native.	Nativity. Foreign.	Race. White.	Race. Colored.
WOOD.						WOOD—Cont'd.					
Centralia	893	621	272	886	(a)	Rudolph	317	211	106	316	(d)
Grand Rapids	1661	1025	636	1656	b3	Saratoga	300	223	77	299	1
Grand Rapids	1115	726	389	1110	b3	Seneca	293	209	84	292	(d)
Lincoln	229	143	86	223	(c)	Sigel	219	106	113	218	1

(a) Also 7 Indians.
(b) Also 2 Indians.
(c) Also 6 Indians.
(d) Also 1 Indian.

TABLE IX.—*Population of Minor Civil Divisions, &c.—WYOMING.*

Counties.	Total.	Nativity. Native.	Nativity. Foreign.	Race. White.	Race. Colored.	Counties.	Total.	Nativity. Native.	Nativity. Foreign.	Race. White.	Race. Colored.
ALBANY. (*) (a)						SWEETWATER. (d)					
Fort Fetterman and vicinity	338	240	98	329	1	Anthony's Saw Mill	11	10	1	11	......
Fort Sanders and vicinity	228	145	83	224	4	Atlantic City	325	221	104	311	4
Laramie and vicinity	828	553	275	792	34	Atlantic Gulch	9	7	2	9	......
Rock Creek and vicinity	80	24	56	80	......	Big Sandy Crossing	14	12	2	14	......
Sherman and vicinity	148	90	58	148	......	Bitter Creek	48	27	21	35	......
Wyoming and vicinity	75	56	19	75	......	Black Buttes	18	8	10	12	......
CARBON. (b)						Bryan	239	150	80	217	2
Carbon	244	88	156	244	......	Croston	22	5	17	8	......
Como	15	4	11	15	......	Green River City	106	68	38	102	1
Dana	22	9	13	22	......	Green River Crossing	4	4	......	4	......
Fort Halleck	40	34	6	37	3	Hallsville	24	7	17	19	......
Fort Fred. Steele	252	135	117	251	1	Hamilton City	75	52	23	75	......
Medicine Bow	105	62	43	105	......	Hermit Gulch	5	3	2	5	......
Percy	32	13	19	32	......	Point of Rocks	65	42	23	65	......
Rawlin's Springs	612	386	226	608	3	Red Desert	20	4	16	8	......
St. Mary's	24	9	15	24	......	Rock Creek Gulch	87	57	30	87	......
Separation	22	5	17	22	......	Rock Springs Coal Company	77	27	50	77	......
LARAMIE. (c)						Rock Springs	40	16	24	38	......
Cheyenne	1450	1043	407	1342	94	Salt Wells	26	14	12	26	......
Fort D. A. Russell	828	449	379	818	10	South Pass City	460	310	150	435	16
Fort Laramie	493	318	175	477	4	Smith's Gulch	159	92	67	159	......
Granite Cañon	39	22	17	39	......	Table Rock	17	2	15	9	......
Pine Bluff	147	66	81	146	1	Union Pacific Railroad	26	9	17	26	......
						Washakie	23	9	14	10	......
						Willow Creek Gulch	16	12	4	15	1

(*) Incomplete; the other principal civil subdivisions were not separately returned.
(a) Albany County: Fort Fetterman and vicinity also includes 8 Indians; Laramie and vicinity, 2 Chinese.
(b) Carbon County: Rawlin's Springs also includes 1 Chinese.
(c) Laramie County: Cheyenne also includes 13 Chinese and 1 Indian; Fort Laramie, 12 Indians.
(d) Sweetwater County: Atlantic City also includes 10 Indians; Bitter Creek, 13 Chinese; Black Buttes, 6 Chinese; Bryan, 16 Chinese and 4 Indians; Creston, 14 Chinese; Green River City, 3 Indians; Hallsville, 5 Chinese; Red Desert, 12 Chinese; Rock Springs, 2 Indians; South Pass City, 8 Chinese and 1 Indian; Table Rock, 8 Chinese; Washakie, 13 Chinese.

TABLE IX.—*Population of Minor Civil Divisions, &c.—WYOMING*—Continued.

Counties.	Total.	NATIVITY.		RACE.	
		Native.	Foreign.	White.	Colored.
UINTAH. (a)					
Aspen	24	12	12	24	......
Bear River City	26	20	6	26	......
Bridger Station	14	4	10	8	......
Byron's Camp	16	10	6	16	......
Carter	35	24	11	33	......
Church Buttes	16	3	13	5	......
Evanston	77	41	36	77	......
Fort Bridger	236	155	81	231	2
Granger	32	6	26	19	......
Ham's Fork	14	13	1	10	......
Millersville	30	30	......	12	......
UINTAH—Cont'd.					
Piedmont	71	40	31	71	......
Rocky Mountain Coal Mine	38	14	24	38	......
Sage Creek Saw Mill	19	17	2	18	1
St. Louis Saw Mill	12	10	2	12	......
Union Pacific Railroad	34	23	11	34	......
White's Saw Mill	22	17	5	22	......
Wyoming Coal Mine	140	50	90	140	......

(a) Uintah County: Bridger Station also includes 6 Chinese; Carter, 2 Chinese; Church Buttes, 11 Chinese; Fort Bridger, 3 Indians; Granger, 13 Chinese; Ham's Fork 4 Indians; Millersville, 18 Indians.

NATIVITY AND NATIONALITY.

TABLE X.—*Population, as Native, Foreign-born, and of Foreign Parentage*—1870–1860–1850.

	States and Territories.	1870.						
		Total population.	Native.	Foreign-born.	Having one or both parents foreign.	Having foreign father.	Having foreign mother.	Having foreign father and foreign mother.
	The United States.	38,558,371	32,991,142	5,567,229	10,892,015	10,521,233	10,105,627	9,734,845
	The States........	38,115,641	32,642,612	5,473,029	10,732,483	10,369,677	9,957,364	9,594,558
1	Alabama	996,992	987,030	9,962	21,844	20,765	18,060	16,981
2	Arkansas	484,471	479,445	5,026	10,617	9,893	8,484	7,760
3	California	560,247	350,416	209,831	323,507	310,927	308,303	295,723
4	Connecticut	537,454	423,815	113,639	203,650	198,958	197,377	192,685
5	Delaware	125,015	115,879	9,136	20,361	19,338	18,311	17,288
6	Florida	187,748	182,781	4,967	9,295	8,734	8,020	7,459
7	Georgia	1,184,109	1,172,982	11,127	23,814	22,901	19,413	18,500
8	Illinois	2,539,891	2,024,693	515,198	986,035	956,711	920,147	890,823
9	Indiana	1,680,637	1,539,163	141,474	341,001	326,312	298,753	284,064
10	Iowa	1,194,020	989,328	204,692	416,139	397,672	379,438	360,971
11	Kansas	364,399	316,007	48,392	87,211	82,848	77,828	73,465
12	Kentucky	1,321,011	1,257,613	63,398	142,720	139,336	130,185	126,799
13	Louisiana	726,915	665,088	61,827	132,011	127,480	118,017	113,486
14	Maine	626,915	578,034	48,881	91,651	84,381	81,128	73,858
15	Maryland	780,894	697,482	83,412	181,369	176,274	164,960	159,865
16	Massachusetts	1,457,351	1,104,032	353,319	626,211	609,836	606,727	590,352
17	Michigan	1,184,059	916,049	268,010	488,159	459,537	444,958	416,336
18	Minnesota	439,706	279,009	160,697	285,516	277,345	273,860	265,689
19	Mississippi	827,922	816,731	11,191	18,756	17,862	15,861	14,967
20	Missouri	1,721,295	1,499,028	222,267	465,125	453,264	428,770	416,909
21	Nebraska	122,993	92,245	30,748	50,017	48,277	46,392	44,652
22	Nevada	42,491	23,690	18,801	25,117	24,222	24,042	23,147
23	New Hampshire	318,300	288,689	29,611	44,592	42,862	42,550	40,820
24	New Jersey	906,096	717,153	188,943	350,316	340,661	330,900	321,245
25	New York	4,382,759	3,244,406	1,138,353	2,225,027	2,161,752	2,106,987	2,043,712
26	North Carolina	1,071,361	1,068,332	3,029	6,464	6,148	4,644	4,328
27	Ohio	2,665,260	2,292,767	372,493	849,815	816,780	764,380	731,345
28	Oregon	90,923	79,323	11,600	20,705	19,320	17,541	16,156
29	Pennsylvania	3,521,951	2,976,642	545,309	1,151,208	1,108,603	1,034,456	991,851
30	Rhode Island	217,353	161,957	55,396	95,090	92,762	92,311	89,983
31	South Carolina	705,606	697,532	8,074	16,449	15,875	14,156	13,582
32	Tennessee	1,258,520	1,239,204	19,316	36,326	35,045	31,861	30,580
33	Texas	818,579	756,168	62,411	107,327	103,713	100,047	96,433
34	Vermont	330,551	283,396	47,155	83,615	79,287	76,482	72,154
35	Virginia	1,225,163	1,211,409	13,754	30,794	29,677	24,751	23,634
36	West Virginia	442,014	424,923	17,091	46,204	43,917	39,077	36,790
37	Wisconsin	1,054,670	690,171	364,499	717,832	700,402	688,129	670,699
	The Territories....	442,730	348,530	94,200	159,532	151,556	148,263	140,287
1	Arizona	9,658	3,849	5,809	6,766	6,612	6,654	6,500
2	Colorado	39,864	33,265	6,599	10,707	10,200	9,854	9,347
3	Dakota	14,181	9,366	4,815	7,319	7,137	6,786	6,604
4	District of Columbia	131,700	115,446	16,254	34,106	32,721	30,568	29,183
5	Idaho	14,999	7,114	7,885	9,305	9,189	9,122	9,006
6	Montana	20,595	12,616	7,979	10,246	9,926	9,682	9,362
7	New Mexico	91,874	86,254	5,620	8,677	8,392	7,636	7,351
8	Utah	86,786	56,084	30,702	59,024	54,649	56,182	51,807
9	Washington	23,955	18,931	5,024	8,382	7,880	7,069	6,567
10	Wyoming	9,118	5,605	3,513	5,000	4,850	4,710	4,560

NOTE.—Of the sums contained in the four columns in order, respectively, fourth, fifth, sixth, and seventh, in this table, that in the seventh is invariably the smallest, and that in the fourth invariably the largest. The sum given in column five may be larger or smaller than that in column six, according to circumstances. It *happens* to be larger in the case of every State, and of each of the Territories except Arizona and Utah, (in the latter case for obvious reasons.) The mathematical proof of column

ABLE X.—*Population, as Native, Foreign-born, and of Foreign Parentage*—1870–1860–1850.

1860.			1850.				
Total population.	Native.*	Foreign-born.	Total population.	Native.*	Foreign-born.	Unknown.	
31, 443, 321	27, 304, 624	4, 138, 697	23, 191, 876	20, 912, 612	2, 244, 602	34, 662	
31, 183, 744	27, 084, 592	4, 099, 152	23, 067, 262	20, 797, 379	2, 235, 489	34, 394	
964, 201	951, 849	12, 352	771, 623	763, 089	7, 509	1, 025	1
435, 450	431, 850	3, 600	209, 897	207, 636	1, 471	790	2
379, 994	233, 466	146, 528	92, 597	70, 340	21, 802	455	3
460, 147	379, 451	80, 696	370, 792	331, 560	38, 518	714	4
112, 216	103, 051	9, 165	91, 532	86, 268	5, 253	11	5
140, 424	137, 115	3, 309	87, 445	84, 665	2, 769	11	6
1, 057, 286	1, 045, 615	11, 671	906, 185	899, 132	6, 488	565	7
1, 711, 951	1, 387, 308	324, 643	851, 470	736, 149	111, 892	3, 429	8
1, 350, 428	1, 232, 144	118, 284	988, 416	930, 458	55, 572	2, 386	9
674, 913	568, 836	106, 077	192, 214	170, 931	20, 969	314	10
107, 206	94, 515	12, 691	......	......	......	......	11
1, 155, 684	1, 095, 885	59, 799	982, 405	949, 652	31, 420	1, 333	12
708, 002	627, 027	80, 975	517, 762	448, 848	68, 233	681	13
628, 279	590, 826	37, 453	583, 169	550, 878	31, 825	466	14
687, 049	609, 520	77, 529	583, 034	531, 476	51, 209	349	15
1, 231, 066	970, 960	260, 106	994, 514	827, 430	164, 024	3, 060	16
749, 113	600, 020	149, 093	397, 654	341, 656	54, 703	1, 295	17
172, 023	113, 295	58, 728	6, 077	4, 097	1, 977	3	18
791, 305	782, 747	8, 558	606, 526	601, 230	4, 788	508	19
1, 182, 012	1, 021, 471	160, 541	682, 044	604, 522	76, 592	930	20
28, 841	22, 490	6, 351	......	......	......	......	21
6, 857	4, 793	2, 064	......	......	......	......	22
326, 073	305, 135	20, 938	317, 976	303, 563	14, 265	148	23
672, 035	549, 245	122, 790	489, 555	429, 176	59, 948	431	24
3, 880, 735	2, 879, 455	1, 001, 280	3, 097, 394	2, 436, 771	655, 929	4, 694	25
992, 622	989, 324	3, 298	869, 039	866, 241	2, 581	217	26
2, 339, 511	2, 011, 262	328, 249	1, 980, 329	1, 757, 746	218, 193	4, 390	27
52, 465	47, 342	5, 123	13, 294	12, 081	1, 022	191	28
2, 906, 215	2, 475, 710	430, 505	2, 311, 786	2, 006, 207	303, 417	2, 162	29
174, 620	137, 226	37, 394	147, 545	123, 564	23, 902	79	30
703, 708	693, 722	9, 986	668, 507	659, 743	8, 707	57	31
1, 109, 801	1, 088, 575	21, 226	1, 002, 717	995, 478	5, 653	1, 586	32
604, 215	560, 793	43, 422	212, 592	194, 433	17, 681	478	33
315, 098	282, 355	32, 743	314, 120	280, 055	33, 715	350	34
1, 219, 630	1, 201, 117	18, 513	1, 421, 661	1, 398, 205	22, 985	471	35
376, 688	360, 143	16, 545	......	......	......	......	36
775, 881	498, 954	276, 967	305, 391	194, 099	110, 477	815	37
259, 577	220, 032	39, 545	124, 614	115, 233	9, 113	268	
......	......	......	......	......	......	......	1
34, 277	31, 611	2, 666	......	......	......	......	2
4, 837	3, 063	1, 774	......	......	......	......	3
75, 080	62, 596	12, 484	51, 687	46, 720	4, 918	49	4
......	......	......	......	......	......	......	5
......	......	......	......	......	......	......	6
93, 516	86, 793	6, 723	61, 547	59, 187	2, 151	209	7
40, 273	27, 519	12, 754	11, 380	9, 326	2, 044	10	8
11, 504	8, 450	3, 144	......	......	......	......	9
......	......	......	......	......	......	......	10

our is by adding columns five and six, and subtracting column seven. The difference between column ve and column seven yields the number having foreign fathers but native mothers. The difference etween column six and column seven yields the number having foreign mothers but native fathers.

* At 1860 and 1850 the nativity of the slaves was not ascertained. In this table they are assumed to ave been native.

TABLE XI.—*Native Population, distributed according to State (or Territory) of Birth*—1870.

	Living in—	BORN IN— The United States.	Alabama.	Arkansas.	California.	Connecticut.	Delaware.	Florida.	Georgia.	Illinois.
	The United States	32, 991, 142	973, 700	287, 832	181, 835	487, 128	133, 419	124, 148	1, 308, 104	1, 479, 410
	The States	32, 642, 612	973, 235	287, 463	180, 491	485, 690	132, 931	124, 031	1, 307, 292	1, 471, 7[illegible]
1	Alabama	987, 030	744, 146	650	16	341	51	2, 764	93, 028	368
2	Arkansas	479, 445	28, 318	232, 881	73	94	43	336	25, 234	5, 679
3	California	350, 416	1, 258	2, 396	169, 904	2, 977	408	134	1, 024	10, 699
4	Connecticut	423, 815	104	5	122	350, 498	147	78	274	521
5	Delaware	115, 879	7	4	11	185	91, 734	17	94	46
6	Florida	182, 781	7, 334	71	4	235	19	109, 554	28, 058	75
7	Georgia	1, 172, 982	12, 230	356	32	588	61	4, 781	1, 033, 962	199
8	Illinois	2, 024, 693	3, 908	2, 245	861	11, 062	1, 885	106	2, 292	1, 189, 5[illegible]
9	Indiana	1, 539, 163	967	451	206	2, 134	1, 969	47	1, 728	16, 5[illegible]
10	Iowa	989, 328	390	397	473	5, 165	876	50	384	65, 391
11	Kansas	316, 007	718	2, 087	207	1, 402	307	22	789	35, 558
12	Kentucky	1, 257, 613	2, 103	980	73	392	191	60	2, 602	4, 085
13	Louisiana	665, 088	20, 446	1, 847	75	317	147	1, 497	15, 909	718
14	Maine	578, 034	23	18	108	442	22	40	72	144
15	Maryland	697, 482	144	50	90	568	6, 876	83	400	296
16	Massachusetts	1, 104, 032	176	22	451	17, 313	315	88	375	972
17	Michigan	916, 049	168	57	298	7, 412	692	57	169	6, 053
18	Minnesota	279, 009	147	65	87	2, 359	170	23	107	10, 97[illegible]
19	Mississippi	816, 731	59, 520	2, 176	55	181	66	673	28, 260	948
20	Missouri	1, 499, 028	5, 243	10, 964	707	2, 070	1, 132	176	3, 845	72, 6[illegible]
21	Nebraska	92, 245	63	85	112	699	60	10	95	9, 6[illegible]
22	Nevada	23, 690	105	103	2, 390	285	72	27	87	1, 144
23	New Hampshire	288, 689	15	5	70	617	14	5	50	191
24	New Jersey	717, 153	116	15	201	5, 448	3, 359	111	400	717
25	New York	3, 244, 406	508	86	861	38, 861	996	321	1, 381	3, 649
26	North Carolina	1, 068, 332	472	88	18	219	58	151	2, 052	77
27	Ohio	2, 292, 767	680	323	297	12, 408	2, 131	76	867	6, 27[illegible]
28	Oregon	79, 323	116	491	1, 710	262	69	9	81	4, 72[illegible]
29	Pennsylvania	2, 976, 642	257	97	328	6, 767	14, 023	113	625	2, 28[illegible]
30	Rhode Island	161, 957	28	1	71	5, 524	197	25	91	139
31	South Carolina	697, 532	363	30	8	240	29	265	2, 884	32
32	Tennessee	1, 239, 204	20, 217	2, 977	49	328	78	122	18, 021	2, 461
33	Texas	756, 168	62, 224	23, 357	163	367	106	1, 931	41, 206	5, 5[illegible]
34	Vermont	283, 596	17	5	70	1, 613	15	12	32	306
35	Virginia	1, 211, 409	456	89	29	417	534	111	539	202
36	West Virginia	424, 923	34	31	19	166	186	10	75	330
37	Wisconsin	690, 171	205	52	214	5, 711	272	28	186	12, 234
	The Territories	348, 530	465	369	1, 342	1, 438	488	117	812	7, 624
1	Arizona	3, 849	28	32	156	30	10	3	24	115
2	Colorado	33, 265	58	90	73	210	27	8	258	1, 818
3	Dakota	9, 366	9	5	8	67	17	5	16	635
4	District of Columbia	115, 446	100	17	62	507	292	54	264	264
5	Idaho	7, 114	26	21	225	59	5	5	23	405
6	Montana	12, 616	35	28	81	131	23	14	73	575
7	New Mexico	86, 254	30	43	23	28	11	4	22	128
8	Utah	56, 084	145	21	308	234	69	11	92	2, 105
9	Washington	18, 931	13	98	412	121	19	5	36	265
10	Wyoming	5, 605	21	11	16	51	15	8	19	404

ABLE XI.—*Native Population, distributed according to State (or Territory) of Birth*—1870.

BORN IN—											
Indiana.	Iowa.	Kansas.	Kentucky.	Louisiana.	Maine.	Maryland.	Massachusetts.	Michigan.	Minnesota.	Mississippi.	
1,369,411	517,631	74,090	1,484,207	564,997	699,834	805,548	1,147,077	572,988	139,031	702,684	
1,365,757	511,863	73,555	1,481,200	564,534	696,742	782,890	1,143,394	571,273	138,288	702,304	
278	38	15	2,580	1,753	185	2,209	370	87	19	10,149	1
2,954	656	458	13,671	4,909	142	1,058	226	212	35	22,082	2
5,190	5,367	279	6,605	1,979	11,261	2,596	15,334	3,032	461	995	3
152	122	29	133	167	1,988	701	17,871	305	66	44	4
37	11	....	20	24	81	7,146	331	19	4	10	5
47	19	11	226	368	261	582	464	35	8	612	6
145	20	21	951	426	262	1,580	635	60	11	1,319	7
86,807	11,384	1,021	67,702	2,272	8,780	12,588	22,156	9,428	1,179	2,607	8
1,048,575	3,473	500	76,524	785	1,215	8,524	3,490	5,694	388	654	9
64,083	428,690	791	14,186	496	5,943	5,972	8,929	8,918	2,683	620	10
30,953	13,073	63,321	15,918	408	1,837	2,067	2,894	4,466	708	529	11
11,687	330	101	1,081,081	1,211	337	3,064	792	243	58	1,775	12
681	69	27	8,320	501,864	428	6,486	885	104	160	31,628	13
40	49	13	34	73	[illegible]	143	11,139	60	95	16	14
194	70	16	269	337	924	629,882	1,212	95	13	164	15
236	260	53	245	346	[illegible]	1,593	903,296	502	186	66	16
12,140	1,486	172	1,719	196	[illegible]	1,265	10,839	507,268	487	101	17
7,438	3,970	51	1,743	185	9,939	719	5,731	3,742	126,491	194	18
575	106	17	8,927	9,417	152	3,250	274	122	10	564,142	19
51,301	22,456	4,940	102,801	4,045	2,316	7,619	5,731	4,570	1,127	3,484	20
6,040	7,611	497	1,873	86	906	649	1,277	1,842	346	135	21
530	492	11	603	195	1,083	298	907	389	24	67	22
32	57	7	50	25	11,404	84	16,510	89	56	18	23
321	179	23	278	342	1,948	3,384	6,068	526	78	93	24
1,256	887	135	1,083	1,375	5,985	5,700	41,355	4,850	417	379	25
95	15	2	259	70	109	481	288	26	3	334	26
17,382	2,837	277	26,230	1,157	2,686	23,292	13,390	6,348	372	890	27
3,451	3,695	211	2,387	98	676	330	746	466	166	79	28
1,440	952	160	1,375	572	3,071	28,910	9,119	1,485	265	272	29
45	24	6	47	27	1,875	687	18,719	66	15	15	30
24	7	2	106	87	118	358	325	16	2	221	31
1,835	259	100	19,867	1,302	218	1,580	566	355	96	15,451	32
2,783	546	193	17,813	27,290	338	2,385	623	220	69	42,537	33
49	69	7	64	29	1,251	78	9,202	162	56	14	34
132	39	20	1,586	294	224	7,344	753	119	6	319	35
408	178	14	2,288	73	176	7,323	453	50	25	39	36
6,414	2,423	114	1,585	190	8,931	1,013	10,403	5,302	2,103	194	37
3,654	5,768	535	2,098	463	3,092	22,658	3,783	1,715	743	380	
69	41	7	107	35	56	52	117	31	1	16	1
809	1,310	269	722	34	362	197	621	528	77	41	2
258	1,044	23	121	13	158	87	143	171	361	9	3
308	115	24	263	173	674	21,751	1,254	220	64	96	4
252	312	22	243	27	242	69	199	69	8	18	5
473	468	63	528	51	333	142	205	218	121	34	6
86	36	28	143	24	68	67	85	32	7	11	7
399	1,492	33	317	27	239	55	492	222	30	125	8
806	749	34	402	59	859	102	399	114	63	17	9
194	201	32	152	20	101	134	178	104	8	13	10

TABLE XI.—*Native Population, distributed according to State (or Territory) of Birth—1870*—Continued.

	Living in—	BORN IN—								
		Missouri.	Nebraska.	Nevada.	New Hampshire.	New Jersey.	New York.	North Carolina.	Ohio.	Oregon.
	The United States	1,045,268	23,234	4,886	367,346	724,075	4,061,348	1,336,040	2,649,296	41,38[illegible]
	The States	1,038,954	22,469	4,810	366,142	722,289	4,044,985	1,334,915	2,640,830	41,29[illegible]
1	Alabama	516	2	......	119	232	1,539	30,290	682	1
2	Arkansas	16,838	27	1	47	152	1,400	18,461	2,209	1
3	California	16,050	237	1,086	2,720	2,598	33,766	1,630	12,735	2,48[illegible]
4	Connecticut	104	6	1	1,688	2,694	29,604	440	928	[illegible]
5	Delaware	32	......	......	56	2,039	1,311	49	132	......
6	Florida	64	5	......	91	132	1,050	6,717	128	......
7	Georgia	227	2	2	141	377	2,243	26,858	366	1
8	Illinois	30,873	208	43	8,213	16,336	133,494	13,169	163,012	19[illegible]
9	Indiana	3,435	109	5	1,011	6,672	20,518	24,790	189,339	60[illegible]
10	Iowa	13,831	874	63	5,066	5,688	73,143	5,090	126,285	16[illegible]
11	Kansas	29,775	639	32	1,158	1,845	18,558	3,612	38,205	9[illegible]
12	Kentucky	4,551	40	35	229	747	4,309	12,877	19,333	16
13	Louisiana	2,925	10	......	137	368	3,913	7,283	1,499	......
14	Maine	23	1	5	9,753	162	1,450	53	160	......
15	Maryland	259	5	1	198	1,853	3,890	993	1,169	1
16	Massachusetts	210	8	6	47,773	1,893	24,658	673	1,457	2[illegible]
17	Michigan	666	36	12	3,633	8,033	231,509	908	62,207	7[illegible]
18	Minnesota	1,447	44	11	3,271	1,348	39,507	438	12,651	2[illegible]
19	Mississippi	2,410	6	......	73	150	1,458	27,941	1,171	4
20	Missouri	874,006	1,225	33	1,384	3,200	31,805	13,755	76,062	9[illegible]
21	Nebraska	4,650	18,530	8	418	633	9,246	341	10,729	1[illegible]
22	Nevada	1,053	19	3,356	289	331	3,265	109	1,858	7[illegible]
23	New Hampshire	37	2	......	242,374	121	2,499	28	212	2
24	New Jersey	267	9	1	1,202	575,245	74,750	400	1,868	1[illegible]
25	New York	912	47	23	9,211	32,408	2,987,776	1,439	7,512	4[illegible]
26	North Carolina	66	1	......	60	261	789	1,028,678	140	......
27	Ohio	2,109	76	9	3,329	13,229	67,594	4,891	1,842,313	3[illegible]
28	Oregon	7,061	152	36	219	268	3,692	457	4,031	37,15[illegible]
29	Pennsylvania	787	41	13	1,858	36,694	87,876	1,002	19,295	2[illegible]
30	Rhode Island	26	14	1	1,242	504	3,932	103	202	......
31	South Carolina	16	......	......	35	93	945	8,282	95	......
32	Tennessee	3,262	10	......	164	405	3,002	51,110	4,320	1[illegible]
33	Texas	18,419	24	7	187	406	2,873	18,655	2,052	2[illegible]
34	Vermont	41	5	2	13,540	193	11,207	25	310	1[illegible]
35	Virginia	264	5	......	270	1,373	4,908	16,868	541	9
36	West Virginia	362	2	2	100	342	1,350	852	12,164	5
37	Wisconsin	1,386	48	13	4,908	3,194	105,697	618	23,164	3[illegible]
	The Territories	6,314	765	76	1,203	1,786	16,363	1,125	8,466	2,0[illegible]
1	Arizona	121	3	......	32	42	481	23	235	6
2	Colorado	1,704	181	8	139	177	2,778	200	2,057	5
3	Dakota	149	59	......	73	76	1,273	40	635	1
4	District of Columbia	102	14	3	473	814	4,597	426	1,042	13
5	Idaho	536	27	3	54	49	804	45	550	348
6	Montana	1,305	56	14	101	118	1,683	56	1,127	97
7	New Mexico	164	7	......	18	40	415	14	274	3
8	Utah	908	272	27	165	322	2,247	215	1,193	4
9	Washington	946	26	10	96	89	1,097	71	866	1,67[illegible]
10	Wyoming	913	117	13	52	60	988	35	547	1

TABLE XI.—*Native Population, distributed according to State (or Territory) of Birth*—1870—Continued.

BORN IN—												
Pennsylvania.	Rhode Island.	South Carolina.	Tennessee.	Texas.	Vermont.	Virginia, and West Virginia.	Wisconsin.	The Territories.	Alaska.	Arizona.	Colorado.	
3, 401, 256	170, 640	924, 774	1, 431, 349	414, 100	420, 978	2, 120, 213	547, 223	231, 129	51	1, 640	7, 579	
3, 390, 451	170, 201	924, 272	1, 429, 767	413, 294	419, 060	2, 103, 353	545, 004	23, 720	40	285	954	
727	39	42, 972	19, 797	640	128	29, 636	55	235	......	......	1	1
1, 147	73	13, 807	66, 565	6, 619	144	11, 851	159	534	......	......	9	2
11, 208	1, 418	851	4, 686	1, 887	3, 500	5, 293	3, 086	2, 067	28	93	60	3
2, 304	7, 897	225	85	47	2, 646	1, 214	234	235	......	......	5	4
8, 764	59	39	27	4	66	450	17	82	......	......	......	5
312	83	22, 116	611	69	122	3, 121	35	84	......	......	......	6
852	151	54, 937	9, 394	253	167	19, 034	45	216	......	......	6	7
98, 614	2, 416	3, 000	47, 524	965	18, 515	35, 743	12, 772	935	......	2	85	8
57, 291	402	2, 170	12, 276	267	2, 987	32, 789	1, 233	362	......	......	14	9
73, 435	914	566	6, 085	235	12, 204	19, 563	24, 309	983	2	3	190	10
19, 287	364	404	6, 209	975	2, 370	9, 906	4, 128	1, 048	4	2	154	11
6, 205	129	2, 204	49, 952	940	261	44, 121	143	188	......	......	1	12
1, 698	102	10, 838	6, 864	4, 713	208	30, 033	114	390	......	......	......	13
396	473	69	20	18	1, 264	329	146	71	......	......	3	14
22, 846	197	579	231	76	243	20, 237	64	3, 229	......	......	......	15
3, 257	14, 356	532	181	72	22, 180	3, 438	521	455	1	2	2	16
28, 507	1, 137	220	687	65	14, 445	2, 984	5, 986	215	......	1	19	17
11, 966	564	80	320	47	6, 815	1, 812	24, 048	385	......	154	10	18
855	46	35, 956	31, 804	1, 145	126	33, 551	122	275	......	......	1	19
35, 384	644	2, 831	70, 212	3, 387	2, 961	51, 306	6, 282	1, 232	1	2	162	20
6, 991	150	81	852	65	1, 050	2, 036	3, 756	633	......	1	90	21
1, 458	131	73	324	73	419	541	330	1, 085	......	1	17	22
307	509	40	32	8	12, 837	186	108	45	1	......	1	23
31, 947	879	494	152	99	1, 390	2, 810	364	434	......	1	1	24
36, 170	6, 993	1, 830	566	232	36, 307	7, 071	2, 555	1, 290	1	2	9	25
674	55	13, 537	3, 505	142	65	15, 425	12	91	......	......	......	26
149, 784	1, 127	1, 135	3, 732	244	9, 055	72, 950	1, 868	736	......	3	13	27
1, 930	72	110	1, 544	86	432	1, 447	434	996	1	4	30	28
2, 726, 712	1, 586	1, 119	669	135	4, 163	18, 936	898	1, 545	......	1	29	29
921	125, 269	101	11	7	941	683	111	203	......	......	2	30
361	97	678, 708	304	57	46	3, 254	11	63	......	......	......	31
4, 074	63	13, 854	261, 347	896	194	43, 397	245	276	1	2	4	32
1, 877	98	17, 717	51, 435	388, 510	248	22, 165	183	871	......	11	4	33
289	374	30	12	8	243, 814	163	235	27	......	......	1	34
4, 046	95	777	4, 117	216	193	1, 163, 822	85	1, 449	......	......	1	35
15, 497	57	100	280	31	149	381, 297	38	250	......	......	1	36
21, 358	1, 152	150	1, 079	61	16, 421	2, 059	450, 272	299	......	......	29	37
10, 805	439	502	1, 582	805	1, 909	25, 860	2, 219	207, 409	11	1, 355	6, 625	
275	16	16	65	114	96	95	18	1, 353	......	1, 240	3	1
1, 532	86	32	287	137	370	520	634	14, 883	......	......	6, 344	2
667	38	9	49	8	200	186	608	2, 141	......	......	3	3
4, 223	136	268	188	61	429	23, 596	119	52, 374	......	......	2	4
416	16	18	109	27	75	175	118	1, 515	......	......	6	5
911	30	36	176	13	185	376	256	2, 147	......	......	99	6
292	15	9	53	284	37	114	17	83, 626	......	100	43	7
1, 315	28	76	405	104	325	287	117	41, 583	......	5	41	8
527	54	28	196	45	163	310	203	7, 149	11	......	18	9
627	20	10	54	13	99	201	129	638	......	1	66	10

TABLE XI.—*Native Population, distributed according to State (or Territory) of birth*—18[70]—Continued.

	Living in—	BORN IN—									
		Dakota.	District of Columbia.	Idaho.	Indian.	Montana.	New Mexico.	Utah.	Washington.	Wyoming.	Not stated, and at sea under United States flag.
	The United States	2, 458	67, 547	1, 499	2, 263	2, 197	92, 286	45, 100	7, 974	535	12, 4[illegible]
	The States	318	14, 982	421	1, 946	374	576	2, 743	945	136	12, 1[illegible]
1	Alabama	......	227	2	1	......	1	3	......	......	37
2	Arkansas	......	81	6	424	3	5	6	......	......	13
3	California	7	458	84	19	65	175	850	207	21	1, 2[illegible]
4	Connecticut	1	216	......	1	3	6	......	3	......	13
5	Delaware	......	79	......	1	......	......	......	2	......	
6	Florida	......	82	1	1	......	......	......	......	......	
7	Georgia	......	200	......	2	1	......	1	5	1	7
8	Illinois	11	724	17	15	20	21	30	6	4	76
9	Indiana	5	295	......	22	4	5	3	9	5	23
10	Iowa	97	174	22	16	51	20	378	21	9	43
11	Kansas	17	204	12	456	37	69	75	11	7	13
12	Kentucky	1	171	......	3	......	4	4	2	2	5
13	Louisiana	......	573	......	17	......	......	......	......	......	22
14	Maine	......	59	......	......	4	2	1	2	......	46
15	Maryland	1	3, 211	......	7	......	7	3	......	......	24
16	Massachusetts	......	422	......	9	......	4	2	9	4	38
17	Michigan	7	157	......	6	3	7	8	4	3	11
18	Minnesota	82	104	1	2	16	2	4	......	10	8
19	Mississippi	......	254	......	16	2	1	1	......	......	77
20	Missouri	33	599	49	97	54	70	151	4	10	80
21	Nebraska	26	78	22	189	22	7	156	2	40	2
22	Nevada	2	38	34	......	21	9	954	7	2	1
23	New Hampshire	......	34	......	3	......	......	5	1	......	4
24	New Jersey	......	413	2	7	......	4	4	1	1	21
25	New York	6	1, 232	1	2	2	20	11	2	2	1, 93
26	North Carolina	......	83	......	5	1	......	1	1	......	1
27	Ohio	5	676	2	10	6	13	3	3	2	67
28	Oregon	......	36	154	51	47	1	56	606	10	3
29	Pennsylvania	4	1, 462	1	17	4	3	6	18	......	64
30	Rhode Island	......	193	......	......	......	4	2	2	......	13
31	South Carolina	......	61	......	1	......	......	......	1	......	4
32	Tennessee	......	221	......	43	......	2	1	1	1	12
33	Texas	4	250	2	486	......	110	4	6	......	41
34	Vermont	......	26	......	......	......	......	......	......	......	[illegible]
35	Virginia	......	1, 436	......	8	......	1	......	2	1	7
36	West Virginia	......	240	......	5	1	......	3	......	......	15
37	Wisconsin	9	213	9	4	7	3	17	7	1	66
	The Territories	2, 140	52, 565	1, 078	317	1, 823	91, 710	42, 357	7, 029	399	32
1	Arizona	......	16	......	......	......	93	1	......	......	......
2	Colorado	4	20	3	1	12	8, 378	67	......	54	24
3	Dakota	2, 088	30	......	3	4	7	4	1	1	1
4	District of Columbia	3	52, 340	......	4	......	11	3	9	2	10
5	Idaho	1	14	946	1	13	1	479	53	1	1
6	Montana	6	62	38	2	1, 683	7	194	28	18	12
7	New Mexico	......	19	......	265	......	83, 175	15	......	......	......
8	Utah	......	9	7	20	37	9	41, 426	2	27	12
9	Washington	2	18	82	1	51	......	31	6, 932	3	11
10	Wyoming	36	37	2	29	13	29	137	4	283	......

[.—*Native White Population, distributed according to State (or Territory) of Birth*—1870.

ng in—	BORN IN—								
	The United States.	Alabama.	Arkansas.	California.	Connecticut.	Delaware.	Florida.	Georgia.	Illinois.
'uited States	28, 095, 665	522, 306	212, 973	173, 792	479, 391	106, 581	61, 568	719, 124	1, 469, 524
States	27, 796, 017	521, 934	212, 630	172, 499	477, 973	106, 114	61, 465	718, 472	1, 461, 928
t...........	511, 718	369, 635	481	15	336	35	1, 956	62, 513	358
s...........	357, 230	20, 883	170, 308	73	94	41	148	18, 080	5, 833
ia..........	339, 199	1, 221	2, 330	162, 003	2, 934	356	119	960	10, 666
cut........	414, 015	92	5	121	341, 254	92	58	214	521
e...........	93, 101	7	3	9	183	74, 540	8	11	44
....	91, 395	5, 142	32	3	233	14	52, 594	17, 900	73
....	628, 173	7, 787	220	31	576	47	2, 667	530, 577	193
....	1, 996, 114	2, 930	1, 918	856	11, 047	1, 871	95	1, 963	1, 181, 106
....	1, 514, 410	812	420	206	2, 131	1, 958	37	1, 580	16, 389
....	983, 543	277	288	472	5, 184	868	55	305	65, 261
....	298, 041	550	1, 104	203	1, 397	302	24	661	35, 454
ty	1, 035, 346	1, 780	888	73	391	180	47	2, 302	3, 960
ia..........	301, 450	10, 708	2, 111	72	305	117	671	7, 874	649
....	576, 097	22	13	108	439	19	35	50	144
d...........	522, 238	111	48	85	555	6, 520	69	278	293
usetts......	1, 090, 843	150	18	446	16, 971	247	57	253	962
n...........	900, 630	72	44	296	7, 382	620	37	102	5, 983
ta..........	277, 570	101	51	87	2, 356	169	23	94	10, 962
ppi.........	371, 915	37, 327	1, 160	49	170	53	348	15, 546	874
....	1, 380, 972	4, 421	9, 846	700	2, 061	1, 106	129	3, 379	72, 324
a...........	91, 376	52	79	112	697	59	9	78	9, 638
....	23, 392	97	100	2, 360	275	71	26	84	1, 141
mpshire	288, 117	15	5	70	617	13	4	30	191
sey.........	686, 589	94	14	195	5, 369	1, 732	82	317	715
rk..........	3, 193, 160	451	79	855	38, 309	710	264	1, 110	3, 633
arolina.....	675, 490	290	75	18	218	53	102	1, 702	74
....	2, 229, 782	272	174	290	12, 370	2, 091	46	434	6, 203
....	78, 711	113	491	1, 649	261	65	9	79	4, 720
vania.......	2, 911, 750	210	85	321	6, 723	10, 879	86	428	2, 263
sland.......	156, 927	21	1	66	5, 312	105	17	75	129
irolina......	281, 894	241	26	7	225	26	111	1, 668	32
ee..........	916, 930	13, 849	2, 120	42	326	68	149	11, 186	2, 399
....	503, 216	41, 663	17, 738	156	353	87	1, 248	26, 396	5, 794
t...........	282, 492	16	4	70	1, 603	15	11	26	267
....	698, 388	381	85	27	412	521	88	377	200
irginia......	406, 951	22	31	19	165	185	9	62	329
in..........	626, 903	109	46	244	5, 703	261	27	160	12, 152
Territories..	299, 618	372	343	1, 293	1, 418	467	103	652	7, 596
....	3, 803	27	29	152	30	10	3	21	115
....	32, 635	43	79	52	210	25	6	240	1, 805
....	8, 275	5	5	8	67	17	5	13	633
of Columbia	72, 107	49	11	60	492	273	45	136	256
....	7, 018	26	21	201	50	5	5	23	399
....	12, 288	34	27	78	130	29	12	71	797
xico........	84, 786	21	11	20	22	11	4	15	122
....	55, 792	138	19	306	232	69	11	88	2, 105
gton........	17, 585	13	98	397	119	19	4	21	965
g...........	5, 350	11	10	16	31	15	8	15	399

TABLE XII.—*Native White Population, distributed according to State (or Territory) of Birth*—1870—Continued.

	Living in—	Born in— Indiana.	Iowa.	Kansas.	Kentucky.	Louisiana.	Maine.	Maryland.	Massachusetts.
	The United States	1,356,938	513,896	69,494	1,211,888	277,136	698,483	593,513	1,138,492
	The States	1,353,298	510,144	68,970	1,209,123	276,750	695,399	582,618	1,134,771
1	Alabama	271	37	15	1,632	1,107	177	471	351
2	Arkansas	2,931	652	442	10,392	2,851	140	405	217
3	California	5,180	5,361	275	6,434	1,887	11,244	2,271	15,213
4	Connecticut	151	120	20	110	120	1,980	377	17,502
5	Delaware	36	11	......	18	17	84	5,291	325
6	Florida	38	19	11	118	236	258	205	434
7	Georgia	140	20	18	671	249	256	544	645
8	Illinois	86,422	12,312	999	63,297	1,876	8,771	12,185	22,111
9	Indiana	1,038,542	3,472	494	67,133	696	1,215	8,421	3,478
10	Iowa	64,006	427,224	781	13,536	461	5,942	5,900	8,912
11	Kansas	30,775	12,990	50,062	13,558	310	1,833	1,946	2,887
12	Kentucky	11,604	330	100	875,415	1,003	329	2,658	779
13	Louisiana	639	67	22	2,315	237,453	405	1,001	825
14	Maine	39	49	13	26	52	549,650	108	11,091
15	Maryland	185	70	16	222	287	422	462,438	1,182
16	Massachusetts	234	260	53	208	286	55,460	840	896,372
17	Michigan	11,357	1,478	162	675	149	3,922	1,062	10,803
18	Minnesota	7,423	3,956	50	1,667	170	9,938	711	5,736
19	Mississippi	546	103	14	3,067	4,598	137	573	263
20	Missouri	51,219	22,383	4,783	92,607	3,112	2,312	6,945	5,694
21	Nebraska	6,035	7,605	481	1,782	79	906	632	1,277
22	Nevada	519	492	11	585	182	1,079	253	988
23	New Hampshire	32	57	7	47	23	11,389	69	16,486
24	New Jersey	318	179	23	255	307	1,941	1,891	6,008
25	New York	1,243	886	134	936	1,235	5,964	3,675	41,062
26	North Carolina	92	15	2	218	44	107	334	278
27	Ohio	16,912	2,824	269	16,480	842	2,679	22,643	13,330
28	Oregon	3,448	3,694	211	2,372	93	676	313	734
29	Pennsylvania	1,426	948	94	1,226	466	3,054	22,384	9,019
30	Rhode Island	39	28	3	38	18	1,837	157	18,522
31	South Carolina	23	6	2	81	37	112	193	303
32	Tennessee	1,794	253	88	13,874	773	210	933	542
33	Texas	2,730	541	155	12,849	15,235	322	965	598
34	Vermont	49	69	7	61	19	1,244	48	9,155
35	Virginia	152	39	20	1,322	253	281	5,665	736
36	West Virginia	408	178	14	2,218	51	176	7,100	432
37	Wisconsin	6,340	2,416	110	1,458	171	8,930	991	10,391
	The Territories	3,640	5,752	524	2,765	383	3,084	10,895	3,721
1	Arizona	69	41	7	107	35	56	51	116
2	Colorado	808	1,308	263	656	28	362	187	618
3	Dakota	255	1,038	23	116	12	158	85	148
4	District of Columbia	303	113	23	185	115	671	10,030	1,294
5	Idaho	252	311	22	236	26	242	65	196
6	Montana	471	466	61	503	44	331	137	293
7	New Mexico	80	36	28	120	21	68	64	85
8	Utah	298	1,490	33	311	27	239	54	492
9	Washington	806	749	34	401	57	857	96	306
10	Wyoming	192	200	30	130	18	100	126	178

XII.—*Native White Population, distributed according to State (or Territory) of Birth*—1870—Continued.

BORN IN—											
Minnesota.	Mississippi.	Missouri.	Nebraska.	Nevada.	New Hampshire.	New Jersey.	New York.	North Carolina.	Ohio.	Oregon.	
137,899	325,319	936,564	23,065	4,831	366,778	697,821	4,016,326	866,416	2,615,264	42,916	
137,365	324,992	930,515	22,333	4,755	365,576	696,059	4,000,141	865,629	2,606,884	40,844	
19	5,717	305	2	......	115	228	1,514	14,256	656	1	1
33	15,058	15,082	25	1	47	150	1,382	13,252	2,092	1	2
461	921	15,759	235	1,083	2,719	2,555	33,526	1,535	12,705	2,452	3
66	36	99	6	1	1,681	2,515	28,728	145	920	7	4
4	9	30	......	......	56	1,959	1,290	29	140	......	5
8	352	47	4	......	91	185	1,015	2,908	122	......	6
11	518	169	2	......	139	367	2,208	19,789	349	1	7
1,171	1,768	26,824	205	43	8,209	16,305	133,290	12,575	162,623	188	8
387	465	3,312	169	5	1,006	6,666	29,486	23,442	188,670	594	9
2,677	431	12,279	867	63	5,031	5,684	79,091	4,982	126,161	165	10
701	387	23,829	633	31	1,157	1,842	18,526	3,192	38,003	98	11
57	1,367	4,023	40	35	229	738	4,270	11,916	19,359	9	12
67	13,791	1,312	10	......	134	345	3,735	2,046	1,313	......	13
95	14	21	1	5	9,730	155	1,421	19	160	......	14
13	122	245	5	1	187	1,816	3,783	696	1,130	1	15
186	50	197	8	6	47,692	1,790	24,031	207	1,385	27	16
480	49	538	34	12	3,632	7,987	231,062	491	61,039	71	17
125,759	149	1,359	91	11	3,271	1,346	39,485	405	12,618	21	18
9	214,236	845	5	......	68	142	1,397	13,430	1,073	4	19
1,114	2,106	728,491	1,221	32	1,381	3,188	31,736	17,644	75,560	95	20
346	117	4,363	18,425	8	418	633	9,241	323	10,709	14	21
24	66	1,035	19	3,313	289	328	3,247	99	1,850	70	22
56	17	37	2	......	212,044	121	2,493	15	212	2	23
78	84	258	9	1	1,195	552,795	73,568	220	1,831	14	24
416	334	887	47	23	9,196	30,941	2,948,883	775	7,426	41	25
3[illegible]	117	56	1	......	60	256	766	648,245	124	......	26
358	374	1,921	76	9	3,317	13,180	67,379	2,065	1,813,069	28	27
166	77	7,032	151	36	219	266	3,070	149	4,029	36,824	28
260	218	763	40	11	1,848	35,213	87,200	502	19,087	20	29
14	9	22	14	1	1,237	432	3,669	38	195	......	30
......	98	11	......	......	35	89	929	5,685	78	......	31
85	6,885	2,511	9	......	163	395	2,960	41,213	4,272	16	32
66	28,639	14,948	23	7	164	386	2,812	11,233	1,961	19	33
56	11	40	5	2	13,519	189	11,235	13	308	10	34
6	233	248	5	......	269	1,361	4,854	10,495	514	5	35
25	31	353	2	2	100	342	1,355	762	12,042	8	36
2,098	106	1,261	47	13	4,908	3,169	105,495	448	23,070	38	37
534	327	6,049	732	76	1,202	1,762	16,185	817	8,380	2,072	
1	16	121	3	......	32	42	480	21	235	4	1
77	32	1,595	184	8	139	177	2,771	188	2,045	4	2
168	9	141	35	......	73	76	1,270	35	633	1	3
64	61	144	11	2	173	793	4,466	151	991	13	4
8	18	533	27	3	54	49	800	44	549	346	5
111	33	1,252	55	13	100	118	1,676	54	1,125	83	6
6	9	146	7	......	18	39	411	10	270	5	7
28	118	901	271	27	165	322	2,242	210	1,125	4	8
63	17	936	25	10	96	86	1,026	71	866	1,610	9
8	11	280	111	13	52	60	983	33	541	1	10

TABLE XII.—*Native White Population, distributed according to State (or Territory) of Birth*—1870—Continued.

	Living in—	BORN IN— Pennsylvania.	Rhode Island.	South Carolina.	Tennessee.	Texas.	Vermont.	Virginia, and West Virginia.	Wisconsin.
	The United States	3,351,722	167,459	418,875	1,106,318	273,903	420,023	1,389,568	545,28[illegible]
	The States	3,341,153	167,032	418,514	1,104,843	273,133	418,125	1,380,668	543,07[illegible]
1	Alabama	695	39	26,909	15,588	418	125	5,412	54
2	Arkansas	1,110	71	8,770	54,999	5,136	142	4,983	15[illegible]
3	California	11,041	1,409	784	4,575	1,866	3,433	4,847	3,0[illegible]
4	Connecticut	2,109	7,805	159	64	46	2,631	439	2[illegible]
5	Delaware	8,444	58	31	6	2	66	262	17
6	Florida	268	72	7,761	370	54	117	576	3[illegible]
7	Georgia	829	143	36,708	8,301	202	164	4,390	4[illegible]
8	Illinois	98,352	2,427	2,701	44,012	913	18,501	31,668	12,[illegible]
9	Indiana	57,224	401	1,990	11,597	260	2,986	31,383	1,2[illegible]
10	Iowa	73,361	914	509	5,779	225	12,195	19,032	24,2[illegible]
11	Kansas	19,220	363	330	5,512	796	2,309	8,763	4,0[illegible]
12	Kentucky	6,130	127	1,893	41,390	883	261	37,171	14[illegible]
13	Louisiana	1,541	94	3,789	2,737	2,374	303	2,359	10[illegible]
14	Maine	386	471	52	11	18	1,250	136	14[illegible]
15	Maryland	22,434	188	430	163	53	241	14,613	6[illegible]
16	Massachusetts	2,939	14,167	308	142	70	22,110	1,124	51[illegible]
17	Michigan	28,211	1,132	103	344	65	14,434	1,721	5,9[illegible]
18	Minnesota	11,945	564	68	276	45	6,811	1,731	24,0[illegible]
19	Mississippi	786	41	19,332	18,520	712	113	5,838	9[illegible]
20	Missouri	35,113	635	2,414	66,352	2,889	2,956	52,297	6,2[illegible]
21	Nebraska	6,964	150	65	809	65	1,049	1,936	3,7[illegible]
22	Nevada	1,436	131	64	315	70	419	494	2[illegible]
23	New Hampshire	303	509	19	26	8	12,923	92	10[illegible]
24	New Jersey	31,397	871	362	128	95	1,389	1,323	36[illegible]
25	New York	34,771	6,900	1,328	477	219	36,177	3,612	2,54[illegible]
26	North Carolina	637	54	8,695	3,274	127	53	9,260	1[illegible]
27	Ohio	148,792	1,114	726	1,908	283	9,034	59,047	1,65[illegible]
28	Oregon	1,919	72	108	1,537	83	432	1,417	43[illegible]
29	Pennsylvania	2,624,965	1,571	576	507	129	4,153	10,766	89[illegible]
30	Rhode Island	738	122,626	67	11	5	938	166	11[illegible]
31	South Carolina	339	86	270,301	244	38	42	729	1[illegible]
32	Tennessee	3,984	62	9,801	766,997	691	192	27,302	2[illegible]
33	Texas	1,762	95	10,559	39,849	254,091	215	8,480	17[illegible]
34	Vermont	983	373	15	9	7	243,272	37	2[illegible]
35	Virginia	3,992	92	551	3,830	185	193	639,230	8[illegible]
36	West Virginia	15,412	57	63	260	31	149	364,086	3[illegible]
37	Wisconsin	21,301	1,148	120	924	59	16,416	1,846	448,74[illegible]
	The Territories	10,569	427	361	1,475	770	1,898	8,900	2,2[illegible]
1	Arizona	273	16	16	62	113	96	91	1[illegible]
2	Colorado	1,532	86	27	256	129	370	467	6[illegible]
3	Dakota	667	38	6	46	7	199	154	60[illegible]
4	District of Columbia	4,027	124	142	137	48	423	6,810	11[illegible]
5	Idaho	415	16	17	109	26	75	166	11[illegible]
6	Montana	897	30	33	171	13	185	330	2[illegible]
7	New Mexico	291	15	8	48	276	36	102	1[illegible]
8	Utah	1,313	28	76	403	103	322	284	11[illegible]
9	Washington	523	54	28	194	41	163	298	2[illegible]
10	Wyoming	611	20	8	48	11	99	160	1[illegible]

TABLE XII.—*Native White Population, distributed according to State (or Territory) of Birth*—1870—Continued.

	BORN IN—													
The Territories.	Alaska.	Arizona.	Colorado.	Dakota.	District of Columbia.	Idaho.	Indian.	Montana.	New Mexico.	Utah.	Washington.	Wyoming.	Not stated, and at sea under United States flag.	
118,393	38	1,515	7,489	1,626	50,503	1,431	1,044	2,071	91,128	44,824	6,869	483	9,372	
28,205	33	277	941	274	11,419	390	1,000	362	550	2,720	921	132	9,186	
189	......	......	1	......	69	2	1	......	1	3	......	......	112	1
350	......	......	9	......	32	5	182	3	5	6	......	......	108	2
2,586	23	89	60	7	363	80	17	65	175	841	204	21	639	3
166	......	......	5	1	103	......	1	3	6	......	3	......	44	4
75	......	......	......	......	71	......	1	......	......	......	2	......	1	5
47	......	......	......	......	45	1	......	......	......	......	......	......	1	6
167	......	......	6	......	113	......	2	1	......	1	4	1	39	7
1,568	......	2	85	11	624	17	10	19	19	30	6	4	741	8
552	......	......	14	5	267	......	22	4	5	3	9	4	219	9
1,394	2	3	186	89	167	22	16	51	18	378	21	9	432	10
764	2	2	151	17	181	12	87	35	65	73	11	6	122	11
211	......	......	1	1	143	......	3	......	4	4	2	2	49	12
167	......	......	......	......	114	......	8	......	......	......	......	......	45	13
70	......	......	3	......	39	......	......	4	2	1	2	......	19	14
3,148	......	......	......	1	2,888	......	7	......	7	3	......	......	242	15
572	1	2	2	......	230	......	9	......	4	2	9	3	310	16
343	......	1	19	4	109	......	6	3	5	8	4	2	182	17
445	......	154	10	53	98	1	2	15	2	4	......	10	96	18
300	......	......	1	......	46	......	4	1	1	......	......	......	247	19
2,031	1	2	160	30	546	44	74	50	58	131	4	10	901	20
626	......	1	90	26	70	11	189	22	7	154	2	40	14	21
1,084	......	1	16	2	32	34	......	21	8	947	7	2	14	22
78	1	......	1	......	29	......	2	......	......	5	1	......	39	23
563	......	1	1	......	337	2	6	......	4	4	1	1	206	24
2,760	1	2	9	5	843	1	2	2	19	11	2	2	1,861	25
72	......	......	......	......	55	......	5	1	......	1	1	......	9	26
1,212	......	3	13	5	529	2	7	5	13	3	2	2	628	27
995	1	4	30	......	30	141	51	46	1	55	590	10	33	28
1,851	......	1	29	4	1,163	1	14	4	3	6	16	......	610	29
181	......	......	2	......	48	......	......	......	3	2	1	......	125	30
72	......	......	......	......	37	......	1	......	......	......	1	......	33	31
193	1	1	4	......	125	......	14	......	2	1	1	1	43	32
697	......	8	1	4	119	2	244	......	109	3	6	......	201	33
27	......	......	1	......	19	......	......	......	......	......	......	......	7	34
1,364	......	......	1	......	1,319	......	4	......	1	......	2	1	36	35
365	......	......	1	......	232	......	5	1	......	3	......	......	123	36
920	......	......	29	9	180	9	4	6	3	17	7	1	635	37
190,188	5	1,238	6,548	1,352	39,048	1,041	44	1,709	90,578	42,104	5,948	351	186	
1,333	......	1,221	3	......	16	......	......	......	93	......	......	......	......	1
14,670	......	......	6,277	2	16	2	......	12	8,229	65	......	43	24	2
1,356	......	......	1	1,307	27	......	3	4	7	4	1	1	1	3
38,931	......	......	2	3	38,889	......	4	......	10	3	9	2	9	4
1,482	......	......	6	1	12	921	1	13	1	478	47	1	1	5
2,028	......	......	98	6	68	34	1	1,588	7	185	23	17	15	6
82,268	......	11	43	......	15	......	2	......	82,191	4	......	......	......	7
41,492	......	5	41	......	8	6	20	36	9	41,211	2	26	129	8
6,063	5	......	18	2	12	76	1	41	......	30	5,862	2	11	9
565	......	1	39	31	31	2	12	13	29	121	4	259	......	10

TABLE XIII.—*Native Colored Population, distributed according to State (or Territory) of Birth*—1870.

	Living in—	BORN IN— The United States.	Alabama.	Arkansas.	California.	Connecticut.	Delaware.	Florida.	Georgia.
	The United States	4,870,364	451,284	74,811	1,205	7,553	26,819	62,574	568,994
	The States	4,825,612	451,191	74,786	1,196	7,534	26,798	62,560	568,764
1	Alabama	475,214	374,418	169		5	16	808	30,514
2	Arkansas	122,126	7,434	62,463			2	188	6,552
3	California	3,835	36	63	1,074	43	52	15	61
4	Connecticut	9,565	12		1	6,091	55	20	60
5	Delaware	22,778		1	2	2	20,214	9	13
6	Florida	91,384	2,192	39	1	2	5	56,958	10,138
7	Georgia	544,770	4,443	136		12	14	2,110	494,364
8	Illinois	28,549	969	327	4	15	14	11	339
9	Indiana	24,517	155	31		3	10	10	148
10	Iowa	5,737	122	109	1	1	8	4	79
11	Kansas	17,066	168	893	2	4	5	4	127
12	Kentucky	222,161	323	92		1	2	13	299
13	Louisiana	363,067	9,738	1,635	3	12	30	826	8,095
14	Maine	1,446	1	5		3	3	5	13
15	Maryland	175,240	33	2	5	13	347	14	122
16	Massachusetts	13 055	26	3	5	338	66	31	122
17	Michigan	10,688	96	13	1	30	72	20	87
18	Minnesota	731	46	9		3	1		13
19	Mississippi	444,007	22,192	1,016	6	5	13	325	12,713
20	Missouri	117,995	821	1,117	6	9	26	47	464
21	Nebraska	782	11	6		2	1	1	17
22	Nevada	328	8	3	20	10	1	1	3
23	New Hampshire	562					1	1	11
24	New Jersey	30,548	22	1	6	79	1,623	29	87
25	New York	50,834	57	7	4	516	285	57	270
26	North Carolina	391,601	182	11		1	5	49	337
27	Ohio	62,887	406	148	7	38	41	30	433
28	Oregon	301	2		27	1	4		9
29	Pennsylvania	64,850	47	12	6	44	3,738	27	197
30	Rhode Island	4,876	7		5	193	92	8	16
31	South Carolina	415,514	122	4	1	15	3	154	1,915
32	Tennessee	322,204	6,368	842	4	2	10	73	6,835
33	Texas	252,634	20,550	5,608	5	14	19	686	14,801
34	Vermont	900	1	1		10		1	6
35	Virginia	512,792	75	4	2	5	13	23	162
36	West Virginia	17,971	12			1	1	1	13
37	Wisconsin	2,068	96	16		11	6	1	26
	The Territories	44,752	93	25	9	19	21	14	160
1	Arizona	21	1	3					3
2	Colorado	450	15	11			2	2	12
3	Dakota	92	4						3
4	District of Columbia	43,325	51	6	2	15	19	9	124
5	Idaho	47			3				
6	Montana	175	1			1		2	1
7	New Mexico	167	7	2					7
8	Utah	113	7	2	1	2			4
9	Washington	179			3	1		1	2
10	Wyoming	180	7	1					4

TABLE XIII.—*Native Colored Population, distributed according to State (or Territory) of Birth*—1870—Continued.

Illinois.	Indiana.	Iowa.	Kansas.	Kentucky.	Louisiana.	Maine.	Maryland.	Massachusetts.	Michigan.	Minnesota.	Mississippi.	
BORN IN—												
9,804	12,131	1,646	4,110	272,227	287,399	1,302	212,027	8,569	4,423	290	376,793	
9,780	12,119	1,634	4,100	271,994	287,319	1,295	200,265	8,507	4,411	287	376,746	
11	7	1	......	948	646	8	1,738	19	1	......	4,431	1
44	23	4	16	3,277	2,058	2	653	9	3	2	7,028	2
23	9	6	4	171	92	17	325	121	15	......	73	3
3	1	2	......	23	47	8	324	277	2	......	8	4
2	1	......	......	2	7	......	1,855	4	......	......	1	5
2	3	......	......	108	132	3	377	10	2	......	260	6
6	5	......	3	280	177	6	1,036	20	......	......	801	7
8,387	385	72	22	4,403	306	9	403	45	85	7	929	8
209	9,811	11	5	9,371	89	......	103	12	46	1	189	9
129	77	1,383	6	647	35	1	72	14	14	6	189	10
52	66	14	3,797	2,360	98	4	121	7	80	7	132	11
45	83	......	1	205,583	208	8	406	13	14	1	408	12
69	42	2	1	6,005	263,956	23	5,485	60	9	93	17,831	13
......	1	......	......	8	21	951	35	48	......	......	2	14
3	9	......	......	47	50	2	167,420	30	......	......	42	15
10	2	......	......	37	60	105	751	6,819	6	......	16	16
70	779	8	8	1,044	47	10	203	36	3,860	2	52	17
17	15	14	1	76	15	1	8	5	6	115	45	18
64	29	3	3	5,860	4,819	15	2,677	11	6	1	319,360	19
292	84	73	150	10,254	933	4	674	37	75	11	1,375	20
15	5	4	15	91	7	......	17	......	4	......	17	21
3	1	......	......	18	13	4	45	9	1	......	1	22
......	......	......	......	3	2	8	15	24	......	......	1	23
2	3	......	......	23	35	7	1,493	60	2	......	9	24
16	13	1	1	147	140	21	2,025	293	25	1	45	25
3	3	......	......	41	26	2	147	10	2	......	187	26
71	470	13	7	9,748	315	7	648	60	90	14	516	27
2	3	1	......	14	5	......	17	12	......	......	2	28
20	14	4	6	149	106	17	6,526	99	14	5	54	29
4	6	......	3	9	10	12	480	195	1	6	6	30
......	1	1	......	25	50	6	165	22	2	1	123	31
61	41	6	12	5,993	569	8	647	24	7	11	8,566	32
60	53	5	37	4,963	12,045	16	1,420	41	7	2	13,895	33
1	......	......	......	3	10	7	30	47	......	......	3	34
2	......	......	......	64	39	3	1,679	17	7	......	86	35
1	......	......	......	70	22	......	223	1	......	......	8	36
81	74	6	2	127	19	......	22	6	25	5	55	37
24	12	12	10	233	80	7	11,762	62	12	3	47	
......	......	......	......	......	......	......	1	1	......	......	......	1
7	1	2	6	66	6	......	12	3	......	......	9	2
1	1	2	......	5	1	......	2	......	......	......	......	3
8	5	2	......	78	58	3	11,720	30	12	......	27	4
1	......	1	......	7	1	......	4	3	......	......	......	5
......	2	2	2	25	[illegible]	2	5	2	......	......	......	6
......	......	......	......	23	3	......	3	......	......	1	2	7
......	1	2	......	6	......	......	1	......	......	2	7	8
2	......	......	......	1	2	1	6	3	......	......	......	9
5	2	1	2	22	2	1	8	......	......	......	2	10

TABLE XIII.—*Native Colored Population, distributed according to State (or Territory) of Birth*—1870—Continued.

	Living in—	BORN IN—												
		Missouri.	Nebraska.	Nevada.	New Hampshire.	New Jersey.	New York.	North Carolina.	Ohio.	Oregon.	Pennsylvania.	Rhode Island.	South Carolina.	Tennessee.
	The United States	108, 635	80	38	559	26, 223	44, 488	468, 262	33, 944	122	49, 503	3, 038	305, 764	324, 841
	The States	108, 376	78	37	556	26, 199	44, 310	467, 954	33, 859	116	49, 268	3, 026	305, 623	324, 734
1	Alabama	211	...	...	4	4	25	16, 034	26	...	32	...	16, 602	4, 208
2	Arkansas	1, 756	2	...	...	2	18	5, 238	107	...	37	2	5, 035	11, 562
3	California	291	2	1	1	43	239	95	30	7	166	8	67	111
4	Connecticut	5	...	...	6	179	858	295	8	...	194	82	66	21
5	Delaware	2	...	...	...	80	12	20	3	...	320	1	8	21
6	Florida	17	1	...	...	7	35	3, 809	6	...	44	11	14, 355	241
7	Georgia	58	...	2	2	10	35	7, 063	17	...	23	8	18, 226	1, 092
8	Illinois	4, 048	3	...	4	31	201	594	389	2	202	19	298	3, 502
9	Indiana	123	...	...	5	16	30	1, 354	687	8	65	1	180	678
10	Iowa	1, 532	6	...	6	4	52	107	118	1	74	...	57	306
11	Kansas	5, 924	5	1	1	3	29	420	179	1	66	1	74	696
12	Kentucky	528	...	...	...	9	39	960	174	1	55	2	311	5, 569
13	Louisiana	1, 613	...	...	3	23	178	5, 237	186	...	157	8	7, 048	4, 127
14	Maine	2	...	...	20	7	28	34	...	...	10	2	17	9
15	Maryland	14	...	...	1	37	107	297	33	...	412	9	149	68
16	Massachusetts	13	...	...	79	103	592	465	42	...	318	185	224	39
17	Michigan	126	...	...	1	46	438	417	1, 167	...	295	5	117	343
18	Minnesota	88	...	...	...	2	21	33	32	...	20	...	12	44
19	Mississippi	1, 565	1	...	5	8	61	14, 511	98	...	69	5	16, 604	13, 984
20	Missouri	85, 501	3	1	3	12	69	1, 111	502	1	269	7	407	3, 858
21	Nebraska	271	53	...	...	...	5	18	20	...	27	...	16	43
22	Nevada	18	...	31	...	3	18	10	8	...	22	...	9	9
23	New Hampshire	...	...	...	329	...	6	13	...	...	4	...	21	6
24	New Jersey	9	...	...	7	22, 443	1, 182	180	17	...	1, 545	8	132	24
25	New York	25	...	...	15	1, 463	38, 504	663	86	1	1, 398	93	502	29
26	North Carolina	10	...	...	...	5	23	379, 231	16	...	36	1	4, 840	210
27	Ohio	178	...	...	12	49	215	2, 820	29, 192	3	988	13	409	1, 786
28	Oregon	29	...	...	...	2	22	8	2	85	11	...	2	7
29	Pennsylvania	24	...	1	4	1, 481	669	410	208	...	41, 740	15	543	162
30	Rhode Island	3	...	...	5	72	261	60	7	...	183	2, 520	34	...
31	South Carolina	5	...	...	...	4	16	2, 597	17	...	21	11	408, 285	60
32	Tennessee	751	...	...	1	10	42	9, 897	148	1	90	1	4, 053	260, 639
33	Texas	3, 470	1	...	23	20	61	7, 421	91	1	115	3	7, 155	11, 472
34	Vermont	1	...	...	20	3	62	12	2	...	6	1	15	3
35	Virginia	16	...	...	1	12	51	6, 373	27	4	54	3	223	297
36	West Virginia	9	...	...	...	...	4	90	122	...	85	...	37	20
37	Wisconsin	120	1	...	...	6	99	62	92	...	55	1	30	155
	The Territories	259	2	1	1	24	178	308	85	6	235	12	141	107
1	Arizona	...	...	...	...	...	1	2	...	...	2	...	...	3
2	Colorado	109	...	...	...	...	7	12	12	...	...	...	5	31
3	Dakota	4	1	...	...	...	3	5	1	...	...	...	3	3
4	District of Columbia	18	...	1	...	21	131	275	51	...	195	12	120	51
5	Idaho	3	...	...	...	...	4	1	1	1	1	...	1	...
6	Montana	52	1	...	1	...	7	2	2	...	14	...	3	5
7	New Mexico	18	...	...	...	1	4	4	4	...	1	...	1	5
8	Utah	7	...	...	...	...	5	5	8	...	2	...	...	1
9	Washington	10	...	...	...	2	11	...	...	5	4	...	...	2
10	Wyoming	38	...	...	...	...	5	2	6	...	16	...	2	6

TABLE XIII.—*Native Colored Population, distributed according to State (or Territory) of Birth*—1870—Continued.

BORN IN—																		
Texas.	Vermont.	Virginia and West Virginia.	Wisconsin.	The Territories.	Alaska.	Arizona.	Colorado.	Dakota.	District of Columbia.	Idaho.	Indian.	Montana.	New Mexico.	Utah.	Washington.	Wyoming.	Not stated, and at sea under U.S. flag.	
140, 072	947	739, 352	926	19, 679	4	4	62	17	17, 036	7	806	20	82	50	110	9	1, 472	
140, 037	936	722, 394	922	5, 899	2	3	11	1	3, 558	4	806	3	19	10	8	3	1, 471	
222	3	24, 223	1	418	....	....	....	....	158	....	....	....	....	....	....	....	200	1
1, 481	2	6, 868	2	266	....	....	....	....	49	1	192	....	....	....	....	....	24	2
26	7	446	....	101	....	1	....	....	93	....	1	....	....	4	1	....	1	3
1	15	734	1	146	....	....	....	....	113	....	....	....	....	....	....	....	33	4
2	....	188	....	8	....	....	....	....	8	....	....	....	....	....	....	....	....	5
15	5	2, 545	....	41	....	....	....	....	37	....	1	....	....	....	....	....	3	6
51	3	14, 642	....	125	....	....	....	....	87	....	....	....	....	....	1	....	37	7
52	14	2, 074	111	131	....	....	....	....	100	....	5	....	2	....	....	....	24	8
7	1	1, 106	9	43	....	....	....	....	28	....	....	....	....	....	....	1	14	9
10	9	506	22	10	....	....	3	....	7	....	....	....	....	....	....	....	....	10
178	....	1, 142	10	395	2	....	3	....	23	....	352	1	1	2	....	1	10	11
57	....	6, 931	3	31	....	....	....	....	26	....	....	....	....	....	....	....	5	12
2, 335	5	27, 673	10	549	....	....	....	....	459	....	6	....	....	....	....	....	84	13
....	5	193	....	23	....	....	....	....	20	....	....	....	....	....	....	....	3	14
23	2	5, 624	....	325	....	....	....	....	323	....	....	....	....	....	....	....	2	15
2	70	2, 313	2	211	....	....	....	....	192	....	....	....	....	....	....	1	18	16
....	11	1, 193	28	63	....	....	....	....	48	....	....	....	2	....	....	....	13	17
2	4	81	13	9	....	....	....	....	6	....	....	....	....	....	....	....	3	18
433	13	27, 713	28	491	....	....	....	....	208	....	11	1	....	1	....	....	270	19
497	5	9, 098	21	178	....	....	2	1	53	3	19	....	12	....	....	....	88	20
....	1	100	....	15	....	....	....	....	8	....	....	....	....	1	....	....	6	21
3	....	47	2	7	....	....	....	....	6	....	....	....	1	....	....	....	....	22
....	13	94	1	9	....	....	....	....	5	....	....	....	....	....	....	....	4	23
4	1	1, 427	....	88	....	....	....	....	76	....	1	....	....	....	....	....	11	24
13	127	3, 458	9	464	....	....	....	....	389	....	....	....	....	....	....	....	75	25
15	10	6, 165	....	33	....	....	....	....	28	....	....	....	....	....	....	....	5	26
40	21	13, 889	17	193	....	....	....	....	147	....	2	....	....	....	1	....	43	27
3	....	30	....	10	....	....	....	....	6	....	....	....	....	1	2	....	1	28
6	10	8, 165	1	335	....	....	....	....	299	....	....	....	....	....	2	....	34	29
2	6	516	....	154	....	....	....	....	145	....	....	....	....	....	1	....	8	30
19	4	2, 525	....	39	....	....	....	....	24	....	....	....	....	....	....	....	15	31
204	2	16, 085	9	181	....	....	....	....	95	....	6	....	....	....	....	....	80	32
134, 306	23	13, 683	10	502	....	2	3	....	131	....	210	....	1	1	....	....	214	33
1	540	106	....	8	....	....	....	....	7	....	....	....	....	....	....	....	1	34
31	....	503, 368	....	152	....	....	....	....	117	....	....	....	....	....	....	....	41	35
....	....	17, 210	1	40	....	....	....	....	8	....	....	....	....	....	....	....	32	36
2	4	213	611	39	....	....	....	....	29	....	....	1	....	....	....	....	9	37
35	11	16, 958	4	13, 780	2	1	51	16	13, 478	3	....	17	63	40	102	6	1	
1	....	4	....	2	....	1	....	....	....	....	....	....	....	1	....	....	....	1
8	....	53	1	58	....	....	45	....	4	....	....	....	6	....	....	3	....	2
1	1	32	....	19	....	....	....	16	3	....	....	....	....	....	....	....	....	3
13	6	16, 785	2	13, 449	....	....	....	....	13, 448	....	....	....	....	....	....	....	1	4
1	....	9	1	4	....	....	....	....	2	2	....	....	....	....	....	....	....	5
....	....	16	....	20	....	....	....	....	4	1	....	15	....	....	....	....	....	6
7	1	12	....	61	....	....	....	....	4	....	....	....	57	....	....	....	....	7
1	3	3	....	43	....	....	....	....	1	....	....	2	....	39	....	1	....	8
1	....	12	....	110	2	....	....	....	6	....	....	....	....	....	102	....	....	9
2	....	32	....	14	....	....	6	....	6	....	....	....	....	....	....	2	....	10

TABLE XIV.—*The Foreign-born Population, distributed according to Place of Birth among the Principal Foreign Countries—1870.*

	Living in—	BORN IN— All foreign countries.	Austria.	Belgium.	Bohemia.	British America.	China.	Denmark.	France.	Germany.
	The United States	5,567,229	30,508	12,553	40,289	493,464	63,042	30,107	116,402	1,690,533
	The States	5,473,029	30,116	12,475	40,071	487,605	55,974	24,574	115,140	1,679,146
1	Alabama	9,962	99	10	29	183	1	80	594	2,482
2	Arkansas	5,026	41	9	21	342	98	55	237	1,563
3	California	209,831	1,078	291	90	10,660	48,826	1,837	8,068	29,701
4	Connecticut	113,639	154	36	95	10,861	11	116	821	12,443
5	Delaware	9,136	8	2	1	112	......	8	127	1,142
6	Florida	4,967	17	8	3	174	1	41	126	397
7	Georgia	11,127	34	21	23	247	4	42	312	2,761
8	Illinois	515,198	2,099	1,071	7,350	32,550	8	3,711	10,911	203,758
9	Indiana	141,474	443	462	141	4,765	6	315	6,363	78,060
10	Iowa	204,692	2,691	650	6,766	17,907	3	2,827	3,130	66,162
11	Kansas	48,392	448	199	105	5,324	......	503	1,274	12,775
12	Kentucky	63,398	146	100	40	1,082	8	53	2,057	30,318
13	Louisiana	61,827	435	220	23	714	71	291	12,341	18,933
14	Maine	48,881	10	11	1	26,788	4	102	137	508
15	Maryland	83,412	266	41	789	644	6	107	649	47,045
16	Massachusetts	353,319	255	104	110	70,055	115	267	1,029	13,072
17	Michigan	268,010	795	832	1,179	89,590	4	1,354	3,121	64,143
18	Minnesota	160,697	2,647	622	2,166	16,698	6	1,910	1,743	41,364
19	Mississippi	11,191	85	10	9	375	16	193	690	2,960
20	Missouri	222,267	1,493	536	3,517	8,448	4	665	6,293	113,618
21	Nebraska	30,748	299	15	1,776	2,635	2	1,129	340	10,954
22	Nevada	18,801	157	28	7	2,365	3,146	208	414	2,181
23	New Hampshire	29,611	9	......	4	12,955	5	11	60	436
24	New Jersey	188,943	686	191	271	2,474	39	510	3,130	54,001
25	New York	1,138,353	3,928	984	2,071	79,042	177	1,701	22,302	316,902
26	North Carolina	3,029	13	6	5	171	4	8	54	904
27	Ohio	372,493	3,699	639	1,429	12,988	12	284	12,781	182,897
28	Oregon	11,600	53	38	36	1,187	3,327	87	308	1,875
29	Pennsylvania	545,309	1,536	399	580	10,022	32	561	8,095	160,146
30	Rhode Island	55,396	19	6	19	10,242	......	24	167	1,201
31	South Carolina	8,074	10	10	1	77	6	50	143	2,754
32	Tennessee	19,316	112	19	37	587	4	88	562	4,539
33	Texas	62,411	1,748	73	781	507	20	159	2,232	23,985
34	Vermont	47,155	2	1	......	28,544	1	21	93	370
35	Virginia	13,754	56	6	31	327	8	23	360	4,050
36	West Virginia	17,091	59	21	1	207	......	21	243	6,232
37	Wisconsin	364,499	4,486	4,804	10,570	25,666	......	5,212	2,704	162,314
	The Territories	94,200	392	78	218	5,859	7,068	5,533	1,262	11,387
1	Arizona	5,809	24	5	2	142	21	19	69	379
2	Colorado	6,599	51	11	15	753	7	77	209	1,456
3	Dakota	4,815	171	1	153	906	......	115	57	563
4	District of Columbia	16,254	26	8	9	290	4	29	231	4,920
5	Idaho	7,885	26	5	1	334	4,268	88	144	329
6	Montana	7,979	36	25	23	1,172	1,943	95	193	1,233
7	New Mexico	5,620	10	5	2	125	......	15	124	582
8	Utah	30,702	4	2	3	687	446	4,957	62	358
9	Washington	5,024	19	11	2	1,121	236	84	113	645
10	Wyoming	3,513	25	5	8	329	143	54	57	652

TABLE XIV.—*The Foreign-born Population, distributed according to Place of Birth among the Principal Foreign Countries—1870*—Continued.

BORN IN—														
Great Britain and Ireland.	Holland.	Hungary.	Italy.	Luxemburg.	Mexico.	Norway.	Poland.	Portugal.	Russia.	Spain.	Sweden.	Switzerland.	West Indies.	
2,626,241	46,802	3,737	17,157	5,802	42,435	114,246	14,436	4,542	4,644	3,764	97,332	75,153	11,570	
2,580,556	46,561	3,649	16,766	5,795	33,920	112,116	14,192	4,510	4,535	3,677	94,447	73,972	11,470	
5,433	14	24	118	......	13	21	38	17	36	98	105	108	69	1
2,162	71	2	30	5	14	19	32	1	24	3	135	104	13	2
78,661	452	102	4,660	11	9,339	1,000	804	2,508	540	405	1,944	2,927	395	3
87,157	99	30	117	......	5	72	83	49	34	27	321	492	191	4
7,600	16	3	5	......	......	......	4	1	3	3	9	33	27	5
1,311	7	2	56	......	41	16	20	18	7	56	30	14	2,256	6
6,701	42	42	50	......	9	14	88	13	32	39	35	103	118	7
192,960	4,180	420	761	733	73	11,880	1,696	76	306	50	29,979	8,980	186	8
42,266	873	36	95	98	17	123	523	13	61	21	2,180	4,287	41	9
65,442	4,513	134	54	1,344	14	17,556	178	3	96	27	10,796	3,937	89	10
19,923	300	38	55	103	63	588	169	4	56	4	4,954	1,328	22	11
27,201	270	107	325	9	31	16	109	3	28	16	112	1,147	39	12
20,819	232	29	1,889	1	409	76	198	125	165	1,130	358	873	1,742	13
20,672	96	......	48	......	4	58	6	72	18	42	91	9	79	14
31,988	236	46	210	......	19	18	145	28	50	49	100	297	384	15
230,878	480	11	454	5	20	302	272	735	154	179	1,386	491	407	16
86,200	12,559	141	110	......	25	1,519	974	31	194	34	2,406	2,116	128	17
30,592	1,855	209	40	1,173	5	35,940	246	......	109	5	20,987	2,162	9	18
4,906	35	10	147	2	32	78	78	3	21	78	970	266	52	19
74,141	1,167	599	936	......	90	297	619	21	140	55	2,302	6,597	135	20
9,616	180	73	44	......	11	506	57	......	27	3	2,332	593	13	21
8,525	44	3	199	......	226	80	50	104	48	75	217	247	25	22
15,805	5	3	9	......	1	55	2	12	2	7	42	11	16	23
120,309	2,944	85	257	7	46	90	279	37	90	71	554	9,061	364	24
674,106	6,426	709	3,592	286	127	975	4,061	237	1,473	818	5,522	7,916	3,127	25
1,601	13	1	19	......	2	5	8	12	11	8	38	80	20	26
140,028	2,018	234	561	329	41	64	526	22	181	31	252	12,727	134	27
3,771	39	8	31	......	51	76	65	48	67	5	205	160	36	28
350,179	819	144	784	72	86	115	777	89	220	146	2,266	5,765	893	29
42,984	45	5	58	......	2	22	13	146	13	12	106	74	67	30
4,206	32	6	63	......	2	......	66	8	31	30	61	45	124	31
11,008	100	87	483	4	17	37	221	5	74	12	349	802	20	32
6,762	54	46	186	......	23,020	403	448	23	62	150	364	599	112	33
17,867	20	......	17	......	5	34	1	9	1	7	83	19	9	34
7,955	231	12	162	......	13	17	42	28	39	27	30	148	61	35
9,710	174	5	34	......	......	1	4	......	11	1	5	325	4	36
90,001	5,990	237	104	1,593	47	40,046	1,290	9	102	13	2,799	6,069	63	37
45,685	241	88	391	7	8,515	2,130	244	32	109	87	2,885	1,181	100	
686	11	6	12	......	4,348	7	11	......	5	4	7	23	5	1
3,307	17	2	16	......	129	40	49	......	10	5	180	140	5	2
1,218	8	3	4	......	6	1,179	3	......	4	3	380	33	3	3
10,021	23	46	182	1	17	5	49	9	22	37	22	175	53	4
1,984	9	4	11	......	46	61	12	10	10	4	91	52	8	5
2,732	18	11	34	5	31	88	55	2	7	3	141	97	8	6
708	3	4	25	......	3,913	5	12	2	12	16	6	42	2	7
20,772	122	1	74	......	8	613	11	2	13	2	1,790	509	3	8
2,191	25	2	24	1	13	104	25	6	21	9	159	50	10	9
1,976	5	9	9	......	4	28	17	1	5	4	109	60	3	10

TABLE XV.—*German Population, distributed according to Place of Birth among the Principal States and Free Cities of Germany*—1870.

	Living in—	BORN IN—					
		All Germany.	Baden.	Bavaria.	Brunswick.	Hamburg.	Hanover.
	The United States	1,690,533	153,366	204,119	4,876	7,829	104,365
	The States	1,679,146	152,316	203,013	4,839	7,674	103,649
1	Alabama	2,482	255	643	10	42	58
2	Arkansas	1,563	148	167	7	4	67
3	California	29,701	2,143	2,547	61	234	2,553
4	Connecticut	12,443	963	1,323	11	110	297
5	Delaware	1,142	109	121	1	16	33
6	Florida	587	31	110	3	15	33
7	Georgia	2,761	131	334	8	46	247
8	Illinois	203,758	15,885	17,554	730	756	20,459
9	Indiana	78,060	8,154	11,500	208	465	3,713
10	Iowa	66,162	4,353	4,869	149	276	5,367
11	Kansas	12,775	931	1,219	28	39	798
12	Kentucky	30,318	4,428	6,294	41	95	3,470
13	Louisiana	18,933	2,861	3,485	36	209	1,194
14	Maine	508	44	40	....	2	9
15	Maryland	47,045	2,471	10,469	279	167	3,520
16	Massachusetts	13,072	1,927	1,244	17	121	408
17	Michigan	64,143	4,437	6,164	86	160	1,243
18	Minnesota	41,364	1,865	2,639	30	90	2,531
19	Mississippi	2,960	207	539	2	28	85
20	Missouri	113,618	11,906	11,197	928	478	17,269
21	Nebraska	10,954	579	394	19	52	586
22	Nevada	2,181	142	180	6	37	52
23	New Hampshire	436	38	46	4	4	5
24	New Jersey	54,001	7,768	6,822	121	321	1,958
25	New York	316,902	26,591	39,859	262	1,813	9,257
26	North Carolina	904	40	142	5	10	49
27	Ohio	182,897	26,058	33,690	328	417	16,442
28	Oregon	1,875	219	336	2	30	134
29	Pennsylvania	160,146	20,579	24,915	218	396	4,019
30	Rhode Island	1,201	110	136	....	10	63
31	South Carolina	2,754	72	121	7	24	513
32	Tennessee	4,539	434	613	....	31	147
33	Texas	23,985	686	837	411	140	1,525
34	Vermont	370	18	23	....	2	7
35	Virginia	4,050	361	583	30	35	208
36	West Virginia	6,232	603	702	302	11	802
37	Wisconsin	162,314	5,409	11,154	450	288	4,604
	The Territories	11,387	1,050	1,106	37	155	716
1	Arizona	379	16	....	....	2	17
2	Colorado	1,456	136	165	6	9	70
3	Dakota	563	60	39	1	23	16
4	District of Columbia	4,920	498	431	20	43	387
5	Idaho	599	50	78	....	11	32
6	Montana	1,233	109	152	....	17	66
7	New Mexico	582	40	59	5	14	38
8	Utah	358	21	98	....	5	2
9	Washington	645	45	79	5	20	38
10	Wyoming	652	75	64	....	8	30

TABLE XV.—*German Population, distributed according to Place of Birth among the Principal States and Free Cities of Germany—1870.*

BORN IN—										
Hessen.	Lübeck.	Mecklenberg.	Nassau.	Oldenburg.	Prussia, (not specified.)	Saxony.	Weimar.	Würtemberg.	Germany, (not specified.)	
131,524	279	39,670	8,962	10,286	506,782	45,256	1,628	127,959	253,632	
130,433	278	39,633	8,925	10,266	503,045	44,777	1,623	126,883	251,792	
109	......	4	6	8	723	49	......	131	450	1
79	1	18	6	1	587	49	......	102	327	2
1,500	13	95	49	110	14,782	622	9	1,401	2,890	3
814	2	36	10	5	3,356	659	10	1,134	3,704	4
122	......	4	1	5	209	31	......	282	148	5
20	......	4	18	1	274	9	......	25	48	6
181	......	8	5	20	936	83	1	130	631	7
16,301	47	7,168	1,210	1,352	82,420	4,788	253	8,872	25,954	8
6,768	42	2,454	707	664	29,076	1,472	73	7,010	5,754	9
3,522	5	2,351	185	664	26,475	1,339	59	3,426	13,122	10
774	5	190	36	52	5,463	355	13	1,108	1,704	11
2,415	1	76	370	1,111	7,028	686	27	2,307	1,969	12
1,055	20	12	27	94	6,348	293	......	956	2,413	13
11	......	......	3	8	164	5	......	10	212	14
8,968	6	52	80	406	12,055	1,533	152	2,637	4,250	15
610	10	46	80	16	3,710	1,119	11	1,056	2,697	16
2,935	5	5,202	228	54	28,660	1,813	82	8,658	4,416	17
1,406	1	955	83	106	23,668	1,003	38	1,738	5,191	18
208	1	5	6	11	880	50	1	128	809	19
8,074	16	619	901	442	46,400	3,180	29	4,917	7,953	20
258	......	257	5	196	6,323	203	......	338	1,744	21
98	3	4	2	2	816	42	2	75	790	22
24	......	1	10	......	71	35	......	13	185	23
5,274	9	413	219	135	16,044	2,444	34	6,362	6,077	24
23,760	57	5,634	854	364	74,729	6,158	168	18,839	108,557	25
43	......	3	6	7	359	27	......	56	157	26
15,917	8	2,582	1,356	3,237	42,979	3,497	96	19,371	16,919	27
140	3	9	9	7	630	65	2	149	140	28
19,403	16	647	730	134	35,247	5,185	264	28,838	19,525	29
79	......	9	7	10	337	93	2	116	229	30
80	......	14	......	51	1,284	49	1	57	481	31
202	1	11	17	11	1,402	224	......	350	1,096	32
1,065	2	466	779	475	13,781	1,240	44	765	1,769	33
36	......	......	......	......	115	7	......	24	138	34
418	1	11	10	3	1,318	169	8	336	559	35
1,097	......	94	15	20	953	169	48	603	813	36
6,661	3	10,179	895	484	103,423	6,023	187	4,443	8,111	37
1,091	1	37	37	20	3,737	479	5	1,076	4,840	
9	......	......	......	......	129	2	......	10	174	1
98	......	6	11	......	674	61	4	178	38	2
33	......	3	......	5	220	30	......	50	92	3
729	......	5	12	9	1,059	238	......	514	975	4
42	......	1	1	......	232	14	......	35	100	5
62	1	2	3	2	486	43	......	98	172	6
51	......	5	3	1	208	31	1	55	71	7
17	......	3	......	......	152	24	......	42	64	8
32	......	7	6	2	312	15	......	47	37	9
18	......	5	1	1	265	21	......	47	117	10

TABLE XVI.—*British Population, distributed according to Place of Birth, as English, Irish, Scotch, and Welsh*—1870.

LIVING IN—	BORN IN— All Great Britain and Ireland.	England.	Ireland.	Scotland.	Wales.	Great Britain (not specified).
The United States	2,626,241	550,924	1,855,827	140,835	74,533	4,122
The States	2,580,556	528,990	1,838,726	136,846	71,907	4,087
Alabama	7,47[illegible]	2,[illegible]	3,893	458	79	21
Arkansas	2,[illegible]	796	1,428	156	84	4
California	78,661	17,699	54,421	4,949	1,517	13
Connecticut	87,157	15,[illegible]	70,630	3,[illegible]	[illegible]	....
Delaware	7,600	1,421	5,907	229	43	....
Florida	1,311	389	737	144	6	35
Georgia	[illegible],701	1,0[illegible]	5,093	420	61	30
Illinois	1[illegible],900	53,871	120,162	15,737	2,146	44
Indiana	42,996	9,945	28,698	2,507	756	590
Iowa	65,442	16,660	40,124	5,248	1,967	1,443
Kansas	19,923	6,161	10,940	1,531	1,021	270
Kentucky	27,951	4,173	21,642	1,013	347	39
Louisiana	20,819	2,811	17,068	814	114	12
Maine	20,672	3,650	15,745	998	279	....
Maryland	31,988	4,855	23,630	2,432	994	77
Massachusetts	259,878	34,099	216,120	9,003	776	88
Michigan	86,200	35,051	42,013	8,552	558	26
Minnesota	30,282	5,670	21,746	2,194	944	28
Mississippi	4,906	1,088	3,359	434	25	....
Missouri	74,141	14,314	54,983	3,253	1,724	37
Nebraska	9,616	3,603	4,999	792	220	2
Nevada	8,725	2,549	5,035	630	301	10
New Hampshire	15,895	2,679	12,190	852	27	165
New Jersey	120,909	27,614	86,784	5,710	904	257
New York	674,106	110,071	528,806	27,282	7,857	90
North Carolina	1,661	490	677	430	10	4
Ohio	140,629	37,561	82,674	7,819	12,939	33
Oregon	3,771	1,347	1,967	394	63	....
Pennsylvania	370,179	69,695	235,798	16,846	27,633	257
Rhode Island	42,884	9,291	31,534	1,948	56	135
South Carolina	4,286	617	3,262	310	15	2
Tennessee	11,098	2,085	8,048	555	311	6
Texas	6,702	2,037	4,031	621	55	19
Vermont	17,867	1,946	14,080	1,240	565	36
Virginia	7,975	1,960	5,191	705	148	2
West Virginia	9,710	1,811	6,832	746	321	....
Wisconsin	90,001	23,192	48,479	6,590	6,550	190
The Territories	45,685	21,934	17,101	3,989	2,626	35
Arizona	686	131	495	54	3	....
Colorado	3,307	1,358	1,685	188	165	1
Dakota	1,218	248	888	77	3	2
District of Columbia	10,021	1,422	8,218	352	29	....
Idaho	1,984	549	986	114	335	9
Montana	2,792	692	1,635	268	197	....
New Mexico	708	120	543	36	9	....
Utah	20,772	16,073	502	2,391	1,783	23
Washington	2,191	791	1,047	309	44	....
Wyoming	1,976	556	1,102	260	58	....

:VII.—*British American Population, distributed according to the Place of Birth among the Principal Geographical Divisions of British America—1870.*

...iving in—	BORN IN— All British America.	Canada.	New Brunswick.	Newfoundland.	Nova Scotia.	Prince Edward's Island.	British America, (not specified.)
...nited States	493,464	414,912	26,737	3,423	33,562	1,361	13,409
...ates	487,605	410,198	26,366	3,402	33,208	1,357	13,074
...	183	145	12	3	16	....	7
...	312	311	7	....	21	2	1
...	10,660	6,977	1,170	72	1,438	54	949
...it	10,861	10,073	315	25	390	....	58
...	112	89	6	1	10	....	6
...	174	122	12	4	32	....	4
...	217	195	20	....	28	1	3
...	32,550	29,919	634	180	816	3	798
...	4,765	4,498	106	16	115	5	25
...	17,907	16,421	391	10	506	48	531
...	5,324	4,639	177	5	187	17	309
...	1,082	924	12	2	32	1	51
...	714	556	36	8	64	....	50
...	26,788	9,437	8,936	463	2,135	125	5,692
...	644	334	79	10	212	....	9
...etts	70,055	38,768	7,063	1,755	19,486	899	2,084
...	89,590	87,487	1,021	37	795	....	250
...	16,698	13,751	1,544	30	787	13	573
...i	375	307	19	4	42	....	3
...	8,448	7,931	201	22	250	....	24
...	2,635	2,338	74	5	183	....	35
...	2,365	1,952	155	5	235	....	18
...pshire	12,955	11,916	239	6	517	22	255
...y	2,474	1,990	113	34	254	4	79
...	79,042	75,578	[illegible]	427	1,608	22	527
...olina	171	151	1	6	13	....	....
...	[illegible]	12,394	[illegible]	37	[illegible]	2	28
...	[illegible]	877	84	16	86	....	124
...nia	10,022	8,522	486	[illegible]	781	13	132
...and	10,242	8,945	181	30	949	69	68
...olina	77	58	5	1	12	....	1
...	587	530	16	4	34	....	3
...	597	485	41	5	31	....	35
...	28,544	28,331	70	5	79	....	59
...	327	233	28	10	40	....	16
...inia	207	177	5	5	13	....	7
...	25,666	22,767	1,789	71	[illegible]	57	260
...erritories	5,859	4,714	371	21	354	4	395
...	142	112	15	....	12	....	3
...	753	664	25	3	49	....	12
...	906	879	19	....	8	....	....
...Columbia	290	229	21	4	31	....	5
...	334	265	23	3	37	2	4
...	1,172	1,057	55	....	34	1	25
...ico	125	111	6	1	7	....	....
...	687	[illegible]	66	1	45	....	9
...on	[illegible]	539	123	5	[illegible]	1	335
...	329	292	18	4	13	....	2

TABLE XVIII.—*Native and Foreign Population, &c.*—Continued.

STATE OF ARKANSAS—Continued.

Counties.	NATIVE.							FOREIGN-BORN.							
	Total.	Born in the State.	Tennessee.	Alabama.	Georgia.	Mississippi.	North Carolina.	Total.	British America.	England and Wales.*	Ireland.	Scotland.	Germany.	France.	Sweden and Norway.
Pike	3783	2104	436	232	310	174	81	5	1	....	......	....	3	....	....
Poinsett	1713	811	358	211	67	51	59	7	....	....	7	....	......	....	....
Polk	3372	1689	330	193	302	217	110	4	....	....	2	....	2	....	....
Pope	8330	4949	1157	212	273	171	647	56	10	7	25	3	8	1	....
Prairie	5337	1927	1106	337	213	470	516	67	9	12	17	2	13	....	10
Pulaski	30370	13809	3985	1379	1230	1306	1208	1696	90	169	598	41	544	52	27
Randolph	7444	3362	1503	176	168	104	177	22	1	....	5	1	3	5	1
Saline	3899	2168	501	209	359	149	120	12	....	3	2	4	11	1	....
Scott	7465	3380	894	628	457	261	183	18	....	4	4	2	8	....	....
Searcy	5610	3290	1177	203	144	82	136	4	....	....	......	2	1	....	....
Sebastian	12292	5298	1650	372	481	344	267	648	19	47	132	10	315	24	7
Sevier	4482	2506	401	338	261	185	144	10	....	5	1	....	4	....	....
Sharpe	5387	2770	1289	172	79	136	185	13	1	1	3	2	5	....	....
St. Francis	6008	2734	1334	489	341	463	340	106	19	13	18	2	12	9	32
Union	10328	5747	244	1565	985	325	380	43	1	8	14	....	5	1	1
Van Buren	5104	2820	1141	132	170	148	196	3	1	....	......	....	1	....	....
Washington	17175	8903	2653	314	343	137	508	91	4	18	25	7	24	2	2
White	10312	4239	2596	720	400	666	606	35	5	8	4	1	12	4	....
Woodruff	6838	2411	1482	473	475	654	423	53	10	5	15	1	14	4	1
Yell	8031	3887	1084	343	822	395	425	17	3	4	2	2	5	....	....

* Also Great Britain not stated: Benton, 1; Craighead, 1; Crawford, 10; Drew, 5; Fulton, 4; Mississippi, 5; Montgomery, 1; Perry, 1.

STATE OF CALIFORNIA.

Counties.	NATIVE.							FOREIGN-BORN.							
	Total.	Born in the State.	New York.	Missouri.	Massachusetts.	Ohio.	Maine.	Total.	British America.	England and Wales.	Ireland.	Scotland.	Germany.	France.	Sweden and Norway.
Alameda	14382	7332	1792	236	968	442	774	9855	733	665	2637	315	1292	283	43
Alpine	485	150	57	18	15	38	32	200	36	37	25	18	19	7	34
Amador	5149	2561	399	378	130	312	143	4133	120	402	490	41	326	152	16
Butte	7428	2720	697	506	181	582	240	3975	154	366	492	98	430	129	35
Calaveras	4677	2699	286	139	177	192	176	4218	70	286	466	51	409	356	43
Colusa	5088	1938	261	650	51	229	70	1077	106	98	246	33	213	20	14
Contra Costa	5791	3146	430	310	209	294	142	2670	206	549	723	214	309	79	42
Del Norte	1580	1058	60	41	24	51	25	412	11	40	71	9	53	7	12
El Dorado	6287	2909	493	231	177	365	173	4022	196	407	418	128	584	151	63
Fresno	4974	3787	71	152	37	58	14	1362	23	149	78	10	59	33	10
Humboldt	4646	1974	323	182	120	217	354	1494	548	180	383	51	138	24	41
Inyo	1164	251	122	64	27	64	36	792	71	76	122	20	122	40	3
Kern	2157	683	91	106	20	61	25	768	31	34	96	13	74	26	9
Klamath	793	368	78	28	24	33	43	893	33	51	137	17	56	6	21
Lake	2483	1060	102	355	18	94	21	486	42	55	171	13	43	3	6
Lassen	1178	365	81	108	28	97	46	149	15	41	35	6	25	3	1
Los Angeles	10984	6921	426	412	162	222	141	4325	65	248	471	65	633	317	28
Marin	3761	1931	383	90	214	104	150	3142	183	181	948	64	273	134	58
Mariposa	2192	1155	128	77	71	68	63	2380	32	219	222	37	148	113	14
Mendocino	6147	2946	305	594	97	202	306	1308	319	108	260	65	160	9	190
Merced	2196	894	132	204	41	62	54	611	42	46	119	11	56	18	6
Monroe	305	64	26	....	16	26	12	125	16	13	22	4	22	1	3

TABLE XVIII.—*Native and Foreign Population, &c.*—Continued.

STATE OF CALIFORNIA—Continued.

…ties.	NATIVE. Total.	Born in the State.	New York.	Missouri.	Massachusetts.	Ohio.	Maine.	FOREIGN-BORN. Total.	British America.	England and Wales.*	Ireland.	Scotland.	Germany.	France.	Sweden and Norway.
	7670	4519	441	443	154	210	134	2306	192	230	441	80	186	121	29
	5394	2438	401	446	155	229	103	1769	114	160	512	55	272	48	49
	10479	5070	886	323	338	541	577	8635	392	2324	1806	158	582	237	89
	6167	2379	651	223	246	339	341	5190	201	549	816	104	571	73	76
	2414	887	213	91	50	160	141	2075	122	248	237	46	159	99	55
	16228	7106	1845	549	698	853	487	10002	542	905	2129	187	1034	170	109
…ino	3328	1661	194	157	16	93	23	660	32	170	78	34	85	18	3
	3743	1629	296	111	108	127	99	1208	122	98	172	36	140	29	11
…o	75754	38491	12612	664	7147	1116	2650	73719	2367	5419	25864	1687	13602	3548	1170
	14824	6578	1149	941	596	586	445	6226	305	535	1581	123	1084	189	55
…spo	3833	2320	132	222	42	129	24	939	56	76	101	34	94	33	5
	3497	1935	381	68	185	92	186	3138	192	197	984	66	258	87	60
…a	6538	4362	319	225	90	187	112	1246	66	134	189	34	118	92	13
	17241	9267	1423	875	514	651	380	9603	690	796	2365	153	1007	481	96
	6758	3619	525	222	221	223	328	1985	187	196	596	66	285	49	35
	2937	1147	197	206	55	186	45	1236	38	85	167	29	209	51	11
	2816	1305	314	66	84	128	172	2803	221	494	496	69	344	106	38
	4321	1763	312	245	60	289	112	2527	62	128	246	35	241	87	24
	11283	4332	1202	797	660	561	390	5608	488	471	2443	176	643	82	53
	15656	6923	1056	1363	342	623	424	4163	565	383	1281	137	642	84	93
	5147	1884	321	565	107	242	154	1352	94	149	317	35	179	44	71
	3949	1492	254	399	44	292	76	1081	61	114	276	50	240	34	33
	2834	1009	209	278	43	130	25	753	41	51	125	19	135	11	10
	1397	712	130	37	32	61	60	1816	45	93	201	20	171	37	20
	3977	1727	183	455	18	106	28	556	39	50	71	18	78	5	5
	4182	2468	265	66	214	82	249	3968	82	386	559	80	389	141	40
	7778	2809	602	806	137	477	128	2121	193	224	489	62	483	30	38
	6141	2760	550	236	139	366	279	4707	167	283	927	73	434	102	23

…at Britain, not stated: Amador, 34; El Dorado, 8; Sacramento, 2; San Francisco, 28; San … Santa Clara, 1.

TERRITORY OF COLORADO.

…ties.	NATIVE. Total.	Born in the Territory.	Territory of New Mexico.	New York.	Ohio.	Illinois.	Missouri.	FOREIGN-BORN. Total.	British America.	England and Wales.*	Ireland.	Scotland.	Germany.	France.	Sweden and Norway.
	5129	825	55	637	471	399	456	1700	142	201	545	46	443	91	59
	482	51	96	39	26	24	72	110	14	9	44	3	25	4	....
	1721	375	1	168	164	153	61	218	38	35	38	6	42	5	29
	1220	191	3	243	94	86	60	376	43	154	80	6	48	12	15
	2489	986	1473	4	4	....	3	15	8	....	2	....	5	4	2
	1721	494	1137	32	8	4	8	58	9	2	22	....	24	4	....
	1088	164	16	106	109	72	115	300	38	47	66	11	71	16	16
	894	160	52	51	105	77	82	93	22	19	19	5	20	3	3
	817	116	45	61	67	91	85	247	15	38	8	1	166	3	....
	3739	664	2	641	288	357	134	1751	146	672	511	44	266	20	27
	333	4	12	50	29	23	37	177	19	14	76	10	30	10	5
	2208	518	1442	12	11	14	22	42	7	4	8	....	3	1	....
	1985	384	5	188	231	184	171	405	101	103	56	10	60	5	41
	413	69	....	46	41	24	21	109	7	16	33	8	25	4	3
	722	127	1	87	99	49	64	116	35	33	12	9	15	3	1

TABLE XVIII.—*Native and Foreign Population, &c.*—Continued.

TERRITORY OF COLORADO—Continued.

Counties.	NATIVE.							FOREIGN-BORN.							
	Total.	Born in the Territory.	Territory of New Mexico.	New York.	Ohio.	Illinois.	Missouri.	Total.	British America.	England and Wales.*	Ireland.	Scotland.	Germany.	France.	Sweden and Norway.
Las Animas	4151	508	3339	25	22	14	56	125	7	6	11	3	19	4	....
Park	332	59	....	36	37	28	25	115	22	31	8	2	20	13	11
Pueblo	2056	341	569	94	76	72	172	209	34	26	46	12	53	5	1
Saguache	281	74	130	8	9	11	8	23	3	1	1	....	16	....	....
Summit	168	13	....	29	26	5	6	90	11	28	14	3	27	....	3
Weld	1316	221	....	221	140	125	46	320	45	84	85	9	76	2	4

* Also Great Britain, not stated: Park, 1.

STATE OF CONNECTICUT.

Counties.	NATIVE.							FOREIGN-BORN.							
	Total.	Born in the State.	New York.	Massachusetts.	Rhode Island.	New Jersey.	Vermont.	Total.	British America.	England and Wales.	Ireland.	Scotland.	Germany.	France.	Sweden and Norway.
Fairfield	77400	60995	11611	1541	207	915	209	17876	387	2157	12019	437	2646	117	97
Hartford	82716	68701	3994	5175	586	434	802	26201	1359	3026	16957	925	3341	164	72
Litchfield	41655	35686	3206	1729	102	87	160	7072	403	940	4706	86	575	230	30
Middlesex	28545	25132	1384	728	160	196	145	7554	213	1020	5418	209	430	19	63
New Haven	91415	76775	6286	3094	208	762	550	29842	1089	3672	19621	711	3906	219	83
New London	53668	45367	1989	1620	2753	184	279	12902	2373	1112	7465	568	943	36	41
Tolland	18469	45264	462	1615	512	56	198	3531	431	636	1511	66	793	30	....
Windham	29947	22578	662	2369	3309	60	303	8571	1606	726	2935	146	109	6	1

TERRITORY OF DAKOTA.

Counties.	NATIVE.							FOREIGN-BORN.							
	Total.	Born in the Territory.	New York.	Iowa.	Pennsylvania.	Illinois.	Ohio.	Total.	British America.	England and Wales.*	Ireland.	Scotland.	Germany.	France.	Sweden and Norway.
Bonbomme	392	42	69	51	34	9	30	216	9	16	22	....	19	1	....
Brookings	151	14	....	2	..		....	12	2	....	....	....	....	....	10
Buffalo	183	58	13	1	13	3	15	63	19	3	18	1	17	3	....
Charles Mix	135	108	3	3	2	....	2	17	12	....	....	....	2	2	....
Clay	1755	329	211	282	160	214	143	806	79	29	53	8	37	12	559
Deuel	25	4	....	....	2	1	....	12	....	....	....	....	....	....	12
Hutchinson	22	2	....	6	1	....	3	15	5	....	7	....	1	....	....

TABLE XVIII.—*Native and Foreign Population, &c.*—Continued.

TERRITORY OF DAKOTA—Continued.

Counties.	NATIVE. Total.	Born in the Territory.	New York.	Iowa.	Pennsylvania.	Illinois.	Ohio.	FOREIGN-BORN. Total.	British America.	England and Wales.*	Ireland.	Scotland.	Germany.	France.	Sweden and Norway.
…e	5	...	...	...	...	1	...	...	...	...	...	...	...	...	...
…oln	476	37	64	87	27	41	38	236	30	4	4	9	14	...	174
…nehaha	200	19	18	19	2	5	12	155	6	3	3	...	2	...	141
…bina	801	605	46	2	31	4	23	412	229	24	70	7	53	5	11
…d	229	21	51	3	15	7	35	108	14	8	54	3	26	1	1
…on	2503	505	334	442	150	230	140	1004	348	42	150	19	24	4	412
…kton	1356	197	240	138	98	102	93	741	54	29	79	8	130	12	224
…rganized portion of …rritory	1133	147	224	8	132	21	161	958	99	93	428	22	238	17	15

* Also Great Britain, not stated: Unorganized portion of Territory, 2.

STATE OF DELAWARE.

Counties.	NATIVE. Total.	Born in the State.	Pennsylvania.	Maryland.	New Jersey.	New York.	Virginia and West Virginia.	FOREIGN-BORN. Total.	British America.	England and Wales.	Ireland.	Scotland.	Germany.	France.	Sweden and Norway.
…t	29284	25280	1151	1556	403	579	56	520	35	102	223	17	117	4	...
…Castle	54996	40450	7277	4039	1418	466	353	8519	70	1318	5670	208	1610	112	8
…ex	31509	29015	336	1551	218	266	41	97	7	41	11	4	15	6	1

DISTRICT OF COLUMBIA.

County.	NATIVE. Total.	Born in the District.	Virginia and West Virginia.	Maryland.	New York.	Pennsylvania.	Massachusetts.	FOREIGN-BORN. Total.	British America.	England and Wales.	Ireland.	Scotland.	Germany.	France.	Norway and Sweden.
…hington	115446	52340	23506	21751	4397	4223	1254	16254	290	1151	8218	352	4920	233	27

TABLE XVIII.—*Native and Foreign Population, &c.*—Continued.

STATE OF FLORIDA.

Counties.	Native. Total.	Born in the State.	Georgia.	South Carolina.	Alabama.	North Carolina.	Virginia and West Virginia.	Foreign-born. Total.	British America.	England and Wales.*	Ireland.	Scotland.	Germany.	France.	Sweden and Norway.
Alachua	17228	8341	1817	6116	249	357	144	100	5	10	27	18	23	6	....
Baker	1320	744	390	129	1	38	12	5	....	3	....	....	2	....	....
Bradford	3665	2720	829	351	7	74	20	6	1	1	1	....	2	....	....
Brevard	1216	437	472	199	96	12	14	....	....	....	....	....	....	....	....
Calhoun	996	694	141	33	69	48	4	2	....	2	....	....	....	....	....
Clay	2081	1383	435	140	13	39	7	17	....	7	1	2	2	2	....
Columbia	7303	4263	1519	1086	37	229	57	32	2	....	6	2	2	....	....
Dade	73	19	13	15	....	1	6	13	1	4	....	....	2	2	....
Duval	11402	6472	1651	1310	133	371	240	519	36	65	74	23	129	21	2
Escambia	7249	3714	351	170	1779	167	235	568	44	56	214	20	108	22	9
Franklin	1104	745	110	40	53	46	42	152	2	3	57	2	26	....	2
Gadsden	9702	6918	1247	661	143	371	201	40	1	5	10	7	12	....	2
Hamilton	5741	3826	1615	549	21	174	43	8	1	....	5	....	2	....	....
Hernando	2920	1692	574	348	147	90	20	18	3	2	5	1	2	....	....
Hillsborough	3137	1924	611	176	146	100	44	79	2	8	12	3	26	6	2
Holmes	1571	789	254	103	371	47	3	1	....	....	....	....	....	....	1
Jackson	9506	6557	1225	177	466	895	119	22	....	3	8	1	9	....	....
Jefferson	13341	9711	1506	1266	59	409	255	57	....	11	9	7	11	4	....
La Fayette	1781	1129	336	77	190	21	5	2	....	....	....	....	....	1	....
Leon	15129	10092	1763	657	188	1272	696	107	7	19	15	7	29	9	....
Levy	1984	1263	294	188	88	56	13	34	....	13	12	1	6	....	1
Liberty	1048	750	130	84	24	....	16	2	....	....	....	....	....	....	....
Madison	11088	6394	1966	1909	174	255	165	33	3	4	5	3	14	2	....
Manatee	1903	1227	395	61	84	33	14	28	....	5	4	1	4	2	2
Marion	10773	5925	957	2828	276	453	186	31	....	3	7	....	11	....	....
Monroe	3140	2429	113	79	23	24	69	2508	28	66	129	20	62	15	17
Nassau	4089	2421	882	264	41	101	86	158	9	32	46	5	36	4	3
Orange	2174	1127	663	151	52	94	16	21	1	9	7	....	1	....	1
Polk	3157	1637	882	384	64	70	36	12	....	....	3	....	....	....	....
Putnam	3734	1916	518	855	84	142	28	87	2	20	20	3	17	3	....
Santa Rosa	3239	1982	182	91	725	67	41	73	7	13	20	2	17	2	4
St. John's	2483	1806	185	139	24	23	37	135	11	19	20	....	26	22	....
Sumter	2945	1424	998	287	142	45	16	7	2	....	1	1	3	....	....
Suwannee	3550	1796	1008	353	96	145	43	6	1	....	2	....	1	....	....
Taylor	1452	890	395	66	58	41	4	1	....	....	....	....	1	....	....
Volusia	1695	691	558	288	9	42	11	27	2	15	4	1	1	....	....
Wakulla	2483	1529	419	225	57	115	56	23	1	2	7	1	5	....	....
Walton	3018	1631	290	117	805	135	19	23	1	4	3	11	4	....	....
Washington	2293	1116	379	54	340	82	5	9	1	1	3	2	1	1	....

* Also Great Britain, not stated: Columbia, 12; Franklin, 9; La Fayette, 1; Liberty, 2; Suwannee, 1.

STATE OF GEORGIA.

Counties.	Native. Total.	Born in the State.	South Carolina.	North Carolina.	Virginia and West Virginia.	Alabama.	Tennessee.	Foreign-born. Total.	British America.	England and Wales.	Ireland.	Scotland.	Germany.	France.	Sweden and Norway.
Appling	5071	4573	326	48	9	6	4	15	...	2	2	....	....	1	1
Baker	6833	5696	645	210	161	56	5	10	...	1	2	....	....	....	....
Baldwin	10545	9642	287	128	276	47	33	83	2	18	36	2	17	5	....
Banks	4972	4405	342	127	36	26	19	1	....	....	1	....	....	....	....
Bartow	16491	12971	2053	622	279	162	343	75	3	30	25	11	5	....	....
Berrien	4510	4139	150	108	20	12	7	8	....	....	6	1	1	....	....

TABLE XVIII.—*Native and Foreign Population, &c.*—Continued.

STATE OF GEORGIA—Continued.

Counties.	NATIVE.							FOREIGN-BORN.							
	Total.	Born in the State.	South Carolina.	North Carolina.	Virginia and West Virginia.	Alabama.	Tennessee.	Total.	British America.	England and Wales.*	Ireland.	Scotland.	Germany.	France.	Sweden and Norway.
Bibb	20492	17732	630	393	663	208	119	763	18	84	284	32	246	29	1
Brooks	8317	7145	458	185	158	53	27	25	....	2	6	1	2	1	....
Bryan	5247	5029	132	7	25	3	9	5	....	....	3	....	....	....	....
Bullock	5599	5470	107	9	2	....	2	11	....	....	7	....	1	....	....
Burke	17648	17255	269	34	84	10	3	31	....	....	13	....	7	1	....
Butts	6927	6655	100	64	57	22	5	14	....	....	4	5	1	....	....
Calhoun	5496	4886	329	87	102	52	4	7	....	1	1	....	1	....	....
Camden	4559	4072	208	33	37	6	1	56	3	9	6	2	6	2	1
Campbell	9151	8490	429	138	39	23	15	25	....	....	22	1	2	....	....
Carroll	11768	10320	583	985	67	390	67	14	....	6	6	1	1	....	....
Catoosa	4395	2912	282	270	66	72	711	14	1	2	6	1	3	1	....
Charlton	1891	1670	42	68	60	1	2	6	....	2	2	....	....	....	....
Chatham	37363	31484	3016	186	430	107	49	3916	67	255	2273	78	884	110	19
Chattahoochee	6052	5327	144	99	239	190	4	7	....	2	3	1	....	....	....
Chattooga	6893	5341	611	234	63	385	224	9	2	2	4	....	1	....	....
Cherokee	10378	8446	1377	351	81	45	48	21	1	12	6	....	1	1	....
Clarke	12818	12010	291	130	188	49	15	123	1	17	24	8	48	4	1
Clay	5469	4717	198	112	87	256	17	24	....	1	4	2	8	....	....
Clayton	5461	4877	273	88	83	84	11	16	....	1	10	....	5	....	....
Clinch	3928	3551	131	66	16	13	30	17	1	3	8	1	3	....	....
Cobb	13757	11859	1190	317	106	55	85	57	1	26	11	2	10	....	....
Coffee	3188	3095	60	17	4	....	2	4	....	1	3	....	....	....	....
Colquitt	1649	1450	76	65	5	20	....	5	....	1	1	....	1	....	....
Columbia	13484	12656	473	148	99	19	11	45	3	7	18	5	6	1	....
Coweta	15835	14006	739	233	405	253	40	40	3	3	10	5	10	3	....
Crawford	7555	7050	213	95	108	61	2	2	....	....	2	....	....	....	....
Dade	3016	1752	85	90	28	255	737	17	1	....	....	4	3	....	....
Dawson	4302	3423	620	234	27	13	38	7	....	3	3	....	....	....	....
Decatur	15126	12103	760	366	290	235	98	57	....	5	11	7	24	3	....
De Kalb	9976	8790	694	207	123	54	34	38	2	2	20	6	3	4	....
Dooly	9773	9020	238	263	161	42	7	17	....	4	6	2	1	....	....
Dougherty	11364	9376	817	275	459	139	34	153	2	22	19	3	79	2	....
Early	6984	5800	314	243	173	218	13	14	1	4	6	....	....	....	....
Echols	1978	1759	120	17	9	5	1	....	....	....	....	....	....	....	....
Effingham	4199	3863	255	25	21	4	....	15	1	4	5	2	1	....	....
Elbert	9233	8571	429	34	136	8	8	16	....	1	6	....	5	1	....
Emanuel	6118	5738	260	50	39	4	2	16	3	3	3	1	2	....	....
Fannin	5421	3697	179	1173	50	10	283	8	....	8	....	....	....	....	....
Fayette	8209	7564	378	130	95	50	9	12	....	1	9	1	1	....	....
Floyd	17070	12811	1364	656	469	1096	342	160	....	37	33	25	35	4	2
Forsyth	7979	6640	889	292	59	37	33	4	....	1	2	....	1	....	....
Franklin	7888	6580	1091	108	49	23	8	5	....	1	....	....	1	....	....
Fulton	32267	26657	1562	610	877	498	527	1179	40	179	470	29	346	24	5
Gilmer	6644	4710	456	1258	23	8	106	....	....	....	....	....	....	....	....
Glascock	2732	2673	26	18	6	5	....	4	....	....	....	1	....	1	....
Glynn	5225	4383	304	60	54	28	5	151	3	24	51	3	15	7	3
Gordon	9239	7298	756	570	178	118	243	29	1	5	14	3	1	1	....
Greene	12424	12013	84	72	151	15	12	30	....	6	7	....	10	....	....
Gwinnett	12417	11177	788	155	209	14	24	14	....	2	7	4	....	....	....
Habersham	6298	5116	719	341	57	19	21	24	....	....	17	....	5	....	....
Hall	9587	8424	858	143	75	21	35	20	....	1	12	5	2	....	....
Hancock	11279	10897	76	115	121	9	9	38	....	3	24	....	8	....	....
Haralson	4000	3419	229	96	28	178	34	4	....	....	2	1	....	....	....
Harris	13270	12222	311	145	303	233	19	8	....	2	1	....	....	....	....
Hart	6781	5506	1098	77	54	20	7	2	....	2	....	....	....	....	....
Heard	7861	7201	183	75	65	301	10	5	1	2	2	....	....	....	....
Henry	10096	9445	362	147	65	29	16	12	....	2	6	....	....	....	....
Houston	20359	17637	1189	474	729	86	57	47	3	9	14	1	9	2	....
Irwin	1836	1733	39	48	8	4	1	1	....	1	....	....	....	....	....
Jackson	11175	10547	347	110	104	16	25	6	....	....	4	....	....	1	....
Jasper	10425	10035	72	53	201	15	10	14	....	1	2	....	5	....	....
Jefferson	12163	11717	142	83	125	12	3	27	1	2	10	1	2	1	1
Johnson	2962	2959	2	....	1	....	....	2	....	....	1	....	1	....	....
Jones	9429	8992	86	155	112	21	16	7	1	3	....	....	....	....	2
Laurens	7820	7579	74	92	50	10	2	14	....	9	5	....	5	....	....
Lee	9555	8799	214	178	247	36	13	12	....	2	3	....	4	....	....
Liberty	7669	7495	83	19	7	6	1	19	....	1	5	....	....	....	....
Lincoln	5409	4953	377	26	31	9	1	5	....	2	1	2	....	....	....
Lowndes	8297	7454	460	105	96	29	9	24	1	1	12	2	5	....	....

TABLE XVIII.—*Native and Foreign Population, &c.*—Continued.

STATE OF GEORGIA—Continued.

Counties.	NATIVE. Total.	Born in the State.	South Carolina.	North Carolina.	Virginia and West Virginia.	Alabama.	Tennessee.	FOREIGN-BORN. Total.	British America.	England and Wales.*	Ireland.	Scotland.	Germany.	France.	Sweden and Norway.
Lumpkin	5151	4293	361	365	37	2	71	10	1	....	4	....	3	....	....
Macon	11430	9759	712	380	390	68	18	28	....	....	4	....	12	1	....
Madison	5227	5019	102	47	46	1	3	....	....	....	....	....	....	....	....
Marion	7991	7199	225	215	182	92	12	9	....	1	5	....	1	....	....
McIntosh	4415	4086	163	42	17	7	1	76	5	11	24	4	13	1	1
Meriwether	13742	13157	245	100	188	23	13	14	....	....	5	3	....	....	....
Miller	3089	2658	181	77	34	63	10	2	....	....	2	....	....	....	....
Milton	4292	3798	302	58	20	24	8	2	....	1	1	....	....	....	....
Mitchell	6613	5382	504	297	196	121	20	20	3	....	5	1	6	....	1
Monroe	17186	16290	227	179	378	25	11	27	2	3	4	1	10	....	....
Montgomery	3569	3374	41	114	21	9	3	17	....	1	7	4	1	....	....
Morgan	10674	9900	145	111	297	30	15	22	1	4	1	1	10	....	....
Murray	6482	4234	522	561	80	49	967	16	....	5	9	....	4	....	....
Muscogee	16240	12305	545	487	726	1513	73	423	16	31	175	42	112	6	....
Newton	14593	13281	550	257	243	98	36	22	....	9	7	1	3	....	....
Oglethorpe	11755	11351	109	37	191	17	24	27	1	4	10	....	7	1	....
Paulding	7635	6655	603	194	30	91	45	4	....	....	2	1	1	....	....
Pickens	5307	4215	529	430	45	20	39	10	....	6	1	....	....	3	....
Pierce	2771	2457	196	45	27	6	....	7	....	....	4	....	2	....	....
Pike	10889	9961	283	172	248	116	30	16	1	3	5	....	5	....	....
Polk	7790	6361	486	168	175	439	99	32	....	20	5	2	3	....	....
Pulaski	11912	10766	274	427	259	57	14	28	2	....	10	2	10	....	....
Putnam	10424	9780	98	124	281	37	15	37	....	2	8	2	19	....	....
Quitman	4140	3583	124	110	75	183	7	10	....	....	5	2	3	....	....
Rabun	3254	2413	373	405	10	3	45	2	....	1	1	....	....	....	....
Randolph	10509	9423	331	252	213	190	28	52	1	1	15	1	15	6	....
Richmond	24051	17560	3950	384	843	187	113	1673	28	131	930	36	367	60	1
Schley	5124	4736	164	89	69	38	....	5	1	1	....	1	....	....	....
Scriven	9137	8257	724	52	47	2	2	38	1	7	7	1	12	1	1
Spalding	10144	9257	247	157	240	83	49	61	1	4	10	2	31	....	....
Stewart	14175	12818	197	249	290	421	35	25	1	1	6	5	10	1	1
Sumter	16478	14742	431	403	506	138	49	81	5	11	21	6	27	1	....
Talbot	11898	11260	242	108	176	66	6	15	....	1	7	....	3	....	....
Taliaferro	4765	4670	13	11	53	3	4	31	....	....	24	....	4	1	1
Tatnall	4827	4629	100	48	22	2	....	33	....	3	5	3	17	....	....
Taylor	7133	6719	138	121	62	51	13	10	....	....	2	1	3	1	....
Telfair	3240	3080	47	80	25	3	....	5	1	....	1	3	....	....	....
Terrell	9025	8119	337	212	144	95	50	28	2	....	10	1	9	....	....
Thomas	14440	11745	446	672	425	195	46	83	1	2	4	5	39	....	....
Towns	2779	1870	115	740	8	4	33	1	....	....	....	....	....	....	....
Troup	17568	15839	318	236	420	691	49	64	....	15	11	6	21	2	....
Twiggs	8538	8254	46	78	130	12	3	7	....	1	5	....	....	1	....
Union	5265	4001	166	943	11	1	128	2	....	1	....	....	1	....	....
Upson	9423	9209	55	53	61	3	27	7	....	1	1	2	3	....	....
Walker	9881	6951	708	550	109	270	1121	44	....	3	3	....	25	....	5
Walton	11036	10772	84	66	51	3	11	2	....	1	....	....	1	....	....
Ware	2280	2117	86	31	7	4	1	6	....	....	1	1	3	....	....
Warren	10500	10264	59	44	70	4	8	45	2	7	16	1	13	....	1
Washington	15805	15496	123	94	36	4	2	37	2	3	10	3	17	1	....
Wayne	2166	2024	58	43	3	4	....	11	....	4	1	....	4	....	1
Webster	4675	4220	244	88	50	38	8	2	....	....	1	1	....	....	....
White	4596	3723	487	307	16	7	28	16	....	2	....	2	....	....	....
Whitfield	10013	6686	966	641	232	120	1222	104	6	5	36	2	34	5	....
Wilcox	2436	2292	51	42	18	7	....	3	....	2	....	1	....	....	....
Wilkes	11734	11196	209	58	165	17	26	62	2	4	24	....	21	1	....
Wilkinson	9366	8873	88	151	236	7	1	17	....	....	6	4	5	....	....
Worth	3774	3428	145	153	21	7	1	4	....	....	1	....	....	....	....

* Also Great Britain, not stated: Chatham, 21; Glascock, 1; Pulaski, 1; Randolph, 5; Whitfield, 10; Worth, 1.

TABLE XVIII.—*Native and Foreign Population, &c.*—Continued.

TERRITORY OF IDAHO.

Counties.	NATIVE.							FOREIGN-BORN.							
	Total.	Born in the Territory.	New York.	Ohio.	Missouri.	Utah.	Pennsylvania.	Total.	British America.	England and Wales.*	Ireland.	Scotland.	Germany.	France.	Sweden and Norway.
Ada	2178	308	199	193	243	19	97	497	49	49	118	13	90	17	18
Alturas	286	37	49	34	14	4	25	403	16	24	25	2	10	2	3
•Boise	1183	187	129	86	69	1	66	2651	95	84	322	18	177	35	35
Idaho	205	21	30	16	10	....	15	644	15	21	47	2	52	45	1
Lemhi	500	24	63	41	37	6	63	479	44	35	135	18	56	13	21
Nez Percés	609	75	76	45	40	3	25	908	42	20	71	4	54	11	6
Oneida	1189	214	163	46	53	444	77	733	18	516	53	35	32	4	31
Owyhee	862	75	142	86	64	2	48	851	42	111	141	12	114	10	18
Shoshone	93	5	22	1	4	....	....	629	13	13	72	3	14	7	19

* Also Great Britain not stated: Ada, 1; Lemhi, 1; Owyhee, 7.

STATE OF ILLINOIS.

Counties.	NATIVE.							FOREIGN-BORN.							
	Total.	Born in the State.	Ohio.	New York.	Pennsylvania.	Indiana.	Kentucky.	Total.	British America.	England and Wales.*	Ireland.	Scotland.	Germany.	France.	Sweden and Norway.
Adams	44622	27746	2652	1431	2055	1075	1902	11740	155	655	1549	88	8809	145	35
Alexander	9163	4181	357	160	179	221	812	1401	70	79	601	21	447	53	7
Bond	11980	8167	811	124	235	422	387	1172	13	110	97	20	494	83	....
Boone	10145	5226	321	2566	370	37	6	2797	403	651	568	249	330	20	528
Brown	11357	7467	1056	147	323	288	803	848	21	96	391	9	270	49	1
Bureau	26182	14073	2631	2420	2308	529	173	6233	429	809	1321	152	1976	77	1214
Calhoun	5347	3523	294	60	108	144	171	1215	35	30	110	5	875	36	1
Carroll	14215	7041	576	1305	3147	193	57	2490	291	278	522	92	1099	34	96
Cass	9711	6990	371	257	232	191	394	1809	34	209	407	75	1078	8	19
Champaign	28725	12274	5832	1433	1330	3384	1096	4012	280	595	1174	116	1348	43	355
Christian	18444	9911	2807	454	705	1138	1042	1919	305	236	609	24	542	114	18
Clark	17800	9725	2800	196	476	2534	731	919	22	76	307	21	406	27	6
Clay	15301	7753	1731	193	260	3013	831	574	27	135	100	19	226	26	14
Clinton	11746	8650	417	238	303	255	259	4539	61	119	236	11	3476	247	3
Coles	24182	12374	3169	313	512	3367	2145	1053	59	135	463	35	284	21	1
Cook	183104	108709	5663	28092	4807	2370	1748	166772	10926	12281	43415	4565	65448	1740	13495
Crawford	13702	8314	2147	87	361	1257	601	127	7	19	35	4	57	3	....
Cumberland	11887	6009	1940	102	233	2188	506	336	7	31	112	10	144	10	5
De Kalb	18671	9748	582	4624	1125	110	28	4594	745	731	1107	137	790	81	893
De Witt	13963	7547	2924	322	327	686	633	805	44	155	407	31	123	14	8
Douglas	12796	5314	2008	232	409	2734	958	688	66	106	150	12	319	13	1
Du Page	11472	7310	193	1566	975	70	19	5213	184	511	427	67	3243	464	130
Edgar	20764	10708	2943	206	592	2873	1637	686	19	94	326	20	187	22	3
Edwards	6565	4855	295	53	86	371	394	1000	2	596	46	11	315	7	....
Effingham	12858	7323	1783	455	376	1377	391	2705	77	117	228	21	2122	58	63
Fayette	18122	11168	2064	400	491	930	657	1516	44	129	296	15	827	35	6
Ford	7105	3167	1118	611	611	623	108	1998	118	330	251	70	381	17	771
Franklin	12580	8783	175	69	111	350	576	72	3	13	16	....	33	2	....
Fulton	30298	20720	4521	1488	3043	1160	890	1903	76	623	547	121	335	29	231
Gallatin	10727	6837	415	65	113	521	881	407	12	56	151	16	142	20	[illegible]
Greene	18630	13157	629	336	259	301	1066	1647	62	337	683	40	403	12	8
Grundy	10944	6213	901	1632	708	230	37	3994	279	965	1198	343	510	22	623

TABLE XVIII.—*Native and Foreign Population, &c.*—Continued.

STATE OF ILLINOIS—Continued.

Counties.	NATIVE. Total.	Born in the State.	Ohio.	New York.	Pennsylvania.	Indiana.	Kentucky.	FOREIGN-BORN. Total.	British America.	England and Wales.	Ireland.	Scotland.	Germany.	France.	Sweden and Norway.
Hamilton	12824	9087	450	36	64	202	777	190	1	29	48	....	104	2	.....
Hancock	31777	18350	2908	1205	1835	1139	1471	4158	145	350	630	109	2110	355	33
Hardin	4920	3167	127	39	45	244	544	184	6	30	12	19	107	2	.....
Henderson	10946	5784	1132	541	731	736	351	1636	64	122	398	52	354	26	493
Henry	25228	13747	2489	2624	2544	517	160	10278	398	1372	993	183	1642	139	5329
Iroquois	21139	10011	2902	1742	917	3111	240	4643	1676	577	718	114	864	135	229
Jackson	17902	11028	579	293	532	399	978	1732	114	441	342	216	459	53	33
Jasper	10707	5602	1323	71	159	2193	668	527	7	35	66	3	254	147	1
Jefferson	17657	11671	625	108	149	594	722	207	25	51	36	13	66	5	5
Jersey	12502	8041	702	388	298	217	325	2532	54	255	1024	55	943	72	5
Jo Daviess	19966	14168	621	1359	1069	193	134	7854	303	1937	2156	123	2799	110	43
Johnson	11186	7197	67	26	28	65	885	62	4	11	33	2	8	3	.....
Kane	28755	15548	599	6651	914	160	49	10336	1285	1534	2317	414	2725	88	1084
Kankakee	16672	10437	893	2074	546	981	77	7680	3813	505	766	91	1907	203	130
Kendall	9715	5451	320	2057	478	116	27	2684	227	630	369	146	578	6	688
Knox	31843	16805	3774	3005	2336	955	716	7679	213	721	1299	406	349	16	4586
Lake	15296	9515	343	2876	293	39	16	5718	367	1041	1608	297	2020	253	33
La Salle	44530	26734	2867	4995	3760	618	189	16262	636	1749	5390	525	4908	749	1582
Lawrence	12176	7396	1634	87	409	1206	544	357	9	51	176	5	78	31	.....
Lee	21067	11069	1000	2614	3167	259	53	6104	528	535	1932	122	2232	152	479
Livingston	25440	13225	3186	2412	2179	921	346	6031	402	942	1545	307	1969	203	311
Logan	20023	11808	3194	570	781	821	938	3030	95	250	794	109	1691	17	37
Macon	24283	12249	3730	731	2063	1523	1279	2198	135	324	780	42	783	46	.....
Macoupin	27946	18686	1096	504	584	545	1878	4780	92	971	1188	85	2144	51	22
Madison	31251	22017	862	616	639	481	554	12880	256	856	1799	290	7422	284	20
Marion	19207	10965	1968	526	533	1037	829	1415	107	239	248	57	621	52	1
Marshall	13858	7846	1505	1000	1183	545	155	3098	185	429	874	202	1089	52	195
Mason	14117	8409	1589	430	887	677	507	2067	47	259	340	19	1314	20	30
Massac	8894	4383	519	43	78	413	1354	687	12	43	20	10	588	7	.....
McDonough	24784	14141	2771	702	1791	855	1439	1725	118	535	420	160	341	17	163
McHenry	19134	10214	448	4790	560	96	24	4028	382	713	1061	207	1187	160	172
McLean	46026	22964	7580	2598	2713	2215	2296	7962	420	952	2949	230	2839	207	50
Menard	10232	6963	438	240	180	351	982	1503	59	82	330	41	804	7	136
Mercer	16508	8529	2096	634	2190	1163	274	2261	109	339	583	85	310	18	793
Monroe	8670	7476	87	68	89	27	83	4312	28	94	432	10	3477	98	.....
Montgomery	22020	14454	1694	520	387	834	1174	2394	67	266	739	74	1092	25	29
Morgan	23805	16254	921	579	553	563	1630	4658	113	1121	1463	197	1062	20	121
Moultrie	9943	5178	1585	86	299	1058	702	442	13	119	171	11	90	8	.....
Ogle	22710	11251	952	3105	3072	190	35	4782	885	424	835	172	2115	21	281
Peoria	35867	21768	3616	2425	2344	834	441	11673	328	1800	3493	344	4399	299	152
Perry	11932	8001	587	239	247	210	480	1791	27	460	387	118	732	9	.....
Piatt	10350	4629	2691	236	427	1026	374	603	35	159	219	23	129	19	8
Pike	28919	18962	2832	692	831	757	1207	1849	63	572	615	61	462	15	5
Pope	10991	6635	169	36	89	257	974	446	11	23	21	12	352	8	.....
Pulaski	8307	3652	372	146	186	163	1112	445	34	37	169	15	159	16	3
Putnam	5248	3020	473	225	665	125	77	1032	41	61	296	11	513	38	48
Randolph	16905	13068	378	191	312	127	377	3954	39	139	577	213	2597	185	4
Richland	11944	6411	2131	157	393	1277	686	859	24	75	113	7	265	71	1
Rock Island	21114	11542	1429	1674	2252	661	288	8669	263	1131	1507	170	2142	77	2127
Saline	12635	8646	364	19	68	317	969	79	2	8	20	1	41	2	1
Sangamon	38575	23465	2609	1509	1177	1225	2615	7777	286	870	3136	178	2565	124	93
Schuyler	15887	10299	1308	314	850	609	824	1532	55	160	624	20	268	27	337
Scott	9354	6576	373	142	209	160	676	1176	45	446	376	35	242	3	5
Shelby	23765	12672	4419	281	888	1898	1193	1711	103	265	289	39	814	31	115
Stark	9475	5102	1192	733	807	257	45	1276	107	308	359	147	158	9	178
St. Clair	32747	25976	620	532	554	372	437	18321	142	1634	2117	231	11878	1324	34
Stephenson	23820	13101	910	1057	5858	143	55	6788	374	413	770	20	4749	160	107
Tazewell	22572	13967	2656	907	1124	760	571	5331	127	390	767	104	3236	310	30
Union	15866	9739	316	176	177	248	502	652	54	87	70	14	348	13	3
Vermilion	28223	13929	4065	593	940	5190	1312	2165	86	494	475	42	888	21	64
Wabash	8290	6195	285	71	280	747	248	551	6	80	28	4	397	16	.....
Warren	20884	10625	2404	1403	2023	951	911	2290	104	371	671	147	225	19	704
Washington	13734	10148	387	297	186	209	458	3865	30	86	295	84	3273	25	10
Wayne	19238	11723	2480	106	514	1411	1159	520	26	127	117	57	155	7	17
White	16241	11371	515	61	128	1617	896	605	18	128	77	25	330	18	.....
Whitesides	22913	10682	1530	3947	3028	496	73	4590	474	669	1380	246	1304	18	228
Will	28426	17647	1374	3989	1541	428	137	14587	824	1898	3085	1092	5763	321	349

TABLE XVIII.—*Native and Foreign Population, &c.*—Continued.

STATE OF ILLINOIS—Continued.

Counties.	NATIVE. Total.	Born in the State.	Ohio.	New York.	Pennsylvania.	Indiana.	Kentucky.	FOREIGN-BORN. Total.	British America.	England and Wales.*	Ireland.	Scotland.	Germany.	France.	Sweden and Norway.
nson	17166	11680	127	34	32	116	898	163	17	31	20	....	91	1	....
bago	22588	11229	816	5029	1038	155	43	6713	1059	1270	1543	604	465	15	1707
ord	14891	8429	1806	709	1221	753	322	4065	70	521	502	50	2335	315	10

› Great Britain not stated: Alexander, 1; Boone, 1; Cook, 23; Hancock, 1; La Salle, 3; Marshall, ›ria, 1; Washington, 1.

STATE OF INDIANA.

Counties.	NATIVE. Total.	Born in the State.	Ohio.	Kentucky.	Pennsylvania.	Virginia and West Virginia.	New York.	FOREIGN-BORN. Total.	British America.	England and Wales.*	Ireland.	Scotland.	Germany.	France.	Sweden and Norway.
	10061	6220	2720	12	644	165	92	1321	11	21	53	2	731	131	1
	34735	21531	7370	93	2324	338	1428	8739	237	367	982	153	5347	1157	25
omew	19700	13558	2299	992	643	341	197	1433	13	60	222	24	960	19	2
	4929	2981	808	69	181	129	178	686	161	85	237	20	108	18	17
rd	6081	3747	1409	38	330	265	65	191	1	22	84	2	74	5	2
	22188	15511	1768	2189	302	650	121	405	12	51	171	8	140	9	1
	8529	5347	1785	424	252	307	32	152	2	25	34	2	69	10	....
	15405	10228	2417	169	1056	477	215	747	46	51	315	8	294	6	4
	21573	13406	3847	283	1488	559	603	2620	199	266	963	39	1012	66	17
	22075	14858	706	3723	468	425	325	2695	69	191	873	32	1262	98	4
	17298	10960	2856	928	840	328	157	1786	38	528	300	281	466	42	25
	17127	12013	2299	481	1075	500	86	203	13	51	80	10	50	5	....
rd	9600	8218	335	556	118	102	46	242	11	18	38	21	91	16	....
s	15840	12268	1097	1177	268	206	104	907	22	17	528	8	192	55	....
rn	19520	15685	1625	579	396	191	285	4596	34	277	602	46	3188	302	3
r	17820	12822	1638	1683	397	394	145	1233	15	54	323	18	733	36	....
b	16303	7919	5420	10	1482	108	659	964	45	135	105	13	541	27	4
re	18329	11919	3671	217	664	1124	139	501	13	48	253	7	122	41	9
	10136	8683	466	483	88	85	28	2461	5	11	5	1	2264	93	....
t	24249	11987	4836	30	3320	318	1545	1777	381	165	157	22	718	50	20
	9712	6406	885	394	355	219	195	764	6	48	364	10	295	19	1
	19605	13966	504	2313	664	350	329	3695	60	527	691	38	1792	406	9
in	15441	10837	1670	582	499	305	197	948	27	58	305	15	274	12	205
n	17295	13418	1875	381	436	244	174	2928	16	174	208	22	2291	112	3
	12212	7519	2717	148	919	295	207	514	35	36	82	13	251	23	....
	16178	12716	429	1012	129	230	105	1193	17	108	229	34	743	43	....
	18173	12057	3512	277	516	525	100	314	11	85	111	20	71	6	2
	19218	13747	2331	938	503	307	101	296	7	67	45	7	130	5	....
on	20491	14426	1899	443	751	407	129	391	12	4	62	4	243	24	7
k	14580	10991	1270	546	262	560	45	543	8	20	183	8	297	12	....
on	18658	15778	154	1343	248	555	32	1255	9	38	40	2	913	208	2
cks	19762	13454	864	2326	163	541	95	515	6	54	343	15	50	2	27
	22532	15214	1973	350	911	1428	164	454	9	94	230	15	88	6	12
l	15542	10736	2455	431	423	300	93	305	19	26	116	3	112	7	3
gton	17746	10474	4637	158	1150	292	311	1290	36	51	133	20	882	67	1
a	17379	13896	1161	906	176	149	125	1395	14	23	146	10	1292	45	....
	6014	3784	1061	120	256	139	156	340	22	58	80	5	136	9	....
	14492	8313	4429	62	506	492	118	508	8	12	57	4	308	63	....
on	26158	20716	1288	2254	440	347	282	3583	21	296	972	299	1092	109	[illegible]

TABLE XVIII.—*Native and Foreign Population, &c.*—Continued.

STATE OF INDIANA—Continued.

Counties.	NATIVE. Total.	Born in the State.	Ohio.	Kentucky.	Pennsylvania.	Virginia and West Virginia.	New York.	FOREIGN-BORN. Total.	British America.	England and Wales.*	Ireland.	Scotland.	Germany.	France.	Sweden and Norway.
Jennings	14644	10998	1234	928	329	918	277	1574	29	85	521	14	757	115	....
Johnson	17882	12512	873	2646	266	421	127	484	21	46	222	17	151	[illegible]	1
Knox	19448	15482	676	809	242	401	200	2114	46	109	276	15	1447	161	....
Kosciusko	22803	12458	6611	64	1854	509	468	728	66	108	132	24	303	30	[illegible]
La Grange	13455	6264	3317	9	1579	105	1107	693	89	195	75	9	246	91	[illegible]
Lake	8742	5431	772	20	348	47	795	3597	194	190	260	15	2432	68	[illegible]
La Porte	20420	12640	1710	135	1092	420	2229	6612	315	429	668	92	4374	72	[illegible]
Lawrence	14391	11123	268	1298	113	279	81	237	8	23	89	4	46	21	[illegible]
Madison	22137	15890	2501	339	693	946	146	633	36	52	338	8	132	13	[illegible]
Marion	59292	36106	7070	5083	2492	1213	1857	12647	346	811	3700	277	6536	295	[illegible]
Marshall	18836	11564	4317	174	1084	303	552	1375	81	59	215	5	744	108	[illegible]
Martin	10816	8175	1093	729	147	146	47	257	3	27	150	2	55	10	1
Miami	19949	12152	4419	223	1211	574	354	1103	41	70	266	15	602	31	11
Monroe	13793	10270	473	1230	142	418	83	375	9	50	181	18	97	9	....
Montgomery	22876	16178	2460	1780	401	729	198	887	28	31	626	24	101	11	2
Morgan	17200	12819	588	1181	139	324	75	328	6	92	116	9	150	6	1
Newton	5380	3028	772	106	215	113	314	440	112	71	87	5	120	7	19
Noble	18889	9439	3695	30	1673	244	936	1500	78	125	140	19	944	47	11
Ohio	5384	4374	232	358	144	76	84	453	5	12	55	4	326	1	....
Orange	13398	10977	119	1151	65	152	31	99	4	23	30	3	31	6	....
Owen	15758	11256	1993	776	516	264	53	379	10	34	67	18	226	7	....
Parke	17295	12847	1169	1262	242	660	147	271	31	73	111	14	30	7	....
Perry	12065	9249	638	1248	161	97	103	2736	13	156	302	24	1310	162	2
Pike	13410	10790	294	1380	62	102	57	369	5	58	24	3	263	13	....
Porter	11103	6718	1377	66	600	137	1138	2839	439	143	527	46	983	20	561
Posey	16931	12883	372	1292	187	151	103	2254	3	203	59	11	1773	152	1
Pulaski	6853	4332	1460	72	456	90	115	948	16	46	131	10	600	61	....
Putnam	20724	14585	763	2828	291	568	159	790	30	63	522	13	135	11	12
Randolph	22302	14897	4220	203	636	565	144	560	21	57	172	4	273	21	....
Ripley	17573	14000	1442	826	282	179	174	3404	19	77	217	16	2745	300	8
Rush	17096	12350	1260	1439	358	369	119	530	13	65	294	4	138	9	1
Scott	7646	5994	340	725	98	120	64	227	7	15	132	11	50	2	1
Shelby	21080	15484	1937	1482	374	423	188	812	10	63	230	14	405	36	4
Spencer	16142	11421	1131	2152	225	161	95	1856	7	62	49	20	1451	131	....
Starke	3546	1977	740	50	220	48	109	342	22	21	54	1	188	5	30
Steuben	12407	5367	3560	8	899	44	1425	447	67	114	76	16	126	11	17
St. Joseph	21750	11880	4026	88	1757	227	1514	3572	293	72	554	45	2011	263	27
Sullivan	18184	13892	1142	1334	171	306	123	269	15	104	55	14	68	6	2
Switzerland	11719	9352	442	932	194	165	214	415	10	41	50	42	201	12	....
Tippecanoe	28141	18333	4184	517	1262	652	895	5374	208	307	1926	72	2114	98	298
Tipton	11731	8936	1014	565	228	318	48	222	2	9	68	5	108	4	20
Union	6030	4209	848	124	235	202	58	291	1	11	193	7	57	....	....
Vanderburgh	23882	16848	1097	3014	428	255	450	9323	40	729	541	63	7207	328	7
Vermillion	10604	7164	1069	353	183	348	46	236	13	39	99	5	70	6	....
Vigo	29842	19313	2959	1645	901	762	638	3707	67	325	1391	55	1588	85	18
Wabash	20809	13150	4228	303	1107	506	292	906	39	66	277	5	450	16	....
Warren	9744	6388	1566	192	380	216	182	460	67	36	171	3	142	1	30
Warrick	16265	12044	433	2206	281	143	8	1388	14	925	63	16	1011	30	4
Washington	18143	15321	236	1015	165	301	106	352	6	117	105	10	94	12	....
Wayne	31099	20324	4204	383	1771	773	475	2949	36	254	956	35	1557	37	1
Wells	13029	7444	3563	82	1101	295	105	556	7	55	105	35	177	16	....
White	9986	6254	1870	217	652	323	212	568	35	57	125	26	273	12	6
Whitley	13553	7377	4066	33	964	201	380	846	11	52	149	4	402	77	7

* Also Great Britain not stated: Allen, 82; Daviess, 75; Decatur, 35; Delaware, 1; Floyd, 29; Fulton, 1; Hamilton, 17; Harrison, 15; Henry, 3; Jackson, 45; Jay, 16; Madison, 17; Marion, 38; Marshall, 1; Montgomery, 30; Ohio, 48; St. Joseph, 89; Warrick, 1; Wayne, 26.

TABLE XVIII.—*Native and Foreign Population, &c.*—Continued.

STATE OF IOWA.

Counties.	NATIVE. Total.	Born in the State.	Ohio.	New York.	Pennsylvania.	Illinois.	Indiana.	FOREIGN-BORN. Total.	British America.	England and Wales.*	Ireland.	Scotland.	Germany.	France.	Sweden and Norway.
....	3678	1141	448	264	215	581	449	304	85	58	48	7	78	4	14
....	4337	1488	781	221	225	450	479	277	43	42	54	4	44	51	9
...ee	11765	6774	675	1119	679	480	254	6103	424	173	1660	92	1253	50	2180
...oso	16111	7170	2157	270	973	809	1685	345	33	82	94	8	99	11	4
...n	1103	396	111	104	76	121	78	100	16	57	9	2	7	2	4
....	18849	6996	2767	1770	1910	1599	1515	3605	321	244	472	159	1409	29	396
...awk	17950	6153	1482	2945	2187	1692	573	3756	671	511	603	111	1428	49	37
....	11676	4255	1370	1042	838	1202	1070	2908	225	367	363	141	474	29	1230
....	10056	3399	604	2052	576	1389	312	2472	257	296	237	49	1506	25	15
...an	14462	5090	1447	2665	1059	1081	553	2632	474	337	958	129	632	37	14
...ista	1181	357	131	203	88	90	55	404	76	59	43	5	24	....	104
....	8527	2693	801	1505	644	937	353	1424	347	222	308	57	376	16	15
....	1348	389	145	184	109	137	70	254	33	47	22	9	75	....	51
....	2134	756	347	147	196	164	124	317	25	26	28	9	30	3	189
....	4699	1480	727	432	319	565	360	765	102	146	107	18	160	3	142
....	17389	7420	3167	1317	2399	708	519	2342	253	113	662	151	985	9	14
...ordo	3767	866	304	812	168	329	88	955	210	133	142	53	153	17	197
...e	1600	459	139	187	200	120	72	367	65	43	92	34	25	3	99
...aw	8039	2972	428	1494	346	677	238	2141	287	183	646	41	521	30	333
....	6462	3238	1546	235	533	705	1063	273	34	51	66	8	84	12	9
....	1304	335	98	228	73	84	96	219	38	60	11	3	51	2	38
....	19250	10700	1253	2119	1237	677	328	8521	425	413	1349	143	4152	103	1327
....	24700	11711	1883	3546	1916	1509	570	10657	1282	457	2695	240	4298	49	564
...d	1970	753	166	233	152	239	72	560	73	82	81	28	65	2	187
....	11139	3005	1558	618	720	848	1932	880	140	91	234	35	138	14	177
....	15023	7290	2111	203	533	684	1833	542	92	53	55	16	188	47	11
....	11634	4806	1927	312	499	823	1231	364	75	90	70	26	72	4	5
...e	14305	6252	1098	2547	1053	833	360	3127	414	426	778	121	976	19	23
...nes	20537	11722	2075	893	1568	854	704	6719	136	488	977	84	3572	119	1039
...on	1196	302	58	237	62	105	12	193	49	26	21	13	23	....	60
...o	25405	17374	912	1749	1071	931	186	13764	498	1267	4237	209	4553	430	61
....	990	311	21	207	55	41	12	402	41	19	16	10	15	....	285
....	14116	5952	1183	2331	1023	999	434	2857	374	353	563	139	622	45	512
....	8965	2666	567	1809	399	616	249	1803	464	228	266	67	619	19	80
...n	3814	1082	436	523	313	386	207	924	157	113	183	18	220	4	172
...t	10589	3716	1143	485	458	1031	1059	585	109	95	135	28	137	4	14
....	4231	1375	614	408	273	455	447	396	94	72	129	16	48	4	21
....	4550	1327	367	605	377	881	117	1849	271	89	95	20	1100	5	7
....	6623	2138	1320	356	399	534	1062	438	35	76	113	23	77	8	26
...n	4931	1700	473	687	408	627	213	1124	155	78	68	19	140	10	596
...k	863	264	87	211	46	67	12	136	26	7	8	9	35	2	30
....	11903	4030	1350	1406	850	1316	791	1781	247	226	251	51	796	20	83
...n	8010	3187	943	656	373	562	634	921	211	206	237	31	144	10	39
....	19752	9317	3456	687	1735	758	1168	1711	121	94	418	20	318	83	429
....	4823	1705	192	975	271	250	87	1459	231	333	372	64	214	15	140
...dt	2090	615	96	463	131	204	34	506	96	56	88	5	75	1	114
....	208	65	19	29	20	25	11	18	....	8	5	....	1	....	....
....	12842	5690	2411	1071	1002	698	562	3802	263	433	775	67	1776	151	88
....	17197	10064	1212	1635	1779	635	278	5422	614	436	1093	78	1899	54	24
....	20421	7328	3615	1074	1835	1571	1929	1695	147	353	331	74	682	16	33
...n	15825	8336	2297	312	1633	671	840	2014	52	148	317	47	398	117	872
....	18573	9874	2450	1181	2182	535	506	6325	215	586	1085	53	1531	119	22
....	16766	7614	2031	2264	1370	735	509	2965	395	253	1059	123	486	17	11
....	17852	8597	2959	406	1112	924	1883	1582	74	111	185	100	982	49	6
....	2780	773	186	632	142	267	62	571	125	50	95	63	124	6	75
....	28409	14730	3126	1194	1647	1278	1290	8801	248	474	1931	152	3896	261	1226
....	26987	12186	3985	2673	2733	1238	1050	4093	313	360	692	127	612	64	23
....	11766	6062	1737	432	1214	449	532	1111	62	187	278	21	374	26	43
....	9817	3931	1591	297	768	880	1229	571	58	80	119	13	103	10	164
....	120	53	6	22	4	9	1	101	...	1	2	....	10	....	85
....	13221	5267	2240	264	823	999	1772	663	70	115	247	35	143	7	19
...a	21091	9104	4523	457	1439	906	2073	1417	86	369	264	30	157	12	135
....	21731	10605	3482	392	1278	1029	2314	2705	46	85	126	42	289	33	8
...l	15463	4672	2690	1347	1233	1617	1460	2113	330	254	228	58	659	44	279
....	7784	3059	1085	364	282	581	587	934	92	192	157	14	362	17	58
....	7190	2354	248	1336	310	444	116	2392	298	255	255	59	419	8	956
....	3077	1064	282	344	187	286	225	577	81	70	66	25	56	12	253
...s	11575	5417	1424	301	746	402	1691	1149	72	145	696	19	71	6	92
...nery	5258	1641	963	281	392	570	606	676	60	86	112	10	72	13	275

TABLE XVIII.—*Native and Foreign Population, &c.*—Continued.

STATE OF IOWA—Continued.

Counties.	NATIVE. Total.	Born in the State.	Ohio.	New York.	Pennsylvania.	Illinois.	Indiana.	FOREIGN-BORN. Total.	British America.	England and Wales.*	Ireland.	Scotland.	Germany.	France.	Sweden and Norway.
Muscatine	17449	8828	2656	1076	1651	602	626	4239	145	284	910	67	2214	69	21
O'Brien	649	151	84	101	46	60	47	66	23	13	11	2	4	....	12
Page	9335	3110	1570	298	852	678	1083	640	95	96	150	33	94	3	159
Palo Alto	989	314	72	145	56	89	12	347	63	23	152	....	34	1	2
Plymouth	1550	327	203	218	115	186	60	649	72	107	81	37	280	16	47
Pocahontas	950	288	44	213	52	90	29	496	84	60	97	26	135	1	79
Polk	23944	9489	3547	1534	1089	1431	2656	3913	246	565	1090	113	840	30	179
Pottawattamie	13070	4535	1207	1138	791	1447	681	3823	318	943	669	126	961	42	277
Poweshiek	13956	4464	2534	1129	1168	1368	796	1625	294	197	421	120	306	19	102
Ringgold	5401	2125	962	134	358	515	668	290	55	44	69	4	33	25	4
Sac	1947	303	126	187	112	85	74	164	39	43	18	8	40	4	[illegible]
Scott	24071	13736	1419	1993	2271	1006	379	14528	415	705	2211	231	9982	109	126
Shelby	2187	847	213	166	168	190	214	363	36	61	20	8	14	1	11
Sioux	392	151	71	17	38	23	26	184	1	1	6	....	42	....	1
Story	9642	3552	1287	748	593	1196	1063	2009	203	109	139	56	129	7	1169
Tama	13296	4694	2135	1396	1330	1104	789	2835	492	255	270	222	589	29	35
Taylor	6766	2379	913	329	427	600	896	223	56	41	23	32	15	20	[illegible]
Union	5534	2190	1048	225	371	511	436	452	46	54	81	11	97	7	138
Van Buren	16746	8543	2865	358	1414	496	815	926	51	136	260	61	253	20	41
Wapello	20168	9410	3347	574	1159	1005	1940	2178	108	239	708	45	468	22	49
Warren	17252	7007	3126	326	909	1220	2264	728	59	116	232	102	171	12	13
Washington	17254	7916	3449	586	1859	613	944	1698	144	66	289	30	413	142	11
Wayne	11001	4273	1794	282	622	1023	1223	286	11	77	54	7	113	2	11
Webster	7467	2757	672	1042	490	934	273	3017	250	125	747	54	441	5	1333
Winnebago	896	334	36	110	18	66	25	666	9	15	2	....	6	3	624
Winneshiek	13811	7511	704	1716	471	653	361	9750	723	278	731	49	1031	90	5311
Woodbury	4653	1387	405	671	356	395	204	1519	232	133	401	38	276	9	332
Worth	1799	753	61	267	57	122	18	1093	46	32	27	21	13	....	886
Wright	2094	643	189	394	126	210	62	298	51	38	61	10	59	16	35

* Also Great Britain not stated: Allamakee, 35; Boone, 1; Bremer, 8; Cedar, 99; Clinton, 679; Davis, 14; Delaware, 211; Fayette, 8; Henry, 144; Johnson, 3; Lee, 31; Linn, 9; Louisa, 73; Montgomery, 4; Palo Alto, 1; Polk, 1; Union, 3; Van Buren, 62; Washington, 55; Wayne, 1; Winneshiek, 1.

STATE OF KANSAS.

Counties.	NATIVE. Total.	Born in the State.	Ohio.	Illinois.	Indiana.	Missouri.	Pennsylvania.	FOREIGN-BORN. Total.	British America.	England and Wales.*	Ireland.	Scotland.	Germany.	France.	Sweden and Norway.
Allen	6365	1044	808	1026	923	368	367	657	86	68	158	8	157	17	126
Anderson	4782	989	847	539	546	243	365	438	51	89	104	22	126	8	....
Atchison	12518	3441	966	660	596	2069	761	2989	298	393	807	91	837	67	120
Barton	....	....	....	....	....	....	....	2	....	....	....	....	2	....	....
Bourbon	13868	2583	1492	2257	1146	1311	825	1208	180	178	329	66	295	33	53
Brown	5083	1372	833	740	355	553	439	840	88	143	152	25	198	15	64
Butler	2859	319	375	474	275	158	179	176	42	50	21	7	40	12	5
Chase	1796	379	220	149	228	47	112	179	11	1	27	10	102	14	8
Cherokee	10443	1143	1141	1878	1282	1018	493	595	112	104	149	22	147	1	27
Clay	2057	328	207	245	218	59	203	885	98	345	28	27	118	5	215
Cloud	1920	202	240	209	172	109	117	403	74	57	50	28	49	9	106
Coffey	5790	1168	913	650	1111	170	252	411	54	110	94	10	70	11	45

TABLE XVIII.—*Native and Foreign Population, &c.*—Continued.

STATE OF KANSAS—Continued.

Counties.	NATIVE.							FOREIGN-BORN.								
	Total.	Born in the State.	Ohio.	Illinois.	Indiana.	Missouri.	Pennsylvania.	Total.	British America.	England and Wales.*	Ireland.	Scotland.	Germany.	France.	Sweden and Norway.
.	1094	138	111	153	150	52	74	81	23	15	7	6	20	2	6
rd	7579	776	946	1680	835	651	436	581	135	82	125	15	168	8	36
	3504	789	426	257	215	183	245	2022	118	415	382	64	408	21	475
son	2176	355	378	271	226	60	222	867	83	79	147	45	287	6	105
ian	12382	3606	1330	639	564	2417	610	1587	96	166	399	28	526	.67	99
s	17786	4226	2133	1053	1567	1331	1437	2806	299	408	478	95	843	154	390
	779	56	112	60	34	112	81	557	16	56	301	22	114	12	3
rth	783	108	87	36	48	78	58	402	34	.....	151	9	84	16	34
	308	13	13	5	8	28	40	119	7	5	44	7	35	3	4
in	9511	1683	1662	1327	947	489	750	874	131	146	153	31	207	31	140
wood	3218	558	434	501	402	249	121	266	53	10	28	8	29	2	84
d	2649	360	251	484	394	250	80	145	19	22	14	10	36	3	34
n	5427	1418	705	375	652	537	280	626	138	96	127	18	175	2	8
on	11800	3133	1090	733	1152	1695	788	726	83	70	211	32	165	14	5
	188	......	45	23	16	13	53	19	3	3	3	1	1	3	5
n	12430	2513	1829	1437	912	1533	647	1254	147	201	388	52	252	35	50
e	9253	920	1132	1778	1446	626	398	720	196	178	104	26	114	19	54
worth	25529	7336	2058	1126	1221	4035	1407	6915	352	585	2548	102	2448	249	85
n	393	52	39	32	36	31	13	123	10	20	31	2	24	1	7
	11647	2463	1295	1830	1061	1081	519	527	126	114	110	18	111	4	16
	7085	1262	1169	727	1012	182	450	929	87	471	103	36	122	6	56
	705	98	77	90	125	19	36	63	5	11	7	4	9	19	2
ll	5407	1155	640	614	359	239	285	1494	259	141	238	51	473	24	171
rson	313	38	45	40	19	20	14	425	8	4	4	2	9	9	364
	10857	2273	1284	1511	1161	1044	528	868	131	130	201	45	274	15	37
ll	411	36	76	66	42	7	18	74	10	14	2	3	5	....	37
omery	7088	608	758	1150	971	702	344	476	91	103	103	16	113	4	25
	1976	454	233	111	87	188	246	249	20	39	63	7	57	6	46
a	5880	1261	732	607	544	317	524	1459	177	166	427	34	417	45	46
	9255	946	1143	1978	1550	598	401	951	199	118	294	40	114	24	121
	....	....	....	....	....	....	....	2	....	....	2	....	....	....	....
	6507	1007	947	760	821	273	641	1141	101	518	112	35	120	25	171
e	26	....	5	1	3	....	1	7	....	6	....	....	1	....	....
	1662	214	206	246	136	73	95	465	101	124	52	12	90	11	38
s	98	3	3	....	2	6	14	81	6	9	38	....	23	3	....
attamie	6304	1873	677	514	700	322	511	1514	139	154	303	29	472	69	280
ic	1105	82	247	104	119	25	89	176	11	42	21	17	11	1	31
	4	....	....	....	....	....	....	1	1	....	....	....	....	....	....
	3931	999	403	280	346	105	275	1174	71	146	83	29	338	4	435
	94	7	6	5	4	13	10	62	5	....	24	9	8	....	....
	2771	436	497	509	164	88	139	1475	79	82	197	47	147	41	801
ck	936	66	149	111	101	64	83	159	41	29	37	5	37	....	....
ee	11657	2309	1817	934	1596	641	854	1464	193	237	234	59	362	48	189
	57	....	9	12	6	4	9	9	....	6	3	....	....	....	....
r	19	2	4	....	4	5	....	3	....	....	2	....	1	....	....
	85	3	12	9	5	9	3	81	1	5	56	1	12	2	....
nsee	2666	687	354	142	235	133	217	696	41	67	28	23	445	12	25
e	321	32	45	18	19	27	39	217	10	23	113	4	51	7	3
gton	3513	563	578	447	382	112	184	568	108	92	65	17	184	9	19
	6255	874	783	1062	858	640	290	439	68	74	40	30	87	11	119
en	3436	544	445	543	463	181	217	391	86	40	47	1	180	6	19
lotte	8766	2018	734	320	313	2180	408	1249	109	122	371	14	442	33	93

o Great Britain not stated: Allen, 1; Atchison, 6; Bourbon, 16; Doniphan, 23; Ellis, 7; Ells-
56; Franklin, 1; Greenwood, 43; Jefferson, 40; Johnson, 3; Marshall, 21; Mitchell, 3; Russell, 8;
ee, 42.

TABLE XVIII.—*Native and Foreign Population, &c.*—**Continued.**

STATE OF KENTUCKY

Counties.	NATIVE. Total.	Born in the State.	Tennessee.	Virginia and West Virginia.	Ohio.	North Carolina.	Indiana.	FOREIGN-BORN. Total.	British America.	England and Wales.	Ireland.	Scotland.	Germany.	France.	Sweden and Norway.
Adair	11058	10143	305	409	5	78	24	7	....	2	3	....	......	......	....
Allen	10287	8389	1287	271	2	136	19	9	....	2	3	....	4	......	....
Anderson	5412	5264	22	82	7	7	12	37	1	....	26	....	8	1	....
Ballard	12484	9196	1718	462	46	232	109	92	17	22	22	....	20	2	1
Barren	17718	15579	1096	671	11	88	31	62	3	2	28	....	23	3	....
Bath	10055	9735	27	216	12	15	9	90	7	2	52	21	......	5	....
Boone	10231	8611	28	428	389	24	449	465	10	11	212	8	200	10	....
Bourbon	14334	13615	85	250	99	13	23	529	16	40	309	12	50	4	1
Boyd	8009	5234	49	1385	814	61	44	564	14	107	164	24	228	14	1
Boyle	9369	8683	77	201	42	42	46	146	4	9	81	9	27	6	....
Bracken	10769	9134	12	159	1085	10	76	640	5	16	205	1	377	13	1
Breathitt	5672	5329	41	181	1	92	5	......	....	....	......	....	......	....	....
Breckenridge	13254	12200	74	418	32	50	202	186	4	6	86	8	66	9	....
Bullitt	7578	6985	63	132	57	22	77	203	1	14	90	3	77	11	....
Butler	9380	7862	891	265	10	141	33	24	2	16	4	....	......	1	....
Caldwell	10735	8845	976	351	14	134	23	91	5	6	59	6	8	2	....
Calloway	9403	6367	1904	303	8	515	2	7	....	....	3	2	1	1	....
Campbell	20270	14053	47	479	3985	19	346	7136	134	790	1272	62	4356	271	8
Carroll	5899	5008	9	143	144	7	404	290	5	25	110	3	125	5	....
Carter	7423	6135	63	867	183	87	6	86	1	42	8	3	27	1	1
Casey	8868	7976	541	170	4	104	15	16	....	5	5	....	6	....	....
Christian	22866	17910	1888	2039	65	373	36	361	12	45	134	6	63	11	....
Clark	10745	10373	55	188	21	9	13	137	6	20	102	....	9	....	....
Clay	8286	7263	408	296	1	202	17	11	....	2	8	....	1	....	....
Clinton	6470	4746	1176	220	18	147	18	27	1	18	6	....	1	....	....
Crittenden	9315	7346	1111	182	25	124	41	66	1	33	14	3	12	1	....
Cumberland	7682	6753	508	224	5	121	10	8	2	1	5	....	......	....	....
Daviess	20108	18891	229	348	105	68	524	606	6	23	138	17	328	34	....
Edmondson	4419	4146	95	91	2	19	21	10	....	3	7	....	......	....	....
Elliott	4132	3557	40	713	27	66	5	1	....	1	......	....	......	....	....
Estill	9102	8061	201	425	124	75	40	96	2	26	53	4	10	....	....
Fayette	25241	22238	177	602	198	50	58	1415	37	138	894	62	207	24	9
Fleming	13147	12303	30	323	155	12	41	251	5	22	203	4	15	1	....
Floyd	7871	6432	106	1060	5	240	4	6	1	2	1	1	......	....	....
Franklin	14755	13309	179	438	103	37	114	545	12	49	343	8	104	9	....
Fulton	5971	3421	1503	150	31	183	55	190	3	8	63	4	105	2	1
Gallatin	4941	4413	27	102	72	3	239	130	1	17	73	....	38	....	....
Garrard	10338	9750	119	237	18	52	24	38	3	2	22	2	9	....	....
Grant	9356	8938	44	135	73	21	47	173	6	3	96	3	56	4	....
Graves	19207	13890	3296	526	25	581	47	101	3	11	46	1	28	9	....
Grayson	11232	10311	239	231	41	63	93	348	6	10	292	6	27	3	....
Green	9369	8839	48	271	3	91	28	10	....	....	4	....	6	....	....
Greenup	10961	8226	48	1004	1090	42	30	502	7	66	173	10	213	15	....
Hancock	6373	5044	16	77	40	16	164	218	8	48	76	5	69	2	....
Hardin	15347	14605	117	141	35	15	89	358	11	35	182	2	105	13	1
Harlan	4415	3747	118	402	2	109	....	......	....	....	......	....	......	....	....
Harrison	12570	11722	32	311	190	12	44	423	10	36	268	3	89	7	....
Hart	13606	12609	299	346	22	125	38	81	2	5	50	7	15	1	....
Henderson	17769	14431	431	764	148	246	875	688	13	59	148	17	375	31	....
Henry	10888	10112	17	150	63	10	78	178	2	6	93	7	59	6	....
Hickman	8319	5494	1776	277	29	110	55	104	10	5	39	8	23	6	1
Hopkins	13765	11612	660	223	19	857	49	62	2	16	19	6	16	2	....
Jackson	4516	3720	390	214	5	145	19	1	....	1	......	....	......	....	....
Jefferson	91143	74587	1233	2083	2270	199	3370	27210	335	1021	6031	316	15766	939	19
Jessamine	8561	8241	22	131	16	16	19	77	4	....	58	3	9	....	....
Johnson	7486	6290	52	962	27	130	....	8	1	5	......	1	......	....	....
Josh Bell	3730	2975	358	235	3	120	13	1	....	....	1	....	......	....	....
Kenton	27010	19055	100	715	4579	32	429	9086	185	898	2616	99	4880	198	12
Knox	8291	6621	806	415	1	361	19	3	....	1	2	....	......	....	....
La Rue	8182	7702	67	176	9	32	41	53	1	4	22	1	18	1	....
Laurel	6008	5027	538	183	4	190	10	7	....	1	6	....	......	....	....
Lawrence	8470	7030	56	1134	59	125	6	27	6	6	2	6	7	....	....
Lee	3949	2621	57	290	1	54	6	6	....	4	1	....	1	....	....
Letcher	4657	4033	29	402	6	128	1	1	....	....	......	....	1	....	....

TABLE XVIII.—*Native and Foreign Population, &c.*—Continued.

STATE OF KENTUCKY—Continued.

nties.	NATIVE.							FOREIGN-BORN.							
	Total.	Born in the State.	Tennessee.	Virginia and West Virginia.	Ohio.	North Carolina.	Indiana.	Total.	British America.	England and Wales.*	Ireland.	Scotland.	Germany.	France.	Sweden and Norway.
....	8973	7476	29	393	680	16	66	142	1	29	43	12	34	13	....
....	10876	10086	180	325	19	76	11	71	2	7	41	[illegible]	3	1	....
....	8064	5893	952	137	64	120	94	136	3	24	62	[illegible]	24	17	....
....	20233	15703	2614	932	31	303	37	106	4	31	120	[illegible]	15	....	....
....	6187	5076	564	117	40	88	19	46	....	13	17	5	5	2	2
....	19391	18658	207	278	28	58	8	152	4	7	125	3	8	1	....
....	4683	4338	16	278	10	30	1	1	....	1	....	....	....	....	....
....	12600	12023	124	163	32	11	25	238	2	19	172	[illegible]	28	4	....
....	9409	7163	1261	161	13	364	52	46	2	2	12	6	7	16	....
....	16935	14968	18	539	794	20	56	1191	10	81	764	15	276	27	....
....	12986	8803	1928	556	179	281	130	1002	22	62	235	11	485	120	6
....	7553	6927	197	139	23	102	73	61	1	5	26	2	23	2	....
....	9379	8361	77	221	36	12	467	106	1	21	21	4	47	7	....
....	1980	1764	17	132	1	50	7	6	....	....	....	1	....	5	....
....	12938	12335	65	281	19	18	32	206	1	18	111	2	11	2	51
....	7927	7085	220	400	4	61	13	7	....	....	1	4	2	....	....
....	9229	6908	1736	276	1	97	26	2	1	....	1	....	....	....	....
y............	7402	6954	16	254	29	37	19	155	2	7	122	....	11	3	....
....	5971	5148	45	644	6	83	8	4	....	....	1	2	1	....	....
....	12420	10741	500	238	20	227	68	218	3	33	140	30	10	1	....
....	14348	13646	69	137	28	6	31	456	8	8	328	5	30	44	....
....	8883	8727	10	50	27	5	6	246	2	7	218	1	11	2	....
....	15389	14339	446	198	24	57	120	172	1	12	69	42	33	5	....
....	8613	7995	63	203	39	25	117	414	2	29	223	3	146	2	....
....	14198	13737	77	156	31	19	64	111	5	11	43	2	46	4	....
....	3886	2992	262	503	5	86	18	3	....	1	1	....	1	....	....
....	13214	11713	20	231	751	37	120	816	17	89	335	5	340	18	9
....	4274	4049	19	167	....	29	1	....	....	....	....	....	....	....	....
....	9557	7317	46	1855	23	307	6	5	1	1	1	....	2	....	....
....	2593	2124	16	95	7	15	7	6	....	4	....	....	....	....	....
....	17634	15582	814	671	5	318	51	36	1	14	6	2	13	....	....
....	5363	5112	5	65	58	1	17	36	....	6	7	....	21	2	....
....	7130	5952	454	417	12	189	38	15	2	3	9	....	1	....	....
....	2989	2851	8	78	18	9	7	2	....	1	1	....	....	....	....
....	5805	5437	152	82	1	61	6	4	....	1	1	1	1	....	....
....	11441	10868	25	221	33	9	37	166	2	11	128	4	14	4	....
....	15341	14317	41	458	40	24	65	392	6	10	297	2	72	3	....
....	9175	6942	1718	285	27	171	12	98	2	13	51	4	28	....	....
....	5851	5700	11	60	1	5	27	102	1	3	85	2	10	....	....
....	8216	7702	90	140	19	26	19	10	....	2	3	....	3	....	....
....	12562	10030	1251	826	17	127	17	50	1	2	33	3	5	3	....
....	13653	10449	1688	922	11	199	10	33	2	1	16	2	7	1	....
....	5497	4771	14	184	48	10	328	89	2	6	20	5	35	9	....
....	13276	11379	405	390	85	164	265	364	6	95	85	25	118	12	....
....	21198	17892	1358	729	113	210	115	544	11	42	306	8	85	36	10
....	12311	12036	11	101	16	28	15	153	9	3	130	....	2	3	....
....	10575	9166	870	272	6	105	18	27	....	2	3	15	5	....	....
....	10001	9261	352	180	27	755	66	33	3	4	5	1	16	3	....
....	8274	7262	670	132	7	127	7	4	....	2	....	....	1	....	....
....	3603	2831	87	586	1	57	8	....	....	....	....	....	....	....	....
....	8110	7802	10	92	21	4	9	130	....	9	101	3	13	....	....

lso Great Britain not stated: Campbell, 1; Daviess, 5; Montgomery, 7; Warren, 7.

TABLE XVIII.—*Native and Foreign Population, &c.*—Continued.

STATE OF LOUISIANA.

Parishes.	NATIVE. Total.	Born in the State.	Mississippi.	Virginia and West Virginia.	Alabama.	Georgia.	South Carolina.	FOREIGN-BORN. Total.	British America.	England and Wales.*	Ireland.	Scotland.	Germany.	France.	Sweden and Norway.
Ascension	11312	9638	167	622	140	24	224	263	2	4	37	2	113	70	....
Assumption	12994	11306	91	664	35	53	52	240	3	8	33	2	34	116	....
Avoyelles	12613	10782	410	494	131	94	137	313	7	12	28	5	31	198	1
Bienville	10601	6286	630	167	882	1432	568	35	....	5	9	....	15	1	1
Bossier	12616	7354	615	532	776	1081	1224	59	1	9	18	5	8	....	7
Caddo	20933	12093	891	933	1853	1299	647	781	24	80	151	29	259	125	13
Calcasieu	6608	5200	513	18	186	111	61	125	9	15	16	2	31	34	1
Caldwell	4804	3054	565	125	379	128	184	16	1	1	4	....	4	4	1
Cameron	1538	1275	90	13	17	12	12	53	....	7	7	....	7	5	8
Carroll	9917	5387	1292	748	268	165	178	193	11	18	31	9	56	11	30
Catahoula	8366	6013	1017	265	213	174	120	109	4	*11	19	5	47	11	3
Claiborne	20125	10949	802	419	1979	3458	706	115	....	27	20	4	51	4	....
Concordia	9878	5844	1535	1174	51	55	107	99	2	7	36	....	22	11	....
De Soto	14868	9090	401	416	2205	971	868	94	3	4	28	7	25	5	1
East Baton Rouge	17043	13261	959	877	100	106	194	773	19	67	176	19	243	136	5
East Feliciana	13214	10995	1113	313	51	58	153	285	11	25	67	9	112	28	....
Franklin	5013	3411	707	192	185	101	57	65	4	10	20	4	19	2	1
Grant	4488	2901	399	204	364	120	203	29	1	2	5	....	14	3	....
Iberia	8685	7647	89	362	78	15	44	357	13	16	30	6	40	200	1
Iberville	12000	9531	197	1145	45	68	94	347	6	7	75	3	80	116	8
Jackson	7631	4375	560	194	917	858	305	15	....	5	3	1	4	2	....
Jefferson	15824	11897	501	1594	169	127	130	1943	3	80	217	15	1025	408	1
Lafayette	10157	9942	26	34	28	4	23	231	13	6	11	....	19	151	3
Lafourche	14412	12613	170	602	86	70	72	307	13	17	46	5	55	108	....
Livingston	3937	3368	206	17	25	36	44	89	5	10	17	2	34	10	....
Madison	8443	4055	1713	806	188	126	138	157	4	11	70	5	26	2	19
Morehouse	9302	5280	870	617	731	331	311	85	2	8	30	1	30	8	....
Natchitoches	17919	12767	773	744	870	848	540	346	9	12	54	3	60	110	5
Orleans	142943	114696	3076	5724	1858	791	1145	48475	309	2090	14693	568	15239	8845	212
Ouachita	11229	7567	566	714	605	423	217	283	7	17	67	6	109	29	18
Plaquemines	9635	7704	146	734	57	49	131	917	23	58	139	14	111	180	27
Point Coupée	12651	10638	700	338	96	120	151	330	7	13	51	4	47	139	1
Rapides	17636	13375	823	901	401	324	166	379	8	27	106	9	118	48	1
Richland	5003	2763	800	204	437	95	87	107	2	8	26	1	17	7	28
Sabine	6418	4101	332	94	572	258	135	38	....	11	4	....	5	1	....
St. Bernard	3273	2650	60	242	26	12	54	280	....	3	39	5	24	104	1
St. Charles	4766	3674	80	570	33	10	35	101	1	3	12	1	26	31	....
St. Helena	5386	4920	272	44	17	33	29	37	....	3	18	3	8	....	3
St. James	9927	8211	182	804	85	39	68	225	3	9	26	1	29	114	1
St. John the Baptist	6606	5963	26	389	10	6	19	156	1	11	10	....	19	86	....
St. Landry	25035	22389	568	504	277	141	134	518	17	31	100	6	112	180	....
St. Martin	9134	8591	66	187	41	14	16	236	4	8	18	....	13	172	....
St. Mary	13349	10731	140	1127	64	61	172	511	13	39	122	10	129	135	9
St. Tammany	5110	4137	434	137	54	43	49	476	8	21	78	9	156	136	3
Tangipahoa	7502	6104	704	156	74	113	72	336	7	30	70	5	124	39	4
Tensas	12151	6166	2466	1483	113	139	179	268	12	29	110	13	53	11	18
Terrebonne	12237	11538	119	300	38	18	46	214	17	6	29	4	38	96	....
Union	11646	6097	399	203	1980	912	271	39	....	4	6	2	19	2	1
Vermillion	4447	4204	43	55	31	3	13	81	4	9	4	1	1	59	2
Washington	3119	2397	737	21	25	50	37	11	....	1	4	1	2	....	....
West Baton Rouge	5028	4392	45	284	25	10	27	86	7	4	24	6	5	32	2
West Feliciana	10321	8884	507	389	26	16	23	178	3	6	46	2	77	23	1
Winn	4935	2758	754	48	549	364	163	19	1	....	6	....	5	1	....

* Also Great Britain not stated: Orleans, 10; Winn, 2.

TABLE XVIII.—*Native and Foreign Population, &c.*—Continued.

STATE OF MAINE.

…nties.	Native. Total.	Born in the State.	Massachusetts.	New Hampshire.	New York.	Vermont.	Rhode Island.	Foreign-born. Total.	British America.	England and Wales.	Ireland.	Scotland.	Germany.	France.	Sweden and Norway.
…in	32236	30050	1085	579	76	150	66	3630	1281	604	1534	90	89	4	5
	22002	21510	194	159	38	51	4	7607	6741	106	673	64	8	3	6
…l	72182	68047	1950	968	339	211	86	9839	3471	1049	4589	281	112	31	58
	18511	17322	663	361	23	51	12	296	210	32	45	3	....	3	....
	35547	34983	313	116	41	9	9	946	395	92	334	33	44	8	4
	50914	48207	1343	672	208	118	54	2289	936	214	926	54	59	12	8
	29745	29036	343	100	62	14	20	1078	351	117	499	37	12	8	12
	24973	24453	262	76	29	22	35	624	276	77	198	23	9	8	5
	32020	30194	908	1402	77	163	22	568	240	184	109	11	7	5	....
	68183	64636	1075	1358	186	144	52	6067	3354	307	3064	109	59	23	8
	13942	13302	194	291	28	42	3	461	306	104	26	8	13	2	....
	17968	17460	256	71	52	18	5	835	372	75	309	24	19	4	2
	33245	31748	543	674	45	90	15	1366	970	91	217	66	2	3	1
	33887	32994	359	322	45	38	19	635	191	49	309	15	12	5	11
…n	36118	35301	408	129	67	25	17	7225	5263	288	1510	90	36	8	7
	55661	51386	1243	2476	134	118	54	4513	2431	540	1343	81	27	10	22

STATE OF MARYLAND.

…nties.	Native. Total.	Born in the State.	Pennsylvania.	Virginia and West Virginia.	Delaware.	New York.	District of Columbia.	Foreign-born. Total.	British America.	England and Wales.*	Ireland.	Scotland.	Germany.	France.	Sweden and Norway.
	30567	24398	2753	2636	26	164	77	7969	171	1959	1847	1558	2312	17	6
…del	23562	22169	180	317	27	230	131	895	11	99	228	20	451	22	11
	264983	237549	7101	9974	647	2255	1477	65758	349	2891	18251	657	40426	503	94
	9840	9794	9	17	....	....	6	25	....	....	5	2	17	....	1
	12026	10347	313	20	1076	101	5	75	4	20	29	3	21	3	....
	27416	25166	1750	213	17	83	35	1203	2	59	276	8	817	13	1
	24814	19052	3295	127	1732	105	15	1000	16	201	598	18	193	23	....
	15661	15402	28	103	13	12	23	77	1	13	33	1	22	2	....
	19426	18796	65	74	336	38	6	32	5	8	6	2	5	....	....
	46161	42740	1667	1081	17	135	117	1411	15	96	387	17	839	14	....
	21399	19661	1107	139	74	112	24	1206	12	108	569	28	463	14	3
	13132	12000	167	397	29	136	73	1018	12	105	445	30	373	14	....
	16780	15177	325	147	846	62	7	322	6	39	126	5	121	4	....
…r	20071	17890	259	954	23	108	507	492	10	45	228	17	150	3	1
…ge's	20609	18717	195	743	32	138	523	529	6	92	170	30	212	....	....
	16054	15015	163	85	620	21	3	117	1	21	36	4	44	....	....
…s	14860	14238	20	472	5	19	34	84	2	9	34	1	36	....	....
	18137	17441	73	374	101	18	3	53	3	6	18	6	14	....	....
	15968	15010	178	106	480	45	12	169	3	15	60	9	77	1	....
…i	33861	28444	3085	1917	7	89	39	851	15	42	268	4	491	13	1
	15765	15129	67	38	506	3	2	37	....	5	22	2	5	1	....
	16390	15678	42	303	202	16	2	29	....	16	3	1	7	....	....

* Also Great Britain not stated: Baltimore, 77.

TABLE XVIII.—*Native and Foreign Population, &c.*—**Continued.**

STATE OF MASSACHUSETTS.

Counties.	NATIVE. Total.	Born in the State.	Maine.	New Hampshire.	New York.	Vermont.	Connecticut.	FOREIGN-BORN. Total.	British America.	England and Wales.*	Ireland.	Scotland.	Germany.	France.	Sweden and Norway.
Barnstable	30925	30022	328	104	102	58	49	1849	362	209	676	39	12	[illegible]	11
Berkshire	49692	37561	133	222	6297	1611	2569	15133	2941	1656	8814	251	833	303	4
Bristol	79574	67687	1221	663	1272	392	654	23312	2474	3047	12654	790	360	52	4
Dukes	3682	3459	116	16	28	3	25	105	5	20	24	1	1	2	1
Essex	157065	128569	10601	12215	1339	1641	507	43778	9326	5606	25357	1734	767	96	231
Franklin	29041	24827	140	865	625	1848	380	3594	720	436	1660	50	664	10	....
Hampden	57610	43667	899	1345	2765	2004	4992	20793	5393	1375	12340	546	844	76	9
Hampshire	35564	30473	261	409	1361	839	1348	8824	2429	590	4833	255	577	19	5
Middlesex	203361	157773	16331	14813	3301	5346	1162	70992	13922	6460	46158	1719	1358	200	273
Nantucket	3920	3751	21	5	60	9	13	203	16	17	103	....	4	6	....
Norfolk	70033	60054	3661	2053	906	816	465	19410	2531	1803	13373	519	708	50	40
Plymouth	58680	54974	1584	557	353	299	151	6085	532	476	4963	132	186	38	181
Suffolk	178514	139332	17165	8533	3693	2713	1074	92388	14892	6706	50099	1971	5718	623	619
Worcester	146365	121120	3030	5973	2526	4601	3924	46351	14512	3402	26066	976	1040	67	82

* Also Great Britain not stated: Berkshire, 65; Middlesex, 6; Norfolk, 7; Suffolk, 2.

STATE OF MICHIGAN.

Counties.	NATIVE. Total.	Born in the State.	New York.	Ohio.	Pennsylvania.	Vermont.	Indiana.	NATIVE-BORN. Total.	British America.	England and Wales.*	Ireland.	Scotland.	Germany.	France.	Sweden and Norway.
Alcona	382	208	122	16	19	6	....	314	230	29	34	11	7	1	9
Allegan	26519	12431	6584	3375	970	640	670	5586	1214	783	505	173	1056	33	32
Alpena	1266	713	230	61	18	21	....	1490	1046	81	128	59	122	7	13
Antrim	1288	616	390	92	40	24	11	697	436	71	48	41	18	3	2
Barry	19982	9224	6346	2352	704	273	292	2217	680	588	292	81	447	18	15
Bay	8868	4666	2692	446	226	85	45	7032	4275	393	697	244	1066	73	15
Bensie	1842	548	516	323	127	83	28	342	161	65	28	21	35	1	17
Berrien	30047	14576	5378	3260	1308	454	1815	5057	1041	494	896	93	2130	53	112
Branch	24518	10314	7875	2701	907	438	698	1706	310	525	334	49	424	11	3
Calhoun	32366	15734	11248	1326	1074	641	216	4203	738	1100	1067	118	1031	27	12
Cass	19677	9948	3107	2208	1077	242	1272	1417	350	264	335	42	298	20	66
Charlevoix	1168	604	326	67	42	27	6	536	361	70	47	20	23	....	1
Cheboygan	1245	817	216	39	18	25	1	951	761	27	65	15	54	4	13
Chippewa	1197	1030	62	15	16	3	8	492	355	23	48	16	31	6	3
Clare	233	83	56	51	9	9	35	113	48	2	25	23	5	1	5
Clinton	20096	10276	5884	2072	543	267	103	2749	730	538	264	56	1044	58	2
Delta	1363	629	245	38	39	30	5	1179	472	82	275	28	166	3	117
Eaton	23622	10824	6629	3596	729	529	302	1549	500	448	263	43	253	14	....
Emmet	1160	1134	9	6	4	1	....	51	24	1	3	....	19	1	1
Genesee	28518	14947	10076	865	493	504	82	5382	2292	1228	1076	200	440	36	8
Grand Traverse	3299	1474	900	301	140	68	57	1144	624	147	107	34	103	12	5
Gratiot	10613	4867	2375	2132	494	130	141	1197	586	231	134	46	139	16	....
Hillsdale	29488	13400	9270	3701	973	400	295	2196	338	718	549	74	416	44	1
Houghton	6010	4735	332	106	49	14	8	7869	1480	1749	2475	153	1380	52	335
Huron	4263	3185	557	217	74	47	17	4786	2440	308	342	229	969	30	27
Ingham	22668	12114	6760	1684	435	424	179	2600	820	559	460	92	607	9	8
Ionia	24027	11693	7425	2263	606	466	247	3654	1088	600	635	130	501	17	5
Iosco	1738	921	474	105	75	32	14	1425	980	90	102	78	141	6	13
Isabella	3540	1446	856	570	290	41	174	373	359	45	61	26	47	13	2
Jackson	31052	16301	10190	1250	647	572	152	4995	1123	1271	1253	211	1010	30	8
Kalamazoo	27106	13155	8635	1626	1050	678	377	4648	859	893	927	168	663	50	9
Kalkaska	237	74	63	33	23	3	3	187	105	39	15	6	7	1	....

TABLE XVIII.—*Native and Foreign Population, &c.*—Continued.

STATE OF MICHIGAN—Continued.

Counties.	NATIVE. Total.	Born in the State.	New York.	Ohio.	Pennsylvania.	Vermont.	Indiana.	FOREIGN-BORN. Total.	British America.	England and Wales.*	Ireland.	Scotland.	Germany.	France.	Sweden and Norway.
nt	38309	19856	11040	2434	1040	785	401	12094	3664	1108	2003	296	1722	60	213
veenaw	2059	1099	88	42	28	6	3	2146	251	851	396	11	522	33	....
ie	401	139	107	51	24	4	31	147	87	9	5	2	39	....	....
eer	15784	9963	4092	325	287	303	35	5561	3748	524	392	398	396	28	3
lanaw	3044	1747	637	214	67	40	29	1532	684	119	117	32	335	29	41
awee	40256	20695	11637	3032	1148	617	257	5339	780	1272	1344	126	1657	43	8
ingston	16895	10497	4786	281	287	242	40	2441	405	700	676	87	541	15	1
kinac	1383	1221	75	13	7	7	....	839	169	14	102	13	20	4	2
comb	20315	14689	3834	256	214	309	31	7301	1867	668	573	169	3670	185	13
nistee	3408	1500	638	222	102	54	54	2666	727	172	218	40	851	24	263
nitou	478	384	56	15	6	2	....	413	65	3	255	2	31	....	40
rquette	5793	3879	810	167	82	86	10	9240	3466	1372	2141	201	763	57	1013
on	2328	1198	424	223	114	41	111	935	353	77	89	19	195	10	148
osta	4200	1819	1116	545	276	47	39	1442	985	115	110	41	99	26	23
nominee	918	332	142	22	16	18	6	873	361	28	65	6	222	15	74
lland	2448	1131	695	162	111	67	16	837	605	63	89	23	41	9	2
saukee	43	19	5	8	4	4	1	67	33	1	3	....	6	....	....
nroe	22760	16948	2899	1180	638	227	80	4783	701	415	494	74	2739	154	6
ntcalm	11708	5170	3315	1556	574	175	282	1921	798	293	142	34	210	4	17
skegon	9449	4480	2413	635	330	132	205	5445	1832	352	593	136	834	21	630
vaygo	6245	2980	1490	694	288	99	312	1049	602	124	112	28	81	6	10
land	34770	21729	8741	502	692	456	50	6097	1578	2068	1346	261	708	41	15
ana	5942	2670	1413	640	297	99	211	1280	533	111	96	40	241	12	133
maw	2	1	1	....	....	....	....	10	7	....	2	1	....	....	....
onagon	1714	1406	84	20	33	10	1	1131	212	347	283	42	168	12	....
eola	1433	541	345	239	98	23	94	658	372	32	34	6	203	2	4
oda	32	10	8	4	6	....	1	38	32	3	3	....	....	....	....
awa	17447	10398	4183	1013	372	276	159	9204	1257	423	567	149	1024	53	89
sque Isle	96	70	17	1	2	3	2	259	86	11	3	2	158	....	....
inaw	24334	14640	6038	1188	525	294	109	14763	6011	900	1522	446	5345	60	25
ilac	6852	5379	884	113	161	65	17	7710	5511	568	720	307	437	34	14
iawassee	17986	9650	5794	956	436	261	51	2872	1018	554	544	116	554	14	1
Clair	21094	16835	3068	422	199	277	28	14967	8113	1031	1803	501	3073	161	38
Joseph	23591	10880	4761	1812	3839	322	855	2684	334	700	291	39	1129	49	44
cola	10261	5144	2843	1046	461	200	32	3453	2332	356	242	85	402	8	....
Buren	26242	11136	8351	2743	791	558	903	2587	971	637	492	96	248	15	19
shtenaw	32708	21028	7592	674	520	439	152	8726	1440	1287	1823	175	3742	89	28
yne	72453	52677	11025	1740	1109	676	243	46585	10005	4828	8751	1960	17060	1180	63
xford	588	204	234	60	14	6	24	62	39	4	2	8	9	....	....

Also Great Britain not stated: Barry, 2; Bay, 1; Calhoun, 1; Clinton, 5; Ingham, 1; Jackson, 2; nt, 4; Montcalm, 1; Oceana, 5; Saginaw, 2; Washtenaw, 2.

STATE OF MINNESOTA.

Counties.	NATIVE. Total.	Born in the State.	New York.	Wisconsin.	Ohio.	Pennsylvania.	Illinois.	FOREIGN-BORN. Total.	British America.	England and Wales.*	Ireland.	Scotland.	Germany.	France.	Sweden and Norway.
kin	178	178	....	....	....	....	....	....	....	....	....	....	....	....	....
oka	2868	1314	294	82	126	77	52	1072	466	48	194	12	96	8	203
ker	185	97	11	7	2	9	7	123	17	....	1	2	....	....	102
trami	73	71	....	....	....	1	....	7	7	....	....	....	....	....	....
nton	1075	415	159	65	47	55	36	483	159	22	83	9	78	14	18
Stone	19	8	....	2				5	....	....	....	....	....	....	5

TABLE XVIII.—*Native and Foreign Population, &c.*—Continued.

STATE OF MINNESOTA—Continued.

Counties.	Native: Total.	Native: Born in the State.	Native: New York.	Native: Wisconsin.	Native: Ohio.	Native: Pennsylvania.	Native: Illinois.	Foreign-born: Total.	Foreign-born: British America.	Foreign-born: England and Wales.*	Foreign-born: Ireland.	Foreign-born: Scotland.	Foreign-born: Germany.	Foreign-born: France.	Foreign-born: Sweden and Norway.
Blue Earth	12148	4239	2121	2087	584	436	452	5134	503	674	523	81	1579	100	1348
Brown	3311	1819	251	468	125	113	165	3085	136	46	83	10	1396	38	589
Carlton	118	50	10	8	6	15	2	168	35	6	25	7	11	8	55
Carver	5668	4368	145	178	235	226	116	5918	65	65	256	3	3108	94	1440
Cass	363	302	9	8	1	5	3	17	11	....	1	1	1	....	2
Chippewa	698	309	75	141	28	17	10	769	38	2	....	4	11	....	691
Chisago	2164	1223	205	98	98	104	98	2194	129	26	106	10	202	12	1674
Clay	49	32	....	....	2	....	1	43	31	2	1	1	5	....	3
Cottonwood	318	76	55	56	23	23	11	216	42	6	7	....	6	....	155
Crow Wing	166	126	11	6	3	1	1	34	26	1	4	1	1	....	....
Dakota	10767	5731	1388	414	439	314	445	5545	644	267	1699	85	1963	53	1006
Dodge	6515	2199	1435	1130	258	294	159	2083	205	141	153	73	191	23	967
Douglas	2316	854	322	265	117	175	109	1923	139	78	68	26	257	6	1227
Faribault	7422	2429	1527	1469	252	335	268	2518	432	171	191	76	660	42	861
Fillmore	15178	7218	2331	1255	691	760	628	9709	637	417	969	170	577	34	6612
Freeborn	6518	2668	1171	956	249	192	266	4060	197	103	391	45	240	10	2683
Goodhue	12164	6270	1771	1103	315	460	479	10454	421	229	506	59	1564	28	7353
Grant	148	86	5	24	1	....	4	192	18	....	1	2	1	....	169
Hennepin	21338	9148	2332	542	948	894	731	10228	2090	392	1896	119	2906	137	2158
Houston	8176	4695	746	641	282	319	267	6760	351	158	1053	87	1261	44	3194
Isanti	865	418	61	38	57	27	12	1170	46	25	14	5	71	....	994
Itasca	92	84	....	....	2	1	....	4	3	....	1	....	....	....	....
Jackson	1192	381	207	205	58	56	59	633	79	30	20	9	47	....	436
Kanabec	85	26	11	1	....	5	1	8	2	5	....	....	....	....	1
Kandiyohi	668	344	53	66	23	15	53	1092	26	11	35	1	13	....	967
Lac qui Parle	108	41	11	7	13	9	13	37	2	4	5	....	5	....	21
Lake	114	91	2	1	6	3	....	21	4	....	....	1	10	....	....
Le Sueur	7710	4125	759	357	571	185	290	3897	253	171	930	24	1288	85	125
Martin	3340	876	819	592	188	129	147	527	193	110	86	19	61	2	45
McLeod	3757	1657	384	350	205	195	202	1886	203	73	110	22	774	25	266
Meeker	3737	1368	370	251	193	153	211	2353	211	39	326	24	162	14	1501
Mille Lac	918	295	137	37	68	29	33	191	93	16	37	2	18	1	21
Monongalia	1463	693	159	191	62	46	78	1698	88	38	50	22	11	2	1465
Morrison	1113	515	134	78	73	34	33	568	253	23	48	9	173	1	9
Mower	7238	2434	1584	676	318	331	317	3209	383	200	416	55	300	9	1790
Murray	185	34	56	41	7	6	11	24	8	1	1	8	....	....	6
Nicollet	4281	2619	349	217	149	129	325	4081	123	95	249	38	1489	39	1659
Nobles	108	25	19	14	1	....	8	9	2	3	1	....	2	....	1
Olmstead	15364	5430	3270	1776	752	847	593	4429	550	362	1128	146	1025	11	1086
Otter Tail	888	352	85	132	95	38	27	1080	28	10	3	19	118	6	829
Pembina	47	33	....	....	....	....	....	17	17	....	....	....	....	....	....
Pine	324	120	40	31	9	42	7	324	42	16	91	5	34	5	127
Pope	1310	560	148	220	32	48	109	1321	134	14	68	26	31	1	1075
Ramsey	13246	6979	1469	345	652	726	444	9839	934	484	2276	74	3644	173	1503
Redwood	1147	341	183	161	62	77	65	682	176	52	32	26	62	....	319
Renville	1808	707	314	199	62	72	101	1411	143	34	146	4	248	3	775
Rice	11349	5096	1783	781	638	404	380	4734	1073	176	1167	72	1017	102	714
Rock	120	13	33	19	12	1	12	18	5	....	3	....	1	....	7
Scott	6025	4390	443	255	307	255	274	4417	256	110	969	41	1690	49	389
Sherburne	1524	526	220	47	72	72	48	526	187	42	72	13	19	1	180
Sibley	3662	2539	229	196	95	144	124	3063	200	41	608	8	1616	11	463
Stearns	8989	4484	788	614	613	309	445	5217	337	123	238	55	3033	333	405
Steele	6088	2024	1436	931	218	197	242	2183	207	123	310	50	655	10	364
Stevens	71	41	6	5	1	5	9	103	7	....	....	....	8	....	86
St. Louis	1708	309	231	139	117	203	56	2853	363	114	408	70	327	24	1410
Todd	1499	427	216	88	87	90	90	537	108	31	22	13	208	11	140
Traverse	13	8	1	....	....	2	....	....	....	....	....	....	....	....	....
Wabashaw	11321	4644	1882	869	472	790	491	4338	585	270	965	167	1573	47	579
Wadena	6	6	....	....	....	....	....	....	....	....	....	....	....	....	....
Waseca	5380	2267	835	1027	212	161	210	2474	146	91	619	32	658	13	803
Washington	6440	3652	765	141	141	261	186	5369	1160	198	602	70	1382	11	1009
Watonwan	1424	474	210	224	52	59	87	1002	95	42	50	8	123	15	642
Wilkin	103	50	7	5	....	2	1	192	30	2	11	4	8	....	122
Winona	15168	6117	2741	1526	791	611	608	7151	641	487	983	132	3230	73	783
Wright	6468	2942	692	170	333	373	274	2989	503	94	424	32	796	55	667

* Also Great Britain not stated: Dakota, 38.

TABLE XVIII.—*Native and Foreign Population, &c.*—Continued.

STATE OF MISSISSIPPI.

…ties.	NATIVE.							FOREIGN-BORN.							
	Total.	Born in the State.	Alabama.	South Carolina.	Virginia and West Virginia.	Tennessee.	Georgia.	Total.	British America.	England and Wales.	Ireland.	Scotland.	Germany.	France.	Sweden and Norway.
....	18408	14144	84	121	1268	237	57	676	14	117	226	28	177	41	2
....	10371	5946	872	308	226	1755	308	60	1	5	17	1	18	7	2
....	10926	9287	30	159	192	49	79	47	4	3	12	1	16	1	....
....	14710	10359	1055	983	221	326	946	66	1	3	24	1	24	....	11
....	9542	4581	388	354	763	810	706	190	14	21	37	6	49	5	28
....	10533	7137	1387	507	105	354	513	28	....	7	6	....	12	....	....
....	20741	14790	1114	636	905	684	677	306	12	25	40	9	126	6	63
....	19651	12283	2743	1578	765	665	715	248	6	27	35	8	37	....	120
....	16943	11670	1827	1304	177	319	755	45	....	5	34	1	2	1	....
....	13175	10431	104	164	814	201	122	211	5	21	58	5	60	36	14
....	7434	4848	1471	269	200	48	250	71	3	4	21	3	12	6	6
....	7039	3577	642	408	376	709	444	103	2	20	39	2	24	2	10
....	20425	17053	504	518	617	240	424	183	2	19	49	5	53	12	3
....	4730	4196	65	126	42	18	87	23	2	1	7	2	......	8	1
....	31701	17782	2133	1374	1573	3878	1801	320	14	64	73	16	71	12	46
....	7467	6663	52	105	146	110	51	31	1	4	8	1	9	....	3
....	2032	1679	186	58	6	3	27	6	....	4	1	....	......	....	....
....	10333	7476	365	394	439	438	254	238	20	29	53	14	49	5	42
....	4025	3364	69	38	32	10	36	214	7	11	35	2	60	56	2
....	5196	3881	118	34	125	34	56	509	11	50	206	11	91	86	12
....	29793	22604	938	843	1801	627	528	695	22	60	274	31	159	53	38
....	19192	14265	761	782	929	457	755	178	15	8	61	....	53	8	19
....	6785	4555	140	443	447	148	75	102	4	14	15	4	29	3	2
....	7808	4899	1389	491	56	316	399	4	....	....	3	1	......	....	....
....	4194	3480	304	37	42	8	56	178	5	20	45	3	25	20	1
....	10824	8182	1255	510	173	74	326	60	....	5	48	1	2	1	....
....	13662	11115	107	200	678	197	93	186	3	19	43	11	92	6	2
....	3306	2685	229	200	9	12	95	7	....	2	......	1	2	....	....
....	12887	8482	1901	641	282	131	446	33	2	2	17	3	4	2	....
....	18538	12136	1359	958	623	1264	824	264	4	16	27	27	41	2	139
....	13364	7395	3050	647	421	181	561	198	7	24	62	7	52	11	2
....	6699	5823	93	136	103	55	155	21	....	2	5	....	11	....	....
....	8466	5527	1139	421	132	152	734	30	1	1	22	1	1	....	....
....	15883	9181	2082	1413	302	953	703	72	2	7	39	5	7	6	2
....	10006	8579	144	237	258	84	166	118	4	13	21	4	58	14	....
....	30176	18753	3616	1552	2248	677	1225	326	17	57	66	30	84	5	45
....	20550	14227	721	652	1117	658	836	398	14	55	123	10	114	20	32
....	4204	4030	13	34	8	1	30	7	1	....	3	....	1	1	1
....	29046	18189	1263	1116	1494	2954	1173	370	8	26	114	21	113	7	43
....	22512	16696	1836	860	864	653	662	119	4	11	24	2	20	1	51
....	7413	4968	988	462	94	118	465	26	....	1	18	1	4	1	....
....	9982	6230	1455	411	194	89	962	85	....	2	65	2	13	1	....
....	20758	13314	3154	1630	919	235	686	147	13	12	38	4	32	4	9
....	14837	9682	1721	1353	621	262	491	54	1	5	13	19	8	2	....
....	20564	13540	1053	1121	905	1355	1111	190	16	19	37	16	27	2	28
....	2688	2475	36	77	8	2	38	6	....	....	......	3	......	....	1
....	10805	9126	78	151	212	68	145	408	6	26	78	16	193	46	3
....	12509	7882	1262	1096	217	646	596	16	1	10	3	1	1	....	....
....	9330	5448	1025	560	149	1093	431	18	4	4	7	....	3	....	....
....	12860	9932	772	344	606	158	342	117	1	12	32	4	27	7	12
....	7817	4713	1346	292	207	134	697	30	....	5	8	1	2	11	....
....	5709	5355	42	95	34	11	103	9	....	....	......	....	1	....	....
....	7110	5256	604	523	112	63	216	16	....	2	7	1	1	3	1
....	4848	3037	322	215	270	148	228	107	4	7	11	2	81	3	28
....	7791	5045	525	370	372	411	362	61	3	4	13	10	17	....	4
....	20681	13125	1227	1650	491	2259	501	46	3	10	26	1	3	....	....
....	7323	3837	1302	372	106	774	350	27	1	6	13	....	4	....	....
....	5305	2490	392	114	224	850	475	53	3	5	22	1	13	3	3
....	25183	18052	351	280	2573	446	272	1586	36	103	663	34	513	56	9
....	14286	9273	319	486	1250	414	368	283	24	13	67	6	97	16	20
....	4192	2945	755	163	46	38	102	14	1	....	4	....	2	2	5
....	12558	10168	63	142	632	154	54	147	6	22	24	5	53	14	....
....	8926	5773	845	1435	154	124	298	58	....	11	42	1	2	....	....
....	12887	8523	896	401	714	798	439	367	11	33	85	19	25	8	170
....	17052	11803	728	533	1360	658	378	227	9	10	90	9	80	7	13

TABLE XVIII.—*Native and Foreign Population, &c.*—Continued.

STATE OF MISSOURI.

Counties.	NATIVE.							FOREIGN-BORN.							
	Total.	Born in the State.	Kentucky.	Ohio.	Illinois.	Tennessee.	Virginia and West Virginia.	Total.	British America.	England and Wales.*	Ireland.	Scotland.	Germany.	France.	Sweden and Norway.
Adair	11072	4904	574	1251	981	260	385	376	68	66	70	4	119	28	9
Andrew	14261	7254	1073	1385	655	338	471	876	84	133	148	43	235	5	8
Atchison	7712	3283	379	799	650	331	240	728	102	45	42	7	430	9	26
Audrain	11720	6133	1630	521	872	131	786	587	44	92	226	15	160	5	4
Barry	10345	4946	415	100	531	1619	340	28	....	17	7	2	1	....	....
Barton	4931	1518	260	483	1025	152	113	156	19	31	21	9	41	11	....
Bates	15422	5383	1259	1585	3423	400	603	538	67	100	99	13	184	20	16
Benton	10198	6166	709	540	552	546	397	1124	26	65	30	15	878	10	....
Bollinger	7823	5677	245	72	352	733	45	330	7	16	37	5	185	4	....
Boone	20139	14990	2616	200	228	177	1093	336	48	30	116	9	113	6	1
Buchanan	28796	15495	2875	1500	1035	527	1258	6313	406	402	2055	165	2286	198	188
Butler	4265	1786	394	73	456	880	111	33	2	2	10	....	14	3	1
Caldwell	10715	4072	588	1440	227	218	445	675	164	176	136	27	131	1	1
Callaway	18108	13317	1507	327	172	329	1806	704	27	63	298	17	254	6	12
Camden	6032	3862	531	138	109	451	120	76	4	31	12	2	24	....	1
Cape Girardeau	11721	11010	475	162	557	836	200	2847	22	45	245	12	2123	75	3
Carroll	16624	9058	1333	1352	975	438	843	822	127	158	184	27	242	15	22
Carter	1444	829	77	15	65	268	15	11	....	4	2	1	4	....	....
Cass	18557	6565	2221	1920	1987	650	803	730	106	122	245	26	170	15	31
Cedar	9370	4919	608	362	626	1055	438	104	17	21	23	3	38	1	1
Chariton	17941	11615	1238	625	905	241	1900	1195	158	132	130	18	550	18	52
Christian	6670	3511	280	88	169	1510	200	37	3	7	20	....	3	2	2
Clarke	12851	5734	922	1442	899	103	680	810	36	122	199	10	395	27	4
Clay	14957	9602	2552	351	233	432	663	607	37	71	240	21	127	14	45
Clinton	13036	6858	1740	1041	549	270	570	1027	77	89	573	39	149	3	97
Cole	8234	5884	354	309	163	192	386	2058	53	57	154	29	1420	89	10
Cooper	18597	12300	1445	754	458	397	1370	2095	42	112	436	27	1241	108	25
Crawford	7589	5135	307	165	239	640	233	393	41	114	127	31	64	3	3
Dade	8798	4256	538	260	554	1664	172	85	21	17	17	2	22	8	1
Dallas	8321	4587	386	359	429	1213	150	62	16	20	5	5	6	4	4
Daviess	14167	7044	1154	1424	779	312	800	243	71	44	49	16	45	2	4
De Kalb	9255	4022	775	1068	512	294	277	603	139	113	70	33	150	3	63
Dent	6253	3573	320	114	239	982	102	104	30	17	20	5	24	3	....
Douglass	3905	2353	193	10	138	555	71	10	4	1	....	....	4	1	....
Dunklin	5958	2110	261	19	311	1800	50	24	1	3	10	1	7	1	....
Franklin	23383	17026	611	688	881	749	685	6715	36	101	572	30	5272	90	7
Gasconade	6817	5076	111	85	62	197	87	3246	3	20	48	1	2609	107	10
Gentry	11298	5822	1058	912	655	510	481	309	71	49	49	37	56	20	....
Greene	20731	10713	926	746	783	3079	581	818	82	157	209	19	168	16	22
Grundy	10276	4519	765	1471	797	185	447	291	65	56	32	9	93	2	11
Harrison	14346	6203	867	1031	1081	311	580	289	35	79	46	33	56	6	1
Henry	16632	7709	1103	1500	1715	432	867	709	93	113	100	19	333	18	17
Hickory	6202	3278	336	338	399	500	242	250	47	31	18	4	49	40	21
Holt	11003	5414	596	1306	551	194	408	649	50	62	121	9	323	14	1
Howard	16679	13167	1219	262	172	101	1027	534	77	31	133	21	242	7	33
Howell	4177	1891	260	51	208	866	54	41	....	10	1	1	25	....	....
Iron	5756	3561	211	158	178	564	176	522	27	61	66	5	313	19	3
Jackson	45916	18906	1505	4655	2000	903	1966	9125	966	810	3898	260	2310	141	676
Jasper	14510	4180	681	1528	1968	756	320	418	66	92	57	43	55	6	73
Jefferson	12671	10210	239	255	382	281	242	2769	24	167	509	26	1547	112	3
Johnson	23665	11165	2195	2174	1447	955	1095	983	101	177	311	31	308	11	4
Knox	10368	4853	958	1104	976	78	544	606	35	39	348	11	127	10	16
Laclede	9030	4536	505	257	672	1353	227	314	13	40	126	21	92	13	20
Lafayette	20692	12518	2409	474	424	537	2300	1931	46	108	397	18	1180	31	15
Lawrence	12829	6454	712	353	852	1712	323	238	25	41	106	3	41	2	14
Lewis	14116	8020	1804	973	767	118	744	968	39	128	147	13	565	16	5
Lincoln	15002	11290	1033	174	285	197	1248	958	8	58	171	5	581	13	....
Linn	14199	6831	976	1073	1170	205	790	1401	370	229	258	65	208	24	140
Livingston	15376	6787	1252	1702	1045	315	747	1354	244	365	324	43	276	40	12
Macon	21198	11832	1873	1476	1018	375	898	2032	147	907	297	35	455	8	102
Madison	5471	3869	208	84	157	482	65	378	13	60	97	7	166	11	5
Maries	5598	3979	249	63	190	520	128	318	1	32	63	3	190	16	....
Marion	21164	12353	1857	870	1186	144	1187	2616	101	331	879	45	1090	15	70
McDonald	5181	2418	225	119	392	818	96	45	4	13	7	....	13	4	....
Mercer	11417	5239	615	1102	392	562	361	140	18	14	52	13	29	....	2
Miller	6189	4080	520	270	215	482	212	127	2	18	8	12	50	5	....
Mississippi	4707	2138	986	56	216	692	95	185	15	22	32	4	84	3	15
Moniteau	10203	6912	442	660	210	367	314	1172	14	79	139	4	780	11	....
Monroe	16821	10601	2838	333	456	64	1237	525	111	66	223	16	77	4	12
Montgomery	9617	6272	630	504	267	185	754	758	34	88	151	9	361	15	2

TABLE XVIII.—*Native and Foreign Population, &c.*—Continued.

STATE OF MISSOURI—Continued.

Counties.	NATIVE. Total.	Born in the State.	Kentucky.	Ohio.	Illinois.	Tennessee.	Virginia and West Virginia.	FOREIGN-BORN. Total.	British America.	England and Wales.*	Ireland.	Scotland.	Germany.	France.	Sweden and Norway.
Morgan	7735	5989	432	401	208	323	375	699	13	50	43	6	544	8	1
New Madrid	6274	4019	405	47	174	875	66	89	4	8	17	9	36	12	....
Newton	12545	5326	702	462	1150	1340	201	270	32	75	35	10	76	7	7
Nodaway	13901	5180	700	1714	1177	373	315	850	66	113	275	26	244	25	4
Oregon	3279	1069	131	24	93	755	34	6	1	....	2	....	4	....	....
Osage	8392	6868	170	125	103	480	250	2401	24	52	133	24	1707	309	6
Ozark	3357	1895	215	23	135	424	43	6	2	1	3	....	....	....	....
Pemiscot	2042	910	193	17	58	514	43	17	1	....	4	1	9	....	....
Perry	8334	7331	187	32	181	157	45	1343	1	8	30	1	1225	198	....
Pettis	17156	8584	1798	1481	1048	439	997	1550	134	144	501	25	586	16	60
Phelps	9092	5317	412	376	398	1149	271	814	43	78	158	24	334	44	21
Pike	22233	15140	1880	564	672	337	2013	843	61	98	202	16	265	17	16
Platte	16359	9896	2567	508	193	505	842	993	60	48	273	20	492	34	10
Polk	12364	6794	760	477	537	1904	315	81	11	16	14	4	21	5	3
Pulaski	4622	2953	223	96	221	484	96	92	2	22	42	1	19	1	4
Putnam	11046	4993	644	1210	761	246	441	171	18	34	48	12	46	3	....
Ralls	10091	6431	1091	312	463	93	608	419	38	80	155	16	110	9	1
Randolph	15317	10446	1788	274	357	296	839	591	55	153	188	33	117	18	7
Ray	18135	11864	1562	527	415	1081	947	565	57	116	187	55	126	6	4
Reynolds	3733	2571	192	59	153	409	62	23	....	5	3	3	5	2	....
Ripley	3121	1575	307	18	148	625	27	54	....	3	22	3	22	1	....
Saline	20677	12712	2143	815	502	524	2245	995	62	43	240	21	501	21	2
Schuyler	8500	4048	569	914	532	280	281	320	47	49	48	6	106	4	1
Scotland	10381	5196	959	845	594	205	792	289	15	45	57	3	155	2	1
Scott	6622	3957	619	152	291	750	63	695	10	14	52	2	313	203	14
Shannon	2333	1485	93	57	142	301	24	6	....	2	....	....	4	....	....
Shelby	9580	5546	949	377	422	87	600	539	104	48	124	10	208	10	1
St. Charles	15783	12377	423	277	378	115	850	5321	83	210	576	23	4255	217	7
St. Clair	6591	3082	384	598	600	283	295	151	20	25	22	7	69	1	1
Ste. Genevieve	7208	6129	114	88	154	258	106	1176	16	22	19	4	926	184	....
St. François	8453	6127	338	182	213	676	201	1289	35	69	370	13	612	53	5
St. Louis	226811	155913	6586	7755	7602	3533	4787	124378	2188	6308	34803	1341	65936	3310	412
Stoddard	8471	4457	510	33	522	1655	59	64	2	7	8	1	31	3	2
Stone	3243	1830	89	62	103	479	44	10	1	3	2	....	3	....	....
Sullivan	11653	5630	792	1066	747	426	500	252	46	32	104	14	32	6	2
Taney	4385	2304	216	121	275	575	145	22	7	7	....	3	2	2	1
Texas	9477	5034	493	194	465	1712	241	141	9	30	23	41	26	2	....
Vernon	11022	4383	993	648	1508	446	556	225	55	48	20	6	66	4	2
Warren	7182	5065	199	121	50	58	396	2491	20	45	118	4	2157	10	9
Washington	11143	8619	367	134	257	516	402	576	48	141	101	21	86	41	....
Wayne	6022	3640	222	50	393	938	104	46	2	18	3	....	17	1	....
Webster	10136	5454	317	165	373	1877	248	208	20	30	162	10	43	4	15
Worth	4906	2004	234	644	475	113	113	98	15	23	19	5	24	4	....
Wright	5613	2991	283	108	273	1034	70	71	....	21	3	....	3	2	41

* Also Great Britain not stated: Cole, 1; Holt, 24; Marion, 4; Phelps, 1; St. François, 1; St. Louis, 6.

TERRITORY OF MONTANA.

Counties.	NATIVE. Total.	Born in the Territory.	New York.	Missouri.	Ohio.	Pennsylvania.	Illinois.	FOREIGN-BORN. Total.	British America.	England and Wales.	Ireland.	Scotland.	Germany.	France.	Sweden and Norway.
Beaver Head	494	37	87	28	52	31	46	292	45	64	55	7	33	....	14
Big Horn	20	....	5	2	5	....	2	12	1	2	5	....	3	....	....
Choteau	379	127	53	27	13	28	18	138	47	9	39	2	24	4	2
Dawson	140	7	16	21	5	12	4	37	11	2	[illegible]	[illegible]	[illegible]	[illegible]	3

TABLE XVIII.—*Native and Foreign Population, &c.*—Continued

TERRITORY OF MONTANA—Continued.

Counties.	NATIVE.							FOREIGN-BORN.								
	Total.	Born in the Territory.	New York.	Missouri.	Ohio.	Pennsylvania.	Illinois.	Total.	British America.	England and Wales.	Ireland.	Scotland.	Germany.	France.	Sweden and Norway.
Deer Lodge	2138	228	285	219	195	168	110	2229	220	227	461	56	253	50	43
Gallatin	1250	164	130	159	110	88	89	328	55	69	68	13	76	15	8
Jefferson	1057	132	116	123	106	70	67	474	55	50	82	19	77	5	35
Lewis and Clarke	2966	312	477	329	260	230	193	2074	153	198	351	40	428	43	68
Madison	1783	357	226	148	151	132	128	901	115	125	139	24	117	19	11
Meagher	941	95	110	134	102	59	61	440	42	76	124	16	103	12	14
Missoula	1442	234	178	115	128	93	79	1112	409	67	303	29	130	46	23

STATE OF NEBRASKA.

Counties.	NATIVE.							FOREIGN-BORN.							
	Total.	Born in the State.	Ohio.	Illinois.	New York.	Iowa.	Pennsylvania.	Total.	British America.	England and Wales.	Ireland.	Scotland.	Germany.	France.	Sweden and Norway.
Adams	12	3	3	2	....	....	....	7	....	5	....	2	....	....	....
Black Bird	26	9	....	1	1	1	3	5	....	1	1	....	....	....	3
Buffalo	100	17	6	....	10	6	24	93	7	35	39	1	10	....	1
Burt	2334	516	295	134	297	241	184	513	79	51	30	16	56	6	240
Butler	1102	112	135	164	141	125	60	188	19	18	98	4	47	2	1
Cass	6843	1550	922	618	525	744	399	1308	108	141	330	36	497	14	114
Cedar	572	191	25	19	77	61	18	460	6	24	14	....	324	27	41
Cheyenne	109	3	6	17	30	1	10	81	14	5	45	2	10	2	....
Clay	48	1	6	5	1	18	8	6	3	1	....	....	2	....	....
Colfax	792	126	134	34	111	47	75	632	179	36	79	31	133	3	21
Cuming	1641	407	103	99	133	118	168	1323	101	51	49	2	788	4	73
Dakota	1627	478	127	97	168	192	199	413	44	28	220	11	64	3	22
Dawson	33	5	4	9	5	1	2	70	10	....	49	2	1	....	4
Dixon	999	199	109	76	138	177	69	346	74	13	122	3	97	....	26
Dodge	2556	575	302	265	351	129	200	1656	89	103	123	73	854	8	300
Douglas	12445	2272	1125	1043	2151	686	1022	7337	446	869	1865	203	1957	80	990
Fillmore	204	8	42	12	16	44	12	34	1	....	2	1	10	....	....
Franklin	16	....	1	....	3	2	2	10	3	....	5	....	1	....	....
Gage	2933	597	429	345	262	212	224	426	71	146	37	10	119	5	5
Grant	286	14	12	22	40	7	44	198	15	17	75	11	51	4	13
Hall	541	198	56	29	69	44	27	516	10	24	70	5	345	3	4
Hamilton	94	11	11	7	9	13	4	36	1	4	1	19	8	....	1
Harrison	384	35	31	28	71	7	37	247	32	27	77	12	42	5	34
Jackson	3	....	....	....	2	....	....	6	3	....	....	....	1	....	1
Jefferson	2085	312	231	269	216	271	140	355	70	50	38	19	122	6	15
Johnson	3063	534	421	670	221	204	225	366	49	53	48	12	170	2	5
Kearney	28	5	2	2	4	1	4	30	....	12	11	....	3	1	1
Lancaster	3337	638	878	573	475	640	450	1737	146	208	395	29	558	14	185
L'Eau qui Court	114	38	2	19	7	4	13	147	2	2	....	....	35	....	....
Lincoln	7	....	1	1	2	....	1	10	....	....	8	....	1	....	....
Lyon	40	....	....	4	9	3	6	38	4	3	15	1	11	....	1
Madison	772	83	51	75	56	120	40	361	31	10	17	3	263	....	....
Merrick	386	76	29	18	87	35	22	171	16	32	47	6	53	....	2
Monroe	130	2	6	11	21	4	31	105	13	9	44	3	28	1	2
Nemaha	6747	1635	819	812	385	422	379	846	108	237	93	28	316	30	4
Nuckolls	3	....	....	....	....	....	....	5	5	....	....	....	....	....	....
Otoe	9609	2186	998	841	766	562	691	2736	44	951	112	78	1173	49	89
Pawnee	3556	762	413	453	279	302	301	615	65	67	79	41	204	4	9
Pierce	44	12	1	....	1	7	....	108	....	....	....	....	108	....	....
Platte	988	301	129	71	121	48	46	911	37	97	191	15	322	10	43

TABLE XVIII.—*Native and Foreign Population, &c.*—Continued.

STATE OF NEBRASKA—Continued.

Counties.	NATIVE. Total.	Born in the State.	Ohio.	Illinois.	New York.	Iowa.	Pennsylvania.	FOREIGN-BORN. Total.	British America.	England and Wales.*	Ireland.	Scotland.	Germany.	France.	Sweden and Norway.
	122	17	11	6	7	37	3	14	1	1	3	....	2	....	6
lson	8253	1917	1033	968	513	502	327	1327	271	125	154	19	737	44	1
	2399	307	391	262	172	392	206	707	32	36	27	8	92	....	9
	2943	690	148	155	219	188	231	670	86	76	167	16	155	12	114
rs	3214	426	465	502	345	292	261	1333	127	78	104	27	213	....	453
	2578	320	296	384	323	347	246	375	44	62	33	19	198	1	9
l	399	58	36	29	18	28	10	237	20	6	4	1	180	2	17
	52	1	2	3	12	1	6	45	4	3	23	....	8	2	1
igton	3442	799	369	323	289	220	254	1010	120	78	111	15	494	12	82
	124	6	8	27	25	4	7	58	7	3	1	2	45	....	....
r	13	3	....	1	....	....	3	3	....	2	1	....	....	....	....
	554	46	60	90	25	78	52	50	6	10	1	3	28	....	....
Indian reserv'n.	41	4	....	....	7	....	10	3	....	1	....	....	1	....	1
nized northwest ory.	13	....	1	3	2	....	1	39	2	3	20	1	8	3	1
nized territory of Madison Co'ty.	152	4	14	27	32	21	9	24	10	5	1	1	1	....	6
bago Indian res'n.	30	1	....	....	6	2	7	1	....	....	....	1	....	....	....

* Also Great Britain not stated: Otoe, 1; Sarpy, 1.

STATE OF NEVADA.

Counties.	NATIVE. Total.	Born in the State.	New York.	California.	Ohio.	Pennsylvania.	Illinois.	FOREIGN-BORN. Total.	British America.	England and Wales.*	Ireland.	Scotland.	Germany.	France.	Sweden and Norway.
ill	140	26	22	10	12	7	9	56	15	6	5	3	10	....	....
s	791	240	66	52	45	23	59	424	119	79	55	20	97	4	7
	2054	144	321	152	186	163	107	1393	170	154	241	54	198	26	34
lda	1065	145	105	86	99	62	66	488	65	70	148	19	77	13	12
ldt	1065	93	131	89	152	75	65	651	51	203	171	26	91	39	9
	1580	206	232	112	109	113	93	1235	91	83	288	24	150	26	19
	2148	192	241	46	126	94	135	837	79	238	230	42	70	18	22
	893	179	130	98	61	56	40	944	147	134	222	34	106	24	13
	760	63	117	38	68	55	36	327	48	46	91	20	40	17	7
	1760	352	209	182	104	90	81	1908	380	168	243	60	145	19	18
	108	2	13	13	14	9	12	25	4	1	5	1	3	....	....
	5557	1244	742	909	363	332	170	5802	486	981	2155	172	613	113	60
e	1997	342	235	239	159	84	113	1094	256	115	210	36	136	24	8
Pino	3772	128	701	364	360	293	158	3417	454	572	971	119	445	91	82

* Also Great Britain not stated: Storey, 9; Washoe, 1.

TABLE XVIII.—*Native and Foreign Population, &c.*—Continued.

STATE OF NEW HAMPSHIRE.

Counties.	NATIVE. Total.	Born in the State.	Massachusetts.	Vermont.	Maine.	New York.	Connecticut.	FOREIGN-BORN. Total.	British America.	England and Wales.*	Ireland.	Scotland.	Germany.	France.	Sweden and Norway.
Belknap	16094	15442	620	401	348	66	19	687	321	44	202	41	9	3	....
Carroll	17156	14708	470	130	1740	37	7	176	114	28	27	4	2	....	....
Cheshire	25463	20534	2291	1770	235	294	112	1802	534	150	1037	34	29	10	....
Coos	12782	9698	331	1281	1283	70	43	2150	1585	137	302	26	6	3	[illegible]
Grafton	36847	30929	1295	3446	500	267	91	2256	1590	135	436	57	12	6	[illegible]
Hillsborough	52766	42533	4943	2328	1446	850	119	11472	4850	792	5135	378	209	12	43
Merrimack	38202	33605	1998	1068	668	384	65	3949	1911	476	1389	90	42	[illegible]	1
Rockingham	44478	38637	2899	355	1940	210	68	2819	678	552	1391	115	34	9	[illegible]
Strafford	26938	22551	869	148	3124	108	92	3285	930	331	1745	119	60	6	15
Sullivan	17043	13737	794	1910	120	216	71	1015	422	61	466	28	27	3	....

* Also Great Britain not stated: Belknap, 58; Grafton, 1; Strafford, 48.

STATE OF NEW JERSEY.

Counties.	NATIVE. Total.	Born in the State.	New York.	Pennsylvania.	Massachusetts.	Connecticut.	Maryland.	FOREIGN-BORN. Total.	British America.	England and Wales.*	Ireland.	Scotland.	Germany.	France.	Sweden and Norway.
Atlantic	12401	10059	635	742	224	66	78	1692	23	221	121	66	1124	36	9
Bergen	23275	16629	5502	215	217	225	26	6840	43	651	2536	189	2204	136	37
Burlington	49507	42667	772	4383	131	119	402	4042	35	561	2206	135	970	39	6
Camden	40592	28642	643	7448	287	134	751	5001	95	992	2435	151	1468	80	13
Cape May	8148	7486	110	350	19	30	40	201	2	38	124	3	27	2	....
Cumberland	32714	26462	1787	1423	330	330	178	1931	101	336	520	66	567	51	3
Essex	97504	78269	13296	1986	1243	1500	335	46335	419	5769	18390	1256	17810	859	82
Gloucester	19865	17309	253	1514	84	65	106	1097	10	156	732	28	672	14	....
Hudson	75903	41953	26651	1608	1379	1131	350	53164	746	5814	25111	1099	17091	953	156
Hunterdon	35066	32504	492	1711	58	53	47	1807	18	277	1233	31	202	38	8
Mercer	38363	32320	1204	3436	211	121	206	8023	63	1771	3851	172	1901	64	11
Middlesex	35908	30769	3373	512	213	275	59	9121	183	942	5285	164	1934	137	82
Monmouth	41496	36293	3228	431	136	155	73	4600	194	438	3140	116	608	64	17
Morris	34530	30833	2271	518	162	163	52	8607	121	3112	4242	189	700	55	65
Ocean	13064	11584	581	211	165	178	19	564	25	132	243	26	104	5	2
Passaic	31068	25049	4455	417	311	196	55	15316	153	3923	6050	1010	1224	271	54
Salem	22884	20733	117	993	19	17	384	1056	11	67	545	10	372	13	1
Somerset	20720	18561	1416	301	64	91	30	2790	21	397	1346	60	874	49	16
Sussex	22069	20380	1068	402	34	30	8	1099	17	155	730	12	134	2	3
Union	30942	21616	6294	893	463	399	132	10917	145	1019	6070	271	2585	199	43
Warren	31046	26427	602	3454	120	78	51	3290	35	514	1808	56	739	21	67

* Also Great Britain not stated: Burlington, 1; Camden, 251; Essex, 1; Hudson, 1; Somerset, 1; Union, 142.

TABLE XVIII.—*Native and Foreign Population &c.*—Continued.

TERRITORY OF NEW MEXICO.

Counties.	NATIVE.							FOREIGN-BORN.							
	Total.	Born in the Territory.	New York.	Pennsylvania.	Texas.	Ohio.	Indian Territory.	Total.	British America.	England and Wales.	Ireland.	Scotland.	Germany.	France.	Sweden and Norway.
Bernalillo	7309	7473	5	9	....	....	....	82	....	2	8	....	22	9	....
Colfax	1725	1109	80	47	21	72	....	267	37	22	87	1	56	9	4
Doña Aña	2856	2321	29	21	174	16	....	3008	2	11	33	....	40	10	....
Grant	592	243	56	33	25	34	....	551	26	29	89	9	55	5	4
Lincoln	1686	1493	28	19	34	23	....	117	4	4	39	2	22	2	1
Mora	7775	7415	57	39	5	36	14	281	13	14	78	11	95	10	2
Rio Arriba	9241	8935	....	3	....	3	249	53	1	....	3	1	10	4	....
San Miguel	15804	15639	26	13	8	9	....	254	15	5	19	....	43	20	....
Santa Aña	2587	2571	....	....	....	....	....	12	....	....	2	....	1	1	....
Santa Fé	9083	9093	40	36	8	24	2	386	9	9	43	1	93	18	....
Socorro	6384	6231	30	23	6	12	....	219	3	16	50	4	55	8	....
Taos	11980	11918	7	2	....	4	....	90	3	5	....	....	21	3	....
Valencia	8732	8472	46	47	3	41	....	361	12	12	92	7	69	10	....

STATE OF NEW YORK.

Counties.	NATIVE.							FOREIGN-BORN.							
	Total.	Born in the State.	Massachusetts.	Connecticut.	Vermont.	Pennsylvania.	New Jersey.	Total.	British America.	England and Wales.*	Ireland.	Scotland.	Germany.	France.	Sweden and Norway.
Albany	93738	89658	1080	512	573	367	296	39314	4361	3450	21366	1088	7909	225	16
Allegany	37268	33392	467	454	624	1094	238	3546	227	551	1897	97	707	17	....
Broome	40058	35067	682	883	225	2101	391	4045	154	476	2881	170	301	17	5
Cattaraugus	38244	33895	717	384	966	1150	117	5665	444	617	2257	269	1821	90	33
Cayuga	50312	46375	797	656	370	452	501	9238	768	1855	5211	345	774	56	19
Chautauqua	50045	42846	1107	717	1287	2364	170	9282	703	1265	2490	211	2150	110	1028
Chemung	30728	26073	456	414	181	2225	598	4553	195	610	2812	115	671	49	3
Chenango	37785	34860	523	1045	202	231	71	2779	138	480	1678	78	228	28	108
Clinton	35270	32091	272	96	2117	55	34	12677	9378	396	2538	131	154	44	5
Columbia	41185	39015	937	464	130	88	95	5850	314	570	3423	91	1195	76	18
Cortland	23285	21611	389	445	152	163	47	1868	127	453	1157	53	55	7	11
Delaware	39503	37567	274	612	87	574	75	3469	92	376	1394	1024	413	45	79
Dutchess	61938	58756	426	1032	148	283	310	12103	153	1367	7927	392	1869	138	22
Erie	117792	108583	1284	844	1493	1570	297	60907	5032	4777	12535	1125	31150	4133	127
Essex	24409	21542	212	84	1982	36	28	4633	2219	329	1954	64	47	11	1
Franklin	23321	19802	227	69	2652	36	6	6950	4671	108	1927	133	11	2	2
Fulton	24549	23935	164	108	133	27	26	2515	87	546	818	108	781	48	8
Genesee	25773	23034	566	654	530	210	89	5833	424	1382	2332	137	1373	102	1
Greene	29346	28509	163	259	46	60	79	2486	245	277	1297	99	487	13	13
Hamilton	2654	2444	26	29	100	17	1	306	61	19	118	19	61	23	....
Herkimer	34144	32638	396	366	157	83	65	5785	266	1357	2657	144	1149	73	5
Jefferson	55379	51704	782	497	1158	138	70	10036	4883	1021	2540	250	912	209	1
Kings	266110	232718	5849	5431	829	3417	6317	153811	2888	20940	78220	4245	40112	2041	1438
Lewis	23467	22341	345	235	253	43	17	5232	919	507	1619	59	1229	681	....
Livingston	32472	29077	440	533	386	802	382	5237	557	736	3395	293	806	24	6
Madison	38706	35790	648	774	379	194	98	4816	351	1464	2423	63	424	98	23
Monroe	84104	77297	1336	1177	903	613	469	33764	4085	4590	10219	658	11663	674	46
Montgomery	30177	29640	103	78	53	42	64	4280	125	439	1650	171	1731	59	27
New York	523198	484100	5995	5140	992	5009	8061	419094	4419	25026	201999	7562	151216	8265	1930
Niagara	37210	33302	453	397	742	735	255	13227	2568	2096	4055	287	3895	157	10
Oneida	84301	78858	1430	1350	601	298	232	25707	1144	7343	9079	720	5664	961	13
Onondaga	80110	74830	1182	1134	655	419	183	24073	2026	3777	10212	260	6348	540	11
Ontario	37758	34628	570	570	319	379	366	7350	475	1623	4303	277	487	60	17
Orange	66643	60789	407	432	60	932	3213	14250	136	2009	9639	432	1677	90	26
Orleans	23446	21397	316	377	530	119	59	4243	569	1510	1581	180	312	22	19

TABLE XVIII.—*Native and Foreign Population, &c.*—Continued.

STATE OF NEW YORK—Continued.

Counties.	NATIVE. Total.	Born in the State.	Massachusetts.	Connecticut.	Vermont.	Pennsylvania.	New Jersey.	FOREIGN-BORN. Total.	British America.	England and Wales.*	Ireland.	Scotland.	Germany.	France.	Sweden and Norway.
Oswego	64686	60840	830	753	913	180	116	13255	4447	1706	5301	310	1009	367	[illegible]
Otsego	46234	44035	509	708	250	173	64	2733	99	990	1250	196	186	5	[illegible]
Putnam	12969	12438	27	291	17	35	64	2451	73	473	1574	67	131	18	24
Queens	54728	51482	419	522	50	294	827	19075	187	1792	8066	406	6553	349	101
Rensselaer	73028	69043	1490	533	1314	231	229	25621	2314	2653	15032	830	3135	137	24
Richmond	22916	20654	288	181	45	210	694	10113	107	1204	5579	209	2245	193	142
Rockland	19863	17938	146	156	32	106	1132	5350	131	496	2972	100	1300	44	79
Saratoga	43820	40791	696	372	911	115	132	7709	779	995	5002	213	570	42	4
Schenectady	17661	17222	105	69	76	35	19	3686	44	474	1207	196	1651	23	5
Schoharie	32439	32072	65	118	45	19	16	901	52	88	418	8	290	23	....
Schuyler	17941	16489	109	266	74	392	383	1048	43	149	709	27	26	19	1
Seneca	23978	21575	172	225	123	682	673	3845	155	737	2326	100	410	38	7
Steuben	61833	56677	475	485	339	2189	703	5884	252	634	3303	169	1392	45	3
St. Lawrence	66607	59403	884	275	4572	78	71	18219	10067	1367	5688	891	108	30	8
Suffolk	42047	40118	233	601	42	118	366	4877	105	805	2355	168	961	62	50
Sullivan	28728	27347	70	306	30	545	295	5822	58	347	2266	176	2450	46	5
Tioga	28670	24604	503	499	156	1940	427	1902	102	298	1178	32	119	93	9
Tompkins	31051	28371	323	460	162	622	544	2127	104	463	1347	76	83	7	12
Ulster	71335	69054	212	285	42	187	280	12740	170	894	7698	165	3415	97	52
Warren	20014	18411	205	114	961	48	20	2578	773	190	1491	67	44	1	....
Washington	41274	37253	452	180	2605	114	29	8294	1999	888	5024	198	124	14	3
Wayne	40299	37571	560	427	341	209	351	7411	660	1698	1828	76	1412	446	6
Westchester	94004	86394	962	2137	214	778	1316	37344	597	3863	21535	1055	8319	333	231
Wyoming	25113	22588	467	417	753	182	64	4051	235	[illegible]	1448	90	1066	388	8
Yates	17840	16333	142	209	136	292	273	1755	105	533	826	99	71	60	9

* Also Great Britain not stated: Albany, 35; Dutchess, 5; Jefferson, 1; Kings, 9; Livingston, 1; Madison, 1; New York, 7; Niagara, 3; Rockland, 1; Steuben, 7; Suffolk, 2; Sullivan, 1; Tioga, 1; Washington, 1; Westchester, 13; Yates, 2.

STATE OF NORTH CAROLINA.

Counties.	NATIVE. Total.	Born in the State.	Virginia and West Virginia.	South Carolina.	Tennessee.	Georgia.	New York.	FOREIGN-BORN. Total.	British America.	England and Wales.*	Ireland.	Scotland.	Germany.	France.	Sweden and Norway.
Alamance	11822	11727	26	4	....	3	10	52	6	5	23	1	17	....	....
Alexander	6868	6860	2	2	2	1	....	....	....	....	....	....	....	....	....
Alleghany	3687	3304	367	....	5	3	1	4	....	1	1	2	....	....	....
Anson	12406	12277	37	62	3	1	1	22	....	6	6	1	....	....	7
Ashe	9509	8866	523	2	127	3	....	4	....	1	2	1	....	....	....
Beaufort	12988	12877	23	3	1	1	94	23	....	4	9	1	12	1	1
Bertie	12947	12845	75	5	1	3	8	3	....	1	....	....	....	1	....
Bladen	12813	12731	15	26	1	12	9	18	....	....	8	6	3	1	....
Brunswick	7727	7377	57	203	....	16	12	27	2	7	10	....	7	....	....
Buncombe	15318	13923	148	721	321	81	19	94	20	3	30	6	9	1	14
Burke	9766	9651	....	29	9	7	5	11	3	1	3	1	3	....	....
Cabarrus	11919	11696	19	101	4	24	5	35	....	7	5	1	19	....	....
Caldwell	8472	8335	21	42	45	10	5	4	....	....	....	....	3	....	1
Camden	5353	5246	82	1	1	4	1	8	1	....	2	2	3	....	....
Carteret	8940	8798	15	5	2	6	15	70	....	10	32	4	16	2	2
Caswell	16072	14633	1363	5	13	10	3	9	....	4	3	....	....	....	....
Catawba	10974	10925	11	7	9	1	....	10	....	....	2	....	6	1	....
Chatham	19648	19609	7	3	2	5	1	75	1	50	21	1	2	....	....
Cherokee	8070	6463	32	146	843	512	3	10	....	9	....	1	....	....	....
Chowan	6438	6349	74	....	....	....	1	12	....	2	5	....	5	....	....
Clay	2459	1917	6	38	85	388	....	2	1	....	1	....	....	....	....
Cleaveland	12084	11870	65	672	33	16	2	12	....	4	3	1	2	....	....

TABLE XVIII.—*Native and Foreign Population, &c.*—Continued.

STATE OF NORTH CAROLINA—Continued.

Counties.	NATIVE. Total.	Born in the State.	Virginia and West Virginia.	South Carolina.	Tennessee.	Georgia.	New York.	FOREIGN-BORN. Total.	British America.	England and Wales.*	Ireland.	Scotland.	Germany.	France.	Sweden and Norway.
ous	8470	8079	50	302	1	4	3	4	...	3	...	1	...	...	...
	20388	19940	64	40	4	15	124	128	8	15	23	9	55	2	1
rland	16915	16709	71	60	2	9	15	120	1	21	10	71	10	4	...
ick	5128	5102	24	...	...	...	...	3	...	2	...	...	1	...	...
	2774	2748	3	1	...	...	11	4	...	2	1	...	1	...	...
on	17372	17235	88	8	2	5	4	42	...	32	4	1	1	...	...
	9615	9247	285	36	3	5	4	5	...	1	...	3	...	...	...
	15499	15446	20	...	4	4	3	43	8	2	14	7	12	...	...
mbe	22906	22215	548	29	7	13	12	64	1	10	10	3	24	1	...
n	13034	12693	172	37	11	41	1	16	...	...	2	1	8	1	...
in	14120	13998	71	4	10	14	3	14	...	1	10	...	...	...	...
	12568	11757	19	748	13	1	2	34	...	7	16	2	6	...	...
	7724	7693	29	...	...	...	...	...	...	...	...	...	...	...	...
lle	24824	23645	1098	2	22	7	9	7	...	...	2	1	1	...	1
	8686	8684	1	...	...	...	...	1	...	...	...	...	1	...	...
d	21585	20877	453	21	13	8	40	151	63	52	3	3	28	1	...
	20395	19753	526	13	14	6	7	13	2	1	8	1	1	...	...
t	8864	8812	22	9	1	5	1	31	1	1	2	24	3	...	...
od	7904	6920	60	581	228	74	...	17	1	...	15	...	...	1	...
son	7685	6378	39	1153	56	22	3	21	...	4	7	7	...	...	...
rd	9262	8736	491	3	1	1	2	11	...	2	3	2	2	1	...
	6441	6427	1	...	...	...	10	4	...	...	...	...	...	...	...
	16908	16658	114	74	8	10	3	23	...	4	1	5	13	...	...
n	6676	5985	37	272	246	109	...	7	...	1	5	...	...	...	1
on	16881	16764	45	3	1	3	10	16	...	3	2	1	1	...	1
	4996	4985	2	3	1	...	...	6	...	2	1	2	1	...	...
	10419	10339	25	7	...	7	2	15	...	6	1	1	4	...	...
n	9553	9208	58	121	11	18	7	20	...	6	3	1	3	2	3
	6610	6061	34	134	191	169	2	5	...	3	...	1	1	...	...
on	8186	7261	69	354	441	23	1	6	...	...	5	...	...	1	...
	9634	9532	54	1	1	...	5	13	1	4	1	...	3	...	...
rell	7546	7346	66	84	24	10	...	46	5	1	24	10	6	...	...
nburg	24047	21241	364	2093	49	38	25	252	...	43	58	36	93	6	...
ll	4703	4524	12	23	120	3	6	2	...	...	...	...	1	...	...
mery	7486	7473	5	6	...	...	...	1	...	...	...	1	...	...	...
	12002	11981	5	7	2	2	1	38	1	2	...	35	...	...	...
	11072	11041	16	...	...	7	2	5	...	1	...	...	2	1	...
anover	27363	25789	405	327	9	72	123	615	17	51	144	35	307	9	5
mpton	14742	14376	341	5	6	1	1	7	2	4	...	...	...	...	...
	7559	7550	...	1	...	1	1	10	...	1	1	4	3	...	...
	17497	17299	98	19	10	4	4	10	1	3	2	1	...	...	1
tank	8102	7802	68	4	...	...	14	29	...	5	3	...	15	1	...
mans	7942	7896	32	...	1	2	1	3	...	...	2	...	1	...	...
	11166	10662	480	...	7	9	...	4	...	...	1	...	2	1	...
	17268	17197	24	5	5	5	10	8	...	...	3	...	5	...	...
	4316	3391	22	853	19	8	...	3	...	...	1	...	...	...	...
ph	17540	17447	39	23	2	2	2	11	...	5	...	3	3	...	...
ond	12827	11863	81	771	9	12	...	55	7	2	5	36	3	1	...
n	16221	15871	27	292	1	6	1	41	...	2	4	22	5	...	...
gham	15689	14414	1103	59	13	16	14	19	2	1	2	6	7	...	...
	16709	16554	95	50	13	8	7	41	2	13	6	7	8	1	...
ford	13113	12540	58	449	21	16	6	8	...	1	1	3	...	1	...
n	16419	16320	30	20	4	3	5	17	1	2	4	5	4	...	...
	8307	8277	7	13	4	2	1	8	...	2	...	...	2	3	...
	11206	10009	1154	3	18	...	...	2	...	1	1	...	...	...	...
	11240	10296	860	13	28	12	5	12	...	1	1	...	2	...	...
lvania	3535	2808	12	661	7	40	...	1	...	...	...	1	...	...	...
l	4166	4137	15	7	...	...	...	7	1	2	2	1	1	...	...
	12200	11002	47	1119	3	19	2	8	1	1	...	1	1	...	1
	35387	34211	557	135	20	42	79	230	9	34	59	19	75	8	1
n	17730	16132	1343	23	14	11	44	34	1	16	7	8	2	1	1
ngton	6508	6478	5	...	...	...	5	8	...	...	3	1	2	...	...
ga	5286	5100	32	31	110	4	2	1	...	...	...	1	...	...	...
	18050	17880	83	32	5	5	6	85	1	3	15	2	49	...	2
	15535	15333	121	14	39	4	...	4	...	...	3	...	1	...	...
	12209	11923	145	71	5	7	11	49	...	1	7	...	16	...	...
	10695	10510	122	25	10	1	2	2	...	...	1	...	1	...	...
	5909	5769	4	6	125	...	...	...	...	...	...	...	...	...	...

* Also Great Britain *not stated*: Edgecombe, 1; New Hanover, 1; Surry, 2.

TABLE XVIII.—*Native and Foreign Population, &c.*—Continued.

STATE OF OHIO.

Counties.	NATIVE. Total.	Born in the State.	Pennsylvania.	Virginia and West Virginia.	New York.	Kentucky.	Maryland.	FOREIGN-BORN. Total.	British America.	England and Wales.	Ireland.	Scotland.	Germany.	France.	Sweden and Norway.
Adams	20209	17237	851	685	62	985	97	541	11	15	217	21	245	21	...
Allen	21557	18639	1222	564	281	100	166	2066	33	331	447	25	812	71	1
Ashland	20718	16018	3408	150	421	7	207	1215	93	123	154	164	574	133	...
Ashtabula	30300	19270	2563	82	1512	16	19	2217	473	810	620	112	163	14	4
Athens	22016	19027	1269	1326	327	40	165	852	54	258	376	20	105	6	...
Auglaize	16860	15177	645	316	112	70	86	5181	22	60	161	1	2721	106	...
Belmont	37100	29096	2263	3432	129	50	911	2614	73	365	1138	75	813	49	...
Brown	28631	24168	550	583	110	2265	126	2171	11	102	379	28	1154	318	...
Butler	33002	27359	1150	488	447	642	328	6910	77	429	1574	101	4145	257	4
Carroll	13700	11895	1193	197	59	3	199	785	10	132	332	37	175	66	...
Champaign	22724	17700	1281	1772	327	287	231	1464	89	134	944	36	193	19	2
Clark	29514	21356	2137	1087	520	765	806	3556	72	438	1741	106	1111	29	2
Clermont	31981	26914	592	538	247	1676	272	2287	47	174	462	65	1191	211	...
Clinton	21232	17880	380	1223	133	447	101	683	5	75	444	16	126	12	...
Columbiana	34514	27101	3310	767	220	32	311	3785	87	1232	1074	486	614	65	15
Coshocton	21768	19279	1120	512	263	13	222	1832	24	363	523	22	671	132	2
Crawford	21714	17151	3033	181	564	15	156	3842	98	188	395	13	2817	167	22
Cuyahoga	81314	61453	2602	556	8107	263	250	50606	3446	8337	12016	1089	19934	438	34
Darke	30397	25136	2167	504	177	145	564	1881	24	52	378	14	1157	217	...
Defiance	13722	11243	890	113	502	27	71	2197	179	85	159	5	1497	102	...
Delaware	23426	18966	1399	661	715	75	251	1749	64	477	689	17	467	24	...
Erie	20786	16753	495	90	1841	70	83	7109	271	573	1367	89	4624	95	12
Fairfield	29190	25027	1538	869	152	42	458	1948	32	119	300	22	1161	110	...
Fayette	16622	13917	332	1317	108	224	68	518	15	22	353	8	135	9	1
Franklin	52482	42275	2541	1919	1591	409	699	10527	351	1238	2341	165	5705	322	3
Fulton	15946	11805	1007	55	1716	8	55	1843	120	240	156	35	513	279	...
Gallia	24389	18923	701	3851	169	136	72	1156	32	575	52	39	360	48	...
Geauga	13179	9400	306	17	1692	10	6	711	123	201	168	20	82	5	1
Greene	26150	19173	981	1868	301	1069	553	1588	51	95	804	84	407	13	...
Guernsey	23016	19605	1842	785	57	13	391	822	15	155	537	23	83	...	...
Hamilton	171871	139033	4598	2439	4227	6818	1319	88490	1255	4492	20251	914	55273	2441	49
Hancock	22546	18894	2383	347	258	19	221	1301	29	68	81	26	899	77	1
Hardin	17117	14567	1042	520	309	77	166	1799	38	150	382	14	678	9	3
Harrison	18218	15853	1280	461	57	7	352	464	6	90	312	15	32	1	...
Henry	11857	10029	673	108	487	9	111	2171	109	150	125	24	1662	79	...
Highland	27993	23786	874	1749	132	416	152	1110	12	101	503	63	237	134	...
Hocking	17062	15245	767	536	102	24	158	863	4	86	217	10	520	17	...
Holmes	16666	14038	1921	160	91	5	116	1611	11	51	116	5	831	252	...
Huron	24552	17291	988	84	3983	42	43	3980	172	833	758	54	1891	135	1
Jackson	19905	16471	1167	1655	66	239	68	1794	12	948	400	23	367	9	1
Jefferson	25943	20535	2715	1568	168	58	471	3245	69	1009	1352	220	531	7	15
Knox	25888	20403	2129	654	473	26	518	1245	39	475	447	29	177	56	1
Lake	14263	9364	514	41	2330	20	12	1672	262	493	747	24	94	6	1
Lawrence	28798	21017	1209	3683	118	2074	78	2582	14	534	745	33	1178	28	...
Licking	33822	26741	1674	1902	836	47	403	2134	51	1048	635	42	505	48	1
Logan	22062	17915	1348	1190	182	193	154	966	65	87	543	52	183	15	...
Lorain	24751	17130	548	267	3218	66	35	5557	339	1684	730	115	2509	79	10
Lucas	32603	22791	1392	178	1174	154	101	14119	1301	1139	3405	168	6804	343	26
Madison	14299	12056	302	763	168	192	171	1344	37	122	908	17	163	8	...
Mahoning	25192	19618	1028	218	405	30	193	5809	107	2078	1897	423	1212	17	1
Marion	14273	11911	1120	298	270	31	141	1911	80	189	432	10	1022	56	4
Medina	18559	12853	1355	65	1808	16	119	1533	139	499	121	36	644	57	3
Meigs	28180	21279	1514	3899	321	145	168	3285	28	1393	236	101	1473	22	...
Mercer	15039	13462	553	245	117	90	80	2215	17	47	93	18	1778	99	...
Miami	30231	24382	2301	856	343	297	585	2509	49	166	580	22	1537	74	...
Monroe	23325	20577	1268	963	66	18	239	2454	...	59	137	15	1962	157	2
Montgomery	53027	41998	4286	1057	898	500	1025	10979	180	573	2008	118	7298	337	25
Morgan	19873	17023	1172	837	97	7	285	490	29	75	201	8	173	1	...
Morrow	17920	14092	1724	427	570	18	229	693	25	152	143	17	300	5	1
Muskingum	41885	34252	2607	2188	362	113	789	3501	44	468	1090	69	1536	207	...
Noble	19285	17075	879	688	70	10	290	661	7	75	166	19	372	17	...
Ottawa	9889	8089	386	45	679	22	27	3475	373	161	242	53	2435	29	9
Paulding	7890	6429	384	154	234	139	44	651	80	76	119	9	224	74	...
Perry	17705	15441	1009	579	69	7	346	748	12	36	469	10	108	65	...
Pickaway	23783	20857	857	962	168	89	281	1092	22	80	377	16	545	20	...
Pike	11548	12382	478	1014	90	152	66	899	5	32	43	6	782	5	...
Portage	22131	16184	1540	95	1354	28	68	2432	195	748	607	100	709	50	2
Preble	20736	16322	878	889	137	383	450	1073	11	36	321	12	467	13	...
Putnam	15033	13322	761	253	191	26	136	2016	15	200	119	6	1314	152	...

TABLE XVIII.—*Native and Foreign Population, &c.*—Continued.

STATE OF OHIO—Continued.

Counties.	Native: Total.	Born in the State.	Pennsylvania.	Virginia and West Virginia.	New York.	Kentucky.	Maryland.	Foreign-born: Total.	British America.	England and Wales.*	Ireland.	Scotland.	Germany.	France.	Sweden and Norway.
	20492	22458	1552	377	743	18	376	3024	107	441	483	71	1676	61	3
	33939	28734	867	2241	222	328	337	3158	30	149	508	62	2188	70	2
	21544	16650	2133	110	1412	28	196	3959	118	318	606	22	2291	229	...
	25727	20294	1436	1313	327	1458	96	3575	22	402	517	40	2176	261	2
	26949	20883	3190	422	1042	19	731	3878	105	119	343	4	2315	281	...
	18485	16216	674	484	149	130	182	2263	30	82	394	21	1221	320	...
	44728	35323	7048	352	606	36	387	7780	92	1060	577	224	3622	1319	5
	28613	21159	3239	119	1090	31	114	6061	369	1855	1280	238	1692	234	11
	30568	22480	4280	181	1272	69	110	8091	331	4462	1676	653	812	75	...
ras	29204	25735	2012	345	227	13	425	4636	43	279	281	30	2438	62	6
	17929	15338	716	673	222	41	191	891	50	103	299	8	328	5	...
t	14507	12234	1026	223	217	50	136	1316	37	283	124	10	722	60	4
	14265	11996	893	743	99	95	109	762	14	105	435	7	160	20	...
	25046	20642	784	934	224	579	197	1643	38	241	638	38	625	36	...
ton	36679	30154	2213	2389	406	98	293	3930	49	374	748	237	2420	54	3
	31988	23987	6638	184	343	9	225	3128	74	231	420	118	1072	433	2
	19484	15247	1889	167	822	21	144	1507	53	126	116	34	698	383	2
	21445	17308	1513	136	1312	23	127	3151	166	567	301	140	1669	113	1
	16842	13500	1593	283	609	12	215	1711	43	85	225	9	977	75	...

Great Britain not stated: Athens, 1; Cuyahoga, 2; Franklin, 1; Hamilton, 4; Lake, 10; Madi- .edina, 1; Portage, 5; Summit, 7; Union, 1.

STATE OF OREGON.

Counties.	Native: Total.	Born in the State.	Missouri.	Illinois.	Ohio.	Iowa.	Indiana.	Foreign-born: Total.	British America.	England and Wales.	Ireland.	Scotland.	Germany.	France.	Sweden and Norway.
	1757	423	196	111	120	126	79	1047	55	49	93	7	68	40	15
	4341	2158	468	222	317	182	159	243	42	49	42	11	62	8	3
as	5436	2553	414	349	331	283	265	557	55	106	129	19	111	20	11
	952	428	34	38	33	20	24	303	39	49	52	13	62	1	45
	744	322	63	45	48	23	34	119	25	20	17	8	20	1	13
	1255	513	68	53	68	61	53	389	1	129	50	23	65	5	51
	426	174	40	36	33	8	13	78	...	14	28	7	8	...	1
	5684	2900	508	298	238	234	260	382	68	58	54	21	47	5	8
	1001	235	76	69	58	28	38	1250	27	35	70	17	83	19	17
	3721	1582	339	182	184	202	145	1057	33	47	97	14	144	24	13
e	817	415	71	33	43	22	23	387	3	15	44	7	38	4	26
	6291	3293	725	428	230	202	238	135	15	25	22	6	44	3	2
	8474	4245	865	543	452	421	494	243	32	51	34	19	74	12	3
	9049	4638	719	594	438	369	408	916	244	151	157	39	193	37	4
ah	8425	3541	328	385	500	261	287	3085	300	400	823	91	629	80	42
	4573	2371	581	313	167	167	141	128	32	26	18	12	21	...	4
k	380	183	18	22	22	27	18	28	6	5	5	2	1	...	5
	2692	683	331	230	162	199	152	294	30	19	30	7	34	14	3
	2338	764	273	167	154	220	127	214	35	19	26	23	30	6	3
	2131	1011	149	123	94	68	68	378	37	32	86	14	81	23	6
ton	4038	2110	297	257	136	268	190	220	58	41	41	9	29	5	5
l	4798	2413	498	234	213	295	295	214	50	50	51	17	21	2	1

TABLE XVIII.—*Native and Foreign Population, &c.*—Continued.

STATE OF PENNSYLVANIA.

Counties.	NATIVE.							FOREIGN-BORN.							
	Total.	Born in the State.	New York.	New Jersey.	Maryland.	Ohio.	Virginia and West Virginia.	Total.	British America.	England and Wales.*	Ireland.	Scotland.	Germany.	France.	Sweden and Norway.
Adams	29622	27559	89	10	1716	26	115	603	7	22	64	....	561	16	1
Allegheny	186307	170915	2102	863	1881	3927	2877	75897	676	11772	25508	2824	30093	2034	74
Armstrong	39828	38947	241	30	78	182	81	3554	84	778	1391	116	1074	30	2
Beaver	32134	29450	291	87	142	1266	367	4014	78	1049	1117	133	1389	101	1
Bedford	28362	27547	52	34	563	53	178	1073	15	289	259	103	369	17	6
Berks	101315	100484	194	131	130	42	122	5386	36	532	982	57	3456	113	9
Blair	34711	33865	99	78	268	60	124	3340	32	339	1491	37	1324	45	16
Bradford	48078	38480	6971	1081	69	78	85	4226	195	750	2560	404	264	19	1
Bucks	60290	56099	320	2137	208	39	130	4046	46	374	2080	63	1346	37	1
Butler	32571	31968	101	45	48	172	74	3939	15	183	1249	78	2067	263	4
Cambria	29470	28758	88	18	228	83	75	7099	33	1848	2210	67	2764	113	7
Cameron	3507	2692	596	38	17	9	10	766	127	42	421	32	50	6	69
Carbon	21180	20629	172	194	21	23	8	6964	26	1456	3577	109	1651	56	18
Centre	32888	32195	242	93	86	52	68	1530	49	301	647	106	308	26	13
Chester	71649	67321	264	451	1529	93	261	6156	64	779	4497	114	583	23	5
Clarion	24917	24546	115	20	32	101	22	1620	16	117	430	36	852	33	2
Clearfield	23651	22851	282	91	74	25	30	2090	183	520	566	114	459	191	....
Clinton	20897	19866	455	68	70	36	41	2314	110	237	963	44	733	14	10
Columbia	26613	26142	132	158	33	18	16	2153	19	708	1050	35	303	18	3
Crawford	56647	43309	8266	368	131	1803	119	7185	957	669	2325	222	2047	491	213
Cumberland	42966	40870	88	39	678	75	819	946	15	79	167	14	606	32	1
Dauphin	56003	53202	196	94	942	111	1029	4737	35	1218	1344	90	1902	32	9
Delaware	32373	28199	282	594	873	53	213	7030	26	2148	4360	206	197	26	1
Elk	6054	5119	586	30	26	9	56	2434	151	212	622	120	933	47	263
Erie	52699	36405	11103	223	103	1424	111	13274	1573	1162	3911	244	5659	252	31
Fayette	41068	38629	77	123	722	343	1415	1616	51	493	596	153	274	20	2
Forest	3560	3003	352	20	19	53	9	450	80	27	150	29	141	8	12
Franklin	44143	40501	42	30	2355	60	979	1222	7	68	171	6	923	29	1
Fulton	9115	8687	19	11	280	13	79	245	....	17	28	5	185	1	5
Greene	25735	23976	15	80	160	182	1202	152	....	24	75	11	31	1	....
Huntingdon	29658	28998	54	54	278	47	106	1393	13	443	656	36	383	20	4
Indiana	34735	34050	120	87	90	91	81	1403	13	189	580	57	523	24	....
Jefferson	20566	19790	439	18	35	98	28	1090	15	123	432	17	427	9	....
Juniata	17175	17039	14	12	38	7	16	215	4	24	75	7	84	6	....
Lancaster	113796	111513	254	165	1109	125	152	7514	21	425	1204	36	5371	136	12
Lawrence	24946	23186	172	80	67	1029	113	2352	77	653	980	95	466	40	....
Lebanon	33341	33190	17	25	41	18	1	755	5	38	215	6	442	7	....
Lehigh	50610	49912	185	236	59	46	24	6186	14	1187	2511	94	2044	56	6
Luzerne	106227	96306	4688	2569	276	289	202	54688	512	17910	24610	2040	8749	193	56
Lycoming	43069	39647	1760	394	354	94	137	4558	279	420	1039	64	2499	138	1
McKean	7676	4506	2616	45	11	35	23	1149	90	119	682	45	106	6	86
Mercer	41942	37554	972	105	179	2363	169	8035	278	2620	2398	1433	1199	59	....
Mifflin	16930	16570	44	49	86	38	36	578	11	136	209	21	180	8	1
Monroe	17356	16379	301	534	36	13	29	1006	11	88	411	9	447	15	3
Montgomery	72322	70199	211	535	377	104	202	9266	60	1483	5179	177	1887	65	12
Montour	12824	12461	99	109	42	22	21	2520	6	1162	757	44	480	23	....
Northampton	55058	52115	197	1944	66	54	58	6374	28	1374	2089	49	2527	86	....
Northumberland	37119	36367	227	121	121	30	51	4325	77	1378	1420	187	1006	24	11
Perry	25026	24713	29	24	113	32	46	421	3	75	104	9	178	3	1
Philadelphia	490398	428250	8865	18157	8238	1381	1233	183624	1488	22549	96698	4175	50754	2479	278
Pike	6940	5210	997	645	3	3	3	1496	8	156	421	34	647	134	6
Potter	10368	6103	3720	96	8	25	6	897	65	58	218	9	419	36	11
Schuylkill	85572	84933	488	245	177	80	96	30856	163	9333	13465	630	6709	291	16
Snyder	15527	15453	12	11	21	5	2	79	2	5	10	....	59	....	....
Somerset	26427	25304	41	11	607	75	277	1799	34	71	462	11	1186	7	1
Sullivan	5201	5010	133	18	1	3	1	900	37	102	424	12	292	21	1
Susquehanna	33519	25583	4681	1179	69	40	31	4004	84	665	2879	97	215	14	21
Tioga	31298	22804	6660	289	34	46	30	3799	150	1405	962	767	358	42	62
Union	15300	15014	74	62	34	12	27	265	7	80	74	5	85	6	....
Venango	42139	32900	5822	313	136	1161	194	5786	1157	855	2395	197	955	58	36
Warren	19991	13534	4910	91	25	268	33	3900	460	410	899	180	458	419	916
Washington	45690	42585	80	68	312	924	1350	2793	41	898	1147	281	363	26	....
Wayne	26469	21543	3523	586	18	22	16	6719	51	1153	3060	52	2139	63	2
Westmoreland	54731	53647	103	73	145	261	272	3988	20	992	1365	338	1105	32	45
Wyoming	13960	12187	996	477	3	9	6	625	11	102	324	5	135	2	18
York	72594	69793	88	29	2216	84	145	3540	15	358	313	32	2711	35	2

* Also Great Britain not stated: Adams, 1; Allegheny, 2; Armstrong, 5; Beaver, 11; Cambria, 12; Centre, 2; Chester, 1; Clearfield, 17; Crawford, 7; Erie, 26; Greene, 9; Huntingdon, 1; Indian… 1 Lawrence, 19; Luzerne, 27; Northumberland, 1; Venango, 1; Warren, 2; Washington, 2; Wayne, 77 Vestmoreland, 13.

TABLE XVIII.—*Native and Foreign Population, &c.*—Continued.

STATE OF RHODE ISLAND.

Counties.	NATIVE. Total.	Born in the State.	Massachusetts.	Connecticut.	New York.	Maine.	New Hampshire.	FOREIGN-BORN. Total.	British America.	England and Wales.*	Ireland.	Scotland.	Germany.	France.	Sweden and Norway.
....	7355	5920	891	117	126	85	22	2066	501	148	1069	66	52	4	3
....	14040	12144	649	609	220	74	51	4535	1865	746	1604	233	14	5	62
....	16786	13839	1185	158	572	120	63	3264	92	558	2164	92	177	46	3
o	105579	77032	15722	3551	2729	1550	1088	43611	7517	7381	25859	1407	867	101	59
on	18197	16314	272	1089	285	46	18	1900	267	513	838	150	91	11	1

* Also Great Britain not stated: Bristol, 155.

STATE OF SOUTH CAROLINA.

Counties.	NATIVE. Total.	Born in the State.	North Carolina.	Virginia and West Virginia.	Georgia.	New York.	Alabama.	FOREIGN-BORN. Total.	British America.	England and Wales.*	Ireland.	Scotland.	Germany.	France.	Sweden and Norway.
....	31035	30632	55	129	129	6	16	94	1	8	45	3	23	1	....
....	23965	23111	130	194	381	6	24	84	1	12	49	4	8	....	1
....	35548	34801	67	188	261	100	1	176	....	27	30	5	73	5	....
....	34200	33634	23	18	205	61	4	159	2	18	33	5	56	6	1
....	83826	81691	304	225	354	429	52	5037	33	260	2209	121	1886	101	24
....	18687	18301	167	158	14	6	4	118	1	4	72	4	22	1	....
ld............	10503	9484	875	51	21	23	8	81	2	39	31	5	......	2	....
....	14012	13940	39	12	7	3	4	26	....	2	8	....	9	1	....
....	25363	25257	36	11	21	1	4	48	1	4	9	3	11	3	....
....	26172	25931	126	40	9	11	13	71	1	7	10	....	29	7	....
....	42328	41135	103	315	548	22	55	158	4	40	30	10	56	1	....
....	19760	19711	16	14	2	2	1	119	2	2	96	3	12	1	....
rn	16102	15892	173	17	18	34	3	59	....	5	16	4	16	....	....
....	22144	21008	475	261	86	24	32	118	1	20	41	27	11	....	4
....	10699	10095	535	27	3	7	2	22	2	7	4	....	2	....	....
....	11695	11451	55	100	8	2	19	59	1	7	12	9	15	....	....
....	12058	11431	536	45	11	6	4	29	2	2	18	2	1	....	....
....	22458	22130	86	149	36	6	6	78	1	5	38	3	20	....	1
....	12949	12733	111	43	16	10	7	39	....	2	7	1	19	....	1
....	22112	21807	269	9	10	7	2	48	....	2	5	9	26	....	....
gh............	11797	11009	725	24	5	2	3	17	....	3	4	4	4	....	....
....	20617	20095	81	310	59	9	6	158	....	5	12	1	93	5	18
....	10404	9811	170	40	315	2	11	132	2	7	33	2	86	....	....
g............	16802	16711	10	48	6	6	4	63	....	4	17	2	26	2	....
....	10250	9965	149	47	67	2	2	10	....	2	5	....	2	....	....
....	22356	21052	300	319	130	103	29	669	13	89	262	48	188	6	....
rg	25704	24560	761	165	68	22	18	80	2	15	27	8	24	....	....
....	25157	24824	199	31	24	11	9	111	2	11	45	7	16	....	10
....	19183	18931	121	73	15	6	4	65	1	9	21	11	14	....	....
urgh	15452	15324	104	8	3	2	1	37	....	4	3	....	21	....	1
....	24177	22341	1481	183	52	6	15	109	2	10	70	9	12	....	....

* Also Great Britain not stated: Kershaw, 1; Laurens, 1.

TABLE XVIII.—*Native and Foreign Population, &c.*—**Continued.**

STATE OF TENNESSEE.

Counties.	NATIVE.							FOREIGN-BORN.							
	Total.*	Born in the State.	North Carolina.	Virginia and West Virginia.	Alabama.	Kentucky.	Georgia.	Total.	British America.	England and Wales.*	Ireland.	Scotland.	Germany.	France.	Sweden and Norway.
Anderson	8025	7803	300	262	8	31	61	79	4	53	10	3	7	1	....
Bedford	24217	21047	740	520	378	156	285	116	2	20	41	2	13	2	....
Benton	8208	7335	475	77	39	85	20	27	2	7	13	1	2	1	....
Bledsoe	4858	4290	150	116	37	47	83	12	....	3	7	1	1	....	....
Blount	14180	12983	608	220	22	28	144	57	1	23	19	7	4	....	....
Bradley	11607	9172	570	276	62	54	993	45	3	5	7	....	26	2	....
Campbell	7416	6635	124	273	15	243	47	20	....	15	8	2	4	....	....
Cannon	10193	9654	315	171	78	55	37	9	....	....	8	....	....	....	....
Carroll	19366	16600	1282	596	87	182	40	81	2	8	49	....	4	4	5
Carter	7887	6630	917	248	10	12	4	22	1	5	11	1	2	....	....
Cheatham	6652	6061	139	155	19	77	27	26	3	2	17	1	1	....	....
Claiborne	9307	7559	352	1074	4	237	15	14	1	3	6	....	4	....	....
Cocke	12436	9836	1595	200	10	23	72	22	1	7	6	6	....	1	....
Coffee	10202	8975	207	204	101	71	166	35	4	7	5	1	16	....	....
Cumberland	3125	2634	203	58	6	75	19	36	3	15	1	4	7	2	2
Davidson	58477	46667	914	2518	1362	1822	869	4420	79	429	2102	145	1031	128	16
Decatur	7728	6585	408	71	85	67	44	44	....	4	20	1	18	1	....
De Kalb	11419	10478	338	254	22	60	80	6	1	....	3	....	....	....	....
Dickson	9280	8137	151	89	35	33	51	60	1	12	21	12	11	1	....
Dyer	13666	11669	641	398	181	111	89	40	4	10	16	1	5	....	....
Fayette	25084	19034	1661	1656	500	181	603	161	18	16	42	6	53	1	16
Fentress	4711	4032	121	62	4	389	6	6	1	1	1	....	....	1	....
Franklin	14776	12023	315	324	787	130	314	194	4	26	21	5	47	27	12
Gibson	25495	21757	1376	591	228	252	236	171	13	20	51	8	46	7	11
Giles	32289	25510	818	1262	2915	234	506	124	3	7	80	....	11	3	....
Grainger	12407	11056	450	547	13	78	19	14	....	7	6	1	....	....	....
Greene	21607	18086	1655	975	8	49	52	61	....	8	35	3	9	....	4
Grundy	3041	2678	55	29	70	12	77	209	....	34	19	13	....	....	1
Hamilton	16659	10594	543	583	405	194	2822	582	17	143	176	22	143	21	10
Hancock	7146	5606	250	1071	8	147	4	2	....	....	2	....	....	....	....
Hardeman	17921	12919	1554	561	478	204	505	133	5	3	75	5	5	4	32
Hardin	11735	9429	390	136	767	120	127	33	5	4	11	4	8	....	....
Hawkins	15808	13247	703	1543	24	93	25	29	1	4	22	....	....	1	....
Haywood	21900	18681	2131	1448	622	266	474	194	9	15	76	14	54	3	9
Henderson	14201	11991	1054	222	172	61	157	16	1	1	10	1	1	....	....
Henry	20304	16793	1412	637	162	754	61	76	3	11	46	3	9	1	1
Hickman	9849	9174	221	93	37	69	38	7	....	1	3	2	1	....	....
Humphreys	9149	8285	162	107	38	77	63	177	1	11	151	....	6	4	....
Jackson	12583	11348	264	143	33	512	50	....	....	....	....	....	....	....	....
Jefferson	19421	16002	1261	936	38	91	159	52	4	16	16	2	8	....	1
Johnson	5849	4155	1332	321	1	7	6	3	....	2	1	....	....	....	....
Knox	28165	23460	1091	1700	143	166	293	825	19	143	288	24	174	30	3
Lake	2389	1784	54	49	16	220	8	39	1	5	11	3	11	3	1
Lauderdale	10789	8102	514	486	340	136	241	49	1	11	13	1	9	1	9
Lawrence	7543	5962	280	133	693	45	101	58	....	17	4	1	24	4	....
Lewis	1985	1791	64	26	14	16	4	1	....	1	....	....	....	....	....
Lincoln	27977	23267	780	562	1727	134	540	73	5	15	45	1	2	....	....
Macon	6631	5817	124	241	15	359	3	2	....	....	1	1	....	....	....
Madison	23271	21218	676	379	115	96	192	209	5	17	109	11	50	2	6
Marion	6771	5172	170	103	426	40	602	70	1	35	27	1	....	....	....
Marshall	16180	14210	639	374	345	84	226	27	1	3	16	....	3	1	....
Maury	36083	31633	1090	919	605	295	575	206	13	30	84	6	46	4	3
McMinn	13953	11561	897	375	60	85	572	16	....	7	4	3	....	....	....
McNairy	12696	9807	1087	179	446	81	139	30	....	3	22	2	2	....	....
Meigs	4505	4061	124	83	8	15	157	6	....	1	3	....	....	....	....
Monroe	12574	11724	388	115	15	16	187	15	2	3	3	....	6	....	....
Montgomery	24340	19478	359	1069	117	2510	97	407	15	42	213	17	83	15	13
Morgan	2849	2562	122	64	5	34	13	120	2	9	5	....	57	....	....
Obion	15515	12520	582	358	214	702	126	69	6	11	27	....	22	2	....
Overton	11293	10004	310	269	16	504	45	4	....	....	4	....	....	....	....
Perry	6875	6228	136	74	157	50	28	50	1	6	4	....	24	10	....
Polk	7153	5263	746	51	27	19	714	216	....	133	6	3	38	6	....
Putnam	8695	7898	302	180	35	128	26	3	....	....	2	....	1	....	....
Rhea	5528	4902	194	130	34	20	115	10	....	2	1	4	2	....	....
Roane	15451	14129	517	294	22	46	182	171	4	63	6	6	73	1	....
Robertson	16088	14803	263	245	60	592	52	78	2	15	42	1	15	2	....
Rutherford	33132	29620	606	1077	504	193	533	157	10	13	44	4	48	2	....
Scott	4048	3429	81	57	9	421	16	6	....	6	....	....	....	....	....
Sequatchie	2337	2010	50	32	33	11	136	8	....	....	....	....	....	....	....

TABLE XVIII.—*Native and Foreign Population, &c.*—Continued.

STATE OF TENNESSEE—Continued.

Counties.	NATIVE.							FOREIGN-BORN.							
	Total.	Born in the State.	North Carolina.	Virginia and West Virginia.	Alabama.	Kentucky.	Georgia.	Total.	British America.	England and Wales.*	Ireland.	Scotland.	Germany.	France.	Sweden and Norway.
Sevier	11021	9947	568	138	19	27	57	7	....	3	2	....	....	....	....
Shelby	68415	41060	2271	4290	2256	1995	1307	7963	266	710	3371	150	2144	242	198
Smith	15979	14907	374	394	22	132	32	15	....	2	10	....	2	1	....
Stewart	11834	9400	388	262	57	933	55	185	4	12	76	9	52	5	5
Sullivan	13119	11034	277	1653	5	18	20	17	....	1	14	....	1	....	....
Sumner	23555	20951	434	604	102	903	71	156	6	25	80	3	24	4	....
Tipton	14691	10813	939	770	255	160	190	193	4	31	114	6	16	1	3
Union	7599	6981	171	295	7	57	13	6	1	3	1	....	1	....	....
Van Buren	2721	2462	59	28	8	18	41	4	1	2	....	....	1	....	....
Warren	12620	10721	434	309	78	138	115	94	8	19	15	2	10	2	3
Washington	16287	13249	1516	1176	3	31	23	30	1	4	5	1	14	1	....
Wayne	10195	8410	292	124	719	98	88	14	1	1	4	....	2	2	....
Weakley	20719	17330	1521	720	130	506	45	36	2	7	18	1	6	1	....
White	9359	8310	351	213	53	81	58	16	....	5	5	3	2	....	....
Williamson	25185	12080	550	1063	313	219	281	143	3	9	103	11	11	1	....
Wilson	25814	23840	550	682	71	178	131	67	5	16	20	3	6	3	....

* Also Great Britain not stated: Benton, 1; Coffee, 1; Davidson, 1; Rutherford, 3.

STATE OF TEXAS.

Counties.	NATIVE.							FOREIGN-BORN.							
	Total.	Born in the State.	Alabama.	Tennessee.	Mississippi.	Georgia.	Louisiana.	Total.	British America.	England and Wales.*	Ireland.	Scotland.	Germany.	France.	Sweden and Norway.
Anderson	9190	4741	1167	667	495	449	276	39	2	2	6	2	6	1	15
Angelina	3976	2150	377	136	474	213	259	9	....	1	3	....	4	....	....
Atascosa	2601	1854	116	134	107	39	60	314	4	7	13	2	28	8	....
Austin	12077	7282	1199	237	463	382	387	3010	4	43	33	17	2111	14	3
Bandera	545	323	20	38	5	11	16	104	2	1	6	8	10	3	....
Bastrop	11032	7030	558	876	480	481	240	1258	9	32	27	9	937	8	....
Bee	1021	679	39	35	50	18	58	61	1	2	34	1	7	4	....
Bell	9687	4328	700	857	704	495	245	84	1	17	12	....	32	4	2
Bexar	10766	8475	111	229	205	88	345	5277	18	45	268	17	1829	346	21
Bexar District	653	173	11	33	13	9	15	424	13	37	137	12	122	15	2
Blanco	1079	738	51	61	57	34	13	108	1	1	1	....	93	....	2
Bosque	4704	2286	364	384	340	291	132	277	1	13	6	....	1	1	250
Bowie	4654	2276	351	334	281	216	160	30	....	5	10	....	14	....	....
Brazoria	7165	4215	347	135	348	266	523	362	6	28	40	7	125	9	4
Brazos	8911	4050	839	450	739	437	680	294	12	27	82	13	84	12	4
Brown	543	336	26	38	24	21	2	1	1	....	....	....	....	....	....
Burleson	7897	3637	891	454	882	266	278	175	6	9	34	5	90	7	....
Burnet	3632	1961	166	392	119	90	38	56	....	8	....	1	42	....	....
Caldwell	6373	3482	513	476	513	226	91	199	6	8	20	2	71	1	....
Calhoun	2774	1616	74	62	90	20	204	669	16	48	94	28	369	32	6
Cameron	4027	3351	28	13	8	11	169	6972	30	56	196	16	150	99	7
Chambers	1438	992	53	26	34	19	131	65	2	14	5	2	19	5	....
Cherokee	11047	5673	1539	1055	559	680	291	32	....	3	5	2	[illegible]	[illegible]	[illegible]

TABLE XVIII.—*Native and Foreign Population, &c.*—Continued.

STATE OF TEXAS—Continued.

Counties.	Native.							Foreign-born.							
	Total.	Born in the State.	Alabama.	Tennessee.	Mississippi.	Georgia.	Louisiana.	Total.	British America.	England and Wales.*	Ireland.	Scotland.	Germany.†	France.	Sweden and Norway.
Coleman	339	173	9	44	12	21	6	8	....	2	4	....	1	....	....
Colin	13941	5782	556	1932	353	413	102	72	5	10	26	5	15	6	....
Colorado	7219	4264	246	557	476	290	164	1107	1	21	21	17	776	79	....
Comal	3282	2015	29	60	30	18	29	2001	....	14	4	1	1878	29	....
Comanche	1000	509	90	68	34	91	24	1	....	....	....	....	1	....	....
Cook	5274	2193	231	606	150	110	52	41	5	3	11	1	15	2	1
Coryell	4113	2003	298	371	279	157	207	11	....	3	6	....	....	....	....
Dallas	13066	5368	514	1462	451	327	161	248	7	39	40	4	27	79	33
Davis	8858	3804	1175	375	308	1839	126	17	....	8	5	....	2	....	....
Demmit	84	64	2	4	4	1	3	25	1	....	....	....	....	....	....
Denton	7212	2994	256	841	205	130	67	39	1	23	6	1	3	3	1
De Witt	5456	3603	169	216	462	150	127	987	5	6	14	....	844	91	....
Duval	393	340	12	....	3	3	12	690	2	8	20	2	9	5	1
Eastland	87	33	4	11	3	4	....	1	....	1	....	....	....	....	....
Ellis	7466	3111	562	1027	464	286	219	48	4	6	12	2	10	6	1
El Paso	2601	2012	19	151	18	16	29	1070	6	3	4	....	15	8	....
Encinal	200	198	....	....	....	....	1	227	....	....	....	....	....	....	....
Erath	1798	986	120	150	80	65	27	3	....	....	1	....	1	....	....
Falls	9702	4231	1148	473	857	402	544	149	3	13	23	4	34	5	10
Fannin	13156	5500	821	1940	372	574	164	51	6	19	8	3	10	2	1
Fayette	13593	8551	855	807	615	540	229	3270	2	41	8	6	2128	30	....
Fort Bend	6050	3569	616	151	335	257	440	164	4	9	27	4	75	6	1
Freestone	8115	3443	1655	410	680	506	314	24	2	4	3	....	11	....	....
Frio	293	192	20	9	13	5	10	16	....	....	3	2	1	1	....
Galveston	11363	5825	545	219	308	199	1324	3927	76	378	735	94	1923	303	23
Gillespie	2278	2088	9	17	7	23	8	1288	1	1	1	....	1245	4	....
Goliad	3350	2156	166	124	180	98	81	278	2	16	18	1	164	22	....
Gonzales	8804	4889	485	483	975	354	254	147	2	19	11	20	75	3	....
Grayson	14310	5705	566	1705	388	414	215	77	9	15	6	7	23	1	....
Grimes	13005	6283	1746	335	708	1228	778	213	3	25	38	16	107	4	1
Guadalupe	6343	3908	269	404	418	200	115	939	3	14	22	7	736	10	1
Hamilton	733	458	66	48	58	19	13	....	....	....	....	....	....	....	....
Hardin	1445	733	200	10	136	179	103	15	....	1	....	....	12	1	....
Harris	14550	7719	789	369	656	482	1309	2825	39	206	341	35	1834	151	18
Harrison	13110	6842	1206	726	611	989	606	131	3	16	11	5	69	10	....
Hays	3881	2138	200	250	250	138	146	207	2	2	5	1	45	6	1
Henderson	6735	3197	961	394	483	405	244	51	1	2	3	....	1	5	35
Hidalgo	768	710	29	9	1	1	8	1619	1	....	1	1	2	7	....
Hill	7429	3016	630	615	815	512	162	21	2	6	4	7	2	1	....
Hood	2564	1304	126	262	89	101	19	21	2	2	2	....	1	....	....
Hopkins	12608	5883	1225	1139	699	807	252	43	2	3	22	3	10	....	1
Houston	8113	4309	786	470	555	431	344	34	2	3	13	2	7	2	....
Hunt	10243	4835	669	1118	411	391	208	48	3	11	6	6	18	1	....
Jack	670	317	23	67	27	14	4	24	2	4	8	....	7	1	1
Jackson	2245	1310	116	60	115	45	106	33	....	....	6	2	15	4	....
Jasper	4211	2491	196	57	192	425	351	7	1	1	1	1	1	....	....
Jefferson	1826	1152	41	24	70	53	302	80	....	15	4	5	49	5	....
Johnson	4900	2119	446	550	401	322	69	23	4	3	3	....	10	....	....
Karnes	1454	914	87	61	152	33	16	251	3	1	3	....	230	2	....
Kaufman	6852	3169	561	652	605	271	212	43	2	15	4	1	4	....	13
Kendall	1061	824	24	33	20	26	29	475	....	9	7	1	386	8	3
Kerr	911	525	24	107	18	14	16	131	3	....	4	1	88	11	....
Kimble	72	47	1	3	....	2	....	....	....	....	....	....	....	....	....
Kinney	740	276	17	28	15	15	85	464	1	4	17	2	4	4	....
Lamar	15707	6488	1128	2351	1086	360	232	83	7	21	18	8	14	....	1
Lampasas	1332	712	60	108	38	65	22	12	1	1	3	....	4	....	....
La Salle	35	24	1	1	....	6	1	34	....	1	....	....	....	....	....
Lavaca	8761	5262	482	423	676	265	388	407	2	14	34	1	257	7	....
Leon	6501	3100	994	329	590	202	411	22	1	6	11	3	....	....	....
Liberty	4325	2306	312	90	184	163	742	89	....	3	19	3	25	18	1
Limestone	8412	4024	969	508	739	446	276	179	7	17	41	6	62	6	14
Live Oak	729	459	33	19	55	12	36	123	....	....	34	4	2	....	....
Llano	1288	871	35	98	10	16	8	91	15	5	....	....	68	....	....
Madison	4038	2160	422	166	318	137	300	23	1	6	7	....	7	....	....
Marion	8160	3364	823	614	287	888	381	402	16	44	80	8	183	25	3
Mason	511	404	15	5	3	8	2	167	....	1	8	....	148	....	....
Matagorda	3131	1836	230	78	129	89	103	246	7	27	25	5	79	5	4

TABLE XVIII.—*Native and Foreign Population, &c.*—Continued.

STATE OF TEXAS—Continued.

Counties.	NATIVE. Total.	Born in the State.	Alabama.	Tennessee.	Mississippi.	Georgia.	Louisiana.	FOREIGN-BORN. Total.	British America.	England and Wales.*	Ireland.	Scotland.	Germany.	France.	Sweden and Norway.
Maverick	766	421	18	14	14	11	24	1125	2	....	4	3	36	10	....
McCulloch	172	100	7	7	9	4	5	1	....	....	1	....	....	....	....
McLennan	13206	5503	1100	1170	977	715	608	294	14	30	43	4	95	10	43
McMullen	217	156	6	6	17	4	7	13	....	....	9	....	....	....	....
Medina	1380	1203	20	23	40	6	7	698	....	1	7	....	336	297	1
Menard	618	132	18	41	13	19	34	49	1	6	11	1	12	....	....
Milam	8917	3820	1341	464	939	448	403	67	2	15	13	2	24	3	1
Montague	898	375	33	72	25	75	8	2	1	....	....	....	1	....	....
Montgomery	6413	3417	1230	194	193	334	282	70	5	7	7	2	36	3	1
Nacogdoches	9555	5658	978	649	448	616	340	59	....	1	6	....	36	3	1
Navarro	8837	3961	771	911	794	410	353	42	2	17	11	3	6	1	....
Newton	2183	1276	128	42	260	101	205	4	....	....	2	....	1	....	....
Nueces	2313	1691	65	44	52	29	90	1662	11	64	176	23	66	15	2
Orange	1237	771	42	22	41	32	222	28	2	6	3	3	12	1	....
Panola	10109	5027	1267	595	419	1138	501	10	....	1	4	....	4	....	....
Parker	4161	2022	121	544	105	180	35	25	4	4	4	2	5	....	....
Polk	8678	4436	1159	123	733	530	487	29	2	1	12	2	7	2	....
Presidio	797	198	19	34	13	16	66	839	....	3	23	3	19	9	....
Red River	10588	4819	605	1198	650	330	242	65	5	9	22	5	20	....	....
Refugio	2080	1320	94	54	75	47	147	244	7	19	80	3	46	11	6
Robertson	9577	4489	1067	540	774	432	422	413	10	39	75	7	150	47	1
Rusk	16849	8212	1876	1384	928	2292	603	67	2	9	27	2	19	1	2
Sabine	3240	1705	205	61	271	411	288	16	....	2	4	3	6	....	....
San Augustine	4176	2746	194	240	214	182	139	20	3	6	5	3	2	....	....
San Patricio	497	331	26	17	17	4	45	105	2	....	39	....	3	1	....
San Saba	1414	806	85	107	60	37	12	11	1	....	4	....	2	....	....
Shackleford	308	91	11	14	5	12	8	147	7	22	63	2	42	3	....
Shelby	5715	3228	584	445	300	370	213	17	....	8	4	....	3	1	....
Smith	16473	7454	2270	1071	932	2369	344	59	4	15	10	4	14	....	5
Starr	1090	897	3	6	1	....	12	3064	12	16	110	4	56	12	3
Stephens	323	194	12	15	12	....	4	7	....	1	3	....	....	....	....
Tarrant	5746	2525	246	634	239	167	49	42	6	6	8	3	6	3	....
Titus	11305	4979	1337	1123	496	1076	217	34	2	6	8	2	6	1	1
Travis	11821	6315	597	1212	399	455	207	1332	27	63	144	38	641	51	130
Trinity	4133	2150	373	103	651	161	285	8	1	1	1	....	1	....	....
Tyler	5002	2381	416	128	562	766	195	8	....	2	....	2	4	....	....
Upshur	12026	5576	1204	763	616	2111	209	13	1	3	5	1	1	....	....
Uvalde	687	439	42	29	15	14	20	164	1	....	12	1	13	2	....
Van Zandt	6456	2896	976	424	560	447	199	38	1	7	5	1	3	2	....
Victoria	4000	2601	115	111	179	69	121	860	4	11	30	2	480	138	5
Walker	9524	4857	1437	300	477	387	532	252	16	24	41	5	56	8	1
Washington	20926	11032	1819	1017	1502	1111	703	2178	14	68	71	25	1701	15	9
Webb	1538	1422	....	1	2	....	....	1077	4	11	52	2	25	16	....
Wharton	3397	1753	251	85	134	346	112	29	....	2	7	1	11	....	....
Williamson	6257	3250	261	604	272	167	115	111	2	7	9	2	11	6	69
Wilson	2215	1580	61	99	112	35	41	341	2	2	2	2	26	5	....
Wise	1439	744	44	139	38	30	7	11	1	3	1	1	3	1	....
Wood	6880	2898	1010	530	488	866	148	14	1	1	....	....	9	2	....
Young	135	61	13	7	4	12	3	....	....	....	....	....	....	....	....
Zapata	321	319	....	....	....	....	....	1167	....	2	....	....	....	2	....
Zavala	99	67	7	....	8	1	....	34	....	....	....	....	....	....	....

* Also Great Britain not stated: Burleson, 7; Harrison, 1; Hays, 8; Medina, 1; Walker, 1.

TABLE XVIII.—*Native and Foreign Population, &c.*—Continued.

TERRITORY OF UTAH.

Counties.	NATIVE.							FOREIGN-BORN.							
	Total.	Born in the Territory.	New York.	Illinois.	Iowa.	Pennsylvania.	Ohio.	Total.	British America.	England and Wales.*	Ireland.	Scotland.	Germany.	France.	Sweden and Norway.
Beaver	1405	1059	31	51	28	22	16	609	10	452	13	67	1	....	4
Box Elder	2795	1782	190	78	104	86	89	2060	55	659	68	95	79	5	142
Cache	6121	4157	131	175	111	68	58	3106	49	1479	24	350	19	8	367
Davis	3010	2289	126	121	65	52	70	1449	30	1273	10	73	1	3	28
Iron	1610	1190	51	62	46	14	33	667	25	460	13	33	5	2	10
Juab	1344	1073	41	43	30	21	19	690	19	518	9	29	9	1	14
Kane	1292	971	56	54	41	14	19	221	12	151	6	9	2	....	2
Millard	1974	1476	88	72	43	26	39	779	21	434	15	39	4	....	45
Morgan	1215	936	36	49	35	70	24	757	11	398	30	27	25	4	99
Piute	54	16	9	....	3	5	2	28	5	13	2	....	2	....	1
Rich	1291	945	54	48	46	16	24	664	17	391	6	15	....	....	58
Rio Virgin	368	241	26	21	11	3	6	82	10	48	....	10	....	....	7
Salt Lake	10894	7898	552	337	190	396	200	7443	118	5096	157	730	84	13	437
San Pete	3890	3200	70	123	102	31	61	2896	31	624	8	60	13	2	476
Sevier	....	....	....	....	....	....	....	19	....	7	....	1	....	....	....
Summit	1448	1019	64	63	29	42	63	1064	28	707	28	92	14	1	93
Tooele	1350	1036	48	69	36	31	35	827	7	462	11	108	5	7	174
Utah	8439	6054	273	359	332	218	180	3764	125	2428	41	276	38	7	265
Wasatch	887	631	20	54	38	12	22	357	10	179	10	100	4	....	11
Washington	2455	1752	91	87	65	37	52	609	33	347	11	32	8	....	21
Weber	5242	3708	290	237	137	151	121	2616	71	1750	40	245	45	10	133

* Also Great Britain not stated: Cache, 17; Salt Lake, 1; Utah, 5.

STATE OF VERMONT.

Counties.	NATIVE.							FOREIGN-BORN.							
	Total.	Born in the State.	New Hampshire.	New York.	Massachusetts.	Connecticut.	Maine.	Total.	British America.	England and Wales.*	Ireland.	Scotland.	Germany.	France.	Sweden and Norway.
Addison	20445	18029	345	1412	287	121	24	3039	2051	105	813	40	15	* 7	....
Bennington	18574	15282	233	1823	866	143	24	2751	812	185	1518	142	61	9	1
Caledonia	19544	16780	1745	153	490	72	174	2891	1911	111	369	248	21	12	....
Chittenden	27002	22629	396	1776	500	102	104	10578	7197	256	2834	161	76	20	11
Essex	5412	3960	966	93	143	11	212	1399	1198	46	137	15	....	....	1
Franklin	23536	21941	282	689	348	93	47	6755	5294	145	1236	45	9	11	1
Grand Isle	3171	2793	51	265	21	11	3	911	801	24	60	23	1	1	....
Lamoille	11544	10290	567	213	297	58	35	904	636	84	162	11	11	....	....
Orange	21943	18711	2020	198	612	141	110	1147	530	222	262	115	6	5	....
Orleans	17273	15069	1288	158	447	67	111	3762	2961	156	351	252	9	3	....
Rutland	33144	27934	607	3016	840	220	112	7507	2671	796	3738	82	84	11	100
Washington	24164	21595	1128	373	719	121	86	2356	1075	95	1119	44	7	5	....
Windham	24781	19785	1510	552	2329	215	95	1255	304	109	749	14	55	4	....
Windsor	33963	29016	2402	576	1303	175	114	2100	1103	177	732	48	15	5	3

* Also Great Britain not stated: Bennington, 1; Caledonia, 5; Orleans, 24; Windham, 6.

TABLE XVIII.—*Native and Foreign Population, &c.*—Continued.

STATE OF VIRGINIA.

…s.	NATIVE. Total.	Born in the State.*	North Carolina.	Maryland.	New York.	Tennessee.	Pennsylvania.	FOREIGN-BORN. Total.	British America.	England and Wales.†	Ireland.	Scotland.	Germany.	France.	Sweden and Norway.
....	20392	19610	6	487	20	....	33	17	1	4	4	1	6	....	....
....	27335	26923	29	51	70	11	65	209	10	42	35	12	84	6	1
....	15772	12984	55	1509	249	12	228	983	15	164	503	26	234	10	3
....	3566	3522	2	12	1	....	22	108	....	9	84	12	1	1	....
....	9673	9549	4	3	57	....	11	205	....	20	6	3	6	1	....
....	14786	14620	13	30	33	7	39	114	3	23	39	18	12	....	....
....	9940	9807	1	4	....	....	16	10	....	8	....	....	1	....	....
....	28376	27812	31	80	20	12	123	387	10	36	218	4	100	6	....
....	3750	3699	5	6	2	2	14	45	1	13	31	....	....	....	....
....	25277	25091	17	12	27	4	26	50	1	4	24	7	10	....	....
....	3986	3834	99	3	....	15	4	14	3	....	9	....	2	....	....
....	11296	11230	2	34	....	1	13	33	....	4	18	....	9	1	....
....	13422	13356	49	....	....	1	....	5	....	....	2	....	3	....	....
....	3777	3541	92	....	....	11	....	....	....	....	....	....	....	....	....
....	13257	13228	5	5	1	....	8	114	....	100	4	1	....	....	....
....	27795	27314	31	104	49	11	119	589	9	49	314	28	148	5	4
....	15076	14791	12	15	121	4	37	52	3	24	15	5	5	....	....
....	9135	8203	849	....	....	18	29	12	....	3	6	....	2	....	....
....	4945	4872	2	1	9	1	6	30	3	15	5	3	3	....	....
....	14488	14362	29	....	57	....	4	25	4	7	5	2	7	....	....
....	18185	17633	124	78	115	8	53	285	6	148	63	17	33	9	....
....	6619	6437	4	60	21	1	50	51	4	8	20	....	15	2	....
....	2938	2918	4	6	....	6	3	4	2	....	....	....	1	....	....
....	12136	11924	7	31	62	1	23	91	4	13	46	1	19	4	1
....	8129	8116	....	2	2	1	6	13	1	2	2	2	6	....	....
....	30215	29139	362	112	201	12	63	487	5	46	190	75	134	6	6
....	7927	7255	73	111	176	1	113	376	8	36	183	28	87	11	1
....	9915	9848	1	28	6	1	7	12	....	6	4	....	1	....	....
....	12525	10474	24	454	624	11	223	427	19	87	219	17	68	3	1
....	19469	18983	13	123	49	9	46	221	1	48	106	11	39	1	....
....	9815	9711	81	4	....	1	2	9	....	2	5	....	2	....	....
....	9862	9802	13	3	1	6	5	13	....	6	2	3	1	....	....
....	18259	18218	15	3	....	7	5	5	....	1	2	....	2	....	....
....	16340	15149	17	325	60	4	574	256	2	31	125	15	65	3	....
....	5848	5782	27	1	1	11	4	27	....	9	16	....	1	....	....
....	10183	9961	7	137	16	....	31	29	1	7	8	1	7	2	....
....	10281	10253	5	8	2	3	2	32	1	12	8	....	10	....	1
....	9562	8290	1175	3	2	52	4	25	....	11	7	....	7	....	....
....	4609	4521	4	8	9	8	38	25	....	3	15	2	5	....	....
....	6359	6126	183	3	1	3	2	3	....	....	3	....	....	....	....
....	27810	27127	618	6	16	10	6	18	....	2	6	1	7	....	....
....	16393	16215	31	33	41	....	21	62	....	7	25	5	9	8	....
....	61820	58682	429	605	629	37	368	4359	45	387	1335	168	1925	173	7
....	12201	11841	422	3	1	3	2	12	1	4	2	....	2	....	....
....	4138	4116	....	5	2	....	4	13	1	2	8	....	1	....	....
....	8307	8217	30	10	18	....	3	13	1	4	2	3	2	1	....
....	4300	4235	11	13	48	2	9	65	1	10	3	47	3	....	....
n	9697	9678	1	2	7	....	1	12	1	1	5	....	5	....	....
....	5726	5637	12	26	5	....	4	16	....	8	1	2	3	....	....
....	7496	7382	....	24	35	1	27	19	1	2	4	1	10	....	....
....	5340	5178	10	86	17	....	10	15	2	1	1	....	6	4	....
....	13261	10838	496	7	....	1385	8	7	....	1	4	....	1	1	....
....	20724	19763	14	412	114	1	124	205	16	46	89	10	32	1	1
....	16259	16186	1	7	29	....	23	73	2	23	15	....	27	2	....
....	10387	10343	7	10	9	2	3	20	2	9	4	....	3	1	....
....	8654	8611	2	5	1	....	14	16	....	....	8	1	5	....	....
....	6196	6102	5	44	28	....	2	4	1	....	....	....	3	....	....
....	21208	20418	729	12	26	13	29	20	5	4	2	5	1	....	1
....	4971	4915	3	28	5	....	4	10	1	....	1	1	3	4	....
....	12495	12372	25	13	2	17	13	61	20	6	10	4	17	4	....
....	11543	10772	534	15	62	....	45	33	....	15	6	....	8	1	....
....	13850	13753	3	12	5	5	25	48	1	10	16	10	2	1	....
....	4314	4249	8	8	10	8	33	37	1	2	7	1	23	1	1
....	45309	38907	3999	682	521	10	269	1393	22	148	609	68	334	34	11
....	8039	7841	17	127	15	....	12	7	....	1	4	....	2	....	....
d..........	6852	6582	1	203	32	1	23	11	....	5	3	1	2	....	....
....	9272	9214	1	2	12	....	28	19	2	11	3	....	2	....	....
....	10336	10111	8	35	89	2	14	60	....	15	16	1	21	2	....
....	8424	8325	2	26	8	....	32	32	....	2	4	4	9	15	....
....	10158	9711	413	2	....	10	2	3	....	2	1	....	....	....	....
....	31287	30215	932	25	17	7	13	56	4	8	16	3	13	3	....

TABLE XVIII.—*Native and Foreign Population, &c.*—Continued.

STATE OF VIRGINIA—Continued.

Counties.	NATIVE.							FOREIGN-BORN.							
	Total.	Born in the State.*	North Carolina.	Maryland.	New York.	Tennessee.	Pennsylvania.	Total.	British America.	England and Wales.†	Ireland.	Scotland.	Germany.	France.	Sweden and Norway.
Powhatan	7640	7583	9	4	8	2	4	27	....	12	5	....	2	1	....
Prince Edward	11931	11739	20	8	56	10	29	73	....	37	17	4	9	1	....
Prince George	7740	7595	37	7	48	1	14	80	9	20	16	7	26	....	1
Princess Anne	8246	6825	1264	62	33	1	26	27	5	6	6	1	......	1	1
Prince William	7362	6633	9	112	180	4	126	142	12	46	49	2	23	2	1
Pulaski	6505	6333	94	14	....	21	7	33	....	....	22	4	6	....	....
Rappahannock	8236	8178	4	18	2	4	7	25	....	4	9	4	7	....	....
Richmond	6476	6315	2	48	13	....	18	27	1	5	8	1	12	....	....
Roanoke	9328	9215	16	34	5	7	14	22	....	1	6	4	9	....	1
Rockbridge	15943	15392	33	44	24	43	19	115	1	21	43	7	18	2	....
Rockingham	23516	23196	11	83	38	2	92	132	2	7	54	....	61	1	....
Russell	11093	10568	261	4	3	126	2	10	....	1	5	1	1	1	....
Scott	13027	11455	435	10	2	809	11	9	1	....	6	1	......	1	....
Shenandoah	14782	14461	3	149	14	2	108	154	7	29	52	4	59	....	....
Smyth	8870	8222	407	9	28	112	12	28	....	11	7	2	6	1	....
Southampton	12268	11915	300	1	4	4	27	17	....	2	8	....	2	2	1
Spottsylvania	11449	10745	5	85	257	8	77	279	20	43	71	22	112	6	....
Stafford	6369	6113	6	66	76	....	29	51	13	6	19	4	8	....	....
Surry	5574	5441	6	....	31	2	40	11	1	....	3	....	4	2	....
Sussex	7876	7772	8	16	46	1	4	9	....	2	......	4	3	....	....
Tazewell	10772	10049	540	7	14	62	1	19	....	4	9	....	2	2	....
Warren	5675	5557	3	36	5	7	43	41	2	4	26	....	8	....	....
Warwick	1666	1611	10	10	3	....	25	6	....	4	2	....	......	....	....
Washington	16737	15025	471	19	16	922	29	79	2	5	41	2	20	....	....
Westmoreland	7634	7437	....	92	17	1	26	28	2	12	4	....	3	6	1
Wise	4781	4089	290	3	1	91	1	4	....	2	1	....	......	....	....
Wythe	11491	11029	306	17	2	44	21	120	1	33	60	....	17	2	....
York	7149	6862	66	35	94	1	18	49	1	3	26	1	9	4	....

* This column includes those born in Virginia and West Virginia.
† Also Great Britain not stated: Henrico, 1; Washington, 1.

TERRITORY OF WASHINGTON.

Counties.	NATIVE.							FOREIGN-BORN.							
	Total.	Born in the Territory.	Oregon.	New York.	Illinois.	Missouri.	Ohio.	Total.	British America.	England and Wales.	Ireland.	Scotland.	Germany.	France.	Sweden and Norway.
Chehalis	381	144	26	16	30	18	23	90	5	7	4	2	1	....	1
Clallam	274	127	....	19	5	5	4	134	38	33	18	20	9	4	2
Clarke	2606	1073	203	120	140	147	124	475	72	49	169	10	108	25	2
Cowlitz	645	263	38	32	30	29	26	85	10	13	22	6	22	3	3
Island	400	147	5	39	17	20	14	226	63	43	40	18	14	5	11
Jefferson	690	248	5	68	6	5	13	578	164	147	68	32	32	6	59
King	1605	586	123	128	76	62	80	516	90	79	110	18	78	6	51
Kitsap	434	106	1	43	8	6	12	432	74	90	66	31	30	11	40
Klikitat	289	91	46	20	14	30	8	40	17	....	11	1	8	....	....
Lewis	779	351	61	31	54	49	31	109	29	17	14	10	17	7	6
Mason	225	73	12	11	8	15	7	64	23	10	16	6	5	1	2
Pacific	591	191	78	36	25	12	39	147	25	24	27	2	19	3	19
Pierce	1144	648	69	62	36	41	40	265	60	47	58	26	34	3	6
Skamania	108	35	14	11	9	6	6	25	4	3	13	....	2	1	1
Snohomish	413	151	8	43	8	6	15	186	57	36	34	13	9	8	13
Stevens	488	280	20	29	8	11	16	246	74	15	41	29	26	4	1
Thurston	1931	672	148	139	148	91	93	315	59	61	51	29	63	3	11
Wahkiakum	190	37	30	11	...	2	17	80	15	9	11	6	7	1	6
Walla-Walla	4692	1254	575	183	315	356	251	608	100	66	165	23	116	18	14
Whatcom	341	193	3	28	5	2	11	193	43	49	39	14	9	3	6
Yakima	410	90	102	16	21	32	22	22	6	2	6	....	7	....	....
"The disputed islands"	295	154	7	19	4	1	12	230	84	33	64	13	29	1	5

TABLE XVIII.—*Native and Foreign Population, &c.*—Continued.

STATE OF WEST VIRGINIA.

Counties.	NATIVE.							FOREIGN-BORN.							
	Total.	Born in the State.*	Pennsylvania.	Ohio.	Maryland.	Kentucky.	New York.	Total.	British America.	England and Wales.	Ireland.	Scotland.	Germany.	France.	Sweden and Norway.
Barbour	10231	9958	97	35	98	4	7	81	3	1	61	1	11	1	....
Berkeley	14261	11901	807	54	1160	4	87	679	6	34	323	4	252	5	....
Boone	4502	4372	9	17	5	25	13	51	1	7	35	6	1	....	....
Braxton	6430	6380	12	7	17	3	1	50	....	....	23	2	24	....	....
Brooke	5066	3744	612	505	85	16	16	398	4	61	199	20	106	3	....
Cabell	6260	5504	67	344	19	143	41	169	4	24	59	1	54	10	....
Calhoun	2926	2804	37	31	23	13	1	13	....	1	2	....	10	....	....
Clay	2196	2148	1	7	....	24	2	....	....	....	....	....	....	....	....
Doddridge	6831	6363	164	103	138	3	7	245	4	3	133	....	61	1	....
Fayette	6615	6459	10	46	6	17	19	32	2	1	24	2	3	....	....
Gilmer	4313	4272	7	6	16	3	3	25	....	13	....	....	12	....	....
Grant	4382	4268	18	9	51	....	18	85	1	1	2	2	71	....	....
Greenbrier	11178	10945	23	24	35	32	12	239	....	19	179	2	8	23	1
Hampshire	7568	7143	140	19	223	4	2	75	....	2	35	1	36	1	....
Hancock	4132	2651	868	504	43	3	15	231	3	63	131	18	15	1	....
Hardy	5477	5299	39	46	57	9	2	41	....	2	2	3	29	....	....
Harrison	16292	15559	318	85	165	10	39	422	10	30	300	35	24	1	....
Jackson	10177	8737	326	848	51	47	75	123	1	29	31	12	27	20	....
Jefferson	12958	11402	429	32	903	27	23	261	....	37	153	7	54	5	1
Kanawha	21662	20383	211	396	52	166	91	687	14	144	228	67	183	8	1
Lewis	9653	9342	87	40	98	4	25	522	6	43	369	11	75	4	....
Lincoln	5039	4576	21	225	2	114	3	14	....	5	2	2	5	....	....
Logan	5117	4789	2	12	....	302	1	7	....	....	....	2	2	1	....
Marion	11917	11104	476	53	154	6	12	190	4	24	124	21	16	....	....
Marshall	14032	10726	1707	921	273	18	65	909	36	99	370	36	342	10	....
Mason	15025	12687	470	1465	37	75	77	953	7	466	194	63	207	7	....
McDowell	1949	1662	1	4	....	172	27	3	....	....	1	....	....	....	....
Mercer	7047	6921	8	9	6	5	4	17	....	9	6	....	1	....	....
Mineral	5906	4899	152	32	741	1	17	426	....	32	245	63	72	1	....
Monongalia	13455	11731	1390	61	178	8	16	92	....	37	29	6	16	3	....
Monroe	11022	10890	8	30	14	4	3	102	....	15	76	6	4	....	....
Morgan	4208	3727	81	5	319	1	28	107	9	3	24	1	64	....	....
Nicholas	4415	4390	1	6	....	3	1	43	6	1	29	3	2	....	....
Ohio	22911	18423	1884	1409	513	51	155	6020	25	524	1594	78	3485	63	....
Pendleton	6449	6429	4	3	9	....	....	6	....	....	4	....	1	....	....
Pleasants	2968	2427	194	292	34	6	4	44	....	12	8	3	18	....	....
Pocahontas	4035	4011	2	1	3	6	1	34	1	....	21	....	3	....	....
Preston	13838	12234	726	67	675	9	21	717	7	115	266	152	166	5	....
Putnam	7655	7021	222	279	10	35	16	139	1	49	59	5	10	5	....
Raleigh	3655	3633	4	2	1	....	....	18	....	....	18	....	....	....	....
Randolph	5426	5262	38	43	33	7	7	137	....	1	113	1	3	....	....
Ritchie	8747	7804	367	269	140	12	29	308	6	27	212	24	33	1	....
Roane	7220	7016	29	56	7	60	1	12	1	....	3	....	8	....	....
Taylor	8883	8052	277	77	332	3	35	484	4	25	297	13	124	15	1
Tucker	1887	1851	5	....	20	....	2	20	....	....	3	8	8	....	....
Tyler	7724	6215	612	730	78	8	23	108	1	7	50	4	29	5	....
Upshur	7938	7714	79	11	20	16	16	85	1	11	64	1	8	....	....
Wayne	7824	6881	47	125	4	668	5	29	5	6	9	2	6	....	....
Webster	1726	1708	1	....	....	12	....	4	....	....	4	....	....	....	....
Wetzel	8281	6482	893	705	100	10	16	314	1	33	104	....	91	3	....
Wirt	4733	3887	295	283	49	21	40	71	3	18	21	1	24	3	....
Wood	17713	13537	1223	1812	331	103	235	1287	30	98	600	57	428	18	2
Wyoming	3168	2864	3	9	....	35	....	3	....	....	3	....	....	....	....

* This column includes those born in Virginia and West Virginia.

TABLE XVIII.—*Native and Foreign Population, &c.*—Continued.

STATE OF WISCONSIN.

Counties.	NATIVE.							FOREIGN-BORN.							
	Total.	Born in the State.	New York.	Ohio.	Pennsylvania.	Vermont.	Illinois.	Total.	British America.	England and Wales.*	Ireland.	Scotland.	Germany.	France.	Sweden and Norway.
Adams	5351	2649	1620	155	201	168	57	1250	127	142	225	26	133	5	337
Ashland	174	148	4	....	1	....	9	47	12	4	18	1	8	....	3
Barron	246	132	25	7	26	8	2	292	127	2	7	1	41	....	98
Bayfield	228	175	22	17	4	2	2	56	23	8	4	23	3	....	1
Brown	14728	11098	1656	292	231	201	216	10440	1687	273	1442	112	2733	68	451
Buffalo	6854	4133	625	142	520	194	210	4269	173	56	242	125	1971	30	556
Burnett	144	100	6	6	....	....	5	562	4	4	1	1	1	....	551
Calumet	7661	5658	931	124	82	130	76	4674	165	167	500	13	3267	51	3
Chippewa	4725	2764	794	224	249	143	128	3586	1437	120	417	39	958	34	420
Clark	2751	1196	632	146	214	60	78	699	226	81	47	18	237	4	79
Columbia	19652	12233	4052	492	491	620	190	9130	511	2046	1332	629	2774	30	1515
Crawford	9612	5808	963	737	527	137	396	3463	397	186	906	48	640	35	764
Dane	33456	22736	4820	802	932	1061	314	10640	684	1631	2955	465	6276	109	6601
Dodge	28708	20034	4172	496	478	764	180	18327	565	1236	2301	256	12656	167	383
Door	2806	1903	400	69	51	21	74	2113	290	89	228	23	426	27	344
Douglas	712	340	103	23	21	4	7	410	133	41	66	6	60	4	93
Dunn	6268	3177	863	374	470	146	241	3220	437	147	227	51	842	17	1336
Eau Claire	7394	3336	1051	179	411	208	131	3375	767	242	487	54	835	34	871
Fond du Lac	31477	20112	6572	580	545	995	361	11796	1754	1291	2572	317	7772	125	156
Grant	28565	19390	2090	1565	1389	317	1004	9414	386	2531	1281	189	3585	83	543
Green	18532	10643	2261	1244	1722	391	607	5070	272	598	942	50	892	30	1017
Green Lake	9098	4533	2247	268	250	353	76	4097	290	507	412	62	2634	7	87
Iowa	15366	12562	792	325	445	72	316	9178	346	3297	1239	86	1447	21	1647
Jackson	5764	2966	1176	229	463	140	170	1923	201	151	137	92	275	29	944
Jefferson	21747	15407	3602	432	257	632	160	12203	369	934	1067	182	8445	41	384
Juneau	9361	5359	1906	458	277	298	192	3011	336	395	1104	81	518	11	379
Kenosha	9066	5959	1650	109	82	235	357	4081	138	650	813	100	2082	39	29
Kewaunee	4642	4208	198	31	40	27	19	5486	159	47	313	16	1611	22	97
La Crosse	11695	6779	1737	502	463	333	290	8602	580	570	488	109	2831	52	2646
La Fayette	15935	11346	1074	632	901	150	756	6724	186	2281	2345	111	729	17	993
Manitowoc	16868	15109	836	151	121	136	109	16496	518	223	1133	52	9515	93	1420
Marathon	3139	2333	263	47	225	46	41	2746	216	49	103	26	2226	19	73
Marquette	5128	3342	860	112	193	216	24	2928	151	252	537	198	1661	1	31
Milwaukee	47697	37183	4756	710	740	478	528	42333	884	1973	4604	502	29019	288	636
Monroe	12512	6722	2808	639	469	458	250	4038	356	510	641	87	1601	38	573
Oconto	4591	2677	817	77	101	90	98	3730	1645	111	422	38	797	23	321
Outagamie	11741	8060	1887	394	239	222	88	6669	796	171	792	85	3292	61	37
Ozaukee	8728	8214	247	30	43	2	38	6836	110	48	475	18	4422	92	98
Pepin	3351	1612	636	191	330	135	95	1308	208	91	118	29	309	27	484
Pierce	7460	3618	1188	366	452	228	188	2498	310	102	422	34	419	16	1052
Polk	2249	931	182	66	112	30	48	1173	191	46	102	19	172	27	483
Portage	7213	4337	1496	110	334	192	98	3121	401	217	369	99	1223	30	795
Racine	15949	11336	2202	299	175	357	209	10791	270	1878	1039	289	3859	82	1068
Richland	13954	6547	1259	2152	700	258	415	1777	168	222	431	46	481	25	257
Rock	30712	15209	7886	868	1262	1171	849	8318	755	1382	2870	490	1142	78	1429
Sauk	17308	9795	2014	1096	754	609	271	6552	386	765	946	103	3433	65	93
Shawano	1688	1133	282	28	45	23	19	1478	111	27	24	5	1096	4	146
Sheboygan	19192	14957	2244	366	160	272	119	*12557	323	302	943	38	8497	119	234
St. Croix	7451	4158	1113	298	305	231	132	3584	816	150	1202	56	224	6	940
Trempealeau	6339	3700	979	209	240	177	158	4393	200	185	286	141	776	22	2231
Vernon	13675	7282	1326	2292	530	248	401	5040	184	189	306	87	661	30	3146
Walworth	20822	11214	6148	321	335	736	438	5150	391	921	1729	148	1173	81	579
Washington	13868	12504	732	132	91	58	40	10051	97	110	882	35	8213	134	40
Waukesha	18368	13304	2854	212	312	440	135	9906	382	2665	1503	397	4082	57	48
Waupaca	11011	6225	2580	331	254	378	155	4528	508	260	517	60	1243	33	1225
Waushara	8702	4358	2136	260	354	354	67	2577	264	708	307	42	818	11	220
Winnebago	25209	14587	5309	662	548	940	372	12070	1358	1531	1399	146	5261	53	772
Wood	2338	1587	427	74	126	46	45	1371	636	42	171	34	229	7	[illegible]

* Also Great Britain not stated: Adams, 2; Columbia, 6; Crawford, 3; Dane, 2; Dodge, 27; Eau Claire, 1; Fond du Lac, 2; Grant, 1; Green Lake, 1; Iowa, 6; Kenosha, 29; La Crosse, 2; La Fayette, 3; Milwaukee, 2; Monroe, 1; Oconto, 5; Racine, 64; Rock, 11; Sauk, 3; Sheboygan, 5; Vernon, 7; Washington, 2; Waukesha, 5.

TABLE XVIII.—*Native and Foreign Population, &c.*—Continued.

TERRITORY OF WYOMING.

Counties.	NATIVE.							FOREIGN-BORN.								
	Total.	Born in the Territory.	New York.	Pennsylvania.	Ohio.	Illinois.	Missouri.	Total.	British America.	England and Wales.	Ireland.	Scotland.	Germany.	France.	Sweden and Norway.
lbany	1296	48	260	131	137	99	66	725	69	106	209	30	165	10	74
rbon	745	25	144	98	65	60	25	690	32	157	208	53	119	6	17
aramie	1898	114	312	208	172	132	133	1050	74	112	457	36	240	28	19
weetwater	1177	79	200	150	127	86	60	739	111	136	168	75	95	9	14
intah	489	27	72	40	46	27	35	307	43	103	60	60	33	4	13

TABLE XIX.—*Native Population of Fifty Principal Cities, according to States (or Territories) of Birth*—1870.

	Living in—	Aggregate population.	BORN IN— The United States.	The State in which each city is situated.	Alabama.	Arkansas.	California.	Connecticut.	Delaware.	Florida.	Georgia.
1	New York, N. Y	942,292	523,198	484,109	199	22	243	5,140	315	101	479
2	Philadelphia, Pa	674,022	490,398	428,250	136	24	139	1,180	9,896	50	316
3	Brooklyn, N. Y	396,099	251,381	219,774	92	7	136	5,264	192	75	380
4	St. Louis, Mo	310,864	198,615	134,221	964	520	126	634	242	86	353
5	Chicago, Ill	298,977	154,420	87,991	218	18	141	2,074	95	13	147
6	Baltimore, Md	267,354	210,870	187,650	66	9	60	338	535	42	218
7	Boston, Mass	250,526	162,540	127,020	55	1	91	967	52	20	61
8	Cincinnati, Ohio	216,239	136,627	111,091	191	81	32	367	96	11	138
9	New Orleans, La	191,418	142,943	114,696	1,858	221	54	170	70	471	791
10	San Francisco, Cal	149,473	75,754	38,491	147	35	(*)	850	149	30	97
11	Buffalo, N. Y	117,714	71,477	65,890	17	1	29	513	12	4	19
12	Washington, D. C	109,199	95,442	42,694	82	16	55	438	240	45	305
13	Newark, N. J	105,059	69,175	55,674	24	2	6	1,006	76	7	61
14	Louisville, Ky	100,753	75,085	60,134	233	71	30	110	36	9	302
15	Cleveland, Ohio	92,829	54,014	40,931	16	3	26	748	19	4	51
16	Pittsburgh, Pa	86,076	58,254	51,567	11	10	9	93	88	4	22
17	Jersey City, N. J	82,546	50,711	27,506	11	1	35	910	62	22	44
18	Detroit, Mich	79,577	44,196	31,935	16	6	23	357	24	11	23
19	Milwaukee, Wis	71,440	37,667	28,561	11	4	8	376	17	1	16
20	Albany, N. Y	69,422	47,215	44,081	8	.....	14	282	6	2	14
21	Providence, R. I	68,904	51,727	37,225	10	1	37	1,820	107	6	43
22	Rochester, N. Y	62,386	41,202	37,734	3	5	10	590	13	1	4
23	Allegheny, Pa	53,180	37,872	34,265	4	3	13	43	42	5	11
24	Richmond, Va	51,038	47,260	44,597	32	1	4	44	27	13	76
25	New Haven, Conn	50,840	36,482	28,394	17	1	19	(*)	56	13	58
26	Charleston, S. C	48,956	44,064	42,202	44	.....	2	75	9	61	328
27	Indianapolis, Ind	48,244	37,587	21,152	50	11	6	164	62	2	63
28	Troy, N. Y	40,465	30,246	27,979	2	.....	8	262	12	1	8
29	Syracuse, N. Y	43,051	29,061	26,878	5	1	4	363	10	1	18
30	Worcester, Mass	41,105	29,139	23,202	3	.....	14	1,048	10	3	17
31	Lowell, Mass	40,928	26,493	16,563	4	1	3	137	.....	2	8
32	Memphis, Tenn	40,226	23,416	18,663	1,001	455	11	72	13	38	659
33	Cambridge, Mass	39,634	27,579	21,150	17	.....	16	206	17	9	30
34	Hartford, Conn	37,180	26,363	20,196	9	.....	13	(*)	3	6	41
35	Scranton, Pa	35,092	19,205	16,353	1	3	9	118	21	1	4
36	Reading, Pa	33,630	30,059	29,396	2	1	.....	19	27	2	1
37	Patterson, N. J	33,579	20,711	16,576	1	1	6	131	4	.....	22
38	Kansas City, Mo	32,260	24,581	8,194	64	84	13	80	43	8	60
39	Mobile, Ala	32,034	27,795	19,547	(*)	28	2	70	15	278	694
40	Toledo, Ohio	31,584	20,485	14,245	9	2	4	204	17	1	8
41	Portland, Me	31,413	24,401	22,164	7	.....	5	58	3	5	21
42	Columbus, Ohio	31,274	23,663	18,317	30	9	.....	148	23	.....	30
43	Wilmington, Del	30,841	25,689	17,720	4	2	5	50	(*)	11	8
44	Dayton, Ohio	30,473	23,050	18,007	6	1	2	92	23	1	8
45	Lawrence, Mass	28,921	16,204	10,084	.....	.....	5	108	.....	.....	5
46	Utica, N. Y	28,804	18,955	17,694	1	1	4	218	6	3	7
47	Charlestown, Mass	28,323	21,399	16,186	9	.....	6	90	8	.....	7
48	Savannah, Ga	28,235	24,564	19,822	74	.....	3	84	7	354	(*)
49	Lynn, Mass	28,233	21,298	18,358	.....	1	3	111	11	1	13
50	Fall River, Mass	26,766	15,288	11,780	1	.....	5	189	.....	1	7

* See column "Born in the State in which each city is situated."

E XIX.—*Native Population of Fifty Principal Cities, according to States (or Territories) of Birth*—1870.

BORN IN—														
Indiana.	Iowa.	Kansas.	Kentucky.	Louisiana.	Maine.	Maryland.	Massachusetts.	Michigan.	Minnesota.	Mississippi.	Missouri.	Nebraska.	Nevada.	
148	51	17	335	552	1,224	2,028	5,995	195	20	104	242	3	5	1
216	108	13	368	292	695	8,238	3,218	143	36	110	237	9	5	2
119	67	15	169	308	1,818	1,086	5,711	190	21	86	150	4	......	3
2,472	1,449	287	5,716	2,493	712	1,677	2,568	812	154	1,467	(*)	50	2	4
2,034	1,069	72	1,665	317	1,657	1,070	6,014	2,303	242	178	1,415	20	12	5
62	22	11	135	177	220	(*)	782	45	6	92	104	4	......	6
39	20	5	60	110	14,858	479	(*)	85	29	9	53	......	......	7
2,822	193	17	5,392	533	220	1,062	1,023	168	32	274	379	3	......	8
294	39	22	2,168	(*)	270	1,720	602	52	147	3,076	1,007	7	......	9
262	175	13	447	851	2,650	876	7,147	305	73	119	664	11	218	10
54	31	6	57	30	160	157	769	320	14	7	27	3	......	11
266	104	22	218	130	598	17,393	1,087	192	49	71	131	13	3	12
53	17	3	36	46	103	227	769	47	8	12	36	......	......	13
3,031	65	23	(*)	351	63	681	279	58	29	225	443	7	30	14
198	47	7	225	43	215	206	1,099	486	14	5	124	1	......	15
102	75	6	194	37	81	931	255	40	11	14	84	1	1	16
25	20	2	35	66	276	266	1,147	63	12	11	37	1	......	17
178	36	11	377	41	216	157	706	(*)	13	12	77	3	......	18
121	51	10	57	17	238	118	798	382	47	16	85	3	......	19
19	2	......	10	14	32	49	591	35	4	6	20	2	2	20
18	8	2	17	10	894	375	6,933	27	7	5	13	13	......	21
47	16	5	20	25	102	99	673	145	4	4	20	......	......	22
74	12	......	89	18	38	424	99	33	2	12	35	......	......	23
12	......	......	32	44	34	524	99	11	1	22	13	......	......	24
22	16	1	48	36	300	177	1,668	24	2	6	23	1	......	25
7	......	......	24	21	26	73	112	6	......	9	1	......	......	26
(*)	145	23	3,217	57	147	453	441	149	23	55	184	8	......	27
5	5	......	10	8	51	44	613	14	3	3	8	......	......	28
29	15	1	15	13	43	46	491	75	10	3	10	......	......	29
4	8	......	9	4	909	77	(*)	12	7	3	9	......	......	30
5	6	6	3	4	3,255	11	(*)	6	5	......	8	1	......	31
288	93	8	1,449	431	37	322	127	77	15	2,578	664	1	......	32
11	6	......	18	17	2,256	93	(*)	14	4	2	19	1	......	33
21	8	1	19	19	249	99	2,272	26	5	6	10	......	......	34
12	5	4	8	2	32	28	117	17	5	2	4	......	......	35
4	3	......	3	9	11	86	43	5	......	......	3	......	......	36
10	7	......	8	16	30	40	205	20	3	1	6	......	......	37
1,224	570	474	1,648	174	109	261	547	491	108	112	(*)	78	......	38
39	6	......	217	687	53	290	134	7	6	874	87	......	......	39
271	18	......	124	9	68	73	345	906	10	6	15	......	1	40
2	2	......	6	4	(*)	18	1,102	6	2	2	1	......	......	41
197	47	7	248	27	58	303	286	51	6	12	35	......	......	42
15	5	......	12	9	46	1,950	177	7	4	1	15	......	......	43
430	32	5	276	20	22	576	186	41	8	27	28	3	......	44
14	3	......	4	5	2,373	13	(*)	7	4	......	3	......	......	45
6	5	......	10	3	21	22	327	21	1	3	4	......	......	46
5	......	1	7	11	2,301	47	(*)	4	2	1	2	......	1	47
1	2	1	30	37	53	111	131	1	......	34	7	......	......	48
6	10	......	7	9	2,118	42	(*)	3	3	......	1	......	......	49
4	2	3	2	2	286	10	(*)	33	3	......	8	......	......	50

* See column "Born in the State in which each city is situated."

TABLE XIX.—*Native Population of Fifty Principal Cities, according to States (or Territories) of Birth*—1870—Continued.

	Living in—	BORN IN—										
		New Hampshire.	New Jersey.	New York.	North Carolina.	Ohio.	Oregon.	Pennsylvania.	Rhode Island.	South Carolina.	Tennessee.	Texas.
1	New York, N. Y	767	8,061	(*)	367	1,235	20	5,090	851	672	164	64
2	Philadelphia, Pa	444	18,157	8,865	455	1,381	4	(*)	348	727	207	47
3	Brooklyn, N. Y	674	6,009	(*)	415	910	1	3,294	916	446	196	63
4	St. Louis, Mo	346	963	9,288	433	7,242	2	6,090	153	298	3,203	218
5	Chicago, Ill	1,339	1,360	24,648	123	5,133	4	4,307	438	113	483	51
6	Baltimore, Md	95	563	2,015	511	528	....	5,124	117	358	95	41
7	Boston, Mass	7,612	341	3,396	156	239	2	752	1,100	174	42	12
8	Cincinnati, Ohio	230	768	3,629	161	(*)	5	3,698	104	119	638	53
9	New Orleans, La	83	214	2,730	848	826	....	1,068	67	1,145	1,096	665
10	San Francisco, Cal	730	861	12,612	123	1,116	219	2,635	489	195	280	78
11	Buffalo, N. Y	152	208	(*)	6	685	....	996	82	20	23	7
12	Washington, D. C	410	710	4,055	319	913	10	3,776	105	200	157	30
13	Newark, N. J	130	(*)	8,252	44	208	2	1,547	101	71	17	10
14	Louisville, Ky	70	163	1,257	154	2,141	2	1,538	23	131	1,103	60
15	Cleveland, Ohio	215	204	5,417	140	(*)	....	1,801	78	42	79	3
16	Pittsburgh, Pa	48	284	1,031	22	1,608	2	(*)	23	29	71	3
17	Jersey City, N. J	168	(*)	17,590	43	203	....	1,201	146	86	19	13
18	Detroit, Mich	187	250	6,008	33	1,251	....	796	57	41	67	3
19	Milwaukee, Wis	156	169	4,138	6	629	2	583	69	12	23	4
20	Albany, N. Y	80	172	(*)	25	86	1	227	50	14	11	1
21	Providence, R. I	558	206	1,675	50	78	....	403	(*)	39	3	2
22	Rochester, N. Y	186	193	(*)	13	191	....	363	73	6	8	4
23	Allegheny, Pa	39	102	535	15	985	....	(*)	20	14	30	7
24	Richmond, Va	17	74	497	386	42	....	281	5	107	36	43
25	New Haven, Conn	178	418	3,445	211	237	....	382	146	48	19	5
26	Charleston, S. C	15	24	403	199	13	....	117	22	(*)	36	10
27	Indianapolis, Ind	100	315	1,608	351	5,100	....	1,830	46	47	287	12
28	Troy, N. Y	108	139	(*)	7	52	....	132	53	16	2	1
29	Syracuse, N. Y	84	91	(*)	19	118	....	243	41	10	8	4
30	Worcester, Mass	1,104	87	709	26	52	....	116	548	21	6	6
31	Lowell, Mass	3,776	16	579	11	37	....	50	127	6	7	1
32	Memphis, Tenn	45	73	752	859	944	....	430	9	427	(*)	74
33	Cambridge, Mass	1,531	56	700	102	83	1	178	181	26	6	1
34	Hartford, Conn	257	182	1,674	22	82	....	216	289	14	10	6
35	Scranton, Pa	30	642	1,570	2	75	....	(*)	26	13	2	3
36	Reading, Pa	3	93	167	6	33	1	(*)	6	3	3	......
37	Paterson, N. J	52	(*)	3,040	10	35	....	300	48	12	3	5
38	Kansas City, Mo	101	157	1,771	101	2,937	2	1,236	44	55	355	74
39	Mobile, Ala	23	50	519	834	111	....	182	13	617	217	58
40	Toledo, Ohio	56	90	2,779	22	(*)	....	676	14	18	28	......
41	Portland, Me	446	19	220	1	11	....	54	40	8	3	......
42	Columbus, Ohio	84	183	1,065	135	(*)	....	1,107	25	15	99	3
43	Wilmington, Del	38	746	315	27	52	....	4,165	30	24	2	1
44	Dayton, Ohio	27	241	636	40	(*)	....	1,614	18	18	107	7
45	Lawrence, Mass	2,252	17	377	9	17	2	30	165	3	4	......
46	Utica, N. Y	44	72	(*)	6	43	....	113	71	10	3	......
47	Charlestown, Mass	1,478	43	396	9	37	10	77	107	11	3	2
48	Savannah, Ga	19	73	643	131	31	....	117	30	2,317	38	5
49	Lynn, Mass	1,870	26	218	13	19	1	89	65	4	2	2
50	Fall River, Mass	145	56	411	6	31	....	74	2,021	4	1	......

* See column "Born in the State in which each city is situated."

TABLE XIX.—*Native Population of Fifty Principal Cities, according to States (or Territories) of Birth—1870*—Continued.

BORN IN—																
Vermont.	Virginia and West Virginia.	Wisconsin.	The Territories.	Alaska.	Arizona.	Colorado.	Dakota.	District of Columbia.	Idaho.	Indian.	Montana.	New Mexico.	Utah.	Washington.	Wyoming.	
992	2,073	170	456	1	1	1	1	441				11				1
365	4,233	125	848		1	3	1	832	1	4	1		2	3		2
802	1,420	129	279					272				3	4			3
382	3,937	668	386			21	6	281	1	5	13	36	22		1	4
2,230	1,191	3,763	330			8	3	301	2		6	6	3	1		5
128	9,073	28	1,300					1,295				2	3			6
2,495	1,048	65	126	1	2			118				4		1		7
247	1,971	140	134					128		2		6				8
99	5,724	65	278					271		5		2				9
661	673	346	373	23	4	1		231	11	1	1	4	21	74	2	10
449	164	97	17			2		13				1	1			11
383	19,924	110	25			2	3	(*)		3		4	3	8	2	12
127	241	49	67					66		1						13
52	1,744	57	50					47		1				2		14
494	457	158	53					53								15
59	1,207	27	95			1		92		1				1		16
162	965	42	73					72				1				17
405	427	178	54					46				5	3			18
411	60	(*)	30			2		26		1		1				19
213	93	22	50					58							1	20
305	353	33	140			1		135				3	1			21
404	63	63	13					13								22
24	623	16	25					25								23
20	(*)	1	153					152		1						24
254	116	27	30					29			1					25
9	187	4	20					20								26
139	691	92	49					46		3						27
580	55	8	23					23								28
194	102	20	13					13								29
965	94	14	22					22								30
1,763	47	18	4					4								31
33	2,225	43	76			2		70		2		1		1		32
496	236	26	40					40								33
318	159	22	59				1	56			2					34
30	30	15														35
5	106		10					8						2		36
27	48	18	7					7								37
251	703	358	129		1	15		97	1		1	5	6	1	2	38
30	1,541	8	51					51								39
158	129	45	3					3								40
112	42	8	15					15								41
127	844	20	34					34								42
17	155	4	48					45		1				2		43
53	348	19	12					9		1		1		1		44
584	78	16	4					4								45
119	9	15	15					15								46
467	38	5	7					7								47
10	352	1	31					29						2		48
211	42	11	5					5								49
94	21	13	5					3		2						50

* See column "Born in the State in which each city is situated."

TABLE XX.—*The Foreign-born Population of Fifty Principal Cities, distributed according to Place of Birth among the Principal Foreign Countries—1870.*

	Living in—	BORN IN— All foreign countries.	Austria.	Belgium.	Bohemia.	British America.	China.	Denmark.	France.	Germany.
1	New York, N. Y	419,094	2,737	323	1,487	4,419	115	682	8,265	[illegible]
2	Philadelphia, Pa	183,624	519	117	101	1,488	17	192	2,479	[illegible]
3	Brooklyn, N. Y	144,718	321	142	91	2,806	18	348	1,694	[illegible]
4	St. Louis, Mo	112,249	731	254	2,652	2,008	1	178	2,786	[illegible]
5	Chicago, Ill	144,557	704	392	6,277	9,648	2	1,243	1,418	[illegible]
6	Baltimore, Md	56,484	215	29	766	301	2	75	437	[illegible]
7	Boston, Mass	87,986	124	31	44	13,818	8	76	615	[illegible]
8	Cincinnati, Ohio	79,612	554	46	123	1,193	4	61	2,093	[illegible]
9	New Orleans, La	48,475	254	134	16	399	24	182	8,845	[illegible]
10	San Francisco, Cal	73,719	476	139	43	2,367	11,729	500	3,547	[illegible]
11	Buffalo, N. Y	46,237	135	37	46	4,174	2	34	2,232	[illegible]
12	Washington, D. C	13,757	26	8	9	239	1	26	193	[illegible]
13	Newark, N. J	35,884	261	45	184	303	5	41	710	[illegible]
14	Louisville, Ky	25,668	69	31	16	321	2	15	860	[illegible]
15	Cleveland, Ohio	38,815	2,155	16	786	2,634	......	49	339	[illegible]
16	Pittsburgh, Pa	27,822	117	9	49	291	......	9	348	[illegible]
17	Jersey City, N. J	31,835	69	43	15	557	2	79	276	[illegible]
18	Detroit, Mich	35,381	161	233	537	7,724	......	19	760	[illegible]
19	Milwaukee, Wis	33,773	574	79	1,435	799	......	116	189	[illegible]
20	Albany, N. Y	22,207	36	17	24	849	1	8	150	[illegible]
21	Providence, R. I	17,177	5	1	5	1,050	......	6	72	[illegible]
22	Rochester, N. Y	21,184	39	4	7	2,658	1	7	475	[illegible]
23	Allegheny, Pa	15,308	109	6	324	166	4	6	619	[illegible]
24	Richmond, Va	3,778	29	1	3	42	......	4	144	[illegible]
25	New Haven, Conn	14,358	54	5	12	344	7	13	133	[illegible]
26	Charleston, S. C	4,892	39	6	......	33	2	16	97	[illegible]
27	Indianapolis, Ind	10,657	14	4	4	305	......	95	237	[illegible]
28	Troy, N. Y	16,219	11	5	5	1,699	1	3	88	[illegible]
29	Syracuse, N. Y	13,990	47	7	8	1,181	......	13	276	[illegible]
30	Worcester, Mass	11,946	12	1	8	1,963	......	......	29	[illegible]
31	Lowell, Mass	14,435	3	1	......	3,039	......	1	28	[illegible]
32	Memphis, Tenn	6,780	14	3	4	232	......	24	207	[illegible]
33	Cambridge, Mass	12,055	9	10	27	2,587	3	10	100	[illegible]
34	Hartford, Conn	10,817	20	1	56	396	1	13	92	[illegible]
35	Scranton, Pa	15,887	4	6	......	125	......	......	64	[illegible]
36	Reading, Pa	3,871	36	......	5	32	......	1	77	[illegible]
37	Paterson, N. J	12,868	48	1	......	128	......	13	237	[illegible]
38	Kansas City, Mo	7,679	44	21	9	824	......	21	111	[illegible]
39	Mobile, Ala	4,239	33	1	......	55	1	21	312	[illegible]
40	Toledo, Ohio	11,099	93	11	5	1,019	......	18	206	[illegible]
41	Portland, Me	7,012	2	......	......	2,041	......	52	23	[illegible]
42	Columbus, Ohio	7,611	20	1	6	194	......	8	234	[illegible]
43	Wilmington, Del	5,152	......	......	......	49	......	3	64	[illegible]
44	Dayton, Ohio	7,423	28	2	43	133	......	4	242	[illegible]
45	Lawrence, Mass	12,717	9	2	......	1,564	1	1	4	[illegible]
46	Utica, N. Y	9,849	25	2	......	263	......	8	287	[illegible]
47	Charlestown, Mass	6,924	1	2	2	1,129	......	14	29	[illegible]
48	Savannah, Ga	3,671	5	......	3	63	......	14	101	[illegible]
49	Lynn, Mass	4,935	1	......	......	1,229	......	2	5	[illegible]
50	Fall River, Mass	11,478	4	2	......	1,326	......	2	3	[illegible]

TABLE XX.—*The Foreign-born Population of Fifty Principal Cities, distributed according to Place of Birth among the Principal Foreign Countries—1870.*

BORN IN—														
Great Britain and Ireland.	Holland.	Hungary.	Italy.	Luxemburg.	Mexico.	Norway.	Poland.	Portugal.	Russia.	Spain.	Sweden.	Switzerland.	West Indies.	
234,594	1,237	521	2,794	19	64	372	2,393	92	1,151	453	1,558	2,178	1,783	1
123,408	390	52	516	10	46	53	146	42	94	107	225	1,791	741	2
97,475	774	70	225	15	22	301	209	54	73	220	1,105	667	725	3
38,961	643	196	786	......	31	59	300	14	86	45	284	2,902	94	4
54,800	1,640	139	552	35	9	6,374	1,205	6	118	22	6,154	1,226	59	5
18,051	144	40	146	......	9	13	127	17	37	33	72	169	337	6
64,787	332	2	264	2	6	137	164	469	102	90	647	201	189	7
23,447	731	37	309	14	15	6	167	1	80	10	39	995	32	8
17,361	186	14	1,571	......	295	37	128	86	111	960	173	668	1,529	9
32,998	190	61	1,622	......	1,220	390	517	199	281	119	780	775	235	10
15,917	287	6	50	20	......	53	135	19	56	13	49	612	20	11
8,505	22	43	175	1	12	2	45	8	18	33	22	146	38	12
17,457	102	30	29	2	2	11	78	3	16	5	44	613	33	13
8,888	106	27	234	......	5	2	52	1	17	6	13	560	7	14
15,452	495	97	35	......	6	6	77	......	35	2	26	704	3	15
17,578	127	11	74	......	4	2	48	1	33	5	28	332	11	16
22,986	110	5	24	......	9	19	32	6	15	14	68	203	82	17
11,937	310	53	35	......	1	15	283	......	89	3	19	462	42	18
5,846	693	43	10	9	4	623	325	1	29	1	90	346	8	19
15,339	378	5	28	32	......	4	22	......	7	9	10	88	9	20
15,113	20	2	27	......	1	18	10	105	10	5	25	34	17	21
9,071	510	3	16	29	......	15	71	2	36	3	20	440	9	22
5,792	7	5	10	......	1	1	7	1	2	4	19	547	6	23
1,699	19	2	100	......	1	1	11	6	31	4	3	19	12	24
11,063	42	2	10	......	2	7	11	2	6	4	64	48	58	25
2,540	6	3	50	......	......	......	23	7	15	24	20	24	97	26
4,318	30	6	18	......	4	5	34	......	3	2	54	210	3	27
13,057	23	5	16	9	1	6	19	3	6	3	14	34	15	28
6,763	29	13	8	......	1	1	370	......	25	2	7	173	......	29
9,479	5	5	27	......	3	32	8	1	1	......	19	6	4	30
11,282	5	......	1	......	1	3	2	4	1	2	16	2	4	31
3,712	34	14	378	1	3	19	47	......	29	4	99	152	8	32
8,550	39	......	19	......	......	16	7	13	3	14	59	25	19	33
8,606	12	15	23	......	......	3	17	......	8	2	16	27	24	34
12,479	3	......	7	......	......	......	13	1	7	1	4	97	11	35
969	10	1	2	1	......	2	......	......	2	......	6	72	1	36
9,378	1,360	......	13	....	14	1	4	......	1	6	36	170	23	37
3,796	26	70	15	......	5	48	15	......	9	2	600	160	7	38
2,559	7	2	78	......	7	12	9	11	10	81	37	82	42	39
3,852	99	3	4	......	3	12	17	1	9	3	12	375	2	40
4,638	9	......	6	......	......	10	1	36	10	19	27	2	25	41
2,809	19	6	14	......	1	2	7	1	3	1	......	194	3	42
4,267	9	......	4	......	......	......	2	1	3	2	7	31	10	43
1,824	13	4	3	1	......	1	18	......	......	1	12	116	3	44
10,616	2	......	2	......	......	5	......	24	2	1	3	4	2	45
6,038	27	5	3	......	1	......	176	......	......	......	4	174	5	46
5,391	1	......	17	......	......	7	2	24	4	9	38	8	8	47
2,524	6	3	20	......	5	2	25	8	1	10	7	22	30	48
3,643	2	......	4	......	1	3	......	......	3	......	1	1	1	49
10,013	2	2	7	......	......	3	......	40	......	......	2	2	1	50

HOOL ATTENDANCE AND ILLITERACY.

TABLE XXI:—*School Attendance and School Ages by States and Territories—1870.*

	States and Territories.	5 TO 18—SCHOOL AGES.*							
		All classes.		Native.		Foreign-born.		White.	
		Male.	Female.	Male.	Female.	Male.	Female.	Male.	Female.
	The United States	6,086,872	5,968,571	5,811,730	5,697,296	275,142	271,175	5,264,6[illegible]	5,151,9[illegible]
	The States	6,027,150	5,907,941	5,756,693	5,641,352	270,457	266,589	5,211,255	5,104,5[illegible]
1	Alabama	173,273	169,703	173,100	169,548	173	155	91,989	88,7[illegible]
2	Arkansas	84,645	80,847	84,530	80,760	115	87	64,515	61,35[illegible]
3	California	71,086	66,043	64,203	62,083	6,883	3,960	66,446	64,34[illegible]
4	Connecticut	69,807	69,155	64,321	63,478	5,486	5,677	68,671	67,94[illegible]
5	Delaware	20,185	19,622	19,944	19,348	241	274	16,376	16,6[illegible]
6	Florida	32,873	31,024	32,626	30,742	247	282	16,985	15,9[illegible]
7	Georgia	206,026	201,490	205,758	201,258	268	232	110,345	108,014
8	Illinois	414,547	404,219	385,164	375,389	29,383	28,830	410,582	400,[illegible]
9	Indiana	287,357	279,818	282,424	274,986	4,933	4,832	283,486	275,9[illegible]
10	Iowa	201,531	193,165	187,839	180,307	13,692	12,858	200,711	192,[illegible]
11	Kansas	55,669	53,041	52,749	50,432	2,920	2,609	52,869	50,[illegible]
12	Kentucky	230,491	224,048	228,727	222,216	1,764	1,832	190,737	185,031
13	Louisiana	112,520	113,594	111,268	112,242	1,252	1,352	59,036	59,1[illegible]
14	Maine	89,233	86,355	85,622	82,659	3,611	3,696	88,917	86,114
15	Maryland	122,932	121,522	120,229	118,870	2,703	2,652	94,785	93,[illegible]
16	Massachusetts	184,640	187,180	166,612	167,613	18,028	19,567	183,151	185,51[illegible]
17	Michigan	181,806	176,724	159,197	154,863	22,609	21,861	179,079	174,0[illegible]
18	Minnesota	72,657	70,008	58,741	56,718	13,916	13,290	72,432	69,[illegible]
19	Mississippi	141,412	137,587	141,047	137,276	365	311	66,248	63,[illegible]
20	Missouri	294,316	283,487	285,539	275,105	8,777	8,382	273,204	262,344
21	Nebraska	17,779	16,744	15,378	14,529	2,401	2,215	17,684	16,618
22	Nevada	2,762	2,575	2,480	2,392	282	183	2,641	2,542
23	New Hampshire	40,073	38,693	37,823	36,182	2,250	2,511	40,000	38,619
24	New Jersey	132,049	130,813	123,899	122,578	8,150	8,235	127,708	126,518
25	New York	613,659	617,329	570,261	571,866	43,398	45,463	607,553	610,[illegible]
26	North Carolina	182,421	177,509	182,318	177,438	103	71	113,413	110,2[illegible]
27	Ohio	425,466	420,505	411,381	406,274	14,085	14,231	415,670	410,[illegible]
28	Oregon	15,035	14,365	14,701	14,197	334	168	14,783	14,[illegible]
29	Pennsylvania	540,133	535,907	516,723	512,610	23,410	23,297	531,904	526,[illegible]
30	Rhode Island	27,834	27,941	24,258	24,139	3,576	3,802	27,256	27,[illegible]
31	South Carolina	118,509	115,406	118,348	115,229	161	177	47,734	46,[illegible]
32	Tennessee	217,922	211,670	217,358	211,022	564	648	161,721	156,061
33	Texas	145,184	139,667	140,690	135,388	4,494	4,279	100,363	95,740
34	Vermont	45,667	44,164	41,577	40,290	4,090	3,874	45,552	44,056
35	Virginia	200,103	196,709	199,665	196,269	438	440	114,561	111,046
36	West Virginia	76,879	73,965	76,262	73,352	617	613	73,915	71,107
37	Wisconsin	178,669	175,347	153,931	151,704	24,738	23,643	178,201	174,879
	The Territories	59,722	60,630	55,037	56,044	4,685	4,586	53,380	53,426
1	Arizona	831	790	302	334	529	456	825	780
2	Colorado	4,605	4,352	4,427	4,174	178	178	4,538	4,251
3	Dakota	1,736	1,631	1,383	1,332	353	299	1,519	1,422
4	Dist. of Columbia	16,954	18,615	16,546	18,117	408	498	11,706	12,373
5	Idaho	897	798	702	725	195	73	754	783
6	Montana	1,134	967	1,067	918	67	49	1,091	936
7	New Mexico	14,440	14,872	14,148	14,541	292	331	14,128	14,518
8	Utah	15,344	15,072	12,904	12,535	2,440	2,517	15,236	15,018
9	Washington	3,332	3,126	3,186	3,007	146	119	3,143	2,948
10	Wyoming	449	407	372	341	77	66	420	356

NOTE.—For remarks on School Attendance, see Table XXVIII.

* Includes persons 5, and excludes persons 18 years of age.

† Also Japanese and Chinese as follows: In the United States, male, 134; female, 6. In California, male, 114; female, 2. In Massachusetts, male, 3; female, 3. In New Jersey, male, 10. In New York, female, 1. In Oregon, male, 7.

Also Indian, (civilized:) In the United States, male, 628; female, 586. In the States, male, 610; female, 566. In California, male, 25; female, 32. In Connecticut, male, 14; female, 17. In Illinois, male, 3; female, 1; in Indiana, male, 13; female, 21. In Iowa, male, 1; female, 1. In Kansas, male, 151; female, 114. In Kentucky, male, 7; female, 13. In Maine, male, 5; female, 5. In Massachusetts, male, 6; female, 11. In Michigan, male, 207; female, 166. In Minnesota, male, 16; female, 16. In Missouri,

TABLE XXI.—*School Attendance and School Ages by States and Territories*—1870.

5 to 18—School ages—Continued.						Attended school.							
Colored.		Chinese.		Indian.					White.		Colored.†		
Male.	Female.	Male.	Female.	Male.	Female.	Total.	Native.	Foreign-born.	Male.	Female.	Male.	Female.	
814,576	806,402	3,666	477	3,995	3,763	6,596,466	6,361,422	235,044	3,326,797	3,087,943	88,594	91,778	
809,197	800,030	3,444	467	3,254	2,944	6,550,808	6,318,890	231,918	3,305,739	3,068,572	86,056	89,125	
81,274	79,882	......	....	10	23	77,139	77,091	48	31,098	30,226	7,502	8,313	1
20,118	19,482	1	....	11	15	62,572	62,546	26	30,138	26,650	2,930	2,854	2
484	464	3,123	449	1,033	790	91,176	87,598	3,578	46,539	44,091	203	170	3
1,104	1,182	......	....	32	31	99,663	95,381	4,282	50,696	47,792	580	564	4
3,809	3,605	......	....	......	......	19,965	19,760	205	9,862	8,908	663	532	5
15,828	15,102	......	....	......	1	12,778	12,757	21	4,195	4,059	2,241	2,283	6
95,676	93,470	......	....	5	6	77,493	77,350	143	33,736	33,346	4,898	5,453	7
3,961	3,992	......	....	4	4	548,225	522,939	25,286	284,084	261,813	1,169	1,155	8
3,830	3,842	......	....	41	55	395,263	391,524	3,739	206,363	185,777	1,620	1,469	9
805	787	......	....	15	5	306,333	293,333	13,000	160,262	145,421	346	315	10
2,641	2,833	......	....	150	125	63,183	61,431	1,752	31,568	29,223	1,011	1,116	11
39,736	38,984	1	....	17	33	181,225	180,063	1,162	91,225	82,278	3,530	4,182	12
53,394	54,304	......	....	90	108	51,259	50,688	571	20,542	19,641	5,467	5,609	13
221	181	......	....	95	58	155,140	152,106	3,034	80,630	74,314	109	77	14
28,137	28,082	......	1	......	......	105,435	103,930	1,505	51,668	46,093	3,808	3,866	15
1,419	1,639	38	....	12	27	287,405	270,369	17,036	143,779	141,755	941	907	16
1,890	1,942	......	....	837	718	264,217	239,865	24,352	136,607	125,754	709	714	17
91	76	......	....	114	109	96,793	83,732	13,061	50,158	46,598	35	40	18
75,084	74,475	......	....	80	65	39,141	39,085	56	17,139	16,264	2,768	2,970	19
21,102	21,125	......	....	10	18	324,348	317,745	6,603	165,792	149,468	4,557	4,523	20
82	111	......	....	13	15	17,956	16,587	1,369	9,437	8,463	30	18	21
22	16	98	12	1	5	2,893	2,796	97	1,451	1,433	6	2	22
69	68	......	....	4	6	65,824	64,366	1,458	34,333	31,423	25	23	23
4,336	4,291	2	....	3	4	158,099	152,009	6,090	79,320	75,428	1,784	1,553	24
6,047	6,463	2	....	57	55	846,796	806,640	40,156	430,731	410,426	2,835	2,733	25
68,800	67,045	......	....	208	240	65,301	65,282	19	28,357	25,511	5,491	5,928	26
9,776	9,632	......	....	20	15	645,639	632,202	13,437	329,367	306,413	5,097	4,747	27
44	35	158	4	50	51	18,096	17,962	134	9,574	8,475	20	8	28
8,223	9,028	1	....	5	4	725,004	706,716	18,288	369,674	347,445	4,023	3,857	29
553	553	......	....	21	25	34,948	32,921	2,027	17,643	16,649	309	309	30
70,737	68,957	......	....	18	19	41,569	41,519	50	12,731	11,961	8,339	8,534	31
56,185	55,602	......	....	10	7	120,710	120,569	141	58,324	51,790	4,938	5,453	32
44,781	43,877	......	1	60	49	65,205	64,384	821	31,508	29,412	2,045	2,144	33
114	107	......	....	1	1	70,199	67,235	2,964	36,765	33,349	58	37	34
85,510	85,644	......	....	32	39	70,871	70,768	103	31,783	28,009	5,105	5,943	35
2,964	2,857	......	....	......	1	82,193	81,786	407	43,278	37,703	634	578	36
290	271	......	....	178	197	260,732	235,835	24,897	135,015	125,281	180	126	37
5,379	6,372	222	10	741	819	45,658	42,532	3,126	21,058	19,371	2,538	2,653	
......	......	......	....	6	10	149	64	85	79	70	......	......	1
34	44	......	....	33	45	2,617	2,482	135	1,376	1,221	12	7	2
7	9	......	....	210	200	1,144	1,008	136	606	522	......	......	3
5,245	6,239	......	....	3	1	19,941	19,552	389	7,505	7,314	2,490	2,623	4
2	2	132	3	9	10	466	416	50	240	218	4	4	5
9	11	19	2	15	18	919	895	24	499	420	......	......	6
9	10	......	....	303	344	1,889	1,830	59	1,095	782	2	1	7
13	18	43	4	32	32	14,632	12,626	2,006	7,616	7,090	6	3	8
47	31	16	1	126	146	3,537	3,323	214	1,864	1,639	14	15	9
13	8	12	....	4	13	364	336	28	178	185	1	......	10

male, 3; female, 5. In Nebraska, male, 3; female, 5. In Nevada, female, 1. In New Jersey, male, 1; female, 3. In New York, male, 25; female, 25. In North Carolina, male, 8; female, 6. In Ohio, male, 7; female, 8. In Oregon, male, 5; female, 7; In Pennsylvania, male, 4; female, 1. In Rhode Island, male, 22; female, 16. In South Carolina, male, 4. In Tennessee, male, 5. In Texas, male, 1; female, 5. In Virginia, male, 14; female, 17. In Wisconsin, male, 60; female, 70. In the Territories, male, 18; female, 20. In Colorado, female, 1. In Dakota, male, 8; female, 8. In New Mexico, male, 5; female, 4. In Utah, male, 1; female, 6. In Washington, male, 4; female, 1.

TABLE XXII.—*School Attendance by States and Territories*—1860.

States and Territories.	ATTENDED SCHOOL.						
				White.		Colored.	
	Total.	Native.	Foreign-born.	Male.	Female.	Male.	Female.
The United States	5,692,954	5,438,784	254,170	2,961,698	2,698,627	16,594	16,0[illegible]
The States	5,672,460	5,420,085	252,375	2,951,275	2,680,234	16,279	15,67[illegible]
Alabama	98,204	97,854	350	52,102	45,988	48	66
Arkansas	42,726	42,684	42	23,354	19,367	3	2
California	25,916	23,539	2,377	13,404	12,350	69	64
Connecticut	89,936	86,120	3,816	45,570	42,988	737	641
Delaware	18,672	18,394	278	9,961	8,461	122	128
Florida	8,503	8,472	31	4,507	3,987	3	6
Georgia	94,687	94,319	368	50,552	44,128	3	4
Illinois	405,121	374,892	30,229	212,838	191,672	264	347
Indiana	338,091	329,961	8,130	179,149	157,820	570	552
Iowa	167,608	157,410	10,198	89,016	78,454	77	61
Kansas	13,332	12,925	407	6,996	6,322	8	6
Kentucky	182,659	180,116	2,543	96,763	85,687	102	107
Louisiana	48,023	45,967	2,056	25,058	22,690	153	122
Maine	189,210	185,877	3,333	99,196	89,722	148	144
Maryland	79,675	77,666	2,009	41,337	36,983	687	668
Massachusetts	249,203	234,280	15,013	125,294	122,384	800	815
Michigan	188,604	174,402	14,202	97,387	90,112	555	550
Minnesota	24,150	20,046	4,104	12,682	11,450	8	10
Mississippi	66,524	66,147	377	35,308	31,214	....	2
Missouri	203,488	196,185	7,303	108,049	95,284	76	79
Nebraska	3,296	3,012	284	1,727	1,567	1	1
Nevada (*a*)	....	....	....	....	....	....	....
New Hampshire	82,934	81,731	1,203	43,453	39,401	49	31
New Jersey	119,216	114,096	5,120	60,620	55,855	1,413	1,3[illegible]
New York	805,550	754,261	51,289	411,913	387,943	2,955	2,730
North Carolina	116,567	116,484	83	62,286	54,148	75	58
Ohio	605,656	583,276	22,380	310,644	289,341	2,857	2,814
Oregon	10,816	10,758	58	5,818	4,996	....	2
Pennsylvania	669,961	648,651	21,310	343,096	319,292	3,882	3,691
Rhode Island	31,568	30,176	1,392	15,818	15,218	276	256
South Carolina	46,590	46,341	249	24,893	21,332	158	207
Tennessee	163,022	162,471	551	87,176	75,794	28	24
Texas	63,625	61,896	1,729	33,989	29,625	4	7
Vermont	79,565	76,797	2,768	41,298	38,152	65	50
Virginia (*b*)	154,963	153,792	1,171	83,393	71,529	21	20
West Virginia	....	....	....	....	....	....	....
Wisconsin	184,709	149,087	35,622	96,628	87,969	62	50
The Territories	20,494	18,699	1,795	10,423	9,393	315	363
Arizona	....	....	....	....	....	....	....
Colorado (*a*)	....	....	....	....	....	....	....
Dakota	270	242	28	140	130	....	....
District of Columbia	9,726	9,338	388	4,566	4,482	315	363
Idaho	....	....	....	....	....	....	....
Montana	....	....	....	....	....	....	....
New Mexico	1,466	1,460	6	880	586	....	....
Utah	7,944	6,602	1,342	4,238	3,706	....	....
Washington	1,088	1,057	31	599	489	....	....
Wyoming	....	....	....	....	....	....	....

(*a*) No returns of School Attendance.
(*b*) Includes West Virginia.

TABLE XXIII.—*School Attendance by States and Territories*—1850.

l Territories.	ATTENDED SCHOOL.						
	Total.	Native.	Foreign-born.	White.		Colored.	
				Male.	Female.	Male.	Female.
ited States....	4,089,507	3,942,081	147,426	2,146,432	1,916,614	13,864	12,597
tes	4,080,436	3,933,163	147,273	2,141,821	1,912,621	13,632	12,362
....	62,846	62,738	108	34,125	28,653	33	35
....	23,361	23,343	18	12,918	10,432	6	5
....	993	976	17	800	192	1	......
....	83,697	81,221	2,476	42,457	39,976	689	575
....	14,403	14,077	326	7,632	6,584	92	95
....	4,812	4,704	108	2,545	2,201	29	37
....	77,016	76,915	101	42,365	34,650	1	......
....	182,292	173,403	8,889	97,945	84,724	162	161
....	220,961	218,227	2,734	119,496	100,538	484	443
....	35,473	34,383	1,090	18,077	16,779	12	5
....	......	......	......	......	......	......	......
....	131,205	129,955	1,250	69,783	61,134	128	160
....	34,057	30,795	3,262	16,903	15,935	619	600
....	186,222	183,051	3,171	97,443	88,498	144	137
....	62,063	60,386	1,677	32,214	28,233	886	730
tts	222,220	211,293	10,927	112,210	108,571	726	713
....	105,961	100,851	5,110	53,546	50,208	106	101
....	209	202	7	105	102	......	2
....	48,803	48,751	52	26,002	22,801	......	......
....	95,285	92,031	3,254	51,146	44,009	23	17
....	......	......	......	......	......	......	......
....	......	......	......	......	......	......	......
hire..........	88,221	86,908	1,223	45,764	42,384	41	32
....	91,601	88,892	2,709	48,065	41,210	1,243	1,083
....	693,321	644,087	49,234	356,602	331,272	2,840	2,607
ina...........	100,808	100,258	550	54,727	45,864	113	104
....	514,809	498,527	16,282	270,254	242,024	1,321	1,210
....	1,877	1,852	25	1,016	859	2	......
ia	504,610	488,823	15,787	263,451	234,660	3,385	3,114
d..............	28,910	27,712	1,198	14,782	13,577	304	247
ina	40,373	40,073	300	21,738	18,555	54	26
....	146,200	146,033	167	78,943	67,187	40	30
....	19,389	18,788	601	10,570	8,799	11	9
....	92,242	88,746	3,496	47,997	44,135	58	32
....	109,775	109,564	211	59,204	50,507	37	27
ia..............	......	......	......	......	......	......	......
....	56,421	45,508	10,913	29,096	27,258	32	35
ritories	9,071	8,918	153	4,611	3,993	232	235
....	......	......	......	......	......	......	......
....	......	......	......	......	......	......	......
....	......	......	......	......	......	......	......
Columbia.....	6,570	6,485	85	3,137	2,966	232	235
....	......	......	......	......	......	......	......
....	......	......	......	......	......	......	......
....	466	464	2	361	105	......	......
....	2,035	1,969	66	1,113	922	......	......
....	......	......	......	......	......	......	......
....	......	......	......	......	......	......	......

(*a*) Includes West Virginia.

TABLE XXIV.—*Illiteracy by States and Territories*—1870.

	States and Territories.	CANNOT READ.	CANNOT WRITE—PERSONS TEN YEARS OF AGE AND UPWARDS.								
		Persons ten years of age and over.	Total.	Native.	Foreign-born.	White. 10 to 15. Male.	White. 10 to 15. Female.	White. 15 to 21. Male.	White. 15 to 21. Female.	White. 21 and over. Male.	White. 21 and over. Female.
	The United States	4528084	5658144	4880271	777873	294422	245690	207578	209533	748970	1145718
	The States	4438206	5552488	4791935	760553	287092	238416	202069	201945	726375	1120261
1	Alabama	349771	383012	382142	870	13214	11016	9642	9757	17429	31001
2	Arkansas	111799	133339	133043	296	7985	6814	6703	7213	13610	21770
3	California	24877	31716	9520	22196	1002	849	1179	839	12362	9837
4	Connecticut	19680	29616	5678	23938	1339	1191	1266	1444	8990	13083
5	Delaware	19356	23100	20631	2469	1045	833	718	632	3466	4599
6	Florida	60238	71803	71235	568	2691	2392	2146	2199	3876	5000
7	Georgia	418553	468593	467503	1090	19843	16654	13101	12911	21899	40531
8	Illinois	86368	133584	90595	42989	6562	5303	7208	6293	40801	56657
9	Indiana	76634	127124	113185	13939	5582	4779	7325	7093	36331	57651
10	Iowa	24115	45671	24979	20692	3401	2457	2044	1636	14782	19825
11	Kansas	16369	24550	20449	4101	1491	1009	1311	908	5994	6175
12	Kentucky	249567	332176	324945	7231	31752	26014	18724	18036	43826	62785
13	Louisiana	257184	276158	268773	7385	7130	6395	4710	4926	12048	15540
14	Maine	13486	19052	7986	11066	1782	1368	1247	1186	6316	6775
15	Maryland	114100	135499	126907	8592	4274	3653	3022	3077	13344	19422
16	Massachusetts	74935	97742	7912	89830	2215	2144	3013	4304	30920	53290
17	Michigan	34613	53127	22547	30580	4728	3294	2973	2125	17543	17986
18	Minnesota	12747	24413	5558	18855	2122	1680	1014	975	8041	10109
19	Mississippi	291718	313310	312483	827	8174	6555	5447	4749	9357	13746
20	Missouri	146771	222411	206827	15584	27509	21864	14735	12731	34780	50124
21	Nebraska	2365	4861	3552	1309	1167	809	317	212	956	1169
22	Nevada	727	872	98	774	8	15	20	10	474	126
23	New Hampshire	7618	9926	1992	7934	456	377	712	700	3361	4225
24	New Jersey	37057	54687	29726	24961	2987	2546	2113	2300	14515	21916
25	New York	163501	239271	70702	168569	10772	9127	8138	10435	73208	116744
26	North Carolina	339789	397690	397573	117	20240	18407	15384	16527	33111	62738
27	Ohio	92720	173172	134102	39070	15064	11372	8568	7491	41439	68449
28	Oregon	2609	4427	3003	1424	572	388	161	109	1085	1096
29	Pennsylvania	131728	222356	126803	95553	5735	4953	8504	9635	61350	116961
30	Rhode Island	15416	21921	4444	17477	1289	1195	1090	1383	5922	10152
31	South Carolina	265892	290379	289726	653	7209	6375	5411	5691	12490	17901
32	Tennessee	290549	364697	362955	1742	20887	17991	15963	17349	37713	62825
33	Texas	189423	221703	203334	18369	11171	8748	7144	6482	17505	19845
34	Vermont	13185	17706	3902	13804	1035	815	1317	1105	6867	6445
35	Virginia	390913	445893	444623	1270	18745	15358	11095	10343	27646	40351
36	West Virginia	48802	81490	78389	3101	10704	9342	5808	5913	15181	24545
37	Wisconsin	35031	55441	14113	41328	5030	4244	2777	2487	17637	22670
	The Territories	89878	105656	88336	17320	7330	7274	5509	7588	22505	25457
1	Arizona	2090	2753	262	2491	177	122	242	254	1167	767
2	Colorado	6297	6823	6568	255	483	487	498	717	2305	2074
3	Dakota	1249	1563	758	805	56	58	44	47	403	306
4	District of Columbia	22845	28719	26501	2218	366	293	150	311	1214	2542
5	Idaho	3293	3388	138	3250	17	19	9	19	315	107
6	Montana	667	918	394	524	69	36	29	29	399	81
7	New Mexico	48836	52220	49311	2909	4530	4893	3956	5734	14892	17135
8	Utah	2515	7363	3334	4029	1539	1289	523	429	1137	2180
9	Washington	1018	1307	804	503	71	58	44	34	437	179
10	Wyoming	468	602	266	336	22	19	14	14	326	86

TABLE XXIV.—*Illiteracy by States and Territories*—1870.

CANNOT WRITE—PERSONS TEN YEARS OF AGE AND UPWARDS.

Colored.					Chinese.*						Indian.						
o 15.	15 to 21.		21 and over.		10 to 15.		15 to 21.		21 and over.		10 to 15.		15 to 21.		21 & over.		
Female.	Male.	Female.	Male.	Female.	Male.	Female.	Male.	Female.	Male.	Female.	Male.	Female.	Male.	Female.	Male.	Female.	
227510	237021	273560	862243	946332	180	13	908	181	5439	474	767	698	782	1082	2495	3525	
226336	235871	271212	854422	935436	144	13	532	163	2693	395	538	451	565	682	2150	2625	
22615	25616	28915	91017	98344	...	...	...	...	...	...	5	12	2	4	16	16	1
4982	5863	6655	23681	22689	3	...	...	...	1	...	3	2	2	...	3	8	2
21	30	34	468	339	130	13	471	147	1730	362	110	71	146	197	701	564	3
62	83	130	627	704	...	...	...	...	...	...	...	2	2	2	7	15	4
860	1054	1011	3765	4205	...	...	...	...	...	...	...	...	...	...	...	...	5
3513	4957	5376	16806	18052	...	...	...	...	...	...	...	...	...	...	5	...	6
31253	31295	34813	100551	112361	...	...	...	...	...	...	2	2	...	2	5	6	7
325	620	619	3969	4082	...	...	...	...	...	...	...	...	...	...	5	5	8
348	530	650	3182	3181	...	...	...	...	...	...	9	7	3	9	30	47	9
38	71	75	635	673	...	...	...	...	...	...	...	...	...	...	...	2	10
314	449	497	2772	2839	...	...	...	...	...	...	8	10	10	22	128	181	11
12067	12157	12769	37889	43277	...	...	...	...	...	...	5	11	1	8	6	18	12
16375	15873	19718	70612	79437	...	...	...	...	41	1	42	31	33	42	119	107	13
3	17	14	69	57	...	...	...	...	...	...	1	1	1	...	...	2	14
6502	7075	8278	27123	32582	...	...	...	...	1	...	...	...	...	...	1	2	15
30	76	147	822	1044	...	...	...	...	2	...	3	...	3	2	2	6	16
199	169	161	1015	941	...	...	...	...	...	...	122	104	152	168	517	760	17
4	11	4	44	37	...	...	...	...	...	...	36	30	32	19	110	143	18
22606	23216	26267	80810	87327	...	...	1	...	15	...	32	27	35	44	102	124	19
5133	5355	6181	18002	20587	...	...	...	...	...	...	2	1	2	6	6	9	20
10	15	21	93	50	...	...	...	...	...	...	4	3	3	2	3	11	21
...	...	...	15	6	2	...	22	4	161	9	...	...	...	...	...	...	22
3	10	8	38	32	...	...	...	...	...	...	...	...	...	...	...	...	23
443	481	551	2881	3509	...	...	...	...	...	...	...	...	1	...	1	2	24
366	585	622	3912	4874	...	...	3	...	10	2	4	6	11	4	30	47	25
19642	21341	23464	68669	76177	...	...	...	...	...	...	85	85	63	89	136	229	26
1115	1372	1398	7531	8076	...	...	...	...	...	...	2	3	3	1	4	10	27
4	4	3	48	28	9	...	35	12	731	21	6	9	12	7	21	63	28
450	719	1096	5758	7469	...	...	...	...	...	...	...	...	...	...	2	3	29
20	63	49	291	421	...	...	...	...	...	...	...	1	1	2	5	11	30
19918	20329	25276	70840	77924	...	...	...	...	...	...	7	2	2	5	11	21	31
15225	16209	18835	55938	63248	...	...	...	...	...	...	2	1	1	...	6	8	32
13366	13070	15040	47235	47583	...	...	...	...	...	...	19	9	16	16	79	52	33
3	16	12	45	37	...	...	...	...	...	...	...	...	1	...	2	3	34
27710	26161	31047	97908	109687	...	...	...	...	1	...	5	10	9	11	37	46	35
804	844	860	3186	3442	...	...	...	...	...	...	...	...	...	...	...	...	36
7	25	16	185	115	...	...	...	...	...	...	24	11	18	20	50	104	37
1174	1150	2288	7821	10896	36	...	376	18	2746	79	229	247	217	400	336	900	
...	...	...	1	...	...	...	...	...	5	...	1	2	2	4	4	5	1
4	13	14	63	48	...	...	...	...	...	...	9	11	18	23	7	45	2
1	3	8	6	12	...	...	...	...	...	...	64	73	58	70	147	206	3
1160	1117	2238	7509	10757	...	...	...	...	...	...	...	...	...	...	...	...	4
...	1	1	4	9	26	...	295	15	2471	65	1	...	2	1	6	4	5
2	2	13	34	15	4	...	12	...	103	10	1	3	5	9	13	47	6
4	7	11	58	24	...	...	...	...	...	...	140	146	110	187	81	307	7
1	...	1	8	10	6	...	54	2	149	4	5	2	6	11	2	3	8
2	4	2	15	9	...	...	...	...	...	...	8	7	14	90	70	261	9
...	3	...	33	12	...	...	15	1	18	...	...	3	2	5	6	22	10

ould appear that some assistant marshals committed the fault of returning as illiterate the who could not write English while they were able to read and write their own language.

TABLE XXV.—*Illiteracy by States and Territories*—1860.

States and Territories.	CANNOT READ AND WRITE—PERSONS TWENTY YEARS OF AGE AND UPWARDS.						
				White.		Colored.	
	Total.	Native.	Foreign-born.	Male.	Female.	Male.	Female.
The United States.	1,218,311	871,418	346,893	467,023	659,552	41,273	50,461
The States	1,177,807	834,503	343,304	449,302	640,172	40,111	48,22
Alabama	38,060	37,302	758	14,517	23,088	192	263
Arkansas	23,665	23,587	78	9,379	14,263	10	13
California	19,693	11,509	8,184	11,835	7,154	497	207
Connecticut	8,833	925	7,908	3,405	5,083	181	164
Delaware	13,169	11,503	1,666	2,838	3,823	3,056	3,452
Florida	5,461	5,150	311	2,378	2,963	48	72
Georgia	44,257	43,550	707	16,900	26,784	255	318
Illinois	59,364	39,748	19,616	24,786	33,251	632	695
Indiana	62,716	55,903	6,813	24,297	36,646	869	904
Iowa	19,951	12,903	7,048	7,806	11,976	92	77
Kansas	3,067	2,695	372	1,228	1,776	25	38
Kentucky	70,040	65,749	4,291	28,742	38,835	1,113	1,350
Louisiana	19,010	15,679	3,331	8,051	9,757	485	717
Maine	8,598	2,386	6,212	4,282	3,270	25	21
Maryland	37,518	33,780	3,738	7,290	8,529	9,904	11,795
Massachusetts	46,921	2,004	44,917	16,969	29,293	291	368
Michigan	18,485	8,170	10,315	8,596	8,845	558	486
Minnesota	4,763	1,055	3,708	2,382	2,369	6	6
Mississippi	15,636	15,136	500	6,256	9,270	50	60
Missouri	60,545	51,173	9,372	24,255	35,405	371	514
Nebraska	634	357	277	317	304	6	7
Nevada	150	40	110	138	5	6	1
New Hampshire	4,717	1,093	3,624	2,023	2,660	15	19
New Jersey	23,081	12,937	10,144	8,436	10,840	1,720	2,085
New York	121,878	26,163	95,715	47,703	68,202	2,653	3,980
North Carolina	74,977	74,877	100	26,024	42,104	3,067	3,788
Ohio	64,828	48,015	16,813	23,997	35,345	2,995	3,191
Oregon	1,511	1,200	311	762	737	7	5
Pennsylvania	81,515	44,930	36,585	27,560	44,596	3,893	5,466
Rhode Island	6,112	1,202	4,910	2,057	3,795	119	141
South Carolina	16,208	15,792	416	5,811	8,981	633	783
Tennessee	72,054	69,262	2,792	27,358	43,001	743	952
Texas	18,476	11,832	6,644	8,514	9,900	25	37
Vermont	8,916	933	7,983	4,467	4,402	27	20
Virginia (a)	86,452	83,300	3,152	31,178	42,877	5,489	6,908
West Virginia	....	....	....	....	....	....	....
Wisconsin	16,546	2,663	13,883	7,465	8,983	53	45
The Territories	40,504	36,915	3,589	17,721	19,380	1,164	2,236
Arizona	....	....	....	....	....	....	....
Colorado	....	....	....	....	....	....	....
Dakota	77	60	17	62	15	....	....
District of Columbia	6,881	4,860	2,021	1,258	2,248	1,151	2,224
Idaho	....	....	....	....	....	....	....
Montana	....	....	....	....	....	....	....
New Mexico	32,785	31,626	1,159	16,008	16,750	12	15
Utah	323	162	161	98	225	....	....
Washington	438	207	231	295	142	1	....
Wyoming	....	....	....	....	....	....	....

(a) Includes West Virginia.

TABLE XXVI.—*Illiteracy by States and Territories*—1850.

…d Territories.	CANNOT READ AND WRITE—PERSONS TWENTY YEARS OF AGE AND UPWARDS.						
	Total.	Native.	Foreign-born.	White.		Colored.	
				Male.	Female.	Male.	Female.
…nited States.	1, 053, 420	858, 306	195, 114	389, 664	573, 234	40, 722	49, 800
States ……	1, 023, 506	829, 407	194, 099	375, 641	560, 502	39, 613	47, 690
……	33, 992	33, 853	139	13, 163	20, 594	108	127
……	16, 935	16, 908	27	6, 810	10, 009	61	55
…a ……	5, 235	2, 318	2, 917	4, 237	881	88	29
…ut ……	5, 306	1, 293	4, 013	2, 037	2, 702	292	275
……	10, 181	9, 777	404	2, 012	2, 524	2, 724	2, 921
……	4, 129	3, 834	295	1, 736	2, 123	116	154
……	41, 667	41, 261	406	16, 552	24, 648	208	259
……	41, 283	35, 336	5, 947	16, 633	23, 421	605	624
……	72, 710	69, 445	3, 265	26, 132	44, 406	1, 024	1, 146
……	8, 153	7, 076	1, 077	2, 929	5, 192	15	18
……							
…y ……	69, 706	67, 359	2, 347	27, 754	38, 933	1, 431	1, 588
…a ……	24, 610	18, 339	6, 271	9, 642	11, 379	1, 038	2, 351
……	6, 282	2, 154	4, 148	3, 259	2, 888	77	58
…l ……	41, 877	38, 426	3, 451	8, 557	12, 258	9, 422	11, 640
…usetts ……	28, 345	1, 861	26, 484	11, 578	15, 961	373	431
……	8, 281	5, 272	3, 009	4, 037	3, 875	201	168
…a. ……	649	259	390	389	260		
…pi ……	13, 528	13, 447	81	5, 522	7, 883	75	48
……	36, 778	34, 917	1, 861	14, 458	21, 823	271	226
……							
……							
…mpshire ……	3, 009	945	2, 064	1, 662	1, 295	26	26
…ey ……	18, 665	12, 787	5, 878	6, 007	8, 241	2, 167	2, 250
…k. ……	98, 722	30, 670	68, 052	39, 178	52, 115	3, 387	4, 042
…rolina ……	80, 423	80, 083	340	26, 230	47, 327	3, 099	3, 758
……	66, 020	56, 958	9, 062	22, 994	38, 036	2, 366	2, 624
……	162	99	63	86	71	3	2
…ania ……	76, 272	51, 283	24, 989	24, 380	42, 548	4, 115	5, 229
…and ……	3, 607	1, 248	2, 359	1, 330	2, 010	130	137
…rolina ……	16, 564	16, 460	104	5, 897	9, 787	421	459
…e. ……	78, 619	78, 114	505	28, 460	49, 053	506	591
……	10, 583	8, 095	2, 488	4, 988	5, 537	34	24
……	6, 240	616	5, 624	3, 601	2, 588	32	19
…(a) ……	88, 520	87, 383	1, 137	30, 244	46, 761	5, 141	6, 374
…ginia ……							
…n. ……	6, 453	1, 551	4, 902	2, 030	3, 431	53	37
…Territories….	29, 914	28, 899	1, 015	14, 023	12, 672	1, 109	2, 110
……							
……							
……							
…f Columbia…	4, 671	4, 349	322	601	856	1, 106	2, 108
……							
……							
…ico ……	25, 089	24, 429	660	13, 334	11, 751	2	2
……	154	121	33	88	65	1	
…son ……							
……							

(a) Includes West Virginia.

TABLE XXVII.—*Population, School Attendance, and Illiteracy of Fifty Principal Cities—1870.*

Cities.	Population.					Attended school.						
									White.		Colored.	
	Total.	Native.	Foreign-born.	White.	Colored.	Total.	Native.	Foreign-born.	Male.	Female.	Male.	Female.
1. *New York (a)*	942292	523198	419094	929199	*b*13072	*c*155693	141677	13926	77183	77085	682	728
1st ward	14463	6441	8022	14239	224	2833	2505	328	1447	1349	18	19
2d ward	1312	651	661	1246	66	123	119	4	55	63	.....	5
3d ward	3715	1752	1963	3657	*e*57	521	500	21	259	262	.....	.....
4th ward	23748	10456	13292	23748	.....	4216	3643	573	2049	2165	2	.....
5th ward	17150	9245	7905	16467	683	2527	2365	162	1232	1269	9	17
6th ward	21153	9444	11709	20950	203	4099	3302	797	2051	2035	5	8
7th ward	44818	24130	20688	44764	54	7820	7071	749	3808	4006	3	3
8th ward	34913	20285	14628	32013	*f*2893	5204	4861	343	2344	2565	131	136
9th ward	47609	33020	14589	46930	*g*678	7451	7164	287	3714	3668	32	57
10th ward	41431	18851	22580	41306	125	6364	5481	883	3179	3169	7	9
11th ward	64230	34805	29425	64142	88	13129	11739	1390	6403	6702	6	18
12th ward	47497	30888	16609	46866	631	11578	10914	664	6302	4946	218	111
13th ward	33364	19288	14076	33153	211	5579	5090	489	2756	2811	6	6
14th ward	26436	13379	13057	25530	906	4964	4487	477	2403	2444	22	65
15th ward	27587	16821	10766	26295	*h*1287	3104	2830	274	1435	1556	46	66
16th ward	48359	29510	18849	47498	861	6911	6493	418	3307	3324	27	53
17th ward	95365	46033	49332	95087	*d*275	16664	14679	1985	8311	8309	18	26
18th ward	59593	32318	27275	59049	*e*544	7186	6513	673	3586	3591	4	5
19th ward	86090	48125	37965	85494	*e*595	12650	11788	862	6388	6252	3	7
20th ward	75407	42660	32747	73700	*e*1706	12468	11421	1047	6067	6232	66	83
21st ward	56703	33402	23301	56128	575	7879	7324	555	3911	3953	7	8
22d ward	71349	41694	29655	70938	410	12333	11388	945	6175	6114	20	23
2. *Philadelphia (a)*	674022	490398	183624	651854	*f*22147	*k*108751	105095	3656	52865	53732	1020	1130
1st ward	25817	20754	5063	25457	360	4638	4516	122	2257	2321	28	28
2d ward	30220	22670	7550	29846	374	4163	4087	76	2006	2114	17	26
3d ward	19149	13574	5575	18406	743	3275	3132	143	1619	1572	32	52
4th ward	20852	14179	6673	18614	2238	3510	3329	181	1572	1688	111	139
5th ward	18736	13344	5392	15560	3176	2402	2306	96	1105	1044	121	132
6th ward	12064	7405	4659	11936	128	1989	1864	125	941	1033	6	9
7th ward	31558	21945	9613	26941	*g*4616	4608	4418	190	1975	2154	213	266
8th ward	22286	15395	6891	19556	2730	2851	2749	102	1255	1361	113	122
9th ward	16629	11313	5316	16314	315	1314	1299	15	677	634	2	1
10th ward	23312	17148	5864	22754	558	3908	3765	143	1839	2030	19	20
11th ward	14845	9289	5556	14810	35	2265	2175	90	1144	1120	.....	1
12th ward	15171	10513	4658	14692	479	2023	2393	30	1247	1327	24	25
13th ward	19956	15517	4439	19640	316	3101	3046	55	1503	1573	11	14
14th ward	22643	18163	4480	21999	*m*644	3077	3006	71	1452	1561	24	40
15th ward	44650	33123	11527	43776	874	8190	7889	301	4142	3840	127	81
16th ward	19256	13503	5753	19172	84	3554	3486	68	1678	1876	.....	.....
17th ward	21347	13128	8219	21074	273	3619	3438	181	1792	1796	11	20
18th ward	26366	20663	5703	26347	19	4711	4551	160	2348	2361	1	1
19th ward	45240	30281	14959	45050	190	8061	7598	463	3987	4042	16	16
20th ward	56642	45711	10931	56004	*n*626	9671	9523	148	4929	4723	9	10
21st ward	13861	9565	4296	13839	22	2342	2216	126	1090	1252	.....	.....
22d ward	22605	16416	6189	22160	445	4005	3902	103	1933	2068	2	2
23d ward	20888	16723	4165	20282	606	2922	2838	84	1465	1408	25	24
24th ward	24932	19134	5798	24518	414	3261	3203	58	1546	1647	38	30
25th ward	18639	13043	5596	18546	93	5324	5113	211	2874	2411	19	20
26th ward	36603	25507	11096	36339	*o*262	5961	5721	240	2876	3045	21	19
27th ward	19385	14036	5349	18033	1352	1789	1771	18	850	879	29	31
28th ward	10370	7856	2514	10189	*p*179	1617	1561	56	763	852	1	1
3. *Brooklyn*	396099	251381	144718	391142	*q*4944	66050	61609	4441	32339	33209	231	271
1st ward	6476	3946	2530	6415	*e*60	1045	974	71	532	512	.....	1
2d ward	9117	4987	4130	9028	89	1473	1338	135	700	764	5	4
3d ward	9984	6610	3374	9802	182	1294	1245	49	591	687	8	8
4th ward	12087	8271	3816	11500	587	1680	1587	93	748	878	21	33

(*a*) At the re-enumerations of the cities of New York and Philadelphia, no return was made in the columns for "School attendance" and "Illiteracy." Consequently these compilations were made from the schedules of the first enumerations, and represent the facts for an aggregate population of 923,944 for the city of New York, and of 657,437 for Philadelphia.

(*b*) Also 9 Indians and 12 Chinese.
(*c*) Including 1 Chinese and 4 Indians.
(*d*) Including 42 Chinese and 16 Indians.
(*e*) Also 1 Chinese.
(*f*) Also 7 Indians.
(*g*) Also 1 Indian.

TABLE XXVII.—*Population, School Attendance, and Illiteracy of Fifty Principal Cities—1870.*

Cannot read—10 and over.	CANNOT WRITE.															
	Total.	Native.	Foreign-born.	White.						Colored.						
				10 to 15.		15 to 21.		21 and over.		10 to 15.		15 to 21.		21 and over.	
				M.	F.	M.	F.	M.	F.	M.	F.	M.	F.	M.	F.
43056	62238	8447	53791	1878	1916	1210	3013	14974	36810	37	63	69	131	687	1392
1748	2562	488	2074	175	144	65	102	719	1318	.....	.....	2	5	16	16
35	58	3	55	1	.....	.....	8	11	37	.....	.....	.....	.....	.....	1
75	123	66	57	58	.....	15	6	3	41	.....	.....	.....	.....	.....	.....
1906	2332	124	2208	28	36	36	73	585	1567	.....	.....	.....	.....	.....	.....
1144	1433	150	1283	4	14	18	50	416	837	.....	4	10	6	27	35
4229	4962	494	4468	181	187	125	205	1492	2027	1	1	1	3	51	56
2999	4862	413	4449	64	66	132	170	1423	2960	.....	.....	1	2	6	18
1473	2063	606	1457	36	45	14	77	401	1015	10	14	14	21	142	272
1175	1790	315	1475	43	66	19	107	325	1098	1	.....	2	10	38	81
848	1160	114	1046	19	18	43	56	329	661	.....	1	.....	.....	7	26
1713	2150	171	1979	37	39	48	67	662	1287	.....	.....	.....	1	4	5
2093	3158	553	2605	119	131	73	298	848	1628	2	6	.....	5	12	36
1244	1967	497	1470	128	175	42	63	399	1084	.....	3	1	3	24	45
3601	4636	726	3910	134	131	107	171	1079	2688	9	10	11	14	126	156
1293	2100	410	1690	64	42	19	186	188	1362	5	5	5	15	51	156
1456	2337	302	2035	23	43	24	161	414	1523	.....	2	1	10	31	105
2105	2937	262	2675	62	65	68	116	619	1966	3	3	1	1	12	21
2158	3714	307	3407	47	49	55	190	750	2512	1	1	8	6	32	63
2140	3349	213	3127	20	40	34	225	797	2159	1	2	2	9	11	39
4092	5695	1145	4550	336	320	127	279	1443	2941	3	7	2	11	62	163
2454	3991	449	3542	66	82	63	148	801	2760	.....	2	5	6	15	46
3075	4868	639	4229	233	203	83	255	1270	2739	1	2	3	3	20	56
26705	42563	13996	28569	665	696	1014	1971	9550	23431	48	99	138	379	1578	2994
945	1565	790	775	60	38	77	86	412	892	1	3	2	2	32	49
1840	2948	1059	1889	135	124	86	94	780	1625	.....	6	4	7	32	55
1064	1400	412	988	14	17	31	60	322	815	.....	3	6	5	56	71
2176	2670	1131	1539	22	30	71	114	640	1029	7	8	26	43	280	400
1162	1459	967	492	4	5	22	34	159	398	6	9	14	58	279	471
663	941	169	772	8	2	10	29	218	607	1	6	.....	6	15	39
2035	3885	1420	2465	54	56	52	112	528	2068	1	9	14	46	302	643
1002	1486	406	1080	3	9	6	61	195	918	5	6	4	24	69	186
749	1244	259	985	11	16	10	65	230	775	.....	1	5	24	16	82
801	1279	314	965	8	20	11	65	206	786	2	2	3	18	30	128
341	525	172	353	4	1	7	25	168	312	.....	.....	.....	.....	3	5
297	419	236	183	3	2	5	21	45	230	2	1	5	7	32	66
647	780	252	528	17	21	20	83	102	440	1	2	4	19	6	65
526	784	337	447	1	9	7	41	120	406	6	8	7	13	52	114
2165	3577	827	2750	32	50	62	199	780	2236	2	7	11	25	64	109
703	1273	548	725	22	26	42	79	304	700	.....	.....	1	2	9	28
862	1450	275	1175	8	5	18	30	423	872	.....	2	3	6	40	43
857	1175	623	552	14	12	43	51	367	686	.....	.....	.....	1	.....	1
1579	2867	932	1935	65	50	84	129	606	1843	2	2	5	5	32	44
1099	1757	531	1226	25	21	36	122	356	1006	3	12	6	27	46	97
747	1733	583	1150	55	63	87	111	431	971	.....	.....	2	.....	4	4
572	1237	225	1012	5	9	15	88	258	723	1	3	2	14	36	82
428	928	358	570	23	38	40	41	220	449	3	1	1	4	47	58
557	995	169	826	12	14	34	65	244	506	.....	2	5	2	8	13
1662	2580	572	2008	39	36	91	87	961	1273	3	2	5	5	30	48
665	874	207	667	14	8	32	44	254	491	.....	.....	1	1	9	20
473	596	193	403	4	4	4	22	125	310	2	3	2	9	47	64
86	138	29	109	.....	5	2	13	36	64	.....	1	.....	6	2	9
(r)9983	16123	1822	14301	287	346	204	897	3247	10398	11	24	21	50	224	413
283	441	13	428	.....	3	3	13	94	326	.....	.....	.....	.....	.....	2
115	147	14	133	1	6	1	15	9	111	.....	.....	.....	.....	1	3
370	718	99	619	5	7	2	79	28	537	1	2	1	16	10	40
67	99	28	71	.....	.....	.....	13	3	73	.....	.....	2	.....	2	6

(h) Also 5 Chinese.
(i) Also 3 Chinese.
(j) Also 12 Chinese, 1 Japanese, and 8 Indians.
(k) Including 4 Indians.
(l) Including 2 Indians.
(m) Also 4 Indians.
(n) Also 12 Chinese.
(o) Also 1 Japanese and 1 Indian.
(p) Also 2 Indians.
(q) Also 6 Indians and 7 Chinese.
(r) Including 1 Chinese.

LE XXVII.—*Population, School Attendance, and Illiteracy of Fi*
1870.

Cities.	POPULATION.					ATTEND		
	Total.	Native.	Foreign-born.	White.	Colored.	Total.	Native.	Foreign-born.
1. *New York* (a)	942292	523198	419094	929199	b13072	c155693	141677	1392
1st ward	14463	6441	8022	14239	224	2833	2503	32
2d ward	1312	651	661	1246	66	123	110	[illegible]
3d ward	3715	1752	1963	3657	c57	521	500	21
4th ward	23748	10456	13292	23748	......	4216	3643	57
5th ward	17150	9245	7905	16467	683	2527	2365	16
6th ward	21153	9444	11709	20950	203	4099	3302	79
7th ward	44818	24130	20688	44764	54	7820	7071	74
8th ward	34913	20285	14628	32013	f2899	5204	4861	34
9th ward	47609	33020	14589	46930	g679	7451	7164	28
10th ward	41431	18851	22580	41306	125	6364	5481	88
11th ward	64230	34805	29425	64142	88	13129	11739	139
12th ward	47497	30888	16609	46866	631	11578	10914	66
13th ward	33364	19288	14076	33153	211	5579	5090	48
14th ward	26436	13379	13057	25530	906	4964	4487	47
15th ward	27587	16821	10766	26295	h1287	3104	2830	27
16th ward	48359	29510	18849	47498	861	6911	6493	41
17th ward	95365	46033	49332	95087	d275	16664	14679	198
18th ward	59593	32318	27275	59049	e544	7186	6513	67
19th ward	86090	48125	37965	85494	e595	12650	11788	86
20th ward	75407	42660	32747	73700	e1706	12468	11421	104
21st ward	56703	33402	23301	56128	575	7879	7324	55
22d ward	71349	41694	29655	70938	410	12333	11388	94
2. *Philadelphia* (a)	674022	490398	183624	651854	f22147	k108751	105095	36
1st ward	25817	20754	5063	25457	360	4638	4516	1
2d ward	30220	23670	7550	29846	374	4163	4087	
3d ward	19149	13574	5575	18406	743	3275	3132	
4th ward	20852	14179	6673	18614	2238	3510	3329	
5th ward	18736	13344	5392	15560	3176	2402	2306	
6th ward	12064	7405	4659	11936	128	1989	1264	
7th ward	31558	21945	9613	26941	g4616	4608	4418	
8th ward	22286	15595	6691	19556	2730	2851	2749	
9th ward	16629	11313	5316	16314	315	1314	1299	
10th ward	23312	17148	5864	22754	558	3908	3765	
11th ward	14845	9289	5556	14810	35	2265	2175	
12th ward	15171	10513	4658	14692	479	2623	2593	
13th ward	19956	15517	4439	19640	316	3101	3046	
14th ward	22643	18163	4480	21999	m643	3077	3006	
15th ward	44650	33123	11527	43776	874	8190	[illegible]	
16th ward	19256	13503	5753	19172	84	3554	[illegible]	
17th ward	21347	13128	8219	21074	273	3619	[illegible]	
18th ward	26366	20663	5703	26347	19	4711	[illegible]	
19th ward	45240	30281	14039	45050	190	8061	[illegible]	
20th ward	56642	45711	10931	56004	n626	9671	[illegible]	
21st ward	13861	9565	4296	13839	22	2342	[illegible]	
22d ward	22605	16416	6189	22160	445	4665	[illegible]	
23d ward	20888	16723	4165	20282	606	[illegible]	[illegible]	
24th ward	24932	19134	5798	24518	414	[illegible]	[illegible]	
25th ward	18639	13043	5596	18546	93	[illegible]	[illegible]	
26th ward	36605	25507	11098	36319	[illegible]	[illegible]	[illegible]	
27th ward	19385	14036	5349	18033	1352	[illegible]	[illegible]	
28th ward	10370	7856	2514	10189	[illegible]	[illegible]	[illegible]	
3. *Brooklyn*	396099	251381	144718	[illegible]	[illegible]	[illegible]	[illegible]	[illegible]
1st ward	6476	3946	[illegible]	[illegible]	[illegible]	[illegible]	[illegible]	[illegible]
2d ward	9117	4087	[illegible]	[illegible]	[illegible]	[illegible]	[illegible]	[illegible]
3d ward	9964	[illegible]	[illegible]	[illegible]	[illegible]	[illegible]	[illegible]	[illegible]
4th ward	12087	[illegible]	[illegible]	[illegible]	[illegible]	[illegible]	[illegible]	[illegible]

(a) At the re-enumerations [illegible]
columns for "School attend[illegible]
the schedules of the first [illegible]
for the city of New York [illegible]

(b) Also 9 Indians [illegible]

(c) Including 1 Chi[illegible]

(d) Including 42 C[illegible]

TABLE XXVII.—*Population, School Attendance, and Illiteracy of Fifty Principal Cities*—1870—Continued.

Cities.	POPULATION.					ATTENDED SCHOOL.						
									White.		Colored.	
	Total.	Native.	Foreign-born.	White.	Colored.	Total.	Native.	Foreign-born.	Male.	Female.	Male.	Female.
3. *Brooklyn*—C'd.												
5th ward	20490	11300	9190	20270	a217	3257	2662	595	1595	1643	6	13
6th ward	28296	16052	12244	28205	b89	5339	4933	406	2341	2998	.....	.....
7th ward	22312	15545	6767	22228	c83	3385	3233	152	1681	1702	1	1
8th ward	9592	5625	3967	9526	66	1349	1316	33	681	668	.....	.....
9th ward	15279	9468	5811	14291	d984	2896	2697	199	1403	1338	72	83
10th ward	34592	21156	13436	31453	139	5438	5137	301	2729	2704	2	3
11th ward	21243	14153	7090	20498	b743	3489	3320	169	1626	1748	48	67
12th ward	18302	9616	8686	18300	2	3632	3256	376	1850	1782	.....	.....
13th ward	18711	13529	5182	18590	121	2896	2791	105	1452	1432	5	7
14th ward	20649	12392	8257	20639	10	4266	3954	312	2156	2110	.....	.....
15th ward	18406	12908	5498	18325	81	3784	3575	209	1843	1925	6	10
16th ward	26438	15298	11140	25863	575	3331	3040	291	1667	1613	33	18
17th ward	17353	12011	5342	17344	9	3235	3052	183	1605	1630	.....	.....
18th ward	11607	7490	4117	11587	20	1995	1882	113	1009	983	.....	3
19th ward	16321	10179	6142	16152	169	2750	2533	217	1397	1333	13	7
20th ward	19179	14187	4992	19016	163	2969	2865	104	1452	1511	.....	6
21st ward	27904	19114	8790	27413	491	4162	4019	143	2097	2049	11	5
22d ward	11761	7544	4217	11697	64	2385	2200	185	1184	1199	.....	2
4. *St. Louis*	310864	198615	112249	288737	e22088	f59089	55963	3126	29033	27260	1420	1354
1st ward	33708	23389	10319	32102	h1604	6970	6605	365	3700	3071	106	93
2d ward	21855	12166	9689	21295	560	3974	3745	229	2143	1756	41	34
3d ward	23878	13341	10537	23110	i753	4502	4168	334	2229	2171	54	47
4th ward	31493	20850	10643	29635	j1857	6711	6479	232	3478	3107	62	64
5th ward	29774	19625	10149	26255	k3512	5141	4939	202	2240	2509	168	224
6th ward	29192	20631	8561	27421	c1770	4981	4761	220	2541	2274	82	84
7th ward	18508	12604	5904	16875	a1630	3784	3608	176	1749	1783	121	131
8th ward	26710	18602	8108	19668	7042	4610	4275	335	1902	1622	613	473
9th ward	22922	13368	9554	22270	h650	4058	3805	253	1982	2010	31	35
10th ward	20623	12298	8325	19432	1191	3573	3371	202	1768	1696	46	63
11th ward	32580	19020	13560	31885	l687	6917	6538	379	3338	3479	50	50
12th ward	19621	12721	6900	18789	832	3868	3669	199	1963	1792	55	58
5. *Chicago*	298977	154420	144557	295281	m3691	50092	40901	9191	24944	24874	121	153
1st ward	6522	3749	2773	6203	319	545	484	61	272	272	1	.....
2d ward	14320	8547	5773	13140	1180	957	852	105	402	477	33	45
3d ward	17681	10008	7673	16240	d1437	2611	2280	331	1218	1244	66	83
4th ward	12174	8166	4008	12077	j96	2115	1919	196	1015	1091	5	4
5th ward	11566	7991	3575	11466	100	2059	1848	211	1000	1058	1	.....
6th ward	19445	9083	10362	19433	12	3502	2810	692	1832	1670	.....	.....
7th ward	13854	5093	8761	13843	11	2678	1734	944	1396	1282	.....	.....
8th ward	22911	10650	12261	22897	14	4939	3887	1052	2541	2398	.....	.....
9th ward	27817	13023	14794	27794	23	4562	3569	993	2301	2253	1	7
10th ward	13771	8752	5019	13649	122	2065	1878	187	966	1099	.....	.....
11th ward	15065	6888	8177	15023	42	1891	1533	358	976	908	4	3
12th ward	13976	8490	5486	13925	51	2524	2144	380	1188	1332	1	3
13th ward	8928	6758	2170	8874	54	1390	1321	69	669	719	1	1
14th ward	9035	5746	3289	8915	120	1892	1678	214	900	979	7	6
15th ward	20361	7634	12727	20341	20	3313	2242	1071	1706	1607	.....	.....
16th ward	14045	6843	7202	14035	10	2961	2345	616	1544	1417	.....	.....
17th ward	18078	8181	9897	18071	7	3491	2820	671	1808	1683	.....	.....
18th ward	17084	6886	10198	17082	2	3035	2330	705	1465	1570	.....	.....
19th ward	8716	4783	3933	8702	14	1561	1421	140	730	831	.....	.....
20th ward	13628	7149	6479	13571	57	2001	1806	195	1015	984	1	1
6. *Baltimore*	267354	210870	56484	227794	b39558	41442	40620	822	19190	18945	1506	1801
1st ward	17263	12299	4964	16815	448	3063	2985	78	1523	1496	24	20
2d ward	14522	8727	5795	13458	c1063	2358	2200	158	1106	1116	75	61

(*a*) Also 3 Indians.
(*b*) Also 1 Indian and 1 Chinese.
(*c*) Also 1 Chinese.
(*d*) Also 4 Indians.
(*e*) Also 38 Indians and 1 Chinese.
(*f*) Including 4 Indians.

TABLE XXVII.—*Population, School Attendance, and Illiteracy of Fifty Principal Cities—* 1870—Continued.

Cannot read—10 and over.	CANNOT WRITE.														
	Total.	Native.	Foreign-born.	White.						Colored.					
				10 to 15.		15 to 21.		21 and over.		10 to 15.		15 to 21.		21 and over.	
				M.	F.	M.	F.	M.	F.	M.	F.	M.	F.	M.	F.
441	1140	107	1033	7	17	22	44	205	798	3	1	......	2	12	20
1040	1632	102	1530	26	16	15	90	357	1102	......	1	1	2	7	6
944	1209	144	1065	30	41	26	135	237	703	1	......	1	4	10	20
20	103	94	9	49	47	1	1	2	3	......	......	......	......	......	......
337	533	213	320	6	4	8	8	115	194	2	8	6	13	70	97
1157	1768	74	1694	10	20	10	121	316	1267	......	3	......	2	2	17
1030	1898	267	1631	25	44	15	130	403	1127	2	4	4	11	50	83
756	1188	77	1111	20	27	20	34	364	723	......	......	......	......	......	......
285	478	38	440	3	5	3	32	83	330	2	2	......	1	5	12
617	779	34	745	15	6	14	10	209	525	......	......	......	......	......	......
32	37	27	10	7	4	1	2	3	7	......	......	......	1	5	7
598	1310	144	1166	7	13	11	15	190	973	......	......	1	2	36	86
332	453	24	429	2	......	12	6	167	265	......	......	......	1	......	......
323	416	128	288	34	51	6	16	85	217	......	......	......	......	3	4
191	208	25	183	3	......	9	7	69	108	......	......	......	......	5	7
318	653	53	600	10	7	9	70	85	455	......	......	1	2	1	13
230	355	58	297	27	19	2	9	70	225	......	1	......	......	1	1
467	558	59	499	......	9	14	38	147	329	......	2	2	3	4	10
15231	g19776	11738	8038	166	231	168	461	3332	5374	160	177	431	610	4567	4084
1005	1669	941	728	28	38	24	54	411	502	15	22	39	30	278	297
675	842	276	566	6	2	11	25	233	321	1	1	5	11	118	108
763	920	375	545	13	17	20	34	148	403	3	2	11	19	109	136
1263	1559	944	615	9	5	16	31	238	427	15	12	33	66	303	404
1935	2625	1823	802	30	52	15	55	326	507	25	36	50	108	699	719
1381	1847	1187	660	30	48	12	114	216	480	[illegible]	32	62	101	426	301
1039	1272	838	434	6	10	3	25	135	312	18	22	21	62	285	372
3649	4476	3408	1068	12	13	11	36	631	610	36	28	158	110	1660	1171
1108	1441	403	1038	12	16	12	30	348	761	2	3	14	16	108	119
761	1042	773	269	2	5	2	8	85	228	11	11	16	53	323	298
791	1026	273	753	4	11	20	24	301	487	7	4	5	17	61	81
861	1057	497	560	14	14	22	25	260	336	3	4	17	17	197	148
7350	a10548	1348	9200	83	91	125	362	3064	5846	7	8	54	52	399	454
280	367	145	222	11	6	4	36	34	165	......	......	19	3	73	16
493	579	320	259	......	......	5	9	140	114	2	3	13	18	118	157
1058	1412	523	889	14	15	22	71	288	556	5	5	18	23	155	237
232	302	35	267	1	0	2	28	56	194	......	......	1	......	10	4
109	196	28	168	1	2	......	10	52	111	......	......	......	3	8	0
1129	1483	20	1463	......	1	13	18	549	900	......	......	......	1	1	......
139	215	6	209	3	1	1	4	80	126	......	......	......	......	......	......
241	333	4	329	1	2	7	8	140	172	......	......	......	......	1	2
1039	1462	49	1413	18	17	14	26	436	950	......	......	......	......	......	1
197	344	72	272	8	7	5	18	81	206	......	......	2	......	9	8
111	137	11	126	......	......	3	3	62	60	......	......	......	......	4	5
86	109	4	105	......	......	2	3	30	62	......	......	......	1	1	1
1	3	2	1	......	1	......	1	......	1	......	......	......	......	......	......
56	76	21	55	......	3	......	1	21	42	......	......	......	......	5	4
455	1126	13	1113	12	10	20	30	351	685	......	......	......	......	2	1
7	11	7	4	......	......	......	......	......	4	......	......	1	1	3	2
313	332	8	324	......	5	1	14	78	229	......	......	......	......	2	3
1050	1594	49	1545	13	13	12	41	527	988	......	......	......	......	......	......
160	227	10	217	......	......	3	14	67	142	......	......	......	......	1	......
154	240	21	219	1	2	2	21	63	130	......	......	......	2	6	4
21503	b28780	23800	4980	420	391	330	493	2516	5120	632	929	822	2218	5966	9041
885	935	436	479	2	3	7	18	275	402	1	17	9	27	65	100
871	1241	921	320	24	29	32	45	200	401	11	13	16	37	170	253

(g) Including 13 Indians.
(h) Also 2 Indians.
(i) Also 15 Indians
(j) Also 1 Indian.
(k) Also 7 Indians.
(l) Also 8 Indians.
(m) Also 5 Indians.
(n) Including 2 Japanese.
(o) Also 3 Chinese.

TABLE XXVII.—*Population, School Attendance, and Illiteracy of Fifty Principal Cities—1870*—Continued.

Cities.	POPULATION.					ATTENDED SCHOOL.						
									White.		Colored.	
	Total.	Native.	Foreign-born.	White.	Colored.	Total.	Native.	Foreign-born.	Male.	Female.	Male.	Female.
6. *Baltimore*—C'd.												
3d ward	15435	12502	2933	13188	2247	2624	2601	23	1214	1231	78	101
4th ward	9430	6857	2573	8677	753	1240	1206	34	615	587	22	16
5th ward	13379	10861	2518	9880	3499	2141	2088	53	900	887	154	191
6th ward	15129	12297	2832	12880	2249	2530	2493	37	1145	1117	125	143
7th ward	16215	12268	3947	15379	836	2847	2748	99	1373	1417	32	25
8th ward	12416	9325	3091	11061	1355	2002	1957	45	1002	942	25	33
9th ward	8275	6115	2160	6820	1455	1315	1298	17	595	624	49	47
10th ward	11059	8757	2302	8514	2545	1365	1341	24	575	553	117	120
11th ward	12221	10534	1687	8641	3580	1638	1633	5	591	720	115	212
12th ward	10576	9333	1243	8684	1892	1280	1268	12	629	576	29	46
13th ward	10387	8637	1750	8562	1825	1411	1398	13	658	618	74	61
14th ward	11584	9366	2218	9928	1656	1467	1454	13	731	619	53	64
15th ward	13854	11246	2608	10645	3209	2183	2176	7	948	935	135	165
16th ward	16689	13503	3186	13454	3235	2638	2601	37	1218	1131	151	138
17th ward	11404	8751	2653	11047	357	2124	2087	37	1033	1057	14	20
18th ward	18987	15101	3886	16326	2661	2900	2833	67	1351	1348	95	106
19th ward	13262	11565	1697	11372	f1889	1719	1700	19	814	792	44	69
20th ward	15267	12826	2441	12463	2804	2597	2553	44	1160	1179	95	163
7. *Boston*	250526	162540	87986	247013	b3496	c45815	42075	3740	22641	22830	179	165
1st ward	25484	16906	8578	25430	54	5659	5067	592	2929	2718	10	2
2d ward	24912	13438	11474	24774	e133	4763	4261	502	2403	2357	2	1
3d ward	14990	9899	5091	14270	720	2251	2051	200	1050	1128	33	40
4th ward	10216	6746	3470	10055	e156	944	850	94	491	450	1	2
5th ward	14166	7939	6227	14123	43	2725	2452	273	1326	1399	....	....
6th ward	11792	8717	3075	10014	f1776	1506	1449	57	641	663	111	91
7th ward	28921	15040	13881	28908	13	6245	5435	810	3132	3113	....	....
8th ward	11278	7821	3457	11238	40	1438	1353	85	723	714	1	....
9th ward	14142	9922	4220	14014	128	2191	2103	88	1049	1129	6	7
10th ward	13097	9437	3660	12925	172	1921	1827	94	905	991	12	13
11th ward	14617	11168	3449	14514	103	2658	2625	33	1141	1514	1	2
12th ward	19880	14027	5853	19832	48	4102	3873	227	2049	2053	....	....
13th ward	8536	5231	3305	8536	......	1772	1691	81	916	856	....	....
14th ward	11385	8259	3126	11349	g31	2367	2227	140	1267	1097	1	....
15th ward	14851	8618	6233	14816	35	2903	2546	357	1457	1446	....	....
16th ward	12259	9372	2887	12215	44	2370	2263	107	1162	1202	1	5
8. *Cincinnati*	216239	136627	79612	210335	h5900	40828	39107	1721	20358	19700	372	398
1st ward	10192	6480	3712	9672	a519	1048	978	70	498	515	17	18
2d ward	3953	2616	1337	3712	241	542	531	11	289	228	17	8
3d ward	8644	5348	3296	8581	63	1135	1041	94	522	611	....	2
4th ward	6002	3560	2442	5621	381	681	671	10	353	303	15	10
5th ward	6286	3833	2453	6115	171	1027	967	60	502	511	3	11
6th ward	8569	5283	3286	8222	347	1735	1641	94	857	832	26	20
7th ward	8092	4617	3475	7967	125	1309	1248	61	796	692	12	9
8th ward	17523	11596	5927	17262	261	3322	3219	103	1647	1638	16	21
9th ward	8816	4890	3926	8784	32	1734	1655	79	851	879	1	3
10th ward	11054	5837	5217	11014	40	2156	2134	22	1111	1041	....	4
11th ward	6247	3976	2271	6228	19	1318	1284	34	690	627	1	....
12th ward	13580	7474	6106	13529	51	2811	2632	179	1378	1428	1	4
13th ward	7480	4584	2896	6388	1092	1536	1450	86	722	662	74	78
14th ward	8836	6026	2810	8286	550	1627	1486	141	830	706	43	48
15th ward	13712	9964	3748	13152	560	2512	2447	65	1191	1256	28	37
16th ward	17483	11631	5852	17183	a299	3431	3300	131	1646	1733	23	29
17th ward	4880	3617	1263	4878	2	997	963	34	520	476	....	1
18th ward	16231	10421	5810	16110	121	3242	3205	37	1639	1589	8	6
19th ward	8883	4951	3932	8876	7	1889	1779	110	1036	853	....	....
20th ward	2350	1620	730	2302	48	449	434	15	231	210	3	5
21st ward	5333	3345	1988	5273	a59	1278	1174	104	665	613	....	....
22d ward	2362	1882	480	1896	466	566	554	12	228	223	51	64

(*a*) Also 1 Indian.
(*b*) Also 12 Indians and 5 Japanese.
(*c*) Including 2 Japanese.
(*d*) Including 4 Indians.

: XXVII.—*Population, School Attendance, and Illiteracy of Fifty Principal Cities—* 1870—Continued.

CANNOT WRITE.

Total.	Native.	Foreign-born.	White.						Colored.					
			10 to 15.		15 to 21.		21 and over.		10 to 15.		15 to 21.		21 and over.	
			M.	F.	M.	F.	M.	F.	M.	F.	M.	F.	M.	F.
1621	1302	229	32	29	9	42	83	245	49	73	76	160	315	508
774	550	224	21	13	7	11	89	167	17	40	24	58	128	199
1602	1576	26	3	5	3	9	13	48	49	58	64	124	476	750
977	912	65	1	5	3	12	28	70	18	27	36	79	251	447
1290	923	367	47	28	31	29	189	488	26	29	20	63	112	228
1183	481	702	7	4	24	28	231	521	4	10	13	48	112	181
1233	947	286	23	21	8	22	88	266	39	44	25	89	187	421
918	904	14	......	2	......	2	7	17	17	33	33	108	187	512
1938	1684	254	6	5	4	28	47	259	22	51	54	176	354	932
1493	1256	237	11	16	3	18	77	180	36	54	42	196	210	650
925	869	56	14	10	3	13	19	65	37	45	31	81	214	393
895	875	20	2	7	......	13	7	32	11	25	34	118	183	463
2119	1994	125	10	19	15	16	61	107	60	93	87	171	595	885
2842	2603	239	76	62	58	62	227	320	116	127	120	227	633	814
1553	1068	485	65	55	67	49	444	660	11	15	8	20	54	99
1602	1218	384	5	2	11	14	182	357	9	32	44	101	356	509
1962	1605	357	64	64	26	42	189	364	54	88	42	157	282	508
1677	1566	111	7	12	19	20	60	171	45	55	44	172	382	690
*d*23420	1427	21993	194	226	207	678	6930	14347	4	5	20	51	334	420
1990	52	1938	2	6	16	39	611	1307	......	......	1	......	4	4
4646	283	4363	120	124	50	99	1710	2492	......	......	......	1	24	14
1696	245	1451	27	29	20	60	451	951	1	2	5	9	71	70
1275	100	1175	29	36	16	81	302	781	......	1	2	3	9	14
1614	18	1596	......	2	2	32	563	1015	......	......	......	......	......	......
914	412	502	......	......	......	28	47	394	3	2	8	21	179	232
3047	21	3026	5	6	24	19	1108	1885	......	......	......	......	......	......
549	14	535	2	3	6	20	123	391	......	......	......	1	......	3
539	40	499	......	1	4	37	99	368	......	......	......	5	11	14
961	71	890	......	3	4	50	261	564	......	......	3	5	23	39
940	40	900	......	......	1	50	71	796	......	......	1	5	3	13
990	14	976	3	2	8	24	357	596	......	......	......	......	......	......
1035	11	1024	4	......	7	31	331	662	......	......	......	......	......	......
834	29	805	......	8	2	39	294	571	......	......	......	......	4	6
1584	53	1531	2	5	25	34	451	1062	......	......	......	......	2	3
806	24	782	......	1	13	26	241	512	......	......	......	1	4	8
*f*8999	2031	6968	99	95	125	304	1968	4494	35	41	54	137	628	1017
716	250	466	7	7	4	4	161	355	2	2	7	10	60	117
180	37	143	1	......	2	17	46	81	......	......	......	2	24	7
250	32	218	5	2	4	6	65	160	......	......	1	......	6	1
719	152	567	1	1	1	4	170	406	......	......	3	4	36	93
261	91	170	......	3	4	13	47	131	......	1	......	3	15	44
676	158	518	1	1	3	12	177	369	1	......	......	4	38	70
183	76	107	3	......	3	5	44	73	......	1	2	7	16	29
416	63	353	1	1	2	11	91	284	......	1	......	3	9	13
225	29	196	1	2	3	2	51	160	......	......	......	1	2	3
......	......	......	......	......	......	......	......	......	......	......	......	......	......	......
66	14	52	......	......	......	4	7	45	......	1	......	......	3	6
40	11	29	......	1	2	1	18	13	......	......	......	......	2	3
1408	526	882	17	15	21	17	290	613	15	12	12	30	154	212
479	228	251	1	......	3	31	53	220	2	4	3	15	38	109
713	303	410	3	8	5	74	68	240	......	3	5	33	52	122
256	60	196	......	2	2	9	65	137	......	1	2	3	16	19
298	103	195	7	3	16	13	126	232	......	......	......	......	......	1
632	214	418	10	22	26	43	184	313	......	......	......	1	15	18
......	......	......	......	......	......	......	......	......	......	......	......	......	......	......
62	60	2	30	25	......	1	......	1	3	2	......	......	......	......
146	40	106	1	......	2	4	41	67	......	1	2	4	15	9
264	205	59	2	......	5	3	20	53	7	6	9	7	62	90

lso 5 Indians.
lso 2 Indians.

(*g*) Also 5 Japanese
(*h*) Also 4 Indians.

TABLE XXVII.—*Population, School Attendance, and Illiteracy of Fifty Principal Cities—1870*—Continued.

Cities.	Population: Total.	Population: Native.	Population: Foreign-born.	Population: White.	Population: Colored.	Attended school: Total.	Attended school: Native.	Attended school: Foreign-born.	Attended school: White: Male.	Attended school: White: Female.	Attended school: Colored: Male.	Attended school: Colored: Female.
8. *Cincinnati*—Con'd.												
23d ward	2357	1465	892	2340	17	564	536	28	280	284	.....	.....
24th ward	1421	1125	296	1421	.....	341	335	6	164	177	.....	.....
ADDITION OF MAY 16, 1870. (a)	1446	977	469	1365	b80	346	332	14	170	153	15	8
Do	484	321	163	483	1	828	795	33	400	427	1	.....
Do	859	618	241	818	41	952	914	38	430	491	2	.....
Do	4602	2875	1727	4552	50	774	739	35	439	320	10	5
Do	4108	2747	1361	4025	83	311	297	14	153	147	4	7
Do	2908	1884	1024	2821	87	1	1	.....	1	.....	.....	.....
Do	1546	1064	482	1459	87	166	165	1	90	75	1	.....
9. *New Orleans*	191418	142943	48475	140923	c50456	28063	27568	495	11661	11377	2446	2579
1st ward	13368	9906	3462	11132	2236	2436	2373	63	1065	1167	96	108
2d ward	18042	13046	4996	14519	3523	3036	2979	57	1236	1571	95	134
3d ward	25146	18430	6716	16914	e8229	3474	3444	30	1323	1305	368	456
4th ward	12921	9367	3554	9083	f3835	1891	1873	18	888	682	175	146
5th ward	17905	12583	5322	12324	g5578	2705	2606	99	1018	1047	305	335
6th ward	11807	8807	3000	8068	3739	1522	1491	31	507	558	168	199
7th ward	18488	15015	3473	10699	h7771	2657	2611	46	880	804	507	466
8th ward	10254	7312	2942	8129	2125	1751	1711	40	741	720	154	136
9th ward	11994	8454	3540	10442	1552	1514	1487	27	799	634	42	38
10th ward	19157	14479	4678	15913	i3236	2683	2648	35	1999	1102	152	130
11th ward	14681	11654	3027	12188	2493	2612	2581	31	1176	1176	112	148
12th ward	4804	3685	1119	3765	1039	38	38	.....	15	20	1	2
13th ward	4594	3853	741	3023	1571	580	570	10	186	237	68	89
14th ward	1438	1232	206	922	516	86	86	.....	38	32	10	6
5th district	6819	5720	1099	3802	j3013	1078	1070	8	400	322	173	183
10. *San Francisco*	149473	75754	73719	136059	k1330	l23714	21972	1742	11855	11613	68	66
1st ward	10767	4316	6451	10385	k77	1030	966	64	518	512	.....	.....
2d ward	11831	6069	5762	11359	k144	2239	2091	148	1095	1131	7	6
3d ward	2964	945	2019	2400	k13	136	117	19	66	68	2	.....
4th ward	16555	5527	11028	10284	k619	1682	1490	192	814	790	33	36
5th ward	2813	1671	1142	2758	k3	85	80	5	55	30	.....	.....
6th ward	9400	3953	5447	6139	k212	1109	944	165	492	592	11	16
7th ward	10379	5179	5200	10228	k13	1336	1250	86	669	664	1	2
8th ward	16503	9474	7029	16006	k88	3043	2930	113	1475	1567	1	.....
9th ward	10689	5965	4724	10420	k49	1954	1760	194	948	1004	2	.....
10th ward	22325	12366	9959	31985	k48	3900	3642	258	1940	1947	2	2
11th ward	22666	12853	9813	21825	k43	4600	4268	332	2446	2127	9	4
12th ward	12581	7436	5145	12270	k21	2600	2434	166	1337	1262	.....	.....
11. *Buffalo*	117714	71477	46237	117018	696	19501	17970	1531	9620	9621	30	30
1st ward	12966	7035	5931	12962	4	2729	2402	327	1296	1432	.....	1
2d ward	8232	5798	2434	8193	39	1168	1108	60	595	567	4	2
3d ward	9411	5916	3495	9377	34	2126	1907	219	1075	1045	2	4
4th ward	8021	4943	3078	7796	225	1389	1326	63	667	692	13	17
5th ward (a)	16838	9592	7246	16670	168	.....	.....	.....	.....	.....	.....	.....
6th ward	11949	6754	5195	11861	88	2616	2491	125	1351	1253	8	4
7th ward	13624	7596	6028	13601	20	2570	2362	208	1344	1226	.....	.....
8th ward	7037	3941	3096	7003	34	441	402	39	213	228	.....	.....
9th ward	6054	4358	1696	6040	14	947	909	38	478	468	.....	1
10th ward	9066	6603	2463	9041	25	1822	1738	84	872	950	.....	.....
11th ward	6738	4200	2538	6722	16	1690	1508	182	835	854	.....	1
12th ward	5280	3158	2122	5265	15	1133	1001	132	643	487	2	.....
13th ward	2498	1583	915	2484	14	870	816	54	431	419	.....	.....

(a) See notes to Table III, page 232.
(b) Also 1 Indian.
(c) Also 16 Indians and 23 Chinese.
(d) Including 16 Chinese and 11 Indians.
(e) Also 3 Chinese.
(f) Also 3 Indians.
(g) Also 1 Indian and 2 Chinese.
(h) Also 4 Indians and 14 Chinese.
(i) Also 8 Indians.
(j) Also 4 Chinese.

E XXVII.—*Population, School Attendance, and Illiteracy of Fifty Principal Cities*—1870—Continued.

CANNOT WRITE.														
			White.						Colored.					
			10 to 15.		15 to 21.		21 and over.		10 to 15.		15 to 21.		21 and over.	
Total.	Native.	Foreign-born.	M.	F.	M.	F.	M.	F.	M.	F.	M.	F.	M.	F.
128	26	102	2	......	3	5	35	78	......	......	....	1	2	2
111	43	68	1	......	1	5	35	69	......	......	....	......	......	......
107	32	75	......	......	2	5	22	56	......	......	1	1	9	10
107	30	77	......	......	1	1	34	57	......	3	1	......	4	6
223	71	152	2	......	5	2	64	110	2	2	....	4	17	15
50	15	35	......	......	4	1	27	11	......	......	1	2	1	3
96	24	72	......	1	1	9	16	46	......	......	1	2	13	7
......	......	......	......	......	......	......	......	......	......	......	....	......	......	......
57	38	19	3	1	......	2	11	14	3	1	4	......	10	8
*d*31826	26376	5450	292	340	214	358	1947	3764	639	805	852	2035	8154	12390
1855	1271	584	7	16	16	33	187	438	21	34	24	85	384	600
2403	2109	294	5	6	7	21	79	251	39	53	58	165	688	1031
6350	5280	1070	96	86	52	76	370	784	145	167	168	341	1679	2381
2427	2224	203	10	10	14	22	88	179	65	67	82	250	601	1038
3878	2853	1025	26	36	35	39	419	575	53	82	102	277	729	1503
2194	1813	381	52	61	11	42	108	242	63	90	49	152	387	937
4353	3664	689	42	54	37	49	270	385	126	143	133	289	1116	1693
577	518	59	1	1	2	6	28	43	......	......	7	22	229	238
889	541	348	7	7	20	22	164	212	4	9	18	48	191	187
2015	1734	281	24	26	2	20	66	216	56	76	68	148	512	799
1227	942	285	......	3	2	7	44	280	12	24	19	62	284	490
520	520	......	2	......	1	1	1	1	9	4	17	39	189	256
1048	900	148	10	16	3	8	79	109	26	41	26	40	302	388
344	297	47	10	18	9	10	28	27	16	13	12	18	100	83
1746	1710	36	......	......	3	2	16	22	4	2	69	99	763	766
*m*8453	509	7944	48	46	121	139	3049	4110	6	......	8	11	165	131
1318	37	1281	12	15	19	9	765	351	......	......	2	......	13	......
602	12	590	6	2	14	13	160	366	......	......	....	......	1	......
182	10	172	1	......	3	3	125	48	......	......	....	......	......	......
1726	242	1484	1	3	37	47	687	704	......	......	3	8	134	101
131	15	116	1	......	6	3	98	23	......	......	....	......	......	......
134	24	110	......	2	1	5	10	88	......	......	1	1	6	13
702	13	689	......	......	2	2	230	419	......	......	1	......	......	3
722	15	707	1	1	......	16	68	445	......	......	1	2	3	9
297	6	291	1	......	1	......	79	215	......	......	....	......	......	1
866	34	832	5	7	7	20	171	573	......	......	....	......	1	1
1238	77	1161	17	13	25	9	504	535	6	......	....	......	5	......
535	24	511	3	3	6	12	153	343	......	......	....	......	2	3
4293	439	3854	41	36	84	137	1439	2445	......	......	2	5	59	45
937	5	932	1	......	2	4	451	479	......	......	....	......	......	......
210	4	206	......	1	......	15	63	128	......	......	....	......	1	......
459	46	413	6	4	9	15	122	292	......	......	....	1	6	4
182	61	121	2	1	3	16	26	83	......	......	1	2	27	21
......	......	......	......	......	......	......	......	......	......	......	....	......	......	......
310	57	253	3	3	6	5	115	147	......	......	1	......	18	12
567	37	530	4	6	12	12	187	345	......	......	....	......	......	1
735	152	583	16	16	35	46	222	393	......	......	....	......	4	3
103	12	91	3	1	2	6	11	77	......	......	....	2	......	1
107	2	105	......	1	......	4	8	94	......	......	....	......	......	......
193	1	192	......	......	1	......	52	140	......	......	....	......	......	......
311	51	260	6	3	11	11	107	167	......	......	....	......	3	3
179	11	168	......	......	3	3	73	100	......	......	....	......	......	......

Also 12,022 Chinese, 8 Japanese, 54 Indians, as follows: 1st ward, 305 Chinese; 2d ward, 323 Chi- Indians; 3d ward, 551 Chinese; 4th ward, 5,649 Chinese, 1 Japanese, 2 Indians; 5th ward, 52 Chi- 6th ward, 3,041 Chinese, 1 Japanese, 7 Indians; 7th ward, 135 Chinese, 3 Indians; 8th ward, 401 se, 3 Japanese, 5 Indians; 9th ward, 212 Chinese, 8 Indians; 10th ward, 284 Chinese, 1 Japanese, 7 s; 11th ward, 781 Chinese, 1 Japanese, 16 Indians; 12th ward, 288 Chinese, 1 Japanese, 1 Indian.

Including 104 Chinese and 8 Indians.

Including 607 *Chinese, 1 Japanese,* and 11 Indians.

(*n*) School attendance and illiteracy not returned by the assistant marshal.

TABLE XXVII.—*Population, School Attendance, and Illiteracy of Fifty Principal Cities—* 1870—Continued.

Cities.	Population.					Attended school.						
									White.		Colored.	
	Total.	Native.	Foreign-born.	White.	Colored.	Total.	Native.	Foreign-born.	Male.	Female.	Male.	Female.
12. *Washington*	109199	95442	13757	73731	a35455	16786	16459	327	6201	6322	2019	2244
1st ward	16652	14526	2126	9294	b7357	2255	2175	80	727	692	413	423
2d ward	18474	16479	1995	11744	c6718	2669	2628	41	819	1015	399	436
3d ward	15527	13585	1942	11343	4184	2235	2224	11	858	898	247	232
4th ward	18900	15428	3472	14424	4476	2854	2755	99	1189	1180	210	275
5th ward	10621	9421	1200	7332	3289	1770	1740	30	728	651	187	204
6th ward	11071	9968	1103	8337	2734	1947	1923	24	821	830	139	157
7th ward	17954	16035	1919	11257	6697	3056	3014	42	1050	1056	434	517
13. *Newark*	105059	69175	35884	103267	d1789	e17319	16275	1044	8639	8537	62	80
1st ward	9599	7584	2015	9404	195	1472	1425	47	730	728	10	4
2d ward	7334	5058	2276	7087	f245	1190	1122	68	552	620	4	13
3d ward	7624	5885	1739	7178	146	1199	1166	33	581	613	3	2
4th ward	5890	3882	2008	5786	104	728	696	32	376	345	5	2
5th ward	8771	5692	3079	8717	54	1518	1413	105	730	784	2	2
6th ward	10240	6018	4222	10119	121	2008	1850	158	1021	973	4	10
7th ward	11987	7443	4544	11874	113	2075	1944	131	1053	1011	6	5
8th ward	6840	4556	2282	6743	b96	1017	950	67	525	480	3	9
9th ward	5458	4391	1067	5344	114	766	759	7	378	385	1	2
10th ward	9229	6455	2771	9039	190	1852	1749	103	901	932	6	13
11th ward	3677	2393	1284	3651	26	689	650	39	360	325	2	2
12th ward	4582	2416	2166	4564	18	635	604	31	311	324	.....	.....
13th ward	13828	7400	6428	13461	367	2170	1947	223	1121	1017	16	16
14. *Louisville*	100753	75085	25668	85796	b14956	15928	15475	453	7067	7700	527	634
1st ward	7439	5164	2275	7128	311	1602	1559	43	768	826	5	3
2d ward	8375	5507	2868	8019	356	1727	1654	73	754	952	12	9
3d ward	9522	6399	3123	8933	589	1777	1709	68	891	803	50	33
4th ward	9387	6922	2465	7519	1868	1184	1154	30	503	511	78	92
5th ward	10010	7733	2277	7638	2372	1639	1622	17	660	753	97	129
6th ward	6042	5083	959	4689	1353	966	939	27	490	425	17	34
7th ward	5341	4040	1301	4458	883	510	491	19	241	238	22	9
8th ward	6734	5286	1448	5440	b1293	1208	1164	44	429	657	36	86
9th ward	7830	6361	1469	5668	2162	1093	1083	10	451	451	89	102
10th ward	11416	8783	2633	9161	2255	1317	1279	38	541	615	77	84
11th ward	13470	9867	3603	12292	1178	2112	2051	61	1002	1032	35	43
12th ward	5187	3940	1247	4851	336	793	770	23	337	437	9	10
15. *Cleveland*	92829	54014	38815	91535	b1293	15854	13698	2156	7728	7990	65	71
1st ward	8521	4963	3558	8148	b372	1364	1161	203	630	690	22	22
2d ward	5618	4021	1597	5529	89	776	722	54	355	408	3	10
3d ward	3290	2349	941	3268	22	210	199	11	90	120	.....	.....
4th ward	9850	6361	3489	9658	192	1767	1677	90	819	919	13	16
5th ward	9725	5457	4268	9698	27	1870	1614	256	936	931	1	2
6th ward	13324	7491	5833	12807	517	1478	1299	179	678	761	22	17
7th ward	5658	2818	2840	5651	7	1232	977	255	605	625	1	1
8th ward	5416	2553	2863	5414	2	1176	870	306	599	577	.....	.....
9th ward	5940	3773	2167	5933	7	1129	986	143	517	612	.....	.....
10th ward	6590	4292	2298	6562	28	1392	1259	133	669	720	1	2
11th ward	8059	4406	3653	8034	25	1679	1522	157	937	739	2	1
12th ward	3812	1777	2035	3812	....	720	549	171	388	332	.....	.....
13th ward	3687	1947	1740	3682	5	693	567	126	345	348	.....	.....
14th ward	1538	525	1013	1538	....	81	50	31	32	49	.....	.....
15th ward	1801	1281	520	1801	....	287	246	41	128	159	.....	.....
16. *Pittsburgh*	86076	58254	27822	84061	2015	14905	13883	1022	7225	7419	126	135
1st ward	4336	2719	1617	4297	39	808	742	66	408	393	2	3
2d ward	3061	2199	862	2965	96	399	387	12	184	214	1	.....
3d ward	2652	1560	1092	2590	62	455	414	41	219	230	3	3
4th ward	3329	2393	936	3303	26	192	173	19	96	92	3	1

(a) Also 13 Indians. (b) Also 1 Indian. (c) Also 12 Indians. (d) Also 1 Indian and 2 Chinese.

XXVII.—*Population, School Attendance, and Illiteracy of Fifty Principal Cities*—1870—Continued.

CANNOT WRITE.

Total.	Native.	Foreign-born.	White. 10 to 15. M.	White. 10 to 15. F.	White. 15 to 21. M.	White. 15 to 21. F.	White. 21 and over. M.	White. 21 and over. F.	Colored. 10 to 15. M.	Colored. 10 to 15. F.	Colored. 15 to 21. M.	Colored. 15 to 21. F.	Colored. 21 and over. M.	Colored. 21 and over. F.
22888	**21130**	**1758**	**256**	**232**	**90**	**221**	**865**	**1918**	**770**	**912**	**874**	**1854**	**6011**	**8885**
4563	4179	384	77	50	16	34	169	366	207	219	174	301	1242	1708
3217	3146	71	3	4	2	23	25	105	12	30	107	294	1004	1608
2873	2590	283	6	13	7	49	76	301	47	100	77	301	686	1210
3318	2747	571	49	50	7	34	168	376	137	148	130	262	708	1240
1823	1798	25	8	2	1	2	16	32	58	72	100	191	569	772
2655	2452	203	73	71	37	49	228	432	129	134	95	193	547	667
4439	4218	221	40	33	20	30	183	306	180	209	191	312	1255	1680
3521	**886**	**2635**	**103**	**115**	**89**	**161**	**821**	**1893**	**7**	**10**	**13**	**22**	**117**	**170**
129	19	110	....	1	1	19	8	91	....	....	....	1	3	5
80	19	61	5	10	5	8	1	51	....	....	....	....	....	....
203	50	153	4	3	....	16	57	98	....	....	....	4	5	16
328	81	247	16	21	8	37	69	158	....	1	3	1	12	8
47	15	32	8	7	3	2	12	15	....	....	....	....	....	....
309	81	228	....	5	5	4	61	178	....	3	1	3	26	23
1026	126	900	25	24	24	28	274	617	1	1	3	1	14	14
2	2	....	....	....	....	1	1	....	....	....	....	....	....	....
58	6	52	....	....	2	6	16	29	....	....	....	1	....	4
590	293	297	27	25	19	15	145	283	5	2	9	4	20	43
327	55	272	9	11	13	20	86	182	1	1	1	....	1	2
3	3	....	1	1	1	....	....	....	....	....	....	....	....	....
419	136	283	8	7	8	11	91	191	....	2	3	7	36	55
14339	**11021**	**3318**	**311**	**300**	**198**	**364**	**1503**	**2638**	**460**	**553**	**495**	**853**	**2641**	**4003**
889	523	366	42	39	38	30	190	337	16	17	17	15	78	70
175	170	5	2	3	1	1	6	13	7	5	6	13	47	71
446	369	77	1	4	2	12	47	77	4	8	15	26	106	144
1660	1344	316	14	20	15	26	153	249	68	58	59	92	391	516
1823	1518	305	8	9	12	53	141	283	56	50	70	120	384	637
1079	1003	76	54	30	11	16	50	63	51	97	51	88	227	341
1061	752	309	21	26	16	42	190	174	22	34	53	83	190	250
1280	977	303	31	38	15	52	103	214	39	60	39	97	214	378
1778	1465	313	25	40	16	40	122	232	68	73	61	122	375	604
1807	1500	307	48	41	11	29	143	237	77	86	85	121	358	571
1496	965	531	33	25	32	36	235	459	45	49	24	57	192	309
845	435	410	32	25	29	27	193	320	7	16	16	19	79	62
(g)4420	**539**	**3881**	**66**	**73**	**101**	**148**	**1429**	**2357**	**3**	**3**	**11**	**16**	**105**	**107**
649	155	494	3	4	16	29	101	309	3	2	9	9	57	46
31	4	27	....	1	....	11	1	18	....	....	....	....	....	....
15	1	14	....	....	....	1	6	8	....	....	....	....	....	....
30	....	30	....	....	....	7	1	22	....	....	....	....	....	....
785	116	669	29	33	23	30	225	439	....	....	....	....	1	5
297	124	173	10	5	7	11	61	111	....	1	1	5	39	46
505	10	495	1	1	9	7	226	260	....	....	....	....	1	....
1094	45	1049	4	11	26	20	417	616	....	....	....	....	....	....
454	42	412	11	11	16	17	173	221	....	....	1	1	3	....
129	6	123	....	....	1	3	33	88	....	....	....	1	1	2
293	24	269	3	3	2	3	84	187	....	....	....	....	3	8
41	9	32	4	1	....	4	9	21	....	....	....	....	....	....
38	1	37	....	....	....	2	13	23	....	....	....	....	....	....
58	1	57	1	3	1	2	19	32	....	....	....	....	....	....
1	1	....	....	....	....	1	....	....	....	....	....	....	....	....
4575	**827**	**3748**	**101**	**70**	**141**	**223**	**1534**	**2177**	**3**	**6**	**7**	**17**	**158**	**138**
668	98	570	15	9	24	57	203	352	1	....	....	2	....	5
97	23	74	1	4	6	23	8	46	1	1	1	....	3	3
76	22	54	1	....	3	5	14	43	....	....	1	1	3	5
192	30	162	4	6	3	29	27	123	....	....	....	....	....	....

(e) Including 1 Chinese. (f) Also 2 Chinese. (g) Including 1 Indian.

TABLE XXVII.—*Population, School Attendance, and Illiteracy of Fifty Principal Cities—1870*—Continued.

Cities.	POPULATION.					ATTENDED SCHOOL.						
									White.		Colored.	
	Total.	Native.	Foreign-born.	White.	Colored.	Total.	Native.	Foreign-born.	Male.	Female.	Male.	Female.
16. *Pittsburgh—Continued.*												
5th ward	4901	2875	2026	4803	98	406	370	36	194	202	4	6
6th ward	7847	5157	2690	7829	18	825	775	50	419	406	....	....
7th ward	4778	3473	1305	4567	211	865	823	42	422	426	6	11
8th ward	5485	4313	1172	4808	677	1191	1120	71	553	534	51	53
9th ward	4935	2786	2149	4902	33	814	735	79	396	418	....	....
10th ward	3198	1910	1288	3197	1	584	525	59	274	310	....	....
11th ward	4859	3674	1185	4463	396	1213	1157	56	547	577	43	46
12th ward	6697	4154	2543	6696	1	1128	986	142	523	605	....	....
13th ward	3329	2372	957	3261	68	817	754	63	423	381	7	6
14th ward	4703	3017	1686	4600	103	893	823	70	446	444	1	2
15th ward	3290	2135	1155	3286	4	642	620	22	323	319	....	....
16th ward	3090	1862	1228	3082	8	557	543	14	284	273	....	....
17th ward	5161	3689	1472	5108	53	1028	994	34	506	518	2	2
18th ward	822	506	316	821	1	152	137	15	67	85	....	....
19th ward	2443	1894	549	2424	19	460	427	33	227	232	....	1
20th ward	2272	1820	452	2216	56	418	392	26	197	218	2	1
21st ward	2502	1931	571	2470	32	502	457	45	252	249	1	....
22d ward	987	774	213	981	6	235	229	6	114	121	....	....
23d ward	1399	1041	358	1392	7	321	300	21	151	170	....	....
17. *Jersey City*	82546	50711	31835	81840	*a*705	13314	11962	1352	6559	6674	43	38
1st ward	5836	3434	2402	5830	26	751	661	90	358	391	1	1
2d ward	6524	3431	3093	6503	21	1025	875	150	508	515	2	....
3d ward	6682	4576	2106	6666	16	1183	1087	96	542	640	1	....
4th ward	7664	5275	2389	7533	131	634	598	36	327	298	6	3
5th ward	6490	4569	1921	6434	56	1103	1023	80	523	573	3	4
6th ward	8380	4360	4020	8234	146	1587	1346	241	769	794	9	15
7th ward	3501	1812	1689	3500	1	450	394	56	221	229	....	....
8th ward	2790	1541	1249	2789	1	343	302	41	187	156	....	....
9th ward	4939	3088	1851	4888	51	714	651	63	349	363	1	1
10th ward	3415	2112	1303	3413	2	666	599	67	336	330	....	....
11th ward	7272	4250	3022	7267	5	1363	1227	136	683	679	1	....
12th ward	5407	3043	2364	5398	9	1044	933	111	539	505	....	....
13th ward	4793	3248	1545	4672	121	942	852	90	483	436	11	12
14th ward	3360	2245	1115	3277	*a*82	607	568	39	284	313	8	2
15th ward	2393	1774	619	2383	10	382	365	17	201	181	....	....
16th ward	3080	1933	1147	3053	27	520	481	39	249	271	....	....
18. *Detroit*	79577	44196	35381	77338	*b*2235	12664	10728	1936	6138	6274	123	129
1st ward	4854	2936	1918	4771	83	598	554	44	308	288	2	....
2d ward	1640	918	722	1591	49	192	173	19	105	83	4	....
3d ward	3996	2311	1685	3813	183	667	610	57	285	370	5	7
4th ward	5595	3060	2535	5131	464	1085	928	157	526	485	37	37
5th ward	9350	6072	3278	9296	54	1227	1097	130	567	653	2	5
6th ward	14276	8122	6154	13589	*b*683	2258	1938	320	1064	1149	20	25
7th ward	8679	4656	4023	8126	553	1498	1271	227	693	707	46	52
8th ward	7582	4329	3253	7575	7	1322	1126	196	624	696	2	....
9th ward	11734	6297	5437	11702	32	2324	1867	457	1140	1184	....	....
10th ward	11871	5495	6376	11744	127	1493	1164	329	826	659	5	3
19. *Milwaukee*	71440	37667	33773	71263	*a*176	14432	12609	1823	7136	7220	5	11
1st ward	7994	4379	3615	7988	*a*5	1860	1671	189	901	956	1	2
2d ward	8360	3991	4369	8354	6	1509	1319	190	765	744	....	....
3d ward	6157	3568	2589	6146	11	1303	1205	98	623	680	....	....
4th ward	7636	5095	2541	7508	128	1323	1240	83	643	670	4	6
5th ward	8725	4656	4069	8722	3	1731	1502	229	868	863	....	....
6th ward	7374	3459	3915	7374	....	1468	1245	223	746	722	....	....
7th ward	7032	4526	2506	7010	22	1593	1516	77	767	823	....	3
8th ward	6625	2940	3685	6624	1	1182	937	245	589	593	....	....
9th ward	11537	5053	6484	11537	....	2463	1974	489	1294	1169	....	....

(*a*) Also 1 Indian. (*b*) Also 4 Indians. (*c*) Including 2 Indians.

TABLE XXVII.—*Population, School Attendance, and Illiteracy of Fifty Principal Cities—1870*—Continued.

Cannot read—10 and over.	CANNOT WRITE.														
	Total.	Native.	Foreign-born.	White.						Colored.					
				10 to 15.		15 to 21.		21 and over.		10 to 15.		15 to 21.		21 and over.	
				M.	F.	M.	F.	M.	F.	M.	F.	M.	F.	M.	F.
470	526	35	491	13	14	15	16	193	273	......	1	......	......	......	1
482	*484	25	459	9	4	5	12	247	207	......	......	......	......	......	......
63	90	38	52	1	1	......	1	20	36	......	......	......	......	15	16
114	140	104	36	......	......	2	2	20	23	......	......	1	8	44	40
312	470	43	427	5	11	21	14	175	229	......	......	......	......	13	2
197	314	41	273	13	4	13	11	101	172	......	......	......	......	......	......
132	135	101	34	......	1	......	1	16	27	......	1	......	4	47	38
363	540	83	457	23	8	21	28	184	276	......	......	......	......	......	......
49	54	34	20	......	......	1	......	16	6	......	2	......	......	18	11
58	76	3	73	......	......	2	......	40	33	......	......	......	......	1	......
130	155	18	137	1	1	3	1	71	76	......	......	......	......	......	2
123	174	18	156	8	2	10	6	64	84	......	......	......	......	......	......
164	201	50	151	6	2	9	5	77	89	......	......	1	2	4	6
37	47	2	45	......	1	2	1	19	24	......	......	......	......	......	......
6	9	5	4	......	......	......	1	2	4	......	......	......	......	2	......
21	33	15	18	1	......	......	3	8	12	......	......	1	......	2	6
71	89	39	50	......	2	1	7	27	39	1	1	2	......	6	3
4	4	......	4	......	......	......	......	2	2	......	......	......	......	......	......
1	1	......	1	......	......	......	......	......	1	......	......	......	......	......	......
3675	4969	852	4117	178	183	72	272	1421	2684	......	10	7	18	47	77
349	371	47	324	19	10	11	20	109	198	......	......	......	1	1	2
455	472	19	453	6	5	5	15	181	257	......	......	......	1	2	......
245	244	13	231	......	2	1	36	44	154	......	1	......	2	......	4
257	370	28	342	1	9	7	19	82	236	......	3	1	1	3	8
326	464	54	410	......	2	3	36	123	288	......	2	......	4	1	5
593	953	273	680	22	21	21	28	326	521	......	2	1	......	5	6
13	14	......	14	......	......	......	3	3	8	......	......	......	......	......	......
44	54	1	53	......	......	......	2	15	37	......	......	......	......	......	......
71	120	12	108	2	2	5	4	45	56	......	......	1	......	3	2
269	372	89	283	41	42	8	14	98	168	......	......	1	......	......	......
98	150	37	113	17	10	......	9	34	77	......	......	1	1	......	1
269	379	144	235	62	68	5	19	70	146	......	......	......	......	1	2
253	350	44	306	......	2	1	21	95	195	......	......	1	2	12	21
215	313	48	265	......	3	1	24	96	154	......	1	......	1	13	20
53	85	8	77	......	3	1	5	21	52	......	......	......	1	......	2
165	258	35	223	2	4	3	17	79	137	......	1	1	4	6	4
4234	c5425	1045	4380	79	77	174	323	1561	2549	9	15	25	47	250	305
306	350	37	313	4	1	12	23	132	156	1	......	1	1	5	14
168	175	16	159	......	......	7	17	52	86	2	......	1	1	7	2
130	190	56	134	1	3	8	20	25	74	......	2	4	8	23	22
209	278	145	133	2	5	7	12	38	73	4	3	1	5	54	74
429	745	72	673	14	22	20	92	173	395	......	3	3	1	8	14
891	1035	352	683	10	11	50	47	277	398	1	7	12	20	107	93
516	518	168	350	1	3	18	25	154	174	......	......	3	10	49	81
340	490	22	468	6	5	3	9	135	329	......	......	......	1	1	1
753	999	92	907	18	15	20	42	316	588	......	......	......	......	......	......
492	645	85	560	23	12	29	36	259	276	1	......	......	......	5	4
1149	1709	108	1594	9	7	35	55	527	1028	1	......	5	2	18	15
213	247	15	232	1	3	5	19	78	141	......	......	......	......	......	......
15	26	5	21	1	1	2	1	7	14	......	......	......	......	......	......
11	10	5	5	4	......	2	2	......	1	......	......	......	......	......	1
229	303	52	251	......	......	5	5	112	141	1	......	5	2	18	14
247	447	19	428	2	2	12	20	104	307	......	......	......	......	......	......
232	245	4	241	......	......	4	1	114	126	......	......	......	......	......	......
1	2	1	1	......	......	......	2	......	......	......	......	......	......	......	......
80	117	4	113	......	......	2	3	40	72	......	......	......	......	......	......
112	305	3	302	1	1	3	2	72	226	......	......	......	......	......	......

TABLE XXVII.—*Population, School Attendance, and Illiteracy of Fifty Principal Cities—1870*—Continued.

Cities.	POPULATION.					ATTENDED SCHOOL.						
									White.		Colored.	
	Total.	Native.	Foreign-born.	White.	Colored.	Total.	Native.	Foreign-born.	Male.	Female.	Male.	Female.
20. *Albany.*(a)	69422	47215	22207	68658	764	10737	10240	497	5179	5307	25	26
1st ward	10884	6372	4512	10801	83	2120	1988	132	1092	1013	7	8
2d ward	6048	4125	1923	6012	36	1128	1078	50	559	568	1	.....
3d ward	4153	3044	1109	4118	35	567	553	14	267	299	.....	1
4th ward	3458	2514	944	3439	19	570	564	6	261	307	1	1
5th ward	1381	916	465	1342	39	100	100	.....	48	52	.....	.....
6th ward	3113	2262	851	3087	26	458	446	12	206	251	1	.....
7th ward	6540	4168	2372	6535	5	1070	1025	45	498	571	1	.....
8th ward (b)	10961	7634	3327	10789	172	.....	.....	.....	.....	.....	.....	.....
9th ward	10018	6439	3579	9949	69	2124	1991	133	1058	1059	2	5
10th ward	12866	9741	3125	12586	280	2600	2495	105	1190	1387	12	11
21. *Providence*	68904	51727	17177	66320	c2559	d11773	11324	449	5868	5541	177	186
1st ward	11927	8159	3768	11446	e480	1962	1863	99	963	927	38	34
2d ward	4607	3592	1015	4081	526	823	810	13	447	278	46	32
3d ward	8912	6416	2496	8658	f245	1242	1171	71	638	558	25	20
4th ward	5504	4110	1394	5424	80	751	729	22	382	364	3	2
5th ward	8077	5832	2245	8020	57	1395	1342	53	665	725	3	2
6th ward	5844	4995	849	5446	g390	912	880	32	441	423	25	21
7th ward	7457	5892	1565	7314	h136	1436	1422	14	685	735	7	9
8th ward	7838	6135	1703	7594	244	1367	1314	53	696	654	8	9
9th ward	8738	6596	2142	8337	401	1885	1793	92	951	877	22	35
22. *Rochester*	62386	41202	21184	61959	427	12586	11802	784	6360	6177	30	19
1st ward	2314	1565	749	2285	29	391	375	16	198	190	3	.....
2d ward	3680	2401	1279	3680	.....	664	609	55	278	386	.....	.....
3d ward	4954	3651	1303	4860	94	1011	971	40	512	494	2	3
4th ward	3487	2592	895	3469	18	631	616	15	333	296	2	.....
5th ward	5718	3661	2057	5700	12	1282	1212	70	659	623	.....	.....
6th ward	4044	2561	1483	4039	5	1004	958	46	471	533	.....	.....
7th ward	3446	2534	912	3396	50	469	445	24	224	242	1	2
8th ward	6757	4445	2312	6644	113	1724	1554	170	904	806	4	10
9th ward	5941	4060	1881	5926	15	1797	1653	144	1043	740	14	.....
10th ward	3310	2237	1073	3278	32	517	494	23	211	306	.....	.....
11th ward	5247	3158	2089	5247	.....	1084	1007	77	553	531	.....	.....
12th ward	4451	2933	1518	4414	37	663	640	21	313	343	4	3
13th ward	5046	2765	2281	5042	4	499	469	30	257	242	.....	.....
14th ward	3991	2639	1352	3973	18	850	799	51	404	445	.....	1
23. *Allegheny*	53180	37872	15308	52018	1162	10333	9846	487	4985	5196	67	85
1st ward	4729	3685	1044	4654	75	1045	1017	28	522	510	4	9
2d ward	9010	6873	2137	8866	144	1871	1800	71	876	981	5	9
3d ward	12507	8395	4112	11824	683	2476	2322	154	1170	1199	51	56
4th ward	10302	7198	3104	10196	106	1617	1572	45	817	794	1	5
5th ward	4457	3694	763	4386	71	782	752	30	359	418	3	2
6th ward	4693	3546	1147	4650	43	909	890	19	435	471	2	1
7th ward	5300	3083	2217	5263	37	1156	1064	92	578	574	1	3
8th ward	2182	1398	784	2179	3	477	429	48	228	249	.....	.....
24. *Richmond*	51038	47260	3778	27928	23110	4616	4582	34	1610	1652	526	828
Clay ward	6101	5654	447	3469	2632	642	642	.....	236	216	73	117
Jefferson ward	13565	12476	1089	7406	6159	910	910	.....	317	353	89	151
Madison ward	11802	10760	1042	6741	5061	1355	1330	25	474	473	145	263
Marshall ward	5276	4976	300	2857	2419	362	362	.....	136	127	43	56
Monroe ward	14294	13394	900	7455	6839	1347	1338	9	447	483	176	241

(a) For an aggregate population of 69,422, being the city as bounded when consisting of ten wards.

(b) School attendance and illiteracy not returned by the assistant marshal.

XXVII.—*Population, School Attendance, and Illiteracy of Fifty Principal Cities*—1870—Continued.

CANNOT WRITE.

Total.	Native.	Foreign-born.	White.						Colored.					
			10 to 15.		15 to 21.		21 and over.		10 to 15.		15 to 21.		21 and over.	
			M.	F.	M.	F.	M.	F.	M.	F.	M.	F.	M.	F.
3736	753	2983	86	88	105	136	1149	2011	2	1	15	7	90	46
1350	211	1139	40	39	34	24	431	742	2	1	...	3	14	20
384	20	364	4	2	1	13	113	249	...	...	...	...	...	2
68	26	42	1	5	6	21	7	28	...	...	...	...	...	...
48	7	41	...	2	1	9	4	30	...	...	...	...	1	1
5	...	5	...	...	...	...	...	5	...	...	...	...	...	...
67	14	53	2	1	2	3	22	37	...	...	...	...	...	...
492	65	427	20	22	10	16	182	242	...	...	...	...	...	...
...	...	...	...	...	...	...	...	...	...	...	...	...	...	...
674	210	464	18	13	28	32	201	370	...	...	...	...	3	9
648	200	448	1	4	23	18	189	308	...	...	15	4	72	14
d5705	934	4771	177	179	117	195	1481	3170	5	8	25	20	140	187
867	107	760	3	3	8	22	259	491	...	...	3	4	34	39
122	9	113	...	1	...	4	9	99	...	...	...	...	2	7
1335	320	1015	102	69	44	36	347	678	4	2	3	4	22	24
707	68	639	8	18	17	35	187	420	...	1	1	...	9	11
800	36	764	2	8	6	30	281	464	...	...	...	...	1	8
214	45	169	1	...	...	7	37	128	1	...	2	3	12	23
59	11	48	4	6	1	1	21	24	...	...	...	...	1	1
775	168	607	37	59	23	41	131	411	...	4	3	3	27	36
826	170	656	20	15	18	19	209	455	...	1	13	6	32	38
1716	364	1352	109	100	42	75	426	916	4	2	3	7	13	19
74	35	39	6	6	3	11	14	22	4	1	1	1	3	2
126	114	12	59	56	1	1	2	7	...	...	...	...	...	...
39	7	32	...	1	...	...	11	23	...	...	...	...	1	3
24	10	14	2	...	2	2	8	9	...	...	...	...	1	...
173	13	160	...	6	1	17	24	121	...	...	...	3	1	...
6	4	2	...	1	1	2	...	1	...	...	...	...	...	1
109	24	85	1	2	2	5	19	71	...	1	1	2	2	3
132	11	121	1	...	4	...	35	87	...	...	...	...	3	2
98	...	98	...	...	...	3	33	62	...	...	...	...	...	...
144	27	117	8	1	5	11	44	71	...	...	...	...	...	4
367	71	296	20	16	16	8	103	204	...	...	...	...	...	...
101	15	86	3	2	2	1	29	59	...	...	1	...	1	3
168	3	165	2	3	3	6	54	100	...	...	...	...	...	...
155	30	125	7	6	2	8	50	79	...	...	...	1	1	1
1197	575	622	30	26	54	82	218	468	3	2	20	25	127	142
173	36	137	...	1	3	20	23	105	...	...	1	3	8	9
258	101	157	6	7	18	9	82	98	1	...	6	...	15	16
452	317	135	8	12	21	20	50	125	1	1	12	11	79	94
92	30	62	2	1	4	3	26	53	...	...	...	...	1	2
89	41	48	1	...	1	11	8	39	...	1	...	6	11	11
77	20	57	...	...	...	2	13	38	...	...	...	4	11	9
25	16	9	6	4	...	7	1	2	1	...	1	1	1	1
31	14	17	7	1	7	1	6	8	...	...	...	...	1	...
16500	16122	378	112	108	65	89	372	582	626	700	794	1545	4984	6523
1942	1824	118	31	23	19	14	100	171	107	111	75	107	519	665
4546	4476	70	46	56	21	38	76	169	223	269	191	455	1259	1743
3378	3359	19	4	7	6	11	9	43	23	30	143	377	1071	1654
1925	1830	95	29	17	15	16	90	90	127	124	67	182	529	619
4709	4633	76	2	5	4	10	97	109	146	166	318	424	1606	1822

lso 25 Indians.
ncluding 1 Indian.

(e) Also 1 Indian.
(f) Also 9 Indians.

(g) Also 8 Indians.
(h) Also 7 Indians.

TABLE XXVII.—*Population, School Attendance, and Illiteracy of Fifty Principal Cities—1870*—Continued.

Cities.	POPULATION.					ATTENDED SCHOOL.						
									White.		Colored.	
	Total.	Native.	Foreign-born.	White.	Colored.	Total.	Native.	Foreign-born.	Male.	Female.	Male.	Female.
25. *New Haven*	50840	36484	14356	49090	a1749	10097	9648	449	5223	4874	98	101
1st ward	8943	7426	1517	7799	1144	2114	2066	48	1256	726	66	65
2d ward	5414	3931	1483	5319	a94	1097	1035	62	593	490	8	6
3d ward	11070	7201	3869	10806	264	2119	1958	161	1025	1066	13	15
4th ward	6331	4754	1577	6222	109	911	880	31	479	425	2	5
5th ward	8625	4910	3715	8611	14	1885	1811	74	935	947	2	1
6th ward	5201	4157	1044	5090	111	960	937	23	446	501	7	6
7th ward	3991	3169	822	3986	5	778	741	34	378	399	....	1
8th ward	1265	994	271	1257	8	233	217	16	111	120	....	2
26. *Charleston*	48956	44064	4892	22749	b26173	c7892	7858	34	2024	2018	1735	2111
1st ward	4132	3562	570	2314	a1817	716	705	11	206	237	115	158
2d ward	4751	4354	397	2167	a2583	655	653	2	169	200	107	179
3d ward	6114	5055	1059	3424	2690	943	933	10	290	296	173	184
4th ward	10691	9636	1055	4885	e5774	1279	1278	1	273	394	273	335
5th ward	6061	5504	557	2287	3774	1035	1027	8	214	180	295	346
6th ward	8785	8248	537	3470	5315	1842	1842	......	471	365	465	541
7th ward	3187	2870	317	2000	1187	473	471	2	147	163	75	88
8th ward	5235	4835	400	2202	3033	949	949	......	254	183	232	280
27. *Indianapolis*	48244	37587	10657	45309	f2931	8851	8479	372	4156	4236	195	264
1st ward	3813	3106	707	3680	133	689	671	18	308	374	2	5
2d ward	5915	4985	930	5559	356	1231	1214	17	609	558	38	96
3d ward	6258	5507	751	5392	g863	1188	1179	9	512	537	56	83
4th ward	5223	4498	725	4249	974	985	954	31	400	414	64	107
5th ward	6996	4839	2157	6778	a217	1333	1212	121	623	674	16	20
6th ward	4254	2921	1333	4198	56	646	615	31	309	332	1	4
7th ward	3797	2762	1035	3772	25	591	558	33	313	275	....	3
8th ward	6361	4716	1645	6224	137	1240	1166	74	611	609	8	12
9th ward	5627	4253	1374	5457	170	948	910	38	471	463	10	4
28. *Troy*	46465	30246	16219	46047	418	6463	6118	345	3077	3333	28	25
1st ward	3780	2569	1211	3593	187	432	416	16	210	205	6	11
2d ward	4201	3006	1195	4107	94	813	774	39	366	428	8	11
3d ward	2214	1617	597	2183	31	294	285	9	147	143	3	1
4th ward	3785	2920	865	3741	41	758	731	27	367	383	7	1
5th ward	3605	2513	1092	3599	6	490	452	38	230	260	....	....
6th ward (h)	3899	2160	1739	3892	7	......	......	......	......	......	....	....
7th ward	7095	4886	2209	7075	20	1309	1244	65	630	679	....	....
8th ward	7131	4089	3042	7113	18	1068	933	135	506	557	4	1
9th ward (h)	6433	3343	3090	6424	9	......	......	......	......	......	....	....
10th ward	4322	3143	1179	4317	5	1299	1283	16	621	678	....	....
29. *Syracuse*	43051	29061	13990	42616	435	8371	7748	623	4092	4240	19	20
1st ward	4074	2839	1235	4073	1	1123	1065	58	564	559	....	....
2d ward	7096	3969	3127	7081	15	1364	1269	95	677	687	....	....
3d ward	2986	1930	1056	2968	18	632	597	35	312	319	....	1
4th ward	7027	4516	2511	7012	15	1251	1124	127	609	641	....	1
5th ward	6326	4449	1877	6319	7	1451	1344	107	708	742	1	....
6th ward	4111	3209	902	4085	26	571	535	36	240	330	....	1
7th ward	7015	4724	2291	6915	100	1020	907	113	485	527	3	5
8th ward	4416	3425	991	4163	253	959	907	52	497	435	15	12
30. *Worcester*	41105	29159	11946	40588	d513	g7526	6850	676	3786	3685	26	26
1st ward	5069	3790	1219	4923	183	906	854	52	476	420	5	2
2d ward	3927	3179	748	3758	169	700	656	44	348	331	7	14

(a) Also 1 Indian.
(b) Also 34 Indians.
(c) Including 4 Indians.
(d) Including 2 Indians.
(e) Also 32 Indians.
(f) Also 4 Indians.

XXVII.—*Population, School Attendance, and Illiteracy of Fifty Principal Cities*—1870—Continued

CANNOT WRITE.

Total.	Native.	Foreign-born.	White.						Colored.					
			10 to 15.		15 to 21.		21 and over.		10 to 15.		15 to 21.		21 and over.	
			M.	F.	M.	F.	M.	F.	M.	F.	M.	F.	M.	F.
2837	428	2409	56	50	29	101	447	1906	4	2	6	11	85	140
424	217	207	2	1	8	13	30	164	4	1	6	10	75	110
123	13	110	......	......	......	7	17	86	......	......	......	......	5	8
796	37	759	......	3	1	21	46	711	......	......	......	......	1	13
171	15	156	1	1	......	27	12	118	......	......	......	......	3	9
828	7	821	1	1	2	13	237	574	......	......	......	......	......	......
58	1	57	......	......	1	5	2	50	......	......	......	......	......	......
396	132	264	49	43	16	13	93	180	......	1	......	1	......	......
41	6	35	3	1	1	2	10	23	......	......	......	......	1	......
d12908	12545	363	65	74	27	45	216	388	416	500	628	1123	3736	5688
1132	1035	97	......	1	4	12	23	104	8	8	43	69	297	562
1377	1376	1	......	......	1	......	2	2	43	60	64	135	407	663
1503	1367	136	1	1	2	4	55	113	8	4	40	84	448	743
2834	2831	3	......	2	......	2	14	8	53	62	128	263	864	1437
1348	1267	81	25	23	5	10	52	57	100	106	62	119	359	430
2597	2588	9	......	5	4	6	18	38	31	40	161	242	865	1187
608	579	29	39	42	9	4	31	38	45	56	25	47	117	155
1509	1502	7	......	......	2	7	21	28	128	164	105	164	379	511
d2869	1646	1223	30	27	75	140	538	1051	18	17	54	80	422	395
134	83	51	2	3	1	12	15	45	3	3	5	8	20	17
288	224	64	2	......	4	9	31	72	6	4	8	21	66	65
569	455	114	5	4	8	30	31	110	6	7	20	29	176	141
304	252	52	1	1	5	11	37	75	1	......	10	10	73	80
664	235	429	7	8	30	33	232	274	......	1	4	5	35	35
187	79	108	2	2	5	10	45	107	1	......	1	2	7	5
76	18	58	......	......	1	1	21	45	......	......	......	......	2	6
397	144	253	3	3	6	16	107	209	......	......	3	4	20	26
250	156	94	8	6	15	18	39	114	1	2	3	1	23	20
1194	137	1057	13	10	16	54	328	746	1	1	......	1	8	16
52	9	43	2	2	......	3	11	32	......	......	......	......	1	1
204	14	190	......	......	......	6	48	138	......	......	......	......	4	8
150	31	119	7	4	1	18	21	91	1	1	......	1	......	5
71	1	70	......	......	......	1	11	58	......	......	......	......	1	......
186	54	132	3	3	7	10	52	107	......	......	......	......	2	2
......	......	......	......	......	......	......	......	......	......	......	......	......	......	......
63	6	57	1	......	2	4	10	46	......	......	......	......	......	......
381	22	359	......	1	6	12	133	229	......	......	......	......	......	......
......	......	......	......	......	......	......	......	......	......	......	......	......	......	......
87	......	87	......	......	......	......	42	45	......	......	......	......	......	......
4663	1437	3226	386	405	204	335	1023	2179	1	3	6	6	62	53
400	46	354	4	8	11	10	144	223	......	......	......	......	......	......
1372	516	856	158	179	78	129	253	570	......	......	......	1	3	1
349	51	298	10	10	12	21	107	180	......	......	1	1	3	4
1351	598	753	204	193	85	99	250	506	......	2	......	......	5	8
322	24	298	3	6	6	10	89	205	......	......	......	......	3	......
133	24	109	......	1	2	24	17	83	......	......	......	1	3	2
470	93	377	5	8	4	28	112	282	1	1	......	......	17	11
266	85	181	2	......	6	14	51	130	......	......	5	3	28	27
2775	116	2659	11	14	66	78	909	1630	1	1	2	4	27	32
385	23	362	1	2	7	21	131	209	......	......	1	2	6	5
188	21	167	1	1	9	4	69	88	......	......	......	1	5	10

(*g*) Also 3 Indians.

(*h*) School attendance and illiteracy not returned by the assistant marshal.

(*i*) Also 4 Japanese.

(*j*) Including 3 Japanese.

(*k*) Also 3 Japanese.

TABLE XXVII.—*Population, School Attendance, and Illiteracy of Fifty Principal Cities—1870*—Continued.

Cities.	POPULATION.					ATTENDED SCHOOL.						
									White.		Colored.	
	Total.	Native.	Foreign-born.	White.	Colored.	Total.	Native.	Foreign-born.	Male.	Female.	Male.	Female.
30. *Worcester*—C'd.												
3d ward	5396	3209	2187	5366	30	959	803	156	501	457	1	....
4th ward	6175	3719	2456	6144	a30	1206	1080	126	573	626	4	3
5th ward	6695	4046	2649	6676	19	1216	1042	174	599	616	....	1
6th ward	6244	4634	1610	6151	93	1207	1124	83	658	538	6	5
7th ward	4481	3777	704	4439	42	883	853	30	402	478	3	....
8th ward	3178	2805	373	3131	47	449	438	11	229	219	....	1
31. *Lowell*	40928	26493	14435	40815	b111	6479	5716	763	3057	3408	7	7
1st ward	5620	3573	2047	5616	4	830	739	91	411	419	....	....
2d ward	6893	4663	2230	6851	42	885	804	81	390	489	2	4
3d ward	7486	4446	3040	7463	b21	1284	1181	103	610	672	....	2
4th ward	8014	5401	2613	7991	23	1286	1090	196	601	680	3	....
5th ward	8710	5642	3068	8705	5	1454	1255	199	691	762	....	1
6th ward	4205	2768	1437	4189	16	740	647	93	354	386	....	....
32. *Memphis*	40226	33446	6780	24755	15471	3033	2987	46	858	993	487	695
1st ward	4883	3522	1361	3490	1393	342	330	12	115	148	33	46
2d ward	2735	1978	757	2090	645	203	203	....	88	86	14	15
3d ward	2251	1676	575	1754	497	126	126	....	46	42	17	21
4th ward	1738	1511	227	1395	343	109	109	....	40	39	9	21
5th ward	2782	2186	596	1967	815	48	42	6	18	17	8	5
6th ward	3612	3196	416	1984	1628	324	319	5	77	89	65	93
7th ward	10278	9117	1161	5198	5080	700	694	6	165	228	129	178
8th ward	5283	4398	885	3603	1680	503	492	11	144	184	71	104
9th ward	2603	2173	430	1620	983	276	276	....	91	84	43	58
10th ward	4061	3689	372	1654	2407	402	396	6	74	76	98	154
33. *Cambridge*	39634	27579	12055	38785	c848	8072	7602	470	4208	3756	56	52
1st ward	6901	5089	1812	6815	86	1734	1688	46	1160	574	....	....
2d ward	10386	7426	2960	9733	c652	1988	1777	211	941	952	50	45
3d ward	9171	5837	3334	9162	9	1858	1780	78	863	995	....	....
4th ward	8865	6495	2370	8783	82	1630	1501	129	815	804	4	7
5th ward	4311	2732	1579	4292	19	862	856	6	429	431	2	....
34. *Hartford*	37180	26363	10817	36232	d946	e6588	6218	370	3312	3193	37	45
1st & 7th w'ds(f)	8621	6772	1849	8346	e274	1629	1561	68	817	783	14	15
2d ward	6337	4566	1771	6111	g225	1206	1161	45	589	601	6	9
3d ward	3930	2898	1032	3847	83	828	800	28	414	396	6	10
4th ward	8233	6128	2105	8146	87	1550	1469	81	720	762	4	4
5th ward	3770	2205	1565	3694	76	581	513	68	304	276	....	1
6th ward	6289	3794	2495	6088	201	794	714	80	408	375	5	6
35. *Scranton*	35092	19205	15887	35043	49	5037	4177	860	2293	2741	2	1
1st ward	1563	969	594	1559	4	214	176	38	101	113	....	....
2d ward	2339	1531	808	2339	....	385	321	64	169	216	....	....
3d ward	2771	1475	1296	2771	....	486	412	74	202	284	....	....
4th ward	4978	2518	2460	4978	....	657	520	137	289	368	....	....
5th ward	4646	2235	2411	4644	2	570	430	140	249	321	....	....
6th ward	2876	1355	1521	2876	....	323	233	90	159	164	....	....
7th ward	1482	794	688	1482	....	195	164	31	81	114	....	....
8th ward	5238	3628	1610	5196	42	686	646	40	341	342	2	1
9th ward	1916	1288	628	1915	1	283	264	19	130	153	....	....
10th ward	808	394	414	808	....	113	95	18	50	63	....	....
11th ward	2080	1007	1073	2080	....	400	341	59	197	203	....	....
12th ward	4395	2011	2384	4393	....	725	575	150	325	400	....	....

(a) Also 1 Japanese.
(b) Also 2 Indians.
(c) Also 1 Indian.
(d) Also 1 Chinese and 1 Indian.

XXVII.—*Population, School Attendance, and Illiteracy of Fifty Principal Cities—1870*—Continued.

CANNOT WRITE.														
			White.						Colored.					
			10 to 15.		15 to 21.		21 and over.		10 to 15.		15 to 21.		21 and over.	
Total.	Native.	Foreign-born.	M.	F.	M.	F.	M.	F.	M.	F.	M.	F.	M.	F.
654	3	651	.....	1	18	6	251	377	.....	.....	.....	.....	.....	1
264	2	262	3	4	4	5	62	186	.....	.....	.....	.....	.....	.....
598	14	584	1	5	14	13	189	372	.....	.....	.....	.....	1	3
410	27	383	4	.....	12	13	138	230	1	1	.....	1	5	5
181	13	168	.....	1	2	2	58	109	.....	.....	.....	.....	4	5
95	13	82	1	.....	.....	14	11	59	.....	.....	1	.....	6	3
2444	99	2345	54	48	105	173	658	1403	.....	.....	1	.....	.....	2
303	12	291	3	4	5	23	81	187	.....	.....	.....	.....	.....	.....
54	6	48	.....	.....	.....	2	18	34	.....	.....	.....	.....	.....	.....
474	6	468	8	5	15	21	137	287	.....	.....	.....	.....	.....	1
846	60	786	38	33	70	86	236	383	.....	.....	.....	.....	.....	.....
605	14	591	5	6	14	38	166	375	.....	.....	1	.....	.....	.....
162	1	161	.....	.....	1	3	20	137	.....	.....	.....	.....	.....	1
9306	8802	504	45	49	34	73	301	415	157	215	373	814	3176	3654
1262	1026	236	15	9	12	25	98	181	28	32	62	87	368	343
445	439	6	7	3	3	3	8	17	14	12	25	55	117	181
367	294	73	.....	2	.....	5	43	39	3	9	15	35	91	125
225	225	.....	.....	1	1	2	1	4	2	10	11	22	73	98
517	487	30	1	4	1	7	25	27	8	8	35	42	212	157
771	746	25	3	4	1	3	17	15	11	9	30	87	260	331
3052	3018	34	5	11	7	17	28	47	55	87	116	307	1062	1310
961	909	52	10	7	3	4	29	41	15	26	25	65	313	423
674	653	21	1	4	3	1	31	19	14	8	24	38	267	261
1032	1005	27	3	4	3	3	21	35	7	14	30	76	413	423
2408	141	2267	9	5	55	70	762	1385	.....	1	.....	13	43	65
334	10	324	1	.....	6	19	95	207	.....	1	.....	1	.....	4
547	96	451	1	1	4	21	108	320	.....	.....	.....	4	36	52
627	1	626	.....	2	2	9	233	381	.....	.....	.....	.....	.....	.....
348	29	319	1	2	6	13	103	200	.....	.....	.....	8	7	8
552	5	547	6	.....	37	8	223	277	.....	.....	.....	.....	.....	1
2577	496	2081	111	122	66	83	732	1264	4	11	4	19	74	67
532	64	468	4	7	14	28	139	279	1	3	1	6	14	16
414	68	346	7	10	5	8	101	242	2	4	2	7	11	15
456	139	317	46	52	6	15	97	206	.....	3	.....	1	16	14
26	2	24	.....	.....	.....	.....	9	15	.....	.....	.....	.....	.....	2
550	132	418	38	41	20	12	131	260	.....	1	1	.....	17	9
599	91	508	16	12	21	20	235	202	1	.....	.....	5	16	11
4620	479	4141	213	109	250	216	1679	2130	.....	.....	1	.....	1	1
178	29	149	9	4	8	12	61	81	.....	.....	1	.....	1	1
267	20	247	12	6	15	11	109	114	.....	.....	.....	.....	.....	.....
742	97	645	45	9	49	24	285	330	.....	.....	.....	.....	.....	.....
729	46	683	22	9	36	33	317	322	.....	.....	.....	.....	.....	.....
616	31	585	9	4	30	31	237	305	.....	.....	.....	.....	.....	.....
540	56	484	35	16	28	14	181	266	.....	.....	.....	.....	.....	.....
275	18	257	11	7	4	2	111	140	.....	.....	.....	.....	.....	.....
170	11	159	2	6	2	30	25	105	.....	.....	.....	.....	.....	.....
76	6	70	2	1	2	9	17	45	.....	.....	.....	.....	.....	.....
68	26	42	9	7	14	6	13	19	.....	.....	.....	.....	.....	.....
23	7	16	.....	1	2	4	6	10	.....	.....	.....	.....	.....	.....
926	132	794	57	39	60	40	317	413	.....	.....	.....	.....	.....	.....

(*e*) Including 1 Indian.
(*f*) 1st and 7th wards, constituting one subdivision, were not separately returned.
(*g*) Also 1 Chinese.

TABLE XXVII.—*Population, School Attendance, and Illiteracy of Fifty Principal Cities*—1870—Continued.

Cities.	Population.					Attended school.						
									White.		Colored.	
	Total.	Native.	Foreign-born.	White.	Colored.	Total.	Native.	Foreign-born.	Male.	Female.	Male.	Female.
36. *Reading*	33930	30059	3871	33611	*a*311	6538	6426	112	3181	3307	27	23
1st ward	2834	2613	221	2834	......	457	454	3	216	240	1	....
2d ward	5530	4767	763	5512	18	993	971	22	479	511	1	2
3d ward	3732	3333	399	3714	18	675	672	3	341	330	4	....
4th ward	2611	2432	179	2590	21	564	561	3	256	298	3	7
5th ward	3205	2948	257	3192	13	626	619	7	287	336	3	....
6th ward	2763	2565	198	2700	63	570	560	10	268	302	....	....
7th ward	3541	3238	303	3514	27	689	680	9	340	347	1	1
8th ward	3690	3282	408	3642	*a*40	684	669	15	333	340	6	5
9th ward	6024	4881	1143	5913	111	1280	1240	40	661	603	8	8
37. *Paterson*	33579	20711	12868	33218	361	5422	4680	742	2688	2699	19	16
1st ward	2904	2217	687	2884	20	517	470	47	261	252	2	2
2d ward	3208	2204	1004	3175	33	535	464	71	276	258	....	1
3d ward	4454	2999	1455	4311	143	767	673	94	366	384	8	9
4th ward	3574	2545	1029	3521	53	620	560	60	274	345	1	....
5th ward	7202	4243	2959	7127	75	1251	1041	210	620	625	5	1
6th ward	4113	2319	1794	4089	24	608	518	90	300	306	1	1
7th ward	3101	1719	1382	3088	13	386	347	39	217	165	2	2
8th ward	4044	1836	2208	4044	......	575	456	119	296	279	....	....
9th ward	979	629	350	979	......	163	151	12	78	85	....	....
38. *Kansas City*	32260	24581	7679	28484	*c*3770	5281	4830	451	2639	2166	235	239
1st ward	11549	9117	2432	10214	*c*1332	2326	2133	193	1268	893	96	69
2d ward	11096	8237	2859	9522	*c*1571	2038	1820	218	953	843	103	139
3d ward	4027	3089	938	3861	166	431	412	19	191	219	13	8
4th ward	5588	4138	1450	4887	701	486	465	21	227	213	23	23
39. *Mobile*	32034	27795	4239	18115	13919	5473	5458	15	1766	1919	788	1000
1st ward	3644	3392	252	1713	1931	557	555	2	150	174	103	130
2d ward	1099	963	136	719	380	152	150	2	71	53	14	14
3d ward	1222	849	373	1029	193	186	186	....	86	82	10	8
4th ward	1799	1435	364	1449	350	390	381	9	140	223	14	13
5th ward	2744	2233	511	1664	1080	423	423	....	151	169	41	62
6th ward	5948	4964	984	3792	2156	984	983	1	368	407	92	117
7th ward	8464	7677	787	2972	5492	1457	1456	1	265	326	375	491
8th ward	7114	6282	832	4777	2337	1324	1324	....	535	485	139	165
40. *Toledo*	31584	20485	11099	30972	612	5558	5236	322	2787	2721	22	28
1st ward	3961	2713	1248	3911	50	836	815	21	423	409	1	3
2d ward	4505	3025	1480	4387	118	753	738	15	350	396	2	5
3d ward	4303	3340	963	4112	191	748	726	22	384	349	9	6
4th ward	4925	2861	2064	4850	75	802	757	45	401	393	5	3
5th ward	5506	3280	2226	5468	38	886	857	29	442	439	1	4
6th ward	1814	1365	449	1811	3	280	271	9	151	129	....	....
7th ward	3680	2407	1273	3635	45	665	639	26	344	317	....	4
8th ward	2890	1494	1396	2798	92	588	433	155	292	289	4	3
41. *Portland*	31413	24401	7012	31078	*f*334	6409	5855	554	3164	3223	15	7
1st ward	5446	3876	1570	5330	116	1314	1166	148	662	647	2	3
2d ward	4274	3121	1153	4112	*f*161	911	803	108	465	430	12	4
3d ward	3164	2734	430	3140	24	585	550	35	279	306	....	....
4th ward	4134	2902	1232	4123	11	820	726	94	385	435	....	....
5th ward	3884	3196	688	3882	2	748	709	39	379	369	....	....
6th ward	4203	3517	686	4196	7	819	773	46	386	432	1	....
7th ward	5767	4584	1183	5754	13	1091	1012	79	544	547	....	....
Island portion	541	471	70	541	......	121	116	5	64	57	....	....

(*a*) Also 8 Indians. (*b*) Including 1 Indian. (*c*) Also 6 Indians.

XXVII.—*Population, School Attendance, and Illiteracy of Fifty Principal Cities*—1870—Continued.

CANNOT WRITE.															
			White.						Colored.						
			10 to 15.		15 to 21.		21 and over.		10 to 15.		15 to 21.		21 and over.	
Total.	Native.	Foreign-born.	M.	F.	M.	F.	M.	F.	M.	F.	M.	F.	M.	F.
*b*2342	1983	359	34	31	80	105	418	1580	1	4	2	7	19	30
11	11			1	1	2	1	6						
425	333	92	2		8	7	27	309						2
183	173	10	1		4	2	40	134					1	1
95	91	1		1	1	1	26	58			1	1	3	3
333	294	39	4	10	11	22	39	240	1	2	1	1		2
14	9	5			1		3	10						
294	208	86	9	12	10	23	40	186		1		3	1	3
386	371	15	7	5	17	20	68	256		1			3	8
601	490	111	11	2	27	22	134	381				2	11	11
2529	904	1625	255	270	104	146	488	1183	7	5	4	8	23	36
38	34	4	14	19	1	3		1						
283	149	134	33	27	12	16	51	133					6	5
59	46	13	16	14	6	3	3	6	1	2	1		4	3
130	70	60	20	28	6	7	4	42	2	1	2	6	4	8
516	175	341	57	64	23	33	76	232	4	2	1	1	7	16
344	114	230	28	20	18	17	74	181				1	2	3
433	136	297	39	32	11	28	102	217						1
589	100	489	33	43	20	33	138	322						
137	80	57	15	23	4	6	40	49						
*c*2315	2089	226	45	36	21	41	88	202	52	79	125	315	681	688
821	792	29	8	13	3	16	12	28	28	33	52	129	232	267
1167	1044	123	36	20	16	20	36	130	21	33	54	153	317	329
49	34	15		1		1	10	11	1		3	5	4	13
278	219	59	1	2	2	4	30	33	2	13	16	28	68	79
9106	8639	467	32	28	36	65	287	556	169	207	286	509	2673	4058
1208	1184	24	2	2	7		16	34	32	27	40	54	383	616
250	246	4			2	2	2	14	1		8	13	82	126
139	137	2	2		1	3	10	23	2	3	11	10	22	52
259	192	67		1		10	36	60	4	7	7	22	28	84
886	741	145	5	5	7	6	62	125	15	31	37	48	235	310
1587	1449	117	12	7	17	21	77	172	38	39	46	130	424	606
3188	3185	3	5	6	3	8	35	42	40	50	74	130	1211	1584
1589	1514	75	6	7	6	15	49	86	37	50	63	102	488	680
161	39	122				5	51	76			1		13	11
70	19	51				5	22	32					7	4
18	7	11					4	7					2	5
8	2	6				1	2	4			1			
21		21				2	6	13						
1	1												1	
35	10	25				1	11	15					3	2
8		8					3	5						
1882	104	1778	29	32	22	54	637	1075	2		4	3	12	12
426	14	412	2	1	5	2	147	255	1		2	1	6	4
248	20	228	5	1	5	1	72	147	1		1	2	5	8
99	35	64	13	22	2	4	13	43			1		1	
582	12	570		3	6	22	230	312						
220		220	1	1	1	10	84	123						
114	3	111				8	22	114						
163	20	143	8	4	2	7	66	81						

) Including 2 Indians. (*c*) Also 3 Indians. (*f*) Also 1 Indian.

TABLE XXVII.—*Population, School Attendance, and Illiteracy of Fifty Principal Cities—1870*—Continued.

Cities.	POPULATION.					ATTENDED SCHOOL.						
									White.		Colored.	
	Total.	Native.	Foreign-born.	White.	Colored.	Total.	Native.	Foreign-born.	Male.	Female.	Male.	Female.
42. *Columbus*	31274	23663	7611	29427	1847	5568	5402	166	2696	2640	93	139
1st ward (*a*)	3045	2400	645	2836	209	....	....	....	....	....	....	....
2d ward	2621	2267	354	2386	235	443	441	2	213	216	5	9
3d ward	2575	2217	358	2451	124	653	648	5	318	327	4	4
4th ward	3671	2957	714	3451	220	787	757	30	350	403	15	17
5th ward	3849	2614	1235	3598	251	769	732	37	396	335	16	[illegible]
6th ward	4728	2899	1829	4672	56	850	818	32	432	395	1	[illegible]
7th ward	3025	2315	710	2950	75	364	356	8	178	185	....	1
8th ward	4361	3425	936	3710	651	1054	1029	25	439	460	52	81
9th ward	3399	2569	830	3373	26	648	621	27	348	299	....	1
43. *Wilmington* (*b*)	30841	25689	5152	27630	3211	4748	4658	90	2139	2380	104	125
44. *Dayton*	30473	23050	7423	29925	548	6200	6003	197	3045	3092	31	32
1st ward	2828	2101	727	2821	7	507	483	24	241	266	....	....
2d ward	2867	2304	563	2800	67	625	616	9	290	330	2	3
3d ward	2744	2239	505	2601	143	439	446	6	222	221	3	6
4th ward	2135	1789	346	2102	33	390	383	7	191	196	2	1
5th ward	2921	2385	536	2908	13	599	591	8	299	298	....	2
6th ward	4116	2996	1120	4084	32	876	837	39	417	456	3	....
7th ward	3611	2278	1333	3586	25	710	670	40	347	362	....	1
8th ward	4006	2806	1200	3831	175	876	843	33	446	400	18	12
9th ward	1619	1436	183	1574	45	393	387	6	202	181	3	7
10th ward	712	613	99	706	6	146	144	2	75	71	....	....
11th ward	2914	2103	811	2912	2	626	603	23	315	311	....	....
45. *Lawrence*	28921	16204	12717	28814	*e*106	4740	3894	846	2305	2431	5	9
1st ward	5183	2999	2184	5170	*e*12	887	719	168	449	434	....	4
2d ward	5516	3145	2371	5498	18	890	744	146	429	461	....	....
3d ward	5849	3025	2824	5828	21	852	675	177	399	450	1	2
4th ward	6451	3504	2947	6432	19	1024	834	190	483	540	....	1
5th ward	3630	2051	1579	3594	36	604	492	112	285	313	4	2
6th ward	2292	1480	812	2292	....	483	430	53	250	233	....	....
46. *Utica*	28804	18955	9849	28583	*d*219	4644	4392	252	2266	2363	9	6
1st ward	1329	957	372	1319	10	176	171	5	85	89	1	1
2d ward	3383	1963	1420	3369	14	448	412	36	230	218	....	....
3d ward	4038	2929	1109	4035	3	640	602	38	301	339	....	....
4th ward	3866	2953	913	3715	151	507	496	11	241	258	6	2
5th ward	2532	1606	926	2530	2	354	348	6	188	166	....	....
6th ward	1938	1137	801	1931	7	374	341	33	186	188	....	....
7th ward	4583	3084	1499	4559	24	926	869	57	454	467	2	3
8th ward	2454	1548	906	2451	3	486	470	16	238	248	....	....
9th ward	4681	2778	1903	4674	*d*5	733	683	50	343	390	....	....
47. *Charlestown*	28323	21399	6924	28196	127	5499	5261	238	2672	2810	7	10
1st ward	10067	7086	2981	10038	29	1753	1676	77	846	906	1	....
2d ward	8277	6530	1747	8264	13	1737	1703	34	861	873	1	2
3d ward	9979	7783	2196	9894	85	2009	1882	127	965	1031	5	8
48. *Savannah* (*c*)	28235	24564	3671	15166	*f*13068	3210	3139	71	1263	1275	324	348
1st district	8002	7047	955	3889	4113	658	650	8	290	210	81	77
2d district	4323	3691	632	2259	2064	537	526	11	237	225	43	32
3d district	8010	7048	962	5275	2735	1002	963	39	404	518	39	41
4th district	7900	6778	1122	3743	*f*4156	1013	1000	13	332	322	161	198

(*a*) School attendance not returned by assistant marshal.
(*b*) Wards were not returned separately.
(*c*) Also 1 Chinese.
(*d*) Also 2 Indians.

XXVII.—*Population, School Attendance, and Illiteracy of Fifty Principal Cities*—1870—Continued.

CANNOT WRITE.

Total.	Native.	Foreign-born.	White.						Colored.					
			10 to 15.		15 to 21.		21 and over.		10 to 15.		15 to 21.		21 and over.	
			M.	F.	M.	F.	M.	F.	M.	F.	M.	F.	M.	F.
1558	970	598	45	35	45	51	298	537	6	17	38	36	222	208
183	157	26	.....	.....	15	1	89	8	.....	.....	10	4	53	3
115	97	18	1	.....	2	8	6	17	.....	1	6	6	31	37
79	55	24	1	1	4	6	3	37	1	1	3	4	9	9
123	99	21	3	3	3	8	8	42	.....	1	1	2	22	30
187	165	22	6	6	5	5	12	40	5	10	12	4	37	45
139	56	83	2	3	8	4	12	92	.....	.....	.....	.....	7	11
211	109	102	7	5	2	6	67	114	.....	.....	3	1	5	1
198	152	46	.....	1	2	4	18	34	.....	4	2	14	52	67
323	80	243	25	16	4	9	83	173	.....	.....	1	1	6	5
3682	2126	1556	81	68	65	79	735	1122	33	68	76	114	511	730
1059	488	571	31	29	30	51	231	531	4	6	10	17	51	68
166	53	113	2	7	7	17	50	82	.....	.....	...	1	.....	.....
96	58	38	1	1	5	9	25	36	.....	.....	2	4	7	6
33	27	6	.....	.....	.....	3	2	9	.....	1	1	1	6	10
67	34	33	4	3	1	.....	12	38	1	1	1	1	2	3
23	12	11	.....	1	1	4	7	7	.....	1	...	1	.....	1
99	43	56	5	1	3	3	13	63	.....	.....	...	.....	3	8
52	16	36	1	.....	1	3	9	27	1	1	1	.....	4	4
182	75	107	1	1	1	2	32	85	2	.....	2	4	23	29
120	82	38	9	13	4	1	21	55	.....	2	2	4	3	6
31	22	9	3	.....	.....	1	6	16	.....	.....	1	1	3	.....
190	66	124	5	2	7	8	54	113	.....	.....	...	.....	.....	1
3483	176	3307	36	63	76	220	835	2212	.....	4	...	3	10	24
515	31	484	7	8	7	31	100	355	.....	2	...	2	1	2
572	18	554	2	3	9	31	133	389	.....	.....	...	.....	1	4
1013	51	962	19	31	32	82	212	627	.....	1	...	.....	4	5
831	30	801	7	16	19	56	226	502	.....	.....	...	.....	1	4
201	23	178	.....	.....	.....	6	57	124	.....	1	...	1	3	9
351	23	328	1	5	9	14	107	215	.....	.....	...	.....	.....	.....
1234	117	1117	22	17	41	53	400	678	.....	.....	...	3	10	10
10	1	9	.....	1	.....	.....	2	7	.....	.....	...	.....	.....	.....
501	13	488	5	4	20	20	186	266	.....	.....	...	.....	.....	.....
28	4	24	.....	.....	2	3	7	16	.....	.....	...	.....	.....	.....
55	20	35	.....	.....	.....	5	9	24	.....	.....	...	3	7	7
.....	.....	.....	.....	.....	.....	.....	.....	.....	.....	.....	...	.....	.....	.....
77	7	70	1	1	5	3	21	44	.....	.....	...	.....	1	1
149	24	125	8	5	3	10	45	75	.....	.....	...	.....	2	1
182	12	170	3	2	4	8	67	97	.....	.....	...	.....	.....	1
232	36	196	5	4	7	4	62	149	.....	.....	...	.....	.....	.....
1348	44	1304	9	15	8	28	480	795	.....	.....	3	.....	5	5
780	29	751	8	14	6	12	266	463	.....	.....	3	.....	4	4
524	12	512	1	1	2	9	206	304	.....	.....	...	.....	1	.....
44	3	41	.....	.....	.....	7	8	28	.....	.....	...	.....	.....	1
*g*9554	9097	457	15	22	32	27	190	389	339	476	503	1148	2522	3881
3271	3096	175	4	7	5	6	75	140	124	168	180	315	926	1312
1249	1204	45	1	2	2	2	16	32	45	61	65	161	311	551
2204	2190	14	.....	.....	3	4	8	11	83	127	146	385	527	910
2830	2607	223	10	13	22	15	100	197	87	120	112	287	758	1108

st, 2d, 3d, and 4th militia districts, the city not being divided into wards.

(*f*) Also 1 Indian.
(*g*) Including 1 Indian.

TABLE XXVII.—*Population, School Attendance, and Illiteracy of Fifty Principal Cities*—1870—Continued.

Cities.	POPULATION.					ATTENDED SCHOOL.						
									White.		Colored.	
	Total.	Native.	Foreign-born.	White.	Colored.	Total.	Native.	Foreign-born.	Male.	Female.	Male.	Female.
49. *Lynn*	28233	23298	4935	27862	371	5326	5135	191	2609	2650	33	25
1st ward	643	604	39	643	.....	171	166	5	71	100	.....	.....
2d ward	1287	1181	106	1282	5	256	251	5	120	136	.....	.....
3d ward	5201	4370	831	5067	134	1071	994	77	530	512	17	12
4th ward	7268	5747	1521	7159	109	1161	1124	37	543	605	4	9
5th ward	6908	5810	1098	6880	28	1245	1236	9	616	627	2	.....
6th ward	6042	4845	1197	5961	81	1245	1193	52	638	509	3	3
7th ward	884	741	143	870	14	177	171	6	91	80	5	1
50. *Fall River*	26766	15288	11478	26635	a106	b5365	4257	1108	2715	2828	6	7
1st ward	6374	3309	3065	6351	23	1393	1026	367	724	667	.....	2
2d ward	5401	2545	2856	5397	7	1029	819	210	515	513	.....	1
3d ward	4760	2508	2252	4741	19	957	725	232	488	467	2	.....
4th ward	4036	2431	1605	3990	c25	791	674	117	382	395	3	2
5th ward	3123	2298	825	3116	d6	629	543	86	322	307	.....	.....
6th ward	3069	2197	872	3040	e26	566	470	96	284	279	1	2

(a) Also 25 Indians. (b) Including 9 Indians. (c) Also 21 Indians.

TABLE XXVII.—*Population, School Attendance, and Illiteracy of Fifty Principal Cities—1870*—Continued.

Cannot read—10 and over.	CANNOT WRITE.															
	Total.	Native.	Foreign-born.	White.						Colored.						
				10 to 15.		15 to 21.		21 and over.		10 to 15.		15 to 21.		21 and over.		
				M.	F.	M.	F.	M.	F.	M.	F.	M.	F.	M.	F.
476	863	96	767	49	37	18	27	202	499	1	......	4	4	9	13
9	37	32	5	12	12	3	......	5	5	......	......	......	......	......	......
12	28	15	13	5	4	......	2	9	5	......	......	......	1	2	......
103	210	25	185	13	11	10	5	55	102	......	......	2	......	5	7
55	225	18	207	17	9	3	16	47	120	1	......	2	3	2	5
130	177	3	174	2	1	2	4	44	123	......	......	......	......	......	1
139	178	3	175	......	......	......	......	40	138	......	......	......	......	......	......
5	8	......	8	......	......	......	......	2	6	......	......	......	......	......	......
2659	4602	593	4009	248	279	273	408	1053	2318	1	1	......	......	5	16
622	829	36	793	11	17	32	71	256	437	......	......	......	......	2	3
646	1210	174	1036	60	75	70	81	267	655	......	1	......	......	......	1
467	912	133	779	61	78	58	78	182	451	......	......	......	......	1	3
515	900	165	735	59	54	59	87	200	439	......	......	......	......	......	2
189	373	52	321	27	30	21	44	63	184	......	......	......	......	......	4
220	378	33	345	30	25	33	47	85	152	1	......	......	......	2	3

(*d*) Also 1 Indian.

(*e*) Also 3 Indians.

SCHOOLS, LIBRARIES, NEWSPAPERS,

AND

CHURCHES.

SCHOOL ATTENDANCE AS EXHIBITED IN TABLES XXI AND XXVIII.

It might be thought that the school attendance stated in the following table should agree precisely with the school attendance exhibited in Table XXI of this volume. A comparison, however, will develop differences often very considerable in the case of nearly all the States and Territories, while a consideration of the character of each table will explain and justify such discrepancies. The returns from which Table XXI is made up are individual. The returns from which the following table is made up are institutional. Table XXI shows the aggregate number of persons in each State and Territory who report themselves to the assistant marshals as having attended school during the census year. Table XXVIII purports to exhibit the record of the schools thus attended.

Inasmuch as the former return is, so far as it is accurate, necessarily an aggregate return, and the latter is generally an average return, (although the idea of averages is rather too nice to be imported into popular inquiries, like those of the census, with any great degree of success,) it is evident that this difference of method would account for differences in figures, and, in some States, for large differences. For example, there are some States in which schools are habitually kept open for the entire year, yet certain classes of the population are able to send their children to school for but a small portion of the time. This is so notorious that the fact needs but to be mentioned to fully justify a statement of school attendance in Table XXVIII considerably below that in Table XXI for all the Middle and Eastern States. Wherever mechanical and manufacturing pursuits are followed to any great extent, the demand for the labor of children becomes so pressing that it is found almost impossible to enforce laws requiring their attendance at school during one or two "quarters," while at the same time it is in precisely these communities that schools are maintained during the entire year.

There are, however, other States in which all classes of the population are so much on an equality in this matter of school attendance that no great differences between Tables XXI and XXVIII are to be expected. These are States in which the expense of schools is only incurred during certain seasons of the year, and, at the same time, from the general desire for instruction on the part of the people, and from the fact that the entire industry of the community practically ceases during the same season, almost all who attend school during the year do so for the whole time for which the schools are open.

The facts and considerations above alluded to would account for an excess, in respect to certain States, of the numbers in Table XXI over those in Table XXVIII, such excess rising in some portions of the country to 20 and 30 per cent., while in other sections it would be reduced to a minimum or would disappear.

It would seem, however, that the school attendance stated in Table XXI should always exceed that stated in Table XXVIII, or at least should never fall below it. That the preponderance should be in the other direction would at first seem impossible and absurd. There are several causes, however, which may produce this result, although they would rarely, if ever, be found to operate in a sufficient degree to overcome the natural preponderance of the numbers in Table XXI over those in Table XXVIII in the Eastern and Middle States.

The first of these causes is found in the fact that the pupils of the private schools are, in the great proportion of instances, identical with the pupils of the public schools. In communities like those previously adverted to, where schools are maintained at the public expense for only a small portion of the year, a system of private schools, often very considerable, is called into existence to supplement the annual course of instruction for those whose lack of gainful occupation and ability to pay the fees of tuition render them desirous of pursuing their studies somewhat beyond the extent of the public provision therefor. A scholar attending one of these schools in summer and a public school in winter would be returned twice for the purposes of Table XXVIII, while appearing only once in Table XXI.

The above remarks are intended to apply to all instances of duplication in Table XXVIII where private schools are used to supplement the course of public instruction, the two classes of schools being substantially of the same grade, and the difference between them being mainly in the season of the year in which they are held and the fact of tuition being paid in the private schools. In addition to this, however, there is occasion for duplication, more or less extensive, in the fact that students every year leave the public schools by hundreds or by thousands in each State, to attend the higher

TABLE XXVIII.—*Schools, All Classes, by States and Territories*—1870.

o the statistics of the schools included in the table add, for the Military Academy of the tes, at West Point, in the State of New York: Teachers, 40; pupils, 229; income from s, $274,489; and for the Naval Academy of the United States, at Annapolis, in the State of Teachers, 67; pupils, 253; income from public funds, $182,424.

erritories.	Number.	TEACHERS. Male.	TEACHERS. Female.	PUPILS. Male.	PUPILS. Female.	INCOME, YEAR ENDED JUNE 1, 1870. Total.	INCOME. From endowment.	INCOME. From taxation and public funds.	INCOME. From other sources, including tuition.
						Dollars.	Dollars.	Dollars.	Dollars.
ted States.	141,629	93,329	127,713	3,621,996	3,587,942	95,402,726	3,663,785	61,746,039	29,992,902
....	2,969	2,372	992	37,223	38,643	976,351	39,500	471,161	465,690
....	1	....	7	72	60	6,000	....	....	6,000
....	1,978	1,653	644	41,939	39,537	691,962	7,300	555,331	119,331
....	1,548	1,054	1,390	45,217	40,290	2,946,308	59,037	1,669,464	1,217,797
....	142	89	99	2,735	2,272	87,915	....	73,375	14,540
....	1,917	695	2,231	51,307	47,314	1,856,279	140,887	1,227,889	487,503
....	35	23	29	694	561	9,284	....	8,364	920
....	375	147	363	9,093	10,482	212,712	....	120,429	92,283
olumbia.	313	183	390	10,149	9,361	811,242	23,000	476,929	311,313
....	377	254	228	6,758	7,892	154,569	6,750	73,642	74,177
....	1,890	1,517	915	32,775	33,375	1,253,299	66,560	114,626	1,072,113
....	25	29	10	602	606	19,938	....	16,178	3,760
....	11,835	10,411	13,645	389,955	377,890	9,970,009	252,569	6,027,510	3,689,930
....	9,073	6,678	4,974	237,664	236,813	2,499,511	50,620	2,126,502	322,389
....	7,496	3,656	5,063	103,665	111,989	3,570,093	63,150	3,347,629	159,314
....	1,689	872	1,063	30,493	29,380	787,226	19,604	678,185	89,437
....	5,149	3,972	2,374	125,734	119,405	2,538,429	393,015	674,992	1,470,422
....	592	926	976	29,854	30,317	1,199,684	34,625	564,988	600,071
....	4,723	2,430	4,556	77,992	84,644	1,106,903	98,626	841,524	166,653
....	1,779	1,498	1,789	55,800	51,584	1,998,215	21,697	1,134,347	842,171
tts	5,726	1,428	6,133	134,777	134,560	4,817,939	383,146	3,183,794	1,250,999
....	5,595	2,996	6,569	138,949	137,678	2,550,018	81,775	2,097,122	371,121
....	2,479	979	1,907	53,166	52,100	1,011,769	2,000	903,101	106,668
....	1,564	1,054	674	22,793	20,658	780,339	11,500	167,414	601,425
....	6,750	5,157	3,871	186,641	183,696	4,340,805	57,567	3,067,449	1,215,789
....	54	34	31	1,027	718	41,170	....	30,434	10,736
....	796	450	390	9,492	8,122	207,560	....	186,435	21,125
....	53	13	71	1,279	1,094	110,493	....	84,273	26,220
hire.......	2,542	653	2,702	33,123	31,554	574,898	59,249	396,901	118,618
....	1,893	1,455	2,434	67,751	62,049	2,982,250	49,000	1,499,550	1,433,700
....	41	38	34	1,014	784	29,896	....	1,200	28,696
....	13,020	8,035	20,883	373,276	488,746	15,936,763	674,732	9,151,023	6,111,028
ina	2,161	1,739	953	32,664	32,294	635,892	9,160	232,104	394,628
....	11,952	10,266	13,323	419,591	371,204	10,244,644	222,074	8,634,815	1,387,755
....	637	484	342	16,753	15,840	218,022	21,500	135,778	87,744
a	11,872	8,507	11,015	428,023	383,840	9,628,119	539,496	7,187,700	1,900,923
d	561	237	714	15,491	17,105	565,012	31,535	348,656	184,821
ne	750	620	483	17,397	20,852	577,953	51,506	282,973	243,474
....	2,794	2,440	1,147	65,979	59,852	1,650,692	79,100	622,461	948,131
....	548	600	106	12,244	10,832	414,880	760	15,230	398,890
....	267	207	201	9,844	11,223	150,447	....	4,151	146,296
....	3,084	1,356	3,804	31,295	31,618	707,293	13,046	523,970	170,276
....	2,024	1,452	1,245	30,878	29,141	1,155,582	47,586	120,148	987,851
....	170	85	112	2,816	2,683	48,305	800	30,326	17,176
ia.......	2,445	2,070	768	55,238	49,711	698,062	15,300	598,124	84,637
....	4,943	2,511	5,444	176,541	167,473	2,600,310	32,959	2,027,876	539,481
....	9	7	8	190	115	8,376	....	2,876	5,500

s of learning, or to undertake courses of technical instruction. In the great f such cases of yearly transfers it would be inevitable that the student should l in the rol both of the school which he had left and of the academy, college, d, or other independent school to which he had gone. Similar reason for n, indeed, would be found in the frequent promotions occurring in the public emselves, wherever a graded system prevails, especially in large cities. , however, to be frankly admitted that the excess of the numbers returned XVIII over those appearing in Table XXI is occasionally due, though in no

TABLE XXIX.—*Schools, Public, by States and Territories*—1870.

States and Territories.	Number.	TEACHERS. Male.	TEACHERS. Female.	PUPILS. Male.	PUPILS. Female.	INCOME, YEAR ENDED JUNE 1, 1870. Total.	INCOME. From endowment.	INCOME. From taxation and public funds.	INCOME. From other sources, including tuition.
						Dollars.	*Dollars.*	*Dollars.*	*Dollars.*
The United States	125,059	74,174	109,024	3,120,052	3,108,008	64,030,673	144,533	58,855,507	5,030,633
Alabama	2,812	2,173	835	33,390	33,873	629,626	8,000	447,156	174,470
Arizona	....	....	....	....	....	....	....	....	....
Arkansas	1,744	1,458	508	37,103	34,942	558,461	7,300	529,881	15,989
California	1,342	767	1,116	39,772	35,755	1,627,733	357	1,519,348	108,028
Colorado	124	81	75	2,552	1,965	75,025	....	73,025	2,000
Connecticut	1,635	452	1,905	45,556	42,893	1,426,846	409	1,216,789	209,648
Dakota	34	22	26	679	544	8,684	....	8,364	320
Delaware	326	107	281	7,694	9,141	127,729	....	120,429	7,300
District of Columbia	216	15	203	5,510	5,672	439,929	3,000	431,929	5,000
Florida	226	169	96	4,674	5,458	76,389	4,000	61,552	10,837
Georgia	246	180	147	5,700	5,450	175,844	7,128	59,293	109,423
Idaho	21	20	6	527	521	16,178	....	16,178	....
Illinois	11,050	8,791	11,306	343,445	334,178	7,810,265	....	5,838,249	1,972,016
Indiana	8,871	6,402	4,640	228,189	217,887	2,063,509	....	2,002,052	61,547
Iowa	7,322	3,381	5,485	100,308	105,615	3,945,352	3,100	3,941,752	500
Kansas	1,663	829	1,035	29,632	28,398	660,635	....	645,532	15,103
Kentucky	4,727	3,468	1,883	111,802	106,438	1,150,451	24,885	604,905	520,661
Louisiana	178	122	337	12,005	13,737	473,707	....	445,683	28,024
Maine	4,565	2,261	4,364	73,393	79,372	843,435	4,116	809,941	29,378
Maryland	1,487	933	1,217	42,927	40,299	1,146,057	4,507	1,039,135	102,415
Massachusetts	5,160	733	5,387	121,572	120,573	3,207,820	27,343	3,069,085	111,392
Michigan	5,414	2,796	6,181	123,984	130,844	2,164,489	....	2,019,622	144,867
Minnesota	2,424	919	1,839	53,171	50,237	895,204	....	870,476	24,728
Mississippi	....	....	....	....	....	....	....	....	....
Missouri	5,906	4,414	2,948	163,582	156,731	3,092,733	5,300	3,007,766	79,667
Montana	45	33	13	965	579	32,925	....	30,434	2,491
Nebraska	781	436	377	9,927	7,825	182,160	....	181,435	725
Nevada	38	9	47	1,065	791	81,273	....	81,273	....
New Hampshire	2,464	510	2,600	30,275	29,133	403,310	1,643	391,991	9,676
New Jersey	1,531	956	2,060	39,763	40,342	1,562,573	....	1,492,608	69,965
New Mexico	5	5	....	84	104	1,000	....	....	1,000
New York	11,678	5,710	18,019	302,373	416,808	8,912,024	13,122	8,385,330	513,572
North Carolina	1,435	1,125	393	21,279	20,633	205,131	600	174,197	30,334
Ohio	11,458	9,306	12,437	389,022	348,671	8,528,145	10,000	8,495,145	23,000
Oregon	594	429	274	15,531	14,291	139,387	3,000	134,648	1,739
Pennsylvania	14,107	7,298	9,820	393,953	351,781	7,292,946	10,000	7,000,111	282,835
Rhode Island	487	165	610	12,736	14,514	355,582	1,085	348,656	5,841
South Carolina	581	429	352	13,082	17,680	279,723	....	270,423	9,300
Tennessee	1,932	1,579	562	43,690	39,370	683,008	1,100	580,416	101,492
Texas	....	....	....	....	....	....	....	....	....
Utah	....	....	....	....	....	....	....	....	....
Vermont	2,830	1,171	3,431	25,872	26,195	516,702	1,366	504,006	11,330
Virginia	122	43	128	4,275	4,425	98,770	1,050	55,425	42,295
Washington	154	75	83	2,456	2,304	33,746	....	30,326	3,420
West Virginia	2,371	1,997	690	53,587	47,906	599,811	1,800	575,324	22,687
Wisconsin	4,850	2,383	5,290	172,950	164,058	2,209,384	350	1,962,741	246,293
Wyoming	4	2	2	100	75	2,876	....	2,876	....

large degree, to the neglect of the assistant marshals to properly ask the question in regard to school attendance prescribed by the act of 1850, or to failure properly to record the answers received.

The States in which, at the Eighth Census, such an excess of school attendance obtained by the canvass of institutions, (as per Table XXVIII of the present publication,) was found to exist, over the attendance obtained by the canvass of families, (Table XXI of the present publication,) were: California, Connecticut, Illinois, Iowa, Maine, Michigan, Minnesota, New Jersey, North Carolina, Ohio, Vermont, and Wisconsin. Those in which such an excess has been found to exist at the present census, are: Arkansas, Florida, Illinois, Indiana, Kentucky, Maine, Minnesota, Missouri, Ohio, Oregon, Pennsylvania, West Virginia, and Wisconsin.

TABLE XXX.—*Schools, Not Public—Classical, Professional, and Technical, by States and Territories—1870.*

States and Territories.	Number.	TEACHERS.		PUPILS.		INCOME, YEAR ENDED JUNE 1, 1870.			
		Male.	Female.	Male.	Female.	Total.	From endowment.	From taxation and public funds.	From other sources, including tuition.
						Dollars.	*Dollars.*	*Dollars.*	*Dollars.*
The United States....	2,545	7,766	5,001	142,810	106,380	17,675,907	3,356,003	2,320,250	11,999,654
Alabama	57	122	85	1,799	2,419	273,355	31,500	22,005	221,850
Arizona	...	...	...	...	...	...	...	...	...
Arkansas	37	51	28	1,235	1,198	55,987	...	25,450	30,537
California	39	189	69	3,140	1,211	1,040,836	58,200	149,516	833,120
Colorado	2	...	12	...	120	5,800	...	...	5,800
Connecticut	11	98	8	1,203	138	265,213	124,008	11,100	130,105
Dakota	...	...	...	...	...	...	...	...	...
Delaware	11	32	31	480	379	53,550	...	...	53,550
District of Columbia	13	102	32	1,488	326	221,310	20,000	45,000	156,310
Florida	10	16	16	318	262	11,005	2,100	4,870	4,035
Georgia	163	267	136	4,756	4,902	385,067	40,300	33,723	311,044
Idaho	...	...	...	...	...	...	...	...	...
Illinois	80	354	217	7,255	4,500	896,372	222,374	161,318	512,680
Indiana	50	184	141	4,936	3,401	366,511	50,620	118,250	197,641
Iowa	71	209	101	3,421	3,032	282,191	60,050	105,877	116,264
Kansas	15	39	39	570	611	119,241	19,604	32,653	66,984
Kentucky	188	361	282	8,706	6,836	1,042,900	366,000	67,374	609,526
Louisiana	48	179	261	2,864	2,328	448,325	34,275	116,400	297,650
Maine	60	133	86	3,208	2,483	202,374	93,010	31,183	78,181
Maryland	72	270	143	4,716	1,847	626,490	14,300	68,212	543,978
Massachusetts	84	406	126	5,264	2,678	1,076,423	355,831	114,709	605,883
Michigan	33	129	187	2,327	3,153	297,155	80,275	77,500	139,380
Minnesota	9	38	13	565	228	76,376	...	32,625	43,751
Mississippi	21	36	42	534	927	96,839	11,500	33,589	51,750
Missouri	106	379	338	6,594	6,226	661,996	51,267	59,683	551,046
Montana	1	...	8	10	40	1,200	...	...	1,200
Nebraska	6	7	6	77	79	16,900	...	5,000	11,900
Nevada	...	...	...	...	...	...	...	...	...
New Hampshire	40	121	50	1,808	1,536	143,966	57,346	5,000	81,620
New Jersey	13	96	10	1,359	212	193,347	49,000	6,942	137,405
New Mexico	4	4	17	251	235	16,750	...	...	16,750
New York	274	1,171	878	25,156	18,572	3,722,193	652,061	466,156	2,603,976
North Carolina	134	202	140	3,659	3,053	234,320	8,200	43,259	182,861
Ohio	167	588	430	12,696	8,397	1,088,899	212,074	139,670	737,155
Oregon	20	44	25	1,002	743	51,123	15,500	1,130	34,493
Pennsylvania	213	812	389	14,321	6,884	1,719,058	465,713	109,589	1,143,756
Rhode Island	5	36	6	984	214	78,550	30,000	...	48,550
South Carolina	33	103	36	1,326	794	206,040	51,506	12,550	141,984
Tennessee	228	390	293	10,188	9,481	647,754	74,300	46,695	526,759
Texas	13	33	24	554	246	33,550	400	14,750	18,400
Utah	4	4	1	70	50	1,300	...	...	1,300
Vermont	46	104	100	2,252	1,944	112,157	11,680	8,537	91,940
Virginia	116	292	88	4,423	2,438	509,437	46,106	63,000	400,331
Washington	3	7	5	169	91	5,988	800	...	5,188
West Virginia	17	43	30	794	878	78,406	13,560	22,800	42,106
Wisconsin	28	115	61	2,312	1,288	307,653	32,603	64,135	210,915
Wyoming	...	...	...	...	...	...	...	...	...

TABLE XXXI.—*Schools, Not Public, other than Classical, Professional, and Technical, by States and Territories—1870.*

States and Territories.	Number.	Teachers. Male.	Teachers. Female.	Pupils. Male.	Pupils. Female.	Income, year ended June 1, 1870. Total.	From endowment.	From taxation and public funds.	From other sources, including tuition.
						Dollars.	*Dollars.*	*Dollars.*	*Dollars.*
The United States	14, 025	11, 389	13, 688	353, 134	373, 554	13, 696, 146	163, 249	570, 282	12, 962, 615
Alabama	100	77	72	2, 034	2, 351	71, 370	......	2, 000	69, 370
Arizona	1	......	7	72	60	6, 000	......	......	6, 000
Arkansas	197	144	108	3, 581	3, 447	73, 514	......	......	73, 514
California	167	98	295	2, 305	3, 324	277, 739	500	600	276, 639
Colorado	16	8	12	203	193	7, 090	......	350	6, 740
Connecticut	271	145	318	4, 548	4, 283	164, 220	16, 470	......	147, 750
Dakota	1	1	3	15	17	600	......	......	600
Delaware	38	8	51	919	902	31, 433	......	......	31, 433
District of Columbia	84	66	155	3, 144	3, 363	150, 003	......	......	150, 003
Florida	141	69	116	1, 796	2, 162	67, 175	650	7, 220	59, 305
Georgia	1, 471	1, 070	632	22, 319	23, 023	692, 388	19, 132	21, 610	651, 646
Idaho	4	3	4	35	85	3, 700	......	......	3, 700
Illinois	705	1, 266	2, 122	39, 255	39, 142	1, 263, 372	30, 195	7, 943	1, 225, 234
Indiana	152	92	193	4, 539	5, 525	69, 401	......	6, 200	63, 201
Iowa	103	66	77	1, 936	3, 342	42, 550	......	......	42, 550
Kansas	11	4	9	291	380	7, 350	......	......	7, 350
Kentucky	234	143	299	5, 226	6, 131	345, 078	2, 130	2, 713	340, 235
Louisiana	366	625	378	14, 695	14, 252	277, 652	350	2, 905	274, 397
Maine	98	36	106	1, 391	2, 789	60, 394	1, 500	400	58, 494
Maryland	220	295	429	8, 157	9, 438	225, 668	2, 890	27, 000	195, 778
Massachusetts	482	269	620	7, 941	11, 309	533, 690	......	......	533, 690
Michigan	148	74	192	2, 638	3, 681	88, 374	1, 500	......	86, 874
Minnesota	46	22	35	1, 430	1, 635	40, 169	2, 000	......	38, 169
Mississippi	1, 543	1, 018	632	22, 259	19, 731	683, 500	......	133, 825	549, 675
Missouri	648	361	585	16, 465	20, 739	586, 076	1, 000	......	585, 076
Montana	8	1	10	52	99	7, 045	......	......	7, 045
Nebraska	9	7	7	188	218	8, 500	......	......	8, 500
Nevada	15	4	24	214	303	29, 220	......	3, 000	26, 220
New Hampshire	38	22	43	1, 040	885	27, 622	300	......	27, 322
New Jersey	349	403	364	26, 629	21, 495	1, 226, 330	......	......	1, 226, 330
New Mexico	35	29	17	679	445	12, 136	......	1, 200	10, 936
New York	1, 068	1, 154	1, 986	45, 747	53, 366	3, 302, 566	9, 549	299, 537	2, 993, 480
North Carolina	592	412	420	7, 726	8, 608	196, 441	360	14, 648	181, 433
Ohio	327	372	456	17, 873	14, 136	627, 600	......	......	627, 600
Oregon	23	11	43	220	806	57, 512	6, 000	......	51, 512
Pennsylvania	552	397	806	19, 749	25, 175	616, 115	63, 763	18, 000	534, 352
Rhode Island	69	36	98	1, 771	2, 377	130, 880	450	......	130, 430
South Carolina	136	88	95	2, 380	2, 378	92, 190	......	......	92, 190
Tennessee	634	471	290	12, 191	11, 001	319, 930	3, 700	2, 350	313, 880
Texas	535	567	82	11, 690	10, 586	381, 330	360	480	380, 490
Utah	263	203	200	9, 774	11, 173	149, 147	......	4, 151	144, 996
Vermont	208	81	253	3, 171	3, 479	78, 433	......	11, 427	67, 006
Virginia	1, 786	1, 117	1, 029	22, 180	22, 278	547, 378	430	1, 723	545, 225
Washington	13	3	24	191	288	8, 568	......	......	8, 568
West Virginia	57	30	48	857	927	19, 844	......	......	19, 844
Wisconsin	56	13	97	1, 279	2, 127	83, 273	......	1, 000	82, 273
Wyoming	5	5	6	90	40	5, 500	......	......	5, 500

TABLE XXXII.—*Schools, All Classes, by States and Territories*—1860.

nd Territories.	Number.	Teachers.	Pupils.	INCOME, YEAR ENDED JUNE 1, 1860. Total.	From endowment.	From taxation and public funds.	From other sources.
				Dollars.	*Dollars.*	*Dollars.*	*Dollars.*
'nited States...	115,224	150,241	5,477,037	34,718,112	2,199,631	19,929,537	12,588,944
....	2,126	2,534	74,649	836,002	59,820	287,610	488,572
....	......	......	......	......	......	......	......
‹	840	934	23,882	194,344	6,500	24,101	163,743
a	508	816	28,654	559,849	17,065	271,646	271,138
....	......	......	......	......	......	......	......
cut	2,007	2,482	92,182	748,474	103,775	311,545	333,154
....	......	......	......	......	......	......	......
, ...	297	405	13,783	124,809	900	62,201	61,708
of Columbia ...	134	274	7,568	215,864	2,000	19,635	194,229
....	235	283	6,518	95,511	2,120	7,080	86,311
....	2,096	2,440	70,464	855,270	50,911	203,862	600,497
....	......	......	......	......	......	......	......
....	8,718	11,666	449,124	2,517,546	199,073	2,053,214	265,259
....	6,841	7,574	318,520	882,688	29,116	653,029	200,543
....	3,916	4,810	171,770	701,116	15,486	600,174	85,456
....	154	189	5,912	50,792	1,210	15,658	33,924
y	4,759	5,395	176,240	1,080,800	66,571	408,730	605,499
a	880	1,388	44,617	1,019,726	219,445	429,222	371,059
....	4,468	5,912	195,327	554,610	38,453	449,607	66,550
d	1,084	1,315	41,580	510,766	69,433	205,319	236,014
usetts	4,461	6,037	232,708	2,230,611	177,338	1,498,650	554,623
n	4,101	6,088	212,705	816,660	14,140	673,783	128,743
a	912	983	33,054	116,702	9,384	80,820	26,498
pi	1,298	1,695	39,800	733,621	59,100	184,507	490,014
....	4,396	5,605	200,280	1,259,130	86,970	574,262	507,907
....	......	......	......	......	......	......	......
a	87	96	3,133	12,219	......	8,626	3,593
....	......	......	......	......	......	......	......
npshire	2,511	3,365	82,373	369,945	35,808	253,340	80,797
sey	1,759	2,508	133,987	858,129	23,406	461,794	372,929
cico	21	33	507	13,149	......	......	13,149
k	11,577	18,878	786,818	5,057,971	119,185	3,284,298	1,654,498
arolina	3,444	3,683	119,734	758,444	45,602	250,974	461,868
....	11,950	17,180	651,661	3,031,770	167,767	2,475,813	388,190
....	259	292	10,269	73,056	6,000	30,577	36,479
ania	12,108	14,646	602,227	3,379,015	238,854	2,465,183	674,978
land	485	782	28,609	235,827	21,781	145,004	69,042
rolina	997	1,268	30,377	690,512	133,755	135,813	420,944
e	3,274	3,831	157,534	1,076,571	36,340	233,888	806,343
....	1,340	1,617	42,943	651,374	14,743	86,369	550,262
....	175	225	5,605	32,738	......	17,130	15,608
....	2,795	3,603	88,928	298,595	5,360	229,429	63,806
....	4,199	4,779	101,471	1,289,819	86,846	234,390	968,583
ton	52	55	1,039	23,976	......	6,575	17,401
ginia	......	......	......	......	......	......	......
n	3,927	4,555	209,908	760,006	35,374	505,089	129,033
g	......	......	......	......	......	......	......

TABLE XXXIII.—*Schools, All Classes, by States and Territories—1850.*

States and Territories.	Number.	Teachers.	Pupils.	INCOME, YEAR ENDED JUNE 1, 1850. Total.	From endowment.	From taxation and public funds.	From other sources.
				Dollars.	*Dollars.*	*Dollars.*	*Dollars.*
The United States	87, 257	105, 858	3, 642, 694	16, 162, 000	923, 763	7, 500, 117	7, 642, 1[illegible]
Alabama	1, 323	1, 630	37, 237	321, 022	9, 916	62, 421	248, 685
Arizona							
Arkansas	446	495	11, 050	74, 800	1, 720	9, 209	63, 871
California	8	7	219	17, 870	6, 600	70	11, 200
Colorado							
Connecticut	1, 862	2, 172	79, 003	430, 896	33, 119	195, 931	201, 776
Dakota							
Delaware	261	324	11, 125	108, 893	1, 425	42, 176	65, 292
District of Columbia	71	196	4, 730	122, 272	2, 300	12, 640	107, 332
Florida	103	122	3, 129	35, 475	1, 900	250	33, 325
Georgia	1, 483	1, 667	43, 299	396, 644	29, 617	39, 179	327, 848
Idaho							
Illinois	4, 141	4, 443	130, 411	403, 138	27, 011	231, 744	144, 383
Indiana	4, 964	5, 154	168, 754	421, 337	25, 340	208, 716	187, 281
Iowa	775	878	30, 767	61, 472	2, 700	35, 627	23, 145
Kansas							
Kentucky	2, 579	3, 006	86, 014	595, 930	51, 053	108, 633	436, 244
Louisiana	812	1, 211	30, 843	619, 006	74, 000	316, 397	228, 609
Maine	4, 176	5, 793	199, 745	380, 683	12, 571	313, 819	54, 293
Maryland	1, 142	1, 585	44, 923	564, 091	16, 554	162, 801	384, 736
Massachusetts	4, 066	5, 049	190, 292	1, 424, 873	88, 599	977, 630	358, 644
Michigan	2, 754	3, 324	112, 382	206, 753	7, 960	143, 158	55, 635
Minnesota	1	1	12	140			140
Mississippi	964	1, 168	26, 236	370, 276	14, 520	71, 911	283, 845
Missouri	1, 783	2, 033	61, 592	383, 469	30, 178	78, 701	274, 590
Montana							
Nebraska							
Nevada							
New Hampshire	2, 489	3, 214	81, 237	221, 146	12, 659	156, 938	51, 549
New Jersey	1, 702	2, 076	88, 244	523, 080	10, 373	141, 486	371, 221
New Mexico	1	1	40				
New York	12, 481	17, 269	727, 156	2, 431, 247	73, 178	1, 384, 929	973, 140
North Carolina	2, 934	3, 162	112, 430	386, 912	28, 822	140, 314	217, 776
Ohio	11, 893	13, 540	502, 826	1, 018, 258	50, 985	631, 197	336, 076
Oregon	32	48	922	24, 815		2, 527	22, 288
Pennsylvania	9, 606	11, 063	440, 743	2, 164, 578	189, 184	1, 367, 959	607, 435
Rhode Island	463	604	24, 881	136, 729	10, 660	93, 730	32, 339
South Carolina	934	1, 115	26, 025	510, 879	21, 350	79, 099	410, 430
Tennessee	2, 944	3, 284	114, 773	415, 792	24, 395	113, 008	278, 389
Texas	448	504	11, 500	84, 472			84, 472
Utah	27			13, 562		8, 200	5, 362
Vermont	2, 854	4, 460	100, 785	246, 604	15, 164	156, 531	74, 909
Virginia	3, 259	3, 617	77, 764	708, 787	49, 525	194, 802	464, 460
Washington							
West Virginia							
Wisconsin	1, 483	1, 623	61, 615	136, 229	385	108, 384	27, 460
Wyoming							

TABLE XXXIV.—*Schools by Classes and Kinds in each State and Territory*—1870.

NOTE.—Each University has been treated as a group of Classical and Professional, or Technical schools. Its statistics have been twice inserted in this table; once, in parts distributed among such special schools and included in the totals of the table; again, in entirety after "Universities," in bold-faced figures, which are not additive. For the sake of economy of space in this Table the word CLASSICAL is used as the name of a Class, instead of "CLASSICAL, PROFESSIONAL, AND TECHNICAL." Parochial includes Charity schools.

STATE OF ALABAMA.

Schools.		Teachers.		Pupils.		
Classes and kinds.	Number.	Male.	Female.	Male.	Female.	Income.
						Dollars.
ALL CLASSES.	2969	2372	992	37223	38643	976351
PUBLIC.	2812	2173	835	33390	33873	629626
Normal	14	13	12	260	228	
High	4	4	2	90	80	629626
Grammar ...	10	6	4	100	100	
Common* ...	2784	2150	817	32940	33465	
CLASSICAL.	57	122	85	1799	2419	275355
Classical.						
Colleges	8	42	21	496	530	108800
Academies..	46	68	64	1231	1855	142750
Professional.						
Medicine ...	1	7	.....	30	......	10000
Theology ...	1	2	.....	21	......	1800
Technical.						
Blind, deaf, & dumb...	1	3	.....	21	34	12005
OTHER.	100	77	72	2034	2351	71370
Day & board'g	83	59	38	1499	1630	70870
Parochial ...	17	18	34	535	721	500

TERRITORY OF ARIZONA.

Classes and kinds.	Number.	Teachers Male.	Teachers Female.	Pupils Male.	Pupils Female.	Income.
ALL CLASSES.	1	.....	7	72	60	6000
NOT PUBLIC.						
Parochial ...	1	.....	7	72	60	6000

STATE OF ARKANSAS.

Classes and kinds.	Number.	Teachers Male.	Teachers Female.	Pupils Male.	Pupils Female.	Income.
ALL CLASSES.	1978	1653	644	41939	39587	681962
PUBLIC.	1744	1458	508	37103	34942	552461
Normal	1	1	2	36	26	10061
High	3	3	3	70	70	3600
Graded †	225	212	77	6170	5717	93500
Ungraded †..	1515	1242	426	30827	29129	445300
CLASSICAL.	37	51	28	1255	1198	55987
Classical.						
Colleges	3	8	2	125	110	7700
Academies..	30	39	22	1102	1042	25387

* Graded and ungraded.

STATE OF ARKANSAS—Continued.

Schools.		Teachers.		Pupils.		
Classes and kinds.	Number.	Male.	Female.	Male.	Female.	Income.
Technical.						*Dollars.*
Blind	1	2	2	10	20	11000
Deaf & dumb	1	1	.....	13	11	10900
Art & music.	2	1	2	5	15	1000
OTHER.	197	144	108	3581	3447	73514
Day & board'g	187	137	104	3484	3334	67214
Parochial ...	10	7	4	97	113	6300

STATE OF CALIFORNIA.

Classes and kinds.	Number.	Teachers Male.	Teachers Female.	Pupils Male.	Pupils Female.	Income.
ALL CLASSES.	1548	1054	1390	45217	40290	2946308
PUBLIC.	1342	767	1116	39772	35755	1627733
Normal	1					
High	16					
Grammar ...	57	767	1116	39772	35756	1627733
Graded †	467					
Ungraded †..	801					
CLASSICAL.	39	189	69	3140	1211	1040836
Universities.	**2**	**15**	**3**	**185**	**65**	**174976**
Classical.						
Colleges	17	108	48	2032	1014	505886
Academies..	5	8	13	115	83	24000
Professional.						
Medicine ...	1	15	.....	140	......	110000
Theology ...	2	16	.....	248	......	125000
Technical.						
Commercial.	2	12	.....	150	......	40,000
Blind	1	2	1	19	17	35640
Deaf & dumb	1	2	.....	38	25	
Art & music.	8	17	7	215	72	51810
Other	2	9	.....	183	......	49500
OTHER.	167	98	205	2305	3324	277739
Day & board'g	154	86	181	1815	2786	243589
Parochial ...	13	12	24	490	538	34150

TERRITORY OF COLORADO.

Classes and kinds.	Number.	Teachers Male.	Teachers Female.	Pupils Male.	Pupils Female.	Income.
ALL CLASSES.	142	89	99	2755	2278	87915
PUBLIC.	124	81	75	2552	1965	75025
Graded †	6	7	18	444	393	22000
Ungraded †..	118	74	57	2108	1572	53025

† Common.

TABLE XXXIV.—*Schools by Classes and Kinds in each State and Territory—1870—Cont'd.*

Classes and kinds.	Schools. Number.	Teachers. Male.	Teachers. Female.	Pupils. Male.*	Pupils. Female.	Income.
TERRITORY OF COLORADO—Continued.						
						Dollars.
CLASSICAL.	2	.....	12	.....	120	5800
Classical.						
Academies..	2	.....	12	.....	120	5800
OTHER.	16	8	12	203	193	7090
Day & board'g	16	8	12	203	193	7090
STATE OF CONNECTICUT.						
ALL CLASSES.	1917	695	2231	51307	47314	1856279
PUBLIC.	1635	452	1905	45556	42893	1426846
Normal	1	2	2	41	39	7500
High	3	10	5	212	200	17593
Common* ...	230	144	781	24371	22946	966425
Ungraded†..	1401	296	1117	20932	19708	435328
CLASSICAL.	11	98	8	1903	138	265213
Universities.	1	61	.....	756	.....	135061
Classical.						
Colleges	3	46	.....	765	.....	134643
Professional.						
Law	1	3	.....	23	.....	1840
Medicine ...	1	8	.....	33	.....	1179
Theology ...	2	9	.....	78	.....	26000
Technical.						
Agricultural	1	21	.....	123	.....	23700
Deaf & dumb	2	10	7	166	118	68851
Idiotic	1	1	1	15	20	9000
OTHER.	271	145	318	4548	4283	164220
Day & board'g	265	140	290	3755	3537	164220
Parochial ...	6	5	28	793	746	....
TERRITORY OF DAKOTA.						
ALL CLASSES.	35	23	29	694	561	9284
PUBLIC.	34	22	26	679	544	8684
Ungraded†..	34	22	26	679	544	8684
NOT PUBLIC.	1	1	3	15	17	600
Parochial ...	1	1	3	15	17	600
STATE OF DELAWARE.						
ALL CLASSES	375	147	363	9093	10482	212712
PUBLIC.	326	107	281	7694	9141	127729
Normal	1	1	6	.....	100	4000
Graded†	12	.....	61	1360	1575	44755
Ungraded†..	313	106	214	6334	7466	78974

Classes and kinds.	Schools. Number.	Teachers. Male.	Teachers. Female.	Pupils. Male.	Pupils. Female.	
STATE OF DELAWARE—Continued.						
						Dollars.
CLASSICAL.	11	32	31	480	379	5330
Classical.						
Colleges	2	7	8	17	120	1850
Academies..	9	25	23	463	259	3500
OTHER.	38	8	51	919	962	31433
Day & board'g	14	4	20	223	259	11572
Parochial ...	24	4	31	696	703	19861
DISTRICT OF COLUMBIA.						
ALL CLASSES.	313	183	390	10142	9361	811282
PUBLIC.	216	15	203	5510	5672	439929
Grammar ...	10	7	5	245	242	439929
Graded†	177	.....	177	4660	4835	
Ungraded†..	29	8	21	605	595	
CLASSICAL.	13	102	32	1488	326	221310
Universities.	3	82	4	1014	90	117310
Classical.						
Colleges	4	46	4	726	76	93509
Academies..	1	.....	24	.....	120	35000
Professional.						
Law	2	7	.....	212	.....	15000
Medicine....	3	32	.....	212	5	13500
Technical.						
Commercial.	2	8	3	274	109	14310
Deaf & dumb	1	9	1	64	16	50000
OTHER.	84	66	155	3144	3363	150003
Day & board'g	61	44	110	1182	1431	117583
Parochial ...	23	22	45	1962	1932	33420
STATE OF FLORIDA.						
ALL CLASSES.	377	254	228	6788	7882	154569
PUBLIC.	236	169	96	4674	5458	78389
Normal	2	5	4	260	215	8500
High	4	4	4	122	97	7500
Graded†	5	4	3	160	210	1900
Ungraded†..	215	156	85	4132	4936	58469
CLASSICAL.	10	16	16	318	262	11005
Classical.						
Academies..	10	16	16	318	262	11005
OTHER.	141	69	116	1796	2162	67175
Day & board'g	135	67	100	1633	1860	61015
Parochial ...	6	2	16	163	302	6160

* Graded and ungraded.

† Common.

TABLE XXXIV.—*Schools by Classes and Kinds in each State and Territory*—1870—Cont'd.

STATE OF GEORGIA.

Schools.		Teachers.		Pupils.		
Classes and kinds.	Number.	Male.	Female.	Male.	Female.	Income.
						Dollars.
ALL CLASSES.	1880	1517	915	32775	33375	1253299
PUBLIC.	246	180	147	5700	5450	175844
Normal	4	4	12	334	323	7867
High	9	12	15	485	409	23350
Grammar ...	26	17	15	523	596	23979
Graded*	18	15	18	849	754	20902
Ungraded* ..	189	132	87	3509	3368	99746
CLASSICAL.	163	267	136	4756	4902	385067
Universities.	3	18	.....	379	.....	31600
Classical.						
Colleges	28	77	56	973	1620	148866
Academies ..	123	152	74	3384	3174	161301
Professional.						
Law	1	2	.....	17	.....	1050
Medicine	2	23	.....	210	.....	40500
Technical.						
Commercial.	3	5	2	120	20	8000
Blind	1	2	2	10	15	11000
Deaf & dumb	1	3	1	22	20	10350
Art & music.	4	3	1	.....	53	4000
OTHER.	1471	1070	632	22319	23023	692388
Day & board'g	1452	1060	610	21965	22583	662933
Parochial ...	19	10	22	354	440	29455

TERRITORY OF IDAHO.

Classes and kinds.	Number.	Teachers, Male.	Teachers, Female.	Pupils, Male.	Pupils, Female.	Income.
ALL CLASSES.	25	23	10	602	606	19938
PUBLIC.	21	20	6	527	521	16178
Grammar ...	1	5	.....	150	60	6325
Ungraded* ..	20	15	6	377	461	9853
NOT PUBLIC.	4	3	4	75	85	3760
Day & board'g	3	1	2	50	55	2060
Parochial ...	1	2	2	25	30	1700

STATE OF ILLINOIS.

Classes and kinds.	Number.	Teachers, Male.	Teachers, Female.	Pupils, Male.	Pupils, Female.	Income.
ALL CLASSES.	11835	10411	13645	389955	377820	9970009
PUBLIC.	11050	8791	11306	343445	334178	7810265
Normal	4	11	6	489	316	} 7810265
High	94	} 8780	} 11300	} 342956	} 333862	
Grammar ...	68					
Graded.*	641					
Ungraded.* .	10243					

STATE OF ILLINOIS—Continued.

Schools.		Teachers.		Pupils.		
Classes and kinds.	Number.	Male.	Female.	Male.	Female.	Income.
						Dollars.
CLASSICAL.	80	354	217	7255	4500	896373
Universities.	6	53	3	1129	148	73131
Classical.						
Colleges	26	190	33	3930	727	271065
Academies ..	32	64	161	1394	3296	257643
Professional.						
Law	2	3	.....	59	3	4335
Medicine ...	2	19	.....	358	.....	36991
Theology ...	9	28	.....	575	.....	112802
Technical.						
Agricultural	2	18	4	276	84	62772
Commercial.	2	17	.....	430	.....	22500
Blind	1	3	2	36	34	25000
Deaf & dumb	1	8	7	137	122	70394
Idiotic	1	.....	4	35	25	21430
Art & music.	2	4	6	25	209	11440
OTHER.	705	1266	2122	39255	39142	1263372
Day & board'g	531	491	1035	21414	20042	966262
Parochial ...	174	775	1087	17841	19100	297110

STATE OF INDIANA.

Classes and kinds.	Number.	Teachers, Male.	Teachers, Female.	Pupils, Male.	Pupils, Female.	Income.
ALL CLASSES.	9073	6678	4974	237654	226813	2499511
PUBLIC.	8871	6402	4640	228189	217887	2063599
Normal	1	3	3	49	54	} 2063599
High	69	106	123	5228	4845	
Common.† ...	371	171	558	17578	18751	
Ungraded.* .	8430	6122	3956	205334	194237	
CLASSICAL.	50	184	141	4936	3401	366511
Universities.	6	66	7	1428	239	67550
Classical.						
Colleges	16	115	28	2431	671	162250
Academies ..	16	26	99	1305	2275	73900
Professional.						
Law	1	2	.....	51	.....	(a)
Medicine ...	1	5	.....	43	.....	2500
Theology ...	2	3	.....	43	.....	(a)
Technical.						
Commercial.	7	15	.....	782	37	24831
Blind	1	3	4	43	57	32500
Deaf & dumb	1	8	5	143	129	60000
Art & music	4	4	5	34	218	8720
Other	1	3	.....	61	12	1720
OTHER.	152	92	193	4539	5525	69401
Day & board'g	124	58	143	2802	3494	47427
Parochial ...	28	34	50	1737	2031	21974

* Common. † Graded and ungraded. (a) Income included in that of Universities.

TABLE XXXIV.—*Schools by Classes and Kinds in each State and Territory*—1870—Cont'd.

STATE OF IOWA.

Schools.		Teachers.		Pupils.		
Classes and kinds.	Number.	Male.	Female.	Male.	Female.	Income.
						Dollars.
ALL CLASSES.	7496	3656	5063	105665	111989	3570093
PUBLIC.	7322	3381	5485	100308	105615	3245352
Normal	1	....	2	13	13	3245352
High	37	38	53	1167	1663	
Grammar	41	27	57	1562	1886	
Graded.*	294	198	587	20715	22408	
Ungraded.*	6949	3118	4786	76851	79645	
CLASSICAL.	71	209	101	3421	3032	282191
Universities.	1	22	3	225	178	30000
Classical.						
Colleges	21	109	30	1685	1376	101950
Academies	34	46	57	1019	1314	55880
Professional.						
Law	1	4	....	25	......	(a)
Medicine	1	7	....	120	......	4000
Theology	4	10	....	64	......	7050
Technical.						
Agricultural	1	8	3	142	49	37611
Commercial	5	12	2	252	63	9200
Blind	1	5	5	46	54	43946
Deaf & dumb	1	5	1	56	35	16004
Art & music	2	3	3	12	141	4550
OTHER.	103	66	77	1936	3342	42550
Day & board'g	100	64	72	1741	3131	38550
Parochial	3	2	5	195	211	4000

STATE OF KANSAS.

Classes and kinds.	Number.	Teachers, Male.	Teachers, Female.	Pupils, Male.	Pupils, Female.	Income.
ALL CLASSES.	1689	872	1083	30493	29389	787226
PUBLIC.	1663	829	1035	29632	28398	660635
Normal	1	2	3	78	83	10000
High	4	5	5	191	140	8000
Grammar	1	2	5	136	144	2700
Graded.*	118	62	137	5576	5714	120325
Ungraded.*	1539	758	885	23651	22317	519610
CLASSICAL.	15	39	39	570	611	119241
Universities.	2	12	1	124	168	19916
Classical.						
Colleges	5	24	3	260	229	61731
Academies	6	6	30	139	256	14900
Technical.						
Agricultural	1	6	2	98	75	21000
Commercial	1	1	....	15	18	627
Blind	1	....	3	8	12	7403
Deaf & dumb	1	2	1	30	21	13580

* Common.
† Graded and ungraded.

STATE OF KANSAS—Continued.

Schools.		Teachers.		Pupils.		
Classes and kinds.	Number.	Male.	Female.	Male.	Female.	Income.
						Dollars.
OTHER.	11	4	9	291	380	7350
Day & board'g	4	....	4	44	71	25
Parochial	7	4	5	247	309	7325

STATE OF KENTUCKY.

Classes and kinds.	Number.	Teachers, Male.	Teachers, Female.	Pupils, Male.	Pupils, Female.	Income.
ALL CLASSES.	5149	3972	2374	125734	119405	2538429
PUBLIC.	4727	3468	1883	111802	106438	1150451
Normal	1	1	3	110	100	1150451
High	23	37	42	1329	1300	
Grammar	19	22	201	6070	7545	
Graded.*	88	98	197	7435	7997	
Ungraded.*	4596	3310	1440	96858	89496	
CLASSICAL.	188	361	282	8706	6836	1042900
Universities.	2	33	....	1092	......	63000
Classical.						
Colleges	42	119	104	3395	2469	431437
Academies (b)	95	146	140	3049	3175	254498
Professional.						
Law	2	6	....	70	......	4344
Medicine	4	24	....	644	......	38000
Theology	5	13	....	263	......	161341
Technical.						
Agricultural	1	10	....	300	......	18365
Commercial	8	16	....	580	7	18001
Blind	1	4	6	32	32	13653
Deaf & dumb	1	3	3	43	37	19100
Idiotic	1	....	3	36	37	16200
Art & music	27	15	26	133	1079	58360
Other	1	5	....	161	.....	9801
OTHER.	234	143	209	5226	6131	345078
Day & board'g	195	128	174	3170	4778	335865
Parochial	39	15	35	2056	1353	9213

STATE OF LOUISIANA.

Classes and kinds.	Number.	Teachers, Male.	Teachers, Female.	Pupils, Male.	Pupils, Female.	Income.
ALL CLASSES.	592	926	976	29854	30317	1198624
PUBLIC.	178	122	337	12095	13737	473707
Normal	1	5	4	75	51	473707
High	5	9	13	182	380	
Grammar	4	3	3	150	150	
Graded *	60	31	228	6572	8421	
Ungraded *	108	74	89	5116	4785	
CLASSICAL.	48	179	261	2864	2328	448345
Universities.	2	42	7	884	326	110450

(a) Income included in that of Universities.
(b) Including the Kentucky Military Institute.

TABLE XXXIV.—*Schools by Classes and Kinds in each State and Territory*—1870—Cont'd.

STATE OF LOUISIANA—Continued.

Classes and kinds.	Schools. Number.	Teachers. Male.	Teachers. Female.	Pupils. Male.	Pupils. Female.	Income.
Classical.						*Dollars.*
Colleges	8	84	16	1139	428	130194
Academies ..	28	33	243	852	1838	198525
Professional.						
Law	1	4	.....	18	......	180
Medicine ...	2	19	.....	94	......	41575
Theology ...	1	3	.....	18	......	4300
Technical.						
Commercial .	4	30	.....	690	......	19700
Blind	1	2	.....	17	6	13000
Deaf & dumb	1	3	1	26	17	17001
Art & music .	2	1	1	10	39	1650
OTHER.	366	625	378	14805	14252	277652
Day & board'g	293	297	251	7234	9008	193692
Parochial ...	73	328	127	7571	5244	83960

STATE OF MAINE.

Classes and kinds.	Schools. Number.	Teachers. Male.	Teachers. Female.	Pupils. Male.	Pupils. Female.	Income.
ALL CLASSES.	4723	2430	4556	77992	84644	1106203
PUBLIC.	4565	2261	4304	73393	79372	843435
Normal	15	11	14	306	453	11824
High	53	55	55	1411	1820	45348
Grammar ...	88	52	116	2061	3745	44103
Graded *	354	114	430	10952	12332	185527
Ungraded * .	4055	2029	3749	57763	61022	556633
CLASSICAL.	60	133	86	3208	2483	202374
Universities.	1	7	.....	68	......	14365
Classical.						
Colleges	4	26	1	295	1	58865
Academies ..	44	76	82	2445	2176	89659
Professional.						
Medicine ...	2	14	.....	121	......	9750
Theology ...	1	4	.....	33	......	8000
Technical.						
Commercial .	5	9	.....	241	114	32500
Art & music .	1	4	3	70	192	3600
OTHER.	98	36	106	1391	2789	60394
Day & board'g	87	34	83	1310	1935	35594
Parochial ...	11	2	23	81	854	24800

STATE OF MARYLAND.

Classes and kinds.	Schools. Number.	Teachers. Male.	Teachers. Female.	Pupils. Male.	Pupils. Female.	Income.
						Dollars.
ALL CLASSES.	1779	1498	1789	55800	51584	1998215
PUBLIC.	1487	933	1217	42927	40299	1140057
Normal	3	4	11	70	195	10580
High	10	18	27	526	898	44475
Grammar ...	49	34	171	3449	3628	233693
Graded *	159	65	348	7851	7699	280422
Ungraded * .	1266	812	660	31031	27879	570887
CLASSICAL.	72	270	143	4716	1847	626490
Universities.	2	19	.....	230	......	16000
Classical.						
Colleges	19	121	2	1782	372	260427
Academies ..	34	57	132	1009	1196	240605
Professional.						
Law	1	2	.....	32	......	3000
Medicine ...	2	20	.....	185	......	8300
Theology ...	4	24	.....	177	......	12000
Technical.						
Agricultural	1	6	.....	98	......	30277
Commercial .	3	11	.....	733	......	21240
Blind	1	2	2	21	24	13500
Deaf & dumb	1	4	2	55	25	21000
Art & music .	6	20	5	624	230	10141
OTHER.	220	295	429	8157	9438	225668
Day & board'g	153	106	226	2600	3472	172333
Parochial ...	67	189	203	5557	5966	53335

STATE OF MASSACHUSETTS.

Classes and kinds.	Schools. Number.	Teachers. Male.	Teachers. Female.	Pupils. Male.	Pupils. Female.	Income.
ALL CLASSES.	5796	1428	6133	134777	134560	4817989
PUBLIC. (a)	5160	753	5387	121572	120573	3207826
Normal	5	9	38	61	990	
High	180	199	195	5804	5711	3207826
Grammar ...	919	292	1162	31095	30603	
Common † ...	4056	253	3992	84612	83269	
CLASSICAL.	84	406	126	5264	2678	1076423
Universities.	1	76	.....	1107	......	255114
Classical.						
Colleges	6	137	.....	1290	......	408126
Academies (b)	50	83	100	1754	1789	285325

* Common.

† Graded and ungraded.

(a) Also 2 charity schools at State almshouses in Hampden and Plymouth Counties; 1 State nautical school in Suffolk County; 1 State industrial school for girls, and 1 State reform school for boys in Worcester County—the last two with 10 male and 20 female teachers, 1,016 male and 260 female pupils, and $137,480 income from taxation and public funds.

(b) Of these 1 is styled "military" academy.

TABLE XXXIV.—*Schools by Classes and Kinds in each State and Territory—1870*—Cont'd.

STATE OF MASSACHUSETTS—Continued.

Classes and kinds.	Schools. Number.	Teachers. Male.	Teachers. Female.	Pupils. Male.	Pupils. Female.	Income.
Professional.						*Dollars.*
Law	1	3	.....	120	......	(a)
Medicine	2	23	2	300	23	a3561
Theology	6	42	.....	232	......	a58340
Technical.						
Agricultural	*1	12	.....	119	......	90303
Commercial	7	25	2	768	118	39058
Blind	1	4	7	83	61	43977
Deaf & dumb	2	.....	7	40	32	20501
Idiotic	1	.....	4	51	39	20629
Art & music	2	27	2	147	643	46500
Dentistry	1	5	.....	16	......	3600
Mining	1	6	.....	10	......	(a)
Other	3	39	.....	334	......	a56503
OTHER.	482	269	620	7941	11309	533690
Day & board'g	468	255	528	6711	6604	533690
Parochial	14	14	92	1230	4705	....

STATE OF MICHIGAN.

Classes and kinds.	Schools. Number.	Teachers. Male.	Teachers. Female.	Pupils. Male.	Pupils. Female.	Income.
ALL CLASSES.	5505	2999	6560	128949	137678	2550018
PUBLIC.	5414	2796	6181	123984	130844	2164489
Normal	3	10	3	301	287	} 2164489
High	37	48	63	600	685	
Grammar	62	31	85	1197	1372	
Graded*	570	411	885	21364	24061	
Ungraded*	4742	2266	5145	100522	104439	
CLASSICAL.	33	129	187	2327	3153	297155
Universities	1	33	.....	1040	32	75000
Classical.						
Colleges	9	66	22	1122	582	98905
Academies	3	4	9	45	140	9722
Professional.						
Law	1	4	.....	290	2	20426
Medicine	1	6	.....	300	18	22252
Theology	1	1	.....	25	......	2000
Technical.						
Agricultural	1	8	.....	114	9	33225
Commercial	6	13	2	259	55	11600
Blind & deaf and dumb.	1	9	5	80	75	37500
Music	10	18	149	92	2272	61465
OTHER.	148	74	192	2638	3681	88374
Day & board'g	119	58	160	1737	2840	75445
Parochial	29	16	32	901	841	12929

STATE OF MINNESOTA.

Classes and kinds.	Schools. Number.	Teachers. Male.	Teachers. Female.	Pupils. Male.	Pupils. Female.	Income.
						Dollars.
ALL CLASSES.	2479	979	1907	55166	52100	1011799
PUBLIC.	2424	919	1830	53171	50237	853304
Normal	3	5	15	185	364	18700
High	9	10	9	348	260	12882
Grammar	61	46	34	1096	1412	30654
Graded*	179	41	245	7450	7801	} 833069
Ungraded*	2172	817	1536	43492	40400	
CLASSICAL.	9	38	13	565	328	76376
Universities	2	11	4	261	148	40000
Classical.						
Colleges	4	27	4	376	148	53090
Academies	3	5	5	82	51	3145
Technical.						
Commercial	1	4	.....	60	......	3000
Blind & deaf and dumb.	1	2	4	47	29	17631
OTHER.	46	22	55	1430	1635	40189
Day & board'g	23	8	20	488	471	18414
Parochial	23	14	35	942	1164	21775

STATE OF MISSISSIPPI.

Classes and kinds.	Schools. Number.	Teachers. Male.	Teachers. Female.	Pupils. Male.	Pupils. Female.	Income.
ALL CLASSES.	1564	1054	674	22793	20658	780339
PUBLIC. (b)	.....	.....	.....	......	......	....
CLASSICAL.	21	36	42	534	927	96639
Universities	1	10	.....	200	......	39500
Classical.						
Colleges	18	32	32	500	792	80700
Academies*	1	3	5	......	123	4450
Professional.						
Law	1	1	.....	25	......	3250
Technical.						
Blind	1	.....	5	9	12	8439
OTHER.	1543	1018	632	22250	19731	683109
Day & board'g	1542	1018	631	22250	19706	683000
Parochial	1	.....	1	......	25	500

* Common.

(a) The income of the several professional schools of the University, except the dental, is included in that of Colleges.

(b) The public-school law of Mississippi was passed in June, 1870. The public funds given to the private schools would seem to be on account of the tuition of indigent pupils under the provisions of law relative to the Chickasaw school-fund.

TABLE XXXIV.—*Schools by Classes and Kinds in each State and Territory*—1870—Cont'd.

STATE OF MISSOURI.

Classes and kinds.	Schools. Number.	Teachers. Male.	Teachers. Female.	Pupils. Male.	Pupils. Female.	Income. Dollars.
ALL CLASSES.	6750	5157	3871	186641	183696	4340805
PUBLIC.	5996	4414	2948	163582	156731	3092730
Normal	5	11	15	206	352	18104
High	45	72	66	2959	3314	72043
Grammar	41	35	42	1461	1638	53199
Graded*	335	220	735	24377	27085	} 294398
Ungraded*	5570	4064	2090	134579	124142	}
CLASSICAL.	106	379	338	6594	6226	661996
Universities.	2	40	17	769	200	106055
Classical.						
Colleges	37	179	82	3183	2584	323835
Academies	45	86	247	1759	3272	204228
Professional.						
Law	1	6	.....	30	1	3000
Medicine	6	67	.....	286	......	24800
Theology	3	10	.....	83	......	10800
Technical.						
Commercial	8	21	.....	780	192	42050
Blind	1	3	4	48	40	21700
Deaf & dumb	2	3	4	50	87	29563
Art & music	3	4	1	75	50	2000
OTHER.	648	364	585	16465	20739	586076
Day & board'g	586	280	490	12019	14797	487176
Parochial	62	84	95	4446	5942	98900

TERRITORY OF MONTANA.

Classes and kinds.	Schools. Number.	Teachers. Male.	Teachers. Female.	Pupils. Male.	Pupils. Female.	Income. Dollars.
ALL CLASSES.	54	34	31	1027	718	41170
PUBLIC.	45	33	13	965	579	32925
Ungraded*	45	33	13	965	579	32925
CLASSICAL.	1	.....	8	10	40	1200
Classical.						
Academies	1	.....	8	10	40	1200
OTHER.	8	1	10	52	99	7045
Day & board'g	7	1	6	52	78	5245
Parochial	1	.....	4	......	21	1800

STATE OF NEBRASKA.

Classes and kinds.	Schools. Number.	Teachers. Male.	Teachers. Female.	Pupils. Male.	Pupils. Female.	Income. Dollars.
ALL CLASSES.	796	430	390	9492	8122	207560
PUBLIC.	781	436	377	9227	7825	182160
High	3	2	3	75	76	2667
Grammar	2	1	2	36	42	1800
Graded*	43	31	16	565	443	15220

STATE OF NEBRASKA—Continued.

Classes and kinds.	Schools. Number.	Teachers. Male.	Teachers. Female.	Pupils. Male.	Pupils. Female.	Income. Dollars.
Ungraded*	733	402	356	8551	7264	162473
CLASSICAL.	6	7	6	77	79	16900
Classical.						
Colleges	1	4	1	26	......	8000
Academies	1	1	2	25	35	1900
Technical.						
Deaf & dumb	1	1	.....	7	4	5000
Art & music	3	1	3	19	40	2000
OTHER.	9	7	7	188	218	8500
Day & board'g	9	7	7	188	218	8500

STATE OF NEVADA.

Classes and kinds.	Schools. Number.	Teachers. Male.	Teachers. Female.	Pupils. Male.	Pupils. Female.	Income. Dollars.
ALL CLASSES.	53	13	71	1279	1094	110493
PUBLIC.	38	9	47	1065	791	81273
Graded*	7	4	18	538	373	27510
Ungraded*	31	5	29	527	418	53763
CLASSICAL.	.....	.....	.....	......	......	....
OTHER.	15	4	24	214	303	29220
Day & board'g	14	4	18	214	208	26220
Parochial	1	.....	6	......	95	3000

STATE OF NEW HAMPSHIRE.

Classes and kinds.	Schools. Number.	Teachers. Male.	Teachers. Female.	Pupils. Male.	Pupils. Female.	Income. Dollars.
ALL CLASSES.	2542	653	2702	33123	31554	574696
PUBLIC.	2464	510	2600	30275	29133	403310
High	18	18	26	744	850	} 403310
Grammar	30	17	38	954	1082	}
Graded*	103	14	117	2875	2925	}
Ungraded*	2313	461	2419	25702	24364	}
CLASSICAL.	40	121	50	1808	1536	143966
Classical.						
Colleges	1	29	.....	280	......	28000
Academies (a)	36	50	50	1367	1529	88377
Professional.						
Medicine	1	11	.....	52	......	2749
Technical.						
Agricultural	1	26	.....	77	......	21065
Commercial	1	2	.....	23	7	3675
OTHER.	38	22	43	1046	885	27622
Day & board'g	21	22	26	426	465	21222
Parochial	17	.....	17	620	420	6400

* Common.

(a) Of these, 1 is styled "military and collegiate institute."

TABLE XXXIV.—*Schools by Classes and Kinds in each State and Territory—1870*—Cont'd.

STATE OF NEW JERSEY.

Schools.		Teachers.		Pupils.		
Classes and kinds.	Number.	Male.	Female.	Male.	Female.	Income.
						Dollars.
ALL CLASSES.	1893	1455	2434	67751	62049	2989250
PUBLIC.	1531	956	2060	39763	40342	1562573
Normal	1	4	4	29	250	10000
Grammar ...	23	51	239	3621	4013	150801
Graded*	156	120	566	14505	13845	511369
Ungraded* ..	1351	781	1251	21608	22234	890393
CLASSICAL.	13	96	10	1350	212	193347
Classical.						
Colleges	4	58	....	553	94	95150
Academies ..	1	....	10	.....	60	6000
Professional.						
Theology ...	4	26	....	247	50	73205
Technical.						
Agricultural	1	4	....	37	......	8483
Commercial	2	8	....	522	8	10500
Other (*a*) ...	1	....	....	.....	.....	......
OTHER.	349	403	364	26629	21495	1226330
Day & board'g	278	315	169	17472	13345	1186669
Parochial ...	71	88	195	9157	8150	39661

TERRITORY OF NEW MEXICO.

Classes and kinds.	Number.	Teachers: Male.	Teachers: Female.	Pupils: Male.	Pupils: Female.	Income.
ALL CLASSES.	41	38	34	1014	784	29886
PUBLIC.	5	5	.....	84	104	1000
Ungraded* ..	5	5	.....	84	104	1000
CLASSICAL.	4	4	17	251	235	16750
Classical.						
Colleges	1	4	.....	251	......	4500
Academies ..	3	.....	17	......	235	12250
OTHER.	35	29	17	679	445	12136
Day & board'g	29	25	9	467	308	7232
Parochial ...	6	4	8	212	137	4904

STATE OF NEW YORK.

Classes and kinds.	Number.	Teachers: Male.	Teachers: Female.	Pupils: Male.	Pupils: Female.	Income.
ALL CLASSES.	13020	8035	20883	373276	488746	15936783
PUBLIC.	11678	5710	18019	302373	416808	8912024
Normal	11	37	77	1251	3014	203194
High	13	69	78	2599	2002	214444
Grammar ...	87	83	547	12022	15301	145478
Graded *	552	752	3919	102031	107209	4071572
Ungraded* ..	11015	4769	13398	184470	289282	4277336

STATE OF NEW YORK—Continued.

Schools.		Teachers.		Pupils.		
Classes and kinds.	Number.	Male.	Female.	Male.	Female.	Income.
						Dollars.
CLASSICAL.	274	1171	878	25156	18572	3722193
Universities.	7	93	18	1032	312	474195
Classical.						
Colleges	94	335	77	4492	1034	1393530
Academies (*b*)	189	445	752	9795	14417	1298654
Professional.						
Law	3	15	.....	330	......	41093
Medicine ...	10	102	3	1408	46	192474
Theology ...	10	36	.....	441	......	148464
Technical.						
Commercial.	23	119	8	6880	816	228042
Blind	2	9	16	117	109	79110
Deaf & dumb	3	14	19	354	253	83107
Idiotic	1	.....	3	49	51	23000
Art & music.	4	58	.....	1085	1844	99285
Mining	1	22	.....	79	......	39290
Other	2	16	.....	126	......	30085
OTHER.	1068	1154	1986	45747	53366	3302566
Day & board'g	819	623	1325	18597	28254	1880277
Parochial ...	249	531	661	27150	25112	1422289

STATE OF NORTH CAROLINA.

Classes and kinds.	Number.	Teachers: Male.	Teachers: Female.	Pupils: Male.	Pupils: Female.	Income.
ALL CLASSES.	2161	1739	953	32664	32294	[illegible]
PUBLIC.	1435	1125	393	21279	20653	205131
Normal	5	4	5	137	190	3571
High	7	7	8	159	139	5450
Grammar ...	9	8	4	264	130	4935
Graded *	29	21	16	657	692	16917
Ungraded* ..	1385	1085	360	20062	19482	174258
CLASSICAL.	134	202	140	3659	3053	234329
Universities.	1	6	.....	40	......	6000
Classical.						
Colleges	22	60	31	694	832	94296
Academies ..	111	135	103	2866	2140	98631
Technical.						
Blind & deaf and dumb.	1	7	6	99	81	41399
OTHER.	592	412	420	7726	8608	196441
Day & board'g	542	378	375	6223	7074	178621
Parochial ...	50	34	45	1503	1534	17820

* Common.

(*a*) The statistics of this school are included in the Agricultural school.

(*b*) Of these 4 are styled "military" academies.

TABLE XXXIV—*Schools by Classes and Kinds in each State and Territory*—1870—Cont'd.

STATE OF OHIO.

Schools.		Teachers.		Pupils.		
Classes and kinds.	Number.	Male.	Female.	Male.	Female.	Income.
						Dollars.
ALL CLASSES.	11952	10266	13323	419391	371204	10244644
PUBLIC. (a)	11458	9306	12437	389022	348671	8528145
Normal	2	12	9	333	190	} 8528145
High	196	211	147	5686	6528	
Graded*	641	430	2138	81855	78039	
Ungraded*	10619	8650	10143	301148	263914	
CLASSICAL.	167	568	430	19696	8397	1088899
Universities.	9	55	2	1147	88	68777
Classical.						
Colleges	33	238	30	4506	1587	300054
Academies	94	204	383	5608	6583	491125
Professional.						
Law	1	3	....	75	......	3750
Medicine	10	56	....	747	......	54800
Theology	11	32	....	344	......	42500
Technical.						
Commercial	15	38	5	1040	......	57000
Blind	1	5	3	55	47	30204
Deaf & dumb	1	11	4	151	115	67171
Idiotic	1	1	5	80	65	42295
OTHER.	327	372	456	17873	14136	627600
Day & board'g	18	10	16	268	380	28000
Parochial	309	362	440	17605	13756	599600

STATE OF OREGON.

Classes and kinds.	Number.	Teachers: Male.	Teachers: Female.	Pupils: Male.	Pupils: Female.	Income.
ALL CLASSES.	637	484	342	16753	15840	248022
PUBLIC.	594	429	274	15531	14291	139387
High	4	9	7	210	192	} 139387
Graded*	31	13	20	1627	1584	
Ungraded*	559	407	247	13694	12515	
CLASSICAL.	20	44	25	1002	743	51123
Universities.	2	7	5	147	151	14680
Classical.						
Colleges	6	16	10	420	319	25650
Academies	10	16	15	507	423	21313
Professional.						
Medicine	1	7	....	15	1	(b)
Technical.						
Agricultural	1	2	....	25	......	960
Commercial	2	3	....	35	......	3200
OTHER.	23	11	43	220	806	57512
Day & board'g	22	10	43	200	806	57212
Parochial	1	1	....	20	......	300

STATE OF PENNSYLVANIA.

Schools.		Teachers.		Pupils.		
Classes and kinds.	Number.	Male.	Female.	Male.	Female.	Income.
						Dollars.
ALL CLASSES	14872	8507	11015	428023	383840	9628119
PUBLIC.	14107	7298	9820	393953	351781	7292946
Normal	19	66	42	2348	1919	194271
High	84	100	44	3180	2440	88983
Grammar	159	86	317	9389	8949	} 1329494
Graded*	2671	930	2877	100747	97950	
Ungraded*	11154	6073	6483	276393	239317	5039898
Soldiers' orphans (c)	20	43	57	1896	1206	440300
CLASSICAL.	213	812	389	14321	6884	1719058
Universities.	6	110	17	1391	170	181830
Classical.						
Colleges (d)	33	249	100	3507	1300	733933
Academies	138	313	263	6010	4977	410017
Professional.						
Medicine	6	63	4	1037	44	129000
Pharmacy	1	3	....	196	......	8000
Theology	11	47	....	408	......	128949
Technical.						
Agricultural	1	8	....	50	......	33000
Commercial	8	44	1	1692	60	81750
Blind	1	14	10	97	86	47500
Deaf & dumb	2	10	3	128	107	46250
Idiotic	1	....	6	108	75	48500
Art & music	2	8	1	62	112	6450
Dentistry	2	17	....	154	......	20000
Other	7	36	1	784	123	32700
OTHER.	552	397	806	19749	25175	616115
Day & board'g	400	246	426	7720	8380	385057
Parochial	152	151	380	12029	16795	231058

STATE OF RHODE ISLAND.

Classes and kinds.	Number.	Teachers: Male.	Teachers: Female.	Pupils: Male.	Pupils: Female.	Income.
ALL CLASSES.	561	237	714	15401	17105	565012
PUBLIC.	487	165	610	12736	14514	355582
High	10	12	37	487	910	12860
Grammar	43	28	91	2147	2025	14727
Graded*	120	15	251	5023	5690	204214
Ungraded*	314	110	231	5079	5889	123781
CLASSICAL.	5	36	6	984	214	78550
Universities.	1	11	....	203	......	45150
Classical.						
Colleges	1	11	....	203	......	45150
Academies	2	10	6	241	174	20400

* Common.

(a) Also 1 State reform school, with 10 male teachers, 150 male pupils, and $25,000 income from public funds.

(b) Income included in Colleges.

(c) Besides these 20 schools there are cared for in 19 other schools nearly 600 children, at an annual expense to the State of about $65,000.

(d) Including the Pennsylvania Military College.

TABLE XXXIV.—*Schools by Classes and Kinds in each State and Territory*—1870—Cont'd.

STATE OF RHODE ISLAND—Continued.

Classes and kinds.	Schools. Number.	Teachers. Male.	Teachers. Female.	Pupils. Male.	Pupils. Female.	Income.
Technical.						*Dollars.*
Commercial	2	15	....	540	40	13000
OTHER.	69	36	98	1771	2377	130880
Day & board'g	63	34	72	820	1076	119380
Parochial	6	2	26	951	1301	11500

STATE OF SOUTH CAROLINA.

Classes and kinds.	Schools. Number.	Teachers. Male.	Teachers. Female.	Pupils. Male.	Pupils. Female.	Income.
ALL CLASSES.	750	620	483	17397	20852	577953
PUBLIC.	581	429	353	13682	17680	279723
Normal	1	3	10	......	500	8000
High	13	16	6	255	297	13800
Grammar	19	27	46	434	600	17500
Common*	548	383	290	12993	16283	240423
CLASSICAL.	33	103	36	1326	794	206040
Universities.	2	9	2	143	73	13000
Classical.						
Colleges	9	40	18	480	275	54800
Academ's (a)	17	30	16	650	504	72825
Professional.						
Law	1	2	....	40	......	8000
Medicine	1	15	....	40	......	11000
Theology	3	13	....	104	......	51415
Technical.						
Blind	1	2	....	8	6	} 8000
Deaf & dumb	1	1	2	4	9	}
OTHER.	136	88	95	2389	2378	92190
Day & board'g	132	83	80	1798	2168	68040
Parochial	4	5	15	591	210	24150

STATE OF TENNESSEE.

Classes and kinds.	Schools. Number.	Teachers. Male.	Teachers. Female.	Pupils. Male.	Pupils. Female.	Income.
ALL CLASSES.	2794	2440	1147	65979	59852	1650692
PUBLIC.	1932	1579	562	43600	39370	683008
Normal	2	3	1	85	65	2100
High	23	20	15	768	762	14950
Grammar	18	22	11	703	539	} 665958
Graded†	145	64	115	3500	4109	}
Ungraded†	1744	1470	420	38544	33895	}

STATE OF TENNESSEE—Continued.

Classes and kinds.	Schools. Number.	Teachers. Male.	Teachers. Female.	Pupils. Male.	Pupils. Female.	Income.
						Dollars.
CLASSICAL.	228	390	293	10188	9481	647754
Universities.	8	52	10	1311	255	80260
Classical.						
Colleges	51	140	86	3082	2497	292030
Academies	152	208	183	6418	6373	247465
Professional.						
Law	1	1	....	80	......	6000
Medicine	1	12	....	60	......	6000
Theology	3	3	....	125	......	5600
Technical.						
Commercial	7	9	....	302	......	19100
Blind	1	1	3	15	23	11809
Deaf & dumb	1	6	1	51	50	26150
Art & music	11	10	22	55	536	36060
OTHER.	634	471	290	12191	11001	319930
Day & board'g	624	461	279	11815	10646	303215
Parochial	10	10	11	376	355	16715

STATE OF TEXAS.

Classes and kinds.	Schools. Number.	Teachers. Male.	Teachers. Female.	Pupils. Male.	Pupils. Female.	Income.
ALL CLASSES.	548	600	106	12244	10832	414880
PUBLIC.	....	....	....	......	......	......
CLASSICAL.	13	33	24	554	246	33550
Universities.	1	6	....	129	......	4800
Classical.						
Colleges (b)	4	16	2	319	103	14500
Academ's (c)	3	12	20	170	120	3500
Professional.						
Law	1	1	....	32	......	800
Medicine (b)	1	....	....	......	......	......
Theology	1	2	....	3	......	(d)
Technical.						
Commer'l (b)	1	....	....	......	......	......
Blind	1	1	1	10	14	5750
Deaf & dumb	1	1	1	20	10	9000
OTHER.	535	567	82	11690	10586	381330
Day & board'g	535	567	82	11690	10586	381330

* Graded and ungraded.

† Common.

(a) Of these 1 is styled "military" academy.

(b) One classical college and 1 medical college in Galveston County, and 1 commercial college in Anderson County, reported without teachers, pupils, or income.

(c) One academy in Harris County and 1 "military" academy in Travis County reported without income.

(d) Income included in Colleges.

TABLE XXXIV.—*Schools by Classes and Kinds in each State and Territory*—1870—Cont'd.

TERRITORY OF UTAH.

Classes and kinds.	Schools. Number.	Teachers. Male.	Teachers. Female.	Pupils. Male.	Pupils. Female.	Income.
						Dollars.
ALL CLASSES.	267	207	201	9844	11223	150447
PUBLIC.	....	....	....	.....	.....	....
CLASSICAL.	4	4	1	70	50	1300
Technical.						
Commercial.	1	1	....	10	10	500
Art & music	3	3	1	60	40	800
OTHER.	263	203	200	9774	11173	149147
Day & board'g	262	201	197	9683	11089	145342
Parochial ...	1	2	3	91	84	3805

STATE OF VERMONT.

Classes and kinds.	Schools. Number.	Teachers. Male.	Teachers. Female.	Pupils. Male.	Pupils. Female.	Income.
ALL CLASSES.	3084	1356	3804	31295	31618	707292
PUBLIC. (*a*)	2830	1171	3451	25872	26195	516702
Normal	3	8	14	142	326	5972
High	11	18	23	369	373	7123
Grammar ...	12	5	16	359	364	14390
Graded *	51	23	99	2667	2676	62572
Ungraded * ..	2753	1117	3299	22335	22456	426715
CLASSICAL.	46	104	100	2252	1944	112157
Universities.	1	15	....	115	.....	17864
Classical.						
Colleges	3	19	....	135	.....	21231
Academies ..	41	74	100	2029	1944	80050
Professional.						
Medicine ...	1	8	....	48	.....	7695
Technical.						
Agricultural	1	3	....	20	.....	3161
OTHER.	208	81	253	3171	3479	78433
Day & board'g	203	80	236	2731	3039	77793
Parochial ...	5	1	17	440	440	640

STATE OF VIRGINIA.

Classes and kinds.	Schools. Number.	Teachers. Male.	Teachers. Female.	Pupils. Male.	Pupils. Female.	Income.
ALL CLASSES.	2024	1432	1245	30878	29141	1155585
PUBLIC.	122	43	128	4275	4425	98770
Normal	4	3	13	109	186	18050
High	3	3	3	96	71	3700
Grammar ...	7	....	7	85	115	2000
Graded * ...	52	4	48	1350	1700	33200
Ungraded * ..	56	33	57	2635	2350	41820

STATE OF VIRGINIA—Continued.

Classes and kinds.	Schools. Number.	Teachers. Male.	Teachers. Female.	Pupils. Male.	Pupils. Female.	Income.
						Dollars.
CLASSICAL.	116	292	88	4423	2438	509437
Universities.	1	27	....	475	.....	88800
Classical.						
Colleges (*b*) ..	14	93	20	1535	562	203329
Academies ..	88	141	65	2201	1826	190592
Professional.						
Law	2	3	....	125	.....	11026
Medicine ...	2	24	....	105	.....	16942
Theology ...	5	14	....	241	.....	24100
Technical.						
Commercial.	2	4	....	70	.....	5480
Blind & deaf and dumb.	1	9	3	71	50	38168
Mining	1	2	....	23	.....	8600
Other	1	2	....	50	.....	11200
OTHER.	1786	1117	1029	22180	22278	547378
Day & board'g	1722	1086	933	20621	19898	505501
Parochial ...	64	31	96	1559	2380	41877

TERRITORY OF WASHINGTON.

Classes and kinds.	Schools. Number.	Teachers. Male.	Teachers. Female.	Pupils. Male.	Pupils. Female.	Income.
ALL CLASSES.	170	85	112	2816	2683	48309
PUBLIC.	154	75	83	2456	2304	33746
Graded *	1	1	1	36	24	936
Ungraded * ..	153	74	82	2420	2280	32810
CLASSICAL.	3	7	5	169	91	5988
Universities.	1	1	3	80	59	3500
Classical.						
Colleges	2	5	3	140	59	4800
Academies ..	1	2	2	29	32	1188
OTHER.	13	3	24	191	288	8568
Day & board'g	11	3	17	135	223	7068
Parochial ...	2	....	7	56	65	1500

STATE OF WEST VIRGINIA.

Classes and kinds.	Schools. Number.	Teachers. Male.	Teachers. Female.	Pupils. Male.	Pupils. Female.	Income.
ALL CLASSES.	2445	2070	768	55238	49711	698061
PUBLIC.	2371	1997	690	53587	47906	599811
Normal	9	4	7	225	230	5800
High	1	2	3	160	170	3300
Grammar ...	6	6	7	129	136	} 76956
Graded *	38	33	104	3642	3644	}
Ungraded * ..	2324	1952	569	49431	43726	513755

* Common.

(*a*) Also, 1 State reform school, with 1 male and 1 female teacher, 120 male pupils, and $6,132 income from public funds.

(*b*) Including the Virginia Military Institute.

TABLE XXXIV.—*Schools by Classes and Kinds in each State and Territory*—1870—Cont'd.

STATE OF WEST VIRGINIA—Continued.

Schools.		Teachers.		Pupils.		
Classes and kinds.	Number.	Male.	Female.	Male.	Female.	Income.
						Dollars.
CLASSICAL.	17	43	30	794	878	78406
Universities.	1	11	.....	170	......	30000
Classical.						
Colleges	6	31	18	599	691	58300
Academies ..	8	8	12	125	187	16856
Technical.						
Commercial.	1	2	.....	34	......	1850
Art & music	1	1	.....	20	......	900
Other	1	1	.....	16	......	500
OTHER.	57	30	48	857	927	19844
Day & board'g	54	28	44	719	797	17364
Parochial ..	3	2	4	108	130	2480

STATE OF WISCONSIN.

Classes and kinds.	Number.	Teachers, Male.	Teachers, Female.	Pupils, Male.	Pupils, Female.	Income.
ALL CLASSES.	4943	2511	5444	176541	167473	2600310
PUBLIC.	4859	2383	5286	172950	164058	2209384
Normal	3					
High	35					
Grammar ..	96	2383	5286	172950	164058	2209384
Graded *	275					
Ungraded* ..	4450					
CLASSICAL.	28	115	61	2312	1288	307653

STATE OF WISCONSIN—Continued.

Schools.		Teachers.		Pupils.		
Classes and kinds.	Number.	Male.	Female.	Male.	Female.	Income.
						Dollars.
Universities.	3	27	10	532	293	[illegible]
Classical.						
Colleges	12	62	37	1430	948	161380
Academies ..	5	6	18	205	246	12850
Professional.						
Law	1	6	.....	13	......	1254
Theology ...	3	19	.....	272	......	5000
Technical.						
Agricult'l (a)	2	8	.....	94	......	9065
Commercial.	3	6	.....	190	21	9230
Blind	1	2	4	26	24	19634
Deaf & dumb	1	6	9	73	49	29000
OTHER.	56	13	97	1279	2127	8323
Day & board'g	38	6	45	421	898	4685
Parochial ...	18	7	52	858	1229	3648

TERRITORY OF WYOMING.

Classes and kinds.	Number.	Teachers, Male.	Teachers, Female.	Pupils, Male.	Pupils, Female.	Income.
ALL CLASSES.	9	7	8	190	115	876
PUBLIC.	4	2	2	100	75	276
Ungraded* ..	4	2	2	100	75	276
NOT PUBLIC.	5	5	6	90	40	600
Day & board'g	5	5	6	90	40	600

* Common.
(a) Including the statistics of a Technical school.

TABLE XXXV.—*Libraries in the United States*—1870, 1860, *and* 1850.

Classes and kinds.	1870		1860		1850	
	Number.	Volumes.	Number.	Volumes.	Number.	Volumes.
ALL CLASSES	164,815	45,528,938	27,730	13,316,379	15,615	4,636,411
NOT PRIVATE	56,015	19,456,518	19,581	8,550,144	15,615	4,636,411
United States, Congressional	1	190,000				
Departmental	14	115,185				
State and territorial	53	633,915				
Town, city, and other municipal	1,101	1,237,430				
Court and law	1,073	425,782				
School, (including university and college)	14,375	3,598,537	10,771	2,743,349	12,280	2,589,725
Sabbath-school	33,580	8,346,153	6,205	2,072,489	1,988	542,321
Church	4,478	1,634,915	537	412,708	130	58,350
Historical, literary, and scientific societies	47	590,002				
Charitable and penal institutions	9	13,890				
Benevolent and secret associations	43	114,581				
Circulating	1,241	2,536,128				
Not specified			2,068	3,321,598	1,217	1,446,015
PRIVATE	108,800	26,072,420	8,149	4,766,235		

REMARKS.—The Statistics of Libraries have never been very creditable to the census of the United States. Such improvement as was practicable with the machinery provided for the collection of these statistics, has been effected at the Ninth Census, and the results will be found in the table, in comparison with the published results of 1860; but no great amount of complacency will be experienced upon a critical examination of the figures. The fact is, the machinery of the census under existing provisions of law, defective as it is in many particulars, is less adapted to work out correct results in this matter of the Statistics of Libraries than in any other use to which it is applied.

In 1860, there were returned, of all kinds, 27,730 libraries, containing 13,316,379 volumes. Of these, 8,149 were returned as private libraries, containing, in the aggregate, 4,766,235 volumes; but for some reason inexplicable at this date, 8,140 of these libraries, containing 4,711,635 volumes, were incorporated in the published table with public libraries, while the nine remaining private libraries, containing 54,600 volumes, were incorporated in the libraries of schools and colleges, as appears by notes to Table XIV (A,) of Vol. I, Ninth Census, (1870,) verified by reference to pages 502 and 505 of the volume on Mortality and Miscellaneous Statistics for the Eighth Census.

At the Ninth Census, (1870,) the total number of libraries returned was 163,353, containing 44,539,184 volumes. Of these, 107,673 were private libraries, containing 25,571,503 volumes. No return under this head was made from the State of Connecticut, the deputy marshal reporting that no exact information could be obtained.

While this increase in the number of private libraries and volumes therein, over the returns of 1860, shows that this portion of the census work has been performed with far greater effort and care on the part of the assistant and deputy marshals charged with the collection of this class of statistics, the results are yet manifestly far below the truth of the case for the whole country, while in respect to certain States the figures of Table XXXVI are almost ludicrously disproportionate.

The only compensation for this failure—for such it must be pronounced in spite of the increase over the returns of former censuses—is found in the consideration that the statistics of private libraries are not, from any proper point of view, among the desirable inquiries of the census. The statistics of the manufacture and importation of books would be far more significant and instructive, while obtained with one-tenth of one per cent. of the effort that would be required to collect accurate statistics of private libraries, based upon any classification that might be adopted.

The last clause of the foregoing sentence intimates a practical difficulty, which, however the methods of the census might be improved, would always render the statistics of private libraries of the least possible value. Unless each one of the two or three hundred thousand private collections of books which might claim admission to such a table as that in contemplation of the census law, were to be personally visited and inspected by a competent judge, it would be impossible to prevent the intrusion into that table of tens of thousands of such collections, without any merit to entitle them to a place there. No matter how carefully assistant marshals might perform this duty, or how fully instructed they might be from the central office, the mere fact of six or seven thousand persons being employed in collecting these statistics would be sufficient to

TABLE XXXVI.—*Libraries by States and Territories—1870.*

	States and Territories.	ALL CLASSES.		LIBRARIES, OTHER THAN PRIVATE.					
				Total.		State and Federal governments.		Town, city, &c.	
		Number.	Volumes.	Number.	Volumes.	Number.	Volumes.	Number.	Volumes.
	The United States	164, 815	45, 528, 938	56, 015	19, 456, 518	68	959, 100	1, 101	1, 237, 430
1	Alabama	1, 430	576, 882	298	86, 577	1	3, 000	4	800
2	Arizona	6	2, 000	1	1, 000	1	1, 000		
3	Arkansas	1, 181	135, 564	293	54, 332	1	12, 500	6	250
4	California	1, 617	474, 299	744	159, 625	1	2, 000	13	18, 278
5	Colorado	175	39, 344	30	11, 385	1	2, 600		
6	Connecticut	63	285, 937	63	285, 937	1	12, 000		
7	Dakota	19	9, 726	5	2, 788	1	2, 238		
8	Delaware	473	183, 423	252	92, 275	1	4, 000		
9	District of Columbia	696	793, 702	127	409, 936	15	305, 185		
10	Florida	253	112, 928	75	25, 374	1	7, 000		
11	Georgia	1, 735	467, 232	545	162, 851	1	16, 000	4	3, 730
12	Idaho	43	10, 625	11	2, 860				
13	Illinois	13, 570	3, 323, 914	3, 705	994, 545	1	10, 000	53	35, 010
14	Indiana	5, 301	1, 125, 553	2, 333	627, 894	1	17, 870	52	39, 029
15	Iowa	3, 540	673, 600	1, 153	377, 851	1	11, 000	23	22, 808
16	Kansas	574	218, 676	190	92, 425			4	4, 100
17	Kentucky	5, 546	1, 909, 230	1, 172	318, 985	2	9, 200	10	13, 436
18	Louisiana	2, 332	847, 406	480	263, 266	2	64, 000	1	10, 000
19	Maine	3, 334	984, 510	1, 462	533, 547	1	20, 000	58	14, 649
20	Maryland	3, 353	1, 713, 483	1, 316	570, 945	2	31, 462	1	41, 500
21	Massachusetts	3, 169	3, 017, 813	1, 544	2, 010, 609	1	30, 000	95	475, 853
22	Michigan*	26, 763	2, 174, 744	3, 002	578, 631	1	31, 265	423	124, 907
23	Minnesota	1, 412	360, 810	587	160, 790	1	10, 000	15	9, 981
24	Mississippi	2, 788	488, 482	537	88, 376	1	7, 000	2	1, 000
25	Missouri	5, 645	1, 065, 638	1, 742	408, 906	1	12, 000	11	8, 097
26	Montana	141	19, 790	13	5, 100	1	400	1	1, 600
27	Nebraska	390	147, 040	171	51, 915			1	200
28	Nevada	314	158, 040	28	41, 940		20, 000		
29	New Hampshire	1, 526	704, 260	670	324, 393		10, 500	32	44, 744
30	New Jersey	2, 413	895, 291	1, 636	535, 679		17, 205	2	20, 000
31	New Mexico	116	39, 425	33	9, 629		4, 000		
32	New York	20, 929	6, 310, 352	13, 771	3, 524, 869		66, 019	130	173, 236
33	North Carolina	1, 746	541, [illegible]15	656	202, 651	3	16, 303	3	2, 316
34	Ohio	17, 790	3, 687, 363	6, 025	1, 334, 363		34, 200	3	61, 000
35	Oregon	2, 361	334, 959	166	61, 532		3, 578	1	1, 161
36	Pennsylvania	14, 849	6, 377, 845	4, 966	3, 049, 247		30, 000	39	22, 586
37	Rhode Island	759	693, 387	334	309, 696		1, 500	10	15, 198
38	South Carolina	1, 663	546, 244	741	149, 224		2, 700		
39	Tennessee	3, 503	802, 112	773	204, 713	1	19, 000	4	1, 337
40	Texas	455	87, 111	135	25, 018	1	2, 000		
41	Utah	133	39, 177	74	31, 493	1	3, 519	3	850
42	Vermont	1, 792	727, 263	736	321, 727	1	14, 158	82	52, 368
43	Virginia	4, 171	1, 107, 313	1, 409	386, 020	2	22, 700	1	753
44	Washington	102	33, 362	30	13, 552	1	5, 400	1	610
45	West Virginia	1, 728	372, 745	638	152, 183	1	3, 093	4	5, 905
46	Wisconsin	2, 883	905, 811	1, 312	378, 680	4	61, 400	9	4, 838
47	Wyoming	31	2, 603	10	1, 103	1	103		

defeat, utterly and hopelessly, all approach to uniformity of treatment. One-half of the assistant marshals would call that a library which the other half would not, or, more probably, nine out of ten such officers would admit everything that claimed to be a library to their lists.

The plan most commonly urged for preventing such a want of uniformity in the collection of the statistics of private libraries is to fix a number of volumes below which no collection of books shall be returned as a library, as, say, 100, 200, 300, or 500 volumes; but it is quite sufficient, without argument, to disprove such a proposition, to indicate the practical difficulties arising from such questions as these: What shall be done with pamphlets and unbound volumes? With children's books? With school-books, old and new? With public documents, State and National? It is not too much to say that if all these classes were to be rejected, nine out of ten collections in the United States, which would otherwise pass into a table of private libraries containing one hundred volumes and over, would be thrown out, while, on the other hand, it is difficult to see what value such a table can have for any use, scientific or popular, if these classes are to be indiscriminately admitted.

TABLE XXXVI.—*Libraries by States and Territories*—1870.

LIBRARIES, OTHER THAN PRIVATE.										PRIVATE.		
Court and law.		School, college, &c.		Sabbath-school and church.		Literary and benevolent associations.		Circulating.				
Number.	Volumes.	Number.	Volumes.	Number.	Volumes.	Number.	Volumes.	Number.	Volumes.	Number.	Volumes.	
1,073	425,782	14,375	3,508,537	33,058	9,981,068	90	704,583	1,241	2,536,128	108,800	26,072,420	
33	7,785	12	23,300	248	51,692	....	......	....	......	1,132	490,305	1
....	......	....	......	....	......	....	......	....	......	5	1,000	2
29	5,747	....	......	253	34,312	....	......	4	1,493	888	81,232	3
46	5,339	288	20,113	364	82,120	1	300	31	22,475	873	314,674	4
2	150	2	2,000	24	5,835	....	......	1	800	145	27,939	5
....	......	5	142,000	....	......	1	14,000	56	117,937	....	(a)	6
....	......	....	......	4	550	....	......	....	......	14	6,938	7
....	......	....	......	246	65,251	....	......	5	26,024	221	91,148	8
4	32,348	....	......	101	42,703	....	......	7	29,700	569	383,766	9
5	4,182	....	......	67	12,470	....	......	2	1,722	178	87,554	10
63	8,610	15	41,100	451	79,116	3	2,400	8	11,805	1,190	304,381	11
1	150	....	......	6	1,510	....	......	4	1,200	32	7,765	12
135	23,832	1,122	140,750	2,308	486,100	7	153,492	79	75,352	9,865	2,399,369	13
92	10,308	1,006	323,391	1,162	229,048	....	......	20	8,248	2,968	497,659	14
11	944	15	18,747	1,084	303,835	1	150	18	20,367	2,387	295,749	15
3	2,050	3	6,500	176	73,225	....	......	4	6,550	384	126,251	16
218	61,590	18	20,675	924	214,084	....	......	....	......	4,374	1,590,245	17
61	31,583	34	37,050	356	100,233	....	......	26	20,400	1,852	584,140	18
19	9,748	25	63,425	1,219	317,652	1	2,500	136	100,273	1,872	450,963	19
20	14,602	72	98,470	1,191	306,752	....	......	30	78,099	2,037	1,142,538	20
18	27,708	20	233,127	1,206	625,565	17	249,800	186	347,556	1,625	1,007,204	21
49	10,359	246	37,734	2,167	321,362	....	......	116	53,704	23,761	1,596,113	22
1	500	1	4,000	544	112,508	2	7,200	23	16,601	825	200,020	23
3	121	1	5,000	523	72,825	....	......	7	2,430	2,251	400,106	24
125	35,104	50	44,825	1,526	285,338	....	......	28	112,450	3,903	566,642	25
....	......	....	......	9	1,800	1	100	1	1,200	128	14,690	26
1	600	....	......	166	50,115	1	......	3	1,000	219	95,125	27
1	250	....	......	18	6,550	....	......	8	15,140	286	116,100	28
7	627	21	30,800	576	171,995	4	16,510	29	47,217	856	379,876	29
....	......	....	......	1,619	423,224	....	......	11	75,250	777	359,612	30
2	210	2	1,200	27	4,010	....	......	1	200	83	29,805	31
26	77,535	9,879	1,165,158	3,589	1,247,790	....	......	141	790,131	7,158	2,785,483	32
24	4,119	14	77,050	609	101,111	....	......	3	1,752	1,090	339,264	33
1	5,000	1,118	426,013	4,896	796,650	1	3,000	5	8,500	11,765	2,353,000	34
1	180	4	4,400	148	43,967	3	1,096	8	7,150	2,195	273,427	35
29	24,051	115	267,223	4,618	2,117,199	48	252,035	86	330,153	9,883	3,328,598	36
5	2,147	12	97,500	274	127,601	....	......	32	65,750	425	383,601	37
3	6,324	4	20,800	731	118,300	....	......	2	1,100	922	397,020	38
3	1,500	10	68,930	738	106,673	....	......	17	7,253	2,732	597,399	39
1	1,000	1	1,200	131	19,318	....	......	1	1,500	320	62,093	40
1	2,000	....	......	61	8,894	....	......	8	16,239	59	7,684	41
4	3,023	58	38,735	555	191,357	....	......	33	20,678	1,056	405,536	42
12	2,117	4	50,000	1,378	257,669	....	......	12	52,781	2,762	721,203	43
....	......	1	400	26	6,842	....	......	1	300	72	19,810	44
6	1,269	3	7,400	621	132,814	....	......	3	1,700	1,090	230,562	45
8	1,010	194	50,492	1,078	222,073	....	......	39	38,867	1,551	527,131	46
....	......	....	......	10	1,000	....	......	....	......	20	1,500	47

(a) No returns of private libraries from Connecticut.

Passing from the private libraries reported in Table XXXVI, to libraries of other descriptions, as returned for the year 1870, a tolerable degree of completeness can fairly be claimed as the result of exceptional efforts in this direction

Omission of some importance have doubtless occurred in the column for circulating libraries, and difference in classification adopted by assistant or deputy marshals have caused some apparent discrepancies in other columns.

It should be said that the class "Libraries of historical, literary, and scientific societies," was intended to include only such libraries belonging to learned societies as are not open to the general public, but are reserved to the exclusive use of members or of a limited number of subscribers. This class fails, therefore, to include many libraries of learned societies which, from the fact of being open to the public freely, or upon terms of such liberality as to make their use practically universal, are, for the purposes of this table, more properly taken as public libraries. For some reason not explained, all libraries of this class for the city and State of New York have been incorporated with other classes.

TABLE XXXVII.—*Newspapers in the United States, by Periods of Issue*—1870.

Periods of issue.	All classes.			Advertising.		Agricultural and horticultural.	
	Number.	Copies annually issued.	Circulation.	Number.	Circulation.	Number.	Circulation.
Total	5,871	1,508,548,250	20,842,475	79	293,450	93	770,752
Daily	574	806,479,570	2,601,547				
Three times a week	107	24,196,380	155,105				
Semi-weekly	115	25,708,488	247,197				
Weekly	4,295	550,921,436	10,594,643	17	30,050	35	305,882
Semi-monthly	96	32,395,680	1,349,820	4	5,200	2	4,800
Monthly	622	67,810,116	5,650,843	53	244,700	56	460,070
Bi-monthly	13	189,900	31,650	2	6,000		
Quarterly	49	846,680	211,670	3	7,500		

TABLE XXXVII.—*Newspapers in the United States, by Periods of Issue*—1870—Continued.

Periods of issue—*Contin'd.*	Benevolent and secret societies.		Commercial and financial.		Illustrated, literary, and miscellaneous.		Devoted to nationality.	
	Number.	Circulation.	Number.	Circulation.	Number.	Circulation.	Number.	Circulation.
Total	81	257,080	142	690,200	503	4,422,235	20	45,150
Daily			8	16,900	8	42,584	2	7,600
Three times a week			2	6,500	2	1,300	2	1,800
Semi-weekly			5	37,000	6	3,133	4	6,700
Weekly	35	84,130	76	327,550	303	2,314,628	11	29,250
Semi-monthly	8	6,700	5	42,200	18	66,500		
Monthly	37	164,750	40	241,450	158	1,927,340		
Bi-monthly			1	1,200	1	10,000	1	400
Quarterly	1	1,500	5	17,400	7	36,750		

TABLE XXXVII.—*Newspapers in the United States, by Periods of Issue*—1870—Continued.

Periods of issue—*Contin'd.*	Political.		Religious.		Sporting.		Technical and professional.	
	Number.	Circulation.	Number.	Circulation.	Number.	Circulation.	Number.	Circulation.
Total	4,333	8,781,220	407	4,764,358	6	73,500	207	744,530
Daily	553	2,531,813					3	3,250
Three times a week	101	145,505						
Semi-weekly	100	200,364						
Weekly	3,565	5,886,668	208	1,385,335	5	58,500	40	132,650
Semi-monthly	8	6,770	40	1,171,250			11	46,400
Monthly	6	10,100	141	2,122,373	1	15,000	130	465,000
Bi-monthly			1	1,000			7	13,050
Quarterly			17	84,400			16	64,120

REMARKS.—In a country where literary as well as business enterprises are so ephemeral as in the United States, it will of course be impossible to secure absolute uniformity between the statistics of newspapers, magazines, and other periodicals, when collected through different agencies, at dates varying ever so little, and upon independent systems of classification.

The newspaper field of the United States has been very thoroughly worked up by

TABLE XXXVIII.—*Newspapers in the United States, by Classes*—1870.

Classes.	All periods of issue.			Daily.		Three times a week.	
	Number.	Copies annually issued.	Circulation.	Number.	Circulation.	Number.	Circulation.
Total	5, 871	1, 508, 548, 250	20, 842, 475	574	2, 601, 547	107	155, 105
Advertising	79	4, 680, 800	293, 450	......	......	......	......
Agricultural and horticultural	93	21, 541, 904	770, 752	......	......	......	......
Benevolent and secret societies	81	6, 518, 560	257, 080	......	......	......	......
Commercial and financial	142	31, 120, 600	690, 200	8	16, 900	2	6, 500
Illustrated, literary, and miscellaneous	503	160, 061, 408	4, 422, 235	8	42, 584	2	1, 300
Nationality, Devoted to	20	4, 671, 000	45, 150	2	7, 000	2	1, 800
Political	4, 333	1, 134, 789, 082	8, 781, 220	553	2, 531, 813	101	145, 505
Religious	407	125, 959, 496	4, 764, 358	......	......	......	......
Sporting	6	3, 222, 000	73, 500	......	......	......	......
Technical and professional	207	15, 974, 400	744, 530	3	3, 250	......	......

TABLE XXXVIII.—*Newspapers in the United States, by Classes*—1870—Continued.

Classes—*Continued.*	Semi-weekly.		Weekly.		Semi-monthly.	
	Number.	Circulation.	Number.	Circulation.	Number.	Circulation.
Total	115	247, 197	4, 295	10, 594, 643	96	1, 349, 820
Advertising	......	......	17	30, 050	4	5, 200
Agricultural and horticultural	......	......	35	305, 882	2	4, 800
Benevolent and secret societies	......	......	35	84, 130	8	6, 700
Commercial and financial	5	37, 000	76	327, 550	5	42, 200
Illustrated, literary, and miscellaneous	6	3, 133	303	2, 334, 628	18	66, 500
Nationality, Devoted to	4	6, 700	11	20, 250	......	......
Political	100	200, 364	3, 565	5, 896, 668	8	6, 770
Religious	......	......	208	1, 385, 335	40	1, 171, 250
Sporting	......	......	5	58, 500	......	......
Technical and professional	......	......	40	152, 650	11	46, 400

TABLE XXXVIII.—*Newspapers in the United States, by Classes*—1870—Continued.

Classes—*Continued.*	Monthly.		Bi-monthly.		Quarterly.	
	Number.	Circulation.	Number.	Circulation.	Number.	Circulation.
Total	622	5, 650, 843	13	31, 650	49	211, 670
Advertising	53	244, 700	2	6, 000	3	7, 500
Agricultural and horticultural	56	460, 070	......	......	......	......
Benevolent and secret societies	37	164, 750	......	......	1	1, 500
Commercial and financial	40	241, 450	1	1, 200	5	17, 400
Illustrated, literary, and miscellaneous	158	1, 927, 340	1	10, 000	7	36, 750
Nationality, Devoted to	......	......	1	400	......	......
Political	6	10, 100	......	......	......	......
Religious	141	2, 122, 373	1	1, 000	17	84, 400
Sporting	1	15, 000	......	......	......	......
Technical and professional	130	465, 060	7	13, 050	16	64, 120

two or three private business firms conducting advertising agencies. The publications of two, at least, of these houses have been carefully consulted in the compilation of this portion of the statistics of the census. Wherever differences have been found to

TABLE XXXIX.—*Newspapers of All Classes, by States and Territories—1870–1860–1850.*

	States and Territories.	ALL CLASSES. 1870 Number.	1870 Copies annually issued.	1870 Circulation.	1860 Number.	1860 Copies annually issued.	1860 Circulation.	1850 Number.	1850 Copies annually issued.	1850 Circulation.
	The United States	5871	1,508,548,250	20,842,475	4051	927,951,548	13,663,409	2526	426,409,978	5,142,177
1	Alabama	89	9,198,980	91,165	96	7,175,444	93,595	60	2,662,741	34,282
2	Arizona	1	14,560	280						
3	Arkansas	56	1,821,860	29,830	37	2,122,224	30,812	9	377,000	7,250
4	California	201	47,472,756	491,903	121	26,111,788	229,893	7	761,200	4,619
5	Colorado	14	1,190,600	12,750						
6	Connecticut	71	17,454,740	203,725	55	9,555,672	95,336	46	4,267,932	52,670
7	Dakota	3	85,904	1,652						
8	Delaware	17	1,607,840	20,860	14	1,010,776	16,144	10	421,200	7,500
9	Dist. of Columbia	22	10,092,800	81,400	13	10,881,100	69,510	18	11,127,238	100,073
10	Florida	23	649,220	10,545	22	1,081,600	15,500	10	319,800	5,750
11	Georgia	110	15,539,724	150,987	105	13,415,444	180,972	51	4,070,868	64,155
12	Idaho	6	200,200	2,750						
13	Illinois	505	113,140,492	1,722,541	286	27,464,764	356,159	107	5,102,276	84,820
14	Indiana	293	26,964,984	363,542	186	10,090,310	159,381	107	4,316,828	63,138
15	Iowa	233	16,403,380	219,090	130	6,589,360	89,240	29	1,512,800	22,500
16	Kansas	97	9,518,176	96,803	27	1,565,540	21,920			
17	Kentucky	89	18,270,160	197,130	77	13,504,044	179,397	62	6,582,838	79,868
18	Louisiana	92	13,755,690	84,165	81	16,948,000	120,650	55	12,416,224	80,288
19	Maine	65	9,867,680	170,690	70	8,333,278	126,169	49	4,203,064	63,439
20	Maryland	88	33,497,778	235,450	57	20,721,472	122,244	68	19,612,724	124,779
21	Massachusetts	259	120,691,266	1,692,124	222	102,000,760	1,368,980	209	64,820,564	718,221
22	Michigan	211	19,686,978	253,774	118	11,606,596	128,848	58	3,247,736	52,690
23	Minnesota	95	9,543,656	110,778	49	2,344,000	32,554			
24	Mississippi	111	4,703,336	71,868	73	9,099,784	88,737	50	1,752,504	30,555
25	Missouri	279	47,980,422	522,866	173	29,741,464	354,607	61	6,195,560	70,235
26	Montana	10	2,860,600	19,580						
27	Nebraska	42	3,388,500	31,600	14	519,000	9,750			
28	Nevada	12	2,572,000	11,300						
29	New Hampshire	51	7,237,588	173,919	20	1,024,400	19,700	38	3,067,552	60,228
30	New Jersey	122	18,625,740	205,500	90	12,801,412	162,016	51	4,098,678	44,521
31	New Mexico	5	137,350	1,525	2	59,800	1,150	2	38,800	1,150
32	New York	835	471,741,744	7,561,497	542	320,930,884	6,034,636	428	115,385,473	1,624,758
33	North Carolina	64	6,684,950	64,820	74	4,862,572	79,374	51	2,020,564	35,222
34	Ohio	395	98,548,814	1,388,367	340	71,767,742	1,121,682	261	30,473,407	339,469
35	Oregon	35	3,657,300	45,750	16	1,074,640	27,620	2	58,968	1,134
36	Pennsylvania	540	211,170,540	3,419,765	367	116,094,480	1,432,695	310	84,898,672	984,777
37	Rhode Island	32	9,721,500	82,050	26	5,289,280	49,690	19	2,756,950	24,472
38	South Carolina	55	8,901,400	80,900	45	3,654,840	53,870	46	7,145,930	53,748
39	Tennessee	91	18,300,844	225,952	83	10,053,152	176,908	50	6,940,750	67,672
40	Texas	112	4,214,800	55,250	89	7,855,808	108,038	34	1,296,924	18,205
41	Utah	10	1,578,400	14,250	2	327,600	6,300			
42	Vermont	47	4,055,300	71,390	31	2,579,080	47,415	35	2,567,662	45,961
43	Virginia (a)	114	13,319,578	143,840	139	26,772,568	301,622	87	9,223,068	87,708
44	Washington	11	396,500	6,785	4	122,250	2,350			
45	West Virginia (a)	59	4,012,400	54,432						
46	Wisconsin	190	28,762,920	313,385	155	10,798,670	139,145	46	2,665,487	33,015
47	Wyoming	6	243,300	1,950						

(a) At 1860 and 1850 Virginia includes West Virginia.

exist between the returns of the assistant or deputy marshals in this particular and the publications of the houses referred to, inquiry has been made into the reason of the excess or deficiency in the census totals, so that, if discrepancies still remain in any case, it is because, after full inquiry, the marshal's return has been held to represent better the facts of the case from the proper point of view of the statistician, or because different dates have been taken for the returns of the census from those on which the statistics of the several business houses conducting these inquiries were collected.

It will readily be seen that considerable differences might be accounted for between statements of this character, bearing date, respectively, 1st of January, 1870, 1st of June, 1870, and 1st of January, 1871, without discrediting any one of such statements. Newspaper enterprises are constantly being started and abandoned in every section of the United States, both in the form of papers under an entirely new name and independent control, and of semi-weekly or weekly issues of long-established journals. It

TABLE XXXIX.—*Newspapers of All Classes, by States and Territories*—1870–1860–1850.

Daily						Tri-weekly						Semi-weekly						
1870		1860		1850		1870		1860		1850		1870		1860		1850		
Number.	Circulation.	Number.	Circulation.	Number.	Circulation.	Number.	Circulation.	Number.	Circulation.	Number.	Circulation.	Number.	Circulation.	Number.	Circulation.	Number.	Circulation.	
574	2,601,547	387	1,478,435	254	758,454	107	155,105	86	107,170	115	75,712	115	247,197	79	175,165	31	33,511	
9	16,420	9	8,820	6	2,804	2	700	6	2,886	5	1,708	2	2,870	1	400			1
																		2
3	1,250					1	300							(a)	1,000			3
33	94,100	22	58,444	4	2,019	4	9,500	2	3,300			4	2,700	3	2,300			4
4	2,200																	5
16	35,730	14	19,100	7	5,654					4	2,400	1	800	1	400			6
																		7
1	1,600											3	3,660	4	3,294	3	600	8
3	24,000	5	32,910	5	19,836	1	2,000	1	4,600	5	7,748			2	3,000			9
						2	820	2	1,400	1	200	1	300	1	2,500			10
13	30,800	12	18,650	5	3,504	5	3,600	5	3,600	3	938	9	5,100	1	900			11
						1	250					1	600					12
39	166,400	23	38,100	8	3,615	10	40,570	6	2,936	4	1,375	4	2,950	2	1,026			13
20	42,300	13	8,881	9	3,720	3	2,300			2	1,250	1	350	5	1,600			14
22	19,800	9	7,700			3	1,650	2	695	2	3,700	1	1,000	2	500			15
12	17,570	3	1,650			4	1,840											16
6	31,900	4	19,500	9	7,237	4	3,500	3	2,750	7	7,213	4	4,100	1	2,000			17
7	34,395	8	41,000	11	32,088	1	800			6	4,433	8	8,500	3	1,850			18
7	10,700	8	8,141	4	3,110	1	350	4	3,978	5	1,942							19
8	82,921	6	53,200	6	50,989	1	5,015	2	6,146	4	3,203	2	1,600					20
21	231,645	17	160,000	22	130,640	1	800	3	2,400	4	2,250	16	41,484	14	40,700	11	19,904	21
16	27,485	8	14,150	3	4,039	3	5,000	1	9,000	2	333			3	9,150			22
6	14,800	4	2,524			5	4,200											23
3	2,300	5	15,370			6	3,650	2	2,500	4	1,573	3	2,400	1	5,000			24
21	86,555	16	44,550	5	10,905	5	13,800	3	7,800	4	1,750							25
3	6,900					1	400											26
7	6,850					1	500							1	1,000			27
5	7,500											2	950					28
7	6,100																	29
20	38,030	15	18,510	6	7,017									1	1,000			30
1	225																	31
87	789,470	74	487,340	51	206,222	5	5,800	7	18,900	8	4,975	22	114,500	10	58,871	13	29,965	32
8	11,795	8	3,550			3	800	1	200	5	2,656	5	5,750	4	2,162			33
26	139,705	24	84,560	26	46,083	8	13,560	8	4,212	10	6,718	3	7,200	4	3,500			34
4	6,330	2	800															35
55	466,070	29	233,550	24	162,635	3	10,000	1	3,900	2	500	2	17,700	3	9,800	1	600	36
6	23,250	5	10,300	5	5,705							1	1,200	1	2,000	2	242	37
5	16,100	2	1,600	7	16,357	4	9,600	4	6,200	5	3,521							38
13	34,630	8	11,300	8	14,218	2	2,300	7	4,509	2	1,707	1	1,000					39
12	3,500	3	5,300			5	2,450	3	9,288	5	3,368	5	3,700					40
3	2,700											3	2,900					41
3	3,190	2	750	2	555											1	2,200	42
16	24,099	15	44,400	15	16,104	7	4,800	5	2,750	12	9,080	8	7,033	11	21,212			43
1	160					1	600											44
4	5,192					2	550											45
14	43,250	14	14,125	6	3,398	2	3,200	8	3,220	4	1,271	3	6,850					46
2	550																	47

(a) No number reported.

is easy to see that a spirited business house, intent upon obtaining intelligence of the first movement of any enterprise of this kind, would be apt to hear of the beginning of such efforts more promptly than of their abandonment, and might embody in its annual statement many periodicals which it would not be desirable to include in the statistics of the census.

A second reason for discrepancies between the census tables and the statements prepared by private advertising agencies, is found in a different point of view, which is necessarily taken in treating the material for such tables for statistical purposes from that occupied by advertising agencies. There are very considerable numbers made of issues in every part of the country, of which it is an open question whether they are properly to be classed as newspapers or not, such as trade circulars, real-estate circulars, periodical prospectuses, sheets intended for gratuitous distribution at places of amusement, and a dozen other forms of advertisement, more or less disguised under a

TABLE XXXIX.—*Newspapers of All Classes, by States and Territories—1870–1860–1850*—Continued.

	States and Territories.	WEEKLY.						SEMI-MONTHLY.				MONTHLY.	
		1870		1860		1850		1870		1850		1870	
		Number.	Circulation.	Number.	Circulation.	Number.	Circulation.	Number.	Circulation.	Number.	Circulation.	Number.	Circulation.
	The United States..	4295	10,594,643	3173	7,581,930	1902	2,944,629	96	1,349,820	95	487,645	622	5,650,843
1	Alabama	76	71,175	77	74,289	48	29,020	..	....	1	750	...	....
2	Arizona	1	280	...	....	...	....	..	....	...	....	...	....
3	Arkansas	48	26,280	37	38,812	9	7,250	..	....	...	....	4	2,000
4	California	140	298,603	89	131,249	3	2,600	1	300	...	....	17	22,200
5	Colorado	9	9,550	...	....	...	....	..	....	...	....	1	1,000
6	Connecticut	43	107,395	37	68,436	30	40,716	2	900	...	....	7	56,400
7	Dakota	3	1,652	...	....	...	....	..	....	...	....	...	....
8	Delaware	12	13,600	16	12,850	7	6,900	..	....	...	....	1	2,000
9	District of Columbia.	12	41,900	4	26,000	8	72,489	..	....	...	....	6	13,500
10	Florida	20	9,425	19	11,600	9	5,550	..	....	...	....	...	....
11	Georgia	73	88,837	73	127,322	37	50,188	2	700	6	9,525	6	21,300
12	Idaho	4	1,900	...	....	...	....	..	....	...	....	...	....
13	Illinois	364	890,913	238	282,997	84	68,768	11	107,900	3	1,800	72	490,808
14	Indiana	233	239,342	160	134,600	95	56,168	6	9,200	1	2,000	28	64,138
15	Iowa	196	187,840	112	76,945	25	17,750	3	3,400	...	....	5	3,950
16	Kansas	78	71,393	24	20,270	...	....	..	....	...	....	3	6,000
17	Kentucky	68	137,930	64	123,947	38	58,712	..	....	8	6,706	7	19,700
18	Louisiana	75	39,970	70	77,800	37	31,667	..	....	...	....	1	500
19	Maine	47	114,600	52	95,510	39	55,887	1	700	...	....	8	42,840
20	Maryland	69	127,314	49	62,898	54	60,867	..	....	1	2,000	8	18,600
21	Massachusetts	153	899,465	145	778,680	126	391,752	11	45,200	3	2,575	48	462,130
22	Michigan	174	192,889	103	92,648	47	32,418	2	1,300	3	5,600	16	27,100
23	Minnesota	79	79,978	45	30,080	...	....	..	....	...	....	5	11,800
24	Mississippi	92	60,018	65	65,867	46	28,922	2	700	...	....	5	2,800
25	Missouri	225	342,361	143	277,357	45	46,280	3	22,000	...	....	23	53,650
26	Montana	6	12,200	...	....	...	....	..	....	...	....	...	....
27	Nebraska	30	22,400	12	7,750	...	....	..	....	...	....	4	1,850
28	Nevada	5	2,850	...	....	...	....	..	....	...	....	...	....
29	New Hampshire	37	75,819	20	19,700	35	58,426	1	25,000	1	650	6	67,000
30	New Jersey	95	120,670	70	131,506	43	36,544	..	....	2	960	7	46,800
31	New Mexico	4	1,300	2	1,150	1	400	..	....	1	750	...	....
32	New York	518	3,388,497	366	2,600,925	308	753,960	21	216,300	9	71,000	163	2,920,810
33	North Carolina	44	43,325	57	65,612	40	29,427	1	1,250	6	3,169	3	1,900
34	Ohio	299	923,502	260	805,810	201	256,427	8	65,050	23	74,235	47	228,750
35	Oregon	26	30,400	12	14,820	2	1,134	..	....	...	....	5	9,000
36	Pennsylvania	385	1,214,395	297	700,961	261	526,142	11	825,100	19	290,500	73	846,730
37	Rhode Island	19	43,950	19	35,990	12	18,525	..	....	...	....	6	13,650
38	South Carolina	42	44,000	35	41,070	27	27,190	..	....	5	4,275	3	10,000
39	Tennessee	65	117,022	61	101,839	36	41,147	1	15,000	...	....	8	54,200
40	Texas	89	45,300	79	90,615	29	14,837	1	300	...	....	...	....
41	Utah	3	8,400	2	6,300	...	....	..	....	...	....	1	250
42	Vermont	43	56,200	28	44,665	30	41,206	..	....	...	....	1	12,000
43	Virginia	60	75,488	103	189,360	55	48,434	4	4,320	3	11,150	10	27,900
44	Washington	10	4,525	4	2,350	...	....	..	....	...	....	2	1,500
45	West Virginia	48	42,390	...	....	...	....	2	3,100	...	....	3	3,200
46	Wisconsin	160	266,000	130	111,400	35	26,846	2	1,900	...	....	9	22,183
47	Wyoming	4	1,400	...	....	...	....	..	....	...	....	...	....

show of presenting news or criticism to the public. Many of these are adapted in a very high degree to the purposes of advertisement, and are, therefore, most properly to be included in the lists of such agencies as those referred to, yet very many of them must be excluded from the tables of the census.

The law requires this report of newspapers and periodicals, on account of their relation to the moral, social, and intellectual condition of the people. To swamp this class of statistics by inconsiderately admitting hundreds of prospectuses, circulars, and advertising sheets, which can possibly have no such relations, would be undoubtedly an abuse. At the same time this subject has been treated liberally, and every periodical has been admitted to these tables which could establish a reasonable claim to be considered as within the purview of the census act.

LE XXXIX.—*Newspapers of All Classes, by States and Territories*—1870-1860-1850—Continued.

…ONTHLY—Continued.			BI-MONTHLY.				QUARTERLY.						ANNUAL.				
1860	1850		1870		1850		1870		1860		1850		1860		1850		
Circulation.	Number.	Circulation.	Number.	Circulation.	Number.	Circulation.	Number.	Circulation.	Number.	Circulation.	Number.	Circulation.	Number.	Circulation.	Number.	Circulation.	
3,411,959	100	740,651	13	31,650	5	8,200	49	211,070	30	101,000	19	25,875	16	807,750	4	47,500	
7,200																	1
																	2
																	3
34,600							2	4,500									4
																	5
500	1	500	1	1,150	1	1,200	1	1,350	2	7,100	2	a2,200					6
																	7
																	8
									1	3,000							9
																	10
29,500									1	1,000							11
																	12
31,100	7	12,267	2	11,000			3	12,000			1	225					13
14,300			2	6,000													14
3,400	2	1,050	2	750			1	700									15
																	16
31,400																	17
	1	12,200															18
18,540	1	2,500					1	1,500									19
	3	7,700															20
353,100	29	113,100			4	7,000	9	11,400	6	21,500	7	6,000	1	3,000	3	45,000	21
3,900	3	10,300															22
																	23
																	24
24,300	7	11,300	1	1,500			1	3,000									25
																	26
1,000																	27
																	28
	2	1,150															29
10,000													1	1,000			30
																	31
2,045,000	36	552,484					19	135,120	10	57,000	3	6,150	6	766,000			32
7,850																	33
218,850			2	2,700			2	7,900			1	6,000	3	4,750			34
4,000									1	(c)			1	8,000			35
464,684			3	8,550			8	31,200	6	6,800	2	1,900	3	13,000	1	2,500	36
1,400																	37
4,500							1	1,200	1	500	2	2,400					38
43,700	4	10,600					1	1,800	2	3,500			1	12,000			39
2,775																	40
																	41
2,000	2	2,000															42
43,900	1	2,000									1	1,000					43
																	44
																	45
10,400	1	1,500															46
																	47

) Also, in Connecticut, one periodical published three times a year, with an annual circulation of 1,500.
) No number reported.
) No circulation reported.

TABLE XL.—*Churches in the United States*—1870–1860–1850.

NOTE.—"Baptist, (other,)" consists of *Free-will, German,* (also called Dunkers or Tunkers—style
"Presbyterian, (other)," consists of *Cumberland, Reformed,* (Synod of the United States,) *Reformed,*

	Denominations.	1870			
		Organizations.	Edifices.	Sittings.	Property.
	ALL DENOMINATIONS	72, 459	63, 082	21, 665, 062	$354, 483, 581
1	Baptist, (regular)	14, 474	12, 857	3, 997, 116	39, 229, 221
2	Baptist, (other)	1, 355	1, 105	363, 019	2, 378, 977
3	Christian	3, 578	2, 822	865, 602	6, 425, 137
4	Congregational	2, 887	2, 715	1, 117, 212	25, 069, 698
5	Episcopal, (Protestant)	2, 835	2, 601	991, 051	36, 514, 549
6	Evangelical Association	815	641	193, 796	2, 301, 650
7	Friends	692	662	224, 664	3, 939, 560
8	Jewish	189	152	73, 265	5, 155, 234
9	Lutheran	3, 032	2, 776	977, 332	14, 917, 747
10	Methodist	25, 278	21, 337	6, 528, 209	69, 854, 121
11	Miscellaneous	27	17	6, 935	135, 650
12	Moravian, (Unitas Fratrum)	72	67	25, 700	709, 100
13	Mormon	189	171	87, 838	656, 750
14	New Jerusalem, (Swedenborgian)	90	61	18, 755	869, 700
15	Presbyterian, (regular)	6, 262	5, 683	2, 198, 900	47, 828, 732
16	Presbyterian, (other)	1, 502	1, 388	499, 344	5, 436, 524
17	Reformed Church in America, (late Dutch Reformed)	471	468	227, 228	10, 359, 255
18	Reformed Church in the United States, (late German Reformed)	1, 256	1, 145	431, 700	5, 775, 215
19	Roman Catholic	4, 127	3, 806	1, 990, 514	60, 985, 566
20	Second Advent	225	140	34, 555	306, 240
21	Shaker	18	18	8, 850	86, 900
22	Spiritualist	95	22	6, 970	100, 150
23	Unitarian	331	310	155, 471	6, 282, 675
24	United Brethren in Christ	1, 445	937	265, 025	1, 819, 810
25	Universalist	719	602	210, 884	5, 692, 325
26	Unknown, (Local Missions)	26	27	11, 925	687, 800
27	Unknown, (Union)	409	552	153, 202	965, 295

REMARKS.—The Statistics of Churches contained in the following tables are believed to be substantially exact, and to present a just view of the organization of the several religious denominations found within the United States and of the accommodation for public worship afforded by each.

It was not to be expected or desired that the account taken in the census of the churches of the country should, in all cases, agree with the statements put forth by religious denominations through their respective official organs. The census has its own proper point of view, and applies, in some respects, different tests from those known to the compilers of year-books or registers.

A church to deserve notice in the census must have something of the character of an institution. It must be known in the community in which it is located. There must be something permanent and tangible to substantiate its title to recognition. No one test, it is true, can be devised that will apply in all cases, yet, in the entire absence of tests, the statistics of the census will be overlaid with fictitious returns to such an extent as to produce the effect of absolute falsehood. It will not do to say that a church without a church-building of its own is, therefore, not a church; that a church without a pastor is not a church; nor even that a church without membership is not a church. There are churches properly cognizable in the census which are without edifices and pastors, and, in rare instances, without a professed membership. Something makes them churches in spite of all their deficiencies. They are known and recognized in the community as churches, and are properly to be returned as such in the census.

On the other hand, there are hundreds of churches borne on the rolls of religious sects having both a legal title to an edifice and a nominal membership, which never gather a congregation together, support no ministry, and conduct none of the services of religion.

Some of the larger religious denominations, either in consequence of their peculiar organization or by reason of special efforts, maintain a careful system of reports and returns, and the statistics of such denominations are accordingly entitled to great consideration.

TABLE XL.—*Churches in the United States*—1870–1860–1850.

·mselves "Brethren,") *Mennonite, Seventh-day, Six-Principle,* and *Winebrencarian.*
eneral Synod of the United States,) *Associated Reformed,* and *United.*

1860			1850			
Churches.	Accommodation.	Property.	Churches.	Accommodation.	Property.	
54,009	19,128,751	$171,397,932	38,061	14,234,825	$87,328,801	
11,221	3,749,551	19,799,378	9,376	3,247,069	11,020,855	1
929	294,667	1,279,736	187	60,112	133,115	2
2,068	681,016	2,518,045	875	303,780	853,386	3
2,234	956,351	13,327,511	1,725	807,335	8,001,995	4
2,145	847,296	21,665,698	1,459	643,598	11,375,010	5
			39	15,479	118,250	6
726	269,084	2,544,507	736	296,323	1,713,767	7
77	34,412	1,135,300	36	18,371	418,600	8
2,128	757,637	5,385,179	1,231	339,701	2,909,711	9
19,883	6,259,799	33,093,371	13,302	4,345,519	14,825,070	10
2	650	4,000	122	36,494	214,530	11
49	20,316	227,450	344	114,988	444,167	12
24	13,500	891,100	16	10,880	84,780	13
58	15,395	321,200	21	5,600	115,100	14
5,061	2,088,838	24,227,350	4,826	2,079,765	14,543,780	15
1,345	477,111	2,613,166	32	10,189	27,550	16
440	211,068	4,453,850	335	182,686	4,116,280	17
676	273,697	2,422,670	341	160,932	993,780	18
2,550	1,404,437	26,774,119	1,222	667,863	9,256,758	19
70	17,120	101,170	25	5,250	11,100	20
12	5,200	41,000	11	5,150	39,500	21
17	6,275	7,500				22
264	138,213	4,338,316	215	138,067	3,280,822	23
			14	4,650	18,600	24
664	235,219	2,856,095	530	215,115	1,778,316	25
			22	9,425	98,950	26
1,366	371,899	1,370,212	999	320,454	915,020	27

METHODIST.

Foremost among these is the Methodist Church, which, by reason of its episcopal rm of government and its scheme of changing periodically the pastors of churches, always in possession, as nearly as it would be possible to effect, of the true condition of s organization in all parts of the country to a late date. Dead churches are not alwed to encumber its rolls, and consequently the list of its several branches present eir exact strength "for duty." This denomination, therefore, affords a high test of e accuracy of the returns of the census; and, notwithstanding that it presents as uch difficulty in the enumeration as any other, the general correspondence between e statements embodied in the minutes of the annual conferences of the principal anches of the church, after making allowance for the known strength of certain inor branches which do not publish official returns, and the statistics of the demination as given in the census, is, taking all the States of the Union together, very ecided. The slight differences that exist are sufficiently explained by differences beveen the dates of the returns and by different rules of construction and classification hich would naturally be adopted in doubtful cases by parties acting independently each other.

There are other denominations, one or two, notably the Baptist, of great importance, which an absence of central control in the government of the churches, and the ant of a thorough system of reports and returns, deprive church statistics of value. is in respect to these, as a rule, that the discrepancies between the claims the denomination and the results of the census are greatest. In all such ses full and searching inquiry has been made; the recognized authorities of the urches interested have been freely consulted; and assistant marshals have been lled on to explain the discrepancy, and to review their own statements. Hundreds letters have been written from the Census Office on this subject; thousands of urches have been inquired for; and where differences, after all has been done, ill exist, it only remains to be said that if this or that denomination has as many urches as it claims, the agents of the census have not been able to find them.

TABLE XLI.—*Churches of All Denominations*—1870–1860–1850.

	States and Territories.	ALL DENOMINATIONS.				
		1870				
		Aggregate population.	Organizations.	Edifices.	Sittings.	Property.
	The United States	38, 558, 371	72, 459	63, 082	21, 665, 062	$354, 483, 581
1	Alabama	996, 992	2, 095	1, 958	510, 810	2, 414, 515
2	Arizona	9, 658	4	4	2, 400	24, 000
3	Arkansas	484, 471	1, 371	1, 141	264, 225	854, 975
4	California	560, 247	643	532	195, 558	7, 404, 235
5	Colorado	39, 864	55	47	17, 495	207, 230
6	Connecticut	537, 454	826	802	338, 735	13, 428, 100
7	Dakota	14, 181	17	10	2, 800	16, 300
8	Delaware	125, 015	267	252	87, 809	1, 893, 950
9	District of Columbia	131, 700	111	112	63, 655	3, 393, 100
10	Florida	187, 748	429	390	78, 920	426, 580
11	Georgia	1, 184, 109	2, 873	2, 698	801, 148	3, 561, 955
12	Idaho	14, 999	15	12	2, 150	18, 200
13	Illinois	2, 539, 891	4, 298	3, 459	1, 201, 403	22, 664, 293
14	Indiana	1, 680, 637	3, 698	3, 106	1, 008, 350	11, 942, 227
15	Iowa	1, 194, 020	2, 763	1, 446	431, 709	5, 730, 352
16	Kansas	364, 399	530	301	102, 135	1, 722, 700
17	Kentucky	1, 321, 011	2, 969	2, 696	878, 039	9, 824, 465
18	Louisiana	726, 915	638	599	213, 955	4, 048, 325
19	Maine	626, 915	1, 328	1, 104	376, 738	5, 200, 653
20	Maryland	780, 894	1, 420	1, 389	499, 770	12, 038, 650
21	Massachusetts	1, 457, 351	1, 848	1, 764	882, 317	24, 488, 985
22	Michigan	1, 184, 059	2, 239	1, 415	456, 226	9, 133, 816
23	Minnesota	439, 706	877	582	158, 266	2, 401, 750
24	Mississippi	827, 922	1, 629	1, 800	485, 398	2, 360, 800
25	Missouri	1, 721, 295	3, 229	2, 082	691, 520	9, 709, 358
26	Montana	20, 595	15	11	3, 850	99, 300
27	Nebraska	122, 993	161	108	32, 210	386, 000
28	Nevada	42, 491	32	19	8, 050	212, 000
29	New Hampshire	318, 300	633	624	210, 090	3, 303, 780
30	New Jersey	906, 096	1, 402	1, 384	573, 303	18, 347, 150
31	New Mexico	91, 874	158	152	81, 560	322, 621
32	New York	4, 382, 759	5, 627	5, 474	2, 282, 876	66, 073, 755
33	North Carolina	1, 071, 361	2, 683	2, 497	718, 310	2, 487, 677
34	Ohio	2, 665, 260	6, 488	6, 284	2, 085, 586	25, 554, 725
35	Oregon	90, 923	220	135	39, 425	471, 100
36	Pennsylvania	3, 521, 951	5, 981	5, 668	2, 332, 288	52, 758, 384
37	Rhode Island	217, 353	295	283	125, 183	4, 117, 200
38	South Carolina	705, 606	1, 457	1, 308	491, 425	3, 276, 988
39	Tennessee	1, 258, 520	3, 180	2, 842	878, 524	4, 697, 675
40	Texas	818, 579	843	647	199, 100	1, 035, 430
41	Utah	86, 786	165	164	86, 110	674, 600
42	Vermont	330, 551	699	744	270, 614	3, 713, 530
43	Virginia	1, 225, 163	2, 582	2, 405	763, 127	5, 277, 368
44	Washington	23, 955	47	36	6, 000*	62, 450
45	West Virginia	442, 014	1, 529	1, 018	297, 315	1, 835, 790
46	Wisconsin	1, 054, 670	1, 864	1, 466	423, 015	4, 890, 781
47	Wyoming	9, 118	12	12	3, 500	46, 000

An analysis of the reports of certain religious denominations, however, is sufficient to explain the discrepancies to the vindication of the census, without further investigation. It is generally found that the aggregate reported by the authorities of the denomination is made up of two classes: first, of churches from which reports have been received up to a recent date, showing an actual organization and an active membership, with church accommodation and a ministry; and, second, of churches, often more numerous, which are deficient in one or all of these respects, in degrees ranging from partial or temporary deprivation to total and habitual destitution. In such cases, the statistics accompanying almost invariably cut in between the highest and lowest figures of the denomination; take in all the churches that are fully officered, organized, and equipped, and add to this number such of the second class as, in spite of deficiencies, answer to the true definition of a church from the point of view of the census, viz, are institutions in the community known and recognized.

TABLE XLI.—*Churches of All Denominations*—1870–1860–1850.

ALL DENOMINATIONS.						
1860			1850			
Churches.	Accommodation.	Property.	Churches.	Accommodation.	Property.	
54, 009	19, 128, 751	$171, 397, 932	38, 061	14, 234, 825	$87, 328, 801	
1, 875	550, 494	1, 930, 499	1, 373	439, 605	1, 131, 616	1
						2
1, 008	216, 183	468, 130	362	60, 226	89, 315	3
293	97, 721	1, 853, 340	28	10, 200	267, 800	4
						5
802	374, 686	6, 354, 205	734	307, 299	3, 555, 194	6
						7
230	68, 560	846, 150	180	55, 741	340, 345	8
68	50, 040	950, 450	46	34, 120	363, 000	9
319	68, 990	284, 390	177	44, 960	165, 400	10
2, 393	763, 812	2, 440, 391	1, 802	627, 197	1, 269, 350	11
						12
2, 424	798, 346	6, 890, 810	1, 223	486, 576	1, 482, 185	13
2, 933	1, 047, 211	4, 065, 274	2, 032	709, 655	1, 529, 585	14
949	256, 891	1, 670, 190	193	43, 083	177, 425	15
97	32, 650	143, 950				16
2, 179	778, 025	3, 928, 620	1, 845	671, 053	2, 252, 448	17
572	206, 196	3, 160, 360	306	109, 615	1, 782, 470	18
1, 167	370, 814	2, 886, 905	945	321, 167	1, 725, 845	19
1, 016	377, 022	5, 516, 150	909	379, 465	3, 947, 884	20
1, 636	737, 905	15, 393, 607	1, 475	691, 823	10, 206, 184	21
807	250, 794	2, 334, 040	309	120, 117	723, 600	22
260	69, 960	478, 200	3	100	900	23
1, 441	445, 965	1, 633, 265	1, 016	294, 104	736, 542	24
1, 577	500, 616	4, 509, 767	880	251, 068	1, 561, 610	25
						26
63	7, 010	42, 715				27
						28
681	231, 363	1, 913, 692	626	237, 417	1, 495, 786	29
1, 123	461, 796	7, 762, 705	813	345, 733	3, 680, 936	30
100	79, 400	429, 460	73	28, 650	94, 100	31
5, 287	2, 155, 828	35, 125, 287	4, 134	1, 913, 854	21, 134, 207	32
2, 270	811, 423	1, 999, 227	1, 795	572, 924	905, 553	33
5, 210	1, 966, 678	12, 988, 312	3, 936	1, 457, 294	5, 793, 099	34
75	19, 230	195, 695	9	3, 133	76, 520	35
5, 337	2, 112, 980	22, 581, 479	3, 566	1, 574, 873	11, 586, 115	36
310	147, 529	3, 308, 350	928	101, 210	1, 251, 400	37
1, 267	451, 256	3, 481, 236	1, 182	460, 450	2, 172, 246	38
2, 311	728, 661	2, 558, 330	2, 014	625, 595	1, 216, 101	39
1, 034	271, 196	1, 095, 254	341	63, 575	204, 930	40
21	12, 950	888, 700	9	4, 200	51, 609	41
697	231, 235	1, 800, 600	599	231, 534	1, 216, 125	42
3, 105	1, 067, 840	5, 439, 605	2, 383	856, 436	2, 856, 075	43
12	4, 775	55, 200				44
						45
1, 070	293, 699	1, 973, 392	365	97, 773	353, 900	46
						47

BAPTIST.

The discrepancies between the returns of the census and the statistics of the church e greatest in the case of the Baptists.

The census of 1860 showed 11,221 "churches." (*a*)

The census of 1870 shows 14,474 church organizations; the increase in the decade ing certainly as large as could have been expected. The statistics of the church, howver, purport to show 17,535 churches in 1870 in the territory covered by the operations the census, (*b*,) a difference against the census of 3,061. But reference to the statistics of the same church shows that in 1869 only 14,084 churches were claimed, exclusive of the States of Delaware and Rhode Island, the District of Columbia, and certain erritories; adding in the number claimed in 1870 for the States and Territories not ported in 1869, to wit, 91, we have as the total churches in 1869, 14,175, (*c*) or 299 less an the census.

TABLE XLII.—*Churches, Fifteen Selected Denominations*—1870.

States and Territories.	BAPTIST.				CHRISTIAN.			
	Organizations.	Edifices.	Sittings.	Property.	Organizations.	Edifices.	Sittings.	Property.
The United States	15, 829	13, 962	4, 360, 135	$41, 608, 198	3, 578	2, 822	865, 602	$6, 425, 137
Alabama	789	772	190, 200	536, 650	19	19	5, 750	18, 650
Arizona								
Arkansas	473	397	103, 800	196, 325	90	63	14, 000	38, 125
California	60	44	16, 775	271, 600	30	22	6, 360	34, 100
Colorado	5	4	835	11, 090	2			
Connecticut	116	120	45, 150	1, 378, 400	4	4	750	6, 500
Dakota	2							
Delaware	8	7	2, 930	131, 000				
District of Columbia	16	16	8, 775	273, 000	1	1	400	5, 000
Florida	127	123	21, 100	53, 400				
Georgia	1, 369	1, 312	3[illegible]9, 165	1, 125, 650	34	33	10, 285	60, 650
Idaho	2	2	175	2, 000				
Illinois	722	571	181, 454	2, 601, 612	350	231	85, 175	681, 450
Indiana	620	521	158, 375	1, 137, 325	455	377	122, 775	810, 635
Iowa	352	165	50, 690	668, 900	113	48	15, 750	134, 450
Kansas	92	56	18, 540	247, 000	35	16	4, 550	45, 300
Kentucky	1, 004	962	288, 936	2, 023, 975	490	436	141, 585	1, 046, 675
Louisiana	227	208	56, 140	346, 500	1	1	800	3, 000
Maine	480	367	117, 189	1, 240, 967	44	20	4, 922	42, 800
Maryland	97	92	20, 780	149, 600	5	5	1, 850	38, 000
Massachusetts	286	295	139, 035	3, 330, 998	31	31	9, 675	198, 400
Michigan	366	232	74, 100	1, 006, 430	38	18	4, 625	51, 550
Minnesota	94	50	12, 435	159, 500	6	6	1, 550	7, 450
Mississippi	665	652	174, 970	582, 325	30	28	7, 325	58, 850
Missouri	805	518	145, 360	1, 005, 708	304	239	68, 545	514, 700
Montana					1			
Nebraska	26	15	5, 400	64, 800	9	4	1, 550	14, 500
Nevada								
New Hampshire	184	172	51, 925	659, 500	19	19	4, 600	42, 400
New Jersey	168	168	63, 113	2, 396, 900	10	10	3, 430	54, 000
New Mexico	1	1	300	800				
New York	902	879	333, 086	7, 602, 275	95	95	28, 175	294, 850
North Carolina	985	938	249, 765	583, 285	66	60	16, 200	24, 377
Ohio	713	702	209, 870	2, 758, 500	681	610	167, 625	1, 366, 900
Oregon	28	16	4, 750	29, 200	26	16	4, 400	25, 000
Pennsylvania	620	589	288, 310	3, 695, 300	97	69	27, 500	584, 100
Rhode Island	109	107	34, 886	877, 400	12	12	3, 050	33, 500
South Carolina	523	471	191, 550	690, 482	2	2	200	400
Tennessee	987	918	255, 376	860, 075	203	167	55, 455	944, 685
Texas	275	211	61, 700	196, 540	18	17	4, 450	11, 650
Utah								
Vermont	131	130	43, 245	506, 700	14	14	4, 350	31, 200
Virginia	849	793	256, 830	1, 345, 048	100	88	29, 225	92, 170
Washington	3				4	1	250	600
West Virginia	325	223	62, 850	200, 855	36	23	6, 400	37, 550
Wisconsin	212	142	42, 980	505, 623	13	5	1, 450	9, 000
Wyoming	1	1	300	4, 000				

If, therefore, the statement of 17,535 churches for 1870 is correct, there must have been a clear addition of 3,360 in the single year intervening, which would be considerably more than the entire addition claimed for the nine years previous, (2,954,) which is wholly unreasonable and incredible.

Proceeding, however, to analyze the aggregate of 17,535, we find that from only 12,600 churches were reports received during the year from which the statement is made up. For 3,273 the figures were taken from the report of the year previous, in the absence of any later advices; and, for 1,662 more, estimates had to be made, in the absence even of returns a year old.

It will be seen here, as has been above indicated, that the census cuts in between the highest claim of the denomination and the number for which positive data can be shown. And in this the census conforms in an eminent degree to the reason of the case, inasmuch as it must be that many of the churches unreported are still in existence, possessing sufficient activity to justify their return by the assistant marshals, while many undoubtedly have, in the natural course of things, ceased to keep up even a form of life.

ABLE XLII.—*Churches, Fifteen Selected Denominations*—1870—Continued.

l Territories.	CONGREGATIONAL.				EPISCOPAL, (PROTESTANT.)			
	Organizations.	Edifices.	Sittings.	Property.	Organizations.	Edifices.	Sittings.	Property.
7nited States .	2,887	2,715	1,117,212	$25,069,698	2,835	2,601	991,051	$36,514,549
	4	2	650	7,300	50	38	15,520	264,600
					15	13	3,095	43,450
	40	36	11,915	282,400	45	38	13,095	398,900
	4	4	1,050	28,200	9	8	2,000	46,040
ut	290	360	133,175	4,728,700	139	147	50,962	3,275,534
	1	1	200	5,000	2	2	350	4,000
					29	27	8,975	246,850
f Columbia	2	1	1,800	115,000	16	16	6,680	583,500
					17	13	4,600	71,100
	10	10	2,800	16,550	35	27	10,080	307,900
					6	4	600	4,000
	212	188	66,137	1,867,800	105	87	30,395	1,496,300
	18	12	4,800	119,900	49	38	10,300	498,500
	187	125	33,925	529,570	58	36	9,584	192,869
	43	26	8,350	152,000	14	9	3,280	57,500
					38	35	15,800	570,300
	9	9	4,650	56,200	36	32	17,100	160,800
	231	219	83,965	1,401,736	25	23	8,975	280,213
	1				153	155	61,480	1,594,800
setts	500	502	269,314	6,293,327	107	99	46,245	2,394,435
	156	114	38,320	742,200	100	79	26,750	911,250
a	57	39	11,400	143,200	64	54	14,595	400,500
pi	2	1	300	1,200	33	33	8,650	203,000
	37	27	12,295	235,700	83	51	20,950	485,650
					2	1	700	5,500
	10	7	2,050	38,500	15	12	3,500	31,000
					5	3	1,100	30,000
ipshire	169	172	67,951	1,150,380	21	22	7,475	283,800
ey	14	9	5,050	335,500	128	122	34,800	2,586,000
ico					3			
k	268	256	111,785	2,732,500	475	465	204,290	7,211,150
rolina	1	1	150	1,500	77	68	22,955	403,450
	198	195	87,150	1,385,585	114	112	51,150	1,343,280
	8	7	2,300	49,500	9	8	1,800	53,200
ania	40	36	14,450	318,200	238	234	94,182	6,703,007
and	27	27	18,500	620,000	42	39	17,155	735,100
rolina	1	1	300	10,000	83	81	35,350	729,600
	3	2	525	14,100	33	31	12,940	269,573
	1	1	500	5,000	32	31	11,400	109,400
					2	2	460	30,800
	183	183	75,925	1,054,400	33	34	11,223	348,100
					185	177	60,105	843,210
on	2	1	250	5,000	4	3	500	7,650
ginia					21	19	7,355	166,500
1	157	140	44,960	610,550	82	70	21,200	380,585
	1	1	300	4,000	3	3	750	10,000

down from the total of the United States to the total for States, (still within e denomination,) we find an even clearer explanation of the same facts. The ncies are mainly in the Southern States, where the conditions of society, es- among the freedmen, are such as would account for even larger differences ist. In Alabama the census reports but 786; the church statistics claim 1,054; n only 489 of these were reports actually received during the year for which rns were made up; 445 were taken from the report the year previous, and 120 tained purely by estimate. In Arkansas the census reports 463; the church s claim 539; but only 122 of these were obtained from the reports of the year 5 were taken from the report of 1869, and 182 were obtained by estimate. In arolina the census reports 951; the church statistics claim 1,235; but of these are obtained from reports of the year, 228 from reports of the year previous, by estimate. In Georgia the census reports 1,364; the church statistics claim nt in 1869 only 1,478 were claimed, while the minutes of the State Baptist ion, held at Cartersville, April 21 and 24, 1871, show but 1,738, included in re 225 taken from the minutes of 1869, 59 taken from the minutes of 1868, and en from the minutes of conventions held before the war. The comparison e carried through all the Southern States with much the same results.

TABLE XLII.—*Churches, Fifteen Selected Denominations*—1870—Continued.

States and Territories.	EVANGELICAL ASSOCIATION.				FRIENDS.			
	Organizations.	Edifices.	Sittings.	Property.	Organizations.	Edifices.	Sittings.	Property.
The United States	815	641	193, 796	$2, 301, 650	692	662	224, 664	$3, 939, 560
Alabama								
Arizona								
Arkansas								
California	1	1	200	5, 000	2	2	500	16, 000
Colorado								
Connecticut					2	3	350	1, 500
Dakota								
Delaware					8	8	3, 425	64, 000
District of Columbia	1	1	800	20, 000	2	1	160	15, 000
Florida								
Georgia								
Idaho								
Illinois	58	55	20, 176	329, 650	5	4	1, 000	13, 400
Indiana	47	40	10, 925	124, 600	81	76	29, 500	263, 800
Iowa	32	11	2, 400	22, 800	82	60	17, 075	125, 800
Kansas	2	1	300	6, 000	7	7	1, 600	13, 300
Kentucky	5	5	3, 000	150, 000				
Louisiana								
Maine								
Maryland	3	3	1, 000	45, 500	22	21	7, 440	151, 700
Massachusetts					29	29	7, 950	91, 000
Michigan	15	11	2, 350	24, 600	10	8	2, 600	8, 850
Minnesota	20	16	3, 875	24, 100				
Mississippi								
Missouri	5	5	1, 800	15, 000	2	2	500	2, 000
Montana								
Nebraska	5	3	600	7, 000				
Nevada								
New Hampshire					13	13	3, 585	15, 500
New Jersey					63	63	28, 730	448, 450
New Mexico								
New York	25	25	7, 300	228, 350	89	87	24, 910	586, 300
North Carolina					28	27	11, 250	21, 465
Ohio	157	140	33, 500	338, 500	91	91	26, 050	218, 770
Oregon	2	2	550	9, 300				
Pennsylvania	256	233	80, 545	712, 800	114	118	43, 725	1, 764, 700
Rhode Island					17	17	5, 514	58, 600
South Carolina					1	1	300	500
Tennessee					5	4	1, 900	4, 800
Texas								
Utah								
Vermont					5	5	1, 280	6, 100
Virginia					12	13	4, 925	33, 625
Washington								
West Virginia	2	1	300	1, 000				
Wisconsin	179	88	24, 175	237, 450	2	2	375	1, 100
Wyoming								

The least impartial consideration of the above facts must convince any one that in the aggregates of this denomination, in the Southern States especially, are included large numbers of congregations "in the bush," properly, it may be, to be reported from a denominational point of view, but hardly to be returned in the census, while there are also included many churches which have been destroyed by the violence of war, or have been merged with other organizations of the same church, or have fallen into hopeless decay, in the natural course of human institutions.

The only one of the Southern States where comparison between the statistics of the census and those of the church, and an analysis of the latter according to the plan above pursued, would induce the belief that the returns of the census, as between the two, were in fault, is the State of Texas, where the conditions attending the recent enumeration were so unfavorable, so almost hopeless, as to prevent the collection of social statistics in any degree satisfactory to the Census Office. The same admission of a failure to fully return the Baptist denomination might seem, at first glance, to be required (though in nothing like the same degree) in respect to the State of Virginia; but a comparison of the results in this State with those for West Virginia establishes the soundness of the statistics of the two States taken together, and justifies the sug-

LE XLII.—*Churches, Fifteen Selected Denominations*—1870—Continued.

rritories.	LUTHERAN.				METHODIST.			
	Organizations.	Edifices.	Sittings.	Property.	Organizations.	Edifices.	Sittings.	Property.
d States.	3, 032	2, 776	977, 332	$14, 917, 747	25, 278	21, 337	6, 528, 209	$69, 854, 121
....	....	....	....	....	991	892	218, 945	787, 965
....	2	2	1, 025	10, 000	583	485	91, 890	276, 850
....	6	6	5, 350	54, 000	184	155	43, 035	677, 625
....	....	....	....	....	14	13	3, 815	50, 800
....	4	3	1, 240	21, 500	184	188	63, 975	1, 834, 025
....	3	3	900	2, 100	5	1	500	1, 200
....	1	1	300	5, 000	173	166	51, 924	781, 000
lumbia ..	10	10	3, 700	223, 000	33	36	20, 860	815, 600
....	....	....	....	....	235	215	42, 600	140, 700
....	11	10	3, 000	57, 100	1, 248	1, 158	327, 343	1, 073, 030
....	....	....	....	....	....	....	....	....
....	230	207	74, 301	1, 043, 476	1, 426	1, 124	357, 073	5, 203, 630
....	195	180	62, 285	619, 600	1, 403	1, 121	346, 125	3, 291, 427
....	79	45	12, 285	113, 950	982	493	142, 655	1, 490, 220
....	9	5	1, 400	12, 500	166	71	53, 525	316, 600
....	7	7	1, 650	16, 000	978	818	244, 918	1, 854, 565
....	3	3	1, 650	28, 000	213	202	52, 990	351, 775
....	4	1	500	800	327	264	82, 530	883, 237
....	88	84	40, 915	875, 100	771	757	231, 530	3, 220, 630
s	2	1	450	20, 000	297	290	117, 325	2, 904, 100
....	96	81	23, 150	360, 650	864	469	140, 290	2, 356, 906
....	135	97	23, 325	222, 150	225	106	38, 690	337, 550
....	10	10	2, 450	12, 300	787	776	208, 203	854, 475
....	94	86	39, 550	768, 000	1, 066	626	185, 420	1, 645, 300
....	....	....	....	....	7	5	1, 430	16, 800
....	14	7	2, 000	27, 900	50	36	10, 150	113, 400
....	....	....	....	....	11	7	2, 630	50, 500
ire........	....	....	....	....	118	118	36, 351	475, 000
....	19	19	6, 750	111, 500	518	518	196, 860	4, 493, 630
....	....	....	....	....	1	1	300	1, 500
....	190	182	70, 133	1, 560, 500	1, 745	1, 702	606, 098	11, 768, 290
ia........	73	70	23, 290	96, 550	1, 193	1, 078	390, 045	775, 805
....	477	476	131, 050	1, 392, 975	2, 161	2, 115	714, 146	6, 540, 910
....	1	1	300	15, 000	97	49	15, 100	113, 400
....	904	841	339, 128	6, 474, 022	1, 286	1, 271	446, 403	7, 510, 675
....	1	1	400	1, 500	33	30	14, 605	371, 300
a	49	44	17, 900	137, 450	611	532	164, 050	652, 100
....	22	22	9, 875	27, 664	1, 339	1, 155	336, 433	1, 506, 153
....	23	21	7, 650	47, 900	355	244	69, 100	251, 140
....	....	....	....	....	2	1	300	1, 200
....	....	....	....	....	180	184	60, 325	884, 530
....	80	73	25, 350	160, 800	1, 011	901	270, 617	1, 449, 565
....	....	....	....	....	16	12	2, 200	21, 650
a	22	21	7, 300	93, 300	879	552	152, 865	723, 015
....	171	156	36, 780	302, 860	508	396	103, 240	973, 018
....	....	....	....	....	2	2	600	8, 000

, the officers charged with the compilation of these statements for denomi-
rposes have, not unnaturally, failed to divide the churches accurately
old and the new State.

CONGREGATIONAL.

to the Congregational Church, again, the difference between the statistics
us and those of the denominational organs is decided, though by no means
as this denomination has never extended its agencies southward with any
e success. The denomination claims 3,121; the census allows 2,887. In
e difference is partially accounted for (probably to the extent of between
y the later date (within the same year) of the statistics of the denomina-
remaining difference is explained by such facts as those contained in the
atistics" of the Congregational Quarterly for January, 1871. Nine hundred
hurches only are there stated to have settled pastors; 1,438 have "acting
29 are supplied by licentiates and ministers of other denominations; and
cant." The differences in respect to this denomination are found mainly
, where the large number of churches without either a stated ministry or

TABLE XLII.—*Churches, Fifteen Selected Denominations*—1870—**Continued.**

States and Territories.	PRESBYTERIAN.				REFORMED CHURCH IN AMERICA. (Late Dutch Reformed.)			
	Organizations.	Edifices.	Sittings.	Property.	Organizations.	Edifices.	Sittings.	Property.
The United States	7, 824	7, 071	2, 698, 244	$53, 265, 256	471	468	227, 228	$10, 330, 25
Alabama	202	200	67, 615	350, 700	......	......	......	......
Arizona	......	......	......	......	......	......	......	......
Arkansas	161	131	33, 600	179, 125	......	......	......	......
California	79	59	21, 798	453, 050	......	......	......	......
Colorado	6	5	1, 200	21, 800	......	......	......	......
Connecticut	7	10	3, 875	195, 300	1	2	1, 300	100, 000
Dakota	......	......	......	......	......	......	......	......
Delaware	32	32	13, 375	384, 500	......	......	......	......
District of Columbia	13	15	9, 250	405, 500	......	......	......	......
Florida	29	29	6, 620	70, 310	......	......	......	......
Georgia	134	123	49, 575	553, 525	......	......	......	......
Idaho	1	......	......	......	......	......	......	......
Illinois	595	523	184, 849	3, 637, 625	14	14	4, 880	150, 200
Indiana	375	357	128, 960	2, 078, 100	2	2	500	8, 200
Iowa	375	222	64, 890	962, 325	4	4	1, 500	25, 000
Kansas	94	62	22, 810	302, 400	......	......	......	......
Kentucky	306	285	100, 750	1, 292, 400	......	......	......	......
Louisiana	37	34	14, 100	185, 450	......	......	......	......
Maine	......	......	......	......	......	......	......	......
Maryland	77	77	32, 415	1, 279, 550	1	1	600	15, 000
Massachusetts	13	10	5, 700	257, 325	......	......	......	......
Michigan	187	142	48, 925	1, 124, 400	26	24	8, 700	190, 150
Minnesota	76	60	16, 956	275, 000	2	2	500	4, 000
Mississippi	262	258	71, 100	470, 200	......	......	......	......
Missouri	476	319	103, 350	1, 385, 750	......	......	......	......
Montana	......	......	......	......	......	......	......	......
Nebraska	24	9	3, 125	48, 300	......	......	......	......
Nevada	5	3	1, 100	18, 500	......	......	......	......
New Hampshire	7	7	3, 170	65, 000	......	......	......	......
New Jersey	251	251	128, 200	3, 623, 025	97	99	, 54, 880	2, 540, 885
New Mexico	1	1	250	7, 000	......	......	......	......
New York	726	705	349, 870	13, 431, 040	304	300	147, 033	7, 076, 250
North Carolina	204	201	77, 155	395, 475	......	......	......	......
Ohio	792	700	293, 945	4, 145, 726	2	2	700	9, 500
Oregon	20	16	5, 675	44, 200	......	......	......	......
Pennsylvania	1, 028	1, 008	423, 850	12, 114, 450	10	10	5, 300	298, 000
Rhode Island	1	1	500	10, 000	......	......	......	......
South Carolina	164	153	67, 100	571, 400	2	2	300	4, 000
Tennessee	556	512	188, 970	1, 258, 335	......	......	......	......
Texas	101	84	27, 600	142, 600	......	......	......	......
Utah	1	......	......	600	......	......	......	......
Vermont	9	9	3, 356	25, 200	......	......	......	......
Virginia	204	200	70, 065	837, 450	1	1	100	350
Washington	3	3	600	5, 500	......	......	......	......
West Virginia	89	76	27, 320	328, 050	......	......	......	......
Wisconsin	98	86	23, 930	308, 070	5	5	1, 015	7, 760
Wyoming	3	3	750	12, 000	......	......	......	......

a "supply," and the large number, also, (often the same churches,) without edifices of their own, afford ample scope for the operation of different rules of construction as to what constitutes a church for census purposes.

The most important discrepancy between the statistics of the denomination and those of the census, within any of the Eastern States, is in the State of Pennsylvania, where the agents of the census report 40 church organizations. The Congregational Quarterly claims 70; 6 only, however, having settled pastors, 31 having "acting pastors," and 33 being "vacant." In the case of 13 of the churches thus reported by the denomination, the Census Office received positive information from the postmasters of the towns or villages where they were said to be severally located that no such churches were in existence. Of the 17 remaining to be accounted for, the Census Office has been able to obtain no information of any kind through correspondence.

In Kentucky, again, the "Quarterly" claims three churches. The returns of the census show none; but in response to inquiries addressed to the pastors of 2 of the churches claimed by the "Quarterly," the Superintendent was informed that the churches should be classed, one as "Christian" and the other as "Baptist." The third is stated by the "Quarterly" to be located at "Camp Nelson," but, as there is neither town nor post-office by that name in the State of Kentucky, the inquiry could

LE XLII.—*Churches, Fifteen Selected Denominations*—1870—Continued.

Territories.	REFORMED CHURCH IN THE UNITED STATES. (Late German Reformed.)				ROMAN CATHOLIC.			
	Organizations.	Edifices.	Sittings.	Property.	Organizations.	Edifices.	Sittings.	Property.
ted States.	1,256	1,145	431,700	$5,775,215	4,127	3,806	1,990,514	$60,985,566
....	......	......	......	......	20	19	6,730	409,000
....	......	......	......	......	4	4	2,400	24,000
....	......	......	......	......	11	11	5,250	82,500
....	......	......	......	......	160	144	66,640	4,092,200
....	......	......	......	......	14	13	8,575	49,300
....	1	1	250	6,000	44	34	26,418	1,469,500
....	......	......	......	......	4	3	850	4,000
....	......	......	......	......	13	8	6,000	170,000
olumbia...	1	1	300	8,500	11	11	9,250	886,000
....	......	......	......	......	10	9	3,950	90,600
....	......	......	......	......	14	11	5,500	294,550
....	......	......	......	......	4	4	575	11,000
....	32	30	7,170	93,600	290	249	136,900	4,010,650
....	34	33	8,680	97,300	204	201	86,830	2,511,700
....	13	13	3,950	46,000	216	165	57,280	1,216,150
....	1	1	275	3,000	37	34	14,605	513,200
....	......	......	......	......	130	123	72,550	2,604,900
....	2	2	600	2,000	103	102	62,525	2,836,800
....	......	......	......	......	32	32	17,822	461,700
....	47	42	19,980	502,150	103	103	62,280	3,001,400
ts........	3	3	950	24,000	196	162	130,415	3,581,085
....	19	10	2,800	24,730	167	148	62,991	2,037,830
....	2	2	400	4,500	154	135	42,370	755,000
....	......	......	......	......	27	27	8,250	165,850
....	11	9	1,900	16,900	184	166	97,550	3,119,450
....	......	......	......	......	5	5	1,700	77,000
....	......	......	......	......	17	11	2,935	34,900
....	......	......	......	......	10	6	3,250	113,000
hire......	......	......	......	......	17	16	8,945	967,500
....	6	6	1,800	17,000	107	107	45,400	1,590,000
....	......	......	......	......	152	149	80,710	313,381
....	9	8	3,450	134,000	455	453	271,285	8,558,150
na........	31	29	9,300	23,400	10	9	3,300	64,100
....	288	266	84,900	887,700	295	295	160,700	3,959,970
....	......	......	......	......	13	14	2,750	94,500
l.........	712	657	270,835	3,746,380	362	319	197,115	6,075,050
l.........	......	......	......	......	22	20	19,108	910,100
na........	......	......	......	......	12	13	10,775	291,500
....	......	......	......	......	21	21	13,850	486,250
....	......	......	......	......	36	36	16,000	264,200
....	......	......	......	......	......	......	......	......
....	......	......	......	......	40	40	25,000	401,500
....	24	16	5,900	38,500	19	17	9,800	343,750
....	......	......	......	......	11	12	1,785	18,400
ia........	2	2	600	15,000	40	37	10,800	221,950
....	18	14	3,200	24,505	320	304	104,000	1,334,450
....	......	......	......	......	2	2	800	8,000

secuted. It may be assumed, however, that the statement of a church at is founded upon a tradition of some local and temporary organization effected war at the large and important camp then formed there.

usas the "Quarterly" reports 2 churches—the census none. For only 1, s the post-office address given by the "Quarterly;" and a letter addressed or of this church was returned to the Census Office by the postmaster, with ation that no church of the denomination existed in that vicinity. In respect r, (which the "Quarterly" admits to be without even a "supply,") no inquiry stituted, for the reason that no address was given. Instances of this char- be multiplied, but the foregoing will suffice.

doubted that in some cases confusion has arisen in returning the three de- is known in the following tables as Congregational, Unitarian, and Univer- ccount of the common use in some sections, and to a limited extent, of the gregational," as expressing merely the form of church government, with- ice to distinctions of theological belief.

UNIVERSALIST.

omination last mentioned by name is also reported much below the number the official organs, by reason probably of the fact that this denomination

TABLE XLII.—*Churches, Fifteen Selected Denominations*—1870—Continued.

States and Territories.	Second Advent.				Unitarian.			
	Organizations.	Edifices.	Sittings.	Property.	Organizations.	Edifices.	Sittings.	Property.
The United States.	225	140	34,555	$306,240	331	310	155,471	$6,282,67[illegible]
Alabama								
Arizona								
Arkansas								
California	3	3	300	4,000	2	2	1,400	151,665
Colorado								
Connecticut	7	7	1,380	8,700	1	1	225	6,000
Dakota								
Delaware					1	1	300	17,000
District of Columbia					1	1	400	30,000
Florida	1							
Georgia								
Idaho								
Illinois	8	5	1,300	7,100	23	17	5,960	492,900
Indiana					1			
Iowa	28	10	2,950	13,050	3	2	715	19,000
Kansas					2	1	400	20,000
Kentucky					1	1	700	75,000
Louisiana					1	1	1,000	3,000
Maine	28	13	3,175	13,050	18	18	9,185	245,000
Maryland					1	1	800	150,000
Massachusetts	15	12	3,400	53,540	180	179	98,306	3,470,575
Michigan	39	21	4,840	44,500	7	4	1,700	42,500
Minnesota	7	1	150	2,100				
Mississippi								
Missouri	1				10	9	3,200	142,900
Montana								
Nebraska					3	3	700	4,500
Nevada								
New Hampshire	21	20	4,405	25,200	23	22	7,830	207,000
New Jersey					1	1	400	10,000
New Mexico								
New York	17	11	3,120	45,650	22	19	8,850	715,200
North Carolina								
Ohio	1	1	300	1,000	8	8	3,100	60,000
Oregon					2	1	250	10,000
Pennsylvania	3	3	725	11,500	4	4	2,050	68,800
Rhode Island	17	14	3,370	28,700	4	4	3,450	229,000
South Carolina					1	1	750	20,000
Tennessee								
Texas								
Utah								
Vermont	15	15	4,450	39,000	4	4	1,900	33,000
Virginia								
Washington	1	1	40	150				
West Virginia	3							
Wisconsin	10	3	650	9,000	7	5	1,900	41,000
Wyoming								

has a larger proportion of congregations without permanent pastors than any other. For example: for the 16 Universalist churches reported in Missouri, only 1 pastor is, according to the New Covenant (a denominational organ) of February 12, 1870, wholly devoted to the ministry.

Of the 13 Universalist churches reported by the denominational Register and Almanac for 1871 as located in Kansas, only 5 claim to have the use of a church edifice; and of these two are known as "Union." The marshal of the district reports that he can only locate 1.

The discrepancies between the church statistics and the returns of the census in the case of the denominations hitherto specifically referred to, are, as will be seen above, susceptible of explanation.

UNITED BRETHREN IN CHRIST.

But the discrepancies which exist between the claims of the denomination and the statements of the census in respect to the church known as United Brethren in Christ, are wholly inexplicable, except upon an assumption of radical and total vice in the statistics of the church.

The denomination claims 3,753 church organizations. The census allows 1,445.

ABLE XLII.—*Churches, Fifteen Selected Denominations*—1870—Continued.

d Territories.	UNITED BRETHREN IN CHRIST.				UNIVERSALIST.			
	Organizations.	Edifices.	Sittings.	Property.	Organizations.	Edifices.	Sittings.	Property.
Jnited States.	1,445	937	265,025	$1,819,810	719	602	210,884	$5,692,325
					6	2	550	1,400
					1	1	200	400
a	3	1	100	500	1	1	160	3,000
cut					14	15	6,850	309,100
					1	1	350	4,000
f Columbia					1			
					5	3	900	900
	125	58	17,995	126,800	52	44	15,225	543,300
	184	121	33,975	188,000	18	15	6,300	73,400
	188	28	10,445	69,250	35	15	4,465	99,525
	24	8	2,200	31,500	1			
y					2	2	400	5,500
a								
					84	65	23,910	434,850
d	36	31	12,100	233,500	2	2	1,000	32,500
setts	1	1	100	500	97	87	35,627	1,613,000
	69	19	4,225	40,800	33	20	5,550	92,200
a	5	2	500	1,000	18	6	1,720	55,000
pi					1	1	400	800
	38	20	5,800	32,000	6	2	900	2,500
a	4				3			
mpshire					24	23	8,812	154,200
sey					5	2	1,100	103,000
xico								
k	7	6	1,850	10,200	124	120	41,610	1,155,950
rolina					2	2	600	700
	370	344	85,350	484,310	78	78	20,750	175,950
	10	2	500	1,200	1			
ania	201	183	60,860	489,300	21	18	6,725	288,500
land					4	4	2,770	220,000
rolina					3	2	850	58,350
e	7	5	1,600	4,100				
					60	60	19,710	220,000
	42	30	7,700	23,300				
ton	3	2	275	3,200				
ginia	94	52	13,800	42,450	4	1	300	1,000
n	34	21	5,650	37,900	12	10	3,150	43,300
g								

discrepancy were wholly or mainly confined to one or two States, it might asonable to charge it to omissions on the part of the agents of the census. But arison of the figures of the census with a statement (*d*) prepared by the agent United Brethren Publishing House, at Dayton, Ohio, (the correctness of the nt being vouched for by one of the bishops of the church,) shows that the claims lenomination so greatly exceed the figures of the census in every State in which s in any considerable strength, as to render it in the highest degree improbable, orally impossible, that the differences arise from the uniform negligence of the of the census in respect to this single church.

undoubtedly true that the erroneous application in some sections, and to a extent, of the name "German Methodists," would explain the occasional omis- societies properly belonging to this denomination; but the effect of this cause elieved to have been considerable at the present census.

thing, also, must be allowed here—more, perhaps, than with denominations ly—for the effect of differing rules of construction as to what constitutes a according as the point of view of the denomination, or that of the census, is in dealing with congregations occasionally gathered in school-houses or in pri- vellings.

But after all reasonable allowance on these several accounts has been made, the Superintendent is compelled, from a careful examination of the subject, involving an extensive correspondence with the agents of the census, as well as with the officers of the church in question, to conclude that the denominational statistics are radically defective. In addition to the decided presumption in favor of the general correctness of the work of the sworn officers of the Government, to which nothing but assertion has been opposed by the representatives of the denomination, this conclusion is strongly supported by two considerations:

First. That the authorities of the denomination admit that they are unable to locate the churches they claim by towns or even by counties. Had such information been furnished, the investigation into the discrepancies existing would not have been dropped until the whole body of such differences had been canvassed by the Census Office, at whatever expense of time and labor. But the absence of anything approaching specific information regarding the location of these churches not only renders it impossible satisfactorily to determine the question at issue, but casts the greatest doubt upon the authority of the denominational statements.

Second. That the number of church organizations claimed by the authorities of the denomination bears an extraordinary and wholly unprecedented relation to the number of communicants reported. The Baptists average 80 communicants to a church organization; the Methodist Episcopal, 90; the Presbyterians, (North,) 98; the Reformed Church in America, 132, the highest average attained; the Evangelical Association, 74, the lowest. But the official organs of the United Brethren in Christ claim 3,753 churches with only 116,523 communicants, or an average of only 31 to a church. When it is considered that nearly if not quite two-thirds of the communicants of churches are, as a rule, women and minor children, we shall have as an average but 10 to 12 communicants among the adult males bearing the burden of the support of a church of this denomination—a most improbable supposition. But if we assume for the church an average number of communicants equal to that shown by the church having, of all those whose statistics on this subject are available, the smallest number, namely, the Evangelical Association, 74 members, we should have for the 116,523 communicants of the United Brethren in Christ, 1,575 churches, or only 130 in excess of the census. If, on the other hand, we assume for the denomination the average of the Reformed Church in America, viz, 132 communicants, we should have but 883 churches, or 562 below the census. If, again, we assume for the calculation the average of either the Baptist or the Methodist Episcopal Church, we should have a result in the first instance almost exactly coinciding with that exhibited in the following table, and in the second falling considerably below the number actually allowed by the census to the church under consideration.

CHRISTIAN, AND DISCIPLES OF CHRIST.

In respect to two denominations, it is admitted that the census fails to make a discrimination required by the facts of the case. From causes, the remedy for which it was not within the power of this office to apply, it became necessary to combine the statistics of the denominations known severally as "Christian" and "Disciples of Christ." The members of the latter denomination, much the stronger of the two, are so frequently termed "Christians," indeed so commonly call themselves by that name, that persons who had not made a study of the subject might readily conclude that the denominations were one and the same, whereas they are, in fact, distinct in official name and style, in organization, and in doctrine.

As an example, not only of the confusion in the popular mind respecting these two churches, but also of the negligence of the officers and members of the several churches in characterizing their own organization and services, it may be mentioned that there is a church belonging to the "Disciples of Christ," within the city of Washington, which is not only commonly, and, indeed, universally spoken of as the "Christian Church," but whose Sunday services are habitually advertised by its own officers in the public prints as those of the "Christian Church," while the edifice in which the congregation worships is inscribed, in conspicuous letters, "Christian Church." It would be wonderful, indeed, when the error is thus daily made by those who should be most interested in maintaining the individuality of the two denominations, if the agents of the census had been found to have preserved the distinction.

Had each or either of these denominations been mainly confined to a distinct section of the Union, special efforts might have resulted in an approximate classification of the data furnished by the assistant marshals. But, in view of the fact that both bodies have their greatest strength in the same States, and oftentimes in the same quarter of the same State, and in view also of the frankly acknowledged inability of the officials of each denomination to whom application for assistance was made to render any practical aid, it was deemed best to follow the precedent established in 1850 and 1860 of merging the two denominations under a single title.

The results here given are believed to present a fair statement of the combined strength of the two denominations.

One of the leading divines of the "Christians" gives the following estimate for that denomination as a whole in the United States, in answer to the inquiries of the Census Office, viz: church organizations, 1,100; church edifices, 1,050; church accommodation, 100,000; value of church property, $735,000.

(a) The principal inquiry, under the head of religion, in the schedule of the census law, viz: "Number of churches," is, unfortunately, ambiguous. As the censuses of 1850 and 1860 were taken, it is impossible to feel any assurance, in any particular case, whether church organizations or church edifices are returned in answer to the inquiry, "Number of churches." In preparation for the Ninth Census, this inquiry was divided into "Number of church organizations. Number of church edifices."

(b) The statistics of the Baptist Church for 1870 are presented in their Year-Book for 1871, in the form of a summary by States, and, also, to a great extent, in detail, by associations within each State. Where differences between the total and the items occur they are supposed to be the result of clerical errors in the preparation of the summary, or of typographical errors in printing it, and the detailed accounts have been assumed to be correct. The total number of churches, as given on page 80 of the Year-Book, is 17,745. An accurate compilation, however, of the details, so far as presented, gives 17,527 churches. To these are to be added 7 and 16, the numbers returned, in the summary only, for Delaware and District of Columbia respectively, and 10 for the difference between the total and the items given for West Virginia, which difference, it is supposed, equals the estimated number of churches belonging to the "Free Salvation" and "Indian Creek" associations, not otherwise accounted for, making a sum of 17,560, from which should be deducted the 25 churches claimed in the Indian Territory, as outside the field covered by the operations of the census, leaving 17,535, as stated above.

(c) On page 80 of the Year-Book the total number of churches for 1869 is stated at 15,143. (See preceding note.)

(d) ***Comparative view of the statistics of the United Brethren in Christ, as determined by officials of the denomination and by the census.***

States.	ORGANIZATIONS.		EDIFICES.		ACCOMMODATION.		PROPERTY.		COMMUNICANTS.
	Church.	Census.	Church.	Census.	Church.	Census.	Church.	Census.	Church.
Total	3,753	1,445	1,429	937	466,936	265,025	$2,454,302	$1,819,810	116,595
California	20	3	2	1	600	100	5,000	500	300
Illinois	391	125	119	58	34,950	17,995	229,750	126,800	12,052
Indiana	634	184	248	121	78,061	33,975	269,664	188,000	20,588
Iowa	298	188	43	28	12,600	10,445	82,775	69,250	6,991
Kansas	150	24	10	8	3,000	2,200	15,000	31,500	3,227
Maryland	67	36	39	34	14,600	12,100	122,650	233,500	2,959
Massachusetts	....	1	....	1	....	100	....	500	....
Michigan	182	69	28	19	8,700	4,225	46,490	40,800	4,500
Minnesota	27	5	1	2	300	500	2,000	1,000	620
Missouri	145	38	5	20	1,500	5,800	7,500	32,000	3,063
Nebraska	....	4	....	....	....	....	....	....	....
New York	70	7	14	6	3,735	1,850	21,600	10,200	1,360
Ohio	836	370	531	344	156,720	85,350	740,840	484,310	32,131
Oregon	42	10	6	2	1,800	500	12,000	1,200	787
Pennsylvania	575	201	280	183	118,170	60,860	777,842	469,300	18,586
Tennessee	13	7	5	5	1,500	1,000	8,000	4,100	447
Virginia	64	42	36	30	13,100	7,700	47,650	23,300	2,459
Washington	7	3	1	2	400	275	2,000	3,200	186
West Virginia	124	94	47	52	13,000	13,800	36,541	42,450	4,231
Wisconsin	88	34	14	21	4,200	5,650	27,000	37,900	2,038

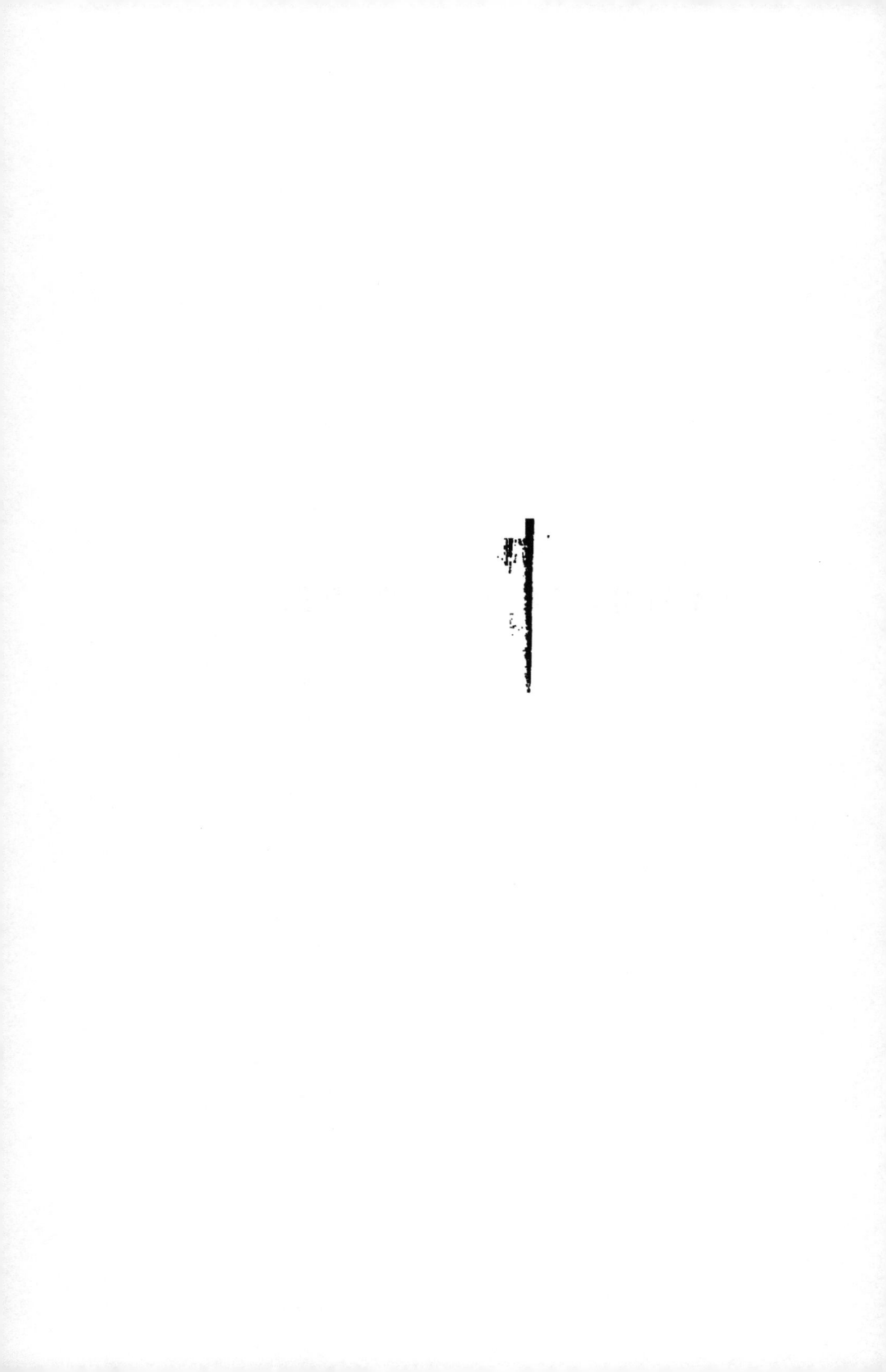

PAUPERISM AND CRIME.

34 c c

TABLE XLIII.—*Pauperism and Crime, with Population by States and Territories—1870.*

	States and Territories.	POPULATION.				
		Total.	White.	Colored.	Native.	Foreign-born.
	The United States	38,558,371	33,589,377	4,880,009	32,991,142	5,567,229
1	Alabama	996,992	521,384	475,510	987,030	9,962
2	Arizona	9,658	9,581	26	3,849	5,809
3	Arkansas	484,471	362,115	122,169	479,445	5,026
4	California	560,247	499,424	4,272	350,416	209,831
5	Colorado	39,864	39,221	456	33,265	6,599
6	Connecticut	537,454	527,549	9,668	423,815	113,639
7	Dakota	14,181	12,887	94	9,366	4,815
8	Delaware	125,015	102,221	22,794	115,879	9,136
9	District of Columbia	131,700	88,278	43,404	115,446	16,254
10	Florida	187,748	96,057	91,689	182,781	4,967
11	Georgia	1,184,109	638,926	545,142	1,172,982	11,127
12	Idaho	14,999	10,618	60	7,114	7,885
13	Illinois	2,539,891	2,511,096	28,762	2,024,693	515,198
14	Indiana	1,680,637	1,655,837	24,560	1,539,163	141,474
15	Iowa	1,194,020	1,188,207	5,762	969,328	204,692
16	Kansas	364,399	346,377	17,108	316,007	48,392
17	Kentucky	1,321,011	1,098,692	222,210	1,257,613	63,398
18	Louisiana	726,915	362,065	364,210	665,088	61,827
19	Maine	626,915	624,809	1,606	578,034	48,881
20	Maryland	780,894	605,497	175,391	697,482	83,412
21	Massachusetts	1,457,351	1,443,156	13,947	1,104,032	353,319
22	Michigan	1,184,059	1,167,282	11,849	916,049	268,010
23	Minnesota	439,706	438,257	759	279,009	160,697
24	Mississippi	827,922	382,896	444,201	816,731	11,191
25	Missouri	1,721,295	1,603,146	118,071	1,499,028	222,267
26	Montana	20,595	18,306	183	12,616	7,979
27	Nebraska	122,993	122,117	789	92,245	30,748
28	Nevada	42,491	38,959	357	23,690	18,801
29	New Hampshire	318,300	317,697	580	288,689	29,611
30	New Jersey	906,096	875,407	30,658	717,153	188,943
31	New Mexico	91,874	90,393	172	86,254	5,620
32	New York	4,382,759	4,330,210	52,081	3,244,406	1,138,353
33	North Carolina	1,071,361	678,470	391,650	1,068,332	3,029
34	Ohio	2,665,260	2,601,946	63,213	2,292,767	372,493
35	Oregon	90,923	86,929	346	79,323	11,600
36	Pennsylvania	3,521,951	3,456,609	65,294	2,976,642	545,309
37	Rhode Island	217,353	212,219	4,980	161,957	55,396
38	South Carolina	705,606	289,667	415,814	697,532	8,074
39	Tennessee	1,258,520	936,119	322,331	1,239,204	19,316
40	Texas	818,579	564,700	253,475	756,168	62,411
41	Utah	86,786	86,044	118	56,084	30,702
42	Vermont	330,551	329,613	924	283,396	47,155
43	Virginia	1,225,163	712,089	512,841	1,211,409	13,754
44	Washington	23,955	22,195	207	18,931	5,024
45	West Virginia	442,014	424,033	17,980	424,923	17,091
46	Wisconsin	1,054,670	1,051,351	2,113	690,171	364,499
47	Wyoming	9,118	8,726	183	5,605	3,513

(*a*) Includes 33 Indians. (*b*) Includes 10 Indians. (*c*) Includes 1 Indian.

PAUPERISM.—The Superintendent, being well aware that the above table will be subject to severe criticism from certain specialists, has thought it best to append a full statement of the plan which has been followed in its construction, as well as to make a frank admission, as has been done in respect to some of the preceding tables of this volume, of occasional errors and deficiencies.

The necessity for a distinct exposition of the rules which govern in the treatment of the subject of Pauperism will be best appreciated after a comparison of the numbers which would respectively be returned under the several classifications possible, and indeed wholly reasonable, in this connection.

Returns from the county poor-houses and the city work and alms houses of the State of New York show that on the 1st of December, 1869, the actual number of the inmates of these institutions was 15,053. On the 1st of December, 1870, the aggregate number

TABLE XLIII.—*Pauperism and Crime, with Population by States and Territories*—1870.

PAUPERISM.							CRIME.						
Number of persons supported during the year ended June 1, 1870.	Cost of annual support. (*Dollars.*)	Receiving support June 1, 1870.					Number of persons convicted during the year ended June 1, 1870.	Number of persons in prison June 1, 1870.					
		Total.	Native.			Foreign-born.		Total.	Native.			Foreign-born.	
			Total.	White.	Colored.				Total.	White.	Colored.		
116,102	10,930,429	76,737	53,939	44,539	a9,400	22,798	36,562	32,901	24,173	16,117	b8,056	8,728	
890	81,459	687	681	354	327	6	1,260	593	585	149	436	8	1
......	......	......	......	......	......	......	29	11	......	......	......	11	2
626	74,917	538	490	288	202	48	344	362	322	137	c185	40	3
2,317	273,147	991	354	351	3	637	1,107	1,574	668	662	6	906	4
73	11,422	19	8	8	......	11	32	19	16	11	5	3	5
1,728	189,918	1,705	1,237	1,123	114	468	450	430	278	215	63	152	6
......	......	......	......	......	......	......	2	3	1	1	......	2	7
556	41,266	453	403	223	180	50	145	66	57	13	44	9	8
303	26,364	279	234	135	99	45	121	143	117	38	79	26	9
147	9,830	147	142	80	62	5	335	179	176	20	156	3	10
2,181	159,793	1,816	1,777	1,270	507	39	1,775	737	723	126	597	14	11
41	7,247	4	3	3	......	1	26	28	18	17	1	10	12
6,054	556,061	2,363	1,254	1,213	41	1,109	1,552	1,795	1,372	1,229	143	423	13
4,657	403,521	3,652	2,790	2,583	207	862	1,374	907	755	691	64	152	14
1,543	175,179	853	542	486	56	311	615	397	287	273	14	110	15
361	46,475	336	190	105	85	146	151	329	262	202	d60	67	16
2,059	160,717	1,784	1,667	963	704	117	603	1,067	968	525	443	99	17
590	53,900	507	409	279	130	98	1,539	845	818	460	358	27	18
4,619	367,009	3,631	3,188	3,149	39	443	431	371	261	255	6	110	19
1,857	163,584	1,612	1,347	781	566	265	868	1,035	967	304	663	68	20
5,636	1,121,604	5,777	5,396	5,323	73	381	1,503	2,526	1,291	1,152	139	1,235	21
3,151	269,682	2,042	853	768	a85	1,189	835	1,095	679	617	d62	416	22
684	66,167	392	126	120	6	266	214	129	73	65	8	56	23
921	96,707	809	793	413	380	16	471	449	421	128	293	28	24
2,424	191,171	1,854	1,415	1,090	325	439	1,503	1,623	1,217	893	324	406	25
164	17,065	23	8	8	......	15	24	16	14	13	1	2	26
93	11,161	92	54	54	......	38	33	69	41	35	9	28	27
196	23,702	54	29	27	2	25	132	99	40	37	3	59	28
2,636	235,126	2,129	1,754	1,739	15	375	182	267	201	199	2	66	29
3,356	283,341	2,390	1,669	1,368	301	721	1,040	1,079	640	483	157	439	30
......	......	......	......	......	......	......	95	24	21	18	3	3	31
26,152	2,661,385	14,100	5,953	5,289	664	8,147	5,473	4,704	2,658	2,323	335	2,046	32
1,706	136,470	1,652	1,647	1,119	528	5	1,311	468	462	132	330	6	33
6,383	566,280	3,674	2,860	2,659	201	814	2,560	1,405	1,018	892	126	387	34
133	24,800	81	62	62	......	19	80	104	67	55	c12	37	35
15,872	1,256,024	8,796	4,822	4,354	468	3,974	3,327	3,231	2,532	2,088	444	699	36
1,046	97,702	634	442	407	35	192	209	180	125	113	12	55	37
2,343	224,805	2,071	1,994	888	1,106	77	1,399	732	714	130	584	18	38
1,349	99,811	1,332	1,280	966	314	52	722	981	902	342	560	79	39
204	21,219	202	177	73	104	25	260	732	602	237	365	130	40
56	6,206	51	20	19	1	31	27	19	19	19	......	......	41
2,008	178,628	1,785	1,262	1,231	31	523	139	193	145	143	2	48	42
3,600	303,081	3,280	3,254	1,942	1,312	26	1,080	1,244	1,232	331	901	12	43
34	5,283	20	15	13	2	5	20	19	8	7	1	11	44
1,102	80,628	994	948	839	109	46	155	191	175	138	37	16	45
1,553	151,181	1,126	390	374	16	736	837	418	215	192	d23	203	46
......	......	......	......	......	......	......	24	13	7	7	......	6	47

(*d*) Includes 2 Indians. (*e*) Includes 3 Indians.

of inmates was 15,352. The date taken for this return, viz, the 1st of December, would probably not show quite so large a number of paupers as a date nearer the close of the winter; but December would certainly exhibit a larger number than any other month of the spring, summer, or autumn, excepting March, and possibly April, and is therefore to be regarded as presenting an unexceptionably fair average for the year.

Yet the books of the same institutions record the admission during the year, whose beginning and ending are thus defined, including those remaining at the beginning of the year, of no less than 59,136 "persons." In addition, the number of persons receiving temporary and partial out-door relief in the State of New York through the year in question (at an expense of $911,855.15) is returned at 101,796, making the total number of "persons" receiving aid from funds appropriated distinctly for the poor, 160,932.

But a still further extension of the list of public pensioners might, upon a possible,

TABLE XLIV.—*Pauperism and Crime, with Population by States and Territories*—1860.

	States and Territories.	POPULATION.				
		Total.	White.	Colored.	Native.	Foreign-born.
	The United States	31,443,321	26,922,537	4,441,830	27,304,624	4,138,697
1	Alabama	964,201	526,271	437,770	951,849	12,352
2	Arkansas	435,450	324,143	111,259	431,850	3,600
3	California	379,994	323,177	4,086	233,466	146,528
4	Colorado	34,277	34,231	46	31,611	2,666
5	Connecticut	460,147	451,504	8,627	379,451	80,696
6	Dakota	4,837	2,576		3,063	1,774
7	Delaware	112,216	90,589	21,627	103,051	9,165
8	District of Columbia	75,080	60,763	14,316	62,596	12,484
9	Florida	140,424	77,746	62,677	137,115	3,309
10	Georgia	1,057,286	591,550	465,698	1,045,615	11,671
11	Illinois	1,711,951	1,704,291	7,628	1,387,308	324,643
12	Indiana	1,350,428	1,338,710	11,428	1,232,144	118,284
13	Iowa	674,913	673,779	1,069	568,836	106,077
14	Kansas	107,206	106,390	627	94,515	12,691
15	Kentucky	1,155,684	919,484	236,167	1,095,885	59,799
16	Louisiana	708,002	357,456	350,373	627,027	80,975
17	Maine	628,279	626,947	1,327	590,826	37,453
18	Maryland	687,049	515,918	171,131	609,520	77,529
19	Massachusetts	1,231,066	1,221,432	9,602	970,960	260,106
20	Michigan	749,113	736,142	6,799	600,020	149,093
21	Minnesota	172,023	169,395	259	113,295	58,728
22	Mississippi	791,305	353,899	437,404	782,747	8,558
23	Missouri	1,182,012	1,063,489	118,503	1,021,471	160,541
24	Nebraska	28,841	28,696	82	22,490	6,351
25	Nevada	6,857	6,812	45	4,793	2,064
26	New Hampshire	326,073	325,579	494	305,135	20,938
27	New Jersey	672,035	646,699	25,336	549,245	122,790
28	New Mexico	93,516	82,924	85	86,793	6,723
29	New York	3,880,735	3,831,590	49,005	2,879,455	1,001,280
30	North Carolina	992,622	629,942	361,522	989,324	3,298
31	Ohio	2,339,511	2,302,808	36,673	2,011,262	328,249
32	Oregon	52,465	52,160	128	47,342	5,123
33	Pennsylvania	2,906,215	2,849,259	56,949	2,475,710	430,505
34	Rhode Island	174,620	170,649	3,952	137,226	37,394
35	South Carolina	703,708	291,300	412,320	693,722	9,986
36	Tennessee	1,109,801	826,722	283,019	1,088,575	21,226
37	Texas	604,215	420,891	182,921	560,793	43,422
38	Utah	40,273	40,125	59	27,519	12,754
39	Vermont	315,098	314,369	709	282,355	32,743
40	Virginia	1,596,318	1,047,299	548,907	1,561,260	35,058
41	Washington	11,594	11,138	30	8,450	3,144
42	Wisconsin	775,881	773,693	1,171	498,954	276,927

* In the opinion of the Superintendent of Census, no use of these figures for purposes of comparison between States and sections, or between the several periods of time covered by this publication, will be justifiable, unless reference is had to the remarks which are beneath the table.

and indeed from its own point of view an entirely reasonable, theory of the case, be claimed and allowed. The immigration commissioners for New York report having expended during the year 1869 $330,000 for the relief of poor immigrants. There was also appropriated from the treasury of the State, or of the city of New York under laws of the State, during the same year, in assistance to hospitals, dispensaries, infirmaries, asylums, &c., the sum of $1,903,075.59.

Allowing for the persons participating in the benefits of these expenditures, we should have the State poor very considerably increased, even above the enormous numbers already expressed.

The number of persons given in the table as "supported during the year," for the State of New York, is 26,152.

The foregoing statements will sufficiently illustrate the importance of having the tables of pauperism for the several States and Territories made up upon a uniform plan.

It was the want of such uniformity of construction, in connection with manifest looseness in the collection of material, which yielded such impossible and altogether

TABLE XLIV.—*Pauperism and Crime, with Population by States and Territories—1860.*

PAUPERISM.					CRIME.				
Number of persons supported during the year ended June 1, 1860.	Cost of annual support. (*Dollars.*)	Receiving support June 1, 1860.			Number of persons convicted during the year ended June 1, 1860.	Number of persons in prison June 1, 1860.			
		Total.	Native.	Foreign-born.		Total.	Native.	Foreign-born.	
*321,665	5,445,143	82,942	50,483	32,459	*98,836	19,086	10,143	8,943	
582	38,830	449	431	18	179	226	183	43	1
289	16,702	178	175	3	200	78	61	17	2
2,183	99,171	293	105	188	915	882	336	546	3
									4
4,044	126,355	2,238	1,548	690	1,473	646	440	197	5
									6
742	22,830	447	331	116	63	27	19	8	7
2,081	12,650	142	95	47	~~[illegible]~~	~~210~~	~~163~~	47	8
168	4,654	107	105	2	33	15	13	2	9
1,451	45,161	1,196	1,106	90	251	111	77	34	10
4,628	196,184	1,856	707	1,149	812	485	313	172	11
3,565	151,851	1,589	1,120	469	1,184	284	129	155	12
2,165	83,737	683	322	361	278	95	61	34	13
21	423	21	7	14	24	31	22	9	14
1,265	71,603	899	749	150	600	232	147	85	15
194	11,395	162	146	16	3,197	849	359	490	16
8,946	226,945	4,618	4,147	471	1,215	255	197	58	17
4,275	75,113	720	621	99	283	116	99	17	18
51,880	579,397	6,503	5,206	1,297	12,732	2,679	1,495	1,184	19
9,104	113,227	1,423	679	744	871	757	505	252	20
350	26,871	156	39	117	33	32	16	16	21
374	26,675	301	270	31	219	53	35	18	22
958	70,445	784	513	271	516	286	166	120	23
30	724	6	3	3	8				24
									25
4,394	153,958	2,311	2,072	239	795	193	138	55	26
8,200	132,646	1,861	1,308	553	1,045	215	124	91	27
					23	10	8	2	28
164,782	1,440,904	19,215	7,666	11,549	52,067	6,882	2,861	4,021	29
1,922	83,486	1,431	1,422	9	450	71	62	9	30
5,953	311,109	14,092	5,700	8,392	6,830	623	265	358	31
50	13,155	25	15	10	29	13	6	7	32
16,463	665,396	7,776	4,495	3,281	2,939	1,161	756	405	33
1,108	42,785	613	445	168	718	181	100	81	34
1,640	65,242	1,439	1,404	35	141	88	57	31	35
3,038	64,771	935	776	159	200	511	433	78	36
139	12,849	122	108	14	214	105	65	40	37
4	344	1	1		24	8	5	3	38
3,387	120,473	1,850	1,510	340	43	119	80	39	39
6,027	208,649	4,534	4,320	214	608	189	163	26	40
7	1,870	2	1	1	15	15	3	12	41
5,256	126,500	1,964	815	1,149	754	353	172	181	42

ational results in the publication of the census of 1860, as New York, with a popula-
on of 3,880,735, having a pauperism of 164,782, (average cost per head less than $9,)
hile Pennsylvania, with a population of 2,906,215, in the same general condition of
ttlement and industry, showed only 16,463 persons supported during the year, (at a
st of something over $40 a head;) Michigan, with a population of only 749,113, hav-
g a pauper list of 9,104, (average, $12,) while Illinois, with a population of 1,711,951,
as returned with only 4,628, (average, $42;) Massachusetts, with a population of
231,066, engaged principally in manufactures, having a pauperism of 51,880, (average,
1,) while Connecticut, also a manufacturing State, with a population of 460,147, was
turned with only 4,044 paupers, (average, $31.) Comparisons like these, which might
extended through pretty much the whole list of the then existing States, show at a
ance that no effort was made at the Eighth Census to impose anything like a uniform
le upon the returns of pauperism; that some States were returned with a pauper-list
ree, five, or ten times as large as States in the same general condition of settlement
d industry, for no other reason than that in one State the aggregate cost of poor-
lief was practically divided by the known cost of sustaining one pauper one year,
d the quotient taken for the number of persons supported during the year, while in
other State all persons entering a work or alms house, for ever so limited a period,
ere included, and, in a third, every person receiving so much as a half ton of coal in

TABLE XLV.—*Pauperism and Crime, with Population by States and Territories*—1850.

	States and Territories.	POPULATION.				
		Total.	White.	Colored.	Native. (†)	Foreign-born. (†)
	The United States	23, 191, 876	19, 553, 068	3, 638, 808	20, 912, 612	2, 244, 602
1	Alabama	771, 623	426, 514	345, 109	763, 089	7, 509
2	Arkansas	209, 897	162, 189	47, 708	207, 636	1, 471
3	California	92, 597	91, 635	962	70, 340	21, 802
4	Connecticut	370, 792	363, 099	7, 693	331, 560	38, 518
5	Delaware	91, 532	71 169	20, 363	86, 268	5, 253
6	District of Columbia	51, 687	37, 941	13, 746	46, 720	4, 968
7	Florida	87, 445	47, 203	40, 242	84, 665	2, 740
8	Georgia	906, 185	521, 572	384, 613	899, 132	6, 488
9	Illinois	851, 470	846, 034	5, 436	736, 149	111, 892
10	Indiana	988, 416	977, 154	11, 262	930, 458	55, 572
11	Iowa	192, 214	191, 881	333	170, 931	20, 969
12	Kentucky	982, 405	761, 413	220, 992	949, 652	31, 420
13	Louisiana	517, 762	255, 491	262, 271	448, 848	68, 233
14	Maine	583, 169	581, 813	1, 356	550, 878	31, 885
15	Maryland	583, 034	417, 943	165, 091	531, 476	51, 209
16	Massachusetts	994, 514	985, 450	9, 064	827, 430	164, 024
17	Michigan	397, 654	395, 071	2, 583	341, 656	54, 703
18	Minnesota	6, 077	6, 038	39	4, 097	1, 977
19	Mississippi	606, 526	295, 718	310, 808	601, 230	4, 728
20	Missouri	682, 044	592, 004	90, 040	604, 522	76, 592
21	New Hampshire	317, 976	317, 456	520	303, 563	14, 265
22	New Jersey	489, 555	465, 509	24, 046	429, 176	59, 948
23	New Mexico	61, 547	61, 525	22	59, 187	2, 151
24	New York	3, 097, 394	3, 048, 325	49, 069	2, 436, 771	655, 929
25	North Carolina	869, 039	553, 028	316, 011	866, 241	2, 581
26	Ohio	1, 980, 329	1, 955, 050	25, 279	1, 757, 746	218, 193
27	Oregon	13, 294	13, 087	207	12, 081	1, 022
28	Pennsylvania	2, 311, 786	2, 258, 160	53, 626	2, 006, 207	303, 417
29	Rhode Island	147, 545	143, 875	3, 670	123, 564	23, 902
30	South Carolina	668, 507	274, 563	393, 944	659, 743	8, 707
31	Tennessee	1, 002, 717	756, 836	245, 881	995, 478	5, 653
32	Texas	212, 592	154, 034	58, 558	194, 433	17, 681
33	Utah	11, 330	11, 330	50	9, 326	2, 044
34	Vermont	314, 120	313, 402	718	280, 055	33, 715
35	Virginia	1, 421, 661	894, 800	526, 861	1, 398, 205	22, 965
36	Wisconsin	305, 391	304, 756	635	194, 099	110, 477

(*) See note (*) on preceding page.
(†) The nativity of 34,662 free persons was not returned on the schedule. For their distribution among the States and Territories, see Table X, page 377.

a hard winter, or a dozen soup-tickets, was set down among the State's poor. While claiming in respect to this as little as in respect to any other class of the statistics of the census, and, indeed, less with respect to this than to almost any other, absolute accuracy, the Superintendent must claim the credit of having attempted to introduce as fully as, with the vicious machinery of the present census law, was possible, discrimination and order into the returns of pauperism.

In a country presenting such wide diversity in the conditions of life, settlement, and industry as the United States, four things would be essential to anything like a complete exhibit of the pauperism of all the States:

First. The number of persons actually inmates of asylums, alms and work houses, on one or more days certain during the year. It would be desirable that three or four dates should be taken for the count. If, however, only a single return could be obtained, the date taken should be as strictly representative of the year as possible. This condition, the day previously indicated as taken for the return in New York, viz, December 1, fairly answers. The census date, June 1, is as little representative as any could be.

Second. The amount of pauperism calculated *impersonally, i. e.*, by dividing the aggregate expenditure for poor-support by the ascertained cost of maintaining, in each State and section by turns, one pauper for one year.

Third. The number of persons who, for any period, however limited, from beginning to close of the year, become inmates of any of the different classes of charitable institutions.

TABLE XLV.—*Pauperism and Crime, with Population by States and Territories*—1850.

PAUPERISM.					CRIME.				
Number of persons supported during the year ended June 1, 1850.	Cost of annual support. (*Dollars.*)	Receiving support June 1, 1850.			Number of persons convicted during the year ended June 1, 1850.	Number of persons in prison June 1, 1850.			
		Total.	Native.	Foreign-born.		Total.	Native.	Foreign-born.	
*134,972	2,954,806	50,353	36,916	13,437	*26,679	6,737	4,326	2,411	
363	17,559	315	306	9	122	70	69	1	1
105	6,888	67	67		25	17	17		2
					1	62	35	27	3
2,337	95,024	1,744	1,463	281	850	310	244	66	4
697	17,730	273	240	33	22	14	14		5
					132	46	26	20	6
76	937	62	58	4	39	11	9	2	7
1,036	27,820	834	825	29	80	43	36	7	8
797	45,213	434	279	155	316	252	164	88	9
1,182	57,500	586.	446	137	175	59	41	18	10
135	5,358	44	27	17	3	5	5		11
1,136	57,543	777	690	87	160	52	41	11	12
423	39,806	106	76	30	297	423	240	183	13
5,503	151,664	3,535	3,209	326	744	100	66	34	14
4,494	71,668	2,001	1,681	320	207	397	325	72	15
15,777	392,715	5,549	4,059	1,490	7,250	1,236	653	583	16
1,190	27,556	429	248	181	659	241	139	102	17
					2	1		1	18
260	18,132	257	245	12	51	46	45	1	19
2,977	53,243	505	251	254	908	180	55	125	20
3,600	157,351	2,184	1,998	186	90	33	25	8	21
2,392	93,110	1,578	1,339	239	603	290	198	92	22
					108	38	37	1	23
59,855	817,336	12,833	5,755	7,078	10,279	1,288	649	639	24
1,931	60,085	1,580	1,567	13	647	44	43	1	25
2,513	95,250	1,673	1,254	419	843	133	102	31	26
					5	5	5		27
11,551	232,138	3,811	2,654	1,157	857	411	296	115	28
2,560	45,837	696	492	204	596	103	58	45	29
1,642	48,337	1,293	1,113	180	46	36	21	15	30
1,005	30,981	591	577	14	81	288	276	12	31
7	438	4	4		19	15	5	10	32
					9	9	6	3	33
3,654	120,462	1,879	1,565	314	79	105	64	41	34
5,118	151,722	4,458	4,356	102	107	313	291	22	35
666	14,743	238	72	106	267	61	26	35	36

Fourth. The number of persons receiving, in any form and in any degree, relief or assistance in money or by supplies at the public expense.

Nothing less than the above would put the statistician, the economist, or the social philosopher, in a position to work out all the relations of the pauperism of such a country as this to the social and economical interests of the people. But unfortunately the census law of 1850 allows the authorities and agents of the census to compass but two of the four points of importance in the consideration of the subject. One of the two is the number of inmates of asylums, alms and work houses on a day certain, corresponding to the first of the series of four just enumerated. The other of the two questions which the law allows may, by the authorities of the census, be made at their discretion to cover any one of the three remaining points, and of necessity must leave the other two uncovered.

The phraseology of the law on this subject, "number supported during the year," is, as usual, ambiguous. It would certainly be within the scope of administrative construction to determine this inquiry to meet any one of the three following points:

First. Number supported during, *i. e.*, throughout, the year. The philological argument is rather in favor of this construction. This would give the *impersonal amount* of pauperism, provided, at least, it were held legitimate, as it clearly might be, to reduce partial to total support at the ascertained cost of the latter.

Second. The number during the year receiving support, greater or less, in public institutions, *i. e.*, receiving support at any time and for any time "during the year," *i. e.*, within the year.

Third. The number receiving support, *i. e.*, assistance at public expense, as above, but without reference to the manner in which such assistance be rendered, whether total support in alms and work houses, or occasional out-door relief.

It being within the discretion of the authorities of the census to direct the one remaining inquiry of the census so as to reach one of these three points, the effort has been made at the present census to bring the returns as nearly as practicable to what may be termed the solid amount of pauperism.

The reasons which controlled the Census Office in selecting this in preference to any other form of returning pauperism were as follows:

First. The most exact single expression possible for the actual pauperism of a country is undoubtedly obtained by dividing the aggregate cost of support by the ascertained cost of supporting one pauper for one year. This gives the *amount* of pauperism, reducing it to a solid form, and affording opportunity for easy and just comparison between States and sections.

Second. The number of "persons" shown, by the records of asylums, alms and work houses, to have been received and discharged during the year, is largely fictitious, sometimes even to the extent of one-half, two-thirds, or five-sixths. An individual of the pauper class will sometimes put in as many appearances during the year at the almhouse, as an individual of the criminal class at the police court; and when he has worn out his welcome at all the institutions of the metropolis, by turns, will make the tour of the provinces. In fact, at many city almshouses, almost the only steady boarders, besides young children, are the insane, the blind, and the crippled. Such facts are too notorious to require extended evidence. An analysis of the returns of the county and city alms and work houses for the State of New York affords a striking illustration. Of the 15,352 inmates on the 1st of December, 1870, 5,517 were stated to be children under sixteen years of age, or to be insane, idiotic, blind, or deaf and dumb. These persons, it may be assumed, did not move about to any appreciable extent, but belonged permanently to the *personnel* of their respective institutions. Deducting these 5,517 from the entire body of inmates, we have but 9,835 who, in the absence of any stated disability, may be assumed, for the purpose of this argument, to belong potentially to the vagabond class of paupers, although large numbers even of these must have been disabled for self-removal by reason of being crippled or maimed. The records of these institutions, however, show that not less than 59,136 "persons" were admitted during the year. Deducting the same 5,517, we have 53,619 entries during the year, to 9,835 actual inmates (not disabled as above) on a day certain, which day, December 1, may be accepted as fairly representative of the year. Such facts as these show how little the record of "admissions" to poor-houses can be taken as affording a just measure of pauperism.

Third. Not only do the difficulties of the work increase almost indefinitely as we seek to carry our inquiries out to determine, free of duplications, the actual number of persons receiving temporary and partial assistance, out of doors, from public funds; but the value of the results diminishes with much the same rapidity. If it were practicable, it would certainly be of curious interest to know the exact number of persons thus relieved in any city or section of the country; but when we consider that the relief thus extended ranges from partial support to the most trifling assistance—a bushel of coal, a few soup-tickets, or even a single dinner, in some cities being scrupulously made a matter of record and report—it must appear plain that these are not the facts in respect to poor-support which are to be obtained at the sacrifice of those which could be used to determine with approximate accuracy the absolute amount of pauperism, its bearing on the social system, and its burden on the industry of the country.

For the reasons above indicated, the Census Office has sought to compass in the preceding table the positive amount of pauperism in each State and Territory, reduced to permanent and entire support. No one who appreciates the lack of system which exists in ninety-nine out of one hundred of even the important communities of this land in respect to matters of this kind, the general absence of well-kept and properly-posted records, and the frequent indifference of officials to statistical or scientific inquiries, will be surprised to find much in this table, after all has been done which the existing law authorizes and enables the Census Office to do, which cannot be said to consist strictly with any single rule.

The cost of support varies greatly in city and in country, and very much also according to the system of poor-relief adopted. The difference between city and country may be stated approximately as follows: Annual cost of support in rural districts, \$75 to \$90; annual cost in cities and large towns, \$90 to \$125. The local system of poor-relief, however, enters, sometimes to equalize these expenditures, and sometimes to exaggerate the differences above indicated. Under a system uniform throughout the State, it happens in more than one State that the paupers in purely rural districts are maintained quite as expensively as the poor of the largest cities.

Unquestionably the most economical method of treating the pauperism of a community is found in the town-farm system. Land, buildings, and farming-tools being provided by the town, only one salary, that of the overseer, requiring to be paid, and the labor of the paupers being employed to the full extent of their physical ability, the annual charge of support in the States using this agency is reduced to a minimum, often not exceeding sixty or even fifty dollars. When it is remembered that an able-bodied laborer, engaged in agriculture in this country, can without difficulty provide food for himself and for three, four, or five persons dependent on him, it will appear wholly reasonable that even the partial and ineffective labor of the pauper on the town farm should so far reduce the cost to the State of his maintenance. In those States, on the other hand, where paupers are gathered into large establishments, with numerous officials and expensive appointments, and with no opportunity for employing the inmates productively, all articles of food and clothing have to be directly purchased by the State, and the cost of support rises to $100, $125, and even $140. In the mining States and Territories, where all articles of merchandise bear high prices, and where the number of paupers to be maintained is not sufficiently large to make it important to rigidly reduce expenditure on this account, the average cost of support rises to even a higher figure.

In addition to the points already discussed, two questions remain as to what elements shall or shall not be included in the Statistics of Pauperism:

First. Shall the amounts expended in the immediate relief of poor immigrants by the immigration commissioners of New York and other large ports of entry be regarded, for the purposes of the following table, as forming a part of the poor-support of those cities and of the States in which they are severally situated? The amount thus expended by the immigration commissioners of New York during the year 1869 was, as already stated, $830,000. The amount so expended at other points must have been considerable.

The Superintendent is disposed to hold that such an expenditure should be regarded merely as incidental to a gigantic system of immigration directly encouraged by the Government. While immigrants continue to arrive at our shores by hundreds of thousands each year, it is a matter of course that some, from sickness, from failure through ignorance to make proper provision, from accidents of one sort and another, and last, not least, from the villainies of the organized hordes of ruffians which beset our immigrant ships, will have occasion, in a wholly strange land, to appeal for temporary assistance to the guardians by law appointed over them. This is hardly pauperism in any proper sense, and until the immigrant has passed from under the control of the commissioners of immigration into the condition of a recognized and registered inmate of some asylum or almshouse, he cannot be said to constitute one of the paupers of the city or the State.

Second. Shall the amounts paid from the treasuries of States, counties, or cities toward the support of charitable institutions of the various classes known to modern philanthropy, hospitals, dispensaries, asylums for the insane, the idiotic, the blind, the deaf and dumb, be included in such tables as the preceding?

Here, again, the best reason of the case seems to be in favor of the stricter construction and the exclusion of these elements as not pertaining to the proper poor-support of the country.

The pauperism of the afflicted classes, inmates of such institutions, is to be regarded as an incident of their several disabilities or infirmities. Some of these persons would undoubtedly be paupers were they not so afflicted; but far more are only paupers because they are thus afflicted, and while thus afflicted. The greater fact, the principal, is properly the one in contemplation; the minor, the incident, may justly be disregarded in such a compilation as the present. One point certainly can be successfully maintained, and it is conclusive of the question, were there nothing else to be said, viz: that the framers of the census law did not have it in contemplation that the beneficiaries of hospitals, dispensaries, and asylums distinctly for the blind, the sick, or the insane would be embraced in the returns of the census.

If it were worth while to accumulate reasons, it might further be said that the inclusion of these classes in the pauperism of the country would be a troublesome precedent in view of the acknowledged fact that nineteen-twentieths of the academies, colleges, and professional schools of the country are, by virtue of their endowments, accumulated often through several generations, rendered mainly eleemosynary, and that not one-half, perhaps not one-fourth of those who now enjoy their advantages could aspire to do so, if required to pay the real cost of what is thus furnished them.

CRIME.

The necessity for a discriminating treatment of the returns of assistant marshals is even more evident in respect to the Statistics of Crime than has been noted in the remarks above upon the Statistics of Pauperism, while on the other hand the difficulties of the subject are found to be much greater.

No single measure can be taken for determining the proportions of crime in the several communities of our country.

It is easy, by a simple arithmetical process, to obtain the *solid amount* of pauperism, but not so of crime. The absence of any effort to reduce to a consistent body the returns on this subject at the last census led to similar misrepresentations of States and sections as have been noted in the published Statistics of Pauperism; Pensylvania, for example, being returned with but 2,930 convictions during the year, while New York, with a population only a little larger and in much the same social and industrial condition, was returned with 58,067, or nearly twenty times as many as Pennsylvania. It would not even require the most casual acquaintance with the communities thus characterized, or stigmatized, to establish the certainty that such statements could not be true. Human nature, with its opportunities and its temptations, does not vary to that extent with two degrees of latitude.

Returns thus out of all proportion were due to the fact that in the former State convictions of crime before courts of record only were taken for the census returns, while in the latter the convictions of police and justices' courts were indifferently admitted. Again, in another class of cases, the returns from one State would be restricted to convictions for grave offenses, without reference to the character of the tribunal, while in a neighboring State convictions for the most petty offenses were equally considered.

In the preparation of the preceding table the effort has been made to reduce the material to something like consistency and uniformity. Of course it is not possible, with the inadequate inquiries authorized to be made by the act of 1850, and with the more inadequate agencies provided for the prosecution of these inquiries, to present the criminal statistics of the States satisfactorily, according to any idea or plan. Even to present the most summary view of the subject with anything approaching success, it would be indispensable that the Census Office be furnished with a statement of the convictions in each State, classified according to the crimes for which convictions were had. This the scheme of enumeration in use in the United States does not provide for. So far as it has been practicable to obtain the information at the Census Office by subsequent correspondence, it has been done without consideration of the amount of labor involved therein, and the preceding table has been corrected accordingly.

Owing to the fact that the constitution of courts of record in the several States varies greatly as to the crimes over which they have jurisdiction, it has not been found practicable to make this table strictly one of convictions for crimes by courts of record. The effort has been, however, to make the returns for each State an equivalent for those of every other, and the results are now submitted with the remark that neither the statements of crime nor those of pauperism *for the year* are regarded as possessing any high degree of statistical authority. They are believed, however, to contain a very much larger amount of exact and of approximate information than it is in the power of any individual or of any other public agency to collect. The numbers reported respectively as receiving poor-support, and as in prison *on the 1st of June*, 1870, are regarded as quite accurately determined. Errors may be found to exist, but an extensive correspondence on the part of the Census Office has established their substantial accuracy and completeness.

From the number in prison have been excluded the inmates of houses of refuge, houses of correction, and institutions of kindred character.

AREAS, FAMILIES, AND DWELLINGS.

TABLE XLVI.—*Areas, Families, and Dwellings*—1870–1860–1850.

	States and Territories.	AREAS.					
		1870 (a)		1860 (b)		1850	
		Square miles.	Persons to a square mile.	Square miles.	Persons to a square mile.	Square miles.	Persons to a square mile.
	The United States	3, 603, 884	10. 70	3, 026, 494	10. 39	2, 980, 959	7. 78
	The States	1, 984, 467	19. 21	1, 723, 029	18. 10	1, 544, 224	14. 94
1	Alabama	50, 722	19. 66	50, 722	19. 01	50, 722	15. 21
2	Arkansas	52, 198	9. 30	52, 198	8. 34	52, 198	4. 02
3	California	188, 981	2. 29	188, 981	2. 01	188, 981	0. 49
4	Connecticut	4, 750	113. 15	4, 750	96. 87	4, 750	78. 53
5	Delaware	2, 120	58. 97	2, 120	52. 93	2, 120	43. 18
6	Florida	59, 268	3. 17	59, 268	2. 65	59, 268	1. 48
7	Georgia	58, 000	20. 42	58, 000	18. 23	58, 000	15. 62
8	Illinois	55, 410	45. 84	55, 410	30. 90	55, 410	15. 37
9	Indiana	33, 809	49. 71	33, 809	39. 94	33, 809	29. 24
10	Iowa	55, 045	21. 69	55, 045	12. 26	55, 045	3. 49
11	Kansas	81, 318	4. 48				
12	Kentucky	37, 680	35. 33	37, 680	30. 94	37, 680	26. 07
13	Louisiana	41, 346	17. 58	41, 346	17. 12	41, 346	12. 52
14	Maine	35, 000	17. 91	35, 000	17. 93	35, 000	16. 61
15	Maryland	11, 124	70. 20	11, 124	61. 76	11, 124	52. 41
16	Massachusetts	7, 800	186. 84	7, 800	157. 83	7, 800	127. 50
17	Michigan	56, 451	20. 97	56, 451	13. 27	56, 451	7. 07
18	Minnesota	83, 531	5. 26	83, 531	2. 10		
19	Mississippi	47, 156	17. 56	47, 156	16. 78	47, 156	12. 86
20	Missouri	65, 350	26. 34	65, 350	18. 09	65, 350	10. 44
21	Nebraska	75, 995	1. 62				
22	Nevada	104, 125	0. 41				
23	New Hampshire	9, 280	34. 30	9, 280	35. 14	9, 280	34. 26
24	New Jersey	8, 320	108. 91	8, 320	80. 77	8, 320	58. 84
25	New York	47, 000	93. 25	47, 000	82. 57	47, 000	65. 90
26	North Carolina	50, 704	21. 13	50, 704	19. 58	50, 704	17. 14
27	Ohio	39, 964	66. 69	39, 964	58. 54	39, 964	49. 55
28	Oregon	95, 274	0. 95	95, 274	0. 55		
29	Pennsylvania	46, 000	76. 56	46, 000	63. 18	46, 000	50. 26
30	Rhode Island	1, 306	166. 43	1, 306	133. 71	1, 306	112. 97
31	South Carolina	34, 000	20. 75	34, 000	20. 70	34, 000	19. 63
32	Tennessee	45, 600	27. 60	45, 600	24. 34	45, 600	21. 99
33	Texas	274, 356	2. 98	274, 356	2. 20	274, 356	0. 77
34	Vermont	10, 212	32. 37	10, 212	30. 86	10, 212	30. 76
35	Virginia	38, 348	31. 95	61, 348	26. 02	61, 348	23. 17
36	West Virginia	23, 000	19. 22				
37	Wisconsin	53, 924	19. 56	53, 924	14. 30	53, 924	5. 66
	The Territories	1, 619, 417	0. 27	1, 303, 465	0. 20	1, 436, 735	0. 09
1	Alaska, (unorganized)	577, 390					
2	Arizona	113, 916	0. 08				
3	Colorado	104, 500	0. 38				
4	Dakota	150, 932	0. 09				
5	District of Columbia	64	2057. 81	64	1173. 13	64	807. 61
6	Idaho	86, 294	0. 17				
7	Indian, (Country) (c)	68, 991		68, 991		195, 274	
8	Kansas			126, 283	0. 85		
9	Minnesota			81, 960		165, 491	0. 04
10	Montana	143, 776	0. 14				
11	Nebraska			351, 558	0. 08	351, 558	
12	New Mexico	121, 201	0. 76	261, 342	0. 36	215, 807	0. 29
13	Oregon					288, 345	0. 05
14	Utah	84, 476	1. 03	220, 196	0. 18	220, 196	0. 05
15	Washington	69, 994	0. 34	193, 071	0. 06		
16	Wyoming	97, 883	0. 09				

NOTES ON AREAS.—(a) The land surface of the United States, 3,603,884 square miles, when increased by the water surface of the great lakes and rivers, brings the total area of the United States to 4,000,000 square miles.

(b) The increase of the total area of the United States at 1860 over 1850 represents that territory acquired from Mexico known as the Gadsden purchase. The increase of the area at 1870 over 1860 expresses the acquisition of Alaska.

(c) The area of the Indian Country at each census includes the area of the unorganized territory which is west of that Country.

NOTES ON FAMILIES AND DWELLINGS.—(d) At the census of 1860 and 1850, the families and dwellings of the free population only were returned. Hence the computations in the above table for those cen-

TABLE XLVI.—*Areas, Families, and Dwellings*—1870-1860-1850—Continued.

FAMILIES.						DWELLINGS.						
1870		1860 (*d*)		1850 (*d*)		1870		1860 (*d*)		1850 (*d*)		
Number.	Persons to a family.	Number.	Persons to a family.	Number.	Persons to a family.	Number.	Persons to a dwelling.	Number.	Persons to a dwelling.	Number.	Persons to a dwelling.	
7,579,363	5.09	5,210,934	5.28	3,598,240	5.56	7,042,833	5.47	4,969,692	5.53	3,362,337	5.94	
7,481,607	5.09	5,147,650	5.28	3,570,683	5.56	6,941,603	5.49	4,912,437	5.54	3,335,269	5.95	
202,704	4.92	96,603	5.48	73,786	5.81	198,327	5.03	96,682	5.47	73,070	5.87	1
96,135	5.04	57,244	5.67	28,461	5.72	93,195	5.20	56,717	5.72	28,252	5.76	2
128,752	4.35	98,767	3.85	24,567	3.77	126,307	4.44	100,328	3.79	23,742	3.90	3
114,981	4.67	94,831	4.85	73,448	5.05	96,880	5.55	83,622	5.50	64,013	5.79	4
22,900	5.46	18,966	5.82	15,439	5.78	22,577	5.54	19,288	5.72	15,290	5.84	5
39,394	4.77	15,090	5.21	9,107	5.20	41,047	4.57	14,132	5.57	9,022	5.34	6
237,830	4.98	109,919	5.41	91,666	5.72	236,436	5.01	109,069	5.46	91,206	5.73	7
474,533	5.35	315,539	5.43	149,153	5.71	464,155	5.47	304,732	5.62	146,544	5.81	8
320,160	5.25	248,664	5.43	171,564	5.76	318,469	5.28	256,946	5.26	170,178	5.81	9
222,430	5.37	124,098	5.44	33,517	5.73	219,846	5.44	131,663	5.13	32,962	5.83	10
72,498	5.03	21,912	4.80	...	...	71,071	5.13	33,278	2.96	...	...	11
232,797	5.67	166,321	5.59	132,920	5.80	224,969	5.87	164,161	5.67	130,769	5.90	12
158,099	4.60	74,725	5.04	54,112	5.04	150,427	4.83	63,992	5.88	49,101	5.56	13
131,017	4.78	120,863	5.20	103,333	5.64	121,953	5.14	115,933	5.42	95,802	6.00	14
140,078	5.57	110,278	5.44	87,384	5.64	129,020	6.02	106,137	5.65	81,708	6.03	15
305,534	4.77	251,287	4.90	192,675	5.16	236,473	6.16	205,319	6.00	152,835	6.51	16
241,006	4.91	144,761	5.17	72,611	5.48	237,036	5.00	150,952	4.96	71,616	5.55	17
82,471	5.33	37,319	4.61	...	...	81,140	5.42	40,926	4.20	...	...	18
166,828	4.96	63,015	5.63	52,107	5.69	164,150	5.04	61,460	5.77	51,681	5.74	19
316,917	5.43	192,073	5.56	100,890	5.89	292,769	5.87	181,069	5.89	96,849	6.14	20
25,075	4.91	...	...	...	...	25,144	4.89	...	...	...	...	21
9,880	4.30	...	...	...	...	12,990	3.27	...	...	...	...	22
72,144	4.41	69,018	4.72	62,287	5.15	67,046	4.75	65,968	4.94	57,339	5.55	23
183,043	4.95	130,348	5.16	89,080	5.50	155,936	5.81	116,353	5.78	81,064	6.04	24
898,772	4.88	758,420	5.12	566,869	5.46	688,559	6.37	615,888	6.30	473,936	6.54	25
205,970	5.20	125,090	5.29	105,451	5.50	202,504	5.29	129,585	5.11	104,996	5.53	26
521,981	5.11	434,134	5.39	348,514	5.68	495,667	5.38	425,672	5.50	336,698	5.69	27
18,504	4.91	11,063	4.74	...	...	19,372	4.69	12,277	4.27	...	...	28
675,408	5.21	524,558	5.54	408,497	5.66	635,680	5.54	515,319	5.64	386,216	5.99	29
46,133	4.71	35,209	4.96	28,216	5.23	34,828	6.24	27,056	6.45	22,379	6.59	30
151,105	4.67	58,642	5.14	52,937	5.36	143,485	4.92	58,220	5.18	52,642	5.39	31
231,365	5.44	149,335	5.59	130,004	5.87	224,816	5.60	147,947	5.64	129,419	5.90	32
154,483	5.30	76,781	5.49	28,377	5.44	141,685	5.78	77,429	5.45	27,988	5.52	33
70,462	4.69	63,781	4.94	52,573	5.36	66,145	5.00	62,977	5.00	56,421	5.57	34
231,574	5.29	201,523	5.49	167,530	5.67	224,947	5.45	207,305	5.33	165,815	5.72	35
78,474	5.63	...	...	...	...	78,854	5.61	...	...	...	...	36
200,155	5.27	147,473	5.26	57,608	5.39	197,008	5.35	154,036	5.04	56,316	5.42	37
97,756	4.48	63,284	4.30	27,557	4.39	101,230	4.37	57,255	5.10	27,068	4.46	
...	...	...	...	...	...	...	...	...	...	...	...	1
2,290	4.22	...	...	...	...	2,822	3.42	...	...	...	...	2
9,358	4.26	10,045	3.41	...	...	10,009	3.98	...	...	...	...	3
3,090	4.59	1,241	3.90	...	...	3,231	4.39	1,361	3.55	...	...	4
25,276	5.21	12,888	5.58	8,343	5.75	23,308	5.65	12,338	5.83	7,917	6.05	5
4,104	3.65	...	...	...	...	4,622	3.25	...	...	...	...	6
...	...	...	...	...	...	...	...	...	...	...	...	7
...	...	...	...	...	...	...	...	...	...	...	...	8
...	...	...	...	1,016	5.98	...	...	...	...	1,002	6.06	9
7,058	2.92	...	...	...	...	9,450	2.18	...	...	...	...	10
...	...	5,931	4.86	...	...	...	...	7,811	3.69	...	...	11
21,449	4.28	20,881	4.48	13,502	4.56	21,053	4.36	21,945	4.26	13,453	4.57	12
...	...	...	...	2,374	5.60	...	...	...	...	2,374	5.60	13
17,210	5.04	*c* 9,500	4.96	2,322	4.90	18,290	4.75	10,763	3.75	2,322	4.90	14
5,673	4.22	2,798	4.44	...	...	6,066	3.95	3,037	3.82	...	...	15
2,248	4.06	...	...	...	...	2,379	3.[illegible]	...	...	...	...	16

…uses respecting persons to a family or to a dwelling have been made on the basis of the free population. The true number of families in the United States at 1860 may be approximated by adding to the total families in the table 748,818, being the families of the slaves, calculated at the average persons (5.28) to a family for the free population of the United States at that census. The number of families thus becomes 5,959,752. By the same process, the families at 1850 become 4,174,555. The dwellings increased for the slaves respectively, at the rate of one dwelling to six slaves, (the estimate adopted at 1850,) become, for 1860, 5,628,652, and, for 1850, 3,896,389.

(*e*) The families and persons to a family for Utah, at 1860, have been obtained by combining the families and population of Utah and Nevada published separately in the report of the Eighth Census. Nevada was not made a Territory until the year 1861.

THE CONSTRUCTION OF THE TABLE OF AREAS.

The construction of the columns of areas in the preceding table has been attended with difficulty, owing to the uncertainty of the official data. As late as 1850, and even at 1860, the reported areas of the Territories and the extreme Western States were mainly estimates, or at best approximate calculations, and even at the present time are not generally the result of completed surveys. For the purposes of this table the areas given in the report of the Commissioner of the General Land Office for the year 1870 have been taken as correct with one exception. In that report the area of Nevada is given as 112,090 square miles. In this area table it has been reduced by 7,965 square miles. The facts relied on to justify this reduction are that the statute erecting Nevada, after fixing its boundaries, provides that the part of California included by the act in Nevada shall not become a part of Nevada until California shall assent to the transfer. California has at no time assented, therefore the area of this strip of land, 7,965 square miles, has been deducted from the reported area of Nevada, and the area of California has not been changed, inasmuch as this tract appears to have been included both in California and Nevada in the table of the General Land Office for the year 1870. Assuming thus the areas of 1870 as standard, the official figures for 1860 and 1850 have been brought to them, where the boundaries of States have remained unchanged. Where transfers of territory have been made it has been sought, in the preceding table, to account accurately for the gain and loss during each decennial period. The principal transfers of areas from one civil division to another, in the columns of the table, are as follows:

The territory given as the Indian Country in the column for 1850, 195,274 square miles, appears at 1860 both as the Indian Country, 68,991 square miles, and as the Territory of Kansas, 126,283 square miles. The latter again at 1870 appears both as the State of Kansas, 81,318 square miles, and as a portion of the Territory of Colorado, 44,965 square miles.

The Territory of Minnesota at 1850, 165,491 square miles, appears at 1860 as the State of Minnesota, 83,531 square miles, and the Territory of Minnesota, 81,960 square miles. The latter appears in 1870 as a portion of the Territory of Dakota.

The Territory of Nebraska was not organized until 1854. The area on the line given to that Territory in the column for 1850, 351,558 square miles, represents the then unorganized portion of the public domain, exclusive of the Indian Country, as tabulated. It was then called the Northwest Territory. It had the same extent as Nebraska, when organized four years later, as the same appears in the column for 1860. The Territory of Nebraska of 1860 appears in 1870 as the entire State of Nebraska, 75,995 square miles, a portion of the Territory of Colorado, 16,035 square miles, a portion of the Territory of Dakota, 68,972 square miles, a portion of the Territory of Montana, 116,269 square miles, and a portion of the Territory of Wyoming, 74,287 square miles.

The Territory of New Mexico at 1850, 215,807 square miles, appears in 1860 with an increase of 45,535 square miles, representing the territory acquired from Mexico by the Gadsden treaty. The area of the Territory in 1860, 261,342 square miles, is represented in 1870 by the whole of the Territory of New Mexico, 121,201 square miles, the whole of the Territory of Arizona, 113,916 square miles, a portion of the State of Nevada, 12,225 square miles, and a portion of the Territory of Colorado, 14,000 square miles.

The Territory of Oregon at 1850, 288,345 square miles, appears in 1860 as the State of Oregon, 95,274 square miles, and the Territory of Washington, 193,071 square miles; the latter in 1870 appears as the whole of the Territory of Washington, 69,994 square miles, the whole of the Territory of Idaho, 86,294 square miles, a portion of the Territory of Montana, 26,901 square miles, and a portion of the Territory of Wyoming, 9,882 square miles.

The Territory of Utah at 1850, 220,196 square miles, appears without change in 1860. In 1870 it appears as the whole of the Territory of Utah, 84,476 square miles, a portion of the Territory of Colorado, 29,500 square miles, a portion of the State of Nevada, 91,900 square miles, and a portion of the Territory of Wyoming, 14,320 square miles. (See Historical Notes, Vol. I, Ninth Census.)

; XLVII.—*Families, Dwellings, and Population in Fifty Principal Cities*—1870.

:ities.	Size.*	FAMILIES.		DWELLINGS.		POPULATION.						
		Number.	Persons to a family.	Number.	Persons to a dwelling.	Population.	Native.	Foreign-born.	White.	Colored.	Chinese.	Indian.
?. Y (*a*).....	20	14, 105	4. 92	8, 748	7. 94	69, 422	47, 215	22, 207	68, 658	764	....	....
y, Pa........	23	10, 147	5. 21	8, 347	6. 37	53, 180	37, 872	15, 308	52, 018	1, 162	....	....
, Md........	6	49, 929	5. 35	40, 350	6. 63	267, 354	210, 870	56, 484	227, 794	39, 558	1	1
lass.........	7	48, 188	5. 20	29, 623	8. 46	250, 526	102, 540	87, 986	247, 013	3, 496	*b*5	12
. N. Y.......	3	80, 066	4. 95	45, 834	8. 64	396, 099	251, 381	144, 718	391, 142	4, 944	7	6
. Y..........	11	22, 325	5. 27	18, 285	6. 44	117, 714	71, 477	46, 237	117, 018	696	....	....
e, Mass....	33	7, 697	5. 02	6, 348	6. 24	39, 634	27, 579	12, 055	38, 785	848	....	1
n, S. C......	26	9, 098	5. 38	6, 861	7. 14	48, 956	44, 064	4, 892	22, 749	26, 173	....	34
wn, Mass....	47	6, 155	4. 60	4, 396	6. 44	28, 323	21, 399	6, 924	28, 196	127	....	....
Ill..........	5	59, 497	5. 03	44, 620	6. 70	298, 977	154, 420	144, 557	295, 281	3, 691	....	5
i, Ohio......	8	42, 937	5. 04	24, 550	8. 81	216, 239	136, 627	79, 612	210, 335	5, 900	....	4
, Ohio.......	15	18, 411	5. 04	16, 692	5. 56	92, 829	54, 014	38, 815	91, 535	1, 293	....	1
, Ohio.......	42	5, 790	5. 40	5, 011	6. 24	31, 274	23, 663	7, 611	29, 427	1, 847	....	....
hio..........	44	6, 109	4. 99	5, 611	5. 43	30, 473	23, 050	7, 423	29, 925	548	....	....
Mich........	18	15, 636	5. 09	14, 688	5. 42	79, 577	44, 196	35, 381	77, 338	2, 235	....	4
r, Mass......	50	5, 210	5. 13	2, 687	9. 96	26, 766	15, 288	11, 478	26, 635	106	....	25
Conn........	34	7, 427	5. 01	6, 688	5. 56	37, 180	26, 363	10, 817	36, 232	946	1	1
lis, Ind.....	27	9, 200	5. 24	7, 820	6. 17	48, 244	37, 587	10, 657	45, 309	2, 931	....	4
ty, N. J.....	17	16, 687	4. 95	9, 867	8. 37	82, 546	50, 711	31, 835	81, 840	705	....	1
ity, Mo......	38	5, 585	5. 78	5, 424	5. 95	32, 260	24, 581	7, 679	28, 484	3, 770	....	6
, Mass.......	45	5, 287	5. 47	3, 443	8. 40	28, 921	16, 204	12, 717	28, 814	106	1	....
, Ky.........	14	19, 177	5. 25	14, 670	6. 87	100, 753	75, 085	25, 668	85, 796	14, 956	....	1
ass..........	31	7, 649	5. 35	6, 362	6. 43	40, 928	26, 493	14, 435	40, 815	111	....	2
ss...........	49	6, 109	4. 63	4, 625	6. 10	28, 233	23, 298	4, 935	27, 862	371	....	....
Tenn........	32	7, 824	5. 14	6, 408	6. 28	40, 226	33, 446	6, 780	24, 755	15, 471	....	....
e, Wis......	19	14, 226	5. 02	13, 048	5. 48	71, 440	37, 667	33, 773	71, 263	176	....	1
la...........	39	6, 301	5. 08	5, 738	5. 58	32, 034	27, 795	4, 239	18, 115	13, 919	....	....
N. J.........	13	21, 631	4. 86	14, 350	7. 32	105, 059	69, 175	35, 884	103, 267	1, 789	2	1
en, Conn....	25	10, 482	4. 85	8, 100	6. 28	50, 840	36, 484	14, 356	49, 090	1, 749	....	1
ans, La......	9	39, 139	4. 89	33, 636	5. 69	191, 418	142, 943	48, 475	140, 923	50, 456	23	16
c, N. Y......	1	185, 789	5. 07	64, 044	14. 72	942, 292	523, 198	419, 094	929, 199	13, 072	12	9
N. J.........	37	7, 048	4. 76	4, 653	7. 22	33, 579	20, 711	12, 868	33, 218	361	....	....
hia, Pa......	2	127, 746	5. 28	112, 366	6. 01	674, 022	490, 398	183, 624	651, 854	22, 147	*c*13	8
h, Pa........	16	16, 182	5. 32	14, 224	6. 05	86, 076	58, 254	27, 822	84, 061	2, 015	....	....
Me..........	41	6, 632	4. 74	4, 836	6. 50	31, 413	24, 401	7, 012	31, 078	334	....	1
e, R. I......	21	14, 775	4. 66	9, 227	7. 46	68, 904	51, 727	17, 177	66, 320	2, 559	....	25
Pa...........	36	6, 932	4. 89	6, 294	5. 39	33, 930	30, 059	3, 871	33, 611	311	....	8
, Va.........	24	9, 792	5. 21	8, 033	6. 35	51, 038	47, 260	3, 778	27, 928	23, 110	....	....
, N. Y.......	22	12, 213	5. 11	11, 649	5. 36	62, 386	41, 202	21, 184	61, 959	427	....	....
isco, Cal....	10	30, 533	4. 89	25, 905	5. 77	149, 473	75, 754	73, 719	136, 059	1, 330	*d*12, 030	54
. Ga.........	48	5, 013	5. 63	4, 561	6. 19	28, 235	24, 564	3, 671	15, 166	13, 068	....	1
Pa...........	35	6, 612	5. 22	5, 646	6. 21	35, 092	19, 205	15, 887	35, 043	49	....	....
Mo..........	4	59, 431	5. 23	39, 675	7. 84	310, 864	198, 615	112, 249	288, 737	22, 088	1	38
N. Y.........	29	8, 677	4. 96	7, 088	6. 07	43, 051	29, 061	13, 990	42, 616	435	....	....
hio..........	40	6, 457	4. 89	6, 069	5. 20	31, 584	20, 485	11, 099	30, 972	612	....	....
?............	28	9, 302	5. 00	5, 893	7. 88	46, 465	30, 246	16, 219	46, 047	418	....	....
Y............	46	5, 793	4. 97	4, 799	6. 00	28, 804	18, 955	9, 849	28, 583	219	....	2
on, D. C.....	12	21, 343	5. 12	19, 545	5. 59	109, 199	95, 442	13, 757	73, 731	35, 455	....	13
on, Del......	43	5, 808	5. 31	5, 396	5. 71	30, 841	25, 689	5, 152	27, 630	3, 211	....	....
r, Mass......	30	8, 658	4. 74	4, 922	8. 35	41, 105	29, 159	11, 946	40, 588	513	*b*4	....

olumn expresses the relative size of the cities in regard to population.
imits.
nese.
iding 1 Japanese.
iding 8 Japanese.

SEX, AND SCHOOL, MILITARY,

AND

CITIZENSHIP AGES.

35 c c

TABLE XLVIII.—*Sex of the Aggregate Population, with General Nativity*—1870.

States and Territories.	ALL RACES.								
				Native.			Foreign-born.		
	Total.	Male.	Female.	Total.	Male.	Female.	Total.	Male.	Female.
The U. S.	38, 558, 371	19, 493, 565	19, 064, 806	32, 991, 142	16, 486, 622	16, 504, 520	5, 567, 229	3, 006, 943	2, 560, 286
Alabama	996, 992	488, 738	508, 254	987, 030	482, 470	504, 560	9, 962	6, 268	[illegible]
Arizona	9, 658	6, 887	2, 771	3, 849	2, 905	944	5, 809	3, 982	[illegible]
Arkansas	484, 471	248, 261	236, 210	479, 445	244, 491	234, 954	5, 026	3, 770	[illegible]
California	560, 247	349, 479	210, 768	350, 416	199, 421	150, 995	209, 831	150, 058	[illegible]
Colorado	39, 864	24, 820	15, 044	33, 265	19, 910	13, 355	6, 599	4, 910	[illegible]
Connecticut	537, 454	265, 270	272, 184	423, 815	207, 014	216, 801	113, 639	58, 256	[illegible]
Dakota	14, 181	8, 878	5, 303	9, 366	5, 562	3, 804	4, 815	3, 316	[illegible]
Delaware	125, 015	62, 628	62, 387	115, 879	57, 963	57, 916	9, 136	4, 665	[illegible]
Dist. of Col.	131, 700	62, 192	69, 508	115, 446	54, 159	61, 287	16, 254	8, 033	[illegible]
Florida	187, 748	94, 548	93, 200	182, 781	91, 573	91, 208	4, 967	2, 975	[illegible]
Georgia	1, 184, 109	578, 955	605, 154	1, 172, 982	572, 126	600, 856	11, 127	6, 830	[illegible]
Idaho	14, 999	12, 184	2, 815	7, 114	5, 054	2, 060	7, 885	7, 130	[illegible]
Illinois	2, 539, 891	1, 316, 537	1, 223, 354	2, 024, 693	1, 033, 161	991, 532	515, 198	283, 376	[illegible]
Indiana	1, 680, 637	857, 994	822, 643	1, 539, 163	779, 009	760, 154	141, 474	78, 985	[illegible]
Iowa	1, 194, 020	625, 917	568, 103	989, 328	510, 864	478, 464	204, 692	115, 053	[illegible]
Kansas	364, 399	202, 224	162, 175	316, 007	171, 248	144, 759	48, 392	30, 976	[illegible]
Kentucky	1, 321, 011	665, 675	655, 336	1, 257, 613	631, 020	626, 593	63, 398	34, 655	[illegible]
Louisiana	726, 915	362, 165	364, 750	665, 088	328, 743	336, 345	61, 827	33, 422	[illegible]
Maine	626, 915	313, 103	313, 812	578, 034	287, 434	290, 600	48, 881	25, 669	[illegible]
Maryland	780, 894	384, 984	395, 910	697, 482	342, 236	355, 246	83, 412	42, 745	[illegible]
Massachus's	1, 457, 351	703, 779	753, 572	1, 104, 032	535, 852	568, 180	353, 319	167, 927	[illegible]
Michigan	1, 184, 059	617, 745	566, 314	916, 049	469, 034	447, 015	268, 010	148, 711	[illegible]
Minnesota	439, 706	235, 299	204, 407	279, 009	145, 190	133, 819	160, 697	90, 109	[illegible]
Mississippi	827, 922	413, 421	414, 501	816, 731	405, 859	410, 872	11, 191	7, 562	[illegible]
Missouri	1, 721, 295	896, 347	824, 948	1, 499, 028	769, 457	729, 571	222, 267	126, 890	[illegible]
Montana	20, 595	16, 771	3, 824	12, 616	9, 562	3, 054	7, 979	7, 209	[illegible]
Nebraska	122, 993	70, 425	52, 568	92, 245	51, 183	41, 062	30, 748	19, 242	11, 506
Nevada	42, 491	32, 379	10, 112	23, 690	16, 808	6, 882	18, 801	15, 571	3, 230
New Hamp.	318, 300	155, 640	162, 660	288, 689	140, 991	147, 698	29, 611	14, 649	14, 962
New Jersey	906, 096	449, 672	456, 424	717, 153	353, 485	363, 668	188, 943	96, 187	92, 756
N. Mexico	91, 874	47, 135	44, 739	86, 254	43, 505	42, 749	5, 620	3, 630	1, 990
New York	4, 382, 759	2, 163, 229	2, 219, 530	3, 244, 406	1, 597, 192	1, 647, 214	1, 138, 353	566, 037	572, 316
N. Carolina	1, 071, 361	518, 704	552, 657	1, 068, 332	516, 684	551, 648	3, 029	2, 020	[illegible]
Ohio	2, 665, 260	1, 337, 550	1, 327, 710	2, 292, 767	1, 138, 971	1, 153, 796	372, 493	198, 579	[illegible]
Oregon	90, 923	53, 131	37, 792	79, 323	43, 952	35, 371	11, 600	9, 179	[illegible]
Pennsylv'ia.	3, 521, 951	1, 758, 499	1, 763, 452	2, 976, 642	1, 468, 318	1, 508, 324	545, 309	290, 181	[illegible]
Rhode Isl'd.	217, 353	104, 756	112, 597	161, 957	78, 656	83, 301	55, 396	26, 100	[illegible]
S. Carolina	705, 606	343, 902	361, 704	697, 532	339, 260	358, 272	8, 074	4, 642	[illegible]
Tennessee	1, 258, 520	623, 347	635, 173	1, 239, 204	611, 727	627, 477	19, 316	11, 620	[illegible]
Texas	818, 579	423, 557	395, 022	756, 168	387, 588	368, 580	62, 411	35, 969	[illegible]
Utah	86, 786	44, 121	42, 665	56, 084	28, 994	27, 090	30, 702	15, 127	[illegible]
Vermont	330, 551	165, 721	164, 830	283, 396	140, 520	142, 876	47, 155	25, 201	21, 954
Virginia	1, 225, 163	597, 058	628, 105	1, 211, 409	589, 038	622, 371	13, 754	8, 020	5, 734
Washington	23, 955	14, 990	8, 965	18, 931	11, 004	7, 927	5, 024	3, 986	1, 038
W. Virginia	442, 014	222, 843	219, 171	424, 923	213, 624	211, 299	17, 091	9, 219	7, 872
Wisconsin	1, 054, 670	544, 886	509, 784	690, 171	349, 547	340, 624	364, 499	195, 339	169, 160
Wyoming	9, 118	7, 219	1, 899	5, 605	4, 258	1, 347	3, 513	2, 961	552

TABLE XLIX.—*Sex of the White Population, with General Nativity*—1870.

...ries.	WHITE.								
				Native.			Foreign-born.		
	Total.	Male.	Female.	Total.	Male.	Female.	Total.	Male.	Female.
.S.	33,589,377	17,029,088	16,560,289	28,095,665	14,086,509	14,009,156	5,493,712	2,942,579	2,551,133
a...	521,384	255,023	266,361	511,718	248,948	262,770	9,666	6,075	3,591
.....	9,581	6,834	2,747	3,803	2,879	924	5,778	3,955	1,823
as.	362,115	186,445	175,670	357,230	182,802	174,428	4,885	3,643	1,242
ia..	499,424	297,648	201,776	339,199	193,310	145,889	160,225	104,338	55,887
o...	39,221	24,465	14,756	32,635	19,565	13,070	6,586	4,900	1,686
icut.	527,549	260,518	267,031	414,015	202,322	211,693	113,534	58,196	55,338
....	12,887	8,255	4,632	8,275	5,040	3,235	4,612	3,215	1,397
re...	102,221	51,148	51,073	93,101	46,491	46,610	9,120	4,657	4,463
Col.	88,278	42,980	45,298	72,107	34,997	37,110	16,171	7,983	8,188
....	96,057	48,953	47,104	91,395	46,136	45,259	4,662	2,817	1,845
....	638,926	311,171	327,755	628,173	304,562	323,611	10,753	6,609	4,144
....	10,618	7,973	2,645	7,018	5,002	2,016	3,600	2,971	629
....	2,511,096	1,301,583	1,209,513	1,996,114	1,018,329	977,785	514,982	283,254	231,728
....	1,655,837	845,307	810,530	1,514,410	766,351	748,059	141,427	78,956	62,471
....	1,188,207	622,786	565,421	983,543	507,752	475,791	204,664	115,034	89,630
....	346,377	193,200	153,177	298,041	162,259	135,782	48,336	30,941	17,395
ky..	1,098,692	557,326	541,366	1,035,346	522,701	512,645	63,346	34,625	28,721
na..	362,065	183,031	179,034	301,450	150,245	151,205	60,615	32,786	27,829
.....	624,809	311,942	312,867	576,097	286,361	289,736	48,712	25,581	23,131
nd	605,497	299,858	305,639	522,238	257,189	265,049	83,259	42,669	40,590
us's	1,443,156	696,925	746,231	1,090,843	529,544	561,299	352,313	167,381	184,932
n..	1,167,282	609,046	558,236	900,630	460,985	439,645	266,652	148,061	118,591
ota..	438,257	234,531	203,726	277,579	144,430	133,149	160,678	90,101	70,577
ppi.	382,896	195,283	187,613	371,915	187,854	184,061	10,981	7,429	3,552
i...	1,603,146	838,290	764,856	1,380,972	711,447	669,525	222,174	126,843	95,331
a...	18,306	14,760	3,546	12,288	9,391	2,897	6,018	5,369	649
ka..	122,117	69,942	52,175	91,376	50,707	40,669	30,741	19,235	11,506
....	38,959	29,284	9,675	23,332	16,576	6,756	15,627	12,708	2,919
mp.	317,697	155,315	162,382	288,117	140,686	147,431	29,580	14,629	14,951
rsey.	875,407	434,588	440,819	686,589	338,476	348,113	188,818	96,112	92,706
co...	90,393	46,553	43,840	84,786	42,931	41,855	5,607	3,622	1,985
rk..	4,330,210	2,137,896	2,192,314	3,193,160	1,572,553	1,620,607	1,137,050	565,343	571,707
lina	678,470	325,705	352,765	675,490	323,718	351,772	2,980	1,987	993
.....	2,601,946	1,305,402	1,296,544	2,229,782	1,106,990	1,122,792	372,164	198,412	173,752
.....	86,929	49,558	37,371	78,711	43,654	35,057	8,218	5,904	2,314
va'a	3,456,609	1,727,392	1,729,217	2,911,750	1,437,446	1,474,304	544,859	289,946	254,913
sl'd.	212,219	102,328	109,891	156,927	76,294	80,633	55,292	26,034	29,258
na..	289,667	140,740	148,927	281,894	136,275	145,619	7,773	4,465	3,308
see..	936,119	466,505	469,614	916,930	454,958	461,972	19,189	11,547	7,642
.....	564,700	297,055	267,645	503,216	261,692	241,524	61,484	35,363	26,121
.....	86,044	43,541	42,503	55,792	28,847	26,945	30,252	14,694	15,558
t..	329,613	165,207	164,406	282,492	140,024	142,468	47,121	25,183	21,938
a....	712,089	348,720	363,369	698,388	340,736	357,652	13,701	7,984	5,717
gton	22,195	14,143	8,052	17,585	10,462	7,123	4,610	3,681	929
inia.	424,033	213,871	210,162	406,951	204,660	202,291	17,082	9,211	7,871
sin..	1,051,351	543,139	508,212	686,903	347,829	339,074	364,448	195,310	169,138
ng..	8,726	6,923	1,803	5,359	4,103	1,256	3,367	2,820	547

TABLE L.—*Sex of the Colored Population, with General Nativity*—1870.

States and Territories.	COLORED, (TOTAL.)								
				Native.			Foreign-born.		
	Total.	Male.	Female.	Total.	Male.	Female.	Total.	Male.	Female.
The United States.	4,880,009	2,393,263	2,486,746	4,870,364	2,387,917	2,482,447	9,645	5,346	4,299
Alabama	475,510	233,677	241,833	475,214	233,484	241,730	296	193	103
Arizona	26	20	6	24	18	6	2	2	......
Arkansas	122,169	61,680	60,489	122,126	61,651	60,475	43	29	14
California	4,272	2,514	1,758	3,835	2,195	1,640	437	319	118
Colorado	456	285	171	450	281	169	6	4	2
Connecticut	9,668	4,632	5,036	9,565	4,574	4,991	103	58	45
Dakota	94	45	49	92	43	49	2	2	......
Delaware	22,794	11,480	11,314	22,778	11,472	11,306	16	8	8
District of Columbia	43,404	19,197	24,207	43,325	19,151	24,174	79	46	33
Florida	91,689	45,594	46,095	91,384	45,436	45,948	305	158	147
Georgia	545,142	267,765	277,377	544,770	267,546	277,224	372	219	153
Idaho	60	42	18	47	29	18	13	13	......
Illinois	28,762	14,934	13,828	28,549	14,814	13,735	213	120	93
Indiana	24,560	12,585	11,975	24,517	12,559	11,958	43	26	17
Iowa	5,762	3,099	2,663	5,737	3,083	2,654	25	16	9
Kansas	17,108	8,566	8,542	17,066	8,538	8,528	42	28	14
Kentucky	222,210	108,304	113,906	222,161	108,277	113,884	49	27	22
Louisiana	364,210	178,784	185,426	363,067	178,216	184,851	1,143	568	575
Maine	1,606	884	722	1,446	799	647	160	85	75
Maryland	175,391	85,123	90,268	175,240	85,045	90,195	151	78	73
Massachusetts	13,947	6,702	7,245	13,055	6,261	6,794	892	441	451
Michigan	11,849	6,192	5,657	10,688	5,645	5,043	1,161	547	614
Minnesota	759	437	322	751	432	319	8	5	3
Mississippi	444,201	217,722	226,479	444,007	217,605	226,402	194	117	77
Missouri	118,071	58,028	60,043	117,995	57,990	60,005	76	38	38
Montana	183	132	51	175	124	51	8	8	......
Nebraska	789	451	338	782	444	338	7	7	......
Nevada	357	239	118	328	218	110	29	21	8
New Hampshire	580	314	266	562	301	261	18	13	5
New Jersey	30,658	15,064	15,594	30,548	15,002	15,546	110	62	48
New Mexico	172	116	56	167	111	56	5	5	......
New York	52,081	25,080	27,001	50,834	24,429	26,405	1,247	651	596
North Carolina	391,650	192,418	199,232	391,601	192,385	199,216	49	33	16
Ohio	63,213	32,090	31,123	62,887	31,926	30,961	326	164	162
Oregon	346	219	127	301	180	121	45	39	6
Pennsylvania	65,294	31,077	34,217	64,859	30,853	34,006	435	224	211
Rhode Island	4,980	2,361	2,619	4,876	2,295	2,581	104	66	38
South Carolina	415,814	203,104	212,710	415,514	202,928	212,586	300	176	124
Tennessee	322,331	156,800	165,531	322,204	156,727	165,477	127	73	54
Texas	253,475	126,278	127,197	252,634	125,731	126,903	841	547	294
Utah	118	63	55	113	59	54	5	4	1
Vermont	924	506	418	900	493	407	24	13	11
Virginia	512,841	248,228	264,613	512,792	248,196	264,596	49	32	17
Washington	207	133	74	179	107	72	28	26	2
West Virginia	17,980	8,972	9,008	17,971	8,964	9,007	9	8	1
Wisconsin	2,113	1,189	924	2,068	1,165	903	45	24	21
Wyoming	183	138	45	180	135	45	3	3	......

TABLE LI.—*Sex of the Blacks, with General Nativity*—1870.

and Territories.	COLORED, (BLACKS.)								
				Native.			Foreign-born.		
	Total.	Male.	Female.	Total.	Male.	Female.	Total.	Male.	Female.
ited States	4, 295, 960	2, 115, 380	2, 180, 580	4, 288, 721	2, 111, 334	2, 177, 387	7, 239	4, 046	3, 193
	433, 698	213, 987	219, 711	433, 416	213, 805	219, 611	282	182	100
	26	20	6	24	18	6	2	2	....
	109, 831	55, 436	54, 395	109, 790	55, 407	54, 383	41	29	12
	2, 712	1, 628	1, 084	2, 444	1, 438	1, 006	268	190	78
	272	181	91	272	181	91	....	....	....
t	6, 992	3, 422	3, 570	6, 932	3, 388	3, 544	60	34	26
	71	36	35	70	35	35	1	1	....
	20, 570	10, 384	10, 186	20, 554	10, 376	10, 178	16	8	8
Columbia	35, 372	15, 827	19, 545	35, 331	15, 803	19, 528	41	24	17
	80, 338	40, 151	40, 187	80, 115	40, 041	40, 074	223	110	113
	501, 814	247, 336	254, 478	501, 442	247, 117	254, 325	372	219	153
	60	42	18	47	29	18	13	13	....
	21, 419	11, 240	10, 179	21, 307	11, 170	10, 137	112	70	42
	17, 548	9, 122	8, 426	17, 519	9, 103	8, 416	29	19	10
	4, 609	2, 502	2, 107	4, 653	2, 492	2, 161	16	10	6
	13, 299	6, 719	6, 580	13, 267	6, 700	6, 567	32	19	13
	177, 499	87, 736	89, 763	177, 464	87, 717	89, 747	35	19	16
	307, 610	152, 298	155, 312	306, 732	151, 846	154, 886	878	452	426
	1, 014	573	441	907	510	397	107	63	44
	151, 463	74, 144	77, 319	151, 355	74, 088	77, 267	108	56	52
etts	9, 686	4, 698	4, 988	9, 092	4, 392	4, 700	594	306	288
	6, 434	3, 481	2, 953	5, 732	3, 147	2, 585	702	334	368
	514	318	196	509	314	195	5	4	1
	398, 798	195, 350	203, 448	398, 607	195, 235	203, 372	191	115	76
	100, 412	49, 879	50, 533	100, 343	49, 845	50, 498	69	34	35
	137	102	35	129	94	35	8	8	....
	738	425	313	733	420	313	5	5	....
	290	199	91	270	183	87	20	16	4
shire	436	249	187	418	236	182	18	13	5
y	27, 105	13, 340	13, 765	26, 998	13, 281	13, 717	107	59	48
o	116	88	28	112	84	28	4	4	....
	46, 498	22, 430	24, 068	45, 444	21, 871	23, 573	1, 054	559	495
olina	354, 209	174, 194	180, 015	354, 164	174, 165	179, 999	45	29	16
	45, 371	23, 166	22, 208	45, 100	23, 024	22, 076	274	142	132
	259	169	90	221	136	85	38	33	5
nia	52, 441	24, 914	27, 527	52, 067	24, 719	27, 348	374	195	179
nd	3, 820	1, 829	1, 991	3, 767	1, 801	1, 966	53	28	25
lina	387, 985	189, 436	198, 549	387, 702	189, 267	198, 435	283	169	114
	292, 029	142, 619	149, 410	291, 911	142, 553	149, 358	118	66	52
	225, 658	112, 622	113, 036	225, 140	112, 295	112, 845	518	327	191
	85	44	41	83	42	41	2	2	....
	677	382	295	656	370	286	21	12	9
	440, 593	214, 758	225, 835	440, 553	214, 731	225, 822	40	27	13
n	56	44	12	45	33	12	11	11	....
inia	13, 640	6, 880	6, 760	13, 633	6, 874	6, 759	7	6	1
	1, 597	904	693	1, 557	884	673	40	20	20
	96	76	20	94	74	20	2	2	....

TABLE LII.—*Sex of the Mulattoes, with General Nativity*—1870.

States and Territories.	COLORED, (MULATTOES.)								
				Native.			Foreign-born.		
	Total.	Male.	Female.	Total.	Male.	Female.	Total.	Male.	Female.
The United States	584, 049	277, 896	306, 153	581, 634	276, 587	305, 047	2, 415	1, 309	1, 106
Alabama	41, 812	19, 690	22, 122	41, 798	19, 679	22, 119	14	11	3
Arizona	......	......	......	......	......	......	......	......	......
Arkansas	12, 338	6, 244	6, 094	12, 336	6, 244	6, 092	2	......	2
California	1, 560	886	674	1, 386	754	632	174	132	42
Colorado	184	104	80	178	100	78	6	4	2
Connecticut	2, 676	1, 211	1, 465	2, 633	1, 187	1, 446	43	24	19
Dakota	23	9	14	22	8	14	1	1	......
Delaware	2, 224	1, 096	1, 128	2, 224	1, 096	1, 128	......	......	......
District of Columbia	8, 032	3, 370	4, 662	7, 994	3, 348	4, 646	38	22	16
Florida	11, 351	5, 443	5, 908	11, 269	5, 395	5, 874	82	48	34
Georgia	43, 328	20, 429	22, 899	43, 328	20, 429	22, 899	......	......	......
Idaho	......	......	......	......	......	......	......	......	......
Illinois	7, 343	3, 694	3, 649	7, 242	3, 644	3, 598	101	50	51
Indiana	7, 012	3, 463	3, 549	6, 998	3, 456	3, 542	14	7	7
Iowa	1, 093	597	496	1, 084	591	493	9	6	3
Kansas	3, 809	1, 847	1, 962	3, 799	1, 838	1, 961	10	9	1
Kentucky	44, 711	20, 569	24, 142	44, 698	20, 562	24, 136	13	7	6
Louisiana	56, 600	26, 486	30, 114	56, 335	26, 370	29, 965	265	116	149
Maine	592	311	281	539	289	250	53	22	31
Maryland	23, 928	10, 979	12, 949	23, 885	10, 957	12, 928	43	22	21
Massachusetts	4, 261	2, 004	2, 257	3, 963	1, 869	2, 094	298	135	163
Michigan	5, 415	2, 715	2, 700	4, 953	2, 500	2, 453	462	215	247
Minnesota	245	120	125	242	118	124	3	2	1
Mississippi	45, 403	22, 372	23, 031	45, 400	22, 370	23, 030	3	2	1
Missouri	17, 659	8, 149	9, 510	17, 652	8, 145	9, 507	7	4	3
Montana	46	30	16	46	30	16	......	......	......
Nebraska	51	26	25	50	25	25	1	1	......
Nevada	67	40	27	58	35	23	9	5	4
New Hampshire	144	65	79	144	65	79	......	......	......
New Jersey	3, 553	1, 724	1, 829	3, 550	1, 721	1, 829	3	3	......
New Mexico	56	28	28	55	27	28	1	1	......
New York	5, 563	2, 633	2, 930	5, 367	2, 539	2, 828	196	94	102
North Carolina	37, 441	18, 224	19, 217	37, 437	18, 220	19, 217	4	4	......
Ohio	17, 839	8, 927	8, 912	17, 787	8, 902	8, 885	52	25	27
Oregon	87	50	37	80	44	36	7	6	1
Pennsylvania	12, 853	6, 163	6, 690	12, 792	6, 134	6, 658	61	29	32
Rhode Island	1, 160	532	628	1, 109	494	615	51	38	13
South Carolina	27, 829	13, 668	14, 161	27, 812	13, 661	14, 151	17	7	10
Tennessee	30, 302	14, 180	16, 122	30, 293	14, 174	16, 119	9	6	3
Texas	27, 817	13, 657	14, 160	27, 494	13, 436	14, 058	323	221	102
Utah	33	19	14	30	17	13	3	2	1
Vermont	247	124	123	244	123	121	3	1	2
Virginia	72, 248	33, 470	38, 778	72, 239	33, 465	38, 774	9	5	4
Washington	151	89	62	134	74	60	17	15	2
West Virginia	4, 340	2, 092	2, 248	4, 338	2, 090	2, 248	2	2	......
Wisconsin	516	285	231	511	281	230	5	4	1
Wyoming	87	62	25	86	61	25	1	1	......

TABLE LIII.—*Sex of the Chinese Population, with General Nativity*—1870.

States and Territories.	CHINESE.								
				Native.			Foreign-born.		
	Total.	Male.	Female.	Total.	Male.	Female.	Total.	Male.	Female.
The United States	a63,254	b58,680	c4,574	d318	d309	200	e62,736	f58,371	c4,365
labama									
rizona	20	20					20	20	
rkansas	98	98					98	98	
alifornia	g49,310	h45,429	c3,881	d487	d290	197	i48,823	j45,130	c3,684
olorado	7	6	1				7	6	1
onnecticut	2	2					2	2	
akota									
elaware									
istrict of Columbia	3	3					3	3	
lorida									
eorgia	1	1					1	1	
daho	4,274	4,148	126	5	3	2	4,269	4,145	124
llinois	1	1					1	1	
ndiana									
owa	3	3					3	3	
ansas									
entucky	1	1					1	1	
ouisiana	71	70	1	2	2		69	68	1
aine	1	1					1	1	
aryland	2	1	1				2	1	1
assachusetts	k97	k96	1				k97	k96	1
ichigan	d2	d2					d2	d2	
innesota									
ississippi	16	16					16	16	
issouri	3	2	1				3	2	1
ontana	1,949	1,826	123	6	2	4	1,943	1,824	119
ebraska									
evada	3,152	2,847	305	9	7	2	3,143	2,840	303
ew Hampshire									
ew Jersey	k15	k13	2				k15	k13	2
ew Mexico									
ew York	29	29					29	29	
orth Carolina									
hio	1	1					1	1	
regon	3,330	3,232	98	4	3	1	3,326	3,229	97
ennsylvania	d14	d11	3				d14	d11	3
hode Island									
outh Carolina	1	1					1	1	
ennessee									
exas	25	17	8	5	2	3	20	15	5
tah	445	429	16				445	429	16
ermont									
irginia	4	4					4	4	
ashington	234	232	2				234	232	2
est Virginia									
isconsin									
yoming	143	138	5				143	138	5

(a) Includes 55 Japanese.
(b) Includes 47 Japanese.
(c) Includes 8 Japanese.
(d) Includes 1 Japanese.
(e) Includes 54 Japanese.
(f) Includes 46 Japanese.
(g) Includes 33 Japanese.
(h) Includes 25 Japanese.
(i) Includes 32 Japanese.
(j) Includes 24 Japanese.
(k) Includes 10 Japanese.

TABLE LIV.—*Sex of the Civilized Indian Population, with General Nativity—1870.*

States and Territories.	INDIAN.								
				Native.			Foreign-born.		
	Total.	Male.	Female.	Total.	Male.	Female.	Total.	Male.	Female.
The United States	25, 731	12, 534	13, 197	24, 595	11, 887	12, 708	1, 136	647	[illegible]
Alabama	98	38	60	98	38	60	......	......	......
Arizona	31	13	18	22	8	14	9	5	4
Arkansas	89	38	51	89	38	51	......	......	......
California	7, 241	3, 888	3, 353	6, 895	3, 626	3, 269	346	202	[illegible]
Colorado	180	64	116	180	64	116	......	......	......
Connecticut	235	118	117	235	118	117	......	......	......
Dakota	1, 200	578	622	999	479	520	201	99	[illegible]
Delaware	......	......	......	......	......	......	......	......	......
District of Columbia	15	12	3	14	11	3	1	1	......
Florida	2	1	1	2	1	1	......	......	......
Georgia	40	18	22	39	18	21	1	......	1
Idaho	47	21	26	44	20	24	3	1	2
Illinois	32	19	13	30	18	12	2	1	1
Indiana	240	102	138	236	99	137	4	3	1
Iowa	48	29	19	48	29	19	......	......	......
Kansas	914	458	456	900	451	449	14	7	7
Kentucky	108	44	64	106	42	64	2	2	......
Louisiana	569	280	289	569	280	289	......	......	......
Maine	499	276	223	491	274	217	8	2	6
Maryland	4	2	2	4	2	2	......	......	......
Massachusetts	151	56	95	134	47	87	17	9	8
Michigan	4, 926	2, 505	2, 421	4, 731	2, 404	2, 327	195	101	94
Minnesota	690	331	359	679	328	351	11	3	8
Mississippi	809	400	409	809	400	409	......	......	......
Missouri	75	27	48	61	20	41	14	7	7
Montana	157	53	104	147	45	102	10	8	2
Nebraska	87	32	55	87	32	55	......	......	......
Nevada	23	9	14	21	7	14	2	2	......
New Hampshire	23	11	12	10	4	6	13	7	6
New Jersey	16	7	9	16	7	9	......	......	......
New Mexico	1, 309	466	843	1, 301	463	838	8	3	5
New York	439	224	215	412	210	202	27	14	13
North Carolina	1, 241	581	660	1, 241	581	660	......	......	......
Ohio	100	57	43	98	55	43	2	2	......
Oregon	318	122	196	307	115	192	11	7	4
Pennsylvania	34	19	15	33	19	14	1	......	1
Rhode Island	154	67	87	154	67	87	......	......	......
South Carolina	124	57	67	124	57	67	......	......	......
Tennessee	70	42	28	70	42	28	......	......	......
Texas	379	207	172	313	163	150	66	44	22
Utah	179	88	91	179	88	91	......	......	......
Vermont	14	8	6	4	3	1	10	5	5
Virginia	229	106	123	229	106	123	......	......	......
Washington	1, 319	482	837	1, 167	435	732	152	47	105
West Virginia	1	......	1	1	......	1	......	......	......
Wisconsin	1, 206	558	648	1, 200	553	647	6	5	1
Wyoming	66	20	46	66	20	46	......	......	......

TABLE LV.—*The Natural Militia, with the Total Male Population*—1870.

States and Territories.	Total male.	18 TO 45—MALE.						
		All classes.	Native.	Foreign-born.	White.	Colored.	Chinese.	Indian.
The United States	19, 493, 565	7, 570, 487	5, 697, 085	1, 873, 402	6, 655, 811	861, 164	48, 666	4, 846
Alabama	488, 738	168, 986	165, 045	3, 941	88, 175	80, 794	....	17
Arizona	6, 887	5, 157	2, 051	3, 106	5, 115	17	19	6
Arkansas	248, 261	94, 873	92, 037	2, 836	70, 253	24, 507	94	19
California	349, 479	194, 935	77, 828	117, 107	154, 200	1, 264	37, 800	1, 071
Colorado	24, 820	15, 166	10, 955	4, 211	14, 936	204	5	21
Connecticut	265, 270	109, 881	71, 349	38, 532	107, 631	2, 207	2	41
Dakota	8, 878	5, 301	2, 808	2, 493	5, 071	32	....	198
Delaware	62, 628	24, 018	21, 097	2, 921	19, 593	4, 425	....	....
District of Columbia	62, 192	26, 824	21, 681	5, 143	18, 486	8, 328	3	7
Florida	94, 548	34, 539	32, 704	1, 835	17, 900	16, 638	....	1
Georgia	578, 955	202, 573	198, 265	4, 308	108, 711	93, 852	1	9
Idaho	12, 184	9, 431	3, 288	6, 143	5, 679	34	3, 708	10
Illinois	1, 316, 537	525, 873	346, 564	179, 309	518, 924	6, 941	....	8
Indiana	857, 994	319, 658	274, 648	45, 010	314, 329	5, 294	....	35
Iowa	625, 917	240, 769	173, 060	67, 709	239, 331	1, 425	3	10
Kansas	202, 224	95, 002	73, 067	21, 935	91, 258	3, 569	....	175
Kentucky	665, 675	239, 483	217, 834	21, 649	202, 093	37, 379	....	11
Louisiana	362, 165	136, 753	115, 851	20, 902	70, 401	66, 158	59	135
Maine	313, 103	118, 940	105, 023	13, 917	118, 403	433	1	103
Maryland	384, 984	144, 695	121, 004	23, 691	112, 613	32, 079	1	2
Massachusetts	703, 779	298, 767	191, 788	106, 979	295, 275	3, 435	38	19
Michigan	617, 745	252, 821	165, 088	87, 733	249, 300	2, 640	2	879
Minnesota	235, 299	94, 238	40, 808	53, 430	93, 848	258	....	132
Mississippi	413, 421	149, 698	144, 574	5, 124	72, 505	77, 069	16	108
Missouri	896, 347	352, 998	267, 459	85, 539	331, 304	21, 680	2	12
Montana	16, 771	12, 418	6, 935	5, 483	11, 531	101	762	24
Nebraska	70, 425	35, 677	22, 257	13, 420	35, 365	302	....	10
Nevada	32, 379	24, 762	11, 109	13, 653	22, 032	154	2, 571	5
New Hampshire	155, 640	60, 684	51, 732	8, 952	60, 504	175	....	5
New Jersey	449, 672	180, 987	118, 871	62, 116	174, 666	6, 307	11	3
New Mexico	47, 135	20, 070	17, 306	2, 764	19, 876	83	....	111
New York	2, 163, 229	881, 500	527, 820	353, 680	869, 403	11, 988	25	84
North Carolina	518, 704	174, 825	173, 610	1, 215	110, 085	64, 534	....	206
Ohio	1, 337, 550	501, 750	387, 360	114, 390	488, 547	13, 180	1	22
Oregon	53, 131	23, 959	16, 837	7, 122	20, 964	119	2, 822	54
Pennsylvania	1, 738, 499	679, 506	506, 438	173, 068	665, 704	13, 780	10	12
Rhode Island	104, 756	44, 377	28, 648	15, 729	43, 187	1, 165	....	25
South Carolina	343, 902	120, 151	117, 545	2, 606	49, 721	70, 407	1	22
Tennessee	623, 347	222, 903	214, 693	8, 210	167, 454	55, 430	....	19
Texas	423, 557	158, 765	136, 894	21, 871	113, 756	44, 894	15	100
Utah	44, 121	14, 603	5, 971	8, 632	14, 173	33	357	40
Vermont	165, 721	62, 459	48, 479	13, 980	62, 206	248	....	5
Virginia	597, 058	206, 658	202, 072	4, 586	123, 124	83, 488	4	42
Washington	14, 990	7, 835	4, 701	3, 134	7, 350	62	207	216
West Virginia	222, 843	76, 832	71, 967	4, 865	73, 492	3, 340	....	....
Wisconsin	544, 886	192, 331	86, 593	105, 738	191, 521	603	....	207
Wyoming	7, 219	6, 056	3, 371	2, 685	5, 816	109	[illegible]	5

TABLE LVI.—*Citizenship, with the Total Male Population.*

States and Territories.	Total male.	21 AND UPWARD—MALE.							21 AND UPWARD.
		All classes.	Native.	Foreign-born.	White.	Colored.	Chinese.	Indian.	Male citizens.
The United States	19,493,565	9,439,206	6,896,623	2,542,583	8,333,719	1,032,475	47,531	5,481	8,425,941
Alabama	488,738	203,315	197,454	5,861	105,474	97,823	.....	18	202,046
Arizona	6,887	5,353	2,213	3,140	5,311	18	19	5	3,397
Arkansas	248,261	104,083	100,598	3,485	77,195	26,789	83	16	100,4[illegible]
California	349,479	227,256	93,327	133,929	186,823	1,731	36,890	1,812	145,[illegible]
Colorado	24,820	16,294	11,722	4,572	16,083	197	6	8	15,515
Connecticut	265,270	150,415	101,628	48,787	147,659	2,700	.....	56	127,4[illegible]
Dakota	8,878	5,724	2,917	2,807	5,426	98	.....	200	[illegible]
Delaware	62,628	30,035	25,806	4,229	24,811	5,224	.....	.....	28,207
District of Columbia	62,192	33,329	26,009	7,320	23,178	10,143	1	7	31,[illegible]
Florida	94,548	39,907	37,365	2,542	21,064	18,842	.....	1	38,854
Georgia	578,955	237,640	231,312	6,328	129,665	107,962	1	12	234,919
Idaho	12,184	10,313	3,680	6,633	6,501	38	3,766	8	5,557
Illinois	1,316,537	625,139	390,735	234,404	617,435	7,694	1	9	542,[illegible]
Indiana	857,994	388,231	318,055	70,176	382,070	6,113	.....	48	376,7[illegible]
Iowa	625,917	290,717	197,852	92,865	289,162	1,542	1	11	255,[illegible]
Kansas	202,224	105,671	79,441	26,230	101,480	3,985	.....	206	[illegible]
Kentucky	665,675	289,471	257,978	31,493	245,133	44,321	.....	17	[illegible]
Louisiana	302,165	174,187	143,156	31,031	87,066	86,913	68	140	[illegible]
Maine	313,103	169,821	149,889	19,932	169,192	497	1	131	[illegible]
Maryland	384,984	184,742	146,684	38,058	145,619	39,120	1	2	[illegible]
Massachusetts	703,779	398,157	260,325	137,832	394,031	4,073	20	33	[illegible]
Michigan	617,745	315,937	201,684	114,253	311,712	3,130	2	1,093	[illegible]
Minnesota	235,299	114,739	45,933	68,806	114,344	246	.....	149	75,[illegible]
Mississippi	413,421	174,845	168,064	6,781	84,784	89,926	15	120	[illegible]
Missouri	896,347	408,206	296,294	111,912	384,314	23,882	2	8	[illegible]
Montana	16,771	13,424	7,450	5,974	12,545	108	742	29	11,[illegible]
Nebraska	70,425	39,080	23,591	15,489	38,782	290	.....	8	[illegible]
Nevada	32,379	26,920	12,278	14,642	24,245	203	2,467	5	16,6[illegible]
New Hampshire	155,640	91,016	80,190	10,826	90,834	176	.....	6	[illegible]
New Jersey	449,672	231,862	149,634	82,228	223,983	7,870	5	4	194,1[illegible]
New Mexico	47,135	23,332	20,153	3,179	23,176	85	.....	71	22,448
New York	2,163,229	1,158,901	670,375	488,526	1,144,165	14,586	23	127	981,567
North Carolina	518,704	217,813	215,974	1,839	139,535	78,019	.....	259	214,[illegible]
Ohio	1,337,550	640,820	466,213	174,607	625,176	15,614	1	29	592,[illegible]
Oregon	53,131	28,616	20,186	8,430	25,640	143	2,789	44	24,[illegible]
Pennsylvania	1,758,499	865,883	614,883	251,000	848,790	17,072	9	12	776,345
Rhode Island	104,756	58,752	38,258	20,494	57,312	1,404	.....	36	43,[illegible]
South Carolina	343,902	148,052	143,774	4,278	62,547	85,475	1	29	146,614
Tennessee	623,347	263,200	252,695	10,505	199,056	64,131	.....	13	259,016
Texas	423,557	184,094	155,428	28,666	132,390	51,575	14	115	169,915
Utah	44,121	18,042	6,509	11,533	17,654	36	316	36	10,147
Vermont	165,721	90,806	72,191	18,615	90,522	278	.....	6	74,[illegible]
Virginia	507,058	269,242	261,948	7,294	161,500	107,691	4	47	266,[illegible]
Washington	14,990	9,241	5,573	3,668	8,750	67	185	239	7,902
West Virginia	222,843	95,317	87,202	8,115	91,345	3,972	.....	..	93,435
Wisconsin	544,886	255,159	98,642	156,517	254,262	642	.....	255	253,077
Wyoming	7,219	6,107	3,355	2,752	5,908	101	97	1	5,297

TABLE LVII.—*School, Military, and Citizenship Ages, with Sex for the School Age and for All Ages, by Counties*—1870.

STATE OF ALABAMA.

NOTE.—Of the school and military ages the first years are inclusive and the last years are exclusive.

Counties.	All ages.			5 to 18.		18 to 45.	21 and upward.	
	Total.	Male.	Female.	Male.	Female.	Male.	Male.	Male citizens.
The State	996,992	488,738	508,254	173,273	169,703	168,986	203,315	202,046
Autauga	11,623	5,656	5,967	1,950	1,968	1,934	2,350	2,348
Baker	6,194	3,061	3,133	1,230	1,122	923	1,072	1,071
Baldwin	6,004	3,085	2,919	999	911	1,137	1,470	1,454
Barbour	29,309	14,258	15,051	5,174	5,004	4,978	5,794	5,763
Bibb	7,469	3,680	3,789	1,350	1,318	1,271	1,494	1,480
Blount	9,945	4,863	5,082	1,827	1,789	1,478	1,814	1,785
Bullock	24,474	12,295	12,179	4,219	4,079	4,546	5,290	5,290
Butler	14,981	7,266	7,715	2,703	2,565	2,442	2,927	2,921
Calhoun	13,980	6,815	7,165	2,558	2,444	2,355	2,719	2,710
Chambers	17,562	8,459	9,103	3,190	3,244	2,754	3,309	3,294
Cherokee	11,132	5,276	5,856	2,040	1,956	1,684	2,074	2,073
Choctaw	12,676	6,260	6,416	2,117	2,130	2,180	2,590	2,517
Clarke	14,663	7,283	7,380	2,647	2,459	2,393	2,895	2,895
Clay	9,560	4,585	4,975	1,790	1,634	1,354	1,664	1,660
Cleburne	8,017	3,847	4,170	1,509	1,453	1,154	1,402	1,401
Coffee	6,171	3,036	3,135	1,196	1,111	929	1,096	1,091
Colbert	12,537	6,179	6,358	2,204	2,126	2,123	2,518	2,516
Conecuh	9,574	4,643	4,931	1,730	1,641	1,478	1,794	1,790
Coosa	11,945	5,722	6,223	2,203	2,130	1,787	2,009	2,009
Covington	4,868	2,333	2,535	917	924	718	869	867
Crenshaw	11,156	5,438	5,718	2,053	1,974	1,766	2,027	2,009
Dale	11,325	5,517	5,808	2,211	2,049	1,713	1,965	1,959
Dallas	40,705	20,026	20,679	6,362	6,275	7,579	9,351	9,258
De Kalb	7,126	3,541	3,585	1,277	1,260	1,203	1,378	1,351
Elmore	14,477	7,195	7,282	2,580	2,452	2,495	3,026	3,018
Escambia	4,041	2,026	2,015	720	681	686	807	800
Etowah	10,109	4,986	5,123	1,794	1,778	1,693	1,935	1,931
Fayette	7,136	3,422	3,714	1,343	1,301	1,056	1,285	1,281
Franklin	8,006	3,930	4,076	1,511	1,472	1,196	1,444	1,389
Geneva	2,959	1,426	1,533	531	562	431	530	517
Greene	18,399	9,101	9,298	3,019	2,982	3,250	3,946	3,943
Hale	21,792	10,958	10,834	3,540	3,629	3,987	4,937	4,905
Henry	14,191	6,840	7,351	2,614	2,509	2,169	2,557	2,551
Jackson	19,410	9,560	9,850	3,498	3,436	3,251	3,740	3,626
Jefferson	12,345	5,919	6,426	2,211	2,230	1,948	2,306	2,294
Lauderdale	15,091	7,383	7,708	2,787	2,588	2,413	2,950	2,925
Lawrence	16,658	8,210	8,448	3,040	2,893	2,771	3,285	3,274
Lee	21,750	10,651	11,099	3,905	3,848	3,546	4,330	4,321
Limestone	15,017	7,385	7,632	2,577	2,478	2,656	3,164	3,157
Lowndes	25,719	12,783	12,936	4,290	4,150	4,518	5,555	5,550
Macon	17,727	8,785	8,942	2,992	2,901	3,132	3,696	3,683
Madison	31,267	15,273	15,994	5,295	5,195	5,294	6,473	6,456
Marengo	26,151	12,896	13,255	4,277	4,296	4,610	5,809	5,804
Marion	6,059	2,880	3,179	1,091	1,139	917	1,084	1,081
Marshall	9,871	4,720	5,151	1,782	1,815	1,487	1,747	1,687
Mobile	49,311	23,936	25,375	7,017	7,609	9,934	12,454	12,364
Monroe	14,214	6,951	7,263	2,522	2,335	2,357	2,811	2,798
Montgomery	43,704	21,515	22,189	6,908	6,856	8,255	10,174	10,162
Morgan	12,187	6,061	6,126	2,236	2,076	2,136	2,466	2,440
Perry	24,975	12,236	12,739	4,230	4,371	4,361	5,355	5,333
Pickens	17,690	8,530	9,160	3,149	3,088	2,835	3,351	3,340
Pike	17,423	8,548	8,875	3,223	3,113	2,848	3,236	3,223
Randolph	12,006	5,730	6,276	2,262	2,141	1,750	2,067	2,066
Russell	21,636	10,892	10,744	3,806	3,592	3,794	4,617	4,572
Sanford	8,893	4,315	4,578	1,647	1,605	1,344	1,564	1,558
Shelby	12,218	5,989	6,229	2,122	2,108	2,065	2,407	2,359
St. Clair	9,360	4,646	4,714	1,684	1,593	1,582	1,809	1,801
Sumter	24,109	11,997	12,112	4,179	4,046	4,153	5,126	5,096
Talladega	18,064	8,706	9,358	3,185	3,182	2,825	3,438	3,425
Tallapoosa	16,963	8,253	8,710	3,261	3,104	2,591	3,030	3,029
Tuscaloosa	20,081	9,810	10,271	3,423	3,365	3,437	4,267	4,200
Walker	6,543	3,171	3,372	1,240	1,297	1,128	1,158	1,158
Washington	3,912	1,930	1,982	732	716	639	751	747
Wilcox	28,377	14,047	14,330	4,815	4,766	5,018	5,986	5,960
Winston	4,155	2,022	2,133	779	746	609	722	721

TABLE LVII.—*School, Military, and Citizenship Ages, &c., by Counties*—1870—Continued.

TERRITORY OF ARIZONA.

Counties.	All ages.			5 to 18.		18 to 45.	21 and upward.	
	Total.	Male.	Female.	Male.	Female.	Male.	Male.	Male citizens.
The Territory	9,658	6,887	2,771	831	790	5,157	5,353	3,397
Mohave	179	162	17	3	2	145	150	118
Pima	5,716	3,855	1,861	589	541	2,795	2,819	1,644
Yavapai	2,142	1,829	313	66	74	1,534	1,664	1,244
Yuma	1,621	1,041	580	173	173	663	720	391

STATE OF ARKANSAS.

Counties.	Total.	Male.	Female.	Male.	Female.	Male.	Male.	Male citizens.
The State	484,471	248,261	236,210	84,645	80,847	94,873	104,083	100,403
Arkansas	8,268	4,328	3,940	1,181	1,099	1,986	2,003	1,980
Ashley	8,042	3,990	4,052	1,420	1,356	1,402	1,588	1,581
Benton	13,831	7,023	6,808	2,582	2,466	2,354	2,790	2,569
Boone	7,032	3,555	3,477	1,391	1,214	1,151	1,330	1,321
Bradley	8,646	4,340	4,306	1,594	1,576	1,516	1,680	1,672
Calhoun	3,853	2,007	1,846	725	673	706	779	765
Carroll	5,780	2,887	2,893	1,071	1,064	941	1,062	1,056
Chicot	7,214	3,755	3,459	1,065	1,029	1,635	1,891	1,578
Clarke	11,953	6,016	5,937	2,150	2,134	2,145	2,393	2,372
Columbia	11,397	5,948	5,449	2,221	2,034	1,959	2,216	2,013
Conway	8,112	4,097	4,015	1,331	1,273	1,616	1,652	1,614
Craighead	4,577	2,298	2,279	836	797	789	852	851
Crawford	8,957	4,580	4,377	1,583	1,533	1,775	1,912	1,586
Crittenden	3,831	2,113	1,718	613	519	1,067	1,133	1,127
Cross	3,915	2,001	1,914	712	643	771	797	792
Dallas	5,707	2,820	2,887	1,051	1,021	939	1,089	1,081
Desha	6,125	3,449	2,676	842	781	1,799	1,803	1,744
Drew	9,960	4,957	5,003	1,757	1,722	1,775	2,035	1,845
Franklin	9,627	5,003	4,624	1,771	1,578	1,930	2,006	1,784
Fulton	4,843	2,401	2,442	916	886	799	883	874
Grant	3,943	1,949	1,994	733	733	638	704	703
Greene	7,573	3,773	3,800	1,387	1,370	1,310	1,429	1,404
Hempstead	13,768	7,121	6,647	2,562	2,402	2,456	2,711	2,687
Hot Springs	5,877	3,049	2,828	946	980	1,211	1,397	1,389
Independence	14,566	7,378	7,188	2,642	2,461	2,685	2,941	2,916
Izard	6,806	3,397	3,409	1,254	1,186	1,150	1,300	1,299
Jackson	7,268	3,805	3,463	1,263	1,194	1,603	1,659	1,653
Jefferson	15,733	8,198	7,535	2,486	2,319	3,589	3,946	3,834
Johnson	9,152	4,683	4,469	1,651	1,594	1,733	1,833	1,730
Lafayette	9,139	4,738	4,401	1,611	1,511	1,767	1,979	1,960
Lawrence	5,981	3,008	2,973	1,067	1,057	1,096	1,232	1,225
Little River	3,236	1,637	1,599	569	584	628	701	606
Madison	8,231	4,161	4,070	1,601	1,453	1,369	1,500	1,437
Marion	3,979	2,049	1,930	772	704	692	749	748
Mississippi	3,633	1,941	1,692	601	581	890	911	905
Monroe	8,336	4,399	3,937	1,348	1,322	1,935	1,979	1,574
Montgomery	2,984	1,466	1,518	543	559	486	538	538
Newton	4,374	2,143	2,231	824	797	720	735	735
Ouachita	12,975	6,542	6,433	2,366	2,216	2,220	2,638	2,635
Perry	2,685	1,391	1,294	493	450	536	584	583
Phillips	15,372	8,025	7,347	2,238	2,091	3,581	4,074	3,993
Pike	3,788	1,917	1,871	734	653	632	688	667
Poinsett	1,720	851	869	308	286	328	340	338
Polk	3,376	1,712	1,664	702	604	515	611	600
Pope	8,386	4,249	4,137	1,437	1,401	1,557	1,695	1,678
Prairie	5,604	2,975	2,629	899	811	1,269	1,411	1,335
Pulaski	32,066	16,994	15,072	4,741	4,859	8,295	8,799	8,422
Randolph	7,466	3,809	3,657	1,410	1,286	1,358	1,466	1,458
Saline	3,911	1,971	1,940	704	685	690	756	750
Scott	7,483	3,790	3,693	1,295	1,290	1,373	1,499	1,490
Searcy	5,614	2,797	2,817	1,084	1,012	903	959	848
Sebastian	12,940	6,725	6,215	2,130	2,136	2,672	2,894	2,705
Sevier	4,492	2,243	2,249	825	800	752	822	861
Sharpe	5,400	2,644	2,756	994	978	898	965	939
St. Francis	6,714	3,543	3,171	1,107	1,065	1,528	1,655	1,607
Union	10,571	5,331	5,240	2,051	1,873	1,658	2,043	2,012
Van Buren	5,107	2,526	2,581	925	940	856	936	887

TABLE LVII.—*School, Military, and Citizenship Ages, &c., by Counties*—1870—Continued.

STATE OF ARKANSAS—Continued.

Counties.	All ages.			5 to 18.		18 to 45.	21 and upward.	
	Total.	Male.	Female.	Male.	Female.	Male.	Male.	Male citizens.
Washington	17,266	8,798	8,468	3,240	2,965	3,028	3,532	3,526
White	10,347	5,245	5,102	1,733	1,814	1,976	2,134	2,109
Woodruff	6,891	3,627	3,264	1,139	1,071	1,659	1,698	1,686
Yell	8,048	4,093	3,955	1,418	1,336	1,566	1,675	1,656

STATE OF CALIFORNIA.

Counties.	All ages.			5 to 18.		18 to 45.	21 and upward.	
	Total.	Male.	Female.	Male.	Female.	Male.	Male.	Male citizens.
The State	560,247	349,479	210,768	71,086	66,043	194,935	237,256	145,802
Alameda	24,237	14,585	9,652	3,100	2,923	8,263	9,165	4,881
Alpine	685	485	200	63	64	307	351	279
Amador	9,582	6,670	2,912	1,053	973	3,771	4,936	2,861
Butte	11,403	7,962	3,441	1,257	1,206	4,917	5,828	3,501
Calaveras	8,895	6,246	2,649	1,073	990	3,231	4,539	2,217
Colusa	6,165	4,031	2,134	790	706	2,380	2,657	2,208
Contra Costa	8,461	5,058	3,403	1,303	1,165	2,453	2,932	2,113
Del Norte	2,022	1,276	746	206	211	728	831	640
El Dorado	10,309	7,042	3,267	1,165	1,164	3,734	5,163	3,265
Fresno	6,336	4,006	2,330	896	660	2,149	2,476	1,532
Humboldt	6,140	3,797	2,343	840	851	1,955	2,362	1,848
Inyo	1,956	1,518	438	148	149	1,052	1,239	877
Kern	2,925	2,000	925	267	229	1,038	1,247	782
Klamath	1,686	1,369	317	110	100	977	1,132	513
Lake	2,969	1,781	1,188	437	455	778	967	846
Lassen	1,327	793	534	189	168	415	473	451
Los Angeles	15,309	8,849	6,460	2,270	2,251	4,300	5,075	3,677
Marin	6,903	5,048	1,855	898	540	3,289	3,464	1,873
Mariposa	4,572	3,294	1,278	436	452	1,898	2,551	1,203
Mendocino	7,545	4,663	2,882	1,089	1,028	2,516	2,788	2,046
Merced	2,807	1,874	933	400	337	1,003	1,202	910
Mono	430	321	109	39	32	202	259	205
Monterey	9,876	5,873	4,003	1,523	1,465	2,869	3,348	2,468
Napa	7,163	4,263	2,900	1,072	938	2,123	2,472	1,954
Nevada	19,134	13,066	6,068	2,146	1,978	7,967	9,338	5,542
Placer	11,357	8,152	3,205	1,150	1,052	4,957	6,122	3,502
Plumas	4,489	3,392	1,097	400	327	2,217	2,656	1,511
Sacramento	26,830	16,876	9,954	3,142	3,038	9,863	11,514	7,419
San Bernardino	3,988	2,324	1,664	666	652	1,028	1,241	1,099
San Diego	4,951	3,055	1,896	611	590	1,690	1,988	1,812
San Francisco	149,473	86,182	63,291	17,856	16,685	49,053	54,728	33,373
San Joaquin	21,050	13,093	7,957	2,985	2,718	7,214	8,323	5,348
San Luis Obispo	4,772	2,930	1,842	809	672	1,308	1,554	1,265
San Mateo	6,635	4,458	2,177	764	670	2,807	3,034	1,487
Santa Barbara	7,784	4,519	3,265	1,272	1,203	2,013	2,484	2,013
Santa Clara	26,246	15,365	10,881	3,722	3,618	7,878	9,190	6,134
Santa Cruz	8,743	5,147	3,596	1,317	1,256	2,439	2,882	2,066
Shasta	4,173	2,839	1,334	622	512	1,404	1,861	1,292
Sierra	5,619	4,046	1,573	517	487	2,653	3,116	2,062
Siskiyou	6,848	4,648	2,200	781	729	2,914	3,214	1,965
Solano	16,871	10,665	6,206	2,062	1,954	6,385	6,982	5,599
Sonoma	19,819	11,574	8,245	3,074	2,974	5,403	6,502	5,084
Stanislaus	6,499	4,247	2,252	925	839	2,351	2,773	2,094
Sutter	5,030	3,208	1,822	715	650	1,783	2,019	1,164
Tehama	3,587	2,357	1,230	512	429	1,359	1,497	980
Trinity	3,213	2,540	673	301	189	1,594	1,990	886
Tulare	4,533	2,645	1,888	641	562	1,202	1,417	1,318
Tuolumne	8,150	5,698	2,452	946	896	2,945	4,148	2,025
Yolo	9,899	6,285	3,614	1,209	1,208	3,551	4,049	3,288
Yuba	10,851	7,364	3,487	1,227	1,089	4,519	5,155	2,310

TABLE LVII.—*School, Military, and Citizenship Ages, &c., by Counties—1870—Continued.*

TERRITORY OF COLORADO.

Counties.	All ages.			5 to 18.		18 to 45.	21 and upward.	
	Total.	Male.	Female.	Male.	Female.	Male.	Male.	Male citizens.
The Territory	39,864	24,820	15,044	4,606	4,352	15,166	16,294	15,515
Arapahoe	6,829	4,406	2,423	647	645	3,040	3,154	2,917
Bent	592	439	153	29	24	302	367	334
Boulder	1,939	1,180	759	233	230	640	738	669
Clear Creek	1,596	1,077	519	150	115	748	890	794
Conejos	2,504	1,303	1,201	441	440	484	574	573
Costilla	1,779	912	867	207	302	305	456	450
Douglas	1,388	1,005	383	117	98	739	753	749
El Paso	987	637	350	121	118	386	425	421
Fremont	1,064	637	427	125	113	370	397	397
Gilpin	5,490	3,539	1,951	523	484	2,363	2,513	2,365
Greenwood	510	417	93	25	17	367	354	350
Huerfano	2,250	1,205	1,045	370	345	517	603	594
Jefferson	2,390	1,521	869	288	256	927	986	941
Lake	522	387	135	48	35	267	303	303
Larimer	838	539	299	81	73	331	351	333
Las Animas	4,276	2,363	1,913	608	595	1,166	1,272	1,197
Park	447	317	130	38	35	218	248	245
Pueblo	2,265	1,471	794	274	215	897	959	959
Saguache	304	189	115	38	44	103	117	116
Summit	258	217	41	13	7	176	190	184
Weld	1,636	1,059	577	169	161	670	714	651

STATE OF CONNECTICUT.

Counties.	Total.	Male.	Female.	5 to 18, Male.	5 to 18, Female.	18 to 45, Male.	21 and upward, Male.	21 and upward, Male citizens.
The State	537,454	265,270	272,184	69,807	69,155	109,891	150,415	127,[illegible]
Fairfield	95,276	46,163	49,113	12,302	12,353	18,897	25,925	22,237
Hartford	109,007	53,957	55,050	14,067	13,910	23,063	30,594	25,[illegible]
Litchfield	48,727	24,558	24,169	6,535	6,197	9,462	14,063	12,[illegible]
Middlesex	36,099	18,453	17,646	4,388	4,429	8,061	11,212	6,[illegible]
New Haven	121,257	60,103	61,154	15,713	15,485	26,317	33,902	[illegible]
New London	66,570	32,677	33,893	8,657	8,720	13,285	17,[illegible]	13,[illegible]
Tolland	22,000	10,733	11,267	2,795	2,732	4,009	6,184	5,[illegible]
Windham	38,518	18,626	19,892	5,290	5,269	6,727	10,049	[illegible]

TERRITORY OF DAKOTA.

Counties.	Total.	Male.	Female.	5 to 18, Male.	5 to 18, Female.	18 to 45, Male.	21 and upward, Male.	21 and upward, Male citizens.
The Territory	14,181	8,879	5,303	1,736	1,631	5,301	5,[illegible]	[illegible]
Bonhomme	608	382	226	37	74	297	[illegible]	[illegible]
Brookings	163	77	86	16	20	40	[illegible]	[illegible]
Buffalo	246	181	65	9	15	150	132	[illegible]
Charles Mix	132	84	68	30	21	[illegible]	[illegible]	[illegible]
Clay	2,621	1,506	1,115	383	377	[illegible]	[illegible]	[illegible]
Deuel	37	19	19	5	[illegible]	[illegible]	[illegible]	[illegible]
Hutchinson	37	25	12	4	4	12	13	13
Jayne	3	3	.....	.....	.....	3	3	3
Lincoln	712	404	308	93	83	[illegible]	[illegible]	[illegible]
Minnehaha	355	213	142	39	33	115	[illegible]	[illegible]
Pembina	1,213	798	431	139	131	[illegible]	[illegible]	[illegible]
Todd	337	262	75	17	15	[illegible]	[illegible]	[illegible]
Union	3,507	1,913	1,594	365	356	[illegible]	[illegible]	[illegible]
Yankton	2,097	1,205	892	252	243	[illegible]	[illegible]	[illegible]
Unorganized portion of Territory	2,301	1,811	490	72	69	1,635	1,[illegible]	1,[illegible]

TABLE LVII.—*School, Military, and Citizenship Ages, &c., by Counties*—1870—Continued.

STATE OF DELAWARE.

Counties.	All ages.			5 to 18.		18 to 45.	21 and upward.	
	Total.	Male.	Female.	Male.	Female.	Male.	Male.	Male citizens.
The State	125,015	62,628	62,387	20,185	19,622	24,018	30,035	28,207
Kent	29,804	15,109	14,695	5,209	4,856	5,348	6,770	6,595
New Castle	63,515	31,447	32,068	9,263	9,415	12,884	16,091	15,060
Sussex	31,696	16,072	15,624	5,713	5,351	5,786	7,174	6,552

DISTRICT OF COLUMBIA.

Counties.	Total.	Male.	Female.	Male.	Female.	Male.	Male.	Male citizens.
Washington	131,700	62,192	69,508	16,954	18,615	26,824	33,329	31,022

STATE OF FLORIDA.

Counties.	Total.	Male.	Female.	Male.	Female.	Male.	Male.	Male citizens.
The State	187,748	94,548	93,200	32,873	31,024	34,530	39,907	38,654
Alachua	17,328	8,665	8,663	3,413	2,950	2,958	2,952	2,915
Baker	1,325	665	660	234	230	237	276	275
Bradford	3,671	1,879	1,792	632	604	639	718	712
Brevard	1,216	703	513	274	186	234	234	225
Calhoun	998	504	494	193	152	158	201	201
Clay	2,098	1,071	1,027	392	391	366	410	402
Columbia	7,335	3,713	3,622	1,439	1,252	1,195	1,408	1,397
Dade	85	53	32	15	11	24	33	28
Duval	11,921	5,909	6,012	1,709	1,781	2,509	3,054	3,000
Escambia	7,817	3,964	3,853	1,131	1,164	1,678	2,027	1,976
Franklin	1,256	572	684	184	209	216	278	277
Gadsden	9,802	4,943	4,859	1,650	1,545	1,856	2,158	2,158
Hamilton	5,749	2,984	2,765	1,139	924	951	1,049	1,049
Hernando	2,938	1,497	1,441	558	488	512	597	574
Hillsborough	3,216	1,661	1,555	605	551	552	655	658
Holmes	1,572	736	836	262	295	237	296	295
Jackson	9,528	4,622	4,906	1,663	1,699	1,591	1,883	1,879
Jefferson	13,398	6,561	6,837	2,302	2,234	2,380	2,758	2,758
La Fayette	1,783	930	853	354	292	311	349	344
Leon	15,236	7,463	7,773	2,418	2,454	2,792	3,435	3,416
Levy	2,018	1,048	970	364	329	383	443	437
Liberty	1,050	535	515	202	175	180	216	216
Madison	11,121	5,480	5,641	1,914	1,917	1,974	2,277	2,260
Manatee	1,931	1,010	921	367	332	331	370	360
Marion	10,804	5,507	5,297	1,907	1,832	1,944	2,251	2,246
Monroe	5,657	2,998	2,659	749	818	1,492	1,719	1,084
Nassau	4,247	2,139	2,108	689	688	837	958	926
Orange	2,195	1,211	984	450	373	436	496	490
Polk	3,169	1,691	1,478	663	548	604	625	590
Putnam	3,821	2,040	1,781	673	632	787	907	896
Santa Rosa	3,312	1,677	1,635	502	522	583	709	709
St. John's	2,618	1,222	1,396	402	419	435	552	531
Sumter	2,952	1,606	1,346	607	478	586	590	576
Suwannee	3,556	1,803	1,753	636	608	642	739	737
Taylor	1,453	729	724	267	247	249	290	284
Volusia	1,723	892	831	310	283	309	405	398
Wakulla	2,506	1,208	1,298	412	448	397	521	519
Walton	3,041	1,508	1,533	568	543	505	612	600
Washington	2,302	1,149	1,153	424	402	379	456	455

TABLE LVII.—*School, Military, and Citizenship Ages, &c., by Counties—1870*—**Continued.**

STATE OF GEORGIA.

Counties.	All ages.			5 to 18.		18 to 45.	21 and upward.	
	Total.	Male.	Female.	Male.	Female.	Male.	Male.	Male citizens.
The State	1,184,109	578,955	605,154	206,026	201,490	202,573	237,640	234,919
Appling	5,086	2,568	2,518	924	879	957	1,023	1,021
Baker	6,843	3,436	3,407	1,095	1,109	1,399	1,512	1,502
Baldwin	10,618	5,358	5,260	1,731	1,723	2,095	2,500	2,472
Banks	4,973	2,393	2,580	917	843	697	863	860
Bartow	16,566	8,208	8,358	2,875	2,873	2,953	3,441	3,374
Berrien	4,518	2,213	2,305	803	822	649	724	722
Bibb	21,255	10,120	11,135	3,007	3,294	4,286	5,129	4,886
Brooks	8,342	4,082	4,260	1,577	1,547	1,385	1,546	1,546
Bryan	5,252	2,619	2,633	978	909	843	937	936
Bullock	5,610	2,759	2,851	1,098	1,078	870	989	983
Burke	17,679	8,944	8,735	3,059	2,791	3,419	3,971	3,937
Butts	6,941	3,369	3,572	1,370	1,312	1,062	1,147	1,143
Calhoun	5,503	2,691	2,812	950	947	991	1,122	1,119
Camden	4,615	2,291	2,324	746	782	827	1,009	1,003
Campbell	9,176	4,431	4,745	1,670	1,650	1,536	1,742	1,740
Carroll	11,782	5,720	6,062	2,202	2,103	1,798	2,068	2,057
Catoosa	4,409	2,159	2,250	758	732	725	845	841
Charlton	1,897	952	945	318	350	365	370	368
Chatham	41,279	19,813	21,466	5,669	6,056	8,757	10,612	10,312
Chattahoochee	6,059	2,973	3,086	1,100	1,021	1,004	1,199	1,190
Chattooga	6,902	3,263	3,639	1,285	1,263	1,063	1,257	1,250
Cherokee	10,399	5,042	5,357	1,946	1,799	1,587	1,930	1,926
Clarke	12,941	6,098	6,843	2,173	2,237	2,111	2,548	2,538
Clay	5,493	2,677	2,816	961	929	904	1,074	1,071
Clayton	5,477	2,686	2,791	978	980	941	1,048	1,031
Clinch	3,945	1,987	1,958	769	709	637	710	707
Cobb	13,814	6,670	7,144	2,431	2,417	2,224	2,725	2,721
Coffee	3,192	1,540	1,652	607	646	461	521	517
Colquitt	1,654	782	872	332	319	207	262	260
Columbia	13,529	6,759	6,770	2,261	2,144	2,425	2,914	2,898
Coweta	15,875	7,678	8,197	2,831	2,765	2,672	3,015	2,905
Crawford	7,557	3,742	3,815	1,346	1,253	1,266	1,477	1,438
Dade	3,033	1,473	1,560	536	533	496	601	596
Dawson	4,369	2,067	2,302	778	774	636	756	749
Decatur	15,183	7,497	7,686	2,659	2,601	2,687	3,058	3,047
De Kalb	10,014	4,851	5,163	1,762	1,681	1,607	1,989	1,969
Dooly	9,790	5,056	4,734	1,969	1,648	1,615	1,836	1,793
Dougherty	11,517	5,803	5,714	1,700	1,702	2,502	2,844	2,836
Early	6,998	3,458	3,540	1,274	1,209	1,105	1,319	1,311
Echols	1,978	966	1,012	373	370	335	373	369
Effingham	4,214	2,106	2,108	741	702	740	905	901
Elbert	9,249	4,612	4,637	1,688	1,474	1,492	1,772	1,764
Emanuel	6,134	3,036	3,098	1,148	1,102	1,032	1,087	1,080
Fannin	5,429	2,669	2,760	999	956	793	962	959
Fayette	8,221	4,010	4,211	1,498	1,425	1,306	1,496	1,490
Floyd	17,230	8,417	8,813	2,961	2,955	3,032	3,557	3,501
Forsyth	7,983	3,856	4,127	1,446	1,383	1,241	1,444	1,425
Franklin	7,893	3,682	4,211	1,378	1,439	1,131	1,425	1,414
Fulton	33,446	16,390	17,056	5,258	5,610	6,899	7,707	7,462
Gilmer	6,644	3,199	3,445	1,212	1,187	968	1,150	1,147
Glascock	2,736	1,344	1,392	494	464	452	510	509
Glynn	5,376	2,665	2,711	805	766	1,056	1,330	1,326
Gordon	9,268	4,575	4,693	1,648	1,594	1,574	1,841	1,804
Greene	12,454	6,177	6,277	2,079	2,055	2,148	2,552	2,543
Gwinnett	12,431	6,099	6,332	2,217	2,124	2,080	2,465	2,461
Habersham	6,322	3,016	3,306	1,085	1,067	915	1,149	1,136
Hall	9,607	4,585	5,022	1,795	1,694	1,402	1,708	1,707
Hancock	11,317	5,696	5,621	2,044	1,911	1,947	2,306	2,288
Haralson	4,004	1,949	2,055	722	712	607	723	719
Harris	13,284	6,532	6,752	2,416	2,320	2,146	2,565	2,561
Hart	6,783	3,275	3,508	1,182	1,147	1,022	1,208	1,205
Heard	7,866	3,843	4,023	1,486	1,395	1,212	1,379	1,366
Henry	10,102	4,919	5,183	1,770	1,742	1,625	1,976	1,974
Houston	20,406	10,188	10,218	3,382	3,323	3,842	4,295	4,236
Irwin	1,837	901	936	351	339	301	319	318
Jackson	11,181	5,407	5,774	2,044	1,902	1,711	2,090	2,044

TABLE LVII.—*School, Military, and Citizenship Ages, &c., by Counties*—1870—Continued.

STATE OF GEORGIA—Continued.

Counties.	All ages.			5 to 18.		18 to 45.	21 and upward.	
	Total.	Male.	Female.	Male.	Female.	Male.	Male.	Male citizens.
Jasper	10, 439	5, 071	5, 365	1, 869	1, 846	1, 694	1, 962	1, 936
Jefferson	12, 190	6, 052	6, 138	2, 159	2, 115	2, 032	2, 403	2, 393
Johnson	2, 964	1, 417	1, 547	571	579	518	550	534
Jones	9, 436	4, 612	4, 824	1, 702	1, 683	1, 613	1, 858	1, 851
Laurens	7, 834	3, 872	3, 962	1, 507	1, 357	1, 267	1, 484	1, 480
Lee	9, 567	4, 873	4, 694	1, 523	1, 465	2, 000	2, 215	2, 205
Liberty	7, 688	3, 703	3, 985	1, 330	1, 350	1, 191	1, 566	1, 558
Lincoln	5, 413	2, 671	2, 742	925	916	910	1, 079	1, 072
Lowndes	8, 321	4, 155	4, 166	1, 576	1, 520	1, 410	1, 549	1, 541
Lumpkin	5, 161	2, 474	2, 687	922	885	752	971	967
Macon	11, 458	5, 469	5, 989	1, 939	2, 037	1, 891	2, 205	2, 197
Madison	5, 227	2, 453	2, 774	902	897	767	937	932
Marion	8, 000	3, 874	4, 126	1, 416	1, 372	1, 295	1, 453	1, 448
McIntosh	4, 491	2, 218	2, 273	730	723	737	980	972
Meriwether	13, 756	6, 771	6, 985	2, 476	2, 321	2, 362	2, 711	2, 680
Miller	3, 091	1, 508	1, 583	563	536	513	569	565
Milton	4, 284	2, 061	2, 223	768	802	645	795	794
Mitchell	6, 633	3, 350	3, 283	1, 162	1, 105	1, 220	1, 348	1, 341
Monroe	17, 213	8, 527	8, 686	3, 084	2, 985	2, 835	3, 363	3, 363
Montgomery	3, 586	1, 760	1, 826	708	667	533	617	582
Morgan	10, 696	5, 249	5, 447	1, 874	1, 863	1, 710	2, 108	2, 102
Murray	6, 500	3, 187	3, 313	1, 210	1, 130	992	1, 218	1, 206
Muscogee	16, 663	7, 725	8, 938	2, 495	2, 702	2, 893	3, 578	3, 558
Newton	14, 615	7, 028	7, 587	2, 596	2, 545	2, 340	2, 765	2, 756
Oglethorpe	11, 782	5, 727	6, 055	2, 086	1, 973	1, 920	2, 271	2, 270
Paulding	7, 639	3, 774	3, 865	1, 490	1, 329	1, 111	1, 374	1, 365
Pickens	5, 317	2, 540	2, 777	950	884	720	941	935
Pierce	2, 778	1, 416	1, 362	470	460	582	550	557
Pike	10, 905	5, 376	5, 529	1, 956	1, 862	1, 796	2, 103	2, 093
Polk	7, 822	3, 873	3, 949	1, 485	1, 347	1, 283	1, 474	1, 463
Pulaski	11, 940	5, 928	6, 012	2, 092	2, 020	2, 083	2, 426	2, 400
Putnam	10, 461	5, 119	5, 342	1, 800	1, 697	1, 737	2, 164	2, 140
Quitman	4, 150	2, 038	2, 112	714	706	735	836	835
Rabun	3, 256	1, 693	1, 633	606	584	478	578	574
Randolph	10, 561	5, 101	5, 460	1, 835	1, 943	1, 809	2, 118	2, 105
Richmond	25, 724	11, 777	13, 947	3, 591	3, 993	4, 651	5, 902	5, 738
Schley	5, 129	2, 520	2, 609	899	874	851	1, 007	991
Scriven	9, 175	4, 527	4, 648	1, 629	1, 635	1, 574	1, 809	1, 796
Spalding	10, 205	4, 887	5, 318	1, 757	1, 734	1, 683	2, 001	2, 001
Stewart	14, 204	6, 985	7, 219	2, 413	2, 454	2, 574	2, 879	2, 867
Sumter	16, 559	8, 167	8, 392	2, 882	2, 804	3, 000	3, 458	3, 431
Talbot	11, 913	5, 827	6, 086	2, 167	2, 081	1, 929	2, 315	2, 309
Taliaferro	4, 796	2, 375	2, 421	847	815	807	982	978
Tatnall	4, 860	2, 445	2, 415	942	921	779	868	830
Taylor	7, 143	3, 491	3, 652	1, 244	1, 217	1, 167	1, 386	1, 380
Telfair	3, 245	1, 611	1, 634	587	605	575	636	631
Terrell	9, 053	4, 499	4, 554	1, 607	1, 516	1, 636	1, 821	1, 817
Thomas	14, 523	7, 054	7, 469	2, 590	2, 609	2, 429	2, 808	2, 800
Towns	2, 780	1, 403	1, 377	553	470	416	493	489
Troup	17, 632	8, 546	9, 086	3, 161	3, 041	2, 952	3, 379	3, 357
Twiggs	8, 545	4, 264	4, 281	1, 506	1, 406	1, 550	1, 725	1, 703
Union	5, 267	2, 629	2, 638	1, 051	888	768	933	929
Upson	9, 430	4, 543	4, 887	1, 682	1, 632	1, 584	1, 863	1, 855
Walker	9, 925	4, 796	5, 129	1, 770	1, 737	1, 577	1, 862	1, 854
Walton	11, 038	5, 321	5, 717	2, 030	1, 956	1, 735	2, 022	2, 014
Ware	2, 286	1, 153	1, 133	448	450	367	390	385
Warren	10, 545	5, 228	5, 317	1, 806	1, 719	1, 789	2, 162	2, 128
Washington	15, 842	7, 833	8, 009	2, 894	2, 696	2, 734	3, 149	3, 142
Wayne	2, 177	1, 071	1, 106	411	405	339	396	390
Webster	4, 677	2, 299	2, 378	842	782	783	895	893
White	4, 606	2, 212	2, 394	834	861	702	816	808
Whitfield	10, 117	4, 907	5, 210	1, 747	1, 748	1, 634	2, 032	2, 003
Wilcox	2, 439	1, 196	1, 243	521	461	342	396	394
Wilkes	11, 796	6, 010	5, 786	1, 986	1, 873	2, 197	2, 600	2, 384
Wilkinson	9, 383	4, 592	4, 791	1, 690	1, 644	1, 574	1, 841	1, 827
Worth	3, 778	1, 867	1, 911	682	632	608	697	693

TABLE LVII.—*School, Military, and Citizenship Ages, &c., by Counties—1870*—**Continued.**

TERRITORY OF IDAHO.

Counties.	All ages.			5 to 18.		18 to 45.	21 and upward.	
	Total.	Male.	Female.	Male.	Female.	Male.	Male.	Male citizens.
The Territory	14, 990	12, 184	2, 815	897	798	9, 430	10, 313	5, 387
Ada	2, 675	1, 795	880	266	262	1, 150	1, 289	[illegible]
Alturas	689	621	68	15	10	543	582	[illegible]
Boise	3, 834	3, 351	483	98	113	2, 818	3, 104	1, 175
Idaho	849	801	48	41	6	660	600	389
Lemhi	988	906	82	23	21	756	855	[illegible]
Nez Percés	1, 607	1, 395	212	107	57	1, 081	1, 139	543
Oneida	1, 922	1, 163	759	262	269	639	713	589
Owyhee	1, 713	1, 455	258	58	39	1, 196	1, 312	[illegible]
Shoshone	722	697	25	27	1	588	629	198

STATE OF ILLINOIS.

Counties.	Total.	Male.	Female.	Male 5 to 18.	Female 5 to 18.	Male 18 to 45.	Male 21 and upward.	Male citizens.
The State	2, 539, 891	1, 316, 537	1, 223, 354	414, 547	404, 219	525, 873	625, 139	542, [illegible]
Adams	56, 362	28, 527	27, 835	8, 963	9, 075	10, 873	13, 587	11, 942
Alexander	10, 564	5, 206	5, 298	1, 499	1, 583	2, 205	2, 636	[illegible]
Bond	13, 152	6, 765	6, 387	2, 289	2, 249	2, 612	2, 983	[illegible]
Boone	12, 942	6, 565	6, 377	2, 064	2, 020	2, 386	3, 235	[illegible]
Brown	12, 205	6, 259	5, 946	2, 168	2, 085	2, 259	2, 763	2, 710
Bureau	32, 415	16, 898	15, 517	5, 459	5, 309	6, 433	7, 911	6, 685
Calhoun	6, 562	3, 562	3, 000	1, 251	1, 089	1, 241	1, 547	1, 304
Carroll	16, 705	8, 700	8, 005	2, 865	2, 742	3, 250	4, 032	[illegible]
Cass	11, 580	6, 089	5, 491	1, 866	1, 742	2, 497	2, 983	2, 790
Champaign	32, 737	17, 423	15, 314	5, 253	5, 064	7, 558	8, 271	7, 610
Christian	20, 363	10, 881	9, 482	3, 373	3, 150	4, 649	5, 149	[illegible]
Clark	18, 719	9, 650	9, 069	3, 326	3, 163	3, 530	4, 273	4, 170
Clay	15, 875	8, 131	7, 744	2, 838	2, 719	3, 004	3, 427	3, 212
Clinton	16, 285	8, 614	7, 671	2, 670	2, 662	3, 487	4, 084	3, 595
Coles	25, 235	12, 984	12, 251	4, 284	4, 349	5, 130	5, 820	5, 647
Cook	349, 966	180, 007	169, 959	47, 001	47, 835	85, 170	97, 645	66, 677
Crawford	13, 889	7, 018	6, 871	2, 579	2, 500	2, 412	2, 859	2, 847
Cumberland	12, 223	6, 274	5, 949	2, 335	2, 137	2, 153	2, 593	[illegible]
De Kalb	23, 265	12, 002	11, 263	3, 646	3, 598	4, 674	5, 915	[illegible]
De Witt	14, 768	7, 845	6, 923	2, 588	2, 333	3, 055	3, 564	3, 445
Douglas	13, 484	7, 118	6, 366	2, 357	2, 141	2, 854	3, 162	[illegible]
Du Page	16, 685	8, 784	7, 901	2, 596	2, 501	3, 358	4, 398	3, 443
Edgar	21, 450	11, 077	10, 373	3, 787	3, 616	4, 227	4, 915	4, 783
Edwards	7, 565	3, 840	3, 725	1, 330	1, 284	1, 426	1, 641	1, 440
Effingham	15, 653	8, 256	7, 397	2, 726	2, 702	3, 253	3, 778	3, 313
Fayette	19, 638	10, 170	9, 468	3, 518	3, 353	3, 904	4, 497	4, 439
Ford	9, 103	5, 039	4, 064	1, 550	1, 326	2, 129	2, 399	2, 010
Franklin	12, 652	6, 484	6, 168	2, 543	2, 314	2, 182	2, 362	2, 332
Fulton	38, 291	19, 739	18, 552	6, 586	6, 194	7, 197	8, 917	8, 595
Gallatin	11, 134	5, 716	5, 418	1, 994	1, 903	2, 138	2, 333	2, 237
Greene	20, 277	10, 677	9, 600	3, 389	3, 251	4, 288	4, 927	4, 730
Grundy	14, 938	7, 741	7, 197	2, 441	2, 387	2, 996	3, 728	3, 119
Hamilton	13, 014	6, 582	6, 432	2, 522	2, 392	2, 223	2, 563	2, 491
Hancock	35, 935	18, 509	17, 426	6, 041	5, 994	6, 785	8, 443	7, 770
Hardin	5, 113	2, 670	2, 443	959	854	939	1, 090	1, 081
Henderson	12, 582	6, 801	5, 781	2, 004	1, 919	2, 887	3, 321	2, 858
Henry	35, 506	18, 487	17, 019	5, 899	5, 426	7, 151	8, 802	7, 396
Iroquois	25, 782	13, 481	12, 301	4, 412	4, 210	5, 243	6, 239	5, 327
Jackson	19, 634	10, 301	9, 273	3, 277	3, 194	4, 298	4, 705	4, 308
Jasper	11, 234	5, 738	5, 496	2, 165	2, 016	1, 927	2, 307	2, 240
Jefferson	17, 864	9, 010	8, 854	3, 251	3, 184	3, 166	3, 646	3, 611
Jersey	15, 054	7, 962	7, 092	2, 425	2, 416	3, 134	3, 867	3, 539
Jo Daviess	27, 820	14, 196	13, 624	4, 894	4, 824	4, 761	6, 511	5, 949
Johnson	11, 248	5, 713	5, 535	2, 125	2, 064	1, 921	2, 156	2, 119
Kane	39, 091	19, 866	19, 225	5, 851	5, 884	7, 900	10, 205	8, 944
Kankakee	24, 352	12, 708	11, 644	4, 246	4, 073	4, 685	5, 678	4, 599
Kendall	12, 399	6, 455	5, 944	1, 985	1, 866	2, 495	3, 195	2, 732
Knox	39, 522	20, 014	19, 508	6, 203	6, 230	8, 082	9, 858	8, 878
Lake	21, 014	10, 696	10, 318	3, 330	3, 366	3, 930	5, 344	4, 731
La Salle	60, 792	31, 228	29, 564	9, 817	9, 898	11, 931	15, 005	12, 675
Lawrence	12, 533	6, 383	6, 150	2, 245	2, 236	2, 334	2, 728	2, 664
Lee	27, 171	14, 220	12, 951	4, 441	4, 343	5, 631	6, 791	6, 590
Livingston	31, 471	16, 662	14, 809	5, 315	5, 012	6, 500	7, 660	6, 891

TABLE LVII.—*School, Military, and Citizenship Ages, &c., by Counties*—1870—Continued.

STATE OF ILLINOIS—Continued.

Counties.	All ages.			5 to 18.		18 to 45.	21 and upward.	
	Total.	Male.	Female.	Male.	Female.	Male.	Male.	Male citizens.
Logan	23,053	12,445	10,608	3,911	3,630	5,172	5,753	4,940
Macon	26,481	13,890	12,591	4,281	4,220	5,756	6,576	6,171
Macoupin	32,726	16,965	15,761	5,549	5,405	6,418	7,757	7,078
Madison	44,131	22,888	21,243	7,153	7,409	9,023	11,005	9,283
Marion	20,622	10,501	10,121	3,479	3,474	4,013	4,751	4,541
Marshall	16,956	8,854	8,102	2,847	2,701	3,447	4,157	3,608
Mason	16,184	8,683	7,501	2,697	2,508	3,645	4,103	3,881
Massac	9,581	4,896	4,685	1,632	1,599	1,781	2,122	2,018
McDonough	26,509	13,546	12,963	4,562	4,444	5,106	6,060	5,923
McHenry	23,762	12,174	11,588	3,752	3,683	4,447	6,057	5,609
McLean	53,988	28,340	25,648	8,662	8,307	11,973	13,606	12,698
Menard	11,735	6,237	5,498	1,883	1,791	2,633	3,014	2,477
Mercer	18,769	9,789	8,980	3,136	3,038	3,785	4,517	4,003
Monroe	12,982	6,815	6,167	2,239	2,230	2,503	3,195	2,743
Montgomery	25,314	13,255	12,059	4,311	4,103	5,426	6,029	5,726
Morgan	28,463	14,579	13,884	4,494	4,630	5,943	7,074	6,386
Moultrie	10,385	5,481	4,904	1,911	1,736	2,153	2,390	2,349
Ogle	27,492	14,355	13,137	4,479	4,194	5,633	6,918	6,239
Peoria	47,540	24,244	23,296	8,034	8,196	9,282	11,311	9,784
Perry	13,723	7,135	6,588	2,400	2,187	2,698	3,116	3,008
Piatt	10,953	5,852	5,101	1,839	1,735	2,405	2,708	2,679
Pike	30,768	15,811	14,957	5,367	5,108	5,945	7,130	6,988
Pope	11,437	5,794	5,643	2,071	1,972	2,043	2,336	2,289
Pulaski	8,752	4,571	4,181	1,249	1,301	1,945	2,265	2,390
Putnam	6,280	3,223	3,057	1,012	1,000	1,264	1,556	1,323
Randolph	20,859	10,889	9,970	3,695	3,453	4,044	4,921	4,706
Richland	12,803	6,439	6,364	2,289	2,314	2,244	2,741	2,667
Rock Island	29,783	15,369	14,414	4,536	4,741	6,297	7,725	5,743
Saline	12,714	6,378	6,336	2,361	2,287	2,157	2,478	2,453
Sangamon	46,352	24,010	22,342	7,331	7,212	10,033	11,788	10,530
Schuyler	17,419	9,479	7,940	2,936	2,677	3,896	4,582	4,509
Scott	10,530	5,557	4,973	1,683	1,598	2,302	2,674	2,497
Shelby	25,476	13,234	12,242	4,609	4,386	5,111	5,743	5,665
Stark	10,751	5,665	5,086	1,810	1,631	2,226	2,690	2,451
St. Clair	51,068	27,325	23,743	8,223	8,220	11,261	13,642	10,690
Stephenson	30,608	15,588	15,020	5,117	5,144	5,587	7,226	5,935
Tazewell	27,903	14,545	13,358	4,402	4,445	5,873	7,001	6,132
Union	16,518	8,367	8,151	2,871	2,761	3,199	3,558	3,410
Vermilion	30,388	15,762	14,626	5,222	5,128	6,144	7,182	6,787
Wabash	8,841	4,427	4,414	1,461	1,540	1,735	1,962	1,909
Warren	23,174	12,100	11,074	3,834	3,601	4,890	5,711	5,181
Washington	17,599	9,157	8,442	3,007	2,877	3,527	4,102	3,763
Wayne	19,758	10,204	9,544	3,669	3,367	3,640	4,091	3,967
White	16,846	8,467	8,379	3,012	2,948	3,075	3,458	3,410
Whitesides	27,503	14,371	13,132	4,491	4,127	5,634	6,989	6,176
Will	43,013	23,221	19,792	6,913	6,570	9,337	11,519	8,930
Williamson	17,329	9,062	8,267	3,782	3,309	3,045	3,271	3,098
Winnebago	29,301	14,762	14,539	4,560	4,534	5,671	7,401	6,068
Woodford	18,956	9,993	8,963	3,232	2,962	3,873	4,697	4,133

STATE OF INDIANA.

Counties.	Total.	Male.	Female.	Male.	Female.	Male.	Male.	Male citizens.
The State	1,680,637	857,994	822,643	287,357	279,818	319,658	388,231	376,780
Adams	11,382	5,711	5,671	2,011	2,053	1,901	2,413	2,282
Allen	43,494	22,474	21,020	7,472	7,126	8,259	10,165	9,227
Bartholomew	21,133	10,763	10,370	3,451	3,654	4,236	4,800	4,852
Benton	5,615	3,113	2,502	1,005	863	1,323	1,395	1,314
Blackford	6,272	3,245	3,027	1,098	1,045	1,182	1,420	1,403
Boone	22,593	11,540	11,053	3,924	3,766	4,273	5,128	5,013
Brown	8,681	4,412	4,269	1,600	1,592	1,447	1,768	1,447
Carroll	16,152	8,346	7,806	2,813	2,620	3,076	3,747	3,746
Cass	24,193	12,472	11,721	3,936	3,929	5,062	6,064	5,704
Clarke	24,770	12,734	12,036	3,970	3,960	4,983	6,160	5,752
Clay	19,084	9,908	9,176	3,189	3,084	3,851	4,538	4,302
Clinton	17,330	8,818	8,512	3,606	3,060	3,201	3,830	3,835
Crawford	9,851	4,978	4,873	1,797	1,724	1,637	2,046	1,883
Daviess	16,747	8,375	8,372	2,861	2,950	3,079	3,609	3,546
Dearborn	24,116	12,162	11,954	4,171	4,080	4,113	5,507	5,383

TABLE LVII.—*School, Military, and Citizenship Ages, &c., by Counties*—1870—**Continued.**

STATE OF INDIANA—Continued.

Counties.	All ages.			5 to 18.		18 to 45.	21 and upward.	
	Total.	Male.	Female.	Male.	Female.	Male.	Male.	Male citizens.
Decatur	19,053	9,698	9,355	3,218	3,132	3,550	4,453	4,216
De Kalb	17,167	8,805	8,362	2,909	2,883	3,225	4,011	3,935
Delaware	19,030	9,763	9,267	3,257	3,064	3,650	4,360	4,329
Dubois	12,597	6,390	6,207	2,315	2,375	2,051	2,583	2,427
Elkhart	26,026	13,318	12,708	4,345	4,181	5,002	6,273	6,183
Fayette	10,476	5,258	5,218	1,620	1,626	2,058	2,654	2,646
Floyd	23,300	11,439	11,861	3,871	3,890	4,136	5,340	4,640
Fountain	16,389	8,535	7,854	2,729	2,679	3,436	4,065	4,008
Franklin	20,223	10,183	10,040	3,418	3,412	3,485	4,672	4,610
Fulton	12,726	6,606	6,120	2,319	2,145	2,355	2,882	2,859
Gibson	17,371	8,893	8,478	3,014	2,931	3,375	3,879	3,806
Grant	18,487	9,461	9,026	3,248	3,166	3,429	4,107	4,093
Greene	19,514	9,782	9,732	3,477	3,494	3,462	4,010	4,007
Hamilton	20,882	10,706	10,176	3,641	3,395	3,959	4,704	4,694
Hancock	15,123	7,740	7,383	2,626	2,503	2,931	3,441	3,438
Harrison	19,913	10,105	9,808	3,588	3,442	3,325	4,192	4,191
Hendricks	20,277	10,363	9,914	3,489	3,360	3,807	4,672	4,623
Henry	22,986	11,688	11,298	3,772	3,702	4,490	5,445	5,397
Howard	15,847	8,005	7,842	2,853	2,880	2,980	3,388	3,356
Huntington	19,036	9,702	9,334	3,357	3,135	3,476	4,319	4,106
Jackson	18,974	9,571	9,403	3,290	3,319	3,571	4,082	4,037
Jasper	6,354	3,226	3,128	1,110	1,109	1,131	1,367	1,351
Jay	15,000	7,626	7,374	2,627	2,511	2,615	3,277	3,260
Jefferson	29,741	15,063	14,678	5,591	5,151	5,105	6,465	6,447
Jennings	16,218	8,117	8,101	2,843	2,833	2,737	3,584	3,326
Johnson	18,366	9,357	9,009	3,078	3,060	3,710	4,244	4,240
Knox	21,562	11,039	10,523	3,813	3,675	4,165	4,772	4,633
Kosciusko	23,531	11,946	11,585	4,163	4,021	4,368	5,375	5,346
La Grange	14,148	7,219	6,929	2,396	2,265	2,706	3,329	3,309
Lake	12,339	6,439	5,900	2,196	2,108	2,224	2,890	2,698
La Porte	27,062	13,970	13,092	4,352	4,310	5,261	6,927	6,063
Lawrence	14,628	7,391	7,237	2,544	2,548	2,648	3,161	3,147
Madison	22,770	11,700	11,070	4,019	3,861	4,377	5,101	5,082
Marion	71,939	36,920	35,019	10,410	10,685	17,131	19,815	19,536
Marshall	20,211	10,420	9,791	3,581	3,355	3,697	4,553	4,501
Martin	11,103	5,696	5,407	1,991	1,905	1,953	2,302	2,295
Miami	21,052	10,750	10,302	3,617	3,517	3,989	4,900	4,849
Monroe	14,168	7,059	7,109	2,428	2,412	2,505	3,116	3,107
Montgomery	23,765	12,301	11,464	3,923	3,757	4,836	5,757	5,716
Morgan	17,528	8,925	8,603	3,100	3,058	3,322	3,891	3,874
Newton	5,829	3,109	2,720	1,063	940	1,206	1,362	1,356
Noble	20,389	10,383	10,006	3,511	3,398	3,777	4,726	4,550
Ohio	5,837	2,944	2,893	981	957	1,072	1,322	1,320
Orange	13,497	6,851	6,646	2,449	2,282	2,351	2,798	2,797
Owen	16,137	8,147	7,990	2,876	2,785	2,930	3,523	3,507
Parke	18,166	9,407	8,759	3,173	2,941	3,549	4,155	4,140
Perry	14,801	7,490	7,311	2,814	2,673	2,327	3,048	2,984
Pike	13,779	7,070	6,709	2,533	2,355	2,515	2,864	2,854
Porter	13,942	7,199	6,743	2,292	2,282	2,646	3,406	2,899
Posey	19,185	9,886	9,299	3,298	3,309	3,696	4,319	4,258
Pulaski	7,801	3,943	3,858	1,420	1,424	1,287	1,682	1,641
Putnam	21,514	11,009	10,505	3,649	3,574	4,263	5,034	4,530
Randolph	22,862	11,618	11,244	3,909	3,855	4,257	5,173	5,133
Ripley	20,977	10,662	10,315	3,895	3,693	3,308	4,498	4,397
Rush	17,626	8,966	8,660	2,884	2,834	3,516	4,262	4,132
Scott	7,873	3,998	3,875	1,425	1,328	1,388	1,710	1,691
Shelby	21,892	11,250	10,642	3,840	3,664	4,282	5,020	5,012
Spencer	17,998	9,247	8,751	3,336	3,108	3,204	3,863	3,816
Starke	3,888	2,076	1,812	768	666	691	848	827
Steuben	12,854	6,593	6,261	2,084	1,956	2,552	3,244	3,190
St. Joseph	25,322	13,061	12,261	4,056	3,984	5,207	6,311	5,608
Sullivan	18,453	9,329	9,124	3,315	3,146	3,392	3,966	3,946
Switzerland	12,134	6,045	6,089	2,114	2,013	2,141	2,720	2,689
Tippecanoe	33,515	17,396	16,119	5,363	5,202	7,207	8,563	7,093
Tipton	11,953	6,117	5,836	2,222	2,080	2,120	2,536	2,534
Union	6,341	3,244	3,097	1,024	918	1,258	1,579	1,577
Vanderburgh	33,145	16,797	16,348	5,244	5,441	6,678	8,021	7,634
Vermillion	10,840	5,639	5,201	1,889	1,712	2,163	2,513	2,507
Vigo	33,549	17,008	16,541	5,383	5,089	6,931	8,191	7,892
Wabash	21,305	10,840	10,465	3,751	3,586	3,916	4,812	4,772
Warren	10,204	5,309	4,895	1,721	1,692	2,096	2,413	2,409
Warrick	17,653	9,098	8,555	3,218	3,006	3,202	3,730	3,685

TABLE LVII.—*School, Military, and Citizenship Ages, &c., by Counties*—1870—Continued.

STATE OF INDIANA—Continued.

Counties.	All ages.			5 to 18.		18 to 45.	21 and upward.	
	Total.	Male.	Female.	Male.	Female.	Male.	Male.	Male citizens.
Washington	18, 495	9, 355	9, 140	3, 245	3, 062	3, 256	3, 971	3, 954
Wayne	34, 048	16, 866	17, 182	5, 374	5, 470	6, 377	8, 286	8, 202
Wells	13, 585	6, 954	6, 631	2, 426	2, 295	2, 420	2, 967	2, 909
White	10, 554	5, 519	5, 035	1, 863	1, 762	2, 012	2, 424	2, 408
Whitley	14, 399	7, 343	7, 056	2, 507	2, 452	2, 609	3, 238	3, 089

STATE OF IOWA.

Counties.	Total.	Male.	Female.	Male.	Female.	Male.	Male.	Male citizens.
The State	1, 194, 020	625, 917	568, 103	201, 531	193, 165	240, 769	290, 717	255, 802
Adair	3, 982	2, 178	1, 804	699	611	898	1, 005	963
Adams	4, 614	2, 470	2, 144	789	708	959	1, 122	1, 100
Allamakee	17, 868	9, 319	8, 549	3, 272	3, 132	3, 030	4, 098	3, 348
Appanoose	16, 456	8, 498	7, 958	3, 004	2, 807	2, 952	3, 483	3, 449
Audubon	1, 212	659	553	183	181	267	320	302
Benton	22, 454	11, 846	10, 608	3, 728	3, 516	4, 750	5, 493	4, 755
Black Hawk	21, 706	11, 381	10, 325	3, 613	3, 478	4, 498	5, 377	4, 774
Boone	14, 584	7, 577	7, 007	2, 424	2, 358	3, 012	3, 540	2, 854
Bremer	12, 528	6, 647	5, 881	2, 202	1, 986	2, 422	3, 048	2, 541
Buchanan	17, 034	8, 869	8, 165	2, 856	2, 804	3, 342	4, 175	3, 804
Buena Vista	1, 585	907	678	220	185	460	507	500
Butler	9, 951	5, 268	4, 683	1, 700	1, 548	2, 016	2, 438	2, 191
Calhoun	1, 602	834	768	245	251	351	498	394
Carroll	2, 451	1, 332	1, 119	397	384	608	642	547
Cass	5, 464	2, 923	2, 541	801	820	1, 337	1, 469	1, 294
Cedar	19, 731	10, 297	9, 434	3, 305	3, 140	3, 918	4, 780	4, 313
Cerro Gordo	4, 722	2, 634	2, 088	668	653	1, 220	1, 434	1, 209
Cherokee	1, 967	1, 156	811	286	253	575	650	573
Chickasaw	10, 180	5, 228	4, 952	1, 810	1, 756	1, 890	2, 374	2, 261
Clarke	8, 735	4, 473	4, 262	1, 506	1, 489	1, 632	1, 949	1, 935
Clay	1, 523	868	655	234	176	403	442	415
Clayton	27, 771	14, 455	13, 316	4, 869	4, 671	4, 960	6, 619	5, 260
Clinton	35, 357	18, 694	16, 663	5, 751	5, 506	7, 530	9, 157	6, 908
Crawford	2, 530	1, 387	1, 143	419	394	585	668	524
Dallas	12, 019	6, 392	5, 627	2, 021	1, 887	2, 542	2, 937	2, 629
Davis	15, 565	7, 898	7, 667	2, 805	2, 704	2, 833	3, 399	3, 316
Decatur	12, 018	6, 197	5, 821	2, 199	2, 060	2, 095	2, 612	2, 550
Delaware	17, 432	8, 998	8, 434	2, 910	2, 941	3, 369	4, 207	3, 611
Des Moines	27, 256	14, 191	13, 065	4, 458	4, 301	5, 554	6, 908	5, 770
Dickinson	1, 389	745	644	233	219	311	369	349
Dubuque	38, 969	20, 013	18, 956	6, 541	6, 631	7, 266	9, 444	7, 655
Emmet	1, 392	757	635	242	190	280	336	276
Fayette	16, 973	8, 744	8, 229	3, 006	3, 001	2, 980	3, 932	3, 422
Floyd	10, 768	5, 705	5, 063	1, 759	1, 687	2, 302	2, 790	2, 491
Franklin	4, 738	2, 560	2, 178	777	736	1, 099	1, 249	1, 079
Fremont	11, 174	5, 980	5, 194	1, 820	1, 776	2, 596	2, 834	2, 758
Greene	4, 627	2, 462	2, 165	763	698	1, 022	1, 149	1, 066
Grundy	6, 399	3, 472	2, 927	1, 034	916	1, 494	1, 639	1, 107
Guthrie	7, 061	3, 758	3, 303	1, 148	1, 123	1, 541	1, 748	[illegible]
Hamilton	6, 055	3, 203	2, 852	1, 041	933	1, 225	1, 476	1, 270
Hancock	999	524	475	169	173	196	238	218
Hardin	13, 684	7, 060	6, 624	2, 209	2, 244	2, 776	3, 317	2, 962
Harrison	8, 931	4, 759	4, 172	1, 439	1, 382	1, 954	2, 254	2, 074
Henry	21, 463	10, 964	10, 499	3, 544	3, 498	4, 024	5, 051	4, 777
Howard	6, 282	3, 399	2, 883	1, 126	957	1, 239	1, 577	1, 422
Humboldt	2, 596	1, 408	1, 188	440	367	578	665	612
Ida	226	124	102	39	35	52	56	56
Iowa	16, 644	8, 671	7, 973	2, 703	2, 641	3, 251	4, 153	3, 642
Jackson	22, 619	11, 688	10, 931	3, 867	3, 940	4, 152	5, 324	4, 535
Jasper	22, 116	11, 601	10, 515	3, 846	3, 490	4, 413	5, 208	4, 997
Jefferson	17, 839	9, 248	8, 591	3, 067	2, 890	3, 361	4, 255	3, 764
Johnson	24, 898	12, 899	11, 999	4, 338	4, 217	4, 618	5, 750	4, 800
Jones	19, 731	10, 273	9, 458	3, 466	3, 296	3, 697	4, 619	4, 101
Keokuk	19, 434	10, 079	9, 355	3, 463	3, 261	3 639	4, 317	4, 128
Kossuth	3, 351	1, 824	1, 527	521	493	801	933	863
Lee	37, 210	19, 625	17, 585	5, 982	5, 884	7, 986	9, 759	8, 216
Linn	31, 080	16, 233	14, 847	5, 348	5, 130	6, 409	7, 554	7, 075
Louisa	12, 877	6, 743	6, 134	2, 191	2, 060	2, 512	3, 108	2, 924
Lucas	10, 388	5, 368	5, 020	1, 831	1, 736	1, 975	2, 312	2, 216

TABLE LVII.—*School, Military, and Citizenship Ages, &c., by Counties*—1870—Continued.

STATE OF IOWA—Continued.

Counties.	All ages.			5 to 18.		18 to 45.	21 and upward.	
	Total.	Male.	Female.	Male.	Female.	Male.	Male.	Male citizens.
Lyon	221	131	90	26	20	64	80	67
Madison	13,884	7,325	6,559	2,394	2,211	2,741	3,207	3,[illegible]
Mahaska	22,508	11,490	11,018	3,919	3,807	4,234	5,087	4,[illegible]
Marion	24,436	12,579	11,857	4,327	4,106	4,315	5,390	4,[illegible]
Marshall	17,576	9,381	8,195	2,872	2,604	3,903	4,467	4,[illegible]
Mills	8,718	4,808	3,910	1,471	1,376	2,062	2,318	2,[illegible]
Mitchell	9,582	5,068	4,514	1,587	1,464	2,066	2,470	2,109
Monona	3,654	1,995	1,659	576	554	871	994	891
Monroe	12,724	6,671	6,053	2,382	2,247	2,286	2,840	2,[illegible]
Montgomery	5,934	3,356	2,578	925	811	1,553	1,685	1,647
Muscatine	21,688	11,175	10,513	3,660	3,541	4,011	5,219	5,058
O'Brien	715	404	311	93	91	212	236	[illegible]
Page	9,975	5,292	4,683	1,743	1,626	2,089	2,346	2,243
Palo Alto	1,336	756	580	208	187	322	378	315
Plymouth	2,199	1,245	954	372	313	582	657	375
Pocahontas	1,446	785	661	220	199	344	415	[illegible]
Polk	27,857	14,527	13,330	4,411	4,394	6,021	6,999	6,[illegible]
Pottawattamie	16,893	9,189	7,704	2,615	2,509	4,304	4,758	3,[illegible]
Poweshiek	15,581	8,456	7,125	2,580	2,369	3,587	4,048	3,679
Ringgold	5,691	2,947	2,744	1,027	986	1,063	1,286	1,[illegible]
Sac	1,411	775	636	205	215	342	303	[illegible]
Scott	38,599	20,157	18,442	6,010	5,964	8,162	10,137	7,131
Shelby	2,540	1,358	1,182	454	403	522	609	516
Sioux	576	320	256	96	98	147	173	[illegible]
Story	11,651	6,088	5,563	2,004	1,933	2,337	2,684	2,[illegible]
Tama	16,131	8,595	7,536	2,715	2,471	3,347	3,951	3,474
Taylor	6,989	3,635	3,354	1,219	1,180	1,320	1,558	1,[illegible]
Union	5,986	3,199	2,787	985	952	1,316	1,480	1,[illegible]
Van Buren	17,672	9,059	8,613	3,052	2,843	3,160	4,129	4,[illegible]
Wapello	22,346	11,669	10,677	3,723	3,656	4,576	5,351	4,[illegible]
Warren	17,980	9,286	8,694	3,162	3,103	3,476	3,989	3,981
Washington	18,952	9,766	9,186	3,308	3,207	3,554	4,379	4,150
Wayne	11,287	5,853	5,434	2,061	1,926	2,027	2,412	2,[illegible]
Webster	10,484	5,598	4,886	1,754	1,658	2,126	2,631	2,421
Winnebago	1,562	820	742	280	254	272	347	[illegible]
Winneshiek	23,570	12,424	11,146	4,027	3,821	4,681	5,722	3,835
Woodbury	6,172	3,477	2,695	817	797	1,886	2,051	1,740
Worth	2,892	1,518	1,374	502	450	545	664	473
Wright	2,392	1,275	1,117	412	386	465	570	514

STATE OF KANSAS.

Counties.	Total.	Male.	Female.	Male.	Female.	Male.	Male.	Male citizens.
The State	364,399	202,224	162,175	55,669	53,041	95,002	105,071	98,049
Allen	7,022	3,957	3,065	1,013	964	1,928	2,124	2,[illegible]
Anderson	5,220	2,826	2,394	858	798	1,204	1,358	1,341
Atchison	15,507	8,484	7,023	2,376	2,430	3,892	4,402	4,185
Barton	2	2	....	....	....	2	2	1
Bourbon	15,076	8,244	6,832	2,344	2,241	3,830	4,197	4,[illegible]
Brown	6,823	3,778	3,045	1,120	977	1,687	1,847	1,565
Butler	3,035	1,792	1,243	446	368	914	1,024	[illegible]
Chase	1,975	1,095	880	306	260	496	547	[illegible]
Cherokee	11,038	6,095	4,943	1,807	1,676	2,730	3,087	2,[illegible]
Clay	2,942	1,675	1,267	430	408	820	906	[illegible]
Cloud	2,323	1,329	994	323	321	663	739	735
Coffey	6,201	3,392	2,809	979	925	1,500	1,668	1,[illegible]
Cowley	1,175	740	435	127	140	431	478	[illegible]
Crawford	8,160	4,541	3,619	1,371	1,221	2,012	2,236	2,[illegible]
Davis	5,526	3,415	2,111	605	584	2,150	2,265	2,[illegible]
Dickinson	3,043	1,852	1,191	404	353	1,056	1,102	1,[illegible]
Doniphan	13,969	7,456	6,513	2,381	2,302	3,009	3,488	3,167
Douglas	20,592	11,066	9,526	3,046	3,069	5,075	5,801	5,574
Ellis	1,336	1,182	154	25	36	1,117	1,095	945
Ellsworth	1,185	838	347	89	77	632	644	601
Ford	427	385	42	11	4	360	353	348
Franklin	10,385	5,609	4,776	1,614	1,508	2,558	2,880	2,544
Greenwood	3,484	1,923	1,561	534	539	905	950	612
Howard	2,794	1,583	1,211	387	409	776	850	[illegible]
Jackson	6,053	3,277	2,776	1,062	993	1,286	1,488	1,417
Jefferson	12,526	6,694	5,832	2,103	2,009	2,694	3,081	2,967

TABLE LVII.—*School, Military, and Citizenship Ages, &c., by Counties*—1870—Continued.

STATE OF KANSAS—Continued.

Counties.	All ages.			5 to 18.		18 to 45.	21 and upward.	
	Total.	Male.	Female.	Male.	Female.	Male.	Male.	Male citizens.
Jewell	207	159	48	17	6	115	124	110
Johnson	13, 684	7, 407	6, 277	2, 222	2, 215	3, 216	3, 632	3, 584
Labette	9, 973	5, 738	4, 235	1, 600	1, 381	2, 777	3, 050	3, 029
Leavenworth	32, 444	17, 504	14, 940	4, 789	4, 808	8, 283	9, 391	9, 044
Lincoln	516	313	203	74	69	166	188	187
Linn	12, 174	6, 466	5, 708	2, 036	1, 942	2, 647	2, 981	2, 892
Lyon	8, 014	4, 510	3, 504	1, 230	1, 114	2, 213	2, 370	2, 214
Marion	768	447	321	112	95	219	234	233
Marshall	6, 901	3, 833	3, 068	1, 010	1, 038	1, 759	1, 983	1, 934
McPherson	738	473	265	90	70	293	312	311
Miami	11, 725	6, 245	5, 480	1, 923	1, 846	2, 581	2, 938	2, 768
Mitchell	485	309	176	55	53	199	216	197
Montgomery	7, 564	4, 380	3, 184	1, 097	1, 019	2, 277	2, 459	2, 358
Morris	2, 225	1, 226	999	328	305	583	640	625
Nemaha	7, 339	4, 285	3, 054	1, 075	1, 034	2, 182	2, 345	2, 043
Neosho	10, 206	5, 739	4, 467	1, 680	1, 450	2, 682	2, 920	2, 805
Ness	2	2	......	......	......	2	2	2
Osage	7, 648	4, 300	3, 348	1, 144	1, 074	2, 072	2, 312	2, 096
Osborne	33	29	4	2	2	22	26	9
Ottawa	2, 127	1, 242	885	308	259	615	693	690
Pawnee	179	146	33	1	5	139	138	137
Pettawattamie	7, 848	4, 349	3, 499	1, 248	1, 165	1, 934	2, 195	1, 953
Republic	1, 281	779	502	209	150	410	448	373
Rice	5	3	2	......	......	3	3	3
Riley	5, 105	2, 800	2, 305	699	684	1, 317	1, 476	1, 947
Russell	156	149	7	3	4	137	127	113
Saline	4, 246	2, 439	1, 807	537	502	1, 347	1, 480	1, 298
Sedgwick	1, 095	763	332	122	92	500	537	537
Shawnee	13, 121	7, 115	6, 006	1, 903	1, 826	3, 444	3, 840	3, 453
Smith	66	55	11	4	......	42	43	38
Sumner	22	18	4	......	3	17	17	17
Trego	166	156	10	1	4	147	142	126
Wabaunsee	3, 362	1, 879	1, 483	514	454	804	953	893
Wallace	538	461	77	20	17	414	403	331
Washington	4, 081	2, 260	1, 821	644	598	984	1, 123	975
Wilson	6, 694	3, 700	2, 994	1, 089	948	1, 647	1, 819	1, 803
Woodson	3, 827	2, 100	1, 727	609	625	907	1, 020	1, 016
Wyandotte	10, 015	5, 215	4, 800	1, 528	1, 574	2, 139	2, 554	2, 317

STATE OF KENTUCKY.

Counties.	Total.	Male.	Female.	5 to 18, Male.	5 to 18, Female.	18 to 45, Male.	21 and upward, Male.	Male citizens.
The State	1, 321, 011	665, 675	655, 336	230, 491	224, 048	239, 483	289, 471	282, 305
Adair	11, 065	5, 513	5, 552	2, 092	2, 034	1, 795	2, 198	2, 091
Allen	10, 296	5, 129	5, 167	1, 867	1, 781	1, 742	2, 084	2, 062
Anderson	5, 449	2, 792	2, 657	995	911	946	1, 204	1, 191
Ballard	12, 576	6, 511	6, 065	2, 351	2, 185	2, 419	2, 690	2, 670
Barren	17, 780	8, 947	8, 833	3, 148	3, 077	3, 227	3, 829	3, 794
Bath	10, 145	5, 114	5, 031	1, 808	1, 723	1, 730	2, 102	2, 157
Boone	10, 696	5, 500	5, 196	1, 773	1, 695	2, 114	2, 660	2, 650
Bourbon	14, 863	7, 589	7, 274	2, 466	2, 342	2, 937	3, 550	3, 512
Boyd	8, 573	4, 309	4, 264	1, 508	1, 543	1, 582	1, 836	1, 754
Boyle	9, 515	4, 768	4, 747	1, 601	1, 584	1, 794	2, 211	2, 209
Bracken	11, 409	5, 821	5, 588	1, 970	1, 894	2, 110	2, 616	2, 592
Breathitt	5, 672	2, 808	2, 864	1, 135	1, 129	892	999	988
Breckenridge	13, 440	6, 873	6, 567	2, 410	2, 246	2, 401	2, 939	2, 920
Bullitt	7, 781	3, 996	3, 785	1, 281	1, 241	1, 532	1, 849	1, 826
Butler	9, 404	4, 728	4, 676	1, 645	1, 595	1, 666	1, 919	1, 910
Caldwell	10, 826	5, 388	5, 438	1, 840	1, 880	1, 954	2, 261	2, 253
Callaway	9, 410	4, 732	4, 678	1, 718	1, 635	1, 663	1, 929	1, 928
Campbell	27, 406	13, 697	13, 709	4, 583	4, 667	4, 953	6, 348	5, 802
Carroll	6, 189	3, 124	3, 065	1, 096	1, 059	1, 128	1, 406	1, 395
Carter	7, 509	3, 920	3, 589	1, 507	1, 291	1, 246	1, 500	1, 495
Casey	8, 884	4, 369	4, 515	1, 628	1, 506	1, 400	1, 725	1, 718
Christian	23, 227	12, 038	11, 189	4, 079	3, 614	4, 597	5, 382	5, 373
Clark	10, 882	5, 490	5, 392	1, 892	1, 793	1, 965	2, 501	2, 491
Clay	8, 297	4, 140	4, 157	1, 617	1, 490	1, 304	1, 514	1, 510
Clinton	6, 497	3, 173	3, 324	1, 285	1, 133	966	1, [illegible]	1, 130
Crittenden	9, 381	4, 734	4, 647	1, 717	1, 661	1, 617	1[illegible]	1, 048

TABLE LVII.—*School, Military, and Citizenship Ages, &c., by Counties*—**1870—Continued.**

STATE OF KENTUCKY—Continued.

Counties.	All ages.			5 to 18.		18 to 45.	21 and upward.	
	Total.	Male.	Female.	Male.	Female.	Male.	Male.	Male citizens.
Cumberland	7,690	3,794	3,896	1,382	1,356	1,304	1,541	1,537
Daviess	20,714	10,698	10,016	3,700	3,457	4,127	4,739	4,510
Edmondson	4,459	2,190	2,269	823	799	747	870	862
Elliott	4,433	2,300	2,133	925	815	719	828	826
Estill	9,198	4,858	4,340	1,721	1,570	1,753	2,056	2,010
Fayette	26,656	13,144	13,512	3,918	4,138	5,196	6,744	6,533
Fleming	13,398	6,787	6,611	2,348	2,269	2,303	3,010	2,980
Floyd	7,877	3,971	3,906	1,531	1,418	1,271	1,443	1,438
Franklin	15,300	7,893	7,407	2,511	2,493	3,141	3,752	3,696
Fulton	6,161	3,160	3,001	1,056	983	1,275	1,405	1,393
Gallatin	5,074	2,616	2,458	883	881	1,000	1,179	1,171
Garrard	10,376	5,192	5,184	1,745	1,720	1,872	2,299	2,106
Grant	9,529	4,885	4,644	1,759	1,604	1,701	2,126	2,101
Graves	19,398	9,861	9,537	3,383	3,367	3,545	4,007	3,991
Grayson	11,580	5,966	5,614	2,076	1,935	2,165	2,492	2,436
Green	9,379	4,642	4,737	1,660	1,634	1,531	1,918	1,914
Greenup	11,463	5,880	5,583	2,023	1,982	2,125	2,527	2,524
Hancock	6,591	3,390	3,201	1,237	1,177	1,171	1,403	1,379
Hardin	15,705	7,999	7,706	2,733	2,681	2,929	3,500	3,473
Harlan	4,415	2,210	2,205	891	815	662	747	743
Harrison	12,993	6,599	6,394	2,221	2,146	2,436	3,009	2,987
Hart	13,687	6,963	6,724	2,452	2,323	2,448	2,919	2,916
Henderson	18,457	9,529	8,928	3,113	2,916	3,830	4,254	4,154
Henry	11,066	5,553	5,513	1,943	2,007	1,928	2,339	2,333
Hickman	8,453	4,290	4,163	1,519	1,425	1,577	1,835	1,805
Hopkins	13,827	6,927	6,900	2,471	2,441	2,463	2,872	2,858
Jackson	4,547	2,318	2,229	872	799	738	856	848
Jefferson	118,953	58,036	60,917	17,913	19,208	23,562	28,958	26,962
Jessamine	8,638	4,396	4,242	1,513	1,451	1,531	2,011	1,989
Johnson	7,494	3,778	3,716	1,464	1,356	1,217	1,384	1,380
Josh Bell	3,731	1,856	1,875	721	667	573	671	670
Kenton	36,096	17,807	18,289	5,760	5,877	6,512	8,315	7,915
Knox	8,294	4,102	4,192	1,503	1,494	1,340	1,560	1,560
La Rue	8,235	4,121	4,114	1,469	1,477	1,408	1,725	1,717
Laurel	6,016	3,036	2,980	1,104	1,010	1,008	1,195	1,187
Lawrence	8,497	4,340	4,157	1,586	1,575	1,444	1,645	1,639
Lee	3,055	1,560	1,495	564	536	533	613	609
Letcher	4,608	2,301	2,307	919	872	717	786	781
Lewis	9,115	4,634	4,481	1,610	1,546	1,559	2,012	1,965
Lincoln	10,947	5,463	5,484	1,864	1,918	1,922	2,389	2,389
Livingston	8,200	4,172	4,028	1,487	1,399	1,521	1,748	1,708
Logan	20,429	10,120	10,309	3,451	3,436	3,606	4,480	4,472
Lyon	6,233	3,249	2,984	1,129	1,047	1,232	1,380	1,345
Madison	19,543	9,905	9,638	3,491	3,452	3,457	4,226	4,153
Magoffin	4,684	2,319	2,365	938	891	713	790	789
Marion	12,838	6,356	6,482	2,203	2,258	2,204	2,823	2,811
Marshall	9,455	4,847	4,608	1,838	1,628	1,661	1,881	1,875
Mason	18,126	8,870	9,256	2,933	3,026	3,169	4,117	4,000
McCracken	13,988	6,994	6,994	2,178	2,271	2,911	3,383	3,278
McLean	7,614	3,894	3,720	1,325	1,334	1,437	1,652	1,650
Meade	9,485	4,844	4,641	1,764	1,616	1,740	2,018	1,992
Menifee	1,986	990	996	355	373	317	385	385
Mercer	13,144	6,568	6,576	2,285	2,208	2,285	2,925	2,900
Metcalfe	7,934	3,931	4,003	1,302	1,324	1,380	1,672	1,663
Monroe	9,231	4,499	4,732	1,655	1,592	1,459	1,763	1,667
Montgomery	7,557	3,797	3,760	1,296	1,217	1,376	1,738	1,725
Morgan	5,975	2,989	2,986	1,168	1,139	974	1,125	1,122
Muhlenburg	12,638	6,458	6,180	2,200	2,138	2,287	2,687	2,621
Nelson	14,804	7,321	7,483	2,590	2,612	2,563	3,273	2,909
Nicholas	9,129	4,755	4,37[illegible]	1,682	1,454	1,656	2,116	2,083
Ohio	15,561	8,083	7,478	2,877	2,615	2,924	3,362	3,345
Oldham	9,027	4,681	4,346	1,554	1,513	1,768	2,163	2,116
Owen	14,309	7,481	6,828	2,577	2,418	2,734	3,250	3,241
Owsley	3,889	1,921	1,968	725	730	630	714	711
Pendleton	14,030	7,183	6,847	2,528	2,452	2,450	3,046	3,018
Perry	4,274	2,175	2,099	855	792	701	785	782
Pike	9,562	4,826	4,736	1,787	1,695	1,524	1,743	1,740
Powell	2,599	1,322	1,277	505	485	427	525	520
Pulaski	17,670	8,698	8,972	3,244	3,168	2,751	3,309	3,306
Robertson	5,399	2,773	2,626	954	934	950	1,140	1,135
Rock Castle	7,145	3,620	3,525	1,276	1,248	1,235	1,461	1,451
Rowan	2,991	1,513	1,478	564	565	469	598	596

TABLE LVII.—*School, Military, and Citizenship Ages, &c., by Counties*—1870—Continued.

STATE OF KENTUCKY—Continued.

Counties.	All ages.			5 to 18.		18 to 45.	21 and upward.	
	Total.	Male.	Female.	Male.	Female.	Male.	Male.	Male citizens.
Russell	5,809	2,876	2,933	1,068	1,023	932	1,179	1,178
Scott	11,607	5,826	5,781	1,917	1,910	2,000	2,676	2,602
Shelby	15,733	8,003	7,730	2,662	2,549	2,857	3,745	3,708
Simpson	9,573	4,889	4,684	1,665	1,558	1,783	2,116	2,091
Spencer	5,956	3,134	2,822	1,077	948	1,136	1,391	1,210
Taylor	8,226	4,050	4,176	1,497	1,449	1,325	1,620	1,618
Todd	12,612	6,261	6,351	2,087	2,161	2,351	2,809	2,796
Trigg	13,686	6,991	6,695	2,536	2,395	2,452	2,822	2,817
Trimble	5,577	2,832	2,745	927	886	1,000	1,284	1,275
Union	13,640	7,095	6,545	2,490	2,257	2,663	3,023	2,911
Warren	21,742	11,061	10,681	3,720	3,600	4,245	5,012	4,972
Washington	12,464	6,285	6,179	2,206	2,110	2,139	2,678	2,670
Wayne	10,602	5,186	5,416	1,972	1,875	1,677	1,959	1,958
Webster	10,937	5,663	5,274	2,127	1,809	1,947	2,201	2,119
Whitley	8,278	4,127	4,151	1,520	1,468	1,380	1,555	1,542
Wolfe	3,603	1,782	1,821	676	695	563	651	651
Woodford	8,240	4,232	4,008	1,379	1,328	1,559	2,033	2,030

STATE OF LOUISIANA.

PARISHES.	Total.	Male.	Female.	5 to 18 Male.	5 to 18 Female.	18 to 45 Male.	21 and upward Male.	Male citizens.
The State	726,915	362,165	364,750	112,520	113,594	136,753	174,187	150,001
Ascension	11,577	5,921	5,656	1,694	1,629	2,144	3,062	2,913
Assumption	13,234	6,706	6,528	2,183	2,104	2,313	3,124	2,979
Avoyelles	12,926	6,638	6,288	2,221	2,170	2,499	2,937	2,696
Bienville	10,636	5,282	5,354	1,871	1,911	1,799	2,062	1,923
Bossier	12,675	6,639	6,036	2,109	1,971	2,614	2,951	2,911
Caddo	21,714	11,079	10,635	3,698	3,952	4,577	5,202	4,870
Calcasieu	6,733	3,528	3,205	1,306	1,144	1,205	1,372	1,273
Caldwell	4,820	2,387	2,433	864	862	797	955	832
Cameron	1,591	807	784	305	312	270	326	323
Carroll	10,110	5,152	4,958	1,351	1,385	2,219	2,744	2,586
Catahoula	8,475	4,201	4,274	1,384	1,393	1,547	1,885	1,847
Claiborne	20,240	10,194	10,046	3,725	3,550	3,338	3,925	3,749
Concordia	9,977	4,983	4,994	1,172	1,142	2,135	2,883	2,843
De Soto	14,962	7,378	7,584	2,586	2,648	2,586	3,108	3,056
East Baton Rouge	17,816	9,013	8,803	2,562	2,602	3,540	4,660	4,341
East Feliciana	13,499	6,635	6,864	2,147	2,264	2,351	2,936	2,810
Franklin	5,078	2,495	2,583	870	877	886	1,020	986
Grant	4,517	2,243	2,274	736	713	806	1,038	1,025
Iberia	9,042	4,622	4,420	1,493	1,494	1,624	2,123	1,956
Iberville	12,347	6,297	6,050	1,798	1,849	2,314	3,219	3,000
Jackson	7,646	3,906	3,740	1,416	1,327	1,309	1,500	1,447
Jefferson	17,767	9,292	8,475	2,481	2,396	3,607	5,009	4,911
Lafayette	10,388	5,222	5,166	1,879	1,740	1,854	2,083	1,905
Latourche	14.719	7,481	7,238	2,368	2,415	2,541	3,484	3,312
Livingston	4,026	2,068	1,958	723	712	722	877	830
Madison	8,600	4,318	4,282	989	1,023	1,840	2,458	2,364
Morehouse	9,387	4,774	4,613	1,623	1,494	1,768	2,028	1,902
Natchitoches	18,265	9,211	9,054	2,866	2,833	3,384	4,384	4,168
Orleans	191,418	90,279	101,139	25,941	28,657	36,817	47,737	38,586
Ouachita	11,582	5,856	5,726	1,814	1,761	2,303	2,715	2,543
Plaquemines	10,552	5,845	4,707	1,497	1,396	2,413	3,272	2,947
Point Coupée	12,981	6,642	6,339	2,024	1,892	2,537	3,318	3,192
Rapides	18,015	9,035	8,980	2,839	2,833	3,252	4,232	4,112
Richland	5,110	2,635	2,475	859	773	1,050	1,182	1,179
Sabine	6,456	3,205	3,251	1,200	1,152	1,068	1,234	1,203
St. Bernard	3,553	1,922	1,631	477	476	748	1,051	951
St. Charles	4,867	2,527	2,340	[illegible]	543	945	1,489	1,439
St. Helena	5,423	2,644	2,779	941	939	913	1,084	1,077
St. James	10,152	5,226	4,926	1,571	1,625	1,764	2,714	2,568
St. John the Baptist	6,762	3,485	3,277	1,047	998	1,180	1,778	1,679
St. Landry	25,553	12,866	12,687	4,483	4,210	4,458	5,495	5,189
St. Martin	9,370	4,802	4,568	1,630	1,504	1,724	2,114	1,948
St. Mary	13,860	7,312	6,548	2,160	2,055	2,857	3,722	3,610
St. Tammany	5,586	2,848	2,738	949	864	846	1,296	1,201
Tangipahoa	7,928	4,021	3,907	1,411	1,350	1,399	1,676	1,577

TABLE LVII.—*School, Military, and Citizenship Ages, &c., by Counties—1870*—**Continued.**

STATE OF LOUISIANA—Continued.

Parishes.	All ages.			5 to 18.		18 to 45.	21 and upward.	
	Total.	Male.	Female.	Male.	Female.	Male.	Male.	Male citizens.
Tensas	12,419	6,293	6,126	1,573	1,566	2,739	3,406	3,329
Terrebonne	12,451	6,406	6,045	2,085	2,091	2,339	3,004	2,956
Union	11,685	5,770	5,915	2,206	2,144	1,909	2,223	2,076
Vermillion	4,528	2,279	2,249	840	793	826	950	939
Washington	3,330	1,657	1,673	677	609	463	573	571
West Baton Rouge	5,114	2,526	2,588	720	788	954	1,310	1,277
West Feliciana	10,499	5,135	5,364	1,638	1,796	1,850	2,317	2,230
Winn	4,954	2,477	2,477	930	867	790	911	876

STATE OF MAINE.

COUNTIES.								
The State	626,915	313,103	313,812	89,233	86,355	118,940	169,821	153,160
Androscoggin	35,866	16,847	19,019	4,652	4,914	6,607	9,358	8,430
Aroostook	29,609	15,540	14,069	5,448	4,972	5,356	6,713	4,633
Cumberland	82,021	40,009	42,012	10,783	10,537	15,952	22,484	19,144
Franklin	18,807	9,434	9,373	2,694	2,527	4,410	5,176	5,021
Hancock	36,495	18,653	17,842	5,610	5,290	7,081	9,698	9,055
Kennebec	53,203	26,399	26,804	6,844	6,513	10,161	15,354	14,815
Knox	30,823	15,584	15,239	4,152	4,231	6,427	8,778	7,886
Lincoln	25,597	12,851	12,746	3,608	3,454	4,624	7,076	6,844
Oxford	33,488	16,845	16,643	4,783	4,680	6,022	9,269	8,843
Penobscot	75,150	38,527	36,623	10,800	10,471	15,539	20,905	18,473
Piscataquis	14,403	7,394	7,009	2,138	2,047	2,773	3,970	3,773
Sagadahoc	18,803	9,176	9,627	2,638	2,541	3,358	5,069	4,838
Somerset	34,611	17,597	17,014	5,191	4,784	6,312	9,470	8,739
Waldo	34,522	17,417	17,105	4,973	4,670	6,457	9,439	8,510
Washington	43,343	21,917	21,426	6,994	6,831	7,912	10,679	8,828
York	60,174	28,913	31,261	7,925	7,903	10,949	16,383	15,368

STATE OF MARYLAND.

The State	780,894	384,984	395,910	122,932	121,522	144,695	184,742	169,865
Allegany	38,536	19,889	18,647	6,302	6,128	7,532	9,151	7,041
Anne Arundel	24,457	12,794	11,663	4,214	3,688	4,985	5,911	5,839
Baltimore	63,387	31,981	31,406	10,535	9,696	11,545	15,347	13,449
Baltimore City	267,354	125,849	141,505	37,402	40,335	50,570	64,398	54,782
Calvert	9,865	4,909	4,956	1,796	1,717	1,667	2,056	1,858
Caroline	12,101	6,043	6,058	2,103	2,032	2,123	2,742	2,735
Carroll	28,619	14,341	14,278	4,654	4,398	4,975	6,898	6,331
Cecil	25,874	13,169	12,705	4,196	3,900	4,859	6,393	6,298
Charles	15,738	7,886	7,852	2,734	2,763	2,749	3,379	3,366
Dorchester	19,458	9,707	9,751	3,384	3,228	3,358	4,412	4,409
Frederick	47,572	23,265	24,307	7,432	7,389	8,370	11,049	10,454
Harford	22,605	11,212	11,393	3,639	3,540	3,958	5,413	5,155
Howard	14,150	7,234	6,916	2,459	2,216	2,619	3,243	3,145
Kent	17,102	8,878	8,224	2,787	2,667	3,554	4,264	4,143
Montgomery	20,563	10,598	9,965	3,339	3,130	3,931	5,061	4,863
Prince George's	21,138	10,852	10,286	3,581	3,334	3,965	5,058	5,018
Queen Anne	16,171	8,265	7,906	2,865	2,597	3,060	3,723	3,723
Saint Mary's	14,944	7,446	7,498	2,565	2,553	2,566	3,267	3,241
Somerset	18,190	9,271	8,919	3,153	2,953	3,381	4,132	4,106
Talbot	16,137	8,136	8,001	2,650	2,526	3,048	3,796	3,770
Washington	34,712	17,150	17,562	5,307	5,253	6,296	8,072	7,798
Wicomico	15,802	7,922	7,880	2,858	2,757	2,732	3,480	3,473
Worcester	16,419	8,187	8,232	2,917	2,722	2,832	3,567	3,549

TABLE LVII.—*School, Military, and Citizenship Ages, &c., by Counties*—1870—Continued.

STATE OF MASSACHUSETTS.

Counties.	All ages.			5 to 18.		18 to 45.	21 and upward.	
	Total.	Male.	Female.	Male.	Female.	Male.	Male.	Male citizens.
The State	1, 457, 351	703, 779	753, 572	184, 640	187, 180	298, 767	398, 157	312, 770
Barnstable	32, 774	16, 035	16, 739	4, 270	4, 000	6, 091	9, 347	8, 819
Berkshire	64, 827	32, 294	32, 533	9, 025	9, 065	12, 698	17, 285	13, 595
Bristol	102, 886	49, 419	53, 467	13, 394	13, 556	19, 777	27, 739	23, 222
Dukes	3, 787	1, 819	1, 968	445	417	673	1, 125	1, 006
Essex	200, 843	95, 498	105, 345	24, 736	25, 446	41, 346	54, 540	44, 051
Franklin	32, 635	16, 362	16, 273	4, 256	4, 100	6, 264	9, 396	8, 312
Hampden	78, 409	37, 382	41, 027	10, 146	10, 378	15, 733	20, 093	15, 677
Hampshire	44, 388	21, 443	22, 945	5, 864	5, 820	8, 308	11, 734	9, 510
Middlesex	274, 353	131, 959	142, 394	33, 668	34, 706	58, 327	75, 274	58, 565
Nantucket	4, 123	1, 825	2, 298	466	421	506	1, 155	1, 154
Norfolk	89, 443	42, 944	46, 499	11, 779	11, 928	16, 890	23, 816	19, 253
Plymouth	65, 365	32, 116	33, 249	8, 345	8, 328	12, 291	18, 588	16, 684
Suffolk	270, 802	129, 482	141, 320	32, 447	33, 461	61, 415	74, 875	51, 943
Worcester	192, 716	95, 201	97, 515	25, 809	25, 534	38, 538	52, 584	40, 889

STATE OF MICHIGAN.

Counties.	Total.	Male.	Female.	Male.	Female.	Male.	Male.	Male citizens.
The State	1, 184, 059	617, 745	566, 314	181, 806	176, 724	252, 821	315, 937	274, 459
Alcona	696	395	301	88	104	211	219	145
Allegan	32, 105	17, 007	15, 098	5, 097	4, 876	6, 809	8, 548	7, 675
Alpena	2, 756	1, 715	1, 041	306	283	1, 084	1, 058	614
Antrim	1, 985	1, 116	869	314	272	473	565	479
Barry	22, 199	11, 637	10, 562	3, 575	3, 348	4, 607	5, 852	5, 628
Bay	15, 900	8, 895	7, 005	2, 306	2, 160	4, 488	4, 837	3, 374
Benzie	2, 184	1, 164	1, 020	305	323	513	638	604
Berrien	35, 104	17, 918	17, 186	5, 457	5, 513	7, 150	8, 930	8, 469
Branch	26, 226	13, 243	12, 983	3, 914	3, 859	5, 091	7, 013	6, 772
Calhoun	36, 569	18, 551	18, 018	5, 290	5, 317	7, 448	9, 869	9, 487
Cass	21, 094	10, 957	10, 137	3, 437	3, 276	4, 184	5, 404	5, 171
Charlevoix	1, 724	942	782	306	280	361	448	424
Cheboygan	2, 196	1, 237	959	349	320	535	624	438
Chippewa	1, 689	932	757	280	251	387	458	393
Clare	366	286	80	34	23	202	222	162
Clinton	22, 845	11, 815	11, 030	3, 620	3, 442	4, 610	5, 813	5, 526
Delta	2, 542	1, 556	986	278	328	921	904	456
Eaton	25, 171	12, 915	12, 256	3, 856	3, 735	5, 150	6, 610	6, 483
Emmet	1, 211	637	574	206	177	200	274	264
Genesee	33, 900	17, 430	16, 470	4, 988	4, 880	7, 112	9, 126	8, 492
Grand Traverse	4, 443	2, 367	2, 076	773	692	872	1, 090	1, 013
Gratiot	11, 810	6, 180	5, 630	2, 038	1, 888	2, 248	2, 875	2, 741
Hillsdale	31, 684	16, 063	15, 621	4, 783	4, 748	6, 234	8, 374	8, 300
Houghton	13, 879	7, 735	6, 144	2, 055	1, 950	3, 618	3, 844	1, 945
Huron	9, 049	5, 024	4, 025	1, 542	1, 436	1, 949	2, 330	1, 387
Ingham	25, 268	13, 081	12, 187	3, 992	3, 717	5, 117	6, 554	6, 365
Ionia	27, 681	14, 421	13, 260	4, 292	3, 982	5, 870	7, 355	6, 979
Iosco	3, 163	1, 894	1, 269	430	365	1, 090	1, 113	677
Isabella	4, 113	2, 214	1, 899	627	684	968	1, 109	1, 017
Jackson	36, 047	19, 053	16, 994	4, 995	4, 932	8, 635	10, 515	9, 772
Kalamazoo	32, 054	16, 519	15, 535	4, 660	4, 670	6, 866	8, 787	8, 191
Kalkaska	424	241	183	70	63	110	134	123
Kent	50, 403	26, 186	24, 217	7, 729	7, 502	10, 764	13, 589	11, 692
Keweenaw	4, 205	2, 333	1, 872	667	650	976	1, 127	892
Lake	548	309	239	96	72	127	160	148
Lapeer	21, 345	11, 077	10, 268	3, 368	3, 337	4, 332	5, 469	4, 990
Leelanaw	4, 576	2, 407	2, 169	828	789	833	1, 088	637
Lenawee	45, 595	22, 911	22, 684	6, 444	6, 555	9, 082	12, 338	11, 103
Livingston	19, 336	10, 053	9, 283	2, 963	2, 817	3, 958	5, 227	5, 041
Mackinac	1, 716	911	805	296	286	351	417	302
Macomb	27, 616	14, 073	13, 543	4, 432	4, 288	4, 964	6, 878	5, 957
Manistee	6, 074	3, 461	2, 613	831	767	1, 850	1, 950	1, 986
Manitou	891	489	402	169	148	165	234	50
Marquette	15, 033	8, 959	6, 074	1, 931	1, 884	5, 127	5, 261	2, 334
Mason	3, 263	1, 811	1, 452	477	478	857	998	886
Mecosta	5, 642	3, 070	2, 572	850	828	1, 402	1, 629	1, 432
Menominee	1, 791	1, 216	575	185	161	830	749	403

TABLE LVII.—*School, Military, and Citizenship Ages, &c., by Counties*—1870—Continued.

STATE OF MICHIGAN—Continued.

Counties.	All ages. Total.	All ages. Male.	All ages. Female.	5 to 18. Male.	5 to 18. Female.	18 to 45. Male.	21 and upward. Male.	21 and upward. Male citizens.
Midland	3,285	1,812	1,473	448	443	671	984	[illegible]
Missaukee	130	76	54	20	14	39	43	41
Monroe	27,483	13,954	13,529	4,680	4,644	4,776	6,380	6,112
Montcalm	13,629	7,269	6,360	2,261	2,039	3,018	3,565	3,321
Muskegon	14,894	8,402	6,492	2,111	1,914	4,250	4,605	2,923
Newaygo	7,294	3,923	3,371	1,198	1,098	1,581	1,915	1,712
Oakland	40,867	21,117	19,750	6,077	5,936	8,582	11,160	10,521
Oceana	7,222	3,939	3,283	1,180	1,041	1,580	1,965	1,772
Ogemaw	12	9	3	....	....	7	8	2
Ontonagon	2,845	1,438	1,407	550	566	434	568	417
Osceola	2,093	1,161	932	333	309	484	580	505
Oscoda	70	49	21	8	5	32	32	15
Ottawa	26,651	14,104	12,547	4,416	4,204	5,345	6,665	5,388
Presque Isle	355	228	127	38	53	136	157	49
Saginaw	39,697	21,003	18,694	5,786	5,748	9,662	11,106	8,165
Sanilac	14,562	7,691	6,871	2,656	2,506	2,667	3,360	2,089
Shiawassee	20,858	10,830	10,028	3,318	3,198	4,297	5,403	5,297
St. Clair	36,661	18,964	17,697	6,386	6,192	6,837	8,733	6,697
St. Joseph	26,275	13,483	12,792	3,952	3,899	5,440	7,073	6,512
Tuscola	13,714	7,257	6,457	2,346	2,152	2,752	3,427	3,039
Van Buren	28,829	14,865	13,964	4,544	4,417	5,842	7,577	7,277
Washtenaw	41,434	21,506	19,928	5,987	5,775	8,838	11,426	10,495
Wayne	119,038	59,916	59,122	17,918	17,951	24,431	30,364	24,097
Wexford	650	343	307	90	84	157	189	189

STATE OF MINNESOTA.

Counties.	All ages. Total.	All ages. Male.	All ages. Female.	5 to 18. Male.	5 to 18. Female.	18 to 45. Male.	21 and upward. Male.	21 and upward. Male citizens.
The State	439,706	235,299	204,407	72,657	70,008	94,238	114,739	75,274
Aitkin	178	94	84	42	29	37	34	3
Anoka	3,940	2,091	1,849	673	615	792	969	623
Becker	308	173	135	39	37	92	102	92
Beltrami	80	40	40	12	13	13	20	15
Benton	1,558	864	694	259	230	333	426	343
Big Stone	24	15	9	5	4	7	5	3
Blue Earth	17,302	9,351	7,951	2,905	2,734	3,824	4,672	3,203
Brown	6,396	3,395	3,001	1,099	1,021	1,201	1,571	1,047
Carlton	286	212	74	21	24	138	178	57
Carver	11,586	6,101	5,485	2,271	2,088	1,693	2,500	1,366
Cass	380	211	169	46	32	115	126	71
Chippewa	1,467	833	634	213	188	380	445	344
Chisago	4,358	2,331	2,027	726	699	907	1,173	507
Clay	92	60	32	10	7	33	38	24
Cottonwood	534	336	198	79	54	176	205	199
Crow Wing	200	122	78	28	21	67	69	67
Dakota	16,312	8,741	7,571	3,003	2,794	3,188	4,034	2,244
Dodge	8,598	4,526	4,072	1,438	1,433	1,754	2,176	1,844
Douglas	4,239	2,278	1,961	602	597	1,014	1,919	553
Faribault	9,940	5,244	4,696	1,638	1,582	2,017	2,453	2,282
Fillmore	24,887	13,221	11,666	4,341	4,183	5,141	6,187	3,358
Freeborn	10,578	5,590	4,988	1,808	1,662	2,081	2,568	2,183
Goodhue	22,618	12,012	10,606	3,782	3,539	4,649	5,698	2,787
Grant	340	202	138	57	46	88	103	7
Hennepin	31,566	16,827	14,739	4,834	4,804	7,504	8,795	6,164
Houston	14,936	7,828	7,108	2,573	2,630	2,849	3,699	2,287
Isanti	2,035	1,075	960	328	328	414	525	474
Itasca	96	58	38	11	13	34	34	11
Jackson	1,825	1,008	817	279	258	448	539	512
Kanabec	93	53	40	13	13	23	28	27
Kandiyohi	1,760	948	812	239	240	421	520	105
Lac qui Parle	145	83	62	17	17	36	39	23
Lake	135	78	57	27	22	33	39	37
Le Sueur	11,607	5,909	6,608	2,143	2,203	1,819	2,499	1,922
Martin	3,867	2,094	1,773	650	568	819	1,009	813
McLeod	5,643	2,975	2,668	854	832	1,100	1,319	947
Meeker	6,090	3,220	2,870	1,013	944	1,258	1,563	1,058
Mille Lac	1,109	598	511	196	183	220	275	248
Monongalia	3,161	1,744	1,417	530	437	647	835	548
Morrison	1,681	956	725	285	256	403	476	388

TABLE LVII.—*School, Military, and Citizenship Ages, &c., by Counties—1870*—Continued.

STATE OF MINNESOTA—Continued.

Counties.	All ages.			5 to 18.		18 to 45.	21 and upward.	
	Total.	Male.	Female.	Male.	Female.	Male.	Male.	Male citizens.
Mower	10,447	5,802	4,645	1,699	1,546	2,577	2,978	2,425
Murray	209	117	92	25	25	52	65	65
Nicollet	8,362	4,434	3,928	1,428	1,353	1,662	2,068	942
Nobles	117	63	54	17	18	33	36	36
Olmsted	19,793	10,435	9,358	3,213	3,163	4,209	5,055	4,077
Otter Tail	1,968	1,084	884	282	281	436	590	149
Pembina	64	31	33	12	19	11	13	12
Pine	648	475	173	56	54	354	347	212
Pope	2,691	1,430	1,261	395	414	604	732	260
Ramsey	23,085	12,021	11,064	3,319	3,469	5,666	6,344	2,995
Redwood	1,829	1,037	792	248	236	528	598	523
Renville	3,219	1,757	1,462	512	494	714	861	527
Rice	16,083	8,399	7,684	2,805	2,646	3,103	3,857	3,159
Rock	138	78	60	16	14	44	53	51
Scott	11,042	5,826	5,216	2,178	2,077	1,772	2,454	1,222
Sherburne	2,050	1,150	900	337	290	499	565	508
Sibley	6,725	3,549	3,176	1,352	1,220	1,060	1,457	650
Stearns	14,206	7,585	6,621	2,311	2,355	2,820	3,576	2,730
Steele	8,271	4,377	3,894	1,354	1,274	1,675	2,127	1,527
Stevens	174	102	72	28	23	53	59	18
St. Louis	4,561	3,525	1,036	328	274	2,789	2,803	1,146
Todd	2,036	1,108	928	343	314	438	545	383
Traverse	13	7	6	1	1	5	6	5
Wabashaw	15,859	8,417	7,442	2,497	2,520	3,558	4,196	3,310
Wadena	6	5	1	1	....	3	3	3
Waseca	7,854	4,154	3,700	1,379	1,322	1,446	1,875	1,267
Washington	11,809	6,733	5,076	1,783	1,685	3,266	3,670	2,096
Watonwan	2,426	1,343	1,083	365	313	613	717	518
Wilkin	295	180	115	36	26	89	106	80
Winona	22,319	11,530	10,789	3,528	3,628	4,648	5,592	4,231
Wright	9,457	4,958	4,499	1,660	1,574	1,691	2,226	1,503

STATE OF MISSISSIPPI.

Counties.	Total.	Male.	Female.	Male 5 to 18.	Female 5 to 18.	Male 18 to 45.	Male 21 and upward.	Male citizens.
The State	827,922	413,421	414,501	141,412	137,587	149,698	174,845	160,737
Adams	19,084	9,275	9,809	2,703	2,711	3,325	4,765	4,740
Alcorn	10,431	5,290	5,141	1,883	1,732	1,910	2,159	2,073
Amite	10,973	5,423	5,550	2,004	1,916	1,700	2,061	2,015
Attala	14,776	7,281	7,495	2,734	2,633	2,433	2,811	2,806
Bolivar	9,732	5,135	4,597	1,337	1,371	2,431	2,638	2,582
Calhoun	10,561	5,297	5,264	1,957	1,850	1,758	2,007	2,005
Carroll	21,047	10,430	10,617	3,568	3,509	3,789	4,364	4,233
Chickasaw	19,899	9,899	10,000	3,622	3,372	3,369	3,978	3,874
Choctaw	16,988	8,376	8,612	3,105	3,001	2,668	3,114	3,090
Claiborne	13,386	6,626	6,760	2,116	2,093	2,382	3,043	3,019
Clark	7,505	3,638	3,867	1,302	1,361	1,212	1,459	1,428
Coahoma	7,144	3,887	3,257	1,065	974	1,853	1,973	1,942
Copiah	20,608	10,229	10,379	3,610	3,520	3,543	4,013	3,900
Covington	4,753	2,316	2,437	870	879	745	852	807
De Soto	32,021	16,320	15,701	5,415	5,177	6,260	6,913	6,612
Franklin	7,498	3,654	3,844	1,347	1,390	1,182	1,392	1,382
Greene	2,038	1,004	1,034	401	378	295	380	369
Grenada	10,571	5,345	5,226	1,734	1,697	2,106	2,418	2,323
Hancock	4,239	2,218	2,021	739	677	927	1,047	972
Harrison	5,795	2,943	2,852	1,057	1,0[illegible]2	1,[illegible]47	1,275	1,183
Hinds	30,488	15,393	15,095	4,984	4,863	5,800	6,829	6,671
Holmes	19,370	9,626	9,744	3,181	3,186	3,619	4,149	4,102
Issaquena	6,887	3,524	3,363	860	906	1,540	1,890	1,809
Itawamba	7,812	3,848	3,964	1,455	1,432	1,270	1,378	1,357
Jackson	4,362	2,287	2,075	732	735	920	1,067	1,056
Jasper	10,884	5,317	5,567	2,035	1,975	1,680	1,961	1,905
Jefferson	13,848	6,690	7,158	2,286	2,353	2,253	2,850	2,802
Jones	3,313	1,619	1,694	676	626	464	538	537
Kemper	12,920	6,445	6,475	2,600	2,273	1,948	2,272	2,253
Lafayette	18,802	9,636	9,166	3,480	3,114	3,467	3,845	3,788
Lauderdale	13,462	6,720	6,742	2,247	2,338	2,404	2,746	2,744
Lawrence	6,720	3,366	3,354	1,257	1,152	1,091	1,258	1,243
Leake	8,496	4,304	4,192	1,649	1,473	1,375	1,585	1,5[illegible]

TABLE LVII.—*School, Military, and Citizenship Ages, &c., by Counties*—1870—**Continued.**

STATE OF MISSISSIPPI—Continued.

Counties.	All ages.			5 to 18.		18 to 45.	21 and upward.	
	Total.	Male.	Female.	Male.	Female.	Male.	Male.	Male citizens.
Lee	15,955	8,028	7,927	2,920	2,700	2,773	3,194	3,15[illegible]
Lincoln	10,184	5,006	5,178	1,831	1,868	1,713	1,960	1,9[illegible]
Lowndes	30,502	15,120	15,382	5,131	5,221	5,839	6,939	[illegible]
Madison	20,948	10,351	10,597	3,450	3,377	3,793	4,514	4,3[illegible]
Marion	4,211	2,119	2,092	774	833	680	773	7[illegible]
Marshall	29,416	14,653	14,763	4,896	4,910	5,446	6,257	6,[illegible]
Monroe	22,631	11,106	11,525	4,081	3,858	3,842	4,507	4,3[illegible]
Neshoba	7,439	3,572	3,867	1,321	1,311	1,121	1,342	1,3[illegible]
Newton	10,067	4,928	5,139	1,763	1,752	1,603	1,857	1,8[illegible]
Noxubee	20,905	10,394	10,511	3,567	3,493	3,806	4,521	4,[illegible]
Oktibbeha	14,891	7,348	7,543	2,680	2,590	2,440	2,945	2,146
Panola	20,754	10,550	10,204	3,543	3,339	4,080	4,514	4,[illegible]
Perry	2,694	1,292	1,402	536	526	401	475	474
Pike	11,303	5,733	5,570	2,103	1,974	1,886	2,234	[illegible]
Pontotoc	12,525	6,095	6,430	2,264	2,280	2,012	2,385	[illegible]
Prentiss	9,348	4,641	4,707	1,709	1,500	1,587	1,753	[illegible]
Rankin	12,977	6,408	6,569	2,280	2,329	2,126	2,491	[illegible]
Scott	7,847	3,870	3,977	1,430	1,400	1,319	1,444	[illegible]
Simpson	5,718	2,937	2,781	1,144	974	956	1,018	[illegible]
Smith	7,126	3,481	3,645	1,306	1,242	1,098	1,257	[illegible]
Sunflower	5,015	2,662	2,353	854	708	1,089	1,258	[illegible]
Tallahatchie	7,852	3,990	3,862	1,270	1,159	1,564	1,774	[illegible]
Tippah	20,727	10,125	10,602	3,718	3,612	3,424	3,899	[illegible]
Tishemingo	7,350	3,715	3,635	1,339	1,366	1,409	1,577	[illegible]
Tunica	5,358	2,918	2,440	804	728	1,396	1,481	[illegible]
Warren	26,769	13,284	13,485	3,273	3,477	5,846	7,258	[illegible]
Washington	14,569	7,698	6,871	1,997	1,881	3,528	4,059	[illegible]
Wayne	4,206	2,075	2,131	719	729	718	819	814
Wilkinson	12,705	6,134	6,571	2,084	2,126	2,058	2,588	2,5[illegible]
Winston	8,984	4,334	4,650	1,659	1,619	1,354	1,646	1,637
Yalabusha	13,254	6,794	6,460	2,314	2,130	2,546	2,938	2,[illegible]
Yazoo	17,279	8,699	8,580	2,572	2,507	3,519	4,118	3,3[illegible]

STATE OF MISSOURI.

Counties.	All ages.			5 to 18.		18 to 45.	21 and upward.	
	Total.	Male.	Female.	Male.	Female.	Male.	Male.	Male citizens.
The State	1,721,295	896,347	824,948	294,316	283,487	352,998	408,206	380,2[illegible]
Adair	11,448	5,892	5,556	2,030	1,997	2,058	2,509	2,4[illegible]
Andrew	15,137	8,014	7,123	2,633	2,479	3,068	3,584	3,448
Atchison	8,440	4,489	3,951	1,382	1,377	1,829	2,036	2,0[illegible]
Audrain	12,307	6,417	5,890	2,171	2,040	2,530	2,888	2,813
Barry	10,373	5,224	5,149	1,970	1,884	1,776	1,936	1,9[illegible]
Barton	5,087	2,698	2,389	860	830	1,114	1,240	1,2[illegible]
Bates	15,960	8,541	7,419	2,730	2,522	3,430	3,858	3,7[illegible]
Benton	11,322	5,850	5,472	2,121	1,993	1,989	2,352	2,277
Bollinger	8,162	4,135	4,027	1,574	1,441	1,456	1,610	1,5[illegible]
Boone	20,765	10,420	10,345	3,657	3,753	3,833	4,540	4,5[illegible]
Buchanan	35,109	19,175	15,934	5,203	5,378	9,383	10,448	9,3[illegible]
Butler	4,298	2,167	2,131	796	792	764	828	[illegible]
Caldwell	11,390	5,959	5,431	1,877	1,771	2,405	2,772	2,6[illegible]
Callaway	19,202	9,916	9,286	3,437	3,183	3,700	4,452	4,2[illegible]
Camden	6,108	3,105	3,003	1,177	1,116	1,022	1,147	1,1[illegible]
Cape Girardeau	17,558	9,003	8,555	3,017	2,927	3,460	3,999	3,6[illegible]
Carroll	17,446	9,237	8,209	3,102	2,897	3,601	4,056	3,9[illegible]
Carter	1,455	733	722	274	276	262	281	275
Cass	19,296	10,408	8,888	3,233	2,945	4,421	4,989	4,757
Cedar	9,474	4,851	4,623	1,752	1,616	1,695	1,806	1,8[illegible]
Chariton	19,136	9,913	9,223	3,479	3,249	3,671	4,290	4,13[illegible]
Christian	6,707	3,374	3,333	1,243	1,204	1,192	1,285	1,2[illegible]
Clarke	13,667	7,050	6,617	2,351	2,290	2,510	3,107	3,0[illegible]
Clay	15,564	8,079	7,485	2,750	2,770	3,085	3,626	[illegible]
Clinton	14,063	7,582	6,481	2,313	2,198	3,291	3,681	[illegible]
Cole	10,292	5,595	4,697	1,700	1,500	2,442	2,744	[illegible]
Cooper	20,692	10,664	10,028	3,568	3,510	3,975	4,842	[illegible]
Crawford	7,982	4,089	3,893	1,455	1,390	1,450	1,646	[illegible]
Dade	8,683	4,430	4,253	1,543	1,543	1,640	1,8[illegible]	[illegible]
Dallas	8,383	4,279	4,104	1,587	484	1,424	1,686	[illegible]
Daviess	14,410	7,497	6,913	2,575	2,[illegible]14	2,699	3,122	[illegible]
De Kalb	9,858	5,277	4,581	1,778	1,569	2,636	2,283	2,1[illegible]
Dent	6,357	3,256	3,101	1,209	1,[illegible]	1,044	1,172	1,1[illegible]
Douglas	3,915	1,941	1,974	749	692	590	664	636

—*School, Military, and Citizenship Ages, &c., by Counties*—1870—Continued.

STATE OF MISSOURI—Continued.

ies.	All ages.			5 to 18.		18 to 45.	21 and upward.	
	Total.	Male.	Female.	Male.	Female.	Male.	Male.	Male citizens.
	5, 982	3, 092	2, 890	1, 148	1, 077	1, 143	1, 160	1, 100
	30, 098	15, 769	14, 329	5, 900	5, 375	5, 437	6, 339	6, 029
	10, 093	5, 312	4, 781	1, 864	1, 730	1, 773	2, 312	2, 138
	11, 607	6, 019	5, 588	2, 100	1, 992	2, 142	2, 484	2, 445
	21, 549	10, 974	10, 575	3, 520	3, 556	4, 419	4, 920	4, 763
	10, 567	5, 441	5, 126	1, 857	1, 787	2, 078	2, 369	2, 110
	14, 635	7, 578	7, 057	2, 755	2, 588	2, 542	3, 002	2, 974
	17, 401	9, 129	8, 272	2, 846	2, 799	3, 735	4, 257	4, 172
	6, 452	3, 302	3, 150	1, 144	1, 117	1, 208	1, 325	1, 307
	11, 652	6, 173	5, 479	1, 988	1, 908	2, 476	2, 793	2, 633
	17, 233	8, 977	8, 256	3, 257	3, 004	3, 211	3, 750	3, 738
	4, 218	2, 150	2, 068	795	776	725	800	793
	6, 278	3, 148	3, 130	1, 065	1, 117	1, 170	1, 359	1, 282
	55, 041	30, 282	24, 759	8, 578	8, 019	14, 633	15, 722	14, 652
	14, 928	7, 893	7, 035	2, 510	2, 392	3, 231	3, 665	3, 576
	15, 380	8, 146	7, 234	2, 785	2, 576	2, 905	3, 649	3, 505
	24, 648	12, 662	11, 986	4, 110	3, 983	5, 017	5, 858	5, 798
	10, 974	5, 735	5, 239	1, 999	1, 866	2, 031	2, 409	2, 190
	9, 380	4, 724	4, 656	1, 667	1, 665	1, 700	1, 913	1, 865
	22, 623	11, 689	10, 934	3, 933	3, 901	4, 487	5, 407	5, 280
	13, 067	6, 634	6, 433	2, 280	2, 203	2, 459	2, 758	2, 713
	15, 114	7, 849	7, 265	2, 782	2, 550	2, 820	3, 442	3, 405
	15, 960	8, 281	7, 679	2, 872	2, 691	3, 022	3, 593	3, 574
	15, 900	8, 219	7, 681	2, 738	2, 686	3, 154	3, 696	3, 588
	16, 730	8, 793	7, 937	2, 843	2, 718	3, 526	4, 079	3, 911
	23, 230	11, 934	11, 296	3, 946	3, 879	4, 557	5, 313	5, 150
	5, 849	3, 015	2, 834	966	994	1, 227	1, 379	1, 374
	5, 916	3, 019	2, 897	1, 138	1, 068	1, 005	1, 178	1, 131
	23, 7[illegible]0	12, 282	11, 408	3, 763	3, 818	5, 097	6, 140	5, 970
	5, [illegible]	2, 667	2, 559	987	922	919	1, 062	1, 061
	11, 557	5, 948	5, 609	2, 202	2, 085	1, 927	2, 277	2, 238
	6, 616	3, 404	3, 212	1, 196	1, 154	1, 189	1, 358	1, 329
	4, 982	2, 692	2, 290	872	798	1, 256	1, 332	1, 018
	11, 375	5, 756	5, 619	2, 025	2, 059	2, 064	2, 465	2, 419
	17, 149	9, 014	8, 135	3, 075	2, 810	3, 364	4, 005	3, 908
	10, 405	5, 272	5, 133	1, 753	1, 779	1, 992	2, 372	2, 306
	8, 434	4, 297	4, 137	1, 610	1, 452	1, 426	1, 763	1, 753
	6, 357	3, 380	2, 977	1, 147	1, 040	1, 404	1, 440	1, 410
	12, 821	6, 689	6, 132	2, 296	2, 156	2, 468	2, 847	2, 816
	14, 751	7, 819	6, 932	2, 572	2, 365	3, 055	3, 487	3, 418
	3, 287	1, 683	1, 604	632	597	537	642	641
	10, 793	5, 641	5, 152	1, 936	1, 831	2, 004	2, 452	2, 148
	3, 363	1, 658	1, 705	622	602	537	592	587
	2, 059	1, 079	980	377	362	426	402	458
	9, 877	5, 004	4, 873	1, 799	1, 794	1, 752	2, 033	1, 997
	18, 706	9, 882	8, 824	2, 987	2, 984	4, 245	4, 750	4, 586
	10, 506	5, 292	5, 214	1, 854	1, 808	1, 881	2, 201	2, 112
	23, 076	11, 829	11, 247	4, 052	3, 922	4, 439	5, 395	5, 308
	17, 352	9, 114	8, 238	3, 000	3, 007	3, 609	4, 284	4, 135
	12, 445	6, 249	6, 196	2, 197	2, 169	2, 244	2, 523	2, 518
	4, 714	2, 440	2, 274	938	829	845	952	950
	11, 217	5, 651	5, 566	1, 999	2, 045	1, 882	2, 276	2, 273
	10, 510	5, 542	4, 968	1 889	1, 784	2, 029	2, 487	2, 459
	15, 908	8, 220	7, 688	2, 713	2, 702	3, 173	3, 725	3, 643
	18, 700	9, 780	8, 920	3, 428	3, 156	3, 655	4, 213	4, 081
	3, 756	1, 847	1, 909	715	734	613	673	664
	3, 175	1, 572	1, 603	642	600	506	577	574
	21, 672	11, 307	10, 365	3, 803	3, 653	4, 385	5, 031	4, 892
	8, 820	4, 499	4, 321	1, 543	1, 582	1, 613	1, 884	1, 855
	10, 670	5, 487	5, 183	2, 013	1, 859	1, 901	2, 313	2, 182
	7, 317	3, 886	3, 431	1, 287	1, 240	1, 590	1, 734	1, 658
	2, 339	1, 152	1, 187	444	422	389	432	437
	10, 119	5, 273	4, 846	1, 835	1, 627	1, 961	2, 342	2, 193
	21, 304	11, 346	9, 958	3, 538	3, 301	4, 513	5, 473	5, 005
	6, 742	3, 445	3, 297	1, 191	1, 200	1, 243	1, 456	1, 442
	8, 384	4, 257	4, 127	1, 566	1, 499	1, 427	1, 804	1, 766
	9, 742	5, 199	4, 543	1, 676	1, 656	2, 110	2, 427	2, 004
	351, 189	183, 356	167, 833	53, 461	52, 775	80, 560	93, 949	77, 085
	8, 535	4, 328	4, 207	1, 628	1, 508	1, 531	1, 657	1, 647
	3, 253	1, 632	1, 621	590	574	567	614	598
	11, 907	6, 078	5, 829	2, 151	2, 113	2, 102	2, 425	2, 412
	4, 407	2, 241	2, 166	870	827	718	811	803
	9, 618	4, 935	4, 683	1, 922	1, 680	1, 647	1, 838	1, [illegible]

TABLE LVII.—*School, Military, and Citizenship Ages, &c., by Counties*—1870—Continued.

STATE OF MISSOURI—Continued.

Counties.	All ages.			5 to 18.		18 to 45.	21 and upward.	
	Total.	Male.	Female.	Male.	Female.	Male.	Male.	Male citizens.
Vernon	11,247	6,038	5,209	1,910	1,827	2,512	2,764	2,719
Warren	9,673	5,219	4,454	1,788	1,629	1,951	2,307	2,088
Washington	11,719	5,868	5,851	1,986	2,096	2,140	2,530	2,339
Wayne	6,068	3,098	2,970	1,185	1,090	1,087	1,169	1,127
Webster	10,434	5,276	5,158	1,876	1,750	1,813	2,051	2,031
Worth	5,004	2,593	2,411	925	881	891	1,019	1,015
Wright	5,684	2,932	2,752	1,039	976	1,042	1,129	1,097

TERRITORY OF MONTANA.

Counties.	Total.	Male.	Female.	Male, 5 to 18.	Female, 5 to 18.	Male, 18 to 45.	Male, 21 and upward.	Male citizens.
The Territory	20,595	16,771	3,824	1,134	967	12,418	13,424	11,522
Beaver Head	722	597	125	46	31	481	523	533
Big Horn	38	26	12			26	26	26
Choteau	517	414	103	22	25	349	364	336
Dawson	177	158	19	2	1	141	149	136
Deer Lodge	4,367	3,773	594	160	127	2,466	2,730	2,622
Gallatin	1,578	1,190	388	134	93	878	917	775
Jefferson	1,531	1,241	290	99	74	969	1,004	869
Lewis and Clarke	5,040	3,998	1,042	292	253	3,250	3,404	2,445
Madison	2,684	1,974	710	183	199	1,132	1,303	1,243
Meagher	1,387	1,162	225	83	66	922	1,007	930
Missoula	2,554	2,238	316	114	98	1,804	1,997	1,627

STATE OF NEBRASKA.

Counties.	Total.	Male.	Female.	Male, 5 to 18.	Female, 5 to 18.	Male, 18 to 45.	Male, 21 and upward.	Male citizens.
The State	122,993	70,425	52,568	17,779	16,744	35,677	39,080	36,169
Adams	19	12	7	2	1	7	7	7
Blackbird	31	19	12	8		7	9	9
Buffalo	193	139	54	22	21	101	94	73
Burt	2,847	1,550	1,297	434	449	665	766	760
Butler	1,290	705	585	182	199	340	374	356
Cass	8,151	4,699	3,452	1,210	1,162	2,290	2,522	2,454
Cedar	1,032	588	444	159	146	261	300	295
Cheyenne	190	148	42	11	6	128	122	118
Clay	54	32	22	10	9	15	18	18
Colfax	1,424	825	599	179	170	436	489	484
Cuming	2,964	1,694	1,270	519	415	757	844	761
Dakota	2,040	1,103	937	347	349	445	546	541
Dawson	103	76	27	16	12	56	59	47
Dixon	1,345	738	607	197	208	314	384	363
Dodge	4,212	2,368	1,844	577	499	1,205	1,360	1,283
Douglas	19,982	12,049	7,933	2,008	2,103	7,976	8,249	7,408
Fillmore	238	131	107	25	32	68	72	67
Franklin	26	21	5	2		17	19	14
Gage	3,359	1,881	1,478	545	497	838	919	887
Grant	484	395	89	23	18	342	338	302
Hall	1,057	647	410	122	126	367	396	356
Hamilton	130	83	47	18	9	40	48	43
Harrison	631	488	143	47	35	395	384	346
Jackson	9	9				9	8	7
Jefferson	2,440	1,417	1,023	363	332	702	774	744
Johnson	3,429	1,800	1,629	571	576	731	842	815
Kearney	58	43	15	4	5	36	36	31
Lancaster	7,074	4,269	2,805	934	872	2,378	2,571	2,067
L'Eau qui Court	261	144	117	36	32	69	80	78
Lincoln	17	15	2			14	15	12
Lyon	78	72	6		1	70	67	54
Madison	1,133	659	474	176	150	303	356	269
Merrick	557	341	216	63	64	180	211	200
Monroe	235	202	33	8	11	178	178	129
Nemaha	7,593	4,057	3,536	1,233	1,201	1,696	1,951	1,883
Nuckolls	8	4	4		2	2	3	2
Otoe	12,345	6,802	5,543	2,043	1,880	3,109	3,438	3,337

VII.—*School, Military, and Citizenship Ages, &c., by Counties*—1870—Continued.

STATE OF NEBRASKA—Continued.

ounties.	All ages.			5 to 18.		18 to 45.	21 and upward.	
	Total.	Male.	Female.	Male.	Female.	Male.	Male.	Male citizens.
....	4, 171	2, 222	1, 949	701	677	889	1, 019	987
....	152	83	69	24	29	45	49	49
....	1, 899	1, 154	745	249	217	611	685	590
....	136	83	53	18	15	42	42	42
ı	9, 780	5, 400	4, 380	1, 782	1, 534	2, 146	2, 398	2, 357
....	3, 106	1, 715	1, 391	509	460	716	840	796
....	2, 913	1, 753	1, 160	463	392	888	942	751
....	4, 547	2, 582	1, 965	594	578	1, 335	1, 472	1, 232
....	2, 953	1, 703	1, 250	453	363	786	801	878
....	636	345	291	110	94	149	166	151
....	97	84	13	6	2	70	72	52
on	4, 452	2, 451	2, 001	622	629	1, 124	1, 282	1, 253
....	182	101	81	19	27	50	62	61
....	16	8	8	....	2	7	7	4
....	604	330	274	87	90	163	183	183
zed Northwest y	52	49	3	....	1	47	45	45
ed Territory west on County........	183	99	84	30	30	44	54	54
Indian reservation	31	20	11	4	3	10	14	14
dian reservation.	44	18	26	5	9	8	8	7

STATE OF NEVADA.

ounties.	All ages: Total.	All ages: Male.	All ages: Female.	5 to 18: Male.	5 to 18: Female.	18 to 45: Male.	21 and upward: Male.	21 and upward: Male citizens.
ate..............	42, 491	32, 379	10, 112	2, 762	2, 575	24, 762	26, 920	18, 652
....	196	142	54	21	12	98	103	92
....	1, 215	886	329	145	102	570	620	306
....	3, 447	2, 776	671	175	158	2, 205	2, 406	1, 832
....	1, 553	1, 253	300	92	82	1, 003	1, 092	743
....	1, 916	1, 548	368	122	89	1, 208	1, 306	960
....	2, 815	2, 204	611	142	136	1, 734	1, 878	1, 455
....	2, 985	2, 119	866	320	300	1, 416	1, 536	1, 248
....	1, 837	1, 389	448	122	114	1, 036	1, 121	694
....	1, 087	887	200	49	44	680	779	693
....	3, 668	2, 798	870	267	219	2, 068	2, 214	1, 085
....	133	115	18	10	7	87	90	80
....	11, 359	7, 864	3, 495	760	835	5, 844	6, 284	4, 334
....	3, 091	2, 173	918	256	254	1, 562	1, 697	1, 175
....	7, 189	6, 225	964	272	223	5, 251	5, 794	3, 935

STATE OF NEW HAMPSHIRE.

ounties.	All ages: Total.	All ages: Male.	All ages: Female.	5 to 18: Male.	5 to 18: Female.	18 to 45: Male.	21 and upward: Male.	21 and upward: Male citizens.
ate..............	318, 300	155, 640	162, 660	40, 073	38, 693	60, 684	91, 016	83, 361
....	17, 681	8, 588	9, 093	2, 120	1, 960	3, 294	5, 240	5, 007
....	17, 332	8, 758	8, 574	2, 468	2, 145	2, 920	4, 066	4, 906
....	27, 265	13, 653	13, 612	3, 537	3, 330	5, 169	7, 903	7, 377
....	14, 932	7, 955	6, 977	2, 032	1, 949	3, 450	4, 453	3, 717
....	39, 103	19, 816	19, 287	5, 049	4, 693	7, 625	11, 614	10, 805
gh................	64, 238	30, 021	34, 217	7, 566	7, 807	12, 504	17, 643	15, 218
....	42, 151	20, 718	21, 433	5, 166	4, 960	8, 086	12, 340	11, 333
n................	47, 297	22, 853	24, 444	6, 074	5, 829	8, 495	13, 314	12, 568
....	30, 243	14, 448	15, 795	3, 854	3, 883	5, 956	8, 310	7, 323
....	18, 058	8, 830	9, 228	2, 207	2, 137	3, 185	5, 233	7, 017

TABLE LVII.—*School, Military, and Citizenship Ages, &c., by Counties*—1870—Continued.

STATE OF NEW JERSEY.

Counties.	All ages.			5 to 18.		18 to 45.	21 and upward.	
	Total.	Male.	Female.	Male.	Female.	Male.	Male.	Male citizens.
The State	906, 096	449, 672	456, 424	132, 049	130, 813	180, 067	231, 862	[illegible]
Atlantic	14, 093	7, 167	6, 926	2, 270	2, 250	2, 511	3, 000	[illegible]
Bergen	30, 122	15, 113	15, 009	4, 158	4, 112	6, 117	8, 211	[illegible]
Burlington	53, 639	26, 175	27, 464	7, 953	7, 938	10, 036	13, 510	[illegible]
Camden	46, 193	22, 704	23, 489	6, 869	6, 713	8, 095	11, 399	[illegible]
Cape May	8, 349	4, 135	4, 214	1, 233	1, 255	1, 540	2, 153	[illegible]
Cumberland	34, 665	17, 626	17, 039	5, 500	5, 225	6, 896	8, 833	[illegible]
Essex	143, 839	70, 058	73, 781	20, 222	20, 333	28, 711	36, 137	[illegible]
Gloucester	21, 562	11, 044	10, 518	3, 439	3, 133	4, 173	5, 494	[illegible]
Hudson	129, 067	64, 022	65, 045	17, 741	18, 195	28, 360	33, 522	[illegible]
Hunterdon	36, 963	18, 320	18, 643	5, 290	5, 338	7, 150	9, 679	[illegible]
Mercer	46, 386	22, 837	23, 549	6, 942	6, 650	9, 001	11, 687	[illegible]
Middlesex	45, 029	22, 427	22, 602	6, 700	6, 479	8, 674	11, 584	[illegible]
Monmouth	46, 195	23, 001	23, 194	7, 031	7, 024	8, 840	11, 503	[illegible]
Morris	43, 137	21, 767	21, 370	6, 313	6, 204	8, 701	11, 377	[illegible]
Ocean	13, 628	7, 042	6, 586	2, 219	1, 985	2, 507	3, 498	[illegible]
Passaic	46, 416	22, 985	23, 431	6, 532	6, 780	9, 543	11, 891	[illegible]
Salem	23, 940	12, 085	11, 855	3, 827	3, 604	4, 542	6, 009	[illegible]
Somerset	23, 510	11, 615	11, 895	3, 392	3, 306	4, 356	6, 162	[illegible]
Sussex	23, 168	11, 663	11, 505	3, 629	3, 470	4, 430	5, 906	[illegible]
Union	41, 859	20, 161	21, 698	5, 445	5, 720	8, 536	10, 909	[illegible]
Warren	34, 336	17, 725	16, 611	5, 344	5, 009	7, 148	8, 943	[illegible]

TERRITORY OF NEW MEXICO.

Counties.	Total.	Male.	Female.	Male, 5 to 18.	Female, 5 to 18.	Male, 18 to 45.	Male, 21 and upward.	Male citizens.
The State	91, 874	47, 135	44, 739	14, 440	14, 872	20, 070	23, 332	22, 443
Bernalillo	7, 591	3, 727	3, 864	1, 216	1, 227	1, 402	1, 785	1, 776
Colfax	1, 992	1, 290	702	185	206	904	931	[illegible]
Doña-Aña	5, 864	2, 875	2, 989	813	919	1, 345	1, 522	[illegible]
Grant	1, 143	850	293	69	59	671	708	[illegible]
Lincoln	1, 803	1, 064	739	214	209	629	693	[illegible]
Mora	8, 056	4, 291	3, 765	1, 293	1, 335	1, 887	2, 157	2, 100
Rio Arriba	9, 294	4, 570	4, 724	1, 580	1, 630	1, 579	1, 971	1, 957
San Miguel	16, 058	8, 305	7, 753	2, 673	2, 596	3, 336	3, 874	[illegible]
Santa Aña	2, 599	1, 278	1, 321	439	422	446	557	[illegible]
Santa Fé	9, 699	4, 742	4, 957	1, 386	1, 651	2, 007	2, 374	[illegible]
Socorro	6, 603	3, 412	3, 191	1, 093	1, 074	1, 543	1, 689	1, 565
Taos	12, 079	5, 960	6, 119	2, 085	2, 163	2, 188	2, 684	2, 661
Valencia	9, 093	4, 771	4, 322	1, 304	1, 381	2, 133	2, 367	2, 304

STATE OF NEW YORK.

Counties.	Total.	Male.	Female.	Male, 5 to 18.	Female, 5 to 18.	Male, 18 to 45.	Male, 21 and upward.	Male citizens.
The State	4, 382, 759	2, 163, 229	2, 219, 530	613, 659	617, 329	881, 500	1, 158, 901	981, 567
Albany	133, 052	64, 775	68, 277	19, 021	19, 624	26, 216	33, 938	[illegible]
Allegany	40, 814	20, 493	20, 321	5, 950	5, 903	7, 711	10, 895	[illegible]
Broome	44, 103	22, 019	22, 084	6, 017	6, 007	8, 813	12, 063	[illegible]
Cattaraugus	43, 909	22, 178	21, 731	6, 525	6, 530	8, 322	11, 630	[illegible]
Cayuga	59, 550	29, 953	29, 597	7, 793	7, 804	12, 348	17, 193	[illegible]
Chautauqua	59, 327	29, 501	29, 826	8, 396	8, 336	11, 420	16, 071	[illegible]
Chemung	35, 281	17, 588	17, 693	5, 040	5, 012	7, 000	9, 379	[illegible]
Chenango	40, 564	20, 379	20, 185	5, 095	5, 044	8, 382	12, 016	[illegible]
Clinton	47, 947	24, 320	23, 627	7, 986	7, 705	8, 440	11, 435	[illegible]
Columbia	47, 044	23, 001	24, 043	6, 368	6, 267	8, 838	12, 626	[illegible]
Cortland	25, 173	12, 549	12, 624	3, 278	3, 257	4, 960	7, 115	[illegible]
Delaware	42, 972	21, 929	21, 043	6, 095	5, 747	8, 577	11, 974	[illegible]
Dutchess	74, 041	36, 368	37, 673	10, 017	10, 160	14, 775	20, 039	[illegible]
Erie	178, 699	89, 530	89, 169	28, 277	28, 250	33, 209	44, 284	[illegible]
Essex	29, 042	14, 719	14, 323	4, 385	4, 461	5, 487	7, 518	6, 772
Franklin	30, 271	14, 991	15, 280	4, 968	4, 822	5, 108	7, 106	6, 126
Fulton	27, 064	13, 349	13, 715	3, 866	3, 849	5, 130	7, 009	6, 678
Genesee	31, 606	15, 703	15, 903	4, 648	4, 397	5, 673	8, 481	7, 654
Greene	31, 832	15, 555	16, 277	4, 344	4, 489	5, 922	8, 550	8, 174
Hamilton	2, 960	1, 638	1, 322	449	396	683	863	774

VII.—*School, Military, and Citizenship Ages, &c., by Counties*—1870—Continued.

STATE OF NEW YORK—Continued.

Counties.	All ages.			5 to 18.		18 to 45.	21 and upward.	
	Total.	Male.	Female.	Male.	Female.	Male.	Male.	Male citizens.
	30,929	20,152	10,777	5,366	5,043	8,196	11,383	10,158
	65,415	32,434	32,981	8,893	8,589	12,644	17,779	15,973
	419,921	202,024	217,897	57,768	59,951	85,694	105,561	83,551
	28,699	14,762	13,937	4,339	4,132	5,554	7,781	7,066
n	38,309	18,919	19,390	5,429	5,439	7,061	10,104	9,115
	43,522	21,920	21,602	5,665	5,557	8,870	12,771	11,769
	117,868	58,105	59,763	17,538	17,499	22,057	29,953	24,792
ery	34,457	17,293	17,164	4,768	4,799	7,062	9,561	8,375
k	942,292	457,117	485,175	122,626	127,727	213,937	249,890	188,276
	50,437	25,010	25,427	7,531	7,602	9,258	12,829	10,634
	110,008	54,022	55,986	15,053	15,318	20,800	29,493	25,964
	104,183	51,960	52,223	14,583	14,578	20,841	28,263	23,646
	45,108	22,348	22,760	6,019	5,970	8,617	12,388	11,263
	80,902	40,146	40,756	11,334	11,220	16,439	21,546	19,062
	27,689	13,752	13,937	3,846	3,802	5,237	7,566	6,964
	77,941	38,907	39,034	11,553	11,580	14,644	20,474	18,173
	48,967	24,432	24,535	6,347	6,038	9,540	14,109	13,498
	15,420	7,652	7,768	2,037	2,138	3,118	4,330	3,659
	73,803	36,717	37,086	10,628	10,593	14,449	19,559	16,019
er	99,549	48,731	50,818	13,956	14,175	19,692	26,200	22,622
d	33,029	16,164	16,865	4,499	4,672	6,296	8,670	7,317
	25,213	12,798	12,415	3,668	3,679	5,121	6,834	5,489
	51,529	25,267	26,262	7,161	7,058	9,260	13,724	12,646
ndy	21,347	10,481	10,866	2,920	3,026	4,001	5,620	5,062
	33,340	16,603	16,737	4,824	4,683	6,236	8,838	8,643
	18,989	9,370	9,619	2,472	2,414	3,661	5,368	5,196
	27,823	13,691	14,132	3,931	3,824	5,201	7,407	7,625
	67,717	34,048	33,669	10,155	9,901	12,903	17,686	16,636
nce	84,826	42,007	42,819	13,088	12,932	15,034	20,806	17,612
	46,924	23,295	23,629	6,708	6,504	8,525	12,689	11,885
	34,550	17,908	16,642	5,775	5,528	6,309	8,804	7,912
	30,572	15,250	15,322	4,085	4,083	6,049	8,577	8,256
s	33,178	16,592	16,586	4,182	4,068	6,983	9,507	9,034
	84,075	42,612	41,463	13,256	13,030	16,413	21,447	19,625
	22,592	11,440	11,152	3,473	3,428	4,275	5,859	5,335
ton	49,568	25,068	24,500	6,983	6,792	9,641	13,566	11,422
	47,710	23,715	23,995	6,746	6,630	8,836	13,025	11,891
ster	131,348	65,739	65,609	19,374	18,821	26,858	34,833	29,055
g	29,164	14,514	14,650	4,040	3,956	5,286	8,022	7,462
	19,595	9,726	9,869	2,522	2,430	3,888	5,502	5,228

STATE OF NORTH CAROLINA.

Counties.	Total.	Male.	Female.	Male.	Female.	Male.	Male.	Male citizens.
State	1,071,361	518,704	552,657	182,421	177,500	174,825	217,813	214,294
e	11,874	5,598	6,276	1,915	1,963	1,858	2,474	2,470
r	6,868	3,183	3,685	1,134	1,125	978	1,228	1,218
y	3,691	1,831	1,860	698	627	548	691	691
	12,428	5,910	6,518	2,125	2,134	1,945	2,360	2,339
	9,573	4,651	4,922	1,798	1,692	1,403	1,773	1,756
	13,011	6,487	6,524	2,150	2,025	2,395	2,964	2,942
	12,950	6,181	6,769	2,177	2,094	2,118	2,627	2,605
	12,831	6,372	6,459	2,252	2,175	2,132	2,618	2,610
k	7,754	3,808	3,946	1,272	1,340	1,328	1,700	1,700
o	15,412	7,519	7,893	2,706	2,630	2,495	3,021	3,009
	9,777	4,601	5,176	1,754	1,692	1,355	1,770	1,757
	11,954	5,762	6,192	2,036	1,931	1,995	2,385	2,381
	8,476	3,954	4,522	1,513	1,512	1,176	1,490	1,488
	5,361	2,738	2,623	918	799	993	1,262	1,255
	9,010	4,472	4,538	1,461	1,430	1,682	2,072	2,071
	16,081	7,896	8,185	2,740	2,649	2,594	3,402	3,357
	10,984	5,093	5,891	1,853	1,972	1,572	2,044	1,971
	19,723	9,518	10,205	3,394	3,332	3,079	4,008	3,955
	8,080	3,903	4,177	1,480	1,444	1,181	1,444	1,440
	6,450	3,049	3,401	998	1,053	1,073	1,391	1,367
	2,461	1,225	1,236	432	396	401	498	496
nd	12,696	6,052	6,644	2,292	2,140	1,875	2,336	2,231
s	8,474	4,436	4,038	1,535	1,504	1,498	1,842	1,674
	20,516	9,842	10,674	2,986	3,036	3,833	4,849	4,816

TABLE LVII.—*School, Military, and Citizenship Ages, &c., by Counties—1870*—Continued.

STATE OF NORTH CAROLINA—Continued.

Counties.	All ages.			5 to 18.		18 to 45.	21 and upward.	
	Total.	Male.	Female.	Male.	Female.	Male.	Male.	Male citizens.
Cumberland	17,035	8,106	8,929	2,839	2,882	2,732	3,400	[illegible]
Currituck	5,131	2,640	2,491	1,013	853	954	1,131	[illegible]
Dare	2,778	1,406	1,372	454	399	332	636	[illegible]
Davidson	17,414	8,415	8,999	2,986	2,869	2,700	3,497	[illegible]
Davie	9,620	4,637	4,983	1,662	1,667	1,515	1,880	[illegible]
Duplin	15,542	7,506	7,946	2,865	2,656	2,380	2,998	[illegible]
Edgecombe	22,970	11,572	11,398	3,482	3,405	4,716	5,988	[illegible]
Forsyth	13,050	6,016	7,034	2,114	2,278	1,867	2,573	[illegible]
Franklin	14,134	6,854	7,280	2,400	2,272	2,146	2,788	[illegible]
Gaston	12,602	5,951	6,651	2,134	1,983	1,883	2,179	[illegible]
Gates	7,724	3,677	4,047	1,428	1,357	1,118	1,443	[illegible]
Granville	24,831	11,972	12,859	4,307	4,112	3,885	5,057	[illegible]
Greene	8,687	4,254	4,433	1,478	1,395	1,478	1,742	[illegible]
Guilford	21,736	10,253	11,483	3,693	3,685	3,354	4,494	[illegible]
Halifax	20,408	10,106	10,302	3,308	3,110	3,700	4,851	[illegible]
Harnett	8,895	4,411	4,484	1,634	1,520	1,424	1,758	[illegible]
Haywood	7,921	3,835	4,086	1,407	1,418	1,290	1,467	[illegible]
Henderson	7,706	3,751	3,955	1,400	1,277	1,168	1,488	[illegible]
Hertford	9,273	4,410	4,863	1,630	1,650	1,444	1,805	[illegible]
Hyde	6,445	3,293	3,152	1,150	1,053	1,168	1,413	1,411
Iredell	16,931	7,908	9,023	2,810	2,745	2,503	3,338	[illegible]
Jackson	6,683	3,298	3,385	1,198	1,214	1,070	1,283	[illegible]
Johnston	16,897	8,358	8,545	2,938	2,787	2,819	3,436	[illegible]
Jones	5,002	2,510	2,492	787	710	940	1,156	[illegible]
Lenoir	10,434	5,084	5,350	1,703	1,726	1,781	2,131	[illegible]
Lincoln	9,573	4,472	5,101	1,632	1,641	1,394	1,803	[illegible]
Macon	6,615	3,197	3,418	1,152	1,137	1,057	1,208	[illegible]
Madison	8,192	4,053	4,139	1,546	1,505	1,243	1,402	[illegible]
Martin	9,647	4,842	4,805	1,655	1,503	1,745	2,180	[illegible]
McDowell	7,592	3,913	3,679	1,359	1,210	1,437	1,650	[illegible]
Mecklenburg	24,299	11,869	12,430	3,919	4,048	4,489	5,394	[illegible]
Mitchell	4,705	2,338	2,373	917	884	712	851	887
Montgomery	7,487	3,584	3,903	1,347	1,208	1,154	1,385	[illegible]
Moore	12,040	5,723	6,317	2,049	1,979	1,864	2,453	[illegible]
Nash	11,077	5,266	5,811	1,869	1,907	1,808	2,169	[illegible]
New Hanover	27,978	13,465	14,513	4,143	4,341	5,293	6,443	[illegible]
Northampton	14,749	7,171	7,578	2,455	2,428	2,480	3,153	[illegible]
Onslow	7,569	3,665	3,904	1,234	1,251	1,314	1,600	[illegible]
Orange	17,507	8,218	9,289	2,937	2,766	2,541	3,549	[illegible]
Pasquotank	8,131	4,010	4,121	1,334	1,350	1,446	1,842	[illegible]
Perquimans	7,945	3,927	4,018	1,337	1,285	1,352	1,697	[illegible]
Person	11,170	5,381	5,789	1,959	1,824	1,727	2,187	2,185
Pitt	17,276	8,514	8,762	2,923	2,814	3,059	3,580	[illegible]
Polk	4,319	2,022	2,297	732	702	626	815	812
Randolph	17,551	8,334	9,217	3,004	2,936	2,725	3,522	3,508
Richmond	12,882	6,434	6,448	2,319	2,144	2,201	2,622	2,611
Robeson	16,262	8,009	8,253	2,895	2,753	2,634	3,276	[illegible]
Rockingham	15,708	7,569	8,139	2,804	2,747	2,413	3,075	[illegible]
Rowan	16,810	7,904	8,906	2,805	2,772	2,635	3,433	3,361
Rutherford	13,121	6,169	6,952	2,311	2,297	1,867	2,409	[illegible]
Sampson	16,436	7,954	8,482	3,002	2,872	2,512	3,060	[illegible]
Stanley	8,315	3,930	4,376	1,510	1,466	1,230	1,477	1,471
Stokes	11,208	5,451	5,757	1,977	1,840	1,743	2,235	2,172
Surry	11,252	5,428	5,824	1,943	1,822	1,737	2,273	[illegible]
Transylvania	3,536	1,701	1,835	615	500	555	704	[illegible]
Tyrrell	4,173	2,096	2,077	710	681	745	930	[illegible]
Union	12,217	5,860	6,357	2,172	2,065	1,844	2,208	2,201
Wake	35,617	17,344	18,273	5,719	5,581	6,268	7,738	7,673
Warren	17,768	8,720	9,048	3,010	2,955	2,723	3,503	[illegible]
Washington	6,516	3,131	3,385	982	986	1,154	1,490	[illegible]
Watauga	5,287	2,571	2,716	887	800	839	1,006	[illegible]
Wayne	18,144	8,915	9,229	3,037	2,854	3,310	3,797	[illegible]
Wilkes	15,539	7,258	8,281	2,802	2,738	2,206	2,795	[illegible]
Wilson	12,258	5,916	6,342	2,037	2,018	2,151	2,462	[illegible]
Yadkin	10,697	5,080	5,617	1,860	1,763	1,581	2,023	[illegible]
Yancey	5,909	2,909	3,000	1,105	1,004	927	1,067	[illegible]

LVII.—*School, Military, and Citizenship Ages, &c., by Counties*—1870—Continued.

STATE OF OHIO.

Counties.	All ages.			5 to 18.		18 to 45.	21 and upward.	
	Total.	Male.	Female.	Male.	Female.	Male.	Male.	Male citizens.
State	2,665,260	1,337,550	1,327,710	425,466	420,525	501,750	640,820	592,350
	20,750	10,297	10,453	3,575	3,452	3,466	4,498	4,323
	23,623	11,949	11,674	4,035	3,918	4,222	5,186	4,961
	21,933	10,830	11,103	3,467	3,471	3,988	5,189	5,043
la	32,517	16,071	16,446	4,501	4,545	5,949	8,696	8,092
	23,768	11,955	11,813	3,967	3,897	4,327	5,374	5,227
	20,041	10,275	9,766	3,600	3,447	3,421	4,367	3,894
	39,714	19,730	19,984	6,403	6,322	7,075	9,279	8,904
	30,802	15,221	15,581	5,192	5,275	5,172	6,752	6,636
	39,912	20,017	19,895	6,279	6,487	7,606	9,765	9,071
	14,491	7,195	7,296	2,367	2,226	2,511	3,408	3,145
ign	24,188	12,151	12,037	3,880	3,707	4,601	5,827	5,628
	32,070	16,201	15,869	4,968	4,932	6,512	8,086	7,791
t	34,268	16,887	17,381	5,534	5,433	6,036	8,073	7,601
	21,914	11,064	10,850	3,613	3,489	4,107	5,093	5,044
ana	38,299	19,064	19,235	5,972	5,760	7,094	9,395	8,677
n	23,600	11,808	11,792	4,008	3,806	4,164	5,330	5,111
d	25,556	12,866	12,690	4,165	4,166	4,721	6,074	5,491
n	132,010	66,725	65,285	18,736	19,434	28,015	34,832	25,165
	32,278	16,612	15,666	5,610	5,319	6,021	7,411	7,244
	15,719	8,047	7,672	2,772	2,592	2,702	3,495	3,321
e	25,175	12,748	12,427	4,076	3,802	4,789	6,204	6,069
	28,188	14,252	13,936	4,459	4,470	5,399	6,973	6,292
	31,138	15,762	15,376	5,380	4,943	5,615	7,179	7,048
	17,170	8,847	8,323	2,831	2,748	3,478	4,094	4,035
l	63,019	31,967	31,052	9,837	9,868	13,069	15,810	14,922
	17,789	9,083	8,706	2,953	2,859	3,350	4,303	3,690
	25,545	12,839	12,706	4,475	4,384	4,424	5,503	5,404
	14,190	7,114	7,076	1,798	1,743	2,899	4,146	4,009
	28,038	14,012	14,026	4,643	4,390	5,221	6,799	6,649
y	23,838	11,609	12,229	3,930	3,908	3,946	5,338	5,258
a	260,370	128,530	131,840	38,691	40,024	52,141	64,612	55,130
	23,847	11,943	11,904	4,127	4,031	4,246	5,326	5,106
	18,714	9,545	9,169	3,256	3,105	3,567	4,301	4,180
l	18,682	9,191	9,491	2,950	2,944	3,201	4,332	4,025
	14,028	7,295	6,733	2,475	2,311	2,597	3,226	3,089
l	29,133	14,468	14,665	4,907	4,804	5,081	6,677	6,545
	17,925	8,987	8,938	3,091	3,146	3,125	3,887	3,815
	18,177	9,103	9,074	3,133	2,930	3,164	4,067	3,852
	28,532	14,503	14,029	4,432	4,079	5,352	7,412	6,587
	21,759	11,125	10,634	3,820	3,623	3,946	4,745	4,648
	29,188	14,211	14,977	4,524	4,584	5,188	6,794	5,980
	26,333	13,060	13,273	3,977	3,950	5,073	6,560	6,443
	15,935	7,785	8,150	2,067	2,221	2,977	4,362	4,051
o	31,380	16,030	15,350	5,754	5,428	5,471	6,627	6,541
	35,756	17,526	18,230	5,348	5,505	6,761	8,786	8,275
	23,028	11,469	11,559	3,755	3,734	4,260	5,416	5,236
	30,308	15,158	15,150	4,463	4,498	5,774	7,870	6,936
	46,722	23,673	23,049	7,037	7,360	10,034	12,027	10,641
	15,633	7,991	7,642	2,566	2,486	3,128	3,816	3,767
g	31,001	15,619	15,382	4,668	4,501	6,164	7,803	6,792
	16,184	8,328	7,856	2,765	2,548	3,162	3,900	3,786
	20,092	9,984	10,108	2,958	2,849	3,641	5,229	4,985
	31,465	15,873	15,592	5,449	5,335	5,509	6,946	6,730
	17,254	8,826	8,428	3,091	2,959	2,956	3,726	3,707
	32,740	16,363	16,377	5,262	5,236	6,101	7,815	7,545
	25,779	12,941	12,838	4,593	4,471	4,235	5,468	5,232
nery	64,006	32,800	31,206	9,863	9,636	13,059	16,565	15,368
	20,363	10,073	10,290	3,287	3,159	3,610	4,690	4,863
	18,583	9,228	9,355	2,900	2,811	3,373	4,532	4,350
um	44,886	21,899	22,987	7,346	7,099	7,671	10,155	9,928
	19,949	10,039	9,910	3,537	3,258	3,416	4,278	4,166
	13,364	7,011	6,353	2,309	2,164	2,678	3,319	2,546
	8,544	4,466	4,078	1,577	1,411	1,561	1,912	1,811
	18,453	9,060	9,393	3,180	3,044	3,014	4,062	3,997
y	24,875	12,728	12,147	4,030	3,915	4,983	5,887	5,796
	15,447	7,711	7,736	2,688	2,700	2,541	3,310	3,236
	24,584	12,311	12,273	3,379	3,260	4,830	6,826	6,501
	21,809	10,847	10,962	3,359	3,423	4,118	5,277	5,198
	17,081	8,687	8,394	3,024	2,848	2,968	3,806	3,737

TABLE LVII.—*School, Military, and Citizenship Ages, &c., by Counties*—1870—Continued.

STATE OF OHIO—Continued.

Counties.	All ages.			5 to 18.		18 to 45.	21 and upward.	
	Total.	Male.	Female.	Male.	Female.	Male.	Male.	Male citizens.
Richland	32, 516	16, 195	16, 321	4, 897	5, 001	6, 307	8, 201	[illegible]
Ross	37, 097	18, 406	18, 691	6, 064	6, 030	6, 590	8, 466	[illegible]
Sandusky	25, 503	12, 936	12, 567	4, 175	4, 262	4, 202	6, 108	[illegible]
Scioto	29, 302	14, 785	14, 517	4, 958	4, 910	5, 387	6, 647	[illegible]
Seneca	30, 827	15, 508	15, 319	5, 158	4, 876	5, 598	7, 339	[illegible]
Shelby	20, 748	10, 525	10, 223	3, 521	3, 486	3, 691	4, 765	[illegible]
Stark	52, 508	26, 444	26, 064	8, 134	8, 176	10, 257	12, 809	[illegible]
Summit	34, 674	17, 441	17, 233	4, 922	5, 076	7, 105	9, 086	[illegible]
Trumbull	38, 659	19, 635	19, 024	5, 644	5, 541	7, 758	10, 190	[illegible]
Tuscarawas	33, 840	17, 013	16, 827	5, 513	5, 572	6, 178	7, 771	[illegible]
Union	18, 730	9, 424	9, 306	3, 083	3, 124	3, 570	4, 418	[illegible]
Van Wert	15, 823	8, 136	7, 687	2, 880	2, 738	2, 806	3, 482	[illegible]
Vinton	15, 027	7, 486	7, 541	2, 633	2, 634	2, 491	3, 162	[illegible]
Warren	26, 689	13, 342	13, 347	4, 038	4, 036	5, 093	6, 714	[illegible]
Washington	40, 609	20, 460	20, 149	6, 844	6, 669	7, 146	9, 209	[illegible]
Wayne	35, 116	17, 467	17, 649	5, 398	5, 456	6, 587	8, 571	[illegible]
Williams	20, 991	10, 730	10, 261	3, 689	3, 433	3, 791	4, 884	[illegible]
Wood	24, 596	12, 566	12, 030	4, 006	4, 066	4, 446	5, 718	[illegible]
Wyandot	18, 553	9, 466	9, 087	3, 135	3, 067	3, 472	4, 456	[illegible]

STATE OF OREGON.

Counties.	Total.	Male.	Female.	Male.	Female.	Male.	Male.	Male citizens.
The State	90, 923	53, 131	37, 792	15, 035	14, 365	23, 959	28, 616	[illegible]
Baker	2, 804	2, 152	652	234	205	1, 480	1, 706	[illegible]
Benton	4, 584	2, 548	2, 036	860	786	946	1, 179	[illegible]
Clackamas	5, 993	3, 345	2, 648	1, 043	1, 012	1, 345	1, 610	[illegible]
Clatstop	1, 255	774	481	166	182	391	495	[illegible]
Columbia	863	518	345	133	131	258	301	[illegible]
Coos	1, 644	1, 078	566	218	212	571	694	514
Curry	504	313	191	67	72	154	200	175
Douglas	6, 066	3, 506	2, 560	1, 107	1, 009	1, 395	1, 731	[illegible]
Grant	2, 251	1, 885	366	129	91	1, 484	1, 583	[illegible]
Jackson	4, 778	3, 031	1, 747	680	638	1, 607	1, 901	[illegible]
Josephine	1, 204	827	377	167	139	452	539	[illegible]
Lane	6, 426	3, 514	2, 912	1, 264	1, 173	1, 266	1, 549	[illegible]
Linn	8, 717	4, 709	4, 008	1, 635	1, 656	1, 711	2, 111	2, 073
Marion	9, 965	5, 384	4, 581	1, 694	1, 794	2, 136	2, 643	2, 557
Multnomah	11, 510	6, 800	4, 710	1, 561	1, 539	3, 641	4, 184	[illegible]
Polk	4, 701	2, 597	2, 104	919	809	925	1, 142	[illegible]
Tillamook	408	228	180	65	70	81	125	[illegible]
Umatilla	2, 916	1, 763	1, 153	473	414	861	974	[illegible]
Union	2, 552	1, 547	1, 005	413	367	734	847	734
Wasco	2, 509	1, 480	1, 029	400	371	688	818	737
Washington	4, 261	2, 391	1, 870	868	773	813	1, 047	[illegible]
Yam Hill	5, 012	2, 741	2, 271	939	922	1, 020	1, 237	[illegible]

STATE OF PENNSYLVANIA.

Counties.	Total.	Male.	Female.	Male.	Female.	Male.	Male.	Male citizens.
The State	3,521,951	1,758,499	1,763,452	540,133	535,907	679,506	865, 883	776, 345
Adams	30, 315	14, 879	15, 436	4, 695	4, 606	5, 171	7, 110	7, 023
Allegheny	262, 204	132, 811	129, 393	40, 549	40, 106	53, 838	64, 240	51, 999
Armstrong	43, 382	22, 157	21, 225	7, 442	6, 992	7, 817	9, 787	9, 253
Beaver	36, 148	18, 025	18, 123	6, 041	5, 677	6, 342	8, 327	7, 339
Bedford	29, 635	14, 925	14, 710	5, 052	4, 894	5, 111	6, 607	6, 410
Berks	106, 701	53, 448	53, 253	16, 593	16, 632	19, 583	25, 615	24, 572
Blair	38, 051	18, 878	19, 173	6, 262	6, 331	6, 885	8, 659	8, 155
Bradford	53, 204	26, 926	26, 278	8, 015	7, 955	10, 251	13, 802	12, 865
Bucks	64, 336	32, 235	32, 101	9, 786	9, 116	11, 361	16, 674	16, 010
Butler	36, 510	18, 351	18, 159	6, 335	6, 251	5, 982	8, 269	7, 803
Cambria	36, 569	18, 601	17, 968	6, 380	6, 203	6, 196	8, 003	6, 361
Cameron	4, 273	2, 408	1, 865	617	608	1, 216	1, 361	1, 023
Carbon	28, 144	14, 711	13, 433	4, 546	4, 554	5, 827	7, 067	5, 994

LVII.—*School, Military, and Citizenship Ages, &c., by Counties*—1870—Continued.

STATE OF PENNSYLVANIA—Continued.

Counties.	All ages.			5 to 18.		18 to 45.	21 and upward.	
	Total.	Male.	Female.	Male.	Female.	Male.	Male.	Male citizens.
	34,418	17,313	17,105	5,713	5,643	6,204	7,880	7,335
	77,805	38,594	39,211	11,580	11,044	14,276	19,951	18,768
	26,537	13,539	12,978	4,093	4,617	4,457	5,792	5,588
	25,741	13,492	12,249	4,282	4,194	5,266	6,164	5,798
	23,211	12,109	11,102	3,596	3,625	5,097	5,997	5,736
	28,766	14,325	14,441	4,658	4,608	5,120	6,702	6,088
	63,832	32,750	31,082	9,801	9,506	13,248	16,098	14,837
nd	43,912	21,336	22,576	6,563	6,697	7,992	10,442	9,901
	60,740	30,155	30,585	9,093	9,139	12,023	14,836	13,931
	39,403	19,507	19,896	6,032	5,727	7,677	9,811	9,024
	8,488	4,793	3,695	1,177	1,218	2,266	2,003	1,995
	65,973	33,435	32,538	9,922	9,692	13,115	17,209	14,911
	43,284	21,395	21,889	7,129	6,883	7,583	9,854	9,348
	4,010	2,219	1,791	587	591	1,062	1,150	1,011
	45,365	22,313	23,052	7,097	6,793	7,973	10,477	10,313
	9,360	4,693	4,667	1,586	1,463	1,488	2,073	2,056
	25,887	12,935	12,952	4,403	4,288	4,563	5,780	5,709
on	31,251	15,499	15,752	5,251	5,228	5,299	6,981	6,671
	36,138	17,729	18,409	5,980	6,003	5,909	7,941	7,796
	21,656	11,030	10,626	3,815	3,816	3,803	4,625	4,330
	17,390	8,697	8,693	3,146	2,964	2,803	3,708	3,664
	121,340	59,172	62,168	18,788	19,032	21,132	28,569	27,619
	27,298	13,440	13,858	4,451	4,450	4,655	6,215	5,814
	34,006	16,806	17,290	5,191	5,162	6,070	8,196	8,016
	56,796	29,047	27,749	8,837	8,618	11,250	14,314	12,647
	160,915	84,785	76,130	24,957	24,307	35,457	41,531	31,017
	47,626	24,227	23,399	7,341	7,377	9,603	11,906	10,976
	8,825	4,598	4,227	1,397	1,341	1,751	2,291	2,063
	49,977	25,413	24,564	8,041	7,830	9,724	12,178	10,275
	17,508	8,677	8,831	2,926	2,773	3,013	3,986	3,456
	18,362	9,401	8,961	3,108	3,039	3,349	4,399	4,214
ery	81,612	40,583	41,029	12,064	11,651	15,318	20,819	19,689
	15,344	7,760	7,584	2,443	2,411	2,920	3,694	3,967
ton	61,432	30,911	30,521	9,615	9,408	11,755	15,164	13,759
erland	41,444	20,971	20,473	6,551	6,473	8,118	9,967	9,046
	25,447	12,778	12,669	4,279	4,163	4,395	5,728	5,575
ia	674,022	390,379	353,643	89,388	93,433	138,526	173,676	149,976
	8,436	4,299	4,137	1,380	1,427	1,484	2,081	1,864
	11,265	5,734	5,531	1,682	1,760	2,125	2,908	2,798
l	116,428	59,555	56,873	19,984	19,738	21,797	26,603	22,433
	15,606	7,773	7,833	2,615	2,544	2,685	3,508	3,487
	28,226	14,411	13,815	4,664	4,681	5,140	6,545	6,056
	6,191	3,262	2,929	1,098	951	1,137	1,486	1,419
nna	37,523	19,172	18,351	5,767	5,413	7,000	9,860	9,143
	35,097	18,034	17,063	5,506	5,323	6,986	9,133	8,100
	15,565	7,651	7,914	2,406	2,338	2,734	3,687	3,652
	47,925	25,625	22,300	6,637	6,697	12,312	13,665	12,314
	23,897	12,813	11,084	3,493	3,366	5,663	6,923	5,954
on	48,483	23,766	24,717	7,455	7,432	8,678	11,692	10,699
	33,188	16,924	16,264	5,534	5,507	5,944	8,001	7,378
land	58,719	29,254	29,465	9,848	9,425	9,814	13,190	12,956
	14,585	7,419	7,166	2,300	2,241	2,797	3,697	3,568
	76,134	37,626	38,508	11,961	11,924	13,250	18,029	17,546

STATE OF RHODE ISLAND.

Counties.	Total.	Male.	Female.	Male.	Female.	Male.	Male.	Male citizens.
State	217,353	104,756	112,597	27,834	27,941	44,377	58,732	43,996
	9,421	4,433	4,988	1,166	1,194	1,795	2,564	2,014
	18,595	8,917	9,678	2,525	2,546	3,426	4,864	3,654
	20,050	9,606	10,444	2,525	2,425	3,899	5,530	4,547
e	149,190	71,840	77,350	18,998	19,102	31,227	40,246	28,702
on	20,097	9,960	10,137	2,020	2,674	4,030	5,548	5,079

TABLE LVII.—*School, Military, and Citizenship Ages, &c., by Counties*—1870—Continued.

STATE OF SOUTH CAROLINA.

Counties.	All ages.			5 to 18.		18 to 45.	21 and upward.	
	Total.	Male.	Female.	Male.	Female.	Male.	Male.	Male citizens.
The State	705,606	343,902	361,704	118,509	115,406	120,151	148,032	146,614
Abbeville	31,129	15,507	15,622	5,657	4,986	5,276	6,127	6,118
Anderson	24,049	11,472	12,577	4,212	4,014	3,606	4,429	4,[illegible]
Barnwell	35,724	18,020	17,704	6,486	5,830	6,270	7,293	7,[illegible]
Beaufort	34,359	16,699	17,660	5,121	5,145	5,983	8,242	8,[illegible]
Charleston	88,863	42,156	46,707	12,660	13,335	16,574	21,396	21,[illegible]
Chester	18,805	9,056	9,749	3,220	3,127	3,029	3,764	3,[illegible]
Chesterfield	10,584	5,128	5,456	1,926	1,832	1,683	2,121	2,[illegible]
Clarendon	14,038	6,876	7,162	2,539	2,416	2,272	2,797	2,773
Colleton	25,410	12,449	12,961	4,058	3,971	4,386	5,656	5,[illegible]
Darlington	26,243	13,837	12,406	4,006	3,858	6,306	6,811	6,[illegible]
Edgefield	42,486	20,760	21,726	7,327	7,177	7,224	8,609	8,[illegible]
Fairfield	19,888	9,742	10,146	3,453	3,330	3,262	4,002	3,[illegible]
Georgetown	16,161	7,688	8,473	2,522	2,552	2,824	3,642	3,[illegible]
Greenville	22,262	10,690	11,572	3,921	3,749	3,331	4,263	4,[illegible]
Horry	10,721	5,268	5,453	1,901	1,918	1,718	2,100	2,[illegible]
Kershaw	11,754	5,746	6,008	2,099	1,954	1,755	2,304	2,[illegible]
Lancaster	12,087	5,853	6,234	2,130	2,014	1,829	2,253	2,[illegible]
Laurens	22,536	10,894	11,642	3,962	3,708	3,612	4,328	4,[illegible]
Lexington	12,988	6,190	6,798	2,254	2,197	2,019	2,541	2,541
Marion	22,160	10,803	11,357	3,902	3,934	3,608	4,251	4,165
Marlborough	11,814	5,894	5,920	2,234	2,037	2,127	2,449	2,[illegible]
Newberry	20,775	10,162	10,613	3,513	3,401	3,552	4,275	4,184
Oconee	10,536	5,034	5,502	1,877	1,809	1,523	1,969	1,[illegible]
Orangeburg	16,865	8,267	8,598	2,864	2,925	2,879	3,456	3,[illegible]
Pickens	10,269	4,898	5,371	1,862	1,782	1,509	1,852	1,[illegible]
Richland	23,025	11,388	11,637	3,502	3,534	4,460	5,578	5,554
Spartanburg	25,784	12,179	13,605	4,514	4,471	3,864	4,889	4,872
Sumter	25,268	12,384	12,884	4,227	4,227	4,186	5,203	5,102
Union	19,248	9,449	9,799	3,497	3,120	3,114	3,785	3,765
Williamsburgh	15,489	7,614	7,875	2,799	2,813	2,472	2,994	2,[illegible]
York	24,286	11,799	12,487	4,235	4,160	3,808	4,741	4,693

STATE OF TENNESSEE.

Counties.	Total.	Male.	Female.	Male (5 to 18).	Female (5 to 18).	Male (18 to 45).	Male (21 and upward).	Male citizens.
The State	1,258,520	623,347	635,173	217,922	211,670	222,903	263,200	259,016
Anderson	8,704	4,357	4,347	1,603	1,443	1,397	1,657	1,622
Bedford	24,333	11,981	12,352	4,338	4,126	4,075	4,923	4,863
Benton	8,234	4,119	4,115	1,565	1,449	1,388	1,567	1,548
Bledsoe	4,870	2,418	2,452	911	840	791	927	920
Blount	14,237	7,077	7,160	2,554	2,366	2,402	2,849	2,829
Bradley	11,652	5,641	6,011	2,018	1,953	1,918	2,347	2,337
Campbell	7,445	3,737	3,708	1,475	1,337	1,161	1,384	1,380
Cannon	10,502	5,151	5,351	1,860	1,876	1,732	2,046	2,042
Carroll	19,447	9,525	9,922	3,341	3,321	3,467	3,922	3,919
Carter	7,909	3,846	4,063	1,420	1,407	1,258	1,511	1,510
Cheatham	6,678	3,339	3,339	1,223	1,166	1,120	1,384	1,380
Claiborne	9,321	4,554	4,767	1,766	1,685	1,403	1,717	1,716
Cocke	12,458	6,012	6,446	2,287	2,252	1,881	2,229	2,214
Coffee	10,237	5,035	5,202	1,818	1,749	1,709	2,088	2,087
Cumberland	3,461	1,713	1,748	674	626	517	654	649
Davidson	62,897	30,996	31,901	9,192	9,684	12,970	15,298	14,156
Decatur	7,772	3,792	3,980	1,455	1,347	1,261	1,425	1,319
De Kalb	11,425	5,642	5,783	2,127	2,066	1,823	2,157	2,148
Dickson	9,340	4,756	4,584	1,677	1,506	1,669	2,042	2,035
Dyer	13,706	6,814	6,892	2,446	2,472	2,492	2,809	2,718
Fayette	26,145	13,165	12,980	4,454	4,331	5,066	5,923	5,821
Fentress	4,717	2,299	2,418	878	831	752	869	855
Franklin	14,970	7,493	7,477	2,808	2,585	2,535	3,015	921
Gibson	25,666	13,163	12,503	4,667	4,249	4,812	5,577	5,515
Giles	32,413	16,176	16,237	5,622	5,206	5,662	6,655	6,596
Grainger	12,421	6,093	6,328	2,300	2,084	1,987	2,405	2,382
Greene	21,668	10,569	11,099	3,791	3,636	3,608	4,319	4,289
Grundy	3,250	1,569	1,681	536	621	564	670	661
Hamilton	17,241	8,655	8,586	2,792	2,663	3,463	3,935	3,894
Hancock	7,148	3,427	3,721	1,314	1,308	1,067	1,249	1,193
Hardeman	18,074	8,929	9,145	3,100	3,103	3,293	3,819	3,786

II.—*School, Military, and Citizenship Ages, &c., by Counties*—1870—Continued.

STATE OF TENNESSEE—Continued.

ntles.	All ages.			5 to 18.		18 to 45.	21 and upward.	
	Total.	Male.	Female.	Male.	Female.	Male.	Male.	Male citizens.
....	11,768	5,743	6,025	2,136	2,117	1,951	2,193	2,189
....	15,837	7,578	8,259	2,755	2,714	2,452	3,020	2,925
....	25,094	12,532	12,562	4,237	4,203	4,645	5,350	5,313
....	14,217	6,974	7,243	2,707	2,590	2,254	2,600	2,566
....	20,380	10,082	10,298	3,616	3,558	3,537	4,178	4,118
....	9,836	4,838	4,998	1,849	1,696	1,554	1,909	1,903
....	9,326	4,640	4,686	1,742	1,600	1,548	1,889	1,875
....	12,583	6,188	6,395	2,395	2,264	1,956	2,341	2,312
....	19,476	9,479	9,997	3,335	3,289	3,152	3,879	3,808
....	5,852	2,855	2,997	1,071	1,044	846	1,078	1,065
....	28,990	14,153	14,837	4,822	4,692	5,153	6,220	6,002
....	2,428	1,291	1,137	424	410	546	581	573
....	10,838	5,552	5,286	1,962	1,829	2,062	2,304	2,287
....	7,601	3,682	3,919	1,373	1,319	1,168	1,425	1,410
....	1,986	961	1,025	372	329	273	355	350
....	28,050	13,936	14,114	5,020	4,722	4,750	5,532	5,475
....	6,633	3,288	3,345	1,156	1,084	1,105	1,345	1,329
....	23,480	11,877	11,603	4,172	3,931	4,602	5,077	5,068
....	6,841	3,396	3,445	1,236	1,187	1,203	1,369	1,351
....	16,207	8,017	8,190	2,847	2,713	2,811	3,305	3,298
....	36,289	17,833	18,456	6,262	6,091	6,159	7,465	7,341
....	13,969	6,714	7,255	2,493	2,479	2,231	2,718	2,711
....	12,726	6,348	6,378	2,281	2,187	2,165	2,504	2,491
....	4,511	2,241	2,270	806	766	732	897	872
....	12,589	6,118	6,471	2,327	2,279	1,986	2,397	2,367
....	24,747	12,219	12,528	4,214	4,167	4,308	5,436	5,391
....	2,969	1,437	1,532	486	512	470	595	590
....	15,584	7,824	7,760	2,812	2,698	2,858	3,255	3,222
....	11,297	5,424	5,873	2,032	2,049	1,693	2,085	2,078
....	6,925	3,438	3,487	1,316	1,176	1,108	1,282	1,271
....	7,369	3,606	3,763	1,310	1,321	1,201	1,407	1,330
....	8,698	4,269	4,429	1,656	1,526	1,327	1,592	1,584
....	5,538	2,722	2,816	1,035	961	855	1,079	1,073
....	15,622	7,660	7,962	2,680	2,696	2,655	3,120	3,062
....	16,166	8,114	8,052	2,916	2,779	2,816	3,458	3,432
....	33,289	16,552	16,737	5,613	5,480	5,922	6,974	6,927
....	4,054	2,028	2,026	771	713	630	720	716
....	2,335	1,171	1,164	411	400	371	456	454
....	11,028	5,393	5,635	2,066	2,088	1,718	1,971	1,946
....	76,378	38,663	37,715	10,462	11,302	18,602	20,903	20,399
....	15,904	7,902	8,002	2,816	2,774	2,620	3,182	3,177
....	12,019	6,130	5,889	2,124	1,997	2,278	2,681	2,671
....	13,136	6,361	6,775	2,204	2,189	2,198	2,749	2,735
....	23,711	11,768	11,943	4,210	3,983	3,970	5,027	5,008
....	14,884	7,586	7,298	2,467	2,347	2,938	3,337	3,295
....	7,605	3,721	3,884	1,351	1,363	1,224	1,432	1,415
....	2,725	1,327	1,398	526	511	423	499	496
....	12,714	6,288	6,426	2,294	2,214	2,054	2,509	2,473
....	16,317	7,951	8,306	2,874	2,787	2,608	3,258	3,240
....	10,209	5,081	5,128	1,880	1,777	1,747	1,949	1,944
....	20,755	10,416	10,339	3,612	3,500	3,688	4,292	4,260
....	9,375	4,581	4,794	1,717	1,593	1,426	1,741	1,722
....	25,328	12,583	12,745	4,225	4,205	4,474	5,336	5,318
....	25,881	12,753	13,128	4,434	4,181	4,575	5,552	5,529

STATE OF TEXAS.

	Total.	Male.	Female.	Male.	Female.	Male.	Male.	Male citizens.
....	818,579	423,557	395,022	145,184	139,667	158,765	184,094	169,238
....	9,229	4,664	4,565	1,737	1,593	1,569	1,883	1,873
....	3,985	1,981	2,004	740	723	644	734	724
....	2,915	1,513	1,402	529	522	559	662	660
....	15,087	7,823	7,264	2,547	2,532	2,800	3,575	3,047
....	649	369	280	109	94	141	164	153
....	12,290	6,467	5,823	2,352	2,134	2,302	2,611	2,425
....	1,082	550	532	195	204	200	225	206
....	9,771	5,099	4,672	1,869	1,743	1,778	2,046	2,038
....	16,043	8,104	7,939	2,893	2,770	2,811	3,502	2,578
ct	1,077	895	182	62	53	765	748	589

TABLE LVII.—*School, Military, and Citizenship Ages, &c., by Counties*—1870—Continued.

STATE OF TEXAS—Continued.

Counties.	All ages.			5 to 18.		18 to 45.	21 and upward.	
	Total.	Male.	Female.	Male.	Female.	Male.	Male.	Male citizens.
Blanco	1,187	625	562	247	216	201	248	241
Bosque	4,981	2,631	2,350	938	868	981	1,085	1,074
Bowie	4,684	2,372	2,312	851	787	864	971	963
Brazoria	7,527	3,913	3,614	1,208	1,153	1,427	1,914	[illegible]
Brazos	9,205	4,726	4,479	1,532	1,555	1,915	2,252	2,167
Brown	544	288	256	107	104	106	112	[illegible]
Burleson	8,072	4,266	3,806	1,398	1,316	1,700	1,871	[illegible]
Burnet	3,688	1,961	1,727	765	655	608	737	[illegible]
Caldwell	6,572	3,374	3,198	1,278	1,191	1,105	1,310	[illegible]
Calhoun	3,443	1,760	1,683	464	546	748	934	[illegible]
Cameron	10,999	5,971	5,028	1,547	1,555	2,970	3,266	[illegible]
Chambers	1,503	770	733	272	262	263	332	[illegible]
Cherokee	11,079	5,556	5,523	2,088	2,004	1,913	2,186	2,176
Coleman	347	217	130	51	45	123	114	114
Collin	14,013	7,246	6,767	2,487	2,439	2,744	3,012	[illegible]
Colorado	8,326	4,258	4,068	1,404	1,435	1,632	1,932	1,785
Comal	5,283	2,788	2,495	1,031	910	823	1,168	911
Comanche	1,001	525	476	209	186	177	206	[illegible]
Cook	5,315	2,794	2,521	1,007	914	1,023	1,141	1,127
Coryell	4,124	2,080	2,044	779	774	696	826	[illegible]
Dallas	13,314	6,900	6,414	2,364	2,297	2,587	2,976	[illegible]
Davis	8,875	4,592	4,283	1,666	1,476	1,512	1,738	[illegible]
Demmit	109	74	35	29	4	29	29	16
Denton	7,251	3,785	3,466	1,301	1,264	1,409	1,597	[illegible]
De Witt	6,443	3,313	3,130	1,195	1,103	1,100	1,387	[illegible]
Duval	1,083	625	458	183	152	250	306	[illegible]
Eastland	88	50	38	12	10	22	22	[illegible]
Ellis	7,514	4,023	3,491	1,308	1,165	1,617	1,768	1,749
El Paso	3,671	2,028	1,643	581	544	967	1,105	[illegible]
Ensinal	427	260	167	76	65	121	148	30
Erath	1,801	941	860	327	315	346	375	365
Falls	9,851	5,122	4,729	1,780	1,732	2,000	2,210	2,975
Fannin	13,207	6,868	6,339	2,454	2,257	2,509	2,811	[illegible]
Fayette	16,863	8,677	8,186	3,137	2,971	2,979	3,682	3,019
Fort Bend	7,114	3,562	3,552	1,054	1,039	1,404	1,765	1,763
Freestone	8,139	4,148	3,991	1,493	1,451	1,488	1,754	1,747
Frio	309	164	145	53	48	73	75	71
Galveston	15,290	7,843	7,447	1,970	2,213	3,846	4,493	3,945
Gillespie	3,566	1,871	1,695	699	691	535	732	[illegible]
Goliad	3,628	1,793	1,835	678	706	590	726	[illegible]
Gonzales	8,951	4,603	4,348	1,680	1,577	1,597	1,858	1,853
Grayson	14,387	7,476	6,911	2,644	2,523	2,829	3,184	3,147
Grimes	13,218	6,954	6,264	2,382	2,138	2,649	3,101	3,056
Guadalupe	7,282	3,771	3,511	1,338	1,314	1,300	1,612	1,565
Hamilton	733	391	342	144	132	141	155	154
Hardin	1,460	740	720	270	257	251	297	285
Harris	17,375	8,762	8,613	2,592	2,702	3,543	4,441	3,903
Harrison	13,241	6,712	6,529	2,241	2,201	2,495	2,926	2,916
Hays	4,088	2,124	1,964	741	699	775	900	854
Henderson	6,786	3,387	3,399	1,239	1,247	1,175	1,297	1,285
Hidalgo	2,387	1,313	1,074	392	356	580	661	112
Hill	7,453	3,867	3,586	1,370	1,358	1,438	1,572	1,553
Hood	2,585	1,362	1,223	487	476	511	595	589
Hopkins	12,651	6,397	6,254	2,353	2,290	2,236	2,512	2,494
Houston	8,147	4,053	4,094	1,509	1,480	1,418	1,632	[illegible]
Hunt	10,291	5,281	5,010	2,104	1,910	1,803	2,020	2,014
Jack	694	374	320	115	121	168	180	170
Jackson	2,278	1,164	1,114	413	384	419	500	481
Jasper	4,218	2,055	2,163	770	764	633	762	738
Jefferson	1,906	956	950	341	348	330	390	379
Johnson	4,923	2,575	2,348	952	850	948	1,053	1,049
Karnes	1,705	959	746	330	274	366	426	423
Kaufman	6,895	3,554	3,341	1,263	1,195	1,299	1,477	1,469
Kendall	1,536	817	719	286	270	279	357	298
Kerr	1,042	598	444	199	151	219	262	236
Kimble	72	41	31	14	7	13	14	11
Kinney	1,204	784	420	119	129	529	553	421
Lamar	15,790	8,025	7,765	2,794	2,768	2,937	3,349	3,291
Lampasas	1,344	724	620	261	219	242	263	263
La Salle	69	43	26	9	8	22	27	12
Lavaca	9,168	4,671	4,497	1,721	1,679	1,618	1,842	1,814
Leon	6,523	3,390	3,133	1,245	1,171	1,198	1,351	1,335

'II.—*School, Military, and Citizenship Ages, &c., by Counties*—1870—Continued.

STATE OF TEXAS—Continued.

unties.	All ages.			5 to 18.		18 to 45.	21 and upward.	
	Total.	Male.	Female.	Male.	Female.	Male.	Male.	Male citizens.
	4,414	2,214	2,200	823	776	746	924	911
	8,591	4,523	4,068	1,579	1,490	1,771	1,978	1,996
	852	497	355	170	124	185	216	162
	1,379	735	644	285	244	230	279	272
	4,061	2,080	1,981	740	712	736	851	851
	8,562	4,453	4,109	1,203	1,301	1,924	2,235	2,078
	678	354	324	194	124	126	156	154
	3,377	1,745	1,632	561	511	648	825	803
	1,951	1,113	838	264	292	626	659	356
	173	97	76	36	31	38	42	42
	13,500	6,880	6,620	2,441	2,422	2,598	3,046	3,006
	230	137	93	41	37	56	62	56
	2,078	1,080	998	368	380	336	457	361
	667	533	134	51	32	439	449	442
	8,984	4,713	4,271	1,677	1,587	1,819	1,955	1,930
	800	487	403	161	152	180	191	190
	6,483	3,338	3,145	1,251	1,112	1,155	1,364	1,348
	9,614	4,806	4,808	1,784	1,728	1,585	1,883	1,871
	8,879	4,623	4,256	1,635	1,603	1,696	1,921	1,908
	2,187	1,101	1,086	418	390	355	421	421
	3,975	2,152	1,823	657	542	891	1,057	696
	1,255	614	641	216	219	227	259	254
	10,119	5,140	4,979	1,895	1,807	1,742	1,981	1,973
	4,186	2,156	2,030	737	742	798	904	897
	8,707	4,305	4,402	1,634	1,590	1,370	1,647	1,636
	1,636	1,142	494	151	142	845	829	575
	10,653	5,382	5,271	1,842	1,810	1,977	2,278	2,270
	2,324	1,259	1,065	388	371	496	687	683
	9,990	5,272	4,718	1,633	1,605	2,379	2,611	2,585
	16,916	8,569	8,347	3,183	3,033	2,963	3,361	3,306
	3,256	1,615	1,641	592	583	509	630	620
no.	4,196	2,092	2,104	798	715	638	792	787
	602	339	263	110	90	138	165	154
	1,425	736	689	276	269	258	287	287
	455	230	225	25	34	179	178	173
	5,732	2,941	2,791	1,064	989	1,005	1,157	1,152
	16,532	8,293	8,239	2,923	2,919	2,939	3,343	3,323
	4,154	2,444	1,710	666	596	1,203	1,317	319
	330	190	140	59	55	88	75	70
	5,788	3,012	2,776	1,066	1,022	1,121	1,263	1,225
	11,339	5,818	5,521	2,054	1,920	2,142	2,345	2,328
	13,153	7,288	5,865	2,061	2,049	3,425	3,832	3,469
	4,141	2,066	2,075	802	741	649	757	749
	5,010	2,554	2,456	1,012	873	784	904	724
	12,039	6,005	6,034	2,197	2,237	2,112	2,372	2,372
	851	476	375	152	132	197	229	174
	6,494	3,290	3,204	1,213	1,215	1,113	1,256	1,219
	4,860	2,415	2,445	830	893	832	1,147	961
	9,776	5,095	4,681	1,636	1,665	1,099	2,348	2,337
	23,104	11,938	11,166	3,811	3,750	4,649	5,522	5,152
	2,615	1,495	1,120	377	352	734	841	415
	3,426	1,720	1,706	511	491	650	816	811
	6,368	3,298	3,070	1,208	1,097	1,141	1,304	1,286
	2,556	1,369	1,187	488	452	456	581	566
	1,450	770	680	282	261	271	297	291
	6,894	3,450	3,444	1,266	1,297	1,248	1,335	1,331
	135	92	43	24	15	45	43	43
	1,488	807	681	246	229	336	380	51
	133	71	62	24	22	34	35	18

TERRITORY OF UTAH.

rritory	86,786	44,121	42,665	15,344	15,072	14,603	18,042	10,147
	2,007	1,010	997	408	381	601	634	326
	4,855	2,842	2,013	724	680	1,070	1,221	816
	8,229	4,068	4,161	1,421	1,404	1,231	1,533	616
	4,459	2,232	2,227	824	836	727	875	348
	2,277	1,123	1,154	407	436	363	450	290
	2,034	1,027	1,007	374	364	300	378	[illegible]

TABLE LVII.—*School, Military, and Citizenship Ages, &c., by Counties—1870*—Continued.

TERRITORY OF UTAH—Continued.

Counties.	All ages.			5 to 18.		18 to 45.	21 and upward.	
	Total.	Male.	Female.	Male.	Female.	Male.	Male.	Male citizens.
Kane	1,513	776	737	341	305	169	240	190
Millard	2,753	1,429	1,324	520	459	434	538	380
Morgan	1,972	995	977	314	369	365	429	133
Piute	82	69	13	7	5	52	57	50
Rich	1,955	1,020	935	330	317	349	399	229
Rio Virgin	430	230	200	101	71	65	83	66
Salt Lake	18,337	9,019	9,318	2,947	3,109	3,072	3,933	2,495
San Pete	6,786	3,274	3,512	1,176	1,215	928	1,294	667
Sevier	19	19	....	5	....	8	12	4
Summit	2,512	1,349	1,163	433	366	516	622	383
Tooele	2,177	1,150	1,018	413	363	371	458	228
Utah	12,203	6,174	6,029	2,207	2,230	1,925	2,388	1,529
Wasatch	1,244	642	602	237	231	203	237	177
Washington	3,064	1,532	1,532	631	615	407	536	400
Weber	7,858	4,112	3,746	1,434	1,316	1,447	1,724	730

STATE OF VERMONT.

Counties.	Total.	Male.	Female.	Male, 5 to 18.	Female, 5 to 18.	Male, 18 to 45.	Male, 21 and upward.	Male citizens.
The State	330,551	165,721	164,830	45,667	44,164	62,459	90,806	74,867
Addison	23,484	11,668	11,816	3,076	3,192	4,338	6,482	5,687
Bennington	21,325	10,678	10,647	2,936	2,868	4,108	5,885	5,173
Caledonia	22,235	11,283	10,952	2,896	2,757	4,372	6,449	4,833
Chittenden	36,480	18,292	18,188	5,665	5,531	7,046	9,164	5,636
Essex	6,811	3,605	3,206	980	883	1,485	1,942	1,455
Franklin	30,291	15,160	15,131	4,568	4,467	5,745	7,651	5,734
Grand Isle	4,082	2,088	1,994	660	640	722	965	793
Lamoille	12,448	6,187	6,261	1,709	1,705	2,260	3,400	3,294
Orange	23,090	11,538	11,552	3,077	2,805	4,043	6,671	6,387
Orleans	21,035	10,724	10,311	3,076	2,974	3,980	5,643	4,709
Rutland	40,651	20,453	20,198	5,780	5,707	7,882	10,885	8,338
Washington	26,520	13,197	13,323	3,633	3,435	4,897	7,364	6,472
Windham	26,036	13,027	13,009	3,148	2,884	4,954	7,872	7,251
Windsor	36,063	17,821	18,242	4,463	4,316	6,627	10,433	9,162

STATE OF VIRGINIA.

Counties.	Total.	Male.	Female.	Male, 5 to 18.	Female, 5 to 18.	Male, 18 to 45.	Male, 21 and upward.	Male citizens.
The State	1,225,163	597,058	628,105	200,103	196,709	206,658	269,242	266,680
Accomack	20,409	10,099	10,310	3,501	3,252	3,495	4,474	4,473
Albemarle	27,544	13,441	14,103	4,496	4,588	4,655	5,986	5,939
Alexandria	16,755	7,819	8,936	2,184	2,496	3,201	4,080	4,027
Alleghany	3,674	1,870	1,804	589	529	668	883	882
Amelia	9,878	4,840	5,038	1,654	1,675	1,611	2,181	2,178
Amherst	14,900	7,365	7,535	2,454	2,386	2,433	3,246	3,173
Appomattox	8,950	4,384	4,566	1,508	1,388	1,400	1,953	1,947
Augusta	28,763	13,996	14,767	4,469	4,538	5,135	6,558	6,542
Bath	3,795	1,954	1,841	614	585	735	931	929
Bedford	25,327	12,422	12,905	4,423	4,127	3,988	5,293	5,281
Bland	4,000	1,955	2,045	695	696	639	813	797
Botetourt	11,329	5,444	5,885	1,826	1,797	1,835	2,476	2,474
Brunswick	13,427	6,506	6,921	2,301	2,263	2,034	2,699	2,686
Buchanan	3,777	1,938	1,839	765	668	521	660	651
Buckingham	13,371	6,558	6,813	2,299	2,195	2,027	2,900	2,856
Campbell	28,384	13,607	14,777	4,450	4,474	4,608	6,371	6,368
Caroline	15,128	7,094	8,034	2,538	2,515	2,264	3,041	3,015
Carroll	9,147	4,407	4,740	1,595	1,601	1,366	1,756	1,727
Charles City	4,975	2,517	2,458	796	784	929	1,911	1,907
Charlotte	14,513	6,992	7,521	2,408	2,515	2,249	3,108	3,093
Chesterfield	18,470	9,023	9,447	2,840	2,844	3,279	4,226	4,236
Clarke	6,670	3,305	3,365	1,080	1,057	1,158	1,498	1,489
Craig	2,942	1,427	1,515	522	483	467	605	601
Culpeper	12,227	6,053	6,174	2,044	1,971	2,026	2,676	2,675
Cumberland	8,142	3,948	4,194	1,329	1,325	1,194	1,765	1,761
Dinwiddie	30,702	14,325	16,377	4,331	4,557	5,379	7,078	7,004
Elizabeth City	8,303	4,258	4,045	1,209	1,184	1,739	2,860	2,001

…VII.—*School, Military, and Citizenship Ages, &c., by Counties*—1870—Continued.

STATE OF VIRGINIA—Continued.

Counties.	All ages.			5 to 18.		18 to 45.	21 and upward.	
	Total.	Male.	Female.	Male.	Female.	Male.	Male.	Male citizens.
	9,927	4,678	5,249	1,710	1,726	1,508	1,989	1,978
	12,952	6,730	6,222	2,072	1,835	2,455	3,272	3,229
	19,690	9,698	9,992	3,249	3,060	3,400	4,385	4,334
	9,824	4,721	5,103	1,704	1,732	1,523	1,883	1,863
	9,875	4,774	5,101	1,610	1,577	1,514	2,113	2,101
	18,264	8,797	9,467	3,296	3,109	2,733	3,590	3,587
	16,596	8,104	8,492	2,628	2,448	2,872	3,835	3,805
	5,875	2,899	2,976	1,031	959	949	1,200	1,189
r	10,211	5,006	5,205	1,690	1,633	1,702	2,227	2,193
l	10,313	5,027	5,286	1,690	1,754	1,591	2,237	2,227
	9,587	4,667	4,920	1,756	1,647	1,418	1,812	1,811
	4,634	2,231	2,403	774	782	697	959	955
	6,362	3,051	3,311	1,047	1,082	1,081	1,338	1,331
	27,828	13,511	14,317	4,640	4,489	4,539	5,848	5,839
	16,455	8,230	8,225	2,863	2,761	2,868	3,724	3,712
	66,179	31,351	34,828	9,039	9,839	12,952	16,552	16,284
	12,303	5,912	6,391	2,232	2,151	1,869	2,293	2,293
	4,151	2,043	2,106	668	638	680	898	891
ight	8,320	4,092	4,228	1,367	1,313	1,445	1,839	1,834
y	4,425	2,149	2,276	609	634	848	1,123	1,089
Queen	9,709	4,565	5,144	1,706	1,704	1,402	1,877	1,873
ge	5,742	2,820	2,922	1,020	1,028	898	1,177	1,165
iam	7,515	3,643	3,872	1,197	1,240	1,286	1,686	1,636
	5,353	2,660	2,605	998	912	826	1,091	1,082
	13,268	6,436	6,832	2,427	2,381	2,035	2,502	2,477
	20,929	10,190	10,739	2,178	3,178	3,654	4,938	4,892
	16,332	7,905	8,427	3,781	2,878	2,555	3,354	3,351
g	10,403	5,120	5,283	1,803	1,701	1,572	2,132	2,115
	8,670	4,151	4,519	1,448	1,486	1,262	1,757	1,746
	6,200	2,979	3,221	1,002	1,024	1,055	1,344	1,339
urg	21,318	10,273	11,045	3,509	3,475	3,134	4,473	4,463
	4,981	2,477	2,504	876	850	840	1,059	1,037
ery	12,556	6,164	6,392	2,138	2,112	2,095	2,617	2,312
id	11,576	5,638	5,938	1,830	1,798	1,941	2,580	2,562
	13,898	6,888	7,010	2,357	2,138	2,176	3,042	3,022
	4,381	2,210	2,171	706	692	809	1,048	1,042
	46,702	22,277	24,425	6,468	6,650	9,244	11,459	11,372
ton	8,046	3,949	4,097	1,254	1,221	1,476	1,913	1,889
erland	6,863	3,262	3,601	1,206	1,201	1,068	1,390	1,385
	9,291	4,535	4,756	1,582	1,592	1,517	2,011	2,005
	10,396	5,102	5,294	1,730	1,694	1,705	2,249	2,246
	8,462	4,116	4,346	1,407	1,392	1,388	1,818	1,810
	10,161	4,912	5,249	1,777	1,650	1,543	1,953	1,940
ia	31,343	15,580	15,763	5,335	5,139	5,509	6,862	6,804
	7,667	3,820	3,847	1,272	1,239	1,235	1,737	1,728
ward	12,004	5,812	6,192	1,915	1,957	1,883	2,690	2,661
orge	7,820	4,043	3,777	1,230	1,067	1,504	1,990	1,990
nno	8,273	4,263	4,010	1,396	1,321	1,579	2,036	2,032
lliam	7,504	3,680	3,824	1,197	1,085	1,320	1,730	1,702
	6,538	3,214	3,324	1,083	1,127	1,112	1,376	1,369
nock	8,261	4,030	4,231	1,304	1,272	1,357	1,834	1,829
	6,503	3,177	3,326	1,185	1,066	1,013	1,353	1,325
	9,350	4,535	4,815	1,478	1,514	1,651	2,049	2,044
ge	16,058	8,140	7,918	2,672	2,468	3,083	3,589	3,578
am	23,668	11,567	12,101	3,944	3,796	4,010	5,154	5,146
	11,103	5,491	5,612	2,056	1,985	1,798	2,187	2,150
	13,036	6,359	6,677	2,375	2,330	1,984	2,406	2,397
th	14,936	7,252	7,684	2,381	2,317	2,503	3,401	3,396
	8,898	4,403	4,495	1,569	1,506	1,446	1,822	1,815
ton	12,285	5,984	6,301	1,924	1,839	2,121	2,718	2,671
nia	11,728	5,464	6,264	1,791	1,852	1,837	2,576	2,532
	6,420	3,123	3,297	1,121	1,074	1,023	1,391	1,383
	5,585	2,886	2,699	939	823	1,082	1,373	1,371
	7,885	3,886	3,999	1,266	1,251	1,413	1,826	1,819
	10,791	5,380	5,411	1,978	1,870	1,670	2,096	2,093
	5,716	2,804	2,912	977	915	917	1,221	1,219
	1,672	849	823	253	230	334	442	438
on	16,816	8,325	8,491	2,809	2,717	2,869	3,529	3,497
land	7,682	3,762	3,920	1,443	1,382	1,187	1,566	1,544
	4,785	2,422	2,363	949	904	720	858	854
	11,611	5,712	5,899	1,990	1,856	1,906	2,391	2,380
	7,198	3,603	3,505	1,181	1,126	1,202	1,635	1,646

TABLE LVII.—*School, Military, and Citizenship Ages, &c., by Counties—1870*—Continued.

TERRITORY OF WASHINGTON.

Counties.	All ages.			5 to 18.		18 to 45.	21 and upward.	
	Total.	Male.	Female.	Male.	Female.	Male.	Male.	Male citizens.
The Territory	23,955	14,990	8,965	3,332	3,126	7,835	9,241	[illegible]
Chehalis	401	238	163	80	66	101	118	115
Clallam	408	267	141	48	46	142	175	[illegible]
Clarke	3,081	1,725	1,356	537	530	658	847	[illegible]
Cowlitz	730	432	298	103	106	199	250	[illegible]
Island	626	435	191	59	72	280	325	215
Jefferson	1,268	937	331	91	91	701	761	577
King	2,120	1,359	761	240	217	769	845	735
Kitsap	866	691	175	50	51	550	573	[illegible]
Klikitat	329	193	136	45	44	92	112	107
Lewis	888	516	372	166	144	208	271	[illegible]
Mason	289	212	77	39	24	120	145	141
Pacific	738	460	278	88	92	241	307	271
Pierce	1,409	810	599	229	239	350	451	[illegible]
Skamania	133	96	37	20	14	48	64	[illegible]
Snohomish	599	448	151	21	31	345	391	334
Stevens	734	509	225	84	68	295	359	[illegible]
Thurston	2,246	1,372	874	315	302	649	823	[illegible]
Wahkiakum	270	190	80	28	27	120	132	[illegible]
Walla-Walla	5,300	3,108	2,192	914	805	1,373	1,576	[illegible]
Whatcom	1,088	731	357	101	93	467	599	374
Yakima	432	261	171	74	64	118	147	143

STATE OF WEST VIRGINIA.

Counties.	Total.	Male.	Female.	Male, 5 to 18.	Female, 5 to 18.	Male, 18 to 45.	Male, 21 and upward.	Male citizens.
The State	442,014	222,843	219,171	76,879	73,965	76,832	95,317	[illegible]
Barbour	10,312	5,197	5,115	1,860	1,805	1,738	2,149	2,137
Berkeley	14,900	7,411	7,489	2,335	2,311	2,609	3,432	[illegible]
Boone	4,553	2,343	2,210	870	782	797	914	[illegible]
Braxton	6,480	3,316	3,164	1,187	1,121	1,117	1,321	[illegible]
Brooke	5,464	2,685	2,779	904	889	909	1,257	[illegible]
Cabell	6,429	3,290	3,139	1,176	1,109	1,130	1,389	[illegible]
Calhoun	2,939	1,510	1,429	555	527	479	581	573
Clay	2,196	1,149	1,047	429	393	347	397	[illegible]
Doddridge	7,076	3,617	3,459	1,303	1,252	1,183	1,417	[illegible]
Fayette	6,647	3,357	3,290	1,260	1,202	1,050	1,335	1,316
Gilmer	4,338	2,188	2,150	820	782	711	850	[illegible]
Grant	4,467	2,277	2,190	763	703	767	964	963
Greenbrier	11,417	5,675	5,742	1,906	1,832	1,892	2,513	[illegible]
Hampshire	7,643	3,816	3,827	1,250	1,119	1,244	1,758	[illegible]
Hancock	4,363	2,183	2,180	702	678	790	1,012	[illegible]
Hardy	5,518	2,746	2,772	924	874	919	1,191	[illegible]
Harrison	16,714	8,333	8,381	2,872	2,761	2,887	3,565	[illegible]
Jackson	10,300	5,254	5,046	1,906	1,789	1,742	2,120	2,101
Jefferson	13,219	6,546	6,673	2,055	1,973	2,446	3,207	3,183
Kanawha	22,349	11,497	10,852	3,826	3,726	4,311	5,124	[illegible]
Lewis	10,175	5,120	5,055	1,783	1,737	1,717	2,178	2,137
Lincoln	5,053	2,546	2,507	930	930	819	985	[illegible]
Logan	5,124	2,640	2,484	944	873	917	1,009	[illegible]
Marion	12,107	6,080	6,027	2,144	2,060	2,042	2,557	[illegible]
Marshall	14,941	7,662	7,279	2,544	2,524	2,742	3,335	[illegible]
Mason	15,978	8,077	7,901	2,856	2,749	2,826	3,391	[illegible]
McDowell	1,952	968	984	378	362	285*	354	[illegible]
Mercer	7,064	3,516	3,548	1,254	1,209	1,130	1,412	1,375
Mineral	6,332	3,216	3,116	1,015	993	1,169	1,469	[illegible]
Monongalia	13,547	6,698	6,849	2,306	2,227	2,347	2,957	[illegible]
Monroe	11,124	5,428	5,696	1,881	1,905	1,863	2,340	2,318
Morgan	4,315	2,254	2,061	750	613	774	984	955
Nicholas	4,458	2,301	2,157	862	749	724	906	905
Ohio	*28,831	14,029	14,802	4,683	4,802	5,243	6,464	6,100
Pendleton	6,455	3,222	3,233	1,144	1,107	1,027	1,327	1,312
Pleasants	3,012	1,590	1,422	529	487	578	673	[illegible]
Pocahontas	4,069	2,056	2,013	664	626	690	933	[illegible]
Preston	14,555	7,338	7,217	2,522	2,442	2,470	3,099	3,057
Putnam	7,794	3,981	3,813	1,381	1,318	1,308	1,657	1,641
Raleigh	3,673	1,839	1,834	692	664	569	697	[illegible]
Randolph	5,563	2,872	2,691	991	887	973	1,219	1,190

TABLE LVII.—*School, Military, and Citizenship Ages, &c., by Counties*—1870—Continued.

STATE OF WEST VIRGINIA—Continued.

Counties.	All ages.			5 to 18.		18 to 45.	21 and upward.	
	Total.	Male.	Female.	Male.	Female.	Male.	Male.	Male citizens.
Ritchie	9,055	4,673	4,382	1,603	1,521	1,615	1,941	1,879
Roane	7,232	3,685	3,547	1,370	1,310	1,191	1,370	1,362
Taylor	9,367	4,720	4,647	1,579	1,497	1,680	2,109	2,058
Tucker	1,907	990	917	361	332	324	393	391
Tyler	7,832	3,950	3,882	1,441	1,354	1,298	1,635	1,606
Upshur	8,023	4,027	3,996	1,387	1,364	1,368	1,714	1,698
Wayne	7,852	4,016	3,836	1,493	1,382	1,364	1,545	1,537
Webster	1,730	880	850	318	291	303	346	345
Wetzel	8,595	4,376	4,219	1,581	1,531	1,416	1,781	1,777
Wirt	4,804	2,532	2,272	815	738	972	1,123	1,110
Wood	19,000	9,544	9,456	3,184	3,180	3,511	4,324	4,223
Wyoming	3,171	1,627	1,544	595	573	509	585	583

STATE OF WISCONSIN.

Counties.	Total.	Male.	Female.	Male 5 to 18.	Female 5 to 18.	Male 18 to 45.	Male 21 and upward.	Male citizens.
The State	1,054,670	544,886	509,784	178,669	175,347	192,331	255,159	203,077
Adams	6,601	3,437	3,164	1,131	1,087	1,129	1,610	1,537
Ashland	221	125	96	27	24	65	77	47
Barron	538	343	195	72	63	201	214	70
Bayfield	344	196	148	38	48	105	126	82
Brown	25,168	13,279	11,889	4,208	4,179	4,774	6,110	4,845
Buffalo	11,123	5,901	5,222	1,899	1,915	2,096	2,647	2,013
Burnett	706	376	330	107	85	148	200	27
Calumet	12,335	6,416	5,919	2,182	2,141	2,070	2,776	1,132
Chippewa	8,311	4,888	3,423	1,260	1,148	2,452	2,785	2,164
Clark	3,450	1,945	1,505	502	472	903	1,021	853
Columbia	28,802	14,856	13,946	4,827	4,687	5,156	7,005	5,611
Crawford	13,075	6,673	6,402	2,366	2,335	2,175	2,872	2,608
Dane	53,096	27,328	25,768	9,191	8,949	9,584	12,713	10,530
Dodge	47,035	24,295	22,740	8,300	7,961	7,864	11,183	8,497
Door	4,919	2,703	2,216	789	757	1,130	1,320	885
Douglas	1,122	666	456	164	147	328	395	201
Dunn	9,488	5,378	4,110	1,576	1,399	2,323	2,694	1,498
Eau Claire	10,769	6,000	4,769	1,474	1,520	3,001	3,289	2,301
Fond du Lac	46,273	23,534	22,739	7,464	7,773	8,108	10,936	9,614
Grant	37,979	19,577	18,402	6,787	6,552	6,601	8,595	8,018
Green	23,611	12,042	11,569	4,040	3,981	4,256	5,546	5,040
Green Lake	13,195	6,681	6,514	2,083	2,163	2,392	3,266	2,448
Iowa	24,544	12,657	11,887	4,565	4,393	4,096	5,369	3,430
Jackson	7,687	4,062	3,625	1,290	1,285	1,591	1,927	1,807
Jefferson	34,040	17,214	16,826	5,887	5,815	5,492	7,860	7,309
Juneau	12,372	6,352	6,020	2,152	2,139	2,145	2,872	1,747
Kenosha	13,147	6,747	6,400	2,086	2,159	2,338	3,331	2,500
Kewaunee	10,128	5,322	4,806	1,883	1,685	1,634	2,269	716
La Crosse	20,297	10,635	9,662	3,186	3,159	4,477	5,387	4,118
La Fayette	22,659	11,670	10,989	4,045	3,920	3,988	5,173	4,898
Manitowoc	33,364	16,886	16,478	6,121	6,180	4,891	7,296	4,247
Marathon	5,885	3,150	2,735	937	946	1,259	1,559	1,495
Marquette	8,056	4,136	3,920	1,461	1,352	1,262	1,857	1,667
Milwaukee	89,930	45,016	44,914	14,054	14,475	16,901	21,900	15,774
Monroe	16,550	8,668	7,882	2,943	2,733	2,963	3,929	3,674
Oconto	8,321	4,922	3,399	1,127	1,011	2,655	2,789	2,151
Outagamie	18,430	9,511	8,919	3,183	3,138	3,276	4,304	3,745
Ozaukee	15,564	8,033	7,531	2,984	2,798	2,194	3,449	2,715
Pepin	4,659	2,467	2,192	803	786	921	1,160	866
Pierce	9,958	5,219	4,739	1,720	1,602	1,861	2,427	2,301
Polk	3,422	1,852	1,570	547	531	690	890	862
Portage	10,634	5,600	5,034	1,750	1,776	2,104	2,678	2,462
Racine	26,740	13,821	12,919	4,350	4,284	5,097	6,752	5,091
Richland	15,731	8,113	7,618	2,923	2,772	2,661	3,439	3,318
Rock	39,030	19,938	19,092	6,162	5,774	7,661	10,087	9,416
Sauk	23,860	12,263	11,597	4,154	3,980	4,086	5,665	4,650
Shawanaw	3,166	1,688	1,478	510	511	642	782	737
Sheboygan	31,749	16,213	15,536	5,793	5,695	4,858	7,072	4,701
St. Croix	11,035	5,755	5,280	1,947	1,832	2,112	2,674	1,531
Trempealeau	10,732	5,634	5,098	1,831	1,818	2,038	2,567	1,985

TABLE LVII.—*School, Military, and Citizenship Ages, &c., by Counties*—1870—Continued.

STATE OF WISCONSIN—Continued.

Counties.	All ages.			5 to 18.		18 to 45.	21 and upward.	
	Total.	Male.	Female.	Male.	Female.	Male.	Male.	Male citizens.
Vernon	18,645	9,724	8,921	3,317	3,121	3,274	4,301	4,037
Walworth	25,972	13,144	12,828	4,087	3,962	4,848	6,754	5,954
Washington	23,919	12,312	11,607	4,438	4,374	3,582	5,330	3,897
Waukesha	28,274	14,488	13,786	4,802	4,626	4,915	6,960	5,4[illegible]
Waupacca	15,539	8,095	7,444	2,725	2,624	2,774	3,743	3,449
Waushara	11,279	5,814	5,465	1,961	1,868	1,936	2,716	2,611
Winnebago	37,279	19,021	18,258	5,856	6,216	7,310	9,417	6,952
Wood	3,912	2,105	1,807	593	601	938	1,094	[illegible]

TERRITORY OF WYOMING.

Counties.	Total.	Male.	Female.	Male.	Female.	Male.	Male.	Male citizens.
The Territory	9,118	7,219	1,899	449	407	6,056	6,107	5,327
Albany	2,021	1,635	386	103	91	1,393	1,387	1,082
Carbon	1,368	1,193	175	47	39	1,071	1,073	976
Laramie	2,957	2,240	717	148	150	1,854	1,877	1,835
Sweetwater	1,916	1,492	424	91	86	1,232	1,258	1,089
Uintah	856	659	197	60	41	506	512	344

OCCUPATIONS.

TABLE LVIII.—*Occupations: Number and Sex of Persons engaged in Each Class, by States and Territories*—1870.

States and Territories.	Population 10 years and over.			Engaged in all classes of occupations.			Engaged in agriculture.		
	Total.	Male.	Female.	Total.	Male.	Female.	Total.	Male.	Female.
The U. S.	28,228,945	14,258,866	13,970,079	12,505,923	10,669,635	1,836,288	5,922,471	5,525,503	396,96[illegible]
Alabama	706,802	340,984	365,818	365,258	275,640	89,618	291,628	226,768	64,8[illegible]
Arizona	8,237	6,148	2,089	6,030	5,734	296	1,285	1,284	1
Arkansas	311,737	175,194	136,543	135,949	120,153	15,796	109,310	100,668	8,64[illegible]
California	430,441	283,740	146,701	238,648	224,868	13,780	47,863	47,580	28[illegible]
Colorado	30,349	19,931	10,418	17,583	17,147	436	6,462	6,462	......
Connecticut	425,896	209,120	216,776	193,421	159,460	33,961	43,653	43,52[illegible]	13[illegible]
Dakota	10,640	7,047	3,593	5,887	5,727	160	2,522	2,522	......
Delaware	92,586	46,274	46,312	40,313	34,306	6,007	15,973	15,907	66
Dist. Col	100,453	46,652	53,801	49,041	35,200	13,841	1,365	1,35[illegible]	1[illegible]
Florida	131,119	65,673	65,446	60,703	50,877	9,826	42,492	36,944	5,5[illegible]
Georgia	835,929	401,547	434,382	444,678	329,185	115,493	336,145	262,152	73,9[illegible]
Idaho	13,189	11,270	1,919	10,879	10,754	125	1,462	1,462	......
Illinois	1,869,606	946,717	922,889	742,015	678,732	63,283	376,441	375,407	1,0[illegible]
Indiana	1,197,936	612,832	585,104	459,369	428,259	31,110	266,777	266,349	428
Iowa	837,950	445,061	392,895	344,276	321,150	23,126	210,263	209,907	3[illegible]
Kansas	258,051	148,152	109,899	123,852	117,343	6,509	73,228	72,918	3[illegible]
Kentucky	930,136	466,762	463,374	414,593	364,300	50,293	261,080	257,436	3,64[illegible]
Louisiana	526,392	261,170	265,222	256,452	198,168	58,284	141,467	114,530	26,9[illegible]
Maine	493,847	245,704	248,143	208,225	179,784	28,441	82,011	81,956	[illegible]
Maryland	575,439	281,294	294,145	258,543	213,691	44,852	80,449	79,197	1,2[illegible]
Massachusetts	1,160,666	554,886	605,780	579,844	451,543	128,301	72,810	72,756	[illegible]
Michigan	873,763	460,408	413,355	404,164	346,717	57,447	187,211	187,036	175
Minnesota	305,568	167,456	138,112	132,657	121,797	10,860	75,157	74,063	94
Mississippi	581,206	288,185	293,021	318,850	232,349	86,501	259,199	193,725	65,4[illegible]
Missouri	1,205,568	632,179	573,389	505,556	466,845	38,711	263,918	262,505	1,[illegible]
Montana	18,170	15,517	2,653	14,048	13,877	171	2,111	2,110	1
Nebraska	88,265	52,588	35,677	43,837	41,943	1,894	23,115	23,083	[illegible]
Nevada	36,655	29,430	7,225	26,911	26,468	443	2,070	2,063	7
N. Hampshire	260,426	126,353	134,073	120,168	96,033	24,135	46,573	46,562	11
New Jersey	680,687	335,819	344,868	296,036	251,625	44,411	63,128	62,943	185
New Mexico	66,464	34,415	32,049	29,361	26,281	3,080	18,668	18,432	236
New York	3,378,959	1,658,504	1,720,455	1,491,018	1,233,979	257,039	374,323	373,455	868
N. Carolina	769,629	365,528	404,101	351,299	292,439	58,860	269,238	211,010	[illegible]
Ohio	1,953,374	976,588	976,786	840,889	757,369	83,520	397,024	396,967	57
Oregon	64,685	39,861	24,824	30,651	29,968	683	13,248	13,232	16
Pennsylvania	2,597,809	1,292,518	1,305,291	1,020,544	886,209	134,335	260,051	258,772	1,27[illegible]
Rhode Island	173,751	82,824	90,927	88,574	66,859	21,715	11,780	11,767	13
S. Carolina	503,763	241,492	262,271	263,301	182,355	80,946	206,654	147,708	58,94[illegible]
Tennessee	890,872	436,154	454,718	367,987	322,585	45,402	267,020	247,953	19,067
Texas	571,075	297,356	273,719	237,126	208,529	28,597	166,753	152,722	14,031
Utah	56,515	28,729	27,786	21,517	20,442	1,075	10,428	10,417	11
Vermont	258,751	129,248	129,503	108,763	95,263	13,500	57,983	57,889	94
Virginia	890,056	427,455	462,601	412,665	337,464	75,201	244,550	228,082	16,468
Washington	17,334	11,611	5,723	9,760	9,524	236	3,771	3,759	12
W. Virginia	308,424	154,234	154,190	115,229	107,076	8,153	73,960	73,725	235
Wisconsin	751,704	391,603	360,101	292,808	267,273	25,535	159,687	158,300	1,387
Wyoming	8,059	6,650	1,409	6,645	6,345	300	165	164	1

THE SCOPE OF THESE TABLES.—The tables of occupations embrace gainful and reputable occupations only. While expressing the employments of more than twelve millions and a half of persons, they do not seek to account for the larger number of those within the same periods of life, who have no recognized occupation for which they receive compensation in the shape of wages or salary, or from which they derive products of a merchantable character. All persons, moreover, whose means of livelihood are criminal, or, in the general judgment of mankind, shameful, are excluded.

The reason for excluding gamblers, prostitutes, keepers of brothels, and such persons from the Tables of Occupations has not been found in any sensitiveness at the mention or recognition of these classes as actually existing in the community, but in the consideration that, from the necessity of the case, the numbers thus reported must be wholly inadequate to the fact, and that a seeming count of them in the census would have the effect to mislead rather than to instruct. Here and there, at the enumeration of the Ninth Census, such persons had the assurance to report themselves by their true designations, or assistant marshals took the responsibility (and in some cases the risk) of writing down the real occupation of members of these classes who had sought to misstate their avocations or to disguise them under ambiguous terms; but an analysis of

ABLE LVIII.—*Occupations: Number and Sex of Persons engaged in Each Class, by States and Territories—1870.*

ENGAGED IN PROFESSIONAL AND PERSONAL SERVICES.			ENGAGED IN TRADE AND TRANSPORTATION.			ENGAGED IN MANUFACTURES, AND MECHANICAL AND MINING INDUSTRIES.		
Total.	Male.	Female.	Total.	Male.	Female.	Total.	Male.	Female.
2,684,793	1,618,121	1,066,672	1,191,238	1,172,540	18,698	2,707,421	2,353,171	353,950
42,125	19,449	22,676	14,435	14,345	90	17,070	15,078	1,992
3,115	2,979	136	591	588	3	1,039	883	156
14,877	8,018	6,859	5,491	5,474	17	6,271	5,992	279
76,112	65,150	10,962	33,165	33,038	127	81,508	79,100	2,408
3,625	3,245	380	2,815	2,813	2	4,681	4,627	54
38,704	21,150	17,554	24,720	24,511	209	86,314	70,276	16,038
2,704	2,562	142	204	204	....	457	439	18
11,389	6,615	4,774	3,437	3,347	90	9,514	8,437	1,077
29,845	17,927	11,918	6,126	5,852	274	11,705	10,071	1,634
10,897	6,892	4,005	3,023	3,016	7	4,291	4,025	266
64,083	27,435	36,648	17,410	17,336	74	27,040	22,262	4,778
1,423	1,310	113	721	720	1	7,273	7,262	11
151,931	99,337	52,594	80,422	79,876	546	133,221	124,112	9,109
80,018	53,466	26,552	36,517	36,371	146	76,057	72,073	3,984
58,484	38,531	19,953	28,210	28,151	59	47,319	44,561	2,758
20,736	15,286	5,450	11,762	11,736	26	18,126	17,403	723
84,024	41,974	42,050	25,292	24,961	331	44,197	39,939	4,258
65,347	36,883	28,464	23,831	23,496	335	25,807	23,259	2,548
36,092	20,683	15,409	28,115	27,880	235	62,007	49,265	12,742
79,226	43,278	35,948	35,542	34,567	975	63,326	56,649	6,677
131,291	75,917	55,374	83,078	81,077	2,001	292,665	231,793	60,872
104,728	52,754	51,974	29,588	29,493	95	82,637	77,434	5,203
28,330	18,920	9,410	10,582	10,559	23	18,588	17,655	933
40,522	20,430	20,092	9,148	9,076	72	9,981	9,118	863
106,903	75,079	31,824	54,885	54,583	302	79,850	74,588	5,262
2,674	2,515	159	1,233	1,232	1	8,030	8,020	10
10,331	8,667	1,664	4,628	4,623	5	5,763	5,570	193
7,431	7,152	279	3,621	3,621	....	13,789	13,632	157
18,528	8,821	9,707	8,514	8,126	388	46,553	32,524	14,029
83,380	54,275	29,105	46,206	45,242	964	103,322	89,165	14,157
7,535	5,542	1,993	863	863	....	2,295	1,444	851
405,339	233,569	171,770	234,581	229,789	4,792	476,775	397,166	79,609
51,290	23,073	28,217	10,179	10,094	85	20,592	18,262	2,330
168,308	104,018	64,290	78,547	77,690	857	197,010	179,394	17,616
6,090	5,522	568	2,619	2,611	8	8,694	8,603	91
283,000	192,674	90,326	121,253	116,714	4,539	356,240	318,049	38,191
19,679	12,349	7,330	10,108	9,878	230	47,007	32,865	14,142
34,383	15,526	18,857	8,470	8,250	220	13,794	10,871	2,923
54,396	30,077	24,319	17,510	17,417	93	29,061	27,138	1,923
40,882	27,168	13,714	13,612	13,576	36	15,879	15,063	816
5,317	4,384	933	1,665	1,648	17	4,107	3,993	114
21,032	9,680	11,352	7,132	7,101	31	22,616	20,593	2,023
98,521	45,407	53,114	20,181	19,992	189	49,413	43,983	5,430
2,207	2,000	207	1,129	1,127	2	2,653	2,638	15
16,699	9,636	7,063	6,897	6,888	9	17,673	16,827	846
58,070	37,898	20,172	21,534	21,342	192	53,517	49,733	3,784
3,170	2,898	272	1,646	1,646	....	1,664	1,637	27

ne schedules soon made it evident that this had not been done, as indeed was not to e expected, with such uniformity as to secure even approximately correct results. All ich titles were, therefore, dropped. Some from these classes may have taken refuge, rough false statements, in one or another of the occupations of good repute (notably ceepers of brothels as "boarding-house keepers," a euphemism familiar to the compil- rs of city directories,) but, as a general rule, where the calling was not correctly given was wholly withheld; and it may therefore be assumed that substantially the whole ody of persons pursuing disreputable and criminal occupations are omitted from these ibles. There are no means known to the Superintendent for accurately calculating ne number thus excluded or excluding themselves.

The number of those who are not accounted for exceeds, as a matter of course, in a ajority of States, the number of those who are returned as pursuing gainful occupa ons.

The following table exhibits the number of persons in each of the six recog- ivisions of the tables, according to age and sex, in comparison with the num- ving inhabitants of each such class:

tes
ls of
vided
s of 16

ed. Of
gainful

TABLE LX.—*Occupations: Nationality (Selected) of Persons engaged in All Classes, by States and Territories*—1870.

States and Territories.	NATIVITY.								
	United States.	Germany.	Ireland.	England and Wales.	Scotland.	British America.	Sweden, Norway, and Denmark.	France.	China and Japan.
Population (a)	22, 921,058	1, 611, 781	1, 769, 375	600, 253	134, 274	470, 476	230, 426	110, 979	[illegible]
The United States.	9, 802, 034	836, 418	947, 234	301, 795	71, 922	180, 318	108, 638	58, 200	[illegible]
Alabama	359, 626	1, 329	2, 438	580	251	10	142	293	......
Arizona	2, 420	355	446	117	45	85	12	54	[illegible]
Arkansas	132, 811	1, 007	958	352	88	112	118	123	[illegible]
California	110, 124	19, 311	30, 783	11, 366	3, 248	4, 836	3, 407	4, 984	[illegible]
Colorado	13, 117	1, 012	1, 230	957	137	294	167	136	[illegible]
Connecticut	138, 804	6, 772	35, 519	6, 141	1, 583	3, 221	270	443	[illegible]
Dakota	3, 104	484	678	185	52	399	730	48	
Delaware	36, 281	629	2, 475	647	99	37	10	66	......
Dist. of Columbia	41, 225	2, 515	3, 908	661	106	81	37	133	3
Florida	58, 437	336	392	299	83	32	72	72	......
Georgia	439, 008	1, 784	2, 541	555	206	92	86	142	1
Idaho	3, 824	529	885	546	90	286	179	119	[illegible]
Illinois	497, 043	97, 810	61, 247	22, 248	7, 691	12, 603	21, 676	4, 961	[illegible]
Indiana	396, 086	35, 524	13, 704	5, 001	1, 240	1, 669	1, 122	2, 392	[illegible]
Iowa	256, 110	30, 772	19, 355	9, 230	2, 435	3, 853	11, 474	1, 488	[illegible]
Kansas	98, 362	6, 970	6, 296	4, 035	941	1, 561	3, 142	707	......
Kentucky	382, 255	15, 666	11, 437	2, 200	518	206	91	954	[illegible]
Louisiana	224, 881	9, 774	8, 290	1, 741	477	369	395	6, 580	[illegible]
Maine	187, 497	294	7, 300	1, 748	463	10, 539	147	69	1
Maryland	219, 296	22, 590	11, 174	2, 742	1, 106	205	142	346	1
Massachusetts	389, 692	7, 966	118, 267	20, 730	5, 098	32, 636	1, 255	967	[illegible]
Michigan	286, 629	32, 282	20, 927	17, 717	4, 647	31, 105	2, 827	1, 619	[illegible]
Minnesota	60, 672	20, 989	10, 703	3, 114	1, 245	5, 261	25, 449	724	......
Mississippi	312, 981	1, 757	1, 591	557	225	83	588	348	1
Missouri	390, 469	58, 500	31, 376	8, 291	1, 791	3, 174	1, 769	2, 635	1
Montana	7, 290	1, 098	1, 436	697	205	1, 034	268	166	[illegible]
Nebraska	27, 592	6, 212	3, 227	1, 952	469	894	2, 116	218	......
Nevada	12, 535	1, 831	3, 546	2, 268	418	1, 754	422	301	[illegible]
New Hampshire	102, 989	258	6, 316	1, 504	524	7, 009	77	58	......
New Jersey	200, 009	29, 311	45, 266	12, 568	2, 668	958	602	1, 069	[illegible]
New Mexico	26, 356	539	489	119	32	31	25	106	......
New York	935, 098	150, 683	264, 858	55, 168	11, 531	31, 945	4, 701	10, 704	[illegible]
North Carolina	349, 696	525	365	323	172	12	20	27	......
Ohio	654, 320	95, 757	43, 712	22, 829	3, 823	5, 023	439	6, 799	[illegible]
Oregon	21, 861	1, 258	1, 314	941	277	524	314	230	[illegible]
Pennsylvania	774, 608	73, 578	111, 398	40, 103	7, 212	3, 163	1, 247	3, 972	[illegible]
Rhode Island	61, 633	925	17, 183	4, 780	940	2, 556	64	85	......
South Carolina	259, 840	1, 121	1, 259	257	148	15	79	52	1
Tennessee	358, 262	2, 495	4, 200	11, 118	318	255	186	299	4
Texas	211, 206	9, 743	2, 317	1, 148	353	451	445	1, 078	[illegible]
Utah	8, 976	321	345	7, 131	1, 021	131	2, 825	41	[illegible]
Vermont	89, 890	194	6, 210	1, 125	447	10, 756	55	52	......
Virginia	407, 093	1, 851	1, 991	844	277	139	47	129	3
Washington	5, 890	545	769	683	236	680	318	90	[illegible]
West Virginia	107, 490	2, 936	3, 057	958	310	39	13	87	......
Wisconsin	134, 930	68, 331	23, 092	17, 159	3, 389	8, 843	19, 891	1, 497	......
Wyoming	3, 716	616	961	444	197	268	151	51	[illegible]

(a) Ten years and over.

occupations: while of 989,516 above the age of 60, 634,837 are accounted for. The difference in the former period (*i. e.*, 16 to 59) is substantially made up, first, by the number of students pursuing courses of instruction beyond the age of 16; second, by the number of persons afflicted with permanent bodily or mental infirmities disqualifying them from participating in the industry of the country; third by the numbers of the criminal and pauper classes. The number of men of this period of life, not disabled, who are not returned as of some specific occupation, by reason of inherited wealth, or of having retired from business, is hardly important enough to be mentioned here. The difference in the latter period (*i. e.*, from 60 upwards) is accounted for by the numbers of persons respectively of the second and third classes just mentioned.

TABLE LXI.—*Occupations: Nationality (Selected) of Persons engaged in Agriculture, by States and Territories*—1870.

States and Territories.	NATIVITY.								
	United States.	Germany.	Ireland.	England and Wales.	Scotland.	British America.	Sweden, Norway, and Denmark.	France.	China and Japan.
The United States.	5,303,363	224,531	138,425	77,173	17,850	48,288	50,480	16,472	2,861
Alabama	290,901	171	276	7	53	1	16	29	....
Arizona	533	49	36	14	6	20	3	7	....
Arkansas	108,390	229	261	115	24	23	41	49	72
California	30,629	2,756	3,803	1,809	663	955	588	572	2,694
Colorado	5,593	229	165	143	34	89	34	31	....
Connecticut	37,540	755	3,823	753	200	362	57	64	....
Dakota	1,247	89	136	50	15	221	657	12	....
Delaware	15,465	75	254	131	16	4	1	19	....
Dist. of Columbia	1,103	136	71	25	15	1	1	3	....
Florida	42,197	53	55	38	24	3	8	14	....
Georgia	335,487	181	269	81	35	13	10	20	....
Idaho	1,046	42	64	182	9	51	37	7	10
Illinois	292,177	37,717	15,617	11,248	2,870	4,479	7,372	2,473	1
Indiana	242,567	14,873	3,506	1,880	428	739	387	1,176	2
Iowa	100,312	16,924	10,668	5,568	1,431	2,435	6,684	836	2
Kansas	61,193	3,395	2,416	2,039	482	876	1,525	360	....
Kentucky	256,528	2,291	1,469	293	73	25	29	185	....
Louisiana	139,381	488	376	133	49	14	54	638	10
Maine	78,514	42	777	214	59	2,377	6	8	....
Maryland	77,250	1,843	913	247	64	10	8	38	....
Massachusetts	61,614	429	7,422	728	240	2,149	40	54	1
Michigan	144,717	12,324	6,680	8,000	1,703	10,781	498	566	....
Minnesota	32,460	12,952	6,205	1,934	697	2,288	15,501	440	....
Mississippi	257,454	410	520	177	68	20	313	57	....
Missouri	240,279	13,976	3,517	2,322	475	1,098	393	403	....
Montana	1,478	96	165	118	25	138	45	19	....
Nebraska	15,481	3,583	892	940	228	441	828	106	....
Nevada	1,412	125	118	131	41	92	51	22	27
New Hampshire	44,215	15	694	299	62	932	1	4	....
New Jersey	54,331	3,139	3,977	847	193	69	62	177	....
New Mexico	18,127	48	27	7	1	....	2	15	....
New York	304,441	16,990	27,923	11,714	2,528	6,601	501	2,273	....
North Carolina	268,876	56	71	86	72	....	4	8	....
Ohio	340,469	25,060	7,513	6,101	991	1,319	125	3,566	2
Oregon	11,856	287	284	274	100	179	45	55	34
Pennsylvania	237,215	9,501	8,014	2,789	670	300	157	782	1
Rhode Island	10,570	40	694	113	32	301	5	1	....
South Carolina	206,173	128	194	60	22	2	30	5	....
Tennessee	265,541	322	632	151	59	38	43	37	....
Texas	155,413	4,226	466	354	116	120	191	383	2
Utah	4,542	57	76	3,354	465	59	1,577	5	....
Vermont	50,920	30	1,998	360	232	4,429	2	9	....
Virginia	213,227	360	460	256	93	37	13	26	3
Washington	2,733	176	235	164	97	207	80	21	....
West Virginia	72,199	607	773	176	49	13	1	31	....
Wisconsin	70,431	37,252	13,914	10,669	2,034	4,043	12,254	810	....
Wyoming	136	4	6	7	5	4	....	2	....

and by the, perhaps, larger number of persons retired from active pursuits by reason of an acquired competence, of support secured from grown children, or of advanced age.

Turning to the table of the occupations of females, (Vol. 1, quarto, Ninth Census,) an analysis of the numbers reported as of specified occupations in the three several periods of life, shows a curious, though probably not significant, rate of progression. In the first period, the females pursuing gainful occupations are to the males as one to three; in the second period as one to six; in the third period as one to twelve.

It would not seem to be difficult to account for the females of each class who are not represented in the Tables of Occupations. The number of female children attending school during the census year, as obtained by the canvass of families, (see Remarks on School Attendance, page 448 of this volume,) was 3,180,313. Assuming, as it is probably fair to do, that two-fifths of the female children under 16 who are reported

TABLE LXII.—*Occupations: Nationality (Selected) of Persons engaged in Personal and Professional Services, by States and Territories—1870.*

States and Territories.	NATIVITY.								
	United States.	Germany.	Ireland.	England and Wales.	Scotland.	British America.	Sweden, Norway, and Denmark.	France.	China and Japan.
The United States	1,858,178	191,212	425,087	49,905	12,672	48,014	29,333	13,102	19,471
Alabama	40,795	246	677	106	51	3	49	80	....
Arizona	1,167	189	328	67	24	37	1	28	13
Arkansas	14,189	169	298	62	16	29	34	21	14
California	29,460	5,016	14,778	2,398	634	1,103	776	1,594	15,86[illegible]
Colorado	2,683	220	345	120	14	46	39	39	6
Connecticut	22,535	1,131	13,332	805	230	341	52	65	6
Dakota	1,309	351	505	121	31	136	67	19	....
Delaware	9,733	164	1,304	124	20	7	1	12	....
Dist. of Columbia	25,817	758	2,650	275	58	39	22	60	3
Florida	10,293	90	203	67	16	7	28	25	....
Georgia	62,337	346	1,076	128	48	28	13	33	....
Idaho	700	115	154	67	17	38	25	12	26[illegible]
Illinois	83,964	22,807	25,140	4,180	1,361	2,723	7,436	893	1
Indiana	65,381	6,514	5,818	670	135	258	411	339	....
Iowa	43,062	5,026	4,159	1,051	229	492	2,443	208	....
Kansas	15,589	1,207	1,703	509	132	255	770	136	....
Kentucky	73,989	3,568	5,350	338	72	60	17	231	4
Louisiana	54,814	2,743	4,381	460	121	122	102	1,559	27
Maine	29,186	48	3,731	296	104	2,640	29	20	....
Maryland	66,062	5,816	6,119	487	151	40	30	131	....
Massachusetts	62,392	1,617	54,370	2,835	801	7,916	239	241	6
Michigan	72,243	7,952	8,030	2,912	974	9,325	1,101	432	....
Minnesota	12,526	3,448	2,809	372	236	1,320	6,323	134	....
Mississippi	39,204	302	495	117	52	25	126	73	....
Missouri	70,419	14,521	15,778	1,614	297	680	794	755	1
Montana	1,465	294	396	122	39	138	23	40	151
Nebraska	5,587	1,427	1,555	402	107	177	095	60	....
Nevada	2,541	421	792	264	88	554	74	107	2,160
New Hampshire	15,372	43	1,636	123	40	998	13	16	....
New Jersey	47,359	6,909	24,486	2,579	515	301	176	330	4
New Mexico	5,819	264	347	70	19	16	14	61	....
New York	207,692	36,814	130,788	9,981	2,915	9,445	1,315	2,537	25
North Carolina	50,952	91	124	43	18	4	7	7	....
Ohio	119,472	22,210	18,441	3,354	569	1,176	89	1,040	1
Oregon	3,968	283	505	189	44	138	98	52	619
Pennsylvania	197,121	20,853	52,513	6,949	1,372	1,060	638	914	15
Rhode Island	10,117	205	7,618	605	148	774	24	46	....
South Carolina	33,720	188	357	42	23	2	20	9	....
Tennessee	51,978	381	1,503	163	38	42	49	73	....
Texas	34,353	1,559	907	260	97	94	105	268	8
Utah	2,126	60	121	1,801	269	11	688	15	73
Vermont	15,520	46	2,102	177	40	3,002	42	29	....
Virginia	97,540	235	524	93	22	26	10	21	....
Washington	1,116	134	257	159	22	147	43	27	16[illegible]
West Virginia	15,094	498	839	123	31	6	3	11	....
Wisconsin	27,618	13,526	5,017	1,987	356	2,135	4,222	272	....
Wyoming	1,716	314	640	142	47	98	57	27	6[illegible]

as pursuing gainful occupations, are also embraced in this total of school attendance,* and, on the other hand, estimating the number of female children of this period of life belonging to the pauper, vagrant, or criminal class at 100,000, we shall have something like 500,000 school attendants among the females of the second period of life. Subtracting this from the total number of females between 16 and 59, we shall have in round numbers 9,750,000 persons, of whom only 1,594,783 appear in the Tables of Occupations, leaving, say, 8,150,000 to be accounted for.

As the considerations remaining to be adduced apply equally to females of the third period of life, we may now add their number to the total already obtained, making the aggregate of females above 16 unaccounted for in the neighborhood of 9,100,000.

* The number of female children embraced in the Tables of Occupations has just been shown to be 191,100. Of these, 73,177 were engaged in agriculture, 1,116 in trade and transportation, 25,664 in manufactures and mining, and 91,143 in personal services, 86,965 of the latter being employed as domestic servants. It is probably within bounds to assume that two-fifths of these were afforded facilities for attending school during some portion of the year.

XIII.—*Occupations: Nationality (Selected) of Persons engaged in Trade and Transportation, by States and Territories—1870.*

d Territories.	NATIVITY.								
	United States.	Germany.	Ireland.	England and Wales.	Scotland.	British America.	Sweden, Norway, and Denmark.	France.	China and Japan.
d States	862,653	112,435	110,004	32,086	8,440	16,565	9,564	8,654	2,250
....	12,253	554	1,054	172	65	5	45	98	....
....	306	41	28	11	6	5	2	8	1
....	4,694	344	243	50	20	24	20	20	....
....	15,957	4,948	3,813	1,537	509	688	884	889	1,861
....	1,941	198	340	87	33	64	21	27	1
t	18,775	705	4,377	391	99	159	63	38	....
....	155	7	7	2	2	14	11	3	....
....	3,160	53	161	41	4	3	2	4	....
lumbia..	4,942	475	505	94	13	15	2	28	....
....	2,377	121	65	51	19	8	24	16	....
....	15,677	781	642	117	52	12	17	35	....
....	448	77	44	20	5	25	11	18	30
....	50,907	10,786	9,624	3,180	874	1,566	1,456	457	....
....	29,204	3,735	2,226	490	119	190	85	193	....
....	19,921	2,563	2,507	695	180	313	1,133	105	....
....	8,338	828	1,328	355	95	157	332	74	....
....	19,649	2,777	2,021	320	97	49	7	161	3
....	14,732	2,884	1,860	630	146	89	128	2,033	1
....	26,090	81	683	183	57	876	62	14	1
....	29,170	3,799	1,768	379	79	44	54	59	4
setts	68,646	916	7,986	1,588	423	2,389	263	148	3
....	20,762	2,731	1,547	1,219	503	1,985	182	197	2
....	6,126	1,072	729	215	92	467	1,095	44	....
i	7,064	598	287	89	45	20	60	136	1
....	35,730	9,109	6,062	1,184	304	589	206	435	....
....	844	117	50	37	11	81	12	25	13
....	3,030	375	464	185	42	100	346	19	....
....	2,274	400	189	107	40	162	39	38	103
pshire...	7,458	32	375	61	8	308	7	1	....
y	33,686	4,348	5,051	1,759	411	153	73	267	4
co	605	123	19	13	1	1	1	9	....
....	151,165	28,069	34,967	8,665	2,344	3,422	1 109	1,577	31
olina...	9,716	281	81	49	26	3	4	3	....
....	55,151	11,245	7,317	2,211	430	716	68	509	1
....	1,794	277	132	120	28	44	35	30	53
nia	93,016	8,684	14,149	3,178	575	354	104	395	4
and.....	8,704	79	848	259	77	78	6	2	....
olina	7,058	738	418	69	48	4	20	14	....
....	15,008	762	1,091	180	56	44	23	64	4
....	10,139	1,583	404	213	48	47	56	204	6
....	1,004	77	47	329	54	21	54	5	....
....	6,140	32	424	47	20	463	....	3	....
....	18,696	562	583	122	47	20	10	40	....
n	625	84	85	94	27	65	83	13	5
inia.....	5,670	384	674	106	22	3	3	8	....
....	12,260	3,848	1,577	1,110	241	558	702	116	....
....	986	150	182	72	43	72	44	9	61

ld at first appear that a clear deduction should be made of one person on of each family returned in the census, in all, 7,579,863. This number must be however, to the extent to which females, the heads of families, and doing all sekeeping that is done for their families, are also returned as of specific occu-

o familiar with factory-towns will doubt that this reduction should be con-; yet we shall probably reach the truth of the case substantially if we cut e number to be considered as accounted for as "keeping house" to 7,400,000.*

t be remembered that this reduction is upon a total of only 1,645,188, the number of females s and upward appearing in the Tables of Occupations. Of this number, 323,791 are engaged ture, 17,582 in trade and transportation, 328,286 in manufactures and mining, and 975,529 in personal and professional services. An examination of the numbers reported under each occupation will lead to the conclusion that many employments, and these quite the most nu- rnish practically no cases whatever of such union of family-housekeeping with paid service . *The number allowed on account of such duplication,* 170,363, appears, from a particular *than from a general view, to be ample.*

TABLE LXV.—*Occupations: The United States by Classes, and severally, with the Periods of Life and Nationality, (Selected,) of Persons occupied*—1870.

	Occupations.	PERSONS OCCUPIED.					
		All ages.			10 to 15.	16 to 59.	60 and over.
		Total.	Males.	Females.	Total.	Total.	Total.
	POPULATION, 10 YEARS AND OVER	28,228,945	14,258,866	13,970,079	3,604,369	20,686,795	1,937,781
	All occupations, (persons engaged in)	12,505,923	10,669,635	1,836,288	739,164	11,081,517	685,242
	AGRICULTURE	5,922,471	5,525,503	396,968	499,558	4,959,890	463,023
1	Agricultural laborers	2,885,996	2,512,664	373,332	499,474	2,287,708	98,814
2	Apiarists	136	136	....	....	124	12
3	Dairymen and dairywomen	3,550	3,133	417	....	3,466	84
4	Farm and plantation overseers	3,609	3,609	....	....	3,493	116
5	Farmers and planters	2,977,711	2,955,030	22,681	....	2,618,000	359,711
6	Florists	1,085	1,046	39	....	1,044	41
7	Gardeners and nurserymen	31,435	31,202	233	....	27,748	3,687
8	Stock-drovers	3,181	3,181	....	....	3,082	99
9	Stock-herders	5,590	5,545	45	....	5,441	149
10	Stock-raisers	6,588	6,558	30	....	6,388	200
11	Turpentine farmers	361	361	....	....	350	11
12	Turpentine laborers	2,117	1,933	184	84	2,018	15
13	Vinegrowers	1,112	1,105	7	....	1,028	84
	PROFESSIONAL & PERSONAL SERVICES	2,684,793	1,618,121	1,166,672	149,491	2,428,147	107,155
14	Actors	2,053	1,361	692	25	2,002	26
15	Apprentices to learned professions	386	341	45	68	318	....
16	Apprentices to barbers	859	853	6	265	594	....
17	Apprentices to dentists	166	165	1	29	137	....
18	Architects	2,017	2,016	1	....	1,969	48
19	Artists, (not specified) (*a*)	2,948	2,663	285	7	2,843	98
20	Auctioneers	2,266	2,254	12	....	2,155	111
21	Authors and lecturers	458	343	115	....	421	37
22	Barbers and hairdressers	23,935	22,756	1,179	315	23,340	280
23	Bath-house keepers	94	89	5	....	82	12
24	Billiard and bowling-saloon keepers	1,220	1,217	3	8	1,202	10
25	Bill-posters	424	424	....	5	406	13
26	Boarding and lodging-house keepers	12,785	5,725	7,060	....	11,772	1,013
27	Boot-blacks	587	587	....	238	340	9
28	Card-writers	33	30	3	....	32	1
29	Chemists, (practicing)	608	608	....	....	579	29
30	Chimney-sweeps	73	73	....	11	59	3
31	Chiropodists	65	63	2	....	60	5
32	Claim agents	693	693	....	....	663	30
33	Clergymen	43,874	43,807	67	....	39,489	4,385
34	Clerks and copyists	6,138	5,891	247	196	5,836	106
35	Clerks in Government offices	8,672	7,729	943	33	8,364	275
36	Clerks in hotels and restaurants	5,243	5,166	77	49	5,147	47
37	Dentists	7,839	7,815	24	....	7,678	163
38	Designers and draughtsmen	934	921	13	3	913	18
39	Domestic servants	975,734	108,380	867,354	109,503	838,409	27,822
40	Employés of companies, (n. s.) (*b*)	848	795	53	14	759	75
41	Employés of Government	14,407	13,806	601	91	13,912	404
42	Employés of hotels and restaurants (*c*)	23,438	17,139	6,299	921	22,263	254
43	Engineers, civil	4,703	4,703	....	1	4,574	128
44	Hostlers	17,586	17,584	2	436	16,770	380
45	Hotel-keepers	26,394	25,529	865	....	24,901	1,493
46	Hunters and trappers	940	938	2	16	847	77
47	Indian scouts, guides, & interpreters	171	171	....	....	162	9
48	Intelligence-office keepers	191	164	27	....	175	16
49	Inventors	352	352	....	....	333	10
50	Janitors	1,709	1,623	146	10	1,592	167
51	Journalists	5,286	5,251	35	....	5,180	106
52	Laborers, (not specified)	1,031,666	1,010,345	21,321	32,159	948,404	51,103

(*a*) See Painters and Sculptors.
(*b*) See Employés of Express, Insurance, Railroad, Street railroad, and Telegraph companies, of Trading and transportation companies, (not specified,) and of Manufacturing establishments, (not specified.)
(*c*) Not clerks.

Second. That it is not deemed practicable, in the United States, to secure that the average enumerator shall, in the course of a canvass necessarily hurried, fill two or

LE LXV.—*Occupations: The United States, by Classes, and severally, with the Periods of Life and Nationality, (Selected,) of Persons occupied*—1870.

NATIVITY.									
United States.	Germany.	Ireland.	England and Wales.	Scotland.	British America.	Sweden, Norway, and Denmark.	France.	China and Japan.	
921, 058	1, 611, 781	1, 769, 375	600, 253	134, 274	470, 476	230, 426	110, 979	60, 174	
802, 034	836, 418	947, 234	301, 795	71, 922	189, 318	109, 658	58, 200	46, 274	
303, 363	224, 531	138, 425	77, 173	17, 850	48, 288	50, 480	16, 472	2, 861	
700, 268	57, 261	43, 398	19, 122	3, 798	20, 589	19, 917	4, 026	1, 760	1
128	4	....	....	....	2	....	2	....	2
1, 831	797	343	91	18	53	34	111	14	3
3, 396	49	59	26	16	5	....	18	1	4
569, 023	150, 114	88, 923	54, 880	13, 039	27, 171	30, 259	11, 459	366	5
522	183	104	135	63	9	6	48	....	6
13, 845	6, 259	5, 079	2, 378	736	318	178	679	676	7
2, 740	190	118	49	16	10	6	15	....	8
3, 320	151	153	141	78	49	50	38	35	9
5, 321	214	222	178	51	75	26	44	....	10
360	....	1	....	....	....	....	....	....	11
2, 111	2	1	1	2	....	....	....	....	12
498	307	24	172	2	7	4	32	3	13
858, 178	191, 212	425, 087	49, 905	12, 672	48, 014	29, 333	13, 102	19, 471	
1, 328	153	99	234	11	35	....	31	95	14
347	14	6	10	....	4	....	1	....	15
685	134	4	12	1	7	....	3	....	16
154	2	1	2	....	5	1	....	....	17
1, 343	261	72	145	65	33	19	35	....	18
2, 029	420	81	176	24	48	14	68	2	19
1, 907	97	96	87	17	19	3	18	....	20
372	32	11	24	4	5	2	2	....	21
16, 377	4, 814	423	381	71	350	67	433	243	22
53	15	2	12	2	....	1	6	....	23
968	107	45	28	4	24	6	19	....	24
353	22	39	14	2	7	....	3	1	25
7, 496	1, 336	2, 173	572	108	349	243	153	112	26
446	16	28	6	....	10	3	11	3	27
19	2	4	6	....	....	1	....	....	28
330	134	26	61	13	5	4	8	....	29
60	6	1	2	1	....	2	....	....	30
47	4	3	5	1	1	....	2	....	31
644	13	9	15	1	4	....	5	....	32
35, 668	2, 745	1, 740	1, 566	318	485	198	416	6	33
5, 341	206	196	186	38	80	8	20	12	34
7, 519	338	379	186	43	64	24	35	....	35
4, 407	280	210	101	14	83	17	27	....	36
7, 299	146	58	116	24	106	9	21	....	37
542	139	48	100	28	18	7	28	....	38
720, 180	42, 866	145, 956	12, 531	3, 399	14, 878	11 287	2, 874	5, 420	39
628	43	97	37	11	6	6	5	1	40
10, 078	987	2, 425	381	133	164	66	64	1	41
15, 598	2, 145	3, 762	504	121	305	197	254	98	42
3, 959	191	167	206	39	42	17	31	....	43
11, 756	1, 365	3, 282	428	91	322	80	89	10	44
19, 416	3, 037	1, 915	831	118	384	104	239	19	45
752	24	13	28	4	92	10	11	....	46
95	11	2	6	....	13	3	8	16	47
111	22	15	8	3	7	4	3	15	48
317	10	3	11	2	6	2	1	....	49
1, 031	154	371	120	25	9	13	21	....	50
4, 411	314	174	183	55	54	90	34	1	51
602, 075	96, 432	229, 199	21, 932	5, 723	25, 394	15, 459	4, 832	9, 436	52

ee thousand subdivisions with appropriate entries without much loss and confusion. assistant marshals are appointed under the American system, nice discriminations respect to industrial relations can hardly be maintained in a sufficient proportion of es to give value to the aggregate results. Of course, accuracy of *definition* is of no ue if the *content* be inadequate. It may even be doubted whether the enumerators

TABLE LXV.—*Occupations: The United States, by Classes, and severally, &c.*—**Continued.**

	Occupations.	PERSONS OCCUPIED.					
		All ages.			10 to 15.	16 to 59.	60 and over.
		Total.	Males.	Females.	Total.	Total.	Total.
53	Lamp-lighters	276	276	....	7	250	19
54	Land-surveyors	2,671	2,671	....	2	2,448	221
55	Launderers and laundresses	60,906	5,297	55,609	548	57,964	2,394
56	Lawyers	40,736	40,731	5	....	38,948	1,788
57	Librarians	213	170	43	1	191	21
58	Livery-stable keepers	8,504	8,493	11	....	8,278	226
59	Marines, (United States)	477	477	....	....	474	3
60	Messengers	8,717	8,637	80	4,093	4,375	249
61	Metallurgists	164	164	....	....	164	....
62	Midwives	1,186	....	1,186	....	766	420
63	Musicians, (professional) (*a*)	6,519	6,346	173	46	6,295	178
64	Naturalists	287	286	1	....	269	18
65	Nurses	10,976	806	10,170	....	9,636	1,340
66	Officers of the Army and Navy	2,286	2,286	....	....	2,207	79
67	Officials of companies, (not spec.) (*b*)	3,410	3,352	58	....	3,199	211
08	Officials of Government	44,743	44,329	414	....	42,058	2,685
69	Painters (*c*)	775	717	58	....	755	20
70	Physicians and surgeons	62,383	61,858	525	....	57,947	4,436
71	Restaurant-keepers	35,185	34,542	643	....	34,457	728
72	Sailors, (United States Navy)	780	780	....	8	765	7
73	Scavengers	301	299	2	1	276	24
74	Sculptors, (*c*)	250	246	4	....	238	12
75	Sextons	1,151	1,144	7	....	938	213
76	Short-hand writers	154	147	7	1	150	3
77	Showmen and showwomen	1,177	1,077	100	16	1,146	15
78	Soldiers, (United States Army)	22,081	22,081	....	....	22,059	22
79	Teachers, (not specified)	126,822	42,775	84,047	336	124,030	2,456
80	Teachers of dancing	149	141	8	....	145	4
81	Teachers of drawing and painting	108	43	65	....	107	1
82	Teachers of music (*a*)	9,491	3,911	5,580	19	9,247	225
83	Translators	21	21	....	....	17	4
84	Veterinary surgeons	1,166	1,166	....	....	1,048	118
83	Whitewashers	2,873	2,482	391	9	2,620	244
	TRADE AND TRANSPORTATION	1,191,238	1,172,540	18,698	14,472	1,149,042	27,724
86	Agents	10,499	10,443	56	19	10,111	369
87	Apprentices in stores	678	673	5	107	559	12
88	Bankers and brokers of money & st'ks	10,631	10,616	15	3	10,137	491
89	Barkeepers	14,362	14,292	70	159	14,043	160
90	Boatmen and watermen	21,332	21,302	30	408	20,484	440
91	Book-keepers & ac'tants in stores (*d*)	31,177	30,884	293	63	30,563	551
92	Canalmen	7,338	7,328	10	639	6,580	119
93	Clerks in stores (*d*)	222,504	216,310	6,194	7,085	213,588	1,831
94	Clerks and book-keepers in banks	7,103	7,081	22	23	6,994	84
95	Clerks and book-keepers in expr's co's	767	767	....	5	758	4
96	Clerks and book-keepers in ins. offices	1,568	1,562	6	13	1,537	18
97	Clerks and book-keep's in rail'd offices	7,374	7,364	10	28	7,300	46
98	Clerks and book-keepers in tel. offices	191	190	1	18	172	1
99	Commercial travelers	7,262	7,230	32	4	7,103	155
100	Draymen, hackmen, teamsters, &c.	120,756	120,560	196	1,427	116,815	2,514
101	Employés of trading & trans'n co's (*e*)	4,152	3,975	177	136	3,918	98
102	Employés of banks, (not clerks)	424	421	3	7	400	17
103	Employés of express co's, (not cl'ks)	8,554	8,549	5	52	8,362	140
104	Employés of insur'ce co's, (not cl'ks)	11,611	11,587	24	2	11,157	452
105	Employés of railroad co's, (not cl'ks)	154,027	153,965	62	874	151,589	1,564
106	Employés of st. railr'd co's, (not cl'ks)	5,103	5,102	1	26	5,054	23
107	Employés of telegraph co's, (not cl'ks)	8,316	7,961	355	260	8,027	29
108	Hucksters	17,362	16,147	1,215	157	16,297	908
109	Laborers	14,882	14,332	550	624	13,911	347
110	Milkmen and milkwomen	3,728	3,635	93	38	3,568	122

(*a*) See Musicians, (professional,) and Teachers of music.
(*b*) See Officials of Express, Insurance, Railroad, Street railroad, and Telegraph companies, (not specified,) and of Manufacturing and mining companies.
(*c*) See Artists, (not specified,) Painters, and Sculptors.
(*d*) See Book-keepers and accountants in stores, Clerks in stores, and Salesmen and saleswomen.
(*e*) Not specified.

of any country are capable of carrying out thoroughly any body of instructions respecting the return of occupations, which require more than the plain and simple character-

…BLE LXV.—*Occupations: The United States, by Classes, and severally, &c.*—Continued.

NATIVITY.									
United States.	Germany.	Ireland.	England and Wales.	Scotland.	British America.	Sweden, Norway, and Denmark.	France.	China and Japan.	
177	34	51	7	....	4	2	....	....	53
2,350	90	85	67	16	28	8	11	....	54
40,814	2,761	11,530	601	205	331	170	397	3,653	55
38,412	513	730	443	122	258	31	58	....	56
191	1	3	12	3	1	1	....	....	57
7,087	427	545	182	34	126	32	28	....	58
320	32	72	20	10	4	5	2	....	59
6,747	435	962	280	56	78	26	43	5	60
97	24	4	13	6	3	6	3	....	61
769	272	40	30	6	4	7	32	....	62
2,663	2,401	351	273	35	66	50	131	36	63
199	32	5	25	3	6	1	8	....	64
8,325	458	1,346	387	92	170	71	54	....	65
1,988	66	124	34	18	17	11	7	....	66
2,888	147	193	85	17	25	13	9	....	67
38,461	1,800	2,534	867	226	302	116	164	4	68
529	114	15	52	5	13	12	15	....	69
55,920	2,362	913	983	268	793	82	308	193	70
14,020	11,877	4,220	1,241	201	628	328	973	66	71
539	30	78	55	12	10	21	5	....	72
110	121	31	6	....	....	....	11	14	73
130	47	15	10	4	....	2	15	....	74
644	152	203	90	10	5	4	12	1	75
117	4	10	12	4	4	3	....	....	76
839	91	42	63	22	20	3	26	2	77
11,478	2,997	4,964	986	328	392	171	210	....	78
116,606	3,215	2,568	1,290	390	1,156	198	696	6	79
112	11	2	8	1	1	2	7	....	80
98	2	1	3	1	....	1	3	....	81
7,246	1,231	162	339	36	125	38	106	....	82
12	2	....	....	....	....	1	1	....	83
744	123	73	141	24	11	17	11	....	84
2,367	323	70	38	3	15	3	15	....	85
862,653	112,435	119,094	32,086	8,440	16,565	9,564	8,654	2,250	
8,816	438	434	391	86	140	37	63	6	86
619	24	6	13	1	2	2	3	....	87
9,004	684	258	311	90	74	15	85	1	88
7,330	3,508	1,824	444	81	221	89	341	4	89
17,499	737	2,019	312	91	326	131	63	....	90
24,494	2,250	1,524	1,250	490	447	74	186	38	91
6,058	293	799	72	13	61	2	19	....	92
181,478	16,886	9,532	5,341	1,537	2,732	1,044	1,166	207	93
6,547	198	91	104	30	30	28	37	....	94
682	8	31	20	5	14	....	4	....	95
1,437	42	24	34	5	12	4	4	....	96
6,387	139	368	257	74	76	11	16	....	97
173	2	7	4	....	4	....	....	....	98
6,203	350	222	235	51	84	27	19	....	99
83,078	11,261	17,925	2,616	630	2,613	457	549	26	100
3,316	222	264	86	28	93	84	16	6	101
360	21	22	13	1	4	1	1	....	102
6,625	556	839	214	43	132	40	22	1	103
10,218	625	205	238	55	196	17	36	....	104
94,505	7,855	37,822	3,860	913	2,857	3,930	381	568	105
3,481	577	763	125	23	66	13	29	....	106
7,577	98	226	164	31	159	21	10	....	107
10,909	2,296	2,214	455	71	138	41	295	55	108
9,234	1,801	2,468	462	142	215	176	76	6	109
2,016	1,026	430	80	31	13	2	51	....	110

…ation of each man's employment in the common phrase of the working people themselves. Certainly, it is not to be thought of in the United States.

The employments reported in the census have been, for the purposes of this publication, brought under four general titles, viz, Agriculture, Manufactures and Mining, Trade and Transportation, Personal and Professional Services, the latter having somewhat *of a residual relation to the* others, and yet in the main a substantial character, *and with limits not hard to define.*

TABLE LXV.—*Occupations: The United States, by Classes, and severally, &c.*—Continued.

	Occupations.	PERSONS OCCUPIED.					
		All ages.			10 to 15.	16 to 59.	60 and over.
		Total.	Males.	Females.	Total.	Total.	Total.
111	Mule-packers	473	473			473	
112	Newspaper criers and carriers	2,002	1,995	7	648	1,299	55
113	Officials of trading & transp'n co's (a)	976	967	9		927	49
114	Officials of banks	2,738	2,738			2,489	249
115	Officials of express companies	75	75			75	
116	Officials of insurance companies	762	762			668	94
117	Officials of railroad companies	1,902	1,902			1,830	72
118	Officials of street railroad companies	88	88			84	4
119	Officials of telegraph companies	72	71	1		71	1
120	Packers	1,421	1,229	192	36	1,325	60
121	Pawnbrokers	384	379	5		376	8
122	Peddlers	16,975	16,697	278	187	16,090	698
123	Pilots	3,649	3,648	1	4	3,500	145
124	Porters in stores and warehouses	16,631	16,631		286	15,964	381
125	Sailors	56,663	56,663		312	54,618	1,733
126	Salesmen and saleswomen (b)	14,203	11,428	2,775	365	13,692	146
127	Shippers and freighters	3,567	3,564	3	9	3,411	147
128	Steamboat men and women	7,975	7,935	40	36	7,840	99
129	Stewards and stewardesses	1,245	1,160	85		1,209	36
130	Toll-gate and bridge keepers	2,253	2,047	206	21	1,829	403
131	Traders and dealers, (not specified)	100,406	97,573	2,833	387	96,067	3,952
132	in agricultural implements	1,939	1,883	56		1,876	63
133	books and stationery	3,392	3,337	55		3,272	120
134	boots and shoes	7,019	6,947	72		6,761	258
135	cabinetware	4,087	4,071	16		3,928	159
136	cigars and tobacco	8,234	8,117	117		8,033	201
137	clothing	7,595	7,532	63		7,369	226
138	cloths and textile fabrics	1,163	1,115	48		1,131	32
139	coal	4,143	4,143			3,959	184
140	coal and wood	2,493	2,485	8		2,367	126
141	cotton	1,701	1,698	3		1,628	73
142	crock'y, china, & stonew'e	1,765	1,703	62		1,693	72
143	drugs and medicines	17,369	17,335	34		16,977	392
144	dry-goods	39,790	39,129	661		38,543	1,247
145	gold & silv'r ware & jew'y	6,402	6,382	20		6,208	194
146	groceries	74,410	73,213	1,197		71,676	2,734
147	hats and caps	3,375	3,360	15		3,161	214
148	ice	1,464	1,463	1		1,431	33
149	iron, tin, and copper wares	9,003	8,981	22		8,766	237
150	leather, hides, and skins	2,261	2,257	4		2,171	90
151	lime	310	310			297	13
152	liquors and wines	11,718	11,612	106		11,504	214
153	live stock	7,723	7,718	5		7,558	165
154	lumber	9,440	9,436	4		9,072	368
155	machinery, (not spec.) (c)	254	254			246	8
156	music and musical instr'ts	848	830	18		823	25
157	newspapers & periodicals	1,455	1,434	21		1,409	46
158	oils, paints, & turpentine	986	985	1		946	40
159	optical instruments	301	301			291	10
160	produce	11,809	11,746	63		11,468	341
161	provisions	7,528	7,474	54		7,233	295
162	real estate	8,933	8,919	14		8,446	487
163	sewing-machines	3,152	3,077	75		3,116	36
164	Undertakers	1,996	1,976	20		1,853	143
165	Weighers, gaugers, and measurers	926	923	3		887	39
166	Wreckers	93	93		2	90	1
	MANUFACTURES AND MINING	2,707,421	2,353,471	353,950	75,643	2,544,438	87,340
167	Agricultural implement makers	3,811	3,786	25	68	3,653	90
168	Artificial flower makers	1,169	218	951	262	894	13

(a) Not specified.
(b) See Book-keepers and accountants in stores, and Clerks in stores.
(c) Not agricultural implements.

The reason for making a common title for Trade and Transportation must be sufficiently evident without explanation.

Mining, which stands in idea between agriculture and manufactures, in that, like agriculture, it obtains the raw material of subsequent industrial processes, while, like

ABLE LXV.—*Occupations: The United States, by Classes, and severally, &c.*—Continued.

NATIVITY.									
United States.	Germany.	Ireland.	England and Wales.	Scotland.	British America.	Sweden, Norway, and Denmark.	France.	China and Japan.	
248	19	21	6	2	22	6	12	39	111
1, 431	285	140	73	13	12	8	15	....	112
861	34	31	29	6	7	3	1	....	113
2, 572	57	29	42	12	12	....	6	....	114
72	....	....	1	....	1	1	....	....	115
696	30	11	9	5	5	....	3	....	116
1, 664	31	110	55	18	12	5	2	....	117
77	4	4	2	....	1	....	....	....	118
64	2	2	1	....	1	1	....	....	119
874	155	218	64	9	39	7	11	11	120
130	107	38	29	3	7	1	10	9	121
7, 072	4, 799	2, 180	571	108	211	78	319	132	122
3, 214	80	138	73	12	42	44	14	....	123
8, 418	2, 888	4, 100	377	122	120	79	164	83	124
42, 004	2, 247	4, 087	2, 170	704	1, 656	1, 710	265	86	125
11, 306	973	1, 025	374	158	184	10	55	....	126
2, 901	112	114	88	32	63	50	24	1	127
6, 519	295	638	189	48	96	51	23	6	128
992	58	73	50	10	19	5	9	1	129
1, 802	90	103	71	15	21	11	9	....	130
74, 381	11, 078	5, 647	2, 992	800	985	376	1, 308	604	131
1, 841	24	13	28	3	12	6	5	....	132
2, 417	324	239	188	65	29	21	32	1	133
4, 903	1, 073	454	277	51	60	16	84	....	134
2, 756	673	258	179	34	62	16	41	....	135
4, 824	2, 352	326	168	38	51	41	99	23	136
3, 415	2, 872	345	263	51	58	14	135	8	137
845	157	72	37	10	10	6	9	....	138
3, 418	297	254	155	31	23	4	15	....	139
1, 710	270	224	73	22	39	13	51	9	140
1, 388	60	119	54	19	7	2	21	....	141
1, 056	264	179	122	28	13	9	23	25	142
14, 273	1, 470	339	607	88	189	64	118	51	143
31, 180	4, 564	1, 505	786	319	242	122	369	4	144
4, 315	1, 084	139	272	52	81	96	100	48	145
46, 226	13, 456	8, 879	2, 075	444	690	232	999	124	146
2, 355	523	231	124	20	16	7	46	1	147
1, 067	180	113	47	8	12	13	7	....	148
7, 313	794	316	250	83	95	24	46	1	149
1, 542	433	109	86	17	17	3	29	....	150
261	17	19	6	4	2	1	....	....	151
4, 559	2, 672	3, 211	387	99	102	45	357	4	152
6, 423	520	382	150	33	82	12	58	1	153
8, 370	336	203	183	62	157	33	29	....	154
231	7	3	6	2	1	2	....	....	155
643	117	12	45	2	4	1	7	....	156
1, 059	128	121	103	14	7	....	10	....	157
783	91	33	38	12	11	2	7	....	158
114	98	12	41	5	2	....	13	....	159
9, 171	1, 056	643	356	78	155	29	69	27	160
6, 077	533	450	167	42	51	4	65	11	161
7, 391	531	425	269	63	77	15	61	2	162
2, 885	88	44	57	24	30	5	5	....	163
1, 480	173	216	74	9	13	6	15	....	164
747	24	97	31	6	7	6	5	....	165
61	3	3	16	3	3	2	....	....	166
1, 777, 840	308, 240	264, 628	142, 631	32, 960	76, 451	20, 281	19, 972	21, 602	
2, 836	210	477	105	32	109	11	15	....	167
828	135	103	28	4	5	3	38	....	168

anufactures, its agencies and forces are chiefly mechanical, not chemical, has, for onvenience mainly, been assigned to the group of Manufactures.

A still stronger consideration of convenience, though with somewhat less clear conderations of propriety, induced the Superintendent to place the fishing industry in e category of Manufactures. The number of persons engaged in the fisheries will ways and inevitably be below the fact, for the reasons, first, that this industry is sually *pursued for a season only*, while, for the remainder of the year, the fisherman

TABLE LXV.—*Occupations: The United States, by Classes, and severally, &c.*—Continued.

	Occupations.	PERSONS OCCUPIED.					
		All ages.			10 to 15.	16 to 59.	60 and over.
		Total.	Males.	Females.	Total.	Total.	Total.
169	Apprentices, (not specified) (*a*)	15,302	15,102	200	2,132	13,170	....
170	Bag-makers	866	520	346	146	710	10
171	Bakers	27,680	27,442	238	537	26,592	531
172	Basket-makers	3,297	3,082	215	100	2,735	412
173	Bell-founders	169	165	4	1	164	4
174	Belting-factory operatives	296	295	1	5	287	4
175	Blacksmiths	141,774	141,774	....	599	135,166	5,999
176	Bleachers, dyers, and scourers	4,901	4,582	319	141	4,532	[illegible]
177	Blind, door, and sash makers	5,155	5,155	....	102	4,987	66
178	Boat-makers	2,101	2,101	....	5	1,990	106
179	Bone and ivory workers	208	208	....	1	200	7
180	Bookbinders and finishers	9,104	6,375	2,729	448	8,496	160
181	Boot and shoe makers	171,127	161,485	9,642	2,328	159,542	9,257
182	Box-factory operatives	6,080	3,857	2,223	600	5,394	86
183	Brass founders and workers	4,694	4,592	102	98	4,486	110
184	Brewers and maltsters	11,246	11,238	8	45	11,037	164
185	Brick and tile makers	26,070	25,996	74	1,456	24,216	398
186	Bridge builders and contractors (*b*)	1,029	1,029	....	....	1,013	16
187	Britannia and japanned ware makers	1,092	987	105	17	1,051	24
188	Broom and brush makers	5,816	5,299	517	289	5,318	209
189	Bronze-workers	79	67	12	1	77	1
190	Builders and contractors, (n. a) (*b*)	7,511	7,508	3	....	7,177	334
191	Butchers	44,354	44,354	....	338	42,841	1,175
192	Button-factory operatives	1,272	736	536	183	1,055	34
193	Cabinetmakers	42,835	42,123	712	886	39,854	2,095
194	Candle, soap, and tallow makers	1,942	1,900	42	80	1,781	81
195	Card and fancy-paper makers	339	118	221	29	306	4
196	Car-makers	2,228	2,228	....	17	2,187	24
197	Carpenters and joiners	344,596	344,596	....	864	329,962	13,770
198	Carpet-bag and satchel makers (*c*)	202	139	63	18	176	8
199	Carpet-makers	15,669	10,292	5,377	522	13,628	1,519
200	Carriage and wagon makers	42,464	42,432	32	208	40,738	1,518
201	Charcoal and lime burners	3,834	3,829	5	29	3,715	90
202	Cheese-makers	3,534	2,750	784	50	3,409	75
203	Cigar-makers (*d*)	28,286	26,442	1,844	1,209	26,893	184
204	Clerks and book-keepers (*e*)	5,861	5,641	220	84	5,697	80
205	Clock-makers	1,779	1,704	75	53	1,635	91
206	Comb-makers	693	595	98	47	618	28
207	Confectioners	8,219	7,607	612	84	7,881	254
208	Coopers	41,789	41,789	....	349	38,830	2,610
209	Copper-workers	2,122	2,118	4	13	2,049	60
210	Cotton-mill operatives (*f*)	111,606	47,208	64,398	19,946	88,840	2,820
211	Curriers, tanners, finishers of leather	28,702	28,642	60	257	26,425	2,020
212	Daguerreotypists and photographers	7,558	7,330	228	32	7,429	97
213	Die-sinkers and stamp-makers	479	477	2	9	459	11
214	Distillers and rectifiers	2,874	2,868	6	....	2,799	75
215	Employés (*e*)	20,242	17,744	2,498	1,302	18,465	475
216	Engineers and firemen	34,233	34,233	....	33	33,857	341
217	Engravers	4,226	4,197	29	48	4,102	76
218	Fertilizer-establishment operatives	316	310	6	2	298	16
219	File makers, cutters, and grinders	1,413	1,401	12	94	1,301	18
220	Fireworks-makers	101	90	11	14	79	8
221	Fishermen and oystermen	27,106	27,071	35	837	24,882	1,387
222	Flax-dressers	1,046	725	321	201	828	17
223	Fur-workers	1,191	836	355	33	1,127	31
224	Galloon, gimp, and tassel makers	569	242	327	74	458	37
225	Gas-works employés	2,086	2,082	4	26	2,020	40
226	Gilders	1,534	1,499	35	22	1,481	31

(*a*) All apprentices to manual trades, whose trades were specified on the schedules, have been included in these tables, with the journeymen of their respective crafts.
(*b*) See Builders and contractors, (not specified;) also Bridge, House, and Railroad builders and contractors.
(*c*) See Trunk and valise makers.
(*d*) See Tobacco-factory operatives.
(*e*) In manufacturing establishments, (not specified.)
(*f*) See Mill and factory operatives, (not specified,) and Woolen-mill operatives.

follows some other gainful avocation under which he will preferably be reported;*

* Often, indeed, fishing is carried on at any season of the year only incidentally to some other occupation from which the family derives its principal support.

[T]ABLE XLV.—*Occupations: The United States, by Classes, and severally, &c.*—Continued.

NATIVITY.									
United States.	Germany.	Ireland.	England and Wales.	Scotland.	British America.	Sweden, Norway, and Denmark.	France.	China and Japan.	
13,209	745	609	332	62	175	30	35	....	169
476	116	131	34	10	5	1	7	70	170
11,167	10,863	2,421	897	487	377	134	628	31	171
2,044	936	74	88	15	31	25	41	1	172
137	6	18	4	2	....	1	1	....	173
225	13	35	16	2	2	....	2	....	174
101,567	14,012	12,339	5,005	1,401	3,712	1,236	866	44	175
2,013	705	1,001	614	165	39	22	162	....	176
3,890	618	171	106	22	161	51	26	45	177
1,743	92	122	72	11	43	1	11	....	178
138	44	10	9	....	....	1	3	....	179
6,460	944	778	498	93	120	53	39	....	180
108,320	28,226	16,998	5,082	1,041	5,506	1,462	1,520	480	181
4,273	918	472	116	33	87	19	34	36	182
2,501	454	1,079	372	125	70	22	45	....	183
2,715	6,780	520	389	73	92	44	271	5	184
15,988	3,340	3,443	731	85	2,200	305	150	62	185
860	23	80	22	9	27	3	3	....	186
655	91	109	120	17	93	2	2	....	187
4,025	747	530	226	52	102	28	30	....	188
24	20	16	4	....	2	....	12	....	189
4,977	483	1,263	404	104	145	36	44	1	190
23,412	13,227	2,646	2,080	247	504	123	1,076	85	191
802	54	263	89	3	54	....	2	....	192
25,293	11,798	1,595	1,020	240	849	632	518	11	193
936	480	304	77	25	28	10	27	22	194
283	16	26	7	2	3	....	1	....	195
1,756	164	151	80	20	98	8	11	....	196
264,531	29,704	16,566	9,784	2,845	11,288	3,500	1,796	155	197
82	82	14	7	5	....	1	3	....	198
8,518	1,725	2,706	1,524	561	302	49	70	1	199
32,244	5,196	1,590	1,162	222	977	288	288	3	200
2,457	306	596	153	26	122	18	88	5	201
3,123	114	53	58	31	70	3	7	....	202
13,833	9,292	547	804	51	177	114	162	1,727	203
4,997	324	202	189	49	42	1	18	1	204
1,351	146	171	64	4	12	1	9	1	205
372	13	71	17	7	10	....	....	....	206
4,350	2,185	477	312	101	114	30	225	6	207
25,903	8,954	3,484	706	232	973	272	580	11	208
997	415	337	164	47	43	51	25	....	209
71,547	1,214	18,713	10,091	1,714	7,683	35	110	3	210
18,005	3,458	4,764	736	256	893	165	160	....	211
6,327	410	146	287	42	165	54	50	5	212
332	39	31	40	9	9	5	9	....	213
1,610	692	334	79	11	23	7	40	....	214
12,549	2,514	2,717	912	205	462	260	143	166	215
24,296	2,098	3,317	2,550	742	653	127	179	....	216
2,288	890	230	434	103	40	18	113	1	217
127	56	70	12	1	35	6	1	....	218
693	183	135	345	11	19	1	12	....	219
69	11	7	9	....	2	1	1	....	220
21,551	564	872	443	95	1,573	345	165	310	221
717	12	187	43	63	19	....	1	....	222
435	372	183	111	8	17	5	17	....	223
446	40	37	20	3	4	3	3	....	224
894	163	816	121	35	23	9	5	1	225
771	382	133	103	30	24	17	22	....	226

[se]cond, that no inconsiderable proportion of the persons actually engaged on the water [i]n this pursuit, at the time of the enumeration, having no families to report them, are [e]ntirely omitted from the census under the American system; third, that where fisheries are carried on in vessels larger than the ordinary row or sail boat, the hands [e]mployed are generally known, not as fishermen, but as sailors. The last statement [h]olds true of the vast majority of all persons who are engaged in the whale, cod, and [m]ackerel fisheries. It is true that, according to the theory of a census of occupations [t]aken in the interest of industrial science mainly, vessels so employed should, with all [t]heir hands, be excluded from the class of transportation and be returned as engaged [in] *the fisheries; but this distinction is one which it appears hopeless to make, at least*

TABLE LXV.—*Occupations: The United States, by Classes, and severally, &c.*—**Continued.**

	Occupations.	PERSONS OCCUPIED.					
		All ages.			10 to 15.	16 to 59.	60 and over.
		Total.	Males.	Females.	Total.	Total.	Total.
285	Powder-makers	575	568	7	1	556	16
286	Printers	39,860	38,365	1,495	1,570	37,813	477
287	Print-works operatives	3,738	2,786	952	599	2,975	164
288	Publishers of books, maps, newspaper	1,577	1,577			1,537	40
289	Pump-makers	1,672	1,672		14	1,564	94
290	Quarrymen	13,589	13,589		548	12,781	260
291	Quartz and stamp mill laborers	617	617		44	569	4
292	Rag-pickers	436	336	100	40	302	94
293	Railroad builders and contractors (*a*)	1,292	1,292			1,273	19
294	Reed and shuttle makers	200	194	6	4	189	7
295	Roofers and slaters	2,750	2,750		27	2,669	54
296	Rope and cordage makers	2,675	2,345	330	292	2,275	108
297	Rubber-factory operatives	3,886	2,035	1,851	143	3,702	41
298	Sail and awning makers	2,309	2,278	31	8	2,193	108
299	Salt-makers	1,721	1,721		56	1,611	54
300	Saw-mill operatives	47,298	47,263	35	797	45,969	532
301	Sawyers	6,939	6,939		18	6,459	462
302	Scale and rule makers	416	390	26	9	399	8
303	Screw-makers	780	434	346	117	655	8
304	Sewing-machine factory operatives	3,881	2,015	1,866	150	3,710	21
305	Sewing-machine operators	3,042	182	2,860	176	2,856	10
306	Shingle and lath makers	3,788	3,704	84	154	3,508	126
307	Ship-carpenters	15,900	15,900		10	15,102	788
308	Ship-smiths	396	396		1	387	8
309	Ship-calkers	3,068	3,068		3	2,950	115
310	Ship-riggers	1,057	1,041	16	1	990	66
311	Shirt, cuff, and collar makers (*b*)	4,080	1,268	2,812	162	3,884	34
312	Shot, cartridge, and fuse makers	186	97	89	12	171	3
313	Silk-mill operatives	3,256	954	2,302	893	2,337	26
314	Spring and axle makers	301	301		7	289	5
315	Starch-makers	229	189	40	12	215	2
316	Stave, shook, and heading makers	1,858	1,825	33	124	1,701	33
317	Steam-boiler makers	6,958	6,953	5	65	6,819	74
318	Steam engine makers	4,172	4,172		5	4,086	81
319	Stereotypers	333	329	4	1	323	9
320	Stove, furnace, and grate makers (*c*)	1,543	1,543		16	1,497	30
321	Straw-workers	2,029	599	1,430	52	1,932	45
322	Sugar makers and refiners	1,609	1,599	10	10	1,568	31
323	Tailors, tailoresses, & seamstresses (*b*)	161,820	64,613	97,207	2,718	153,977	5,125
324	Tinners	30,524	30,507	17	449	29,581	494
325	Tool and cutlery makers	5,351	5,255	96	181	5,072	98
326	Trunk and valise makers (*d*)	1,845	1,831	14	63	1,751	31
327	Tobacco-factory operatives (*e*)	11,985	9,695	2,290	2,496	9,319	170
328	Truss-makers	74	64	10		72	2
329	Type founders and cutters	649	556	93	64	577	8
330	Umbrella and parasol makers	1,439	749	690	67	1,338	34
331	Upholsterers	5,736	5,558	178	67	5,548	121
332	Wheelwrights	20,942	20,942		15	19,153	1,774
333	Whip-makers	609	491	118	12	561	36
334	Window-shade makers	245	219	26	6	236	3
335	Wire makers and workers	1,834	1,753	81	72	1,741	21
336	Woodchoppers	8,338	8,338		130	7,931	277
337	Wood turners and carvers	7,947	7,903	41	84	7,665	198
338	Woolen-mill operatives (*f*)	58,836	36,060	22,776	7,427	50,212	1,197

(*a*) See Builders and contractors, (not specified;) also Bridge and House builders and contracters.
(*b*) See Milliners, dress, and mantua makers, Shirt, cuff, and collar makers, and Tailors, tailoresses, and seamstresses.
(*c*) See Iron-foundry operatives.
(*d*) See Carpet-bag and satchel makers.
(*e*) See Cigar-makers.
(*f*) See Cotton mill operatives and Mill and factory operatives, (not specified.)

broad reasons are found in the very form of a census taken under existing laws in the United States, one of which explains the first class of discrepancies, while the other covers the ground of the second. As these discrepancies are capital in their extent, they require to be discussed at some length.

ᴀʙʟᴇ LXV.—*Occupations: The United States, by Classes, and severally, &c.*—Continued.

NATIVITY.									
United States.	Germany.	Ireland.	England and Wales.	Scotland.	British America.	Sweden, Norway, and Denmark.	France.	China and Japan.	
290	26	148	37	12	25	4	2	22	285
31, 208	2, 249	2, 856	1, 652	409	803	122	161	23	286
1, 674	47	1, 078	573	141	89	2	10	....	287
1, 353	50	47	69	13	17	2	7	....	288
1, 465	66	39	44	10	31	4	4	....	289
6, 020	1, 301	4, 031	1, 258	140	436	203	54	....	290
156	119	98	89	8	68	15	32	3	291
203	108	68	2	....	....	1	8	....	292
999	22	167	27	19	40	7	6	....	293
156	5	9	21	6	1	....	....	....	294
1, 707	219	483	193	75	38	5	10	....	295
1, 535	431	414	121	63	34	8	15	2	296
2, 383	347	778	103	24	224	5	9	....	297
1, 679	81	168	111	31	79	114	17	....	298
799	251	460	20	14	123	11	21	16	299
33, 527	3, 404	1, 793	689	304	4, 894	1, 176	135	40	300
5, 764	480	231	107	28	209	15	37	19	301
290	43	44	18	4	15	....	2	....	302
558	17	158	30	6	5	....	....	....	303
2, 614	195	742	190	28	44	4	22	....	304
2, 337	77	470	71	17	52	5	6	....	305
3, 136	146	53	39	13	260	26	5	....	306
11, 720	644	1, 176	545	295	1, 072	252	74	1	307
283	3	66	20	5	10	3	3	....	308
2, 346	82	312	93	32	151	19	10	....	309
495	65	175	129	42	26	78	12	....	310
2, 970	277	557	110	33	53	5	17	....	311
155	10	17	4	....	....	....	....	....	312
2, 258	78	233	432	33	35	4	73	....	313
165	32	58	19	8	10	....	4	....	314
80	57	79	12	....	1	....	....	....	315
1, 353	286	69	32	7	59	10	28	....	316
3, 177	585	1, 907	732	307	139	21	45	....	317
2, 549	375	427	464	134	82	34	62	....	318
211	25	43	23	13	4	1	12	....	319
963	264	192	70	9	30	1	10	....	320
1, 880	13	83	29	4	18	....	2	....	321
360	893	213	32	9	5	7	21	9	322
94, 875	33, 200	18, 009	4, 785	1, 196	2, 795	1, 961	1, 496	145	323
22, 337	3, 835	1, 732	1, 019	241	529	155	264	13	324
3, 012	672	560	606	51	346	11	40	....	325
966	549	176	44	8	24	8	19	....	326
10, 266	936	451	96	10	24	6	36	1	327
49	14	3	7	....	1	....	....	....	328
457	57	67	37	15	3	....	5	....	329
988	134	239	38	....	9	1	15	....	330
2, 832	1, 683	437	313	70	96	99	100	....	331
17, 477	1, 416	652	419	111	520	65	103	3	332
479	44	41	29	1	7	2	7	....	333
178	45	9	1	1	4	2	....	....	334
832	172	541	195	19	47	4	6	....	335
6, 201	322	196	100	30	735	88	81	419	336
4, 271	2, 210	450	347	80	153	93	155	....	337
32, 083	2, 664	12, 231	6, 609	1, 306	3, 175	69	138	97	338

First, however, it needs to be stated just what constitutes a discrepancy. A failure the numbers reported in the one place and in the other to balance exactly is not a screpancy. On the contrary, this is to be expected; and if the numbers are found be in excess in the proper set of tables, and to be in excess to only the proper extent, iis furnishes a statistical proof of a high character. The tables in which the numbers iould thus be generally found in excess are the Occupation Tables. The reason for ie excess being found in these Tables and not in the others is, that the schedule of anufactures gives an *average* return of the number of "hands employed," while the atistics of occupations are taken from a count of individuals upon the population hedule, and *present, therefore, a maximum* return, embracing, as they do, artisans of every class out of employment, temporarily disabled, or for some other reason not included in the actual return of any establishment.

The degree to which such excess should extend will depend, within certain limits, upon the nature of the special occupation, as well as upon the general condition of manufacturing industry throughout the country at the time. It should rarely, however, fall below six per cent. in any trade at any time, and it should quite as rarely go above sixteen per cent.

Whenever, therefore, the numbers returned in the Tables of Occupations do not exceed those under the same titles in the Tables of Manufactures by at least six per cent., and, on the other hand, whenever the former exceed the latter by more than sixteen per cent., there a discrepancy must be admitted.

And, first, of those cases where the numbers in the Tables of Occupations do not exceed those in the Tables of Manufactures by six per cent., or even fall below them.

Instances of this kind are principally confined to the returns of factory operatives. At the present census these instances are sufficiently marked to require explanation.*

A portion of these omissions, undoubtedly, may be accounted for by the large number (41,619) returned under the head of "Mill and factory operatives not specified," as well as by the number (20,242) of "Employés of manufacturing establishments not specified;" but, in the main, the explanation of the discrepancies is found in the fact, heretofore adverted to, that women and children employed in factories are omitted in large numbers.

Second. Those instances where the numbers appearing in the Tables of Occupations exceed those in the Tables of Manufactures by more than the probable or possible difference between a maximum and an average return. Unlike the class first noted, these discrepancies affect mainly the statistics of those occupations which are pursued singly, or by twos and threes, out of large mills and factories, and even, in a considerable degree, out of shops. Discrepancies of this character in no degree discredit the statistics of occupations. They arise from the fact that the return of "Productive Industry," under the census law of 1850, is not, as indeed it was not intended to be, a complete return of the mechanical production of the country.

The census attempts the enumeration of mechanical industry only as it is carried on in shops, and thus fails to embrace that large body of individual labor which is not attached to distinct "establishments of productive industry." Moreover, the census law establishes a mimimum (namely, the value of $500 annually) below which the production of shops shall not be returned; behind which unfortunate exception a host of minor establishments, producing in the neighborhood of $500, take refuge and thus escape enumeration.

The scope of these omissions may be seen in the tables on pages 664 and 665 of Volume I of the Ninth Census. Larger omissions occurred at the census of 1860, (see Vol. I, Ninth Census, p. 665.)

The effect of this wholesale omission of the production of certain trades upon the aggregate value of manufacturing and mechanical products in the country has been discussed in the quarto volume on Industry.

Inasmuch at it is not the Tables of Occupations which suffer from the comparison, it will not be necessary to pursue inquiry further into this class of discrepancies in the present connection. The Tables of Occupations are incontestably accurate, in a high degree, in respect to these common trades.

An exception.—In making such comparisons as the foregoing, between the Tables of Occupations and those of Manufactures, care should be used that the titles taken for the purpose really correspond. In some cases, even those in which the apparent correspondence is the strongest, the quantities are in fact not commensurable. An example may be found in the brick and tile manufacture. It would seem, at first glance, that the "hands employed" should answer exactly to the "brick and tile makers" in the Tables of Occupations; but, in fact, a considerable portion of the hands employed in large brick-yards, exceeding, indeed, not infrequently, the number of craftsmen, are classed and known as common laborers, and are so returned in the census. The table on page 666 of Vol. I, Ninth Census, will show the scope of this exception. It will be seen that, while in two or three minor cases the number returned on the Tables of Occupations exceeds, as we are accustomed to expect, the number in the Tables of Manufactures, the proportion of common laborers employed in brickyards where that branch of manufacture becomes considerable, (notably in the larger manufacturing States,) is so great as to raise the numbers in the latter tables considerably above those in the former.

Incomplete subdivision of employments.—In addition to the apparent deficiencies or discrepancies which have been noted, one general remark will suffice in explanation of

* At the census of 1860 the discrepancies of this kind were still more numerous and far more extensive. A single example will suffice. The Tables of Occupations characterize but a little over two thousand persons as connected with the woolen and worsted manufactures, while the Tables of Manufactures show that considerably more than forty thousand persons were engaged, upon the average, in these branches of manufacturing industry.

many of the entries in the tables, in respect to the accuracy of which question may naturally arise.

It must be borne in mind that the number of persons who are reported under a certain specified occupation does not necessarily embrace all the persons who perform the duties usually associated with that title, but only those who discharge such duties to the exclusion of other gainful occupations, or, at least, as their principal or sole professed means of support.

The organization of labor and the subdivision of industry vary in respect to completeness and minuteness with each successive community. As communities advance in industrial character, functions become separated, and distinct occupations become recognized. This country, from its peculiar conditions, presents almost every degree between the two extremes of industrial development in this particular. It is common to find on the returns from the present Territories, and even some of the present States of the Union, such entries as these: "Carpenter and miner," "Blacksmith and carpenter," "Blacksmith and miner." In many of the communities of the land it is difficult to draw distinctions much finer than those between the agricultural, the mining, the mechanical, and the commercial pursuit or profession. Indeed, even this is not always practicable, since it is matter of notoriety that in many of the States of the Union, and those not among the newest, the occupations of carpenter and farmer, or blacksmith and farmer, or farmer and fisherman, are frequently united in one person. In large and more prosperous communities a clear separation between such incongruous occupations takes place; yet, still, the carpenter, for instance, in nine out of ten counties in the United States, performs half a dozen functions which, in cities, are recognized as belonging to distinct trades.

The same general process occurs in agricultural, commercial, and professional employments; thus, the tables show 100,406 traders and dealers whose branch of trade is not specified.

The want of specifications in the case of this 100,406 is not due to the neglect of assistant marshals, but to the fact that these persons so characterized are actually selling agricultural implements, books and stationery, boots and shoes, &c., &c., through pretty much the entire line of articles sold by those other dealers whose departments are defined because the communities in which they dwell and deal are sufficiently large to allow of the subdivision of trade.

If, therefore, we look at those occupations which emerge as distinct employments only in communities where the organization of industry and the subdivision of labor are carried to a high degree, the number of persons engaged will appear to be impossibly small, unless the above considerations are borne carefully in mind.

ANOMALOUS ENTRIES.—Other seeming discrepancies, which demand at least an allusion here, occur where persons are returned as of certain special occupations in States where it is notorious that the industries represented are not carried on; or, again, where persons, not more than one, two, or five in number, are returned in a State under a description which implies a large body of workmen, as (in illustration of both these classes) when Ohio is returned as having one silk-mill operative, it being difficult to see how one operative could justify a silk-factory in Ohio, and it being, moreover, notorious, as matter of fact, that the manufacture of silk is not carried on in that State. An adequate explanation of all cases of this general nature is found in the consideration that the census takes account of persons where they are actually residing, and assigns them to their habitual occupation, whether it is being at the time pursued or not.

In the enumeration of tens of thousands of persons out of health, or out of employment, traveling, or visiting friends in other States, it is inevitable that such apparent anomalies should arise.

Nota Bene.—Each employment specified in the following tables must be understood in connection with the class or grand division of industry under which it is placed. To many, and, indeed, most of the specifications of occupation, this warning, in the nature of the case, does not apply.

Others, however, will be misinterpreted without a reference to the more general title. Thus, "clerks and copyists" appear under the head "personal and professional services," to the number of 6,138. These are clerks to lawyers, clerks to civil engineers, copyists not attached to commercial houses or manufacturing establishments, &c. "Clerks" also appear under the head of "Manufactures and Mining," so far as persons are employed in a purely clerical capacity in those banches of industry; while, under the title of "Trade and Transportation," "clerks" appear several times as "clerks in stores," "clerks in banks," "clerks in railroad-offices," &c. In such cases, "cross-references" will generally be found between the several parts of the tables where these entries occur.

TABLE LXVI.—*Occupations: Fifty Cities—Periods of Life of Persons engaged in Each Class—1870.*

	Fifty cities.	ALL CLASSES OF OCCUPATION.				AGRICULTURE.			
		Total.	10 to 15.	16 to 59.	60 and over.	Total.	10 to 15.	16 to 59.	60 and over.
	Total	2, 128, 608	60, 497	2, 012, 049	56, 062	22, 636	648	20, 146	1, 842
1	Albany, N. Y	21, 376	326	20, 423	627	194	....	187	7
2	Allegheny, Pa	25, 558	1, 056	23, 921	581	141	2	127	12
3	Baltimore, Md	94, 737	2, 927	88, 669	3, 141	735	7	668	60
4	Boston, Mass	102, 740	1, 494	98, 164	3, 082	499	4	460	35
5	Brooklyn, N. Y	139, 195	4, 197	131, 499	3, 499	565	5	538	22
6	Buffalo, N. Y	39, 686	998	37, 785	903	665	4	611	50
7	Cambridge, Mass	15, 036	208	14, 143	685	138	....	112	26
8	Charleston, S. C	18, 705	449	17, 164	1, 092	331	6	274	51
9	Charlestown, Mass	11, 169	44	10, 972	153	28	....	28	....
10	Chicago, Ill	112, 960	2, 903	108, 263	1, 794	533	7	481	45
11	Cincinnati, Ohio	77, 923	2, 729	73, 140	2, 054	1, 420	36	1, 302	82
12	Cleveland, Ohio	30, 211	459	29, 144	608	330	5	298	27
13	Columbus, Ohio	11, 625	371	10, 889	365	123	107	16	....
14	Dayton, Ohio	10, 689	403	9, 864	422	128	8	110	10
15	Detroit, Mich	51, 340	186	50, 952	202	278	....	270	8
16	Fall River, Mass	12, 882	1, 535	10, 911	436	351	11	275	65
17	Hartford, Conn	13, 339	113	12, 870	356	357	3	354	....
18	Indianapolis, Ind	18, 615	282	18, 079	254	210	2	198	10
19	Jersey City, N. J	26, 412	487	25, 366	559	311	1	299	11
20	Kansas City, Mo	12, 967	400	12, 386	181	237	5	227	5
21	Lawrence, Mass	14, 731	883	13, 581	267	124	1	103	20
22	Louisville, Ky	35, 800	1, 501	33, 150	1, 149	331	15	278	38
23	Lowell, Mass	20, 793	883	19, 109	801	206	8	165	33
24	Lynn, Mass	11, 807	103	11, 249	456	199	4	160	35
25	Memphis, Tenn	12, 614	128	12, 355	131	325	....	315	10
26	Milwaukee, Wis	23, 119	510	22, 067	542	244	3	207	34
27	Mobile, Ala	12, 186	367	11, 295	524	138	2	109	27
28	Newark, N. J	37, 468	1, 724	34, 234	1, 510	291	7	240	44
29	New Haven, Conn	17, 962	78	17, 515	369	279	....	252	27
30	New Orleans, La	66, 032	1, 846	61, 779	2, 407	1, 319	4	1, 218	97
31	New York, N. Y	350, 556	8, 456	336, 507	5, 593	1, 401	20	1, 338	43
32	Paterson, N. J	18, 375	1, 149	11, 750	476	181	9	157	15
33	Philadelphia, Pa	217, 685	7, 684	202, 127	7, 874	3, 690	173	3, 185	332
34	Pittsburgh, Pa	29, 854	1, 281	27, 815	758	444	7	404	33
35	Portland, Me	10, 695	29	10, 560	106	74	....	65	9
36	Providence, R. I	26, 266	938	24, 195	1, 133	249	12	206	31
37	Reading, Pa	11, 522	727	10, 425	370	50	....	47	3
38	Richmond, Va	18, 545	967	17, 019	559	311	12	263	36
39	Rochester, N. Y	21, 927	859	20, 229	839	274	16	246	12
40	San Francisco, Cal	68, 352	1, 021	66, 688	643	1, 000	10	969	21
41	Savannah, Ga	11, 350	463	9, 208	1, 679	154	....	121	33
42	Scranton, Pa	12, 509	802	11, 422	285	95	....	85	10
43	St. Louis, Mo	108, 691	3, 034	103, 934	1, 723	810	9	763	38
44	Syracuse, N. Y	16, 987	578	15, 793	616	259	14	219	26
45	Toledo, Ohio	13, 025	184	12, 606	235	110	....	101	9
46	Troy, N. Y	16, 526	344	15, 524	658	205	16	176	13
47	Utica, N. Y	10, 443	467	9, 419	557	180	13	147	20
48	Washington, D. C	41, 188	1, 256	38, 334	1, 598	284	....	244	40
49	Wilmington, Del	12, 908	338	11, 889	681	1, 268	62	1, 061	145
50	Worcester, Mass	16, 527	331	15, 667	529	567	18	467	82

E LXVI.—*Occupations: Fifty Cities—Periods of Life of Persons engaged in Each Class—* 1870.

	SONAL AND PROFESSIONAL.			TRADE AND TRANSPORTATION.				MANUFACTURES, MECHANICAL AND MINING INDUSTRIES.				
l.	10 to 15.	16 to 59.	60 and over.	Total.	10 to 15.	16 to 59.	60 and over.	Total.	10 to 15.	16 to 59.	60 and over.	
7	22,331	712,750	24,306	476,451	7,589	458,394	10,468	870,134	29,929	820,759	19,446	
4	204	6,918	342	4,343	40	4,197	106	9,375	82	9,121	172	1
3	390	9,013	231	3,810	64	3,663	83	11,964	591	11,118	255	2
0	1,838	32,039	1,353	23,914	363	22,223	628	35,538	719	33,719	1,100	3
7	602	35,096	1,479	25,997	331	25,069	597	38,977	467	37,539	971	4
0	1,312	40,230	1,378	38,166	692	36,597	877	57,544	2,188	54,134	1,222	5
5	413	15,068	454	7,250	120	7,003	127	15,836	461	15,103	272	6
7	67	4,533	237	2,830	37	2,630	163	7,231	104	6,868	259	7
9	382	8,986	631	3,496	24	3,315	157	4,929	87	4,589	253	8
1	14	3,829	58	2,751	15	2,710	26	4,489	15	4,405	69	9
3	831	40,302	930	29,806	646	28,832	328	40,558	1,419	38,648	491	10
6	881	23,977	808	16,865	374	16,043	448	33,972	1,438	31,818	716	11
1	110	7,445	236	8,212	91	7,994	127	13,878	253	13,407	218	12
9	144	3,504	181	2,420	31	2,327	62	5,163	89	4,952	122	13
1	90	2,708	163	2,145	67	2,003	75	5,455	238	5,043	174	14
4	124	34,414	126	6,002	7	5,970	25	10,396	55	10,298	43	15
1	16	1,502	93	1,327	22	1,227	78	9,593	1,486	7,907	200	16
9	35	4,607	107	2,659	22	2,545	92	5,574	53	5,364	157	17
6	151	6,445	110	4,783	26	4,710	47	6,916	103	6,726	87	18
0	211	9,145	224	7,172	93	6,945	134	9,349	182	8,977	190	19
8	268	5,363	117	2,806	37	2,751	18	4,176	90	4,045	41	20
1	12	1,781	87	1,212	15	1,188	9	11,514	854	10,509	151	21
9	959	13,764	606	7,652	87	7,403	162	12,488	440	11,705	343	22
2	25	3,050	307	1,899	21	1,802	76	15,306	829	14,092	385	23
9	12	1,831	106	1,519	3	1,463	53	8,140	83	7,795	262	24
2	126	5,244	82	3,811	....	3,795	16	3,026	2	3,001	23	25
3	187	7,858	218	5,355	74	5,193	88	9,257	246	8,809	202	26
4	335	6,359	330	2,979	22	2,861	96	2,045	8	1,906	71	27
6	303	7,664	449	5,932	205	5,498	229	22,829	1,209	20,832	788	28
0	18	5,275	147	3,688	30	3,611	47	8,555	30	8,377	148	29
5	1,408	28,345	1,482	17,404	178	16,826	400	16,074	256	15,390	428	30
9	2,807	110,373	2,079	88,611	1,360	85,875	1,376	145,285	4,269	138,921	2,095	31
7	34	2,701	182	1,677	90	1,521	66	8,600	1,016	7,371	213	32
9	2,045	59,031	2,793	43,960	970	41,555	1,435	106,166	4,496	98,356	3,314	33
7	369	10,351	357	5,963	141	5,682	140	12,370	764	11,378	228	34
1	20	3,357	44	3,198	9	3,171	18	4,002	....	3,967	35	35
5	161	7,890	281	5,439	151	4,919	369	12,243	614	11,180	449	36
1	317	3,643	191	1,609	32	1,517	60	5,712	378	5,218	116	37
7	469	7,488	370	3,387	40	3,285	62	6,520	446	5,983	91	38
6	195	5,357	324	4,955	125	4,675	155	10,822	523	9,951	348	39
0	689	26,793	278	17,558	69	17,350	139	22,034	253	21,576	205	40
6	430	5,659	977	1,862	1	1,554	307	2,268	32	1,874	362	41
1	126	3,454	161	1,776	33	1,734	9	6,807	643	6,149	105	42
8	1,345	39,270	803	28,219	431	27,441	347	38,244	1,249	36,460	535	43
3	168	4,785	270	3,641	100	3,458	83	7,864	296	7,331	237	44
2	105	5,508	149	2,808	22	2,767	19	4,345	57	4,230	58	45
5	236	5,123	276	3,169	47	3,008	114	7,517	45	7,217	255	46
7	56	2,775	256	1,973	48	1,844	81	5,203	350	4,653	200	47
9	1,059	24,034	1,016	5,296	114	5,013	169	9,499	83	9,043	373	48
0	131	4,419	267	1,506	22	1,403	81	5,314	120	5,006	188	49
9	48	4,334	157	2,339	47	2,228	64	9,082	218	8,038	226	50

TABLE LXVII.—*Occupations: Fifty Cities—Nationality (Selected) of Persons engaged in All Classes—1870.*

Cities.	SELECTED NATIVITY.								
	United States.	Germany.	Ireland.	England and Wales.	Scotland.	British America.	Sweden, Norway, and Denmark.	France.	China and Japan.
Total	1,124,326	317,375	428,825	84,561	21,653	34,840	14,552	22,283	9,171
Albany, N. Y	12,174	2,780	4,912	708	189	386	5	77	......
Allegheny, Pa	15,284	5,697	2,468	852	320	62	21	353	......
Baltimore, Md	68,005	16,938	7,348	1,040	227	90	104	287	1
Boston, Mass	54,482	3,164	31,701	3,106	979	7,026	562	344	......
Brooklyn, N. Y	66,197	19,310	38,107	8,812	2,003	1,200	1,067	816	11
Buffalo, N. Y	22,046	10,003	3,426	1,350	395	1,190	32	864	......
Cambridge, Mass	8,900	477	3,613	522	163	1,099	54	49	......
Charleston, S. C	16,793	866	779	90	37	6	22	27	......
Charlestown, Mass	7,730	144	2,501	190	71	396	43	17	......
Chicago, Ill	39,755	25,778	22,337	5,688	2,066	4,065	7,213	747	......
Cincinnati, Ohio	34,817	26,991	10,686	2,041	450	478	50	1,001	1
Cleveland, Ohio	11,932	8,701	5,048	2,275	325	933	72	183	......
Columbus, Ohio	7,347	2,248	1,116	489	74	90	8	105	......
Dayton, Ohio	6,677	2,699	737	214	47	54	8	122	......
Detroit, Mich	34,501	7,036	3,802	1,747	947	2,795	29	373	......
Fall River, Mass	5,970	25	3,263	2,528	216	816	6	2	......
Hartford, Conn	9,066	699	2,711	366	166	194	15	39	......
Indianapolis, Ind	13,078	2,641	1,835	384	136	149	96	138	......
Jersey City, N. J	10,592	3,740	8,968	1,809	537	183	120	133	......
Kansas City, Mo	8,746	1,090	1,736	342	84	239	307	76	......
Lawrence, Mass	5,729	325	5,021	2,359	419	845	6	3	......
Louisville, Ky	22,510	7,510	3,999	487	165	100	17	420	2
Lowell, Mass	13,042	31	5,787	712	207	965	19	15	......
Lynn, Mass	9,091	11	1,832	182	31	648	5	2	......
Memphis, Tenn	9,318	967	1,422	272	81	94	68	114	......
Milwaukee, Wis	6,670	10,798	1,989	840	235	232	369	98	......
Mobile, Ala	10,129	424	881	195	83	3	44	154	......
Newark, N. J	18,759	8,439	6,702	1,994	382	193	44	412	......
New Haven, Conn	10,590	1,368	5,175	445	128	95	45	63	......
New Orleans, La	41,201	7,990	7,237	1,116	337	263	251	4,737	16
New York, N. Y	132,733	78,410	106,362	13,064	4,284	2,286	1,582	4,300	84
Paterson, N. J	6,319	823	2,930	1,785	491	56	31	150	......
Philadelphia, Pa	137,746	23,565	43,073	8,541	1,657	387	202	1,026	......
Pittsburgh, Pa	15,339	4,684	6,983	1,797	310	76	23	176	......
Portland, Me	7,691	58	1,732	249	80	745	69	16	......
Providence, R. I	17,276	492	6,280	1,174	307	514	30	38	......
Reading, Pa	9,534	1,399	277	185	21	2	3	45	......
Richmond, Va	16,863	829	539	137	60	20	4	60	......
Rochester	12,104	3,759	2,878	1,111	211	1,174	22	211	......
San Francisco, Cal	22,480	8,987	15,129	3,138	991	948	1,388	2,228	9,054
Savannah, Ga	9,482	438	1,186	90	35	14	22	44	......
Scranton, Pa	4,679	1,609	3,436	2,400	190	58	3	42	......
St. Louis, Mo	48,421	31,724	18,040	3,124	712	658	341	1,481	1
Syracuse, N. Y	9,308	2,709	3,057	778	84	591	14	139	......
Toledo, Ohio	5,638	3,718	2,281	404	85	390	24	126	......
Troy, N. Y	8,286	769	5,547	686	208	854	21	62	......
Utica, N. Y	5,314	1,456	1,871	1,224	96	143	7	142	......
Washington, D. C	34,344	2,170	3,423	602	151	69	34	113	1
Wilmington, Del	9,577	679	1,991	471	83	9	7	42	......
Worcester, Mass	9,953	207	4,671	437	97	957	23	19	......

LXVIII.—*Occupations: Fifty Cities—Nationality (Selected) of Persons engaged in Agriculture*—1870.

Cities.	SELECTED NATIVITY.								
	United States.	Germany.	Ireland.	England and Wales.	Scotland.	British America.	Sweden, Norway, and Denmark.	France.	China and Japan.
al	12,812	4,124	3,076	1,032	325	229	78	461	29
, N. Y	96	31	48	15	2	1	......	1	......
ny, Pa	50	52	20	5	3	1	......	3	......
re, Md	555	104	50	13	5	1	......	3	......
Mass	242	16	189	12	3	28	2	3	......
n, N. Y	227	133	133	47	11	2	1	10	......
, N. Y	337	155	42	50	14	21	......	19	......
dge, Mass	57	7	56	4	3	9	......	1	......
ton, S. C	280	18	23	3	1	......	1	3	......
town, Mass	22	......	6	......	......	......	......	......	......
, Ill	151	186	84	42	17	9	21	3	......
nati, Ohio	483	781	85	25	9	......	......	14	......
nd, Ohio	93	134	41	41	9	3	......	2	......
ms, Ohio	59	49	4	5	......	1	......	2	......
, Ohio	82	29	4	4	......	......	......	5	......
, Mich	101	66	45	37	14	9	......	4	......
ver, Mass	282	......	37	19	1	......	......	......	......
d, Conn	248	9	76	16	5	1	1	1	......
polis, Ind	171	26	3	4	3	......	......	1	......
City, N. J	72	57	121	39	17	......	......	2	......
City, Mo	181	15	7	10	2	12	1	1	......
ce, Mass	68	2	44	3	4	3	......	......	......
lle, Ky	226	72	10	4	1	......	......	4	......
Mass	129	......	40	3	4	28	2	......	......
Mass	138	......	45	6	3	7	......	......	......
is, Tenn	294	6	13	5	......	......	6	......	......
kee, Wis	45	141	28	10	3	......	2	2	......
Ala	105	8	19	2	1	......	......	2	......
k, N. J	100	116	46	13	5	3	......	4	......
aven, Conn	112	14	115	11	10	......	15	2	......
rleans, La	860	184	36	10	2	......	1	201	......
ork, N. Y	407	554	274	61	25	6	4	38	......
on, N. J	101	18	24	11	2	......	3	1	......
lphia, Pa	2,683	320	450	127	63	5	1	21	......
rgh, Pa	180	124	72	46	9	1	......	4	......
d, Me	45	1	18	8	2	......	......	......	......
ence, R. I	146	......	83	8	8	4	......	......	......
g, Pa	36	12	......	1	1	......	......	......	......
nd, Va	294	6	6	2	3	......	......	......	......
ter, N. Y	181	31	18	28	2	14	......	......	......
ancisco, Cal	280	130	230	53	23	11	8	64	29
ah, Ga	135	6	10	......	......	......	......	......	......
on, Pa	59	8	7	18	1	......	......	2	......
is, Mo	280	337	75	33	11	6	5	20	......
se, N. Y	132	42	37	35	2	7	......	2	......
, Ohio	56	24	9	17	2	......	......	1	......
N. Y	143	8	37	8	5	3	......	......	......
N. Y	68	23	32	48	......	1	2	2	......
ngton, D. C	199	44	22	5	7	1	......	3	......
ngton, Del	1,064	18	125	47	3	......	1	9	......
ster, Mass	437	8	68	15	4	31	1	1	......

TABLE LXIX.—*Occupations: Fifty Cities—Nationality (Selected) of Persons engaged in Personal and Professional Services—1870.*

Cities.	SELECTED NATIVITY.								
	United States.	Germany.	Ireland.	England and Wales.	Scotland.	British America.	Sweden, Norway, and Denmark.	France.	China and Japan.
Total	374, 458	96, 369	227, 037	17, 253	4, 453	10, 030	4, 897	6, 550	5, 16[illegible]
Albany, N. Y	3, 990	1, 014	2, 104	136	38	99	3	28	......
Allegheny, Pa	5, 973	2, 003	1, 074	218	61	18	9	110	......
Baltimore, Md	25, 549	4, 533	4, 412	246	61	21	16	83	......
Boston, Mass	13, 319	855	19, 096	802	238	2, 273	126	193	......
Brooklyn, N. Y	15, 534	4, 522	19, 832	1, 474	357	264	338	168	1
Buffalo, N. Y	8, 176	4, 153	2, 191	437	112	454	11	257	......
Cambridge, Mass	2, 078	97	2, 169	85	24	339	9	11	......
Charleston, S. C	9, 505	129	275	17	4	5	7	1	......
Charlestown, Mass	1, 884	49	1, 721	44	23	106	14	6	......
Chicago, Ill	12, 656	8, 678	12, 351	1, 359	615	1, 172	2, 776	297	......
Cincinnati, Ohio	10, 287	7, 626	6, 381	489	99	117	9	365	......
Cleveland, Ohio	2, 658	2, 290	1, 877	357	58	197	17	64	......
Columbus, Ohio	2, 248	813	628	120	13	15	1	27	......
Dayton, Ohio	1, 659	783	378	32	11	22	1	37	......
Detroit, Mich	27, 739	2, 936	2, 085	434	243	1, 080	9	131	......
Fall River, Mass	630	2	781	96	13	87	......	......	......
Hartford, Conn	3, 040	202	1, 299	74	42	39	3	14	......
Indianapolis, Ind	4, 492	766	1, 176	88	16	27	45	34	......
Jersey City, N. J	2, 670	925	5, 410	337	79	24	33	23	......
Kansas City, Mo	3, 635	368	1, 179	93	22	85	230	31	......
Lawrence, Mass	736	17	884	94	21	115	1	1	......
Louisville, Ky	10, 417	1, 986	2, 383	80	22	21	4	127	2
Lowell, Mass	1, 477	14	1, 385	94	25	376	1	5	......
Lynn, Mass	1, 008	2	802	15	2	119	1	......	......
Memphis, Tenn	4, 352	175	679	51	13	23	25	36	......
Milwaukee, Wis	1, 972	5, 369	1, 004	146	35	58	97	38	......
Mobile, Ala	6, 238	142	414	62	28	2	17	35	......
Newark, N. J	3, 069	1, 538	3, 297	246	20	65	9	68	......
New Haven, Conn	2, 192	293	2, 799	95	24	8	......	16	......
New Orleans, La	22, 187	2, 303	4, 062	354	96	81	78	1, 197	7
New York, N. Y	36, 884	16, 388	54, 282	2, 840	832	549	348	1, 248	29
Paterson, N. J	748	199	1, 268	236	65	19	2	21	......
Philadelphia, Pa	33, 682	5, 234	22, 104	1, 635	325	98	141	258	......
Pittsburgh, Pa	4, 356	1, 895	4, 019	430	99	30	10	74	......
Portland, Me	1, 675	14	1, 235	100	29	325	17	7	......
Providence, R. I	3, 911	79	3, 837	189	63	201	5	18	......
Reading, Pa	3, 197	661	187	44	13	......	2	19	......
Richmond, Va	7, 839	186	241	20	6	2	1	15	......
Rochester, N. Y	3, 166	845	1, 199	188	31	294	......	54	......
San Francisco, Cal	8, 090	2, 430	8, 299	891	191	237	285	917	5, 1[illegible]
Savannah, Ga	6, 255	134	596	27	4	8	10	14	......
Scranton, Pa	930	599	1, 773	332	44	13	2	11	......
St. Louis, Mo	17, 820	9, 657	10, 672	868	145	186	157	508	1
Syracuse, N. Y	2, 538	728	1, 496	198	16	158	3	33	......
Toledo, Ohio	1, 860	1, 950	1, 420	119	15	158	5	58	......
Troy, N. Y	1, 695	182	3, 315	151	51	172	6	31	......
Utica, N. Y	1, 194	473	1, 019	278	8	42	1	30	......
Washington, D. C	22, 661	677	2, 298	262	55	34	21	50	1
Wilmington, Del	2, 893	409	1, 252	202	29	5	1	9	......
Worcester, Mass	1, 801	37	2, 388	68	14	127	......	4	......

LXX.—*Occupations: Fifty Cities—Nationality (Selected) of Persons engaged in Trade and Transportation*—1870.

Cities.	SELECTED NATIVITY.								
	United States.	Germany.	Ireland.	England and Wales.	Scotland.	British America.	Sweden, Norway, and Denmark.	France.	China and Japan.
al	295, 019	69, 160	65, 107	16, 719	4, 574	6, 090	3, 374	5, 155	761
N. Y	2, 965	363	726	158	34	59	1	9	......
y Pa	2, 376	665	468	105	94	6	1	42	......
, Md	18, 034	3, 168	1, 360	283	57	32	51	52	1
Iass	19, 008	529	3, 859	746	196	984	191	62	......
, N. Y	23, 931	4, 095	6, 192	2, 128	403	275	254	206	7
N. Y	5, 002	1, 078	335	269	102	227	11	166	......
ge, Mass	2, 238	92	233	75	21	147	8	2	......
n, S. C	2, 603	488	288	33	17	......	9	7	......
wn, Mass	2, 388	19	199	32	9	93	6	2	......
Ill	14, 915	5, 424	4, 312	1, 453	475	883	1, 094	173	......
i, Ohio	9, 379	4, 763	1, 551	405	84	122	13	287	......
l, Ohio	4, 170	1, 621	1, 487	440	72	227	22	34	......
s, Ohio	1, 789	275	168	95	20	22	1	18	......
Ohio	1, 562	379	119	32	7	9	1	19	......
Mich	2, 935	1, 056	652	393	207	658	10	63	......
r, Mass	912	11	252	105	10	21	3	1	......
Conn	2, 186	101	293	32	17	9	1	2	......
olis, Ind	3, 629	620	292	69	28	69	7	28	......
ty, N. J	4, 062	929	1, 345	444	163	42	34	33	......
ity, Mo	2, 202	903	219	40	8	70	14	16	......
, Mass	892	6	215	52	20	20	1	......	......
, Ky	5, 168	1, 624	522	104	30	17	1	87	......
Iass	1, 519	10	235	41	10	76	3	......	......
ss	1, 397	3	79	17	3	19	1	......	......
, Tenn	2, 744	411	308	80	19	13	5	36	......
e, Wis	2, 227	1, 698	414	262	84	75	105	19	......
la	2, 359	141	244	59	25	......	20	51	......
N. J	4, 002	921	560	216	46	32	3	66	......
en, Conn	2, 861	208	522	47	12	16	3	8	......
ans, La	9, 815	2, 456	1, 708	389	124	87	97	1, 548	1
k, N. Y	43, 317	18, 181	18, 490	3, 585	986	624	528	927	24
N. J	978	102	331	155	41	5	6	12	......
hia, Pa	32, 409	3, 379	6, 035	1, 344	231	72	25	156	......
gh, Pa	3, 909	733	951	189	27	8	3	24	......
Mo	2, 732	19	199	48	16	135	22	4	......
ce, R. I	4, 747	50	415	113	54	22	6	1	......
Pa	1, 441	130	11	19	......	......	......	5	......
l, Va	2, 805	309	144	32	10	8	2	23	......
r, N. Y	3, 196	601	607	196	42	194	4	25	......
cisco, Cal	6, 599	3, 356	2, 760	993	349	212	734	578	728
, Ga	1, 333	130	332	28	16	......	7	11	......
Pa	1, 220	162	242	107	19	7	......	2	......
Mo	15, 895	6, 893	3, 018	728	169	167	44	300	......
, N. Y	2, 453	302	455	129	16	50	3	18	......
hio	1, 558	612	352	79	37	79	6	26	......
Y	2, 304	153	484	61	27	108	7	4	......
Y	1, 367	137	216	153	20	7	......	13	......
ton, D. C	4, 204	433	469	89	13	13	2	21	......
ton, Del	1, 281	44	124	40	4	......	1	4	......
r, Mass	1, 981	17	232	27	10	55	3	4	......

TABLE LXXI.—*Occupations: Fifty Cities—Nationality (Selected) of Persons engaged in Manufacturing, Mechanical, and Mining Industries*—1870.

Cities.	SELECTED NATIVITY.								
	United States.	Germany.	Ireland.	England and Wales.	Scotland.	British America.	Sweden, Norway, and Denmark.	France.	China and Japan.
Total	442, 037	177, 722	133, 605	49, 557	12, 301	18, 491	6, 203	10, 117	3, 2[illegible]
Albany, N. Y	5, 123	1, 372	2, 034	399	115	227	1	39	......
Allegheny, Pa	6, 885	2, 977	906	524	162	37	11	198	......
Baltimore, Md	23, 867	9, 133	1, 526	498	104	36	37	89	......
Boston, Mass	21, 913	1, 764	8, 557	1, 546	542	3, 741	243	156	......
Brooklyn, N. Y	26, 505	10, 560	11, 950	5, 163	1, 142	650	474	432	1
Buffalo, N. Y	8, 511	4, 617	858	603	167	488	10	422	......
Cambridge, Mass	4, 596	281	1, 155	358	115	604	37	35	......
Charleston, S. C	4, 405	231	193	37	15	1	5	16	......
Charlestown, Mass	3, 436	76	575	114	39	198	23	9	......
Chicago, Ill	12, 033	11, 490	5, 590	2, 834	959	2, 001	3, 322	334	......
Cincinnati, Ohio	14, 668	13, 821	2, 669	1, 122	258	239	28	505	1
Cleveland, Ohio	5, 011	4, 647	1, 643	1, 437	186	506	33	63	......
Columbus, Ohio	3, 251	1, 1[illegible]	316	269	41	52	6	58	......
Dayton, Ohio	3, 374	1, 508	236	146	29	23	6	61	......
Detroit, Mich	3, 816	2, 978	1, 020	883	483	1, 048	10	155	......
Fall River, Mass	4, 156	12	2, 193	2, 308	192	708	3	1	......
Hartford, Conn	3, 592	387	1, 043	244	102	145	10	22	......
Indianapolis, Ind	4, 786	1, 229	364	223	80	53	44	69	......
Jersey City, N. J	3, 768	1, 829	2, 063	989	278	117	53	75	......
Kansas City, Mo	2, 728	504	338	199	52	72	72	28	......
Lawrence, Mass	4, 033	300	3, 878	2, 210	374	701	4	2	......
Louisville, Ky	6, 699	3, 828	1, 075	299	112	62	12	202	......
Lowell, Mass	9, 917	7	4, 127	574	168	485	13	10	......
Lynn, Mass	6, 548	6	906	144	23	503	3	2	......
Memphis, Tenn	1, 928	375	332	136	49	58	32	42	......
Milwaukee, Wis	2, 426	4, 590	543	422	113	99	165	41	......
Mobile, Ala	1, 427	133	204	72	29	1	7	66	......
Newark, N. J	11, 588	5, 864	2, 799	1, 519	311	93	32	274	......
New Haven, Conn	5, 434	853	1, 739	292	82	71	27	37	......
New Orleans, La	8, 339	3, 047	1, 431	363	115	95	75	1, 791	8
New York, N. Y	52, 125	43, 287	33, 316	6, 575	2, 441	1, 107	702	2, 147	40
Paterson, N. J	4, 492	504	1, 307	1, 383	383	32	20	116	......
Philadelphia, Pa	68, 972	14, 632	14, 484	5, 435	1, 038	212	35	581	......
Pittsburgh, Pa	6, 894	1, 932	1, 941	1, 132	175	37	10	74	......
Portland, Me	3, 239	24	280	93	33	285	30	5	......
Providence, R. I	8, 472	363	1, 945	864	183	287	19	17	......
Reading, Pa	4, 860	596	79	121	7	2	1	21	......
Richmond, Va	5, 865	328	148	83	41	10	1	22	......
Rochester, N. Y	5, 561	2, 282	1, 054	699	133	672	18	132	......
San Francisco, Cal	7, 511	3, 071	3, 840	1, 201	428	488	361	729	3, 1[illegible]
Savannah, Ga	1, 759	168	248	35	15	6	5	19	......
Scranton, Pa	2, 470	840	1, 414	1, 943	126	38	1	27	......
St. Louis, Mo	14, 426	14, 837	4, 275	1, 495	387	299	135	653	......
Syracuse, N. Y	4, 185	1, 577	1, 069	416	50	367	8	86	......
Toledo, Ohio	2, 164	1, 132	500	189	31	153	13	41	......
Troy, N. Y	4, 144	426	1, 711	466	125	571	8	27	......
Utica, N. Y	2, 685	824	604	743	68	93	4	97	......
Washington, D. C	7, 377	1, 016	634	246	76	21	11	39	......
Wilmington, Del	4, 339	208	490	182	47	4	4	20	......
Worcester, Mass	5, 734	145	1, 983	327	69	684	19	10	......

THE BLIND, DEAF AND DUMB, INSANE, AND IDIOTIC.

TABLE LXXII.—*The Blind, with Race and Sex*—1870.

[N. B.—W, White; B, Black; M, Mulatto; C, Chinese; I, Indian.]

States and Territories.	Aggregate.	Total.		W.		B.		M.		C.		I.	
		M.	F.	M.	F.	M.	F.	M.	F.	M.	F.	M.	F.
The United States	20,320	11,343	8,977	9,640	7,326	1,518	1,448	166	189	4	....	15	14
The States	20,011	11,149	8,862	9,477	7,240	1,495	1,427	158	183	4	....	15	12
Alabama	611	344	267	192	156	139	101	13	10	....	....	....	....
Arkansas	333	166	167	131	139	32	24	3	3	....	....	....	1
California	179	120	59	113	56	....	2	....	1	4	....	3	....
Connecticut	252	138	114	129	112	5	2	4	....	....	....	....	....
Delaware	68	26	42	17	25	9	16	....	1	....	....	....	....
Florida	88	45	43	24	14	18	28	3	1	....	....	....	....
Georgia	740	376	364	217	199	157	154	2	11	....	....	....	....
Illinois	1,042	599	443	595	439	3	4	1	....	....	....	....	....
Indiana	991	541	450	521	441	15	7	5	2	....	....	....	....
Iowa	465	268	197	267	195	1	2	....	....	....	....	....	....
Kansas	128	69	59	53	49	12	9	2	1	....	....	2	....
Kentucky	978	515	463	412	367	83	79	19	17	....	....	1	....
Louisiana	447	262	185	113	65	134	95	15	25	....	....	....	....
Maine	324	207	117	206	117	....	....	1	....	....	....	....	....
Maryland	427	219	208	171	152	43	48	5	8	....	....	....	....
Massachusetts	761	432	329	422	322	8	3	2	4	....	....	....	....
Michigan	418	262	156	251	148	....	2	3	1	....	....	8	5
Minnesota	103	59	44	59	44	....	....	....	....	....	....	....	....
Mississippi	474	254	220	121	91	122	119	11	8	....	....	....	2
Missouri	904	503	401	457	340	42	54	4	7	....	....	....	....
Nebraska	22	12	10	12	10	....	....	....	....	....	....	....	....
Nevada	4	2	2	2	2	....	....	....	....	....	....	....	....
New Hampshire	206	118	88	118	85	....	3	....	....	....	....	....	....
New Jersey	317	178	139	166	125	12	12	....	2	....	....	....	....
New York	2,213	1,295	918	1,273	895	22	22	....	....	....	....	....	1
North Carolina	835	429	406	270	270	147	119	12	14	....	....	....	3
Ohio	1,366	772	594	746	572	20	18	6	4	....	....	....	....
Oregon	35	23	12	22	12	1	....	....	....	....	....	....	....
Pennsylvania	1,767	1,022	745	998	724	17	19	7	2	....	....	....	....
Rhode Island	121	66	55	63	51	3	2	....	2	....	....	....	....
South Carolina	451	232	219	95	93	131	117	6	9	....	....	....	....
Tennessee	876	444	432	353	313	77	109	14	10	....	....	....	....
Texas	404	229	175	157	117	62	52	9	6	....	....	1	....
Vermont	189	123	66	123	66	....	....	....	....	....	....	....	....
Virginia	895	455	440	272	214	175	192	8	34	....	....	....	....
West Virginia	168	95	73	87	60	5	13	3	....	....	....	....	....
Wisconsin	409	249	160	249	160	....	....	....	....	....	....	....	....
The Territories	309	194	115	163	86	23	21	8	6	....	....	....	2
Arizona	1	1	....	1	....	....	....	....	....	....	....	....	....
Colorado	26	18	8	18	8	....	....	....	....	....	....	....	....
Dakota	5	3	2	3	2	....	....	....	....	....	....	....	....
District of Columbia	78	43	35	12	8	23	21	8	6	....	....	....	....
Idaho	4	2	2	2	2	....	....	....	....	....	....	....	....
Montana	....	....	....	....	....	....	....	....	....	....	....	....	....
New Mexico	159	104	55	104	53	....	....	....	....	....	....	....	2
Utah	29	17	12	17	12	....	....	....	....	....	....	....	....
Washington	5	4	1	4	1	....	....	....	....	....	....	....	....
Wyoming	2	2	....	2	....	....	....	....	....	....	....	....	....

REMARKS.—It is held by many persons conversant with the special subject, that the returns of the census in respect to the blind and the deaf and dumb, and also, in a higher degree, to the insane and the idiotic, are always, and necessarily, considerably below the fact. F. B. Sanborn, esq., of Massachusetts, late secretary of the board of charities for that commonwealth, has advanced the opinion that the numbers reported in the census, be it State or National, rarely embrace more than sixty or seventy per cent. of their respective classes.

The Superintendent certainly can claim not to be bigoted in his defense of the accuracy of the census as taken under existing laws, nor does he desire to exhibit a disposition to close, were it in his power, the discussion of this question by a dogmatic denial of the charge of large omissions in the returns of the Afflicted Classes of our population at the census.

It is fair to say, however, that the opinion referred to would appear to have been formed, in advance of anything like a general and systematic investigation, from impressions derived from casual observation or partial inquiry, and therefore to have hardly authority enough to withstand positive official statements.

TABLE LXXIII.—*The Blind, with Nativity*—1870.

d Territories.	Total living in the State.	Born in the State and living in it.	Born in other States and living in the State.	Born in foreign countries and living in the State. (Foreign.)	Total born in the State and living in the United States. (Native.)	Born in the State and living in it.	Born in the State and living in other States.
ted States	20, 320	10, 653	6, 390	3, 277	a17, 001	10, 653	a6, 348
;os.	20, 011	10, 474	6, 296	3, 241	16, 794	10, 474	6, 320
... .	611	270	326	15	411	270	141
....	333	101	228	4	129	101	28
....	179	51	63	65	55	51	4
....	252	180	38	34	345	180	165
....	68	47	11	10	93	47	46
....	88	22	58	8	25	22	3
....	740	486	238	16	728	486	242
....	1, 042	320	460	202	424	320	104
....	991	406	480	105	546	406	140
....	465	67	302	96	93	67	26
....	128	4	116	8	6	4	2
....	978	660	281	37	1, 045	660	385
....	447	193	194	60	226	193	33
....	324	254	43	27	310	254	56
....	427	333	35	59	595	333	262
ts	761	450	97	214	612	450	162
....	418	76	219	123	92	76	16
....	103	10	51	42	13	10	3
....	474	178	288	8	247	178	69
....	904	317	462	125	399	317	82
....	22	1	17	4	2	1	1
....	4	....	3	1	....	....	....
hire	206	155	31	20	258	155	103
....	317	201	46	70	353	201	152
....	2, 213	1, 171	293	749	1, 753	1, 171	582
na	835	791	40	4	1, 364	791	573
....	1, 366	513	589	264	855	513	342
....	35	5	23	7	7	5	2
a	1, 767	1, 126	211	430	1, 631	1, 126	505
l	121	81	14	26	129	81	48
na	451	412	22	17	789	412	377
....	876	507	353	16	874	507	367
....	404	70	284	50	81	70	11
....	189	110	51	28	265	110	155
....	895	837	38	20	b1, 945	837	1, 108
ia	168	....	c153	15	....	....	....
....	409	69	138	202	94	69	25
ritorics	309	179	94	36	207	179	28
....	1	....	....	1	....	....	....
....	26	1	23	2	1	1	....
....	5	1	3	1	1	1	....
Columbia	78	20	53	5	26	20	6
....	4	....	3	1	....	....	....
....	....	....	....	....	....	....	....
....	159	154	....	5	175	154	21
....	29	2	7	20	3	2	1
....	5	1	3	1	1	1	....
....	2	....	2	....	....	....	....

s not include 5 born in Indian Territory and 37 the State of whose birth is unknown.
luding 127 living in West Virginia.
luding 127 born in Virginia.

e time the above tables were sent to press, the sole attempt, known to the ndent, which had been made to supply absolute data by which to test the re- e census in this particular, was in Massachusetts, where a list, bearing a indefinite date, but formed between the State census of 1865 and the Federal 1870, had been prepared, of the deaf and dumb of the commonwealth. contains an aggregate of 821 names. Examination, however, shows that two or three years, names were added from time to time to complete it, only were, during that time, stricken from the roll, as lost by death or by removal State. Of course, among so large a number as 821, the casualities for such a 'd *not but have been far* more numerous. It would certainly be fair to assume a

TABLE LXXIV.—*The Deaf and Dumb, with Race and Sex*—1870.

[N. B.—W, White; B, Black; M, Mulatto; C, Chinese; I, Indian.]

States and Territories.	Aggregate.	Total.		W.		B.		M.		C.		I.	
		M.	F.	M.	F.	M.	F.	M.	F.	M.	F.	M.	F.
The United States.....	16,205	8,916	7,289	8,206	6,701	613	495	93	90	....	....	4	3
The States	15,983	8,780	7,203	8,087	6,626	600	487	89	88	....	....	4	2
Alabama	401	205	196	130	132	72	56	3	8	....	....	....	....
Arkansas	265	142	123	131	105	8	16	3	2	....	....	....	....
California	141	79	62	79	60	......	2	....	....	....	....	....	....
Connecticut	475	267	208	264	206	3	1	....	1	....	....	....	....
Delaware	61	34	27	29	25	5	2	....	....	....	....	....	....
Florida	48	29	19	20	12	8	3	1	4	....	....	....	....
Georgia	326	168	158	117	120	42	34	8	4	....	....	1	....
Illinois	833	484	349	479	344	4	5	1	....	....	....	....	....
Indiana	872	467	405	402	403	2	......	2	2	....	....	1	....
Iowa	549	315	234	314	234	1	......	....	....	....	....	....	....
Kansas	121	72	49	68	46	3	......	....	3	....	....	1	....
Kentucky	723	365	358	320	314	39	31	6	13	....	....	....	....
Louisiana	197	105	92	81	73	20	13	4	6	....	....	....	....
Maine	299	158	141	158	141	......	......	....	....	....	....	....	....
Maryland	384	229	155	191	120	28	29	10	6	....	....	....	....
Massachusetts	538	303	235	300	233	2	2	1	....	....	....	....	....
Michigan	455	258	197	258	196	......	......	....	1	....	....	....	....
Minnesota	166	99	67	99	66	......	......	....	....	....	....	....	1
Mississippi	245	145	100	82	52	56	45	6	3	....	....	1	....
Missouri	790	389	401	366	385	19	14	4	2	....	....	....	....
Nebraska	55	22	33	22	33	......	......	....	....	....	....	....	....
Nevada	4	2	2	2	2	......	......	....	....	....	....	....	....
New Hampshire	170	92	78	92	78	......	......	....	....	....	....	....	....
New Jersey	231	125	106	122	100	3	6	....	....	....	....	....	....
New York	1,783	984	799	979	789	5	10	....	....	....	....	....	....
North Carolina	619	358	261	257	185	89	62	12	14	....	....	....	....
Ohio	1,339	709	630	700	623	5	3	4	4	....	....	....	....
Oregon	23	13	10	13	9	......	......	....	....	....	....	....	1
Pennsylvania	1,433	777	656	775	650	2	4	....	2	....	....	....	....
Rhode Island	64	40	24	38	24	2	......	....	....	....	....	....	....
South Carolina	212	118	94	67	55	45	34	6	5	....	....	....	....
Tennessee	570	304	266	250	226	48	39	6	1	....	....	....	....
Texas	232	146	86	121	64	23	21	2	1	....	....	....	....
Vermont	148	78	70	78	70	......	......	....	....	....	....	....	....
Virginia	534	298	236	223	178	65	52	10	6	....	....	....	....
West Virginia	218	125	93	124	90	1	3	....	....	....	....	....	....
Wisconsin	459	276	183	276	183	......	......	....	....	....	....	....	....
The Territories	222	136	86	119	75	13	8	4	2	....	....	....	1
Arizona	......	......	......	......	......	......	......	....	....	....	....	....	....
Colorado	4	1	3	1	3	......	......	....	....	....	....	....	....
Dakota	4	2	2	2	2	......	......	....	....	....	....	....	....
District of Columbia	134	92	42	76	32	13	8	3	2	....	....	....	....
Idaho	1	1	......	1	......	......	......	....	....	....	....	....	....
Montana	5	1	4	1	3	......	......	....	....	....	....	....	1
New Mexico	48	30	18	30	18	......	......	....	....	....	....	....	....
Utah	18	4	14	4	14	......	......	....	....	....	....	....	....
Washington	6	3	3	3	3	......	......	....	....	....	....	....	....
Wyoming	2	2	......	1	......	......	......	1	....	....	....	....	....

rate of mortality among the afflicted classes not below that of the community generally, after excluding infants of an age too early to allow such infirmities as are being considered to become developed and recognized.

Still further scrutiny of the list shows that the actual statement of the individual case in no small proportion of instances fails to bear out the title of the list itself. Thus, of the total of 821 persons, only 692 are distinctly and in terms put down as "deaf and dumb," while 41 appear as "dumb," 14 as "mute," 73 as "deaf," and 1 simply as "idiotic."

The Superintendent does not take the responsibility of saying that none of the persons reported as "mute" or as "dumb," or even of the larger number reported under the more questionable title of "deaf," were not deaf-mutes or deaf and dumb; but it is certainly fair to demand, in a list prepared solely with a view to this single consideration, something like accuracy of definition; and if accuracy of definition cannot be attained in so simple a matter, what reason to expect accuracy of description?

But the reductions above indicated are not the only ones to which this list must be subjected before it can fairly be put in comparison with the census returns of Massachusetts

TABLE LXXV.—*The Deaf and Dumb, with Nativity*—1870.

States and Territories.	Total living in the State.	Born in the State and living in it.	Born in other States and living in the State.	Born in foreign countries and living in the State. (Foreign.)	Total born in the State and living in the United States. (Native.)	Born in the State and living in it.	Born in the State and living in other States.
The United States	16,205	11,367	3,502	1,336	a14,792	11,367	a3,425
The States	15,983	11,264	3,404	1,315	14,679	11,264	3,415
Alabama	401	292	101	8	376	292	84
Arkansas	265	143	121	1	177	143	34
California	141	87	43	11	88	87	1
Connecticut	475	221	236	18	273	221	52
Delaware	61	58	1	2	70	58	12
Florida	48	32	16	....	36	32	4
Georgia	326	286	38	2	385	286	99
Illinois	833	405	298	130	528	405	123
Indiana	872	584	240	48	760	584	176
Iowa	549	175	296	78	216	175	41
Kansas	121	13	97	11	18	13	5
Kentucky	723	632	79	12	797	632	165
Louisiana	197	164	25	8	188	164	24
Maine	299	276	13	10	366	276	90
Maryland	384	341	21	22	422	341	81
Massachusetts	538	383	78	77	571	383	188
Michigan	455	183	183	89	208	183	25
Minnesota	166	54	63	49	58	54	4
Mississippi	245	164	77	4	210	164	46
Missouri	790	484	254	52	569	484	85
Nebraska	55	7	44	4	9	7	2
Nevada	4	1	3	....	1	1	....
New Hampshire	170	139	19	12	195	139	56
New Jersey	231	171	36	24	268	171	97
New York	1,783	1,370	184	229	1,761	1,370	391
North Carolina	619	597	22	....	693	597	96
Ohio	1,339	1,038	180	121	1,367	1,038	329
Oregon	23	11	11	1	15	11	4
Pennsylvania	1,433	1,229	85	119	1,495	1,229	266
Rhode Island	64	36	19	9	61	36	25
South Carolina	212	206	4	2	284	206	78
Tennessee	570	497	69	4	649	497	152
Texas	232	98	116	18	111	98	13
Vermont	148	121	16	11	222	121	101
Virginia	534	519	13	2	b943	519	424
West Virginia	218	....	c212	6	....	....	....
Wisconsin	439	247	91	121	289	247	42
The Territories	222	103	98	21	113	103	10
Arizona	....	....	....	....	....	....	....
Colorado	4	1	3	....	1	1	....
Dakota	4	2	2	....	2	2	....
District of Columbia	134	45	81	8	48	45	3
Idaho	1	....	1	....	....	....	....
Montana	5	1	2	2	1	1	....
New Mexico	48	46	....	2	49	46	3
Utah	18	7	3	8	11	7	4
Washington	6	1	5	....	1	1	....
Wyoming	2	....	1	1	....	....	....

(a) Does not include 77 the State of whose birth is unknown.
(b) Including 196 living in West Virginia.
(c) Including 196 born in Virginia.

or 1860 and 1870. From entries in red ink, it appears that 117 names were added to he list, on account of the deaf and dumb of Massachusetts, found in 1867 among the nmates of the asylum for the deaf and dumb at Hartford, Connecticut. But by the ensus law the pupils of the Hartford asylum are required to be returned on the chedules for Connecticut, as having their "usual place of abode" therein; and, as a natter of fact, 118 persons, deaf and dumb, born in Massachusetts, were returned by he proper assistant marshal of Hartford, on the 1st of June, 1870, and will be found in he above tables. If, therefore, the 117, added as above to the Massachusetts list, e subtracted from the total number who were distinctly and in terms reported to the tate board of charities as "*deaf and dumb*," we shall have but 575 who were, at any *ate that may be taken as the* date of the list, whether 1866, 1867, or 1868, fairly sub-

TABLE LXXVI.—*The Insane, with Race and Sex*—1870.

[N. B.—W, White; B, Black; M, Mulatto; C, Chinese; I, Indian.]

States and Territories.	Aggregate.	Total.		W.		B.		M.		C.		I.	
		M.	F.	M.	F.	M.	F.	M.	F.	M.	F.	M.	F.
The United States...	37,432	18,219	19,213	17,424	18,186	676	929	79	90	31	4	9	4
The States...	36,836	17,811	19,025	17,045	18,018	650	915	78	84	31	4	7	4
Alabama	555	275	280	240	191	33	84	2	5				
Arkansas	161	78	83	66	71	12	11						1
California	1,146	835	311	789	304	15	2			29	4	2	1
Connecticut	772	356	416	349	411	5	2	1	2			1	1
Delaware	65	36	29	34	24	2	5						
Florida	29	15	14	10	8	4	6					1	
Georgia	634	309	325	253	252	50	72	6	1				
Illinois	1,625	794	831	790	825	4	4		2				
Indiana	1,504	748	756	739	747	6	4	3	5				
Iowa	742	378	364	378	364								
Kansas	131	67	64	64	64	3							
Kentucky	1,245	672	573	628	515	40	56	4	2				
Louisiana	451	220	231	168	155	47	65	5	11				
Maine	792	359	433	359	432		1						
Maryland	733	368	365	331	331	36	32	1	2				
Massachusetts	2,662	1,238	1,424	1,229	1,413	7	11	2					
Michigan	814	376	438	374	435	2	3						
Minnesota	302	158	144	154	144	3						1	
Mississippi	245	118	127	82	71	31	55	5	1				
Missouri	1,263	616	647	599	618	15	27	2	2				
Nebraska	28	17	11	17	11								
Nevada	2	1	1	1	1								
New Hampshire	548	233	315	233	315								
New Jersey	918	407	511	401	500	6	11						
New York	6,353	2,707	3,646	2,678	3,595	28	50					1	1
North Carolina	779	380	399	335	335	40	57	5	7				
Ohio	3,414	1,612	1,802	1,584	1,757	24	41	4	4				
Oregon	122	83	39	78	38	1	1	2		2			
Pennsylvania	3,895	1,944	1,951	1,904	1,906	37	38	3	7				
Rhode Island	312	141	171	141	170		1						
South Carolina	333	158	175	127	111	29	60	2	4				
Tennessee	925	450	475	402	404	43	64	5	7				
Texas	270	120	141	104	107	21	32	4	2				
Vermont	721	350	371	348	371	1		1					
Virginia	1,125	595	530	475	393	99	117	20	20			1	
West Virginia	374	198	176	192	173	5	3	1					
Wisconsin	846	390	456	389	456	1							
The Territories*	596	408	188	379	168	26	14	1	6			2	
Arizona	1	1		1									
Colorado	12	7	5	7	5								
Dakota	3	2	1	2	1								
District of Columbia	479	341	138	312	118	26	14	1	6			2	
Idaho	1	1		1									
Montana	2	1	1	1	1								
New Mexico	50	28	22	28	22								
Utah	25	10	15	10	15								
Washington	23	17	6	17	6								
Wyoming													

ject to enumeration within the State of Massachusetts, according to the conditions of the census law. The number returned by the assistant marshals to the Census Office, on the 1st of June, 1870, was 538. The difference would be easily accounted for by the failure, already indicated, to follow up on the State list the changes from death or removal; and were this cause not sufficient, it would neither be an unfair nor a violent assumption that a list thus prepared by piecemeal, and exhibiting so much looseness both of definition and construction, might contain other important errors which would need to be corrected before the positive count of the census could be discredited through its instrumentality.

Since the corresponding tables of Vol. I (quarto, Nos. X to XIX) were sent to press, this office has received, by favor of the secretary of the Illinois State board of charities, the lists, prepared for or by that board, of the insane and the idiotic of that State. The list of idiotic has not been examined for the purposes of these remarks; but the list of insane has been subjected to a careful comparison with the returns of the census, name by name. This comparison exhibits such an utter want of correspondence, at nearly every point, as not only renders criticism impossible, but is, in itself, wholly inexplicable. The list of the board of charities contains 2,376 names. Eighty-eight might be deducted on various accounts: duplication, 41; death, 14; recovery of reason, 31, and removal from the

TABLE LXXVII.—*The Insane, with Nativity*—1870.

and Territories.	Total living in the State.	Born in the State and living in it.	Born in other States and living in the State.	Born in foreign countries and living in the State. (Foreign.)	Total born in the State and living in the United States. (Native.)	Born in the State and living in it.	Born in the State and living in other States.
United States	37,432	17,898	8,263	11,221	a25,372	17,898	a7,474
States	36,836	17,787	8,045	10,954	25,237	17,787	7,450
	555	313	223	19	417	313	104
	101	41	118	2	64	41	23
	1,146	25	363	738	33	25	8
ut.	772	478	128	166	734	478	256
	65	47	9	9	95	47	48
	29	10	18	1	24	10	14
	634	508	114	12	667	508	159
	1,625	324	606	695	471	324	147
	1,504	604	619	281	792	604	188
	742	44	400	298	70	44	26
	131	3	87	41	7	3	4
	1,245	864	218	163	1,302	864	438
	451	198	126	127	254	198	56
	799	678	34	80	838	678	160
	733	497	96	140	714	497	217
setts	2,662	1,446	361	855	1,824	1,446	378
	814	140	388	286	178	140	38
	309	11	119	179	15	11	4
d	245	118	118	9	198	118	80
	1,263	342	489	432	441	342	99
	28	....	10	18	1	....	1
	2	....	....	2	....	....	....
pshire	548	401	37	60	567	401	166
y	918	506	61	351	717	506	211
	6,353	2,612	595	3,146	3,862	2,612	1,250
olina	779	760	15	4	1,032	760	272
	3,414	1,638	865	911	2,269	1,638	631
	122	4	84	34	4	4	....
nia	3,895	2,451	348	1,096	3,149	2,451	698
nd	312	189	41	82	282	189	93
olina	333	308	13	12	539	308	231
	925	689	211	25	1,010	689	321
	270	53	176	41	65	53	12
	721	357	259	105	546	357	189
	1,125	1,082	25	18	c1,988	1,082	906
ginia	374	....	b336	38	....	....	....
	846	46	202	538	68	46	22
Territories	596	111	218	267	135	111	24
	1	....	....	1	....	....	....
	12	....	11	1	....	....	....
	3	....	1	2	....	....	....
Columbia	479	61	181	237	80	61	19
	1	....	....	1	....	....	....
	2	....	2	....	....	....	....
co	50	48	....	2	52	48	4
	25	2	8	15	3	2	1
on	23	....	15	8	....	....	....
	....	....	....	....	....	....	....

(a) Does not include 789 the State of whose birth is unknown.
(b) Including 303 born in Virginia.
(c) Including 303 living in West Virginia.

In addition to the above, 6 are characterized as "idiotic," 32 are indicated ·ks as "probably recovered," "friends feel hopeful," &c., and 24 are marked d," which word is supposed to refer to the action of those in charge of asylums nstify a doubt as to the fact of insanity. But after all reasonable allowance accounts, there would probably remain something like 2,250 insane persons in by the count of the State board of charities. Only 1,621 insane persons were by the assistant marshals in the census, leaving the difference unaccounted on the mere statement of such a difference, it might reasonably be assumed assistant marshals of Illinois had failed to properly characterize, as insane otherwise reported upon their schedules. But a critical examination of the *and a comparison of* names dispose of this assumption and leave the difference *explicable,* except upon the ground of radical and total vice in one or the

TABLE LXXVIII.—*The Idiotic, with Race and Sex*—1870.

[N. B.—W, White; B, Black; M, Mulatto; C, Chinese; I, Indian.]

States and Territories.	Aggregate.	Total.		W.		B.		M.		C.		I.	
		M.	F.	M.	F.	M.	F.	M.	F.	M.	F.	M.	F.
The United States...	24, 527	14, 485	10, 042	12, 574	8, 750	1, 632	1, 111	270	175	4	1	5	5
The States..........	24, 395	14, 406	9, 989	12, 519	8, 705	1, 612	1, 107	266	172	4	1	5	4
Alabama	721	418	303	236	169	165	109	17	5				
Arkansas	289	181	108	146	78	30	27	5	3				
California	87	56	31	48	29	2		1	1	4	1	1	
Connecticut	341	191	150	185	148	3	2	3					
Delaware	69	39	30	28	20	11	10						
Florida	100	55	45	34	29	20	12	1	4				
Georgia	871	488	383	294	223	185	149	9	11				
Illinois	1, 244	754	490	744	484	7	3	3	2				1
Indiana	1, 360	790	570	785	561	2	5	3	4				
Iowa	533	316	217	316	217								
Kansas	109	64	45	60	39	4	3		2				1
Kentucky	1, 141	670	471	540	397	106	60	24	14				
Louisiana	286	185	101	97	42	72	46	16	13				
Maine	628	371	257	370	257	1							
Maryland	362	218	144	146	93	60	42	12	9				
Massachusetts	778	494	284	490	281	3	2	1	1				
Michigan	613	377	236	373	233		1	3	2			1	
Minnesota	134	79	55	79	55								
Mississippi	485	295	190	146	93	130	88	18	9			1	
Missouri	779	442	337	396	303	32	30	13	4			1	
Nebraska	25	19	6	19	6								
Nevada	2	1	1	1	1								
New Hampshire	325	198	127	198	127								
New Jersey	436	256	180	246	171	8	8	2	1				
New York	2, 486	1, 387	1, 099	1, 379	1, 083	7	15	1	1				
North Carolina	976	558	418	375	290	163	116	20	12				
Ohio	2, 338	1, 345	993	1, 299	972	29	15	17	6				
Oregon	55	36	19	35	19			1					
Pennsylvania	2, 250	1, 355	895	1, 336	877	14	14	5	4				
Rhode Island	123	76	47	73	46	3	1						
South Carolina	465	279	186	174	111	98	68	7	7				
Tennessee	1, 091	624	467	469	363	136	89	19	15				
Texas	451	291	160	180	93	100	53	11	12				2
Vermont	325	213	112	213	112								
Virginia	1, 130	691	439	428	280	212	131	51	28				
West Virginia	427	266	161	254	151	9	8	3	2				
Wisconsin	560	328	232	327	232							1	
The Territories......	132	79	53	55	45	20	4	4	3				1
Arizona													
Colorado	3	2	1	2	1								
Dakota	3	1	2	1	2								
District of Columbia	50	38	12	15	5	20	4	3	3				
Idaho	1		1		1								
Montana	1		1		1								
New Mexico	46	25	21	24	20			1					1
Utah	23	10	13	10	13								
Washington	5	3	2	3	2								
Wyoming													

other of the two lists being compared. Out of the total number of 2,376 names on the State list and 1,621 names on the census list, only 721 are found to be common to the two lists. Thus the State list contains 1,655 names which are not on the census, while the census contains 900 names which are not upon the State list. In the view of such monstrous discrepancies, it would be reasonable to assume that, inasmuch as the returns of the census are made by sworn officials visiting each house and family by turn, while the list of the State board of charities would appear to have been made up by no class of officials, and even by no distinct class of persons, the board must have been imposed upon, either through negligence or design on the part of its correspondents. This, which would appear to be the natural presumption upon the first statement of such discrepancies, is confirmed and rendered almost certain by the results of a careful search which has been instituted with a view to ascertaining whether the names of persons appearing on the State list as "insane" but not returned as such by assistant marshals, are to be found at all, in any connection, upon the schedules of the census, which, it should be stated, purport to present the name and personal description of every man, woman, and child in the community. Three hundred and ninety-nine names thus borne upon the State list as "insane," belonging to one hundred and

TABLE LXXIX.—*The Idiotic, with Nativity*—1870.

...nd Territories.	Total living in the State.	Born in the State and living in it.	Born in other States and living in the State.	Born in foreign countries and living in the State. (Foreign.)	Total born in the State and living in the United States. (Native.)	Born in the State and living in it.	Born in the State and living in other States.
United States	24, 527	17, 970	4, 912	1, 645	a22, 727	17, 970	a4, 737
States	24, 395	17, 900	4, 860	1, 629	22, 649	17, 900	4, 749
....	721	532	188	1	713	532	181
....	289	135	154	....	168	135	33
....	87	36	34	17	39	36	3
...t	341	287	29	25	332	287	45
....	69	58	9	2	74	58	16
....	100	57	43	....	62	57	5
....	871	782	88	1	967	782	185
....	1, 244	561	507	176	719	561	158
....	1, 360	861	421	78	1, 093	861	232
....	533	164	300	69	200	164	36
....	109	8	93	8	13	8	5
....	1, 141	970	154	17	1, 221	970	251
....	286	226	54	6	262	226	36
....	628	597	16	15	625	507	28
....	362	329	20	13	419	329	90
...etts	778	649	67	62	742	649	93
....	613	291	226	96	329	291	38
....	134	20	69	45	23	20	3
...i	485	304	180	1	385	304	81
....	779	401	314	64	502	401	101
....	25	3	18	4	3	3	....
....	2	....	1	1	....	....	....
...shire	325	289	24	12	324	289	35
...y	436	352	47	37	467	352	115
....	2, 486	2, 054	125	307	*2, 565	2, 054	511
...olina	976	955	21	....	1, 161	955	206
....	2, 338	1, 807	367	164	2, 306	1, 807	499
....	55	16	33	6	18	16	2
...nia	2, 250	1, 898	192	160	2, 247	1, 898	349
...nd	123	101	13	9	133	101	32
...olina	465	454	11	....	618	454	164
....	1, 091	940	147	4	1, 219	940	279
....	451	163	249	39	180	163	17
....	325	274	25	26	343	274	69
....	1, 130	1, 095	34	1	c1, 899	1, 095	804
...inia	427	....	b420	7	....	....	....
....	560	231	173	156	278	231	47
Territories	132	70	46	16	78	70	8
....	....	....	....	....	....	....	....
....	3	....	3	....	1	....	1
....	3	....	3	....	....	....	....
... Columbia	50	21	26	3	24	21	3
....	1	....	1	....	....	....	....
....	1	....	1	....	....	....	....
...co	46	42	....	4	45	42	3
....	23	6	9	8	7	6	1
...n	5	1	3	1	1	1	....
....	....	....	....	....	....	....	....

...s not include 150 the State of whose birth is unknown, 1 at sea, and 4 in Indian Territory.
...uding 389 born in Virginia.
...uding 389 living in West Virginia.

...hree towns and cities, were sought for throughout the entire body of the ...f their respective towns, covering a population of about half a million. Of ...ber only forty-five were found reported, as of any condition, on the schedules; ... considerable proportion of cases, no family of the same surname was found ...o town to which the State list assigned the person for whose name search was

... in contrast to facts like the above, it is stated that the census as an agency, ... State or National, is always steadily consistent with itself in respect to the ... of the Afflicted Classes, never departing far from the ratios exhibited in the ...bles, it must, the Superintendent thinks, be admitted that the figures of the ...e *entitled to full credence,* until impeached by evidence more carefully and ...*cally gathered than any yet presented.*

;ALTH, TAXATION, AND PUBLIC INDEBTEDNESS.

Valuation.—The schedule commonly known as the Social Statistics Schedule, annexed to the act of 1850, proposes ten distinct subjects of inquiry, viz: Valuation; Taxation; Churches; Schools; Libraries; Newspapers; Wages; Crops; Pauperism; and Crime. Of these ten heads, one, viz, Crops, was, as explained in the remarks which preface the Population volume of this census, stricken out of the schedule, as its proposed scope is more fully covered by the investigations of another office, viz: the Department of Agriculture. The place which it formerly occupied upon the schedule was devoted to an inquiry into State, county, and municipal indebtedness.

The results of the inquiries in respect to churches, libraries, schools, newspapers, pauperism, and crime, as bearing on the moral, social, and intellectual condition of the people, will be found in connection with the Statistics of Population. The Tables of Valuation, Taxation, and Indebtedness, constituting a part of the Industrial Statistics of the census, have been grouped with the Statistics of Production in the volume on Industry, and an abridgment of them will be found in the pages immediately following.

That part of the Social Statistics Schedule of 1850 which is devoted to the subject of Valuation has always been understood to require—

FIRST. A positive statement of the value of Real Property as *assessed* for purposes of State or local taxation.

SECOND. A positive statement of the value of Personal Property as *assessed* for purposes of State or local taxation.

THIRD. An *estimate*, by the officer making the return, of the True Value of both species of property combined. The phraseology of the schedule in this matter is most unfortunate, but it has always been understood (interpreted is hardly the word) to mean what is given above.

Inasmuch as the laws of some States exempt large amounts of personal property from taxation, while in others large classes of real property are so exempted; inasmuch, moreover, as the customs of assessment vary greatly in different States, and oftentimes in the several counties of the same State—in some the taxable value of the property not exempted by law being fixed at no more than a third of its recognized selling price; in others, at fifty, sixty, seventy, eighty, or ninety per cent.—it will be seen that the result of the first two inquiries is not to obtain the wealth of the several States and Territories, but to present merely the actual basis of State or local taxation: the amount, namely, in each State, county, or town, upon which a tax of five, ten, or fifteen dollars in the thousand might be levied. The utter want of uniformity in this matter of assessment for purposes of taxation cannot be too strongly insisted on. Without a knowledge of the laws in each community in respect to exemptions, as well as a knowledge of the customs of assessment in each, assessed values must always bear a very uncertain relation to real wealth.

That, then, which the first two inquiries under this head do not attempt to obtain, namely, the Real Wealth of the several States and Territories, it is sought to reach by means of estimates to be made by the officer immediately charged with the collection of the Social Statistics of the district or subdivision; and the results of this effort will be found in the proper column of the tables following.

As estimates on no subject can have any authority excepting such as is derived from confidence in the persons making them, or, if such estimates are put forth impersonally, then from confidence in the methods pursued, it is but right that it should be stated by what class of officers this part of the census work has been performed, and under what instructions from the central office they have acted. At the best, these figures represent but the opinion of one man, or of a body of men, in each State, acting under advice in the collection of material and in the calculation of the several elements of the public wealth.

From the following States and judicial districts the return of Social Statistics was made by a single deputy marshal specially commissioned for that duty, viz: California, Connecticut, Delaware, Indiana, Iowa, Kansas, Kentucky, Louisiana, Massachusetts, Michigan, Mississippi, Nebraska, Nevada, New Jersey, Eastern New York, Southern New York, North Carolina, Ohio, Oregon, Western Pennsylvania, South Carolina, Texas, Vermont, Wisconsin, Wyoming, and District of Columbia.

From each of the following States and judicial districts the returns of the Social Statistics were made by two or more deputy marshals specially commissioned for the service, viz: Alabama, Illinois, Missouri, Northern New York, and Eastern Pennsylvania.

In the following States and judicial districts the collection of the Social Statistics was, by the United States marshal, in his discretion, intrusted chiefly to the regular assistant marshals, each in his own subdivision, viz: Arkansas, Florida, Georgia, Maine, Maryland, Minnesota, New Hampshire, Rhode Island, Virginia, West Virginia, Arizona, Colorado, Dakota, Idaho, Montana, New Mexico, Utah, and Washington.

Where the duty of making these estimates of the true value of all species of property was charged upon assistant marshals, the merit of such estimates will, of course, depend upon the character of the marshal's general line of appointments. Where assistant marshals were selected from among the best citizens of the district their estimates, based on a more intimate local knowledge than was otherwise attainable, and with the advantage of a thorough personal canvass of the immediate region concerned, may be assumed to be reasonably just and close to all the facts and conditions of the case. The advantage of committing this duty to one or two officers in a State was found in the considerations—first, that this plan secured a greater uniformity of treatment; second, that, with the smaller number of persons engaged, it was practicable for the Census Office to confer more frequently and minutely with them in respect to difficulties encountered, and to communicate information or suggestions bearing on the subject; third, that it was possible by this method to secure officers of a distinctly higher grade for the performance of this duty.

The latter consideration was of prime importance for the purposes of a true valuation of the realized wealth of the country. Some of the gentlemen who consented to act in this capacity are of national reputation, while nearly all the appointees of this class brought to the work special qualifications and exceptional opportunities for the investigation.

The two points particularly dwelt upon in instructions from the Census Office in this matter of valuation were, first, the undervaluation of real estate in assessments for taxation; second, the large classes of personal property which,

(*a*) By State or Federal laws are exempt from taxation; or,

(*b*) By the habits of assessment are disregarded, (notably furniture, apparel, and equipage, and small amounts of money in hand or in bank;) or,

(*c*) By evasion or fraud escape assessment.

The investigations under the first head, as they have become known to the Census Office, have been searching and comprehensive. It is a great mistake to suppose that a uniform per cent. can be taken by which to advance the assessed values of real property throughout the country, or even throughout any one State, to reach the true selling-price. Not only are the variations to be calculated very great in every State, even after the nominal equalization which, in a few States, is effected by State boards constituted for the purpose, but the variations as between States are such as to deprive random statements as to the amount of undervaluation of all authority whatever. There are States in which the assessed value of the whole body of real estate does not fall short of its selling-price in a favorable market by more than ten per cent. In others the true value exceeds the assessed value by two hundred per cent., and even more; while between these extremes States are ranged without any perceptible order, certainly without any means of determining *a priori* their place in the scale. Hence, to say generally, as is so often done in discussions of the realized wealth of the country, "Add 30 per cent. for undervaluation," is the merest trifling. It is possible, however, so to conduct investigations in regard to each important section, by turn, as to reach results of real value, even though they take no more authoritative form than that of estimates. But that this should be so, it is necessary that they should be the estimates of judicious and well-informed men, known to have canvassed the whole field, with access to all official data existing, and acting in constant conference with each other and with a central office.

In a few States, notably several of the former slave States, both property and industry are in such a condition of uncertainty that it has only been possible to deal with the question roughly and approximately; but speaking generally for the majority of the States, and for the vast majority of the property of the country, the additions to be made to assessed values, on account of the undervaluation of real estate, have been calculated with great nicety by competent investigators.

No such accurate methods could, of course, be applied to the determination of the question how much should be added to the assessed valuation of the country on account of the exemption or escape of personal property from taxation. The result reached must, at best, be characterized rather as an *impression* than an *opinion;* but so long as this work was to be done at all, it was highly desirable that the impression should come from a study of the subject, and not from guessing at elements which had never been seriously considered.

One remark more will be appropriate before submitting these tables to criticism. No attempt has been made to eliminate that portion of the personal property of the country which is based on the value of real estate. To that extent, therefore, there is a duplication of wealth. The reasons why it was not deemed expedient to undertake the work of reducing the aggregate valuation of real and personal property by the amount of the latter, which merely represents the former, were as follows:

First. This duplication follows the general rule of State and municipal taxation. In nearly all the States of the Union land and buildings are taxed to their full (assumed) value, without deduction on account of mortgages, while the mortgages are also taxed at their full value. To obtain the aggregate value of both species of property, this duplication being admitted, is, therefore, to obtain the basis of possible taxation on prevailing methods of taxation, better than by excluding such duplicated values.

Second. This personal property representing real property is not always, perhaps not generally, *owned in the immediate* community where the real property is situated. *Its exclusion, therefore,* while it would more accurately present the realized wealth of

TABLE LXXX.—*Valuation of Property*—1870–1860–1850.

NOTE.—It has not been thought advisable to attempt a valuation of the property of the General Go[illegible] June, 1870, as appears in the report of the Secretary of the Treasury, was $411,255,470. The nation[illegible] Secretary of the Treasury, was $2,406,562,372; adding these amounts to the proper columns in this table, $3,271,874,768.

	States and Territories.	Total population, 1870.	Total population, 1860.	Total population, 1850.	1870		
					ASSESSED.		
					Total.	Real estate.	Personal estate.
					Dollars.	*Dollars.*	*Dollars.*
	The United States.	38, 558, 371	31, 443, 321	23, 191, 876	14, 178, 986, 732	9, 914, 780, 825	4, 264, 205, 907
	The States	38, 115, 641	31, 183, 744	23, 067, 262	14, 021, 297, 071	9, 804, 637, 402	4, 216, 659, 6[illegible]
1	Alabama	996, 992	964, 201	771, 623	155, 582, 595	117, 223, 043	38, 359, 5[illegible]
2	Arkansas	484, 471	435, 450	209, 897	94, 528, 843	63, 102, 304	31, 4[illegible]
3	California	560, 247	379, 994	92, 597	269, 644, 068	176, 527, 160	93, 116, [illegible]
4	Connecticut	537, 454	460, 147	370, 792	425, 433, 237	204, 110, 509	221, [illegible]
5	Delaware	125, 015	112, 216	91, 532	64, 787, 223	48, 744, 783	16, 042, 4[illegible]
6	Florida	187, 748	140, 424	87, 445	32, 480, 843	20, 197, 69[illegible]	12, 283, 1[illegible]
7	Georgia	1, 184, 09	1, 057, 286	906, 185	227, 219, 519	143, 948, 216	83, 271, 3[illegible]
8	Illinois	2, 539, 89[illegible]	, 711, 951	851, 470	482, 899, 575	348, 433, 906	134, 465, 6[illegible]
9	Indiana	1, 680, 637	1, 350, 428	988, 416	663, 455, 044	460, 120, 974	203, 334, 0[illegible]
10	Iowa	1, 191, 792	674, 913	192, 214	302, 515, 418	226, 610, 638	75, 904, 7[illegible]
11	Kansas	364, 399	107, 206	....	92, 125, 861	65, 499, 365	26, [illegible]
12	Kentucky	1, 321, 01[illegible]	1, 155, 684	982, 405	409, 544, 294	311, 479, 694	98, 064, 6[illegible]
13	Louisiana	726, 915	708, 002	517, 762	253, 371, 890	191, 343, 376	62, 028, 5[illegible]
14	Maine	626, 915	628, 279	583, 169	204, 253, 780	134, 580, 157	69, 673, 6[illegible]
15	Maryland	780, 894	687, 049	583, 034	423, 834, 918	286, 910, 332	136, 924, 5[illegible]
16	Massachusetts	1, 457, 351	1, 231, 066	994, 514	1, 591, 983, 112	901, 937, 841	690, 045, 2[illegible]
17	Michigan	1, 184, 059	749, 113	397, 654	272, 242, 917	224, 663, 667	47, 579, 2[illegible]
18	Minnesota	439, 706	172, 023	6, 077	84, 135, 332	62, 079, 587	22, 055, 7[illegible]
19	Mississippi	827, 922	791, 305	606, 526	177, 278, 890	118, 278, 460	59, 000, 4[illegible]
20	Missouri	1, 721, 295	1, 182, 012	682, 044	556, 129, 969	418, 527, 535	137, 602, 4[illegible]
21	Nebraska	122, 993	28, 841	....	54, 584, 616	38, 365, 999	16, 218, 6[illegible]
22	Nevada	42, 491	6, 857	....	25, 740, 973	14, 594, 722	11, 146, 2[illegible]
23	New Hampshire	318, 300	326, 073	317, 976	149, 065, 290	85, 231, 288	63, 834, 0[illegible]
24	New Jersey	906, 096	672, 035	489, 555	624, 868, 971	448, 832, 127	176, 036, 844
25	New York	4, 382, 759	3, 880, 735	3, 097, 394	1, 967, 001, 185	1, 532, 720, 907	434, 280, 279
26	North Carolina	1, 071, 361	992, 622	869, 039	130, 378, 622	83, 322, 012	47, 056, 610
27	Ohio	2, 665, 260	2, 339, 511	1, 980, 329	1, 167, 731, 697	707, 846, 836	4[illegible], 884, 861
28	Oregon	90, 923	52, 465	13, 294	31, 798, 510	17, 674, 202	14, 124, 308
29	Pennsylvania	3, 521, 791	2, 906, 215	2, 311, 786	1, 313, 236, 042	1, 071, 680, 934	241, 555, 108
30	Rhode Island	217, 353	174, 620	147, 545	244, 278, 854	132, 876, 581	111, 402, 273
31	South Carolina	705, 606	703, 708	668, 507	183, 913, 337	119, 494, 675	64, 418, 662
32	Tennessee	1, 258, 520	1, 109, 801	1, 002, 717	253, 782, 161	223, 035, 375	30, 746, 786
33	Texas	818, 579	604, 215	212, 592	149, 732, 929	97, 186, 568	52, 546, 361
34	Vermont	330, 551	315, 098	314, 120	102, 548, 528	80, 993, 100	21, 555, 428
35	Virginia	1, 225, 163	1, 219, 630	1, 421, 661	365, 439, 917	279, 116, 017	86, 323, 900
36	West Virginia	442, 014	376, 688	....	140, 538, 273	95, 924, 774	44, 613, 499
37	Wisconsin	1, 054, 670	775, 881	305, 391	333, 209, 838	252, 322, 107	80, 887, 731
	The Territories	442, 730	259, 577	124, 614	157, 689, 661	110, 143, 363	47, 546, 29[illegible]
1	Arizona	9, 658	....	....	1, 410, 295	538, 355	871, 940
2	Colorado	39, 864	34, 277	....	17, 338, 101	8, 840, 811	8, 497, 290
3	Dakota	14, 181	4, 837	....	2, 924, 489	1, 693, 923	1, 230, 766
4	Distr't of Columbia	131, 700	75, 080	51, 687	74, 271, 693	71, 437, 468	2, 834, 225
5	Idaho	14, 999	....	....	5, 292, 205	1, 926, 565	3, 365, 640
6	Montana	20, 595	....	....	9, 943, 411	2, 728, 128	7, 215, 283
7	New Mexico	91, 874	93, 516	61, 547	17, 784, 014	9, 917, 091	7, 866, 923
8	Utah	86, 786	40, 273	11, 380	12, 565, 842	7, 047, 881	5, 517, 961
9	Washington	23, 955	11, 594	....	10, 642, 863	5, 146, 776	3, 496, 087
10	Wyoming	9, 118	....	....	5, 516, 748	863, 665	4, 653, 083

the country as a whole, would lead to the grossest misrepresentations as between sections and States. Hundreds of millions are owned in the East in the form of mortgages on the real estate of the West. If these gigantic amounts are to be excluded from such tables as the following, they must be excluded *as personal property* from the valuations of the Eastern States. But to do so would be in the highest degree unjust. The wealth of these States consists in the value of their own real estate, their manufacturing, commercial, and banking capital, their furniture, apparel, and equipage, *plus* the claims they have upon the lands, buildings, and railways of the newer States.

Third. Even were it desirable, in view of the two considerations here presented, to eliminate the element of duplicated valuations, it will appear, on reflection, clear that

TABLE LXXX.—*Valuation of Property*—1870–1860–1850.

ernment. The total of receipts into the National Treasury for the fiscal year ended on the 30th day of debt, less the amount in the Treasury on the 1st day of June, 1870, as appears in the statement of the the aggregate public income of the country becomes $588,520,435, and the aggregate public indebtedness

1870	1860				1850	
TRUE.	ASSESSED.			TRUE.	TRUE.	
Real and personal estate.	Total.	Real estate.	Personal estate.	Real and personal estate.	Real and personal estate.	
Dollars. 30,068,518,507	*Dollars.* 12,084,560,005	*Dollars.* 6,973,006,049	*Dollars.* 5,111,553,956	*Dollars.* 16,159,616,068	*Dollars.* 7,135,780,228	
29,822,535,140	12,014,083,525	6,930,727,680	5,083,353,845	16,086,519,771	7,115,600,800	
201,855,841	432,198,762	155,034,089	277,164,673	495,237,078	228,204,332	1
156,394,691	180,211,330	63,254,740	116,956,590	219,256,473	39,841,025	2
638,767,017	139,654,667	66,906,631	72,748,036	207,874,613	22,161,872	3
774,631,524	341,256,976	191,478,842	149,778,134	444,274,114	155,707,980	4
97,180,833	39,767,233	26,273,803	13,493,430	46,242,181	21,062,556	5
44,163,655	68,929,685	21,722,810	47,206,875	73,101,500	22,862,270	6
268,169,207	618,232,387	179,801,441	438,430,946	645,895,237	335,425,714	7
2,121,680,579	389,207,372	287,219,940	101,987,432	871,860,282	156,265,006	8
1,268,180,543	411,042,424	291,829,992	119,212,432	528,835,371	202,650,264	9
717,644,750	205,166,983	149,433,423	55,733,560	247,338,265	23,714,638	10
188,892,014	22,518,232	16,088,602	6,429,630	31,327,895	....	11
604,318,552	528,212,693	277,925,054	250,287,639	666,043,112	301,628,456	12
323,125,666	435,787,265	280,704,988	155,082,277	602,118,568	233,998,764	13
348,155,671	154,380,388	86,717,716	67,662,672	190,211,600	122,777,571	14
643,748,976	297,135,238	65,341,438	231,793,800	376,919,944	219,217,364	15
2,132,148,741	777,157,816	475,413,165	301,744,651	815,237,433	573,342,286	16
719,208,118	163,533,005	123,605,084	39,927,921	257,163,983	59,787,255	17
228,909,590	32,018,773	25,291,771	6,727,002	52,294,413	....	18
209,197,345	509,472,912	157,836,737	351,636,175	607,324,911	228,951,130	19
1,284,922,897	266,935,851	153,450,577	113,485,274	501,214,398	137,247,707	20
69,277,483	7,426,949	5,732,145	1,694,804	9,131,056	....	21
31,134,012	....	....	....	....	....	22
252,624,112	193,810,089	59,638,346	64,171,743	156,310,860	103,652,835	23
940,976,064	296,682,492	151,161,942	145,520,550	467,918,324	200,000,000	24
6,500,841,264	1,390,464,638	1,069,658,080	320,806,558	1,843,338,517	1,080,309,216	25
260,757,244	292,297,602	116,366,573	175,931,029	358,739,399	226,800,472	26
2,235,430,300	959,867,101	687,518,121	272,348,980	1,193,898,422	504,726,120	27
51,558,932	19,024,915	6,279,602	12,745,313	28,930,637	5,063,474	28
3,808,340,112	719,253,335	561,192,980	158,060,355	1,416,501,818	722,486,120	29
296,965,646	125,104,305	83,778,204	41,326,101	135,337,588	80,508,794	30
208,146,989	489,319,128	129,772,684	359,546,444	548,138,754	288,257,694	31
498,237,724	382,495,200	219,991,180	162,504,020	493,903,892	201,246,686	32
159,052,542	267,792,335	112,476,013	155,316,322	365,200,614	52,740,473	33
235,349,553	84,758,619	65,639,973	19,118,646	122,477,170	92,205,049	34
409,588,133	657,021,336	417,952,228	239,069,108	793,249,681	430,701,082	35
190,651,491	(b)	....	....	....	....	36
702,307,329	185,945,489	148,238,766	37,706,723	273,671,668	42,056,595	37
245,983,367	70,476,480	42,278,369	28,198,111	73,096,207	20,179,428	
3,440,791	....	....	....	....	....	1
20,243,303	....	....	....	....	....	2
5,599,752	....	....	....	....	....	3
126,873,618	41,084,945	33,097,542	7,987,403	41,084,945	14,018,874	4
6,552,681	....	....	....	....	....	5
15,184,522	....	....	....	....	....	6
31,349,793	20,838,780	7,018,260	13,820,520	20,813,768	5,174,471	7
16,159,995	4,158,020	286,504	3,871,516	5,596,118	986,083	8
13,562,164	4,394,735	1,876,063	2,518,672	5,601,466	....	9
7,016,748	....	....	....	....	....	10

the difficulties in the way of anything approaching an accurate determination of the amount to be excluded would be almost insuperable.

On all these accounts it was believed that it would be far more satisfactory to aggregate the totals of real and of personal property as separately obtained, without any inquiry how far the value of one merely represents the value of the other.

Public indebtedness.—It is, of course, impossible to introduce into such statements of public indebtedness as are contained in Table LXXXII and in the last division of Table LXXXIII anything like uniformity in the treatment of contingent liabilities.

In some States *the treasury is contingently liable, in an amount far exceeding the proper debt of the State,* for the payment (in some cases of the principal and in others

TABLE LXXXI.—*Taxation*—1870-1860.

States and Territories.	Aggregate population.	1870				1860
		Total.	State.	County.	Town, city, &c.	Total.
		Dollars.	*Dollars.*	*Dollars.*	*Dollars.*	*Dollars.*
The United States	38, 558, 371	280, 591, 521	68, 051, 298	77, 746, 115	134, 794, 108	94, 186, 746
The States	38, 115, 641	277, 802, 495	67, 786, 674	76, 849, 111	133, 166, 710	93, 774, 421
Alabama	996, 992	2, 982, 932	1, 456, 024	1, 122, 971	403, 937	851, 171
Arkansas	484, 471	2, 866, 890	950, 894	1, 738, 760	177, 236	635, [illegible]
California	560, 247	7, 817, 115	2, 540, 383	5, 068, 041	208, 691	2, 981, 122
Connecticut	537, 454	6, 064, 843	1, 875, 024	20, 113	4, 169, 706	1, 015, [illegible]
Delaware	125, 015	418, 092	83, 666	189, 994	144, 432	a285, 891
Florida	187, 748	496, 166	248, 768	168, 389	79, 009	129, [illegible]
Georgia	1, 184, 109	2, 627, 029	945, 394	906, 270	775, 365	797, [illegible]
Illinois	2, 539, 891	21, 825, 008	3, 620, 681	5, 242, 137	12, 962, 190	6, 121, [illegible]
Indiana	1, 680, 637	10, 791, 121	2, 943, 078	4, 654, 466	3, 193, 577	3, 701, [illegible]
Iowa	1, 191, 792	9, 055, 614	832, 918	3, 052, 931	5, 169, 765	2, 372, [illegible]
Kansas	364, 399	2, 673, 992	809, 608	1, 160, 138	704, 246	195, [illegible]
Kentucky	1, 321, 011	5, 730, 118	2, 254, 413	1, 307, 833	2, 167, 872	2, 148, [illegible]
Louisiana	726, 915	7, 060, 722	2, 671, 693	4, 109, 999	270, 030	4, [illegible]
Maine	626, 915	5, 348, 645	1, 350, 305	315, 199	3, 683, 141	2, 257, [illegible]
Maryland	780, 894	6, 632, 842	1, 781, 252	1, 542, 218	3, 309, 372	2, 15[illegible]
Massachusetts	1, 457, 351	24, 922, 900	7, 408, 962	653, 500	16, 860, 438	7, [illegible]
Michigan	1, 184, 059	5, 412, 957	306, 332	1, 565, 163	3, 451, 442	1, [illegible]
Minnesota	439, 706	2, 648, 372	511, 126	1, 070, 944	1, 066, 302	[illegible]
Mississippi	827, 922	3, 736, 432	1, 309, 655	2, 299, 699	127, 078	954, [illegible]
Missouri	1, 721, 295	13, 908, 498	2, 778, 697	4, 402, 227	6, 727, 574	4, [illegible]
Nebraska	122, 993	1, 027, 327	262, 505	753, 022	11, 800	91, [illegible]
Nevada	42, 491	820, 308	298, 411	498, 062	23, 835	....
New Hampshire	318, 300	3, 255, 793	955, 126	318, 666	1, 982, 001	1, 261, [illegible]
New Jersey	906, 096	7, 416, 724	373, 046	2, 397, 348	4, 646, 330	1, 457, [illegible]
New York	4, 382, 759	48, 550, 308	8, 720, 156	15, 102, 761	24, 727, 391	15, 363, [illegible]
North Carolina	1, 071, 361	2, 352, 809	1, 200, 854	923, 604	228, 351	1, 044, [illegible]
Ohio	6, 665, 260	23, 526, 548	4, 727, 318	6, 501, 941	12, 297, 289	9, 611, 081
Oregon	90, 923	580, 956	177, 653	362, 753	40, 550	199, [illegible]
Pennsylvania	3, 521, 791	24, 531, 397	5, 800, 172	4, 263, 898	14, 467, 327	8, [illegible]
Rhode Island	217, 353	2, 170, 152	489, 253	....	1, 680, 899	656, 133
South Carolina	705, 606	2, 767, 675	1, 321, 837	575, 005	870, 833	1, [illegible]
Tennessee	1, 258, 520	3, 381, 579	1, 056, 261	1, 302, 836	1, 022, 482	1, 102, 780
Texas	818, 579	1, 129, 577	589, 363	312, 335	227, 879	533, 265
Vermont	330, 551	1, 547, 128	588, 792	40, 329	918, 007	908, [illegible]
Virginia	1, 225, 163	4, 613, 798	2, 847, 635	842, 069	924, 094	3, 672, [illegible]
West Virginia	442, 014	1, 722, 158	734, 722	555, 885	431, 551	....
Wisconsin	1, 054, 670	5, 387, 970	874, 677	1, 507, 605	3, 005, 688	2, 330, 011
The Territories	442, 730	2, 789, 026	264, 624	897, 004	1, 627, 398	412, 325
Arizona	9, 658	31, 323	7, 782	23, 541	....	....
Colorado	39, 864	362, 197	63, 425	267, 201	31, 571	....
Dakota	14, 181	13, 867	1, 269	12, 598	....	(b)
District of Columbia	131, 700	1, 581, 569	....	49, 975	1, 531, 594	280, 21[illegible]
Idaho	14, 999	174, 711	40, 594	132, 171	1, 946	....
Montana	20, 595	198, 527	38, 131	157, 396	3, 000	....
New Mexico	91, 874	61, 014	34, 115	26, 101	798	23, 7[illegible]
Utah	86, 786	167, 355	39, 402	80, 419	47, 534	65, 0[illegible]
Washington	23, 955	163, 992	33, 743	119, 294	10, 955	57, 311
Wyoming	9, 118	34, 471	6, 163	28, 308	....	....

(*a*) Returns of taxation incomplete. (*b*) No returns of taxation.

of the interest) of bonds issued by, or in aid of, railroad and other companies; the security given for the payment of such obligations at maturity, by the companies themselves, varying in quality from the highest to the lowest. It is hardly necessary to say that the same difficulty attends the statement of the debt of the United States, by reason of the aid extended by the Government in the construction of certain railroads.

A second obstacle to uniformity in such statements is found in the fact that in many States the bonds of the State are held in trust, in large amounts, by officers representing various special interests of the State itself. For example, the securities of the educational funds in one-half the States consist largely, if not principally, of State bonds. To determine in which of these States, at any future time, or under all reasonable contingencies, provision would be made for the payment of the interest or principal, and in which of the States, in times of financial embarrassment or under possible political conditions, the interests of education would be left to suffer, would be invidious even if it were practicable, but will be seen at a glance to be wholly impracticable and hopeless.

TABLE LXXXII.—*Public Indebtedness*—1870.

ates and Territories.	STATE.			COUNTY.		TOWN, CITY, ETC.	
	Total.	For which bonds have been issued.	All other.	For which bonds have been issued.	All other.	For which bonds have been issued.	All other.
	Dollars.	*Dollars.*	*Dollars.*	*Dollars.*	*Dollars.*	*Dollars.*	*Dollars.*
he United States	868, 676, 758	324, 747, 959	28, 118, 739	157, 955, 880	29, 609, 660	271, 119, 668	57, 124, 852
he States	864, 785, 067	324, 747, 959	28, 118, 739	157, 197, 873	29, 099, 180	269, 460, 661	56, 160, 665
bama	13, 277, 154	5, 382, 800	3, 093, 218	1, 457, 128	247, 045	2, 773, 900	321, 063
ansas	4, 151, 152	3, 050, 000	409, 557	247, 333	289, 316	122, 096	32, 850
fornia	18, 069, 082	3, 311, 500	117, 527	9, 808, 404	4, 009, 307	815, 764	26, 580
necticut	17, 088, 906	7, 275, 900	....	....	6, 103	6, 837, 417	2, 969, 486
aware	526, 125	....	....	116, 375	23, 500	384, 250	2, 000
ida	2, 185, 838	1, 012, 372	276, 325	365, 514	77, 527	331, 000	123, 100
rgia	21, 733, 712	6, 544, 500	....	300, 386	261, 349	14, 383, 315	264, 162
ois	42, 191, 869	4, 890, 937	....	10, 729, 192	2, 088, 730	23, 724, 835	758, 175
ana	7, 818, 710	4, 167, 507	....	620, 926	506, 343	2, 342, 067	181, 867
a	8, 043, 133	534, 498	....	2, 279, 729	1, 453, 200	1, 941, 966	1, 833, 740
sas	6, 442, 282	1, 341, 975	251, 331	3, 547, 800	189, 101	824, 075	288, 000
tucky	18, 953, 484	3, 076, 480	816, 000	6, 305, 864	807, 780	7, 361, 727	585, 633
isiana	53, 087, 441	22, 560, 233	2, 461, 501	847, 526	479, 109	18, 123, 010	8, 616, 062
ne	16, 624, 624	8, 067, 900	....	240, 300	33, 853	6, 108, 344	2, 174, 227
yland	29, 032, 577	13, 317, 475	....	1, 305, 395	260, 384	14, 097, 856	51, 467
sachusetts	69, 211, 538	27, 128, 164	1, 142, 717	30, 000	677, 123	26, 530, 150	13, 694, 384
higan	6, 725, 231	2, 385, 028	....	1, 006, 150	269, 329	2, 687, 925	376, 799
nesota	2, 788, 797	350, 000	....	343, 383	129, 311	1, 845, 497	120, 606
sissippi	2, 594, 415	100, 000	1, 696, 230	344, 596	311, 969	120, 950	20, 650
souri	46, 909, 865	17, 866, 000	....	10, 265, 419	1, 553, 593	15, 782 100	1, 442, 753
raska	2, 089, 264	36, 300	211, 000	1, 563, 530	206, 034	70, 400	2, 000
ada	1, 986, 093	500, 000	142, 894	576, 937	410, 496	327, 776	28, 000
Hampshire	11, 153, 373	2, 752, 200	65, 669	372, 700	372, 370	2, 364, 114	5, 226, 320
Jersey	22, 854, 304	2, 996, 200	....	6, 222, 921	712, 394	11, 710, 162	1, 212, 627
York	159, 808, 234	32, 409, 144	....	39, 923, 185	10, 756, 590	66, 363, 637	10, 355, 669
th Carolina	32, 474, 036	29, 900, 045	....	931, 256	801, 517	659, 248	181, 970
	22, 241, 988	9, 732, 078	....	3, 893, 000	344, 543	8, 272, 367	....
gon	218, 486	106, 583	....	51, 386	54, 517	500	5, 500
nsylvania	89, 027, 131	31, 111, 662	....	48, 762, 038	411, 812	7, 882, 377	859, 242
de Island	5, 938, 642	2, 913, 500	....	....	....	2, 571, 965	453, 177
th Carolina	13, 075, 229	7, 665, 909	....	....	97, 112	5, 312, 208	....
nessee	48, 827, 191	31, 892, 144	6, 647, 658	2, 283, 042	446, 617	5, 534, 050	2, 023, 680
as	1, 613, 907	....	508, 641	195, 595	231, 271	524, 600	153, 800
mont	3, 594, 700	1, 002, 500	....	8, 042	....	1, 470, 094	1, 114, 064
ginia	55, 921, 255	39, 208, 225	8, 092, 614	980, 498	385, 268	6, 743, 800	420, 850
st Virginia	561, 767	(a)	....	251, 733	78, 100	205, 872	26, 062
consin	5, 903, 532	68, 200	2, 183, 857	960, 600	116, 528	2, 300, 247	274, 100
he Territories	3, 891, 691	....	....	758, 007	510, 490	1, 650, 007	964, 187
zona	10, 500	....	....	4, 000	6, 500	....	....
orado	681, 158	....	....	620, 000	58, 829	....	2, 320
kota	5, 761	....	....	1, 250	4, 421	....	90
trict of Columbia	2, 596, 545	....	....	....	....	1, 640, 584	955, 961
ho	222, 621	....	....	33, 739	184, 783	2, 542	1, 557
ntana	278, 719	....	....	77, 706	198, 513	....	2, 500
Mexico	7, 560	....	....	....	7, 560	....	....
h	....	....	....	....	....	....	....
ashington	88, 827	....	....	21, 312	49, 884	15, 881	1, 750
oming	....	....	....	....	....	....	....

(a) Included in Virginia.

n view of the difficulties thus briefly stated, (and others might be cited,) it has en thought best to express the debt of each State in the following tables at the ount recognized by the proper officers and authorities of the State as constituting debt, and to accompany the statement by such explanations and such additional ormation as may be necessary to enable any person so disposed to work out the tement of indebtedness upon a uniform rule, either inclusive or exclusive of all ntingent liabilities, (without reference to the quality of the security;) or, again, her inclusive or exclusive of all sums owing from the treasury to some department the State itself. It is true that this plan may involve considerable differences in treatment of the subject of State liability, due not so much to differences in the aracter of the security in the several cases, as to the somber or sanguine disposition the officers immediately in charge, or to temporary embarrassments, or to the tradins of an auditor's or a comptroller's office. [For special remarks respecting each ate and Territory, see pages 6 and 7 of Vol. II., Ninth Census.]

TABLE LXXXIII.—*Valuation, Taxation, and Public Indebtedness by Counties*—1870.

STATE OF ALABAMA.

Counties.	VALUATION.		TAXATION NOT NATIONAL.				PUBLIC DEBT.	
	Assessed valuation of real and personal estate.	True valuation of real and personal estate.	All.	State.	County.	Town, city, &c.	County.	Town, city, &c.
	Dollars.	*Dollars.*	*Dollars.*	*Dollars.*	*Dollars.*	*Dollars.*	*Dollars.*	*Dollars.*
The State	155, 582, 595	201, 855, 841	2, 982, 932	1, 436, 024	1, 122, 971	403, 937	1, 704, 173	3, 094, 96[illegible]
Autauga	1, 867, 040	2, 379, 744	29, 998	15, 996	14, 002			
Baker	388, 144	512, 291	7, 263	4, 352	2, 911			
Baldwin	1, 015, 457	1, 220, 827	13, 770	8, 201	5, 569		2, 500	
Barbour	4, 574, 427	5, 953, 446	113, 541	44, 296	69, 245		340, 100	
Bibb	878, 867	1, 130, 089	12, 942	8, 328	4, 614		2, 520	
Blount	757, 893	961, 690	17, 482	7, 497	5, 770	4, 215	3, 000	
Bullock	4, 090, 919	5, 380, 830	55, 014	27, 638	19, 916	7, 460	1, 000	25, 000
Butler	1, 794, 867	2, 471, 910	31, 161	17, 795	13, 366		12, 500	
Calhoun	1, 702, 258	2, 679, 635	32, 322	16, 252	16, 070		5, 000	
Chambers	1, 687, 876	2, 218, 770	27, 371	14, 713	12, 658		172, 000	
Cherokee	1, 368, 353	1, 809, 405	23, 019	12, 163	10, 856		5, 000	
Choctaw	1, 104, 975	1, 452, 755	16, 547	10, 335	6, 212			
Clarke	1, 224, 414	1, 620, 064	21, 136	11, 953	9, 183			
Clay	603, 592	801, 268	10, 347	5, 821	4, 526			
Cleburne	444, 381	568, 634	7, 667	4, 469	3, 198		4, 000	
Coffee	352, 217	467, 036	10, 566	3, 987	6, 579		9, 870	
Colbert	1, 834, 723	2, 178, 058	29, 288	16, 229	13, 059		10, 000	
Conecuh	960, 383	1, 252, 635	16, 760	9, 550	7, 210		7, 270	
Coosa	943, 875	1, 246, 203	17, 029	9, 950	7, 079		500	
Covington	190, 222	252, 788	4, 329	2, 190	2, 139		1, 336	
Crenshaw	791, 719	1, 046, 027	14, 632	8, 694	5, 938		4, 008	
Dale	907, 980	1, 198, 152	18, 039	9, 528	8, 511		5, 000	
Dallas	9, 779, 577	12, 722, 277	210, 233	88, 408	75, 825	46, 000		342, 000
De Kalb	654, 629	872, 358	12, 259	6, 875	5, 384		5, 000	
Elmore	2, 307, 687	2, 931, 364	39, 984	21, 664	18, 320			
Escambia	268, 622	345, 616	5, 530	3, 516	2, 014			
Etowah	991, 797	1, 168, 222	16, 863	9, 854	7, 009		8, 000	
Fayette	629, 417	775, 693	10, 733	6, 079	4, 651		10, 000	
Franklin	793, 939	3, 302, 081	28, 800	8, 988	19, 812		9, 000	
Geneva	202, 933	268, 633	3, 542	2, 021	1, 521			
Greene	3, 614, 226	4, 708, 610	57, 368	33, 107	20, 304	3, 957	80, 000	20, 000
Hale	4, 388, 825	5, 717, 318	78, 377	39, 461	32, 916	6, 000		19, 000
Henry	1, 404, 241	1, 852, 582	24, 688	14, 147	10, 541		9, 000	
Jackson	1, 935, 239	2, 137, 200	31, 802	18, 979	12, 823		16, 500	
Jefferson	1, 350, 630	1, 557, 197	22, 010	12, 667	9, 343		7, 500	
Lauderdale	3, 179, 565	3, 442, 526	49, 373	28, 718	20, 655		19, 062	3, 433
Lawrence	1, 827, 672	3, 000, 000	35, 758	18, 294	17, 264	200	4, 000	
Lee	2, 229, 037	2, 922, 373	38, 604	19, 559	16, 685	2, 360	200, 000	50, 000
Limestone	2, 693, 056	3, 351, 651	44, 651	24, 542	20, 109			
Lowndes	3, 287, 616	4, 283, 954	49, 311	30, 922	18, 389		5, 009	325
Macon	2, 699, 659	3, 530, 490	47, 331	25, 210	20, 246	1, 875		25
Madison	7, 970, 675	8, 000, 000	127, 481	73, 262	54, 219		149, 000	
Marengo	3, 399, 176	4, 481, 437	90, 715	48, 854	41, 861		8, 376	1, 500
Marion	291, 293	683, 191	7, 275	3, 161	4, 114			
Marshall	1, 028, 782	1, 325, 737	17, 491	9, 537	7, 954		15, 000	
Mobile	23, 743, 719	30, 510, 869	496, 890	201, 341	91, 780	203, 769	100, 200	2, 095, 45[illegible]
Monroe	1, 444, 753	1, 874, 108	22, 204	14, 078	8, 126			
Montgomery	12, 931, 881	16, 614, 637	347, 426	125, 923	95, 003	126, 500	50, 020	538, 000
Morgan	1, 500, 304	1, 910, 641	22, 723	14, 366	8, 357		2, 509	
Perry	4, 721, 530	6, 156, 480	69, 861	43, 624	26, 237		12, 000	
Pickens	1, 482, 010	1, 953, 971	25, 771	14, 656	11, 115			
Pike	1, 699, 337	2, 245, 440	29, 030	16, 286	12, 744			
Randolph	882, 332	1, 170, 408	13, 555	8, 595	4, 960		103, 630	
Russell	2, 635, 477	3, 483, 797	45, 603	25, 837	19, 766		23, 007	
Sanford	800, 000	1, 000, 000	12, 435	6, 435	6, 000		5, 000	
Shelby	1, 202, 069	1, 580, 501	21, 176	12, 425	8, 751		11, 500	
St. Clair	645, 906	841, 937	11, 684	6, 633	5, 051		8, 000	
Sumter	3, 164, 590	4, 156, 041	63, 539	31, 079	31, 645	815	35, 000	
Talladega	3, 541, 690	4, 632, 823	58, 268	31, 658	26, 610			
Tallapoosa	1, 992, 911	2, 624, 321	45, 095	19, 309	25, 000	786	200, 000	
Tuscaloosa	2, 690, 789	3, 501, 072	41, 898	21, 539	20, 359			
Walker	549, 470	725, 128	9, 859	5, 508	4, 351		11, 000	
Washington	311, 129	406, 189	5, 280	2, 950	2, 333			
Wilcox	3, 036, 656	3, 975, 671	53, 647	30, 831	22, 816		10, 000	
Winston	190, 167	300, 000	3, 577	2, 183	1, 391		1, 300	

LXXXIII.—*Valuation, Taxation, and Public Indebtedness by Counties*—1870—Cont'd.

TERRITORY OF ARIZONA.

ities.	VALUATION.		TAXATION, NOT NATIONAL.				PUBLIC DEBT.	
	Assessed valuation of real and personal estate.	True valuation of real and personal estate.	All.	Territory.	County.	Town, city, &c.	County.	Town, city, &c.
	Dollars.	*Dollars.*	*Dollars.*	*Dollars.*	*Dollars.*	*Dollars.*	*Dollars.*	*Dollars.*
erritory	1,410,295	3,440,791	31,323	7,782	23,541	....	10,500	....
....	125,000	175,000	2,892	964	1,928	....	1,500	....
....	821,700	2,702,196	18,000	4,500	13,500	....	4,000	....
i (a)...	....	....	....	....	....	....	....	....
....	463,595	563,595	10,431	2,318	8,113	....	5,000	....

(a) No report.

STATE OF ARKANSAS.

ities.	VALUATION.		TAXATION, NOT NATIONAL.				PUBLIC DEBT.	
	Assessed valuation of real and personal estate	True valuation of real and personal estate.	All.	State.	County.	Town, city, &c.	County.	Town, city, &c.
	Dollars.	*Dollars.*	*Dollars.*	*Dollars.*	*Dollars.*	*Dollars.*	*Dollars.*	*Dollars.*
tate....	94,528,843	156,394,691	2,866,890	950,894	1,738,760	177,236	536,649	154,946
as......	1,768,946	2,830,313	....	....	....	....	15,000	....
....	1,607,986	2,266,189	41,142	17,023	24,119	....	6,000	....
....	2,158,242	3,095,197	35,989	24,412	11,577	....	....	....
....	810,522	1,883,225	28,834	8,776	20,058	....	13,000	....
....	1,197,458	2,963,280	53,917	12,658	41,259	....	3,478	....
....	459,193	734,708	11,958	5,072	6,886	....	....	....
....	612,502	1,468,360	15,116	6,305	8,811	....	4,368	....
....	2,550,006	4,080,009	25,233	25,233	....	....	....	....
....	2,136,363	3,281,683	83,641	22,723	53,585	7,333	....	....
ia......	1,743,826	2,208,721	55,811	19,628	36,183	....	5,000	....
....	1,459,038	3,517,900	37,676	14,313	23,363	....	....	....
ad.....	687,820	687,820	20,542	7,237	13,305	....	1,000	....
al......	1,519,688	2,431,501	42,941	14,950	27,991	....	21,895	....
len.....	1,299,320	2,078,925	26,352	8,108	18,241	....	....	....
....	976,562	1,562,499	30,145	10,112	19,868	165	2,500	....
....	704,526	1,117,145	21,955	7,657	14,298	....	3,000	....
....	1,445,084	2,756,956	14,421	16,660	27,761	....	15,000	....
....	2,107,117	2,235,968	73,472	22,358	44,327	6,787	....	....
n.......	1,618,637	1,676,461	56,402	16,901	39,501	....	2,000	....
....	620,225	971,825	14,715	6,756	7,959	....	2,500	....
....	372,842	483,926	20,539	4,563	12,165	3,811	....	....
....	1,184,217	1,891,746	35,841	11,321	24,520	....	....	....
ead....	2,458,043	3,932,868	104,658	26,165	78,493	....	....	....
ings...	859,547	1,625,952	18,533	9,075	9,458	....	16,500	....
dence..	2,537,357	4,059,770	64,396	21,858	33,637	901	9,000	....
....	820,965	1,726,745	14,991	9,016	5,975	....	2,500	....
....	1,279,523	2,714,042	43,678	13,641	27,837	2,200	15,006	700
n......	5,362,772	8,673,689	198,783	60,443	122,522	15,818	36,314	7,546
....	1,298,982	2,078,372	44,314	13,861	30,453	....	....	....
te......	1,892,580	3,333,290	41,528	19,381	22,147	....	1,200	....
ne......	1,207,550	1,932,693	21,024	12,509	8,515	....	....	....
iver...	592,505	1,289,241	33,492	6,197	27,295	....	9,200	....
n.......	591,433	1,643,576	15,831	6,961	8,870	....	7,000	....
....	612,686	767,785	18,690	6,873	10,617	1,200	2,000	....
ppi....	774,987	1,164,201	15,794	8,220	7,574	....	4,100	....
....	1,403,671	4,488,380	44,631	15,156	29,475	....	....	....
mery...	250,154	640,000	8,303	2,839	5,464	....	5,341	....
....	321,378	471,415	10,573	3,866	6,707	....	4,010	....
a.......	2,204,387	4,070,547	74,564	23,057	43,077	8,430	100	5,400
....	592,958	799,132	22,592	6,141	16,451	....	3,600	....

TABLE LXXXIII.—*Valuation, Taxation, and Public Indebtedness by Counties*—1870—Cont'd.

STATE OF ARKANSAS—Continued.

Counties.	VALUATION.		TAXATION, NOT NATIONAL.				PUBLIC DEBT.	
	Assessed valuation of real and personal estate.	True valuation of real and personal estate.	All.	State.	County.	Town, city, &c.	County.	Town, city, &c.
	Dollars.	*Dollars.*	*Dollars.*	*Dollars.*	*Dollars.*	*Dollars.*	*Dollars.*	*Dollars.*
Phillips	4, 978, 476	9, 600, 000	180, 452	54, 458	125, 994	....	50, 000	....
Pike	433, 960	631, 450	9, 715	5, 280	4, 435	....	6, 859	....
Poinsett	360, 000	576, 000	....	....	....	....	2, 600	....
Polk	123, 659	294, 887	11, 848	2, 766	9, 082	....	15, 060	....
Pope	1, 410, 112	2, 256, 179	28, 869	14, 769	14, 100	....	....	....
Prairie	1, 583, 849	2, 534, 157	58, 490	16, 206	31, 938	10, 346	4, 000	....
Pulaski	9, 903, 324	15, 967, 059	414, 463	98, 628	242, 440	73, 395	120, 288	120, 000
Randolph	906, 968	1, 451, 148	31, 861	10, 141	21, 720	....	....	....
Saline	477, 048	747, 953	21, 680	5, 274	9, 641	6, 765	....	....
Scott	756, 170	737, 056	11, 981	8, 201	3, 780	....	....	....
Searcy	534, 745	855, 591	12, 645	5, 961	6, 684	....	400	....
Sebastian	2, 904, 549	4, 501, 632	111, 875	29, 740	69, 135	13, 000	35, 000	21, 50
Sevier	1, 007, 316	1, 606, 052	36, 637	10, 448	26, 189	....	15, 496	....
Sharpe	670, 668	1, 040, 000	17, 810	7, 203	10, 607	....	4, 000	....
St. Francis	1, 719, 497	1, 923, 491	37, 912	17, 738	20, 174	....	3, 000	....
Union	1, 934, 122	2, 880, 000	79, 600	20, 247	32, 668	26, 685	12, 500	....
Van Buren	449, 165	718, 663	11, 642	5, 105	6, 537	....	....	....
Washington	4, 141, 619	6, 626, 589	65, 244	24, 885	40, 359	....	....	....
White	2, 559, 340	3, 718, 631	67, 708	25, 902	41, 806	....	....	....
Woodruff	1, 432, 841	2, 880, 000	43, 932	15, 276	28, 656	....	42, 000	....
Yell	2, 139, 799	3, 209, 698	39, 509	21, 641	17, 468	400	9, 000	....

STATE OF CALIFORNIA.

Counties.	VALUATION.		TAXATION, NOT NATIONAL.				PUBLIC DEBT.	
	Assessed valuation of real and personal estate.	True valuation of real and personal estate.	All.	State.	County.	Town, city, &c.	County.	Town, city, &c.
	Dollars.	*Dollars.*	*Dollars.*	*Dollars.*	*Dollars.*	*Dollars.*	*Dollars.*	*Dollars.*
The State	269, 644, 068	638, 767, 017	7, 817, 115	2, 540, 383	5, 068, 041	208, 691	13, 817, 711	842, 34
Alameda	11, 786, 471	23, 622, 500	255, 764	101, 952	153, 812	....	34, 000	132, 60
Alpine	346, 525	346, 525	11, 399	2, 997	8, 402	....	20, 920	....
Amador	1, 952, 941	4, 428, 490	48, 237	18, 944	29, 293	....	165, 000	....
Butte	3, 784, 014	6, 222, 830	102, 167	32, 731	69, 436	....	269, 000	....
Calaveras	1, 124, 208	1, 791, 749	56, 210	10, 905	45, 305	....	222, 117	....
Colusa	4, 339, 041	8, 696, 068	94, 335	37, 532	53, 803	3, 000	50, 000	1, 000
Contra Costa	3, 926, 585	6, 678, 953	92, 309	38, 088	54, 221	....	15, 581	....
Del Norte	486, 584	718, 645	13, 135	4, 013	9, 122	....	14, 000	....
El Dorado	2, 143, 941	3, 153, 256	64, 958	18, 545	42, 450	3, 963	267, 056	56, 150
Fresno	3, 013, 598	3, 774, 295	63, 735	26, 066	37, 669	....	....	....
Humboldt	2, 166, 540	4, 132, 318	67, 268	18, 739	48, 529	....	27, 540	....
Inyo	630, 769	1, 119, 095	19, 483	6, 116	13, 367	....	33, 525	....
Kern	1, 770, 068	3, 168, 360	42, 745	15, 310	27, 435	....	31, 000	....
Klamath	411, 361	525, 875	11, 369	3, 554	7, 815	....	24, 245	....
Lake	709, 954	1, 266, 290	21, 287	6, 132	15, 155	....	4, 386	....
Lassen	522, 880	936, 065	14, 975	4, 519	10, 456	....	32, 580	....
Los Angeles	6, 667, 940	11, 556, 757	184, 367	57, 677	86, 637	40, 053	277, 056	204, 60
Marin	3, 774, 755	7, 080, 058	93, 042	32, 648	60, 394	....	73, 000	....
Mariposa	1, 197, 473	1, 329, 775	36, 458	10, 357	26, 101	....	92, 000	....
Mendocino	2, 212, 523	3, 681, 895	59, 736	22, 125	37, 611	....	60, 434	....
Merced	2, 239, 206	4, 194, 513	46, 236	19, 366	26, 870	....	....	....
Mono	316, 708	361, 960	9, 491	2, 732	6, 759	....	20, 000	....
Monterey	5, 659, 457	9, 318, 821	149, 994	48, 954	99, 049	2, 000	22, 000	500
Napa	4, 027, 624	12, 569, 515	89, 487	34, 839	54, 648	....	311, 390	....
Nevada	6, 870, 972	10, 918, 255	137, 417	59, 433	77, 984	....	70, 000	25, 000
Placer	4, 437, 145	6, 318, 325	115, 363	37, 715	77, 648	....	343, 000	....
Plumas	1, 232, 359	2, 201, 165	28, 354	10, 609	17, 745	....	58, 650	....

XXXIII.—*Valuation, Taxation, and Public Indebtedness by Counties*—1870—Cont'd.

STATE OF CALIFORNIA—Continued.

es.	VALUATION.		TAXATION, NOT NATIONAL.				PUBLIC DEBT.	
	Assessed valuation of real and personal estate.	True valuation of real and personal estate.	All.	State.	County.	Town, city, &c.	County.	Town, city, &c.
	Dollars.	*Dollars.*	*Dollars.*	*Dollars.*	*Dollars.*	*Dollars.*	*Dollars.*	*Dollars.*
o....	11,173,794	38,870,795	268,168	96,652	171,516	....	1,900,000	....
rdino	1,197,270	2,302,315	27,715	10,356	16,771	588	14,929	....
.....	4,526,296	4,480,456	129,675	39,151	90,524	....	110,000	....
isco .	102,087,989	263,056,512	3,144,307	883,061	2,261,246	....	7,458,647	....
in ...	7,842,770	23,472,805	352,920	66,663	286,257	....	314,302	222,000
bispo	1,694,508	3,389,016	46,004	14,657	31,347	....	27,875	1,250
.....	1,942,031	23,286,825	69,687	16,798	20,798	32,001	31,500	....
bara .	1,614,087	10,896,021	47,613	16,140	31,473	....	....	....
a	11,841,703	39,877,413	313,220	102,430	143,284	67,506	361,600	1,600
z.....	2,586,963	6,216,475	77,606	25,093	52,513	....	61,144	1,200
.....	1,073,981	1,844,307	27,598	10,417	17,181	....	44,132	....
.....	1,832,143	2,267,679	47,543	15,848	31,695	....	48,660	....
.....	3,669,475	4,002,047	83,511	31,740	51,771	....	55,600	....
.....	6,945,726	19,357,710	202,813	56,954	141,490	4,369	257,000	22,000
.....	11,305,277	15,535,418	283,125	97,790	170,921	14,414	....	14,414
.....	3,206,057	6,739,115	59,309	27,732	31,577	....	7,800	....
.....	2,103,602	3,707,648	85,826	20,405	65,421	....	2,500	71,000
.....	2,444,858	3,667,286	57,818	23,592	34,226	....	87,855	....
.....	596,161	1,076,465	16,780	5,156	11,624	....	59,000	....
.....	2,501,968	3,844,990	60,045	21,642	38,403	....	40,000	....
.....	1,186,231	1,895,845	54,149	10,260	43,889	....	96,669	....
.....	4,453,473	12,889,847	96,416	38,522	57,894	....	80,000	....
.....	4,066,137	5,887,764	144,392	33,172	68,513	40,707	211,000	89,000
buted unties	....	....	191,554	191,554	....	....	....	....

TERRITORY OF COLORADO.

es.	VALUATION.		TAXATION, NOT NATIONAL.				PUBLIC DEBT.	
	Assessed valuation of real and personal estate.	True valuation of real and personal estate.	All.	Territory.	County.	Town, city, &c.	County.	Town, city, &c.
	Dollars.	*Dollars.*	*Dollars.*	*Dollars.*	*Dollars.*	*Dollars.*	*Dollars.*	*Dollars.*
ritory	17,338,101	20,243,303	362,197	63,425	267,201	31,571	678,829	2,329
.....	4,731,860	5,500,000	115,859	18,600	97,259	....	520,000	....
.....	351,248	351,248	225	....	225	....	....	....
.....	1,123,055	1,623,055	14,599	3,369	11,230	....	20,000	....
k....	1,100,112	1,210,224	16,600	3,300	11,000	2,300	7,000	....
.....	200,000	200,000	2,050	550	1,500	....	3,000	....
.....	260,000	260,000	1,850	600	1,250	....	1,500	....
.....	575,281	803,041	9,032	3,612	5,420	....	....	....
.....	665,117	872,130	10,528	2,632	7,896	....	2,329	2,329
.....	466,809	580,270	8,432	1,945	6,487	....	2,500	....
.....	2,735,216	3,008,737	64,880	8,218	27,391	29,271	....	....
d (a)	447,024	586,032	10,281	3,576	6,705	....	....	....
.....	480,000	480,000	4,408	1,075	3,333	....	1,200	....
.....	1,034,738	1,200,900	30,967	4,692	26,275	....	104,600	....
.....	185,190	185,190	5,540	940	4,600	....	....	....
.....	174,037	232,000	17,900	500	17,400	....	....	....
as....	457,932	700,000	12,064	2,886	9,178	....	7,393	....
.....	175,569	175,569	3,605	526	3,079	....	....	....
.....	1,041,251	1,084,020	17,945	4,486	13,459	....	8,003	....
.....	155,415	155,415	1,005	247	758	....	150	....
.....	123,926	136,318	1,610	371	1,239	....	957	....
.....	854,381	900,054	12,817	1,300	11,517	....	....	....

(a) Organized since June, 1870; real estate reported as never having been assessed.

TABLE LXXXIII.—*Valuation, Taxation, and Public Indebtedness by Counties*—1870—Cont'd.

STATE OF CONNECTICUT.

Counties.	VALUATION.		TAXATION, NOT NATIONAL.				PUBLIC DEBT.	
	Assessed valuation of real and personal estate.	True valuation of real and personal estate.	All.	State.	County.	Town, city, &c.	County.	Town, city, &c.
	Dollars.	*Dollars.*	*Dollars.*	*Dollars.*	*Dollars.*	*Dollars.*	*Dollars.*	*Dollars.*
The State	425, 433, 237	774, 631, 524	6, 064, 843	1, 875, 024	20, 113	4, 169, 706	6, 103	9, 806, 903
Fairfield	54, 042, 116	194, 940, 524	712, 838	119, 818	12, 885	580, 135	....	957, 331
Hartford	79, 051, 800	203, 756, 068	1, 291, 828	169, 151	2, 338	1, 120, 339	500	3, 846, 957
Litchfield	26, 447, 170	53, 843, 564	362, 658	59, 234	1, 153	302, 271	715	587, [illegible]
Middlesex	16, 047, 490	38, 422, 380	290, 067	35, 922	3, 737	250, 408	....	1, 383, [illegible]
New Haven	81, 606, 191	174, 531, 318	1, 347, 196	174, 548	....	1, 172, 648	....	1, 540, 115
New London	39, 495, 179	87, 262, 960	533, 814	85, 078	....	448, 736	3, 332	1, 193, 147
Tolland	9, 133, 166	18, 834, 346	161, 040	21, 236	....	139, 804	882	199, 495
Windham	16, 730, 373	39, 032, 361	192, 969	37, 604	....	155, 365	674	93, 442
Not distributed among counties	102, 879, 749	34, 000, 000	1, 172, 433	1, 172, 433	....	....	....	....

TERRITORY OF DAKOTA.

Counties.	VALUATION.		TAXATION, NOT NATIONAL.				PUBLIC DEBT.	
	Assessed valuation of real and personal estate.	True valuation of real and personal estate.	All.	Territory.	County.	Town, city, &c.	County.	Town, city, &c.
	Dollars.	*Dollars.*	*Dollars.*	*Dollars.*	*Dollars.*	*Dollars.*	*Dollars.*	*Dollars.*
The Territory	2, 924, 489	5, 599, 752	13, 867	1, 269	12, 598	....	5, 671	90
Bonhomme	160, 000	335, 000	335	16	319	....	1, 250	....
Buffalo	61, 900	61, 900	....	....	....	....	....	....
Charles Mix	73, 300	73, 300	....	....	....	....	....	....
Clay	500, 000	1, 145, 443	4, 276	263	4, 013	....	....	....
Hutchinson	18, 750	18, 750	....	....	....	....	....	....
Jayne (*a*)	....	....	....	....	....	....	....	....
Lincoln	59, 864	89, 796	....	....	....	....	421	90
Minnehaha (*a*)	....	....	....	....	....	....	....	....
Pembina	119, 425	119, 425	....	....	....	....	....	....
Todd	21, 250	21, 250	....	....	....	....	....	....
Union	910, 000	910, 000	3, 035	435	2, 600	....	3, 000	....
Yankton	1, 000, 000	2, 561, 388	6, 221	555	5, 666	....	1, 000	....
Unorganized portion of Territory	....	263, 500	....	....	....	....	....	....

(*a*) No report.

STATE OF DELAWARE.

Counties.	VALUATION.		TAXATION, NOT NATIONAL.				PUBLIC DEBT.	
	Assessed valuation of real and personal estate.	True valuation of real and personal estate.	All.	State.	County.	Town, city, &c.	County.	Town, city, &c.
	Dollars.	*Dollars.*	*Dollars.*	*Dollars.*	*Dollars.*	*Dollars.*	*Dollars.*	*Dollars.*
The State	64, 787, 223	97, 180, 833	418, 092	83, 666	189, 991	141, 432	139, 875	386, 250
Kent	12, 892, 133	19, 338, 199	55, 961	14, 000	37, 761	4, 200	23, 500	11, 000
New Castle	37, 894, 383	56, 841, 574	298, 009	60, 000	102, 777	135, 232	86, 375	374, 250
Sussex	14, 000, 707	21, 001, 060	64, 122	9, 666	49, 456	5, 000	30, 000	1, 000

TABLE LXXXIII.—*Valuation, Taxation, and Public Indebtedness by Counties*—1870—Cont'd.

DISTRICT OF COLUMBIA.

Cities, &c.	VALUATION.		TAXATION, NOT NATIONAL.				PUBLIC DEBT.	
	Assessed valuation of real and personal estate.	True valuation of real and personal estate.	All.	District.	County.	Town, city, &c.	County.	Town, city, &c.
	Dollars.	*Dollars.*	*Dollars.*	*Dollars.*	*Dollars.*	*Dollars.*	*Dollars.*	*Dollars.*
The District	74, 271, 693	126, 873, 618	1, 581, 569	....	49, 975	1, 531, 594	....	2, 596, 545
Georgetown....	6, 242, 695	7, 242, 695	84, 276	....	....	84, 276	....	232, 660
Washington	62, 476, 098	113, 358, 023	1, 447, 318	....	....	1, 447, 318	....	2, 363, 885
Remainder of the District..	5, 552, 900	6, 272, 900	49, 975	....	49, 975	....	....	....

STATE OF FLORIDA.

Counties.	VALUATION.		TAXATION, NOT NATIONAL.				PUBLIC DEBT.	
	Assessed valuation of real and personal estate.	True valuation of real and personal estate.	All.	State.	County.	Town, city, &c.	County.	Town, city, &c.
	Dollars.	*Dollars.*	*Dollars.*	*Dollars.*	*Dollars.*	*Dollars.*	*Dollars.*	*Dollars.*
The State....	32, 480, 843	44, 163, 655	496, 186	248, 768	168, 389	79, 009	443, 041	454, 100
Alachua........	1, 497, 401	3, 000, 000	19, 838	10, 961	6, 477	2, 400	4, 000	....
Baker	98, 414	162, 000	1, 167	767	400	....	600	....
Bradford.......	446, 797	446, 797	4, 402	3, 402	1, 000	....	500	....
Brevard........	240, 000	240, 000	(*)	(*)	(*)	(*)	15, 000	....
Calhoun........	136, 419	220, 000	838	590	248	....	1, 500	....
Clay	280, 000	290, 000	2, 100	1, 400	700	....	800	....
Columbia.......	1, 499, 204	1, 499, 204	19, 485	11, 000	7, 335	1, 150	102, 350	....
Dade	14, 800	14, 800	135	90	45	....	....	....
Duval..........	3, 373, 649	4, 531, 586	60, 556	24, 229	8, 493	27, 843	1, 100	77, 000
Escambia.......	2, 815, 895	2, 815, 895	59, 458	19, 911	9, 603	29, 944	6, 500	308, 000
Franklin.......	227, 285	227, 285	2, 577	1, 727	475	375	....	550
Gadsden	1, 280, 606	1, 650, 000	16, 183	10, 557	5, 626	....	7, 300	....
Hamilton	718, 763	718, 763	9, 397	5, 397	4, 000	....	2, 500	....
Hernando.......	474, 782	474, 782	6, 119	3, 585	2, 534	....	2, 000	....
Hillsborough...	525, 600	700, 000	4, 378	2, 229	2, 149	....	....	....
Holmes.........	50, 968	153, 365	1, 661	985	676	....	500	....
Jackson........	2, 000, 000	2, 000, 000	15, 000	10, 000	5, 000	....	6, 000	....
Jefferson......	2, 082, 503	3, 000, 000	32, 593	15, 393	16, 000	1, 200	80, 000	....
La Fayette	221, 262	221, 262	3, 571	1, 707	1, 299	567	2, 100	....
Leon	2, 996, 860	7, 000, 000	63, 064	22, 449	34, 783	5, 832	81, 500	....
Levy	414, 896	450, 000	5, 886	3, 074	2, 812	....	4, 500	....
Liberty........	198, 499	198, 499	2, 030	1, 485	545	....	1, 500	....
Madison	1, 213, 796	1, 603, 736	14, 549	9, 114	5, 435	....	83, 000	....
Manatee	429, 748	429, 748	4, 182	3, 282	900	....	....	....
Marion	1, 687, 725	2, 225, 000	19, 217	12, 673	6, 544	....	8, 000	....
Monroe	1, 069, 736	1, 604, 604	17, 124	8, 397	6, 134	2, 593	....	....
Nassau.........	907, 633	1, 163, 704	19, 039	8, 082	6, 957	4, 000	1, 850	8, 550
Orange	448, 180	448, 180	4, 355	3, 355	1, 000	....	3, 330	....
Polk	349, 028	349, 028	5, 672	2, 572	3, 100	....	3, 100	....
Putnam.........	944, 318	944, 318	11, 910	6, 904	5, 006	....	2, 000	....
Santa Rosa.....	843, 862	2, 150, 000	13, 332	6, 242	6, 340	750	3, 000	....
St. John's.....	745, 205	752, 598	12, 349	5, 479	5, 893	977	....	....
Sumter	345, 479	345, 479	3, 328	2, 615	713	....	8, 000	....
Suwannee.......	492, 725	516, 657	6, 840	3, 710	1, 750	1, 380	3, 150	....
Taylor	132, 825	150, 000	1, 448	1, 048	400	....	....	....
Volusia........	435, 932	508, 902	6, 767	3, 717	3, 050	....	2, 561	....
Wakulla	317, 403	317, 403	3, 632	2, 422	1, 210	....	2, 500	....
Walton	243, 611	250, 000	3, 719	1, 919	1, 800	....	1, 200	....
Washington	279, 634	300, 000	4, 118	2, 161	1, 957	....	900	....
Not distributed among counties	....	....	14, 096	14, 096	....	....	....	....

* None returned.

TABLE LXXXIII.—*Valuation, Taxation, and Public Indebtedness by Counties*—1870—Cont'd.

STATE OF GEORGIA.

Counties.	Valuation.		Taxation, not national.				Public debt.	
	Assessed valuation of real and personal estate.	True valuation of real and personal estate.	All.	State.	County.	Town, city, &c.	County.	Town, city, &c.
	Dollars.	*Dollars.*	*Dollars.*	*Dollars.*	*Dollars.*	*Dollars.*	*Dollars.*	*Dollars.*
The State..	227,219,519	268,169,207	2,627,029	945,394	906,270	775,365	561,735	14,64[illegible]
Appling	658,016	798,265	3,361	2,211	1,150			
Baker	806,825	1,179,945	5,984	3,059	2,925			
Baldwin	1,484,252	1,484,252	28,587	5,717	22,870		91,000	
Banks	470,665	525,186	3,621	1,621	2,000		650	
Bartow	3,324,746	3,804,988	30,302	11,712	14,640	3,950	8,300	850
Berrien	634,800	838,451	3,800	2,587	1,213			
Bibb	7,839,339	9,222,508	117,497	31,493	42,597	43,407		514,[illegible]
Brooks	1,983,259	1,983,259	11,676	7,781	3,895		460	
Bryan	565,371	565,371	5,353	3,212	2,141		800	
Bullock	852,943	1,200,000	6,800	3,800	3,000		3,100	
Burke	2,022,968	2,178,000	28,000	10,000	18,000		23,000	
Butts	755,492	834,323	10,643	3,068	7,575		5,000	
Calhoun	818,404	1,500,000	8,530	3,472	4,658	400	2,750	
Camden	1,100,000	1,100,000	3,000	2,000	500	500	1,000	600
Campbell	1,378,730	1,890,500	16,558	12,158	4,400			
Carroll	1,620,971	1,800,000	11,459	6,710	4,749		500	
Catoosa	928,873	928,873	6,000	2,000	4,000		4,000	
Charlton	234,850	400,000	1,300	1,000	300			
Chatham	22,749,322	25,257,940	350,254	96,415	52,880	200,959		2,[illegible],592
Chattahoochee	931,511	1,208,110	8,330	3,400	4,930		1,500	
Chattooga	1,199,210	1,400,000	9,758	4,879	4,879		850	
Cherokee	1,099,988	1,099,988	10,507	5,042	5,465		3,000	
Clarke	3,353,238	4,844,900	30,100	13,000	13,500	3,600	43,300	7,650
Clay	839,079	1,095,891	6,800	3,700	2,500	600	800	
Clayton	841,786	841,786	9,995	2,906	7,089		4,500	
Clinch	575,331	823,389	2,902	1,800	1,102		1,300	
Cobb	2,785,404	2,785,404	23,519	11,847	9,772	1,900	2,077	500
Coffee	490,860	490,860	2,196	1,890	306		175	
Colquitt	204,047	204,047	1,312	547	765		132	
Columbia	1,838,758	1,840,453	8,053	7,321	732		1,000	
Coweta	2,601,782	5,096,936	23,997	12,831	8,166	3,000	1,200	
Crawford	988,997	1,200,000	3,900	1,900	2,000		2,000	
Dade	792,922	792,922	5,480	2,740	2,740		1,270	
Dawson	441,713	441,713	2,738	1,711	1,027		200	
Decatur	2,068,633	2,673,165	99,929	8,000	20,188	71,741	18,638	104,000
De Kalb	1,641,003	1,805,213	9,000	5,200	3,800		2,600	
Dooly	1,555,285	2,131,695	7,000	5,000	2,000			
Dougherty	3,771,406	3,914,826	40,233	16,978	11,850	11,405	5,787	2,850
Early	1,032,478	1,136,752	5,005	2,962	2,043			
Echols	234,976	350,000	3,232	2,394	838		2,400	400
Effingham	647,975	647,975	3,564	2,403	1,161			
Elbert	1,332,978	1,500,000	11,236	7,206	4,030			
Emanuel	884,110	884,110	5,150	2,450	2,600	100	3,000	100
Fannin	426,680	426,680	3,098	1,271	1,827		1,000	
Fayette	909,360	1,122,264	11,639	4,656	6,983		1,095	
Floyd	4,739,197	5,943,216	52,164	18,082	18,082	16,000		3,000
Forsyth	867,350	1,024,743	5,128	2,772	2,356			
Franklin	813,018	968,893	7,828	3,828	4,000		1,000	
Fulton	13,768,967	15,039,400	71,652	14,836	13,375	43,441	8,000	9,935,[illegible]
Gilmer	444,716	681,150	3,906	2,108	1,798		7,500	
Glascock	384,246	384,246	4,000	1,639	2,361		325	
Glynn	1,619,534	1,619,534	22,433	6,907	9,526	6,000	14,500	124,[illegible]
Gordon	1,688,866	2,922,000	11,520	6,350	4,970	200		
Greene	2,054,629	2,200,000	16,700	9,000	5,200	2,500	7,000	
Gwinnett	1,488,352	1,488,352	9,808	5,082	4,726		3,504	
Habersham	508,862	522,835	3,748	2,499	1,249		1,807	
Hall	1,067,560	1,253,191	7,720	4,207	3,513		51,200	
Hancock	2,465,053	2,465,053	17,745	10,572	6,173	1,000		
Haralson	374,437	374,437	3,119	1,559	1,560		1,550	
Harris	1,975,802	1,975,802	12,552	5,931	6,621		4,770	
Hart	656,061	656,061	6,280	3,156	3,124		2,470	
Heard	1,004,522	1,232,544	8,750	3,500	5,250		1,600	
Henry	1,545,142	1,545,142	17,053	7,890	9,163			
Houston	3,601,185	4,300,442	45,873	17,401	27,272	1,200	3,000	600
Irwin	330,341	330,341	1,810	1,303	507			
Jackson	1,132,634	1,532,634	6,000	4,530	1,470		6,000	
Jasper	1,171,500	2,781,332	11,400	5,700	5,700		3,000	
Jefferson	1,523,207	1,523,207	13,647	5,099	7,348	1,500	2,[illegible]	

XXIII.—*Valuation, Taxation, and Public Indebtedness by Counties*—1870—Cont'd.

STATE OF GEORGIA—Continued.

	VALUATION.*		TAXATION, NOT NATIONAL.				PUBLIC DEBT.	
	Assessed valuation of real and personal estate.	True valuation of real and personal estate.	All.	State.	County.	Town, city, &c.	County.	Town, city, &c.
	Dollars.	Dollars.	Dollars.	Dollars.	Dollars.	Dollars.	Dollars.	Dollars.
....	419,113	419,113	3,191	1,276	1,915	....	....	....
....	1,397,312	1,529,629	10,907	6,157	4,750	....	....	....
....	1,244,372	1,244,372	10,564	6,022	4,542	....	....	....
....	1,880,252	1,880,252	23,791	9,727	14,064	....	....	....
....	625,702	625,702	4,148	2,074	2,074	....	....	....
....	641,097	1,371,492	5,344	3,200	2,144	....	....	....
....	1,350,404	1,350,404	13,530	6,503	6,027	1,000	1,184	400
....	406,612	604,976	3,000	1,200	1,800	....	240	....
....	1,964,703	1,964,703	10,406	5,936	4,470	....	....	....
....	643,175	643,175	4,146	2,073	2,073	....	....	....
....	1,320,070	1,320,070	11,054	4,913	6,141	....	....	....
....	600,388	1,173,700	8,295	3,300	3,795	1,200	3,800	1,700
....	1,725,038	2,084,072	14,400	6,000	8,000	400	....	....
....	323,440	1,000,000	5,200	800	4,400	....	500	....
....	547,334	547,334	3,604	1,802	1,802	....	3,850	....
....	1,146,023	1,146,023	10,235	4,549	5,686	....	2,000	....
....	2,428,536	2,428,536	34,632	10,412	23,303	917	22,000	....
y...	565,036	565,036	2,[illegible]	1,162	1,102	....	1,500	....
....	1,766,552	1,766,552	13,247	6,205	6,205	837	6,500	....
....	1,023,693	1,228,431	7,405	4,829	2,576	....	1,851	....
....	7,612,735	7,612,735	175,952	30,381	45,571	100,000	50,147	400,000
....	2,636,984	2,694,994	18,804	12,312	5,792	700	....	....
....	1,530,508	1,729,152	14,115	5,646	8,469	....	5,000	....
....	819,082	819,082	5,747	3,698	2,049	....	200	....
....	454,125	500,000	2,560	1,280	1,280	....	....	....
....	346,872	418,033	3,256	988	2,268	....	2,000	....
....	1,825,619	1,827,179	17,200	8,838	8,362	....	....	....
....	1,407,475	1,562,945	10,096	4,408	5,288	400	2,000	....
....	1,628,164	1,760,000	18,164	7,766	9,798	600	5,000	....
....	1,545,199	1,858,367	16,157	7,557	8,000	600	5,345	....
....	732,826	770,000	5,769	2,569	3,125	75	....	....
....	274,184	293,142	2,590	1,300	1,290	....	1,500	....
....	2,147,030	3,104,981	20,798	9,527	8,280	2,991	4,200	....
....	14,075,615	19,473,131	325,545	60,617	54,928	210,000	....	1,395,250
....	907,402	1,016,548	6,672	2,224	4,448	....	2,200	....
....	733,150	850,000	5,900	2,600	3,200	100	5,000	....
....	2,039,339	2,039,339	21,500	3,250	3,250	15,000	4,000	50,500
....	1,981,723	2,629,093	18,771	9,958	8,063	750	....	....
....	3,559,395	4,139,723	50,491	16,110	23,550	10,831	8,000	3,435
....	1,425,141	1,830,101	18,011	5,146	12,865	....	10,000	....
....	615,209	781,063	3,400	1,800	1,600	....	....	....
....	768,041	875,000	4,486	3,236	1,250	....	....	....
....	890,904	900,000	2,700	900	1,800	....	300	....
....	465,450	465,450	2,858	1,655	1,203	....	1,900	....
....	1,606,199	1,606,199	15,397	6,674	7,523	1,200	3,000	700
....	2,122,905	2,122,905	29,147	9,511	16,917	2,719	6,790	....
....	211,794	406,326	1,845	1,045	800	....	650	....
....	2,965,363	4,997,356	27,932	11,767	11,990	4,175	....	....
....	1,047,611	1,110,291	12,443	4,148	8,295	....	....	....
....	449,122	569,910	3,194	2,259	935	....	1,200	....
....	1,872,403	1,872,403	13,100	5,000	8,000	100	1,000	....
....	1,638,878	1,907,643	8,548	5,515	3,033	....	125	....
....	1,647,847	1,864,953	17,429	7,522	9,907	....	9,116	....
....	362,398	402,504	1,500	800	700	....	600	....
....	972,103	1,619,238	5,400	2,700	2,300	400	1,600	600
n....	2,413,827	2,413,827	26,917	8,811	17,056	1,050	13,000	300
....	305,118	400,251	2,040	1,217	486	337	600	....
....	930,221	1,664,007	5,100	4,000	1,100	....	....	....
....	452,854	580,382	3,767	2,126	1,641	....	....	....
....	1,922,169	1,922,169	14,350	6,550	3,800	4,000	875	....
....	334,429	488,967	3,402	2,248	1,124	30	400	....
....	2,254,231	2,254,231	14,285	9,335	3,750	1,200	....	200
....	1,675,225	3,325,918	20,174	7,799	11,725	650	14,952	650
....	519,272	687,963	2,150	750	1,400	....	....	....
uted nties	....	....	65,710	65,710	....	....	....	....

TABLE LXXXIII.—*Valuation, Taxation, and Public Indebtedness by Counties.*—1870—Cont'd.

TERRITORY OF IDAHO.

Counties.	Valuation.		Taxation, not national.				Public debt.	
	Assessed valuation of real and personal estate.	True valuation of real and personal estate.	All.	Territory.	County.	Town, city, &c.	County.	Town, city, &c.
	Dollars.	*Dollars.*	*Dollars.*	*Dollars.*	*Dollars.*	*Dollars.*	*Dollars.*	*Dollars.*
The Territory	5, 292, 205	6, 552, 681	174, 711	40, 594	132, 171	1, 946	218, 522	4, 000
Ada	918, 141	1, 041, 391	29, 490	7, 315	20, 199	1, 946		4, 000
Alturas	148, 078	500, 000	4, 660		4, 660		33, 739	
Boise	1, 405, 017	1, 405, 017	44, 960	11, 240	33, 720		70, 000	
Idaho	198, 928	198, 928	3, 653		3, 653		5, 000	
Lemhi (*a*)	178, 716	178, 716	7, 348	2, 507	4, 841			
Nez Percé	449, 011	732, 775	22, 385	8, 649	19, 736		33, 088	
Oneida	176, 000	528, 000	6, 118	1, 391	4, 727		9, 000	
Owyhee	1, 747, 384	1, 747, 384	39, 952	7, 191	32, 761		64, 000	
Shoshone (*a*)	70, 930	220, 470	10, 145	2, 271	7, 874		3, 695	

(*a*) No further information could be obtained.

STATE OF ILLINOIS.

Counties.	Valuation.		Taxation, not national.				Public debt.	
	Assessed valuation of real and personal estate.	True valuation of real and personal estate.	All.	State.	County.	Town, city, &c.	County.	Town, city, &c.
	Dollars.	*Dollars.*	*Dollars.*	*Dollars.*	*Dollars.*	*Dollars.*	*Dollars.*	*Dollars.*
The State	482, 899, 575	2,121,680,579	21, 825, 008	3, 620, 681	5, 242, 137	12, 962, 190	12, 817, 922	24, 483, 010
Adams	13, 198, 067	50, 748, 596	287, 279	85, 657	56, 481	145, 141	420, 000	1, 228, 290
Alexander	1, 558, 305	6, 212, 820	118, 538	10, 130	37, 422	70, 986	16, 000	312, 705
Bond	2, 428, 725	9, 706, 196	83, 047	15, 760	40, 244	27, 043	102, 500	3, 600
Boone	2, 401, 180	11, 700, 000	69, 501	15, 603	8, 898	45, 000		
Brown	1, 681, 779	6, 727, 024	81, 292	10, 931	39, 992	30, 369	120, 000	
Bureau	7, 015, 962	25, 000, 000	266, 931	45, 619	51, 960	169, 352		36, 000
Calhoun	648, 423	2, 593, 216	21, 183	4, 214	9, 667	7, 302		
Carroll	2, 982, 296	12, 265, 000	146, 226	19, 417	50, 977	75, 832	76, 300	6, 300
Cass	2, 730, 828	10, 901, 844	91, 530	17, 754	27, 511	46, 265	60, 815	94, 000
Champaign	4, 696, 045	22, 719, 680	276, 590	36, 938	87, 224	152, 428	290, 000	342, 900
Christian	4, 430, 083	17, 800, 332	124, 739	28, 926	32, 381	63, 432	132, 000	94, 000
Clark	2, 655, 640	10, 367, 636	61, 413	17, 261	18, 739	25, 413	188, 000	
Clay	2, 206, 341	9, 043, 612	85, 067	14, 808	38, 930	32, 229	160, 000	
Clinton	2, 560, 796	10, 507, 676	78, 922	16, 704	34, 666	27, 552	60, 000	
Coles	4, 150, 075	17, 642, 432	158, 386	26, 951	34, 618	96, 817	60, 000	30, 000
Cook	85, 684, 584	575, 000, 000	8, 167, 556	556, 971	1, 351, 669	6, 258, 916	3, 665, 000	14, 103, 000
Crawford	1, 731, 070	6, 899, 724	42, 218	11, 234	6, 245	24, 739		
Cumberland	1, 600, 306	6, 389, 756	44, 422	10, 402	17, 242	16, 778	16, 000	
De Kalb	4, 505, 978	23, 769, 785	196, 383	29, 216	35, 843	131, 324	62, 405	
De Witt	2, 509, 698	10, 026, 668	98, 942	16, 313	24, 015	58, 614		89, 900
Douglas	2, 348, 453	9, 393, 804	93, 290	15, 240	33, 703	44, 347	85, 000	
Du Page	2, 982, 330	10, 500, 000	79, 647	19, 378	17, 031	43, 238	10, 000	
Edgar	4, 288, 539	17, 338, 040	125, 225	27, 875	36, 817	60, 533	45, 000	
Edwards	1, 174, 116	4, 694, 988	21, 258	7, 632	6, 559	7, 067		
Effingham	2, 377, 510	9, 366, 308	71, 626	15, 453	22, 147	34, 026	6, 000	95, 000
Fayette	2, 761, 196	10, 732, 132	80, 215	17, 948	17, 468	44, 799	1, 000	45, 000
Ford	2, 146, 175	8, 563, 736	71, 047	13, 950	20, 425	36, 672	12, 000	
Franklin	1, 212, 029	4, 858, 756	37, 165	7, 878	17, 681	11, 603	8, 500	
Fulton	6, 531, 430	26, 070, 096	218, 086	42, 454	68, 498	107, 128	221, 000	30, 000
Gallatin	1, 235, 497	4, 940, 056	55, 912	6, 398	31, 601	17, 913	25, 000	
Greene	3, 931, 120	15, 724, 516	103, 506	25, 552	31, 355	46, 599	60, 400	13, 000
Grundy	3, 257, 451	10, 628, 165	87, 197	21, 128	18, 989	47, 080	2, 180	3, 750
Hamilton	1, 205, 719	4, 821, 792	40, 787	7, 837	21, 780	11, 170	15, 841	
Hancock	6, 072, 201	23, 936, 008	188, 281	39, 469	57, 503	91, 309	220, 400	

e LXXXIII.—*Valuation, Taxation, and Public Indebtedness by Counties*—1870—Cont'd.

STATE OF ILLINOIS—Continued.

...nties.	VALUATION.*		TAXATION, NOT NATIONAL.				PUBLIC DEBT.	
	Assessed valuation of real and personal estate.	True valuation of real and personal estate.	All.	State.	County.	Town, city, &c.	County.	Town, city, &c.
	Dollars.	*Dollars.*	*Dollars.*	*Dollars.*	*Dollars.*	*Dollars.*	*Dollars.*	*Dollars.*
l	424,743	1,688,572	13,582	2,761	6,418	4,403	21,406	....
rson	2,783,641	9,247,374	76,344	18,094	30,535	27,715	75,000	35,000
....	6,849,208	30,000,000	221,509	44,538	28,338	148,633	6,000	193,470
is	5,454,928	12,462,687	158,083	35,423	30,500	92,160	55,000	14,000
n	3,139,971	12,559,880	89,045	20,410	43,135	25,500	10,064	....
....	1,432,990	5,706,832	42,254	9,283	8,341	24,630	4,100	....
on	2,860,912	11,391,676	87,589	27,640	32,210	27,739	103,000	500
....	2,972,915	11,891,272	71,736	19,324	30,414	21,998	35,000	3,500
iess	3,337,731	11,796,500	103,172	21,695	31,496	49,979	49,154	200,000
n	980,659	3,922,632	20,969	6,374	15,979	7,616	22,442	....
....	7,740,757	32,890,389	252,492	50,201	33,723	168,478	2,000	104,500
kee	3,536,848	14,068,480	137,201	22,884	21,388	92,929	28,000	130,000
l	2,487,049	10,801,080	67,850	16,131	32,762	18,963	105,000	90,000
....	7,681,747	26,094,620	206,379	49,931	51,046	105,402	56,900	100,000
....	2,877,519	18,930,128	36,410	18,646	11,179	6,585	....	6,000
o	11,493,697	42,972,474	382,489	74,508	115,676	192,245	150,500	262,000
nce	1,847,770	7,391,080	45,621	12,011	16,326	17,284	30,000	....
....	4,759,195	12,398,156	207,225	30,840	63,710	112,675	113,300	80,000
ston	6,762,063	19,178,415	275,484	43,959	38,265	193,260	72,626	135,000
....	4,797,206	19,133,108	152,402	31,182	42,540	78,680	300,000	375,000
....	5,113,189	20,456,232	181,254	33,235	53,131	94,888	....	63,000
pin	6,863,906	27,541,624	189,013	44,615	45,047	99,351	1,464,000	44,000
n	10,692,365	40,745,328	183,092	69,500	86,734	26,858	139,000	262,378
....	3,742,042	14,798,036	105,711	24,331	39,325	42,035	....	....
ll	3,052,368	15,408,890	107,985	19,837	28,431	59,717	100,000	130,000
....	3,622,207	13,759,592	139,030	23,427	44,554	71,049	211,500	45,000
....	805,208	3,268,424	24,447	5,234	10,966	8,247	3,400	2,800
ough	5,450,944	20,466,036	152,084	35,347	68,770	47,967	75,000	70,000
ry	4,689,437	14,464,748	87,002	30,406	36,674	19,922	100,000	....
n	11,249,494	44,920,108	511,186	72,993	118,706	319,427	500,000	980,000
l	2,348,070	9,376,840	77,021	15,266	34,565	27,190	55,000	1,700
....	4,293,826	19,909,852	88,425	27,906	40,604	19,915	111,000	75,200
....	1,804,482	7,217,260	73,225	11,738	28,568	32,919	9,971	800
nnery	4,444,562	17,779,564	109,759	28,781	35,427	45,551	50,000	51,000
l	7,552,936	29,885,936	199,294	49,094	100,610	49,561	236,000	280,000
e	1,824,117	7,296,464	48,983	12,156	7,535	29,292	....	....
....	5,642,452	23,685,654	191,763	36,675	21,651	133,437	15,000	....
....	9,475,030	47,039,994	509,837	61,588	153,784	294,465	330,200	1,285,000
....	1,890,894	7,536,748	62,423	12,248	30,987	19,188	17,083	....
....	2,587,819	10,363,636	96,773	16,821	14,541	65,411	....	195,000
....	5,417,025	21,097,652	196,163	35,211	67,461	93,491	256,000	152,000
....	1,071,508	4,286,392	38,048	6,964	18,043	13,041	27,493	1,140
i	660,479	2,627,296	22,071	4,239	5,816	12,016	48,000	68,000
a	1,134,790	5,488,875	33,223	7,376	6,521	19,326	....	....
ph	3,459,721	13,831,636	90,647	22,488	35,794	32,365	59,725	....
d	1,972,205	7,850,268	51,248	12,819	7,381	31,048	....	....
land	4,645,670	12,548,601	203,551	30,197	75,879	97,475	143,680	100,000
....	1,029,525	4,118,104	31,741	6,692	11,207	13,842	11,350	....
ion	12,995,035	51,133,532	649,503	84,342	214,716	350,445	268,500	1,092,172
r	2,524,184	10,275,584	85,532	16,369	31,747	37,416	110,250	35,000
....	1,625,219	6,483,364	70,407	10,564	32,425	27,418	96,076	30,000
....	4,698,369	18,146,580	122,006	30,451	31,720	50,835	....	3,000
....	2,283,584	7,795,364	119,145	14,843	34,737	69,545	36,000	271,000
....	9,140,021	37,622,084	248,171	59,410	70,504	118,257	20,000	233,000
ison	5,332,053	23,054,272	223,522	34,658	59,942	130,922	....	80,600
ll	5,919,124	23,165,560	214,077	38,474	84,989	90,614	375,000	258,000
....	1,683,236	6,733,348	51,625	10,832	15,001	25,702	....	....
on	6,797,194	26,426,852	156,485	44,061	29,964	80,400	2,600	100,000
a	1,082,243	4,328,972	28,085	7,035	9,344	11,706	....	19,500
....	4,769,276	5,187,544	168,234	31,001	44,750	92,482	50,000	10,000
gton	3,086,899	12,319,788	70,402	20,065	31,848	18,489	200,000	....
....	2,382,105	9,528,420	80,330	15,448	37,745	27,137	202,411	25,000
....	1,911,335	7,603,116	51,942	12,424	15,879	23,639	....	....
ides	5,208,005	18,845,560	191,309	33,741	33,343	124,313	18,791	14,173
....	6,906,882	28,516,120	270,037	44,895	62,344	162,798	47,755	75,000
ison	1,320,184	5,560,292	51,938	8,533	18,208	25,197	27,795	....
bago	5,898,921	23,175,720	145,779	37,812	30,660	68,307	....	160,000
rd	3,052,884	3,881,548	118,446	23,744	31,101	63,603	16,500	50,000
tributed counties	....	....	469,809	469,809	....	....	....	....

TABLE LXXXIII.—*Valuation, Taxation, and Public Indebtedness by Counties—1870*—Cont'd.

STATE OF INDIANA.

Counties.	VALUATION.		TAXATION, NOT NATIONAL.				PUBLIC DEBT.	
	Assessed valuation of real and personal estate.	True valuation of real and personal estate.	All.	State.	County.	Town, city, &c.	County.	Town, city, &c.
	Dollars.	*Dollars.*	*Dollars.*	*Dollars.*	*Dollars.*	*Dollars.*	*Dollars.*	*Dollars.*
The State..	663, 455, 041	1,268,180,543	10, 791, 121	2, 943, 078	4, 654, 466	3, 193, 577	1, 127, 269	2, 583, 934
Adams	2, 761, 720	3, 761, 720	84, 615	13, 101	55, 234	16, 280		
Allen	13, 063, 509	39, 193, 500	374, 851	58, 595	132, 893	183, 363	45, 000	510, 000
Bartholomew	9, 496, 200	12, 661, 600	125, 298	41, 259	35, 586	48, 453		27, 300
Benton	3, 278, 195	8, 000, 000	50, 232	14, 273	20, 995	14, 964	9, 000	
Blackford	1, 392, 535	4, 250, 000	33, 315	6, 719	16, 932	9, 664	25, 000	6, 000
Boone	8, 311, 620	18, 000, 000	92, 774	38, 065	22, 603	32, 106		
Brown	1, 327, 187	2, 000, 000	29, 470	6, 712	15, 015	7, 743	5, 000	
Carroll	6, 954, 905	14, 000, 000	145, 170	74, 514	41, 732	28, 924	28, 000	
Cass	9, 659, 185	20, 000, 000	123, 584	42, 750	42, 892	37, 942	3, 000	65, 000
Clarke	9, 660, 654	20, 000, 000	179, 695	43, 270	45, 140	91, 285		
Clay	5, 216, 579	12, 000, 000	68, 769	21, 387	26, 082	21, 300		
Clinton	6, 948, 060	15, 000, 000	138, 029	33, 925	79, 772	24, 332		
Crawford	1, 641, 010	3, 000, 000	27, 212	8, 312	16, 253	2, 647	5, 000	
Daviess	5. 437, 525	10, 875, 050	70, 547	24, 844	23, 171	22, 532		
Dearborn	8, 812, 870	13, 219, 300	145, 468	39, 097	64, 054	42, 317	22, 000	105, 000
Decatur	6, 959, 430	11, 000, 000	117, 480	33, 925	66, 078	17, 477		
De Kalb	3, 886, 892	11, 600, 678	83, 848	18, 731	27, 159	37, 958	10, 001	
Delaware	8, 163, 515	15, 000, 000	208, 443	36, 873	55, 237	116, 333	37, 000	2, 200
Dubois	3, 052, 190	6, 000, 000	49, 543	14, 260	18, 909	16, 374		
Elkhart	11, 285, 772	33, 857, 000	187, 756	46, 900	66, 600	74, 256	75, 000	37, 000
Fayette	7, 579, 870	12, 678, 780	80, 996	33, 137	13, 247	34, 612		36, 250
Floyd	9, 836, 973	14, 755, 458	122, 233	43, 370	72, 745	6, 118	38, 609	40, 635
Fountain	6, 798, 525	10, 000, 000	144, 393	32, 637	69, 371	42, 385		
Franklin	8, 220, 770	20, 000, 000	141, 831	36, 957	64, 612	40, 262		
Fulton	3, 106, 150	4, 659, 225	65, 613	14, 956	23, 296	27, 361	35, 115	
Gibson	9, 333, 167	20, 000, 000	126, 114	41, 140	51, 351	33, 623		
Grant	5, 644, 210	13, 110, 570	120, 321	26, 571	59, 417	34, 333	2, 000	
Greene	6, 137, 205	10, 000, 000	61, 073	11, 081	20, 756	29, 236	2, 213	
Hamilton	7, 576, 730	18, 000, 000	146, 185	34, 534	70, 651	41, 000		42, 000
Hancock	6, 111, 370	10, 000, 000	71, 608	27, 608	20, 654	23, 346		15, 150
Harrison	4, 894, 250	9, 000, 000	67, 979	23, 334	25, 738	18, 907	33, 500	
Hendricks	11, 499, 172	20, 000, 000	157, 547	50, 679	52, 412	54, 456	38, 114	
Henry	10, 087, 780	20, 000, 000	196, 178	47, 473	121, 278	27, 427		
Howard	5, 185, 975	12, 000, 000	92, 626	24, 157	42, 095	26, 374		
Huntington	4, 534, 545	10, 000, 000	98, 975	21, 761	70, 522	6, 692	74, 873	10, 907
Jackson	8, 121, 218	20, 000, 000	104, 501	35, 508	44, 865	24, 128	3, 000	
Jasper	2, 361, 449	5, 000, 000	34, 584	11, 204	12, 331	11, 049	2, 000	
Jay	3, 360, 755	8, 000, 000	67, 500	16, 096	29, 474	21, 930		
Jefferson	8, 973, 659	13, 000, 000	131, 618	40, 270	60, 003	31, 345	42, 004	
Jennings	4, 211, 591	9, 000, 000	67, 543	19, 800	27, 569	20, 174		
Johnson	9, 913, 065	15, 006, 000	183, 476	42, 601	108, 114	32, 761	25, 000	
Knox	8, 049, 570	10, 503, 000	129, 461	35, 985	55, 453	38, 023	18, 300	37, 000
Kosciusko	7, 517, 640	15, 000, 000	119, 500	35, 000	43, 000	41, 500		15, 000
La Grange	10, 906, 975	20, 000, 000	66, 140	23, 697	20, 195	22, 248	1, 435	
Lake	2, 979, 705	8, 930, 115	45, 684	6, 311	16, 616	22, 757		
La Porte	10, 251, 936	20, 000, 000	163, 197	45, 253	78, 829	39, 115		5, 000
Lawrence	7, 825, 000	12, 000, 000	*103, 471	34, 700	41, 000	27, 771		13, 000
Madison	8, 118, 145	16, 236, 290	98, 228	33, 284	40, 590	24, 354	22, 504	
Marion	41, 058, 045	75, 000, 000	699, 317	178, 374	234, 943	286, 000		155, 000
Marshall	5, 203, 010	10, 000, 000	89, 965	26, 655	38, 330	24, 980		
Martin	2, 217, 719	4, 470, 876	36, 827	10, 781	13, 392	12, 654	9, 065	
Miami	5, 356, 555	12, 600, 000	96, 897	25, 832	44, 949	26, 116	64, 000	42, 000
Monroe	6, 005, 774	6, 800, 000	102, 841	26, 550	33, 750	42, 541		
Montgomery	12, 563, 680	20, 000, 000	177, 473	55, 646	87, 518	34, 309		
Morgan	8, 320, 400	12, 000, 000	128, 558	36, 396	53, 532	38, 630	30, 000	
Newton	4, 763, 206	7, 500, 000	114, 200	21, 200	73, 000	20, 000	18, 000	
Noble	5, 737, 500	17, 272, 500	79, 788	27, 203	25, 845	26, 740		
Ohio	1, 689, 903	2, 505, 320	34, 280	7, 839	20, 880	5, 561	11, 110	
Orange	4, 828, 231	10, 000, 000	60, 737	21, 950	20, 296	18, 491	10, 000	
Owen	5, 482, 250	8, 223, 375	76, 991	25, 143	33, 788	18, 060		
Parke	9, 912, 150	15, 746, 300	133, 140	43, 846	42, 563	46, 731		
Perry	2, 323, 685	5, 000, 000	60, 432	14, 725	29, 847	15, 860	21, 838	
Pike	3, 265, 240	5, 000, 000	64, 444	16, 278	31, 453	16, 713	8, 000	2, 000
Porter	4, 942, 965	14, 828, 895	101, 628	24, 787	38, 992	37, 849		30, 000
Posey	8, 005, 045	9, 451, 086	89, 998	36, 064	26, 964	26, 970		16, 000
Pulaski	1, 911, 215	2, 500, 000	36, 778	9, 667	14, 980	12, [illegible]	4, 515	8, 600

LE LXXXIII.—*Valuation, Taxation, and Public Indebtedness by Counties*—1870—Cont'd.

STATE OF INDIANA—Continued.

ounties.	VALUATION.		TAXATION, NOT NATIONAL.				PUBLIC DEBT.	
	Assessed valuation of real and personal estate.	True valuation of real and personal estate.	All.	State.	County.	Town, city, &c.	County.	Town, city, &c.
	Dollars.	*Dollars.*	*Dollars.*	*Dollars.*	*Dollars.*	*Dollars.*	*Dollars.*	*Dollars.*
am	12, 252, 215	16, 819, 900	153, 201	53, 958	57, 295	41, 948	....	....
olph	8, 067, 725	13, 446, 208	120, 903	37, 418	30, 373	53, 112	....	....
y	3, 874, 075	8, 000, 000	63, 836	15, 354	46, 169	2, 313	9, 300	....
	12, 286, 780	15, 000, 000	122, 257	52, 749	20, 790	48, 718	6, 000	15, 700
	1, 702, 830	3, 400, 000	24, 317	7, 136	8, 666	8, 515	5, 000	....
y	10, 773, 225	25, 709, 275	205, 278	47, 554	148, 566	9, 158	2, 380	12, 267
er	5, 321, 515	12, 000, 000	97, 100	24, 400	44, 000	28, 700	50, 000	....
e	943, 904	1, 200, 000	24, 150	5, 150	11, 500	7, 500	14, 000	....
en	3, 024, 846	9, 350, 000	60, 735	14, 636	22, 679	23, 420	1, 500	....
seph	10, 496, 885	20, 000, 000	127, 046	46, 845	38, 172	42, 029	23, 000	75, 000
van	5, 875, 800	8, 000, 000	72, 849	27, 592	25, 706	19, 551	....	....
erland	3, 683, 005	10, 940, 015	66, 761	17, 183	31, 337	18, 241	10, 000	....
ecanoe	20, 857, 915	45, 000, 000	356, 901	91, 233	200, 003	65, 665	....	....
n	2, 905, 120	4, 000, 000	54, 538	12, 613	27, 193	14, 732	17, 500	....
a	4, 555, 290	10, 665, 870	61, 542	20, 189	20, 716	20, 637	....	....
erburgh	13, 736, 100	30, 000, 000	452, 410	61, 052	227, 380	163, 978	65, 000	818, 169
illion	4, 795, 000	10, 000, 000	114, 621	21, 333	79, 435	13, 853	18, 000	....
	22, 000, 000	30, 000, 000	213, 977	71, 400	85, 600	56, 977	16, 000	100, 000
ash	6, 107, 575	14, 169, 092	116, 795	38, 342	42, 122	36, 331	....	....
en	6, 410, 435	10, 000, 000	101, 539	26, 282	35, 257	40, 000	6, 000	....
ick	5, 144, 975	8, 500, 000	142, 718	23, 920	79, 444	39, 354	5, 000	15, 000
ington	7, 213, 947	15, 000, 000	37, 774	12, 401	20, 668	4, 705	....	....
ne	20, 231, 500	35, 000, 000	246, 847	86, 474	149, 608	10, 765	32, 400	240, 000
a	2, 718, 920	6, 000, 000	81, 823	13, 340	49, 392	19, 091	50, 000	4, 000
e	4, 251, 635	5, 314, 545	74, 506	19, 211	33, 406	21, 889	12, 093	21, 156
ley	4, 110, 290	12, 000, 000	67, 720	19, 761	25, 431	22, 528	4, 900	....
istributed g counties	....	....	169, 026	169, 026	....	....	....	....

STATE OF IOWA.

ounties.	VALUATION.		TAXATION, NOT NATIONAL.				PUBLIC DEBT.	
	Assessed valuation of real and personal estate.	True valuation of real and personal estate.	All.	State.	County.	Town, city, &c.	County.	Town, city, &c.
	Dollars.	*Dollars.*	*Dollars.*	*Dollars.*	*Dollars.*	*Dollars.*	*Dollars.*	*Dollars.*
he State..	302, 515, 418	717, 644, 750	9, 055, 614	832, 918	3, 052, 931	5, 169, 765	3, 732, 929	3, 775, 706
r	2, 200, 178	5, 332, 342	40, 558	4, 400	5, 187	30, 971	4, 339	36, 158
as	1, 224, 319	3, 125, 437	23, 941	2, 446	7, 613	13, 880	4, 362	....
akee	2, 300, 019	4, 656, 370	91, 722	4, 600	30, 265	56, 857	15, 000	....
noose	3, 179, 748	5, 048, 703	75, 796	6, 359	28, 263	41, 174	8, 000	....
ubon	1, 072, 563	2, 686, 250	14, 803	2, 145	7, 855	4, 803	2, 734	....
on	4, 570, 779	13, 584, 774	121, 960	9, 141	36, 053	76, 766	....	....
Hawk	4, 531, 428	11, 333, 447	167, 870	9, 062	51, 346	107, 462	32, 939	23, 500
e	3, 620, 835	8, 946, 870	104, 874	7, 259	46, 859	50, 756	65, 857	....
er	2, 122, 246	10, 000, 000	61, 130	4, 244	21, 755	35, 131	5, 000	....
anan	4, 116, 615	6, 126, 184	112, 464	8, 233	41, 520	62, 711	728	....
a Vista	608, 374	742, 500	26, 564	1, 216	13, 426	11, 922	14, 000	....
r	2, 229, 415	6, 028, 670	119, 751	4, 458	20, 693	94, 600	3, 776	....
mn	962, 793	2, 406, 982	31, 690	1, 925	9, 177	20, 578	....	....
ll	1, 698, 937	5, 210, 447	65, 569	3, 397	29, 133	33, 039	122, 000	....
	2, 104, 176	4, 082, 832	51, 659	4, 208	16, 923	30, 528	....	....
r	5, 757, 836	22, 662, 408	109, 181	11, 515	41, 628	56, 038	20, 022	6, 000
Gordo	1, 788, 974	4, 341, 522	59, 234	3, 577	20, 132	35, 525	....	....
okee	323, 575	440, 000	19, 384	647	4, 708	13, 969	4, 000	....
kasaw	1, 849, 147	4, 435, 947	69, 860	3, 698	45, 665	20, 497	8, 707	....
o	2, 344, 706	3, 512, 039	47, 788	4, 689	12, 423	30, 610	2, 500	....

TABLE LXXXIII.—*Valuation, Taxation, and Public Indebtedness by Counties*—1870—Cont'd.

STATE OF IOWA—Continued.

Counties.	VALUATION.		TAXATION, NOT NATIONAL.				PUBLIC DEBT.	
	Assessed valuation of real and personal estate.	True valuation of real and personal estate.	All.	State.	County.	Town, city, &c.	County.	Town, city, &c.
	Dollars.	*Dollars.*	*Dollars.*	*Dollars.*	*Dollars.*	*Dollars.*	*Dollars.*	*Dollars.*
Clay	317, 172	430, 000	18, 834	634	9, 060	9, 140	10, 000	....
Clayton	5, 650, 976	16, 865, 841	212, 772	11, 301	59, 840	141, 631	14, 523	46, 542
Clinton	8, 083, 075	29, 207, 080	178, 052	16, 166	71, 575	90, 311	....	77, 6[illegible]
Crawford	1, 732, 210	1, 865, 479	49, 635	3, 464	17, 216	28, 955	356	....
Dallas	3, 701, 218	9, 253, 045	88, 367	7, 402	34, 237	46, 738	....	....
Davis	3, 587, 939	7, 172, 928	87, 374	7, 175	19, 432	60, 767	....	....
Decatur	2, 222, 080	4, 710, 407	80, 051	4, 441	26, 734	48, 873	5, 266	....
Delaware	3, 983, 013	7, 260, 016	118, 040	7, 966	33, 518	76, 556	....	4, 223
Des Moines	7, 730, 341	20, 846, 251	167, 955	15, 500	107, 845	44, 610	160, 000	....
Dickinson	121, 563	529, 527	6, 559	243	2, 118	4, 198	15, 000	....
Dubuque	9, 703, 598	27, 472, 620	224, 699	19, 407	117, 737	87, 555	156, 928	....
Emmett	192, 767	435, 126	8, 666	385	2, 613	5, 668	11, 000	....
Fayette	3, 350, 444	10, 051, 332	108, 041	6, 700	39, 985	61, 356	8, 000	....
Floyd	2, 307, 760	6, 565, 548	98, 413	4, 615	27, 479	66, 319	20, 350	....
Franklin	1, 541, 361	2, 076, 657	9, 695	3, 082	6, 613	....	3, 000	....
Fremont	3, 042, 675	7, 102, 950	72, 966	6, 085	22, 450	44, 431	10, 000	....
Greene	2, 292, 890	5, 500, 000	75, 779	4, 585	27, 132	44, 062	40, 000	....
Grundy	1, 837, 344	3, 660, 342	41, 814	3, 674	18, 254	19, 886	3, 000	....
Guthrie	2, 456, 531	3, 028, 353	62, 079	4, 913	19, 668	37, 498	....	....
Hamilton	1, 687, 896	3, 623, 420	42, 638	3, 375	14, 440	21, 823	....	....
Hancock	948, 774	2, 000, 000	33, 805	1, 897	12, 403	19, 505	....	....
Hardin	2, 698, 444	5, 398, 088	88, 773	5, 396	31, 670	51, 707	23, 000	....
Harrison	2, 904, 275	8, 652, 242	77, 091	5, 808	26, 857	44, 426	8, 210	....
Henry	4, 911, 434	11, 027, 166	98, 380	9, 822	26, 750	61, 808	350, 000	2, 450
Howard	1, 426, 727	4, 131, 132	45, 754	2, 853	42, 901	....	27, 000	....
Humboldt	628, 092	1, 577, 730	45, 088	1, 256	10, 425	33, 407	....	....
Ida	1, 943, 956	3, 887, 912	21, 642	3, 887	15, 291	2, 464	15, 000	....
Iowa	3, 880, 744	7, 309, 300	77, 423	7, 761	41, 127	28, 535	142, 350	....
Jackson	4, 527, 515	12, 000, 000	96, 122	9, 055	40, 251	46, 816	17, 000	2, 1[illegible]
Jasper	5, 643, 502	13, 451, 747	141, 885	11, 287	51, 566	79, 032	4, 067	....
Jefferson	3, 540, 568	7, 743, 612	76, 043	7, 082	26, 332	42, 629	....	....
Johnson	6, 353, 424	15, 000, 000	172, 227	12, 707	47, 361	112, 159	168, 328	121, 1[illegible]
Jones	4, 611, 771	9, 487, 096	115, 761	9, 224	27, 876	78, 661	....	....
Keokuk	3, 530, 576	5, 648, 922	85, 859	7, 062	25, 974	52, 823	....	....
Kossuth	663, 947	1, 515, 151	33, 921	1, 328	11, 907	20, 686	18, 000	....
Lee	9, 135, 286	20, 000, 000	255, 764	18, 271	82, 014	155, 479	380, 000	1, 552, 560
Linn	8, 001, 716	15, 412, 248	258, 374	16, 004	49, 737	192, 633	....	2, 000
Louisa	3, 141, 915	10, 000, 000	89, 832	6, 284	24, 876	58, 672	225, 000	362
Lucas	2, 580, 809	3, 852, 123	57, 773	5, 162	23, 052	29, 559	4, 000	....
Lyon (a)	....	....	....	....	....	....	....	....
Madison	3, 682, 975	9, 046, 990	102, 941	7, 366	47, 624	47, 951	....	....
Mahaska	5, 704, 368	15, 761, 135	123, 525	11, 409	48, 019	64, 097	....	....
Marion	4, 566, 877	12, 389, 902	185, 596	9, 134	39, 097	137, 365	5, 000	290
Marshall	3, 913, 883	9, 544, 035	128, 763	7, 828	44, 457	76, 478	6, 380	232
Mills	2, 787, 302	7, 146, 750	57, 833	5, 575	22, 374	29, 884	3, 406	....
Mitchell	2, 035, 384	6, 117, 072	83, 703	4, 071	42, 634	36, 998	70, 000	....
Monona	1, 719, 530	3, 462, 446	61, 514	3, 440	13, 422	44, 652	5, 000	....
Monroe	3, 007, 408	4, 147, 024	52, 069	6, 015	21, 606	24, 448	10, 000	....
Montgomery	1, 150, 458	2, 540, 283	47, 420	2, 301	18, 994	26, 125	6, 034	....
Muscatine	6, 945, 710	17, 471, 995	153, 975	13, 892	98, 511	41, 569	158, 000	365, 000
O'Brien	316, 995	350, 000	11, 410	634	6, 973	3, 803	....	....
Page	2, 457, 124	7, 325, 921	74, 752	4, 915	25, 027	44, 810	....	....
Palo Alto	342, 976	1, 259, 426	22, 755	686	9, 572	12, 497	....	....
Plymouth	242, 701	369, 967	17, 628	486	5, 245	11, 897	3, 852	....
Pocahontas	601, 004	1, 630, 140	14, 408	1, 202	6, 578	6, 628	1, 129	....
Polk	7, 577, 312	18, 943, 280	580, 588	15, 155	104, 881	460, 552	69, 764	430, 000
Pottawattamie	7, 884, 476	19, 711, 180	167, 462	15, 769	75, 190	76, 503	414, 931	108, 086
Poweshiek	3, 914, 493	7, 600, 000	141, 884	7, 830	41, 246	92, 808	106, 000	330
Ringgold	1, 542, 390	3, 866, 745	33, 193	3, 085	9, 269	20, 839	....	....
Sac	1, 194, 467	2, 986, 167	98, 579	2, 389	22, 066	74, 124	18, 000	....
Scott	8, 920, 146	22, 412, 960	236, 611	17, 841	116, 655	102, 115	92, 100	930, 000
Shelby	1, 661, 949	2, 355, 333	54, 601	3, 324	15, 401	35, 876	2, 252	....
Sioux	386, 667	717, 192	12, 089	774	11, 315	....	7, 000	....
Story	2, 490, 613	6, 277, 342	100, 166	4, 982	27, 926	67, 258	28, 748	....
Tama	4, 459, 201	12, 962, 492	118, 517	8, 919	33, 186	76, 412	....	....
Taylor	2, 069, 665	4, 472, 377	53, 835	4, 140	18, 102	31, 593	10, 000	....
Union	1, 565, 203	2, 214, 065	40, 383	3, 131	14, 053	23, 199	....	....

(a) No report.

TABLE LXXXIII.—*Valuation, Taxation, and Public Indebtedness by Counties*—1870—Cont'd.

STATE OF IOWA—Continued.

Counties.	VALUATION.		TAXATION, NOT NATIONAL.				PUBLIC DEBT.	
	Assessed valuation of real and personal estate.	True valuation of real and personal estate.	All.	State.	County.	Town, city, &c.	County.	Town, city, &c.
	Dollars.	*Dollars.*	*Dollars.*	*Dollars.*	*Dollars.*	*Dollars.*	*Dollars.*	*Dollars.*
Van Buren	6, 016, 586	8, 705, 415	79, 620	12, 034	30, 607	36, 979	....	608
Wapello	5, 684, 386	8, 556, 779	141, 920	11, 369	43, 445	87, 106	33, 000	14, 143
Warren	4, 382, 816	10, 914, 000	145, 212	8, 766	39, 540	96, 906	87, 500	....
Washington	4, 852, 306	12, 250, 000	188, 772	9, 705	31, 189	147, 878	308, 000	....
Wayne	2, 321, 287	6, 216, 838	49, 296	4, 649	24, 507	20, 140	5, 000	....
Webster	2, 740, 330	8, 000, 000	135, 689	5, 481	32, 099	98, 109	60, 000	....
Winnebago	587, 160	1, 061, 348	21, 581	1, 174	9, 943	10, 464	12, 000	....
Winneshiek	3, 205, 387	9, 600, 000	92, 075	6, 411	43, 439	42, 225	....	....
Woodbury	2, 408, 251	4, 816, 502	101, 573	4, 817	46, 974	49, 782	55, 000	....
Worth	870, 253	1, 305, 380	18, 763	1, 741	8, 666	8, 356	4, 431	....
Wright	1, 033, 264	2, 251, 134	37, 285	2, 107	16, 040	19, 138	2, 000	....
Not distributed among counties	....	....	227, 894	227, 894	....	....	....	....

STATE OF KANSAS.

Counties.	VALUATION.		TAXATION, NOT NATIONAL.				PUBLIC DEBT.	
	Assessed valuation of real and personal estate.	True valuation of real and personal estate.	All.	State.	County.	Town, city, &c.	County.	Town, city, &c.
	Dollars.	*Dollars.*	*Dollars.*	*Dollars.*	*Dollars.*	*Dollars.*	*Dollars.*	*Dollars.*
The State	92, 125, 861	188, 892, 014	2, 673, 992	809, 608	1, 160, 138	704, 246	3, 736, 901	1, 112, 075
Allen	1, 408, 948	2, 913, 422	22, 670	12, 328	8, 728	1, 614	12, 000	75, 000
Anderson	1, 941, 065	3, 342, 026	24, 855	17, 010	7, 480	365	200, 000	....
Atchison	4, 503, 727	7, 450, 234	185, 603	39, 407	48, 696	97, 500	87, 122	225, 000
Barton (*a*)	....	....	....	....	....	....	....	....
Bourbon	4, 193, 357	5, 119, 236	118, 644	39, 599	842	31, 203	186, 900	....
Brown	2, 022, 287	4, 340, 800	39, 721	17, 695	7, 803	14, 223	100, 000	....
Butler	822, 174	1, 200, 000	14, 119	7, 194	5, 825	1, 100	....	....
Chase	879, 884	3, 870, 000	27, 498	7, 698	4, 800	15, 000	....	....
Cherokee	912, 318	5, 142, 711	24, 982	7, 982	17, 000	....	1, 200	....
Clay	474, 712	474, 712	12, 153	4, 153	5, 000	3, 000	2, 000	....
Cloud	165, 907	485, 771	3, 121	1, 451	1, 670	....	....	....
Coffey	1, 844, 148	3, 550, 300	25, 197	17, 011	7, 286	900	....	9, 000
Cowley (*a*)	....	....	....	....	....	....	....	....
Crawford	500, 000	4, 820, 115	9, 877	4, 812	5, 065	....	9, 476	....
Davis	1, 507, 024	3, 105, 200	46, 889	13, 973	15, 134	17, 782	31, 331	....
Dickinson	1, 322, 377	2, 600, 000	43, 140	11, 570	10, 000	21, 570	30, 200	....
Doniphan	3, 251, 423	4, 414, 534	82, 473	28, 476	47, 168	6, 829	334, 000	....
Douglas	6, 851, 728	11, 277, 000	115, 952	59, 952	56, 000	....	300, 000	230, 000
Ellis	253, 468	253, 656	2, 635	2, 217	418	....	....	....
Ellsworth	398, 402	398, 402	6, 886	3, 486	3, 400	....	....	....
Ford (*b*)	....	....	....	....	....	....	....	....
Franklin	3, 183, 837	4, 575, 322	110, 858	27, 858	38, 000	45, 000	258, 000	....
Greenwood	1, 554, 920	3, 220, 400	21, 820	13, 605	8, 215	....	....	....
Howard (*c*)	....	949, 340	....	....	....	....	300	....
Jackson	1, 569, 586	3, 966, 425	44, 270	13, 733	14, 055	16, 482	....	....
Jefferson	3, 234, 142	6, 929, 856	127, 106	28, 298	49, 204	49, 604	12, 500	....
Jewell (*a*)	....	....	....	....	....	....	....	....
Johnson	3, 146, 749	6, 123, 201	72, 923	27, 534	37, 650	7, 739	10, 892	....
Labette	1, 117, 215	4, 110, 510	35, 331	9, 775	11, 572	13, 984	9, 010	....
Leavenworth	10, 370, 644	23, 476, 311	667, 743	90, 743	375, 000	202, 000	957, 550	500, 000
Lincoln (*c*)	....	398, 992	....	....	....	....	....	....
Linn	2, 906, 877	5, 002, 650	47, 710	25, 435	22, 275	....	....	....

(*a*) New county; reported as never having been assessed.
(*b*) No report.
(*c*) New county; no further information could be obtained.

TABLE LXXXIII.—*Valuation, Taxation, and Public Indebtedness by Counties*—1870—Cont'd.

STATE OF KANSAS—Continued.

Counties.	VALUATION.		TAXATION, NOT NATIONAL.				PUBLIC DEBT.	
	Assessed valuation of real and personal estate.	True valuation of real and personal estate.	All.	State.	County.	Town, city, &c.	County.	Town, city, &c.
	Dollars.	*Dollars.*	*Dollars.*	*Dollars.*	*Dollars.*	*Dollars.*	*Dollars.*	*Dollars.*
Lyon	3,916,927	6,672,291	64,846	34,273	19,340	11,233	425,000	3,[illegible]
Marion	225 465	640,320	6,318	1,972	3,272	1,074	....	....
Marshall	1,694,859	3,109,233	31,583	14,830	11,169	5,584	4,000	10,[illegible]
McPherson	226,911	789,631	5,770	1,985	3,355	430	100	[illegible]
Miami	3,459,997	5,876,543	101,971	30,274	40,446	31,251	160,000	....
Mitchell (a)	....	....	....	....	....	....	....	....
Montgomery	163,061	1,596,564	1,426	1,426	....	....	1,000	....
Morris	1,231,000	2,312,135	21,621	10,771	8,850	2,000	6,300	....
Nemaha	2,094,015	3,998,654	59,396	18,332	8,371	32,693	....	25,[illegible]
Neosho	817,882	4,219,876	25,436	7,156	9,140	9,140	....	5,[illegible]
Ness (b)	....	....	....	....	....	....	....	....
Osage	2,071,142	3,876,123	31,872	18,122	11,625	2,125	153,000	....
Osborne (b)	....	....	....	....	....	....	....	....
Ottawa	720,831	1,123,456	10,307	6,307	3,000	1,000	....	....
Pawnee (a)	....	....	....	....	....	....	....	....
Pottawattamie	2,024,119	3,567,890	47,849	17,711	30,138	....	2,500	....
Republic	192,845	1,987,654	4,687	1,687	3,000	....	678	....
Rice (b)	....	....	....	....	....	....	....	....
Riley	1,394,762	3,267,980	41,802	12,204	14,601	14,997	11,700	....
Russell (b)	....	....	....	....	....	....	....	....
Saline	1,838,999	2,897,879	26,220	16,091	7,564	2,565	56,999	....
Sedgwick (c)	....	910,000	....	....	....	....	....	....
Shawnee	4,654,690	8,313,830	101,218	40,728	51,170	9,320	208,000	....
Smith (b)	....	....	....	....	....	....	....	....
Sumner (a)	....	....	....	....	....	....	....	....
Trego (a)	....	....	....	....	....	....	....	....
Wabaunsee	884,097	1,987,654	22,385	7,735	14,650	....	8,700	....
Wallace (b)	....	....	....	....	....	....	....	....
Washington	720,210	1,7[illegible]5,432	8,801	5,601	3,200	....	6,000	....
Wilson	556,970	1,811,332	12,342	4,873	6,280	1,189	....	....
Woodson	545,311	1,600,411	13,202	4,771	7,681	750	10,500	....
Wyandotte	2,258,849	3,656,000	100,764	19,764	48,000	33,000	140,000	30,[illegible]

(a) New county; reported as never having been assessed.
(b) No report.
(c) New county; no further information could be obtained.

STATE OF KENTUCKY.

Counties.	VALUATION.		TAXATION NOT NATIONAL.				PUBLIC DEBT.	
	Assessed valuation of real and personal estate.	True valuation of real and personal estate.	All.	State.	County.	Town, city, &c.	County.	Town, city, &c.
	Dollars.	*Dollars.*	*Dollars.*	*Dollars.*	*Dollars.*	*Dollars.*	*Dollars.*	*Dollars.*
The State	409,544,294	604,318,552	5,730,118	2,254,413	1,307,833	2,167,872	7,173,644	7,887,[illegible]
Adair	1,768,973	2,000,000	10,823	7,960	2,263	600	1,300	5[illegible]
Allen	1,818,615	1,906,720	12,139	8,183	3,638	318	....	....
Anderson	1,511,100	2,305,870	8,799	6,799	2,000	....	2,000	....
Ballard	2,190,588	2,800,000	17,069	9,857	7,212	....	11,000	....
Barren	3,353,784	4,897,008	30,319	15,092	5,327	9,900	....	125,000
Bath	2,694,168	8,107,584	47,102	12,123	34,979	....	154,450	....
Boone	5,006,925	6,666,666	26,031	22,531	3,500	....	3,000	....
Bourbon	11,982,749	23,000,000	87,953	53,922	20,400	13,631	110,000	123,333
Boyd	2,239,177	2,239,177	13,776	10,076	3,700	....	3,[illegible]	....

LXXXIII.—*Valuation, Taxation, and Public Indebtedness by Counties*—1870—Cont'd.

STATE OF KENTUCKY—Continued.

...ties.	VALUATION.		TAXATION, NOT NATIONAL.				PUBLIC DEBT.	
	Assessed valuation of real and personal estate.	True valuation of real and personal estate.	All.	State.	County.	Town, city, &c.	County.	Town, city, &c.
	Dollars.	*Dollars.*	*Dollars.*	*Dollars.*	*Dollars.*	*Dollars.*	*Dollars.*	*Dollars.*
....	4,123,535	6,560,437	34,659	18,555	16,104	....	89,000	2,500
....	3,900,888	5,000,000	45,053	17,553	27,500	....	60,000	15,000
t	489,848	650,780	3,946	2,204	1,742	....	....	....
ridge ..	3,584,226	4,000,000	28,334	16,129	12,205	....	10,600	....
....	2,419,859	5,000,000	14,654	10,889	3,600	165	....	....
....	1,566,207	2,802,920	13,047	7,047	6,000	....	1,400	....
l	2,206,472	3,225,000	47,429	9,929	35,500	2,000	410,000	....
y	1,976,765	2,000,000	14,095	8,695	4,000	1,200	4,000	....
ll	8,724,696	8,724,696	115,970	39,261	20,824	55,885	175,000	....
....	2,207,236	3,815,214	17,932	9,932	6,000	2,000	220,000	....
....	1,535,033	1,535,509	13,199	6,907	6,142	150	75,000	....
....	1,432,361	5,897,638	8,382	6,445	1,937	....	....	....
n	5,294,945	7,000,000	72,367	23,827	40,240	8,300	291,254	54,689
....	6,296,610	10,000,000	84,171	28,334	53,337	2,500	154,000	1,250
....	886,808	886,808	5,065	3,990	1,075	....	....	....
....	870,279	1,000,000	6,274	3,916	2,358	....	1,800	....
len.....	1,769,651	2,000,000	20,255	7,963	11,292	1,000	6,735	....
land ...	1,254,948	1,901,100	9,937	5,647	4,290	....	3,732	....
....	7,825,750	9,787,086	59,015	35,215	11,800	12,000	307,350	75,000
son	874,224	874,224	5,433	3,933	1,500	....	....	....
....	363,693	500,000	3,326	1,636	1,690	....	....	....
....	1,520,726	2,027,426	9,241	6,843	2,398	....	....	....
....	14,790,457	20,231,996	294,165	66,557	75,869	151,739	400,000	300,000
....	4,337,841	4,345,280	45,220	19,520	25,000	700	....	....
....	685,255	685,255	5,583	3,083	2,500	....	3,200	....
1.......	4,923,176	4,923,176	74,154	22,154	29,000	23,000	79,493	131,500
....	1,434,348	3,755,571	9,202	6,454	2,748	....	....	40,000
....	1,862,731	3,060,520	13,832	8,382	4,700	750	11,250	2,000
....	3,836,809	8,133,619	30,465	17,265	12,000	1,200	348,188	2,500
....	2,841,682	3,400,000	19,050	12,787	6,263	....	....	....
....	3,732,053	4,359,720	28,794	16,794	12,000	....	22,000	....
....	1,606,960	2,000,000	23,316	7,231	16,085	....	200,000	....
....	1,219,873	2,725,460	9,309	5,489	3,820	....	400	....
....	2,949,187	2,949,187	34,891	13,271	19,922	1,698	11,060	....
....	1,752,300	2,373,488	16,541	7,885	8,158	498	10,800	....
....	3,728,882	11,287,860	30,494	16,779	3,792	9,923	210,000	75,000
....	405,596	475,000	3,195	1,825	1,370	....	2,500	....
n.......	6,720,070	7,000,000	52,355	30,240	19,465	2,650	20,000	....
....	2,535,940	2,535,940	17,655	11,411	6,244	....	....	....
on	6,454,182	7,000,000	109,043	29,043	23,000	57,000	13,000	378,000
....	5,262,399	6,000,000	29,680	23,680	4,500	1,500	....	10,000
n	1,788,027	2,000,000	23,843	8,046	8,297	7,500	3,870	50,000
....	2,477,296	2,642,569	30,547	11,147	17,700	1,700	150,000	....
....	355,385	800,000	3,436	1,599	1,837	....	600	....
n.......	76,414,971	116,616,325	1,857,492	343,867	113,625	1,400,000	64,000	5,006,000
ne	4,049,579	6,000,000	58,223	18,223	30,000	10,000	100,000	....
....	684,049	821,122	6,588	3,078	3,510	....	3,509	....
ll	264,944	1,349,919	2,492	1,192	1,300	....	2,300	....
....	14,229,850	28,406,690	276,034	64,034	4,000	208,000	600	900,000
....	905,231	1,200,000	7,201	4,073	3,128	....	100,688	....
....	1,542,417	1,542,417	11,019	6,940	4,079	....	....	....
....	864,922	1,000,000	6,382	3,892	2,490	....	....	....
e	1,152,310	1,500,000	16,309	5,185	10,324	800	18,095	1,694
....	395,290	425,000	4,250	1,778	1,672	800	....	....
....	310,502	500,000	2,888	1,388	1,500	....	2,000	....
....	2,349,340	2,879,237	17,482	10,572	6,910	....	21,000	....
....	4,483,920	4,483,920	33,261	20,177	13,084	....	2,500	....
ton.....	1,509,182	2,000,000	18,547	6,791	11,316	440	5,875	....
....	4,269,135	5,638,566	35,211	19,211	13,000	3,000	247,000	23,000
....	937,574	1,138,171	9,236	4,219	4,017	1,000	204,939	....
....	8,177,420	8,227,500	68,884	36,798	32,086	....	498,000	....
....	559,856	1,715,631	4,843	2,519	2,324	....	4,291	....
....	3,223,991	5,513,587	42,715	14,507	12,089	16,119	50,000	18,000
l.......	1,487,155	1,550,000	13,567	6,692	6,875	....	6,500	....
....	8,171,205	11,473,959	122,138	36,770	28,684	56,684	126,000	124,150
ken	5,284,846	8,000,000	68,418	23,781	5,068	39,569	607,500	305,000
....	1,564,823	2,499,411	11,641	7,041	4,400	200	....	56,000
....	2,165,548	2,800,000	12,744	9,744	3,000	....	280	....
....	190,773	190,773	2,156	543	1,613	....	....	....

TABLE LXXXIII.—*Valuation, Taxation, and Public Indebtedness by Counties*—1870—Cont'd.

STATE OF KENTUCKY—Continued.

Counties.	VALUATION.		TAXATION, NOT NATIONAL.				PUBLIC DEBT.	
	Assessed valuation of real and personal estate.	True valuation of real and personal estate.	All.	State.	County.	Town, city, &c.	County.	Town, city, &c.
	Dollars.	*Dollars.*	*Dollars.*	*Dollars.*	*Dollars.*	*Dollars.*	*Dollars.*	*Dollars.*
Mercer	4,129,231	5,350,692	27,602	18,581	9,021	....	....	....
Metcalfe	1,301,095	1,838,427	12,054	5,854	6,000	200	16,000	....
Monroe	1,217,072	1,400,000	9,476	5,476	4,000	....	4,000	....
Montgomery	3,546,027	7,000,000	59,557	15,957	42,000	1,000	200,000	[illegible]
Morgan	718,267	1,000,000	6,932	3,232	3,700	....	3,200	....
Muhlenburg	2,462,757	2,462,757	19,700	11,082	8,618	....	400,000	....
Nelson	5,339,210	12,300,000	31,426	24,026	5,600	1,800	140,000	[illegible]
Nicholas	3,090,350	4,500,000	31,406	13,906	2,500	15,000	2,500	15,[illegible]
Ohio	3,343,006	4,090,827	23,224	15,043	8,181	....	30,320	....
Oldham	3,194,252	8,061,786	16,268	14,374	1,894	....	4,800	....
Owen	2,588,130	2,671,635	16,346	11,646	4,700	....	3,000	....
Owsley	517,601	714,392	4,351	2,326	2,025	....	1,700	....
Pendleton	2,894,389	2,980,342	27,378	13,024	14,354	....	90,000	....
Perry	330,033	851,571	2,685	1,485	1,200	....	3,000	....
Pike	910,007	1,388,208	7,041	4,095	2,946	....	....	....
Powell	343,819	450,307	3,235	1,547	1,688	....	3,000	....
Pulaski	2,258,090	3,516,232	17,471	10,161	6,800	510	....	
Robertson	1,025,147	1,025,147	9,005	4,613	4,092	300	1,500	....
Rock Castle	1,033,551	1,033,551	8,250	4,650	3,600	....	3,200	....
Rowan	388,688	460,000	2,849	1,749	1,100	....	750	....
Russell	1,057,697	1,057,697	8,459	4,759	3,700	....	3,300	....
Scott	6,722,370	7,394,207	59,300	30,250	29,050	....	3,400	....
Shelby	8,569,998	20,000,000	84,476	38,564	42,302	3,610	316,000	....
Simpson	2,533,749	5,500,000	65,401	11,401	33,000	21,000	33,000	21,[illegible]
Spencer	2,693,561	3,991,005	16,121	12,121	4,000	....	3,300	....
Taylor	1,402,094	2,000,000	7,009	6,309	700	....	10,940	2,[illegible]
Todd	2,803,846	5,500,000	25,450	12,617	11,475	1,358	13,042	....
Trigg	2,498,423	3,390,440	19,621	11,242	7,804	575	17,013	....
Trimble	1,739,680	2,086,308	9,705	7,828	1,877	....	1,400	....
Union	3,396,183	3,396,183	23,746	15,282	8,464	....	....	....
Warren	7,072,222	9,045,529	65,833	31,825	20,008	14,000	186,000	32,[illegible]
Washington	3,564,004	6,194,852	23,450	16,038	7,412	....	4,000	....
Wayne	1,419,585	2,000,000	9,988	6,388	3,600	....	....	....
Webster	1,578,643	2,000,000	13,819	7,103	6,716	....	....	....
Whitley	986,852	2,000,000	7,436	4,436	3,000	....	....	....
Wolfe	381,325	457,515	4,612	1,715	2,897	....	18,940	....
Woodford	5,981,130	5,981,130	37,607	26,915	8,892	1,800	10,000	....
Not distributed am'g counties	....	....	411,543	411,543	....	....	....	....

STATE OF LOUISIANA.

Parishes.	VALUATION.		TAXATION, NOT NATIONAL.				PUBLIC DEBT.	
	Assessed valuation of real and personal estate.	True valuation of real and personal estate.	All.	State.	Parish.	Town, city, &c.	Parish.	Town, city, &c.
	Dollars.	*Dollars.*	*Dollars.*	*Dollars.*	*Dollars.*	*Dollars.*	*Dollars.*	*Dollars.*
The State	253,371,860	323,125,666	7,060,722	2,671,693	4,109,999	279,030	1,336,635	36,739,072
Ascension	1,957,204	2,580,685	46,657	20,657	25,000	1,000	10,500	17,000
Assumption	2,278,831	2,938,474	50,308	25,308	21,000	4,000	10,500	2,500
Avoyelles	2,250,157	3,005,209	46,363	16,363	27,500	2,500	30,500	....
Bienville	874,554	1,066,065	17,790	12,290	3,500	2,000	....	....
Bossier	2,376,047	3,168,062	31,092	9,092	18,000	4,000	11,000	20,000
Caddo	2,860,313	3,813,850	98,369	36,069	18,300	44,000	....	20,000
Calcasieu	920,355	1,227,130	18,550	8,170	10,380	....	2,500	1,000

LXXXIII.—*Valuation, Taxation, and Public Indebtedness by Counties*—1870—Cont'd.

STATE OF LOUISIANA—Continued.

ishes.	VALUATION.		TAXATION, NOT NATIONAL.				PUBLIC DEBT.	
	Assessed valuation of real and personal estate.	True valuation of real and personal estate.	All.	State.	Parish.	Town, city, &c.	Parish.	Town, city, &c.
	Dollars.	*Dollars.*	*Dollars.*	*Dollars.*	*Dollars.*	*Dollars.*	*Dollars.*	*Dollars.*
ll	651, 087	868, 249	17, 318	5, 818	5, 500	6, 000	14, 150	1, 000
m	173, 700	321, 100	1, 800	1, 800	....	....	....	....
	3, 194, 035	3, 194, 035	78, 209	13, 209	60, 000	5, 000	20, 000	....
ula	1, 233, 562	1, 233, 562	28, 500	10, 500	10, 000	8, 000	20, 000	1, 000
no	1, 247, 750	1, 663, 667	28, 210	15, 710	10, 000	2, 500	10, 000	3, [illegible]
dia	2, 940, 731	3, 920, 974	110, 285	30, 285	50, 000	30, 000	364, 800	29, 000
o	1, 696, 091	2, 200, 788	57, 178	20, 571	20, 407	16, 200	10, 000	1, 000
Baton ge	2, 673, 428	3, 697, 904	106, 887	38, 700	25, 468	42, 719	237, 345	56, [illegible]
eliciana	1, 424, 426	1, 809, 368	39, 968	14, 868	15, 000	10, 100	15, 000	1, [illegible]
in	588, 358	784, 477	13, 468	4, 668	8, 000	800	9, 000	1, [illegible]
	688, 743	918, 324	10, 022	7, 022	3, 000	....	2, 000	[illegible]
	2, 297, 845	3, 063, 793	47, 415	18, 723	13, 692	15, 000	....	....
le	3, 949, 958	5, 266, 624	75, 979	33, 880	39, 599	2, 500	40, 000	....
n	711, 029	944, 372	17, 976	8, 576	5, 400	4, 000	10, 000	....
on	13, 220, 480	17, 627, 306	151, 157	102, 157	27, 000	22, 000	9, 000	45, [illegible]
tte	880, 571	1, 177, 440	18, 724	9, 670	7, 554	1, 500	1, 500	....
che	3, 381, 038	3, 381, 038	47, 403	29, 344	14, 612	3, 447	10, 000	15, 000
ston	491, 165	654, 886	12, 770	5, 094	7, 676	....	8, 508	....
n	981, 907	1, 309, 209	68, 852	13, 852	55, 000	....	....	....
ouse	1, 986, 789	2, 659, 082	61, 101	16, 101	45, 000	....	18, 000	....
toches	2, 986, 153	3, 983, 404	75, 525	23, 165	46, 800	5, 560	30, 788	4, 000
	146, 718, 888	185, 625, 187	4, 191, 417	1, 141, 417	3, 050, 000	....	....	26, 500, 000
ta	3, 511, 160	4, 681, 546	28, 227	19, 477	7, 000	1, 750	....	1, 000
mines	2, 283, 000	2, 930, 966	30, 417	12, 481	17, 936	....	10, 000	....
oupée	1, 362, 025	1, 396, 000	26, 851	11, 851	15, 000	....	43, 000	....
e	3, 012, 486	4, 016, 648	98, 894	17, 209	79, 664	2, 021	23, 000	14, 500
nd	852, 574	1, 136, 765	27, 504	10, 019	8, 135	8, 750	9, 980	....
	377, 490	503, 320	10, 187	5, 287	4, 900	....	4, 000	....
nard	971, 590	1, 295, 483	33, 664	9, 664	24, 000	....	47, 000	....
rles	1, 776, 425	2, 368, 566	40, 934	17, 254	23, 680	....	12, 000	....
ena	531, 022	720, 029	10, 120	4, 499	5, 388	233	....	7, 000
ies	3, 188, 678	4, 251, 570	48, 969	33, 969	15, 000	....	33, 000	....
hn the ist	3, 162, 927	3, 217, 236	85, 430	22, 172	63, 258	....	7, 064	....
dry	3, 272, 980	4, 363, 973	112, 500	45, 000	60, 000	7, 500	20, 000	2, 000
tin	3, 560, 534	4, 747, 378	45, 380	21, 380	22, 000	2, 000	30, 000	....
y	3, 086, 071	4, 114, 761	41, 782	30, 682	9, 000	2, 100	5, 000	....
amany	447, 698	447, 698	10, 044	1, 544	7, 000	1, 500	10, 000	....
ahoa	1, 650, 400	2, 200, 000	29, 229	9, 288	14, 441	5, 500	10, 000	....
	2, 165, 338	2, 887, 117	29, 989	27, 181	2, 808	....	70, 000	....
onno	3, 167, 338	4, 193, 117	41, 282	30, 382	10, 400	500	4, 300	....
	1, 257, 911	1, 480, 028	44, 868	14, 638	27, 730	2, 500	13, 000	1, 000
lion	930, 166	1, 240, 221	26, 400	7, 750	17, 800	850	8, 000	3, 000
ngton	207, 347	226, 690	5, 413	1, 768	3, 645	....	15, 000	....
Baton ge	2, 937, 419	3, 916, 616	34, 882	28, 782	6, 100	....	19, 000	....
Feliciana	1, 205, 518	1, 440, 290	40, 657	13, 657	16, 000	11, 000	20, 000	....
	818, 538	1, 091, 384	17, 106	11, 380	5, 726	....	....	....
tributed counties	....	....	570, 694	570, 694	....	....	....	....

TABLE LXXXIII.—*Valuation, Taxation, and Public Indebtedness by Counties—1870*—Cont'd.

STATE OF MAINE.

Counties.	VALUATION.		TAXATION, NOT NATIONAL.				PUBLIC DEBT.	
	Assessed valuation of real and personal estate.	True valuation of real and personal estate.	All.	State.	County.	Town, city, &c.	County.	Town, city, &c.
	Dollars.	*Dollars.*	*Dollars.*	*Dollars.*	*Dollars.*	*Dollars.*	*Dollars.*	*Dollars.*
The State	204,253,780	348,155,671	5,348,645	1,350,305	315,199	3,683,141	274,153	8,282,5[illegible]
Androscoggin	13,275,063	23,163,709	392,025	105,634	23,530	262,861	112,400	[illegible]
Aroostook	3,553,439	5,184,179	100,035	30,026	10,944	50,065	....	[illegible]
Cumberland	47,008,189	84,068,337	1,151,658	293,852	86,546	771,260	72,500	[illegible]
Franklin	3,994,278	8,057,012	137,515	34,795	9,278	93,442	1,834	[illegible]
Hancock	9,071,720	12,058,753	217,387	45,408	10,725	161,254	....	[illegible]
Kennebec	20,694,918	31,078,916	471,155	126,144	29,988	315,023	70	[illegible]
Knox	10,106,670	15,121,850	253,489	63,121	11,224	179,144	9,250	[illegible]
Lincoln	5,426,063	9,718,573	172,138	41,205	8,570	122,357	....	[illegible]
Oxford	8,506,842	13,926,318	231,470	59,448	8,791	163,231	250	[illegible]
Penobscot	20,607,586	31,688,437	602,127	136,349	30,606	435,082	....	[illegible]
Piscataquis	3,572,049	6,545,030	148,699	29,096	4,183	115,420	....	[illegible]
Sagadahoc	10,904,049	14,371,779	250,879	66,294	15,187	169,398	65,000	[illegible]
Somerset	8,754,414	13,187,909	236,363	66,025	9,357	160,981	620	[illegible]
Waldo	8,378,346	17,471,527	236,597	60,627	14,519	161,451	....	[illegible]
Washington	10,029,549	26,615,048	247,639	57,486	13,555	176,598	12,200	[illegible]
York	20,310,614	35,898,294	499,469	134,795	28,100	336,574	....	[illegible]

STATE OF MARYLAND.

Counties.	VALUATION.		TAXATION, NOT NATIONAL.				PUBLIC DEBT.	
	Assessed valuation of real and personal estate.	True valuation of real and personal estate.	All.	State.	County.	Town, city, &c.	County.	Town, city, &c.
	Dollars.	*Dollars.*	*Dollars.*	*Dollars.*	*Dollars.*	*Dollars.*	*Dollars.*	*Dollars.*
The State	423,834,918	643,748,976	6,632,842	1,781,252	1,542,218	3,309,372	1,565,779	14,149,3[illegible]
Allegany	9,521,884	24,328,620	113,545	18,092	76,175	19,278	....	130,000
Anne Arundel	9,822,454	10,237,999	103,875	18,908	70,132	14,835	....	30,000
Baltimore	237,806,530	401,634,738	3,892,646	458,776	211,764	3,222,106	121,000	13,562,4[illegible]
Calvert	2,112,879	3,100,000	20,706	4,014	16,692	....	....	....
Caroline	4,101,939	4,239,452	42,249	7,793	34,456	....	....	....
Carroll	17,080,159	21,366,192	112,239	32,870	76,860	2,500	65,625	....
Cecil	13,252,030	14,703,747	130,876	25,510	103,366	2,000	....	....
Charles	3,062,738	4,351,302	37,135	5,896	31,239	....	6,200	....
Dorchester	6,056,563	7,228,875	68,984	11,658	56,326	1,000	50,000	....
Frederick	26,435,079	32,920,117	242,200	50,888	150,679	40,693	203,800	[illegible]
Harford	12,271,766	12,917,526	109,525	23,623	85,902	....	6,000	2,000
Howard	6,478,365	9,509,640	57,818	12,470	45,348	....	76,387	300
Kent	7,827,151	13,090,185	84,728	15,067	69,661	....	143,287	....
Montgomery	7,629,057	8,992,534	76,948	14,685	62,263	....	....	....
Prince George's	8,782,240	8,782,240	97,620	16,686	77,284	3,650	....	....
Queen Anne	8,307,896	9,145,779	81,295	15,993	64,802	500	128,793	457
Saint Mary's	2,936,834	2,936,834	34,434	5,633	28,781	....	....	....
Somerset	3,602,302	5,000,000	38,474	6,934	31,340	200	81,337	....
Talbot	7,645,956	10,705,297	73,532	14,719	56,203	2,610	....	....
Washington	20,185,928	27,550,552	155,936	38,858	117,078	....	650,000	96,500
Wicomico	4,422,290	4,422,290	54,728	8,513	46,215	....	....	....
Worcester	4,492,858	6,585,057	38,301	8,649	29,652	....	33,350	630
Not distributed among counties	....	....	964,988	964,988	....	....	....	....

.XXXIII.—*Valuation, Taxation, and Public Indebtedness by Counties*—1870—Cont'd.

STATE OF MASSACHUSETTS.

ies.	VALUATION.		TAXATION, NOT NATIONAL.				PUBLIC DEBT.	
	Assessed valuation of real and personal estate.	True valuation of real and personal estate.	All.	State.	County.	Town, city, &c.	County.	Town, city, &c.
	Dollars.	*Dollars.*	*Dollars.*	*Dollars.*	*Dollars.*	*Dollars.*	*Dollars.*	*Dollars.*
ate....	1,591,983,112	2,132,148,741	24,922,900	7,408,962	653,500	16,860,438	707,123	40,233,534
le.....	14,871,480	18,824,039	270,087	61,948	13,000	195,139	3,338	186,755
e......	37,128,919	50,381,804	460,673	99,355	35,000	326,318	248,315	474,926
....	80,425,791	105,522,355	1,416,898	342,498	60,000	1,014,400	....	1,402,033
....	2,230,737	2,894,285	44,154	7,344	4,000	32,810	13,662	71,728
....	135,230,821	214,438,507	2,287,845	444,098	100,000	1,743,747	238,808	4,424,465
....	14,846,886	20,927,226	322,801	60,550	20,000	242,251	....	303,831
ı......	51,333,673	73,611,670	839,452	164,887	36,500	638,065	....	646,430
re	26,298,838	35,655,080	430,223	89,411	25,000	315,812	45,000	357,088
x	225,802,314	384,665,298	3,365,607	656,837	160,000	2,548,860	125,000	6,028,539
et.....	1,977,013	2,230,095	43,038	13,217	....	29,821	....	43,381
....	80,475,030	150,922,635	1,326,946	318,048	60,000	948,898	....	648,794
h......	31,811,883	39,722,335	593,605	140,929	40,000	412,676	24,000	312,145
....	597,630,891	836,683,247	8,669,808	1,729,845	....	6,939,963	....	22,598,301
r	117,063,100	195,671,745	1,969,955	398,277	100,000	1,471,678	9,000	2,674,429
ibuted ounties	174,855,736	....	2,881,718	2,881,718	....	....	....	....

STATE OF MICHIGAN.

ies.	VALUATION.		TAXATION, NOT NATIONAL.				PUBLIC DEBT.	
	Assessed valuation of real and personal estate.	True valuation of real and personal estate.	All.	State.	County.	Town, city, &c.	County.	Town, city, &c.
	Dollars.	*Dollars.*	*Dollars.*	*Dollars.*	*Dollars.*	*Dollars.*	*Dollars.*	*Dollars.*
ate....	272,242,917	719,208,118	5,412,937	396,332	1,565,163	3,451,442	1,275,479	3,064,724
....	1,073,551	2,147,102	18,295	790	8,619	8,886	6,000	4,400
....	10,530,089	15,795,133	57,480	7,626	21,530	28,324	....	10,087
....	1,488,730	2,977,460	22,303	2,243	11,910	8,150	....	10,000
....	460,433	920,866	11,308	724	4,243	6,341	....	1,535
....	5,587,424	11,174,848	55,322	4,348	19,731	31,243	5,000	21,165
....	2,670,198	10,680,792	148,831	3,211	51,000	94,620	57,150	95,825
....	307,413	461,119	8,979	323	5,308	3,288	....	1,150
....	6,396,244	25,584,976	173,390	10,397	50,010	112,983	27,445	24,702
....	4,344,008	17,376,032	107,549	8,984	20,462	78,103	150	....
....	7,520,950	30,083,800	191,873	15,861	37,956	138,056	....	218,791
....	4,358,572	17,434,288	52,242	9,085	20,613	22,544	3,680	1,044
dix....	208,030	208,030	3,906	....	1,209	2,697	700	237
an	448,140	448,140	12,661	196	4,808	7,665	2,000	....
a......	220,838	331,257	3,664	216	1,040	2,408	....	....
....	....	....	....	....	....	....	....	....
....	3,421,665	10,264,995	82,743	5,387	28,000	40,356	20,000	19,825
....	315,000	945,000	7,154	329	3,725	3,100	4,900	....
....	4,397,614	13,192,842	127,095	5,734	20,709	100,652	75,000	83,800
....	144,115	144,115	1,446	149	989	308	....	145
....	6,032,374	18,097,122	137,516	9,942	41,514	86,060	19,000	57,355
raverse	1,159,530	1,739,295	22,973	897	8,004	14,072	9,675	8,953
....	2,686,474	4,029,711	24,926	2,099	13,867	8,941	5,000	1,919
....	6,707,952	20,123,856	123,335	11,356	27,112	84,867	....	....
n	1,917,595	3,835,190	80,937	4,161	47,800	28,896	60,700	3,500
....	1,190,602	3,571,986	22,896	1,082	8,139	13,075	....	....
....	8,921,812	13,382,718	70,800	5,737	26,257	38,866	43,872	11,280
....	4,247,790	12,743,370	47,515	8,737	17,855	20,923	2,000	170,000
....	1,518,400	3,036,818	38,724	1,408	13,821	23,433	9,000	25,000
....	1,424,705	2,137,057	24,263	1,375	10,100	12,782	5,000	[illegible]

(a) No report.

TABLE LXXXIII.—*Valuation, Taxation, and Public Indebtedness by Counties—1870*—Cont'd.

STATE OF MICHIGAN—Continued.

Counties.	VALUATION.		TAXATION, NOT NATIONAL.				PUBLIC DEBT.	
	Assessed valuation of real and personal estate.	True valuation of real and personal estate.	All.	State.	County.	Town, city, &c.	County.	Town, city, &c.
	Dollars.	*Dollars.*	*Dollars.*	*Dollars.*	*Dollars.*	*Dollars.*	*Dollars.*	*Dollars.*
Jackson	10, 767, 060	30, 763, 020	113, 545	16, 323	29, 506	67, 716	10, 500	[illegible]
Kalamazoo	14, 008, 280	26, 004, 560	190, 081	12, 804	61, 631	46, 646	50, 000	[illegible]
Kalkaska (a)								
Kent	8, 617, 615	34, 470, 460	236, 709	15, 252	73, 677	147, 779	66, 800	[illegible]
Keweenaw	1, 122, 916	2, 945, 832	26, 574	3, 224	11, 250	14, 100	14, 000	
Lake (a)								
Lapeer	2, 872, 202	11, 488, 808	48, 767	6, 032	19, 957	22, 758	3, 950	24, 686
Leelanaw	458, 227	687, 340	8, 609	494	2, 749	5, 520		
Lenawee	10, 987, 220	32, 961, 607	88, 401	22, 536	47, 072	18, 793		73, 686
Livingston	3, 496, 541	6, 118, 940	30, 753	8, 040	14, 154	8, 581	5, 939	
Mackinac	410, 934	616, 401	4, 885	479	1, 600	2, 800		
Macomb	5, 804, 072	23, 456, 288	73, 081	11, 050	32, 373	26, 658		
Manistee	1, 102, 865	4, 411, 460	33, 997	1, 043	16, 544	16, 340	6, 000	[illegible]
Manitou	113, 550	113, 550	1, 443	193	350	900		
Marquette	2, 807, 782	5, 410, 872	101, 888	2, 884	24, 508	74, 496	17, 000	[illegible]
Mason	939, 200	1, 389, 300	10, 796	623	7, 152	3, 021		[illegible]
Mecosta	2, 391, 637	3, 587, 455	24, 275	1, 557	6, 100	16, 618	1, 000	[illegible]
Menominee	541, 650	1, 694, 950	7, 151	565	5, 097	1, 489	1, 250	[illegible]
Midland	3, 107, 568	6, 215, 130	44, 911	2, 414	31, 076	11, 421	17, 900	[illegible]
Missaukee (a)								
Monroe	4, 488, 345	8, 976, 690	39, 841	8, 858	22, 442	8, 541	9, 200	[illegible]
Montcalm	1, 579, 750	4, 739, 250	55, 131	2, 619	12, 986	39, 526	12, 500	[illegible]
Muskegon	3, 485, 887	6, 971, 774	102, 017	3, 399	42, 179	58, 446	20, 000	[illegible]
Newaygo	1, 576, 603	3, 153, 206	23, 171	2, 028	11, 000	10, 143	4, 500	[illegible]
Oakland	9, 600, 819	28, 802, 457	175, 902	19, 750	36, 295	119, 857		[illegible]
Oceana	1, 792, 118	3, 584, 236	46, 775	1, 237	17, 931	27, 607		[illegible]
Ogemaw (a)								
Ontonagon	943, 618	1, 887, 236	32, 168	1, 894	13, 250	17, 094	6, 800	[illegible]
Osceola	966, 922	966, 922	2, 347		558	1, 789	7, 000	[illegible]
Oscoda (a)								
Ottawa	2, 224, 662	11, 123, 310	137, 674	4, 496	73, 621	59, 557	23, 150	[illegible]
Presque Isle (a)								
Saginaw	9, 011, 423	18, 022, 846	427, 530	10, 257	53, 771	362, 902	219, 099	[illegible]
Sanilac	3, 547, 074	3, 547, 074	37, 299	3, 180	17, 735	16, 384	5, 000	[illegible]
Shiawassee	2, 282, 000	9, 128, 000	106, 011	4, 860	17, 609	83, 542	12, 000	[illegible]
St. Clair	4, 630, 058	13, 890, 174	69, 661	8, 094	37, 040	24, 527	4, 350	[illegible]
St. Joseph	12, 722, 564	19, 083, 846	108, 009	11, 846	23, 602	72, 561		[illegible]
Tuscola	1, 850, 644	5, 551, 932	78, 939	3, 109	13, 558	62, 272	1, 215	[illegible]
Van Buren	12, 880, 480	12, 880, 480	118, 046	6, 322	15, 000	96, 724		[illegible]
Washtenaw	11, 166, 346	33, 499, 038	108, 464	22, 062	42, 664	43, 738		[illegible]
Wayne	27, 221, 630	96, 054, 196	1, 071, 079	53, 000	197, 480	820, 500	400, 000	[illegible]
Wexford	931, 279	931, 279	13, 110		4, 691	8, 419		[illegible]

(a) No report.

STATE OF MINNESOTA.

Counties.	VALUATION.		TAXATION, NOT NATIONAL.				PUBLIC DEBT.	
	Assessed valuation of real and personal estate.	True valuation of real and personal estate.	All.	State.	County.	Town, city, &c.	County.	Town, city, &c.
	Dollars.	*Dollars.*	*Dollars.*	*Dollars.*	*Dollars.*	*Dollars.*	*Dollars.*	*Dollars.*
The State	84, 135, 332	228, 909, 500	2, 646, 372	511, 126	1, 070, 944	1, 065, 302	472, 694	[illegible]
Aitkin	45, 000	750, 573						
Anoka	854, 354	2, 179, 542	25, 748	4, 260	10, 798	10, 681	11, 929	[illegible]
Becker	373, 000	750, 573						
Beltrami	53, 000	112, 276						
Benton	482, 279	546, 151	12, 175	[illegible]	[illegible]	[illegible]		[illegible]

:E LXXXIII.—*Valuation, Taxation, and Public Indebtedness by Counties*—1870—Cont'd.

STATE OF MINNESOTA—Continued.

nnties.	VALUATION.		TAXATION, NOT NATIONAL.				PUBLIC DEBT.	
	Assessed valuation of real and personal estate.	True valuation of real and personal estate.	All.	State.	County.	Town, city, &c.	County.	Town, city, &c.
	Dollars.	*Dollars.*	*Dollars.*	*Dollars.*	*Dollars.*	*Dollars.*	*Dollars.*	*Dollars.*
one (a)	....	....	....	....	....	....	....	....
:arth	3,548,869	10,214,178	90,192	17,744	53,334	19,114	62,333	166,224
ı	715,024	2,161,440	24,704	3,566	7,851	13,287	2,300	2,396
n	110,970	221,940	....	....	....	....	....	....
r	1,265,394	4,430,230	36,522	6,327	15,185	15,010	10,330	4,589
....	105,000	115,862	....	....	....	....	....	....
ewa (a)	....	....	....	....	....	....	....	....
go	958,188	2,697,084	18,886	6,284	6,289	6,313	....	....
....	2,023	3,860	....	....	....	....	....	....
wood (a)	....	....	....	....	....	....	....	....
Wing	100,000	163,664	800	200	600	....	....	....
a	3,795,615	9,123,030	137,200	18,978	37,956	80,266	60,000	130,000
....	2,626,379	4,864,084	49,513	8,169	16,369	24,975	3,000	91,000
as	678,916	1,835,532	14,097	3,393	6,789	3,915	1,995	....
ult	1,100,435	4,029,792	36,938	5,502	9,903	21,533	....	33,909
re	4,030,366	11,798,390	56,397	20,151	32,252	3,994	12,500	61,000
rn	1,619,284	4,234,492	43,077	6,364	11,454	25,259	....	65,000
ue.	4,755,423	11,883,754	142,742	23,777	52,294	66,671	26,669	42,574
(a)	....	....	....	....	....	....	....	....
pin	6,532,049	16,446,212	350,549	32,660	224,160	93,729	53,000	310,000
on	2,038,636	6,142,752	42,370	10,193	10,193	21,984	....	....
....	129,382	648,070	3,682	647	2,071	964	1,150	....
....	70,000	120,260	....	....	....	....	....	....
on	128,043	442,756	4,980	640	3,700	640	4,700	....
ec	169,931	571,282	1,638	862	776	....	....	....
yohi	97,413	1,015,534	2,922	682	974	1,266	125	....
i Parle (a)	....	....	....	....	....	....	....	....
....	35,147	99,202	550	172	137	241	....	....
ur	1,508,984	3,683,750	36,330	6,822	12,264	17,244	....	5,500
ı	143,000	1,091,402	7,035	1,135	4,400	1,500	3,000	3,800
d	787,623	2,132,688	17,733	3,938	7,870	5,945	300	1,500
r	571,000	1,940,704	14,307	2,946	5,597	5,764	....	....
Lac	285,717	934,100	3,956	1,417	1,417	1,122	....	....
galia	239,132	478,264	3,934	1,181	2,000	753	....	....
ion	578,509	2,802,526	11,419	2,893	6,941	1,585	7,000	....
....	2,326,385	6,159,658	81,000	9,820	19,637	51,523	13,000	24,250
y (a)	....	....	....	....	....	....	....	....
t	1,544,721	4,142,602	39,453	6,724	18,826	13,903	1,200	15,000
(a)	....	....	....	....	....	....	....	....
d	4,518,616	12,032,368	120,045	31,649	18,073	70,323	....	22,000
Tail (a)	....	....	....	....	....	....	....	....
na (a)	....	....	....	....	....	....	....	....
....	335,432	486,184	8,387	1,677	3,020	3,690	....	....
....	348,479	1,111,032	11,587	1,743	4,917	4,927	....	....
y	8,808,567	25,816,920	406,762	78,167	202,689	125,906	100,411	812,014
od	467,204	1,342,572	8,439	2,336	4,672	1,431	....	....
le	225,143	1,209,252	6,084	926	4,165	993	1,000	....
....	3,365,075	8,737,906	62,663	15,790	25,264	21,609	....	10,200
a)	....	....	....	....	....	....	....	....
....	1,361,875	3,460,992	41,409	6,809	19,747	14,853	6,600	....
rne	468,998	1,277,612	14,712	2,591	6,218	5,903	....	....
....	873,978	2,566,300	32,460	4,474	6,495	21,491	6,000	11,000
s	2,178,965	5,992,280	77,459	10,894	23,968	42,597	27,600	24,900
....	2,042,397	4,896,666	49,004	8,857	16,858	23,289	....	28,000
s	59,690	118,380	....	....	....	....	....	....
is	220,693	2,043,087	7,955	1,038	4,663	2,254	3,605	1,607
....	244,080	962,368	5,985	1,217	2,437	2,331	302	....
rse	7,900	16,870	....	....	....	....	....	....
haw	3,900,000	7,418,044	119,000	22,000	32,000	65,000	5,000	51,000
a	7,500	15,640	....	....	....	....	....	....
a	1,241,862	3,225,322	36,651	6,209	13,150	17,292	1,084	8,000
ngton	3,003,421	8,026,898	87,577	15,022	30,035	42,520	45,000	14,180
wan	211,451	937,694	3,250	1,057	1,536	666	....	....
ı	90,800	180,720	....	....	....	....	....	....
a	4,673,612	13,051,776	150,804	23,369	51,411	85,114	....	23,000
t	1,100,460	3,011,798	18,101	5,502	9,368	3,231	1,500	2,700
stributed counties.	....	....	60,070	60,070	....	....	....	....

(a) No report.

TABLE LXXXIII.—*Valuation, Taxation, and Public Indebtedness by Counties*—1870—Cont'd.

STATE OF MISSISSIPPI.

Counties.	VALUATION.		TAXATION, NOT NATIONAL.				PUBLIC DEBT.	
	Assessed valuation of real and personal estate.	True valuation of real and personal estate.	All.	State.	County.	Town, city, &c.	County.	Town, city, &c.
	Dollars.	*Dollars.*	*Dollars.*	*Dollars.*	*Dollars.*	*Dollars.*	*Dollars.*	*Dollars.*
The State..	177, 278, 890	209, 197, 345	3, 736, 432	1, 309, 655	2, 299, 699	127, 078	656, 565	141, [illegible]
Adams	5, 912, 426	6, 000, 000	120, 514	33, 290	59, 224	28, 000	68, 877	[illegible]
Alcorn	2, 239, 014	2, 239, 014	36, 661	14, 271	22, 390			
Amite	2, 654, 338	2, 654, 338	61, 516	16, 549	42, 467	2, 500	4, 000	
Attala	2, 418, 678	2, 872, 720	40, 383	16, 197	24, 186		6, 000	
Bolivar	4, 669, 040	4, 333, 977	80, 563	28, 037	52, 526		6, 500	
Calhoun	1, 377, 830	4, 500, 000	23, 563	9, 785	13, 778		5, 000	
Carroll	4, 102, 564	4, 856, 000	67, 851	26, 146	41, 705			
Chickasaw	4, 033, 780	4, 033, 780	69, 352	25, 992	43, 360		7, 000	
Choctaw	2, 347, 262	2, 364, 006	57, 450	16, 374	41, 076			
Claiborne	3, 734, 092	3, 772, 020	75, 475	23, 090	49, 475	3, 000	5, 000	4, [illegible]
Clark	1, 977, 910	2, 333, 575	45, 416	12, 749	29, 667	3, 000	17, 000	3, [illegible]
Coahoma	3, 567, 577	4, 100, 460	61, 318	21, 183	40, 135		29, 608	
Copiah	4, 367, 800	4, 367, 878	92, 427	26, 801	64, 426	1, 200	2, 500	
Covington	497, 034	497, 034	13, 667	3, 727	9, 940		2, 000	
De Soto	8, 607, 150	8, 607, 150	155, 690	52, 189	103, 501			
Franklin	933, 034	1, 060, 412	15, 951	6, 621	9, 330			
Greene	158, 392	158, 392	3, 399	1, 340	2, 059			
Grenada	1, 926, 226	1, 926, 226	48, 693	12, 503	36, 190			
Hancock	785, 044	784, 146	12, 503	5, 635	6, 868			
Harrison	1, 208, 492	1, 567, 450	12, 954	6, 912	6, 042			
Hinds	7, 397, 322	9, 486, 776	140, 204	36, 986	83, 218	20, 000	50, 000	
Holmes	4, 615, 570	5, 413, 514	91, 143	29, 679	58, 464	3, 000	18, 000	1, 100
Issaquena	2, 629, 748	2, 629, 748	122, 622	15, 930	105, 192	1, 500		
Itawamba	1, 164, 856	1, 178, 900	19, 484	7, 834	11, 650		5, 000	
Jackson	976, 410	1, 000, 000	13, 531	6, 208	7, 323			
Jasper	1, 089, 672	1, 090, 229	13, 236	7, 788	5, 448			
Jefferson	2, 356, 114	2, 356, 114	65, 780	15, 656	47, 124	3, 000	7, 500	
Jones	199, 520	200, 000	2, 243	997	1, 246			
Kemper	1, 343, 530	2, 000, 000	22, 326	9, 901	12, 425		7, 500	
Lafayette	3, 339, 716	3, 339, 716	48, 859	21, 312	25, 047	2, 500	5, 000	
Lauderdale	2, 804, 944	2, 804, 944	84, 222	17, 516	61, 706	5, 000	5, 000	1, 000
Lawrence	796, 966	1, 917, 084	18, 935	5, 980	11, 955	1, 000		
Leake	1, 299, 698	1, 299, 698	27, 836	8, 982	15, 854	3, 000	3, 000	
Lee	2, 559, 254	2, 972, 413	45, 938	16, 508	29, 430		37, 000	
Lincoln	1, 546, 722	1, 546, 722	29, 635	10, 303	19, 332			
Lowndes	6, 215, 131	6, 749, 043	147, 612	38, 739	88, 873	20, 000	210, 000	100, 000
Madison	4, 694, 480	6, 066, 125	104, 672	29, 256	70, 416	5, 000	18, 000	
Marion	392, 666	392, 666	10, 349	2, 989	7, 360			
Marshall	6, 609, 988	6, 609, 988	126, 174	41, 768	76, 658	6, 748	10, 000	
Monroe	3, 876, 604	4, 473, 262	85, 484	26, 213	54, 271	5, 000	2, 500	
Neshoba	921, 378	921, 378	21, 066	6, 630	13, 436	1, 000	6, 900	
Newton	1, 103, 027	1, 213, 329	16, 648	5, 515	11, 133		12, 000	
Noxubee	3, 930, 064	5, 704, 250	82, 719	26, 664	53, 055	3, 000	5, 000	3, 000
Oktibbeha	1, 894, 164	2, 781, 253	51, 930	14, 046	37, 884		5, 000	
Panola	5, 001, 366	5, 001, 368	58, 192	32, 185	25, 007	1, 000		
Perry	256, 338	256, 338	4, 281	2, 038	2, 243			
Pike	2, 838, 888	2, 838, 888	57, 716	16, 554	41, 162		3, 500	
Pontotoc	3, 461, 255	3, 701, 079	55, 433	22, 313	33, 120			
Prentiss	1, 630, 384	2, 065, 087	25, 574	10, 900	14, 674			
Rankin	2, 660, 924	2, 743, 440	56, 667	17, 118	39, 249	300	3, 000	200
Scott	1, 220, 828	1, 487, 310	26, 200	8, 078	17, 522	600	3, 000	300
Simpson	434, 274	696, 560	9, 787	3, 709	6, 078		4, 000	
Smith	750, 320	750, 320	9, 266	5, 515	3, 751		4, 750	350
Sunflower	1, 782, 513	4, 068, 670	24, 182	10, 814	13, 368			
Tallahatchie	1, 361, 530	3, 228, 400	24, 092	9, 115	14, 977			
Tippah	3, 443, 262	6, 272, 817	64, 461	23, 528	40, 933		16, 000	
Tishemingo	1, 178, 038	4, 619, 062	19, 518	7, 738	11, 780			
Tunica	2, 934, 012	3, 080, 737	31, 630	16, 960	14, 670		20, 000	
Warren	9, 815, 338	9, 815, 338	227, 167	58, 505	163, 432	5, 230	23, 550	6, 500
Washington	4, 218, 994	6, 191, 200	77, 357	25, 729	50, 628	1, 000	3, 700	500
Wayne	355, 938	356, 684	5, 005	3, 225	1, 780			
Wilkinson	2, 212, 616	2, 212, 616	88, 760	15, 351	71, 909	1, 500	4, 200	1, 350
Winston	1, 298, 602	1, 298, 602	17, 029	8, 913	8, 116		5, 000	
Yalabusha	2, 502, 524	4, 133, 707	35, 028	16, 260	18, 768		5, 000	
Yazoo	6, 645, 716	7, 188, 392	140, 497	40, 810	99, 687			
Not distributed among counties			191, 596	191, 596				

: LXXXIII.—*Valuation, Taxation, and Public Indebtedness by Counties*—1870—Cont'd.

STATE OF MISSOURI.

...nties.	VALUATION.		TAXATION, NOT NATIONAL.				PUBLIC DEBT.	
	Assessed valuation of real and personal estate.	True valuation of real and personal estate.	All.	State.	County.	Town, city, &c.	County.	Town, city, &c.
	Dollars.	*Dollars.*	*Dollars.*	*Dollars.*	*Dollars.*	*Dollars.*	*Dollars.*	*Dollars.*
State....	556,129,960	1,284,922,897	13,908,498	2,718,697	4,402,227	6,787,574	11,819,012	17,224,853
....	2,535,901	10,202,000	41,350	12,680	22,679	6,000	76,000	....
v	5,483,340	8,000,000	107,171	27,416	54,755	25,000	115,000	....
on	2,673,778	5,000,000	42,797	13,369	24,402	4,936	3,000	....
n	5,102,127	8,503,407	68,402	25,510	62,952	....	1,500	....
....	1,205,492	2,500,000	19,572	6,027	6,904	6,641	20	....
....	1,466,220	3,000,000	34,854	7,331	26,199	1,324	10,000	....
....	5,506,256	8,000,000	126,637	27,331	55,028	44,078	20,000	....
....	3,225,796	4,000,000	51,729	16,129	21,600	14,000	....	....
er	1,554,295	2,106,000	11,784	7,771	4,013	....	1,942	....
....	6,363,103	15,000,000	212,555	31,815	142,740	38,000	429,500	10,000
an.......	12,175,579	20,000,000	1,218,747	60,877	182,870	975,000	460,000	500,000
....	787,148	1,100,000	7,878	3,943	3,935	....	60,000	....
ll	3,237,374	7,000,000	58,472	16,186	23,517	18,709	25,000	....
ay	5,317,779	10,000,000	141,241	26,588	81,079	33,574	456,000	7,500
a........	1,156,128	1,500,000	19,089	5,780	11,102	2,207	7,981	....
irardeau.	4,200,135	10,105,000	76,465	21,000	17,000	38,465	3,500	226,000
....	4,246,574	9,000,000	83,495	21,232	39,469	22,794	104,000	20,900
....	516,588	980,000	14,802	2,582	12,220	....	24,000	....
....	7,068,736	12,000,000	199,316	35,360	110,456	53,500	20,600	282,500
....	1,455,747	2,000,000	24,529	7,378	13,824	3,327	5,700	....
on.......	4,342,547	9,500,000	130,073	21,712	63,361	45,000	241,000	25,000
an	986,948	1,800,000	16,742	4,934	6,845	4,963	10,000	....
....	4,270,535	10,560,000	67,129	21,352	44,777	1,000	125,000	14,000
....	6,291,235	8,000,000	145,556	28,556	67,000	50,000	150,000	....
....	4,302,905	8,000,000	75,327	21,414	33,038	20,875	14,000	....
....	4,115,612	7,000,000	92,321	18,321	21,000	53,000	29,000	29,700
....	5,856,362	10,000,000	176,614	29,281	79,603	67,730	421,264	171,350
rd	2,344,233	2,800,000	31,132	11,721	13,411	6,000	....	....
....	2,069,116	3,000,000	33,853	10,345	10,335	13,173	6,000	....
....	1,364,120	2,300,000	28,841	6,820	16,265	5,756	7,200	....
s........	3,678,833	9,000,000	74,795	18,394	31,401	25,000	150,000	....
b	2,203,193	5,000,000	55,915	11,015	32,600	12,300	7,000	....
....	1,083,648	1,900,000	29,913	5,418	11,738	12,757	3,657	....
s	329,015	1,000,000	6,253	2,208	4,045	....	10,808	....
n	678,677	1,650,000	12,804	3,394	8,000	1,500	17,000	2,500
in.......	4,863,449	15,550,000	89,837	24,317	65,520	....	283,191	....
ade	2,643,087	5,650,770	22,259	13,214	9,045	....	....	....
....	2,489,301	4,500,000	48,164	12,196	16,800	19,168	....	....
....	6,281,339	9,500,000	91,357	31,692	21,665	38,000	15,000	18,500
y	2,396,127	4,000,000	79,388	11,980	46,408	21,000	200,000	50,000
on.......	4,740,321	7,500,000	78,646	23,701	34,697	20,248	4,000	1,600
....	6,133,822	9,000,000	86,591	30,769	33,822	22,000	100,000	....
y	1,221,911	2,000,000	17,446	6,109	7,493	3,844	1,000	....
....	4,056,724	8,000,000	83,751	20,283	59,468	4,000	37,500	....
d	5,429,003	9,000,000	117,677	27,145	69,727	20,805	280,000	....
....	496,048	1,000,000	6,960	2,480	2,480	2,000	1,715	....
....	1,952,167	12,406,100	18,867	9,761	9,106	....	18,000	....
n	16,103,332	38,000,000	617,179	80,516	95,535	441,128	146,086	850,000
....	4,177,446	6,000,000	90,830	20,887	40,421	29,531	20,000	20,000
on.......	3,686,599	8,108,520	72,794	18,432	35,791	18,571	57,842	920
n	7,879,509	18,000,000	156,214	39,398	66,816	50,000	100,000	125,000
....	3,038,515	4,500,100	54,760	15,292	39,468	....	14,000	....
e	1,397,172	3,000,000	24,898	6,985	12,506	5,407	110,000	....
tte	8,357,976	20,000,000	278,856	41,789	186,386	50,681	959,900	335,000
aco	2,210,646	3,000,000	39,148	11,089	8,845	19,214	....	....
....	4,784,225	13,206,000	97,789	23,921	67,868	6,000	50,000	13,000
a	3,827,350	10,000,000	38,345	19,136	18,584	625	7,366	....
....	3,264,709	6,500,000	66,740	16,370	16,370	34,000	52,000	....
ston.....	4,602,531	7,000,000	156,785	23,012	68,919	64,854	104,894	47,000
....	4,973,880	10,000,000	157,439	24,869	82,076	50,494	320,579	66,000
on	1,836,411	8,210,000	26,682	9,182	15,000	2,500	22,000	....
....	1,047,584	1,600,000	11,547	5,236	3,311	3,000	3,000	....
....	8,287,875	15,750,000	201,439	41,439	60,000	100,000	35,000	425,000
ald	790,573	1,500,000	12,610	3,952	5,100	3,758	4,000	....
....	2,269,391	4,000,000	72,020	11,346	47,665	13,615	203,000	....
....	1,498,940	2,100,000	18,265	7,518	6,739	4,008	....	....
ippi	*1,079,636*	*4,125,000*	13,508	5,398	8,000	200	....	....

TABLE LXXXIII.—*Valuation, Taxation, and Public Indebtedness by Counties—1870*—Cont'd.

STATE OF MISSOURI—Continued.

Counties.	VALUATION.		TAXATION, NOT NATIONAL.				PUBLIC DEBT.	
	Assessed valuation of real and personal estate.	True valuation of real and personal estate.	All.	State.	County.	Town, city, &c.	County.	Town, city, &c.
	Dollars.	*Dollars.*	*Dollars.*	*Dollars.*	*Dollars.*	*Dollars.*	*Dollars.*	*Dollars.*
Moniteau	3,502,529	7,000,000	74,012	17,512	26,500	30,000	102,000	....
Monroe	4,855,009	10,550,000	87,314	24,314	57,000	6,000	251,800	10,000
Montgomery	3,126,315	9,550,000	60,631	15,631	20,000	25,000	16,000	....
Morgan	2,348,310	3,500,000	54,209	13,551	27,158	13,500	112,000	....
New Madrid	845,952	5,650,000	18,220	4,229	13,111	880	25,500	....
Newton	2,155,565	4,600,000	30,611	11,011	8,100	11,500	....	....
Nodaway	5,501,332	8,400,000	107,427	27,506	49,071	30,850	85,000	....
Oregon	693,117	1,125,000	8,660	3,465	4,820	375	6,600	....
Osage	1,892,936	3,000,000	36,260	9,454	18,738	8,074	10,000	....
Ozark	183,550	500,000	5,102	917	3,597	588	5,300	[illegible]
Pemiscot	300,647	850,000	4,008	1,503	2,505	....	....	....
Perry	2,220,711	4,650,000	26,603	11,103	8,500	7,000	7,000	400
Pettis	6,277,908	12,000,000	224,754	31,389	123,365	70,000	560,000	....
Phelps	2,871,494	5,000,000	77,263	14,357	37,906	25,000	50,000	....
Pike	7,331,100	15,550,000	128,256	36,655	66,946	24,655	460,921	145,000
Platte	6,362,353	13,000,000	629,157	31,811	62,346	535,000	339,567	....
Polk	2,735,520	4,500,000	45,368	13,677	13,691	18,000	5,000	....
Pulaski	712,715	1,000,000	8,908	3,563	3,563	1,782	8,500	....
Putnam	2,568,378	3,500,000	65,119	12,841	39,778	12,500	13,800	....
Ralls	4,331,047	10,250,000	103,655	21,655	25,000	57,000	25,750	75,000
Randolph	3,466,559	6,000,000	83,020	17,332	34,688	31,000	26,000	....
Ray	6,699,964	10,000,000	95,290	33,490	43,197	18,603	215,576	....
Reynolds	904,241	1,000,000	15,161	4,521	10,640	....	14,000	....
Ripley	769,824	1,500,000	15,070	3,850	11,220	....	24,000	....
Saline	9,210,870	13,000,000	138,854	46,054	50,000	42,800	21,600	22,000
Schuyler	1,965,867	8,550,000	56,150	9,829	34,313	12,008	49,404	4,900
Scotland	2,038,826	8,250,000	53,944	10,194	43,750	....	38,000	16,500
Scott	1,964,341	7,650,000	19,642	9,821	9,821	....	....	....
Shannon	778,222	1,850,000	17,921	3,891	14,030	....	8,000	....
Shelby	2,655,213	8,850,000	29,213	13,276	15,937	....	3,448	....
St. Charles	6,716,860	15,650,000	108,584	33,744	47,840	27,000	37,000	25,730
St. Clair	2,653,422	4,000,000	63,834	13,297	28,187	22,350	9,000	....
Ste. Genevieve	1,647,598	4,550,000	35,113	8,237	26,876	....	....	10,000
St. François	1,970,685	12,550,000	29,654	9,853	19,801	....	....	....
St. Louis	187,345,420	511,035,000	4,523,861	936,727	623,849	2,963,285	2,962,000	13,613,000
Stoddard	1,245,069	9,550,000	24,225	6,225	8,000	10,000	26,000	....
Stone	274,379	500,000	5,456	1,430	2,826	1,200	....	....
Sullivan	2,325,895	4,000,000	45,095	11,629	22,138	11,328	1,000	....
Taney	288,721	500,000	6,203	1,443	3,760	1,000	10,600	....
Texas	906,820	2,500,000	19,009	4,534	9,975	4,500	5,000	....
Vernon	3,012,752	10,000,000	65,091	15,063	30,028	20,000	21,300	....
Warren	2,161,706	8,650,000	51,409	10,808	25,814	14,787	11,801	....
Washington	2,398,300	4,550,000	27,882	11,991	14,991	900	....	....
Wayne	1,296,243	5,550,000	19,507	6,485	13,022	....	13,400	....
Webster	1,559,201	3,000,000	25,427	7,796	11,342	6,289	11,000	....
Worth	1,210,787	1,600,000	20,593	6,053	9,540	5,000	....	....
Wright	833,580	1,700,000	9,730	4,167	3,063	2,500	1,200	....

TERRITORY OF MONTANA.

Counties.	VALUATION.		TAXATION, NOT NATIONAL.				PUBLIC DEBT.	
	Assessed valuation of real and personal estate.	True valuation of real and personal estate.	All.	Territory.	County.	Town, city, &c.	County.	Town, city, &c.
	Dollars.	*Dollars.*	*Dollars.*	*Dollars.*	*Dollars.*	*Dollars.*	*Dollars.*	*Dollars.*
The Territory	9,943,411	15,184,522	198,527	38,131	157,396	3,000	270,219	2,500
Beaver Head	406,212	528,511	8,937	1,625	7,312	....	7,000	....
Big Horn (a)	....	....	....	....	....	....	....	....
Choteau	345,000	475,000	4,324	1,002	3,322	....	1,750	....

(a) No report.

LE LXXXIII.—*Valuation, Taxation, and Public Indebtedness by Counties*—1870—Cont'd.

TERRITORY OF MONTANA—Continued.

Counties.	VALUATION. Assessed valuation of real and personal estate.	VALUATION. True valuation of real and personal estate.	TAXATION, NOT NATIONAL. All.	TAXATION, NOT NATIONAL. Territory.	TAXATION, NOT NATIONAL. County.	TAXATION, NOT NATIONAL. Town, city, &c.	PUBLIC DEBT. County.	PUBLIC DEBT. Town, city, &c.
	Dollars.	*Dollars.*	*Dollars.*	*Dollars.*	*Dollars.*	*Dollars.*	*Dollars.*	*Dollars.*
son	100, 300	144, 400	....	....	....	....	....	....
r Lodge	1, 431, 678	1, 500, 000	23, 617	4, 435	19, 182	....	92, 006	....
atin	715, 893	894, 866	13, 869	2, 863	11, 006	....	20, 000	....
rson	500, 000	500, 000	6, 515	1, 861	4, 654	....	4, 763	....
is & Clarke	3, 438, 484	5, 242, 430	79, 665	13, 745	65, 920	....	70, 000	....
ison	1, 604, 691	4, 131, 648	43, 800	10, 800	30, 000	3, 000	43, 700	2, 500
gher	696, 610	696, 610	7, 000	....	7, 000	....	20, 000	....
oula	706, 543	1, 071, 057	10, 800	1, 800	9, 000	....	17, 000	....

STATE OF NEBRASKA.

Counties.	VALUATION. Assessed valuation of real and personal estate.	VALUATION. True valuation of real and personal estate.	TAXATION, NOT NATIONAL. All.	TAXATION, NOT NATIONAL. State.	TAXATION, NOT NATIONAL. County.	TAXATION, NOT NATIONAL. Town, city, &c.	PUBLIC DEBT. County.	PUBLIC DEBT. Town, city, &c.
	Dollars.	*Dollars.*	*Dollars.*	*Dollars.*	*Dollars.*	*Dollars.*	*Dollars.*	*Dollars.*
e State	54, 584, 616	69, 277, 483	1, 027, 327	262, 505	753, 022	11, 800	1, 769, 564	72, 400
ms	89, 876	89, 876	539	539	....	....	....	....
kbird (a)	....	....	....	....	....	....	....	....
alo	784, 569	784, 569	12, 976	4, 752	8, 224	....	800	....
	1, 103, 849	1, 471, 796	2, 736	1, 156	1, 580	....	....	....
er	144, 893	217, 341	1, 738	869	869	....	....	....
	3, 109, 856	3, 199, 856	45, 500	18, 500	27, 000	....	200, 000	50, 000
ar	328, 000	437, 333	4, 670	1, 970	2, 700	....	....	....
yenne	209, 260	279, 013	19, 800	2, 600	17, 200	....	700	....
(a)	....	....	....	....	....	....	....	....
ax	1, 123, 409	1, 497, 878	17, 952	3, 328	14, 024	....	17, 060	....
ding	1, 282, 653	1, 282, 653	14, 659	1, 479	13, 180	....	9, 200	....
ota	610, 730	814, 206	12, 824	3, 664	9, 160	....	16, 000	5, 000
son (a)	....	....	....	....	....	....	....	....
n	492, 497	656, 662	14, 560	1, 360	13, 200	....	700	....
ge	2, 776, 000	2, 776, 000	74, 319	15, 500	58, 819	....	170, 000	....
glas	13, 541, 707	18, 055, 609	284, 239	74, 197	210, 042	....	410, 917	....
nore (a)	....	....	....	....	....	....	....	....
nklin (a)	....	....	....	....	....	....	....	....
e	1, 227, 265	1, 636, 355	24, 544	6, 136	18, 408	....	800	....
nt (a)	....	....	....	....	....	....	....	....
	858, 405	1, 287, 607	20, 105	4, 842	15, 263	....	15, 000	....
milton	533, 164	533, 164	3, 198	3, 198	....	....	....	....
rison (a)	....	....	....	....	....	....	....	....
kson (a)	....	....	....	....	....	....	....	....
erson	723, 198	964, 237	13, 169	2, 894	6, 275	4, 000	800	2, 400
nson	966, 994	1, 289, 325	17, 642	5, 883	11, 759	....	4, 932	....
rney (a)	....	....	....	....	....	....	....	....
caster	1, 505, 790	1, 505, 790	50, 446	7, 096	38, 350	5, 000	61, 000	....
u qui Court	62, 915	62, 915	1, 500	314	1, 186	....	480	....
coln	2, 061, 569	2, 748, 758	33, 004	10, 327	22, 677	....	11, 000	....
n (a)	....	....	....	....	....	....	....	....
lison	143, 236	143, 236	696	200	496	....	....	....
rick	1, 155, 700	1, 409, 600	5, 282	3, 000	2, 282	....	600	....
roe (a)	....	....	....	....	....	....	....	....
maha	2, 778, 208	3, 707, 610	56, 952	16, 669	40, 283	....	....	....
kolls (a)	....	....	....	....	....	....	....	....
	4, 834, 389	6, 445, 852	23, 000	7, 000	16, 000	....	390, 000	....
nee	1, 161, 258	1, 548, 344	10, 200	3, 200	7, 000	....	27, 500	....
ce	21, 960	21, 960	131	131	....	....	....	....
te	1, 174, 296	2, 348, 592	21, 476	6, 956	13, 800	720	23, 600	....

(a) No report.

TABLE LXXXIII.—*Valuation, Taxation, and Public Indebtedness by Counties*—1870—Cont'd.

STATE OF NEBRASKA—Continued.

Counties.	VALUATION.		TAXATION, NOT NATIONAL.				PUBLIC DEBT.	
	Assessed valuation of real and personal estate.	True valuation of real and personal estate.	All.	State.	County.	Town, city, &c.	County.	Town, city, &c.
	Dollars.	*Dollars.*	*Dollars.*	*Dollars.*	*Dollars.*	*Dollars.*	*Dollars.*	*Dollars.*
Polk (a)								
Richardson	4, 125, 000	5, 500, 000	73, 300	15, 300	58, 000		38, 700	
Saline	487, 845	650, 460	10, 244	2, 927	7, 317		300	
Sarpy	1, 217, 628	1, 217, 628	32, 659	8, 659	24, 000		18, 000	
Saunders	1, 342, 684	2, 000, 000	42, 716	6, 039	34, 597	2, 080	40, 000	15, 000
Seward	197, 005	295, 507	6, 000	6, 000			75, 300	
Stanton	252, 073	300, 000	5, 960	1, 279	4, 681		150	
Taylor (a)								
Washington	1, 702, 767	1, 702, 767	65, 096	12, 359	52, 737		235, 005	
Wayne	219, 984	219, 984	1, 319	1, 319				
Webster (a)								
York	143, 984	175, 000	2, 176	863	1, 313			

(a) No report.

STATE OF NEVADA.

Counties.	VALUATION.		TAXATION, NOT NATIONAL.				PUBLIC DEBT.	
	Assessed valuation of real and personal estate.	True valuation of real and personal estate.	All.	State.	County.	Town, city, &c.	County.	Town, city, &c.
	Dollars.	*Dollars.*	*Dollars.*	*Dollars.*	*Dollars.*	*Dollars.*	*Dollars.*	*Dollars.*
The State	25, 740, 973	31, 134, 012	820, 308	298, 411	498, 062	23, 835	987, 423	355, 776
Churchill	393, 627	524, 836	10, 923	4, 428	6, 495		11, 000	
Douglas	762, 864	762, 864	24, 793	9, 536	15, 257		12, 000	
Elko	2, 264, 724	3, 397, 086	82, 707	29, 507	53, 200		90, 329	
Esmeralda	880, 682	1, 174, 242	29, 723	9, 908	19, 815		22, 500	
Humboldt	1, 751, 348	2, 335, 131	49, 038	19, 703	29, 335		25, 000	
Lander	4, 766, 947	4, 766, 947	132, 283	53, 628	54, 820	23, 835		
Lincoln	253, 474	253, 474	7, 351	3, 549	3, 802		9, 000	
Lyon	1, 546, 023	1, 546, 023	51, 866	19, 325	32, 541		27, 200	
Nye	967, 707	967, 707	32, 176	10, 887	21, 289		32, 107	
Ormsby	1, 572, 434	2, 096, 578	68, 640	19, 655	48, 985		236, 563	
Roop (a)								
Storey	4, 757, 961	6, 343, 948	155, 962	54, 916	101, 046		430, 000	327, 776
Washoe	2, 397, 300	2, 397, 300	65, 926	26, 970	38, 956		21, 844	
White Pine	3, 425, 882	4, 567, 876	108, 920	36, 399	72, 521		63, 880	28, 000

(a) No report.

LE LXXXIII.—*Valuation, Taxation, and Public Indebtedness by Counties*—1870—Cont'd.

STATE OF NEW HAMPSHIRE.

Counties.	VALUATION.		TAXATION, NOT NATIONAL.				PUBLIC DEBT.	
	Assessed valuation of real and personal estate.	True valuation of real and personal estate.	All.	State.	County.	Town, city, &c.	County.	Town, city, &c.
	Dollars.	*Dollars.*	*Dollars.*	*Dollars.*	*Dollars.*	*Dollars.*	*Dollars.*	*Dollars.*
ıe State....	149, 065, 290	252, 624, 112	3, 255, 793	955, 126	318, 666	1, 982, 001	745, 070	7, 590, 434
knap.......	6, 451, 190	10, 751, 983	90, 319	25, 968	15, 000	49, 351	29, 000	441, 620
roll.........	5, 748, 334	10, 457, 441	135, 262	23, 136	24, 325	87, 801	40, 000	384, 751
shire.......	13, 837, 491	23, 062, 485	306, 985	55, 698	35, 000	216, 287	74, 671	627, 145
....	4, 722, 934	11, 176, 643	125, 037	19, 008	16, 500	89, 529	78, 854	249, 315
fton........	15, 872, 157	26, 453, 595	380, 796	62, 832	30, 002	287, 962	114, 500	1, 196, 614
sborough ..	35, 430, 425	59, 050, 708	618, 570	142, 614	43, 149	432, 807	84, 349	1, 213, 970
rimack	19, 964, 590	33, 274, 316	388, 562	81, 408	37, 000	270, 154	58, 853	1, 112, 425
kingham ..	23, 815, 602	39, 691, 670	381, 993	96, 246	67, 000	218, 747	137, 700	1, 214, 088
fford.......	14, 361, 430	23, 935, 710	317, 473	57, 420	30, 690	229, 363	99, 120	770, 856
ivan	8, 861, 737	14, 769, 561	155, 670	35, 670	20, 000	100, 000	27, 323	379, 650
distributed among counties........	....	....	355, 126	355, 126	....	....	....	....

STATE OF NEW JERSEY.

Counties.	VALUATION.		TAXATION, NOT NATIONAL.				PUBLIC DEBT.	
	Assessed valuation of real and personal estate.	True valuation of real and personal estate.	All.	State.	County.	Town, city, &c.	County.	Town, city, &c.
	Dollars.	*Dollars.*	*Dollars.*	*Dollars.*	*Dollars.*	*Dollars.*	*Dollars.*	*Dollars.*
he State....	624, 868, 971	940, 976, 064	7, 416, 724	373, 046	2, 397, 348	4, 646, 330	6, 935, 315	12, 922, 789
antic.......	4, 732, 470	6, 687, 491	36, 767	3, 003	22, 164	11, 600	27, 370	....
gen	26, 820, 026	35, 649, 660	118, 384	14, 515	56, 169	47, 700	523, 100	....
lington.....	32, 615, 883	46, 984, 047	249, 962	18, 093	149, 999	81, 870	254, 400	....
nden	19, 914, 699	31, 328, 534	252, 489	11, 489	121, 000	120, 000	333, 100	214, 000
e May......	3, 800, 810	5, 509, 383	36, 627	2, 228	11, 529	22, 870	....	50, 600
nberland ...	14, 470, 374	21, 776, 415	123, 276	7, 276	60, 000	56, 000	127, 950	....
ex..........	104, 461, 370	160, 269, 082	1, 495, 418	58, 730	453, 027	983, 661	2, 010, 000	3, 110, 000
ucester	14, 090, 600	18, 737, 720	43, 561	8, 561	25, 000	10, 000	....	44, 200
lson........	85, 133, 272	135, 139, 369	2, 395, 378	54, 903	376, 830	1, 963, 645	940, 700	5, 133, 514
nterdon.....	34, 638, 501	48, 142, 051	239, 027	18, 704	140, 561	79, 762	83, 938	....
rcer	36, 698, 639	62, 364, 494	304, 780	19, 064	67, 616	218, 100	298, 000	587, 000
dlesex	33, 638, 839	53, 355, 097	295, 493	15, 316	158, 000	122, 177	569, 052	210, 000
nmouth.....	37, 024, 819	50, 948, 795	203, 904	27, 780	131, 864	44, 260	407, 700	2, 000
ris	27, 326, 757	38, 567, 026	105, 896	16, 105	60, 000	29, 791	62, 136	19, 485
an	5, 395, 341	6, 884, 378	65, 375	3, 375	20, 000	42, 000	10, 000	20, 000
saic	26, 365, 584	43, 177, 638	405, 000	24, 205	120, 000	260, 795	250, 000	743, 000
m..........	22, 354, 567	32, 392, 190	144, 874	12, 085	80, 829	51, 960	179, 169	2, 500
erset	22, 469, 420	30, 420, 071	170, 437	15, 571	40, 000	114, 866	75, 000	37, 790
sex	16, 950, 655	22, 446, 043	82, 995	11, 670	38, 866	32, 450	10, 000	....
on	28, 719, 642	50, 219, 382	533, 594	14, 943	232, 324	286, 327	733, 700	2, 678, 700
rren........	27, 237, 703	39, 887, 178	113, 487	15, 430	31, 570	66, 487	40, 000	70, 000

TABLE LXXXIII.—*Valuation, Taxation, and Public Indebtedness by Counties—1870*—Cont'd.

TERRITORY OF NEW MEXICO.

Counties.	VALUATION.		TAXATION, NOT NATIONAL.				PUBLIC DEBT.	
	Assessed valuation of real and personal estate.	True valuation of real and personal estate.	All.	Territory.	County.	Town, city, &c.	County.	Town, city, &c.
	Dollars.	*Dollars.*	*Dollars.*	*Dollars.*	*Dollars.*	*Dollars.*	*Dollars.*	*Dollars.*
The Territory	17,784,014	31,349,793	61,014	34,115	26,101	798	7,560	....
Bernalillo	1,941,645	2,350,000	6,738	3,725	3,013	....	250	....
Colfax	2,503,385	6,171,135	6,105	3,225	2,880	....	1,959	....
Doña Aña	786,493	1,250,000	1,064	853	211	....	....	....
Grant	167,195	1,342,400	428	343	85	....	....	....
Lincoln	258,201	570,351	2,595	1,476	1,119	....	....	....
Mora	1,095,149	2,190,907	4,565	2,153	2,412	....	860	....
Rio Arriba	418,398	675,000	1,688	938	750	....	1,224	....
San Miguel	2,205,850	4,250,000	10,405	6,240	4,165	....	747	....
Santa Aña	309,114	750,000	281	225	56	....	....	....
Santa Fé	2,608,865	4,250,000	15,145	8,034	6,313	798	....	....
Socorro	3,150,984	3,500,000	4,212	2,347	1,865	....	1,000	....
Taos	807,863	1,550,000	3,088	1,756	1,332	....	930	....
Valencia	1,530,672	2,500,000	4,700	2,800	1,900	....	500	....

STATE OF NEW YORK.

Counties.	VALUATION.		TAXATION, NOT NATIONAL.				PUBLIC DEBT.	
	Assessed valuation of real and personal estate.	True valuation of real and personal estate.	All.	State.	County.	Town, city, &c.	County.	Town, city, &c.
	Dollars.	*Dollars.*	*Dollars.*	*Dollars.*	*Dollars.*	*Dollars.*	*Dollars.*	*Dollars.*
The State	1,967,001,185	6,500,841,264	48,550,308	8,720,156	15,102,761	24,727,391	50,679,784	76,719,3[illegible]
Albany	47,669,879	152,055,765	1,722,764	202,552	499,475	1,020,737	1,368,450	2,800,00[illegible]
Allegany	8,538,033	23,893,857	102,885	47,909	19,320	35,656	17,500	....
Broome	8,047,186	21,521,822	194,664	44,356	99,053	51,255	138,920	350,2[illegible]
Cattaraugus	7,537,102	20,620,578	78,675	40,689	30,624	7,362	15,000	....
Cayuga	21,068,698	65,120,255	397,973	124,594	173,015	100,364	154,623	817,05[illegible]
Chautauqua	15,606,765	48,007,170	228,543	87,067	71,629	69,847	....	351,00[illegible]
Chemung	8,483,747	22,374,820	252,123	47,135	94,615	110,373	41,660	34,00[illegible]
Chenango	11,346,922	28,396,584	316,712	58,780	63,023	194,909	136,000	446,00[illegible]
Clinton	5,792,745	12,327,960	190,462	34,781	78,607	77,074	83,450	....
Columbia	21,853,412	45,603,545	359,881	131,288	96,176	132,417	190,000	220,91[illegible]
Cortland	6,953,909	11,374,827	163,965	35,239	105,625	23,101	162,422	129,97[illegible]
Delaware	8,575,096	23,305,734	165,568	49,605	34,289	81,674	20,000	1,014,00[illegible]
Dutchess	29,690,511	90,903,798	463,780	217,412	123,577	122,791	316,800	923,16[illegible]
Erie	52,894,543	162,098,478	2,171,167	297,531	273,490	1,600,146	1,372,100	2,031,5[illegible]
Essex	5,131,258	10,262,516	82,745	28,149	14,490	40,106	96,396	74,8[illegible]
Franklin	5,801,114	17,403,342	71,898	29,980	22,870	19,048	25,000	20,00[illegible]
Fulton	3,483,316	11,714,680	133,598	20,598	69,000	44,000	50,000	20,00[illegible]
Genesee	15,511,112	45,355,321	273,412	82,468	147,211	43,733	109,800	8,00[illegible]
Greene	5,606,576	25,173,279	141,330	29,109	75,599	36,622	503,641	38,40[illegible]
Hamilton	747,160	1,494,320	26,914	2,819	6,847	17,248	40,000	....
Herkimer	9,089,064	30,931,054	183,153	58,575	42,128	82,450	35,000	85,00[illegible]
Jefferson	15,127,745	40,019,235	463,560	88,510	202,371	172,679	862,500	290,00[illegible]
Kings	194,106,451	700,000,000	6,726,548	869,013	1,623,763	4,233,772	4,265,000	20,00[illegible]
Lewis	3,962,902	11,129,312	106,287	23,857	23,183	59,247	2,000	....
Livingston	16,041,631	44,086,217	153,172	81,028	41,480	30,664	....	100,00[illegible]
Madison	11,228,350	13,349,705	206,356	59,518	50,000	96,838	....	1,160,30[illegible]
Monroe	35,806,316	82,561,640	992,704	195,831	305,226	491,647	1,194,100	634,36[illegible]
Montgomery	6,664,002	19,992,006	379,162	48,382	93,901	236,879	232,096	....
New York	928,283,464	3,484,268,700	22,074,594	2,834,501	7,713,607	11,526,486	28,985,800	54,436,18[illegible]
Niagara	15,081,938	44,959,654	252,043	83,086	144,069	24,808	259,000	12,00[illegible]
Oneida	28,748,360	45,912,258	387,480	154,112	80,368	153,000	45,000	733,00[illegible]
Onondaga	32,553,095	99,658,400	814,219	180,277	291,397	342,545	959,500	379,80[illegible]
Ontario	18,424,684	56,948,816	280,695	102,164	147,776	30,755	147,550	14,00[illegible]
Orange	30,414,407	86,267,635	592,275	172,307	142,112	277,[illegible]	[illegible]	863,454
Orleans	10,627,231	31,532,509	149,059	66,852	[illegible]	11,368	[illegible]	....
Oswego	14,965,135	44,094,043	417,708	84,848	150,[illegible]	182,718	[illegible]	[illegible]

LXXXIII.—*Valuation, Taxation, and Public Indebtedness by Counties*—1870—Cont'd.

STATE OF NEW YORK—Continued.

ties.	VALUATION.		TAXATION, NOT NATIONAL.				PUBLIC DEBT.	
	Assessed valuation of real and personal estate.	True valuation of real and personal estate.	All.	State.	County.	Town, city, &c.	County.	Town, city, &c.
	Dollars.	*Dollars.*	*Dollars.*	*Dollars.*	*Dollars.*	*Dollars.*	*Dollars.*	*Dollars.*
....	12, 674, 303	30, 474, 171	282, 223	66, 296	26, 919	189, 008	4, 260	776, 500
....	5, 632, 163	13, 192, 769	63, 089	30, 811	9, 577	22, 701	....	23, 000
....	24, 561, 645	26, 026, 645	210, 137	178, 386	9, 567	22, 184	817, 000	122, 600
ier.....	30, 516, 528	110, 939, 126	904, 738	163, 530	232, 225	508, 983	2, 035, 300	1, 119, 010
id	7, 716, 630	14, 444, 276	290, 623	37, 767	184, 531	68, 325	900, 000	45, 000
d......	6, 912, 530	10, 979, 456	115, 798	50, 248	22, 448	43, 102	22, 684	15, 533
....	12, 683, 725	36, 797, 898	423, 937	71, 264	80, 835	271, 838	901, 967	100, 000
tady ..	5, 550, 301	15, 651, 240	148, 164	29, 837	37, 984	80, 343	....	26, 000
e	5, 293, 821	9, 948, 844	154, 517	33, 452	51, 022	70, 043	57, 400	....
....	3, 784, 076	9, 901, 295	131, 419	16, 624	70, 380	44, 415	64, 300	11, 504
....	9, 685, 738	33, 479, 935	102, 579	56, 278	40, 237	66, 064	19, 800	5, 000
....	13, 738, 127	36, 573, 915	195, 223	60, 779	95, 229	39, 215	50, 000	....
ence ..	16, 005, 328	51, 074, 369	353, 698	86, 296	189, 274	78, 128	500, 000	183, 000
....	11, 431, 957	30, 317, 006	205, 762	83, 700	27, 000	95, 062	....	67, 000
....	2, 995, 464	15, 076, 043	166, 089	17, 702	76, 909	71, 478	60, 000	470, 816
....	5, 534, 529	15, 025, 923	197, 438	32, 571	78, 876	85, 991	400, 000	444, 000
as	7, 680, 703	19, 078, 639	104, 629	43, 120	21, 675	39, 834	7, 652	300, 000
....	13, 358, 355	45, 536, 460	610, 482	91, 988	219, 039	299, 455	1, 491, 500	1, 539, 151
....	2, 793, 295	7, 989, 885	60, 600	15, 000	18, 600	27, 000	25, 500	100, 000
gton ...	15, 215, 096	45, 345, 288	157, 621	65, 791	45, 347	46, 483	63, 000	67, 800
....	14, 799, 455	46, 081, 326	184, 292	85, 889	49, 214	49, 189	17, 700	17, 000
ster ...	50, 928, 652	158, 410, 460	1, 264, 877	329, 677	243, 984	691, 216	768, 554	2, 348, 794
g......	9, 151, 644	27, 717, 538	90, 666	49, 703	17, 700	23, 263	....	....
....	7, 887, 261	14, 858, 922	83, 006	43, 958	27, 212	11, 836	....	....
ributed counties	....	....	270, 567	270, 567	....	....	....	....

STATE OF NORTH CAROLINA.

ties.	VALUATION.		TAXATION, NOT NATIONAL.				PUBLIC DEBT.	
	Assessed valuation of real and personal estate.	True valuation of real and personal estate.	All.	State.	County.	Town, city, &c.	County.	Town, city, &c.
	Dollars.	*Dollars.*	*Dollars.*	*Dollars.*	*Dollars.*	*Dollars.*	*Dollars.*	*Dollars.*
State..	130, 378, 622	260, 757, 244	2, 352, 809	1, 200, 854	923, 604	228, 351	1, 732, 773	841, 218
o......	1, 631, 020	3, 262, 040	21, 393	14, 710	6, 533	150	8, 000	....
er.....	652, 908	1, 305, 816	11, 143	6, 180	4, 963	....	....	....
y	524, 777	1, 049, 554	5, 488	3, 765	1, 723	....	5, 500	....
....	1, 415, 202	2, 830, 404	24, 849	12, 173	12, 676	....	133, 000	....
....	833, 209	1, 666, 418	18, 845	7, 576	11, 269	....	4, 000	....
....	1, 508, 035	3, 016, 070	33, 804	15, 523	16, 425	1, 856	5, 000	1, 694
....	1, 998, 179	3, 996, 358	16, 235	7, 683	6, 597	1, 955	20, 000	....
....	1, 239, 700	2, 479, 400	18, 654	11, 566	6, 088	1, 000	10, 000	1, 000
ck.....	924, 426	1, 848, 852	23, 073	8, 949	14, 124	....	3, 000	3, 000
o	1, 905, 057	3, 810, 114	23, 851	16, 738	7, 113	....	15, 000	1, 500
....	1, 015, 506	2, 031, 012	14, 242	9, 693	4, 049	500	70, 000	200
....	2, 320, 916	4, 641, 832	49, 305	20, 778	28, 527	....	....	....
....	953, 982	1, 907, 964	12, 056	8, 475	3, 581	....	7, 000	200
....	394, 109	788, 218	7, 770	4, 295	3, 475	....	4, 000	....
....	644, 497	1, 288, 994	11, 342	6, 745	3, 097	1, 500	86, 000	2, 500
....	1, 528, 279	3, 056, 558	34, 077	13, 091	20, 986	....	3, 000	....
....	1, 579, 918	3, 159, 836	20, 059	13, 976	5, 883	200	....	....
....	2, 457, 791	4, 915, 582	30, 967	21, 045	9, 922	....	20, 000	....
....	683, 666	1, 367, 332	16, 164	6, 394	9, 770	....	16, 000	....
....	524, 646	1, 049, 292	12, 634	6, 239	6, 395	....	4, 000	1, 000
....	168, 609	337, 218	3, 041	1, 788	1, 253	....	3, 615	....
nd....	1, 420, 450	2, 840, 900	17, 739	12, 129	5, 630	....	....	....
s......	797, 754	1, 595, 508	14, 128	8, 797	5, 331	....	3, 000	....
....	*2, 091, 019*	*4, 182, 038*	39, 923	18, 575	27, 348	14, 000	194, 919	20, 000
nd ...	*2, 163, 705*	*4, 327, 410*	22, 501	22, 501	....	....	100, 000	132, 000

TABLE LXXXIII.—*Valuation, Taxation, and Public Indebtedness by Counties—1870*—Cont'd.

STATE OF NORTH CAROLINA—Continued.

Counties.	VALUATION.		TAXATION, NOT NATIONAL.				PUBLIC DEBT.	
	Assessed valuation of real and personal estate.	True valuation of real and personal estate.	All.	State.	County.	Town, city, &c.	County.	Town, city, &c.
	Dollars.	*Dollars.*	*Dollars.*	*Dollars.*	*Dollars.*	*Dollars.*	*Dollars.*	*Dollars.*
Currituck	581, 899	1, 163, 798	9, 004	6, 238	2, 766	....	88, 000	....
Dare (a)	....	....	....	....	....	....	....	....
Davidson	2, 113, 842	4, 227, 684	28, 248	19, 521	8, 727	....	4, 500	....
Davie	1, 036, 954	2, 073, 908	13, 629	9, 329	4, 000	300	....	....
Duplin	1, 164, 960	2, 329, 920	19, 434	11, 801	7, 633	....	4, 000	....
Edgecombe	4, 525, 041	9, 050, 082	61, 771	41, 357	17, 114	3, 300	12, 000	2, [illegible]
Forsyth	2, 160, 658	4, 321, 316	28, 550	19, 040	6, 688	2, 822	1, 000	1, 5[illegible]
Franklin	1, 822, 006	3, 644, 012	31, 159	15, 601	15, 558	....	8, 000	....
Gaston	1, 149, 302	2, 298, 604	20, 052	13, 298	6, 754	....	5, 375	....
Gates	610, 966	1, 221, 932	16, 911	8, 198	8, 713	....	4, 000	....
Granville	3, 419, 077	6, 838, 154	56, 565	29, 001	23, 564	4, 000	8, 081	4, [illegible]
Greene	1, 209, 873	2, 419, 746	22, 748	11, 833	10, 915	....	....	....
Guilford	3, 695, 151	7, 390, 302	48, 950	34, 379	14, 571	....	40, 000	1, [illegible]
Halifax	2, 713, 175	5, 426, 350	36, 248	23, 893	12, 355	....	21, 000	....
Harnett	745, 815	1, 491, 630	10, 309	6, 905	3, 404	....	600	....
Haywood	804, 192	1, 608, 384	10, 827	7, 452	3, 375	....	3, 350	....
Henderson	1, 083, 707	2, 167, 414	13, 755	9, 370	4, 185	200	....	....
Hertford	1, 068, 105	2, 136, 210	25, 768	9, 901	15, 867	....	8, 000	....
Hyde	576, 776	1, 153, 552	9, 096	6, 154	2, 942	....	6, 000	....
Iredell	2, 039, 936	4, 079, 872	24, 921	16, 678	8, 243	....	....	6, [illegible]
Jackson	564, 857	1, 129, 714	12, 736	5, 130	7, 606	....	3, 800	....
Johnston	1, 888, 022	3, 776, 044	35, 966	18, 260	13, 206	4, 500	22, 500	1, 7[illegible]
Jones	687, 540	1, 375, 080	21, 165	6, 410	14, 755	....	2, 500	....
Lenoir	1, 168, 883	2, 337, 766	21, 738	11, 505	10, 233	....	45, 000	....
Lincoln	1, 370, 792	2, 741, 584	17, 981	12, 042	5, 314	625	8, 000	565
Macon	598, 624	1, 197, 248	16, 877	6, 470	10, 407	....	4, 850	....
Madison	408, 940	817, 880	7, 903	4, 770	3, 133	....	5, 219	....
Martin	1, 578, 912	3, 157, 824	27, 306	14, 368	12, 138	800	900	1, 5[illegible]
McDowell	722, 500	1, 445, 000	9, 704	6, 647	3, 057	....	17, 000	....
Mecklenburg	4, 305, 923	8, 611, 846	120, 604	43, 317	63, 006	14, 281	85, 813	17, 0[illegible]
Mitchell	330, 246	660, 492	6, 178	3, 205	2, 973	....	2, 000	....
Montgomery	719, 080	1, 438, 160	9, 885	6, 746	3, 139	....	10, 000	....
Moore	950, 560	1, 901, 120	12, 845	8, 759	4, 086	....	7, 500	....
Nash	1, 317, 850	2, 635, 700	18, 410	12, 798	5, 612	....	5, 500	....
New Hanover	4, 996, 465	9, 992, 930	236, 750	61, 999	64, 751	110, 000	91, 684	511, 6[illegible]
Northampton	2, 377, 100	4, 754, 200	33, 113	21, 546	11, 567	....	9, 800	....
Onslow	854, 175	1, 708, 350	12, 711	8, 097	4, 614	....	....	....
Orange	2, 040, 903	4, 081, 806	27, 685	18, 805	8, 880	....	....	....
Pasquotank	1, 118, 414	2, 236, 828	21, 702	10, 948	10, 754	....	11, 000	800
Perquimans	946, 114	1, 892, 228	26, 067	8, 617	17, 450	....	4, 100	....
Person	1, 294, 321	2, 588, 642	29, 185	11, 639	17, 546	....	....	....
Pitt	1, 949, 137	3, 898, 274	25, 482	17, 323	8, 159	....	1, 200	....
Polk	425, 878	851, 756	5, 283	3, 703	1, 580	....	1, 600	10
Randolph	2, 322, 805	4, 645, 610	31, 245	19, 406	11, 839	....	5, 000	30, 57[illegible]
Richmond	1, 426, 905	2, 853, 810	25, 099	12, 769	12, 330	....	76, 000	610
Robeson	1, 471, 181	2, 942, 362	25, 611	15, 408	9, 623	580	25, 000	....
Rockingham	2, 330, 465	4, 660, 930	41, 598	20, 111	21, 487	....	15, 000	....
Rowan	2, 396, 306	4, 792, 612	48, 250	24, 011	9, 739	14, 500	6, 500	9, 000
Rutherford	1, 321, 351	2, 642, 702	18, 949	11, 850	7, 099	....	99, 000	....
Sampson	1, 285, 111	2, 570, 222	22, 352	12, 590	9, 762	....	6, 000	900
Stanley	682, 613	1, 365, 226	17, 606	6, 505	11, 101	....	6, 500	....
Stokes	1, 045, 122	2, 090, 244	14, 218	9, 760	4, 458	....	35, 000	....
Surry	1, 302, 930	2, 605, 860	16, 687	11, 574	5, 113	....	4, 500	....
Transylvania	375, 978	751, 956	6, 683	3, 548	3, 135	....	....	....
Tyrrell	405, 036	810, 072	10, 214	4, 308	5, 906	....	3, 500	....
Union	1, 686, 923	3, 373, 846	48, 883	14, 690	34, 011	182	49, 500	....
Wake	6, 129, 676	12, 259, 352	50, 867	573	294	50, 000	16, 623	85, 000
Warren	1, 898, 361	3, 796, 722	29, 334	17, 246	10, 988	1, 100	14, 058	....
Washington	621, 297	1, 242, 594	10, 645	6, 764	3, 881	....	....	....
Watauga	482, 489	964, 978	11, 382	4, 702	6, 680	....	3, 000	3, 000
Wayne	2, 737, 752	5, 475, 504	39, 168	25, 268	13, 900	....	6, 000	....
Wilkes	1, 067, 865	2, 135, 730	16, 684	9, 902	6, 782	....	20, 000	....
Wilson	1, 478, 116	2, 956, 232	39, 807	14, 638	25, 169	....	8, 500	700
Yadkin	965, 803	1, 931, 606	13, 176	8, 990	4, 186	....	4, 186	....
Yancy	430, 506	861, 012	5, 386	3, 363	2, 023	....	....	....
Not distributed among counties	....	....	40, 441	40, 441	....	....	....	....

(a) No report; lately formed from the counties of Currituck, Hyde, and Tyrrell, and its statistics here included in those counties.

E LXXXIII.—*Valuation, Taxation, and Public Indebtedness by Counties*—1870—Cont'd.

STATE OF OHIO.

Counties.	VALUATION.		TAXATION, NOT NATIONAL.				PUBLIC DEBT.	
	Assessed valuation of real and personal estate.	True valuation of real and personal estate.	All.	State.	County.	Town, city, &c.	County.	Town, city, &c.
	Dollars.	*Dollars.*	*Dollars.*	*Dollars.*	*Dollars.*	*Dollars.*	*Dollars.*	*Dollars.*
State....	1,167,731,697	2,235,430,300	23,526,548	4,727,318	6,501,941	12,297,289	4,237,543	8,272,367
s	6,054,949	9,535,481	83,427	24,220	27,247	31,960	....	....
....	6,738,802	12,664,050	151,444	26,955	65,049	59,447	....	....
nd	10,384,386	16,067,439	145,851	41,537	47,519	56,795	....	....
bula	11,665,433	19,425,000	190,136	46,262	50,736	84,138	....	....
s	5,614,777	10,471,263	135,275	20,448	86,032	28,795	200,000	....
izo.......	4,919,270	8,642,293	102,308	19,677	37,147	45,484	....	....
nt	15,599,664	29,547,000	246,331	62,309	88,707	95,225	78,000	....
....	10,553,494	15,961,419	182,359	42,213	60,150	80,190	20,000	....
....	24,818,393	42,050,000	385,680	96,451	68,722	220,507	....	100,000
l.........	5,961,890	13,650,000	80,287	23,848	32,782	23,657	....	....
paign	15,950,717	19,648,235	224,711	68,802	62,144	98,765	22,000	....
....	19,462,494	37,905,000	316,898	77,850	69,272	169,776	115,000	24,150
ont	13,368,560	22,611,631	219,393	63,474	65,038	90,881	....	....
n	12,534,719	20,733,702	158,945	50,139	33,382	75,424	200,000	....
biana.....	16,291,000	36,257,471	232,638	65,164	73,141	100,333	....	....
ston......	10,495,020	20,791,461	156,242	41,980	57,722	56,540	....	....
ord	11,669,147	24,786,902	197,611	46,677	54,056	96,878	....	....
oga.......	53,480,729	106,575,000	1,638,770	213,959	178,508	1,246,303	75,000	2,101,255
....	12,498,531	30,436,350	213,531	49,994	77,955	85,582	50,000	....
ce	3,182,083	7,940,596	89,476	12,728	48,526	28,222	....	....
aro	11,205,548	25,035,973	185,158	44,822	68,100	72,236	100,000	....
....	9,664,954	15,276,166	187,918	38,666	47,299	101,953	....	....
eld	15,150,430	27,305,235	239,615	60,601	90,903	88,111	240,000	....
te........	11,318,358	16,637,986	144,697	45,273	36,218	63,206	100,000	....
lin.......	35,370,292	66,546,900	660,818	141,481	179,173	340,164	....	....
a.........	2,754,858	6,616,103	93,715	11,019	48,544	34,152	....	....
....	5,977,943	9,415,259	111,764	23,912	28,027	50,825	10,000	....
n	6,521,874	11,029,795	104,816	26,087	48,914	29,815	....	....
o	19,008,345	31,498,478	325,091	76,033	122,831	126,827	40,000	....
sey	8,336,496	12,557,368	152,250	33,345	72,944	45,961	100,000	....
ton	165,702,518	341,250,000	4,836,315	662,810	647,159	3,526,346	500,000	5,020,000
ck........	7,765,869	18,064,333	158,055	31,063	65,679	61,313	....	....
a	5,393,521	26,741,519	168,643	21,582	57,639	89,422	....	....
on	9,412,732	13,619,073	138,129	37,651	51,289	49,189	....	150,000
....	2,268,643	6,417,713	91,773	9,075	32,668	50,030	....	....
and	14,317,018	24,243,858	211,429	57,268	74,503	79,658	....	....
ng	3,752,883	8,423,962	75,281	15,012	29,648	30,621	....	....
s	7,174,280	11,630,473	106,698	28,692	39,459	38,542	....	....
....	13,946,984	26,831,575	215,787	55,787	79,749	80,251	....	....
on	4,264,994	8,400,000	82,811	17,059	27,722	38,030	100,000	....
on	13,647,217	28,931,260	260,003	54,589	88,015	117,399	250,000	....
....	12,773,687	23,702,975	167,742	51,095	57,238	59,409	....	....
....	7,867,554	14,171,449	105,857	31,470	35,361	39,056	....	....
nce.......	6,717,973	11,334,186	160,953	26,872	67,180	66,901	....	....
g.........	20,534,736	38,487,990	315,200	82,139	117,895	115,166	45,000	125,000
....	10,042,520	22,177,673	192,791	40,170	97,363	55,258	....	....
....	12,932,350	24,879,670	172,894	51,729	46,562	74,603	....	....
....	12,892,020	32,287,500	560,150	51,568	95,270	413,312	27,543	401,962
on	10,975,910	22,036,807	251,779	43,903	48,826	159,050	....	....
ding	12,860,317	27,510,000	244,197	51,441	69,373	123,383	....	....
a	9,227,890	18,649,693	155,666	36,911	66,031	52,724	100,000	....
a	9,316,852	20,712,540	109,358	37,414	26,442	45,502	....	....
....	7,654,023	15,437,670	155,250	30,616	53,152	71,482	....	....
r	3,421,897	5,515,078	85,325	13,688	42,549	29,088	....	....
....	17,478,998	30,927,538	275,657	69,915	81,825	123,917	180,000	....
o	5,335,439	8,047,939	102,687	21,342	47,526	33,819	....	....
omery.....	36,802,170	68,775,000	771,483	147,209	191,388	432,886	135,000	....
n	7,234,631	10,282,582	109,583	28,939	38,999	41,645	....	....
w.........	8,794,319	18,254,095	128,005	35,177	35,787	57,041	....	....
ngum	21,608,188	25,031,981	397,820	86,433	129,648	181,739	500,000	....
....	4,928,001	8,810,543	78,631	19,712	34,822	24,097	....	....
s	3,130,484	4,601,810	93,111	12,522	32,571	48,018	....	....
ng........	1,690,047	4,725,600	78,290	6,760	30,189	41,341	....	....
....	6,070,653	13,247,480	82,216	24,283	26,885	31,048	....	....
way.......	17,425,346	36,562,734	276,277	69,701	106,683	99,893	200,000	....
....	4,644,514	9,660,000	78,238	18,578	28,215	31,445	....	....
e.........	14,228,943	19,919,420	196,176	56,916	55,700	83,569	....	....

TABLE LXXXIII.—*Valuation, Taxation, and Public Indebtedness by Counties*—1870—Cont'd.

STATE OF OHIO—Continued.

Counties.	VALUATION.		TAXATION, NOT NATIONAL.				PUBLIC DEBT.	
	Assessed valuation of real and personal estate.	True valuation of real and personal estate.	All.	State.	County.	Town, city, &c.	County.	Town, city, &c.
	Dollars.	*Dollars.*	*Dollars.*	*Dollars.*	*Dollars.*	*Dollars.*	*Dollars.*	*Dollars.*
Preble	14,313,830	29,665,461	194,270	57,255	42,636	94,379	....	....
Putnam	3,717,326	8,472,206	115,939	14,869	58,314	42,756	....	....
Richland	16,975,048	24,184,794	329,402	67,900	119,862	141,640	....	....
Ross	20,243,401	32,824,329	403,385	80,974	167,008	155,403	350,000	30,00[illegible]
Sandusky	8,158,521	17,353,597	169,982	32,634	74,829	62,519	....	....
Scioto	9,836,834	19,624,631	242,430	39,347	98,368	104,715	100,000	130,0[illegible]
Seneca	13,064,235	23,133,987	200,209	52,257	60,871	87,081	....	....
Shelby	7,432,233	15,487,565	143,365	29,728	69,234	44,403	....	....
Stark	21,971,600	47,884,648	424,546	87,886	147,449	189,211	60,00[illegible]	....
Summit	16,853,683	39,661,650	306,585	67,415	57,276	181,894	90,000	....
Trumbull	15,116,557	34,941,818	229,691	60,466	59,938	109,287	....	....
Tuscarawas	12,446,836	20,200,145	217,350	49,787	83,489	84,074	....	....
Union	7,065,113	14,115,946	151,307	28,260	54,309	68,738	....	....
Van Wert	3,751,239	7,513,867	98,330	15,005	49,842	33,483	50,000	....
Vinton	3,685,480	5,583,937	70,032	14,742	27,333	27,957	....	....
Warren	17,969,571	35,496,536	265,020	71,878	92,278	100,864	....	....
Washington	11,423,750	17,161,659	235,227	44,895	95,606	94,726	200,000	150,0[illegible]
Wayne	17,269,399	28,213,234	243,680	69,079	72,292	102,309	....	....
Williams	4,175,253	11,406,819	99,768	16,701	48,251	34,816	....	....
Wood	4,737,217	11,908,537	154,135	18,949	67,076	68,110	....	....
Wyandot	6,924,274	12,749,284	126,200	27,699	62,8[illegible]0	35,619	....	....
Not distributed among counties	....	....	51,480	51,480	....	....	....	....

STATE OF OREGON.

Counties.	VALUATION.		TAXATION, NOT NATIONAL.				PUBLIC DEBT.	
	Assessed valuation of real and personal estate.	True valuation of real and personal estate.	All.	State.	County.	Town, city, &c.	County.	Town, city, &c.
	Dollars.	*Dollars.*	*Dollars.*	*Dollars.*	*Dollars.*	*Dollars.*	*Dollars.*	*Dollars.*
The State	31,798,510	51,558,932	580,956	177,653	362,753	40,550	105,903	6,[illegible]
Baker	1,093,695	1,093,695	14,105	2,875	11,230	....	21,539	....
Benton	1,134,000	2,268,000	19,833	7,974	11,859	....	1,006	....
Clackamas	1,533,000	3,000,000	37,638	11,138	21,000	5,500	1,300	4,000
Clatsop	449,502	900,000	6,571	2,283	2,288	2,000	....	....
Columbia	260,890	350,000	3,947	1,147	2,800	....	2,500	....
Coos	450,503	960,000	9,427	3,103	6,324	....	3,801	....
Curry	110,500	200,000	2,016	911	1,105	....	....	....
Douglas	1,812,425	3,000,000	33,155	8,986	24,169	....	2,704	....
Grant	433,830	578,440	13,964	2,621	11,343	....	4,762	....
Jackson	1,385,0[illegible]	1,500,000	35,878	7,378	26,0[illegible]0	2,500	1,410	....
Josephine	220,000	300,000	13,473	1,073	12,400	....	2,250	....
Lane	1,702,755	2,100,000	26,035	11,177	14,008	850	9,000	....
Linn	2,9[illegible]0,600	5,5[illegible]0,000	43,964	20,964	23,000	....	14,000	....
Marion	3,175,600	6,325,000	49,684	21,254	28,430	....	....	....
Multnomah	7,146,0[illegible]	11,500,000	146,334	36,192	82,642	27,500	....	....
Polk	1,518,511	2,500,000	26,998	8,776	18,222	....	629	....
Tillamook	50,000	118,000	839	439	400	....	....	....
Umatilla	1,668,507	1,668,507	22,780	4,535	18,245	....	15,701	....
Union	768,169	1,500,000	16,958	4,892	12,066	....	9,441	300
Wasco	1,463,587	1,500,000	23,242	6,372	14,670	2,200	15,890	1,500
Washington	1,098,645	2,197,290	15,742	5,871	9,871	....	....	....
Yam Hill	1,256,920	2,500,000	18,373	7,692	10,681	....	....	....

LXXXIII.—*Valuation, Taxation, and Public Indebtedness by Counties*—1870—Cont'd.

STATE OF PENNSYLVANIA.

ties.	VALUATION.		TAXATION, NOT NATIONAL.				PUBLIC DEBT.	
	Assessed valuation of real and personal estate.	True valuation of real and personal estate.	All.	State.	County.	Town, city, &c.	County.	Town, city, &c.
	Dollars.	*Dollars.*	*Dollars.*	*Dollars.*	*Dollars.*	*Dollars.*	*Dollars.*	*Dollars.*
ate ...	1,313,236,042	3,808,340,112	24,531,397	5,800,172	4,963,898	14,467,327	49,173,850	8,741,619
......	5,763,021	20,552,000	140,662	4,662	49,562	86,432	31,000	....
ly	46,196,430	355,181,070	1,434,653	50,775	461,304	922,574	2,488,502	4,042,619
ng....	4,383,743	26,021,220	92,582	3,482	31,370	57,730	27,630	23,310
......	6,006,213	31,065,895	135,507	4,926	62,108	68,493	5,000	9,253
......	4,377,508	19,222,505	73,696	3,727	34,650	35,369	6,100	7,094
......	105,076,716	155,000,000	121,745	16,942	30,803	74,000	147,640	737,734
......	6,887,550	30,594,870	152,291	3,596	48,001	100,605	37,000	52,006
......	5,922,585	35,535,510	161,061	5,543	25,060	133,538	....	22,645
......	19,354,252	68,942,801	367,742	15,334	184,068	168,340	60,000	57,000
......	5,449,871	27,292,655	95,775	2,723	35,765	57,287	10,000	3,285
......	2,265,844	11,329,220	123,649	2,500	41,906	79,183	35,250	17,397
......	1,311,116	4,200,000	50,550	345	41,655	8,550	15,400	4,400
......	3,448,489	20,475,600	80,180	3,400	32,760	44,020	45,000	....
......	5,977,418	25,063,560	145,767	4,356	69,569	71,842	35,500	19,661
......	27,075,534	70,000,000	440,490	24,046	130,101	286,283	641,972	197,357
......	2,817,819	12,786,020	55,926	2,104	19,573	34,249	....	689
d......	2,140,287	10,374,050	141,661	1,656	118,199	21,806	19,800	2,094
......	4,600,000	18,400,000	79,949	2,246	36,800	40,903	36,000	15,820
a......	4,499,384	21,327,400	121,505	2,123	26,453	92,929	....	22,025
l......	8,677,036	47,772,970	238,101	6,982	96,660	134,450	209,353	66,918
and ...	15,287,212	48,504,000	203,395	10,715	72,500	120,180	32,000	52,750
......	17,661,385	59,873,460	427,307	11,888	162,208	253,211	217,810	408,800
e......	25,216,870	30,871,402	244,483	14,405	92,564	137,514	504,478	219,734
......	1,257,133	6,177,050	29,875	335	3,684	25,856	....	7,677
......	8,629,067	50,139,728	370,990	9,795	116,408	244,787	22,450	792,352
......	12,656,516	57,767,680	147,750	5,833	55,957	85,960	18,200	49,735
......	628,057	3,233,765	32,413	326	30,521	1,566	28,000	....
......	12,023,250	34,943,580	108,075	9,775	62,300	96,000	27,000	9,500
......	1,208,012	6,040,050	17,814	644	8,111	9,059	....	222
......	3,729,080	16,955,650	64,967	2,676	25,940	36,351	....	10,028
don....	6,421,212	30,240,360	100,711	3,317	32,508	64,886	....	13,850
......	3,311,401	26,491,208	88,047	3,501	34,208	50,338	90,000	3,882
......	2,315,498	10,979,210	142,649	1,560	97,610	43,479	50,700	4,201
......	3,180,444	15,902,220	20,588	2,039	13,211	14,338	....	8,929
r......	118,085,470	170,000,000	330,809	34,685	198,782	97,342	157,525	420,478
o......	5,261,427	22,256,500	180,460	4,143	118,881	57,436	317,633	2,120
......	10,921,099	33,713,719	126,038	6,871	43,920	75,247	14,000	....
......	12,575,667	44,681,022	188,806	9,957	124,113	54,736	283,713	181,347
......	18,703,116	174,032,720	332,868	12,348	94,632	225,888	107,350	101,226
g......	6,122,860	32,538,850	206,703	4,240	63,506	228,957	209,450	678,219
......	1,414,483	6,415,110	25,244	716	11,733	12,795	....	11,650
......	7,758,407	32,767,560	171,856	5,615	96,385	69,856	58,000	18,101
......	4,525,860	21,380,610	64,743	2,920	31,126	30,699	10,000	4,475
......	1,744,294	8,134,164	39,067	1,327	17,442	20,298	14,000	....
nery...	31,167,152	88,093,750	376,094	21,412	105,951	248,731	109,504	....
......	2,631,104	15,786,624	52,939	1,424	18,418	33,097	38,145	10,040
pton ..	13,803,562	51,711,205	236,839	14,630	116,733	105,476	80,000	....
berl'nd	6,244,855	31,224,425	130,589	4,982	42,000	83,607	1,850	24,575
......	3,392,500	9,120,400	84,062	2,642	27,140	54,280	27,000	28,000
phia ...	515,515,958	1,206,254,747	8,442,890	185,907	....	8,256,983	42,103,866	....
......	1,008,900	3,863,728	10,844	727	7,769	11,348	3,700	....
......	1,294,200	5,507,790	41,080	889	18,760	21,431	26,000	11,945
ll	20,083,543	91,358,166	389,607	11,026	179,133	198,848	75,000	....
......	3,380,048	10,126,209	44,600	2,305	17,013	25,282	2,500	500
......	5,118,293	23,307,510	74,513	3,915	27,233	43,345	....	4,101
......	532,421	2,289,040	18,473	406	4,507	13,470	1,000	5,552
nna ..	3,336,060	16,680,300	128,957	3,729	32,361	92,867	20,000	18,016
......	7,070,056	34,141,020	148,170	2,769	60,221	85,160	100,000	37,512
......	4,774,760	22,000,675	40,477	3,385	8,836	37,256	....	1,365
......	5,017,405	30,004,430	184,376	3,324	67,176	113,876	130,000	65,250
......	2,186,386	10,931,930	119,917	2,813	71,687	45,417	6,000	5,498
ton ..	13,857,878	69,288,390	180,692	8,663	65,545	106,684	127,500	71,014
......	2,361,989	14,091,168	53,920	1,561	16,646	35,713	....	....
reland	10,059,779	44,637,173	209,245	7,415	64,530	137,300	8,000	38,494
g......	1,960,651	9,353,330	46,710	1,421	30,544	14,745	14,900	5,530
......	15,641,660	60,215,000	238,059	13,836	97,123	127,100	227,500	16,000
ributed coun-	*60,868,190*	....	5,179,572	5,179,572	....	....	....	....

TABLE LXXXIII.— ***Valuation, Taxation, and Public Indebtedness by Counties*—1870—Cont'd.**

STATE OF RHODE ISLAND.

Counties.	VALUATION.		TAXATION, NOT NATIONAL.				PUBLIC DEBT.	
	Assessed valuation of real and personal estate.	True valuation of real and personal estate.	All.	State.	County.	Town, city, &c.	County.	Town, city, &c.
	Dollars.	*Dollars.*	*Dollars.*	*Dollars.*	*Dollars.*	*Dollars.*	*Dollars.*	*Dollars.*
The State....	244, 278, 854	296, 965, 646	2, 170, 152	489, 253	....	1, 680, 899	....	3, 0[illegible]
Bristol........	9, 490, 270	13, 288, 962	68, 167	18, 527	....	49, 640	....	22, 3[illegible]
Kent........	12, 779, 322	17, 849, 153	99, 999	35, 311	....	64, 688	....	[illegible]
Newport........	28, 121, 006	36, 978, 740	160, 227	16, 741	....	143, 486	....	[illegible]
Providence....	149, 088, 320	209, 984, 497	1, 696, 728	328, 980	....	1, 367, 748	....	1, 7[illegible]
Washington....	14, 091, 435	18, 864, 294	81, 049	25, 712	....	55, 337	....	[illegible]
Not distributed among counties........	30, 708, 501	....	63, 982	63, 982	....	....	....	....

STATE OF SOUTH CAROLINA.

Counties.	VALUATION.		TAXATION, NOT NATIONAL.				PUBLIC DEBT.	
	Assessed valuation of real and personal estate.	True valuation of real and personal estate.	All.	State.	County.	Town, city, &c.	County.	Town, city, &c.
	Dollars.	*Dollars.*	*Dollars.*	*Dollars.*	*Dollars.*	*Dollars.*	*Dollars.*	*Dollars.*
The State....	183, 913, 337	208, 146, 989	2, 767, 675	1, 321, 837	575, 005	870, 833	97, 112	5, 312, [illegible]
Abbeville......	7, 165, 354	7, 361, 095	80, 419	40, 524	17, 914	21, 981	....	....
Anderson......	5, 770, 180	5, 968, 134	60, 680	39, 667	17, 522	3, 491	....	....
Barnwell......	9, 682, 451	9, 941, 090	73, 833	46, 442	24, 549	2, 842	2, 000	....
Beaufort......	4, 414, 476	11, 669, 471	49, 000	27, 000	22, 000	....	15, 000	....
Charleston.....	47, 316, 445	60, 524, 654	1, 304, 006	345, 700	138, 000	820, 306	....	5, 137, 2[illegible]
Chester......	5, 442, 272	5, 557, 272	67, 578	48, 858	18, 720	....	....	....
Chesterfield...	2, 414, 785	2, 500, 815	31, 140	22, 837	8, 303	....	....	....
Clarendon.....	2, 508, 083	2, 559, 560	31, 832	23, 524	8, 308	....	....	....
Colleton......	4, 892, 454	5, 117, 454	56, 406	29, 498	26, 908	....	....	....
Darlington.....	4, 719, 282	4, 850, 282	47, 192	23, 596	23, 596	....	35, 412	....
Edgefield......	8, 422, 281	8, 578, 424	70, 647	50, 138	20, 509	....	13, 000	....
Fairfield......	5, 007, 542	5, 142, 542	37, 500	25, 000	12, 500	....	....	....
Georgetown...	2, 935, 338	2, 980, 338	38, 482	28, 343	10, 139	....	....	....
Greenville....	5, 043, 130	5, 362, 358	61, 169	43, 962	14, 654	2, 533	....	....
Horry......	1, 436, 501	1, 556, 500	12, 000	7, 500	4, 500	....	500	....
Kershaw......	3, 148, 161	3, 245, 161	42, 717	31, 533	11, 184	....	....	....
Lancaster.....	1, 933, 910	2, 012, 810	17, 153	11, 318	5, 835	....	8, 000	....
Laurens......	4, 429, 017	4, 504, 017	38, 626	25, 339	13, 287	....	....	....
Lexington.....	3, 464, 197	3, 517, 197	38, 929	28, 949	9, 980	....	....	....
Marion......	4, 582, 914	4, 682, 914	57, 408	41, 981	15, 427	....	....	....
Marlborough..	2, 346, 978	2, 401, 298	31, 197	23, 205	7, 992	....	....	....
Newberry.....	4, 839, 344	4, 984, 344	41, 703	24, 196	14, 507	3, 000	21, 000	....
Oconee......	2, 316, 649	2, 385, 649	19, 886	12, 937	6, 949	....	2, 200	....
Orangeburg....	8, 909, 915	9, 039, 915	93, 571	68, 453	25, 118	....	....	....
Pickens......	1, 386, 002	1, 411, 002	23, 601	6, 941	....	16, 660	....	....
Richland......	7, 807, 020	8, 127, 020	84, 897	62, 117	22, 780	....	....	175, [illegible]
Spartanburg...	4, 088, 823	4, 336, 940	48, 913	34, 938	13, 975	....	....	....
Sumter......	5, 201, 101	5, 337, 100	68, 478	50, 579	17, 899	....	....	....
Union......	4, 221, 279	4, 287, 180	55, 716	37, 936	17, 780	....	....	....
Williamsburgh.	3, 159, 638	3, 159, 638	35, 519	26, 066	9, 453	....	....	....
York......	4, 905, 815	5, 035, 815	42, 583	27, 866	14, 717	....	....	....
Not distributed among counties........	....	....	4, 894	4, 894	....	....	....	....

:LXXXIII.—*Valuation, Taxation, and Public Indebtedness by Counties*—1870—Cont'd.

STATE OF TENNESSEE.

unties.	VALUATION.		TAXATION, NOT NATIONAL.				PUBLIC DEBT.	
	Assessed valuation of real and personal estate.	True valuation of real and personal estate.	All.	State.	County.	Town, city, &c.	County.	Town, city, &c.
	Dollars.	*Dollars.*	*Dollars.*	*Dollars.*	*Dollars.*	*Dollars.*	*Dollars.*	*Dollars.*
State..	253,782,161	498,237,724	3,381,579	1,056,261	1,302,836	1,022,482	2,720,659	7,557,730
on......	1,133,312	2,335,442	13,494	2,266	11,228	....	100,000	....
l........	6,019,234	8,205,820	21,910	12,038	6,872	3,000	....	5,000
....	875,955	1,830,343	7,026	1,751	5,275	....	2,000	....
....	706,537	1,712,553	3,668	1,413	2,255	....	2,255	....
....	2,550,337	5,746,681	13,801	5,110	5,584	3,107	71,280	....
....	2,379,641	3,073,428	12,678	4,759	2,271	5,848	3,965	1,000
ll......	730,074	1,049,333	8,948	1,501	5,495	1,952	4,000	....
....	1,407,438	1,759,297	8,363	2,814	5,549	....	1,000	....
....	3,241,910	4,354,230	14,443	6,483	7,560	400	7,000	....
....	769,456	1,463,246	3,846	1,538	2,308	....	....	....
am	1,027,676	1,284,593	4,110	2,055	2,055	....	540	....
no......	848,336	1,597,450	7,836	1,696	6,140	....	18,000	....
....	958,052	2,732,248	5,268	1,916	3,352	....	3,905	....
....	1,608,640	2,500,000	11,064	3,217	7,847	....	4,000	....
rland ...	384,857	1,314,338	2,568	770	1,798	....	....	....
on......	25,854,650	64,636,618	479,914	51,709	77,563	350,642	760,000	2,050,000
r	820,336	1,765,457	4,020	1,640	2,380	....	2,380	....
b	1,322,854	1,626,517	6,319	2,651	3,668	....	300	....
n	1,187,708	3,166,858	5,437	2,375	3,062	....	....	....
....	3,501,816	6,264,588	17,003	7,003	10,000	....	14,000	....
e.......	4,632,440	11,244,681	72,977	9,264	60,648	3,065	3,000	1,500
ss......	362,029	533,382	4,217	724	3,493	....	2,000	....
in......	2,131,359	5,013,643	28,372	4,262	21,453	2,657	600	....
....	5,495,949	13,065,700	28,824	10,991	12,833	5,000	1,090	800
....	6,682,175	16,705,415	31,864	13,364	15,000	3,500	32,000	....
er......	1,848,358	3,103,494	9,566	3,696	5,870	....	2,400	....
....	3,036,989	8,442,414	15,090	6,073	9,017	....	....	....
y.......	497,988	1,000,000	2,278	995	1,283	....	4,250	....
on	3,112,108	5,343,794	77,424	6,224	36,200	35,000	....	....
k	586,194	1,267,268	3,113	1,172	1,941	....	3,000	....
nan	3,741,068	4,302,227	18,482	7,482	9,000	2,000	9,000	250
....	1,755,142	3,034,690	6,360	3,510	2,850	....	2,500	....
ns	2,467,334	4,721,907	18,208	4,934	13,274	....	62,760	....
od	6,043,537	17,184,118	33,863	12,087	15,168	6,608	....	....
rson....	1,817,956	3,672,018	11,914	3,635	8,279	....	12,000	....
....	2,643,480	4,943,565	20,223	5,286	13,237	1,700	30,000	....
an	1,415,411	2,493,478	9,830	2,830	7,000	....	5,000	....
hreys....	926,890	1,158,612	6,791	1,853	4,938	....	5,000	....
n	1,211,471	1,920,993	4,843	2,422	2,421	....	5,000	....
on	3,153,975	5,190,112	24,761	6,307	18,454	....	....	....
n	364,762	2,041,641	6,764	729	6,035	....	8,000	....
....	7,243,595	9,520,113	83,125	14,487	18,638	50,000	228,290	....
....	1,396,179	1,528,139	4,542	2,445	2,097	....	16,000	....
dale	1,861,419	2,942,568	20,863	3,722	17,141	....	1,500	12,500
nce.....	922,506	1,250,000	4,730	1,845	1,845	1,040	3,030	688
....	215,831	5,554,153	2,288	1,560	728	....	10,500	....
n.......	4,202,496	7,580,748	26,754	8,404	16,350	2,000	....	....
....	786,584	1,024,281	1,573	1,573	....	....	....	....
n	4,720,162	8,930,525	37,940	9,440	22,000	6,500	8,500	....
....	1,090,978	1,272,605	7,367	2,181	5,186	....	3,206	....
ll......	2,545,544	6,250,000	6,591	5,091	1,500	....	....	....
....	8,605,967	17,496,571	47,289	17,643	20,146	9,500	....	....
n.......	2,803,260	3,740,346	12,138	5,606	5,432	1,100	....	....
ry	2,737,449	2,837,449	21,377	10,743	10,634	....	....	....
....	1,021,123	1,021,123	4,421	2,042	2,379	....	1,500	....
e.......	2,276,559	3,074,973	14,935	4,553	10,382	....	....	....
omery...	4,898,720	15,000,000	68,797	9,797	41,000	18,000	328,000	155,000
n.......	258,846	653,013	2,818	517	2,301	....	100	....
....	2,099,109	3,791,294	20,368	4,545	13,823	2,000	5,000	....
n.......	1,097,725	1,261,160	8,939	2,195	6,744	....	6,000	....
....	1,490,081	2,793,901	10,547	2,980	7,567	....	1,200	....
....	1,178,386	1,541,204	8,912	2,356	6,556	....	....	....
n.......	728,341	2,125,005	1,456	1,456	....	....	4,000	....
....	766,424	1,824,193	3,532	1,532	2,000	....	....	....
....	3,096,263	6,029,190	15,046	6,192	8,854	....	....	....
son	2,939,387	4,517,051	16,758	5,878	10,257	623	....	2,500
ford	*7,075,872*	*12,500,000*	42,451	14,151	21,225	7,075	....	50,000

TABLE LXXXIII.—*Valuation, Taxation, and Public Indebtedness by Counties—1870—Cont'd.*

STATE OF TENNESSEE—Continued.

Counties.	VALUATION.		TAXATION, NOT NATIONAL.				PUBLIC DEBT.	
	Assessed valuation of real and personal estate.	True valuation of real and personal estate.	All.	State.	County.	Town, city, &c.	County.	Town, city, &c.
	Dollars.	*Dollars.*	*Dollars.*	*Dollars.*	*Dollars.*	*Dollars.*	*Dollars.*	*Dollars.*
Scott	252, 671	732, 937	1, 508	505	1, 003		1, 000	
Sequatchie	251, 235	967, 113	2, 731	502	2, 240		2, 500	
Sevier	1, 151, 686	2, 721, 058	7, 988	2, 303	5, 685			
Shelby	35, 064, 924	47, 412, 873	932, 823	70, 129	375, 813	486, 881	791, 380	5, 271, [illegible]
Smith	2, 798, 752	7, 002, 306	8, 624	5, 597	3, 027		11, 700	
Stewart	1, 280, 930	4, 803, 487	10, 061	2, 561	7, 500		11, 000	
Sullivan	2, 114, 021	3, 977, 109	16, 268	4, 229	11, 239	800		
Sumner	5, 846, 078	14, 615, 194	24, 786	11, 691	13, 095		30, 000	
Tipton	2, 788, 063	3, 094, 749	27, 510	5, 576	19, 380	2, 554	5, 175	1, [illegible]
Union	777, 386	2, 017, 653	4, 102	1, 554	2, 548			
Van Buren	211, 007	263, 771	25, 722	422	25, 300		1, 800	
Warren	2, 022, 397	3, 791, 994	11, 788	4, 044	5, 544	2, 200		1, [illegible]
Washington	2, 779, 155	8, 039, 246	13, 731	5, 558	7, 673	500		
Wayne	1, 279, 393	1, 561, 178	7, 116	2, 558	4, 258	300	2, 068	
Weakley	2, 978, 066	5, 086, 875	70, 628	5, 956	61, 482	3, 190	4, 500	2, [illegible]
White	861, 976	2, 387, 500	4, 923	1, 723	2, 960	240	10, 500	
Williamson	6, 924, 612	15, 562, 792	33, 879	13, 840	16, 330	3, 500	23, 000	1, [illegible]
Wilson	5, 064, 486	12, 500, 000	52, 237	10, 128	42, 109		36, 000	
Not distributed among counties			541, 897	541, 897				

STATE OF TEXAS.

Counties.	VALUATION.		TAXATION, NOT NATIONAL.				PUBLIC DEBT.	
	Assessed valuation of real and personal estate.	True valuation of real and personal estate.	All.	State.	County.	Town, city, &c.	County.	Town, city, &c.
	Dollars.	*Dollars.*	*Dollars.*	*Dollars.*	*Dollars.*	*Dollars.*	*Dollars.*	*Dollars.*
The State	149, 732, 929	159, 052, 542	1, 129, 577	589, 363	312, 335	227, 879	426, 866	678, [illegible]
Anderson	1, 583, 726	1, 068, 141	9, 077	6, 274	2, 803			
Angelina	301, 702	323, 497	2, 550	1, 700	850			
Archer (a)	205, 072	205, 072						
Atascosa	818, 378	925, 847	3, 535	2, 357	1, 178			
Austin	2, 382, 372	2, 497, 870	14, 725	9, 817	4, 908		4, 000	
Bandera	136, 249	146, 181	1, 151	737	231	186		
Bastrop	1, 993, 760	2, 100, 947	13, 403	8, 602	4, 301	500	8, 000	[illegible]
Baylor (a)	34, 428	34, 428						
Bee (b)								
Bell	1, 184, 415	1, 255, 533	7, 353	4, 902	2, 451			
Bexar	3, 963, 951	4, 281, 072	32, 383	10, 152	5, 076	17, 155		
Blanco	228, 566	249, 599	1, 079	754	325		500	
Bosque	767, 870	830, 969	3, 816	2, 544	1, 272		454	
Bowie	544, 361	575, 031	4, 810	3, 207	1, 603			
Brazoria	1, 626, 379	1, 681, 554	9, 569	6, 379	3, 190		79, 000	
Brazos	1, 381, 050	1, 493, 571	15, 677	6, 451	3, 226	6, 000	24, 000	1, [illegible]
Brown (b)								
Burleson	945, 345	999, 060	5, 170	3, 447	1, 723			
Burnet	450, 896	484, 718	2, 639	1, 426	713	500	1, 400	
Caldwell	1, 152, 841	1, 229, 084	8, 404	5, 603	2, 801			
Calhoun	1, 478, 231	1, 009, 616	11, 755	7, 037	3, 518	1, 200		4, 000
Cameron	1, 633, 012	1, 731, 972	18, 825	9, 817	4, 908	4, 100	20, 000	
Chambers	306, 561	325, 435	1, 058	705	339			
Cherokee	864, 452	917, 284	6, 185	4, 123	2, 062			
Coleman (b)								
Collin	2, 643, 787	2, 784, 695	12, 624	8, 416	4, 208			
Colorado	1, 877, 734	1, 978, 675	14, 281	9, 520	4, 761		2, 000	12, 000

(a) Unorganized. (b) No report.

: LXXXIII.—*Valuation, Taxation, and Public Indebtedness by Counties*—1870—Cont'd.

STATE OF TEXAS—Continued.

...ties.	VALUATION.		TAXATION, NOT NATIONAL.				PUBLIC DEBT.	
	Assessed valuation of real and personal estate.	True valuation of real and personal estate.	All.	State.	County.	Town, city, &c.	County.	Town, city, &c.
	Dollars.	*Dollars.*	*Dollars.*	*Dollars.*	*Dollars.*	*Dollars.*	*Dollars.*	*Dollars.*
....	1,215,880	1,220,536	8,428	4,578	2,788	1,062	10,100	2,300
...che (a)								
....	635,419	681,467	4,017	2,320	1,697			
....	650,364	698,376	4,005	2,767	1,238		400	
....	2,853,265	2,997,238	12,325	8,217	4,108			
....	682,210	703,435	5,968	3,995	1,993		14,000	
...t (b)								
....	1,360,485	1,419,309	5,487	4,298	1,189		1,000	
...t	1,441,929	1,520,711	9,970	6,647	3,323		6,000	
...(b)								
...nd (b)								
....	1,391,054	1,474,419	2,250	1,500	750			
...o	422,449	454,301	4,731	3,154	1,577			
...l (a)	19,457	19,457						
....	579,936	607,567	2,434	1,488	946		2,000	
....	1,349,972	1,403,508	7,253	4,835	2,418		2,500	
....	1,911,693	1,994,170	9,988	6,659	3,329			
...o	3,456,952	3,730,255	26,509	11,280	12,729	2,000	1,200	200
...end	1,182,889	1,238,995	16,548	4,515	2,267	9,776	8,000	
...one	1,041,131	1,116,034	13,395	6,930	6,465		2,000	
...)								
...ton	15,301,641	16,379,724	159,027	52,685	26,342	80,000		250,000
...ie	659,709	704,820	7,240	3,826	1,914	1,500	2,000	
....	795,102	835,401	5,147	3,431	1,716			
...es	1,548,365	1,648,715	11,444	5,963	2,981	2,500	3,500	
...on	1,865,895	1,962,168	11,020	7,347	3,673		13,000	
...a	1,973,085	2,076,264	11,043	7,362	3,681			
...lupe	1,646,030	1,736,444	8,714	5,809	2,905			
...ton (b)								
....	88,837	95,954	553	369	184		10,100	
....	9,970,102	10,816,897	116,181	37,454	18,727	60,000	80,000	400,000
...on	2,764,205	2,912,043	20,841	10,561	5,280	5,005	15,000	300
...ll (a)	183,419	183,419						
....	608,873	643,520	2,850	1,927	923			
...rson	617,703	658,648	5,181	3,454	1,727		9,000	
...o	264,380	282,424	3,194	1,133	2,061		650	
....	1,213,058	1,295,927	6,156	4,104	2,052		1,900	
....	375,922	411,504	1,977	1,351	626		3,000	
...ns	1,167,787	1,196,237	7,711	5,141	2,570			
...on	1,600,656	1,663,911	12,026	8,017	4,009			
....	1,169,677	1,252,256	7,443	4,962	2,481			
....	254,222	273,003	3,526	2,351	1,175		2,136	
...on	847,457	912,318	3,405	2,270	1,135		1,258	
...(b)			855		855		2,021	
...son	613,528	671,405	2,283	1,522	761			
...on	1,011,777	1,080,496	4,224	2,816	1,408		3,700	
...s	613,482	678,513	3,095	2,063	1,032			
...an	960,910	1,026,535	7,291	4,861	2,430			
...ll	338,803	360,245	2,499	1,666	833			
....	188,067	203,697	1,302	868	434			
...e (b)								
...y (b)								
...(a)	91,464	91,464						
....	2,104,606	2,206,391	13,407	8,938	4,469		3,500	
...nsas	264,984	288,120	1,083	722	361			
...le (b)								
...a	1,433,697	1,519,510	9,705	6,470	3,235			
...(b)							852	
...y	510,236	533,983	2,544	1,696	848		4,350	
...tone	1,252,026	1,328,368	10,933	7,289	3,644		1,000	
...ak (b)			600		800		1,700	
....	294,993	332,243	1,319	879	440		700	
...on	534,018	574,026	4,474	2,983	1,491		1,200	
...n	2,063,728	2,206,099	21,206	8,804	4,402	8,000		
....	164,980	184,343	1,779	1,186	593			
...gorda	704,323	750,753	6,021	2,681	3,340		1,000	
...rick (b)								
...lloch (b)								

(a) Unorganized. (b) No report.

TABLE LXXXIII.—*Valuation, Taxation, and Public Indebtedness by Counties—1870*—Cont'd.

STATE OF TEXAS—Continued.

Counties.	VALUATION.		TAXATION, NOT NATIONAL.				PUBLIC DEBT.	
	Assessed valuation of real and personal estate.	True valuation of real and personal estate.	All.	State.	County.	Town, city, &c.	County.	Town, city, &c.
	Dollars.	*Dollars.*	*Dollars.*	*Dollars.*	*Dollars.*	*Dollars.*	*Dollars.*	*Dollars.*
McLennan	2, 527, 428	2, 637, 910	18, 473	8, 982	4, 491	5, 000		
McMullen (*a*)								
Medina	513, 224	552, 423	4, 229	2, 819	1, 410		2, 000	
Menard (*a*)								
Milam	941, 200	991, 541	5, 303	3, 535	1, 768			
Montague	190, 302	206, 247	837	558	279			
Montgomery	745, 130	775, 714	4, 523	3, 015	1, 508		8, 000	
Nacogdoches	1, 802, 648	1, 865, 231	10, 070	6, 380	3, 690		2, 200	
Navarro	1, 969, 141	2, 064, 282	9, 907	6, 605	3, 302			
Newton (*a*)								
Nueces	1, 218, 451	1, 330, 573	7, 363	4, 109	2, 054	1, 200	1, 500	
Orange	261, 975	276, 733	1, 372	918	454		800	
Palo Pinto (*a*)								
Panola	750, 617	792, 947	4, 875	3, 247	1, 628		1, 000	
Parker	873, 532	938, 129	5, 907	3, 938	1, 969		2, 000	
Polk	724, 059	761, 518	8, 016	3, 811	4, 205		3, 000	
Presidio (*a*)								
Red River	1, 186, 020	1, 237, 822	8, 687	5, 791	2, 896			
Refugio	509, 965	657, 296	2, 284	1, 523	761			
Robertson	959, 011	999, 245	11, 402	7, 601	3, 801			
Rusk	1, 300, 489	1, 382, 090	9, 795	6, 530	3, 265			
Sabine	276, 609	292, 170	1, 945	1, 297	648			
San Augustine	1, 175, 897	1, 210, 619	5, 874	3, 916	1, 958			
San Patricio (*a*)			606		606		3, 745	
San Saba	449, 554	498, 922	1, 783	1, 189	594			
Shackleford (*a*)								
Shelby	524, 339	556, 407	3, 963	2, 642	1, 321		2, 500	
Smith	1, 740, 994	1, 841, 230	10, 023	5, 682	2, 841	1, 500		
Starr	687, 872	750, 434	3, 619	2, 413	1, 206			
Stephens (*a*)								
Tarrant	1, 079, 627	1, 145, 457	6, 008	4, 005	2, 003		2, 700	
Throckmorton	246, 842	246, 842						
Titus (*b*)	1, 183, 080	1, 242, 203	9, 480	6, 320	3, 160		1, 500	
Travis	5, 000, 127	5, 281, 356	36, 362	16, 241	8, 121	12, 000	10, 100	7, 000
Trinity	244, 773	266, 716	3, 893	2, 595	1, 298		5, 000	
Tyler	308, 734	331, 019	2, 246	1, 497	749		1, 500	
Upshur	1, 381, 308	1, 458, 345	10, 545	7, 030	3, 515			
Uvalde	438, 538	491, 323	3, 251	2, 171	1, 080			
Van Zandt	507, 685	544, 435	3, 282	2, 185	1, 097			
Victoria	1, 167, 747	1, 231, 405	12, 364	5, 576	2, 788	4, 000		
Walker	1, 351, 084	1, 432, 380	8, 965	5, 977	2, 988		5, 000	
Washington	4, 424, 669	4, 578, 381	29, 922	17, 615	8, 307	4, 000	1, 800	1, 000
Webb	334, 634	367, 245	2, 744	1, 696	848	200		
Wharton	411, 460	440, 120	4, 216	2, 811	1, 405		10, 000	
Williamson	1, 549, 490	1, 665, 978	12, 027	8, 018	4, 009		2, 500	
Wilson	408, 585	439, 271	2, 919	1, 946	973		3, 000	
Wise	266, 069	291, 072	1, 203	802	401			
Wood	669, 787	712, 412	5, 265	3, 510	1, 755		9, 000	
Young (*b*)	330, 840	330, 840						
Zapata	242, 294	267, 642	1, 130	753	377			
Zavala (*a*)								

(*a*) No report. (*b*) Unorganized.

LE LXXXIII.—*Valuation, Taxation, and Public Indebtedness by Counties—1870*—Cont'd.

TERRITORY OF UTAH.

unties.	VALUATION.		TAXATION, NOT NATIONAL.				PUBLIC DEBT.	
	Assessed valuation of real and personal estate.	True valuation of real and personal estate.	All.	Territory.	County.	Town, city, &c.	County.	Town, city, &c.
	Dollars.	*Dollars.*	*Dollars.*	*Dollars.*	*Dollars.*	*Dollars.*	*Dollars.*	*Dollars.*
Territory	12, 565, 842	16, 159, 995	107, 355	39, 402	80, 419	47, 534	....	....
r..........	95, 000	118, 750	1, 500	750	750	....	....	....
Elder	500, 000	600, 000	5, 000	1, 250	3, 750	....	....	....
....	728, 195	873, 000	7, 281	1, 820	5, 461	....	....	....
....	648, 655	648, 655	12, 971	1, 621	4, 864	6, 486	....	....
....	275, 000	343, 750	3, 257	690	2, 060	507	....	....
....	272, 641	340, 801	2, 960	1, 480	1, 480	....	....	....
....	248, 000	269, 105	2, 420	210	210	2, 000	....	....
rd	250, 000	502, 855	3, 850	1, 250	1, 250	1, 350	....	....
an	320, 000	320, 000	5, 750	650	2, 800	2, 300	....	....
(a)	....	....	....	....	....	....	....	....
....	307, 950	307, 950	1, 286	643	643	....	....	....
Virgin.....	40, 575	40, 575	352	176	176	....	....	....
Lake.......	4, 210, 990	5, 614, 653	38, 657	10, 527	10, 527	17, 603	....	....
Pete.......	386, 385	1, 134, 987	7, 517	960	2, 897	3, 654	....	....
r (a)	....	....	....	....	....	....	....	....
ilt........	263, 592	263, 592	3, 100	1, 100	1, 100	900	....	....
o.	371, 736	464, 670	4, 216	1, 858	1, 858	500	....	....
....	1, 252, 096	1, 649, 431	14, 247	6, 260	6, 260	1, 727	....	....
tch	145, 027	145, 027	1, 600	500	500	600	....	....
ington ...	500, 000	772, 194	39, 308	2, 818	29, 000	7, 490	....	....
r..........	1, 750, 000	1, 750, 000	12, 083	4, 833	4, 833	2, 417	....	....

(a) No report.

STATE OF VERMONT.

unties.	VALUATION.		TAXATION, NOT NATIONAL.				PUBLIC DEBT.	
	Assessed valuation of real and personal estate.	True valuation of real and personal estate.	All.	State.	County.	Town, city, &c.	County.	Town, city, &c.
	Dollars.	*Dollars.*	*Dollars.*	*Dollars.*	*Dollars.*	*Dollars.*	*Dollars.*	*Dollars.*
State....	102, 548, 528	235, 349, 553	1, 547, 128	588, 792	40, 329	918, 007	8, 042	2, 584, 158
on	8, 133, 537	18, 649, 575	93, 157	46, 041	870	46, 246	....	56, 708
ngton	5, 732, 586	13, 927, 385	110, 688	33, 556	....	77, 132	....	464, 486
onia......	7, 397, 995	18, 092, 569	113, 832	42, 302	....	71, 470	....	253, 345
enden	11, 706, 766	18, 347, 263	122, 916	65, 502	1, 674	55, 740	....	229, 776
....	1, 744, 049	4, 537, 927	21, 355	10, 215	....	11, 140	....	4, 493
lin.......	8, 680, 912	14, 913, 887	112, 150	49, 499	....	62, 651	....	298, 421
l Isle.....	1, 082, 389	2, 408, 000	9, 331	6, 212	....	3, 119	....	2, 355
ille.......	3, 104, 872	6, 015, 609	51, 013	18, 711	....	32, 302	....	235, 546
ro	6, 021, 463	16, 863, 356	121, 316	39, 000	....	82, 316	....	102, 218
ns........	5, 421, 080	12, 570, 640	77, 304	31, 959	....	45, 345	....	44, 134
nd	13, 853, 476	35, 349, 109	219, 035	78, 461	30, 073	110, 501	....	234, 149
ington ...	7, 941, 202	18, 614, 189	131, 679	46, 074	....	85, 605	....	180, 905
ham......	8, 025, 683	22, 016, 328	155, 005	49, 816	2, 002	103, 187	....	104, 064
sor	12, 448, 518	33, 073, 716	208, 347	71, 384	5, 710	131, 253	8, 042	371, 503

TABLE LXXXIII.—*Valuation, Taxation, and Public Indebtedness by Counties*—1870—Cont'd.

STATE OF VIRGINIA.

Counties.	Valuation.		Taxation, not national.				Public debt.	
	Assessed valuation of real and personal estate.	True valuation of real and personal estate.	All.	State.	County.	Town, city, &c.	County.	Town, city, &c.
	Dollars.	*Dollars.*	*Dollars.*	*Dollars.*	*Dollars.*	*Dollars.*	*Dollars.*	*Dollars.*
The State	365, 439, 917	409, 588, 133	4, 613, 798	2, 847, 635	842, 069	924, 094	1, 365, 766	7, 164, [illegible]
Accomack	4, 033, 435	4, 033, 435	36, 903	29, 007	7, 926			
Albemarle	10, 886, 680	13, 242, 985	80, 984	66, 425	9, 050	5, 500		15, [illegible]
Alexandria	6, 082, 337	6, 082, 337	58, 203	43, 654	14, 549			967, [illegible]
Alleghany	1, 391, 005	1, 391, 005	9, 018	7, 398	1, 620			
Amelia	2, 431, 576	2, 546, 059	33, 088	17, 088	16, 000		16, 000	
Amherst	2, 670, 461	2, 697, 891	32, 061	19, 061	13, 000		45, 000	
Appomattox	1, 478, 767	1, 478, 767	17, 503	12, 810	4, 693		2, 937	
Augusta	16, 292, 184	16, 292, 184	125, 963	104, 605	16, 000	5, 358		27, [illegible]
Bath	1, 231, 500	1, 231, 500	9, 580	8, 601	979			
Bedford	5, 473, 365	5, 712, 936	54, 988	37, 998	16, 990			
Bland	797, 432	797, 432	7, 995	5, 196	2, 799			
Botetourt	3, 744, 317	3, 744, 317	33, 325	22, 435	10, 890		1, 200	
Brunswick	1, 694, 550	1, 877, 603	23, 981	14, 032	9, 949			
Buchanan	455, 457	455, 457	3, 528	2, 196	1, 332			
Buckingham	2, 358, 394	2, 358, 394	27, 442	19, 059	8, 383			
Campbell	9, 004, 674	12, 053, 612	142, 669	66, 911	10, 758	65, 000	1, 000	[illegible]
Caroline	3, 806, 160	5, 510, 230	31, 685	26, 207	5, 478			
Carroll	819, 917	1, 188, 402	10, 676	6, 818	3, 858			
Charles City	904, 594	1, 057, 545	11, 967	8, 593	3, 374			
Charlotte	3, 112, 863	3, 500, 000	35, 897	26, 265	9, 632			
Chesterfield	5, 275, 667	5, 275, 667	46, 141	35, 930	7, 000	3, 211		37, [illegible]
Clarke	3, 674, 914	4, 307, 215	29, 583	24, 866	4, 717			
Craig	831, 619	1, 258, 332	8, 814	6, 086	2, 728		2, 728	
Culpeper	4, 403, 046	4, 403, 046	28, 789	24, 890	3, 899		5, 422	1, [illegible]
Cumberland	2, 047, 042	2, 047, 042	21, 440	15, 552	5, 888		6, 000	
Dinwiddie	11, 265, 579	12, 664, 915	127, 997	93, 178	12, 214	22, 605		996, 2[illegible]
Elizabeth City	1, 194, 358	1, 194, 358	22, 282	10, 379	11, 903		8, 967	
Essex	1, 518, 317	2, 199, 701	21, 466	14, 258	7, 208		7, 208	
Fairfax	5, 568, 284	8, 244, 307	40, 090	27, 308	12, 782			
Fauquier	11, 724, 455	12, 490, 980	83, 279	66, 691	14, 088	2, 500	12, 884	2, 000
Floyd	1, 381, 806	1, 755, 320	14, 127	8, 490	5, 637		6, 500	
Fluvanna	2, 301, 231	2, 460, 918	21, 912	16, 012	5, 900			
Franklin	2, 478, 896	2, 726, 584	25, 091	19, 962	5, 129			
Frederick	8, 025, 565	9, 100, 000	70, 385	46, 135	7, 450	16, 800	7, 250	25, 74[illegible]
Giles	1, 478, 312	1, 656, 369	13, 983	8, 239	5, 744			
Gloucester	2, 040, 136	2, 040, 136	18, 574	15, 634	2, 940			
Goochland	2, 528, 775	2, 528, 775	32, 846	19, 004	13, 842		10, 000	
Grayson	1, 061, 891	1, 643, 831	12, 363	8, 226	4, 137			
Greene	1, 067, 147	1, 100, 777	10, 516	7, 395	3, 121			
Greenville	980, 232	1, 339, 725	14, 298	6, 298	8, 000		9, 000	
Halifax	5, 431, 795	5, 785, 610	65, 744	39, 955	25, 789		9, 000	
Hanover	3, 035, 207	3, 062, 098	32, 598	24, 712	7, 886			
Henrico	41, 310, 061	41, 310, 061	809, 604	279, 032	21, 572	509, 000		2, 111, 3[illegible]
Henry	1, 388, 640	1, 773, 108	27, 971	14, 113	13, 858		20, 000	
Highland	1, 579, 573	1, 900, 000	13, 115	9, 661	3, 454		2, 000	
Isle of Wight	1, 630, 461	1, 735, 481	17, 751	11, 951	5, 800			
James City	1, 071, 477	1, 133, 050	13, 581	8, 981	4, 600			
King and Queen	1, 466, 660	1, 916, 713	16, 429	12, 938	3, 491			
King George	1, 511, 329	1, 511, 329	16, 632	10, [illegible]	5, 750			
King William	1, 695, 742	1, 954, 244	19, 051	13, 201	5, 850			
Lancaster	929, 661	1, 867, 538	10, 413	8, 357	2, 056			
Lee	1, 808, 495	2, 500, 000	22, 852	14, 311	8, 541		60, 000	
Loudon	16, 584, 414	16, 584, 414	113, 742	84, 303	29, 439			10, 000
Louisa	3, 653, 300	3, 653, 300	49, 592	27, 092	22, 500		15, 000	
Lunenburg	1, 428, 800	1, 428, 800	19, 993	12, 419	7, 574			
Madison	2, 424, 903	2, 467, 530	20, 542	15, 696	4, 846		10, 400	
Matthews	968, 326	968, 326	12, 244	8, 584	3, 660			
Mecklenburg	2, 855, 779	6, 090, 785	41, 717	27, 147	14, 570			
Middlesex	905, 396	1, 005, 170	10, 117	7, 919	2, 198		400	
Montgomery	3, 314, 183	4, 703, 030	28, 330	21, 336	7, 000			
Nansemond	2, 195, 619	2, 195, 619	23, 358	15, 918	6, 840	600	2, 250	
Nelson	3, 024, 640	3, 890, 454	33, 833	20, 158	13, 675			
New Kent	1, 091, 774	1, 091, 774	12, 546	7, 578	4, 968		4, 968	
Norfolk	18, 045, 487	20, 512, 605	356, 418	107, 542	17, 800	231, 076	18, 924	1, 855, 741
Northampton	1, 727, 347	1, 727, 347	18, 406	11, 906	6, 500			
Northumberl'd	1, 229, 443	2, 600, 000	11, 701	9, 483	2, 218			
Nottoway	1, 582, 525	2, 353, 911	25, 769	13, 769	12, 000		3, 000	

:LXXXIII.—*Valuation, Taxation, and Public Indebtedness by Counties*—1870—Cont'd.

STATE OF VIRGINIA—Continued.

...nties.	VALUATION.		TAXATION, NOT NATIONAL.				PUBLIC DEBT.	
	Assessed valuation of real and personal estate.	True valuation of real and personal estate.	All.	State.	County.	Town, city, &c.	County.	Town, city, &c.
	Dollars.	*Dollars.*	*Dollars.*	*Dollars.*	*Dollars.*	*Dollars.*	*Dollars.*	*Dollars.*
	3, 595, 977	4, 178, 177	28, 675	23, 063	5, 612	....	....	....
	2, 912, 764	3, 503, 840	25, 254	17, 254	8, 000	....	6, 000	....
	1, 291, 131	1, 291, 131	18, 727	9, 669	9, 058	....	236, 000	....
...vania	6, 182, 572	6, 182, 572	95, 822	51, 978	28, 000	15, 844	158, 650	87, 858
...an	2, 133, 314	2, 161, 272	22, 509	14, 509	8, 000	....	23, 345	....
...Edward	2, 440, 625	2, 897, 982	26, 558	17, 908	5, 950	2, 700	....	....
...George	1, 786, 334	1, 792, 904	18, 653	13, 609	5, 044	....	6, 714	....
...s Anne	2, 055, 203	2, 055, 203	20, 717	12, 717	8, 000	....	....	....
...William	3, 202, 696	3, 202, 696	30, 156	19, 350	10, 806	....	....	....
	2, 087, 318	3, 797, 918	18, 365	13, 822	4, 543	....	....	....
...annock	2, 795, 840	3, 200, 000	24, 493	19, 493	5, 000	....	....	....
...nd	1, 263, 458	1, 263, 458	12, 680	9, 097	3, 583	....	3, 411	....
...o	3, 725, 047	3, 725, 047	27, 325	22, 325	4, 600	400	....	1, 500
...idgo	7, 258, 604	7, 258, 604	68, 244	43, 643	17, 601	7, 000	10, 790	14, 166
...gham	10, 136, 588	13, 443, 160	94, 380	62, 880	25, 000	6, 500	165, 000	5, 000
	1, 896, 159	2, 129, 922	17, 411	13, 911	3, 500	....	....	....
	1, 700, 294	1, 700, 294	16, 811	12, 365	4, 446	....	30, 000	....
...doah	5, 401, 157	6, 728, 100	46, 982	33, 482	13, 500	....	11, 000	....
	2, 796, 768	2, 810, 080	28, 869	18, 369	10, 500	....	19, 600	....
...npton	2, 117, 570	2, 117, 570	24, 939	15, 305	9, 634	....	200, 000	....
...lvania	3, 473, 197	5, 926, 132	60, 226	28, 438	4, 788	27, 000	5, 938	253, 000
...l	1, 749, 545	2, 000, 000	15, 027	12, 627	2, 400	....	....	....
	1, 153, 934	1, 153, 934	14, 136	7, 889	6 247	....	....	....
	1, 273, 979	1, 343, 560	17, 375	9, 752	7 623	....	100, 000	....
...ll	2, 364, 597	2, 364, 597	18, 284	14, 263	4, 021	....	....	....
...1	2, 442, 201	2, 637, 184	22, 501	14, 731	7, 770	....	45, 000	....
...ok	494, 289	494, 289	3, 298	3, 298	....	....	....	....
...gton	5, 172, 190	5, 899, 881	49, 615	32, 155	17, 460	....	54, 780	....
...oreland	1, 569, 991	1, 879, 492	17, 963	13, 092	4, 871	....	....	....
	502, 871	708, 342	6, 065	3, 265	2, 800	....	....	....
	3, 989, 602	4, 041, 571	41, 491	25, 491	13, 000	3, 000	1, 500	13, 008
	896, 725	896, 725	12, 777	8, 096	4, 681	....	....	....
...tributed counties	....	....	371, 893	371, 893	....	....	....	....

TERRITORY OF WASHINGTON.

...nties.	VALUATION.		TAXATION, NOT NATIONAL.				PUBLIC DEBT.	
	Assessed valuation of real and personal estate.	True valuation of real and personal estate.	All.	Territory.	County.	Town, city, &c.	County.	Town, city, &c.
	Dollars.	*Dollars.*	*Dollars.*	*Dollars.*	*Dollars.*	*Dollars.*	*Dollars.*	*Dollars.*
...erritory	10, 642, 863	13, 562, 164	163, 992	33, 743	119, 294	10, 955	71, 196	17, 631
...is	152, 829	202, 829	1, 834	338	1, 496	....	50	....
	98, 722	216, 155	1, 964	296	1, 668	....	2, 000	....
	677, 272	803, 029	15, 330	4, 063	11, 267	....	16, 000	....
	265, 925	354, 566	5, 695	1. 848	3, 847	....	1, 937	....
	366, 268	366, 268	4, 165	1, 098	3, 067	....	2, 000	....
...on	467, 847	709, 870	8, 294	1, 403	5, 146	1, 735	4, 187	1, 348
	1, 002, 389	1, 113, 765	7, 029	2, 338	4, 691	....	6, 000	1, 500
	1, 050, 000	1, 050, 000	12, 700	2, 700	10, 000	....	....	....
...t	204, 046	204, 046	2, 548	1, 224	1, 324	....	1, 000	....
	347, 424	626, 125	6, 865	1, 042	5, 823	....	4, 871	....
	196, 000	196, 000	3, 600	600	3, 000	....	....	....
	517, 630	600, 000	4, 472	659	3, 813	....	250	....
	455, 047	505, 607	9, 112	1, 308	7, 804	....	6, 062	....
...nia	158, 439	158, 439	2, 217	950	1, 267	....	335	....

TABLE LXXXIII.—*Valuation, Taxation, and Public Indebtedness by Counties—1870*—Cont'd.

TERRITORY OF WASHINGTON—Continued.

Counties.	VALUATION.		TAXATION, NOT NATIONAL.				PUBLIC DEBT.	
	Assessed valuation of real and personal estate.	True valuation of real and personal estate.	All.	Territory.	County.	Town, city, &c.	County.	Town, city, &c.
	Dollars.	*Dollars.*	*Dollars.*	*Dollars.*	*Dollars.*	*Dollars.*	*Dollars.*	*Dollars.*
Snohomish	138, 570	138, 570	2, 810	415	2, 395	....	500	....
Stevens	134, 320	201, 480	2, 540	432	2, 108	....	6, 500	....
Thurston	1, 185, 471	2, 483, 650	25, 387	3, 556	15, 411	6, 420	12, 354	13, 0[illegible]
Wahkiakum	305, 210	375, 000	290	145	145	....	2, 185	....
Walla-Walla	2, 550, 244	3, 187, 555	40, 432	7, 645	29, 987	2, 800	....	1, 7[illegible]
Whatcom	177, 158	177, 158	3, 646	531	3, 115	....	5, 000	....
Yakima	192, 052	192, 052	3, 072	1, 152	1, 920	....	....	....

STATE OF WEST VIRGINIA.

Counties.	VALUATION.		TAXATION, NOT NATIONAL.				PUBLIC DEBT.	
	Assessed valuation of real and personal estate.	True valuation of real and personal estate.	All.	State.	County.	Town, city, &c.	County.	Town, city, &c.
	Dollars.	*Dollars.*	*Dollars.*	*Dollars.*	*Dollars.*	*Dollars.*	*Dollars.*	*Dollars.*
The State	140, 538, 273	190, 651, 491	1, 722, 158	734, 722	555, 885	431, 551	329, 833	231, 934
Barbour	1, 993, 733	3, 882, 280	15, 133	9, 042	2, 847	3, 244	....	6, 100
Berkeley	6, 386, 218	7, 373, 664	55, 704	27, 396	24, 423	3, 885	7, 000	....
Boone	710, 419	810, 419	15, 796	3, 322	9, 591	2, 883	....	....
Braxton	1, 174, 286	2, 000, 000	17, 694	5, 426	8, 438	3, 830	....	....
Brooke	2, 716, 622	8, 980, 134	20, 484	10, 718	3, 689	6, 077	16, 000	10, 000
Cabell	1, 917, 805	2, 048, 420	22, 150	8, 750	7, 900	5, 500	10, 500	3, 900
Calhoun	417, 068	577, 791	10, 867	2, 266	4, 381	4, 220	....	....
Clay	327, 680	347, 680	4, 395	1, 534	1, 480	1, 381	....	800
Doddridge	1, 694, 638	2, 567, 851	19, 884	6, 036	3, 646	10, 202	4, 000	....
Fayette	1, 208, 458	1, 643, 242	9, 076	5, 949	1, 152	1, 975	....	....
Gilmer	815, 729	919, 133	14, 935	4, 029	6, 906	4, 000	....	....
Grant	1, 830, 905	2, 436, 000	23, 431	7, 672	5, 562	10, 197	....	....
Greenbrier	4, 306, 053	5, 741, 404	41, 836	18, 810	8, 103	14, 923	....	....
Hampshire	2, 221, 669	2, 531, 198	28, 394	10, 161	7, 293	10, 940	3, 331	100
Hancock	2, 374, 828	4, 060, 127	13, 621	8, 115	3, 060	2, 446	....	....
Hardy	2, 304, 548	3, 057, 547	17, 821	9, 434	8, 387	....	1, 230	....
Harrison	7, 174, 751	8, 500, 000	70, 124	27, 362	13, 997	28, 765	2, 487	....
Jackson	2, 514, 026	2, 514, 026	30, 609	10, 800	12, 119	7, 690	2, 600	....
Jefferson	7, 911, 775	12, 206, 135	88, 843	30, 872	49, 136	8, 835	1, 250	....
Kanawha	5, 962, 157	7, 953, 876	99, 101	29, 101	30, 000	40, 000	10, 000	....
Lewis	2, 662, 241	3, 327, 800	23, 063	12, 018	10, 045	1, 000	10, 000	....
Lincoln	1, 118, 360	1, 848, 390	24, 041	5, 194	11, 847	7, 000	10, 170	1, 561
Logan	367, 653	827, 414	10, 942	1, 078	7, 490	2, 374	....	....
Marion	4, 712, 036	5, 280, 000	29, 497	17, 781	11, 330	386	....	....
Marshall	4, 641, 981	7, 543, 945	67, 970	17, 722	15, 144	35, 104	....	....
Mason	6, 232, 173	7, 900, 000	72, 805	25, 150	22, 000	25, 655	1, 200	2, 000
McDowell	196, 754	196, 754	3, 268	1, 022	1, 800	446	....	....
Mercer	1, 370, 861	1, 370, 861	13, 557	5, 906	3, 651	4, 000	....	....
Mineral	3, 043, 810	3, 798, 256	26, 913	12, 333	9, 259	5, 321	9, 450	1, 000
Monongalia	4, 445, 727	4, 445, 727	77, 733	18, 695	48, 038	11, 000	....	....
Monroe	3, 274, 571	4, 854, 509	27, 533	14, 679	12, 354	500	....	....
Morgan	1, 922, 698	1, 922, 698	14, 561	5, 403	7, 462	1, 696	....	....
Nicholas	901, 397	1, 054, 391	7, 207	4, 305	2, 902	....	1, 800	446
Ohio	14, 835, 845	17, 535, 518	198, 769	72, 439	50, 637	75, 693	143, 320	....
Pendleton	1, 574, 950	2, 099, 950	18, 527	5, 930	4, 723	7, 874	....	....
Pleasants	736, 109	794, 399	3, 329	3, 329	....	....	2, 200	....
Pocahontas	1, 423, 351	1, 721, 080	8, 715	6, 112	1, 243	1, 360	....	....
Preston	3, 525, 577	5, 871, 378	30, 814	14, 125	16, 689	....	10, 000	7, 847
Putnam	1, 667, 917	2, 223, 890	27, 538	8, 358	9, 173	10, 007	....	....
Raleigh	654, 956	663, 208	11, 251	3, 251	8, 000	....	1, 800	....
Randolph	1, 275, 210	2, 062, 602	18, 466	5, 944	10, 522	2, 000	....	....

TABLE LXXXIII.—*Valuation, Taxation, and Public Indebtedness by Counties*—1870—Cont'd.

STATE OF WEST VIRGINIA—Continued.

Counties.	VALUATION.		TAXATION, NOT NATIONAL.				PUBLIC DEBT.	
	Assessed valuation of real and personal estate.	True valuation of real and personal estate.	All.	State.	County.	Town, city, &c.	County.	Town, city, &c.
	Dollars.	*Dollars.*	*Dollars.*	*Dollars.*	*Dollars.*	*Dollars.*	*Dollars.*	*Dollars.*
Ritchie	2, 337, 676	2, 454, 267	15, 748	8, 957	2, 492	4, 299	8, 688	955
Roane	1, 120, 196	1, 469, 196	12, 913	5, 314	6, 699	....	....	....
Taylor	3, 179, 430	7, 230, 818	31, 711	12, 691	8, 134	10, 886	....	6, 925
Tucker	385, 964	505, 285	7, 190	1, 706	3, 590	1, 894	....	....
Tyler	1, 743, 082	2, 287, 738	17, 158	7, 721	9, 437	....	7, 187	....
Upshur	2, 225, 334	2, 990, 505	13, 024	9, 449	1, 287	2, 338	....	....
Wayne	1, 874, 318	1, 874, 318	11, 667	8, 147	3, 520	....	....	....
Webster	524, 145	551, 005	8, 501	2, 396	5, 550	555	....	....
Wetzel	1, 782, 386	1, 857, 159	28, 948	7, 383	11, 953	9, 612	3, 400	....
Wirt	1, 064, 379	1, 064, 379	22, 094	4, 715	7, 821	9, 558	28, 214	300
Wood	6, 820, 664	10, 000, 000	81, 848	32, 815	19, 033	30, 000	34, 000	190, 000
Wyoming	873, 025	873, 025	3, 646	3, 646	....	....	....	....
Not distributed among counties	....	....	132, 213	132, 213	....	....	....	....

STATE OF WISCONSIN.

Counties.	VALUATION.		TAXATION, NOT NATIONAL.				PUBLIC DEBT.	
	Assessed valuation of real and personal estate.	True valuation of real and personal estate.	All.	State.	County.	Town, city, &c.	County.	Town, city, &c.
	Dollars.	*Dollars.*	*Dollars.*	*Dollars.*	*Dollars.*	*Dollars.*	*Dollars.*	*Dollars.*
The State	333, 209, 838	702, 307, 329	5, 387, 970	874, 677	1, 507, 605	3, 005, 688	1, 077, 128	2, 574, 347
Adams	933, 035	1, 446, 320	23, 948	1, 194	10, 654	12, 100	....	....
Ashland	83, 640	167, 280	1, 437	237	1, 200	....	....	....
Barron	325, 761	665, 478	417	417	....	....	....	....
Bayfield	351, 109	375, 956	5, 501	276	2, 500	2, 725	....	....
Brown	4, 066, 254	12, 163, 888	58, 515	5, 515	17, 000	36, 000	21, 600	46, 000
Buffalo	1, 171, 815	3, 439, 838	37, 968	2, 968	25, 000	10, 060	....	....
Burnett	166, 695	538, 832	5, 172	435	1, 896	2, 841	....	....
Calumet	1, 382, 341	5, 420, 501	56, 450	3, 970	17, 050	35, 430	....	7, 300
Chippewa	3, 102, 626	9, 776, 984	28, 519	10, 019	12, 000	6, 500	30, 000	....
Clark	1, 737, 245	5, 266, 317	30, 157	6, 157	15, 000	9, 000	25, 000	....
Columbia	9, 934, 812	17, 420, 017	135, 649	12, 053	33, 571	90, 025	....	44, 000
Crawford	2, 095, 927	5, 148, 510	55, 023	3, 652	51, 371	....	....	2, 500
Dane	20, 568, 011	38, 607, 272	287, 072	39, 072	48, 000	200, 000	25, 000	150, 000
Dodge	16, 750, 322	34, 132, 064	156, 531	24, 352	40, 000	92, 179	....	....
Door	717, 887	1, 625, 012	26, 826	2, 226	14, 600	10, 000	....	6, 000
Douglas	658, 230	1, 414, 422	28, 971	1, 354	19, 348	8, 269	2, 000	....
Dunn	2, 421, 530	4, 556, 920	40, 573	4, 550	12, 280	23, 743	....	....
Eau Claire	2, 367, 953	5, 238, 944	77, 592	4, 132	12, 905	60, 555	15, 000	5, 300
Fond du Lac	13, 327, 835	35, 861, 740	222, 998	25, 998	57, 000	140, 000	90, 000	150, 423
Grant	11, 306, 146	30, 651, 881	105, 802	23, 802	22, 000	60, 000	....	....
Green	8, 999, 490	18, 849, 605	79, 216	13, 821	31, 259	34, 136	....	....
Green Lake	7, 362, 929	9, 340, 000	65, 695	10, 695	15, 000	40, 000	....	21, 000
Iowa	6, 458, 695	17, 941, 107	109, 351	13, 307	40, 000	56, 044	150, 000	20, 000
Jackson	1, 441, 706	3, 175, 109	35, 345	3, 241	13, 078	19, 026	25, 000	....
Jefferson	10, 647, 202	20, 742, 580	163, 295	15, 366	33, 324	114, 605	....	467, 000
Juneau	2, 212, 580	3, 817, 146	39, 336	826	13, 510	25, 000	2, 000	....
Kenosha	5, 825, 331	12, 622, 543	58, 967	11, 417	17, 550	30, 000	4, 000	400, 000
Kewaunee	559, 890	2, 811, 831	32, 179	1, 330	6, 000	24, 849	....	....
La Crosse	4, 970, 348	12, 893, 938	70, 170	9, 982	20, 188	40, 000	....	34, 500
La Fayette	6, 613, 075	14, 383, 814	144, 180	12, 150	57, 878	74, 152	9, 600	20, 000
Manitowoc	3, 297, 189	11, 316, 963	70, 593	9, 793	28, 800	32, 000	10, 000	....
Marathon	1, 407, 245	3, 805, 712	28, 611	3, 156	25, 455	....	34, 000	75, 000
Marquette	1, 032, 866	1, 464, 227	16, 163	1, 163	8, 000	7, 000	2, 000	1, 800
Milwaukee	51, 275, 012	88, 422, 711	1, 100, 072	57, 690	271, 100	771, 282	500, 000	[illegible]
Monroe	3, 635, 143	5, 038, 162	55, 999	5, 685	20, 314	30, 000	....	....

TABLE LXXXIII.—*Valuation, Taxation, and Public Indebtedness by Counties*—1870—Cont'd.

STATE OF WISCONSIN—Continued.*

Counties.	VALUATION.		TAXATION, NOT NATIONAL.				PUBLIC DEBT.	
	Assessed valuation of real and personal estate.	True valuation of real and personal estate.	All.	State.	County.	Town, city, &c.	County.	Town, city, &c.
	Dollars.	*Dollars.*	*Dollars.*	*Dollars.*	*Dollars.*	*Dollars.*	*Dollars.*	*Dollars.*
Oconto	1,619,900	11,044,316	55,540	4,540	13,000	38,000	....	15,5[illegible]
Outagamie	2,212,945	10,904,395	81,677	4,794	36,884	40,000	....	3,[illegible]
Ozaukee	3,279,109	5,797,248	39,060	5,125	21,935	12,000	....	16,[illegible]
Pepin	819,880	1,377,426	11,478	1,314	5,164	5,000	....	....
Pierce	2,606,925	5,373,602	69,114	4,610	25,390	39,114	....	....
Polk	931,835	1,950,365	32,150	1,470	1,791	28,883	....	....
Portage	1,734,788	4,022,646	35,451	4,092	17,359	14,000	....	....
Racine	9,543,281	20,827,105	83,571	15,571	18,000	50,000	....	450,0[illegible]
Richland	2,114,117	6,180,000	61,244	5,244	6,000	50,000	....	....
Rock	21,393,939	40,900,000	297,986	32,657	80,548	154,781	....	150,0[illegible]
Sauk	5,551,700	13,200,000	77,003	9,003	28,000	40,000	14,528	6,17[illegible]
Shawanaw	348,329	2,809,159	7,042	1,342	1,500	4,200	9,000	....
Sheboygan	7,908,365	14,626,613	125,255	10,120	45,935	69,200	100,000	182,2[illegible]
St. Croix	3,550,813	7,796,551	75,851	8,613	17,230	50,008	....	12,6[illegible]
Trempeleau	1,866,355	3,660,594	26,456	788	7,668	18,000	....	....
Vernon	3,161,558	9,429,411	36,128	6,543	14,542	15,041	....	....
Walworth	14,873,235	29,560,600	140,471	22,006	23,465	95,000	....	160,00[illegible]
Washington	6,210,164	11,810,144	54,932	10,082	19,850	25,000	....	....
Waukesha	14,793,202	25,660,000	82,707	19,348	29,359	34,000	1,000	....
Waupaca	2,499,570	4,152,550	45,188	4,296	22,892	18,000	....	....
Waushara	1,621,870	3,784,244	26,370	2,370	4,000	20,000	....	....
Winnebago	14,437,299	25,625,512	125,716	17,791	39,925	68,000	....	....
Wood	902,767	1,402,374	33,990	1,652	12,338	20,000	8,000	10,00[illegible]
Not distributed among counties	....	....	339,297	339,297	....	....	....	....

* The Territory of Wyoming was not returned in this respect by counties.

AGRICULTURE.

TABLE LXXXIV.—*Farms: Number and Acreage*—1870–1860–1850.

	States and Territories.	LAND IN FARMS—ACRES.					
		Total.			Improved.		
		1870	1860	1850	1870	1860	1850
	The United States..	407, 735, 041	407, 212, 538	293, 560, 614	188, 921, 099	163, 110, 720	113, 032, 614
1	Alabama	14, 961, 178	19, 104, 545	12, 137, 681	5, 062, 204	6, 385, 724	4, 435, 614
2	Arizona	21, 807	....	....	14, 585	....	....
3	Arkansas	7, 597, 296	9, 573, 706	2, 598, 214	1, 859, 821	1, 983, 313	781, 530
4	California	11, 427, 105	8, 730, 034	3, 893, 985	6, 218, 133	2, 468, 034	32, 454
5	Colorado	320, 346	....	....	95, 594	....	....
6	Connecticut	2, 364, 416	2, 504, 264	2, 383, 879	1, 646, 752	1, 830, 807	1, 768, 178
7	Dakota	302, 376	26, 448	....	42, 645	2, 115	....
8	Delaware	1, 052, 322	1, 004, 295	956, 144	698, 115	637, 065	580, 862
9	District of Columbia	11, 077	34, 263	27, 454	8, 266	17, 474	16, 267
10	Florida	2, 373, 541	2, 920, 228	1, 595, 289	736, 172	654, 213	349, 049
11	Georgia	23, 647, 941	26, 650, 490	22, 821, 379	6, 831, 856	8, 062, 758	6, 378, 479
12	Idaho	77, 139	....	....	26, 603	....	....
13	Illinois	25, 882, 861	20, 911, 989	12, 037, 412	19, 329, 952	13, 096, 374	5, 039, 545
14	Indiana	18, 119, 648	16, 388, 292	12, 793, 422	10, 104, 279	8, 242, 183	5, 046, 543
15	Iowa	15, 541, 793	10, 069, 907	2, 736, 064	9, 396, 467	3, 792, 792	824, 682
16	Kansas	5, 656, 879	1, 778, 400	....	1, 971, 003	405, 468	....
17	Kentucky	18, 660, 106	19, 163, 261	16, 949, 748	8, 103, 850	7, 644, 208	5, 968, 270
18	Louisiana	7, 025, 817	9, 298, 576	4, 989, 043	2, 045, 640	2, 707, 108	1, 590, 025
19	Maine	5, 838, 058	5, 727, 671	4, 555, 393	2, 917, 793	2, 704, 133	2, 039, 596
20	Maryland	4, 512, 579	4, 835, 571	4, 634, 350	2, 914, 007	3, 002, 267	2, 797, 905
21	Massachusetts	2, 730, 283	3, 398, 724	3, 356, 012	1, 736, 221	2, 155, 512	2, 133, 436
22	Michigan	10, 019, 142	7, 030, 834	4, 383, 890	5, 096, 939	3, 476, 296	1, 929, 110
23	Minnesota	6, 483, 828	2, 711, 968	28, 881	2, 322, 102	556, 250	5, 035
24	Mississippi	13, 121, 113	15, 839, 684	10, 490, 419	4, 209, 146	5, 065, 755	3, 444, 358
25	Missouri	21, 707, 220	19, 984, 810	9, 732, 670	9, 130, 615	6, 246, 871	2, 938, 425
26	Montana	139, 537	....	....	84, 674	....	....
27	Nebraska	2, 073, 781	631, 214	....	647, 031	118, 789	....
28	Nevada	208, 510	56, 118	....	92, 644	14, 132	....
29	New Hampshire	3, 605, 994	3, 744, 625	3, 392, 414	2, 334, 487	2, 367, 034	2, 251, 488
30	New Jersey	2, 989, 511	2, 983, 525	2, 752, 946	1, 976, 474	1, 944, 441	1, 767, 991
31	New Mexico	833, 549	1, 414, 909	290, 571	143, 007	149, 274	166, 201
32	New York	22, 190, 810	20, 974, 958	19, 119, 084	15, 627, 206	14, 358, 403	12, 408, 964
33	North Carolina	19, 835, 410	23, 762, 969	20, 996, 983	5, 258, 742	6, 517, 284	5, 453, 975
34	Ohio	21, 712, 420	20, 472, 141	17, 997, 493	14, 469, 133	12, 625, 394	9, 851, 493
35	Oregon	2, 389, 252	2, 060, 539	432, 808	1, 116, 290	896, 414	132, 857
36	Pennsylvania	17, 994, 200	17, 012, 140	14, 923, 347	11, 515, 965	10, 463, 296	8, 628, 619
37	Rhode Island	502, 308	521, 224	553, 938	289, 030	335, 128	356, 487
38	South Carolina	12, 105, 280	16, 195, 919	16, 217, 700	3, 010, 539	4, 572, 060	4, 072, 651
39	Tennessee	19, 581, 214	20, 669, 165	18, 984, 022	6, 843, 278	6, 795, 337	5, 175, 173
40	Texas	18, 396, 523	25, 344, 028	11, 496, 339	2, 964, 836	2, 650, 781	643, 976
41	Utah	148, 361	89, 911	46, 849	118, 755	77, 219	16, 333
42	Vermont	4, 528, 804	4, 274, 414	4, 125, 822	3, 073, 257	2, 823, 157	2, 601, 409
43	Virginia	18, 145, 911	31, 117, 036	26, 152, 311	8, 165, 040	11, 437, 821	10, 360, 135
44	Washington	649, 139	366, 156	....	192, 016	81, 869	....
45	West Virginia	8, 528, 394	....	....	2, 580, 254	....	....
46	Wisconsin	11, 715, 321	7, 893, 587	2, 976, 658	5, 899, 343	3, 746, 107	1, 045, 499
47	Wyoming	4, 341	....	....	338	....	....

REMARKS UPON THE STATISTICS OF AGRICULTURE.

Extracts from the pamphlet of "Instructions to Assistant Marshals" in explanation of these tables:

"FARMS, for the purposes of the Agricultural Schedule, include all considerable nurseries, orchards, and market-gardens, which are owned by separate parties, which are cultivated for pecuniary profit, and employ as much as the labor of one able-bodied workman during the year. Mere cabbage and potato patches, family vegetable-gardens, and ornamental lawns, not constituting a portion of a farm for general agricultural purposes, will be excluded. No farm will be reported of less than three acres, *unless* five hundred dollars' worth of produce has actually been sold off from it during the year. The latter proviso will allow the inclusion of many market-gardens in the neighborhood of large cities, where, although the area is small, a high state of cultivation is maintained and considerable values are produced. A farm is what is owned or leased by one man and cultivated under his care. A distant wood-lot or sheep-pasture, even if in another subdivision, is to be treated as a part of the farm; but wherever there is a resident overseer, or a manager, there a farm is to be reported.

TABLE LXXXIV.—*Farms: Number and Acreage*—1870-1860-1850.

LAND IN FARMS—ACRES.			Percentage of unimproved land in farms to total land in farms.			AVERAGE SIZE OF FARMS.			
Unimproved.						Acres.			
1870	1860	1850	1870	1860	1850	1870	1860	1850	
218, 813, 942	244, 101, 818	180, 528, 000	53. 7	59. 9	61. 5	153	199	203	
9, 898, 974	12, 718, 821	7, 702, 067	66. 2	66. 6	63. 5	222	346	289	1
7, 222	....	....	33. 1	....	....	127	....	....	2
5, 737, 475	7, 590, 393	1, 816, 684	75. 5	79. 3	69. 9	154	245	146	3
5, 208, 972	6, 262, 000	3, 861, 531	45. 6	71. 7	99. 2	482	466	4, 466	4
224, 752	....	....	70. 2	....	....	184	....	....	5
717, 664	673, 457	615, 701	30. 4	26. 9	25. 8	93	99	106	6
230, 731	24, 333	....	85. 9	92. 0	....	176	215	....	7
354, 207	367, 230	375, 282	33. 7	36. 6	39. 2	138	151	158	8
3, 411	16, 789	11, 187	29. 2	49. 0	40. 7	56	144	103	9
1, 637, 369	2, 266, 015	1, 246, 240	69. 0	77. 6	78. 1	232	444	371	10
16, 816, 085	18, 587, 732	16, 442, 900	71. 1	69. 7	72. 0	338	430	441	11
50, 536	....	....	65. 5	....	....	186	....	....	12
6, 552, 909	7, 815, 615	6, 997, 867	25. 3	32. 6	58. 1	128	146	158	13
8, 015, 369	8, 146, 109	7, 746, 879	44. 2	49. 7	60. 6	112	124	136	14
6, 145, 326	6, 277, 115	2, 911, 382	30. 5	62. 2	69. 9	134	165	185	15
3, 685, 876	1, 372, 932	....	65. 2	77. 2	....	148	171	....	16
10, 556, 256	11, 519, 053	10, 961, 478	56. 6	60. 1	64. 7	158	211	227	17
4, 960, 177	6, 591, 468	3, 399, 018	70. 9	70. 9	68. 1	247	536	372	18
2, 920, 265	3, 023, 538	2, 515, 797	50. 0	52. 8	55. 2	98	103	97	19
1, 608, 572	1, 833, 304	1, 836, 445	35. 4	37. 9	39. 6	167	190	212	20
994, 062	1, 183, 212	1, 222, 576	36. 4	35. 4	36. 1	103	94	99	21
4, 922, 203	3, 554, 538	2, 454, 780	49. 1	50. 5	56. 0	101	113	129	22
4, 161, 726	2, 155, 718	23, 846	64. 2	79. 5	82. 6	139	149	184	23
8, 911, 967	10, 773, 929	7, 046, 061	67. 9	68. 0	67. 2	193	370	309	24
12, 576, 605	13, 737, 939	6, 794, 245	57. 9	68. 7	69. 8	146	215	179	25
54, 863	....	....	39. 3	....	....	164	....	....	26
1, 426, 750	512, 425	....	68. 8	81. 2	....	160	226	....	27
115, 866	41, 986	....	55. 5	74. 8	....	201	617	....	28
1, 271, 507	1, 377, 591	1, 140, 926	35. 3	36. 8	33. 3	122	123	116	29
1, 013, 037	1, 039, 084	984, 955	33. 9	34. 9	35. 7	98	108	115	30
690, 542	1, 265, 635	124, 370	82. 8	89. 4	42. 8	186	278	77	31
6, 563, 604	6, 616, 555	6, 710, 120	29. 6	31. 5	35. 1	103	106	112	32
14, 576, 668	17, 245, 685	15, 543, 008	73. 5	72. 6	74. 0	212	316	369	33
7, 243, 287	7, 846, 747	8, 146, 000	33. 4	38. 3	45. 2	111	114	125	34
1, 272, 902	1, 164, 125	299, 951	53. 3	56. 5	69. 3	315	355	372	35
6, 478, 235	6, 548, 844	6, 294, 728	36. 0	38. 5	42. 2	103	109	117	36
213, 278	186, 096	197, 451	42. 5	35. 7	35. 6	94	96	103	37
9, 094, 741	11, 623, 859	12, 145, 049	75. 1	71. 8	74. 9	233	488	541	38
12, 737, 936	13, 873, 828	13, 808, 849	65. 1	67. 1	72. 7	166	251	261	39
15, 431, 687	22, 693, 247	10, 852, 363	83. 9	80. 5	94. 3	301	591	942	40
29, 606	12, 692	30, 516	20. 0	14. 1	65. 1	30	25	51	41
1, 455, 547	1, 451, 257	1, 524, 413	32. 1	34. 0	30. 9	134	135	139	42
9, 960, 871	19, 679, 215	15, 792, 176	55. 0	63. 2	60. 3	246	324	340	43
457, 123	284, 287	....	70. 4	77. 6	....	208	275	....	44
5, 948, 140	....	....	69. 7	....	....	214	....	....	45
5, 815, 978	4, 147, 420	1, 931, 159	50. 5	52. 5	64. 8	114	114	148	46
4, 003	....	....	92. 2	....	....	25	....	....	47

"By 'Improved Land' is meant cleared land used for grazing, grass, or tillage, or ing fallow. Irreclaimable marshes and considerable bodies of water will be exclu ed in giving the area of a farm improved and unimproved. In reporting 'Live-ock,' columns 12, 13, and 14, sucking-pigs, spring-lambs, and calves will be omitted.

"In the 'Produce of the year' will be included the total of all crops, &c., whether nsumed at home or sold off the farm.

"By 'Clover and grass seed' is intended only that which has been cleaned for use or epared for market.

"Under 'Home manufactures' is to be included the value of all articles manufactured the farm, whether for home use or for sale, when the same has not been reported among e products of industry, (Schedule No. 4.) The value of materials *purchased* for such anufactures will be deducted.

"The total value of 'Annual production,' column 52, is intended to exhibit the total sults of all the labor of the farm during the year, whether in the production of crops, additions to stock, in fencing, or in improvements of any description, so far as the me are due to farm labor. Building, fencing, &c., by professional mechanics, will t be included. Neither will a speculative rise of land, nor an enhancement of values the opening of railroads, &c., be reckoned in the annual production of the farm."

TABLE LXXXV.—*Values of Farms, Farming Implements, and Machinery—1870–1860–1850.*

States and Territories.	1870		1860		1850	
	Of farms.	Of farming implements and machinery.	Of farms.	Of farming implements and machinery.	Of farms.	Of farming implements and machinery.
	Dollars.	*Dollars.*	*Dollars.*	*Dollars.*	*Dollars.*	*Dollars.*
The United States	9,262,803,861	336,878,429	6,645,045,007	246,118,141	3,271,575,426	151,587,638
Alabama	67,739,036	3,286,924	175,824,622	7,433,178	64,323,224	5,125,663
Arizona	161,340	20,105				
Arkansas	40,029,698	2,237,409	91,649,773	4,175,326	15,265,245	1,601,296
California	141,240,028	5,316,690	48,726,804	2,558,506	3,874,041	103,483
Colorado	3,385,748	272,604				
Connecticut	124,241,382	3,246,599	90,830,005	2,339,481	72,726,422	1,892,541
Dakota	2,085,265	142,612	96,445	15,574		
Delaware	46,712,870	1,201,644	31,426,357	817,883	18,880,031	510,279
District of Columbia	3,800,230	39,450	2,989,267	54,408	1,730,460	40,220
Florida	9,947,920	505,074	16,435,727	900,669	6,323,109	658,795
Georgia	94,559,468	4,614,701	157,072,803	6,844,387	95,753,445	5,894,150
Idaho	492,860	50,295				
Illinois	920,506,346	34,576,587	408,944,033	17,235,472	96,133,290	6,405,561
Indiana	634,804,189	17,676,591	356,712,175	10,457,897	136,385,173	6,704,444
Iowa	*392,662,441	20,509,582	119,899,547	5,327,033	16,657,567	1,172,869
Kansas	90,327,040	4,053,312	12,258,239	727,694		
Kentucky	311,238,916	8,572,896	291,496,955	7,474,573	155,021,262	5,169,037
Louisiana	68,215,421	7,159,333	204,789,662	18,648,225	75,814,398	11,576,938
Maine	102,961,951	4,809,113	78,688,525	3,298,327	54,861,748	2,284,557
Maryland	170,369,684	5,268,676	145,973,677	4,010,529	87,178,545	2,463,443
Massachusetts	116,432,784	5,000,879	123,255,948	3,894,998	109,076,347	3,209,584
Michigan	398,240,578	13,711,979	160,836,495	5,819,832	51,872,446	2,891,371
Minnesota	97,847,442	6,721,120	27,505,922	1,018,183	161,948	15,981
Mississippi	81,716,576	4,456,633	190,760,367	8,826,512	54,738,634	5,762,927
Missouri	392,908,047	15,596,426	230,632,126	8,711,508	63,225,543	3,981,525
Montana	729,193	145,438				
Nebraska	30,242,186	1,549,716	3,878,326	205,664		
Nevada	1,485,505	163,718	302,340	11,081		
New Hampshire	80,589,313	3,459,943	69,689,761	2,683,012	55,245,997	2,314,125
New Jersey	257,523,376	7,887,991	180,250,338	5,746,567	120,237,511	4,425,503
New Mexico	2,260,139	121,114	2,707,386	192,917	1,653,922	77,900
New York	1,272,857,766	45,997,712	803,343,593	29,166,695	554,546,642	22,084,926
North Carolina	78,211,083	4,082,111	143,301,065	5,873,942	67,891,766	3,931,532
Ohio	1,054,465,226	25,692,787	678,132,991	17,538,832	358,758,603	12,750,585
Oregon	22,352,989	1,293,717	15,200,593	952,313	2,849,170	183,423
Pennsylvania	1,043,481,582	35,658,196	662,050,707	22,442,842	407,876,099	14,722,541
Rhode Island	21,574,968	726,246	19,550,553	586,791	17,070,802	497,201
South Carolina	44,808,763	2,282,946	139,652,508	6,151,657	82,431,684	4,136,354
Tennessee	218,743,747	8,199,487	271,358,985	8,465,792	97,851,212	5,360,210
Texas	60,149,950	3,396,793	88,101,320	6,259,452	16,550,008	2,151,704
Utah	2,297,922	291,390	1,333,355	242,889	311,799	84,288
Vermont	139,367,075	5,250,279	94,289,045	3,665,955	63,367,227	2,739,282
Virginia	213,020,845	4,924,036	371,761,661	9,392,296	216,401,543	7,021,772
Washington	3,978,341	280,551	2,217,842	190,402		
West Virginia	101,604,381	2,112,937				
Wisconsin	300,414,064	14,239,364	131,117,164	5,758,847	28,528,563	1,641,568
Wyoming	18,187	5,723				

The Census agricultural year.—The first question, logically, which arises in respect to what purports to be a statement of annual production, viz: "What is the year covered by the report?" is one which it is impossible to answer in respect to the tables of agricultural production in the census of the United States. The schedule annexed to and made a part of the law of 1850 requires the products of each farm in the United States "for the year ending June 1." But there is no agricultural year ending June 1. The division made by the law is a purely artificial one, and cuts the agricultural year in twain.

As a matter of fact, as the census under existing laws always has been and always will be taken, the production returned is not the production of any one year distinctly, but is made up, without any determinable proportion, indifferently from the production of two years.

The enumeration at the Ninth Census, for example, beginning upon the 1st of June, 1870, assistant marshals obtain for a month or two the production of 1869 in the main, although in some sections many of the crops (notably hay, wool, and some of the grain crops) are already so far advanced that the farmer is quite as likely to estimate his an-

SHEEP AND WOOL.

[To illustrate the remarks on page 696. See also tables on pages 698 and 708.]

States and Territories.	SHEEP.		WOOL, (pounds.)		AVERAGE.	
	1870	1860	1870	1860	1870	1860
United States	28, 477, 951	22, 471, 275	100, 102, 387	60, 264, 913	3. 52	2. 68
I. Total	1, 450, 155	1, 779, 767	6, 643, 387	6, 578, 094	4. 58	4. 82
Maine	434, 666	452, 472	1, 774, 168	1, 495, 060	4. 08	3. 30
New Hampshire	248, 760	310, 534	1, 129, 442	1, 160, 222	4. 54	3. 74
Vermont	580, 347	752, 201	3, 102, 137	3, 118, 950	5. 35	4. 15
Massachusetts	78, 560	114, 829	306, 659	377, 267	3. 90	3. 29
Rhode Island	23, 938	32, 624	77, 328	90, 699	3. 23	2. 78
Connecticut	83, 884	117, 107	254, 129	335, 896	3. 03	2. 87
II. Total	4, 248, 357	4, 550, 245	17, 991, 085	15, 097, 958	4. 23	3. 31
New York	2, 181, 578	2, 617, 855	10, 599, 225	9, 454, 474	4. 86	3. 61
Pennsylvania	1, 794, 301	1, 631, 540	6, 561, 722	4, 752, 522	3. 66	2. 91
New Jersey	120, 067	135, 228	336, 600	349, 250	2. 80	2. 58
Delaware	22, 714	18, 857	58, 316	50, 201	2. 57	2. 66
Maryland	129, 697	155, 765	435, 213	491, 511	3. 36	3. 16
III. Total	4, 502, 060	4, 239, 810	10, 543, 920	197, 711	2. 31	2. 17
Virginia	370, 145	10, 043, 269	877, 110	2, 510, 019	2. 37	2. 41
District of Columbia	604	40	....	100	0. 00	2. 50
West Virginia	552, 327	....	1, 593, 541	....	2. 89	....
North Carolina	463, 435	546, 749	799, 667	853, 473	1. 73	1. 63
Kentucky	936, 765	938, 990	2, 234, 450	2, 329, 105	2. 39	2. 48
Tennessee	826, 783	773, 317	1, 389, 762	1, 405, 236	1. 68	1. 82
Missouri	1, 352, 001	937, 445	3, 649, 390	2, 069, 778	2. 70	2. 21
IV. Total	2, 039, 354	2, 636, 442	3, 316, 901	5, 068, 513	1. 63	1. 92
South Carolina	124, 594	233, 509	156, 314	427, 102	1. 25	1. 83
Georgia	419, 465	512, 618	846, 947	946, 227	2. 02	1. 85
Florida	26, 599	30, 158	37, 562	59, 171	1. 41	1. 96
Alabama	241, 934	370, 156	381, 253	775, 117	1. 58	2. 09
Mississippi	232, 732	352, 632	288, 285	665, 959	1. 24	1. 89
Louisiana	118, 602	181, 253	140, 428	290, 847	1. 18	1. 60
Texas	714, 351	753, 363	1, 251, 328	1, 493, 738	1. 75	1. 98
Arkansas	161, 077	202, 753	214, 784	410, 382	1. 33	2. 02
V. Total	12, 284, 438	7, 203, 783	47, 902, 618	20, 832, 927	3. 90	2. 89
Ohio	4, 928, 635	3, 546, 767	20, 539, 643	10, 608, 927	4. 17	2. 99
Indiana	1, 612, 680	991, 175	5, 029, 023	2, 552, 318	3. 12	2. 57
Illinois	1, 568, 286	769, 135	5, 739, 249	1, 989, 567	3. 66	2. 59
Iowa	855, 493	250, 041	2, 967, 043	660, 858	3. 47	2. 55
Michigan	1, 985, 906	1, 271, 743	8, 726, 145	3, 960, 888	4. 39	3. 11
Wisconsin	1, 069, 282	332, 954	4, 090, 670	1, 011, 933	3. 83	3. 04
Minnesota	132, 343	13, 044	401, 185	20, 388	3. 03	1. 56
Kansas	109, 088	17, 569	335, 005	24, 746	3. 07	1. 41
Nebraska	22, 725	2, 355	74, 655	3, 302	3. 29	1. 40
VI. Total	3, 149, 194	1, 184, 587	12, 662, 802	2, 922, 270	4. 02	2. 46
Washington	44, 063	10, 157	162, 713	19, 819	3. 69	1. 95
Oregon	318, 123	86, 052	1, 080, 638	219, 012	3. 40	2. 55
California	2, 768, 187	1, 088, 002	11, 391, 743	2, 683, 109	4. 12	2. 47
Nevada	11, 018	376	27, 029	330	2. 45	0. 88
Arizona	803	....	679	....	0. 85	....
VII. Total	811, 393	867, 641	1, 041, 198	567, 410	1. 28	0. 65
Idaho	1, 021	....	3, 415	....	3. 34	....
Montana	2, 024	....	100	....	0. 05	....
Dakota	1, 901	193	8, 810	....	4. 63	....
Wyoming	6, 409	....	30, 000	....	4. 68	....
Utah	59, 672	37, 332	109, 018	74, 765	1. 83	2. 00
Colorado	120, 928	....	204, 925	....	1. 69	....
New Mexico	619, 438	830, 116	684, 930	492, 645	1. 11	0. 59

ual production (it must be remembered that few of the statistics of production are obtained as transcripts from actual accounts) from his impressions in regard to the growing crop, as by recalling the experience of the previous year. As the enumeration progresses through September and October, the crop of 1870 is returned in increasing pro-

TABLE LXXXVI.—*Values of Farm Productions and Wages*—1870–1860–1850.

	States and Territories.	1870						
		All farm productions, including betterments and additions to stock.	Animals slaughtered, or sold for slaughter.	Home manufactures.	Forest products.	Market-garden products.	Orchard products.	Wages paid during the year, including value of board.
		Dollars.	*Dollars.*	*Dollars.*	*Dollars.*	*Dollars.*	*Dollars.*	*Dollars.*
	The United States	2, 447, 538, 658	398, 956, 376	23, 423, 332	36, 808, 277	20, 719, 229	47, 335, 189	310, 286, 28[illegible]
1	Alabama	67, 522, 335	4, 670, 146	1, 124, 513	85, 933	139, 636	37, 590	11, 651, [illegible]
2	Arizona	277, 998	9, 400	....	....	2, 850	....	[illegible]
3	Arkansas	40, 701, 699	3, 843, 923	807, 573	34, 225	55, 697	157, 219	[illegible]
4	California	49, 856, 024	6, 112, 503	301, 491	566, 017	1, 059, 779	1, 384, 480	[illegible]
5	Colorado	2, 335, 106	252, 394	57, 658	....	55, 020	9	[illegible]
6	Connecticut	26, 482, 150	4, 881, 858	53, 297	1, 224, 107	599, 718	535, 594	[illegible]
7	Dakota	495, 657	22, 066	1, 677	700	500	....	[illegible]
8	Delaware	8, 171, 667	997, 403	33, 070	111, 810	198, 075	1, 226, 893	[illegible]
9	District of Columbia	319, 517	455	750	....	112, 034	6, 781	[illegible]
10	Florida	8, 909, 746	520, 966	131, 693	7, 965	31, 983	53, 639	[illegible]
11	Georgia	80, 390, 228	6, 854, 382	1, 113, 080	1, 281, 623	193, 206	352, 926	[illegible]
12	Idaho	637, 797	57, 932	34, 730	....	24, 577	725	[illegible]
13	Illinois	210, 860, 585	56, 718, 944	1, 408, 015	1, 087, 144	765, 992	3, 571, 789	[illegible]
14	Indiana	122, 914, 302	30, 246, 962	605, 639	2, 645, 679	487, 479	2, 858, 086	[illegible]
15	Iowa	114, 386, 441	25, 781, 223	521, 404	1, 200, 468	244, 963	1, 075, 169	[illegible]
16	Kansas	27, 630, 651	4, 156, 386	156, 910	368, 947	129, 013	158, 046	[illegible]
17	Kentucky	87, 477, 374	24, 121, 861	1, 683, 972	574, 994	527, 329	1, 231, 385	[illegible]
18	Louisiana	52, 006, 622	817, 831	64, 416	92, 596	170, 969	142, 129	[illegible]
19	Maine	33, 470, 044	4, 939, 071	450, 988	1, 531, 741	966, 397	674, 569	[illegible]
20	Maryland	35, 343, 927	4, 621, 418	63, 608	613, 209	1, 039, 782	1, 319, 405	[illegible]
21	Massachusetts	32, 192, 378	4, 324, 658	79, 378	1, 616, 818	1, 980, 231	939, 854	[illegible]
22	Michigan	81, 508, 623	11, 711, 624	338, 008	2, 559, 682	352, 658	3, 447, 985	[illegible]
23	Minnesota	33, 446, 400	3, 076, 650	174, 046	311, 528	115, 234	15, 818	[illegible]
24	Mississippi	73, 137, 953	4, 090, 818	505, 298	39, 975	61, 735	71, 018	[illegible]
25	Missouri	103, 035, 759	23, 626, 784	1, 737, 606	793, 343	406, 655	2, 617, 462	[illegible]
26	Montana	1, 676, 660	169, 092	155, 357	918	33, 130	....	[illegible]
27	Nebraska	8, 604, 742	854, 850	36, 951	36, 307	30, 649	9, 932	[illegible]
28	Nevada	1, 659, 713	104, 471	2, 329	36, 700	31, 235	900	[illegible]
29	New Hampshire	22, 473, 547	3, 720, 243	234, 062	1, 743, 944	119, 297	743, 552	[illegible]
30	New Jersey	42, 725, 198	6, 982, 162	144, 016	352, 704	2, 978, 250	1, 295, 282	[illegible]
31	New Mexico	1, 905, 060	224, 765	19, 592	500	64, 132	13, 609	[illegible]
32	New York	253, 526, 153	28, 225, 720	1, 621, 621	6, 689, 179	3, 432, 354	8, 347, 417	[illegible]
33	North Carolina	57, 845, 940	7, 983, 132	1, 603, 513	1, 069, 115	48, 499	394, 749	[illegible]
34	Ohio	198, 256, 907	40, 498, 375	1, 371, 409	2, 719, 140	1, 289, 272	5, 843, 679	[illegible]
35	Oregon	7, 122, 790	1, 365, 737	87, 376	239, 220	105, 371	310, 041	[illegible]
36	Pennsylvania	183, 946, 027	28, 412, 903	1, 503, 754	2, 670, 370	1, 810, 016	4, 208, 094	[illegible]
37	Rhode Island	4, 761, 163	755, 532	37, 847	254, 683	316, 133	43, 036	[illegible]
38	South Carolina	41, 909, 402	2, 507, 149	312, 191	167, 233	127, 459	47, 960	[illegible]
39	Tennessee	86, 472, 847	15, 856, 880	2, 773, 829	335, 317	301, 093	571, 520	[illegible]
40	Texas	49, 185, 170	4, 835, 284	293, 308	66, 841	74, 924	60, 172	[illegible]
41	Utah	1, 973, 142	172, 382	56, 891	800	8, 700	43, 938	[illegible]
42	Vermont	34, 647, 027	4, 320, 619	181, 268	1, 238, 929	42, 225	682, 241	[illegible]
43	Virginia	51, 774, 801	8, 375, 975	556, 307	686, 862	505, 117	891, 231	[illegible]
44	Washington	2, 111, 902	292, 280	28, 890	19, 705	74, 462	71, 863	215, 3[illegible]
45	West Virginia	23, 379, 692	4, 914, 792	615, 412	363, 668	69, 974	848, 773	1, 903, 7[illegible]
46	Wisconsin	78, 027, 032	11, 914, 643	338, 423	1, 327, 618	226, 665	810, 268	8, 186, 110
47	Wyoming	42, 760	11, 712	175	....	....	....	3, 075

portions, earlier in some parts of the country than in others, and earlier in respect to some crops than to others in the same section. As the work is protracted through November and December, and, through the utter want of control at the central office, is allowed to drag, in some counties, through January and February, the crop of 1870 becomes the only one that is in contemplation of either the farmer or the assistant marshal in filling up the agricultural schedule.

Number and size of farms.—The preparation of the tables distributing the total number of farms returned at the census into classes, according to the number of acres of improved land in each, has been attended with unusual difficulty at the present census, in consequence of the extraordinary and wholly anomalous condition of agriculture at the South. The plantations of the old slave States are squatted all over by the former slaves, who hold small portions of the soil, often very loosely determined as to extent, under almost all varieties of tenure.

In the instructions to assistant marshals in preparation for the census, and during the early days of the enumeration, efforts were made to impose something like a rule

TABLE LXXXVI.—*Values of Farm Productions and Wages*—1870-1860-1850.

1860				1850				
Animals slaughtered, or sold for slaughter.	Home manufactures.	Market-garden products.	Orchard products.	Animals slaughtered.	Home manufactures.	Market-garden products.	Orchard products.	
Dollars. 213, 618, 692	*Dollars.* 24, 546, 876	*Dollars.* 16, 159, 498	*Dollars.* 19, 991, 885	*Dollars.* 111, 703, 142	*Dollars.* 27, 493, 644	*Dollars.* 5, 280, 030	*Dollars.* 7, 723, 186	
10, 237, 131	1, 817, 520	163, 062	223, 312	4, 823, 485	1, 934, 120	84, 821	15, 408	1
....	....	....	....	....	....	....	....	2
3, 878, 990	1, 019, 240	37, 845	56, 025	1, 163, 313	638, 217	17, 150	40, 141	3
3, 449, 823	255, 653	1, 161, 855	754, 236	107, 173	7, 000	75, 275	17, 700	4
....	....	....	....	....	....	....	....	5
3, 181, 992	48, 954	337, 025	508, 848	2, 202, 266	192, 252	196, 874	175, 118	6
375	....	....	....	....	....	....	....	7
573, 075	17, 591	37, 797	114, 225	373, 665	38, 121	12, 714	46, 574	8
55, 440	440	139, 408	9, 080	9, 038	2, 075	67, 222	14, 843	9
1, 193, 904	63, 259	20, 828	21, 259	514, 685	75, 582	8, 721	1, 280	10
10, 908, 204	1, 431, 413	201, 916	176, 048	6, 339, 762	1, 838, 908	76, 500	92, 770	11
....	....	....	....	....	....	....	....	12
15, 032, 433	923, 220	387, 027	1, 126, 323	4, 972, 286	1, 155, 902	127, 494	446, 049	13
9, 824, 204	986, 393	546, 153	1, 258, 942	6, 567, 935	1, 631, 039	72, 864	324, 940	14
4, 430, 030	317, 690	169, 870	118, 377	821, 164	221, 292	8, 848	8, 434	15
558, 174	24, 748	31, 641	658	....	....	....	....	16
11, 640, 738	2, 095, 578	458, 245	604, 849	6, 462, 598	2, 459, 128	303, 120	106, 230	17
2, 085, 330	502, 100	413, 169	114, 330	1, 458, 990	139, 232	148, 329	22, 359	18
2, 780, 179	490, 786	194, 006	501, 767	1, 646, 773	513, 599	122, 387	342, 865	19
2, 821, 510	67, 003	530, 221	252, 196	1, 954, 800	111, 828	200, 869	164, 051	20
2, 915, 045	245, 886	1, 397, 623	925, 519	2, 500, 924	205, 333	600, 020	463, 995	21
4, 093, 362	142, 756	145, 883	1, 122, 074	1, 328, 327	340, 947	14, 738	132, 650	22
751, 544	7, 981	174, 704	649	2, 840	....	150	....	23
7, 809, 153	1, 382, 144	124, 281	254, 718	3, 636, 582	1, 164, 020	46, 250	50, 405	24
9, 844, 449	1, 984, 262	346, 405	810, 975	3, 367, 106	1, 674, 705	99, 454	514, 711	25
....	....	....	....	....	....	....	....	26
97, 790	15, 995	10, 582	125	....	....	....	....	27
9, 385	300	2, 225	....	....	....	....	....	28
3, 787, 500	251, 052	76, 256	557, 934	1, 522, 873	393, 455	56, 810	248, 563	29
4, 120, 276	27, 588	1, 541, 995	429, 402	2, 638, 552	112, 781	475, 242	607, 268	30
347, 105	26, 406	17, 664	19, 651	88, 125	6, 033	6, 679	8, 231	31
15, 841, 404	717, 898	3, 381, 596	3, 726, 380	13, 573, 883	1, 280, 333	912, 047	1, 761, 950	32
10, 414, 546	2, 045, 372	75, 063	643, 688	5, 767, 866	2, 086, 522	39, 462	34, 348	33
14, 725, 945	596, 197	907, 513	1, 929, 309	7, 439, 243	1, 712, 196	214, 004	695, 921	34
648, 465	46, 278	75, 605	478, 479	164, 530	....	90, 241	1, 271	35
13, 309, 375	544, 728	1, 384, 968	1, 479, 937	8, 219, 848	749, 132	688, 714	723, 389	36
711, 723	7, 824	140, 291	83, 691	667, 486	26, 495	98, 298	63, 994	37
6, 072, 822	815, 117	187, 348	213, 989	3, 502, 637	909, 525	47, 286	35, 108	38
12, 430, 768	3, 174, 977	303, 226	305, 003	6, 401, 765	3, 137, 790	97, 183	52, 894	39
5, 143, 635	584, 217	178, 374	48, 047	1, 110, 137	266, 984	12, 354	12, 503	40
244, 802	66, 851	9, 830	9, 281	67, 985	1, 392	23, 868	....	41
2, 610, 800	63, 334	24, 802	211, 693	1, 861, 336	267, 710	18, 853	315, 255	42
11, 491, 027	1, 576, 627	589, 467	800, 650	7, 502, 986	2, 156, 312	183, 047	177, 137	43
80, 909	33, 506	24, 399	20, 619	....	....	....	....	44
....	....	....	....	....	....	....	....	45
3, 365, 261	127, 092	208, 730	78, 600	920, 178	43, 624	32, 142	4, 823	46
....	....	....	....	....	....	....	....	47

which should govern in the returns of agriculture at the South; but after a weary and unprofitable struggle the Superintendent was fain to accept whatever could be obtained in regard to the agriculture of that region, without greatly criticising the form in which it came. To have insisted upon a logical treatment of the subject would have been equivalent to giving up the agricultural statistics of the year.

For the reasons above stated it became necessary to distribute among the several classes, in the tables under discussion, a great number of farms, in each of the former slave States, of undetermined acreage. The plan adopted has been to treat all such farms as being of more than three* and less than ten acres. Undoubtedly, in ninety-nine out of every hundred instances, this assumption answered to the real facts of the case. Of the remainder it is enough to say that nothing better could be done with them under the most unfortunate circumstances attending the enumeration.

* Less than three acres not constituting a farm for census purposes, with a single class of exceptions only occurring in the immediate neighborhood of large cities, with land in a high state of cultivation.

TABLE LXXXVII.—*Principal Cereal Productions*—1870-1860-1850.

	States and Territories.	1870						
		WHEAT.						
		Spring.	Winter.	Rye.	Indian corn.	Oats.	Barley.	Buckwheat.
		Bushels.	*Bushels.*	*Bushels.*	*Bushels.*	*Bushels.*	*Bushels.*	*Bushels.*
	The United States..	112,549,733	175,195,893	16,918,795	760,944,549	282,107,157	29,761,305	9,821,7
1	Alabama	201,086	833,982	18,977	16,977,948	770,866	5,174	16
2	Arizona	27,052	....	....	32,041	25	55,077	....
3	Arkansas	72,347	669,329	27,645	13,382,145	528,777	1,921	26
4	California	16,676,702	....	26,275	1,221,222	1,757,507	8,783,490	21,92
5	Colorado	255,939	2,535	5,235	231,903	332,940	35,141	1
6	Connecticut	2,085	36,050	229,057	1,570,364	1,114,595	26,458	148,15
7	Dakota	170,460	202	....	133,140	114,327	4,118	17
8	Delaware	137	895,340	10,222	3,010,390	554,382	1,729	1,3
9	District of Columbia	....	3,782	3,724	28,020	8,500	....	[illegible]
10	Florida	....	....	545	2,225,056	114,204	12	....
11	Georgia	308,890	1,818,127	82,549	17,646,459	1,904,601	5,640	42
12	Idaho	73,725	1,925	1,750	5,750	100,119	72,316	....
13	Illinois	10,133,207	19,995,198	2,456,578	129,921,395	42,780,851	2,480,400	168,862
14	Indiana	161,991	27,585,231	457,468	51,094,538	8,590,409	356,262	60,2
15	Iowa	28,708,312	727,380	505,807	68,935,065	21,005,142	1,960,779	109,432
16	Kansas	1,314,522	1,076,676	85,207	17,025,525	4,097,925	98,405	27,2
17	Kentucky	38,532	5,690,172	1,108,933	50,091,006	6,620,103	238,486	3,443
18	Louisiana	1,157	8,749	984	7,596,628	17,782	1,296	9
19	Maine	274,593	4,200	34,115	1,089,888	2,351,354	658,816	466,63
20	Maryland	1,095	5,773,408	307,089	11,701,817	3,221,643	11,315	77,867
21	Massachusetts	17,574	17,074	239,227	1,397,807	797,664	133,071	52,049
22	Michigan	268,810	15,996,963	144,508	14,086,238	8,954,466	834,558	436,7
23	Minnesota	18,789,188	76,885	78,088	4,743,117	10,678,261	1,032,024	52,438
24	Mississippi	66,638	207,841	14,852	15,637,316	414,586	3,973	1,619
25	Missouri	1,093,905	13,222,021	559,532	66,034,075	16,578,313	269,240	36,2
26	Montana	177,535	3,649	1,141	330	149,367	85,756	9
27	Nebraska	2,109,321	15,763	13,532	4,736,710	1,477,562	216,481	3,471
28	Nevada	147,987	80,879	310	9,660	55,916	205,452	9
29	New Hampshire	189,222	4,390	47,420	1,277,768	1,146,451	105,822	100,034
30	New Jersey	2,099	2,299,334	566,775	8,745,384	4,009,830	8,283	353,98
31	New Mexico	338,930	13,892	42	640,823	67,660	3,876	1
32	New York	1,831,330	10,344,132	2,478,125	16,462,825	35,293,625	7,434,621	3,904,030
33	North Carolina	405,218	2,454,641	352,006	18,454,215	3,220,105	3,186	20,109
34	Ohio	256,400	27,625,759	846,890	67,501,144	25,347,549	1,715,221	180,341
35	Oregon	1,794,494	546,252	3,890	72,138	2,029,909	210,736	1,645
36	Pennsylvania	322,328	19,350,639	3,577,641	34,702,006	36,478,585	529,562	2,532,173
37	Rhode Island	586	196	20,214	311,957	157,010	33,559	1,444
38	South Carolina	317,700	465,910	36,165	7,614,207	613,593	4,752	312
39	Tennessee	375,400	5,813,516	223,335	41,343,614	4,513,315	75,068	77,437
40	Texas	66,173	348,239	28,521	20,554,538	762,663	44,351	44
41	Utah	543,487	14,986	1,312	95,557	65,650	49,117	17
42	Vermont	438,155	16,548	73,346	1,690,882	3,602,430	117,333	415,096
43	Virginia	7,389	7,391,398	582,264	17,649,304	6,857,555	7,259	45,0
44	Washington	186,180	30,863	4,453	21,781	258,169	55,787	31
45	West Virginia	3,395	2,480,148	277,746	8,197,865	2,413,749	30,263	82,916
46	Wisconsin	24,375,435	1,230,909	1,325,294	15,033,998	20,180,016	1,645,019	408,897
47	Wyoming	....	....	....	....	100	....	....

A comparison of the number of acres of land in farms in 1870 with that in 1860 will show that the only States in which there has been a falling off in the amount under cultivation are, first, those in which slavery existed in 1860, and in which conditions growing out of the change in the system of labor have prevented a complete rehabilitation of agricultural industry; or, second, those of New England, in which the decrease is mainly due to the extension of manufacturing towns and villages; or, third, as in the case of New Mexico and Virginia, where territory has been set off to create new States or Territories.

The limitations of agricultural statistics.—The agricultural statistics of the United States, under the present census law, being obtained by the visitation of each farm in turn, attain a high degree of accuracy in respect to all crops which are of considerable importance, either for the whole country or for the particular section under enumeration.

The above qualification expresses quite exactly the principal limitation of the agricultural statistics of the United States. The census has little authority in respect to minor productions. Where a crop is of small importance, or is only occasionally cultivated, the assistant marshal will naturally and almost inevitably fail to put the question at every house. The farmer, on the other hand, on account of its little import-

TABLE LXXXVII.—*Principal Cereal Productions*—1870-1860-1850.

1860						
Wheat.	Rye.	Indian corn.	Oats.	Barley.	Buckwheat.	
Bushels. 173, 104, 924	*Bushels.* 21, 101, 380	*Bushels.* 838, 792, 742	*Bushels.* 172, 643, 185	*Bushels.* 15, 825, 898	*Bushels.* 17, 571, 818	
1, 218, 444	72, 457	33, 226, 282	682, 179	15, 135	1, 347	1
....	....	....	....	....	....	2
957, 601	78, 092	17, 823, 588	475, 268	3, 158	509	3
5, 928, 470	52, 140	510, 708	1, 043, 006	4, 415, 426	76, 887	4
....	....	....	....	....	....	5
52, 401	618, 702	2, 059, 835	1, 522, 218	20, 813	300, 107	6
945	700	20, 269	2, 540	....	115	7
912, 941	27, 209	3, 892, 337	1, 040, 910	3, 646	16, 355	8
12, 760	6, 919	80, 840	29, 548	175	445	9
2, 808	21, 306	2, 834, 391	46, 890	8, 369	....	10
2, 544, 913	115, 532	30, 776, 293	1, 231, 817	14, 682	2, 023	11
....	....	....	....	....	....	12
23, 837, 023	951, 281	115, 174, 777	15, 220, 029	1, 036, 338	324, 117	13
16, 848, 267	463, 495	71, 588, 919	5, 317, 831	382, 245	396, 989	14
8, 449, 403	183, 022	42, 410, 686	5, 887, 645	467, 103	215, 705	15
194, 173	3, 833	6, 150, 727	88, 325	4, 716	41, 575	16
7, 394, 809	1, 055, 260	64, 043, 633	4, 617, 029	270, 685	18, 928	17
32, 208	36, 065	16, 853, 745	89, 377	224	160	18
233, 870	123, 287	1, 546, 071	2, 988, 939	802, 108	239, 519	19
6, 103, 480	518, 901	13, 444, 922	3, 959, 298	17, 350	212, 338	20
119, 783	388, 085	2, 157, 063	1, 180, 075	134, 891	183, 202	21
8, 336, 368	514, 129	12, 444, 676	4, 036, 980	307, 868	529, 910	22
2, 186, 993	121, 411	2, 941, 952	2, 176, 002	109, 668	28, 052	23
587, 925	39, 474	29, 057, 682	221, 235	1, 875	1, 099	24
4, 227, 586	293, 262	72, 892, 157	3, 680, 870	228, 502	182, 292	25
....	....	....	....	....	....	26
147, 807	2, 495	1, 482, 080	74, 502	1, 108	12, 224	27
3, 631	98	460	1, 082	1, 597	....	28
238, 965	128, 247	1, 414, 628	1, 329, 233	121, 103	89, 996	29
1, 763, 218	1, 439, 497	9, 723, 336	4, 539, 132	24, 915	877, 386	30
434, 309	1, 300	709, 304	7, 246	6, 099	6	31
8, 681, 105	4, 786, 905	20, 061, 049	35, 175, 134	4, 186, 668	5, 126, 307	32
4, 743, 706	436, 856	30, 078, 564	2, 781, 860	3, 445	35, 924	33
15, 119, 047	683, 686	73, 543, 190	15, 409, 234	1, 663, 868	2, 370, 650	34
826, 776	2, 704	76, 122	885, 673	26, 254	2, 749	35
13, 042, 165	5, 474, 788	28, 196, 821	27, 387, 147	530, 714	5, 572, 024	36
1, 131	28, 259	461, 497	244, 453	40, 993	3, 573	37
1, 285, 631	89, 091	15, 065, 606	936, 974	11, 490	602	38
5, 459, 268	257, 989	52, 089, 926	2, 267, 814	25, 144	14, 481	39
1, 478, 345	111, 860	16, 500, 702	985, 889	67, 562	1, 349	40
384, 892	754	90, 482	63, 211	9, 976	68	41
437, 037	139, 271	1, 525, 411	3, 630, 267	79, 211	225, 415	42
13, 130, 977	944, 330	38, 319, 999	10, 186, 720	68, 846	478, 090	43
86, 219	144	4, 712	134, 334	4, 021	707	44
....	....	....	....	....	....	45
15, 657, 458	888, 544	7, 517, 300	11, 059, 260	707, 307	38, 987	46
....	....	....	....	....	....	47

ance among the products of the year, will fail to mention it, and the result will be an inadequate representation of that crop.

So general and positive is the law of the human mind under which such omissions take place, that some of the inquiries of the Agricultural Schedule might just as well be dropped. The results are hardly worth publishing, and, if taken without the present qualification, are calculated only to deceive.

This much is true, however, that certain crops which are only rarely cultivated, and that in small amounts, in the great majority of States, and are therefore in those States inadequately represented, become of importance in some single section and are there returned with reasonable completeness. If, then, due allowance be made for the omissions in the sections where the crop is of little account, a very tolerable result for the entire country may be reached.

This frank admission in regard to the slight value of the statistics of the census in respect to the minor crops should have no effect to disparage the authority of its statements in respect to the staple products of the country as a whole, or of any section. The very laws of mind by which the former lose even the slight attention they deserve, give the strongest assurance for the general completeness and correctness of the latter.

TABLE LXXXVII.—*Principal Cereal Productions—1870–1860–1850*—Continued.

	States and Territories.	1850						
		Wheat.	Rye.	Indian corn.	Oats.	Barley.	Buckwheat.	
		Bushels.	*Bushels.*	*Bushels.*	*Bushels.*	*Bushels.*	*Bushels.*	
	The United States...	100, 485, 944	14, 188, 813	592, 071, 104	146, 584, 179	5, 167, 015	8, 956, 912	
1	Alabama	294, 044	17, 261	28, 754, 048	2, 965, 696	3, 958	346	1
2	Arizona							2
3	Arkansas	199, 639	8, 047	8, 893, 939	656, 183	177	175	3
4	California	17, 328		12, 236		9, 712		4
5	Colorado							5
6	Connecticut	41, 762	600, 893	1, 935, 043	1, 258, 738	19, 099	229, 297	6
7	Dakota							7
8	Delaware	482, 511	8, 066	3, 145, 542	604, 518	56	8, 615	8
9	District of Columbia	17, 370	5, 509	65, 230	8, 134	75	378	9
10	Florida	1, 027	1, 152	1, 996, 809	66, 586		55	10
11	Georgia	1, 088, 534	53, 750	30, 080, 099	3, 820, 044	11, 501	[illegible]	11
12	Idaho							12
13	Illinois	9, 414, 575	83, 364	57, 646, 984	10, 087, 241	110, 795	184, [illegible]	13
14	Indiana	6, 214, 458	78, 792	52, 964, 363	5, 655, 014	45, 483	149, [illegible]	14
15	Iowa	1, 530, 581	19, 916	8, 656, 799	1, 524, 345	25, 093	52, [illegible]	15
16	Kansas							16
17	Kentucky	2, 142, 822	415, 073	58, 672, 591	8, 201, 311	95, 343	16, [illegible]	17
18	Louisiana	417	475	10, 266, 373	89, 637		[illegible]	18
19	Maine	296, 259	102, 916	1, 750, 056	2, 181, 037	151, 731	104, [illegible]	19
20	Maryland	4, 494, 680	226, 014	10, 749, 858	2, 242, 151	745	103, [illegible]	20
21	Massachusetts	31, 211	481, 021	2, 345, 490	1, 165, 146	112, 385	105, [illegible]	21
22	Michigan	4, 925, 889	105, 871	5, 641, 420	2, 866, 056	75, 249	472, [illegible]	22
23	Minnesota	1, 401	125	16, 725	30, 582	1, 216	[illegible]	23
24	Mississippi	137, 990	9, 606	22, 446, 552	1, 503, 288	228	1, [illegible]	24
25	Missouri	2, 981, 652	44, 268	36, 214, 537	5, 278, 079	9, 631	23, [illegible]	25
26	Montana							26
27	Nebraska							27
28	Nevada							28
29	New Hampshire	185, 658	183, 117	1, 573, 670	973, 381	70, 256	65, [illegible]	29
30	New Jersey	1, 601, 190	1, 255, 578	8, 759, 704	3, 378, 063	6, 492	878, [illegible]	30
31	New Mexico	196, 516		365, 411	5	5	[illegible]	31
32	New York	13, 121, 498	4, 148, 182	17, 858, 400	26, 552, 814	3, 585, 059	3, 183, [illegible]	32
33	North Carolina	2, 130, 102	229, 563	27, 941, 051	4, 052, 078	2, 735	16, [illegible]	33
34	Ohio	14, 487, 351	425, 918	59, 078, 695	13, 472, 742	354, 358	638, [illegible]	34
35	Oregon	211, 943	106	2, 918	61, 214			35
36	Pennsylvania	15, 367, 691	4, 805, 160	19, 835, 214	21, 538, 156	165, 584	2, 193, [illegible]	36
37	Rhode Island	49	26, 409	539, 201	215, 232	18, 875	1, [illegible]	37
38	South Carolina	1, 066, 277	43, 790	16, 271, 454	2, 322, 155	4, 583	[illegible]	38
39	Tennessee	1, 619, 386	89, 137	52, 276, 223	7, 703, 086	2, 737	19, [illegible]	39
40	Texas	41, 729	3, 108	6, 028, 876	199, 017	4, 776	59	40
41	Utah	107, 702	210	9, 899	10, 900	1, 799	332	41
42	Vermont	535, 955	176, 233	2, 032, 396	2, 307, 734	42, 150	209, 819	42
43	Virginia	11, 212, 616	458, 930	35, 254, 319	10, 179, 144	25, 437	214, [illegible]	43
44	Washington							44
45	West Virginia							45
46	Wisconsin	4, 286, 131	81, 253	1, 988, 979	3, 414, 672	209, 692	79, 878	46
47	Wyoming							47

A second limitation of the agricultural statistics of the census is found in the inapplicability of the schedule to sections in the condition of the several Territories, as also of the State of Texas, and some portions of the States of California, Kansas, and Nebraska. That schedule was framed wholly with reference to the agricultural requirements of the older States, where the land is divided up into well-defined farms, and the operations of a comparatively advanced agriculture are systematically carried on. It is utterly inadequate to represent the grazing industry of the great plains beyond the Missouri, and the results in respect to this region might, perhaps, have been omitted from the publication with credit to the census.

Wool.—The census statistics of wool for the Seventh and Eighth Censuses have been severely criticised by "the trade" on account of the low average clip per head reported throughout the country, and more especially in certain of the States.

It is doubtful whether the average yield of wool, as shown by the ratio between the number of sheep returned in the census and the number of pounds of wool returned, will ever reach the average weight of fleece as reckoned by the trade. This is due, unquestionably, in part to the fact that the average taken by the wool-brokers for the

HORSES AND NEAT CATTLE.

[To be read with the remarks on page 708. See also the table on page 708.]

s and Territories.	HORSES.			NEAT CATTLE.		
	Total.	On farms.	Not on farms.	Total.	On farms.	Not on farms.
tal	8,690,219	7,142,849	1,547,370	28,074,582	23,800,609	4,273,973
a	92,807	78,962	13,845	500,206	471,893	28,313
	4,432	335	4,097	38,632	5,132	33,500
as	102,240	92,013	10,227	379,023	357,935	21,088
ia	241,146	192,273	48,873	669,280	631,398	37,882
	13,317	6,446	6,871	159,456	70,736	88,720
icut	54,139	34,935	19,204	231,094	218,013	13,081
	3,243	2,514	729	56,724	12,467	44,257
e	18,633	16,770	1,863	53,990	49,990	4,000
of Columbia	6,029	533	5,496	1,801	801	1,000
	14,451	11,902	2,549	453,451	390,915	62,536
	110,237	81,777	28,460	809,667	697,903	111,764
	2,775	2,151	624	59,996	10,456	49,540
	1,017,646	853,738	163,908	1,944,573	1,715,586	228,987
	551,203	497,883	53,320	1,182,988	1,026,184	156,804
	482,786	433,642	49,144	1,137,045	1,006,235	130,810
	152,000	117,786	34,214	998,347	373,967	624,380
y	351,200	317,034	34,166	812,380	700,327	112,053
a	62,584	59,025	3,559	383,364	330,532	52,832
	79,782	71,514	8,268	428,826	343,061	85,765
d	102,216	89,696	12,520	231,399	215,359	16,040
usetts	86,266	41,039	45,227	271,315	219,052	52,263
a	253,670	228,302	25,368	635,134	547,529	87,605
ta	102,678	93,011	9,667	365,241	310,379	54,862
pi	104,600	90,221	14,379	581,247	501,075	80,172
	545,822	493,969	51,853	1,269,065	1,153,695	115,370
	6,733	5,289	1,444	82,380	36,738	45,642
a	33,901	30,511	3,390	392,716	79,928	312,788
	14,400	7,520	6,880	40,969	31,516	9,453
mpshire	43,335	39,095	4,240	236,169	222,801	13,368
sey	103,663	79,708	23,955	229,086	197,488	31,598
xico	26,500	5,033	21,467	186,301	57,534	128,767
k	856,241	536,861	319,380	2,086,230	2,045,324	40,906
rolina	114,406	102,763	11,643	618,263	521,162	97,101
	704,664	609,722	94,942	1,521,421	1,436,217	85,204
	64,625	51,702	12,923	150,246	120,197	30,049
ania	611,488	460,339	151,149	1,505,897	1,344,551	161,346
land	11,113	7,770	3,343	40,105	34,375	5,730
rolina	54,052	44,105	9,947	289,207	249,303	39,904
ee	273,200	247,254	25,946	682,318	643,696	38,622
	574,641	424,504	150,137	3,990,158	3,494,043	496,115
	14,281	11,068	3,213	190,934	39,180	151,754
	69,015	65,015	4,000	346,501	320,835	25,666
	168,938	152,899	16,039	573,152	511,743	61,409
ton	13,923	11,138	2,785	51,979	47,254	4,725
rginia	99,362	90,479	8,883	337,881	301,680	36,201
in	270,083	252,019	18,064	831,953	693,294	138,659
g	3,753	584	3,169	36,472	11,130	25,342

es of this comparison is the average under favorable conditions. Still, it must nitted, as the result of candid investigation, that the figures of the trade have uch nearer to the truth than those of the census, in this particular, in the great y of States. In certain of the States, however, (notably those of the South,) ust be taken with the statements of the trade. It is not questioned that single of sheep, receiving adequate care and attention, and kept with a view to the oduct, in any one of these States, might, under fortunate conditions, yield an weight of fleece equal to what is claimed. But a very extensive correspond- onducted by the Census Office—more extensive, unquestionably, than any nducted by private parties—enables the statement to be made with confidence some of the Southern States a large portion of the sheep owned are not kept view to the wool product, and are actually not sheared. So general is this as ce the aggregate clip in those States more nearly to the figures of the census those of the trade.

l the States, however, where sheep are kept in considerable numbers for the the wool crop, and in the Northern and Western States generally, there is no hat *the return of wool in* previous censuses has been partial, and the average *therefore, brought below* the undoubted facts of the case. This has been due

TABLE LXXXVIII.—*Principal Fibrous Productions*—1870–1860–1850.

	States and Territories.	1870				
		Cotton.	Flax.	Hemp.	Silk cocoons.	Wool.*
		*Bales.**	*Pounds.*	*Tons.*	*Pounds.*	*Pounds.*
	The United States	3, 011, 996	27, 133, 034	12, 746	3, 937	100, 102, [illegible]
1	Alabama	429, 482	37			[illegible]
2	Arizona					[illegible]
3	Arkansas	247, 968	490			214, [illegible]
4	California	34	31, 740	200	3, 587	11, [illegible]
5	Colorado					204, [illegible]
6	Connecticut		300			[illegible]
7	Dakota					[illegible]
8	Delaware		878			[illegible]
9	District of Columbia					
10	Florida	39, 789				37, [illegible]
11	Georgia	473, 934	983		14	[illegible], 947
12	Idaho					[illegible]
13	Illinois	465	2, 204, 606	174		5, [illegible]
14	Indiana	3	37, 771	22		5, [illegible]
15	Iowa		695, 518	4		2, [illegible]
16	Kansas	7	1, 040	35		[illegible]
17	Kentucky	1, 080	237, 268	7, 777	45	2, [illegible]
18	Louisiana	350, 832			1	[illegible]
19	Maine		5, 435			1, [illegible]
20	Maryland		30, 760			[illegible]
21	Massachusetts		930	2		[illegible]
22	Michigan		240, 110			8, [illegible]
23	Minnesota		122, 571			[illegible]
24	Mississippi	564, 938	100	3	31	[illegible]
25	Missouri	1, 246	10, 613	2, 816	3	3, [illegible]
26	Montana					[illegible]
27	Nebraska		54			74, 655
28	Nevada	106				[illegible]
29	New Hampshire		177			1, [illegible]
30	New Jersey		234, 061	5		[illegible]
31	New Mexico					[illegible]
32	New York		3, 670, 818	6		10, [illegible]
33	North Carolina	144, 935	59, 552		95	[illegible]
34	Ohio		17, 880, 624	25		20, [illegible]
35	Oregon		40, 474			1, [illegible]
36	Pennsylvania		815, 906	571	1	6, 561, [illegible]
37	Rhode Island					77, [illegible]
38	South Carolina	224, 500				136, [illegible]
39	Tennessee	181, 842	80, 930	1, 033	153	1, [illegible]
40	Texas	350, 628	25	5		1, [illegible]
41	Utah	22	10			[illegible]
42	Vermont		12, 899			3, [illegible], 137
43	Virginia	183	130, 750	31	7	877, 110
44	Washington					[illegible]
45	West Virginia	2	82, 276	37		1, [illegible]
46	Wisconsin		497, 398			4, [illegible]
47	Wyoming					[illegible]

* Four hundred pounds each.

partly to the fact that all wool used in "Domestic manufactures" (as returned upon the Agricultural Schedule under the law of 1850) is properly excluded, in order to avoid a duplication of value; also, to the fact that the aggregate number of sheep is made up in part of very small flocks, or single animals, whose product of wool is so inconsiderable that it is never marketed, or, if marketed, escapes mention among the farm productions of the year; also, to the fact that large numbers of sheep are sold to butchers, who in turn sell the wool on the skin, making no return of any portion of their industry upon the Schedule of Agriculture; also, probably, to the fact that in spite of instructions from the Census Office, a considerable number of spring lambs are included in the report of sheep, thus reducing the average yield; also, probably, to the fact that a portion of the wool returned was either cleaned before being sold from the farm, or was stated by the farmer "discounted," according to the usual loss in cleaning. Of these five causes, the second and third are by far the most influential. For the purpose of ascertaining the extent of omissions to return wool where sheep

TABLE LXXXVIII.—*Principal Fibrous Productions*—1870–1860–1850.

1860					1850					
Cotton.	Flax.	Hemp.	Silk cocoons.	Wool. †	Cotton.	Flax.	Hemp.	Silk cocoons.	Wool.	
Bales. *	*Pounds.*	*Tons.*	*Pounds.*	*Pounds.*	*Bales.* *	*Pounds.*	*Tons.*	*Pounds.*	*Pounds.*	
5,387,052	4,720,145	74,493	11,944	60,264,913	2,469,093	7,709,676	34,871	10,843	52,516,959	
989,955	111		315	775,117	564,429	3,921		167	657,118	1
										2
367,393	3,821	447	5	410,382	65,344	12,291	15	38	182,595	3
				2,683,109					5,590	4
										5
	1,187	3	18	335,896		17,928		328	497,454	6
										7
	8,112			50,201		11,174			57,768	8
				100					585	9
65,153		1		59,171	45,131	50		6	23,247	10
701,840	3,303	31	72	946,227	499,091	5,387		813	990,019	11
										12
1,482	48,235	1,502	1,545	1,989,567		160,063		47	2,150,113	13
	97,119	4,222	575	2,552,318	14	584,469		387	2,610,287	14
	30,226	651	124	660,858		92,660		246	373,898	15
61	1,135	44	40	24,746						16
	728,234	39,409	340	2,329,105	758	2,100,116	17,787	1,281	2,297,433	17
777,738		1		290,847	178,737			29	109,897	18
	2,997	50	73	1,495,060		17,081		252	1,364,034	19
	14,481	272	3	491,511		35,686	63	39	477,438	20
	165			377,267		1,102		7	586,136	21
	4,128	776	12	3,960,888		7,152		108	2,043,283	22
	1,983	109	52	20,388					85	23
1,202,507	50		10	665,959	484,292	665	7	2	539,619	24
41,188	109,837	19,267	127	2,069,778		527,160	16,028	186	1,627,164	25
										26
		9	120	3,302						27
				330						28
	1,347	81	1	1,160,222		7,632		191	1,108,476	29
	42,651	430		349,250		182,965		23	375,396	30
19				492,645					32,901	31
	1,518,025	5	250	9,454,474		940,577	4	1,774	10,071,301	32
145,514	216,490	3,016	338	883,473	73,845	503,796	39	229	970,738	33
	882,423	1,212	7,394	10,608,927		446,932	150	1,552	10,196,371	34
	162	1		219,012		640			29,686	35
	312,368	46	163	4,752,522		530,307	44	285	4,481,570	36
				90,699		85			120,602	37
353,412	344	1	20	427,102	300,901	333		123	487,233	38
296,464	164,294	2,243	71	1,405,236	194,532	308,131	595	1,923	1,364,378	39
431,463	115	170	27	1,493,738	58,072	1,048		22	131,917	40
136	4,343	114		74,765		550			9,222	41
	7,007			3,118,950		20,852		268	3,400,717	42
12,727	487,808	15	225	2,510,019	3,947	1,000,450	139	517	2,860,765	43
				19,819						44
										45
	21,644	356	15	1,011,933		62,393			253,963	46
										47

† See table on page 691.

are reported, the Agricultural Schedules of 1860 for the State of Iowa have been carefully examined, with the result that 2,416 farms, with an aggregate of 24,067 sheep, (out of a total of 259,041,) were found for which no production of wool was returned. In a very small proportion of these cases the sheep may have been brought upon the farms after shearing-time, and consequently their product would be embraced in the return of other farms; but, after all reasonable deduction on this account, the fact would still remain that no product of wool was returned for at least eight per cent. of the sheep owned in this State at the last census. [For table of sheep and wool with the average clip at the censuses of 1870 and 1860, see page 691.]

Horses and cattle not upon farms.—The census law of 1850 makes no provision for enumerating live stock not found upon farms. As a consequence, the returns on the Agricultural Schedule fail to include the large number of horses and yoke-oxen which are kept in cities, towns, and villages for draught or driving, and also to include the not inconsiderable number of milch-cows found in cities, towns, and villages, as above,

TABLE LXXXIX.—*Hay, Hops, Rice, and Tobacco*—1870–1860–1850.

	States and Territories.	1870			
		Hay.	Hops.	Rice.	Tobacco.
	The United States	*Tons.* 27, 316, 048	*Pounds.* 25, 456, 669	*Pounds.* 73, 635, 021	*Pounds.* 262, 735, 341
1	Alabama	10, 613	32	222, 945	152, 742
2	Arizona	109			109
3	Arkansas	6, 839	25	73, 021	594, 886
4	California	551, 773	625, 064		63, 809
5	Colorado	19, 787			250
6	Connecticut	563, 328	1, 004		8, 328, 798
7	Dakota	13, 347			
8	Delaware	41, 890	800		250
9	District of Columbia	2, 019			
10	Florida	17		401, 687	157, 405
11	Georgia	10, 518	2	22, 277, 380	288, 596
12	Idaho	6, 985	21		
13	Illinois	2, 747, 339	104, 032		5, 249, 274
14	Indiana	1, 076, 768	63, 884		9, 325, 392
15	Iowa	1, 777, 339	171, 113		71, 792
16	Kansas	490, 289	396		33, 241
17	Kentucky	204, 399	947		105, 305, 869
18	Louisiana	8, 776		15, 854, 012	15, 541
19	Maine	1, 053, 415	296, 850		15
20	Maryland	223, 119	2, 800		15, 785, 339
21	Massachusetts	597, 455	61, 910		7, 312, 885
22	Michigan	1, 290, 923	828, 269		5, 385
23	Minnesota	695, 053	222, 065		8, 247
24	Mississippi	8, 324		374, 627	61, 012
25	Missouri	615, 611	19, 297		12, 320, 483
26	Montana	18, 727			680
27	Nebraska	169, 354	100		5, 988
28	Nevada	33, 855			25
29	New Hampshire	612, 648	99, 469		155, 334
30	New Jersey	521, 975	19, 033		40, 871
31	New Mexico	4, 209			8, 587
32	New York	5, 614, 205	17, 558, 681		2, 349, 798
33	North Carolina	83, 540	238	2, 059, 281	11, 150, 087
34	Ohio	2, 289, 565	101, 236		18, 741, 973
35	Oregon	75, 357	9, 745		3, 847
36	Pennsylvania	2, 848, 219	90, 688		3, 467, 539
37	Rhode Island	89, 045	249		796
38	South Carolina	10, 665	1, 507	32, 304, 825	34, 805
39	Tennessee	116, 582	565	3, 399	21, 465, 452
40	Texas	18, 982	51	63, 844	59, 706
41	Utah	27, 305	322		
42	Vermont	1, 020, 669	527, 927		72, 671
43	Virginia	109, 883	10, 099		37, 086, 364
44	Washington	30, 233	6, 162		1, 634
45	West Virginia	224, 164	1, 031		2, 046, 452
46	Wisconsin	1, 287, 651	4, 630, 155		960, 813
47	Wyoming	3, 180			

as well as those belonging to persons following commercial, mechanical, or professional pursuits in agricultual regions.

At the census of 1850 no effort appears to have been made to supplement the returns of live stock on the Agricultural Schedules by any calculation or estimate of the number not upon farms.

At the census of 1860 assistant marshals were requested, each in his own subdivision, to prepare estimates of the number of animals, of each recognized class, not found upon farms in the course of enumeration. This request appears to have been quite generally complied with. The results will be found upon page 192 of the Agricultural volume of that census.

No effort of this kind has been made at the present census; but the Superintendent has sought to place himself in possession of all statistical data of a positive character in existence upon this subject, and by comparison of these data, and with consideration of the varying conditions of settlement and employment in each section, to prepare himself to make an intelligent estimate of the number of horses and of neat cattle, respectively, omitted from enumeration by reason of the defect noted in the census

TABLE LXXXIX.—*Hay, Hops, Rice, and Tobacco*—1870–1860–1850.

1860				1850				
Hay.	Hops.	Rice.	Tobacco.	Hay.	Hops.	Rice.	Tobacco.	
Tons. 19,083,896	*Pounds.* 10,991,996	*Pounds.* 187,167,032	*Pounds.* 434,209,461	*Tons.* 13,838,642	*Pounds.* 3,497,029	*Pounds.* 215,313,497	*Pounds.* 199,752,655	
62,211	507	493,465	232,914	32,685	276	2,312,252	164,990	1
......	......	......	......	......	......	......	......	2
9,356	146	16,831	989,980	3,976	137	63,179	218,936	3
305,655	80	2,140	3,150	2,038	......	......	1,000	4
......	......	......	......	......	......	......	......	5
502,425	959	......	6,000,133	516,131	554	......	1,267,624	6
855	......	......	10	......	......	......	......	7
36,973	414	......	9,699	30,150	348	......	......	8
3,180	15	......	15,200	2,279	15	......	7,800	9
11,478	......	223,704	828,815	2,510	14	1,075,090	998,614	10
46,448	199	52,507,652	919,318	23,449	261	38,950,691	423,924	11
......	......	......	......	......	......	......	......	12
1,774,554	7,254	......	6,885,262	601,952	3,551	......	841,394	13
622,426	27,884	......	7,093,378	403,230	92,796	......	1,044,620	14
813,173	2,078	......	303,168	89,055	8,242	......	6,041	15
56,232	197	......	20,349	......	......	......	......	16
158,476	5,899	......	108,126,840	113,747	4,309	5,688	55,501,196	17
52,721	27	6,331,257	39,940	23,752	125	4,425,349	26,878	18
975,803	102,987	......	1,583	755,889	40,120	......	......	19
191,744	2,943	......	38,410,965	157,956	1,870	......	21,407,497	20
665,331	111,301	......	3,233,198	651,807	121,595	......	138,246	21
768,256	60,602	716	121,090	404,934	10,663	......	1,245	22
179,482	132	3,296	38,938	2,019	......	......	......	23
32,901	248	609,082	159,141	12,504	473	2,719,856	49,960	24
401,070	2,265	9,767	25,086,196	116,925	4,130	700	17,113,784	25
......	......	......	......	......	......	......	......	26
24,458	41	......	3,636	......	......	......	......	27
2,213	......	......	......	......	......	......	......	28
642,741	130,428	......	18,581	598,854	257,174	......	50	29
508,726	3,722	......	149,485	435,950	2,133	......	310	30
1,113	......	......	7,041	......	......	......	8,467	31
3,564,793	9,671,931	......	5,764,582	3,728,79[illegible]	2,536,299	......	83,189	32
181,365	1,767	7,593,976	32,853,250	145,653	9,246	5,465,868	11,984,786	33
1,564,502	27,533	......	25,092,581	1,443,142	63,731	......	10,454,449	34
27,986	493	......	405	373	8	......	325	35
2,245,413	43,191	......	3,181,586	1,842,970	22,088	......	912,651	36
82,722	50	......	705	74,818	277	......	......	37
87,587	122	119,100,528	104,412	20,925	26	159,930,613	74,285	38
143,499	1,581	40,372	43,448,097	74,091	1,032	258,854	20,148,932	39
11,865	123	26,031	97,914	8,354	7	88,203	66,897	40
19,235	545	......	......	4,805	50	......	70	41
940,178	638,677	......	12,245	866,153	288,023	......	......	42
445,133	10,024	8,225	123,968,312	369,098	11,506	17,154	56,803,227	43
4,580	44	......	10	......	......	......	......	44
......	......	......	......	......	......	......	......	45
855,037	135,587	......	87,340	275,662	15,930	......	1,268	46
......	......	......	......	......	......	......	......	47

aw. In some cases statistical data of a high character were accessible in the form of State censuses, or reports of State auditors made up from the returns of local assessors. The number of such animals in nearly fifty important cities was accurately determined by reports from the police authorities, and many towns and villages, and some rural counties in States not furnishing other official data, were canvassed with reference to this subject. The known habits and conditions of settlement, society, and occupation in each State became also elements of great importance in these computations. The result of these processes will be found in the table on page 697. The large relative falling off in the live stock of the country between 1860 and 1870 is due in great part, if not entirely, to the tremendous waste of four years of war.

Cheese and wine.—It should be observed that the cheese returned among the productions of agriculture includes only the cheese made upon the farm. The product of cheese-factories will be found in the proper place in the Statistics of Manufactures.

In the same manner the production of wine will be found both in the tables of agriculture and manufactures, according as the wine is made upon the farm or vineyard,

TABLE LXXXIX.—*Hay, Hops, Rice, and Tobacco*—1870-1860-1850.

	States and Territories.	1870			
		Hay.	Hops.	Rice.	Tobacco.
		Tons.	*Pounds.*	*Pounds.*	*Pounds.*
	The United States	27,316,048	25,456,669	73,635,021	262,735,341
1	Alabama	10,613	32	222,945	152,742
2	Arizona	109			100
3	Arkansas	6,839	25	73,021	594,886
4	California	551,773	625,064		63,809
5	Colorado	19,787			899
6	Connecticut	563,328	1,004		8,328,798
7	Dakota	13,347			
8	Delaware	41,890	800		250
9	District of Columbia	2,019			
10	Florida	17		401,687	157,405
11	Georgia	10,518	2	22,277,380	288,596
12	Idaho	6,985	21		
13	Illinois	2,747,339	104,032		5,249,274
14	Indiana	1,076,768	63,884		9,325,392
15	Iowa	1,777,339	171,113		71,792
16	Kansas	490,289	396		33,241
17	Kentucky	204,399	947		105,305,869
18	Louisiana	8,776		15,854,012	15,541
19	Maine	1,053,415	296,850		15
20	Maryland	223,119	2,800		15,785,339
21	Massachusetts	597,455	61,910		7,312,885
22	Michigan	1,290,923	828,269		5,385
23	Minnesota	695,053	222,065		8,247
24	Mississippi	8,324		374,627	61,012
25	Missouri	615,611	19,297		12,320,483
26	Montana	18,727			680
27	Nebraska	169,354	100		5,988
28	Nevada	33,855			25
29	New Hampshire	612,648	99,469		155,334
30	New Jersey	521,975	19,033		40,871
31	New Mexico	4,209			8,587
32	New York	5,614,205	17,558,681		2,349,798
33	North Carolina	83,540	238	2,059,281	11,150,087
34	Ohio	2,289,565	101,236		18,741,973
35	Oregon	75,357	9,745		3,847
36	Pennsylvania	2,848,219	90,688		3,467,539
37	Rhode Island	89,045	249		796
38	South Carolina	10,665	1,507	32,304,825	34,805
39	Tennessee	116,582	565	3,399	21,465,452
40	Texas	18,982	51	63,844	59,706
41	Utah	27,305	322		
42	Vermont	1,020,669	527,927		72,671
43	Virginia	199,883	10,999		37,086,364
44	Washington	30,233	6,162		1,698
45	West Virginia	224,164	1,031		2,046,452
46	Wisconsin	1,287,651	4,630,155		960,813
47	Wyoming	3,180			

as well as those belonging to persons following commercial, mechanical, or professional pursuits in agricultual regions.

At the census of 1850 no effort appears to have been made to supplement the returns of live stock on the Agricultural Schedules by any calculation or estimate of the number not upon farms.

At the census of 1860 assistant marshals were requested, each in his own subdivision, to prepare estimates of the number of animals, of each recognized class, not found upon farms in the course of enumeration. This request appears to have been quite generally complied with. The results will be found upon page 192 of the Agricultural volume of that census.

No effort of this kind has been made at the present census; but the Superintendent has sought to place himself in possession of all statistical data of a positive character in existence upon this subject, and by comparison of these data, and with consideration of the varying conditions of settlement and employment in each section, to prepare himself to make an intelligent estimate of the number of horses and of neat cattle, respectively, omitted from enumeration by reason of the defect noted in the census

TABLE LXXXIX.—*Hay, Hops, Rice, and Tobacco*—1870-1860-1850.

1860				1850				
Hay.	Hops.	Rice.	Tobacco.	Hay.	Hops.	Rice.	Tobacco.	
Tons. 19, 083, 896	*Pounds.* 10, 991, 996	*Pounds.* 187, 167, 032	*Pounds.* 434, 209, 461	*Tons.* 13, 838, 642	*Pounds.* 3, 497, 029	*Pounds.* 215, 313, 497	*Pounds.* 199, 752, 655	
62, 211	507	493, 465	232, 914	32, 685	276	2, 312, 252	164, 990	1
....	....	....	....	....	....	....	....	2
9, 356	146	16, 831	989, 980	3, 976	157	63, 179	218, 936	3
305, 655	80	2, 140	3, 150	2, 038	....	....	1, 000	4
....	....	....	....	....	....	....	....	5
502, 425	959	....	6, 000, 133	516, 131	554	....	1, 267, 624	6
855	....	....	10	....	....	....	....	7
36, 973	414	....	9, 699	30, 159	348	....	....	8
3, 180	15	....	15, 200	2, 279	15	....	7, 800	9
11, 478	....	223, 704	828, 815	2, 510	14	1, 075, 090	998, 614	10
46, 448	199	52, 507, 652	919, 318	23, 449	261	38, 950, 691	423, 924	11
....	....	....	....	....	....	....	....	12
1, 774, 554	7, 254	....	6, 885, 262	601, 952	3, 551	....	841, 394	13
622, 426	27, 884	....	7, 993, 378	403, 230	92, 796	....	1, 044, 620	14
813, 173	2, 078	....	303, 168	89, 055	8, 242	....	6, 041	15
56, 232	197	....	20, 349	....	....	....	....	16
158, 476	5, 899	....	108, 126, 840	113, 747	4, 309	5, 688	55, 501, 196	17
52, 721	27	6, 331, 257	39, 940	25, 752	125	4, 425, 349	26, 878	18
975, 803	102, 987	....	1, 583	755, 889	40, 120	....	....	19
191, 744	2, 943	....	38, 410, 965	157, 956	1, 870	....	21, 407, 497	20
665, 331	111, 301	....	3, 233, 198	651, 807	121, 595	....	138, 246	21
768, 256	60, 602	716	121, 099	404, 934	10, 663	....	1, 245	22
179, 482	132	3, 286	38, 938	2, 019	....	....	....	23
32, 901	248	809, 082	159, 141	12, 504	473	2, 719, 856	49, 960	24
401, 070	2, 265	9, 767	25, 086, 196	116, 925	4, 130	700	17, 113, 784	25
....	....	....	....	....	....	....	....	26
24, 458	41	....	3, 636	....	....	....	....	27
2, 213	....	....	....	....	....	....	....	28
642, 741	130, 428	....	18, 581	598, 854	257, 174	....	50	29
508, 726	3, 722	....	149, 485	435, 950	2, 133	....	310	30
1, 113	....	....	7, 041	....	....	....	8, 467	31
3, 564, 793	9, 671, 931	....	5, 764, 582	3, 728, 797	2, 536, 299	....	83, 189	32
181, 365	1, 767	7, 593, 976	32, 853, 250	145, 653	9, 246	5, 465, 868	11, 984, 786	33
1, 564, 502	27, 533	....	25, 092, 581	1, 443, 142	63, 731	....	10, 454, 449	34
27, 986	493	....	405	373	8	....	325	35
2, 245, 413	43, 191	....	3, 181, 586	1, 842, 970	22, 088	....	912, 651	36
22, 722	50	....	705	74, 818	277	....	....	37
87, 587	122	119, 100, 528	104, 412	20, 925	26	159, 930, 613	74, 285	38
143, 499	1, 581	40, 372	43, 448, 097	74, 091	1, 032	258, 854	20, 148, 932	39
11, 865	123	26, 031	97, 914	8, 354	7	88, 203	66, 897	40
19, 235	545	....	....	4, 805	50	....	70	41
940, 178	638, 677	....	12, 245	866, 153	288, 023	....	....	42
445, 133	10, 024	8, 225	123, 968, 312	369, 098	11, 506	17, 154	56, 803, 227	43
4, 580	44	....	10	....	....	....	....	44
....	....	....	....	....	....	....	....	45
855, 037	135, 587	....	87, 340	275, 662	15, 930	....	1, 268	46
....	....	....	....	....	....	....	....	47

law. In some cases statistical data of a high character were accessible in the form of State censuses, or reports of State auditors made up from the returns of local assessors. The number of such animals in nearly fifty important cities was accurately determined by reports from the police authorities, and many towns and villages, and some rural counties in States not furnishing other official data, were canvassed with reference to this subject. The known habits and conditions of settlement, society, and occupation in each State became also elements of great importance in these computations. The result of these processes will be found in the table on page 697. The large relative falling off in the live stock of the country between 1860 and 1870 is due in great part, if not entirely, to the tremendous waste of four years of war.

Cheese and wine.—It should be observed that the cheese returned among the productions of agriculture includes only the cheese made upon the farm. The product of cheese-factories will be found in the proper place in the Statistics of Manufactures.

In the same manner the production of wine will be found both in the tables of agriculture and manufactures, according as the wine is made upon the farm or vineyard,

TABLE XC.—*Sugar and Molasses*—1870–1860–1850.

	States and Territories.	1870					
		SUGAR.			MOLASSES.		
		Cane.	Sorghum.	Maple.	Cane.	Sorghum.	Maple.
		Hhds.	*Hhds.*	*Pounds.*	*Gallons.*	*Gallons.*	*Gallons.*
	The United States	87,043	24	28,443,645	6,593,323	16,050,089	921,057
1	Alabama	31			166,009	267,269	3
2	Arizona						
3	Arkansas	92		1,185	72,008	147,203	73
4	California					333	
5	Colorado						
6	Connecticut			14,266		6,832	168
7	Dakota					1,230	
8	Delaware					65,908	
9	District of Columbia						
10	Florida	952			344,339		
11	Georgia	644			553,192	374,027	
12	Idaho						
13	Illinois			136,873		1,960,473	10,378
14	Indiana			1,332,332		2,026,212	287,880
15	Iowa		15	146,490		1,218,636	2,315
16	Kansas			938		449,409	212
17	Kentucky			269,416		1,740,453	48,673
18	Louisiana	80,706			4,585,150	180	
19	Maine			160,805			28,470
20	Maryland			70,464		28,563	374
21	Massachusetts			399,800			2,326
22	Michigan			1,781,855		94,686	32,637
23	Minnesota			216,467		38,735	12,722
24	Mississippi	49		125	152,161	67,509	
25	Missouri	49		116,980		1,730,171	16,317
26	Montana						
27	Nebraska			10		77,598	
28	Nevada					3,651	
29	New Hampshire			1,800,704			16,884
30	New Jersey			419		17,424	5
31	New Mexico					1,765	
32	New York			6,692,040		7,832	46,048
33	North Carolina	35		21,257	33,888	621,855	418
34	Ohio			3,469,128		2,023,427	332,612
35	Oregon			11			30
36	Pennsylvania		9	1,545,917		213,373	38,385
37	Rhode Island					20	
38	South Carolina	1,055		2	436,882	183,585	
39	Tennessee	1,410		134,968	3,629	1,254,701	4,843
40	Texas	2,020			246,062	174,509	5,032
41	Utah					67,446	
42	Vermont			8,894,302			12,023
43	Virginia			245,093		329,155	11,400
44	Washington					612	
45	West Virginia			490,606		780,829	28,209
46	Wisconsin			507,192		74,478	31,218
47	Wyoming						

and consequently by agricultural labor, or in large establishments of a purely manufacturing character.

Animals slaughtered.—For the same reasons that the statistics of agriculture are uniformly inadequate for the Territories, and for sections of Kansas, Nebraska, California, and perhaps the whole of Texas, the returns of "Animals slaughtered and sold for slaughter" from those regions will fail generally to include the flocks and herds that graze over fields and plains not embraced in defined farms. Thus the aggregate of all the returns under this head for the Territories and for the States named is only $17,171,046.

Unfortunately there are not sufficient data within reach to enable one to form even an estimate of the values thus omitted. There is also a considerable loss in the older States from the fact that large numbers of cattle are sold from farms to traders and speculators, to be turned into beef at one time or another, as occasion may serve or necessity require, or the market justify, while yet the farmer cannot properly report them as "Sold for slaughter," as he can know nothing of the plans of the purchaser.

Notwithstanding this liability to omission, the returns under this head for 1870 show

TABLE XC.—*Sugar and Molasses*—1870-1860-1850.

1860					1850			
SUGAR.		MOLASSES.			SUGAR.			
Cane.	Maple.	Cane.	Sorghum.	Maple.	Cane.	Maple.	Molasses.	
Hhds. 230, 982	*Pounds.* 40, 120, 205	*Gallons.* 14, 963, 996	*Gallons.* 6, 749, 123	*Gallons.* 1, 597, 580	*Hhds.* 247, 577	*Pounds.* 34, 253, 436	*Gallons.* 12, 700, 896	
175	228	85, 115	55, 653		8, 242	643	83, 428	1
								2
	3, 077		115, 604	124		9, 330	18	3
			552	6				4
								5
	44, 259		395	2, 277		50, 796	665	6
			20					7
			1, 013				50	8
								9
1, 669		436, 357			2, 750		352, 893	10
1, 167	991	546, 749	103, 490	20	1, 642	50	216, 150	11
								12
	134, 193		806, 589	20, 048		248, 904	8, 354	13
	1, 541, 761		881, 049	292, 908		2, 921, 192	180, 325	14
	315, 436		1, 211, 512	11, 405		78, 407	3, 162	15
	3, 742		87, 656	2				16
	380, 941		356, 705	140, 076	284	437, 405	30, 079	17
221, 726		13, 439, 772			226, 001	255	10, 931, 177	18
	306, 742			32, 079		93, 542	3, 167	19
	63, 281		907	2, 404		47, 740	1, 430	20
	1, 006, 078			15, 307		795, 525	4, 693	21
	4, 051, 822		86, 953	78, 998		2, 439, 794	19, 823	22
	370, 669		14, 178	23, 038		2, 950		23
506	99	10, 016	1, 427		368		18, 318	24
402	142, 028	22, 305	796, 111	18, 289		178, 910	5, 636	25
								26
	122		23, 497	275				27
								28
	2, 255, 012			43, 833		1, 298, 863	9, 811	29
	3, 455		396	8, 088		2, 197	954	30
			1, 950				4, 236	31
	10, 816, 419		516	131, 843		10, 357, 484	56, 539	32
38	30, 845	12, 494	263, 475	17, 759		27, 932	704	33
	3, 345, 508		779, 076	370, 512		4, 588, 209	197, 308	34
			315				24	35
	2, 767, 335		22, 749	114, 310		2, 326, 525	50, 652	36
			20			28	4	37
198	205		51, 041		671	200	15, 904	38
2	115, 620	2, 830	706, 663	74, 372	248	158, 557	7, 223	39
5, 099		408, 358	112, 412		7, 351		441, 918	40
			25, 475	40			58	41
	9, 897, 781			16, 253		6, 349, 357	5, 997	42
	938, 103		221, 270	99, 605		1, 227, 665	40, 322	43
								44
								45
	1, 584, 451		19, 854	83, 118		610, 976	9, 874	46
								47

handsome increase from the last census, aggregating $398,956,376, against $213,618,692 ported in 1860.

The cotton crop.—From the joint effect of two of the causes above indicated, viz, the omalous conditions of land in the Southern States, and the splitting of the agricul- ral year by the artificial date given to the enumerations of the census, it might be pected that the return of the cotton crop in the census would be peculiarly liable to jection. The aggregate crop returned to the Census Office has been 3,011,996 bales. aking into account the period fixed for the enumeration, (June 1, 1870,) it will be seen at this is substantially the crop which was planted between February and May, 1869, rvested between September, 1869, and February, 1870, and marketed between Sep- mber, 1869, and September, 1870. It should be added that the bale recognized in the nsus law of 1850 was the bale of 400 pounds.

Aggregate value of farm production.—The inquiry by which this value was obtained as, as explained in the report of the Superintendent, prefixed to the Population volume, troduced into the Agricultural Schedule at the present census.

The reasons which appeared to justify this innovation were found in the difficulty

TABLE XCI.—*Potatoes, Peas and Beans, Beeswax, Honey, and Domestic Wine, by States and Territories—1870–1860.*

	States and Territories.	1870					
		Irish potatoes.	Sweet potatoes.	Peas and beans.	Beeswax.	Bees' honey.	Domestic wine.
		Bushels.	*Bushels.*	*Bushels.*	*Pounds.*	*Pounds.*	*Gallons.*
	The United States...	143,337,473	21,709,824	5,746,027	631,129	14,702,815	3,092,330
1	Alabama	162,512	1,871,360	156,574	22,767	320,674	5,156
2	Arizona	575	16	3,417	....	....	....
3	Arkansas	422,196	890,631	47,376	12,789	276,884	3,734
4	California	2,049,227	202,035	380,010	4,903	294,326	1,814,656
5	Colorado	121,442	60	7,500	....	....	67
6	Connecticut	2,789,894	867	13,038	1,326	32,158	27,414
7	Dakota	50,177	....	456	6	110	....
8	Delaware	362,724	85,309	3,123	800	33,151	1,552
9	District of Columbia	27,367	5,790	40	....	....	900
10	Florida	10,218	789,456	64,846	6,052	50,884	661
11	Georgia	197,101	2,021,562	410,020	31,233	610,877	21,927
12	Idaho	64,534	....	610	....	....	....
13	Illinois	10,944,790	322,041	115,854	46,262	1,547,178	111,882
14	Indiana	5,399,044	150,705	35,526	12,049	395,278	19,479
15	Iowa	5,914,620	34,292	42,313	2,225	853,213	37,518
16	Kansas	2,342,988	49,533	13,109	2,208	110,827	14,889
17	Kentucky	2,391,062	802,114	119,926	32,557	1,171,500	82,389
18	Louisiana	67,695	1,023,706	26,888	2,363	37,646	578
19	Maine	7,771,009	354	264,502	5,253	155,640	7,047
20	Maryland	1,632,205	218,706	57,556	3,439	118,938	11,568
21	Massachusetts	3,025,446	917	24,690	1,[illegible]95	25,299	10,956
22	Michigan	10,318,799	3,651	349,365	14,[illegible]71	280,325	21,832
23	Minnesota	1,943,063	1,594	46,601	3,963	92,006	1,750
24	Mississippi	214,189	1,743,432	176,417	9,390	199,581	3,055
25	Missouri	4,238,361	241,253	43,986	35,248	1,156,444	326,173
26	Montana	91,477	....	2,414	....	....	....
27	Nebraska	739,984	762	3,332	707	28,114	470
28	Nevada	129,249	....	414	....	363	711
29	New Hampshire	4,515,419	160	58,375	2,668	56,944	2,446
30	New Jersey	4,705,439	1,530,784	56,221	2,021	60,636	24,970
31	New Mexico	3,102	....	28,856	....	....	19,686
32	New York	28,547,593	10,656	1,152,541	86,333	896,286	82,607
33	North Carolina	738,803	3,071,840	332,749	109,054	1,404,040	62,348
34	Ohio	11,192,814	230,295	45,443	22,488	763,124	212,912
35	Oregon	481,710	1,970	12,575	1,207	66,858	1,751
36	Pennsylvania	12,889,367	131,572	39,574	27,033	796,989	97,165
37	Rhode Island	669,408	142	9,920	498	6,290	765
38	South Carolina	83,252	1,342,165	460,378	11,404	194,253	13,179
39	Tennessee	1,124,337	1,205,683	194,535	51,685	1,039,550	15,778
40	Texas	208,383	2,188,041	42,654	13,255	275,169	6,216
41	Utah	323,645	163	9,291	13	575	3,131
42	Vermont	5,157,428	96	95,242	5,235	142,932	1,03[illegible]
43	Virginia	1,293,853	865,882	162,102	26,438	505,239	26,283
44	Washington	280,719	425	15,790	629	25,636	235
45	West Virginia	1,053,507	46,984	31,449	9,917	376,907	6,093
46	Wisconsin	6,646,129	2,220	388,425	9,945	299,341	9,357
47	Wyoming	617	....	4	....	....	....

which has attended, and the ill-success which has followed, every attempt to reach anything like the true aggregate value of the farm production of the United States by means of the incomplete, and withal somewhat fragmentary, data furnished in the amounts given in the census of certain crops, embracing, it is true, almost all of the staples of the country, and some of less importance, yet far from covering the entire field of American agriculture.

Whenever efforts have been made to fix an average price for each of these reported products, and to supplement the statement by the value of the minor and miscellaneous products of the year, the result has invariably been a failure, more or less conspicuous. No estimate of the agricultural productions of the United States is known to the Superintendent which is entitled to much more than the credit of good intentions.

The cause of this failure is not found alone in the want of data by which to reach the sum of the numerous and, in a few cases, the considerable elements of production which are not recognized on the schedules of the census. The degree of error to which estimates in respect to these are liable is perhaps not greater than the probable error in calculations of value from quantity in the case of the products which do appear on

TABLE XCI.—*Potatoes, Peas and Beans, Beeswax, Honey, and Domestic Wine, by States and Territories—1870–1860.*

1860						
Irish potatoes.	Sweet potatoes.	Peas and beans.	Beeswax.	Bees' honey.	Domestic wine.	
Bushels. 111,148,867	*Bushels.* 42,095,026	*Bushels.* 15,061,995	*Pounds.* 1,322,787	*Pounds.* 23,366,357	*Gallons.* 1,627,192	
491,646	5,439,917	1,482,036	100,987	47,233	18,267	1
....	....	....	....	....	....	2
418,010	1,566,540	440,472	50,949	806,327	1,004	3
1,789,463	214,307	165,574	584	12,276	246,518	4
....	....	....	....	....	....	5
1,833,148	2,710	25,864	4,371	62,730	46,783	6
9,489	....	286	....	....	....	7
377,931	142,213	7,438	1,093	66,137	683	8
31,693	5,606	3,749	24	510	118	9
18,766	1,129,759	363,217	10,899	115,520	336	10
303,789	6,508,541	1,765,214	61,505	953,915	27,646	11
....	....	....	....	....	....	12
5,540,390	306,154	108,028	56,730	1,346,803	50,690	13
3,866,647	299,516	79,902	34,525	1,224,489	102,895	14
2,806,720	51,362	41,081	34,296	917,877	3,309	15
296,335	9,965	9,827	1,181	16,944	583	16
1,756,531	1,037,557	288,346	68,339	1,768,692	179,948	17
294,655	2,060,981	431,148	20,970	255,481	2,912	18
6,374,617	1,435	246,915	8,769	314,685	3,164	19
1,264,429	236,740	34,407	6,960	193,354	3,222	20
3,201,901	616	45,246	3,289	59,125	20,915	21
5,261,245	38,492	165,128	41,632	769,282	14,427	22
2,565,485	792	18,988	1,544	34,285	412	23
414,320	4,563,873	1,954,666	42,603	708,237	7,262	24
1,990,850	335,102	107,990	79,190	1,585,983	27,827	25
....	....	....	....	....	....	26
162,188	168	5,029	142	5,843	671	27
5,686	200	15	....	....	....	28
4,137,543	161	79,454	4,936	125,142	9,401	29
4,171,690	1,034,832	27,674	8,130	185,925	21,083	30
5,223	180	38,514	....	....	8,260	31
26,447,394	7,529	1,609,339	121,020	2,369,751	61,407	32
830,565	6,140,039	1,932,204	170,495	2,055,969	54,064	33
8,695,101	304,445	102,511	53,786	1,459,601	568,617	34
303,319	335	34,407	179	821	2,603	35
11,687,467	103,187	123,090	52,569	1,402,128	38,621	36
542,909	946	7,698	540	5,261	507	37
226,735	4,115,688	1,728,074	40,479	526,077	24,964	38
1,182,005	2,604,672	547,803	98,892	1,519,390	13,566	39
174,182	1,846,612	341,961	28,123	394,273	14,199	40
141,101	....	2,535	....	....	60	41
5,253,498	623	70,654	8,794	212,150	2,923	42
2,292,398	1,960,817	515,168	94,860	1,431,591	40,808	43
163,594	18	10,850	564	5,256	179	44
....	....	....	....	....	....	45
3,818,309	2,396	99,484	8,008	207,294	6,278	46
....	....	....	....	....	....	47

the schedules. It is no exaggeration to say that to fix a true average price for any crop cultivated in as many as half of the States of the Union, would be a work of not less difficulty than to fix the true center of population of the United States. That this would be so, were scientific precision required, would probably not be questioned. But it may be thought that it would yet be practicable roughly to determine the average price of such an article, with such limits of error only as would be inappreciable when applied to the entire crop, or would be offset by errors in an opposite direction during the further course of such calculations. Such, however, is far from being the fact. There is no crop named on the census schedules, cultivated in as large a number of States as that mentioned, for which an average farm-price could be fixed with the least approach to accuracy, while from the degree of uncertainty that prevails in respect to the entire schedule, as well as in regard to the elements omitted from enumeration, an error of from five hundred to a thousand millions would be pretty much a matter of course.

In the foregoing remarks reference is made to such estimates as have sought to obtain

TABLE XCI.—*Potatoes, Peas and Beans, Beeswax, Honey, and Domestic Wine*—1850.

States and Territories.	1850				
	Irish potatoes.	Sweet potatoes.	Peas and beans.	Beeswax and honey.	Domestic wine.
	Bushels.	*Bushels.*	*Bushels.*	*Pounds.*	*Gallons.*
The United States	65, 797, 896	38, 268, 148	9, 219, 901	14, 853, 790	221, 249
Alabama	246, 001	5, 475, 204	892, 701	897, 021	220
Arizona	....	....	....	....	....
Arkansas	193, 832	788, 149	285, 738	192, 338	35
California	9, 292	1, 000	2, 292	....	58, 055
Colorado	....	....	....	....	....
Connecticut	2, 689, 725	80	19, 090	93, 304	4, 269
Dakota	....	....	....	....	....
Delaware	240, 542	65, 443	4, 120	41, 248	145
District of Columbia	28, 292	3, 497	7, 754	550	863
Florida	7, 828	757, 226	135, 359	18, 971	10
Georgia	227, 379	6, 986, 428	1, 142, 011	732, 514	796
Idaho	....	....	....	....	....
Illinois	2, 514, 861	157, 433	82, 814	869, 444	2, 997
Indiana	2, 083, 337	201, 711	35, 773	935, 329	14, 055
Iowa	276, 120	6, 243	4, 775	321, 711	420
Kansas	....	....	....	....	....
Kentucky	1, 492, 487	998, 179	202, 574	1, 158, 019	8, 093
Louisiana	95, 632	1, 428, 453	161, 732	96, 701	15
Maine	3, 436, 040	....	205, 541	189, 618	724
Maryland	764, 939	208, 993	12, 816	74, 802	1, 431
Massachusetts	3, 585, 384	....	43, 709	59, 508	4, 688
Michigan	2, 359, 897	1, 177	74, 254	359, 232	1, 654
Minnesota	21, 145	200	10, 002	80	....
Mississippi	261, 482	4, 741, 795	1, 072, 757	397, 460	407
Missouri	939, 006	335, 505	46, 017	1, 328, 972	10, 563
Montana	....	....	....	....	....
Nebraska	....	....	....	....	....
Nevada	....	....	....	....	....
New Hampshire	4, 304, 919	....	70, 856	117, 140	344
New Jersey	3, 207, 236	508, 015	14, 174	156, 694	1, 811
New Mexico	3	....	15, 688	2	2, 363
New York	15, 398, 368	5, 629	741, 546	1, 755, 830	9, 172
North Carolina	620, 318	5, 095, 709	1, 584, 252	512, 289	11, 058
Ohio	5, 057, 769	187, 991	60, 168	804, 275	48, 207
Oregon	91, 326	....	6, 566	....	....
Pennsylvania	5, 980, 732	52, 172	55, 231	839, 509	25, 590
Rhode Island	651, 029	....	6, 846	6, 347	1, 013
South Carolina	136, 494	4, 337, 469	1, 026, 900	216, 281	5, 880
Tennessee	1, 067, 844	2, 777, 716	369, 321	1, 036, 572	92
Texas	94, 645	1, 332, 158	179, 350	380, 825	99
Utah	43, 968	60	289	10	....
Vermont	4, 951, 014	....	104, 649	249, 422	659
Virginia	1, 316, 933	1, 813, 634	521, 579	880, 767	5, 408
Washington	....	....	....	....	....
West Virginia	....	....	....	....	....
Wisconsin	1, 402, 077	879	20, 657	131, 005	113
Wyoming	....	....	....	....	....

the value of the agricultural products of the country to the agricultural interest purely; the value of the farm production to the farmer; the value of the crops of the United States before the elements of transportation and exchange have been introduced. It is easy, from daily quotations, to reach an average price of any single commodity in any one of the principal markets of the country; it is even possible to reach an average price, which shall be based not only on the several market averages attained, but also, to a reasonable extent, upon the amount sold at each such local average; but to tell how much of the aggregate value thus reached has remained in the hands of the farmer is quite another matter.

The Superintendent has no desire to pursue this subject further than to show at once the novelty and the importance of this new feature of the census; nor is it necessary to multiply illustrations to accomplish this result. It is sufficient barely to allude to such notorious facts as corn selling in New England at 90 cents and being burned for fuel in Iowa; wheat selling at $1.35 in New York, and for 45 cents in Minnesota; beef

TABLE XCII.—*Clover, Grass, and Flaxseed*—1870-1860-1850.

nd Territories.	1870			1860			1850		
	SEED.			SEED.			SEED.		
	Clover.	Flax.	Grass.	Clover.	Flax.	Grass.	Clover.	Flax.	Grass.
	Bushels.	*Bushels.*	*Bushels.*	*Bushels.*	*Bushels.*	*Bushels.*	*Bushels.*	*Bushels.*	*Bushels.*
United States..	639,657	1,730,444	583,188	956,188	566,867	900,040	468,978	562,312	416,831
....	77	2	139	244	68	630	138	60	547
....	....	....	....	....	....	....	....	....	....
s	42	104	143	95	545	3,168	90	321	436
ia	1,353	13,294	976	....	....	....	....	....	....
....	....	....	....	90	....	286	....	....	....
icut	1,725	4	4,471	....	....	....	13,841	703	16,628
....	....	....	....	13,671	100	13,024	....	....	....
e	2,228	356	60	302	....	....	2,525	904	1,403
of Columbia ...	....	....	....	3,595	2,126	1,165	3	....	....
....	....	....	....	....	....	....	....	....	2
....	143	48	540	....	....	....	132	622	498
....	....	....	14	635	96	1,914	....	....	....
....	10,486	280,043	153,464	....	....	....	3,427	10,787	14,380
....	61,168	401,931	17,377	18,831	8,670	101,273	18,320	36,888	11,951
....	2,473	88,621	53,432	60,726	119,420	34,914	342	1,950	2,096
....	334	1,553	8,023	3,454	5,921	69,366	....	....	....
y	2,551	14,637	35,896	103	11	3,043	3,230	75,801	21,481
a	1	....	....	2,308	28,875	68,561	2	....	97
....	5,255	227	3,859	1	....	700	9,097	580	9,214
d	35,040	1,541	2,609	48,849	419	6,306	15,217	2,446	2,561
usetts	252	52	464	30,811	1,570	3,105	1,002	72	5,085
n	49,918	5,528	2,500	1,295	7	4,852	16,980	519	9,285
ta	126	18,635	3,045	54,408	341	8,045	....	....	....
ppi	6	2	82	432	118	3,122	84	26	533
....	2,494	10,391	12,246	8	3	1,064	619	13,696	4,346
....	....	....	31	2,216	4,636	55,713	....	....	....
a	....	404	133	....	....	....	....	....	....
....	7	....	64	5	2	705	....	....	....
mpshire	607	6	1,775	....	....	....	829	189	8,071
rsey	26,306	6,095	72,401	12,690	30	5,569	23,280	16,525	63,051
xico	....	....	....	39,205	3,241	85,408	....	....	....
rk	98,837	92,519	57,225	....	....	....	88,222	57,963	96,493
arolina	651	6,756	1,002	106,934	56,991	81,625	576	38,196	1,275
....	102,355	631,894	48,811	332	20,008	3,008	103,197	188,880	37,310
....	10	10,988	1,210	243,489	242,420	54,990	4	....	22
vania	200,679	15,621	50,642	1,433	6	3,883	125,030	41,728	53,913
sland	954	....	1,938	247,351	24,198	57,193	1,328	....	3,708
arolina	5,830	....	1,878	1,221	....	4,237	376	55	30
ee	8,564	4,612	11,153	28	313	38	5,096	18,904	9,118
....	7	2	497	8,572	9,302	42,113	10	26	....
....	....	....	5	585	....	5,228	2	5	....
t	785	444	4,613	3	33	149	760	939	14,936
....	11,367	9,699	12,709	2,445	331	11,587	29,727	52,318	23,428
gton	179	....	1,387	36,962	32,691	53,063	....	....	....
rginia	3,939	2,393	3,868	7	30	311	....	....	....
sin	2,906	112,019	13,016	....	....	....	483	1,191	5,003
ng	....	....	....	3,852	4,256	26,512	....	....	....

ng $7 a hundred on the hoof in the East, while cattle are being slaughtered for hides in Texas.

total value of farm production reached in the above tables is believed to be ect, for the great majority of the States and counties of the Union, as any statis- esult can be expected to be. Here and there an assistant marshal may have d this portion of his duty; but in general the work has been well done. The t of each farm has been estimated upon the spot at its actual worth to the , the officer of the Government and the owner of the land sitting down together ke out the statement. The aggregation of these results for two million six hun- nd fifty thousand farms yields a total which must be taken as the most accurate aination of the value of the agricultural production of the country ever attained.

TABLE XCIII.—*Live Stock on Farms*—1870*-1860.

	States and Territories.	1870							
		Value of all live stock.	Horses.	Mules and asses.	Milch cows.	Working oxen.	Other cattle.	Sheep.	Swine.
		Dollars.	*Number.*	*Number.*	*Number.*	*Number.*	*Number.*	*Number.*	*Number.*
	The United States	1,525,276,457	7,145,370	1,125,415	8,935,332	1,319,271	13,566,005	28,477,951	25,134,[illegible]
1	Alabama	26,690,095	80,770	76,675	170,640	59,176	257,347	241,934	719,[illegible]
2	Arizona	143,996	335	401	938	587	3,607	803	[illegible]
3	Arkansas	17,222,506	92,013	36,202	128,959	35,387	193,589	161,077	841,129
4	California	37,964,732	192,273	17,533	164,093	5,944	461,361	2,768,187	444,617
5	Colorado	2,871,102	6,446	1,173	25,017	5,566	40,153	120,928	5,509
6	Connecticut	17,545,038	34,935	190	98,889	39,639	79,485	83,884	51,983
7	Dakota	779,952	2,514	225	4,151	2,125	6,191	1,901	2,[illegible]
8	Delaware	4,257,323	16,770	3,584	24,082	6,868	19,020	22,714	[illegible]
9	Dist. Columbia	114,916	533	124	657	6	138	604	[illegible]
10	Florida	5,212,157	11,902	8,835	61,922	6,292	322,701	26,599	[illegible]
11	Georgia	30,156,317	81,777	87,426	231,310	54,332	412,261	419,465	[illegible]
12	Idaho	520,580	2,151	371	4,171	582	5,763	1,021	[illegible]
13	Illinois	149,756,698	853,738	85,075	640,321	19,766	1,055,499	1,568,286	2,703,[illegible]
14	Indiana	83,776,782	497,883	43,259	393,736	14,088	618,360	1,612,680	1,[illegible]
15	Iowa	82,987,133	433,642	25,485	369,811	22,058	614,366	855,493	1,353,[illegible]
16	Kansas	23,173,185	117,786	11,786	123,440	20,774	229,753	109,088	[illegible]
17	Kentucky	66,287,343	317,034	99,230	247,615	69,719	382,993	936,765	1,[illegible]
18	Louisiana	15,929,188	50,738	61,338	102,076	32,596	200,589	118,602	[illegible]
19	Maine	23,357,129	71,514	336	139,259	60,530	143,272	434,[illegible]	[illegible]
20	Maryland	18,433,698	89,696	9,830	94,794	22,491	98,074	129,697	[illegible]
21	Massachusetts	17,049,228	41,039	103	114,771	24,430	79,851	78,560	[illegible]
22	Michigan	49,809,869	228,302	2,353	250,859	36,499	260,171	1,985,906	417,[illegible]
23	Minnesota	20,118,841	93,011	2,350	121,467	43,176	145,736	132,343	148,[illegible]
24	Mississippi	29,940,238	90,221	85,886	173,899	58,146	269,030	232,732	814,[illegible]
25	Missouri	84,285,273	493,969	111,502	398,515	65,825	689,355	1,352,001	2,306,[illegible]
26	Montana	1,818,693	5,289	475	12,432	1,761	22,545	2,024	2,[illegible]
27	Nebraska	6,551,185	30,511	2,632	28,940	5,931	45,057	22,725	[illegible]
28	Nevada	1,445,449	7,520	990	6,174	2,443	22,899	11,018	3,[illegible]
29	New Hampshire	13,246,545	39,095	37	90,583	40,513	91,705	248,760	33,[illegible]
30	New Jersey	21,443,463	79,708	8,853	133,331	3,830	60,327	120,067	148,[illegible]
31	New Mexico	2,389,157	5,033	6,141	16,417	19,774	21,343	619,438	11,[illegible]
32	New York	175,882,712	536,861	4,407	1,350,661	64,141	630,522	2,181,578	518,251
33	North Carolina	21,993,967	102,763	50,684	196,731	45,408	279,023	463,435	1,075,215
34	Ohio	120,300,528	609,722	16,063	654,390	23,606	758,221	4,928,635	1,728,[illegible]
35	Oregon	6,828,675	51,702	2,581	48,325	2,441	69,431	318,123	119,455
36	Pennsylvania	115,647,075	460,339	18,009	706,437	30,048	608,066	1,794,301	867,548
37	Rhode Island	3,135,132	7,770	43	18,806	5,821	9,748	23,938	14,607
38	South Carolina	12,443,510	44,105	41,327	98,693	17,685	132,925	124,594	395,[illegible]
39	Tennessee	55,084,075	247,254	102,983	243,197	63,970	336,529	826,783	1,828,[illegible]
40	Texas	37,425,194	424,504	61,322	428,048	132,407	2,933,588	714,351	1,202,445
41	Utah	2,149,814	11,068	2,679	17,563	3,479	18,138	59,672	3,150
42	Vermont	23,888,835	65,015	232	180,285	27,809	112,741	580,347	46,[illegible]
43	Virginia	28,187,669	152,899	20,903	188,471	45,987	277,285	370,145	674,670
44	Washington	2,103,343	11,138	943	16,938	9,181	28,135	44,063	17,491
45	West Virginia	17,175,420	90,479	2,139	104,434	18,937	178,309	552,327	[illegible]
46	Wisconsin	45,310,882	252,019	4,195	308,377	53,615	331,302	1,069,282	512,778
47	Wyoming	441,795	584	283	707	922	6,501	6,409	146

* For live stock on and off Farms, see p. 697.

TABLE XCIII.—*Live Stock on Farms*—1870–1860.

1860								
...stock.	Horses.	Mules and asses.	Milch cows.	Working oxen.	Other cattle.	Sheep.	Swine.	
...ars.	*Number.*	*Number.*	*Number.*	*Number.*	*Number.*	*Number.*	*Number.*	
...29, 915	6, 249, 174	1, 151, 148	8, 585, 735	2, 254, 911	14, 779, 373	22, 471, 275	33, 512, 867	
...11, 711	127, 063	111, 687	230, 537	88, 316	434, 543	370, 156	1, 748, 321	1
								2
...96, 977	140, 198	57, 358	171, 003	78, 707	318, 089	202, 753	1, 171, 630	3
...85, 017	160, 610	3, 681	205, 407	26, 004	948, 731	1, 088, 002	456, 396	4
								5
...11, 079	33, 276	82	98, 877	47, 939	95, 091	117, 107	75, 120	6
...39, 116	84	19	286	348	167	193	287	7
...44, 706	16, 562	2, 294	22, 595	9, 530	25, 596	18, 857	47, 848	8
...09, 640	641	122	639	69	198	40	1, 099	9
...53, 356	13, 446	10, 910	92, 974	7, 361	287, 725	30, 158	271, 742	10
...72, 734	130, 771	101, 069	299, 688	74, 487	631, 707	512, 618	2, 036, 116	11
								12
...01, 225	563, 736	38, 539	522, 634	90, 380	970, 799	769, 135	2, 502, 308	13
...55, 539	520, 677	28, 893	363, 553	117, 687	588, 144	991, 175	3, 099, 110	14
...76, 293	175, 088	5, 734	189, 802	56, 964	293, 322	259, 041	934, 820	15
...32, 450	20, 344	1, 496	28, 550	21, 551	43, 354	17, 569	138, 224	16
...68, 237	355, 704	117, 634	269, 215	108, 999	437, 845	938, 990	2, 330, 595	17
...46, 940	78, 703	91, 762	129, 662	60, 358	326, 787	181, 253	634, 525	18
...37, 533	60, 637	104	147, 314	79, 792	149, 827	452, 472	54, 783	19
...57, 853	93, 406	9, 829	99, 463	34, 524	119, 254	155, 765	387, 756	20
...37, 744	47, 786	108	144, 492	38, 221	97, 201	114, 829	73, 948	21
...14, 771	136, 917	330	179, 543	61, 686	238, 615	1, 271, 743	372, 386	22
...42, 841	17, 065	377	40, 344	27, 568	51, 345	13, 044	101, 371	23
...91, 692	117, 571	110, 723	207, 646	105, 603	416, 660	352, 632	1, 532, 768	24
...93, 673	361, 874	80, 941	345, 243	166, 588	657, 153	937, 445	2, 354, 425	25
								26
...28, 771	4, 449	469	6, 995	12, 594	17, 608	2, 355	25, 369	27
...77, 638	541	134	947	620	3, 904	376	3, 571	28
...24, 627	41, 101	10	94, 880	51, 512	118, 075	310, 534	51, 935	29
...34, 693	79, 707	6, 362	138, 818	10, 067	89, 909	135, 228	236, 089	30
...39, 746	10, 066	11, 291	34, 369	25, 266	29, 094	830, 116	10, 313	31
...56, 296	503, 725	1, 553	1, 123, 634	121, 703	727, 817	2, 617, 855	910, 178	32
...40, 805	150, 661	51, 388	228, 623	48, 511	416, 676	546, 749	1, 883, 214	33
...94, 819	625, 346	7, 194	676, 585	63, 078	895, 077	3, 546, 767	2, 251, 653	34
...46, 255	36, 772	980	53, 170	7, 469	93, 492	86, 052	81, 615	35
...72, 726	437, 654	8, 882	673, 547	60, 371	685, 575	1, 631, 540	1, 031, 266	36
...42, 044	7, 121	10	19, 700	7, 857	11, 548	32, 624	17, 478	37
...34, 465	81, 125	56, 456	163, 938	22, 629	320, 209	233, 509	965, 779	38
...11, 425	290, 882	126, 345	249, 514	102, 158	413, 060	773, 317	2, 347, 321	39
...25, 447	325, 698	63, 334	601, 540	172, 492	2, 761, 736	753, 363	1, 371, 532	40
...16, 707	4, 565	851	11, 967	9, 168	12, 959	37, 332	6, 707	41
...11, 989	69, 071	43	174, 667	42, 639	153, 144	752, 201	52, 912	42
...13, 049	287, 579	41, 015	330, 713	97, 872	615, 882	1, 043, 269	1, 509, 919	43
...09, 911	4, 772	159	9, 660	2, 571	16, 228	10, 157	6, 383	44
								45
...07, 375	116, 180	1, 030	203, 001	93, 652	225, 207	332, 954	344, 055	46
....	....	....	....	....	....	....	....	47

TABLE XCIII.—*Live Stock on Farms*—1850.

States and Territories.	1850							
	Value of all live stock.	Horses.	Mules and asses.	Milch cows.	Working oxen.	Other cattle.	Sheep.	Swine.
	Dollars.	*Number.*	*Number.*	*Number.*	*Number.*	*Number.*	*Number.*	*Number.*
The United States	544,180,516	4,336,719	559,331	6,385,094	1,700,744	9,693,069	21,723,220	30,354,213
Alabama	21,690,112	128,001	59,895	227,791	66,961	433,263	371,880	1,904,540
Arizona	......	......	......	......	......	......	......	......
Arkansas	6,647,969	60,197	11,559	93,151	34,239	165,320	91,256	836,727
California	3,351,058	21,719	1,666	4,280	4,780	253,599	17,574	2,776
Colorado	......	......	......	......	......	......	......	......
Connecticut	7,467,490	26,879	49	85,461	46,988	80,226	174,181	76,472
Dakota	......	......	......	......	......	......	......	......
Delaware	1,849,281	13,852	791	19,248	9,797	24,166	27,503	56,261
District of Columbia	71,643	824	57	813	104	123	150	1,635
Florida	2,880,058	10,848	5,002	72,876	5,794	182,415	23,311	209,453
Georgia	25,728,416	151,331	57,379	334,223	73,286	690,019	560,435	2,168,617
Idaho	......	......	......	......	......	......	......	......
Illinois	24,209,258	267,653	10,573	294,671	76,156	541,209	894,043	1,915,907
Indiana	22,478,555	314,299	6,599	284,554	40,221	389,891	1,122,493	2,263,776
Iowa	3,689,275	38,536	754	45,704	21,892	69,025	149,960	323,247
Kansas	......	......	......	......	......	......	......	......
Kentucky	29,661,436	315,682	65,609	247,475	62,274	442,763	1,102,091	2,891,163
Louisiana	11,152,275	89,514	44,849	105,576	54,968	414,798	110,333	597,301
Maine	9,705,726	41,721	55	133,556	83,893	125,890	451,577	54,598
Maryland	7,997,634	75,684	5,644	86,856	34,135	98,595	177,902	352,911
Massachusetts	9,647,710	42,216	34	130,099	46,611	83,284	188,651	81,119
Michigan	8,008,734	58,506	70	99,676	55,350	119,471	746,435	205,847
Minnesota	92,859	860	14	607	655	740	80	734
Mississippi	19,403,662	115,460	54,547	214,231	83,485	436,254	304,929	1,582,734
Missouri	19,887,580	225,319	41,667	230,169	112,168	449,173	762,511	1,702,625
Montana	......	......	......	......	......	......	......	......
Nebraska	......	......	......	......	......	......	......	......
Nevada	......	......	......	......	......	......	......	......
New Hampshire	8,871,901	34,233	19	94,277	59,027	114,606	384,756	63,487
New Jersey	10,679,291	63,955	4,089	118,736	12,070	80,455	160,488	250,370
New Mexico	1,494,629	5,079	8,654	10,635	12,257	10,085	377,271	7,314
New York	73,570,499	447,014	963	931,324	178,909	767,406	3,453,241	1,018,252
North Carolina	17,717,647	148,693	25,259	221,799	37,309	434,402	595,249	1,812,813
Ohio	44,121,741	463,397	3,423	544,499	65,381	749,067	3,942,929	1,964,770
Oregon	1,876,189	8,046	420	9,427	8,114	24,188	15,382	30,235
Pennsylvania	41,500,053	350,398	2,259	530,224	61,527	562,195	1,822,357	1,040,366
Rhode Island	1,532,637	6,168	1	18,698	8,139	9,375	44,296	19,509
South Carolina	15,060,015	97,171	37,483	193,244	20,507	563,935	285,551	1,065,503
Tennessee	29,978,016	270,636	75,303	250,456	86,255	414,051	811,591	3,104,800
Texas	10,412,927	76,760	12,463	217,811	51,285	61,018	100,530	692,022
Utah	546,968	2,429	325	4,861	5,266	2,489	3,262	914
Vermont	12,643,228	61,057	218	146,128	48,577	154,143	1,014,122	66,296
Virginia	33,656,659	272,403	21,483	317,619	89,513	669,137	1,310,004	1,829,843
Washington	......	......	......	......	......	......	......	......
West Virginia	......	......	......	......	......	......	......	......
Wisconsin	4,897,385	30,179	156	64,339	42,801	76,293	124,896	159,276
Wyoming	......	......	......	......	......	......	......	......

TABLE XCIV.—*Dairy Products*—1870-1860-1850.

...nd Territories.	1870			1860		1850	
	DAIRY PRODUCTS.			DAIRY PRODUCTS.		DAIRY PRODUCTS.	
	Butter.	Cheese.	Milk sold.	Butter.	Cheese.	Butter.	Cheese.
	Pounds.	*Pounds.*	*Gallons.*	*Pounds.*	*Pounds.*	*Pounds.*	*Pounds.*
...nited States...	514,092,683	53,492,153	235,500,599	459,681,372	103,663,927	313,345,306	105,535,893
...ia	3,213,753	2,732	104,657	6,028,478	15,923	4,008,811	31,412
...a	800	14,500	4,800	....	....	....	....
...as	2,753,931	2,110	31,350	4,067,556	16,810	1,854,239	30,088
...nia	7,969,744	3,395,074	3,693,021	3,095,035	1,343,689	705	150
...o	392,920	33,626	19,520	....	....	....	....
...ticut	6,716,007	2,031,194	6,253,250	7,620,912	3,898,411	6,498,119	5,363,277
...	209,735	1,830	....	2,170	....	....	....
...re	1,171,963	315	738,663	1,430,502	6,579	1,055,308	3,187
...of Columbia	4,495	....	126,077	18,835	....	14,872	1,500
...	100,989	25	3,002	408,855	5,280	371,498	18,015
...	4,499,572	4,292	109,139	5,439,765	15,587	4,640,559	46,976
...	111,480	4,464	11,250	....	....	....	....
...	36,083,405	1,661,703	9,258,545	28,052,551	1,848,557	12,526,543	1,278,225
...	22,915,385	283,807	936,983	18,306,651	605,795	12,881,535	624,564
...	27,512,179	1,087,741	688,800	11,953,666	918,635	2,171,188	209,840
...	5,022,758	226,607	196,662	1,093,497	29,045	....	....
...ky	11,874,978	115,219	1,345,779	11,716,609	190,400	9,947,523	213,954
...na	322,405	11,747	833,928	1,444,742	6,153	683,069	1,957
...	11,636,482	1,152,590	1,374,091	11,687,781	1,799,862	9,243,811	2,434,454
...nd	5,014,729	6,732	1,520,101	5,265,295	8,342	3,806,160	3,975
...husetts	6,559,161	2,245,873	15,284,057	8,297,936	5,294,090	8,071,370	7,088,142
...an	24,400,185	670,804	2,277,122	15,503,482	1,641,897	7,065,878	1,011,492
...ota	9,522,010	233,977	208,130	2,957,673	199,314	1,100	....
...ippi	2,613,521	3,099	17,052	5,006,610	4,427	4,346,234	21,191
...ri	14,455,825	204,090	857,704	12,704,837	259,633	7,834,359	203,572
...a	408,080	25,603	105,186	....	....	....	....
...ka	1,539,535	46,142	95,059	342,541	12,342	....	....
...	110,880	....	63,850	7,700	....	....	....
...ampshire	5,965,080	849,118	2,352,884	6,956,764	2,232,092	6,977,056	3,196,563
...rsey	8,266,023	38,229	5,373,323	10,714,447	182,172	9,487,210	365,756
...exico	12,912	27,239	813	13,259	37,240	111	5,848
...rk	107,147,526	22,769,964	135,775,919	103,097,280	48,548,289	79,766,094	49,741,413
...Carolina	4,297,834	75,185	17,145	4,735,495	51,119	4,146,290	95,921
...	50,266,372	8,169,486	22,275,344	48,543,162	21,618,893	34,449,379	20,819,542
...	1,418,373	79,333	107,367	1,000,157	105,379	211,464	36,980
...lvania	60,834,644	1,145,209	14,411,729	58,653,511	2,508,556	39,878,418	2,505,034
...Island	941,199	81,976	1,944,044	1,021,767	181,511	995,670	316,508
...Carolina	1,461,980	169	241,815	3,177,934	1,543	2,981,850	4,970
...see	9,571,069	142,240	415,786	10,017,787	135,575	8,139,585	177,681
...	3,712,747	34,342	62,771	5,850,583	275,128	2,344,900	95,299
...	310,335	69,603	11,240	316,046	53,331	83,309	30,998
...nt	17,844,396	4,830,700	3,835,840	15,900,359	8,215,030	12,137,980	8,720,834
...a	6,979,269	71,743	266,812	13,464,722	280,852	11,089,359	436,292
...gton	407,306	17,465	21,060	153,092	12,146	....	....
...irginia	5,044,475	32,429	144,895	....	....	....	....
...sin	22,473,036	1,591,798	2,059,105	13,611,328	1,104,300	3,633,750	400,283
...ng	1,200	....	4,980	....	....	....	....

TABLE XCV.—*Selected Statistics of Agriculture by Counties*—1870.

STATE OF ALABAMA.

	Counties.	Improved land.	Value of farms.	Total (estimated) value of all farm productions, including betterments and additions to stock.	LIVE STOCK. Value of all live stock.	Horses.	Mules and asses.	Milch cows.	Working oxen.	Sheep.	Swine.
		Acres.	*Dollars.*	*Dollars.*	*Dolls.*	*No.*	*No.*	*No.*	*No.*	*No.*	*No.*
1	Autauga	92, 012	1, 122, 059	995, 114	369, 056	897	1, 174	2, 439	539	1, 677	7, 18[illegible]
2	Baker	31, 852	284, 378	349, 587	237, 442	1, 008	295	2, 485	887	4, 767	9, 171
3	Baldwin	4, 919	140, 550	81, 210	124, 137	223	151	2, 438	249	3, 724	2, 745
4	Barbour	185, 727	2, 374, 493	3, 186, 725	669, 972	1, 442	2, 430	2, 926	1, 157	2, 436	15, 7[illegible]
5	Bibb	24, 575	295, 110	273, 777	147, 400	519	383	1, 939	414	2, 961	3, 6[illegible]
6	Blount	56, 349	649, 291	572, 045	435, 315	1, 651	633	3, 235	1, 703	9, 507	15, 9[illegible]
7	Bullock	115, 310	2, 468, 172	2, 008, 451	715, 225	1, 277	2, 381	3, 277	918	2, 732	11, 04[illegible]
8	Butler	75, 685	927, 827	983, 066	363, 962	1, 017	1, 642	2, 344	751	2, 281	11, 9[illegible]
9	Calhoun	68, 234	1, 324, 105	713, 006	339, 112	1, 186	980	2, 061	615	3, 441	9, 3[illegible]
10	Chambers	198, 945	1, 286, 665	1, 258, 874	454, 123	1, 382	1, 457	2, 895	836	3, 861	9, 7[illegible]
11	Cherokee	61, 408	1, 267, 036	665, 213	371, 513	1, 406	772	2, 262	765	5, 835	11, 7[illegible]
12	Choctaw	79, 502	946, 850	908, 562	409, 209	1, 313	941	3, 133	1, 356	2, 940	14, 0[illegible]
13	Clarke	61, 549	156, 165	840, 160	374, 706	1, 146	873	3, 708	1, 224	4, 3[illegible]	12, 6[illegible]
14	Clay	37, 348	453, 791	593, 139	310, 795	959	561	2, 580	1, 282	8, 994	10, 27[illegible]
15	Cleburne	42, 267	497, 820	460, 501	263, 116	960	524	1, 976	1, 067	3, 871	10, 6[illegible]
16	Coffee	30, 546	308, 110	511, 588	214, 622	617	321	2, 142	965	4, 059	9, 4[illegible]
17	Colbert	57, 190	910, 627	677, 646	306, 808	1, 190	799	1, 623	520	2, 735	8, 9[illegible]
18	Conecuh	20, 563	240, 795	275, 675	172, 132	425	283	1, 760	493	2, 2[illegible]	4, [illegible]
19	Coosa	64, 905	610, 653	1, 040, 736	472, 805	1, 406	1, 184	3, 779	1, 353	4, 542	12, 6[illegible]
20	Covington	14, 048	123, 443	315, 418	158, 667	462	90	1, 796	722	4, 250	7, 07[illegible]
21	Crenshaw	74, 115	684, 870	970, 227	351, 618	1, 173	697	2, 843	1, 182	2, 610	14, 2[illegible]
22	Dale	76, 083	437, 060	832, 351	393, 579	1, 109	796	2, 752	1, 097	4, 717	17, 6[illegible]
23	Dallas	168, 156	3, 112, 373	2, 753, 591	740, 737	1, 339	3, 496	2, 784	611	1, 508	7, 791
24	De Kalb	44, 188	534, 924	404, 203	328, 799	1, 363	397	2, 369	1, 263	6, 627	13, 094
25	Elmore	73, 524	924, 020	1, 514, 157	440, 747	944	1, 411	2, 706	683	1, 716	8, 9[illegible]
26	Escambia	7, 783	36, 999	146, 195	147, 226	372	111	2, 253	481	3, 582	4, 6[illegible]
27	Etowah	37, 277	750, 420	543, 142	249, 043	923	479	1, 726	619	4, 950	8, 6[illegible]
28	Fayette	40, 897	325, 385	498, 094	313, 271	1, 450	423	2, 534	1, 242	6, 354	10, 9[illegible]
29	Franklin	41, 036	488, 593	539, 049	309, 542	1, 382	499	2, 156	938	3, 705	8, 0[illegible]
30	Geneva	12, 758	125, 304	201, 548	148, 288	408	66	2, 148	685	4, 922	8, 674
31	Greene	127, 856	1, 560, 652	1, 154, 762	498, 944	1, 077	2, 101	2, 145	577	2, 576	6, 674
32	Hale	165, 966	2, 639, 207	2, 029, 383	702, 218	1, 176	2, 734	2, 494	994	2, 626	9, 019
33	Henry	106, 863	895, 419	1, 061, 838	474, 760	1, 240	1, 061	3, 551	1, 396	3, 953	22, 18[illegible]
34	Jackson	77, 086	1, 510, 268	1, 062, 130	620, 263	3, 541	814	3, 737	2, 062	9, 745	25, 9[illegible]
35	Jefferson	56, 964	1, 140, 947	607, 967	430, 702	1, 754	686	3, 094	1, 414	5, 437	13, 7[illegible]
36	Lauderdale	93, 625	1, 405, 630	849, 029	500, 471	2, 380	1, 115	2, 964	777	5, 984	16, 196
37	Lawrence	144, 224	1, 413, 224	1, 350, 431	669, 507	2, 570	1, 816	3, 748	863	5, 095	18, 0[illegible]
38	Lee	120, 765	1, 405, 738	1, 412, 750	472, 696	1, 265	1, 927	3, 444	831	2, 019	10, 2[illegible]
39	Limestone	115, 730	1, 816, 510	1, 231, 157	502, 739	2, 213	1, 479	2, 188	642	3, 960	13, 5[illegible]
40	Lowndes	126, 185	2, 271, 911	2, 176, 738	644, 753	1, 081	2, 706	1, 904	644	706	8, 465
41	Macon	125, 944	1, 486, 811	1, 221, 587	415, 079	872	1, 653	2, 201	692	820	4, 99[illegible]
42	Madison	139, 305	2, 194, 834	1, 935, 501	704, 036	3, 319	1, 911	3, 383	770	4, 062	17, 624
43	Marengo	141, 368	2, 819, 711	3, 034, 675	770, 674	1, 377	3, 629	4, 116	1, 140	1, 763	16, 531
44	Marion	18, 315	80, 438	149, 365	138, 122	662	158	1, 269	665	2, 909	5, 76[illegible]
45	Marshall	48, 353	692, 799	611, 809	390, 242	1, 609	560	2, 614	1, 215	5, 343	12, 3[illegible]
46	Mobile	13, 824	548, 730	393, 777	228, 520	451	492	3, 214	518	3, 013	5, 567
47	Monroe	53, 175	768, 867	921, 752	394, 212	1, 068	975	3, 134	1, 134	3, 2[illegible]	10, 746
48	Montgomery	222, 200	3, 793, 895	3, 403, 382	833, 199	1, 823	4, 250	3, 027	846	980	13, 909
49	Morgan	80, 749	1, 183, 488	837, 236	453, 375	2, 462	666	2, 944	924	4, 902	14, 844
50	Perry	97, 977	1, 455, 175	1, 476, 555	491, 609	929	2, 160	2, 291	564	2, 374	7, 969
51	Pickens	76, 816	799, 785	1, 078, 078	377, 537	1, 125	1, 546	2, 202	642	4, 055	8, 339
52	Pike	97, 885	1, 314, 779	1, 284, 584	539, 227	1, 615	1, 323	3, 521	1, 379	2, 672	24, 43[illegible]
53	Randolph	62, 023	620, 331	718, 695	370, 810	1, 313	845	3, 062	1, 751	7, 485	14, 819
54	Russell	114, 781	1, 721, 442	2, 236, 179	498, 304	824	2, 410	2, 672	317	890	6, 540
55	Sanford	42, 465	304, 250	643, 059	301, 749	1, 462	496	2, 518	1, 187	6, 784	11, 463
56	Shelby	48, 376	516, 136	692, 911	311, 018	1, 174	652	2, 680	1, 060	3, 524	9, 78[illegible]
57	St. Clair	34, 055	401, 174	391, 114	252, 095	970	452	1, 621	622	3, 578	8, 773
58	Sumter	141, 784	1, 684, 953	1, 513, 982	513, 788	1, 242	1, 957	2, 097	988	2, 949	8, 024
59	Talladega	81, 579	940, 662	1, 084, 387	400, 156	922	1, 786	1, 801	687	2, 355	6, 947
60	Tallapoosa	88, 902	488, 967	1, 055, 798	406, 999	1, 224	1, 198	2, 736	1, 092	3, 528	12, 79[illegible]
61	Tuscaloosa	77, 007	1, 105, 677	1, 346, 815	454, 982	1, 245	1, 378	2, 768	934	6, 139	11, 046
62	Walker	23, 454	206, 480	282, 415	216, 724	963	326	2, 107	712	1, 795	8, 309
63	Washington	14, 778	155, 020	160, 312	164, 741	403	214	2, 626	454	2, 389	5, 024
64	Wilcox	165, 907	2, 347, 868	2, 550, 667	957, 754	1, 702	3, 418	4, 722	1, 003	2, 897	17, 020
65	Winston	17, 847	119, 410	298, 475	175, 028	708	132	1, 798	1, 063	3, 550	10, 985

TABLE XCV.—*Selected Statistics of Agriculture by Counties*—1870.

STATE OF ALABAMA.

Wheat. Winter.	Indian corn.	Oats.	Tobacco.	Cotton.	Wool.	Potatoes. Irish.	Potatoes. Sweet.	Butter.	
PRODUCED.									
Bushels.	*Bushels.*	*Bushels.*	*Pounds.*	*Bales.*	*Pounds.*	*Bushels.*	*Bushels.*	*Pounds.*	
672	191, 158	5, 568	285	7, 965	2, 060	2, 154	36, 660	25, 542	1
11, 282	131, 311	6, 238	3, 256	1, 360	7, 634	425	29, 571	46, 293	2
....	31, 025	....	50	87	9, 864	17	19, 411	4, 870	3
....	364, 304	3, 648	....	17, 011	1, 266	15	42, 734	300	4
4, 157	82, 620	13, 645	490	3, 973	3, 934	352	14, 554	7, 395	5
26, 956	266, 553	12, 779	5, 682	950	14, 088	4, 769	31, 578	83, 055	6
97	389, 791	13, 632	....	17, 972	656	239	33, 021	50	7
....	251, 512	4, 126	....	5, 854	2, 737	1, 233	60, 116	12, 365	8
76, 804	238, 451	29, 030	1, 500	3, 098	4, 840	3, 807	16, 776	88, 463	9
38, 295	205, 099	35, 921	....	7, 868	1, 395	580	94, 734	51, 358	10
67, 776	231, 946	27, 683	7, 470	1, 807	10, 179	4, 938	24, 675	83, 785	11
....	227, 715	1, 495	215	6, 439	3, 356	4, 133	47, 626	29, 146	12
....	227, 031	490	175	5, 713	789	....	49, 550	9, 780	13
38, 422	196, 886	17, 005	9, 005	1, 143	6, 948	28	8, 297	123, 464	14
24, 641	186, 763	19, 853	10, 997	833	6, 496	1, 868	15, 679	83, 965	15
64	121, 352	4, 253	1, 052	2, 004	6, 737	817	28, 254	61	16
12, 148	291, 402	14, 347	215	3, 936	4, 026	4, 190	5, 308	6, 735	17
15	92, 177	815	170	1, 539	3, 731	73	12, 550	800	18
35, 389	262, 683	20, 513	5, 634	3, 893	6, 980	1, 687	30, 508	91, 961	19
....	63, 389	465	330	689	7, 078	210	16, 264	....	20
10	263, 615	2, 565	317	4, 638	2, 847	351	45, 320	280	21
60	225, 364	14, 444	3, 258	4, 273	5, 045	306	49, 728	41, 291	22
257	436, 701	18, 101	130	24, 819	1, 926	5, 567	35, 908	63, 192	23
36, 879	209, 994	12, 088	6, 707	205	11, 909	8, 241	20, 488	91, 042	24
10, 330	198, 371	18, 078	115	7, 295	2, 547	335	32, 560	57, 673	25
....	30, 390	240	175	605	9, 965	30	31, 665	10, 780	26
....	181, 034	9, 300	4, 441	1, 383	13, 791	2, 321	16, 745	58, 057	27
8, 310	201, 228	13, 283	3, 254	1, 909	13, 194	1, 957	27, 702	97, 350	28
180	264, 136	7, 055	6, 656	2, 072	6, 142	4, 490	10, 584	31, 061	29
....	53, 642	4, 990	6, 094	420	9, 001	494	22, 039	13, 121	30
1, 265	207, 782	2, 038	....	9, 910	2, 498	863	22, 080	81, 187	31
360	384, 420	5, 240	....	18, 573	9, 759	325	26, 462	74, 257	32
....	248, 470	5, 670	126	7, 127	3, 411	8	48, 988	....	33
42, 355	506, 777	26, 952	11, 107	2, 339	16, 809	12, 281	19, 995	121, 075	34
14, 919	251, 184	9, 336	10	1, 470	8, 135	687	24, 195	31, 566	35
10, 417	447, 155	12, 526	1, 714	5, 457	11, 643	4, 603	4, 908	34, 306	36
17, 071	519, 673	14, 217	6, 324	9, 243	8, 297	7, 005	14, 143	174, 063	37
35, 816	244, 955	44, 005	....	11, 591	1, 779	4, 845	58, 827	112, 391	38
23, 851	404, 435	10, 102	9, 582	7, 319	4, 880	17, 922	15, 427	115, 982	39
637	433, 187	16, 901	....	18, 369	383	1, 689	23, 225	55, 517	40
50	168, 661	31, 690	282	11, 872	1, 854	30	20, 755	45, 894	41
23, 011	674, 625	13, 221	8, 736	12, 180	5, 730	10, 386	22, 437	78, 373	42
4	598, 938	11, 532	370	23, 614	2, 135	1, 733	38, 691	164, 391	43
326	90, 429	2, 644	1, 010	463	9, 691	5, 066	15, 546	25, 335	44
13, 988	187, 491	9, 445	5, 477	2, 340	8, 093	2, 990	14, 797	47, 995	45
....	61, 350	185	80	317	7, 532	10, 394	67, 116	1, 148	46
10	232, 486	3, 011	10	6, 172	4, 568	1, 418	44, 788	43, 037	47
28	602, 549	3, 045	....	25, 517	201	2, 074	25, 648	3, 403	48
23, 336	333, 332	17, 701	1, 110	4, 389	6, 747	5, 116	19, 902	70, 886	49
419	841, 985	1, 935	....	13, 449	695	200	13, 800	....	50
4, 259	254, 251	11, 686	....	8, 263	3, 799	744	19, 662	28, 482	51
....	309, 965	4, 416	....	7, 192	3, 123	....	64, 451	21, 725	52
48, 531	264, 448	20, 707	7, 677	2, 246	13, 262	1, 144	37, 758	125, 066	53
792	272, 221	26, 770	210	20, 796	662	1, 206	52, 146	18, 975	54
15, 926	219, 437	14, 128	4, 600	1, 825	9, 924	1, 045	31, 619	72, 157	55
19, 321	221, 618	26, 189	3, 710	2, 194	6, 283	2, 602	22, 358	73, 099	56
29, 351	157, 268	7, 895	1, 293	1, 244	4, 451	693	8, 633	32, 077	57
472	334, 110	1, 822	....	11, 646	2, 513	2, 784	14, 941	45, 270	58
69, 321	284, 783	42, 821	225	5, 697	5, 784	772	14, 469	53, 167	59
48, 468	267, 764	33, 353	75	5, 446	10, 439	....	26, 236	....	60
7, 551	343, 509	7, 718	1, 960	6, 458	8, 194	220	41, 282	120, 010	61
6, 204	158, 810	2, 420	1, 213	928	3, 243	1, 371	33, 553	36, 652	62
....	57, 034	....	625	1, 803	5, 103	303	14, 260	315	63
1	660, 978	1, 725	189	20, 005	2, 611	1, 472	91, 460	47, 428	64
3, 178	94, 165	2, 162	7, 954	205	5, 259	1, 834	16, 157	42, 759	65

TABLE XCV.—*Selected Statistics of Agriculture*—1870—Continued.

STATE OF ARKANSAS.

	Counties.	Improved land.	Value of farms.	Total (estimated) value of all farm productions, including betterments and additions to stock.	LIVE STOCK.						
					Value of all live stock.	Horses.	Mules and asses.	Milch cows.	Working oxen.	Sheep.	Swine.
		Acres.	*Dollars.*	*Dollars.*	*Dollars.*	*No.*	*No.*	*No.*	*No.*	*No.*	*No.*
1	Arkansas	30, 363	965, 012	967, 367	364, 094	1, 677	923	1, 956	340	794	12, [illegible]
2	Ashley	59, 952	718, 592	982, 419	428, 654	1, 511	1, 298	3, 700	951	2, 295	12, [illegible]
3	Benton	50, 767	677, 035	536, 876	467, 608	4, 330	829	3, 337	540	7, 987	24, [illegible]
4	Boone	28, 816	601, 945	451, 736	337, 883	2, 247	307	2, 161	1, 170	5, 537	22, [illegible]
5	Bradley	42, 313	607, 980	798, 778	351, 714	1, 656	786	3, 536	493	2, 544	16, [illegible]
6	Calhoun	20, 572	258, 884	296, 079	189, 715	726	391	1, 475	251	1, 634	8, [illegible]
7	Carroll	19, 942	224, 617	173, 324	223, 770	1, 937	202	1, 435	755	4, 590	14, [illegible]
8	Chicot	34, 181	1, 484, 065	806, 094	259, 446	449	988	1, 005	220	871	2, [illegible]
9	Clarke	39, 257	620, 390	1, 212, 359	427, 393	1, 874	767	3, 165	790	3, 945	21, [illegible]
10	Columbia	61, 114	624, 595	808, 931	263, 776	1, 042	944	2, 217	347	5, 472	13, [illegible]
11	Conway	28, 984	1, 055, 071	818, 328	440, 479	2, 282	580	3, 195	1, 292	4, 402	27, [illegible]
12	Craighead	18, 432	346, 086	333, 738	200, 540	1, 016	249	1, 733	671	2, 396	8, [illegible]
13	Crawford	24, 026	748, 524	921, 921	228, 753	2, 617	451	1, 736	471	2, 724	16, [illegible]
14	Crittenden	18, 242	443, 335	197, 278	154, 334	593	556	894	231	300	4, [illegible]
15	Cross	15, 458	306, 067	351, 576	137, 148	763	347	1, 108	341	580	6, [illegible]
16	Dallas	30, 911	358, 539	482, 556	182, 702	839	419	1, 772	270	1, 818	11, [illegible]
17	Desha	33, 202	976, 504	721, 345	288, 678	864	1, 018	1, 397	256	312	7, [illegible]
18	Drew	40, 325	567, 745	940, 412	299, 734	1, 284	998	3, 079	613	3, 628	12, 613
19	Franklin	35, 896	818, 329	856, 233	369, 607	2, 561	503	3, 113	988	3, 240	27, 823
20	Fulton	14, 435	309, 397	311, 437	175, 234	1, 318	186	1, 382	861	3, 711	7, 859
21	Grant	13, 038	151, 317	345, 535	137, 914	748	255	1, 367	287	2, 022	8, 770
22	Greene	19, 513	381, 480	347, 819	172, 423	1, 173	313	1, 365	587	2, 757	8, 292
23	Hempstead	51, 279	733, 528	1, 336, 606	553, 453	1, 706	1, 354	3, 325	228	1, 986	23, 391
24	Hot Springs	18, 663	208, 837	393, 645	183, 221	964	270	1, 678	463	1, 779	11, 384
25	Independence	58, 842	1, 236, 732	1, 267, 717	505, 596	3, 370	819	4, 050	1, 496	5, 387	22, 787
26	Izard	31, 409	400, 145	606, 577	341, 784	2, 293	393	2, 501	1, 392	4, 413	17, 270
27	Jackson	20, 555	648, 361	632, 880	228, 633	890	370	1, 386	350	855	7, 062
28	Jefferson	70, 883	2, 460, 271	2, 003, 090	576, 138	2, 211	1, 936	3, 231	677	1, 079	17, 063
29	Johnson	31, 953	912, 064	813, 528	516, 091	3, 341	584	2, 958	964	3, 135	18, 906
30	Lafayette	68, 108	1, 215, 616	974, 551	350, 548	1, 406	1, 476	2, 779	501	1, 392	11, 466
31	Lawrence	6, 787	164, 890	169, 390	89, 362	526	113	639	208	331	5, 471
32	Little River	10, 843	289, 337	483, 583	233, 624	892	598	2, 853	286	393	4, 409
33	Madison	32, 863	623, 845	481, 729	291, 185	2, 336	241	2, 036	760	6, 783	26, 283
34	Marion	12, 020	149, 545	204, 441	105, 148	843	97	849	441	2, 983	7, 952
35	Mississippi	12, 573	477, 166	434, 210	292, 647	095	465	1, 347	290	563	6, 263
36	Monroe	31, 852	1, 286, 794	1, 227, 703	299, 874	1, 256	893	1, 925	379	624	10, 210
37	Montgomery	9, 664	133, 835	112, 074	89, 857	570	102	945	381	1, 318	5, 762
38	Newton	14, 256	226, 030	163, 349	178, 005	1, 148	100	1, 232	781	2, 355	14, 136
39	Ouachita	66, 852	837, 802	1, 239, 252	470, 280	1, 550	1, 179	3, 574	686	5, 382	24, 600
40	Perry	8, 763	242, 765	201, 283	114, 221	742	175	919	363	1, 240	7, [illegible]
41	Phillips	49, 947	1, 943, 465	1, 935, 109	445, 663	1, 267	1, 605	1, 778	310	647	8, 830
42	Pike	12, 966	200, 697	233, 889	118, 619	798	209	1, 390	320	2, 068	9, 861
43	Poinsett	5, 388	100, 945	105, 278	52, 104	301	131	526	225	389	3, 379
44	Polk	5, 669	67, 070	106, 335	68, 347	611	113	747	321	1, 267	5, 849
45	Pope	26, 892	669, 301	656, 201	244, 538	1, 461	409	1, 897	586	3, 826	13, 137
46	Prairie	13, 101	356, 045	244, 320	125, 966	537	308	983	174	532	4, 680
47	Pulaski	62, 702	2, 633, 509	2, 046, 937	687, 559	2, 388	1, 913	4, 341	682	2, 288	24, 977
48	Randolph	25, 109	448, 330	430, 669	260, 747	1, 896	229	2, 057	759	5, 363	17, 431
49	Saline	18, 820	311, 603	367, 500	189, 464	779	259	1, 518	202	2, 049	11, 221
50	Scott	30, 320	394, 421	809, 814	305, 188	2, 514	296	3, 057	1, 218	2, 268	21, 733
51	Searcy	18, 773	309, 501	315, 320	237, 232	1, 512	200	1, 619	1, 073	2, 711	15, 682
52	Sebastian	38, 926	1, 190, 008	1, 013, 071	488, 090	3, 060	670	4, 284	1, 040	2, 788	35, 846
53	Sevier	17, 379	312, 220	405, 773	125, 250	757	363	1, 472	226	2, 507	8, 65[illegible]
54	Sharpe	24, 735	365, 760	460, 255	210, 038	1, 704	240	2, 004	945	4, 837	9, 541
55	St. Francis	22, 175	355, 410	740, 420	241, 889	1, 014	659	1, 662	368	924	8, 060
56	Union	66, 932	794, 650	1, 005, 653	341, 279	1, 290	1, 007	3, 071	817	4, 697	14, 810
57	Van Buren	16, 556	269, 730	390, 571	194, 556	1, 029	178	1, 410	665	2, 574	11, 559
58	Washington	73, 145	2, 037, 060	762, 535	573, 122	4, 667	1, 130	4, 133	742	7, 597	33, 431
59	White	45, 924	532, 877	900, 131	417, 211	2, 096	838	3, 192	483	3, 933	21, 586
60	Woodruff	25, 665	529, 450	609, 900	152, 805	661	569	1, 659	274	735	7, 157
61	Yell	22, 773	734, 354	734, 978	221, 573	1, 397	297	1, 809	616	2, 200	14, 224

TABLE XCV.—*Selected Statistics of Agriculture*—1870—Continued.

STATE OF ARKANSAS.

PRODUCED.										
Wheat.		Indian corn.	Oats.	Tobacco.	Cotton.	Wool.	Potatoes.		Butter.	
Spring.	Winter.						Irish.	Sweet.		
hels.	*Bushels.*	*Bushels.*	*Bushels.*	*Pounds.*	*Bales.*	*Pounds.*	*Bushels.*	*Bushels.*	*Pounds.*	
200	......	217, 450	......	......	12, 315	40	17, 327	28, 598	3, 250	1
.....	243	201, 905	2, 905	460	7, 856	2, 543	4, 559	34, 269	55, 284	2
.....	84, 779	340, 046	40, 569	35, 280	1	13, 740	18, 595	9, 866	98, 246	3
295	41, 645	341, 042	22, 837	56, 365	206	9, 449	12, 394	10, 027	92, 958	4
.....	4, 726	222, 825	2, 930	2, 460	5, 177	2, 408	5, 095	48, 356	55, 701	5
20	235	109, 705	835	125	2, 593	91	10	13, 746	474	6
.....	20, 438	172, 696	10, 483	15, 545	17	3, 825	5, 041	2, 797	45, 447	7
.....	......	85, 462	130	......	10, 187	20	56	5, 092	100	8
, 083	749	356, 428	1, 025	200	6, 531	6, 422	6, 009	30, 907	94, 843	9
.....	3, 149	245, 388	5, 203	100	5, 565	7. 306	5, 300	48, 024	665	10
119	9, 320	269, 945	11, 601	7, 127	3, 954	5, 070	9, 644	13, 633	55, 686	11
.....	7, 619	122, 395	7, 960	13, 238	1, 208	3, 587	6, 464	12, 498	......	12
.....	9, 746	237, 702	16, 090	3, 302	2, 366	2, 877	13, 448	12, 634	61, 863	13
.....	......	76, 340	......	200	6, 841	......	3, 032	3, 012	350	14
.....	513	77, 408	3, 971	215	1, 719	757	2, 235	6, 461	19, 782	15
185	435	124, 449	355	290	2, 555	618	500	14, 575	30, 188	16
.....	380	94, 797	100	......	8, 166	167	7, 041	11, 387	25, 062	17
.....	8, 828	222, 140	9, 850	430	6, 661	2, 497	3, 470	32, 775	1, 118	18
, 304	1, 781	323, 444	4, 918	5, 674	4, 796	3, 584	13, 520	23, 689	71, 092	19
75	18, 416	141, 925	10, 598	22, 750	276	5, 197	3, 587	2, 870	21, 395	20
110	3, 548	105, 664	3, 716	3, 919	1, 145	3, 178	2, 678	22, 147	48, 118	21
111	10, 779	208, 352	10, 623	16, 912	983	4, 649	7, 691	12, 904	30, 742	22
, 488	120	683, 425	2, 713	875	10, 664	40	7, 261	40, 541	13, 152	23
, 047	4, 749	196, 848	4, 244	4, 845	843	2, 927	5, 543	15, 851	59, 667	24
.....	38, 653	508, 005	30, 820	21, 336	5, 613	8, 178	17, 574	21, 483	139, 225	25
686	19, 390	303, 242	17, 358	24, 975	1, 568	6, 885	11, 107	13, 435	92, 686	26
7	933	115, 215	1, 346	33	3, 996	895	4, 981	4, 105	50, 395	27
42	188	303, 125	1, 673	......	18, 390	485	667	3, 840	215	28
, 919	9, 945	275, 185	21, 159	11, 915	4, 489	4, 290	7, 048	16, 890	70, 493	29
50	24	247, 004	140	......	9, 572	192	2, 462	22, 303	18, 055	30
.....	285	47, 450	1, 545	375	1, 023	778	2, 864	1, 646	15, 867	31
.....	......	136, 500	......	......	4, 966	......	......	......	......	32
.....	68, 779	374, 171	17, 973	14, 080	8	13, 110	23, 059	10, 763	160, 187	33
, 301	11, 521	115, 169	4, 121	19, 361	302	3, 352	3, 906	3, 010	39, 024	34
.....	23	120, 700	100	......	3, 587	425	7, 416	3, 780	31, 412	35
335	48	184, 358	396	100	7, 334	370	1, 208	8, 205	260	36
.....	3, 072	93, 739	2, 596	3, 044	273	2, 051	1, 897	5, 100	19, 252	37
.....	9, 830	160, 825	7, 741	13, 645	......	4, 435	7, 074	3, 944	43, 292	38
.....	1, 311	279, 589	2, 258	235	6, 407	8, 398	2, 902	20, 680	20, 933	39
431	1, 138	85, 115	3, 631	3, 297	980	1, 275	2, 664	4, 902	15, 607	40
.....	3, 180	293, 849	2, 675	9, 000	18, 002	......	654	2, 371	40	41
, 734	906	122, 358	3, 275	2, 474	1, 109	4, 061	2, 985	10, 842	21, 329	42
60	558	36, 670	935	......	892	314	2, 532	4, 147	18, 760	43
2, 153	33	75, 883	5, 349	6, 906	259	2, 049	3, 070	7, 713	1, 126	44
, 363	......	225, 152	10, 834	1, 015	3, 070	718	6, 306	8, 114	42, 797	45
354	532	81, 618	2, 417	11, 335	3, 332	945	4, 398	4, 671	3, 718	46
919	8, 754	516, 519	16, 442	......	14, 891	897	26, 252	41, 743	161, 370	47
30	16, 733	265, 990	18, 293	11, 130	686	7, 643	7, 820	7, 257	57, 450	48
, 066	824	186, 040	8, 689	3, 816	603	3, 438	5, 874	15, 899	69, 292	49
7, 913	5, 228	304, 408	9, 940	30, 411	678	3, 128	1, 338	5, 223	71, 530	50
, 067	20, 894	263, 812	11, 852	25, 008	2, 180	4, 389	6, 715	7, 212	2, 990	51
55	18, 463	362, 019	16, 084	28, 289	2, 215	3, 494	13, 703	25, 453	142, 347	52
.....	1, 919	123, 045	2, 108	3, 367	2, 189	3, 761	2, 823	11, 873	23, 075	53
70	13, 373	200, 090	13, 447	13, 166	1, 046	6, 617	5, 951	7, 709	56, 600	54
357	280	141, 911	880	......	3, 757	506	2, 440	8, 859	32, 760	55
.....	641	232, 038	2, 956	......	6, 181	8, 238	5, 650	56, 623	44, 471	56
.....	3, 921	165, 710	11, 116	7, 264	1, 038	2, 270	6, 199	6, 104	52, 985	57
135	156, 486	580, 687	71, 938	116, 176	81	14, 876	40, 229	18, 502	136, 648	58
.....	5, 567	323, 603	21, 039	8, 217	4, 925	6, 880	11, 613	21, 816	75, 875	59
50	110	145, 495	105	......	5, 880	544	1, 957	1, 772	18, 780	60
213	13, 589	200, 075	11, 890	4, 404	3, 671	2, 999	6, 269	15, 932	97, 302	61

TABLE XCV.—*Selected Statistics of Agriculture*—1870—Continued.

STATE OF CALIFORNIA.

	Counties.	Improved land.	Value of farms.	Total (estimated) value of all farm productions, including betterments and additions to stock.	LIVE STOCK.					
					Value of all live stock.	Horses.	Mules and asses.	Milch cows.	Working oxen.	Sheep.
		Acres.	*Dollars.*	*Dollars.*	*Dollars.*	*No.*	*No.*	*No.*	*No.*	*No.*
1	**Alameda**	178, 661	**16, 747, 770**	2, 310, 062	1, 119, 435	6, 947	647	3, 663	36	46, 692
2	Alpine	12, 365	82, 800	165, 490	264, 700	500	15	868	8	57, 165
3	Amador	41, 534	480, 400	363, 983	280, 587	1, 686	141	1, 471	68	23, 914
4	Butte	187, 995	2, 423, 300	1, 445, 591	851, 856	4, 315	272	2, 330	56	76, 864
5	Calaveras	41, 000	221, 245	389, 388	401, 639	1, 781	75	1, 995	61	35, 214
6	Colusa	223, 337	4, 408, 064	2, 011, 830	1, 872, 830	5, 905	670	2, 666	14	173, 962
7	Contra Costa	279, 100	4, 936, 635	1, 421, 895	953, 346	7, 033	658	5, 366	23	25, 538
8	**Del Norte**	9, 877	165, 950	60, 617	65, 888	394	37	707	88	657
9	El Dorado	73, 823	672, 295	498, 443	449, 430	2, 098	120	3, 809	188	17, 387
10	Fresno	24, 536	629, 705	229, 068	680, 010	3, 074	263	1, 009	437	139, 677
11	Humboldt	89, 851	1, 244, 775	537, 212	727, 660	4, 329	460	5, 691	282	12, 669
12	Inyo	4, 988	148, 520	157, 221	228, 368	1, 514	98	783	110	521
13	Kern	9, 060	339, 650	192, 925	419, 125	1, 685	163	628	118	90, 200
14	Klamath	3, 309	69, 850	117, 949	78, 735	284	368	372	33	17
15	Lake	17, 508	713, 100	316, 928	314, 210	1, 984	175	1, 827	72	16, 387
16	Lassen	37, 353	297, 800	295, 385	354, 241	2, 022	61	1, 791	48	708
17	Los Angeles	234, 883	4, 245, 885	939, 859	1, 177, 805	9, 632	635	2, 468	48	247, 663
18	Marin	247, 186	5, 532, 313	1, 625, 171	1, 398, 556	2, 671	115	18, 655	244	2, 087
19	Mariposa	24, 184	346, 500	695, 330	239, 571	1, 110	112	923	117	18, 448
20	Mendocino	62, 043	1, 364, 643	616, 373	676, 257	4, 405	488	3, 431	143	49, 820
21	**Merced**	474, 735	2, 324, 112	754, 769	1, 428, 876	2, 362	661	872	119	46, 583
22	Mono	9, 190	84, 300	88, 822	107, 130	723	32	545	101	101
23	Monterey	150, 291	5, 150, 298	1, 640, 107	2, 036, 652	8, 017	403	9, 370	139	298, 877
24	Napa	38, 539	1, 998, 190	509, 846	350, 160	1, 755	311	1, 128	97	6, 006
25	Nevada	7, 974	508, 750	371, 605	181, 270	786	21	1, 148	24	504
26	**Placer**	71, 057	994, 200	1, 263, 275	341, 770	1, 767	107	1, 563	69	26, 396
27	Plumas	66, 131	441, 510	380, 051	542, 345	1, 440	186	3, 465	220	12, 042
28	**Sacramento**	318, 639	5, 052, 160	2, 674, 169	1, 504, 770	9, 462	528	9, 050	105	113, 294
29	San Bernardino	7, 129	191, 242	133, 140	151, 530	970	109	622	10	18, 121
30	San Diego	10, 963	782, 662	160, 920	545, 277	5, 687	723	1, 298	839	16, 443
31	San Francisco	3, 792	5, 817, 400	846, 754	280, 355	611	1	3, 169	1	1
32	San Joaquin	428, 061	7, 874, 365	4, 376, 675	1, 692, 119	14, 139	776	6, 999	50	79, 889
33	San Luis Obispo	457, 846	1, 869, 673	767, 715	1, 559, 818	4, 485	469	4, 813	61	194, 909
34	San Mateo	44, 626	3, 397, 701	1, 190, 793	745, 543	3, 228	359	5, 140	269	6, 535
35	Santa Barbara	40, 026	5, 323, 963	847, 902	947, 840	3, 777	319	2, 166	88	189, 334
36	Santa Clara	168, 315	12, 092, 722	2, 700, 125	1, 487, 076	7, 926	270	7, 363	18	49, 085
37	Santa Cruz	38, 352	1, 870, 800	381, 195	319, 375	1, 729	101	2, 168	503	819
38	Shasta	22, 332	324, 973	209, 698	206, 119	1, 473	157	1, 207	79	3, 520
39	Sierra	13, 204	170, 950	189, 230	116, 285	464	64	887	43	402
40	Siskiyou	66, 674	724, 755	567, 573	880, 365	4, 654	462	2, 631	114	12, 844
41	Solano	360, 536	10, 170, 758	3, 170, 535	1, 532, 905	6, 852	1, 046	4, 123	43	41, 890
42	Sonoma	**402**, 026	10, 079, 183	2, 509, 718	2, 178, 996	10, 616	1, 110	14, 960	392	58, 387
43	Stanislaus	**389, 239**	4, 302, 840	2, 718, 030	1, 382, 943	10, 137	1, 139	2, 271	17	118, 469
44	Sutter	**197, 966**	2, 072, 288	918, 417	611, 798	4, 754	334	3, 623	100	35, 078
45	Tehama	**185, 390**	**1, 353**, 815	880, 234	908, 047	3, 069	267	2, 137	11	130, 868
46	Trinity	**2, 307**	78, 550	88, 325	64, 478	185	23	425	30	130
47	Tulare	35, 028	812, 900	818, 910	1, 164, 817	4, 590	270	2, 039	54	147, 301
48	Tuolumne	18, 736	296, 365	268, 256	284, 195	1, 283	203	1, 681	48	39, 117
49	Yolo	307, 139	8, 720, 586	3, 022, 355	1, 283, 494	8, 739	1, 206	3, 688	51	83, 087
50	Yuba	79, 231	1, 350, 827	906, 224	573, 927	3, 194	283	2, 909	53	12, 540

TABLE XCV.—*Selected Statistics of Agriculture*—1870—Continued.

STATE OF CALIFORNIA.

PRODUCED.										
					Potatoes.			Dairy products.		
Wheat.*	Indian corn.	Oats.	Barley.	Wool.	Irish.	Sweet.	Wine.	Butter.	Cheese.	
Bushels.	*Bushels.*	*Bushels.*	*Bushels.*	*Pounds.*	*Bushels.*	*Bushels.*	*Gallons.*	*Pounds.*	*Pounds.*	
854,888	27,288	69,080	668,975	138,975	114,053	2,205	2,785	198,910	430	1
1,294	308	3,113	8,260	281,700	6,005	....	....	57,290	50	2
16,678	36,700	130	51,815	73,010	9,898	1,060	54,105	43,700	950	3
746,162	16,490	6,140	329,698	351,023	2,043	268	27,919	24,445	3,000	4
8,341	4,535	....	37,395	129,025	6,635	400	99,860	66,357	3,545	5
701,174	2,330	420	386,468	1,086,590	1,708	364	170	37,577	500	6
925,054	290	67,025	358,350	58,800	1,020	....	10,330	153,936	64,890	7
7,423	505	14,955	2,550	3,471	20,495	....	....	35,853	....	8
3,997	581	268	8,642	50,096	4,693	....	118,831	215,530	27,601	9
19,765	3,930	....	18,875	191,594	4,208	1,650	....	5,600	400	10
32,284	10,022	137,022	31,907	51,867	372,924	140	5	112,580	850	11
13,629	22,915	2,175	4,903	....	6,336	....	....	20,940	....	12
13,700	3,575	590	26,270	281,100	6,050	420	....	3,150	....	13
2,360	1,505	2,375	530	72	9,648	10	560	6,275	200	14
87,016	11,615	3,894	67,946	58,046	5,154	....	16	84,268	63,340	15
12,904	205	36,497	93,926	75	6,170	....	....	59,494	1,700	16
18,210	454,896	253	153,080	962,603	20,407	3,310	531,710	25,636	300	17
57,880	320	297,744	37,755	6,692	157,245	....	800	2,107,755	381,300	18
4,275	455	350	8,135	87,816	1,712	100	295	8,290	....	19
95,639	6,878	129,971	64,670	178,493	83,473	....	500	62,092	330	20
218,162	14,456	750	142,436	231,072	13,830	11,330	10,815	232,530	229,298	21
6,144	325	4,173	12,704	7,000	4,982	....	....	35,085	4,100	22
744,093	3,570	21,411	681,115	1,054,316	69,850	1,200	5,200	423,385	713,550	23
264,240	10,190	3,780	34,890	20,789	2,458	785	46,745	56,860	....	24
585	306	190	200	....	5,548	....	10,183	50,741	1,600	25
102,402	1,000	2,510	57,261	109,033	2,208	3,345	61,209	72,125	850	26
15,212	190	63,474	16,345	13,023	14,848	....	....	234,725	....	27
196,135	62,280	10,910	589,513	515,213	72,055	148,920	74,797	439,835	88,050	28
10,356	12,250	50	51,906	71,075	1,542	785	48,730	21,510	7,000	29
32,947	9,330	260	18,743	9,250	3,572	85	1,000	11,528	2,300	30
....	....	....	500	....	128,800	....	....	....	....	31
2,360,925	37,350	600	1,027,016	86,700	7,095	2,300	21,165	292,060	23,111	32
38,864	25,982	780	126,604	903,863	5,741	550	....	156,340	341,250	33
107,049	278	294,318	171,207	12,625	329,875	....	500	285,460	469,295	34
20,200	158,374	514	187,871	996,200	26,530	3,350	6,275	81,088	34,500	35
1,188,137	13,084	15,134	405,575	179,465	31,764	100	85,150	179,675	525,290	36
115,687	22,795	56,690	72,155	3,100	34,253	245	14,550	120,955	120,225	37
29,569	2,455	2,227	54,636	15,820	9,748	1,735	19,287	30,150	2,190	38
7,794	....	8,250	10,415	....	8,451	....	400	39,200	....	39
116,107	3,167	131,383	55,138	43,850	17,066	....	525	95,800	2,300	40
1,949,418	3,750	5,442	443,400	306,817	1,950	960	54,780	119,969	4,000	41
618,425	145,792	323,961	195,456	230,394	369,154	107	308,496	1,060,266	246,900	42
1,650,725	15,700	....	632,950	749,263	1,750	....	5,140	52,625	....	43
673,749	26,513	4,150	452,911	196,657	1,612	9,480	14,630	117,875	....	44
404,722	625	3,801	108,323	445,450	260	350	33,000	68,185	....	45
9,898	795	1,460	735	....	5,658	....	....	8,820	200	46
53,605	9,750	....	85,110	660,645	8,685	2,100	5,430	37,490	200	47
21,920	137	40	7,995	48,525	5,260	....	51,590	26,760	350	48
2,025,612	2,140	1,320	499,926	437,048	15,520	2,930	10,250	186,929	18,750	49
147,347	33,245	27,867	270,271	63,425	9,256	1,442	76,743	100,695	8,280	50

* Distinction of "spring" and "winter" not wado in tho roturns of wheat from California.

TABLE XCV.—*Selected Statistics of Agriculture*—1870—Continued.

STATE OF CONNECTICUT.

	Counties.	Improved land.	Value of farms.	Total (estimated) value of all farm productions, including betterments and additions to stock.	LIVE STOCK. Value of all live stock.	Horses.	Milch cows.	Working oxen.	Sheep.	Swine.
		Acres.	*Dollars.*	*Dollars.*	*Dollars.*	*No.*	*No.*	*No.*	*No.*	*No.*
1	Fairfield	199, 762	25, 038, 719	3, 891, 312	2, 670, 137	5, 652	14, 214	5, 285	6, 092	[illegible]
2	Hartford	278, 436	28, 289, 153	6, 220, 911	3, 259, 387	7, 002	16, 657	5, 742	8, 009	[illegible]
3	Litchfield	342, 308	19, 344, 295	4, 456, 676	3, 484, 593	6, 076	22, 514	6, 482	17, 824	[illegible]
4	Middlesex	82, 016	6, 932, 828	1, 504, 256	1, 046, 838	1, 838	5, 031	3, 938	4, 735	[illegible]
5	New Haven	192, 563	17, 256, 347	3, 614, 178	2, 284, 658	4, 752	10, 841	5, 050	8, 591	[illegible]
6	New London	227, 162	12, 878, 346	2, 895, 417	2, 144, 279	3, 916	13, 116	5, 711	20, 565	[illegible]
7	Tolland	133, 856	6, 308, 423	1, 654, 198	1, 112, 221	2, 401	6, 432	3, 436	7, 902	[illegible]
8	Windham	190, 649	8, 193, 206	2, 245, 202	1, 548, 925	3, 238	10, 064	3, 995	10, 176	[illegible]

STATE OF DELAWARE.

	Counties.	Improved land.	Value of farms.	Total (estimated) value of all farm productions, including betterments and additions to stock.	LIVE STOCK. Value of all live stock.	Horses.	Mules and asses.	Milch cows.	Working oxen.	Sheep.	Swine.
		Acres.	*Dollars.*	*Dollars.*	*Dollars.*	*No.*	*No.*	*No.*	*No.*	*No.*	*No.*
1	Kent	216, 958	13, 167, 760	2, 322, 817	1, 184, 690	5, 232	1, 436	6, 222	1, 274	5, 316	[illegible]
2	New Castle	203, 167	24, 573, 079	4, 004, 098	2, 074, 132	7, 464	863	11, 733	1, 364	5, 185	[illegible]
3	Sussex	277, 990	8, 972, 031	1, 844, 752	998, 501	4, 074	1, 265	6, 127	4, 250	12, 213	[illegible]

STATE OF FLORIDA.

	Counties.	Improved land.	Value of farms.	Total (estimated) value of all farm productions, including betterments and additions to stock.	LIVE STOCK. Value of all live stock.	Horses.	Mules and asses.	Milch cows.	Working oxen.	Sheep.	Swine.
		Acres.	*Dollars.*	*Dollars.*	*Dollars.*	*No.*	*No.*	*No.*	*No.*	*No.*	*No.*
1	Alachua	45, 934	1, 550, 079	624, 622	394, 890	1, 535	539	3, 147	181	3, 195	6, 684
2	Baker	2, 579	37, 640	30, 354	40, 860	117	24	1, 531	1	84	1, 786
3	Bradford	12, 158	133, 632	116, 616	106, 467	375	110	2, 843	62	1, 833	4, 816
4	Brevard	5, 385	21, 000	153, 250	386, 950	191	149	......	......	......	4, 538
5	Calhoun	5, 311	51, 970	87, 050	46, 458	96	70	1, 264	230	633	3, 641
6	Clay	2, 678	70, 418	34, 844	41, 082	130	38	1, 238	46	236	1, 986

TABLE XCV.—*Selected Statistics of Agriculture*—1870—Continued.

STATE OF CONNECTICUT.

PRODUCED.											
Wheat.									Dairy products.		
Spring.	Winter.	Rye.	Indian corn.	Oats	Barley.	Buckwheat.	Tobacco.	Wool.	Butter.	Cheese.	
Bushels.	*Bushels.*	*Bushels.*	*Bushels.*	*Bushels.*	*Bushels.*	*Bushels.*	*Pounds.*	*Pounds.*	*Pounds.*	*Pounds.*	
321	12,991	46,457	285,683	172,482	727	21,843	100,047	15,256	880,261	29,511	1
218	6,240	69,387	217,502	119,335	388	17,203	5,830,200	25,925	1,301,352	103,436	2
766	6,058	50,444	236,900	257,606	1,909	27,561	1,048,569	51,750	1,617,830	1,307,396	3
162	5,650	17,101	85,451	40,352	478	7,731	600,327	13,644	404,620	10,610	4
157	4,201	56,868	234,331	106,372	7,726	17,639	103,562	24,751	804,246	28,261	5
99	265	16,846	247,302	174,300	5,590	17,546	10,000	64,758	803,406	95,613	6
253	626	15,800	101,721	76,574	1,888	17,121	531,309	21,530	386,763	80,671	7
89	21	16,094	161,414	167,574	7,752	22,100	5,685	36,526	517,509	375,696	8

STATE OF DELAWARE.

PRODUCED.										
Wheat.					Potatoes.					
Winter.	Rye.	Indian corn.	Oats.	Wool.	Irish.	Sweet.	Wine.	Butter.	Hay.	
Bushels.	*Bushels.*	*Bushels.*	*Bushels.*	*Pounds.*	*Bushels.*	*Bushels.*	*Gallons.*	*Pounds.*	*Tons.*	
321,954	6,391	885,178	145,238	15,195	81,788	25,418	1,238	221,212	7,239	1
504,187	1,089	1,002,519	353,371	17,555	193,636	6,501	120	765,746	31,490	2
69,199	2,742	1,122,603	55,779	25,566	87,300	53,390	194	185,005	3,161	3

STATE OF FLORIDA.

PRODUCED.										
							Potatoes.		Molasses.	
Indian corn.	Oats.	Rice.	Tobacco.	Cotton.	Wool.	Peas and beans.	Irish.	Sweet.	Cane.	
Bushels.	*Bushels.*	*Pounds.*	*Pounds.*	*Bales.*	*Pounds.*	*Bushels.*	*Bushels.*	*Bushels.*	*Gallons.*	
168,580	8,450	300	....	2,474	7,788	23	615	18,264	22,906	1
10,403	1,715	72	....	83	163	....	....	6,150	3,075	2
45,708	6,170	555	....	295	3,096	....	149	13,273	8,518	3
38,650	....	6,450	....	....	....	4,000	....	38,700	....	4
25,970	180	6,237	13,822	178	1,423	1,427	640	13,950	8,141	5
13,188	1,380	75	....	65	683	122	56	5,322	6,690	6

TABLE XCV.—*Selected Statistics of Agriculture*—1870—Continued.

STATE OF FLORIDA—Continued.

	Counties.	Improved land.	Value of farms.	Total (estimated) value of all farm productions, including betterments and additions to stock.	Value of all live stock.	LIVE STOCK.					
						Horses.	Mules and asses.	Milch cows.	Working oxen.	Sheep.	Swine.
		Acres.	Dollars.	Dollars.	Dollars.	No.	No.	No.	No.	No.	No.
7	Columbia	32,002	423,945	369,710	209,597	733	318	3,562	50	1,654	[illegible]
8	Duval	7,804	647,881	122,010	155,517	328	135	1,620	311	214	[illegible]
9	Escambia	1,077	47,725	51,250	71,520	111	34	914	100	3,392	[illegible]
10	Franklin	237	4,260	4,795	4,210	9	......	50	21	70	[illegible]
11	Gadsden	66,234	601,481	509,635	212,454	691	603	2,319	550	1,695	[illegible]
12	Hamilton	27,720	256,150	263,345	89,008	290	333	800	7	15	[illegible]
13	Hernando	7,964	210,232	500,554	309,810	427	101	2,894	223	542	[illegible]
14	Hillsborough	5,345	151,368	337,964	134,586	406	52	3,123	130	15	[illegible]
15	Holmes	3,986	22,158	73,531	57,619	116	20	1,112	241	1,237	[illegible]
16	Jackson	40,052	342,080	529,420	165,911	440	516	1,974	621	1,429	[illegible]
17	Jefferson	73,113	1,044,805	904,921	258,698	494	1,025	1,635	261	956	[illegible]
18	La Fayette	6,902	66,195	104,086	62,331	200	32	2,020	117	......	[illegible]
19	Leon	87,656	1,225,418	892,458	321,713	427	1,296	1,625	320	715	[illegible]
20	Levy	5,603	81,270	89,955	60,619	296	32	2,407	38	66	[illegible]
21	Liberty	4,976	42,165	54,245	32,350	70	32	670	186	946	[illegible]
22	Madison	51,747	668,078	509,482	210,590	361	760	1,904	83	1,371	[illegible]
23	Manatee	2,811	36,858	48,196	212,526	330	19	2,840	267	56	[illegible]
24	Marion	139,672	828,795	862,896	275,905	637	936	3,035	306	442	[illegible]
25	Monroe	81	11,100	10,200	63,735	26	2	93	4	109	[illegible]
26	Nassau	4,155	132,213	89,653	88,834	125	57	70	265	777	[illegible]
27	Orange	4,698	174,900	82,126	124,845	254	85	3,962	173	......	[illegible]
28	Polk	15,395	56,600	198,505	221,860	417	525	......	......	......	[illegible]
29	Putnam	7,530	248,286	173,880	82,676	247	108	1,055	82	360	2,710
30	Santa Rosa	1,740	11,135	27,700	22,342	46	2	438	118	492	[illegible]
31	St. John's	1,977	115,705	66,798	64,074	309	40	22	99	42	[illegible]
32	Sumter	16,070	95,110	177,330	171,300	512	300	......	......	......	[illegible]
33	Suwannee	11,834	134,935	161,318	79,644	237	177	1,875	71	363	[illegible]
34	Taylor	5,653	44,050	69,827	64,634	117	72	1,040	51	67	[illegible]
35	Volusia	3,813	146,120	68,088	87,119	186	50	3,102	88	107	4,014
36	Wakulla	11,806	88,148	109,329	64,031	184	119	1,617	39	299	[illegible]
37	Walton	6,803	56,585	151,833	147,244	287	50	2,770	650	2,537	[illegible]
38	Washington	5,671	67,390	77,470	59,528	145	64	1,321	279	729	[illegible]

STATE OF GEORGIA.

	Counties.	Improved land.	Value of farms.	Total (estimated) value of all farm productions, including betterments and additions to stock.	Value of all livestock.	LIVE STOCK.					
						Horses.	Mules and asses.	Milch cows.	Working oxen.	Sheep.	Swine.
		Acres.	Dollars.	Dollars.	Dollars.	No.	No.	No.	No.	No.	No.
1	Appling	19,906	138,475	250,506	272,275	536	129	5,841	304	8,336	14,906
2	Baker	67,330	424,058	607,728	167,182	320	900	1,492	221	1,519	3,938
3	Baldwin	47,122	407,566	638,018	140,903	332	560	828	231	871	2,604
4	Banks	26,311	297,816	240,611	108,817	578	210	947	418	2,840	3,471
5	Bartow	79,309	1,959,589	823,200	343,414	1,045	974	1,682	352	4,190	11,794
6	Berrien	21,691	132,772	340,059	255,768	636	214	3,687	257	7,016	[illegible]
7	Bibb	35,705	1,388,734	1,045,633	249,587	342	1,008	1,105	147	260	[illegible]
8	Brooks	60,520	913,551	669,289	278,253	491	777	2,618	335	4,924	[illegible]
9	Bryan	29,037	342,916	251,925	171,950	527	218	1,291	104	1,934	5,631
10	Bullock	38,875	189,255	333,500	268,464	992	263	4,538	109	5,677	15,949
11	Burke	145,884	1,490,497	1,477,811	390,374	1,007	1,630	4,277	169	932	11,157

TABLE XCV.—*Selected Statistics of Agriculture*—1870—Continued.

STATE OF FLORIDA—Continued.

PRODUCED.										
							Potatoes.		Molasses.	
Indian corn.	Oats.	Rice.	Tobacco.	Cotton.	Wool.	Peas and beans.	Irish.	Sweet.	Cane.	
Bushels.	*Bushels.*	*Pounds.*	*Pounds.*	*Bales.*	*Pounds.*	*Bushels.*	*Bushels.*	*Bushels.*	*Gallons.*	
103, 317	24, 798	2, 519	900	1, 264	1, 843	6, 101	844	32, 316	15, 526	7
32, 737	100	7, 700	200	8	100	626	300	35, 273	2, 305	8
7, 020	....	35, 050	....	....	3, 905	302	592	13, 970	1, 276	9
....	555	2, 865	....	....	....	....	....	540	2, 249	10
145, 165	16, 075	32, 785	118, 799	3, 258	1, 220	1, 432	1, 019	40, 930	42, 334	11
83, 930	6, 185	....	....	1, 592	....	7, 395	....	2, 235	1, 840	12
41, 354	1, 027	34, 682	2, 124	162	1, 224	1, 464	15	16, 680	6, 356	13
33, 332	20	75	....	2, 443	....	453	....	27, 663	5, 629	14
18, 424	1, 900	76, 285	2, 570	116	1, 273	225	....	7, 035	4, 480	15
130, 780	2, 025	39, 280	4, 202	3, 391	178	8, 292	30	25, 005	27, 972	16
238, 728	4, 400	4, 306	50	6, 051	1, 043	420	649	15, 163	21, 773	17
28, 435	789	....	....	192	....	288	12	10, 180	3, 269	18
258, 432	999	2, 150	400	6, 518	783	1, 626	225	34, 035	27, 099	19
26, 500	1, 250	....	200	273	190	40	....	11, 380	3, 620	20
10, 865	1, 545	13, 660	800	120	3, 686	1, 007	....	11, 675	5, 418	21
161, 105	4, 129	....	....	4, 470	450	4, 287	....	13, 885	23, 111	22
12, 727	....	71, 452	435	29	....	....	....	21, 652	544	23
129, 596	3, 355	500	....	3, 858	....	....	1, 248	23, 968	....	24
605	....	2, 000	....	....	100	....	....	1, 650	....	25
24, 058	75	1, 900	....	19	984	1, 264	555	17, 614	4, 198	26
16, 213	....	49	125	306	....	1, 563	65	18, 490	4, 856	27
97, 225	....	14, 200	....	346	....	....	....	87, 470	11, 450	28
16, 592	641	1, 125	125	162	1, 045	683	1, 052	11, 673	4, 823	29
6, 872	993	27, 845	1, 025	42	430	63	....	1, 887	1, 328	30
7, 630	250	1, 000	....	....	....	975	869	15, 235	3, 457	31
67, 278	670	8, 800	....	501	....	1, 820	....	112, 620	13, 650	32
50, 934	19, 404	1, 905	750	511	95	10, 741	873	17, 670	17, 427	33
20, 625	200	....	250	214	49	332	....	9, 535	4, 369	34
11, 220	....	63	550	134	125	3, 093	260	15, 417	5, 039	35
47, 274	822	2, 800	861	258	375	921	51	8, 726	10, 727	36
35, 574	3, 312	1, 827	1, 627	299	4, 125	3, 522	85	19, 164	9, 525	37
34, 900	100	475	7, 590	107	1, 786	335	5	13, 061	9, 319	38

STATE OF GEORGIA.

PRODUCED.										
Wheat.							POTATOES.			
Spring.	Winter.	Indian corn.	Oats.	Tobacco.	Cotton.	Wool.	Irish.	Sweet.	Butter.	
Bushels.	*Bushels.*	*Bushels.*	*Bushels.*	*Pounds.*	*Bales.*	*Pounds.*	*Bushels.*	*Bushels.*	*Pounds.*	
....	....	63, 063	39, 508	935	152	20, 870	244	38, 106	12, 106	1
....	....	153, 986	595	....	5, 556	3, 250	....	5, 684	....	2
....	3, 553	89, 857	1, 335	....	4, 036	1, 923	759	13, 285	19, 330	3
....	11, 314	114, 167	11, 069	434	398	4, 620	1, 474	12, 263	22, 372	4
86, 939	49, 708	239, 197	36, 284	350	2, 833	7, 633	3, 093	9, 045	72, 925	5
....	....	76, 976	41, 184	4, 114	671	19, 016	449	55, 875	16, 136	6
....	1, 060	148, 060	4, 310	....	6, 283	564	460	46, 075	42, 460	7
100	....	171, 190	45, 716	125	3, 466	4, 281	1, 571	32, 445	14, 017	8
....	....	38, 909	28, 560	....	412	4, 350	760	30, 834	2, 808	9
....	....	81, 556	22, 799	....	1, 000	11, 187	7	21, 034	14, 941	10
100	184	203, 733	4, 113	....	14, 290	625	1, 329	18, 347	9, 905	11

TABLE XCV.—*Selected Statistics of Agriculture*—1870—Continued.

STATE OF GEORGIA—Continued.

	Counties.	Improved land.	Value of farms.	Total (estimated) value of all farm productions, including betterments and additions to stock.	LIVE STOCK.						
					Value of all live stock.	Horses.	Mules and asses.	Milch cows.	Working oxen.	Sheep.	Swine.
		Acres.	*Dollars.*	*Dollars.*	*Dollars.*	*No.*	*No.*	*No.*	*No.*	*No.*	*No.*
12	Butts	71,727	616,335	584,640	216,366	661	580	1,319	267	1,568	6,[illegible]
13	Calhoun	49,039	529,930	498,675	159,022	209	696	870	218	1,304	3,[illegible]
14	Camden	10,332	283,199	280,173	137,076	296	134	2,073	530	685	3,[illegible]
15	Campbell	49,574	796,235	669,954	192,605	424	828	1,104	343	2,731	3,[illegible]
16	Carroll	53,893	915,093	607,120	250,261	849	725	2,354	977	5,484	11,[illegible]
17	Catoosa	28,446	542,538	230,625	130,877	542	283	834	225	2,447	4,[illegible]
18	Charlton	5,013	88,415	173,732	112,212	228	60	2,044	219	899	6,[illegible]
19	Chatham	22,154	2,157,630	1,257,617	188,410	312	681	902	87	236	1,[illegible]
20	Chattahoochee	43,326	682,530	599,218	176,237	235	781	896	196	261	4,[illegible]
21	Chattooga	41,286	763,725	317,035	173,671	803	525	1,004	327	3,[illegible]	8,[illegible]
22	Cherokee	53,322	704,048	391,611	182,796	725	501	1,466	469	4,715	9,[illegible]
23	Clarke	50,925	871,100	601,369	206,705	647	578	1,254	453	2,340	4,[illegible]
24	Clay	43,503	491,581	513,654	159,070	375	464	845	197	903	4,[illegible]
25	Clayton	36,993	421,921	258,209	116,774	292	383	683	199	1,042	2,[illegible]
26	Clinch	10,923	90,245	169,077	127,680	263	109	3,201	100	1,616	7,[illegible]
27	Cobb	54,438	1,238,766	811,810	344,750	893	799	1,764	617	2,843	10,[illegible]
28	Coffee	11,669	111,540	190,580	221,671	403	157	3,925	317	16,636	12,[illegible]
29	Colquitt	9,120	77,912	109,059	91,261	183	93	1,804	85	9,061	6,349
30	Columbia	104,464	1,136,235	1,025,498	354,419	910	1,219	2,058	539	1,[illegible]	7,[illegible]
31	Coweta	127,123	1,637,893	1,248,607	371,856	861	1,477	2,025	419	2,540	8,[illegible]
32	Crawford	51,187	646,555	679,373	222,125	403	973	1,257	221	971	7,[illegible]
33	Dade	14,548	496,307	153,863	109,865	483	150	615	254	1,744	4,[illegible]
34	Dawson	27,939	348,012	206,876	105,282	531	308	1,014	492	3,976	6,[illegible]
35	Decatur	79,918	805,560	859,548	315,178	742	870	3,412	1,073	5,831	10,[illegible]
36	De Kalb	40,289	1,124,168	550,009	268,893	733	666	1,406	512	2,302	6,[illegible]
37	Dooly	56,832	802,516	530,903	255,624	657	826	1,630	409	5,992	10,104
38	Dougherty	91,130	1,739,470	1,398,330	393,565	374	1,360	1,168	261	317	3,[illegible]
39	Early	47,681	469,250	513,702	193,961	363	593	1,600	298	2,364	6,[illegible]
40	Echols	9,946	95,300	96,822	72,706	186	155	1,387	100	993	5,[illegible]
41	Effingham	19,346	100,485	115,279	137,085	294	283	2,101	79	1,238	8,162
42	Elbert	64,549	865,410	683,275	302,054	1,051	609	1,848	757	3,325	7,[illegible]
43	Emanuel	41,528	314,549	438,143	336,924	1,094	256	4,013	612	14,988	15,461
44	Fannin	19,591	301,030	133,546	118,705	645	63	1,375	750	5,123	7,[illegible]
45	Fayette	55,618	858,221	515,414	189,501	538	659	1,157	324	2,241	5,[illegible]
46	Floyd	76,447	2,331,144	975,43[illegible]	418,160	1,085	1,142	2,145	681	3,854	11,[illegible]
47	Forsyth	29,216	273,299	178,137	88,661	304	278	618	189	1,452	3,[illegible]
48	Franklin	36,925	571,583	347,981	187,842	1,093	327	1,630	834	4,963	5,[illegible]
49	Fulton	26,711	1,037,600	469,052	200,587	414	716	1,204	516	727	6,[illegible]
50	Gilmer	23,636	252,525	323,068	183,368	764	214	1,922	1,125	6,461	10,[illegible]
51	Glascock	25,479	162,590	235,820	89,559	289	255	556	255	871	4,[illegible]
52	Glynn	12,936	260,210	110,009	42,262	105	66	872	175	257	[illegible]
53	Gordon	49,337	1,511,430	576,618	214,235	936	518	1,231	444	4,036	7,[illegible]
54	Greene	51,789	1,059,700	763,855	215,700	829	993	1,384	301	2,240	5,[illegible]
55	Gwinnett	104,923	925,718	638,014	270,252	1,058	719	1,855	549	6,115	8,[illegible]
56	Habersham	20,298	165,845	269,719	141,802	695	175	1,354	729	4,729	7,[illegible]
57	Hall	50,218	588,055	412,902	208,718	700	545	1,386	619	5,905	7,[illegible]
58	Hancock	78,841	1,090,348	1,163,398	286,956	656	938	1,430	629	1,634	5,[illegible]
59	Haralson	18,845	291,600	297,792	105,079	354	237	900	501	1,992	5,[illegible]
60	Harris	98,271	1,298,789	1,129,127	405,370	964	1,537	2,647	634	1,922	9,[illegible]
61	Hart	37,625	191,909	432,698	165,959	871	313	1,522	735	3,437	4,[illegible]
62	Heard	66,246	1,031,224	591,408	246,990	637	744	1,231	406	3,012	6,[illegible]
63	Henry	82,551	1,073,010	922,821	309,849	860	1,125	1,897	424	3,523	7,[illegible]
64	Houston	154,433	2,539,566	2,250,743	659,000	834	2,730	1,502	429	947	10,[illegible]
65	Irwin	8,143	73,829	114,417	116,794	257	76	2,232	172	7,372	7,[illegible]
66	Jackson	50,050	847,616	712,444	269,792	1,143	663	1,904	600	6,273	8,[illegible]
67	Jasper	57,571	938,380	884,708	384,976	977	1,091	1,729	609	1,885	8,[illegible]
68	Jefferson	104,484	1,036,830	1,000,519	277,825	643	1,023	1,508	463	4,440	8,[illegible]
69	Johnson	20,443	132,580	226,025	78,707	374	130	680	177	1,306	4,[illegible]
70	Jones	83,820	874,176	709,305	231,309	479	891	1,082	360	1,250	6,[illegible]
71	Laurens	93,183	853,466	650,538	315,253	1,037	586	2,507	653	8,502	9,[illegible]
72	Lee	82,058	992,374	1,013,891	222,927	187	1,141	852	292	658	2,[illegible]
73	Liberty	67,093	681,656	558,291	339,589	1,078	251	5,026	646	3,[illegible]	14,[illegible]
74	Lincoln	29,402	331,907	455,525	143,709	462	508	1,054	264	1,300	3,[illegible]
75	Lowndes	62,926	842,935	581,034	317,448	691	780	3,243	306	3,473	14,[illegible]
76	Lumpkin	19,803	304,895	188,527	100,416	323	244	831	385	2,383	5,[illegible]
77	Macon	92,749	1,067,361	1,134,431	288,557	511	1,201	1,288	275	1,147	6,[illegible]

TABLE XCV.—*Selected Statistics of Agriculture*—1870—Continued.

STATE OF GEORGIA—Continued.

PRODUCED.										
Wheat.							Potatoes.			
	Winter.	Indian corn.	Oats.	Tobacco.	Cotton.	Wool.	Irish.	Sweet.	Butter.	
le.	Bushels.	Bushels.	Bushels.	Pounds.	Bales.	Pounds.	Bushels.	Bushels.	Pounds.	
35	23,290	126,339	....	80	2,926	2,407	3,546	19,380	55,393	12
45	....	101,517	5,546	....	3,843	2,619	514	11,243	14,065	13
..	....	28,532	456	155	145	630	562	19,187	10,953	14
78	....	159,502	17,126	195	2,621	5,462	....	583	48,200	15
.	40,981	215,338	8,997	100	1,964	6,600	958	29,640	113,083	16
..	43,366	90,855	19,909	78	96	5,201	182	718	40,679	17
..	....	23,250	3,474	85	118	1,291	261	18,008	9,435	18
..	....	55,220	725	....	63	762	10,945	42,680	....	19
..	2,331	107,453	5,503	....	4,374	562	1,158	16,130	23,520	20
75	58,232	145,403	17,802	735	901	5,821	3,021	16,786	38,170	21
..	59,064	168,529	22,786	18,407	347	7,882	1,034	11,911	53,797	22
..	18,103	134,951	27,335	785	3,069	3,390	2,510	13,112	30,881	23
40	255	85,014	5,417	120	3,220	1,916	1,115	18,124	24,005	24
..	13,814	64,319	8,714	....	1,221	1,387	89	6,924	29,511	25
..	....	41,605	21,054	....	330	2,784	....	22,589	11,395	26
00	56,996	215,522	23,182	382	1,972	4,150	2,296	20,351	130,650	27
..	....	49,022	19,949	397	261	42,366	39	45,996	6,116	28
..	....	24,139	6,801	1,276	327	24,468	....	11,834	6,430	29
..	8,699	121,160	11,864	....	7,434	3,124	1,604	15,092	46,311	30
31	....	224,070	26,586	225	9,793	4,628	1,732	19,828	64,933	31
..	5,406	116,326	3,558	....	4,720	1,983	....	15,806	24,627	32
..	26,637	65,488	3,673	545	....	3,841	2,946	2,375	27,703	33
41	22,172	102,066	4,824	11,845	19,690	6,576	1,441	7,705	27,715	34
..	....	215,040	23,055	48,614	5,444	10,738	497	52,115	24,535	35
40	27,645	156,125	14,922	230	1,709	6,906	880	10,928	25,898	36
80	842	149,987	9,485	....	4,132	10,503	9	20,881	....	37
..	30	228,223	12,365	....	14,034	1,032	163	8,806	3,465	38
..	12	129,092	11,201	598	3,461	7,310	831	22,614	23,881	39
..	....	41,814	7,947	30	457	1,761	166	16,957	1,783	40
..	....	55,854	3,189	....	294	1,868	50	15,922	1,573	41
36	....	140,435	13,268	267	3,035	5,616	2,904	9,961	71,364	42
25	50	103,705	21,399	2,540	1,376	35,778	495	24,353	15,057	43
..	3,947	113,754	6,210	7,972	....	10,805	5,646	4,517	31,513	44
46	....	104,486	11,916	....	2,951	3,737	78	8,448	28,895	45
..	96,464	245,091	43,229	140	3,182	6,451	6,503	14,249	120,314	46
..	19,881	68,075	9,769	815	217	2,790	201	4,394	4,432	47
..	18,863	173,007	14,151	725	637	7,894	190	12,335	60,447	48
63	19,921	134,996	10,207	15	866	1,315	10,002	31,598	43,854	49
..	8,103	160,099	12,333	19,481	2	12,045	8,396	13,546	67,128	50
5	8,826	52,886	865	....	1,394	1,629	156	8,222	7,187	51
..	....	15,589	330	....	167	253	49	6,774	5,349	52
..	96,181	233,785	15,827	10,231	354	8,536	2,261	11,214	80,316	53
..	24,651	132,635	9,735	....	5,699	2,871	602	13,971	63,020	54
..	55,102	206,210	31,707	1,242	1,391	9,378	1,171	16,964	65,787	55
..	5,409	132,824	5,915	25,127	79	9,001	3,567	16,297	83,241	56
..	39,663	212,656	20,081	14,144	288	9,287	3,315	15,315	62,101	57
21	7,657	141,630	17,794	....	9,624	4,963	70	26,404	87,220	58
..	17,780	86,352	7,209	4,581	308	4,656	1,369	6,772	49,947	59
..	24,226	255,976	16,312	....	8,163	3,600	25	62,914	28,375	60
86	....	112,656	11,566	4,381	1,320	5,751	532	12,158	41,025	61
99	22,272	151,435	11,230	160	3,508	5,316	311	13,406	41,085	62
68	42,920	166,210	16,619	....	4,888	5,596	308	22,714	52,173	63
29	2,807	363,895	7,450	....	3,819	831	40	40,107	27,320	64
25	40	97,875	15,165	....	153	16,510	....	23,220	2,671	65
..	35,200	218,780	25,990	2,563	1,825	9,625	373	10,636	56,115	66
..	24,274	185,870	11,077	2,209	5,937	3,002	2,341	15,543	70,099	67
..	11,949	211,528	9,014	....	6,885	5,329	97	22,514	16,961	68
09	....	47,229	....	....	1,558	3,446	348	7,168	730	69
62	5,729	108,945	6,815	....	5,188	1,408	1,239	14,354	14,669	70
07	1,075	175,298	6,988	....	4,305	22,728	459	18,229	9,079	71
00	328	155,565	9,816	....	10,179	1,243	160	13,230	....	72
..	....	131,845	58,096	....	2,090	5,917	1,407	95,325	15,939	73
..	10,113	75,606	21,275	....	2,587	2,353	2,352	7,918	27,330	74
..	16	166,570	47,373	....	2,799	8,071	880	37,258	21,212	75
35	8,876	82,013	8,828	12,297	1	5,083	2,693	7,620	39,072	76
20	110	184,877	1,700	....	9,391	1,381	154	21,487	25,534	77

TABLE XCV.—*Selected Statistics of Agriculture*—1870—Continued.

STATE OF GEORGIA—Continued.

	Counties.	Improved land.	Value of farms.	Total (estimated) value of all farm productions, including betterments and additions to stock.	Value of all live stock.	LIVE STOCK. Horses.	Mules and asses.	Milch cows.	Working oxen.	Sheep.	Swine.
		Acres.	*Dollars.*	*Dollars.*	*Dollars.*	*No.*	*No.*	*No.*	*No.*	*No.*	*No.*
78	Madison	13, 286	123, 905	151, 129	71, 988	390	119	437	277	2, 101	2, 05[illegible]
79	Marion	50, 360	578, 295	767, 934	270, 483	514	1, 002	1, 404	321	1, 260	7, 0[illegible]
80	McIntosh	15, 193	438, 054	430, 482	95, 233	188	98	1, 800	144	684	4, 1[illegible]
81	Meriwether	73, 699	510, 380	1, 078, 290	373, 648	994	1, 763	2, 473	437	3, 220	10, 6[illegible]
82	Miller	20, 086	224, 782	266, 625	147, 860	454	289	1, 871	268	3, 995	6, 6[illegible]
83	Milton	33, 945	422, 380	185, 937	196, 345	457	337	818	262	1, 921	4, 3[illegible]
84	Mitchell	58, 132	779, 085	638, 100	205, 356	459	721	2, 133	334	2, 092	7, 1[illegible]
85	Monroe	75, 219	1, 712, 229	1, 383, 147	489, 582	1, 041	1, 789	2, 173	589	1, 754	11, 0[illegible]
86	Montgomery	20, 664	255, 402	234, 103	240, 707	598	186	3, 339	502	9, 853	9, 3[illegible]
87	Morgan	41, 896	606, 603	620, 277	210, 568	636	721	1, 144	364	1, 363	3, 7[illegible]
88	Murray	34, 862	806, 756	396, 853	141, 196	659	252	1, 067	410	3, 025	5, 4[illegible]
89	Muscogee	37, 441	1, 097, 480	849, 455	245, 672	456	841	1, 257	228	334	3, 7[illegible]
90	Newton	123, 651	1, 329, 917	994, 082	351, 001	968	1, 112	1, 936	489	3, 602	7, 2[illegible]
91	Oglethorpe	103, 931	975, 891	1, 109, 340	379, 521	1, 478	635	2, 144	803	4, 314	9, 3[illegible]
92	Paulding	33, 734	509, 064	457, 566	169, 423	543	379	1, 378	605	2, 882	8, 3[illegible]
93	Pickens	25, 271	223, 894	284, 168	121, 126	495	261	1, 271	683	4, 168	6, 8[illegible]
94	Pierce	9, 745	91, 185	113, 641	134, 367	371	38	2, 242	83	2, 292	7, 9[illegible]
95	Pike	93, 625	1, 073, 293	954, 712	281, 305	701	1, 113	1, 652	461	1, 817	6, 2[illegible]
96	Polk	38, 905	908, 923	411, 200	108, 812	463	444	788	318	1, 916	4, 4[illegible]
97	Pulaski	88, 592	590, 240	1, 026, 775	382, 337	855	940	2, 868	595	6, 767	12, 3[illegible]
98	Putnam	45, 639	1, 085, 455	955, 720	298, 323	464	1, 100	1, 541	465	1, 538	4, 3[illegible]
99	Quitman	42, 185	487, 773	458, 780	144, 913	287	473	764	132	438	2, 9[illegible]
100	Rabun	16, 654	182, 974	121, 297	92, 333	481	470	1, 170	453	4, 086	6, 6[illegible]
101	Randolph	77, 700	890, 155	817, 656	294, 043	574	962	1, 533	347	1, 143	9, 5[illegible]
102	Richmond	32, 827	795, 314	408, 319	145, 399	342	507	739	158	378	3, 71[illegible]
103	Schley	54, 210	697, 827	510, 430	177, 900	317	621	627	195	486	4, 37[illegible]
104	Scriven	66, 991	395, 851	985, 576	209, 788	609	565	3, 067	482	3, 225	9, 41[illegible]
105	Spalding	56, 593	792, 376	670, 531	190, 480	400	728	1, 169	192	1, 321	4, 25[illegible]
106	Stewart	163, 172	1, 745, 412	1, 575, 996	420, 449	703	1, 933	1, 739	540	1, 150	8, 27[illegible]
107	Sumter	110, 440	1, 893, 170	1, 724, 681	457, 041	634	1, 796	1, 768	455	822	12, 62[illegible]
108	Talbot	141, 114	962, 631	964, 861	301, 526	631	1, 325	2, 021	486	1, 093	9, 30[illegible]
109	Taliaferro	23, 107	514, 358	411, 719	144, 053	543	381	865	188	1, 220	3, 71[illegible]
110	Tatnall	19, 258	207, 061	218, 707	312, 804	699	700	4, 567	380	12, 030	13, 42[illegible]
111	Taylor	51, 267	618, 965	815, 703	220, 695	348	654	1, 320	430	1, 159	6, 32[illegible]
112	Telfair	21, 900	159, 889	275, 266	199, 772	497	150	2, 563	438	8, 475	7, 47[illegible]
113	Terrell	55, 570	603, 325	776, 940	254, 290	444	983	982	264	1, 069	6, 12[illegible]
114	Thomas	94, 395	990, 380	1, 077, 804	381, 812	907	1, 026	3, 375	622	9, 605	14, 916
115	Towns	14, 289	149, 280	125, 982	85, 297	458	138	802	211	2, 575	4, 18[illegible]
116	Troup	114, 117	1, 571, 308	1, 220, 715	355, 190	680	1, 698	1, 519	432	1, 293	6, 51[illegible]
117	Twiggs	127, 428	665, 028	781, 629	242, 989	473	1, 046	1, 172	452	794	6, 2[illegible]
118	Union	22, 517	367, 950	206, 190	143, 932	800	204	1, 622	697	6, 345	9, 72[illegible]
119	Upson	5, 057	883, 429	925, 791	257, 330	510	1, 047	1, 238	468	1, 193	7, 55[illegible]
120	Walker	63, 889	1, 202, 175	627, 874	324, 015	1, 608	787	1, 939	559	5, 673	12, 41[illegible]
121	Walton	50, 468	483, 819	837, 535	288, 025	1, 288	753	2, 054	602	4, 219	9, 5[illegible]
122	Ware	6, 922	83, 863	93, 079	102, 962	244	94	2, 192	81	1, 845	7, 0[illegible]
123	Warren	57, 906	1, 364, 913	981, 906	288, 594	963	819	1, 479	743	2, 269	7, 7[illegible]
124	Washington	112, 556	1, 042, 836	1, 664, 902	469, 169	1, 485	1, 427	2, 704	1, 287	4, 557	21, 6[illegible]
125	Wayne	6, 804	59, 700	57, 780	119, 600	257	25	2, 703	297	480	4, 9[illegible]
126	Webster	36, 301	283, 975	437, 397	143, 262	270	586	580	127	438	4, 6[illegible]
127	White	17, 737	284, 098	163, 118	115, 120	486	205	784	298	2, 341	4, 17[illegible]
128	Whitfield	43, 062	966, 354	426, 120	223, 622	974	383	1, 569	605	4, 350	7, 4[illegible]
129	Wilcox	17, 749	165, 289	202, 468	143, 386	447	135	1, 627	259	8, 998	7, 4[illegible]
130	Wilkes	69, 897	1, 182, 489	972, 825	357, 894	1, 109	1, 011	2, 337	779	3, 482	9, 4[illegible]
131	Wilkinson	62, 949	850, 663	738, 954	323, 096	953	703	1, 948	573	1, 558	11, 3[illegible]
132	Worth	32, 750	201, 845	305, 678	195, 718	476	388	2, 898	235	5, 306	10, 24[illegible]

TABLE XCV.—*Selected Statistics of Agriculture*—1870—Continued.

STATE OF GEORGIA—Continued.

PRODUCED.										
Vheat.		Indian corn.	Oats.	Tobacco.	Cotton.	Wool.	POTATOES.		Butter.	
	Winter.						Irish.	Sweet.		
ls.	Bushels.	Bushels.	Bushels.	Pounds.	Bales.	Pounds.	Bushels.	Bushels.	Pounds.	
31	...	49,523	7,382	...	732	3,815	...	1,225	9,680	78
23	...	163,298	1,589	700	5,439	1,629	594	20,967	15,050	79
..	...	23,638	2,225	...	403	776	324	26,438	7,805	80
..	33,098	200,830	23,776	370	8,230	5,949	...	27,648	83,480	81
..	...	76,783	11,968	515	1,684	6,015	258	13,867	11,370	82
..	24,896	93,095	15,331	258	215	3,048	762	9,015	24,026	83
20	50	150,526	26,240	...	4,708	6,276	...	21,382	39,860	84
..	36,917	241,251	21,286	...	10,434	2,819	4,709	35,188	68,692	85
..	...	70,405	15,852	...	391	21,353	...	11,437	10,261	86
..	19,820	129,948	14,325	...	4,868	3,121	169	8,019	38,968	87
41	43,228	151,286	11,121	7,698	288	5,810	1,813	5,540	40,851	88
44	2,096	103,117	10,205	105	5,150	616	2,790	29,560	53,147	89
20	38,394	102,587	31,974	288	5,770	5,871	1,544	23,455	67,455	90
..	28,958	181,368	22,880	1,205	5,907	6,457	6,760	21,532	106,249	91
..	29,779	153,132	12,887	1,825	1,322	3,846	2,402	12,974	57,995	92
..	25,209	191,447	3,850	20,285	14,739	8,382	1,360	13,816	46,914	93
..	...	33,896	14,506	100	250	4,445	143	39,960	5,901	94
..	30,135	182,045	18,368	1,412	5,676	3,355	1,715	24,745	51,116	95
..	45,497	126,750	23,410	60	2,001	3,774	2,075	4,898	36,320	96
25	268	215,375	13,646	80	6,617	15,444	3,344	20,432	17,320	97
20	10,320	160,661	7,872	100	7,326	3,328	2,497	14,848	29,047	98
..	958	79,610	4,151	...	3,880	538	50	15,615	15,196	99
29	...	71,376	1,488	4,208	...	5,541	2,704	3,915	19,868	100
15	...	184,940	3,584	...	5,748	2,215	577	25,457	34,465	101
32	2,178	77,895	2,002	...	2,017	1,222	1,739	18,544	8,128	102
..	3,899	88,058	728	...	3,657	1,550	937	19,626	13,897	103
44	350	153,242	7,629	...	3,086	9,901	1,219	30,789	3,406	104
..	18,634	125,984	17,164	...	3,630	2,532	2,480	16,381	90,790	105
..	6,051	271,288	4,760	...	13,643	1,780	486	26,103	44,343	106
97	747	280,379	22,085	252	12,823	1,056	1,488	40,924	61,031	107
..	18,372	200,645	12,940	...	7,020	1,471	2,284	27,786	27,977	108
56	8,062	78,815	5,567	...	3,024	2,279	1,142	8,530	24,793	109
..	...	74,684	28,117	...	314	23,834	325	25,386	13,978	110
..	5,962	119,209	6,491	485	3,559	2,103	766	16,344	19,096	111
..	...	62,429	15,823	627	704	19,829	60	20,569	12,725	112
..	443	158,130	13,973	35	6,163	2,218	967	22,898	19,887	113
40	30	248,618	58,962	2,593	6,092	24,022	1,392	58,187	31,467	114
..	5,096	61,990	8,927	4,659	...	4,874	2,557	3,405	18,861	115
..	26,645	162,946	34,514	...	9,963	2,256	3,594	29,290	38,205	116
..	709	164,145	350	...	6,189	2,051	2,193	18,163	19,858	117
10	7,571	139,127	12,099	20,268	...	12,458	7,791	9,098	50,155	118
50	26,444	168,164	9,166	...	4,835	5,188	3,531	17,186	22,695	119
53	107,748	226,194	28,547	3,268	261	13,319	4,903	18,022	71,837	120
..	46,772	178,553	34,022	...	3,536	6,160	831	20,365	81,219	121
..	...	28,474	8,535	413	124	3,713	112	20,993	2,690	122
98	5,739	117,518	12,549	200	7,605	4,787	2,268	32,415	27,203	123
44	23	313,487	3,877	50	11,338	8,024	303	43,590	36,152	124
..	...	19,597	7,092	216	9	816	153	18,017	6,042	125
40	1,381	86,810	150	25	3,167	895	397	11,041	14,958	126
18	...	80,811	8,067	4,686	...	4,076	1,218	8,829	22,475	127
30	48,760	135,007	33,120	9,673	10	7,211	3,851	10,563	97,510	128
	8	47,130	11,870	739	700	17,839	31	15,866	2,869	129
50	22,617	171,378	37,742	...	6,882	5,598	115	16,970	79,469	130
10	58	182,164	4,257	...	5,115	3,747	854	32,919	26,286	131
..	22	84,194	13,381	1,298	2,051	16,065	567	24,219	6,108	132

TABLE XCV.—*Selected Statistics of Agriculture*—1870—Continued.

STATE OF ILLINOIS.

	Counties.	Improved land.	Value of farms.	Total (estimated) value of all farm productions, including betterments and additions to stock.	LIVE STOCK.						
					Value of all live stock.	Horses.	Mules and asses.	Milch cows.	Working oxen.	Sheep.	Swine.
		Acres.	*Dollars.*	*Dollars.*	*Dollars.*	*No.*	*No.*	*No.*	*No.*	*No.*	*No.*
1	Adams	287, 926	21, 202, 263	4, 654, 410	2, 816, 750	14, 370	3, 018	10, 759	85	26, 949	[illegible]
2	Alexander	13, 836	546, 256	268, 959	120, 047	488	197	496	141	1, 007	[illegible]
3	Bond	145, 045	6, 570, 103	1, 454, 850	925, 370	6, 481	613	3, 618	10	10, 239	[illegible]
4	Boone	137, 307	6, 916, 863	1, 270, 276	1, 049, 107	6, 309	95	7, 088	10	20, 810	[illegible]
5	Brown	57, 062	3, 149, 005	460, 981	442, 100	3, 431	501	2, 256	27	9, 525	[illegible]
6	Bureau	392, 611	18, 286, 039	3, 936, 439	3, 150, 413	19, 193	533	13, 590	......	9, 079	[illegible]
7	Calhoun	37, 684	1, 991, 145	626, 364	344, 311	2, 365	337	1, 710	438	1, 550	[illegible]
8	Carroll	186, 864	8, 265, 045	2, 672, 966	1, 519, 090	9, 813	136	7, 984	......	7, 348	[illegible]
9	Cass	92, 902	4, 591, 535	1, 071, 951	672, 190	3, 513	594	2, 281	7	4, 235	[illegible]
10	Champaign	419, 368	16, 634, 591	4, 505, 875	3, 129, 038	16, 529	1, 496	8, 565	472	17, 312	[illegible]
11	Christian	241, 472	10, 769, 555	2, 195, 504	1, 717, 801	9, 229	1, 640	4, 470	179	15, 585	[illegible]
12	Clark	118, 594	5, 028, 245	1, 239, 976	831, 944	6, 320	573	4, 169	69	23, 607	[illegible]
13	Clay	146, 922	4, 581, 916	1, 175, 541	831, 482	5, 437	901	3, 830	379	20, 189	[illegible]
14	Clinton	150, 177	5, 976, 205	1, 524, 284	827, 144	5, 903	1, 041	3, 739	32	5, 356	17, 911
15	Coles	208, 337	9, 186, 010	2, 169, 192	1, 579, 113	9, 397	987	5, 448	107	20, 546	[illegible]
16	Cook	348, 824	22, 873, 349	4, 033, 256	2, 612, 441	12, 770	127	23, 063	55	[illegible]	[illegible]
17	Crawford	105, 505	3, 920, 349	1, 157, 358	684, 200	6, 374	351	3, 179	61	23, 762	[illegible]
18	Cumberland	75, 342	2, 529, 650	519, 013	441, 129	3, 570	347	2, 388	152	12, 132	[illegible]
19	De Kalb	334, 502	13, 988, 325	2, 903, 762	2, 230, 356	13, 044	302	14, 619	[illegible]	24, [illegible]	[illegible]
20	De Witt	168, 539	9, 852, 110	1, 990, 119	1, 530, 592	7, 873	746	4, 351	156	21, 796	[illegible]
21	Douglas	147, 633	4, 906, 353	1, 180, 055	986, 233	5, 681	668	3, 907	131	10, 555	[illegible]
22	Du Page	164, 874	9, 525, 290	1, 708, 512	1, 182, 194	6, 247	104	10, 888	22	26, 939	[illegible]
23	Edgar	265, 458	10, 328, 996	2, 368, 421	2, 307, 567	10, 294	893	6, 666	345	42, 788	[illegible]
24	Edwards	58, 912	1, 677, 047	612, 221	327, 927	2, 952	451	2, 045	36	14, 401	[illegible]
25	Effingham	120, 343	4, 375, 776	1, 379, 455	793, 648	4, 907	522	4, 316	376	13, 228	[illegible]
26	Fayette	187, 196	5, 868, 725	2, 115, 593	1, 291, 793	8, 898	862	6, 261	266	21, 234	[illegible]
27	Ford	141, 228	6, 316, 265	1, 001, 129	969, 456	4, 889	533	3, 069	176	2, 625	[illegible]
28	Franklin	80, 749	2, 159, 079	1, 099, 576	749, 598	4, 306	1, 482	3, 280	577	18, 196	[illegible]
29	Fulton	228, 132	14, 213, 531	3, 092, 067	2, 243, 228	12, 825	654	8, 510	73	29, 078	57, 965
30	Gallatin	49, 572	1, 795, 075	665, 821	411, 301	3, 016	567	2, 095	766	7, 204	14, 985
31	Greene	175, 408	11, 007, 844	2, 507, 350	1, 347, 532	9, 034	1, 231	4, 479	127	13, 690	[illegible]
32	Grundy	193, 999	7, 739, 878	1, 043, 965	1, 113, 149	7, 264	219	6, 770	2	3, 845	[illegible]
33	Hamilton	88, 996	1, 977, 070	1, 131, 953	631, 732	4, 603	727	3, 349	1, 124	20, 117	[illegible]
34	Hancock	311, 517	15, 338, 171	2, 611, 161	2, 393, 702	14, 115	2, 258	9, 437	48	20, 562	[illegible]
35	Hardin	28, 117	755, 518	235, 462	216, 909	1, 201	307	1, 057	902	3, 390	[illegible]
36	Henderson	140, 954	7, 719, 414	2, 717, 950	1, 470, 221	7, 075	691	4, 485	52	6, 146	[illegible]
37	Henry	265, 904	12, 152, 900	2, 959, 687	1, 944, 279	11, 960	549	8, 872	14	6, 266	[illegible]
38	Iroquois	322, 510	11, 932, 462	1, 578, 845	2, 283, 926	12, 716	746	10, 345	57	14, 986	21, 764
39	Jackson	78, 548	3, 239, 360	1, 208, 989	617, 961	4, 429	1, 034	3, 230	494	9, 011	[illegible]
40	Jasper	90, 867	2, 469, 866	733, 027	624, 868	4, 170	338	2, 946	291	17, 330	[illegible]
41	Jefferson	118, 951	3, 375, 968	1, 100, 632	855, 660	6, 006	1, 878	3, 908	389	22, 759	[illegible]
42	Jersey	94, 147	6, 065, 415	1, 445, 440	827, 323	4, 531	658	2, 978	50	4, 532	[illegible]
43	Jo Daviess	156, 517	8, 831, 353	2, 538, 195	1, 617, 521	8, 528	207	10, 309	35	17, 517	[illegible]
44	Johnson	57, 820	1, 457, 105	736, 631	392, 012	2, 247	926	1, 846	557	9, 563	[illegible]
45	Kane	240, 120	13, 322, 455	2, 632, 137	1, 892, 252	8, 923	180	16, 034	35	36, 188	[illegible]
46	Kankakee	312, 182	12, 522, 509	1, 970, 196	2, 067, 847	13, 514	514	12, 075	7	4, 397	[illegible]
47	Kendall	164, 004	9, 583, 619	1, 490, 171	1, 203, 225	7, 275	182	5, 982	4	12, 230	[illegible]
48	Knox	330, 829	18, 807, 671	3, 929, 613	3, 194, 166	18, 247	930	10, 997	24	16, 137	[illegible]
49	Lake	207, 779	10, 698, 599	2, 265, 727	1, 632, 632	8, 087	94	12, 167	100	67, 763	[illegible]
50	La Salle	533, 724	25, 274, 479	5, 502, 502	3, 906, 367	24, 673	524	17, 605	94	17, 200	[illegible]
51	Lawrence	87, 828	3, 421, 020	969, 491	651, 633	4, 375	376	3, 053	29	15, 422	[illegible]
52	Lee	322, 212	12, 822, 993	3, 001, 570	2, 334, 963	12, 150	281	12, 825	90	12, 239	[illegible]
53	Livingston	377, 505	14, 246, 593	1, 981, 993	2, 171, 727	13, 897	851	10, 225	19	6, 766	[illegible]
54	Logan	321, 709	16, 168, 686	3, 623, 501	2, 435, 541	12, 204	1, 015	6, 319	73	7, 776	[illegible]
55	Macon	265, 259	10, 132, 379	2, 808, 166	1, 608, 466	8, 375	1, 344	4, 943	84	10, 602	[illegible]
56	Macoupin	291, 059	13, 128, 576	2, 439, 466	1, 831, 772	12, 926	2, 007	6, 907	70	17, 670	[illegible]
57	Madison	257, 032	18, 194, 701	3, 727, 065	1, 831, 004	12, 194	3, 070	7, 734	92	8, 027	[illegible]
58	Marion	173, 081	5, 611, 010	1, 563, 488	1, 024, 806	6, 605	890	4, 457	305	14, 511	[illegible]
59	Marshall	166, 057	9, 320, 164	1, 615, 758	1, 400, 831	9, 798	273	5, 533	13	5, 517	[illegible]
60	Mason	209, 453	10, 109, 200	2, 304, 803	1, 293, 818	6, 541	1, 988	4, 217	142	1, 968	[illegible]
61	Massac	25, 151	726, 259	345, 947	133, 439	762	430	948	199	2, 297	[illegible]
62	McDonough	261, 635	13, 907, 711	2, 294, 082	2, 088, 995	11, 402	1, 318	6, 890	44	14, 750	[illegible]
63	McHenry	230, 566	11, 843, 688	3, 294, 277	2, 071, 933	10, 382	195	16, 378	140	64, 331	[illegible]
64	McLean	494, 978	21, 863, 621	4, 860, 898	4, 129, 814	19, 943	1, 524	11, 663	206	25, [illegible]	[illegible]
65	Menard	131, 173	7, 944, 895	2, 237, 505	1, 617, 389	6, 840	921	3, 341	56	11, 113	[illegible]
66	Mercer	222, 809	10, 788, 303	2, 848, 387	1, 740, 348	10, 984	770	7, 655	9	11, 278	[illegible]

TABLE XCV.—*Selected Statistics of Agriculture*—1870—Continued.

STATE OF ILLINOIS.

Produced.										
Wheat.							Potatoes.			
Spring.	Winter.	Rye.	Indian corn.	Oats.	Barley.	Wool.	Irish.	Butter.	Hay.	
Bushels.	*Bushels.*	*Bushels.*	*Bushels.*	*Bushels.*	*Bushels.*	*Pounds.*	*Bushels.*	*Pounds.*	*Tons.*	
16,191	947,616	20,989	1,432,905	750,074	8,320	104,855	198,511	756,866	31,770	1
....	42,658	30	244,220	21,627	....	3,509	13,270	....	264	2
700	368,625	6,240	1,064,052	461,097	....	37,259	13,668	108,542	19,388	3
241,042	309	35,871	466,985	579,127	52,335	80,508	167,311	555,159	31,323	4
13,276	117,502	4,742	337,769	70,852	....	20,439	22,604	72,614	5,633	5
465,236	724	43,811	3,030,404	987,426	98,732	45,633	234,580	580,287	62,099	6
15	221,298	186	234,041	26,234	416	4,619	29,980	35,700	1,914	7
418,073	260	25,721	1,367,965	775,100	123,466	32,650	133,949	532,486	25,610	8
12,165	127,054	2,772	1,146,980	168,784	1,027	12,049	20,351	80,690	4,136	9
109,577	123,001	45,752	3,924,730	721,375	18,384	66,986	206,018	716,430	44,800	10
18,360	504,041	10,722	1,883,336	383,821	8,082	63,247	86,161	193,572	22,964	11
....	195,118	7,308	614,582	212,628	80	69,468	49,737	218,799	18,076	12
1,894	85,737	3,221	1,019,904	269,945	313	47,546	41,297	215,416	12,967	13
500	610,888	1,619	813,237	446,324	20	8,897	76,297	169,055	11,585	14
2,651	154,485	8,825	2,133,111	315,954	5,057	59,017	161,985	260,409	22,371	15
144,296	4,904	20,171	570,427	1,584,225	50,973	57,372	444,554	1,088,903	129,210	16
60	212,934	15,497	581,964	136,255	30	72,931	26,841	164,193	11,697	17
550	84,697	14,798	403,075	171,860	62	32,421	18,734	68,653	9,372	18
298,059	190	21,018	1,023,849	987,074	289,447	104,974	199,478	915,804	68,665	19
106,493	11,695	11,540	1,311,635	216,750	9,525	90,016	88,190	341,456	20,289	20
7,083	65,461	9,017	1,680,225	225,074	272	29,406	65,265	198,283	15,201	21
106,096	693	7,532	331,981	860,809	72,062	153,611	141,590	548,453	52,430	22
13,282	247,360	37,508	2,107,615	290,079	1,185	164,105	88,508	457,104	36,638	23
....	122,703	528	352,371	129,152	....	48,703	14,528	32,533	7,374	24
77	195,716	19,750	620,247	380,073	235	35,650	54,671	210,155	11,360	25
....	351,310	25,328	962,525	497,395	192	54,446	73,845	393,710	20,844	26
42,571	1,008	11,577	565,671	154,589	3,391	13,465	39,636	262,646	23,446	27
365	111,324	5,195	653,290	222,426	98	48,956	27,068	64,556	4,835	28
193,669	223,930	131,711	1,508,763	261,390	3,746	105,259	96,207	458,873	27,545	29
....	83,093	512	509,491	27,164	65	18,051	22,657	7,953	2,252	30
....	577,400	415	1,051,313	64,029	82	70,854	50,435	195,992	20,001	31
21,700	150	4,930	295,971	269,332	774	16,775	51,451	438,309	37,116	32
129	92,347	11,672	735,252	203,464	20	42,776	28,402	195,246	6,397	33
181,378	232,750	133,533	1,510,401	579,509	1,300	74,586	92,863	443,770	36,062	34
13	32,306	865	172,651	26,901	6	7,683	105,707	589	166	35
161,112	69,062	96,430	1,712,901	229,286	4,119	23,317	59,711	267,268	12,326	36
462,379	445	35,766	2,541,683	668,367	65,760	40,991	156,734	644,494	37,229	37
57,160	10,480	23,259	790,810	430,746	11,328	54,495	87,197	358,672	63,947	38
820	329,036	524	611,951	149,931	2,426	29,326	68,481	167,334	4,353	39
....	87,808	9,165	461,345	149,214	300	43,465	21,755	18,845	10,739	40
....	100,553	5,934	887,981	285,949	200	52,957	52,309	150,298	10,460	41
....	558,367	....	519,120	71,779	932	13,226	39,330	180,078	11,650	42
282,758	555	7,185	1,286,326	874,016	22,889	66,650	201,015	655,681	34,372	43
....	92,191	2,468	343,298	74,525	30	21,663	19,764	99,725	2,327	44
182,826	325	23,018	674,333	785,608	137,407	173,264	211,048	758,893	73,255	45
103,466	480	12,935	637,399	772,408	11,426	36,760	118,451	714,666	73,585	46
90,681	1,249	5,163	681,207	468,890	12,439	39,884	79,365	386,050	23,740	47
267,764	7,654	113,547	2,708,319	787,952	19,723	53,885	147,909	658,074	53,014	48
168,914	221	5,870	517,353	699,069	21,852	318,042	222,234	927,533	76,337	49
271,181	2,193	48,308	3,077,028	509,642	86,635	68,801	325,953	1,240,386	97,273	50
....	264,134	1,121	656,363	131,386	1,350	41,220	33,855	93,941	7,701	51
450,793	2,260	14,829	1,656,978	963,197	154,665	44,107	210,873	753,149	57,506	52
129,206	1,339	26,163	1,182,696	659,300	11,419	27,979	93,788	809,020	64,013	53
198,056	40,963	37,232	4,221,640	490,226	14,543	30,448	130,015	482,755	31,297	54
55,239	196,813	29,223	2,214,468	454,648	20,277	57,639	117,050	159,426	19,963	55
160	861,398	2,404	1,051,544	459,417	2,092	88,080	60,964	291,608	42,493	56
550	1,207,181	3,685	2,127,540	474,232	6,577	24,899	667,460	298,988	26,068	57
....	173,632	14,517	1,034,037	389,446	6,880	40,285	37,080	81,014	21,249	58
106,129	900	36,135	1,122,903	362,604	16,936	20,819	98,236	290,077	21,455	59
73,261	125,028	49,182	2,648,720	272,660	2,747	4,084	71,345	231,960	8,943	60
....	72,316	544	183,126	22,097	163	5,908	13,125	42,505	2,034	61
273,871	36,146	52,401	1,362,490	280,717	3,120	31,310	71,476	413,416	27,424	62
401,790	970	29,264	1,145,005	910,397	77,456	200,022	303,467	910,226	71,742	63
211,801	10,955	39,824	3,723,379	911,127	36,072	116,738	219,558	887,578	77,841	64
36,152	45,793	4,289	1,973,880	235,091	1,155	37,511	41,456	237,575	13,323	65
289,991	13,203	40,778	2,054,962	452,889	5,026	52,088	94,241	376,797	28,180	66

TABLE XCV.—*Selected Statistics of Agriculture*—1870—Continued.

STATE OF ILLINOIS—Continued.

	Counties.	Improved land.	Value of farms.	Total (estimated) value of all farm productions, including betterments and additions to stock.	LIVE STOCK.						
					Value of all live stock.	Horses.	Mules and asses.	Milch cows.	Working oxen.	Sheep.	Swine.
		Acres.	*Dollars.*	*Dollars.*	*Dollars.*	*No.*	*No.*	*No.*	*No.*	*No.*	*No.*
67	Monroe	92, 810	5, 355, 430	1, 407, 966	608, 903	4, 205	999	2, 715	51	2, 020	11, [illegible]
68	Montgomery	276, 682	7, 961, 130	2, 493, 642	1, 450, 605	12, 447	1, 483	6, 400	54	12, 881	34, [illegible]
69	Morgan	293, 450	18, 818, 839	4, 482, 802	3, 875, 150	10, 330	1, 974	5, 648	465	15, 040	44, [illegible]
70	Moultrie	144, 220	5, 803, 602	1, 732, 864	1, 105, 444	6, 274	699	3, 254	281	20, 531	22, [illegible]
71	Ogle	316, 883	15, 669, 702	3, 442, 692	2, 530, 290	13, 525	298	12, 932	64	18, 295	33, [illegible]
72	Peoria	170, 729	10, 291, 236	1, 671, 970	1, 239, 646	8, 839	401	6, 318	35	6, 760	25, [illegible]
73	Perry	93, 754	3, 716, 079	958, 420	621, 825	4, 527	815	3, 095	60	10, 255	14, [illegible]
74	Piatt	94, 454	3, 530, 998	1, 089, 661	696, 031	3, 483	334	1, 986	181	3, 180	12, [illegible]
75	Pike	233, 785	14, 508, 922	3, 118, 876	2, 073, 538	11, 047	1, 880	7, 657	81	18, 688	51, [illegible]
76	Pope	55, 980	1, 286, 325	657, 723	381, 222	2, 217	790	1, 848	1, 016	9, 557	12, [illegible]
77	Pulaski	19, 319	810, 661	330, 712	170, 498	871	199	842	363	1, 380	5, [illegible]
78	Putnam	37, 271	2, 258, 709	466, 554	402, 594	2, 420	90	1, 406	35	1, 987	5, [illegible]
79	Randolph	140, 764	8, 127, 306	2, 270, 199	1, 050, 616	6, 972	1, 209	4, 619	87	12, 180	24, [illegible]
80	Richland	75, 079	2, 984, 050	733, 924	459, 737	3, 254	416	2, 723	79	12, 447	12, [illegible]
81	Rock Island	155, 214	7, 636, 949	1, 787, 283	1, 347, 059	7, 985	342	7, 471	23	5, 067	[illegible]
82	Saline	72, 309	1, 571, 920	671, 036	482, 080	3, 467	1, 109	2, 888	907	15, 018	20, [illegible]
83	Sangamon	421, 748	25, 388, 118	4, 557, 711	3, 777, 044	16, 395	3, 046	8, 897	190	29, 749	76, [illegible]
84	Schuyler	96, 195	5, 429, 725	1, 230, 491	929, 902	6, 479	587	4, 192	63	15, 419	23, [illegible]
85	Scott	85, 331	5, 918, 724	1, 126, 237	690, 972	3, 257	446	2, 151	28	6, 077	17, [illegible]
86	Shelby	310, 179	10, 918, 768	2, 911, 557	2, 141, 612	13, 059	1, 271	7, 513	386	62, 868	43, [illegible]
87	Stark	138, 129	7, 226, 929	1, 596, 615	1, 258, 735	7, 080	289	4, 093	......	4, 226	[illegible]
88	St. Clair	231, 117	19, 556, 277	3, 302, 620	1, 401, 325	8, 457	2, 565	6, 338	96	3, 782	29, [illegible]
89	Stephenson	254, 857	14, 678, 439	3, 136, 474	1, 786, 210	11, 441	216	10, 723	31	18, 346	34, [illegible]
90	Tazewell	229, 126	11, 854, 646	2, 320, 048	1, 768, 989	10, 312	489	6, 194	21	7, 501	34, [illegible]
91	Union	75, 832	3, 383, 201	1, 295, 237	619, 053	3, 919	901	2, 907	1, 079	9, 342	25, 14[illegible]
92	Vermillion	360, 251	14, 080, 111	3, 426, 816	3, 159, 545	15, 282	1, 122	9, 681	321	67, 890	50, 17[illegible]
93	Wabash	54, 063	2, 335, 340	730, 464	317, 779	2, 122	123	1, 707	14	8, 312	10, [illegible]
94	Warren	266, 187	14, 430, 489	3, 794, 801	2, 725, 214	14, 230	1, 215	8, 358	58	12, 735	52, 19[illegible]
95	Washington	177, 592	5, 518, 910	1, 859, 140	837, 674	6, 220	1, 333	3, 798	34	8, 037	20, [illegible]
96	Wayne	147, 352	2, 981, 095	2, 105, 082	1, 870, 439	7, 890	1, 296	5, 843	873	28, 967	30, [illegible]
97	White	92, 398	3, 264, 489	1, 192, 005	724, 874	4, 696	1, 022	3, 697	594	17, 085	24, [illegible]
98	Whitesides	289, 809	12, 632, 720	3, 085, 329	2, 497, 554	14, 944	232	13, 129	8	11, 108	37, [illegible]
99	Will	419, 442	20, 654, 783	3, 965, 271	3, 091, 825	17, 433	431	18, 193	23	16, 409	21, [illegible]
100	Williamson	128, 448	2, 514, 981	1, 706, 997	938, 097	5, 129	1, 667	4, 016	1, 047	20, 971	30, [illegible]
101	Winnebago	241, 373	12, 125, 217	2, 513, 513	1, 732, 461	10, 116	219	1, 023	65	24, 767	19, [illegible]
102	Woodford	225, 504	9, 742, 750	2, 288, 375	1, 665, 830	9, 002	190	6, 300	54	1, 331	43, 64[illegible]

STATE OF INDIANA.

	Counties.	Improved land.	Value of farms.	Total (estimated) value of all farm productions, including betterments and additions to stock.	LIVE STOCK.						
					Value of all live stock.	Horses.	Mules and asses.	Milch cows.	Working oxen.	Sheep.	Swine.
		Acres.	*Dollars.*	*Dollars.*	*Dollars.*	*No.*	*No.*	*No.*	*No.*	*No.*	*No.*
1	Adams	76, 020	3, 453, 733	622, 343	521, 997	4, 667	29	4, 429	34	21, 337	13, 354
2	Allen	155, 211	12, 696, 007	1, 976, 523	1, 282, 233	8, 740	94	8, 644	210	36, 323	23, 417
3	Bartholomew	131, 355	9, 748, 630	2, 035, 730	1, 040, 804	6, 189	1, 048	4, 372	79	15, 838	38, 546
4	Benton	133, 812	4, 300, 560	1, 228, 660	781, 020	3, 115	314	1, 906	140	5, 143	8, 566
5	Blackford	30, 863	1, 524, 040	342, 115	284, 844	2, 646	77	1, 720	20	7, 890	5, 863
6	Boone	126, 942	8, 974, 665	3, 814, 552	1, 309, 597	7, 902	637	5, 147	40	23, 095	27, 109
7	Brown	41, 825	1, 205, 152	359, 069	253, 611	2, 062	191	1, 391	143	8, 404	7, 100
8	Carroll	97, 350	7, 420, 307	1, 317, 588	816, 058	5, 175	104	4, 268	60	19, 942	18, 338
9	Cass	88, 381	7, 077, 945	1, 328, 609	749, 476	4, 980	129	4, 361	44	18, 186	14, 706
10	Clarke	106, 511	6, 980, 128	1, 101, 173	804, 357	4, 475	570	4, 024	129	11, 767	22, 325

TABLE XCV.—*Selected Statistics of Agriculture*—1870—Continued.

STATE OF ILLINOIS—Continued.

PRODUCED.										
Wheat.							Potatoes.			
	Winter.	Rye.	Indian corn.	Oats.	Barley.	Wool.	Irish.	Butter.	Hay.	
els.	*Bushels.*	*Bushels.*	*Bushels.*	*Bushels.*	*Bushels.*	*Pounds.*	*Bushels.*	*Pounds.*	*Tons.*	
....	651,767	1,425	543,718	152,251	1,276	5,323	67,119	103,083	5,243	67
59	744,891	3,296	1,527,898	668,424	9,871	54,608	66,515	276,734	20,871	68
196	357,523	5,535	3,198,835	198,724	1,015	77,156	68,105	295,798	29,671	69
128	196,436	6,670	1,753,141	263,992	3,231	56,679	59,263	247,264	9,214	70
038	5,580	157,504	1,787,066	141,540	317,462	95,138	207,784	875,036	41,637	71
261	31,843	99,592	969,224	334,892	10,228	8,485	108,039	254,482	22,036	72
....	350,446	1,016	384,446	338,760	4	33,209	36,514	111,982	5,057	73
382	39,762	9,248	1,629,725	130,610	350	12,510	33,675	106,476	9,455	74
130	1,057,497	25,303	1,399,188	161,419	2	71,638	54,736	385,672	17,216	75
....	70,457	2,309	315,958	67,886	12	19,334	58,326	96,796	1,461	76
....	44,922	222	195,735	16,511	143	2,967	24,652	695	988	77
137	796	7,707	334,259	86,519	8,104	10,571	73,088	47,699	5,080	78
450	1,031,022	3,235	510,080	414,487	3,098	35,731	107,049	109,184	11,097	79
....	150,268	3,401	482,594	204,634	....	31,612	13,263	87,166	11,422	80
541	2,279	20,003	1,450,653	276,575	36,980	17,239	192,531	563,122	31,299	81
200	83,011	568	531,516	69,793	....	29,274	24,247	198,462	3,149	82
304	247,658	23,073	4,388,763	397,718	33,485	117,736	183,029	554,196	50,682	83
221	165,724	20,841	440,975	119,359	435	52,532	33,784	213,030	13,361	84
18	266,105	930	752,771	13,462	180	21,194	12,457	45,570	4,735	85
526	452,015	23,686	2,082,578	637,812	2,686	222,042	136,938	368,649	23,687	86
639	....	30,534	1,149,878	316,726	7,034	20,789	51,932	295,683	19,933	87
550	1,562,621	1,008	1,423,121	476,851	48,192	5,347	265,169	336,362	10,438	88
394	2,118	135,362	1,615,679	960,620	165,266	69,251	230,948	757,458	36,507	89
417	72,410	50,027	2,062,053	505,841	43,210	29,292	108,984	285,323	27,564	90
....	180,231	1,737	679,753	124,473	170	24,653	95,352	93,545	3,365	91
806	249,558	52,476	2,818,027	436,051	4,255	278,554	172,558	632,624	52,553	92
....	202,201	....	421,361	110,793	....	23,744	20,428	39,335	6,497	93
290	5,712	72,212	2,982,853	601,054	2,481	52,718	85,152	420,268	36,037	94
....	672,486	2,576	836,115	533,398	....	22,136	64,592	251,529	12,491	95
266	164,689	8,665	1,179,291	404,482	1,111	72,355	69,873	233,295	20,130	96
....	184,321	418	870,521	119,653	170	42,702	27,291	142,362	6,056	97
455	264	31,658	2,162,943	880,838	89,078	40,660	219,476	732,591	54,833	98
286	1,996	8,030	1,131,458	1,868,682	44,568	62,442	224,843	1,397,805	106,196	99
176	170,787	6,228	635,710	180,986	2,528	43,908	38,901	16,728	3,059	100
606	2,468	137,985	1,237,406	808,933	75,018	95,194	266,272	640,827	23,010	101
139	108,307	20,426	2,154,185	744,581	57,776	5,824	87,994	305,326	30,701	102

STATE OF INDIANA.

PRODUCED.										
Wheat.							Potatoes.			
	Winter.	Rye.	Indian corn.	Oats.	Barley.	Wool.	Irish.	Butter.	Hay.	
els.	*Bushels.*	*Bushels.*	*Bushels.*	*Bushels.*	*Bushels.*	*Pounds.*	*Bushels.*	*Pounds.*	*Tons.*	
7	172,326	7,282	96,168	88,697	1,137	62,957	20,499	227,303	12,408	1
,282	428,470	17,761	273,344	212,944	4,235	106,778	100,930	543,329	28,377	2
....	491,424	1,729	1,529,675	111,839	3,045	47,590	67,352	221,080	9,370	3
,066	37,447	11,942	458,857	121,842	685	29,097	22,425	103,900	6,659	4
3	82,760	2,150	75,346	14,567	300	24,068	8,321	111,106	3,734	5
100	388,252	14,337	749,482	22,075	1,492	68,607	48,278	261,816	9,041	6
....	83,656	2,504	197,734	61,139	....	24,498	17,779	67,754	2,348	7
115	521,574	1,523	401,635	65,738	5,433	69,452	36,834	236,988	7,475	8
40	401,114	8,204	312,434	90,835	8,665	56,444	55,077	310,588	10,516	9
....	119,368	3,111	612,192	136,295	756	31,030	103,206	224,376	9,020	10

TABLE XCV.—*Selected Statistics of Agriculture*—1870—Continued.

STATE OF INDIANA—Continued.

	Counties.	Improved land.	Value of farms.	Total (estimated) value of all farm productions, including betterments and additions to stock.	LIVE STOCK. Value of all live stock.	Horses.	Mules and asses.	Milch cows.	Working oxen.	Sheep.	Swine.
		Acres.	Dollars.	Dollars.	Dollars.	No.	No.	No.	No.	No.	No.
11	Clay	90,039	4,790,525	839,311	646,962	4,927	463	3,686	66	20,437	[illegible]
12	Clinton	149,402	10,666,922	2,332,868	1,115,284	7,763	941	5,890	138	25,537	[illegible]
13	Crawford	61,256	1,501,154	472,697	339,248	2,778	971	2,307	428	10,223	[illegible]
14	Daviess	109,231	5,849,692	1,427,251	953,692	5,909	760	4,122	120	25,205	[illegible]
15	Dearborn	108,834	6,337,095	1,260,392	798,875	4,507	469	4,621	158	6,017	[illegible]
16	Decatur	136,270	8,809,318	1,850,579	1,368,785	6,230	1,338	4,491	129	13,810	[illegible]
17	De Kalb	100,431	8,063,488	1,380,809	920,078	5,839	89	5,587	213	34,964	[illegible]
18	Delaware	133,491	10,025,183	1,746,273	1,187,038	6,849	387	4,546	60	23,783	[illegible]
19	Dubois	69,155	1,964,964	855,952	437,174	3,428	227	2,061	430	12,730	[illegible]
20	Elkhart	148,671	15,060,300	1,577,840	1,086,212	7,804	207	6,370	125	24,147	[illegible]
21	Fayette	85,856	6,705,061	1,305,672	749,882	3,601	385	2,631	22	8,105	[illegible]
22	Floyd	40,042	2,697,946	478,138	252,894	1,780	102	2,002	24	2,815	[illegible]
23	Fountain	115,993	7,399,502	1,424,378	1,099,281	6,578	805	3,977	6	26,389	[illegible]
24	Franklin	139,164	8,999,998	1,830,314	1,083,342	6,049	441	6,032	194	11,284	[illegible]
25	Fulton	78,219	4,497,625	805,167	627,353	4,700	112	3,817	113	14,940	[illegible]
26	Gibson	106,169	6,261,688	1,501,322	842,355	5,206	865	3,795	108	15,038	[illegible]
27	Grant	123,550	8,531,699	1,596,862	1,130,750	6,942	250	5,052	112	25,290	[illegible]
28	Greene	124,962	4,701,180	1,301,518	898,558	6,464	475	4,530	162	30,341	[illegible]
29	Hamilton	125,984	9,840,058	1,746,085	1,347,230	7,647	373	5,630	40	21,796	[illegible]
30	Hancock	98,833	7,721,401	1,482,245	877,629	5,946	204	3,986	14	13,440	[illegible]
31	Harrison	141,665	5,044,381	1,147,821	787,341	6,155	406	5,226	234	15,760	[illegible]
32	Hendricks	129,838	12,195,484	1,722,832	1,645,701	7,550	1,176	5,492	221	21,460	[illegible]
33	Henry	147,479	12,464,507	2,369,670	1,439,242	6,694	949	4,985	74	17,089	[illegible]
34	Howard	63,222	3,889,797	801,829	491,664	3,803	203	2,687	180	14,393	[illegible]
35	Huntington	105,453	7,573,192	1,283,204	832,861	5,902	131	5,094	38	21,038	[illegible]
36	Jackson	131,148	6,009,099	1,385,856	888,900	5,842	944	4,821	170	16,604	34,733
37	Jasper	55,060	2,355,095	555,409	715,390	3,119	137	3,192	105	7,038	[illegible]
38	Jay	94,194	5,337,530	1,013,961	815,640	6,046	198	4,192	44	24,938	[illegible]
39	Jefferson	138,106	6,537,858	1,404,476	1,096,634	6,406	720	5,289	284	18,921	[illegible]
40	Jennings	104,622	4,156,608	1,131,264	683,596	4,837	639	4,012	224	17,085	[illegible]
41	Johnson	124,161	9,957,789	2,369,818	1,312,462	6,319	787	4,279	41	13,775	[illegible]
42	Knox	117,501	5,621,066	1,586,760	971,152	6,415	814	4,632	167	18,907	[illegible]
43	Kosciusko	133,227	10,714,620	1,586,170	1,114,108	7,964	149	6,504	230	29,909	[illegible]
44	La Grange	111,102	9,470,313	1,287,567	855,631	5,217	82	4,211	132	31,958	[illegible]
45	Lake	114,102	5,132,015	968,925	1,023,341	5,560	121	7,694	185	11,637	8,326
46	La Porte	160,060	11,368,264	1,843,529	1,082,302	7,297	380	6,135	238	15,031	[illegible]
47	Lawrence	137,026	4,892,988	844,365	969,229	5,206	1,516	3,564	380	19,984	[illegible]
48	Madison	133,190	9,399,441	2,219,502	1,229,996	7,677	225	5,145	35	22,829	[illegible]
49	Marion	138,859	19,398,062	2,811,844	1,488,105	7,483	1,064	6,494	108	13,173	27,959
50	Marshall	90,981	6,930,262	966,347	748,845	5,166	202	4,987	421	15,216	[illegible]
51	Martin	64,381	2,106,149	617,928	387,564	3,267	375	2,357	256	17,071	[illegible]
52	Miami	106,676	8,223,410	1,539,845	1,034,784	6,509	360	5,111	82	20,706	[illegible]
53	Monroe	102,442	4,003,023	892,560	762,954	4,612	814	3,451	263	18,272	18,614
54	Montgomery	164,979	14,480,217	2,370,176	1,965,390	9,466	1,222	6,590	122	[illegible]	[illegible]
55	Morgan	133,615	8,563,855	1,699,704	1,240,651	6,142	512	4,375	184	[illegible]	[illegible]
56	Newton	88,380	2,658,840	481,320	580,881	2,814	258	2,362	35	3,320	[illegible]
57	Noble	113,016	8,885,080	1,526,561	940,774	6,067	163	5,456	239	30,464	[illegible]
58	Ohio	34,550	2,732,000	439,790	228,105	1,234	223	1,150	31	2,748	4,342
59	Orange	136,355	3,840,305	798,463	811,996	4,798	596	3,724	301	17,390	25,164
60	Owen	132,763	5,840,995	1,024,706	964,191	5,815	583	4,532	210	30,985	[illegible]
61	Parke	167,788	9,763,397	1,973,990	1,570,744	7,384	801	5,104	135	31,583	[illegible]
62	Perry	54,829	1,656,150	561,188	329,524	2,770	183	2,520	612	9,013	15,224
63	Pike	84,404	2,825,819	937,068	628,399	4,311	498	3,041	386	17,331	26,413
64	Porter	110,891	4,813,202	820,630	813,150	5,087	184	4,405	151	15,200	[illegible]
65	Posey	110,182	6,279,709	1,688,097	814,196	5,383	1,052	4,101	162	9,422	[illegible]
66	Pulaski	65,038	2,467,985	865,293	510,396	2,576	131	2,341	130	7,823	[illegible]
67	Putnam	166,889	12,154,422	1,612,814	2,182,097	8,274	2,416	5,729	227	34,227	[illegible]
68	Randolph	151,191	10,111,013	1,731,541	1,242,842	8,485	259	6,094	29	25,154	[illegible]
69	Ripley	129,320	6,180,650	1,188,305	868,063	6,439	609	6,127	274	18,358	[illegible]
70	Rush	194,777	12,939,663	2,244,472	1,690,645	7,799	770	5,122	113	15,921	[illegible]
71	Scott	54,393	1,768,050	457,578	387,705	2,342	390	1,503	76	[illegible]	8,815
72	Shelby	137,861	12,080,675	2,281,933	1,347,027	7,739	510	5,202	24	14,250	[illegible]
73	Spencer	106,462	3,844,803	1,053,676	601,282	4,802	684	3,711	436	14,054	[illegible]
74	Starke	15,148	777,972	218,548	179,015	739	55	1,017	267	1,482	[illegible]
75	Steuben	80,144	5,940,275	1,245,946	785,260	4,122	67	3,822	900	[illegible]	11,332
76	St. Joseph	123,976	10,807,848	1,467,265	872,554	5,700	198	5,537	245	[illegible]	[illegible]
77	Sullivan	120,724	5,633,817	1,200,945	979,300	6,912	650	4,892	62	[illegible]	[illegible]

TABLE XCV.—*Selected Statistics of Agriculture*—1870—Continued.

STATE OF INDIANA—Continued.

PRODUCED.										
Wheat.							Potatoes.			
	Winter.	Rye.	Indian corn.	Oats.	Barley.	Wool.	Irish.	Butter.	Hay.	
ls.	*Bushels.*	*Bushels.*	*Bushels.*	*Bushels.*	*Bushels.*	*Pounds.*	*Bushels.*	*Pounds.*	*Tons.*	
32	192,086	6,197	367,654	93,068	1,269	50,965	50,472	150,252	10,558	11
231	535,183	8,076	980,891	140,389	4,520	87,861	53,270	502,253	10,767	12
18	64,419	695	234,458	63,609	....	27,736	29,631	82,419	3,744	13
60	251,863	3,916	702,642	98,530	400	63,382	39,895	208,468	9,648	14
828	169,828	12,371	448,793	156,314	50,122	18,777	66,506	331,232	18,697	15
...	382,304	3,400	960,167	72,712	3,270	43,725	51,074	194,402	12,034	16
32	348,908	2,015	219,566	198,945	1,879	117,802	77,899	444,407	20,440	17
18	451,484	4,799	674,477	63,546	1,681	76,251	45,387	422,108	10,774	18
200	120,436	2,623	373,817	110,868	6,122	34,738	24,796	45,738	4,318	19
59	541,943	6,842	268,538	108,430	732	71,453	148,527	446,269	20,888	20
...	271,150	2,027	635,454	56,348	6,527	31,208	26,118	93,874	5,524	21
29	47,413	988	124,807	66,110	439	7,486	71,634	93,243	4,509	22
...	413,786	2,014	574,426	59,681	75	90,028	58,600	257,196	10,679	23
70	396,704	6,677	771,074	143 148	21 727	40,353	59,562	369,005	9,267	24
37	278,108	4,942	142,684	38,909	630	45,734	41,897	229,108	13,246	25
...	437,260	725	757,933	39,807	1,367	37,440	22,979	102,812	7,564	26
...	374,574	9,107	540,453	68,349	871	84,824	41,657	375,244	9,448	27
...	190,647	5,340	784,195	101,410	680	79,319	39,639	160,958	7,833	28
...	548,039	1,821	972,660	74,164	1,905	62,206	65,094	336,215	9,791	29
...	440,212	979	810,496	42,050	2,455	141,244	47,149	234,379	6,308	30
68	255,779	2,196	507,072	171,700	1,585	37,403	156,259	196,377	7,912	31
...	376,992	2,319	975,825	53,501	75	70,233	47,620	218,526	12,180	32
...	601,721	1,305	1,152,164	98,677	5,615	64,953	52,599	384,451	10,090	33
20	287,855	7,370	356,401	34,031	1,484	46,429	37,668	121,777	4,250	34
5	367,516	5,872	288,840	81,425	1,332	66,257	42,635	320,098	12,079	35
40	191,437	3,644	861,520	143,737	319	**47,648**	65,894	259,131	8,307	36
643	22,068	11,613	111,882	79,606	120	22,928	20,673	126,132	23,129	37
154	281,781	5,383	216,090	96,139	1,564	78,866	24,106	290,459	10,852	38
105	207,804	4,904	466,246	131,321	40,028	35,707	98,952	408,565	20,933	39
...	147,879	802	402,268	88,242	766	48,293	41,236	232,299	12,903	40
...	544,917	1,378	1,240,220	20,550	665	45,363	50,392	300,915	6,376	41
...	376,950	3,217	959,209	55,767	900	56,237	46,215	137,185	7,331	42
60	528,442	3,499	276,820	73,591	369	86,430	75,755	448,364	18,005	43
54	445,677	1,646	344,882	58,488	1,517	120,461	119,563	243,649	18,139	44
804	15,594	*6,242	189,947	364,008	4,754	49,989	73,516	537,820	40,994	45
886	504,132	9,331	394,294	148,311	4,348	47,277	151,812	320,766	22,333	46
...	139,340	6,583	591,824	127,640	....	55,843	30,220	213,125	5,764	47
...	541,669	3,804	1,028,150	74,637	2,650	73,475	62,184	322,487	10,385	48
75	613,192	2,103	1,305,988	78,246	2,042	37,439	220,885	378,963	17,464	49
297	319,561	5,285	193,005	50,534	1,222	39,526	84,994	243,583	13,689	50
100	102,188	4,591	300,680	72,394	....	39,561	21,588	120,481	3,241	51
747	484,070	4,653	417,930	100,757	5,545	66,643	61,627	372,457	17,560	52
...	130,043	4,227	454,275	105,415	263	49,798	42,146	253,078	7,311	53
800	705,372	7,537	1,004,706	89,500	2,015	149,826	69,409	391,403	18,104	54
...	328,131	6,213	1,188,229	63,439	265	61,471	48,402	229,355	8,185	55
500	8,212	12,278	142,096	111,333	693	8,456	18,855	155,755	14,824	56
327	437,748	2,768	224,958	139,624	4,536	107,236	77,005	430,240	19,171	57
...	61,833	12,213	221,565	10,224	13,581	8,658	89,370	18,245	6,489	58
...	156,622	1,080	498,740	145,600	....	45,495	25,532	245,381	3,904	59
...	202,512	14,863	602,098	100,216	100	86,612	48,064	168,606	9,253	60
...	502,270	3,378	982,628	48,391	601	110,813	65,004	314,099	14,512	61
792	52,432	342	288,705	62,495	1,774	17,345	83,918	74,300	5,544	62
...	107,262	493	566,709	53,084	257	40,112	21,624	121,671	4,067	63
930	119,645	4,433	212,331	178,886	65	52,721	66,332	220,998	21,841	64
320	393,610	126	931,936	80,633	38,321	23,748	30,041	118,498	7,027	65
797	82,843	12,035	60,512	25,186	146	22,266	50,102	147,015	17,442	66
375	297,422	4,907	988,919	68,565	70	125,320	54,650	332,383	15,990	67
232	534,771	3,645	740,051	147,992	2,882	73,010	35,753	349,327	9,908	68
63	204,932	4,264	441,645	131,771	2,985	48,912	81,345	380,911	19,504	69
15	666,992	211	1,333,421	69,236	873	63,227	58,359	389,592	11,038	70
716	41,040	969	213,475	69,235	145	28,007	24,667	131,080	5,729	71
...	669,509	1,570	1,509,448	40,227	12,754	39,494	61,361	414,863	8,574	72
...	123,663	6,161	682,374	98,510	5,409	21,416	74,150	3,367	7,878	73
623	11,826	4,516	36,104	3,931	....	4,436	36,587	81,145	7,716	74
503	232,313	2,047	352,200	97,719	520	117,337	89,949	280,472	16,861	75
255	503,502	8,353	223,045	76,846	755	25,506	112,196	332,577	19,910	76
...	297,452	4,621	706,801	93,736	173	67,640	42,431	176,279	9,305	77

TABLE XCV.—*Selected Statistics of Agriculture*—1870—Continued.

STATE OF INDIANA—Continued.

	Counties.	Improved land.	Value of farms.	Total (estimated) value of all farm productions, including betterments and additions to stock.	LIVE STOCK.						
					Value of all live stock.	Horses.	Mules and asses.	Milch cows.	Working oxen.	Sheep.	Swine.
		Acres.	*Dollars.*	*Dollars.*	*Dollars.*	*No.*	*No.*	*No.*	*No.*	*No.*	*No.*
78	Switzerland	86, 667	5, 196, 800	828, 176	543, 460	3, 526	320	2, 626	89	8, 473	9, 407
79	Tippecanoe	190, 567	12, 533, 574	2, 176, 885	1, 606, 212	9, 095	696	5, 836	79	16, 310	27, 290
80	Tipton	46, 667	3, 064, 500	701, 112	448, 215	2, 967	132	2, 050	88	10, 762	11, 860
81	Union	58, 733	6, 095, 475	1, 391, 285	642, 424	2, 469	139	1, 884	32	4, 215	16, 955
82	Vanderburgh	66, 913	4, 241, 775	913, 340	483, 667	2, 856	1, 185	3, 254	202	3, 157	12, 223
83	Vermillion	87, 558	4, 148, 925	892, 741	597, 764	3, 551	292	2, 278	37	13, 532	14, 047
84	Vigo	127, 664	8, 766, 583	1, 695, 229	1, 076, 912	7, 206	673	4, 767	107	19, 009	23, 118
85	Wabash	121, 578	8, 727, 365	1, 550, 156	1, 088, 990	6, 658	192	5, 256	27	21, 464	22, 195
86	Warren	131, 455	5, 806, 901	1, 583, 014	1, 014, 702	4, 126	324	2, 557	57	13, 006	14, 746
87	Warrick	103, 241	4, 402, 735	1, 236, 835	758, 912	5, 008	943	3, 457	439	16, 479	21, 736
88	Washington	166, 578	6, 909, 183	1, 308, 059	1, 048, 750	6, 378	1, 125	5, 235	197	18, 290	23, 176
89	Wayne	158, 574	14, 394, 696	1, 833, 842	1, 362, 920	7, 189	252	5, 442	33	11, 960	34, 396
90	Wells	86, 794	6, 113, 709	1, 124, 641	816, 517	5, 206	89	4, 643	34	21, 723	15, 470
91	White	109, 741	4, 666, 108	850, 417	884, 977	4, 292	329	3, 701	80	13, 020	7, 298
92	Whitley	83, 948	6, 473, 308	1, 072, 044	772, 023	5, 064	61	5, 403	151	21, 263	12, 397

STATE OF IOWA.

	Counties.	Improved land.	Value of farms.	Total (estimated) value of all farm productions, including betterments and additions to stock.	LIVE STOCK.						
					Value of all live stock.	Horses.	Mules and asses.	Milch cows.	Working oxen.	Sheep.	Swine.
		Acres.	*Dollars.*	*Dollars.*	*Dollars.*	*No.*	*No.*	*No.*	*No.*	*No.*	*No.*
1	Adair	35, 329	1, 527, 586	221, 892	366, 091	1, 943	116	1, 461	166	3, 308	3, 071
2	Adams	27, 270	1, 385, 963	358, 207	352, 304	1, 656	158	1, 488	184	4, 348	2, 510
3	Allamakee	112, 149	4, 301, 936	1, 752, 249	1, 005, 201	5, 413	65	5, 735	1, 046	7, 457	17, 927
4	Appanoose	135, 402	5, 631, 209	1, 672, 620	1, 255, 375	6, 669	615	5, 934	573	29, 810	24, 183
5	Audubon	9, 872	473, 407	194, 558	147, 366	593	115	619	52	708	1, 172
6	Benton	254, 856	8, 710, 034	2, 155, 748	1, 731, 218	8, 878	394	8, 000	108	6, 127	21, 921
7	Black Hawk	223, 426	8, 100, 998	2, 180, 803	1, 434, 060	7, 456	243	6, 407	199	4, 479	13, 436
8	Boone	113, 243	3, 438, 031	952, 806	883, 027	3, 740	264	3, 636	406	11, 788	10, 802
9	Bremer	139, 519	4, 486, 291	1, 162, 744	878, 483	4, 946	88	5, 101	319	5, 923	9, 424
10	Buchanan	177, 781	6, 021, 232	1, 597, 375	1, 161, 162	6, 563	198	6, 130	430	10, 687	16, 006
11	Buena Vista	5, 546	272, 924	92, 525	91, 824	299	29	374	319	249	172
12	Butler	90, 788	3, 294, 701	1, 061, 249	668, 304	3, 922	77	3, 439	105	3, 952	6, 522
13	Calhoun	6, 475	215, 000	62, 840	66, 325	378	23	317	136	360	679
14	Carroll	13, 894	456, 044	100, 400	139, 829	745	55	503	129	649	1, 523
15	Cass	16, 141	820, 231	261, 739	259, 660	954	50	868	22	1, 386	1, 839
16	Cedar	254, 219	10, 473, 122	2, 754, 614	1, 988, 500	8, 533	373	9, 194	43	7, 461	31, 896
17	Cerro Gordo	26, 724	1, 269, 175	308, 679	284, 471	1, 515	38	1, 435	188	1, 914	1, 542
18	Cherokee	9, 739	401, 025	182, 680	143, 716	530	55	559	463	73	353
19	Chickasaw	66, 925	3, 542, 015	1, 072, 554	705, 017	3, 558	42	4, 736	887	4, 830	6, 206
20	Clarke	63, 162	2, 214, 809	717, 255	667, 935	3, 654	319	2, 938	121	12, 073	11, 349
21	Clay	4, 993	173, 215	77, 163	96, 409	364	31	404	322	220	290
22	Clayton	196, 775	9, 267, 968	2, 949, 917	1, 786, 393	8, 988	363	8, 761	620	11, 691	23, 186
23	Clinton	323, 182	12, 964, 845	3, 909, 589	2, 530, 023	14, 520	381	13, 564	42	9, 633	39, 465
24	Crawford	20, 011	986, 740	236, 555	205, 379	921	40	952	208	2, 029	1, 083
25	Dallas	78, 858	3, 579, 844	953, 829	849, 113	4, 139	337	3, 323	161	8, 778	10, 370
26	Davis	145, 665	5, 690, 432	1, 622, 328	1, 354, 714	7, 450	878	5, 994	183	36, 364	26, 929
27	Decatur	65, 659	2, 609, 576	1, 352, 239	698, 018	4, 298	280	3, 444	304	19, 168	15, 053
28	Delaware	222, 307	8, 200, 888	2, 452, 654	1, 611, 499	8, 501	216	9, 312	241	11, 395	27, 376
29	Des Moines	147, 210	8, 709, 607	1, 758, 025	1, 447, 455	8, 350	648	6, 558	50	15, 426	26, 198
30	Dickinson	5, 473	225, 950	94, 740	81, 470	345	9	491	246	284	332
31	Dubuque	181, 049	9, 141, 827	2, 949, 075	1, 668, 855	8, 425	293	10, 434	202	9, [illegible]	37, 223

TABLE XCV.—*Selected Statistics of Agriculture*—1870—Continued.

STATE OF INDIANA—Continued.

PRODUCED.										
Wheat.							Potatoes.			
Spring.	Winter.	Rye.	Indian corn.	Oats.	Barley.	Wool.	Irish.	Butter.	Hay.	
Bushels.	*Bushels.*	*Bushels.*	*Bushels.*	*Bushels.*	*Bushels.*	*Pounds.*	*Bushels.*	*Pounds.*	*Tons.*	
149	132,716	15,020	309,183	27,970	13,324	20,964	125,878	174,821	19,446	78
2,502	550,175	6,270	909,367	177,578	3,040	54,286	94,516	267,971	16,654	79
20	149,802	10,723	357,835	21,487	180	30,648	25,413	179,905	4,892	80
....	261,895	20	417,555	59,400	2,407	13,514	16,527	160,540	2,699	81
80	180,565	238	553,925	56,361	13,318	2,805	54,842	115,502	9,852	82
50	261,196	2,440	508,322	54,257	166	44,595	33,167	145,253	9,659	83
....	354,132	6,322	832,372	96,179	1,209	56,637	144,319	316,076	13,950	84
93	537,790	1,769	443,901	73,456	582	64,331	51,279	382,374	11,157	85
7,023	135,319	5,663	442,874	122,153	300	46,653	27,033	107,505	16,195	86
....	150,746	2,286	601,054	123,143	1,072	30,979	43,799	185,408	11,282	87
3	213,375	942	681,399	253,229	70	48,386	33,803	320,309	8,546	88
....	470,641	184	1,000,160	165,100	9,842	42,038	77,290	319,950	9,214	89
48	237,962	10,980	177,030	82,524	681	63,336	27,758	360,709	12,413	90
5,350	167,962	14,650	215,808	119,424	404	56,758	55,687	227,304	20,994	91
50	290,456	2,913	192,813	88,505	2,223	63,266	42,454	257,517	12,199	92

STATE OF IOWA.

PRODUCED.										
Wheat.						Potatoes.	Dairy products.			
Spring.	Winter.	Indian corn.	Oats.	Barley.	Wool.	Irish.	Butter.	Cheese.	Hay.	
Bushels.	*Bushels.*	*Bushels.*	*Bushels.*	*Bushels.*	*Pounds.*	*Bushels.*	*Pounds.*	*Pounds.*	*Tons.*	
66,508	....	200,591	38,430	437	17,719	13,070	53,930	....	2,676	1
60,660	156	253,261	40,327	900	16,905	25,321	77,067	2,305	8,490	2
675,236	212	560,814	331,035	25,474	19,367	73,512	394,613	10,320	18,873	3
114,679	19,732	986,280	322,256	1,109	83,784	57,740	484,147	5,174	22,650	4
26,174	....	98,150	7,100	95	6,018	2,993	29,872	1,035	3,457	5
1,254,947	....	1,516,420	468,543	68,103	18,674	97,941	570,126	4,615	32,473	6
1,306,824	....	902,128	507,340	11,310	17,226	109,771	506,844	7,770	29,235	7
176,069	300	727,831	151,272	7,373	20,825	63,541	256,549	25,920	22,019	8
327,638	....	423,362	387,658	15,493	20,101	77,349	400,791	14,100	26,550	9
719,581	....	617,310	534,530	16,385	39,990	85,222	531,519	16,365	28,667	10
7,780	....	9,085	6,450	215	436	4,617	26,475	50	151	11
598,553	4	422,448	261,000	5,423	15,732	46,739	268,273	26,519	16,351	12
26,327	....	36,589	14,430	640	1,077	1,667	8,927	....	1,149	13
68,830	....	65,758	12,525	....	1,858	3,947	14,625	....	2,189	14
54,524	5	235,500	23,144	532	550	13,867	56,185	3,880	7,061	15
632,751	127	2,203,802	723,312	141,182	35,087	92,937	741,650	28,636	38,820	16
138,592	....	97,930	136,556	2,944	4,508	12,115	98,267	35,025	8,119	17
10,797	....	21,896	6,584	....	....	6,178	20,755	1,050	4,277	18
417,849	....	386,723	334,521	22,762	13,426	62,462	422,338	8,970	34,651	19
125,304	8	374,588	129,595	1,102	37,209	31,863	203,170	17,060	14,889	20
15,382	....	12,105	13,099	15	700	4,414	25,565	175	3,684	21
1,067,199	6,028	940,784	623,459	57,254	33,491	135,794	716,298	8,970	31,290	22
954,000	175	2,493,660	912,469	199,072	44,209	231,348	989,806	10,570	52,706	23
78,538	....	131,635	35,431	455	9,918	13,236	50,139	....	6,468	24
240,004	....	939,600	91,884	1,805	32,196	38,012	201,368	500	16,724	25
91,783	64,034	1,142,635	296,013	430	111,137	55,135	346,277	4,159	18,835	26
76,304	6,934	401,879	124,120	216	67,430	37,617	198,897	3,205	14,343	27
695,137	....	981,010	677,012	49,515	41,243	116,877	674,506	101,545	42,700	28
118,808	92,426	887,138	208,833	7,647	69,850	98,269	478,878	25,145	24,457	29
21,871	....	5,267	20,541	1,700	945	7,220	26,555	630	3,267	30
494,857	387	1,311,789	834,320	75,739	31,384	163,881	437,149	28,020	37,393	31

TABLE XCV.—*Selected Statistics of Agriculture*—1870—Continued.

STATE OF IOWA—Continued.

	Counties.	Improved land.	Value of farms.	Total (estimated) value of all farm productions, including betterments and additions to stock.	LIVE STOCK.						
					Value of all live stock.	Horses.	Mules and asses.	Milch cows.	Working oxen.	Sheep.	Swine.
		Acres.	*Dollars.*	*Dollars.*	*Dollars.*	*No.*	*No.*	*No.*	*No.*	*No.*	*No.*
32	Emmett	6,526	395,975	99,890	109,840	378	15	759	343	1,031	27
33	Fayette	124,647	4,590,802	1,363,841	843,586	4,901	163	5,527	476	11,771	14,1[illegible]
34	Floyd	79,706	3,807,985	1,609,631	682,068	4,093	60	3,472	222	6,244	6,5[illegible]
35	Franklin	51,207	1,906,673	591,748	399,087	2,370	63	1,863	224	1,802	3,4[illegible]
36	Fremont	98,343	4,769,850	2,110,845	1,198,230	4,411	699	4,686	219	5,174	[illegible]
37	Greene	33,759	1,285,286	394,810	305,993	1,774	198	1,300	224	3,875	5,62[illegible]
38	Grundy	108,483	3,459,275	841,088	618,543	3,667	110	2,881	122	2,972	4,11[illegible]
39	Guthrie	46,778	1,872,900	424,693	423,005	2,692	71	2,077	74	9,460	8,5[illegible]
40	Hamilton	36,946	1,640,590	425,025	364,430	1,968	40	1,990	301	[illegible]	2,9[illegible]
41	Hancock	6,024	286,190	68,700	70,369	377	15	375	110	411	[illegible]
42	Hardin	97,890	4,757,912	998,258	898,996	5,191	166	4,153	132	3,857	10,53[illegible]
43	Harrison	54,150	3,011,350	932,698	758,476	3,431	147	4,202	183	5,[illegible]	[illegible]
44	Henry	176,285	8,243,369	2,174,772	1,516,670	9,400	60[illegible]	7,003	144	30,805	30,8[illegible]
45	Howard	44,235	2,109,075	615,810	445,276	2,175	37	2,734	431	1,[illegible]	2,[illegible]
46	Humboldt	14,453	780,093	242,424	170,568	999	19	1,021	180	[illegible]	1,[illegible]
47	Ida	2,011	75,460	31,381	34,867	138	4	130	86	[illegible]	[illegible]
48	Iowa	139,753	5,422,071	1,526,481	1,222,559	6,564	386	6,481	403	8,806	21,[illegible]
49	Jackson	176,683	8,021,360	3,017,572	1,872,904	8,043	178	9,991	156	10,67[illegible]	34,[illegible]
50	Jasper	198,411	8,870,354	2,550,058	1,781,682	8,506	586	6,658	168	15,8[illegible]	[illegible]
51	Jefferson	163,276	7,611,811	1,711,007	1,418,704	9,150	607	6,365	149	29,[illegible]	[illegible]
52	Johnson	228,919	8,496,044	2,864,412	1,829,265	9,989	690	9,028	85	16,975	[illegible]
53	Jones	213,399	7,786,975	2,214,146	1,430,598	7,791	202	9,736	37	7,72[illegible]	18,7[illegible]
54	Keokuk	176,975	8,170,684	2,267,488	1,887,444	11,253	771	8,207	285	27,551	[illegible]
55	Kossuth	12,488	630,580	227,639	161,965	891	35	874	151	[illegible]	1,1[illegible]
56	Lee	175,662	7,750,525	1,948,977	1,448,287	8,993	970	7,959	48	21,44[illegible]	[illegible]
57	Linn	227,019	10,364,525	3,371,939	2,220,945	11,465	398	10,887	105	15,650	[illegible]
58	Louisa	144,172	6,721,425	1,855,863	1,467,690	7,255	416	5,987	71	12,835	[illegible]
59	Lucas	107,996	3,550,464	895,109	802,585	4,665	414	3,690	204	17,210	17,5[illegible]
60	Lyon	604	31,080	14,460	8,569	30	3	66	40	5	[illegible]
61	Madison	126,243	3,516,431	1,644,035	1,142,054	5,459	503	4,337	179	20,183	19,[illegible]
62	Mahaska	201,651	8,103,098	2,027,540	1,735,433	8,924	933	6,979	272	31,652	[illegible],501
63	Marion	173,129	8,376,390	2,355,831	1,617,209	8,975	685	7,162	249	25,074	41,[illegible]
64	Marshall	200,816	6,863,379	1,808,258	1,184,168	7,494	312	5,219	80	3,952	21,537
65	Mills	81,889	3,564,201	1,215,629	880,702	4,122	345	3,638	118	3,354	13,965
66	Mitchell	55,724	2,165,450	537,995	453,962	2,600	39	2,986	239	2,440	2,603
67	Monona	28,822	799,210	355,905	422,220	1,413	75	2,410	269	4,043	2,7[illegible]
68	Monroe	100,453	4,682,189	1,531,809	1,089,687	5,122	414	4,687	466	21,168	21,739
69	Montgomery	30,284	1,373,765	476,059	302,311	1,461	135	1,256	158	4,503	10,2[illegible]
70	Muscatine	204,261	9,490,715	2,005,772	1,674,159	9,238	555	7,101	26	7,173	24,504
71	O'Brien	3,146	82,070	27,600	41,490	182	12	123	179	......	44
72	Page	80,941	3,562,383	912,001	913,544	4,645	372	3,899	76	7,532	14,619
73	Palo Alto	4,852	195,053	105,692	101,202	349	10	760	257	106	357
74	Plymouth	11,274	277,749	119,291	125,750	561	40	533	301	101	336
75	Pocahontas	7,078	330,930	49,913	99,312	374	18	596	366	7	803
76	Polk	151,014	6,667,664	2,113,188	1,421,866	6,726	492	5,818	96	9,03[illegible]	28,69[illegible]
77	Pottawattamie	46,043	2,471,865	805,992	586,654	3,040	144	3,134	115	2,193	6,6[illegible]
78	Poweshiek	151,419	6,107,700	1,507,608	1,282,205	7,064	507	5,223	125	8,395	25,102
79	Ringgold	41,919	1,664,735	591,950	580,050	2,612	204	2,306	191	14,219	8,764
80	Sac	9,070	429,933	160,981	111,436	402	29	404	269	341	391
81	Scott	235,741	11,744,695	2,747,995	1,932,358	9,386	847	9,846	4	3,721	[illegible]
82	Shelby	16,368	797,800	349,091	264,761	1,199	91	1,151	98	2,806	2,060
83	Sioux	1,237	20,630	15,150	24,303	104	12	109	53	36	18
84	Story	42,474	1,908,980	453,407	407,708	1,580	54	2,253	40	3,163	5,3[illegible]
85	Tama	167,563	6,540,221	1,745,772	1,350,223	7,959	251	6,073	376	4,547	17,646
86	Taylor	46,895	2,212,586	518,842	592,739	2,744	175	2,539	91	9,952	10,568
87	Union	28,675	1,233,983	416,087	357,037	2,058	128	1,557	71	4,675	5,231
88	Van Buren	128,615	5,538,664	1,758,720	1,241,738	7,137	704	5,850	81	38,112	25,[illegible]
89	Wapello	132,373	5,861,913	1,658,005	1,217,715	6,826	635	5,163	223	25,193	27,3[illegible]
90	Warren	142,942	7,461,356	2,492,151	1,587,609	7,830	453	5,660	127	24,[illegible]	31,5[illegible]
91	Washington	197,390	8,135,408	1,786,789	1,571,064	8,653	683	7,165	308	19,618	38,866
92	Wayne	95,783	3,154,245	1,161,527	843,481	4,418	406	3,027	114	18,730	14,14[illegible]
93	Webster	37,175	1,852,565	664,032	472,668	2,435	111	2,357	463	3,169	3,304
94	Winnebago	3,955	203,030	53,704	57,490	236	7	390	142	518	411
95	Winneshiek	243,975	8,119,041	2,888,944	1,648,947	6,782	98	8,713	1,054	11,373	17,33[illegible]
96	Woodbury	12,475	707,900	318,705	231,405	873	77	1,254	252	706	1,37[illegible]
97	Worth	14,030	738,641	223,474	202,406	846	18	1,309	363	1,580	1,363
98	Wright	18,323	682,665	212,609	187,838	947	33	998	171	783	1,2[illegible]

TABLE XCV.—*Selected Statistics of Agriculture*—1870—Continued.

STATE OF IOWA—Continued.

PRODUCED.										
Wheat.						Potatoes.	Dairy products.			
Spring.	Winter.	Indian corn.	Oats.	Barley.	Wool.	Irish.	Butter.	Cheese.	Hay.	
Bushels.	*Bushels.*	*Bushels.*	*Bushels.*	*Bushels.*	*Pounds.*	*Bushels.*	*Pounds.*	*Pounds.*	*Tons.*	
29, 621	....	12, 816	27, 819	1, 899	3, 690	9, 320	57, 025	5, 297	6, 948	32
478, 538	....	448, 028	395, 075	29, 553	38, 290	58, 652	434, 868	7, 525	27, 327	33
565, 990	....	310, 119	293, 591	8, 373	24, 938	42, 606	251, 718	5, 463	18, 517	34
268, 231	....	189, 133	149, 810	3, 366	4, 228	26, 312	130, 382	1, 250	12, 008	35
60, 921	600	1, 650, 863	58, 122	4, 475	7, 991	66, 206	147, 311	12, 115	1, 686	36
98, 891	32	226, 965	54, 967	3, 062	5, 192	18, 951	81, 201	120	6, 862	37
621, 322	....	345, 717	201, 733	13, 360	14, 157	38, 995	154, 107	24, 800	14, 576	38
164, 012	....	447, 380	73, 827	1, 861	35, 180	12, 873	120, 390	350	10, 405	39
126, 977	1	214, 818	80, 206	3, 279	1, 907	26, 323	153, 755	4, 730	14, 715	40
18, 918	....	19, 541	30, 231	430	1, 304	2, 729	22, 175	....	2, 087	41
496, 347	....	640, 510	250, 139	5, 510	12, 464	45, 077	256, 357	17, 125	18, 785	42
194, 499	100	664, 510	103, 207	1, 285	13, 047	42, 167	223, 615	16, 650	23, 661	43
137, 804	81, 670	1, 095, 846	231, 631	4, 194	129, 187	99, 459	490, 181	13, 634	27, 991	44
221, 514	....	120, 234	263, 258	13, 357	5, 153	30, 713	408, 351	4, 476	14, 880	45
59, 101	....	107, 950	60, 316	1, 659	4, 009	12, 416	83, 985	8, 450	9, 133	46
9, 239	....	8, 510	6, 058	35	....	2, 511	8, 640	....	1, 887	47
530, 898	250	1, 281, 123	267, 049	21, 741	31, 877	111, 882	499, 379	3, 784	30, 703	48
428, 490	1, 023	1, 485, 250	807, 511	21, 518	42, 000	168, 701	724, 366	77, 750	33, 742	49
773, 359	70	2, 102, 366	270, 631	10, 823	40, 865	185, 736	570, 285	9, 830	28, 454	50
153, 716	81, 063	1, 100, 560	242, 364	2, 247	107, 394	72, 637	403, 782	4, 505	20, 335	51
501, 254	1, 897	2, 147, 570	491, 137	21, 553	69, 790	104, 889	504, 573	32, 902	40, 650	52
476, 020	19	1, 606, 640	682, 260	15, 198	37, 104	111, 216	733, 645	33, 121	37, 936	53
335, 307	7, 479	1, 297, 459	236, 410	10, 180	91, 713	97, 943	517, 663	8, 320	35, 833	54
32, 258	....	65, 137	67, 825	2, 294	1, 540	10, 449	86, 131	1, 300	7, 442	55
165, 486	95, 320	1, 187, 322	272, 134	28, 838	93, 030	132, 176	451, 724	110, 092	24, 060	56
707, 868	....	2, 261, 647	702, 110	18, 327	49, 921	157, 251	893, 190	24, 350	51, 207	57
193, 385	27, 780	931, 263	100, 452	2, 674	51, 425	74, 788	383, 926	2, 986	25, 880	58
135, 433	3, 632	507, 322	174, 889	3, 220	50, 100	54, 274	307, 894	6, 835	14, 680	59
400	....	1, 250	900	....	....	710	4, 565	....	375	60
257, 144	887	1, 453, 684	140, 639	1, 294	71, 909	62, 231	302, 835	5, 202	20, 758	61
351, 204	3, 528	1, 861, 282	197, 109	1, 794	138, 512	127, 145	582, 402	4, 336	28, 139	62
309, 729	4, 685	2, 110, 900	189, 331	5, 293	83, 820	152, 763	499, 153	10, 315	21, 522	63
921, 860	700	1, 239, 631	308, 671	8, 229	20, 934	99, 881	405, 972	1, 398	25, 439	64
162, 821	80	1, 380, 055	191, 569	11, 451	11, 652	80, 074	182, 755	2, 845	16, 471	65
564, 849	45	150, 847	358, 105	33, 804	8, 906	36, 141	194, 060	3, 000	15, 415	66
82, 990	....	285, 457	50, 346	824	18, 783	24, 026	85, 611	4, 700	16, 132	67
144, 300	15, 515	734, 692	185, 173	233	72, 052	64, 073	282, 452	8, 237	21, 206	68
59, 712	....	323, 168	37, 393	....	18, 492	23, 991	87, 220	190	9, 079	69
331, 292	1, 855	1, 208, 640	380, 250	96, 049	28, 090	147, 005	380, 382	12, 368	29, 841	70
4, 648	....	500	8, 909	404	....	....	....	....	....	71
68, 907	520	1, 001, 054	123, 457	110	22, 213	58, 856	188, 699	1, 750	16, 332	72
19, 475	....	22, 336	19, 976	....	273	6, 500	45, 525	60	7, 432	73
34, 761	....	22, 048	22, 741	970	404	15, 480	....	....	....	74
18, 413	....	32, 860	11, 015	260	....	4, 753	39, 265	1, 750	4, 864	75
366, 163	260	1, 779, 875	176, 399	17, 253	15, 992	132, 172	382, 606	11, 511	25, 533	76
148, 257	608	611, 528	88, 108	6, 100	5, 692	81, 800	200, 491	3, 970	19, 326	77
709, 501	225	1, 435, 557	189, 362	19, 778	28, 127	78, 981	286, 630	10, 451	22, 783	78
40, 194	187	340, 735	79, 159	313	52, 850	27, 894	163, 485	5, 958	14, 325	79
37, 090	....	42, 207	38, 831	....	2, 584	7, 770	30, 120	50	10	80
629, 927	27	1, 855, 226	538, 109	638, 440	13, 635	361, 073	702, 706	55, 640	34, 376	81
43, 489	....	155, 320	25, 594	10	11, 103	9, 922	61, 834	600	6, 492	82
....	....	....	....	....	144	....	....	....	....	83
131, 022	....	390, 395	97, 938	808	8, 918	25, 034	132, 249	29, 010	13, 730	84
1, 053, 447	720	1, 103, 371	282, 591	23, 588	17, 080	88, 616	407, 567	7, 685	25, 854	85
56, 768	84	438, 089	85, 886	203	33, 868	38, 507	120, 167	2, 720	14, 174	86
57, 978	239	250, 063	65, 145	....	19, 022	27, 707	92, 797	1, 340	9, 817	87
84, 291	147, 536	906, 874	255, 820	526	129, 303	73, 322	443, 586	11, 212	22, 948	88
163, 716	41, 334	1, 054, 570	166, 356	3, 016	82, 511	86, 156	314, 300	2, 028	20, 487	89
404, 208	2, 264	1, 925, 914	169, 217	4, 670	74, 957	114, 885	382, 568	7, 941	24, 517	90
324, 522	8, 531	1, 028, 564	268, 027	6, 415	66, 864	67, 107	457, 010	20, 879	31, 240	91
103, 666	6, 036	560, 828	184, 331	1, 946	50, 370	39, 260	230, 975	3, 650	19, 291	92
155, 285	5	301, 176	98, 702	2, 657	8, 829	25, 323	221, 990	6, 760	23, 378	93
23, 914	....	8, 040	12, 545	532	1, 476	1, 985	17, 305	200	3, 351	94
1, 479, 331	....	700, 191	822, 400	99, 095	42, 233	77, 325	810, 126	14, 995	42, 246	95
44, 667	....	99, 740	40, 653	1, 876	415	25, 040	22, 845	....	10, 433	96
97, 156	....	49, 472	71, 107	1, 097	5, 226	9, 161	94, 290	250	9, 830	97
72, 538	....	85, 284	55, 859	1, 968	3, 734	8, 652	63, 354	2, 840	8, 033	98

TABLE XCV.—*Selected Statistics of Agriculture*—1870—Continued.

STATE OF KANSAS.

	Counties.	Improved land.	Value of farms.	Total (estimated) value of all farm productions, including betterments and additions to stock.	LIVE STOCK.						
					Value of all live stock.	Horses.	Mules and asses.	Milch cows.	Working oxen.	Sheep.	Swine.
		Acres.	*Dollars.*	*Dollars.*	*Dollars.*	*No.*	*No.*	*No.*	*No.*	*No.*	*No.*
1	Allen	30,474	1,412,870	435,572	364,006	1,717	136	1,842	172	1,670	[illegible]
2	Anderson	29,598	1,343,358	442,653	460,046	2,711	203	2,796	204	2,950	[illegible]
3	Atchison	82,593	3,525,775	1,204,733	793,741	3,793	618	4,055	142	1,084	[illegible]
4	Bourbon	98,069	4,783,865	1,187,729	780,151	5,423	562	5,299	765	4,362	[illegible]
5	Brown	30,174	2,245,711	454,232	628,520	3,004	283	2,767	68	2,590	[illegible]
6	Butler	10,839	544,230	107,411	284,285	987	148	1,082	292	2,601	[illegible]
7	Chase	9,810	940,697	178,286	279,964	1,189	60	1,201	98	1,253	[illegible]
8	Cherokee	61,428	2,063,517	848,675	574,269	3,581	443	3,002	1,757	2,064	[illegible]
9	Clay	10,885	624,990	188,725	234,869	1,034	81	1,154	321	42	[illegible]
10	Cloud	90,371	572,910	153,044	220,978	894	113	842	363	614	[illegible]
11	Coffey	34,798	1,953,215	528,077	790,146	2,762	187	3,459	284	11,917	[illegible]
12	Cowley	2,381	295,917	163,151	118,950	701	60	619	375	1,130	[illegible]
13	Crawford	60,181	2,676,500	709,767	640,476	3,304	435	3,014	1,466	2,005	[illegible]
14	Davis	45,006	760,530	553,860	304,735	1,308	56	1,539	701	127	[illegible]
15	Dickinson	12,396	636,112	181,152	265,418	1,153	83	1,494	148	206	[illegible]
16	Doniphan	88,028	3,962,347	1,625,724	918,480	4,124	721	3,868	636	4,586	[illegible]
17	Douglas	94,852	6,689,989	3,514,452	1,240,913	6,614	434	6,656	233	[illegible]	[illegible]
18	Ellsworth	2,476	113,470	53,492	67,985	187	80	298	128	92	[illegible]
19	Franklin	78,324	3,438,800	974,590	765,900	3,706	314	3,818	391	5,182	[illegible]
20	Greenwood	20,161	997,453	342,868	331,815	1,638	64	2,323	191	3,575	[illegible]
21	Howard	2,251	91,880	56,157	75,341	243	23	502	108	592	[illegible]
22	Jackson	41,833	2,386,640	641,441	635,244	3,484	221	3,349	81	2,657	[illegible]
23	Jefferson	97,583	4,363,943	1,031,237	1,142,748	6,313	654	6,215	452	4,072	[illegible]
24	Jewell	964	47,7[illegible]	20,350	8,347	35	6	35	44	3	[illegible]
25	Johnson	119,528	4,300,355	1,172,387	836,905	4,798	681	4,518	536	3,691	[illegible]
26	Labette	40,782	1,851,390	457,907	538,623	2,644	451	2,538	1,990	2,910	[illegible]
27	Leavenworth	100,191	5,207,554	1,407,381	944,695	4,480	689	4,701	711	3,406	[illegible]
28	Lincoln	1,226	69,150	6,960	33,436	130	11	305	53	22	[illegible]
29	Linn	93,198	3,576,846	977,132	832,029	5,362	476	4,955	407	8,463	[illegible]
30	Lyon	38,253	2,551,968	513,781	674,945	3,108	169	4,188	80	3,214	[illegible]
31	Marion	3,601	185,760	95,728	107,699	407	16	537	261	485	[illegible]
32	Marshall	33,868	1,545,383	568,849	468,748	2,534	173	3,025	490	2,379	[illegible]
33	McPherson	3,608	270,770	39,436	72,210	253	21	340	354	36	[illegible]
34	Miami	88,928	4,069,390	891,307	861,145	4,913	557	4,774	358	3,929	[illegible]
35	Mitchell	30,192	98,250	5,131	56,377	189	40	141	120	......	[illegible]
36	Montgomery	21,653	821,800	288,159	337,771	1,629	329	1,595	1,348	674	[illegible]
37	Morris	10,506	549,946	165,542	181,086	1,033	121	1,165	34	682	[illegible]
38	Nemaha	41,723	1,996,630	536,817	638,993	3,307	156	3,405	209	3,501	[illegible]
39	Neosho	38,915	1,472,533	422,882	368,161	1,981	215	2,257	883	1,712	[illegible]
40	Osage	29,178	1,943,030	398,571	599,530	2,782	217	3,339	527	381	[illegible]
41	Osborne	3,780	7,200	......	3,130	20	1	5	10	......	......
42	Ottawa	11,441	559,240	188,048	290,747	922	75	1,151	219	827	[illegible]
43	Pottawattamie	31,782	1,891,220	803,439	653,376	3,404	168	3,526	204	3,346	[illegible]
44	Republic	5,613	373,700	130,698	100,376	463	61	351	248	325	[illegible]
45	Rice	13	2,600	1,340	1,412	5	......	10	4	4	[illegible]
46	Riley	28,366	1,808,615	502,384	483,128	2,290	189	2,192	318	2,190	[illegible]
47	Saline	19,756	1,185,962	317,187	311,096	1,425	135	1,867	595	128	[illegible]
48	Sedgwick	3,459	266,790	171,797	76,832	407	79	183	102	307	[illegible]
49	Shawnee	43,259	3,485,760	764,228	671,997	3,461	216	3,562	144	1,832	[illegible]
50	Smith	407	25,300	9,600	5,760	25	3	17	58	......	[illegible]
51	Wabaunsee	16,875	973,080	234,845	334,490	1,983	97	2,692	151	862	[illegible]
52	Washington	9,819	453,290	165,307	148,416	735	56	837	229	432	[illegible]
53	Wilson	14,893	703,240	262,776	261,682	1,210	108	1,597	[illegible]	2,368	[illegible]
54	Woodson	10,024	398,810	151,220	170,672	870	54	1,248	125	2,214	[illegible]
55	Wyandotte	20,711	1,298,807	350,114	181,031	1,022	233	990	212	492	[illegible]

TABLE XCV.—*Selected Statistics of Agriculture*—1870—Continued.

STATE OF KANSAS.

PRODUCED.										
Wheat.							Potatoes.			
Spring.	Winter.	Rye.	Indian corn.	Oats.	Barley.	Wool.	Irish.	Butter.	Hay.	
Bushels.	*Bushels.*	*Bushels.*	*Bushels.*	*Bushels.*	*Bushels.*	*Pounds.*	*Bushels.*	*Pounds.*	*Tons.*	
3, 863	23, 871	990	187, 225	115, 708	137	6, 431	23, 333	90, 588	9, 801	1
4, 115	31, 654	3, 614	206, 989	77, 779	587	12, 913	21, 591	93, 485	9, 087	2
4, 230	67, 548	3, 496	808, 195	191, 000	5, 079	2, 964	204, 602	194, 894	15, 534	3
2, 040	143, 139	2, 081	706, 607	266, 320	884	12, 103	81, 527	255, 218	20, 789	4
36, 613	26, 006	400	614, 268	128, 136	4, 679	9, 633	57, 961	131, 257	12, 582	5
4, 757	587	727	38, 915	2, 406	....	60	1, 640	2, 620	4, 465	6
40, 593	6, 668	1, 504	104, 626	26, 748	255	3, 847	8, 879	41, 145	8, 605	7
1, 778	53, 014	1, 454	291, 916	68, 059	291	7, 094	25, 603	95, 340	18, 883	8
35, 659	1, 045	45	95, 145	6, 090	....	....	13, 335	30, 070	5, 356	9
21, 779	15	....	76, 105	4, 735	9	5, 272	11, 609	25, 871	3, 224	10
39, 636	8, 109	1, 397	268, 218	90, 190	129	36, 702	26, 879	140, 602	14, 275	11
6, 000	2, 490	2, 380	38, 720	10, 200	1, 215	5, 686	3, 400	4, 412	1, 786	12
1, 111	33, 271	213	285, 500	56, 785	464	7, 071	34, 368	130, 319	14, 745	13
31, 170	15, 380	3, 061	160, 125	21, 130	700	225	18, 285	58, 525	11, 431	14
36, 452	18, 860	917	97, 615	21, 628	200	545	10, 349	41, 161	11, 115	15
48, 614	109, 503	5, 309	1, 326, 968	148, 676	28, 822	12, 632	206, 705	194, 396	6, 640	16
39, 932	25, 110	2, 639	1, 065, 113	415, 129	3, 161	6, 043	193, 983	293, 376	19, 482	17
2, 175	....	20	12, 167	1, 456	140	....	4, 393	10, 096	1, 604	18
4, 392	40, 079	538	618, 840	181, 515	1, 320	20, 498	54, 618	185, 640	17, 644	19
24, 723	10, 726	1, 411	173, 590	24, 492	100	5, 179	14, 774	55, 285	10, 485	20
1, 988	2, 778	105	26, 795	2, 710	....	2, 085	2, 304	7, 200	150	21
28, 345	13, 238	1, 460	486, 940	137, 894	789	6, 769	52, 497	145, 698	16, 273	22
10, 011	22, 291	1, 190	1, 257, 790	210, 040	912	9, 994	142, 405	261, 161	18, 925	23
										24
50, 557	21, 278	5, 684	1, 074, 186	335, 056	13, 730	9, 250	112, 046	219, 358	16, 309	25
702	27, 812	500	128, 543	32, 489	258	5, 749	13, 484	69, 218	5, 956	26
6, 515	25, 132	1, 272	1, 133, 188	193, 851	3, 757	14, 380	295, 986	254, 837	19, 796	27
1, 778	8	....	9, 536	....	....	180	320	1, 950	319	28
4, 337	112, 364	3, 282	728, 814	300, 880	10	25, 544	80, 683	233, 214	7, 133	29
100, 704	11, 449	506	342, 855	106, 006	587	14, 986	32, 004	129, 120	16, 740	30
6, 139	1, 583	....	20, 827	1, 879	....	1, 371	1, 814	12, 745	3, 555	31
156, 887	3, 863	726	333, 505	45, 476	1, 432	9, 076	42, 488	125, 303	12, 885	32
4, 314	824	....	40, 540	2, 818	....	....	3, 458	7, 800	1, 444	33
13, 224	41, 372	814	764, 145	268, 500	4, 517	11, 243	71, 242	240, 323	14, 147	34
666	....	....	6, 250	58	....	....	215	....	....	35
193	688	25	12, 665	753	....	425	1, 443	....	1, 555	36
21, 602	19, 832	395	89, 815	15, 341	95	2, 108	17, 549	30, 590	4, 991	37
98, 773	13, 839	26, 840	358, 871	107, 737	4, 205	12, 018	50, 074	200, 460	17, 167	38
40	27, 426	495	199, 997	48, 241	368	2, 215	27, 522	59, 025	4, 943	39
14, 033	7, 168	283	221, 880	30, 740	1, 180	1, 550	25, 518	99, 398	10, 396	40
										41
29, 377	1, 869	1, 374	100, 680	5, 100	427	3, 155	12, 475	33, 169	5, 851	42
87, 307	9, 128	453	468, 445	112, 407	4, 527	14, 534	51, 254	152, 422	18, 719	43
8, 626	....	....	16, 820	160	....	....	4, 705	13, 790	1, 079	44
							20	....	125	45
68, 446	9, 720	293	405, 277	57, 753	5, 909	8, 215	43, 086	111, 590	15, 740	46
57, 842	9, 744	3, 251	225, 048	20, 931	1, 511	....	30, 220	40, 331	10, 862	47
445	....	....	6, 632	1, 100	....	2, 000	1, 290	100	6	48
37, 577	9, 149	910	602, 475	60, 853	1, 545	7, 006	84, 636	238, 005	19, 122	49
										50
46, 123	17, 328	641	220, 365	38, 243	1, 784	3, 411	35, 669	69, 685	11, 640	51
50, 650	526	611	123, 124	18, 484	661	1, 117	16, 109	53, 182	5, 284	52
2, 749	21, 835	590	126, 795	24, 578	100	3, 185	12, 112	52, 720	5, 583	53
3, 917	9, 395	1, 011	81, 950	35, 336	294	8, 293	9, 173	45, 199	4, 382	54
733	17, 962	120	233, 905	24, 129	1, 615	248	52, 339	40, 865	1, 589	55

TABLE XCV.—*Selected Statistics of Agriculture*—1870—Continued.

STATE OF KENTUCKY.

	Counties.	Improved land.	Value of farms.	Total (estimated) value of all farm productions, including betterments and additions to stock.	LIVE STOCK. Value of all live stock.	Horses.	Mules and asses.	Milch cows.	Working oxen.	Sheep.	Swine.
		Acres.	*Dollars.*	*Dollars.*	*Dollars.*	*No.*	*No.*	*No.*	*No.*	*No.*	*No.*
1	Adair	79, 249	1, 224, 168	622, 516	522, 824	3, 326	585	2, 497	672	13, 107	[illegible]
2	Allen	77, 733	878, 504	908, 227	628, 335	3, 332	1, 512	2, 336	796	12, 516	[illegible]
3	Anderson	50, 409	1, 397, 857	548, 248	464, 511	2, 782	514	1, 518	346	5, 229	[illegible]
4	Ballard	72, 420	1, 537, 482	1, 353, 235	692, 670	2, 651	1, 562	2, 520	1, 076	7, 041	[illegible]
5	Barren	135, 618	3, 045, 915	1, 249, 486	970, 557	5, 985	1, 210	3, 736	1, 048	19, 913	[illegible]
6	Bath	116, 847	5, 199, 829	1, 120, 340	1, 247, 057	4, 178	2, 199	2, 879	1, 139	8, 343	[illegible]
7	B one	105, 927	8, 601, 330	1, 552, 670	1, 177, 142	4, 709	621	2, 918	106	11, 278	[illegible]
8	Bourbon	155, 304	15, 945, 373	2, 541, 896	2, 474, 323	5, 214	5, 119	3, 870	508	11, 639	[illegible]
9	Boyd	19, 129	732, 584	279, 523	177, 261	850	90	954	598	3, 842	[illegible]
10	Boyle	62, 760	3, 671, 986	748, 793	730, 132	2, 335	1, 703	1, 496	294	3, 211	[illegible]
11	Bracken	75, 575	3, 158, 884	1, 043, 908	502, 484	3, 760	157	2, 067	209	3, 443	12, 718
12	Breathitt	21, 735	437, 469	198, 701	168, 790	835	65	1, 494	837	7, 629	[illegible]
13	Breckenridge	107, 833	2, 155, 576	1, 451, 942	685, 732	3, 672	934	2, 565	863	13, 525	[illegible]
14	Bullitt	58, 757	2, 056, 652	600, 009	397, 544	2, 472	500	1, 688	222	4, 801	[illegible]
15	Butler	55, 947	1, 011, 750	475, 976	410, 718	2, 733	612	2, 206	963	10, 663	[illegible]
16	Caldwell	87, 497	1, 448, 191	803, 169	481, 957	2, 377	1, 275	2, 010	750	9, 226	[illegible]
17	Callaway	60, 883	1, 194, 590	778, 798	468, 203	2, 192	1, 503	2, 186	566	8, 685	[illegible]
18	Campbell	46, 227	2, 991, 854	578, 422	346, 744	2, 384	238	2, 173	55	2, 793	7, 616
19	Carroll	46, 838	1, 806, 127	454, 562	352, 905	2, 058	356	1, 282	323	3, 495	[illegible]
20	Carter	40, 056	587, 800	370, 524	293, 356	1, 805	205	1, 747	727	8, 614	[illegible]
21	Casey	61, 042	1, 197, 906	554, 075	488, 291	2, 780	513	1, 972	773	12, 047	[illegible]
22	Christian	140, 349	5, 528, 778	1, 701, 015	909, 412	3, 923	2, 777	3, 325	342	11, 942	[illegible]
23	Clark	118, 684	7, 292, 615	1, 528, 664	1, 629, 243	4, 046	1, 897	3, 901	1, 174	8, 054	[illegible]
24	Clay	33, 488	635, 570	364, 519	319, 043	1, 274	415	2, 385	1, 029	9, 921	[illegible]
25	Clinton	41, 063	505, 023	335, 634	257, 673	1, 626	225	1, 534	846	6, 741	[illegible]
26	Crittenden	64, 604	1, 295, 646	552, 851	489, 879	2, 552	1, 041	2, 027	1, 031	12, 092	[illegible]
27	Cumberland	40, 781	939, 691	447, 332	210, 965	1, 427	212	1, 075	698	6, 789	[illegible]
28	Daviess	115, 001	4, 816, 889	1, 631, 639	885, 243	5, 184	1, 077	3, 363	685	12, 368	[illegible]
29	Edmondson	29, 079	450, 117	223, 524	237, 769	1, 602	155	1, 246	283	6, 852	[illegible]
30	Elliott	25, 387	327, 361	203, 966	144, 405	908	58	1, 083	573	6, 835	[illegible]
31	Estill	47, 048	1, 298, 840	486, 627	450, 836	1, 956	596	1, 871	972	6, 146	[illegible]
32	Fayette	125, 246	15, 234, 119	2, 347, 247	2, 140, 012	5, 522	2, 354	3, 753	429	7, 477	[illegible]
33	Fleming	119, 414	3, 842, 873	1, 052, 149	940, 964	4, 705	1, 254	2, 915	401	9, 562	[illegible]
34	Floyd	27, 958	712, 547	330, 044	250, 640	1, 405	99	2, 295	1, 559	11, 287	[illegible]
35	Franklin	62, 205	2, 651, 192	633, 214	459, 251	2, 651	478	1, 642	242	4, 170	[illegible]
36	Fulton	31, 365	1, 994, 154	512, 442	369, 586	1, 293	793	1, 210	241	3, 799	[illegible]
37	Gallatin	45, 266	2, 046, 600	420, 300	352, 170	1, 754	246	962	163	3, 229	[illegible]
38	Garrard	91, 014	3, 777, 902	652, 304	800, 811	3, 135	1, 442	2, 321	685	4, 410	[illegible]
39	Grant	80, 440	3, 562, 505	993, 590	784, 864	3, 790	375	2, 364	401	7, 253	[illegible]
40	Graves	104, 725	3, 168, 722	1, 560, 415	917, 174	3, 935	2, 311	3, 681	1, 284	13, 876	[illegible]
41	Grayson	80, 414	1, 182, 435	686, 745	492, 782	3, 172	376	2, 816	921	14, 543	[illegible]
42	Green	68, 323	958, 818	523, 666	434, 753	2, 540	610	1, 869	650	8, 925	[illegible]
43	Greenup	19, 893	1, 078, 840	262, 058	140, 358	747	96	533	233	2, 086	[illegible]
44	Hancock	47, 131	1, 310, 317	808, 390	309, 187	1, 961	375	1, 249	299	5, 099	[illegible]
45	Hardin	125, 178	2, 453, 229	1, 013, 871	648, 414	4, 693	736	3, 108	630	14, 736	[illegible]
46	Harlan	23, 527	398, 583	123, 654	156, 894	779	97	1, 600	524	5, 933	[illegible]
47	Harrison	117, 186	4, 755, 752	989, 917	1, 001, 963	5, 966	1, 924	2, 845	309	8, 627	[illegible]
48	Hart	81, 249	1, 766, 083	955, 515	608, 686	3, 601	673	2, 830	824	13, 365	[illegible]
49	Henderson	101, 706	3, 322, 516	1, 371, 942	653, 440	2, 667	1, 656	2, 664	616	7, 681	[illegible]
50	Henry	99, 747	4, 279, 326	882, 863	667, 401	3, 595	573	2, 376	180	6, 369	[illegible]
51	Hickman	35, 006	1, 178, 430	448, 180	294, 198	1, 385	858	1, 286	448	5, 010	[illegible]
52	Hopkins	85, 955	1, 052, 974	775, 797	642, 030	3, 511	1, 426	2, 867	634	14, 619	[illegible]
53	Jackson	20, 610	305, 815	205, 430	150, 792	774	113	1, 124	410	5, 730	6, 748
54	Jefferson	152, 494	17, 253, 897	2, 631, 076	1, 304, 615	6, 360	1, 369	6, 263	114	7, 080	[illegible]
55	Jessamine	70, 201	3, 518, 055	435, 390	580, 234	2, 504	1, 016	1, 543	210	3, 483	[illegible]
56	Johnson	32, 020	590, 875	333, 347	900, 814	1, 120	81	1, 537	1, 088	8, 105	[illegible]
57	Josh Bell	18, 344	261, 366	145, 499	113, 785	670	63	1, 089	400	2, 890	[illegible]
58	Kenton	66, 742	6, 294, 885	1, 218, 688	494, 522	2, 847	301	2, 698	118	5, 598	[illegible]
59	Knox	43, 663	716, 351	303, 661	250, 990	1, 212	311	1, 534	720	8, 372	[illegible]
60	La Rue	66, 144	1, 744, 402	578, 473	463, 541	2, 046	418	1, 783	254	9, 064	[illegible]
61	Laurel	42, 470	561, 226	379, 616	234, 326	1, 351	231	1, 537	511	7, 617	[illegible]
62	Lawrence	32, 863	592, 678	293, 701	195, 476	1, 054	77	1, 474	1, 361	8, 454	[illegible]
63	Lee	10, 637	235, 380	71, 030	77, 480	349	38	514	189	1, 973	2, 646
64	Letcher	19, 579	278, 019	165, 434	130, 977	736	46	1, 592	620	6, 444	[illegible]
65	Lewis	34, 336	699, 396	273, 990	226, 438	1, 430	144	1, 070	308	4, 125	[illegible]
66	Lincoln	73, 460	4, 002, 549	616, 781	845, 332	2, 678	1, 706	2, 153	763	7, 422	13, 157

TABLE XCV.—*Selected Statistics of Agriculture*—1870—Continued.

STATE OF KENTUCKY.

PRODUCED.										
Vheat.							Potatoes.			
Winter.	Rye.	Indian corn.	Oats.	Tobacco.	Wool.	Irish.	Sweet.	Butter.		
Bushels.	*Bushels.*	*Bushels.*	*Bushels.*	*Pounds.*	*Pounds.*	*Bushels.*	*Bushels.*	*Pounds.*		
44, 877	466	347, 472	80, 284	1, 231, 665	21, 153	17, 153	13, 380	107, 985	1	
55, 844	151	390, 883	96, 647	747, 489	24, 011	1, 599	1, 219	133, 487	2	
35, 086	19, 539	300, 963	33, 004	15, 165	18, 425	2, 240	204	112, 341	3	
70, 719	3, 061	577, 739	28, 223	2, 863, 455	12, 001	18, 198	17, 220	97, 914	4	
111, 747	4, 716	603, 541	179, 609	2, 473, 939	40, 492	24, 468	24, 152	247, 771	5	
46, 053	23, 092	869, 631	108, 945	9, 810	25, 480	21, 318	1, 152	266, 546	6	
93, 424	32, 621	770, 505	86, 441	279, 740	36, 661	81, 518	2, 240	198, 511	7	
71, 514	67, 739	1, 229, 515	114, 762	750	47, 585	29, 961	2, 015	163, 850	8	
11, 718	454	168, 199	17, 968	10, 915	7, 708	12, 598	2, 094	42, 506	9	
99, 227	14, 789	272, 505	58, 115	2, 615	13, 056	9, 484	1, 708	83, 433	10	
29, 850	20, 610	440, 530	22, 533	4, 188, 039	9, 133	18, 575	2, 725	138, 360	11	
4, 066	529	166, 729	8, 205	5, 768	11, 633	11, 224	2, 565	14, 275	12	
57, 021	5, 734	526, 080	129, 703	3, 338, 471	30, 031	22, 918	4, 952	139, 207	13	
34, 752	1, 176	337, 320	82, 739	500	16, 498	8, 487	835	61, 408	14	
13, 875	77	340, 115	60, 506	1, 008, 582	20, 583	10, 676	7, 057	64, 775	15	
56, 847	661	438, 600	26, 667	2, 221, 899	18, 727	11, 674	10, 571	84, 886	16	
33, 770	698	417, 410	9, 228	1, 924, 502	13, 598	10, 353	15, 474	66, 040	17	
17, 772	9, 084	166, 509	60, 500	76, 568	7, 030	66, 989	8, 319	98, 217	18	
38, 236	4, 778	263, 020	19, 027	669, 875	12, 640	26, 965	185	20, 114	19	
13, 189	1, 372	282, 091	41, 507	....	17, 175	19, 184	4, 217	107, 589	20	
16, 765	8, 748	356, 850	42, 747	145, 982	22, 469	15, 794	8, 121	116, 841	21	
242, 980	2, 881	778, 533	65, 577	5, 384, 137	28, 727	19, 042	22, 800	155, 725	22	
38, 692	36, 636	774, 210	38, 810	7, 816	32, 886	20, 161	3, 230	137, 150	23	
7, 841	988	281, 499	25, 138	17, 787	17, 673	17, 774	4, 843	67, 984	24	
28, 770	337	198, 602	37, 881	117, 238	14, 946	12, 395	9, 547	70, 821	25	
21, 196	1, 551	403, 948	17, 487	1, 970, 776	21, 995	13, 510	4, 556	64, 405	26	
20, 523	969	243, 840	43, 300	1, 304, 366	9, 945	6, 321	5, 440	64, 948	27	
68, 681	4, 982	1, 085, 492	65, 394	6, 273, 067	34, 001	29, 764	7, 859	173, 244	28	
11, 698	863	172, 998	23, 684	414, 840	11, 779	7, 231	4, 278	46, 257	29	
8, 261	1, 340	171, 389	21, 600	9, 945	11, 981	12, 024	3, 011	54, 346	30	
7, 910	2, 112	376, 792	25, 645	15, 952	14, 024	14, 095	4, 808	157, 380	31	
76, 102	42, 628	1, 117, 196	176, 276	2, 160	28, 421	49, 432	6, 474	157, 742	32	
52, 657	26, 466	686, 538	78, 242	305, 254	27, 854	26, 483	3, 399	219, 970	33	
8, 069	1, 162	338, 009	26, 325	13, 202	19, 859	17, 795	6, 007	57, 168	34	
28, 924	19, 337	423, 295	53, 638	123, 250	16, 366	16, 472	1, 407	82, 429	35	
40, 844	15	438, 014	2, 945	383, 636	4, 534	5, 690	4, 029	31, 109	36	
46, 675	5, 140	277, 140	23, 890	157, 050	9, 210	32, 070	120	....	37	
83, 807	25, 207	578, 697	84, 456	32, 115	14, 889	14, 163	2, 106	86, 842	38	
41, 974	20, 384	611, 568	31, 059	164, 295	17, 958	17, 668	465	137, 407	39	
96, 453	2, 800	842, 445	24, 424	4, 774, 195	27, 103	14, 959	24, 259	158, 380	40	
25, 448	2, 056	377, 005	80, 953	859, 769	32, 221	20, 792	8, 420	149, 001	41	
34, 098	919	281, 827	47, 231	1, 375, 091	14, 674	9, 407	6, 817	87, 222	42	
29, 842	842	164, 650	26, 864	3, 757	5, 382	9, 498	1, 075	21, 853	43	
12, 016	1, 098	376, 915	23, 930	1, 679, 384	8, 310	8, 882	1, 042	5, 561	44	
137, 623	16, 546	566, 830	114, 127	284, 178	30, 149	11, 105	2, 573	115, 363	45	
2, 266	797	158, 410	12, 207	6, 218	10, 324	12, 636	4, 927	58, 558	46	
61, 432	42, 386	719, 315	85, 914	281, 704	31, 961	20, 604	1, 109	153, 756	47	
81, 923	7, 842	449, 286	62, 785	2, 315, 212	26, 250	20, 204	16, 680	132, 382	48	
47, 381	1, 843	739, 652	31, 118	6, 600, 506	19, 985	19, 641	6, 164	84, 174	49	
56, 602	25, 516	591, 528	63, 913	1, 375, 364	26, 501	16, 986	1, 787	114, 160	50	
48, 090	220	350, 860	6, 005	570, 287	10, 416	9, 647	2, 380	53, 650	51	
25, 506	90	464, 879	48, 240	3, 012, 053	24, 849	11, 424	10, 642	114, 798	52	
4, 537	650	137, 181	14, 361	13, 111	10, 043	11, 141	3, 741	51, 540	53	
102, 820	12, 454	1, 050, 729	368, 328	9, 574	35, 263	377, 382	104, 862	312, 233	54	
79, 467	30, 176	469, 505	58, 740	500	14, 175	13, 644	3, 633	78, 915	55	
9, 482	1, 620	256, 256	30, 310	14, 481	13, 798	13, 341	4, 962	81, 082	56	
3, 608	667	105, 465	12, 883	9, 005	6, 548	8, 222	3, 020	42, 357	57	
33, 558	30, 870	374, 165	69, 489	360, 983	16, 538	80, 545	7, 307	226, 128	58	
13, 305	1, 532	214, 369	36, 670	6, 722	14, 348	11, 290	5, 304	78, 427	59	
61, 537	11, 890	314, 424	70, 807	368, 100	18, 776	10, 346	5, 254	110, 964	60	
14, 136	1, 133	136, 259	45, 043	17, 784	13, 600	11, 597	4, 313	46, 304	61	
11, 227	932	222, 659	29, 782	11, 935	12, 918	16, 620	4, 115	11, 236	62	
2, 239	385	68, 463	7, 367	3, 976	4, 249	4, 725	2, 947	1, 370	63	
4, 656	1, 755	124, 478	10, 744	6, 582	10, 631	11, 167	3, 146	44, 596	64	
18, 620	2, 561	163, 150	23, 085	48, 807	10, 069	12, 674	1, 700	66, 725	65	
61, 303	16, 148	321, 428	72, 611	7, 168	17, 840	13, 499	2, 564	160, 806	66	

TABLE XCV.—*Selected Statistics of Agriculture*—1870—Continued.

STATE OF KENTUCKY—Continued.

	Counties.	Improved land.	Value of farms.	Total (estimated) value of all farm productions, including betterments and additions to stock.	LIVE STOCK.						
					Value of all live stock.	Horses.	Mules and asses.	Milch cows.	Working oxen.	Sheep.	Swine.
		Acres.	Dollars.	Dollars.	Dollars.	No.	No.	No.	No.	No.	No.
67	Livingston	40, 912	826, 057	505, 762	323, 213	1, 429	701	1, 430	780	6, 344	[illegible]
68	Logan	139, 036	6, 084, 554	1, 697, 441	1, 065, 901	4, 807	2, 618	3, 357	289	11, 865	[illegible]
69	Lyon	32, 475	316, 605	364, 663	234, 363	1, 116	578	1, 131	507	3, 486	[illegible]
70	Madison	224, 377	8, 981, 032	1, 493, 485	1, 948, 277	6, 957	4, 287	5, 664	2, 010	11, 777	[illegible]
71	Magoffin	24, 664	493, 366	208, 579	199, 324	1, 063	55	1, 532	948	6, 130	[illegible]
72	Marion	106, 573	3, 530, 976	1, 015, 252	630, 555	3, 398	1, 138	2, 070	422	7, 578	[illegible]
73	Marshall	59, 134	1, 193, 005	767, 763	437, 841	1, 331	1, 019	2, 187	974	10, 532	[illegible]
74	Mason	119, 021	5, 897, 634	1, 280, 306	797, 401	4, 132	1, 361	2, 798	259	5, 629	[illegible]
75	McCracken	40, 593	1, 643, 148	652, 105	304, 971	1, 350	687	1, 392	319	4, 110	[illegible]
76	McLean	42, 640	1, 214, 143	538, 667	341, 608	1, 919	481	1, 533	253	7, 347	[illegible]
77	Meade	77, 652	1, 906, 109	777, 663	478, 707	3, 209	825	1, 791	509	7, 460	[illegible]
78	Menifee	9, 760	191, 129	73, 890	71, 885	384	22	467	227	2, 116	[illegible]
79	Mercer	94, 842	4, 022, 702	949, 552	753, 714	3, 733	907	2, 220	174	7, 694	[illegible]
80	Metcalfe	47, 776	916, 599	522, 661	397, 050	2, 327	334	1, 368	459	8, 701	[illegible]
81	Monroe	68, 685	720, 680	790, 429	434, 517	4, 686	415	2, 148	935	11, 505	[illegible]
82	Montgomery	83, 606	5, 038, 849	447, 118	1, 019, 791	2, 660	1, 402	1, 977	705	5, 215	[illegible]
83	Morgan	37, 827	624, 545	296, 066	278, 770	1, 502	113	662	1, 090	10, 102	[illegible]
84	Muhlenburg	76, 993	1, 645, 030	655, 050	506, 818	2, 985	1, 290	2, 961	737	13, 959	[illegible]
85	Nelson	126, 556	5, 246, 296	1, 500, 855	1, 285, 584	5, 406	1, 542	3, 364	327	11, 096	[illegible]
86	Nicholas	88, 314	3, 593, 935	873, 260	791, 548	4, 314	1, 729	2, 477	332	9, 032	[illegible]
87	Ohio	114, 749	2, 185, 083	1, 250, 008	770, 298	5, 325	899	3, 801	1, 300	21, 308	[illegible]
88	Oldham	86, 605	4, 919, 320	1, 304, 111	678, 745	3, 164	788	2, 028	135	9, 226	[illegible]
89	Owen	127, 320	4, 034, 405	1, 259, 639	991, 828	5, 589	629	3, 074	896	11, 104	[illegible]
90	Owsley	23, 366	417, 133	127, 062	162, 200	796	128	1, 119	637	4, 139	[illegible]
91	Pendleton	82, 724	2, 602, 376	654, 425	681, 031	4, 269	294	2, 774	478	7, 307	[illegible]
92	Perry	17, 537	271, 803	289, 044	136, 067	644	74	1, 637	823	7, 025	[illegible]
93	Pike	30, 816	854, 777	522, 734	343, 104	1, 455	89	3, 087	1, 943	7, 670	[illegible]
94	Powell	11, 544	306, 560	101, 074	97, 265	458	107	396	228	1, 851	[illegible]
95	Pulaski	128, 307	1, 773, 628	1, 069, 237	800, 918	4, 354	1, 187	4, 631	1, 655	21, 579	[illegible]
96	Robertson	35, 553	1, 115, 462	432, 430	299, 862	1, 931	141	961	170	2, 289	[illegible]
97	Rock Castle	46, 115	725, 857	243, 406	239, 722	1, 638	278	1, 648	671	6, 625	[illegible]
98	Rowan	19, 474	329, 165	174, 850	134, 805	721	61	720	419	3, 321	[illegible]
99	Russell	40, 329	531, 009	269, 889	265, 717	1, 499	181	1, 416	694	7, 171	[illegible]
100	Scott	100, 484	5, 342, 521	1, 123, 521	891, 035	3, 728	1, 413	2, 242	355	7, 743	[illegible]
101	Shelby	164, 879	10, 023, 460	1, 954, 678	1, 607, 670	6, 781	2, 092	4, 191	242	9, 436	[illegible]
102	Simpson	69, 004	2, 800, 058	787, 662	447, 841	2, 091	921	1, 311	116	7, 410	13, 951
103	Spencer	74, 992	2, 963, 479	588, 538	540, 074	3, 018	538	1, 935	72	4, 330	[illegible]
104	Taylor	67, 974	1, 309, 712	561, 467	375, 289	2, 414	437	[illegible]	340	8, 046	[illegible]
105	Todd	94, 144	7, 923, 969	983, 833	552, 169	2, 363	1, 789	2, 000	142	7, 300	[illegible]
106	Trigg	80, 664	1, 880, 044	1, 080, 483	688, 008	2, 673	1, 908	2, 440	667	9, 439	[illegible]
107	Trimble	35, 856	1, 191, 509	369, 062	327, 461	1, 906	376	1, 064	284	3, 043	6, 519
108	Union	72, 621	2, 852, 215	1, 136, 178	649, 430	2, 800	934	2, 130	528	7, 816	14, 976
109	Warren	134, 874	5, 991, 918	1, 577, 859	1, 225, 792	5, 901	2, 449	3, 965	920	16, 344	[illegible]
110	Washington	130, 480	4, 349, 657	938, 372	1, 075, 104	5, 087	1, 816	3, 108	463	10, 635	[illegible]
111	Wayne	94, 380	1, 198, 460	587, 683	539, 209	2, 739	488	3, 017	1, 376	15, 659	[illegible]
112	Webster	66, 344	1, 075, 452	630, 474	475, 385	2, 965	1, 048	2, 253	584	10, 549	[illegible]
113	Whitley	58, 464	685, 940	330, 021	342, 663	1, 804	462	2, 802	1, 364	10, 507	15, 816
114	Wolfe	20, 862	354, 100	183, 971	126, 367	629	60	860	455	3, 274	3, 419
115	Woodford	67, 118	5, 698, 160	827, 961	830, 937	3, 070	1, 413	1, 903	153	4, 417	9, 335

TABLE XCV.—*Selected Statistics of Agriculture*—1870—Continued.

STATE OF KENTUCKY—Continued.

PRODUCED.										
Wheat.							Potatoes.			
Spring.	Winter.	Rye.	Indian corn.	Oats.	Tobacco.	Wool.	Irish.	Sweet.	Butter.	
Bush.	*Bushels.*	*Bushels.*	*Bushels.*	*Bushels.*	*Pounds.*	*Pounds.*	*Bushels.*	*Bushels.*	*Pounds.*	
44	27, 481	270	308, 298	30, 726	1, 066, 578	11, 996	23, 735	5, 805	44, 512	67
85	251, 964	921	931, 666	143, 927	2, 707, 571	30, 833	18, 036	23, 937	172, 001	68
......	15, 505	106	263, 925	6, 191	854, 212	5, 684	7, 603	4, 955	52, 520	69
153	33, 696	49, 271	1, 115, 061	88, 162	16, 600	26, 757	39, 493	7, 014	265, 616	70
......	5, 971	1, 482	174, 591	17, 488	7, 624	13, 774	10, 660	2, 972	45, 537	71
......	92, 530	19, 073	395, 170	72, 812	132, 293	22, 102	16, 676	5, 136	193, 397	72
275	40, 433	1, 998	478, 241	38, 346	1, 416, 282	16, 786	16, 891	19, 508	138, 881	73
555	72, 295	51, 450	765, 000	45, 076	1, 593, 156	19, 178	41, 731	2, 096	106, 329	74
......	31, 543	951	273, 914	20, 767	1, 545, 050	7, 079	18, 690	11, 985	84, 991	75
47	26, 937	449	271, 508	50, 506	2, 262, 037	17, 580	11, 022	5, 466	61, 665	76
44	67, 647	7, 726	464, 674	122, 136	539, 000	22, 656	40, 662	4, 136	94, 440	77
......	1, 760	131	73, 725	10, 662	4, 503	4, 417	4, 111	975	406	78
256	146, 276	23, 949	495, 775	66, 001	2, 695	33, 584	14, 551	2, 145	123, 042	79
5, 370	33, 448	1, 679	276, 207	62, 462	1, 310, 381	17, 718	9, 000	8, 506	84, 350	80
14	37, 353	798	747, 660	112, 275	674, 696	33, 353	13, 649	11, 299	121, 854	81
......	31, 651	16, 259	542, 710	43, 945	3, 232	17, 902	16, 285	1, 558	87, 244	82
......	10, 479	1, 899	226, 751	34, 139	16, 800	20, 960	17, 678	5, 436	89, 717	83
......	36, 544	77	364, 513	86, 880	1, 821, 988	27, 091	9, 195	10, 689	76, 389	84
290	148, 074	22, 085	774, 315	151, 569	....	28, 282	25, 583	2, 759	205, 289	85
364	39, 033	24, 638	665, 795	68, 304	83, 994	25, 796	17, 820	1, 295	163, 448	86
......	40, 321	449	577, 371	96, 268	3, 392, 633	42, 567	28, 033	16, 870	177, 229	87
50	52, 883	8, 130	514, 745	127, 650	301, 225	25, 718	38, 332	2, 196	124, 560	88
......	57, 248	21, 439	695, 608	53, 085	2, 890, 670	32, 491	28, 584	731	187, 200	89
......	8, 398	1, 571	103, 055	20, 072	8, 779	7, 446	9, 265	4, 094	43, 073	90
60	37, 143	19, 355	578, 932	46, 560	1, 651, 593	24, 948	29, 453	1, 139	161, 343	91
......	3, 304	132	135, 454	4, 266	5, 202	10, 007	9, 446	1, 635	24, 406	92
......	13, 401	2, 292	332, 802	25, 035	17, 157	16, 811	21, 244	14, 607	81, 966	93
......	2, 105	490	88, 022	5, 080	3, 938	5, 201	3, 537	1, 245	30, 237	94
......	43, 918	1, 848	466, 379	176, 016	47, 749	37, 341	34, 790	21, 709	279, 716	95
1, 988	7, 925	11, 176	242, 426	16, 667	1, 648, 201	7, 382	7, 807	408	84, 675	96
......	10, 539	899	216, 816	35, 077	23, 445	10, 949	14, 077	3, 007	92, 675	97
......	2, 786	698	112, 040	15, 950	11, 295	7, 072	8, 618	2, 667	56, 275	98
......	13, 027	215	224, 262	43, 431	89, 484	15, 189	12, 430	6, 969	66, 416	99
49	47, 721	26, 774	573, 626	76, 156	32, 900	31, 329	516	41	70, 499	100
28	171, 534	62, 097	1, 125, 787	156, 935	240, 435	37, 512	32, 099	1, 417	229, 050	101
......	107, 242	47	402, 379	73, 682	1, 072, 401	14, 572	7, 433	11, 436	72, 004	102
......	105, 211	16, 470	436, 875	35, 885	5, 500	15, 383	9, 548	632	119, 748	103
50	27, 694	1, 365	239, 581	55, 867	1, 209, 830	17, 040	11, 959	8, 749	95, 860	104
75	178, 762	875	445, 275	57, 373	2, 620, 193	18, 925	8, 819	13, 490	65, 260	105
......	99, 371	1, 250	589, 820	16, 114	3, 614, 363	18, 442	14, 805	18, 832	83, 308	106
40	31, 808	2, 088	209, 060	38, 216	658, 465	10, 676	12, 647	237	24, 870	107
......	82, 892	1, 004	771, 186	34, 398	2, 096, 260	19, 402	3, 533	1, 581	69, 731	108
......	190, 904	1, 480	978, 247	185, 509	2, 035, 159	39, 669	19, 964	21, 452	53, 183	109
713	115, 188	40, 437	643, 588	84, 742	34, 975	31, 944	22, 405	2, 887	150, 997	110
......	44, 255	986	414, 607	79, 962	45, 782	29, 910	24, 228	14, 787	214, 086	111
......	39, 771	347	221, 332	21, 765	3, 511, 649	21, 994	9, 602	7, 310	42, 660	112
......	6, 913	896	251, 872	34, 587	18, 866	20, 827	20, 544	10, 348	128, 219	113
......	4, 145	1, 159	106, 152	15, 734	9, 144	8, 572	8, 070	3, 355	72, 121	114
30	98, 938	25, 942	516, 625	79, 888	....	21, 503	8, 766	392	69, 700	115

TABLE XCV.—*Selected Statistics of Agriculture*—1870—Continued.

STATE OF LOUISIANA.

	Parishes.	Improved land.	Value of farms.	Total (estimated) value of all farm productions, including betterments and additions to stock.	LIVE STOCK.						
					Value of all live stock.	Horses.	Mules and asses.	Milch cows.	Working oxen.	Sheep.	Swine.
		Acres.	*Dollars.*	*Dollars.*	*Dollars.*	*No.*	*No.*	*No.*	*No.*	*No.*	*No.*
1	Ascension	40, 091	1, 475, 633	684, 563	272, 716	682	1, 769	1, 163	144	765	[illegible]
2	Assumption	39, 895	1, 953, 395	1, 579, 831	364, 753	474	1, 931	649	216	215	[illegible]
3	Avoyelles	38, 525	1, 525, 955	2, 148, 874	340, 836	1, 385	978	3, 136	672	1, 965	[illegible]
4	Bienville	59, 449	442, 648	1, 225, 100	320, 895	1, 313	947	2, 786	845	4, 340	[illegible]
5	Bossier	60, 381	1, 633, 983	1, 534, 020	449, 618	1, 553	1, 364	2, 788	504	1, 917	[illegible]
6	Caddo	75, 813	1, 911, 256	1, 810, 926	564, 475	844	3, 597	2, 173	447	2, 157	[illegible]
7	Calcasieu	4, 719	83, 800	100, 120	99, 340	886	76	1, 347	836	1, 900	[illegible]
8	Caldwell	16, 146	260, 275	402, 644	184, 322	873	467	1, 488	577	2, 643	[illegible]
9	Cameron	2, 808	68, 055	253, 077	135, 677	1, 343	24	1, 165	411	3, 840	[illegible]
10	Carroll	44, 448	2, 376, 630	1, 025, 238	303, 613	683	1, 424	1, 504	220	772	[illegible]
11	Catahoula	46, 509	1, 009, 831	735, 095	407, 531	1, 449	931	3, 062	1, 229	1, 751	[illegible]
12	Claiborne	130, 186	1, 494, 346	1, 986, 546	591, 248	1, 863	2, 220	4, 144	805	8, 195	[illegible]
13	Concordia	87, 273	3, 168, 500	1, 935, 405	491, 491	1, 035	2, 280	1, 079	536	109	4, 017
14	De Soto	110, 132	1, 190, 596	1, 702, 430	435, 451	1, 334	1, 618	3, 110	1, 258	4, 906	[illegible]
15	East Baton Rouge	50, 355	1, 719, 591	1, 131, 336	363, 302	1, 296	1, 275	3, 203	583	3, 470	[illegible]
16	East Feliciana	73, 545	886, 420	1, 044, 376	276, 440	1, 147	890	2, 155	677	2, 284	[illegible]
17	Franklin	11, 994	396, 594	299, 098	149, 325	713	395	1, 402	332	994	[illegible]
18	Grant	28, 135	464, 444	490, 650	238, 361	651	460	1, 097	432	895	[illegible]
19	Iberia	19, 244	1, 429, 025	475, 352	142, 746	1, 271	834	1, 834	711	3, 511	[illegible]
20	Iberville	32, 812	1, 334, 675	1, 341, 809	309, 632	377	1, 938	622	226	1, 483	[illegible]
21	Jackson	41, 094	225, 414	584, 569	201, 358	912	729	1, 955	602	3, 192	[illegible]
22	Jefferson	17, 806	1, 333, 700	437, 168	148, 655	195	828	394	48	336	21
23	Lafayette	58, 105	1, 118, 526	852, 093	457, 526	4, 322	944	4, 804	1, 880	6, 881	[illegible]
24	Lafourche	32, 820	1, 998, 950	1, 176, 819	298, 779	324	1, 812	567	219	236	221
25	Livingston	10, 465	200, 629	202, 725	169, 195	935	150	2, 712	498	3, 110	[illegible]
26	Madison	42, 284	1, 757, 403	1, 830, 593	355, 598	896	1, 605	756	193	73	[illegible]
27	Morehouse	35, 731	1, 011, 421	973, 183	365, 197	1, 136	1, 326	2, 510	528	2, 570	[illegible]
28	Natchitoches	81, 732	1, 939, 575	1, 525, 476	633, 879	2, 949	1, 845	3, 527	1, 644	5, 442	[illegible]
29	Orleans	4, 603	859, 012	614, 128	173, 690	295	336	1, 617	25	11	[illegible]
30	Ouachita	40, 571	1, 588, 070	1, 356, 348	301, 283	828	1, 498	1, 606	509	1, 951	[illegible]
31	Plaquemines	36, 777	3, 808, 300	1, 906, 846	417, 552	914	1, 648	1, 116	843	236	1, 111
32	Point Coupée	38, 166	1, 611, 037	1, 065, 173	302, 325	612	1, 537	1, 586	160	1, 257	[illegible]
33	Rapides	63, 265	1, 580, 915	1, 482, 594	450, 945	2, 225	1, 976	3, 748	1, 218	3, 848	[illegible]
34	Richland	16, 932	523, 947	529, 762	237, 285	958	653	2, 829	419	1, 843	[illegible]
35	Sabine	16, 576	223, 805	264, 270	140, 152	736	222	1, 521	627	1, 512	[illegible]
36	St. Bernard	7, 648	438, 700	183, 333	41, 350	104	214	135	146	56	[illegible]
37	St. Charles	15, 330	920, 800	881, 895	193, 670	327	1, 287	186	136	258	[illegible]
38	St. Helena	33, 673	373, 708	354, 261	161, 281	807	395	1, 823	720	1, 858	[illegible]
39	St. James	26, 513	2, 097, 131	1, 224, 294	294, 901	370	2, 447	558	255	367	[illegible]
40	St. John the Baptist	19, 880	1, 621, 127	1, 182, 746	240, 718	337	1, 570	431	254	294	[illegible]
41	St. Landry	80, 452	2, 258, 502	1, 556, 290	666, 414	5, 843	2, 052	8, 455	3, 049	9, 398	[illegible]
42	St. Martin	33, 776	1, 021, 150	523, 258	347, 700	2, 413	1, 372	3, 101	937	3, 769	[illegible]
43	St. Mary	43, 564	4, 710, 540	1, 534, 154	432, 234	958	1, 861	1, 077	839	1, 704	[illegible]
44	St. Tammany	1, 978	38, 900	86, 170	39, 100	192	51	918	406	1, 499	[illegible]
45	Tangipahoa	16, 708	320, 181	331, 863	199, 964	772	147	1, 480	687	3, 457	[illegible]
46	Tensas	77, 724	3, 223, 840	2, 493, 250	517, 091	1, 211	2, 404	1, 049	518	1, 043	[illegible]
47	Terrebonne	36, 693	2, 742, 325	1, 317, 410	422, 255	676	1, 798	696	468	470	[illegible]
48	Union	47, 236	550, 311	893, 917	370, 578	1, 400	1, 138	2, 741	674	5, 502	[illegible]
49	Vermillion	11, 524	278, 975	177, 738	266, 810	2, 056	121	3, 183	989	1, 502	[illegible]
50	Washington	11, 140	63, 908	230, 589	77, 088	618	70	1, 448	405	2, 732	[illegible]
51	West Baton Rouge	21, 628	1, 646, 255	596, 810	155, 135	379	733	483	145	442	[illegible]
52	West Feliciana	28, 810	913, 595	785, 610	197, 602	671	940	1, 013	253	1, 152	894
53	Winn	21, 927	139, 117	344, 177	210, 706	985	286	2, 144	698	2, 354	15, 734

TABLE XCV.—*Selected Statistics of Agriculture*—1870—Continued.

STATE OF LOUISIANA.

PRODUCED.										
					Potatoes.			Sugar.	Molasses.	
Indian corn.	Rice.	Tobacco.	Cotton.	Wool.	Irish.	Sweet.	Butter.	Cane.	Cane.	
Bushels.	*Pounds.*	*Pounds.*	*Bales.*	*Pounds.*	*Bushels.*	*Bushels.*	*Pounds.*	*Hhds.*	*Gallons.*	
160, 542	15, 926	....	981	1, 993	1, 053	4, 010	....	6, 423	308, 587	1
246, 929	17, 229	500	263	10	2, 109	11, 050	....	9, 558	490, 135	2
175, 330	78, 365	808	10, 139	....	770	24, 985	....	325	25, 600	3
192, 164	....	....	7, 253	8, 951	20	27, 621	....	....	445	4
987, 660	....	....	13, 506	3, 834	615	11, 422	....	....	....	5
384, 834	....	5, 220	26, 387	1, 040	7, 720	56, 705	11, 733	....	20	6
39, 950	29, 400	....	605	....	90	29, 380	....	28	1, 130	7
75, 741	....	63	4, 157	2, 928	362	15, 512	715	....	....	8
14, 451	....	....	696	3, 300	....	7, 518	....	14	800	9
148, 525	....	....	20, 384	150	1, 320	12, 765	17, 230	....	....	10
76, 165	....	....	8, 872	140	95	6, 528	175	....	480	11
475, 374	245	312	14, 900	15, 389	3, 270	95, 914	20, 835	....	....	12
68, 950	....	....	26, 712	....	1, 560	4, 350	....	....	....	13
321, 365	....	....	15, 809	....	300	2, 280	....	....	700	14
185, 133	427	50	8, 967	5, 598	3, 163	32, 075	26, 780	833	59, 497	15
167, 962	5, 900	....	10, 252	5, 854	98	26, 263	875	....	240	16
35, 794	....	....	3, 498	310	236	6, 804	....	....	....	17
58, 786	150	90	4, 377	409	105	9, 948	....	....	....	18
115, 843	12, 500	....	1, 297	7, 930	135	12, 414	....	1, 854	102, 495	19
168, 645	....	....	1, 178	....	....	1, 333	....	4, 907	323, 600	20
132, 224	4	285	4, 097	3, 412	801	29, 603	18, 750	....	20	21
67, 460	969, 620	....	456	600	8, 071	7, 640	....	2, 196	136, 200	22
238, 020	221, 600	340	6, 234	14, 385	3, 803	47, 043	40, 166	128	6, 715	23
181, 095	1, 691, 410	....	5	....	3, 729	11, 624	....	7, 128	366, 685	24
46, 595	20, 900	300	1, 426	4, 573	476	20, 923	520	135	3, 518	25
170, 477	....	....	17, 189	100	50	12, 964	150	....	....	26
180, 032	....	....	11, 154	1, 077	1, 265	17, 399	55, 950	....	....	27
231, 746	....	75	15, 671	3, 189	779	12, 356	....	2	90	28
14, 357	198	....	....	....	2, 468	4, 540	1, 800	751	17, 910	29
211, 505	....	....	14, 239	1, 987	1, 224	17, 124	3, 481	....	....	30
55, 280	8, 630, 026	....	11	472	2, 543	4, 569	6, 730	7, 723	421, 562	31
138, 010	....	130	9, 744	460	184	3, 619	100	1, 548	113, 210	32
261, 579	....	12	9, 133	8, 868	3, 020	54, 276	15, 855	3, 324	212, 860	33
95, 225	....	25	6, 051	3, 235	597	19, 839	14, 218	....	75	34
74, 520	....	240	2, 350	746	56	15, 032	....	....	882	35
12, 775	190, 480	....	61	....	3, 553	32, 767	....	686	42, 580	36
129, 564	2, 238, 200	....	207	648	890	1, 798	....	3, 914	217, 120	37
91, 265	....	....	3, 284	3, 875	....	38, 961	....	....	....	38
91, 105	934, 915	3, 450	3, 041	200	574	1, 985	....	6, 265	347, 722	39
106, 884	632, 670	....	....	....	1, 702	252	....	4, 962	346, 100	40
368, 897	33, 375	1, 350	14, 205	5, 026	719	58, 811	1, 000	1, 988	118, 110	41
192, 840	....	....	3, 428	440	537	9, 808	....	1, 494	75, 740	42
186, 842	69, 327	....	67	200	370	11, 882	2, 600	6, 591	341, 445	43
8, 795	26, 225	150	34	3, 186	994	13, 266	5, 533	36	600	44
64, 021	57, 030	180	1, 642	9, 071	1, 278	35, 809	20, 423	1	2, 234	45
94, 500	....	....	25, 371	1, 650	1, 834	13, 050	170	....	....	46
209, 050	233, 000	....	130	....	246	9, 947	1, 420	6, 537	366, 282	47
230, 282	....	....	6, 675	4, 660	285	50, 445	28, 860	....	....	48
111, 995	421, 501	50	969	....	....	22, 087	....	259	10, 165	49
33, 729	12, 807	427	533	5, 173	512	14, 903	9, 055	....	3, 844	50
24, 955	....	....	2, 445	300	315	873	400	806	50, 740	51
66, 029	....	....	7, 967	1, 461	750	10, 200	2, 670	290	29, 500	52
87, 540	1, 562	1, 482	2, 680	3, 596	969	18, 022	14, 161	....	732	53

TABLE XCV.—*Selected Statistics of Agriculture*—1870—Continued.

STATE OF MAINE.

	Counties.	Improved land.	Value of farms.	Total (estimated) value of all farm productions, including betterments and additions to stock.	LIVE STOCK.					
					Value of all live stock.	Horses.	Milch cows.	Working oxen.	Sheep.	Swine.
		Acres.	*Dollars.*	*Dollars.*	*Dollars.*	*No.*	*No.*	*No.*	*No.*	*No.*
1	Androscoggin	161, 777	6, 558, 570	1, 587, 089	1, 203, 806	3, 645	7, 872	2, 996	12, 281	[illegible]
2	Aroostook	133, 024	3, 010, 130	1, 845, 600	1, 027, 442	5, 072	7, 190	1, 681	24, 369	[illegible]
3	Cumberland	249, 617	13, 029, 330	3, 016, 347	2, 014, 435	5, 925	13, 354	4, 890	13, 413	[illegible]
4	Franklin	213, 913	4, 866, 019	1, 820, 510	1, 525, 040	4, 096	7, 108	4, 321	57, 093	[illegible]
5	Hancock	103, 536	3, 032, 269	1, 208, 946	802, 934	1, 958	5, 777	2, 399	20, 084	[illegible]
6	Kennebec	280, 994	12, 076, 918	3, 497, 195	2, 373, 079	7, 563	13, 252	5, 481	31, 975	[illegible]
7	Knox	72, 987	3, 189, 372	981, 377	685, 852	1, 785	4, 608	1, 652	10, 600	[illegible]
8	Lincoln	109, 738	4, 480, 419	1, 308, 362	929, 996	2, 260	6, 136	3, 656	13, 898	[illegible]
9	Oxford	273, 369	7, 570, 084	2, 609, 766	2, 033, 740	6, 001	13, 105	7, 262	35, [illegible]	[illegible]
10	Penobscot	297, 263	10, 394, 213	3, 880, 532	2, 608, 451	9, 263	14, 815	4, 372	46, 425	[illegible]
11	Piscataquis	110, 726	2, 940, 458	1, 266, 909	904, 124	2, 938	4, 714	2, 250	21, 805	[illegible]
12	Sagadahoc	63, 587	2, 760, 001	752, 504	530, 176	1, 340	3, 125	1, 068	8, 151	[illegible]
13	Somerset	302, 615	8, 482, 979	3, 297, 786	2, 432, 029	7, 222	11, 132	5, 886	78, 400	[illegible]
14	Waldo	228, 842	7, 058, 828	2, 458, 174	1, 690, 602	5, 116	8, 861	3, 913	31, 347	[illegible]
15	Washington	59, 220	2, 138, 232	1, 073, 194	692, 979	2, 139	5, 341	1, 446	15, 211	[illegible]
16	York	247, 565	11, 435, 103	2, 865, 753	1, 903, 384	5, 191	12, 869	6, 649	14, 356	[illegible]

STATE OF MARYLAND.

	Counties.	Improved land.	Value of farms.	Total (estimated) value of all farm productions, including betterments and additions to stock.	LIVE STOCK.						
					Value of all live stock.	Horses.	Mules and asses.	Milch cows.	Working oxen.	Sheep.	Swine.
		Acres.	*Dollars.*	*Dollars.*	*Dollars.*	*No.*	*No.*	*No.*	*No.*	*No.*	*No.*
1	Allegany	106, 865	4, 930, 230	1, 141, 418	829, 767	4, 002	95	5, 580	50	17, 232	8, 06[illegible]
2	Anne Arundel	140, 936	6, 369, 913	1, 817, 407	799, 384	4, 075	660	2, 926	1, 733	5, 345	11, [illegible]
3	Baltimore	226, 040	29, 181, 762	3, 447, 945	1, 867, 543	7, 482	1, 575	10, 819	432	5, 511	16, 73[illegible]
4	Calvert	74, 936	2, 100, 526	568, 237	284, 738	1, 814	79	1, 280	1, 409	3, 109	4, 7[illegible]
5	Caroline	109, 628	3, 866, 480	848, 275	412, 585	2, 155	528	2, 253	463	2, 836	6, 6[illegible]
6	Carroll	201, 533	11, 751, 860	2, 719, 378	1, 472, 970	6, 564	447	8, 945	28	5, 279	19, 9[illegible]
7	Cecil	136, 432	10, 894, 291	2, 288, 360	1, 108, 396	4, 824	572	5, 797	1, 085	4, 579	9, 76[illegible]
8	Charles	97, 745	2, 694, 212	823, 314	324, 357	2, 004	463	1, 676	1, 772	3, 872	6, 9[illegible]
9	Dorchester	78, 265	3, 156, 240	822, 793	402, 849	1, 678	155	2, 379	1, 789	4, 401	8, 4[illegible]
10	Frederick	287, 750	19, 463, 749	4, 094, 567	2, 054, 773	11, 860	351	11, 907	88	9, 817	29, [illegible]
11	Harford	134, 321	9, 325, 375	1, 926, 321	1, 152, 058	4, 247	597	5, 748	1, 166	5, 612	11, [illegible]
12	Howard	96, 960	6, 167, 584	1, 283, 395	638, 380	2, 958	267	3, 100	391	2, 516	8, 4[illegible]
13	Kent	140, 013	9, 401, 750	2, 110, 903	999, 742	4, 535	523	3, 518	911	6, 154	12, [illegible]
14	Montgomery	162, 143	5, 480, 453	1, 845, 788	946, 010	5, 211	363	4, 691	544	6, 812	13, [illegible]
15	Prince George's	125, 045	7, 358, 111	1, 340, 947	659, 620	3, 434	532	2, 620	1, 947	4, 906	9, 9[illegible]
16	Queen Anne	1, 237	6, 183, 808	1, 487, 863	758, 667	3, 703	586	3, 121	1, 201	5, 373	9, 9[illegible]
17	Saint Mary's	100, 656	3, 211, 181	843, 548	561, 604	2, 577	172	2, 260	2, 122	3, 982	11, [illegible]
18	Somerset	63, 664	2, 754, 645	550, 786	336, 189	1, 235	299	1, 683	1, 602	3, 199	7, 6[illegible]
19	Talbot	106, 499	5, 848, 480	1, 246, 475	694, 597	3, 298	570	3, 309	882	6, 044	9, 41[illegible]
20	Washington	78, 748	3, 884, 800	2, 500, 233	311, 648	8, 423	108	6, 310	......	9, 268	20, [illegible]
21	Wicomico	95, 361	2, 882, 280	743, 521	313, 682	1, 521	451	1, 911	1, 347	5, 766	6, [illegible]
22	Worcester	69, 176	3, 461, 948	822, 453	444, 199	2, 086	437	2, 921	2, 208	8, 094	11, [illegible]

TABLE XCV.—*Selected Statistics of Agriculture*—1870—Continued.

STATE OF MAINE.

PRODUCED.										
eat.						Potatoes.	Dairy products.			
Winter.	Rye.	Indian corn.	Oats.	Barley.	Wool.	Irish.	Butter.	Cheese.	Hay.	
Bushels.	*Bushels.*	*Bushels.*	*Bushels.*	*Bushels.*	*Pounds.*	*Bushels.*	*Pounds.*	*Pounds.*	*Tons.*	
54	3, 787	72, 344	96, 413	20, 404	48, 665	371, 391	559, 213	179, 858	50, 787	1
201	2, 553	4, 242	532, 151	4, 879	86, 173	380, 701	523, 510	21, 011	48, 052	2
240	3, 767	154, 360	77, 406	31, 656	48, 295	510, 207	1, 060, 811	69, 844	88, 461	3
29	968	64, 267	151, 032	12, 611	257, 369	325, 513	562, 470	101, 007	71, 211	4
47	131	5, 971	34, 396	32, 798	72, 827	221, 379	531, 907	10, 506	32, 653	5
163	2, 101	111, 246	170, 371	122, 627	137, 231	733, 026	1, 176, 423	154, 727	113, 153	6
226	2, 635	15, 445	12, 276	25, 259	45, 859	190, 676	395, 960	26, 515	28, 014	7
55	1, 545	28, 255	21, 766	48, 175	48, 820	241, 625	537, 885	2, 165	44, 185	8
20	9, 005	181, 319	201, 746	3, 873	142, 444	701, 615	923, 641	207, 048	90, 679	9
1, 849	2, 144	73, 944	361, 355	90, 763	188, 273	1, 201, 558	1, 363, 921	92, 581	116, 323	10
79	112	36, 142	140, 652	35, 485	80, 753	352, 915	420, 362	57, 419	41, 187	11
30	428	18, 225	15, 849	21, 051	29, 416	103, 928	264, 862	1, 683	25, 060	12
86	1, 965	106, 657	296, 185	92, 767	366, 442	988, 179	796, 238	163, 349	113, 481	13
858	1, 085	40, 594	146, 738	78, 791	126, 724	680, 971	876, 494	31, 386	81, 417	14
58	131	953	35, 997	12, 427	47, 072	237, 102	526, 913	406	30, 190	15
205	1, 758	175, 924	57, 021	24, 348	47, 865	530, 223	1, 115, 782	32, 995	78, 632	16

STATE OF MARYLAND.

PRODUCED.									
Vheat.						Potatoes.			
Winter.	Rye.	Indian corn.	Oats.	Tobacco.	Wool.	Irish.	Sweet.	Butter.	
Bushels.	*Bushels.*	*Bushels.*	*Bushels.*	*Pounds.*	*Pounds.*	*Bushels.*	*Bushels.*	*Pounds.*	
70, 034	45, 090	116, 062	206, 580	....	47, 935	68, 373	100	337, 639	1
126, 451	8, 767	500, 359	65, 888	3, 020, 955	21, 521	47, 647	20, 392	142, 632	2
264, 568	31, 182	856, 754	375, 063	1, 941	18, 772	201, 754	3, 294	544, 888	3
38, 023	3, 965	178, 400	28, 740	3, 158, 200	12, 106	2, 412	100	32, 018	4
130, 728	17, 295	342, 971	37, 948	....	9, 397	27, 302	17, 141	98, 591	5
467, 586	35, 257	716, 887	425, 019	225, 800	19, 012	118, 072	5, 621	823, 759	6
365, 818	670	683, 683	305, 307	....	14, 102	110, 839	5, 287	445, 720	7
73, 028	8, 269	221, 726	50, 813	2, 102, 739	11, 428	10, 037	925	53, 878	8
122, 460	3, 079	311, 039	35, 100	....	15, 368	19, 996	10, 118	65, 949	9
1, 133, 623	54, 995	1, 380, 420	250, 060	274, 369	34, 533	138, 484	1, 860	877, 784	10
244, 835	3, 241	650, 789	303, 164	....	10, 469	140, 523	209	209, 140	11
128, 276	11, 200	415, 719	204, 877	182, 980	9, 427	97, 929	2, 480	189, 646	12
473, 601	139	723, 824	143, 653	....	26, 550	44, 003	3, 331	155, 974	13
309, 418	25, 234	638, 047	171, 242	630, 000	17, 880	179, 502	259	188, 334	14
79, 181	23, 849	518, 131	57, 411	3, 665, 034	12, 997	60, 179	8, 009	69, 658	15
326, 828	5, 415	605, 975	59, 167	....	22, 581	26, 845	9, 467	107, 422	16
152, 630	814	274, 457	44, 379	2, 522, 917	9, 809	8, 525	1, 117	48, 922	17
40, 719	85	251, 883	100, 110	14	9, 090	105, 009	42, 026	42, 929	18
302, 078	71	515, 122	38, 825	....	29, 695	41, 770	10, 725	99, 008	19
930, 246	28, 394	737, 980	142, 880	....	42, 224	90, 885	2, 084	393, 070	20
12, 103	58	405, 627	17, 693	370	14, 333	31, 214	29, 127	48, 308	21
20, 574	20	606, 944	157, 700	....	19, 924	60, 845	44, 836	39, 460	22

TABLE XCV.—*Selected Statistics of Agriculture*—1870—Continued.

STATE OF MASSACHUSETTS.

	Counties.	Improved land.	Value of farms.	Total (estimated) value of all farm productions, including betterments and additions to stock.	LIVE STOCK.					
					Value of all live stock.	Horses.	Milch cows.	Working oxen.	Sheep.	Swine.
		Acres.	*Dollars.*	*Dollars.*	*Dollars.*	*No.*	*No.*	*No.*	*No.*	*No.*
1	Barnstable	10,780	436,500	164,064	110,215	239	544	224	626	[illegible]
2	Berkshire	239,388	12,106,277	3,063,468	2,179,606	5,028	15,834	2,128	27,195	4,2[illegible]
3	Bristol	73,977	6,737,831	1,660,002	840,809	2,068	5,671	1,603	2,281	3,7[illegible]
4	Dukes	13,779	324,900	56,280	63,555	150	383	174	4,716	[illegible]
5	Essex	115,448	10,576,299	2,579,654	1,251,183	3,177	9,076	2,319	1,254	4,[illegible]
6	Franklin	225,933	9,241,187	3,108,969	1,736,157	4,245	8,779	2,627	15,959	[illegible]
7	Hampden	177,228	9,888,002	3,297,007	1,575,871	3,585	10,200	2,718	6,751	4,[illegible]
8	Hampshire	207,636	11,543,877	3,719,471	1,773,101	4,478	9,514	2,034	10,173	5,[illegible]
9	Middlesex	181,727	19,544,230	5,297,365	2,306,538	5,836	16,887	2,107	983	8,1[illegible]
10	Nantucket	2,860	123,360	108,203	67,053	153	441	35	1,219	[illegible]
11	Norfolk	60,797	7,186,306	1,524,100	712,424	2,070	5,289	689	508	3,[illegible]
12	Plymouth	53,598	4,552,483	1,014,709	545,703	1,637	3,263	1,324	1,986	2,1[illegible]
13	Suffolk	3,678	1,070,250	267,615	72,560	190	376	26	5	[illegible]
14	Worcester	370,326	22,493,282	6,351,411	3,814,303	7,583	28,314	6,342	4,904	7,[illegible]

STATE OF MICHIGAN.

	Counties.	Improved land.	Value of farms.	Total (estimated) value of all farm productions, including betterments and additions to stock.	LIVE STOCK.					
					Value of all live stock.	Horses.	Milch cows.	Working oxen.	Sheep.	Swine.
		Acres.	*Dollars.*	*Dollars.*	*Dollars.*	*No.*	*No.*	*No.*	*No.*	*No.*
1	Alcona	319	23,400	7,245	6,650	14	24	16	......	51
2	Allegan	100,722	8,734,527	1,880,755	1,159,887	5,375	5,884	1,212	33,626	8,[illegible]
3	Alpena	502	39,800	12,758	5,896	25	21	......	......	18
4	Antrim	4,486	405,860	100,565	52,619	99	262	194	28	[illegible]
5	Barry	141,822	9,510,440	1,864,573	1,301,541	5,944	5,994	1,336	53,260	9,[illegible]
6	Bay	7,723	688,860	178,553	93,873	478	700	167	223	453
7	Benzie	4,806	435,090	86,877	44,459	161	205	128	15	151
8	Berrien	132,752	14,958,851	2,676,107	1,201,161	6,448	5,967	543	26,118	16,[illegible]
9	Branch	150,262	12,238,801	2,024,066	1,349,294	7,704	7,313	391	60,877	14,[illegible]
10	Calhoun	219,319	16,727,160	3,206,325	1,917,377	8,708	8,459	398	102,010	15,[illegible]
11	Cass	161,328	12,220,821	2,203,229	1,217,739	7,142	5,648	106	36,770	22,[illegible]
12	Charlevoix	2,692	244,350	56,435	28,602	67	127	122	39	415
13	Cheboygan	1,423	108,420	37,716	20,585	62	63	26	129	36
14	Chippewa	2,149	59,858	50,485	16,278	67	97	32	63	80
15	Clare	401	21,700	8,808	3,035	8	17	20	......	32
16	Clinton	113,578	9,248,012	2,151,159	1,321,970	5,313	6,020	1,076	44,895	10,151
17	Delta	759	18,950	11,163	7,540	34	33	[illegible]	16	33
18	Eaton	115,843	8,611,210	1,808,256	1,237,767	5,526	6,423	1,061	49,733	10,943
19	Emmet	2,524	73,275	28,519	22,065	228	[illegible]	28	44	321
20	Genesee	173,035	12,671,110	2,029,802	1,600,772	7,486	8,850	1,573	79,306	9,[illegible]
21	Grand Traverse	13,607	1,009,720	278,418	164,350	449	827	463	290	643
22	Gratiot	46,581	3,355,425	786,512	515,784	2,072	3,288	1,309	11,536	4,[illegible]
23	Hillsdale	198,042	14,938,430	2,926,903	1,856,674	8,996	10,567	452	89,457	17,[illegible]
24	Houghton	2,064	58,985	65,586	16,000	97	40	21	1	52
25	Huron	25,567	1,463,855	454,147	289,887	694	1,788	1,197	2,576	1,933
26	Ingham	127,324	9,685,863	1,980,878	1,386,393	5,954	6,535	1,200	62,407	11,[illegible]
27	Ionia	155,073	12,000,828	2,534,487	1,553,888	6,514	7,424	1,844	78,541	10,[illegible]
28	Iosco	647	55,500	10,203	8,185	43	38	13	......	[illegible]
29	Isabella	14,116	1,086,190	269,502	165,450	568	867	630	1,911	1,375

TABLE XCV.—*Selected Statistics of Agriculture*—1870—Continued.

STATE OF MASSACHUSETTS.

PRODUCED.										
heat.						Potatoes.	Dairy products.			
Winter.	Rye.	Indian corn.	Oats.	Tobacco.	Wool.	Irish.	Butter.	Cheese.	Hay.	
Bush.	*Bushels.*	*Bushels.*	*Bushels.*	*Pounds.*	*Pounds.*	*Bushels.*	*Pounds.*	*Pounds.*	*Tons.*	
5	2,648	12,069	4,019	....	2,700	11,246	32,935	1,755	3,872	1
651	33,903	156,384	248,642	22,810	119,574	355,670	1,038,751	1,114,343	84,790	2
515	7,928	82,256	40,003	....	5,704	237,675	223,986	11,725	27,091	3
......	167	7,011	2,321	....	12,969	8,045	14,224	625	1,746	4
406	9,256	94,033	27,427	800	3,517	310,807	335,885	22,782	50,299	5
7,967	23,327	150,538	76,533	2,473,265	70,882	221,633	906,543	73,375	63,456	6
1,110	63,518	145,728	74,617	1,095,423	18,737	267,702	716,979	242,046	51,859	7
4,539	36,706	157,939	64,572	3,720,587	43,832	274,008	1,003,427	136,086	61,734	8
231	20,350	190,965	56,302	....	2,228	443,099	560,136	8,465	74,678	9
......	117	7,921	2,045	....	3,503	7,424	99,838	....	2,177	10
153	6,717	46,136	7,734	....	1,289	132,734	170,295	7,676	24,920	11
698	8,924	50,462	20,080	....	5,723	94,766	197,129	19,434	17,525	12
......	3,054	2,479	....	....	....	20,672	3,136	....	3,123	13
799	20,612	224,886	173,349	....	16,001	639,305	1,275,897	605,561	130,185	14

STATE OF MICHIGAN.

PRODUCED.										
Wheat.						Potatoes.			Sugar.	
Winter.	Indian corn.	Oats.	Barley.	Buckwheat.	Wool.	Irish.	Butter.	Hay.	Maple.	
Bushels.	*Bushels.*	*Bushels.*	*Bushels.*	*Bushels.*	*Pounds.*	*Bushels.*	*Pounds.*	*Tons.*	*Pounds.*	
60	....	1,970	....	....	....	1,805	....	146	....	1
336,558	376,974	205,219	20,973	10,724	129,223	267,795	476,065	27,453	127,336	2
....	....	2,380	36	30	....	6,430	200	127	....	3
5,157	10,605	4,270	309	331	43	45,008	22,920	500	16,268	4
574,873	373,420	212,857	12,568	9,748	230,554	244,579	623,171	28,899	138,698	5
9,358	8,458	10,008	140	142	424	26,505	65,245	3,534	....	6
8,400	15,079	3,601	252	1,416	55	48,263	18,870	658	40,508	7
448,749	469,705	178,217	453	4,636	90,769	282,503	548,959	27,654	47,044	8
419,030	454,593	185,707	7,993	10,100	277,261	322,145	684,639	35,601	62,037	9
741,394	729,832	304,872	62,366	9,347	449,651	389,738	824,058	47,052	965	10
626,234	670,013	175,665	1,699	2,630	143,913	302,058	443,182	34,078	42,278	11
2,261	5,155	3,251	211	638	....	31,310	10,780	232	18,066	12
....	30	8,285	30	9	448	8,484	7,225	349	3,390	13
6	65	2,085	39	....	190	9,227	3,674	940	2,760	14
108	290	400	....	29	....	4,240	1,615	217	260	15
495,363	274,606	285,419	17,871	8,603	196,444	227,140	796,970	29,369	78,500	16
294	....	4,365	....	....	....	4,170	....	145	....	17
325,729	231,955	300,308	16,876	5,651	221,732	177,313	749,464	31,212	204,028	18
418	4,452	5,972	53	115	100	25,801	3,190	99	40,730	19
531,805	326,637	410,561	23,884	18,634	375,877	288,829	910,876	48,041	13,472	20
26,939	26,708	15,218	909	4,812	913	94,174	84,950	3,544	23,875	21
125,798	81,655	64,923	881	6,889	44,903	95,354	306,436	13,297	59,009	22
529,829	879,032	271,732	18,336	14,815	385,031	294,364	866,352	43,807	59,096	23
33	....	8,595	303	....	....	22,040	....	703	....	24
54,586	4,836	50,194	439	381	10,097	99,005	131,265	7,597	1,638	25
469,504	382,164	233,594	16,207	9,117	281,562	240,324	779,496	36,606	43,301	26
665,317	366,811	284,314	27,572	12,246	317,261	316,487	656,369	34,271	120,870	27
....	45	1,355	....	139	....	8,395	....	88	....	28
95,789	18,984	21,382	58	1,555	6,346	39,001	87,854	4,268	16,545	29

TABLE XCV.—*Selected Statistics of Agriculture*—1870—Continued.

STATE OF MICHIGAN—Continued.

	Counties.	Improved land.	Value of farms.	Total (estimated) value of all farm productions, including betterments and additions to stock.	LIVE STOCK.					
					Value of all live stock.	Horses.	Milch cows.	Working oxen.	Sheep.	Swine.
		Acres.	*Dollars.*	*Dollars.*	*Dollars.*	*No.*	*No.*	*No.*	*No.*	*No.*
30	Jackson	255,610	18,324,020	3,593,297	2,443,749	10,201	8,946	551	130,289	[illegible]
31	Kalamazoo	201,689	17,255,839	2,887,376	1,695,748	[illegible]	7,182	405	76,699	[illegible]
32	Kalkaska	462	40,000	9,587	6,880	5	43	32	17	66
33	Kent	202,160	16,592,422	2,955,404	1,990,697	8,386	9,695	2,009	63,360	[illegible]
34	Keweenaw	408	13,990	6,670	3,950	24	17	......	......	16
35	Lake	640	43,600	13,079	6,992	7	47	36	26	22
36	Lapeer	110,042	8,022,633	1,825,137	1,181,879	4,973	5,301	1,011	52,191	[illegible]
37	Leelanaw	10,976	719,581	251,738	128,022	468	618	282	236	[illegible]
38	Lenawee	263,197	21,158,168	4,821,811	2,897,101	12,138	15,772	367	112,633	[illegible]
39	Livingston	179,292	10,829,325	2,381,063	1,631,019	7,185	7,092	947	103,527	[illegible]
40	Mackinac	371	9,200	8,225	4,330	16	42	2	......	[illegible]
41	Macomb	155,904	12,283,257	2,276,223	1,614,700	7,983	9,027	381	64,305	[illegible]
42	Manistee	2,629	229,100	85,868	36,999	101	200	132	42	[illegible]
43	Manitou	1,747	25,510	22,994	15,960	39	124	28	63	118
44	Marquette	310	14,500	17,870	5,890	13	27	6	......	27
45	Mason	4,344	337,720	62,119	49,302	162	273	207	28	72
46	Mecosta	10,893	1,002,961	239,543	131,161	385	600	477	917	740
47	Menominee	179	7,100	4,484	2,690	10	22	10	20	19
48	Midland	5,211	391,300	122,305	61,225	257	315	127	298	254
49	Monroe	124,147	9,656,840	2,317,318	1,232,894	7,601	7,982	455	38,932	13,67[illegible]
50	Montcalm	48,480	3,343,891	794,605	470,423	1,827	2,256	953	13,485	3,34[illegible]
51	Muskegon	20,357	1,364,695	297,996	192,112	800	975	366	2,530	1,543
52	Newaygo	21,939	1,202,300	364,366	194,069	784	1,007	422	2,940	1,997
53	Oakland	336,060	25,554,239	5,154,231	3,073,040	12,991	13,668	480	162,832	19,67[illegible]
54	Oceana	11,476	779,500	147,152	143,276	433	663	394	926	1,602
55	Ogemaw	136	2,500	4,650	3,450	9	1	6	......	14
56	Ontonagon	7,562	829,580	60,857	30,670	107	165	27	16	109
57	Osceola	4,811	433,330	90,997	65,767	146	331	302	320	451
58	Oscoda	150	6,500	3,445	2,209	8	2	6	......	3
59	Ottawa	81,702	7,568,445	1,975,1[illegible]	1,060,667	4,324	6,514	1,346	14,943	7,795
60	Saginaw	33,153	2,820,883	731,799	420,220	1,894	3,077	821	5,258	3,216
61	Sanilac	45,965	2,244,420	847,421	454,853	1,941	3,265	1,419	9,182	3,769
62	Shiawassee	111,390	8,123,000	1,915,143	1,181,149	4,718	5,864	1,480	45,536	8,398
63	St. Clair	105,080	6,915,877	1,591,116	1,028,804	6,398	8,014	1,245	32,587	9,439
64	St. Joseph	184,188	14,803,721	2,288,868	1,253,301	7,302	5,792	117	46,129	21,0[illegible]
65	Tuscola	48,345	3,387,540	837,945	578,710	2,163	3,333	1,356	9,428	3,712
66	Van Buren	125,445	10,885,465	2,189,000	1,258,204	6,271	5,702	1,101	32,955	13,29[illegible]
67	Washtenaw	284,711	22,156,160	4,912,618	2,581,973	11,215	11,272	334	187,059	19,474
68	Wayne	171,792	17,986,185	3,033,019	1,830,309	10,118	11,927	462	42,683	12,63[illegible]
69	Wexford	1,425	89,900	34,818	15,531	44	77	56	2	32

TABLE XCV.—*Selected Statistics of Agriculture*—1870—Continued.

STATE OF MICHIGAN—Continued.

PRODUCED.										
Wheat.						Potatoes.			Sugar.	
Winter.	Indian corn.	Oats.	Barley.	Buckwheat.	Wool.	Irish.	Butter.	Hay.	Maple.	
Bushels.	*Bushels.*	*Bushels.*	*Bushels.*	*Bushels.*	*Pounds.*	*Bushels.*	*Pounds.*	*Tons.*	*Pounds.*	
825, 318	750, 146	239, 021	62, 546	11, 924	616, 238	401, 558	1, 021, 831	62, 090	....	30
844, 254	143, 817	226, 942	13, 066	4, 183	209, 532	312, 777	714, 969	40, 784	33, 778	31
423	405	30	30	20	36	5, 435	2, 025	43	4, 446	32
703, 425	405, 281	343, 556	22, 724	18, 179	251, 721	480, 909	862, 309	47, 983	86, 336	33
....	....	715	30	....	....	2, 010	100	215	....	34
542	1, 610	829	....	479	50	5, 110	6, 300	99	16, 705	35
333, 455	241, 266	300, 735	37, 585	12, 305	241, 179	138, 984	646, 757	29, 835	16, 278	36
21, 651	19, 989	15, 322	1, 556	2, 771	836	84, 343	53, 971	1, 607	37, 056	37
684, 266	964, 306	402, 396	36, 804	16, 332	550, 426	302, 402	1, 467, 408	68, 332	21, 694	38
671, 502	454, 923	247, 801	40, 481	16, 779	455, 540	293, 832	751, 357	43, 027	7, 415	39
....	....	468	113	....	....	2, 001	2, 445	139	4, 760	40
361, 862	317, 358	529, 417	30, 014	20, 454	322, 189	264, 553	888, 184	42, 689	1, 108	41
4, 428	10, 509	4, 743	225	949	183	29, 360	12, 730	565	8, 495	42
770	330	2, 312	....	....	217	7, 210	7, 305	268	....	43
....	30	8, 800	....	....	....	3, 100	2, 580	99	300	44
4, 161	12, 261	9, 457	273	871	....	37, 515	5, 640	636	3, 175	45
19, 515	15, 734	27, 805	220	1, 347	....	53, 729	47, 510	3, 176	12, 075	46
420	....	735	....	....		1, 200	....	40	....	47
3, 271	6, 838	11, 224	150	461	1, 140	23, 482	31, 175	2, 498	2, 400	48
248, 921	399, 583	260, 913	9, 393	27, 314	154, 421	268, 373	894, 265	44, 896	1, 930	49
136, 233	117, 163	63, 925	8, 018	6, 772	69, 541	178, 010	43, 340	13, 141	50, 755	50
28, 895	28, 629	24, 028	434	4, 365	8, 568	72, 335	55, 872	5, 658	17, 927	51
37, 296	42, 378	25, 999	515	3, 731	8, 726	66, 746	109, 064	5, 977	46, 298	52
1, 129, 186	1, 143, 443	752, 359	133, 867	42, 588	703, 876	707, 936	1, 654, 621	79, 709	4, 359	53
19, 610	40, 397	11, 011	313	4, 432	1, 733	73, 007	4, 200	2, 369	3, 499	54
....	150	1, 300	....	....	....	1, 200	....	50	....	55
101	48	8, 711	373	....	....	8, 097	14, 019	1, 437	150	56
3, 122	6, 087	9, 532	64	653	874	37, 467	16, 490	2, 532	11, 298	57
....	....	2, 000	....	....	....	600	....	10	....	58
217, 626	215, 043	164, 643	11, 836	9, 751	51, 453	253, 826	618, 130	23, 148	80, 840	59
36, 561	43, 349	52, 295	1, 999	3, 261	16, 086	86, 999	318, 275	14, 926	9, 251	60
76, 222	8, 273	145, 396	4, 811	3, 356	32, 503	103, 999	250, 832	14, 901	2, 481	61
469, 720	262, 861	202, 510	17, 341	9, 947	192, 612	240, 102	491, 606	32, 464	32, 999	62
154, 167	102, 066	368, 034	16, 089	13, 211	128, 020	210, 848	663, 610	39, 477	4, 651	63
754, 445	654, 712	91, 184	2, 458	6, 700	203, 223	400, 201	483, 104	31, 227	5, 997	64
111, 109	82, 880	84, 475	650	6, 409	40, 635	122, 102	359, 136	14, 996	8, 899	65
385, 205	572, 578	159, 835	1, 258	10, 050	121, 106	304, 465	646, 908	26, 615	68, 619	66
1, 049, 130	874, 822	418, 138	120, 543	15, 267	906, 011	350, 409	1, 248, 586	76, 678	1, 000	67
232, 815	413, 284	477, 321	28, 068	28, 295	204, 543	440, 569	891, 305	57, 367	3, 835	68
3, 635	2, 585	1, 910	103	602	....	8, 190	8, 305	243	9, 870	69

TABLE XCV.—*Selected Statistics of Agriculture*—1870—Continued.

STATE OF MINNESOTA.

	Counties.	Improved land.	Value of farms.	Total (estimated) value of all farm productions, including betterments and additions to stock.	LIVE STOCK.					
					Value of all live stock.	Horses.	Milch cows.	Working oxen.	Sheep.	Swine.
		Acres.	*Dollars.*	*Dollars.*	*Dollars.*	*No.*	*No.*	*No.*	*No.*	*No.*
1	Aitkin	6	500	400	330	3	1	......	......	......
2	Anoka	8,434	421,379	123,215	138,944	625	978	277	1,745	[illegible]
3	Becker	267	6,300	3,243	4,360	15	19	12	36	6
4	Benton	2,553	73,450	37,765	30,138	99	217	71	201	[illegible]
5	Big Stone	13	65	299	1,670	......	7	10	10	2
6	Blue Earth	102,295	5,133,375	1,415,075	886,048	4,402	4,734	1,690	6,690	[illegible]
7	Brown	33,821	1,493,537	333,061	318,060	1,209	2,155	1,202	995	[illegible]
8	Carver	34,047	2,637,526	867,331	513,100	1,691	4,170	1,969	5,501	[illegible]
9	Cass	74	850	1,770	1,360	10	4	2	......	......
10	Chippewa	9,524	45,365	57,088	90,604	158	584	616	[illegible]	[illegible]
11	Chisago	8,004	477,720	211,638	163,325	387	1,027	373	1,357	[illegible]
12	Clay	22	1,598	1,106	2,085	10	13	10	......	15
13	Cottonwood	782	43,600	14,900	12,420	46	74	85	30	[illegible]
14	Crow Wing	380	5,950	6,362	9,075	39	35	16	......	[illegible]
15	Dakota	162,503	5,226,820	2,509,758	1,014,741	5,480	4,806	799	3,063	[illegible]
16	Dodge	74,540	2,933,717	1,017,813	577,198	2,877	3,208	1,003	[illegible]	[illegible]
17	Douglas	13,982	589,050	190,291	168,758	523	1,071	884	1,017	[illegible]
18	Faribault	68,027	2,916,985	732,645	587,898	2,995	3,235	1,351	4,127	[illegible]
19	Fillmore	185,087	6,636,880	2,664,398	1,409,805	6,558	8,092	2,035	10,342	[illegible]
20	Freeborn	69,048	3,077,225	856,233	665,956	3,136	4,468	1,710	5,057	[illegible]
21	Goodhue	217,028	6,723,190	2,269,040	1,331,058	6,766	6,485	1,819	6,241	6,671
22	Grant	864	40,835	9,264	16,924	46	133	108	106	33
23	Hennepin	64,704	4,164,074	1,400,479	802,159	3,633	5,361	1,318	5,672	[illegible]
24	Houston	67,824	2,706,140	964,512	518,650	2,917	3,614	790	4,607	[illegible]
25	Isanti	7,614	225,751	95,477	85,921	225	660	426	975	[illegible]
26	Jackson	5,391	261,815	90,650	59,576	237	469	288	413	[illegible]
27	Kanabec	30	1,000	700	600	3	2	2	......	......
28	Kandiyohi*	6,199	266,221	45,720	77,733	221	563	355	742	[illegible]
29	Lac qui Parle	268	1,355	2,243	8,655	17	54	59	25	[illegible]
30	Lake	111	16,000	3,500	1,430	6	11	12	7	[illegible]
31	Le Sueur	37,245	2,614,215	907,789	574,377	2,088	3,695	1,678	5,233	[illegible]
32	Martin	10,453	1,073,755	258,080	239,240	1,114	1,267	719	749	[illegible]
33	McLeod	21,447	1,107,763	295,219	290,165	1,102	2,483	1,225	3,480	[illegible]
34	Meeker	21,538	1,136,565	411,917	263,249	963	1,871	1,145	2,906	[illegible]
35	Mille Lac	1,784	86,410	40,514	33,860	95	249	118	155	170
36	Monongalia	17,376	495,995	160,828	167,018	567	1,299	734	2,468	649
37	Morrison	3,497	107,221	62,383	56,116	235	353	171	570	583
38	Mower	65,522	2,674,775	949,145	516,132	2,821	3,073	930	1,945	2,973
39	Murray	413	15,100	6,400	5,850	17	38	40	115	10
40	Nicollet	50,828	1,907,475	645,855	365,841	1,879	3,189	788	1,619	[illegible]
41	Olmsted	202,008	7,308,111	2,877,800	1,362,321	7,576	6,496	1,300	4,918	[illegible]
42	Otter Tail	3,632	151,281	36,539	54,853	155	539	443	[illegible]	411
43	Pine	45	5,000	1,900	2,050	15	6	2	11	30
44	Pope	12,646	493,833	161,386	113,372	360	942	720	964	790
45	Ramsey	10,224	1,083,950	514,884	164,037	618	1,099	113	298	1,357
46	Redwood	1,074	48,600	17,417	15,473	48	90	30	[illegible]	47
47	Renville	9,728	343,490	96,643	116,999	404	993	823	[illegible]	[illegible]
48	Rice	94,475	3,584,355	1,291,392	777,420	3,775	4,240	1,191	7,907	[illegible]
49	Rock	463	10,700	6,650	6,075	17	34	34	9	11
50	Scott	46,566	2,204,115	673,973	516,568	2,042	4,262	1,307	3,863	6,654
51	Sherburne	7,877	486,950	157,573	129,560	412	716	270	1,112	542
52	Sibley	31,275	1,468,800	536,376	412,565	1,726	3,531	1,238	3,666	3,990
53	Stearns	55,182	2,740,575	789,885	603,931	2,313	4,399	2,568	6,174	[illegible]
54	Steele	47,738	1,974,300	546,701	375,185	1,971	2,846	706	2,785	2,006
55	Stevens	745	37,300	15,811	9,840	36	89	55	32	53
56	Todd	3,762	219,370	71,672	52,171	74	337	243	378	373
57	Traverse	20	400	1,000	200	2	......	......	......	2
58	Wabashaw	136,500	5,997,080	2,139,397	989,948	5,385	4,374	957	2,819	[illegible]
59	Wadena	6	250	650	1,450	......	6	2	......	......
60	Waseca	49,259	1,995,036	648,297	410,602	2,043	2,593	1,106	2,617	[illegible]
61	Washington	48,471	2,681,780	790,181	383,650	1,699	2,074	281	2,179	[illegible]
62	Watonwan	16,720	617,350	176,188	136,108	528	702	601	446	815
63	Wilkin	906	23,003	43,455	17,160	44	113	162	11	44
64	Winona	136,584	5,893,010	1,883,873	1,141,203	5,478	5,167	1,063	3,287	[illegible]
65	Wright	23,631	1,131,256	309,251	252,292	1,082	2,050	928	2,612	[illegible]

Table XCV.—Selected Statistics of Agriculture—1870—Continued.

STATE OF MINNESOTA.

Produced.											
Wheat.						Potatoes.	Dairy products.			Sugar.	
Spring.	Winter.	Indian corn.	Oats.	Barley.	Wool.	Irish.	Butter.	Cheese.	Hay.	Maple.	
Bushels.	*Bushels.*	*Bushels.*	*Bushels.*	*Bushels.*	*Pounds.*	*Bushels.*	*Pounds.*	*Pounds.*	*Tons.*	*Pounds.*	
....	....	38	....	....	....	440	....	....	....	880	1
27, 393	....	36, 838	17, 715	481	5, 246	15, 672	51, 240	1, 055	7, 919	60	2
2, 850	....	330	1, 553	....	106	40	....	....	....	....	3
3, 541	....	5, 036	7, 672	314	1, 261	5, 312	17, 620	5, 125	1, 535	767	4
							910	....	75	....	5
794, 092	1, 787	198, 060	407, 575	35, 146	22, 586	65, 393	487, 971	12, 090	18, 994	2, 968	6
213, 900	70	34, 525	156, 768	24, 448	1, 986	24, 566	94, 993	2, 070	16, 520	910	7
298, 355	497	122, 140	140, 375	33, 987	10, 313	54, 207	211, 497	1, 230	19, 694	8, 798	8
....	....	330	1, 209	....	....	900	....	....	....	....	9
9, 118	200	3, 550	2, 465	450	1, 365	158	64, 030	....	4, 993	....	10
32, 620	237	13, 603	39, 596	1, 848	3, 688	16, 975	100, 975	1, 483	6, 242	2, 117	11
....	....	....	....	....	....	300	300	....	....	....	12
311	....	295	215	....	....	245	3, 100	....	539	....	13
		3, 265				1, 550	970	....	....	....	14
1, 435, 361	513	210, 286	634, 806	33, 877	7, 874	93, 387	457, 400	3, 450	22, 744	....	15
634, 741	....	81, 277	384, 528	47, 150	20, 808	36, 569	277, 667	10, 021	19, 863	....	16
59, 375	....	6, 570	65, 568	3, 934	1, 992	36, 884	90, 574	324	10, 708	3, 325	17
562, 940	....	137, 496	394, 992	25, 786	12, 712	29, 321	259, 645	17, 891	15, 398	60	18
1, 687, 424	610	389, 956	976, 281	108, 335	27, 137	92, 402	595, 114	17, 645	28, 903	300	19
537, 358	1, 040	134, 638	326, 766	7, 188	15, 000	53, 814	380, 652	2, 340	35, 712	....	20
1, 815, 403	200	209, 790	825, 301	81, 678	21, 298	85, 399	470, 201	16, 967	31, 468	375	21
1, 552	....	100	2, 273	25	174	1, 730	8, 368	....	881	....	22
378, 943	120	259, 418	226, 361	11, 326	12, 034	98, 863	333, 146	7, 341	25, 454	89, 414	23
605, 358	18, 199	249, 761	227, 688	31, 182	14, 286	32, 065	229, 183	6, 790	14, 776	....	24
15, 367	658	8, 699	11, 860	57	2, 607	11, 544	58, 331	175	5, 432	20	25
24, 150	....	6, 405	24, 366	392	1, 328	7, 637	35, 510	1, 110	4, 203	1, 110	26
100	....	100	200	....	....	150	300	100	....	50	27
20, 161	....	488	7, 832	651	2, 025	5, 586	25, 963	100	3, 823	....	28
....	....	....	....	....	100	....	6, 010	....	....	....	29
220	....	....	....	20	....	650	....	....	445	....	30
246, 987	1, 622	264, 298	152, 682	18, 692	18, 652	61, 580	320, 985	945	18, 510	48, 667	31
99, 565	....	39, 149	107, 042	5, 262	2, 210	25, 004	114, 473	1, 190	11, 680	....	32
149, 296	155	48, 381	96, 487	10, 914	11, 470	31, 855	168, 428	11, 072	16, 932	3, 510	33
134, 337	810	28, 974	92, 592	10, 492	7, 878	39, 913	142, 771	685	15, 320	20	34
7, 889	31	9, 572	9, 131	96	380	5, 163	22, 667	....	1, 917	2, 947	35
77, 154	....	4, 930	48, 959	4, 766	10, 515	22, 158	67, 047	2, 482	10, 209	....	36
11, 927	....	9, 345	18, 987	756	1, 491	13, 668	20, 005	....	2, 462	100	37
673, 017	....	118, 771	463, 085	39, 975	7, 670	63, 244	295, 896	2, 130	18, 151	....	38
835	....	720	592	200	....	855	3, 900	150	340	....	39
315, 671	132	83, 256	264, 565	32, 411	5, 389	36, 158	250, 844	11, 163	24, 446	476	40
2, 117, 054	30	340, 223	996, 364	114, 056	18, 082	126, 668	654, 455	16, 480	31, 319	950	41
8, 406	....	942	6, 701	37	343	8, 784	14, 525	....	4, 262	483	42
86	....	110	460	....	43	360	500	....	133	....	43
53, 721	....	1, 925	44, 395	2, 231	2, 757	20, 528	65, 375	1, 310	8, 567	....	44
53, 883	438	38, 020	53, 868	9, 015	1, 500	33, 697	91, 185	10, 700	5, 600	600	45
5, 400	....	2, 240	6, 978	470	900	1, 880	5, 275	2, 900	882	....	46
43, 289	....	6, 537	27, 659	3, 610	1, 735	14, 761	40, 185	610	9, 731	....	47
529, 383	1, 823	227, 931	348, 543	36, 773	20, 607	57, 862	364, 200	15, 311	33, 615	24, 991	48
130	....	400	600	....	....	480	2, 900	....	433	....	49
362, 196	300	186, 012	165, 247	15, 667	13, 446	39, 292	319, 142	1, 500	19, 700	916	50
26, 257	200	37, 036	17, 797	643	2, 556	17, 987	53, 610	12, 250	8, 303	....	51
237, 706	....	142, 060	221, 416	34, 545	19, 600	52, 049	310, 217	1, 200	32, 659	....	52
305, 049	65	78, 627	447, 193	23, 856	17, 701	120, 865	323, 085	10, 435	28, 930	680	53
385, 214	....	82, 040	230, 421	12, 709	7, 172	36, 625	208, 249	2, 950	19, 928	600	54
2, 064	....	235	3, 234	50	111	1, 613	8, 280	....	877	....	55
15, 907	....	3, 814	18, 012	1, 065	1, 054	13, 736	25, 683	160	3, 339	3, 045	56
		300				400	....	....	100	....	57
1, 476, 643	3, 650	312, 697	669, 410	89, 125	4, 416	97, 700	370, 729	4, 830	11, 618	....	58
		100				28	....	....	....	....	59
400, 058	230	98, 478	208, 243	8, 754	6, 206	30, 092	224, 227	4, 184	20, 445	2, 803	60
444, 311	100	113, 650	267, 086	42, 155	6, 806	45, 686	118, 392	3, 501	6, 430	....	61
75, 865	....	6, 391	46, 068	2, 125	988	11, 171	43, 095	280	6, 383	....	62
465	....	....	4, 425	139	....	8, 390	9, 825	....	1, 510	....	63
1, 315, 012	42, 942	273, 477	598, 871	64, 311	10, 615	79, 074	478, 495	6, 760	16, 944	....	64
133, 850	236	69, 572	97, 282	7, 630	6, 964	51, 748	115, 675	1, 490	6, 961	8, 615	65

TABLE XCV.—*Selected Statistics of Agriculture*—1870—Continued.

STATE OF MISSISSIPPI.

	Counties.	Improved land.	Value of farms.	Total (estimated) value of all farm productions, including betterments and additions to stock.	LIVE STOCK.						
					Value of all live stock.	Horses.	Mules and asses.	Milch cows.	Working oxen.	Sheep.	Swine.
		Acres.	*Dollars.*	*Dollars.*	*Dollars.*	*No.*	*No.*	*No.*	*No.*	*No.*	*No.*
1	Adams	143,644	4,184,447	1,866,035	731,113	1,489	1,792	2,242	876	1,678	[illegible]
2	Alcorn	41,300	891,190	646,626	398,515	1,477	778	2,440	919	3,446	14,158
3	Amite	81,880	1,164,842	1,204,595	585,986	1,902	1,107	3,859	1,516	4,697	14,781
4	Attala	74,960	1,197,213	1,485,058	648,718	1,788	1,937	4,463	1,466	7,106	22,749
5	Bolivar	39,629	1,449,525	1,301,937	306,664	720	1,478	1,414	261	707	4,571
6	Calhoun	62,223	1,016,025	1,078,975	525,360	1,820	1,153	3,186	1,123	5,934	20,962
7	Carroll	115,479	1,833,972	1,846,746	776,153	1,809	2,552	4,346	1,505	3,955	22,388
8	Chickasaw	89,210	1,311,563	1,758,691	745,739	2,306	2,193	4,067	1,104	4,980	22,613
9	Choctaw	73,514	511,163	1,130,930	598,280	2,276	1,567	4,173	1,697	7,618	25,892
10	Claiborne	89,178	1,638,551	1,436,167	655,976	2,006	2,048	3,450	1,242	2,261	8,886
11	Clark	15,983	84,008	178,351	88,950	336	246	879	454	1,092	3,738
12	Coahoma	28,959	2,002,295	1,018,884	310,971	517	939	1,184	474	241	5,066
13	Copiah	115,408	1,762,750	1,910,971	790,744	2,677	2,049	4,188	1,788	5,845	20,622
14	Covington	21,062	145,670	347,152	192,100	965	209	1,979	980	3,766	8,963
15	De Soto	191,692	4,670,763	3,110,589	1,367,827	4,339	4,408	6,648	937	4,700	36,315
16	Franklin	32,257	589,363	603,247	271,880	977	541	2,297	1,291	2,275	8,698
17	Greene	4,552	29,065	95,114	146,478	400	58	2,402	456	4,357	7,398
18	Grenada	56,828	1,006,960	900,563	385,493	832	1,108	1,976	716	2,039	9,429
19	Hancock	1,347	15,000	147,320	51,075	159	55	792	226	1,458	2,385
20	Harrison	1,074	36,050	36,007	78,135	168	.....	564	28	1,765	4,621
21	Hinds	165,553	2,717,004	2,900,112	809,876	1,714	2,905	4,274	1,034	4,179	14,330
22	Holmes	93,691	1,725,089	1,960,981	607,943	1,110	2,343	2,962	741	2,680	10,496
23	Issaquena	35,286	1,723,230	1,027,590	238,225	562	931	619	313	395	1,675
24	Itawamba	29,901	364,342	429,901	279,137	1,420	429	2,235	829	6,130	9,736
25	Jackson	1,291	21,010	55,537	57,790	150	28	788	263	4,020	3,098
26	Jasper	66,710	577,783	708,661	482,712	1,704	841	3,621	1,335	4,104	18,418
27	Jefferson	62,509	1,121,638	1,343,617	555,015	1,681	1,964	3,215	1,584	2,118	7,086
28	Jones	11,860	69,080	134,099	143,011	608	61	1,804	558	3,773	7,784
29	Kemper	55,419	722,560	829,751	378,811	1,140	902	2,118	890	3,174	10,316
30	Lafayette	89,230	1,857,047	2,125,337	799,900	2,334	2,322	4,515	1,016	6,281	31,516
31	Lauderdale	43,704	566,767	552,560	284,179	895	561	2,040	828	2,314	7,278
32	Lawrence	32,539	352,156	460,186	246,096	1,051	342	1,718	1,046	4,014	8,668
33	Leake	46,837	553,212	622,313	291,535	1,017	702	2,317	1,062	3,473	11,528
34	Lee	72,208	1,463,074	1,357,712	660,509	3,099	1,688	4,025	892	6,689	23,442
35	Lincoln	34,605	534,964	593,380	274,550	1,121	444	2,084	1,018	4,144	8,882
36	Lowndes	145,134	2,079,973	2,014,219	621,244	1,122	3,042	2,595	640	2,006	11,693
37	Madison	212,782	2,907,357	2,150,451	840,006	1,817	2,862	4,635	1,120	4,237	12,128
38	Marion	19,955	218,966	198,325	186,517	797	137	2,206	670	4,827	8,574
39	Marshall	189,031	4,309,221	2,468,237	1,098,167	2,809	4,058	5,885	718	4,719	37,157
40	Monroe	95,312	1,431,399	1,498,490	656,688	1,934	2,084	3,458	783	4,472	19,586
41	Neshoba	31,682	386,938	532,888	361,869	1,549	513	2,813	1,393	4,469	11,774
42	Newton	48,894	487,292	609,692	341,130	1,256	643	2,737	1,238	4,205	12,909
43	Noxubee	159,707	2,383,491	2,168,970	927,052	1,511	3,308	3,131	843	2,570	19,196
44	Oktibbeha	84,662	1,063,890	1,273,304	482,037	1,237	1,705	2,296	521	2,105	14,355
45	Panola	103,567	3,030,587	2,145,996	724,079	2,147	2,361	3,085	760	2,952	17,385
46	Perry	7,752	87,755	137,415	146,663	554	123	3,160	883	6,898	6,928
47	Pike	32,261	635,414	575,419	236,048	1,162	323	1,777	929	4,145	7,566
48	Pontotoc	67,209	1,160,335	940,724	597,551	2,229	1,533	4,151	892	6,999	23,322
49	Prentiss	40,266	795,547	635,483	315,429	1,492	568	1,945	658	5,100	12,146
50	Rankin	46,777	979,486	1,057,675	463,772	1,327	1,083	3,088	1,315	4,729	13,238
51	Scott	38,613	355,877	533,128	282,938	988	567	2,343	956	2,399	11,489
52	Simpson	23,934	212,090	365,850	193,640	871	299	1,631	1,237	4,211	7,733
53	Smith	31,242	164,452	401,429	250,787	1,065	332	2,027	948	3,694	11,254
54	Sunflower	30,264	1,227,452	743,393	337,105	839	849	1,728	451	184	7,337
55	Tallahatchie	38,420	1,130,222	841,179	336,108	842	954	1,824	596	908	7,406
56	Tippah	104,057	1,416,000	1,726,136	855,097	3,116	2,010	5,171	1,306	9,942	32,629
57	Tishemingo	28,068	486,172	524,188	273,618	1,117	430	2,091	933	4,547	9,153
58	Tunica	14,141	829,115	497,618	158,453	240	645	413	148	33	1,812
59	Warren	145,951	2,621,780	3,186,971	711,114	1,875	2,839	1,963	478	1,023	5,576
60	Washington	70,119	6,002,270	3,818,040	798,862	1,240	3,716	2,101	881	1,089	9,175
61	Wayne	12,256	123,523	118,834	149,800	442	134	1,594	402	1,615	4,506
62	Wilkinson	62,044	987,323	1,189,743	482,848	2,220	1,537	2,889	1,331	2,078	6,946
63	Winston	39,862	351,807	469,014	266,907	975	639	1,986	767	4,218	10,733
64	Yalabusha	52,430	990,780	760,903	333,443	841	1,146	1,851	633	3,002	8,232
65	Yazoo	111,232	2,890,611	2,227,854	896,591	1,938	2,775	3,040	1,136	1,838	11,851

TABLE XCV.—*Selected Statistics of Agriculture*—1870—Continued.

STATE OF MISSISSIPPI.

PRODUCED.										
Wheat.						Potatoes.			Molasses.	
Spring.	Winter.	Indian corn.	Tobacco.	Cotton.	Wool.	Irish.	Sweet.	Butter.	Cane.	
Bushels.	Bushels.	Bushels.	Pounds.	Bales.	Pounds.	Bushels.	Bushels.	Pounds.	Gallons.	
385	...	177,307	...	20,140	3,336	2,284	26,469	11,035	...	1
70	11,527	226,057	440	2,546	3,260	7,705	14,842	71,906	17,039	2
...	...	254,784	570	8,276	4,141	3,293	53,702	17,102	652	3
340	9,204	337,402	1,146	8,912	9,735	4,391	35,150	128,063	...	4
...	...	182,728	...	15,571	...	1,070	6,255	18,915	240	5
...	6,119	303,405	225	4,329	9,218	1,811	31,800	127,180	...	6
2,432	4,389	433,245	819	14,135	4,274	4,637	29,794	25,923	...	7
1,463	5,206	478,406	5,117	8,892	6,390	2,113	36,314	150,962	9,939	8
...	7,844	432,751	580	5,637	10,578	253	9,534	97,283	2,574	9
...	...	179,187	...	14,776	835	10,266	18,330	20,190	...	10
...	...	62,721	265	1,142	1,155	774	12,922	9,265	2,330	11
...	...	151,985	...	11,456	...	...	300	...	...	12
...	...	408,003	253	15,653	7,439	3,738	55,725	38,446	...	13
8	66	109,813	1,902	1,605	6,136	1,240	28,042	13,702	3,844	14
2,781	22,967	741,363	12,500	24,118	6,206	20,387	72,977	191,543	1,365	15
...	...	124,846	...	5,079	3,927	1,648	28,035	19,939	545	16
...	...	21,473	...	1	9,085	594	13,877	6,707	593	17
1,530	993	191,675	160	6,479	2,854	3,041	19,548	58,916	...	18
...	...	3,394	...	...	...	...	...	...	...	19
...	...	9,345	...	18	3,868	...	12,625	...	...	20
15	129	410,553	18	27,394	5,511	3,505	58,304	50,343	317	21
...	557	352,623	...	19,027	1,010	673	16,433	3,195	...	22
...	...	82,825	...	15,821	65	...	5,105	...	...	23
...	7,053	172,363	...	1,865	6,748	316	24,942	...	...	24
...	...	5,377	...	...	11,058	...	9,460	500	...	25
...	300	255,858	186	4,273	3,815	794	42,225	48,814	...	26
...	...	204,464	170	13,719	2,624	4,650	31,386	33,235	...	27
...	...	43,187	1,411	315	7,347	955	20,503	9,495	243	28
838	313	218,350	3,353	4,964	4,729	4,650	36,995	64,010	372	29
4,208	3,656	470,305	...	9,007	2,441	4,692	23,772	26,300	1,920	30
...	10	140,250	...	3,683	1,223	410	23,908	38,493	...	31
...	...	140,917	45	2,782	6,602	213	21,869	15,731	6,813	32
681	1,313	157,648	977	4,181	5,015	3,642	21,259	39,855	5,803	33
1,744	722	443,901	480	8,224	6,938	4,664	76,470	187,963	13,117	34
...	...	144,364	907	3,850	5,765	2,218	25,052	22,821	1,794	35
710	11,697	429,280	...	16,073	297	151	12,084	1,575	50	36
149	432	320,602	250	19,269	7,733	6,306	45,623	77,588	440	37
...	...	69,691	50	793	7,421	344	22,268	13,164	4,949	38
291	18,830	765,466	4,500	18,379	3,362	9,736	29,111	81,350	855	39
1,085	11,164	415,153	1,280	8,562	3,505	1,742	55,651	47,380	40	40
...	2,284	176,189	2,971	2,492	6,471	212	27,624	...	...	41
50	2,442	201,704	242	3,399	5,650	168	30,262	42,030	1,311	42
2,789	830	516,155	735	15,473	1,492	3,353	30,835	69,044	25,000	43
4,342	856	334,463	2,046	6,288	3,763	2,915	23,627	48,787	1,705	44
17,834	12,574	390,767	100	15,764	4,058	36,531	58,395	15,230	433	45
...	...	51,310	40	164	12,106	212	27,109	300	426	46
...	...	151,891	210	4,133	8,267	2,285	28,546	8,253	5,529	47
...	13,057	371,719	...	4,524	6,582	1,778	31,408	66,266	16,923	48
3,278	3,457	239,406	2,424	2,604	6,603	1,742	12,132	67,832	1,526	49
12	75	217,708	...	8,705	3,279	125	32,134	26,325	...	50
309	1,298	131,775	...	3,560	160	...	...	3,466	...	51
...	100	72,832	15	2,134	5,797	3,241	29,520	28,860	...	52
54	303	144,688	963	2,411	5,666	1,556	28,286	22,488	...	53
...	...	155,672	785	7,028	495	4,797	21,091	35,146	...	54
...	1,867	203,425	60	6,760	625	4,075	13,620	33,165	585	55
6,129	31,300	582,988	6,248	6,397	15,457	7,237	43,125	188,439	17,572	56
35	4,284	188,836	3,999	1,397	6,957	4,849	18,578	94,627	...	57
...	4,500	82,153	...	6,424	50	2,376	2,203	8,677	...	58
...	...	213,073	25	32,175	485	5,157	66,227	4,701	...	59
2,000	700	248,991	800	35,902	80	1,255	5,132	7,530	...	60
...	...	46,819	150	740	707	295	12,047	580	421	61
...	...	158,859	...	12,430	536	1,234	25,487	19,577	...	62
936	3,798	151,238	1,195	1,964	5,674	998	19,100	38,248	4,825	63
140	365	241,138	...	5,167	626	3,772	11,880	5,961	40	64
...	...	290,448	400	26,047	853	5,171	35,509	9,100	34	65

Table XCV.—*Selected Statistics of Agriculture*—1870—Continued.

STATE OF MISSOURI.

	Counties.	Improved land.	Value of farms.	Total (estimated) value of all farm productions, including betterments and additions to stock.	LIVE STOCK.					
					Value of all live stock.	Horses.	Mules and asses.	Milch cows.	Working oxen.	Sheep.
		Acres.	Dollars.	Dollars.	Dollars.	No.	No.	No.	No.	No.
1	Adair	96, 339	3, 292, 980	804, 109	732, 055	4, 761	724	4, 401	448	16, 22
2	Andrew	111, 414	6, 366, 656	1, 479, 071	1, 041, 068	5, 711	1, 295	4, 390	172	12, 197
3	Atchison	68, 298	3, 513, 482	1, 089, 750	853, 870	3, 359	709	3, 837	300	6, 449
4	Audrain	191, 087	5, 131, 435	1, 467, 751	1, 495, 611	6, 245	1, 716	4, 630	241	10, 929
5	Barry	37, 518	1, 092, 010	486, 660	111, 668	3, 350	387	2, 378	903	8, 736
6	Barton	41, 056	1, 343, 689	364, 215	335, 419	1, 983	229	1, 755	854	3, 367
7	Bates	113, 579	5, 022, 564	1, 201, 717	1, 251, 484	7, 331	1, 038	5, 567	1, 141	11, 294
8	Benton	79, 940	2, 448, 509	575, 239	737, 991	5, 825	1, 035	4, 780	955	15, 685
9	Bollinger	42, 009	1, 346, 550	586, 032	412, 408	2, 579	386	2, 173	826	9, 868
10	Boone	222, 296	5, 883, 432	1, 212, 831	1, 345, 424	7, 218	2, 709	5, 441	619	21, 037
11	Buchanan	91, 495	5, 882, 120	1, 377, 826	893, 309	4, 642	1, 709	3, 871	330	8, 729
12	Butler	14, 794	437, 272	725, 824	217, 973	1, 300	187	1, 355	661	2, 680
13	Caldwell	115, 998	5, 150, 055	1, 139, 002	1, 130, 073	5, 212	907	3, 571	312	12, 806
14	Callaway	174, 990	5, 863, 926	1, 649, 405	1, 643, 821	8, 767	2, 953	7, 139	937	30, 830
15	Camden	19, 852	492, 558	275, 150	225, 828	2, 030	290	1, 544	672	6, 874
16	Cape Girardeau	99, 131	3, 525, 398	1, 343, 984	789, 400	5, 454	1, 415	3, 862	635	15, 297
17	Carroll	130, 418	4, 974, 203	1, 369, 854	1, 314, 147	7, 442	1, 787	5, 729	600	17, 171
18	Carter	6, 191	153, 686	68, 625	69, 413	417	45	470	334	1, 18
19	Cass	176, 135	7, 883, 939	1, 629, 529	1, 512, 560	8, 053	1, 441	5, 366	840	9, 167
20	Cedar	35, 678	1, 429, 938	335, 229	405, 082	3, 069	472	2, 347	588	7, 73
21	Chariton	118, 932	4, 581, 355	1, 406, 286	1, 078, 502	6, 169	1, 973	5, 290	586	15, 69
22	Christian	32, 738	1, 127, 415	388, 750	336, 214	2, 601	374	1, 826	874	7, 071
23	Clarke	100, 697	3, 627, 710	**746, 619**	845, 117	5, 655	781	4, 653	94	18, 97
24	Clay	159, 896	7, 168, 052	2, 032, 770	1, 434, 775	5, 884	1, 562	3, 979	514	17, 39
25	Clinton	131, 446	5, 565, 385	**1, 200, 096**	**1, 142,** 325	6, 095	1, 504	4, 224	201	14, 09
26	Cole	72, 642	**1, 172, 440**	**316, 411**	**266,** 800	1, 570	697	1, 520	55	4, 70
27	Cooper	156, 334	7, 679, 556	**1, 820, 125**	**1, 428, 891**	6, 971	2, 607	5, 383	414	21, 20
28	Crawford	39, 543	1, 237, 629	423, 538	412, **824**	2, 573	544	2, 474	1, 048	9, 38
29	Dade	44, 885	1, 933, 005	614, 210	535, 793	3, 544	625	2, 509	562	11, 47
30	Dallas	38, 991	775, 056	400, 849	389, 895	3, 292	565	2, 167	904	9, 66
31	Daviess	108, 664	3, 543, 211	1, 072, 329	1, 282, 684	8, 465	1, 338	5, 831	253	25, 65
32	De Kalb	84, 248	3, 299, 869	**589, 518**	760, 446	4, 894	610	3, 665	275	11, 60
33	Dent	22, 950	764, 040	302, 180	271, 236	1, 241	183	1, 547	685	6, 86
34	Douglas	12, 840	226, 210	148, 450	**150, 191**	1, 289	127	970	672	2, 80
35	Dunklin	20, 997	352, 911	413, 985	243, 862	1, 211	324	1, 097	760	2, 62
36	Franklin	120, 666	7, 579, 265	2, 551, 992	1, 257, 615	6, 804	2, 175	7, 477	771	16, 79
37	Gasconade	47, 690	2, 941, 185	876, 764	520, 283	3, 270	766	3, 311	658	8, 39
38	Gentry	83, 950	3, 430, 754	1, 063, 431	886, 268	5, 516	529	4, 014	248	18, 73
39	Greene	93, 095	4, 062, 269	1, 466, 776	921, 912	6, 752	1, 645	4, 661	861	22, 49
40	Grundy	89, 892	2, 942, 289	624, 801	806, 316	5, 241	731	4, 137	329	18, 89
41	Harrison	109, 489	3, 515, 584	1, 230, 095	1, 260, 488	7, 781	791	5, 989	299	31, 60
42	Henry	148, 462	6, 024, 430	1, 279, 095	841, 721	7, 066	1, 256	5, 262	784	12, 16
43	Hickory	39, 191	1, 250, 389	398, 778	480, 933	3, 543	602	2, 569	632	8, 26
44	Holt	70, 826	3, 654, 270	1, 084, 745	767, 053	3, 551	903	3, 924	348	7, 76
45	Howard	128, 342	5, 006, 825	1, 400, 936	932, 766	5, 799	2, 425	4, 103	450	19, 15
46	Howell	12, 934	363, 950	167, 229	152, 850	1, 132	108	1, 004	862	2, 707
47	Iron	15, 477	580, 870	171, 090	129, 352	690	168	919	331	3, 17
48	Jackson	195, 134	**10, 349,** 680	1, 615, 990	1, 356, 802	6, 961	1, 703	5, 294	669	11, 01
49	Jasper	81, 266	3, 588, 880	941, 921	748, 684	4, 795	654	3, 429	1, 031	11, 444
50	Jefferson	70, 361	4, 923, 823	1, 155, 612	787, 926	4, 639	1, 374	4, 739	1, 235	10, 722
51	**Johnson**	197, 491	11, 835, 733	2, 417, 873	2, 024, 087	9, 732	2, 137	7, 161	712	16, 865
52	Knox	154, 710	3, 937, 436	1, 104, 198	1, 502, 512	7, 215	901	5, 417	304	24, 73
53	Laclede	31, 091	1, 097, 560	489, 277	362, 214	2, 854	427	2, 065	1, 115	7, 980
54	Lafayette	166, 608	8, 623, 785	1, 806, 904	1, 446, 638	6, 983	2, 760	5, 541	736	12, 244
55	Lawrence	85, 283	2, 634, 050	1, 438, 725	907, 485	6, 917	991	4, 043	714	12, 444
56	Lewis	138, 126	5, 239, 259	1, 264, 502	1, 006, 610	6, 304	1, 402	5, 036	166	21, 13
57	Lincoln	135, 423	5, 133, 736	1, 729, 562	1, 387, 573	7, 228	1, 216	5, 299	318	18, 712
58	Linn	103, 120	5, 095, 497	1, 145, 623	934, 659	5, 662	710	4, 602	541	17, 192
59	Livingston	94, 918	4, 843, 993	1, 264, 080	876, 915	5, 182	1, 033	4, 250	287	14, 262
60	Macon	140, 087	5, 283, 315	1, 506, 693	1, 415, 071	7, 765	1, 491	6, 635	871	22, 737
61	Madison	18, 298	591, 757	197, 079	162, 710	1, 101	345	1, 014	499	4, 10
62	**Maries**	29, 935	910, 452	342, 565	323, 361	2, 720	566	1, 998	729	8, 095
63	Marion	99, 544	5, 412, 589	899, 262	1, 032, 124	6, 340	1, 145	4, 306	163	14, 976
64	**McDonald**	21, 958	726, 827	244, 583	223, 370	1, 839	224	1, 338	497	3, 851
65	Mercer	81, 353	2, 822, 948	907, 586	865, 576	5, 153	468	4, 416	320	25, 441
66	Miller	40, 664	1, 005, 740	308, 835	371, 4[illegible]	2, 9[illegible]	504	2, 474	729	11, 504
67	Mississippi	21, 109	630, 71[illegible]	406, 735	247, 2[illegible]	[illegible]	[illegible]	1, 17[illegible]	[illegible]	[illegible]

TABLE XCV.—*Selected Statistics of Agriculture*—1870—Continued.

STATE OF MISSOURI.

PRODUCED.										
Wheat.								Potatoes.			
	Winter.	Rye.	Indian corn.	Oats.	Tobacco.	Wool.	Irish.	Sweet.	Butter.	
s.	*Bushels.*	*Bushels.*	*Bushels.*	*Bushels.*	*Pounds.*	*Pounds.*	*Bushels.*	*Bushels.*	*Pounds.*	
74	23, 407	10, 849	356, 105	210, 832	8, 535	48, 463	38, 274	172	187, 709	1
51	58, 074	5, 982	1, 086, 375	178, 332	5, 941	31, 825	102, 967	1, 339	187, 663	2
75	1, 242	1, 100	1, 312, 030	69, 666	265	18, 266	48, 263	59	127, 826	3
30	40, 225	4, 630	648, 963	292, 435	6, 850	28, 223	34, 056	780	241, 855	4
10	70, 729	330	322, 808	55, 348	56, 586	14, 104	16, 787	4, 282	83, 877	5
12	21, 324	696	245, 460	38, 347	6, 192	10, 584	18, 818	942	76, 432	6
16	100, 437	2, 916	910, 266	168, 621	21, 199	25, 350	47, 118	809	193, 836	7
37	122, 765	1, 846	358, 959	120, 918	36, 238	30, 238	24, 740	484	159, 167	8
1	51, 285	1, 354	395, 953	135, 980	32, 210	18, 011	21, 351	4, 866	177, 908	9
83	234, 557	14, 981	1, 096, 114	260, 019	149, 634	74, 552	21, 909	719	83, 833	10
18	223, 336	698	1, 070, 517	157, 611	5, 390	18, 642	122, 051	3, 416	63, 530	11
15	10, 799	86	185, 009	12, 018	48, 245	4, 380	5, 142	3, 277	1, 146	12
15	97, 825	7, 408	728, 121	217, 040	337	36, 374	59, 872	288	206, 150	13
39	167, 336	7, 993	971, 715	405, 294	338, 228	89, 890	45, 229	2, 325	205, 233	14
29	42, 981	1, 377	181, 288	23, 415	25, 507	12, 553	9, 486	721	....	15
90	259, 865	419	538, 437	136, 601	55, 045	30, 081	41, 086	7, 338	145, 680	16
18	208, 321	8, 016	1, 205, 966	192, 829	256, 578	41, 821	57, 453	986	186, 278	17
..	4, 992	571	73, 250	7, 311	28, 550	2, 504	1, 398	802	11, 351	18
23	175, 606	3, 427	1, 711, 952	202, 472	19, 281	22, 680	82, 859	4, 274	252, 508	19
..	59, 377	622	326, 060	49, 588	37, 465	15, 792	17, 070	2, 004	15, 147	20
77	189, 724	11, 312	919, 288	205, 914	2, 993, 981	39, 833	65, 593	1, 003	219, 697	21
00	56, 074	978	216, 185	45, 260	16, 132	9, 271	9, 958	2, 606	7, 910	22
15	49, 054	55, 336	505, 152	239, 298	1, 231	60, 196	33, 815	412	181, 507	23
20	193, 194	2, 985	1, 844, 270	199, 604	31, 040	57, 738	83, 277	5, 617	253, 865	24
53	44, 607	3, 650	1, 147, 395	239, 598	41, 805	44, 714	62, 758	874	200, 688	25
..	115, 299	100	165, 350	60, 668	2, 700	9, 857	24, 589	33	41, 774	26
77	383, 569	2, 455	1, 210, 533	412, 809	34, 731	78, 571	68, 052	3, 952	227, 001	27
10	64, 220	4, 150	242, 906	66, 882	5, 885	14, 974	16, 265	1, 107	51, 173	28
..	78, 016	762	416, 307	109, 553	22, 004	26, 482	17, 898	3, 430	92, 688	29
16	57, 513	544	290, 388	79, 698	14, 990	19, 554	14, 810	1, 947	66, 894	30
18	70, 844	6, 268	624, 012	244, 963	15, 077	64, 338	47, 620	481	211, 787	31
15	12, 151	621	521, 955	125, 923	6, 900	26, 805	44, 184	430	140, 795	32
..	55, 024	2, 834	215, 603	53, 042	26, 770	13, 922	16, 539	1, 572	56, 588	33
..	13, 794	1, 585	102, 975	18, 050	10, 029	5, 468	5, 072	863	22, 206	34
..	5, 267	25	256, 620	2, 633	2, 835	3, 750	7, 568	8, 050	32, 516	35
48	582, 073	1, 367	853, 297	351, 340	783, 270	62, 988	114, 934	7, 573	273, 789	36
..	222, 850	7, 414	260, 178	163, 717	5, 810	18, 922	31, 738	767	82, 600	37
40	6, 725	7, 955	640, 951	135, 555	18, 178	52, 641	44, 929	387	177, 834	38
13	171, 153	713	859, 953	256, 096	29, 382	37, 491	47, 626	9, 212	159, 245	39
55	50, 177	13, 138	427, 818	186, 184	19, 425	48, 207	37, 666	76	123, 251	40
03	24, 668	14, 831	756, 607	210, 521	20, 075	86, 415	55, 400	748	370, 359	41
81	239, 647	515	1, 167, 590	298, 581	7, 450	14, 662	34, 117	2, 112	181, 945	42
75	42, 221	307	271, 582	65, 573	42, 164	17, 698	16, 715	927	105, 040	43
01	14, 220	3, 945	1, 321, 620	91, 994	3, 275	19, 225	61, 402	551	155, 100	44
50	399, 830	8, 003	917, 335	152, 490	788, 132	66, 554	42, 422	1, 747	126, 216	45
..	15, 356	160	115, 728	8, 454	9, 996	3, 058	3, 456	1, 000	20, 320	46
59	10, 662	651	90, 385	28, 141	1, 056	4, 903	9, 137	548	3, 700	47
98	275, 486	4, 535	1, 504, 439	173, 229	70, 312	11, 729	91, 419	2, 724	237, 623	48
51	86, 607	2, 257	528, 591	133, 016	10, 400	38, 753	33, 418	2, 853	209, 967	49
20	149, 278	5, 316	534, 705	134, 279	25, 235	18, 152	76, 278	6, 386	152, 934	50
82	462, 308	3, 228	1, 946, 741	356, 351	18, 700	43, 256	106, 731	930	367, 464	51
28	34, 417	9, 435	573, 603	251, 812	10, 600	62, 890	40, 837	....	....	52
89	66, 904	889	317, 154	57, 835	31, 750	16, 773	27, 872	1, 378	86, 940	53
90	414, 777	8, 442	1, 576, 126	268, 881	113, 735	33, 100	91, 345	4, 023	154, 045	54
10	135, 528	2, 125	621, 495	222, 723	21, 770	24, 514	40, 225	2, 924	148, 164	55
72	127, 482	30, 783	526, 611	347, 145	10, 006	57, 325	35, 412	756	47, 515	56
94	329, 285	2, 850	754, 257	295, 007	891, 727	52, 396	32, 658	1, 655	209, 177	57
22	74, 589	20, 408	472, 135	228, 473	58, 255	43, 697	52, 853	1, 026	179, 263	58
84	123, 673	14, 768	756, 428	248, 535	323, 362	292, 694	57, 817	797	239, 507	59
06	71, 750	19, 472	857, 327	411, 510	355, 767	55, 407	72, 834	4, 373	412, 146	60
..	11, 431	808	155, 352	45, 156	17, 887	7, 869	8, 949	1, 830	48, 419	61
09	78, 834	4, 003	163, 479	72, 075	17, 672	15, 152	8, 887	96	41, 633	62
47	230, 475	8, 621	305, 256	158, 715	33, 438	41, 481	25, 936	318	22, 700	63
..	34, 160	39	136, 712	27, 099	10, 466	3, 947	9, 736	6, 159	19, 314	64
00	25, 668	9, 669	472, 730	160, 081	17, 550	57, 000	42, 969	1, 046	234, 074	65
29	91, 889	2, 650	256, 141	69, 977	10, 436	22, 482	12, 475	1, 517	31, 773	66
..	5, 225	....	491, 990	4, 593	6, 160	642	9, 625	1, 392	1, 489	67

TABLE XCV.—*Selected Statistics of Agriculture*—1870—Continued.

STATE OF MISSOURI—Continued.

	Counties.	Improved land.	Value of farms.	Total (estimated) value of all farm productions, including betterments and additions to stock.	LIVE STOCK. Value of all live stock.	Horses.	Mules and asses.	Milch cows.	Working oxen.	Sheep.	Swine.
		Acres.	*Dollars.*	*Dollars.*	*Dollars.*	*No.*	*No.*	*No.*	*No.*	*No.*	*No.*
68	Moniteau	98,029	3,616,803	934,000	770,120	5,004	1,314	3,741	418	17,187	23,2[illegible]
69	Monroe	226,132	9,412,406	1,455,046	1,818,517	9,765	2,989	5,813	206	25,533	30,3[illegible]
70	Montgomery	77,711	2,865,995	676,207	573,108	3,377	866	2,943	231	10,330	14,0[illegible]
71	Morgan	66,076	1,537,375	502,111	400,856	3,409	1,063	2,771	575	10,398	11,6[illegible]
72	New Madrid	35,385	776,800	581,230	329,190	1,150	1,031	1,744	699	465	13,1[illegible]
73	Newton	47,283	1,834,208	613,760	451,589	3,134	407	2,496	894	6,511	16,67[illegible]
74	Nodaway	111,803	5,067,785	1,104,383	1,387,184	6,715	1,070	5,964	356	15,661	36,4[illegible]
75	Oregon	15,745	366,260	188,636	133,895	960	118	747	549	3,139	8,8[illegible]
76	Osage	55,702	2,519,865	793,685	600,063	3,535	1,431	3,962	644	12,144	22,5[illegible]
77	Ozark	7,692	175,623	120,115	128,270	949	84	806	493	2,122	6,2[illegible]
78	Pemiscot	8,919	193,985	214,470	163,798	791	197	1,167	351	635	9,37[illegible]
79	Perry	63,458	2,080,920	1,198,830	465,300	3,068	676	2,592	268	8,859	17,6[illegible]
80	Pettis	198,024	7,475,790	1,535,401	1,194,483	7,060	2,012	5,376	614	17,9[illegible]	25,7[illegible]
81	Phelps	33,930	1,296,090	408,796	362,930	2,219	357	2,291	1,499	8,912	15,8[illegible]
82	Pike	174,840	8,256,252	2,032,574	1,641,721	8,091	3,079	5,760	168	22,6[illegible]	39,6[illegible]
83	Platte	112,237	7,116,577	1,811,355	1,323,017	6,595	1,476	4,482	535	11,702	35,9[illegible]
84	Polk	74,680	2,596,553	732,084	714,673	5,433	1,092	4,055	875	16,681	22,41[illegible]
85	Pulaski	15,148	551,385	245,341	198,217	1,481	135	1,271	661	3,686	10,15[illegible]
86	Putnam	79,965	2,127,123	763,788	719,049	5,320	515	4,137	353	26,227	21,7[illegible]
87	Ralls	94,794	4,504,516	746,196	855,772	4,715	1,150	3,668	108	11,470	16,6[illegible]
88	Randolph	163,991	4,310,300	1,037,471	1,092,195	7,155	2,203	4,380	425	21,770	25,71[illegible]
89	Ray	136,790	5,728,321	1,424,917	1,380,694	9,009	2,155	5,469	677	20,580	38,5[illegible]
90	Reynolds	16,556	291,284	279,896	199,692	1,075	102	1,210	650	4,810	9,9[illegible]
91	Ripley	10,933	277,510	204,760	139,179	1,086	157	937	447	2,989	10,47[illegible]
92	Saline	200,799	9,354,974	2,695,617	1,651,961	8,083	3,279	7,171	788	16,310	46,2[illegible]
93	Schuyler	54,561	1,933,568	565,135	496,691	3,686	1,002	3,206	245	15,961	11,9[illegible]
94	Scotland	109,447	3,556,785	996,945	1,095,085	5,898	919	5,326	137	29,957	24,84[illegible]
95	Scott	32,542	1,081,580	526,053	302,608	1,780	764	1,777	536	3,225	17,3[illegible]
96	Shannon	8,404	216,205	121,813	91,931	637	41	657	527	2,549	6,3[illegible]
97	Shelby	77,849	2,579,765	664,269	860,810	3,741	541	3,504	239	13,088	14,2[illegible]
98	St. Charles	131,012	8,560,516	1,967,370	1,041,250	5,788	1,815	4,863	56	10,527	31,3[illegible]
99	St. Clair	45,492	1,175,957	326,324	421,041	2,284	280	2,137	641	5,773	8,4[illegible]
100	Ste. Genevieve	37,221	1,161,505	372,780	228,799	1,967	452	1,805	555	4,997	11,06[illegible]
101	St. François	41,946	1,195,510	457,207	353,615	1,927	732	1,945	512	9,459	17,217
102	St. Louis	132,556	28,409,635	3,566,476	1,333,793	7,037	2,229	8,216	206	6,692	27,19[illegible]
103	Stoddard	36,646	916,070	506,127	38,507	2,295	396	2,560	1,286	6,765	26,55[illegible]
104	Stone	11,744	265,407	135,335	130,577	1,298	89	905	285	3,085	10,72[illegible]
105	*Sullivan	89,435	2,679,579	1,271,731	1,016,346	6,171	665	5,024	498	25,369	17,770
106	Taney	11,376	275,806	185,741	161,374	1,163	136	1,025	398	3,189	9,300
107	Texas	31,387	1,008,853	322,979	344,632	2,061	243	2,399	1,951	7,393	15,24[illegible]
108	Vernon	71,214	3,560,020	620,329	968,536	4,168	697	4,202	1,065	6,822	15,09[illegible]
109	Warren	70,523	3,375,930	1,377,990	704,815	3,567	948	3,52[illegible]	79	8,016	21,9[illegible]
110	Washington	38,650	1,303,240	443,367	425,210	2,573	832	2,696	931	7,630	16,0[illegible]
111	Wayne	27,469	735,177	436,209	266,653	1,781	207	1,636	84[illegible]	7,133	16,25[illegible]
112	Webster	38,686	1,261,832	575,960	435,153	3,318	737	2,467	1,127	10,345	15,8[illegible]
113	Worth	45,125	1,803,383	325,387	548,865	2,897	419	2,[illegible]1	257	10,375	13,5[illegible]
114	Wright	22,186	608,918	356,317	278,718	1,931	250	1,5[illegible]	1,139	6,647	14,9[illegible]

TABLE XCV.—*Selected Statistics of Agriculture*—1870—Continued.

STATE OF MISSOURI—Continued.

PRODUCED.										
Wheat.							Potatoes.			
…	Winter.	Rye.	Indian corn.	Oats.	Tobacco.	Wool.	Irish.	Sweet.	Butter.	
…els.	*Bushels.*	*Bushels.*	*Bushels.*	*Bushels.*	*Pounds.*	*Pounds.*	*Bushels.*	*Bushels.*	*Pounds.*	
209	204,380	1,217	502,917	204,036	53,706	42,688	32,274	582	178,283	68
333	109,733	13,628	589,127	304,275	187,091	68,772	26,921	1,106	245,975	69
504	73,646	2,700	543,112	297,035	203,170	38,083	9,227	331	16,973	70
31	83,092	1,319	228,175	138,259	2,470	23,468	16,424	84	41,333	71
....	3,990	....	717,495	2,875	....	330	5,135	1,720	12,326	72
18	67,707	466	359,945	81,045	16,480	10,387	26,982	6,879	90,824	73
099	725	2,072	1,276,460	122,491	50	34,972	66,061	80	203,347	74
....	15,363	940	127,001	16,114	8,180	5,091	3,600	2,477	35,376	75
4	222,169	1,057	426,563	97,320	119,617	23,422	32,329	229	100,018	76
25	9,512	523	121,724	7,143	18,613	4,185	4,094	2,092	1,021	77
80	90	100	210,145	905	3,505	633	2,719	1,367	9,442	78
....	230,674	352	331,375	112,234	3,480	18,292	22,961	1,021	91,627	79
511	269,734	3,195	920,178	312,416	9,958	48,989	55,250	1,538	146,905	80
90	70,097	2,744	239,504	62,510	13,902	14,436	23,121	620	82,548	81
220	437,789	1,190	699,522	232,828	632,552	69,791	25,905	2,452	253,545	82
290	175,770	2,958	1,470,861	152,114	400	24,577	62,046	2,587	311,495	83
175	117,824	366	552,612	155,661	11,610	32,957	22,897	4,028	150,221	84
....	28,037	765	201,019	20,873	9,020	7,150	9,353	231	78,580	85
326	22,982	11,798	458,582	146,152	39,200	63,800	33,651	1,328	194,098	86
65	158,663	1,386	292,534	125,677	2,005	32,533	15,740	693	127,793	87
937	78,601	22,361	594,372	209,013	873,776	63,623	29,250	2,365	150,737	88
145	186,591	1,900	1,245,233	177,461	190,355	42,374	27,550	1,564	122,774	89
....	13,382	1,363	168,255	17,680	13,385	6,607	6,531	718	48,000	90
....	17,725	100	142,485	14,214	1,830	4,105	5,958	3,365	41,961	91
595	384,050	6,589	2,106,043	323,806	215,475	47,018	78,470	2,200	339,108	92
356	23,371	10,399	279,460	125,442	22,094	47,717	28,155	125	129,451	93
700	38,162	30,035	736,703	350,516	10,972	110,698	44,635	611	327,960	94
....	77,020	60	428,857	19,291	6,440	4,932	20,915	1,744	3,985	95
....	7,243	229	104,725	7,496	9,045	3,294	4,724	1,685	25,129	96
429	38,829	4,173	297,982	161,559	....	36,596	9,694	214	146,905	97
416	760,564	3,031	968,161	278,235	146,754	41,003	96,716	907	158,268	98
102	34,958	177	200,368	56,180	2,410	10,376	9,551	18	41,155	99
875	151,353	3,854	180,350	78,197	5,970	10,327	14,744	1,121	27,340	100
....	63,632	2,300	247,581	125,803	9,490	20,460	18,438	2,910	66,133	101
75	453,951	3,191	1,023,978	280,783	14,570	15,537	377,316	24,748	286,615	102
278	34,223	85	384,051	17,259	118,534	9,138	15,345	14,363	37,688	103
200	12,822	85	121,735	14,340	3,205	3,521	3,932	1,692	27,817	104
451	31,016	15,826	412,624	164,614	26,619	70,094	38,754	621	234,065	105
....	6,375	443	135,577	11,075	13,223	4,844	4,161	1,333	48,250	106
....	51,778	4,087	256,252	29,876	44,349	13,238	16,318	318	67,231	107
416	56,518	302	476,230	98,793	3,927	15,450	32,153	255	145,775	108
205	251,982	7,944	729,010	415,375	296,745	32,475	55,373	555	209,662	109
....	38,627	6,225	261,633	86,809	5,000	14,684	20,398	828	69,709	110
....	23,819	1,272	293,569	31,121	47,054	11,803	8,380	3,739	54,309	111
16	73,565	1,279	288,918	76,568	143,162	18,536	17,872	3,241	97,705	112
621	1,955	3,702	375,035	71,816	5,624	32,834	31,396	301	105,809	113
625	41,691	1,352	247,735	29,286	37,551	11,726	13,109	1,023	36,799	114

TABLE XCV.—*Selected Statistics of Agriculture*—1870—Continued.

STATE OF NEBRASKA.

	Counties.	Improved land.	Value of farms.	Total (estimated) value of all farm productions, including betterments and additions to stock.	LIVE STOCK.						
					Value of all live stock.	Horses.	Mules and asses.	Milch cows.	Working oxen.	Sheep.	Swine.
		Acres.	*Dollars.*	*Dollars.*	*Dollars.*	*No.*	*No.*	*No.*	*No.*	*No.*	*No.*
1	Adams	416	8,940	7,605	27,293	21	5	40	32	3	[illegible]
2	Buffalo	295	4,685	6,097	9,860	19	......	76	6	35	6
3	Burt	25,451	1,040,787	322,951	258,106	1,134	57	1,143	244	1,161	1,[illegible]
4	Butler	9,260	317,800	60,760	101,050	574	55	460	238	478	66[illegible]
5	Cass	65,195	2,886,152	1,408,405	614,858	3,310	183	2,748	150	2,098	7,41[illegible]
6	Cedar	5,324	244,030	133,880	104,623	224	7	557	279	436	12[illegible]
7	Clay	......	......	......	......	......	......	......	......	......	......
8	Colfax	4,141	104,127	68,256	75,295	231	55	351	74	105	[illegible]
9	Cuming	21,293	865,645	205,949	169,896	831	60	720	345	820	2,0[illegible]
10	Dakota	9,564	777,985	253,587	206,393	761	48	1,073	223	58	9[illegible]
11	Dawson	......	......	......	......	......	......	......	......	......	......
12	Dixon	4,996	187,279	67,081	96,511	362	34	525	189	134	44[illegible]
13	Dodge	35,392	1,520,300	150,505	327,276	1,382	183	1,264	301	598	2,3[illegible]
14	Douglas	30,333	2,515,905	560,525	339,005	1,595	104	1,509	42	31	2,6[illegible]
15	Fillmore	......	......	......	......	......	......	......	......	......	......
16	Franklin	......	......	......	......	......	......	......	......	......	......
17	Gage	19,324	1,018,940	323,192	212,896	1,068	96	835	304	1,979	2,0[illegible]
18	Grant	......	......	......	......	......	......	......	......	......	......
19	Hall	5,807	258,600	111,025	105,051	262	16	646	74	846	[illegible]
20	Hamilton	1,122	43,400	14,645	12,111	71	1	44	16	4	[illegible]
21	Harrison	......	......	......	......	......	......	......	......	......	......
22	Jackson	......	......	......	......	......	......	......	......	......	......
23	Jefferson	8,737	355,490	79,774	110,502	528	50	507	215	791	71[illegible]
24	Johnson	11,237	541,825	187,383	120,328	671	58	533	91	299	1,44[illegible]
25	Jones	......	......	......	......	......	......	......	......	......	......
26	Kearney	......	......	......	......	......	......	......	......	......	......
27	Lancaster	37,805	2,136,053	578,414	374,029	1,614	196	1,178	508	905	2,[illegible]
28	L'Eau qui Court	797	51,850	25,425	20,610	57	7	169	46	73	2[illegible]
29	Lincoln	......	......	......	......	......	......	......	......	......	......
30	Lyon	......	......	......	......	......	......	......	......	......	......
31	Madison	3,912	150,350	71,450	48,963	209	11	194	104	317	21
32	Merrick	3,485	131,670	53,845	43,149	118	4	298	54	478	308
33	Monroe	......	......	......	......	......	......	......	......	......	......
34	Nemaha	10,760	540,950	276,131	142,466	728	70	539	29	454	1,463
35	Nuckolls	......	......	......	......	......	......	......	......	......	......
36	Otoe	77,162	3,765,270	701,778	584,910	2,935	372	2,608	267	1,333	5,956
37	Pawnee	29,052	1,542,530	395,266	354,081	1,642	59	1,660	206	847	2,615
38	Pierce	......	......	......	......	......	......	......	......	......	......
39	Platte	10,342	396,390	204,687	168,275	552	34	835	266	427	762
40	Polk	718	27,500	8,035	11,315	56	2	63	26	......	156
41	Richardson	73,939	3,669,350	875,429	748,223	3,924	280	3,829	183	3,712	12,74[illegible]
42	Saline	4,114	162,150	35,912	58,725	340	17	257	75	696	384
43	Sarpy	29,707	1,820,461	479,315	312,817	1,531	49	1,422	8	160	1,96[illegible]
44	Saunders	41,441	615,530	210,022	186,973	800	81	583	406	1,351	1,3[illegible]
45	Seward	23,513	781,460	286,417	214,566	1,214	172	718	542	509	1,29[illegible]
46	Stanton	3,115	159,609	26,727	27,521	88	16	109	90	45	214
47	Taylor	......	......	......	......	......	......	......	......	......	......
48	Washington	35,093	1,426,060	371,445	319,190	1,431	226	1,269	179	1,478	2,50[illegible]
49	Wayne	......	......	......	......	......	......	......	......	......	......
50	York	4,189	153,802	43,524	44,994	208	26	158	108	74	2[illegible]

TABLE XCV.—*Selected Statistics of Agriculture*—1870—Continued.

STATE OF NEBRASKA.

PRODUCED.										
Wheat.						Potatoes.	Dairy products.			
Spring.	Winter.	Indian corn.	Oats.	Barley.	Wool.	Irish.	Butter.	Cheese.	Hay.	
Bushels.	*Bushels.*	*Bushels.*	*Bushels.*	*Bushels.*	*Pounds.*	*Bushels.*	*Pounds.*	*Pounds.*	*Tons.*	
1,270	...	425	1,515	706	...	400	790	...	1,071	1
155	...	5,400	640	...	...	830	1,645	560	490	2
134,062	...	157,152	73,724	512	3,829	18,167	56,969	9,499	9,036	3
18,668	...	21,030	9,350	25	1,195	6,050	12,210	...	2,261	4
223,770	900	674,558	137,986	4,015	5,653	78,107	171,262	3,325	11,971	5
24,555	...	16,900	11,675	668	1,550	12,190	41,950	...	3,214	6
...	...	...	...	...	...	...	...	...	...	7
13,439	90	27,164	15,017	540	...	8,354	20,350	...	2,203	8
91,381	...	80,786	60,955	11,809	3,076	20,694	29,762	...	6,708	9
55,708	602	66,255	25,835	3,841	50	27,450	69,950	100	11,635	10
...	...	...	...	...	...	...	...	...	...	11
27,923	...	19,725	9,507	663	210	11,135	25,532	50	4,574	12
86,181	...	123,466	116,252	4,146	...	13,927	9,069	3,300	...	13
84,545	...	208,820	89,766	6,555	...	44,809	100,595	...	11,381	14
...	...	...	...	...	...	...	...	...	...	15
...	...	...	...	...	...	...	...	...	...	16
129,203	30	146,180	42,586	580	10,192	20,122	35,840	5,650	5,316	17
...	...	...	...	...	...	...	...	...	...	18
17,781	...	49,443	44,350	12,609	2,923	8,355	36,681	13,400	3,753	19
3,291	251	1,660	2,566	939	...	710	1,931	...	197	20
...	...	...	...	...	...	...	...	...	...	21
...	...	...	...	...	...	...	...	...	...	22
24,847	...	72,230	4,070	...	1,269	15,199	19,850	...	2,182	23
81,454	...	113,495	32,914	865	984	21,341	58,107	2,250	4,545	24
...	...	...	...	...	...	...	...	...	...	25
...	...	...	...	...	...	...	...	...	...	26
132,613	574	134,400	73,239	4,489	5,204	32,118	94,018	300	7,974	27
1,309	...	3,610	996	89	314	3,210	7,615	...	1,012	28
...	...	...	...	...	...	...	...	...	...	29
...	...	...	...	...	...	...	...	...	...	30
24,929	...	8,105	15,330	1,169	551	3,907	15,130	100	1,662	31
9,999	...	13,024	31,579	3,035	1,350	5,029	13,205	...	1,548	32
...	...	...	...	...	...	...	...	...	...	33
33,715	75	224,695	35,831	1,370	1,287	16,140	49,425	100	3,015	34
...	...	...	...	...	...	...	...	...	...	35
174,658	400	632,160	109,063	120,832	5,180	97,062	60,180	1,275	14,248	36
122,971	278	232,720	74,431	1,152	3,875	30,577	75,187	400	8,709	37
...	...	...	...	...	...	...	...	...	...	38
43,905	...	65,290	40,230	2,250	1,781	18,330	57,625	1,700	5,879	39
1,509	...	1,540	450	...	...	530	300	...	75	40
187,828	12,315	1,003,010	143,006	3,560	10,749	98,056	164,358	740	15,398	41
19,061	...	33,570	2,747	14	2,099	5,809	11,885	...	1,051	42
95,233	...	231,075	91,387	12,135	...	39,578	107,655	16	7,465	43
55,652	50	86,545	28,827	430	4,630	15,273	41,525	50	5,730	44
58,579	...	58,637	31,620	1,234	1,921	18,488	35,601	2,477	5,205	45
15,640	...	9,255	6,548	368	25	3,630	8,645	...	943	46
...	...	...	...	...	...	...	...	...	...	47
164,611	...	203,695	108,971	5,672	4,758	40,617	97,032	330	8,978	48
...	...	...	...	...	...	...	...	...	...	49
8,876	...	10,700	4,399	1,149	...	3,680	7,656	100	825	50

TABLE XCV.—*Selected Statistics of Agriculture*—1870—Continued.

STATE OF NEVADA.

	Counties.	Improved land.	Value of farms.	Total (estimated) value of all farm productions, including betterments and additions to stock.	LIVE STOCK. Value of all live stock.	Horses.	Mules and asses.	Milch cows.	Working oxen.	Sheep.	Swine.
		Acres.	*Dollars.*	*Dollars.*	*Dollars.*	*No.*	*No.*	*No.*	*No.*	*No.*	*No.*
1	Churchill	2,965	16,230	24,110	49,585	130	5	137	2	4	[illegible]
2	Douglas	14,274	218,765	214,770	147,530	1,014	156	862	117	502	[illegible]
3	Elko	2,970	62,300	113,450	85,965	202	61	465	348	......	[illegible]
4	Esmeralda	20,180	168,150	162,300	194,550	2,191	52	528	12	......	......
5	Humboldt	5,186	158,970	101,210	108,130	365	78	418	365	700	[illegible]
6	Lander	2,357	67,740	205,112	211,980	507	101	570	317	1,507	[illegible]
7	Lincoln	8,097	66,980	68,709	139,760	581	158	500	273	1,674	[illegible]
8	Lyon	2,335	22,300	35,295	18,535	93	10	120	......	......	[illegible]
9	Nye	4,465	32,670	52,774	42,822	139	20	332	112	......	[illegible]
10	Ormsby	4,957	256,850	163,026	77,968	254	27	291	124	32	[illegible]
11	Pah Ute	3,150	43,300	136,355	62,405	234	179	311	125	55	[illegible]
12	Roop	755	29,050	4,300	51,750	262	17	236	46	5	[illegible]
13	Storey	......	......	......	......	......	......	......	......	......	......
14	Washoe	16,338	221,800	152,173	89,284	492	11	820	86	815	[illegible]
15	White Pine	5,315	120,400	226,129	165,185	966	106	575	516	5,650	[illegible]

STATE OF NEW HAMPSHIRE.

	Counties.	Improved land.	Value of farms.	Total (estimated) value of all farm productions, including betterments and additions to stock.	LIVE STOCK. Value of all live stock.	Horses.	Milch cows.	Working oxen.	Sheep.	Swine.
		Acres.	*Dollars.*	*Dollars.*	*Dollars.*	*No.*	*No.*	*No.*	*No.*	*No.*
1	Belknap	155,421	4,934,900	1,069,518	1,023,092	2,146	4,640	3,570	10,053	[illegible]
2	Carroll	176,191	4,963,413	1,702,204	1,256,076	3,018	6,801	5,122	9,059	[illegible]
3	Cheshire	266,180	7,151,499	1,895,960	1,509,765	3,645	7,162	3,211	30,237	[illegible]
4	Coos	120,674	3,647,955	1,395,063	945,478	3,147	5,119	2,259	14,766	[illegible]
5	Grafton	442,738	12,106,924	4,034,671	2,738,807	7,135	12,748	6,685	86,621	[illegible]
6	Hillsborough	283,874	11,073,395	3,102,108	1,824,315	4,748	12,466	3,997	11,820	[illegible]
7	Merrimack	335,882	12,096,577	3,120,292	2,000,764	4,887	10,430	5,619	34,479	[illegible]
8	Rockingham	235,605	13,418,030	2,833,228	1,753,277	4,771	20,129	4,326	7,960	[illegible]
9	Strafford	102,412	5,127,390	1,146,464	767,964	1,923	4,227	2,602	4,027	[illegible]
10	Sullivan	221,310	6,069,230	1,574,039	1,367,007	3,615	6,832	3,122	39,078	[illegible]

TABLE XCV.—*Selected Statistics of Agriculture*—1870—Continued.

STATE OF NEVADA.

PRODUCED.										
Wheat.							Potatoes.			
Spring.	Winter.	Rye.	Indian corn.	Oats.	Barley.	Wool.	Irish.	Butter.	Hay.	
Bushels.	*Bushels.*	*Bushels.*	*Bushels.*	*Bushels.*	*Bushels.*	*Pounds.*	*Bushels.*	*Pounds.*	*Tons.*	
50	......	......	......	400	7,145	2,224	440	500	559	1
12,781	......	......	970	37,714	40,331	......	20,405	43,870	7,758	2
4,385	......	......	......	1,458	30,560	......	9,841	1,700	406	3
121,600	62,800	......	......	800	103,920	......	1,980	......	4,405	4
4,419	......	......	......	450	30,209	1,400	5,504	5,050	2,219	5
1,128	235	......	......	2,062	29,307	4,600	17,599	20,950	2,245	6
......	2,995	......	6,080	......	4,200	4,690	260	4,420	1,169	7
......	......	55	545	555	......	......	1,765	2,600	792	8
1,314	......	......	......	1,390	14,200	......	7,065	4,750	1,138	9
2,160	1,545	80	1,245	2,270	9,320	......	22,945	8,450	901	10
......	10,430	......	......	......	2,900	165	......	......	546	11
......	......	......	......	......	4,300	......	......	......	......	12
......	......	......	......	......	......	......	......	......	......	13
......	2,874	175	820	8,825	17,250	......	17,570	9,690	5,399	14
......	......	......	......	......	1,750	13,950	23,875	8,900	6,318	15

STATE OF NEW HAMPSHIRE.

PRODUCED.											
Wheat.							Potatoes.	Dairy products.			
Spring.	Winter.	Rye.	Indian corn.	Oats.	Barley.	Wool.	Irish.	Butter.	Cheese.	Hay.	
Bushels.	*Bushels.*	*Bushels.*	*Bushels.*	*Bushels.*	*Bushels.*	*Pounds.*	*Bushels.*	*Pounds.*	*Pounds.*	*Tons.*	
20,745	129	1,862	90,687	37,837	2,817	38,549	220,705	397,036	81,298	36,149	1
17,022	12	1,860	106,383	59,853	970	32,766	327,694	504,194	16,481	43,052	2
3,468	1,901	7,165	146,040	104,601	19,889	110,529	263,791	531,601	63,278	56,975	3
15,708	......	2,284	19,227	185,674	2,363	63,666	811,569	419,462	31,578	40,795	4
56,680	1,122	8,221	198,165	390,172	9,138	446,197	1,078,208	1,095,623	189,602	140,220	5
15,030	350	10,070	163,801	74,716	15,677	42,441	349,692	718,696	58,261	68,089	6
31,018	385	5,068	189,788	103,525	6,489	144,673	472,131	743,386	191,298	78,278	7
7,997	68	6,639	165,843	51,316	21,003	28,240	456,227	674,208	74,226	65,604	8
5,092	30	1,968	59,761	13,938	13,531	15,752	248,681	302,149	42,667	28,903	9
16,462	402	2,983	138,071	124,819	13,945	206,629	286,721	576,725	100,429	54,583	10

TABLE XCV.—*Selected Statistics of Agriculture*—1870—Continued.

STATE OF NEW JERSEY.

	Counties.	Improved land.	Value of farms.	Total (estimated) value of all farm productions, including betterments and additions to stock.	LIVE STOCK.						
					Value of all live stock.	Horses.	Mules and asses.	Milch cows.	Working oxen.	Sheep.	Swine.
		Acres	*Dollars.*	*Dollars.*	*Dollars.*	*No.*	*No.*	*No.*	*No.*	*No.*	*No.*
1	Atlantic	18, 432	2, 628, 540	361, 918	153, 163	727	95	953	30	274	1, 3[illegible]
2	Bergen	69, 082	19, 143, 150	1, 405, 968	842, 598	3, 535	292	4, 076	513	473	2, 9[illegible]
3	Burlington	180, 775	23, 616, 049	4, 908, 639	2, 229, 183	6, 407	1, 25[illegible]	14, 796	91	16, 6[illegible]	15, 7[illegible]
4	Camden	67, 739	8, 793, 480	2, 072, 298	708, 479	2, 838	543	4, 555	13	990	6, [illegible]
5	Cape May	21, 402	1, 683, 430	318, 609	196, 100	816	4	1, 545	13	392	1, 3[illegible]
6	Cumberland	74, 241	9, 515, 930	2, 254, 906	831, 735	3, 439	314	4, 444	58	3, 221	5, 6[illegible]
7	Essex	20, 964	8, 810, 100	806, 638	403, 680	1, 426	23	2, 858	191	114	1, 1[illegible]
8	Gloucester	98, 122	10, 800, 430	3, 161, 117	974, 159	4, 574	348	5, 523	6	2, 704	10, 3[illegible]
9	Hudson	1, 762	3, 134, 000	312, 920	73, 457	252	7	335	7	3	2[illegible]
10	Hunterdon	223, 059	21, 797, 348	3, 885, 830	2, 337, 936	9, 520	689	12, 983	119	22, 790	15, 3[illegible]
11	Mercer	108, 400	14, 102, 100	2, 332, 203	1, 195, 593	4, 464	660	6, 801	42	9, 384	6, 7[illegible]
12	Middlesex	115, 021	16, 896, 100	2, 178, 202	1, 206, 797	4, 888	719	6, 135	223	3, 449	6, 6[illegible]
13	Monmouth	156, 777	22, 280, 815	3, 736, 215	1, 711, 606	6, 035	1, 254	8, 033	55	14, 099	10, 8[illegible]
14	Morris	130, 204	15, 000, 520	2, 127, 211	1, 401, 712	5, 170	316	8, 595	808	8, 770	7, 0[illegible]
15	Ocean	23, 653	3, 218, 500	563, 770	286, 995	982	346	1, 755	70	1, 470	2, 3[illegible]
16	Passaic	46, 253	7, 174, 170	653, 829	585, 908	1, 539	179	3, 299	704	1, 686	1, 0[illegible]
17	Salem	122, 021	13, 661, 904	2, 991, 792	1, 227, 814	5, 155	630	7, 362	10	6, 668	2, 6[illegible]
18	Somerset	157, 276	17, 189, 580	2, 731, 190	1, 524, 405	6, 263	638	9, 992	168	7, 302	7, 8[illegible]
19	Sussex	157, 403	13, 264, 703	2, 526, 710	1, 660, 947	4, 230	171	17, 376	502	3, 976	14, 41[illegible]
20	Union	27, 349	8, 893, 600	684, 898	373, 354	1, 428	35	2, 780	163	469	1, 11[illegible]
21	Warren	155, 939	15, 918, 927	2, 710, 115	1, 557, 812	6, 020	282	9, 145	48	14, 362	12, 3[illegible]

STATE OF NEW YORK.

	Counties.	Improved land.	Value of farms.	Total (estimated) value of all farm productions, including betterments and additions to stock.	LIVE STOCK.					
					Value of all live stock.	Horses.	Milch cows.	Working oxen.	Sheep.	Swine.
		Acres.	*Dollars.*	*Dollars.*	*Dollars.*	*No.*	*No.*	*No.*	*No.*	*No.*
1	Albany	248, 562	22, 382, 713	4, 104, 540	2, 485, 578	9, 150	12, 480	1, 160	31, 315	7, 54[illegible]
2	Allegany	354, 804	18, 232, 213	4, 319, 981	3, 597, 066	11, 705	27, 849	1, 672	79, 054	7, 85[illegible]
3	Broome	244, 424	17, 653, 310	3, 828, 791	2, 898, 638	7, 547	24, 649	1, 386	20, 134	8, 20[illegible]
4	Cattaragus	362, 605	22, 914, 176	5, 224, 297	4, 192, 522	10, 687	44, 463	2, 220	26, 739	10, 73[illegible]
5	Cayuga	334, 376	32, 712, 555	5, 706, 417	3, 995, 019	14, 453	21, 332	626	58, 915	14, 92[illegible]
6	Chautauqua	425, 220	33, 061, 755	6, 103, 495	4, 880, 586	13, 244	46, 990	1, 530	40, 404	13, 4[illegible]
7	Chemung	145, 824	11, 714, 795	2, 275, 058	1, 695, 347	5, 217	12, 257	843	15, 257	6, 9[illegible]
8	Chenango	400, 690	27, 048, 542	7, 030, 507	5, 151, 660	10, 389	51, 294	913	26, 472	9, 5[illegible]
9	Clinton	224, 898	10, 067, 945	2, 499, 589	1, 655, 867	7, 883	10, 972	364	40, 391	4, 7[illegible]
10	Columbia	313, 762	26, 450, 746	4, 640, 317	2, 992, 311	9, 101	14, 030	2, 622	53, 798	8, 8[illegible]
11	Cortland	231, 875	16, 832, 124	3, 737, 081	3, 185, 010	6, 808	32, 905	397	12, 503	6, 2[illegible]
12	Delaware	438, 159	23, 435, 701	6, 384, 043	4, 741, 357	10, 295	46, 699	2, 866	33, 481	9, 55[illegible]
13	Dutchess	376, 302	39, 732, 863	5, 524, 291	4, 744, 712	10, 397	27, 209	4, 826	35, 422	13, 54[illegible]
14	Erie	425, 927	34, 577, 979	6, 748, 527	4, 677, 925	16, 154	40, 323	887	33, 394	17, 04[illegible]
15	Essex	235, 984	6, 843, 040	1, 835, 568	1, 515, 379	5, 664	8, 026	743	62, 664	2, 9[illegible]
16	Franklin	192, 392	9, 650, 833	2, 697, 647	1, 738, 339	6, 816	17, 138	732	25, 130	4, 6[illegible]
17	Fulton	152, 099	7, 772, 385	2, 053, 662	1, 547, 673	4, 001	11, 197	910	16, 099	5, 2[illegible]
18	Genesee	232, 624	21, 185, 076	4, 080, 086	2, 521, 990	10, 411	10, 485	226	73, 884	8, 4[illegible]
19	Greene	231, 406	14, 734, 775	3, 051, 687	2, 131, 582	5, 902	14, 825	1, 564	12, 778	6, 17[illegible]
20	Hamilton	23, 892	613, 488	201, 158	195, 628	606	1, 063	395	3, 748	51[illegible]

TABLE XCV.—*Selected Statistics of Agriculture*—1870—Continued.

STATE OF NEW JERSEY.

PRODUCED.										
Wheat.							Potatoes.			
Spring.	Winter.	Rye.	Indian corn.	Oats.	Buckwheat.	Wool.	Irish.	Sweet.	Butter.	
Bushels.	Bushels.	Bushels.	Bushels.	Bushels.	Bushels.	Pounds.	Bushels.	Bushels.	Pounds.	
63	7, 135	3, 349	47, 488	1, 921	1, 492	199	31, 702	18, 514	33, 036	1
50	8, 738	31, 719	146, 140	45, 533	24, 009	706	209, 162	135	323, 919	2
....	200, 120	102, 411	983, 879	175, 738	11, 251	47, 247	581, 955	114, 517	494, 769	3
....	85, 284	27, 036	320, 774	17, 808	829	3, 210	376, 369	113, 523	206, 775	4
....	19, 064	171	86, 218	6, 648	157	1, 095	22, 360	21, 193	68, 319	5
....	140, 549	4, 314	507, 539	98, 079	10, 756	11, 262	203, 856	216, 987	209, 140	6
5	7, 574	6, 249	66, 192	22, 107	4, 049	....	73, 060	20	125, 213	7
....	123, 181	20, 334	457, 236	27, 543	4, 244	8, 122	411, 872	762, 024	334, 574	8
....	300	597	2, 575	942	20	....	2, 534	....	950	9
215	340, 178	26, 729	1, 021, 251	902, 737	41, 527	67, 863	86, 807	526	965, 243	10
40	149, 198	16, 505	545, 547	428, 143	11, 415	25, 425	222, 207	9, 724	500, 342	11
7	106, 151	15, 967	423, 843	271, 332	11, 772	8, 639	248, 830	12, 391	418, 434	12
689	175, 784	46, 567	760, 479	180, 461	3, 282	41, 582	1, 263, 403	50, 892	415, 307	13
96	80, 871	23, 776	608, 024	290, 721	40, 764	18, 361	168, 611	273	535, 274	14
....	9, 273	13, 768	106, 969	10, 228	3, 380	4, 425	52, 719	8, 760	75, 926	15
27	2, 695	15, 223	68, 407	36, 467	13, 308	6, 487	87, 950	....	159, 418	16
....	259, 777	5, 345	756, 342	164, 678	5, 957	11, 656	350, 955	220, 574	373, 849	17
....	218, 766	12, 872	561, 136	700, 515	6, 731	22, 457	86, 684	....	587, 093	18
24	64, 508	105, 306	432, 776	268, 477	72, 870	11, 959	81, 006	....	1, 455, 788	19
33	5, 306	4, 215	94, 618	36, 948	4, 312	355	61, 544	....	114, 763	20
920	294, 882	84, 252	747, 981	322, 804	72, 858	45, 557	81, 823	131	867, 831	21

STATE OF NEW YORK.

PRODUCED.											
Wheat.								Potatoes.	Dairy products.		
Spring.	Winter.	Rye.	Indian corn.	Oats.	Barley.	Buckwheat.	Wool.	Irish.	Butter.	Cheese.	
Bush.	Bushels.	Bush.	Bushels.	Bushels.	Bushels.	Bushels.	Pounds.	Bushels.	Pounds.	Pounds.	
6, 320	8, 539	129, 535	165, 350	784, 146	37, 205	160, 504	137, 641	637, 058	1, 142, 783	10, 985	1
36, 945	98, 776	16, 434	135, 850	800, 600	29, 558	96, 354	410, 168	384, 687	1, 908, 721	220, 880	2
15, 911	47, 292	10, 708	202, 095	623, 661	2, 465	136, 085	72, 137	450, 028	2, 961, 378	31, 540	3
29, 065	25, 861	9, 271	160, 602	763, 387	18, 801	29, 754	110, 063	340, 803	2, 700, 265	889, 132	4
8, 321	613, 916	2, 459	703, 148	916, 168	732, 140	65, 758	324, 792	397, 747	2, 392, 238	75, 573	5
36, 426	82, 423	972	254, 110	755, 451	43, 927	14, 097	193, 891	314, 873	5, 049, 037	773, 830	6
28, 067	134, 367	13, 547	215, 305	480, 161	50, 491	116, 152	48, 983	138, 573	1, 203, 401	49, 110	7
5, 781	13, 637	5, 212	228, 921	584, 429	10, 091	33, 308	117, 546	398, 045	5, 319, 814	280, 114	8
31, 317	93	16, 514	106, 256	520, 609	23, 159	92, 443	151, 525	844, 703	965, 608	61, 022	9
2, 239	1, 693	426, 408	336, 281	942, 307	11, 053	108, 971	233, 196	678, 480	1, 227, 274	22, 173	10
7, 145	18, 293	1, 883	151, 810	389, 667	27, 704	26, 378	59, 160	244, 527	3, 431, 135	826, 273	11
9, 030	2, 467	26, 120	126, 097	689, 084	4, 345	162, 585	130, 472	432, 443	6, 135, 715	42, 578	12
1, 208	86, 713	174, 194	509, 608	700, 100	15, 092	45, 229	135, 275	403, 687	1, 232, 252	35, 946	13
18, 991	367, 202	58, 283	346, 122	1, 125, 339	246, 551	21, 804	158, 353	643, 932	2, 149, 358	503, 073	14
18, 792	1, 058	11, 726	100, 662	317, 790	5, 791	49, 184	260, 800	406, 122	993, 974	46, 998	15
34, 936	113	20, 249	69, 005	362, 540	15, 521	47, 548	106, 270	1, 068, 083	1, 628, 045	47, 271	16
617	3, 913	12, 938	107, 428	303, 914	8, 925	62, 178	56, 761	200, 949	667, 152	255, 473	17
8, 236	714, 138	2, 686	428, 710	509, 690	380, 466	21, 447	461, 337	275, 717	883, 721	86, 246	18
8, 745	2, 712	72, 016	138, 889	378, 422	2, 338	97, 947	52, 147	276, 787	1, 538, 203	1, 752	19
94	260	113	5, 781	21, 980	447	6, 392	8, 873	46, 317	78, 312	17, 030	20

TABLE XCV.—*Selected Statistics of Agriculture*—1870—Continued.

STATE OF NEW YORK—Continued.

	Counties.	Improved land.	Value of farms.	Total (estimated) value of all farm productions, including betterments and additions to stock.	LIVE STOCK.				
					Value of all live stock.	Horses.	Milch cows.	Working oxen.	Sheep.
		Acres.	*Dollars.*	*Dollars.*	*Dollars.*	*No.*	*No.*	*No.*	*No.*
21	Herkimer	296, 629	27, 429, 169	5, 707, 902	4, 422, 250	8, 299	48, 547	278	6, 964
22	Jefferson	554, 155	33, 432, 152	8, 276, 348	5, 809, 161	15, 564	72, 920	557	26, 390
23	Kings	11, 031	6, 808, 865	1, 097, 392	289, 216	1, 241	1, 148	8	......
24	Lewis	233, 704	15, 181, 008	3, 837, 797	2, 635, 706	6, 547	32, 298	1, 120	8, 384
25	Livingston	292, 713	25, 674, 042	5, 121, 380	3, 284, 779	11, 509	11, 109	352	113, 933
26	Madison	307, 324	26, 568, 018	5, 842, 436	4, 059, 272	10, 084	36, 088	523	24, 928
27	Monroe	350, 575	43, 077, 031	7, 522, 571	4, 337, 656	17, 151	16, 163	277	70, 546
28	Montgomery	209, 234	19, 455, 515	3, 966, 268	2, 794, 451	7, 606	26, 317	294	12, 884
29	New York	1, 149	9, 144, 475	373, 534	188, 750	323	284	2	......
30	Niagara	249, 870	25, 621, 272	4, 871, 319	2, 746, 917	12, 218	11, 594	154	53, 382
31	Oneida	496, 463	40, 166, 660	8, 818, 277	6, 290, 803	15, 231	65, 264	1, 100	25, 812
32	Onondaga	360, 147	37, 222, 291	6, 910, 394	4, 563, 992	15, 162	29, 394	508	63, 265
33	Ontario	321, 875	31, 471, 539	5, 933, 074	3, 709, 077	13, 324	11, 729	328	131, 465
34	Orange	305, 071	35, 558, 445	7, 005, 900	4, 672, 529	10, 498	43, 830	1, 463	6, 980
35	Orleans	188, 961	18, 693, 109	3, 386, 468	1, 924, 016	8, 883	7, 731	244	49, 615
36	Oswego	323, 252	22, 956, 268	5, 292, 437	3, 979, 463	12, 057	35, 820	1, 523	20, 154
37	Otsego	450, 742	33, 512, 709	6, 870, 260	5, 308, 286	13, 462	45, 603	849	43, 408
38	Putnam	91, 495	10, 732, 460	1, 847, 098	1, 184, 962	2, 184	10, 220	1, 460	2, 119
39	Queens	112, 703	26, 720, 700	4, 605, 626	1, 789, 195	7, 733	8, 627	569	3, 838
40	Rensselaer	301, 498	25, 601, 729	4, 383, 412	2, 812, 000	9, 372	16, 813	1, 358	54, 998
41	Richmond	11, 879	4, 328, 609	306, 663	229, 230	756	841	174	23
42	Rockland	31, 089	5, 933, 900	629, 237	408, 906	1, 604	2, 271	222	221
43	Saratoga	313, 714	21, 339, 426	4, 072, 943	2, 856, 984	9, 200	15, 779	1, 261	40, 513
44	Schenectady	103, 726	7, 115, 793	1, 326, 709	974, 985	3, 816	6, 185	168	7, 938
45	Schoharie	278, 733	18, 494, 894	3, 831, 478	2, 811, 382	8, 634	23, 256	1, 488	29, 293
46	Schuyler	142, 440	11, 819, 673	2, 512, 275	1, 554, 379	5, 665	7, 440	389	40, 235
47	Seneca	167, 360	18, 294, 264	3, 415, 736	1, 975, 353	8, 314	7, 073	130	27, 063
48	Steuben	478, 710	26, 678, 047	6, 284, 820	4, 846, 858	15, 042	30, 329	2, 993	145, 645
49	St. Lawrence	664, 823	37, 661, 214	9, 598, 071	6, 739, 900	24, 126	87, 293	1, 612	62, 632
50	Suffolk	132, 033	16, 324, 870	2, 813, 462	1, 930, 587	7, 112	9, 269	570	14, 412
51	Sullivan	155, 563	8, 182, 347	2, 382, 749	1, 937, 616	4, 168	13, 987	4, 369	12, 352
52	Tioga	185, 116	13, 431, 805	2, 952, 907	2, 072, 537	6, 402	16, 424	933	19, 668
53	Tompkins	221, 989	19, 007, 784	3, 867, 070	2, 639, 018	8, 804	16, 402	762	35, 372
54	Ulster	279, 140	21, 051, 469	4, 215, 729	2, 535, 689	8, 928	17, 640	3, 261	14, 119
55	Warren	126, 622	4, 648, 455	1, 319, 897	966, 055	3, 158	5, 944	1, 222	20, 333
56	Washington	353, 761	29, 113, 663	4, 924, 103	3, 263, 426	10, 222	18, 352	554	102, 045
57	Wayne	284, 451	27, 020, 485	5, 110, 301	3, 371, 486	13, 284	16, 208	589	53, 942
58	Westchester	177, 052	36, 861, 860	3, 332, 680	2, 491, 893	5, 828	17, 321	3, 062	2, 391
59	Wyoming	282, 926	17, 717, 480	3, 967, 573	3, 004, 076	9, 520	24, 331	375	56, 823
60	Yates	101, 660	15, 118, 257	2, 940, 115	1, 906, 532	6, 692	6, 511	136	71, 439

TABLE XCV.—*Selected Statistics of Agriculture*—1870—Continued.

STATE OF NEW YORK—Continued.

PRODUCED.										
Wheat.							Potatoes.	Dairy products.		
Winter.	Rye.	Indian corn.	Oats.	Barley.	Buckwheat.	Wool.	Irish.	Butter.	Cheese.	
Bushels.	*Bush.*	*Bushels.*	*Bushels.*	*Bushels.*	*Bushels.*	*Pounds.*	*Bushels.*	*Pounds.*	*Pounds.*	
8,844	7,350	128,953	551,179	60,288	41,806	25,918	367,805	1,212,051	5,101,654	21
46,816	36,609	221,531	1,058,227	415,704	23,837	104,450	507,349	4,883,508	2,543,654	22
5,355	1,341	44,600	3,375	400	....	....	547,375	1,540	....	23
5,034	9,546	38,414	445,667	69,828	16,055	32,631	353,016	2,080,259	977,547	24
869,829	13,498	579,313	779,189	465,363	42,140	605,341	313,274	1,069,300	39,322	25
144,476	1,282	286,284	737,824	133,016	29,273	129,813	418,990	1,575,027	280,776	26
1,050,448	37,370	802,261	1,217,955	480,968	19,471	385,443	990,998	1,631,050	39,558	27
58,941	11,714	175,654	662,516	86,605	100,769	58,847	194,041	1,174,822	1,514,482	28
....	....	....	....	....	....	....	6,135	....	....	29
941,963	38,399	396,642	790,243	215,988	17,973	296,458	236,026	1,392,038	57,596	30
58,897	18,561	377,906	968,215	113,462	45,764	100,456	878,434	3,651,127	1,228,459	31
551,200	6,758	566,558	1,119,263	541,770	51,249	339,740	589,816	2,375,577	821,562	32
784,633	11,373	727,661	898,568	557,084	37,204	743,306	584,259	1,288,820	96,493	33
102,941	66,625	459,343	412,625	442	28,335	16,832	394,732	1,403,409	33,800	34
540,224	7,023	306,972	430,768	142,785	23,063	266,292	245,097	793,562	23,092	35
53,328	37,714	312,903	540,842	28,295	55,752	81,200	513,203	2,720,914	1,089,228	36
23,391	24,274	250,901	990,727	41,003	130,692	199,937	626,836	3,566,286	828,439	37
2,599	9,375	89,934	49,673	50	9,302	3,707	101,595	277,759	240	38
83,103	58,576	535,796	164,599	7,063	24,685	11,254	733,652	362,250	95	39
2,552	187,383	211,968	717,845	11,747	49,702	235,406	1,504,209	1,271,128	365,414	40
4,110	3,427	35,083	12,001	625	368	....	34,863	29,154	....	41
4,864	12,944	57,046	30,781	....	11,987	655	85,694	144,588	300	42
12,854	173,509	381,541	581,674	20,700	144,985	194,792	1,236,831	1,426,308	83,277	43
3,207	53,730	103,533	233,199	43,465	67,651	29,393	392,902	557,770	18,025	44
46,735	82,432	113,097	750,091	40,127	231,230	126,903	329,488	2,190,068	112,421	45
207,153	21,408	178,074	520,160	269,945	118,986	221,749	137,896	853,374	40,579	46
536,011	3,054	490,366	627,190	409,340	22,995	166,416	182,704	812,811	3,160	47
314,522	72,792	344,299	1,538,117	207,024	286,102	700,704	543,677	2,834,636	233,438	48
12,078	35,295	174,840	1,077,345	196,421	57,078	281,962	1,217,809	8,419,605	1,710,082	49
184,548	35,436	515,099	322,069	11,404	20,800	47,168	551,341	564,766	2,280	50
5,023	49,025	181,551	231,934	593	130,421	22,011	236,881	1,183,642	1,425	51
82,484	14,643	229,395	622,379	5,320	167,674	79,432	398,770	1,907,767	75,204	52
256,940	21,167	422,411	737,741	236,183	143,917	169,867	273,941	1,834,029	27,960	53
41,042	107,502	394,004	447,837	1,120	132,515	41,505	688,435	1,631,956	273	54
1,366	14,365	92,322	127,261	124	55,142	78,653	275,701	533,467	26,245	55
5,802	105,932	384,702	761,489	6,021	58,479	507,183	2,141,464	1,606,457	225,002	56
467,827	8,367	635,309	924,719	408,962	29,707	299,907	429,791	1,615,325	136,186	57
23,280	31,457	263,211	196,846	289	9,531	6,479	425,626	430,737	1,200	58
198,210	6,912	193,249	514,862	164,958	42,314	355,661	243,624	1,561,291	709,935	50
378,096	28,375	337,983	507,165	354,067	30,608	402,176	169,692	670,272	41,614	60

TABLE XCV.—*Selected Statistics of Agriculture*—1870—Continued.

STATE OF NORTH CAROLINA.

	Counties.	Improved land.	Value of farms.	Total (estimated) value of all farm productions, including betterments and additions to stock.	LIVE STOCK.					
					Value of all live stock.	Horses.	Mules and asses.	Milch cows.	Working oxen.	Sheep.
		Acres.	*Dollars.*	*Dollars.*	*Dollars.*	*No.*	*No.*	*No.*	*No.*	*No.*
1	Alamance	80, 543	772, 989	809, 915	286, 347	2, 039	478	2, 823	137	7, 270
2	Alexander	32, 137	550, 708	292, 268	167, 033	837	419	1, 620	320	5, 061
3	Alleghany	45, 298	526, 862	934, 368	179, 217	1, 032	128	1, 904	386	7, 136
4	Anson	54, 535	699, 925	1, 102, 066	225, 263	876	895	2, 116	815	[illegible]
5	Ashe	60, 147	847, 548	346, 441	260, 234	1, 761	201	3, 308	604	11, 505
6	Beaufort	35, 161	481, 471	496, 161	178, 311	706	339	2, 469	440	[illegible]
7	Bertie	78, 713	1, 036, 101	862, 509	264, 096	1, 063	724	2, 454	579	3, 453
8	Bladen	28, 332	222, 227	371, 113	190, 884	478	360	2, 380	621	4, 398
9	Brunswick	21, 019	376, 432	291, 062	161, 030	372	168	2, 777	892	3, 555
10	Buncombe	66, 135	1, 703, 115	771, 337	459, 808	1, 966	907	4, 151	307	12, 330
11	Burke	33, 275	595, 096	604, 705	175, 390	800	602	1, 719	230	4, 798
12	Cabarrus	72, 492	1, 205, 471	831, 267	322, 933	1, 797	1, 035	2, 469	62	4, 067
13	Caldwell	42, 686	856, 910	390, 002	228, 798	868	526	2, 223	643	5, 970
14	Camden	34, 836	531, 296	337, 789	123, 773	576	177	828	151	1, 073
15	Carteret	10, 836	179, 290	151, 038	72, 529	542	100	935	290	1, 099
16	Caswell	74, 204	1, 129, 700	849, 462	249, 262	1, 543	747	2, 126	166	2, 765
17	Catawba	39, 203	607, 424	350, 252	152, 563	1, 252	597	1, 458	45	4, 644
18	Chatham	122, 750	1, 169, 981	1, 103, 148	660, 297	2, 561	1, 470	5, 410	301	15, 531
19	Cherokee	26, 858	480, 909	203, 743	160, 325	841	194	2, 042	906	6, 093
20	Chowan	36, 637	542, 278	410, 458	106, 089	451	291	637	110	581
21	Clay	13, 991	323, 965	174, 323	131, 155	587	223	945	292	3, 154
22	Cleaveland	76, 099	686, 785	581, 919	254, 297	1, 301	1, 002	2, 577	228	8, 036
23	Columbus	25, 785	161, 127	691, 123	121, 507	368	219	1, 960	854	5, 383
24	Craven	45, 089	844, 404	821, 567	265, 883	897	440	2, 484	787	4, 203
25	Cumberland	37, 332	637, 362	536, 984	230, 620	743	558	2, 025	295	4, 724
26	Currituck	39, 687	510, 874	411, 790	140, 070	711	108	1, 154	228	2, 409
27	Dare	278	14, 193	8, 100	3, 655	27	3	44	16	6
28	Davidson	111, 230	1, 395, 298	1, 126, 404	373, 136	2, 850	798	3, 702	186	13, 440
29	Davie	42, 878	626, 542	403, 674	135, 922	896	296	1, 215	70	3, 351
30	Duplin	83, 957	649, 750	809, 962	302, 520	1, 176	466	3, 100	994	[illegible]
31	Edgecombe	108, 019	3, 353, 471	2, 348, 276	501, 020	1, 164	1, 919	1, 403	877	1, 656
32	Forsyth	114, 126	1, 173, 202	557, 778	200, 524	1, 546	405	2, 166	99	6, 606
33	Franklin	82, 926	944, 916	883, 898	298, 383	1, 442	604	2, 503	1, 018	3, 621
34	Gaston	62, 591	1, 294, 000	817, 672	324, 946	1, 218	1, 166	2, 709	98	7, 362
35	Gates	53, 382	451, 750	341, 079	137, 820	774	158	1, 353	314	1, 663
36	Granville	149, 968	2, 007, 031	1, 021, 975	446, 556	2, 722	733	4, 073	732	8, 021
37	Greene	55, 450	1, 534, 503	842, 785	205, 963	779	642	982	512	1, 345
38	Guilford	156, 567	2, 093, 277	1, 066, 207	473, 921	2, 790	905	4, 791	615	13, 302
39	Halifax	146, 700	2, 875, 197	1, 546, 965	489, 377	1, 456	1, 473	2, 347	1, 499	2, 156
40	Harnett	29, 114	509, 679	425, 288	102, 288	588	352	1, 791	482	3, 793
41	Haywood	35, 750	591, 148	358, 520	273, 096	1, 357	366	2, 539	325	7, 844
42	Henderson	42, 569	1, 015, 192	469, 231	239, 719	825	360	2, 249	858	6, 235
43	Hertford	53, 499	730, 355	962, 322	222, 196	915	357	1, 174	467	2, 259
44	Hyde	24, 655	861, 775	227, 614	66, 940	378	99	681	332	978
45	Iredell	74, 240	1, 434, 977	745, 445	333, 925	1, 920	980	2, 738	166	9, 723
46	Jackson	24, 882	415, 733	308, 737	188, 347	1, 022	170	2, 136	590	5, 028
47	Johnston	76, 829	871, 903	613, 921	365, 894	1, 366	788	3, 253	1, 649	5, 653
48	Jones	30, 021	330, 495	190, 435	75, 814	251	256	683	230	1, 610
49	Lenoir	71, 896	731, 917	968, 716	200, 955	722	684	1, 300	502	1, 785
50	Lincoln	57, 376	828, 644	451, 857	179, 367	1, 022	681	1, 739	50	4, 971
51	Macon	34, 795	510, 612	353, 442	270, 548	1, 307	413	2, 379	679	7, 848
52	Madison	32, 804	527, 216	274, 004	175, 426	739	319	1, 912	447	6, 670
53	Martin	48, 830	1, 061, 956	518, 026	173, 503	696	566	1, 232	435	2, 253
54	McDowell	31, 496	581, 325	205, 709	124, 483	618	500	1, 348	163	3, 054
55	Mecklenburg	103, 602	2, 645, 482	1, 352, 673	580, 286	2, 117	1, 822	3, 353	143	5, 403
56	Mitchell	18, 385	258, 205	177, 089	135, 803	665	99	1, 416	244	5, 142
57	Montgomery	46, 296	411, 125	399, 202	186, 142	1, 144	321	2, 278	331	8, 320
58	Moore	58, 971	380, 188	717, 766	272, 729	1, 435	644	3, 616	522	10, 072
59	Nash	52, 534	608, 289	534, 590	181, 109	845	444	1, 443	911	2, 619
60	New Hanover	46, 493	651, 180	634, 083	230, 450	683	410	2, 456	605	3, 736
61	Northampton	104, 697	1, 746, 833	1, 123, 120	341, 766	1, 317	806	1, 022	913	2, 955
62	Onslow	37, 618	349, 640	372, 019	142, 230	469	323	1, 700	431	1, 849
63	Orange	73, 745	977, 308	737, 196	287, 631	2, 006	622	3, 216	294	7, 171
64	Pasquotank	44, 616	1, 274, 945	683, 372	179, 106	738	329	1, 016	417	702
65	Perquimans	47, 806	796, 648	534, 499	144, 663	733	374	1, 101	298	847
66	Person	49, 763	442, 203	528, 069	232, 992	1, 383	[illegible]	[illegible]	313	4, 829

TABLE XCV.—*Selected Statistics of Agriculture*—1870—Continued.

STATE OF NORTH CAROLINA.

PRODUCED.									
heat.							Potatoes.		
Winter.	Indian corn.	Oats.	Rice.	Tobacco.	Cotton.	Wool.	Irish.	Sweet.	
Bushels.	*Bushels.*	*Bushels.*	*Pounds.*	*Pounds.*	*Bales.*	*Pounds.*	*Bushels.*	*Bushels.*	
86, 284	177, 772	66, 274	....	155, 570	3	9, 711	13, 444	11, 451	1
20, 142	137, 207	37, 865	15	19, 499	1	11, 693	11, 099	12, 581	2
7, 988	43, 309	21, 496	....	802	....	14, 191	8, 779	78	3
32, 620	149, 726	46, 851	....	579	4, 311	6, 538	3, 584	25, 569	4
16, 341	120, 545	42, 350	....	381	....	23, 211	13, 732	....	5
1, 773	179, 994	3, 674	59, 206	3, 245	1, 987	2, 501	3, 893	102, 626	6
1, 541	300, 314	11, 522	60	790	5, 055	6, 284	9, 759	54, 599	7
57	86, 986	3, 214	38, 187	789	146	6, 151	882	68, 123	8
12	56, 211	10	748, 418	528	119	3, 775	1, 890	129, 168	9
66, 492	324, 566	43, 799	....	30, 689	1	24, 347	19, 416	4, 728	10
26, 528	217, 049	31, 010	835	25, 204	8	6, 569	10, 093	12, 342	11
79, 412	268, 560	47, 590	....	....	2, 703	11, 669	6, 948	7, 819	12
24, 455	207, 731	35, 313	690	27, 000	....	10, 462	19, 194	18, 057	13
2, 823	329, 660	10, 430	....	30	58	2, 845	7, 186	24, 635	14
1, 487	32, 260	165	210	....	774	50	60	58, 715	15
80, 597	237, 257	93, 646	....	2, 262, 053	1	4, 800	8, 615	12, 546	16
14, 682	142, 876	41, 553	....	25	22	10, 483	4, 540	5, 177	17
123, 712	304, 881	124, 632	100	52, 210	1, 593	12, 803	21, 409	43, 677	18
3, 618	162, 529	18, 098	....	19, 392	70	12, 578	10, 702	8, 368	19
....	137, 647	9, 730	33	189	1, 331	779	4, 740	41, 130	20
6, 061	79, [illegible]	14, 408	....	13, 113	....	5, 811	4, 618	5, 507	21
42, 654	236, 232	67, 794	....	415	520	15, 842	4, 431	37, 882	22
18	65, 972	209	216, 964	2, 430	119	7, 993	1, 791	79, 307	23
1, 657	241, 084	5, 966	55, 386	4, 765	3, 809	4, 780	5, 254	112, 217	24
1, 085	142, 203	13, 491	87	50	484	7, 589	1, 146	57, 361	25
745	270, 699	1, 150	....	....	64	4, 308	14, 380	69, 708	26
....	2, 425	15	....	....	....	....	230	3, 185	27
152, 693	287, 355	120, 459	....	38, 937	100	29, 262	19, 326	16, 300	28
47, 866	186, 821	39, 721	....	247, 555	3	5, 427	1, 323	1, 183	29
402	291, 633	1, 470	**155, 509**	275	1, 785	9, 522	4, 379	135, 581	30
6, 102	488, 800	48, 573	10, 400	65	18, 361	2, 107	7, 410	58, 055	31
66, 518	173, 146	76, 569	....	238, 262	....	9, 749	13, 083	11, 003	32
23, 238	241, 435	31, 659	467	36, 243	3, 356	5, 022	8, 992	30, 135	33
64, 468	338, 023	79, 717	....	3, 640	762	14, 763	9, 288	16, 415	34
9, 412	158, 070	6, 915	....	....	151	1, 441	6, 500	54, 186	35
110, 209	306, 113	115, 593	....	2, 134, 228	277	13, 527	16, 484	34, 298	36
5, 098	223, 988	5, 517	2, 505	393	6, 268	2, 547	5, 924	44, 531	37
132, 783	308, 347	169, 847	50	177, 782	21	31, 461	22, 521	23, 468	38
819	353, 808	25, 367	....	200	11, 716	3, 914	8, 491	28, 169	39
3, 200	125, 410	8, 717	....	6, 225	334	7, 586	2, 564	64, 290	40
40, 734	206, 998	26, 879	....	18, 692	....	15, 299	11, 126	699	41
4, 019	212, 914	21, 101	197	22, 886	1	14, 434	14, 960	7, 377	42
5, 430	189, 079	13, 857	....	....	2, 686	4, 661	12, 392	49, 807	43
21, 319	**163, 916**	11, 633	171, 548	100	235	2, 227	1, 107	8, 923	44
67, 687	315, 972	108, 657	100	67, 071	408	13, 233	9, 552	11, 357	45
13, 560	156, 050	10, 668	....	11, 697	....	10, 634	13, 235	7, 116	46
1, 322	246, 338	14, 402	....	....	4, 108	5, 344	1, 761	132, 277	47
....	96, 383	2, 111	5, 790	6, 030	1, 196	3, 203	1, 7[illegible]9	14, 139	48
3, 373	195, 785	3, 983	27, 690	543	4, 804	2, 746	6, 343	45, 036	49
....	190, 226	52, 396	....	3, 137	242	6, 184	7, 914	12, 572	50
21, 229	163, 199	19, 970	....	26, 739	....	14, 964	10, 837	10, 225	51
29, 749	167, 971	19, 108	....	15, 924	....	12, 007	7, 596	1, 322	52
1, 925	206, 384	3, 264	125	....	3, 607	2, 420	3, 820	47, 709	53
11, 909	176, 364	11, 580	....	300	....	8, 866	5, 394	4, 135	54
65, 596	454, 864	75, 990	....	5, 171	6, 067	8, 014	12, 159	18, 774	55
12, 530	72, 860	21, 311	....	5, 636	....	8, 725	8, 483	527	56
....	118, 589	39, 177	....	13, 992	632	23, 782	8, 863	22, 155	57
56, 328	170, 450	45, 545	....	21, 731	930	14, 209	9, 277	52, 906	58
5, 643	152, 506	14, 356	....	1, 738	3, 697	1, 869	2, 102	24, 907	59
....	133, 176	540	398, 925	....	70	11, 629	4, 192	94, 713	60
13, 572	320, 924	36, 860	....	8, 300	7, 320	3, 348	11, 861	43, 435	61
....	117, 420	125	10, 500	....	881	3, 734	2, 632	62, 186	62
86, 249	193, 161	92, 061	....	530, 442	383	11, 106	18, 157	18, 550	63
21, 786	434, 985	11, 504	....	....	110	1, 077	7, 311	24, 937	64
34, 282	310, 135	27, 519	2	682	593	1, 891	3, 908	32, 851	65
53, 824	138, 085	78, 181	....	1, 2[illegible]7, 150	....	6, 784	9, 150	10, [illegible]	66

TABLE XCV.—*Selected Statistics of Agriculture*—1870—Continued.

STATE OF NORTH CAROLINA—Continued.

	Counties.	Improved land.	Value of farms.	Total (estimated) value of all farm productions, including betterments and additions to stock.	LIVE STOCK.						
					Value of all live stock.	Horses.	Mules and asses.	Milch cows.	Working oxen.	Sheep.	Swine.
		Acres.	*Dollars.*	*Dollars.*	*Dollars.*	*No.*	*No.*	*No.*	*No.*	*No.*	*No.*
67	Pitt	97,342	1,896,965	1,437,592	408,807	1,668	1,074	2,398	900	2,260	[illegible]
68	Polk	16,239	347,606	200,317	97,085	358	261	874	336	1,851	4,[illegible]
69	Randolph	120,272	1,518,108	832,027	448,810	2,844	772	4,787	839	17,101	[illegible]
70	Richmond	51,316	670,193	669,567	222,054	871	768	2,346	381	2,247	13,[illegible]
71	Robeson	77,741	552,220	808,704	314,629	1,152	741	2,915	928	8,396	18,[illegible]
72	Rockingham	76,534	1,401,765	748,671	280,587	1,237	817	2,722	340	4,759	11,[illegible]
73	Rowan	93,440	1,408,361	822,346	352,313	2,654	899	3,529	62	7,663	15,[illegible]
74	Rutherford	52,210	760,471	580,582	228,458	1,142	747	1,966	475	6,496	9,[illegible]
75	Sampson	83,662	513,191	913,875	393,747	1,441	605	3,378	1,149	6,732	22,[illegible]
76	Stanley	41,598	352,580	308,067	175,992	1,333	332	1,725	192	5,705	9,[illegible]
77	Stokes	41,420	613,079	470,116	190,541	916	504	1,862	432	5,482	12,[illegible]
78	Surry	52,899	830,837	446,128	215,008	1,129	364	2,178	820	6,414	11,[illegible]
79	Transylvania	15,096	340,007	156,478	94,968	504	196	1,197	329	4,721	6,[illegible]
80	Tyrrell	17,514	215,896	188,260	65,143	306	149	752	187	1,539	4,[illegible]
81	Union	71,982	378,056	716,987	455,206	1,624	981	3,501	860	8,973	12,[illegible]
82	Wake	119,021	1,816,048	1,714,152	557,305	2,108	1,396	3,895	1,186	6,758	23,[illegible]
83	Warren	110,173	1,608,848	1,573,218	367,719	1,426	658	2,677	1,100	3,409	15,[illegible]
84	Washington	21,215	393,907	296,822	113,199	483	211	941	214	1,606	6,[illegible]
85	Watauga	28,240	239,638	209,278	148,283	812	123	1,957	585	7,039	6,[illegible]
86	Wayne	94,390	1,680,473	1,433,330	339,233	1,162	916	2,091	722	4,102	16,[illegible]
87	Wilkes	82,102	986,086	448,754	272,114	1,529	465	3,318	1,132	8,352	16,[illegible]
88	Wilson	55,412	1,159,690	828,264	259,411	841	683	1,141	677	2,176	9,[illegible]
89	Yadkin	50,988	670,688	570,089	228,879	1,435	479	2,283	331	5,941	12,[illegible]
90	Yancey	23,826	218,651	113,726	116,311	760	190	1,963	290	5,518	[illegible]

STATE OF OHIO.

	Counties.	Improved land.	Value of farms.	Total (estimated) value of all farm productions, including betterments and additions to stock.	LIVE STOCK.						
					Value of all live stock.	Horses.	Mules and asses.	Milch cows.	Working oxen.	Sheep.	Swine.
		Acres.	*Dollars.*	*Dollars.*	*Dollars.*	*No.*	*No.*	*No.*	*No.*	*No.*	*No.*
1	Adams	152,591	5,715,694	1,528,105	913,945	6,140	338	4,520	580	16,335	20,[illegible]
2	Allen	119,287	8,117,216	1,565,908	1,049,034	6,918	195	5,964	90	38,503	22,[illegible]
3	Ashland	189,500	14,121,144	3,968,925	1,596,684	7,702	107	10,299	32	77,308	21,[illegible]
4	Ashtabula	271,276	15,378,315	2,737,930	2,324,215	8,228	88	20,470	539	43,804	5,[illegible]
5	Athens	153,673	7,414,708	1,607,698	1,040,544	5,363	102	5,368	792	57,498	14,[illegible]
6	Auglaize	94,764	6,429,025	3,068,288	804,990	5,631	170	5,214	98	29,678	18,[illegible]
7	Belmont	221,457	16,572,733	2,950,783	1,977,415	9,207	116	7,718	797	162,787	22,[illegible]
8	Brown	199,862	9,376,576	2,196,181	1,215,710	8,113	440	6,326	231	19,269	28,[illegible]
9	Butler	191,028	21,452,774	3,807,719	1,430,912	8,181	306	6,472	28	6,637	27,[illegible]
10	Carroll	183,075	11,939,575	1,685,624	1,434,712	5,628	90	6,314	177	131,069	16,[illegible]
11	Champaign	159,300	14,501,483	3,100,264	1,507,074	7,696	389	5,463	69	38,103	20,[illegible]
12	Clark	168,680	15,492,266	2,798,833	1,569,299	6,716	275	5,570	65	54,225	23,[illegible]
13	Clermont	187,046	14,229,016	2,503,790	1,310,254	8,107	716	6,837	42	12,702	25,[illegible]
14	Clinton	160,132	11,144,679	2,498,142	1,589,975	7,919	486	5,390	69	38,896	32,[illegible]
15	Columbiana	221,714	17,419,789	2,623,912	2,050,642	8,827	116	9,519	101	131,367	15,[illegible]
16	Coshocton	221,228	12,051,120	2,131,943	1,537,465	8,836	109	8,022	216	132,173	22,[illegible]
17	Crawford	156,417	11,634,697	2,227,371	1,329,321	7,170	57	7,001	34	73,771	[illegible]
18	Cuyahoga	197,730	20,270,197	2,398,792	1,396,653	6,902	84	15,641	92	25,875	7,[illegible]
19	Darke	195,236	14,438,481	3,015,830	1,502,227	9,942	216	9,089	233	20,235	31,[illegible]
20	Defiance	83,153	5,588,757	1,136,810	661,608	5,025	68	4,933	121	24,271	10,676
21	Delaware	189,496	14,233,665	2,056,380	1,511,889	7,705	190	6,770	[illegible]	[illegible]	[illegible]
22	Erie	117,276	11,190,256	1,820,362	844,178	4,813	35	4,700	[illegible]	[illegible]	[illegible]

TABLE XCV.—*Selected Statistics of Agriculture*—1870—Continued.

STATE OF NORTH CAROLINA—Continued.

Produced.										
Wheat.								Potatoes.		
Spring.	Winter.	Indian corn.	Oats.	Rice.	Tobacco.	Cotton.	Wool.	Irish.	Sweet.	
Bushels.	*Bushels.*	*Bushels.*	*Bushels.*	*Pounds.*	*Pounds.*	*Bales.*	*Pounds.*	*Bushels.*	*Bushels.*	
859	10, 538	498, 662	7, 635	4, 513	190	8, 814	2, 013	5, 823	71, 735	67
116	3, 692	117, 060	5, 937	....	1, 881	14	2, 551	1, 963	5, 279	68
22	137, 405	264, 924	95, 681	....	24, 399	....	26, 050	18, 880	23, 125	69
6, 640	12, 964	131, 855	21, 350	....	140	5, 130	2, 032	785	43, 364	70
1, 304	968	138, 545	9, 603	69, 486	653	2, 109	14, 081	5, 495	84, 784	71
59	53, 236	218, 469	103, 528	....	1, 441, 971	....	7, 101	16, 159	16, 057	72
44, 955	81, 798	289, 400	119, 132	....	54, 810	520	9, 699	10, 263	8, 748	73
1, 953	22, 452	272, 485	39, 678	130	13, 119	122	9, 509	7, 087	26, 474	74
1, 617	1, 022	281, 381	8, 775	19, 837	7, 523	1, 231	11, 437	1, 662	141, 373	75
63, 575	....	118, 788	42, 037	....	12, 459	201	8, 494	5, 294	10, 435	76
2	33, 448	171, 214	36, 353	....	844, 145	....	6, 381	11, 246	9, 953	77
....	26, 701	190, 171	39, 321	....	254, 226	....	12, 690	14, 707	15, 368	78
....	372	95, 633	190	....	6, 301	....	18, 884	8, 142	3, 101	79
737	....	105, 308	2, 418	17, 804	....	507	2, 355	4, 097	22, 544	80
39, 499	40, 435	203, 032	72, 308	....	8, 262	1, 196	12, 444	8, 167	16, 945	81
28, 373	32, 223	379, 363	80, 804	6, 933	93, 874	7, 015	11, 371	10, 365	99, 976	82
75	47, 409	256, 803	49, 500	24	731, 045	1, 818	6, 774	9, 409	23, 941	83
....	2, 413	152, 038	4, 104	13, 256	75	1, 087	1, 738	5, 297	28, 309	84
143	6, 020	75, 944	18, 724	....	3, 617	....	13, 850	11, 381	940	85
883	8, 530	297, 546	12, 216	22, 996	1, 905	5, 617	8, 348	5, 016	75, 220	86
55	24, 079	202, 590	43, 691	....	32, 236	4	12, 040	16, 460	12, 796	87
....	8, 690	212, 770	10, 588	33	1, 898	5, 225	3, 241	4, 280	36, 353	88
15	42, 094	223, 856	63, 159	....	98, 493	42	11, 123	12, 172	10, 139	89
....	20, 514	113, 683	28, 207	....	5, 211	....	8, 980	791	164	90

STATE OF OHIO.

Produced.										
Wheat.							Potatoes.	Dairy products.		
Spring.	Winter.	Rye.	Indian corn.	Oats.	Barley.	Wool.	Irish.	Butter.	Cheese.	
Bushels.	*Bushels.*	*Bushels.*	*Bushels.*	*Bushels.*	*Bushels.*	*Pounds.*	*Bushels.*	*Pounds.*	*Pounds.*	
....	162, 677	2, 123	772, 899	156, 073	4, 370	52, 208	39, 542	434, 664	885	1
1, 128	314, 036	21, 671	374, 017	209, 209	2, 985	125, 897	52, 905	466, 482	6, 220	2
492	467, 192	8, 052	537, 798	551, 243	17, 755	344, 197	117, 416	668, 473	418, 011	3
8, 359	181, 832	4, 218	382, 556	537, 632	2, 440	197, 464	363, 957	1, 134, 877	1, 193, 089	4
468	123, 277	2, 187	619, 447	96, 012	110	201, 593	78, 721	513, 864	22, 265	5
2, 116	264, 640	13, 046	379, 015	245, 277	34, 584	76, 630	36, 354	246, 085	3, 280	6
5, 796	299, 409	6, 237	1, 181, 615	481, 803	48, 763	674, 178	142, 569	830, 906	1, 454	7
207	199, 398	17, 740	926, 168	196, 305	11, 987	62, 756	95, 510	519, 771	3, 063	8
....	627, 377	1, 864	1, 716, 802	229, 621	277, 016	25, 856	113, 135	548, 878	2, 194	9
56	210, 952	23, 699	417, 864	520, 663	10, 106	538, 589	75, 819	600, 785	225	10
75	724, 285	3, 943	1, 289, 472	244, 073	12, 938	169, 060	74, 277	344, 401	56, 950	11
244	600, 488	18, 295	1, 204, 559	227, 904	14, 820	259, 742	94, 539	449, 334	14, 480	12
99	181, 433	13, 850	878, 027	325, 755	5, 492	39, 425	308, 006	769, 133	625	13
234	329, 568	1, 764	1, 583, 907	109, 238	6, 428	142, 221	64, 682	348, 150	9, 700	14
197	269, 093	25, 175	566, 242	653, 001	11, 010	573, 561	163, 484	848, 882	45, 425	15
380	332, 011	13, 692	1, 098, 184	401, 308	2, 716	547, 709	108, 471	676, 102	2, 585	16
2, 598	481, 918	7, 755	424, 383	461, 905	12, 968	310, 505	78, 498	583, 528	40, 090	17
29, 667	47, 821	19, 707	350, 702	419, 176	5, 831	105, 173	484, 724	786, 430	1, 204, 111	18
293	791, 910	20, 933	1, 063, 030	330, 352	51, 854	63, 623	70, 101	738, 243	653	19
151	246, 242	1, 329	146, 810	128, 111	2, 087	72, 215	70, 825	366, 211	[illegible]	20
7, 084	234, 941	7, 489	992, 760	206, 688	1, 683	475, 301	116, 613	630, 327	[illegible]	21
21, 616	218, 258	3, 300	550, 026	307, 080	22, 865	169, 905	258, 900	330, 358	[illegible]	22

TABLE XCV.—*Selected Statistics of Agriculture*—1870—Continued.

STATE OF OHIO—Continued.

	Counties.	Improved land.	Value of farms.	Total (estimated) value of all farm productions, including betterments and additions to stock.	LIVE STOCK. Value of all live stock.	Horses.	Mules and asses.	Milch cows.	Working oxen.	Sheep.
		Acres.	Dollars.	Dollars.	Dollars.	No.	No.	No.	No.	No.
23	Fairfield	212, 323	17, 952, 097	3, 450, 967	1, 823, 526	8, 728	426	7, 956	138	40, 13
24	Fayette	181, 677	15, 603, 109	4, 206, 842	2, 142, 121	7, 235	528	4, 889	555	31, 39
25	Franklin	201, 313	18, 051, 454	3, 495, 139	2, 019, 368	10, 565	206	7, 841	105	40, 54
26	Fulton	92, 578	7, 189, 890	1, 482, 634	868, 685	4, 924	76	6, 043	268	33, 35
27	Gallia	152, 135	6, 476, 596	1, 447, 320	887, 489	4, 689	222	4, 944	1, 151	23, 74
28	Geauga	182, 650	10, 647, 181	2, 087, 878	1, 713, 580	4, 622	118	18, 674	200	19, 81
29	Greene	165, 485	14, 868, 341	2, 877, 165	1, 549, 739	7, 585	390	5, 741	43	29, 32
30	Guernsey	208, 513	11, 233, 520	2, 043, 431	1, 533, 597	7, 047	127	6, 411	298	151, 64
31	Hamilton	158, 028	27, 723, 353	4, 305, 248	1, 521, 390	8, 531	530	12, 413	111	3, 64
32	Hancock	168, 120	11, 880, 938	2, 375, 421	1, 431, 473	9, 313	109	8, 078	02	56, 62
33	Hardin	95, 497	5, 859, 176	1, 297, 821	796, 664	5, 385	250	4, 272	109	42, 40
34	Harrison	157, 408	11, 972, 620	1, 978, 051	1, 431, 790	4, 844	93	4, 477	301	180, 18
35	Henry	57, 380	4, 440, 804	907, 291	548, 041	3, 764	48	3, 958	210	14, 69
36	Highland	220, 677	12, 115, 509	2, 477, 864	1, 662, 084	9, 227	828	6, 743	251	25, 86
37	Hocking	131, 088	5, 394, 776	1, 155, 242	834, 598	5, 062	191	4, 903	312	36, 36
38	Holmes	161, 029	10, 869, 136	1, 752, 353	1, 049, 314	7, 015	105	7, 006	35	62, 49
39	Huron	198, 110	13, 940, 257	2, 642, 468	1, 618, 845	8, 550	133	10, 113	129	92, 68
40	Jackson	129, 742	5, 050, 415	1, 206, 387	862, 546	4, 294	195	4, 490	830	24, 43
41	Jefferson	166, 205	15, 328, 050	2, 354, 643	1, 711, 544	5, 577	36	5, 429	188	154, 66
42	Knox	242, 595	17, 571, 640	3, 061, 468	1, 814, 755	9, 429	105	8, 542	57	145, 61
43	Lake	102, 821	9, 287, 628	1, 368, 588	900, 766	3, 598	40	5, 409	68	22, 90
44	Lawrence	73, 443	2, 892, 997	917, 726	446, 916	2, 522	111	2, 316	912	8, 51
45	Licking	278, 611	20, 116, 813	3, 471, 261	2, 544, 819	9, 993	201	8, 319	197	220, 96
46	Logan	145, 372	11, 179, 380	1, 988, 384	1, 267, 263	7, 439	240	5, 586	234	54, 47
47	Lorain	228, 458	17, 506, 545	3, 068, 127	2, 551, 333	8, 811	66	21, 444	105	73, 14
48	Lucas	64, 697	8, 020, 342	1, 126, 254	666, 994	3, 875	28	4, 346	166	11, 02
49	Madison	176, 812	10, 713, 942	2, 079, 324	1, 644, 404	5, 626	519	3, 462	217	70, 81
50	Mahoning	179, 866	14, 288, 062	2, 168, 583	1, 719, 516	7, 312	109	8, 688	304	68, 05
51	Marion	146, 245	8, 317, 109	1, 685, 801	1, 263, 210	6, 715	99	4, 897	95	89, 61
52	Medina	193, 950	13, 454, 343	2, 439, 460	1, 871, 744	7, 588	37	15, 621	43	69, 74
53	Meigs	124, 794	6, 576, 131	1, 468, 313	860, 472	4, 929	211	5, 360	825	28, 44
54	Mercer	110, 030	5, 229, 599	1, 090, 590	874, 507	6, 518	149	5, 816	98	26, 66
55	Miami	163, 410	16, 650, 827	2, 993, 974	1, 265, 435	8, 126	157	6, 208	13	16, 12
56	Monroe	176, 110	6, 988, 721	1, 866, 730	1, 154, 392	7, 060	91	8, 358	1, 235	42, 19
57	Montgomery	188, 813	21, 660, 408	3, 628, 371	1, 461, 893	9, 183	108	8, 775	40	7, 09
58	Morgan	159, 628	8, 205, 440	1, 918, 771	1, 223, 275	6, 637	112	5, 795	674	78, 00
59	Morrow	168, 225	12, 689, 310	2, 008, 435	1, 483, 215	7, 985	116	7, 653	66	118, 29
60	Muskingum	264, 966	15, 611, 814	3, 326, 284	1, 890, 529	9, 430	137	9, 379	659	145, 95
61	Noble	165, 155	9, 219, 017	1, 810, 835	1, 242, 629	7, 023	133	5, 822	650	64, 22
62	Ottawa	40, 221	2, 857, 146	791, 807	380, 525	2, 816	14	2, 695	114	21. 48
63	Paulding	23, 850	1, 311, 290	335, 544	214, 949	1, 662	24	1, 693	117	5, 97
64	Perry	177, 856	9, 300, 643	1, 863, 241	1, 243, 442	6, 241	95	6, 340	461	85, 29
65	Pickaway	250, 570	21, 538, 927	4, 215, 401	2, 343, 915	10, 285	543	6, 491	874	24, 62
66	Pike	103, 100	3, 939, 154	979, 376	653, 145	4, 174	268	3, 080	330	14, 26
67	Portage	207, 750	14, 550, 729	2, 669, 520	1, 903, 773	6, 373	56	17, 135	197	45, 38
68	Preble	169, 594	14, 467, 232	2, 793, 214	1, 345, 878	7, 297	136	6, 309	40	10, 19
69	Putnam	77, 671	5, 011, 785	1, 512, 806	783, 632	5, 437	79	5, 242	56	23, 26
70	Richland	211, 025	17, 917, 080	2, 951, 341	1, 721, 428	8, 580	111	8, 979	44	71, 09
71	Ross	215, 731	13, 801, 113	3, 287, 765	1, 765, 097	8, 035	340	5, 532	754	24, 41
72	Sandusky	142, 420	12, 246, 110	1, 042, 887	1, 063, 767	7, 643	66	7, 064	98	41, 96
73	Scioto	85, 074	4, 163, 879	1, 104, 920	560, 887	3, 577	289	3, 281	508	9, 56
74	Seneca	216, 900	17, 933, 407	2, 794, 509	1, 625, 558	10, 302	86	9, 261	55	89, 10
75	Shelby	125, 557	8, 661, 641	1, 944, 059	1, 002, 645	6, 566	125	5, 404	25	27, 80
76	Stark	245, 365	21, 139, 051	3, 385, 641	2, 023, 606	10, 653	56	12, 135	45	81, 30
77	Summit	171, 255	14, 527, 726	2, 511, 048	1, 563, 462	5, 947	22	13, 127	64	36, 69
78	Trumbull	254, 832	16, 677, 276	2, 737, 736	2, 499, 718	8, 067	129	19, 811	265	47, 16
79	Tuscarawas	237, 722	15, 676, 102	2, 901, 896	1, 892, 630	9, 188	135	10, 077	252	128, 30
80	Union	140, 107	10, 628, 135	2, 027, 847	1, 364, 583	6, 876	258	5, 073	92	75, 92
81	Van Wert	69, 869	4, 379, 086	744, 841	585, 954	4, 364	92	4, 340	102	19, 78
82	Vinton	94, 765	3, 340, 474	959, 033	639, 767	3, 205	212	3, 066	612	29, 40
83	Warren	176, 077	17, 773, 860	3, 203, 875	1, 596, 373	7, 801	238	6, 487	31	19, 71
84	Washington	184, 506	10, 432, 746	2, 212, 994	1, 307, 071	7, 047	122	7, 669	1, 148	61, 76
85	Wayne	241, 936	23, 005, 031	3, 138, 220	2, 151, 273	11, 430	155	12, 218	132	69, 22
86	Williams	128, 397	8, 518, 564	1, 506, 359	962, 499	6, 761	69	6, 682	242	39, 77
87	Wood	117, 193	8, 375, 993	1, 023, 020	1, 029, 633	6, 982	81	7, 000	237	33, 03
88	Wyandot	122, 940	8, 132, 510	1, 616, 824	1, 053, 120	5, 398	[illegible]	4, 422	[illegible]	77, 90

TABLE XCV.—*Selected Statistics of Agriculture*—1870—Continued.

STATE OF OHIO—Continued.

PRODUCED.											
Wheat.								Potatoes.	Dairy products.		
Spring.	Winter.	Rye.	Indian corn.	Oats.	Barley.	Wool.	Irish.	Butter.	Cheese.		
Bushels.	*Bushels.*	*Bushels.*	*Bushels.*	*Bushels.*	*Bushels.*	*Pounds.*	*Bushels.*	*Pounds.*	*Pounds.*		
390	553,525	12,721	1,706,216	242,380	24,431	175,239	116,231	609,348	544	23
833	159,687	30,068	2,055,926	66,841	....	134,739	50,929	361,725	310	24
6,027	417,139	15,871	1,826,313	246,217	13,910	144,018	323,525	638,319	1,500	25
200	238,006	3,392	199,725	176,248	475	150,421	106,686	512,290	113,552	26
7	192,551	1,735	626,033	135,688	323	65,293	132,358	438,623	11,005	27
13,177	51,638	4,986	179,319	337,686	1,072	105,811	185,731	619,742	458,384	28
34	643,946	10,671	1,527,647	152,747	22,491	109,591	83,270	370,179	125	29
880	174,162	11,669	685,758	325,676	3,281	617,551	81,885	696,183	1,025	30
157	162,450	22,706	1,246,726	268,089	96,970	12,266	562,537	773,387	126,400	31
315	513,868	5,536	701,222	286,822	2,868	240,468	80,763	765,744	4,118	32
904	240,913	5,272	270,909	147,562	141	140,021	33,717	277,068	110	33
337	155,351	9,006	588,216	283,959	7,937	820,615	67,996	616,628	320	34
48	175,103	3,745	145,522	78,190	2,219	80,482	67,347	207,973	9,460	35
83	415,287	4,236	1,110,437	153,324	877	81,832	50,278	517,622	5,336	36
....	132,714	5,805	498,660	108,726	1,207	130,000	54,432	387,395	1,810	37
3,286	348,218	15,021	569,895	538,383	18,275	246,520	102,117	589,193	11,311	38
45,385	427,191	2,335	777,083	519,905	17,015	445,909	109,312	809,801	60,842	39
....	90,127	1,718	469,920	119,534	....	69,162	53,637	390,898	655	40
380	215,334	7,034	630,196	430,384	44,263	664,512	122,530	561,047	12,180	41
596	385,650	20,389	1,223,270	440,130	5,799	676,603	97,201	709,366	660	42
7,150	77,009	2,559	236,771	202,948	13,758	99,058	700,910	409,550	21,540	43
81	115,977	1,644	523,858	71,987	105	19,336	52,052	187,174	2,030	44
2,765	329,616	20,046	1,556,341	359,617	3,502	1,061,513	145,305	858,152	17,365	45
975	543,151	3,483	803,782	159,630	1,269	207,486	56,333	452,813	5,000	46
29,659	177,859	5,662	563,083	412,949	25,062	405,478	267,928	1,148,946	864,172	47
985	119,910	2,735	242,502	135,157	2,237	54,067	200,052	314,533	3,715	48
1,657	71,497	12,734	1,164,121	73,741	528	348,114	37,572	206,244	40,525	49
1,218	174,689	11,847	361,439	449,385	5,590	295,467	124,758	963,557	45,539	50
6,418	278,601	3,090	635,291	196,639	1,565	337,617	53,720	439,226	2,360	51
16,634	188,274	13,620	393,696	537,217	9,668	408,891	148,911	975,938	416,958	52
5	140,262	2,975	479,933	102,980	1,635	91,034	163,132	489,087	35,847	53
96	338,193	14,659	341,775	244,289	9,368	94,742	34,208	373,956	2,565	54
....	858,886	5,856	1,293,096	379,415	71,804	55,181	82,521	489,132	725	55
362	160,680	15,954	629,846	306,425	1,099	158,066	98,676	524,887	56,062	56
28	823,975	9,407	1,088,781	409,804	83,002	23,047	142,425	650,826	702	57
51	192,650	3,725	613,837	137,546	891	313,372	71,821	593,454	5,733	58
3,460	204,254	8,635	615,679	342,300	2,930	532,348	92,452	652,684	3,720	59
23	336,961	9,998	1,198,677	313,240	1,665	605,194	185,130	815,562	950	60
158	179,557	7,035	853,950	172,210	565	247,534	61,771	510,903	12,785	61
1,888	83,972	658	115,850	58,511	2,729	68,241	43,368	203,812	300	62
42	56,513	2,763	55,499	23,938	226	19,107	20,002	135,131	350	63
320	196,032	4,975	681,612	132,208	3,820	374,331	76,050	623,153	527	64
723	444,623	22,161	2,867,598	95,008	1,945	80,392	72,654	301,290	3,660	65
77	62,738	4,509	740,557	108,178	4,240	36,832	57,957	215,631	2,385	66
2,887	182,430	18,270	356,953	426,814	33,635	200,308	263,449	807,636	714,787	67
....	700,475	2,334	973,686	298,315	32,497	36,119	55,264	507,313	580	68
374	237,212	16,292	434,948	105,896	305	78,605	69,639	330,078	704	69
1,050	587,525	19,458	621,381	700,830	33,081	269,981	113,877	883,005	22,050	70
1,014	326,844	13,639	2,313,529	90,983	4,458	85,402	98,134	334,391	5,778	71
3,576	479,087	5,856	341,002	389,233	11,107	162,063	186,491	549,492	500	72
....	85,518	180	699,736	116,376	9,474	21,647	81,924	221,304	200	73
3,702	915,202	7,361	641,640	605,519	9,063	332,973	141,819	801,181	1,100	74
668	494,831	6,679	586,424	363,349	23,835	164,538	51,737	397,470	176	75
56	806,016	8,207	796,914	769,530	175,667	316,900	189,486	1,238,428	45,018	76
4,042	333,889	10,972	688,651	435,771	79,456	167,293	186,815	856,265	372,991	77
534	112,942	16,229	383,662	433,407	293	213,572	156,912	1,102,581	1,368,505	78
143	509,152	20,520	723,659	683,594	18,192	496,414	133,705	917,708	97,112	79
2,380	206,280	3,941	808,275	156,436	720	390,281	60,341	451,407	43,624	80
497	146,222	25,768	162,280	90,379	870	57,781	35,617	270,789	4,315	81
....	44,292	2,366	342,211	59,824	10	104,934	41,052	215,714	6,900	82
....	427,674	4,650	1,487,121	281,210	157,273	68,242	130,061	574,554	440	83
....	206,549	19,476	675,616	245,414	....	236,230	216,297	702,600	22,706	84
1,066	708,033	10,307	920,537	897,965	43,537	297,383	166,354	1,117,442	41,290	85
148	308,951	1,567	317,760	234,225	1,550	144,635	89,792	571,752	4,690	86
2,665	253,880	5,481	300,272	232,364	5,494	126,064	131,600	562,80[illegible]	4,8[illegible]	87
2,708	385,322	4,471	451,887	178,712	1,815	311,964	50,308	342,142	[illegible]	88

TABLE XCV.—*Selected Statistics of Agriculture*—1870—Continued.

STATE OF OREGON.

	Counties.	Improved land.	Value of farms.	Total (estimated) value of all farm productions, including betterments and additions to stock.	Value of all live stock.	LIVE STOCK. Horses.	Mules and asses.	Milch cows.	Working oxen.	Sheep.
		Acres.	*Dollars.*	*Dollars.*	*Dollars.*	*No.*	*No.*	*No.*	*No.*	*No.*
1	Baker	13,010	73,580	84,616	77,096	287	20	605	17	560
2	Benton	30,307	1,489,433	417,063	367,579	2,263	126	2,665	70	12,957
3	Clackamas	23,520	1,143,900	319,556	242,536	869	108	1,329	229	5,220
4	Clatsop	2,249	164,710	50,214	51,997	147	4	517	89	1,208
5	Columbia	2,033	194,160	71,244	68,593	307	28	724	158	1,602
6	Coos	3,421	203,350	163,102	94,954	347	48	949	193	236
7	Curry	3,183	80,290	69,849	88,301	373	47	925	63	7,722
8	Douglas	132,657	1,791,723	674,094	720,015	5,265	369	4,948	173	94,963
9	Grant	10,963	128,800	122,579	166,959	507	30	1,384	74	1,154
10	Jackson	27,391	322,570	105,995	175,497	1,404	161	1,007	14	2,108
11	Josephine	5,182	68,800	24,775	27,100	48	1	120	.....	214
12	Lane	190,920	2,499,297	619,603	666,521	4,874	219	5,158	132	52,745
13	Linn	185,345	3,630,068	782,915	648,423	4,249	176	4,005	21	41,171
14	Marion	61,990	1,937,458	417,834	217,714	1,707	90	1,830	56	12,760
15	Multnomah	19,672	1,188,950	318,839	160,300	838	60	1,966	181	2,583
16	Polk	125,444	2,182,410	555,045	475,908	3,863	122	3,092	29	16,046
17	Tillamook	1,020	67,050	36,030	24,285	86	1	374	34	278
18	Umatilla	27,518	394,570	514,816	945,205	13,712	246	7,317	305	29,960
19	Union	47,066	444,000	285,936	452,199	2,204	237	3,585	358	2,791
20	Wasco	17,184	302,075	287,702	305,761	2,432	208	1,291	100	6,858
21	Washington	24,714	1,219,650	430,158	226,959	1,718	105	1,503	77	6,135
22	Yam Hill	161,481	2,826,145	770,765	564,773	4,202	166	3,031	68	18,851

STATE OF PENNSYLVANIA.

	Counties.	Improved land.	Value of farms.	Total (estimated) value of all farm productions, including betterments and additions to stock.	Value of all live stock.	LIVE STOCK. Horses.	Milch cows.	Working oxen.	Sheep.
		Acres.	*Dollars.*	*Dollars.*	*Dollars.*	*No.*	*No.*	*No.*	*No.*
1	Adams	214,546	14,611,060	3,228,241	1,722,610	8,148	11,068	3	6,097
2	Allegheny	292,089	56,448,818	4,433,043	3,015,224	12,157	17,316	74	77,320
3	Armstrong	230,915	13,681,426	2,299,674	1,915,150	10,313	11,683	85	40,308
4	Beaver	176,861	14,198,713	2,069,312	1,576,277	5,882	7,901	130	98,300
5	Bedford	197,250	9,495,119	1,765,574	1,298,205	8,249	8,079	89	21,746
6	Berks	374,560	43,638,465	9,150,789	4,544,490	16,783	32,112	37	5,610
7	Blair	98,285	8,098,146	1,405,706	798,164	4,322	4,242	4	8,372
8	Bradford	366,851	25,158,245	5,561,375	4,262,095	12,131	35,243	2,223	36,257
9	Bucks	315,833	40,289,213	8,232,569	4,357,108	14,679	28,572	58	7,404
10	Butler	273,128	18,230,848	3,125,482	2,467,001	11,521	16,078	222	67,831
11	Cambria	93,438	4,834,076	1,140,447	833,361	4,519	6,537	255	16,389
12	Cameron	6,485	1,332,188	302,418	73,220	254	394	82	1,042
13	Carbon	25,782	1,484,210	350,416	202,974	885	1,316	33	515
14	Centre	152,338	13,565,198	2,052,317	1,332,555	6,588	6,484	190	18,017
15	Chester	374,739	46,737,682	8,554,928	5,192,517	14,086	32,670	3,371	13,069
16	Clarion	162,742	7,784,127	1,710,279	1,317,708	6,718	7,877	650	29,844
17	Clearfield	116,218	5,931,360	1,889,767	931,661	4,497	5,677	327	18,408
18	Clinton	54,852	4,797,040	1,015,876	530,152	2,512	2,784	93	6,045
19	Columbia	136,710	9,015,460	1,840,189	1,064,968	4,718	5,615	164	6,823
20	Crawford	328,555	21,905,661	4,525,489	3,702,266	13,911	24,247	1,919	59,954
21	Cumberland	239,784	22,474,577	3,576,854	1,909,461	10,178	11,423	7	7,861
22	Dauphin	172,586	19,033,433	3,034,199	1,660,572	7,002	10,208	5	4,462
23	Delaware	80,436	19,288,727	2,938,587	1,665,657	4,219	[illegible]	454	2,142
24	Elk	16,124	1,019,820	407,047	206,706	689	1,277	[illegible]	[illegible]
25	Erie	279,868	23,991,607	4,720,295	2,930,156	11,117	25,140	1,183	[illegible]

TABLE XCV.—*Selected Statistics of Agriculture*—1870—Continued.

STATE OF OREGON.

PRODUCED.										
Wheat.						Potatoes.	Dairy products.			
Spring.	Winter.	Indian corn.	Oats.	Barley.	Wool.	Irish.	Butter.	Cheese.	Hay.	
Bushels.	*Bushels.*	*Bushels.*	*Bushels.*	*Bushels.*	*Pounds.*	*Bushels.*	*Pounds.*	*Pounds.*	*Tons.*	
2,306	......	15	37,426	17,739	2,775	7,377	17,615	400	1,944	1
175,322	21,276	2,343	146,235	7,414	68,970	38,320	100,880	5,530	4,176	2
10,675	37,975	200	58,017	1,255	15,028	34,613	46,935	......	2,716	3
220	75	12	2,007	......	4,945	15,130	23,115	938	688	4
1,554	65	1,169	2,200	254	4,382	10,337	25,195	100	1,850	5
1,634	1,168	1,859	3,386	1,182	644	19,165	22,130	300	644	6
1,306	515	1,274	2,001	740	24,110	4,319	16,510	......	149	7
17,773	86,473	26,956	188,761	22,737	321,643	24,250	75,583	5,250	6,573	8
16,779	680	143	23,426	22,172	8,000	13,925	22,300	6,000	1,193	9
440	14,786	6,000	47,800	8,020	1,015	......	8,180	300	1,814	10
......	100	230	4,900	......	550	200	2,600	......	173	11
220,932	3,838	2,760	235,722	24,087	167,893	32,455	155,214	18,230	5,381	12
342,323	136,971	5,834	343,298	21,917	108,714	30,295	167,680	6,470	6,475	13
102,731	129,360	1,078	164,087	5,199	51,169	37,464	70,836	7,730	3,405	14
4,674	320	1,473	11,892	3,724	4,626	60,490	115,549	11,260	6,138	15
274,614	28,794	300	199,405	7,805	55,203	22,933	142,778	330	6,128	16
2,099	800	......	2,719	896	1,527	9,340	29,340	65	764	17
18,379	9,830	9,788	56,634	11,782	97,564	24,413	72,730	8,200	3,394	18
60,435	900	640	69,660	29,666	8,154	26,877	84,030	1,875	6,752	19
8,418	2,181	9,045	26,593	7,203	38,106	12,962	43,901	1,840	2,330	20
97,454	59,733	525	183,151	4,724	29,920	23,915	72,118	1,645	5,409	21
364,425	10,473	493	219,939	11,627	65,100	31,610	103,168	2,830	7,261	22

STATE OF PENNSYLVANIA.

PRODUCED.											
Wheat.								Potatoes.	Dairy products.		
Spring.	Winter.	Rye.	Indian corn.	Oats.	Barley.	Buckwheat.	Wool.	Irish.	Butter.	Cheese.	
Bush.	*Bushels.*	*Bushels.*	*Bushels.*	*Bushels.*	*Bush.*	*Bush.*	*Pounds.*	*Bushels.*	*Pounds.*	*Lbs.*	
......	494,346	33,425	737,019	636,828	255	2,156	20,977	1,005,303	957,020	760	1
697	324,434	78,372	674,916	1,111,260	69,946	4,406	308,475	769,144	1,223,744	2,256	2
172	298,020	135,257	680,314	883,846	1,120	56,423	126,068	100,761	964,020	1,672	3
327	174,181	50,800	404,233	532,625	21,540	16,937	421,907	193,425	936,107	5,430	4
......	338,074	118,091	405,261	376,296	1,177	35,491	60,705	104,657	457,241	208	5
1,306	929,347	281,867	1,267,194	1,425,157	411	4,902	11,859	400,846	2,658,031	3,045	6
20	259,509	64,839	339,922	266,348	19,275	7,025	19,666	85,938	294,879	100	7
97,023	188,675	33,901	505,341	1,114,120	12,753	382,581	122,253	541,198	3,704,709	40,258	8
30	525,710	94,095	1,325,626	1,208,717	455	7,341	17,516	372,979	2,861,557	125,479	9
703	293,761	179,577	453,894	1,099,163	4,637	113,994	234,220	187,984	1,447,093	2,695	10
2,307	54,431	47,385	153,252	346,991	3,569	21,852	47,545	89,368	428,273	1,238	11
......	2,658	4,906	21,795	17,152	310	6,690	2,129	20,535	49,210	100	12
......	18,646	18,286	55,097	62,493	20	12,301	1,230	47,496	81,976	......	13
110	475,035	63,108	1,044,760	389,028	37,256	8,629	53,448	117,403	521,090	......	14
......	753,803	12,481	1,540,125	1,034,430	1,581	2,446	31,776	404,303	2,848,243	8,526	15
457	151,715	99,339	251,183	607,290	2,200	46,139	88,787	57,678	565,070	1,315	16
144	68,580	52,117	245,260	375,053	550	43,426	57,072	62,050	451,942	1,337	17
15	147,032	29,165	458,716	909,813	4,064	12,654	17,149	55,203	218,250	......	18
9	240,750	50,610	589,472	406,031	......	82,676	22,327	182,124	468,398	......	19
24,213	233,036	26,537	574,538	924,392	1,215	73,134	230,664	293,750	2,046,252	196,039	20
44	809,002	43,851	1,106,633	1,131,724	11,222	834	28,139	160,688	858,471	2,712	21
......	492,637	56,327	714,886	727,535	334	1,970	9,963	210,650	766,126	1,680	22
100	121,298	6,200	379,417	135,052	2,417	14	1,001	197,295	1,143,051	4,460	23
733	2,026	6,372	12,234	61,573	116	2,982	7,108	35,694	108,739	......	24
22,490	885,825	4,523	531,524	743,106	100,014	27,464	170,225	415,985	1,896,701	165,739	25

TABLE XCV.—*Selected Statistics of Agriculture*—1870—Continued.

STATE OF PENNSYLVANIA—Continued.

	Counties.	Improved land.	Value of farms.	Total (estimated) value of all farm productions, including betterments and additions to stock.	LIVE STOCK.					
					Value of all live stock.	Horses.	Milch cows.	Working oxen.	Sheep.	Swine.
		Acres.	*Dollars.*	*Dollars.*	*Dollars.*	*No.*	*No.*	*No.*	*No.*	*No.*
26	Fayette	235,006	18,250,958	2,779,685	2,093,444	8,318	8,404	433	65,261	[illegible]
27	Forest	10,890	619,398	202,985	127,114	444	635	163	2,087	[illegible]
28	Franklin	265,517	23,775,174	3,912,032	2,270,161	11,278	10,503	6	9,031	[illegible]
29	Fulton	86,955	2,565,042	652,655	474,654	2,945	3,200	217	6,879	[illegible]
30	Greene	230,504	13,554,374	2,294,308	1,875,272	7,278	7,369	1,363	121,135	[illegible]
31	Huntingdon	186,818	9,445,678	1,968,703	1,434,648	7,098	7,120	54	17,780	[illegible]
32	Indiana	256,023	12,945,069	2,640,875	2,174,542	11,586	12,661	241	44,054	[illegible]
33	Jefferson	104,220	5,362,623	1,433,269	941,012	4,855	5,391	348	20,089	[illegible]
34	Juniata	97,509	6,351,175	1,097,639	635,850	4,215	4,204	22	6,315	[illegible]
35	Lancaster	402,833	70,724,908	11,845,008	6,044,215	21,409	31,368	1,142	11,821	[illegible]
36	Lawrence	148,509	11,614,044	1,776,093	1,373,251	6,245	7,650	166	61,373	[illegible]
37	Lebanon	139,481	19,016,808	3,160,020	1,020,335	6,895	9,131	14	2,687	[illegible]
38	Lehigh	181,097	23,555,476	3,085,841	1,949,157	7,816	11,591	4	3,122	[illegible]
39	Luzerne	194,115	21,565,724	3,224,040	2,056,063	7,431	12,306	1,014	12,051	[illegible]
40	Lycoming	163,892	11,212,366	1,966,770	1,244,900	5,591	7,597	584	10,[illegible]	[illegible]
41	McKean	28,164	1,566,250	434,900	372,162	1,178	2,199	504	7,[illegible]	[illegible]
42	Mercer	260,109	22,048,299	3,358,557	2,784,612	11,390	15,507	458	68,008	[illegible]
43	Mifflin	97,687	9,133,277	1,544,981	808,039	4,373	3,908	20	7,538	[illegible]
44	Monroe	85,663	4,459,114	964,023	677,047	2,870	4,260	246	3,974	[illegible]
45	Montgomery	256,909	40,902,030	7,959,263	3,835,237	13,281	31,179	72	3,[illegible]	[illegible]
46	Montour	53,182	4,615,655	1,187,494	419,606	1,692	2,340	4	2,[illegible]	[illegible]
47	Northampton	170,062	20,991,169	3,402,260	1,900,042	7,999	10,841	13	5,562	[illegible]
48	Northumberland	147,129	12,430,987	2,347,216	1,113,983	5,406	6,117	4	5,602	[illegible]
49	Perry	136,809	8,750,895	2,793,127	948,988	4,885	5,501	147	7,119	[illegible]
50	Philadelphia	37,518	18,945,000	2,231,366	639,695	2,605	4,159	14	370	[illegible]
51	Pike	27,303	2,213,325	487,387	309,090	832	2,142	371	1,237	[illegible]
52	Potter	56,307	2,942,348	842,684	672,291	1,819	4,350	901	12,539	[illegible]
53	Schuylkill	109,135	8,643,655	2,212,273	951,979	3,712	5,883	35	3,100	[illegible]
54	Snyder	92,580	5,769,403	1,209,819	651,113	3,964	3,900	8	3,367	[illegible]
55	Somerset	249,615	12,043,715	2,173,581	1,666,233	8,273	13,811	101	32,343	[illegible]
56	Sullivan	36,689	1,658,109	496,694	351,901	1,074	2,705	604	6,976	[illegible]
57	Susquehanna	290,997	16,707,011	3,808,075	3,277,763	8,282	24,533	1,871	35,700	[illegible]
58	Tioga	187,305	10,923,925	2,753,129	2,071,117	6,148	16,017	1,716	22,723	[illegible]
59	Union	70,752	7,891,977	1,195,362	658,911	3,271	3,565	......	2,639	[illegible]
60	Venango	122,874	7,211,006	1,470,969	1,150,153	5,113	6,963	350	32,764	[illegible]
61	Warren	83,762	6,976,674	1,534,757	1,063,533	3,599	7,422	720	15,337	[illegible]
62	Washington	409,863	39,015,006	4,526,239	3,938,335	12,421	12,280	517	495,621	[illegible]
63	Wayne	110,718	8,816,220	1,795,465	1,731,055	3,832	11,096	2,797	16,46[illegible]	[illegible]
64	Westmoreland	342,083	28,210,826	4,176,690	3,028,081	15,144	16,349	48	47,958	[illegible]
65	Wyoming	87,953	6,633,160	1,216,747	822,811	2,987	5,814	540	6,857	[illegible]
66	York	411,341	36,358,484	6,443,180	4,013,452	14,707	23,269	297	14,06[illegible]	[illegible]

STATE OF RHODE ISLAND.

	Counties.	Improved land.	Value of farms.	Total (estimated) value of all farm productions, including betterments and additions to stock.	LIVE STOCK.					
					Value of all live stock.	Horses.	Milch cows.	Working oxen.	Sheep.	Swine.
		Acres.	*Dollars.*	*Dollars.*	*Dollars.*	*No.*	*No.*	*No.*	*No.*	*No.*
1	Bristol	8,922	1,320,950	261,295	118,823	399	664	187	473	[illegible]
2	Kent	48,245	2,614,465	631,934	391,832	1,081	2,380	735	1,505	[illegible]
3	Newport	49,743	4,803,680	808,593	728,450	1,426	3,659	1,620	10,930	[illegible]
4	Providence	95,415	9,245,106	2,140,477	1,218,505	3,323	8,056	1,369	1,667	[illegible]
5	Washington	86,699	3,590,767	828,804	677,582	1,541	4,047	1,910	9,338	[illegible]

TABLE XCV.—*Selected Statistics of Agriculture*—1870—Continued.

STATE OF PENNSYLVANIA—Continued.

PRODUCED.										
Wheat.							Potatoes.	Dairy products.		
Winter.	Rye.	Indian corn.	Oats.	Barley.	Buckwheat.	Wool.	Irish.	Butter.	Cheese.	
Bushels.	*Bushels.*	*Bushels.*	*Bushels.*	*Bush.*	*Bush.*	*Pounds.*	*Bushels.*	*Pounds.*	*Lbs.*	
301, 970	22, 768	824, 268	633, 897	5, 758	16, 877	287, 752	70, 665	691, 623	3, 250	26
2, 474	5, 802	17, 538	38, 465	23	6, 946	6, 615	15, 260	72, 948	500	27
888, 727	47, 047	948, 618	731, 911	9, 162	1, 784	31, 162	146, 753	900, 710	356	28
102, 144	43, 202	142, 176	163, 705	....	14, 572	30, 441	40, 081	171, 741	1, 003	29
254, 393	26, 606	749, 520	438, 223	1, 880	7, 638	444, 489	53, 712	750, 135	3, 569	30
388, 659	78, 480	503, 807	410, 479	4, 325	20, 009	54, 110	148, 679	465, 027	690	31
307, 516	97, 550	652, 263	906, 256	589	71, 477	125, 891	77, 367	1, 100, 925	7, 874	32
78, 299	64, 678	200, 484	390, 151	....	46, 632	56, 021	54, 506	497, 951	246	33
230, 624	9, 198	329, 231	347, 054	489	4, 454	16, 938	69, 520	299, 575	....	34
2, 077, 363	88, 245	2, 820, 825	1, 943, 577	15, 329	3, 146	20, 092	419, 755	2, 462, 376	82, 614	35
234, 810	21, 493	349, 353	547, 783	18, 604	30, 832	208, 127	119, 777	716, 229	9, 310	36
538, 308	70, 188	627, 881	678, 614	194	70	5, 206	95, 835	569, 199	1, 870	37
380, 945	102, 147	549, 480	530, 632	2, 538	10, 596	8, 769	279, 718	915, 818	150	38
101, 405	115, 339	368, 537	475, 988	625	197, 160	38, 555	573, 322	1, 068, 565	40, 306	39
271, 361	39, 820	535, 158	470, 619	2, 105	66, 780	25, 804	103, 425	429, 500	....	40
4, 637	1, 978	22, 620	97, 984	79	3, 190	28, 016	54, 983	197, 200	1, 810	41
339, 424	24, 850	639, 743	883, 965	1, 040	68, 625	246, 639	149, 124	1, 516, 067	101, 530	42
322, 835	10, 851	365, 806	322, 487	833	3, 991	20, 457	73, 211	415, 115	15, 500	43
37, 062	72, 424	175, 040	113, 470	95	79, 165	12, 039	103, 816	298, 168	....	44
340, 873	150, 156	1, 026, 865	791, 272	1, 638	631	5, 609	456, 345	3, 104, 748	195, 057	45
111, 384	7, 330	176, 941	179, 518	....	8, 849	6, 750	54, 241	192, 048	....	46
473, 295	122, 584	707, 494	539, 067	4, 123	23, 838	14, 271	282, 038	843, 541	....	47
335, 165	37, 520	510, 418	463, 634	171	25, 130	15, 759	227, 658	486, 128	....	48
286, 725	29, 508	417, 235	435, 885	40	9, 305	20, 449	115, 264	366, 221	291	49
53, 405	19, 886	189, 325	63, 884	8	1, 668	300	350, 139	132, 566	550	50
5, 850	22, 369	56, 815	28, 654	....	29, 592	3, 217	71, 910	161, 179	75	51
7, 354	3, 383	32, 098	245, 763	232	30, 701	52, 460	97, 621	475, 600	14, 109	52
115, 631	86, 410	267, 560	288, 356	279	18, 776	6, 685	253, 636	383, 495	943	53
247, 381	12, 752	255, 831	283, 841	....	6, 203	9, 366	73, 178	241, 246	....	54
133, 788	142, 515	92, 277	559, 616	4, 306	49, 779	60, 177	84, 445	1, 344, 522	30	55
10, 976	5, 678	42, 942	76, 141	....	34, 453	21, 219	42, 507	229, 972	165	56
18, 653	31, 117	311, 218	628, 061	734	177, 864	108, 584	341, 717	2, 380, 649	8, 890	57
91, 368	8, 874	236, 313	564, 684	17, 117	116, 263	89, 788	282, 618	1, 574, 825	65, 889	58
202, 039	6, 217	297, 513	318, 154	20	2, 728	8, 538	75, 374	262, 936	....	59
67, 830	24, 610	216, 733	535, 899	1, 112	63, 267	92, 566	75, 355	566, 405	5, 026	60
15, 159	13, 749	98, 850	253, 380	2, 660	25, 763	50, 806	128, 078	739, 853	11, 042	61
445, 159	27, 243	1, 467, 904	1, 062, 408	128, 367	765	1, 862, 752	187, 516	1, 178, 306	1, 562	62
688	15, 075	95, 433	215, 459	....	92, 364	49, 526	255, 335	1, 055, 076	3, 014	63
675, 770	43, 886	1, 168, 498	1, 358, 208	5, 605	15, 739	178, 650	148, 248	1, 206, 845	270	64
66, 849	38, 334	187, 213	250, 048	62	124, 983	18, 615	236, 525	449, 532	2, 043	65
1, 129, 500	121 035	1, 531, 541	1, 444, 763	2, 354	44, 092	39, 095	248, 461	1, 734, 895	615	66

STATE OF RHODE ISLAND.

PRODUCED.											
	Wheat.						Potatoes.	Dairy products.			
	Winter.	Rye.	Indian corn.	Oats.	Barley.	Wool.	Irish.	Butter.	Cheese.	Hay.	
ls.	*Bushels.*	*Bushels.*	*Bushels.*	*Bushels.*	*Bushels.*	*Pounds.*	*Bushels.*	*Pounds.*	*Pounds.*	*Tons.*	
..	8	1, 576	13, 521	5, 934	1, 348	1, 029	34, 996	26, 715	298	2, 551	1
..	....	5, 152	31, 707	4, 955	2, 809	4, 742	94, 035	103, 227	21, 037	10, 234	2
..	152	1, 540	92, 975	76, 980	16, 661	39, 044	92, 878	266, 775	9, 164	17, 229	3
43	8	9, 887	85, 114	15, 386	9, 900	3, 330	329, 482	296, 128	30, 235	[illegible]	4
45	28	2, 039	88, 640	53, 755	2, 831	29, 183	118, 017	248, 354	21, 962	[illegible]	5

TABLE XCV.—*Selected Statistics of Agriculture*—1870—Continued.

STATE OF SOUTH CAROLINA.

	Counties.	Improved land.	Value of farms.	Total (estimated) value of all farm productions, including betterments and additions to stock.	LIVE STOCK. Value of all live stock.	Horses.	Mules and asses.	Milch cows.	Working oxen.	Sheep.
		Acres.	*Dollars.*	*Dollars.*	*Dollars.*	*No.*	*No.*	*No.*	*No.*	*No.*
1	Abbeville	128, 040	2, 911, 932	2, 573, 683	677, 490	1, 960	2, 662	4, 443	752	6, 1
2	Anderson	96, 228	1, 286, 980	1, 578, 850	609, 507	2, 350	1, 596	4, 994	1, 032	10, 5
3	Barnwell	383, 140	4, 589, 974	4, 099, 460	1, 001, 545	3, 389	3, 453	8, 185	623	4, 1
4	Beaufort	150, 260	2, 554, 149	2, 220, 266	500, 192	1, 721	1, 341	4, 219	365	1, 9
5	Charleston	168, 393	2, 984, 178	2, 854, 955	433, 011	1, 044	1, 220	2, 565	353	2, 8
6	Chester	233, 112	1, 449, 709	1, 060, 860	425, 505	1, 292	1, 781	2, 550	38	1, 9
7	Chesterfield	41, 694	752, 373	692, 791	225, 542	804	441	2, 606	1, 458	3, 3
8	Clarendon	103, 868	1, 281, 350	882, 673	381, 077	996	795	3, 314	359	1, 5
9	Colleton	100, 698	2, 050, 731	936, 166	464, 362	1, 679	642	4, 264	57	3, 3
10	Darlington	151, 064	1, 918, 489	2, 783, 257	674, 752	2, 550	1, 847	2, 918	1, 224	2, 2
11	Edgefield	173, 514	2, 135, 331	2, 331, 041	798, 305	3, 134	3, 459	6, 596	466	6, 9
12	Fairfield	85, 164	2, 214, 870	1, 658, 581	553, 634	1, 142	2, 556	2, 891	491	1, 3
13	Georgetown	15, 817	678, 089	1, 274, 157	77, 763	189	179	961	515	1, 1
14	Greenville	68, 589	983, 053	882, 200	344, 262	1, 556	1, 184	3, 561	869	7, 6
15	Horry	27, 026	130, 428	365, 773	193, 626	471	122	3, 347	1, 733	7, 5
16	Kershaw	36, 946	761, 831	540, 604	178, 477	501	651	1, 432	306	1, 9
17	Lancaster	38, 982	615, 726	837, 966	206, 601	642	725	1, 539	345	2, 3
18	Laurens	99, 614	1, 000, 789	1, 469, 545	452, 261	1, 741	2, 037	3, 071	171	5, 6
19	Lexington	56, 062	585, 344	694, 422	34, 876	1, 568	954	3, 204	506	4, 4
20	Marion	82, 851	1, 445, 276	1, 147, 392	417, 976	1, 419	957	3, 633	1, 138	4, 4
21	Marlborough	76, 142	1, 505, 200	1, 172, 464	288, 660	916	919	1, 637	222	9
22	Newberry	74, 221	1, 943, 846	2, 576, 390	384, 450	1, 259	1, 754	2, 379	51	2, 8
23	Oconee	28, 245	679, 918	196, 482	174, 735	818	286	1, 578	777	4, 8
24	Orangeburg	102, 985	965, 031	840, 474	435, 150	1, 527	1, 077	2, 521	428	2, 1
25	Pickens	36, 557	808, 357	425, 631	225, 076	1, 170	481	1, 819	564	4, 8
26	Richland	56, 797	886, 138	697, 197	267, 132	623	990	1, 367	400	1, 0
27	Spartanburg	97, 675	1, 147, 446	1, 349, 178	612, 158	2, 465	1, 791	5, 451	720	11, 3
28	Sumter	65, 816	1, 473, 258	922, 343	208, 025	905	1, 126	1, 699	271	1, 0
29	Union	86, 728	1, 235, 951	1, 207, 112	473, 573	1, 674	1, 830	3, 446	215	4, 5
30	Williamsburgh	51, 432	316, 278	320, 772	249, 501	764	452	3, 034	1, 105	3, 4
31	York	92, 879	1, 516, 639	1, 316, 715	474, 337	1, 856	2, 007	3, 467	131	5, 0

STATE OF TENNESSEE.

	Counties.	Improved land.	Value of farms.	Total (estimated) value of all farm productions, including betterments and additions to stock.	LIVE STOCK. Value of all live stock.	Horses.	Mules and asses.	Milch cows.	Working oxen.	Sheep.
		Acres.	*Dollars.*	*Dollars.*	*Dollars.*	*No.*	*No.*	*No.*	*No.*	*No.*
1	Anderson	50, 750	1, 045, 727	344, 492	337, 678	1, 783	261	1, 893	636	6, 0
2	Bedford	143, 537	7, 511, 259	2, 037, 652	1, 471, 421	6, 255	2, 372	4, 568	716	25, 2
3	Benton	46, 443	463, 607	599, 786	372, 297	747	819	2, 028	1, 075	7, 7
4	Bledsoe	33, 873	702, 890	387, 703	231, 915	1, 137	236	1, 354	498	5, 5
5	Blount	91, 740	2, 410, 825	986, 532	540, 884	2, 847	476	2, 488	813	10, 8
6	Bradley	74, 597	2, 077, 861	639, 655	448, 542	2, 181	730	2, 455	638	9, 1
7	Campbell	40, 042	897, 182	350, 291	253, 685	390	235	1, 488	684	6, 6
8	Cannon	59, 149	1, 671, 572	1, 088, 168	680, 805	3, 366	1, 202	2, 487	1, 046	12, 1
9	Carroll	127, 515	3, 077, 511	1, 791, 796	910, 255	3, 517	2, 265	4, 076	857	10, 8
10	Carter	36, 386	1, 022, 276	275, 355	193, 166	1, 033	167	1, 326	239	5, 4
11	Cheatham	43, 213	758, 535	379, 496	341, 920	1, 450	890	1, 529	293	4, 8
12	Claiborne	47, 847	979, 459	254, 175	320, 016	1, 752	187	2, 112	824	9, 5

TABLE XCV.—*Selected Statistics of Agriculture*—1870—Continued

STATE OF SOUTH CAROLINA.

PRODUCED.										
Wheat.								Potatoes.	Molasses.	
Spring.	Winter.	Indian corn.	Oats.	Rice.	Tobacco.	Cotton.	Wool.	Sweet.	Cane.	
Bushels.	*Bushels.*	*Bushels.*	*Bushels.*	*Pounds.*	*Pounds.*	*Bales.*	*Pounds.*	*Bushels.*	*Gallons.*	
10, 657	53, 435	315, 399	56, 312	1, 600	280	13, 924	5, 791	10, 995	1, 787	1
65, 937	11, 232	409, 628	34, 213	13, 865	4, 087	5, 274	15, 397	13, 225	269	2
869	58, 417	781, 054	70, 106	1, 544, 784	....	24, 910	1, 951	227, 566	300, 240	3
236	378	285, 532	1, 392	9, 069, 130	16	7, 486	1, 477	118, 036	1, 007	4
....	....	170, 087	1, 915	4, 329, 217	329	5, 512	2, 257	62, 984	....	5
....	33, 210	169, 379	22, 496	....	....	7, 042	4, 869	13, 464	20	6
355	21, 566	118, 129	22, 530	1, 785	4, 696	2, 457	6, 416	52, 732	....	7
160	437	218, 417	2, 347	813, 012	....	5, 016	169	75, 330	....	8
....	399	207, 927	6, 746	8, 742, 271	....	2, 335	4, 542	52, 825	8, 005	9
2, 811	12, 497	484, 076	28, 392	44, 154	999	34, 591	309	170, 070	....	10
8, 605	44, 552	412, 259	77, 370	....	....	17, 553	9, 981	29, 896	....	11
175	27, 830	218, 054	16, 269	3, 000	....	14, 024	10	474	....	12
....	....	14, 094	50	5, 324, 970	....	61	740	7, 644	....	13
28, 739	15, 682	355, 526	23, 698	2, 880	5, 987	1, 864	9, 186	92, 499	3, 521	14
5	35	62, 039	79	417, 507	1, 891	74	7, 317	72, 232	507	15
6, 234	155	108, 420	3, 875	30, 530	....	4, 161	1, 070	16, 595	....	16
13, 511	2, 361	100, 113	16, 135	....	67	3, 414	1, 756	7, 933	768	17
33, 022	19, 224	277, 364	35, 192	....	85	7, 077	9, 068	19, 947	9, 934	18
305	46, 078	180, 729	13, 584	32, 275	134	2, 534	4, 990	33, 647	5, 408	19
2, 047	343	190, 326	11, 412	415, 382	195	6, 910	5, 772	58, 103	30	20
5, 107	1, 214	158, 088	20, 748	17, 077	116	8, 643	993	42, 356	823	21
41, 849	65	152, 232	27, 701	480	....	9, 836	5, 778	14, 072	5, 959	22
2, 812	7, 721	138, 903	5, 903	23, 660	2, 927	810	8, 099	8, 950	4, 573	23
6, 186	2, 100	263, 739	698	952, 378	....	6, 449	3, 680	31, 846	5, 041	24
4, 926	16, 004	214, 759	8, 277	2, 300	3, 824	489	6, 416	13, 523	....	25
624	4, 231	121, 495	3, 118	26, 823	25	5, 453	1, 082	12, 805	564	26
59, 068	14, 715	525, 698	36, 106	....	3, 207	2, 851	15, 345	30, 247	....	27
....	655	189, 039	1, 859	245, 325	1	7, 212	825	36, 113	....	28
19, 628	16, 658	314, 981	18, 491	....	5, 282	8, 537	6, 502	30, 610	2, 822	29
65	651	103, 487	445	249, 800	....	1, 791	5, 702	37, 011	5	30
3, 774	54, 065	353, 174	46, 114	....	657	6, 010	8, 834	18, 435	25, 799	31

STATE OF TENNESSEE.

PRODUCED.										
Wheat.								Potatoes.	Sugar.	
Spring.	Winter.	Rye.	Indian corn.	Oats.	Tobacco.	Cotton.	Wool.	Sweet.	Cane.	
Bushels.	*Bushels.*	*Bushels.*	*Bushels.*	*Bushels.*	*Pounds.*	*Bales.*	*Pounds.*	*Bushels.*	*Hhds.*	
....	23, 932	290	262, 664	73, 441	15, 578	....	12, 884	11, 063	....	1
170	212, 752	10, 486	1, 010, 642	104, 801	19, 290	869	35, 516	17, 408	....	2
3, 415	22, 338	105	357, 403	18, 986	412, 435	696	10, 288	19, 926	....	3
68	21, 966	2, 078	201, 667	21, 550	14, 226	....	11, 465	4, 714	....	4
548	107, 971	774	384, 583	104, 501	675	....	18, 178	3, 520	30	5
2, 761	109, 580	76	239, 490	41, 727	10, 628	....	14, 826	12, 810	....	6
....	18, 401	239	127, 145	65, 908	8, 509	2	12, 035	2, 455	200	7
387	79, 133	3, 167	564, 330	96, 870	30, 750	54	21, 451	7, 045	160	8
....	93, 872	70	777, 922	4, 206	10, 840	5, 023	13, 044	371	....	9
....	37, 169	4, 094	132, 097	63, 396	1, 140	....	7, 978	2, 781	....	10
140	19, 432	281	274, 052	44, 585	419, 265	62	8, 179	7, 609	....	11
....	33, 901	1, 125	204, 840	59, 039	4, 827	....	15, 300	3, 150	....	12

TABLE XCV.—*Selected Statistics of Agriculture*—1870—Continued.

STATE OF TENNESSEE—Continued.

	Counties.	Improved land.	Value of farms.	Total (estimated) value of all farm productions, including betterments and additions to stock.	LIVE STOCK.					
					Value of all live stock.	Horses.	Mules and asses.	Milch cows.	Working oxen.	Sheep.
		Acres.	*Dollars.*	*Dollars.*	*Dollars.*	*No.*	*No.*	*No.*	*No.*	*No.*
13	Cocke	67, 332	1, 523, 952	352, 850	433, 768	1, 994	525	2, 830	1, 145	9, 7
14	Coffee	55, 307	2, 414, 115	598, 277	468, 201	2, 506	503	1, 881	509	8, 1
15	Cumberland	16, 174	414, 435	227, 074	175, 339	527	103	964	521	4, 4
16	Davidson	126, 481	12, 186, 365	1, 967, 907	1, 269, 870	5, 646	2, 228	5, 428	138	12, 2
17	Decatur	41, 205	564, 677	577, 609	311, 117	1, 238	628	1, 436	754	5, 6
18	De Kalb	54, 405	1, 549, 156	710, 808	548, 285	2, 737	653	2, 002	1, 183	11, 4
19	Dickson	50, 534	1, 381, 330	533, 057	366, 935	1, 622	997	1, 917	655	6, 9
20	Dyer	83, 724	1, 950, 346	1, 528, 585	862, 591	3, 855	1, 562	3, 531	923	8, 8
21	Fayette	152, 766	3, 901, 190	2, 974, 576	1, 085, 136	3, 839	4, 073	4, 534	405	3, 8
22	Fentress	29, 059	527, 275	219, 302	194, 839	942	148	1, 380	822	5, 0
23	Franklin	94, 716	2, 784, 364	1, 012, 197	925, 000	2, 945	750	3, 043	948	8, 8
24	Gibson	132, 669	4, 890, 576	3, 327, 523	1, 319, 242	5, 631	2, 955	5, 470	533	14, 1
25	Giles	182, 894	6, 717, 824	2, 690, 754	1, 736, 504	7, 672	3, 456	6, 536	1, 383	18,
26	Grainger	82, 518	1, 680, 266	553, 925	433, 913	2, 233	350	2, 248	1, 000	9, 7
27	Greene	162, 034	4, 526, 184	1, 200, 990	890, 043	4, 644	856	5, 279	1, 026	21, 1
28	Grundy	12, 274	429, 190	356, 108	104, 140	504	99	521	298	1,
29	Hamilton	68, 958	2, 416, 203	571, 856	445, 340	1, 875	563	2, 393	796	6, 7
30	Hancock	39, 778	692, 815	334, 031	244, 673	1, 263	98	1, 514	661	7,
31	Hardeman	138, 112	3, 335, 409	2, 154, 818	793, 203	2, 684	2, 202	3, 146	1, 007	7, 1
32	Hardin	51, 005	1, 293, 203	740, 785	502, 919	1, 993	670	2, 670	1, 383	8,
33	Hawkins	116, 798	2, 348, 287	815, 053	593, 066	3, 192	417	3, 705	1, 298	16,
34	Haywood	75, 949	1, 885, 796	1, 403, 495	662, 705	2, 172	1, 889	2, 681	331	5,
35	Henderson	92, 520	1, 920, 885	1, 168, 172	732, 510	2, 816	1, 679	3, 649	1, 308	10,
36	Henry	110, 172	2, 645, 294	1, 337, 686	915, 425	3, 658	2, 722	3, 600	882	10,
37	Hickman	57, 329	1, 411, 409	975, 199	536, 926	2, 374	1, 790	2, 600	549	6,
38	Humphreys	44, 018	1, 603, 934	648, 819	512, 133	1, 971	914	2, 355	1, 094	8,
39	Jackson	68, 834	1, 075, 086	631, 496	533, 605	2, 984	435	2, 780	2, 040	15,
40	Jefferson	118, 132	3, 694, 155	993, 655	652, 822	3, 210	461	3, 097	768	11,
41	Johnson	28, 393	763, 190	237, 671	210, 240	951	142	1, 601	369	6,
42	Knox	135, 960	4, 502, 445	1, 116, 430	840, 287	4, 907	913	4, 543	744	13,
43	Lake	13, 379	882, 411	398, 348	125, 802	511	381	615	236	[illegible]
44	Lauderdale	53, 728	2, 536, 980	1, 197, 975	594, 020	1, 992	1, 123	2, 799	605	3,
45	Lawrence	33, 337	803, 486	574, 891	353, 641	1, 743	544	1, 867	771	5,
46	Lewis	9, 168	211, 140	107, 804	84, 064	329	209	443	165	1,
47	Lincoln	189, 562	6, 521, 190	2, 066, 342	2, 155, 474	7, 968	3, 431	6, 934	1, 371	27,
48	Macon	42, 690	639, 731	1, 143, 735	424, 090	2, 233	561	1, 509	800	8,
49	Madison	94, 169	3, 953, 675	1, 001, 143	956, 719	2, 849	3, 195	3, 931	101	3,
50	Marion	33, 211	989, 080	499, 367	356, 903	1, 571	265	1, 977	1, 014	5,
51	Marshall	114, 602	3, 707, 071	1, 204, 956	1, 229, 100	6, 202	2, 598	3, 881	396	16,
52	Maury	196, 242	10, 686, 999	2, 682, 211	2, 015, 355	8, 464	5, 346	6, 735	693	21,
53	McMinn	98, 734	2, 350, 882	856, 632	530, 128	2, 336	713	2, 653	703	9,
54	McNairy	64, 596	1, 139, 310	943, 156	615, 521	2, 338	1, 149	2, 999	827	9,
55	Meigs	41, 204	729, 108	266, 338	213, 550	996	254	1, 069	336	4, 3
56	Monroe	101, 976	2, 253, 045	829, 515	419, 798	2, 334	485	2, 539	536	8, 3
57	Montgomery	136, 395	4, 472, 162	1, 706, 506	873, 256	3, 023	2, 569	3, 272	562	8, 0
58	Morgan	12, 248	261, 952	102, 877	133, 759	515	71	940	473	4, 3
59	Obion	75, 416	2, 437, 755	1, 564, 292	871, 179	3, 742	1, 671	3, 716	1, 169	10, 5
60	Overton	82, 963	1, 357, 263	623, 539	570, 079	3, 450	434	3, 360	1, 643	17, 2
61	Perry	29, 286	991, 673	499, 295	384, 690	1, 706	804	1, 971	928	5, 3
62	Polk	34, 648	887, 695	317, 949	160, 998	715	364	1, 057	540	4, 6
63	Putnam	51, 315	812, 779	637, 645	419, 792	2, 218	339	2, 166	1, 364	10, 4
64	Rhea	32, 723	996, 474	717, 797	262, 190	1, 152	243	1, 455	542	5, 3
65	Roane	102, 502	2, 587, 423	619, 768	520, 488	3, 390	604	3, 064	827	10, 5
66	Robertson	140, 641	4, 291, 516	1, 359, 245	970, 816	3, 908	2, 461	3, 000	134	11, 1
67	Rutherford	181, 447	10, 153, 110	2, 260, 874	1, 519, 939	7, 953	3, 493	5, 862	496	17, 1
68	Scott	20, 682	298, 248	181, 869	176, 947	824	69	1, 400	579	6, 5
69	Sequatchie	15, 505	382, 060	150, 180	146, 756	655	104	680	298	2, 9
70	Sevier	57, 338	1, 444, 930	308, 498	364, 923	1, 954	257	2, 264	574	9, 5
71	Shelby	164, 431	9, 987, 974	4, 169, 342	1, 418, 349	4, 221	4, 676	6, 629	542	5, 7
72	Smith	120, 332	3, 182, 929	1, 278, 068	1, 006, 202	4, 857	1, 239	3, 715	1, 979	17, 5
73	Stewart	47, 382	803, 838	637, 559	461, 870	1, 579	994	2, 158	1, 007	8, 9
74	Sullivan	104, 306	2, 434, 169	655, 732	593, 487	3, 384	202	3, 405	208	15, 6
75	Sumner	181, 189	5, 167, 581	1, 690, 216	1, 435, 431	7, 582	3, 078	5, 378	687	20, 4
76	Tipton	67, 370	2, 236, 745	1, 458, 235	600, 109	1, 879	1, 851	2, 784	184	4, 6
77	Union	46, 435	904, 320	505, 506	231, 235	1, 451	118	1, 264	460	6, 3

TABLE XCV.—*Selected Statistics of Agriculture*—1870—Continued.

STATE OF TENNESSEE—Continued.

	PRODUCED.									
	Wheat.							Potatoes.	Sugar.	
	Winter.	Rye.	Indian corn.	Oats.	Tobacco.	Cotton.	Wool.	Sweet.	Cane.	
ls.	Bushels.	Bushels.	Bushels.	Bushels.	Pounds.	Bales.	Pounds.	Bushels.	Hhds.	
1	79, 006	1, 023	388, 867	45, 259	17, 741	....	15, 074	6, 218	....	13
..	43, 075	10, 226	300, 503	25, 462	13, 387	30	12, 597	11, 726	....	14
..	1, 585	2, 241	42, 377	9, 115	13, 098	....	8, 497	2, 367	....	15
63	82, 303	10, 442	832, 982	131, 550	21, 490	1, 416	30, 310	62, 854	....	16
80	19, 159	146	314, 653	20, 540	44, 630	1, 159	9, 796	15, 913	....	17
13	81, 399	1, 492	486, 823	32, 259	87, 076	12	20, 480	9, 156	....	18
94	7, 336	721	319, 085	58, 810	462, 130	9	15, 028	12, 554	....	19
12	74, 078	738	749, 175	7, 523	412, 440	4, 908	3, 314	2, 931	....	20
08	6, 578	34	627, 271	9, 450	840	20, 131	3, 305	26, 077	....	21
03	10, 236	1, 232	109, 084	24, 067	16, 990	....	9, 044	4, 901	....	22
28	77, 529	3, 229	467, 757	68, 371	9, 983	229	16, 294	9, 915	....	23
34	116, 835	....	1, 067, 775	12, 118	97, 300	9, 815	12, 677	60, 275	....	24
51	111, 184	5, 895	2, 054, 163	70, 512	40, 655	8, 367	34, 259	28, 074	....	25
..	78, 146	1, 971	353, 260	86, 005	16, 646	....	15, 089	8, 045	....	26
..	238, 716	818	496, 659	149, 518	41, 585	....	39, 511	11, 331	12	27
30	11, 601	689	73, 373	11, 242	2, 147	47	3, 158	3, 652	....	28
06	103, 110	3, 846	353, 700	44, 963	855	1	12, 912	1, 480	....	29
..	22, 956	2, 407	204, 190	41, 308	9, 978	....	13, 967	3, 489	....	30
75	24, 755	1, 180	586, 508	19, 799	5, 600	7, 884	9, 920	32, 143	....	31
04	19, 662	131	484, 721	15, 151	300	2, 026	10, 275	10, 472	....	32
..	138, 968	1, 083	466, 470	112, 306	12, 370	....	26, 124	4, 956	....	33
11	38, 296	452	522, 921	9, 717	40	10, 510	10, 118	31, 037	....	34
16	38, 458	446	547, 805	17, 397	15, 134	4, 191	15, 923	30, 736	....	35
60	98, 375	554	767, 220	26, 816	1, 715, 001	2, 385	16, 450	31, 882	....	36
16	22, 120	1, 221	514, 554	34, 202	18, 935	755	14, 953	15, 226	....	37
15	27, 668	958	491, 355	29, 907	113, 177	107	14, 622	17, 829	....	38
37	29, 909	4, 160	530, 276	54, 314	713, 578	9	26, 311	12, 863	191	39
20	135, 738	1, 947	527, 853	132, 453	10, 182	71	21, 892	9, 280	....	40
..	16, 484	13, 397	85, 782	34, 682	7, 557	....	11, 333	646	....	41
..	151, 232	7, 201	548, 546	259, 047	26, 532	2	26, 328	24, 243	....	42
..	1, 000	....	414, 570	1, 892	....	32	815	4, 382	....	43
..	18, 669	100	443, 809	5, 465	2, 100	6, 337	447	5, 602	....	44
38	29, 183	1, 004	189, 695	22, 095	32, 417	522	10, 598	9, 301	....	45
74	4, 025	163	73, 315	3, 472	5, 677	120	3, 040	3, 004	....	46
22	192, 175	13, 989	1, 233, 960	72, 179	31, 837	3, 745	48, 113	23, 103	....	47
28	30, 497	696	256, 483	60, 756	950, 768	1, 988	13, 605	9, 340	20	48
30	48, 408	287	692, 910	9, 781	....	9, 255	8, 592	9, 734	....	49
60	28, 074	1, 979	265, 100	27, 989	17, 487	724	9, 157	10, 662	....	50
17	123, 416	18, 526	591, 358	83, 601	12, 788	2, 063	34, 553	16, 556	....	51
58	122, 026	5, 812	1, 449, 935	61, 387	14, 245	9, 367	35, 544	24, 962	127	52
[illegible]	43, 326	702	350, 833	77, 810	4, 862	4	17, 858	13, 102	....	53
21	26, 378	363	370, 431	18, 362	6, 338	3, 347	13, 509	22, 028	....	54
..	29, 603	452	176, 733	18, 776	200	456	4, 396	3, 497	....	55
71	113, 382	1, 178	415, 010	56, 367	2, 875	....	15, 324	9, 208	....	56
45	168, 978	6, 838	810, 194	62, 378	4, 856, 378	21	14, 009	33, 490	....	57
29	1, 532	2, 212	52, 642	15, 548	7, 944	....	9, 197	3, 415	....	58
..	91, 130	216	917, 445	21, 919	645, 937	2, 256	17, 082	33, 607	....	59
17	43, 102	1, 897	394, 026	69, 957	187, 331	16	25, 585	14, 514	....	60
01	336	301	368, 045	9, 312	5, 944	495	10, 429	6, 254	....	61
73	35, 353	1, 519	152, 425	17, 192	1, 160	....	7, 639	4, 575	....	62
..	39, 330	2, 088	332, 254	37, 854	131, 856	....	10, 092	11, 581	....	63
..	32, 639	2, 459	187, 970	36, 034	10, 276	6	9, 088	6, 185	....	64
83	74, 331	1, 527	504, 590	112, 029	350	....	14, 027	11, 609	....	65
14	157, 404	937	559, 020	149, 019	2, 103, 322	11	19, 387	27, 455	1	66
25	152, 020	13, 746	807, 443	63, 514	1, 300	8, 412	23, 225	24, 299	....	67
24	726	1, 001	88, 311	17, 793	9, 283	....	12, 560	4, 200	....	68
..	12, 472	2, 035	103, 010	6, 915	9, 353	....	5, 904	4, 102	....	69
..	63, 483	1, 575	260, 214	42, 460	13, 997	6	16, 109	7, 308	....	70
33	14, 692	287	940, 796	7, 697	950	32, 434	1, 264	50, 747	....	71
57	126, 004	3, 833	888, 078	72, 528	2, 250, 202	8	32, 674	15, 163	654	72
..	31, 380	430	428, 311	26, 623	1, 191, 620	1, 809	16, 135	18, 746	....	73
00	132, 247	5, 650	302, 227	176, 387	16, 307	....	27, 026	7, 844	....	74
40	163, 074	7, 222	1, 155, 914	233, 837	909, 568	170	38, 860	25, 074	....	75
..	30, 579	108	446, 771	18, 681	170	10, 052	5, 195	18, 380	....	76
..	29, 615	735	168, 579	69, 799	14, 189	884	10, 673	....	....	77

TABLE XCV.—*Selected Statistics of Agriculture*—1870—Continued.

STATE OF TENNESSEE—Continued.

	Counties.	Improved land.	Value of farms.	Total (estimated) value of all farm productions, including betterments and additions to stock.	LIVE STOCK.					
					Value of all live stock.	Horses.	Mules and asses.	Milch cows.	Working oxen.	Sheep.
		Acres.	*Dollars.*	*Dollars.*	*Dollars.*	*No.*	*No.*	*No.*	*No.*	*No.*
78	Van Buren	26,414	370,120	236,262	143,041	718	112	766	406	3,2
79	Warren	85,844	2,454,908	751,645	570,221	3,218	666	2,781	906	12,49
80	Washington	106,646	3,228,291	882,804	605,797	3,620	297	3,604	462	13,20
81	Wayne	56,957	1,201,233	766,893	645,740	2,500	962	2,898	1,585	9,67
82	Weakley	113,457	3,453,713	1,393,025	1,024,853	3,914	2,673	4,062	1,047	13,03
83	White	64,361	1,203,790	673,072	377,622	2,345	349	2,122	866	8,14
84	Williamson	155,471	6,528,324	2,504,875	1,403,202	7,194	3,121	5,060	379	15,22
85	Wilson	163,834	7,147,654	2,195,087	1,919,019	9,682	4,150	5,185	584	24,06

STATE OF TEXAS.

	Counties.	Improved land.	Value of farms.	Total (estimated) value of all farm productions, including betterments and additions to stock.	LIVE STOCK.					
					Value of all live stock.	Horses.	Mules and asses.	Milch cows.	Working oxen.	
		Acres.	*Dollars.*	*Dollars.*	*Dollars.*	*No.*	*No.*	*No.*	*No.*	
1	Anderson	43,413	399,740	427,988	237,458	1,680	558	3,797	1,040	
2	Angelina	13,808	209,030	268,990	184,828	1,191	195	4,601	859	1
3	Atascosa	4,772	74,453	75,710	418,515	6,370	125	4,656	919	8
4	Austin	76,619	1,724,465	1,392,667	664,958	5,768	1,331	10,009	4,473	7
5	Bandera	1,156	21,250	22,057	31,132	281	7	898	363	3
6	Bastrop	46,210	1,387,995	658,725	396,915	6,781	1,339	6,895	2,611	1
7	Bee	452	16,090	9,435	36,110	260	2	78	31	1
8	Bell	27,927	614,605	472,986	390,300	7,425	469	4,430	1,494	9
9	Bexar	5,546	256,120	326,597	364,284	4,615	338	4,156	1,315	8
10	Blanco	3,690	90,736	66,077	99,524	2,074	71	1,367	705	3
11	Bosque	21,038	380,355	454,317	431,045	8,071	570	4,829	1,320	5
12	Bowie	18,360	223,347	331,261	126,295	772	405	1,501	337	
13	Brazoria	38,181	1,435,070	557,284	374,250	2,775	1,776	2,207	695	1
14	Brazos	22,046	109,765	823,791	266,946	2,172	458	2,852	879	8
15	Brown	408	6,450	18,422	75,869	77	6	373	71	
16	Burleson	24,814	578,649	733,635	307,498	3,117	472	4,110	1,710	6
17	Burnet	13,510	326,540	189,911	213,370	2,726	225	3,023	787	5
18	Caldwell	39,547	500,331	169,369	197,247	3,842	396	3,331	1,400	4
19	Calhoun	451	55,730	35,478	57,438	927	29	402	30	2
20	Cameron	4,354	102,920	157,770	444,900	5,488	771	928	1,144	7
21	Chambers	5,365	137,407	53,630	136,703	1,444	54	1,205	334	1,
22	Cherokee	43,206	465,947	660,298	343,385	2,448	795	4,182	878	1,
23	Coleman	150	2,450	13,660	53,286	13	4	71	27	
24	Collin	51,728	3,002,800	994,160	882,510	10,668	1,592	5,065	1,627	4,
25	Colorado	30,244	493,890	335,115	342,130	2,751	606	4,370	1,379	2,
26	Comal	13,850	632,950	260,350	214,347	3,993	532	5,978	2,806	1,
27	Comanche	1,543	40,595	28,326	98,334	275	65	427	259	
28	Cook	20,159	688,565	320,480	424,565	3,479	431	3,015	994	3,
29	Coryell	11,831	210,537	233,214	239,131	3,469	195	3,046	836	2,
30	Dallas	65,300	1,578,915	783,166	816,567	12,459	1,387	8,452	2,245	6,
31	Davis	53,903	406,566	1,066,633	255,723	1,156	841	2,584	545	3,
32	Demmit	510	3,860	79,050	72,147	199	......	3,230	16	
33	Denton	19,778	585,972	341,604	488,247	6,195	312	2,863	776	3,
34	De Witt	22,884	478,823	225,673	369,621	5,529	761	5,547	1,555	17,
35	Duval	740	19,321	26,522	75,735	2,622	......	438	14	34,
36	Eastland	16	230	4,392	17,987	40	......	41	......	
37	Ellis	28,201	633,232	412,826	462,573	7,387	776	3,892	975	3,

TABLE XCV.—*Selected Statistics of Agriculture*—1870—Continued.

STATE OF TENNESSEE—Continued.

PRODUCED.									
...heat.							Potatoes.	Sugar.	
Winter.	Rye.	Indian corn.	Oats.	Tobacco.	Cotton.	Wool.	Sweet.	Cane.	
Bushels.	*Bushels.*	*Bushels.*	*Bushels.*	*Pounds.*	*Bales.*	*Pounds.*	*Bushels.*	*Hhds.*	
14,002	422	104,033	4,456	9,858	135	6,006	4,216	15	78
72,280	1,072	339,250	56,348	27,446	105	24,212	17,152	....	79
170,934	6,439	290,388	148,383	22,896	....	26,694	3,656	....	80
47,428	1,500	484,861	19,314	26,769	1,101	17,856	14,927	....	81
136,173	211	879,544	1,945	2,599,590	7	20,056	10,282	....	82
55,181	1,158	347,944	22,129	21,816	84	15,735	13,301	....	83
181,726	4,662	1,010,443	99,933	80,415	3,815	29,944	20,555	....	84
239,950	3,189	1,173,201	151,067	332,901	1,205	36,854	33,302	....	85

STATE OF TEXAS.

PRODUCED.									
...heat.					Potatoes.			Molasses.	
Winter.	Indian corn.	Tobacco.	Cotton.	Wool.	Irish.	Sweet.	Butter.	Cane.	
Bushels.	*Bushels.*	*Pounds.*	*Bales.*	*Pounds.*	*Bushels.*	*Bushels.*	*Pounds.*	*Gallons.*	
35	177,285	890	4,016	1,893	1,716	22,136	40,381	....	1
....	86,640	2,478	1,654	2,395	2,327	23,194	52,275	6,193	2
....	36,371	....	6	22,877	122	11,839	18,182	....	3
....	445,584	3,682	11,967	19,302	13,368	65,745	100,867	....	4
....	15,673	....	....	5,530	20	716	9,095	....	5
....	356,874	....	8,728	6,690	130	710	....	....	6
....	4,690	....	1	6,708	....	2,000	200	....	7
3,236	358,360	....	2,896	10,575	800	14,296	85,945	....	8
190	81,997	....	117	7,910	268	3,409	22,952	....	9
200	42,830	....	233	6,178	200	2,215	40,977	....	10
38,615	260,946	....	2,165	1,885	1,660	8,556	84,242	....	11
....	104,805	200	2,990	..,259	782	11,923	18,524	....	12
....	207,881	....	2,988	4,740	3,362	23,051	....	92,450	13
400	205,864	....	6,927	8,001	5,690	38,597	36,639	....	14
....	11,000	....	....	1,560	....	70	1,000	....	15
....	223,929	....	6,423	14,200	3,274	20,627	25,407	....	16
6,001	142,900	....	408	13,870	55	6,189	45,460	....	17
....	120,965	50	1,692	3,065	1,130	12,039	33,142	....	18
....	4,165	....	....	17,490	920	2,432	6,200	....	19
....	38,487	....	118	14,450	....	....	....	....	20
....	23,759	....	105	2,944	1,721	15,200	5,067	585	21
1,773	292,181	115	5,185	1,424	2,140	30,230	25,480	3,391	22
....	5,050	....	....	350	....	65	4	....	23
31,513	674,565	2,642	4,371	14,136	3,214	32,159	204,915	....	24
....	130,423	831	2,796	4,928	2,648	14,442	40,165	1,400	25
1,968	169,250	....	1,303	455	106	8,913	69,305	....	26
3,145	39,292	....	28	950	84	1,722	....	....	27
12,724	211,939	325	308	1,486	1,310	22,664	76,809	....	28
5,518	109,900	....	378	8,015	452	3,407	34,061	1,174	29
58,318	557,508	30	3,834	12,282	1,812	25,541	86,795	....	30
202	256,505	380	5,966	3,807	4,984	36,228	53,595	....	31
....	550	....	....	600	....	....	....	....	32
9,475	173,510	1,220	674	6,285	2,831	11,826	37,409	....	33
....	107,896	....	541	21,275	4,402	13,583	55,523	....	34
....	....	....	....	110,950	....	....	....	....	35
....	250	....	....	....	....	....	....	....	36
11,338	*312,843*	....	2,960	2,650	1,100	8,273	180	....	37

TABLE XCV.—*Selected Statistics of Agriculture*—1870—Continued.

STATE OF TEXAS—Continued.

	Counties.	Improved land.	Value of farms.	Total (estimated) value of all farm productions, including betterments and additions to stock.	LIVE STOCK.					
					Value of all live stock.	Horses.	Mules and asses.	Milch cows.	Working oxen.	Sheep.
		Acres.	*Dollars.*	*Dollars.*	*Dollars.*	*No.*	*No.*	*No.*	*No.*	*No.*
38	El Paso	50	800	326	300	5	......	2	......	
39	Ensinal	2, 660	5, 510	19, 030	16, 305	335	6	335	68	5, 7
40	Erath	5, 858	151, 378	119, 988	307, 865	1, 703	49	1, 298	412	2, 3
41	Falls	32, 988	549, 704	1, 080, 186	363, 236	5, 269	828	2, 405	843	2, 5
42	Fannin	46, 097	1, 302, 250	750, 436	621, 794	7, 041	1, 138	6, 032	1, 416	5, 6
43	Fayette	76, 041	2, 117, 213	1, 232, 740	915, 033	6, 650	1, 252	10, 836	4, 321	10, 0
44	Fort Bend	31, 258	924, 241	595, 193	390, 084	3, 207	1, 301	2, 193	776	5
45	Freestone	47, 558	692, 461	659, 420	411, 576	3, 640	894	4, 931	1, 804	1, 6
46	Frio	322	11, 030	14, 390	211, 810	1, 273	10	1, 945	53	5, 2
47	Galveston	2, 326	245, 900	77, 241	52, 890	390	108	717	53	5
48	Gillespie	6, 878	174, 001	161, 787	140, 475	880	375	3, 927	1, 837	2, 1
49	Goliad	6, 257	105, 484	56, 755	57, 686	794	93	917	225	4, 8
50	Gonzales	33, 841	608, 972	301, 184	637, 973	8, 977	461	8, 833	2, 747	5, 7
51	Grayson	48, 918	1, 315, 148	724, 649	579, 893	7, 324	1, 149	4, 840	1, 704	5, 9
52	Grimes	71, 436	991, 807	1, 024, 575	526, 530	3, 569	1, 305	5, 779	4, 765	3, 7
53	Guadalupe	28, 929	627, 948	342, 433	386, 504	6, 859	737	6, 061	2, 358	3, 9
54	Hamilton	2, 596	26, 160	151, 550	109, 622	991	38	1, 653	218	
55	Hardin	3, 866	46, 880	67, 900	38, 382	492	30	1, 246	250	
56	Harris	14, 016	605, 732	270, 757	284, 463	2, 833	300	4, 561	1, 204	5,
57	Harrison	76, 187	863, 851	878, 745	214, 240	899	1, 095	2, 396	393	2,
58	Hays	7, 792	207, 897	162, 577	101, 929	2, 448	166	1, 863	582	1,
59	Henderson	26, 240	187, 080	336, 551	253, 687	1, 538	419	5, 109	984	1,
60	Hidalgo	1, 098	74, 200	50, 460	139, 188	3, 459	44	4, 496	504	11,
61	Hill	23, 296	1, 030, 420	551, 562	726, 366	7, 632	527	5, 816	1, 008	3,
62	Hood	9, 574	174, 100	279, 701	274, 942	3, 442	220	3, 348	573	2,
63	Hopkins	42, 371	1, 037, 789	874, 987	568, 393	6, 210	745	6, 381	1, 571	10,
64	Houston	6, 746	57, 180	128, 651	55, 101	297	118	728	209	
65	Hunt	41, 065	780, 140	735, 109	779, 394	9, 941	977	9, 672	2, 077	7,
66	Jack	323	9, 040	10, 155	15, 925	81	......	79	30	
67	Jackson	10, 816	152, 613	82, 623	78, 555	956	89	708	243	
68	Jasper	23, 114	245, 344	273, 175	125, 029	884	126	2, 088	586	2,
69	Jefferson	1, 484	61, 092	34, 781	90, 619	1, 758	56	743	204	
70	Johnson	18, 413	331, 054	192, 716	215, 204	6, 343	315	2, 549	669	1,
71	Karnes	3, 443	45, 620	337, 161	328, 776	8, 380	325	2, 330	417	4,
72	Kaufman	14, 942	487, 055	292, 583	281, 550	2, 605	164	3, 033	675	2,
73	Kendall	3, 617	116, 960	75, 766	92, 465	1, 345	72	2, 337	1, 073	4,
74	Kerr	3, 712	99, 052	74, 827	97, 204	486	35	2, 511	847	4,
75	Kimble	18	180	2, 050	7, 700	13	......	59	......	......
76	Kinney	2, 610	57, 605	26, 575	95, 230	186	16	665	424	6,
77	Lamar	43, 494	1, 058, 936	821, 789	473, 301	5, 037	1, 090	5, 196	1, 061	3,
78	Lampasas	3, 611	62, 140	61, 077	103, 536	713	40	552	262	1,
79	La Salle	......	......	8, 828	39, 600	140	......	......	......	5,
80	Lavaca	36, 987	1, 025, 101	621, 966	692, 937	5, 970	1, 058	21, 012	2, 553	10,
81	Leon	32, 265	370, 852	527, 871	298, 541	2, 405	629	5, 263	1, 414	1,
82	Liberty	11, 279	319, 662	241, 656	176, 253	2, 190	218	2, 706	714	1,
83	Limestone	34, 846	1, 121, 390	418, 720	420, 559	6, 000	620	844	1, 519	3,
84	Live Oak	4, 801	63, 839	38, 091	310, 372	5, 010	85	611	102	5,
85	Llano	1, 624	42, 210	31, 751	106, 000	443	21	1, 687	233	4,
86	Madison	15, 166	206, 175	266, 345	190, 920	2, 233	338	3, 186	927	5,
87	Marion	27, 819	412, 591	196, 025	85, 117	362	362	943	298	
88	Mason	1, 131	29, 530	27, 795	61, 820	183	39	2, 588	229	1,
89	Matagorda	16, 007	364, 817	261, 521	333, 483	2, 341	808	1, 395	471	8,
90	Maverick	1, 388	44, 235	26, 200	162, 200	294	12	797	508	17,
91	McCulloch	97	2, 920	2, 922	4, 835	20	......	148	8	
92	McLennan	36, 148	356, 734	816, 205	475, 962	7, 506	608	3, 774	1, 131	7,
93	McMullen	173	4, 500	395	95, 800	341	3	128	10	5,
94	Medina	5, 504	118, 570	82, 628	326, 305	1, 586	124	8, 264	4, 337	
95	Menard	147	15, 050	19, 985	61, 950	209	4	831	63	
96	Milam	32, 644	505, 584	553, 792	398, 881	4, 543	674	4, 106	1, 564	6,
97	Montague	2, 615	63, 960	63, 547	95, 005	383	34	687	1, 002	
98	Montgomery	35, 412	702, 398	351, 943	228, 761	1, 929	532	4, 184	1, 381	1, 4
99	Nacogdoches	35, 646	499, 311	558, 104	291, 868	1, 971	560	3, 607	995	2, 4
100	Navarro	47, 042	1, 078, 152	965, 891	654, 826	9, 241	1 151	4, 875	2, 450	7, 1
101	Newton	10, 580	136, 255	253, 100	92, 937	556	95	1, 370	387	1, 4
102	Nueces	14, 367	288, 149	224, 539	1, 063, 658	18, 504	675	1, 911	170	82, 3
103	Orange	984	28, 063	18, 905	33, 736	501	9	725	111	
104	Panola	61, 359	1, 031, 615	1, 407, 730	304, 025	1, 739	1, 178	3, 806	653	4, 4
105	Parker	5, 926	136, 475	102, 070	108, 973	1, 497	21	1, 922	353	
106	Polk	30, 344	311, 426	607, 993	241, 631	1, 856	644	3, 492	1, 224	

TABLE XCV.—*Selected Statistics of Agriculture*—1870—Continued.

STATE OF TEXAS—Continued.

PRODUCED.										
[W]heat.						Potatoes.			Molasses.	
…	Winter.	Indian corn.	Tobacco.	Cotton.	Wool.	Irish.	Sweet.	Butter.	Cane.	
…s.	*Bushels.*	*Bushels.*	*Pounds.*	*Bales.*	*Pounds.*	*Bushels.*	*Bushels.*	*Pounds.*	*Gallons.*	
90	....	....	....	....	....	....	....	....	....	38
..	....	50	....	....	9,556	....	....	....	....	39
71	9,560	78,109	....	167	3,842	257	1,751	100	....	40
..	....	403,094	....	14,	8,531	3,322	31,424	3,152	....	41
33	15,345	476,563	20	5,	8,801	3,043	23,193	123,835	....	42
..	187	459,392	1,331	10,	16,280	8,081	34,206	144,196	....	43
..	....	233,505	....	4,	1,305	2,365	20,867	20,111	28,960	44
..	....	197,431	....	6,	960	1,328	26,015	38,112	....	45
..	....	8,080	....	....	13,948	....	300	900	....	46
..	....	2,905	....		....	384	16,205	2,175	....	47
75	15,213	82,135	50	....	4,447	218	5,931	38,842	3,257	48
..	....	37,640	....		9,946	688	5,977	3,650	....	49
15	....	203,591	....	2,	478	697	28,932	37,419	210	50
34	35,534	577,540	7,875	2,	8,798	3,371	39,411	111,840	9,301	51
..	....	336,690	....	10,	4,165	1,348	60,966	47,081	....	52
..	25	197,889	....	2,	6,556	225	13,556	....	....	53
..	3,330	27,150	....		2,445	253	1,550	19,775	....	54
..	....	26,385	....		740	316	15,240	2,600	5,235	55
..	....	90,977	....	1,	4,067	5,543	38,895	31,566	2,730	56
13	....	233,019	....	8,	2,215	1,443	23,004	10,365	....	57
11	....	92,420	....	1,	5,349	238	7,838	32,310	....	58
..	150	156,804	....	2,	828	1,906	23,075	34,543	....	59
..	....	7,380	....		....	....	340	300	....	60
..	1,743	295,668	....	3,	8,572	8,750	2,301	76,818	....	61
..	1,714	192,540	....		7,346	3,479	11,352	45,155	....	62
35	1,004	340,676	235	5,	22,549	3,436	44,872	108,884	....	63
..	....	33,163	100		1,236	17	5,779	8,042	....	64
25	1,127	342,411	2,465	4,	7,963	2,319	31,480	163,267	32	65
..	....	6,750	....		....	35	295	200	....	66
..	....	36,125	....		....	622	6,770	....	556	67
..	....	90,377	10,998	1,	2,982	962	25,550	128	7,969	68
..	....	15,282	25		150	35	8,880	....	1,103	69
59	5,435	155,435	230	1,	1,571	324	7,297	1,615	....	70
..	....	35,965	....		8,065	....	2,330	5,410	....	71
59	2,038	179,658	....	1,910	3,092	135	11,700	1,097	....	72
56	889	51,243	1,745	....	8,781	22	2,737	26,458	....	73
..	3,196	43,781	....	7	10,963	24	2,001	19,005	....	74
..	....	150	....	....	....	....	....	....	....	75
..	....	17,320	....	....	8,950	550	....	5,500	....	76
12	5,278	474,361	2,035	6,753	3,093	3,978	16,347	29,110	....	77
25	2,427	45,487	....	28	4,593	30	1,191	12,630	....	78
..	....	....	....	....	26,000	....	....	....	....	79
..	30	261,815	4,748	3,528	19,508	5,569	47,287	5,332	....	80
..	....	160,906	100	4,897	2,594	1,687	24,505	44,998	....	81
..	....	98,087	....	1,881	1,647	858	21,896	550	1,063	82
60	110	190,609	....	3,414	10,608	787	13,741	....	25	83
..	....	1,875	....	....	....	....	....	....	....	84
..	350	23,504	....	7	12,179	25	255	300	177	85
..	....	84,006	662	2,729	9,360	1,106	8,296	21,430	....	86
..	....	73,118	....	....	....	4,140	8,345	....	....	87
..	53	7,740	....	....	5,510	1	593	6,945	439	88
..	....	94,095	150	1,590	12,285	500	13,777	22,225	115	89
..	100	8,315	....	....	24,060	....	300	4,800	....	90
..	....	1,270	....	....	125	....	75	1,530	70	91
78	33	502,500	100	8,820	2,564	2,137	21,280	8,904	....	92
..	....	....	....	....	1,000	....	....	....	....	93
40	....	87,240	....	....	....	45	421	350	....	94
..	....	930	....	....	800	....	630	1,300	....	95
35	15	201,117	....	5,143	21,881	1,436	21,391	37,549	....	96
14	2,150	41,715	....	15	1,416	310	1,777	21,200	1,319	97
..	....	163,290	2,283	3,485	660	2,541	41,945	....	....	98
..	108	217,861	....	4,531	2,642	150	35,113	62,334	....	99
66	200	219,865	....	4,077	2,935	505	5,150	....	....	100
..	....	51,303	53	1,001	1,228	....	11,890	....	4,574	101
..	....	3,000	....	....	199,650	190	925	3,388	....	102
..	....	8,720	....	67	1,350	....	5,905	400	580	103
24	....	*306,665*	2,240	9,367	5,984	5,806	66,898	60,280	890	104
39	*13,606*	*70,685*	....	13	20	1,253	3,790	90,050	....	105
0	*2*	*206,326*	1,843	4,548	3,398	1,633	45,151	33,865	17,[illegible]	106

TABLE XCV.—*Selected Statistics of Agriculture*—1870—Continued.

STATE OF TEXAS—Continued.

	Counties.	Improved land.	Value of farms.	Total (estimated) value of all farm productions, including betterments and additions to stock.	LIVE STOCK.					
					Value of all live stock.	Horses.	Mules and asses.	Milch cows.	Working oxen.	Sheep.
		Acres.	Dollars.	Dollars.	Dollars.	No.	No.	No.	No.	No.
107	Red River	50, 964	909, 268	763, 358	392, 797	2, 522	1, 242	3, 813	868	1, 7[illegible]
108	Refugio	5, 400	135, 300	136, 870	592, 745	9, 949	1, 002	1, 556	584	4, 85[illegible]
109	Robertson	97, 207	742, 965	293, 475	190, 335	897	547	1, 854	505	5, 15[illegible]
110	Rusk	78, 250	562, 829	1, 555, 718	389, 450	1, 904	1, 337	4, 085	711	3, 60[illegible]
111	Sabine	17, 653	136, 000	267, 058	123, 892	831	188	1, 634	983	1, 59[illegible]
112	San Augustine	19, 752	131, 363	328, 886	173, 804	913	331	2, 576	791	1, 22[illegible]
113	San Patricio	2, 417	43, 800	49, 375	189, 450	4, 973	341	393	166	2, 84[illegible]
114	San Saba	2, 377	124, 561	64, 789	114, 045	183	49	1, 244	260	1, 46[illegible]
115	Shackleford	320	480	200	4, 550	16	1	20	14	.....
116	Shelby	31, 649	178, 553	440, 358	240, 816	1, 597	372	3, 219	1, 058	2, 17[illegible]
117	Smith	75, 466	1, 382, 113	1, 256, 126	421, 896	1, 988	1, 189	4, 975	858	2, 78[illegible]
118	Starr	200	1, 375	1, 450	18, 320	110	13	625	60	3, 50[illegible]
119	Stephens	105	2, 850	43, 570	147, 160	167	2	186	75	1[illegible]
120	Tarrant	22, 387	496, 047	228, 837	350, 637	6, 953	429	4, 099	1, 049	4, 9[illegible]
121	Titus	53, 012	1, 133, 072	899, 135	467, 387	3, 437	916	4, 507	1, 000	3, 7[illegible]
122	Travis	83, 270	1, 897, 960	1, 121, 946	611, 579	6, 584	1, 337	6, 952	8, 991	12, 0[illegible]
123	Trinity	16, 151	172, 214	323, 020	175, 400	1, 318	200	4, 872	778	1, 6[illegible]
124	Tyler	17, 040	250, 806	372, 175	192, 287	1, 303	180	3, 117	822	3, 1[illegible]
125	Upshur	63, 804	590, 238	928, 687	370, 570	2, 703	960	4, 247	891	2, 2[illegible]
126	Uvalde	1, 205	35, 410	42, 850	129, 900	162	6	228	270	4, 9[illegible]
127	Van Zandt	22, 195	502, 267	494, 357	238, 577	2, 422	280	4, 157	986	2, 4[illegible]
128	Victoria	11, 247	240, 743	182, 191	320, 242	5, 047	531	2, 044	652	5, 4[illegible]
129	Walker	34, 224	311, 566	603, 808	232, 000	1, 680	764	2, 904	1, 142	2, 5[illegible]
130	Washington	122, 833	3, 765, 786	1, 872, 244	879, 871	7, 313	2, 162	10, 944	5, 922	8, 2[illegible]
131	Webb	6, 120	17, 640	165, 178	131, 599	1, 259	77	2, 947	591	71, 7[illegible]
132	Wharton	22, 126	332, 345	162, 521	73, 094	667	603	562	300	
133	Williamson	18, 329	389, 239	217, 321	341, 794	7, 948	378	3, 481	1, 006	12, 0[illegible]
134	Wilson	10, 907	153, 961	85, 048	189, 669	5, 481	102	2, 619	921	4[illegible]
135	Wise	3, 537	70, 420	45, 250	91, 176	532	17	633	178	6[illegible]
136	Wood	30, 053	510, 834	606, 210	284, 006	2, 226	400	3, 396	796	2, 5[illegible]
137	Young	190	1, 200	8, 840	49, 100	88	3	162	24	[illegible]
138	Zapata	10, 442	106, 939	10, 268	108, 731	4, 119	171	3, 716	455	34, 9[illegible]
139	Zavala	108	2, 600	2, 550	13, 800	38	......	10	8	

STATE OF VERMONT.

	Counties.	Improved land.	Value of farms.	Total (estimated) value of all farm productions, including betterments and additions to stock.	LIVE STOCK.				
					Value of all live stock.	Horses.	Milch cows.	Working oxen.	Sheep.
		Acres.	Dollars.	Dollars.	Dollars.	No.	No.	No.	No.
1	Addison	278, 170	16, 001, 518	3, 055, 768	2, 304, 419	6, 595	16, 442	1, 143	[illegible]
2	Bennington	127, 006	6, 340, 195	1, 160, 545	887, 167	2, 529	5, 659	524	32, 0[illegible]
3	Caledonia	235, 955	8, 438, 065	2, 609, 673	1, 729, 437	5, 217	10, 650	2, 377	27, 1[illegible]
4	Chittenden	218, 670	14, 783, 045	3, 098, 404	2, 116, 498	4, 977	21, 941	1, 014	17, 0[illegible]
5	Essex	58, 516	1, 873, 965	791, 092	431, 300	1, 383	2, 543	995	5, 7[illegible]
6	Franklin	276, 963	16, 663, 492	3, 236, 782	2, 294, 070	6, 025	27, 624	1, 377	20, 0[illegible]
7	Grand Isle	36, 872	2, 579, 795	497, 750	297, 331	1, 285	1, 437	12	16, 0[illegible]
8	Lamoille	106, 638	5, 675, 180	1, 520, 590	1, 060, 330	2, 703	8, 886	1, 375	9, 3[illegible]
9	Orange	291, 318	10, 205, 063	2, 900, 786	2, 091, 368	5, 778	10, 661	3, 912	77, 81[illegible]
10	Orleans	196, 456	8, 949, 310	2, 552, 519	1, 697, 469	5, 184	14, 125	1, 961	22, 4[illegible]
11	Rutland	301, 499	14, 231, 525	3, 458, 102	2, 314, 499	5, 623	19, 504	1, 227	83, 6[illegible]
12	Washington	238, 113	11, 305, 586	3, 666, 376	2, 071, 255	5, 564	17, 154	2, 632	26, 1[illegible]
13	Windham	308, 975	9, 127, 096	2, 619, 542	2, 094, 566	4, 818	9, 665	4, 337	42, 4[illegible]
14	Windsor	398, 106	13, 193, 240	3, 479, 098	2, 499, 130	7, 334	13, 894	4, 923	117, [illegible]

TABLE XCV.—*Selected Statistics of Agriculture*—1870—Continued.

STATE OF TEXAS—Continued.

PRODUCED.											
Wheat.						Potatoes.			Molasses.		
Spring.	Winter.	Indian corn.	Tobacco.	Cotton.	Wool.	Irish.	Sweet.	Butter.	Cane.		
Bushels.	*Bushels.*	*Bushels.*	*Pounds.*	*Bales.*	*Pounds.*	*Bushels.*	*Bushels.*	*Pounds.*	*Gallons.*		
6	1, 518	385, 840	100	....	3, 069	435	1, 830	1, 865	....	107	
....	....	41, 555	....	....	13, 955	2, 679	20, 504	....	....	108	
....	....	140, 083	....	4, 833	1, 385	1, 453	700	1, 216	....	109	
201	787	347, 561	....	12, 752	8, 718	8, 487	73, 556	108, 301	750	110	
31	130	86, 839	527	1, 722	1, 766	235	19, 680	13, 802	1, 918	111	
25	30	110, 007	335	2, 598	1, 135	180	10, 082	1, 050	7, 033	112	
....	....	21, 325	....	....	7, 325	863	9, 010	....	....	113	
70	1, 534	49, 710	....	7	3, 518	....	3, 187	9, 862	1, 870	114	
....	....	400	....	....	....	....	....	....	....	115	
....	....	168, 827	....	4, 090	1, 216	185	21, 416	16	566	116	
342	985	420, 646	1, 125	9, 322	3, 494	8, 555	54, 987	109, 856	1, 878	117	
....	....	....	....	....	....	....	....	....	....	118	
....	....	600	....	....	75	....	....	....	....	119	
3, 988	25, 599	203, 595	2, 953	728	6, 059	1, 478	12, 995	41, 664	....	120	
15	239	382, 029	135	7, 039	4, 338	5, 378	48, 343	7, 950	1, 000	121	
607	60	498, 710	....	16, 769	1, 717	168	88, 210	56, 792	....	122	
....	....	94, 240	1, 620	2, 205	1, 913	1, 826	31, 083	48, 260	7, 156	123	
....	....	121, 723	....	2, 236	4, 850	493	41, 580	19, 540	22, 905	124	
15	438	326, 681	205	7, 362	1, 129	2, 108	40, 806	51, 816	433	125	
....	....	18, 225	....	2	4, 800	....	1, 820	5, 550	....	126	
....	316	194, 879	....	2, 926	4, 088	903	29, 935	81, 089	....	127	
....	....	71, 078	....	205	14, 871	2, 331	8, 129	10, 822	184	128	
....	....	186, 401	....	5, 524	2, 359	2, 003	35, 536	38, 226	3, 805	129	
....	....	663, 252	....	22, 452	12, 044	11, 814	59, 092	157, 237	....	130	
....	....	865	....	....	119, 260	....	....	....	....	131	
....	....	143, 900	....	1, 217	....	165	8, 540	....	....	132	
4, 426	7, 421	208, 574	....	913	22, 518	247	5, 086	2, 520	....	133	
....	....	52, 712	....	358	....	96	12, 116	34, 410	....	134	
2, 322	3, 497	26, 750	....	21	1, 302	331	2, 575	14, 850	1, 276	135	
603	692	201, 547	525	3, 919	1, 803	904	33, 033	11, 925	3, 131	136	
....	....	1, 700	....	....	....	....	....	....	....	137	
....	....	7, 945	....	....	37, 675	....	....	....	....	138	
....	....	450	....	....	....	....	....	100	....	139	

STATE OF VERMONT.

PRODUCED.												
Wheat.								Potatoes.	Dairy products.			
Spring.	Winter.	Rye.	Indian corn.	Oats.	Barley.	Buckwheat.	Wool.	Irish.	Butter.	Cheese.		
Bushels.	*Bushels.*	*Bushels.*	*Bushels.*	*Bushels.*	*Bushels.*	*Bushels.*	*Pounds.*	*Bushels.*	*Pounds.*	*Pounds.*		
49, 067	8, 658	13, 201	144, 257	334, 446	7, 218	28, 211	495, 771	317, 043	1, 723, 437	546, 047	1	
7, 379	50	7, 561	108, 537	161, 876	6, 379	18, 379	146, 419	196, 791	412, 092	416, 655	2	
49, 309	22	1, 179	68, 622	355, 938	11, 031	49, 084	130, 295	466, 680	1, 246, 309	20, 057	3	
44, 160	1, 266	11, 804	163, 597	286, 615	14, 381	21, 768	87, 256	333, 858	1, 761, 543	1, 374, 387	4	
6, 103	....	1, 746	13, 613	107, 589	732	22, 015	24, 132	229, 941	233, 285	23, 980	5	
49, 361	70	5, 857	116, 826	308, 587	14, 275	13, 793	92, 178	335, 122	2, 984, 520	510, 226	6	
17, 581	1, 199	205	21, 073	105, 431	7, 454	26, 876	83, 838	51, 509	160, 653	11, 388	7	
18, 219	38	2, 740	61, 836	168, 103	2, 777	20, 224	50, 022	333, 185	984, 378	39, 199	8	
51, 920	32	2, 939	174, 261	316, 148	5, 699	76, 826	498, 749	490, 715	1, 062, 104	105, 295	9	
56, 418	14	3, 017	54, 589	369, 319	21, 376	38, 796	110, 476	598, 307	1, 738, 526	67, 079	10	
21, 421	1, 771	7, 939	180, 780	246, 092	3, 462	22, 127	425, 216	617, 094	1, 190, 645	1, 369, 844	11	
29, 431	89	3, 651	127, 480	395, 424	4, 801	30, 988	121, 195	393, 841	2, 218, 224	92, 547	12	
4, 119	111	3, 980	185, 673	163, 122	12, 688	6, 186	233, 772	353, 836	1, 045, 473	92, 095	13	
33, 667	3, 234	7, 527	278, 736	283, 740	5, 060	39, 823	602, 818	439, 416	1, 083, 207	161, 911	14	

TABLE XCV.—*Selected Statistics of Agriculture*—1870—Continued.

STATE OF VIRGINIA.

	Counties.	Improved land.	Value of farms.	Total (estimated) value of all farm productions, including betterments and additions to stock.	Value of all live stock.	LIVE STOCK. Horses.	Mules and asses.	Milch cows.	Working oxen.	Sheep.
		Acres.	Dollars.	Dollars.	Dollars.	No.	No.	No.	No.	No.
1	Accomack	78,556	2,657,265	1,118,430	320,628	2,209	210	2,600	1,080	3,53
2	Albemarle	196,309	5,928,975	1,133,157	519,523	3,418	523	3,065	996	4,87
3	Alexandria	6,914	660,875	97,024	38,831	201	51	293	.....	1
4	Alleghany	23,423	744,820	177,263	111,247	623	32	837	75	1,72
5	Amelia	109,009	1,725,061	391,862	150,385	748	461	1,162	320	1,62
6	Amherst	130,593	1,987,119	626,433	257,219	1,983	268	2,297	491	1,5
7	Appomattox	109,111	1,540,199	277,281	171,866	964	360	1,411	494	1,7
8	Augusta	222,843	10,232,552	2,130,430	1,086,917	7,599	64	6,232	108	8,2
9	Bath	37,913	1,394,270	153,906	194,584	1,081	49	1,357	182	3,0
10	Bedford	174,099	3,373,549	1,158,684	449,558	3,194	583	3,995	578	5,9
11	Bland	30,082	663,119	150,067	130,153	958	35	1,105	103	3,8
12	Botetourt	73,691	2,748,574	478,607	282,089	2,044	78	1,984	123	3,3
13	Brunswick	75,337	694,602	546,397	199,222	859	432	1,540	707	2,5
14	Buchanan	14,055	293,994	130,526	114,847	503	79	1,565	186	5,4
15	Buckingham	123,273	1,998,752	410,218	204,713	1,138	464	1,819	1,078	2,9
16	Campbell	144,813	3,048,166	858,333	402,923	1,877	542	2,591	422	3,5
17	Caroline	137,176	2,350,064	410,346	220,953	1,263	539	1,733	806	1,9
18	Carroll	57,656	638,494	363,993	198,798	1,200	83	2,186	836	8,6
19	Charles City	41,438	991,352	271,086	128,661	355	496	880	200	6
20	Charlotte	116,802	2,401,030	688,314	279,475	1,035	748	1,715	739	3,2
21	Chesterfield	60,855	2,315,669	430,588	232,861	925	697	1,560	160	2,1
22	Clarke	73,253	4,014,970	500,764	272,641	1,769	87	1,499	80	6,2
23	Craig	27,107	861,052	192,248	157,156	958	9	1,049	25	3,1
24	Culpeper	165,789	4,041,710	583,550	351,697	2,338	271	2,563	628	10,1
25	Cumberland	77,239	1,170,312	338,062	138,077	684	377	851	406	1,0
26	Dinwiddie	86,573	1,324,876	464,837	150,128	903	442	1,626	323	1,3
27	Elizabeth City	12,213	577,229	210,249	51,120	280	107	416	94	1
28	Essex	91,509	1,652,972	325,096	161,611	624	340	1,125	909	1,8
29	Fairfax	103,099	5,885,840	939,230	515,823	2,811	224	3,907	343	2,4
30	Fauquier	288,546	9,581,485	1,634,898	1,219,331	5,811	199	5,325	1,198	12,1
31	Floyd	68,627	1,000,650	582,824	307,542	1,846	25	2,769	823	7,9
32	Fluvanna	64,484	1,306,339	416,242	199,270	1,138	287	1,648	646	1,6
33	Franklin	109,514	1,674,512	896,106	424,533	2,410	331	3,550	736	8,[illegible]
34	Frederick	134,160	4,494,430	994,911	558,575	3,990	43	3,405	74	6,0
35	Giles	40,102	979,272	239,051	178,738	1,295	35	1,346	93	4,4
36	Gloucester	56,777	1,128,473	295,401	187,358	868	198	1,707	1,272	1,9
37	Goochland	135,445	1,607,600	324,781	347,005	670	538	1,324	457	1,3
38	Grayson	65,389	1,039,544	428,100	325,839	2,056	125	2,947	479	11,8
39	Greene	43,585	841,995	216,060	110,336	1,016	54	885	83	1,1
40	Greenville	51,991	909,097	395,822	116,265	393	336	766	363	1,0
41	Halifax	183,771	2,545,790	1,132,251	358,473	1,939	987	2,713	1,207	3,8
42	Hanover	130,193	3,295,587	671,824	329,492	1,468	983	2,175	326	2,2
43	Henrico	62,029	5,195,650	724,845	216,497	830	735	1,391	22	3
44	Henry	66,559	819,920	492,127	197,707	865	336	1,747	314	3,4
45	Highland	53,491	1,811,700	277,655	418,905	1,903	11	2,112	264	7,9
46	Isle of Wight	56,317	1,143,148	373,989	146,407	829	248	1,226	582	1,5
47	James City	15,071	311,647	135,780	70,025	298	120	497	224	4
48	King and Queen	75,646	981,885	341,542	163,503	770	236	1,690	1,289	2,0
49	King George	60,404	1,320,987	286,004	146,018	843	246	956	537	8
50	King William	71,848	1,728,298	418,498	195,474	805	528	1,217	473	1,6
51	Lancaster	34,432	849,895	112,316	91,498	560	105	716	642	7
52	Lee	75,731	2,184,205	647,474	377,280	2,314	110	2,581	818	11,3
53	London	201,888	10,877,006	2,097,904	1,168,311	5,572	82	5,749	620	8,9
54	Louisa	122,974	2,564,753	624,693	272,220	1,734	475	2,375	1,159	2,0
55	Lunenburg	94,967	801,238	370,871	169,321	1,109	341	1,497	625	2,6
56	Madison	72,312	1,753,087	488,760	236,832	1,597	119	1,730	352	3,0
57	Matthews	25,376	825,169	120,670	66,077	380	56	970	621	9
58	Mecklenburg	133,357	2,197,841	804,125	316,754	1,479	767	2,557	1,081	5,4
59	Middlesex	32,834	583,200	160,908	81,666	426	126	777	453	1,2
60	Montgomery	79,573	2,976,295	667,378	396,701	1,867	83	2,240	452	[illegible],9
61	Nansemond	56,338	1,197,737	498,329	174,514	1,017	283	1,392	371	1,3
62	Nelson	105,982	3,042,768	641,075	338,206	1,952	244	2,246	707	3,0
63	New Kent	29,115	644,940	191,842	88,361	358	215	661	169	3
64	Norfolk	46,655	2,755,457	718,827	177,980	1,028	339	1,144	94	6
65	Northampton	68,728	1,609,493	553,348	170,347	1,238	160	1,217	247	1,1
66	Northumberland	51,238	1,129,160	423,235	120,391	703	151	1,178	1,209	1,7

TABLE XCV.—*Selected Statistics of Agriculture*—1870—Continued.

STATE OF VIRGINIA.

PRODUCED.										
Wheat.							Potatoes.			
-pring.	Winter.	Rye.	Indian corn.	Oats.	Tobacco.	Wool.	Irish.	Sweet.	Butter.	
-hels.	*Bushels.*	*Bushels.*	*Bushels.*	*Bushels.*	*Pounds.*	*Pounds.*	*Bushels.*	*Bushels.*	*Pounds.*	
175	535	100	530,560	336,860	....	7,991	97,730	212,507	40,284	1
....	218,545	2,812	384,851	180,461	1,781,619	16,947	10,135	2,591	52,295	2
....	3,161	1,573	21,679	5,527	65	29	6,940	736	3,805	3
43	24,800	4,784	50,695	31,991	25,747	4,241	4,386	5	40,690	4
....	64,549	58	70,509	62,688	1,037,721	3,158	5,005	3,580	47,768	5
25	75,040	2,237	160,655	117,608	1,285,471	3,327	15,813	3,900	109,773	6
....	33,825	20	76,708	65,858	656,944	3,627	6,456	4,790	50,868	7
313	462,963	20,835	280,380	234,492	2,000	23,201	28,090	498	333,335	8
....	30,033	5,531	49,252	23,552	....	8,355	5,691	16	33,292	9
100	165,460	7,831	258,995	249,799	1,956,157	13,188	22,306	11,169	200,506	10
....	16,518	4,064	42,057	28,392	2,440	10,819	3,582	....	36,098	11
....	152,799	2,325	95,986	92,307	196,459	8,619	8,086	1,034	98,557	12
....	44,309	....	166,892	68,283	1,121,480	3,386	7,391	9,801	50,335	13
....	3,184	3,047	82,624	14,990	6,424	7,997	6,726	3,973	71,855	14
6	76,688	58	112,336	96,314	809,937	5,517	8,036	5,357	78,557	15
....	77,057	2,534	226,690	175,733	1,761,901	5,961	15,106	7,359	71,978	16
....	63,462	11,050	214,968	30,194	417,848	2,747	5,103	2,770	8,718	17
...	13,382	25,080	91,772	42,658	9,557	16,797	10,837	1,345	74,803	18
....	55,269	175	111,244	47,578	2,200	2,433	6,412	4,995	32,906	19
47	75,147	172	194,260	118,931	1,964,736	6,838	7,585	5,500	98,170	20
....	46,408	708	150,485	74,475	194,510	....	15,543	13,580	62,833	21
....	234,858	6,151	211,628	59,618	....	26,443	8,130	45	85,339	22
....	23,854	11,772	44,242	31,486	15,750	7,148	4,276	113	48,080	23
64	105,528	3,842	361,654	78,568	2,836	39,603	16,644	1,770	83,974	24
....	72,082	....	64,257	42,945	956,855	2,212	3,369	2,598	34,658	25
50	39,819	424	170,712	57,079	844,504	2,092	8,123	8,894	37,421	26
....	10,820	20	78,646	6,717	....	....	15,024	13,879	1,164	27
....	47,577	3,252	264,605	14,757	140	5,205	1,670	360	27,340	28
14	59,968	9,240	295,330	120,072	50	4,961	71,227	4,923	178,345	29
....	269,952	11,001	824,947	180,591	2,205	39,493	37,010	637	194,986	30
14	29,396	41,515	112,789	93,692	157,467	18,995	16,033	136	119,180	31
....	77,486	265	126,448	67,247	894,023	3,878	3,142	1,905	61,397	32
....	77,722	11,340	241,919	178,231	1,696,549	14,986	23,218	10,036	165,490	33
....	239,698	14,225	182,672	76,743	825	26,928	22,661	488	230,178	34
....	53,598	12,633	105,402	23,474	30,653	10,299	3,420	179	39,676	35
....	21,966	107	207,240	25,856	949	4,880	10,673	9,110	20,175	36
....	76,177	310	101,402	72,630	405,215	3,990	370	162	6,485	37
....	30,060	42,704	109,938	63,695	6,401	25,326	12,313	129	91,543	38
....	36,060	6,895	84,033	37,886	262,030	2,905	3,314	1,299	26,362	39
....	5,524	30	112,392	13,509	33,200	1,903	3,475	7,572	12,671	40
900	122,863	4,614	387,227	168,970	3,838,284	4,681	5,950	7,896	55,480	41
....	122,593	1,330	225,517	119,211	449,434	5,502	29,278	35,775	72,013	42
589	80,913	1,150	127,166	80,601	11,175	334	37,634	10,228	46,005	43
....	23,651	9,302	154,794	75,229	1,129,617	4,973	7,030	6,996	27,335	44
....	25,133	6,605	26,075	11,755	....	37,913	5,743	....	71,557	45
,021	428	2	160,733	17,823	....	....	17,957	30,411	....	46
....	10,350	....	64,128	8,238	135	876	6,804	5,071	11,809	47
....	28,172	3,583	204,906	19,771	70	4,007	8,138	7,665	30,733	48
....	34,463	5,737	144,807	11,652	2,662	2,166	5,304	1,545	29,322	49
....	68,256	2,991	236,530	33,030	28,850	2,535	17,045	8,309	37,095	50
....	12,978	190	108,940	22,544	....	827	908	722	50	51
...	81,620	3,645	367,790	66,831	....	21,864	12,108	6,116	132,547	52
....	537,026	9,257	842,128	120,811	....	34,592	32,750	551	167,363	53
15	126,338	920	151,042	126,387	930,226	4,916	7,231	[illegible]	75,914	54
....	38,529	....	107,174	77,394	963,673	4,738	2,936	4,210	33,667	55
....	105,833	9,451	240,240	54,884	60,650	6,054	7,217	2,852	46,705	56
....	3,268	110	104,867	13,577	....	1,054	587	254	190	57
....	83,033	247	243,506	123,492	2,166,628	8,815	11,288	12,512	147,590	58
....	19,650	515	86,967	11,420	30	2,518	2,111	[illegible]	13,754	59
1	100,760	16,252	146,723	78,168	204,747	13,737	12,273	[illegible]	[illegible]	60
70	5,335	50	228,057	22,466	....	1,931	22,169	[illegible]	306	61
....	77,166	6,007	186,858	98,771	1,199,182	6,629	12,707	4,354	111,524	62
....	20,719	89	92,676	19,959	8,600	75	2,836	4,829	8,305	63
50	55	....	348,821	2,888	....	774	60,212	43,918	187	64
....	2,747	351	266,594	139,668	....	2,372	61,616	79,689	20,132	65
....	20,061	251	158,483	22,871	135	3,507	8,210	10,185	10,680	66

TABLE XCV.—*Selected Statistics of Agriculture*—1870—Continued.

STATE OF VIRGINIA—Continued.

	Counties.	Improved land.	Value of farms.	Total (estimated) value of all farm productions, including betterments and additions to stock.	LIVE STOCK. Value of all live stock.	Horses.	Mules and asses.	Milch cows.	Working oxen.	Sheep.
		Acres.	*Dollars.*	*Dollars.*	*Dollars.*	*No.*	*No.*	*No.*	*No.*	*No.*
67	Nottoway	69, 454	1, 225, 536	323, 513	105, 857	466	316	760	345	9
68	Orange	96, 734	799, 148	495, 220	285, 963	1, 942	125	1, 791	502	3, 3
69	Page	48, 744	1, 935, 974	401, 002	236, 778	1, 965	48	1, 450	17	2, 5
70	Patrick	59, 414	351, 975	400, 533	177, 276	975	277	2, 196	624	5, 0
71	Pittsylvania	239, 018	3, 390, 720	1, 599, 734	475, 411	2, 926	1, 310	5, 031	1, 175	5, 6
72	Powhatan	59, 540	1, 449, 229	488, 968	102, 073	628	447	982	374	2, 0
73	Prince Edward	76, 912	1, 797, 300	356, 035	157, 092	692	519	1, 241	528	1, 6
74	Prince George	55, 551	969, 513	383, 683	118, 163	490	533	663	137	6
75	Princess Anne	46, 940	1, 412, 328	622, 815	275, 533	1, 299	239	1, 538	76	3, 0
76	Prince William	69, 737	2, 193, 552	414, 568	304, 892	1, 496	107	1, 976	498	4, 2
77	Pulaski	61, 250	2, 500, 533	177, 489	351, 530	1, 104	8	1, 147	131	2, 0
78	Rappahannock	84, 135	1, 847, 386	577, 985	358, 766	2, 087	71	1, 904	190	3, 6
79	Richmond	50, 206	1, 000, 685	321, 724	82, 485	552	87	993	1, 063	1, 1
80	Roanoke	69, 533	3, 235, 520	567, 955	301, 285	1, 846	178	1, 916	98	2, 3
81	Rockbridge	100, 794	3, 950, 537	722, 273	440, 347	2, 288	107	2, 378	59	3, 4
82	Rockingham	184, 134	9, 218, 089	1, 557, 971	1, 050, 409	6, 505	27	5, 401	40	8, 0
83	Russell	74, 209	1, 662, 746	410, 249	469, 105	2, 251	469	2, 874	334	13, 1
84	Scott	70, 449	1, 181, 395	344, 502	324, 857	2, 528	191	2, 991	560	13, 4
85	Shenandoah	114, 931	4, 409, 310	893, 058	516, 015	3, 466	65	3, 495	8	6, 6
86	Smyth	56, 478	1, 755, 188	306, 282	261, 854	1, 395	158	1, 846	130	4, 5
87	Southampton	123, 059	1, 203, 975	539, 316	203, 942	909	464	1, 385	669	2, 5
88	Spottsylvania	65, 324	1, 789, 206	311, 739	157, 948	906	352	1, 368	511	1, 9
89	Stafford	46, 090	1, 490, 483	255, 864	158, 226	942	153	1, 408	402	1, 4
90	Surry	34, 069	750, 957	212, 622	91, 862	452	227	724	287	1, 0
91	Sussex	68, 064	772, 499	300, 131	122, 601	546	268	876	349	1, 3
92	Tazewell	63, 404	2, 374, 906	347, 905	422, 581	2, 025	205	2, 562	281	9, 5
93	Warren	55, 269	2, 041, 435	524, 506	230, 197	1, 526	34	1, 268	31	5, 1
94	Warwick	10, 489	412, 360	48, 535	27, 430	140	61	246	58	
95	Washington	145, 802	3, 435, 203	942, 725	575, 073	4, 292	442	4, 404	347	13, 3
96	Westmoreland	58, 850	1, 298, 843	261, 239	141, 165	663	126	1, 243	1, 304	2, 0
97	Wise	24, 696	509, 894	121, 144	142, 860	779	64	1, 749	394	6, 2
98	Wythe	85, 387	2, 442, 561	319, 753	359, 187	2, 176	71	2, 376	254	7, 4
99	York	20, 665	484, 734	176, 478	112, 595	433	107	951	501	7

STATE OF WEST VIRGINIA.

	Counties.	Improved land.	Value of farms.	Total (estimated) value of all farm productions, including betterments and additions to stock.	LIVE STOCK. Value of all live stock.	Horses.	Mules and asses.	Milch cows.	Working oxen.	Sheep.
		Acres.	*Dollars.*	*Dollars.*	*Dollars.*	*No.*	*No.*	*No.*	*No.*	*No.*
1	Barbour	95, 668	3, 226, 800	664, 062	658, 275	3, 113	69	3, 622	421	11, 7
2	Berkeley	111, 857	5, 487, 717	1, 120, 041	496, 532	3, 358	40	3, 050	24	9, 2
3	Boone	14, 762	268, 899	168, 449	120, 213	565	34	1, 356	446	3, 9
4	Braxton	32, 240	878, 588	247, 372	218, 990	1, 558	30	2, 049	375	9, 9
5	Brooke	54, 856	3, 548, 075	582, 593	265, 944	1, 230	6	1, 060	70	46, 5
6	Cabell	26, 860	1, 391, 833	297, 673	146, 412	765	56	833	685	4, 0
7	Calhoun	11, 315	332, 762	132, 114	81, 350	496	21	686	188	3, 2
8	Clay	7, 798	166, 282	121, 524	63, 096	341	14	722	129	2, 6
9	Doddridge	37, 758	1, 586, 866	409, 541	300, 950	1, 815	33	1, 987	362	7, 1

TABLE XCV.—*Selected Statistics of Agriculture*—1870—Continued.

STATE OF VIRGINIA—Continued.

PRODUCED.										
Wheat.							Potatoes.			
Spring.	Winter.	Rye.	Indian corn.	Oats.	Tobacco.	Wool.	Irish.	Sweet.	Butter.	
Bushels.	*Bushels.*	*Bushels.*	*Bushels.*	*Bushels.*	*Pounds.*	*Pounds.*	*Bushels.*	*Bushels.*	*Pounds.*	
20	37,887	....	82,686	55,754	653,296	2,006	3,924	3,386	37,135	67
820	116,756	47	185,604	83,286	46,460	10,772	6,526	247	58,938	68
....	128,552	18,583	93,765	24,249	3,435	9,527	8,283	1,025	43,932	69
....	9,657	12,984	147,329	50,937	323,886	8,096	17,166	8,205	85,545	70
783	124,576	6,832	307,657	252,787	4,282,511	....	20,332	9,145	28,189	71
....	70,804	646	74,896	72,046	541,430	5,541	2,434	1,036	33,850	72
....	43,820	....	87,440	67,445	960,700	....	7,544	4,484	51,791	73
....	47,282	....	164,050	31,390	1,800	2,408	8,485	6,986	11,912	74
1,500	1,331	....	398,105	21,985	400	7,105	19,975	30,416	25,112	75
....	47,726	1,989	167,250	70,063	1,616	13,356	9,625	764	108,668	76
10	38,401	7,023	96,690	27,301	18,580	9,605	6,120	....	53,100	77
....	103,112	10,755	304,040	44,297	23,918	15,036	13,144	1,069	87,426	78
....	29,769	2,986	121,680	9,781	1,736	1,913	5,059	4,433	23,057	79
....	203,226	8,167	86,943	89,558	280,550	4,365	8,417	625	120,980	80
....	214,800	7,137	119,518	85,564	186,469	9,156	13,280	966	131,092	81
....	375,688	36,251	251,754	140,896	232	27,571	20,542	4,347	307,668	82
....	40,985	9,443	205,968	56,216	17,282	27,100	7,983	1,259	124,631	83
....	53,583	4,403	222,254	68,730	16,557	24,249	8,544	4,361	95,354	84
....	239,045	19,860	154,313	81,023	....	18,757	14,658	1,278	165,338	85
....	44,681	9,756	96,829	66,323	1,575	10,514	6,049	26	64,910	86
403	988	1,219	218,858	13,683	25	3,587	10,088	24,927	18,660	87
115	55,935	1,655	104,210	50,832	132,502	4,527	6,404	2,543	30,678	88
....	30,763	2,157	99,057	39,586	1,070	3,174	8,900	399	40,707	89
210	700	....	85,995	9,495	....	1,104	15,773	3,381	....	90
30	3,083	66	118,305	21,357	16,100	1,833	7,223	9,818	21,528	91
....	38,020	6,242	155,133	69,189	5,026	19,812	9,675	95	95,175	92
....	100,197	15,317	122,700	27,252	1,117	16,072	3,680	391	59,144	93
....	4,350	....	35,794	7,653	....	....	4,210	2,217	....	94
1	106,520	10,863	351,732	183,147	27,864	28,936	11,383	2,486	187,010	95
....	29,896	3,125	189,381	25,585	4,245	3,497	901	350	812	96
....	6,844	4,443	90,187	17,953	8,128	12,482	9,842	1,522	75,213	97
....	71,913	17,913	115,175	79,234	478	19,827	17,057	3	86,144	98
....	3,289	94	107,103	12,060	410	1,277	12,416	12,954	18,411	99

STATE OF WEST VIRGINIA.

PRODUCED.										
Wheat.							Potatoes.	Dairy products.		
Spring.	Winter.	Rye.	Indian corn.	Oats.	Tobacco.	Wool.	Irish.	Butter.	Cheese.	
Bushels.	*Bushels.*	*Bushels.*	*Bushels.*	*Bushels.*	*Pounds.*	*Pounds.*	*Bushels.*	*Pounds.*	*Pounds.*	
297	42,008	3,935	173,195	43,367	4,776	31,973	14,596	157,317	1,728	1
....	296,975	6,265	297,639	107,588	....	41,147	17,738	239,493	50	2
....	2,585	1,398	129,630	13,667	6,213	9,699	12,043	55,784	....	3
....	20,019	2,883	130,690	29,908	....	18,507	9,028	34,733	....	4
325	45,559	1,445	185,576	81,135	....	185,105	45,850	110,307	....	5
....	42,592	2,675	167,600	31,586	135,410	8,676	17,398	28,674	....	6
28	5,354	849	52,202	8,357	2,181	6,555	6,160	24,640	....	7
249	1,955	657	39,093	11,497	3,175	5,731	2,411	30,595	....	8
....	15,879	4,196	113,064	18,723	17,568	17,441	14,167	113,649	1,236	9

STATE OF WEST VIRGINIA—Continued.

TABLE XCV.—*Selected Statistics of Agriculture*—1870—Continued.

	Counties.	Improved land.	Value of farms.	Total (estimated) value of all farm productions, including betterments and additions to stock.	LIVE STOCK.					
					Value of all live stock.	Horses.	Mules and asses.	Milch cows.	Working oxen.	Sheep.
		Acres.	Dollars.	Dollars.	Dollars.	No.	No.	No.	No.	No.
10	Fayette	36, 410	1, 164, 172	393, 195	225, 085	1, 317	46	2, 267	436	8, 709
11	Gilmer	20, 721	620, 749	190, 092	102, 509	2, 114	10	1, 295	271	6, 100
12	Grant	63, 145	1, 381, 852	477, 725	363, 399	1, 435	5	1, 739	44	7, 551
13	Greenbrier	95, 099	4, 152, 216	690, 154	553, 856	2, 805	58	3, 201	496	13, 88
14	Hampshire	77, 873	1, 924, 264	524, 221	381, 454	2, 380	35	2, 673	21	8, 31
15	Hancock	30, 947	2, 317, 814	347, 055	218, 840	835	12	869	72	26, 33
16	Hardy	43, 675	1, 722, 337	400, 128	288, 204	1, 163	24	1, 360	146	4, 17
17	Harrison	147, 488	6, 935, 258	1, 302, 545	1, 267, 287	5, 040	67	4, 906	706	15, 81
18	Jackson	49, 903	1, 620, 335	510, 780	370, 271	2, 558	64	2, 289	608	13, 61
19	Jefferson	92, 245	6, 883, 804	1, 139, 166	581, 038	3, 694	131	2, 489	91	6, 58
20	Kanawha	59, 459	3, 097, 767	774, 582	413, 450	2, 426	167	3, 400	1, 078	9, 87
21	Lewis	75, 878	2, 417, 175	649, 527	564, 196	2, 515	28	2, 962	482	10, 92
22	Lincoln	15, 613	393, 511	136, 803	89, 626	547	10	950	448	3, 87
23	Logan	14, 149	355, 009	143, 462	116, 372	589	57	1, 376	903	4, 50
24	Marion	37, 410	1, 440, 408	134, 811	247, 090	907	27	1, 110	173	4, 99
25	Marshall	78, 852	3, 511, 574	857, 854	530, 730	3, 109	32	3, 076	515	37, 50
26	Mason	67, 010	2, 980, 122	654, 570	544, 554	2, 563	162	2, 332	833	9, 88
27	McDowell	4, 592	85, 834	51, 125	39, 500	189	18	546	86	1, 30
28	Mercer	47, 313	1, 110, 793	303, 500	297, 648	1, 667	44	2, 722	989	8, 29
29	Mineral	59, 119	1, 406, 707	445, 144	277, 600	1, 333	21	1, 534	14	6, 42
30	Monongalia	112, 045	4, 724, 358	1, 141, 914	871, 260	4, 238	36	4, 606	761	17, 37
31	Monroe	104, 760	3, 423, 584	590, 143	567, 053	2, 555	58	3, 006	281	11, 51
32	Morgan	32, 729	700, 364	266, 436	142, 792	882	6	1, 112	27	2, 68
33	Nicholas	24, 455	641, 456	315, 854	185, 532	1, 073	13	1, 600	324	8, 17
34	Ohio	46, 059	4, 061, 879	687, 379	418, 466	1, 637	12	1, 585	200	47, 20
35	Pendleton	54, 041	1, 326, 476	326, 656	328, 164	1, 767	13	2, 270	50	9, 94
36	Pleasants	17, 098	578, 465	141, 247	98, 257	620	17	638	120	2, 91
37	Pocahontas	43, 329	1, 379, 774	224, 697	358, 239	1, 815	55	2, 440	266	10, 82
38	Preston	102, 062	2, 541, 651	730, 462	613, 369	3, 596	32	4, 526	187	22, 33
39	Putnam	36, 044	1, 419, 585	323, 132	251, 049	1, 463	80	1, 565	813	6, 29
40	Raleigh	20, 969	422, 896	147, 916	119, 184	827	20	1, 545	274	5, 46
41	Randolph	50, 036	1, 469, 878	270, 656	369, 158	1, 525	36	1, 970	245	8, 32
42	Ritchie	46, 119	1, 676, 082	511, 910	299, 199	1, 970	33	2, 079	383	11, 60
43	Roane	34, 921	965, 212	317, 150	241, 585	1, 540	43	1, 858	507	12, 97
44	Taylor	53, 815	2, 311, 085	502, 070	390, 939	1, 685	11	1, 791	170	6, 00
45	Tucker	13, 078	361, 970	95, 403	112, 583	493	8	637	75	2, 60
46	Tyler	45, 019	1, 781, 480	392, 653	330, 777	1, 897	96	1, 566	308	12, 11
47	Upshur	59, 812	2, 341, 034	510, 337	383, 509	2, 039	17	2, 329	257	8, 00
48	Wayne	39, 554	1, 025, 269	451, 455	259, 327	1, 398	121	1, 827	1, 837	9, 72
49	Webster	6, 945	151, 720	53, 079	49, 607	359	7	643	127	2, 01
50	Wetzel	34, 202	1, 460, 361	457, 563	255, 597	1, 629	13	1, 641	400	9, 54
51	Wirt	29, 061	625, 354	237, 307	143, 163	954	13	954	251	4, 18
52	Wood	63, 281	3, 625, 905	715, 860	392, 720	2, 745	62	2, 763	497	10, 41
53	Wyoming	9, 805	178, 980	106, 615	80, 420	345	16	1, 042	165	2, 82

STATE OF WEST VIRGINIA—Continued.

TABLE XCV.—*Selected Statistics of Agriculture*—1870—Continued.

PRODUCED.										
Wheat.							Potatoes.	Dairy products.		
Spring.	Winter.	Rye.	Indian corn.	Oats.	Tobacco.	Wool.	Irish.	Butter.	Cheese.	
...hels.	*Bushels.*	*Bushels.*	*Bushels.*	*Bushels.*	*Pounds.*	*Pounds.*	*Bushels.*	*Pounds.*	*Pounds.*	
13	13, 304	3, 003	123, 220	41, 991	188, 165	16, 331	11, 350	72, 182	1, 070	10
65	9, 765	2, 402	106, 036	17, 592	15, 931	12, 736	7, 138	44, 929	270	11
65	31, 566	8, 255	52, 350	10, 503	519	20, 680	7, 536	67, 587	....	12
....	50, 214	7, 734	181, 381	92, 295	3, 176	34, 051	13, 928	174, 865	2, 145	13
....	76, 832	21, 885	120, 325	46, 769	285	26, 658	13, 800	114, 948	1, 764	14
....	34, 270	11, 749	83, 180	68, 494	....	128, 642	34, 578	70, 588	60	15
10	33, 432	8, 939	114, 567	13, 283	....	13, 566	7, 069	39, 057	590	16
10	83, 463	4, 551	327, 261	56, 183	17, 098	45, 662	26, 028	276, 955	4, 282	17
....	59, 845	3, 587	272, 044	48, 521	96, 265	29, 850	50, 397	87, 052	....	18
5	468, 836	7, 620	336, 287	44, 077	140	28, 699	24, 305	120, 374	....	19
413	45, 587	728	406, 226	96, 268	412, 460	20, 457	44, 300	163, 142	5	20
....	41, 174	3, 956	191, 556	31, 776	51, 470	26, 055	16, 071	113, 259	315	21
....	6, 260	1, 696	104, 961	12, 054	56, 083	7, 151	....	48, 271	10	22
200	1, 784	496	125, 273	4, 142	3, 912	6, 296	7, 957	29, 182	12	23
10	26, 528	1, 109	63, 643	29, 819	....	12, 780	2, 493	22, 927	336	24
129	131, 509	7, 363	364, 743	211, 602	20	119, 579	54, 781	204, 480	320	25
150	115, 200	598	456, 990	43, 464	58, 600	22, 833	84, 534	5, 002	330	26
....	675	460	31, 586	3, 615	3, 000	2, 404	2, 310	15, 597	....	27
....	25, 756	5, 597	114, 746	43, 184	117, 420	18, 713	10, 867	109, 355	550	28
....	50, 915	13, 257	71, 895	29, 331	....	23, 406	8, 891	52, 078	125	29
54	111, 751	5, 130	301, 328	148, 072	2, 733	55, 856	23, 772	345, 573	1, 030	30
....	52, 817	11, 320	170, 721	59, 062	123, 221	26, 694	12, 164	163, 540	690	31
....	27, 697	9, 217	58, 142	19, 835	1, 068	7, 564	10, 915	41, 183	....	32
....	10, 242	1, 331	101, 300	38, 365	840	18, 838	6, 247	164, 990	560	33
844	41, 432	3, 795	225, 465	97, 372	....	175, 124	46, 748	120, 135	....	34
....	37, 984	10, 594	50, 228	14, 538	....	26, 273	8, 692	56, 876	980	35
....	15, 283	1, 290	67, 580	14, 596	11, 910	6, 441	15, 925	110	....	36
....	14, 901	6, 334	46, 512	22, 343	2, 966	24, 137	8, 623	65, 740	2, 015	37
305	33, 390	20, 581	145, 004	189, 070	1, 673	58, 388	24, 063	193, 233	110	38
40	39, 980	1, 340	232, 126	49, 879	472, 765	14, 992	26, 918	63, 061	50	39
....	7, 509	1, 660	73, 657	16, 278	5, 769	11, 332	6, 720	41, 635	30	40
....	8, 969	2, 493	59, 758	33, 237	2, 133	17, 706	10, 006	90, 840	903	41
7	25, 503	35, 635	146, 235	40, 033	9, 907	26, 828	19, 538	116, 094	355	42
....	24, 087	2, 479	160, 912	28, 489	16, 885	24, 176	15, 200	100, 379	300	43
25	28, 659	2, 075	95, 439	45, 166	2, 250	17, 233	10, 305	97, 223	1, 792	44
....	1, 409	1, 294	27, 813	14, 726	....	6, 093	2, 083	26, 769	....	45
....	41, 262	2, 316	157, 302	42, 480	47, 969	26, 704	21, 159	108, 080	860	46
10	29, 948	6, 055	108, 494	21, 422	11, 190	21, 857	11, 448	127, 158	5, 555	47
135	23, 192	402	294, 863	27, 131	58, 230	17, 022	21, 759	68, 967	218	48
....	1, 196	866	21, 075	4, 689	2, 508	4, 598	2, 340	14, 563	463	49
6	37, 164	4, 484	193, 111	66, 122	47, 050	23, 392	19, 209	119, 393	1, 100	50
....	15, 532	1, 025	128, 836	37, 988	8, 712	9, 515	17, 809	44, 000	130	51
....	68, 190	5, 929	327, 506	80, 839	21, 890	24, 830	138, 230	215, 576	....	52
....	2, 150	973	57, 899	11, 073	889	5, 630	5, 962	32, 329	160	53

TABLE XCV.—*Selected Statistics of Agriculture*—1870—Continued.

STATE OF WISCONSIN.

	Counties.	Improved land.	Value of farms.	Total (estimated) value of all farm productions, including betterments and additions to stock.	LIVE STOCK. Value of all live stock.	Horses.	Milch cows.	Working oxen.	Sheep.
		Acres.	*Dollars.*	*Dollars.*	*Dollars.*	*No.*	*No.*	*No.*	*No.*
1	Adams	45, 230	1, 205, 135	510, 024	327, 914	1, 633	2, 578	909	7, 734
2	Ashland	175	17, 400	2, 150	985	1	6	9	
3	Barron	1, 014	25, 590	23, 180	12, 235	23	49	67	40
4	Bayfield	10	1, 060	725	400	2	2		
5	Brown	51, 884	2, 655, 608	860, 127	459, 797	2, 479	4, 267	1, 404	5, 216
6	Buffalo	59, 197	2, 412, 645	1, 362, 865	755, 744	3, 028	3, 871	1, 283	5, 926
7	Burnett	1, 164	33, 170	29, 963	9, 805	34	182	100	146
8	Calumet	62, 194	3, 879, 810	766, 848	500, 578	2, 776	4, 186	1, 571	9, 488
9	Chippewa	22, 268	740, 047	336, 763	172, 821	928	1, 466	802	916
10	Clark	8, 992	645, 460	227, 185	127, 673	202	705	580	506
11	Columbia	251, 814	10, 422, 097	2, 913, 397	1, 577, 953	9, 758	9, 659	893	49, 413
12	Crawford	54, 556	1, 985, 630	820, 513	560, 004	3, 149	3, 779	1, 128	7, 921
13	Dane	396, 900	21, 111, 053	5, 706, 491	2, 939, 893	19, 416	17, 891	1, 016	65, 391
14	Dodge	321, 597	21, 279, 847	4, 650, 142	2, 411, 499	13, 550	16, 311	1, 571	59, 138
15	Door	11, 452	429, 043	183, 318	103, 639	331	805	586	246
16	Douglas	234	66, 760	4, 950	3, 225	14	11	8	2
17	Dunn	44, 931	1, 571, 834	669, 969	437, 200	1, 567	2, 813	1, 254	4, 182
18	Eau Claire	35, 070	1, 340, 385	576, 390	295, 540	1, 458	1, 834	361	1, 864
19	Fond du Lac	285, 777	17, 161, 131	3, 547, 091	2, 010, 577	11, 621	14, 273	1, 907	66, 084
20	Grant	273, 850	11, 662, 855	3, 629, 805	2, 216, 899	13, 901	13, 312	1, 017	24, 936
21	Green	250, 998	10, 269, 402	2, 800, 041	2, 204, 543	9, 744	11, 474	154	39, 477
22	Green Lake	97, 149	5, 622, 125	1, 536, 438	810, 298	4, 108	4, 353	726	31, 501
23	Iowa	167, 581	8, 222, 321	2, 333, 720	1, 628, 744	9, 871	10, 064	497	13, 756
24	Jackson	35, 630	1, 181, 810	485, 144	294, 648	1, 677	2, 011	605	3, 088
25	Jefferson	228, 409	11, 716, 020	2, 822, 127	1, 575, 251	8, 409	11, 701	932	49, 118
26	Juneau	51, 665	1, 963, 725	683, 448	392, 605	2, 040	2, 846	1, 047	8, 406
27	Kenosha	142, 139	6, 073, 921	1, 457, 696	982, 512	4, 707	7, 169	88	49, 277
28	Kewaunee	31, 944	1, 391, 975	435, 258	277, 912	842	2, 497	1, 940	1, 546
29	La Crosse	77, 703	3, 537, 085	1, 059, 983	603, 150	3, 486	4, 438	727	9, 288
30	La Fayette	207, 887	10, 278, 217	2, 804, 349	1, 678, 709	10, 353	10, 461	105	18, 770
31	Manitowoc	131, 292	7, 029, 669	1, 458, 135	1, 085, 479	4, 460	9, 351	4, 095	16, 403
32	Marathon	12, 146	592, 540	138, 942	98, 310	273	1, 331	947	1, 482
33	Marquette	62, 219	1, 680, 355	697, 709	401, 345	2, 220	3, 429	1, 163	16, 488
34	Milwaukee	90, 358	10, 284, 555	1, 734, 926	768, 593	4, 577	6, 757	235	5, 796
35	Monroe	76, 590	3, 631, 240	1, 346, 555	727, 489	3, 232	4, 621	1, 628	12, 341
36	Oconto	9, 736	474, 700	232, 983	95, 712	352	522	289	274
37	Outagamie	74, 886	4, 426, 800	904, 021	592, 315	3, 064	4, 819	1, 488	10, 815
38	Ozaukee	83, 966	5, 230, 670	952, 902	639, 269	3, 690	5, 641	951	5, 482
39	Pepin	19, 900	745, 285	260, 834	224, 732	958	1, 298	491	2, 746
40	Pierce	41, 702	1, 950, 350	586, 475	391, 880	1, 562	2, 436	902	3, 536
41	Polk	8, 987	513, 130	167, 368	126, 155	976	834	373	745
42	Portage	58, 961	1, 769, 417	643, 856	382, 402	1, 427	3, 024	1, 663	8, 542
43	Racine	174, 591	8, 447, 746	1, 638, 609	1, 231, 932	5, 395	7, 257	191	37, 620
44	Richland	72, 649	3, 202, 165	1, 005, 318	656, 606	3, 719	4, 668	1, 117	21, 014
45	Rock	318, 811	16, 746, 851	4, 034, 563	2, 306, 395	13, 995	12, 652	140	62, 193
46	Sauk	137, 629	6, 277, 290	1, 856, 973	1, 008, 226	6, 030	7, 250	1, 063	18, 766
47	Shawanaw	7, 891	352, 425	137, 633	75, 428	254	582	431	735
48	Sheboygan	159, 912	8, 929, 086	2, 077, 812	1, 233, 511	6, 403	10, 487	2, 690	31, 734
49	St. Croix	103, 953	3, 666, 305	1, 214, 620	635, 875	3, 032	3, 232	920	1, 435
50	Trempealeau	67, 896	2, 256, 870	895, 446	603, 808	2, 784	3, 537	1, 226	9, 536
51	Vernon	97, 254	3, 748, 290	1, 433, 527	836, 360	4, 676	5, 560	1, 694	21, 456
52	Walworth	221, 790	11, 804, 180	2, 763, 409	1, 760, 946	11, 244	9, 743	266	97, 324
53	Washington	147, 565	9, 328, 575	1, 928, 664	137, 797	6, 700	8, 459	1, 570	16, 808
54	Waukesha	218, 984	14, 238, 070	2, 715, 212	1, 789, 084	9, 660	10, 515	625	72, 339
55	Waupacca	58, 139	2, 501, 805	747, 926	478, 063	1, 796	3, 606	1, 614	10, 378
56	Waushara	59, 760	1, 997, 300	843, 228	424, 284	1, 978	3, 137	1, 351	11, 771
57	Winnebago	152, 819	9, 436, 356	2, 210, 718	1, 204, 631	6, 103	7, 911	836	37, 707
58	Wood	6, 556	248, 938	167, 628	81, 472	291	594	369	440

TABLE XCV.—*Selected Statistics of Agriculture*—1870—Continued.

STATE OF WISCONSIN.

PRODUCED.											
Wheat.								Potatoes.	Dairy products.		
Spring.	Winter.	Rye.	Indian corn.	Oats.	Barley.	Buckwheat.	Wool.	Irish.	Butter.	Cheese.	
Bushels.	*Bushels.*	*Bushels.*	*Bushels.*	*Bushels.*	*Bushels.*	*Bushels.*	*Pounds.*	*Bushels.*	*Pounds.*	*Pounds.*	
122, 161	1, 293	60, 701	114, 320	88, 831	2, 596	25, 435	22, 668	64, 343	277, 530	8, 521	1
....	....	....	....	330	....	....	....	530	260	....	2
1, 665	....	600	965	10, 130	100	50	160	1, 850	4, 975	....	3
....	....	....	....	....	....	....	....	550	50	....	4
90, 481	73, 746	16, 498	13, 152	133, 953	4, 674	832	10, 837	68, 329	309, 838	50	5
494, 695	72, 469	11, 234	195, 372	316, 383	44, 912	3, 852	28, 330	65, 885	264, 685	19, 320	6
2, 553	....	....	545	1, 349	66	....	265	1, 955	5, 896	....	7
301, 359	38, 621	2, 072	42, 344	175, 294	12, 479	711	34, 801	41, 196	305, 386	3, 895	8
125, 739	5, 766	6, 216	32, 751	166, 944	11, 707	1, 515	2, 849	67, 890	51, 436	100	9
5, 922	6, 181	670	9, 511	34, 997	2, 938	172	1, 901	17, 317	74, 876	....	10
1, 517, 052	280	40, 844	528, 541	678, 907	51, 745	18, 156	108, 255	202, 068	706, 516	33, 093	11
173, 360	18, 309	947	261, 879	160, 939	7, 557	3, 644	23, 854	79, 649	226, 277	....	12
2, 535, 048	808	15, 602	938, 128	1, 490, 663	148, 791	10, 479	252, 525	348, 220	1, 242, 953	43, 416	13
2, 285, 640	8, 898	25, 009	629, 020	909, 648	96, 233	7, 650	229, 984	354, 744	1, 153, 272	12, 939	14
16, 493	18, 092	4, 353	1, 486	22, 103	1, 649	38	698	43, 157	56, 861	....	15
10	....	....	....	690	140	....	....	1, 540	....	....	16
196, 790	7, 556	12, 671	71, 574	233, 404	20, 409	4, 387	8, 378	45, 069	209, 830	1, 330	17
205, 112	715	4, 243	69, 964	294, 493	18, 336	1, 953	5, 075	29, 011	124, 365	400	18
1, 575, 800	39, 466	11, 988	287, 400	879, 515	60, 735	11, 248	274, 137	242, 961	1, 095, 482	61, 303	19
912, 828	1, 627	5, 705	1, 744, 398	1, 433, 020	44, 316	6, 077	75, 821	288, 017	861, 028	18, 577	20
541, 114	745	25, 469	947, 105	743, 019	15, 107	5, 226	139, 110	184, 195	909, 485	358, 830	21
613, 622	625	17, 702	251, 822	300, 814	18, 416	11, 809	119, 214	91, 343	362, 594	40, 575	22
760, 131	35	4, 408	705, 792	803, 951	40, 867	3, 767	48, 758	145, 141	547, 388	3, 722	23
194, 119	17, 835	8, 359	68, 547	271, 066	15, 129	5, 007	6, 744	38, 718	140, 154	470	24
676, 791	1, 924	34, 374	579, 233	470, 466	50, 310	11, 526	203, 408	296, 103	908, 119	84, 201	25
178, 959	13, 345	16, 892	115, 393	197, 005	3, 756	12, 573	26, 904	97, 755	221, 003	3, 420	26
214, 422	145	13, 092	269, 036	359, 343	45, 473	5, 767	242, 616	134, 463	480, 509	308, 600	27
77, 106	42, 959	21, 123	755	73, 554	6, 029	238	4, 853	58, 866	124, 091	252	28
549, 027	32, 458	21, 789	192, 503	286, 126	25, 985	2, 922	27, 179	66, 526	248, 638	22, 165	29
516, 850	50	3, 017	1, 294, 453	1, 519, 202	75, 802	3, 101	65, 089	198, 327	689, 355	22, 760	30
436, 036	81, 110	92, 881	2, 865	386, 759	30, 176	410	44, 421	108, 180	575, 319	4, 412	31
32, 533	2, 794	1, 478	131	76, 482	3, 281	42	4, 336	22, 164	....	....	32
144, 386	176	77, 488	116, 049	77, 881	234	17, 392	49, 508	68, 950	240, 408	1, 440	33
238, 032	100	48, 271	169, 996	297, 874	54, 923	4, 934	13, 779	214, 916	647, 590	17, 706	34
368, 402	110, 045	14, 717	183, 119	291, 469	10, 375	11, 636	39, 228	91, 836	391, 476	9, 150	35
10, 147	11, 966	2, 337	2, 683	25, 481	147	433	533	36, 300	46, 300	....	36
183, 015	168, 605	2, 992	55, 862	199, 167	3, 105	1, 802	35, 445	66, 051	282, 342	17, 710	37
312, 761	1, 512	72, 017	28, 305	258, 442	36, 520	821	15, 807	84, 349	395, 003	1, 100	38
94, 631	3, 359	4, 774	108, 232	79, 378	7, 419	5, 086	7, 917	27, 187	125, 010	1, 400	39
330, 954	175	2, 715	81, 353	171, 393	24, 551	929	9, 179	47, 512	121, 038	790	40
40, 831	198	458	10, 839	52, 564	1, 217	895	2, 142	15, 366	68, 203	....	41
206, 344	7, 123	58, 657	63, 909	153, 294	5, 233	6, 721	25, 911	112, 707	198, 693	7, 492	42
339, 601	135	10, 252	376, 398	393, 127	25, 983	7, 090	164, 321	164, 219	610, 228	1, 795	43
100, 153	89, 747	7, 453	345, 787	183, 952	2, 681	10, 407	68, 573	108, 926	316, 734	25, 544	44
864, 883	165	120, 965	1, 137, 304	1, 173, 714	204, 998	26, 864	264, 446	443, 151	1, 043, 169	86, 110	45
476, 278	11, 138	24, 522	410, 710	510, 125	21, 990	25, 010	61, 081	210, 518	513, 080	6, 004	46
11, 191	16, 081	3, 144	7, 996	27, 631	450	254	1, 964	20, 273	20, 970	100	47
497, 290	107, 241	93, 165	75, 198	418, 083	56, 767	21, 810	127, 241	138, 786	710, 010	120, 005	48
823, 678	....	1, 623	42, 461	447, 775	27, 664	1, 058	3, 343	61, 972	229, 615	1, 625	49
502, 853	13, 341	9, 734	141, 275	241, 408	17, 533	2, 878	37, 242	47, 699	341, 043	7, 863	50
482, 638	69, 956	2, 829	290, 846	445, 526	30, 709	3, 570	61, 633	82, 349	484, 741	1, 965	51
603, 632	1, 461	41, 210	830, 179	698, 033	113, 835	30, 137	443, 995	294, 157	639, 516	79, 327	52
693, 056	23, 631	75, 767	216, 382	393, 543	64, 303	4, 524	57, 458	192, 995	632, 214	4, 540	53
647, 945	3, 660	64, 525	518, 798	501, 443	58, 034	29, 287	308, 071	406, 134	864, 215	33, 585	54
125, 033	71, 549	24, 312	103, 300	111, 357	3, 825	10, 129	33, 301	96, 489	283, 563	5, 295	55
193, 607	8, 135	64, 206	143, 099	106, 383	752	21, 951	42, 769	91, 391	321, 706	9, 514	56
723, 189	22, 323	10, 216	190, 397	364, 143	11, 544	2, 992	135, 648	87, 366	721, 265	99, 387	57
7, 484	1, 175	6, 948	14, 536	17, 430	493	1, 691	875	28, 468	46, 643	....	58

MANUFACTURES, MINING, AND FISHERIES.

TABLE XCVI.—*Manufactures, by Totals of States and Territories*—1870.

	States and Territories.	Establishments.	STEAM-ENGINES.		WATER-WHEELS.	
			Horse-power.	Number.	Horse-power.	Number.
	The United States	252, 148	1, 215, 711	40, 191	1, 130, 431	51, 01[illegible]
1	Alabama	2, 188	7, 740	295	11, 011	734
2	Arizona	18	80	5	10	1
3	Arkansas	1, 079	6, 101	256	1, 545	12[illegible]
4	California	3, 984	18, 493	604	6, 877	271
5	Colorado	256	1, 433	49	792	31
6	Connecticut	5, 128	25, 979	711	54, 395	1, 9[illegible]
7	Dakota	17	248	9	76	6
8	Delaware	800	4, 313	164	4, 290	234
9	District of Columbia	952	789	54	1, 100	15
10	Florida	659	3, 172	196	588	79
11	Georgia	3, 836	10, 826	405	27, 417	1, 7[illegible]
12	Idaho	101	311	11	295	16
13	Illinois	12, 597	73, 091	2, 330	12, 953	53[illegible]
14	Indiana	11, 847	76, 851	2, 881	23, 518	1, 0[illegible]
15	Iowa	6, 566	25, 298	899	14, 249	7[illegible]
16	Kansas	1, 477	6, 360	254	1, 789	[illegible]
17	Kentucky	5, 390	31, 928	1, 147	7, 040	43[illegible]
18	Louisiana	2, 557	24, 924	887	142	23
19	Maine	5, 550	9, 465	354	70, 108	2, 76[illegible]
20	Maryland	5, 812	13, 961	531	18, 461	937
21	Massachusetts	13, 212	78, 502	2, 396	105, 854	3, 157
22	Michigan	9, 435	70, 956	2, 215	34, 895	1, 500
23	Minnesota	2, 270	7, 085	246	13, 054	434
24	Mississippi	1, 731	10, 019	384	2, 453	[illegible]
25	Missouri	11, 871	48, 418	1, 638	6, 644	3[illegible]
26	Montana	201	822	33	795	46
27	Nebraska	670	1, 865	63	1, 446	67
28	Nevada	330	6, 007	120	2, 538	34
29	New Hampshire	3, 342	8, 787	280	68, 291	2, 312
30	New Jersey	6, 636	32, 307	984	25, 832	1, 13[illegible]
31	New Mexico	182	252	13	659	[illegible]
32	New York	36, 206	126, 107	4, 664	208, 256	9, 011
33	North Carolina	3, 642	6, 941	306	26, 211	1, [illegible]
34	Ohio	22, 773	129, 577	4, 586	44, 746	2, 157
35	Oregon	969	2, 471	88	5, 806	2[illegible]
36	Pennsylvania	37, 200	221, 936	6, 230	141, 982	7, 603
37	Rhode Island	1, 850	23, 546	402	18, 481	456
38	South Carolina	1, 584	4, 537	210	10, 395	700
39	Tennessee	5, 317	18, 467	732	19, 514	1, 340
40	Texas	2, 399	11, 214	540	1, 830	116
41	Utah	533	331	21	2, 169	192
42	Vermont	3, 270	6, 425	186	44, 897	1, 9[illegible]
43	Virginia	5, 933	8, 410	396	41, 202	2, [illegible]
44	Washington	269	1, 411	38	1, 412	52
45	West Virginia	2, 444	17, 136	509	10, 195	6[illegible]
46	Wisconsin	7, 013	30, 509	926	33, 714	1, 2[illegible]
47	Wyoming	32	310	13	34	2

The scope of these statistics.—The above tables purport to exhibit the production of every mill, factory, or shop in the United States in which any class of mechanical industry is carried on to the extent of producing the value of $500 a year. Inasmuch as, with ruling prices of labor and materials, few able-bodied artisans working ten months in the year but produce to the value of $500, these tables should comprise all the results of substantially all the manufacturing and mechanical industry in the country. Between this, the theory of the case, and the facts exposed to criticism in the above tables, will be found a difference so great as only to be accounted for by a full explanation of the mode of collecting these statistics. (See page 372 *et seq.* of Vol. III, Ninth Census.)

The period covered by the returns.—It needs to be borne carefully in mind, in the use of the above tables, that the period covered by the returns is the twelve months from June 1, 1869, to May 31, 1870, inclusive. The fluctuations of productive industry are so incessant and so extensive, that it is necessary to fix precisely the period covered by any statement before tests can be applied to ascertain its completeness and accuracy. Especially in the United States, where these fluctuations are far greater than in older manufacturing countries, is it essential to observe this caution. It often happens that e comparison of two twelve-months periods, having so many as ten or eleven months in

TABLE XCVI.—*Manufactures, by Totals of States and Territories*—1870.

HANDS EMPLOYED.				CAPITAL.	WAGES.	MATERIALS.	PRODUCTS.	
All.	Males above 16.	Females above 15.	Youth.	Dollars.	Dollars.	Dollars.	Dollars.	
2,053,996	1,615,598	323,770	114,628	2,118,208,769	775,584,343	2,488,427,242	4,232,325,442	
8,248	7,196	664	388	5,714,032	2,227,968	7,592,837	13,040,644	1
84	84			150,700	45,580	110,090	185,410	2
3,206	3,077	47	82	1,782,913	673,963	2,536,998	4,629,234	3
25,392	24,040	873	479	39,728,202	13,136,722	35,351,193	66,594,556	4
876	874	2		2,835,605	528,221	1,593,290	2,852,820	5
89,523	61,684	20,810	7,029	95,281,278	38,987,187	86,419,579	161,065,474	6
91	89		2	79,200	21,106	105,997	178,570	7
9,710	7,705	1,199	806	10,839,093	3,692,195	10,206,397	16,791,382	8
4,685	4,333	216	136	5,021,925	2,007,600	4,754,883	9,292,173	9
2,749	2,670	20	59	1,679,930	989,592	2,330,873	4,685,403	10
17,871	15,078	1,498	1,295	13,930,125	4,844,508	18,583,731	31,196,115	11
265	264		1	742,300	112,372	691,785	1,047,624	12
82,979	73,045	6,717	3,217	94,368,057	31,100,244	127,600,077	205,620,672	13
58,852	54,412	2,272	2,168	52,052,425	18,366,780	63,135,492	108,617,278	14
25,032	23,395	951	685	22,420,183	6,893,292	27,682,096	46,534,322	15
6,844	6,599	118	127	4,319,060	2,377,511	6,112,163	11,775,833	16
30,636	27,687	1,159	1,790	29,277,809	9,444,524	29,497,535	54,625,809	17
30,071	23,637	4,210	2,224	18,313,974	4,593,470	12,412,023	24,161,905	18
49,180	34,310	13,448	1,422	39,796,190	14,282,205	49,379,757	79,497,521	19
44,860	34,061	8,278	2,521	36,438,729	12,682,817	46,897,032	76,593,613	20
279,380	179,032	86,229	14,119	231,677,862	118,051,886	334,413,982	553,912,568	21
63,694	58,347	2,941	2,406	71,712,283	21,205,355	68,142,515	118,394,676	22
11,290	10,892	259	139	11,993,729	4,052,837	13,842,902	23,110,700	23
5,941	5,500	191	250	4,501,714	1,547,428	4,364,206	8,154,758	24
65,354	53,904	3,884	5,566	80,257,244	31,055,445	115,533,269	206,213,429	25
701	697	2	2	1,794,300	370,843	1,316,331	2,494,511	26
2,665	2,558	81	26	2,169,963	1,429,913	2,902,074	5,738,512	27
2,859	2,856	3		5,127,790	2,498,473	10,315,984	15,870,539	28
40,783	25,829	12,775	2,179	36,023,743	13,823,091	44,577,967	71,038,249	29
75,552	58,115	11,198	6,239	79,606,719	32,648,409	103,415,245	169,237,732	30
427	423	1	3	1,450,695	167,281	880,957	1,489,868	31
351,800	267,378	63,795	20,627	366,994,320	142,466,758	452,065,452	785,194,651	32
13,622	11,339	1,422	861	8,140,473	2,195,711	12,824,693	19,021,327	33
137,202	119,686	11,575	5,941	141,923,964	49,066,488	157,131,697	269,713,610	34
2,884	2,753	67	64	4,376,849	1,120,173	3,419,756	6,877,387	35
319,487	256,543	43,712	19,232	406,821,845	127,976,594	421,197,673	711,894,344	36
49,417	28,804	11,752	5,861	66,557,322	19,354,256	73,154,109	111,418,354	37
8,141	7,099	578	464	5,400,418	1,543,715	5,856,736	9,858,981	38
19,412	17,663	1,089	660	15,595,295	5,390,630	19,657,027	34,362,636	39
7,927	7,450	157	320	5,284,110	1,787,835	6,273,193	11,517,302	40
1,534	1,465	43	26	1,391,898	395,365	1,238,252	2,343,019	41
18,686	16,301	1,872	513	20,329,637	6,264,581	17,007,769	32,184,606	42
26,974	22,175	2,259	2,540	18,455,400	5,343,099	23,832,384	38,364,322	43
1,096	1,025	1		1,893,674	574,936	1,435,128	2,851,052	44
11,672	10,728	287	657	11,084,520	4,322,164	14,503,701	24,102,201	45
43,910	40,296	2,114	1,500	41,981,872	13,575,642	45,851,266	77,214,326	46
502	500	1	1	889,400	347,578	280,156	765,424	47

ommon, will exhibit important differences caused by the eleventh or twelfth month, r both.

Capital invested in manufactures.—The census returns of capital invested in manu-actures are entirely untrustworthy and delusive. The inquiry is one of which it is ot too much to say, that it ought never to be embraced in the schedules of the cen-us; not merely for the reason that the results are, and must remain, wholly worthless, he inquiry occupying upon the schedules the place of some technical question which night be made to yield information of great value, but, also, because the inquiry in espect to capital creates more prejudice and arouses more opposition to the progress f the enumeration than all the other inquiries of the manufacturing schedule united. t is, in fact, the one question which manufacturers resent as needlessly obtrusive, while, at the same time, it is perhaps the one question in respect to their business which manufacturers, certainly the majority of them, could not answer to their own atisfaction, even if disposed. No man in business knows what he is worth—far less an say what portion of his estate is to be treated as capital. With respect, indeed, to orporations having a determinate capital stock, the difficulty of making a correct eturn in this particular becomes very much reduced; yet, even here, the difference aused by returning such capital stock at its nominal value on the one hand, or at its ctual selling-price on the other, whether above or below par, might easily make

TABLE XCVII.—*Manufactures, by Totals of States and Territories—1860.*

States and Territories.	Establishments.	Hands employed.			Capital.	Wages.	Materials.	Products.
		All.	Male.	Female.	Dollars.	Dollars.	Dollars.	Dollars.
The United States	140, 433	1, 311, 246	1, 040, 349	270, 897	1, 009, 855, 715	378, 878, 966	1, 031, 605, 092	1, 885, [illegible]
Alabama	1, 459	7, 889	6, 792	1, 097	9, 098, 181	2, 132, 940	5, 489, 963	10, 588, [illegible]
Arkansas	518	1, 877	1, 831	46	1, 316, 610	554, 240	1, 280, 503	[illegible]
California	8, 468	49, 226	49, 171	55	22, 043, 096	28, 402, 287	27, 051, 674	[illegible]
Connecticut	3, 019	64, 469	44, 002	20, 467	45, 590, 430	19, 026, 196	40, 909, 090	[illegible]
Delaware	615	6, 421	5, 465	956	5, 452, 887	1, 905, 754	6, 028, 918	[illegible]
Dist. of Columbia	429	3, 148	2, 653	495	2, 905, 865	1, 139, 154	2, 884, 185	[illegible]
Florida	185	2, 454	2, 297	157	1, 874, 125	619, 840	874, 506	[illegible]
Georgia	1, 890	11, 575	9, 492	2, 083	10, 890, 875	2, 925, 145	9, 986, 532	[illegible]
Illinois	4, 268	22, 968	22, 489	479	27, 548, 563	7, 637, 921	35, 558, 782	[illegible]
Indiana	5, 323	21, 295	20, 563	732	18, 451, 121	6, 318, 335	27, 142, 597	[illegible]
Iowa	1, 939	6, 307	6, 142	165	7, 247, 130	1, 922, 417	8, 612, 259	[illegible]
Kansas	344	1, 735	1, 700	35	1, 084, 935	880, 346	1, 444, 975	[illegible]
Kentucky	3, 450	21, 258	19, 587	1, 671	20, 256, 579	6, 020, 082	22, 295, 759	[illegible]
Louisiana	1, 744	8, 789	7, 873	916	7, 151, 172	3, 683, 679	6, 738, 486	[illegible]
Maine	3, 810	34, 619	24, 827	9, 792	22, 044, 020	8, 368, 691	21, 553, 066	[illegible]
Maryland	3, 083	28, 403	21, 630	6, 773	23, 230, 608	7, 190, 672	25, 494, 007	[illegible]
Massachusetts	8, 176	217, 421	146, 268	71, 153	132, 792, 327	56, 960, 913	135, 053, 721	[illegible]
Michigan	3, 448	23, 190	22, 144	1, 046	23, 808, 226	6, 735, 047	17, 635, 611	[illegible]
Minnesota	562	2, 123	2, 104	19	2, 388, 310	712, 214	1, 904, 070	[illegible]
Mississippi	976	4, 775	4, 572	203	4, 384, 492	1, 618, 320	3, 146, 636	[illegible]
Missouri	3, 157	19, 681	18, 628	1, 053	20, 034, 220	6, 669, 916	23, 849, 941	[illegible]
Nebraska	107	336	334	2	266, 575	105, 330	237, 215	[illegible]
New Hampshire	2, 592	32, 340	18, 379	13, 961	23, 274, 094	8, 110, 561	20, 539, 857	[illegible]
New Jersey	4, 173	56, 027	43, 198	12, 829	40, 521, 048	16, 277, 337	11, 429, 100	[illegible]
New Mexico	82	1, 074	1, 044	30	2, 008, 350	341, 306	367, 892	[illegible]
New York	22, 624	230, 112	176, 885	53, 227	172, 895, 652	65, 446, 759	214, 813, 061	[illegible]
North Carolina	3, 689	14, 217	12, 102	2, 115	9, 693, 703	2, 689, 441	10, 203, 228	[illegible]
Ohio	11, 123	75, 602	65, 749	9, 853	57, 295, 303	22, 302, 989	69, 800, 270	121, 691, [illegible]
Oregon	309	978	968	10	1, 337, 238	635, 256	1, 431, 952	[illegible]
Pennsylvania	22, 363	222, 132	182, 593	39, 539	190, 055, 904	60, 369, 165	153, 477, 698	290, 121, [illegible]
Rhode Island	1, 191	32, 490	20, 795	11, 695	21, 278, 295	8, 760, 125	19, 858, 515	40, 711, [illegible]
South Carolina	1, 230	6, 994	6, 096	898	6, 931, 756	1, 380, 027	5, 198, 881	8, 615, [illegible]
Tennessee	2, 572	12, 528	11, 582	946	14, 426, 261	3, 370, 687	9, 416, 514	17, 987, [illegible]
Texas	983	3, 449	3, 338	111	3, 272, 450	1, 162, 756	3, 367, 372	6, 577, [illegible]
Utah	148	389	380	9	443, 356	231, 701	439, 512	900, 153
Vermont	1, 883	10, 497	8, 563	1, 934	9, 498, 617	3, 004, 986	7, 608, 858	14, 637, [illegible]
Virginia	5, 385	36, 174	32, 606	3, 568	26, 935, 560	8, 544, 117	30, 840, 531	50, 652, [illegible]
Washington	52	870	866	4	1, 296, 200	453, 601	502, 021	1, 406, [illegible]
Wisconsin	3, 064	15, 414	14, 641	773	15, 831, 581	4, 268, 708	17, 137, 334	27, 849, [illegible]

a difference of 50 or 75 per cent. in the aggregate amount of capital stated for any branch of industry.

Where, however, business is carried on outside of incorporated companies, the difficulty of obtaining even an approximate return of capital, resulting from the nature of the inquiry itself, irrespective of the reluctance of manufacturers, becomes such as to render success hopeless. So numerous are the constructions, possible and even reasonable, in respect to what constitutes manufacturing capital, that anything like harmony or consistency of treatment is not to be expected of a large body of officials pursuing their work independently of each other. The Superintendent is free to confess that he would be puzzled to furnish a definition (fit for practical use by enumerators) of manufacturing capital, or, even in a single case, with complete access to the books of a manufacturing establishment conducted by two or more partners, and with the frankest exhibit of the assets, both of the firm and of the individuals thereof, to make up a statement of the capital of the concern, in respect to which he would feel any assurance. When to such difficulties in the nature of the subject is added the reluctance of manufacturers to answer an inquiry of this character, it may fairly be assumed, in advance of any enumerations, that the results will be of the slightest possible value.

It is greatly to be regretted that the census should be incumbered by an inquiry yielding so little, yet provoking so much opposition to the progress of the general work.

The aggregate amount of capital invested in manufactures in the United States, as by the following tables, is $2,118,208,769. It is doubtful whether this sum represents one-fourth of the capital actually contributing to the annual gross product of $4,232,325,442.

It is a pity, and may almost be said to be a shame, that statistical information, in

TABLE XCVIII.—*Manufactures, by Totals of States and Territories*—1850.

NOTE.—This table is an exact reproduction of Table 4 of the Abstract of Manufactures at the Seventh Census. [Senate Ex. Doc. No. 39, 2d session 35th Congress.] The table is arithmetically imperfect, and it is not known whether the errors are in the items or total of the table, or in both. The true total line of the items as printed is: Establishments, 123,029; hands employed, total, 958,079; male, 732,157; female. 225,922; capital, $533,245,351; wages, $236,750,461; materials, $555,174,320; products. $1,019,109,616.

States and Territories.	Establishments.	HANDS EMPLOYED.			CAPITAL.	WAGES.	MATERIALS.	PRODUCTS.
		All.	Male.	Female	Dollars.	Dollars	Dollars	Dollars.
The United States	123,025	957,059	731,137	225,922	533,245,351	236,755,464	555,123,822	1,019,106,616
Alabama	1,026	4,936	4,397	539	3,450,606	1,105,824	2,224,960	4,528,876
Arkansas	261	842	812	30	305,015	159,876	215,789	537,908
California	1,003	3,964	3,964	......	1,006,197	3,717,180	1,201,154	12,862,522
Connecticut	3,737	50,731	34,248	16,483	25,876,648	12,435,984	21,608,971	47,114,585
Delaware	531	3,888	3,237	651	2,978,945	936,924	2,864,607	4,649,296
District of Columbia	403	2,370	2,034	336	1,001,575	757,584	1,405,871	2,690,258
Florida	103	991	876	115	547,060	199,452	220,611	668,335
Georgia	1,522	8,368	6,650	1,718	5,456,483	1,709,664	3,404,917	7,082,075
Illinois	3,162	11,559	11,066	493	6,217,765	3,204,330	8,959,327	16,534,272
Indiana	4,392	14,440	13,748	692	7,750,402	3,728,844	10,369,700	18,725,423
Iowa	522	1,707	1,687	20	1,292,875	473,016	2,356,881	3,551,783
Kentucky	3,609	21,476	19,576	1,900	11,810,462	5,106,048	12,165,075	21,710,212
Louisiana	1,008	6,217	5,458	759	5,032,424	2,033,928	2,459,508	6,779,417
Maine	3,974	28,020	21,853	6,167	14,699,152	7,485,588	13,553,144	24,661,057
Maryland	3,725	30,212	22,729	7,483	14,934,450	7,403,832	17,690,836	33,043,892
Massachusetts	8,852	177,461	107,784	69,677	88,940,292	41,954,736	85,856,771	157,743,994
Michigan	2,033	9,344	8,990	354	6,563,660	2,717,124	6,136,328	11,169,002
Minnesota	5	63	63	......	91,000	18,540	24,300	58,300
Mississippi	947	3,154	3,046	108	1,815,820	771,528	1,275,771	2,912,068
Missouri	2,923	15,808	14,880	928	8,576,607	4,692,648	12,798,351	24,324,418
New Hampshire	3,211	27,092	14,103	12,989	18,242,114	6,123,876	12,745,466	23,164,503
New Jersey	4,207	37,830	29,068	8,762	22,293,258	9,364,740	22,011,871	39,851,256
New Mexico	23	81	81	......	68,300	20,772	110,220	249,010
New York	23,553	199,349	147,737	51,612	99,904,405	49,131,000	134,655,674	237,507,249
North Carolina	2,663	14,601	12,473	2,128	7,456,860	2,383,456	4,602,501	9,111,050
Ohio	10,622	51,491	47,054	4,437	29,019,538	13,467,156	34,678,019	62,692,279
Oregon	52	285	285	......	843,600	388,620	809,560	2,236,640
Pennsylvania	21,605	146,766	124,688	22,078	94,473,810	37,163,232	87,206,377	155,044,910
Rhode Island	864	20,967	12,923	8,044	12,935,676	5,047,060	13,186,703	22,117,688
South Carolina	1,430	7,066	5,992	1,074	6,053,265	1,127,712	2,787,534	7,045,477
Tennessee	2,887	12,039	11,080	959	6,527,729	2,247,492	5,166,886	9,725,608
Texas	309	1,066	1,042	24	539,290	322,368	394,642	1,168,538
Utah	14	51	51	......	44,400	9,984	337,381	291,220
Vermont	1,849	8,445	6,894	1,551	5,001,377	2,202,348	4,172,552	8,570,920
Virginia	4,740	29,110	25,790	3,320	18,109,143	5,434,476	18,101,131	29,602,507
Wisconsin	1,262	6,089	5,798	291	3,382,148	1,712,496	5,414,931	9,293,068

many respects, of high authority and accuracy, should be discredited by association with statements so flagrantly false, even to the least critical eye; yet, as the manufacturing schedule annexed to the act of 1850 requires this return, and as there is a vague popular notion that the statement of capital in this connection is of real and great importance, (instead of being, as it is, at the best, of the least consequence,) the Superintendent does not feel at liberty to withhold the results from publication; but he feels not only authorized but required by the facts of the case to brand them as he has here done, in order that no one may be deceived by the show of authority they present.

The relation of wages to product.—In reference to certain of the common trades, it needs to be stated, in explanation, that the apparently inadequate amount of wages reported is due to the fact that a very large body of labor is included which is not represented in the wages column. Thus, the statistics of carpentering show that, for a total production of $132,901,432, (the value of materials being $65,943,115,) the amount of wages paid was only $29,169,588. The consideration above noted is sufficient to account for the seeming deficiency, inasmuch as the labor of proprietors of establishments in this line (certainly not less than 17,142, and probably rising to 20,000) was compensated, not out of the wages paid, but out of the profits of the business. In some branches of industry the number of "hired hands" is even less than the number of artisans working in their own shops, and, hence, receiving no wages, but living off the profits of manufacture.

Relation of materials to product.—The relation of materials to product, in the Statistics

[Continued on page 810.]

TABLE XCIX.—*The United States, by Specified Industries*—1870.

	Mechanical and manufacturing industries.	Establishments.	STEAM-ENGINES.		WATER-WHEELS.	
			Horse-power.	Number.	Horse-power.	Number.
	All industries	252, 148	1, 215, 711	40, 191	1, 130, 431	[illegible]
1	Acid, pyroligneous (*a*)	5			15	[illegible]
2	sulphuric (*a*)	4	29	3	16	[illegible]
3	Agricultural implements	2, 076	15, 873	676	10, 209	[illegible]
4	Alarms, burglar and till	5	3			
5	Ammunition, cartridges	8	110	3	13	
6	Artificial eyes	1				
7	feathers, flowers, and fruits	54				
8	limbs	24	10	1		
9	Artists' materials (*b*)	8	40	4		
10	Ashes, pot and pearl	105	16	1		
11	Awnings and tents	45				
12	Babbitt metal and solder	8	2			
13	Bagging, flax, hemp, and jute	33	785	15	535	[illegible]
14	Bags, paper	30	321	17	127	
15	other than paper	39	239	14	125	
16	Baking-powders	30	80	5	10	
17	Bark, ground	33	513	13	169	
18	Base-ball goods	5				
19	Baskets	127	553	21	220	
20	Bee-hives	15	11	2	31	
21	Bellows	13	15	2		
22	Bells	31	55	8	150	
23	Belting and hose, (leather)	91	302	13	42	
24	Billiard and bagatelle tables, cues and materials	39	86	4		
25	Blacking	32	91	8		
26	Blacksmithing	26, 364	747	69	628	
27	Bleaching and dyeing	250	4, 278	101	1, 384	
28	straw-goods	11	10	1		
29	Blocks and spars	9	78	7	15	
30	Blueing	11	60	1		
31	Boats	174	1, 446	45	13	
32	Bookbinding	500	773	77		
33	Boot and shoe findings	271	310	32	223	
34	Boots and shoes	23, 428	2, 902	267	167	
35	Bottling, malt liquors and mineral waters	20				
36	Boxes, cheese	194	547	40	2, 318	[illegible]
37	cigar	104	200	17	73	
38	fancy	15	50	2	64	
39	wooden, packing	489	4, 303	195	2, 642	[illegible]
40	tobacco	13	83	3	48	
41	paper	234	122	16	177	
42	Brass and copper tubing	3	80	2		
43	founding and finishing	275	1, 882	146	266	
44	rolled	11	360	4	235	
45	ware (*c*)	30	489	13	335	
46	Bread, crackers, and other bakery products	3, 550	2, 370	187	218	
47	Brick	3, 114	10, 333	372	218	
48	Bridge-building	64	1, 034	36	40	
49	Bronze castings	9	45	2		
50	Brooms and whisk-brushes	635	178	6	118	
51	Brushes, (not whisk)	157	257	18	21	
52	Building-stone, artificial	12	40	2		
53	Butchering	509	247	18	6	
54	Buttons	64	281	31	316	
55	Calcium-lights	2	13	2		
56	Candles, adamantine and wax	4	60	2		
57	Cards, playing	5	62	4		
58	other than playing	13	117	7		
59	Carpentering and building	17, 142	4, 654	289	1, 140	
60	Carpets, rag	471	60	2	24	
61	other than rag	215	3, 017	45	702	
62	Carriage trimmings	41	71	6	55	
63	Carriages and sleds, children's	53	366	92	291	
64	wagons	11, 847	4, 169	279	4, 651	[illegible]
65	Car fixtures and trimmings	3	55	3		
66	Cars, railroad and repairs (*d*)	170	5, 609	134	163	

(*a*) *Acid, sulphuric*, includes 1 establishment, having 1 steam-engine of 6 horse-power, 18 males ab[ove] sixteen, $80,000 capital, $20,000 wages, $21,600 materials, and $90,000 products, styled *Acids, (not speci[fied])* in Table IX (B) of Connecticut. The remainder of *Acids, (not specified,)* in Connecticut is here inclu[ded] in *Acids, pyroligneous*.

TABLE XCIX.—*The United States, by Specified Industries*—1870.

HANDS EMPLOYED.				CAPITAL.	WAGES.	MATERIALS.	PRODUCTS.	
All.	Males above 16.	Females above 15.	Youth.	Dollars.	Dollars.	Dollars.	Dollars.	
2, 053, 996	1, 615, 598	323, 770	114, 628	2, 118, 208, 769	775, 584, 343	2, 488, 427, 242	4, 232, 325, 442	
29	29			31, 500	9, 464	27, 400	68, 280	1
73	73			162, 000	55, 900	51, 280	212, 150	2
25, 249	24, 634	12	603	34, 834, 600	12, 151, 504	21, 473, 925	52, 066, 875	3
46	44		2	72, 000	31, 864	27, 780	91, 000	4
462	242	214	6	570, 430	344, 515	532, 095	976, 366	5
3	3			2, 000	600	200	3, 000	6
1, 451	400	842	209	418, 650	276, 331	369, 004	986, 125	7
78	70	1	7	122, 300	36, 079	59, 894	166, 416	8
50	38	3	9	43, 800	20, 062	21, 680	94, 150	9
278	277		1	175, 183	41, 454	193, 081	327, 671	10
219	162	49	8	132, 475	87, 424	371, 677	625, 269	11
34	33		1	152, 650	15, 610	246, 513	309, 900	12
3, 170	1, 718	863	589	3, 158, 101	958, 106	2, 624, 682	4, 507, 664	13
444	205	206	33	473, 100	134, 932	1, 053, 463	1, 483, 963	14
1, 097	486	502	109	1, 200, 500	452, 517	3, 827, 678	8, 261, 679	15
235	167	58	10	294, 450	88, 107	600, 691	895, 433	16
133	131		2	322, 760	47, 069	194, 491	372, 829	17
118	25	69	24	24, 500	26, 836	34, 091	72, 605	18
920	755	73	92	376, 945	224, 878	158, 109	594, 739	19
33	32		1	15, 350	3, 172	8, 459	21, 452	20
117	110		7	101, 200	67, 360	106, 735	257, 675	21
389	329	47	13	517, 000	185, 751	512, 537	1, 023, 010	22
808	784	8	16	2, 118, 577	454, 187	3, 231, 204	4, 558, 043	23
505	493	2	10	805, 000	383, 768	650, 864	1, 692, 943	24
305	134	158	13	266, 750	107, 450	422, 716	817, 768	25
52, 982	52, 527	9	446	15, 977, 992	9, 246, 549	13, 223, 907	41, 828, 296	26
4, 172	3, 279	680	213	5, 006, 950	1, 783, 449	53, 166, 634	58, 571, 493	27
100	66	34		17, 100	29, 000	52, 505	108, 010	28
64	62		2	66, 250	31, 914	28, 565	95, 095	29
54	36	11	7	52, 500	17, 975	37, 423	92, 100	30
2, 381	2, 350	1	30	1, 665, 193	1, 225, 996	1, 214, 016	3, 300, 775	31
7, 697	3, 972	3, 175	550	5, 319, 410	3, 095, 821	8, 026, 870	14, 077, 309	32
2, 773	1, 045	1, 442	286	858, 560	792, 957	1, 817, 028	3, 389, 091	33
135, 889	113, 415	19, 113	3, 361	48, 994, 366	51, 972, 712	93, 582, 528	181, 644, 090	34
89	82	1	6	47, 300	28, 470	56, 100	157, 163	35
694	662	11	21	424, 375	125, 012	242, 937	570, 840	36
783	486	139	158	274, 610	242, 130	477, 499	960, 222	37
146	101	26	19	44, 300	36, 314	39, 199	112, 500	38
4, 509	4, 084	195	230	3, 571, 942	1, 909, 088	4, 236, 745	8, 222, 433	39
100	95		5	32, 325	34, 218	110, 380	171, 630	40
4, 486	1, 104	3, 062	320	1, 148, 025	1, 222, 338	1, 553, 777	3, 917, 159	41
121	114		7	203, 600	60, 434	345, 875	500, 000	42
3, 377	3, 102	39	236	4, 783, 585	1, 731, 306	3, 293, 629	6, 855, 756	43
448	228	210	10	502, 800	233, 484	704, 870	1, 254, 966	44
757	540	87	130	1, 243, 450	386, 008	907, 908	1, 849, 013	45
14, 136	12, 508	842	686	10, 025, 966	5, 353, 184	22, 211, 856	36, 907, 704	46
43, 293	39, 541	258	3, 494	20, 504, 238	10, 768, 853	7, 413, 097	29, 028, 359	47
2, 090	2, 069		21	2, 973, 250	1, 123, 353	3, 239, 771	5, 476, 175	48
187	156	29	2	539, 300	111, 714	63, 375	220, 400	49
5, 206	3, 056	992	1, 158	2, 015, 602	1, 268, 875	3, 672, 837	6, 622, 265	50
2, 425	1, 481	522	422	1, 683, 993	691, 405	1, 312, 897	2, 694, 823	51
67	67			203, 100	32, 570	53, 945	163, 400	52
1, 881	1, 851	11	19	2, 099, 905	546, 346	11, 039, 928	13, 686, 061	53
1, 912	617	949	346	1, 013, 700	580, 380	751, 183	1, 778, 893	54
11	11			56, 000	6, 800	4, 100	16, 000	55
49	38	1	10	216, 500	18, 380	36, 260	89, 275	56
276	74	178	24	620, 000	90, 896	442, 800	765, 000	57
377	161	195	21	364, 600	156, 240	422, 000	754, 000	58
67, 864	67, 306	5	553	25, 110, 428	29, 169, 588	65, 943, 115	132, 901, 432	59
1, 016	874	116	26	310, 744	141, 148	498, 595	1, 005, 327	60
12, 098	6, 808	4, 316	974	12, 540, 750	4, 681, 718	13, 577, 993	21, 761, 573	61
453	241	176	36	396, 150	144, 278	214, 544	590, 878	62
913	780	89	44	746, 628	407, 327	495, 281	1, 432, 833	63
54, 928	54, 280	76	572	36, 563, 095	21, 272, 730	22, 787, 341	65, 362, 837	64
122	102	20		122, 000	69, 568	73, 061	208, 000	65
15, 931	15, 690	20	221	16, 632, 792	9, 659, 992	18, 117, 707	31, 070, 734	66

(*b*) Includes *Crayons* of Table IX (B.)
(*c*) Includes *Brass ornaments* of Table IX (B.)
(*d*) Comprises *Car-repairing*, *Cars, railroad, horse*, and *Cars, railroad, steam*, of Table IX (B.)

TABLE XCIX.—*The United States, by Specified Industries*—1870—Continued.

	Mechanical and manufacturing industries.	Establishments.	STEAM-ENGINES.		WATER-WHEELS.	
			Horse-power.	Number.	Horse-power.	Number.
67	Cement	45	1,190	23	909	[illegible]
68	Charcoal and coke (a)	167	270	16	96	[illegible]
69	Cheese	1,313	1,872	261	119	[illegible]
70	Chocolate	9	290	7	210	[illegible]
71	Chromos and lithographs	91	186	20	....	....
72	Cider	547	514	48	2,048	17[illegible]
73	Clock-cases	5	4	2	63	[illegible]
74	materials	15	34	4	92	[illegible]
75	Clocks	26	502	12	277	[illegible]
76	Clothing, children's	20	....	....	....	....
77	men's	7,838	457	37	96	[illegible]
78	women's	1,847	35	4	125	[illegible]
79	Coal-oil, refined	170	4,214	198	....	....
80	Coffee and spices, roasted and ground	156	1,638	117	134	[illegible]
81	Coffins	642	359	19	183	[illegible]
82	Collars and cuffs, paper	33	269	21	118	[illegible]
83	Combs	37	175	9	224	[illegible]
84	Confectionery	949	550	41	23	[illegible]
85	Cooperage	4,961	3,653	153	2,644	14[illegible]
86	Copper, milled and smelted	27	3,944	43	39	[illegible]
87	rolled	7	1,000	6	750	[illegible]
88	Coppersmithing (b)	65	129	10	60	[illegible]
89	Cordage and twine	201	2,381	36	664	[illegible]
90	Cordials and sirups	33	27	4	....	....
91	Cork-cutting	27	147	11	14	[illegible]
92	Costumes	4	....	....	....	....
93	Cotton goods, (not specified) (c)	819	44,874	402	94,253	1,1[illegible]
94	batting and wadding	27	240	14	161	[illegible]
95	thread, twine, and yarns	123	2,093	40	4,820	[illegible]
96	Croquet sets	8	80	3	38	[illegible]
97	Crucibles	10	155	7	....	....
98	Cutlery	82	953	40	1,054	[illegible]
99	and edge-tools, (not specified)	102	452	21	1,547	[illegible]
100	Dentistry, mechanical	650	6	2	....	....
101	Dentists' materials	10	32	2	....	....
102	Drain-pipe	68	339	15	110	[illegible]
103	Drugs and chemicals (d)	292	3,637	114	445	[illegible]
104	Dye woods, stuffs, and extracts	19	1,004	22	565	[illegible]
105	Edge-tools and axes	97	1,292	36	4,431	[illegible]
106	Emery, reduced and ground	5	145	5	100	[illegible]
107	wheels	6	22	2	75	[illegible]
108	Enameling	12	218	11	....	....
109	Engraving	157	151	13	....	....
110	and stencil-cutting	136	13	4	10	[illegible]
111	Envelopes (e)	22	129	14	30	[illegible]
112	Explosives and fireworks	21	72	3	60	[illegible]
113	Fancy articles	13	77	2	22	[illegible]
114	Fans	6	14	2	....	....
115	Feathers, cleaned, dressed, and dyed	19	32	2	....	....
116	Fences, patent	4	25	2	8	[illegible]
117	Fertilizers, (not plaster, ground)	126	2,307	69	644	[illegible]
118	Files	121	780	30	216	[illegible]
119	Fire-arms	46	1,323	27	365	[illegible]
120	Fish, cured and packed	75	28	5	5	[illegible]
121	and oysters, canned	17	267	6	....	....
122	Flax, dressed	90	502	28	1,064	[illegible]
123	and linen goods (f)	10	593	7	1,105	[illegible]
124	Flouring and grist mill products	22,573	168,736	5,383	407,950	21,2[illegible]
125	Food preparations, animal	85	426	32	87	[illegible]
126	vegetable	33	308	9	340	[illegible]
127	vermicelli and macaroni	6	19	3	....	....
128	Fruits and vegetables, canned and preserved	97	742	45	....	....
129	Furniture, (not specified)	5,423	14,811	764	6,920	[illegible]
130	chairs	529	3,203	117	4,740	[illegible]
131	iron bedsteads	2	6	1	....	....
132	refrigerators	27	114	6	24	[illegible]
133	Furs, dressed	182	76	6	10	[illegible]
134	Galvanizing	9	48	4	....	....
135	Gas	390	2,747	160	21	[illegible]

(a) For *Coke*, see Ohio and Pennsylvania, Table IX (B.)
(b) Includes Fire-extinguishers of Table IX (B.)
(c) Includes Comfortables of Table IX (B.)

TABLE XCIX.—*The United States, by Specified Industries*—1870—Continued.

HANDS EMPLOYED.				CAPITAL.	WAGES.	MATERIALS.	PRODUCTS.	
All.	Males above 16.	Females above 15.	Youth.	Dollars.	Dollars.	Dollars.	Dollars.	
1, 632	1, 508	....	124	1, 521, 500	631, 993	773, 192	2, 033, 893	67
3, 473	3, 436	....	37	2, 393, 083	1, 294, 707	1, 204, 779	3, 161, 104	68
4, 607	3, 272	1, 279	56	3, 690, 075	706, 566	14, 089, 284	16, 771, 665	69
199	104	87	8	377, 000	78, 700	665, 149	946, 250	70
1, 399	1, 244	56	99	1, 533, 725	837, 732	735, 810	2, 515, 684	71
1, 472	1, 439	4	29	766, 256	144, 334	892, 820	1, 537, 214	72
68	65	1	2	53, 700	27, 784	71, 479	111, 430	73
207	172	29	6	197, 250	101, 790	160, 568	401, 180	74
1, 330	1, 177	66	87	882, 700	805, 340	818, 409	2, 509, 643	75
1, 449	895	553	1	332, 300	210, 700	677, 475	1, 009, 875	76
106, 679	46, 934	58, 466	1, 279	49, 891, 080	30, 535, 879	86, 117, 231	147, 650, 378	77
11, 696	1, 105	10, 247	344	3, 520, 218	2, 513, 956	6, 837, 978	12, 900, 583	78
1, 870	1, 834	1	35	6, 770, 383	1, 184, 559	21, 450, 189	26, 942, 287	79
1, 220	1, 054	100	66	3, 846, 210	670, 983	8, 171, 837	11, 266, 413	80
2, 365	2, 292	42	31	2, 592, 862	1, 011, 397	1, 412, 078	4, 026, 989	81
2, 064	493	1, 448	123	1, 659, 275	575, 000	1, 367, 513	3, 042, 650	82
675	511	113	51	429, 825	221, 318	232, 587	668, 889	83
5, 825	4, 151	1, 225	449	4, 995, 293	2, 091, 826	8, 703, 560	15, 922, 643	84
23, 314	22, 764	20	530	9, 798, 847	7, 819, 813	12, 831, 796	26, 863, 734	85
1, 082	982	1	99	3, 158, 500	577, 129	10, 715, 400	11, 684, 123	86
266	266	....	....	1, 608, 750	183, 875	1, 777, 585	2, 390, 460	87
643	571	4	68	739, 550	362, 554	798, 304	1, 722, 167	88
3, 698	2, 115	779	804	3, 530, 470	1, 234, 272	5, 739, 608	8, 979, 382	89
258	185	51	22	527, 100	118, 847	505, 398	955, 271	90
482	245	121	116	347, 400	144, 518	426, 739	754, 530	91
28	8	19	1	17, 600	2, 775	3, 400	9, 500	92
129, 442	40, 746	66, 870	21, 826	133, 238, 797	37, 280, 856	106, 307, 962	168, 457, 353	93
244	159	31	54	276, 800	78, 876	533, 451	720, 117	94
6, 077	2, 052	2, 938	1, 087	7, 392, 295	1, 743, 651	5, 135, 303	8, 726, 217	95
121	104	4	13	51, 000	50, 900	74, 220	172, 980	96
119	112	....	7	699, 000	127, 188	538, 712	1, 117, 463	97
2, 111	1, 896	150	65	2, 246, 830	973, 854	762, 029	2, 882, 803	98
[illegible], 317	2, 070	76	171	1, 880, 717	1, 157, 904	862, 014	2, 739, 998	99
1, 020	991	15	14	621, 762	184, 272	441, 534	1, 634, 844	100
346	264	72	10	838, 290	242, 836	181, 908	579, 364	101
758	733	2	23	977, 375	316, 521	415, 360	1, 294, 256	102
4, 729	4, 026	452	251	12, 750, 800	2, 141, 238	11, 681, 405	19, 417, 194	103
548	517	5	26	1, 227, 500	300, 755	1, 275, 434	2, 053, 300	104
3, 520	3, 470	11	39	4, 219, 205	1, 997, 795	2, 413, 555	5, 482, 539	105
25	25	....	....	157, 000	17, 320	70, 650	153, 760	106
41	41	....	....	282, 500	31, 222	53, 840	156, 300	107
274	253	13	8	393, 000	137, 385	718, 394	1, 070, 783	108
1, 407	1, 047	269	91	1, 744, 795	1, 022, 090	452, 072	2, 093, 482	109
431	381	5	45	244, 000	155, 968	103, 035	500, 644	110
910	245	627	38	875, 000	316, 158	1, 288, 139	2, 277, 541	111
363	208	82	73	600, 100	196, 497	307, 369	880, 150	112
191	82	94	15	172, 650	65, 435	77, 627	188, 830	113
117	31	43	43	28, 000	23, 426	37, 279	92, 100	114
583	290	272	21	474, 050	144, 097	467, 200	850, 925	115
45	45	....	....	30, 100	3, 440	21, 655	48, 400	116
2, 501	2, 470	19	12	4, 395, 948	766, 712	3, 808, 025	5, 815, 118	117
1, 581	1, 356	59	166	1, 659, 370	638, 982	468, 303	1, 649, 394	118
3, 297	3, 152	33	112	4, 016, 902	2, 490, 774	1, 100, 999	5, 582, 258	119
854	673	142	39	391, 695	181, 105	841, 205	1, 502, 591	120
1, 587	751	554	282	574, 800	266, 409	940, 302	1, 471, 300	121
765	700	13	52	524, 701	209, 943	382, 534	815, 010	122
1, 746	473	759	514	2, 325, 250	424, 946	1, 121, 467	2, 178, 775	123
58, 448	57, 795	91	562	151, 565, 376	14, 577, 533	367, 392, 122	444, 985, 143	124
582	512	55	15	672, 656	276, 437	1, 548, 480	2, 328, 790	125
559	211	331	17	618, 216	177, 062	746, 899	1, 186, 202	126
37	34	....	3	35, 200	17, 100	43, 338	107, 472	127
5, 869	1, 658	3, 434	777	2, 335, 925	771, 643	3, 094, 846	5, 425, 677	128
40, 554	38, 023	657	1, 874	35, 740, 029	17, 001, 379	21, 669, 837	57, 926, 547	129
12, 462	6, 975	3, 168	2, 319	7, 643, 884	3, 522, 940	3, 979, 743	10, 567, 104	130
15	15	....	....	16, 000	9, 000	11, 181	28, 570	131
267	260	....	7	548, 000	141, 212	192, 409	566, 463	132
2, 903	1, 306	1, 525	72	3, 472, 267	1, 042, 305	4, 816, 122	8, 903, 052	133
146	141	....	5	206, 000	88, 650	584, 996	796, 326	134
8, 723	8, 705	....	18	71, 773, 694	6, 546, 734	10, 869, 373	32, 048, 851	135

(*d*) Includes *Burning-fluid*, ("*Phosgene*,") and *Copperas* of Table IX (B.)
(*e*) Includes the item of Table IX (B.) (Massachusetts,) there erroneously styled Stationery.
(*f*) Includes *Linen thread* of Table IX (B.)

TABLE XCIX.—*The United States, by Specified Industries*—1870—Continued.

	Mechanical and manufacturing industries.	Establishments.	STEAM-ENGINES.		WATER-WHEELS.	
			Horse-power.	Number.	Horse-power.	Number.
136	Gasometers	2	7	2	....	....
137	Gas-retorts	5	122	3	....	....
138	and lamp fixtures	39	661	27	50	
139	Gilding	40	....	....	....	....
140	Glass, cut	29	180	21	....	....
141	plate	5	52	2	4	
142	stained	18	44	3	....	....
143	ware, (not specified)	114	1,044	55	42	
144	window	35	381	20	110	
145	Gloves and mittens	221	3	1	86	
146	Glue	70	1,049	27	2	
147	Gold and silver, reduced and refined	12	506	10	....	....
148	Gold leaf and foil	51	98	4	....	....
149	Grease and tallow	62	233	13	....	....
150	Grindstones	10	136	6	....	....
151	Gunpowder	33	943	16	2,779	
152	Gunsmithing	615	76	15	103	
153	Hair-cloth	5	15	1	170	
154	work	230	55	3	7	
155	Hand-stamps	8	5	1	2	
156	Hardware	580	5,616	243	3,398	
157	saddlery	155	689	29	260	
158	Hat materials	62	433	11	138	
159	Hats and caps	483	2,112	64	186	
160	Hatters' tools	7	17	3	8	
161	Heating-apparatus	59	239	18	....	....
162	Hemlock-bark extract	2	140	2	....	....
163	Hides and tallow	12	84	6	....	....
164	Hinges, wrought and cast	6	135	4	....	....
165	Hones and whetstones	39	126	10	380	
166	Hooks and eyes	9	3	1	54	
167	Hoop-skirts and corsets	194	359	13	2	
168	Hosiery	248	2,223	81	4,275	
169	Hubs, spokes, bows, shafts, wheels, and felloes	302	4,796	189	1,912	
170	Hunting and fishing tackle	33	258	8	72	
171	Ice, (by patented process)	4	72	4	....	....
172	India-rubber and elastic goods	56	4,412	49	1,864	
173	Ink, printing	16	248	13	55	
174	writing	25	8	1	....	....
175	Instruments, professional and scientific (*a*)	135	207	32	125	
176	Iron, pigs	386	58,866	509	5,034	
177	castings, (not specified)	2,328	25,907	1,345	8,169	
178	stoves, heaters, and hollow ware	326	5,732	248	491	
179	blooms	82	2,710	31	3,174	
180	forged and rolled	306	85,383	821	9,347	
181	anchors and cable chains	18	162	8	240	
182	bolts, nuts, washers, and rivets	93	2,480	69	743	
183	nails and spikes, cut and wrought	142	10,775	101	2,503	
184	pipe, wrought	22	1,715	26	25	
185	railing, wrought (*b*)	74	197	27	3	
186	ship-building and marine engines	1	100	2	....	....
187	Ivory work	20	205	13	75	
188	Japanned ware	21	42	3	....	....
189	Jewelry, (not specified)	681	805	78	111	
190	and instrument cases	29	3	2	....	....
191	Kaolin and ground earths	52	529	15	672	
192	Kindling-wood	70	827	48	30	
193	Lamp-black	9	43	3	....	....
194	Lamps, lanterns, and locomotive head-lights	40	154	16	10	
195	Lapidary work	13	10	1	22	
196	Lasts	60	465	32	180	
197	Lead, bar and sheet	5	46	2	35	
198	pigs	62	431	20	201	
199	pipe	17	453	15	....	....
200	shot	7	170	5	....	....
201	Leather, tanned	4,237	19,572	1,045	14,202	
202	curried	3,083	2,992	174	887	
203	morocco, tanned and curried	113	683	48	16	
204	patent and enameled	26	354	14	45	
205	dressed skins	110	206	15	626	
206	Leather-board	8	80	4	495	

(*a*) Includes Globes, terrestrial and celestial, of Table IX (B.)

TABLE XCIX.—*The United States, by Specified Industries*—1870—Continued.

HANDS EMPLOYED.				CAPITAL.	WAGES.	MATERIALS.	PRODUCTS.	
All.	Males above 16.	Females above 15.	Youth.	Dollars.	Dollars.	Dollars.	Dollars.	
30	30	....	....	35,000	15,000	74,000	140,000	136
177	176	....	1	863,000	142,280	356,846	665,225	137
2,469	2,089	257	123	2,723,194	1,232,424	1,626,579	[illegible],061,778	138
213	189	3	21	100,250	102,824	122,523	335,527	139
285	257	2	26	136,700	157,576	178,526	470,875	140
200	195	....	5	195,700	132,410	86,708	355,250	141
170	156	10	4	148,800	99,739	90,277	297,480	142
12,308	8,494	666	3,148	10,385,882	5,953,423	4,376,897	14,300,949	143
2,859	2,403	37	419	3,244,560	1,503,277	1,490,760	3,811,308	144
4,058	1,127	2,894	37	2,340,550	980,549	1,884,146	3,998,521	145
800	685	27	88	1,954,800	309,673	832,961	1,709,605	146
165	164	....	1	292,000	110,118	673,020	848,801	147
613	373	189	51	412,905	264,408	621,773	1,411,431	148
442	359	62	21	841,080	184,787	5,114,868	6,035,845	149
236	226	....	10	83,800	59,600	33,853	163,700	150
939	926	4	9	4,060,400	570,279	2,270,747	4,011,839	151
1,082	1,062	7	13	605,770	228,879	227,151	959,602	152
244	87	154	3	535,500	81,850	351,822	467,750	153
1,651	597	940	114	766,875	416,294	883,421	1,971,839	154
29	28	....	1	14,100	10,350	10,721	42,700	155
14,236	11,713	1,179	1,344	13,869,315	6,845,640	9,188,064	22,237,389	156
2,566	2,129	184	253	1,482,225	1,062,059	1,257,947	3,227,123	157
1,014	722	146	146	1,168,635	537,287	2,074,959	3,225,763	158
16,173	8,847	6,301	1,025	6,489,571	6,574,490	12,262,107	24,848,167	159
27	24	2	1	30,175	12,900	18,015	44,190	160
1,141	1,121	....	20	1,605,830	853,516	1,424,345	3,425,150	161
37	37	....	....	85,000	19,500	32,630	185,300	162
138	135	1	2	164,000	39,000	526,754	743,040	163
189	176	3	10	136,500	77,425	120,587	284,750	164
286	216	52	18	155,150	80,260	74,960	258,942	165
185	72	67	46	185,000	72,646	90,655	269,582	166
4,345	1,138	2,921	286	1,707,600	1,045,188	2,276,577	4,758,290	167
14,788	4,252	7,991	2,545	10,931,260	4,429,085	9,835,823	18,411,564	168
3,721	3,599	5	117	4,050,609	1,544,896	2,204,713	5,285,157	169
485	379	63	43	601,775	150,355	194,156	090,994	170
97	96	....	1	434,000	40,600	82,165	258,250	171
6,025	3,030	2,649	346	7,486,600	2,559,877	7,434,742	14,566,374	172
135	132	....	3	343,300	100,187	353,711	600,329	173
160	101	32	27	276,230	45,962	176,399	366,473	174
1,173	1,049	58	66	1,838,391	649,921	417,165	1,724,257	175
27,554	26,962	54	538	56,145,326	12,475,250	43,498,017	69,640,498	176
37,980	36,701	48	1,231	47,745,241	20,679,793	39,178,481	76,453,553	177
13,325	12,740	....	585	19,833,720	8,156,121	9,044,069	23,389,665	178
2,902	2,819	2	81	4,506,733	1,195,964	5,685,466	7,647,054	179
47,891	45,977	22	1,892	59,119,094	27,002,829	83,834,268	128,062,627	180
359	338	....	21	276,480	165,582	353,824	634,200	181
4,423	3,632	89	702	4,263,227	1,665,426	4,021,070	7,191,151	182
7,770	6,062	381	1,327	9,091,912	3,961,172	18,792,383	24,823,996	183
2,129	1,988	....	141	5,311,095	1,155,910	4,872,907	7,369,194	184
630	605	....	25	405,200	321,101	533,116	1,268,756	185
352	352	....	....	750,000	210,000	187,000	472,000	186
272	236	33	3	586,450	172,968	635,435	1,080,210	187
158	127	19	12	140,600	64,810	83,189	216,145	188
10,091	8,141	1,545	405	11,787,956	4,433,235	9,187,364	22,104,032	189
183	153	16	14	79,900	65,108	65,061	216,997	190
262	253	1	8	306,366	101,213	163,874	388,054	191
701	523	2	176	562,750	253,150	486,642	930,294	192
56	56	....	....	93,000	20,734	107,565	193,800	193
558	490	36	32	689,300	286,843	403,295	995,289	194
88	81	5	2	34,400	38,800	37,184	107,300	195
510	484	2	24	330,800	262,212	137,657	665,703	196
39	39	....	....	246,000	23,500	693,789	747,700	197
589	577	....	12	2,191,600	237,628	2,807,074	3,499,183	198
160	160	....	....	2,054,500	115,020	9,303,869	12,861,959	199
55	47	1	7	330,000	32,755	989,189	1,218,354	200
20,784	20,423	98	263	42,720,505	7,934,416	63,069,491	86,170,883	201
10,027	9,907	57	63	12,303,785	4,154,114	43,565,593	54,191,167	202
3,006	2,740	182	84	3,854,072	1,678,226	6,693,060	9,997,460	203
528	509	....	19	906,000	341,445	3,211,749	4,018,115	204
898	844	16	38	1,340,450	397,574	2,099,735	2,859,972	205
94	87	5	2	268,000	36,360	135,675	242,500	206

(*b*) Includes *Fire-escapes* of Table IX (B.)

TABLE XCIX.—*The United States, by Specified Industries*—1870—Continued.

	Mechanical and manufacturing industries.	Establishments.	STEAM-ENGINES. Horse-power.	STEAM-ENGINES. Number.	WATER-WHEELS. Horse-power.	WATER-WHEELS. Number.
207	Lightning-rods	25	47	6		
208	Lime	1,001	425	17	56	1
209	Liquors, distilled	719	12,853	411	811	[illegible]
210	malt	1,972	10,438	726	334	[illegible]
211	vinous	398	39	4		
212	Locksmithing and bellhanging	191	63	7		
213	Looking-glasses	11	25	2		
214	Looking-glass and picture frames	320	1,107	49	93	4
215	Lumber, planed	1,113	25,668	848	3,651	[illegible]
216	sawed	25,817	314,774	11,199	326,728	16,[illegible]
217	staves, shooks, and headings	15	110	5	53	1
218	Machinery, (not specified)	1,737	17,429	981	6,707	[illegible]
219	cotton and woolen	338	3,383	146	2,543	115
220	fire-engines	9	25	3	413	[illegible]
221	railroad-repairing	150	5,760	160	282	[illegible]
222	steam engines and boilers	663	11,076	515	764	[illegible]
223	Malt	208	1,159	82	220	11
224	Maps and atlases	18			29	1
225	Marble and stone work, (not specified)	923	4,231	141	1,406	34
226	monuments and tombstones	1,049	853	43	135	13
227	Masonry, brick and stone	2,264	32	4		
228	Matches	75	359	29	449	19
229	Mats and rugs	15	26	3		
230	Meat, cured and packed, (not specified)	17	128	6		
231	packed, beef	36	225	15		
232	pork	206	1,861	86		
233	Meters, gas and water	1	20	1		
234	gas	12	172	11		
235	water	2	5	1		
236	Military goods	6	24	3		
237	Millinery (a)	1,668	18	4		
238	Millstones	19	125	5		
239	Millwrighting	189	71	9	116	10
240	Mineral and soda waters	387	165	23	3	1
241	Mops and dusters	4	3	1	14	1
242	Musical instruments, (not specified)	83	207	10	355	19
243	melodeons, house-organs and materials	22	135	7	23	2
244	organs and materials	76	328	19	58	4
245	pianos and materials	156	889	36	23	3
246	Mucilage and paste	7	18	4		
247	Mustard, ground	15	79	11		
248	Needles and pins	39	126	13	370	20
249	Nets, fish and seine	9			20	1
250	Nickel, smelted	1	50	1		
251	Nitro-glycerine	3	32	2		
252	Oars	25	238	10	99	5
253	Oil, animal	58	396	24		
254	fish	101	1,081	57	30	2
255	lubricating	3	5	1		
256	vegetable, (not specified)	16	199	7	103	6
257	castor	6	191	8		
258	cotton-seed	26	1,142	21	65	2
259	essential	118	34	7		
260	linseed	77	1,825	39	843	36
261	Oil-cloth, silk	1				
262	Oil floor-cloth	34	424	25		
263	Painting	3,040	19	3		
264	Paints, (not specified)	68	1,731	57	365	9
265	lead and zinc	75	5,054	83	242	10
266	Paper, (not specified)	163	3,002	68	6,424	229
267	printing	235	5,269	144	17,354	454
268	wrapping	225	2,572	67	11,652	352
269	writing	46	731	10	6,144	146
270	Paper-hangings	15	348	18	40	1
271	Paperhanging	79				
272	Patent medicines and compounds	319	477	24	20	1
273	Patterns and models	165	398	58	25	3
274	Paving-materials	8	145	5		
275	Pencils, lead	7	265	6		
276	indelible	1	8	1		
277	Penholders, wooden	4	2	1	60	2
278	Pens and pencils, gold	21	56	3	5	1

(a) Includes the item of Table IX (B,) there erroneously called Lace.

TABLE XCIX.—*The United States, by Specified Industries*—1870—Continued.

HANDS EMPLOYED.				CAPITAL.	WAGES.	MATERIALS.	PRODUCTS.	
All.	Males above 16.	Females above 15.	Youth.	Dollars.	Dollars.	Dollars.	Dollars.	
204	185	....	19	510,275	83,110	458,799	1,374,631	207
6,430	6,402	3	45	5,344,154	1,936,158	4,458,542	8,917,405	208
5,131	5,068	6	57	15,545,116	2,019,810	19,729,432	36,191,133	209
12,443	12,320	29	94	48,779,435	6,758,602	28,177,684	55,706,643	210
1,486	1,426	32	28	2,334,394	230,650	1,203,172	2,225,238	211
555	518	1	36	229,955	160,799	170,168	608,149	212
206	193	....	13	229,000	106,772	197,061	488,800	213
3,587	2,976	196	415	2,590,020	1,623,653	2,466,313	5,962,235	214
13,640	13,064	52	524	18,007,041	6,222,076	28,728,348	42,179,702	215
149,671	145,926	682	3,263	143,309,082	39,966,817	103,102,393	209,852,527	216
126	121	....	5	94,150	42,345	241,037	306,800	217
30,781	30,183	93	505	40,383,960	17,812,493	22,573,692	54,429,634	218
8,918	8,438	326	154	10,603,424	4,632,913	5,246,874	13,311,118	219
838	831	....	7	986,000	307,414	913,833	1,636,580	220
20,015	19,886	6	123	23,222,761	12,541,818	11,952,840	27,565,650	221
22,962	22,444	8	510	25,987,452	12,572,244	19,734,404	41,576,264	222
1,640	1,634	....	6	8,017,248	700,624	9,002,094	12,016,515	223
181	101	65	15	380,500	87,562	120,162	393,447	224
13,190	12,974	12	204	11,287,677	7,601,471	8,034,858	21,316,860	225
5,719	5,650	8	61	4,942,063	2,490,296	3,709,518	8,916,654	226
11,043	10,931	....	112	2,546,425	4,271,700	7,015,782	14,587,185	227
2,556	600	1,089	858	1,521,802	616,714	1,179,666	3,540,008	228
158	113	16	29	88,400	55,600	135,728	257,981	229
499	257	165	77	1,549,100	173,180	2,531,552	3,760,809	230
435	423	4	8	496,700	111,595	1,524,680	1,950,306	231
5,551	5,375	22	154	20,078,987	1,722,326	46,577,864	56,429,831	232
75	75	....	....	100,000	70,000	170,000	420,000	233
577	569	6	2	936,000	366,240	435,155	1,000,190	234
12	12	....	....	15,000	6,700	6,508	32,000	235
91	69	12	10	98,200	66,426	141,550	262,630	236
7,205	864	6,106	235	2,425,926	1,156,531	3,365,132	6,513,222	237
317	316	....	1	813,100	191,913	378,575	819,350	238
507	503	....	4	153,120	208,817	384,787	850,941	239
2,383	2,128	16	239	3,462,360	923,703	1,687,931	4,222,278	240
40	17	23	....	16,800	8,700	30,790	49,875	241
1,059	1,019	21	19	1,351,600	631,634	932,657	2,019,464	242
401	393	8	....	408,000	264,485	233,767	596,685	243
1,566	1,535	20	11	1,775,850	1,139,780	743,351	2,960,165	244
4,141	4,054	19	68	6,019,311	3,071,392	2,924,777	8,320,594	245
21	19	....	2	21,500	8,900	81,887	125,850	246
94	92	....	2	105,950	43,086	198,835	307,009	247
656	373	226	57	616,050	286,023	355,407	955,854	248
80	34	39	7	101,325	20,648	105,108	157,057	249
33	33	....	....	55,000	9,900	48,110	66,190	250
34	30	2	2	39,500	24,100	127,660	225,700	251
191	186	3	2	158,798	61,210	45,845	178,139	252
543	464	45	34	2,072,532	298,975	7,582,576	9,728,667	253
1,487	1,468	12	7	1,490,131	277,895	2,782,361	3,993,139	254
9	8	....	1	12,200	4,200	67,050	87,500	255
111	111	....	....	353,400	60,138	544,909	772,524	256
94	76	....	18	479,800	46,950	537,250	757,700	257
664	639	10	15	1,225,350	292,032	1,333,631	2,205,610	258
2,365	2,365	....	....	145,475	32,864	274,058	631,445	259
945	924	11	10	3,862,956	458,387	7,216,414	8,881,962	260
2	2	....	....	500	400	300	1,400	261
1,411	1,343	17	51	2,237,000	687,288	2,548,768	4,211,579	262
10,964	10,728	28	208	2,797,306	4,169,839	4,990,475	13,244,498	263
1,008	968	9	31	3,742,150	550,463	3,988,106	5,720,738	264
1,932	1,865	29	38	7,414,250	1,016,574	7,480,022	11,211,647	265
2,770	1,902	741	127	5,001,820	1,028,208	3,478,709	6,436,817	266
8,167	5,107	2,553	507	16,771,920	3,400,038	16,120,363	25,200,417	267
3,111	2,462	475	174	6,276,600	1,249,821	4,420,240	7,706,317	268
3,862	1,450	2,384	28	6,314,674	1,470,446	6,009,751	9,363,384	269
869	558	145	166	1,415,500	329,267	1,315,106	2,165,540	270
422	372	12	38	368,648	227,366	395,237	992,895	271
2,436	1,667	631	138	6,667,684	1,017,795	7,319,752	16,257,790	272
867	705	132	30	634,715	408,248	235,933	1,211,191	273
189	174	....	15	139,500	119,400	219,075	447,080	274
156	61	95	....	241,150	48,150	44,510	160,800	275
4	4	....	....	20,000	3,000	13,000	20,000	276
24	19	5	....	32,500	7,700	11,391	34,096	277
242	199	30	13	268,250	133,556	181,740	467,380	278

TABLE XCIX.—*The United States, by Specified Industries*—1870—Continued.

	Mechanical and manufacturing industries.	Establishments.	STEAM-ENGINES.		WATER-WHEELS.	
			Horse-power.	Number.	Horse-power.	Number.
279	Pens, steel	3	38	2		
280	Percussion-caps	2			100	
281	Perfumery, cosmetics, and fancy soaps	64	122	8		
282	Photographic apparatus	10	16	4		
283	Photographs	1,090				
284	Pipes, tobacco	31	323	15	15	
285	Plaster, ground	321	1,967	44	4,388	
286	Plastering	691	54	2	80	
287	Plated ware	203	1,229	61	650	
288	Plumbing and gasfitting	705	356	36	12	
289	Pocket-books	60	1	1		
290	Polishing preparations	21	85	4	33	
291	Portable forges	4	12	1		
292	Preserves and sauces	30	67	8		
293	Printers' fixtures	21	15	3	28	
294	Printing cotton and woolen goods	42	7,158	130	2,695	
295	Printing and publishing, (not specified) (a)	311	2,698	187	20	
296	book	40	458	28		
297	newspaper	1,199	3,135	302	74	
298	job	609	1,440	174	15	
299	Pumps	465	1,379	102	958	
300	Putty	13	74	6		
301	Quartz, milled	296	8,210	175	4,398	
302	Quicksilver, smelted	4	64	1	12	
303	Regalia and society banners and emblems	29	31	5		
304	Roofing-materials (b)	198	442	27	274	
305	Saddlery and harness	7,607	172	12	43	
306	Safes, doors, and vaults, (fire-proof)	65	659	35	10	
307	Sails	179				
308	Saleratus	4	41	3		
309	Salt	282	3,278	192	44	
310	ground	15	277	10	32	
311	Saltpeter	2	10	1		
312	Sand and emery paper and cloth	4	190	2		
313	Sash, doors, and blinds	1,605	27,061	990	7,758	
314	Saws	72	1,303	40	246	
315	Scales and balances	49	508	16	205	
316	School slates and slate pencils	22	108	4	234	
317	Screws	18	978	11	158	
318	Sewing-machine fixtures	20	490	13	75	
319	Sewing-machines	49	1,688	37	145	
320	Ship building, ship materials, and repairs (c)	762	3,311	119	109	
321	Shoddy	56	284	16	1,487	
322	Shoe-pegs	26	257	10	365	
323	Shovels and spades	13	614	11	540	
324	Show-cases	47	9	2		
325	Silk goods, (not specified)	53	672	27	457	
326	sewing and twist	35	450	28	332	
327	Silverware	55	361	35	10	
328	Skewers, wooden, for butchers and packers	2			45	
329	Small beer	52	4	1		
330	Soap and candles	614	3,909	158	20	
331	Soap-stone stoves, fire-places, sinks, and cisterns	9	50	1	87	
332	Soda-water apparatus	13	97	9		
333	Spectacles and eye-glasses	31	51	9	2	
334	Starch	195	983	40	3,564	
335	Steel, (not specified)	5	700	8	75	
336	Bessemer	3	3,200	19	100	
337	cast	20	7,537	55	75	
338	forged	2	100	1		
339	Steel springs	41	976	27	207	
340	Stereotyping and electrotyping	36	91	8		
341	Stone and earthen ware	777	1,586	82	122	
342	Straw goods	75	341	24	35	
343	Sugar and molasses, raw cane	713	18,330	529		
344	refined cane	59	9,635	119		
345	beet and grape	2	260	12		
346	sorghum	317	272	17	138	
347	Sumac, ground	19	208	10	85	
348	Tar and turpentine	227	177	26	15	
349	Taxidermy	8				

(a) Includes Albums, photograph, of Table IX (B.)
(b) Includes Coal tar, of Table IX (B.) District of Columbia.

TABLE XCIX.—*The United States, by Specified Industries*—1870—Continued.

HANDS EMPLOYED.				CAPITAL.	WAGES.	MATERIALS.	PRODUCTS.	
All.	Males above 16.	Females above 15.	Youth.	Dollars.	Dollars.	Dollars.	Dollars.	
257	47	195	15	175,000	60,000	49,943	180,000	279
140	53	46	41	145,000	76,500	153,800	290,000	280
727	320	371	36	1,172,900	260,415	892,219	2,029,582	281
196	134	60	2	245,400	103,000	174,253	831,975	282
2,800	2,260	452	88	1,995,280	786,702	1,094,491	3,643,887	283
481	360	35	86	178,600	214,924	93,899	447,330	284
1,513	1,488	3	22	2,341,260	533,407	1,430,140	2,691,851	285
2,464	2,404	......	60	353,462	900,395	907,524	2,659,025	286
4,235	3,425	654	156	4,586,125	2,350,169	3,771,981	8,142,150	287
4,783	4,582	1	200	3,731,667	2,277,644	5,167,323	10,394,471	288
733	394	293	46	351,225	293,258	467,922	1,108,380	289
98	73	16	9	370,800	37,087	214,696	323,015	290
25	25	......	......	20,900	11,730	13,975	53,930	291
335	195	121	19	411,100	113,427	844,770	1,242,836	292
86	80	......	6	55,200	33,931	32,640	118,119	293
8,894	6,092	1,393	1,409	13,367,553	3,438,089	46,373,358	54,446,044	294
10,668	8,718	1,231	719	16,839,993	7,156,332	11,398,131	28,995,214	295
1,390	920	352	118	2,128,903	760,275	1,525,773	3,568,823	296
13,130	11,343	718	1,069	14,947,887	8,168,515	8,709,632	25,393,029	297
5,555	4,458	499	598	6,007,354	2,710,234	2,966,709	8,511,934	298
1,905	1,817	7	81	1,[illegible]55,894	663,594	970,547	2,818,457	299
93	91	......	2	231,600	42,590	264,250	395,250	300
2,973	2,973	......	......	10,910,822	2,460,631	12,446,974	18,386,406	301
256	248	......	8	3,500,000	181,000	837,800	1,027,680	302
410	150	237	23	251,650	114,702	307,296	626,476	303
1,919	1,884	13	22	2,448,680	883,341	1,293,116	3,257,403	304
23,557	22,716	375	466	13,935,961	7,046,207	16,068,310	32,709,981	305
1,639	1,599	1	39	2,075,200	917,263	967,810	2,728,336	306
908	836	44	28	583,290	455,575	1,239,346	2,255,446	307
63	63	......	......	140,700	33,530	164,660	231,647	308
2,921	2,858	7	56	6,561,615	1,147,910	1,760,670	4,890,629	309
146	115	25	6	515,670	69,166	205,039	376,160	310
10	10	......	......	22,000	4,800	57,410	66,280	311
82	62	4	16	980,956	45,450	146,165	349,068	312
20,379	19,496	43	840	21,239,809	10,059,812	17,581,814	36,625,806	313
1,595	1,457	8	130	2,883,391	995,609	1,332,891	3,175,289	314
1,003	955	7	41	1,019,500	668,451	920,870	2,823,816	315
339	271	11	57	384,020	113,236	81,435	208,853	316
1,582	924	476	182	9,147,880	664,408	1,248,135	3,425,473	317
1,130	1,075	11	44	761,800	638,973	585,909	1,749,858	318
7,291	6,709	334	248	8,759,431	5,142,248	3,055,786	14,097,446	319
11,063	10,978	2	83	9,102,335	5,594,686	8,252,394	17,910,328	320
632	419	171	42	815,950	198,372	1,098,603	1,768,592	321
279	175	98	6	169,900	78,051	63,736	264,847	322
849	837	2	10	757,100	489,100	1,424,944	2,445,526	323
353	340	1	12	178,300	219,384	419,466	838,699	324
4,176	1,269	2,203	704	4,019,630	1,328,389	4,126,821	7,066,487	325
2,523	465	1,368	690	2,223,500	624,917	4,197,752	5,672,875	326
815	747	59	9	1,282,550	542,113	1,222,428	2,344,357	327
18	11	7	......	20,000	11,400	3,100	23,000	328
166	138	5	23	101,250	34,412	80,108	225,376	329
4,422	3,828	309	285	10,454,860	1,925,951	15,232,587	22,535,337	330
74	74	......	......	127,500	38,444	98,325	189,115	331
307	300	1	6	424,150	140,751	304,246	813,075	332
258	237	10	11	183,825	133,555	183,830	429,859	333
2,072	1,712	317	43	2,741,675	900,719	3,884,909	5,994,422	334
168	165	......	3	1,305,000	158,200	253,250	654,000	335
329	329	......	......	858,000	176,000	1,373,812	1,818,220	336
1,893	1,842	4	47	3,979,400	1,256,632	3,417,928	6,936,566	337
47	42	......	5	203,000	60,300	121,013	201,200	338
1,021	996	......	25	2,426,500	601,706	1,662,920	2,928,993	339
766	659	15	92	1,033,200	446,532	290,774	1,075,080	340
6,116	5,059	316	741	5,294,398	2,247,173	1,702,705	6,045,536	341
14,925	1,988	12,594	343	2,119,350	2,122,870	3,661,760	7,282,086	342
21,299	15,723	3,797	1,779	10,248,475	1,230,119	6,069,271	10,383,368	343
4,597	4,494	20	83	20,545,220	3,177,288	96,899,431	108,941,911	344
116	66	25	25	67,350	8,090	90,740	119,720	345
1,169	1,038	51	80	143,057	39,616	162,207	344,098	346
85	84	1	......	167,450	31,325	164,702	207,180	347
2,638	2,526	81	31	902,225	476,284	2,146,090	3,585,225	348
18	18	......	......	20,200	5,700	11,464	26,650	349

(*a*) Includes *Oakum*, of Table IX, (B.)

TABLE XCIX.—*The United States, by Specified Industries*—1870—Continued.

	Mechanical and manufacturing industries.	Establishments.	STEAM-ENGINES.		WATER-WHEEL[S]	
			Horse-power.	Number.	Horse-power.	Numb[er.]
350	Tin, copper, and sheet-iron ware	6,646	1,236	68	270	
351	Tobacco and cigars	61	352	30	10	
352	chewing and smoking, and snuff	512	2,320	146	362	2
353	cigars	4,631	16	2	30	1
354	Toys and games	49	57	7	270	
355	Trunks, valises, and satchels	222	358	15	55	
356	Trusses, bandages, and supporters	36	31	4	9	
357	Type-founding	31	166	11	....	....
358	Umbrella furniture	10	135	8	....	....
359	Umbrellas and canes	83	65	3	30	
360	Upholstery	609	198	16	88	
361	materials (*a*)	47	827	16	704	
362	Varnish	59	95	5	....	....
363	Vault lights, (of iron and glass)	2	6	1	....	....
364	Veneering	10	324	6	45	
365	Vinegar	181	201	21	34	
366	Washing-machines and clothes-wringers	64	351	13	290	
367	Watch and clock repairing	1,103	1	1	10	
368	cases	49	5	3	....	....
369	materials	10	13	2	33	
370	Watches	37	145	4	....	....
371	Weaving, (not specified)	8	....	....	....	....
372	Whalebone and rattan, prepared	5	4	3	10	
373	Wheelbarrows	23	213	10	297	
374	Wheelwrighting	3,613	554	32	983	
375	Whips	43	117	4	17	
376	and canes	60	25	3	108	
377	Willow ware (*b*)	168	25	2	28	
378	Wire	32	2,082	23	745	
379	insulated	2	....	....	10	
380	work (*c*)	141	470	22	422	
381	Wood brackets, moldings, and scrolls	65	1,375	54	101	
382	Wooden ware	269	2,293	76	3,366	1
383	Wood pulp	8	....	....	1,069	
384	turned and carved (*d*)	733	3,830	221	4,323	
385	miscellaneous articles	117	418	20	727	
386	Wool-carding and cloth-dressing	1,001	3,768	202	6,223	
387	Woolen goods	1,938	32,195	855	52,906	1,
388	Worsted goods	102	3,382	71	4,634	
389	Zinc, smelted and rolled	11	134	4	100	
390	statuary and building ornaments	2	10	1	....	....

(*a*) Includes *Curled hair, Elastic sponge, Excelsior, (shaved wood,)* and *Husks, prepared*, of Table IX
(*b*) Includes 1 establishment only, (in Michigan,) producing also *Rustic ornaments*.

of Industry, needs to be carefully borne in mind; otherwise the most mistaken vi of the importance of the several branches of industry will result.

The manufacturing, mechanical, mining, and fishing industries may be groupe respect of the value of materials into five classes:

First. Those industries in which the subject-matter of labor is taken as of no va and the value of the "materials" reported is made up of the mechanical and ch ical appliances with which that subject-matter is treated. This is true of pretty m the entire body of mining and fishing industries. The ores in the rock or in the the fish in the sea, are taken, and properly so, as of no value for the purposes of t statistics. The royalty paid to the owner of the mine in the one case, the license ta out by the fisherman in the other, are not included in the value of materials. In s cases the appliances, chemical or mechanical, are of the simplest kind, and are sumed in very small quantities; in others, they become very extensive and costly; through all this class, it remains true, as a rule, that it is labor, and the risk and of capital, which make up the chief cost of production.

Second. Those industries in which the subject-matter is of a distinct and immed commercial value, but the property does not reside in the person who treats it. these cases, still, the value of the subject-matter treated is not embraced in the ret of materials. A familiar illustration is that of horse-shoeing. It would be the hei of absurdity for the smith, for example, to return the value of unshod horses among

TABLE XCIX.—*The United States, by Specified Industries*—1870—Continued.

HANDS EMPLOYED.				CAPITAL.	WAGES.	MATERIALS.	PRODUCTS.	
All.	Males above 16.	Females above 15.	Youth.	Dollars.	Dollars.	Dollars.	Dollars.	
25,883	24,201	631	991	21,027,876	9,516,357	19,067,015	40,636,811	350
1,431	838	319	274	1,767,100	546,538	1,782,829	3,337,274	351
20,368	9,750	4,860	5,758	11,788,714	4,670,095	20,351,607	36,258,177	352
26,049	21,409	2,615	2,025	11,368,516	9,098,709	12,522,171	32,166,593	353
615	357	184	74	312,800	182,255	159,946	579,865	354
3,479	2,798	457	224	2,185,964	1,810,798	3,315,038	7,725,488	355
275	154	110	11	154,305	101,070	108,512	363,205	356
1,331	729	413	189	1,704,785	720,105	819,938	2,180,001	357
578	292	236	50	367,900	219,482	293,547	724,034	358
2,618	648	1,784	186	1,737,757	837,560	1,926,056	4,098,032	359
4,757	3,212	1,259	286	4,688,049	1,679,217	4,740,572	9,379,310	360
575	453	40	82	2,028,612	233,575	1,031,929	1,544,612	361
415	410	2	3	2,168,740	252,059	3,311,097	4,991,405	362
19	19	....	....	7,500	14,700	14,703	41,600	363
94	74	20	....	229,550	45,310	129,918	241,750	364
569	553	3	13	1,079,079	174,699	1,216,694	1,934,842	365
462	424	14	24	811,182	200,912	454,562	1,379,827	366
2,025	1,966	13	46	1,355,170	459,492	332,729	1,827,993	367
703	619	73	11	730,500	555,018	1,152,979	2,333,340	368
47	45	2	....	22,150	22,500	12,320	61,021	369
1,816	1,202	592	22	2,666,133	1,304,304	412,783	2,819,080	370
27	25	2	....	2,450	455	6,639	10,145	371
55	33	12	10	18,000	26,000	169,644	262,000	372
238	204	8	26	243,750	111,390	166,420	472,790	373
6,989	6,915	11	63	2,839,316	1,353,474	1,907,418	5,846,943	374
377	220	124	33	332,031	124,261	173,391	475,651	375
584	401	177	6	551,530	260,283	330,111	767,467	376
859	565	68	226	208,755	171,213	143,634	510,930	377
1,733	1,475	226	32	2,520,800	1,078,184	2,955,925	5,030,581	378
11	10	1	....	12,000	4,800	8,960	27,817	379
2,526	1,316	1,053	157	1,667,900	719,633	1,548,006	2,959,227	380
747	714	3	30	832,275	434,640	636,423	1,472,042	381
3,169	2,708	67	394	2,814,592	1,210,268	1,623,694	4,142,194	382
111	111	....	....	191,000	60,178	29,500	172,350	383
4,103	3,777	103	223	2,751,544	1,499,565	1,648,008	4,959,191	384
715	673	11	31	481,495	257,451	388,549	1,018,047	385
2,318	1,986	173	159	1,740,249	260,419	3,504,052	4,675,986	386
77,870	40,852	27,531	9,487	97,173,432	26,648,272	93,406,884	151,298,196	387
12,920	3,864	7,152	1,904	10,085,778	4,368,857	14,808,198	22,090,331	388
316	302	1	13	620,020	150,516	764,508	1,167,947	389
38	36	....	2	38,500	19,000	24,115	56,500	390

(*c*) Includes *Telegraph supplies* (mainly wire) of Table IX (B.)
(*d*) Includes the item of Table IX (B,) (Connecticut,) there erroneously styled *Stationery*.

"materials," and the value of the same, when shod, in his product. The census assigns, as the materials of his industry, merely the coal, iron, steel, &c., used, and, as the value of his product, merely the price of the personal service he renders, plus the cost of those materials. In the same category are many of the trades. The returns in respect to the industries of painting, plastering, and plumbing, for example, do not take into account the value of the houses, stores, factories, &c., before and after these operations, but regard only the added value given as the product, and, in the same way, only the paints, the plaster and lime, the tubing, iron, and brass-ware, &c., used, as the "materials" of these industries.

Third. Those industries in which the entire value of the subject-matter is carried into the value of "materials," and appears again in the product enhanced by the value of labor, by the charges for the use of capital, for rent, freight, &c.; but in which the value of such subject-matter is small, compared to the cost of labor. The cabinet-maker takes a few dollars' worth of woods, coarse or fine, and works this material up into articles bearing ten times the value. The cutler takes a few pounds of steel, and produces edged or pointed instruments of high cost, because of the time and skill required in their fabrication. In all these cases the value of the product is not greatly enhanced by the fact that the entire subject-matter of the industry is included.

Fourth. Industries which are otherwise under the same conditions as those of the third class, but in which the value of the materials approaches, or even moderately exceeds, *the value of the labor* employed, and becomes thus an important element in the

[Continued on page 847.]

TABLE C.—*Manufactures, by Totals of Counties, in each State and Territory*—1870.

THE STATE OF ALABAMA.

Counties.	Establishm'ts.	Steam-engines.	Water-wheels.	All hands.	Males above 16.	Females above 15.	Youth.	Capital. (Dollars.)	Wages. (Dollars.)	Materials. (Dollars.)	Products. (Dollars.)
Autauga	32	2	21	397	215	104	78	287, 600	127, 203	382, 881	67
Baker	16		16	24	24			20, 400	1, 485	60, 323	
Baldwin	15	5	2	450	402	41	7	115, 150	130, 360	98, 305	22
Barbour	46	7	24	185	185			163, 175	63, 740	610, 856	78
Bibb	19	7	9	73	59		14	53, 760	13, 652	64, 076	11
Blount	32	1	14	58	58			31, 890	3, 346	60, 371	8
Bullock	19	9	7	55	55			69, 000	14, 770	112, 607	14
Butler	99	5	13	236	229	3	4	81, 080	38, 850	111, 165	26
Calhoun	60	8	27	176	175	1		165, 720	36, 795	194, 488	32
Chambers	14		4	27	27			18, 075	4, 780	90, 887	10
Cherokee	65	4	33	195	194	1		100, 407	31, 139	179, 255	28
Choctaw	25	6	4	50	46	4		18, 850	3, 125	37, 596	
Clarke	19	1	6	35	35			10, 205	3, 550	21, 525	
Clay	31		23	66	65	1		28, 703	3, 551	80, 398	
Cleburne	14		18	35	35			22, 100	5, 176	29, 865	
Colbert	36	11	2	124	111	5	8	78, 790	26, 400	67, 884	1
Conecuh	16	2	8	24	24			21, 900	3, 528	31, 938	
Coosa	9		11	58	18	25	15	51, 700	8, 798	83, 602	1
Crenshaw	10	1	2	25	25			9, 100	2, 625	11, 750	
Dale	53	1	34	103	100	1	2	40, 100	12, 875	123, 570	1
Dallas	41	16	6	166	161		5	115, 650	54, 687	134, 060	2
De Kalb	8		6	14	14			10, 205	640	8, 550	
Elmore	54	2	32	427	204	133	90	511, 125	94, 975	308, 114	4
Etowah	25	6	13	129	116	4	9	54, 850	22, 855	152, 234	2
Fayette	13		7	23	23			13, 600	1, 500	10, 308	
Franklin	41	3	16	74	71	1	2	24, 911	5, 898	51, 241	
Greene	10	5		23	23			15, 800	4, 550	27, 520	
Hale	43	9	10	124	122	2		67, 691	20, 780	113, 690	2
Henry	23		15	52	52			11, 700	7, 425	32, 838	
Jackson	60	7	18	134	133		1	52, 125	18, 133	107, 050	1
Jefferson	22		19	41	41			45, 800	5, 460	150, 215	1
Lauderdale	45	2	21	105	105			45, 050	12, 900	80, 404	1
Lawrence	33	4	3	59	58		1	22, 955	9, 240	75, 791	1
Lee	39	2	28	106	106			86, 375	16, 140	187, 757	2
Limestone	21	3	13	70	59	8	3	39, 600	9, 511	51, 030	1
Lowndes	32	10	2	62	62			46, 150	11, 020	113, 230	1
Macon	32	7	3	120	120			62, 550	27, 450	97, 573	1
Madison	93	10	21	419	337	58	24	167, 440	103, 839	254, 334	5
Marengo	92	16	10	226	221	5		72, 810	43, 975	125, 932	2
Marion	1		1	24	10	8	6	11, 000	4, 800	41, 000	
Marshall	29		17	47	47			26, 079	4, 120	51, 770	
Mobile	272	32	2	1, 373	1, 220	130	23	1, 099, 435	645, 205	1, 300, 574	2, 7
Monroe	4		1	9	9			6, 300	1, 350	13, 400	
Montgomery	59	22		368	360	8		386, 425	230, 350	347, 809	6
Morgan	1			2	1	1		500	50	400	
Perry	5	5		18	18			13, 800	4, 650	81, 000	1
Pickens	32	8	9	94	70	18	6	46, 900	17, 090	71, 595	1
Pike	14	2	4	41	41			10, 600	13, 550	12, 425	
Randolph	33		33	113	73	20	20	98, 050	20, 150	152, 161	1
Russell	36	12	8	143	142	1		56, 400	30, 735	94, 847	1
Sanford	37		33	60	60			21, 930	1, 904	37, 655	
Shelby	40	11	7	413	393	4	16	372, 285	125, 206	109, 415	3
St. Clair	9	1	6	27	27			18, 916	1, 670	47, 950	
Talladega	26	2	15	74	74			75, 120	14, 515	50, 490	
Tallapoosa	69		31	136	136			51, 375	15, 700	96, 099	1
Tuscaloosa	87	8	21	336	236	46	54	419, 930	66, 378	310, 872	4
Walker	3		1	7	7			3, 300	800	5, 625	
Washington	9	2	7	19	19			9, 500	3, 170	13, 850	
Wilcox	65	18	4	138	137	1		71, 495	19, 756	215, 497	2

THE TERRITORY OF ARIZONA.

Counties.	Establishm'ts.	Steam-engines.	Water-wheels.	All hands.	Males above 16.	Females above 15.	Youth.	Capital. (Dollars.)	Wages. (Dollars.)	Materials. (Dollars.)	Products. (Dollars.)
Mohave, (see Yuma)											
Pima	8	2	1	53	53			42, 600	30, 280	79, 640	1
Yavapai (a)											
Yuma and Mohave	10	3		31	31			108, 100	15, 300	30, 450	

(a) Returned as having no manufactures.

TABLE C.—*Manufactures, by Totals of Counties, &c.*—1870—Continued.

THE STATE OF ARKANSAS.

ounties.	Establishm'ts.	Steam-engines.	Water-wheels.	All hands.	Males above 16.	Females above 15.	Youth.	Capital. (*Dollars.*)	Wages. (*Dollars.*)	Materials. (*Dollars.*)	Products. (*Dollars.*)
sas (a)											
' (a)											
	33	5	9	81	80	1		95,950	15,950	102,942	159,112
	16		4	21	21			4,200	530	20,523	32,188
y	16	6		58	58			15,450	16,550	32,417	62,796
n	7	2		14	14			7,400	1,000	10,444	17,145
	11	5	6	60	55	5		54,000	9,575	80,780	146,229
(a)											
	35	7	2	73	73			37,555	15,470	117,720	176,250
bia	17	8		26	26			21,343	3,870	24,725	33,440
y	8	4	2	25	25			6,750	1,660	5,300	13,150
ead	2	2		5	5			2,700	515	16,200	18,375
rd	16	3	1	57	44	3	10	22,382	8,780	27,974	63,518
iden (a)											
	9	6		40	40			7,650	3,108	21,083	32,944
	12	1	4	26	26			7,300	2,455	20,733	29,837
	24	1		43	43			12,950	3,685	12,094	27,450
	34	7		62	62			64,750	4,020	37,883	61,751
in	12	8		54	50		4	52,500	12,156	81,610	122,387
	7	1	9	16	15		1	15,600	3,110	14,000	20,860
	6	3		26	26			7,750	1,970	18,207	23,202
)	19	4	2	31	30	1		13,683	3,190	54,972	65,614
tead	37	7		79	79			31,075	12,732	83,504	131,003
rings	22	3	5	46	46			17,950	3,090	57,650	86,570
ndence	51	5	17	107	107			61,445	12,190	120,939	187,853
	13	2	4	35	35			12,982	6,920	24,464	45,477
n	12	3		54	54			25,375	13,065	31,863	76,795
on	19	12		107	104		3	97,200	18,630	183,300	197,710
on	10	4		32	32			18,850	10,150	24,550	74,790
tto	14	1		21	21			9,350	500	9,455	25,300
nce (a)											
River	2	2		17	17			10,000	6,100	5,000	18,200
on	6		3	13	13			6,550	1,450	10,025	14,980
a	20	2	5	41	41			24,900	5,240	10,325	36,375
sippi	5	5		34	34			10,500	3,550	4,850	13,500
e	31	7		100	98		2	52,745	15,000	30,995	77,307
omery	6		3	12	12			7,750	875	3,746	5,909
n (a)											
ita	86	18	13	263	256		7	210,850	60,245	159,327	352,969
(a)											
s	46	11	1	145	138	5	2	57,100	29,021	66,689	161,201
	5	3	1	13	13			20,000	5,040	15,180	25,262
tt (a)											
	8	1	5	13	13			4,750	210	8,963	11,175
	9	6	1	39	39			17,350	5,700	54,624	70,725
)	4	4		43	43			34,600	23,400	31,700	75,060
i	77	18	2	438	377	26	35	240,135	184,524	250,880	688,003
lph	15	4	7	19	19			19,550	1,490	35,380	48,629
	14	2	5	33	32		1	8,550	1,735	12,680	19.945
	10	6		26	26			10,450	4,695	14,880	28,129
	3		2	7	5		2	2,775		1,875	3,400
ian	93	13		243	226	6	11	91,970	48,262	106,002	215,381
	12	2		25	25			6,700	4,810	115,150	133,350
)	7		6	21	21			10,600	2,400	16,645	23,600
ncis	32	4	1	72	72			19,890	13,500	32,390	88,020
	12	5		26	26			12,600	5,200	23,700	34,950
uren	4			16	16			9,000	2,200	4,275	17,750
ngton	47	5	7	111	109		2	71,800	23,685	204,992	275,742
	34	14		136	134		2	51,475	19,995	31,567	88,310
uff	19	7		57	57			27,833	10,895	99,686	129,836
	10	7	1	42	42			18,450	9,850	10,050	39,250

THE STATE OF CALIFORNIA.

ounties.	Establishm'ts.	Steam-engines.	Water-wheels.	All hands.	Males above 16.	Females above 15.	Youth.	Capital. (*Dollars.*)	Wages. (*Dollars.*)	Materials. (*Dollars.*)	Products. (*Dollars.*)
da	120	21	1	648	630	13	5	455,750	287,830	544,592	1,163,914
)	10	1	3	20	19	1		20,075	6,135	3,625	22,752
or	89	16	10	384	384			646,250	173,915	907,394	1,588,494
	45	18	6	286	285		1	442,200	144,730	659,175	977,937
ras	246	15	26	569	568		1	234,920	139,598	104,224	606,150
	32	5		78	78			63,850	44,317	147,753	[illegible]

(*a*) Returned as having no manufactures.

TABLE C.—*Manufactures, by Totals of Counties, &c.*—1870—Continued.

THE STATE OF CALIFORNIA—Continued.

Counties.	Establishm'ts.	Steam-engines.	Water-wheels.	All hands.	Males above 16.	Females above 15.	Youth.	Capital. (Dollars.)	Wages. (Dollars.)	Materials. (Dollars.)	Products. (Dollars.)
Contra Costa	35	2	....	63	63	......	.....	36, 640	31, 775	40, 694	[illegible]
Del Norte	29	5	3	65	65	......	.....	77, 430	16, 803	65, 290	[illegible]
El Dorado	62	13	16	259	257	2	.....	248, 422	86, 909	254, 664	[illegible]
Fresno	7	2	1	113	112	1	.....	272, 800	79, 900	412, 025	[illegible]
Humboldt	35	11	2	316	303	5	8	495, 400	158, 887	325, 259	[illegible]
Inyo	27	3	5	104	104	......	.....	231, 120	51, 180	213, 795	[illegible]
Kern	11	5	4	71	71	......	.....	128, 700	22, 985	68, 918	[illegible]
Klamath	8	3	4	137	137	......	.....	90, 600	56, 006	96, 832	[illegible]
Lake	22	5	2	153	153	......	.....	301, 725	67, 510	145, 415	[illegible]
Lassen	10	....	4	16	16	......	.....	18, 150	1, 905	11, 200	[illegible]
Los Angeles	79	6	5	621	621	......	.....	648, 570	154, 100	294, 958	[illegible]
Marin	25	1	1	396	396	......	.....	235, 900	88, 250	148, 336	[illegible]
Mariposa	18	10	3	110	110	......	.....	203, 950	70, 074	86, 702	[illegible]
Mendocino	85	18	8	876	875	1	.....	1, 114, 550	358, 700	412, 768	1, 6
Merced	5	....	7	13	13	......	.....	43, 300	3, 500	53, 330	
Mono	8	1	6	29	28	1	.....	27, 600	12, 180	40, 345	
Monterey	35	5	....	98	93	......	.....	133, 100	30, 305	109, 306	1
Napa	4	1	....	16	16	......	.....	25, 700	3, 740	128, 561	
Nevada	137	21	7	597	595	2	.....	501, 260	247, 704	571, 161	1,
Placer	66	10	10	344	344	......	.....	271, 625	101, 270	232, 743	
Plumas	28	6	10	112	112	[illegible]	.....	148, 700	59, 450	233, 041	
Sacramento	182	28	....	1, 159	1, 091	13	55	1, 761, 179	1, 107, 428	1, 964, 847	3,
San Bernardino	20	4	2	104	103	1	.....	75, 275	32, 300	68, 583	
San Diego	5	2	1	23	21	2	.....	22, 200	7, 667	29, 768	
San Francisco	1, 223	207	....	12, 377	11, 252	737	388	24, 170, 956	7, 238, 528	20, 046, 321	37,
San Joaquin	149	10	....	455	453	2	.....	421, 025	238, 476	497, 009	1,
San Luis Obispo	10	3	1	34	34	......	.....	36, 900	13, 480	47, 633	
San Mateo	75	11	4	283	281	2	.....	230, 270	105, 225	132, 116	
Santa Barbara	24	....	....	105	94	9	2	170, 900	25, 450	27, 948	
Santa Clara	171	23	5	761	741	6	14	3, 828, 900	369, 625	1, 566, 725	2,
Santa Cruz	76	24	13	704	704	......	.....	1, 292, 550	336, 607	810, 449	1,
Shasta	40	2	16	119	119	......	.....	190, 775	37, 915	77, 669	
Sierra	42	9	13	200	200	......	.....	364, 990	90, 755	367, 099	
Siskiyou	47	6	17	108	108	......	.....	169, 100	32, 269	103, 071	
Solano	101	6	....	303	296	7	.....	434, 200	144, 780	416, 953	
Sonoma	234	33	8	954	944	8	2	726, 080	328, 884	740, 470	1,
Stanislaus	18	1	2	40	40	......	.....	212, 350	20, 700	147, 274	
Sutter (a)	.....	.....	.....	.....	.....	.....	.....	.....	.....	.....	.....
Tehama	11	3	6	141	89	52	.....	140, 000	52, 700	705, 244	
Trinity	22	....	11	50	50	......	.....	48, 450	16, 520	20, 390	
Tulare	14	2	6	60	60	......	.....	58, 100	16, 150	55, 445	
Tuolumne	25	6	12	105	105	......	.....	148, 600	44, 480	130, 627	
Yolo	103	8	1	306	300	3	3	265, 525	109, 857	285, 502	
Yuba	114	12	9	512	507	5	.....	731, 590	267, 268	797, 814	1,

THE TERRITORY OF COLORADO.

Counties.	Establishm'ts.	Steam-engines.	Water-wheels.	All hands.	Males above 16.	Females above 15.	Youth.	Capital. (Dollars.)	Wages. (Dollars.)	Materials. (Dollars.)
Arapahoe	92	10	1	316	315	1	.....	246, 700	221, 290	427, 205
Bent (a)	.....	.....	.....	.....	.....	.....	.....	.....	.....	.....
Boulder	21	5	5	58	53	......	.....	36, 300	23, 250	130, 575
Clear Creek	4	2	....	23	23	......	.....	125, 550	28, 000	114, 00[illegible]
Conejos	2	....	2	3	3	......	.....	17, 500	1, 110	3, 300
Costilla	2	....	2	5	5	......	.....	14, 000	1, 275	5, 650
Douglas	1	1	....	21	20	1	.....	7, 500	6, 000	5, 150
El Paso	8	5	3	87	87	......	.....	61, 500	36, 100	54, 900
Fremont	7	....	1	11	11	......	.....	17, 400	8, 400	25, 310
Gilpin	30	13	1	153	153	......	.....	2, 030, 400	123, 813	499, 935
Greenwood (a)	.....	.....	.....	.....	.....	.....	.....	.....	.....	.....
Huerfano	4	....	....	4	4	......	.....	3, 000	250	1, 340
Jefferson	27	9	5	74	74	......	.....	145, 650	37, 232	157, 915
Lake	7	1	3	22	22	......	.....	12, 050	8, 326	9, 650
Larimer	7	2	3	31	31	......	.....	35, 410	8, 925	38, 925
Las Animas	12	....	2	17	17	......	.....	21, 405	4, 290	49, 419
Park	8	1	2	21	21	......	.....	16, 700	5, 300	10, 390
Pueblo	10	....	1	28	28	......	.....	42, 700	13, 490	67, 656
Saguache (a)	.....	.....	.....	.....	.....	.....	.....	.....	.....	.....
Summit	2	....	....	2	2	......	.....	650	.....	630
Weld	3	....	....	5	5	......	.....	1, 200	1, 250	1, 300

(a) Returned as having no manufactures.

TABLE C.—*Manufactures, by Totals of Counties, &c.*—1870—Continued.

THE STATE OF CONNECTICUT.

[Cou]nties.	Establishm'ts.	Steam-engines.	Water-wheels.	All hands.	Males above 16.	Females above 15.	Youth.	Capital. (*Dollars.*)	Wages. (*Dollars.*)	Materials. (*Dollars.*)	Products. (*Dollars.*)
....	754	129	176	13,844	10,218	3,074	552	12,145,097	6,580,593	12,552,187	23,499,004
....	1,031	183	415	19,106	13,789	4,085	1,232	21,259,828	9,316,592	17,542,785	35,039,324
l	609	27	317	4,846	3,800	795	251	5,362,490	1,964,975	5,613,473	9,918,506
x	429	37	147	4,503	3,356	872	275	4,614,630	1,877,636	3,937,528	7,719,537
en	940	225	253	23,306	16,927	4,918	1,461	29,445,641	11,549,919	22,054,303	45,156,181
don	703	77	223	10,624	7,219	2,701	704	11,279,402	3,896,885	12,279,363	19,797,065
....	238	15	164	3,909	2,119	1,499	291	3,177,931	1,295,846	5,643,279	8,907,799
l	424	20	293	9,385	4,256	2,866	2,263	7,996,259	2,504,741	6,796,661	11,028,056

THE TERRITORY OF DAKOTA.

[Counties.]	Establishm'ts.	Steam-engines.	Water-wheels.	All hands.	Males above 16.	Females above 15.	Youth.	Capital.	Wages.	Materials.	Products.
no	2	2	....	18	18	......	......	13,000	8,000	7,500	22,500
s (a)											
a)											
Mix (a)											
....	4	3	2	25	25	......	......	22,500	4,234	28,672	55,720
....											
ion (a)											
....											
a)											
ha (a)											
(a)											
....											
....	6	4	4	30	28	......	2	14,900	4,472	57,200	75,050
....	4	....	....	15	15	......	......	26,800	3,900	10,900	21,800
ized portion of Territory.	1	....	....	3	3	......	......	2,000	500	1,725	3,500

THE STATE OF DELAWARE.

[Counties.]	Establishm'ts.	Steam-engines.	Water-wheels.	All hands.	Males above 16.	Females above 15.	Youth.	Capital.	Wages.	Materials.	Products.
....	186	37	39	1,104	739	317	48	519,868	182,890	691,031	1,169,132
tle	459	101	114	8,161	6,528	879	754	9,995,175	3,440,371	9,184,544	15,093,131
....	155	26	81	445	438	3	4	324,050	68,934	330,822	529,119

THE DISTRICT OF COLUMBIA.

[Counties.]	Establishm'ts.	Steam-engines.	Water-wheels.	All hands.	Males above 16.	Females above 15.	Youth.	Capital.	Wages.	Materials.	Products.
rict	952	54	15	4,685	4,333	216	136	5,021,925	2,007,600	4,754,883	9,292,173

THE STATE OF FLORIDA.

[Counties.]	Establishm'ts.	Steam-engines.	Water-wheels.	All hands.	Males above 16.	Females above 15.	Youth.	Capital.	Wages.	Materials.	Products.
....	130	25	4	337	334	......	3	50,275	25,180	174,744	288,480
....	3	2	....	3	3	......	......	3,200	....	2,367	3,400
....	7	3	....	24	24	......	......	18,540	4,000	39,900	58,151
(a)											
....	15	....	7	20	20	......	......	5,050	1,545	6,850	15,800
....	2	....	....	3	3	......	......	900	350	1,500	2,475
....	10	4	....	24	23	......	1	10,600	4,900	14,000	26,230
....											
....	105	13	....	739	727	5	7	419,450	350,480	1,090,425	1,883,225
....	28	12	2	252	244	......	8	125,975	115,456	232,380	472,325
....	6	1	....	24	24	......	......	16,225	6,300	6,050	24,625
....	36	1	16	59	50	......	......	25,800	4,125	39,525	65,164
l	7	1	3	17	17	......	......	4,750	5,900	35,150	43,575
o (a)											
ugh	5	2	1	52	35	......	17	28,600	14,200	33,230	93,573
a)											
....	61	4	8	90	90	......	......	29,800	5,720	38,175	73,150
....	23	5	4	47	47	......	......	24,775	5,750	37,048	57,358

(*a*) Returned as having no manufactures.

TABLE C.—*Manufactures, by Totals of Counties*

THE STATE OF FLORIDA—C

Counties.	Establishm'ts.	Water-wheels.	Steam-engines.	All hands.	Males above 16.	Females above 15.	Youth.	Capital.
La Fayette (a)								
Leon	30	12	2	187	176	6	5	31
Levy	5	3		45	37	4	4	1
Liberty	6		2	18	18			
Madison	16	6	22	96	90	3	3	7
Manatee (a)								
Marion	7	2		19	13	2	4	
Monroe	22			300	299		1	27
Nassau	15	6		78	78			7
Orange	8	1	2	12	12			
Polk	5		2	7	7			
Putnam	6	3	3	27	27			1
Santa Rosa	9	8		92	92			4
St. John's	5	2		22	22			1
Sumter	6	1	2	15	15			
Suwannee	4	2		26	20		6	1
Taylor	7	1	4	11	11			
Volusia	2	1	1	2	2			
Wakulla	17	1	7	17	17			
Walton	4	3	1	23	23			
Washington	42	1	6	61	61			1

THE STATE OF GEORG

Counties.	Establishm'ts.	Water-wheels.	Steam-engines.	All hands.	Males above 16.	Females above 15.	Youth.	Capital.
Appling (a)								
Baker	12	7	5	34	34			1
Baldwin	30	4	10	189	106	40	43	12
Banks	13		13	25	25			
Bartow	59	8	35	314	309	3	2	15
Berrien	7		6	12	12			
Bibb	94	16	13	979	869	66	44	80
Brooks	12	4	2	27	24		3	1
Bryan	5	1	2	6	6			
Bullock	6		2	8	8			
Burke	22	1	10	61	61			2
Butts	17		12	37	37			4
Calhoun	17	2	6	40	39	1		2
Camden	17	9		222	197	7	18	37
Campbell	56	5	39	161	146	10	5	8
Carroll	91	2	82	168	146	11	11	10
Catoosa	21		15	50	49		1	4
Charlton	8	2		121	113	2	6	3
Chatham	98	29		1,362	1,300	3	59	1, 14
Chattahoochee	23		18	47	44		3	3
Chattooga	32	1	14	62	62			3
Cherokee	22		20	42	41		1	4
Clarke	51	2	26	639	296	236	107	50
Clay	40		24	90	85	3	2	3
Clayton	27	3	15	69	68		1	2
Clinch	1	1		25	25			
Cobb	60	12	34	353	239	69	45	53
Coffee (a)								
Colquitt (a)								
Columbia (a)								
Coweta	55	10	59	205	171	20	14	14
Crawford	14		9	30	29		1	1
Dade	8	2	7	31	31			1
Dawson	3		3	6	6			
Decatur	32	4	17	73	73			3
De Kalb	54	7	43	254	226	17	11	21
Dooly	13	5	7	55	55			2
Dougherty	19	3		70	70			5
Early	17	3	7	55	34	8	13	5
Echols	8		7	19	18		1	
Effingham	7	6	9	52	52			1
Elbert	15		10	115	64	47	4	20
Emanuel	9	6	4	137	114	11	12	6
Fannin	2		2	12	12			3
Fayette	15	1	11	36	36			3
Floyd	121	20	43	612	522	14	76	3

(a) Returned as having no manu

TABLE C.—*Manufactures, by Totals of Counties, &c.*—1870—Continued.

THE STATE OF GEORGIA—Continued.

…ties.	Establishm't's.	Water-wheels.	Steam-engines.	All hands.	Males above 16.	Females above 15.	Youth.	Capital. (*Dollars.*)	Wages. (*Dollars.*)	Materials. (*Dollars.*)	Products. (*Dollars.*)
....	20	1	14	60	60	......	....	31, 115	8, 706	79, 746	121, 469
....	17	7	4	32	32	......	....	17, 140	2, 625	43, 243	53, 280
....	74	8	6	1, 016	846	44	126	434, 560	445, 150	1, 183, 708	2, 001, 965
....	21	....	18	41	41	......	....	8, 625	1, 645	17, 800	21, 842
....	3	1	2	12	12	......	....	17, 500	1, 300	20, 900	24, 700
....	24	8	....	173	173	......	....	116, 500	92, 800	183, 058	655, 070
....	97	4	38	171	168	3	....	55, 965	18, 666	191, 791	317, 435
....	23	6	8	167	97	35	35	162, 450	34, 020	197, 675	281, 925
....	53	3	36	130	127	......	3	69, 390	15, 037	108, 221	161, 740
…m	21	....	13	39	37	......	2	19, 800	3, 020	28, 408	42, 791
....	73	....	51	133	125	3	5	50, 095	10, 155	321, 662	418, 922
....	14	5	8	192	72	82	38	82, 150	30, 215	155, 279	210, 167
....	17	....	14	34	33	......	1	7, 650	1, 687	56, 031	73, 784
....	26	2	36	70	70	......	....	65, 200	14, 052	133, 490	162, 770
....	35	....	24	81	64	7	10	33, 130	3, 743	73, 177	90, 916
....	22	1	17	46	45	......	1	42, 800	4, 608	68, 397	98, 730
....	7	....	3	15	15	......	....	11, 400	3, 060	19, 510	28, 500
....	54	5	14	218	161	36	21	210, 310	40, 748	186, 680	314, 915
....	....	....	....	....	....	......	....	....	....	....	....
....	26	....	18	53	52	1	....	41, 860	4, 400	80, 855	111, 150
....	37	3	10	80	80	......	....	39, 630	10, 280	122, 180	171, 190
....	17	1	12	45	43	......	2	42, 940	6, 800	32, 528	47, 853
…(a)	....	....	....	....	....	......	....	....	....	....	....
....	32	2	8	86	84	1	1	73, 257	15, 920	147, 712	200, 633
....	16	4	4	59	59	......	....	24, 200	13, 500	124, 205	167, 200
....	3	1	4	17	17	......	....	18, 000	4, 000	28, 872	45, 630
....	16	3	6	28	28	......	....	19, 800	2, 110	42, 062	50, 295
....	51	8	18	174	174	......	....	100, 304	22, 440	132, 304	196, 784
....	22	7	10	66	66	......	....	37, 100	6, 355	40, 940	63, 760
....	10	....	3	27	27	......	....	42, 600	3, 820	34, 799	49, 706
....	8	....	5	20	20	......	....	14, 250	2, 450	23, 100	31, 167
....	9	....	6	24	24	......	....	18, 500	5, 030	88, 260	104, 216
....	12	....	7	27	27	......	....	18, 400	4, 012	34, 790	41, 200
....	36	10	1	325	322	3	....	140, 525	75, 800	307, 075	482, 100
…ner	32	2	15	69	67	2	....	46, 850	9, 025	90, 917	129, 350
....	7	....	6	15	15	......	....	10, 500	1, 850	11, 400	29, 410
....	6	....	3	10	10	......	....	11, 000	100	28, 554	37, 656
....	9	4	....	37	37	......	....	10, 400	5, 475	29, 770	44, 406
....	61	1	18	124	120	......	4	94, 980	19, 765	97, 368	145, 852
…ry (a)	....	....	....	....	....	......	....	....	....	....	....
....	42	2	10	103	103	......	....	59, 025	23, 615	123, 330	191, 975
....	27	....	12	46	45	......	1	28, 855	3, 650	59, 749	74, 925
....	108	12	28	1, 341	784	324	233	1, 889, 770	350, 604	929, 185	1, 856, 660
....	85	1	49	294	199	61	34	185, 215	42, 566	255, 842	386, 725
…o	23	1	13	58	57	1	....	51, 900	11, 975	131, 380	169, 584
....	31	1	21	74	69	2	3	29, 250	8, 424	66, 340	94, 603
....	15	....	13	50	34	3	13	35, 100	6, 280	34, 388	54, 203
....	13	7	4	217	217	......	....	143, 450	75, 970	45, 427	314, 420
....	53	5	20	192	183	1	8	95, 925	46, 465	132, 340	227, 606
....	19	1	12	43	43	......	....	44, 600	6, 841	106, 452	127, 491
....	37	16	9	221	190	11	20	99, 100	50, 856	160, 990	324, 216
....	21	1	11	55	55	......	....	38, 950	13, 218	100, 992	148, 684
....	10	1	8	29	29	......	....	24, 675	5, 720	93, 770	116, 872
....	....	....	....	....	....	......	....	....	....	....	....
....	17	2	2	60	58	......	2	27, 850	10, 075	28, 950	52, 550
....	97	12	47	1, 280	1, 178	78	24	1, 345, 155	517, 230	1, 695, 765	2, 614, 405
....	11	....	7	20	20	......	....	11, 600	2, 670	14, 141	20, 087
....	13	5	8	41	41	......	....	18, 800	4, 220	63, 800	87, 925
....	58	2	7	189	175	4	10	99, 250	54, 343	147, 578	265, 964
....	78	4	35	198	163	26	9	76, 745	34, 970	163, 706	252, 260
....	50	5	20	199	193	5	1	139, 000	56, 320	290, 413	414, 657
....	21	1	16	46	45	......	1	26, 950	5, 125	64, 163	85, 285
....	14	1	4	40	40	......	....	15, 100	4, 550	30, 913	44, 022
....	....	....	....	....	....	......	....	....	....	....	....
....	40	....	27	127	160	11	16	76, 740	20, 075	491, 355	632, 585
....	3	3	....	29	26	3	....	9, 000	6, 900	9, 150	23, 000
....	26	9	6	223	207	......	16	118, 000	96, 225	303, 696	433, 753
....	15	6	....	39	39	......	....	37, 655	7, 512	37, 295	54, 877
....	10	....	10	19	19	......	....	6, 750	....	13, 010	16, 377
....	157	5	36	338	290	28	20	238, 745	62, 835	287, 486	556, 452
....	10	4	3	51	51	......	....	28, 750	6, 250	63, 255	98, 880
....	11	....	9	16	16	......	....	14, 200	1, 325	25, 187	99, 610

(a) Returned as having no manufactures.

TABLE C.—*Manufactures, by Totals of Counties, &c.*—1870—Continued.

THE STATE OF GEORGIA—Continued.

Counties.	Establishm'ts.	Steam-engines.	Water-wheels.	All hands.	Males above 16.	Females above 15.	Youth.	Capital. (*Dollars.*)	Wages. (*Dollars.*)	Materials. (*Dollars.*)
Upson	32	....	16	221	122	50	49	481, 800	39, 088	195, 863
Walker	42	1	16	85	78	......	7	32, 537	4, 323	90, 007
Walton	42	2	14	159	89	50	20	141, 945	19, 425	210, 988
Ware (*a*)	....	....	....	....	....	......	....	....	....	....
Warren	14	3	13	168	71	50	47	160, 300	34, 390	215, 258
Washington	107	6	23	180	180	......	....	65, 470	23, 350	112, 867
Wayne	3	1	2	21	21	......	....	7, 800	525	5, 700
Webster	7	....	7	13	11	2	....	14, 350	1, 200	31, 608
White	23	....	14	28	27	......	1	10, 700	1, 980	16, 163
Whitfield	88	7	30	290	260	3	27	119, 860	40, 893	332, 302
Wilcox	8	....	3	9	9	......	....	4, 296	634	4, 794
Wilkes	48	3	24	134	127	......	7	58, 905	20, 119	137, 748
Wilkinson	42	2	9	85	85	......	....	38, 910	15, 080	83, 472
Worth	8	....	8	19	19	......	....	8, 750	2, 175	20, 830

THE TERRITORY OF IDAHO.

Counties.	Establishm'ts.	Steam-engines.	Water-wheels.	All hands.	Males above 16.	Females above 15.	Youth.	Capital. (*Dollars.*)	Wages. (*Dollars.*)	Materials. (*Dollars.*)
Ada	30	1	7	64	64	......	....	116, 675	28, 500	208, 704
Alturas	2	....	1	6	6	......	....	150, 500	3, 400	48, 020
Boise	38	3	3	85	85	......	....	130, 200	26, 425	64, 959
Idaho	5	....	2	8	8	......	....	6, 700	1, 973	882
Lemhi	2	....	1	3	3	......	....	725	624	940
Nez Percés	6	1	....	21	21	......	....	24, 550	4, 100	10, 685
Oneida	2	....	....	11	11	......	....	12, 500	2, 800	3, 080
Owyhee	13	6	2	63	62	......	1	302, 600	44, 400	353, 015
Shoshone	3	....	....	4	4	......	....	850	150	1, 500

THE STATE OF ILLINOIS.

Counties.	Establishm'ts.	Steam-engines.	Water-wheels.	All hands.	Males above 16.	Females above 15.	Youth.	Capital. (*Dollars.*)	Wages. (*Dollars.*)	Materials. (*Dollars.*)
Adams	381	70	1	2, 962	2, 379	179	404	2, 858, 840	1, 071, 147	3, 416, 092
Alexander	48	16	....	316	312	4	....	321, 770	118, 446	409, 056
Bond	10	9	....	46	46	......	....	81, 700	15, 950	67, 600
Boone	162	6	15	435	377	56	2	196, 500	112, 059	346, 777
Brown	58	6	2	174	171	3	....	89, 275	49, 556	58, 349
Bureau	97	15	2	306	304	......	2	344, 425	92, 928	340, 572
Calhoun	50	6	....	80	76	......	4	34, 000	3, 990	50, 216
Carroll	81	3	11	237	226	4	7	170, 000	62, 351	275, 683
Cass	22	10	....	107	92	12	3	130, 200	40, 655	194, 385
Champaign	132	26	....	691	670	15	6	429, 370	181, 750	739, 116
Christian	40	11	....	183	172	4	7	202, 575	52, 710	757, 272
Clark	104	20	1	283	269	14	....	160, 568	52, 671	260, 440
Clay	80	20	....	193	186	7	....	180, 948	26, 052	190, 579
Clinton	58	11	2	197	197	......	....	505, 650	54, 273	600, 066
Coles	84	29	1	463	435	22	6	334, 000	131, 680	669, 108
Cook	1 440	482	2	31, 105	24, 705	4, 652	1, 748	39, 372, 276	13, 045, 286	60, 362, 188
Crawford	46	19	2	145	138	6	1	110, 000	23, 877	177, 338
Cumberland	57	22	....	166	158	7	1	79, 920	17, 301	125, 365
De Kalb	73	12	1	347	341	5	1	439, 900	122, 660	336, 492
De Witt	127	11	5	297	281	15	1	153, 768	52, 034	242, 203
Douglas	44	5	....	134	125	6	3	49, 675	26, 799	75, 206
Du Page	154	8	10	420	416	2	2	438, 890	100, 268	377, 725
Edgar	182	15	....	420	392	27	1	195, 210	108, 404	444, 370
Edwards	23	3	....	52	52	......	....	26, 770	12, 798	31, 667
Effingham	98	25	1	261	261	......	....	174, 900	56, 850	345, 853
Fayette	162	36	2	400	390	8	2	232, 500	84, 950	420, 845
Ford	35	1	....	77	71	6	....	52, 920	18, 142	50, 758
Franklin	16	8	....	54	54	......	....	44, 800	15, 290	64, 282
Fulton	143	46	12	562	529	26	7	713, 699	173, 809	776, 678
Gallatin	29	11	....	127	123	1	3	137, 500	60, 350	179, 128
Greene	81	16	1	359	345	11	3	279, 750	102, 025	305, 228
Grundy	41	9	....	168	167	......	1	132, 300	57, 350	182, 424
Hamilton	130	11	....	227	212	12	3	100, 550	14, 881	187, 770
Hancock	185	35	....	664	599	31	34	579, 120	155, 495	646, 118
Hardin	7	1	....	20	20	......	....	5, 620	2, 500	17, 475
Henderson	82	12	9	325	320	3	2	219, 825	94, 642	381, 271
Henry	134	12	1	483	452	15	16	330, 785	97, 306	454, 056
Iroquois	56	18	....	226	222	2	2	180, 700	75, 245	[illegible]

(*a*) Returned as having no manufactures.

TABLE C.—*Manufactures, by Totals of Counties, &c.*—1870—Continued.

THE STATE OF ILLINOIS—Continued.

nties.	Establishm'ts.	Steam-engines.	Water-wheels.	All hands.	Males above 16.	Females above 15.	Youth.	Capital. (*Dollars.*)	Wages. (*Dollars.*)	Materials. (*Dollars.*)	Products. (*Dollars.*)
....	58	29	....	261	253	1	7	250, 362	87, 966	274, 199	603, 015
....	41	14	2	93	91	......	2	63, 125	11, 493	94, 340	154, 567
....	49	15	....	144	138	4	2	94, 150	30, 381	220, 064	334, 992
....	42	11	....	185	184	......	1	292, 550	58, 561	497, 637	686, 094
ss	133	18	13	786	736	29	21	830, 375	243, 254	685, 870	1, 252, 515
....	41	6	....	71	70	1	....	34, 015	6, 600	77, 030	126, 635
....	131	14	85	2, 735	2, 438	271	26	4, 040, 012	1, 390, 446	2, 357, 832	4, 693, 397
o	114	5	17	301	277	24	....	1, 077, 710	72, 326	477, 265	735, 639
....	52	2	7	192	181	11	....	231, 250	60, 675	235, 324	411, 080
....	369	56	4	1, 989	1, 843	107	39	1, 505, 535	774, 635	1, 345, 453	2, 835, 937
....	84	13	1	304	272	18	14	257, 700	78, 565	469, 643	692, 928
....	206	28	27	1, 349	1, 305	15	29	1, 691, 030	585, 373	1, 335, 356	2, 690, 152
3	18	7	1	57	55	2	....	44, 800	8, 900	151, 965	205, 073
....	45	4	19	486	383	56	47	733, 500	237, 620	1, 340, 864	2, 066, 295
n	57	23	2	287	225	32	30	249, 100	52, 990	303, 554	465, 963
....	142	21	4	469	430	19	....	407, 500	138, 040	543, 748	997, 026
....	138	21	1	653	625	13	15	770, 455	247, 874	873, 861	1, 559, 629
1	123	29	....	528	497	15	16	529, 325	163, 883	1, 255, 762	1, 681, 591
....	373	47	1	1, 644	1, 528	36	80	1, 751, 414	586, 789	2, 644, 499	4, 794, 490
....	198	33	....	633	619	13	1	602, 287	255, 978	470, 848	935, 046
....	147	19	....	592	544	33	15	1, 049, 685	156, 083	951, 332	1, 303, 502
....	110	6	2	301	275	26	....	187, 500	63, 790	306, 152	545, 678
....	20	12	....	242	236	......	6	205, 500	77, 420	236, 019	437, 562
gh	60	17	2	206	196	......	10	137, 100	52, 215	278, 257	473, 974
....	138	22	13	405	392	13	....	382, 535	102, 473	451, 354	698, 199
....	179	32	....	1, 510	1, 417	39	54	2, 305, 030	769, 244	1, 915, 365	3, 367, 647
....	102	17	1	373	355	7	11	214, 100	90, 670	324, 486	578, 735
....	73	7	3	209	207	......	2	131, 425	55, 772	139, 084	250, 527
....	62	10	....	173	172	1	....	278, 450	55, 275	589, 442	737, 720
ery	179	35	1	832	799	33	....	896, 395	374, 273	964, 567	1, 641, 842
....	127	20	....	636	567	50	19	866, 145	234, 208	667, 527	1, 287, 441
....	30	8	....	84	76	3	5	124, 510	19, 994	104, 560	161, 127
....	90	8	7	260	248	8	4	239, 905	60, 705	282, 776	442, 711
....	334	69	1	2, 668	2, 477	135	56	3, 472, 550	1, 303, 843	5, 702, 080	8, 844, 493
....	52	5	....	126	126	......	....	102, 335	37, 760	147, 205	235, 357
....	6	1	1	22	22	......	....	20, 500	4, 112	31, 647	44, 284
....	237	38	6	700	606	35	59	630, 810	142, 518	870, 333	1, 415, 577
....	42	13	....	78	77	1	....	63, 400	12, 712	100, 530	171, 408
....	23	25	....	436	421	1	14	523, 000	167, 450	212, 918	544, 447
....	36	2	....	67	67	......	....	39, 800	12, 915	75, 477	134, 146
....	121	23	...	441	426	14	1	561, 705	137, 706	1, 383, 082	1, 846, 130
....	101	13	1	237	223	13	1	151, 785	50, 770	363, 577	520, 313
nd	253	48	22	2, 488	2, 383	57	48	3, 388, 270	1, 081, 113	3, 128, 102	5, 602, 443
....	32	8	....	72	71	......	1	53, 400	13, 270	117, 320	175, 493
a	215	38	1	959	918	25	16	834, 130	393, 343	890, 230	1, 806, 986
....	80	21	8	321	298	20	3	284, 500	67, 875	346, 400	578, 037
....	72	15	....	239	239	......	....	133, 870	43, 031	166, 644	330, 121
....	83	23	3	275	247	22	6	277, 600	72, 863	503, 162	782, 473
....	57	7	1	144	139	2	3	152, 455	28, 862	143, 666	222, 990
....	440	74	....	2, 638	2, 521	8	109	2, 816, 300	1, 239, 197	5, 421, 991	7, 985, 410
on	98	18	21	461	425	17	19	425, 110	146, 887	389, 643	734, 051
....	125	29	4	811	760	31	20	835, 295	312, 526	1, 190, 862	1, 958, 718
....	137	32	2	430	417	5	8	238, 490	109, 629	530, 987	878, 876
a	156	24	10	513	479	24	10	437, 213	115, 603	396, 144	727, 137
....	95	22	....	262	256	5	1	170, 550	53, 255	248, 708	418, 185
....	93	17	2	377	372	3	2	269, 680	125, 561	397, 201	740, 089
ton	89	23	....	334	329	4	1	588, 850	111, 390	1, 419, 427	1, 835, 322
....	256	31	....	657	586	18	53	201, 615	111, 630	665, 991	1, 139, 811
....	62	18	2	200	195	1	4	191, 876	46, 289	332, 362	509, 047
es	298	11	30	1, 027	890	116	12	973, 199	282, 392	1, 010, 862	1, 846, 083
....	154	27	30	1, 665	1, 644	16	5	1, 615, 400	407, 337	1, 492, 012	2, 565, 907
on	98	13	....	198	194	3	1	103, 400	30, 983	189, 361	356, 885
go	139	7	87	1, 182	1, 040	106	36	1, 911, 475	585, 028	1, 535, 474	3, 063, 346
l	118	10	2	249	249	......	....	194, 780	54, 430	294, 711	486, 250

TABLE C.—*Manufactures, by Totals of Counties, &c.*—1870—Continued.

THE STATE OF INDIANA.

Counties.	Establishm'ts.	Steam-engines.	Water-wheels.	All hands.	Males above 16.	Females above 15.	Youth.	Capital. (*Dollars.*)	Wages. (*Dollars.*)	Materials. (*Dollars.*)	Products. (*Dollars.*)
Adams	84	17	2	232	221	4	7	123, 025	33, 728	143, 768	22
Allen	369	110	30	3, 264	2, 986	115	163	2, 761, 891	1, 355, 752	3, 803, 866	6, 45
Bartholomew	100	29	16	450	395	40	15	573, 950	122, 720	540, 874	87
Benton	19	....	....	36	33	3	....	10, 575	1, 489	12, 100	25
Blackford	37	9	1	139	124	....	15	119, 916	17, 350	112, 853	19
Boone	151	53	6	617	560	22	35	356, 215	117, 215	518, 249	88
Brown	21	15	....	96	96	....	....	35, 340	22, 055	45, 455	16
Carroll	143	25	37	522	491	20	11	349, 980	91, 153	343, 270	70
Cass	228	38	34	1, 809	1, 746	43	20	1, 113, 745	577, 824	1, 476, 415	2, 3
Clarke	151	45	8	1, 999	1, 934	35	30	1, 513, 175	815, 619	2, 191, 377	3, 63
Clay	94	40	9	736	698	7	31	781, 645	309, 084	1, 330, 011	1, 9
Clinton	210	41	8	662	655	7	....	467, 035	128, 642	592, 508	9
Crawford	43	13	3	130	130	....	....	85, 125	22, 057	90, 229	15
Daviess	140	23	5	445	413	11	21	266, 641	119, 519	353, 437	5
Dearborn	142	36	2	1, 382	1, 253	79	50	1, 317, 908	345, 547	1, 571, 634	2, 54
Decatur	114	23	13	390	364	17	9	245, 296	81, 935	308, 501	6
De Kalb	100	25	10	366	358	....	8	211, 225	57, 115	216, 992	3
Delaware	80	24	24	315	305	2	8	373, 000	74, 796	407, 984	6
Dubois	51	7	2	125	119	4	2	71, 550	16, 303	154, 900	2
Elkhart	219	38	48	873	805	64	4	780, 330	212, 364	842, 057	1, 4
Fayette	84	19	14	362	333	14	15	349, 867	101, 113	330, 077	5
Floyd	182	76	3	1, 958	1, 659	100	199	2, 504, 495	952, 999	2, 143, 571	4, 0
Fountain	124	21	23	361	356	4	1	246, 685	75, 733	329, 863	6
Franklin	257	34	39	816	779	33	4	555, 355	178, 274	682, 925	1, 3
Fulton	62	18	11	182	180	1	1	117, 900	31, 128	314, 601	4
Gibson	88	31	5	380	373	....	7	361, 905	99, 775	595, 329	9
Grant	170	42	26	392	379	4	9	231, 840	45, 983	365, 598	6
Greene	74	22	6	217	212	2	3	124, 760	23, 930	177, 831	3
Hamilton	157	18	8	530	520	1	9	354, 375	86, 323	722, 241	1, 2
Hancock	108	20	....	341	333	3	5	174, 295	77, 486	217, 340	4
Harrison	139	26	20	382	367	....	15	210, 678	45, 461	442, 595	6
Hendricks	166	39	1	568	505	43	20	274, 264	90, 941	343, 173	6
Henry	200	38	22	596	589	7	....	437, 167	107, 470	594, 653	9
Howard	88	52	5	378	375	....	3	245, 850	63, 986	396, 012	5
Huntington	166	51	18	653	629	17	7	451, 710	132, 283	453, 941	8
Jackson	118	36	11	457	420	20	17	392, 590	92, 191	384, 742	6
Jasper	13	3	2	34	34	....	....	17, 900	8, 540	26, 001	
Jay	84	23	3	215	211	4	....	135, 360	27, 486	205, 723	3
Jefferson	244	40	8	1, 108	1, 038	38	32	886, 330	349, 422	1, 290, 689	2, 1
Jennings	106	34	4	378	369	4	5	239, 085	75, 971	283, 091	4
Johnson	208	34	9	825	742	56	27	648, 118	184, 799	843, 841	1, 3
Knox	90	20	3	457	452	5	....	298, 205	119, 134	572, 836	8
Kosciusko	92	55	14	458	437	5	16	478, 025	131, 070	417, 228	7
La Grange	72	21	26	233	225	4	4	274, 850	44, 036	194, 086	4
Lake	111	3	6	252	220	18	14	142, 055	39, 361	161, 225	3
La Porte	111	30	23	883	677	24	182	653, 340	260, 655	699, 841	1, 2
Lawrence	17	5	8	55	48	....	7	75, 200	11, 750	69, 047	1
Madison	127	37	9	446	433	7	6	377, 807	119, 335	463, 017	8
Marion	740	149	25	6, 167	5, 526	365	276	8, 303, 185	2, 972, 941	9, 776, 656	16, 6
Marshall	101	66	9	475	468	5	2	437, 980	111, 186	537, 375	9
Martin	76	12	10	280	245	4	31	173, 785	39, 706	235, 325	3
Miami	156	48	27	611	575	30	6	633, 770	170, 483	559, 954	9
Monroe	111	31	9	404	363	30	11	294, 915	83, 426	448, 664	7
Montgomery	191	42	44	852	774	52	26	702, 320	191, 788	663, 969	1, 1
Morgan	164	43	9	514	492	10	12	314, 770	92, 422	415, 200	7
Newton	19	4	1	63	57	6	....	50, 900	11, 670	51, 125	
Noble	229	37	7	721	664	33	24	420, 768	143, 701	465, 234	9
Ohio	41	14	3	167	137	22	8	79, 925	33, 750	143, 565	2
Orange	88	26	10	336	303	18	15	183, 490	42, 739	301, 119	4
Owen	163	30	14	374	367	6	1	175, 375	42, 243	280, 333	4
Parke	139	36	17	490	474	8	8	379, 800	79, 310	508, 990	7
Perry	79	35	2	832	501	122	209	580, 950	231, 727	494, 595	8
Pike	46	14	....	110	110	....	....	75, 897	21, 418	99, 377	1
Porter	98	24	11	386	352	22	12	357, 875	88, 585	390, 916	5
Posey	106	22	3	318	303	10	5	309, 665	89, 425	875, 525	1, 1
Pulaski	33	7	8	86	84	....	2	56, 365	11, 531	95, 925	1
Putnam	123	33	8	525	509	12	4	444, 007	102, 272	768, 149	1, 1
Randolph	135	47	12	385	377	7	1	276, 640	60, 929	398, 797	6
Ripley	171	55	1	582	549	7	26	377, 312	123, 327	499, 830	8
Rush	120	23	3	414	378	21	12	330, 040	79, 918	290, 950	5
Scott	32	15	....	110	110	....	....	52, 575	21, 536	86, 226	1
Shelby	138	28	16	477	451	7	19	365, 010	140, 465	434, 378	8
Spencer	123	27	4	329	291	14	24	229, 790	[illegible]	355, 471	6
Starke	4	....	1	4	4	....	....	8, 000	320	12, 850	

TABLE C.—*Manufactures, by Totals of Counties, &c.*—1870—Continued.

THE STATE OF INDIANA—Continued.

ounties.	Establishm'ts.	Steam-engines.	Water-wheels.	All hands.	Males above 16.	Females above 15.	Youth.	Capital. (Dollars.)	Wages. (Dollars.)	Materials. (Dollars.)	Products. (Dollars.)
n	67	17	14	138	134	4	....	146, 600	28, 887	221, 551	352, 768
eph	270	36	66	2, 483	2, 348	76	59	2, 705, 900	958, 873	2, 253, 113	4, 444, 284
n	79	34	....	318	314	3	1	174, 480	59, 784	525, 865	803, 160
rland	129	19	3	318	300	7	11	120, 510	46, 901	143, 982	386, 748
anoe	340	44	34	2, 139	2, 000	88	51	1, 782, 055	736, 652	2, 512, 211	4, 069, 217
	42	18	1	169	160	4	5	123, 150	38, 411	212, 561	334, 524
	41	12	10	124	115	4	5	118, 500	36, 973	157, 335	270, 697
burgh	281	75	1	2, 817	2, 446	210	161	3, 308, 600	1, 186, 118	2, 703, 476	5, 341, 517
lion	39	13	....	172	156	11	5	173, 985	50, 265	265, 923	371, 450
	213	57	4	1, 868	1, 781	35	52	1, 279, 555	879, 364	2, 371, 559	4, 102, 154
h	180	41	27	596	571	21	4	551, 335	119, 384	543, 207	861, 554
n	40	4	7	105	105	......	....	72, 525	12, 984	140, 881	192, 594
k	56	13	....	126	124	2	....	104, 990	26, 055	215, 382	296, 873
ngton	204	44	17	603	551	28	24	359, 864	63, 828	611, 878	921, 121
	205	40	42	1, 473	1, 405	59	9	2, 029, 185	589, 936	1, 037, 050	2, 967, 796
	155	43	6	396	383	10	3	282, 840	50, 136	373, 775	613, 195
	23	2	13	92	82	3	7	84, 090	18, 064	136, 461	176, 942
y	103	42	6	398	392	6	....	201, 484	65, 585	226, 491	442, 194

THE STATE OF IOWA.

Counties.	Establishm'ts.	Steam-engines.	Water-wheels.	All hands.	Males above 16.	Females above 15.	Youth.	Capital. (Dollars.)	Wages. (Dollars.)	Materials. (Dollars.)	Products. (Dollars.)
	3	2	1	15	15	......	....	4, 200	3, 976	2, 633	8, 204
	23	4	3	76	71	3	2	42, 900	14, 438	89, 921	155, 519
kee	94	11	25	317	305	6	6	373, 799	81, 385	454, 292	679, 549
oso	160	35	1	435	419	8	8	193, 174	70, 754	316, 138	523, 705
on	13	3	2	20	20	......	....	7, 000	1, 457	22, 428	36, 175
	11	7	....	39	38	......	1	58, 900	11, 500	110, 680	176, 315
Hawk	84	7	24	442	396	37	9	537, 410	155, 554	691, 138	1, 034, 771
	72	27	3	321	310	1	10	254, 682	85, 646	207, 805	388, 417
	135	15	8	381	368	8	5	248, 555	63, 333	232, 349	419, 338
nan	111	3	19	460	460	......	....	169, 315	123, 910	287, 737	607, 001
Vista	5	....	1	9	9	......	....	4, 530	1, 425	6, 900	14, 700
	49	2	20	118	114	4	....	115, 642	21, 772	167, 869	253, 566
n	1	....	1	3	3	......	....	4, 500	....	5, 400	8, 442
	3	1	3	14	14	......	....	30, 500	3, 200	87, 660	116, 846
	30	....	4	74	73	1	....	34, 600	24, 860	51, 855	97, 756
	54	2	3	123	118	5	....	96, 825	19, 244	104, 681	177, 002
ordo	37	....	6	79	73	4	2	51, 885	13, 108	80, 668	136, 625
ce	3	....	2	8	8	......	....	8, 900	1, 410	5, 262	9, 025
saw (a)	....	....	....	....	....	......	....	....	....	....	....
	32	7	....	108	95	13	....	68, 850	15, 818	152, 335	211, 070
	4	....	2	8	8	......	....	6, 250	1, 040	52, 321	63, 583
a	244	25	46	766	714	26	26	668, 565	194, 115	833, 869	1, 377, 967
	108	32	21	1, 245	1, 120	15	100	2, 086, 610	492, 250	1, 422, 276	2, 522, 205
rd	26	1	4	66	65	......	1	33, 510	8, 125	35, 816	58, 883
	33	5	4	77	77	......	....	99, 225	16, 845	87, 131	145, 695
	68	20	....	192	178	7	7	97, 960	31, 231	208, 350	322, 529
r	39	20	6	129	111	17	1	119, 050	19, 845	255, 439	404, 323
re	84	6	19	315	287	21	7	280, 918	64, 003	255, 918	434, 306
oines	138	16	1	1, 102	1, 025	23	54	861, 621	469, 870	1, 178, 997	2, 010, 299
son (a)	....	....	....	....	....	......	....	....	....	....	....
ue	297	45	35	1, 780	1, 570	106	104	1, 636, 775	613, 016	1, 802, 856	3, 308, 399
(a)	....	....	....	....	....	......	....	....	....	....	....
	35	7	41	158	158	......	....	205, 480	33, 891	575, 693	796, 209
	39	5	13	174	171	......	3	90, 570	48, 350	187, 752	283, 668
in	11	1	1	28	26	......	2	17, 800	6, 245	18, 618	34, 725
nt	202	16	1	468	454	8	6	225, 440	84, 165	696, 527	1, 090, 545
	23	3	3	79	79	......	....	42, 900	22, 300	104, 400	172, 830
	29	....	1	36	36	......	....	8, 615	300	5, 270	16, 600
	24	1	11	75	61	14	....	101, 700	17, 500	100, 360	154, 938
on	57	5	7	175	169	6	7	67, 870	20, 179	77, 172	143, 963
k (a)	....	....	....	....	....	......	....	....	....	....	....
	12	1	20	42	36	3	3	103, 850	11, 065	212, 515	387, 380
on	24	4	7	93	85	5	3	103, 325	18, 050	133, 305	212, 185
	163	24	16	489	484	5	....	310, 070	119, 767	933, 990	1, 549, 818
d	32	....	7	69	60	9	....	54, 350	8, 310	52, 279	86, 292
ldt	30	....	6	79	76	3	....	64, 550	17, 155	182, 957	273, 565
	1	....	....	10	10	......	....	1, 500	1, 500	1, 000	3, 000
	46	5	6	278	252	22	4	139, 600	41, 619	218, 111	358, [illegible]

(a) Returned as having no manufactures.

TABLE C.—*Manufactures, by Totals of Counties, &c.*—1870—Continued.

THE STATE OF IOWA—Continued.

Counties.	Establishm'ts.	Steam-engines.	Water-wheels.	All hands.	Males above 16.	Females above 15.	Youth.	Capital. (*Dollars.*)	Wages. (*Dollars.*)	Materials. (*Dollars.*)	Products. (*Dollars.*)
Jackson	316	15	55	705	674	17	14	737, 280	131, 460	916, 989	[illegible]
Jasper	95	17	3	289	284	1	4	178, 570	57, 098	296, 4[illegible]	[illegible]
Jefferson	47	14	3	190	184	1	5	168, 050	34, 095	177, 819	[illegible]
Johnson	135	11	16	554	502	42	10	494, 725	146, 571	503, 199	[illegible]
Jones	138	4	15	291	276	15		138, 110	43, 479	213, 032	[illegible]
Keokuk	105	22	15	248	229	14	5	176, 005	39, 120	336, 278	[illegible]
Kossuth	39		2	98	95	3		39, 325	13, 414	86, 497	[illegible]
Lee	368	50	1	1, 671	1, 563	76	32	1, 272, 227	530, 291	1, 436, 742	[illegible]
Linn	249	25	24	861	838	22	1	723, 850	235, 387	952, 505	[illegible]
Louisa	95	9	1	238	220	10	8	104, 067	23, 921	172, 033	[illegible]
Lucas	11	2		58	58			31, 400	19, 003	23, 759	[illegible]
Lyon (*a*)											
Madison	47	15	11	149	138	8	3	159, 318	27, 990	167, 239	[illegible]
Mahaska	68	13	17	251	238	12	1	259, 300	74, 975	254, 214	[illegible]
Marion	62	25	1	228	207	7	14	207, 395	43, 050	262, 374	[illegible]
Marshall	90	7	12	251	244	6	1	258, 475	70, 300	177, 222	[illegible]
Mills	69	9	11	216	215		1	128, 110	46, 220	145, 910	[illegible]
Mitchell	60	12	4	165	147	17	1	158, 400	42, 100	246, 970	[illegible]
Monona	10	5		56	56			15, 400	11, 400	20, 138	[illegible]
Monroe	63	18		163	159	4		103, 680	29, 121	204, 608	[illegible]
Montgomery	19	2	9	48	48			75, 050	11, 215	49, 798	[illegible]
Muscatine	216	21	1	971	914	28	29	805, 419	287, 015	956, 404	[illegible]
O'Brien (*a*)											
Osceola (*a*)											
Page	17	3	7	43	43			60, 525	14, 514	152, 234	[illegible]
Palo Alto	4		1	11	11			2, 700	1, 100	3, 150	
Plymouth	1		2	2	2			8, 000	400	3, 900	
Pocahontas (*a*)											
Polk	178	38	2	961	914	27	20	1, 107, 675	362, 465	1, 083, 887	[illegible]
Pottawattamie	20	5	3	115	113	2		159, 100	55, 080	202, 030	[illegible]
Poweshiek	34	5		111	110		1	65, 950	28, 730	99, 265	[illegible]
Ringgold	23	3	2	40	39		1	20, 750	2, 875	21, 929	[illegible]
Sac	12		2	29	29			15, 200	3, 950	20, 697	[illegible]
Scott	341	53	1	1, 951	1, 732	100	119	2, 217, 750	633, 701	2, 008, 740	[illegible]
Shelby	17	2	2	27	27			17, 010	1, 502	42, 287	[illegible]
Sioux (*a*)											
Story	31	5	4	71	71			68, 635	14, 420	116, 634	[illegible]
Tama	82	7	9	217	207	9	1	275, 691	38, 177	196, 521	[illegible]
Taylor	30	7		72	65		7	44, 735	8, 525	136, 263	[illegible]
Union	28	5		77	70	7		37, 995	13, 971	94, 418	[illegible]
Van Buren	103	11	22	379	317	45	17	287, 125	94, 288	555, 945	[illegible]
Wapello	161	30		685	643	29	13	939, 975	229, 047	1, 040, 060	[illegible]
Warren	85	25	5	312	290	18	4	151, 400	46, 181	321, 568	[illegible]
Washington	79	11	8	217	214	2	1	216, 120	51, 910	332, 657	[illegible]
Wayne	87	10		201	194	6	1	66, 990	17, 112	96, 860	[illegible]
Webster	29	7	3	126	121	4	1	154, 500	39, 000	109, 500	[illegible]
Winnebago	1	1		2	2			4, 000	500	14, 100	[illegible]
Winneshiek	141	1	39	513	474	39		520, 400	127, 553	559, 587	[illegible]
Woodbury	26	4	2	175	175			136, 700	97, 700	140, 034	[illegible]
Worth	8		4	14	14			30, 400	3, 375	30, 707	[illegible]
Wright	7	2	3	15	15			11, 450	400	17, 499	[illegible]

THE STATE OF KANSAS.

Counties.	Establishm'ts.	Steam-engines.	Water-wheels.	All hands.	Males above 16.	Females above 15.	Youth.	Capital. (*Dollars.*)	Wages. (*Dollars.*)	Materials. (*Dollars.*)	Products. (*Dollars.*)
Allen	12	6		61	61			45, 400	21, 617	43, 781	[illegible]
Anderson	14	2		49	49			39, 320	12, 841	55, 186	[illegible]
Atchison	95	7	2	400	369	10	21	264, 790	157, 231	333, 675	[illegible]
Barton (*a*)											
Bourbon	105	14		497	466	21	10	264, 160	236, 634	630, 090	[illegible]
Brown	15			28	28			8, 190	5, 620	29, 489	[illegible]
Butler	3	3		20	20			8, 000	3, 700	14, 200	[illegible]
Chase	14	3	6	44	44			36, 050	10, 100	63, 880	[illegible]
Cherokee	36	5	7	174	167	5	2	71, 965	35, 301	100, 097	[illegible]
Clay	2	2		8	8			6, 000	2, 700	17, 350	[illegible]
Cloud	11	3		29	29			14, 182	5, 725	19, 723	[illegible]
Coffey	39	6	3	160	156	3	1	68, 835	33, 291	135, 380	[illegible]
Cowley	6	2		12	12			10, 400	2, 800	14, 500	[illegible]
Crawford	21	3		84	83	1		23, 400	16, 295	51, 720	[illegible]

(*a*) Returned as having no manufactures.

TABLE C.—*Manufactures, by Totals of Counties, &c.*—1870—Continued.

THE STATE OF KANSAS—Continued.

ounties.	Establishm'ts.	Steam-engines.	Water-wheels.	All hands.	Males above 16.	Females above 15.	Youth.	Capital. (*Dollars.*)	Wages. (*Dollars.*)	Materials. (*Dollars.*)	Products. (*Dollars.*)
	26	2	1	170	169		1	44, 200	50, 020	58, 892	134, 702
ason	6	1	2	23	23			31, 635	5, 792	65, 667	99, 418
han	60	19	1	264	255	7	2	174, 171	63, 196	476, 931	704, 973
as	119	15		496	468	20	8	444, 500	199, 161	435, 884	864, 677
a)											
rth	3			12	12			2, 200	8, 532	10, 722	25, 800
a)											
lin	46	12		163	152	8	3	86, 750	40, 800	164, 205	317, 962
wood	16	5	1	56	56			28, 600	8, 961	38, 527	70, 757
d (a)											
n	17	4		32	32			18, 100	3, 260	37, 499	62, 170
on	32	7	4	111	106	1	4	56, 650	17, 560	80, 338	126, 840
(a)											
n	15	2		61	61			45, 160	17, 764	66, 893	122, 345
e	23	10		119	119			81, 150	42, 888	80, 250	175, 700
nworth	220	23	2	1, 238	1, 162	25	51	1, 187, 148	544, 589	1, 101, 743	2, 411, 073
n (a)											
	80	10	4	178	175		3	73, 310	38, 868	245, 676	403, 486
	11	3	5	73	61	2	10	92, 950	21, 677	97, 997	165, 748
n	2			5	5			700	760	758	3, 450
all	44	2	5	106	106			136, 890	25, 095	196, 964	301, 480
erson (a)											
l	27	11		93	93			31, 300	15, 720	71, 483	127, 576
ell (a)											
omery	14	11		97	97			34, 200	16, 690	56, 091	131, 925
a	12	2		59	59			16, 860	9, 020	36, 553	68, 660
ha	8	1		25	22		3	6, 860	1, 955	4, 415	11, 395
o	21	9	1	110	107	1	2	44, 425	22, 484	73, 527	150, 544
a)											
	21	4		65	65			56, 450	19, 250	72, 615	128, 510
ne (a)											
a	7	1	2	14	14			7, 900	2, 600	19, 055	31, 340
se (a)											
wattamie	31	3	6	87	87			153, 210	19, 588	109, 089	160, 900
lic	3			6	6			1, 400	2, 000	3, 426	9, 988
s)											
	63	4		202	191	7	4	83, 860	80, 235	96, 202	288, 345
ll (a)											
	10	1		32	31	1		50, 955	10, 235	33, 020	68, 185
rick	1	1		6	6			3, 000	2, 500	13, 000	18, 200
nee	62	8		354	346	6	2	184, 660	154, 655	363, 312	798, 394
(a)											
r (a)											
(a)											
unsee	9	2	2	31	31			20, 700	6, 770	19, 575	28, 320
ce (a)											
ington	9	2	5	20	20			23, 300	3, 720	28, 457	46, 674
n	11	11		62	62			37, 600	13, 915	28, 296	58, 813
son	3	1	3	13	13			28, 000	3, 885	55, 700	81, 800
dotte	32	11		895	895			163, 535	350, 521	340, 737	755, 061

THE STATE OF KENTUCKY.

ounties.	Establishm'ts.	Steam-engines.	Water-wheels.	All hands.	Males above 16.	Females above 15.	Youth.	Capital. (*Dollars.*)	Wages. (*Dollars.*)	Materials. (*Dollars.*)	Products. (*Dollars.*)
	37	6	7	85	78		7	29, 900	7, 440	142, 308	190, 640
	25	14	4	87	85	1	1	52, 950	8, 930	50, 113	61, 898
rson	48	9	4	81	80		1	41, 800	10, 572	95, 662	148, 883
d	42	9	3	99	97	1	1	58, 955	11, 450	38, 991	71, 090
n	67	9	10	154	154			70, 995	21, 183	114, 903	197, 384
	25	3		54	52		2	13, 610	7, 790	23, 569	48, 884
	54	7	1	137	132	1	4	158, 222	26, 610	257, 824	472, 663
on	73	7	5	293	283	7	3	482, 075	108, 585	321, 589	662, 519
	69	21		362	331	5	26	258, 245	117, 065	364, 407	670, 454
	77	6	3	206	198	3	5	106, 010	54, 509	198, 344	338, 994
en	46	7		92	88	1	3	32, 700	7, 250	43, 609	98, 840
hitt	12		5	18	18			12, 350	2, 550	6, 002	14, 614
enridge	73	9	7	123	121		2	54, 550	13, 083	87, 225	152, 814
s	40	18	2	264	264			422, 655	71, 963	169, 894	388, 114
y	36	12	6	82	82			41, 080	8, 085	48, 173	71, 774
ell	55	9	5	160	144	10	6	90, 415	21, 190	98, 720	167, 646
ay	21	4	5	94	78		16	45, 200	12, 170	69, 779	153, [illegible]
bell	63	26		1, 077	1, 021	2	54	1, 411, 050	560, 540	1, 687, [illegible]	[illegible]

(a) Returned as having no manufactures.

TABLE C.—*Manufactures, by Totals of Counties, &c.*—1870—Continued.

THE STATE OF KENTUCKY—Continued.

Counties.	Establishm'ts.	Steam-engines.	Water-wheels.	All hands.	Males above 16.	Females above 15.	Youth.	Capital. (*Dollars.*)	Wages. (*Dollars.*)	Materials. (*Dollars.*)	Products. (*Dollars.*)
Carroll	25	6	2	74	68	4	2	63, 805	17, 520	104, 730	12
Carter	7	3	1	181	181	.....	.....	272, 100	25, 160	88, 290	16
Casey	24	9	.....	56	49	.....	7	22, 045	6, 791	43, 526	6
Christian	52	8	4	149	145	2	2	103, 950	34, 582	223, 721	36
Clark	63	11	10	142	138	1	3	87, 160	25, 205	92, 732	22
Clay	13	1	2	56	55	1	.....	23, 200	12, 470	15, 891	3
Clinton	30	4	7	60	59	1	.....	24, 280	4, 360	47, 782	6
Crittenden	5	3	.....	13	13	.....	.....	5, 750	1, 470	11, 130	1
Cumberland	21	9	.....	44	44	.....	.....	16, 575	5, 900	33, 485	5
Daviess	125	30	2	559	509	23	27	441, 138	136, 641	415, 704	79
Edmondson	16	4	2	36	35	.....	1	14, 945	4, 000	19, 255	3
Elliott	3	1	.....	6	6	.....	.....	15, 000	2, 100	16, 900	9
Estill	50	12	11	543	518	.....	25	864, 581	83, 338	197, 204	34
Fayette	197	25	7	1, 516	1, 273	112	131	1, 121, 825	496, 843	1, 404, 996	2, 5
Fleming	54	9	6	118	115	2	1	68, 400	19, 860	63, 998	1
Floyd	4	.....	.....	4	4	.....	.....	1, 400	300	2, 074	
Franklin	90	21	10	893	831	39	23	1, 089, 170	244, 284	960, 740	1, 9
Fulton	27	8	.....	88	85	2	1	34, 925	7, 485	70, 778	1
Gallatin	11	3	1	29	29	.....	.....	21, 600	5, 300	86, 554	1
Garrard	61	6	5	121	121	.....	.....	66, 040	11, 580	120, 279	1
Grant	35	13	.....	65	65	.....	.....	43, 825	8, 045	83, 030	1
Graves	34	9	1	110	98	8	4	55, 600	19, 095	85, 757	1
Grayson	69	4	14	120	117	3	.....	63, 290	10, 800	97, 232	1
Green	33	2	7	66	66	.....	.....	45, 650	8, 080	67, 653	1
Greenup	28	16	3	533	533	.....	.....	1, 027, 300	150, 062	504, 190	7
Hancock	33	12	.....	101	101	.....	.....	55, 402	21, 500	136, 829	2
Hardin	74	8	10	206	201	.....	5	90, 205	35, 575	139, 650	2
Harlan	1	.....	1	2	2	.....	.....	2, 500	200	200	
Harrison	108	28	8	438	434	2	2	793, 225	85, 394	419, 144	8
Hart	56	4	6	118	117	.....	1	59, 410	10, 635	105, 468	1
Henderson	41	12	.....	210	196	2	12	228, 250	68, 500	204, 945	3
Henry	54	8	.....	109	104	2	3	72, 715	15, 124	84, 852	1
Hickman	18	9	1	62	62	.....	.....	37, 075	10, 425	70, 335	1
Hopkins	12	2	.....	36	33	.....	3	17, 800	4, 760	61, 739	
Jackson	14	.....	10	14	14	.....	.....	4, 250	.....	14, 350	
Jefferson	801	187	10	11, 589	10, 039	692	858	11, 129, 291	4, 464, 040	10, 369, 556	20, 3
Jessamine	22	4	4	101	98	2	1	77, 060	21, 680	84, 636	1
Johnson	10	2	5	13	12	.....	1	10, 100	1, 675	17, 990	
Josh Bell	4	.....	4	6	6	.....	.....	1, 874	310	4, 424	
Kenton	160	47	2	1, 727	1, 450	25	252	2, 145, 966	769, 651	1, 993, 755	3, 5
Knox	8	.....	4	24	24	.....	.....	13, 000	2, 472	18, 517	
La Rue	23	9	5	101	101	.....	.....	85, 750	20, 200	72, 339	1
Laurel	7	4	1	20	20	.....	.....	21, 000	1, 750	38, 100	
Lawrence	11	1	.....	19	19	.....	.....	8, 774	1, 450	10, 305	
Lee	9	5	3	19	19	.....	.....	10, 550	1, 917	11, 775	
Letcher (*a*)	.....	.....	.....	.....	.....	.....	.....	.....	.....	.....	.....
Lewis	25	7	3	93	91	.....	2	71, 150	13, 925	182, 675	2
Lincoln	64	15	6	209	202	4	3	90, 350	21, 929	152, 907	2
Livingston	18	9	.....	83	74	.....	9	90, 775	15, 515	52, 496	
Logan	94	16	12	261	240	11	10	235, 570	44, 145	385, 188	5
Lyon	11	11	1	217	217	.....	.....	413, 000	151, 000	352, 188	5
Madison	103	15	8	302	296	6	.....	286, 375	59, 930	428, 784	7
Magoffin	6	4	.....	10	10	.....	.....	7, 000	2, 265	23, 140	
Marion	64	14	2	201	189	10	2	288, 708	46, 995	338, 777	5
Marshall	44	10	3	95	90	2	3	45, 722	9, 090	276, 105	3
Mason	64	8	1	534	418	40	76	526, 527	174, 980	526, 238	9
McCracken	114	15	.....	592	519	23	50	558, 490	190, 080	728, 639	1, 2
McLean	34	6	2	90	87	1	2	56, 135	13, 345	88, 987	1
Meade	49	7	11	180	143	26	11	253, 760	52, 497	131, 251	2
Menifee	9	5	2	31	30	.....	1	13, 750	2, 345	4, 221	
Mercer	39	7	7	204	149	24	31	71, 000	22, 843	138, 373	2
Metcalfe	33	13	6	70	64	.....	6	29, 230	4, 511	43, 235	
Monroe	42	11	11	95	86	.....	9	37, 745	5, 293	76, 269	1
Montgomery	9	4	.....	68	68	.....	.....	104, 500	26, 950	85, 979	1
Morgan	9	3	1	91	91	.....	.....	76, 000	26, 300	69, 435	1
Muhlenburg	35	10	4	95	94	.....	1	42, 750	14, 476	78, 772	1
Nelson	101	23	3	267	266	1	.....	138, 675	41, 758	224, 393	4
Nicholas	25	10	.....	91	88	.....	3	90, 800	15, 000	111, 629	1
Ohio	45	7	2	101	97	.....	4	47, 150	10, 350	69, 188	1
Oldham	24	8	.....	64	64	.....	.....	49, 900	13, 350	53, 021	1
Owen	109	14	9	189	179	3	7	86, 470	20, 436	111, 946	2
Owsley	6	2	1	12	12	.....	.....	7, 500	1, 800	9, 652	
Pendleton	75	19	8	206	197	.....	9	173, 660	49, 375	390, 748	7

(*a*) Returned as having no manufactures.

TABLE C.—*Manufactures, by Totals of Counties, &c.*—1870—Continued.

THE STATE OF KENTUCKY—Continued.

Counties.	Establishm'ts.	Steam-engines.	Water-wheels.	All hands.	Males above 16.	Females above 15.	Youth.	Capital. (*Dollars.*)	Wages. (*Dollars.*)	Materials. (*Dollars.*)	Products. (*Dollars.*)
Perry (*a*)											
Pike	6	2		8	8			9, 000	1, 350	8, 620	11, 417
Powell	3	3		26	17	3	6	9, 500	2, 700	6, 000	20, 000
Pulaski	72	10	40	160	160			64, 559	14, 397	153, 446	216, 147
Robertson	21	6	1	45	45			14, 935	4, 675	23, 043	38, 151
Rock Castle	12	11		99	98		1	50, 000	15, 704	44, 150	71, 825
Rowan	5	3		22	22			39, 900	6, 900	8, 312	11, 737
Russell	9	3	1	28	26	2		18, 050	4, 275	18, 795	32, 295
Scott	11	1		21	21			26, 650	1, 300	9, 824	18, 475
Shelby	125	19	7	315	298	16	1	190, 825	55, 925	255, 181	458, 400
Simpson	39	8	3	135	122	9	4	117, 700	32, 345	169, 086	263, 980
Spencer	7	2	1	23	23			17, 800	4, 000	33, 340	79, 980
Taylor	28	6	3	62	61		1	27, 095	6, 040	42, 850	80, 701
Todd	37	6	5	74	74			53, 084	11, 090	104, 951	160, 351
Trigg	37	10	2	246	231		15	223, 750	61, 506	118, 707	240, 635
Trimble	5	3	2	11	11			8, 100	1, 150	2, 776	5, 512
Union	54	11		127	117	6	4	96, 350	21, 530	84, 623	149, 934
Warren	84	7	7	290	259	11	20	236, 025	88, 063	248, 345	479, 865
Washington	43	11	4	99	99			69, 836	9, 486	90, 478	138, 056
Wayne	21	2	16	50	50			36, 000	4, 850	121, 031	149, 166
Webster	19	3		53	53			12, 230	5, 960	11, 610	28, 900
Whitley	18		13	27	27			19, 100	860	26, 463	35, 374
Wolfe	11		7	19	18	1		4, 625	800	23, 375	30, 269
Woodford	57	12	8	280	271	6	3	214, 900	76, 850	209, 960	627, 405

THE STATE OF LOUISIANA.

PARISHES.	Establishm'ts.	Steam-engines.	Water-wheels.	All hands.	Males above 16.	Females above 15.	Youth.	Capital. (*Dollars.*)	Wages. (*Dollars.*)	Materials. (*Dollars.*)	Products. (*Dollars.*)
Ascension	88	40		1, 900	1, 317	456	127	1, 748, 050	300, 188	516, 554	1, 016, 365
Assumption	95	73		1, 916	1, 442	253	221	762, 050	232, 458	506, 689	1, 187, 737
Avoyelles	21	10		183	153	26	4	94, 800	8, 925	28, 090	70, 390
Bienville	12	6	1	25	25			22, 200	4, 750	101, 050	118, 600
Bossier	5	4		30	27		3	19, 500	9, 354	21, 579	35, 930
Caddo	29	7		182	176	1	5	280, 700	120, 155	181, 939	402, 175
Calcasieu	15	11	4	119	119			92, 200	44, 197	102, 050	206, 500
Caldwell	2	2		7	7			2, 700	1, 250	3, 200	5, 600
Carroll (*a*)											
Catahoula (*a*)											
Claiborne	32	11	3	148	110	15	23	155, 663	41, 070	175, 105	268, 315
Concordia (*a*)											
De Soto	37	10		125	125			40, 950	31, 410	48, 952	128, 050
East Baton Rouge	38	17		794	602	134	58	601, 375	122, 160	204, 430	411, 376
East Feliciana	145	7		333	197		136	48, 575	6, 460	84, 538	156, 985
Grant	10	2		25	21		4	11, 650	1, 280	9, 650	13, 174
Iberia	36	9		327	264	31	32	185, 400	48, 780	38, 680	209, 270
Iberville	60	60		2, 054	1, 510	402	142	286, 885	87, 562	323, 104	713, 590
Jackson	19	6		45	45			20, 175	4, 499	12, 203	25, 198
Jefferson	11	7		278	202	55	21	291, 000	49, 050	122, 520	294, 700
Lafayette	73	3		217	174	3	40	57, 095	20, 908	48, 967	106, 300
Lafourche	84	67		2, 851	1, 833	714	304	631, 300	102, 985	440, 052	1, 014, 370
Livingston	8	3	1	30	30			11, 100	6, 892	24, 070	50, 150
Madison (*a*)											
Morehouse	14	3		33	30		3	15, 500	6, 350	8, 110	35, 300
Natchitoches	5	4		21	21			15, 500	4, 050	7, 700	21, 000
Orleans	911	117		5, 640	5, 084	352	201	5, 751, 985	2, 554, 554	4, 566, 543	9, 980, 278
Ouachita	39	2		124	121	1	2	45, 250	27, 500	32, 425	103, 450
Plaquemines	38	35		2, 245	1, 597	355	293	309, 550	97, 070	835, 298	1, 295, 235
Point Coupée	33	21		578	550	4	24	327, 765	28, 084	124, 273	243, 397
Rapides	24	19	1	586	337	193	56	287, 400	35, 110	288, 974	436, 300
Richland	10	4		35	35			5, 270	2, 602	19, 965	67, 800
Sabine	3	1		12	10		2	9, 200	2, 250	4, 116	15, 850
St. Bernard	10	8		230	158	60	12	257, 600	13, 350	68, 759	115, 130
St. Charles	23	23		527	395	132		410, 700	22, 560	280, 077	443, 814
St. Helena (*a*)											
St. James	68	62		1, 968	1, 490	336	142	1, 290, 027	61, 794	654, 192	1, 016, 747
St. John the Baptist	49	41		1, 210	1, 138	49	23	1, 336, 800	46, 235	486, 835	748, 490
St. Landry	48	21		361	360		1	111, 409	23, 575	136, 114	282, 225
St. Martin	30	17		811	502	171	138	261, 000	41, 780	201, 570	369, 340
St. Mary	155	56		1, 608	1, 479	113	16	1, 079, 228	93, 082	427, 809	801, 966
St. Tammany	69	7		239	210	29		23, 750	20, 267	52, 900	[illegible]

(*a*) Returned as having no manufactures.

TABLE C.—*Manufactures, by Totals of Counties, &c.*—1870—Continued.

THE STATE OF LOUISIANA—Continued.

Parishes.	Establishments.	Steam-engines.	Water-wheels.	All hands.	Males above 16.	Females above 15.	Youth.	Capital. (Dollars.)	Wages. (Dollars.)	Materials. (Dollars.)	Products. (Dollars.)
Tangipahoa	22	11	3	257	239	......	18	161,700	117,494	121,310	[illegible]
Tensas	4	....	....	6	6	......	....	550	300	1,900	4,[illegible]
Terrebonne	91	66	....	1,757	1,287	307	163	527,775	63,565	1,001,519	1,[illegible]
Union	25	9	....	65	61	2	2	22,150	8,230	27,375	[illegible]
Vermillion	13	....	....	62	52	10	....	43,700	4,900	21,421	[illegible]
Washington	10	....	10	16	16	......	....	3,500	1,126	3,550	[illegible]
West Feliciana	43	3	....	82	71	6	5	24,956	5,755	38,175	[illegible]
Winn	6	2	....	9	9	......	....	7,450	930	6,272	[illegible]

THE STATE OF MAINE.

COUNTIES.	Establishments.	Steam-engines.	Water-wheels.	All hands.	Males above 16.	Females above 15.	Youth.	Capital. (Dollars.)	Wages. (Dollars.)	Materials. (Dollars.)	Products. (Dollars.)
Androscoggin	314	19	150	8,502	3,908	4,045	549	8,066,929	2,549,723	9,247,520	14,[illegible]
Aroostook	178	....	86	407	382	19	6	947,245	57,180	323,335	[illegible]
Cumberland	676	84	145	6,870	4,910	1,495	465	6,121,547	2,634,[illegible]	10,905,522	16,537,[illegible]
Franklin	196	5	112	643	595	40	8	399,337	121,316	361,056	712,[illegible]
Hancock	278	11	138	1,751	1,616	126	9	1,111,676	488,739	998,860	2,[illegible]
Kennebec	470	24	231	3,932	2,947	923	62	3,947,135	1,290,924	3,867,031	7,[illegible]
Knox	244	3	32	2,340	2,149	137	54	1,920,965	672,379	2,216,084	3,[illegible]
Lincoln	309	32	96	1,332	1,246	62	24	587,280	164,781	510,593	1,012,[illegible]
Oxford	325	10	209	1,493	1,125	342	26	850,247	252,721	1,512,963	2,[illegible]
Penobscot	850	81	418	5,975	5,213	722	40	4,658,390	1,802,[illegible]	6,738,435	10,538,[illegible]
Piscataquis	129	4	112	539	419	118	2	816,325	139,[illegible]	488,426	[illegible]
Sagadahoc	107	27	51	914	844	61	9	718,300	305,519	910,359	1,561,[illegible]
Somerset	348	5	250	1,722	1,302	397	23	1,017,960	355,923	1,402,586	2,458,744
Waldo	374	12	190	1,603	1,241	351	11	705,110	329,853	1,035,541	1,789,[illegible]
Washington	327	8	250	2,831	2,724	98	9	2,277,920	975,466	2,435,739	4,223,[illegible]
York	425	29	261	8,326	3,689	4,512	125	6,350,524	2,120,709	6,365,589	10,339,[illegible]

THE STATE OF MARYLAND.

Counties.	Establishments.	Steam-engines.	Water-wheels.	All hands.	Males above 16.	Females above 15.	Youth.	Capital. (Dollars.)	Wages. (Dollars.)	Materials. (Dollars.)	Products. (Dollars.)
Allegany	304	48	50	1,523	1,437	24	62	2,124,450	511,345	1,190,573	2,403,[illegible]
Anne Arundel	86	3	15	208	192	6	10	127,650	45,557	169,197	[illegible]
Baltimore (a)	2,759	293	123	33,182	23,944	7,107	2,131	26,049,040	10,352,078	36,144,425	59,[illegible]
Calvert	7	3	2	269	169	60	40	110,100	35,156	50,555	163,[illegible]
Caroline	65	7	26	165	162	......	3	141,525	24,050	159,860	245,[illegible]
Carroll	449	9	169	991	971	11	9	585,970	99,678	726,645	1,130,[illegible]
Cecil	140	24	71	899	792	68	39	1,242,700	301,875	1,201,259	2,113,[illegible]
Charles	12	3	7	37	37	......	....	27,050	5,162	29,096	[illegible]
Dorchester	74	2	26	256	194	62	....	130,940	28,161	129,819	[illegible]
Frederick	550	24	140	1,703	1,614	72	17	1,694,712	313,758	2,262,012	3,253,[illegible]
Harford	125	7	40	368	342	25	1	550,575	59,506	415,935	642,[illegible]
Howard	111	1	24	693	377	254	62	654,315	137,719	712,400	1,057,[illegible]
Kent	149	8	10	500	402	68	30	187,025	69,477	275,115	460,[illegible]
Montgomery	109	5	20	351	351	......	....	277,027	54,474	299,609	431,[illegible]
Prince George's	50	7	11	480	279	152	58	347,925	97,317	427,694	[illegible]
Queen Anne	64	7	9	626	362	252	12	240,195	32,001	252,001	486,[illegible]
St. Mary's	14	2	8	56	55	1	....	65,930	5,797	58,788	[illegible]
Somerset	64	16	5	253	249	......	4	93,975	35,675	97,872	215,[illegible]
Talbot	89	12	5	287	264	22	1	137,320	45,256	149,501	272,[illegible]
Washington	393	19	99	1,355	1,230	93	32	1,300,075	294,293	1,760,396	2,593,[illegible]
Wicomico	94	14	52	329	318	1	10	173,100	44,306	233,499	418,[illegible]
Worcester	104	17	19	320	320	......	....	177,810	70,176	150,850	[illegible]

THE STATE OF MASSACHUSETTS.

Counties.	Establishments.	Steam-engines.	Water-wheels.	All hands.	Males above 16.	Females above 15.	Youth.	Capital. (Dollars.)	Wages. (Dollars.)	Materials. (Dollars.)	Products. (Dollars.)
Barnstable	182	2	10	819	679	78	62	668,365	267,305	359,654	1,358,613
Berkshire	517	81	380	9,841	5,836	2,916	1,089	11,306,213	3,689,001	13,650,547	20,444,[illegible]
Bristol	581	252	148	22,048	13,372	6,357	2,319	22,930,528	8,941,489	25,604,345	41,721,[illegible]
Dukes	15	1	1	86	85	1	.....	96,000	28,830	47,152	105,[illegible]
Essex	2,821	421	184	48,158	30,680	15,701	1,777	29,777,160	21,360,153	63,203,907	96,[illegible]
Franklin	372	23	284	3,249	2,704	474	71	2,620,381	1,296,766	2,306,576	4,[illegible]
Hampden	687	97	262	17,119	9,192	6,593	1,334	16,942,490	6,878,516	17,749,440	30,[illegible]
Hampshire	433	43	249	7,575	4,038	2,545	992	7,053,085	2,747,131	7,115,452	13,445,778
Middlesex	1,876	436	351	49,822	30,697	17,732	1,373	43,528,466	20,767,[illegible]	72,[illegible]	113,[illegible]

(a) Including Baltimore City.

TABLE C.—*Manufactures, by Totals of Counties, &c.*—1870—Continued.

THE STATE OF MASSACHUSETTS—Continued.

Counties.	Establishm'ts.	Steam-engines.	Water-wheels.	All hands.	Males above 16.	Females above 15.	Youth.	Capital. (*Dollars.*)	Wages. (*Dollars.*)	Materials. (*Dollars.*)	Products. (*Dollars.*)
Nantucket	51	....	....	117	95	22	....	66,900	13,165	43,470	96,768
Norfolk	658	100	179	18,545	11,015	6,837	693	9,548,750	6,333,067	15,353,909	25,836,394
Plymouth	608	111	243	11,267	9,836	1,154	277	5,992,500	4,876,066	12,415,216	19,852,796
Suffolk	2,546	485	13	43,550	31,221	11,922	407	47,311,906	22,748,730	59,384,305	111,380,840
Worcester	1,863	335	853	47,184	29,582	13,877	3,725	33,835,118	18,103,782	44,131,647	74,579,759

THE STATE OF MICHIGAN.

Counties.	Establishm'ts.	Steam-engines.	Water-wheels.	All hands.	Males above 16.	Females above 15.	Youth.	Capital. (*Dollars.*)	Wages. (*Dollars.*)	Materials. (*Dollars.*)	Products. (*Dollars.*)
Alcona	4	3	1	87	87	....	....	356,500	28,000	61,390	119,550
Allegan	270	55	99	1,647	1,507	38	102	1,196,303	440,769	1,262,661	2,264,451
Alpena	26	17	3	650	616	14	20	876,800	274,512	494,203	913,949
Antrim	6	1	13	168	160	....	8	264,428	44,908	100,306	169,722
Barry	93	20	26	276	253	6	17	266,825	60,649	317,121	502,098
Bay	156	76	2	2,067	1,953	21	93	3,312,100	791,783	2,481,621	4,368,328
Benzie	10	3	6	40	40	....	....	41,100	11,350	27,162	46,568
Berrien	162	52	41	933	898	5	30	1,046,875	320,793	1,153,602	2,030,930
Branch	204	60	28	696	661	22	13	684,125	177,284	447,160	861,034
Calhoun	260	41	61	1,448	1,386	60	2	1,625,550	525,657	2,615,327	3,849,099
Cass	182	42	48	570	531	25	14	525,280	90,700	496,857	816,914
Charlevoix	2	2	....	23	23	....	....	45,000	10,000	19,950	43,000
Cheboygan	35	6	3	300	268	4	28	377,850	100,841	139,570	347,649
Chippewa	9	2	....	43	34	3	6	14,525	4,514	7,948	20,330
Clare (*a*)	....	....	....	....	....	....	....	....	....	....	....
Clinton	114	32	18	433	416	1	16	363,495	95,027	481,741	722,071
Delta	5	....	1	248	248	....	....	465,300	123,400	81,830	264,349
Eaton	174	50	34	610	593	6	11	493,330	134,494	458,965	849,123
Emmet	4	1	2	12	12	....	....	7,100	1,240	4,875	8,064
Genesee	413	86	62	2,069	1,952	77	40	2,078,750	554,351	2,268,991	3,860,508
Grand Traverse	20	4	16	159	155	2	2	169,700	37,548	132,954	232,499
Gratiot	42	11	16	196	195	1	....	184,700	51,702	136,612	260,504
Hillsdale	200	59	38	707	669	37	1	595,925	142,522	633,243	1,064,297
Houghton	70	34	....	805	710	1	94	1,516,890	421,651	6,003,498	7,322,897
Huron	60	37	....	868	863	1	4	1,086,650	259,350	514,117	1,011,294
Ingham	376	68	26	1,333	1,077	66	190	668,205	234,660	967,811	1,596,156
Ionia	147	34	41	821	785	9	27	793,730	222,176	698,746	1,224,274
Iosco	19	13	....	511	505	....	6	1,095,200	205,800	395,100	734,969
Isabella	9	2	5	25	25	....	....	47,850	2,000	56,866	70,370
Jackson	357	40	37	1,946	1,837	100	9	2,191,775	607,077	2,381,112	3,880,797
Kalamazoo	251	36	52	1,297	1,195	83	19	1,512,545	440,544	1,975,542	3,163,245
Kalkaska (*a*)	....	....	....	....	....	....	....	....	....	....	....
Kent	434	67	97	3,236	2,933	219	84	3,184,805	1,207,426	2,703,787	5,417,347
Keweenaw	12	12	1	85	81	4	....	322,700	32,223	464,707	588,860
Lake (*a*)	....	....	....	....	....	....	....	....	....	....	....
Lapeer	153	39	39	707	682	9	16	546,525	167,140	580,615	985,854
Leelanaw	12	4	8	47	47	....	....	45,200	17,384	79,774	140,760
Lenawee	585	138	56	2,510	2,346	131	33	2,226,831	813,825	2,359,606	4,265,925
Livingston	130	21	20	372	364	6	2	315,800	75,094	347,825	541,046
Mackinac	12	....	3	91	91	....	....	94,650	32,660	34,433	98,940
Macomb	220	51	21	1,017	915	26	76	676,160	230,658	781,606	1,379,312
Manistee	50	24	3	1,053	1,043	4	6	1,333,100	373,431	1,004,369	1,717,312
Manitou (*a*)	....	....	....	....	....	....	....	....	....	....	....
Marquette	41	13	15	1,272	1,270	1	1	1,743,200	767,522	1,122,870	2,382,737
Mason	15	11	3	362	351	....	11	853,200	80,764	254,950	571,035
Mecosta	7	2	5	27	26	....	1	54,000	7,300	79,204	114,474
Menominee	7	5	....	521	517	4	....	1,056,800	252,160	278,952	609,737
Midland	16	11	....	175	167	1	7	124,700	75,200	129,257	247,825
Missaukee (*a*)	....	....	....	....	....	....	....	....	....	....	....
Monroe	222	48	34	856	783	19	54	704,305	191,121	586,958	1,137,874
Montcalm	157	46	41	801	744	34	23	690,410	187,727	425,826	834,931
Muskegon	125	60	22	2,004	1,997	....	7	3,053,350	828,686	2,690,794	4,825,152
Newaygo	47	11	24	237	228	....	9	296,668	61,546	191,654	324,033
Oakland	230	27	64	776	746	30	....	888,650	212,420	1,200,110	1,741,948
Oceana	18	10	12	161	161	....	....	374,200	74,264	142,243	304,100
Ogemaw (*a*)	....	....	....	....	....	....	....	....	....	....	....
Ontonagon	13	3	....	21	21	....	....	21,486	845	5,881	12,891
Osceola	6	....	3	13	13	....	....	18,700	2,000	8,200	17,114
Oscoda (*a*)	....	....	....	....	....	....	....	....	....	....	....
Ottawa	159	40	8	866	799	35	32	854,530	247,820	925,531	1,598,086
Presque Isle (*a*)	....	....	....	....	....	....	....	....	....	....	....
Saginaw	412	146	10	4,461	4,263	52	146	6,703,150	1,623,487	1,839,976	8,094,799

(*a*) Returned as having no manufactures.

TABLE C.—*Manufactures, by Totals of Counties, &c.*—1870—Continued.

THE STATE OF MICHIGAN—Continued.

Counties.	Establishm'ts.	Steam-engines.	Water-wheels.	All hands.	Males above 16.	Females above 15.	Youth.	Capital. (Dollars.)	Wages. (Dollars.)	Materials. (Dollars.)	Products. (Dollars.)
Sanilac	65	27	4	340	340	.....	.....	852, 608	92, 837	363, 807	672, 55[illegible]
Schoolcraft	6	5	3	640	640	.....	.....	513, 000	232, 650	242, 000	[illegible]
Shiawassee	101	17	29	358	343	14	1	404, 075	85, 525	462, 118	[illegible]
St. Clair	229	55	12	1, 240	1, 152	32	56	1, 058, 745	380, 806	1, 100, 687	1, [illegible]
St. Joseph	284	21	90	1, 200	1, 113	60	27	1, 033, 784	254, 880	1, 189, 545	1, [illegible]
Tuscola	90	32	19	336	318	11	7	247, 930	62, 497	277, 187	[illegible]
Van Buren	182	68	37	990	949	6	35	1, 154, 815	252, 479	1, 095, 577	1, [illegible]
Washtenaw	544	58	113	1, 942	1, 707	207	28	1, 717, 670	470, 434	2, 419, 136	3, [illegible]
Wayne	1, 191	247	25	13, 989	11, 543	1, 454	992	14, 732, 160	5, 375, 213	15, 336, 359	26, 217, 6[illegible]
Wexford (a)	.....	.....	.....	.....	.....	.....	.....	.....	.....	.....	.....

THE STATE OF MINNESOTA.

Counties.	Establishm'ts.	Steam-engines.	Water-wheels.	All hands.	Males above 16.	Females above 15.	Youth.	Capital. (Dollars.)	Wages. (Dollars.)	Materials. (Dollars.)	Products. (Dollars.)
Aitkin (a)	.....	.....	.....	.....	.....	.....	.....	.....	.....	.....	.....
Anoka	15	2	4	201	200	1	.....	237, 700	69, 610	123, 073	279, 5[illegible]
Becker (a)	.....	.....	.....	.....	.....	.....	.....	.....	.....	.....	.....
Beltrami (a)	.....	.....	.....	.....	.....	.....	.....	.....	.....	.....	.....
Benton	5	.....	.....	9	9	.....	.....	4, 600	500	1, 148	5, 3[illegible]
Big Stone (a)	.....	.....	.....	.....	.....	.....	.....	.....	.....	.....	.....
Blue Earth	54	9	11	192	191	.....	1	225, 900	67, 567	345, 524	5[illegible]
Brown	36	4	3	85	85	.....	.....	78, 300	25, 310	70, 894	135, 1[illegible]
Carlton	1	1	.....	6	6	.....	.....	3, 000	3, 400	2, 400	6, [illegible]
Carver	42	11	1	190	189	1	.....	107, 150	38, 908	176, 087	[illegible]
Cass (a)	.....	.....	.....	.....	.....	.....	.....	.....	.....	.....	.....
Chippewa (a)	.....	.....	.....	.....	.....	.....	.....	.....	.....	.....	.....
Chisago	51	6	5	160	152	2	6	121, 450	35, 710	85, 315	177, 867
Clay (a)	.....	.....	.....	.....	.....	.....	.....	.....	.....	.....	.....
Cottonwood (a)	.....	.....	.....	.....	.....	.....	.....	.....	.....	.....	.....
Crow Wing (a)	.....	.....	.....	.....	.....	.....	.....	.....	.....	.....	.....
Dakota	77	5	11	260	260	.....	.....	250, 537	75, 084	446, 572	641, 873
Dodge	29	1	7	61	60	.....	1	82, 990	10, 666	240, 628	295, 732
Douglas	13	3	.....	48	48	.....	.....	34, 550	10, 906	52, 757	90, 441
Faribault	24	2	2	78	77	1	.....	55, 900	14, 280	46, 073	61, 797
Fillmore	78	3	32	232	213	19	.....	301, 625	61, 181	454, 062	644, 873
Freeborn	33	.....	3	63	60	3	.....	57, 775	12, 230	51, 742	90, 393
Goodhue	114	15	20	480	464	6	10	577, 823	138, 725	814, 924	1, 200, 69[illegible]
Grant (a)	.....	.....	.....	.....	.....	.....	.....	.....	.....	.....	.....
Hennepin	314	16	100	3, 221	3, 054	136	31	3, 908, 550	1, 436, 302	3, 913, 214	6, 810, 970
Houston	58	1	18	204	193	2	9	299, 575	76, 160	896, 786	1, 038, 79[illegible]
Isanti	6	2	3	17	17	.....	.....	12, 600	2, 928	10, 200	15, 400
Itasca (a)	.....	.....	.....	.....	.....	.....	.....	.....	.....	.....	.....
Jackson	3	.....	3	9	9	.....	.....	11, 000	2, 500	14, 300	24, 000
Kanabec	2	.....	2	6	6	.....	.....	6, 300	1, 100	2, 500	4, 600
Kandiyohi (a)	.....	.....	.....	.....	.....	.....	.....	.....	.....	.....	.....
Lac qui Parle (a)	.....	.....	.....	.....	.....	.....	.....	.....	.....	.....	.....
Lake	3	.....	3	15	15	.....	.....	2, 750	4, 822	3, 240	10, 600
Le Sueur	51	17	7	184	179	1	4	142, 275	35, 950	234, 465	407, 023
Martin	7	1	3	19	19	.....	.....	18, 100	3, 620	23, 656	48, 880
McLeod	15	2	7	35	35	.....	.....	37, 000	4, 915	52, 870	88, 945
Meeker	13	1	20	38	37	1	.....	54, 800	8, 510	118, 700	130, 345
Mille Lac	7	2	3	33	33	.....	.....	26, 950	6, 738	27, 364	45, 897
Monongalia	4	.....	6	9	9	.....	.....	11, 000	1, 900	39, 839	53, 325
Morrison	3	.....	3	7	7	.....	.....	6, 050	2, 500	3, 690	8, 355
Mower	32	6	.....	93	92	1	.....	79, 800	23, 050	140, 340	222, 490
Murray (a)	.....	.....	.....	.....	.....	.....	.....	.....	.....	.....	.....
Nicollet	47	7	1	177	167	2	8	121, 550	43, 820	150, 678	265, 419
Nobles (a)	.....	.....	.....	.....	.....	.....	.....	.....	.....	.....	.....
Olmsted	153	7	26	373	373	.....	.....	267, 100	92, 595	499, 997	783, 518
Otter Tail	1	1	.....	9	9	.....	.....	10, 000	4, 000	4, 000	11, 200
Pembina (a)	.....	.....	.....	.....	.....	.....	.....	.....	.....	.....	.....
Pine	8	6	3	97	94	3	.....	51, 800	34, 550	63, 040	146, 390
Pope (a)	.....	.....	.....	.....	.....	.....	.....	.....	.....	.....	.....
Ramsey	88	6	2	985	932	16	37	1, 401, 112	520, 459	812, 020	1, 612, 378
Redwood	6	.....	4	23	23	.....	.....	24, 050	3, 300	23, 647	40, 596
Renville	5	.....	3	16	16	.....	.....	14, 800	2, 870	14, 420	27, 160
Rice	133	23	22	475	442	29	4	574, 300	128, 689	974, 738	1, 447, 685
Rock (a)	.....	.....	.....	.....	.....	.....	.....	.....	.....	.....	.....
Scott	81	7	6	240	234	.....	6	180, 464	77, 704	210, 032	381, 334
Sherburne	6	1	3	71	71	.....	.....	53, 100	16, 400	31, 985	61, 755

(a) Returned as having no manufactures.

TABLE C.—*Manufactures, by Totals of Counties, &c.*—1870—Continued.

THE STATE OF MINNESOTA—Continued.

Counties.	Establishm'ts.	Steam-engines.	Water-wheels.	All hands.	Males above 16.	Females above 15.	Youth.	Capital. (*Dollars.*)	Wages. (*Dollars.*)	Materials. (*Dollars.*)	Products. (*Dollars.*)
Sibley	20	9	3	80	79	1		44, 600	19, 950	51, 951	91, 400
Stearns	118	9	19	467	450	12	5	254, 420	145, 560	266, 097	548, 165
Steele	12	3		59	59			34, 500	22, 275	30, 625	79, 321
Stevens (*a*)											
St. Louis	16	5		188	188			53, 100	101, 600	95, 076	262, 000
Todd	2		1	6	6			5, 400	400	1, 575	2, 950
Traverse (*a*)											
Wabashaw	175	8	13	340	332	8		257, 067	69, 965	398, 567	652, 810
Wadena (*a*)											
Waseca	28	2		60	60			45, 925	8, 051	57, 244	82, 167
Washington	89	17	10	761	755	4	2	841, 040	237, 228	617, 336	1, 131, 949
Watonwan	4	1	1	13	13			17, 500	2, 800	46, 500	59, 900
Wilkin	1	1		30	30			50, 000	26, 000	2, 500	67, 000
Winona	160	20	30	810	785	10	15	876, 449	310, 699	1, 018, 895	1, 811, 064
Wright	18	3	7	55	55			48, 100	8, 850	79, 585	113, 820

THE STATE OF MISSISSIPPI.

Counties.	Establishm'ts.	Steam-engines.	Water-wheels.	All hands.	Males above 16.	Females above 15.	Youth.	Capital. (*Dollars.*)	Wages. (*Dollars.*)	Materials. (*Dollars.*)	Products. (*Dollars.*)
Adams	69	3		227	219	3	5	128, 460	46, 046	72, 922	192, 540
Alcorn	31	13	1	88	88			65, 650	21, 350	64, 443	133, 388
Amite	14		5	18	18			7, 965	1, 300	10, 720	19, 555
Attala	43	7	6	81	81			45, 650	14, 284	99, 315	140, 922
Bolivar	4	4		5	5			7, 300	200	2, 300	2, 900
Calhoun	50	6	6	95	94		1	33, 950	7, 820	85, 182	144, 082
Carroll	49	13	1	199	141	27	31	270, 140	37, 024	94, 443	158, 952
Chickasaw	51	11	3	110	108		2	52, 325	13, 745	100, 397	147, 715
Choctaw	14	2	2	24	24			9, 375	5, 085	19, 842	31, 473
Claiborne (*a*)											
Clark	18	8	4	173	104	25	44	57, 625	39, 800	108, 637	193, 410
Coahoma	5			15	15			2, 400	6, 900	10, 100	23, 600
Copiah	58	22	4	352	256	42	54	614, 485	106, 896	206, 015	456, 585
Covington	11	2	9	23	23			4, 550	1, 450	16, 615	24, 276
De Soto	75	17	1	177	172	2	3	73, 325	25, 710	114, 216	188, 650
Franklin	6	5		21	21			8, 400	2, 450	6, 126	14, 700
Greene	12	6	6	43	43			12, 725	9, 000	24, 400	45, 873
Grenada	19	6		39	39			51, 550	10, 050	29, 605	52, 700
Hancock	9	10	1	244	241	3		106, 000	206, 000	46, 600	315, 400
Harrison	19	20		208	208			117, 600	48, 900	61, 742	157, 700
Hinds	55	14		204	201		3	134, 655	68, 042	157, 538	344, 904
Holmes	21	8		75	73	1	1	37, 750	15, 325	27, 300	74, 330
Issaquena	11			32	32			2, 700	6, 100	11, 678	27, 080
Itawamba (*a*)											
Jackson	9	7		186	161	8	17	246, 100	48, 280	263, 050	406, 280
Jasper	9	4		10	10			4, 800	700	3, 612	11, 162
Jefferson	13			19	19			8, 085	3, 340	8, 495	18, 375
Jones (*a*)											
Kemper	27	3	9	51	51			31, 400	8, 200	56, 635	87, 390
Lafayette	37	6	23	102	102			51, 100	18, 700	291, 200	390, 800
Lauderdale (*a*)											
Lawrence	11		9	17	17			9, 400	770	7, 793	15, 385
Leake	6	4	2	23	15	4	4	9, 900	3, 310	11, 668	21, 460
Lee	9	1		43	38		5	9, 600	9, 170	20, 660	37, 480
Lincoln	44	15	18	175	172	1	2	92, 332	14, 595	62, 409	152, 737
Lowndes	75	18	10	368	315	22	11	376, 007	74, 398	245, 565	412, 097
Madison	33	11		145	138		7	71, 380	23, 732	65, 424	106, 426
Marion (*a*)											
Marshall	103	8	13	192	188	2	2	111, 365	41, 970	86, 279	225, 568
Monroe	4	3		17	16		1	20, 000	7, 680	110, 300	149, 220
Neshoba	3	1	1	5	5			4, 500	1, 400	9, 300	12, 212
Newton	23	8	6	122	120		2	42, 340	26, 258	57, 411	136, 591
Noxubee	38	8	2	153	120	15	18	158, 118	23, 672	149, 531	210, 959
Oktibbeha	32	8		76	76			30, 135	6, 303	44, 517	71, 059
Panola	39	11	2	119	116	1	2	31, 950	22, 907	74, 762	129, 909
Perry	14		8	19	19			5, 400	1, 100	9, 260	15, 630
Pike	43	9	13	108	108			50, 120	16, 200	43, 796	103, 648
Pontotoc	30	5	3	62	62			28, 775	6, 505	49, 878	86, 690
Prentiss	15	5	3	43	42		1	21, 700	4, 620	24, 720	41, 690
Rankin	11	3	1	29	29			9, 500	4, 660	13, 085	24, 392
Scott	24	6	1	58	53		5	36, 200	7, 825	43, 480	74, 550

(*a*) Returned as having no manufactures.

TABLE C.—*Manufactures, by Totals of Counties, &c.*—1870—Continued.

THE STATE OF MISSISSIPPI—Continued.

Counties.	Establishm'ts.	Steam-engines.	Water-wheels.	All hands.	Males above 16.	Females above 15.	Youth.	Capital. (Dollars.)	Wages. (Dollars.)	Materials. (Dollars.)	Products. (Dollars.)
Simpson	14	2	10	25	25	.....	.....	10, 900	3, 550	19, 425	[illegible]
Smith	8	2	5	14	14	.....	.....	9, 300	450	17, 780	[illegible]
Sunflower	8	3	....	29	29	.....	.....	46, 400	3, 532	15, 900	[illegible]
Tallahatchie	22	8	....	55	55	.....	.....	38, 405	13, 150	34, 886	[illegible]
Tippah	68	6	31	103	103	.....	.....	43, 935	15, 530	139, 200	[illegible]
Tishemingo	22	8	1	136	112	13	11	82, 880	29, 338	81, 138	[illegible]
Tunica (a)											
Warren	212	14	....	498	478	15	5	609, 818	179, 970	674, 165	1, [illegible]
Washington	2	....	....	7	7	.....	.....	10, 000	3, 000	9, 000	[illegible]
Wayne	2	2	....	20	20	.....	.....	18, 000	5, 000	1, 800	[illegible]
Wilkinson	7	2	....	15	15	.....	.....	4, 700	2, 790	11, 300	[illegible]
Winston	1	1	1	20	5	5	10	60, 000	2, 906	16, 150	[illegible]
Yalabusha	51	12	3	384	381	.....	3	226, 089	211, 848	206, 849	[illegible]
Yazoo	18	3	1	40	38	2	.....	27, 500	6, 592	13, 347	41, [illegible]

THE STATE OF MISSOURI.

Counties.	Establishm'ts.	Steam-engines.	Water-wheels.	All hands.	Males above 16.	Females above 15.	Youth.	Capital. (Dollars.)	Wages. (Dollars.)	Materials. (Dollars.)	Products. (Dollars.)
Adair	66	21	2	188	179	6	3	122, 345	24, 345	137, 634	[illegible]
Andrew	74	13	13	171	165	5	1	80, 185	23, 112	188, 528	[illegible]
Atchison	53	11	7	183	183	.....	.....	82, 406	34, 820	122, 011	[illegible]
Audrain	135	7	....	290	260	25	5	127, 055	44, 825	177, 482	[illegible]
Barry	6	....	4	15	15	.....	.....	23, 000	3, 640	44, 250	[illegible]
Barton	32	5	....	80	80	.....	.....	38, 805	15, 325	60, 871	[illegible]
Bates	64	17	....	163	157	4	2	100, 928	42, 674	128, 373	[illegible]
Benton	29	4	3	55	54	1	.....	45, 300	6, 005	55, 701	[illegible]
Bollinger	28	5	6	76	76	.....	.....	41, 100	14, 264	59, 379	[illegible]
Boone	129	20	2	366	359	5	2	193, 952	93, 555	516, 236	[illegible]
Buchanan	135	31	....	964	915	14	35	1, 083, 050	483, 240	2, 140, 286	3, 434, [illegible]
Butler	13	1	2	24	24	.....	.....	10, 175	2, 070	17, 778	[illegible]
Caldwell	65	8	1	166	166	.....	.....	66, 560	22, 590	119, 523	[illegible]
Callaway	113	24	....	240	235	2	3	131, 119	28, 456	162, 172	[illegible]
Camden	12	1	5	28	28	.....	.....	21, 702	3, 645	84, 439	104, 197
Cape Girardeau	189	31	9	504	493	2	9	406, 875	76, 284	577, 430	907, [illegible]
Carroll	57	9	4	196	196	.....	.....	106, 175	38, 319	372, 015	551, [illegible]
Carter	8	1	1	16	16	.....	.....	21, 430	2, 500	4, 059	8, 533
Cass	67	15	1	249	246	.....	3	179, 205	54, 168	218, 094	410, 677
Cedar	10	....	7	22	22	.....	.....	31, 000	2, 300	35, 837	[illegible]
Chariton	86	14	7	192	191	1	.....	156, 645	33, 590	222, 421	[illegible]
Christian	22	4	9	75	71	1	3	44, 600	11, 230	182, 355	[illegible]
Clarke	44	5	1	91	88	2	1	36, 090	9, 370	55, 505	95, 446
Clay	92	20	....	325	281	32	12	341, 245	110, 835	405, 436	[illegible]
Clinton	81	10	....	227	227	.....	.....	114, 925	43, 158	215, 815	[illegible]
Cole	47	11	....	371	371	.....	.....	240, 050	90, 848	212, 150	501, [illegible]
Cooper	67	14	2	227	221	3	3	179, 250	60, 495	277, 091	[illegible]
Crawford	48	3	16	73	72	.....	1	38, 155	5, 400	91, 100	[illegible]
Dade	30	2	6	61	59	1	1	32, 155	11, 455	112, 854	[illegible]
Dallas	10	2	1	26	25	1	.....	7, 800	5, 765	24, 320	[illegible]
Daviess	60	11	7	123	123	.....	.....	68, 080	16, 045	122, 791	214, 917
De Kalb	12	1	....	21	21	.....	.....	12, 250	1, 650	7, 947	18, [illegible]
Dent	16	1	5	34	34	.....	.....	19, 000	3, 000	44, 725	64, [illegible]
Douglas	4	2	2	20	20	.....	.....	14, 100	4, 590	19, 800	[illegible]
Dunklin	7	2	....	19	19	.....	....	7, 150	2, 456	10, 425	[illegible]
Franklin	650	29	14	2, 062	2, 002	23	37	1, 037, 725	671, 110	1, 075, 936	2, 218, [illegible]
Gasconade	40	8	....	87	81	.....	6	90, 050	9, 721	96, 656	178, [illegible]
Gentry	101	19	4	245	235	6	4	104, 533	27, 241	215, 960	356, 673
Greene	96	16	12	431	414	.....	17	244, 720	158, 822	541, 638	933, 795
Grundy	29	12	4	88	87	.....	1	89, 800	12, 290	104, 796	144, [illegible]
Harrison	85	16	6	186	184	2	.....	99, 772	33, 515	221, 637	358, 974
Henry	91	11	3	256	238	15	3	167, 650	60, 015	357, 310	585, 115
Hickory	19	5	9	50	50	.....	.....	29, 475	4, 931	71, 154	98, 277
Holt	64	17	6	177	164	13	.....	135, 050	52, 950	311, 115	548, 970
Howard	29	5	....	96	94	2	.....	117, 300	22, 856	142, 719	209, [illegible]
Howell	2	....	....	5	5	.....	.....	1, 100	475	136	1, [illegible]
Iron	39	10	....	352	342	.....	10	774, 925	121, 985	224, 719	435, [illegible]
Jackson	687	41	1	3, 145	3, 007	83	55	1, 671, 525	1, 406, 348	3, 203, 589	6, 197, 182
Jasper	23	4	7	91	90	1	.....	179, 200	28, 930	130, 300	[illegible]
Jefferson	79	11	6	227	216	2	9	276, 810	38, 483	243, 933	409, 254
Johnson	66	14	....	224	220	.....	4	178, 409	64, 875	316, 080	[illegible]
Knox	179	15	3	396	369	18	9	146, 005	63, 923	199, 932	370, [illegible]

(a) Returned as having no manufactures.

TABLE C.—*Manufactures, by Totals of Counties, &c.*—1870—Continued.

THE STATE OF MISSOURI—Continued.

Counties.	Establishm'ts.	Steam-engines.	Water-wheels.	All hands.	Males above 16.	Females above 15.	Youth.	Capital. (*Dollars.*)	Wages. (*Dollars.*)	Materials. (*Dollars.*)	Products. (*Dollars.*)
Laclede	28	5	4	83	83	.....	....	32, 105	11, 004	50, 916	94, 713
Lafayette	118	24	....	410	406	3	1	286, 745	100, 604	276, 509	803, 352
Lawrence	91	12	11	199	199	.....	....	111, 915	24, 100	356, 065	493, 890
Lewis	165	8	2	497	375	6	116	196, 570	85, 636	392, 101	677, 943
Lincoln	94	25	1	187	176	1	10	111, 120	20, 754	169, 191	270, 285
Linn	87	8	5	180	171	6	3	96, 700	36, 856	109, 897	228, 328
Livingston	89	16	....	288	278	7	3	170, 310	77, 871	204, 058	409, 935
Macon	110	39	....	273	253	7	13	157, 385	65, 243	486, 532	789, 684
Madison	31	2	4	66	65	1	....	37, 550	10, 970	38, 112	77, 785
Maries	11	2	3	23	21	2	....	15, 328	1, 300	28, 997	37, 806
Marion	147	32	1	1, 209	1, 127	22	60	907, 975	565, 559	1, 520, 730	2, 447, 102
McDonald	19	1	7	34	34	.....	....	28, 585	4, 700	117, 550	140, 720
Mercer	26	7	3	64	64	.....	....	21, 950	5, 810	50, 898	79, 035
Miller	21	5	5	61	61	.....	....	37, 000	5, 050	92, 377	127, 430
Moniteau	49	7	....	141	138	.....	3	100, 330	21, 855	123, 634	242, 337
Monroe	74	25	1	183	173	5	5	130, 360	32, 420	224, 655	349, 731
Montgomery	15	5	....	47	47	.....	....	36, 000	7, 450	45, 025	78, 069
Morgan	23	4	9	72	72	.....	....	45, 200	9, 789	155, 556	218, 001
New Madrid	5	3	....	22	22	.....	....	7, 550	5, 600	4, 621	17, 460
Newton	66	10	8	200	197	.....	3	109, 722	35, 691	212, 480	360, 112
Nodaway	116	14	9	237	237	.....	....	114, 680	24, 000	183, 062	314, 970
Oregon	13	1	8	33	33	.....	....	16, 300	4, 150	32, 056	50, 193
Osage	40	13	2	117	104	.....	13	84, 930	14, 596	182, 603	262, 855
Ozark	2	....	2	9	9	.....	....	3, 600	650	6, 000	7, 548
Perry	81	13	9	163	157	2	4	207, 355	28, 600	365, 442	582, 890
Pettis	60	9	....	194	194	.....	....	229, 710	91, 257	250, 178	467, 207
Phelps	30	7	10	441	428	10	3	298, 790	140, 912	486, 899	780, 739
Pike	160	32	....	754	631	30	93	696, 750	192, 910	988, 740	1, 685, 807
Platte	83	25	3	292	283	6	3	663, 830	73, 695	692, 680	951, 862
Polk	17	5	3	55	54	1	....	22, 875	6, 985	31, 210	56, 880
Pulaski	5	....	5	11	11	.....	....	12, 500	2, 020	41, 500	53, 785
Putnam	39	10	2	139	114	9	16	35, 050	10, 865	31, 666	72, 868
Ralls	18	10	....	58	58	.....	....	34, 000	4, 110	44, 946	65, 690
Randolph	50	18	....	180	173	1	6	111, 300	27, 571	149, 497	218, 675
Ray	69	23	1	246	246	.....	....	120, 750	48, 276	143, 507	269, 216
Reynolds	11	....	7	19	18	.....	1	15, 450	2, 150	14, 454	24, 750
Ripley	5	....	4	17	15	.....	2	11, 500	2, 100	19, 523	26, 190
Saline	84	20	1	220	212	2	6	148, 095	44, 215	227, 548	398, 579
Schuyler	39	23	....	118	117	.....	1	51, 945	12, 669	130, 067	203, 216
Scotland	70	16	....	168	162	6	....	88, 270	31, 650	138, 712	258, 472
Scott	22	7	....	89	89	.....	....	39, 570	18, 220	54, 980	108, 290
Shannon	11	1	8	15	15	.....	....	7, 100	470	8, 500	11, 580
Shelby	91	11	3	211	188	20	3	106, 975	20, 640	185, 794	301, 445
St. Charles	116	48	....	852	852	.....	....	2, 006, 230	386, 692	2, 394, 123	3, 269, 840
St. Clair	16	4	1	38	38	.....	....	28, 150	5, 300	47, 809	72, 645
Ste. Genevieve	19	7	3	82	82	.....	....	191, 500	24, 120	380, 609	454, 019
St. François	32	14	3	163	161	.....	2	308, 524	63, 347	401, 948	753, 315
St. Louis	4, 579	425	....	40, 856	32, 484	3, 455	4, 917	60, 357, 001	24, 221, 717	87, 388, 252	158, 761, 013
Stoddard	25	4	....	66	66	.....	....	28, 350	8, 830	44, 668	78, 600
Stone	6	3	2	24	24	.....	....	9, 600	4, 622	27, 965	40, 506
Sullivan	59	10	3	142	135	1	6	69, 100	19, 161	167, 620	263, 425
Taney	4	1	1	14	14	.....	....	6, 950	2, 167	17, 200	24, 300
Texas	34	7	9	124	106	10	8	47, 450	19, 843	45, 325	91, 164
Vernon	25	9	....	88	88	.....	....	45, 950	27, 393	77, 855	142, 214
Warren	211	14	....	307	299	.....	8	119, 110	16, 135	135, 917	283, 027
Washington	69	18	22	341	331	.....	10	1, 489, 325	88, 791	473, 325	700, 838
Wayne	6	2	2	17	17	.....	....	11. 800	2, 025	30, 160	52, 732
Webster	57	11	2	144	136	1	7	65, 660	24, 058	113, 962	192, 600
Worth	22	2	....	50	49	.....	1	25, 000	4, 300	13, 396	40, 020
Wright	10	2	1	22	22	.....	....	8, 900	1, 363	9, 542	18, 155

THE TERRITORY OF MONTANA.

Counties.	Establishm'ts.	Steam-engines.	Water-wheels.	All hands.	Males above 16.	Females above 15.	Youth.	Capital. (*Dollars.*)	Wages. (*Dollars.*)	Materials. (*Dollars.*)	Products. (*Dollars.*)
Beaver Head	15	2	....	36	36	.....	....	41, 900	11, 500	77, 380	174, 300
Big Horn (*a*)	....	....	....	.....	.....	.....	....	....	....	....	....
Choteau	1	....	....	2	2	.....	....	4, 000	900	800	3, 000
Dawson	1	....	....	1	1	.....	....	400	....	200	1, 000
Deer Lodge	13	6	7	121	121	.....	....	382, 100	35, 000	188, 235	323, 691
Gallatin	31	1	9	63	63	.....	....	85, 810	32, 173	135, 833	267, 829
Jefferson	18	5	9	70	70	.....	....	80, 770	14, 165	39, 845	120, 949
Lewis and Clarke	43	12	3	224	220	2	2	436, 450	204, 060	515, 183	929, 368
Madison	43	5	10	107	107	.....	....	671, 550	47, 200	136, 497	312, 108
Meagher	23	2	1	47	47	.....	....	39, 270	12, 350	66, 458	[illegible]
Missoula	*13*	....	7	30	30	.....	....	52, 050	12, 895	155, 900	215, 400

TABLE C.—*Manufactures, by Totals of Counties, &c.*—1870—Continued.

THE STATE OF NEBRASKA.

Counties.	Establishm'ts.	Steam-engines.	Water-wheels.	All hands.	Males above 16.	Females above 15.	Youth.	Capital. (Dollars.)	Wages. (Dollars.)	Materials. (Dollars.)	Products. (Dollars.)
Adams (a)											
Blackbird (a)											
Buffalo (a)											
Burt	20	4		45	45			17,660	5,140	38,254	[illegible]
Butler	2		1	6	6			6,500	1,620	100	[illegible]
Calhoun (a)											
Cass	34	1	5	89	89			101,700	21,483	130,402	[illegible]
Cedar	14	1	8	35	35			30,550	9,450	55,664	[illegible]
Cheyenne (a)											
Clay (a)											
Colfax	9		1	19	19			18,100	4,780	37,341	[illegible]
Cuming	11	2	2	36	36			57,700	9,247	92,913	[illegible]
Dakota	37	4	3	90	90			65,520	27,790	124,195	[illegible]
Dawson (a)											
Dixon	24	2	4	41	41			34,450	7,200	70,065	[illegible]
Dodge	23		2	73	73			46,175	23,409	53,132	[illegible]
Douglas	229	14	3	1,572	1,483	72	17	1,127,555	1,120,570	1,254,323	[illegible]
Fillmore (a)											
Fort Randall (a)											
Franklin (a)											
Gage	2		1	7	7			27,000	5,500	33,000	[illegible]
Grant (a)											
Green (a)											
Hall	19	3	2	29	28	1		49,475	5,825	34,173	[illegible]
Hamilton (a)											
Harrison (a)											
Jackson (a)											
Jefferson	6	1	5	18	18			15,200	3,600	11,440	[illegible]
Johnson	10		2	25	25			30,525	7,256	23,449	[illegible]
Jones (a)											
Kearney (a)											
Lancaster	7		2	23	22	1		47,000	8,670	31,710	[illegible]
L'Eau qui Court	2	1		5	5			4,100	1,500	3,300	[illegible]
Lincoln (a)											
Lyon (a)											
Madison (a)											
Merrick (a)											
Monroe (a)											
Nemaha	9	4	5	30	30			40,100	9,222	79,446	[illegible]
Nuckolls (a)											
Otoe	58	6	2	177	170	1	6	151,600	80,620	271,676	[illegible]
Pawnee	21	1	1	47	45	2		21,883	6,325	55,192	[illegible]
Pierce (a)											
Platte	22			41	37	3	1	13,800	8,550	45,360	[illegible]
Polk (a)											
Richardson	34	3	5	102	102			91,160	27,535	198,584	[illegible]
Saline	7		3	11	11			6,850	800	9,503	[illegible]
Sarpy	12	6	1	22	22			39,400	6,800	29,420	[illegible]
Saunders	1		1	4	4			33,000	1,600	20,760	[illegible]
Seward	26	1	8	55	55			40,700	9,300	56,144	[illegible]
Shorter (a)											
Stanton (a)											
Taylor (a)											
Washington	22	6		63	60	1	2	52,260	16,121	142,468	[illegible]
Wayne (a)											
Webster (a)											
York (a)											

THE STATE OF NEVADA.

Counties.	Establishm'ts.	Steam-engines.	Water-wheels.	All hands.	Males above 16.	Females above 15.	Youth.	Capital. (Dollars.)	Wages. (Dollars.)	Materials. (Dollars.)	Products. (Dollars.)
Churchill (a)											
Douglas	5		6	82	82			79,000	50,300	33,600	[illegible]
Elko	21	2		56	55	1		70,100	32,300	51,770	[illegible]
Esmeralda	44	11	2	259	259			229,400	128,600	375,870	[illegible]
Humboldt	5	5		44	44			110,000	48,960	305,298	[illegible]
Lander	4	7		191	191			657,500	223,884	700,236	[illegible]
Lincoln	15	2	1	68	68			162,300	28,000	207,876	[illegible]
Lyon	24	16	9	387	387			537,500	382,950	1,128,009	[illegible]
Nye	10	9		146	146			150,500	46,100	43,500	[illegible]
Ormsby	76	8	9	368	366	2		640,240	259,359	1,235,491	[illegible]
Storey	73	27	2	624	624			1,036,200	730,715	3,604,343	[illegible]
Washoe	31	8	5	266	266			411,050	203,481	456,565	[illegible]
White Pine	22	25		368	368			1,044,000	363,824	2,173,246	[illegible]

(a) Returned as having no manufactures.

TABLE C.—*Manufactures, by Totals of Counties, &c.*—1870—Continued.

THE STATE OF NEW HAMPSHIRE.

Counties.	Establishm'ts.	Steam-engines.	Water-wheels.	All hands.	Males above 16.	Females above 15.	Youth.	Capital. (Dollars.)	Wages. (Dollars.)	Materials. (Dollars.)	Products. (Dollars.)
nap	147	11	132	1, 800	1, 034	671	95	1, 257, 125	568, 925	1, 849, 464	2, 962, 617
oll	125	8	62	475	433	39	3	462, 832	130, 866	755, 292	1, 151, 304
shire	364	26	321	3, 213	2, 546	572	95	2, 896, 295	1, 229, 893	3, 317, 652	5, 910, 774
l	287	21	262	1, 389	1, 339	41	9	1, 068, 515	265, 715	812, 490	1, 368, 767
ton	646	19	464	3, 299	2, 681	542	76	2, 362, 735	823, 463	2, 955, 893	5, 012, 033
sborough	564	76	361	14, 389	7, 627	5, 887	875	13, 443, 890	5, 026, 180	17, 586, 821	25, 330, 611
rimack	414	26	272	4, 429	3, 042	1, 145	242	4, 896, 995	1, 747, 620	4, 294, 447	7, 627, 676
kingham	424	56	159	3, 710	2, 449	1, 079	182	3, 019, 420	1, 124, 581	3, 111, 795	5, 484, 238
fford	176	31	103	6, 538	3, 687	2, 320	531	5, 301, 711	2, 442, 827	8, 533, 454	13, 709, 511
van	195	6	176	1, 541	991	479	71	1, 314, 225	463, 701	1, 450, 659	2, 480, 718

THE STATE OF NEW JERSEY.

Counties.	Establishm'ts.	Steam-engines.	Water-wheels.	All hands.	Males above 16.	Females above 15.	Youth.	Capital. (Dollars.)	Wages. (Dollars.)	Materials. (Dollars.)	Products. (Dollars.)
ntic	80	6	35	469	355	78	36	381, 500	136, 324	433, 575	799, 464
en	180	50	56	1, 401	1, 110	139	152	1, 357, 200	507, 661	4, 163, 487	5, 325, 072
ington	339	30	88	3, 283	2, 555	573	155	2, 272, 075	1, 240, 405	2, 896, 937	4, 884, 438
den	329	59	26	3, 836	2, 842	500	494	3, 507, 295	1, 470, 517	5, 902, 246	8, 330, 013
May	27	7	9	122	119		3	88, 550	29, 830	147, 012	218, 640
berland	295	44	39	4, 184	2, 602	1, 125	457	2, 573, 800	1, 357, 766	3, 716, 878	6, 314, 577
x	1, 198	291	43	22, 156	17, 344	3, 333	1, 479	22, 606, 662	11, 537, 270	29, 255, 062	52, 108, 958
cester	166	12	23	1, 255	1, 174		81	1, 386, 310	436, 616	1, 002, 491	1, 798, 168
son	333	93		5, 624	4, 909	383	332	11, 718, 400	3, 280, 526	17, 229, 632	24, 256, 017
terdon	614	29	142	2, 273	1, 878	261	134	2, 136, 681	677, 657	3, 025, 765	4, 754, 085
cer	475	78	65	5, 100	4, 007	535	558	5, 022, 782	2, 092, 349	4, 981, 541	8, 881, 074
llesex	250	49	36	3, 513	2, 555	535	423	4, 231, 320	1, 349, 701	2, 623, 080	5, 372, 563
mouth	302	15	42	2, 192	1, 492	615	85	1, 735, 225	463, 160	1, 580, 685	2, 605, 176
ris	280	24	104	1, 851	1, 626	147	78	1, 783, 100	847, 035	2, 800, 775	4, 644, 951
n	69	5	29	331	287	23	21	424, 210	122, 213	469, 177	717, 107
aic	218	62	97	9, 632	5, 934	2, 300	1, 398	8, 176, 400	3, 882, 440	11, 859, 780	19, 958, 728
n	289	18	44	1, 056	840	123	93	1, 359, 377	293, 629	1, 563, 365	2, 277, 791
rset	264	14	59	1, 072	851	145	76	1, 210, 690	322, 571	1, 514, 662	2, 551, 709
ex	249	13	61	661	619	25	17	868, 669	168, 861	997, 157	1, 455, 104
n	315	44	27	2, 754	2, 599	130	25	3, 570, 450	1, 384, 293	3, 440, 423	5, 986, 512
ren	358	41	197	2, 787	2, 417	228	142	3, 191, 023	1, 047, 585	3, 811, 489	5, 996, 965

THE TERRITORY OF NEW MEXICO.

Counties.	Establishm'ts.	Steam-engines.	Water-wheels.	All hands.	Males above 16.	Females above 15.	Youth.	Capital. (Dollars.)	Wages. (Dollars.)	Materials. (Dollars.)	Products. (Dollars.)
alillo	5	1	2	12	12			31, 400	3, 150	10, 475	18, 170
x	5	1		34	34			172, 000	30, 000	194, 265	265, 150
-Aña	7	3	3	18	18			42, 000	7, 080	121, 020	191, 851
t	4	4		28	28			49, 000	16, 500	66, 834	93, 387
oln	3		3	23	23			16, 000	10, 200	13, 200	30, 000
	20	1	5	68	68			136, 100	19, 600	157, 430	309, 600
Arriba (*a*)											
Miguel	64		11	80	80			44, 045	13, 930	72, 353	161, 842
a Aña	2			4	4			450	250	600	1, 100
a Fé	31	2	9	103	100		3	890, 550	49, 011	135, 650	235, 272
rro	9	1	4	21	20	1		22, 150	5, 060	21, 900	44, 836
	3		3	10	10			20, 800	9, 560	63, 320	94, 000
ncia	26		2	26	26			17, 200	2, 940	23, 910	44, 660

THE STATE OF NEW YORK.

Counties.	Establishm'ts.	Steam-engines.	Water-wheels.	All hands.	Males above 16.	Females above 15.	Youth.	Capital. (Dollars.)	Wages. (Dollars.)	Materials. (Dollars.)	Products. (Dollars.)
ny	721	149	82	14, 495	9, 255	3, 852	1, 388	16, 031, 268	5, 956, 157	13, 439, 705	24, 785, 921
gany	494	108	118	1, 764	1, 653	76	35	1, 329, 290	383, 727	1, 929, 913	3, 005, 737
me	340	65	148	2, 309	2, 174	92	43	2, 410, 616	878, 649	3, 571, 072	5, 592, 910
raugus	594	102	213	1, 979	1, 828	119	32	2, 300, 835	483, 288	2, 607, 704	4, 002, 720
ga	473	46	176	4, 112	3, 536	301	275	5, 152, 779	1, 440, 123	3, 617, 068	7, 378, 333
tanqua	737	127	200	3, 505	3, 126	310	69	3, 489, 740	973, 099	2, 848, 668	5, 308, 459
mung	346	74	59	2, 118	1, 912	115	91	2, 503, 170	894, 798	3, 500, 928	5, 925, 471
ango	450	25	182	1, 545	1, 360	137	48	1, 277, 766	320, 371	1, 398, 646	2, 237, 804
on	438	24	400	3, 798	3, 415	180	203	3, 103, 920	1, 022, 615	3, 300, 214	5, 272, 750
nbia	483	28	131	3, 551	2, 437	742	372	5, 033, 505	1, 045, 636	3, 900, 371	6, 737, 568
and	264	27	95	977	917	54	6	978, 600	253, 314	1, 068, 900	1, 642, 631

(*a*) Returned as having no manufactures.

TABLE C.—*Manufactures, by Totals of Counties, &c.*—1870—**Continued.**

THE STATE OF NEW YORK—Continued.

Counties.	Establishm'ts.	Steam-engines.	Water-wheels.	All hands.	Males above 16.	Females above 15.	Youth.	Capital. (Dollars.)	Wages. (Dollars.)	Materials. (Dollars.)	Products. (Dollars.)
Delaware	439	19	260	1,336	1,274	58	4	1,365,120	263,717	1,476,030	[illegible]
Dutchess	602	71	130	6,021	4,342	935	744	6,604,866	2,476,251	8,187,736	[illegible]
Erie	1,429	276	228	13,274	11,357	960	957	13,043,790	4,946,414	15,274,440	[illegible]
Essex	171	17	107	1,553	1,511	13	29	2,897,614	611,830	2,171,020	[illegible]
Franklin	366	13	197	1,316	1,197	113	6	1,172,400	229,944	1,567,206	[illegible]
Fulton	311	10	121	3,865	1,812	2,020	33	2,943,897	1,129,474	3,602,003	[illegible]
Genesee	284	27	61	980	858	91	31	976,365	210,507	1,229,946	[illegible]
Greene	235	22	72	1,799	1,446	203	150	1,939,140	541,037	1,822,076	[illegible]
Hamilton	14	1	13	160	154	2	4	183,400	64,950	418,691	[illegible]
Herkimer	592	45	237	4,112	3,237	630	245	4,776,168	1,603,417	5,163,269	[illegible]
Jefferson	737	41	364	3,455	2,776	555	124	3,813,092	941,944	4,753,521	[illegible]
Kings	1,043	286	1	18,545	14,033	2,715	1,797	25,287,981	9,273,994	39,899,971	[illegible]
Lewis	336	50	211	1,487	1,378	94	15	2,110,325	412,554	2,274,611	[illegible]
Livingston	321	26	77	1,432	1,316	84	32	1,469,294	420,077	1,680,257	[illegible]
Madison	736	48	183	2,488	2,095	280	113	2,149,286	592,548	3,238,770	[illegible]
Monroe	1,160	116	165	11,549	9,050	1,570	920	10,951,090	4,438,714	14,506,631	[illegible]
Montgomery	337	43	102	2,523	1,769	493	251	3,445,060	861,928	4,603,732	[illegible]
New York	7,624	1,261	16	129,577	91,305	32,981	5,991	129,952,262	63,824,049	178,696,939	[illegible]
Niagara	421	40	93	2,483	2,181	171	131	2,908,605	803,771	3,541,018	[illegible]
Oneida	1,075	125	390	11,175	7,096	3,150	929	11,508,438	3,610,637	10,873,468	[illegible]
Onondaga	1,215	138	257	9,682	8,073	1,100	509	10,814,028	3,606,686	11,322,620	[illegible]
Ontario	413	41	123	1,503	1,376	91	36	1,442,825	342,795	1,603,814	[illegible]
Orange	574	68	85	5,234	4,039	816	379	5,413,620	2,125,874	6,060,125	[illegible]
Orleans	259	24	55	980	867	55	58	914,150	283,886	1,437,014	[illegible]
Oswego	968	81	504	5,615	4,803	535	277	8,783,232	1,760,425	11,431,168	[illegible]
Otsego	805	31	250	2,440	1,932	346	162	1,826,328	460,777	2,130,003	[illegible]
Putnam	107	8	46	833	774	43	16	647,018	368,409	1,033,296	[illegible]
Queens	336	35	26	2,534	2,170	244	120	2,326,965	1,017,928	2,516,256	[illegible]
Rensselaer	792	123	198	15,588	9,664	4,605	1,319	12,354,181	5,804,555	15,980,083	[illegible]
Richmond	134	19	3	1,033	912	88	33	1,730,955	444,507	3,567,083	[illegible]
Rockland	119	33	24	1,976	1,671	139	166	1,076,775	754,608	992,049	[illegible]
Saratoga	455	24	209	4,135	3,138	673	324	5,705,575	1,448,075	3,989,121	[illegible]
Schenectady	111	14	21	1,638	1,386	161	91	897,820	634,163	1,587,350	[illegible]
Schoharie	295	12	136	851	765	65	21	741,540	134,941	831,294	[illegible]
Schuyler	258	38	63	829	802	22	5	823,242	179,078	1,031,110	[illegible]
Seneca	276	19	85	2,352	1,847	416	89	3,262,462	787,760	2,787,702	[illegible]
Steuben	566	123	128	2,636	2,514	48	74	3,141,570	854,380	3,238,738	[illegible]
St. Lawrence	687	36	503	2,922	2,672	150	100	3,631,081	821,429	3,697,952	[illegible]
Suffolk	247	24	40	1,352	1,130	134	88	1,288,310	343,812	1,157,286	[illegible]
Sullivan	355	15	219	1,334	1,325	6	3	1,536,264	387,472	2,771,128	[illegible]
Tioga	328	52	118	1,355	1,318	26	11	1,543,200	423,873	1,570,197	[illegible]
Tompkins	364	58	138	1,668	1,509	129	30	1,867,650	518,930	2,345,680	[illegible]
Ulster	690	58	271	5,245	4,748	162	335	4,938,201	2,093,750	5,767,084	[illegible]
Warren	130	9	82	919	915	4	.....	1,376,240	334,004	1,372,077	[illegible]
Washington	427	28	211	2,714	2,453	172	89	3,561,980	928,398	2,927,615	[illegible]
Wayne	588	108	75	4,109	3,916	128	65	1,869,868	478,278	1,950,371	[illegible]
Westchester	567	89	63	9,162	7,152	893	1,117	8,464,058	3,666,800	8,307,681	[illegible]
Wyoming	350	48	98	1,117	1,023	79	15	1,103,335	237,401	1,562,249	[illegible]
Yates	208	26	49	761	684	68	9	699,167	191,230	738,654	[illegible]

THE STATE OF NORTH CAROLINA.

Counties.	Establishm'ts.	Steam-engines.	Water-wheels.	All hands.	Males above 16.	Females above 15.	Youth.	Capital. (Dollars.)	Wages. (Dollars.)	Materials. (Dollars.)	Products. (Dollars.)
Alamance	49	1	35	522	225	251	46	403,500	94,167	425,858	651,07[illegible]
Alexander	6	6	.....	25	11	14	.....	8,500	1,400	16,953	22,4[illegible]
Alleghany	19	.....	19	32	29	2	1	13,100	2,495	35,621	40,3[illegible]
Anson	43	1	13	95	86	2	7	79,116	17,873	110,493	162,5[illegible]
Ashe (a)	.....	.....	.....	.....	.....	.....	.....	.....	.....	.....	.....
Beaufort	45	9	11	349	343	.....	6	261,900	65,199	78,043	195,7[illegible]
Bertie	18	2	8	42	42	.....	.....	25,900	6,065	49,443	62,7[illegible]
Bladen	31	21	3	197	195	.....	2	207,300	33,550	137,988	223,64[illegible]
Brunswick	8	2	.....	52	52	.....	.....	41,200	12,015	86,626	143,16[illegible]
Buncombe	72	.....	39	150	145	5	.....	111,675	22,024	251,734	327,60[illegible]
Burke	52	2	40	103	101	2	.....	42,200	7,425	90,797	122,6[illegible]
Cabarrus	87	3	47	211	155	42	11	156,125	17,191	319,853	400,16[illegible]
Caldwell	51	2	39	87	87	.....	.....	38,450	4,050	76,952	92,6[illegible]
Camden	17	3	3	47	47	.....	.....	12,570	5,540	45,785	67,6[illegible]
Carteret	28	5	1	93	93	.....	.....	59,000	13,550	65,000	142,91[illegible]
Caswell	39	.....	15	166	142	15	9	56,731	10,485	98,677	157,4[illegible]
Catawba	16	1	11	89	42	37	10	78,900	10,874	63,670	98,7[illegible]
Chatham	69	4	35	146	146	.....	.....	139,000	15,575	283,106	337,2[illegible]

(a) Returned as having no manufactures.

TABLE C.—*Manufactures, by Totals of Counties, &c.*—1870—Continued.

THE STATE OF NORTH CAROLINA—Continued.

Counties.	Establishm'ts.	Steam-engines.	Water-wheels.	All hands.	Males above 16.	Females above 15.	Youth.	Capital. (*Dollars.*)	Wages. (*Dollars.*)	Materials. (*Dollars.*)	Products. (*Dollars.*)
Cherokee	12	1	3	51	51	.....	....	8, 125	5, 129	8, 925	17, 279
Chowan	13	3	1	29	29	.....	....	19, 555	2, 256	30, 544	42, 385
Clay (a)	....	....	....	....	....	.....	....	....	....	....	....
Cleaveland	84	2	57	199	173	21	5	124, 900	25, 625	203, 250	292, 196
Columbus	32	4	10	92	92	.....	....	48, 900	12, 550	165, 200	253, 680
Craven	58	23	1	276	267	.....	9	148, 700	70, 800	280, 743	501, 873
Cumberland	90	5	33	502	369	101	32	272, 070	101, 036	539, 563	828, 715
Currituck	7	6	1	39	31	4	1	36, 500	5, 250	8, 110	18, 300
Dare (a)	....	....	....	....	....	.....	....	....	....	....	....
Davidson	102	14	49	303	271	8	24	190, 740	48, 350	780, 305	903, 266
Davie	32	2	15	176	136	30	10	54, 945	17, 076	120, 507	171, 949
Duplin	42	3	35	90	89	1	....	26, 970	10, 622	159, 134	224, 646
Edgecombe	27	13	4	235	194	25	16	139, 225	43, 696	145, 934	287, 762
Forsyth	24	4	5	187	137	36	14	119, 600	40, 084	141, 743	240, 687
Franklin	29	2	25	70	69	.....	1	76, 050	9, 195	129, 535	176, 980
Gaston	19	1	13	165	81	72	12	95, 700	21, 875	152, 067	201, 037
Gates	4	....	3	16	16	.....	....	7, 000	1, 850	7, 920	12, 750
Granville	162	6	53	637	488	65	84	209, 095	40, 370	291, 470	467, 204
Greene	21	5	14	48	48	.....	....	18, 600	7, 950	53, 065	78, 937
Guilford	114	5	58	427	340	36	51	238, 443	45, 385	434, 371	598, 135
Halifax	25	5	17	62	62	.....	....	47, 000	4, 835	58, 228	72, 724
Harnett	23	....	12	94	92	1	1	25, 650	8, 404	86, 160	120, 400
Haywood	5	....	1	13	13	.....	....	6, 950	550	5, 210	8, 415
Henderson	60	1	30	101	94	2	5	26, 348	7, 126	48, 107	81, 403
Hertford	15	3	13	65	49	2	14	23, 550	12, 191	52, 993	78, 697
Hyde	8	1	2	14	13	.....	1	8, 550	1, 000	27, 740	33, 325
Iredell	31	2	16	135	69	33	33	86, 350	9, 945	143, 617	175, 300
Jackson	11	....	3	16	16	.....	....	6, 125	1, 246	9, 285	14, 530
Johnston	56	7	39	205	178	10	17	86, 920	21, 027	80, 589	136, 122
Jones	8	2	6	17	17	.....	....	3, 200	1, 170	17, 625	24, 450
Lenoir	16	6	7	41	41	.....	....	41, 400	11, 132	63, 110	94, 094
Lincoln	65	6	61	294	262	32	....	184, 625	69, 503	207, 515	319, 025
Macon (a)	....	....	....	....	....	.....	....	....	....	....	....
Madison	4	....	6	9	9	.....	....	8, 150	1, 132	26, 570	39, 787
Martin	18	4	9	198	198	.....	....	35, 000	23, 710	28, 500	63, 000
McDowell	21	1	15	45	45	.....	....	20, 880	4, 000	37, 046	46, 686
Mecklenburg	199	12	60	603	504	76	23	453, 568	122, 965	675, 495	1, 183, 302
Mitchell (a)	....	....	....	....	....	.....	....	....	....	....	....
Montgomery	53	....	45	127	106	6	15	62, 750	8, 415	84, 516	117, 626
Moore	124	1	60	225	223	2	....	92, 250	15, 580	220, 390	289, 042
Nash	5	....	3	6	6	.....	....	12, 000	710	2, 400	3, 500
New Hanover	93	16	6	869	822	16	31	913, 220	387, 300	1, 427, 829	2, 069, 804
Northampton	58	2	18	135	135	.....	....	45, 040	9, 400	80, 081	114, 316
Onslow	16	1	10	38	38	.....	....	20, 300	4, 815	46, 670	56, 042
Orange	92	1	46	296	227	39	30	201, 857	31, 120	276, 385	420, 970
Pasquotank	2	....	2	4	4	.....	....	10, 000	400	5, 200	8, 600
Perquimans	37	9	5	77	77	.....	....	33, 600	12, 330	58, 193	91, 775
Person	37	2	18	166	105	12	49	101, 250	9, 430	112, 130	145, 325
Pitt	32	10	5	99	95	.....	4	38, 900	18, 312	98, 600	178, 735
Polk	26	....	13	36	33	.....	3	12, 400	2, 725	28, 593	38, 503
Randolph	141	7	83	592	340	180	72	342, 680	76, 503	557, 087	718, 705
Richmond	37	....	14	316	304	10	2	93, 630	53, 010	177, 330	277, 820
Robeson	58	1	32	218	218	.....	....	73, 250	30, 960	155, 548	264, 878
Rockingham	44	2	14	278	148	62	68	93, 900	23, 442	151, 883	207, 451
Rowan	92	3	59	248	218	17	13	174, 155	36, 016	250, 711	358, 399
Rutherford	57	....	53	76	76	.....	....	46, 575	2, 650	102, 078	122, 747
Sampson	34	1	27	61	60	.....	1	16, 425	6, 679	25, 198	38, 603
Stanley	15	3	12	31	31	.....	....	42, 000	2, 940	91, 350	103, 850
Stokes	36	....	12	204	106	52	46	45, 700	6, 710	56, 487	79, 503
Surry	36	....	19	218	133	66	19	191, 450	18, 216	120, 231	182, 620
Transylvania (a)	....	....	....	....	....	.....	....	....	....	....	....
Tyrrell	17	6	....	83	83	.....	....	12, 325	5, 346	25, 109	33, 539
Union	61	1	45	89	88	.....	1	58, 050	12, 390	135, 823	193, 664
Wake	145	9	99	597	559	18	20	395, 935	171, 289	109, 395	808, 345
Warren	59	7	40	220	206	1	13	131, 800	32, 003	231, 126	343, 051
Washington	3	2	....	55	55	.....	....	20, 900	13, 500	70, 000	94, 400
Watauga (a)	....	....	....	....	....	.....	....	....	....	....	....
Wayne	17	5	3	68	63	.....	5	21, 725	5, 776	36, 720	55, 918
Wilkes	22	....	22	50	43	5	2	19, 375	2, 495	39, 206	47, 084
Wilson	46	6	26	136	134	.....	2	85, 000	28, 643	156, 086	247, 616
Yadkin	52	....	31	133	105	11	17	42, 400	5, 761	69, 507	97, 047
Yancy	8	....	1	8	8	.....	....	2, 600	....	4, 421	6, 308

(a) Returned as having no manufactures.

TABLE C.—*Manufactures, by Totals of Counties, &c.*—1870—Continued.

THE STATE OF OHIO.

Counties.	Establishm'ts.	Steam-engines.	Water-wheels.	All hands.	Males above 16.	Females above 15.	Youth.	Capital. (*Dollars.*)	Wages. (*Dollars.*)	Materials. (*Dollars.*)	Products. (*Dollars.*)
Adams	140	41	18	314	300	5	9	234, 351	31, 417	387, 543	558, [illegible]
Allen	259	62	10	984	906	67	11	569, 181	271, 331	364, 612	1, 092, [illegible]
Ashland	165	31	35	501	490	11	.....	429, 029	138, 394	558, 036	973, [illegible]
Ashtabula	375	115	52	998	925	66	7	755, 985	182, 994	1, 040, 794	1, 622, [illegible]
Athens	99	18	18	310	294	4	12	372, 885	68, 381	345, 768	531, [illegible]
Auglaize	87	33	9	454	431	17	6	383, 087	132, 431	473, 378	778, [illegible]
Belmont	278	64	33	1, 375	1, 246	39	90	1, 000, 945	478, 064	1, 223, 125	2, 057, [illegible]
Brown	178	42	18	624	596	8	20	445, 493	160, 471	500, 665	853, [illegible]
Butler	470	38	86	2, 474	2, 141	244	89	3, 219, 869	844, 165	3, 921, 381	6, 106, [illegible]
Carroll	144	20	8	312	307	4	1	139, 256	30, 290	151, 434	277, [illegible]
Champaign	217	34	31	751	687	55	9	696, 105	211, 905	830, 282	1, 343, [illegible]
Clark	196	32	35	1, 983	1, 835	87	61	2, 088, 949	963, 439	2, 036, 154	4, 132, [illegible]
Clermont	345	36	22	1, 121	863	170	88	330, 986	176, 084	548, 175	1, 098, [illegible]
Clinton	177	34	7	430	402	17	11	185, 925	61, 221	402, 570	641, [illegible]
Columbiana	427	86	35	1, 858	1, 583	108	157	1, 817, 555	600, 298	1, 504, 393	2, 807, [illegible]
Coshocton	172	11	29	439	419	14	6	221, 658	80, 770	393, 884	623, [illegible]
Crawford	350	59	4	1, 449	1, 373	62	14	1, 124, 959	401, 035	820, 672	1, 607, 911
Cuyahoga	149	274	55	10, 063	8, 690	791	582	13, 645, 018	4, 339, 065	16, 861, 357	27, 049, [illegible]
Darke	271	56	16	816	784	9	23	463, 651	144, 309	582, 240	1, 096, [illegible]
Defiance	107	30	14	554	542	10	2	440, 185	165, 968	599, 872	987, [illegible]
Delaware	282	52	23	1, 025	878	127	20	775, 315	242, 879	725, 059	1, 290, [illegible]
Erie	678	40	6	2, 801	2, 654	106	41	2, 533, 093	937, 911	2, 378, 069	4, 563, [illegible]
Fairfield	285	30	35	1, 095	983	97	15	611, 963	236, 736	760, 611	1, 342, [illegible]
Fayette	133	12	6	383	351	17	15	176, 610	85, 169	368, 991	613, [illegible]
Franklin	582	91	11	4, 588	3, 745	483	360	3, 379, 915	1, 580, 699	3, 523, 964	6, 978, [illegible]
Fulton	99	34	2	272	260	12	.....	213, 050	57, 713	316, 494	522, 115
Gallia	107	37	17	661	610	45	6	637, 536	130, 982	873, 857	1, 186, [illegible]
Geauga	192	31	38	461	410	51	.....	266, 825	45, 296	718, 191	951, [illegible]
Greene	264	26	51	1, 031	985	93	53	794, 878	260, 014	1, 277, 713	2, 017, [illegible]
Guernsey	187	26	17	410	377	29	4	257, 024	61, 825	339, 795	547, [illegible]
Hamilton	2, 469	511	36	37, 344	28, 450	6, 445	2, 449	42, 646, 152	15, 601, 289	44, 876, 148	78, 905, [illegible]
Hancock	196	62	9	650	645	3	2	395, 002	115, 640	672, 675	1, 011, 906
Hardin	112	57	1	509	496	6	7	333, 000	112, 229	424, 087	825, [illegible]
Harrison	152	25	12	365	343	18	4	239, 790	47, 205	339, 944	549, 691
Henry	113	31	13	457	419	11	27	232, 265	72, 775	309, 846	579, 221
Highland	172	33	11	537	507	22	8	477, 360	123, 203	533, 182	901, 112
Hocking	92	16	18	255	249	5	1	250, 400	58, 300	219, 742	399, 737
Holmes	78	7	23	196	184	8	4	214, 420	17, 869	204, 236	301, 794
Huron	206	54	23	801	787	9	5	942, 480	235, 135	1, 173, 034	1, 840, [illegible]
Jackson	122	34	16	1, 596	1, 556	11	26	1, 403, 915	491, 223	939, 205	1, 680, [illegible]
Jefferson	260	67	30	1, 670	1, 465	110	95	2, 371, 745	710, 815	2, 622, 727	4, 062, 017
Knox	280	31	39	1, 089	1, 022	59	8	805, 020	309, 282	1, 271, 283	2, 023, 680
Lake	249	34	32	705	657	21	11	589, 475	191, 533	801, 973	1, 322, [illegible]
Lawrence	116	58	4	2, 621	2, 559	8	57	2, 452, 850	1, 087, 945	2, 202, 282	4, 015, [illegible]
Licking	276	39	20	1, 039	961	45	33	872, 610	306, 993	928, 244	1, 625, [illegible]
Logan	236	29	36	635	612	21	2	480, 953	121, 391	604, 560	1, 001, [illegible]
Lorain	341	71	22	1, 251	1, 128	85	38	771, 105	298, 580	950, 517	1, 620, [illegible]
Lucas	209	10	21	2, 204	1, 823	162	219	3, 172, 155	936, 126	3, 891, 674	5, 889, [illegible]
Madison	117	13	9	328	282	36	10	175, 316	72, 546	202, 149	405, [illegible]
Mahoning	253	113	39	1, 980	1, 904	2	74	3, 432, 015	1, 133, 789	4, 843, 251	7, 313, [illegible]
Marion	135	31	3	393	362	28	3	298, 938	97, 751	357, 594	643, [illegible]
Medina	196	53	10	463	421	33	9	404, 428	83, 671	427, 607	747, 617
Meigs	225	78	33	1, 460	1, 382	35	43	1, 603, 162	462, 089	960, 181	1, 912, [illegible]
Mercer	157	25	7	331	298	16	17	146, 930	33, 125	196, 476	382, [illegible]
Miami	277	36	58	1, 243	1, 138	71	34	1, 456, 607	429, 896	1, 677, 887	2, 958, [illegible]
Monroe	298	38	24	495	456	13	26	226, 875	49, 217	371, 728	566, [illegible]
Montgomery	602	109	119	4, 873	4, 432	210	231	6, 624, 865	2, 114, 843	6, 647, 709	11, 474, [illegible]
Morgan	150	27	46	477	408	35	34	416, 360	97, 105	177, 361	748, [illegible]
Morrow	163	32	31	393	370	22	1	302, 248	82, 777	301, 826	581, [illegible]
Muskingum	331	58	47	2, 210	1, 956	169	85	1, 930, 745	837, 258	2, 078, 888	3, 092, 992
Noble	160	27	15	322	298	17	7	110, 947	23, 136	244, 046	326, [illegible]
Ottawa	80	34	.....	410	377	.....	33	304, 849	92, 734	285, 816	574, [illegible]
Paulding	39	19	8	261	255	.....	6	287, 650	65, 315	238, 317	379, [illegible]
Perry	125	17	9	302	290	1	11	139, 003	31, 867	216, 958	354, [illegible]
Pickaway	110	16	20	344	340	4	.....	312, 060	91, 755	404, 443	689, [illegible]
Pike	89	20	9	271	257	2	12	221, 489	47, 810	282, 282	414, [illegible]
Portage	238	53	29	1, 277	1, 222	41	14	805, 939	508, 281	970, 320	1, 858, [illegible]
Preble	202	31	33	721	671	32	18	495, 015	125, 506	571, 160	960, [illegible]
Putnam	112	37	6	289	279	1	9	219, 935	50, 325	223, 076	387, [illegible]
Richland	372	55	53	1, 551	1, 478	57	16	1, 783, 530	585, 879	1, 033, 545	3, 002, [illegible]
Ross	208	10	25	1, 475	1, 401	47	27	1, 154, 817	555, 958	1, 515, 742	2, 567, [illegible]
Sandusky	217	51	13	819	824	20	5	725, 817	242, 690	956, 900	1, 562, [illegible]
Scioto	178	16	9	1, 843	1, 695	85	63	1, 637, 710	782, 224	2, 175, 969	3, 302, 144
Seneca	236	67	11	1, 084	973	90	21	956, 345	282, 929	983, 109	[illegible]

TABLE C.—*Manufactures, by Totals of Counties, &c.*—1870—Continued.

THE STATE OF OHIO—Continued.

Counties.	Establishm'ts.	Steam-engines.	Water-wheels.	All hands.	Males above 16.	Females above 15.	Youth.	Capital. (*Dollars.*)	Wages. (*Dollars.*)	Materials. (*Dollars.*)	Products. (*Dollars.*)
Shelby	153	30	14	505	471	24	10	333, 385	106, 753	340, 990	696, 133
Stark	504	117	49	3, 767	3, 662	38	67	5, 753, 325	1, 624, 961	4, 650, 729	8, 712, 522
Summit	513	81	62	3, 427	3, 107	260	60	4, 289, 047	1, 528, 610	4, 615, 547	8, 769, 486
Trumbull	413	130	43	2, 307	2, 087	67	153	2, 331, 638	753, 459	3, 379, 445	5, 113, 915
Tuscarawas	372	39	50	1, 262	1, 232	26	4	1, 332, 865	396, 547	1, 206, 165	2, 106, 488
Union	120	31	10	359	349	6	4	244, 450	76, 122	324, 276	547, 914
Van Wert	92	38	7	427	375	5	47	329, 630	110, 052	427, 291	703, 005
Vinton	82	18	28	603	597	......	6	601, 075	147, 302	485, 172	736, 591
Warren	173	14	30	543	509	22	12	544, 432	131, 002	595, 389	940, 654
Washington	254	47	29	1, 063	1, 002	21	40	774, 638	390, 320	1, 457, 471	2, 341, 913
Wayne	347	71	38	1, 449	1, 357	82	10	1, 240, 250	370, 863	1, 295, 720	2, 457, 174
Williams	129	37	6	475	448	25	2	344, 060	90, 194	342, 940	583, 692
Wood	168	73	5	531	527	2	2	415, 140	100, 643	426, 308	733, 436
Wyandot	118	39	10	375	354	17	4	246, 665	76, 455	295, 173	524, 167

THE STATE OF OREGON.

Counties.	Establishm'ts.	Steam-engines.	Water-wheels.	All hands.	Males above 16.	Females above 15.	Youth.	Capital. (*Dollars.*)	Wages. (*Dollars.*)	Materials. (*Dollars.*)	Products. (*Dollars.*)
Baker	33	1	8	74	73	......	1	55, 675	24, 450	66, 254	154, 055
Benton	63	6	22	119	118	1	......	124, 750	30, 960	84, 315	186, 588
Clackamas	31	1	21	164	142	2	20	317, 100	96, 760	427, 290	638, 070
Clarke (*a*)	......	......	......	......	......	......	......	......	......	......	......
Clatsop	19	2	5	80	72	3	5	58, 940	24, 830	40, 953	100, 403
Columbia	14	4	5	59	58	1	......	93, 105	21, 395	32, 238	76, 433
Coos	8	3	......	71	71	......	......	101, 850	50, 325	92, 977	197, 041
Curry (*a*)	......	......	......	......	......	......	......	......	......	......	......
Douglas	56	2	25	112	110	2	......	152, 900	26, 050	98, 014	217, 970
Grant	22	2	7	54	54	......	......	86, 882	15, 017	36, 768	86, 545
Jackson	8	......	6	26	23	......	3	25, 250	10, 113	31, 906	53, 590
Josephine (*a*)	......	......	......	......	......	......	......	......	......	......	......
Lane	47	1	18	111	109	2	......	116, 325	22, 855	69, 235	164, 239
Lewis (*a*)	......	......	......	......	......	......	......	......	......	......	......
Linn	120	12	23	226	222	4	......	289, 617	64, 418	302, 075	577, 655
Marion	38	10	16	193	167	6	20	572, 200	103, 800	319, 440	689, 488
Multnomah	307	30	6	1, 142	1, 092	46	4	1, 573, 875	521, 247	1, 297, 847	2, 698, 817
Polk	47	3	12	96	94	......	2	127, 460	26, 292	88, 941	213, 491
Tillamook	1	......	1	1	1	......	......	1, 500	......	300	750
Umatilla	13	3	4	57	57	......	......	31, 125	21, 675	32, 572	90, 775
Umpqua (*a*)	......	......	......	......	......	......	......	......	......	......	......
Union	21	2	11	56	56	......	......	139, 500	17, 450	80, 019	167, 731
Wasco	14	1	5	35	35	......	......	30, 000	6, 076	14, 917	30, 617
Washington	32	......	19	61	59	......	2	74, 550	5, 607	44, 847	90, 097
Yam Hill	75	5	22	147	140	......	7	404, 185	27, 853	258, 848	443, 032

THE STATE OF PENNSYLVANIA.

Counties.	Establishm'ts.	Steam-engines.	Water-wheels.	All hands.	Males above 16.	Females above 15.	Youth.	Capital. (*Dollars.*)	Wages. (*Dollars.*)	Materials. (*Dollars.*)	Products. (*Dollars.*)
Adams	502	14	169	1, 214	1, 172	23	19	686, 028	123, 801	863, 892	1, 415, 126
Allegheny	1, 844	595	15	34, 228	29, 139	1, 723	3, 366	54, 303, 474	18, 493, 124	52, 165, 657	88, 780, 414
Armstrong	276	65	59	1, 806	1, 654	61	91	3, 265, 233	732, 544	2, 901, 551	4, 337, 357
Beaver	500	64	51	2, 412	1, 984	172	256	2, 562, 430	771, 697	2, 049, 913	4, 024, 083
Bedford	369	14	131	943	915	22	6	1, 372, 515	182, 020	1, 113, 090	1, 587, 024
Berks	1, 414	310	205	8, 991	7, 671	701	619	11, 182, 603	2, 711, 231	10, 646, 049	16, 243, 433
Blair	440	49	79	3, 624	3, 453	70	101	4, 145, 430	1, 485, 501	3, 704, 301	6, 428, 366
Bradford	531	69	262	1, 531	1, 497	18	16	1, 636, 705	350, 162	1, 645, 690	2, 738, 395
Bucks	739	41	183	3, 425	2, 770	577	78	2, 808, 968	817, 292	2, 909, 773	4, 732, 118
Butler	387	59	65	808	767	34	7	671, 189	97, 474	885, 836	1, 330, 032
Cambria	373	158	164	3, 464	3, 438	8	18	2, 377, 072	1, 501, 908	6, 201, 631	8, 641, 813
Cameron	44	20	10	325	317	3	5	420, 645	127, 090	541, 951	896, 810
Carbon	161	16	64	1, 612	1, 515	55	42	2, 460, 250	758, 397	1, 846, 802	2, 955, 783
Centre	362	32	122	1, 451	1, 375	26	50	1, 830, 346	462, 486	1, 876, 951	3, 047, 674
Chester	996	54	354	6, 548	5, 985	292	261	5, 277, 501	1, 997, 615	7, 650, 940	11, 494, 543
Clarion	279	47	107	974	945	22	7	785, 776	194, 910	793, 134	1, 355, 506
Clearfield	245	33	98	726	721	1	4	1, 298, 857	182, 405	609, 792	1, 109, 405
Clinton	241	63	85	1, 532	1, 482	40	10	978, 005	628, 744	2, 153, 087	3, 646, 586
Columbia	258	26	143	901	839	17	45	1, 200, 735	312, 474	2, 021, 374	2, 706, 990
Crawford	743	160	163	3, 646	3, 491	107	48	4, 091, 166	1, 905, 603	5, 887, 388	10, 1[illegible]

(*a*) Returned as having no manufactures.

TABLE C.—*Manufactures, by Totals of Counties, &c.*—1870—Continued.

THE STATE OF PENNSYLVANIA—Continued.

Counties.	Establishm'ts.	Steam-engines.	Water-wheels.	All hands.	Males above 16.	Females above 15.	Youth.	Capital. (*Dollars.*)	Wages. (*Dollars.*)	Materials. (*Dollars.*)	Products. (*Dollars.*)
Cumberland	449	39	103	1,669	1,434	201	34	2,144,945	385,150	2,030,789	[illegible]
Dauphin	587	167	102	4,865	4,451	234	180	6,357,520	1,928,486	9,248,5[illegible]	[illegible]
Delaware	314	79	72	6,448	3,811	1,503	1,131	5,927,187	2,155,554	6,845,504	[illegible]
Elk	81	36	47	661	657	1	3	1,070,000	217,388	921,679	[illegible]
Erie	928	173	161	4,664	4,164	253	247	5,717,993	1,927,184	5,646,425	[illegible]
Fayette	432	90	104	2,003	1,881	66	56	2,509,875	700,022	1,929,278	[illegible]
Forest	37	7	25	256	243	.....	13	506,640	92,192	171,302	[illegible]
Franklin	529	37	170	2,106	1,971	81	54	2,438,271	430,138	2,258,792	[illegible]
Fulton	65	9	31	166	165	.....	1	387,810	36,073	337,418	[illegible]
Greene	162	74	92	421	402	10	9	454,008	81,970	323,5[illegible]	[illegible]
Huntingdon	324	21	150	1,359	1,249	9	101	2,087,052	353,507	1,590,506	[illegible]
Indiana	173	66	129	1,086	1,044	14	28	918,220	199,321	822,4[illegible]	[illegible]
Jefferson	232	49	112	700	695	3	2	743,160	153,148	677,792	[illegible]
Juniata	204	6	80	395	380	13	2	374,550	38,569	437,792	[illegible]
Lancaster	1,616	122	361	8,166	6,479	1,089	598	9,504,102	2,037,841	9,100,637	[illegible]
Lawrence	181	44	47	1,432	1,335	56	41	1,579,135	616,411	2,382,635	[illegible]
Lebanon	481	52	65	2,229	2,099	75	55	2,876,725	627,258	2,646,049	[illegible]
Lehigh	694	107	139	5,345	4,857	296	192	10,276,247	2,361,339	10,226,622	[illegible]
Luzerne	886	171	351	8,232	7,702	190	340	9,380,272	3,012,48[illegible]	9,518,72[illegible]	[illegible]
Lycoming	608	131	218	4,106	4,025	66	15	7,875,938	1,408,22[illegible]	5,320,2[illegible]	[illegible]
McKean	36	19	28	227	227	.....	.....	288,100	60,870	195,306	[illegible]
Mercer	458	161	129	2,435	2,301	65	69	3,023,677	1,079,278	4,347,036	[illegible]
Mifflin	194	27	54	693	668	8	17	1,058,054	220,859	1,057,371	[illegible]
Monroe	254	14	100	815	783	16	16	1,525,275	251,004	1,477,036	[illegible]
Montgomery	1,089	170	190	8,475	6,114	1,620	741	9,050,983	2,901,448	10,674,495	[illegible]
Montour	158	54	15	2,290	2,191	30	69	2,745,216	1,011,858	3,181,116	[illegible]
Northampton	655	81	140	5,765	5,253	329	183	7,099,283	2,493,226	8,166,049	[illegible]
Northumberland	424	55	58	1,941	1,812	69	60	2,348,186	731,792	2,744,803	[illegible]
Perry	282	35	103	1,037	951	18	68	1,438,174	299,300	1,743,001	[illegible]
Philadelphia	8,184	1611	59	137496	95,421	32,687	9,388	174,016,674	58,780,130	190,825,713	322,004,517
Pike	67	1	49	259	255	.....	4	552,900	88,902	470,271	[illegible]
Potter	41	13	16	163	159	4	.....	195,550	39,639	120,490	[illegible]
Schuylkill	844	88	80	5,042	4,606	303	133	4,420,081	1,699,954	5,734,578	[illegible]
Snyder	98	9	47	307	293	7	7	117,638	52,672	434,818	[illegible]
Somerset	496	15	160	1,128	1,100	12	16	731,309	133,966	735,375	[illegible]
Sullivan	83	8	61	247	247	.....	.....	367,555	69,743	209,740	[illegible]
Susquehanna	376	40	155	1,636	1,612	19	5	6,501,315	643,955	1,865,795	[illegible]
Tioga	282	48	91	1,123	1,099	22	2	1,025,203	326,501	1,186,270	[illegible]
Union	106	12	41	664	637	17	10	751,463	203,007	673,171	[illegible]
Venango	278	65	43	1,061	1,018	32	11	1,122,640	551,847	3,304,681	[illegible]
Warren	450	100	212	1,773	1,729	44	.....	2,549,510	491,805	1,532,438	[illegible]
Washington	402	108	55	1,230	1,119	56	55	1,018,054	309,661	1,152,623	[illegible]
Wayne	254	24	176	1,488	1,460	8	20	2,485,775	493,466	2,317,792	[illegible]
Westmoreland	390	108	55	1,201	1,146	18	37	1,614,225	275,085	1,649,660	[illegible]
Wyoming	194	11	101	491	491	.....	.....	505,005	120,515	672,133	[illegible]
York	1,111	63	350	4,027	3,667	226	134	3,251,490	934,928	4,029,981	[illegible]

THE STATE OF RHODE ISLAND.

Counties.	Establishm'ts.	Steam-engines.	Water-wheels.	All hands.	Males above 16.	Females above 15.	Youth.	Capital. (*Dollars.*)	Wages. (*Dollars.*)	Materials. (*Dollars.*)	Products. (*Dollars.*)
Bristol	71	26	1	2,337	1,311	739	287	2,006,400	807,865	3,232,231	[illegible]
Kent	168	31	73	4,934	2,385	1,513	1,036	5,951,025	1,624,842	9,801,377	[illegible]
Newport	184	22	6	1,314	1,015	226	73	993,350	550,866	1,311,183	[illegible]
Providence	1,303	294	268	37,160	22,072	10,953	4,135	54,485,967	15,097,233	55,117,483	[illegible]
Washington	121	26	108	3,732	2,021	1,381	330	3,120,580	1,273,450	3,661,835	[illegible]

THE STATE OF SOUTH CAROLINA.

Counties.	Establishm'ts.	Steam-engines.	Water-wheels.	All hands.	Males above 16.	Females above 15.	Youth.	Capital. (*Dollars.*)	Wages. (*Dollars.*)	Materials. (*Dollars.*)	Products. (*Dollars.*)
Abbeville	102	6	25	197	196	.....	1	114,646	24,470	180,648	[illegible]
Anderson	78	.....	40	225	168	38	19	138,650	28,958	409,854	[illegible]
Barnwell	154	15	107	408	408	.....	.....	176,825	38,241	204,289	[illegible]
Beaufort	31	10	4	126	120	3	3	74,350	17,575	41,913	[illegible]
Charleston	224	54	2	2,579	2,493	23	63	1,538,539	616,962	1,264,731	[illegible]
Chester	33	1	13	74	74	.....	.....	38,300	13,966	192,923	[illegible]
Chesterfield	69	2	62	112	110	.....	2	125,450	8,680	102,862	[illegible]
Clarendon	20	1	11	32	31	.....	1	29,156	4,935	39,740	[illegible]
Colleton	12	8	.....	86	85	1	.....	23,850	18,255	23,011	[illegible]

TABLE C.—*Manufactures, by Totals of Counties, &c.*—1870—Continued.

THE STATE OF SOUTH CAROLINA—Continued.

Counties.	Establishm'ts.	Steam-engines.	Water-wheels.	All hands.	Males above 16.	Females above 15.	Youth.	Capital. (Dollars.)	Wages. (Dollars.)	Materials. (Dollars.)	Products. (Dollars.)
Darlington	23	6	11	80	80			99, 550	28, 990	78, 415	121, 298
Edgefield	64	20	47	780	397	233	150	1, 103, 250	231, 249	586, 779	1, 316, 807
Fairfield	87	4	11	144	144			32, 110	10, 560	44, 715	98, 977
Georgetown	12	6		176	150	4	13	59, 100	35, 975	232, 550	376, 575
Greenville	48	17	11	329	164	103	62	208, 285	45, 893	256, 402	351, 875
Horry	28	3	11	174	154		20	82, 075	31, 495	198, 980	265, 096
Kershaw	6		3	11	11			6, 850	1, 770	5, 013	11, 122
Lancaster	26	1	12	46	45		1	31, 118	6, 387	92, 830	114, 160
Laurens	65		37	124	112	8	4	79, 500	14, 285	159, 023	220, 645
Lexington	34	6	32	206	123	60	20	184, 850	21, 430	164, 585	265, 143
Marion	17	2	6	131	122	5	4	83, 800	16, 270	91, 515	158, 317
Marlborough	23	1	17	53	53			28, 240	7, 350	68, 000	84, 742
Newberry	9	3	6	18	18			16, 400	2, 375	99, 500	109, 650
Oconee	18	3	6	70	67		3	17, 750	6, 550	19, 057	32, 851
Orangeburg	23	4	10	61	60		1	17, 935	8, 985	39, 225	75, 354
Pickens	56	1	40	93	84	6	3	32, 380	2, 105	84, 668	100, 051
Richland	69	22	29	493	481		12	537, 129	112, 191	263, 899	536, 999
Spartanburg	95		62	431	259	91	81	247, 445	49, 910	292, 369	457, 152
Sumter	44	6	19	237	234	3		59, 051	30, 843	107, 997	178, 257
Union	55	2	39	125	125			93, 680	16, 939	227, 300	318, 076
Williamsburgh	17	4		369	369			62, 650	62, 661	102, 357	226, 658
York	42	4	18	154	153		1	97, 585	28, 380	180, 582	238, 297

THE STATE OF TENNESSEE.

Counties.	Establishm'ts.	Steam-engines.	Water-wheels.	All hands.	Males above 16.	Females above 15.	Youth.	Capital. (Dollars.)	Wages. (Dollars.)	Materials. (Dollars.)	Products. (Dollars.)
Anderson	22	2	15	43	42		1	25, 350	3, 303	49, 411	66, 944
Bedford	30	8	10	241	191	35	15	139, 700	42, 227	243, 318	358, 542
Benton	21	2	3	50	50			23, 705	7, 370	75, 188	102, 924
Bledsoe	26		7	40	40			13, 905	1, 988	34, 546	46, 879
Blount	58	2	29	161	129	28	4	188, 437	24, 871	210, 928	327, 990
Bradley	17		12	41	39		2	52, 500	7, 750	164, 565	203, 705
Campbell	26	3	14	59	59			25, 605	6, 595	27, 221	44, 967
Cannon	2			3	3			3, 000	400	4, 283	6, 032
Carroll	100	6	33	157	154	1	2	74, 746	11, 685	374, 232	476, 646
Carter	32		24	127	124	1	2	88, 600	15, 000	110, 234	161, 613
Cheatham	35	15	9	131	131			123, 700	24, 360	102, 518	191, 731
Claiborne	41		29	75	74		1	22, 500	7, 661	63, 901	92, 543
Cocke	54	1	31	100	100			41, 630	10, 620	93, 976	141, 867
Coffee	60	5	13	143	134	8	1	205, 278	20, 816	210, 770	345, 098
Cumberland	24	1	13	36	36			14, 250	2, 400	25, 300	35, 093
Davidson (a)	373	82	12	2, 613	2, 311	129	173	2, 513, 677	1, 059, 255	2, 849, 745	5, 331, 293
Decatur	20	2	9	249	187	21	41	213, 900	72, 155	120, 751	277, 367
De Kalb	44	5	10	94	90	2	2	69, 847	14, 876	191, 968	256, 079
Dickson	31	9	4	308	288		20	190, 150	125, 650	141, 469	333, 610
Dyer	24	9		96	95		1	71, 425	16, 415	107, 529	157, 268
Fayette	29	2	5	59	59			56, 400	10, 260	122, 870	173, 200
Fentress	14		9	16	16			4, 340	770	22, 969	29, 800
Franklin	59	7	25	187	160	17	10	152, 143	35, 025	198, 810	296, 392
Gibson	232	31	11	549	517	11	21	275, 687	110, 994	680, 987	1, 148, 022
Giles	166	20	15	506	438	39	29	229, 994	69, 167	338, 918	592, 294
Grainger	29	2	18	67	67			46, 150	9, 144	57, 038	81, 450
Greene	106	2	60	301	297	2	2	200, 440	66, 571	243, 458	436, 042
Grundy	13	3	1	81	61		20	25, 450	13, 150	26, 825	47, 250
Hamilton	58	13	21	541	540	1		475, 155	253, 133	639, 677	1, 012, 335
Hancock	21		14	36	33	3		20, 310	1, 367	28, 469	37, 541
Hardeman	33	5	25	102	101		1	92, 400	19, 630	297, 475	399, 480
Hardin	39	9	12	133	125	4	4	70, 085	23, 761	129, 641	201, 340
Hawkins	22	3	9	49	45	4		47, 400	8, 489	55, 929	84, 439
Haywood	33	12	1	106	106			94, 900	31, 740	67, 690	140, 796
Henderson	49	13	15	88	79		9	42, 310	6, 137	82, 907	118, 419
Henry	92	15	27	281	218	53	10	184, 481	50, 507	241, 127	391, 745
Hickman	23	4	9	79	56	16	7	116, 145	11, 955	133, 336	184, 500
Humphreys	25	6	5	95	87	6	2	143, 850	19, 105	115, 988	196, 744
Jackson	16	7	4	33	33			19, 100	1, 986	49, 894	73, 972
Jefferson	46	6	25	151	148		3	368, 055	17, 114	112, 598	180, 178

(*a*) In addition to the industries of this table, the assistant marshal of Davidson County returned the State penitentiary as an establishment employing 640 hands, (principally convicts,) and three steam-engines of 125 horse-power, using materials of the value of $280,000, and producing agricultural implements, furniture, iron castings, machinery, rope and bagging, and stone quarried, to the value of *$500,000.*

TABLE C.—*Manufactures, by Totals of Counties, &c.*—1870—Continued.

THE STATE OF TENNESSEE—Continued.

Counties.	Establishm'ts.	Steam-engines.	Water-wheels.	All hands.	Males above 16.	Females above 15.	Youth.	Capital. (Dollars.)	Wages. (Dollars.)	Materials. (Dollars.)	Products. (Dollars.)
Johnson	42	....	34	103	101	2	....	44,075	14,359	57,738	[illegible]
Knox	82	11	38	436	405	15	16	449,915	150,625	542,946	[illegible]
Lake	4	1	....	9	9	....	....	2,400	1,140	11,240	[illegible]
Lauderdale	77	10	1	148	145	1	2	55,025	21,644	106,[illegible]	[illegible]
Lawrence	37	....	20	309	132	123	54	306,150	52,560	193,659	[illegible]
Lewis	15	....	6	22	21	....	1	5,400	540	9,680	[illegible]
Lincoln	185	17	44	507	479	18	10	223,236	56,564	504,947	[illegible]
Macon	31	7	9	69	69	....	....	32,275	5,028	63,199	[illegible]
Madison	107	12	10	392	377	15	....	137,265	82,935	136,385	[illegible]
Marion	5	3	2	21	21	....	....	20,000	6,280	29,000	[illegible]
Marshall	54	13	12	162	162	....	....	63,130	12,080	178,225	[illegible]
Maury	158	28	21	480	454	10	16	390,000	77,446	261,087	[illegible]
McMinn	50	2	42	174	140	34	....	130,650	31,232	195,604	[illegible]
McNairy	3	....	....	5	5	....	....	1,275	644	1,[illegible]	3,[illegible]
Meigs	13	1	5	27	27	....	....	14,705	2,100	32,614	[illegible]
Monroe	86	1	35	118	116	2	[illegible]	49,810	4,650	85,486	[illegible]
Montgomery	108	22	19	506	499	7	....	408,675	158,077	712,613	1,[illegible]
Morgan	7	1	2	19	16	2	1	5,950	2,170	9,468	[illegible]
Obion	41	14	4	124	122	....	2	80,170	25,882	92,315	[illegible]
Overton	15	3	7	40	38	2	....	11,500	2,105	18,375	[illegible]
Perry	21	2	8	49	46	2	1	66,750	16,340	165,201	[illegible]
Polk	16	1	10	216	215	....	1	188,100	67,070	466,480	[illegible]
Putnam (a)	....	....	....	....	....	....	....	....	....	....	....
Rhea	27	....	21	54	54	....	....	25,950	4,410	81,125	[illegible]
Roane	144	14	63	330	324	19	6	256,280	56,080	243,264	[illegible]
Robertson	121	26	17	352	351	....	1	250,300	53,436	300,541	[illegible]
Rutherford	64	9	17	252	235	....	17	187,250	71,945	466,188	[illegible]
Scott	2	....	1	2	2	....	....	1,400	....	620	[illegible]
Sequatchie	3	....	3	6	6	....	....	8,000	750	17,625	[illegible]
Sevier	9	1	6	21	21	....	....	19,020	1,450	22,863	[illegible]
Shelby	757	76	2	3,236	2,858	334	44	3,155,957	1,627,438	2,738,062	[illegible]
Smith	29	10	7	67	66	....	1	47,750	4,824	93,547	[illegible]
Stewart	22	8	4	434	430	....	4	664,055	106,497	192,810	[illegible]
Sullivan	112	5	78	225	224	1	....	124,850	12,908	185,212	[illegible]
Sumner	135	25	14	412	339	43	30	285,750	73,016	440,688	[illegible]
Tipton	37	21	1	106	106	....	....	46,000	23,644	119,664	[illegible]
Union	15	....	9	36	36	....	....	24,730	4,900	53,732	78,085
Van Buren	2	....	2	4	4	....	....	1,150	250	6,323	7,500
Warren	80	5	45	288	212	41	35	248,075	53,212	270,529	402,302
Washington	97	1	59	270	269	....	1	102,713	33,901	138,100	224,354
Wayne	69	12	30	230	220	3	7	248,137	55,318	293,929	434,365
Weakley	20	11	12	128	105	22	1	100,800	27,550	82,972	153,042
White	41	1	18	66	64	....	2	54,795	4,510	124,285	162,465
Williamson	76	17	5	277	270	....	7	102,621	58,556	180,025	329,533
Wilson	147	29	11	424	395	12	17	286,534	69,191	703,985	1,167,071

THE STATE OF TEXAS.

Counties.	Establishm'ts.	Steam-engines.	Water-wheels.	All hands.	Males above 16.	Females above 15.	Youth.	Capital. (Dollars.)	Wages. (Dollars.)	Materials. (Dollars.)	Products. (Dollars.)
Anderson	47	10	7	154	138	2	14	61,619	28,610	80,540	152,3[illegible]
Angelina (a)	....	....	....	....	....	....	....	....	....	....	....
Atascosa (a)	....	....	....	....	....	....	....	....	....	....	....
Austin	105	22	....	213	192	8	13	70,765	16,900	81,198	164,457
Bandera	4	....	3	8	8	....	....	4,500	940	4,370	7,480
Bastrop	34	28	....	184	158	10	16	100,300	45,873	65,075	151,880
Bee (a)	....	....	....	....	....	....	....	....	....	....	....
Bell	45	5	7	90	90	....	....	87,125	16,290	57,024	110,385
Bexar	25	3	3	75	75	....	....	56,390	27,510	41,378	132,000
Bexar District	4	....	....	10	10	....	....	14,940	4,440	14,600	18,440
Blanco (a)	....	....	....	....	....	....	....	....	....	....	....
Bosque	13	2	1	30	30	....	....	12,950	3,600	40,124	57,011
Bowie	7	2	....	15	15	....	....	8,300	1,900	1,440	8,405
Brazoria	3	3	....	54	52	....	2	13,000	17,500	48,615	133,400
Brazos	11	1	....	63	59	....	4	39,200	19,400	22,540	60,960
Brown (a)	....	....	....	....	....	....	....	....	....	....	....
Buchanan (a)	....	....	....	....	....	....	....	....	....	....	....
Burleson	10	1	....	18	18	....	....	2,000	1,430	6,156	12,[illegible]
Burnet	16	2	3	27	27	....	....	13,725	1,450	16,940	27,[illegible]
Caldwell	13	2	5	37	36	....	1	21,200	8,785	23,260	42,[illegible]

(a) Returned as having no manufactures.

TABLE C.—*Manufactures, by Totals of Counties, &c.*—1870—Continued.

THE STATE OF TEXAS—Continued.

Counties.	Establishm'ts.	Steam-engines.	Water-wheels.	All hands.	Males above 16.	Females above 15.	Youth.	Capital. (Dollars.)	Wages. (Dollars.)	Materials. (Dollars.)	Products. (Dollars.)
Calhoun	33	6	....	142	140	....	2	83, 150	39, 664	248, 276	351, 989
Cameron	83	....	....	142	132	5	5	41, 275	20, 125	40, 425	100, 135
Cass (a)											
Chambers (a)											
Cherokee	5	....	1	9	9	....	....	2, 750	1, 300	2, 200	5, 950
Clay (a)											
Coleman (a)											
Collin	46	3	....	78	78	....	....	50, 195	6, 845	74, 800	127, 220
Colorado	29	4	....	58	56	....	2	27, 700	8, 516	34, 601	69, 948
Comal	84	2	7	202	168	19	15	147, 640	28, 647	99, 696	180, 026
Comanche (a)											
Cook	4	1	....	15	15	....	....	15, 500	2, 500	41, 000	56, 000
Coryell (a)											
Dallas	44	13	1	118	118	....	....	106, 322	25, 715	174, 592	279, 983
Davis	22	12	1	59	59	....	....	31, 600	6, 540	42, 000	64, 100
Dawson (a)											
Demmit (a)											
Denton	4	2	....	9	9	....	....	27, 800	2, 100	29, 000	34, 150
De Witt	39	9	....	68	66	1	1	34, 962	5, 651	54, 851	93, 850
Duval (a)											
Eastland (a)											
Ellis	21	8	3	94	94	....	....	57, 700	32, 700	108, 370	178, 672
El Paso	1	1	....	6	4	2	....	4, 000	1, 500	6, 000	8, 400
Encinal (a)											
Erath	4	1	....	8	8	....	....	6, 262	1, 100	8, 829	13, 065
Falls	24	7	....	65	65	....	....	20, 700	8, 737	27, 584	62, 950
Fannin	54	4	....	99	99	....	....	36, 408	10, 175	61, 322	106, 333
Fayette	41	26	....	129	129	....	....	28, 375	15, 771	53, 606	124, 198
Fort Bend	36	11	....	243	161	20	62	62, 745	9, 017	91, 929	107, 594
Freestone	24	11	....	57	57	....	....	35, 250	3, 800	56, 800	80, 450
Frio (a)											
Galveston	91	12	....	533	492	13	28	710, 950	253, 770	678, 989	1, 214, 814
Gillespie	7	2	....	27	24	....	3	26, 000	3, 740	51, 200	67, 106
Goliad	1	....	....	2	2	....	....	1, 000	....	1, 338	1, 600
Gonzales	28	6	....	78	75	....	3	36, 750	15, 090	59, 190	130, 360
Grayson	53	10	2	119	117	....	2	97, 483	16, 173	146, 547	210, 325
Grimes	26	5	....	92	92	....	....	29, 300	23, 800	19, 050	79, 730
Guadalupe	26	7	1	60	60	....	....	20, 875	5, 910	35, 340	67, 015
Hamilton	1	1	....	4	4	....	....	3, 000	1, 000	600	3, 120
Hardin	3	....	....	5	5	....	....	700	500	700	2, 900
Harris	64	19	1	583	472	34	77	723, 890	160, 246	273, 348	578, 707
Harrison	25	10	....	95	95	....	....	43, 750	27, 590	27, 899	124, 904
Hays	10	1	5	18	18	....	....	12, 000	1, 210	8, 140	19, 846
Henderson	23	4	3	51	44	....	7	34, 625	4, 420	24, 406	49, 037
Hidalgo (a)											
Hill	26	....	2	36	36	....	....	25, 800	5, 250	29, 450	64, 600
Hood	3	....	1	7	7	....	....	6, 750	600	15, 750	20, 200
Hopkins	36	15	....	85	85	....	....	58, 010	13, 148	76, 179	119, 564
Houston (a)											
Hunt	34	3	....	59	57	....	2	17, 718	4, 237	134. 401	176, 286
Jack	9	....	....	16	16	....	....	5, 375	1, 300	5, 880	18, 850
Jackson (a)											
Jasper	10	....	3	16	16	....	....	5, 950	1, 290	4, 833	10, 646
Jefferson	14	2	....	63	59	4	....	20, 500	8, 035	11, 270	31, 652
Johnson (a)											
Karnes (a)											
Kaufman	27	3	....	40	40	....	....	14, 460	3, 300	14, 820	33, 110
Kendall	18	1	1	30	30	....	....	11, 645	1, 585	6, 146	14, 685
Kerr	11	1	5	30	30	....	....	18, 200	4, 860	23, 855	34, 651
Kimble (a)											
Kinney (a)											
Lamar	59	5	....	164	153	....	11	64, 405	20, 289	66, 291	131, 538
Lampasas	10	....	3	29	26	....	3	6, 785	1, 375	6, 527	14, 930
La Salle (a)											
Lavaca	20	4	2	35	35	....	....	19, 400	4, 568	10, 449	24, 915
Leon	12	1	2	19	19	....	....	5, 400	815	23, 310	30, 500
Liberty	13	2	....	43	43	....	....	14, 425	1, 160	6, 066	11, 455
Limestone	13	4	....	22	22	....	....	16, 350	2, 550	8, 590	15, 757
Live Oak (a)											
Llano (a)											
Madison	10	3	....	12	12	....	....	4, 100	915	5, 145	9, 700
Marion	33	13	....	298	291	7	....	338, 962	171, 425	410, 051	756, 250

(a) Returned as having no manufactures.

TABLE C.—*Manufactures, by Totals of Counties, &c.*—1870—Continued.

THE STATE OF TEXAS—Continued.

Counties.	Establishm'ts.	Steam-engines.	Water-wheels.	All hands.	Males above 16.	Females above 15.	Youth.	Capital. (Dollars.)	Wages. (Dollars.)	Materials. (Dollars.)	Products. (Dollars.)
Mason (a)											
Matagorda	7	1		64	60	1	3	35, 750	8, 830	38, 709	[illegible]
Maverick	1			1	1			150		300	[illegible]
McCulloch (a)											
McLennan	43	11		183	180		3	118, 000	58, 270	151, 150	[illegible]
McMullen (a)											
Medina	4	1	1	10	10			12, 600	2, 160	11, 151	[illegible]
Menard (a)											
Milam	32	10		84	82		2	38,	7, 332	39, 997	[illegible]
Montague	1	1		2	2			4,	300	800	[illegible]
Montgomery	39	17	4	170	154	11	5	80,	38, 970	64, 070	[illegible]
Nacogdoches	7	3	1	14	14			8, 100	1, 490	9, 550	[illegible]
Navarro	16	12		49	49			38, 572	6, 935	130, 592	[illegible]
Newton (a)											
Nueces	10	4		109	108	1		62, 320	24, 050	109, 861	[illegible]
Orange	7	2		74	72		2	18, 650	19, 225	22, 700	[illegible]
Palo Pinto (a)											
Panola	13	7		21	21			14, 000	3, 200	20, 650	[illegible]
Parker	10	2		34	34			33, 350	7, 200	47, 475	[illegible]
Polk	27	5	6	50	50			20, 675	2, 095	17, 447	[illegible]
Presidio (a)											
Red River	45	17		165	165			89,	39, 585	73, 037	[illegible]
Refugio	13	6		89	87	2		101,	38, 450	418, 155	[illegible]
Robertson	20	3		78	78			28,	10, 450	87, 600	[illegible]
Rusk	38	10	2	83	83			40,	10, 240	32, 128	[illegible]
Sabine	17	1	3	27	27			15,	2, 500	22, 405	[illegible]
San Augustine	18	2	2	34	34			16,	2, 973	15, 817	[illegible]
San Patricio	2	1		6	6			5,	2, 100	70, 230	[illegible]
San Saba	5	1		8	8			9,		2, 227	[illegible]
Shackleford (a)											
Shelby	17	4	1	53	51		2	22,	4, 509	28, 250	40, 585
Smith	38	8	6	129	129			69,	20, 080	76, 920	121, 175
Starr (a)											
Stephens (a)											
Tarrant	27	4	1	48	47	1		13,	2, 050	21, 030	37, 625
Throckmorton (a)											
Titus	20	13	1	97	94		3	59,	16, 850	49, 150	82, 670
Travis	91	11	3	303	286	4	13	178,	121, 252	187, 545	464, 065
Trinity (a)											
Tyler	7		1	11	11			4,	1, 375	4, 515	8, 335
Upshur	18	6	2	70	70			29,	17, 618	44, 496	108, 500
Uvalde	2	1		8	8			10,	3, 000	11, 500	23, 000
Van Zandt	14	3	1	39	39			20,	9, 668	45, 561	83, 440
Victoria	25	4		103	98	1	4	51,	15, 833	107, 595	149, 875
Walker	13	5		214	199	11	4	160,	45, 558	175, 660	333, 530
Washington	39	16	1	90	89		1	48,	20, 345	58, 437	121, 150
Webb	1			2	2				120	90	340
Wharton (a)											
Williamson	11		1	15	15			6, 700	800	26, 185	37, 730
Wilson (a)											
Wise (a)											
Wood	36	12	5	134	129		5	89, 620	36, 520	105, 514	312, 855
Young	1			5	5			4, 000	300	475	900
Zapata (a)											
Zavala	1		1	1	1			500		300	300

THE TERRITORY OF UTAH.

Counties.	Establishm'ts.	Steam-engines.	Water-wheels.	All hands.	Males above 16.	Females above 15.	Youth.	Capital. (Dollars.)	Wages. (Dollars.)	Materials. (Dollars.)	Products. (Dollars.)
Beaver	18	2	10	70	50	20		77, 700	23, 300	148, 945	216, 450
Box Elder	21	1	4	69	67		2	55, 250	23, 065	60, 378	94, 100
Cache	36		17	62	62			46, 350	8, 371	42, 407	75, 222
Davis	15		6	23	23			71, 350	6, 500	21, 450	37, 995
Iron	12	1	9	30	30			26, 700	12, 800	56, 621	102, 404
Juab	21		6	29	29			16, 425	5, 540	39, 360	69, 326
Kane	4		4	8	8			13, 400	1, 900	7, 700	11, 790
Millard	11		6	26	26			26, 500	4, 125	23, 070	38, 596
Morgan	9	3	6	59	59			69, 500	18, 200	72, 800	132, 400
Piute (a)											
Rich	48		2	62	62			34, 925	4, 100	32, 108	66, 770

(a) Returned as having no manufactures.

TABLE C.—*Manufactures, by Totals of Counties, &c.*—1870—Continued.

THE TERRITORY OF UTAH—Continued.

Counties.	Establishm'ts.	Steam-engines.	Water-wheels.	All hands.	Males above 16.	Females above 15.	Youth.	Capital. (*Dollars.*)	Wages. (*Dollars.*)	Materials. (*Dollars.*)	Products. (*Dollars.*)
Rio Virgin	1	....	1	2	2	......	....	5, 000	800	2, 882	15, 096
Salt Lake	92	5	19	456	430	16	10	390, 150	134, 085	214, 539	498, 254
San Pete	64	....	29	151	145	......	6	99, 375	32, 908	131, 796	249, 323
Sevier (*a*)	....	....	....	....	....	......	....	......	......	......	......
Summit	13	1	8	33	33	......	....	21, 265	8, 809	15, 977	40, 540
Tooele	5	1	4	13	13	......	....	7, 400	2, 524	34, 610	58, 307
Utah	114	3	38	256	247	2	7	138, 510	38, 376	185, 269	337, 319
Wasatch	4	....	2	33	33	......	....	38, 063	23, 332	26, 350	57, 402
Washington	33	3	11	90	90	......	....	113, 533	18, 840	79, 410	160, 113
Weber	12	1	10	62	56	5	1	140, 500	27, 700	42, 600	94, 350
THE STATE OF VERMONT.											
Addison	342	4	149	1, 275	1, 172	48	55	1, 111, 170	379, 825	1, 102, 150	1, 950, 775
Bennington	237	18	143	2, 128	1, 556	467	105	2, 946, 225	823, 810	1, 658, 702	3, 820, 330
Caledonia	246	12	211	1, 376	1, 295	78	3	1, 506, 975	637, 503	1, 424, 908	3, 173, 036
Chittenden	300	31	100	3, 451	3, 017	337	97	3, 760, 520	1, 085, 453	3, 643, 707	6, 537, 230
Essex	77	8	80	665	649	13	3	642, 230	177, 269	383, 156	734, 739
Franklin	213	13	109	1, 133	1, 080	47	6	833, 400	411, 518	1, 104, 393	1, 802, 849
Grand Isle	12	....	2	38	32	..	6	7, 185	3, 137	7, 537	22, 417
Lamoille	106	4	81	251	236	15	....	229, 775	44, 050	251, 134	403, 825
Orange	212	3	167	580	547	19	14	492, 370	125, 453	660, 414	1, 054, 566
Orleans	188	9	141	651	624	14	13	542, 980	156, 000	634, 689	1, 093, 346
Rutland	377	32	199	2, 307	2, 145	84	78	3, 190, 855	922, 867	1, 874, 200	3, 714, 795
Washington	215	11	161	1, 122	998	115	9	1, 082, 510	370, 931	1, 144, 800	1, 876, 565
Windham	278	23	158	1, 409	1, 219	175	15	1, 413, 452	471, 180	1, 177, 884	2, 310, 942
Windsor	467	18	283	2, 300	1, 731	460	109	2, 569, 990	655, 495	1, 940, 086	3, 759, 271
THE STATE OF VIRGINIA.											
Accomack	116	5	21	171	171	......	....	25, 560	5, 850	57, 990	100, 599
Albemarle	99	4	55	263	236	12	15	242, 130	63, 022	325, 884	481, 111
Alexandria	126	18	....	731	622	83	26	422, 270	248, 034	523, 120	909, 026
Alleghany	29	2	15	80	55	25	....	24, 450	4, 600	55, 456	75, 730
Amelia	30	3	14	49	49	......	....	34, 525	4, 840	79, 605	100, 174
Amherst	91	3	34	238	238	......	....	80, 460	37, 246	328, 944	456, 715
Appomattox	53	9	17	167	167	......	....	41, 460	14, 555	116, 951	158, 530
Augusta	264	14	102	648	631	13	4	497, 655	74, 946	674, 340	985, 554
Bath	15	....	15	18	18	......	....	27, 450	500	31, 182	39, 187
Bedford	164	5	87	483	400	29	54	175, 500	46, 213	287, 374	421, 017
Bland	7	....	8	12	12	......	....	7, 650	423	12, 010	17, 096
Botetourt	22	....	15	125	118	......	7	125, 100	35, 478	160, 046	272, 136
Brunswick	23	1	21	52	52	......	....	45, 700	4, 520	163, 990	240, 254
Buchanan	19	....	16	20	20	......	....	3, 400	240	13, 443	16, 435
Buckingham	58	3	28	112	112	......	....	57, 975	7, 570	129, 897	171, 807
Campbell	164	3	32	687	673	5	9	673, 181	195, 369	728, 224	1, 165, 398
Caroline	46	6	25	139	139	......	....	81, 740	14, 312	86, 709	145, 395
Carroll	53	....	38	100	98	......	2	33, 199	5, 152	54, 747	81, 780
Charles City	12	7	4	94	94	......	....	35, 900	13, 575	47, 900	82, 800
Charlotte	40	....	29	53	53	......	....	56, 212	9, 595	145, 084	180, 429
Chesterfield	37	4	31	1, 569	1, 100	267	202	939, 050	211, 960	1, 042, 856	1, 522, 928
Clarke	105	1	16	163	163	......	....	60, 405	15, 369	121, 905	230, 612
Craig	9	....	6	14	14	......	....	9, 720	2, 864	14, 347	24, 546
Culpeper	45	5	21	142	138	4	....	43, 445	35, 790	124, 700	216, 246
Cumberland	21	2	16	28	28	......	....	35, 825	3, 640	60, 408	84, 533
Dinwiddie	170	22	36	3, 122	1, 649	791	682	1, 556, 423	613, 804	2, 653, 533	4, 195, 281
Elizabeth City	13	3	....	44	44	......	....	23, 300	10, 700	33, 855	77, 845
Essex	20	4	8	81	81	......	....	51, 500	7, 295	51, 520	92, 060
Fairfax	94	10	19	224	218	......	6	147, 937	26, 586	238, 697	334, 004
Fauquier	151	6	57	293	291	......	2	120, 905	32, 386	192, 197	320, 842
Floyd	105	....	60	132	132	......	....	70, 500	2, 690	114, 235	151, 298
Fluvanna	37	2	10	103	97	......	6	56, 350	19, 922	171, 935	276, 503
Franklin	93	....	46	201	156	13	32	111, 240	8, 452	159, 114	223, 070
Frederick	149	3	68	312	286	14	12	325, 848	49, 915	504, 041	757, 124
Giles	11	....	2	18	18	......	....	9, 350	2, 543	12, 438	[illegible]
Gloucester	23	6	8	106	97	......	9	52, 275	20, 972	61, 925	153, 409

(*a*) Returned as having no manufactures.

TABLE C.—*Manufactures, by Totals of Counties, &c.*—1870—Continued.

THE STATE OF VIRGINIA—Continued.

Counties.	Establishm'ts.	Steam-engines.	Water-wheels.	All hands.	Males above 16.	Females above 15.	Youth.	Capital. (Dollars.)	Wages. (Dollars.)	Materials. (Dollars.)	Products. (Dollars.)
Goochland	22	1	19	45	45	......	.....	21, 800	6, 164	78, 997	108
Grayson	41	....	30	53	51	1	1	30, 007	1, 605	61, 948	[illegible]
Greene	25	2	14	41	41	......	.....	25, 080	2, 453	37, 992	[illegible]
Greenville	15	....	8	42	42	......	.....	25, 075	2, 100	34, 503	3
Halifax	77	8	43	165	162	......	3	72, 096	15, 823	151, 897	28
Hanover	30	4	31	101	99	1	1	51, 800	12, 925	85, 821	11
Henrico	595	61	34	7, 456	5, 926	662	868	5, 503, 525	2, 055, 185	6, 720, 104	11, 43
Henry	20	1	4	174	91	4	79	83, 300	14, 430	74, 001	14
Highland	45	....	9	58	57	......	1	35, 225	2, 358	51, 039	7
Isle of Wight	21	6	13	98	98	......	.....	56, 330	22, 335	89, 108	14
James City	20	2	3	46	46	......	.....	24, 900	3, 975	27, 751	6
King and Queen	30	1	19	58	58	......	.....	78, 470	9, 985	77, 446	11
King George	17	....	6	21	21	......	.....	24, 550	2, 260	40, 245	5
King William	44	3	23	102	97	......	5	78, 000	9, 970	100, 770	13
Lancaster	16	4	8	51	46	3	2	20, 190	5, 385	24, 368	4
Lee	86	....	56	120	120	......	.....	51, 800	12, 248	120, 355	16
Loudon	101	4	56	347	342	2	3	264, 359	38, 132	331, 425	4
Louisa	75	3	37	271	222	11	38	182, 125	30, 350	185, 507	30
Lunenburg	27	1	9	52	52	......	.....	25, 855	4, 228	61, 870	8
Madison	42	2	24	85	85	......	.....	35, 950	7, 260	87, 975	10
Matthews	5	2	2	16	16	......	.....	11, 250	2, 000	6, 820	1
Mecklenburg	62	2	20	127	124	1	2	83, 215	18, 694	171, 176	23
Middlesex	13	1	8	23	21	1	1	23, 700	2, 720	37, 900	5
Montgomery	60	2	27	157	154	1	2	84, 420	16, 065	118, 525	19
Nansemond	26	5	14	116	116	......	.....	56, 950	21, 259	47, 780	10
Nelson	76	1	32	108	107	......	1	95, 705	13, 895	144, 805	19
New Kent	15	5	10	60	58	2	.....	41, 400	9, 360	47, 875	8
Norfolk	99	18	1	858	809	22	27	894, 180	315, 642	499, 270	1, 10
Northampton	11	11	....	59	59	......	.....	55, 500	7, 400	37, 960	6
Northumberland	22	4	14	75	75	......	.....	37, 500	9, 456	26, 250	51
Nottoway	17	1	6	37	36	......	1	39, 350	6, 070	38, 814	6
Orange	68	8	22	214	210	4	.....	118, 720	29, 588	161, 254	27
Page	104	6	35	592	555	3	34	598, 900	99, 397	294, 492	45
Patrick	8	....	1	179	85	41	53	54, 250	7, 675	47, 615	7
Pittsylvania	134	2	51	847	505	115	227	257, 368	99, 363	622, 703	1, 09
Powhatan	29	1	10	75	45	20	10	63, 825	3, 355	49, 498	6
Prince Edward	53	1	18	79	79	......	.....	44, 567	12, 909	59, 183	93
Prince George	9	5	4	74	74	......	.....	32, 000	14, 760	44, 248	8
Princess Anne	29	11	1	121	120	1	.....	38, 175	16, 875	77, 528	19
Prince William	14	1	17	45	39	6	.....	100, 300	9, 000	84, 448	12
Pulaski	40	1	17	158	157	......	1	142, 650	62, 110	76, 933	194
Rappahannock	70	....	32	157	156	......	1	60, 525	16, 435	153, 981	21
Richmond	17	2	12	28	28	......	.....	17, 530	4, 900	48, 665	6
Roanoke	37	....	15	90	90	......	.....	86, 250	18, 886	140, 639	1
Rockbridge	52	5	39	108	107	1	.....	189, 817	32, 990	226, 776	32
Rockingham	171	4	93	456	425	4	27	437, 700	64, 256	493, 763	75
Russell	43	....	15	53	53	......	.....	20, 570	2, 123	34, 998	54
Scott	14	....	1	28	26	......	2	4, 225	1, 070	9, 872	15
Shenandoah	74	3	32	274	268	4	2	251, 000	59, 400	257, 955	470
Smyth	32	1	15	69	60	7	2	101, 325	11, 880	82, 266	134
Southampton	23	3	14	77	76	1	.....	48, 700	13, 769	59, 630	12
Spottsylvania	48	4	10	212	162	28	22	525, 850	72, 574	325, 649	53
Stafford	14	4	9	82	37	15	30	27, 975	14, 950	68, 615	10
Surry	8	6	2	71	71	......	.....	24, 950	13, 750	11, 675	4
Sussex	22	3	10	60	60	......	.....	22, 525	21, 400	76, 075	1
Tazewell	23	....	11	39	35	4	.....	32, 675	4, 660	73, 150	9
Warren	91	1	52	138	138	......	.....	101, 080	19, 375	201, 298	2
Warwick	3	1	2	9	9	......	.....	11, 000	1, 800	26, 000	3
Washington	252	7	89	557	514	35	8	273, 555	41, 966	492, 157	76
Westmoreland	16	4	6	58	57	1	.....	30, 775	10, 325	59, 464	8
Wise	1	....	1	2	2	......	.....	1, 000	200	5, 000	6
Wythe	45	1	21	170	152	......	18	84, 225	22, 020	111, 388	18
York	7	5	3	36	34	2	.....	30, 700	6, 617	155, 248	19

THE TERRITORY OF WASHINGTON.

Counties.	Establishm'ts.	Steam-engines.	Water-wheels.	All hands.	Males above 16.	Females above 15.	Youth.	Capital. (Dollars.)	Wages. (Dollars.)	Materials. (Dollars.)	Products. (Dollars.)
Chehalis (*a*)	....	....	....	....	....	......	.....	......	......	......	......
Clallam (*a*)	....	....	....	....	....	......	.....	......	......	......	......
Clarke	27	....	9	39	39	......	.....	39, 425	3, 700	27, 386	49
Cowlitz	6	1	1	42	42	......	.....	84, 000	[illegible]	31, 944	66

(*a*) Returned as having no manufactures.

TABLE C.—*Manufactures, by Totals of Counties, &c.*—1870—Continued.

THE TERRITORY OF WASHINGTON—Continued.

...ounties.	Establishm'ts.	Steam-engines.	Water-wheels.	All hands.	Males above 16.	Females above 15.	Youth.	Capital. (*Dollars.*)	Wages. (*Dollars.*)	Materials. (*Dollars.*)	Products. (*Dollars.*)
	10	5		74	74			63, 600	42, 746	72, 338	152, 107
...on	11	4		134	134			98, 900	97, 820	138, 094	347, 350
	34	12		123	123			110, 350	57, 370	140, 846	305, 287
	6	4		125	125			850, 000	195, 000	625, 000	1, 108, 000
...t	1		1	4	4			5, 000	1, 080	1, 125	3, 350
	4		4	4	4			9, 300	930	5, 300	8, 600
	1		1	7	7			8, 000	4, 000	12, 000	20, 000
	11	4	3	76	76			115, 350	28, 700	31, 234	71, 912
	16	4	4	34	34			85, 650	5, 330	18, 165	35, 722
...nia	1		1	2	2			4, 000	800	750	3, 050
...nish	6		1	11	11			3, 102	960	2, 500	8, 825
...s	6		3	9	9			21, 747	2, 680	14, 695	30, 854
...on	26	1	8	74	73	1		112, 100	18, 980	78, 995	138, 761
...akum	1			1	1			200		460	900
...Walla	80	3	15	197	197			261, 655	67, 400	212, 872	420, 883
...om	13		1	70	70			21, 295	20, 720	21, 424	70, 045
...a (*a*)											
...isputed Isl-(*a*)											

THE STATE OF WEST VIRGINIA.

...ounties.	Establishm'ts.	Steam-engines.	Water-wheels.	All hands.	Males above 16.	Females above 15.	Youth.	Capital. (*Dollars.*)	Wages. (*Dollars.*)	Materials. (*Dollars.*)	Products. (*Dollars.*)
...ir	53	6	24	101	100		1	86, 675	9, 826	98, 595	139, 125
...ey	161	10	41	625	616	5	4	676, 888	218, 478	698, 492	1, 101, 525
	2	2		17	17			9, 000	8, 500	32, 500	56, 000
...n	13	3	16	51	43	5	3	42, 000	7, 900	50, 470	89, 720
	49	11	12	122	113	6	3	103, 100	38, 680	112, 225	200, 738
	19	2	1	50	50			29, 140	8, 913	23, 261	48, 000
...n	2		4	4	4			5, 000	800	4, 800	6, 000
	9		12	9	9			2, 700		8, 170	10, 527
...dge	50	13	21	178	174		4	74, 325	29, 510	65, 676	149, 293
...e	25	1	30	30	30			16, 250	1, 872	29, 025	38, 444
	8	3	5	13	13			21, 570	980	7, 525	11, 770
	60		20	79	73		6	43, 300	4, 330	55, 002	85, 901
...rier	56	4	28	134	106	26	2	67, 350	18, 533	159, 165	233, 663
...hire	56	3	34	117	115		2	59, 977	9, 895	90, 457	137, 459
...ck	55	26	5	306	279		27	267, 470	86, 220	108, 691	260, 550
	40	1	21	88	87	1		44, 500	9, 375	57, 715	91, 706
...on	127	21	23	277	270	1	6	195, 125	55, 935	194, 570	352, 259
...n	60	17	10	158	145	5	8	100, 995	24, 862	102, 356	239, 716
...on	108	8	38	405	393	3	9	520, 800	79, 742	958, 842	1, 375, 603
...ha	164	69	21	812	787	9	16	852, 715	233, 761	580, 242	1, 097, 729
	31	2		49	48	1		24, 130	5, 770	27, 324	53, 870
...n	2		5	3	3			1, 400		3, 433	4, 153
	3		3	4	4			2, 300		2, 550	3, 500
	29	8	10	103	91	8	4	184, 100	33, 200	235, 306	334, 080
...all	44	11	4	427	422	3	2	230, 870	262, 517	949, 919	1, 468, 921
	53	52		779	749		30	1, 262, 390	345, 469	685, 359	1, 955, 138
...well (*a*)											
...r	4		2	5	5			4, 000	600	8, 960	11, 204
...l	25	2	5	75	75			56, 525	21, 770	69, 325	117, 532
...galia	115	17	27	178	175	3		148, 750	28, 271	208, 001	329, 714
...e	21		18	43	39	4		44, 150	5, 189	65, 998	87, 020
...n	14	3	8	41	40	1		56, 270	8, 900	89, 965	140, 212
...as	14		13	20	20			34, 900	2, 345	69, 410	79, 733
	286	67	2	3, 997	3, 399	165	433	4, 011, 590	2, 170, 327	6, 836, 387	10, 765, 859
...ton	26		18	34	31		3	27, 628	2, 860	64, 823	79, 171
...nts	35	2	12	95	95			26, 702	17, 700	43, 330	79, 870
...ontas	22		14	28	28			20, 400	1, 720	41, 835	50, 482
...n	97	22	38	560	527	20	13	535, 025	199, 895	242, 782	532, 407
...n	19	6	7	50	50			29, 800	5, 562	34, 425	50, 230
...h (*a*)											
...iph	25	1	14	42	37		5	32, 350	855	34, 802	45, 881
	69	13	41	203	202	1		123, 835	47, 046	154, 837	259, 702
	20	7	3	35	35			13, 400	3, 930	50, 400	74, 025
	86	21	9	336	306	4	26	271, 090	85, 223	167, 603	340, 130
...r	7		4	14	14			7, 950	3, 800	10, 758	16, 760
	33	11	10	92	70	11	11	77, 900	15, 292	73, 100	132, 878
...r	49	3	23	64	64			50, 160	2, 034	97, 341	124, 656

(*a*) Returned as having no manufactures.

TABLE C.—*Manufactures, by Totals of Counties, &c.*—1870—Continued.

THE STATE OF WEST VIRGINIA—Continued.

Counties.	Establishm'ts.	Steam-engines.	Water-wheels.	All hands.	Males above 16.	Females above 15.	Youth.	Capital. (Dollars.)	Wages. (Dollars.)	Materials. (Dollars.)
Wayne (a)	....	....	....	....	....	....	....	....	....	....
Webster	3	....	3	6	6	....	....	2,000	400	5,204
Wetzel	21	11	3	77	72	1	4	46,800	19,960	41,743
Wirt	43	6	11	75	75	....	....	56,035	11,712	45,868
Wood	131	41	6	644	605	4	35	471,100	170,855	640,631
Wyoming	1	....	1	2	2	....	....	10,000	150	4,410

THE STATE OF WISCONSIN.

Counties.	Establishm'ts.	Steam-engines.	Water-wheels.	All hands.	Males above 16.	Females above 15.	Youth.	Capital. (Dollars.)	Wages. (Dollars.)	Materials. (Dollars.)
Adams	18	3	11	113	112	1	....	77,850	17,546	104,333
Ashland (a)	....	....	....	....	....	....	....	....	....	....
Barron (a)	....	....	....	....	....	....	....	....	....	....
Bayfield	3	3	1	85	85	....	....	65,000	39,000	40,500
Brown	168	72	22	1,880	1,779	35	66	1,416,440	582,336	971,195
Buffalo	96	....	7	209	207	1	1	151,595	40,495	440,901
Burnett (a)	....	....	....	....	....	....	....	....	....	....
Calumet	65	8	7	203	203	....	....	116,600	24,603	75,043
Chippewa	90	12	18	1,063	1,063	....	....	1,127,840	258,450	701,463
Clark	31	9	6	152	150	....	2	113,450	30,395	54,655
Columbia	109	10	24	447	368	67	12	469,840	105,312	464,080
Crawford	40	4	10	163	153	10	....	166,230	31,100	138,030
Dane	153	10	26	545	534	10	1	504,055	139,389	583,215
Dodge	331	34	32	1,671	1,622	26	23	1,949,120	281,606	1,289,597
Door	17	6	....	193	193	....	....	198,970	49,780	89,239
Douglas	17	3	....	60	57	1	2	39,340	32,801	56,142
Dunn	70	7	28	733	708	11	14	298,900	325,425	463,000
Eau Claire	111	35	16	1,055	1,041	8	6	1,265,774	367,532	712,092
Fond du Lac	300	58	28	2,325	2,129	142	54	2,435,001	721,298	2,397,593
Grant	176	14	42	595	567	17	11	627,131	131,832	717,087
Green	201	10	38	710	644	63	3	470,035	197,067	671,494
Green Lake	147	11	10	488	445	39	4	323,480	106,544	594,997
Iowa	200	10	5	607	553	23	31	709,235	112,012	588,130
Jackson	22	3	18	272	272	....	....	278,050	115,042	320,400
Jefferson	300	38	68	1,560	1,395	80	85	1,398,034	375,118	1,601,226
Juneau	66	11	16	639	632	7	....	590,015	239,735	422,341
Kenosha	74	16	1	605	531	13	61	622,195	261,259	852,016
Kewaunee	40	8	10	302	299	3	....	284,985	84,268	304,647
La Crosse	76	19	11	708	694	13	1	959,050	426,175	551,754
La Fayette	95	2	17	257	252	5	....	171,700	49,706	336,515
Manitowoc	130	41	38	872	837	12	23	895,876	247,802	1,607,831
Marathon	42	8	27	450	448	2	....	386,550	113,160	332,054
Marquette	44	....	40	115	110	3	2	107,350	21,136	168,768
Milwaukee	828	126	14	8,433	7,197	600	576	8,109,109	3,400,172	11,649,995
Monroe	108	15	27	510	487	23	....	480,600	134,122	559,814
Oconto	44	26	5	1,526	1,459	51	16	1,606,600	535,318	976,544
Outagamie	58	9	21	533	472	50	11	609,540	186,525	674,970
Ozaukee	96	7	17	321	317	....	4	421,775	73,290	619,276
Pepin	30	4	10	170	169	1	....	171,550	45,650	74,564
Pierce	63	6	26	214	213	1	....	234,900	74,080	176,972
Polk	9	1	4	36	36	....	....	37,700	9,975	38,545
Portage	80	13	39	427	427	....	....	463,565	73,177	302,717
Racine	211	33	15	1,882	1,726	86	70	1,912,725	769,250	2,141,519
Richland	69	6	32	201	200	1	3	171,780	36,379	209,043
Rock	301	15	39	1,707	1,530	138	39	1,771,260	536,529	2,145,938
Sauk	136	9	61	508	474	32	2	512,665	130,247	457,431
Shawanaw	11	5	1	86	86	....	....	54,000	13,100	39,529
Sheboygan	372	26	60	1,474	1,219	152	103	940,310	342,087	1,010,325
St. Croix	109	11	33	350	346	3	1	314,500	70,505	354,540
Trempealeau	60	2	12	111	111	....	....	133,337	13,031	116,877
Vernon	66	3	33	176	176	....	....	189,950	30,480	328,286
Walworth	186	9	24	752	712	32	8	770,230	239,906	723,928
Washington	195	10	32	497	464	16	17	439,005	50,720	618,406
Waukesha	276	13	45	622	596	9	17	589,215	92,449	634,056
Waupacca	113	11	52	488	424	37	27	393,875	96,625	515,359
Waushara	49	6	16	141	133	8	....	103,450	26,550	186,329
Winnebago	239	79	72	3,005	2,583	219	203	2,851,650	919,512	3,416,107
Wood	46	14	17	658	654	3	1	475,710	112,062	227,817

(a) Returned as having no manufactures.

TABLE C.—*Manufactures, by Totals of Counties, &c.*—1870—Continued.

THE TERRITORY OF WYOMING.

Counties.	Establishm'ts.	Steam-engines.	Water-wheels.	All hands.	Males above 16.	Females above 15.	Youth.	Capital. (*Dollars.*)	Wages. (*Dollars.*)	Materials. (*Dollars.*)	Products. (*Dollars.*)
Albany	7			138	138			64, 900	63, 430	53, 774	129, 050
Carbon	3	2		84	84			470, 000	99, 872	38, 586	138, 458
Laramie	10	2		133	133			226, 000	99, 901	79, 358	226, 173
Sweetwater	7	5	2	69	67	1	1	74, 500	27, 000	66, 320	134, 100
Uintah	5	4		78	78			54, 000	57, 375	42, 118	137, 643

[*Continued from page* 811.]

final value of the product as reported, enhancing the apparent production of the industry in a high degree. Here come in the great body of the industries known technically as the "manufactures" of the country, the mill and factory industries, whose productions appear oftentimes enormous, as compared with those of bodies of craftsmen more skilled, and receiving higher wages, and do so merely because of the high cost of the materials consumed in the former case.

Fifth. Industries in which the value of the materials far exceeds all the other elements in the cost of production combined, and thus carries up the apparent product of these industries to a very high point, although, in fact, comparatively little value has been added by these operations, and only a small number of artisans or laborers supported.

The reduction of gold and silver, calico-printing, bleaching and dyeing, the currying of leather, the packing of meat, the refining of sugar and molasses, and the production of flour and meal, are among the most important industries of this class.

The distribution of the industries embraced in Table VIII (B,) as nearly as possible, according to the classification just indicated,* yields the following instructive results:

Relation of Wages and Materials to Product in Manufacturing, Mechanical, Mining, and Fishing industry.

Class.	Hands.	Wages.	Materials.	Product.
I	169, 691	$73, 438, 952	$14, 418, 908	$143, 136, 692
II	110, 504	35, 689, 883	67, 850, 482	154, 692, 177
III	388, 924	167, 118, 533	183, 543, 034	535, 487, 704
IV	1, 453, 056	541, 078, 362	1, 529, 537, 058	2, 701, 440, 948
V	101, 504	31, 734, 815	707, 361, 378	841, 005, 063
	2, 223, 679	849, 060, 545	2, 502, 710, 860	4, 375, 762, 584

Class.	Excess of product over materials.	Excess of product over wages and materials.	Wages in $100 of product.	Materials in $100 of product.	Wages & materials in $100 of product.	Product per capita, gross.	Product per capita, deducting materials.
I	$128, 717, 784	$55, 278, 832	$51. 30	$10. 07	$61. 37	$843. 51	$758. 54
II	86, 841, 695	51, 151, 812	23. 07	43. 86	66. 93	1, 400. 00	785. 87
III	351, 944, 670	184, 826, 137	31. 20	34. 28	65. 48	1, 376. 84	904. 92
IV	1, 171, 903, 890	630, 825, 528	20. 29	56. 62	76. 91	1, 859. 10	806. 51
V	133, 643, 685	101, 908, 870	3. 77	84. 10	87. 87	8, 285. 44	1, 316. 64
	1, 873, 051, 724	1, 023, 991, 179	19. 40	57. 19	76. 59	1, 967. 80	842. 32

* Two common trades, each of which belongs partly to the second and partly to some other class, were divided for this purpose, in such proportions as seemed due. All the other industries in Table VIII (B) were assigned entire to one class or another, according to the principles indicated in the text. The lines of division taken for the third, fourth, and fifth classes were, 1st, where the value of the materials is less than two-fifths of that of the ultimate product; 2d, where the value of the materials is from two-fifths to four-fifths of that of the ultimate product; and, 3d, where the value of the materials is over four-fifths *of that of the ultimate* product.

[Continued on page 872.]

TABLE CI.—*Manufactures, in each State and Territory, by Selected Industries*—1870.

NOTE.—In the construction of this Table, to save space, two classes of Industries have been excluded: (1.) Those which may be called "neighborhood industries," *i. e.*, when production is presumably for use and consumption within their immediate locality. These industries are blacksmithing, custom boot and shoe making, butchering, carpentering, brick and stone masonry, the manufacture of gas, locksmithing and bell-hanging, millwrighting, house-painting, paperhanging, photographing, plastering, plumbing and gas-fitting, watch and clock repairing, wheelwrighting, mechanical dentistry, custom grist-milling, and the sawing of lumber at small mills producing under $2,500 annually. (2.) All industries, in any State or Territory, whose aggregate annual product for such State or Territory falls short of $250,000.

THE STATE OF ALABAMA.

Mechanical and manufacturing industries.	Establishm'ts.	Steam-engines.	Water-wheels.	All hands.	Males above 16.	Females above 15.	Youth.	Capital. (*Dollars.*)	Wages. (*Dollars.*)	Materials. (*Dollars.*)	Products. (*Dollars.*)
Carriages and wagons	93	1	1	311	309	....	2	137900	104153	91674	310031
Cotton goods	13	3	14	1032	303	445	284	931000	216679	764965	10[illegible]
Flouring-mill products	102	(*)	(*)	269	(*)	(*)	(*)	399096	52795	1213998	167[illegible]
Iron, castings	18	13	3	140	137	....	3	177100	96022	152271	[illegible]
Lumber	125	(*)	(*)	1068	(*)	(*)	(*)	647400	396511	508405	[illegible]
Machinery, (not engines & boilers)	11	4	4	135	130	2	3	333870	80250	138456	[illegible]
Printing and publishing	15	1	....	187	160	25	2	123300	150530	107158	[illegible]
Tar and turpentine	12	....	....	602	540	55	7	86200	120000	84155	[illegible]

THE STATE OF ARKANSAS.

Mechanical and manufacturing industries.	Establishm'ts.	Steam-engines.	Water-wheels.	All hands.	Males above 16.	Females above 15.	Youth.	Capital. (*Dollars.*)	Wages. (*Dollars.*)	Materials. (*Dollars.*)	Products. (*Dollars.*)
Flouring-mill products	28	(*)	(*)	65	(*)	(*)	(*)	118300	12638	250914	[illegible]
Lumber	108	(*)	(*)	717	(*)	(*)	(*)	523256	211460	520260	1307[illegible]

THE STATE OF CALIFORNIA.

Mechanical and manufacturing industries.	Establishm'ts.	Steam-engines.	Water-wheels.	All hands.	Males above 16.	Females above 15.	Youth.	Capital. (*Dollars.*)	Wages. (*Dollars.*)	Materials. (*Dollars.*)	Products. (*Dollars.*)
Bags, other than paper	8	1	....	113	96	14	3	106500	53125	334500	501310
Boots and shoes	46	....	....	968	838	107	23	346249	500812	743855	1598[illegible]
Boxes, wooden, (not cigar)	8	4	....	195	195	....	....	169500	109886	183014	[illegible]
Bread and other bakery products	74	4	....	320	311	7	2	280740	186376	632713	1165[illegible]
Brick	34	....	....	610	610	....	....	226200	128139	109778	407[illegible]
Carriages and wagons	84	2	....	640	630	....	10	780150	417336	439404	[illegible]
Cars, freight and passenger	3	1	....	80	80	....	....	270000	72171	104550	[illegible]
Clothing	177	....	....	757	406	346	5	351881	379432	984452	[illegible]
Coffee & spices, roasted & ground	13	7	....	92	91	....	1	149200	44640	329865	[illegible]
Confectionery	18	1	....	65	52	6	7	123700	35165	136944	[illegible]
Cooperage	51	4	1	259	253	....	6	255425	136792	185343	474[illegible]
Cordage and twine	2	2	....	162	162	....	....	350000	76000	668300	[illegible]
Drugs and chemicals	21	7	....	190	190	....	....	488900	68498	349691	617[illegible]
Flouring-mill products	93	(*)	(*)	622	(*)	(*)	(*)	2383000	356421	6946129	843[illegible]
Furniture	48	9	....	285	282	2	1	237050	199121	224784	624[illegible]
Gold and silver, reduced and refined	2	1	....	35	35	....	....	110000	35000	3750086	[illegible]
Gunpowder	3	2	2	75	75	....	....	513000	61380	209798	[illegible]
Iron, forged and rolled	2	3	....	129	129	....	....	381470	78511	201920	[illegible]
Iron, castings	31	28	....	727	686	....	41	897000	434845	712351	13[illegible]
Jewelry	29	2	....	173	159	....	14	320350	87122	187708	[illegible]
Lead, shot	1	1	....	12	12	....	....	150000	7560	208500	[illegible]
Leather, tanned	45	8	1	207	204	2	1	322550	92411	480411	751[illegible]
Leather, curried	27	2	....	55	53	1	1	110950	19373	357743	[illegible]
Liquors, distilled	16	2	2	75	71	1	....	386200	30789	402194	109[illegible]
Liquors, malt	96	22	6	389	388	....	1	1118070	227242	696215	1641[illegible]
Liquors, vinous	139	2	....	752	741	9	2	658420	90659	[illegible]	[illegible]
Lumber	256	(*)	(*)	4268	(*)	(*)	(*)	4110040	6847666	2570111	[illegible]
Machinery, (not specified)	29	21	2	404	401	....	3	766600	673253	667667	16[illegible]
Machinery, railroad repairing	1	1	....	80	80	....	....	45600	83800	227200	[illegible]
Machinery, steam engines & boilers	17	13	....	586	561	....	25	564050	536645	704840	[illegible]
Marble and stone work	38	2	....	216	214	....	2	144525	139995	130233	[illegible]
Matches	6	1	....	55	53	....	2	20750	19634	116600	[illegible]
Meat, packed, pork	6	....	....	33	33	....	....	141000	13600	193311	[illegible]
Molasses and sugar, refined	3	4	....	255	255	....	....	1300000	160000	3245050	[illegible]
Printing and publishing	82	14	....	847	766	18	63	1217100	788725	670810	[illegible]
Quartz, milled	114	39	68	676	676	....	....	1749272	436241	1927281	3405[illegible]
Quicksilver, smelted	4	1	1	256	248	....	8	3500000	180000	837800	[illegible]
Saddlery and harness	187	1	....	693	688	3	2	550125	283411	446831	[illegible]
Sash, doors, and blinds	23	15	3	391	378	....	13	295100	230690	305839	[illegible]
Ship build'g, repair'g, & materials	21	1	....	82	82	....	....	57650	70640	129277	[illegible]
Soap and candles	21	7	....	80	80	....	....	192000	42592	431340	[illegible]

* Not separately compiled.

TABLE CI.—*Manufactures, in each State and Territory, by Selected Industries*—1870—Cont'd.

THE STATE OF CALIFORNIA—Continued.

Mechanical and manufacturing industries.	Establishm'ts.	Steam-engines.	Water-wheels.	All hands.	Males above 16.	Females above 15.	Youth.	Capital. (*Dollars.*)	Wages. (*Dollars.*)	Materials. (*Dollars.*)	Products. (*Dollars.*)
Tin, copper, and sheet-iron ware	133	1	....	368	335	1	32	394850	202541	363909	782224
Tobacco, cigars	88	....	....	1834	1791	....	43	681345	523555	778126	1909917
Trunks, valises, and satchels	11	3	....	141	136	4	1	72800	91600	107950	280375
Woolen goods	5	6	1	659	584	31	44	1785000	230200	608141	1102754

THE TERRITORY OF COLORADO.

Mechanical and manufacturing industries.	Establishm'ts.	Steam-engines.	Water-wheels.	All hands.	Males above 16.	Females above 15.	Youth.	Capital. (*Dollars.*)	Wages. (*Dollars.*)	Materials. (*Dollars.*)	Products. (*Dollars.*)
Flouring-mill products	17	(*)	(*)	48	(*)	(*)	(*)	154200	32800	425266	593506
Lumber	29	(*)	(*)	219	(*)	(*)	(*)	135000	86176	169875	380260
Quartz, milled	15	14	2	89	89	....	....	2094900	86680	574585	769324

THE STATE OF CONNECTICUT.

Mechanical and manufacturing industries.	Establishm'ts.	Steam-engines.	Water-wheels.	All hands.	Males above 16.	Females above 15.	Youth.	Capital. (*Dollars.*)	Wages. (*Dollars.*)	Materials. (*Dollars.*)	Products. (*Dollars.*)
Agricultural implements	38	4	50	593	591	2	....	1061100	328718	455849	1183947
Ammunition	4	2	1	377	207	170	....	480430	312515	477595	833000
Bells	12	....	10	221	173	42	6	223500	88095	144974	340100
Belting and hose, (leather)	8	1	1	108	107	....	1	290500	70900	667000	850500
Bleaching and dyeing	18	2	2	188	146	42	....	150100	81352	2541985	2849743
Bookbinding	10	4	....	261	89	171	1	149046	97495	385081	552410
Boots and shoes	38	2	1	1918	1267	589	62	475700	543631	990646	1930652
Boxes, paper	30	1	1	346	94	244	8	116550	99728	156041	333345
Brass founding and finishing	16	5	1	378	346	23	9	504600	177641	365567	737725
Brass, rolled	1	....	2	69	55	6	8	115000	44000	128200	336252
Brass ware	12	4	8	416	355	39	22	785000	244300	694630	1331013
Bread and other bakery products	33	4	....	227	202	19	6	114300	104386	482685	739730
Brick	71	2	2	716	703	3	10	250180	196508	97895	458951
Brushes	5	2	1	81	50	27	4	522500	26702	183637	270621
Buttons	21	7	14	623	201	321	101	418100	170571	278825	563433
Carpets, other than rag	3	8	....	1185	451	514	220	1530000	432031	1307397	2027136
Carriage trimmings	7	4	2	187	92	81	14	187000	64473	102643	251997
Carriages and wagons	205	7	24	2341	2321	11	9	2282810	1402034	1798299	4164480
Cars, freight and passenger	7	5	....	206	206	....	....	323272	160550	136409	399459
Clock cases and materials	18	4	15	267	229	30	8	249650	126190	222036	502110
Clocks	10	7	12	1204	1067	63	74	759000	736290	713518	2245043
Clothing	244	10	3	3414	999	2372	43	1250220	1138149	2666068	4481250
Confectionery	13	1	....	111	82	26	3	100100	51344	194306	339353
Copper, rolled	2	1	1	86	86	....	....	500000	58875	761200	925400
Coppersmithing	2	....	1	50	45	2	3	80000	33500	89610	250000
Cotton goods	111	15	177	12086	4443	4734	2909	12710700	3246783	8818651	14026334
Cutlery	8	4	3	339	278	55	6	348750	150360	101035	388100
Cutlery and edge-tools, (see Edge-tools and axes)	33	5	35	1449	1281	64	104	957800	762203	506182	1711795
Drugs and chemicals	6	8	8	261	259	....	2	486200	134000	945435	1289845
Edge-tools and axes	7	3	33	590	576	7	7	911675	361110	534385	959011
Envelopes	2	1	1	115	41	73	1	90000	42000	258225	344183
Fertilizers	14	2	8	151	151	....	....	117000	65125	248224	373375
Fire-arms, small arms	8	8	8	1607	1521	30	56	1793770	1100668	315247	2222873
Flouring-mill products	150	(*)	(*)	351	(*)	(*)	(*)	796850	146449	2461729	2946010
Furniture	56	8	10	825	671	16	138	817850	356628	441620	1103620
Gas and lamp **fixtures**	5	3	1	378	214	124	40	314000	169700	204475	592915
Gunpowder	2	4	33	153	153	....	....	635000	120660	588075	761000
Hardware	145	67	75	7246	5646	908	692	6863395	3549840	5122759	12111034
Hardware, saddlery	10	4	2	475	331	112	32	275250	198982	222052	561000
Hat materials	6	3	1	101	76	6	19	193500	43016	457100	600000
Hats and caps	33	17	2	2464	1500	828	136	1153300	1019108	1894647	3740871
Hooks and eyes	9	1	5	185	72	67	46	185000	72646	90655	269582
Hoop-skirts and corsets	14	3	1	529	131	304	94	195700	117175	251530	491997
Hosiery	14	7	12	1333	364	751	218	1159700	431089	625391	1251742
India-rubber and elastic goods	13	11	16	1946	980	931	35	2345000	761434	2355488	4239329
Iron, forged and rolled	15	11	14	523	510	....	13	550000	315630	680575	1191140
Iron bolts, nuts, washers, & rivets	15	7	11	626	490	40	96	860000	327208	486774	1111502
Iron, pig	7	....	7	159	159	....	....	780000	92614	716933	949125
Iron, castings	83	38	24	2458	2338	23	97	3006650	1444345	1748035	4156044
Ivory-work	6	3	6	161	127	33	1	325500	100030	320730	511750
Leather, tanned	39	4	17	158	156	2	....	324650	66302	580747	739625
Leather, curried	30	1	1	66	66	....	....	862006	25745	[illegible]	[illegible]

* Not separately compiled.

TABLE C I.—*Manufactures, in each State and Territory, by Selected Industries—1870*—Continued.

THE STATE OF CONNECTICUT—Continued.

Mechanical and manufacturing industries.	Establishments.	Steam-engines.	Water-wheels.	All hands.	Males above 16.	Females above 15.	Youth.	Capital. (*Dollars.*)	Wages. (*Dollars.*)	Materials. (*Dollars.*)	Products. (*Dollars.*)
Liquors, malt	12	1	1	79	75	....	4	130070	30200	184771	[illegible]
Lumber, planed	5	(*)	(*)	75	(*)	(*)	(*)	80000	52230	470750	[illegible]
Lumber, sawed	146	(*)	(*)	480	(*)	(*)	(*)	522425	120276	761758	[illegible]
Machinery, (not specified)	77	36	29	1758	1744	7	7	2542141	1100000	969963	[illegible]
Machinery, cotton and woolen	16	5	10	252	242	10	....	357020	130654	137670	[illegible]
Machinery, railroad repairing	4	3	....	326	321	4	1	505100	185150	147672	[illegible]
Machinery, steam engines & boiler	11	12	1	414	413	....	1	937500	276869	362175	[illegible]
Marble & stone work, (not specified)	21	2	....	234	234	....	....	167910	141701	108010	[illegible]
Meat, packed, pork	4	3	....	56	56	....	....	217000	41000	723000	[illegible]
Monuments and tombstones	37	1	7	310	306	....	4	240900	187438	242857	[illegible]
Musical instruments and materials	14	4	6	299	278	21	....	511000	202563	527441	[illegible]
Needles and pins	16	3	12	400	212	149	39	483900	180688	294017	[illegible]
Oil, fish	23	15	1	492	485	7	....	304000	92055	199358	[illegible]
Paper, (not specified)	21	1	31	259	214	37	8	513500	95834	276782	[illegible]
Paper, printing	18	4	29	437	223	202	12	854100	200336	932230	146740
Paper, wrapping	18	2	31	185	163	17	5	574100	85509	480325	[illegible]
Paper, writing	6	3	26	616	349	267	....	1046346	315318	1637929	213650
Percussion caps	2	....	2	140	53	46	41	145000	76500	153600	[illegible]
Plated ware	32	19	19	2107	1671	359	77	2337500	1201552	2005090	[illegible]
Printing and publishing	42	21	2	672	550	91	31	701329	367151	379757	109440
Pumps	7	4	....	179	142	....	37	213700	70225	151423	[illegible]
Saddlery and harness	106	....	1	603	547	47	9	253563	265636	450371	[illegible]
Sash, doors, and blinds	31	16	13	539	537	1	1	522900	316075	335825	[illegible]
Screws	5	2	2	348	328	19	1	767880	202959	87815	47125
Sewing machine fixtures	3	3	....	225	199	6	20	142000	135600	155680	330000
Sewing machines	6	10	2	2300	2031	149	120	2350000	1649246	1200335	361900
Ship build'g, repair'g, & materials	34	4	....	438	438	....	....	355600	263416	345410	[illegible]
Shoddy	18	....	17	106	84	14	8	128950	31368	302636	[illegible]
Silk goods	23	11	20	1703	466	1003	234	1414130	569425	2049834	331445
Soap and candles	21	5	1	108	91	14	3	208925	38638	299013	[illegible]
Steel, (not specified)	2	3	2	61	60	....	1	600000	57000	[illegible]	[illegible]
Steel springs	7	5	3	276	264	....	12	311000	180700	385710	64000
Straw goods	3	2	....	1010	255	755	....	401000	270108	[illegible]	[illegible]
Tin, copper, and sheet iron ware	120	1	3	968	854	91	23	[illegible]	[illegible]	[illegible]	[illegible]
Tobacco, cigars	100	....	....	719	523	164	32	[illegible]	305109	[illegible]	[illegible]
Washing mach's & clothes wringers	3	1	1	111	105	6	....	[illegible]	[illegible]	[illegible]	[illegible]
Wire	10	5	3	[illegible]	313	14	1	[illegible]	171923	[illegible]	[illegible]
Wire work	8	[illegible]	9	127	71	37	19	252000	58350	[illegible]	[illegible]
Wood, turned and carved	42	[illegible]	37	318	289	21	8	214500	132940	[illegible]	[illegible]
Woolen goods	[illegible]	52	120	[illegible]	[illegible]	[illegible]	[illegible]	[illegible]	[illegible]	[illegible]	1756516
Worsted goods	[illegible]	[illegible]	2	[illegible]	[illegible]	191	[illegible]	[illegible]	[illegible]	[illegible]	[illegible]

THE STATE OF DELAWARE.

Mechanical and manufacturing industries.	Establishments.	Steam-engines.	Water-wheels.	All hands.	Males above 16.	Females above 15.	Youth.	Capital. (*Dollars.*)	Wages. (*Dollars.*)	Materials. (*Dollars.*)	Products. (*Dollars.*)
Boots and shoes	[illegible]	2		[illegible]	[illegible]	7	[illegible]	[illegible]	[illegible]	[illegible]	[illegible]
Carriages and wagons	[illegible]	1	....	[illegible]	[illegible]	[illegible]	[illegible]	[illegible]	[illegible]	[illegible]	[illegible]
Cars, freight and passenger	3	1		[illegible]	[illegible]		[illegible]	[illegible]	[illegible]	[illegible]	[illegible]
Cotton goods	[illegible]	[illegible]	[illegible]	[illegible]	[illegible]	[illegible]	[illegible]	[illegible]	[illegible]	[illegible]	[illegible]
Flouring-mill products	[illegible]			[illegible]				[illegible]	[illegible]	[illegible]	[illegible]
Gunpowder	[illegible]			[illegible]				[illegible]	[illegible]	[illegible]	[illegible]
Iron, forged and rolled	[illegible]	[illegible]	1		[illegible]		[illegible]	[illegible]	[illegible]	[illegible]	[illegible]
Iron, castings	[illegible]	[illegible]			[illegible]			[illegible]	[illegible]	[illegible]	[illegible]
Leather, [illegible]	[illegible]	[illegible]		[illegible]	[illegible]	[illegible]	[illegible]	[illegible]	[illegible]	[illegible]	[illegible]
Leather, [illegible]	[illegible]	[illegible]		[illegible]		[illegible]		[illegible]	[illegible]	[illegible]	[illegible]
Lumber, [illegible]				[illegible]				[illegible]	[illegible]	[illegible]	[illegible]
Machinery, steam engines & boilers				[illegible]	[illegible]		[illegible]	[illegible]	[illegible]	[illegible]	[illegible]
Matches				[illegible]	[illegible]			[illegible]	[illegible]	[illegible]	[illegible]
[illegible] & materials								[illegible]	[illegible]	[illegible]	[illegible]
[illegible]									[illegible]	[illegible]	[illegible]

THE DISTRICT OF COLUMBIA.

TABLE CI.—*Manufactures, in each State and Territory, by Selected Industries*—1870—Cont'd.

THE STATE OF FLORIDA.

Mechanical and manufacturing industries.	Establishm'ts.	Steam-engines.	Water-wheels.	All hands.	Males above 16.	Females above 15.	Youth.	Capital. (*Dollars.*)	Wages. (*Dollars.*)	Materials. (*Dollars.*)	Products. (*Dollars.*)
Lumber	70	(*)	(*)	985	(*)	(*)	(*)	687674	309367	1109549	2158920
Tobacco, cigars	13	....	....	254	254	....	....	257500	204910	92840	572350

THE STATE OF GEORGIA.

Mechanical and manufacturing industries.	Establishm'ts.	Steam-engines.	Water-wheels.	All hands.	Males above 16.	Females above 15.	Youth.	Capital. (*Dollars.*)	Wages. (*Dollars.*)	Materials. (*Dollars.*)	Products. (*Dollars.*)
Brick	41	3	....	860	696	19	145	132500	146487	94981	420109
Carriages and wagons	178	2	7	676	656	1	10	267295	187715	243605	664512
Cotton goods	34	4	59	2846	1147	1080	619	3433265	611868	2504758	3648973
Flouring-mill products	141	(*)	(*)	433	(*)	(*)	(*)	963254	108832	3075671	3903004
Iron, forged and rolled	3	7	....	250	235	....	15	215860	170766	541050	855856
Iron, castings, (not specified)	20	14	2	209	203	....	6	166750	97430	139473	411897
Leather	186	5	10	316	310	1	5	186247	47758	418793	572306
Lumber, planed	7	7	....	239	236	....	3	89500	130250	341600	571200
Lumber, sawed	193	(*)	(*)	2047	(*)	(*)	(*)	1267737	556260	1437866	3340683
Machinery, (not specified)	25	14	4	326	302	4	20	264400	164962	323867	614058
Machinery, railroad repairing	7	7	....	596	584	....	12	466000	475832	387410	866072
Printing and publishing	45	8	....	428	392	3	33	416798	282222	144291	929151
Tobacco, chew'g, smok'g, and snuff	5	....	....	196	93	40	63	78700	76592	201520	365074
Woolen goods	11	1	11	490	190	185	115	894435	116538	179084	358583

THE TERRITORY OF IDAHO.

Mechanical and manufacturing industries.	Establishm'ts.	Steam-engines.	Water-wheels.	All hands.	Males above 16.	Females above 15.	Youth.	Capital. (*Dollars.*)	Wages. (*Dollars.*)	Materials. (*Dollars.*)	Products. (*Dollars.*)
Quartz, milled	8	4	3	52	52	....	....	465300	41530	406720	523100

THE STATE OF ILLINOIS.

Mechanical and manufacturing industries.	Establishm'ts.	Steam-engines.	Water-wheels.	All hands.	Males above 16.	Females above 15.	Youth.	Capital. (*Dollars.*)	Wages. (*Dollars.*)	Materials. (*Dollars.*)	Products. (*Dollars.*)
Agricultural implements	294	91	14	3935	3911	1	23	5350978	1813835	3598897	8860300
Bagging	2	....	4	113	37	34	42	125000	38000	136000	290000
Bags, paper	3	3	....	39	20	17	2	75000	15350	189100	270000
Bookbinding	34	2	....	329	176	124	29	189450	130957	676208	980575
Boots and shoes	88	....	....	1274	1197	50	27	1527448	600600	1151215	2298136
Boxes, wooden	14	11	1	256	223	7	26	144000	84000	210860	387395
Bread and other bakery products	128	8	....	537	476	36	25	363575	195231	885528	1732885
Brick	240	23	....	3203	2936	3	264	1018140	678945	381010	1638764
Brooms and whisk-brushes	69	....	....	243	230	1	12	84080	57331	139196	295231
Carriages and wagons	1165	37	5	4847	4825	1	21	3429426	1775946	2213297	6019291
Cars, freight and passenger	5	3	....	849	848	....	1	959000	501978	492235	1010007
Cheese	69	19	....	197	173	24	....	191400	32721	440890	557356
Clothing	458	....	1	6652	2724	3921	7	2777255	1887555	5178284	8407005
Coffee and spices, roasted & ground	7	6	....	69	64	1	4	249000	42576	661475	798851
Confectionery	24	5	....	462	272	81	109	314050	161601	1355431	1948710
Cooperage	391	4	....	2037	2030	2	5	763637	679779	1226819	2501531
Cordials and sirups	5	1	....	72	39	26	7	60000	18980	204500	271625
Cotton goods	5	3	2	98	26	31	41	151000	25500	177525	279000
Flouring-mill products	681	(*)	(*)	3581	(*)	(*)	(*)	12031600	1704779	32000825	39413618
Food preparations, animal	8	3	....	77	60	14	3	56500	33854	152390	252778
Furniture	371	71	4	2349	2166	19	164	1885731	946294	1011328	2982522
Grease and tallow	5	1	....	130	55	62	13	234500	42420	1270430	1412900
Hardware	4	4	....	132	117	2	13	96000	56632	120345	251269
Iron, forged and rolled	8	23	....	1749	1634	....	115	2390000	1069082	1917422	3430746
Iron, nails & spikes, cut & wrought	4	1	1	192	159	....	33	156200	110785	554750	804644
Iron, castings, (not specified)	109	66	13	1793	1758	....	35	2167885	937927	2094020	3788953
Iron, castings, stoves, heaters, and hollow ware	9	7	....	364	361	....	3	595000	242500	310210	714100
Lead pipe	1	1	....	17	17	....	....	100000	8852	480635	588410
Leather, tanned	53	23	1	418	415	1	2	896750	203315	1492878	2013774
Leather, curried	44	3	....	334	334	....	....	386550	169129	1748299	2134389
Lime	35	1	....	417	413	....	4	290575	149291	234993	541021
Liquors, distilled	45	48	....	958	957	....	1	2513000	550116	4875011	7288731
Liquors, malt	148	77	....	997	994	1	2	4884900	481026	2023366	4154224
Lumber, planed	54	(*)	(*)	1872	(*)	(*)	(*)	2173800	837861	5368117	7322369
Lumber, sawed	356	(*)	(*)	2630	(*)	(*)	(*)	2246066	[illegible]	[illegible]	[illegible]

* Not separately compiled.

TABLE CI.—*Manufactures, in each State and Territory, by Selected Industries*—1870—Cont'd.

THE STATE OF ILLINOIS—Continued.

Mechanical and manufacturing industries.	Establishm'ts.	Steam-engines.	Water-wheels.	All hands.	Males above 16.	Females above 15.	Youth.	Capital. (Dollars.)	Wages. (Dollars.)	Materials. (Dollars.)	Products. (Dollars.)
Machinery, (not specified)	80	50	6	1697	1645	5	47	2449000	1062373	1238683	[illegible]
Machinery, railroad repairing	15	18	....	2169	2167	....	2	2068800	1228506	921667	[illegible]
Machinery, steam engines & boilers	36	21	2	837	827	....	10	957800	469891	613651	[illegible]
Malt	17	4	....	99	99	....	....	626000	42548	669547	[illegible]
Marble and stone work, (not spec.)	34	15	....	1336	1291	....	45	593850	625020	494135	[illegible]
Meat, packed, pork	33	28	....	2236	2205	....	31	6021000	448500	16836541	[illegible]
Millinery	121	....	....	353	8	343	2	118385	38041	130568	[illegible]
Mineral and soda waters	38	1	....	217	198	1	18	222000	69828	186320	[illegible]
Monuments and tombstones	88	1	....	381	374	....	7	208700	156744	196443	[illegible]
Musical instruments and materials	13	2	....	170	168	1	1	201800	119586	80900	[illegible]
Oil, animal	8	1	....	121	68	38	15	269500	52850	1301800	[illegible]
Oil, vegetable, linseed	9	7	1	155	150	....	5	545500	64650	924282	[illegible]
Paints	4	3	....	70	70	....	....	368000	33850	471875	[illegible]
Paper, printing	6	3	13	249	173	65	11	470000	94570	392435	[illegible]
Paper, wrapping	10	4	21	171	129	33	9	342000	71950	139108	[illegible]
Patent medicines and compounds	16	1	....	111	73	31	7	208850	23940	110681	[illegible]
Printing and publishing, (not spec.)	2	2	....	53	44	5	4	68000	37000	210440	[illegible]
Printing and publishing, book	8	8	....	181	140	8	33	271000	114700	205630	[illegible]
Printing and publishing, newspaper	70	23	....	745	667	32	46	543050	405011	448382	[illegible]
Printing, job	49	12	....	410	315	19	76	371700	183069	127599	[illegible]
Pumps	29	9	4	154	153	....	1	230091	64396	128923	[illegible]
Saddlery and harness	687	....	....	1932	1919	6	7	1086815	515460	1341062	[illegible]
Sash, doors, and blinds	94	69	9	1407	1350	....	57	1140350	666765	990395	[illegible]
Ship build'g, repair'g, and materials	13	4	....	309	304	....	5	290200	156739	188100	[illegible]
Soap and candles	24	14	....	205	160	17	28	740500	83596	937938	[illegible]
Stone and earthen ware	45	4	....	310	296	4	10	204575	122350	40104	[illegible]
Tin, copper, and sheet-iron ware	478	4	....	1528	1452	34	42	1137082	520335	1025356	[illegible]
Tobacco, chew'g, smok'g, and snuff	37	13	....	1659	753	258	648	917550	436475	1517945	[illegible]
Tobacco, cigars	237	....	....	1025	873	33	119	1047070	345269	528977	[illegible]
Trunks, valises, and satchels	10	....	....	154	134	12	8	126000	80580	155530	317100
Upholstery	24	....	....	195	125	29	41	126950	70912	166292	[illegible]
Varnish	4	....	....	27	27	....	....	225000	21750	193886	[illegible]
Vinegar	19	3	....	62	61	1	....	266100	27053	187325	[illegible]
Watches	3	1	....	471	284	190	....	860900	350600	80250	[illegible]
Woolen goods	85	72	19	1680	992	465	223	2023193	531151	1610625	[illegible]

THE STATE OF INDIANA.

Mechanical and manufacturing industries.	Establishm'ts.	Steam-engines.	Water-wheels.	All hands.	Males above 16.	Females above 15.	Youth.	Capital. (Dollars.)	Wages. (Dollars.)	Materials. (Dollars.)	Products. (Dollars.)
Agricultural implements	124	33	6	1268	1257	....	11	1622769	484596	951714	[illegible]
Boats	9	8	....	301	291	....	10	156250	194853	166986	[illegible]
Boots and shoes	88	....	....	689	664	17	8	327275	289092	445660	[illegible]
Bread and other bakery products	101	10	....	334	316	12	6	225300	94009	415766	[illegible]
Brick	275	5	....	2009	1896	....	113	536792	331598	207386	[illegible]
Carriages and wagons	770	15	5	3325	3295	2	28	2196485	1044146	1276233	[illegible]
Cars, freight and passenger	10	9	....	1403	1384	....	19	623333	834124	1039340	[illegible]
Clothing	267	....	....	1649	985	652	12	781659	508527	1326017	[illegible]
Confectionery	30	....	....	107	91	13	3	59825	32286	180034	[illegible]
Cooperage	357	10	....	1868	1837	....	31	611037	584211	950743	[illegible]
Cotton goods	4	7	2	504	119	179	206	551500	113200	548675	[illegible]
Flouring-mill products	611	(*)	(*)	2301	(*)	(*)	(*)	6711239	735183	17290717	[illegible]
Furniture, (not specified)	319	65	15	2780	2519	32	229	2346373	1110660	1267081	[illegible]
Furniture, chairs	33	10	1	416	263	37	116	210626	125734	141098	[illegible]
Glass ware	3	1	....	448	351	2	95	410000	290000	321500	[illegible]
Hubs and other wagon material	33	31	1	593	561	4	28	719800	230788	317764	[illegible]
Iron, forged and rolled	9	42	....	989	947	....	42	1588000	528592	1984668	[illegible]
Iron, nails & spikes, cut & wrought	2	2	....	67	62	....	5	98000	37767	250000	[illegible]
Iron, pig	4	8	....	189	185	....	4	425000	159400	825435	[illegible]
Iron, castings, (not specified)	96	54	7	949	928	....	21	1281582	470733	1619851	[illegible]
Iron, castings, stoves, heaters, and hollow ware	9	7	....	254	254	....	....	390600	141400	243863	[illegible]
Leather, tanned	197	31	1	514	503	2	9	875740	142469	905347	[illegible]
Leather, curried	156	10	....	319	315	....	4	303810	84981	909778	[illegible]
Liquors, distilled	36	19	1	280	277	....	3	658838	126150	1358196	[illegible]
Liquors, malt	99	33	1	443	440	1	2	1117400	175730	627576	[illegible]
Lumber, planed	53	(*)	(*)	512	(*)	(*)	(*)	687600	212621	717734	[illegible]
Lumber, sawed	1307	(*)	(*)	7814	(*)	(*)	(*)	5113116	1752898	5148619	[illegible]
Machinery, (not specified)	62	36	4	1148	1143	....	5	1047376	628774	632089	[illegible]
Machinery, railroad repairing	3	3	....	453	453	....	....	427000	154800	110360	[illegible]
Machinery, steam engines & boilers	33	19	....	1006	996	....	10	1352716	578653	1350104	[illegible]
Marble and stone work, (not spec'd)	31	11	....	235	234	....	1	141900	143256	162355	[illegible]

* Not separately compiled.

TABLE CI.—*Manufactures, in each State and Territory, by Selected Industries*—1870—Cont'd.

THE STATE OF INDIANA—Continued.

Mechanical and manufacturing industries.	Establishm'ts.	Steam-engines.	Water-wheels.	All hands.	Males above 16.	Females above 15.	Youth.	Capital. (Dollars.)	Wages. (Dollars.)	Materials. (Dollars.)	Products. (Dollars.)
Meat, packed, pork	11	6	....	452	452	....	....	1598000	92862	2262737	2780021
Monuments and tombstones	63	2	....	281	278	....	3	149365	86018	136459	329823
Oil, vegetable, linseed	7	5	3	75	73	....	2	380000	24022	514969	600912
Paper, printing	10	5	22	294	194	91	9	393000	100145	327802	581302
Printing and publishing	69	20	....	810	704	26	80	754952	511330	513617	1408142
Saddlery and harness	436	....	....	1333	1314	....	19	625680	321212	806903	1654341
Sash, doors, and blinds	59	50	5	640	637	....	3	663650	291856	536004	1029404
Sewing-machine fixtures	2	1	1	201	201	....	....	251000	130000	171200	500900
Starch	3	2	1	130	101	....	29	220000	46500	256780	348575
Tin, copper, and sheet-iron ware	322	....	....	996	986	5	5	751005	275017	620560	1293206
Tobacco, chew'g, smok'g, and snuff	15	2	....	147	84	33	30	134700	39165	187113	354734
Tobacco, cigars	133	....	....	670	607	16	47	258565	235078	294314	793581
Wood, turned and carved	25	16	3	293	270	....	23	213823	81042	121068	280439
Woolen goods	146	97	54	2395	1386	706	303	3770513	717176	2595604	4212737

THE STATE OF IOWA.

Mechanical and manufacturing industries.	Establishm'ts.	Steam-engines.	Water-wheels.	All hands.	Males above 16.	Females above 15.	Youth.	Capital. (Dollars.)	Wages. (Dollars.)	Materials. (Dollars.)	Products. (Dollars.)
Agricultural implements	55	27	1	552	546	....	6	543040	182138	401371	829965
Boots and shoes	53	....	....	323	318	5	....	126600	134148	188919	423283
Bread and other bakery products	58	3	....	159	154	3	2	134075	33232	177177	315330
Brick	116	....	....	971	944	1	26	168030	192995	96849	425919
Carriages and wagons	449	17	....	1662	1660	1	1	1086882	566222	739240	1952143
Clothing	196	....	....	726	449	276	1	307305	184470	563042	1003732
Cooperage	136	2	....	425	423	....	2	122378	116812	233458	452388
Flouring-mill products	306	(*)	(*)	1298	(*)	(*)	(*)	4351233	469546	9385363	12298882
Furniture	223	22	6	959	889	8	62	670525	295343	340124	981691
Iron, castings	44	33	1	272	270	....	2	359514	137512	252994	532780
Liquors, malt	101	18	1	405	405	....	....	1238134	131571	422148	992848
Lumber, planed	17	(*)	(*)	165	(*)	(*)	(*)	174800	76338	688384	838130
Lumber, sawed	322	(*)	(*)	2963	(*)	(*)	(*)	3536231	931715	3115081	5399315
Machinery, railroad repairing	5	5	1	336	336	....	....	96000	181063	162348	345018
Machinery, steam engines & boilers	15	8	....	170	166	....	4	167160	97340	145429	302395
Meat, packed, pork	10	4	....	328	317	1	10	927150	45170	1064100	1190400
Printing and publishing	67	9	....	544	472	27	45	378775	257308	178212	648752
Saddlery and harness	325	....	....	879	874	1	4	417615	208232	591272	1110852
Sash, doors, and blinds	31	19	1	321	302	....	19	318967	141920	180273	467586
Tin, copper, and sheet-iron ware	231	....	....	609	606	....	3	369470	164609	365418	758011
Tobacco, cigars	71	....	....	319	289	5	25	152050	117983	154845	377773
Woolen goods	68	37	32	1038	645	291	102	1382784	264061	929132	1561341

THE STATE OF KANSAS.

Mechanical and manufacturing industries.	Establishm'ts.	Steam-engines.	Water-wheels.	All hands.	Males above 16.	Females above 15.	Youth.	Capital. (Dollars.)	Wages. (Dollars.)	Materials. (Dollars.)	Products. (Dollars.)
Flouring-mill products	68	(*)	(*)	319	(*)	(*)	(*)	980200	155446	2007786	2638790
Furniture	52	6	....	206	199	1	6	119105	90696	89473	285181
Iron, castings	5	3	....	123	114	....	9	135986	77334	136660	326420
Lumber, sawed	154	(*)	(*)	1012	(*)	(*)	(*)	584565	266707	788120	1664319
Machinery	8	9	....	841	835	....	6	189514	375679	293316	686387
Printing and publishing	21	2	....	216	195	8	13	125500	141044	102161	335650
Saddlery and harness	76	....	....	272	268	....	4	217205	92655	212473	425928
Tin, copper, and sheet-iron ware	73	....	....	230	228	....	2	142050	80661	159478	356003

THE STATE OF KENTUCKY.

Mechanical and manufacturing industries.	Establishm'ts.	Steam-engines.	Water-wheels.	All hands.	Males above 16.	Females above 15.	Youth.	Capital. (Dollars.)	Wages. (Dollars.)	Materials. (Dollars.)	Products. (Dollars.)
Agricultural implements	44	10	....	624	567	....	57	633025	287590	673176	1384917
Bagging	11	2	....	1228	993	102	133	756000	301240	1077300	1752120
Bookbinding	4	....	....	133	78	43	12	100000	68000	258425	353200
Boots and shoes	45	....	....	400	356	39	5	237350	185652	193044	540182
Bread and other bakery products	35	2	....	150	124	12	14	104375	51298	198320	356468
Brick	40	3	....	507	399	....	108	120575	101026	69078	278218
Bridge-building	2	2	....	120	120	....	....	150000	71000	182325	535000
Carriages and wagons	325	3	....	1250	1229	1	20	577405	439076	440170	1339909
Cement	2	2	4	265	223	....	42	350200	160480	90000	302000
Clothing	167	....	....	907	566	335	6	479107	240304	641113	1181158
Confectionery	19	....	....	96	83	8	5	103100	32626	176411	252311
Cooperage	95	2	....	383	368	....	15	125663	[illegible]	[illegible]	[illegible]

* Not separately compiled.

TABLE CI. *Manufactures, in each State and Territory, by Selected Industries—1870—Cont'd.*

THE STATE OF KENTUCKY—Continued.

Mechanical and manufacturing industries.	Establishm'ts.	Steam-engines.	Water-wheels.	All hands.	Males above 16.	Females above 15.	Youth.	Capital. (Dollars.)	Wages. (Dollars.)	Materials. (Dollars.)	Products. (Dollars.)
Cotton goods	5	5	1	269	77	71	121	465000	57951	375048	[illegible]
Flouring-mill products	190	(*)	(*)	660	(*)	(*)	(*)	1657725	197875	4121857	[illegible]
Furniture	90	16	....	967	827	12	128	750355	412872	545472	[illegible]
Glass ware	3	2	....	436	315	4	117	370000	233631	170350	[illegible]
Iron, forged and rolled	6	24	....	876	864	.....	12	1125008	582283	1307064	[illegible]
Iron, pig	19	22	....	1565	1521	.....	44	2979000	417948	1923034	[illegible]
Iron, castings, (not specified)	25	21	....	895	850	.....	45	1457431	494985	1350249	[illegible]
Iron, castings, stoves, heaters, and hollow ware	7	6	....	493	471	.....	22	505060	298000	370500	[illegible]
Leather, tanned	100	15	1	293	282	1	10	566421	70968	741192	[illegible]
Leather, curried	82	....	....	155	154	.....	1	157916	41849	556805	[illegible]
Liquors, distilled	141	95	6	1033	1024	3	6	2670700	257732	1852096	[illegible]
Liquors, malt	35	28	1	193	192	.....	1	584900	102630	365612	[illegible]
Lumber, planed	14	(*)	(*)	218	(*)	(*)	(*)	279225	124024	305589	[illegible]
Lumber, sawed	264	(*)	(*)	1651	(*)	(*)	(*)	1259908	387389	1597519	[illegible]
Machinery, (not specified)	18	9	....	517	507	5	5	409150	229085	380008	[illegible]
Machinery, steam engines & boilers	10	9	....	228	228	.....	.....	339000	236000	331719	[illegible]
Monuments and tombstones	30	1	....	227	221	.....	6	246250	91654	225494	[illegible]
Paints, lead and zinc	2	2	....	40	40	.....	.....	215000	20000	191350	[illegible]
Printing and publishing	31	9	....	441	359	35	47	507000	288720	310092	[illegible]
Saddlery and harness	212	1	....	635	612	4	19	403348	193855	403619	[illegible]
Sash, doors, and blinds	8	6	....	154	147	.....	7	133300	74604	279246	[illegible]
Tin, copper, and sheet-iron ware	127	3	....	531	509	1	21	550710	275061	465749	[illegible]
Tobacco, chew'g, smok'g, and snuff	32	11	....	900	400	159	341	602601	212752	826153	[illegible]
Tobacco, cigars	70	....	....	359	314	5	40	197380	140563	187643	[illegible]
Wool-carding and cloth-dressing	89	36	18	198	183	2	13	117347	17023	311009	[illegible]
Woolen goods	36	29	5	485	271	135	79	583102	142350	530619	[illegible]

THE STATE OF LOUISIANA.

Mechanical and manufacturing industries.	Establishm'ts.	Steam-engines.	Water-wheels.	All hands.	Males above 16.	Females above 15.	Youth.	Capital. (Dollars.)	Wages. (Dollars.)	Materials. (Dollars.)	Products. (Dollars.)
Bread and other bakery products	98	4	....	365	339	9	17	87250	134196	516435	[illegible]
Brick	22	1	....	401	296	70	35	117250	94600	58752	[illegible]
Cars, freight and passenger	5	3	....	222	222	.....	.....	175060	195115	122985	[illegible]
Clothing	111	....	....	441	213	225	3	85115	108986	174995	[illegible]
Cooperage	89	....	....	388	386	.....	2	85865	102750	73612	[illegible]
Cotton goods	4	4	....	246	123	57	66	592000	60000	161485	[illegible]
Flouring-mill products	79	(*)	(*)	91	(*)	(*)	(*)	176000	13640	386145	[illegible]
Ice, by patented process	2	2	....	91	90	.....	1	422000	39000	78485	[illegible]
Iron, castings	15	13	....	385	373	.....	12	367500	250100	196414	[illegible]
Liquors, malt	12	8	....	93	91	2	.....	165850	42240	142225	[illegible]
Lumber, planed	7	(*)	(*)	165	(*)	(*)	(*)	91500	99300	276200	[illegible]
Lumber, sawed	89	(*)	(*)	782	(*)	(*)	(*)	410800	259925	465727	[illegible]
Machinery, steam engines & boilers	8	8	....	189	186	.....	3	314500	150490	192310	[illegible]
Molasses and sugar	606	597	....	21156	15583	3797	1776	10239525	1227479	6052367	[illegible]
Molasses and sugar, refined	3	13	....	141	141	.....	.....	365000	77000	490378	[illegible]
Oil, vegetable, cotton-seed	6	3	....	183	173	2	8	351550	74100	192112	[illegible]
Ship build'g, repair'g, & materials	11	5	....	101	101	.....	.....	207700	127500	69915	[illegible]
Tobacco, cigars	42	....	....	272	268	.....	4	58100	12344	127043	[illegible]

THE STATE OF MAINE.

Mechanical and manufacturing industries.	Establishm'ts.	Steam-engines.	Water-wheels.	All hands.	Males above 16.	Females above 15.	Youth.	Capital. (Dollars.)	Wages. (Dollars.)	Materials. (Dollars.)	Products. (Dollars.)
Bleaching and dyeing	11	2	1	155	119	19	17	261700	64136	2569467	2707000
Boots and shoes	85	6	3	2165	1511	[illegible]	22	677300	771066	[illegible]	[illegible]
Bread and other bakery products	92	9	....	138	128	7	3	117500	58309	244675	[illegible]
Brick	110	2	....	[illegible]	[illegible]	2	2	[illegible]	[illegible]	127231	[illegible]
Carriages and wagons	291	2	[illegible]	[illegible]	[illegible]	.....	5	[illegible]	356207	[illegible]	[illegible]
Clothing	161	....	....	[illegible]	[illegible]	[illegible]	63	[illegible]	[illegible]	1891501	[illegible]
Coal-oil, rectified	2	[illegible]	....	[illegible]	[illegible]	.....	.....	[illegible]	90060	516097	[illegible]
Cooperage	217	3	7	[illegible]	[illegible]	.....	1	211350	132745	[illegible]	[illegible]
Cotton goods	23	2	[illegible]	[illegible]	[illegible]	[illegible]	[illegible]	[illegible]	[illegible]	[illegible]	[illegible]
Edge tools and axes	9	1	11	[illegible]	[illegible]	.....	.....	214750	111382	113767	[illegible]
Fish, cured and packed	40	....	1	[illegible]	[illegible]	127	14	[illegible]	[illegible]	[illegible]	[illegible]
Flouring-mill products	66	(*)	(*)	[illegible]	(*)	(*)	(*)	[illegible]	[illegible]	[illegible]	[illegible]
Furniture	[illegible]	5	32	461	[illegible]	62	31	[illegible]	[illegible]	[illegible]	[illegible]
Iron, forged and rolled	4	[illegible]	[illegible]	[illegible]	[illegible]	.....	15	[illegible]	[illegible]	[illegible]	[illegible]
Iron, castings	47	21	17	512	[illegible]	.....	3	[illegible]	247472	[illegible]	[illegible]
Leather, tanned	123	[illegible]	[illegible]	781	772	1	8	1600740	[illegible]	[illegible]	[illegible]
Leather, curried	[illegible]	[illegible]	[illegible]	[illegible]	[illegible]	.....	3	[illegible]	64244	[illegible]	[illegible]
Lime	43	....	....	759	759	.....	.....	[illegible]	[illegible]	[illegible]	[illegible]

* Not separately compiled.

TABLE CI.—*Manufactures, in each State and Territory, by Selected Industries*—1870—Cont'd.

THE STATE OF MAINE—Continued.

Mechanical and manufacturing industries.	Establishm'ts.	Steam-engines.	Water-wheels.	All hands.	Males above 16.	Females above 15.	Youth.	Capital. (Dollars.)	Wages. (Dollars.)	Material. (Dollars.)	Products. (Dollars.)
Lumber, planed	11	(*)	(*)	110	(*)	(*)	(*)	98000	37900	221320	294500
Lumber, sawed	570	(*)	(*)	7157	(*)	(*)	(*)	6020394	2383134	6494805	10712160
Machinery, (not specified)	37	13	14	307	307	....	....	275822	150826	174370	438814
Machinery, cotton and woolen	19	6	13	595	568	22	5	895064	223085	343133	693643
Machinery, railroad repairing	3	2	....	224	224	....	....	317600	132400	175900	387083
Machinery, steam engines & boilers	11	10	....	219	216	3	....	269400	118924	82762	272883
Marble and stone work, (n. s.)	58	....	....	580	579	1	....	149541	305250	222014	777615
Meat, cured and packed, (n. s.)	2	1	....	201	42	87	72	150600	34200	129280	432000
Molasses and sugar, refined	3	3	....	185	185	....	....	775000	117050	2958113	3142132
Oil floor-cloth	6	5	....	297	293	4	....	525000	149500	850200	1314000
Paper, printing	9	....	23	320	175	134	11	284000	116641	694673	957607
Printing and publishing	31	29	....	361	225	96	40	292562	161756	116037	422132
Saddlery and harness	142	1	1	485	377	65	43	160650	93501	159219	306890
Sails	37	....	....	155	148	6	1	99840	59164	260909	387834
Sash, doors, and blinds	49	8	35	371	364	....	7	320000	140751	182667	438039
Ship build'g, repair'g, and materials	113	4	....	1802	1802	....	....	904473	627135	1263821	2358445
Tin, copper, and sheet-iron ware	125	....	....	383	381	....	2	226630	105125	165361	308747
Vegetables, canned	3	2	....	308	112	109	87	348000	82500	247000	605000
Wool-carding and cloth-dressing	62	2	50	136	127	9	....	87610	13518	223985	288373
Woolen goods	56	2	78	2925	1471	1244	210	4092685	1035483	3761715	6150680

THE STATE OF MARYLAND.

Mechanical and manufacturing industries.	Establishm'ts.	Steam-engines.	Water-wheels.	All hands.	Males above 16.	Females above 15.	Youth.	Capital. (Dollars.)	Wages. (Dollars.)	Material. (Dollars.)	Products. (Dollars.)
Agricultural implements	34	14	2	295	295	....	....	281300	117311	276257	549085
Bags, other than paper	2	1	....	88	25	63	....	60000	23000	330000	430000
Boots and shoes	68	2	....	1631	1279	335	17	464300	676701	905102	1997768
Boxes, wooden, (not cigar)	18	10	1	186	183	....	3	63600	58476	152738	260380
Brass founding and finishing	5	4	....	136	108	....	28	58000	61559	85676	255435
Bread and other bakery products	159	7	....	488	434	17	37	374195	124168	765914	1280399
Brick	73	5	....	2051	1919	1	131	1063300	588283	236963	1191545
Brooms and whisk-brushes	11	....	....	218	90	....	128	70575	35836	185704	277938
Carriages and wagons	133	....	1	681	669	....	12	297650	227170	219132	667157
Clothing	323	....	....	7453	3635	3793	25	2284825	1135426	3785993	5970713
Coal-oil, rectified	8	8	....	55	55	....	....	198000	23120	546171	647389
Coffee and spices, roasted & ground	4	4	....	29	29	....	....	139600	16123	312570	360535
Confectionery	52	1	3	279	235	37	7	249585	73450	475704	733431
Cooperage	88	2	....	745	734	....	11	290134	275217	415037	873789
Copper, milled and smelted	1	1	....	127	121	1	5	800000	96500	1098665	1016500
Cotton goods, (not specified)	22	8	21	2860	688	1452	720	2734250	671033	3409426	4832808
Fertilizers	15	6	7	126	119	....	7	432800	44827	522886	632358
Flouring-mill products	151	(*)	(*)	431	(*)	(*)	(*)	1429700	100785	3231982	3772630
Fruits and vegetables, canned	19	7	....	1985	801	902	282	603800	263419	1028818	1527230
Furniture	137	16	....	1134	1099	2	33	847970	450824	572778	1399488
Iron, forged and rolled	7	23	15	1444	1390	....	54	983000	709922	1300315	3573212
Iron, pig	14	12	7	859	839	....	20	2005000	255941	1286881	2143089
Iron, castings	43	30	....	695	686	....	9	784135	215605	453370	928094
Leather, tanned	69	21	3	281	275	3	3	792430	94180	926406	1265388
Leather, curried	50	2	....	163	161	1	1	232145	53131	494075	623308
Liquors, distilled	8	7	3	63	63	....	....	220700	30228	381236	889981
Liquors, malt	32	10	....	208	208	....	....	583500	103644	510492	665743
Lumber, planed	6	(*)	(*)	128	(*)	(*)	(*)	211000	57088	304796	472015
Lumber, sawed	110	(*)	(*)	726	(*)	(*)	(*)	720100	223308	514744	1184565
Machinery, (not specified)	22	17	2	343	341	....	2	372700	175744	323646	581391
Machinery, steam engines & boilers	7	7	....	341	330	....	11	435000	174527	182730	373475
Malt	3	3	....	54	54	....	....	145050	20780	208428	339500
Meat, packed, pork	1	1	....	25	25	....	....	125000	14000	556200	595000
Molasses and sugar, refined	4	7	....	437	432	....	5	952000	198551	6394569	7007857
Monuments and tombstones	24	5	....	274	267	....	7	228250	126467	143896	375597
Musical instruments and materials	9	1	....	384	377	....	7	594000	249348	317570	674600
Oil, vegetable	2	2	1	43	43	....	....	145000	18900	371400	478125
Oysters and fish, canned	13	5	....	1531	699	532	280	553300	256719	922402	1418900
Paints, (not specified)	2	2	....	41	41	....	....	65000	20000	300000	387500
Paints, lead and zinc	3	3	....	69	69	....	....	355000	44500	465148	640000
Paper, printing	12	4	17	266	146	102	18	1121800	86116	445498	823000
Patent medicines and compounds	14	....	....	97	77	20	....	201350	27333	131850	288850
Printing and publishing, (n. s.)	40	25	....	665	614	10	41	802800	404305	334556	1179988
Printing, job	27	14	....	250	202	9	39	181350	101947	165048	381581
Saddlery and harness	135	....	....	420	411	....	9	207385	109806	267007	530033
Sash, doors, and blinds	17	13	....	262	253	4	5	282425	149014	214284	418506
Ship build'g, repair'g, and materials	31	4	....	313	313	....	....	172500	116836	196723	357404
Soap and candles	13	3	....	99	93	....	6	230030	38392	[illegible]	[illegible]

* Not separately compiled.

TABLE CI.—*Manufactures, in each State and Territory, by Selected Industries*—1870—Cont'd

THE STATE OF MARYLAND—Continued.

Mechanical and manufacturing industries.	Establishm'ts.	Steam-engines.	Water-wheels.	All hands.	Males above 16.	Females above 15.	Youth.	Capital. (Dollars.)	Wages. (Dollars.)	Materials. (Dollars.)	Products. (Dollars.)
Tin, copper and sheet-iron ware	183	1		956	875	20	61	663500	318742	901901	[illegible]
Tobacco, chew'g, smok'g, and snuff	13	9		346	142	149	55	496400	82046	251911	[illegible]
Tobacco, cigars	269			1034	924	51	59	409100	304502	409603	[illegible]
Woolen goods	28	2	28	309	235	65	9	198045	79739	214364	[illegible]

THE STATE OF MASSACHUSETTS.

Mechanical and manufacturing industries.	Establishm'ts.	Steam-engines.	Water-wheels.	All hands.	Males above 16.	Females above 15.	Youth.	Capital. (Dollars.)	Wages. (Dollars.)	Materials. (Dollars.)	Products. (Dollars.)
Agricultural implements	37	8	31	477	471	2	4	499400	243112	487460	[illegible]
Belting and hose, leather	16	3	1	85	85			903500	43434	[illegible]	[illegible]
Bleaching and dyeing	32	19	4	1387	1048	297	42	1063650	608348	[illegible]	[illegible]
Bookbinding	65	10		1078	483	577	18	492300	478310	588070	[illegible]
Boot and shoe findings	170	22	3	1612	591	868	153	372030	450358	1204420	[illegible]
Boots and shoes	1123	200	18	51167	39365	10773	1029	19148645	24955827	50509201	[illegible]
Boxes, packing	110	55	59	917	859	36	22	779840	401637	915962	[illegible]
Boxes, paper	39	5		753	129	610	14	202425	180267	252267	[illegible]
Brass and copper tubing	1	2		115	110		5	200000	57290	340800	[illegible]
Brass founding and finishing	30	10	2	430	401	8	21	218550	191414	405361	[illegible]
Bread and other bakery products	144	21		1087	976	89	22	758650	552215	2128676	3130172
Brick	107	28	3	2901	2802		99	2433310	765168	978508	2251984
Brooms and whisk-brushes	33			168	166	1	1	79475	54775	[illegible]	[illegible]
Brushes	13	6	1	639	420	208	11	199600	178332	297671	[illegible]
Buttons	9	3	6	557	137	349	71	272500	187808	199170	511175
Carpets, other than rag	6	9	5	2200	841	1323	36	3250000	832954	[illegible]	[illegible]
Carriages and sleds, children's	10	1	7	150	124	26		102425	60750	90567	251180
Carriages and wagons	326	10	23	2914	2888	15	11	1729091	1480959	[illegible]	[illegible]
Cars, freight and passenger	6	5		866	866			1245000	636760	[illegible]	[illegible]
Cheese, (factory)	23			66	49	16	1	85300	15399	281768	321900
Chocolate	4	3	9	148	72	76		300000	61006	576414	[illegible]
Chromos and lithographs	7	2		166	157	1	8	127800	103700	91185	[illegible]
Clothing, men's	446	8		9878	3031	6730	117	5096764	3815742	11913317	[illegible]
Clothing, women's	116			959	62	882	15	190820	248262	[illegible]	1512613
Coal-oil, rectified	8	11		155	150		5	466000	121940	791828	[illegible]
Coffee and spices, roasted & ground	19	16	1	131	106	25		407500	63504	448070	[illegible]
Coffins	33	1		160	153	7		130650	73737	88576	[illegible]
Collars and cuffs, paper	9	7	6	329	57	265	7	983625	108650	[illegible]	[illegible]
Combs	20	4	15	526	392	90	44	320950	170540	193458	[illegible]
Confectionery	63	6		549	363	181	5	309745	227778	873718	[illegible]
Cooperage	93	11	32	850	836	6	8	438475	383934	[illegible]	[illegible]
Copper, milled and smelted	1	1		97	97			500000	50200	466374	[illegible]
Copper, rolled	2	2	5	100	100			668750	62000	499105	[illegible]
Coppersmithing	8	3		92	92			91000	60500	93798	[illegible]
Cordage and twine	32	10	9	988	643	231	114	600900	395273	1961410	[illegible]
Cordials and sirups	3			29	17	12		103000	27100	87122	[illegible]
Cotton goods	194	114	336	43596	13713	24128	5755	44832375	13612025	[illegible]	[illegible]
Cutlery	12	3	22	1140	1056	74	10	1135400	601247	357238	[illegible]
Drugs and chemicals	22	7		354	301	45	8	1230800	190545	1152780	[illegible]
Dye-woods and dye-stuffs, ground	2	6		45	45			93000	21750	[illegible]	[illegible]
Edge-tools and axes	17	3	19	479	479			628240	293346	477040	[illegible]
Envelopes	5	4		187	36	138	13	90500	64450	314964	[illegible]
Fertilizers	8	5	3	116	146			516100	82500	478450	[illegible]
Fire-arms, small-arms	12	8	3	464	439	3	22	546800	388679	96108	[illegible]
Fish, cured and packed	13	4		65	65			75500	19375	86572	[illegible]
Flax and linen goods	3	2	8	817	292	317	208	982000	223421	336170	[illegible]
Flouring-mill products	185	(*)	(*)	606	(*)	(*)	(*)	1763700	224360	7028875	[illegible]
Food preparations, animal	8	5	1	65	63	2		80000	21915	175584	[illegible]
Furniture	324	80	120	9794	6200	2622	972	6124875	3560751	4863950	[illegible]
Furs, dressed	16	1		146	48	96	2	257900	40160	202570	[illegible]
Gas and lamp fixtures	4	2		218	199	13	6	150000	122200	179468	[illegible]
Glass ware	11	6		1570	1130	376	64	1205000	669520	531634	[illegible]
Glass, window	3	1	2	494	403	37	54	883560	257200	127390	[illegible]
Glue	15	5		143	142	1		240600	70750	220799	[illegible]
Hardware	119	56	40	1757	1668	57	32	1903050	929738	891065	[illegible]
Hats and caps	50	16		3290	953	2225	112	855000	985304	1846566	[illegible]
Heating apparatus	5	4		124	124			116500	66600	142950	[illegible]
Hoop-skirts and corsets	13	4		664	93	563	8	197800	170561	349225	[illegible]
Hosiery	32	13	18	2415	844	1404	167	1570500	848864	1515396	[illegible]
Hubs and other wagon material	23	10	9	256	255		1	228800	123080	284387	[illegible]
India-rubber and elastic goods	16	10	6	1405	492	818	95	1920600	580723	1554006	[illegible]
Instrum'ts, professional & scientific	12	3	1	202	185	10	7	647000	119450	87470	[illegible]
Iron, forged and rolled	29	51	35	2390	2385		5	2760125	1327673	[illegible]	[illegible]

* Not separately compiled.

TABLE CI.—*Manufactures, in each State and Territory, by Selected Industries*—1870—Cont'd.

THE STATE OF MASSACHUSETTS—Continued.

Mechanical and manufacturing industries.	Establishm'ts.	Steam-engines.	Water-wheels.	All hands.	Males above 16.	Females above 16.	Youth.	Capital. (*Dollars.*)	Wages. (*Dollars.*)	Materials. (*Dollars.*)	Products. (*Dollars.*)
Iron, bolts, nuts, washers, and rivets	6	2	1	990	958	27	5	213600	68225	170586	343280
Iron, nails & spikes, cut & wrought	49	27	44	2458	2026	333	99	2600850	1050230	4082775	5986144
Iron, pipe, wrought	5	3	1	335	332	....	3	325000	219500	976218	1407000
Iron, pig	4	4	2	421	421	....	....	700000	334541	446823	722225
Iron, castings, (not specified)	101	63	36	2749	2712	1	36	2496900	1640402	2574320	5285154
Iron, castings, stoves, heaters, and hollow ware	18	12	8	965	952	....	13	940500	646401	555675	1781548
Jewelry	50	33	10	1642	1241	334	67	972500	786650	825523	2342025
Lasts	20	16	2	208	207	1	....	146000	135960	68617	313768
Lead pipe	1	....	....	14	14	....	....	310000	8400	481200	616650
Leather, tanned	138	75	37	1424	1416	....	8	3130850	756467	8025578	9984497
Leather, curried	196	99	8	3194	3168	11	15	3163076	1812052	14969920	19211330
Leather, morocco, tanned & curried	40	23	3	744	703	21	20	998900	450200	2315800	3158020
Leather, patent and enameled	6	2	1	133	133	....	....	177000	105220	660150	911600
Liquors, distilled	11	6	2	66	66	....	....	312900	42477	571702	774821
Liquors, malt	18	6	1	230	230	....	....	959600	133040	866177	1542487
Looking-glass and picture frames	56	5	1	433	415	8	10	347900	220718	538668	1122211
Lumber, planed	66	(*)	(*)	1152	(*)	(*)	(*)	1685500	752881	3782801	5153170
Lumber, sawed	365	(*)	(*)	1672	(*)	(*)	(*)	1714700	500808	1912907	3138277
Machinery, (not specified)	200	118	66	3626	3577	31	18	4105600	2116494	2570666	6733102
Machinery, cotton and woolen	95	52	30	2816	2607	183	26	2940750	1575017	2258392	4821314
Machinery, railroad repairing	3	3	....	1101	1043	....	58	708500	635835	812825	1898894
Machinery, steam engines & boilers	42	37	3	1357	1346	5	6	1843000	878901	1335073	2973432
Marble and stone work, (n. s.)	49	9	1	1365	1363	....	2	993500	820111	879838	2178450
Matches	8	....	7	147	53	88	6	82700	41140	115441	574117
Meat, cured and packed, (n. s.)	2	1	....	131	56	75	....	103500	50140	300500	401500
Meat, packed, pork	7	2	....	77	77	....	....	140000	39660	801848	1067060
Millinery	87	2	....	544	70	464	10	189100	133268	382047	707914
Mineral and soda waters	25	....	....	203	202	....	1	127500	87043	120377	383786
Molasses and sugar, refined	4	14	....	460	460	....	....	2200000	226848	6944395	7665485
Monuments and tombstones	61	4	1	499	499	....	....	412340	249733	419147	879969
Musical instruments and materials	60	23	14	2193	2173	16	4	3247436	1800082	1142304	4453794
Oil, fish	9	11	....	152	152	....	....	482000	57133	1970232	2578176
Oil, linseed	2	2	....	69	67	2	....	200000	47500	914000	1003610
Paints, (not specified)	9	6	4	73	68	1	4	112500	41790	141855	340672
Paints, lead and zinc	7	9	....	193	187	6	....	585000	101700	1223448	1637500
Paper, (not specified)	17	7	40	364	227	130	7	558100	144903	555139	1052784
Paper, printing	25	11	108	1173	728	398	47	1858700	549190	3052971	4319924
Paper, wrapping	23	8	55	416	332	66	18	914500	181752	769769	1289178
Paper, writing	30	4	98	2602	862	1723	17	4387828	979000	3638470	6025595
Patent medicines and compounds	36	3	....	294	188	91	15	827800	107064	921964	1447990
Plated ware	37	11	2	786	620	152	14	493775	387387	402722	1012100
Pocket-books	12	....	....	297	100	196	1	111850	112710	250172	482000
Preserves and sauces	5	2	....	137	51	86	....	155000	34000	463000	602276
Printing cotton and woolen goods	11	33	8	2996	2006	726	264	2894653	1110055	15420530	17325150
Printing, and publishing (n. s.)	18	5	....	435	381	36	18	520400	268533	308611	1702740
Printing and publishing, book	3	3	....	311	224	87	....	268000	177456	372860	1205000
Printing and publishing, newspaper	52	23	....	1135	916	135	84	2545400	991530	1433835	4005425
Printing, job	89	20	1	1092	898	179	15	1634650	515016	420544	1477811
Roofing materials	26	2	1	196	196	....	....	272300	95541	323543	526408
Saddlery and harness	247	1	....	1008	917	84	7	614375	413256	719526	1503994
Safes, doors, and vaults, (fire-proof)	6	3	....	201	201	....	....	288000	112300	221700	500000
Sails	46	....	....	214	207	7	....	111400	95355	291864	503385
Sash, doors, and blinds	58	26	18	912	903	3	6	752000	556077	1052577	1997905
Screws	4	1	1	65	64	1	....	1011060	37000	234484	723000
Sewing-machines	6	5	1	1033	1009	12	12	2677800	686432	641725	1927310
Ship build'g, repair'g, and materials	98	18	....	1166	1164	....	2	1192350	727173	902845	2070201
Shoddy	17	3	20	189	127	44	18	298000	63000	326311	529375
Shovels and spades	5	6	18	654	647	2	5	371100	376000	1080144	1890526
Show-cases	5	....	....	70	70	....	....	33000	43100	164320	254000
Silk goods	9	6	7	433	97	286	70	412000	154300	937000	1402500
Silver ware	10	5	1	210	190	19	1	239000	150400	232161	493633
Soap and candles	96	15	....	451	443	7	1	717130	197040	1309819	1923464
Soda-water apparatus	6	4	....	86	86	....	....	199000	53200	121200	429575
Straw goods	39	18	2	11441	1113	10003	325	1361400	1411350	2503070	4869514
Tin, copper, and sheet-iron ware	300	4	....	1584	1534	36	14	1284000	766485	1384095	2785674
Tobacco, cigars	128	....	....	968	740	216	12	447085	426044	678129	1521511
Trunks, valises, and satchels	18	....	....	181	157	24	....	143700	95982	147729	407400
Type-founding	4	1	....	214	99	105	10	115000	104100	55575	252000
Upholstery	77	....	....	901	621	271	9	978655	461909	1234157	2424457
Varnish	8	....	....	39	39	....	....	124500	23884	463302	597687
Watches	3	1	....	758	497	249	12	980000	610024	175909	1281160
Whips and canes	38	2	6	452	282	167	3	480750	209059	259431	604367
Wire	6	10	14	910	848	62	....	1418500	[illegible]	1226822	[illegible]

* Not separately compiled.

TABLE [illegible].—[illegible]

THE STATE OF MASSACHUSETTS—Continued.

Mechanical and manufacturing industries.	Establishments.	Steam-engines.	Water-wheels.	All hands.	Males above 16.	Females above 15.	Youth.	Capital. (Dollars.)	Wages. (Dollars.)	Materials. (Dollars.)	Products. (Dollars.)
Wire work	26	2	7	[illegible]	215	[illegible]	43	[illegible]	[illegible]	240944	[illegible]
Wood brackets, moldings, & scroll	7	6	2	137	[illegible]	1	3	[illegible]	[illegible]	137020	[illegible]
Wooden ware	25	5	25	402	377	17	18	[illegible]	[illegible]	[illegible]	[illegible]
Wood, turned and carved	78	17	50	397	367	[illegible]	19	[illegible]	[illegible]	[illegible]	[illegible]
Woolen goods	182	91	210	[illegible]	10751	[illegible]	[illegible]	[illegible]	[illegible]	[illegible]	[illegible]
Worsted goods	35	19	25	[illegible]	1625	3190	439	[illegible]	[illegible]	[illegible]	[illegible]

THE STATE OF MICHIGAN.

Mechanical and manufacturing industries.	Establishments.	Steam-engines.	Water-wheels.	All hands.	Males above 16.	Females above 15.	Youth.	Capital. (Dollars.)	Wages. (Dollars.)	Materials. (Dollars.)	Products. (Dollars.)
Agricultural implements	161	52	20	969	960	...	9	1251756	362344	714923	[illegible]
Boots and shoes	81	1	...	830	755	68	5	578172	372844	587104	[illegible]
Bread, and other bakery products	82	8	...	306	298	1	7	291672	95251	459716	[illegible]
Brick	136	25	...	1584	1505	21	58	438800	275331	128685	[illegible]
Carriages and wagons	531	8	6	2289	2255	...	4	1649860	761764	862903	[illegible]
Cars, freight and passenger	3	4	...	823	809	2	12	615223	490659	687292	[illegible]
Clothing	288	...	...	2593	1352	1171	70	1098650	696881	1444596	[illegible]
Confectionery	14	...	...	89	72	14	3	57400	30794	179769	[illegible]
Cooperage	291	6	...	1139	1137	...	2	438165	325096	530706	[illegible]
Copper, milled and smelted	19	37	...	636	512	...	94	1301000	350909	8499496	[illegible]
Flouring mill products	315	(*)	(*)	1389	(*)	(*)	(*)	5369700	519848	14522834	[illegible]
Furniture	210	60	21	2365	1969	129	267	2067020	660179	679612	[illegible]
Iron, forged and rolled	3	12	...	465	426	...	39	725000	239164	446000	[illegible]
Iron, pig	17	15	7	1625	1625	...	...	2528000	844259	1651102	[illegible]
Iron, castings, (not specified)	106	98	19	1101	1088	...	13	1571447	519433	[illegible]	[illegible]
Leather, tanned	99	47	9	478	474	1	3	897047	192150	1167876	1606311
Leather, curried	73	...	...	249	248	1	...	395493	89799	833360	[illegible]
Liquors, malt	128	25	2	481	473	1	7	1327441	102768	598898	[illegible]
Looking-glasses and picture frames	9		...	330	151	45	134	97125	90989	111083	[illegible]
Lumber, planed	58	(*)	(*)	488	(*)	(*)	(*)	630650	192157	710165	[illegible]
Lumber, sawed	1180	(*)	(*)	18817	(*)	(*)	(*)	26086415	6274374	14045223	[illegible]
Machinery, (not specified)	63	34	3	685	682	2	1	808666	371965	687740	[illegible]
Machinery, steam engines & boilers	31	[illegible]	[illegible]	412	401	...	11	476713	211076	369913	[illegible]
Meat, packed, pork	4	...	...	33	33	...	...	170000	12050	[illegible]	[illegible]
Millinery	111	...	...	409	16	374	19	132706	49555	197542	[illegible]
Monuments and tombstones	50	3	...	242	240	...	2	176175	82966	119663	[illegible]
Paper, printing	4	13	...	170	89	78	3	215000	50900	257580	[illegible]
Plaster, ground	22	8	13	240	234	...	6	687100	98702	166691	[illegible]
Printing and publishing	65	19	...	726	633	28	65	697777	393999	392104	1071523
Saddlery and harness	288	1	...	824	821	...	3	460436	197497	413637	[illegible]
Salt	65	39	...	858	826	2	30	1717500	331239	410561	1176811
Sash, doors, and blinds	150	107	33	1305	1273	...	32	1279200	564959	834232	[illegible]
Ship build'g, repair'g, and materials	26	6	...	637	637	...	...	547000	233031	271064	[illegible]
Tin, copper, and sheet-iron ware	260	1	...	835	819	...	16	487515	256595	437995	[illegible]
Tobacco and cigars	6	4	...	205	90	73	42	228500	67105	445660	[illegible]
Tobacco, chew'g, smok'g and snuff	9	9	...	470	169	152	149	847500	160250	697904	1131743
Tobacco, cigars	99			581	501	24	56	225202	214575	304741	[illegible]
Wooden ware	17	16	...	297	174	25	28	324200	69774	87795	[illegible]
Wood, turned and carved	43	27	5	282	262	...	20	206825	85292	92703	[illegible]
Woolen goods	38	16	28	585	354	190	41	858200	174872	530064	[illegible]

THE STATE OF MINNESOTA.

Mechanical and manufacturing industries.	Establishments.	Steam-engines.	Water-wheels.	All hands.	Males above 16.	Females above 15.	Youth.	Capital. (Dollars.)	Wages. (Dollars.)	Materials. (Dollars.)	Products. (Dollars.)
Agricultural implements	27	9	2	167	166	...	1	196712	72520	92036	[illegible]
Boots and shoes	29	...	...	212	208	4	...	97400	103990	231427	[illegible]
Carriages and wagons	102	4	1	444	442	...	2	[illegible]	183094	170119	[illegible]
Cars, freight and passenger	1	...	1	75	75	...	...	150000	52800	735500	[illegible]
Clothing	61	...	...	227	202	25	...	166250	[illegible]	144406	310667
Cooperage	62	1	1	338	334	...	4	120020	130137	219293	[illegible]
Flouring-mill products	112	(*)	(*)	531	(*)	(*)	(*)	2176765	231097	4028404	[illegible]
Furniture	85	8	2	308	250	2	6	302550	142981	117427	[illegible]
Liquors, malt	65	2	...	225	223	...	2	450750	[illegible]	161812	[illegible]
Lumber	157	(*)	(*)	2818	(*)	(*)	(*)	[illegible]	[illegible]	2404125	[illegible]
Machinery, railroad repairing	1	3	1	452	450	...	...	[illegible]	378962	499112	[illegible]
Machinery, steam engines & boilers	8	3	3	241	233	...	...	[illegible]	118798	[illegible]	[illegible]
Printing and publishing, newspaper	2	2	...	211	164	12	35	[illegible]	[illegible]	[illegible]	[illegible]
Saddlery and harness	93	1	...	299	298	...	1	165475	[illegible]	184771	[illegible]
Sash, doors, and blinds	27	15	3	254	254	...	...	[illegible]	127917	[illegible]	[illegible]
Tin, copper, and sheet-iron ware	78	...	...	235	223	...	2	[illegible]	[illegible]	154841	[illegible]

* Not separately compiled.

TABLE CI.—*Manufactures, in each State and Territory, by Selected Industries*—1870—Cont'd.

THE STATE OF MISSISSIPPI.

Mechanical and manufacturing industries.	Establishm'ts.	Steam-engines.	Water-wheels.	All hands.	Males above 16.	Females above 15.	Youth.	Capital. (Dollars.)	Wages. (Dollars.)	Materials. (Dollars.)	Products. (Dollars.)
Carriages and wagons	85	4	....	203	201	....	2	138495	91469	74911	269031
Flouring-mill products	45	(*)	(*)	113	(*)	(*)	(*)	171518	18472	356734	468576
Lumber	156	(*)	(*)	1643	(*)	(*)	(*)	1012382	521396	804193	2020145

THE STATE OF MISSOURI.

Mechanical and manufacturing industries.	Establishm'ts.	Steam-engines.	Water-wheels.	All hands.	Males above 16.	Females above 15.	Youth.	Capital. (Dollars.)	Wages. (Dollars.)	Materials. (Dollars.)	Products. (Dollars.)
Agricultural implements	38	14	....	537	497	....	40	791435	403847	699376	1588108
Bagging	2	2	....	333	103	116	114	1200000	235000	423100	750000
Bags, other than paper	6	3	....	320	101	153	66	511000	192600	1464100	5037250
Boats	5	10	....	226	212	....	14	350200	192300	196850	537000
Boots and shoes	182	....	....	960	856	23	81	505200	562703	1102118	2363701
Boxes, packing	8	2		86	69	....	17	123500	49700	124600	280100
Brass founding and finishing	10	5		147	129	....	18	203500	91270	101175	292500
Bread and other bakery products	217	6		894	700	60	125	697615	473499	2061826	3160053
Brick	186	7		2198	2077	2	119	1198431	652610	440639	3148884
Bridge-building	7	22		385	385	....	....	1515100	268300	1540305	2072030
Brooms and whisk-brushes	33	....		202	175	2	25	130235	114225	425144	746043
Brushes	14	....		188	100	9	79	104200	92620	113550	298000
Carriages and wagons	331	5		2170	2094	2	74	1594679	949609	1306587	3253734
Cars, freight and passenger	3	5		736	691	....	45	660000	558700	1312000	2200150
Chromos and lithographs		....		65	54	....	11	85000	54200	67000	252500
Clothing, men's	507	....		3470	2323	1003	144	2298025	1821950	3619435	7971968
Clothing, women's	157	....		884	31	793	60	261050	209275	634850	1080170
Confectionery	20	5		306	205	49	52	290250	186800	602240	1274855
Cooperage	291	3		1536	1411	4	121	851430	670635	1107107	2234581
Coppersmithing	1	1		128	68	2	58	200000	100000	250000	500000
Cordage and twine	17	....		145	101	....	44	87780	57480	164380	272400
Cotton goods, (not specified)	3	3		361	107	154	100	489200	120300	481745	798050
Flouring-mill products	385	(*)	(*)	2170	(*)	(*)	(*)	7644322	954986	22383777	26332160
Furniture	271	32		2021	1691	8	322	2670630	1068901	1638418	3830749
Hardware, saddlery	12	2		194	188	....	6	85200	98700	181650	374800
Hats and caps	9	....		120	72	27	21	85700	69700	271700	396600
Iron, forged and rolled	2	7		401	385		16	1007143	330000	826750	1455000
Iron nails & spikes, cut & wrought	1	2		47	32		15	142857	30000	237250	294000
Iron, pig	9	15	2	1123	1045	....	78	1914000	836780	1375766	2991618
Iron castings, (not specified)	23	15		397	394	....	3	321000	258210	766162	1182255
Iron castings, stoves, heaters, and hollow ware	18	21		1580	1351	....	229	2787500	1186674	1431475	2981350
Lead, bar and sheet	1	1	....	22	22	....	....	200000	16000	622500	650000
Lead, pig	31	9	11	194	194	....	....	1428600	49220	454288	642831
Leather, tanned	50	4	....	164	162	....	2	135242	78528	252359	403432
Leather, curried	30	....	....	76	76	....	....	54008	33297	277875	371496
Lightning-rods	6	....	....	45	45	....	....	106000	28500	151300	632000
Lime	23	1	....	187	183	....	4	182875	101050	216064	462900
Liquors, distilled	16	5	....	110	105		5	413400	56115	535786	917450
Liquors, malt	87	50	....	788	774		14	4631050	507973	2377028	6319548
Liquors, vinous	190	....	....	483	473		10	680875	79125	663811	934442
Lumber, planed	18	(*)	(*)	210	(*)	(*)	(*)	306000	97406	587559	843335
Lumber, sawed	477	(*)	(*)	2898	(*)	(*)	(*)	2656710	928699	3192056	5838127
Machinery, (not specified)	15	5	....	106	105		1	139886	60920	118450	264400
Machinery, railroad repairing	3	2	....	272	272		....	135000	187800	131436	319836
Machinery, steam engines & boilers	32	32	....	1421	1289		132	2079900	1100100	1806064	3825100
Malt	10	6	....	71	71	....	....	455000	40000	551870	706550
Marble & stone work, (not specified)	89	6	....	554	525	....	29	341260	396270	476315	1177505
Matches	5	4	....	189	41	66	79	110500	58900	104375	546400
Meat, packed, beef	4	....	....	101	99	....	2	105000	18075	236945	311200
Meat, packed, pork	23	15	....	952	859	....	93	4042000	412963	10361999	13021995
Millinery	85	....	....	393	5	355	33	150075	96246	221718	432796
Mineral and soda waters	20	5	....	164	126	4	34	96200	72920	77040	254375
Molasses and sugar, refined	1	10	....	302	252	....	50	2000000	175000	3667000	4135250
Monuments and tombstones	36	1	....	154	152	1	1	117900	71870	94817	268850
Oil, animal	3	4	....	77	68	....	9	525000	62500	2866100	4100000
Oil, vegetable, castor	1	2	....	38	38	....	....	325000	30000	355000	500000
Paints, (not specified)	10	12	....	235	223	....	12	987500	162281	1550516	2090850
Patent medicines and compounds	25	2	....	312	225	29	58	1049000	207140	771093	2073875
Printing and publishing, (n. s.)	28	16	....	1188	941	132	115	1797300	890050	1819270	3837830
Printing, newspaper	32	6	....	534	481	6	47	364700	304185	370859	994577
Printing, job	25	5	....	218	163	11	44	212100	125900	206675	436800
Saddlery and harness	390	....	....	1842	1664	3	175	2025164	892518	3189730	5424626
Sails	7	....	....	80	32	29	19	87000	40400	162450	299850

* Not separately compiled.

TABLE CI.—*Manufactures, in each State and Territory, by Selected Industries*—1870—Cont'd.

THE STATE OF MISSOURI—Continued.

Mechanical and manufacturing industries.	Establishm'ts.	Steam-engines.	Water-wheels.	All hands.	Males above 16.	Females above 15.	Youth.	Capital. (Dollars.)	Wages. (Dollars.)	Materials. (Dollars.)	Products. (Dollars.)
Sash, doors, and blinds	25	24	....	601	542	.....	59	1185000	459288	1300000	[illegible]
Saws	2	2	....	58	57	.....	1	230000	50000	173000	[illegible]
Soap and candles	13	8	....	274	178	42	54	1075400	159850	1288392	[illegible]
Tin, copper, and sheet-iron ware	353	.....	....	1386	1258	.....	128	1240405	623195	1369206	[illegible]
Tobacco, chew'g, smok'g, and snuff	65	13	....	1971	888	382	701	2444700	874860	4480306	[illegible]
Tobacco, cigars	318	.....	....	1417	1102	16	299	586600	611867	803687	[illegible]
Trunks, valises, and satchels	25	.....	....	282	238	.....	44	188100	168404	198490	[illegible]
Upholstery	46	.....	....	245	191	24	30	150250	97300	163800	[illegible]
Wooden ware	5	2	1	184	119	.....	65	131100	120700	140800	[illegible]
Wool-carding and cloth-dressing	118	39	22	288	258	5	23	188124	30944	508416	[illegible]
Woolen goods	38	28	4	430	290	80	60	528400	106464	340697	[illegible]

THE TERRITORY OF MONTANA.

Mechanical and manufacturing industries.	Establishm'ts.	Steam-engines.	Water-wheels.	All hands.	Males above 16.	Females above 15.	Youth.	Capital. (Dollars.)	Wages. (Dollars.)	Materials. (Dollars.)	Products. (Dollars.)
Flouring-mill products	7	(*)	(*)	19	(*)	(*)	(*)	92000	17900	271090	[illegible]
Lumber	29	(*)	(*)	152	(*)	(*)	(*)	135000	79635	171098	[illegible]
Quartz, milled	34	17	15	234	234	.....	....	1184900	81525	509571	[illegible]

THE STATE OF NEBRASKA.

Mechanical and manufacturing industries.	Establishm'ts.	Steam-engines.	Water-wheels.	All hands.	Males above 16.	Females above 15.	Youth.	Capital. (Dollars.)	Wages. (Dollars.)	Materials. (Dollars.)	Products. (Dollars.)
Flouring-mill products	41	(*)	(*)	139	(*)	(*)	(*)	431500	55836	770679	[illegible]
Machinery, railroad repairing	4	3	....	701	701	.....	....	363810	601411	196012	[illegible]

THE STATE OF NEVADA.

Mechanical and manufacturing industries.	Establishm'ts.	Steam-engines.	Water-wheels.	All hands.	Males above 16.	Females above 15.	Youth.	Capital. (Dollars.)	Wages. (Dollars.)	Materials. (Dollars.)	Products. (Dollars.)
Gold and silver, reduced and refined	1	2	....	40	40	.....	....	50000	36000	206000	[illegible]
Iron, castings, (not specified)	5	5	....	114	114	.....	....	101000	133500	263416	[illegible]
Lead, pig	9	9	....	181	181	.....	....	438000	109900	557962	[illegible]
Lumber	20	13	9	330	330	.....	....	199000	156430	142450	[illegible]
Machinery, (not specified)	3	....	....	53	53	.....	....	48000	67200	92850	[illegible]
Quartz, milled	93	84	22	1637	1637	.....	....	3869500	1693135	8527843	[illegible]

THE STATE OF NEW HAMPSHIRE.

Mechanical and manufacturing industries.	Establishm'ts.	Steam-engines.	Water-wheels.	All hands.	Males above 16.	Females above 15.	Youth.	Capital. (Dollars.)	Wages. (Dollars.)	Materials. (Dollars.)	Products. (Dollars.)
Agricultural implements	24	2	24	184	181	.....	3	174550	78305	77714	[illegible]
Boots and shoes	78	7	....	2777	2239	513	25	919435	1177067	2215788	[illegible]
Brick	57	9	....	544	544	.....	....	131805	112040	88570	[illegible]
Carpets, other than rag	3	....	1	170	72	79	19	310000	55730	226288	[illegible]
Carriages and wagons	116	4	38	782	780	1	1	598555	356692	329532	[illegible]
Cars, freight and passenger	2	4	....	190	190	.....	....	200000	100000	256250	[illegible]
Clothing	87	1	....	848	181	667	....	263240	215740	483420	870144
Cotton goods	36	7	94	12542	3752	7490	1300	13332710	3989853	12318267	[illegible]
Flouring-mill products	32	(*)	(*)	98	(*)	(*)	(*)	291400	32350	1160922	[illegible]
Furniture, (not specified)	58	10	36	1104	1045	26	33	731300	495673	676332	[illegible]
Furniture, chairs	21	....	22	221	216	4	1	220600	102460	91268	[illegible]
Hosiery	28	1	31	1081	344	624	113	855460	405003	881646	[illegible]
Iron, forged and rolled	2	5	1	111	111	.....	....	131000	57400	301860	[illegible]
Iron, castings	26	10	14	506	505	.....	1	500760	285165	458796	[illegible]
Leather, tanned	72	21	53	410	408	.....	2	875800	160109	1566950	[illegible]
Leather, curried	42	1	7	219	219	.....	....	312600	100599	1432419	[illegible]
Liquors, malt	4	3	....	113	113	.....	....	276810	53800	373156	[illegible]
Lumber	399	(*)	(*)	2144	(*)	(*)	(*)	1921854	658421	2270103	[illegible]
Machinery, (not specified)	36	6	28	397	368	3	6	341150	190786	165206	[illegible]
Machinery, cotton and woolen	31	2	24	386	342	20	24	272450	149932	126389	[illegible]
Machinery, fire-engines	1	....	2	365	365	.....	....	300000	46497	477133	[illegible]
Machinery, railroad repairing	4	7	....	664	664	.....	....	368000	395544	505364	[illegible]
Paper, (not specified)	14	8	25	310	210	93	7	418000	111973	511642	[illegible]
Paper, printing	7	1	16	190	125	65	....	444000	74800	359240	[illegible]
Paper, wrapping	11	2	25	148	120	24	4	217000	53700	209490	[illegible]
Printing cotton and woolen goods	3	6	3	635	538	77	20	678000	273925	4118453	[illegible]
Printing and publishing	45	5	3	302	235	61	6	336400	118904	115770	[illegible]
Saddlery and harness	85	....	....	260	258	1	1	133540	80401	[illegible]	[illegible]
Sash, doors, and blinds	28	7	23	354	343	1	10	243450	159130	[illegible]	[illegible]

* Not separately compiled.

TABLE CI.—*Manufactures, in each State and Territory, by Selected Industries*—1870—Cont'd.

THE STATE OF NEW HAMPSHIRE—Continued.

Mechanical and manufacturing industries.	Establishm'ts.	Steam-engines.	Water-wheels.	All hands.	Males above 16.	Females above 15.	Youth.	Capital. (*Dollars.*)	Wages. (*Dollars.*)	Materials. (*Dollars.*)	Products. (*Dollars.*)
Starch	66	8	58	294	292	....	2	246200	23381	308695	405342
Tin, copper, and sheet-iron ware	57	....	....	191	190	....	1	137650	64115	123760	261675
Wooden ware	60	4	67	416	395	3	18	273400	114848	140322	449220
Woolen goods	66	9	106	3729	1811	1549	369	4598800	1353992	5264520	8703307
Worsted goods	2	....	3	1161	355	700	106	700000	378017	1032118	1447423

THE STATE OF NEW JERSEY.

Mechanical and manufacturing industries.	Establishm'ts.	Steam-engines.	Water-wheels.	All hands.	Males above 16.	Females above 15.	Youth.	Capital. (*Dollars.*)	Wages. (*Dollars.*)	Materials. (*Dollars.*)	Products. (*Dollars.*)
Agricultural implements	30	8	6	366	366	....	....	517250	181687	202361	633875
Bagging	4	2	2	484	100	292	92	363600	135721	414129	621245
Bleaching and dyeing	12	7	4	285	207	53	25	281450	113875	4572429	4889695
Boots and shoes	67	2	....	1990	1594	313	53	777900	1025674	1333590	2830322
Boxes, packing	22	5	2	215	194	5	16	366150	107750	461319	624464
Bread and other bakery products	138	6	....	550	455	21	74	357500	196645	900922	1377336
Brick	118	35	....	2366	2245	7	114	1486500	679157	483965	1695530
Carriages and wagons	267	1	2	1830	1817	3	10	1236150	838563	787368	2281643
Cars, freight and passenger	6	7	1	978	978	....	....	1841040	654707	988481	1670427
Clothing	230	1	....	2550	963	1560	27	1069275	715981	2008985	3346125
Coffee and spices, roasted & ground	11	7	....	59	52	2	5	220900	34096	471834	591390
Confectionery	26	....	....	118	77	31	10	49375	35350	165249	276544
Cooperage	37	1	....	238	230	....	8	104380	109795	262385	403612
Copper, rolled	1	2	5	43	43	....	....	150000	35000	300000	500000
Cordage and twine	12	3	3	376	173	121	82	434850	99939	648472	872546
Cotton goods, (not specified)	14	10	13	2249	773	986	490	1550000	629171	1266702	2326167
Cotton thread, twine, and yarn	14	5	10	1373	321	859	193	1217500	387580	731932	1739061
Crucibles	3	2	....	36	33	....	3	455000	83688	278857	562463
Drugs and chemicals	9	5	1	109	108	....	1	447700	62660	385902	531300
Enameling	5	8	....	195	187	....	8	330000	88114	641916	899333
Fertilizers	10	8	....	262	260	2	....	368150	137350	450180	661650
Flouring-mill products	325	(*)	(*)	1058	(*)	(*)	(*)	3712900	308417	9117459	10557070
Fruits & veg'bles, canned & pres'd.	10	7	....	1098	166	787	145	242000	109152	330707	555675
Furniture	95	9	2	481	452	3	26	387600	185463	222035	562784
Glass ware	8	8	....	1627	1284	1	342	1277000	657311	579913	1564127
Glass, window	11	14	....	1116	882	....	234	1164500	467683	637763	1241599
Hardware	49	17	4	1168	946	54	168	937700	605352	519692	1457135
Hardware saddlery	31	6	1	612	552	35	25	348200	324365	200783	725260
Hat materials	9	4	4	231	178	45	8	237010	93892	171012	303550
Hats and caps	64	1	....	2785	1936	697	152	550100	1414004	2469179	5007270
Hosiery	4	2	2	722	136	271	315	575500	193200	188030	568900
Hubs and other wagon material	31	23	7	331	329	....	2	477800	168657	294291	610800
India-rubber and elastic goods	12	13	6	807	456	287	64	1034200	346638	1281967	2224839
Iron, forged and rolled	21	36	12	2032	1928	....	104	2123097	1249930	3430350	5297808
Iron bolts, nuts, washers, and rivets	6	4	2	140	103	....	37	149000	49190	145574	261791
Iron nails & spikes, cut & wrought	6	9	4	534	442	....	92	537839	256675	1480850	1769812
Iron pipe, wrought	3	3	....	273	250	....	23	396595	131700	501712	722000
Iron, pig	6	8	2	360	349	....	11	1405000	241611	1125261	1546965
Iron, castings	86	47	25	2089	1989	9	91	2476541	1191639	2138484	4012805
Jewelry	39	16	....	1502	1223	143	136	1844900	942081	1622201	3315679
Leather, tanned	67	27	10	617	571	31	15	1275387	347760	2444205	3110657
Leather, curried	61	2	....	279	278	....	1	658600	220314	2444170	2932401
Leather, morocco, tanned & curried	5	....	....	117	110	2	5	199500	82500	328635	525049
Leather, patent and enameled	15	9	....	285	280	....	5	548000	188465	2312956	2738941
Linen, thread	1	....	1	440	40	200	200	130000	55600	425470	602000
Liquors, distilled	56	9	9	153	147	....	6	187930	16987	167360	454734
Liquors, malt	46	34	....	528	522	....	6	2912300	329139	1650113	3219484
Looking-glass and picture frames	5	3	1	280	159	60	61	260500	102529	89571	289000
Lumber, planed	9	(*)	(*)	131	(*)	(*)	(*)	256600	76780	325334	553953
Lumber, sawed	185	(*)	(*)	938	(*)	(*)	(*)	2074650	353230	1610382	2543839
Machinery, (not specified)	64	39	17	1160	1135	....	25	2546500	640342	794406	1772342
Machinery, cotton and woolen	13	4	8	433	428	....	5	410000	213374	270398	556037
Machinery, railroad repairing	9	11	2	2978	2977	....	1	2887300	1982316	1878370	5528167
Machinery, steam engines & boilers	16	14	....	583	576	....	7	823500	340971	458085	961577
Marble and stone work, (n. s.)	31	2	....	447	444	....	3	254700	229272	209577	567723
Meat, packed, pork	9	4	....	116	116	....	....	183600	86150	279723	394100
Molasses and sugar, refined	3	4	....	404	404	....	....	645000	272000	10046744	11199740
Oakum	5	3	1	117	97	....	20	265500	46506	331540	447900
Oil, vegetable, castor	1	4	....	43	25	....	18	150000	15000	178000	250000
Oil floor-cloth	9	7	....	343	342	1	....	667000	201500	564245	943400
Paints, lead and zinc	8	15	1	395	390	2	3	1395000	222930	722304	1203082
Paper, (not specified)	17	11	25	215	142	43	30	427500	83241	271863	554230
Paper, printing	6	5	5	230	140	83	16	700000	101704	368821	558900
Paper, wrapping	9	4	19	138	109	27	2	313500	63514	300814	498191

* Not separately compiled.

TABLE CI.—*Manufactures, in each State and Territory, by Selected Industries*—1870—Cont'd.

THE STATE OF NEW JERSEY—Continued.

Mechanical and manufacturing industries.	Establishm'ts.	Steam-engines.	Water-wheels.	All hands.	Males above 16.	Females above 15.	Youth.	Capital. (*Dollars.*)	Wages. (*Dollars.*)	Materials. (*Dollars.*)	Products. (*Dollars.*)
Paper-hangings	1	1	....	107	70	12	25	160000	38000	137936	[illegible]
Plated ware	9	1	....	49	45	1	3	103300	34526	200783	[illegible]
Printing cotton and woolen goods	5	41	4	789	549	108	132	1024100	368629	4359633	[illegible]
Printing and publishing	39	10	....	369	346	4	28	450500	201101	211159	[illegible]
Roofing materials	13	1	2	82	69	13	....	212930	35349	135419	[illegible]
Saddlery and harness	170	2	....	1213	1166	35	12	694610	460716	859660	[illegible]
Sash, doors, and blinds	79	60	6	1210	1126	25	59	1246700	682535	1019425	[illegible]
Ship build'g, repair'g, and materials	47	3	....	385	385	....	....	287350	200694	253313	[illegible]
Shoddy	5	2	5	180	113	63	4	174000	48000	205348	[illegible]
Silk goods, (not specified)	15	8	5	1652	523	657	472	1259000	404609	1937258	[illegible]
Silk, sewing and twist	15	8	8	1188	210	547	431	919503	292227	1857917	[illegible]
Soap and candles	21	10	....	395	342	....	53	1170700	181854	1281320	[illegible]
Steel, cast	4	7	1	293	279	4	10	500000	190000	573310	[illegible]
Steel springs	6	5	....	158	158	....	....	287600	89697	251431	[illegible]
Stone and earthen ware	30	14	1	1206	763	144	299	1175800	443025	372669	[illegible]
Tin, copper, and sheet-iron ware	143	3	....	759	754	....	5	738196	348563	879985	[illegible]
Tobacco and cigars	4	3	....	181	133	26	22	344500	68700	270719	[illegible]
Tobacco, cigars	185	1	1	663	562	43	58	296980	187442	311036	[illegible]
Trunks, valises, and satchels	13	8	....	1350	944	330	76	757400	771150	1575305	[illegible]
Varnish	17	....	....	81	81	....	....	558300	44065	601216	[illegible]
Vegetables, canned	12	6	....	491	68	339	84	362500	44458	173655	[illegible]
Watches	2	2	....	404	267	130	7	700000	231250	47085	[illegible]
Wire-work	3	5	1	132	109	5	18	310250	74000	152660	[illegible]
Woolen goods	27	15	25	1090	520	402	168	1169200	331442	1299316	[illegible]
Worsted goods	5	2	3	281	109	107	65	198000	98000	292240	[illegible]

THE TERRITORY OF NEW MEXICO.

Mechanical and manufacturing industries.	Establishm'ts.	Steam-engines.	Water-wheels.	All hands.	Males above 16.	Females above 15.	Youth.	Capital. (*Dollars.*)	Wages. (*Dollars.*)	Materials. (*Dollars.*)	Products. (*Dollars.*)
Flouring-mill products	23	(*)	(*)	51	(*)	(*)	(*)	158600	22000	340993	[illegible]
Quartz, milled	7	6	1	83	83	....	....	1019800	57000	23419	[illegible]

THE STATE OF NEW YORK.

Mechanical and manufacturing industries.	Establishm'ts.	Steam-engines.	Water-wheels.	All hands.	Males above 16.	Females above 15.	Youth.	Capital. (*Dollars.*)	Wages. (*Dollars.*)	Materials. (*Dollars.*)	Products. (*Dollars.*)
Agricultural implements	337	106	116	4953	4678	1	274	[illegible]	2513317	[illegible]	[illegible]
Artificial flowers	36	....	....	1110	350	607	153	[illegible]	[illegible]	[illegible]	[illegible]
Awnings and tents	17	....	....	89	65	21	3	59275	[illegible]	[illegible]	[illegible]
Bags, paper	12	4	1	111	41	55	15	70000	[illegible]	[illegible]	[illegible]
Bags, other than paper	8	4	1	408	192	202	14	[illegible]	[illegible]	[illegible]	[illegible]
Baking-powders	9	3	....	105	64	36	5	[illegible]	[illegible]	[illegible]	[illegible]
Banners, flags, and regalias	8	2	....	139	77	52	10	[illegible]	[illegible]	[illegible]	[illegible]
Bells	5	5	....	58	57	....	1	[illegible]	[illegible]	[illegible]	[illegible]
Belting and hose, (leather)	10	4	....	210	207	....	3	[illegible]	[illegible]	[illegible]	[illegible]
Billiard and bagatelle tables and materials	11	2	....	170	167	....	3	[illegible]	[illegible]	[illegible]	[illegible]
Bleaching and dyeing	[illegible]	11	1	[illegible]	292	[illegible]	[illegible]	[illegible]	[illegible]	[illegible]	[illegible]
Boats	25	3	1	374	370	1	3	[illegible]	[illegible]	[illegible]	[illegible]
Bookbinding	[illegible]	2	....	[illegible]	1231	[illegible]	[illegible]	[illegible]	[illegible]	[illegible]	[illegible]
Boot and shoe findings	31	1	....	321	[illegible]	[illegible]	11	[illegible]	[illegible]	[illegible]	[illegible]
Boots and shoes	[illegible]	[illegible]	[illegible]	[illegible]	[illegible]	[illegible]	[illegible]	[illegible]	[illegible]	[illegible]	[illegible]
Boxes, cheese	[illegible]	22	117	[illegible]	[illegible]	7	15	[illegible]	[illegible]	[illegible]	[illegible]
Boxes, cigar	23	6	1	217	[illegible]	[illegible]	[illegible]	[illegible]	[illegible]	[illegible]	[illegible]
Boxes, packing	[illegible]	47	[illegible]	1121	[illegible]	[illegible]	[illegible]	[illegible]	[illegible]	[illegible]	[illegible]
Boxes, paper	[illegible]	1	2	[illegible]	[illegible]	[illegible]	[illegible]	[illegible]	[illegible]	[illegible]	[illegible]
Brass castings and finishings	[illegible]	32	....	[illegible]	780	7	42	[illegible]	[illegible]	[illegible]	[illegible]
[illegible]	2	....	....	[illegible]	113	[illegible]	....	[illegible]	[illegible]	[illegible]	[illegible]
Bread and other bakery products	710	3	2	[illegible]	[illegible]	[illegible]	132	[illegible]	[illegible]	[illegible]	[illegible]
[illegible]	326	[illegible]	1	[illegible]	[illegible]	81	[illegible]	[illegible]	[illegible]	[illegible]	[illegible]
[illegible]	[illegible]	[illegible]	[illegible]	[illegible]	[illegible]	[illegible]	[illegible]	[illegible]	[illegible]	[illegible]	[illegible]
[illegible]	4	[illegible]	....	[illegible]	[illegible]	[illegible]	[illegible]	[illegible]	[illegible]	[illegible]	[illegible]
[illegible]	[illegible]	[illegible]	....	[illegible]	[illegible]	[illegible]	[illegible]	[illegible]	[illegible]	[illegible]	[illegible]
[illegible]	[illegible]	[illegible]	[illegible]	[illegible]	[illegible]	[illegible]	[illegible]	[illegible]	[illegible]	[illegible]	[illegible]
[illegible]	[illegible]	[illegible]	1	174	[illegible]	[illegible]	[illegible]	[illegible]	[illegible]	[illegible]	[illegible]
[illegible]	[illegible]	[illegible]	[illegible]	[illegible]	[illegible]	[illegible]	[illegible]	[illegible]	[illegible]	[illegible]	[illegible]
[illegible]	[illegible]	[illegible]	....	[illegible]	[illegible]	....	1	[illegible]	[illegible]	[illegible]	[illegible]
[illegible]	[illegible]	[illegible]	[illegible]	[illegible]	[illegible]	[illegible]	[illegible]	[illegible]	[illegible]	[illegible]	[illegible]
[illegible]	[illegible]	[illegible]	....	[illegible]	[illegible]	....	[illegible]	[illegible]	[illegible]	[illegible]	[illegible]
[illegible]	[illegible]	1	[illegible]	[illegible]	[illegible]	....	1	[illegible]	[illegible]	[illegible]	[illegible]
[illegible]	[illegible]	[illegible]	11	[illegible]	[illegible]	[illegible]	[illegible]	[illegible]	[illegible]	[illegible]	[illegible]

* Not separately compiled.

I.—*Manufactures, in each State and Territory, by Selected Industries*—1870—Cont'd.

THE STATE OF NEW YORK—Continued.

…al and manufacturing industries.	Establishm'ts.	Steam-engines.	Water-wheels.	All hands.	Males above 16.	Females above 15.	Youth.	Capital. (Dollars.)	Wages. (Dollars.)	Materials. (Dollars.)	Products. (Dollars.)
nd lithographs	24	7	....	363	321	8	34	327400	243200	198415	607850
	274	25	99	769	760	4	5	326521	46986	369759	606524
hildren's	4	....	....	1194	796	398	....	156000	144100	355045	550000
ien's	1526	4	1	26090	12235	13671	184	14205043	8195780	27349298	44718491
vomen's	446	4	....	4700	709	3805	186	1526434	1078893	2310674	4830425
ctified	19	20	....	183	180	....	3	699500	109607	2236149	2702680
ices, roasted & ground	29	25	2	309	279	3	27	1513600	211095	3105260	4706900
	104	5	5	581	555	13	13	748900	315060	467478	1240569
l cuffs, (not specified)	11	6	....	1329	366	911	52	271650	255450	514350	1174200
l cuffs, linen	15	11	....	2703	132	2560	11	577000	630228	633096	1656878
l cuffs, paper	4	3	1	175	26	99	50	144000	131600	128528	367600
ery	157	13	....	1398	955	385	58	1377700	489514	1820988	3942391
	870	31	47	4332	4195	4	133	2223366	1359083	2558920	4945434
thing	18	3	....	174	173	....	1	173500	79023	166717	283450
id twine	45	6	7	1006	399	278	329	812450	288420	818669	1553329
id sirups	11	....	....	86	62	11	13	310700	36825	167230	287150
ls	81	40	82	9144	2608	4546	1990	8511336	2026131	6990626	11178211
d edge-tools, (see edge-axes)	13	3	7	397	324	10	63	473400	191916	133202	462246
	18	5	....	215	210	....	5	333700	91387	160931	384686
chemicals	57	30	1	1046	832	146	68	2299700	510285	2227243	4578857
and dye-stuffs, ground	3	3	....	240	224	....	16	675000	160850	494457	888800
and axes	24	5	34	1143	1116	1	26	1129400	608784	586808	1558545
	33	8	....	850	553	252	45	1472025	765580	326076	1410498
	8	5	....	355	99	233	23	463500	147600	572100	1142500
leaned, dressed, and dyed	16	1	....	479	253	205	21	272750	99097	365800	693595
	11	6	....	168	167	....	1	213900	61355	158070	289011
	20	4	9	429	350	14	65	341350	150530	128139	397076
small-arms	11	3	6	849	827	....	22	1112300	748200	521618	1890957
ed	46	3	42	253	246	2	5	189780	54180	166545	284385
ill products	944	(*)	(*)	3810	(*)	(*)	(*)	16844970	1448537	44055830	52636861
rations, animal	17	7	3	208	181	21	6	340900	153304	756100	1099944
rations, vegetable	12	4	12	336	63	269	4	181700	75230	210260	301369
ned and preserved	10	7	....	278	114	131	33	210500	88680	812620	1059150
	917	135	142	9634	8896	233	505	9078363	4785673	6129079	16275111
ed	72	3	....	2029	974	1000	55	2183917	823744	3828297	7028488
	2	2	....	160	159	....	1	800000	128000	320000	575000
mp fixtures	17	12	....	812	753	32	27	937300	449040	479042	1397000
	15	13	....	139	139	....	20	82500	98276	100546	270600
	32	8	1	1824	1153	117	554	829666	679004	533477	1709364
low	7	2	....	390	344	....	46	360000	171849	182307	453659
mittens	144	1	3	3112	893	2192	27	2071350	842484	1668993	3507795
nd foil	27	1	....	288	184	69	35	190005	126180	169135	681289
l tallow	16	6	....	110	104	....	6	201800	47320	2803055	3316207
r	5	....	13	108	108	....	....	270000	64159	244789	547519
	77	2	....	803	290	449	64	248600	179810	351763	811632
	113	38	22	1811	1591	39	181	1980385	815871	923435	2484787
saddlery	20	6	3	469	344	32	93	333000	191270	251392	661610
als	35	2	1	603	414	90	99	657900	375038	1194974	1977350
aps	135	11	3	5267	3061	1728	478	2363083	2188110	4213353	8708723
paratus	10	5	....	288	283	....	5	345500	242020	518412	1011345
s and corsets	46	5	....	2480	736	1581	163	1079000	615334	1349367	2866619
	60	11	52	3741	1061	1899	781	3318700	1122890	3391840	5528742
other wagon material	47	18	30	311	311	....	....	324550	116799	128385	370784
id fishing tackle	20	5	2	271	191	44	36	363100	100466	161182	538750
er and elastic goods	10	9	7	1008	643	330	35	1777000	489500	1316803	3076720
, professional & scientific	48	14	....	480	425	31	24	480528	268779	149539	617388
is	22	5	32	1020	998	....	22	1614883	358135	1626264	2171106
d and rolled	47	55	36	5503	5304	....	199	6143700	2841147	11489147	16834480
nuts, washers, and rivets	15	13	6	479	380	3	96	620300	219002	811454	1250137
& spikes, cut & wrought	15	6	6	464	349	4	111	415000	177209	857290	1141030
g, wrought	31	13	....	328	318	....	10	211700	183195	325098	734367
	39	37	23	2121	2117	....	4	5732116	1095450	5548925	7928463
gs, (not specified)	423	211	108	8769	8423	13	333	9372118	5024413	8205735	17252226
gs, stoves, heaters, and are	63	47	11	3853	3770	....	83	5749383	2400716	2244394	6741210
t	9	8	....	91	90	....	1	253950	64910	298030	462850
	215	4	....	3618	2957	623	38	5124250	826481	3927612	9757856
ood	35	26	....	511	357	....	154	408600	191814	339972	659845
lanterns	11	2	1	152	134	5	13	180500	92060	128714	377976
	2	1	....	30	30	....	....	140000	16750	916350	970500
	8	7	....	60	60	....	....	910000	57408	7623490	10738800
	2	1	....	13	10	....	3	23000	9020	[illegible]	[illegible]
aned	624	239	368	6064	6005	8	51	13226940	2609052	19118186	[illegible]

* Not separately compiled.

TABLE CI.—*Manufactures, in each State and Territory, by Selected Industries*—1870—Cont'd.

THE STATE OF NEW YORK—Continued.

Mechanical and manufacturing industries.	Establishm'ts.	Steam-engines.	Water-wheels.	All hands.	Males above 16.	Females above 15.	Youth.	Capital. (*Dollars.*)	Wages. (*Dollars.*)	Materials. (*Dollars.*)	Products. (*Dollars.*)
Leather, curried	325	12	12	1011	989	15	7	1639388	439253	5186494	[illegible]
Leather, morocco, tanned & curried	22	8	....	552	520	10	22	605900	293865	792724	[illegible]
Leather, dressed skins	29	4	17	442	417	5	20	584150	210685	1454347	[illegible]
Lime	119	7	1	991	980	....	11	1079860	310230	503479	[illegible]
Liquors, distilled	50	16	8	333	333	....	....	1377640	125772	1829574	[illegible]
Liquors, malt	281	150	8	2942	2907	6	29	12425322	2067908	9194243	[illegible]
Liquors, vinous	9	2	....	56	52	4	....	480700	26800	108448	[illegible]
Looking-glass and picture frames	84	19	1	1128	1006	6	116	713200	548665	830422	[illegible]
Lumber, planed	153	(*)	(*)	1910	(*)	(*)	(*)	2910336	880944	4532328	[illegible]
Lumber, sawed	1683	(*)	(*)	11358	(*)	(*)	(*)	12031561	3116230	10449784	[illegible]
Machinery, (not specified)	326	171	91	5985	5865	9	111	7884366	3395771	4454321	[illegible]
Machinery, fire-engines	5	2	5	347	340	....	7	560000	192500	380750	[illegible]
Machinery, railroad repairing	7	10	....	678	664	2	12	535919	386773	391133	[illegible]
Machinery, steam engines & boilers	103	84	16	4478	4381	....	97	4930645	2492453	3766318	[illegible]
Malt	91	26	10	824	818	....	6	3647066	323698	4338458	[illegible]
Maps and atlases	6	....	1	130	76	42	12	326000	73600	100048	[illegible]
Marble and stone work, (u. s.)	172	27	5	3188	3160	1	27	2831750	2272403	2313177	[illegible]
Matches	13	5	3	619	141	304	174	433422	102208	259685	[illegible]
Meters, (not specified)	1	1	....	75	75	....	....	100000	70000	170000	[illegible]
Meters, gas	3	3	....	295	293	....	2	613000	208000	146255	[illegible]
Millinery	213	....	....	1676	485	1106	85	429276	233477	779578	[illegible]
Millstones	5	1	....	75	74	....	1	423000	44200	153275	[illegible]
Mineral and soda waters	81	2	1	694	639	3	52	2180250	332910	640974	[illegible]
Molasses and sugar, refined	18	32	....	864	858	....	6	6375000	1229956	37247730	[illegible]
Monuments and tombstones	161	6	2	967	958	4	5	1125010	449467	684382	[illegible]
Musical instrum'ts & material, (n. s)	14	4	....	120	109	3	8	88800	82296	95347	[illegible]
Musical instruments, organs and materials	19	5	2	353	346	1	6	429400	264189	203580	[illegible]
Musical instruments, pianos and materials	89	17	....	2387	2312	19	56	2825950	1650049	1099006	[illegible]
Oil, animal	11	6	....	88	88	....	....	242800	61268	97348	117763
Oil, fish	17	12	1	193	186	5	2	197000	35840	225425	[illegible]
Oil, vegetable, essential	68	2	....	2195	2195	....	....	120215	24591	230543	[illegible]
Oil, vegetable, linseed	9	2	8	225	218	7	....	576600	142980	2141300	[illegible]
Oil floor-cloth	12	9	....	487	476	2	9	624000	221468	610648	[illegible]
Paints	11	10	1	230	209	8	13	760000	122380	719032	[illegible]
Paints, lead and zinc	12	12	2	342	340	....	2	1057500	202312	1687290	[illegible]
Paper, (not specified)	28	6	27	527	244	246	37	760000	161374	[illegible]	[illegible]
Paper, printing	68	20	125	2310	1521	501	288	4421800	1092352	[illegible]	[illegible]
Paper, wrapping	78	10	120	963	779	112	72	1841800	382456	1053194	[illegible]
Paper, writing	5	1	11	285	121	153	11	340500	77900	322375	[illegible]
Paper-hangings	7	6	1	354	122	125	107	318000	157255	626732	[illegible]
Patent medicines and compounds	60	4	1	646	399	225	22	1572250	263714	1631680	[illegible]
Patterns and models	41	16	2	362	228	122	12	237050	159522	95010	[illegible]
Paving materials	4	3	....	168	153	....	15	78000	107500	113500	[illegible]
Pencils and pens, gold	7	2	....	142	125	10	7	215000	108400	122230	[illegible]
Perfumery and fancy soaps	15	2	....	259	102	151	6	457300	98885	378261	[illegible]
Photographic apparatus	4	2	....	124	92	31	1	193500	79760	126358	[illegible]
Pipes, tobacco	18	12	1	313	224	23	66	124850	139244	64700	[illegible]
Plaster, ground	152	20	106	817	800	3	14	1018750	289940	834218	[illegible]
Plated ware	38	13	1	314	243	57	14	550450	143351	237342	[illegible]
Pocket-books	31	....	....	338	225	79	34	198400	150247	[illegible]	[illegible]
Preserves and sauces	14	5	....	140	94	31	15	147000	33880	352975	[illegible]
Printing of cotton and woolen goods	4	4	1	590	379	61	150	280000	297500	2781000	3317109
Printing and publishing, (n. s.)	18	6	1	1861	1313	395	153	1612500	1257550	2531380	[illegible]
Printing and publishing, book	18	14	....	755	448	229	78	1495257	400294	852008	[illegible]
Printing & publishing, newspaper	159	74	3	2557	2231	75	251	3029350	1700970	2679488	[illegible]
Printing, job	102	40	....	1128	917	85	126	1264910	548135	612674	[illegible]
Pumps	70	15	19	407	373	7	27	438550	149724	168249	[illegible]
Roofing materials	31	2	3	221	219	....	2	155000	108610	201574	[illegible]
Saddlery and harness	1010	3	....	3239	3100	90	49	1743080	928082	1597540	[illegible]
Safes, doors, and vaults, (fire-proof)	19	11	1	584	564	1	19	808400	284151	161172	[illegible]
Sails	32	....	....	161	160	1	....	92000	111550	181565	[illegible]
Salt	93	4	....	528	528	....	....	1584211	204226	494854	[illegible]
Sash, doors, and blinds	315	142	111	3632	3406	....	226	3637966	1783954	2880073	[illegible]
Saws	16	9	2	486	451	5	30	1050300	265338	295082	[illegible]
Scales and balances	14	4	1	323	291	....	32	387403	180812	140367	[illegible]
Screws	3	2	....	121	81	15	25	79500	61700	170470	[illegible]
Sewing-machine fixtures	5	4	....	536	526	....	10	292000	281667	191124	[illegible]
Sewing machines	12	11	3	3131	2882	167	82	2727576	2189640	[illegible]	[illegible]
Ship build'g, repair'g, and materials	200	22	2	2448	2440	....	8	2449350	1427709	2437459	[illegible]
Show-cases	20	2	....	155	150	1	4	77800	109678	132534	317511
Silk goods, (not specified)	7	6	....	107	51	49	7	129500	76200	117580	[illegible]
Silk, sewing and twist	7	2	5	632	103	364	165	671000	[illegible]	[illegible]	[illegible]

* Not separately compiled.

CI.—*Manufactures, in each State and Territory, by Selected Industries*—1870—Cont'd.

THE STATE OF NEW YORK—Continued.

…nical and manufacturing industries.	Establishm'ts.	Steam-engines.	Water-wheels.	All hands.	Males - above 16.	Females above 16.	Youth.	Capital. (*Dollars.*)	Wages. (*Dollars.*)	Materials. (*Dollars.*)	Products. (*Dollars.*)
…are	20	16	....	338	308	25	5	551900	237840	570193	1096100
…l candles	97	32	....	1019	897	68	54	2360575	506982	3913419	6125018
…ter apparatus	2	2	....	162	160	....	2	156150	57361	119006	252500
…	72	22	68	1348	1031	314	3	1895375	776855	2929018	4678413
…ot specified)	3	5	....	107	105	....	2	705000	101200	134200	370000
…essemer	1	3	1	112	112	....	....	300000	72000	293812	413220
…rings	7	7	1	241	239	....	2	417000	142000	247730	512500
…d earthen ware	42	7	2	514	421	48	45	656900	213371	154286	561392
…oods	18	2	....	1413	518	886	9	177800	306136	389890	1006000
…per, and sheet-iron ware	932	26	1	5013	4517	160	336	4372821	1977487	3848557	8130044
… and cigars	24	16	2	710	394	146	170	844600	272154	854289	1543363
…, chew'g, smok'g, and snuff	27	22	3	3823	1283	1579	961	2677311	984406	5406151	8671475
…, cigars	1072	....	....	5710	4951	339	420	2704135	2494310	3503186	8725821
… valises, and satchels	39	4	2	378	283	57	38	357889	191297	336302	728766
…anding	12	6	....	592	308	195	89	892000	322470	570218	1289252
…a furniture	5	4	....	211	127	73	9	122400	87763	96947	284184
…as and canes	28	1	....	1096	259	702	135	624050	439750	756620	1776639
…ery	116	6	....	1600	1070	434	96	1941700	478501	1600374	2923251
…	8	3	....	128	123	2	3	679040	73300	1339898	1846700
…	49	10	3	197	191	....	6	338300	54692	332467	523800
…ases	33	....	....	511	444	60	7	554500	435900	796000	1734500
…	3	1	....	210	60	150	....	52200	201783	408897	759400
…ork	40	7	....	1129	492	596	41	328150	280970	357038	815210
…rackets, moldings, & scrolls	30	26	2	281	262	1	18	261500	179332	288760	627250
… ware	56	9	32	420	395	5	20	421670	139251	211287	479168
…urned and carved	145	43	65	651	618	1	32	577145	314447	334913	919116
…rding and cloth-dressing	75	3	66	155	136	10	9	128275	12795	483972	554840
… goods	188	35	208	8679	4381	2992	1306	9972857	2824344	8348693	14152645

THE STATE OF NORTH CAROLINA.

…nical and manufacturing industries.	Establishm'ts.	Steam-engines.	Water-wheels.	All hands.	Males - above 16.	Females above 16.	Youth.	Capital. (*Dollars.*)	Wages. (*Dollars.*)	Materials. (*Dollars.*)	Products. (*Dollars.*)
…s and wagons	130	2	1	462	455	....	7	141785	105448	107853	340484
…goods	33	3	31	1453	258	916	279	1030900	182951	963809	1345052
…-mill products	227	(*)	(*)	483	(*)	(*)	(*)	620400	64325	1913812	2232404
…, sawed	104	(*)	(*)	1176	(*)	(*)	(*)	757800	296234	794411	1500539
… turpentine	147	21	....	959	957	1	1	472100	184839	1552577	2338309
… chew'g, smok'g, and snuff	110	....	....	1464	762	332	370	375832	102144	390627	717765
…elted and rolled	1	....	....	17	17	....	....	4500	6500	437245	522000

THE STATE OF OHIO.

…nical and manufacturing industries.	Establishm'ts.	Steam-engines.	Water-wheels.	All hands.	Males - above 16.	Females above 16.	Youth.	Capital. (*Dollars.*)	Wages. (*Dollars.*)	Materials. (*Dollars.*)	Products. (*Dollars.*)
…tural implements	219	110	15	5124	5026	....	98	7570320	2841518	5240550	11907366
…	7	4	3	497	211	189	97	348501	137545	289053	563799
…and hose, (leather)	4	2	....	70	54	6	10	90600	37114	240745	334463
… and bagatelle tables and …ials	2	....	....	86	83	....	3	103000	62346	130996	276034
…	46	12	....	762	762	....	....	674418	360429	295895	851060
…ding	37	5	....	526	242	156	128	352250	197326	485086	922934
…d shoes	164	4	....	2026	1686	305	35	790025	946084	1294925	2866803
…acking	12	9	....	168	161	3	4	285462	87584	198225	321005
…nding and finishing	22	15	1	236	207	....	29	258950	118013	158035	384715
…d other bakery products	279	16	....	975	884	55	36	495522	284332	1288604	2202818
…	331	27	1	2409	2275	5	129	633660	462758	294420	1252857
…uilding	17	3	....	427	423	....	4	319700	201592	339410	803391
… and whisk-brushes	78	....	3	283	259	2	22	86185	64646	224261	371296
…	15	2	....	536	245	131	160	102379	91958	166525	324352
…s and wagons	1221	18	4	5094	5024	4	66	2964783	1671070	1537164	5049580
…ight and passenger	11	9	....	1462	1460	2	....	1355970	917565	1365699	2555855
…l	23	1	....	1056	1032	....	24	311400	356830	205473	682087
…	195	45	4	759	571	187	1	474970	116635	1875711	2287804
…s and lithographs	4	2	....	122	101	4	17	223000	99500	94800	312000
…	953	....	....	11810	5456	6106	248	4884134	2502268	7961165	13194998
… rectified	25	24	....	270	268	....	2	757000	157359	4496163	5388473
…d spices, roasted & ground	13	10	....	123	105	13	5	294700	60394	571494	726877
…	62	5	1	303	292	9	2	378303	116670	132662	473069
…onery	61	2	....	380	237	89	54	300900	119799	462060	739409
…ge	658	32	2	3206	3148	3	55	1108957	1105530	1729417	3554171
… and twine	18	2	1	245	164	22	59	109186	75701	147660	307692

* Not separately compiled.

TABLE CI.—*Manufactures, in each State and Territory, by Selected Industries*—1870—Cont'd.

THE STATE OF OHIO—Continued.

Mechanical and manufacturing industries.	Establishm'ts.	Steam-engines.	Water-wheels.	All hands.	Males above 16.	Females above 15.	Youth.	Capital. (*Dollars.*)	Wages. (*Dollars.*)	Materials. (*Dollars.*)	Products. (*Dollars.*)
Cotton goods	7	5	3	462	216	147	99	555700	113520	491704	[illegible]
Drain-pipe	23	4	3	218	213	2	3	109520	66938	45604	[illegible]
Drugs and chemicals	16	8	...	151	120	8	23	456900	71640	293922	[illegible]
Edge-tools and axes	11	10	1	223	223	...	...	383300	113064	172224	[illegible]
Fish, cured and packed	14	...	...	266	258	5	3	117500	80250	360530	[illegible]
Flax, dressed	27	16	23	358	307	11	40	240900	113628	136509	[illegible]
Flouring-mill products	699	(*)	(*)	2415	(*)	(*)	(*)	8507388	[illegible]	[illegible]	[illegible]
Food preparations, vegetable	9	3	...	132	110	11	11	350566	59621	367749	[illegible]
Furniture	615	141	13	6279	5263	295	721	5618565	2492042	2156832	[illegible]
Glass, plate	3	1	...	148	148	...	...	175000	123410	[illegible]	[illegible]
Glass ware	6	2	...	308	192	5	111	140900	110435	103918	[illegible]
Grease and tallow	8	1	...	46	46	...	...	198215	17434	259512	[illegible]
Gunpowder	2	2	7	55	55	...	...	270000	36720	123925	[illegible]
Hardware	23	12	1	399	350	10	39	400560	168578	332465	[illegible]
Hardware, saddlery	16	3	...	308	307	...	1	174720	83700	227382	[illegible]
Heating apparatus	7	...	...	125	124	...	1	285000	85700	101066	[illegible]
Hubs and other wagon material	58	53	5	1301	1251	...	50	1303150	548647	685190	[illegible]
Iron, rolled and forged	38	101	3	4670	4400	...	270	6636659	2791560	8435585	[illegible]
Iron bolts, nuts, washers, & rivets	10	7	1	389	252	1	136	367560	117583	372288	[illegible]
Iron nails & spikes, cut & wrought	10	13	...	370	255	...	115	841241	198140	1807402	[illegible]
Iron, pig	65	89	...	4582	4571	...	11	7437826	2035520	7056405	[illegible]
Iron castings, (not specified)	215	14	17	3073	2993	...	80	5656879	1757360	3509056	[illegible]
Iron castings, stoves, heaters, and hollow ware	53	43	2	1967	1933	...	34	2616750	1100866	1195424	[illegible]
Jewelry	20	1	...	267	212	31	24	146364	167025	156514	[illegible]
Leather, tanned	495	106	7	1265	1239	...	26	2171108	379178	2768493	[illegible]
Leather, curried	387	6	...	796	785	3	8	1057733	251413	2332218	[illegible]
Lime	63	...	...	284	281	...	3	178762	81971	178748	[illegible]
Liquors, distilled	63	67	10	735	729	...	6	2229700	362987	4371289	[illegible]
Liquors, malt	199	91	1	1305	1296	2	7	5337272	748540	2711270	[illegible]
Liquors, vinous	38	...	...	124	106	8	10	369905	25300	179775	[illegible]
Looking glass and picture frames	13	2	...	239	156	62	21	219525	106900	86925	[illegible]
Lumber, planed	110	(*)	(*)	948	(*)	(*)	(*)	1066652	442963	1124600	[illegible]
Lumber, sawed	1179	(*)	(*)	5687	(*)	(*)	(*)	4679488	1312564	4927217	[illegible]
Machinery, (not specified)	142	95	23	2251	2204	...	50	3395885	1244973	1880786	[illegible]
Machinery, railroad repairing	13	18	...	1862	1862	...	...	2417281	1117110	1130339	[illegible]
Machinery, steam engines & boilers	72	70	1	2311	2270	...	41	2826120	1301640	2626406	[illegible]
Malt	31	12	1	166	166	...	...	965228	77301	843812	[illegible]
Marble & stone work, (not specified)	79	31	3	927	914	...	13	1085125	410680	439674	[illegible]
Meat, packed, pork	58	10	...	830	816	1	13	3792490	341951	[illegible]	[illegible]
Millinery	159	...	...	578	23	527	28	198900	82878	[illegible]	[illegible]
Monuments and tombstones	118	7	...	677	670	...	7	661445	[illegible]	[illegible]	[illegible]
Oil, animal	11	6	...	148	132	7	9	501000	71822	1353186	[illegible]
Oil, vegetable, cotton seed	4	2	2	48	47	...	1	78000	[illegible]	[illegible]	[illegible]
Oil, vegetable, linseed	23	9	13	202	198	2	2	[illegible]	[illegible]	[illegible]	[illegible]
Paints, lead and zinc	11	13	2	185	179	8	3	[illegible]	111280	[illegible]	[illegible]
Paper, (not specified)	6	7	4	165	121	30	14	277600	67100	191621	[illegible]
Paper, printing	17	30	22	785	416	322	47	1064800	[illegible]	1711145	[illegible]
Paper, wrapping	20	13	23	368	276	61	31	870066	144770	[illegible]	[illegible]
Patent medicines and compounds	17	1	...	154	101	53	...	417400	[illegible]	[illegible]	[illegible]
Printing and publishing, (n. s.)	43	25	...	1433	1125	[illegible]	72	[illegible]	948721	856444	[illegible]
Printing and publishing, newspaper	90	15	1	633	[illegible]	27	44	[illegible]	[illegible]	231071	[illegible]
Printing, job	45	15	...	313	245	29	40	[illegible]	[illegible]	271651	[illegible]
Saddlery and harness	787	...	...	1999	1967	6	26	[illegible]	[illegible]	[illegible]	[illegible]
Safes, doors and vaults, fire-proof	3	3	...	310	302	...	8	[illegible]	[illegible]	[illegible]	[illegible]
Salt	40	40	2	437	424	...	13	[illegible]	[illegible]	[illegible]	[illegible]
Sash, doors and blinds	122	113	7	2078	[illegible]	4	77	[illegible]	[illegible]	[illegible]	[illegible]
Saws	6	[illegible]	7	142	126	1	[illegible]	[illegible]	[illegible]	[illegible]	[illegible]
Sewing machines	7	5	...	[illegible]	[illegible]	1	[illegible]	[illegible]	[illegible]	[illegible]	[illegible]
Soap and candles	[illegible]	11	...	[illegible]	[illegible]	72	[illegible]	[illegible]	[illegible]	[illegible]	[illegible]
Stone and earthen ware	175	2	[illegible]	1244	[illegible]	[illegible]	[illegible]	[illegible]	[illegible]	[illegible]	[illegible]
Tin, copper, and sheet-iron ware	152	4	...	2313	[illegible]	[illegible]	64	[illegible]	711421	[illegible]	[illegible]
Tobacco and cigars	11	[illegible]	...	178	107	[illegible]	[illegible]	[illegible]	[illegible]	[illegible]	[illegible]
Tobacco, chewing, smoking, & snuff	[illegible]	[illegible]	3	[illegible]	[illegible]	[illegible]	[illegible]	[illegible]	[illegible]	[illegible]	[illegible]
[illegible]	4	1	...	[illegible]	[illegible]	[illegible]	[illegible]	[illegible]	[illegible]	[illegible]	[illegible]
[illegible]	[illegible]	...	...	274	[illegible]	[illegible]	13	[illegible]	[illegible]	[illegible]	[illegible]
[illegible]	[illegible]	2	...	[illegible]	[illegible]	[illegible]	[illegible]	[illegible]	[illegible]	[illegible]	[illegible]
[illegible]	[illegible]	1	...	[illegible]	[illegible]	[illegible]	[illegible]	[illegible]	[illegible]	[illegible]	[illegible]
[illegible]	[illegible]	1	...	[illegible]	[illegible]	...	...	[illegible]	[illegible]	[illegible]	[illegible]
[illegible]	[illegible]	[illegible]	4	[illegible]	[illegible]	[illegible]	[illegible]	[illegible]	[illegible]	[illegible]	[illegible]
[illegible]	[illegible]	[illegible]	4	[illegible]	[illegible]	...	14	[illegible]	[illegible]	[illegible]	[illegible]
[illegible]	[illegible]	[illegible]	[illegible]	[illegible]	[illegible]	[illegible]	[illegible]	[illegible]	[illegible]	[illegible]	[illegible]

* Not separately compiled.

TABLE CI.—*Manufactures, in each State and Territory, by Selected Industries*—1870—Cont'd.

THE STATE OF OREGON.

Mechanical and manufacturing industries.	Establishm'ts.	Steam-engines.	Water-wheels.	All hands.	Males above 16.	Females above 15.	Youth.	Capital. (*Dollars.*)	Wages. (*Dollars.*)	Materials. (*Dollars.*)	Products. (*Dollars.*)
Flouring-mill products	43	(*)	(*)	121	(*)	(*)	(*)	738000	78086	993338	1530989
Lumber	80	(*)	(*)	489	(*)	(*)	(*)	751062	236860	341242	928576
Woolen goods	6	....	6	173	125	7	41	380500	112113	221545	492857

THE STATE OF PENNSYLVANIA.

Mechanical and manufacturing industries.	Establishm'ts.	Steam-engines.	Water-wheels.	All hands.	Males above 16.	Females above 15.	Youth.	Capital. (*Dollars.*)	Wages. (*Dollars.*)	Materials. (*Dollars.*)	Products. (*Dollars.*)
Agricultural implements	226	104	43	2286	2248	....	38	3387049	1025618	1278805	3652295
Bags, paper	7	2	....	76	18	58	....	91000	18292	220508	281000
Belting and hose, (leather)	15	....	....	99	97	2	....	336300	50942	356300	510312
Blacking	9	5	....	184	56	117	11	151000	62250	254087	466322
Bleaching and dyeing	78	34	2	709	629	47	53	1212840	352887	6087364	7285114
Bookbinding	91	19	....	1877	930	803	144	1640807	674254	1919981	3588623
Boot and shoe findings	24	1	....	295	127	162	6	130350	89458	151036	319819
Boots and shoes	335	11	....	8330	5801	2231	298	4240523	3513182	4734136	11002587
Boxes, paper	30	5	....	987	187	714	86	192400	214133	226291	635351
Boxes, wooden, (not cigar)	39	6	....	237	219	....	18	109250	110414	271021	599658
Brass founding and finishing	63	37	....	826	786	1	39	2118985	395780	1100167	2030055
Bread, and other bakery products	809	25	....	2494	2299	90	105	1920290	783411	3195678	5597291
Brick	458	68	3	7443	6219	4	1220	4530783	2537691	1330527	6071209
Bridge-building	4	3	1	429	416	....	13	275500	240500	628811	948856
Brooms and whisk-brushes	31	....	....	205	192	....	13	74760	53266	200985	340145
Brushes	61	5	....	635	416	100	122	436864	180293	296717	628827
Buttons	18	16	....	360	150	127	83	170800	116174	141165	360200
Cards, other than playing	4	3	....	102	34	53	15	189000	26850	206900	276500
Carpets, rag	212	....	2	472	436	24	12	168974	63055	247379	460450
Carpets, other than rag	184	16	1	4941	3688	905	348	3026500	1870527	5619448	9758171
Carriages and wagons	1449	35	21	6252	6199	5	48	4322517	2220441	2111361	6682302
Cars, freight and passenger	49	34	1	4076	3975	14	87	3763804	2193857	5532736	9288041
Cheese, (factory)	27	9	....	93	75	17	1	109750	19074	205367	268702
Chromos and lithographs	34	5	....	464	421	28	15	584900	232532	193378	765184
Clothing, children's	12	....	....	114	38	76	....	130000	36700	261230	351600
Clothing, men's	1364	2	....	17073	7781	9017	275	9709039	4758807	12036899	21853319
Clothing, women's	102	....	....	1049	83	939	27	519384	244765	524336	1158237
Coal-oil, rectified	89	105	....	957	932	1	21	4006433	638563	12345899	15251223
Coffee & spices, roasted & ground	26	18	....	217	172	40	5	446400	96101	1327800	1646171
Coffins	91	3	....	409	398	8	3	500000	179214	184721	653718
Coke	18	10	....	494	494	....	....	1146043	274877	550066	1048711
Confectionery	268	6	....	1137	824	236	77	1130905	390535	1195851	2491332
Cooperage	474	20	11	2256	2171	1	84	1084385	945437	1502537	3209470
Copper, rolled	1	1	....	30	30	....	....	250000	25000	211280	276000
Cordage and twine	17	6	4	373	200	96	77	771834	150512	1012966	1701511
Cork-cutting	10	6	....	268	108	89	71	196000	63436	236541	403735
Cotton goods	143	119	45	12762	3881	6103	2778	12575221	3510534	10749472	17565028
Crucibles	5	4	....	57	57	....	....	189000	28400	224860	457000
Curled hair	5	2	....	170	119	25	26	1633100	99950	597677	827620
Cutlery	22	15	3	378	324	16	38	577480	113608	232672	537442
Dentists' materials	6	1	....	322	244	68	10	797000	234500	140250	512500
Drugs and chemicals	82	27	2	1812	1543	133	136	6060300	826037	5346834	8451991
Edge-tools and axes	20	9	15	602	597	3	2	742500	384144	398695	830723
Engraving	31	2	....	233	197	14	22	137000	109244	58269	268910
Envelopes	6	4	....	245	61	180	1	230000	60408	136850	313600
Explosives and fireworks	2	....	....	31	31	....	....	315000	98322	155500	460000
Fertilizers	33	17	7	414	413	1	....	1507500	216626	700975	1635200
Files	20	6	1	323	265	17	41	277700	108247	110122	383274
Flouring-mill products	1251	(*)	(*)	3275	(*)	(*)	(*)	12154637	826500	26893253	31124017
Food preparations, animal	17	8	....	104	86	17	1	129000	34537	270497	396286
Fruits and vegetables, canned	7	4	....	425	73	352	....	230000	80200	203435	488004
Furniture	948	100	31	5684	5458	107	119	5005053	2130868	2826060	6082530
Furs, dressed	45	....	....	459	161	288	10	628850	114426	498718	961388
Galvanizing	4	4	....	111	106	....	5	169000	68300	466296	639526
Gas and lamp fixtures	9	7	....	919	825	58	36	1134894	441484	423447	1171783
Glass ware	42	27	....	5590	3668	122	1800	5843816	3095597	2016705	7407135
Glass, window	10	2	....	645	560	....	85	598000	412345	315293	894190
Glue	12	1	1	152	121	6	25	1042300	75328	246888	509157
Gold leaf and foil	8	1	....	198	99	84	15	153100	72311	178058	308522
Grease and tallow	8	3	....	50	50	....	....	136175	37678	442591	602706
Gunpowder	15	5	13	184	184	....	....	752900	77045	558546	873033
Hardware, (with saddlery hardw're)	87	37	1	1177	917	67	103	1120929	490312	810306	1777285
Hats and caps	81	18	5	1650	989	558	103	1035663	703088	1248231	2813766
Heating apparatus	27	3	....	342	339	....	3	511580	252190	413487	1157086
Hides and tallow	4	....	....	18	18	....	....	78000	9690	364804	418300

* Not separately compiled.

TABLE CI.—*Manufactures, in each State and Territory, by Selected Industries—1870—Cont'd.*

THE STATE OF PENNSYLVANIA—Continued.

Mechanical and manufacturing industries.	Establishm'ts.	Steam-engines.	Water-wheels.	All hands.	Males above 16.	Females above 15.	Youth.	Capital. (Dollars.)	Wages. (Dollars.)	Materials. (Dollars.)	Products. (Dollars.)
Hosiery	76	44	....	4899	1325	2672	902	[illegible]	[illegible]	[illegible]	[illegible]
Hubs and other wagon material	40	26	11	274	264	1	9	350525	105759	[illegible]	[illegible]
Instrum'ts, professional & scientific	30	7	....	226	199	8	19	334033	105541	[illegible]	[illegible]
Iron, blooms	43	21	36	1473	1422	2	49	2446000	[illegible]	[illegible]	[illegible]
Iron, forged and rolled	135	368	33	21865	20074	20	871	[illegible]	[illegible]	[illegible]	[illegible]
Iron, bolts, nuts,					1230	18	305	1792900	[illegible]	1700315	[illegible]
Iron, nails & spikes, cut & wrought	31	22	1	2036	1594	22	420	[illegible]	1106214	[illegible]	[illegible]
Iron, pipe, wroug	8	16	....	1288	1195	....	93	4200000	702710	[illegible]	[illegible]
Iron, ship-buildin gines											
Iron, pig	136	252	46	10861	10629	10	222	[illegible]	[illegible]	[illegible]	[illegible]
Iron, castings, (not specified)	443	294	59	7587	7270	2	396	[illegible]	[illegible]	[illegible]	[illegible]
Iron, castings, stoves, heaters, and hollow ware	81	60	4	2052	1897	....	155	3912200	1130751	[illegible]	[illegible]
Jewelry	65	8	....	720	601	64	55	917093	280417	708931	[illegible]
Lead pipe	2	2	....	37	37	....	....	600000	23000	170000	[illegible]
Leather, tanned	890	294	132	4650	4559	25	66	11800046	1683479	[illegible]	[illegible]
Leather, curried	558	13	1	1080	1067	7	6	1830461	[illegible]	1479451	[illegible]
Leather, morocco, tanned & curried	25	7	....	1002	892	87	23	[illegible]	[illegible]	2051813	[illegible]
Leather, dressed skins	22	3	....	148	136	8	4	344500	[illegible]	[illegible]	[illegible]
Lightning-rods	3	1	....	81	70	....	11	152100	[illegible]	[illegible]	[illegible]
Lime	403	[illegible]	1	1821	1811	....	10	[illegible]	[illegible]	[illegible]	[illegible]
Liquors, distilled	108	77	4	512	510	1	1	2504857	[illegible]	[illegible]	[illegible]
Liquors, malt	246	90	4	1583	1569	2	12	[illegible]	773267	[illegible]	[illegible]
Looking-glass and picture frames	47	9	....	616	589	....	27	[illegible]	[illegible]	[illegible]	[illegible]
Lumber, planed	166	(*)	(*)	1791	(*)	(*)	(*)	2915316	941877	[illegible]	[illegible]
Lumber, sawed	1583	(*)	(*)	11452	(*)	(*)	(*)	[illegible]	4139361	[illegible]	[illegible]
Machinery, (not specified)	276	192	11	6774	6600	25	149	9405012	3656044	[illegible]	[illegible]
Machinery, cotton and woolen	27	21	1	857	818	29	10	1584300	395301	707202	[illegible]
Machinery, railroad repairing	23	98	1	5373	5337	....	36	[illegible]	[illegible]	[illegible]	[illegible]
Machinery, steam engines & boilers	151	127	5	4686	4559	....	127	5843118	2597144	[illegible]	[illegible]
Malt	21	12	....	253	253	....	....	1246300	[illegible]	[illegible]	[illegible]
Marble and stone work, (n. s.)	150	21	4	1950	1924	....	26	[illegible]	[illegible]	[illegible]	[illegible]
Matches	9	5	....	262	41	81	140	[illegible]	11750	[illegible]	[illegible]
Meat, cured and packed, (n. s.)	9	4	....	120	118	....	2	1270000	76560	[illegible]	[illegible]
Meat, packed, pork	13	8	....	195	189	....	6	1543000	[illegible]	[illegible]	[illegible]
Meters, gas	4	3	....	180	177	3	....	200000	108740	[illegible]	[illegible]
Millinery	238	1	....	1288	94	1158	36	[illegible]	[illegible]	[illegible]	[illegible]
Mineral and soda waters	42	3	....	246	212	....	34	177550	[illegible]	[illegible]	[illegible]
Molasses and sugar, refined	15	25	....	1241	1240	....	1	5619000	[illegible]	[illegible]	[illegible]
Monuments and tombstones	158	6	1	716	710	....	6	[illegible]	[illegible]	[illegible]	[illegible]
Musical instruments and materials	32	5	....	409	401	2	6	605500	[illegible]	211714	[illegible]
Oil, animal	12	6	....	60	59	....	1	389000	[illegible]	[illegible]	[illegible]
Oil, vegetable, linseed	15	8	6	145	144	....	1	716100	[illegible]	[illegible]	[illegible]
Oil floor-cloth	4	4	....	227	175	10	42	390000	[illegible]	[illegible]	[illegible]
Paints, (not specified)	13	11	1	192	191	....	1	871000	[illegible]	507707	[illegible]
Paints, lead and zinc	23	22	3	561	523	18	20	2177250	261022	[illegible]	[illegible]
Paper, (not specified)	31	21	21	471	368	87	16	[illegible]	[illegible]	[illegible]	[illegible]
Paper, printing	29	29	45	1178	805	343	30	[illegible]	[illegible]	[illegible]	[illegible]
Paper, wrapping	15	9	15	173	144	21	8	[illegible]	[illegible]	[illegible]	[illegible]
Paper, writing	3	2	7	209	63	146	....	[illegible]	53000	[illegible]	[illegible]
Paper-hangings	5	11	....	397	357	8	32	[illegible]	[illegible]	[illegible]	[illegible]
Patent medicines and compounds	61	6	....	441	283	141	[illegible]	[illegible]	[illegible]	[illegible]	[illegible]
Perfumery and fancy soaps	19	6	....	253	123	119	11	[illegible]	[illegible]	[illegible]	[illegible]
Plaster and plaster work	53	5	39	179	178	....	1	[illegible]	66312	[illegible]	[illegible]
Plated ware	32	9	....	304	208	61	35	[illegible]	[illegible]	[illegible]	[illegible]
Printing cotton and woolen goods	7	25	2	868	569	70	229	[illegible]	[illegible]	[illegible]	[illegible]
Printing and publishing	307	118	....	5364	4482	491	391	[illegible]	3197649	[illegible]	[illegible]
Pumps	43	13	5	159	148	....	11	[illegible]	[illegible]	[illegible]	[illegible]
Roofing materials	58	17	9	910	905	....	5	[illegible]	[illegible]	[illegible]	[illegible]
Saddlery and harness	903	1	....	2488	2431	26	31	[illegible]	[illegible]	[illegible]	[illegible]
Safes, doors, and vaults, (fire-proof)	10	6	....	177	175	....	2	[illegible]	111010	[illegible]	[illegible]
Sand and emery paper and cloth	1	1	....	55	40	....	15	[illegible]	35000	[illegible]	[illegible]
Sash, doors, and blinds	204	145	27	2732	2667	2	63	[illegible]	[illegible]	[illegible]	[illegible]
Saws	11	11	....	682	609	2	71	[illegible]	[illegible]	[illegible]	[illegible]
Sewing machines	8	4	....	325	320	2	3	[illegible]	[illegible]	[illegible]	[illegible]
Ship build'g, repair'g, and materials	106	30	1	2174	2155	....	19	[illegible]	[illegible]	[illegible]	[illegible]
Shovels and spades	7	4	3	186	181	....	....	[illegible]	[illegible]	[illegible]	[illegible]
Silk goods, (not specified)	8	5	....	817	243	559	15	[illegible]	[illegible]	[illegible]	[illegible]
Silk, sewing and twist	9	2	....	119	23	96	....	[illegible]	[illegible]	[illegible]	[illegible]
Silver ware	9	7	....	156	141	13	2	[illegible]	[illegible]	[illegible]	[illegible]
Soap and candles	96	25	....	748	627	80	41	[illegible]	[illegible]	[illegible]	[illegible]
Steel, Bessemer	2	16	....	217	217	....	....	[illegible]	[illegible]	[illegible]	[illegible]
Steel, cast	14	46	1	[illegible]	1512	....	37	[illegible]	[illegible]	[illegible]	[illegible]

* Not separately compiled.

TABLE CI.—*Manufactures, in each State and Territory, by Selected Industries*—1870—Cont'd.

THE STATE OF PENNSYLVANIA—Continued.

Mechanical and manufacturing industries.	Establishm'ts.	Steam-engines.	Water-wheels.	All hands.	Males above 16.	Females above 15.	Youth.	Capital. (*Dollars.*)	Wages. (*Dollars.*)	Materials. (*Dollars.*)	Products. (*Dollars.*)
Steel, springs	10	7	....	198	192	....	6	1226000	122202	566023	990763
Stereotyping and electrotyping	11	3	....	558	466	12	80	938000	320934	149150	792700
Stone and earthen ware	198	18	....	1374	1206	43	125	1477240	448315	534808	1659747
Tin, copper, and sheet-iron ware	974	15	....	3631	3315	189	127	3202477	1206277	2423749	5311810
Tobacco, chew'g, smok'g, and snuff	25	8	1	411	172	84	155	420800	115830	276181	854245
Tobacco, cigars	975	....	....	5775	3959	1411	405	1966395	1460359	1982445	5276628
Trunks, valises, and satchels	28	....	....	257	232	19	6	162875	127412	245982	478377
Umbrella furniture	1	4	....	360	164	155	41	244500	130719	196600	429850
Umbrellas and canes	27	1	....	1355	302	1003	50	1016682	343260	1051926	2049793
Upholstery	95	4	....	741	403	283	55	686888	212165	613589	1311743
Varnish	5	1	....	21	21	....	..	123000	12500	129435	336000
Watch-cases	10	3	....	136	128	6	2	145000	89685	275962	443160
Wire	6	3	4	159	153	....	6	422000	89341	513908	667133
Wire-work	29	1	1	238	160	59	19	207100	70425	171485	330240
Wood brackets, moldings, & scrolls	12	10	....	117	115	1	1	137600	63882	105036	257947
Wooden ware	19	7	3	242	177	....	65	398825	92670	185824	502915
Wood, turned and carved	158	52	29	955	836	45	74	553748	337772	320669	1105470
Wool-carding and cloth-dressing	61	9	47	237	162	46	29	210750	49114	285157	395608
Woolen goods	403	184	226	12578	5699	5032	1847	14066785	4340066	17325849	27361897
Worsted goods	31	28	1	3868	1318	1743	807	3350078	1363334	4932940	7883038
Zinc, smelted and rolled	3	2	....	172	172	....	....	283520	94816	165708	341547

THE STATE OF RHODE ISLAND.

Mechanical and manufacturing industries.	Establishm'ts.	Steam-engines.	Water-wheels.	All hands.	Males above 16.	Females above 15.	Youth.	Capital. (*Dollars.*)	Wages. (*Dollars.*)	Materials. (*Dollars.*)	Products. (*Dollars.*)
Bleaching and dyeing	18	14	7	780	618	108	54	1471000	316994	13842026	15138723
Boots and shoes	16	1	....	306	260	45	1	70000	114475	267595	437254
Bread and other bakery products	25	3	....	180	165	3	12	140000	75302	339229	541324
Carriages and wagons	55	....	8	270	267	1	2	148900	115182	112720	314139
Clothing	100	....	....	1244	431	779	34	509475	383159	787664	1448066
Copper, milled and smelted	1	1	....	25	25	....	....	65000	15000	256110	335920
Cotton goods	142	72	186	16910	5697	8060	3153	18885300	5240333	13325938	22139203
Drugs and chemicals	17	13	3	376	333	43	....	394600	133460	389175	642346
Files	8	4	....	220	199	2	19	749700	122184	102715	373992
Fire-arms, small-arms	1	1	....	153	141	....	12	170000	121515	85659	298017
Flax and linen goods	1	2	....	250	75	125	50	1000000	71500	122000	374400
Flouring-mill products	28	(*)	(*)	82	(*)	(*)	(*)	133400	19660	1119633	1281887
Furniture	18	5	....	290	210	9	71	166450	112200	112412	311620
Gas and lamp fixtures	3	2	....	90	78	10	2	134000	29000	316192	387500
Hair-cloth	2	....	4	148	77	68	3	525000	62008	324921	414310
Hardware	6	2	....	322	273	16	33	394500	154000	256524	649600
India-rubber and elastic goods	2	6	....	845	455	275	115	403000	378582	901053	1804868
Iron, forged and rolled	5	10	....	261	223	....	38	585000	159000	522436	753500
Iron, nails & spikes, cut & wrought	4	4	....	179	137	3	39	250200	131162	293994	450188
Iron, castings, stoves, heaters, and hollow ware	17	13	2	927	909	....	18	1224000	512025	622061	1416103
Jewelry	71	11	2	1579	1191	331	57	1850400	948201	1358831	3043846
Leather, tanned	8	5	2	101	101	....	....	283000	47400	673344	741103
Leather, curried	6	....	....	112	112	....	....	263000	61045	793954	1087161
Machinery, cotton and woolen	70	34	13	3087	3005	25	57	3583060	1770371	1112715	4316376
Marble and stone work, (not spec.)	19	2	....	584	556	10	18	159150	328711	145887	676594
Meat, packed, pork	3	1	....	29	28	....	1	65000	16000	319040	343572
Molasses and sugar, refined	2	5	....	153	152	....	1	258000	46500	1431575	1600980
Oil, vegetable, cotton-seed	1	1	....	60	56	4	....	150000	49050	365000	500000
Plated ware	9	2	....	380	363	14	3	634700	317400	564900	1212240
Printing cotton and woolen goods	9	20	1	2996	2035	351	610	6770000	1028000	14604962	17842480
Printing and publishing, (not spec.)	11	10	....	269	192	8	69	203600	133350	123098	328210
Sash, doors, and blinds	10	5	4	136	131	....	5	132000	77350	251555	402004
Screws	2	3	....	972	426	433	113	7080000	353800	718465	1882318
Soap and candles	15	2	....	89	88	....	1	234200	35785	328156	494500
Tin, copper, and sheet-iron ware	51	....	....	229	220	3	6	156700	91285	140464	319973
Wash'g-mach's & clothes-wringers	3	1	1	72	58	4	10	259000	34300	93275	265900
Woolen goods	65	28	70	6363	3354	2198	811	8167500	2228402	8089946	12558117
Worsted goods	11	15	2	1531	290	986	255	2300000	631090	1736210	2835950

THE STATE OF SOUTH CAROLINA.

Mechanical and manufacturing industries.	Establishm'ts.	Steam-engines.	Water-wheels.	All hands.	Males above 16.	Females above 15.	Youth.	Capital. (*Dollars.*)	Wages. (*Dollars.*)	Materials. (*Dollars.*)	Products. (*Dollars.*)
Cotton goods, (not specified)	12	....	14	1123	289	508	326	1337000	257680	761480	[illegible]
Fertilizers	2	3	....	825	825	....	....	350000	23000	365000	[illegible]

* Not separately compiled.

TABLE CI.—*Manufactures, in each State and Territory, by Selected Industries*—1870—Cont'd

THE STATE OF SOUTH CAROLINA—Continued.

Mechanical and manufacturing industries.	Establishm'ts.	Steam-engines.	Water-wheels.	All hands.	Males above 16.	Females above 15.	Youth.	Capital. (*Dollars.*)	Wages. (*Dollars.*)	Materials. (*Dollars.*)	Products. (*Dollars.*)
Flouring-mill products	91	(*)	(*)	182	(*)	(*)	(*)	171150	29619	672549	[illegible]
Lumber	83	(*)	(*)	850	(*)	(*)	(*)	400650	178340	522105	[illegible]
Machinery, (not specified)	11	7	1	220	207	....	13	137502	104500	102717	[illegible]
Printing and publishing	13	8	....	182	143	15	24	129550	127100	54725	[illegible]
Tar and turpentine	54	3	1	876	843	16	17	205425	123645	422378	[illegible]

THE STATE OF TENNESSEE.

Mechanical and manufacturing industries.	Establishm'ts.	Steam-engines.	Water-wheels.	All hands.	Males above 16.	Females above 15.	Youth.	Capital. (*Dollars.*)	Wages. (*Dollars.*)	Materials. (*Dollars.*)	Products. (*Dollars.*)
Bread and other bakery products	29	1	....	106	104	1	1	50000	50415	151987	[illegible]
Carriages and wagons	220	5	1	818	815	....	3	495280	297546	330152	[illegible]
Cars, freight and passenger	4	4	....	194	194	....	....	160000	133412	140212	[illegible]
Clothing	180	....	....	487	212	274	1	178440	155135	229294	[illegible]
Copper, milled and smelted	2	1	1	188	188	....	....	150000	62000	369470	[illegible]
Cotton goods	28	9	21	890	252	463	175	970650	175156	595789	941542
Flouring-mill products	216	(*)	(*)	675	(*)	(*)	(*)	1390942	161118	4472830	[illegible]
Furniture	89	11	9	485	427	....	58	231310	119260	[illegible]	[illegible]
Iron, forged and rolled	18	3	17	337	334	....	3	253750	130883	139696	[illegible]
Iron, pig	14	11	8	1122	1038	20	64	1103750	379324	439937	[illegible]
Iron, castings	33	16	4	316	312	....	4	331302	166501	246504	555111
Leather, tanned	209	9	8	453	440	2	11	451097	87619	660335	[illegible]
Leather, curried	180	2	....	309	300	....	3	249568	62636	737070	[illegible]
Liquors, distilled	44	21	1	213	199	....	14	215650	30983	171460	[illegible]
Lumber, planed	20	(*)	(*)	186	(*)	(*)	(*)	160575	82300	341300	[illegible]
Lumber, sawed	318	(*)	(*)	1949	(*)	(*)	(*)	1168125	483407	1238543	[illegible]
Machinery, (not specified)	21	12	....	211	208	....	3	224900	106785	[illegible]	327430
Oil, vegetable, cotton-seed	4	4	....	161	157	4	....	190000	75000	272000	[illegible]
Printing and publishing	39	13	....	457	402	21	34	518300	347433	276256	[illegible]
Saddlery and harness	161	....	....	421	418	....	3	248405	143070	313935	[illegible]
Sash, doors, and blinds	11	6	2	162	137	....	25	127100	93330	228042	[illegible]
Tin, copper, and sheet-iron ware	76	....	....	289	283	1	5	250350	112078	183009	437551
Wool-carding and cloth-dressing	133	22	72	265	237	19	9	185793	17860	367623	[illegible]

THE STATE OF TEXAS.

Mechanical and manufacturing industries.	Establishm'ts.	Steam-engines.	Water-wheels.	All hands.	Males above 16.	Females above 15.	Youth.	Capital. (*Dollars.*)	Wages. (*Dollars.*)	Materials. (*Dollars.*)	Products. (*Dollars.*)
Carriages and wagons	115	1	....	325	321	....	4	130585	81162	94588	299124
Cotton goods, (not specified)	4	4	....	291	184	52	55	496000	68211	216519	[illegible]
Flouring-mill products	20	(*)	(*)	62	(*)	(*)	(*)	86200	14800	188775	[illegible]
Hides and tallow	6	6	....	112	109	1	2	65000	25450	115500	[illegible]
Lumber	192	(*)	(*)	1301	(*)	(*)	(*)	634859	339426	548430	[illegible]
Meat, packed, beef	15	13	....	275	266	4	5	200500	70223	809290	[illegible]
Saddlery and harness	138	....	....	292	285	....	7	153320	55941	176518	[illegible]
Sash, doors, and blinds	10	8	....	118	117	....	1	140000	69804	153326	[illegible]
Tin, copper, and sheet-iron ware	71	....	....	237	224	2	11	154136	82068	140222	[illegible]

THE TERRITORY OF UTAH.

Mechanical and manufacturing industries.	Establishm'ts.	Steam-engines.	Water-wheels.	All hands.	Males above 16.	Females above 15.	Youth.	Capital. (*Dollars.*)	Wages. (*Dollars.*)	Materials. (*Dollars.*)	Products. (*Dollars.*)
Lumber	72	(*)	(*)	474	(*)	(*)	(*)	303000	131124	250770	[illegible]

THE STATE OF VERMONT.

Mechanical and manufacturing industries.	Establishm'ts.	Steam-engines.	Water-wheels.	All hands.	Males above 16.	Females above 15.	Youth.	Capital. (*Dollars.*)	Wages. (*Dollars.*)	Materials. (*Dollars.*)	Products. (*Dollars.*)
Agricultural implements	45	4	45	372	367	2	3	518150	138327	212964	[illegible]
Boots and shoes	29	1	....	331	280	44	7	141584	137050	240687	[illegible]
Carriages and sleds	169	13	84	823	808	14	1	574670	304081	236236	[illegible]
Cars, freight and passenger	2	1	....	250	246	2	2	175000	120000	332470	[illegible]
Cheese	28	8	....	92	64	28	....	107700	18305	365028	[illegible]
Clothing	63	....	....	372	132	227	13	162570	80415	217946	[illegible]
Cotton goods, (not specified)	8	1	12	451	125	242	84	670000	125000	292269	[illegible]
Flouring-mill products	81	(*)	(*)	235	(*)	(*)	(*)	764550	70244	[illegible]	2071534
Furniture, (not specified)	47	5	24	413	386	....	27	439175	184135	200190	[illegible]
Furniture, chairs	33	5	36	322	290	21	12	262200	120382	111373	[illegible]
Hosiery	7	....	7	331	89	216	26	303000	[illegible]	[illegible]	[illegible]
Iron, castings	26	8	15	244	244	....	....	[illegible]	[illegible]	[illegible]	[illegible]

* Not separately compiled.

TABLE CI.—*Manufactures, in each State and Territory, by Selected Industries*—1870—Cont'd.

THE STATE OF VERMONT—Continued.

Mechanical and manufacturing industries.	Establishm'ts.	Steam-engines.	Water-wheels.	All hands.	Males above 16.	Females above 15.	Youth.	Capital. (*Dollars.*)	Wages. (*Dollars.*)	Materials. (*Dollars.*)	Products. (*Dollars.*)
Leather, tanned	86	11	69	321	317	4	....	620743	113415	967840	1249942
Leather, curried	64	3	12	137	137	....	....	156390	44730	619045	762571
Lumber, planed	13	(*)	(*)	1331	(*)	(*)	(*)	2000600	333000	1544215	2326228
Lumber, sawed	347	(*)	(*)	2050	(*)	(*)	(*)	2501036	667029	1504139	3142307
Machinery, (not specified)	37	4	35	401	401	....	....	714233	226210	259728	756080
Marble and stone work, (not spec.)	29	7	19	650	619	....	31	1138000	322205	414481	960984
Musical instruments and materials	9	1	....	204	199	5	....	302000	120200	96390	348999
Saddlery and harness	123	....	....	280	280	....	....	140375	63788	127724	286071
Sash, doors, and blinds	43	9	40	331	311	....	20	286900	131759	234556	518123
Scales and balances	2	2	9	363	363	....	....	280000	336283	529630	1629000
Tin, copper, and sheet-iron ware	97	1	1	339	332	5	2	358150	98983	227522	505005
Woolen goods	43	8	63	1829	896	746	187	2297500	640753	1881955	3550962

THE STATE OF VIRGINIA.

Mechanical and manufacturing industries.	Establishm'ts.	Steam-engines.	Water-wheels.	All hands.	Males above 16.	Females above 15.	Youth.	Capital. (*Dollars.*)	Wages. (*Dollars.*)	Materials. (*Dollars.*)	Products. (*Dollars.*)
Agricultural implements	37	9	5	267	267	....	....	187128	102886	153694	403457
Bread and other bakery products	43	2	....	163	146	8	9	58675	46100	203864	308984
Carriages and wagons	186	1	....	563	557	2	4	157565	121842	117872	389663
Cars, freight and passenger	7	7	1	469	469	....	....	1205600	258578	330458	613036
Clothing	146	....	....	381	197	176	8	80145	75285	197762	396191
Cotton goods, (not specified)	11	2	19	1741	921	507	313	1128000	229750	937830	1435800
Flouring-mill products	282	(*)	(*)	720	(*)	(*)	(*)	2648050	277450	4776572	6581396
Furniture	126	6	4	311	303	2	6	132542	58025	72492	280838
Iron, forged and rolled	12	....	21	696	696	....	....	810200	329025	1298575	1994146
Iron, nails & spikes, cut & wrought	1	....	2	160	160	....	....	125000	85000	224200	350000
Iron, pig	18	10	11	1036	982	4	50	828700	271220	276173	619880
Iron, castings	54	15	19	541	529	....	12	554215	190275	323768	769274
Leather, tanned	172	5	7	313	307	....	6	211790	43907	331138	408149
Leather, curried	146	2	....	194	193	....	1	90694	18802	259958	328894
Liquors, distilled	49	4	1	140	139	1	....	238635	23341	183595	415980
Lumber, sawed	173	(*)	(*)	1456	(*)	(*)	(*)	596789	281254	642951	1609966
Machinery, (not specified)	26	13	3	443	421	....	22	604727	172723	217906	511485
Printing and publishing	36	6	2	332	305	3	24	249300	193616	148688	429968
Tin, copper, and sheet-iron ware	80	....	....	251	239	1	11	120357	64431	125646	296998
Tobacco, chew'g, smok'g, and snuff	94	25	2	7414	4256	1311	1847	1361700	1149331	4039372	6935249
Woolen goods	19	1	20	203	121	51	31	391500	56527	208614	352829

THE TERRITORY OF WASHINGTON.

Mechanical and manufacturing industries.	Establishm'ts.	Steam-engines.	Water-wheels.	All hands.	Males above 16.	Females above 15.	Youth.	Capital. (*Dollars.*)	Wages. (*Dollars.*)	Materials. (*Dollars.*)	Products. (*Dollars.*)
Flouring-mill products	11	(*)	(*)	24	(*)	(*)	(*)	145500	14080	188298	222728
Lumber, planed	4	(*)	(*)	55	(*)	(*)	(*)	105000	30000	377000	605000
Lumber, sawed	19	(*)	(*)	417	(*)	(*)	(*)	1174800	381760	565044	1267310

THE STATE OF WEST VIRGINIA.

Mechanical and manufacturing industries.	Establishm'ts.	Steam-engines.	Water-wheels.	All hands.	Males above 16.	Females above 15.	Youth.	Capital. (*Dollars.*)	Wages. (*Dollars.*)	Materials. (*Dollars.*)	Products. (*Dollars.*)
Carriages and wagons	50	5	1	243	229	....	14	210295	100330	85889	303690
Clothing, men's	41	....	....	291	193	98	....	111848	84310	229566	399049
Coal-oil, rectified	10	19	....	82	81	....	1	125050	22850	320235	432850
Cooperage	101	6	....	549	545	....	4	125632	140243	233583	488476
Flouring-mill products	68	(*)	(*)	179	(*)	(*)	(*)	810300	50678	1880546	2239799
Iron, forged and rolled	9	15	....	1498	1462	2	34	1185860	1016087	2424646	4025620
Iron, nails & spikes, cut & wrought	8	8	....	1156	769	9	378	988000	722460	3689207	4065000
Iron, pig	5	5	1	317	297	....	20	434000	179720	243300	577200
Iron, castings, (not specified)	16	11	....	148	145	....	3	286900	81988	159224	291972
Iron, castings, stoves, heaters, and hollow ware	8	7	....	137	136	....	1	175200	85700	110870	274100
Leather, tanned	104	13	4	220	213	1	6	362890	47454	374292	527016
Leather, curried	74	2	....	108	106	....	2	93489	21438	252386	313829
Lumber	144	(*)	(*)	1156	(*)	(*)	(*)	877700	330431	602861	1344512
Salt	18	72	1	661	652	4	5	1631000	290600	384835	1507605
Tobacco, cigars	42	....	....	177	144	12	21	40875	67899	70206	268348
Woolen goods	29	16	19	250	143	75	30	183900	55590	222275	370101

* Not separately compiled.

TABLE CI.—*Manufactures, in each State and Territory, by Selected Industries*—1870—Cont'd.

THE STATE OF WISCONSIN.

Mechanical and manufacturing industries.	Establishments.	Steam-engines.	Water-wheels.	All hands.	Males above 16.	Females above 15.	Youth.	Capital. (*Dollars.*)	Wages. (*Dollars.*)	Materials. (*Dollars.*)	Products. (*Dollars.*)
Agricultural implements	82	31	6	1387	1360	3	24	1494700	663392	966749	[illegible]
Boats	7	3	....	208	208	....	....	54400	139200	79055	[illegible]
Boots and shoes	78	....	....	927	903	21	3	637047	343754	656319	[illegible]
Bread and other bakery products	39	4	....	191	184	1	6	127250	58152	256631	[illegible]
Brick	79	12	....	1133	1086	2	45	456050	198445	125361	[illegible]
Carriages and wagons	485	22	2	2184	2134	....	50	1252476	762705	900170	[illegible]
Clothing	263	....	....	1902	1065	810	27	1096575	539701	1308947	[illegible]
Coffee & spices, roasted and ground.	4	3	....	32	24	....	8	92410	22140	249031	[illegible]
Cooperage	250	3	1	717	699	....	18	207040	160083	291904	[illegible]
Flouring-mill products	306	(*)	(*)	1344	(*)	(*)	(*)	4397400	442906	13416127	[illegible]
Furniture	188	30	21	1844	1588	151	105	1793505	578880	515053	[illegible]
Iron, forged and rolled	1	....	....	642	630	....	12	100000	374078	753439	[illegible]
Iron, pig	6	6	1	592	592	....	....	865000	122580	511645	[illegible]
Iron, castings, (not specified)	66	35	7	561	553	....	11	634000	310506	589497	[illegible]
Iron, castings, stoves, heaters, and hollow ware	8	5	2	155	143	....	12	126500	61846	139002	[illegible]
Lead, pig	13	....	6	91	91	....	....	91000	28908	459929	[illegible]
Leather, tanned	85	40	5	577	573	....	4	906181	229010	1478142	[illegible]
Leather, curried	70	2	....	322	317	5	....	407906	126789	2010090	[illegible]
Lime	53	1	....	312	312	....	....	228180	81072	159801	30729
Liquors, distilled	8	7	....	104	102	....	2	171000	30850	222415	[illegible]
Liquors, malt	176	27	2	835	819	9	7	2108150	258908	935046	[illegible]
Lumber, planed	22	(*)	(*)	223	(*)	(*)	(*)	217000	80492	392800	[illegible]
Lumber, sawed	544	(*)	(*)	10905	(*)	(*)	(*)	11054795	3710068	7239813	[illegible]
Machinery, (not specified)	41	22	9	311	311	....	....	312024	156018	232160	[illegible]
Machinery, steam engines & boilers	17	12	....	448	447	....	1	521000	236866	245887	[illegible]
Paper	6	3	7	207	156	46	5	445000	83536	225197	[illegible]
Printing and publishing	66	9	....	613	527	44	42	513250	274125	375267	[illegible]
Saddlery and harness	269	....	1	672	665	....	7	312211	135385	344867	[illegible]
Sash, doors, and blinds	81	62	16	1381	1278	....	103	1413793	502170	887929	[illegible]
Soap and candles	16	4	....	69	57	3	9	103430	18327	178401	[illegible]
Tin, copper, and sheet-iron ware	225	....	....	605	590	2	13	388339	148299	350784	[illegible]
Tobacco, chewing and smoking	4	4	....	128	60	10	58	190000	43000	251000	[illegible]
Tobacco, cigars	109	....	....	597	509	6	82	308230	173694	258854	[illegible]
Wooden ware	6	3	10	361	295	....	66	188700	131800	150136	[illegible]
Woolen goods	48	9	46	736	469	205	62	1211289	225611	581063	1115646

* Not separately compiled.

[Continued from page 847.]

Examination of the table within the text on page 847 shows that the first class of industries, with a reported gross product of $143,000,000, yields a net product only $5,000,000 less than that of the fifth class, which has a gross product of $841,000,000, while the wages paid in the first class exceed those paid in the fifth by 131 per cent. Nothing, perhaps, could set in a stronger light the necessity of considering all statements of manufacturing production in connection with the value of materials consumed and the cost of labor. Here are two groups of industries, the one reaching the gigantic total of $841,000,000, the other aggregating but one-sixth as much; yet the latter makes a clear addition to the wealth of the country equal to 96 per cent. of the net production of the former, and actually pays more than twice as much in wages.

The calculations which have been added to show the number of dollars' worth of wages and of materials, separately and combined, in each hundred dollars of product, and also the average value of production, gross and net, to each hand employed, are well worth studying.

It appears that the value of the materials consumed in the several groups of industries range from $10.07 to $84.10 in each $100 of product; that the amount of wages ranges (going, so to speak, in the opposite direction) from $51.30 to $3.77 in each $100 of product, while the gross product per capita ranges from $843.51 to $8,285.44, and the net product ranges from $758.54 to $1,316.64. The reason for these astonishing differences is not found chiefly in any difference in the quality of labor, or in the more extensive application of machinery in one class than in another, but, almost wholly, in the treatment of this subject of the materials consumed in the successive industries and classes of industries.

Defects of the census law.—The Tables of Manufacturing Industry probably show more clearly than any other conspicuous portion of these volumes the importance of additional legislation in respect to the census. The industry of the United States has

[Continued on page 885.]

ABLE CII.—*Groups of Principal Industries, by States and Territories*—1870.

—Each of these groups is a combination of certain of the Industries specified in Table XCIX. nbinations as are here attempted must, at the best, fall short of theoretical exactness, and in es will be found only approximately correct. For example, in dealing with the group of indusducing building-materials, it is wholly impracticable to separate from the manufactures of iron ts which go to the building of houses, stores, factories, bridges, &c., and the group is, thereincomplete to just this extent. Again, in the group dealing with the preparation of food for sign elements are manifestly included to a small extent, as in the case of provender for horses e, embraced in the productions of grist and flouring mills. Many other such instances might . Still, it is believed that these combinations will be found highly convenient for many of the to which the statistics of production are applied, and that substantial accuracy may be for the results, after the one broad exception has been made as to the completeness of the elating to the common trades of carpentering, painting, plastering, and plumbing.

BRASS, CAST AND ROLLED, AND BRASS-WARE.

s Brass and copper tubing, (chiefly brass;) Brass founding and finishing; Brass, rolled; and Brass-ware.]

d Territories.	Establishm'ts.	Steam-engines.	Water-wheels.	All hands.	Capital. (Dollars.)	Wages. (Dollars.)	Materials. (Dollars.)	Products. (Dollars.)
nited States ..	319	165	20	4,703	6,793,435	2,411,232	5,252,282	10,459,735
....	1	....	....	2	300	200	5,014	7,500
a..............	7	6	....	100	71,600	61,139	59,390	187,500
cut	29	9	10	863	1,494,600	465,941	1,188,397	2,404,990
of Columbia..	1	1	....	32	3,600	11,000	14,002	59,500
....	5	4	....	115	111,800	68,020	61,693	180,500
....	9	8	....	54	71,000	26,670	47,532	103,200
....	1	1	....	6	3,000	2,000	800	5,200
....	1	....	....	4	300	2,000	1,105	4,055
y	3	2	....	11	9,550	3,000	8,159	17,700
a..............	2	1	....	7	2,800	2,500	1,872	6,500
....	9	4	1	27	40,000	9,530	39,712	71,559
d..............	5	4	....	136	58,000	61,559	85,676	255,435
usetts..........	32	12	3	550	422,550	250,486	748,561	1,259,305
n..............	6	2	1	43	31,650	20,415	29,088	59,880
....	10	5	....	147	203,500	91,270	101,175	292,500
mpshire	3	2	....	45	19,000	25,000	46,510	92,500
sey..............	21	6	2	287	236,950	125,065	285,558	499,194
k	67	38	....	985	1,139,200	537,036	992,290	1,991,707
arolina..........	1	....	....	2	200	300	356	900
....	24	15	1	241	202,950	119,613	162,885	394,015
vania	68	39	2	899	2,205,985	425,140	1,157,622	2,144,055
sland	8	4	....	123	369,000	71,316	200,861	393,000
arolina	1	....	....	2	4,500	864	332	3,000
ee	1	1	....	9	20,000	7,000	6,500	16,000
....	1	....	....	3	5,000	1,368	2,000	3,500
....	1	....	....	2	200	300	375	800
rginia	1	....	....	1	200	500	92	740
in	1	1	....	7	6,000	2,000	4,725	5,000

BUILDING, (NOT MARINE.)

s Bridge-building; Carpentering and building; Marble and stone work; Masonry, brick and stone; Painting; Paperhanging; Plastering; and Plumbing and gasfitting.]

d Territories.	Establishm'ts.	Steam-engines.	Water-wheels.	All hands.	Capital. (Dollars.)	Wages. (Dollars.)	Materials. (Dollars.)	Products. (Dollars.)
nited States ..	24,908	511	117	112,820	49,168,863	49,741,376	95,694,685	201,572,541
a	158	1	....	408	64,895	153,025	179,444	509,383
....	2	....	....	5	3,000	2,040	1,950	4,500
s	73	....	....	156	23,920	35,730	72,582	210,139
a..............	368	11	....	1,075	398,770	630,096	868,378	2,100,212
....	35	....	....	130	63,100	96,250	121,980	303,210
cut	589	10	2	3,108	1,087,120	1,607,935	2,603,650	5,435,305
o	40	2	....	323	207,100	140,741	213,482	450,376
of Columbia..	138	....	....	1,607	405,050	543,551	936,144	1,905,618
....	134	2	....	321	56,600	134,670	370,335	636,435
....	231	1	....	797	214,180	231,611	475,017	1,168,933
....	14	....	....	18	1,775	2,200	16,245	35,400
....	1,437	27	....	5,809	1,950,722	2,240,953	4,342,563	9,410,073
....	1,317	21	....	4,245	786,413	1,196,130	2,081,734	4,916,500
....	1,159	3	....	3,083	418,716	700,795	1,855,319	3,729,440
....	250	2	....	1,084	254,082	394,545	985,578	1,991,717
y	421	7	....	1,503	328,275	328,583	1,233,647	2,808,641
a..............	223	5	....	569	131,265	193,329	[illegible]	875,745
....	466	2	5	1,755	404,388	688,920	[illegible]	2,178,543

TABLE CII.—*Groups of Principal Industries, by States and Territories*—1870—Continued.

BUILDING, (NOT MARINE)—Continued.

States and Territories.	Establishm'ts.	Steam-engines.	Water-wheels.	All hands.	Capital. (Dollars.)	Wages. (Dollars.)	Materials. (Dollars.)	Products. (Dollars.)
Maryland	337	2	1	1,487	624,707	509,590	1,557,694	2,735,[illegible]
Massachusetts	1,618	55	10	11,221	4,161,562	6,331,031	9,663,646	20,534,[illegible]
Michigan	1,070	19	5	4,416	1,298,618	1,525,156	2,801,667	5,746,[illegible]
Minnesota	315	5	......	903	157,170	347,708	715,596	1,412,[illegible]
Mississippi	219	2	......	369	111,928	74,832	458,855	[illegible]
Missouri	2,304	33	......	9,516	4,971,057	4,397,371	12,606,879	25,158,[illegible]
Montana	14	......	1	21	4,830	6,025	19,220	43,[illegible]
Nebraska	117	......	......	285	66,155	113,387	356,850	631,[illegible]
Nevada	26	......	......	55	13,450	46,960	32,425	104,[illegible]
New Hampshire	179	4	7	800	544,075	344,331	457,068	1,070,[illegible]
New Jersey	786	27	2	5,190	2,187,142	2,693,513	5,616,181	10,406,[illegible]
New Mexico	43	......	......	56	16,600	9,725	20,063	48,[illegible]
New York	2,711	93	37	16,326	8,851,068	8,616,229	13,535,674	30,348,[illegible]
North Carolina	116	3	2	326	83,180	72,232	89,771	248,[illegible]
Ohio	2,415	56	3	8,668	2,915,681	2,793,449	5,514,905	11,675,[illegible]
Oregon	150	1	......	396	96,195	115,609	280,938	619,[illegible]
Pennsylvania	3,023	70	10	17,681	12,100,831	8,502,775	18,431,997	38,348,344
Rhode Island	279	16	1	2,923	1,072,555	1,632,245	2,[illegible],974	4,727,[illegible]
South Carolina	75	......	1	476	297,535	85,197	182,838	369,15[illegible]
Tennessee	420	5	1	1,099	299,644	278,207	610,244	1,473,[illegible]
Texas	160	3	......	437	196,105	144,307	362,070	725,[illegible]
Utah	56	......	......	72	13,705	14,300	44,510	[illegible]
Vermont	247	10	26	1,205	1,224,935	459,758	628,147	1,483,[illegible]
Virginia	366	6	1	1,095	209,992	264,667	562,602	1,297,[illegible]
Washington	46	......	......	74	18,535	20,820	45,310	103,[illegible]
West Virginia	140	3	......	410	127,495	117,460	172,064	467,201
Wisconsin	621	4	2	1,857	502,742	533,439	1,082,417	2,516,[illegible]

BUILDING-MATERIALS.

[Includes Brick; Building-stone, artificial; Cement; Glass, window; Lumber, planed and sawed; Paints and putty; Paints, lead and zinc; Roofing-materials; Sash, doors, and blinds; and Marble and stone quarrying.]

States and Territories.	Establishm'ts.	Steam-engines.	Water-wheels.	All hands.	Capital. (Dollars.)	Wages. (Dollars.)	Materials. (Dollars.)	Products. (Dollars.)
The United States	33,207	13,751	17,220	251,582	233,005,203	78,126,900	173,198,451	356,140,945
Alabama	308	120	130	1,724	858,605	444,325	635,838	1,731,863
Arizona	1	1	......	16	5,000	6,000	1,600	10,000
Arkansas	229	130	24	1,260	799,975	305,971	628,769	1,571,703
California	373	220	125	5,508	4,779,640	2,294,261	2,931,622	7,528,777
Colorado	42	25	11	299	191,450	113,511	197,800	465,429
Connecticut	524	53	398	3,682	3,166,171	1,533,123	1,981,269	4,673,249
Dakota	10	9	2	68	37,400	14,256	32,772	72,240
Delaware	105	44	52	830	678,116	246,205	409,317	873,667
District of Columbia	24	12	......	586	248,600	195,450	252,950	600,840
Florida	111	70	15	1,187	785,290	448,620	1,184,738	2,303,960
Georgia	600	205	339	4,310	2,099,193	1,013,630	2,136,618	5,251,429
Idaho	11	5	6	50	70,750	19,524	21,877	61,190
Illinois	956	623	34	10,937	7,934,468	3,524,026	9,531,638	17,349,245
Indiana	2,314	1,607	310	13,231	8,283,615	2,916,816	7,363,442	16,339,97[illegible]
Iowa	733	439	122	5,487	4,750,265	1,502,947	4,300,438	7,098,[illegible]
Kansas	230	156	22	1,534	763,105	365,848	850,426	1,905,451
Kentucky	632	406	105	3,726	2,838,286	965,267	2,750,409	5,541,315
Louisiana	193	151	7	1,757	852,470	542,295	946,690	2,116,[illegible]
Maine	1,339	103	1,704	10,560	7,989,163	3,143,156	7,474,631	13,[illegible]
Maryland	516	133	278	4,361	3,409,755	1,424,304	2,423,696	5,374,161
Massachusetts	982	210	740	9,642	9,597,499	3,953,457	9,840,608	17,646,6[illegible]
Michigan	1,931	1,320	594	23,556	29,716,300	7,473,489	16,206,170	35,849,5[illegible]
Minnesota	294	137	127	3,694	3,851,348	1,121,371	2,555,695	5,112,1[illegible]
Mississippi	291	204	48	2,229	1,283,017	636,844	963,443	2,420,[illegible]
Missouri	1,096	616	87	7,686	7,234,771	2,748,026	7,654,054	16,030,614
Montana	36	12	21	118	153,675	88,091	177,648	453,0[illegible]
Nebraska	71	30	18	341	189,100	77,576	137,498	361,6[illegible]
Nevada	23	15	9	357	220,800	178,356	162,030	507,0[illegible]
New Hampshire	841	77	1,025	4,678	3,022,898	1,206,542	2,879,276	5,512,829
New Jersey	544	175	274	7,049	8,990,790	2,864,188	5,168,518	10,484,[illegible]
New Mexico	12	2	10	63	47,100	35,425	40,063	121,[illegible]
New York	4,814	1,090	3,809	32,876	29,136,304	10,130,828	23,452,802	45,955,711
North Carolina	550	146	341	2,624	1,2[illegible]	449,893	1,079,[illegible]	2,231,913
Ohio	3,000	1,910	595	15,765	12,698,019	4,160,129	9,[illegible]	[illegible]
Oregon	191	50	140	812	1,070,462	313,403	418,418	[illegible]

TABLE CII.—*Groups of Principal Industries, by States and Territories*—1870—Continued.

BUILDING-MATERIALS—Continued.

States and Territories.	Establishm'ts.	Steam-engines.	Water-wheels.	All hands.	Capital. (Dollars.)	Wages. (Dollars.)	Materials. (Dollars.)	Products. (Dollars.)
Pennsylvania	4, 857	1, 541	3, 220	33, 797	43, 546, 667	12, 016, 906	27, 270, 756	55, 630, 364
Rhode Island	93	25	69	583	538, 000	172, 298	426, 163	801, 642
South Carolina	238	88	114	1, 415	722, 525	230, 536	632, 559	1, 313, 470
Tennessee	775	334	294	3, 818	2, 320, 546	839, 032	2, 098, 175	4, 584, 906
Texas	366	236	31	2, 170	1, 106, 216	516, 489	864, 111	2, 452, 771
Utah	100	18	75	566	349, 300	144, 283	270, 991	673, 731
Vermont	793	74	844	5, 510	7, 145, 601	1, 665, 013	3, 610, 450	7, 428, 470
Virginia	662	211	386	2, 850	1, 211, 408	460, 691	980, 072	2, 504, 047
Washington	62	33	27	580	1, 428, 402	428, 760	970, 309	1, 950, 655
West Virginia	380	167	186	1, 892	1, 374, 825	468, 253	793, 707	1, 839, 714
Wisconsin	941	482	452	15, 505	14, 015, 913	4, 622, 986	8, 934, 993	18, 387, 399
Wyoming	8	6	......	213	110, 500	104, 500	99, 000	268, 000

BUILDING, (MARINE.)

[Includes boats; Iron ship-building and marine engines; Oakum; Oars; Blocks and spars; Ship-building, ship-materials and repairs.]

States and Territories.	Establishm'ts.	Steam-engines.	Water-wheels.	All hands.	Capital. (Dollars.)	Wages. (Dollars.)	Materials. (Dollars.)	Products. (Dollars.)
The United States	971	183	14	14, 051	11, 742, 576	7, 123, 806	9, 727, 820	21, 956, 337
California	21	1	......	82	57, 650	70, 640	126, 277	254, 500
Connecticut	36	5	2	457	369, 600	267, 316	361, 710	913, 320
Delaware	5	3	......	771	435, 500	364, 026	476, 815	1, 003, 100
District of Columbia	5	1	......	17	11, 000	5, 556	3, 357	13, 800
Florida	8	1	......	20	8, 125	4, 050	16, 825	30, 125
Georgia	2	......	......	11	1, 800	3, 800	7, 372	14, 700
Illinois	13	4	......	309	296, 200	156, 739	188, 100	440, 338
Indiana	9	8	......	301	156, 250	194, 853	166, 899	424, 390
Iowa	3	......	......	51	16, 020	13, 500	8, 905	43, 930
Kentucky	8	1	......	56	33, 100	14, 396	20, 045	56, 500
Louisiana	14	5	......	104	297, 700	127, 500	69, 915	326, 230
Maine	116	4	......	1, 810	908, 173	620, 335	1, 267, 146	2, 365, 745
Maryland	34	4	......	323	176, 300	118, 596	136, 343	373, 534
Massachusetts	116	21	1	1, 239	1, 243, 850	749, 123	937, 504	2, 149, 371
Michigan	28	8	......	645	551, 000	236, 031	274, 114	717, 384
Minnesota	4	......	......	12	3, 450	2, 750	2, 030	7, 100
Missouri	5	10	......	226	330, 200	192, 300	196, 850	537, 000
New Hampshire	6	1	......	31	16, 200	9, 600	23, 063	40, 950
New Jersey	53	7	1	516	574, 650	256, 200	592, 653	1, 040, 582
New York	233	28	7	2, 909	2, 757, 000	1, 630, 516	2, 701, 082	5, 616, 120
North Carolina	3	2	......	23	23, 500	10, 480	1, 580	18, 000
Ohio	53	18	......	811	712, 918	377, 693	305, 445	897, 260
Oregon	2	......	......	2	700	......	836	1, 955
Pennsylvania	140	35	3	2, 726	2, 394, 840	1, 332, 840	1, 578, 105	3, 777, 483
Rhode Island	15	3	......	66	41, 400	28, 400	27, 990	86, 750
South Carolina	7	2	......	27	26, 800	11, 740	12, 525	45, 650
Tennessee	1	1	......	50	10, 000	35, 000	20, 000	150, 000
Texas	4	......	......	19	2, 500	10, 150	10, 031	21, 925
Vermont	4	1	......	95	137, 000	87, 000	63, 250	157, 900
Virginia	7	2	......	41	24, 950	11, 450	10, 670	42, 700
Washington	6	......	......	27	11, 600	10, 796	10, 828	28, 675
West Virginia	3	4	......	66	38, 000	21, 400	50, 500	80, 300
Wisconsin	7	3	......	208	54, 400	139, 200	59, 055	273, 000

COPPER MILLED, AND SMELTED, AND WROUGHT.

[Includes Copper, milled and smelted; Copper, rolled; and Coppersmithing.

States and Territories.	Establishm'ts.	Steam-engines.	Water-wheels.	All hands.	Capital. (Dollars.)	Wages. (Dollars.)	Materials. (Dollars.)	Products. (Dollars.)
The United States	99	59	17	1, 991	5, 506, 800	1, 123, 558	13, 201, 989	15, 796, 730
Arizona	1	1	......	2	50, 000	400	3, 200	5, 000
California	6	1	......	23	12, 500	15, 320	16, 171	61, 550
Connecticut	4	1	2	136	580, 000	92, 375	850, 810	1, 173, 400
Delaware	1	......	......	12	10, 000	6, 000	7, 730	14, 725
Illinois	2	2	......	16	9, 500	7, 600	16, 542	31, 888
Maryland	9	1	3	164	851, 700	109, 250	1, 125, 366	1, 879, 195

TABLE CII.—*Groups of Principal Industries, by States and Territories*—1870—Continued.

COPPER MILLED, AND SMELTED, AND WROUGHT—Continued.

States and Territories.	Establishments.	Steam-engines.	Water-wheels.	All hands.	Capital. (Dollars.)	Wages. (Dollars.)	Materials. (Dollars.)	Products. (Dollars.)
Massachusetts	12	6	6	294	1,262,250	173,450	1,060,017	1,491,90
Michigan	19	37	......	636	1,591,000	350,909	8,499,496	9,900,5[illegible]
Missouri	1	1	......	128	200,000	100,000	250,000	500,00
New Jersey	2	2	5	47	151,600	37,000	303,000	306,00
New York	18	3	......	171	173,500	79,023	166,717	283,6[illegible]
North Carolina	2	......	......	6	4,000	1,850	4,305	9,[illegible]
Ohio	1	......	......	4	2,500	1,150	32,800	39,5[illegible]
Oregon	1	......	......	4	2,000	2,000	500	4,00
Pennsylvania	13	2	......	113	386,950	63,831	302,555	467,55
Rhode Island	1	1	......	25	65,000	15,000	256,110	335,90
Tennessee	5	1	1	197	152,300	66,900	395,070	525,17
Wisconsin	1	......	......	10	2,000	1,500	900	5,30

FIRE-ARMS AND AMMUNITION.

[Includes Ammunition; Cartridges; Gunpowder; Lead, shot; Fire-arms; Gunsmithing.]

States and Territories.	Establishments.	Steam-engines.	Water-wheels.	All hands.	Capital. (Dollars.)	Wages. (Dollars.)	Materials. (Dollars.)	Products. (Dollars.)
The United States	709	66	152	5,835	9,583,502	3,067,202	5,140,181	12,748,419
Alabama	16	......	......	26	18,225	4,485	5,032	22,850
Arkansas	8	......	......	9	4,650	300	2,065	6,950
California	21	3	2	111	680,100	77,510	425,448	831,977
Colorado	4	......	......	6	7,100	3,000	3,800	11,000
Connecticut	20	14	43	2,171	2,930,600	1,547,643	1,384,167	3,840,523
Delaware	1	3	40	318	1,400,000	150,000	418,854	737,800
District of Columbia	3	......	......	6	2,600	2,100	1,180	5,82[illegible]
Florida	3	......	......	3	2,100	......	1,225	4,400
Georgia	21	......	......	30	13,215	4,050	4,105	26,289
Idaho	1	......	......	1	2,500	......	500	2,000
Illinois	51	1	......	83	107,500	17,910	183,134	274,911
Indiana	37	......	......	51	18,275	5,862	11,926	43,505
Iowa	19	1	......	31	35,350	6,350	79,370	120,310
Kansas	7	......	......	11	3,350	4,500	2,025	7,200
Kentucky	20	......	......	28	7,775	2,985	6,629	20,410
Louisiana	9	......	......	21	3,860	7,050	3,805	15,300
Maine	5	1	......	14	9,600	2,700	1,884	8,500
Maryland	8	1	......	31	47,250	9,766	61,015	78,554
Massachusetts	24	11	15	570	859,500	438,551	255,770	1,203,477
Michigan	33	2	......	53	43,750	7,730	7,836	37,775
Minnesota	11	......	......	12	6,325	900	1,950	9,91[illegible]
Mississippi	15	......	......	20	9,925	2,330	4,482	19,084
Missouri	46	......	......	108	66,100	36,974	51,725	157,78[illegible]
Montana	4	......	......	8	1,960	3,325	1,100	9,200
Nebraska	2	......	......	5	6,500	2,700	1,055	7,100
Nevada	4	......	......	7	2,000	2,400	2,600	6,906
New Hampshire	6	2	......	11	6,700	1,230	2,045	7,50[illegible]
New Jersey	5	......	......	56	41,150	36,180	6,870	54,740
New York	64	9	20	1,093	1,500,650	861,257	1,203,333	3,052,311
North Carolina	14	......	......	22	4,825	2,450	3,754	14,484
Ohio	44	2	8	113	267,940	43,769	134,170	316,653
Oregon	5	......	......	6	8,100	500	1,807	6,000
Pennsylvania	80	11	17	158	1,189,612	191,117	711,941	1,254,25[illegible]
Rhode Island	2	1	......	155	170,500	122,115	85,959	300,517
South Carolina	4	......	......	6	950	500	380	4,60[illegible]
Tennessee	25	......	1	61	42,400	16,185	37,602	105,056
Texas	21	......	......	25	5,700	600	2,927	19,275
Utah	3	......	......	6	1,200	1,450	1,525	7,060
Vermont	4	1	......	7	3,300	1,700	1,102	4,663
Virginia	15	1	......	29	12,275	8,610	3,155	24,400
Washington	1	......	......	1	600	......	500	1,250
West Virginia	5	......	......	8	2,000	200	911	4,671
Wisconsin	15	2	6	38	35,550	11,218	16,578	61,305

CII.—*Groups of Principal Industries, by States and Territories*—1870—Continued.

FOOD AND FOOD PREPARATIONS.

les Bread, crackers, and other bakery products; Butchering; Cheese; Chocolate; Coffee and
asted and ground; Fish, cured and packed; Fish and oysters, canned; Flouring and grist mill
; Food preparations, animal; Food preparations, vegetable; Food preparations, vermicelli and
ii; Fruits and vegetables, canned; Meat, cured and packed; Meat, packed, beef; Meat,
pork; Mustard, ground; Preserves and sauces. This table does not include cheese made on
r butter.]

d Territories.	Establishm'ts.	Steam-engines.	Water-wheels.	All hands.	Capital. (*Dollars.*)	Wages. (*Dollars.*)	Materials. (*Dollars.*)	Products. (*Dollars.*)
nited States ..	28, 727	6, 199	21, 263	96, 883	198, 871, 861	25, 786, 682	482, 162, 947	600, 365, 571
....	627	129	554	1, 245	1, 214, 906	192, 469	4, 062, 516	4, 989, 095
....	3	1	1	24	20, 600	16, 200	49, 540	78, 210
s..............	277	114	99	615	482, 201	68, 152	1, 390, 323	1, 683, 031
a..............	224	90	59	1, 215	3, 268, 240	665, 289	8, 731, 210	11, 400, 170
....	25	6	17	65	193, 000	38, 620	451, 146	638, 136
cut	332	21	314	947	1, 618, 758	296, 439	5, 122, 095	6, 215, 822
....	2	......	4	5	13, 000	2, 450	60, 600	80, 990
e..............	120	13	108	770	898, 404	116, 418	1, 902, 626	2, 400, 914
of Columbia..	100	2	11	360	779, 640	109, 808	1, 773, 709	2, 270, 262
....	147	46	64	290	130, 925	35, 751	448, 057	572, 288
....	1, 122	106	1, 227	2, 456	3, 143, 918	360, 132	9, 282, 456	11, 362, 775
....	3	......	6	10	72, 000	6, 800	162, 500	211, 010
....	1, 217	794	368	8, 041	23, 219, 897	2, 797, 035	57, 811, 034	71, 368, 408
....	1, 118	545	630	4, 144	10, 444, 471	1, 105, 573	23, 555, 587	29, 180, 601
....	595	205	542	2, 431	6, 877, 998	692, 972	13, 319, 500	17, 292, 945
....	129	62	39	465	1, 096, 650	185, 191	2, 317, 403	3, 033, 140
y..............	740	320	321	1, 939	2, 869, 443	395, 403	6, 802, 239	8, 474, 902
a..............	355	40	16	959	426, 781	188, 253	1, 265, 349	1, 807, 648
....	360	24	396	1, 807	1, 805, 170	383, 247	5, 465, 180	7, 219, 133
d..............	738	55	511	5, 236	4, 625, 615	870, 947	9, 523, 318	12, 132, 288
usetts	559	88	410	3, 005	4, 407, 944	1, 182, 636	15, 672, 183	19, 189, 021
n..............	650	174	719	2, 445	7, 607, 072	784, 048	19, 348, 286	22, 961, 907
ta	261	40	281	943	3, 105, 340	356, 756	6, 354, 276	7, 940, 648
pi	372	133	166	727	641, 693	86, 684	1, 723, 058	2, 066, 567
....	1, 062	501	257	5, 190	13, 960, 507	2, 058, 695	37, 775, 166	49, 319, 754
....	17	......	8	44	141, 200	31, 400	409, 692	555, 714
a..............	90	20	49	270	686, 500	109, 574	1, 345, 517	1, 895, 098
....	13	4	3	31	50, 200	6, 650	85, 725	113, 770
mpshire	217	10	389	479	730, 040	107, 400	2, 664, 814	2, 992, 025
sey..........	682	58	525	3, 706	5, 879, 600	827, 597	13, 071, 666	16, 135, 831
xico	39	4	30	86	225, 800	35, 261	446, 602	732, 467
k..............	3, 315	384	2, 419	13, 361	28, 768, 512	4, 275, 275	72, 854, 252	91, 192, 499
arolina	1, 429	74	1, 351	2, 708	2, 612, 830	255, 382	6, 473, 956	7, 647, 297
....	2, 082	683	1, 185	7, 557	17, 295, 632	2, 012, 098	41, 582, 420	50, 256, 841
....	78	8	61	233*	1, 202, 745	129, 551	1, 445, 064	2, 233, 547
ania	4, 034	656	3, 281	10, 526	26, 536, 455	2, 601, 513	53, 365, 509	66, 564, 919
land	113	17	51	422	510, 930	148, 814	2, 675, 474	3, 191, 365
arolina........	641	80	537	1, 209	872, 014	130, 591	2, 753, 633	3, 322, 292
se..............	1, 089	187	885	2, 328	2, 980, 584	376, 248	8, 988, 748	11, 130, 688
....	571	249	85	1, 566	1, 384, 888	251, 136	3, 180, 885	4, 094, 613
....	74	......	77	130	430, 408	44, 930	582, 955	782, 846
....	258	20	436	674	1, 471, 750	152, 289	3, 868, 204	4, 608, 191
....	1, 608	37	1, 644	2, 862	5, 400, 721	397, 128	10, 791, 656	13, 068, 348
ton	25	2	19	46	220, 147	18, 000	226, 013	337, 207
rginia	492	92	436	803	1, 551, 607	103, 283	3, 326, 180	4, 007, 237
in	722	105	669	2, 508	6, 997, 725	776, 597	17, 947, 625	21, 613, 111

TURE AND HOUSE-FIXTURES, (EXCLUSIVE OF STOVES AND HOLLOW-WARE.)

s Furniture, (not specified;) Chairs; Iron bedsteads; Refrigerators; Looking-glasses; and Looking-glass and picture frames.]

d Territories.	Establishm'ts.	Steam-engines.	Water-wheels.	All hands.	Capital. (*Dollars.*)	Wages. (*Dollars.*)	Materials. (*Dollars.*)	Products. (*Dollars.*)
nited States ..	6, 312	939	596	57, 091	46, 766, 933	23, 304, 956	28, 516, 544	75, 539, 719
....	21	......	1	40	21, 755	10, 860	12, 063	35, 694
s..............	23	1	......	65	20, 675	17, 390	20, 753	70, 616
a..............	57	9	......	319	273, 550	218, 281	246, 035	776, 412
....	4	......	......	14	14, 600	11, 590	40, 100	76, 000
cut..........	71	11	10	932	873, 050	412, 624	531, 442	1, 994, 898
....	7	......	1	44	78, 500	17, 702	13, 879	57, 791

TABLE CII.—*Groups of Principal Industries, by States and Territories—1870—Continu*

FURNITURE AND HOUSE-FIXTURES, (EXCLUSIVE OF STOVES AND HOLLO WARE)—Continued.

States and Territories.	Establishm'ts.	Steam-engines.	Water-wheels.	All hands.	Capital. (Dollars.)	Wages. (Dollars.)	Materials. (Dollars.)	Products. (Dollars.)
District of Columbia	33	......	......	65	27,725	21,582	36,945	9
Florida	8	......	......	16	4,250	4,580	4,150	1
Georgia	77	4	11	267	85,900	70,037	65,875	21
Idaho	1	......	......	2	1,000	......	800	1
Illinois	382	73	4	2,440	1,923,931	986,294	1,042,130	3,07
Indiana	356	75	16	3,206	2,565,809	1,235,844	1,414,074	3,63
Iowa	226	22	6	964	672,325	296,043	342,014	9
Kansas	53	6	......	208	120,605	91,096	89,973	2
Kentucky	92	17	......	992	760,355	422,872	553,472	1,4
Louisiana	28	1	......	72	21,500	24,600	44,005	9
Maine	106	6	32	476	196,200	131,516	137,007	41
Maryland	152	16	......	1,242	896,270	489,294	631,088	1,53
Massachusetts	381	86	121	10,259	6,497,775	3,799,469	5,422,627	12,74
Michigan	255	64	24	2,695	2,164,745	751,168	790,697	2,23
Minnesota	87	8	2	401	302,900	143,281	137,977	45
Mississippi	24	1	......	50	18,720	6,328	50,498	6
Missouri	280	32	......	2,074	2,745,180	1,099,001	1,709,718	4,00
Montana	2	......	......	4	1,000	3,200	545	
Nebraska	17	......	......	29	22,605	11,313	18,835	4
Nevada	8	......	......	17	23,900	11,200	17,300	3
New Hampshire	81	10	59	1,377	974,485	614,133	782,765	1,77
New Jersey	100	12	3	761	648,100	287,992	311,606	85
New Mexico	1	......	......	1	1,000	......	100	
New York	1,006	155	143	10,885	9,895,063	5,399,410	7,046,019	18,37
North Carolina	54	1	5	133	31,520	19,737	16,870	6
Ohio	629	143	13	6,519	5,839,590	2,598,942	2,243,120	7,06
Oregon	30	5	8	60	59,600	15,292	35,233	8
Pennsylvania	999	109	34	6,350	5,686,553	2,775,026	3,355,908	9,3
Rhode Island	18	5	......	290	166,450	112,290	112,412	31
South Carolina	12	......	......	20	7,165	2,200	3,539	1
Tennessee	94	11	9	494	237,610	121,860	150,460	41
Texas	55	4	......	141	98,400	44,190	109,817	21
Utah	26	1	8	84	33,150	26,895	20,291	6
Vermont	81	10	60	738	701,875	304,797	312,563	88
Virginia	128	6	4	316	133,542	58,797	73,128	2
Washington	4	......	......	11	9,350	1,700	3,075	
West Virginia	47	5	1	155	84,850	50,460	33,930	14
Wisconsin	196	30	21	1,863	1,823,805	583,980	531,606	1,5

IRON AND MANUFACTURES OF IRON.

[Includes Iron anchors and cable chains; Iron, bolts, nuts, washers, and rivets; Iron, blooms; castings, stoves, heaters, and hollow-ware; Iron, forged and rolled; Iron, pig; Iron railing, wro Iron pipe, wrought; Iron, ship-building and marine-engines.]

States and Territories.	Establishm'ts.	Steam-engines.	Water-wheels.	All hands.	Capital. (Dollars.)	Wages. (Dollars.)	Materials. (Dollars.)	Products. (Dollars.)
The United States	3,726	3,086	898	137,545	198,356,116	73,027,976	193,208,218	322,1
Alabama	22	20	5	455	566,100	197,440	207,286	5
Arkansas	2	1	......	9	3,500	3,500	4,800	
California	34	32	......	863	1,291,470	519,356	920,614	1,7
Colorado	1	1	......	18	25,000	20,000	32,500	
Connecticut	122	57	57	3,795	5,210,650	2,200,797	3,658,411	7,4
Delaware	26	32	3	837	1,224,042	414,626	1,398,677	2,0
District of Columbia	6	5	......	85	219,200	45,982	63,640	1
Georgia	30	23	6	546	407,810	290,496	705,598	1,3
Idaho	1	1	......	3	3,000	1,200	1,975	
Illinois	133	102	14	4,067	5,284,385	2,312,471	4,452,495	8,1
Indiana	120	111	7	2,394	3,695,282	1,308,135	4,690,032	7,1
Iowa	41	33	1	272	359,514	137,512	252,904	5
Kansas	5	3	......	123	135,986	77,334	136,660	3
Kentucky	60	83	......	3,906	6,280,431	1,831,466	4,372,885	7,9
Louisiana	15	13	......	385	367,500	250,100	196,414	5
Maine	53	31	22	1,004	1,297,384	537,830	1,444,096	2,4
Maryland	70	68	22	3,033	3,804,635	1,191,868	3,096,691	6,7
Massachusetts	168	136	94	8,098	7,569,125	4,253,586	9,316,478	16,3
Michigan	217	136	26	3,243	4,874,447	1,623,206	3,309,556	5,9
Minnesota	19	11	3	158	229,500	73,434	184,883	3
Mississippi	17	10	1	170	177,550	45,150	[illegible]	[illegible]

TABLE CII.—*Groups of Principal Industries, by States and Territories*—1870—Continued.

IRON AND MANUFACTURES OF IRON—Continued.

States and Territories.	Establishm'ts.	Steam-engines.	Water-wheels.	All hands.	Capital. (*Dollars.*)	Wages. (*Dollars.*)	Materials. (*Dollars.*)	Products. (*Dollars.*)
Missouri	60	59	5	3, 681	6, 130, 643	2, 709, 514	4, 542, 613	8, 889, 723
Montana	1	1	......	5	8, 000	5, 000	14, 600	25, 000
Nebraska	3	3	......	68	67, 840	72, 194	107, 181	106, 518
Nevada	5	5	......	114	101, 000	133, 500	263, 416	641, 250
New Hampshire	30	16	16	681	689, 760	372, 665	891, 906	1, 557, 368
New Jersey	125	98	41	4, 913	6, 567, 733	2, 874, 651	7, 372, 213	11, 888, 459
New York	646	384	217	22, 244	29, 588, 800	12, 199, 073	30, 449, 479	53, 272, 049
North Carolina	52	17	25	329	227, 425	92, 531	137, 945	248, 855
Ohio	393	361	24	14, 943	22, 852, 774	7, 905, 101	20, 852, 520	35, 625, 157
Oregon	4	3	......	39	28, 000	25, 500	29, 360	65, 000
Pennsylvania	892	1, 045	179	47, 134	78, 768, 802	24, 080, 024	80, 657, 261	122, 605, 296
Rhode Island	24	23	2	1, 207	1, 818, 000	678, 145	1, 157, 477	2, 196, 705
South Carolina	13	6	6	124	116, 251	47, 310	56, 097	158, 615
Tennessee	68	32	30	1, 807	1, 782, 142	679, 767	841, 646	2, 093, 932
Texas	6	5	......	30	54, 000	17, 350	44, 070	77, 000
Vermont	29	8	20	290	386, 200	132, 147	329, 743	580, 020
Virginia	89	25	58	2, 414	2, 318, 635	833, 660	2, 027, 590	3, 605, 940
Washington	2	2	......	5	16, 200	1, 150	2, 658	8, 500
West Virginia	38	38	1	2, 100	2, 081, 900	1, 364, 195	2, 938, 040	5, 168, 892
Wisconsin	81	46	13	1, 953	1, 725, 500	869, 010	1, 985, 474	3, 290, 023

LEAD.

[Includes Lead, bar and sheet; Lead, pig; Lead, pipe; and Lead, shot.]

States and Territories.	Establishm'ts.	Steam-engines.	Water-wheels.	All hands.	Capital. (*Dollars.*)	Wages. (*Dollars.*)	Materials. (*Dollars.*)	Products. (*Dollars.*)
The United States	91	42	24	843	4, 822, 100	408, 903	13, 793, 921	18, 327, 196
California	2	1	......	27	190, 000	22, 560	408, 500	477, 000
Illinois	5	2	3	49	177, 000	24, 877	818, 179	980, 690
Iowa	4	3	2	17	37, 000	5, 980	126, 172	163, 850
Maryland	1	1	......	12	42, 000	2, 550	58, 715	82, 354
Massachusetts	4	......	1	29	351, 000	15, 400	542, 692	696, 350
Missouri	34	12	11	228	1, 681, 100	73, 930	1, 204, 788	1, 450, 831
Nevada	9	9	......	181	438, 000	109, 900	557, 962	894, 600
New York	12	9	......	103	1, 073, 000	83, 178	8, 938, 740	12, 180, 300
Ohio	2	2	......	16	35, 000	8, 900	90, 184	139, 000
Pennsylvania	3	2	......	41	650, 000	24, 000	550, 000	678, 000
Rhode Island	1	1	......	4	47, 000	2, 750	24, 360	28, 099
Virginia	1	......	1	42	10, 000	6, 000	22, 700	43, 720
Wisconsin	13	......	6	91	91, 000	28, 908	450, 929	514, 402

LEATHER.

[Includes Leather, tanned; Leather, curried; Leather, dressed skins; Leather, morocco, tanned and curried; and Leather, patent and enameled.]

States and Territories.	Establishm'ts.	Steam-engines.	Water-wheels.	All hands.	Capital. (*Dollars.*)	Wages. (*Dollars.*)	Materials. (*Dollars.*)	Products. (*Dollars.*)
The United States	7, 569	1, 296	940	35, 243	61, 124, 812	14, 505, 775	118, 569, 634	157, 237, 597
Alabama	141	2	3	278	205, 769	48, 028	263, 744	412, 335
Arkansas	35	......	......	52	32, 100	5, 260	52, 777	83, 091
California	70	10	1	262	433, 500	111, 784	838, 154	1, 174, 924
Connecticut	75	8	18	336	592, 850	157, 747	990, 820	1, 317, 030
Delaware	28	13	......	609	930, 018	318, 035	1, 451, 022	2, 050, 846
District of Columbia	3	3	......	32	85, 000	10, 700	89, 272	146, 475
Florida	3	......	......	11	8, 000	3, 500	8, 000	13, 800
Georgia	180	5	10	316	186, 247	47, 758	418, 793	572, 316
Illinois	98	26	1	754	1, 286, 300	372, 944	3, 211, 197	4, 150, 338
Indiana	353	41	1	833	1, 179, 550	227, 430	1, 815, 125	2, 461, 549
Iowa	35	1	......	55	38, 175	6, 825	70, 823	94, 449
Kansas	6	......	......	11	6, 300	2, 000	22, 427	26, 427
Kentucky	182	15	1	448	724, 340	118, 816	1, 297, 997	1, 693, 974
Louisiana	10	......	......	20	16, 550	3, 430	17, 920	82, 450
Maine	200	30	93	1, 020	1, 864, 949	360, 126	3, 956, 839	4, 911, 781
Maryland	125	23	3	547	1, 120, 125	195, 911	1, 516, 861	2, 084, 696
Massachusetts	386	202	50	5, 553	7, 577, 926	3, 152, 399	26, 106, 013	33, 457, 975
Michigan	173	53	9	734	1, 307, 540	285, 749	2, 013, 156	2, 089, 408
Minnesota	12	2	......	30	34, 400	11, 150	79, 747	[illegible]

TABLE CII.—*Groups of Principal Industries, by States and Territories*—1870—Continued.

LEATHER—Continued.

States and Territories.	Establishm'ts.	Steam-engines.	Water-wheels.	All hands.	Capital. (Dollars.)	Wages. (Dollars.)	Materials. (Dollars.)	Products. (Dollars.)
Mississippi	56	......	3	101	49,660	13,293	184,367	262,723
Missouri	80	4	......	240	189,250	113,825	530,234	834,948
New Hampshire	126	22	66	667	1,223,800	271,638	3,037,894	3,744,236
New Jersey	148	38	10	1,298	2,679,487	839,039	7,529,966	9,307,942
New York	1,002	264	397	8,109	16,147,378	3,580,855	26,573,801	36,569,880
North Carolina	222	5	8	308	150,828	31,830	265,390	364,360
Ohio	892	115	7	2,115	3,304,841	652,919	5,755,276	7,338,992
Oregon	24	1	4	59	47,400	18,700	98,393	147,283
Pennsylvania	1,495	317	133	6,880	15,317,785	2,587,699	20,793,080	28,690,496
Rhode Island	14	5	2	213	546,000	108,445	1,467,298	1,898,364
South Carolina	65	......	8	127	40,200	13,386	106,225	166,025
Tennessee	396	12	8	769	705,665	152,775	1,401,705	1,851,632
Texas	56	......	......	90	54,843	11,935	77,068	117,911
Utah	37	......	3	56	45,300	11,405	59,353	91,680
Vermont	155	14	82	475	837,133	166,995	1,609,857	2,052,913
Virginia	318	7	7	507	302,484	62,799	591,090	790,442
Washington	10	......	2	16	17,000	4,700	36,161	51,389
West Virginia	178	15	4	328	456,379	68,892	626,678	840,245
Wisconsin	174	43	6	984	1,369,740	375,013	3,575,051	4,503,081

LIQUORS.

[Includes Liquors, distilled; Liquors, malt; and Liquors, vinous.]

States and Territories.	Establishm'ts.	Steam-engines.	Water-wheels.	All hands.	Capital. (Dollars.)	Wages. (Dollars.)	Materials. (Dollars.)	Products. (Dollars.)
The United States	3,089	1,141	112	19,060	66,658,945	9,009,062	49,110,288	94,123,014
Alabama	2	1	......	3	3,275	710	1,280	3,400
Arizona	1	......	......	5	10,000	3,000	5,000	10,000
Arkansas	2	......	......	5	3,300	310	1,300	2,000
California	251	26	8	1,216	2,162,690	348,690	1,362,340	3,342,934
Colorado	10	2	......	17	49,900	13,850	11,490	47,420
Connecticut	38	6	29	151	232,000	45,438	329,045	488,065
Dakota	2	......	......	7	12,000	1,700	5,075	9,500
Delaware	2	1	......	13	31,000	3,300	17,800	28,101
District of Columbia	13	6	......	58	108,600	24,150	87,873	168,950
Georgia	3	1	1	18	16,500	5,880	16,215	34,925
Idaho	9	1	1	24	48,550	9,700	17,288	49,139
Illinois	198	125	......	1,967	7,416,200	1,032,928	6,904,727	12,058,935
Indiana	135	52	2	723	1,776,238	301,880	1,985,772	3,353,536
Iowa	108	22	1	458	1,322,634	147,961	491,289	1,191,249
Kansas	16	4	......	72	195,600	27,500	79,730	236,194
Kentucky	176	123	7	1,226	3,255,600	360,371	2,217,708	[illegible]
Louisiana	14	11	......	123	190,850	51,740	175,425	[illegible]
Maine	6	3	......	25	102,270	10,300	165,377	[illegible]
Maryland	40	17	3	271	804,900	133,872	891,728	[illegible]
Massachusetts	31	12	3	298	1,274,500	175,517	1,438,799	[illegible]
Michigan	129	26	2	496	1,402,441	171,768	679,323	[illegible]
Minnesota	65	2	......	225	450,550	68,386	161,812	[illegible]
Mississippi	3	2	......	7	5,300	950	2,718	[illegible]
Missouri	293	55	......	1,381	5,725,325	733,213	3,596,625	[illegible]
Montana	15	2	1	35	68,500	14,255	47,460	[illegible]
Nebraska	16	4	......	53	137,400	22,990	95,589	[illegible]
Nevada	18	......	......	46	86,300	26,400	45,726	[illegible]
New Hampshire	5	3	......	114	279,810	53,800	373,234	[illegible]
New Jersey	103	43	9	682	3,130,449	346,026	1,827,163	[illegible]
New Mexico	3	1	......	7	26,500	5,155	9,775	[illegible]
New York	340	177	16	3,331	14,283,662	2,220,480	11,132,265	[illegible]
North Carolina	12	2	1	67	57,050	9,025	98,261	[illegible]
Ohio	300	158	11	2,164	8,536,872	1,143,827	7,262,334	[illegible]
Oregon	16	1	1	36	66,250	14,360	35,385	[illegible]
Pennsylvania	356	167	8	2,110	9,571,253	993,354	5,512,053	[illegible]
Rhode Island	4	4	......	27	147,500	13,200	64,718	[illegible]
South Carolina	2	......	......	9	8,250	2,600	5,600	[illegible]
Tennessee	50	23	1	217	273,350	53,983	241,218	[illegible]
Texas	28	4	......	77	118,300	28,836	85,678	[illegible]
Utah	4	1	1	8	63,850	4,260	8,574	[illegible]
Virginia	55	10	1	172	525,535	34,291	233,340	[illegible]
West Virginia	21	8	1	422	363,541	51,188	202,515	[illegible]
Washington	9	1	2	15	32,900	7,160	18,235	[illegible]
Wisconsin	185	34	2	949	2,282,150	290,158	1,139,461	[illegible]

TABLE CII.—*Groups of Principal Industries, by States and Territories*—1870—Continued.

LUMBER.

[Includes Lumber, planed: Lumber, sawed; and Lumber, staves, shooks, and headings.]

States and Territories.	Establishm'ts.	Steam-engines.	Water-wheels.	All hands.	Capital. (*Dollars.*)	Wages. (*Dollars.*)	Materials. (*Dollars.*)	Products. (*Dollars.*)
The United States	26, 945	12, 052	16, 755	163, 637	161, 500, 273	46, 231, 238	132, 071, 778	252, 339, 029
Alabama	289	115	129	1, 498	785, 405	385, 695	601, 513	1, 504, 683
Arizona	1	1	......	16	5, 000	6, 000	1, 600	10, 000
Arkansas	216	127	24	1, 124	719, 200	261, 086	593, 559	1, 411, 253
California	313	204	122	4, 484	4, 230, 540	1, 911, 084	2, 429, 919	6, 279, 914
Colorado	34	24	11	229	147, 700	89, 111	174, 325	393, 870
Connecticut	400	22	382	987	869, 191	296, 220	1, 421, 715	2, 123, 118
Dakota	10	9	2	68	37, 400	14, 256	32, 772	72, 280
Delaware	83	34	52	333	343, 924	78, 523	271, 656	466, 941
District of Columbia	5	5	......	114	89, 000	38, 400	125, 500	207, 000
Florida	105	69	15	1, 122	757, 090	422, 020	1, 163, 968	2, 236, 780
Georgia	539	194	336	3, 215	1, 807, 973	797, 878	1, 958, 127	4, 615, 575
Idaho	10	4	6	47	50, 750	17, 924	20, 177	56, 850
Illinois	580	519	25	5, 020	4, 780, 730	1, 668, 233	7, 576, 567	11, 837, 234
Indiana	1, 946	1, 541	305	10, 084	6, 772, 423	2, 141, 191	6, 359, 036	13, 698, 859
Iowa	566	420	121	3, 973	4, 126, 801	1, 078, 700	4, 010, 126	6, 661, 700
Kansas	195	154	22	1, 161	642, 955	282, 662	822, 028	1, 736, 381
Kentucky	579	393	101	2, 756	2, 013, 211	608, 157	2, 119, 730	4, 245, 759
Louisiana	160	142	7	1, 222	634, 220	384, 365	797, 138	1, 643, 037
Maine	1, 117	87	1, 667	8, 635	6, 722, 675	2, 491, 072	7, 111, 298	1, 718, 122
Maryland	402	105	276	1, 396	1, 297, 400	321, 619	995, 490	1, 976, 328
Massachusetts	711	117	712	3, 447	3, 741, 429	1, 322, 681	5, 848, 876	8, 712, 240
Michigan	1, 641	1, 181	561	20, 576	27, 701, 300	6, 597, 110	15, 090, 191	33, 078, 241
Minnesota	220	122	124	3, 010	3, 454, 540	905, 550	2, 376, 21	4, 538, 804
Mississippi	274	200	48	1, 992	1, 174, 117	588, 906	877, 093	2, 229, 017
Missouri	828	598	87	4, 120	3, 554, 770	1, 130, 584	4, 026, 744	7, 220, 452
Montana	32	12	20	162	149, 000	80, 965	172, 598	431, 957
Nebraska	50	30	18	202	152, 200	47, 102	118, 975	278, 205
Nevada	20	13	9	330	199, 000	156, 430	142, 450	447, 500
New Hampshire	736	68	1, 002	3, 447	2, 481, 193	741, 653	2, 520, 347	4, 380, 622
New Jersey	300	48	264	1, 311	2, 538, 000	451, 865	2, 026, 836	3, 330, 769
New Mexico	12	2	10	63	47, 100	55, 425	40, 083	121, 225
New York	3, 685	818	3, 664	17, 370	18, 066, 567	4, 324, 768	15, 803, 232	27, 570, 569
North Carolina	533	137	341	2, 421	1, 229, 450	404, 733	1, 046, 228	2, 107, 313
Ohio	2, 372	1, 752	585	9, 332	7, 404, 581	2, 027, 172	6, 638, 293	12, 754, 925
Oregon	173	41	138	717	953, 262	275, 285	380, 373	1, 072, 061
Pennsylvania	3, 922	1, 250	3, 169	19, 286	27, 802, 710	6, 220, 393	19, 022, 221	35, 262, 590
Rhode Island	83	15	67	219	166, 500	45, 126	193, 164	305, 138
South Carolina	229	83	114	1, 231	602, 425	214, 126	660, 499	1, 232, 005
Tennessee	724	320	291	3, 101	1, 791, 616	660, 904	1, 789, 582	3, 919, 237
Texas	327	227	31	1, 764	883, 491	393, 129	653, 474	1, 974, 101
Utah	96	16	75	543	339, 000	139, 833	266, 647	662, 731
Vermont	656	42	797	4, 124	4, 880, 051	1, 064, 025	3, 290, 206	6, 069, 725
Virginia	609	201	380	2, 300	983, 486	347, 698	872, 887	2, 130, 705
Washington	53	31	25	535	1, 396, 102	420, 210	964, 009	1, 923, 685
West Virginia	348	150	185	1, 613	1, 160, 950	393, 368	783, 405	1, 676, 539
Wisconsin	753	403	435	12, 724	11, 703, 345	3, 840, 301	7, 841, 891	15, 744, 989
Wyoming	8	6	......	213	110, 500	104, 500	99, 000	268, 000

PAPER.

[Includes Paper, (not specified:) Paper, printing; Paper, wrapping; Paper, writing; and Paper-hangings.]

States and Territories.	Establishm'ts.	Steam-engines.	Water-wheels.	All hands.	Capital. (*Dollars.*)	Wages. (*Dollars.*)	Materials. (*Dollars.*)	Products. (*Dollars.*)
The United States	684	307	1, 173	18, 779	35, 780, 514	7, 477, 780	31, 311, 169	50, 842, 445
Alabama	1	1	1	29	150, 000	20, 000	73, 000	124, 000
California	2	1	1	28	48, 000	17, 000	43, 025	89, 700
Colorado	1	......	1	3	12, 000	475	980	2, 250
Connecticut	66	10	120	1, 497	2, 988, 046	703, 727	3, 327, 266	4, 874, 291
Delaware	1	......	2	21	50, 000	8, 500	41, 500	78, 000
District of Columbia	1	......	2	25	50, 000	10, 400	36, 620	81, 580
Georgia	3	1	4	89	170, 000	29, 838	105, 346	184, 083
Illinois	19	8	35	484	909, 000	199, 510	624, 213	1, 120, 586
Indiana	17	9	29	398	540, 000	130, 561	421, 807	780, 152
Iowa	5	2	10	89	230, 500	33, 600	41, 064	90, 885
Kentucky	2	4	1	56	190, 000	28, 500	79, 490	157, 500

TABLE CII.—*Groups of Principal Industries, by States and Territories*—1870—Continued.

PAPER—Continued.

States and Territories.	Establishm'ts.	Steam-engines.	Water-wheels.	All hands.	Capital. (*Dollars.*)	Wages. (*Dollars.*)	Materials. (*Dollars.*)	Products. (*Dollars.*)
Maine	12	......	28	382	399, 000	146, 477	864, 153	[illegible]
Maryland	26	5	33	338	1, 206, 000	110, 589	505, 431	[illegible]
Massachusetts	97	30	301	4, 566	7, 723, 628	1, 859, 317	8, 017, 967	[illegible]
Michigan	11	15	11	261	376, 000	79, 000	287, 040	[illegible]
Minnesota	2	......	3	72	130, 000	32, 150	70, 075	[illegible]
Missouri	1	1	......	19	30, 000	12, 000	12, 000	[illegible]
New Hampshire	32	11	66	648	1, 079, 000	240, 473	1, 080, 372	[illegible]
New Jersey	33	21	49	699	1, 600, 700	286, 459	1, 078, 784	[illegible]
New York	186	43	284	4, 439	7, 682, 100	1, 805, 237	7, 358, 790	[illegible]
North Carolina	5	......	9	89	98, 000	30, 650	87, 983	[illegible]
Ohio	44	50	51	1, 438	2, 957, 800	554, 407	2, 601, 637	[illegible]
Oregon	1	......	1	12	4, 000	9, 000	13, 250	[illegible]
Pennsylvania	83	72	91	2, 428	5, 747, 040	878, 678	3, 837, 191	[illegible]
Rhode Island	1	1	......	23	30, 000	8, 000	40, 000	[illegible]
South Carolina	2	5	1	43	409, 000	12, 600	46, 400	[illegible]
Tennessee	3	1	3	69	120, 000	26, 400	78, 400	[illegible]
Utah	1	......	1	4	15, 000	2, 000	1, 002	[illegible]
Vermont	12	2	22	174	233, 700	55, 883	142, 078	[illegible]
Virginia	4	......	6	77	401, 000	31, 427	144, 189	[illegible]
West Virginia	4	11	......	72	156, 000	31, 386	57, 929	[illegible]
Wisconsin	6	3	7	207	445, 000	83, 536	225, 197	[illegible]

PRINTING AND PUBLISHING.

[Includes Printing and publishing, (not specified;) Printing and publishing, book; Printing and publishing, newspaper; Printing, job; Maps and atlases; and Photograph albums; does not include Book-binding.]

States and Territories.	Establishm'ts.	Steam-engines.	Water-wheels.	All hands.	Capital. (*Dollars.*)	Wages. (*Dollars.*)	Materials. (*Dollars.*)	Products. (*Dollars.*)
The United States	2, 177	691	15	30, 924	40, 304, 727	18, 882, 918	24, 729, 407	[illegible]
Alabama	15	1	......	187	123, 300	150, 330	107, 158	[illegible]
Arkansas	14	1	......	77	38, 000	36, 950	24, 398	[illegible]
California	82	14	......	847	1, 217, 100	788, 725	670, 840	[illegible]
Colorado	9	......	......	32	37, 000	38, 053	22, 450	[illegible]
Connecticut	42	21	2	672	701, 329	367, 151	379, 757	[illegible]
Delaware	6	4	......	56	90, 000	26, 722	41, 892	[illegible]
District of Columbia	14	10	......	343	746, 500	209, 541	254, 315	[illegible]
Florida	5	1	......	41	32, 000	22, 100	14, 112	[illegible]
Georgia	45	8	......	428	416, 798	282, 222	144, 291	[illegible]
Illinois	130	45	......	1, 398	1, 258, 650	743, 580	1, 066, 139	[illegible]
Indiana	69	20	......	810	754, 952	511, 330	513, 617	[illegible]
Iowa	67	9	......	544	378, 775	257, 308	178, 212	[illegible]
Kansas	21	2	......	216	125, 500	141, 044	102, 161	[illegible]
Kentucky	32	9	......	443	509, 500	289, 720	311, , 492	[illegible]
Louisiana	9	......	......	41	28, 800	23, 000	11, 960	[illegible]
Maine	34	20	......	361	292, 562	161, 756	116, 037	[illegible]
Maryland	67	39	......	915	1, 044, 150	506, 252	499, 604	[illegible]
Massachusetts	162	51	1	2, 973	4, 968, 450	1, 953, 435	2, 535, 850	[illegible]
Michigan	65	19	......	786	697, 777	393, 999	302, 104	[illegible]
Minnesota	20	2	......	241	267, 000	137, 892	113, 503	[illegible]
Mississippi	11	2	......	60	74, 700	44, 450	30, 387	[illegible]
Missouri	105	27	......	1, 940	2, 374, 300	1, 320, 135	2, 396, 804	[illegible]
Montana	4	1	......	31	96, 700	51, 040	18, 618	[illegible]
Nebraska	10	2	......	94	92, 100	70, 010	40, 463	[illegible]
Nevada	1	......	......	6	3, 000	5, 000	850	[illegible]
New Hampshire	45	5	3	302	336, 400	118, 904	115, 770	[illegible]
New Jersey	39	10	......	378	450, 500	201, 101	211, 159	[illegible]
New Mexico	2	......	......	13	11, 000	6, 200	10, 606	[illegible]
New York	303	134	5	6, 431	7, 728, 017	3, 980, 549	6, 785, 518	[illegible]
North Carolina	9	2	......	120	43, 600	68, 954	50, 912	[illegible]
Ohio	187	58	1	2, 409	2, 635, 050	1, 355, 956	1, 437, 066	[illegible]
Oregon	11	......	......	68	42, 350	52, 400	41, 787	[illegible]
Pennsylvania	318	119	......	5, 497	10, 782, 492	3, 236, 011	5, 079, 163	[illegible]
Rhode Island	14	10	......	269	203, 600	133, 350	123, 098	[illegible]
South Carolina	13	8	......	182	129, 550	127, 100	54, 725	[illegible]
Tennessee	40	13	......	459	523, 300	348, 233	276, 658	[illegible]
Texas	29	3	......	168	108, 375	83, 780	47, 563	[illegible]
Vermont	20	6	1	177	172, 600	76, 364	70, 815	[illegible]
Virginia	36	6	2	332	249, 300	193, 616	148, 688	[illegible]
West Virginia	5	......	......	18	4, 600	1, 650	1, 698	[illegible]
Wisconsin	60	9	......	613	513, 250	274, 125	375, 267	[illegible]
Wyoming	1	......	......	6	1, 800	2, 880	2, 500	[illegible]

ΙΙ.—*Groups of Principal Industries, by States and Territories*—1870—Continued.

TEXTILES.

ıdes Cotton goods; Flax and linen goods; Carpets; Woolen goods; and Worsted goods.]

ıl Territories.	Establishm'ts.	Steam-engines.	Water-wheels.	All hands.	Capital. (*Dollars.*)	Wages. (*Dollars.*)	Materials. (*Dollars.*)	Products. (*Dollars.*)
ıited States..	4, 709	1, 638	3, 431	243, 731	265, 084, 095	75, 628, 743	238, 393, 905	380, 913, 815
....	27	4	24	1, 073	953, 375	221, 560	822, 303	1, 178, 765
....	15	6	4	48	45, 500	10, 970	69, 562	101, 252
....	6	6	1	663	1, 786, 000	232, 600	609, 184	1, 107, 854
·ut	234	59	310	20, 947	27, 232, 500	6, 660, 964	21, 480, 702	34, 024, 228
....	20	8	17	1, 131	1, 550, 400	306, 536	1, 099, 450	1, 642, 965
ıf Columbia..	2	......	......	4	4, 500	700	2, 108	3, 575
....	1	......	......	1	500	....	150	500
....	80	6	107	3, 409	4, 369, 850	734, 006	2, 772, 934	4, 120, 496
....	135	94	23	1, 863	3, 116, 223	562, 760	1, 892, 896	3, 154, 431
....	190	119	62	2, 988	4, 375, 458	839, 913	3, 232, 605	5, 119, 739
....	100	46	30	1, 115	1, 443, 224	271, 207	1, 009, 102	1, 669, 471
....	9	6	1	91	96, 000	30, 682	86, 105	153, 150
/...........	132	70	24	956	1, 106, 399	217, 324	1, 207, 576	1, 813, 463
....	6	4	......	275	626, 000	69, 500	180, 532	282, 345
....	144	6	214	12, 564	14, 040, 255	3, 632, 198	10, 787, 985	18, 363, 824
l	74	10	54	3, 238	2, 962, 645	764, 182	3, 670, 705	5, 327, 661
ısetts	427	240	617	72, 464	72, 548, 475	23, 636, 614	71, 619, 650	112, 763, 211
....	65	24	37	694	1, 020, 215	205, 769	670, 796	1, 228, 446
a	11	2	6	148	246, 850	45, 992	108, 840	221, 362
pi	16	7	7	381	946, 750	90, 633	203, 134	381, 768
....	169	70	26	1, 101	1, 212, 119	202, 108	1, 339, 108	2, 078, 913
npshire	121	16	216	17, 715	19, 054, 060	5, 805, 817	19, 023, 675	27, 692, 588
ey	106	34	55	5, 669	4, 458, 175	1, 580, 677	4, 089, 965	7, 434, 521
ifco	1	......	1	20	65, 000	2, 000	12, 775	21, 000
k	422	93	372	21, 969	23, 137, 703	7, 023, 374	19, 151, 712	31, 473, 172
ırolina	85	6	73	1, 702	1, 268, 700	222, 052	1, 130, 306	1, 643, 690
....	287	129	115	2, 882	3, 637, 354	695, 025	2, 657, 196	4, 239, 450
....	9	......	9	179	389, 200	112, 213	227, 595	505, 857
ınia	1, 038	357	322	34, 869	33, 413, 904	11, 199, 030	39, 142, 645	63, 436, 186
land	219	117	258	25, 054	30, 352, 800	8, 174, 325	23, 280, 096	37, 907, 670
rolina	27	......	27	1, 176	1, 362, 900	261, 495	783, 707	1, 564, 396
e	176	41	99	1, 318	1, 344, 518	237, 936	1, 009, 526	1, 638, 386
....	24	11	......	391	593, 250	88, 489	303, 336	527, 566
....	18	......	16	122	265, 400	54, 340	105, 323	216, 405
....	81	9	103	2, 357	3, 007, 150	775, 703	2, 266, 633	4, 200, 819
....	80	4	85	2, 030	1, 564, 373	288, 515	1, 256, 120	1, 924, 752
·ginia	77	22	48	322	236, 700	60, 628	314, 071	486, 268
n	75	12	50	812	1, 249, 664	230, 906	693, 737	1, 970, 677

TOBACCO.

ludes Tobacco, chewing, smoking, and snuff; Tobacco and cigars; and Tobacco, cigars.]

ıl Territories.	Establishm'ts.	Steam-engines.	Water-wheels.	All hands.	Capital. (*Dollars.*)	Wages. (*Dollars.*)	Materials. (*Dollars.*)	Products. (*Dollars.*)
ıited States..	5, 204	178	26	47, 848	24, 924, 330	14, 315, 342	34, 656, 607	71, 762, 044
....	14	......	......	35	9, 950	9, 785	9, 290	33, 850
s	4	......	......	14	11, 500	5, 900	6, 800	19, 800
a	91	3	......	1, 838	709, 345	534, 755	807, 081	1, 967, 717
cut	103	2	1	734	418, 230	307, 709	447, 718	1, 148, 494
)	19	1	4	157	266, 750	52, 288	155, 955	270, 296
ıf Columbia...	44	......	......	109	36, 715	27, 919	35, 583	96, 550
....	13	......	......	254	257, 500	204, 910	98, 840	572, 350
....	20	......	......	254	118, 700	92, 247	231, 304	475, 874
....	274	13	......	2, 684	1, 964, 020	781, 744	2, 046, 922	4, 319, 716
....	148	2	......	817	393, 265	274, 243	481, 427	1, 148, 315
....	74	2	......	423	254, 550	151, 483	214, 355	590, 373
....	27	......	......	135	66, 100	62, 405	83, 806	223, 800
y	102	11	......	1, 289	860, 071	353, 315	1, 013, 798	2, 097, 005
a	48	5	......	358	190, 400	145, 149	205, 363	578, 890
....	12	......	......	74	27, 000	29, 286	48, 775	91, 447
i	284	9	......	1, 387	910, 000	389, 784	664, 279	1, 772, 257
ısetts	136	......	2	1, 050	507, 885	459, 844	737, 438	1, 670, 932
ı	114	13	......	1, 256	1, 301, 202	441, 930	1, 448, 305	2, 572, 522
a	14	......	......	57	38, 400	19, 546	30, 260	72, 869
pi	1	......	......	7	200	100	666	1, [illegible]
....	383	13	......	3, 388	3, 031, 360	1, 486, 727	5, 925, 995	10, 415, [illegible]

TABLE CII.—*Groups of Principal Industries, by States and Territories—1870*—Continued.

TOBACCO—Continued.

States and Territories.	Establishm'ts.	Steam-engines.	Water-wheels.	All hands.	Capital. (*Dollars.*)	Wages. (*Dollars.*)	Materials. (*Dollars.*)	Products. (*Dollars.*)
Nebraska	12			43	29,400	28,416	60,539	109,734
New Hampshire	12			60	31,675	26,390	32,037	79,521
New Jersey	194	4	8	877	714,960	267,992	624,823	1,985,929
New York	1,123	38	5	10,243	6,226,046	3,750,870	9,763,626	18,940,658
North Carolina	111			1,465	375,882	102,144	391,027	718,765
Ohio	452	23	3	3,719	1,487,499	1,104,247	2,545,139	5,307,591
Oregon	2			8	4,200	3,700	2,800	6,850
Pennsylvania	1,005	10	1	6,229	2,517,795	1,501,789	2,292,781	6,234,493
Rhode Island	34			178	54,900	50,145	92,355	197,445
South Carolina	1			15	10,000	6,500	7,000	25,000
Tennessee	18			73	42,200	19,520	45,775	110,125
Texas	18			56	12,730	9,089	11,600	34,735
Vermont	7			42	31,350	25,800	43,178	87,888
Virginia	131	25	2	7,534	1,391,925	1,184,418	4,082,181	7,054,770
West Virginia	45			198	46,775	69,559	72,933	277,573
Wisconsin	114	4		759	573,230	246,604	544,854	1,222,032

WEAR, ARTICLES OF.

[Includes Clothing, men's; Clothing, women's; Clothing, children's; Boots and shoes; Hats and caps; Collars and cuffs, paper; Gloves and mittens; Hoop-skirts and corsets; and Hosiery.]

States and Territories.	Establishm'ts.	Steam-engines.	Water-wheels.	All hands.	Capital. (*Dollars.*)	Wages. (*Dollars.*)	Materials. (*Dollars.*)	Products. (*Dollars.*)
The United States	34,312	488	175	297,141	123,866,220	98,837,550	214,841,378	398,264,118
Alabama	190	1		387	163,385	75,672	151,948	391,573
Arkansas	51			132	33,350	37,181	46,939	129,130
California	623	1		2,463	945,435	1,082,550	2,026,868	4,268,228
Colorado	21			26	9,250	11,240	14,175	44,950
Connecticut	586	39	19	10,157	4,344,720	3,346,565	6,662,684	12,285,465
Delaware	110	2		660	234,103	190,807	372,695	735,333
District of Columbia	228			613	183,200	178,466	310,927	754,006
Florida	43			80	20,740	20,936	39,356	92,314
Georgia	284		1	714	198,460	158,951	309,897	708,834
Idaho	15			27	15,200	6,985	11,630	33,267
Illinois	1,686	1	1	11,677	5,072,670	3,059,390	7,399,008	13,136,625
Indiana	1,275			4,424	1,649,606	1,170,777	2,441,299	5,021,762
Iowa	736			2,047	724,398	488,504	1,111,701	2,235,294
Kansas	154			468	229,802	154,463	227,384	526,002
Kentucky	593			2,089	938,478	558,089	1,085,657	2,336,042
Louisiana	325			997	215,535	248,565	340,628	896,194
Maine	566	7	3	7,469	1,549,928	1,429,960	4,185,417	6,746,218
Maryland	1,162	2		10,838	3,081,060	2,076,953	5,189,216	9,198,525
Massachusetts	3,060	258	43	72,392	28,475,347	33,448,772	68,386,356	118,482,947
Michigan	1,075	1		5,304	2,465,181	1,372,696	2,681,133	5,424,665
Minnesota	237			780	335,439	266,652	495,316	865,172
Mississippi	121			209	58,776	38,032	89,768	230,945
Missouri	1,829	1		7,261	3,763,169	3,050,141	6,452,738	13,044,634
Montana	13			27	10,700	17,350	18,097	36,090
Nebraska	87			203	103,720	87,145	108,088	302,327
Nevada	29			58	26,900	29,770	44,830	119,370
New Hampshire	390	9	31	5,346	2,194,615	1,879,651	4,458,017	8,942,279
New Jersey	884	6	2	9,190	3,236,830	3,580,755	6,274,054	12,567,121
New Mexico	11			14	4,200	1,520	4,049	10,265
New York	5,415	77	61	68,292	32,567,917	21,425,932	52,606,619	96,549,347
North Carolina	139			386	134,004	76,272	177,533	380,712
Ohio	3,354	4		18,804	7,077,726	4,405,402	10,932,729	20,082,905
Oregon	86			174	82,255	38,141	90,088	214,022
Pennsylvania	5,683	76	5	41,758	20,939,599	11,908,755	24,070,802	48,729,076
Rhode Island	213	2	2	1,945	783,285	599,126	1,249,542	2,317,840
South Carolina	73			176	32,760	24,864	46,208	131,022
Tennessee	495			1,212	369,641	340,154	482,315	1,286,454
Texas	131			264	75,510	52,840	101,663	272,218
Utah	49			154	42,420	29,770	33,934	90,870
Vermont	286	1	7	1,470	756,749	391,094	770,440	1,924,796
Virginia	653			1,295	246,771	186,714	475,256	1,058,146
Washington	18			38	18,680	8,510	16,054	44,558
West Virginia	296			760	202,543	152,193	376,001	760,712
Wisconsin	1,032			4,346	2,244,443	1,129,525	2,479,583	4,673,600
Wyoming	5			15	7,700	9,686	22,017	50,140

[*Continued from page 872.*]

now attained to such dimensions, and has come to embrace so diversified and complicated interests, as to require peremptorily a system of statistical investigations substantially new, both as to the scope and the details of inquiry, and as to the methods and agencies of enumeration. Outgrown and ineffective as is the census law of 1850 in almost all particulars, it is nowhere so painfully and almost ludicrously inadequate as in the canvass of the national industry.

Of the total amount paid for the collection of the Statistics of Manufacture in "Schedule 4," more than a fifth was expended for returns relating to carpentering, blacksmithing, coopering, painting, plastering, and plumbing, not one of which industries, though far better returned than ever before, was reported with sufficient completeness even to furnish the data for a computation of the true production of the trade, so that, after this expenditure, one is still obliged to resort to the Tables of Occupations for the material from which to estimate the production of this group of industries. The money thus thrown away would have served, if placed under the control of the Department of the Interior for the salaries of experts and for the traveling expenses of special agents, to make the statistics of the larger industries complete and correct in the highest attainable degree, creditable to the census as a national work, and invaluable to the statesman, the political economist, and the practical man of business. At the same time, a well-trained statistician can, in a few hours, from the Tables of Occupations, reach a far more satisfactory result in respect to the products of the minor trades than is to be obtained by manipulating the partial returns of the trades themselves. In a word, the returns of manufactures should be restricted to those industries which are carried on in considerable establishments, and are susceptible of a thorough, complete, and detailed enumeration.

Second. The returns of manufactures, having been thus restricted, should be far more specific, and should be made to conform to the advance in the practical arts within the last twenty years, and to the requirements of modern statistical science. The additional facts thus to be elicited should not be industrial merely, but such also as are of social and sanitary importance. The Manufacturing Tables of the census ought to be so full of technical information as to become the hand-book of manufacturers, while, at the same time, they might be made so pregnant with truths important to the economist and the statesman as to become a hand-book of social and political philosophy. With no more authority of law than might have been contained in five lines of the statutes, and with not a dollar of expense above what has been incurred in making this unsatisfactory exhibit of the national industries, such an enumeration of the manufactures of the country might have been effected at the Ninth Census.

Third. The enumeration of all the manufacturing industries, which are of sufficient importance to be taken at all in the census, should be charged upon special agents or deputies, who should be in the widest sense experts, who should be liberally compensated; who should have ample authority to prosecute the stated inquiries of the census; and each of whom should be assigned to the enumeration of a single specific industry, or of a limited number of cognate industries, over a large extent of territory. To reduce the subjects of inquiry given each such agent, while extending his field of inquiry over entire cities, States, and sections, affords the true means of securing at once closeness of scrutiny and comprehensiveness of survey.

Fourth. The canvass of manufacturing industries should be conducted through means of schedules, special successively to each of the industries to be enumerated. This is demanded, not less for the convenience of the public than in the interest of the census itself, in order to accuracy and economy of enumeration.

At the census of 1860, the return of "kinds and quantities," both of materials and of products, required by the act of 1850, was enforced more or less completely in respect to each one of the 140,433 establishments enumerated;* while, in the case of only 6,336 establishments, (excluding, as in 1870, coal and iron mines,) were the returns of "kinds and quantities" tabulated. At the census of 1870, in the manifest uselessness and, indeed, impracticability of returning the kinds and quantities of materials or products in a form allowing of a systematic tabulation, the instructions to assistant marshals were so drawn as to excuse from this duty the proprietors of at least 115,000 establishments of productive industry. Eighty-five thousand and forty-two are published in one of the following tables, with the kinds and quantities of materials and products stated in detail. In respect to the remainder, the returns of "kinds and quantities" were not used, either from the inadequacy or irregularity of the statements made, or because the materials and products were found, upon an attempt at compilation, not to be of a character to repay the expense of tabulation, or to justify the space required in publication.

To increase the ratio of establishments in respect of which quantitative statements of materials and of products are supplied in the census, from $4\frac{1}{2}$ per cent., as in 1860,

*Exception must be made to the extent of 5,000 gold mines, in the State of California, which were estimated for at the Census Office.

[Continued on page 940.]

TABLE CIII.—*Manufactures: Special Statistics for Principal Industries*—1870.

AGRICULTURAL IMPLEMENTS.

	States and Territories.	Establishments.	STEAM-ENGINES. Horse-power.	STEAM-ENGINES. Number.	WATER-WHEELS. Horse-power.	WATER-WHEELS. Number.	All hands.	Capital.	Wages.	Materials.
								Dollars.	*Dollars.*	*Dollars.*
	The United States	2,076	15,873	676	10,209	426	25,249	34,834,600	12,151,504	21,473,925
1	Alabama	3	......	...	......	...	9	3,800	1,975	1,849
2	Arkansas	1	15	1	......	...	16	12,500	1,340	5,050
3	California	10	48	3	......	...	68	79,450	43,725	43,370
4	Connecticut	38	136	4	1,278	50	593	1,061,100	328,718	455,649
5	Delaware	10	58	5	23	2	56	57,800	18,850	13,864
6	Georgia	10	70	3	130	5	59	39,550	12,436	23,904
7	Illinois	294	2,575	91	620	14	3,935	5,350,978	1,813,835	3,598,897
8	Indiana	124	860	33	165	6	1,268	1,622,769	484,526	951,714
9	Iowa	55	457	27	20	1	552	543,040	182,138	401,372
10	Kansas	3	12	1	......	...	29	30,750	8,951	10,163
11	Kentucky	44	270	10	......	...	624	633,025	287,590	673,[illegible]
12	Louisiana	1	5	...	......	...	15	5,000	5,000	5,000
13	Maine	32	31	2	505	24	219	241,250	72,742	86,430
14	Maryland	34	189	14	10	2	295	281,300	117,311	276,257
15	Massachusetts	37	221	8	964	31	477	499,400	243,112	487,460
16	Michigan	164	948	52	317	20	969	1,254,759	362,844	714,933
17	Minnesota	27	126	9	50	2	167	190,712	72,520	92,656
18	Mississippi	11	24	3	......	...	34	21,150	8,950	22,586
19	Missouri	38	325	14	......	...	537	791,435	403,847	690,376
20	Montana	1	......	...	......	...	1	500	100	440
21	Nebraska	2	......	...	......	...	9	3,800	3,210	10,579
22	New Hampshire	24	26	2	458	24	184	174,550	78,505	77,714
23	New Jersey	30	139	8	208	6	366	517,250	181,687	202,361
24	New York	337	2,529	106	2,722	116	4,953	7,824,656	2,513,377	4,594,316
25	North Carolina	20	31	5	16	1	78	34,520	16,914	34,348
26	Ohio	219	3,581	110	283	15	5,124	7,570,320	2,841,518	5,940,550
27	Oregon	4	8	1	21	1	10	15,700	3,800	7,075
28	Pennsylvania	286	2,041	104	581	43	2,286	3,387,949	1,025,618	1,278,805
29	Rhode Island	5	15	1	154	4	81	252,500	37,450	42,806
30	Tennessee	25	102	10	6	2	110	62,900	36,717	49,782
31	Texas	12	......	...	......	...	44	12,559	13,370	18,165
32	Vermont	45	162	4	1,251	45	372	518,150	138,327	212,964
33	Virginia	37	157	9	323	5	267	187,128	102,886	153,694
34	West Virginia	11	53	5	15	1	55	57,650	24,283	19,640
35	Wisconsin	83	669	31	89	6	1,387	1,494,700	663,392	966,739

BAGGING: FLAX, HEMP, AND JUTE.

	States.	Establishments.	STEAM-ENGINES. Horse-power.	STEAM-ENGINES. Number.	WATER-WHEELS. Horse-power.	WATER-WHEELS. Number.	MACHINES. Looms.	MACHINES. Spindles.	MACHINES. Cards.	MACHINES. Hackles.	HANDS EMPLOYED. All.	HANDS EMPLOYED. Males above 16.	HANDS EMPLOYED. Females above 15.	HANDS EMPLOYED. Youth.
							No.	*No.*	*No.*	*No.*				
	The United States	33	785	15	535	11	466	5,103	63	289	3,170	1,718	863	589
1	Illinois	2	......	......	175	4	14	356	....	...	113	37	34	42
2	Kentucky	11	130	2	......	......	117	346	....	289	1,228	993	102	133
3	Massachusetts	2	140	2	......	......	20	1,720	26	....	234	213	6	15
4	Missouri	2	145	2	......	......	62	95	....	....	333	103	116	114
5	New Jersey	4	75	2	170	2	70	1,690	5	....	484	100	292	92
6	New York	4	90	2	70	2	42	202	8	....	209	45	84	80
7	Ohio	7	185	4	120	3	46	694	14	....	497	211	189	97
8	Pennsylvania	1	20	1	......	......	26	......	10	....	72	16	40	16

TABLE CIII.—*Manufactures: Special Statistics for Principal Industries*—1870.

AGRICULTURAL IMPLEMENTS.

PRODUCTS.												
Cane-mills.	Clover-hullers.	Corn-planters.	Corn-shellers.	Cotton-plant'rs.	Cultivators.	Fanning-mills.	Grain-cradles.	Grain-drills.	Hand-rakes.	Harrows.	Harvesters.	
No. 108	*No.* 5,206	*No.* 21,700	*No.* 12,941	*No.* 2,000	*No.* 88,740	*No.* 19,772	*No.* 103,646	*No.* 32,033	*Dozens.* 207,310	*No.* 9,150	*No.* 3,566	
......	......	......	......	......	......	......	......	......	......	145	......	1
......	......	......	......	......	......	......	......	......	......	......	......	2
......	......	......	......	......	95	......	......	......	......	251	......	3
......	......	......	......	......	230	......	300	......	7,167	50	......	4
......	......	......	......	......	18	......	......	50	......	......	......	5
......	......	......	......	2,000	......	33	......	......	......	50	......	6
......	......	15,244	1,262	......	42,945	1,626	......	4,750	......	1,890	2,860	7
......	......	......	196	......	1,030	1,076	39,324	5,931	3,888	1,088	......	8
......	......	......	......	......	2,700	3,027	......	......	......	300	......	9
......	......	......	......	......	......	......	......	......	......	95	......	10
100	......	......	50	......	50	50	57	......	......	92	......	11
......	......	......	......	......	......	......	......	......	......	......	......	12
[illegible]	......	......	......	......	1,437	......	......	......	4,200	8	......	13
......	40	100	1,290	......	625	200	2,040	505	371	475	......	14
......	......	1,000	1,700	......	2,200	......	2,400	......	13,530	800	700	15
......	......	......	1,150	......	13,636	2,410	16,536	240	140,100	650	......	16
......	......	......	......	......	156	1,940	......	580	......	30	......	17
......	......	......	......	......	......	......	......	......	......	......	......	18
......	......	3,500	......	......	100	680	......	100	......	30	......	19
......	......	......	......	......	......	8	......	......	......	......	......	20
......	......	......	......	......	......	......	......	......	......	......	......	21
......	......	......	100	......	492	......	......	......	6,710	140	......	22
......	......	......	63	......	1,412	......	110	......	54	75	......	23
......	206	100	664	......	11,492	4,481	34,539	2,068	10,447	994	6	24
8	......	......	158	......	......	......	......	......	......	......	......	25
......	......	1,100	1,026	......	5,683	1,425	2,428	11,793	3,450	6	......	26
......	......	......	......	......	......	10	......	......	......	......	......	27
......	4,958	665	4,547	......	821	1,660	4,972	1,881	1,801	25	......	28
......	......	......	......	......	300	......	......	......	200	100	......	29
......	......	......	85	......	......	266	......	......	......	200	......	30
......	......	......	......	......	25	......	......	......	......	......	......	31
......	......	......	......	......	415	......	......	......	6,292	......	......	32
......	......	......	250	......	300	105	100	885	......	1,595	......	33
......	......	......	400	......	2,007	50	840	......	......	1	......	34
......	......	......	......	......	571	725	......	3,250	100	60	......	35

BAGGING: FLAX, HEMP, AND JUTE.

Capital.	Wages.	MATERIALS.							
		American hemp.	Tow.	Jute.	Jute yarn.	Flax.	All other materials.	All materials.	
Dollars. 3,168,104	*Dollars.* 958,106	*Tons.* 7,060	*Tons.* 3,058	*Tons.* 5,601	*Tons.* 112	*Tons.* 4,672	*Dollars.* 109,413	*Dollars.* 2,624,682	
125,000	38,000	......	......	......	......	1,725	......	136,000	1
756,000	301,240	6,292	......	105	......	357	2,400	1,077,300	2
225,000	53,000	......	......	1,130	......	......	......	106,000	3
1,200,000	285,000	768	......	......	......	2,[illegible]90	18,600	423,100	4
363,600	135,721	......	......	3,688	......	......	24,960	414,199	5
100,000	35,600	......	......	768	......	......	41,500	131,900	6
348,501	137,545	......	3,058	......	......	......	19,553	289,053	7
40,000	22,000	......	......	......	112	......	2,400	47,900	8

TABLE CIII.—*Manufactures: Special Statistics for Principal Industries*—1870—Cont'd.

AGRICULTURAL IMPLEMENTS—Continued.

	States and Territories.	Products—Continued.								
		Hay and straw cutters.	Hay forks.	Hoes.	Horse-powers.	Horse-rakes.	Lawn-mowers.	Mowers.	Plows.	Reapers.
		No.	*No.*	*Dozens.*	*No.*	*No.*	*No.*	*No.*	*No.*	*No.*
	The United States.	30, 879	1, 298, 260	135, 139	4, 541	89, 619	2, 536	39, 486	864, 947	60, 382
1	Alabama								200	
2	Arkansas									
3	California		500					50	867	175
4	Connecticut	5, 380	86, 000	30, 350		4, 780		4, 025	18, 091	
5	Delaware					9	36		1, 278	54
6	Georgia								1, 190	
7	Illinois	3, 634	66, 000		654	6, 475		170	236, 783	1, 341
8	Indiana	1, 808	147, 600	9, 400	97			4	62, 700	25
9	Iowa	300	200			25			25, 314	8
10	Kansas								1, 235	
11	Kentucky	475		12	100			350	147, 189	
12	Louisiana								1, 000	
13	Maine		8, 400	2, 000		1, 520		23	32, 229	[illegible]
14	Maryland		30	50	61	400		164	10, 608	
15	Massachusetts	8, 050	102, 600	40, 000	73	3, 013		2, 050	14, 600	
16	Michigan	162	96, 000	7, 000	706	10, 932		20	20, 794	
17	Minnesota					38			5, 980	
18	Mississippi								10, 450	
19	Missouri								52, 490	34, 200
20	Montana									
21	Nebraska								425	
22	New Hampshire				6			1, 025	1, 760	
23	New Jersey	1, 750	300		192	752		1, 473	12, 700	802
24	New York	1, 766	308, 823	27, 000	1, 505	15, 541	2, 500	19, 005	28, 809	12, 895
25	North Carolina	93			21				12, 650	
26	Ohio	4, 190	144, 000	2, 085	380	30, 004		4, 691	61, 941	7, 455
27	Oregon								125	
28	Pennsylvania	271	203, 807	11, 000	573	5, 276		6, 094	52, 096	1, 633
29	Rhode Island					60			600	
30	Tennessee								16, 064	
31	Texas								2, 180	
32	Vermont		131, 000	6, 200	173	1, 385		202	2, 030	
33	Virginia	3, 000		42		225			21, 545	
34	West Virginia					12		50	2, 290	
35	Wisconsin					172			6, 734	1, 540

BAGGING: FLAX, HEMP, AND JUTE—Concluded.

	States.	Products.					
		Bagging.	Gunny-cloth.	Cloth.	Yarn.	All other products.	All products.
		Yards.	*Yards.*	*Pounds.*	*Pounds.*	*Dollars.*	*Dollars.*
	The United States	12, 287, 922	1, 215, 000	942, 864	767, 296	473, 260	4, 507, 664
1	Illinois	560, 000					290, 000
2	Kentucky	4, 950, 200				473, 260	1, 752, 120
3	Massachusetts	50, 000	1, 000, 000				210, 000
4	Missouri	2, 488, 000					750, 000
5	New Jersey	1, 000, 000	180, 000	942, 864	767, 296		621, 245
6	New York	860, 000	35, 000				215, 500
7	Ohio	2, 029, 722					563, 799
8	Pennsylvania	350, 000					105, 000

TABLE CIII.—*Manufactures: Special Statistics for Principal Industries*—1870—Cont'd.

AGRICULTURAL IMPLEMENTS—Continued.

PRODUCTS—Continued.												
Reapers and mowers combined.	Rollers and scrapers.	Seed-sowers.	Scythes.	Scythe-snaths.	Separators.	Shovels.*	Sickles.	Stump-pullers.	Thrashers.	Other products.	All products.	
No. 50,645	*No.* 4,803	*No.* 6,900	*No.* 881,244	*No.* 17,680	*No.* 1,131	*Doz.* 25,756	*Doz.* 300	*No.* 124	*No.* 22,931	*Dollars.* 5,206,789	*Dollars.* 52,066,875	
										7,500	10,050	1
										12,000	12,000	2
										49,450	118,540	3
			342,000							*138,239	1,183,947	4
									14	13,430	41,325	5
									6	6,500	77,450	6
11,500	1,405				175					449,641	8,880,390	7
1,460	762		72,000		240				647	158,245	2,128,794	8
									206	215,750	829,965	9
										8,714	31,252	10
					55				154	78,630	1,384,917	11
											14,000	12
			44,400	780		11,000			135	68,115	231,991	13
	80								81	181,829	549,085	14
		750	49,200							103,601	1,033,590	15
	694					6			806	407,658	1,569,596	16
									1	42,223	267,841	17
										4,575	51,800	18
5									8,021	96,970	1,588,108	19
										1,000	1,640	20
											17,000	21
		5,300	86,400							12,545	254,470	22
									290	122,578	633,875	23
21,027	997	850	186,300		101				4,101	879,604	11,847,037	24
									50	17,125	82,110	25
24,518					25				5,610	1,036,315	11,907,366	26
									2	8,300	19,950	27
1,135				3,900	15	14,500	300	124	2,067	777,339	3,652,295	28
			95,544						24	12,040	92,464	29
										28,605	132,772	30
										6,295	42,420	31
			5,400	13,000	20				183	120,858	523,669	32
									384	56,485	403,457	33
						250			41	8,100	58,281	34
	865				500				99	76,530	2,393,428	35

Shovels and Spades made in Establishments not producing other Agricultural Implements—1870.

States.	Establishments.	Steam-engines.	Water-wheels.	All hands.	Capital.	Wages.	Materials.	PRODUCTS.				
								Shovels.		Spades.		All products.
					Dolls.	*Dolls.*	*Dollars.*	*Doz.*	*Dollars.*	*Doz.*	*Dolls.*	*Dollars.*
The United States	13	11	21	849	757,100	489,100	1,424,944	190,910	2,150,666	29,986	294,860	2,445,526
Massachusetts	5	6	18	654	371,100	376,000	1,080,144	134,226	1,585,666	22,986	234,860	1,820,526
New York	1	1	....	9	10,000	5,000	20,000	4,167	40,000	......	......	40,000
Pennsylvania	7	4	3	186	376,000	108,100	324,800	52,517	525,000	7,000	60,000	585,000

TABLE CIII.—*Manufactures: Special Statistics for I*

BOOTS AND SHOE

	States and Territories.	Establishments.	MACHINES. Sewing.	MACHINES. Pegging.	HANDS EMPLOYED. All.	HANDS EMPLOYED. Males above 16.	HANDS EMPLOYED. Females above 15.	HANDS EMPLOYED. Youth.
	The United States	3,151	12,394	901	91,702	70,658	18,208	[illegible]
1	**Alabama**	6	6	...	38	38	......	...
2	**Arkansas**	2	3	...	12	11	1	...
3	**California**	46	148	2	968	833	107	
4	**Colorado**	1	1	...	3	3	......	...
5	**Connecticut**	38	193	7	1,918	1,267	580	
6	**Delaware**	6	57	4	221	146	70	
7	**Dist. of Columbia**	5	2	...	34	32	2	...
8	**Georgia**	11	12	6	97	88	3	...
9	**Illinois**	88	137	4	1,274	1,197	50	[illegible]
10	**Indiana**	88	100	7	689	664	17	
11	**Iowa**	53	50	3	323	318	5	...
12	**Kansas**	11	9	...	73	73	......	...
13	**Kentucky**	45	24	1	400	356	39	
14	**Louisiana**	8	20	3	135	132	3	...
15	**Maine**	85	325	14	2,105	1,544	539	[illegible]
16	**Maryland**	68	257	...	1,631	1,279	335	[illegible]
17	**Massachusetts**	1,123	7,042	636	51,167	39,365	10,773	[illegible]
18	**Michigan**	81	105	...	830	757	68	
19	**Minnesota**	29	32	...	212	208	4	...
20	**Mississippi**	6	2	...	35	35	......	...
21	**Missouri**	182	284	...	960	856	23	[illegible]
22	**Montana**	5	3	...	15	15	......	...
23	**Nebraska**	7	8	...	43	43	......	...
24	**Nevada**	4	3	1	9	9	......	...
25	**New Hampshire**	78	279	24	2,777	2,229	513	[illegible]
26	**New Jersey**	67	285	2	1,990	1,504	343	[illegible]
27	**New York**	341	1,135	150	11,409	8,287	2,057	[illegible]
28	**North Carolina**	6	21	4	91	74	8	[illegible]
29	**Ohio**	164	331	3	2,026	1,636	305	[illegible]
30	**Oregon**	2	4	...	10	10	......	...
31	**Pennsylvania**	335	1,287	15	8,330	5,801	2,231	[illegible]
32	**Rhode Island**	16	33	9	306	260	45	
33	**South Carolina**	2	1	...	8	8	......	...
34	**Tennessee**	23	31	3	165	152	10	
35	**Texas**	5	1	...	21	21	......	...
36	**Utah**	2	2	...	17	17	......	...
37	**Vermont**	20	34	5	331	280	44	
38	**Virginia**	8	5	...	61	57	3	
39	**Washington**	2	2	...	10	10	......	...
40	**West Virginia**	3	7	...	20	20	......	...
41	**Wisconsin**	78	105	...	927	903	21	
42	**Wyoming**	1	1	...	5	5	......	...

* Includes all establishments yielding an annual production

MOTIVE POWER.—*Steam-engines, horse-power and number:* cut, 19 and 2; Delaware, 15 and 2; Maine, 38 and 6; Marylan Michigan, 10 and 1; New Hampshire, 97 and 7; New Jersey, and 4; Pennsylvania, 59 and 11; Rhode Island, 10 and 1; Ve

Water-wheels, horse-power and number: United States, 163 and 3; Massachusetts, 94 and 18; New York, 20 and 2.

TABLE CIII.--*Manufactures: Special Statistics for Principal Industries*—1870—Cont'd.

BOOTS AND SHOES.

MATERIALS—Continued.			PRODUCTS.						
Other leather.	All other materials.	All materials.	Boots.		Shoes.		All other products.†	All products.	
Pounds.	*Dollars.*	*Dollars.*	*Pairs.*	*Dollars.*	*Pairs.*	*Dollars.*	*Dollars.*	*Dollars.*	
[illegible]3, 785, 443	11, 388, 900	80, 502, 718	14, 318, 529	50, 231, 470	66, 308, 715	93, 846, 206	2, 611, 179	146, 704, 055	
2, 825	1, 355	17, 625	1, 405	17, 560	5, 260	16, 928	8, 250	42, 888	1
225	350	4, 400	1, 250	14, 850	600	2, 400	2, 250	19, 500	2
122, 088	219, 341	745, 455	103, 441	619, 922	576, 549	901, 311	17, 120	1, 538, 353	3
200	250	2, 250	300	3, 000	625	2, 575	1, 925	7, 500	4
30, 637	213, 110	990, 646	160, 090	680, 581	806, 810	1, 258, 871	200	1, 939, 652	5
1, 900	126, 192	200, 354	824	8, 440	152, 648	372, 940	1, 040	382, 420	6
7, 850	1, 610	21, 075	2, 912	31, 168	3, 725	24, 130	1, 650	56, 948	7
1, 900	4, 571	78, 172	2, 775	24, 624	68, 080	127, 940	6, 890	159, 454	8
57, 209	138, 983	1, 151, 215	365, 563	1, 701, 164	186, 128	442, 344	154, 628	2, 298, 136	9
65, 367	61, 704	445, 660	126, 202	768, 027	75, 485	177, 051	56, 714	1, 001, 792	10
30, 331	25, 236	188, 919	45, 261	322, 456	18, 449	63, 362	37, 465	423, 283	11
3, 675	4, 405	48, 235	11, 089	87, 980	3, 780	15, 608	11, 040	114, 628	12
41, 101	36, 508	193, 044	47, 053	343, 633	57, 473	186, 077	10, 472	540, 182	13
4, 400	2, 158	62, 803	3, 300	35, 300	59, 100	98, 000	3, 000	136, 300	14
442, 066	340, 981	1, 949, 989	154, 754	611, 812	1, 934, 405	2, 532, 935	10, 474	3, 155, 221	15
38, 600	171, 030	905, 102	77, 497	522, 506	793, 355	1, 452, 186	23, 076	1, 997, 768	16
8, 068, 275	6, 618, 441	50, 509, 201	10, 129, 910	29, 164, 594	45, 443, 049	56, 840, 464	560, 387	86, 565, 445	17
111, 757	66, 108	587, 104	146, 416	863, 741	121, 421	322, 779	62, 610	1, 249, 130	18
35, 784	10, 633	231, 497	56, 009	253, 755	55, 853	118, 213	23, 960	395, 928	19
2, 462	1, 750	21, 521	2, 110	24, 320	7, 674	24, 654	2, 624	51, 598	20
75, 197	46, 453	1, 102, 118	158, 009	1, 567, 033	148, 466	600, 865	195, 803	2, 363, 701	21
200	2, 500	11, 210	1, 745	28, 350	60	650	6, 450	35, 450	22
2, 050	6, 018	34, 550	5, 738	63, 974	3, 691	19, 188	21, 538	104, 700	23
275	1, 400	9, 650	1, 389	26, 460	75	750	1, 290	28, 500	24
272, 333	267, 796	2, 815, 788	63, 850	210, 100	3, 256, 771	4, 567, 420	2, 500	4, 780, 020	25
531, 322	202, 110	1, 333, 590	125, 950	850, 304	945, 932	1, 896, 358	83, 460	2, 830, 322	26
2, 366, 818	1, 368, 380	9, 383, 167	1, 531, 179	6, 141, 503	5, 815, 126	10, 732, 242	939, 303	17, 813, 048	27
20, 500	4, 360	92, 391	1, 150	5, 200	96, 290	162, 401	....	167, 601	28
267, 306	364, 443	1, 294, 925	185, 238	1, 194, 966	668, 561	1, 562, 353	109, 484	2, 866, 803	29
1, 200	140	3, 365	900	10, 000	1, 000	6, 000	1, 000	17, 000	30
902, 302	934, 341	4, 734, 136	481, 927	2, 412, 394	4, 552, 274	8, 438, 986	151, 207	11, 002, 587	31
24, 328	26, 225	267, 595	24, 366	135, 110	187, 096	287, 094	....	437, 254	32
960	359	6, 709	466	5, 724	2, 050	10, 500	1, 176	17, 400	33
12, 940	5, 606	83, 044	13, 290	125, 350	31, 804	93, 080	18, 750	237, 180	34
1, 500	3, 150	14, 980	2, 531	26, 872	1, 997	8, 931	1, 700	37, 503	35
....	256	4, 166	525	4, 185	2, 800	8, 200	....	12, 385	36
40, 825	47, 891	240, 687	102, 075	400, 929	100, 150	141, 000	5, 860	547, 789	37
4, 281	1, 863	29, 009	4, 665	30, 280	10, 004	33, 118	7, 386	70, 784	38
234	570	5, 307	1, 100	12, 000	1, 075	2, 375	1, 500	15, 875	39
1, 430	615	10, 995	3, 200	20, 900	1, 550	4, 450	1, 400	26, 750	40
173, 470	59, 508	656, 319	169, 072	828, 403	117, 280	287, 677	65, 597	1, 181, 677	41
8, 320	200	15, 150	2, 000	32, 000	200	1, 600	....	33, 600	42

† Chiefly repairing.

TABLE CIII.—*Manufactures: Special Statistics for Principal Industries*—1870—Con.

BRICK AND TILE.

	States and Territories.	Establishments.	Steam-engines. Horse-power.	Steam-engines. Number.	Water-wheels. Horse-power.	Water-wheels. Number.	Hands employed. All.	Hands employed. Males above 16.	Hands employed. Females above 15.	Hands employed. [illegible]
	The United States	3,137	10,453	376	328	22	43,511	39,754	260	[illegible]
1	Alabama	12					157	131	3	
2	Arkansas	6					77	68		
3	California	31					610	610		
4	Colorado	6	20	1			63	63		
5	Connecticut	71	40	2	20	2	716	703	3	
6	Delaware	14	82	4			365	327		
7	District of Columbia	13	160	5			427	419		
8	Florida	4					55	49		
9	Georgia	41	61	3			860	696	19	
10	Illinois	240	700	23			3,203	2,936	2	
11	Indiana	275	92	5			2,009	1,896		
12	Iowa	116					971	914	1	
13	Kansas	27					270	248		
14	Kentucky	40	29	3			507	389		
15	Louisiana	22	20	1			401	286	70	
16	Maine	110	175	3			773	769	2	
17	Maryland	73	116	5			2,051	1,919	1	
18	Massachusetts	107	823	28	44	3	2,901	2,802		
19	Michigan	136	609	27			1,584	1,505	21	
20	Minnesota	38					377	377		
21	Mississippi	12					139	120	1	
22	Missouri	186	255	7			2,198	2,077	2	
23	Montana	2					8	8		
24	Nebraska	17					109	108	1	
25	Nevada	1					9	9		
26	New Hampshire	57	55	2			514	514		
27	New Jersey	118	1,119	35			2,366	2,245	7	
28	New York	320	2,807	87	89	10	6,728	6,161	41	
29	North Carolina	8					96	79		
30	Ohio	354	636	31	118	4	2,627	2,488	7	
31	Oregon	5					43	43		
32	Pennsylvania	458	1,868	68	57	3	7,443	6,219	4	1
33	Rhode Island	3	100	4			224	216		
34	South Carolina	4	15	1			38	33	5	
35	Tennessee	34	80	2			442	349	3	
36	Texas	24	24	1			268	218	3	
37	Utah	1					6	6		
38	Vermont	18	7	1			166	162		
39	Virginia	22	9	1			251	190	20	
40	Washington	5					34	33	1	
41	West Virginia	24	432	14			262	213		
42	Wisconsin	79	179	12			1,133	1,086	2	

TABLE CIII.—*Manufactures: Special Statistics for Principal Industries*—1870—Cont'd.

BRICK AND TILE.

CAPITAL.	WAGES.	MATERIALS.	PRODUCTS.					
Dollars.	Dollars.	Dollars.	Common brick.	Fire-brick.	Pressed brick.	All other products, including tile and drain pipe.	All products.	
			Thousand.	*Thousand*	*Thousand*	*Dollars.*	*Dollars.*	
20,613,738	10,835,791	7,458,701	2,801,832	60,072	37,428	1,887,335	29,302,016	
29,800	36,030	17,930	13,650	....	....	400	164,530	1
23,775	18,875	4,150	4,564	....	....	....	41,000	2
226,200	128,139	166,750	53,120	....	....	....	407,800	3
28,000	16,900	10,200	3,700	30	....	4,500	40,550	4
250,180	196,508	97,895	50,796	400	....	6,800	458,951	5
210,692	114,186	49,806	16,463	....	125	32,000	218,496	6
91,700	124,750	62,400	26,870	....	....	....	257,800	7
17,500	22,300	18,250	4,300	....	....	....	57,000	8
132,500	146,487	94,981	40,860	300	....	....	420,109	9
1,018,140	678,945	381,010	224,553	80	....	33,000	1,638,764	10
536,792	331,598	207,386	87,972	1,450	....	333,300	984,264	11
168,030	192,995	96,849	56,340	....	....	350	425,919	12
41,450	43,777	23,789	12,668	....	....	....	106,845	13
120,575	101,026	69,078	39,250	900	....	25	278,218	14
147,250	94,600	58,783	23,870	....	....	....	264,300	15
322,370	134,208	127,231	63,975	....	550	1,200	405,893	16
1,063,300	588,283	256,963	113,287	1,100	....	8,000	1,191,545	17
2,435,310	765,168	978,508	172,064	3,040	12,000	84,600	2,251,984	18
438,800	275,331	128,665	99,840	75	....	93,340	681,480	19
116,525	69,746	52,835	22,295	....	....	....	178,840	20
27,200	13,838	6,370	4,195	....	....	....	34,191	21
1,198,451	632,610	446,639	195,300	5,500	2,865	4,300	3,148,884	22
675	1,126	450	225	....	....	....	4,500	23
22,900	20,874	16,823	6,225	....	....	....	61,865	24
800	3,000	900	350	....	....	....	4,500	25
131,805	112,040	88,570	39,571	2,800	124	2,500	313,831	26
1,886,560	679,157	483,965	149,011	9,755	....	227,460	1,695,530	27
3,416,280	1,886,424	1,265,299	538,353	5,614	2,434	324,340	4,483,202	28
20,350	10,160	15,620	6,268	....	....	....	55,660	29
743,160	529,696	340,024	142,778	4,447	....	565,090	1,526,514	30
10,400	9,284	2,670	2,917	....	....	....	21,242	31
4,559,783	2,337,691	1,530,527	428,640	24,581	18,900	127,880	6,071,209	32
231,000	44,372	32,300	15,800	....	....	100	154,000	33
5,100	3,560	7,400	1,950	....	....	....	23,300	34
78,785	68,768	66,686	30,080	....	....	....	225,000	35
82,175	49,636	54,017	16,720	....	....	....	172,670	36
1,200	600	300	100	....	....	....	1,000	37
72,450	31,620	18,910	9,150	....	220	7,500	76,380	38
61,250	31,303	22,600	9,881	....	10	2,500	96,034	39
5,500	3,900	1,250	845	....	....	....	9,560	40
182,975	67,835	28,562	11,910	....	....	26,950	130,050	41
456,050	198,445	125,361	61,126	....	200	1,200	509,606	42

TABLE CIII.—*Manufactures: Special Statistics for Pri*

CHEESE, (FACTOR

	States and Territories.	men	Steam-engines.		Water-wheels.		All.
				Number.	Horse-power.	Number.	
	The United States	1,313	1,872	261	119	16	
1	Alabama						
2	Arizona						
3	Arkansas						
4	California						
5	Colorado						
6	Connecticut	7	10	1			
7	Dakota						
8	Delaware						
9	District of Columbia						
10	Florida						
11	Georgia						
12	Idaho						
13	Illinois	69	155	19	[illegible]		
14	Indiana	17					
15	Iowa	14	10	1			
16	Kansas	1					
17	Kentucky	4	22	2			
18	Louisiana						
19	Maine						
20	Maryland						
21	Massachusetts	23					
22	Michigan	30	30	6			
23	Minnesota	2	12	1			
24	Mississippi						
25	Missouri						
26	Montana						
27	Nebraska	5					
28	Nevada						
29	New Hampshire	2	5	1			
30	New Jersey	8			5	1	
31	New Mexico						
32	New York	818	1,026	160	74	11	2,93
33	North Carolina	3					
34	Ohio	195	317	45	40	4	
35	Oregon	1					
36	Pennsylvania	27	72	9			
37	Rhode Island						
38	South Carolina						
39	Tennessee						
40	Texas						
41	Utah						
42	Vermont	28	64	8			
43	Virginia	2					
44	Washington						
45	West Virginia						
46	Wisconsin	54	49	[illegible]			
47	Wyoming						

.E CIII.—*Manufactures: Special Statistics for Principal Industries*—1870—Cont'd.

CHEESE, (FACTORY.)

MATERIALS.			PRODUCTS.			MILCH COWS AND DAIRY PRODUCTS.*				
	Other materials.	All materials.	Cheese.	Other products.	All products.	Milch cows.	Butter.	Cheese.	Milk sold.	
...ns.	*Dolls.*	*Dollars.*	*Pounds.*	*Dolls.*	*Dollars.*	*Number.*	*Pounds.*	*Pounds.*	*Gallons.*	
,405	567,535	14,089,284	109,435,229	61,096	16,771,665	8,935,332	514,092,683	53,492,153	235,500,599	
....	......	......	......	......	......	170,640	3,213,753	2,732	104,657	1
....	......	......	......	......	......	938	800	14,500	4,800	2
....	......	......	......	......	......	128,959	2,753,931	2,119	31,350	3
....	......	......	......	......	......	164,093	7,969,744	3,395,074	3,693,021	4
,000	80	480	4,000	......	1,280	25,017	392,926	33,626	19,520	5
,410	962	27,400	231,700	......	38,024	98,889	6,716,007	2,031,194	6,253,250	6
....	......	......	......	......	......	4,151	209,735	1,850	......	7
....	......	......	......	......	......	24,082	1,171,963	315	758,603	8
....	......	......	......	......	......	657	4,495	......	126,077	9
....	......	......	......	......	......	61,922	100,989	25	3,002	10
....	......	......	......	......	......	231,310	4,499,572	4,292	109,139	11
....	......	......	......	......	......	4,171	111,480	4,464	11,250	12
,119	22,002	440,890	4,072,301	1,000	537,356	640,321	36,083,405	1,661,703	9,258,543	13
,625	293	11,686	107,680	......	16,076	393,736	22,915,385	283,807	936,983	14
,893	1,093	25,579	256,900	......	44,590	369,811	27,512,179	1,087,741	688,800	15
,000	......	1,500	15,000	......	2,700	123,440	5,622,758	226,607	196,662	16
,000	1,185	27,685	240,000	......	42,000	247,615	11,874,978	115,219	1,345,772	17
....	......	......	......	......	......	102,076	322,405	11,747	833,928	18
....	......	......	......	......	......	139,259	11,636,482	1,152,590	1,374,091	19
....	......	......	......	......	......	94,794	5,014,729	6,732	1,520,101	20
,238	13,451	281,768	1,885,436	......	321,900	114,771	6,559,161	2,245,873	15,284,057	21
,031	3,222	186,989	1,650,997	70	239,659	250,859	24,400,185	670,804	2,277,122	22
,500	75	4,525	37,500	......	5,850	121,467	9,522,010	233,977	208,130	23
....	......	......	......	......	......	173,899	2,613,521	3,099	17,052	24
,765	48	828	9,785	......	1,943	398,515	14,455,825	204,090	857,704	25
,000	28	328	2,000	......	800	12,432	408,080	25,603	105,186	26
,300	170	4,040	32,400	1,950	7,270	28,940	1,539,535	46,142	95,059	27
....	......	......	......	......	......	6,174	110,860	......	63,850	28
,000	90	3,690	23,250	......	4,650	90,583	5,965,080	849,118	2,332,884	29
,107	650	43,643	440,107	2,875	52,147	133,331	8,266,023	38,229	5,373,323	30
....	......	......	......	......	......	16,417	12,912	27,249	813	31
,176	403,402	10,372,598	78,006,048	20,471	12,164,065	1,350,661	107,147,526	22,769,964	135,775,919	32
,630	450	6,474	48,800	......	9,760	196,731	4,297,834	75,185	17,145	33
,503	60,410	1,875,711	15,984,390	450	2,287,804	654,390	50,266,372	8,169,486	22,275,344	34
,000	109	5,959	40,000	......	8,400	48,325	1,418,373	79,333	107,367	35
,369	33,027	205,367	1,647,467	33,780	268,702	706,437	60,834,644	1,145,209	14,411,729	36
....	......	......	......	......	......	18,806	941,199	81,976	1,944,044	37
....	......	......	......	......	......	98,693	1,461,980	169	241,815	38
....	......	......	......	......	......	243,197	9,571,069	142,240	415,786	39
....	......	......	......	......	......	428,048	3,712,747	34,342	62,771	40
....	......	......	......	......	......	17,563	310,335	69,608	11,240	41
,126	15,630	365,928	2,984,179	......	445,323	180,285	17,844,396	4,830,700	3,835,840	42
,300	100	1,500	12,500	......	2,310	188,471	6,979,269	71,741	266,812	43
....	......	......	......	......	......	16,938	407,306	17,465	21,060	44
....	......	......	......	......	......	104,434	5,044,475	32,429	144,895	45
,313	11,051	194,716	1,696,783	500	249,056	308,377	22,473,036	1,591,798	2,059,105	46
....	......	......	......	......	......	707	1,200	......	4,980	47

* From the Agricultural Tables.

TABLE CIII.—*Manufactures: Special Statistics for Principal Industries*—1870—Cont'd.

COTTON GOODS.

	States and Territories.	Establishments.	Steam-engines. Horse-power.	Steam-engines. Number.	Water-wheels. Horse-power.	Water-wheels. Number.	Machines. Looms.	Machines. Frame-spindles.	Machines. Mule-spindles.	Hands employed. All.	Hands employed. Males above 16.	Hands employed. Females above 15.	Hands employed. Youth.
	The United States.	956	47,117	448	99,191	1,240	157,310	3,694,477	3,437,938	135,369	42,790	69,637	22,942
1	Alabama	13	175	3	824	14	632	19,802	8,244	1,032	303	445	[illegible]
2	Arkansas	2	15	1	10	1	......	125	1,000	17	8	3	6
3	Connecticut	111	860	15	10,840	177	11,943	294,760	302,382	12,086	4,443	4,7[illegible]	[illegible]
4	Delaware	6	500	5	370	6	771	18,634	10,900	736	245	[illegible]	[illegible]
5	Georgia	34	290	4	2,920	50	1,887	74,148	11,454	2,846	1,147	1,0[illegible]	[illegible]
6	Illinois	5	47	3	90	2	16	1,856	......	98	26	31	[illegible]
7	Indiana	4	1,084	7	80	2	448	17,360	......	504	119	179	[illegible]
8	Iowa	1	6	1	......	......	......	......	......	6	3	3	......
9	Kentucky	5	330	5	60	1	72	7,060	674	209	77	71	[illegible]
10	Louisiana	4	255	4	......	......	292	10,200	2,884	246	123	57	[illegible]
11	Maine	23	390	2	8,018	85	9,902	230,594	200,178	9,439	2,606	6,2[illegible]	[illegible]
12	Maryland	22	1,510	8	1,991	21	1,947	82,212	6,900	2,860	698	1,4[illegible]	[illegible]
13	Massachusetts	191	17,217	111	32,310	335	55,343	1,255,532	1,363,980	43,512	13,694	24,06[illegible]	[illegible]
14	Mississippi	5	270	3	96	3	172	2,526	1,000	265	78	[illegible]	[illegible]
15	Missouri	3	375	3	......	......	415	16,015	700	361	107	12[illegible]	[illegible]
16	New Hampshire	36	915	7	17,777	94	19,091	447,795	302,048	12,542	3,732	[illegible]	[illegible]
17	New Jersey	27	1,799	15	1,260	22	2,176	107,542	93,038	3,514	1,086	1,7[illegible]	[illegible]
18	New York	81	4,898	40	5,202	82	17,218	131,380	361,193	9,144	2,608	4,5[illegible]	1,9[illegible]
19	North Carolina	33	120	3	1,533	34	618	37,957	1,940	1,453	258	[illegible]	[illegible]
20	Ohio	7	305	5	81	3	208	14,390	8,920	462	216	[illegible]	[illegible]
21	Pennsylvania	138	7,440	116	1,983	44	12,862	232,598	201,718	12,730	3,8[illegible]	6,0[illegible]	2,7[illegible]
22	Rhode Island	139	7,391	71	10,726	186	18,075	503,797	539,445	16,745	5,583	8,0[illegible]	3,1[illegible]
23	South Carolina	12	......	......	955	14	745	34,683	257	1,123	299	[illegible]	[illegible]
24	Tennessee	28	470	9	676	21	313	22,465	5,438	890	252	[illegible]	[illegible]
25	Texas	4	268	4	......	......	235	8,478	400	291	184	[illegible]	[illegible]
26	Utah	3	......	......	39	3	11	1,020	......	16	10	[illegible]	[illegible]
27	Vermont	8	50	1	600	12	628	16,532	12,230	451	125	[illegible]	[illegible]
28	Virginia	11	210	2	750	19	1,310	76,116	1,000	1,741	921	[illegible]	[illegible]

CARPETS, OTHER THAN RAG.

	States and Territories.	Establishments.	Steam-engines. Horse-power.	Steam-engines. Number.	Water-wheels. Horse-power.	Water-wheels. Number.	Machines. Combing-machines.	Machines. Cards, sets.	Machines. Hand-looms.	Machines. Power-looms.	Hands employed. All.	Hands employed. Males above 16.	Hands employed. Females above 15.	Hands employed. Youth.
	The United States.	215	3,017	45	702	18	100	211	3,975	1,451	12,098	6,898	4,316	[illegible]
1	Connecticut	3	800	8	......	......	31	22	50	247	1,185	451	514	[illegible]
2	District of Columbia	1	......	......	......	......	......	......	3	......	2	2	......	......
3	Maryland	1	......	......	15	1	......	1	12	......	12	8	2	2
4	Massachusetts	6	303	9	100	5	54	66	49	429	2,200	841	1,323	36
5	New Hampshire	3	1	......	200	1	6	9	20	21	170	72	79	19
6	New Jersey	2	30	1	120	2	......	17	30	24	147	76	43	[illegible]
7	New York	13	1,333	11	265	8	......	87	646	669	3,424	1,659	1,444	321
8	Pennsylvania	184	550	16	2	1	9	38	3,161	61	4,941	3,688	905	348
9	Wisconsin	2	......	......	......	......	......	1	4	......	17	11	6	......

.E CIII.—*Manufactures: Special Statistics for Principal Industries*—1870—Cont'd.

COTTON GOODS.

		MATERIALS.					PRODUCTS.		
	Wages.	Cotton.	Cotton-yarn.*	Cotton-waste.	Mill supplies.	All materials.	Sheetings, shirtings, and twilled goods.	Lawns and fine muslins.	
rs.	*Dollars.*	*Pounds.*	*Pounds.*	*Pounds.*	*Dollars.*	*Dollars.*	*Yards.*	*Yards.*	
291	39,044,132	398,308,257	6,222,189	5,234,260	10,910,672	111,736,936	478,204,513	34,533,462	
000	216,679	3,249,523	....	....	28,484	764,965	4,518,403	....	1
000	4,100	66,400	....	....	500	13,780	....	....	2
700	3,246,783	31,747,309	....	....	780,329	8,818,651	52,655,693	8,338,677	3
000	190,069	2,587,615	....	400,900	80,795	704,733	2,396,000	....	4
265	611,868	10,921,176	....	....	89,401	2,504,758	13,739,847	....	5
000	25,500	857,000	....	....	15,325	177,525	....	....	6
500	113,260	2,070,318	....	....	42,405	542,875	3,831,059	....	7
500	275	20,000	....	....	150	4,950	....	....	8
000	57,951	1,584,625	....	....	16,820	375,048	....	....	9
000	60,600	748,525	....	....	11,200	161,485	438,860	....	10
685	2,565,197	25,887,771	....	....	614,979	6,746,780	65,614,092	....	11
250	671,933	12,693,647	....	....	119,876	3,409,426	18,839,625	2,358,454	12
375	13,589,305	130,654,040	526,144	3,744,000	3,325,419	37,371,599	22,123,147	12,434,858	13
500	61,833	580,764	....	....	10,824	123,568	407,788	....	14
200	120,300	2,196,600	....	....	51,745	481,745	2,150,000	....	15
710	3,989,853	41,469,719	....	4,000	1,702,691	12,318,867	89,326,701	75,000	16
000	1,009,351	7,920,035	325,000	....	246,506	1,964,758	4,174,000	2,442,000	17
336	2,626,131	24,783,351	53,000	867,260	650,743	6,990,626	25,382,532	1,327,336	18
900	182,951	4,238,276	....	....	45,933	963,809	2,954,607	....	19
700	113,520	2,226,400	....	....	8,625	493,704	1,294,500	....	20
720	3,496,986	32,953,318	4,816,608	219,000	1,208,363	10,724,038	65,706,865	....	21
300	5,224,650	44,630,787	501,437	....	1,756,982	13,268,315	77,973,206	7,557,137	22
000	257,680	4,756,823	....	....	11,129	761,462	8,273,900	....	23
650	178,156	2,872,582	....	....	21,645	595,789	1,976,450	....	24
000	68,211	1,077,118	....	....	15,719	216,519	739,778	....	25
000	6,300	23,500	....	....	501	7,051	700	....	26
000	125,000	1,235,652	....	....	21,486	292,269	142,000	....	27
000	229,750	4,255,383	....	....	31,837	937,820	12,544,820	....	28

* Also *Cotton-Warps*: Pennsylvania, 136,100 pounds.

CARPETS, OTHER THAN RAG.

		MATERIALS.							
	Wages.	Cotton.	Cotton and linen yarns.	Jute or flax.	Wool.	Woolen yarn.	All other materials.	All materials.	
s.	*Dollars.*	*Pounds.*	*Pounds.*	*Pounds.*	*Pounds.*	*Pounds.*	*Dollars.*	*Dollars.*	
750	4,681,718	974,440	1,140,737	3,691,909	25,139,999	7,835,934	1,577,032	13,577,993	
000	432,031	....	....	1,800	2,691,038	....	413,077	1,307,397	1
400	600	....	500	....	....	1,600	562	1,747	2
000	5,080	....	....	....	21,000	....	1,000	7,300	3
000	832,954	250,040	413,330	961,974	10,813,264	....	476,848	3,256,628	4
000	55,730	....	....	....	615,428	....	48,068	226,288	5
000	60,412	....	....	....	297,367	....	24,197	111,497	6
750	1,423,784	402,000	....	1,500,000	8,401,332	....	372,583	3,046,863	7
500	1,870,527	321,900	726,907	1,228,135	2,299,320	7,834,354	240,420	5,619,448	8
100	600	500	....	....	1,250	....	175	825	9

TABLE CIII.—*Manufactures: Special Statistics for Principal Industries*—1870—Cont'd.

COTTON GOODS—Continued.

	States and Territories.	PRODUCTS—Continued.							
		Print cloth.	Yarn, not woven.	Spool-thread.	Warps.	Bats, wicking, and wadding.	Table-cloths, quilts, and counterpanes.	Seamless bags.	Cordage, lines, and twines.
		Yards.	*Pounds.*	*Dozens.*	*Yards.*	*Pounds.*	*No.*	*Number.*	*Pounds.*
	The United States	489, 250, 053	30, 301, 067	11, 560, 241	73, 018, 045	11, 118, 127	133, 892	2, 767, 060	5, 067, 45[illegible]
1	Alabama		548, 750	105, 724					33, 1[illegible]
2	Arkansas								
3	Connecticut	34, 279, 875	1, 281, 780	3, 397, 130	11, 367, 661	1, 232, 305		173, 900	1, 370, 7[illegible]
4	Delaware		1, 475, 600			171, 428			
5	Georgia		4, 097, 167			2, 696	10, 000		214, 3[illegible]
6	Illinois				1, 305, 000	330, 000			79, 00[illegible]
7	Indiana		74, 880		3, 600, 000	100, 000			
8	Iowa					18, 000			
9	Kentucky		637, 000		530, 000	131, 000		12, 230	6[illegible], 00[illegible]
10	Louisiana		112, 000	4, 000					5, 00[illegible]
11	Maine		490, 450		78, 000	265, 400	137, 629	933, 470	72, 0[illegible]
12	Maryland		1, 247		90, 55[illegible]		190, 000		325, 4[illegible]
13	Massachusetts	229, 613, 105	2, 108, 952	2, 595, 358	33, 712, 996	3, 773, 664	127, 424		924, 16[illegible]
14	Mississippi	1, 712	275, 461						
15	Missouri		1, 044, 000		14, 000	173, 000			147, 0[illegible]
16	New Hampshire	40, 843, 060	132, 200			277, 02[illegible]	850	1, 595, 700	[illegible]
17	New Jersey	11, 000, 000	1, 729, 075	1, 650, 000	3, 120, 950	219, 800			
18	New York	82, 335, 813	250, 076		5, 097, 000	1, 659, 170			[illegible] 79[illegible]
19	North Carolina		2, 180, 062		1, 486, 000	2, 000			
20	Ohio		957, 900		810, 000	121, 000			79, 00[illegible]
21	Pennsylvania	9, 704, 795	4, 510, 486		2, 944, 335	872, 56[illegible]	23, 020		121, 00[illegible]
22	Rhode Island	75, 183, 628	6, 155, 692	3, 311, 200	6, 281, 150	1, 367, 800	4, 969	50, 000	1, 165, 0[illegible]
23	South Carolina		808, 781		260, 000	150, 000			
24	Tennessee		1, 220, 098	466, 829		289, 650		1, 700	56, 0[illegible]
25	Texas		46, 175						100, 00[illegible]
26	Utah		21, 280			1, 575			
27	Vermont	6, 287, 136			2, 320, 400				
28	Virginia		132, 975						

CARPETS, OTHER THAN RAG—Concluded.

	States and Territories.	PRODUCTS.								
		Brussels.	Felt.	Ingrain, 2 and 3 ply.	Jute.	Tapestry.	Velvet.	Venetian.	All other products.	All products.
		Yards.	*Yards.*	*Yards.*	*Yards.*	*Yards.*	*Yards.*	*Yards.*	*Dolls.*	*Dollars.*
	The United States	806, 505	586, 000	16, 024, 711	500, 000	1, 711, 000	107, 000	1, 350, 017	670, 047	21, 761, 573
1	Connecticut	162, 505	29, 000	1, 519, 045						2, 027, 136
2	Dist. of Columbia			1, 273					1, 000	2, 600
3	Maryland			10, 000				5, 000		11, 00[illegible]
4	Massachusetts	514, 000		1, 969, 560		811, 000	17, 000		180, 000	4, 187, 52[illegible]
5	New Hampshire			113, 600					179, 800	299, 70[illegible]
6	New Jersey			118, 720					62, 706	193, 6[illegible]
7	New York	100, 000	500, 000	2, 805, 288		900, 000	90, 000	30, 000	36, 544	4, 976, 8[illegible]
8	Pennsylvania		57, 000	10, 385, 725	500, 000			1, 315, 017	209, 997	9, 758, 171
9	Wisconsin			1, 500						1, 7[illegible]

TABLE CIII.—*Manufactures: Special Statistics for Principal Industries*—1870—Cont'd.

COTTON GOODS—Continued.

PRODUCTS—Continued.										
Flannel.	Thread.	Ginghams and checks.	Cotton-waste.	Tape and webbing.	Seamless bags.	Cassimeres, cottonades, and jeans.	Other products.	All products.		
Yards.	*Pounds.*	*Yards.*	*Pounds.*	*Pounds.*	*Pounds.*	*Yards.*	*Pounds.*	*Pounds.*	*Dollars.*	
8, 390, 050	906, 068	39, 275, 244	7, 921, 449	484, 400	405, 585	13, 940, 895	10, 811, 028	349, 314, 592	177, 489, 739	
		1, 039, 321					12, 000	2, 843, 000	1, 088, 767	1
	53, 125							53, 125	22, 562	2
		1, 671, 309	510, 717	430, 400	175, 585		111, 786	27, 296, 710	14, 026, 334	3
		306, 600					420, 400	2, 437, 649	1, 060, 898	4
	421, 416	1, 653, 434					4, 000	9, 596, 800	3, 648, 973	5
					185, 000			739, 000	279, 000	6
							113, 337	1, 779, 481	778, 047	7
								18, 000	7, 000	8
								1, 389, 000	498, 960	9
		926, 000						629, 025	251, 550	10
						1, 889, 600	844, 000	23, 627, 155	11, 844, 181	11
		564, 240					4, 900	10, 496, 677	4, 852, 808	12
6, 864, 954	407, 527	13, 690, 000	6, 610, 160	54, 000			1, 233, 057	113, 803, 458	59, 493, 153	13
		206, 202					2, 892	529, 573	234, 445	14
					45, 000		2, 900	1, 949, 900	798, 050	15
442, 696		1, 845, 199				5, 260, 000		35, 003, 432	16, 999, 672	16
		880, 000	662, 145				300, 000	6, 723, 748	4, 015, 768	17
			25, 927			1, 500, 000	635, 253	22, 113, 630	11, 178, 211	18
	24, 000							3, 444, 166	1, 345, 052	19
			112, 500					1, 918, 000	681, 835	20
1, 082, 400		15, 101, 170				5, 288, 795	608, 410	32, 494, 857	17, 490, 080	21
							6, 516, 386	38, 503, 000	22, 049, 203	22
								4, 125, 210	1, 529, 937	23
						2, 500	2, 007	2, 381, 477	941, 542	24
		1, 261, 769					600	887, 695	374, 598	25
								23, 195	16, 803	26
								1, 051, 000	546, 510	27
		130, 000						3, 456, 569	1, 435, 800	28

TABLE CIII.—*Manufactures: Special Statistics for Principal Industries*—1870—Cont'd.

FLOURING AND GRIST MILL PRODUCTS.

	States and Territories.	Establishments.	Steam-engines. Horse-power.	Steam-engines. Number.	Water-wheels. Horse-power.	Water-wheels. Number.	Runs of stone.	Daily capacity.	All hands employed.	Capital.	Wages.
							No.	*Bushels.*	*No.*	*Dollars.*	*Dollars.*
	The United States.	22,573	168,736	5,383	407,950	21,213	48,051	3,271,128	58,448	151,565,376	14,577,53[illegible]
1	Alabama	613	2,560	120	7,740	554	925	42,174	1,208	1,191,856	177,5[illegible]
2	Arizona	2	25	1	10	1	3	160	22	20,000	15,8[illegible]
3	Arkansas	272	2,537	111	1,186	99	357	18,497	607	477,151	67,2[illegible]
4	California	115	3,406	77	1,874	50	311	51,794	690	2,590,400	384,9[illegible]
5	Colorado	20	117	6	521	17	48	4,735	54	185,700	34,5[illegible]
6	Connecticut	276	420	8	6,251	312	573	32,878	502	1,165,358	128,3[illegible]
7	Dakota	2	......	......	31	4	5	400	5	13,000	2,450
8	Delaware	103	302	11	1,923	108	248	13,088	277	777,554	60,874
9	District of Columbia.	9	......	......	1,010	11	48	6,280	70	655,000	34,310
10	Florida	138	578	46	361	64	162	6,532	247	119,075	23,751
11	Georgia	1,097	2,246	104	17,887	1,227	1,776	82,333	2,356	3,103,918	337,864
12	Idaho	3	......	......	85	6	4	850	10	72,000	6,800
13	Illinois	941	28,877	726	8,963	368	2,420	321,533	4,457	14,826,562	1,861,47[illegible]
14	Indiana	962	16,676	524	13,667	630	2,381	194,336	3,214	8,515,627	896,717
15	Iowa	502	7,236	195	10,172	542	1,137	121,666	1,867	5,765,758	605,865
16	Kansas	106	1,880	62	1,172	39	213	21,152	413	1,036,800	171,916
17	Kentucky	696	9,019	314	5,197	321	1,166	82,560	1,686	2,660,968	325,247
18	Louisiana	248	1,133	31	100	16	254	11,840	526	270,781	31,15[illegible]
19	Maine	265	200	6	8,191	395	635	40,587	550	944,350	115,30[illegible]
20	Maryland	518	892	30	9,815	511	1,129	50,963	1,101	2,790,700	178,73[illegible]
21	Massachusetts	316	1,810	32	9,013	390	522	70,224	855	2,171,314	271,248
22	Michigan	516	6,274	156	18,036	719	1,366	152,112	1,938	6,902,675	646,504
23	Minnesota	216	1,087	38	7,694	281	507	61,314	790	2,900,915	293,0[illegible]
24	Mississippi	363	2,751	133	1,872	166	469	26,376	710	636,813	85,6[illegible]
25	Missouri	804	16,471	478	4,341	257	1,529	154,591	3,160	8,913,842	1,105,980
26	Montana	8	......	......	203	8	14	830	26	122,000	25,100
27	Nebraska	60	610	19	1,088	49	110	10,016	183	591,900	72,016
28	Nevada	7	70	4	55	3	13	1,062	18	47,200	4,350
29	New Hampshire	195	320	7	6,853	389	454	25,221	388	669,340	74,914
30	New Jersey	486	1,520	27	11,108	524	1,312	75,734	1,310	4,466,400	346,2[illegible]
31	New Mexico	36	47	4	420	30	45	2,574	80	222,550	34,111
32	New York	1,610	6,338	199	57,223	2,389	4,668	386,510	5,193	20,936,[illegible]	1,687,234
33	North Carolina	1,415	1,500	74	18,739	1,351	2,288	83,791	2,660	2,564,520	244,813
34	Ohio	1,396	18,834	588	26,564	1,181	3,567	231,490	3,932	11,334,932	965,72[illegible]
35	Oregon	64	216	6	2,108	64	130	18,562	165	1,116,825	90,431
36	Pennsylvania	2,985	13,733	572	60,192	3,280	8,019	343,495	6,427	20,393,620	1,272,146
37	Rhode Island	66	253	12	1,199	51	95	7,823	143	188,430	29,006
38	South Carolina	624	1,242	79	7,209	537	963	36,116	1,138	835,814	109,3[illegible]
39	Tennessee	1,058	4,641	184	12,150	885	1,702	90,394	2,218	2,891,484	322,331
40	Texas	533	4,686	230	1,219	85	696	35,065	1,124	1,066,893	136,353
41	Utah	74	......	......	990	77	108	7,009	130	430,408	44,9[illegible]
42	Vermont	220	336	9	8,386	436	600	41,139	500	1,231,050	103,2[illegible]
43	Virginia	1,556	739	35	29,546	1,644	2,749	121,751	2,592	5,324,846	346,8[illegible]
44	Washington	20	45	2	560	19	28	1,539	37	188,300	15,270
45	West Virginia	476	2,071	92	6,719	436	828	34,493	770	1,539,257	94,61[illegible]
46	Wisconsin	581	4,939	89	18,275	669	1,412	149,230	2,031	6,574,650	668,847

The construction of the above table is wholly peculiar, as respects the relation between materials and products. This peculiarity of form is due to the desire of the Superintendent to exhibit the flouring interest proper of the country distinct from the custom-work of the ordinary "grist-mill." In reading this table it needs to be borne in mind that while the amount of grain specified under the head of materials embraces all that was ground for individual owners, as well as what was ground on the venture of the proprietors of mills, the amounts of flour, meal, &c., enumerated in the product only embrace the production of flouring as distinguished from grist mills. The difference between the amount of grain (of the several kinds) which would be required to produce the amounts of the several kinds of flour, meal, &c., specified in the product, and the total amount of grain actually reported under the head of materials, yields the quantity ground for individual owners. The statements respectively of the total value of materials and of the total value of the product include *all* grain ground, whether as custom-work or on personal venture, and, again, all flour, meal, &c., produced, whether for individual owners or otherwise. The table has been annotated according to this statement, but it has been apprehended that in a hasty use of the figures the caution conveyed by the notes might be overlooked. To repeat: The amount of grain specified under the head of materials includes all the work of all the grist and flouring mills returned in the census, and the value given is the value of all the materials consumed.

TABLE CIII.—*Manufactures: Special Statistics for Principal Industries*—1870—Cont'd.

FLOURING AND GRIST MILL PRODUCTS.

MATERIALS.				PRODUCTS.						
Grain.		Mill supplies.	All materials.	Buckwheat-flour.*	Rye-flour.*	Wheat-flour.*	Corn-meal.*	Feed.*	All products.	
Bushels.	*Dollars.*	*Dollars.*	*Dollars.*	*Cwt.*	*Bbls.*	*Barrels.*	*Bushels.*	*Cwt.*	*Dollars.*	
366, 548, 969	362, 314, 526	5, 077, 596	367, 392, 122	404, 461	444, 251	32, 079, 144	31, 193, 962	29, 407, 465	444, 985, 143	
3, 298, 848	3, 985, 523	3, 818	3, 989, 341	......	......	36, 780	630, 289	27, 994	4, 827, 470	1
28, 000	48, 100	....	48, 100	......	......	4, 726	600	3, 400	75, 000	2
1, 393, 617	1, 380, 153	2, 130	1, 382, 283	......	......	14, 064	61, 115	8, 751	1, 670, 416	3
8, 127, 131	7, 090, 541	314, 410	7, 404, 951	152	1, 429	1, 193, 288	119, 094	1, 344, 710	9, 036, 386	4
344, 787	439, 706	1, 210	440, 916	......	......	52, 670	14, 425	28, 409	616, 856	5
3, 231, 717	3, 348, 444	4, 520	3, 352, 964	3, 447	9, 588	50, 850	1, 189, 872	204, 829	3, 966, 328	6
75, 000	60, 600	....	60, 600	......	......	7, 800	500	6, 360	80, 990	7
1, 600, 682	1, 739, 662	7, 188	1, 746, 850	......	110	136, 110	413, 290	93, 109	2, 067, 401	8
903, 522	1, 286, 100	....	1, 286, 100	......	733	191, 982	47, 378	106, 471	1, 543, 576	9
396, 458	410, 266	1, 591	411, 857	......	......	12	16, 670	300	508, 388	10
7, 173, 693	9, 163, 040	26, 538	9, 189, 578	......	10	228, 035	933, 994	107, 956	11, 202, 029	11
84, 200	162, 500	....	162, 500	......	......	14, 000	4, 200	13, 682	211, 010	12
38, 178, 736	34, 489, 217	941, 499	35, 430, 716	5, 663	46, 756	5, 131, 587	2, 119, 642	3, 232, 039	43, 876, 775	13
21, 425, 856	20, 144, 958	457, 273	20, 602, 231	7, 475	3, 021	2, 455, 632	1, 145, 446	1, 481, 494	25, 371, 322	14
17, 623, 604	11, 760, 989	200, 455	11, 961, 444	10, 360	9, 702	1, 342, 912	586, 235	853, 468	15, 635, 345	15
2, 667, 331	2, 244, 384	14, 574	2, 258, 958	540	4, 754	255, 477	296, 160	141, 865	2, 938, 215	16
7, 231, 617	6, 327, 734	101, 500	6, 429, 234	......	3, 165	465, 698	772, 804	278, 607	7, 886, 734	17
578, 103	602, 052	5, 812	607, 864	......	......	....	425, 843	....	726, 287	18
3, 419, 233	3, 833, 080	4, 290	3, 837, 370	960	640	78, 241	1, 263, 686	70, 814	4, 415, 998	19
5, 131, 288	5, 794, 475	33, 996	5, 828, 471	9, 331	6, 542	500, 324	203, 781	315, 531	6, 786, 459	20
7, 804, 878	8, 743, 924	25, 002	8, 768, 926	7, 135	55, 168	132, 359	4, 539, 527	343, 360	9, 720, 374	21
16, 891, 910	17, 658, 718	262, 777	17, 921, 495	10, 956	3, 759	963, 101	610, 103	1, 508, 180	21, 174, 247	22
8, 226, 852	6, 070, 540	19, 466	6, 090, 006	1, 453	525	895, 410	52, 749	451, 306	7, 534, 575	23
1, 585, 704	1, 708, 157	8, 133	1, 716, 290	......	......	4, 870	149, 269	16, 489	2, 053, 567	24
24, 255, 846	23, 693, 114	1, 198, 104	24, 891, 218	1, 410	4, 097	3, 182, 309	2, 389, 692	2, 088, 227	31, 837, 352	25
200, 630	366, 070	220	366, 290	......	500	26, 693	50	6, 687	480, 859	26
1, 507, 843	1, 057, 267	52, 232	1, 109, 499	1, 694	165	150, 513	25, 280	94, 204	1, 516, 150	27
73, 550	80, 100	....	80, 100	......	......	8, 036	2, 420	7, 606	97, 920	28
2, 113, 762	2, 495, 209	845	2, 496, 054	60	400	16, 540	528, 670	31, 540	2, 747, 973	29
10, 276, 682	10, 627, 486	7, 156	10, 634, 642	36, 163	33, 355	500, 905	1, 634, 829	1, 204, 628	12, 593, 148	30
358, 810	437, 131	4, 396	441, 527	......	......	42, 122	27, 015	35, 786	725, 292	31
45, 663, 123	50, 329, 077	277, 327	50, 606, 404	185, 440	133, 273	4, 235, 144	4, 207, 375	5, 032, 298	60, 237, 220	32
5, 522, 936	6, 430, 058	5, 052	6, 435, 110	160	396	55, 584	430, 229	58, 045	7, 583, 133	33
25, 541, 270	26, 095, 838	402, 939	26, 498, 777	15, 710	17, 115	3, 073, 473	1, 107, 661	2, 895, 727	31, 692, 210	34
1, 849, 623	1, 274, 286	8, 201	1, 282, 487	3	15	325, 496	6, 595	195, 007	1, 972, 444	35
40, 755, 503	41, 644, 132	119, 123	41, 763, 255	71, 691	78, 028	2, 518, 495	1, 710, 768	3, 680, 253	49, 476, 246	36
1, 288, 398	1, 486, 558	33, 269	1, 519, 827	......	167	65, 240	626, 314	44, 537	1, 728, 704	37
2, 003, 513	2, 658, 071	5, 352	2, 663, 423	......	187	22, 699	179, 014	13, 587	3, 180, 247	38
9, 385, 700	8, 684, 899	108, 162	8, 793, 061	74	175	443, 611	841, 736	388, 688	10, 767, 388	39
2, 236, 634	1, 858, 079	17, 226	1, 875, 305	......	85	11, 305	152, 824	5, 975	2, 421, 047	40
517, 288	582, 955	....	582, 955	......	......	10, 482	1, 600	14, 022	782, 846	41
3, 060, 427	3, 323, 504	9, 940	3, 333, 444	6, 733	4, 223	80, 257	535, 902	68, 425	3, 895, 058	42
9, 945, 828	10, 469, 199	35, 453	10, 504, 652	787	2, 197	583, 325	833, 557	307, 492	12, 649, 276	43
287, 957	214, 038	3, 040	217, 078	8	......	47, 014	4, 315	22, 654	321, 103	44
3, 084, 525	3, 291, 356	1, 234	3, 292, 590	5, 990	5, 157	241, 208	145, 966	47, 108	3, 933, 902	45
19, 196, 354	16, 723, 236	352, 143	17, 075, 379	21, 066	18, 214	2, 282, 745	205, 498	1, 925, 845	20, 419, 877	46

NOTE.—In addition to the above products, California produced 243,700 bushels barley-meal; Maine, 14,282; Michigan, 3,375; New Jersey, 16,000; New York, 22,795; Ohio, 36,220; Utah, 400; Wisconsin, ,080. Of hominy, Florida produced 3,000 bushels; Indiana, 41,230; Maryland, 22,110; New Jersey, 0,000; New York, 326,400; North Carolina, 31,200; Ohio, 40,790.

Excluding flour, meal, &c., from grain ground for individual owners.

On the other hand, the amounts of the several kinds of flour, meal, &c., specified in the product only embrace the production of mills grinding for market; but the value given in the product covers the production of both classes of establishments. No such distinction as the above was attempted in the publications of the census of 1860, and the values given, both for materials and products, therefore, embrace both classes of establishments. The fact that in a few States and Territories the number of mills exceeds the aggregate number of steam-engines and water-wheels returned, is due, firstly, to the use of wind-mills in some sections and the employment of horses for power in others; and, secondly, to the fact that in some of the Southern States a cane-mill and a grist-mill frequently take their power from the same wheel. The latter is very generally the case in Louisiana. In South Carolina 22 flour-mills are returned as operated by horse-power; in Texas, 50 mills are returned as driven by horses, 17 by oxen, and 5 by wind. In addition to the products specified in the table, New York is returned as producing 1,550 bushels oat-meal, New Jersey 100,000 bushels, Vermont 8,500 bushels, Wisconsin 2,400 bushels.

TABLE CIII.—*Manufactures: Special Statistics for Principal Industries* 1870—Cont'd.

HOSIERY.

	States.	Establishments.	Steam-engines: Horse-power.	Steam-engines: Number.	Water-wheels: Horse-power.	Water-wheels: Number.	Machines: Sets cards.	Machines: Knitting-looms.	Machines: Knitting-machines.	Machines: Sewing-machines.	Machines: Spindles.	Hands employed: All.	Hands employed: Males above 16.	Hands employed: Females above 15.	Hands employed: Youth.
	The United States	248	2,223	81	4,275	124	519	438	5,625	1,668	148,385	14,788	4,252	7,993	[illegible]
1	Connecticut	14	367	7	193	12	70	9	436	293	18,050	1,333	364	731	[illegible]
2	Illinois	3	......	...	......	....	1	....	19	1	12	27	4	21	2
3	Indiana	5	......	...	......	....	....	....	9	1	......	26	7	18	1
4	Iowa	2	......	...	......	....	....	....	......	......	......	6	3	3	...
5	Maryland	1	......	...	......	....	....	....	2	......	......	3	2	1	...
6	Massachusetts	32	408	13	718	18	79	180	1,116	312	19,331	2,415	844	1,404	167
7	Minnesota	1	......	...	......	....	....	1	......	......	......	1	1	...	...
8	Missouri	7	......	...	......	....	....	....	33	......	......	61	19	41	1
9	New Hampshire	28	12	1	868	31	58	20	832	102	17,175	1,081	344	624	113
10	New Jersey	4	235	2	75	2	13	147	11	138	6,480	722	136	571	[illegible]
11	New York	60	376	14	2,220	52	230	20	746	620	49,441	3,741	1,061	1,890	[illegible]
12	Ohio	5	......	...	......	....	....	10	7	......	......	22	16	6	...
13	Pennsylvania	76	825	44	......	....	39	46	2,332	148	9,796	4,899	1,325	2,672	[illegible]
14	Rhode Island	3	......	...	42	2	6	5	33	......	1,800	120	37	64	19
15	Vermont	7	......	...	150	7	23	....	49	53	26,300	331	89	216	[illegible]

INDIA-RUBBER AND ELASTIC GOODS.

	States.	Establishments.	Steam-engines: Horse-power.	Steam-engines: Number.	Water-wheels: Horse-power.	Water-wheels: Number.	Machines: Looms.	Machines: Spindles.	Hands employed: All.	Hands employed: Males above 16.	Hands employed: Females above 15.	Hands employed: Youth.
							No.	No.				
	The United States	56	4,412	49	1,864	35	663	4,100	6,025	3,030	2,649	3[illegible]
1	Connecticut	13	1,183	11	981	16	294	4,100	1,946	980	931	[illegible]
2	Maine	1	......	....	......	....	....	......	9	1	6	[illegible]
3	Massachusetts	16	698	10	255	6	369	......	1,405	492	818	[illegible]
4	Missouri	1	......	....	......	....	....	......	4	2	2	...
5	New Jersey	12	936	13	80	6	....	......	807	456	287	[illegible]
6	New York	10	845	9	548	7	....	......	1,008	643	330	[illegible]
7	Pennsylvania	1	......	....	......	....	....	......	1	1	......	...
8	Rhode Island	2	750	6	......	....	....	......	845	455	275	1[illegible]

TABLE CIII.—*Manufactures: Special Statistics for Principal Industries*—1870—Cont'd.

HOSIERY.

Capital.	Wages.	Materials. Cotton.	Cotton yarn.	Domestic wool.	Foreign wool.	Shoddy.	Woolen yarn.	All other materials.	All materials.	
Dollars.	*Dollars.*	*Pounds.*	*Pounds.*	*Pounds.*	*Pounds.*	*Pounds.*	*Pounds.*	*Dollars.*	*Dollars.*	
[illegible], 931, 260	4, 429, 085	11, 463, 503	2, 188, 722	5, 304, 655	292, 300	189, 857	2, 229, 777	1, 110, 909	9, 835, 823	
[illegible], 159, 700	431, 089	791, 673	31, 250	362, 794	76, 000	10, 000	66, 063	126, 015	625, 391	1
1, 800	1, 800	....	100	600	....	....	5, 100	....	5, 775	2
4, 050	540	....	....	....	....	....	2, 575	325	2, 842	3
5, 200	1, 200	....	600	....	....	....	300	350	1, 510	4
100	....	....	500	....	....	....	500	....	760	5
1, 570, 500	848, 864	1, 350, 100	499, 894	879, 900	25, 000	....	249, 356	151, 917	1, 515, 326	6
150	....	....	....	....	....	....	200	....	200	7
15, 700	15, 600	....	15, 600	....	....	....	24, 400	2, 350	27, 040	8
855, 400	405, 003	905, 500	40, 735	840, 250	40, 500	....	....	143, 863	881, 646	9
575, 500	193, 200	214, 200	2, 500	230, 000	....	....	1, 000	40, 570	188, 030	10
3, 318, 700	1, 122, 890	7, 019, 839	100, 000	2, 018, 022	150, 800	179, 857	50, 500	524, 420	3, 391, 840	11
9, 400	5, 250	....	....	....	....	....	10, 600	....	10, 360	12
2, 979, 000	1, 280, 270	797, 400	1, 467, 543	713, 800	....	....	1, 819, 183	87, 208	2, 925, 323	13
133, 000	33, 200	....	30, 000	113, 000	....	....	....	6, 341	68, 541	14
303, 000	90, 179	384, 789	....	146, 289	....	....	....	27, 633	191, 219	15

INDIA-RUBBER AND ELASTIC GOODS.

Capital.	Wages.	Materials. Cloth.	Cotton.	Rubber.	Silk.	Yarn.	All other materials.	All materials.	
Dollars.	*Dollars.*	*Yards.*	*Pounds.*	*Pounds.*	*Pounds.*	*Pounds.*	*Dollars.*	*Dollars.*	
7, 486, 600	2, 559, 877	2, 934, 575	2, 391, 451	8, 433, 320	2, 990	294, 418	1, 003, 793	7, 434, 742	
2, 345, 000	761, 434	325, 500	2, 201, 950	2, 473, 902	....	39, 000	592, 889	2, 355, 488	1
4, 000	2, 200	....	....	....	....	....	20, 425	20, 425	2
1, 920, 600	580, 723	372, 300	126, 501	1, 038, 393	1, 490	255, 418	100, 739	1, 534, 006	3
2, 000	800	....	....	....	....	....	1, 500	1, 500	4
1, 034, 200	346, 638	761, 377	2, 000	1, 260, 795	....	....	142, 054	1, 284, 967	5
1, 777, 000	489, 500	951, 490	61, 000	2, 745, 470	1, 500	....	58, 096	1, 316, 803	6
800	....	....	....	....	....	....	500	500	7
403. 000	378, 582	523, 908	....	894, 760	....	....	127, 590	901, 053	8

TABLE CIII.—*Manufactures: Special Statistics for Principal Industries*—1870—Cont'd.

HOSIERY—Concluded.

	States.	PRODUCTS.								
		Cotton hose and half hose.	Shirts, drawers, and jackets.	Gloves and mittens.	Opera hoods and scarfs.	Shawls.	Stockinet.	Woolen and mixed hose and half hose.	All other products.	All products.
		Doz. pairs.	*Dozen.*	*Pairs.*	*Dozen.*	*Dozen*	*Yards.*	*Doz. p'rs.*	*Dolls.*	*Dollars.*
	The United States	1, 299, 342	1, 132, 189	206, 800	426, 749	14, 947	289, 372	2, 970, 170	369, 784	18, 411, 564
1	Connecticut	....	102, 461	......	......	......	111, 562	62, 253	5, 700	1, 251, 742
2	Illinois	....	....	......	......	......	......	1, 800	......	8, 800
3	Indiana	....	18	500	......	......	......	1, 118	750	5, 450
4	Iowa	....	....	......	......	......	......	80	2, 327	2, 887
5	Maryland	....	....	......	......	......	......	333	......	1, 000
6	Massachusetts	387, 985	77, 751	140, 400	......	......	148, 210	586, 287	225, 336	3, 213, 461
7	Minnesota	....	....	......	......	......	......	50	......	500
8	Missouri	....	1, 120	......	......	......	......	27, 165	2, 350	54, 650
9	New Hampshire	185, 760	4, 250	1, 500	......	......	......	617, 700	770	1, 757, 445
10	New Jersey	20, 000	42, 500	......	......	......	......	22, 500	......	568, 900
11	New York	....	794, 213	6, 000	700	......	......	170, 427	30, 150	5, 522, 742
12	Ohio	....	....	......	......	......	......	17, 800	......	23, 100
13	Pennsylvania	705, 597	49, 876	58, 400	418, 349	13, 167	100	1, 459, 536	87, 401	5, 306, 738
14	Rhode Island	....	500	......	7, 700	1, 780	29, 500	....	15, 000	137, 000
15	Vermont	....	50, 500	......	......	......	......	3, 121	......	551, 129

INDIA-RUBBER AND ELASTIC GOODS—Concluded.

	States.	PRODUCTS.								
		Belting and hose.	Boots and shoes.	Car-springs.	Coats.	Fabrics.	Packing.	Suspenders.	All other products.	All products.
		Pounds.	*Pairs.*	*Pounds.*	*No.*	*Yards.*	*Lbs.*	*Dozen.*	*Dollars.*	*Dollars.*
	The United States	906, 000	5, 402, 666	1, 250, 000	30, 000	1, 256, 687	91, 127	552, 500	5, 140, 691	14, 566, 374
1	Connecticut	......	2, 155, 120	......	......	......	......	294, 400	1, 325, 552	4, 239, 329
2	Maine	......	......	......	......	......	......	9, 000	......	31, 500
3	Massachusetts	......	1, 127, 700	......	......	692, 187	......	172, 600	688, 076	3, 183, 218
4	Missouri	......	......	......	......	......	......	1, 500	......	4, 500
5	New Jersey	......	1, 070, 102	......	30, 000	64, 500	......	......	1, 067, 538	2, 224, 839
6	New York	906, 000	150, 000	1, 250, 000	......	500, 000	91, 127	75, 000	1, 205, 001	3, 076, 720
7	Pennsylvania	......	......	......	......	......	......	......	1, 400	1, 400
8	Rhode Island	......	899, 744	......	......	......	......	......	853, 124	1, 804, 86[illegible]

TABLE CIII.—*Manufactures: Special Statistics for Principal Industries*—1870—Cont'd.

IRON BLOOMS.

States.	Establishments.	Steam-engines.		Water-wheels.		Hands employed.			
		Horse-power.	Number.	Horse-power.	Number.	All.	Males above 16.	Females above 15.	Youth.
The United States	82	2,710	31	3,174	84	2,902	2,819	2	81
Kentucky	1	80	2	....	......	50	50	......	......
Massachusetts	1	....	......	40	3	7	7	......	......
Mississippi	1	....	......	10	1	5	5	......	......
Missouri	1	....	......	33	2	132	132	......	......
New Jersey	1	....	......	....	......	6	6	......	......
New York	22	245	5	1,380	32	1,020	998	......	22
North Carolina	2	80	1	20	1	15	15	......	......
Ohio	1	50	1	....	......	18	18	......	......
Pennsylvania	43	2,145	21	1,563	36	1,473	1,422	2	49
South Carolina	2	....	......	22	1	9	9	......	......
Tennessee	2	60	1	20	1	26	26	......	......
Virginia	5	50	......	86	7	141	131	......	10

IRON BLOOMS—Continued.

States.	Capital.	Wages.	Materials.					
			Iron-ore.		Pig-iron.		Scrap-iron.	
	Dollars.	*Dollars.*	*Tons.*	*Dollars.*	*Tons.*	*Dollars.*	*Tons.*	*Dollars.*
The United States	4,506,733	1,195,964	45,168	382,533	100,881	3,795,030	14,695	488,950
Kentucky	100,000	37,500	....	....	900	32,200	300	12,000
Massachusetts	6,000	3,000	....	....	....	....	300	9,600
Mississippi	5,000	750	....	....	65	1,500	....	....
Missouri	44,000	38,250	....	....	1,600	64,000	....	....
New Jersey	15,000	2,500	....	....	400	16,500	....	....
New York	1,614,883	358,135	35,544	274,092	12,859	499,150	11,000	330,000
North Carolina	36,000	2,800	558	2,326	....	....	....	....
Ohio	10,000	8,500	....	....	1,050	37,750	....	....
Pennsylvania	2,446,600	707,589	9,036	105,950	80,725	3,012,610	3,095	137,350
South Carolina	12,000	1,106	....	....	147	5,880	....	....
Tennessee	91,750	1,700	30	165	240	10,000	....	....
Virginia	125,500	34,140	....	....	2,895	115,460	....	....

IRON BLOOMS—Continued.

States.	Materials—Continued.						Products.	
	Charcoal.		Coal.		All other materials.	All materials.	Blooms.	All products.
	Bushels.	*Dollars.*	*Tons.*	*Dollars.*	*Dollars.*	*Dollars.*	*Tons.*	*Dollars.*
The United States	6,898,447	602,689	143,496	379,904	36,340	5,685,466	110,808	7,647,054
Kentucky	27,000	2,000	1,500	7,000	500	53,700	1,054	94,860
Massachusetts	15,000	1,500	....	....	100	11,200	250	17,000
Mississippi	....	....	10	80	....	1,585	60	3,000
Missouri	....	....	3,937	22,750	1,250	88,000	1,500	140,000
New Jersey	50,000	5,800	....	....	....	22,300	300	25,000
New York	4,427,918	392,387	32,463	113,935	16,680	1,626,264	36,016	2,171,166
North Carolina	78,500	3,325	....	....	1,050	6,701	150	11,822
Ohio	70,000	4,900	500	1,000	100	43,750	700	56,000
Pennsylvania	1,908,308	176,841	105,000	234,429	16,120	3,683,300	68,238	4,881,431
South Carolina	23,400	1,150	....	....	....	7,030	133	8,475
Tennessee	16,640	1,856	....	....	540	12,561	175	[illegible]
Virginia	191,681	12,930	86	690	....	[illegible]	[illegible]	[illegible]

TABLE CIII.—*Manufactures: Special Statistics for Principal Industries*—1870—Cont

IRON, ROLLED.

	States.	Establishments.	Steam-engines. Horse-power.	Steam-engines. Number.	Water-wheels. Horse-power.	Water-wheels. Number.	All hands.	Capital.	Wages.	Materials. Pig-iron.	
								Dollars.	*Dollars.*	*Tons.*	*Doll*
	The United States..	310	80, 958	744	8, 126	162	44, 662	54, 774, 615	25, 192, 635	1, 123, 707	38, 7
1	Alabama	1	500	3	......	....	14	3, 000	1, 800	350	1
2	California	2	225	3	......	....	129	381, 470	78, 511	....	....
3	Connecticut	5	685	6	50	6	235	245, 000	149, 751	50	
4	Delaware	4	660	11	65	1	275	512, 200	157, 000	6, 600	2
5	Georgia	2	470	5	......	....	225	195, 860	163, 766	10, 550	3
6	Illinois	6	3, 675	22	......	....	1, 582	2, 245, 000	984, 022	15, 618	5
7	Indiana	8	3, 215	41	......	....	977	1, 576, 000	521, 672	22, 326	8
8	Kentucky	6	1, 450	24	......	....	876	1, 125, 000	582, 283	20, 534	7
9	Maine	3	680	8	120	4	438	520, 000	262, 958	10, 314	3
10	Maryland	7	1, 332	23	460	15	1, 444	983, 000	709, 922	27, 645	6
11	Massachusetts	19	4, 910	38	615	25	2, 274	2, 378, 000	1, 140, 475	57, 303	2, 3
12	Michigan	1	1, 900	10	......	....	433	672, 600	221, 764	....	....
13	Missouri	2	656	7	......	....	401	1, 0[illegible]7, 143	330, 000	17, 000	(
14	New Jersey	12	2, 280	28	790	10	1, 670	1, 813, 097	1, 040, 510	34, 041	1,
15	New York	27	6, 781	41	3, 047	28	4, 653	5, 008, 400	2, 362, 890	86, 088	3,
16	North Carolina	10	......	....	183	7	45	15, 700	5, 844	186	
17	Ohio	29	11, 066	97	60	1	4, 431	6, 100, 409	2, 644, 985	137, 330	4,
18	Pennsylvania	120	35, 423	354	1, 082	24	21, 221	27, 177, 986	11, 880, 450	584, 106	19,
19	Rhode Island	3	425	5	......	....	138	410, 600	93, 500	4, 350	
20	South Carolina	2	......	....	28	2	15	20, 000	2, 500	165	
21	Tennessee	18	370	3	565	17	337	253, 750	130, 882	2, 900	
22	Vermont	1	......	....	100	1	13	35, 000	7, 000	....	....
23	Virginia	12	......	....	961	21	696	810, 200	329, 025	16, 130	
24	West Virginia	9	4, 155	15	......	....	1, 498	1, 185, 800	1, 016, 987	62, 572	2,
25	Wisconsin	1	100	....	......	....	642	100, 000	374, 078	7, 549	

IRON, FORGED.

	States.	Establishments.	Steam-engines. Horse-power.	Steam-engines. Number.	Water-wheels. Horse-power.	Water-wheels. Number.	Hands employed. All.	Hands employed. Males above 16.	Hands employed. Females above 15.	Hands employed. Youth.	Capital.	
											Dollars.	*D*
	The United States..	104	4, 587	85	1, 461	51	3, 568	3, 437	......	131	4, 620, 959	1, 9
1	Connecticut	11	380	5	269	9	309	305	......	4	310, 000	1
2	Delaware	2	17	2	......	....	30	20	......	10	32, 000	
3	Georgia	1	75	2	......	....	25	20	......	5	20, 000	
4	Illinois	3	76	2	......	....	217	207	......	10	170, 000	
5	Indiana	1	35	1	......	....	12	10	......	2	12, 000	
6	Maine	3	106	2	40	1	54	54	......	......	65, 000	
7	Massachusetts	14	563	14	240	18	357	352	......	5	449, 125	9
8	Michigan	2	140	2	......	....	32	31	......	1	52, 400	
9	Missouri	1	16	1	......	....	20	20	......	......	20, 000	
10	New Hampshire	2	315	5	10	1	111	111	......	......	131, 000	
11	New Jersey	9	345	8	27	2	362	321	......	41	310, 000	9
12	New York	23	960	15	280	9	902	871	......	31	1, 197, 300	3
13	Ohio	11	160	5	40	2	342	335	......	7	561, 350	1
14	Pennsylvania	19	995	16	535	9	692	672	......	20	1, 115, 784	3
15	Rhode Island	2	404	5	......	....	123	108	......	15	175, 000	

…E CIII.—*Manufactures: Special Statistics for Principal Industries*—1870—Cont'd.

IRON, ROLLED.

MATERIALS—Continued.									
…rap-iron.	Blooms.		Ore.*		Coal.		All other materials.	All materials.	
Dollars.	*Tons.*	*Dollars.*	*Tons.*	*Dollars.*	*Tons.*	*Dollars.*	*Dollars.*	*Dollars.*	
19, 254, 180	132, 912	8, 465, 662	145, 689	976, 835	2, 028, 415	9, 629, 306	1, 359, 360	79, 176, 646	
....	....	....	....	....	300	900	....	14, 900	1
156, 665	....	....	....	....	4, 174	41, 740	3, 515	201, 920	2
292, 900	....	....	....	....	9, 060	77, 650	5, 009	377, 550	3
158, 822	198	17, 907	1, 100	11, 550	13, 900	91, 800	12, 135	499, 714	4
9, 000	....	....	....	....	26, 191	134, 300	....	518, 050	5
430, 377	5, 954	260, 000	5, 000	40, 000	110, 689	510, 917	....	1, 819, 228	6
888, 550	....	....	....	....	61, 810	206, 223	64, 583	1, 968, 518	7
265, 406	3, 058	165, 588	....	....	43, 104	161, 118	24, 498	1, 367, 064	8
468, 767	....	....	....	....	20, 328	150, 211	23, 708	1, 026, 390	9
3, 100	1, 835	143, 490	....	....	53, 660	260, 700	10, 030	1, 300, 315	10
929, 452	2, 300	231, 594	3, 850	46, 780	87, 201	613, 472	97, 963	4, 237, 743	11
201, 000	1, 550	77, 500	....	....	10, 000	72, 500	30, 000	381, 000	12
					38, 928	101, 750	45, 000	826, 750	13
1, 146, 484	2, 402	159, 783	15, 595	48, 872	78, 986	455, 957	93, 789	3, 049, 417	14
3, 497, 031	17, 895	972, 400	31, 292	214, 944	199, 481	970, 290	118, 910	9, 714, 807	15
	100	8, 322			620	2, 920	60	18, 411	16
1, 761, 091	992	43, 750	21, 747	116, 189	309, 262	998, 411	213, 447	8, 016, 590	17
8, 092, 085	96, 433	6, 384, 128	58, 773	487, 732	1, 384, 110	4, 261, 597	497, 336	38, 896, 771	18
49, 000	....	....	....	....	6, 713	46, 834	32, 332	284, 436	19
					160	1, 500	....	11, 975	20
18, 755	15	1, 200	8, 332	10, 708	5, 286	29, 973	....	139, 696	21
14, 000	....	....	....	....	500	4, 500	1, 250	10, 750	22
614, 020	....	....	....	....	30, 305	130, 443	2, 562	1, 298, 575	23
					107, 687	143, 645	85, 222	2, 424, 646	24
237, 675	....	....	....	....	25, 960	160, 952	....	753, 430	25

* Also puddled bar, New York, 17,480 tons, valued at $787,800.

IRON, FORGED.

MATERIALS.											
…oms.	Coal.		Pig-iron.		Scrap-iron.		Wrought iron.		Other materials.	All materials.	
Dollars.	*Tons.*	*Dollars.*	*Tons.*	*Dollars.*	*Tons.*	*Dollars.*	*Tons.*	*Dollars.*	*Dollars.*	*Dollars.*	
…01, 852	82, 214	457, 571	93, 350	657, 696	19, 651	778, 844	23, 172	1, 765, 029	750, 454	5, 011, 446	
77, 744	3, 612	30, 652	500	20, 000	1, 386	53, 875	......	....	39, 848	322, 119	1
......	260	1, 900	40	1, 396	......	......	233	21, 300	2, 520	27, 116	2
......	500	3, 000	......	......			309	20, 000	......	23, 000	3
......	2, 112	9, 124	......	......	1, 080	32, 400	850	64, 770	3, 900	110, 194	4
......	1, 000	4, 000	......	......	316	12, 000	......	....	150	16, 150	5
......	730	6, 300	1, 270	43, 800	......	......	50	3, 750	2, 950	56, 800	6
46, 298	8, 681	68, 150	250	11, 700	4, 125	162, 375	250	22, 000	33, 390	343, 913	7
......	2, 200	14, 000	150	6, 000	1, 100	44, 000	......	....	1, 000	65, 000	8
15, 750	1, 800	6, 000	......	......					4, 000	25, 750	9
......	3, 030	24, 260	40	1, 600	1, 700	69, 000	......	....	207, 000	301, 860	10
......	7, 900	56, 050	......	......	4, 893	196, 200	1, 444	112, 300	16, 383	380, 933	11
......	14, 253	100, 877	1, 400	47, 900	2, 735	107, 000	18, 380	1, 397, 500	201, 153	1, 854, 430	12
07, 900	7, 180	29, 375	50	1, 800	520	20, 800	......	....	186, 920	446, 795	13
27, 160	24, 456	73, 883	85, 650	363, 500	1, 796	81, 194	1, 656	123, 409	30, 240	799, 380	14
27, 000	4, 500	30, 000	4, 000	160, 000	......	......	......	....	21, 000	238, 000	15

TABLE CIII.—*Manufactures: Special Statistics for Principal Industries*—1870—Cont'd.

IRON, ROLLED—Concluded.

	States.	PRODUCTS.									
		Bar.	Plate.	Sheet.	Puddled, bar.	Rails.	Skelp-iron.	Rolled car-axles.	Rod-iron.	All other products.	All products.
		Tons.	*Tons.*	*Tons.*	*Tons.*	*Tons.*	*Tons.*	*No.*	*Tons.*	*Dollars.*	*Dollars.*
	The United States.	488, 234	309, 995	74, 753	33, 631	331, 605	2, 217	34, 821	26, 087	4, 000, 650	[illegible]
1	Alabama	300	......	......	......			......	......	......	[illegible]
2	California	3, 000	......	......	......			......	......	......	[illegible]
3	Connecticut	4, 725	......	......	......			......	2, 725	......	[illegible]
4	Delaware	6, 200	1, 407	500	......	......		......	200	......	[illegible]
5	Georgia	8, 105	309	......	......	......		......	......		[illegible]
6	Illinois	750	7, 100	300	......	17, 611	......	......	......	1, 118, 536	[illegible]
7	Indiana	10, 870	3, 600	......	......	19, 235	......	......	......	227, 020	[illegible]
8	Kentucky	15, 116	5, 450	1, 947	......	3, 966	......	......	1, 256	40, 000	[illegible]
9	Maine	4, 192	191	......	......	12, 750	......	......	5	......	[illegible]
10	Maryland	4, 983	4, 947	4, 100	......	27, 190	......	......	......	9, 000	[illegible]
11	Massachusetts	21, 325	26, 428	......	35	15, 000	......	......	6, 292	431, 700	[illegible]
12	Michigan	1, 250	1, 450	150	......	4, 550	......	......	......		[illegible]
13	Missouri	3, 500	5, 800	4, 000	......				......	220, 000	[illegible]
14	New Jersey	13, 524	22, 768	1, 482	......	14, 657	......	100	2, 176	225, 000	[illegible]
15	New York	73, 747	4, 563	2, 500	12, 320	79, 701	......	......	8, 337	497, 074	[illegible]
16	North Carolina	229	25, 293	......	......						[illegible]
17	Ohio	68, 718	30, 316	11, 796	......	30, 552	......	106	1, 323	278, 140	[illegible]
18	Pennsylvania	233, 854	113, 847	47, 353	21, 276	281, 445	2, 217	34, 615	......	204, 189	[illegible]
19	Rhode Island	1, 965	......	625	......	......	......	......	1, 825	......	[illegible]
20	South Carolina	100	30								[illegible]
21	Tennessee	5, 392	50	......	......	......	......	......	......	......	[illegible]
22	Vermont	......	325	......	......	......	......	......	......	......	[illegible]
23	Virginia	2, 671	6, 050	......	......	8, 700	......	......	950	750, 000	[illegible]
24	West Virginia	4, 318	50, 071	......	......	......	......	......	998	......	[illegible]
25	Wisconsin	......	......	......	......	16, 248	......	......	......	......	[illegible]

IRON, FORGED—Concluded.

	States.	PRODUCTS.									
		Anchors.	Axles.	Chains.	Horseshoes.	Railroad chairs and clamps.	Railroad screw spikes.	Shafting.	Spikes.	Other products.	All products.
		Tons.	*Tons.*	*Tons.*	*Tons.*	*Tons.*	*Tons.*	*Tons.*	*Tons.*	*Tons.*	*Dollars.*
	The United States	1, 605	17, 944	3, 449	14, 270	3, 315	600	145	40, 360	21, 660	8, 385, 669
1	Connecticut	320	2, 425	......	......	......	......	......	......	495	641, 140
2	Delaware	......	232	......	......	......	......	......	......	......	47, 536
3	Georgia	......	......	......	......	......	......	......	300	......	31, 306
4	Illinois	......	918	......	......	......	......	......	......	......	985, 275
5	Indiana	......	140	......	......	......	......	135	......	......	27, 500
6	Maine	385	300	......	......	......	......	10	10	125	93, 800
7	Massachusetts	496	1, 330	......	......	......	......	......	......	2, 730	689, 000
8	Michigan	......	800	130	......	......	......	......	......	125	102, 250
9	Missouri	104	......	......	......	......	......	......	......	106	60, 000
10	New Hampshire	......	33	......	......	......	......	......	......	2, 200	455, 000
11	New Jersey	......	1, 240	1, 005	......	......	......	......	......	3, 612	686, 250
12	New York	300	4, 823	790	11, 000	1, 050	600	......	......	6, 230	2, 827, 255
13	Ohio	......	3, 300	398	......	......	......	......	......	860	763, 471
14	Pennsylvania	......	2, 403	1, 126	......	2, 265	......	......	40, 050	5, 117	1, 324, 996
15	Rhode Island	......	......	......	3, 270	......	......	......	......	......	350, 000

CIII.—*Manufactures: Special Statistics for Principal Industries*—1870—Cont'd.

IRON, PIG.

...ates.	Establishments.	Blast-furnaces.	Daily capacity in tons of melted metal.	Steam-engines. Horse-power.	Steam-engines. Number.	Water-wheels. Horse-power.	Water-wheels. Number.	Hands employed.	Capital. Dollars.	Wages. Dollars.	Materials. Iron-ore. Tons.	Materials. Iron-ore. Dollars.
...ited States..	386	574	8,357	58,866	509	5,034	141	27,554	56,145,323	12,475,250	4,303,847	24,745,445
....	3	3	33	240	4	125	2	301	386,000	97,018	11,350	30,175
...nt	7	8	70	......	..	153	7	150	780,000	92,614	42,585	338,127
....	4	5	5	20	1	22	3	49	12,200	11,600	2,362	11,225
....	4	5	105	1,725	8	......	...	180	425,000	159,400	51,150	426,050
....	19	29	384	2,370	28	......	...	1,565	2,979,000	417,948	126,562	670,278
....	14	21	191	736	12	200	7	850	2,005,000	255,941	138,067	758,510
...setts.......	4	6	64	330	4	130	2	421	700,000	334,541	36,340	190,150
....	17	27	287	1,229	15	95	7	1,625	2,528,000	844,250	119,415	719,596
...d	1	1	8	20	1	......	...	98	60,000	9,700	800	3,000
....	9	13	232	1,925	15	33	2	1,123	1,914,000	856,780	126,212	586,293
...y..........	6	12	193	1,100	8	250	2	300	1,405,000	241,611	101,633	583,725
....	39	81	842	4,510	37	1,191	23	2,121	5,732,116	1,095,450	446,945	2,609,794
...olina.......	11	15	21	35	3	150	10	126	68,675	42,129	3,174	12,461
....	65	84	1,383	10,158	89	......	...	4,582	7,437,826	2,035,520	558,664	3,763,282
...nia	136	199	4,076	32,303	252	1,184	46	10,861	26,376,059	5,014,455	2,337,286	13,277,325
...olina.......	2	2	6	......	...	61	2	15	20,000	3,500	600	2,000
....	14	23	192	710	11	590	8	1,122	1,103,750	379,384	64,088	178,635
....	2	4	9	......	...	80	4	33	85,000	9,860	2,500	12,000
....	18	21	82	440	10	551	11	1,036	828,700	271,220	47,168	108,258
...ginia	5	7	68	220	5	20	1	317	434,000	179,720	36,940	206,850
....	6	6	86	795	6	190	4	592	865,000	122,580	49,106	257,491

IRON, PIG—Continued.

...ates.	Materials—Continued. Anthracite coal. Tons.	Anthracite coal. Dollars.	Charcoal.* Tons.	Charcoal.* Dollars.	All other materials. Dollars.	All materials. Dollars.	Products. Pig-iron. Tons.	Pig-iron. Dollars.
...ited States..	2,233,410	9,992,296	635,519	5,575,833	2,566,834	45,498,017	2,052,821	69,640,498
....	....	....	1,579	9,940	....	40,115	6,250	210,258
...nt	....	....	23,404	326,800	52,006	716,933	16,855	949,125
....	....	....	800	3,880	....	15,105	1,220	47,212
....	114,438	343,085	....	....	56,300	825,435	30,443	1,191,834
....	40,128	103,774	48,106	344,043	32,430	1,223,034	57,943	2,182,482
....	26,600	193,100	25,430	230,202	102,822	1,286,881	54,204	2,143,089
...setts.......	4,000	35,000	15,881	206,872	14,801	446,823	16,416	722,225
....	4,872	31,039	93,085	894,411	6,056	1,651,102	79,279	2,911,515
...i	50	480	....	....	....	3,480	450	18,000
....	28,000	300,000	40,627	395,305	61,418	1,375,766	80,090	2,991,618
...y..........	84,625	444,312	4,400	41,000	56,224	1,125,261	54,652	1,546,965
....	357,887	2,017,940	41,870	479,027	264,564	5,548,925	223,725	7,922,463
...olina.......	....	....	3,197	18,746	123	31,330	1,422	54,169
....	47,593	266,309	175,104	1,479,350	438,815	7,056,405	306,363	10,956,938
...nia	1,518,127	6,206,414	87,612	599,216	1,366,982	22,638,492	1,033,272	32,636,410
...olina.......	....	....	400	1,600	....	3,600	180	8,250
....	1,550	5,923	29,751	250,859	4,500	439,937	28,688	1,147,707
....	....	....	2,050	24,925	1,350	38,275	1,200	66,000
....	....	....	26,916	165,297	100	276,173	17,233	619,820
...ginia	....	....	600	2,400	1,000	243,300	16,950	577,200
....	5,540	44,920	14,707	101,900	107,334	511,645	25,986	737,268

...*Coke:* Kentucky, 5,000 tons, $32,500; Maryland, 438 tons, $2,187; Pennsylvania, 38,432 tons, ... United States, 43,870 tons, $196,647.

...*tuminous Coal*, United States, (total,) 843,866 tons, $2,420,962; Kentucky, 16,000 tons, $40,000; ...8,938 tons, $32,750; New York, 53,986 tons, $177,600; Ohio, 374,770 tons, $1,108,649; Pennsyl-...,002 tons, $1,026,395; Virginia, 470 tons, $2,518; West Virginia, 26,700 tons, $33,050.

TABLE CIII.—*Manufactures: Special Statistics for Principal Industries*—1870—Cont'd.

IRON, CAST.

	States and Territories.	Establishments.	STEAM-ENGINES. Horse-power.	STEAM-ENGINES. Number.	WATER-WHEELS. Horse-power.	WATER-WHEELS. Number.	MACHINES. Cupola-furnaces.	MACHINES. Daily capacity in tons of melted metal.	HANDS EMPLOYED. All.	HANDS EMPLOYED. Males above 16.	HANDS EMPLOYED. Females above 15.	HANDS EMPLOYED. Youth.
	The United States..	2, 654	31, 640	1, 593	8, 660	434	2, 945	9, 814	51, 305	49, 441	48	1, 816
1	Alabama	18	200	13	54	3	19	39	140	137	....	3
2	Arkansas	2	18	1	......	......	2	2	9	9	....	......
3	California	31	577	28	......	......	42	129	727	686	....	41
4	Colorado	1	15	1	......	......	1	2	18	18	....	......
5	Connecticut	83	1, 425	38	559	24	111	468	2, 458	2, 338	23	97
6	Delaware	18	241	17	10	2	24	111	471	435	....	36
7	District of Columbia	5	53	5	......	......	5	9	83	82	....	1
8	Georgia	23	237	15	38	3	28	83	247	238	....	9
9	Idaho	1	7	1	......	......	1	1	3	3	....	......
10	Illinois	118	1, 662	73	217	13	131	462	2, 157	2, 119	....	38
11	Indiana	105	1, 131	61	253	7	109	425	1, 203	1, 182	....	21
12	Iowa	44	342	33	10	1	46	106	272	270	....	2
13	Kansas	5	37	3	......	......	7	20	123	114	....	9
14	Kentucky	32	678	27	......	......	39	281	1, 388	1, 321	....	67
15	Louisiana	15	168	13	......	......	17	30	385	373	....	12
16	Maine	47	360	21	229	17	49	170	512	509	....	3
17	Maryland	43	447	30	10	......	45	135	695	686	....	9
18	Massachusetts	119	1, 270	75	764	44	162	526	3, 714	3, 664	1	49
19	Michigan	196	1, 522	108	240	19	202	397	1, 101	1, 088	....	13
20	Minnesota	18	73	11	75	3	19	39	118	118	....	......
21	Mississippi	15	191	9	......	......	16	35	67	65	....	2
22	Missouri	41	1, 112	36	9	1	......	......	1, 977	1, 745	....	232
23	Montana	1	20	1	......	......	1	1	5	5	....	......
24	Nebraska	3	81	3	......	......	4	11	68	68	....	......
25	Nevada	5	172	5	......	......	7	19	114	114	....	......
26	New Hampshire	26	191	10	303	14	34	81	506	505	....	1
27	New Jersey	86	1, 237	47	1, 054	25	97	474	2, 089	1, 989	9	91
28	New York	485	5, 334	258	2, 415	119	586	1, 932	12, 622	12, 193	13	416
29	North Carolina	29	178	13	152	7	29	45	143	139	....	4
30	Ohio	268	3, 826	157	485	19	285	713	5, 060	4, 946	....	114
31	Oregon	4	24	3	......	......	4	8	39	39	....	......
32	Pennsylvania	524	6, 543	354	939	63	563	2, 455	9, 639	9, 156	2	481
33	Rhode Island	17	443	13	35	2	26	101	927	909	....	18
34	South Carolina	7	57	6	10	1	7	9	85	81	....	4
35	Tennessee	33	330	16	35	4	34	43	316	312	....	4
36	Texas	6	84	5	......	......	7	9	30	30	....	......
37	Vermont	26	134	8	245	15	27	44	244	244	....	......
38	Virginia	54	245	15	388	19	57	127	541	529	....	12
39	Washington	2	25	2	......	......	2	1	5	5	....	......
40	West Virginia	24	354	18	......	......	23	89	285	281	....	4
41	Wisconsin	74	596	40	131	9	77	182	719	696	....	23

TABLE CIII.—*Manufactures: Special Statistics for Principal Industries*—1870—Cont'd.

IRON, CAST.

CAPITAL.	WAGES.	MATERIALS.						
Dollars.	Dollars.	Pig-iron.		Scrap-iron.		Coal.		
		Tons.	*Dollars.*	*Tons.*	*Dollars.*	*Tons.*	*Dollars.*	
67, 578, 961	28, 835, 914	982, 488	37, 677, 042	144, 586	3, 869, 969	662, 941	3, 853, 669	
177, 100	98, 622	1, 577	73, 170	1, 075	33, 550	2, 176	23, 921	1
3, 500	3, 500	30	1, 300	100	2, 000	80	1, 500	2
897, 000	434, 845	11, 506	443, 883	716	20, 335	6, 630	123, 850	3
25, 000	20, 000	....	....	350	28, 000	400	4, 000	4
3, 006, 650	1, 444, 345	36, 537	1, 470, 027	2, 964	82, 015	22, 229	173, 665	5
592, 275	227, 761	17, 923	705, 064	201	5, 226	4, 970	30, 289	6
219, 000	45, 782	925	36, 250	600	18, 200	910	6, 740	7
179, 750	108, 130	2, 150	87, 177	1, 256	36, 357	1, 638	16, 389	8
3, 000	1, 200	18	1, 080	....	....	15	270	9
2, 762, 885	1, 200, 127	43, 681	1, 872, 692	10, 114	267, 566	29, 348	218, 882	10
1, 672, 182	612, 133	38, 638	1, 545, 035	5, 346	144, 654	25, 430	129, 160	11
359, 514	137, 512	3, 576	159, 393	1, 978	50, 229	1, 709	22, 518	12
135, 986	77, 334	1, 937	95, 780	442	11, 550	690	10, 190	13
2, 052, 431	782, 985	38, 415	1, 533, 781	3, 771	93, 145	21, 684	85, 340	14
367, 500	250, 100	2, 947	116, 910	895	20, 775	5, 786	43, 124	15
712, 384	247, 472	6, 839	263, 888	2, 138	54, 174	3, 468	31, 347	16
784, 135	215, 805	8, 421	313, 091	3, 581	94, 979	5, 487	37, 463	17
3, 437, 400	2, 286, 803	63, 728	2, 397, 518	9, 382	274, 477	32, 850	293, 455	18
1, 571, 447	519, 433	17, 462	753, 412	5, 422	154, 963	9, 647	113, 511	19
109, 500	50, 934	1, 473	66, 290	802	26, 680	728	8, 282	20
112, 550	34, 700	785	24, 339	437	12, 174	378	3, 377	21
3, 108, 500	1, 444, 884	41, 767	1, 672, 290	5, 942	174, 225	43, 097	162, 679	22
8, 000	5, 000	20	4, 800	40	5, 000	60	2, 250	23
67, 840	72, 194	1, 845	59, 410	130	5, 240	439	5, 679	24
101, 000	133, 500	3, 173	190, 380	140	5, 300	963	28, 260	25
500, 760	285, 165	6, 684	240, 781	2, 750	91, 086	7, 798	82, 575	26
2, 476, 541	1, 191, 689	50, 477	1, 778, 610	4, 911	131, 910	26, 632	163, 798	27
13, 121, 501	7, 425, 129	222, 959	7, 955, 649	33, 115	840, 247	109, 098	789, 099	28
107, 050	41, 758	902	36, 994	1, 236	31, 270	864	7, 211	29
8, 273, 629	2, 858, 166	93, 788	3, 801, 531	17, 095	458, 596	83, 772	353, 556	30
28, 000	25, 500	625	21, 570	60	200	347	4, 990	31
14, 872, 073	4, 952, 788	214, 117	7, 947, 228	18, 688	469, 636	184, 197	657, 466	32
1, 224, 000	512, 025	13, 111	534, 305	100	2, 500	5, 630	45, 703	33
64, 251	40, 210	415	22, 600	230	5, 880	250	2, 012	34
331, 392	166, 501	4, 017	168, 235	1, 994	47, 940	4, 279	25, 199	35
54, 000	17, 350	575	28, 770	116	3, 500	495	7, 950	36
266, 200	115, 267	4, 366	207, 507	1, 288	34, 343	2, 395	24, 613	37
554, 235	199, 275	5, 547	199, 788	2, 995	79, 141	6, 242	42, 521	38
16, 200	1, 150	61	1, 610	15	390	12	168	39
462, 100	167, 488	5, 285	225, 830	1, 377	28, 597	3, 716	7, 770	40
760, 500	372, 352	14, 186	610, 074	794	23, 910	6, 402	62, 697	41

TABLE CIII.—*Manufactures: Special Statistics for Principal Industries*—1870—Cont'

IRON, CAST—Continued.

	States and Territories.	MATERIALS—Continued.		PRODUCTS.		
		All other materials.	All materials.	Car-wheels.	Railing.	Hollow ware.
		Dollars.	*Dollars.*	*Number.*	*Feet.*	*Dolla*
	The United States	2, 821, 870	48, 222, 550	473, 108	1, 530, 581	3, 00
1	Alabama	21, 630	152, 271	373	5, 000	1,
2	Arkansas		4, 800			
3	California	124, 286	712, 354	300	100	64,
4	Colorado	500	32, 500			
5	Connecticut	22, 328	1, 748, 035	10, 000	608, 006	25
6	Delaware	20, 760	761, 339	40, 000	3, 000	
7	District of Columbia	1, 850	63, 040			
8	Georgia	9, 520	149, 443	2, 105		17,
9	Idaho	625	1, 975			
10	Illinois	45, 090	2, 404, 230	27, 170		235
11	Indiana	44, 807	1, 863, 656	63, 127	15, 200	68
12	Iowa	20, 854	252, 994	730	100	
13	Kansas	19, 140	136, 660			12
14	Kentucky	8, 483	1, 720, 749	2, 560		134
15	Louisiana	15, 605	196, 414	10		
16	Maine	11, 497	360, 906		3, 000	
17	Maryland	7, 837	453, 370	1, 056	230	3
18	Massachusetts	164, 545	3, 129, 995	100		187
19	Michigan	55, 135	1, 077, 021	14, 483		
20	Minnesota	1, 556	102, 808			2
21	Mississippi	15, 294	55, 184		1, 140	
22	Missouri	188, 443	2, 197, 637	33, 968	103, 000	286
23	Montana	2, 550	14, 600			
24	Nebraska	36, 852	107, 181			
25	Nevada	39, 476	263, 416			
26	New Hampshire	44, 354	438, 796	3, 000	2, 160	5
27	New Jersey	64, 166	2, 138, 484	19, 896	2, 500	113
28	New York	865, 134	10, 450, 129	65, 689	622, 577	553
29	North Carolina	6, 028	81, 503	900		
30	Ohio	150, 827	4, 764, 510	42, 366	28, 665	479
31	Oregon	2, 600	29, 360			
32	Pennsylvania	727, 112	9, 801, 442	125, 905	122, 469	749
33	Rhode Island	40, 453	622, 961			
34	South Carolina	3, 000	33, 492			4
35	Tennessee	5, 220	246, 594	972	2, 800	3
36	Texas	3, 850	44, 070			
37	Vermont	5, 055	271, 718	6, 388	10, 000	3
38	Virginia	2, 312	323, 762	5, 300	700	4
39	Washington	490	2, 658			
40	West Virginia	7, 897	270, 094	1, 680		
41	Wisconsin	14, 709	720, 399	5, 030		15

TABLE CIII.—*Manufactures: Special Statistics for Principal Industries*—1870—Cont'd.

IRON, CAST—Continued.

PRODUCTS—Continued.									
Malleable iron castings.	Hot-air furnaces.	Cook'g ranges.	Stoves.	Agricultural castings.	Architectural castings.	Machine castings.	Miscellaneous castings.	All products.	
Dollars. 2,597,096	*Number.* 15,351	*Number.* 5,450	*Number.* 1,985,177	*Tons.* 40,168	*Tons.* 27,845	*Tons.* 107,791	*Tons.* 535,395	*Dollars.* 99,843,218	
							2,103	326,890	1
							140	10,000	2
		190	808	57		3,368	7,045	1,329,961	3
							315	55,000	4
462,936			14,550	15		2,524	24,596	4,156,944	5
			250	79			4,448	1,085,557	6
							1,310	131,405	7
			1,200				2,567	443,297	8
							17	4,940	9
76,000			55,575	2,963	3,025	3,848	27,153	4,503,053	10
10,000		3	28,082			5,759	16,043	3,067,708	11
			6,750				3,911	532,780	12
			10,000				1,020	326,420	13
			52,544	3,710			26,830	3,222,943	14
	50					636	2,889	552,470	15
	50		3,407	27		1,080	6,611	772,965	16
			1,092	355		2,243	6,360	928,094	17
138,500	4,652	1,350	67,070	620		2,357	50,348	7,046,702	18
4,000			14,046	5,133		5,642	5,545	2,082,532	19
	24		110				2,117	244,202	20
			250				1,096	126,082	21
170,000	370	850	124,840	200	2,445	426	13,824	4,163,605	22
							50	25,000	23
							1,763	196,518	24
							2,964	641,250	25
	264		12,520	5		2,795	4,009	914,568	26
374,800	35		4,633	1,305		1,748	41,197	4,012,805	27
870,800	7,652		422,694	13,320	20,975	33,966	77,640	23,993,436	28
12,000				449			1,150	157,571	29
170,000	50	100	228,579	5,445	1,400	7,376	48,817	10,539,400	30
						80	525	65,000	31
254,160	4	1,157	194,121	4,821		30,589	118,304	18,758,295	32
49,000	2,000	1,800	15,575				8,109	1,416,105	33
900						135	270	119,750	34
			650	143		1,974	2,253	555,111	35
							632	77,000	36
4,000			850	96		200	3,134	491,520	37
			1,890	1,059			5,344	769,274	38
							67	8,500	39
			15,872	40		1,045	1,575	566,072	40
			7,210	275			10,695	1,423,193	41

TABLE CIII.—*Manufactures: Special Statistics for Principal Industries*—1870—Cont'd.

LEAD, PIG.

	States.	Establishments.	Steam-engines. Horse-power.	Steam-engines. Number.	Water-wheels. Horse-power.	Water-wheels. Number.	Machines. Furnaces.	Machines. Capacity, tons.	Hands employed. All.	Hands employed. Males above 16.	Hands employed. Females above 15.	Hands employed. Youth.	Capital. Dollars.
	The United States	62	431	20	201	23	4	8	589	577	......	12	2,191,000
1	California	1	......	......	......	......	......	......	15	15	......	......	40,000
2	Illinois	3	......	......	8	3	......	......	25	25	......	......	27,000
3	Iowa	2	5	1	10	2	4	8	11	11	......	......	17,000
4	Missouri	31	203	9	81	11	......	......	194	194	......	......	1,422,000
5	Nevada	9	215	9	......	......	......	......	181	181	......	......	438,000
6	New York	2	8	1	......	......	......	......	30	30	......	......	140,000
7	Virginia	1	......	......	40	1	......	......	42	30	......	12	16,000
8	Wisconsin	13	......	......	62	6	......	......	91	91	......	......	91,000

LEATHER, CURRIED.

	States and Territories.	Establishments.	Steam-engines. Horse-power.	Steam-engines. Number.	Wat'r-wh'ls. Horse-power.	Wat'r-wh'ls. Number.	Hands employed. All.	Hands employed. Males above 16.	Hands employed. Females ab. 15.	Hands employed. Youth.	Capital. Dollars.	Wages. Dollars.	Materials. Leather. Sides.	Materials. Leather. Dollars.
	The United States	3,023	2,992	174	887	55	10,027	9,907	57	63	12,303,785	4,154,114	9,131,330	33,784,271
1	Alabama	58	....	...	15	1	97	94	2	1	60,508	15,340	48,572	110,082
2	Arkansas	14	....	...	....	..	18	18	...	...	10,175	1,275	10,841	24,616
3	Connecticut	30	8	1	20	1	66	66	...	...	86,200	25,745	31,550	145,912
4	California	27	36	2	....	..	55	53	1	1	110,950	19,373	84,862	292,873
5	Delaware	7	43	3	....	..	70	52	9	9	96,024	34,323	43,530	213,229
6	Georgia	86	10	1	20	2	126	126	...	...	72,924	18,727	76,545	195,655
7	Illinois	44	39	3	....	..	334	334	...	...	386,550	169,129	415,893	1,436,651
8	Indiana	156	147	10	....	..	319	315	...	4	303,810	84,981	224,889	780,296
9	Iowa	16	....	...	....	..	20	20	...	...	13,775	2,065	6,310	17,429
10	Kansas	3	....	...	....	..	5	5	...	...	3,150	1,000	4,304	10,553
11	Kentucky	82	40	...	....	..	155	154	...	1	157,916	41,848	143,248	522,309
12	Louisiana	2	....	...	....	..	2	2	...	...	2,400	....	800	1,600
13	Maine	76	109	2	126	8	219	216	...	3	238,209	64,244	200,713	709,233
14	Maryland	50	15	2	....	..	163	161	1	1	238,145	53,131	91,142	367,685
15	Massachusetts	196	1,350	99	85	8	3,194	3,168	11	15	3,163,076	1,812,052	3,370,319	11,674,785
16	Michigan	73	82	5	5	..	249	248	1	...	395,493	89,799	163,507	651,064
17	Minnesota	5	4	1	....	..	10	10	...	...	9,200	2,385	5,682	20,067
18	Mississippi	25	....	...	9	2	36	36	...	...	19,575	4,916	53,960	92,448
19	Missouri	30	....	...	....	..	76	76	...	...	54,008	35,297	55,190	174,988
20	New Hampshire	49	30	1	96	7	219	219	...	...	312,600	100,599	248,436	986,743
21	New Jersey	61	48	2	20	..	279	278	...	1	658,600	220,314	357,625	2,158,655
22	New York	325	272	12	249	12	1,011	989	15	7	1,639,388	439,253	865,178	3,504,227
23	North Carolina	101	4	...	14	..	119	119	...	...	60,186	12,297	59,345	122,954
24	Ohio	387	210	6	....	..	796	785	3	8	1,057,733	251,413	733,380	2,381,644
25	Oregon	10	....	...	....	..	21	21	...	...	11,700	6,575	14,350	40,066
26	Pennsylvania	558	254	13	20	1	1,080	1,067	7	6	1,830,461	298,981	728,578	3,301,244
27	Rhode Island	6	....	...	....	..	112	112	...	...	263,000	61,045	158,350	592,520
28	South Carolina	31	....	...	27	1	55	53	2	...	16,075	5,287	17,850	49,656
29	Tennessee	186	65	2	2	..	309	306	...	3	249,568	62,656	217,659	607,969
30	Texas	22	....	...	....	..	28	28	...	...	17,367	4,015	20,821	35,467
31	Utah	15	....	...	....	..	17	17	...	...	10,700	3,115	10,745	26,306
32	Vermont	64	56	3	179	12	137	137	...	...	176,390	44,730	126,155	464,257
33	Virginia	146	13	2	....	..	194	193	...	1	90,694	18,802	88,467	224,171
34	West Virginia	74	37	2	....	..	108	106	...	2	93,489	21,438	54,723	211,905
35	Washington	5	....	...	....	..	6	6	...	...	6,450	1,175	5,175	16,554
36	Wisconsin	70	114	2	....	..	322	317	5	...	407,206	126,789	394,637	1,610,545

TABLE CIII.—*Manufactures: Special Statistics for Principal Industries*—1870—Cont'd.

LEAD, PIG.

WAGES.	MATERIALS.								PRODUCTS.		
Dollars.	Ore.		Coal.		Wood.		All other.	All.	Pig.		
Dollars.	*Tons.*	*Dollars.*	*Tons.*	*Dollars.*	*Cords.*	*Dollars.*	*Dollars.*	*Dollars.*	*Tons.*	*Dollars.*	
237, 628	52, 293	2, 288, 198	8, 518	51, 600	7, 001	24, 946	242, 330	2, 807, 074	21, 515	3, 499, 183	
15, 000	....	....	....	....	....	....	....	200, 000	1, 900	200, 000	1
8, 400	1, 850	159, 050	....	....	....	....	4, 420	163, 470	1, 083	182, 280	2
3, 450	450	40, 500	....	....	125	650	225	41, 375	310	50, 850	3
49, 220	6, 602	434, 136	518	2, 850	3, 994	8, 076	9, 226	454, 288	4, 397	642, 831	4
109, 900	27, 575	442, 512	....	....	1, 190	7, 700	107, 750	557, 962	4, 083	894, 600	5
16, 750	9, 150	750, 000	8, 000	48, 750	....	....	117, 600	916, 350	6, 336	970, 500	6
6, 000	2, 000	20, 000	....	....	300	1, 200	1, 500	22, 700	252	43, 720	7
28, 902	4, 666	442, 000	....	....	1, 392	7, 320	1, 609	450, 929	3, 154	514, 402	8

LEATHER, CURRIED.

MATERIALS—Continued.						PRODUCTS.			
Oil.		Skins.		All other materials.	All materials.	Leather.	Skins.	All products.	
Gallons.	*Dollars.*	*Number.*	*Dollars.*	*Dollars.*	*Dollars.*	*Sides.*	*Number.*	*Dollars.*	
2, 089, 754	1, 642, 495	4, 084, 980	6, 833, 215	1, 305, 612	43, 565, 593	9, 133, 330	4, 084, 967	54, 191, 167	
3, 113	3, 387	7, 247	12, 406	478	126, 354	48, 572	7, 247	172, 949	1
815	835	1, 940	3, 740	241	29, 452	10, 841	1, 940	40, 493	2
9, 247	7, 979	23, 215	70, 419	6, 458	230, 768	31, 550	23, 215	291, 691	3
18, 187	16, 332	25, 463	46, 010	2, 529	357, 743	84, 862	25, 463	423, 678	4
3, 300	2, 713	1, 425	7, 258	2, 124	225, 384	43, 530	1, 425	279, 962	5
7, 223	7, 320	11, 650	21, 521	1, 476	225, 972	76, 545	11, 650	288, 346	6
86, 997	68, 232	87, 065	228, 621	14, 705	1, 748, 299	415, 893	87, 065	2, 134, 389	7
41, 956	35, 187	63, 747	88, 263	6, 042	909, 778	224, 888	63, 747	1, 151, 307	8
1, 945	2, 168	10, 095	14, 427	....	34, 021	6, 310	10, 095	41, 310	9
470	505	640	1, 075	....	12, 433	4, 304	640	14, 499	10
15, 275	14, 442	9, 127	17, 374	2, 684	556, 805	143, 248	9, 127	683, 668	11
95	95	....	....	....	1, 695	800	....	2, 200	12
54, 254	36, 407	62, 135	143, 780	5, 382	894, 862	200, 713	62, 135	1, 082, 554	13
17, 731	14, 102	46, 164	100, 365	11, 923	494, 075	91, 142	46, 164	623, 308	14
945, 329	648, 027	1, 055, 087	1, 722, 583	924, 527	14, 969, 920	3, 370, 319	1, 055, 087	19, 211, 330	15
41, 730	35, 784	238, 030	132, 938	13, 594	833, 380	163, 507	238, 030	1, 064, 297	16
1, 480	1, 610	2, 453	4, 255	30	25, 932	5, 682	2, 453	30, 765	17
2, 740	2, 803	5, 176	8, 360	....	103, 611	53, 960	5, 176	133, 316	18
17, 171	17, 490	64, 540	83, 897	1, 500	277, 875	55, 190	64, 540	371, 496	19
79, 704	59, 927	116, 402	361, 760	29, 989	1, 438, 419	248, 436	116, 402	1, 720, 520	20
120, 722	105, 151	48, 020	117, 968	63, 014	2, 444, 170	357, 625	48, 020	2, 932, 401	21
158, 922	131, 338	1, 028, 850	1, 473, 955	76, 804	5, 186, 494	865, 178	1, 028, 850	6, 310, 222	22
5, 777	5, 895	6, 364	11, 034	888	149, 771	59, 345	6, 351	180, 195	23
148, 468	137, 467	210, 882	380, 510	33, 597	2, 933, 218	733, 380	210, 882	3, 522, 100	24
2, 636	2, 590	6, 200	11, 145	610	55, 005	14, 350	6, 200	73, 688	25
139, 953	130, 783	518, 439	903, 742	50, 685	4, 479, 454	728, 578	518, 430	5, 429, 833	26
15, 750	17, 863	132, 304	170, 783	8, 788	793, 954	158, 350	132, 304	1, 087, 161	27
1, 471	1, 563	4, 034	6, 615	321	58, 155	17, 850	4, 034	80, 247	28
29, 025	20, 008	63, 575	106, 000	3, 093	737, 070	217, 659	63, 575	922, 641	29
1, 138	1, 189	2, 585	3, 943	60	40, 659	20, 821	2, 585	57, 387	30
1, 129	2, 107	2, 090	6, 220	362	34 995	10, 745	2, 090	41, 639	31
29, 361	24, 456	70, 913	127, 789	1, 843	619, 045	126, 155	70, 913	762, 571	32
9, 445	8, 889	13, 345	24, 397	2, 495	250, 952	88, 467	13, 345	328, 294	33
7, 149	7, 587	20, 627	31, 748	1, 846	252, 386	54, 723	20, 627	313, 220	34
865	898	3, 062	5, 249	310	23, 397	5, 175	3, 062	26, 934	35
78, 190	69, 356	122, 089	293, 065	37, 124	2, 010, 090	394, 637	122, 089	2, 360, 347	36

TABLE CIII.—*Manufactures: Special Statistics for Principal Industries*—1870—Cont'd.

LEATHER, TANNED.

	States and Territories.	Establishments.	STEAM-ENGINES.		WATER-WHEELS.		HANDS EMPLOYED.				CAPITAL.	WAGES.
			Horse-power.	Number.	Horse-power.	Number.	All.	Males above 16.	Females above 15.	Youth.	Dollars.	Dollars.
	The United States	4,237	19,572	1,045	14,202	855	20,784	20,423	98	263	42,730,565	7,934,416
1	Alabama	83	18	2	35	2	181	168	5	8	146,171	32,668
2	Arkansas	21	.....	.....	.....	.....	34	33	....	1	21,925	3,965
3	Connecticut	39	50	4	279	17	158	156	2	....	324,650	66,382
4	California	43	113	8	2	1	207	204	2	1	322,550	92,411
5	Delaware	10	63	3	.....	.....	85	75	8	2	227,000	35,223
6	Dist. of Columbia	2	38	2	.....	.....	25	25	....	....	75,000	8,710
7	Florida	3	.....	.....	.....	.....	11	11	....	....	8,000	3,510
8	Georgia	100	62	4	79	8	190	184	1	5	113,323	29,631
9	Illinois	33	529	23	5	1	418	415	1	2	826,750	203,315
10	Indiana	197	535	31	5	1	514	503	2	9	875,740	144,469
11	Iowa	17	3	1	.....	.....	32	32	....	....	23,350	4,300
12	Kansas	3	.....	.....	.....	.....	6	6	....	....	3,150	1,000
13	Kentucky	100	237	15	1	1	293	282	1	10	576,424	76,962
14	Louisiana	7	.....	.....	.....	.....	16	16	....	....	13,800	2,250
15	Maine	123	552	28	1,313	85	781	772	1	8	1,606,740	255,882
16	Maryland	69	271	21	35	3	281	275	3	3	792,430	94,160
17	Massachusetts	138	1,584	75	478	37	1,424	1,416	....	8	3,150,850	754,467
18	Michigan	99	838	47	189	9	478	474	1	3	867,017	192,150
19	Minnesota	7	4	1	.....	.....	20	20	....	....	25,200	8,765
20	Mississippi	31	.....	.....	5	1	65	63	....	2	30,085	8,377
21	Missouri	50	115	4	.....	.....	164	162	....	2	135,242	73,588
22	New Hampshire	72	375	21	925	53	410	408	....	2	875,800	100,109
23	New Jersey	67	385	27	110	10	617	571	31	15	1,273,387	347,760
24	New York	624	5,384	239	7,086	368	6,064	6,005	8	51	13,286,940	2,029,052
25	North Carolina	121	54	5	52	8	189	183	....	6	99,642	19,533
26	Ohio	495	1,622	106	94	7	1,265	1,239	....	26	2,171,108	379,178
27	Oregon	14	10	1	22	4	38	38	....	....	35,700	12,125
28	Pennsylvania	890	5,341	294	2,164	132	4,650	4,559	25	66	11,800,046	1,683,479
29	Rhode Island	8	135	5	27	2	101	101	....	....	283,000	47,400
30	South Carolina	34	.....	.....	43	7	72	70	....	2	24,125	8,099
31	Tennessee	200	230	9	66	8	453	440	2	11	451,097	87,619
32	Texas	34	.....	.....	.....	.....	62	61	....	1	37,476	7,920
33	Utah	22	.....	.....	21	3	39	36	....	3	34,600	8,290
34	Vermont	86	200	11	979	69	321	317	4	....	620,743	113,415
35	Virginia	172	73	5	105	7	313	307	....	6	211,790	43,997
36	West Virginia	104	185	13	31	4	220	213	1	6	362,890	47,454
37	Washington	5	.....	.....	20	2	10	10	....	....	10,550	3,525
38	Wisconsin	85	566	40	31	5	577	573	....	4	906,184	222,010

TABLE CIII.—*Manufactures: Special Statistics for Principal Industries*—1870—Cont'd.

LEATHER, TANNED.

MATERIALS.						PRODUCTS.			
Bark.		Hides.	Skins.	All other materials.	All materials.	Leather.	Skins.	All products.	
Cords.	*Dollars.*	*Number.*	*Number.*	*Dollars.*	*Dollars.*	*Sides.*	*Number.*	*Dollars.*	
1, 255, 346	9, 089, 303	8, 783, 752	9, 664, 148	1, 631, 234	63, 069, 491	17, 577, 404	9, 794, 148	86, 169, 883	
5, 236	22, 353	40, 685	10, 441	4, 634	137, 390	81, 370	10, 441	239, 386	1
771	3, 474	7, 542	2, 120	580	23, 325	15, 084	2, 120	42, 528	2
5, 293	49, 385	20, 723	648, 956	11, 406	580, 747	41, 446	648, 956	732, 625	3
6, 214	72, 672	79, 703	198, 063	11, 598	480, 411	159, 406	198, 063	751, 046	4
1, 184	18, 079	18, 227	81, 425	18, 999	171, 746	36, 434	81, 425	244, 993	5
1, 100	15, 200	9, 500	3, 000	1, 072	80, 772	19, 000	3, 000	134, 475	6
185	1, 100	2, 400	200	150	8, 000	4, 800	200	13 800	7
5, 463	26, 555	48, 307	11, 866	6, 604	192, 821	96, 614	11, 866	283, 960	8
21, 657	191, 179	230, 255	265, 425	27, 270	1, 492, 078	460, 510	265, 425	2, 013, 774	9
21, 413	162, 914	151, 603	108, 575	10, 912	905, 347	303, 206	108, 575	1, 310, 242	10
842	4, 231	4, 715	14, 218	1, 544	35, 577	9, 430	14, 218	50, 139	11
230	1, 840	2, 152	640	585	9, 994	4, 304	640	11, 928	12
13, 240	133, 092	115, 396	88, 002	13, 293	741, 192	230, 792	88, 002	1, 009, 926	13
359	2, 172	3, 500	500	442	15, 585	7, 000	500	27, 250	14
63, 470	428, 467	432, 300	669, 850	96, 889	3, 021, 127	864, 600	669, 850	3, 779, 227	15
17, 504	161, 298	98, 901	53, 308	7, 413	926, 406	197, 802	53, 308	1, 265, 388	16
76, 132	1, 047, 145	1, 253, 507	288, 864	472, 010	8, 025, 578	2, 507, 01	288, 864	9, 984, 497	17
26, 199	172, 614	163, 181	572, 338	27, 501	1, 167, 876	326, 362	572, 338	1, 606, 311	18
2, 485	6, 462	7, 99	1, 41	1, 970	53, 815	15, 982	1, 13	76, 242	19
1, 638	5, 552	32, 275	6, 276	452	80, 756	64, 550	6, 276	129, 407	20
3, 050	22, 035	35, 582	70, 047	13, 729	252, 350	71, 164	170, 047	463, 452	21
22, 029	202, 75	195, 268	156, 814	14, 801	1, 366, 950	390, 536	156, 81	1, 965, 576	22
25, 951	268, 71	10, 447	510, 472	135, 755	2, 444, 205	420, 894	510, 472	3, 110, 657	23
467, 080	2, 685, 669	2, 615, 442	4, 035, 524	371, 581	19, 118, 186	5, 230, 884	4, 065, 524	26, 968, 320	24
4, 491	16, 373	41, 586	7, 492	4, 769	124, 619	83, 172	7, 492	184, 113	25
54, 208	471, 039	401, 874	390, 24	66, 927	2, 768, 493	803, 748	390, 124	3, 714, 232	26
1, 265	7, 440	9, 850	6, 300	503	43, 388	19, 700	6, 300	73, 555	27
322, 119	2, 360, 587	1, 808, 760	993, 002	181, 240	13, 994, 036	3, 617, 520	993, 002	19, 828, 323	28
375	5, 750	100, 300	96, 304	63, 624	673, 314	200, 600	96, 304	741, 103	29
911	3, 908	13, 124	4, 241	1, 096	48, 070	26, 248	4, 24	85, 778	30
16, 132	86, 105	137, 240	69, 485	11, 740	660, 335	274, 480	69, 485	921, 497	31
1, 149	5, 047	13, 655	2, 848	2, 395	36, 429	27, 210	2, 848	60, 524	32
404	6, 597	7, 457	2, 647	521	24, 358	14, 914	2, 647	43, 964	33
16, 497	121, 257	138, 631	117, 953	20, 847	967, 840	277, 262	117, 953	1, 249, 942	34
8, 930	58, 206	70, 549	19, 232	6, 703	331, 138	141, 098	19, 232	462, 149	35
9, 858	72, 486	59, 135	29, 173	2, 940	374, 292	118, 270	29, 173	527, 016	36
415	4, 110	2, 950	3, 186	56	12, 764	5, 900	3, 186	24, 465	37
29, 867	165, 618	204, 039	123, 824	16, 584	1, 478, 142	408, 078	123, 824	2, 013, 093	38

TABLE III. *Manufactures: Special Statistics of Principal Industries* — [illegible]

LUMBER SAWED.

	States and Territories.	Establishments.	STEAM-ENGINES. Horse-power.	Number.	WATER-WHEELS. Horse-power.	Number.	SAWS.* Number.	HANDS EMPLOYED. All.	Males above 16.	Females above 15.	Youths.
	The United States	[illegible]	314,[illegible]	11,5[illegible]	[illegible]	[illegible]	[illegible]	[illegible]	[illegible]	[illegible]	[illegible]
1	Alabama	[illegible]	2,051	[illegible]	1,9[illegible]	[illegible]	[illegible]	[illegible]	[illegible]	[illegible]	[illegible]
2	Arizona	1	10	1	....	....	[illegible]	[illegible]	[illegible]	[illegible]	...
3	Arkansas	311	3,144	[illegible]	[illegible]	[illegible]	[illegible]	[illegible]	[illegible]	[illegible]	[illegible]
4	California	[illegible]	6,7[illegible]	[illegible]	2,[illegible]	[illegible]	[illegible]	[illegible]	[illegible]	[illegible]	[illegible]
5	Colorado	[illegible]	[illegible]	[illegible]	[illegible]	11	[illegible]	[illegible]	[illegible]	1	...
6	Connecticut	[illegible]	434	[illegible]	6,[illegible]	[illegible]	[illegible]	[illegible]	[illegible]	...	
7	Dakota	[illegible]	[illegible]	[illegible]	[illegible]	[illegible]	13	[illegible]	[illegible]	...	[illegible]
8	Delaware	[illegible]	[illegible]	[illegible]	[illegible]	[illegible]	[illegible]	[illegible]	[illegible]	...	[illegible]
9	Dist. of Columbia	1	[illegible]	1	....	....	[illegible]	[illegible]	[illegible]	...	[illegible]
10	Florida	104	2,4[illegible]	[illegible]	167	[illegible]	[illegible]	[illegible]	[illegible]	[illegible]	[illegible]
11	Georgia	[illegible]	[illegible]	[illegible]	4,7[illegible]	[illegible]	[illegible]	[illegible]	[illegible]	[illegible]	[illegible]
12	Idaho	10	[illegible]	4	[illegible]	[illegible]	11	[illegible]	[illegible]	...	...
13	Illinois	511	12,[illegible]	[illegible]	[illegible]	[illegible]	[illegible]	[illegible]	[illegible]	[illegible]	[illegible]
14	Indiana	1,[illegible]	34,[illegible]	1,[illegible]	[illegible]	[illegible]	[illegible]	[illegible]	[illegible]	[illegible]	[illegible]
15	Iowa	545	12,[illegible]	401	2,[illegible]	[illegible]	1,[illegible]	[illegible]	[illegible]	[illegible]	[illegible]
16	Kansas	[illegible]	3,[illegible]	154	[illegible]	[illegible]	[illegible]	1,[illegible]	1,[illegible]	1	[illegible]
17	Kentucky	[illegible]	9,443	[illegible]	1,7[illegible]	101	[illegible]	[illegible]	[illegible]	[illegible]	[illegible]
18	Louisiana	[illegible]	3,350	134	[illegible]	7	[illegible]	1,4[illegible]	1,[illegible]	[illegible]	[illegible]
19	Maine	1,[illegible]	3,213	76	[illegible]	1,[illegible]	4,[illegible]	[illegible]	[illegible]	[illegible]	[illegible]
20	Maryland	301	2,373	[illegible]	3,[illegible]	[illegible]	[illegible]	1,[illegible]	1,[illegible]	...	[illegible]
21	Massachusetts	644	2,019	64	13,910	[illegible]	1,[illegible]	[illegible]	[illegible]	...	[illegible]
22	Michigan	1,571	41,216	1,13[illegible]	12,4[illegible]	[illegible]	7,[illegible]	[illegible]	[illegible]	[illegible]	[illegible]
23	Minnesota	[illegible]	4,5[illegible]	114	3,[illegible]	[illegible]	1,012	[illegible]	[illegible]	[illegible]	[illegible]
24	Mississippi	[illegible]	[illegible]	[illegible]	419	[illegible]	[illegible]	[illegible]	1,[illegible]	[illegible]	[illegible]
25	Missouri	[illegible]	14,[illegible]	[illegible]	1,7[illegible]	[illegible]	1,[illegible]	3,[illegible]	[illegible]	11	[illegible]
26	Montana	31	[illegible]	11	[illegible]	[illegible]	40	[illegible]	[illegible]	...	...
27	Nebraska	[illegible]	[illegible]	[illegible]	[illegible]	[illegible]	[illegible]	[illegible]	[illegible]	...	...
28	Nevada	[illegible]	[illegible]	11	315	[illegible]	[illegible]	[illegible]	[illegible]	...	...
29	New Hampshire	[illegible]	1,[illegible]	[illegible]	21,101	[illegible]	[illegible]	[illegible]	[illegible]	[illegible]	[illegible]
30	New Jersey	[illegible]	1,31[illegible]	[illegible]	4,6[illegible]	[illegible]	[illegible]	1,145	1,[illegible]	...	[illegible]
31	New Mexico	12	[illegible]	[illegible]	153	10	[illegible]	[illegible]	[illegible]	...	...
32	New York	3,510	20,[illegible]	[illegible]	73,[illegible]	[illegible]	[illegible]	[illegible]	14,[illegible]	[illegible]	[illegible]
33	North Carolina	[illegible]	3,517	[illegible]	4,5[illegible]	341	[illegible]	[illegible]	[illegible]	[illegible]	[illegible]
34	Ohio	2,[illegible]	36,[illegible]	1,[illegible]	9,[illegible]	[illegible]	3,17[illegible]	[illegible]	[illegible]	[illegible]	[illegible]
35	Oregon	[illegible]	1,[illegible]	40	2,916	[illegible]	[illegible]	[illegible]	[illegible]	[illegible]	4
36	Pennsylvania	3,7[illegible]	33,[illegible]	1,[illegible]	[illegible]	3,13[illegible]	[illegible]	17,4[illegible]	17,[illegible]	[illegible]	[illegible]
37	Rhode Island	[illegible]	321	14	1,1[illegible]	66	115	[illegible]	[illegible]	[illegible]	[illegible]
38	South Carolina	[illegible]	2,315	[illegible]	1,7[illegible]	114	[illegible]	1,[illegible]	1,[illegible]	[illegible]	[illegible]
39	Tennessee	[illegible]	7,3[illegible]	[illegible]	4,[illegible]	[illegible]	[illegible]	2,[illegible]	[illegible]	[illegible]	[illegible]
40	Texas	[illegible]	4,710	[illegible]	[illegible]	31	[illegible]	1,[illegible]	1,714	[illegible]	[illegible]
41	Utah	[illegible]	[illegible]	16	[illegible]	[illegible]	[illegible]	541	[illegible]	...	[illegible]
42	Vermont	[illegible]	1,[illegible]	[illegible]	19,731	[illegible]	1,[illegible]	2,[illegible]	2,[illegible]	[illegible]	[illegible]
43	Virginia	[illegible]	4,[illegible]	[illegible]	6,[illegible]	[illegible]	741	2,[illegible]	[illegible]	[illegible]	[illegible]
44	Washington	46	1,0[illegible]	[illegible]	[illegible]	24	179	474	474	...	...
45	West Virginia	343	3,4[illegible]	144	2,572	[illegible]	453	1,515	1,[illegible]	...	[illegible]
46	Wisconsin	[illegible]	16,119	[illegible]	11,6[illegible]	427	4,12[illegible]	12,461	11,7[illegible]	[illegible]	[illegible]
47	Wyoming	[illegible]	151	6	....	....	[illegible]	213	[illegible]	[illegible]	[illegible]

* Including shingles, staves, &c., shaved.

TABLE CIII.—*Manufactures: Special Statistics for Principal Industries*—1870—Cont'd.

LUMBER, SAWED.

CAPITAL.	WAGES.	MATERIALS.	PRODUCTS.					
Dollars.	Dollars.	Dollars.	Laths.	Lumber.	Shingles.	Staves, shooks, headings, &c.	All products.	
			Thousand.	*M feet.*	*Thousand.*	*Dollars.*	*Dollars.*	
143, 493, 232	40, 009, 162	103, 343, 430	1, 295, 091	12, 755, 543	3, 265, 516	10, 473, 681	210, 159, 327	
744, 005	337, 195	520, 513	1, 115	97, 199	1, 422	18, 341	1, 359, 083	1
5, 000	6, 000	1, 600	....	1, 200	....	....	10, 000	2
694, 400	255, 186	546, 059	2, 200	78, 692	4, 747	....	1, 344, 403	3
3, 856, 440	1, 629, 626	1, 986, 119	2, 877	318, 817	103, 547	94, 580	5, 227, 064	4
122, 700	78, 711	117, 075	2, 710	13, 625	3, 675	....	324, 370	5
775, 391	242, 990	940, 665	813	56, 482	15, 510	16, 451	1, 341, 038	6
37, 400	14, 256	32, 772	....	3, 894	....	....	72, 280	7
290, 434	70, 823	229, 856	100	18, 858	....	56, 356	405, 041	8
1, 500	1, 800	20, 000	....	....	....	30, 000	30, 000	9
755, 000	421, 820	1, 163, 238	1, 400	158, 524	....	....	2, 235, 780	10
1, 718, 473	667, 628	1, 616, 527	1, 883	245, 141	1, 560	....	4, 044, 375	11
50, 750	17, 924	20. 177	....	1, 490	400	....	56, 850	12
2, 542, 530	817, 212	2, 163, 655	13, 650	245, 910	40, 928	123, 205	4, 546, 769	13
5, 975, 746	1, 901, 612	5, 563, 985	11, 202	656, 400	73, 707	1, 456, 233	12, 324, 755	14
3, 925, 031	995, 962	3, 302, 782	47, 884	325, 285	97, 928	97, 775	5, 794, 285	15
642, 955	282, 662	822, 028	320	74, 163	12, 108	6, 814	1, 736, 381	16
1, 724, 686	482, 683	1, 805, 591	8, 050	214, 074	13, 573	142, 675	3, 662, 086	17
541, 800	284, 953	519, 938	8	76, 459	....	6, 668	1, 212, 637	18
6, 614, 875	2, 449, 132	6, 872, 723	266, 889	639, 167	364, 201	1, 263, 613	11, 395, 747	19
1, 055, 600	259, 551	674, 858	5, 849	96, 165	3, 869	64, 477	1, 591, 471	20
2, 054, 869	569, 300	2, 065, 375	873	197, 377	36, 486	391, 838	3, 556, 870	21
26, 990, 450	6, 400, 283	14, 347, 661	304, 054	2, 251, 613	658, 741	1, 332, 922	31, 946, 396	22
3, 311, 140	880, 028	2, 193, 965	49, 768	242, 390	127, 813	88, 861	4, 299, 162	23
1, 153, 917	580, 056	828, 793	651	160, 584	5, 530	....	2, 160, 667	24
3, 241, 670	1, 031, 513	3, 428, 235	12, 970	329, 676	10, 442	104, 236	6, 363, 112	25
146, 000	80, 965	172, 098	400	12, 571	2, 356	546	430, 957	26
152, 900	47, 102	118, 975	....	13, 824	900	....	278, 205	27
193, 500	153, 930	135, 450	75	35, 025	700	....	432, 500	28
2, 428, 193	725, 304	2, 471, 427	10, 383	253, 434	52, 225	321, 959	4, 286, 142	29
2, 238, 900	369, 835	1, 612, 802	3, 167	101, 829	3, 624	135, 066	2, 745, 317	30
47, 100	35, 425	40, 083	....	6, 909	....	....	121, 225	31
15, 110, 981	3, 438, 601	11, 228, 613	87, 999	1, 310, 066	372, 183	1, 646, 811	21, 238, 228	32
1, 175, 950	379, 611	970, 294	1, 530	124, 938	13, 817	123, 990	2, 000, 243	33
6, 191, 679	1, 535, 909	5, 038, 678	15, 238	557, 237	59, 632	1, 001, 669	10, 235, 180	34
913, 262	261, 785	358, 273	7, 346	75, 193	....	11, 086	1, 014, 211	35
24, 804, 304	5, 261, 576	14, 940, 096	95, 592	1, 629, 631	275, 273	766, 995	28, 938, 985	36
101, 200	39, 826	157, 079	....	12, 732	5, 119	6, 500	257, 258	37
583, 425	209, 806	581, 499	2, 500	95, 098	1, 200	450	1, 197, 005	38
1, 622, 741	578, 364	1, 446, 782	5, 370	204, 751	11, 337	14, 365	3, 390, 667	39
870, 491	390, 149	644, 274	623	106, 897	30, 209	....	1, 960, 851	40
338, 500	139, 533	260, 047	1, 138	19, 741	8, 061	120	661, 431	41
2, 872, 451	729, 925	1, 731, 516	6, 672	241, 687	28, 502	217, 293	3, 525, 122	42
979, 386	343, 823	860, 949	4, 258	144, 225	614	8, 225	2, 111, 055	43
1, 285, 202	388, 830	580, 259	17, 000	128, 743	10, 450	1, 500	1, 307, 585	44
961, 950	349, 368	682, 180	197, 871	76, 375	5, 600	295, 470	1, 478, 309	45
11, 448, 545	3, 755, 089	7, 422, 866	102, 663	1, 098, 190	806, 807	620, 591	15, 130, 719	46
110, 500	104, 500	69, 000	....	3, 260	750	....	268, 000	47

TABLE CIII.—*Manufactures: Special Statistics for Principal Industries*—1870—Cont'd.

MUSICAL INSTRUMENTS.

	States.	Establishments.	Steam-engines.		Water-wheels.		Hands employed.				Capital.	Wages.
			Number.	Horse-power.	Number.	Horse-power.	All.	Males above 16.	Females above 15.	Youth.	Dollars.	Dollars.
	The United States	337	1, 559	72	459	28	7, 167	7, 001	68	98	9, 554, 761	5, 107, 291
1	Alabama	1	......	......	......	......	1	1	......	......	50	......
2	California	3	......	......	......	......	5	5	......	......	5, 100	2, 000
3	Connecticut	13	95	4	108	6	299	278	21	......	511, 000	202, 563
4	Illinois	13	80	2	......	......	170	168	1	1	901, 800	119, 586
5	Indiana	3	60	2	......	......	59	59	......	......	130, 000	47, 800
6	Iowa	3	......	......	......	......	5	5	......	......	3, 600	1, 700
7	Kentucky	2	10	1	......	......	51	48	......	3	55, 000	28, 000
8	Louisiana	2	......	......	......	......	5	5	......	......	325	1, 850
9	Maine	9	......	......	13	2	31	31	......	......	24, 250	11, 550
10	Maryland	9	50	1	......	......	384	377	......	7	594, 000	249, 348
11	Massachusetts	60	550	23	243	14	2, 193	2, 173	16	4	3, 247, 436	1, 800, 082
12	Michigan	12	5	......	......	......	87	86	......	1	72, 550	51, 400
13	Missouri	11	......	......	......	......	71	67	......	4	174, 400	60, 800
14	New Hampshire	11	10	1	60	4	73	73	......	......	36, 800	36, 850
15	New Jersey	7	20	1	......	......	110	110	......	......	82, 300	76, 437
16	New York	122	404	26	35	2	2, 860	2, 767	23	70	3, 344, 150	1, 997, 134
17	Ohio	16	42	3	......	......	115	114	......	1	127, 650	50, 560
18	Oregon	2	......	......	......	......	2	2	......	......	1, 700	......
19	Pennsylvania	32	128	5	......	......	409	401	2	6	605, 500	288, 031
20	Rhode Island	1	15	1	......	......	18	18	......	......	20, 000	9, 000
21	Tennessee	1	30	1	......	......	2	2	......	......	150	450
22	Vermont	2	60	1	......	......	204	199	5	......	302, 000	120, 200
23	Wisconsin	1	......	......	......	......	13	12	......	1	15, 000	12, 000

NAILS AND TACKS.

	States.	Establishments.	Steam-engines.		Water-wheels.		Hands employed.				Capital.	Wages.
			Horse-power.	Number.	Horse-power.	Number.	All.	Males above 16.	Females above 15.	Youth.	Dollars.	Dollars.
	The United States	119	9, 955	91	2, 149	56	7, 353	5, 610	434	1, 309	8, 043, 112	3, 721, 099
1	Connecticut	1	......	......	10	1	44	28	7	9	50, 000	21, 000
2	Delaware	1	......	......	......	......	2	2	......	......	175	400
3	Illinois	1	40	3	......	......	138	108	......	30	90, 000	70, 000
4	Indiana	2	422	2	......	......	67	62	......	5	98, 000	37, 767
5	Maine	1	......	......	30	1	2	2	......	......	10, 000	900
6	Massachusetts	43	1, 562	23	1, 289	40	2, 213	1, 725	389	99	1, 912, 950	908, 290
7	Missouri	1	160	2	......	......	47	32	......	15	142, 957	30, 000
8	New Jersey	6	928	9	295	4	534	442	......	92	537, 839	256, 675
9	New York	15	189	6	285	6	464	349	4	111	415, 000	177, 200
10	Ohio	6	957	6	......	......	316	211	......	105	751, 091	178, 040
11	Pennsylvania	27	2, 895	27	115	1	2, 020	1, 578	22	420	2, 649, 000	1, 100, 536
12	Rhode Island	4	462	4	5	......	179	137	3	39	250, 200	131, 162
13	Tennessee	1	10	1	......	......	8	2	......	6	8, 000	1, 000
14	Vermont	1	......	......	20	1	3	3	......	......	15, 000	700
15	Virginia	1	......	......	100	2	160	160	......	......	125, 000	85, 000
16	West Virginia	8	2, 330	8	......	......	1, 156	769	9	378	988, 000	722, 460

TABLE CIII.—*Manufactures: Special Statistics for Principal Industries*—1870—Cont'd.

MUSICAL INSTRUMENTS.

MATERIALS.	PRODUCTS.										
Dollars.	Melodeons.		Pianos.		Church organs.		House organs.		All other products.	All products.	
	No.	Dollars.	No.	Dollars.	No.	Dollars.	No.	Dollars.	Dollars.	Dollars.	
1, 834, 552	3, 247	252, 655	24, 306	8, 225, 204	699	913, 100	28, 963	2, 873, 923	1, 641, 026	13, 905, 908	
590									1, 500	1, 500	1
4, 322			24	9, 000					1, 800	10, 800	2
527, 441	1, 231	74, 400	325	98, 000			2, 347	264, 324	427, 675	864, 399	3
80, 200	20	2, 200	72	26, 600	10	21, 200	2. 460	264, 000	15, 200	329, 200	4
54, 500			420	190, 000					800	190, 800	5
1, 350			2	800			5	600	2, 500	3, 900	6
28, 000			241	95, 000						95, 000	7
500									3, 000	3, 000	8
17, 387	167	11, 596					171	21, 531	19, 700	52, 827	9
317, 570			1, 624	651, 000	7	18, 400			5, 200	674, 600	10
, 142, 394	30	4, 500	7, 419	2, 485, 035	343	338, 700	12, 502	1, 075, 789	549, 770	4, 453, 794	11
50, 810	35	1, 750	12	8, 000	5	6, 000	1, 202	134, 200	4, 450	154, 400	12
66, 340			282	101, 100	27	29, 500			12, 700	153, 300	13
32, 881	603	34, 429					195	17, 811	42, 430	94, 670	14
73, 360			132	44, 500			1, 345	140, 041	3, 200	187, 741	15
, 998, 833	490	47, 155	12, 181	4, 001, 219	191	425, 700	4, 536	507, 645	471, 196	5, 452, 915	16
84, 560	618	71, 520	75	24, 050	1	2, 500	547	59, 240	20, 315	177, 625	17
350									1, 800	1, 800	18
241, 714			1, 497	400, 900	15	36, 100	232	25, 848	56, 790	609, 638	19
5, 000	38	3, 230					178	15, 770		19, 000	20
150									1, 000	1, 000	21
96, 390	15	1, 875					3, 183	347, 124		348, 999	22
10, 000					8	25, 000				25, 000	23

NAILS AND TACKS.

MATERIALS.						PRODUCTS.				
Plate-iron.	Rod-iron.	Bar-iron.	Coal.	All other materials.	All materials.	Nails.	Tacks.	All other products.	All products.	
Tons.	*Tons.*	*Tons.*	*Tons.*	*Dollars.*	*Dollars.*	*Tons.*	*Tons.*	*Dollars.*	*Dollars.*	
30, 225	10, 742	2, 980	99, 718	517, 954	17, 786, 072	207, 882	13, 855	1, 409, 876	23, 101, 082	
45	182		90		29, 000		202		71, 514	1
	4				425	4			1, 816	2
6, 100			5, 000	38, 250	415, 000	6, 000			540, 000	3
3, 600			1, 700		250, 000	3, 390			304, 550	4
191	5		100		16, 390	195			19, 636	5
37, 102	3, 357		10, 076	214, 596	3, 810, 355	27, 457	7, 050	574, 766	5, 285, 244	6
3, 200			5, 000	2, 000	237, 250	3, 000			294, 000	7
19, 706	894		2, 903	55, 211	1, 480, 850	20, 362	18		1, 769, 812	8
4, 652	2, 215	2, 980	3, 190	63, 649	857, 299	8, 584		73, 170	1, 141, 030	9
24, 716			2, 574	62, 102	1, 650, 997	22, 629		41, 191	1, 908, 531	10
69, 677	3, 000		33, 385	34, 096	4, 826, 239	57, 834	4, 590	640, 749	6, 291, 636	11
5, 000	87			48, 050	293, 994	4, 842	45		450, 188	12
50			40		3, 000	50			5, 000	13
25			10		1, 875	25			3, 125	14
4, 000			50		294, 200	3, 950			350, 000	15
52, 071	998		35, 600		3, 689, 207	49, 560	1, 930	80, 000	4, 665, 000	16

TABLE CIII. *Manufactures: Special Statistics for Principal Industries—1870—Cont.*

PRINTS.

	States.	Establishments.	STEAM-ENGINES. Horse-power.	Number.	WATER-WHEELS. Horse-power.	Number.	Printing-machines.	HANDS EMPLOYED. All.	Males above 16.	Females above 15.	Youth.	CAPITAL. Dollars.	WAGES. Dollars.
	The United States	42	7,158	130	2,635	19	240	8,894	6,092	1,393	1,409	13,367,553	3,48[illegible]
1	Iowa	1					1	5	5			4,000	[illegible]
2	Maine	1						10	6		4	1,500	4,[illegible]
3	Massachusetts	11	1,806	33	1,165	8		2,996	2,006	726	264	2,894,653	1,110,[illegible]
4	New Hampshire	3	350	6	580	3	32	635	538	77	20	678,000	273,[illegible]
5	New Jersey	5	600	41	280	4	34	789	549	108	132	1,024,400	369,[illegible]
6	New York	4	850	4	500	1	22	590	379	61	150	280,000	297,[illegible]
7	Pennsylvania	7	1,317	25	70	2	60	868	569	70	229	1,695,000	351,[illegible]
8	Rhode Island	9	2,925	20	100	1	90	2,996	2,035	351	610	6,770,000	1,092,[illegible]
9	West Virginia	1	10	1			1	5	5			20,000	1,[illegible]

SALT.

	States and Territories.	Establishments.	STEAM-ENGINES. Horse-power.	Number.	WATER-WHEELS. Horse-power.	Number.	MACHINES. Blocks.	Boilers.	Capacity.	Grainers.	Kettles.	Capacity.	Pans.	Capacity.	Vats.	Area in square feet.
							No.	No.	Galls.	No.	No.	Gallons.	No.	Galls.	No.	
	United States	282	3,278	192	44	3	402	7	1,200	2	12,879	1,273,207	470	797,286	24,525	4,496[illegible]
1	California	8													8	4[illegible]
2	Colorado	1					5				6	7,000				
3	Florida	6									13	2,980			90	531
4	Idaho	1					1	1	1,000		1					
5	Illinois	1	25	1			2						10	18,290	6	
6	Indiana	1					36				16	3,600				
7	Kansas	1	8	1											33	5[illegible]
8	Kentucky	4						4			149	14,900				
9	Louisiana	1	30	1												
10	Massachusetts	9													2,755	[illegible]
11	Michigan	65	756	39			76				3,749	1,031,700			3,461	36[illegible]
12	New York	93	78	4			147				8,091	10,287			18,106	2,5[illegible]
13	Ohio	40	849	46	40	2	131				678	98,990	431	729,745		
14	Pennsylvania	27	313	28			4				33	55,900	25	49,131	2	
15	Texas	3									143	47,850				
16	Utah	1						2	200							
17	Virginia	2											4	12		
18	West Virginia	18	1,219	72	4	1				2					64	

TABLE CIII.—*Manufactures: Special Statistics for Principal Industries*—1870—Cont'd.

PRINTS.

MATERIALS.						PRODUCTS.				
Print cloth.	Delaines.	Chemicals and dyes.	Mill supplies.	All other materials.	All materials.	Prints.	Delaines.	All other products.	All products.	
Yards.	*Yards.*	*Dollars.*	*Dollars.*	*Dollars.*	*Dollars.*	*Yards.*	*Yards.*	*Dollars.*	*Dollars.*	
453, 809, 251	27, 710, 213	7, 204, 370	1, 581, 471	749, 510	46, 373, 358	453, 809, 251	27, 710, 213	625, 910	54, 446, 044	
105, 620	....	7, 500	700	....	23, 200	105, 620	....	....	26, 400	1
....	....	12, 000	3, 000	52, 000	67, 000	....	....	100, 000	100, 000	2
107, 838, 117	19, 575, 213	3, 286, 978	225, 644	414, 650	15, 490, 530	107, 838, 117	19, 575, 213	140, 000	17, 325, 150	3
24, 930, 000	8, 135, 000	696, 850	225, 076	147, 360	4, 118, 433	24, 930, 000	8, 135, 000	173, 410	4, 670, 333	4
50, 179, 514	....	561, 406	247, 250	135, 500	4, 359, 653	50, 179, 514	....	212, 500	5, 005, 997	5
50, 030, 000	....	40, 500	20, 000	....	2, 784, 600	50, 030, 000	....	....	3, 317, 100	6
53, 022, 000	....	508, 699	208, 137	....	4, 958, 960	53, 022, 000	....	....	6, 113, 584	7
167, 509, 000	....	1, 995, 428	650, 664	....	14, 604, 982	167, 509, 000	....	....	17, 842, 480	8
175, 000	....	5, 000	1, 000	....	36, 000	175, 000	....	....	45, 000	9

SALT.

HANDS EMPLOYED.				CAPITAL.	WAGES.	MATERIALS.						PRODUCTS.		
All.	Males above 16.	Females above 15.	Youth.	Dollars.	Dollars.	Coal.		Wood.		All other materials.	All materials.	All products.		
						Tons.	*Dolls.*	*Cords.*	*Dolls.*	*Dolls.*	*Dollars.*	*Bushels.*	*Dollars.*	
2, 953	2, 890	7	56	6, 561, 615	1, 146, 910	468, 368	696, 713	45, 035	11, 420	576, 502	1, 760, 670	17, 606, 105	4, 818, 229	
84	84	...	...	66, 500	13, 400	....	....	....	....	....	....	174, 855	48, 150	1
8	8	...	...	10, 000	1, 600	....	....	600	1, 800	....	1, 800	7, 560	4, 600	2
22	22	...	...	6, 050	3, 000	....	....	770	....	....	820	25, 130	10, 950	3
8	8	...	...	12, 000	2, 000	....	....	500	1, 200	1, 000	2, 200	13, 400	10, 0[illegible]0	4
26	26	...	...	50, 000	24, 000	3, 300	3, 300	....	....	9, 000	12, 300	54, 000	45, 000	5
4	4	...	...	2, 000	200	....	....	100	200	....	200	1, 020	600	6
4	4	...	...	50, 000	1, 000	....	....	35	175	100	275	10, 000	6, 000	7
40	39	1	...	16, 500	10, 070	....	5, 520	....	....	....	5, 520	64, 600	20, 920	8
57	57	...	...	120, 000	35, 000	210	1, 240	420	1, 680	1, 750	4, 670	128, 000	57, 600	9
18	18	...	...	27, 300	1, 875	....	....	....	....	....	250	22, 846	11, 550	10
858	826	2	30	1, 717, 500	331, 239	....	....	30, 390	....	374, 391	410, 561	3, 981, 316	1, 176, 811	11
528	528	...	..	1, 584, 211	204, 236	117, 617	493, 050	....	....	1, 795	494, 854	4, 977, 720	925, 709	12
437	424	...	13	1, 085, 904	161, 420	142, 302	193, 594	....	....	159, 328	352, 922	2, 898, 649	773, 492	13
159	153	...	6	171, 700	57, 980	36, 851	....	25	125	29, 138	83, 293	579, 970	167, 312	14
29	27	...	2	10, 000	8, 800	....	....	3, 050	5, 600	....	5, 600	29, 936	29, 900	15
2	2	...	...	650	300	....	....	40	240	....	240	1, 926	720	16
8	8	...	...	300	....	....	....	105	400	....	400	2, 063	1, 250	17
661	652	4	5	1, 631, 000	290, 800	167, 998	....	....	....	....	324, 855	4, 633, 750	1, 507, 605	18

TABLE CIII. *Manufactures: Special Statistics for Principal Industries*—1870—Continued.

SEWING-MACHINES.

	States.	Establishments.	Steam-engines. Horse-power.	Steam-engines. Number.	Water-wheels. Horse-power.	Water-wheels. Number.	Hands employed. All.	Hands employed. Males above 16.	Hands employed. Females above 15.	Hands employed. Youth.
	The United States	49	1,688	37	145	6	7,291	6,709	334	248
1	Connecticut	6	585	10	30	2	2,300	2,031	149	120
2	Illinois	1					2	2		
3	Maryland	5					12	12		
4	Massachusetts	6	250	5	30	1	1,033	1,009	12	12
5	New Jersey	1					5	4		1
6	New York	12	692	11	85	3	3,131	2,882	167	82
7	Ohio	7	80	5			306	292	4	10
8	Oregon	1					2	2		
9	Pennsylvania	8	60	4			325	320	2	3
10	Rhode Island	1	18	1			170	150		20
11	Vermont	1	3	1			5	5		

SILK.

	States.	Establishments.	Steam-engines. Horse-power.	Steam-engines. Number.	Water-wheels. Horse-power.	Water-wheels. Number.	Machines. Looms.	Machines. Spoolers.*	Machines. Winders.*	Hands employed. All.	Hands employed. Males above 16.	Hands employed. Females above 15.	Hands employed. Youth.	Capital. Dollars.	Wages. Dollars.
	The United States	86	1,122	48	785	45	1,251	2,427	3,038	6,649	1,734	3,529	1,386	6,231,130	1,942,286
1	Connecticut	23	401	11	300	20	255	170	139	1,703	466	1,003	234	1,414,130	529,425
2	Massachusetts	9	75	6	90	7	5	84	520	453	97	286	70	412,000	154,306
3	New Hampshire	1			20	1		4	2	15	5	10		5,000	1,600
4	New Jersey	28	425	16	246	11	308	2,071	2,251	2,790	733	1,162	895	2,166,500	625,916
5	New York	14	135	8	121	5	216	69	63	739	154	413	172	809,500	392,345
6	Pennsylvania	10	86	7			467	27	61	936	266	655	15	1,420,000	236,400
7	Vermont	1			8	1		2	2	13	13			4,000	2,400

STEEL.

	States.	Establishments.	Steam-engines. Horse-power.	Steam-engines. Number.	Water-wheels. Horse-power.	Water-wheels. Number.	All hands.	Capital. Dollars.	Wages. Dollars.	Materials. Pig iron.	Materials. Blooms.	Materials. Bar iron.	Materials. Scrap iron.
										Tons.	Tons.	Tons.	Tons.
	The United States	30	11,[illegible]	83	250	6	2,[illegible]	6,345,400	1,651,132	27,732	10,[illegible]	11,[illegible]	[illegible]
1	Connecticut	2	555	3	75	3	61	600,000	57,400	500	375		[illegible]
2	Massachusetts	1	200	1			36	150,000	[illegible]		500		
3	New Jersey	4	[illegible]	[illegible]	40	1	[illegible]	500,000	[illegible]	[illegible]	[illegible]	3,770	[illegible]
4	New York	5	1,125	9	100	1	234	1,030,000	[illegible]	7,[illegible]		1,[illegible]	[illegible]
5	Pennsylvania	18	8,917	[illegible]	35	1	1,813	4,065,400	1,290,[illegible]	18,[illegible]	[illegible]	[illegible]	7,[illegible]

Repairs [illegible]

* Also [illegible] in New Jersey [illegible]; Spindles, in New Jersey [illegible], in Pennsylvania 3,900; [illegible] in the United States [illegible], and Braiders, in Pennsylvania 30.

TABLE CIII.—*Manufactures: Special Statistics for Principal Industries*—1870—Cont'd.

SEWING-MACHINES.

CAPITAL.	WAGES.	MATERIALS.	PRODUCTS.				
Dollars.	Dollars.	Dollars.	Sewing-machines.		All other products.*	All products.	
			Number.	*Dollars.*	*Dollars.*	*Dollars.*	
8, 759, 431	5, 142, 248	3, 055, 786	578, 919	13, 638, 706	458, 740	14, 097, 446	
2, 350, 000	1, 649, 246	1, 200, 335	203, 500	3, 479, 500	139, 500	3, 619, 000	1
300	550	300	....	....	2, 000	2, 000	2
1, 405	4, 500	1, 350	....	....	7, 300	7, 300	3
2, 677, 800	680, 432	641, 725	74, 647	1, 921, 510	5, 800	1, 927, 310	4
5, 000	2, 080	232	....	....	4, 500	4, 500	5
2, 727, 576	2, 189, 640	888, 066	243, 406	6, 636, 500	263, 640	6, 920, 140	6
171, 350	286, 200	94, 163	36, 916	718, 496	2, 200	720, 696	7
1, 500	300	300	....	....	1, 000	1, 000	8
721, 500	201, 300	188, 928	16, 450	672, 700	12, 800	685, 500	9
100, 000	120, 000	40, 000	3, 000	180, 000	20, 000	200, 000	10
3, 000	2, 000	387	1, 000	10, 000	....	10, 000	11

SILK.

MATERIALS.					PRODUCTS.							
Raw silk.	Silk-yarn.	Chemicals.	Other materials.	All materials.	Silk goods.	Silk ribbon.	Machine-silk.	Spool-silk.	Silk-thread.	All other products.	All products.	
Pounds.	*Lbs.*	*Dollars.*	*Dolls.*	*Dollars.*	*Yards.*	*Yards.*	*Lbs.*	*Lbs.*	*Lbs.*	*Dollars.*	*Dollars.*	
684, 488	48, 456	209, 224	853, 796	7, 817, 559	1, 026, 422	3, 224, 264	370, 031	127, 590	19, 000	3, 880, 357	12, 210, 662	
175, 839	......	81, 674	407, 727	2, 049, 834	636, 282	447, 664	145, 702	36, 790	......	....	3, 314, 845	1
101, 650	......	46, 500	23, 930	937, 000	....	160, 000	82, 800	68, 900	......	....	1, 402, 500	2
2, 000	......	350	....	14, 350	....	....	2, 000	....	......	....	25, 000	3
239, 727	22, 440	43, 800	90, 555	2, 678, 161	352, 100	1, 294, 600	55, 529	13, 400	......	2, 182, 784	3, 998, 964	4
111, 843	......	....	24, 805	1, 211, 385	....	22, 000	77, 500	7, 500	......	644, 573	1, 826, 073	5
32, 429	26, 016	36, 700	306, 664	919, 024	38, 040	1, 300, 000	6, 500	....	19, 000	1, 053, 000	1, 632, 900	6
1, 000	......	200	115	7, 805	....	....	......	1, 000	......	....	10, 380	7

STEEL.

MATERIALS—Cont'd.			PRODUCTS.										
Coal.	All other materials.	All materials.	Puddled steel.		Blistered steel.		Bessemer steel.		Cast steel.		All other products.	All products.	
Tons.	*Dolls.*	*Dollars.*	*Tons.*	*Dolls.*	*Tons.*	*Dolls.*	*Tons.*	*Dollars.*	*Tons.*	*Dollars.*	*Dolls.*	*Dollars.*	
209, 488	654, 026	5, 166, 003	1, 185	218, 500	1, 100	230, 000	19, 403	1, 818, 220	28, 069	7, 286, 188	57, 078	9, 609, 986	
5, 000	1, 200	119, 050	......	....	......	....	......	....	1, 000	275, 000	......	275, 000	1
1, 000	....	60, 000	......	....	......	....	......	....	400	120, 000	13, 750	133, 750	2
16, 000	40, 000	573, 310	......	....	1, 000	200, 000	......	....	4, 703	1, 201, 778	......	1, 401, 778	3
10, 039	19, 179	456, 712	......	....	100	30, 000	5, 903	413, 220	1, 345	391, 000	......	834, 220	4
177, 449	593, 647	3, 956, 931	1, 185	218, 500	......	....	13, 500	1, 405, 000	20, 621	5, 298, 410	43, 328	6, 965, 238	5

‡ Two establishments, using 2 water-wheels of 4 horse-power, employing 42 females and 8 youths, and $12,000 capital, paying $11,020 wages, using $507,014 materials, producing $528,700, appearing on Table IX (B,) included in "Silk, sewing and twist," are excluded from this table, as they do not manufacture, *but simply wind sewing-silk and twist.*

TABLE CIII.—*Manufactures: Special Statistics for Principal Industries*—1870—Cont'd.

SUGAR AND MOLASSES, (CANE,) REFINED.

States.	Establishments.	Steam-engines. Horse-power.	Steam-engines. Number.	Hands employed. All.	Hands employed. Males above 16.	Hands employed. Females above 15.	Hands employed. Youth.	Capital. Dollars.	Wages. Dollars.
The United States	59	9,655	119	4,597	4,494	20	83	20,545,220	3,177,[illegible]
California	3	725	4	255	255	......	......	1,300,000	166,000
Louisiana	3	116	13	141	141	......	......	365,000	75,000
Maine	3	240	3	185	185	......	......	775,000	117,000
Maryland	4	1,250	7	437	432	......	5	985,000	198,351
Massachusetts	4	900	14	460	400	......	......	2,200,000	226,848
Missouri	1	320	10	302	252	......	50	2,000,000	175,000
New Jersey	3	517	4	404	404	......	......	645,000	272,000
New York	18	2,051	32	864	858	......	6	6,375,000	1,229,956
Pennsylvania	15	3,011	25	1,241	1,240	......	1	5,619,000	663,408
Rhode Island	2	437	5	153	152	......	1	258,000	46,500
Texas	3	88	2	155	115	20	20	50,220	7,025

SUGAR AND MOLASSES, (CANE,) REFINED—Continued.

States.	Materials. Coal. Tons.	Fuel. Dollars.	Molasses. Gallons.	Molasses. Dollars.	Sugar. Pounds.	Sugar. Dollars.	All other materials. Dollars.	All materials. Dollars.
The United States	89,325	721,227	23,952,131	7,748,967	804,408,427	44,350,661	2,847,151	96,898,431
California	15,000	137,000	......	......	35,000,000	2,980,000	108,050	3,225,050
Louisiana	......	......	630,000	250,000	3,971,125	232,078	14,300	496,378
Maine	......	......	3,470,000	1,450,000	13,931,260	1,457,159	50,954	2,958,113
Maryland	......	......	1,324,121	473,480	52,398,051	5,784,959	136,130	6,394,569
Massachusetts	......	312,300	......	......	62,479,008	6,632,095	......	6,944,395
Missouri	......	......	60,000	......	30,960,000	......	200,000	3,667,000
New Jersey	......	......	1,267,597	507,599	100,000,000	9,000,000	539,145	10,046,744
New York	72,825	......	5,416,000	......	342,957,409	......	977,70	37,247,730
Pennsylvania	......	271,927	11,438,333	5,067,888	161,410,674	18,264,370	813,797	24,417,982
Rhode Island	1,500	......	316,080	......	1,300,000	......	7,075	1,431,575
Texas	......	......	......	......	......	......	......	69,235

SUGAR AND MOLASSES, (CANE,) REFINED—Continued.

States.	Products. Molasses, refined. Gallons.	Molasses, refined. Dollars.	Sugar, refined. Pounds.	Sugar, refined. Dollars.	Sirup, refined. Gallons.	Sirup, refined. Dollars.	All products. Dollars.
The United States	839,560	425,762	754,010,051	52,132,669	18,168,279	7,810,066	108,941,911
California	......	......	28,176,618	3,519,660	572,711	384,385	3,904,045
Louisiana	810,000	405,000	1,758,900	238,085	......	......	643,085
Maine	......	......	19,027,376	2,533,907	847,062	608,225	3,142,132
Maryland	......	......	49,416,750	6,498,608	1,018,163	509,240	7,007,857
Massachusetts	......	......	50,971,600	6,218,175	1,723,945	1,447,310	7,665,485
Missouri	......	......	24,455,500	......	547,000	......	4,135,250
New Jersey	......	......	84,202,000	10,174,200	1,571,000	1,025,545	11,199,745
New York	......	......	297,749,314	......	3,591,095	......	42,837,184
Pennsylvania	......	......	186,365,593	22,895,650	8,052,863	3,825,357	26,751,018
Rhode Island	......	......	11,489,000	......	244,440	......	1,680,990
Texas	29,560	20,762	398,300	54,375	......	......	75,137

TABLE CIII.—*Manufactures: Special Statistics for Principal Industries*—1870—Cont'd.

SUGAR AND MOLASSES, (CANE,) RAW.

States.	Establishments.	Steam-engines.	All hands.	Capital.	Wages.	Materials.	PRODUCTS. Molasses.		Sugar.		All products.
				Dollars.	*Dollars.*	*Dollars.*	*Gallons.*	*Dollars.*	*Hhds.*	*Dollars.*	*Dollars.*
United States	713	399	21, 299	10, 248, 475	1, 230, 119	6, 069, 271	4, 368, 687	2, 265, 860	77, 317	8, 117, 508	10, 383, 368
Florida	27	2	143	8, 950	2, 640	16, 604	1, 500	730	407	40, 760	41, 510
Louisiana	686	307	21, 156	10, 239, 525	1, 227, 479	6, 052, 667	4, 367, 187	2, 265, 110	76, 910	8, 076, 748	10, 341, 858

TAR AND TURPENTINE.

States.	Establishments.	STEAM-ENGINES. Horse-power.	Number.	WATER-WHEELS. Horse-power.	Number.	HANDS EMPLOYED. All.	Males above 16.	Females above 15.	Youth.	Capital.	Wages.	Materials.
										Dollars.	*Dollars.*	*Dollars.*
United States	227	177	26	15	1	2, 638	2, 526	81	31	902, 225	476, 284	2, 146, 090
Alabama	12					602	540	55	7	86, 200	120, 000	84, 155
Florida	2	3	1			18	18			16, 000	5, 900	9, 308
Georgia	4	20	1			138	133	2	3	63, 000	28, 000	39, 672
Louisiana	5					5	5			500		900
Mississippi	1					27	20	7		28, 000	6, 000	1, 500
Missouri	2					13	10		3	31, 000	7, 900	35, 400
North Carolina	147	49	21			959	957	1	1	472, 100	184, 839	1, 552, 577
South Carolina	54	105	3	15	1	876	843	16	17	205, 425	123, 645	422, 378

TAR AND TURPENTINE—Continued.

States.	PRODUCTS. Resin.		Tar.		Turpentine.		All other products.	All products.
	Barrels.	*Dollars.*	*Barrels.*	*Dollars.*	*Barrels.*	*Dollars.*	*Dollars.*	*Dollars.*
United States	646, 243	1, 279, 699	12, 002	46, 828	6, 004, 887	2, 194, 498	64, 200	3, 585, 225
Alabama	53, 175	112, 150			409, 950	168, 053		280, 203
Florida	5, 252	12, 488	2, 869	8, 508	8, 740	5, 120		26, 116
Georgia	13, 840	35, 050			160, 400	60, 920		95, 970
Louisiana			833	2, 500				2, 500
Mississippi	1, 900	3, 750			12, 000	4, 800		8, 550
Missouri			8, 000	35, 000	32, 000	8, 000	16, 500	59, 500
North Carolina	456, 131	861, 222	300	820	3, 799, 449	1, 428, 567	47, 700	2, 338, 309
South Carolina	115, 945	255, 039			1, 582, 348	519, 038		774, 077

TABLE CIII.—*Manufactures: Special Statistics for Principal Industries*—1870—Cont'd.

*TOBACCO, CIGARS.

	States and Territories.	Establishments.	Steam-engines. Horse-power.	Steam-engines. Number.	Water-wheels. Horse-power.	Water-wheels. Number.	Hands employed. All.	Hands employed. Males above 16.	Hands employed. Females above 15.	Hands employed. Youth.	Capital. Dollars.	Wages. Dollars.
	The United States	4,631	16	2	30	1	26,049	21,409	2,615	2,025	11,[illegible] 516	9,[illegible]
1	Alabama	14	....	....	....	....	35	34	......	1	9,[illegible]	[illegible]
2	Arkansas	2	....	....	....	....	7	7	......	......	5,[illegible]	[illegible]
3	California	88	....	....	....	....	1,834	1,791	......	43	661,345	523,[illegible]
4	Connecticut	100	....	....	....	....	719	523	164	32	409,[illegible]	303,10[illegible]
5	Delaware	17	....	....	....	....	130	65	33	32	56,770	40,[illegible]
6	District of Columbia	44	....	....	....	....	109	101	1	7	36,715	27,919
7	Florida	13	....	....	....	....	254	254	......	......	257,500	244,919
8	Georgia	15	....	....	....	....	58	47	8	3	40,000	15,655
9	Illinois	217	....	....	....	....	1,025	873	33	119	1,047,070	345,269
10	Indiana	133	....	....	....	....	670	607	16	47	25[illegible],565	235,07[illegible]
11	Iowa	71	....	....	....	....	319	289	5	25	152,050	117,983
12	Kansas	27	....	....	....	....	135	120	1	14	66,100	62,405
13	Kentucky	70	....	....	....	....	389	344	5	40	197,380	140,563
14	Louisiana	42	....	....	....	....	272	268	......	4	58,900	112,344
15	Maine	12	....	....	....	....	74	57	16		27,000	29,296
16	Maryland	260	....	....	....	....	1,034	924	51	59	409,100	304,502
17	Massachusetts	128	....	....	....	....	968	740	216	12	447,085	426,044
18	Michigan	99	....	....	....	....	581	501	24	56	225,202	214,575
19	Minnesota	14	....	....	....	....	57	55	..	2	38,400	19,546
20	Missouri	318	....	....	....	....	1,417	1,192	16	209	586,660	611,867
21	Nebraska	12	....	....	....	....	43	39	..	4	29,400	28,416
22	New Hampshire	12	....	....	....	....	69	54	15		31,675	26,390
23	New Jersey	185	10	1	30	1	663	562	43	58	296,980	187,442
24	New York	1,072	....	....	....	....	5,710	4,951	339	420	2,704,135	2,494,310
25	North Carolina	1	....	....	....	....	1	1	..		50	....
26	Ohio	406	6	1	....	....	2,499	2,053	137	309	826,309	709,937
27	Oregon	2	....	....	....	....	8	8	......	......	4,200	3,700
28	Pennsylvania	975	....	....	....	....	5,775	3,959	1,411	405	1,966,395	1,460,359
29	Rhode Island	34	....	....	....	....	178	118	56	4	54,900	50,115
30	South Carolina	1	....	....	....	....	15	15	......	......	10,000	6,500
31	Tennessee	8	....	....	....	....	27	27	......	......	15,500	14,970
32	Texas	17	....	....	....	....	41	36	4	4	8,530	8,459
33	Vermont	7	....	....	....	....	42	38	2	2	31,350	25,600
34	Virginia	35	....	....	....	....	111	103	1	10	29,425	30,500
35	West Virginia	42	....	....	....	....	177	141	12	21	40,875	67,899
36	Wisconsin	109	....	....	....	....	597	509	6	82	308,230	173,694

* Under the general head of Tobacco in Table VIII (B) appear three specifications: "Tobacco and cigars;" "Tobacco, chewing and smoking, and snuff;" "Tobacco, cigars." For the purpose of Table X, the first class has been divided between the two remaining classes, so that the total production under the head of Tobacco, in Table X, is accounted for under the two heads of "Tobacco" and "Cigars."

TABLE CIII.—*Manufactures: Special Statistics for Principal Industries*—1870—Cont'd.

TOBACCO, CIGARS.

Materials.				Products.				
Tobacco-leaf.		All other materials.	All materials.	Cigars.		All other products.	All products.	
Pounds. 26, 008, 463	*Dollars.* 12, 500, 530	*Dollars.* 459, 004	*Dollars.* 13, 047, 370	*Thousands.* 935, 868	*Dollars.* 28, 299, 067	*Dollars.* 21, 467	*Dollars.* 33, 373, 685	
23, 230	9, 290	....	9, 290	864	33, 850	....	33, 850	1
6, 000	3, 200	....	3, 200	325	....	....	14, 000	2
1, 550, 240	762, 473	15, 953	778, 426	48, 812	1, 909, 917	....	1, 909, 917	3
667, 868	429, 608	12, 055	441, 663	28, 435	....	....	1, 133, 665	4
134, 832	42, 666	2, 510	45, 176	5, 482	....	....	131, 578	5
69, 607	34, 758	825	35, 583	2, 669	....	....	96, 550	6
232, 400	98, 340	500	98, 840	8, 520	....	....	572, 350	7
57, 639	29, 388	387	29, 775	1, 980	....	....	110, 800	8
958, 809	532, 942	14, 887	547, 829	36, 412	1, 346, 347	1, 900	1, 348, 247	9
608, 681	288, 563	5, 751	294, 314	20, 355	....	....	793, 581	10
239, 924	148, 401	7, 029	154, 845	9, 208	....	4, 000	377, 773	11
122, 988	81, 491	2, 315	83, 806	4, 891	....	....	223, 800	12
316, 901	185, 730	1, 913	187, 643	13, 015	....	....	449, 336	13
515, 782	122, 043	5, 000	127, 043	14, 785	....	....	417, 010	14
61, 704	47, 477	1, 298	48, 775	2, 770	....	....	91, 447	15
858, 955	405, 500	7, 237	412, 737	34, 524	1, 114, 988	....	1, 114, 988	16
1, 243, 071	674, 971	42, 560	717, 531	43, 074	1, 504, 553	2, 948	1, 507, 501	17
553, 642	389, 346	2, 947	392, 293	21, 208	931, 736	420	932, 156	18
55, 000	....	1, 350	30, 260	1, 300	....	....	72, 880	19
1, 351, 067	775, 291	41, 904	817, 195	47, 157	2, 084, 093	....	2, 084, 093	20
115, 394	59, 163	1, 376	60, 539	2, 386	....	294	109, 734	21
48, 050	....	2, 451	32, 037	1, 978	....	....	79, 521	22
634, 271	337, 171	16, 246	353, 417	24, 263	826, 029	....	826, 029	23
6, 102, 510	3, 610, 077	88, 981	3, 699, 058	205, 174	9, 258, 722	5, 800	9, 264, 522	24
800	....	....	400	40	....	....	1, 000	25
2, 671, 134	943, 865	72, 395	1, 016, 260	83, 930	2, 766, 868	....	2, 766, 868	26
3, 600	2, 700	100	2, 800	180	....	....	6, 850	27
5, 337, 133	1, 904, 439	90, 119	1, 994, 558	211, 919	5, 319, 748	500	5, 320, 248	28
127, 614	83, 796	8, 559	92, 355	5, 360	....	....	197, 445	29
9, 000	7, 000	....	7, 009	4, 000	....	....	25, 000	30
34, 296	....	400	30, 525	1, 470	....	....	65, 325	31
22, 220	9, 675	325	10, 000	597	25, 765	5, 370	31, 135	32
61, 291	42, 928	250	43, 178	1, 942	....	....	87, 800	33
83, 587	41, 756	960	42, 716	3, 381	118, 606	....	118, 606	34
501, 045	68, 501	2, 410	70, 911	21, 840	272, 813	235	273, 048	35
628, 479	327, 981	7, 411	335, 392	21, 423	695, 032	....	695, 032	36

This change involved the separation of the cigars produced in establishments whose main productions consisted of chewing or smoking tobacco. Thus the aggregate of the two classes, as by Table X, agree with the aggregate of the three classes, as by Table VIII (B.)

† Includes 8 establishments manufacturing cigaretos in Cameron County.

TABLE CIII.—*Manufactures: Special Statistics for Principal Industries*—1870—Cont'd.

*TOBACCO, CHEWING AND SMOKING, AND SNUFF.

	States.	Establishments.	STEAM-ENGINES.		WATER-WHEELS.		HANDS EMPLOYED.				CAPITAL.	WAGES.	MATERIALS.	
			Horse-power.	Number.	Horse-power.	Number.	All.	Males above 16.	Females above 15.	Youth.	Dollars.	Dollars.	Tobacco leaf.	
													Pounds.	Dollars.
	United States	573	2,072	176	372	25	21,799	10,588	5,179	6,032	13,555,814	5,216,633	106,062,313	[illegible]
1	Arkansas	2					7	4	1	2	6,500	400	25,500	3,00
2	California	3	53	3			24	14	4	6	28,000	11,200	99,000	21,89
3	Connecticut	3	7	2	5	1	15	11	1	3	8,500	4,600	26,490	6,03
4	Delaware	2	10	1	50	4	27	27			210,000	12,085	943,126	109,54
5	Georgia	5					196	93	40	63	78,700	76,592	1,609,213	188,48
6	Illinois	37	240	13			1,659	753	258	648	917,550	436,475	9,782,860	1,294,40
7	Indiana	15	14	2			147	84	33	30	134,700	39,165	1,507,703	122,32
8	Iowa	3	32	2			104	56	16	32	102,500	33,500	375,000	53,00
9	Kentucky	32	174	11			900	400	159	341	662,691	212,752	5,233,412	683,36
10	Louisiana	6	24	5			86	74		12	131,500	32,805	478,000	75,70
11	Maryland	15	172	9			353	148	150	55	500,900	85,282	2,235,750	214,42
12	Massachusetts	8			30	2	82	44	34	4	60,800	33,800	136,631	16,93
13	Michigan	15	209	13			675	259	225	191	1,076,000	227,355	4,407,306	932,90
14	Mississippi	1					7	3	1	3	200	100	500	60
15	Missouri	65	944	13			1,971	888	382	701	2,444,700	874,860	9,593,591	3,732,37
16	New Jersey	9	46	3	118	7	214	165	27	22	418,000	80,550	1,103,929	222,42
17	New York	51	776	38	70	5	4,533	1,677	1,725	1,131	3,521,911	1,256,560	24,613,432	517,42
18	North Carolina	110					1,464	762	332	370	375,832	102,144	3,371,553	
19	Ohio	46	260	22	10	3	1,220	503	376	341	661,130	334,310	7,149,742	1,438,60
20	Pennsylvania	30	94	10	20	1	454	211	88	155	551,400	131,430	2,062,968	226,376
21	Tennessee	10					46	32	6	8	26,700	4,550	432,275	
22	Texas	1					12	10		2	4,200	630	13,500	1,600
23	Virginia	96	239	25	60	2	7,420	4,262	1,311	1,847	1,362,500	1,150,828	29,413,584	3,324,35
24	West Virginia	3					21	15		6	5,900	1,660	11,838	1,795
25	Wisconsin	5	78	4			162	93	10	59	265,000	73,000	2,035,320	209,462

*Under the general head of Tobacco in Table VIII (B) appear three specifications: "Tobacco and cigars," "Tobacco, chewing and smoking, and snuff;" "Tobacco, cigars." For the purposes of Table X, the first class has been divided between the two remaining classes, so that the total production under the head of Tobacco, in Table X, is accounted for under the two heads of "Tobacco" and "Cigars." This change involved the separation of the cigars produced in establishments whose main productions consisted of chewing or smoking tobacco. Thus the aggregate of the two classes, as by Table X, agree with the aggregate of the three classes, as by Table VIII (B.)

TABLE CIII.—*Manufactures: Special Statistics for Principal Industries*—1870—Cont'd.

TOBACCO, CHEWING AND SMOKING, AND SNUFF.

MATERIALS—Con'd.		PRODUCTS.								
All other materials.	All materials.	Tobacco, chewing.		Tobacco, smoking.		† Snuff.		All other products.	All products.	
Dollars.	*Dollars.*	*Pounds.*	*Dollars.*	*Pounds.*	*Dollars.*	*Pounds.*	*Dollars.*	*Dolls.*	*Dollars.*	
2,966,004	21,600,237	66,705,769	28,942,472	‡24,762,211	7,431,999	‡2,867,191	954,884	15,600	38,388,359	
600	3,600	15,800	5,800	....	....	....	....	.....	5,800	1
6,855	28,655	48,000	48,000	20,000	7,600	....	....	2,200	57,800	2
....	6,055	9,445	6,112	10,934	8,217	....	....	.....	14,829	3
1,235	110,779	....	....	18,000	5,400	701,676	133,318	.....	138,718	4
12,126	201,520	780,874	364,261	4,063	813	....	....	.....	365,074	5
204,693	1,499,093	3,786,134	1,477,044	4,453,540	1,478,716	1,145	234	6,475	2,971,469	6
64,785	187,113	307,205	259,270	147,913	22,074	....	....	.....	354,734	7
6,510	59,510	247,000	106,600	158,000	36,000	....	....	.....	142,600	8
205,767	826,155	3,798,600	1,445,029	35,000	8,820	....	....	.....	1,647,669	9
2,620	78,330	....	....	445,200	155,080	16,000	6,800	.....	161,880	10
37,115	251,542	172,659	58,587	1,856,433	529,203	251,450	69,479	.....	657,269	11
8,952	19,907	27,804	25,631	73,225	21,657	65,900	26,143	.....	73,431	12
103,108	1,056,012	2,202,414	1,161,636	2,015,946	473,694	10,174	5,037	.....	1,640,367	13
66	666	3,500	1,050	....	....	....	....	.....	1,050	14
716,426	4,468,800	6,735,362	6,209,593	3,300,938	1,967,918	223,900	154,000	.....	8,331,511	15
8,977	271,405	411,800	262,450	315,700	94,400	293,700	102,350	.....	459,200	16
893,117	6,064,568	15,506,408	8,195,819	5,788,706	1,132,017	1,114,350	345,498	.....	9,676,136	17
25,706	390,627	2,217,453	645,299	239,904	72,446	....	....	.....	717,765	18
90,182	1,528,872	4,534,946	2,085,056	2,048,729	440,467	30,200	15,200	.....	2,540,723	19
61,847	288,223	1,061,645	....	729,106	238,173	158,696	96,825	.....	914,245	20
....	15,250	55,872	....	775	400	....	....	.....	44,800	21
....	1,600	9,000	3,600	....	....	....	....	.....	3,600	22
515,070	4,039,465	24,324,028	6,319,735	1,572,499	469,454	....	....	6,925	6,936,164	23
227	2,022	2,700	1,890	3,500	2,450	....	....	.....	4,525	24
....	209,462	467,000	260,000	1,525,000	267,000	....	....	.....	527,000	25

† **Also,** *Tobacco, stemmed, strips, and dried-leaf:* United States, 2,497,600 pounds, $279,000; Indiana, 944,600 pounds, $73,390; Kentucky, 1,451,000 pounds, $193,810; Tennessee, 102,000 pounds, $11,800.

‡ The amounts of tobacco and snuff paying duty under the internal revenue acts, during the fiscal year ended June 30, 1870, were as follows: Of snuff, 1,168,070 pounds; of tobacco, chewing and other, 99,120,005 pounds. These amounts are inclusive of the quantities of the several articles imported, which were, for the same fiscal year—of snuff, 16,767 pounds; of tobacco, 5,981,863 pounds; leaving the amounts manufactured in the United States as follows: of snuff, 1,151,303 pounds; of tobacco, 93,138,142 pounds. The returns of the census for the year ended May 31, 1870, as will be seen above, exhibit a production of snuff, 2,867,191 pounds; of tobacco, 93,965,520 pounds.

TABLE CIII.—*Manufactures: Special Statistics for Principal Industries*—1870—Cont'd.

WOOLEN GOODS.

	States and Territories.	Establishments.	Steam-engines. Horse-power.	Steam-engines. Number.	Water-wheels. Horse-power.	Water-wheels. Number.	Machines. Cards.	Machines. Daily capacity in carded wool.	Machines. Broad looms.	Machines. Narrow looms.	Machines. Spindles.
							Sets.	*Pounds.*	*No.*	*No.*	*Number.*
	The United States	2,891	35,900	1,051	50,332	2,092	8,366	857,392	14,039	20,144	1,845,4[illegible]
1	Alabama	14	12	1	160	10	24	1,836	....	2	330
2	Arkansas	13	75	5	22	3	17	1,448	....	....	....
3	California	5	435	6	40	1	46	8,000	163	22	3,8[illegible]
4	Connecticut	108	2,258	32	6,142	131	660	70,085	1,190	1,703	17[illegible],470
5	Delaware	11	130	3	275	11	30	2,475	53	174	8,75[illegible]
6	Florida	1	2	....	....	....	1	50	....	....	....
7	Georgia	46	86	2	908	48	72	5,454	6	389	14,45[illegible]
8	Illinois	109	2,437	91	483	21	250	21,302	210	423	36,9[illegible]
9	Indiana	175	2,977	112	1,244	60	346	32,467	232	948	57,0[illegible]
10	Iowa	85	1,126	45	1,037	30	199	19,482	133	241	31,462
11	Kansas	9	200	6	20	1	24	1,270	9	20	1,616
12	Kentucky	125	1,651	65	247	23	298	17,768	34	226	10,509
13	Louisiana	2	50	....	....	....	12	800	20	80	4,000
14	Maine	107	140	2	4,453	121	331	33,020	962	199	63,209
15	Maryland	31	50	2	468	31	60	4,158	57	91	12,368
16	Massachusetts	185	5,421	94	12,270	243	1,367	159,421	4,469	3,374	47[illegible],785
17	Michigan	54	619	22	660	37	116	[illegible],430	74	158	15,650
18	Minnesota	10	21	2	266	6	19	2,103	17	22	2,664
19	Mississippi	14	169	4	42	4	17	[illegible],405	....	30	344
20	Missouri	156	1,674	67	383	26	258	21,162	68	115	10,371
21	New Hampshire	77	583	9	4,879	110	351	41,550	909	690	117,057
22	New Jersey	29	627	15	474	26	81	10,700	182	421	23,457
23	New Mexico	1	....	....	50	1	1	100	4	1	240
24	New York	252	2,040	38	7,405	270	615	84,470	1,344	1,127	162,540
25	North Carolina	52	84	3	334	39	78	5,698	11	86	2,[illegible]06
26	Ohio	223	2,960	122	1,982	112	334	28,376	300	752	52,7[illegible]
27	Oregon	9	....	....	360	9	21	3,955	65	25	4,3[illegible]
28	Pennsylvania	457	5,679	192	5,030	269	1,317	140,362	2,226	6,394	316,[illegible]
29	Rhode Island	65	2,175	26	3,288	70	474	64,639	652	1,710	157,0[illegible]
30	South Carolina	15	3	....	160	13	25	1,458	2	7	350
31	Tennessee	148	481	32	773	78	177	10,307	20	60	3,614
32	Texas	20	134	7	6	....	29	1,855	14	16	1,070
33	Utah	15	....	....	137	13	19	1,475	11	20	1,4[illegible]
34	Vermont	65	630	8	2,270	84	175	18,070	379	201	47,71[illegible]
35	Virginia	68	32	2	1,132	66	116	8,011	61	76	6,2[illegible]
36	West Virginia	71	599	22	732	48	132	10,152	50	70	6,[illegible]
37	Wisconsin	64	310	12	1,238	59	131	11,013	112	110	16,44[illegible]

TABLE CIII.—*Manufactures: Special Statistics for Principal Industries*—1870—Cont'd.

WOOLEN GOODS.

HANDS EMPLOYED.				CAPITAL.	WAGES.	MATERIALS.					
All.	Males above 16.	Females above 15.	Youth.	Dollars.	Dollars.	Cotton.	Shoddy.	Warp, cotton.	Warp.	Wool, domestic.	
						Pounds.	*Pounds.*	*Yards.*	*Pounds.*	*Pounds.*	
80,053	42,728	27,682	9,643	98,824,531	26,877,575	17,571,929	19,372,062	1,312,560	140,733	154,767,005	
41	38	1	2	22,375	4,881	2,000	....	....	....	196,550	1
31	29	......	2	32,500	6,870	....	....	....	....	115,330	2
659	584	31	44	1,785,000	230,200	100,000	1,860	....	....	1,928,030	3
7,297	4,257	2,381	659	12,496,000	2,860,370	2,138,911	2,398,417	....	....	13,798,545	4
399	186	110	103	384,500	115,137	185,000	96,930	....	....	533,739	5
1	1	......	......	500	....	....	....	....	....	550	6
563	251	191	121	936,585	122,138	165,000	....	....	....	620,937	7
1,736	1,040	468	228	2,902,443	535,185	151,650	....	....	....	3,560,829	8
2,469	1,450	711	308	3,821,913	726,113	513,595	....	....	....	4,949,461	9
1,098	685	293	110	1,440,484	269,432	23,148	1,225	....	....	2,273,428	10
91	56	24	11	96,000	30,682	1,300	....	....	....	200,000	11
683	454	137	92	700,449	150,373	275,250	....	....	....	1,639,367	12
29	22	3	4	34,000	8,900	1,500	....	....	....	50,325	13
3,042	1,582	1,250	210	4,167,745	1,047,151	669,363	....	....	....	7,338,591	14
327	247	67	13	205,245	82,019	37,885	1,000	....	....	500,291	15
20,550	10,761	7,439	2,350	20,633,400	7,298,302	2,813,449	5,994,110	....	....	37,146,190	16
667	408	208	51	1,011,050	202,813	3,550	....	....	....	1,391,869	17
146	77	60	9	246,600	45,592	....	....	....	....	254,857	18
116	34	31	51	195,250	28,800	32,700	....	....	....	134,790	19
718	548	85	85	716,524	137,408	25,500	....	....	....	1,979,671	20
3,750	1,832	1,549	369	4,616,100	1,355,147	1,079,120	1,380,000	1,312,560	....	8,785,862	21
1,094	524	402	168	1,171,200	334,642	247,398	27,600	....	102,893	2,191,178	22
20	20	......	......	65,000	2,000	....	4,000	....	....	50,000	23
8,812	4,498	2,999	1,315	10,087,282	2,834,326	624,877	432,900	....	22,135	16,146,873	24
249	151	81	17	237,800	39,101	10,000	....	....	....	355,093	25
2,243	1,340	669	234	3,010,969	559,414	175,464	....	....	....	3,910,034	26
179	129	8	42	389,200	112,213	....	....	....	....	943,400	27
12,764	5,825	5,066	1,873	14,238,835	4,373,628	6,969,201	7,866,861	....	....	21,349,389	28
6,363	3,354	2,198	811	8,167,500	2,228,402	1,090,139	919,000	....	....	12,249,720	29
53	32	13	8	25,900	3,815	1,300	700	....	....	55,696	30
428	342	61	25	373,868	62,780	101,449	2,062	....	4,200	1,030,153	31
100	80	16	4	97,250	20,278	....	....	....	....	278,045	32
106	58	39	9	223,400	48,040	8,320	....	....	....	276,000	33
1,870	930	751	189	2,317,900	644,524	77,600	225,967	....	....	3,470,667	34
278	190	56	32	435,375	58,765	27,260	....	....	....	741,000	35
316	207	79	30	236,100	39,828	....	....	....	7,170	673,003	36
775	506	205	64	1,242,269	229,306	....	....	....	4,335	1,027,169	37

TABLE CIII.—*Manufactures: Special Statistics for Principal Industries*—1870—Cont'd.

WOOLEN GOODS—Continued.

	States and Territories.	MATERIALS—Continued.						PRODUCTS.	
		Wool, foreign.	Yarn, cotton.	Yarn, woolen.	Chemicals and dye-stuffs.	All other materials.	All materials.	Blankets.	Blankets, horse.
		Pounds.	*Pounds.*	*Pounds.*	*Dollars.*	*Dollars.*	*Dollars.*	*Pairs.*	*No.*
	United States	17, 311, 824	3, 263, 949	2, 573, 419	5, 833, 346	5, 670, 250	96, 432, 601	2, 000, 439	56, [illegible]
1	Alabama					350	57, 338		
2	Arkansas					890	55, 782		
3	California				53, 481	32, 175	608, 141	80, 930	
4	Connecticut	3, 025, 272			566, 679	751, 947	11, 090, 825	124, 476	18, 7[illegible]
5	Delaware	12, 435			19, 248	53, 564	392, 614	70	
6	Florida						150		
7	Georgia				275	18, 156	268, 176		
8	Illinois				109, 279	87, 907	1, 701, 323	44, 434	
9	Indiana	80, 157			168, 728	109, 369	2, 684, 315	56, 83[illegible]	
10	Iowa				72, 107	46, 290	998, 073	17, 080	
11	Kansas				4, 380	11, 160	86, 105	4, 500	
12	Kentucky				24, 815	28, 777	831, 628	4, 223	
13	Louisiana				250	900	19, 047		
14	Maine	382, 727			209, 842	220, 830	3, 958, 759	174, 650	14, [illegible]
15	Maryland	450			9, 145	4, 940	233, 924	5, 548	1[illegible]
16	Massachusetts	7, 201, 948			1, 871, 127	1, 707, 296	24, 876, 318	493, 785	
17	Michigan				32, 107	23, 848	659, 700	615	
18	Minnesota				8, 474	3, 755	108, 540	3, 504	
19	Mississippi				500	5, 226	79, 566		
20	Missouri				10, 818	24, 233	849, 313	6, 908	
21	New Hampshire	793, 433			431, 897	163, 977	5, 310, 622	184, 809	
22	New Jersey	92, 240		300	55, 610	91, 262	1, 215, 016	1, 255	1, [illegible]
23	New Mexico				1, 975		12, 775	1, 750	
24	New York	898, 447	102, 682	24, 360	448, 653	655, 171	8, 535, 316	110, 555	24, 6[illegible]
25	North Carolina				5, 681	6, 059	166, 427		
26	Ohio	62, 200		4, 500	122, 542	110, 045	1, 968, 629	32, 118	
27	Oregon				9, 845	6, 298	227, 595	27, 960	
28	Pennsylvania	3, 214, 850	3, 161, 267	2, 544, 259	955, 800	459, 479	17, 457, 913	699, 766	
29	Rhode Island	412, 247			388, 650	851, 102	8, 029, 948		
30	South Carolina				550	140	22, 238	450	
31	Tennessee				4, 008	10, 682	503, 737	2, 987	
32	Texas				1, 400	1, 425	86, 817	2, 809	
33	Utah				1, 350	2, 221	98, 272	1, 105	
34	Vermont	1, 120, 680			87, 329	156, 197	1, 937, 370	100	
35	Virginia	1, 200			11, 974		317, 800	827	
36	West Virginia				7, 932	5, 115	307, 051	3, 005	
37	Wisconsin	14, 218			48, 695	19, 564	685, 368	3, 290	

TABLE CIII.—*Manufactures: Special Statistics for Principal Industries*—1870—Cont'd.

WOOLEN GOODS—Continued.

PRODUCTS—Continued.										
Beavers.	Cloth, cassimeres, and doeskins.	Cloth, felted.	Cloths, negro.	Cottonade.	Coverlids.	Flannels.	Frocking.	Hosiery.	Jeans.	
Yards. 261, 208	*Yards.* 63, 340, 612	*Yards.* 1, 941, 865	*Yards.* 1, 932, 382	*Yards.* 75, 000	*No.* 226, 744	*Yards.* 58, 965, 286	*Yards.* 75, 000	*Dozens.* 21, 460	*Yards.* 24, 489, 985	
......	......	......	......	......	......	......	......	......	......	1
......	......	......	......	......	......	......	......	......	......	2
......	231, 260	......	......	......	......	278, 501	......	4, 000	......	3
......	10, 637, 028	731, 065	......	......	......	1, 563, 000	......	......	1, 280, 000	4
......	276, 332	......	......	......	......	730	......	......	590, 000	5
......	......	......	......	......	......	......	......	......	......	6
......	119, 574	......	......	......	......	......	......	......	177, 155	7
......	663, 498	......	......	......	......	1, 219, 642	......	410	813, 573	8
......	727, 504	......	18, 000	......	......	1, 672, 774	......	......	2, 193, 086	9
......	483, 199	......	......	......	......	509, 044	......	......	106, 959	10
......	22, 380	......	......	......	......	19, 000	......	......	28, 380	11
......	41, 585	2, 000	......	......	......	63, 232	......	......	1, 244, 578	12
......	......	......	......	......	......	......	......	......	......	13
261, 208	1, 983, 656	1, 500	......	......	......	2, 019, 729	......	......	......	14
......	64, 490	2, 500	......	......	......	31, 327	......	......	4, 610	15
......	21, 819, 879	285, 000	......	......	......	22, 321, 684	......	......	......	16
......	668, 468	......	......	......	......	253, 028	......	......	1, 400	17
......	105, 996	......	......	......	......	74, 190	......	......	......	18
......	......	......	......	......	......	......	......	......	......	19
......	94, 610	......	......	......	......	171, 200	......	......	137, 990	20
......	2, 481, 416	184, 200	......	......	......	13, 141, 565	75, 000	16, 000	......	21
......	1, 385, 668	1, 500	......	......	......	634, 746	......	......	126, 652	22
......	1, 500	......	......	......	......	2, 000	......	......	2, 000	23
......	6, 427, 758	680, 000	......	......	......	2, 175, 078	......	......	15, 000	24
......	100, 000	......	......	......	......	1, 690	......	......	153, 452	25
......	469, 403	......	......	......	......	1, 464, 832	......	......	993, 926	26
......	148, 095	......	......	......	......	334, 300	......	......	......	27
......	3, 938, 277	54, 100	200, 000	......	226, 744	6, 809, 565	......	1, 050	14, 171, 662	28
......	7, 483, 598	......	1, 714, 382	75, 000	......	1, 625, 000	......	......	2, 187, 156	29
......	......	......	......	......	......	......	......	......	13, 000	30
......	4, 158	......	......	......	......	3, 919	......	......	145, 692	31
......	10, 100	......	......	......	......	......	......	......	......	32
......	11, 000	......	......	......	......	58, 650	......	......	4, 000	33
......	1, 978, 007	......	......	......	......	2, 018, 533	......	......	......	34
......	276, 610	......	......	......	......	19, 235	......	......	3, 000	35
......	59, 623	......	......	......	......	135, 445	......	......	89, 306	36
......	625, 940	......	......	......	......	343, 627	......	......	7, 478	37

TABLE CIII.—*Manufactures: Special Statistics for Principal Industries*—1870—Cont'd.

WOOLEN GOODS—Continued.

	States and Territories.	Products—Continued.						
		Kerseys.	Linseys.	Repellants.	Robes, carriage.	Rolls	Satinets.	Shawls.
		Yards.	*Yards.*	*Yards.*	*No.*	*Pounds.*	*Yards.*	*Number.*
	The United States ..	5,506,902	14,130,274	2,663,767	22,500	8,685,069	14,072,559	2,312,3[illegible]
1	Alabama	8,500				67,916		
2	Arkansas					102,400		
3	California							
4	Connecticut		960,000			8,536	4,093,967	160,71[illegible]
5	Delaware	96,000				10,000		
6	Florida					500		
7	Georgia	444,200				220,686		
8	Illinois		7,425			410,806	15,672	22,333
9	Indiana	18,600	26,290			474,318	183,977	100
10	Iowa	2,200	6,800			350,696	44,750	380
11	Kansas					56,300		
12	Kentucky		47,712			757,227	1,300	112
13	Louisiana					22,536		
14	Maine	30,900		1,707,767	22,500	530,961		33,300
15	Maryland	380,400	3,980				16,720	
16	Massachusetts	9,600				23,500	7,701,880	565,435
17	Michigan	4,000	200			211,600	16,300	60
18	Minnesota					36,000		
19	Mississippi	6,000	152,891					
20	Missouri		21,500			1,169,499	5,350	4,000
21	New Hampshire	1,001,000				110,075	720,567	
22	New Jersey			384,000		19,000	171,823	
23	New Mexico							
24	New York	44,093	16,000			739,676	261,800	365,023
25	North Carolina		22,971			198,6[illegible]		
26	Ohio	4,150	19,160			751,518	273,219	15,000
27	Oregon					23,320		
28	Pennsylvania	1,648,375	10,718,994	406,000		549,213	181,580	670,690
29	Rhode Island	1,658,725	1,991,258	54,000		5,490	220,000	1[illegible],000
30	South Carolina					39,238		
31	Tennessee		23,167			730,900	5,000	400
32	Texas	87,500	7,500			156,280		
33	Utah	2,000	17,000			87,370		
34	Vermont			112,000		127,936	75	160,000
35	Virginia	37,669	32,175			269,086	42,850	
36	West Virginia	23,000	54,751			224,745		
37	Wisconsin		500			374,187	15,000	35,000

TABLE CIII.—*Manufactures: Special Statistics for Principal Industries*—1870—Cont'd.

WOOLEN GOODS—Continued.

PRODUCTS—Continued.										
Skirts, balmoral.	Skirts, balmoral.	Tweeds and twills.	Warp.	Yarn.	Yarn, hosiery.	Yarn, shoddy.	Goods not specified.	Miscellaneous articles.	All products.	
Yards.	*Dollars.*	*Yards.*	*Pounds.*	*Pounds.*	*Pounds.*	*Pounds.*	*Yards.*	*Dollars.*	*Dollars.*	
280,000	1,217,800	2,853,458	122,000	14,156,237	223,000	1,569,000	162,000	3,251,368	155,405,358	
				107,800					89,998	1
									78,690	2
								129,342	1,102,754	3
		650,000		461,550				166,963	17,371,048	4
			122,000	20,500				921	576,067	5
									500	6
				49,000					471,523	7
		29,909		549,088				50,303	2,849,249	8
		38,540		709,517				94,209	4,329,711	9
				339,485				5,009	1,647,606	10
				40,000					153,150	11
				21,440				12,625	1,312,458	12
								15,795	30,795	13
				8,600				53,685	6,398,881	14
				72,100					427,596	15
280,000		808,920		1,235,161				192,944	39,502,542	16
		13,000		78,174				16,172	1,204,868	17
				9,350				7,429	219,862	18
				2,087				8,100	147,323	19
		5,000		289,525				3,764	1,256,213	20
		32,000		485,600				27,130	8,766,104	21
				187,100				13,664	1,903,825	22
								1,500	21,000	23
		96,000		564,033			162,000	1,430,639	14,394,786	24
									298,638	25
		119,340		689,706				56,661	3,287,699	26
		18,000		1,000					505,857	27
	1,217,800	1,006,749		7,696,889	223,000	1,569,000		874,828	27,580,586	28
				233,500				50,040	12,558,117	29
									34,459	30
				79,002					696,844	31
				400					152,968	32
				1,000					199,600	33
		26,000		6,400				3,575	3,619,459	34
				5,800				5,010	488,352	35
				116,382				20,450	475,763	36
		10,000		105,048				10,570	1,250,467	37

TABLE CIII.—*Manufactures: Special Statistics for Princi*

WORSTED GOODS.

	States.	STEAM.			WATER-WHEELS.			
					power.			
							No.	
	The United States	102			4, 634		7, 334	
1	Connecticut		128	4	65	2	1, 069	
2	Maine				60	1	500	
3	Massachusetts	35	730	19	2, 579	25	1, 980	
4	New Hampshire	2			1, 525	3	......	....
5	New Jersey		65	2	75	3	300	....
6	New York		5	1	120	2	47	
7	Ohio							
8	Pennsylvania	31	,211	28	25	1	977	
9	Rhode Island		,208	15	140	2	161	
10	Vermont							
11	Wisconsin							

WORSTED GOODS—Contin

	States.	MATERIALS—Continued.			
		Cotton yarn.	Woolen yarn.	Worsted yarn.	All materials.
		Pounds.	*Pounds.*	*Pounds.*	*Dollars*
	The United States	2, 146, 500	46, 240	1, 958, 880	14, 308, 1
1	Connecticut	....	....	37, 000	330, 6
2	Maine	....	25, 000	....	55, 0
3	Massachusetts	1, 116, 000	6, 240	505, 200	5, 663, 0
4	New Hampshire	....	....	....	1, 032, 1
5	New Jersey	105, 000	15, 000	75, 000	292, 2
6	New York	300	....	20, 450	94, 2
7	Ohio	....	....	198, 000	151, 2
8	Pennsylvania	925, 000	....	860, 380	4, 932, 9
9	Rhode Island	....	....	260, 850	1, 736, 2
10	Vermont	200	....	....	18, 6
11	Wisconsin	....	....	2, 000	2, 0

TABLE CIII.—*Manufactures: Special Statistics for Principal Industries*—1870—Cont'd.

WORSTED GOODS.

HANDS EMPLOYED.						MATERIALS.					
All.	Males above 16.	Females above 15.	Youth.	Capital.	Wages.	Chemicals, &c.	Cotton.	Shoddy.	Domestic wool.	Foreign wool.	
				Dollars.	*Dollars.*	*Dollars.*	*Pounds.*	*Lbs.*	*Pounds.*	*Pounds.*	
12,920	3,864	7,152	1,904	10,085,778	4,368,857	1,250,016	2,463,808	12,342	13,317,319	3,836,982	
370	96	191	83	495,000	120,700	120,800	69,000	......	45,000	145,000	1
62	10	37	15	20,000	18,000	....	100,600	......	....	....	2
5,275	1,626	3,199	450	2,839,500	1,678,462	541,465	876,868	......	6,163,816	2,175,234	3
1,161	335	700	106	700,000	378,017	68,231	591,874	......	1,077,915	560,008	4
281	109	107	65	198,000	98,000	29,400	55,000	......	185,000	90,740	5
251	42	140	69	112,200	57,600	14,900	56,800	......	66,000	6,000	6
86	11	41	34	56,000	14,750	7,740	....	......	....	....	7
3,868	1,318	1,743	807	3,350,078	1,363,334	234,038	107,266	12,342	4,359,588	500,000	8
1,531	290	986	255	2,300,000	634,090	241,960	607,000	......	1,400,000	360,000	9
25	5	8	12	13,000	5,104	462	....	......	20,000	....	10
10	2	......	8	2,000	800	....	....	......	....	....	11

WORSTED GOODS—Continued.

PRODUCTS.											
Fancy goods.	Shawls.	Shirts and drawers.	Balmoral skirts.	Other skirting.	Webbing and tape.	Worsted dress goods.	Woolen yarn.	Worsted yarn.	Zephyr goods.	All products.	
Dollars.	*No.*	*Doz.*	*Yards.*	*Yards.*	*Yards.*	*Yards.*	*Pounds.*	*Pounds.*	*Lbs.*	*Dollars.*	
1,974,957	111,404	4,080	433,288	51,851	2,096,000	12,057,006	284,100	4,047,750	3,900	22,090,331	
....	....	......	....	....	....	....	....	....	......	591,000	1
....	....	......	....	....	....	....	....	....	......	85,000	2
804,757	....	......	86,880	....	....	2,983,206	....	1,935,686	......	8,280,541	3
67,000	....	......	....	....	....	....	....	486,964	......	1,447,422	4
....	15,000	......	261,000	....	2,000,000	....	....	21,800	......	518,980	5
87,400	....	......	....	....	....	....	....	....	......	237,400	6
....	....	......	....	....	....	....	....	....	......	180,000	7
900,100	96,404	4,080	85,408	51,851	96,000	9,073,800	201,600	1,581,000	3,900	7,883,938	8
19,700	....	......	....	....	....	....	82,500	....	......	2,835,950	9
....	....	......	....	....	....	....	....	19,300	......	25,000	10
6,000	....	......	....	....	....	....	....	....	......	6,000	11

TABLE CIV.—*Mining, including Quarrying, Oil-boring, and Peat-cutting*—1870.

THE UNITED STATES—BY STATES AND TERRITORIES.

States and Territories.	Establishments.	Steam-engines.	Water-wheels.	HANDS EMPLOYED.					CAPITAL.	WAGES.	MATERIALS.	PRODUCTS.
				All.	Men above ground.	Men under ground.	Boys above ground.	Boys under ground.	Dollars.	Dollars.	Dollars.	Dollars.
The United States	7974	4131	134	154328	66178	77221	6916	4013	222384654	74464044	14275631	152598994
Alabama	3	1	...	72	34	33	5	...	39600	29970	946	72536
Arizona	4	...	...	45	18	27	...	...	6500	13700	1485	24500
California	1046	42	70	7589	5442	2128	19	...	20079975	3953638	1355304	8281633
Colorado	53	15	2	575	284	291	...	...	2835835	375125	68068	858674
Connecticut	23	13	1	1507	1507	...	...	...	1436100	780120	45802	1227402
Delaware	2	2	...	26	26	...	...	...	89210	4950	1510	10600
Georgia	10	...	1	126	118	4	4	...	145800	28073	2929	49800
Idaho	254	5	2	1692	1518	174	...	...	1088640	503266	231763	1998341
Illinois	356	102	...	7504	2204	5159	141	...	4814123	3606913	448338	6962901
Indiana	72	27	...	1723	579	1056	88	...	610692	754964	73092	1137172
Iowa	131	6	...	1628	629	986	13	...	736224	676714	88262	1063464
Kansas	26	1	...	351	347	4	...	...	179130	128100	6550	174628
Kentucky	35	5	...	925	602	275	47	1	761450	312486	31083	509865
Louisiana	1	...	...	2	2	...	...	...	100	250	250	1000
Maine	57	5	...	733	724	...	9	...	397768	356775	34710	621738
Maryland	80	32	2	3801	1209	2515	32	45	25369730	1839952	205547	3444183
Massachusetts	65	23	1	1595	1450	132	13	...	944250	899743	147361	1403568
Michigan	44	111	...	6381	1980	4381	20	...	9962874	3727633	926119	7190118
Minnesota	9	...	...	51	51	...	...	...	18500	17665	5650	35350
Missouri	142	40	...	3423	1644	1685	94	...	3489250	1938792	570781	3472513
Montana	683	1	...	3534	3362	172	...	...	2518613	1381699	733901	4030435
Nebraska	7	...	...	38	36	...	2	...	14850	12550	3154	30130
Nevada	139	41	2	2866	809	2057	...	...	32253400	2900872	1636865	11106452
New Hampshire	21	1	...	334	323	11	...	...	203450	201129	13452	322805
New Jersey	49	53	7	2496	975	1492	29	...	2501700	1376957	232819	2554475
New Mexico	17	...	...	177	95	82	...	...	2384000	107550	33138	343250
New York	454	54	8	5177	4054	1094	29	...	4696091	2259088	422955	4324631
North Carolina	17	3	...	482	273	193	16	...	1853100	153220	37807	638302
Ohio	535	121	...	11241	5358	5537	346	...	9017197	4682571	437714	7751544
Oregon	168	...	...	880	861	19	...	...	321520	79022	29930	417797
Pennsylvania	3086	3120	17	81215	26088	45454	5790	3883	81660276	38815276	6069917	75200390
Rhode Island	2	2	...	75	28	42	5	...	80000	33000	4100	30000
South Carolina	5	...	2	148	130	18	...	...	137000	17460	5170	19888
Tennessee	22	4	3	1239	655	473	111	...	944829	378913	21425	776292
Texas	1	...	...	2	2	...	...	...	150	750	...	900
Utah	6	1	...	25	5	20	...	...	44800	25550	5985	14950
Vermont	54	22	11	1143	906	165	72	...	2194700	484937	58969	905410
Virginia	27	20	2	997	554	441	2	...	1113000	248270	31067	409914
West Virginia	185	177	...	1527	784	646	28	69	2554499	821513	170741	2538531
Washington	3	2	...	90	30	60	...	...	307200	71069	13499	102064
Wisconsin	80	7	3	701	406	294	1	...	737728	233981	38582	510882
Wyoming	3	1	...	192	76	101	...	15	261000	232800	49254	850000

[*Continued from page* 885.]

to 34 per cent., as in 1870, may fairly be claimed as a marked success. But, to effect this object, an amount of clerical labor has been expended which has been simply enormous. Tens of thousands of letters from the Census Office were required to obtain the material for complete and comparative statements of production for the trades and branches of industry which are embraced in Table CIII of this Compendium.

The fatal defect of the "general blank" in this particular is, that each proprietor of establishment is left to fill out the columns, "kinds," "quantities," "values," twice—once for materials and once for products—according to his own judgment or inclination.

He has no idea how much particularity is desired, or how fully his neighbors and rivals in business will report their operations. If he really wishes to comply with the intentions of the law, he is at a loss to decide as to the best method of classifying the materials and products of his industry. The determination of this question, which is a matter for careful consideration by the best-informed statisticians, is thrown by turns upon each one of 250,000 manufacturers. No reasonable number of precise and specific questions could cause one-half the trouble which is involved in filling these

ABLE CV.—*The Statistics of Fisheries, exclusive of the Whale Fishery*—1870.

THE UNITED STATES—BY STATES AND TERRITORIES.

nd Terri- ies.	Establishments.	HANDS EMPLOYED.				CAPITAL.	WAGES.	MATERIALS.	PRODUCTS.
		Total.	Males above 16.	Females above 15.	Youth.	Dollars.	Dollars.	Dollars.	Dollars.
ted States	2,140	20,504	19,970	324	210	7,469,575	3,449,331	1,642,276	11,096,522
	1	2	2			500	150	200	1,200
	1	3	3			300	440	1,000	2,200
	87	198	194		4	30,790	6,800	30,200	150,260
cut	171	1,128	1,099		29	421,775	184,932	38,717	769,799
	9	46	46			5,600	1,540		7,350
	43	150	149		1	75,000	22,040	26,939	101,528
	1	3	3			750	500		1,200
	14	42	40	2		5,500	4,340	1,460	17,495
	2	8	5	3		4,150	200	450	1,800
	1	3	2	1		500		500	1,200
	2	4	4			196	20	10	1,840
y	6	13	13			2,300	400	325	4,330
	4	16	12		4	800	3,400	403	9,092
	237	2,461	2,441	4	16	891,798	339,942	216,928	979,610
l	157	783	769	12	2	118,729	52,667	3,085	190,550
isetts	237	8,993	8,953		40	4,287,871	2,291,370	1,001,891	6,215,325
	242	1,159	1,122	27	10	363,957	137,324	101,008	567,576
	2	4	3		1	180			1,100
sey	204	947	935		12	231,231	80,541	1,387	374,912
k	338	755	751	2	2	135,875	35,824	21,483	235,750
rolina	42	1,606	1,276	265	65	211,100	80,748	40,041	265,839
	106	565	565			262,600	71,762	14,512	383,121
	18	87	87			27,940	18,956	27,068	54,758
ania	34	169	169			24,048	14,112	550	38,114
land	35	227	220		7	67,500	10,244	17,360	124,505
e	1	8	8			2,000	1,440		3,000
	1	3	3			350	550		1,650
	26	606	603	3		54,812	30,927	9,804	87,482
ton	17	234	218	4	12	165,565	27,520	46,166	289,746
n	105	379	373	1	5	117,458	58,142	47,289	214,190

mns of the general schedule of manufactures. A similar difficulty, though not ing to the same degree, is found in the return of power and machinery upon eral schedule.

esult of all this is, that some manufacturers, out of conscientiousness, or from a erest in securing a complete and correct census of their industry, will make iswers even more full and explicit than is necessary; while others will put in as possible, disregarding, perhaps, the plainest and most natural divisions be- he classes of products and materials. Each man's inclinations are thus made .sure of his duty, and uniformity of practice becomes impossible. Where there iformity of practice, there can be no comparison and no tabulation of results. ernative presented to the Census Office by returns of industry so irregular and d, is either to drop the whole and accept the failure of the effort to obtain information of the highest economical and social value, or else, by a most ex- laborious, and thankless correspondence, to elicit the information which would en given as a matter of course, and without extra trouble to any one, on sched- ecially adapted to the industries in the enumeration of which they were to be

ll this uncertainty, vexation, and confusion to enumerator, enumerated, and r, the special schedule offers a clear and easy remedy, substituting for the diverse nts and inclinations of a thousand manufacturers a single straight rule by which govern themselves, knowing that they are doing all that will be required of a rule, too, which, by making compilation a mere work of transcription, would save ten or twenty times more in clerical service than the trifling additional cost of printing involved.

For the treatment of the following topics affecting the Tables of Manufactures, see quarto Volume III, (Wealth and Industry,) Ninth Census:

O

Lightning Source UK Ltd.
Milton Keynes UK
UKHW050640201218
334046UK00006BA/145/P

9 780428 461461